ROTHMANS
FOOTBALL
YEARBOOK
1992-93

EDITOR: JACK ROLLIN

HEADLINE

First published in 1992
by HEADLINE BOOK PUBLISHING PLC

10 9 8 7 6 5 4 3 2 1

Cover photograph Left: Paul Ince (Manchester United); right: Gary McAllister (Leeds United) (*Action Images*)

British Library Cataloguing in Publication Data
Rothmans Football Yearbook.—1992–93
1. Association Football—Serials
796.334′05

ISBN 0 7472 0715 1 (hardback)
0 7472 7905 5 (softback)

Printed and bound in Great Britain by
BPCC Hazells Ltd
Member of BPCC Ltd

HEADLINE BOOK PUBLISHING PLC
Headline House
79 Great Titchfield Street
London W1P 7FN

CONTENTS

INTRODUCTION

The 23rd edition of Rothmans Football Yearbook continues the policy of covering as much of the world game as possible, with the emphasis again on the domestic scene. As in recent editions, every one of the Football League clubs has a full page photograph of the 1991–92 squad and six pages in all devoted to each team. The recently returned club Colchester United are also featured. This edition also shows a significant increase in the number of overall pages.

Transfer fees for players moving between League clubs are again indicated, but only tribunal transactions are officially published and the others are those universally reported at the time. For each of the League clubs there are new stories in the 'Did You Know' category.

On the international scene, the directory of nations in FIFA again includes full addresses, there is full coverage of the 1992 European Championship, fixtures for the 1994 World Cup and results to date in that competition. There is also a short directory of the venues for the USA in 1994.

For the first time there are pages devoted to women's football both at domestic and international level which acknowledge the growth in this section of the game.

Again because of the many changes in the Laws of the Game, the latest amendments are included at the end of the existing laws.

The Editor would like to thank Maurice Golesworthy for historical notes on the clubs, Alan Elliott for the Scottish section and Norman Barrett for the Milestones diary. Thanks are also due to John English, whose painstaking and conscientious reading of the proofs has been of invaluable assistance in the preparation of the book as well as editorial assistance from Glenda Meeson, Sara Thompson and Christine Forrest.

The Editor would also like to pay tribute to the various organisations who have helped to make this edition complete, especially Sheila Murphy of the Football League, Mike Foster of the FA Premier League and the secretaries of all the Football League and Scottish League clubs for their kind co-operation. The ready availability of Football League secretary David Dent and his staff to answer queries was as usual most appreciated especially Ian Cotton and Chris Hull and thanks are due in equal measure to the Scottish Football League.

ACKNOWLEDGEMENTS

The Editor would also like to express his appreciation of the following individuals and organisations for their co-operation: Glynis Firth, Sandra Whiteside, Lorna Parnell, Debbie Birch and Jenny Nash (all from the Football League), David C. Thompson of The Scottish League, Malcolm Stammers (FA of Wales), Alan Dick, Malcolm Brodie, Bob Hennessy, Peter Hughes (English Schools FA), W. P. Goss (AFA), Ken Scott for GM Vauxhall Conference information, Rev. Nigel Sands, Edward Grayson, Ken Goldman, Andy Howland and Don Aldridge.

Special appreciation is due to Lorraine Jerram of Headline Book Publishing plc for her patience, understanding and support as well as encouragement and also thanks to former colleagues Caroline North and Sarah Barratt.

Finally sincere thanks to the production staff at Page Bros (Norwich) Ltd for their efforts in the production of this book which was much appreciated in the final stages.

EDITORIAL

Association Football was once the people's game. Now it belongs to the times and the sky's the limit. The passing of the old style Football League deserves a suitable period of mourning, but the birth of a competition of such stature as the FA Premier League, must be encouraged whatever the misgivings attendant upon it.

This is no underprivileged infant, offering a begging bowl; the newcomer was born clutching a lucrative £304 million dish from BSkyB and the BBC over five years. But for the armchair fan it may well become an expensive hobby for the luxury of watching its development twice a week with hints of pay-to-view in the future. He must now put his money where his house is . . . This is unless he decides to stay with ITV and its intermittent schedule of Division One fare, from the economy size Football League, or go continental via Channel 4, to view the likes of exiles Paul Gascoigne, Des Walker and David Platt in the Italian League. There will also be the return of recorded highlights on the BBC. One recent opinion poll reported only three percent of non-satellite owners were prepared to invest. But we know about lies, damn lies and polls.

The revolution which brought about the formation of a super league did not achieve its original aim of an 18-club top division to allow the international team to breathe. Did anyone expect it? Fewer fixtures would in reality present problems for clubs, footballers and spectators alike. The fans would have to pay more or the players accept reduced salaries because of the loss of clubs' income, unless finance outside the game continues to grow despite the recession. And will other smaller clubs follow Aldershot into reduced circumstances?

On another front the England manager Graham Taylor was right when he said that once the League season ends and the FA Cup is out of the way, everyone expects the national side to be up and running for either of the major competitions, the European Championship or the World Cup. But averaging 12 games a season, the international fixture list is itself a formidable addition to the demands on players with clubs in the top echelon of the game.

This coming season will see a further attempt at the prevention of time-wasting with the introduction of a measure to prevent the goalkeeper being brought into action by his own players from up to half the length of the field, by restricting his right to handle the ball at all times. But it was the over-protection of the goalkeeper which caused the original problem. The penalty area has long since become a 'no-go' area when the goalkeeper is in possession.

Off the field, the implementation of the Taylor Report will cost top clubs millions of pounds as they shrink to all-seater capacities by 1994–95. They will claim increased prices of admission are necessary for this reason and that the income from television is insufficient to cover all outgoing costs. But the fans will see it in a different light.

The game is again at the crossroads and it will be a testing time for the FA Premier League. The new body and the Football League must bury their differences and act as neighbours, home and away, with both subject to paying the bill, as the cost of policing the game soars. While arrests at grounds were down last season for the third year in a row, with arrests and ejections at 8556 compared with 9190 the season before, the figures do not represent statistics outside stadia and for those who travel to matches by public transport, there remain too many instances of misbehaviour. Moreover that underlying current of unpleasantness which erupted in Sweden during the European Championship made it obvious that hooliganism is being contained over here, not eradicated. England fans who cause trouble abroad also watch games in England. Hosting the 1996 tournament will be an expensive experience as the FA has already noted.

Alas, there are now so many people in authority who have no personal experience of watching large scale, non-policed football in a less enlightened age, they accept the present, citing it as society's curse and wrongly assuming football has always had a problem of spectator indiscipline on a scale comparable with recent decades. Life's hour glass cannot be upturned, but the encouragement of family participation and the community in football has to be the way forward – if the price is right.

ROTHMANS FOOTBALL AWARDS

Rothmans Football Awards are presented to clubs and players who have achieved success and enriched the game during the past season. They also reveal the wide ranging nature of the book itself.

BURNLEY FOOTBALL CLUB won the championship of the Fourth Division in 1991–92 and erased the memory of how near they came to losing their Football League status in 1987. It was only on the last day of that season that they managed to beat Leyton Orient and stay in Division Four. From that moment interest in the club has grown and support at home and away has been the envy of many clubs in higher divisions. This befits a club which is proud to have been one of the founder members of the Football League in 1888 and now intends to further improve its standing. The basis for optimism is in place.

COLCHESTER UNITED FOOTBALL CLUB achieved a double last season, winning the GM Vauxhall Conference to regain its position in the Football League and taking the FA Trophy. They return to the League fold after two years absence. The club made its name as FA Cup giant-killers in the years immediately after the Second World War and entered the old Third Division (South) in 1950. Cup fighting traditions remained and reached a peak in 1971 when they defeated Leeds United 3-2 in a fifth round FA Cup tie at Layer Road. Last season they were unbeaten in their last 12 League games.

STEVE McMANAMAN was born in Liverpool and raised as an Evertonian. But he is now an established member of Liverpool Football Club and gave a stunning second-half performance on the flanks in the 1992 FA Cup Final. He toyed with, then tortured the Sunderland defence with his confident running, close control and natural swerve. All this at the age of 20. He had the unusual experience of making as many England Under-21 appearances in his first season as he achieved in the Football League – just two in 1990–91. A versatile attacker he can play on either flank or in the middle.

GORDON STRACHAN is no stranger to winning awards but his leadership by example enabled Leeds United to win the Football League championship in 1991–92. At the age of 35 he was an inspirational captain displaying the stamina and enthusiasm of a younger man. This was achieved despite a niggling back injury which forced him out of Scotland's European Championship final team in Sweden. He has won Player of the Year awards on either side of the border in a career with Dundee, Aberdeen, Manchester United and Leeds. Last season provided another milestone for him.

KAREN WALKER of England was outstanding in women's football last season for the highly successful Doncaster Belles. She finished as leading scorer in the National League with 36 goals and her feat of scoring a hat-trick or more in every round of the cup may not be repeated by anyone who follows her in the future. Her total of cup goals reached 22 and she failed to score in only one game in 1991–92. The Belles had such appeal that they remained unbeaten in both senior competitions, in what was the inaugural season for a national league.

IAN WRIGHT was the leading scorer in Football League matches in 1991–92 with 29 goals, five of which were scored while with Crystal Palace, the remaining 24 coming from his efforts for Arsenal. He joined the Highbury club in September for a fee of £2.5 million and the move enhanced his already strong reputation as a sharp, incisive marksman. His haul included four against Everton and three against Southampton. He considered Arsenal to be the most effective First Division team in the last three months of the season and much credit must go to the England striker for their marked improvement during this period.

MILESTONES DIARY 1991–92

June 1991

14   **Sixteen First Division clubs** sign a document of intent to join the **Premier League**; 3 do not vote and only 3 are against. In the **Queen's Birthday Honours**, there are **knighthoods** for **FA chairman Bert Millichip** and **Everton chairman** and former **League president Philip Carter**, while **Nottingham Forest** manager **Brian Clough** gets the OBE. **Rangers** pay **Hibs £1m** for keeper **Andy Goram**.

15   **Kaiserslautern** win the **German Bundesliga**.

16   **Bobby Robson's PSV Eindhoven** win the **Dutch championship**.

17   **Trevor Francis** is named **Sheffield Wednesday manager**. **Alan Murray** takes over at **Hartlepool** from **Cyril Knowles**, who has undergone his third **brain operation**.

18   **Lou Macari** leaves **Birmingham City** to become **Stoke manager**.

19   **Liam Brady** ends **Celtic manager's** job. The FA unveil their 119-page **Blueprint for the Future of Football**: It includes the establishment of an **FA-governed Premier League** for 1992–93 of **22 clubs** reducing to **18**; a minimum requirement for Premier League clubs of a **20,000 all-seat stadium**; **live TV coverage** of a Premier League match every week and of all **England's internationals**; and a new **Football League of 70 clubs**, 22 in the First Division, 24 in the Second and 24 in the Third.

20   As news of a **Sugar-Venables** victory in the struggle for **Spurs** emerges, Second Division **Blackburn** make a **£2m** bid for **Gary Lineker**. **England** fail to reach the last eight of the **World Youth Cup**.

21   The Football League Executive Staffs' Association (**FLESA**) is reorganized as the **Institute of Football Management and Administration**, with separate branches for managers, coaches, administrators and commercial managers. **England** make an official complaint to **FIFA** over the goalless draw played out by **Spain** and **Syria** that eliminated them from the **World Youth Cup** in Portugal.

22   A **£7.25m takeover of Spurs** is finally signed, with **Terry Venables** as non-executive managing director and **Alan Sugar** as non-executive chairman, each putting up the money equally.

24   **Glasgow Rangers** sign Soviet midfielder **Alexei Mikhailichenko** from Italian champions **Sampdoria** for a **Scottish record £2m**. **Colin Todd** resigns as manager of **Middlesbrough**.

25   **Colin Todd** cites **board interference** as reason for his resignation. **UEFA** confirm new structure of **European Cup**, with **last eight** to be split into **groups of four** to produce finalists.

28   **Fifteen First Division clubs** meeting at Lancaster Gate agree to **resign** from the **Football League**, with the others expected to follow suit. **FA Cup ties** that end in a **draw** after the **first replay** are to be decided on **penalties**. Players sent off for **'serious foul play'** (the so-called **'professional foul'**) will be **banned for one match** instead of three. **Everton's Norman Whiteside**, 26, **retires** after a vain struggle against a knee injury. **Terry Yorath** is invited to become **full-time manager of Wales**. **Bobby Charlton loses his place** on the **FA Council**.

29   As the number of **First Division clubs resigning** from the League reaches **20**, their newly elected **chairman**, public relations adviser **Rick Parry**, confirms they will either **follow the FA or go it alone**.

30   The **FA's summer meeting** in Torquay fails to shed any light on the continuing saga of the proposed new **'Super League'** even though all **22 First Division clubs** are now committed to **resigning** from the **Football League**. **Portugal** beat **Brazil** on **penalties** to win the **World Youth Cup**.

July

2   **Martin Dobson** is new **Bristol Rovers manager**, leaving GM Conference club **Northwich Victoria** after only four weeks in charge. After talks with **Birmingham City**, **Peter Shilton** will not become manager.

3   **Aston Villa** sign **Dalian Atkinson** from **Real Sociedad** for **£1.6m**.

8   **Arsenal, Manchester United** and **Spurs** sign a lucrative deal with **ITV** for **exclusive coverage** of their **home ties in Europe** this season. **Chelsea** sign **Paul Elliott** from **Celtic** for **£1.4m**.

9   A **League transfer tribunal** rules that **Leeds** must pay **Chelsea £1.3m** for **Tony Dorigo** and **Southampton £1.6m** for **Rod Wallace**.

10   After nine years as **Charlton manager**, **Lennie Lawrence** moves on to **Middlesbrough**.

12   **Liverpool** complete the signing of **Mark Wright** from **Derby** for **£2.2m**.

13   Ailing **Brazil** plumb the depths with a **2-0 defeat** by **Colombia** in the **South American Championships**.

14   **Liverpool** pip **Everton** and **Forest** to sign **Dean Saunders** from **Derby** for a **British record £2.9m**.

15   **Germany** beat **Norway 3-1** after extra time in the final of the **European Women's Championship**.

16   Thanks to a last-minute goal, **Brazil** beat **Ecuador 3-1** and qualify on goal difference for the semi-finals of the **South American Championships**. **Don Howe** returns to **Wimbledon** as **coach**.

17   The majority of **First Division clubs** sign a **'founder members document'** locking them into a new **Premier League**; the **Second Division clubs**, who are not consulted, are reminded that they will not figure in the new plans but are offered **three-up** promotion while the **Premier League** has 22 clubs.

18   **Nottingham Forest** sign **Teddy Sheringham** from **Millwall** for **£2m** and **Celtic** complete the signing of **Tony Cascarino** from **Aston Villa** for **£1.1m**. In the High Court, the **FA** successfully apply for the hearing of the **League's £9m-plus damages claim** to be **delayed** until the courts decide whether their plans for a breakaway **Premier League** are legal.

20   **David Platt** signs for Italian club **Bari**, who pay **Villa** a **British record £5.5m**.

22   **Liverpool's Ian Rush** has his Achilles' tendon encased in plaster and will **miss start of season**. **Charlton** confirm that **The Valley** will **not be ready** for the start of the new season.

23 **Spurs** promote chief coach and former manager **Peter Shreeves** to **team manager**, with full responsibility for team selection under **Terry Venables**. **Leeds** announce **record sponsorship** deal of **£7.1m** over five years with **Admiral** sportswear.

24 Home Office figures show **arrests fell by 31 per cent** and **ejections by 27 per cent** last season. **Charlton** appoint two **player-coaches**, Alan Curbishley and Steve Gritt, to replace **Lennie Lawrence**; the club will play their **first three home matches at Upton Park**. **Real Madrid** bid **£4.4m** for **Forest's Des Walker**.

25 **West Brom's Graham Roberts** escapes punishment for **failing a drugs test** in March, but the **FA** warn that in future players could expect **strong action** even if **drugs** are taken innocently.

31 **Robert Maxwell** completes sale of **Derby County** to consortium led by new chairman **Brian Fearn**.

August

1 **Everton** sign **Peter Beardsley** from **Liverpool** for **£1m**. Crystal Palace manager Steve Coppell launches **attack** on FA's **Premier League** proposals.

2 **Liverpool** sell another star, **Steve Staunton** going to **Aston Villa** for **£1.1m**.

4 **Sampdoria** win the **Makita International** tournament at Highbury, **beating Arsenal on penalties**.

5 **Manchester United** sign **Paul Parker** from QPR for **£2m**.

6 **Manchester City** pay Wimbledon **£2.5m** for **Keith Curle**, a **British record** for a **defender**, and sell **Mark Ward** to **Everton** for **£1.3m**. **Exeter** appoint **Alan Ball** as **manager**. **Coventry fine and transfer-list Kenny Sansom, Trevor Peake** and **Lloyd McGrath** for a drinking session on their Scottish tour last week. **Harry Cavan** is re-elected **president** of the **Irish FA** for a world-record **33rd year**.

8 Former **manager Graeme Souness** pays **Glasgow Rangers £1.25m** to bring **Mark Walters** to **Liverpool**.

9 **Birmingham** appoint **Terry Cooper manager**.

10 **Arsenal** and **Spurs** draw 0-0 and share the **Charity Shield**. **Terry Fenwick** making a comeback for Spurs after two years. Scottish champions **Rangers** open the new season with a **6-0** mauling of **St Johnstone**, helped by a **Mark Hateley hat-trick**. The **1991 Football Offences Act** comes into effect – **throwing objects** on to the pitch or at spectators, **running on to the pitch** without good reason, or **chanting** racist or indecent **slogans** are now all punishable by **heavy fines** and **exclusion** from matches.

11 The **FA** withdraw **England's** bid for the **1998 World Cup** finals to concentrate on their application for the **1996 European Championships**. **Over 33,000** turn up at **Old Trafford** in a **testimonial** for **Sir Matt Busby**, paying **£250,000** to see **Manchester United draw 1-1** with a **Republic of Ireland XI**.

12 A lengthy meeting of the **Football League management committee** ends in stalemate because, with the four members of the proposed **Premier League** ineligible to vote, they cannot form a quorum.

13 The **Third** and **Fourth Division** clubs, while recognizing the inevitability of the new **Premier League**, warn they will **boycott the FA Cup** if their position is undermined. **Wimbledon coach Don Howe resigns**. **Crystal Palace** and **Wimbledon** have to postpone their first home matches because building work at **Selhurst Park** is behind schedule.

14 **Spurs** sign **Gordon Durie** from **Chelsea** for **£2m**. **Sheffield Wednesday** sign **England goalkeeper Chris Woods** from **Glasgow Rangers** for **£1.2m**.

15 Former Walker Cup golfer **Dr David Marsh** is **Everton's new chairman**, replacing **Sir Philip Carter** who steps down after 13 years. **Glasgow Rangers** sell **Trevor Steven** to **Olympique Marseille** for a **Scottish record £5m** and pay **Everton £1.2m** for **Stuart McCall**. At the launch of the **22nd** *Rothmans Football Yearbook*, FA chief **Graham Kelly** offers the **Football League** the chance to come under the **FA's** umbrella, operating side by side with the **Premier League**. Meanwhile the **League's** reconvened **management committee** meeting again fails to reach agreement with **League president Bill Fox** still insisting that the **Premier League** will never happen.

16 The **22 First Division clubs** hand in their **resignations** to the **Football League**, which is preparing to start the new season virtually leaderless and without a management committee.

17 The **opening** of the **Football League season** is overshadowed by the behind-the-scenes wrangling, as **Sunderland chairman Bob Murray** circulates all **League clubs** with unconvincing plans to isolate the proposed **Premier League** members, while the **FA** threaten to charge players who, backed by the **PFA, refuse mandatory drug tests**. Action on the field produces one more goal than last season's start, thanks largely to **Crewe's 7-4 win at newcomers Barnet**. **Seven players are sent off.**

18 **Bob Murray** keeps on the warpath, promising to back any **strike** called by the **PFA** over the proposed **Premier League**. Scottish FA secretary **Jim Farry** blames player ignorance of the **new laws** for the spate of **sendings-off (16)** in the first week of their season.

19 The **Football League farce** continues . . . assistant secretary **Andy Williamson** welcomes growing support for **Sunderland's** plans to isolate the **breakaway clubs**, but **League** commercial director **Trevor Phillips** warns the **militant Second Division clubs** that they would face financial ruin.

20 The **Football League** go to the **High Court** for the appointment of an **administrator** to run the collapsed **management committee** – chief executive **Arthur Sandford** and **Ian Watt** of accountants Peat Marwick McLintock are appointed as **joint receivers** and managers of the **League** until 2 October. **Barnet** host another goal glut, **drawing 5-5 with Brentford** in the first round of the **Rumbelows Cup**.

21 **Spurs** mark their return to **Europe** with a **1-0 win** over part-timers **Sparkasse Stockerau** in Vienna in the Preliminary round of the **Cup-Winners' Cup**. In the Italian Cup, **David Platt** marks his debut for **Bari** by **missing a penalty** in their embarrassing, **goalless home draw** with **Third Division Empoli**.

22 The **Football League** confirms that **Sunderland's** proposal to **halt relegation and promotion** from and to the new **Premier League** cannot begin this season. **Charlton** learn that **The Valley** will not now be ready until the New Year and face League action.

23 John Barnes of Liverpool undergoes an **Achilles' tendon operation** which will keep him out for at least a month. **Terry Fenwick** of **Spurs** is bailed until next month on a **drink-driving charge.**

24 After three games, **Manchester City** are the only **First Division** club with a **100 per cent record. Barnet** chalk up their **first ever win** in the **Football League** with a **1-0** victory at **Mansfield. Aberdeen** and **Hearts** maintain their **100 per cent record** in **Scotland** after four matches.

26 Compulsory **drug testing** is suspended after a clear-the-air meeting between the **FA, PFA** and the **Association of Managers and Secretaries.**

27 **Arsenal's first win** of the season, **2-0** over **Luton**, is marred by **Anders Limpar's dismissal.**

28 **Manchester United** leapfrog over neighbours **City** to the **top** of the **First Division** thanks to a late **McClair goal** against **Oldham. Stuart Pearce** collects the **PFA Fair Play award** for **Nottingham Forest** and is then **sent off** for swearing as they go down **3-1** at home to **Spurs. Manager Brian Clough** threatens to quit **Forest** if a ground-sharing scheme with **Notts County** materializes. The **League** allow **Charlton** to extend their **ground-sharing** agreement with **West Ham** for at least another three months. **Vernon Edwards,** former **doctor** to the **England** team, **dies.**

29 **David Moores** takes over as **chairman** of **Liverpool** as **Noel White** steps down.

30 **Liverpool**, despite a mounting **injury problem**, beat **Everton 3-1** and move up to within a point of **Manchester United**, who are **held at home by Leeds**, while **Arsenal end Manchester City's unbeaten record. Aberdeen** and **Hearts** stay **top** in **Scotland** despite figuring in **goalless draws. Nottingham Forest** sign winger **Kingsley Black** from **Luton** for **£1.5m. Ghana** beat **Spain 1-0** in **Italy** to win the **Under-17 World Cup.** Former **England** and **Spurs** back **Cyril Knowles** dies at 47.

September

2 **Spurs suspend Paul Walsh** indefinitely after an incident when he was substituted at a reserve game that left **team manager Ray Clemence** with **facial injuries. Blackburn dismiss manager** of 4½ years **Don Mackay. Maidstone manager Graham Carr** resigns. **Graham Taylor** includes **Arsenal's Paul Merson** and **Spurs' Paul Stewart** in his **squad** to play **Germany** next week.

4 A **1-0 win** over **Stockerau** at White Hart Lane puts **Spurs** through to the 1st round of the **European Cup-Winners' Cup 2-0** on aggregate. In **Division Four, Barnet** win **6-0** at **Lincoln.**

5 **FA** chief **Graham Kelly** threatens to take **court action** and possibly **shut down** this season's **League competition** if the **League** continue to **oppose** the proposed **Premier League.**

7 Lowest **First Division** attendance since the war, **3,231**, sees **Wimbledon** beat **Luton 3-0** at Selhurst Park. **Arsenal** go down **2-1** to **Coventry**, their first **League home defeat** for 18 months. The **last 100 per cent record** in the **League** goes as **Third Division Birmingham** are **held 1-1** at **Reading. Hearts** go top in **Scotland** as **Aberdeen** lose **4-0** at home to lowly **St Johnstone.**

9 The **FA** agree to the **League's** insistence on **three-up and three-down** but find their various cash demands unacceptable; they give the **League** until **2pm** tomorrow to accept their proposals.

10 **Graham Taylor** picks tour success **John Salako** (Palace) to face **Germany** tomorrow in a friendly at Wembley. In an **Under-21 friendly England** beat **Germany 2-1** at Scunthorpe, while **Scotland U-21s** win a **European** group match **3-0** away to **Switzerland.** The **FA** receive a **setback** when the **22 First Division** clubs change sides in the debate over the **League's** demands.

11 **Germany** beat **England 1-0**, while in other friendlies **Wales** beat **Brazil 1-0** at Cardiff Arms Park and **Ireland** win **2-1** in **Hungary. Scotland** draw their crucial **European Championship** match in **Switzerland** from two goals down so stay one point behind the Swiss but with a game in hand. **Northern Ireland** beat the **Faeroes 5-0** in **Sweden.** Both the **FA** and the **League** serve notice of further **court actions.**

12 **Crystal Palace chairman Ron Noades** makes some controversial generalities in a **TV documentary** about **black footballers** in Britain which fails to get to grips with **racism** at football grounds.

14 **Ron Noades** apologizes in the **Palace** programme for his **TV** comments about **black players.** Performance of the day goes to **Third Division Huddersfield** who take a point after being **4-0** down at **Bury.**

15 The **PFA** are to report **Palace chairman Ron Noades** to the **FA** for 'bringing the game into disrepute'.

16 Yet another meeting of **FA, League** and **First Division** representatives ends in **stalemate**, the sticking point being the **amount of League compensation.** Three **Leicester fans** successfully **sue Millwall** for the 'extremely poor view' from the away enclosure at **the Den** and **win a refund** of a third of their admission money and travelling expenses.

17 **Spurs** go down **1-0** to **Hajduk Split** in the first leg of their **Cup-Winners' Cup** tie, played in **Austria** because of the civil strife in **Yugoslavia.** The **PFA withdraw** their complaint against **Ron Noades** after a **further apology** and 'the matter is now closed'.

18 **Arsenal** and **Liverpool** celebrate their return to **Europe** with **6-1 wins** over **FK Austria** and **Kuusysi Lahti (Finland)**, respectively, with **Alan Smith (Arsenal)** and **Dean Saunders (Liverpool)** both hitting **4 goals.** But **Manchester United** are held to a **goalless draw** by **Athinaikos** in Athens and **Glasgow Rangers** lose **1-0** to **Sparta** in Prague. **Cork City** gain a creditable **home draw** against **Bayern Munich.** Meanwhile **FA chairman Sir Birt Millichip** threatens to suspend **League competition** unless an agreement on the **Premier League** can be reached. **Diego Maradona** receives a **suspended 14-month jail sentence** in **Italy** for **drug offences.**

19 The **FA** and the **League** finally end more than four months of wrangling, as the **League** accept payments of **£2m** from the **FA** and **£1m** from the **Premier League** clubs for the next five years, as opposed to the annual **£6m** they had demanded for 50 years. **Liverpool's John Barnes** is to have an **Achilles' tendon operation.** A **UEFA statute** change will allow **Israeli clubs** to play in **European** competitions.

20 **Spurs' Terry Fenwick** is **jailed** for four months on **drink-drive** charges.

21 **Gary Lineker scores 4** for **Spurs** in their **5-3 win over Wimbledon** at Selhurst Park. **Manchester United** and **Arsenal** also hit **5** as **46 goals** are registered in the **First Division**, including a **hat-trick** for **Peter Beardsley** in **Everton's 3-0** defeat of **Coventry**.

23 The new **Premier League**, run by the **FA**, becomes official and will **begin in 1992**, as the **League's Rule 11**, stipulating a three-year period of notice for resignation from the League, is finally **revoked** on a **51½ to 9** vote. The so-called **Super League** will have **22 clubs** reducing to **20**. **Arsenal** pay **Crystal Palace £2.5m** for England striker **Ian Wright**.

24 **Wimbledon** chalk-up another unfortunate **attendance record**, this time in the **Rumbelows League Cup**, only **2,081** seeing their **2-1 defeat** by **Third Division** Peterborough, the **lowest gate** to watch a **First Division club** at home in the League Cup. Andy Ritchie scores **4** in **Oldham's 7-1 hammering** of **Torquay**. **Dunfermline beat Airdrie on penalties** to reach the **Skol Cup final**.

25 **Third Division** sides have a field day in the **Rumbelows** first-leg matches – **Stoke draw 2-2 at Liverpool, Birmingham 2-2 at Luton**, and **Swansea beat Spurs 1-0** at the Vetch Field. **Chelsea** are held **1-1** at home by **Second Division** Tranmere. **Ian Wright** scores on his debut in **Arsenal's 1-1 draw** at **Leicester**. **Hibs beat Rangers 1-0** in the second **Skol Cup semi-final**.

26 **Crystal Palace sign Marco Gabbiadini** from Sunderland for **£1.8m** to replace **Ian Wright**. **England** and **Arsenal** winger **Joe Hulme dies** at 87.

27 The **FA** finally – and two months late – **sanction the League season**.

28 A late **Bryan Robson winner** at Spurs takes **Manchester United 6 points clear** at the top of the **First Division** and an **Ian Wright hat-trick** in **Arsenal's 4-0 win** at **Southampton** helps the slow-starting champions into third spot. **Aberdeen beat Rangers 2-0** at Ibrox to go **second** behind **Hearts**, whose **2-1 victory** at **Falkirk** makes it five out of five away from home. **Spurs' Paul Gascoigne** is taken to **hospital** after an **incident** in a **Newcastle nightclub**.

29· **Gascoigne** has a further **operation** on his **knee**, setting back his recovery another two months and jeopardizing his **move to Lazio**.

October

1 **Monaco thrash Swansea 8-0** in the **Cup-Winners' Cup (10-1 agg.)**. In the **UFEA Cup**, brave **Cork** hold out for 75 minutes against **Bayern Munich** in Germany before **going down 2-0** and out 3-1 on aggregate, while an **away draw** is enough to see **Celtic** through against **Ekeren of Belgium**. **Leeds** lose their **unbeaten record** in the First Division, going down **1-0** to Crystal Palace. In a remarkable **Zenith Cup** match, **Tranmere beat Newcastle** on penalties after a **6-6 draw** after extra time.

2 All the **English sides in Europe** progress to the next round, **1-0 defeats** for **Arsenal** and **Liverpool** making only small dents in their huge first-leg margins. But **Manchester United** come through **2-0** against **Athinaikos** only after being held to a **goalless draw** at Old Trafford over 90 minutes, and **Spurs' 2-0 victory** is just enough to beat **Hajduk Split**. But **Rangers** got out of the **Champions Cup**, **losing on away goals** despite beating Sparta Prague 2-1, and **Motherwell** suffer a similar fate in the **Cup-Winners' Cup**. **Aberdeen** complete Scotland's misery, **crashing out** of the **UEFA Cup 3-0** on aggregate, while all three **Northern Ireland** representatives are also **eliminated**. **UEFA Cup** holders **Inter Milan** go out to **Boavista** of Portugal. **Wimbledon** record the **lowest First Division attendance** since the war – **3,121** against **Sheffield Wednesday**. **Crystal Palace** and England winger **John Salako** is ruled out for three months after an **operation** for **damaged ligaments** sustained against **Leeds**.

3 **Liverpool** captain **Ronnie Whelan** returns to hospital for a second **operation** on his damaged **knee**. **John McGrath** becomes Halifax manager following the dismissal of **Jim McCalliog**.

4 Manager **Martin Dobson** leaves Bristol Rovers by mutual consent after only 11 games in charge.

5 With leaders **Manchester United** playing tomorrow, **Leeds** creep to within three points, although bottom club **Sheffield United** almost claw back a four-goal deficit. **Tony Cottee** hits a **hat-trick** as **Everton beat Spurs 3-1**. **Second Division** leaders **Middlesbrough lose 2-1** to bottom club **Bristol Rovers**, **Newcastle** now go to **bottom**. **Aberdeen** lead the **Scottish Premier Division** as **Hearts** are **beaten 3-1** by **Celtic**, for whom substitute **Tony Cascarino** scores his **first goal** and is **sent off**.

6 **Liverpool** hold **Manchester United** to a goalless draw at Old Trafford, where **Liverpool's Gary Ablett** and **United's Mark Hughes** are **sent off**.

7 **Bryan Robson** is **recalled** to **England's** injury-depleted **squad** for the **European Championship** game against **Turkey**, while **manager Graham Taylor slams FA** plans for a **22-club Premier League** next season. **Wimbledon** appoint **Peter Withe** manager. **Manchester City** winger **David White** breaks a **shoulder** in training and is out for six weeks.

8 Four months after leading **Torquay** back to the **Third Division**, manager **John Impey** is **sacked** together with his **assistant John Turner**. **John Aldridge's** controversial **penalty** for Tranmere helps knock **Chelsea** out of the **Rumbelows Cup**, while **Wimbledon** go out to Peterborough. **Hibs** lose their first game of the season **4-2** to **Rangers**, who go top of the **Scottish Premier Division**.

9 In the **Rumbelows Cup**, **Grimsby** eliminate Aston Villa on away goals. **Liverpool** scrape through **3-2** at brave **Stoke**, but **Port Vale** beat **First Division** Notts County on away goals.

10 The **first meeting** of the **Premier League** takes place and **task forces** are set up to work on rules and constitution. With a serious injury problem in central defence, **Graham Taylor** calls **Spurs' Gary Mabbutt** into the **England squad**. **England's travel** is to be **sponsored by American Airlines** to the tune of £100,000 a year.

12 No First Division football because of Wednesday's internationals. **Second Division Blackburn Rovers** grab the headlines, announcing their **new manager, Kenny Dalglish**, with **Ray Harford** as his **assistant**, and the pair see their **new club beat Plymouth 5-2**. In the **Third Division**, former Southampton star **Steve Moran scores four** for **Exeter**. In Scotland, **Hearts** scrape a **late winner** at home to bottom club **Dunfermline**. **Rangers win 3-2** at **St Johnstone**, but their respective **managers, Walter Smith** and **Alex Totten**, are to be **reported to the police** for a clash in the players' tunnel at half-time.

15 Southampton's **Alan Shearer** keeps up his goalscoring record at **Under-21** level with **both goals** in **England's 2-0** defeat of **Turkey** at Reading, but the result is academic as **Poland** earlier **clinched** the **group** with a **2-0** victory over the **Republic of Ireland**. **Scotland's Under-21s** win **3-1** in **Romania**. **Liverpool's injury crisis** worsens with keeper **Mike Hooper out** for two months. **Azeglio Vicini** is forced to **resign** after five years as **Italy's coach**.

16 In the third and final hearing relating to the **1985 Heysel disaster**, Belgium's highest court **confirms** the earlier **convictions** of former **UEFA** secretary-general **Hans Bangerter** (three-month suspended sentence for gross negligence) and **UEFA** itself (ordered to compensate victims of the tragedy and their families). In the **European Championships** qualifying groups, the **Republic of Ireland's 3-3 draw** in **Poland** after leading 3-1 and **England's** disappointing **1-0** defeat of **Turkey** at Wembley mean that England have to get a point in their last game in Poland to go through. **Scotland's 1-0** defeat in **Romania** now leaves **Switzerland favourites** to qualify from **Group 2**, and **Germany's 4-1** defeat of **Wales** give them the edge in Group 5. **Wales's Dean Saunders** is **sent off**.

18 **Arrigo Sacchi** is appointed **Italy's coach**.

19 Champions **Arsenal** hold League leaders **Manchester United** to **1-1 draw** at Old Trafford. In **Scotland**, **Rangers** beat **Hearts 2-0** to take their place at the top.

21 **Millwall** sack manager **Steve Harrison**, the **England coach**, for **'personal misconduct'**. Aberdeen manager **Alex Smith** is **banned** from the touchline for a year and fined £1,000 for an **offence against** the referee in a **Skol Cup** tie against Airdrie in August. **England's 1966 World Cup** winning squad get together to celebrate the **25th anniversary** of their triumph; manager **Sir Alf Ramsey** criticizes not only the performance of the current **England side** against Turkey, but also the **team selection**.

22 **Celtic**, the only Scottish side through to the **2nd round of European** matches, **crash 5-1** to **Neuchatel** in the **UEFA Cup** first leg, with **Egyptian** international **Hossam Hassan** scoring 4 for the Swiss side. Mighty **Bayern Munich** suffer a similar humiliation, **going down 6-2** to **BK 1903 Copenhagen**.

23 A mixed night for English clubs in **Europe** sees **Arsenal** hold **Benfica 1-1** in Lisbon in the **Champions' Cup** and **Spurs** beat **FC Porto 3-1** in the **Cup-Winners' Cup**, while holders of the latter trophy **Manchester United go down 3-0** to **Atletico** in **Madrid**, conceding two goals in the last three minutes, and **Liverpool lose 2-0 to Auxerre** in France in the **UEFA Cup**. In domestic football, **Coventry player-manager Terry Butcher**, making a **comeback** after nine months out with injury, is **sent off** in a **Zenith Cup** match against **Aston Villa**, and **York** sack **manager John Bird**.

24 **Steve Harrison** joins coaching staff at **Crystal Palace**.

25 **Wales** captain **Kevin Ratcliffe** is out for four weeks after a knee **operation**.

26 **Manchester United** lose the only **unbeaten record** in the League, with **3-2** defeat at **Sheffield Wednesday**, and **lose top spot** to **Leeds**, who beat **Oldham 1-0** thanks to a **Brian Kilcline own goal** and **lead** the **League** for the first time since the days of **Don Revie**, 17 years ago. Other divisional leaders to be toppled are **West Bromwich**, losing their lead in the **Third** to **Birmingham**, who beat them **1-0** at the Hawthorns in front of **26,168**, the fifth biggest gate of the day in England. **Rangers** retain the lead in **Scotland** on goal difference despite being **held at Ibrox by Falkirk**. **Celtic** win **5-0 away to St Mirren**, whose **manager David Hay** threatens to **withhold** his players' **wages**.

27 **Hibs** beat **Dunfermline 2-0** at Hampden Park in the **final** of the **Skol Cup** to record their first major success for 19 years. **Steve Harrison resigns** his post as **England coach**.

29 **Liverpool** are again **held 2-2** at Anfield in the **Rumbelows Cup** by a Potteries side, this time **Port Vale**. **Rangers** lose **3-2 to Dundee United**, but **stay top** of the **Scottish Premier** on goal difference.

30 **Arsenal** are dumped out of the **Rumbelows Cup 1-0 by Coventry** at Highfield Road. Holders **Sheffield Wednesday** are **held 1-1** at home by **Southampton**, while last year's runners-up **Manchester United scramble a 3-1 victory** over **Portsmouth** at Old Trafford. **Aberdeen beat Motherwell 3-1** and go **top** of the **Scottish Premier** on goal difference from **Hearts**.

31 **Crystal Palace's Steve Coppell** is the latest **manager** to join the call for a **reduction** in the number of **teams** in the **Premier League**.

November

2 Thanks to the televising of **rugby's World Cup**, **21 clubs** suffer their **lowest gate** of the season. Only **89 goals** are scored in the **44 League matches**, one of them, the winner for **Maidstone** against **Hereford**, from a **punt** by keeper Iain Hesford – in front of the **season's lowest gate** to date, **846**. Only **9 goals** are scored in the **11 First Division** games. **Manchester United** go back to **top** of the League with a **2-0** home victory over bottom club **Sheffield United** as **Leeds** play a goalless draw at Wimbledon. **Manager Billy Bremner resigns** from the League's bottom club, **Doncaster**. **Hearts** return to the **top** in Scotland with a **1-1 draw at Hibs** as all five at the top fail to win.

4 Not in **England's squad** for the vital **European Championship** match in **Poland**, **Bryan Robson** announces his **retirement** from **international football**. **Graham Taylor** also **omits Chris Waddle** and **Trevor Steven**, both on duty for **Marseille** three days before the match, and **includes Andy Gray**, **Tony Daley**, **Andy Sinton** and **Keith Curle**. **Andy Roxburgh** restores **Richard Gough** to the **Scotland squad**. **Glasgow Rangers** sign **Dale Gordon** from Norwich for **£1.2m**. A meeting of **First Division clubs** (nine attend) come out **against** the suggestion of **full-time professional referees** for the **Premier League**.

5 **Robert Maxwell** is **found dead** in the sea after going missing from his yacht off Tenerife. **John Ward**, England Under-21 and **'B' team coach**, takes over at **York City**.

6 Of the **British hopes** in action in **Europe**, only **Liverpool go through** to the next round. **Arsenal** **lose** in extra time to **Benfica**, while **Manchester United** and **Celtic** find their first-leg deficits too much for them, **Liverpool**, however, get the 3 goals they need to **beat Auxerre 3-2 on aggregate**. A **goalless draw** at **Charlton** is enough to take **Swindon** to the **top** of the Second Division.

7   **Spurs** reach the **last eight** of the **European Cup-Winners' Cup** with a **goalless draw** in **Oporto**. With England's ranks further depleted by injuries in European matches, **Graham Taylor** drafts **Chelsea's** central defender **Paul Elliott** and **Arsenal's Davis Rocastle** into his **squad**. The FA seek a firm commitment from clubs entering the **Premier League** to rapid reduction to an **18-team competition**. A **League meeting** at Walsall, with 70 of the 72 clubs attending, backs a **'Blueprint for the Future'**, put forward by commercial director **Trevor Phillips**, calling for a **voting structure based on region** rather than division, and a distribution of **cash based on League position**. **Celtic sign Middlesbrough** defender **Tony Mowbray** for **£1m** and announce an eight-year **sponsorship** with **Umbro International** worth **£11m**. **Doncaster** appoint first-team coach **Steve Beaglehole** as new **manager**. The **FA fine Nottingham Forest's Steve Hodge** and **Sheffield United manager Dave Bassett** for making insulting remarks to match officials.

9   No First Division games, but the other divisions get **new leaders** – **Cambridge** in the **Second**, **Brentford** the **Third** and **Barnet** the **Fourth**. **Hearts** stay top in Scotland. **Dale Gordon** scores two on his debut for **Rangers**, who **win 5-0** at **Dunfermline**.

11 **Bradford** sack manager **John Docherty**. Former **Football League president** and **Newcastle United chairman Lord Westwood** dies at 83.

13 **England qualify** for the **European Championship** finals thanks to a late **Lineker** equalizer in **Poland**, which makes unbeaten **Ireland's 3-1 victory** in **Turkey** superfluous. **Romania beat Switzerland 1-0** to keep **Scotland's hopes alive**, but the Scots' inability to score more than **4 goals against San Marino** means that **Romania** can pip them if they win by 2 goals in **Bulgaria** next week. A late **Paul Bodin penalty** gives **Wales victory** over **Luxembourg**, but they need **Belgium to beat Germany** if they are to go through. In other groups **Yugoslavia** qualify at the expense of **Denmark**, 2–1 victors over **Northern Ireland**, and the **USSR** reach the finals, leaving **Italy eliminated**.

14 **Kenny Dalglish** signs **Everton** striker **Mike Newell** for **Blackburn** for **£1.1m**. The **First Division clubs** produce the **basis** of the **Premier League rule book**, a five-page draft, the contents of which are not revealed except that the **League** will definitely **start** with **22 members**.

15 **Hayes** of the **Diadora League** become the season's first **giant-killers**, beating **Fulham 2-0** at Craven Cottage in the first round of the **FA Cup**. **Coventry player-manager Terry Butcher** is to **retire** from playing because of an arthritic knee.

16 **Leeds beat QPR 2-0** to go back on **top** of **Division One** as **Manchester United** are **held 0-0** in the derby at **Maine Road**. More **giant-killing** in the **FA Cup**, with **Enfield winning 1-0** at **Aldershot** and **Crawley humbling Northampton 4-2** to reach the second round for the first time. Seven other **non-League** sides earn **replays** against League opposition, notably **Slough**, who **hold Reading 3-3** with two goals in injury time, and **Telford** who **draw 0-0** at **Stoke**. On the other side of the coin, both **Lincoln United** and **Harlow** suffer **7-0 drubbings** by **Huddersfield** and **Peterborough**, respectively. **Second Division Grimsby** go out **2-1** at **Blackpool**. **Chesterfield** have three players sent off in their **2-1 defeat** at **Darlington**. In Scotland, **Hearts** stay **top** by **beating Celtic 3-1**.

17 In the **first Sheffield Division One derby** for 23 years, **United beat Wednesday 2-0** at Bramall Lane to ease themselves off the bottom of the table.

18 **Everton** sign Scotland striker **Mo Johnston** from **Rangers** for **£1.5m**.

19 A **Brian McClair** goal gives **Manchester United** a **1-0 victory** in the **Super Cup** over **European Champions Red Star Belgrade** at Old Trafford. **Geoff Thomas** heads a late extra-time equalizer for **Crystal Palace** at Selhurst Park to again **deny Third Division Birmingham** victory in their **Rumbelows** third round tie. **Rangers' 3-0 victory** at **Hibs** in the only **Scottish Premier League** game puts them back on **top**. **Coventry manager Terry Butcher** sacks right-hand men **Mick Mills** and **Brian Eastick** on new chairman **Peter Robins's** orders. **Liverpool's Ian Rush** needs a cartilage **operation** and **Manchester City's Peter Reid** has two **cracked ribs**.

20 **Scotland qualify** for the **European finals** as **Romania** fail to beat **Bulgaria**, but **Germany's 1-0 win** in **Belgium** means that **Wales** are virtually **out**. **Gary Lineker** announces a lucrative **deal** with **Japanese** side **Grampus Eight** which means he will **leave Spurs** at the end of the season. **Rumbelows Cup** holders **Sheffield Wednesday** go out **1-0** at **Southampton**, while in other third round replays **Liverpool** and **Manchester City** both **win away**. **Don Howe** becomes **Terry Butcher's new coach** at **Coventry**. **Hearts win 2-0** at **Aberdeen** to take over from **Rangers** at the **top** of the **Scottish Premier**, while at the bottom **Dunfermline** chalk up their **first win**, **1-0 at Falkirk**. Former **Derby** star **Jack Stamps dies** at 72.

21 **Derby County** changes hands for the second time in five months as local businessman **Lionel Pickering** buys a **controlling interest**; he takes over as vice-chairman, with **Brian Fearn** staying in the chair. A **discussion document** prepared jointly by **Aberdeen** and **Rangers** is put before the **Scottish League** management committee, with proposals for **eight-team play-offs** for the title and European places after a **four-week shutdown in January**, and free Saturdays to accommodate international matches.

22 **FIFA** confirm that the newly independent Baltic states of **Estonia**, **Latvia** and **Lithuania**, who joined in 1923 and never resigned, would be **recognized** and entered in the **1994 World Cup**.

23 With **Leeds** not playing, **Manchester United** go back on **top**, beating **West Ham 2-1** at Old Trafford in front of **47,185**, the **League's largest crowd** so far this season. **Sheffield United** chalk up their **first win at Spurs** since 1975 to climb off the bottom. They are emulated, even more sensationally, in the **Third Division**, by **Swansea**, who, with no goals and only one point from their previous seven away matches, **win 6-4 at Bradford**. But the shock of the day is provided in **Scotland** by struggling **St Mirren**, **1-0 winners over Rangers** at Ibrox.

24 **Leeds** go back on **top**, outclassing **Aston Villa**, who had won their previous five League games, by **4-1** at Villa Park.

26 **Rotherham** make **FA Cup history** as the first side ever to **win a tie on penalties, beating Scunthorpe 7-6** after their 1st-round replay is drawn 3-3. **Non-League Telford United beat Third Division Stoke 2-1** in another replay. **Brian Talbot resigns** as both **manager** and **managing director** of Aldershot, whose **financial difficulties** are threatening the existence of the club. The **Football Licensing Authority** contradict the League's assertion that all grounds are now safe, and **warn** that many **clubs do not have a safety officer.**

27 In the **UEFA Cup, Liverpool beat Swarovski Tirol 2-0** in Innsbruck, with both goals from **Dean Saunders**. Two **non-League** sides beat League opposition in **Cup replays**, both after extra time, **Witton 2-1** at Halifax and **Yeovil 1-0** at Walsall, Yeovil chalking up their **14th victory** over **League clubs** to equal **Altrincham's** record. In the second **FA Cup** shoot-out, **Exeter keeper Kevin Miller saves two penalties** and then **scores the winner** himself to eliminate **Colchester**. An independent valuer sets the price of **Stamford Bridge** at **£22.8m**, which **Chelsea** must find by the end of January if they wish to stay there. **Aldershot** are given nine days to pay half their £92,000 **tax bill** or **face being wound up. Bobby Robson** receives an **apology** in the High Court from the *Today* newspaper and is awarded costs and undisclosed **damages for libel.**

28 *World Soccer's* **Player of the Year** is French star **Jean-Pierre Papin (Marseille)**, with **Mark Hughes (Wales** and **Manchester United)** named **fourth**, the best from Britain. **Gary Lineker's** eight-week-old **son** is **seriously ill** in hospital.

29 **Arsenal's Ian Wright, David Seaman** and **Paul Merson** are **charged** with **misconduct** by the **FA** after a police report of **crowd incidents** following their match at **Oldham** on 16 November. **Gary Lineker's** baby **son** is diagnosed as suffering from the rare acute myeloid **leukaemia**.

30 **Gordon Taylor** warns of a possible players' **strike** if the **FA** continue to ignore the players' views over the proposed **Premier League. Leeds** stay **top** with a late **1-0 win** over **Everton** despite having **Chris Fairclough sent off**, while **Manchester United win 3-1** at **Crystal Palace**. In **China**, a **60,000** crowd see the **United States beat Norway 2-1** to win the first ever **women's World Soccer Championship**.

December

1 **Arsenal beat Spurs 2-0** at Highbury in the live televised match.

2 **PFA chief Gordon Taylor** gets unanimous support at the annual meeting for a **players' strike** if the FA don't include them in negotiations, a major grievance being the **treatment of the smaller clubs**. The **Football League** elect **Newcastle's Gordon McKeag** as **chairman** and set up five '**strategy groups**'.

3 **Third Division** giant-killers **Peterborough beat Liverpool 1-0** in the **Rumbelows Cup. Manchester City** go down **2-1** at **Middlesbrough**, and **Crystal Palace** finally **dispose of Birmingham**. **West Ham fine Martin Allen** a week's wages for a **late tackle** on **Carlton Palmer** that left the **Sheffield Wednesday** player with a badly bruised leg on Saturday. **Fulham** part company with **manager Alan Dicks**, and **Ray Lewington** takes temporary charge. **Cliff Bastin** of England and Arsenal **dies** aged 79.

4 **Leeds win 4-1** at **Everton** in the **Rumbelows Cup**, while **Manchester United beat Oldham 2-0** and **Spurs win 2-1** at **Coventry**, **Norwich 2-1** at **West Ham**. In **Scotland**, **Rangers' 3-2 victory** at **Aberdeen** takes them a point closer to **Hearts**, held at home by **Falkirk**.

6 **FIFA** confirm that the **European World Cup qualifying competition** will consist of **five groups of six teams** and **one of seven**, and give permission for matches to start as soon as countries wish. **Spurs supremo Alan Sugar** says the club's **debts** are **down** to a manageable level and announces a proposed **£7m rights issue**. **Paul Gascoigne** is given a **conditional discharge** in a Newcastle court on an assault charge. **Northampton players** boycott training in **protest** over late payment of their wages.

7 **Leeds**, a point ahead, and **Manchester United**, both with good wins, open up a 9-point gap at the top of **Division One** and are **drawn against each other** in both the quarter-finals of the **Rumbelows Cup** and the third round of the **FA Cup**; both ties and a League clash will take place at **Elland Road** over a period of 11 days. In the **Cup**, **Kettering** are the only **non-League** club to **beat League** opposition, winning **2-1** at struggling **Maidstone**. In **Scotland**, **Hearts** and **Rangers** both **win** again.

8 In the **World Cup qualifying draw**, England are set to meet **Poland** and **Turkey** again in a group that also includes the **Netherlands** and **Norway**, while **Scotland** are drawn in **Italy's** group, the two **Irelands** with **Spain** and **Denmark** in the seven-team group, and **Wales** with **Belgium, Czechoslovakia** and **Romania**. Germany captain **Lothar Matthäus** is the first 'official' **World Footballer of the Year**, gaining 128 points in FIFA's poll of international coaches, with **France's Jean-Pierre Papin** (113) 2nd and **England's Gary Lineker** (40) 3rd. The new **Premier League** appoint **Barclays Bank** chairman **Sir John Quinton** as **unpaid, non-executive chairman**. **Red Star Belgrade** beat **Colo Colo (Chile) 3-0** in Tokyo to win the **World Club Championship**.

9 **Blackburn chairman** and **Football League president Bill Fox**, 63, **dies** after a short illness. **Oxford**, having lost the financial support of the Maxwell family, put all **28 players** on the **transfer list** as 4 directors resign, although **Kevin Maxwell** remains as **chairman**. **Bradford City** appoint **Frank Stapleton player-manager**. **FIFA** announce that all international **referees must speak English**.

10 The **Second Division** top-of-the-table clash between **Cambridge** and **Blackburn** is abandoned goalless at half-time owing to frost, which also causes the postponement of several minor cup matches.

11 Another **European hit-trick** for **Dean Saunders** sees **Liverpool** cruise through to the **UEFA Cup** last eight with a **4-0** (6-0 aggregate) victory over **Swarovski Tirol**, **Barry Venison** scoring the fourth on his comeback as a late substitute after being sidelined with injury for 10 months. **Rick Parry**, chief executive designate of the new **Premier League**, confirms a future reduction to **20 teams**.

Millwall agree the **sale of The Den** for **£5.2m** and announce plans for a new **multi-purpose stadium** for 1993–94.

13   **Graeme Souness** persuades **Michael Thomas** to join **Liverpool** for **£1.5m** from **Arsenal**, with a gentleman's agreement that he can play on the Continent if the opportunity arises.

14   Frost and fog in the South bite into the **League** programme, causing **16 postponements**. **Spurs** hold **Leeds 1-1** at Elland Road to end a run of six home wins. **Blackburn go top of Division Two**, above **Cambridge** and **Middlesbrough**, whose game is postponed. **Brentford** only draw at bottom club **Torquay**, where **three players are sent off** (two from Brentford), but stay **top** of **Division Three**. In **Scotland**, leaders **Hearts** and **Rangers** both **win 3-1**.

15   **Manchester United** go back **top** of **Division One**, a point ahead of **Leeds** with a game in hand, after a convincing **3-1 win** at Stamford Bridge. In his programme notes, **Chelsea chairman Ken Bates** slams **Graham Taylor** for arranging an **England B fixture** just before the heavy Christmas schedule. PFA chief **Gordon Taylor** again **castigates** the **Premier League** officials, notably **Sir John Quinton**.

16   **Torquay** defender **John Uzzell**, whose **career** is **threatened** after a facial injury received in Saturday's game against **Brentford**, lodges a formal **complaint** with the police **against Brentford's Gary Blissett**, who was sent off after the incident.

17   **Non-League Farnborough Town** earn a 3rd-round tie with **West Ham**, winning their **FA Cup** replay against **Torquay 4-3**, although they almost blow a four-goal lead in the last 15 minutes. **Palace** and **Forest** will meet in the last eight of the **Rumbelows Cup** after both win away ties **1-0**. **Manchester United** are to **ban away fans** next season while the Stretford End is being converted to an all-seater stand.

18   **Gary Lineker** returns for **Spurs**, who **lose 2-1** at home to **Liverpool**, now 4th in the table. **England B** beat a **Spanish Olympic XI 1-0** in Castellon, **Arsenal's Paul Merson** shaking off a bout of gastro-enteritis to hit the **winner**. **Germany** beat **Luxembourg 4-0** to ensure their **European Championship** qualification above **Wales**. **Brighton manager Barry Lloyd** is made **managing director**. Former **England** and **Sheffield Wednesday** inside-forward **Ronnie Starling dies** at 82.

19   The **Football League** announce their new **three-tiered structure**, headed by a **board of six directors** appointed on a **regional basis**, with an **executive committee** comprising the **senior officers** of the **League** and **Gordon Taylor** of the **PFA** if he accepts the invitation, and a **consultative committee** embracing **people** from a **wider area** of the game. **West Ham** get the local council go-ahead for a **£15.5m development** of Upton Park.

20   **Luton's 1-0 win** over **Coventry** is their first in 15 League matches, but they still remain rooted at the bottom. **Leeds** slap a **life ban** on **19 hooligans** who were convicted for their part in the May 1990 disturbance at **Bournemouth**. **Gordon Taylor** accepts the **League's** invitation to join their new **executive committee**. **AC Milan** pay **Atletico Madrid** a **world record £11.5m** for **Yugoslav** midfielder **Dejan Savicevic**, who will collect about **£7m** over four years.

21   Eight more **postponements**, including **Manchester United's** game with **Villa** due to a waterlogged pitch, reduce an already abbreviated Saturday programme. **Ian Wright**, returning for **Arsenal** after injury, scores all **4 goals** against **Everton**, making it 13 in 12 games since his transfer. **Birmingham** go **top** of **Division Three**, above **Brentford**, who play tomorrow. In **Division Four, Barnet** beat leaders **Mansfield 2-0**, leaving **Burnley** to go **top**. Only 5 of the 19 games in **Scotland** survive, but both **Hearts** and **Rangers win** to stretch their lead to 9 and 7 points respectively above third-placed **Celtic**.

22   **Leeds' goalless draw** at **Forest** takes them level with **Manchester United** at the **top**, but behind on goal difference, while in **Division Two Cambridge's 1-1** draw at **Southend** sees them do likewise behind **Blackburn**. **Brentford** go **top** of **Division Three** with a **3-0 win** over **Exeter**.

26   **Manchester United's 6-3 win** at **Oldham** gives them a 2-point advantage over **Leeds,** who are held **3-3** by **Southampton** at Elland Road. Bottom club **Luton** beat **Arsenal 1-0** to record their second win in seven days. **Forest's Nigel Clough** is **sent off** for the **first time** in his career, at White Hart Lane. In **Division Two, Middlesbrough win** at **Newcastle** and join leaders **Blackburn** and **Cambridge**, who both **draw**, on 41 points at the top. Likewise, in **Division Three, West Brom win** at **Wigan** and join **Brentford** and **Birmingham** on 42 points at the top. The top four clubs in **Division Four** all lose.

27   **Don Mackay**, sacked by Blackburn in September, becomes **Fulham manager** and retains caretaker **Ray Lewington** as assistant. **Arsenal's Anders Limpar** is out for six weeks with a **broken jaw**.

28   With the two leaders doing battle tomorrow, **First Division** interest is at the other end, as **Luton** climb off the bottom with their **third successive victory, 2-0** over **Chelsea** for whom **Tommy Boyd** is **sent off** for a 'professional foul'. **Arsenal's Andy Linighan** is similarly **dismissed** as the champion's hopes of retaining their title take another nosedive with a **1-0 defeat by Manchester City** who go 4th. **Cambridge** go back on **top** of **Division Two** without playing, as leaders **Blackburn lose 2-1** to **Ipswich**, now **3rd**, and **Middlesbrough**, the 4th club on 41 points, **crash 4-0 to Portsmouth**. **West Brom's 1-1 draw** at **Exeter** puts them **top** of **Division Three** as **Brentford** and **Birmingham lose**. In **Scotland**, **Hearts' win 5-0** at **St Johnstone**, who **lose keeper Lindsay Hamilton** after 22 minutes for a 'professional foul', while **Rangers** just **beat** bottom club **Dunfermline 2-1** at Ibrox.

29   **Manchester United** stay **top** of **Division One** thanks to a **1-1** draw at Elland Road in this first of three 'clashes of the Titans', a late **Mel Sterland** penalty for **Leeds** equalizing **Neil Webb's** 47th minute goal. In **Division Two** it is **Blackburn's** turn to go back on **top** without playing, as **Cambridge lose 1-0** at home to the rapidly improving **Watford**.

30   **Sunderland** manager **Denis Smith** goes after 4½ years and assistant **Malcolm Crosby** is appointed **caretaker**. **Terry Venables** announces that **Spurs'** debts of £21m have been **reduced to £5m**.

31   In the **New Year Honours List, England** and **Preston** legend **Tom Finney** is 'promoted' to **CBE** and **England captain Gary Lineker** of **Spurs** earns an **OBE**. As dealing in **Spurs'** shares recommences, they settle at 100p, **up 9p** from the suspended price of 15 months ago.

January 1992

1 **Leeds** go **top** of **Division One** with a **3-1 win** at **West Ham** and stay there as **Manchester United** sensationally **go down 4-1 to QPR** in their late kick-off match at Old Trafford, **Dennis Bailey** hitting them with a hat-trick. In **Division Two**, **Southend** briefly go **top**, **beating Newcastle 4-0** in an early kick-off, but **Blackburn** regain their lead with a **2-1 victory over Cambridge**. **Brentford** regain the lead in **Division Three** thanks to **West Brom's shock 3-2 defeat at home to Fulham**, for whom **Sean Farrell** scores all 3. **Burnley** open up a **5-point lead** in **Division Four**. Lowly **Maidstone** register their first away win of the season, **5-0 at Cardiff**. **Rangers' 3-1 win** at **Celtic** narrows the gap in Scotland to a single point and they are briefly top before **Hearts regain the lead**. **Aldershot's** survival seems assured as new **chairman Simon Hume-Kendall**, who will resign his post as Crystal Palace director, promises to clear their Inland Revenue debts.

2 **Chelsea's Vinny Jones** is fined £1,500 by the FA for making obscene gestures at the Highbury crowd in October. **Liverpool's Ian Rush** needs further knee surgery and will be out for another six weeks.

3 **Sheffield United's Simon Tracey** and **Carl Bradshaw** refuse to pay FA fines for alleged gestures to the crowd at the **Sheffield Wednesday** match in November. **Gary Lineker's** son is no longer critical.

4 Lowly **Wrexham**, last season's 92nd club, **knock out champions Arsenal 2-1** in the **3rd round** of the **FA Cup**. **Middlesbrough beat Manchester City** and **Leicester** are another Second Division side to beat one from the First, a last-minute goal seeing them through to the 4th round for the first time in eight years against **Crystal Palace**, who have **Eric Young sent off** in the first half. Non-League **Kettering** and **Crawley** are **thrashed by** Second Division sides, **Blackburn** and **Brighton**, but the two home **non-Leaguers draw** — **Woking with Hereford** and **Farnborough**, having transferred their tie to Upton Park, with **West Ham**. Other notable performances include **Hartlepool's draw at Ipswich**, **Orient's at Oldham** and **Cambridge's at Coventry**. In **Division Four**, **Mansfield win at York** and move to within 2 points of **Burnley**, who hold **Derby 2-2** in the **Cup**. In Scotland, **Hearts win 2-1 at Celtic** and restore their 2-point lead over **Rangers**, who have **Oleg Kuznetsov sent off** but draw **0-0 at Airdrie**.

5 The big game at Elland Road is postponed because of a waterlogged pitch so **Leeds and Manchester United must replay** on the 15th. Cup-holders **Spurs draw 0-0 at Villa Park**, **Carl Saunders** scores **4 of Bristol Rovers' 5 against Plymouth**, and **Charlton come** from behind to **beat Barnet 3-1**.

6 **John Barnes**, back after 4 months, **hits 3 in Liverpool's 4-0 Cup victory at Crewe**. **Coventry**, desperate for Premier League football next season, **sack player-manager Terry Butcher** after only 14 months in charge after failing to negotiate a new manager-only contract.

7 Terry Butcher's assistant at Coventry, **Don Howe**, unwilling to fill in as caretaker, **becomes manager** on an 18-month contract. **PFA chief Gordon Taylor** has talks with **Premier League chairman Sir John Quinton** and is encouraged by a 'positive response', to the PFA's requirements.

8 In the **Rumbelows Cup quarter-finals**, **Manchester United and Spurs** win from behind, **United 3-1 at Leeds and Spurs 2-1 over Norwich**. **Nigel Clough** scores a late equalizer for **Forest at Crystal Palace**, and **Peterborough** holds out for a **goalless draw with Middlesbrough**. The **FA fine Arsenal's Ian Wright £1,500** and **Paul Merson £500**, with warnings as to their future conduct, for incidents concerning the **Oldham** crowd which were reported by the police; **David Seaman is cleared.**

9 The **Premier League** argument re-emerges as the **Football League accuse the FA** of reneging on their agreement. **Billy Bingham's** part-time contract as **Northern Ireland manager** is extended to 1994.

10 **Northern Ireland appoint Jimmy Nicholl assistant manager**, to be groomed as Bingham's successor.

11 An **Andrei Kanchelskis** goal is enough for **Manchester United to beat Everton** at Old Trafford and go back on **top of the First Division**. The **Second Division** battle for places in the Premier League continues to rage, with only 5 points separating the top 7 clubs, who are still led by **Blackburn**, **4-0 winners over Bristol City**. Mid-table **Sunderland's 6-2 thrashing of Millwall**, helped by **3 from** record signing **Don Goodman**, is their third win running since **Malcolm Crosby** became caretaker boss. **Mansfield** take over at the **top of Division Four** from **Burnley, who crash 5-2 at Blackpool**. In Scotland, **Hearts lose 4-0 at Aberdeen**, their first home defeat of the season, having conceded only 6 goals in their previous 13 home matches. **Rangers beat Hibs 2-0 to go top** on goal difference.

12 **Leeds**, without **Strachan and Batty**, climb back **on top** in style, **Lee Chapman hitting 3** in their **6-1 victory**, the biggest home League defeat in **Sheffield Wednesday's** history. **The First Division** clubs confirm that the new league will be called the **FA Premier League.**

13 Both **FIFA** and **UEFA** recognize the successor to the **USSR Football Federation**, which will compete as the **Commonwealth of Independent States**. Former **QPR and Cambridge** forward **Mick Leach dies** at 44.

14 A night of FA Cup replays sees holders **Spurs go out 1-0 to Aston Villa**. Other recent Cup-winners eliminated by the same score are **Wimbledon, beaten at home by Bristol City**, and **Coventry, downed by a last-minute own goal**. Another fine display against **West Ham at Upton Park** by **Farnborough is thwarted** by an 89th-minute goal from **Trevor Morley**, and **Hereford** need extra time to **dispose of** the other non-Leaguers **Woking**. The **ties at Newcastle and Derby are abandoned** owing to fog. **West Brom defender Frank Sinclair**, on loan from **Chelsea**, is found **guilty of misconduct** by an FA disciplinary committee, **fined and banned** for nine matches for the incident during the December 28 game against **Exeter** when a clash of heads left **referee Paul Alcock** injured.

15 **Leeds go out of the FA Cup** to a **Mark Hughes** goal and lose **Lee Chapman** with a **broken wrist** as **Manchester United** complete their ascendancy over their rivals despite being outplayed for most of the match. **Newcastle's Gordon McKeag** is elected league president.

18 The **First Division top two** are both held 1-1, **Leeds** at home to **Crystal Palace** and **Manchester United** away to **Notts County**. **Charlton** bring off the performance of the day, coming **from 3 down at Newcastle to win 4-3**. Thanks to a **Mike Conroy hat-trick**, **Burnley beat Gillingham 4-1** and

regain the **Fourth Division lead**. In Scotland, **Rangers go 2 points clear** as **Hearts** lose again.

19 **Wimbledon sack Peter Withe** after 3 months in charge and only 1 win in 17 games, putting reserve-team manager **Joe Kinnear in charge** for the rest of the season.

20 **Villa manager Ron Atkinson fines keeper Les Sealey** for his behaviour on Saturday following the award of a goal to **Sheffield Wednesday**.

21 The **FA reject a £2m offer** from brewers **Bass** to sponsor this season's **Cup** final and semi-finals.

22 **Manchester United go back on top** with a **1-0 home win over Villa**. **Newcastle lose** their **Cup replay** at home to **Bournemouth** on penalties after having **Alan Thompson sent off**. The two quarter-final **Rumbelows Cup replays** are postponed owing to frost. **Rangers knock Aberdeen out of the Scottish Cup**, 1-0 at Pittodrie. **Sheffield Wednesday striker Nigel Jemson** is hurt in a **car crash**.

23 **Robert Rosario of Coventry** and **John Keeley of Oldham** have their **Cup-final ticket allocation stopped** for three years for failing to follow FA guidelines for the distribution of their tickets. The **Parliamentary All-Party Football Committee** urge a rethink on **all-seater stadiums** for **Third and Fourth Division** clubs because of the cost. **Gary Lineker** gets the go-ahead to continue playing despite **arthritis in a big toe**. The Inland Revenue serve a **winding-up petitition** on **Doncaster**.

25 With six 4th-round ties called off through frost and four scheduled for tomorrow and Monday, only six **FA Cup matches** are played, including the 3rd-round replay in which **Derby beat Bolton 2-0**. Giant-killers **Wrexham draw 2-2 at West Ham**, the only First Division side in action. **Brentford beat Preston 1-0** to take a **5-point lead in Division Three**, as **West Brom lose** a two-goal lead at home **to Swansea**, whose sub **Steve Thornber scores 3** in the last 13 minutes, leaving West Brom manager **Bobby Gould** to address a disgruntled crowd at the request of the police. Honours in the **Scottish Cup** go to non-Leaguers **Huntley and Caledonian**, who beat the **Second Division 1 and 2, Dumbarton and Clyde**, respectively, 2-0 away and 3-1.

26 **Clive Allen's goal against Everton puts Chelsea through** to the **FA Cup 5th round**, where the only definite tie is **Forest, 2-0 winners over Hereford**, against **Bristol City**. **Ivory Coast beat Ghana 11-10 on penalties** to win the **African Nations Cup**.

27 **Manchester United draw their FA Cup tie 0-0 at Southampton**. French 'bad boy' **Eric Cantona joins Sheffield Wednesday** on a week's trial. **Crystal Palace transfer-list unsettled Andy Gray**. **Reconstruction plans** for the **Scottish League** are **rejected** by a full meeting of the clubs.

29 **Liverpool's threat** to the leaders is confirmed as they **overcome Arsenal 2-0** at Anfield and move to within 8 points of **Manchester United**, who have a game in hand.

30 **Crystal Palace sell Marco Gabbiadini to Derby for £1.2m** — a loss of £600,000 after only four months.

February

1 **Leeds beat Notts County 3-0** and return to the **top** as **Manchester United are held 1-1 at Arsenal**. **Liverpool's charge** is **halted by Chelsea**, whose 2-1 win is their first at Anfield since 1935. **Sheffield United** move out of the relegation zone with a **shock 5-2 win at Forest**. **Blackburn, Southend and Ipswich all win** to open up a **5-point gap** at the top of **Division Two**, while bottom club Oxford beat fellow strugglers **Newcastle 5-2**. **West Brom beat Brentford 2-0** to narrow the gap at the top of **Divsion Three**. **Rangers win 1-0 at Hearts** to open up a **4-point lead** in Scotland.

2 French striker **Eric Cantona signs on loan for Leeds** after walking out on **Sheffield Wednesday**.

3 In a private report based on replies from 61 League clubs, **Dr Simon Pitt claims** that the **League clubs** are collectively **over £130m in debt** and warns that more than a dozen clubs face extinction. He blames the spiralling costs of players' wages, signing-on fees and transfers, and serious underestimation of the costs of implementing the **Taylor Report**.

4 **Middlesbrough beat Sheffield Wednesday** at Hillsborough in the **FA Cup 4th round** and **Notts County beat Blackburn**, who have **David Speedie sent off** along with County captain **Phil Turner**. **West Ham win** their replay **at Wrexham 1-0**. The **FA Premier League** reaches a compromise with the **First Division clubs**, leaving the reduction from 22 to 20 till 1994–95.

5 Tremendous action and drama in the **Cup** sees favourites **Manchester United** become the **first Division One side to go out on penalties** as **Southampton hero Tim Flowers** saves from **Ryan Giggs** at Old Trafford. In 4th-round ties, **Dwight Yorke scores 3** in Aston Villa's 4-3 win at Derby and has two penalties saved by **Peter Shilton**, but follows up to score from the first. **Bristol Rovers hold Liverpool 1-1** at Twerton Park. **Teddy Sheringham scores 3** as Nottingham Forest beat Crystal Palace 4-2 in the **Rumbelows Cup** replay. In the **Scottish Cup John Robertson scores all 3** in Hearts' 3-0 win over St Mirren, who have two men sent off. **Newcastle manager Ossie Ardiles is sacked and Kevin Keegan takes over**. Swansea and former **Welsh international Alan Davies**, 30, is found **dead** in his car.

7 **Bob Paisley leaves the Liverpool board** because of ill health.

8 **Manchester United are held** at home 1-1 by **Sheffield Wednesday**, but go **top** on goal difference as **Leeds lose 2-0 at Oldham**, only their second League defeat. **Blackburn and Ipswich** have good wins in Division Two, but **Keegan's Newcastle** steal the headlines with a **3-0 win over Bristol City**. **West Brom win 3-0 at Birmingham** to go **top of Division Three** above **Brentford**, shock 3-0 losers at home to lowly **Bury**. **Burnley** open up a **5-point gap in Division Four**. **Aldershot** go ahead with their game against **Walsall** despite warnings that they are breaking company law by 'trading when insolvent'.

9 **Spurs draw 1-1 at Nottingham Forest** in their **Rumbelows Cup semi-final** first leg. **Doncaster Belles** make it 11 wins out of 11 to take the first **women's National League** title.

10 **Liverpool's Rob Jones** is in **England's** 30-strong squad for the senior and B games against **France**, along with **Southampton's Matthew Le Tissier** and **Alan Shearer**. **Aberdeen sack manager Alex Smith**, and appoint **Willie Miller** from the coaching staff.

11 **Liverpool**, a goal down at half-time, **beat Bristol Rovers 2-1** in a **4th-round Cup replay** at Anfield.
Blackburn beat Derby 2-0 to go **4 points clear in Division Two** with a game in hand. **Burnley** open
up a **7-point lead in Division Four**. **West Ham's** relaunched **bond scheme** is **rejected** by their fans,
who call for a national demonstration against all-seat stadiums. **Aldershot's directors** give the
beleaguered club new hope by **waiving their financial claims**.

12 **Middlesbrough beat Peterborough 1-0** in the much postponed **Rumbelows Cup replay** and will meet
Manchester United in the semi-finals. **Stoke beat West Brom 1-0** to go **top of Division Three**.

13 **Football League** chief executive **Arthur Sandford will quit** in June, with compensation agreed for
the remaining 2½ years of his £80,000-a-year contract. **Liverpool** sign a **record shirt sponsorship
deal** with **Carlsberg**, worth **£4m** over four years.

14 The **FA Premier League** draw up an agreed **constitution** and confirm the appointment of **Rick
Parry as chief executive** until August, with the first fixtures set for 15 August.

15 **Norwich** and **Nottingham Forest** enjoy **3-goal wins** in the **5th round** of the **FA Cup**, while in **Division
One Arsenal slam Sheffield Wednesday 7-1** with a record 6 goals in 18 minutes late in the game.
Thanks to a **David Speedie hat-trick**, **Blackburn** come from behind to **beat Newcastle 3-1** and go **7
points clear in Division Two**. **Brentford scrape a 3-2 win over Torquay** and go **top of Division Three**.
Hearts and Rangers both come back to **win 2-1 in the Scottish Cup 4th round**, while **Highland
League Inverness Caledonian hold St Johnstone 2-2**.

16 All three **First Division** sides survive away ties against sides from lower divisions in the **Cup**, **Villa**
winning **2-1 at Swindon**, **Southampton** losing a two-goal lead in the last 11 minutes at **Bolton**, and
Liverpool being held **0-0 at Ipswich**.

18 **England beat France 3-0** in a B international. The Devon and Cornwall **police** are to **charge**
Brentford's **Gary Blissett** with causing grievous bodily harm as a result of an incident in December's
game at **Torquay** after which **John Uzzell** needed facial surgery.

19 **Southampton's Alan Shearer** scores a debut goal as **England win 2-0** at Wembley to inflict **France's
first defeat** for 20 games. **Lineker**, coming on as substitute, **scores his 47th international goal**.
Liverpool's Rob Jones, who began the season with **Crewe**, and **Everton's Martin Keown** also make
their **debuts** in England's starting line-up. In other friendlies, **Scotland beat N. Ireland 1-0** and the
Republic suffer their first loss in Dublin for 25 games, **going down 1-0 to Wales**. The **FA fine
Liverpool's Michael Thomas** £3,000 for criticism of his former manager, **Arsenal's George Graham**,
while **Villa keeper Les Sealey** receives a **four-match ban** and a £2,000 fine for his outburst at the
end of the game with **Sheffield Wednesday**.

20 The **FA Council** approve the formation of the **FA Premier League**. **Aston Villa sign defender Earl
Barrett from Oldham for £1.7m**. Three **managers** are **fined** for comments to referees, **Crystal
Palace's Steve Coppell**, **Wimbledon's Joe Kinnear** and **Notts County's Neil Warnock**.

22 With **Leeds** playing tomorrow, **Manchester United** take a **4-point lead in Division One** after beating
Palace 2-0. **Stoke beat Brentford 2-1** to go **top of Division Three**. Joint **Fourth Division**
leaders **Burnley and Blackpool** play out a **1-1 draw** in front of 18,183 at Turf Moor.

23 **Everton hold Leeds 1-1** at Goodison Park.

24 **Bristol City**, 20th in **Division Two**, sack manager **Jimmy Lumsden**. **Darlington**, bottom of **Division
Three**, sack manager **Frank Gray**.

25 **Cambridge beat Second Division leaders Blackburn 2-1** and go third.

26 In **5th-round FA Cup** replays, **Liverpool** and **Southampton** both need extra time at home before
winning 3-2, against **Ipswich** and **Bolton**, respectively, while **Sunderland win 3-2 at West Ham** and
Portsmouth 4-2 at Middlesbrough. A late **Mark Hughes equalizer** prevents a shock **Chelsea** win at
Old Trafford and takes **Manchester United 4 points clear of Leeds** again. **Chelsea** are ordered by
the **High Court** to **pay £22.85m for Stamford Bridge** or risk eviction.

28 A second win this week for **Cambridge, 6-1 over Bristol Rovers**, takes them second in **Division
Two**.

29 In the first serious act of **hooliganism** for two years, a pitch invasion at **Birmingham** after **Third
Division leaders Stoke equalize** stops the game for 20 minutes before the last 35 seconds are played
in an empty ground. The trouble has **Birmingham** manager **Terry Cooper** considering his future
with the club and **chairman Samesh Kumar** in despair, although he alleges 'some scandalous
decisions by the referee', **Roger Wiseman**, who is struck by a spectator. Another **referee** under
fire is **Stephen Lodge** at Anfield, where **Liverpool** manager **Graeme Souness** calls him 'a disgrace'.
Justin Fashanu of Torquay, one of three players **sent off at West Brom**, expresses disgust at the
way referee **Jim Parker** handled the game. And there is a 200-strong **pitch protest at West Ham**
against their **bond scheme**. **Leeds beat Luton 2-0** to close the **First Division** gap to 2 points as
Manchester United are held **0-0 at Coventry**. **Ipswich** close the **Division Two** gap to **3 points**, **beating
Plymouth 2-0**, while **Blackburn are held** at home by lowly **Oxford**. **Rangers beat Airdrie 5-0** in
Scotland and open up a **7-point** lead over **Hearts**, beaten 2-1 at home by **Celtic**.

March

1 A terrorist **bomb** on a railway line near **White Hart Lane** and the threat of another inside **Spurs'**
ground holds up the start of the **Rumbelows Cup** semi-final second leg for over an hour, but,
despite this and a morass of a ground, **Nottingham Forest** win a classic match **2-1** after extra time.

2 **Peter Shilton** joins Plymouth from Derby as player-manager. The **FA charge Birmingham** with
misconduct after Saturday's pitch invasion. Former **Blackpool** star **Jackie Mudie dies**, aged 62.

3 **Leeds**, held **0-0 at home** by Villa, miss their chance to go back on top of **Division One**, while **West
Ham lose 1-0 at Southampton** and replace them at the bottom. **Brentford go top of Division Three**,
Blackpool of Division Four, as **Burnley crash 3-0 at Gillingham**. **Barnet fans** collect £600 for
Aldershot's unpaid players before thrashing them **5-0**.

4 No joy for English sides in **Europe**, as **Spurs and Liverpool lose** their 1st leg ties. **Manchester**

United draw **0-0 at Middlesbrough** in the 1st leg of their **Rumbelows Cup** semi-final. **Stoke** go back on **top of Division Three** on goal difference.

5   **Blackburn** sign Roy Wegerle from QPR for **£1m** to replace the injured **Mike Newell** (broken leg).

7   **Portsmouth** beat **Nottingham Forest 1-0** to reach the **FA Cup semi-finals. Leeds** win **3-1** at Spurs to go back on **top of Division One. Ipswich** move up to **Blackburn's** shoulders on goal difference in **Divsion Two.** Both **Division Three** leaders lose **3-2, Stoke at home** to lowly **Hull** and **Brentford at Preston. Burnley** beat **Barnet 3-0** and go back on **top of Division Four**.

8   **Liverpool** beat **Villa 1-0** at Anfield to reach the **FA Cup semi-finals.** In Scotland, **Hearts** beat **Falkirk 3-1** to reach the semis, where **Rangers and Celtic** are paired.

9   **Sunderland** take **Chelsea** to a **replay** with a late equalizer at Stamford Bridge in their 6th-round **Cup** tie. **Bristol City appoint Denis Smith manager.**

10 **David O'Leary** plays his **700th game** for **Arsenal. Blackburn** scrape a home **draw with Southend,** while **Newcastle** climb out of the immediate relegation zone with a **2-0 win** at 3rd-placed **Cambridge.** Wins for **Blackpool and Mansfield** in **Division Four** take them past **Burnley,** whose game at **York** is postponed because of the **death** earlier of a **17-year-old apprentice Ben Lee** in an accident at Turf Moor.

11 An extra-time goal from **Ryan Giggs** takes **Manchester United to Wembley** as they **beat Middlesbrough 2-1** in the **Rumbelows Cup** semi-final 2nd leg. Further good news for United comes from Loftus Road as **QPR** beat **Leeds 4-1. Leeds,** who have **Chris Whyte sent off** near the end, still **lead Division One** by 2 points but **Manchester** now have three games in hand. In **Division Three,** leaders **Stoke** and 3rd-placed **West Brom** both **lose 2-1** at home to lowly opposition.

12 **Liverpool striker Dean Saunders is suspended** for 3 matches for an elbowing incident in the Cup against **Bristol Rovers** highlighted by BBC cameras, and will miss the semi-final.

14 **Leeds** bounce back with a **5-1 win over Wimbledon,** aided by a **Lee Chapman hat-trick,** but **Manchester United** keep the gap at 2 points with a **2-1 win** at in-form **Sheffield United. Blackburn** stretch their **lead in Division Two** to 3 points thanks to a **3-0 victory at Brighton,** while **Ipswich** are **held** at home by **Leicester. Newcastle** continue their **revival** under **Keegan** with a **3-1 win** over **Swindon,** but **Keegan fuels talk of resignation** by leaving immediately for Heathrow. **Stoke win at Huddersfield** to take a 3-point lead in **Division Three,** as **Brentford go down 4-3** at home to **Bradford.**

15 Chairman **Sir John Hall** keeps **Keegan** at Newcastle, pledging **£0.5m** of his own money for players.

16 **Graham Taylor** brings back **Glasgow Rangers striker Mark Hateley** for **England's** friendly against **Czechoslovakia** after nearly 4 years. The **FA** get tough on the resale of **Cup final tickets, censuring Spurs** for their negligent distribution of tickets last season and penalizing various individuals and organizations for irregularities in ticket handling, including **Gordon Banks** and **Nottingham Forest striker Lee Glover.**

17 The **referee** assaulted at **Birmingham, Roger Wiseman, withdraws** from the list for the season because of **mental stress. Millwall manager Bruce Rioch resigns.** The **government** extend the reduction on **pools betting duty** to the turn of the century, a £100m boost for the **Football Trust,** who allocate clubs money for ground improvements. **David O'Leary is sent off** for the first time in his career, along with two team-mates and an opponent in **Arsenal's** reserve-team match at QPR.

18 The last British clubs, **Spurs and Liverpool,** go out of Europe. **Sunderland and Norwich** reach the **FA Cup semi-finals** with **2-1 replay wins** over **Chelsea** and **Southampton,** respectively, the latter having **Le Tissier** and **Horne sent off. Manchester United lose 1-0** at **Nottingham Forest** but still have two games in hand over **Division One** leaders **Leeds. Aldershot FC are wound up** in the High Court with debts of **£1.2m. Millwall appoint Mick McCarthy caretaker-manager.**

19 The **FA** ban **Sheffield United's Carl Bradshaw** for three games for a punch thrown at **Chelsea's Vinny Jones** in the Cup tie last month, and caught on camera. **Derby** complete the **signing of Notts County's Tommy Johnson** for **£1.3m** after having him on a week's loan.

20 **Aldershot** persuade the High Court to freeze their winding-up order for 12 hours so they can **fulfil their Fourth Division fixture at Cardiff;** they **lose 2-0.** Former **Arsenal and Wales keeper Jack Kelsey** dies at 62, **John Oakes,** who played for **Charlton** in the 1946 Cup final, **dies** at 86.

21 **Manchester United** falter again, **held 0-0 by Wimbledon** at Old Trafford, and are 1 point behind **Leeds.** In Division Two, **Blackburn lose 2-0** at home to **Charlton,** but stay top as their nearest challengers, **Cambridge and Ipswich,** play a **1-1 draw. Steve Bull** scores his **195th goal** for Wolves to overhaul **John Richards'** club **record.** Local derbies in Scotland reduce **Rangers'** lead over **Hearts** to 5 points, as **Celtic win 2-0 at Ibrox** and **Hearts 2-1 at Hibs. Dunfermline,** with only 15 points, are **relegated** with 6 games still to play.

22 **Leeds draw 1-1 at Arsenal** and go 2 points ahead of **Manchester United,** who have two games in hand.

23 Ballot papers are sent to all **First Division PFA members** asking whether they are prepared to boycott live TV games or even strike. **Southend accept manager David Webb's resignation.**

24 An **Alan Smith** goal gives **England B** a **1-0 win** in Czechoslovakia, while **Arsenal** team-mate **Paul Merson** is selected for the **senior side** along with the recalled **Mark Hateley** of **Rangers. Scotland Under-21s** make a remarkable comeback at Pittodrie from 3-1 down to **beat Germany 4-3** (5-4 on aggregate) and go through to the UEFA semi-finals.

25 **England draw 2-2 in Czechoslovakia,** while in other friendlies **Ireland beat Switzerland 2-1** and **Finland hold the Scots 1-1** at a deserted Hampden. **Aldershot** finally lose their fight for survival, becoming the first club since **Accrington Stanley** in 1962 to **fold** during the season; their results this season are expunged from the records, putting **Burnley above Blackpool** on goal difference.

26 **Chelsea chairman Ken Bates** spends **£3m** to buy a 27 per cent share in Cabra Estates, the club's landlords.

27 PFA chief executive **Gordon Taylor rejects a Premier League 'peace formula'** and a players' strike moves closer.

28 **Leeds, held 0-0** at home by bottom club **West Ham**, stay **top of Division One** as **Manchester United draw 0-0 at QPR**, but suffer a blow as full-back **Mel Sterland is ruled out** for the rest of the season. **Gordon Durie scores 3 in Spurs' 4-3 win over Coventry** to lift them clear of relegation danger. **Ipswich** take over at the **top of Division Two**, beating **Derby** 2-1 as leaders **Blackburn go down 2-1 at Barnsley**, where the home club manager **Mel Machin** and **Blackburn assistant Ray Harford** are involved in a post-match **scuffle**. In **Division Four**, **Burnley** scrape past **Maidstone 2-1** to open up a 3-point lead as their nearest challengers slip. **Mark Hateley scores twice** but twists his back in **Rangers' 2-1 win at St Johnstone** and will probably miss the Cup semi-final against **Celtic**. Canadian businessman **Fergus McCann** announces a **£17m** package for a **new Celtic stadium**.

29 **Manchester United** players clean up the **major PFA awards** for the second year running, **Gary Pallister** being voted **Player of the Year** and **Ryan Giggs Young Player of the Year**.

31 **Manchester United's 3-1 win at Norwich** takes them a point ahead of **Leeds** with still a game in hand. **Ipswich** go **4 points clear in Division Two** with a **2-0 win over Barnsley** as **Blackburn lose again**, **2-0 to** bottom club **Port Vale**. Aided by a **Mutch hat-trick**, **Wolves slam** relegation-haunted **Newcastle 6-2**. In **Division Three**, **Stockport beat WBA 3-0** to edge within a point of the lead as **Stoke are held 1-1 at Fulham**. An **Ally McCoist goal** on half-time against **Celtic** puts **Rangers** into the **Scottish Cup final**, despite having **Robertson sent off** after only **6 minutes**.

April

1 A **Lineker hat-trick** in **Spurs' 3-0 win** puts **West Ham** in deeper trouble.

3 The administrators in charge of debt-ridden **Northampton sack manager Theo Foley** along with nine players and two other staff. **Birmingham are fined £50,000** and ordered to play **two games behind closed doors** as a result of the **pitch invasion** after the game against Stoke in February. Meanwhile **Stoke** increase their **lead in Division Three** to 4 points.

4 **Leeds are hammered 4-0 at Maine Road**. **Villa** come from two down to **beat Spurs 5-2** at White Hart Lane. **Hearts and Airdrie draw** their Scottish **Cup semi-final** 0-0. **Celtic** move into **second place** in the Premier League above Hearts on goal difference.

5 Lowly **Second Division Sunderland beat Norwich 1-0** to reach the **FA Cup semi-final**, and only a last-gasp equalizer in extra time by 10-man **Liverpool** prevents **Portsmouth** joining them.

6 Liverpool manager **Graeme Souness**, 39, enters hospital for a **triple heart bypass** and **Ronnie Moran takes temporary charge**. PFA members give chief executive **Gordon Taylor** overwhelming **support** (548 to 37) for any necessary action involving the refusal to play in televised matches.

7 **Manchester United are held** by neighbours **City 1-1** at Old Trafford despite the **dismissal of City's Pointon**. Two **Lineker** goals at **Notts County** makes **Spurs** virtually **safe** and **County almost certain** for the drop. **Ipswich beat Wolves 2-1** to go **7 points clear in Division Two**. In Scotland, a **McCoist hat-trick** helps **Rangers beat Falkirk 4-1** to retain their 5-point lead.

8 **Sunderland lose 3-2 at Leicester** and remain under threat of **relegation** from **Division Two**.

9 **Birmingham chairman Samesh Kumar** is charged with **misconduct** by the FA. **Liverpool** grant a **testimonial** to **Wayne Harrison**, the teenager who went to Anfield for £250,000 in 1985 but was forced to retire through injury without making a senior appearance for them.

11 Another eight **dismissals** in the **Barclays League** takes the season's total to **246** in domestic competitions, passing the previous **record** of 242 sent off in 1982–83. **Leeds beat Chelsea 3-0** to go a point above **Manchester United** who now have two games in hand. **Paul Merson** scores a **hat-trick** in **Arsenal's 4-1 defeat of Palace**. **Ipswich beat Newcastle 3-2** to stretch their **Division Two lead to 10 points**. **St Mirren hold Hearts to a 0-0** draw at Tynecastle Park but are **relegated**.

12 **Manchester United win the Rumbelows Cup**, **1-0 against Nottingham Forest** at Wembley; both club captains, **Bryan Robson** and **Stuart Pearce**, miss the game through injury.

13 **Liverpool** finally get past **Portsmouth** — **on penalties** — to reach the **FA Cup final**, after a 0-0 draw at Villa Park, **Portsmouth's McLoughlin** having struck the bar after 87 minutes.

14 In **Division Two**, Cup finalists **Sunderland** ease their relegation worries, inflicting the heaviest defeat of the season, **3-0, on Ipswich**, who nevertheless retain their 10-point lead, **Blackburn losing** at home again, **2-1 to Wolves**. The leaders of Divisions Three and Four, **Stoke and Burnley**, without a game, lose their place to **Birmingham and Blackpool**, respectively. **Airdrie beat Hearts on penalties** after a 1-1 draw to reach the **Scottish Cup final**.

15 In the **European Cup**, **Panathinaikos** score their first goal in Group A to hold **Sampdoria** away, but the Italians still go through to meet **Barcelona, 2-1 winners** over **Benfica**, in the Wembley final.

16 **Manchester United beat Southampton 1-0** to go **two points ahead of Leeds** with a game in hand. **Liverpool manager Graeme Souness** is back in **intensive care** after suffering a relapse — this after public protests at his dealings with *The Sun*, in which he was pictured kissing his girlfriend on the day Liverpool held a memorial service for the fans who died in the **Hillsborough disaster**.

18 Away **draws** for **Manchester United at Luton** and **Leeds at Liverpool** maintain the status quo in **Division One**, while a **1-0 win for Sheffield Wednesday at Southampton** takes them to within 3 points of **Leeds**. It's almost curtains for **West Ham** as they go **down 2-0 at Manchester City**, but **Notts County win 1-0 at Norwich**. **Ipswich lose again** in **Division Two**, 2-1 at Bristol City, while below them **Leicester win 1-0 at Blackburn**, who suffer their 6th successive defeat to drop out of the play-off zone behind **Charlton**. In Scotland, **Rangers clinch the Premier League** with a **4-0 win over St Mirren**, **Ally McCoist** scoring two and being voted **Scottish Footballer of the Year**.

20 **Manchester United** suffer a disastrous Easter Monday **home defeat**, **2-1 to their Rumbelows victims Nottingham Forest**, and are now a **point behind Leeds**, **2-0 victors over Coventry**, but with still a game in hand. **Arsenal** continue their late, but futile, unbeaten run with a **4-0 victory over Liverpool**, the Merseysiders' **heaviest defeat** for nine years. **West Ham lose 2-0** at home to **Palace** and are relegated. In **Division Two**, with the top three playing tomorrow, **Derby** move into 3rd with a **4-1** defeat of **Newcastle**, who have **three men sent off** and drop into the last three as **Plymouth win**.

21 In **Division Two, Ipswich**, held at home by Grimsby, **fail to clinch promotion. Leicester**, 2-1 victors over **Cambridge**, cut their lead to 3 points.

22 ~~Manchester United squander their last game in hand, going down 1-0 to relegated West Ham;~~ they are still a **point behind Leeds** with two games left.

23 **Gary Lineker** wins the **Footballer of the Year** award for the second time.

25 **Notts County** lose at **Manchester City** and are **relegated. Luton** keep their **hopes alive** by winning, but **so do Coventry. Norwich**, after seven successive defeats, gain a **point against Wimbledon** to ensure Premier League status next season. With the top two playing tomorrow, **Sheffield Wednesday** are **held 1-1 at Crystal Palace** and blow their chance of joining Leeds at the top, but earn a place in **next season's UEFA Cup**. A **draw at Oxford** is enough to earn faltering **Ipswich promotion**, but **Leicester lose 2-0 at Charlton** and are in danger of losing automatic promotion, as **Derby, Middlesbrough, Cambridge and Blackburn all win**. At the other end of the table, **Newcastle** claw their way towards safety with a **last-gasp win over Portsmouth**. In **Division Three, Birmingham** go 4 points ahead of Stoke and **win promotion**, relegating **Shrewsbury** in the process. **Stoke lose 1-0** at home to lowly **Chester**, leaving the way open for **Brentford**, who play tomorrow. In **Division Four**, a **draw for Burnley at Carlisle** virtually assures them of **promotion**.

26 **Leeds win the League title** a week early with a **3-2 victory at Sheffield United** thanks to a **Brian Gayle own goal** and **Manchester United's 2-0 defeat at Anfield**.

27 A **player's strike is averted** as the **PFA** accept a minimum of **£1.5m TV revenue** from the **Premier League**, a 50 per cent increase on the previous offer.

28 In a **World Cup** qualifier, **Northern Ireland** lose a two-goal lead and **are held 2-2** at home by 'new' nation **Lithuania**, while **England B draw 1-1 with CIS** (ex-Soviets) **B** in Moscow. **Aston Villa's Tony Daley** is a surprise choice in **England's side** to face CIS in tomorrow's senior friendly. **Paul Gascoigne** comes through his first full-scale practice match unscathed. **Middlesbrough beat Grimsby 2-0** to go **2nd in Division Two** and assure themselves of at least a play-off place. Leaders **Birmingham** fail to clinch the **Third Division** championship, **going down 3-0 at Wigan. Burnley win 2-1 at York** to clinch the **Fourth Division title**, while **Rotherham's 3-0 win at Wrexham** lifts them into **2nd place**.

29 **Lineker** scores his **48th goal** for **England** to give them the lead **against CIS** in Moscow, but it needs a **Trevor Steven** equalizer in the end to save England from defeat. In other friendlies, **Ireland beat USA 4-1** and **Wales draw 1-1 in Austria**. A late goal gives **Sweden a 1-0 aggregate victory** over **Scotland** in the UEFA Under-21 semi-finals. In the **UEFA Cup final first leg**, Ajax come away from Torino with a **2-2 draw**.

30 Newcastle manager **Kevin Keegan transfer-lists** striker **Mick Quinn**, fines him and drops him from Saturday's vital match at Leicester following critical remarks in a newspaper.

May
1 **Norwich manager David Stringer resigns** after 4½ years in charge and is offered a seat on the board. **Ivan Golac resigns as Torquay manager**, accusing the club of lack of ambition.

2 The **last full Saturday** of the season sees most issues resolved. **Luton go down**, losing at Notts County 2-1 after leading, so **Coventry stay up** despite losing at Villa. **Leeds**, who beat Norwich 1-0, finish 4 points ahead of Manchester United, 3-1 winners over Spurs. Lineker's 86th minute consolation **goal** is not enough for the First Division's 'Golden Boot', which is snatched by Ian Wright, who scores twice in injury time to chalk up a **hat-trick in Arsenal's 5-1 drubbing of Southampton** and take his League tally to **29 goals** and Arsenal's to 81, **equal top with Barnet** in the League. In **Division Two, Middlesbrough win 2-1 at Wolves** in a game almost postponed by an early morning arson attack and despite having **Mohan sent off** and then going a goal down; they earn **promotion** at the expense of **Derby**, 2-1 winners over Swindon. **A David Speedie hat-trick** at **Plymouth** earns a **play-off place for Blackburn**, but **Charlton lose anyway**. Of the bottom three, only **Oxford escape relegation**, with a **2-1 win at Tranmere**, condemning **Plymouth** to the drop, along with **Brighton**, defeated 3-1 at champions Ipswich, and **Port Vale. Brentford steal the Third Division title** with a **1-0 win at Peterborough** as leaders **Birmingham lose**. At the other end of the table, **Exeter** are slammed 5-2 by bottom club **Darlington**, but **stay up** thanks to **Bury's 2-0 defeat at Preston**. In **Division Four**, a home point for **Rotherham** is enough to **win promotion** behind champions **Burnley. Mansfield beat Rochdale 2-1** to snatch the third **promotion** place from **Blackpool**. Good wins for **Crewe** and **Scunthorpe** ensure **play-off places** with **Blackpool**, but **Barnet's 4-1 win at York** means **Rochdale** must beat **Burnley** in the only remaining match to gain the last play-off spot. Big wins for runaway leaders **Colchester** and **Wycombe** in the **GM Vauxhall Conference** mean **Colchester** get back **into the League** on goal difference, with the next club 21 points adrift of their **record 94 points**. Another **two McCoist goals in Rangers' 2-0 win at Aberdeen** confirms him as Scotland's leading scorer and **Rangers as champions by 9 points. Celtic lose 2-1** at home to **Hibs**, allowing **Hearts** to grab the **UEFA Cup place**. In **Division One**, where the top three play the bottom three, **champions Dundee lose 2-1** at home to **relegated Montrose**. Also **promoted** are **Partick**, who scrape a **draw** at home to bottom club **Forfar. Hamilton beat Meadowbank 2-0** but need another two goals to pip Partick. In **Division Two**, a home point is enough to give **Dumbarton the title**; they are accompanied upwards by **Cowdenbeath** whose 0-0 draw at Alloa keeps **Alloa** in 3rd place.

3 **Leeds' Gordon Strachan**, forced to take a complete summer break because of his back problem, **quits international football**.

5 A temporary **stand collapses in Corsica** before the **French Cup** semi-final between **Bastia and Marseille**, causing **many deaths**. **UEFA award the 1996 European Championships to England**. **West Brom**, as expected, **sack manager Bobby Gould**, and **chairman John Silk steps down** in favour of Trevor Summers. **Burnley win 3-1** at Rochdale **to put Barnet in the play-offs**.

6 **Werder Bremen beat Monaco 2-0** in the **European Cup-Winners' Cup final** at Lisbon. **Des Walker** signs a two-year **contract worth £3m** with Italian club **Sampdoria**, who pay **Forest** the cut-price £1.5m stipulated in Walker's contract.

8 **John Barnes** fails a fitness test and will **miss** tomorrow's **Cup final**, but **Steve McManaman** is **back** to take his place in the **Liverpool** side. Manager **Graeme Souness** is discharged from hospital. West Brom appoint **Ossie Ardiles** manager. **Colin Murphy** will **take over** from **David Webb** as **Southend manager** in July. **Manager Phil Neal leaves Bolton** after 6½ years. **Torquay** make youth development officer **Paul Compton manager**. **Howard Wilkinson** of Leeds is named **Barclays Manager of the Year**.

9 **Liverpool**, with **McManaman** outstanding in the second half, **beat Sunderland 2-0 to win the FA Cup**. **Rangers** bring off the **Scottish double**, beating **Airdrie 2-1** in a lack-lustre **Cup final**.

10 In the **Division Two play-offs**, **Blackburn** recover from 2-0 down and will **take a 4-2 lead to Derby**, while **Leicester draw 1-1 at Cambridge**. **Barnet beat Blackpool 1-0** in a **Division Four** play-off tie, but **manager Barry Fry** claims he has been **sacked by chairman Stan Flashman** following a bust-up in the dressing-room after the game.

11 **Newcastle chairman Sir John Hall** takes a **51 per cent controlling interest** in the club. **Ossie Ardiles** appoints his former Spurs boss **Keith Burkinshaw** as his **assistant at West Brom**.

12 **England beat Hungary 1-0** in a friendly in Budapest; the **Under-21s draw 2-2**.

13 **Ajax draw 0-0 with Torino** and **win the UEFA Cup** on away goals. **Leicester slam Cambridge 5-0** to reach the **Second Division play-off final**. **Blackburn lose 2-1** at Derby and **David Speedie** is **attacked by spectators**, but **Blackburn go through**. In Division Three, **Stockport hold Stoke and go through 2-1**. **Blackpool will meet Scunthorpe** in the **Fourth Division final**. Liverpool censure manager **Graeme Souness** for his indiscreet deals with *The Sun*, but confirm he will remain in charge and announce an end to the 'unfortunate matter'. **Rangers** captain **Richard Gough** is appointed **captain of Scotland**.

14 **Peterborough** reach the **Third Division** play-offs **final**. Kevin Maxwell sells his **Oxford United** shares to **Biomass Recycling Ltd**, who promise to make Oxford the League's first 'green' club. **Portsmouth win the PFA Fair Play Award**.

15 **Spurs sack manager Peter Shreeves** — for the second time. **Liverpool's** young right-back **Rob Jones** is **ruled out of the England squad** because of injury.

16 **Liverpool captain Mark Wright**, who stayed to celebrate their Cup final victory last week instead of travelling with England to Hungary, is **omitted** from the team to face **Brazil** at Wembley. Manager **Graham Taylor selects David Platt** to partner **Gary Lineker** up front. Hearts striker **John Robertson** is injured in training and has to **return from Scotland's tour** of North America.

17 **England** struggle to **hold Brazil 1-1** at Wembley and **Lineker misses a penalty. Scotland beat the United States 1-0**.

18 The **FA Premier League** strike a record five-year **£304m TV deal** with **BSkyB and the BBC**, allowing Sky to show 60 live matches a season, on Sunday afternoons and Monday evenings, and the BBC to show highlights both Saturday evenings and midweek.

19 The **Parliamentary All-Party Football Committee** chairman Tom Pendry files a report recommending a **reassessment of the Taylor Report**, particularly in respect of all-seater stadiums.

20 An extra-time goal by Dutch star **Ronald Koeman** gives **Barcelona a 1-0 victory** over **Sampdoria** at Wembley and the **European Cup at last**. In a **World Cup** qualifier, **Wales lose 5-1 to Romania**.

21 A row brews up over the **FA Premier League TV deal**, with **ITV calling for it to be scrapped** and leading club managers talking of rebellion. Newcastle manager **Kevin Keegan** ends speculation and **signs a new 3-year contract**. The touring **Scots beat Canada 3-1**.

22 **ITV** are to **seek an injunction** to halt the TV deal with Sky and the BBC.

23 **Blackpool beat Scunthorpe on penalties** in the **Fourth Division play-off** final at Wembley. **John Barnes** passes a fitness test and **will go to Sweden**.

24 **Peterborough beat Stockport 2-1** in the **Third Division** play-off final.

25 **Blackburn beat Leicester 1-0** in the **Second Division** play-off final at Wembley to return to the top flight after 26 years. **Rangers' Gary Stevens replaces** the injured **Lee Dixon** at right-back in the **England squad**. Wales manager **Terry Yorath's** 15-year-old **son Daniel**, about to start an apprenticeship with Leeds, **dies** suddenly after a kickabout at his home.

26 **Ireland** open their **World Cup** qualifying campaign with **a 2-0 victory over Albania** in Dublin. **ITV's High Court plea** for a two-week freeze on the Premier League football deal **fails**. **Bobby Gould returns to Coventry** as **joint manager** with **Don Howe**.

27 **Derby sign Luton midfielder Mark Pembridge for £1.25m**. **Terry Venables** appoints **Doug Livermore** and **Ray Clemence** from the **Spurs** staff to **first-team coach and assistant**, respectively.

28 **Graham Taylor** brings **sports psychologist John Gardner** into the **England party** in Sweden. The **BBC beat ITV** to another TV deal, **winning the right** to screen **Liverpool's Cup-Winners' Cup** matches next season.

29 **Bruce Rioch** is appointed **Bolton manager. West Ham chairman Martin Cearns steps down** in favour of **Terence Brown**.

30 **New laws** to take effect from 25 July include **penalizing the goalkeeper** with an **indirect free-kick** if he **handles a deliberate pass from a team-mate**. The UN decision to impose trade and sporting sanctions on war-torn **Yugoslavia** means they **will be replaced as England's first opponents** in the forthcoming **European Championships by Denmark**. In friendlies, **Holland beat Wales 4-0** and the **United States shock Ireland 3-1**.

June

1 **Graham Taylor** unveils **England's team** and tactics for Sweden with the **eleven** for the last warm-up game, **against Finland**, which has a **sweeper, Mark Wright**, behind **Walker** and **Keown**, and **Barnes** up front with **Lineker** in a **1-4-3-2 line-up**. **Norwich** name reserve-team coach **Mike Walker as manager.**

2 **Northern Ireland** hold world champions **Germany** to a **1-1 draw** in a friendly at Bremen.

3 The unfortunate **John Barnes** ruptures an Achilles' tendon after 10 minutes of **England's 2-1 win in Finland** and is **out of the European Championships**, with the **injured Gary Stevens** also doubtful; **Platt** scores both goals. **Scotland draw 0-0 in Norway. Wales lose 1-0 to Argentina** in Japan.

4 **Ireland are beaten 2-0 by Italy** in the US and have keeper **Pat Bonner sent off** for a 'professional foul'. In a deal worth a minimum **£25m over four years**, **ITV** acquire exclusive **TV rights** for **highlights of Football League** and **Rumbelows Cup** matches and **live coverage of Rumbelows semi-finals and final**. They will also cover **Leeds and Manchester** exclusively **in Europe** next season.

5 In the inaugural meeting of the **new Football League**, the old **Second, Third and Fourth Divisions** become the **First (24 clubs), Second (24)** and **Third (23)** Divisions, respectively, with **one vote per club**. The first new rules include **scrapping goal difference in favour of goals 'for'** (if equal, then goals 'against' and then a play-off), clubs will be **rewarded financially** on a scale relating to **success**, and **managers and assistants** must **remain seated** during matches. UEFA permit **England** to draft **Andy Sinton** and **Keith Curle** into their squad to replace the injured Barnes and Stevens. The **League's £24m deal with ITV** over four years will include some **live coverage of Sunday games**.

7 Another **blow for England** as **Mark Wright** suffers a recurrence of his **Achilles' tendon injury**; **Graham Taylor** is furious with **Liverpool** for neglecting to let him know, but the club's chief executive **Peter Robinson** denies Taylor's charges; **Arsenal's Tony Adams** is put on **stand-by**. In friendly tournaments, **Wales beat Japan 1-0** despite having **Iwan Roberts sent off**, and in Boston **Ireland beat Portugal 2-0**, while the **USA's 1-1 draw** with **Italy** is enough to **win the US Cup**.

8 A specialist does not rule **Mark Wright** out of the **European Championships**, and an injection may enable him to play in the later stages. **David Platt's** move from **Bari to Juventus** is finalized.

9 **Bournemouth** manager **Harry Redknapp calls it a day** after nearly 9 years in charge.

10 The **European Championships open** with a **1-1 draw** between hosts **Sweden and France** in Group 1. **Cardiff** are up **for sale** for **£2m. Napoli sign Uruguayan Daniel Fonseca** from **Cagliari** in a **£7m** deal, and **Roma** sign **Serbian Senisa Mihajlovic** from **Red Star Belgrade** for **£4m**.

11 **England and Denmark draw 0-0** in Group 1. In the black at last following **Gascoigne's transfer**, **Spurs** sign a new **£1.9m deal** with sponsors **Holsten**. **Charlton** launch a **£1.5m Valley Investment Plan** in an attempt to return to The Valley by October. **Iain Munro** replaces **Bill McLaren** as **Hamilton** manager.

12 **Holland** are the first Euro **winners**, relieved to knock back a **brave Scottish effort** with a **late goal** from **Bergkamp** in Group 2. **Germany** scrape a **draw with CIS**, equalizing with a last-gasp free-kick, but **lose captain Rudi Völler** with a broken arm.

INDEX TO SELECTED DIARY ITEMS

REVIEW OF THE SEASON

With seven days remaining in the Football League season, there was every prospect of a photo-finish to the championship involving Leeds United and Manchester United; the possibility of the strongly-running Sheffield Wednesday coming through if the two pacesetters stumbled, had just eased. A Mark Bright goal two minutes from the end of Crystal Palace's game with Wednesday for a 1-1 draw, had left the field open to the other two clubs.

Alas, someone forgot to follow the script. Manchester United duly lost 2-0 at Liverpool after Leeds had won a midday comedy of derby errors with Sheffield United, more in keeping with 'It's a Knockout' than a championship clincher.

Those who criticised the standard of play in what was the last Football League championship – as we have come to know it in over 100 years – were given ample scope for argument by this match. Alan Cork scrambled a goal for the Blades in the 28th minute, but Leeds equalised when Gary Speed's shot bounced off Rodney Wallace, who knew nothing about what had happened. That was a minute before half-time and in the 64th minute Jon Newsome put Leeds ahead from a diving header from Gary McAllister's corner, finishing up off the pitch as the ball crossed the line. But four minutes later Sheffield were level when Lee Chapman, in his own penalty area, contrived to score an own goal from John Pemberton's low shot. The pantomime season having arrived early, closed in the 77th minute when Brian Gayle, under pressure, headed the ball over the head of injured goalkeeper Mel Rees, who had hobbled out to the edge of the penalty area. Leeds won 3-2.

To judge Leeds' achievement in winning their first title since 1974 on this performace would be grossly unfair. They proved themselves to be the more consistent team, though it was agreed Manchester United snatched runner-up position from the mouth of the champions. All this despite the omens having been firmly on their side. Unbeaten until losing 3-2 at Sheffield Wednesday on October 26 it proved to be unlucky 13 for United. But they were the last Football League club to lose in 1991–92 and the previous two occasions which had seen them in a similar position, had ended happily enough. In 1974–75 after nine unbeaten games at the start, they went on to win the Second Division title and in 1956–57 they survived a dozen without loss and took the League championship itself.

Leeds had previously won the title in 1974 in some style. Twenty-nine games undefeated. This time apart from a few odd lapses, they gave little away at the back. John Lukic in goal was as cool as ever, Mel Sterland forceful at right-back, Chris Fairclough and Chris Whyte, resolute and tough in the middle, Tony Dorigo, signed from Chelsea, ever ready to show his pace on the left flank. The combative David Batty supplied the threat in midfield, McAllister flitted around, threading menace when it was least expected, while Speed operated with alacrity on the wing or in midfield. Gordon Strachan, 35, was an inspirational captain and revealed a level of stamina inconsistent with his age. Up front, that much travelled target man Chapman accumulated a tidy crop of goals while Wallace provided the freer, foraging role around him.

At the helm was the dour, determined manager Howard Wilkinson, not given to reckless conversation, words without meaning or wandering thought processes. His single-minded approach was amply rewarded. Wilkinson's most frivolous signing came late on when he took Eric Cantona, virtually sight unseen after a trial at Sheffield Wednesday. The controversial Frenchman was an instant hit with the players and supporters alike. Though used chiefly as a substitute, he possessed the confidence and ability to accelerate past opponents with finesse. Moreover he made things happen. On April 11 against Chelsea, he took the ball on his chest, controlled it superbly, outwitted two defenders and rifled home from an acute angle for a goal which had even Wilkinson going misty-eyed. Here the manager revealed his true belief: it's better to win the title well, but it's better to win it than not at all.

While one side of the Pennines was celebrating, the other was in mourning for yet another Manchester United near-achievement in the championship. Alex Ferguson saw United's iron grip slip. From September 7 until losing 1-0 at rock-bottom West Ham on April 22, the destiny of the title remained in their grasp. Hopes of a double having wrested the Rumbelows Cup, faded in disappointment.

Arsenal surrendered their champions crown early on, but there was no doubt that had they been able to knuckle down to matters before going out of the FA Cup at Wrexham on January 4, their challenge might have been more certain. As it was, they lost just one League game afterwards. Meanwhile Liverpool had problems on the field and off it. Injuries deprived the club of players of the calibre of John Barnes, Ian Rush and Ronnie Whelan for long periods. Barnes scored only one League goal, Rush three, including his first ever over Manchester United. Manager Graeme Souness underwent successful heart surgery and Ronnie Moran took over in his absence. A 4-0 defeat at Arsenal was their heaviest reverse for nine years. Consolation came in the FA Cup success.

Jon Newsome is surrounded by enthusiastic colleagues after scoring for Leeds United in what proved to be the League Championship clinching game at Sheffield United. (Allsport)

Sandwiched between Arsenal and Liverpool came Manchester City who beat Leeds 4-0 as late on as April 4, but were erratic and had several poor spells. Lying sixth on January 1 after losing 2-1 at Norwich, Aston Villa scored only one goal in the next 11 games but still finished seventh. Nottingham Forest, ever capable of Brian Clough's brand of stylish attacking football, twice beat Manchester United, but looked distinctly ordinary at others. They did win the ZDS Cup. Dave Bassett's famous escape plans were formulated earlier for Sheffield United, starting in earnest with a 4-2 win at Southampton on January 11, but Crystal Palace never recovered from the loss of Ian Wright, transferred to Arsenal, finding goals increasingly elusive.

Queen's Park Rangers reserved their best performance for New Year's Day, giving Manchester United a 4-1 drubbing at Old Trafford in a run of 11 without defeat. They also beat Leeds 4-1 on March 11. Everton, seventh on March 14, slipped to 12th but Wimbledon survived again without undue problems, though it requried a change of managership at one stage. Chelsea won 2-1 at Liverpool on February 1 to go sixth, but fell away.

Gary Lineker contributed almost half of Tottenham Hotspur's total of goals – 28 of 58 – despite missing seven games. Spurs home record was the worst in the club's history and they lost 11 times at White Hart Lane. A defence-backed recovery helped Southampton, but having conceded only six goals in the previous 15 games, they let in five in a second-half at Arsenal in the last game. Only seven different players scored their League goals. For Oldham, it was an undistinguised season and Norwich reserved their best performances for the FA Cup. Coventry were sixth on October 26 but scored only once in the last seven games and failed to score at all in 21. They did manage two more points than relegated Luton, who failed to win away and also found difficulty in scoring goals.

After some early encouragement, Notts County were never out of the bottom two from March and West Ham were in trouble after losing 3-0 at Notts County on December 28 and a 4-0 win over Norwich on April 11 proved a false dawn.

In the Second Division, Ipswich won the championship, ironically under former Hammers boss John Lyall. Yet after a confident opening they endured eight games without a win including three successive defeats. Nerves set in near the end, but they overcame them. In contrast, Middlesbrough had a run of eight without loss after an indifferent start, but held on to top spot despite the odd lapse until losing 2-1 at Barnsley on November 5. With games in hand they won five of their last six fixtures. Derby surged unbeaten in the last eight to finish third, but Leicester, after appearing to time their thrust to perfection lost the last two matches. Cambridge United's widely criticised Route One approach still helped to put them on top after a 2-1 win at Ipswich on November 9. Injuries hindered them but so did inconsistency.

Blackburn's traditional second half of the season slump produced six successive defeats but after a 2-2 draw at Tranmere, Kenny Dalglish's expensive outfit edged back into the play-offs. However Charlton spoiled a run of ten without defeat by losing their last two and after hovering on the brink of the play-offs themselves, Swindon transferred Duncan Shearer to Blackburn in March and never scored more than one goal in a game afterwards.

Portsmouth chased promotion and a Wembley Cup Final but lost out both times. Their reward was a well merited Fair Play Award. Watford's season was salvaged with only one defeat in the last 13 and though Wolves were 21st on November 23 they did improve. An early kick-off had Southend top for a couple of hours on February 1, but they became unsettled after manger David Webb announced his intention to leave in the summer. Brett Angell scored in seven successive games for them.

Bristol Rovers were as low as 21st themselves on the turn of the year, but gained from two stout performances against Liverpool in the FA Cup. Despite 40 League and Cup goals from ex-Merseyside favourite John Aldridge, Tranmere could only manage 14th place and Millwall were never higher than 11th. Barnsley, never in the top half, still managed a win over Ipswich and Bristol City turned the corner with the arrival of Andy Cole on loan from Arsenal and Leroy Rosenior from West Ham. In the last ten games they contributed 13 of 17 goals scored.

Sunderland's FA Cup run threatened their First Division status, but they managed to pick up sufficient points including a 3-0 win over Ipswich. Grimsby were never far from the danger zone and the last 14 games yielded only seven goals. Kevin Keegan's stint in charge of Newcastle started in 23rd place with a 3-0 win over Bristol City, but five successive defeats made it appear ominous for a time. Oxford looked a good tip for relegation until beating Swindon 5-3 on March 7, yet not even Peter Shilton could save Plymouth and Brighton were never out of the bottom five from December. Port Vale finished at the foot after a disastrous run of 17 without a win and a 2-0 win over Blackburn was merely a momentary relief.

Brentford emerged as Third Division champions despite an average spell with which to begin. They were top on October 5, suffered four consecutive defeats in March but eneded with six successive wins. Birmingham, with problems in several positions necessitating the use of 33 different players including five goalkeepers, still stabilized at the right moment. Top scorer Nigel Gleghorn was the only ever present player. Huddersfield made the play-offs after remaining unbeaten in the last eight, scoring 17 and conceding just two goals. Stoke headed the division for nearly two months but then one point from a possible nine cost them dearly. They did win the Autoglass Trophy over Stockport who scored freely but found the net in only two of their last six matches. The second of these brought a 2-0 win over Birmingham on the last day.

Peterborough lost 3-0 at Stockport on December 14 and went 15 without defeat to mid-March but they had no success in the next five, recovering only to lose the last game 1-0 to Brentford. West Bromwich beat Birmingham 3-0 on February 8 to lead the others, then collapsed, winning only four more games. They used 34 players. Middle of the table Bournemouth produced a belated effort which was not sustained and Fulham's defence had its moments, one of six games without conceding a goal. Leyton Orient's home record survived until February 8 but three more defeats followed at Brisbane Road. Hartlepool had their highest placing in Division Three at 11th and it might have been better but for a spell of only two goals in seven outings. Reading's attack failed into April with no goals in five consecutive games before scoring six against Torquay, but several youngsters were given senior opportunities at Elm Park. The arrival of Andy Walker from Celtic promised better things for Bolton and he responded with 15 of the 26 goals scored. But the side entered the last match with a run of ten without a win.

Hull's two faces were shown by 11 games and no win to February 1, then only one reverse in 12. The last four games were won without losing a goal. After struggling all season, Wigan lost just two of the last 11 games while Bradford were 21st in the middle of January before a nine-game sequence around March improved matters. Preston were one place worse off on March 14 after losing 3-0 at home to Chester, but pulled their game together and Chester themselves escaped after a run of 12 without a win at one time. Swansea were unable to win any of their last 11 and Exeter, who used 35 players, slid with just one point from the last possible 24 but remained in the division. Bury had a wretched second half of the season and went down with Shrewsbury, who suffered a club record 17 games without a win, Torquay whose highlight was two successive 1-0 wins and Darlington, never off the bottom from mid-February.

In Division Four on December 21, Burnley beat ill-fated Aldershot 2-1 at the Recreation Ground to go top and spurred on by their formidable support at home and away, never suffered two consecutive defeats afterwards and were worthy champions. Rotherham finished runners-up showing consistent form all season, but perhaps more of it after the turn of the year. Mansfield were never lower than fourth at any one time and Blackpool made the play-offs a point below

Happy line-up of Barclays League 1991–1992 top managers: Left to right: Divisional Managers of the Season John Lyall (Ipswich), Division Two; Phil Holder (Brentford), Division Three; Howard Wilkinson (Leeds United), Barclays Bank Manager of the Year; Brian Flynn, accepting on behalf of Jimmy Mullen (Burnley), Division Four & Dave Bassett (Sheffield United), winner of the new Barclays Bank Special Achievement Award. (Copyright Barclays Bank)

the Stags. Dave Bamber again took the Seasiders scoring honours but the side slipped from top to fourth despite a run of 14 without defeat. Scunthorpe beat Blackpool 2-1 on December 28 but failed to capitalize on it, though they had a late run dropping only two out of 24 points. Crewe drew 1-1 at Burnley on September 7 to lead the field, but often found scoring goals a problem.

Freescoring newcomers Barnet were briefly top on November 9 but were let down by poor away form, though oddly enough won 4-1 at York on the last day to secure a play-off berth. Rochdale could have overhauled Barnet by beating Burnley on May 5, but lost 3-0, three successive defeats costing them a real chance in April. Chris Pike and Carl Dale scored 44 goals between them for Cardiff but the team still finished ninth. Fathoming out Lincoln was difficult: they scored only 19 goals in the first 26 matches, hit four and five in the next two and let in just a couple in the last eight.

Gillingham's consistency was simply one of being an average team in the middle of the table and Scarborough, who used 32 players, seemed to be on the threshold of improvement on January 4 after a 2-0 win at Rotherham. Alas the weather hit them badly and it was a month before they played again only to lose 5-1 at Barnet. Chesterfield suffered a goal famine until Steve Norris arrived from Halifax and Wrexham's best form in the League coincided with their sensational cup win over Arsenal. Walsall, who once ousted the Gunners from the same competition in 1933, never shook off a middle of the table look.

Northampton had a promising run of ten games without defeat, but pressing financial worries forced them to sell Tony Adcock and Bobby Barnes to Peterborough and Hereford's season tailed off after they had been as high as fourth in early November. Maidstone, with their own fiscal failings, rallied briefly before scoring only three times in the last eight games. Nine games without a win led York to 19th. Halifax were unable to score in exactly half of their games to illustrate their plight but Doncaster escaped bottom place even though they went 17 games without a win at one period. They left the cellar to Carlisle who had won 3-0 at Doncaster on the first day of the season. Aldershot bowed out in March, the fans finding some money for players who were not being paid, yet both bodies apparently willing to stagger on even longer in such extraordinary circumstances.

Transfers Continued from Page 614

		From	To	Fee
12	Johnson, Thomas	Notts County	Derby County	
25	Kerr, Dylan	Blackpool	Leeds United (Tr. back)	
25	Kruszynski, Zbigniew	Wimbledon	Brentford	
26	Lange, Anthony S.	Wolverhampton Wanderers	Portsmouth	
26	Lee, David J.	Chelsea	Plymouth Argyle	
26	Loram, Mark J.	Torquay United	Stockport County	
19	Lowe, David A.	Ipswich Town	Port Vale	
5	McClelland, John	Leeds United	Notts County	
5	McKeown, Gary J.	Arsenal	Shrewsbury Town	
26	Marshall, Colin	Barnsley	Scarborough	
12	Mauchlen, Alistair H.	Leicester City	Leeds United	
16	Maxwell, Alistair	Motherwell	Bolton Wanderers	
19	Mendonca, Clive P.	Sheffield United	Grimsby Town	
4	Morris, Andrew D.	Chesterfield	Exeter City	
4	Morrow, Stephen J.	Arsenal	Barnet	
4	Nevin, Patrick K. F.	Everton	Tranmere Rovers	
26	Petterson, Andrew K.	Luton Town	Ipswich Town	
7	Peyton, Gerry J.	Bolton Wanderers	Everton (Tr. back)	
26	Peyton, Gerry J.	Everton	Norwich City	
26	Pollitt, Michael F.	Bury	Lincoln City	
10	Pressman, Kevin P.	Sheffield Wednesday	Stoke City	
26	Rees, Melvyn	Norwich City	West Bromwich Albion (Tr. back)	
19	Reid, Paul R.	Leicester City	Bradford City	
26	Salman, Danis M. M.	Plymouth Argyle	Peterborough United	
26	Samways, Mark	Doncaster Rovers	Scunthorpe United	
25	Sealey, Leslie J.	Aston Villa	Coventry City	
5	Shepstone, Paul T.	Blackburn Rovers	York City	
26	Stiles, John C.	Doncaster Rovers	Rochdale	
27	Thomas, Roderick C.	Watford	Gillingham	
26	Trollope, Paul J.	Swindon Town	Torquay United	
26	Varadi, Imre	Leeds United	Luton Town	
19	Waddock, Gary P.	Queens Park Rangers	Swindon Town	
26	Whyte, David A.	Crystal Palace	Charlton Athletic	
5	Williams, Andrew	Leeds United	Notts County	
26	Willis, James A.	Leicester City	Bradford City	

April 1992

22	Nicholson, Shane M.	Lincoln City	Derby County	

Temporary Transfers

1	Brown, Kevan	Aldershot	Portsmouth	
15	Day, Mervyn R.	Luton Town	Leeds United (Tr. back)	
2	Gilkes, Earl G. M.	Southampton	Reading (Tr. back)	
1	Hoult, Matthew J.	Blackburn Rovers	Aston Villa	
28	Hoult, Russell	Blackpool	Leicester City (Tr. back)	
10	Key, Lance	Sheffield Wednesday	York City	
21	Whitworth, Neil A.	Barnsley	Manchester United (Tr. back)	

May 1992

Temporary Transfer

6	Varadi, Imre	Luton Town	Leeds United (Tr. back)	

Summer moves:

Andy Gray, Crystal Palace to Tottenham H; Darren Anderton, Portsmouth to Tottenham H; Dean Austin, Southend U to Tottenham H; Peter Beadle, Gillingham to Tottenham H; Warren Joyce, Preston NE to Plymouth Arg; Paul Bracewell, Sunderland to Newcastle U; Steve Castle, Leyton Orient to Plymouth Arg; Ryan Cross, Plymouth Arg to Hartlepool U; Paul Dalton, Hartlepool U to Plymouth Arg; Matt Elliott, Torquay U to Scunthorpe U; Ian Hamilton, Scunthorpe U to WBA; Mark Hine, Scunthorpe U to Doncaster R; Paul Holmes, Torquay U to Birmingham C; Mike Jeffrey, Bolton W to Doncaster R; Tony McCarthy, Shelbourne to Millwall; Andy May, Bristol C to Millwall; Mark Pembridge, Luton T to Derby Co; Shaun Rouse, Rangers to Bristol C; Mark Samways, Doncaster R to Scunthorpe U; David Thompson, Millwall to Bristol C; Paul Walsh, Tottenham H to Portsmouth; Darren Wassall, Nottingham F to Derby Co; John Colquhoun, Millwall to Sunderland; Graham Harbey, WBA to Stoke C; Tom Jones, Swindon T to Reading; Craig Maskell, Reading to Swindon T; Jon Narbett, Hereford U to Oxford U; Phil Parkinson, Bury to Reading.

INTRODUCTION TO THE CLUB SECTION

The full page team photographs which appear on the first of each club's six pages in this section of the yearbook were taken at the beginning of the 1991–92 season, and therefore relate to the season covered by this edition's statistics.

The third and fourth pages of each club's section give a complete record of the League season for the club concerned, including date, venue, opponents, result, half-time score, League position, goalscorers, attendance and complete line-ups, including substitutes where used, for every League game in the 1991–92 season. These two pages also include consolidated lists of goalscorers for the club in League, Rumbelows Cup and FA Cup matches and a summary of results in the two main domestic cups. The full League history of the club, a complete list of major honours won and best placings achieved, and a note of the team's first and second choice colours appears on the second page of this section. The colours are checked with the clubs, but please note that second choice colours may vary during the season.

Note also that the League position shown after each League result is recalculated as at every Saturday night plus full holiday programmes, but the position after mid-week fixtures will not normally be updated. Please be advised that the attendance figures quoted for each League game are those which appeared in the Press at the time, whereas the attendance statistics published on pages 618 and 619 are those issued officially by the Football League after the season has been completed. However, the figures for each League game are those used by the Football League in its weekly bulletin, in conjunction with the *Sunday Telegraph* and Jack Rollin's column in that newspaper.

On the fourth page of each club's section, the total League appearances for the season are listed at the foot of each player's column. Substitutes are inserted as numbers 12 and 14 where they actually came on to play. The players taken off are respectively given an asterisk (*) and a dagger (†). But in order to give the chart a uniform appearance, where only one substitute has played the number 12 will have been used.

In the totals at the foot of each column, substitute appearances are listed separately below the '+' sign, but have been amalgamated in the totals which feature in the player's historical section on the final page for each club. Thus these appearances include those as substitute.

The final pages for each club list all the players included on the Football League's 'Retained' list, which is published at the end of May. Here you will find each player's height and weight, where known, plus birthplace, birthdate and source, together with total League appearances and goals for each club he has represented. Full names of all other players retained including trainees, non-contract players and schoolboys are also given. In addition more club information is added on these pages including items of interest from the club's history and a list of previous managers.

No appearances or goals are credited in matches against Aldershot in the Fourth Division, but those goals scored in the various cup competitions are included. Aldershot's record is shown up to the time they were forced to withdraw, but the appearances and goals for their players are not shown in the accumulated version.

Any transfers which take place between the publication of the League's Retained list and this book going to press will be included in the transfer section between pages 607 and 614, but the player's details will remain under the club which retained him at the end of the season. An asterisk * by a player's name on the fifth and sixth pages means that he was given a free transfer at the end of the 1991–92 season, a dagger † against a name means that he is a non-contract player, and a double dagger ‡ indicates that the player's registration was cancelled during the season. An § indicates either a Trainee or an Associated Schoolboy who has made Football League appearances.

The play-offs in the Football League are listed separately on pages 592 and 593. Appearances made by players in these play-offs will *not* be included in their career totals.

Four pages have been included for Colchester United, the 93rd club in the Football League.

Editor's note: In the Scottish League, substitutes where used are listed as 12 and 14. The second player to be taken off is also picked out with a dagger.

30

ALDERSHOT 1991–92 *Back row (left to right):* Steve Wignall (Physiol), Robert Reinelt, Peter Terry, Jon Flower, John Granville, Charlie Henry, Mark Ogley, George Berry, Jason Tucker.
Front row: Mark Rees, David Puckett, Ian McDonald (Player-Manager), Kevan Brown, Phil Heath.

Diadora Division 3   **ALDERSHOT TOWN**

Recreation Ground, High St, Aldershot GU11 1TW. Telephone Aldershot (0252) 20211. Shotsline: 0891 446834.

Ground capacity: 5000.

Record attendance: 19,138 v Carlisle U, FA Cup 4th rd (replay), 28 January 1970.

Record receipts: £22,949.66 v Sheffield W, Littlewoods Cup 2nd rd, 2nd leg, 3 October 1989.

Pitch measurements: 116yd × 72yd.

President: Arthur English.

Chairman: T. Owens.

Directors: P. Bloomfield, G. Brookland (Supporters Club representative), M. Grant, D. Hunt, J. McGinty, K. Prentice.

Team Manager: Steve Wignall. *Hon. Doctor:* A. Gillespie FRCS.

Secretary: P. Bridgeman. *Youth Development Officer:* P. Bevis. *Press & PRO:* N. Fryer.

Year Formed: 1926. Re-formed 1992 as Aldershot Town (1992) Ltd. Turned Professional: 1927. Ltd Co.: 1927.

Former Names: Aldershot Town, Aldershot c.1937.

Club Nickname: 'Shots'.

Record League Victory: 8-1 v Gateshead, Division 4, 13 September 1958 – Marshall; Henry, Jackson; Mundy, Price, Gough; Walters, Stepney (3), Lacey (3), Matthews (2), Tyrer.

Record Cup Victory: 7-0 v Chelmsford, FA Cup, 1st rd, 28 November 1931 – Robb; Twine, McDougall (1); Norman Wilson, Gardiner, Middleton (1); Blackbourne, Stevenson (1), Thorn (3), Hopkins (1), Edgar. 7-0 v Newport (I of W), FA Cup, 2nd rd, 8 December 1945 – Reynolds; Horton, Sheppard; Ray, White, Summerbee; Sinclair, Hold (1), Brooks (5), Fitzgerald, Hobbs (1).

Record Defeat: 1-10 v Southend U, Leyland Daf Cup, Pr rd, 6 November 1990.

Most League Points (2 for a win): 57, Division 4, 1978–79.

Most League points (3 for a win): 75, Division 4, 1983–84.

Most League Goals: 83, Division 4, 1963–64.

Highest League Scorer in Season: John Dungworth, 26, Division 4, 1978–79.

Most League Goals in Total Aggregate: Jack Howarth, 171, 1965–71 and 1972–77.

Most Capped Player: Peter Scott, 1 (10), Northern Ireland.

Most League Appearances: Murray Brodie, 461, 1970–83.

Record Transfer Fee Received: £150,000 from Wolverhampton W for Tony Lange, July 1989.

Record Transfer Fee Paid: £54,000 to Portsmouth for Colin Garwood, February 1980.

Football League Record: 1932 Elected to Division 3 (S); 1958–73 Division 4; 1973–76 Division 3; 1976–87 Division 4; 1987–89 Division 3; 1989–92 Division 4; 1992– Diadora Division 3.

Honours: Football League: best season: 8th, Division 3, 1973–74. *FA Cup:* best season: 5th rd, 1932–33, 5th rd replay, 1978–79. *Football League Cup:* best season: 3rd rd replay, 1984–85.

Colours: Red shirts (blue trim), white shorts (red flash), blue stockings (white trim). Away strip: White shirts (red trim), blue shorts (white flash), red stockings (blue trim).

ALDERSHOT 1991–92 LEAGUE RECORD

Match No.	Date		Venue	Opponents		Result	H/T Score	Lg. Pos.	Goalscorers	Atten-dance
1	Aug	24	A	Burnley	L	0-2	0-0	21		5877
2		31	H	Maidstone U	W	3-0	2-0	15	Heath, Puckett, Rees	1864
3	Sep	3	A	Crewe Alex	L	0-4	0-2	—		3624
4		6	H	Carlisle U	D	2-2	2-1	—	Bertschin, Puckett	2149
5		14	A	Scarborough	W	2-0	2-0	12	Cooper, Puckett	1564
6		17	A	Wrexham	D	0-0	0-0	—		1774
7		20	H	Halifax T	L	1-3	1-1	—	Hopkins	2695
8		28	A	Chesterfield	L	1-2	1-0	17	Puckett	2801
9	Oct	4	H	Rochdale	D	1-1	0-1	—	Bertschin	2443
10		12	A	Hereford U	L	0-1	0-1	19		3332
11		18	H	Rotherham U	L	0-1	0-0	—		2370
12		26	A	Walsall	L	1-3	0-1	22	Hopkins	3025
13	Nov	2	A	Lincoln C	D	0-0	0-0	22		1737
14		5	H	Blackpool	L	2-5	1-2	—	Henry, Groves (og)	1685
15		8	H	Cardiff C	L	1-2	1-2	—	Berry	2174
16		23	A	York C	L	0-1	0-1	22		2050
17		30	A	Gillingham	L	1-3	0-1	22	Ogley	2566
18	Dec	14	H	Doncaster R	D	0-0	0-0	22		1467
19		21	H	Burnley	L	1-2	0-0	22	Henry	2567
20		28	A	Maidstone U	W	2-1	1-1	22	Stewart, Puckett	1506
21	Jan	1	H	Crewe Alex	L	0-2	0-0	22		2161
22		3	H	Scunthorpe U	D	0-0	0-0	—		1929
23		11	A	Mansfield T	L	0-3	0-0	22		2933
24		17	H	Barnet	L	0-1	0-0	—		2922
25	Feb	1	A	Rotherham U	L	0-2	0-0	22		3717
26		4	A	Northampton T	L	0-1	0-1	—		2547
27		8	H	Walsall	D	1-1	0-0	22	Puckett	2078
28		11	H	Gillingham	D	0-0	0-0	—		2986
29		15	A	Doncaster R	L	0-1	0-1	22		1568
30		21	H	Mansfield T	L	1-3	1-2	—	Puckett	2076
31		29	A	Scunthorpe U	L	0-1	0-0	23		2576
32	Mar	3	A	Barnet	L	0-5	0-3	—		2038
33		7	H	Northampton T	L	1-4	1-1	23	Joyce	1374
34		10	A	Blackpool	L	0-1	0-0	—		3728
35		14	H	Lincoln C	L	0-3	0-3	23		1473
36		20	A	Cardiff C	L	0-2	0-1	—		6006

Final League Position: —

GOALSCORERS

League (21): Puckett 7, Bertschin 2, Henry 2, Hopkins 2, Berry 1, Cooper 1, Heath 1, Joyce 1, Ogley 1, Rees 1, Stewart 1, own goals 1.
Rumbelows Cup (2): Bertschin 1, Puckett 1.
FA Cup (0).

Granville	Brown	Cooper	Henry	Flower	Whitlock	Rees	Puckett	Bertschin	Ogley	Stewart	Burvill	Heath	Hopkins	Talbot	Berry	Randall	Stapleton	Cole	Hucker	McDonald	Phillips S	Terry	Halbert	Baker	Reinelt	Tucker	Parks	Osgood	Match No.
1	2	3	4	5	6	7	8	9	10*	11†	12	14																	1
1	2	3	10	5†	6	7*	8	9	12	11			4	14															2
1	2	3	10	5	6	7*	8	9	12	11			4																3
1	2	3	10†	5	6	7	8	9	14	12		11*	4																4
1	2	3	10			7	8	9†	5		12	11	4*		6	14													5
1	2	3	10			7	8		5			11	4		6			9											6
1	2	3	10			7	8		5	12		14	11*	4	6					9†									7
1	2	3	10	9		7	8		5			11	4		6														8
	2	3				7	8	9	5				4		6	10		1	11										9
1	2	3	9	12		7	8		5				4		6	10		11*											10
1	2	3	9	11		7	8		5*	12			4		6	10													11
1	2	3	4		12		9	5				7	11		6	10				8*									12
1	2	3	4	5		7*	8	9	10			11			6							12							13
1	2	3†	4	5			8	9	6			11	14*		10							7	12						14
1	2		4	5			8	9				11	14		6	10		3	7*	12									15
1	2		5			7	12	9*	4			14	11†		6	10		3	8										16
1	2	12	5		6	7†	8	9	4			14					10*	3	11										17
1	2		5	10			8	9	4	12		11*			6			3				7							18
1	2	3	5	10			8		4			11			6							7	9						19
1	2	3†10		5			8		4	11		12	14		6							7	9*						20
1	2		10	5	12		8	9	4*11			3			6							7							21
1	2		10	5	12		8	9†	4*11			14	3		6							7							22
1	2		10	5	6*		8	9†		11		14	3							4		7	12						23
1	2		10*	5			8	9	4	11†		14								3		6	7	12					24
1	2		9	5		7*	8		4			11	12		6					10		3							25
1	2		9	5		7†12			4			14			6					3	10		11	8*					26
1	2		9	5		11*	8		4			12			6					3	10					7			27
1	2		9	5		11	8		4*						6					3	10			12		7			28
1	2		9	5		7*	8		4			11			6					3	10			12					29
1	2		9	5			8		4			11			6					3	10					7			30
1	2		9	5			8		4			11			6					3	10		7						31
	2		9	5			8		4			11			6					3	10		7					1	32
		2 10	9						4			11								3	8		7	6				1	33
	2	8	9						4			11								3	10		7	6				1	34
	2	8	9	12					4*			11								3†	10		7	6				1	35
	2	8	9	5											6*					12	10		7	11†				1	36
30	36	20	35	23	8	19	29	17	30	6	1	15	20	—	25	8	1	1	1	17	5	14	—	9	9	4	3	5	

+ 1s   + 2s   + 2s   + 3s   + 1s + 5s + 3s + 10s 4s + 1s   + 1s   + 1s + 2s 1s + 2s 2s

Joyce—Match No. 33(5) 34(5) 35(5) 36(3); Tomlinson—Match No. 35(14) 36(14); Hutchinson—Match No. 36(14).

Rumbelows Cup	First Round	Peterborough U (a)		1-3
		(h)		1-2
FA Cup	First Round	Enfield (h)		0-1

ALDERSHOT

Player and Position	Ht	Wt	Birth Date	Birth Place	Source	Clubs	League App	League Gls
Goalkeepers								
John Granville	6 0	12 07	6 5 56	Tobago	Slough	Slough	—	—
						Millwall	6	—
						Los Angeles	—	—
						Wycombe	—	—
						Aldershot	—	—
Steve Osgood†	6 0	12 00	20 1 62	Surrey	Farnborough	Aldershot	1	—
Defenders								
Kevan Brown	5 9	11 08	2 1 66	Andover		Southampton	—	—
						Brighton & HA	53	—
						Aldershot	110	2
						Portsmouth (loan)	—	—
Leigh Cooper	5 8	10 09	7 5 61	Reading	Apprentice	Plymouth Arg	323	15
						Aldershot	33	2
Alex Fisher‡	5 11	12 08	30 1 73	Southampton	Trainee	Aldershot	2	—
John Flower	6 4	15 04	9 12 64	Northampton	Corby T	Sheffield U	—	—
						Aldershot	32	2
Tony Hopkins	5 9	11 05	17 2 71	Pontypool	Trainee	Newport Co	6	—
						Bristol C	—	—
						Aldershot	10	—
Anthony Joyce†	5 11	11 00	24 9 71	Wembley	Trainee	QPR	—	—
						Aldershot	3	—
Chris Tomlinson			10 7 70	Aldershot	British Univs	Aldershot	—	—
Jason Tucker‡	5 11	11 00	3 2 73	Isleworth	Trainee	Aldershot	1	—
Mark Whitlock‡	6 0	12 02	14 3 61	Portsmouth	Apprentice	Southampton	61	1
						Grimsby T (loan)	8	—
						Aldershot (loan)	14	—
						Bournemouth	99	1
						Reading	27	—
						Aldershot	29	2
Midfield								
Steve Baker	5 5	10 05	2 12 61	Newcastle	Apprentice	Southampton	73	—
						Burnley (loan)	10	—
						Leyton Orient	112	6
						Bournemouth	6	—
						Aldershot	—	—
Glen Burvill‡	5 9	10 10	26 10 62	Canning Town	Apprentice	West Ham U	—	—
						Aldershot	65	15
						Reading	30	—
						Fulham (loan)	9	2
						Aldershot	195	23
Charlie Henry‡	5 11	12 08	13 2 62	Acton	Apprentice	Swindon T	223	26
						Torquay U (loan)	6	1
						Northampton T (loan)	4	1
						Aldershot	81	18
Ian McDonald†	5 9	11 09	10 5 53	Barrow	Apprentice	Barrow	35	2
						Workington	42	4
						Liverpool	—	—
						Colchester U (loan)	5	2
						Mansfield T	56	4
						York C	175	29
						Aldershot	340	49
Brian Talbot‡	5 10	12 00	21 7 53	Ipswich	Apprentice	Ipswich T	177	25
						Arsenal	254	40
						Watford	48	8
						Stoke C	54	5
						WBA	74	5
						Fulham	5	1
						Aldershot	10	—

ALDERSHOT

Foundation: It was through the initiative of Councillor Jack White, a local newsagent who immediately captured the interest of the Town Clerk D. Llewellyn Griffiths, that Aldershot Town was formed in 1926. Having established a limited liability company under the chairmanship of Norman Clinton, an Aldershot resident and chairman of the Hampshire County FA they rented the Recreation Ground from the Aldershot Borough Council.

First Football League game: 27 August, 1932, Division 3(S), v Southend U (h) L 1-2 – Robb; Wade, McDougall; Lawson, Spence, Middleton; Proud, White, Gamble, Douglas, Fishlock (1).

Did you know: Aldershot's record run of scoring in consecutive League games is 31 from 1 April 1961 to 25 November 1961 inclusive. This included a 2-0 win over Accrington Stanley which was subsequently deleted when that club resigned from the League.

Managers (and Secretary-managers)
Angus Seed 1927–37, Bill McCracken 1937–49, Gordon Clark 1950–55, Harry Evans 1955–59, Dave Smith 1959–71 (GM from 1967), Tommy McAnearney 1967–68, Jimmy Melia 1968–72, Tommy McAnearney 1972–81, Len Walker 1981–84, Ron Harris (GM) 1984–85, Len Walker 1985–91, Brian Talbot 1991–92, Ian McDonald 1992.

Player and Position	Ht	Wt	Birth Date	Birth Place	Source	Clubs	League App	League Gls
Forwards								
Keith Bertschin‡	6 1	11 08	25 8 56	Enfield	Barnet	Ipswich T	32	8
						Birmingham C	118	29
						Norwich C	114	29
						Stoke City	88	29
						Sunderland	36	7
						Walsall	55	9
						Chester C	19	—
						Aldershot	—	—
Michael Cole*	5 11	11 04	3 9 66	Stepney	Amateur	Ipswich T	38	3
						Port Vale (loan)	4	1
						Fulham	48	4
						Aldershot	—	—
Paul Coombs	5 11	12 07	4 9 70	Bristol	QPR	Aldershot	16	1
Paul Halbert	5 9	11 00	28 10 73	St Albans	Trainee	Aldershot	3	—
Philip Heath*	5 9	12 02	24 11 64	Stoke	Apprentice	Stoke C	156	17
						Oxford U	37	1
						Cardiff C	11	1
						Aldershot	—	—
Grant Hutchinson			23 2 73	St Peter's		Aldershot	—	—
Wayne Parks			21 6 74	Brighton	Trainee	Aldershot	—	—
Stewart Phillips*	6 0	11 07	30 12 61	Halifax	Amateur	Hereford U	293	83
						WBA	15	4
						Swansea C	20	1
						Hereford U	37	10
						Wrexham	3	1
						Aldershot	—	—
Mark Rees	5 10	11 10	13 10 61	Smethwick	Apprentice	Walsall	237	37
						Rochdale (loan)	3	—
						Shamrock R	2	—
						Aldershot	—	—
Robert Reinelt	5 10	11 05	11 3 74	Epping	Trainee	Aldershot	5	—

ARSENAL 1991–92 *Back row (left to right):* Gary Lewin (Physiotherapist), Pat Rice (Youth Team Coach), Andy Linighan, David Seaman, Tony Adams, Steve Bould, Alan Smith, Colin Pates, Stewart Houston (First Team Coach), George Armstrong (Reserve Team Coach).
Front row: Craig McKernon, Michael Thomas, Paul Davis, Kevin Campbell, Lee Dixon, Anders Limpar, George Graham (Manager), David Hillier, Siggi Jonsson, Perry Groves, David Rocastle, Paul Merson, Nigel Winterburn.

FA Premier

ARSENAL

Arsenal Stadium, Highbury, London N5. Telephone 071-226 0304. Recorded information on 071-359 0131. Commercial and Marketing 359-0808. Clubline 0898 20 20 20. Mail Order 354 8397.

Ground capacity: 28,000.

Record attendance: 73,295 v Sunderland, Div 1, 9 March 1935.

Record receipts: £233,595 v Everton, Littlewoods Cup semi-final, 24 February 1988.

Pitch measurements: 110yd × 71yd.

Chairman: P. D. Hill-Wood.

Vice-chairman: D. Dein.

Directors: Sir Robert Bellinger CBE, DSC, R. G. Gibbs, C. E. B. L. Carr, R. C. S. Carr, D. Fiszman.

Managing Director: K. J. Friar.

Manager: George Graham. *Assistant Manager/Coach:* Stewart Houston. *Physio:* Gary Lewin. *Reserve Coach:* George Armstrong. *Youth Coach:* Pat Rice. *Secretary:* K. J. Friar. *Assistant Secretary:* David Miles. *Commercial Manager:* John Hazell. *Marketing Manager:* Phil Carling.

Year Formed: 1886. Turned Professional: 1891. Ltd Co.: 1893.

Former Grounds: 1886–87, Plumstead Common; 1887–88, Sportsman Ground; 1888–90, Manor Ground; 1890–93, Invicta Ground; 1893–1913, Manor Ground; 1913, Highbury.

Former Names: 1886, Dial Square; 1886–91, Royal Arsenal; 1891–1914, Woolwich Arsenal.

Club Nickname: 'Gunners'.

Record League Victory: 12-0 v Loughborough T, Division 2, 12 March 1900 – Orr; McNichol, Jackson; Moir, Dick (2), Anderson (1); Hunt, Cottrell (2), Main (2), Gaudie (3), Tennant (2).

Record Cup Victory: 11-1 v Darwen, FA Cup, 3rd rd, 9 January 1932 – Moss; Parker, Hapgood; Jones, Roberts, John; Hulme (2), Jack (3), Lambert (2), James, Bastin (4).

Record Defeat: 0-8 v Loughborough T, Division 2, 12 December 1896.

Most League Points (2 for a win): 66, Division 1, 1930–31.

Most League points (3 for a win): 83, Division 1, 1990–91.

Most League Goals: 127, Division 1, 1930–31.

Highest League Scorer in Season: Ted Drake, 42, 1934–35.

Most League Goals in Total Aggregate: Cliff Bastin, 150, 1930–47.

Most Capped Player: Kenny Sansom, 77 (86), England.

Most League Appearances: David O'Leary, 547, 1975–92.

Record Transfer Fee Received: £1,500,000 from Liverpool for Michael Thomas, November 1991.

Record Transfer Fee Paid: £2,500,000 to Crystal Palace for Ian Wright, September 1991.

Football League Record: 1893 Elected to Division 2; 1904–13 Division 1; 1913–19 Division 2; 1919–92 Division 1; 1992– FA Premier League.

Honours: Football League: Division 1 – Champions 1930–31, 1932–33, 1933–34, 1934–35, 1937–38, 1947–48, 1952–53, 1970–71, 1988–89, 1990–91; Runners-up 1925–26, 1931–32, 1972–73; Division 2 – Runners-up 1903–04. *FA Cup:* Winners 1929–30, 1935–36, 1949–50, 1970–71, 1978–79; Runners-up 1926–27, 1931–32, 1951–52, 1971–72, 1977–78, 1979–80. *Double Performed:* 1970–71. *Football League Cup:* Winners 1986–87; Runners-up 1967–68, 1968–69, 1987–88. **European Competitions:** *Fairs Cup:* 1963–64, 1969–70 (winners), 1970–71; *European Cup:* 1971–72, 1991–92; *UEFA Cup:* 1978–79, 1981–82, 1982–83; *European Cup-Winners' Cup:* 1979–80 (runners-up).

Colours: Red shirts with white sleeves, white shorts, red stockings. **Change colours:** Yellow shirts, navy blue shorts, yellow stockings.

ARSENAL 1991–92 LEAGUE RECORD

Match No.	Date		Venue	Opponents	Result		H/T Score	Lg. Pos.	Goalscorers	Attendance
1	Aug	17	H	QPR	D	1-1	0-1	—	Merson	38,099
2		20	A	Everton	L	1-3	0-1	—	Winterburn	31,200
3		24	A	Aston Villa	L	1-3	1-1	21	Smith	29,684
4		27	H	Luton T	W	2-0	1-0	—	Merson, Smith	25,898
5		31	H	Manchester C	W	2-1	0-1	12	Smith, Limpar	35,009
6	Sep	3	A	Leeds U	D	2-2	1-0	—	Smith 2	29,396
7		7	H	Coventry C	L	1-2	0-1	15	Adams	28,142
8		14	A	Crystal Palace	W	4-1	1-0	10	Campbell 2, Smith, Thomas	24,228
9		21	H	Sheffield U	W	5-2	4-0	7	Smith, Dixon (pen), Groves, Rocastle, Campbell	30,244
10		28	A	Southampton	W	4-0	1-0	3	Rocastle, Wright 3	18,050
11	Oct	5	H	Chelsea	W	3-2	1-2	3	Dixon (pen), Wright, Campbell	42,074
12		19	A	Manchester U	D	1-1	1-1	4	Rocastle	46,594
13		26	H	Notts Co	W	2-0	0-0	4	Smith, Wright	30,011
14	Nov	2	H	West Ham U	L	0-1	0-0	5		33,539
15		16	A	Oldham Ath	D	1-1	0-0	6	Wright	15,681
16		23	A	Sheffield W	D	1-1	0-1	6	Bould	32,174
17	Dec	1	H	Tottenham H	W	2-0	0-0	—	Wright, Campbell	38,892
18		8	A	Nottingham F	L	2-3	0-1	—	Merson, Smith	22,095
19		21	H	Everton	W	4-2	3-2	6	Wright 4	29,684
20		26	A	Luton T	L	0-1	0-0	7		12,655
21		28	A	Manchester C	L	0-1	0-0	7		32,325
22	Jan	1	H	Wimbledon	D	1-1	0-1	7	Merson	26,839
23		11	H	Aston Villa	D	0-0	0-0	7		31,413
24		18	A	QPR	D	0-0	0-0	7		20,497
25		29	A	Liverpool	L	0-2	0-1	—		33,753
26	Feb	1	H	Manchester U	D	1-1	1-1	8	Rocastle	41,703
27		8	A	Notts Co	W	1-0	1-0	8	Smith	11,221
28		11	H	Norwich C	D	1-1	0-0	—	Merson	22,352
29		15	H	Sheffield W	W	7-1	1-1	6	Smith, Campbell 2, Limpar 2, Merson, Wright	26,805
30		22	A	Tottenham H	D	1-1	0-0	6	Wright	33,124
31	Mar	10	H	Oldham Ath	W	2-1	1-0	—	Wright, Merson	22,096
32		14	A	West Ham U	W	2-0	1-0	6	Wright 2	22,640
33		22	H	Leeds U	D	1-1	0-0	—	Merson	27,844
34		28	A	Wimbledon	W	3-1	2-0	5	Parlour, Wright, Campbell	11,299
35		31	H	Nottingham F	D	3-3	1-2	—	Dixon (pen), Merson, Adams	27,036
36	Apr	4	A	Coventry C	W	1-0	1-0	4	Campbell	14,133
37		8	A	Norwich C	W	3-1	1-0	—	Wright 2 (1 pen), Campbell	12,971
38		11	H	Crystal Palace	W	4-1	3-1	4	Merson 3, Campbell	36,016
39		18	A	Sheffield U	D	1-1	0-1	4	Campbell	25,034
40		20	H	Liverpool	W	4-0	3-0	4	Hillier, Wright 2, Limpar	38,517
41		25	A	Chelsea	D	1-1	0-0	4	Dixon	26,003
42	May	2	H	Southampton	W	5-1	0-0	4	Campbell, Wright 3 (1 pen), Smith	37,702

Final League Position: 4

GOALSCORERS

League (81): Wright 24 (2 pens), Campbell 13, Merson 12, Smith 12, Dixon 4 (3 pens), Limpar 4, Rocastle 4, Adams 2, Bould 1, Groves 1, Hillier 1, Parlour 1, Thomas 1, Winterburn 1.
Rumbelows Cup (3): Wright 2, Merson 1.
FA Cup (1): Smith 1.

Seaman	Dixon	Winterburn	Hillier	O'Leary	Adams	Campbell	Davis	Smith	Merson	Limpar	Rocastle	Groves	Linighan	Thomas	Pates	Wright	Bould	Carter	Parlour	Lydersen	Morrow	Heaney	Match No.
1	2	3	4	5*	6	7†	8	9	10	11	12	14											1
1	2	3	4*	5	6		8	9	10	11†	7	14	12										2
1	2	3		5†	6		8	9	10	11	7*	14	4	12									3
1	2	3			6		8	9	10	11	7		5	4									4
1	2	3			6	12	8	9	10	11†	7*		5	4	14								5
1	2	3	7		6	11	8	9	10		12		5	4*									6
1	2	3	14		6	4	8*	9	10	11†	7		5	12									7
1	2	3	4†	14	6	11	8*	9	10		7		5	12									8
1	2	3†	14		6	4	8	9	10	11*	7		5	12									9
1	2	3			6	12		9	10*	11	7		5	4		8							10
1	2	3	14		6	12		9	10	11*	7		5	4		8†							11
1	2	3	4		6	11		9	10		7					8	5						12
1	2	3	4		6	11*		9	10		7	12				8	5						13
1	2	3	4*		6			9	10	11	7	12				8	5						14
1	2	3	4	14	6			9	10	11*	7	12				8	5†						15
1	2	3	4*	12	6			9	10	11	7					8	5						16
1	2	3	4	12	6			9	10	11	7*	14				8†	5						17
1	2	3	4	12	6		8	9	10	11†	7	14					5*						18
1	2	3	4	12	6			9	10†	11	7*	14				8	5						19
1	2	3	4	12	6			9	10	11*	7					8	5						20
1	2	3	4*		6	11		9	10		7	12	14			8	5†						21
1	2	3	4	12	6			9	10		7					8*	5	11					22
1	2	3	4	5	6		8	9	10*		7				12			11					23
1	2	3	4	5	6			9	10		7					8		11					24
1	2	3		5*	6			9	10		7	14				8	12	11	4†				25
1	2	3	4		6			9	10	12	7†	14				8	5	11*					26
1	2	3†	4	12	6			9	10	11*	7					8	5	14					27
1	2	3†	4	12	6			9	10	11*	7					8	5	14					28
1	2	3	4	12	6			9*	10	11	7					8	5						29
1	2	3	4†	14	6			9	10	11	7*	12				8	5						30
1	2	3	4	12	6			9	10	11*	7					8	5						31
1	2	3	4	12	6			9†	10	11*	7	14				8	5						32
1	2	3	4†		6			9	10	11	7*	12				8	5	14					33
1	2	3	4		6			9	10†	11*		12				8	5	7	14				34
1	2	3	4		6			9	10	11	7†	12				8*	5	14					35
1	2	3†	4	12	6			9	10	11*			14			8	5	7					36
1	2†		4	12	6			9	10	11*	7					8	5			3	14		37
1		3†	4	12	6			9	10	11*	7					8	5			2	14		38
1		3	4	12	6		8	9	10	11*	7						5			2	12		39
1		3	4	12	6			9	10	11	7					8	5			2*			40
1	2	3	4		6			9	10*	11†	7	14				8	5						41
1	2	3	4		6			9	10*	11†	7	14				8	5	12					42

Totals:

42	38	41	27	11	35	22	12	33	41	23	36	5	15	6	9	30	24	5	2	5	—	—	
			+14s	+9s		+6s	+1s	+6s	+3s	+8s	+2s	+4s	+2s			+1s	+1s	+4s	+2s	+2s	+1s		

Rumbelows Cup	Second Round	Leicester C (a) 1-1
		(h) 2-0
	Third Round	Coventry C (a) 0-1
FA Cup	Third Round	Wrexham (a) 1-2

ARSENAL

Goalkeepers

Player				Birthplace		Club	Apps	Gls
Allan Miller	6 3	14 07	29 3 70	Epping	Trainee	Arsenal	—	—
						Plymouth Arg (loan)	13	—
						WBA (loan)	3	—
						Birmingham C (loan)	15	—
David Seaman	6 4	14 10	19 9 63	Rotherham	Apprentice	Leeds U	—	—
						Peterborough U	91	—
						Birmingham C	75	—
						QPR	141	—
						Arsenal	80	—
James Will	6 2	13 13	7 10 72	Turriff	Trainee	Arsenal	—	—
						Sheffield U (loan)	—	—

Defenders

Player				Birthplace		Club	Apps	Gls
Tony Adams	6 3	13 11	10 10 66	London	Apprentice	Arsenal	249	20
Steve Bould	6 4	14 02	16 11 62	Stoke	Apprentice	Stoke C	183	6
						Torquay U (loan)	9	—
						Arsenal	112	3
Lee Dixon	5 8	11 08	17 3 64	Manchester	Local	Burnley	4	—
						Chester C	57	1
						Bury	45	5
						Stoke C	71	5
						Arsenal	153	15
Craig Gaunt	5 11	12 02	31 3 73	Nottingham	Trainee	Arsenal	—	—
Justin Lee	5 6	11 05	19 9 73	Hereford	Trainee	Arsenal	—	—
Andy Linighan	6 4	13 10	18 8 62	Hartlepool	Smiths BC	Hartlepool U	110	4
						Leeds U	66	3
						Oldham Ath	87	6
						Norwich C	86	8
						Arsenal	27	—
Pal Lydersen	6 0	14 01	10 9 65	Norway	IK Start	Arsenal	7	—
Craig McKernon‡	5 9	11 00	23 2 68	Gloucester	Apprentice	Mansfield T	94	—
						Arsenal	—	—
Scott Marshall	6 1	12 05	1 5 73	Edinburgh	Trainee	Arsenal	—	—
Steve Morrow	5 11	12 02	2 7 70	Belfast	Trainee	Arsenal	2	—
						Reading (loan)	10	—
						Watford (loan)	8	—
						Reading (loan)	3	—
						Barnet (loan)	1	—
David O'Leary	6 1	13 09	2 5 58	London	Apprentice	Arsenal	547	10
Colin Pates	6 0	13 00	10 8 61	Mitcham	Apprentice	Chelsea	281	10
						Charlton Ath	38	—
						Arsenal	14	—
						Brighton & HA (loan)	17	—
Ken Webster	5 8	13 02	2 3 73	Hammersmith	Trainee	Arsenal	—	—
Nigel Winterburn	5 8	11 04	11 12 63	Coventry	Local	Birmingham C	—	—
						Oxford U	—	—
						Wimbledon	165	8
						Arsenal	170	4

Midfield

Player				Birthplace		Club	Apps	Gls
Steve Clements	5 10	11 10	26 9 72	Slough	Trainee	Arsenal	—	—
Paul Davis	5 10	10 13	9 12 61	London	Apprentice	Arsenal	319	29
Mark Flatts	5 6	9 08	14 10 72	Islington	Trainee	Arsenal	—	—
David Hillier	5 10	12 05	19 12 69	Blackheath	Trainee	Arsenal	43	1
Siggi Jonsson‡	5 11	11 11	27 9 66	Akranes, Iceland	Akranes FC	Sheffield W	67	4
						Barnsley (loan)	5	—
						Arsenal	8	—
Matthew Joseph*			30 9 72	Bethnal Green	Trainee	Arsenal	—	—
Gary McKeown*	5 10	11 07	19 10 70	Oxford	Trainee	Arsenal	—	—
						Shrewsbury T (loan)	8	1
Ray Parlour	5 10	11 12	7 3 73	Romford	Trainee	Arsenal	6	1
David Rocastle	5 9	12 10	2 5 67	Lewisham	Apprentice	Arsenal	218	24
Ian Selley	5 9	10 01	14 6 74	Surrey	Trainee	Arsenal	—	—

ARSENAL

Foundation: Formed by workers at the Royal Arsenal, Woolwich in 1886 they began as Dial Square (name of one of the workshops) and included two former Nottingham Forest players Fred Beardsley and Morris Bates. Beardsley wrote to his old club seeking help and they provided the new club with a full set of red jerseys and a ball. The club became known as the "Woolwich Reds" although their official title soon after formation was Woolwich Arsenal.

First Football League game: 2 September, 1893, Division 2, v Newcastle U (h) D 2-2 – Williams; Powell, Jeffrey; Devine, Buist, Howat; Gemmell, Henderson, Shaw (1), Elliott (1), Booth.

Did you know: Considering their remarkable record of success, it may be surprising to note that the only season in which they were undefeated at home before the double-winning campaign of 1970–71 was 1903–04 – the first time they won promotion from Division 2.

Managers (and Secretary-managers)
Sam Hollis 1894–97, Tom Mitchell 1897–98, George Elcoat 1898–99, Harry Bradshaw 1899–1904, Phil Kelso 1904–08, George Morrell 1908–15, Leslie Knighton 1919–25, Herbert Chapman 1925–34, George Allison 1934–47, Tom Whittaker 1947–56, Jack Crayston 1956–58, George Swindin 1958–62, Billy Wright 1962–66, Bertie Mee 1966–76, Terry Neill 1976–83, Don Howe 1984–86, George Graham May 1986–.

Forwards

John Bacon	5 11	11 05	23 3 73	Dublin	Trainee	Arsenal	—	—
Kevin Campbell	6 1	13 08	4 2 70	Lambeth	Trainee	Arsenal	69	24
						Leyton Orient (loan)	16	9
						Leicester C (loan)	11	5
Jimmy Carter	5 10	11 01	9 11 65	London	Apprentice	Crystal Palace	—	—
						QPR	—	—
						Millwall	110	11
						Liverpool	5	—
						Arsenal	6	—
Andrew Cole	5 11	11 02	15 10 71	Nottingham	Trainee	Arsenal	1	—
						Fulham (loan)	13	3
						Bristol C (loan)	12	8
Paul Dickov	5 5	11 05	1 11 72	Livingston	Trainee	Arsenal	—	—
Perry Groves	5 11	12 07	19 4 65	London	Apprentice	Colchester U	156	26
						Arsenal	155	21
Martin Hayes	6 0	11 08	21 3 66	Walthamstow	Apprentice	Arsenal	102	26
						Celtic	—	—
						Wimbledon (loan)	2	—
Neil Heaney	5 9	11 09	3 11 71	Middlesbrough	Trainee	Arsenal	1	—
						Hartlepool U (loan)	3	—
						Cambridge U (loan)	13	2
Anders Limpar	5 8	11 07	24 9 65	Sweden	Cremonese	Arsenal	63	15
Paul Merson	6 0	13 02	20 3 68	London	Apprentice	Arsenal	167	50
						Brentford (loan)	7	—
Paul Read	5 11	12 06	25 9 73	Harlow	Trainee	Arsenal	—	—
Paul Shaw	5 11	12 02	4 9 73	Burnham	Trainee	Arsenal	—	—
Alan Smith	6 2	12 13	21 11 62	Birmingham	Alvechurch	Leicester C	191	73
						Arsenal	189	79
						Leicester C (loan)	9	3
Ian Wright	5 9	11 08	3 11 63	Woolwich	Greenwich B	Crystal Palace	225	89
						Arsenal	30	24

Trainees
Brissett, Jason C; Campbell Stuart J; Charlton, John L; Clarke, Adrian J; Connolly, Anthony; Harford, Paul R. T; Kirby, Ryan M; McCardle, Mark; McDonald, Christopher; O'Brien, Roy J; Rust, Nicholas C. I; Swain, Joel T; Zumrutel, Soner.

Associated Schoolboys
Black, Michael J; Clarke, Albert; Dennis, Kevin; Dowson, Keith S; Howell, Jamie; Hughes, Stephen J; Owen, Dafydd; Reynolds, Stuart; Taylor, Ross E; Wynter, Jermaine.

Associated Schoolboys who have accepted the club's offer of a Traineeship/Contract
Hall, Graeme B; McGowan, Gavin G; Rawlins, Matthew; Rose, Matthew.

ASTON VILLA 1991–92 *Back row (left to right):* Bryan Small, Derek Mountfield, Ugo Ehiogu, Kent Nielsen, Les Sealey, Nigel Spink, Ivo Stas, Paul Mortimer, Chris Price, Kevin Richardson.

Centre row: Jim Barron (Coach), Ian Ormondroyd, Neil Cox, Ian Olney, Dalian Atkinson, Cyrille Regis, Kevin Gage, Mark Blake, Steve Staunton, Andy Gray (Assistant Manager).

Front row: Jim Walker (Physiotherapist), Dwight Yorke, Stuart Gray, Shaun Teale, Ron Atkinson (Manager), Gary Penrice, Gordon Cowans, Tony Daley, Roger Spry (Fitness Consultant).

FA Premier **ASTON VILLA**

Villa Park, Trinity Rd, Birmingham B6 6HE. Telephone 021-327 2299. Commercial Dept. 021-327 5399. Clubcall: 0898 121148. Ticketline: 0898 121848. Ticket Office 021 327 5353.

Ground capacity: 40,312.

Record attendance: 76,588 v Derby Co, FA Cup 6th rd, 2 March 1946.

Record receipts: £385,678 Everton v Norwich C, FA Cup semi-final, 15 April 1989.

Pitch measurements: 115yd × 75yd.

President: H. J. Musgrove.

Chairman: H. D. Ellis.

Directors: J. A. Alderson, Dr D. H. Targett, P. D. Ellis.

Manager: Ron Atkinson.

Assistant Managers: Jim Barron. *First Team Coach:* Dave Sexton.

Secretary: Steven Stride. *Physio:* Jim Walker. *Youth Coach:* Richard Money. *Commercial Manager:* Abdul Rashid. *Director of Youth:* Dave Richardson. *Chief Scout:* Brian Whitehouse. *Fitness Consultant:* Roger Spry.

Year Formed: 1874. Turned Professional: 1885. Ltd Co.: 1896.

Former Grounds: 1874–76, Aston Park; 1876–97, Perry Barr; 1897, Villa Park.

Club Nickname: 'The Villans'.

Record League Victory: 12-2 v Accrington S, Division 1, 12 March 1892 – Warner; Evans, Cox; Harry Devey, Jimmy Cowan, Baird; Athersmith (1), Dickson (2), John Devey (4), L. Campbell (4), Hodgetts (1).

Record Cup Victory: 13-0 v Wednesbury Old Ath, FA Cup, 1st rd, 30 October 1886 – Warner; Coulton, Simmonds; Yates, Robertson, Burton (2); R. Davis (1), A. Brown (3), Hunter (3), Loach (2), Hodgetts (2).

Record Defeat: 1-8 v Blackburn R, FA Cup, 3rd rd, 16 February 1889.

Most League Points (2 for a win): 70, Division 3, 1971–72.

Most League points (3 for a win): 78, Division 2, 1987–88.

Most League Goals: 128, Division 1, 1930–31.

Highest League Scorer in Season: 'Pongo' Waring, 49, Division 1, 1930–31.

Most League Goals in Total Aggregate: Harry Hampton, 215, 1904–15 and Billy Walker, 213, 1919–34.

Most Capped Player: Peter McParland, 33 (34), Northern Ireland.

Most League Appearances: Charlie Aitken, 561, 1961–76.

Record Transfer Fee Received: £5,500,000 from Bari for David Platt, August 1991.

Record Transfer Fee Paid: £1,700,000 to Oldham Ath for Earl Barrett, February 1992.

Football League Record: 1888 Founder Member of the League; 1936–38 Division 2; 1938–59 Division 1; 1959–60 Division 2; 1960–67 Division 1; 1967–70 Division 2; 1970–72 Division 3; 1972–75 Division 2; 1975–87 Division 1; 1987–88 Division 2; 1988–92 Division 1; 1992– FA Premier League.

Honours: Football League: Division 1 – Champions 1893–94, 1895–96, 1896–97, 1898–99, 1899–1900, 1909–10, 1980–81; Runners-up 1888–89, 1902–03, 1907–08, 1910–11, 1912–13, 1913–14, 1930–31, 1932–33, 1989–90; Division 2 – Champions 1937–38, 1959–60; Runners-up 1974–75, 1987–88; Division 3 – Champions 1971–72. *FA Cup:* Winners 1887, 1895, 1897, 1905, 1913, 1920, 1957; Runners-up 1892, 1924. *Double Performed:* 1896–97. *Football League Cup:* Winners 1961, 1975, 1977; Runners-up 1963, 1971. **European Competitions:** *European Cup:* 1981–82 (winners), 1982–83; *UEFA Cup:* 1975–76, 1977–78, 1983–84, 1990– 91. *World Club Championship:* 1982–83; *European Super Cup:* 1982–83 (winners).

Colours: Claret shirts, blue trim, white shorts, claret and blue trim, blue stockings, claret trim. **Change colours:** White shirts, purple/black trim, black shorts, white stockings.

ASTON VILLA 1991–92 LEAGUE RECORD

Match No.	Date		Venue	Opponents	Result		H/T Score	Lg. Pos.	Goalscorers	Atten- dance
1	Aug	17	A	Sheffield W	W	3-2	1-2	—	Regis, Atkinson, Staunton	36,749
2		21	H	Manchester U	L	0-1	0-1			39,995
3		24	H	Arsenal	W	3-1	1-1	4	Staunton (pen), Penrice, Daley	29,684
4		28	A	West Ham U	L	1-3	0-0	—	Daley	23,644
5		31	A	Southampton	D	1-1	1-1	11	Richardson	16,161
6	Sep	4	H	Crystal Palace	L	0-1	0-1	—		20,740
7		7	H	Tottenham H	D	0-0	0-0	14		33,096
8		14	A	Liverpool	D	1-1	1-1	16	Richardson	38,400
9		18	A	Chelsea	L	0-2	0-1	—		17,182
10		21	H	Nottingham F	W	3-1	0-1	15	Blake, Richardson, Yorke	28,506
11		28	H	Coventry C	L	0-1	0-1	16		17,851
12	Oct	5	H	Luton T	W	4-0	1-0	14	Richardson, Regis, Yorke, Mortimer	18,722
13		19	A	Everton	W	2-0	1-0	8	Regis, Daley	27,688
14		26	H	Wimbledon	W	2-1	2-0	6	Olney, Yorke	16,928
15	Nov	2	A	QPR	W	1-0	1-0	6	Yorke	10,642
16		16	H	Notts Co	W	1-0	1-0	4	Yorke	23,020
17		24	H	Leeds U	L	1-4	0-1	—	Yorke	23,666
18		30	A	Oldham Ath	L	2-3	1-1	5	Blake, Regis	15,370
19	Dec	7	H	Manchester C	W	3-1	2-0	5	Regis, Yorke, Daley	26,265
20		14	A	Sheffield U	L	0-2	0-1	5		18,401
21		26	H	West Ham U	W	3-1	2-0	6	Yorke, Daley, Richardson	31,959
22		28	H	Southampton	W	2-1	1-0	5	Regis, Yorke	23,094
23	Jan	1	A	Norwich C	L	1-2	0-0	6	Regis	15,318
24		11	A	Arsenal	D	0-0	0-0	6		31,413
25		18	H	Sheffield W	L	0-1	0-0	6		28,036
26		22	A	Manchester U	L	0-1	0-0	—		45,022
27	Feb	2	H	Everton	D	0-0	0-0	—		17,451
28		8	A	Wimbledon	L	0-2	0-1	8		5534
29		22	H	Oldham Ath	W	1-0	0-0	7	Regis	20,509
30		29	A	Manchester C	L	0-2	0-1	8		28,268
31	Mar	3	A	Leeds U	D	0-0	0-0	—		28,896
32		10	A	Notts Co	D	0-0	0-0	—		8389
33		14	H	QPR	L	0-1	0-0	11		19,630
34		21	A	Crystal Palace	D	0-0	0-0	12		15,368
35		28	H	Norwich C	W	1-0	0-0	10	Staunton	16,985
36		31	H	Sheffield U	D	1-1	0-0	—	Regis	15,745
37	Apr	4	A	Tottenham H	W	5-2	2-2	8	Richardson, Olney, Yorke, Daley, Regis	26,370
38		11	H	Liverpool	W	1-0	0-0	7	Daley	35,755
39		18	A	Nottingham F	L	0-2	0-1	9		22,800
40		20	H	Chelsea	W	3-1	1-0	9	Staunton, McGrath, Parker	19,269
41		25	A	Luton T	L	0-2	0-1	9		11,178
42	May	2	H	Coventry C	W	2-0	2-0	7	Regis, Yorke	31,984

Final League Position: 7

GOALSCORERS

League (48): Regis 11, Yorke 11, Daley 7, Richardson 6, Staunton 4 (1 pen), Blake 2, Olney 2, Atkinson 1, McGrath 1, Mortimer 1, Parker 1, Penrice 1.
Rumbelows Cup (1): Teale 1.
FA Cup (7): Yorke 5, Froggatt 1, Parker 1.

Spink	Mountfield	Staunton	Teale	McGrath	Richardson	Yorke	Regis	Atkinson	Cowans	Mortimer	Penrice	Olney	Ehiogu	Daley	Price	Kubicki	Ormondroyd	Nielsen	Blake	Sealey	Small	Parker	Froggatt	Breitkreutz	Carruthers	Barrett	Cox	Beinlich	Match No.
1	2	3	4	5	6	7	8	9*	10	11	12																		1
1	2	3	4	5	6	7	9		10	11*	8	12																	2
1		3*	4	5	6	14	9		10	11	8†			2	7	12													3
1			4	5	6	12	9		10	11	8			2	7	3*													4
1		3	4	5	6		8	9	10	11				7		2													5
1		3	4	5	6		9		10	11	8*			7		2	12												6
1		3	4	5	6		8	9	10	11				7		2													7
1		3	4	5	6	12	8	9†	10	11				7*		2	14												8
1		3	4	5	6	7	9*		10†	11	12	8				2	14												9
1		3	4	5	6	7	9†			14	12	8*				2	10	11											10
1		3	4	5	6	7	9				12	11*	10			2	8												11
1		3	4	5	6	7	8	9	10		12					2	11*												12
			4	5	6	11	8	9						7		2		10		1	3								13
		3	4	5	6	11	8					9		7		2		10		1									14
		3	4	5	6	11†	8	12				9*	14	7		2		10		1									15
		3	4	5	6	11*	8	12				9†	14	7		2		10		1									16
		3	4	5	6	11	8	9	12					7		2		10*		1									17
		3	4	5	6	11	9		10			12				2			7	1	8*								18
		3	4	5	6	11*	9					12		7		2			8	1		10							19
		3	4	5	6	11	9					12		7		2			8*	1		10							20
		3	4	5	6	11*	9							7		2			8	1		10	12						21
		3*	4	5	6	11	9							7		2	12		8	1		10							22
			4	5	6	11	9					12		7	3	2			8*	1		10							23
			4	5	6	11	9							7		2			8	1	3	10							24
		3	4	5	6	11	9							7		2			8*	1		10	12						25
		3*	4	5	6	11	9							7		2			8	1		10	12						26
		3	4	5	6	11	9*					12		7		2			8	1		10							27
			4	5	6	11	9							7		2			8	1	3*	10	12						28
		3	4	5	6		9									2			8	1		10	11	7					29
		3	4	5	6	8*	9							7						1		10	11	12	2				30
1		3	4	5	6		9							7					8			10	11			2			31
1		3	4	5	6	10*	9					12		7					8				11			2			32
1		3	4	5	6	14	9†					10		7					8				11*			2			33
1		3	4	5	6	11*	9					12		7					8			10				2			34
1		3	4	5	6	11*	9					14		7†					8*			10	12			2			35
1		3	4	5	6	12	9							7					8*			10	11			2			36
1		3	4	5	6	11†	9					12		7*					8			10				2	14		37
1			4	5	6		9							7					8		3	10	11*			2	12		38
1		3	4	5	6		9†							7					8			10	11*			2	12	14	39
1		3	4	5	6		9							7					8			10	11*			2	12		40
		3	4	5	6		9					12		7					8		10*		11			2			41
1		3	4	5	6	10*	9					12		7					8				11			2			42
23	2	37	42	41	42	27	39	11	10	10	5	14	4	29	2	23	—	3	14	18	8	25	6	7	2	13	4	—	

Substitute appearances: Regis +5s; Atkinson +3s, Cowans +2s, Mortimer +2s, Penrice +3s, Olney +6s, Ehiogu +4s, Daley +5s, Price +1s; Ormondroyd +1s, Nielsen +3s; Breitkreutz +3s, Carruthers +1s, Barrett +1s; Cox +3s, Beinlich +2s.

Bosnich—Match No. 41(1).

Rumbelows Cup	Second Round	Grimsby T (a)	0-0
		(h)	1-1
FA Cup	Third Round	Tottenham H (h)	0-0
		(a)	1-0
	Fourth Round	Derby Co (a)	4-3
	Fifth Round	Swindon T (a)	2-1
	Sixth Round	Liverpool (a)	0-1

ASTON VILLA

Player and Position	Ht	Wt	Birth Date	Birth Place	Source	Clubs	League App	Gls
Goalkeepers								
Mark Bosnich†	6 2	13 07	13 1 72	Sydney, Australia		Manchester U	3	—
						Sydney Croatia	—	—
						Aston Villa	1	—
Glen Livingstone	6 2	14 01	13 10 72	Birmingham	Trainee	Aston Villa	—	—
Michael Oakes	6 1	12 07	30 10 73	Northwich	Trainee	Aston Villa	—	—
Les Sealey	6 1	12 08	29 9 57	Bethnal Green	Apprentice	Coventry C	158	—
						Luton T	207	—
						Plymouth Arg (loan)	6	—
						Manchester U (loan)	2	—
						Manchester U	31	—
						Aston Villa	18	—
						Coventry C (loan)	2	—
Nigel Spink	6 1	14 06	8 8 58	Chelmsford	Chelmsford C	Aston Villa	306	—
Defenders								
Earl Barrett	5 10	11 00	28 4 67	Rochdale	Apprentice	Manchester C	3	—
						Chester C (loan)	12	—
						Oldham Ath	183	7
						Aston Villa	13	—
Chris Boden	5 09	11 00	13 10 73	Wolverhampton	Trainee	Aston Villa	—	—
Darrell Duffy*	5 11	11 00	18 1 71	Birmingham	Trainee	Aston Villa	1	—
Dariusz Kubicki	5 10	11 07	6 6 63	Warsaw	Legia Warsaw	Aston Villa	23	—
Craig Liddle‡	5 10	12 03	21 10 71	Perkinsville	Trainee	Aston Villa	—	—
Paul McGrath	6 0	13 02	4 12 59	Ealing	St Patrick's Ath	Manchester U	163	12
						Aston Villa	111	2
Kent Nielsen (To Aarhus Dec 1991)	6 2	14 01	28 12 61	Frederiksberg	Brondby	Aston Villa	79	4
Bryan Small	5 9	11 08	15 11 71	Birmingham	Trainee	Aston Villa	8	—
Ivo Stas‡	6 2	14 00	10 2 65	Ostrava	Banik Ostrava	Aston Villa	—	—
Steve Staunton	5 11	11 02	19 1 69	Drogheda	Dundalk	Liverpool	65	—
						Bradford C (loan)	8	—
						Aston Villa	37	4
Shaun Teale	6 0	13 07	10 3 64	Southport	Weymouth	Bournemouth	100	4
						Aston Villa	42	—
Midfield								
Mark Blake	5 11	12 03	16 12 70	Nottingham	Trainee	Aston Villa	30	2
						Wolverhampton W (loan)	2	—
Matthias Breitkreutz	5 09	11 03	12 5 71	Crivitz	Borussia Borsig	Aston Villa	8	—
Russell Bullivant‡	6 0	11 09	6 9 72	Birmingham	Trainee	Aston Villa	—	—
Neil Cox	5 11	12 10	8 10 71	Scunthorpe	Trainee	Scunthorpe U	17	1
						Aston Villa	7	—
Richard Crisp	5 7	10 05	23 5 72	Wordsley		Aston Villa	—	—
Ugo Ehiogu	6 1	12 00	3 11 72	London	Trainee	WBA	2	—
						Aston Villa	8	—
Steve Froggatt	5 10	11 00	9 3 73	Lincoln	Trainee	Aston Villa	9	—
Garry Parker	5 10	11 00	7 9 65	Oxford	Apprentice	Luton T	42	3
						Hull C	84	8
						Nottingham F	103	17
						Aston Villa	25	1
Kevin Richardson	5 9	11 02	4 12 62	Newcastle	Apprentice	Watford	39	2
						Arsenal	96	5
						Aston Villa	42	6

ASTON VILLA

Foundation: Cricketing enthusiasts of Villa Cross Wesleyan Chapel, Aston, Birmingham decided to form a football club during the winter of 1873–74. Football clubs were few and far between in the Birmingham area and in their first game against Aston Brook St. Mary's Rugby team they played one half rugby and the other soccer. In 1876 they were joined by a Scottish soccer enthusiast George Ramsay who was immediately appointed captain and went on to lead Aston Villa from obscurity to one of the country's top clubs in a period of less than 10 years.

First Football League game: 8 September, 1888, Football League, v Wolverhampton W, (a) D 1-1 – Warner; Cox, Coulton; Yates, H. Devey, Dawson; A. Brown, Green (1), Allen, Garvey, Hodgetts.

Did you know: The coal mines have provided many top-class footballers and in 1893 Aston Villa's secretary, Fred Rinder, actually went down the pit at Hednesford to clinch the signing of outside-left Steve Smith – a star of the side that won the League Championship four times in five years at the end of the last century.

Managers (and Secretary-managers)
George Ramsay 1884–1926*, W. J. Smith 1926–34*, Jimmy McMullan 1934–35, Jimmy Hogan 1936–44, Alex Massie 1945–50, George Martin 1950–53, Eric Houghton 1953–58, Joe Mercer 1958–64, Dick Taylor 1965–67, Tommy Cummings 1967–68, Tommy Docherty 1968–70, Vic Crowe 1970–74, Ron Saunders 1974–82, Tony Barton 1982–84, Graham Turner 1984–86, Billy McNeill 1986–87, Graham Taylor 1987–90, Dr. Jozef Venglos 1990–91, Ron Atkinson June 1991–.

Forwards

Name				Birthplace	Source	Club	Apps	Gls
Dalian Atkinson	6 1	12 10	21 3 68	Shrewsbury		Ipswich T	60	18
						Sheffield W	38	10
						Real Sociedad	—	—
						Aston Villa	14	1
Stefan Beinlich	5 11	11 02	13 1 72	Berlin	Borussia Borsig	Aston Villa	2	—
Trevor Berry			1 8 74	Surrey	Trainee	Aston Villa	—	—
Nigel Callaghan‡	5 9	10 09	12 9 62	Singapore	Apprentice	Watford	222	41
						Derby Co	76	10
						Aston Villa	26	1
						Derby Co (loan)	12	1
						Watford (loan)	12	1
						Huddersfield T (loan)	8	—
Martin Carruthers	5 11	11 07	7 8 72	Nottingham	Trainee	Aston Villa	3	—
Tony Daley	5 9	10 05	18 10 67	Birmingham	Apprentice	Aston Villa	193	28
Neil Davis	5 08	11 00	15 8 73	Bloxwich	Redditch U	Aston Villa	—	—
Dave Farrell	5 11	11 02	11 11 71	Birmingham	Redditch U	Aston Villa	—	—
Graham Fenton	5 10	11 03	22 5 74	Wallsend	Trainee	Aston Villa	—	—
Ian Olney	6 1	11 03	17 12 69	Luton	Trainee	Aston Villa	88	16
Mark Parrott	5 11	11 00	14 3 71	Cheltenham	Trainee	Aston Villa	—	—
David Platt	5 10	11 12	10 6 66	Chadderton	Chadderton	Manchester U	—	—
						Crewe Alex	134	55
						Aston Villa	121	50
Cyrille Regis	6 0	13 06	9 2 58	Mariapousoula	Hayes	WBA	237	82
						Coventry C	238	47
						Aston Villa	39	11
Lee Williams	5 7	11 00	3 2 73	Birmingham	Trainee	Aston Villa	—	—
Dwight Yorke	5 10	11 12	3 12 71	Tobago	St Clairs CS	Aston Villa	52	13

Trainees
Browne, Paul; Cowe, Steven M; Evans, Darren; Goodwin, Craig; Harrison, Garry M; Hodgson, Shaun D; Hutson, Otis; King, Ian J; McCallum, Matthew; McLaughlin, Scott; McNamara, Philip J; Pearce, Christopher J; Pearce, Dennis A; Pitcher, Steven; Scimeca, Riccardo; Williams, Graeme E.

Associated Schoolboys
Bailey, Russell; Barrett, Neil R; Boxall, Michael K; Brock, Stuart A.; Brown, Ian S; Burchell, Lee A; Byfield, Darren; Collins, Lee D; Evans, Paul D; Hendrie, Lee A; Hines, Leslie D; Jaszczun, Antony J; Leek, Brian; Miley, Jonathan H; Moore, David; Peters, Mark P; Petty, Ben J; Pugh, Mark R; Rachel, Adam; Senior, Marc A; Shaw, Gareth R.

Associated Schoolboys who have accepted the club's offer of a Traineeship/Contract
Aston, Lee A; Finney, Nicki D. J; Wiltshire, John M.

48

BARNET 1991-92 *Back row (left to right):* Gordon Ogbourne (Kit Manager), Carl Hoddle, David Howell, Kenny Lowe, Mick Bodley, Richard Nugent, Mark Flashman, Gary Phillips, Steve Berryman, Nicky Evans, Gary Poole, Gary Blackford, Roger Willis, Jonathan Hunt, Andy McDade (Physiotherapist).
Front row: Gary Bull, Dominic Naylor, Tony Lynch, Frank Murphy, Mark Carter, Barry Fry (Manager), Edwin Stein, Derek Payne, Hakan Hayrettin, Geoff Cooper, Duncan Horton.

(Photograph by kind permission of Colorsport)

Division 3

BARNET

Underhill Stadium, Barnet Lane, Barnet, Herts EN5 2BE. Telephone 081-441 6932. Clubcall: 0898 121544.

Ground capacity: 9000.

Record attendance: 11,026 v Wycombe Wanderers. FA Amateur Cup 4th Round 1951–52.

Record receipts: £31,202 v Portsmouth FA Cup 3rd Round 5th January 1991.

Pitch measurements: 110yd × 72yd.

Chairman: S. Flashman.

Managing Director: T. Hill.

Directors: J. Quill, L. Rose, L. Wise.

Manager: Barry Fry.

Assistant Manager: Edwin Stein.

Physio: Andy McDade.

Secretary: Bryan Ayres.

Commercial Manager.

Year Formed: 1888. Turned Professional: 1965. Ltd Co.: Ltd Co.

Former Grounds: Queens Road (1888–1901) Totteridge Lane (1901–07).

Former Names: 1906–19 Barnet Alston FC.

Club Nickname: The Bees.

Record League Victory: 6-0 v Lincoln C (away), Division 4, 4 September 1991 – Pape; Poole, Naylor, Bodley, Howell, Evans (1), Willis (1), Murphy (1), Bull (2), Lowe, Showler. (1 og).

Record Defeat: 4-7 v Crewe Alex, Division 4, 17 August 1991.

Most League points (3 for a win): 69, Division 4, 1991–92.

Most League Goals: 81, Division 4, 1991–92.

Highest League Scorer in Season: Gary Bull, 20, Division 4, 1991–92.

Most League Goals in Total Aggregate: Gary Bull, 20, 1991–92.

Most Capped Player: None.

Most League Appearances: Gary Bull, 42, 1991–92.

Record Transfer Fee Received: £350,000 from Wimbledon for Andy Clarke, February 1991.

Record Transfer Fee Paid: £40,000 to Barrow for Kenny Lowe, January 1991 and £40,000 to Runcorn for Mark Carter, February 1991.

Football League Record: Promoted to Division 4 from GMVC 1991; 1991–92 Division 4; 1992– Division 3.

Honours: Football League: best season 7th, Division 4, 1991 FA Amateur Cup Winners 1945–46, GM Vauxhall N-›92. Conference Winners 1990–91. *FA Cup:* best season: never past 3rd rd. *League Cup:* best season: never past 1st rd.

Colours: Amber shirts, black shorts, black stockings. **Change colours:** white shirts, white shorts, white stockings.

BARNET 1991–92 LEAGUE RECORD

Match No.	Date		Venue	Opponents	Result		H/T Score	Lg. Pos.	Goalscorers	Atten- dance
1	Aug	17	H	Crewe Alex	L	4-7	2-3	—	Bull 2, Carter 2	5090
2		24	A	Mansfield T	W	2-1	2-1	12	Bull, Carter	2668
3		31	H	Hereford U	W	1-0	0-0	6	Willis	2860
4	Sep	4	A	Lincoln C	W	6-0	2-0	—	Bull 2, Murphy, Willis, Finney (og), Evans	3067
5		7	A	Northampton T	D	1-1	0-1	3	Bull	4339
6		14	H	Doncaster R	W	1-0	1-0	3	Bull	3762
7		17	H	Scunthorpe U	W	3-2	1-1	—	Carter, Willis, Bull (pen)	3094
8		21	A	Gillingham	D	3-3	2-2	2	Wilson, Lowe, Bull	4864
9		28	H	Cardiff C	W	3-1	2-1	2	Showler, Bull 2 (1 pen)	4000
10	Oct	5	A	Walsall	L	0-2	0-2	4		4981
11		12	H	York C	W	2-0	0-0	2	Murphy 2	4474
12		19	H	Blackpool	W	3-0	1-0	2	Willis, Poole, Showler	5085
13		26	A	Scarborough	W	4-0	2-0	2	Showler, Willis 2, Bull	1942
14	Nov	2	A	Wrexham	L	0-1	0-1	2		1886
15		5	H	Carlisle U	W	4-2	0-1	—	Howell, Poole, Bull, Carter	2983
16		9	H	Halifax T	W	3-0	1-0	1	Bull, Lowe, Willis	4837
17		23	A	Rochdale	L	0-1	0-1	2		3033
18		30	H	Chesterfield	L	1-2	0-1	4	Carter	3725
19	Dec	21	H	Mansfield T	W	2-0	1-0	3	Showler, Willis	4209
20		26	A	Crewe Alex	L	0-3	0-2	3		4736
21		28	A	Hereford U	D	2-2	2-2	3	Howell, Carter	4654
22	Jan	1	H	Lincoln C	W	1-0	1-0	2	Bull	3739
23		8	A	Maidstone U	D	1-1	0-1	—	Carter	1988
24		11	H	Rotherham U	L	2-5	0-3	4	Carter, Bull (pen)	3552
25	Feb	8	A	Scarborough	W	5-1	2-0	3	Horton, Willis, Lowe, Carter, Bull	2851
26		11	A	Chesterfield	L	2-3	1-1	—	Bodley, Horton	3076
27		15	H	Maidstone U	W	3-2	2-0	3	Showler, Willis, Carter	2871
28		18	A	Blackpool	L	2-4	2-2	—	Kerr (og), Showler	5149
29		22	A	Rotherham U	L	0-3	0-1	4		3841
30	Mar	7	A	Burnley	L	0-3	0-1	7		12,018
31		10	A	Carlisle U	W	3-1	2-0	—	Carter, Horton, Willis	1888
32		14	H	Wrexham	W	2-0	0-0	5	Carter, Murphy	2917
33		21	A	Halifax T	L	1-3	0-0	5	Murphy	1756
34		24	H	Burnley	D	0-0	0-0	—		4881
35		28	H	Rochdale	W	3-0	2-0	6	Bull 2 (1 pen), Carter	3099
36		31	A	Doncaster R	L	0-1	0-1	—		1247
37	Apr	4	H	Northampton T	W	3-0	1-0	6	Carter 2, Showler	2816
38		11	A	Scunthorpe U	D	1-1	1-0	6	Howell	3361
39		18	H	Gillingham	W	2-0	1-0	5	Payne, Carter	4049
40		20	A	Cardiff C	L	1-3	0-2	5	Cooper	7720
41		25	H	Walsall	L	0-1	0-1	7		3207
42	May	2	A	York C	W	4-1	0-0	7	Bull, Carter 2, Willis	2643

Final League Position: 7

GOALSCORERS

League (81): Bull 20 (4 pens), Carter 19, Willis 12, Showler 7, Murphy 5, Horton 3, Howell 3, Lowe 3, Poole 2, Bodley 1, Cooper 1, Evans 1, Payne 1, Wilson 1, own goals 2.
Rumbelows Cup (6): Bull 2, Carter 2, Evans 2.
FA Cup (10): Carter 5, Bull 2, Evans 1, Naylor 1, Showler 1.

Phillips	Blackford	Cooper	Horton	Bodley	Johnson	Showler	Carter	Bull	Lowe	Evans	Murphy	Stein	Naylor	Hoddle	Willis	Poole	Pape	Howell	Hayrettin	Tomlinson	Wilson	Nugent	Lynch	Joseph	Payne	Hunt	Cawley	Nethercott	Match No.
1	2	3*	4	5†	6	7	8	9	10	11	12	14																	1
1	2		4			11	8	9	10				3	5	6	7													2
			4	6		11	8*	9	10				3	7†	12	2	1	5			14								3
			4			11		9	10	6	8		3		7	2	1	5											4
	14		4			11	8†	9	10*	6			3		7	2	1	5			12								5
			4			11*	8	9	10	6			3	7†		2	1	5			12	14							6
	12		4	6*		11	8	9	10				3		7	2†	1				14	5							7
	12		4			11	8	9	10†				3		6	2	1	5*			7				14				8
			4			11	8†	9	10				3	12	6*	2	1	5			7				14				9
			4†			11		9	10				3	12	6	2	1	5			7		14	8*					10
			4			11		9	10*	12			3		6	2	1	5			7				8				11
	14		4			11		9	10	12			3		6	2	1	5*			7				8†				12
	14		4			11	12	9	10†				3		6	2	1	5			7*				8				13
	14		4			11	12	9	10				3		6*	2†	1	5			7				8				14
	14		4			11	12	9	10*				3		6	2	1	5			7				8†				15
			4			11	8*	9	10†				3	12	6	2	1	5			7	14							16
	12		4			11	8*	9	10†14				3		6	2	1	5			7								17
	14	10†	4			11	8	9	12				3		6	2	1	5			7*								18
		6	4			11†	8	9	10*				3	12		2	1	5			7				14				19
		6	4*			11	8	9	10				3	12		2	1	5†			7				14				20
		10*	4			11	12	9	14		8		3†		6	2	1	5			7								21
		11†	4				8	9	10*	12			3		6	2	1	5			7				14				22
	14	3	4				8†	9		7	12		10		6*	2	1	5							11				23
		3				11	8	9	12	10†			4		6*	2	1	5			7				14				24
		6	4			11†	8*	9	10	12			3		7	2	1								14		5		25
		6	4			11	8	9	10*				3		7	2	1								12		5		26
			4			11*	8	9	10				3		7†	2	1	14			6				12			5	27
		6	4			11	8	9	14				3			2†	1	5			7				12			10*	28
		6	4*			11	8	9†14			12		3			2	1	5			7				12			10	29
1		6	4†			11	8	9					12			2					7*				14				30
1	3	6	4			11†	8	9					10	7*	2		5	12							14				31
1	3	6	4			11†	8	9	12	14			10*	7	2		5												32
1	3	6*	4			11†	8	9	12	14			10	7	2		5												33
	3		4			11†		9	12				10	8	2*	1	5				7				6	14			34
	3	6	4			11	8	9					10*	7†		1	5				2				12	14			35
	3	6	4			11	8*	9	12				7†	14		1	5				2				10				36
	3	6	4			11	8	9	10*					2†		1	5						12	7					37
	3	6	4			11	8	9					7	2		1	5								10				38
	3	6				11*	8†	9	12				7	2		1	5						14		10				39
	3	6					8	9	12		14		7†	2		1	5						11		10				40
	3					11†	8	9	6*12				7	2		1	5	14							10		4		41
	3	6				11†	8	9	12				4	14	2	1	5				10*				7				42
6	2	13	24	36	2	39	32	42	26	7	3	—	26	10	33	39	36	34	—	—	23	2	1	1	13	2	3	3	
+4s	+1s	+5s			+4s				+10s	+2s	+12s	+1s	+3s	+5s	+1s			+4s	+3s	+2s		+5s		+1s	+1s	+12s			

Morrow—Match No. 30(3); Barnett—Match No. 30(5) 37(14) 39(4) 40(4*).

Rumbelows Cup	First Round	Brentford (h)	5-5
		(a)	1-3
FA Cup	First Round	Tiverton (h)	5-0
	Second Round	Enfield (a)	4-1
	Third Round	Charlton Ath (a)	1-3

BARNET

Player and Position	Ht	Wt	Date	Birth Place	Source	Clubs	League App	Gls
Goalkeepers								
Steve Berryman†			26 12 66	Blackburn		Hartlepool U	1	—
						Exeter C	—	—
						Cambridge U	1	—
						Barnet	—	—
Andy Pape			22 3 62	London	Enfield	Barnet	36	—
Gary Phillips†	6 0	14 00	20 9 61	St Albans	Barnet	WBA	—	—
						Brentford	143	—
						Reading	24	—
						Hereford U (loan)	6	—
						Barnet	6	—
Defenders								
Gary Blackford†			25 9 68	Redhill		Barnet	6	—
Mickey Bodley	5 11	12 00	14 9 67	Hayes	Apprentice	Chelsea	6	1
						Northampton T	20	—
						Barnet	36	1
Peter Cawley†	6 4	13 00	15 9 65	London	Chertsey	Wimbledon	1	—
						Bristol R (loan)	10	—
						Fulham (loan)	5	—
						Bristol R	3	—
						Southend U	7	1
						Exeter C	7	—
						Barnet	3	—
Geoff Cooper‡	5 10	11 00	27 12 60	Kingston	Bognor Regis	Brighton & H A	7	—
						Barnet	14	1
Duncan Horton	5 10	11 00	18 2 67	Maidstone	Welling	Barnet	29	3
David Howell*	6 0		10 10 58	London	Enfield	Barnet	34	3
Richard Nugent†	6 02	13 00	20 3 64	Birmingham	St Albans	Barnet	2	—
Gary Poole*	6 0	11 00	11 9 67	Stratford	School	Tottenham H	—	—
						Cambridge U	43	—
						Barnet	40	2
Paul Wilson*	5 09	10 11	26 9 64	London	Barking	Barnet	25	1
Midfield								
Dave Barnett	6 1	12 08	16 4 67	London	Windsor & Eton	Colchester U	20	—
						WBA	—	—
						Walsall	5	—
						Barnet	4	—
Hakan Hayrettin†			4 2 70	Enfield	Trainee	Leyton Orient	—	—
						Barnet	4	—
Carl Hoddle†	6 0	11 00	8 3 67	Harlow	Bishop's Stortford	Leyton Orient	28	2
						Barnet	13	—
Rob Johnson†	5 6	9 12	22 2 62	Bedford	Apprentice	Luton T	97	1
						Lincoln C (loan)	4	—
						Leicester C	25	—
						Barnet	2	—
Ken Lowe	6 1	12 06	6 11 64	Sedgefield	Barrow	Hartlepool U	54	3
						Barrow	—	—
						Scarborough	4	—
						Barnet	36	3
Dominic Naylor	5 9	11 07	12 8 62	Watford	Trainee	Watford	—	—
						Halifax T	6	1
						Barnet	26	—
Derek Payne†	5 07	10 00	26 4 67	Edgware	Hayes	Barnet	14	1
Paul Showler			10 10 66	Doncaster	Altrincham	Barnet	39	7
Edwin Stein*	5 10		28 9 55	Cape Town	Dagenham	Barnet	1	—
Roger Willis	6 1	11 06	17 6 67	Sheffield		Grimsby T	9	—
						Barnet	38	12

BARNET

Foundation: Barnet Football Club was formed in 1888, disbanded in 1901. A club known as Alston Works FC was then formed and in 1906 changed its name to Barnet Alston FC. In 1912 it combined with The Avenue to become Barnet and Alston.

First Football League game: 17 August, 1991, Division 4, v Crewe Alex (h) L 4-7 – Phillips; Blackford, Cooper (Murphy), Horton, Bodley (Stein), Johnson, Showler, Carter (2), Bull (2), Lowe, Evans.

Did you know: As a Southern League side Barnet reached the FA Cup third round twice in three seasons in the early 1970s. They lost 1-0 to Colchester at home in 1970–71 and after holding QPR to a goalless draw at Loftus Road in 1972–73 they were beaten 3-0 in the replay.

Managers: (since 1946) Lester Finch, George Wheeler, Dexter Adams, Tommy Coleman, Gerry Ward, Gordon Ferry, Brian Kelly, Bill Meadows, Barry Fry, Roger Thompson, Don McAllister, Barry Fry July 1986–.

Player and Position	Ht	Wt	Birth Date	Birth Place	Source	Clubs	League App	Gls
Forwards								
Gary Bull	5 9	11 07	12 6 66	West Bromwich		Southampton	—	—
						Cambridge U	19	4
						Barnet	42	20
Mark Carter	5 9	11 00	17 12 60	Liverpool	Runcorn	Barnet	36	19
Nicky Evans	6 0	12 00	6 7 58	Bedford	Wycombe	Barnet	9	1
Jonathan Hunt†			2 11 71	London		Barnet	14	—
Francis Joseph†	5 10	12 00	6 3 60	Kilburn	Hillingdon B	Wimbledon	51	14
						Brentford	110	44
						Wimbledon (loan)	5	1
						Reading	11	2
						Bristol R (loan)	3	—
						Aldershot (loan)	10	2
						Sheffield U	13	3
						Gillingham	18	1
						Crewe Alex	16	2
						Fulham	4	—
						Barnet	1	—
Tony Lynch†	5 8	10 08	20 1 66	Paddington	Trainee	Brentford	45	6
						Wealdstone	—	—
						Barnet	12	—
Frank Murphy*	5 9		1 6 59	Glasgow	Kettering	Barnet	15	5
David Tomlinson	5 08	11 00	13 12 68	Rotherham	Apprentice	Sheffield W	1	—
						Rotherham U	9	—
						Boston U	—	—
						Barnet	3	—

54

BARNSLEY 1991–92 *Back row (left to right):* Mel Machin (Team Manager), Gareth Williams, Brendan O'Connell, Colin Hoyle, Carlie Bishop, Lee Butler, Steve Davis, Philip Whitehead, Andy Saville, Philip Gridelet, John Pearson, Wayne Bullimore, John Deehan (First Team Coach).
Front row: Neil Redfearn, Mark Robinson, Ian Banks, Brian McCord, Andy Rammell, Deiniol Graham, Mark Smith, Dean Connelly, David Currie, Colin Marshall, Owen Archdeacon, Paul Cross.

Division 1 **BARNSLEY**

Oakwell Ground, Grove St, Barnsley. Telephone Barnsley (0226) 295353. Clubcall: 0898 121152. Commercial Office: 0226 286718. Fax No: 0226 201000

Ground capacity: 26,584 (15,000 under cover).

Record attendance: 40,255 v Stoke C, FA Cup 5th rd, 15 February 1936.

Pitch measurements: 110yd × 75yd.

President: Arthur Raynor.

Vice-presidents.

Chairman: J. A. Dennis.

Directors: C. B. Taylor (Vice-chairman), C. H. Harrison, M. R. Hayselden, S. Manley.

Team Manager: Mel Machin. *Physio:* Andrew Thomas. *Secretary:* Michael Spinks. *Commercial Manager:* Gerry Whewall.

Year Formed: 1887. Turned Professional: 1888. Ltd Co.: 1899.

Former Names: Barnsley St Peter's, 1887–89.

Club Nickname: 'The Tykes', 'Reds' or 'Colliers'.

Record League Victory: 9-0 v Loughborough T, Division 2, 28 January 1899 – Greaves; McCartney, Nixon; Porteous, Burleigh, Howard; Davis (4), Hepworth (1), Lees (1), McCullough (1), Jones (2). 9-0 v Accrington S, Division 3 (N), 3 February 1934 – Ellis; Cookson, Shotton; Harper, Henderson, Whitworth; Spence (2), Smith (1), Blight (4), Andrews (1), Ashton (1).

Record Cup Victory: 6-0 v Blackpool, FA Cup, 1st rd replay, 20 January 1910 – Mearns; Downs, Ness; Glendinning, Boyle (1), Utley; Bartrop, Gadsby (1), Lillycrop (2), Tufnell (2), Forman. 6-0 v Peterborough U, League Cup, 1st rd, 2nd leg, 15 September 1981 – Horn; Joyce, Chambers, Glavin (2), Banks, McCarthy, Evans, Parker (2), Aylott (1), McHale, Barrowclough (1).

Record Defeat: 0-9 v Notts Co, Division 2, 19 November 1927.

Most League Points (2 for a win): 67, Division 3 (N), 1938–39.

Most League points (3 for a win): 74, Division 2, 1988–89.

Most League Goals: 118, Division 3 (N), 1933–34.

Highest League Scorer in Season: Cecil McCormack, 33, Division 2, 1950–51.

Most League Goals in Total Aggregate: Ernest Hine, 123, 1921–26 and 1934–38.

Most Capped Player: Gerry Taggart, 11, Northern Ireland.

Most League Appearances: Barry Murphy, 514, 1962–78.

Record Transfer Fee Received: £1,500,000 from Nottingham F for Carl Tiler, May 1991.

Record Transfer Fee Paid: £175,000 to Barnet for Phil Gridelet, September 1990.

Football League Record: 1898 Elected to Division 2; 1932–34 Division 3 (N); 1934–38 Division 2; 1938–39 Division 3 (N); 1946–53 Division 2; 1953–55 Division 3 (N); 1955–59 Division 2; 1959–65 Division 3; 1965–68 Division 4; 1968–72 Division 3; 1972–79 Division 4; 1979–81 Division 3; 1981–92 Division 2; 1992– Division 1.

Honours: Football League: best season: 3rd, Division 2, 1914–15, 1921–22; Division 3 (N) – Champions 1933–34, 1938–39, 1954–55; Runners-up 1953–54; Division 3 – Runners-up 1980–81; Division 4 – Runners-up 1967–68; Promoted 1978–79. *FA Cup:* Winners 1912; Runners-up 1910. *Football League Cup:* best season: 5th rd, 1981–82.

Colours: Red shirts, white trim, white shorts, red stockings. **Change colours:** White shirts, black shorts, black stockings.

BARNSLEY 1991–92 LEAGUE RECORD

Match No.	Date		Venue	Opponents		Result	H/T Score	Lg. Pos.	Goalscorers	Atten-dance
1	Aug	17	A	Plymouth Arg	L	1-2	0-1	—	Pearson	6352
2		20	H	Sunderland	L	0-3	0-2	—		12,454
3		24	H	Brighton & HA	L	1-2	1-1	24	O'Connell	6066
4		27	A	Port Vale	D	0-0	0-0	—		6229
5		31	A	Swindon T	L	1-3	1-0	23	Banks	7449
6	Sep	3	H	Watford	L	0-3	0-1	—		6500
7		7	A	Derby Co	D	1-1	0-1	23	Saville	10,559
8		14	H	Ipswich T	W	1-0	0-0	21	Currie	6786
9		17	H	Leicester C	W	3-1	1-1	—	Rammell, Taggart, Redfearn (pen)	9318
10		21	A	Tranmere R	L	1-2	0-1	21	Banks	8482
11		28	H	Millwall	L	0-2	0-1	21		6544
12	Oct	5	A	Wolverhampton W	W	2-1	0-1	20	Saville, O'Connell	14,082
13		12	H	Portsmouth	W	2-0	1-0	19	Taggart, Graham	6579
14		19	H	Bristol C	L	1-2	0-1	19	Currie	6566
15		26	A	Cambridge U	L	1-2	0-0	21	Rammell	5534
16	Nov	2	A	Oxford U	W	1-0	1-0	18	Redfearn	3419
17		5	H	Middlesbrough	W	2-1	2-0	—	Rammell, Taggart	6525
18		9	H	Bristol R	L	0-1	0-0	17		6688
19		16	A	Blackburn R	L	0-3	0-1	19		13,797
20		23	A	Southend U	L	1-2	0-0	20	Saville	5060
21		30	H	Newcastle U	W	3-0	3-0	19	Saville, Robinson, Rammell	9648
22	Dec	7	A	Charlton Ath	D	1-1	0-0	18	Redfearn (pen)	4581
23		14	H	Grimsby T	W	4-1	2-0	15	Currie, Archdeacon 2, Saville	6856
24		22	A	Watford	D	1-1	1-0	—	Robinson	7522
25		26	H	Port Vale	D	0-0	0-0	15		8843
26		28	H	Swindon T	D	1-1	0-1	16	Rammell	8357
27	Jan	1	A	Sunderland	L	0-2	0-1	18		16,107
28		11	H	Brighton & HA ·	L	1-3	0-2	19	Currie	6107
29		18	H	Plymouth Arg	L	1-3	0-3	21	Saville	5322
30	Feb	1	A	Bristol C	W	2-0	0-0	21	Archdeacon, O'Connell	9508
31		8	H	Cambridge U	D	0-0	0-0	17		6196
32		15	H	Southend U	W	1-0	0-0	16	O'Connell	5328
33		22	A	Newcastle U	D	1-1	0-0	17	Currie	27,670
34		29	H	Charlton Ath	W	1-0	0-0	14	Archdeacon	6050
35	Mar	7	A	Grimsby T	W	1-0	1-0	13	Archdeacon	6913
36		14	H	Oxford U	W	1-0	0-0	13	Currie	5436
37		21	A	Bristol R	D	0-0	0-0	14		5665
38		28	H	Blackburn R	W	2-1	0-1	12	Smith, Rammell	13,346
39		31	A	Ipswich T	L	0-2	0-1	—		14,148
40	Apr	4	A	Derby Co	L	0-3	0-2	16		10,121
41		11	A	Leicester C	L	1-3	1-0	17	Currie	14,438
42		13	A	Middlesbrough	W	1-0	0-0	—	Redfearn	12,743
43		18	H	Tranmere R	D	1-1	1-1	16	Archdeacon	5811
44		22	A	Millwall	D	1-1	1-1	—	Rammell	5703
45		26	H	Wolverhampton W	W	2-0	1-0	14	Bullimore, Rammell	7244
46	May	2	A	Portsmouth	L	0-2	0-0	16		11,169

Final League Position: 16

GOALSCORERS

League (46): Rammell 8, Currie 7, Archdeacon 6, Saville 6, O'Connell 4, Redfearn 4 (2 pens), Taggart 3, Banks 2, Robinson 2, Bullimore 1, Graham 1, Pearson 1, Smith 1.
Rumbelows Cup (2): O'Connell 1, Pearson 1.
FA Cup (0).

Whitehead	Bishop	Williams	Banks	Davis	Taggart	O'Connell	Rammell	Pearson	McCord	Graham	Fleming	Connelly	Smith	Butler	Robinson	Cross	Redfearn	Currie	Archdeacon	Saville	Bullimore	Whitworth	Liddell	Match No.
1	2	3	4	5	6	7	8	9	10*	11	12													1
1	2	3	4	5	6*	7	8	9	11†	10	12	14												2
1	2		4	5	6	7	8	9*	12	10	11	3												3
10			4		6	7	8	9		11			5	1	2	3								4
10			4		6	7	8	9*		12	11		5	1	2	3								5
10			4	5	6	7	8				9	2	11*	1	12	3								6
	2				4*	6	7	8†	12			3	5	1				9	10	11	14			7
					4	6	7	12				3	5	1	2		8	10	11	9*				8
					4	6	7	9				3	5	1	2		8	10*	11	12				9
					4	6	7*	9	10			3	5	1	2		8		11	12				10
					4*	6	7	9				3	5	1	2		8	10	11	12				11
					12	6	7	11	9			4		1	2		8	10*	3	5				12
12						6	7	11	9	10		4		1	2		8			3*	5			13
		14				6	7	11	9*	12		4		1	2		8	10		3	5†			14
		9				6	7	11				4	5	1	2		8	10*	3					15
		9*				6	7	11				4	5	1	2		8	12	3		10			16
		9				6	7	11				4	5	1	2		8	10	3					17
5		9				6	7	11				12	4*	1	2		8	10	3					18
	14	9*				6	7	11	12			4	5	1	2		8	10†	3					19
10						6		11				4*	5	1	2		8	12	3	9	7			20
			3			6			10*			2	5	1		7	8	12	11	9	4			21
			3			6					12	2	5	1		7	8	10*	11	9	4			22
			3	14		6					12	2	5	1		7	8†	10*	11	9	4			23
			3			6					12	2	5	1		7	8	10*	11	9	4			24
			3			6					12	2	5	1		7	8	10	11	9	4*			25
			14	3		6			10			2*	5	1		7	8	12	11	9†	4			26
			3*	14		6			10			2	5	1		7	8	12	11	9	4†			27
			3			6	7*	9				12	5	1		2†	8	10	11	14	4			28
			3	5		6	12	7				14	2†	1			8	10	11	9	4*			29
			3	8		6	7				9	4	5	1	2			10	11					30
			3	8		6	7*				9	4	5	1	2			10	11	12				31
			3*	8		6	7				9†	4	5	1	2		14	10	11	12				32
				8	3*		7†		14			4	5	1	2			9	10	11	12	6		33
			3	8			7	12	14			4*	5	1	2			10	11	9†		6		34
			3	8	4		7						5	1	2			10	11		9	6		35
			4	3	8		7						5	1	2			9	10	11		6		36
			4	3	8		7						5	1	2			9	10	11		6		37
			4	3	8		7	12					5	1	2			9	10*	11		6		38
			3	8*		4†	7		10			14	5	1	2			9	12	11		6		39
			3*	8			7		10		14	4	5	1	2			9	12	11		6†		40
				8†			7*	3			12	4	5	1	2			9	10	11	14	6		41
					3		7*	12				4	5	1	2			9	10	11	8	6		42
			14		3†		7*	10			12	4	5	1	2			9		11	8	6		43
				6	3			12	10*			4	5	1	2			9	7	11	8			44
				6	12			3*	10			4	5	1	2			9	7	11	8			45
				6*	3				10		12	4	5	1	2			9	7†	11	8		14	46
3	25	15	23	8	38	34	31	8	1	8	40	2	37	43	40	3	35	30	40	14	17	11	—	
+3s	+2s	+3s	+1s		+2s	+6s	+2s	+2s	+13s	+2s	+1s	+1s			+1s			+1s	+7s		+8s	+1s	+1s	

Rumbelows Cup	Second Round	Blackpool (a)	0-1
		(h)	2-0
	Third Round	Middlesbrough (a)	0-1
FA Cup	Third Round	Norwich C (a)	0-1

BARNSLEY

Goalkeepers

Lee Butler	6 2	14 02	30 5 66	Sheffield	Haworth Coll	Lincoln C	30	—
						Aston Villa	8	—
						Hull C (loan)	4	—
						Barnsley	43	—
Phil Whitehead	6 2	13 00	17 12 69	Halifax		Halifax T	42	—
						Barnsley	3	—
						Halifax T (loan)	9	—
						Scunthorpe U (loan)	9	—

Defenders

Charlie Bishop	6 0	12 01	16 2 68	Nottingham	Apprentice	Stoke C	—	—
						Watford	—	—
						Bury	114	6
						Barnsley	28	—
Steve Davis	6 0	12 07	26 7 65	Birmingham	Apprentice	Stoke C	—	—
						Crewe Alex	145	1
						Burnley	147	11
						Barnsley	9	—
Nicholas Eaden	6 00	12 00	12 12 72	Sheffield	Trainee	Barnsley	—	—
Gary Fleming	5 9	11 07	17 2 67	Londonderry	Apprentice	Nottingham F	74	—
						Manchester C	14	—
						Notts Co (loan)	3	—
						Barnsley	98	—
Brian McCord	5 10	11 06	24 8 68	Derby	Apprentice	Derby Co	5	—
						Barnsley	43	2
Mark Smith	6 2	13 11	21 3 60	Sheffield	Apprentice	Sheffield W	282	16
						Plymouth Arg	82	6
						Barnsley	100	10
Gerry Taggart	6 1	12 03	18 10 70	Belfast	Trainee	Manchester C	12	1
						Barnsley	89	7
Allan Wilkinson‡	6 0	10 07	14 9 72	Barnsley	Trainee	Barnsley	—	—

Midfield

Ian Banks*	5 11	12 12	9 1 61	Mexborough	Apprentice	Barnsley	164	37
						Leicester C	93	14
						Huddersfield T	78	17
						Bradford C	30	3
						WBA	4	—
						Barnsley	96	7
Wayne Bullimore	5 9	10 06	12 9 70	Sutton-in-Ashfield	Trainee	Manchester U	—	—
						Barnsley	18	1
Mark Burton	5 8	11 07	7 5 73	Barnsley	Trainee	Barnsley	—	—
Dino Connelly	5 9	10 08	6 1 70	Glasgow	Trainee	Arsenal	—	—
						Barnsley	12	—
						Wigan Ath (loan)	12	2
Phil Gridelet	5 11	12 00	30 4 67	Edgware	Barnet	Barnsley	4	—
Neil Hodgkinson*	5 10	12 00	31 7 73	Dewsbury	Trainee	Barnsley	—	—
Colin Marshall‡	5 5	9 05	1 11 69	Glasgow	Trainee	Barnsley	4	—
						Wrexham (loan)	3	—
						Scarborough (loan)	4	1
Neil Redfearn	5 10	12 04	20 6 65	Dewsbury	Apprentice	Nottingham F	—	—
						Bolton W	35	1
						Lincoln C (loan)	10	1
						Lincoln C	90	12
						Doncaster R	46	14
						Crystal Palace	57	10
						Watford	24	3
						Oldham Ath	62	16
						Barnsley	36	4
Mark Robinson	5 9	11 08	21 11 68	Manchester	Trainee	WBA	2	—
						Barnsley	108	5

Forwards

Owen Archdeacon	5 7	11 00	4 3 66	Greenock	Gourock U	Celtic	76	7
						Barnsley	106	11

BARNSLEY

Foundation: Many clubs owe their inception to the church and Barnsley are among them, for they were formed in 1887 by the Rev. T. T. Preedy, curate of Barnsley St. Peter's and went under that name until a year after being admitted to the Second Division of the Football League in 1898.

First Football League game: 1 September, 1898, Division 2, v Lincoln C (a) L 0-1 – Fawcett; McArtney, Nixon; King, Burleigh, Porteous; Davis, Lees, Murray, McCullough, McGee.

Did you know: In 1932–33 Barnsley signed an inside-forward from West Stanley named Jackie Smith who was barely 5ft 3in tall and nicknamed "Peter Pan" or "Tiny". Despite his lack of height he scored 12 goals in each of his two seasons with the club, many with his head.

Managers (and Secretary-managers)
Arthur Fairclough 1898–1901*, John McCartney 1901–04*, Arthur Fairclough 1904–12, John Hastie 1912–14, Percy Lewis 1914–19, Peter Sant 1919–26, John Commins 1926–29, Arthur Fairclough 1929–30, Brough Fletcher 1930–37, Angus Seed 1937–53, Tim Ward 1953–60, Johnny Steele 1960–71 (continued as GM), John McSeveney 1971–72, Johnny Steele (GM) 1972–73, Jim Iley 1973–78, Allan Clarke 1978–80, Norman Hunter 1980–84, Bobby Collins 1984–85, Allan Clarke 1985–89, Mel Machin December 1989–.

Name	Ht	Wt	Born	Birthplace	Signed from	Club	Apps	Gls
David Currie	5 11	12 09	27 11 62	Stockton	Local	Middlesbrough	113	31
						Darlington	76	33
						Barnsley	80	30
						Nottingham F	8	1
						Oldham Ath	31	3
						Barnsley	37	7
John Deehan*	5 11	13 00	8 8 57	Solihull	Apprentice	Aston Villa	110	42
						WBA	47	5
						Norwich C	162	62
						Ipswich T	49	11
						Manchester C	—	—
						Barnsley	11	2
Deiniol Graham	5 10	10 05	4 10 69	Cannock	Trainee	Manchester U	2	—
						Barnsley	21	1
Colin Hoyle	5 11	12 03	15 1 72	Derby	Trainee	Arsenal	—	—
						Chesterfield (loan)	3	—
						Barnsley	—	—
Michael Jackson‡	5 7	9 04	11 4 73	Barnsley	Trainee	Barnsley	—	—
Andrew Liddell	5 8	10 05	28 6 73	Leeds	Trainee	Barnsley	—	—
Brendan O'Connell	5 10	10 09	12 11 66	London		Portsmouth	—	—
						Exeter C	81	19
						Burnley	64	17
						Huddersfield T (loan)	11	1
						Barnsley	92	15
John Pearson	6 2	13 02	1 9 63	Sheffield	Apprentice	Sheffield W	105	24
						Charlton Ath	61	15
						Leeds U	99	12
						Rotherham U (loan)	11	5
						Barnsley	10	1
						Hull C (loan)	15	—
Andy Rammell	5 10	11 07	10 2 67	Nuneaton	Atherstone U	Manchester U	—	—
						Barnsley	77	20
Gareth Williams	5 10	11 08	12 3 67	Isle of Wight	Gosport	Aston Villa	12	—
						Barnsley	17	—
Corrie Winks*	5 11	11 07	7 4 73	Mexborough	Trainee	Barnsley	—	—

Trainees
Degnan, Lee A; Driver, Christopher; Eaton, Barry; Feeney, Mark A; Firth, Lee; Gregg, John H; Hanby, Robert J; Lumb, Richard M; Mercer, Mark S; Morgan, Gregory D; Peacock, Dennis J; Watson, David N.

Associated Schoolboys
Barwise, Andrew J; Bennett, Troy; Bochenski, Simon; Brooke, David; Craft, Adrian; Dobson, Stephen P; Fearon, Dean A; Green, Simon; Gregory, Andrew; Halstead, Peter; Hughes, Russell; Jackson, Christopher D; Jebson, Carl M; Newsam, Andrew; Pettinger, Paul A; Rawson, Neil; Shelley, Steven; Skelton, Ian S; Sollitt, Adam; Standish, Mark A; Wainwright, Jonathan M; Widdowson, Steven; Yates, Kevin.

BIRMINGHAM CITY 1991–92 *Back row (left to right):* Nigel Gleghorn, Nigel Larkins, Martin Hicks, Martin Thomas, John Gayle, Richard Williams, Matthew Fox, Ian Clarkson, Trevor Matthewson.
Centre row: Andy Dale, Mark Harrison, Mark Yates, Dean Peer, Paul Mardon, Richard Naylor, Brian Gray, Paul Masefield, Stuart Brown, Sean Francis, Eamon Dolan, Brendon Devery.
Front row: David Foye, Eric Hogan, Andy Harris, Paul Tait, Folorunso Okenla, Mark Rutherford, Mark Cougan, Simon Sturridge, John Frain, Ian Rodgerson.

Division 1   **BIRMINGHAM CITY**

St Andrews, Birmingham B9 4NH. Telephone 021-772 0101/ 2689. Lottery office/Souvenir shop: 021-772 1245. Clubcall: 0898 121188. Fax No: 021 766 7866. Club Soccer Shop: 021 766 8274

Ground capacity: 28,235.
Record attendance: 66,844 v Everton, FA Cup 5th rd, 11 February 1939.
Record receipts: £116,372.50 v Nottingham Forest, FA Cup 5th rd, 20 February 1988.
Pitch measurements: 115yd × 75yd.
Directors: S. Kumar BA (Chairman), R. Kumar BSC (Vice-chairman), B. Kumar MSC, J. F. Wiseman, T. Cooper, B. Slater.
General Manager: E. Partridge.
Manager: Terry Cooper. *Coach/Assistant Manager:* Ian Atkins. *Physio:* Paul Heath. *Commercial Manager:* Joan Hill. *Secretary:* Alan G. Jones BA, MBA.
Year Formed: 1875. Turned Professional: 1885. Ltd Co.: 1888.
Former Grounds: 1875, waste ground near Arthur St; 1877, Muntz St, Small Heath; 1906, St Andrews.
Former Names: 1875–88, Small Heath Alliance; 1888, dropped 'Alliance'; became Birmingham 1905; became Birmingham City 1945.
Club Nickname: 'Blues'.
Record League Victory: 12-0 v Walsall T Swifts, Division 2, 17 December 1892 – Charnley; Bayley, Jones; Ollis, Jenkyns, Devey; Hallam (2), Walton (3), Mobley (3), Wheldon (2), Hands (2). 12-0 v Doncaster R, Division 2, 11 April 1903 – Dorrington; Goldie, Wassell; Beer, Dougherty (1), Howard; Athersmith (1), Leonard (3), McRoberts (1), Wilcox (4), Field (1). Aston. (1 og).
Record Cup Victory: 9-2 v Burton W, FA Cup, 1st rd, 31 October 1885 – Hedges; Jones, Evetts (1); F. James, Felton, A. James (1); Davenport (2), Stanley (4), Simms, Figures, Morris (1).
Record Defeat: 1-9 v Sheffield W, Division 1, 13 December 1930 and v Blackburn R, Division 1, 5 January 1895.
Most League Points (2 for a win): 59, Division 2, 1947–48.
Most League points (3 for a win): 82, Division 2, 1984–85.
Most League Goals: 103, Division 2, 1893–94 (only 28 games).
Highest League Scorer in Season: Joe Bradford, 29, Division 1, 1927–28.
Most League Goals in Total Aggregate: Joe Bradford, 249, 1920–35.
Most Capped Player: Malcolm Page, 28, Wales.
Most League Appearances: Frank Womack, 491, 1908–28.
Record Transfer Fee Received: £975,000 from Nottingham F for Trevor Francis, February 1979.
Record Transfer Fee Paid: £350,000 to Derby Co for David Langan, June 1980.
Football League Record: 1892 elected to Division 2; 1894–96 Division 1; 1896–1901 Division 2; 1901–02 Division 1; 1902–03 Division 2; 1903–08 Division 1; 1908–21 Division 2; 1921–39 Division 1; 1946–48 Division 2; 1948–50 Division 1; 1950–55 Division 2; 1955–65 Division 1; 1965–72 Division 2; 1972–79 Division 1; 1979–80 Division 2; 1980–84 Division 1; 1984–85 Division 2; 1985–86 Division 1; 1986–89 Division 2; 1989–92 Division 3; 1992– Division 1.
Honours: Football League: Division 1 best season: 6th, 1955–56; Division 2 – Champions 1892–93, 1920–21, 1947–48, 1954–55; Runners-up 1893–94, 1900–01, 1902–03, 1971–72, 1984–85. Division 3 Runners-up 1991–92. *FA Cup:* Runners-up 1931, 1956. *Football League Cup:* Winners 1963. *Leyland Daf Cup:* Winners 1991. **European Competitions:** *European Fairs Cup:* 1955–58, 1958–60 (runners-up), 1960–61 (runners-up), 1961–62.
Colours: Royal blue shirts, white shorts, blue stockings with white trim. **Change colours:** All white.

BIRMINGHAM CITY 1991–92 LEAGUE RECORD

Match No.	Date		Venue	Opponents	Result		H/T Score	Lg. Pos.	Goalscorers	Atten- dance
1	Aug	17	H	Bury	W	3-2	2-1	—	Gleghorn, Gayle, Okenla	9033
2		24	A	Fulham	W	1-0	1-0	3	Rodgerson	4762
3		31	H	Darlington	W	1-0	1-0	1	Sturridge	8768
4	Sep	3	A	Hull C	W	2-1	0-0	—	Sturridge, Rodgerson	4801
5		7	A	Reading	D	1-1	1-1	2	Sturridge	6649
6		14	H	Peterborough U	D	1-1	0-0	1	Cooper	9408
7		17	H	Chester C	W	3-2	2-2	—	Sturridge, Frain (pen), Gleghorn	8154
8		21	A	Hartlepool U	L	0-1	0-1	2		4643
9		28	H	Preston NE	W	3-1	1-1	2	Matthewson, Gleghorn, Rodgerson	8760
10	Oct	5	A	Shrewsbury T	D	1-1	1-0	2	Gleghorn	7035
11		12	H	Stockport Co	W	3-0	2-0	1	Cooper, Drinkell, Donowa	12,634
12		19	H	Wigan Ath	D	3-3	1-2	2	Sturridge, Gleghorn, Rodgerson	9662
13		26	A	WBA	W	1-0	0-0	1	Drinkell	26,168
14	Nov	2	H	Torquay U	W	3-0	1-0	1	Gleghorn (pen), Sturridge, Donowa	9478
15		6	A	Brentford	D	2-2	1-1	—	Sturridge, Cooper	8798
16		9	A	Huddersfield T	L	2-3	0-1	2	Gleghorn, Matthewson	11,688
17		23	H	Exeter C	W	1-0	0-0	2	Gleghorn	11,319
18		30	H	Bradford C	W	2-0	1-0	2	Peer, Gleghorn	10,468
19	Dec	14	A	Bournemouth	L	1-2	0-1	2	Paskin	6048
20		21	H	Fulham	W	3-1	1-0	1	Gleghorn, Rodgerson 2	8877
21		26	A	Darlington	D	1-1	0-1	2	Rodgerson	4421
22		28	A	Bury	L	0-1	0-0	3		4254
23	Jan	1	H	Hull C	D	2-2	1-1	2	Paskin, Gleghorn	12,983
24		4	A	Stoke C	L	1-2	0-0	2	Beckford	18,914
25		11	H	Leyton Orient	D	2-2	0-1	3	Cooper, Paskin	10,445
26		18	A	Swansea C	W	2-0	1-0	2	Rodgerson, Rowbotham	4147
27	Feb	8	H	WBA	L	0-3	0-2	4		27,508
28		11	A	Bradford C	W	2-1	1-0	—	Gleghorn, Sturridge	7008
29		15	H	Bournemouth	L	0-1	0-0	5		10,898
30		22	A	Leyton Orient	D	0-0	0-0	6		5995
31		29	H	Stoke C	D	1-1	1-0	5	Frain (pen)	22,162
32	Mar	3	H	Swansea C	D	1-1	1-0	—	Rowbotham	9475
33		10	H	Brentford	W	1-0	1-0	—	Matthewson	13,290
34		17	A	Bolton W	'D	1-1	1-0	—	Rodgerson	7329
35		21	H	Huddersfield T	W	2-0	1-0	6	Sturridge, Gleghorn	12,482
36		24	A	Torquay U	W	2-1	0-1	—	Rowbotham, Matthewson	2446
37		28	A	Exeter C	L	1-2	1-1	3	Hicks	5479
38		31	A	Peterborough U	W	3-2	1-1	—	Frain (pen), Sturridge, Matthewson	12,081
39	Apr	4	H	Reading	W	2-0	2-0	2	Rowbotham, Frain (pen)	12,229
40		11	A	Chester C	W	1-0	0-0	2	Gleghorn	4895
41		14	H	Bolton W	W	2-1	2-1	—	Frain (pen), Rennie	14,440
42		18	H	Hartlepool U	W	2-1	0-0	1	Matthewson, Gleghorn	13,698
43		21	A	Preston NE	L	2-3	0-2	—	Gleghorn, Rennie	7738
44		25	A	Shrewsbury T	W	1-0	1-0	1	Gleghorn	19,868
45		28	A	Wigan Ath	L	0-3	0-2	—		5950
46	May	2	A	Stockport Co	L	0-2	0-2	2		7840

Final League Position: 2

GOALSCORERS

League (69): Gleghorn 17 (1 pen), Sturridge 10, Rodgerson 9, Matthewson 6, Frain 5 (5 pens), Cooper 4, Rowbotham 4, Paskin 3, Donowa 2, Drinkell 2, Rennie 2, Beckford 1, Gayle 1, Hicks 1, Okenla 1, Peer 1.
Rumbelows Cup (13): Gleghorn 5, Peer 3, Rodgerson 2, Hicks 1, Sturridge 1, Yates 1.
FA Cup (0).

Thomas	Clarkson	Matthewson	Frain	Hicks	Mardon	Rodgerson	Gayle	Peer	Gleghorn	Sturridge	Yates	Okenla	Dolan	Donowa	Aylott	Cooper	Jones	Atkins	Tait	Drinkell	Carter	Paskin	Cheesewright	Hogan	Miller	Rowbotham	Beckford	Francis	Match No.
1	2	3*	4	5	6	7	8†	9	10	11	12	14																	1
1	2		3	5	6	7		9	10	11	4	12	8*																2
1	2		3	5	6	7	8*	9	10	11	12	4																	3
1	2		3	5	6	7		9	10	11						4		8											4
1	2		3	5	6	7*		9	10	11						4		8		12									5
1	2		3	5	6†			9	10	11	7*					4		8		12	14								6
1	2		3	5	6	7		9	10	11						4		8											7
1	2		3	5	6	7		9	10	11						4		8											8
1	2	3	8	5	6	7			10	11					9	4													9
1	2	3	8	5	6	7			10	11	14				9†	4*												12	10
1	2	3	8	5	6	7			10	11				12		4						9*							11
1	2	3	8	5	6	7			10	11	14			12		4†						9*							12
1	2	3	8	5	6				10	11			7			4				9									13
1	2	3	8	5	6				10	11			7			4				9									14
1	2	3	8	5	6			14	12	10		11	7			4*				9†									15
1	2	3	8	5	6	7			4*	10	11				9	12													16
	2	5	3		6	7			4*	10	11				9			8					1	12					17
	2	5	3		6	7			4	10	11*				9			8					1	12					18
	2	5	3	12	6	7			4	10		11			9†			8*					1	14					19
	2	5	3		6	7			4	10	11							8		9					1				20
	2	5	3		6	7			4	10	11			12				8*		9					1				21
	2	12	3	5	6	7			4*	10	11							8		9					1				22
		3	2	5	6	7				10	11*	12			8†	4	14			9					1				23
		3	2	5	6*	7				10	12					4				9					1		8	11	24
	2	6	3	5		7			8	10	12					4				9					1		11*		25
	2	6	3	5		7			8*	10						4				9					1		11	12	26
	2	6	3	5		7	14		10	12					9	4*									1		8	11	27
	2	6		5		7			10	11*					9	4			3						1		8	12	28
	2	6		5		7			10	11					9*	4			3†14						1		8	12	29
	2	11		5		7			10	4					9				3	8					1				30
	2		3	5	6	7			10	11*	12†							8							1		9		31
	2		3	5	6	7			10		12							8†							1		9	14	32
	2	6	3	5		7			10	11*	12†					14		8							1		9		33
		6	3	5	2	7			10		12						11	8*							1		9		34
	2	3	8	5	6	7			10	11*	12																9		35
		3	8	5	6	7			10	11																	9		36
	2	3	8	5	6*	7			10	11	12																9†		37
	2	6	3	5		7*			10	11						8											9		38
	2	6	3	5					10	11*						8											9	12	39
	2	6	3	5					10	11						8											9*		40
2*	6	3		5	14	7†			10	11						8											9		41
	2	6	3	5				7	10	11						8											9		42
	2	6	3	5	12			14	10	11						8				9*							7†		43
	2	6	3	5	12	7			10	11						8											9*		44
	2	6	3	5	9*	7			10	11†						8											12		45
	2	6	3	5	14	7			10	12						8											9†		46

Totals: 16 42 35 44 41 31 38 2 18 46 38 1 2 1 20 2 27 — 5 10 5 2 8 1 — 15 21 2 —

Substitute appearances: +1s +1s +4s +1s +1s +3s +2s +1s +5s +1s +6s +6s +1s +3s +2s +2s +1s +1s +2s +3s

Rennie—Match No. 30(6) 31(4) 32(4) 33(4) 34(4) 35(4) 36(4) 37(4) 38(4) 39(4) 40(4) 41(4) 42(4) 43(4) 44(4) 45(4) 46(4); Dearden—Match No. 35(1) 36(1) 37(1) 38(1) 39(1) 40(1) 41(1) 42(1) 43(1) 44(1) 45(1) 46(1); O'Neill—Match No. 31(14) 32(11*) 39(7) 40(12); Sale—Match No. 37(14) 38(12) 40(7) 41(12) 45(14) 46(11*).

Rumbelows Cup	First Round	Exeter C (a)	1-0
		(h)	4-0
	Second Round	Luton T (a)	2-2
		(h)	3-2
	Third Round	Crystal Palace (h)	1-1
		(a)	1-1
		(a)	1-2
FA Cup	First Round	Torquay U (a)	0-3

BIRMINGHAM CITY

Player and Position	Ht	Wt	Birth Date	Birth Place	Source	Clubs	League App	League Gls
Goalkeepers								
Martin Thomas	6 1	13 00	28 11 59	Senghennydd	Apprentice	Bristol R	162	—
						Cardiff C (loan)	15	—
						Tottenham H (loan)	—	—
						Southend U (loan)	6	—
						Newcastle U (loan)	3	—
						Newcastle U	115	—
						Middlesbrough (loan)	4	—
						Birmingham C	139	—
Dean Williams†	6 0	11 07	5 1 72	Lichfield	Trainee	Birmingham C	4	—
Richard Williams*	5 10	11 02	I3 3 73	Nuneaton	Trainee	Birmingham C	—	—
Defenders								
Ian Clarkson	5 11	12 00	4 12 70	Birmingham	Trainee	Birmingham C	108	—
Mark Coogan‡	5 7	10 04	19 5 73	Birmingham	Trainee	Birmingham C	—	—
Matthew Fox	6 0	13 00	13 7 71	Birmingham	Trainee	Birmingham C	14	—
Martin Hicks	6 3	13 06	27 2 57	Stratford on Avon	Stratford T	Charlton Ath	—	—
						Reading	500	23
						Birmingham C	42	1
Nigel Larkins*			6 4 72	Burton-on-Trent	Trainee	Birmingham C	—	—
Paul Mardon	6 0	11 10	14 9 69	Bristol	Trainee	Bristol C	42	—
						Doncaster (loan)	3	—
						Birmingham C	35	—
Trevor Matthewson	6 1	12 05	12 2 63	Sheffield	Apprentice	Sheffield W	3	—
						Newport Co	75	—
						Stockport Co	80	—
						Lincoln C	43	2
						Birmingham C	128	10
Dean Peer	6 2	12 00	8 8 69	Dudley	Trainee	Birmingham C	107	1
Ian Rodgerson	5 8	11 05	9 4 66	Hereford	Local	Hereford U	100	6
						Cardiff C	99	4
						Birmingham C	64	11
Midfield								
Ian Atkins	6 0	12 03	16 1 57	Birmingham	Apprentice	Shrewsbury T	278	58
						Sunderland	77	6
						Everton	7	1
						Ipswich T	77	4
						Birmingham C	101	6
Steven Brown*	5 11	11 06	6 11 72	Birmingham	Trainee	Birmingham C	—	—
Mark Cooper	5 8	11 04	18 12 68	Wakefield	Trainee	Bristol C	—	—
						Exeter C	50	12
						Southend U (loan)	5	—
						Birmingham C	33	4
Brendon Devery‡	6 0	11 00	12 9 72		Trainee	Birmingham C	—	—
David Foy	6 1	12 00	20 10 72	Coventry	Trainee	Birmingham C	—	—
John Frain	5 7	11 10	8 10 68	Birmingham	Apprentice	Birmingham C	172	15
Brian Gray*	5 11	11 00	25 11 72	Birmingham	Trainee	Birmingham C	—	—
Mark Harrison‡			7 8 73	Birmingham	Trainee	Birmingham C	—	—
Paul Jones			6 2 74	Solihull	Trainee	Birmingham C	1	—
Richard Naylor*	5 7	10 10	15 4 73	Birmingham	Trainee	Birmingham C	—	—
David Rennie	6 0	12 00	29 8 64	Edinburgh	Apprentice	Leicester C	21	1
						Leeds U	101	5
						Bristol C	104	8
						Birmingham C	17	2
Darren Rowbotham	5 10	11 05	22 10 66	Cardiff	Trainee	Plymouth Arg	46	2
						Exeter C	118	47
						Torquay U	14	3
						Birmingham C	22	4

BIRMINGHAM CITY

Foundation: In 1875 cricketing enthusiasts who were largely members of Trinity Church, Bordesley, determined to continue their sporting relationships throughout the year by forming a football club which they called Small Heath Alliance. For their earliest games played on waste land in Arthur Street, the team included three Edden brothers and two James brothers.

First Football League game: 3 September, 1892, Division 2, v Burslem Port Vale (h) W 5-1 – Charsley; Bayley, Speller; Ollis, Jenkyns, Devey; Hallam (1), Edwards (1), Short (1), Wheldon (2), Hands.

Did you know: In the FA Cup third round in January 1928 at St Andrews, non-league Peterborough & Fletton United were leading 3-1 at the interval but Birmingham's ace goalscorer Joe Bradford scored a winning hat-trick in the second half.

Managers (and Secretary-managers)
Alfred Jones 1892–1908*, Alec Watson 1908–1910, Bob McRoberts 1910–15, Frank Richards 1915–23*, Bill Beer 1923–27, Leslie Knighton 1928–33, George Liddell 1933–39, Harry Storer 1945–48, Bob Brocklebank 1949–54, Arthur Turner 1954–58, Pat Beasley 1959–60, Gil Merrick 1960–64, Joe Mallett 1965, Stan Cullis 1965–70, Fred Goodwin 1970–75, Willie Bell 1975–77, Sir Alf Ramsey 1977–78, Jim Smith 1978–82, Ron Saunders 1982–86, John Bond 1986–87, Garry Pendrey 1987–89, Dave Mackay 1989–1991, Lou Macari 1991, Terry Cooper August 1991–.

Player and Position	Ht	Wt	Birth Date	Place	Source	Clubs	League App	Gls
Forwards								
Jason Beckford	5 9	12 04	14 2 70	Manchester	Trainee	Manchester C	20	1
						Blackburn R (loan)	4	—
						Birmingham C	4	1
						Port Vale (loan)	5	1
Andrew Dale‡	6 1	12 04	15 12 72	West Bromwich	Trainee	Birmingham C	—	—
Louie Donowa	5 9	11 00	24 9 64	Ipswich	Apprentice	Norwich C	62	11
						Stoke C (loan)	4	1
						Coruna	—	—
						Willem II	—	—
						Ipswich T	23	1
						Bristol C	24	3
						Birmingham C	26	2
Sean Francis*	5 10	11 09	1 8 72	Birmingham	Trainee	Birmingham C	6	—
John Gayle	6 4	13 01	30 7 64	Birmingham	Burton Albion	Wimbledon	20	2
						Birmingham C	25	7
Nigel Gleghorn	6 0	12 13	12 8 62	Seaham	Seaham Red Star	Ipswich T	66	11
						Manchester C	34	7
						Birmingham C	131	32
Eric Hogan			17 12 71	Cork	Cobh Ramblers	Birmingham C	1	—
Alan O'Neill			27 8 73	Cork	Cobh Ramblers	Birmingham C	4	—
Folorunso Okenla			9 10 67	Nigeria	Trainee	Birmingham C	7	1
Mark Rutherford	5 11	11 00	25 3 72	Birmingham	Trainee	Birmingham C	5	—
Mark Sale*	6 5	13 08	27 2 72	Burton-on-Trent	Trainee	Stoke C	2	—
						Cambridge U	—	—
						Birmingham C	6	—
Simon Sturridge	5 8	10 00	9 12 69	Birmingham	Trainee	Birmingham C	130	29
Paul Tait	6 1	10 00	31 7 71	Sutton Coldfield	Trainee	Birmingham C	54	5

Trainees
Adams, Carl A; Aston, David E; Baker, Lewis M; Bignott, Marcus; Fowkes, Graeme L; Green, Andrew P; Halford, John D; Higgins, Matthew P; McKeever, Scott J; Morley, Jamie D; O'Connor, David W. P; Potter, Graham S; Powell, Mark J; Quinn, Stephen J; Robinson, Steven E; Scott, Richard P; Shevlin, Thomas M; Wall, Mario K; Wratten, Adam P.

Associated Schoolboys
Bloxham, Robert S; Bunch, James; Donald, Marcus; Evans, Richard J; Gardiner, Nathan; Hancocks, Benjamin S. J; Hiles, Paul; Hughes, Lee R; Jones, Ian; McKenzie, Christy; Plant, Philip; Rea, Simon; Round, Steven C; Weston, Richard; Williams, Jamie P.

BLACKBURN ROVERS 1991–92. *Back row (left to right):* Tony Dobson, David May, Bobby Mimms, Darren Collier, Terry Gennoe, Robert Dewhurst, Steve Livingstone.
Centre row: Craig Skinner, Jason Wilcox, Lee Richardson, Steve Agnew, Richard Brown, Keith Hill, Lenny Johnrose, Mark Atkins, Stuart Munro, Peter Thorne, Nicky Reid.
Front row: Peter Baah, John Buttenworth, Alan Irvine, Chris Sulley, Matthew Holt, Paul Shepstone, Howard Gayle, Simon Garner, Kevin Moran, Scott Sellars, Mike Duxbury, Darren Donnelly.

FA Premier **BLACKBURN ROVERS**

ARTE ET LABORE

Ewood Park, Blackburn BB2 4JF. Telephone Blackburn (0254) 55432.

Ground capacity: 19,947.

Record attendance: 61,783 v Bolton W, FA Cup 6th rd, 2 March, 1929.

Record receipts: £108,883 v Derby Co, play-off semi-final 1st leg, 10 May, 1992.

Pitch measurements: 115yd × 76yd.

Chairman: R. D. Coar BSC.

Vice-chairman: T. W. Ibbotson LLB.

Directors: K. C. Lee, I. R. Stanners, G. R. Root FCMA, R. L. Matthewman.

Manager: Kenny Dalglish.

Assistant Manager: Ray Harford. *Reserve Team Manager:* Asa Hartford.

Physio: M. Pettigrew. *Commercial Manager:* Ken Beamish.

Secretary: John W. Howarth FAAI.

Year Formed: 1875. Turned Professional: 1880. Ltd Co.: 1897.

Former Grounds: 1875, Brookhouse Ground; 1876, Alexandra Meadows; 1881, Leamington Road; 1890, Ewood Park.

Former Names: Blackburn Grammar School OB.

Club Nickname: 'Blue and Whites'.

Record League Victory: 9-0 v Middlesbrough, Division 2, 6 November 1954 – Elvy; Suart, Eckersley; Clayton, Kelly, Bell; Mooney (3), Crossan (2), Briggs, Quigley (3), Langton (1).

Record Cup Victory: 11-0 v Rossendale, FA Cup 1st rd, 13 October 1884 – Arthur; Hopwood, McIntyre; Forrest, Blenkhorn, Lofthouse; Sowerbutts (2), J. Brown (1), Fecitt (4), Barton (3), Birtwistle (1).

Record Defeat: 0-8 v Arsenal, Division 1, 25 February 1933.

Most League Points (2 for a win): 60, Division 3, 1974–75.

Most League points (3 for a win): 77, Division 2, 1987–88, 1988–89.

Most League Goals: 114, Division 2, 1954–55.

Highest League Scorer in Season: Ted Harper, 43, Division 1, 1925–26.

Most League Goals in Total Aggregate: Simon Garner, 168, 1978–92.

Most Capped Player: Bob Crompton, 41, England.

Most League Appearances: Derek Fazackerley, 596, 1970–86.

Record Transfer Fee Received: £600,000 from Manchester C for Colin Hendry, November 1989.

Record Transfer Fee Paid: £1,100,000 to Everton for Mike Newell, November 1991.

Football League Record: 1888 Founder Member of the League; 1936–39 Division 2; 1946–48 Division 1; 1948–58 Division 2; 1958–66 Division 1; 1966–71 Division 2; 1971–75 Division 3; 1975–79 Division 2; 1979–80 Division 3; 1980–92 Division 2; 1992– FA Premier League.

Honours: Football League: Division 1 – Champions 1911–12, 1913–14; Division 2 – Champions 1938–39; Runners–up 1957–58; Division 3 – Champions 1974–75; Runners-up 1979–80. *FA Cup:* Winners 1884, 1885, 1886, 1890, 1891, 1928; Runners-up 1882, 1960. *Football League Cup:* Semi-final 1961–62. *Full Members' Cup:* Winners 1986–87.

Colours: Blue and white halved shirts, white shorts, blue stockings. **Change colours:** Black & red striped shirts, black shorts, black stockings with red turnovers.

BLACKBURN ROVERS 1991–92 LEAGUE RECORD

Match No.	Date	Venue	Opponents	Result	H/T Score	Lg. Pos.	Goalscorers	Attendance
1	Aug 17	H	Portsmouth	D	1-1	0-0	—	Moran	11,118
2	24	A	Bristol C	L	0-1	0-1	21		11,317
3	31	H	Ipswich T	L	1-2	0-1	21	Speedie	8898
4	Sep 4	A	Derby Co	W	2-0	1-0	—	Wilcox, Speedie	12,078
5	7	A	Sunderland	D	1-1	1-1	18	Speedie	17,043
6	14	H	Port Vale	W	1-0	1-0	14	Speedie	10,225
7	17	H	Watford	W	1-0	1-0	—	Richardson	9452
8	21	A	Leicester C	L	0-3	0-2	15		13,287
9	28	H	Tranmere R	D	0-0	0-0	15		11,449
10	Oct 5	A	Millwall	W	3-1	1-0	11	Speedie, Johnrose, Garner	8026
11	12	H	Plymouth Arg	W	5-2	2-0	7	Moran, Garner 2, Speedie 2 (1 pen)	10,830
12	19	A	Swindon T	L	1-2	1-0	9	Speedie	10,717
13	26	H	Grimsby T	W	2-1	1-1	8	Garner, Atkins	11,096
14	Nov 2	H	Brighton & HA	W	1-0	0-0	8	Livingstone (pen)	9877
15	5	A	Southend U	L	0-3	0-1	—		4860
16	9	A	Charlton Ath	W	2-0	1-0	8	Sellars, Speedie	7114
17	16	H	Barnsley	W	3-0	1-0	5	Speedie, Wilcox, Newell	13,797
18	23	A	Newcastle U	D	0-0	0-0	5		23,639
19	30	H	Middlesbrough	W	2-1	1-1	4	Newell (pen), Atkins	15,541
20	Dec 7	A	Oxford U	W	3-1	2-0	3	Sellars, Cowans, Garner	5924
21	14	H	Bristol R	W	3-0	3-0	1	Atkins 2, Sellars	12,295
22	26	A	Wolverhampton W	D	0-0	0-0	1		18,277
23	28	A	Ipswich T	L	1-2	1-0	2	Wright	17,675
24	Jan 1	H	Cambridge U	W	2-1	0-0	1	Speedie, Reid	15,001
25	11	H	Bristol C	W	4-0	3-0	1	Newell 2, Scott (og), Speedie	12,964
26	18	A	Portsmouth	D	2-2	1-0	1	Speedie 2	20,106
27	Feb 1	H	Swindon T	W	2-1	0-1	1	Hendry, Speedie	14,887
28	8	A	Grimsby T	W	3-2	3-1	1	Price, Sellars, Wilcox	10,014
29	11	H	Derby Co	W	2-0	0-0	—	Price, Atkins	15,350
30	15	H	Newcastle U	W	3-1	1-1	1	Speedie 3	19,511
31	22	A	Middlesbrough	D	0-0	0-0	1		19,353
32	25	A	Cambridge U	L	1-2	0-2	—	Hendry	7857
33	29	H	Oxford U	D	1-1	1-1	1	Sellars (pen)	13,917
34	Mar 7	A	Bristol R	L	0-3	0-2	1		6313
35	10	H	Southend U	D	2-2	1-2	—	Price, Speedie	14,404
36	14	A	Brighton & HA	W	3-0	2-0	1	Speedie, Hendry, Wegerle	10,845
37	21	H	Charlton Ath	L	0-2	0-0	1		14,844
38	28	A	Barnsley	L	1-2	1-0	2	Shearer	13,346
39	31	A	Port Vale	L	0-2	0-1	—		10,384
40	Apr 11	A	Watford	L	1-2	1-1	4	Wegerle	10,522
41	14	H	Wolverhampton W	L	1-2	1-0	—	Sellars	14,114
42	18	H	Leicester C	L	0-1	0-0	7		18,075
43	20	A	Tranmere R	D	2-2	1-1	6	Wilcox, Newell (pen)	13,705
44	25	A	Millwall	W	2-1	0-0	7	Newell, Atkins	12,820
45	29	H	Sunderland	D	2-2	1-0	—	Hendry, Sellars	15,079
46	May 2	A	Plymouth Arg	W	3-1	2-1	6	Speedie 3	17,459

Final League Position: 6

GOALSCORERS

League (70): Speedie 23 (1 pen), Sellars 7 (1 pen), Atkins 6, Newell 6 (2 pens), Garner 5, Hendry 4, Wilcox 4, Price 3, Moran 2, Wegerle 2, Cowans 1, Johnrose 1, Livingstone 1 (1 pen), Reid 1, Richardson 1, Shearer 1, Wright 1, own goals 1.
Rumbelows Cup (1): own goal 1.
FA Cup (5): Newell 3, Cowans 1, Speedie 1.

Mimms	Atkins	Sulley	Agnew	Moran	Dobson	Irvine	Richardson	Livingstone	Speedie	Sellars	Garner	Gayle	Reid	May	Munro	Shepstone	Wilcox	Skinner	Duxbury M	Johnrose	Brown	Hill	Baah	Wright	Hendry	Newell	Cowans	Beardsmore	Match No.
1	2	3	4	5	6	7	8*	9†	10	11	12	14																	1
1	2	3	8	5	6		12	9*	10	11†	14		4	7															2
1	2			6			8	9				7	4	5	3	10*	11	12											3
1	8	3		5			4		9		12	14	6				11*	7†	2	10									4
1	8	3		5			4		9		12		6*				11	7	2	10									5
1	8	3		5			4*		9		12						11	7	2	10									6
1	8	3		5			4†		9		12	14	6				11	7	2	10*									7
1	8*	3†		5			4		9		12	14	6				11	7	2	10									8
1			5	3			4	12	9		8		14	6			11*	7†	2	10									9
1	14			3			12	4		9			10†				7*	2	8		5	11							10
1	3			8†			7*	11	12	9	14	10	4	6				2			5								11
1	3			6			14	8	10*	9	11	12		4			7†	2			5								12
1	2*			6			7	4	9†	8	11	10	12				14				5	3							13
1	2			6			7*	4	14	8	11	10	12				9†				5	3							14
1	2			6	14		10*	8	9	11†12			4	7							5	3							15
1	8			6			4		9	11	10*	12					7				2			3	5				16
1	8			6			4		9*11	12							7	14	2					3†	5	10			17
1	8			6			4		9	11	12						7				2	3				5*10			18
1	8			6					11	9*	12						7				2	5		3		10	4		19
1	8			14					11†10*	12							7				2	6		3	5	9	4		20
1	8			6					11*10	12							7				2			3	5	9	4		21
1	8			6					12	10*							7				2	14		3	5†	9	4	11	22
1	8†			6			14		10								7				2	11*		3	5	9	4	12	23
1	8			6					10		12						7				2	11		3	5*	9	4		24
1	8*			6†					10	11	12						7				2	5		3	14	9	4		25
1				6					9*11			8					7	12			2	5		3†14		10	4		26
1	8			6					9	11	12		7†								2	5		3	14	10*	4		27
1	8			6					9*11								7					5		3	12	10	4		28
1	8*								9	11†12							7				14	5		3	6	10	4		29
1	8								9	12							7				11	5		3	6	10*	4		30
1	8								9*10								7				11	5		3	6		4		31
1	8			3					12		10*		2†				7				11	5	14	6			4		32
1	12			14					9*	11	10						7†					5		3	6		4		33
1	12			14					9	11†							7					5		3	6		4*		34
1	8			7					9		12						11†5							3	6		4		35
1	8			7*					9†								11	5						3	6		4		36
1	8				7†				9	12							11	5						3	6		4		37
1	8								9	11†							14	5						3	6		4		38
1	8			14					9†11									5						3	6		4		39
1	14			2					11*			9					12	5						3	6	12	4		40
	9			2					11								7	5						3	6	12	4		41
1	9			2			14		11								7	5						3	6	12	4†		42
1	8			5			12		11								7	2						3	6	9†	4*		43
1	8			5			12		14 11								7†	2						3	6	9			44
1	8			5			4		9*11								7	2†						3	6	10			45
1	8			5			12		9*11								7†	2						3	6	10	4		46
45	40	7	2	37	4	4	18	6	34	28	14	1	8	12	1	1	33	7	5	7	24	31	1	32	26	18	26	1	

+ (substitute appearances):

4s — 4s 1s 2s 6s 4s 2s 2s 11s 3s 13s — 5s 2s — 2s 1s — 1s 4s 2s — 1s

Price—Match No. 28(2) 29(2) 30(2) 31(2) 33(2) 34(2) 35(2) 36(2) 37(2) 38(2) 39(2) 45(14) 46(14); Sherwood—Match No. 31(12) 32(9) 33(8) 34(8) 35(14) 36(14) 37(14) 38(7*) 39(7*) 40(7+) 44(4*); Wegerle—Match No. 34(10) 35(10*) 36(10) 37(10*) 38(12) 39(12) 40(10) 41(10) 42(10) 43(10) 44(10) 45(12); Shearer—Match No. 38(10) 39(10) 40(8) 41(8*) 42(8*) 43(14); Dickins—Match No. 41(1).

Rumbelows Cup	First Round	Hull C (h)		1-1
		(a)		0-1
FA Cup	Third Round	Kettering (h)		4-1
	Fourth Round	Notts Co (a)		1-2

BLACKBURN ROVERS

Goalkeepers

Name	Ht	Wt	Born	Birthplace	Source	Club	Apps	Gls
Darren Collier	6 0	12 06	1 12 67	Stockton	Middlesbrough	Blackburn R	27	—
Matt Dickins	6 4	14 00	3 9 70	Sheffield	Trainee	Sheffield U	—	—
						Leyton Orient (loan)	—	—
						Lincoln C	27	—
						Blackburn R	1	—
Terry Gennoe*	6 2	13 03	16 3 53	Shrewsbury	Bricklayers Sp	Bury	3	—
						Blackburn R (loan)	—	—
						Leeds U (loan)	—	—
						Halifax T	78	—
						Southampton	36	—
						Everton (loan)	—	—
						Crystal Palace (loan)	3	—
						Blackburn R	289	—
Bobby Mimms	6 2	12 13	12 10 63	York	Apprentice	Halifax T		
						Rotherham U	83	—
						Everton	29	—
						Notts Co (loan)	2	—
						Sunderland (loan)	4	—
						Blackburn R (loan)	6	—
						Manchester C (loan)	3	—
						Tottenham H	37	—
						Aberdeen (loan)	6	—
						Blackburn R	67	—

Defenders

Name	Ht	Wt	Born	Birthplace	Source	Club	Apps	Gls
Mark Atkins	6 1	12 00	14 8 68	Doncaster	School	Scunthorpe U	48	2
						Blackburn R	173	23
Richard Brown			13 1 67	Nottingham	Ilkeston T	Sheffield W	—	—
						Kettering T	—	—
						Blackburn R	26	—
						Maidstone U (loan)	3	—
John Butterworth*	5 11	11 04	13 4 73	Oldham	Trainee	Blackburn R	—	—
Robert Dewhurst	6 3	13 01	10 9 71	Keighley	Trainee	Blackburn R	13	—
						Darlington (loan)	11	1
Tony Dobson	6 1	12 10	5 2 69	Coventry	Apprentice	Coventry C	54	1
						Blackburn R	22	—
Colin Hendry	6 1	12 02	7 12 65	Keith	Islavale	Dundee	41	2
						Blackburn R	102	22
						Manchester C	63	5
						Blackburn R	30	4
Keith Hill	6 0	11 03	17 5 69	Bolton	Apprentice	Blackburn R	95	3
David May	6 0	12 00	24 6 70	Oldham	Trainee	Blackburn R	49	1
Kevin Moran	5 11	12 09	29 4 56	Dublin	Pegasus (Eire)	Manchester U	231	21
						Sporting Gijon	—	—
						Blackburn R	92	5
Stuart Munro	5 8	10 05	15 9 62	Falkirk	Bo'ness U	St Mirren	1	—
						Alloa	60	6
						Rangers	179	3
						Blackburn R	2	—
Chris Price	5 7	10 02	30 3 60	Hereford	Apprentice	Hereford U	330	27
						Blackburn R	83	11
						Aston Villa	111	2
						Blackburn R	13	3
Chris Sulley	5 8	10 00	3 12 59	Camberwell	Apprentice	Chelsea	—	—
						Bournemouth	206	3
						Dundee U	7	—
						Blackburn R	134	3

Midfield

Name	Ht	Wt	Born	Birthplace	Source	Club	Apps	Gls
Steve Agnew	5 9	10 06	9 11 65	Shipley	Apprentice	Barnsley	194	29
						Blackburn R	2	—
Gordon Cowans	5 9	10 07	27 10 58	Durham	Apprentice	Aston Villa	286	42
						Bari	—	—
						Aston Villa	117	7
						Blackburn R	26	1
Matthew Holt*	5 06	10 05	9 9 72	Oldham	Trainee	Blackburn R	—	—
						Aston Villa (loan)	—	—
Nicky Reid	5 10	12 04	30 10 60	Ormston	Apprentice	Manchester C	217	2
						Blackburn R	174	9

BLACKBURN ROVERS

Foundation: It was in 1875 that some Public School old boys called a meeting at which the Blackburn Rovers club was formed and the colours blue and white adopted. The leading light was John Lewis, later to become a founder of the Lancashire FA, a famous referee who was in charge of two FA Cup Finals, and a vice-president of both the FA and the Football League.

First Football League game: 15 September, 1888, Football League, v Accrington (h) D 5-5 – Arthur; Beverley, James Southworth; Douglas, Almond, Forrest; Beresford (1), Walton, John Southworth (1), Fecitt (1), Townley (2).

Did you know: Because of a clash of colours in the 1890 FA Cup Final with Sheffield Wednesday, Rovers played in white evening dress shirts which they bought after their arrival in London.

Managers (and Secretary-managers)
Thomas Mitchell 1884–96*, J. Walmsley 1896–1903*, R. B. Middleton 1903–25, Jack Carr 1922–26 (TM under Middleton to 1925), Bob Crompton 1926–31 (Hon. TM), Arthur Barritt 1931–36 (had been Sec. from 1927), Reg Taylor 1936–38, Bob Crompton 1938–41, Eddie Hapgood 1944–47, Will Scott 1947, Jack Bruton 1947–49, Jackie Bestall 1949–53, Johnny Carey 1953–58, Dally Duncan 1958–60, Jack Marshall 1960–67, Eddie Quigley 1967–70, Johnny Carey 1970–71, Ken Furphy 1971–73, Gordon Lee 1974–75, Jim Smith 1975–78, Jim Iley 1978, John Pickering 1978–79, Howard Kendall 1979–81, Bobby Saxton 1981–86, Don Mackay 1987–91, Kenny Dalglish October 1991–.

Name				Birthplace	Source	Clubs	Apps	Gls
Lee Richardson	5 11	11 00	12 3 69	Halifax	School	Halifax T	56	2
						Watford	41	1
						Blackburn R	62	3
Scott Sellars	5 7	9 10	27 11 65	Sheffield	Apprentice	Leeds U	76	12
						Blackburn R	202	35
Paul Shepstone	5 8	10 06	8 11 70	Coventry	Atherstone U	Coventry C	—	—
						Birmingham C	—	—
						Blackburn R	26	1
						York C (loan)	2	—
Tim Sherwood	6 1	11 04	6 2 69	St Albans	Trainee	Watford	32	2
						Norwich C	71	10
						Blackburn R	11	—
Alan Wright	5 4	9 04	28 9 71	Ashton Under Lyne		Blackpool	98	—
						Blackburn R	33	1
Forwards								
Peter Baah*	5 9	10 04	1 5 73	Littleborough	Trainee	Blackburn R	1	—
Darren Donnelly	5 10	11 06	28 12 71	Liverpool	Trainee	Blackburn R	2	—
Simon Garner	5 9	11 12	23 11 59	Boston	Apprentice	Blackburn R	484	168
Howard Gayle	5 10	10 09	18 5 58	Liverpool	Local	Liverpool	4	1
						Fulham (loan)	14	—
						Birmingham C (loan)	13	1
						Newcastle U (loan)	8	2
						Birmingham C	33	8
						Sunderland	48	4
						Stoke C	6	2
						Blackburn R	116	29
Alan Irvine*	5 9	11 03	12 7 58	Glasgow	Glasgow BC	Queen's Park	88	9
						Everton	60	4
						Crystal Palace	109	12
						Dundee U	24	3
						Blackburn R	58	3
Steve Livingstone	6 1	12 07	8 9 69	Middlesbrough	Trainee	Coventry C	31	5
						Blackburn R	28	10

Continued on page 591

Trainees
Ainscough, Paul B; Berry, Ian J; Berry, James S; Cullen, Anthony S; Grunshaw, Steven J; Hitchen, Lee A ; Lindsay, Scott W; McGarry, Ian J; Metcalf, Joshua H; Moss, Lee A; O'Shaughnessy, Brendan J; Pickup, Jonathan J; Ridgway, Alec D; Scott, Andrew M.

Associated Schoolboys
Baxter, Lee S; Gaston, Karl S; Hitchen, Steven J; Jones, Stuart J; Lowery, Simon P; Marsden, Shaun C; McCrone, Christopher P; McLean, James L; Moores, Nicholas S; Ormerod, Brett R; Whealing, Anthony J; Wojciechowicz, Alexander.

Associated Schoolboys who have accepted the club's offer of a Traineeship/Contract
Bardsley, Christopher J; Gifford, Andrew J; Gill, Wayne J; Goodall, Daniel J; Sweeney, Damian; Thornton, Scott L.

72

BLACKPOOL 1991–92 *Back row (left to right)*: Grant Leitch, Ian Gore, Andy Garner, Paul Groves, David Eyres, Mark Taylor, Tony Rodwell. *Centre row*: Steve Redmond, Trevor Sinclair, Paul Stoneman, Phil Horner, Carl Richards, Steve McIlhargey, Dave Bamber, Dave Lancaster, Chris Hedworth, Mike Davies, Neil Bailey. *Front row*: Alan Wright, Mark Murray, Gary Brook, Billy Ayre, Dave Burgess, Andy Gouck, Nigel Hawkins.

Division 2   **BLACKPOOL**

Bloomfield Rd Ground, Blackpool FY1 6JJ. Telephone Blackpool (0253) 404331. Fax No: 0253 405011

Ground capacity: 10,337.

Record attendance: 38,098 v Wolverhampton W, Division 1, 17 September 1955.

Record receipts: £72,949 v Tottenham H, FA Cup 3rd rd, 5 January 1991.

Pitch measurements: 111yd × 73yd.

President: C. A. Sagar BEM.

Chairman: Owen J. Oyston.

Vice-chairman: G. Aloor.

Managing Director: David Hatton.

Directors: J. Allitt, W. Ayre, J. Crowther LLB, G. Warburton, J. Wilde MBE, Mrs V. Oyston.

Manager: Bill Ayre. *Secretary:* Jean Miskelly. *Commercial Manager:* Geoffrey Warburton. *Physio:* Stephen Redmond.

Year Formed: 1887. Turned Professional: 1887. Ltd Co.: 1896.

Former Grounds: 1887, Raikes Hall Gardens; 1897, Athletic Grounds; 1899, Raikes Hall Gardens; 1899, Bloomfield Road.

Former Names: 'South Shore' combined with Blackpool in 1899, twelve years after the latter had been formed on the breaking up of the old 'Blackpool St John's' club.

Club Nickname: 'The Seasiders'.

Record League Victory: 7-0 v Preston NE (away), Division 1, 1 May 1948 – Robinson; Shimwell, Crosland; Buchan, Hayward, Kelly; Hobson, Munro (1), McIntosh (5), McCall, Rickett (1).

Record Cup Victory: 7-1 v Charlton Ath, League Cup, 2nd rd, 25 September 1963 – Harvey; Armfield, Martin; Crawford, Gratrix, Cranston; Lea, Ball (1), Charnley (4), Durie (1), Oakes (1).

Record Defeat: 1-10 v Small Heath, Division 2, 2 March 1901 and v Huddersfield T, Division 1, 13 December 1930.

Most League Points (2 for a win): 58, Division 2, 1929–30.

Most League points (3 for a win): 86, Division 4, 1984–85.

Most League Goals: 98, Division 2, 1929–30.

Highest League Scorer in Season: Jimmy Hampson, 45, Division 2, 1929–30.

Most League Goals in Total Aggregate: Jimmy Hampson, 247, 1927–38.

Most Capped Player: Jimmy Armfield, 43, England.

Most League Appearances: Jimmy Armfield, 568, 1952–71.

Record Transfer Fee Received: £633,333 from Manchester C for Paul Stewart, March 1987.

Record Transfer Fee Paid: £116,666 to Sunderland for Jack Ashurst, October 1979.

Football League Record: 1896 Elected to Division 2; 1899 Failed re-election; 1900 Re-elected; 1900–30 Division 2; 1930–33 Division 1; 1933–37 Division 2; 1937–67 Division 1; 1967–70 Division 2; 1970–71 Division 1; 1971–78 Division 2; 1978–81 Division 3; 1981–85 Division 4; 1985–90 Division 3; 1990–92 Division 4; 1992– Division 2.

Honours: Football League: Division 1 – Runners-up 1955–56; Division 2 – Champions 1929–30; Runners-up 1936–37, 1969–70; Division 4 – Runners-up 1984–85. *FA Cup:* Winners 1953; Runners-up 1948, 1951. *Football League Cup:* Semi-final 1962. *Anglo-Italian Cup:* Winners 1971; Runners-up 1972.

Colours: Tangerine shirts with navy and white trim, white shorts, tangerine stockings with white tops. **Change colours:** White shirts with navy and tangerine trim, tangerine shorts, tangerine stockings with navy and white tops.

BLACKPOOL 1991–92 LEAGUE RECORD

Match No.	Date		Venue	Opponents	Result		H/T Score	Lg. Pos.	Goalscorers	Attendance
1	Aug	17	H	Walsall	W	3-0	1-0	—	Horner, Eyres, Garner	4141
2		24	A	Carlisle U	W	2-1	2-1	1	Bamber, Rodwell	4369
3		31	H	Scunthorpe U	W	2-1	1-1	1	Hicks (og), Groves	3273
4	Sep	3	A	York C	L	0-1	0-0	—		2686
5		7	A	Mansfield T	D	1-1	0-1	5	Bamber	2629
6		14	H	Cardiff C	D	1-1	1-1	7	Horner	3931
7		17	H	Gillingham	W	2-0	1-0	—	Bamber 2	3035
8		20	A	Doncaster R	W	2-0	2-0	—	Bamber, Taylor	2428
9		28	H	Rotherham U	W	3-0	1-0	1	Eyres, Groves, Rodwell	5356
10	Oct	5	A	Northampton T	D	1-1	1-0	1	Sinclair	3355
11		13	H	Lincoln C	W	3-0	1-0	—	Horner, Groves (pen), Bamber	5086
12		19	A	Barnet	L	0-3	0-1	3		5085
13	Nov	2	H	Scarborough	D	1-1	1-1	5	Groves	3057
14		9	A	Chesterfield	D	1-1	0-0	4	Taylor	4917
15		19	A	Wrexham	W	4-0	2-0	—	Sinclair 2, Bamber 2	2842
16		23	H	Crewe Alex	L	0-2	0-1	4		4534
17		30	H	Halifax T	W	3-0	3-0	3	Groves, Bamber 2	3118
18	Dec	14	A	Rochdale	L	2-4	1-2	4	Garner, Rodwell	2892
19		21	A	Carlisle U	W	1-0	0-0	4	Bamber	3440
20		26	A	Walsall	L	2-4	0-2	4	Eyres, Bamber	4675
21		28	A	Scunthorpe U	L	1-2	1-1	4	Groves	4271
22	Jan	1	H	York C	W	3-1	2-0	4	Eyres, Bamber, Gouck	3534
23		4	A	Maidstone U	D	0-0	0-0	4		1774
24		11	H	Burnley	W	5-2	2-0	3	Rodwell 2, Kerr, Garner, Bamber	8007
25		18	A	Hereford U	W	2-1	1-1	3	Bamber 2	3008
26	Feb	8	A	Wrexham	D	1-1	1-1	2	Garner	4053
27		12	A	Halifax T	W	2-1	2-0	—	Bamber, Rodwell	2158
28		15	H	Rochdale	W	3-0	3-0	2	Gouck, Groves, Eyres	4632
29		18	H	Barnet	W	4-2	2-2	—	Bamber, Groves, Rodwell, Eyres	5149
30		22	A	Burnley	D	1-1	1-1	2	Bamber	18,183
31		29	H	Maidstone U	D	1-1	1-1	2	Garner	4136
32	Mar	3	H	Hereford U	W	2-0	0-0	—	Bamber, Groves	3560
33		14	A	Scarborough	W	2-1	2-1	1	Eyres, Bamber	1965
34		21	H	Chesterfield	W	3-1	3-1	1	Davies, Rodwell, Bamber	4447
35		28	A	Crewe Alex	L	0-1	0-0	2		4913
36		31	A	Cardiff C	D	1-1	1-1	—	Bamber	8430
37	Apr	4	H	Mansfield T	W	2-1	1-1	2	Bamber 2	6055
38		11	A	Gillingham	L	2-3	1-1	2	Eyres, Horner	3684
39		14	H	Doncaster R	W	1-0	0-0	—	Eyres (pen)	4353
40		20	A	Rotherham U	L	0-2	0-1	3		8992
41		25	H	Northampton T	W	1-0	0-0	2	Bamber	5915
42	May	2	A	Lincoln C	L	0-2	0-1	4		7884

Final League Position: 4

GOALSCORERS

League (71): Bamber 26, Eyres 9 (1 pen), Groves 9 (1 pen), Rodwell 8, Garner 5, Horner 4, Sinclair 3, Gouck 2, Taylor 2, Davies 1, Kerr 1, own goals 1.
Rumbelows Cup (8): Bamber 6, Groves 1, own goal 1.
FA Cup (2): Bamber 1, Groves 1.

McIlhargey	Davies	Wright	Groves	Stoneman	Gore	Rodwell	Horner	Bamber	Garner	Eyres	Richards	Gouck	Hedworth	Sinclair	Briggs	Taylor	Burgess	Murray	Brook	Mitchell	Bonner	Kerr	Kearton	Leitch	Cook	Match No.
1	2†	3	4	5	6	7	8*	9	10	11	12	14														1
1	2	3	4	5	6	7		9	10	11		8														2
1	2	3	4		6	7	5	9	10	11	12	8*														3
1	2	3	4	5†	6	7	8	9	10*	11	12	14														4
1	2	3	4		6	7	8	9	10	11					5											5
1	2	3	4		6	7	8	9	10*	11				12	5											6
1	2	3	4		6	7	8	9*	14	11		10†		12	5											7
1	2	3*	4		6	7	8	9		11		10		12	5											8
1	2	3	4		6	7	8	9		11		10			5											9
1	2	3	4		6	7	8	9		11		10			5											10
1	2	3	4		6	7	8	9		11		10			5											11
1	2†	3	4	14	6	7	8	9		11		10*		12	5											12
1			4		6	7	8	9		11			14	12	5		2	10†	3*							13
1	14	3	4		6	7		9		11		10		12	5*		2		8							14
1	14	3	4		6	7	8*	9		11		10		12	5		2†									15
1	14	3	4		6†	7	8*	9		11		10		12	5		2									16
1	2	3	4			7		9	14	11		6	10*	12	5				8†							17
1	2†	3	4		6	7		9		11		8*	10	12	5				14							18
1		3	4		6	7		9		11		8	10		5		2									19
1		3	4		6	7		9	14	11		8†	10*	12	5		2									20
1		3	4		6	7		9		11		10			5		2		8							21
1		3	4		6	7		9	10	11		8			5		2									22
1		3	4		6	7		9	10	11		8			5											23
		3	4		6	7		9	10	11		8			5								1			24
	2		4		6	7		9	10	11		8			5							3	1			25
	2*		4		6	7		9	10	11		8		12	5							3	1			26
	2		4		6	7		9	10	11		8			5							3	1			27
	2		4		6	7*	14	9	10	11		8†		12	5							3	1			28
	2		4		6	7		9	10	11		8			5							3	1			29
	2		4		6	7*		9	10	11		8		12	5							3	1			30
	2		4		6		12	9	10	11		8*			5						7†	3	1	14		31
	2		4		6		8	9†	10*	11			14	12	5						7	3	1			32
	2		4		6	7	8	9	10*	11				12	5							3	1			33
	2		4		6	7	8	9	10	11				12	5*							3	1	14†		34
			4		6	7	8	9	10	11					5		2						1		3	35
			4		6	7*	8	9	10	11				12	5		2						1		3	36
	2		4		6	7*	8	9	10	11					5								1	12	3	37
1	2*		4	14	6	7	8	9	10	11				12	5†										3	38
1			4	5	6	7	8	9	10*	11				12			2								3	39
1			4		6	7†	8	9	10	11			14	12	5		2								3*	40
1	12		4	5	6	7†	8	9		11		10*					2							14	3	41
1			4	5	6	7	8	9		11		10					2								3	42
28	26	12	42	17	41	40	25	42	27	41	—	20	4	15	24	2	16	2	1	—	2	12	14	1	8	
				+3s			+2s		+2s	+3s	+3s	+4s			+12s		+8s				+1s	+1s		+5s		

Rumbelows Cup First Round Mansfield T (a) 3-0
(h) 4-2
Second Round Barnsley (h) 1-0
(a) 0-2
FA Cup First Round Grimsby T (h) 2-1
Second Round Hull C (h) 0-1

BLACKPOOL

Player and Position	Ht	Wt	Birth Date	Birth Place	Source	Clubs	League App	Gls
Goalkeepers								
Steve McIlhargey	6 0	11 07	28 8 63	Ferryhill	Blantyre Celtic	Walsall	—	—
						Rotherham U (loan)	—	—
						Blackpool	94	—
Defenders								
Gary Briggs	6 3	12 10	8 5 58	Leeds	Apprentice	Middlesbrough	—	—
						Oxford U	420	18
						Blackpool	71	2
Dave Burgess	5 10	11 02	20 1 60	Liverpool	Local	Tranmere R	218	1
						Grimsby T	69	—
						Blackpool	81	1
Chris Hedworth*	6 1	10 11	5 1 64	Newcastle	Apprentice	Newcastle U	9	—
						Barnsley	25	—
						Halifax T	38	—
						Blackpool	24	—
Philip Horner	6 1	12 07	10 11 66	Leeds	School	Leicester C	10	—
						Rotherham U (loan)	4	—
						Halifax T	72	4
						Blackpool	66	11
Jamie Murphy			25 2 73	Manchester	Trainee	Blackpool	—	—
Mark Murray			13 6 73	Manchester	Trainee	Blackpool	2	—
Paul Stoneman			26 2 73	Whitley Bay	Trainee	Blackpool	19	—
Midfield								
Mark Bonner			7 6 74	Ormskirk	Trainee	Blackpool	3	—
James Booth*			11 11 68	Sheffield	Trainee	Blackpool	—	—
Mark Bradshaw‡	5 10	11 05	7 6 69	Ashton	Trainee	Blackpool	42	1
						York C (loan)	1	—
Mitch Cook*	5 10	12 00	15 10 61	Scarborough	Scarborough	Darlington	34	4
						Middlesbrough	6	—
						Scarborough	81	10
						Halifax T	54	2
						Scarborough (loan)	9	1
						Darlington (loan)	9	1
						Darlington	27	3
						Blackpool	8	—
Michael Davies	5 8	10 00	19 1 66	Stretford	Apprentice	Blackpool	255	15
Ian Gore	5 11	12 04	10 1 68	Liverpool	Southport	Blackpool	137	—
Andy Gouck			8 6 72	Blackpool	Trainee	Blackpool	37	3
Paul Groves	5 11	11 05	28 2 66	Derby	Burton Alb	Leicester C	16	1
						Lincoln C (loan)	8	1
						Blackpool	107	21
Neil Mitchell§			7 11 74	Lytham	Trainee	Blackpool	1	—
Trevor Sinclair	5 10	11 02	2 3 73	Dulwich	Trainee	Blackpool	67	4
Forwards								
Dave Bamber	6 3	13 10	1 2 59	St Helens	Manchester Univ	Blackpool	86	29
						Coventry C	19	3
						Walsall	20	7
						Portsmouth	4	1
						Swindon T	106	31
						Watford	18	3
						Stoke C	43	8
						Hull C	28	5
						Blackpool	65	43
Richie Bond			27 10 65	Blyth	Blyth S	Blackpool	—	—

BLACKPOOL

Foundation: Old boys of St. John's School who had formed themselves into a football club decided to establish a club bearing the name of their town and Blackpool FC came into being at a meeting at the Stanley Arms Hotel in the summer of 1887. In their first season playing at Raikes Hall Gardens, the club won both the Lancashire Junior Cup and the Fylde Cup.

First Football League game: 5 September, 1896, Division 2, v Lincoln C (a) L 1-3 – Douglas; Parr, Bowman; Stuart, Stirzaker, Norris; Clarkin, Donnelly, R. Parkinson, Mount (1), J. Parkinson.

Did you know: On 15 March 1902 Blackpool's regular goalkeeper missed the team's train at Preston en route for a Second Division game at Leicester and honorary secretary Tom Barcroft went in goal. Blackpool were beaten only 1-0.

Managers (and Secretary-managers)
Tom Barcroft 1903–33* (Hon. Sec.), John Cox 1909–11, Bill Norman 1919–23, Maj. Frank Buckley 1923–27, Sid Beaumont 1927–28, Harry Evans 1928–33 (Hon. TM), Alex "Sandy" Macfarlane 1933–35, Joe Smith 1935–58, Ronnie Suart 1958–67, Stan Mortensen 1967–69, Les Shannon 1969–70, Bob Stokoe 1970–72, Harry Potts 1972–76, Allan Brown 1976–78, Bob Stokoe 1978–79, Stan Ternent 1979–80, Alan Ball 1980–81, Allan Brown 1981–82, Sam Ellis 1982–89, Jimmy Mullen 1989–90, Graham Carr 1990, Bill Ayre December 1990–.

Player and Position	Ht	Wt	Birth Date	Birth Place	Source	Clubs	League App	Gls
Gary Brook‡	5 10	12 04	9 5 64	Dewsbury	Frickley Ath	Newport Co	14	2
						Scarborough	64	15
						Blackpool	30	6
						Notts Co (loan)	1	—
						Scarborough (loan)	8	—
David Eyres	5 10	11 00	26 2 64	Liverpool	Rhyl	Blackpool	112	22
Andy Garner	6 0	12 01	8 3 66	Chesterfield	Apprentice	Derby Co	71	17
						Blackpool	154	37
Nigel Hawkins*	5 9	10 07	7 9 68	Bristol	Apprentice	Bristol C	18	2
						Blackpool	7	—
Andy Howard‡			15 3 73	Southport	Trainee	Liverpool	—	—
						Blackpool	—	—
Grant Leitch			31 10 72	South Africa		Blackpool	6	—
Carl Richards‡	6 0	13 00	12 1 60	Jamaica	Enfield	Bournemouth	71	15
						Birmingham C	19	2
						Peterborough U	20	5
						Blackpool	41	8
						Maidstone U (loan)	4	2
Tony Rodwell	5 11	11 02	26 8 62	Southport	Colne Dynamoes	Blackpool	85	15

Trainees
Beech, Christopher S; Bonner, Mark; Horsfield, Damien J; Irvine, Jonathan A; Little, Glen; Mitchell, Neil N; Morris, Andrew; Morris, Neil A; Proctor, Alistair; Stoddard, John A; Trickett, Andrew; Wood, Timothy.

Associated Schoolboys
Birkman, Peter L; Blacow, Iain C; Carroll, David; Croasdale, Peter J; Gawthorpe, Neil J; Hargreaves, Boyd M; Shaw, Richard E; Trafford, Craig A; Woodall, Alan C.

Associated Schoolboys who have accepted the club's offer of a Traineeship/Contract
Sheppard, James H; Thompson, Paul D.

BOLTON WANDERERS 1991–92 *Back row (left to right):* Barry Cowdrill, Paul Comstive, Mark Winstanley, Alan Stubbs, Julian Darby, Andy Roscoe.
First row: Mark Seagraves, Tony Philliskirk, Kevin Rose, Dave Felgate, Tony Cunningham, David Reeves, Mark Came.
Second row: Dean Crombie (Youth Development Officer), Nicky Spooner, Mike Jeffrey, Phil Brown, Stuart Storer, Scott Green, Steve Thompson, David Burke, Ewan Simpson (Physiotherapist).
Front row: Darren Oliver, Mark Patterson, Steve Carroll (Reserve Team Manager), Phil Neal (Manager), Mick Brown (Assistant Manager/Coach), Neil Fisher, Sammy Lee.

Division 2   **BOLTON WANDERERS**

Burnden Park, Bolton B13 2QR. Telephone Bolton (0204) 389200. Information Service: Bolton 21101. Commercial Dept. (0204) 24518.

Ground capacity: 24,772.

Record attendance: 69,912 v Manchester C, FA Cup 5th rd, 18 February 1933.

Record receipts: £113,396 v Southampton, FA Cup 5th rd, 16 February 1992.

Pitch measurements: 113yd × 76yd.

President: Nat Lofthouse.

Chairman: G. Hargreaves.

Directors: P. A. Gartside, G. Ball, G. Seymour, G. Warburton, W. B. Warburton.

Team Manager: Bruce Rioch. *Physio:* E. Simpson. *Chief Executive & Secretary:* Des McBain. *Commercial Manager:* T. Holland.

Year Formed: 1874. Turned Professional: 1880. Ltd Co.: 1895.

Former Grounds: Park Recreation Ground and Cockle's Field before moving to Pike's Lane ground 1881; 1895, Burnden Park.

Former Names: 1874–77, Christ Church FC; 1877 became Bolton Wanderers.

Club Nickname: 'The Trotters'.

Record League Victory: 8-0 v Barnsley, Division 2, 6 October 1934 – Jones; Smith, Finney; Goslin, Atkinson, George Taylor; George T. Taylor (2), Eastham, Milsom (1), Westwood (4), Cook. (1 og).

Record Cup Victory: 13-0 v Sheffield U, FA Cup, 2nd rd, 1 February 1890 – Parkinson; Robinson (1), Jones; Bullough, Davenport, Roberts; Rushton, Brogan (3), Cassidy (5), McNee, Weir (4).

Record Defeat: 0-7 v Manchester C, Division 1, 21 March 1936.

Most League Points (2 for a win): 61, Division 3, 1972–73.

Most League points (3 for a win): 83, Division 3, 1990–91.

Most League Goals: 96, Division 2, 1934–35.

Highest League Scorer in Season: Joe Smith, 38, Division 1, 1920–21.

Most League Goals in Total Aggregate: Nat Lofthouse, 255, 1946–61.

Most Capped Player: Nat Lofthouse, 33, England.

Most League Appearances: Eddie Hopkinson, 519, 1956–70.

Record Transfer Fee Received: £340,000 from Birmingham C for Neil Whatmore, August 1981.

Record Transfer Fee Paid: £350,000 to WBA for Len Cantello, May 1979.

Football League Record: 1888 Founder Member of the League; 1899–1900 Division 2; 1900–03 Division 1; 1903–05 Division 2; 1905–08 Division 1; 1908–09 Division 2; 1909–10 Division 1; 1910–11 Division 2; 1911–33 Division 1; 1933–35 Division 2; 1935–64 Division 1; 1964–71 Division 2; 1971–73 Division 3; 1973–78 Division 2; 1978–80 Division 1; 1980–83 Division 2; 1983–87 Division 3; 1987–88 Division 4; 1988 –92 Division 3; 1992– Division 2.

Honours: Football League: Division 1 best season: 3rd, 1891–92, 1920–21, 1924–25; Division 2 – Champions 1908–09, 1977–78; Runners-up 1899–1900, 1904–05, 1910–11, 1934–35; Division 3 – Champions 1972–73. *FA Cup:* Winners 1923, 1926, 1929, 1958; Runners-up 1894, 1904, 1953. *Football League Cup:* Semi-final 1976–77. *Freight Rover Trophy:* Runners-up 1986. *Sherpa Van Trophy:* Winners 1989.

Colours: White shirts, navy blue shorts, red stockings, blue and white tops. **Change colours:** All yellow.

BOLTON WANDERERS 1991–92 LEAGUE RECORD

Match No.	Date		Venue	Opponents	Result	H/T Score	Lg. Pos.	Goalscorers	Atten- dance
1	Aug	17	H	Huddersfield T	D 1-1	0-1	—	Philliskirk	7606
2		24	A	Swansea C	D 1-1	1-1	15	Reeves	3578
3		31	H	Leyton Orient	W 1-0	0-0	9	Reeves	5058
4	Sep	3	A	Darlington	L 2-3	0-3	—	Philliskirk, Reeves	3384
5		7	H	WBA	W 3-0	1-0	5	Philliskirk 2, Brown M	7980
6		14	A	Bournemouth	W 2-1	1-0	5	Reeves, Brown P	5614
7		17	A	Bradford C	D 4-4	1-0	—	Darby 2, Patterson (pen), Reeves	5669
8		21	H	Wigan Ath	D 1-1	0-1	7	Darby	6923
9		28	A	Brentford	L 2-3	0-2	9	Reeves, Darby	5658
10	Oct	5	A	Torquay U	W 1-0	1-0	6	Green	5092
11		12	A	Stoke C	L 0-2	0-1	9		12,420
12		19	H	Fulham	L 0-3	0-1	14		5152
13		26	A	Chester C	W 1-0	0-0	11	Darby	1867
14	Nov	2	H	Reading	D 1-1	0-0	11	Philliskirk (pen)	3632
15		5	A	Stockport Co	D 2-2	2-1	—	Philliskirk 2 (1 pen)	4860
16		9	A	Bury	D 1-1	1-0	11	Brown M	5886
17		23	H	Preston NE	W 1-0	0-0	8	Reeves	7033
18		30	A	Shrewsbury T	W 3-1	1-1	7	Philliskirk (pen), Kelly, Reeves	3937
19	Dec	14	H	Hull C	W 1-0	0-0	7	Philliskirk (pen)	5273
20		26	A	Leyton Orient	L 1-2	1-0	8	Green	4896
21		28	A	Huddersfield T	L 0-1	0-1	9		11,884
22	Jan	1	H	Darlington	W 2-0	0-0	7	Fisher, Philliskirk	5841
23		11	A	Exeter C	D 2-2	1-1	8	Philliskirk, Walker	3336
24		18	A	Hartlepool U	D 2-2	0-1	8	Walker, Darby	6129
25	Feb	1	A	Fulham	D 1-1	0-1	9	Walker	3804
26		8	H	Chester C	D 0-0	0-0	10		6609
27		11	H	Shrewsbury T	W 1-0	1-0	—	Walker	5276
28		22	H	Exeter C	L 1-2	1-1	11	Walker	5631
29		29	A	Peterborough U	L 0-1	0-0	13		6270
30	Mar	3	A	Hartlepool U	W 4-0	3-0	—	Kelly, Walker 2, Brown M	2244
31		10	H	Stockport Co	D 0-0	0-0	—		7635
32		14	A	Reading	L 0-1	0-1	15		3515
33		17	H	Birmingham C	D 1-1	0-1	—	Brown P	7329
34		21	H	Bury	W 2-1	1-0	13	Walker 2	7619
35		24	H	Peterborough U	W 2-1	2-1	—	Walker, Charlery (og)	5421
36		28	A	Preston NE	L 1-2	0-1	12	Philliskirk	7327
37		31	H	Bournemouth	L 0-2	0-1	—		4995
38	Apr	4	A	WBA	D 2-2	1-1	12	Walker, Stubbs	10,287
39		7	H	Swansea C	D 0-0	0-0	—		3535
40		11	A	Bradford C	D 1-1	1-0	12	Walker	4892
41		14	A	Birmingham C	L 1-2	1-2	—	Walker	14,440
42		18	A	Wigan Ath	D 1-1	0-1	12	Spooner	3557
43		20	H	Brentford	L 1-2	0-2	12	Walker	4382
44		25	A	Torquay U	L 0-2	0-1	13		2178
45		29	A	Hull C	L 0-2	0-1	—		3997
46	May	2	H	Stoke C	W 3-1	0-1	13	Patterson, Seagraves, Walker	10,000

Final League Position: 13

GOALSCORERS

League (57): Walker 15, Philliskirk 12 (4 pens), Reeves 8, Darby 6, Brown M 3, Brown P 2, Green 2, Kelly 2, Patterson 2 (1 pen), Fisher 1, Seagraves 1, Spooner 1, Stubbs 1, own goals 1.
Rumbelows Cup (6): Darby 3, Kelly 1, Patterson 1, Philliskirk 1.
FA Cup (12): Philliskirk 3 (2 pens), Reeves 3, Walker 3, Burke 1, Darby 1, Green 1.

Felgate	Brown P	Cowdrill	Kelly	Seagraves	Stubbs	Green	Thompson	Reeves	Philliskirk	Darby	Brown M	Rose	Burke	Storer	Winstanley	Patterson	Jeffrey	Dibble	Came	Kennedy	Fisher	Walker	Spooner	Peyton	Charnley	Maxwell	Lydiate	Match No.
1	2	3	4	5	6	7*	8	9	10	11	12																	1
	2		4	5	6		8	9	10	11		1	3	7														2
	2		4	5*		12		9	10	11	7	1	3		6	8												3
	2		4	5				9	10	11	7	1	3*		6	8	12											4
	2		4	5				9	10	11	7		3		6	8		1										5
	2		4	5		12		9	10	11	7*		3		6	8		1										6
	2		4	5*		12		9	10	11	7		3		6	8		1										7
	2		4*		6	12		9	10	11	7†		3	14		8		1			5							8
	2		4*		6	7		9	10	11		1	3	12		8					5							9
	2		4		6	10		9		11			3	7		8		1			5							10
	2		4	14	6	10*		9		11	7		3†	12		8		1			5							11
	2		4	5	6	12		9	10	11	7		3*			8		1										12
	2		4	5		12		14	10	11	7†		3		6	8*		1			9							13
	2		4	5				9	10	11	7		3		6	8		1										14
	2		4	5		12		9	10	11	7		3		6	8*		1										15
	2		4	5				9	10	11	7		3		6	8		1										16
	2		4	5			8	9	10	11	7		3		6			1										17
	2		4	5		12	8	9	10	11	7		3		6*			1										18
1	2		4	5			8	9*	10	11	7		3	12	6													19
1	2		4	5				9	10	11	7*		3	12	6	8												20
1	2		4	5		12		9	10	11			3	7*	6	8												21
1	2*		4	5		12		9	10	11			3	7†	6	8					14							22
1			4	5		7	2		10	11			3		6	8			12			9*						23
1			4	5		7	2		10	11			3		6	8						9						24
1			4	5		7*			10	11	12	14	3		6	8†						9	2					25
1			4	5		7*			10	11	12		3		6	8†			14			9	2					26
1			4	5		7†			10*	11	12	14	3		6	8						9	2					27
14			4†	5		7			10	11	12		3		6	8						9	2*	1				28
1			4	5		7			10	11	12		3		6	8*						9	2					29
1	2		4	5		7			10	11			3		6	8						9						30
1	2		4†	5		7			10	11*	12		3	14	6	8						9						31
1	2		4	5		7†			10	11	12		3*		6	8						9						32
1	2		4*	5		7			10	11	12		3		6	8†						9	14					33
1	2		4	5		7			10*	11	12		3		6	8						9						34
1	2		4	5		7			10	11			3		6	8						9						35
1	2		4	5		7*			10	11	12		3		6							9				8		36
1	2		4	5		7			10	11	12		3†	14	6							9				8*		37
1			4	5		7†			10	11	12		3	14	6							9	2			8*		38
1			4	5		7			10	11*	12		3		6	8						9	2					39
			4	5		7			10	11			3		6	8						9	2		1			40
14			4	5		7			10†	11	12		3*		6	8						9	2		1			41
7			4	5					10	11	12		3*		6	8						9	2		1			42
1		3	4*	5					10	11	12				6	8			7			9	2					43
1		3	4*	5					10	11	12				6	8			7			9	2					44
1		3	4	5	6				10	11	12					8			7*			9	2					45
1		3	4	5		7			10	11						8						9	2				6	46
25	35	1	31	39	26	26	2	24	42	42	23	4	37	4	27	36	1	13	18	1	4	23	14	1	3	3	1	

Substitute appearances: Brown P +2s; Seagraves +1s; Stubbs +6s; Green +11s; Reeves +11s; Philliskirk +1s; Darby +2s; Brown M +4s; Winstanley +5s; Came +1s; Walker +3s; Spooner +1s; Peyton +1s.

Rumbelows Cup	First Round	York C (h)	2-2
		(a)	2-1
	Second Round	Nottingham F (a)	0-4
		(h)	2-5
FA Cup	First Round	Emley (at Huddersfield) (a)	3-0
	Second Round	Bradford C (h)	3-1
	Fourth Round	Brighton & HA (h)	2-1
	Fifth Round	Southampton (h)	2-2
		(a)	2-3

BOLTON WANDERERS

Player and Position	Ht	Wt	Date	Birth Place	Source	Clubs	League App	Gls
Goalkeepers								
David Felgate	6 2	13 10	4 3 60	Bl Ffestiniog	Blaenau	Bolton W	—	—
						Rochdale (loan)	35	—
						Bradford C (loan)	—	—
						Crewe Alex (loan)	14	—
						Rochdale (loan)	12	—
						Lincoln C	198	—
						Cardiff C (loan)	4	—
						Grimsby T (loan)	12	—
						Grimsby T	12	—
						Rotherham U (loan)	—	—
						Bolton W	238	—
Ally Maxwell On loan from Motherwell						Bolton W	3	—
Defenders								
Stephen Birks‡			7 7 73	Fleetwood	Trainee	Bolton W	—	—
Phil Brown	5 11	11 06	30 5 59	South Shields	Local	Hartlepool U	217	8
						Halifax T	135	19
						Bolton W	174	7
David Burke	5 10	10 13	6 8 60	Liverpool	Apprentice	Bolton W	69	1
						Huddersfield T	189	3
						Crystal Palace	81	—
						Bolton W	51	—
Mark Came	6 0	12 13	14 9 61	Exeter	Winsford U	Bolton W	191	7
Julian Darby	6 0	11 04	3 10 68	Bolton		Bolton W	244	32
Jason Lydiate	5 11	12 07	29 10 71	Manchester	Trainee	Manchester U	—	—
						Bolton W	1	—
Phil Neal‡	5 11	12 02	20 2 51	Irchester	Apprentice	Northampton T	186	29
						Liverpool	455	41
						Bolton W	64	3
Darren Oliver	5 8	10 05	1 11 71	Liverpool		Bolton W	—	—
Mark Seagraves	6 1	12 10	22 10 66	Bootle	Local	Liverpool	—	—
						Norwich C (loan)	3	—
						Manchester C	42	—
						Bolton W	72	1
Nicky Spooner	5 8	11 00	5 6 71	Manchester	Trainee	Bolton W	15	1
Alan Stubbs	6 2	12 12	6 10 71	Kirkby	Trainee	Bolton W	55	1
Mark Winstanley	6 1	12 04	22 1 68	St Helens	Trainee	Bolton W	170	2
Midfield								
Steven Coffey‡			2 11 72	Farnworth	Trainee	Bolton W	—	—
Neil Fisher	5 8	11 00	7 11 70	St Helens	Trainee	Bolton W	7	1
Tony Kelly	5 10	11 09	1 10 64	Liverpool	Apprentice	Liverpool	—	—
						Derby Co	—	—
						Wigan Ath	101	15
						Stoke C	36	4
						WBA	26	1
						Chester C (loan)	5	—
						Colchester U (loan)	13	2
						Shrewsbury T	101	15
						Bolton W	31	2
Sammy Lee*	5 7	10 01	7 2 59	Liverpool	Apprentice	Liverpool	197	13
						QPR	30	—
						Osasuna	—	—
						Southampton	2	—
						Bolton W	4	—
Jason McAteer	5 10	10 05	18 6 71	Liverpool	Marine	Bolton W	—	—

BOLTON WANDERERS

Foundation: In 1874 boys of Christ Church Sunday School, Blackburn Street, led by their master Thomas Ogden, established a football club which went under the name of the school and whose president was Vicar of Christ Church. Membership was 6d (2cp). When their president began to lay down too many rules about the use of church premises, the club broke away and formed Bolton Wanderers in 1877, holding their earliest meetings at the Gladstone Hotel.

First Football League game: 8 September, 1888, Football League, v Derby C (h), L 3-6 – Harrison; Robinson, Mitchell; Roberts, Weir, Bullough, Davenport (2), Milne, Coupar, Barbour, Brogan (1).

Did you know: David Jack scored in a club record eight consecutive FA Cup ties for Bolton in 1922–23 to 1923–24, a total of ten goals.

Managers (and Secretary-managers)
Tom Rawthorne 1874–85*, J. J. Bentley 1885–86*, W. G. Struthers 1886–87*, Fitzroy Norris 1887*, J. J. Bentley 1887–95*, Harry Downs 1895–96*, Frank Brettell 1896–98*, John Somerville 1898–1910, Will Settle 1910–15, Tom Mather 1915–19, Charles Foweraker 1919–44, Walter Rowley 1944–50, Bill Ridding 1951–68, Nat Lofthouse 1968–70, Jimmy McIlroy 1970, Jimmy Meadows 1971, Nat Lofthouse 1971 (then admin. man. to 1972), Jimmy Armfield 1971–74, Ian Greaves 1974–80, Stan Anderson 1980–81, George Mulhall 1981–82, John McGovern 1982–85, Charlie Wright 1985, Phil Neal 1985–92, Bruce Rioch May 1992–.

Name	Ht	Wt	Birthdate	Birthplace	Signed from	Club	Apps	Gls
Mark Patterson	5 6	10 10	24 5 65	Darwen	Apprentice	Blackburn R	101	20
						Preston NE	55	19
						Bury	42	10
						Bolton W	55	4
Andrew Roscoe	5 11	12 00	4 6 73	Liverpool	Trainee	Liverpool	—	—
						Bolton W	—	—
Forwards								
Mike Brown	5 9	10 12	8 2 68	Birmingham		Shrewsbury T	190	9
						Bolton W	27	3
Chic Charnley On loan from St Mirren						Bolton W	3	—
Scott Green	6 0	11 12	15 1 70	Walsall	Trainee	Derby Co	—	—
						Bolton W	83	10
Mike Jeffrey	5 9	10 06	11 8 71	Liverpool	Trainee	Bolton W	15	—
						Doncaster R (loan)	11	6
Tony Philliskirk	6 1	11 03	10 2 65	Sunderland	Amateur	Sheffield U	80	20
						Rotherham U (loan)	6	1
						Oldham Ath	10	1
						Preston NE	14	6
						Bolton W	131	49
David Reeves	6 0	11 05	19 11 67	Birkenhead	Heswell	Sheffield W	17	2
						Scunthorpe U (loan)	4	2
						Scunthorpe U (loan)	6	4
						Burnley (loan)	16	8
						Bolton W	120	28
Stuart Storer	5 11	11 08	16 1 67	Harborough		Mansfield T	1	—
						Birmingham C	8	—
						Everton	—	—
						Wigan Ath (loan)	12	—
						Bolton W	120	12
Andy Walker	5 08	10 08	6 4 65	Glasgow	Baillieston J	Motherwell	76	17
						Celtic	108	30
						Newcastle U (loan)	2	—
						Bolton W	24	15

Trainees
Bragg, Lee E; Clarke, Christopher J; Foster, Neil; Gerard, Steven M; Hassall, Jonathan; Jackson, Justin J; Jones, Andrew E. J; Leedham, Paul; Lewin, Craig; Mason, Andrew J; McKay, Andrew S; Smith, Barry; Smith, Marcus; Strange, Stephen A.

Associated Schoolboys
Evans, Robert T. D; Holden, Martin J; Leather, Ian; Leyland, Simon M; Livesey, Mathew D; Longworth, Michael S; Purdom, Dominic P; Redmond, Brendan; Stratulis, Andrew P; Sumner, Mark; Wiggans, Andrew.

AFC BOURNEMOUTH 1991–92   *Back row (left to right)*: Andy Jones, George Lawrence, Denny Mundee, Sean O'Driscoll, Wayne Fereday, Paul Morrell.
Centre row: John Kirk (Trainer), Kevin Bond, Mark Morris, Alec Watson, Vince Bartram, John Williams, Jimmy Quinn, Efan Ekoku, David Coleman, Steve Hardwick (Physiotherapist).
Front row: Tony Pulis (Player/Coach), Steve Baker, Matthew Holmes, Keith Rowland, Harry Redknapp (Manager), Jimmy Case (Captain), Richard Cooke, Shaun Brooks, Terry Shanahan (Assistant Manager).

Division 2   **AFC BOURNEMOUTH**

Dean Court Ground, Bournemouth. Telephone Bournemouth (0202) 395381. Fax No: (0202) 309797

Ground capacity: 11,428.

Record attendance: 28,799 v Manchester U, FA Cup 6th rd, 2 March 1957.

Record receipts: £33,723 v Manchester U, FA Cup 3rd rd, 7 January 1984.

Pitch measurements: 112yd × 75yd.

Chairman: N. Hayward.

Managing Director.

Directors: B. E. Willis (Vice-chairman), E. G. Keep, G. M. C. Hayward, C. W. Legg, K. Gardiner.

Chief Executive: Annie Bassett.

Secretary: Keith MacAlister.

Manager: Tony Pulis. *Coach:* David Williams. *Trainer:* J. Kirk. *Physio:* Steve Hardwick. *Assistant Manager:* Terry Shanahan.

Year Formed: 1899. Turned Professional: 1912. Ltd Co.: 1914.

Former Grounds: 1899–1910, Castlemain Road, Pokesdown; 1910, Dean Court.

Former Names: Boscombe St Johns, 1890–99; Boscombe FC, 1899–1923; Bournemouth & Boscombe Ath FC, 1923–71.

Club Nickname: 'Cherries'.

Record League Victory: 7-0 v Swindon T, Division 3 (S), 22 September 1956 – Godwin; Cunningham, Keetley; Clayton, Crosland, Rushworth; Siddall (1), Norris (2), Arnott (1), Newsham (2), Cutler (1). 10-0 win v Northampton T at start of 1939–40 expunged from the records on outbreak of war.

Record Cup Victory: 11-0 v Margate, FA Cup, 1st rd, 20 November 1971 – Davies; Machin (1), Kitchener, Benson, Jones, Powell, Cave (1), Boyer, MacDougall (9 incl. 1p), Miller, Scott (De Garis).

Record Defeat: 0-9 v Lincoln C, Division 3, 18 December 1982.

Most League Points (2 for a win): 62, Division 3, 1971 –72.

Most League points (3 for a win): 97, Division 3, 1986–87.

Most League Goals: 88, Division 3 (S), 1956–57.

Highest League Scorer in Season: Ted MacDougall, 42, 1970–71.

Most League Goals in Total Aggregate: Ron Eyre, 202, 1924–33.

Most Capped Player: Colin Clarke, 6 (35), Northern Ireland.

Most League Appearances: Ray Bumstead, 412, 1958–70.

Record Transfer Fee Received: £465,000 from Manchester C for Ian Bishop, August 1989.

Record Transfer Fee Paid: £210,000 to Gillingham for Gavin Peacock, August 1989.

Football League Record: 1923 Elected to Division 3 (S). Remained a Third Division club for record number of years until 1970; 1970–71 Division 4; 1971–75 Division 3; 1975–82 Division 4; 1982–87 Division 3; 1987–90 Division 2; 1990–92 Division 3; 1992– Division 2.

Honours: Football League: Division 3 – Champions 1986–87; Division 3 (S) – Runners-up 1947–48. Promotion from Division 4 1970–71 (2nd), 1981–82 (4th). *FA Cup:* best season: 6th rd, 1956–57. *Football League Cup:* best season: 4th rd, 1962, 1964. *Associate Members' Cup:* Winners 1984.

Colours: Red and black striped shirts, white shorts, white stockings. **Change colours:** Blue and black striped shirts, white shorts, white stockings.

AFC BOURNEMOUTH 1991–92 LEAGUE RECORD

Match No.	Date		Venue	Opponents		Result	H/T Score	Lg. Pos.	Goalscorers	Atten- dance
1	Aug	17	H	Darlington	L	1-2	0-0	—	Morris	6210
2		24	A	Stoke C	D	1-1	1-1	18	Quinn	10,011
3		31	H	Hull C	D	0-0	0-0	19		5015
4	Sep	3	A	Preston NE	D	2-2	1-0	—	Holmes, Case	3170
5		7	A	Chester C	W	1-0	0-0	13	O'Driscoll	1117
6		14	H	Bolton W	L	1-2	0-1	19	Quinn	5614
7		17	H	Shrewsbury T	W	1-0	0-0	—	Morris	4454
8		21	A	Huddersfield T	D	0-0	0-0	13		6802
9		27	H	Fulham	D	0-0	0-0	—		6450
10	Oct	5	A	Reading	D	0-0	0-0	14		4033
11		12	H	Hartlepool U	W	2-0	1-0	11	Holmes, Quinn	4817
12		19	A	Leyton Orient	D	1-1	1-0	12	Quinn	3878
13		26	H	Bradford C	L	1-3	0-1	15	Quinn	4445
14	Nov	1	H	Stockport Co	W	1-0	0-0	—	Morris	4649
15		6	A	Torquay U	L	0-1	0-0	—		1884
16		8	A	Swansea C	L	1-3	0-1	—	Quinn	2698
17		22	H	Brentford	D	0-0	0-0	—		4764
18		30	A	Bury	W	1-0	1-0	13	Mundee	1886
19	Dec	14	H	Birmingham C	W	2-1	1-0	10	Wood, Quinn	6048
20		21	H	Stoke C	L	1-2	1-1	12	Wood	5436
21		26	A	Hull C	W	1-0	0-0	10	Quinn	4741
22		28	A	Darlington	D	0-0	0-0	10		3172
23	Jan	1	H	Preston NE	W	1-0	1-0	10	Wood	5508
24		11	A	WBA	L	0-4	0-1	12		10,932
25		18	H	Wigan Ath	W	3-0	0-0	11	Bond, Wood, Quinn	4338
26	Feb	1	H	Leyton Orient	L	0-1	0-1	12		6544
27		8	A	Bradford C	L	1-3	0-1	12	Quinn	5820
28		11	H	Bury	W	4-0	1-0	—	Quinn, Mundee, Ekoku 2	3558
29		15	A	Birmingham C	W	1-0	0-0	10	Quinn	10,898
30		22	H	WBA	W	2-1	1-0	9	Wood, Ekoku	7721
31		29	A	Exeter C	W	3-0	1-0	9	Quinn 2 (1 pen), Morrell	4538
32	Mar	3	A	Wigan Ath	L	0-2	0-1	—		1790
33		7	H	Peterborough U	L	1-2	1-1	9	Shearer	5379
34		10	H	Torquay U	W	2-1	2-0	—	Quinn, Ekoku	4083
35		13	A	Stockport Co	L	0-5	0-3	—		3576
36		20	H	Swansea C	W	3-0	2-0	—	Ekoku 2, Wood	4385
37		24	H	Exeter C	W	1-0	1-0	—	Quinn	4959
38		29	A	Brentford	D	2-2	0-1	—	Holmes, Ekoku	7605
39		31	A	Bolton W	W	2-0	1-0	—	Ekoku, Wood	4995
40	Apr	3	A	Chester C	W	2-0	1-0	—	Wood, Ekoku	5974
41		8	A	Peterborough U	L	0-2	0-2	—		4910
42		11	A	Shrewsbury T	W	2-1	0-1	6	Quinn, Ekoku	2586
43		14	H	Huddersfield T	D	1-1	1-0	—	Wood	7655
44		20	A	Fulham	L	0-2	0-0	6		7619
45		25	H	Reading	W	3-2	1-1	7	Quinn 2 (2 pen), Ekoku	6486
46	May	2	A	Hartlepool U	L	0-1	0-0	8		2612

Final League Position: 8

GOALSCORERS

League (52): Quinn 19 (3 pens), Ekoku 11, Wood 9, Holmes 3, Morris 3, Mundee 2, Bond 1, Case 1, Morrell 1, O'Driscoll 1, Shearer 1.
Rumbelows Cup (8): Jones 2, Quinn 2, Cooke 1, Lawrence 1, Morrell 1, Watson 1.
FA Cup (7): Bond 2, Mundee 2 (2 pens), Quinn 2, Wood 1.

Bartram	Baker	Morrell	Morris	Watson	O'Driscoll	Cooke	Jones	Quinn	Case	Holmes	Rowland	Mundee	Bond	Fereday	Mitchell	Lawrence	Wood	McGorry	Statham	Ekoku	Brooks	Shearer	Puckett	Pulis	Match No.
1	2	3	4	5	6†	7	8	9*10		11	12	14													1
1	2	3	4	5	6	12	8†	9	10	11*			14	7											2
1	7	3†	4	5	6	12	8	9	10	11*			14	2											3
1	2	3	4	5	6	12	8†	9	10	11			14	7*											4
1	7	3	4	5	6		8	9	10	11†			14		2*12										5
1		3	4	5	6	12	8†	9	10	11*			14	2	7										6
1			4	5	6		12	9	10	11	3	8	2	7*											7
1			4	5	6	7*		9	10	11	3	8	2			12									8
1			4	5	6*	7		9	10	11	3	8	2†14			12									9
1 12			4	5	6			9		11*	3	8	2				7 10								10
1			4	5	6	10		9		11*	3	8	2				7 12								11
1			4		6	7*		9	10	11	3	5	2				8 12								12
1			4	5		7		9	10	11*	3	12	2				8 6								13
1			4		5			9	10	11	3	2	7				8 6								14
1			4		6			9	10	11	3	5	2	7*			8 12								15
1			4	5	14			9	10	11†	3	7*	2	12			8 6								16
1			4		6			9	10	11	3	7*	2				8	5							17
1			4		6			9	10	11	3	7*	2				8	5 12							18
1			4		6	12		9	10	11	3	5	2				8	7*							19
1			4		6	7		9	10	11*	3	5	2	14	12		8†								20
1			4		6	12		9	10	11	3	5	2				8†	14 7*							21
1			4		6			9	10	11*	3	5	2				8	12 7							22
1			4		6	12		9*10	14		3	5	2				8	7†11							23
1			4		6				10	11*	3	5	2			12	8	9 7							24
1			4		12			9	10	6	3	5	2				8	11 7*							25
1	14		4		6	12		9	10	8†	3	5	2					11* 7							26
1	3		4		6	12		9	10†14	11*	5	2					8	7							27
1	5		4		6	7		9		10	3	11	2†				8*	14 12							28
1	5				6	7		9	12	10†	3	4	2*	14			8	11							29
1	5		4		6	7			10*11	3		2		14	12†	8	9								30
1	5		4		10†	7*		9		6	3	14	2				8	11	12						31
1	5		4			7		9		6	3	2				12	8†14	11	10*						32
1	5*		4			7		9		6	3	8	2					11	10 12						33
1			4		10	7*		9	12	6	3	2	5				8	11							34
1			4		7			9*10†	6		3	2	5				8	11			12 14				35
1	5		4		12			9	10	6	3		2				8	11			7*				36
1	5		4		12	7*		9	10	6	3		2				8	11							37
1	5		4		7	12		9	10	6	3*		2				8	11							38
1	3		4		5	7†		9	10	6	12 14		2				8	11*							39
1	3		4		5	7*		9	10	6			12	2			8	11							40
1	3		4		5			9	10	6	12		2*				8	11			7				41
1	3		4	2	5			9	10	6	12						8*	11			7				42
1	3		4	5	7				10	6			2				8	11			9*12				43
1	3		4	2	5	6†		9	10*14		12						8	11			7				44
1				5	12	7		9	10*	6	3	2	4				8	11							45
1	5			2	7†			9	10*	6	3	12	4				8	11			14				46
46	5	23	43	15	40	20	6	43	38	43	34	28	38	3	1	2	35	4	2	24	6	6	1	—	
	+	+			+	+	+						+	+	+			+		+	+	+	+	+	
	1s	1s			4s	11s	1s						2s	3s	3s	13s		2s		4s	6s	4s	4s	1s	

Rumbelows Cup	First Round	Cardiff C (a)	2-3
		(h)	4-1
	Second Round	Middlesbrough (a)	1-1
		(h)	1-2
FA Cup	First Round	Bromsgrove (h)	3-1
	Second Round	Brentford (h)	2-1
	Third Round	Newcastle U (h)	0-0
		(a)	2-2
		Bournemouth won 4-3 on penalties	
	Fourth Round	Ipswich T (a)	0-3

AFC BOURNEMOUTH

Player and Position	Ht	Wt	Birth Date	Birth Place	Source	Clubs	League App	Gls
Goalkeepers								
Vincent Bartram	6 2	13 04	7 8 68	Birmingham	Amateur	Wolverhampton W	5	—
						Blackpool (loan)	9	—
						WBA (loan)	—	—
						Bournemouth	46	—
Peter Guthrie‡	6 1	12 13	10 10 61	Newcastle	Weymouth	Tottenham H	—	—
						Swansea C (loan)	14	—
						Charlton Ath (loan)	—	—
						Barnet	—	—
						Bournemouth	10	—
Peter Huckert†	6 2	12 12	28 10 59	London	Apprentice	QPR	160	—
						Cambridge U (loan)	—	—
						Oxford U	66	—
						WBA (loan)	7	—
						Manchester U (loan)	—	—
						Millwall	—	—
						Aldershot	27	—
						Bournemouth	—	—
Defenders								
Kevin Bond*	6 0	13 07	22 6 57	London	Apprentice	Bournemouth	—	—
						Norwich C	142	12
						Seattle S	—	—
						Manchester C	110	11
						Southampton	140	6
						Bournemouth	126	4
Paul Morrell	5 11	13 05	23 3 61	Poole	Weymouth	Bournemouth	322	8
Mark Morris	6 0	11 10	26 9 62	Morden	Apprentice	Wimbledon	168	9
						Aldershot (loan)	14	—
						Watford	41	1
						Sheffield U	56	3
						Bournemouth	43	3
Alex Watson	6 0	10 12	6 4 68	Liverpool	Apprentice	Liverpool	4	—
						Derby Co (loan)	5	—
						Bournemouth	38	3
Midfield								
Shaun Brooks	5 7	11 00	9 10 62	London	Apprentice	Crystal Palace	54	4
						Orient	148	26
						Bournemouth	128	13
Jimmy Case*	5 9	12 07	18 5 54	Liverpool	S Liverpool	Liverpool	186	23
						Brighton & HA	127	10
						Southampton	215	10
						Bournemouth	40	1
David Coleman†	5 7	10 08	8 4 67	Salisbury		Bournemouth	50	2
						Colchester U (loan)	6	1
Ian Hedges‡			5 2 69	Bristol	Gloucester C	Bournemouth	—	—
Dan Holmes†			13 6 72	Clophill	Trainee	Middlesbrough	—	—
						Bournemouth	—	—
Paul Mitchell			20 10 71	Bournemouth	Trainee	Bournemouth	7	—
David Morris†	5 11	12 00	19 11 71	Plumstead	Trainee	Bournemouth	1	—
Sean O'Driscoll*	5 8	11 03	1 7 57	Wolverhampton	Alvechurch	Fulham	148	13
						Bournemouth (loan)	19	1
						Bournemouth	344	18
Tony Pulis*	5 10	11 08	16 1 58	Newport	Apprentice	Bristol R	85	3
						Happy Valley, HK	—	—
						Bristol R	45	2
						Newport Co	77	—
						Bournemouth	74	3
						Gillingham	16	—
						Bournemouth	16	1
Keith Rowland			1 9 71	Portadown	Trainee	Bournemouth	37	—
Forwards								
Richard Cooke	5 6	9 00	4 9 65	Islington	Apprentice	Tottenham H	11	2
						Birmingham C (loan)	5	—
						Bournemouth	72	16
						Luton T	17	1
						Bournemouth	41	2
Efan Ekoku	6 1	12 00	8 6 67	Manchester	Sutton U	Bournemouth	48	14
Matt Holmes	5 7	10 07	1 8 69	Luton		Bournemouth	114	8
						Cardiff C (loan)	1	—
George Lawrence*	5 10	12 02	14 9 62	London	Apprentice	Southampton	10	1
						Oxford U (loan)	15	4
						Oxford U	63	21
						Southampton	68	11
						Millwall	28	4
						Bournemouth	75	5

AFC BOURNEMOUTH

Foundation: There was a Bournemouth FC as early as 1875, but the present club arose out of the remnants of the Boscombe St John's club (formed 1890). The meeting at which Boscombe FC came into being was held at a house in Gladstone Road in 1899. They began by playing in the Boscombe and District Junior League.

First Football League game: 25 August, 1923, Division 3(S), v Swindon T (a), L 1-3 – Heron; Wingham, Lamb; Butt, C. Smith, Voisey; Miller, Lister (1), Davey, Simpson, Robinson.

Did you know: One of Bournemouth's most remarkable away victories was at Merthyr in Division 3 (S) on 5 March 1927. The score was 4-4 with 20 minutes remaining, Jack Phillips having scored all Merthyr's goals. But with Bournemouth centre-forward Ronnie Eyre completing his hat-trick, Bournemouth ran out 6-4 winners.

Managers (and Secretary-managers)
Vincent Kitcher 1914–23*, Harry Kinghorn 1923–25, Leslie Knighton 1925–28, Frank Richards 1928–30, Billy Birrell 1930–35, Bob Crompton 1935–36, Charlie Bell 1936–39, Harry Kinghorn 1939–47, Harry Lowe 1947–50, Jack Bruton 1950–56, Fred Cox 1956–58, Don Welsh 1958–61, Bill McGarry 1961–63, Reg Flewin 1963–65, Fred Cox 1965–70, John Bond 1970–73, Trevor Hartley 1974–78, John Benson 1975–78, Alec Stock 1979–80, David Webb 1980–82, Don Megson 1983, Harry Redknapp 1983–92, Tony Pulis July 1992–.

Player and Position	Ht	Wt	Birth Date	Birth Place	Source	Clubs	League App	Gls
Brian McGorry	5 10	11 00	16 4 70	Liverpool	Weymouth	Bournemouth	8	—
Denny Mundee	5 10	11 00	10 10 68	Swindon	Apprentice	QPR	—	—
						Swindon T	—	—
						Bournemouth	74	4
						Torquay U (loan)	9	—
David Puckett	5 7	10 05	29 10 60	Southampton	Apprentice	Southampton	95	14
						Nottingham F (loan)	—	—
						Bournemouth	35	14
						Stoke C (loan)	7	—
						Swansea (loan)	8	3
						Aldershot	113	50
						Bournemouth	4	—
Jimmy Quinn	6 1	12 00	18 11 59	Belfast	Oswestry T	Swindon T	49	10
						Blackburn R	71	17
						Swindon T	64	30
						Leicester C	31	6
						Bradford C	35	14
						West Ham U	47	18
						Bournemouth	43	19
Peter Shearer	6 0	11 06	4 2 67	Birmingham	Apprentice	Birmingham C	4	—
						Rochdale	1	—
						Cheltenham T	—	—
						Bournemouth	51	6
Paul Wood	5 9	10 01	1 11 64	Middlesbrough	Apprentice	Portsmouth	47	6
						Brighton & HA	92	8
						Sheffield U	28	3
						Bournemouth (loan)	21	—
						Bournemouth	35	9

Trainees
Bibbo, Salvatore; Butcher, Gareth L; Elliot, Steven M; Kerr, Stuart P; Mean, Scott; Morgan, Scott; Moss, Neil G; Murray, Robert J; Shanahan, John A; Smith, Paul; Wake, Nathan.

**Non-Contract
Holmes, Daniel G; Masters, Neil B; Morris, David K; Phillips, Brett S.

Associated Schoolboys
Eastland, Robert L; Ferrett, Christopher A; Hill, Lee D; Kydd, Peter R; McGregor, Christopher N; Musgrove, Neil S; Richards, Carl D; Taylor, Mark R; Town, David E; Wooding, Nathan S.

Associated Schoolboys who have accepted the club's offer of a Traineeship/Contract
Barfoot, Stuart J; Champion, Neil B; Jones, Mark D.

**Non-Contract Players who are retained must be re-signed before they are eligible to play in League matches.

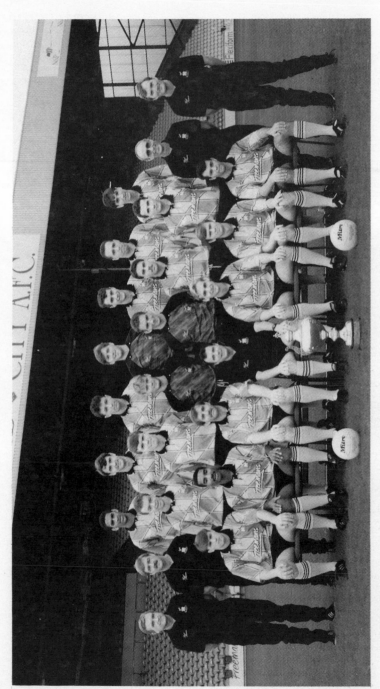

BRADFORD CITY 1991–92   *Back row (left to right):* Philip Babb, Gavin Oliver, Stephen Torpey, Paul Tomlinson, Scott Bairstow, Brian Tinnion, Brian Mitchell.
Centre row: Bob Pearson (Assistant Manager), Steve Smith (Youth Development Officer), Michael McHugh, Mark Leonard, Steven Dickinson, Mark Evans, Sean McCarthy,
Mark Stuart, Brian Edwards (Physiotherapist), Leighton James (Coach).
Front row: Paul Jewell, Wesley Reid, Robbie James, John Docherty (Manager), Lee Duxbury, Alan Dowson, Craig Lawford.

Division 2 **BRADFORD CITY**

Valley Parade Ground, Bradford BD8 7DY. Telephone Bradford (0274) 306062 (Office); (0274) 307050 (Ticket Office).

Ground capacity: 14,352.

Record attendance: 39,146 v Burnley, FA Cup 4th rd, 11 March 1911.

Record receipts: £59,250 v Tottenham H, FA Cup 3rd rd, 7 January 1989.

Pitch measurements: 110yd × 76yd.

Chairman: D. Simpson.

Vice-chairman: D. Thompson FCA.

Directors: P. Wilkowski, D. Taylor FCA, M. Woodhead, T. Goddard.

Associate Directors: M. Smith, M. Scott, P. Brearley, H. Williams.

Manager: Frank Stapleton.

Assistant Manager: Stuart Pearson.

Youth Coach: Steve Smith.

Physio: Brian Edwards.

Secretary: Terry Newman.

Chief Commercial Executive: Keith Hanvey.

Year Formed: 1903. Turned Professional: 1903. Ltd Co.: 1908.

Club Nickname: 'The Bantams'.

Record League Victory: 11-1 v Rotherham U, Division 3 (N), 25 August 1928 – Sherlaw; Russell, Watson; Burkinshaw (1), Summers, Bauld; Harvey (2), Edmunds (3), White (3), Cairns, Scriven (2).

Record Cup Victory: 11-3 v Walker Celtic, FA Cup, 1st rd (replay), 1 December 1937 – Parker; Rookes, McDermott; Murphy, Mackie, Moore; Bagley (1), Whittingham (1), Deakin (4 incl. lp), Cooke (1), Bartholomew (4).

Record Defeat: 1-9 v Colchester U, Division 4, 30 December 1961.

Most League Points (2 for a win): 63, Division 3 (N), 1928–29.

Most League points (3 for a win): 94, Division 3, 1984–85.

Most League Goals: 128, Division 3 (N), 1928–29.

Highest League Scorer in Season: David Layne, 34, Division 4, 1961–62.

Most League Goals in Total Aggregate: Bobby Campbell, 121, 1981–84, 1984–86.

Most Capped Player: Harry Hampton, 9, Northern Ireland.

Most League Appearances: Cec Podd, 502, 1970–84.

Record Transfer Fee Received: £850,000 from Everton for Stuart McCall, June 1988.

Record Transfer Fee Paid: £290,000 to Newcastle U for Peter Jackson, October 1988.

Football League Record: 1903 Elected to Division 2; 1908–22 Division 1; 1922–27 Division 2; 1927–29 Division 3 (N); 1929–37 Division 2; 1937–61 Division 3; 1961–69 Division 4; 1969–72 Division 3; 1972–77 Division 4; 1977–78 Division 3; 1978–82 Division 4; 1982–85 Division 3; 1985–90 Division 2; 1990–92 Division 3; 1992– Division 2.

Honours: Football League: Division 1 best season: 5th, 1910–11; Division 2 – Champions 1907–08; Division 3 – Champions 1984–85; Division 3 (N) – Champions 1928–29; Division 4 – Runners-up 1981–82. *FA Cup:* Winners 1911 (first holders of the present trophy). *Football League Cup:* best season: 5th rd, 1965, 1989.

Colours: Amber and claret diamond shirts, black shorts, amber stockings. **Change colours:** All blue.

BRADFORD CITY 1991–92 LEAGUE RECORD

Match No.	Date		Venue	Opponents	Result	H/T Score	Lg. Pos.	Goalscorers	Attendance
1	Aug	17	H	Stoke C	W 1-0	1-0	—	Tinnion	7556
2		25	A	Huddersfield T	L 0-1	0-1	—		9234
3		31	H	Hartlepool U	D 1-1	0-0	12	Tinnion (pen)	5872
4	Sep	3	A	Leyton Orient	D 1-1	0-1	—	Tinnion	3435
5		7	A	Preston NE	D 1-1	0-0	15	Stuart	4160
6		14	H	Chester C	D 1-1	0-1	15	Stuart	4843
7		17	H	Bolton W	D 4-4	0-1	—	Stuart, Babb, Torpey, Tinnion	5669
8		21	A	Reading	W 2-1	1-1	10	Babb, Reid W	3765
9		28	H	Shrewsbury T	W 3-0	0-0	6	Torpey 2, Reid W	5324
10	Oct	5	A	Stockport Co	L 1-4	1-2	13	Tinnion (pen)	5825
11		12	H	Fulham	L 3-4	1-3	16	Tinnion 2, Babb	5143
12		19	H	Torquay U	W 2-0	0-0	10	Duxbury L, Babb	4543
13		26	A	Bournemouth	W 3-1	1-0	9	Torpey, Richards, Tinnion	4445
14	Nov	2	H	Brentford	L 0-1	0-0	10		5359
15		6	A	Exeter C	L 0-1	0-0	—		2625
16		9	A	Peterborough U	L 1-2	0-1	13	Robinson (og)	9224
17		23	H	Swansea C	L 4-6	1-4	15	McCarthy, Duxbury L, Torpey 2	5728
18		30	A	Birmingham C	L 0-2	0-1	17		10,468
19	Dec	14	H	WBA	D 1-1	1-0	17	McCarthy	7195
20		22	H	Huddersfield T	D 1-1	0-1	—	Jewell	10,050
21		26	A	Hartlepool U	L 0-1	0-1	19		5412
22		28	A	Stoke C	D 0-0	0-0	19		12,208
23	Jan	1	H	Leyton Orient	D 1-1	1-1	19	Jewell	6810
24		4	H	Bury	D 1-1	1-0	20	Torpey	6354
25		11	A	Wigan Ath	L 1-2	1-2	21	Torpey	2548
26		18	H	Hull C	W 2-1	0-0	17	James (pen), McCarthy	6369
27	Feb	1	A	Torquay U	D 1-1	0-1	17	McCarthy	2243
28		8	A	Bournemouth	W 3-1	1-0	17	McCarthy 2, Jewell	5820
29		11	H	Birmingham C	L 1-2	0-1	—	Reid W	7008
30		15	A	WBA	D 1-1	1-1	19	James (pen)	12,607
31		22	H	Wigan Ath	D 1-1	0-0	19	Johnson (og)	5621
32		29	A	Bury	W 1-0	0-0	17	Jewell	2983
33	Mar	3	A	Hull C	D 0-0	0-0	—		4224
34		7	H	Darlington	L 0-1	0-1	18		5579
35		10	H	Exeter C	D 1-1	0-0	—	Jewell	4170
36		14	A	Brentford	W 4-3	2-1	16	McCarthy 2, Torpey, Duxbury L	6791
37		21	H	Peterborough U	W 2-1	2-0	16	McCarthy, James (pen)	6896
38		28	A	Swansea C	D 2-2	1-2	16	Duxbury L, Willis	3748
39		31	A	Chester C	D 0-0	0-0	—		1149
40	Apr	4	H	Preston NE	D 1-1	1-0	16	Jewell	6044
41		7	A	Darlington	W 3-1	2-1	—	McCarthy 2, Duxbury L	1946
42		11	A	Bolton W	D 1-1	0-1	14	McCarthy	4892
43		18	H	Reading	W 1-0	0-0	13	McCarthy	5492
44		21	A	Shrewsbury T	L 2-3	0-2	—	McCarthy 2	2707
45		25	H	Stockport Co	W 1-0	0-0	12	McCarthy	7099
46	May	2	A	Fulham	L 1-2	1-2	16	Torpey	8671

Final League Position: 16

GOALSCORERS

League (62): McCarthy 16, Torpey 10, Tinnion 8 (2 pens), Jewell 6, Duxbury L 5, Babb 4, James 3 (3 pens), Reid W 3, Stuart 3, Richards 1, Willis 1, own goals 2.
Rumbelows Cup (5): Duxbury L 2 (1 pens), Leonard 1, Stuart 1, Tinnion 1 (1 pen).
FA Cup (2): Tinnion 2.

Tomlinson	Mitchell	Dowson	James	Oliver	Gardner	Babb	Duxbury L	Torpey	Tinnion	Stuart	Leonard	Reid W	Morgan	McCarthy	Richards	Jewell	McHugh	Stapleton	Williams	Duxbury M	Evans	Howe	Blake	Reid P	Willis	Match No.
1	2	3	4	5	6	7	8	9	10	11																1
1	2	3	4	5	6	7	8	9	10	11*	12															2
1	2	3	4	5	6	7†	8	9	10	11*	12		14													3
1	2	3	4	5	6	7	8	9	10			11														4
1	2	3	4	5	6	7	8	9		11	10															5
1	2†	3	4	5	6	7*	8	9	11	12	14	10														6
1	2	3	4	5*	6	7	8	9†	11	12	14	10														7
1	2	3	4		6	7*	8	9	11	12		5	10													8
1	2	3	4		6	7	8	9	11			5	10													9
1	2	3	4		6	7	8	9	10			5	11													10
1	2	3	4		6	7	8	9	10			5*	11	12												11
1	2	3	4	5		7	8	9	10	11				6												12
1		3	4		6	7	8	9	10		11		2		5											13
1		3	4		6	7*	8	9	10†		11		2	12	5	14										14
1		3*	4		6	7	8	9	10	12	11		2		5											15
1			4			7	8	9	10		11		2	5		3	6									16
1		3	4	5*	6		8	9	10	12	11		2†	7		14										17
1	2		4	5*	6		8	9	10	12		7		3		11										18
1	2		4			6	8	9	10	11		5		7		3										19
1	2		4.			6	8	9	10		5	7		11		3										20
1	2		4			6	8	9	10*12			5	7†	11		14	3									21
1	2					6	8	9				5		7		11		10	4	3						22
1	2					6	8	9				5	12	7		11		10	4	3*						23
1	2					6	8	9				5		7		11		10	4	3						24
1	2					6	8*	9				5	12	11		10		4	3			7				25
	2					6	8	9*				5	4	10		11		12	3	7	1					26
1	2					6	8					5*	4	10		11		9	3	7						27
1	2					6	8					5*	4	10		11	14	12	3	7			9†			28
1	2					6	8					4		10	12	11	14	5	3*	7			9†			29
1	2					6	8	12				9	4*	10		11		5	3	7						30
1	8*14	2				6	7	12						10	5	11		9	3			4†				31
1	2					6	7		8					4		10		11	9	3					5	32
1	2					6	7		8*	12				4		10		11	9	3					5	33
1	2					6	7		8					4		10*12		11	9	3					5	34
1	2					6	7		8					4		10		11	9	3					5	35
1	12	2				6	7		8					4*		10		11	9	3					5	36
1	2					6	7		8			9		10		3		4						11	5	37
1	2					6	7		8			9		10		3		4					11		5	38
1	2					6	7		8	12		9		10		3		4					11		5*	39
1	2					6	7		8	12		9		10		3		4					11*		5	40
1	2					6	7		8	12		9		10*		3		4					11		5	41
1	2					6	7		8	12		9		10		3		4					11		5*	42
1	2					6	7*		8	12		9		10		3		4					11		5	43
1	2					6	7		8		11	9		10		3		4							5	44
1	2					6	7		8			9		10		3		4	11						5	45
1	2					6	7		8			9		10	12	3		4	11*						5	46
45	20	16	43	10	14	46	46	41	21	9	15	17	9	27	5	28	5	25	22	16	1	3	6	7	9	
		+2s								+2s	+5s	+7s	+4s	+2s	+2s	+2s	+2s	+2s	+4s	+2s						

Rumbelows Cup   First Round   Stockport Co (a)   1-1
                                                    (h)   3-1
                       Second Round   West Ham U (h)   1-1
                                                    (a)   0-4
FA Cup   First Round   Bury (a)   1-0
                       Second Round   Bolton W (a)   1-3

BRADFORD CITY

Player and Position	Ht	Wt	Birth Date	Birth Place	Source	Clubs	League App	Gls
Goalkeepers								
Stephen Dickinson*	6 1	12 00	1 2 73	Bradford	Trainee	Bradford C	—	—
						Blackpool (loan)	—	—
Mark Evans*	6 0	11 08	24 8 70	Leeds	Trainee	Bradford C	12	—
Paul Tomlinson	6 2	12 10	22 2 64	Brierley Hill	Amateur	Sheffield U	37	—
						Birmingham C (loan)	11	—
						Bradford C	209	—
Defenders								
Philip Babb	6 0	12 03	30 11 70	Lambeth		Millwall	—	—
						Bradford C	80	14
Scott Bairstow	6 1		1 6 72	Bradford		Bradford C	—	—
Alan Dowson	5 8	10 06	17 6 70	Gateshead	Trainee	Millwall	1	—
						Fulham (loan)	4	—
						Bradford C	18	—
Mike Duxbury	5 9	11 02	1 9 59	Accrington	Apprentice	Manchester U	299	6
						Blackburn R	27	—
						Bradford C	16	—
Steve Gardner‡	5 9	12 08	3 7 68	Teeside	Trainee	Manchester U	—	—
						Burnley	95	—
						Glossop	—	—
						Bradford C	14	—
Brian Mitchell‡	6 2	13 00	30 7 63	Stonehaven	King Street	Aberdeen	65	1
						Bradford C	178	9
Gavin Oliver	6 0	12 10	6 9 62	Felling	Apprentice	Sheffield W	20	—
						Tranmere R (loan)	17	1
						Brighton & HA (loan)	16	—
						Bradford C	227	7
Dean Richards§			9 6 74	Bradford	Trainee	Bradford C	7	1
Brian Tinnion	6 0	11 05	23 2 68	Newcastle	Apprentice	Newcastle U	32	2
						Bradford C	118	19
Gary Williams	5 9	11 01	17 6 60	Wolverhampton	Apprentice	Aston Villa	240	—
						Walsall (loan)	9	—
						Leeds U	39	3
						Watford	42	—
						Bradford C	22	—
Midfield								
David Campbell‡	5 9	10 09	2 6 65	Eglington	Oxford BC (NI)	Nottingham F	41	3
						Notts Co (loan)	18	2
						Charlton Ath	30	1
						Plymouth Arg (loan)	1	—
						Bradford C	35	4
						Shamrock R (loan)	—	—
Lee Duxbury	5 10	11 07	7 10 69	Skipton	Trainee	Bradford C	104	11
						Rochdale (loan)	10	—
Craig Lawford	5 10	11 00	25 11 72	Dewsbury	Trainee	Bradford C	1	—
Martin McGinley*			11 11 72	Glasgow	Trainee	Bradford C	—	—
Darren Morgan*	5 6	9 05	5 11 67	Camberwell	Apprentice	Millwall	43	2
						Bradford C (loan)	2	—
						Peterborough U (loan)	5	—
						Bradford C	11	—
Wesley Reid (To Airdrie March 1992)	5 8	11 03	10 9 68	Lewisham	Trainee	Arsenal	—	—
						Millwall	6	—
						Bradford C	35	3
Forwards								
Jeremy Howe§			5 9 73	Stancliffe	Trainee	Bradford C	3	—

BRADFORD CITY

Foundation: Bradford was a rugby stronghold around the turn of the century but after Manningham RFC held an archery contest to help them out of financial difficulties in 1903, they were persuaded to give up the handling code and turn to soccer. So they formed Bradford City and continued at Valley Parade. Recognising this as an opportunity for spreading the dribbling code in this part of Yorkshire, the Football League immediately accepted the new club's first application for membership of the Second Division.

First Football League game: 1 September, 1903, Division 2, v Grimsby T (a), L 0-2 – Seymour; Wilson, Halliday; Robinson, Millar, Farnall; Guy, Beckram, Forrest, McMillan, Graham.

Did you know: In the first half of their record-breaking goalscoring season of 1928–29, City tried six different centre-forwards before signing Bert Whitehurst from Liverpool in February. He then went on to score 24 goals in the last 15 games, four more than all the others had scored in the first 27 of the season.

Managers (and Secretary-managers)
Robert Campbell 1903–05, Peter O'Rourke 1905–21, David Menzies 1921–26, Colin Veitch 1926–28, Peter O'Rourke 1928–30, Jack Peart 1930–35, Dick Ray 1935–37, Fred Westgarth 1938–43, Bob Sharp 1943–46, Jack Barker 1946–47, John Milburn 1947–48, David Steele 1948–52, Albert Harris 1952, Ivor Powell 1952–55, Peter Jackson 1955–61, Bob Brocklebank 1961–64, Bill Harris 1965–66, Willie Watson 1966–69, Grenville Hair 1967–68, Jimmy Wheeler 1968–71, Bryan Edwards 1971–75, Bobby Kennedy 1975–78, John Napier 1978, George Mulhall 1978–81, Roy McFarland 1981–82, Trevor Cherry 1982–87, Terry Dolan 1987–89, Terry Yorath 1989–90, John Docherty 1990–91, Frank Stapleton December 1991–.

Robbie James	5 11	13 00	23	3 57	Swansea	Apprentice	Swansea C	394	99
							Stoke C	48	6
							QPR	87	4
							Leicester C	23	—
							Swansea C	90	16
							Bradford C	89	6
Paul Jewell	5 8	10 08	28	9 64	Liverpool	Apprentice	Liverpool	—	—
							Wigan Ath	137	35
							Bradford C	137	18
Sean McCarthy	6 0	12 02	12	9 67	Bridgend	Bridgend	Swansea C	91	25
							Plymouth Arg	70	19
							Bradford C	71	29
Michael McHugh	5 11	11 00	3	4 71	Donegal		Bradford C	10	—
Frank Stapleton	6 0	13 01	10	7 56	Dublin	Apprentice	Arsenal	225	75
							Manchester U	223	60
							Ajax	4	—
							Derby Co	10	1
							Le Havre	—	—
							Blackburn R	81	13
							Aldershot	—	—
							Huddersfield T	5	—
							Bradford C	27	—
Mark Stuart	5 8	11 02	15	12 66	Hammersmith	QPR schoolboy	Charlton Ath	107	28
							Plymouth Arg	57	11
							Ipswich T (loan)	5	2
							Bradford C	29	5
Stephen Torpey	6 2	12 11	8	12 70	Islington	Trainee	Millwall	7	—
							Bradford C	72	17
Darren Treacy	5 10	12 09	6	9 70	Lambeth	Trainee	Millwall	7	—
							Bradford C	16	2

Trainees
Coy, Paul T; Crabtree, Anthony M; Cressey, Matthew A; Dale, Michael; Delahaye, Scott; Hart, Aiden M; Howe, Jeremy R; Margerison, Lee; Owen, Gary; Partridge, Scott M; Richards, Dean I; Summerscales, Lee J; Tomkinson, Alan P; Wilson, Richard J.

Associated Schoolboys
Aldred, Andrew J; Brannan, Michael L; Burgess, Stuart M; Crowther, Andrew J; Crowther, Mathew; Elam, Lee P. G; Ellis, John; Gibson, Jamie A; Holland, Martyn P; Holmes, Richard M; Jackson, Scott; Lowe, Anthony; Mazurke, Shane; McFatter, Robin C; Morrell, Michael J; Polli, Sam; Proctor, James A; Reed, Daniel; Richardson, Christopher; Riches, Phillip V; Simpson, Anthony K; Smith, Christopher P; Stabb, Christopher J; Taylor, Adam.

Associated Schoolboys who have accepted the club's offer of a Traineeship/Contract
Benn, Wayne; Blair, David A; Carss, Anthony J; Grayston, Neil J; Hamilton, Derick V; Lynch, Michael; Stuttard, Andrew J; Tomlinson, Graeme M.

BRENTFORD 1991–92 *Back row (left to right):* Dean Holdsworth, Jamie Bates, Keith Millen, Ashley Bayes, Graham Benstead, Terry Evans, Gary Blissett, Kevin Godfrey. *Centre row:* Joe Gadston (Youth Team Manager), Paul Buckle, Robert Peters, Simon Line, Simon Ratcliffe, Marcus Gayle, Andy Driscoll, Roy Clare (Physiotherapist). *Front row:* Billy Manuel, Richard Cadette, Wilf Rostron (Assistant Manager), Phil Holder (Manager), Neil Smillie, Keith Jones, Mark Turner.

Division 1 **BRENTFORD**

Griffin Park, Braemar Rd, Brentford, Middlesex TW8 0NT. Telephone 081-847 2511. Commercial Dept: 081-560 6062. Press Office: 081-574 3047. Clubcall: 0898 121108.

Ground capacity: 12,500.

Record attendance: 39,626 v Preston NE, FA Cup 6th rd, 5 March 1938.

Record receipts: £80,000 v Fulham, Division 3, 26 April, 1992.

Pitch measurements: 110yd × 73yd.

President: W. Wheatley.

Life Vice-president: F. Edwards.

Chairman: G. V. Potter.

Vice-chairman: E. J. Radley-Smith.

Directors: R. J. J. Blindell LLB, D. Tana, M. M. Lange.

Chief Executive: K. A. Loring.

Deputy President: E. S. J. White.

Manager: Phil Holder. *Assistant Manager:* Wilf Rostron. *Coach:* Graham Pearce. *Physio:* Roy Clare. *Youth Team Manager:* Joe Gadston. *Community Liaison Officer:* Martyn Spong. *Secretary:* Polly Kates. *Press Officer/Programme Editor:* Eric White (081-574 3047).

Year Formed: 1889. Turned Professional: 1899. Ltd Co.: 1901.

Former Grounds: 1889–91, Clifden Road; 1891–95, Benns Fields, Little Ealing; 1895–98, Shotters Field; 1898–1900, Cross Road, S. Ealing; 1900–04, Boston Park; 1904, Griffin Park.

Club Nickname: 'The Bees'.

Record League Victory: 9-0 v Wrexham, Division 3, 15 October 1963 – Cakebread; Coote, Jones; Slater, Scott, Higginson; Summers (1), Brooks (2), McAdams (2), Ward (2), Hales (1). (1 og).

Record Cup Victory: 7-0 v Windsor & Eton (away), FA Cup, 1st rd, 20 November 1982 – Roche; Rowe, Harris (Booker); McNichol (1), Whitehead, Hurlock (2), Kamara, Bowles, Joseph (1), Mahoney (3), Roberts.

Record Defeat: 0-7 v Swansea T, Division 3 (S), 8 November 1924 and v Walsall, Division 3 (S), 19 January 1957.

Most League Points (2 for a win): 62, Division 3 (S), 1932–33 and Division 4, 1962–63.

Most League points (3 for a win): 82, Division 3, 1991–92.

Most League Goals: 98, Division 4, 1962–63.

Highest League Scorer in Season: Jack Holliday, 38, Division 3 (S), 1932–33.

Most League Goals in Total Aggregate: Jim Towers, 153, 1954–61.

Most Capped Player: John Buttigieg, Malta.

Most League Appearances: Ken Coote, 514, 1949–64.

Record Transfer Fee Received: £350,000 from QPR for Andy Sinton, March 1989.

Record Transfer Fee Paid: £167,000 to Hibernian for Eddie May, July 1989.

Football League Record: 1920 Original Member of Division 3; 1921–33 Division 3 (S); 1933–35 Division 2; 1935–47 Division 1; 1947–54 Division 2; 1954–62 Division 3 (S); 1962–63 Division 4; 1963–66 Division 3; 1966–72 Division 4; 1972–73 Division 3; 1973–78 Division 4; 1978–92 Division 3; 1992– Division 1.

Honours: Football League: Division 1 best season: 5th, 1935–36; Division 2 – Champions 1934–35; Division 3 – Champions 1991–92; Division 3 (S) – Champions 1932–33; Runners-up 1929–30, 1957–58; Division 4 – Champions 1962–63. *FA Cup:* best season: 6th rd, 1938, 1946, 1949, 1989. *Football League Cup:* best season: 4th rd, 1982–83. *Freight Rover Trophy* – Runners-up 1985.

Colours: Red and white striped shirts, black shorts, red stockings with black tops. **Change colours:** All blue.

BRENTFORD 1991–92 LEAGUE RECORD

Match No.	Date	Venue	Opponents	Result		H/T Score	Lg. Pos.	Goalscorers	Attendance
1	Aug 17	H	Leyton Orient	W	4-3	1-1	—	Holdsworth 3, Evans	6156
2	24	A	Exeter C	W	2-1	2-0	2	Gayle, Blissett	3518
3	31	H	Huddersfield T	L	2-3	1-1	8	Jones, Godfrey	5459
4	Sep 3	A	Hartlepool U	L	0-1	0-0	—		3660
5	7	A	Shrewsbury T	L	0-1	0-0	16		3193
6	14	H	Reading	W	1-0	0-0	8	Cadette	5775
7	17	H	Hull C	W	4-1	4-0	—	Evans, Smillie, Buckley (og), Holdsworth	4586
8	21	A	Darlington	W	2-1	2-1	5	Smillie, Holdsworth	3900
9	28	H	Bolton W	W	3-2	2-0	3	Holdsworth 2, Gayle	5658
10	Oct 5	A	Fulham	W	1-0	1-0	1	Evans	7710
11	12	H	Peterborough U	W	2-1	1-0	2	Evans, Smillie	7705
12	19	H	WBA	L	1-2	0-1	3	Gayle	8575
13	26	A	Bury	W	3-0	2-0	2	Holdsworth 2, Gayle	2280
14	Nov 2	A	Bradford C	W	1-0	0-0	2	Smillie	5359
15	6	H	Birmingham C	D	2-2	1-1	—	Smillie, Blissett	8798
16	9	H	Wigan Ath	W	4-0	1-0	1	Blissett 2, Holdsworth 2	6675
17	22	A	Bournemouth	D	0-0	0-0	—		4764
18	30	H	Swansea C	W	3-2	0-2	1	Holdsworth, Ratcliffe, Blissett	6669
19	Dec 14	A	Torquay U	D	1-1	1-0	1	Godfrey	2475
20	22	H	Exeter C	W	3-0	2-0	—	Blissett 2, Gayle	7226
21	26	A	Huddersfield T	L	1-2	0-1	1	Blissett (pen)	10,605
22	28	A	Leyton Orient	L	2-4	2-2	2	Luscombe 2	7333
23	Jan 1	H	Hartlepool U	W	1-0	0-0	1	Holdsworth	7103
24	4	A	Stockport Co	L	1-2	1-0	1	Francis (og)	4421
25	11	H	Stoke C	W	2-0	1-0	1	Luscombe, Holdsworth	9004
26	18	A	Chester C	D	1-1	1-0	1	Booker	1447
27	25	H	Preston NE	W	1-0	1-0	1	Evans	7559
28	Feb 1	A	WBA	L	0-2	0-2	1		15,984
29	8	H	Bury	L	0-3	0-2	3		6789
30	11	A	Swansea C	D	1-1	1-0	—	Millen	3582
31	15	A	Torquay U	W	3-2	1-0	1	Booker, Blissett, Bates	6079
32	22	A	Stoke C	L	1-2	0-1	2	Blissett	16,417
33	29	H	Stockport Co	W	2-1	2-1	2	Smillie, Holdsworth	7484
34	Mar 3	H	Chester C	W	2-0	1-0	—	Blissett, Holdsworth (pen)	6869
35	7	A	Preston NE	L	2-3	2-2	2	Smillie, Buckle	3548
36	10	A	Birmingham C	L	0-1	0-1	—		13,290
37	14	H	Bradford C	L	3-4	1-2	2	Evans, Blissett, Holdsworth	6791
38	20	A	Wigan Ath	L	1-2	0-1	—	Holdsworth	2371
39	29	H	Bournemouth	D	2-2	1-0	—	Godfrey, Blissett	7605
40	Apr 1	A	Reading	D	0-0	0-0	—		5660
41	4	H	Shrewsbury T	W	2-0	1-0	4	Holdsworth, Evans	5561
42	11	A	Hull C	W	3-0	1-0	4	Holdsworth 2, Blissett	3770
43	17	H	Darlington	W	4-1	3-0	—	Holdsworth 2, Toman (og), Blissett	8383
44	20	A	Bolton W	W	2-1	2-0	3	Evans, Spooner (og)	4382
45	26	H	Fulham	W	4-0	4-0	—	Holdsworth, Gayle, Blissett, Ratcliffe	12,071
46	May 2	A	Peterborough U	W	1-0	1-0	1	Blissett	14,539

Final League Position: 1

GOALSCORERS

League (81): Holdsworth 24 (1 pen), Blissett 17 (1 pen), Evans 8, Smillie 7, Gayle 6, Godfrey 3, Luscombe 3, Booker 2, Ratcliffe 2, Bates 1, Buckle 1, Cadette 1, Jones 1, Millen 1, own goals 4.
Rumbelows Cup (15): Holdsworth 6, Cadette 4, Godfrey 3, Evans 1, Manuel 1.
FA Cup (7): Holdsworth 4, Bates 1, Blissett 1, Sealy 1.

	Bayes	Ratcliffe	Rostron	Bates	Evans	Buckle	Jones	Godfrey	Holdsworth	Cadette	Smillie	Blissett	Gayle	Benstead	Manuel	Peters	Millen	Suckling	Sealy	Booker	Luscombe	Statham	Driscoll	Finnigan	Hughton	Kruszynski	Match No.
1	1	2†	3	4	5	6	7	8	9*	10	11	12	14														1
		14		4	5	6	7	8	9		11	10	2*	1	3†	12											2
		14		4	5	6*		8	9	11	10	12	1	3	2†												3
		2		4	5	6		8	9	10*	11	12	7†	1	3	14											4
		6		4	5	12	7*	8	9	10	2	11†		1	3	14											5
		2		4	5		7	9	12	11	10†	8*			3	14	6										6
		2		4	5		7	9	10*	11	12	8		1	3		6										7
		2		4	5		7	9	10*	11	12	8		1	3†	14	6										8
		6		2	5		7	9	10*	11	12	8		1	3		4										9
		6		2	5		7	8	10*	11		9		1	3	12	4										10
	12	6		2	5	3	8	9	10	11	7*						4	1									11
	12	6		2	5		7		10*	11	14	8			3		4	1	9†								12
	6			2	5		7	9*		11	10	8			3		4	1	12								13
	6	8		2	5		7	9		11	10				3		4	1									14
	6	12		2	5		7*	9		11	10	8			3		4	1									15
	6			2	5		7	9		11	10	8*			3		4	1	12								16
	6			2	5		12	9		11		8*			3		4	1	7	10							17
	6	11*		2	5	14	8†	9			10	12			3		4	1	7								18
		2		5	8		3	9*		11	10	6	1		12	4		7									19
	6	3		2	5	12	8			11*	10	14	1			4		7		9†							20
	6	11		2	5	8	3				10	9	1			4		7*		12							21
	6	3†		2	5	11	8*	12		10			1		14		4		7		9						22
	6			2	12		8	9		11			1		3	14	4		7	5*	10†						23
	6			2	5		8	9		11			1		3*		4		12	10	7						24
	6			2	5		12	9		11	10†	14	1		3*		4			8	7						25
	6				5			9		11	10		1		3		4			8	7	2					26
	6	3		5	12			9		11		10	1				4			8	7*	2					27
	6	3		5				9		11		10	1		14		4		12	8†	7*	2					28
	6†	3*		5				9		11	10	7	1		14		4			8		2	12				29
		6		5	14			9*		11	10	12	1		3†		4			8		2		7			30
	14			3	5			9		11	10	12	1		6		4			8†		2		7*			31
	6			2	5			9		11	10†	12	1		3		4		14	8				7*			32
	6			2	5			9		11	10	7†	1		3*		4		14	12		8					33
	6				5			9		11	10*	7	1				4		12	8		2		3			34
	6			4	5	8		9		11	10	7	1									2		3			35
	6†			5	14		7	9		11		12	1						4	8	10*	2		3			36
				4	5	12		9		11	10		1		6†				14	8	7*	2		3			37
	8			4	5		7	9		11	10*		1		6†				14	12		2		3			38
	6			3	5		7	9		11	10	12	1		8*							2			4		39
	6				5			9		11	10	7	1				4					2		3	8		40
	6			2	5			9		11	10	7	1		14		4*			12				3	8†		41
	6			2	5			9		11	10	7*	1		14		4†			12				3	8		42
	6			4	5	12		9		11	10	7*	1		14							2		3	8†		43
	6			4	5	12†		9		11	10*	7	1		14							2		3	8		44
	6				5			9		11	10	7	1				4					2		3	8		45
	6	12			5			9†		11	10*	7	1		14		4					2		3	8		46
	1	31	15	41	44	8	6	26	40	10	44	31	28	37	27	1	34	8	9	14	10	18	—	3	12	8	
		+3s	+3s		+7s			+5s	+1s	+1s		+6s	+10s		+8s	+8s			+9s	+2s	+3s		+1s				

BRENTFORD

Goalkeepers

Ashley Bayes			19 4 72	Lincoln	Trainee	Brentford	2	—
Graham Benstead	6 1	13 07	20 8 63	Aldershot	Apprentice	QPR	—	—
						Norwich C (loan)	1	—
						Norwich C	15	—
						Colchester U (loan)	18	—
						Sheffield U (loan)	8	—
						Sheffield U	39	—
						Brentford	82	—

Defenders

Jamie Bates	6 1	12 12	24 2 68	London	Trainee	Brentford	172	6
Jason Cousins‡	6 0	11 06	4 10 70	Hillingdon	Trainee	Brentford	21	—
Terry Evans	6 5	15 01	12 4 65	London	Hillingdon B	Brentford	218	23
Tony Finnigan‡	6 0	12 00	17 10 62	Wimbledon	Fulham	Crystal Palace	105	10
						Blackburn R	36	—
						Hull C	18	1
						Swindon T	3	—
						Brentford	3	—
Mark Fleming‡	5 9	10 11	11 8 69	Hammersmith	Trainee	QPR	3	—
						Brentford	35	1
Marcus Gayle	6 2	12 13	27 9 70	Hammersmith	Trainee	Brentford	83	12
Chris Hughton*	5 7	11 05	11 12 58	West Ham	Amateur	Tottenham H	297	12
						West Ham U	33	—
						Brentford	12	—
Simon Line‡	6 0	13 00	1 11 71	York	Trainee	Crystal Palace	—	—
						Brentford	—	—
Billy Manuel	5 5	10 00	28 6 69	Hackney	Apprentice	Tottenham H	—	—
						Gillingham	87	5
						Brentford	35	—
Keith Millen	6 2	12 04	26 9 66	Croydon	Juniors	Brentford	262	13
Tim O'Shea†	5 11	11 04	12 11 66	London	School	Tottenham H	3	—
						Newport Co (loan)	10	—
						Leyton Orient	9	1
						Gillingham	114	2
						Brentford	—	—
Rob Peters	5 8	11 02	18 5 71	Kensington	Trainee	Brentford	17	1
Simon Ratcliffe	5 11	11 09	8 2 67	Davyhulme	Apprentice	Manchester U	—	—
						Norwich C	9	—
						Brentford	116	7
Wilf Rostron	5 7	11 11	29 9 56	Sunderland	Apprentice	Arsenal	17	2
						Sunderland	76	17
						Watford	317	22
						Sheffield W	7	—
						Sheffield U	36	3
						Brentford	40	2
Brian Statham	5 11	11 00	21 5 69	Zimbabwe	Apprentice	Tottenham H	24	—
						Reading (loan)	8	—
						Bournemouth (loan)	2	—
						Brentford	18	—
Mark Turner*	5 8	10 04	30 6 73	Chiswick	Trainee	Brentford	—	—

Midfield

Bob Booker	6 2	12 04	25 1 58	Watford	Bedmond Sp	Brentford	251	41
						Sheffield U	109	13
						Brentford	16	2
Paul Buckle	5 8	10 08	16 12 70	Hatfield	Trainee	Brentford	52	1
Adam King†	5 11	11 12	4 10 69	Hillingdon	Trainee	West Ham U	—	—
						Plymouth Arg	16	—
						Bristol R (loan)	—	—
						Brentford	—	—
Neil Smillie	5 6	10 07	19 7 58	Barnsley	Apprentice	Crystal Palace	83	7
						Brentford (loan)	3	—
						Brighton & HA	75	2
						Watford	16	3
						Reading	39	—
						Brentford	151	17

BRENTFORD

Foundation: Formed as a small amateur concern in 1889 they were very successful in local circles. They won the championship of the West London Alliance in 1893 and a year later the West Middlesex Junior Cup before carrying off the Senior Cup in 1895. After winning both the London Senior Amateur Cup and the Middlesex Senior Cup in 1898 they were admitted to the Second Division of the Southern League.

First Football League game: 28 August, 1920, Division 3, v Exeter C (a), L 0-3 – Young; Rosier, Hodson; Amos, Levitt, Elliott; Henery, Morley, Spredbury, Thompson, Smith.

Did you know: In 1937–38 Brentford fielded a forward line of internationals in the First Division – Idris Hopkins (Wales), Bill Scott (England), Dave McCulloch (Scotland), George Eastham (England) and Bobby Reid (Scotland).

Managers (and Secretary-managers)
Will Lewis 1900–03*, Dick Molyneux 1903–06, W. G. Brown 1906–08, Fred Halliday 1908–26 (only secretary to 1922), Ephraim Rhodes 1912–15, Archie Mitchell 1921–22, Harry Curtis 1926–49, Jackie Gibbons 1949–52, Jimmy Blain 1952–53, Tommy Lawton 1953, Bill Dodgin Snr 1953–57, Malcolm Macdonald 1957–65, Tommy Cavanagh 1965–66, Billy Gray 1966–67, Jimmy Sirrel 1967–69, Frank Blunstone 1969–73, Mike Everitt 1973–75, John Docherty 1975–76, Bill Dodgin Jnr 1976–80, Fred Callaghan 1980–84, Frank McLintock 1984–87, Steve Perryman 1987–90, Phil Holder September 1990–.

Forwards

Paul Birch	6 0	12 05	3 12 68	Reading	Trainee	Arsenal	—	—
						Portsmouth	—	—
						Brentford	18	2
Gary Blissett	6 1	11 13	29 6 64	Manchester	Altrincham	Crewe Alex	122	39
						Brentford	187	58
Richard Cadette (To Falkirk Jan 1992)	5 8	11 07	21 3 65	Hammersmith	Wembley	Orient	21	4
						Southend U	90	48
						Sheffield U	28	7
						Brentford	87	20
						Bournemouth (loan)	8	1
Andy Driscoll*	5 7	10 13	21 10 71	Staines	Trainee	Brentford	14	2
Kevin Godfrey	5 10	10 11	24 2 60	Kennington	Apprentice	Leyton Orient	285	63
						Plymouth Arg (loan)	7	1
						Brentford	119	17
Dean Holdsworth	5 11	11 04	8 11 68	London	Trainee	Watford	16	3
						Carlisle U (loan)	4	1
						Port Vale (loan)	6	2
						Swansea C (loan)	5	1
						Brentford (loan)	7	1
						Brentford	110	53
Lee Luscombe	6 0	12 04	16 7 71	Guernsey	Trainee	Southampton	—	—
						Brentford	13	3
Tony Sealy	5 8	11 08	7 5 59	London	Apprentice	Southampton	7	—
						Crystal Palace	24	5
						Port Vale (loan)	17	6
						QPR	63	18
						Port Vale (loan)	6	4
						Fulham (loan)	5	1
						Fulham	20	9
						Leicester C	39	7
						Bournemouth (loan)	13	2
						Braga	—	—
						Brentford	12	4
						Swindon T	—	—
						Bristol R	37	7
						Brentford	18	—

Trainees
Aouf, Tamer H; Brady, Christopher J; Brown, Matthew J; Bunce, Nathan; Burton, Jamie R; Clubb, Matthew C; Dickson, Christopher M; Dunkley, Kerry M. J; Grace, Darren M; Hutchings, Carl E; Hynes, Michael C; Johnson, Michael S; Mason, Neil; Price, Paul J; Ravenscroft, Craig; Smart, Lee A; Sparks, Christopher R; Tripp, Daniel E; Udaw, Emem; White, Ian J; Winyard, Alfred P.

Associated Schoolboys
Adams, Russell; Brown, Stewart; Campbell, Corey A; Christophe, Stephen J; Cleary, Kevin J; Daldy, Neil F; Edgeley, David C; Evans, Luke; Genus, Marlon H; Marsh, Simon T; Pelton, Daryl; Whall, Scott T; Wright, Simon.

BRIGHTON AND HOVE ALBION 1991–92 *Back row (left to right):* John Robinson, Bryan Wade, Gary Chivers, Nicky Bissett, Stefan Iovan, Robert Codner, Clive Walker. *Centre row:* Larry May (Reserve Team Coach), Malcolm Stuart (Physiotherapist), Gary Nelson, Gary O'Reilly, Perry Digweed, Mark Beeney, Mike Small, John Byrne, Ted Streeter (Youth Development Officer), Martin Hinshelwood (Coach). *Front row:* John Crumplin, Ian Chapman, Russel Bromage, Barry Lloyd (Manager), Dean Wilkins, Derek McGrath, Mark Barham.

Division 2   **BRIGHTON & HOVE ALBION**

Goldstone Ground, Old Shoreham Rd, Hove, Sussex BN3 7DE. Telephone Brighton (0273) 739535. Commercial Dept: (0273) 778230. Ticket office (0273) 778855. Shop (0273) 26412. Recorded information (team & ticket news etc): Seagull Line 0898 800609.

Ground capacity: 18,647.

Record attendance: 36,747 v Fulham, Division 2, 27 December 1958.

Record receipts: £109,615 v Crawley T, FA Cup 3rd rd, 4 January 1992.

Pitch measurements: 112yd × 75yd.

Chairman: G. A. Stanley.

Vice-chairman: R. A. Bloom.

President: G. A. Stanley.

Directors: B. E. Clarke, W. A. Archer, D. Sullivan, B. D. Lloyd (managing).

Manager: Barry Lloyd.

Secretary: Steve Rooke. *Chief Executive:* Ron Pavey. *Coach:* Martin Hinshelwood. *Physio:* Malcolm Stuart. *Marketing Manager:* Terry Gill. *Lottery Manager:* Dave Treagus.

Year Formed: 1900. Turned Professional: 1900. Ltd Co.: 1904.

Former Grounds: 1900, Withdean; 1901, County Ground; 1902, Goldstone Ground.

Former Names: Brighton & Hove Rangers.

Club Nickname: 'The Seagulls'.

Record League Victory: 9-1 v Newport C, Division 3 (S), 18 April 1951 – Ball; Tennant (1p), Mansell (1p); Willard, McCoy, Wilson; Reed, McNichol (4), Garbutt, Bennett (2), Keene (1). 9-1 v Southend U, Division 3, 27 November 1965 – Powney; Magill, Baxter; Leck, Gall, Turner; Gould (1), Collins (1), Livesey (2), Smith (3), Goodchild (2).

Record Cup Victory: 10-1 v Wisbech, FA Cup, 1st rd, 13 November 1965 – Powney; Magill, Baxter; Collins (1), Gall, Turner; Gould, Smith (2), Livesey (3), Cassidy (2), Goodchild (1). (1 og).

Record Defeat: 0-9 v Middlesbrough, Division 2, 23 August 1958.

Most League Points (2 for a win): 65, Division 3 (S), 1955–56 and Division 3, 1971–72.

Most League points (3 for a win): 84, Division 3, 1987–88.

Most League Goals: 112, Division 3 (S), 1955–56.

Highest League Scorer in Season: Peter Ward, 32, Division 3, 1976–77.

Most League Goals in Total Aggregate: Tommy Cook, 113, 1922–29.

Most Capped Player: Stefan Iovan, 34, Romania.

Most League Appearances: 'Tug' Wilson, 509, 1922–36.

Record Transfer Fee Received: £900,000 from Liverpool for Mark Lawrenson, August 1981.

Record Transfer Fee Paid: £500,000 to Manchester U for Andy Ritchie, October 1980.

Football League Record: 1920 Original Member of Division 3; 1921–58 Division 3 (S); 1958–62 Division 2; 1962–63 Division 3; 1963–65 Division 4; 1965–72 Division 3; 1972–73 Division 2; 1973–77 Division 3; 1977–79 Division 2; 1979–83 Division 1; 1983–87 Division 2; 1987–88 Division 3; 1988– Division 2.

Honours: Football League: Division 1 best season: 13th 1981–82; Division 2 – Runners-up 1978–79; Division 3 (S) – Champions 1957–58; Runners-up 1953–54, 1955–56; Division 3 – Runners-up 1971–72, 1976–77, 1987–88; Division 4 – Champions 1964–65. *FA Cup:* Runners-up 1982–83. *Football League Cup:* best season: 5th rd, 1978–79.

Colours: Blue and white vertical striped shirts, matching shorts with red trim, blue stockings. **Change colours:** Red and white patterned shirts, matching shorts, red stockings.

BRIGHTON & HOVE ALBION 1991–92 LEAGUE RECORD

Match No.	Date		Venue	Opponents	Result		H/T Score	Lg. Pos.	Goalscorers	Atten- dance
1	Aug	17	H	Tranmere R	L	0-2	0-2	—		9679
2		20	A	Bristol C	L	1-2	0-1	—	Bissett	11,299
3		24	A	Barnsley	W	2-1	1-1	16	Wade, Barham (pen)	6066
4		31	H	Wolverhampton W	D	3-3	2-2	17	O'Reilly, Barham, Robinson	10,621
5	Sep	4	A	Millwall	W	2-1	1-1	—	Byrne, Codner	9266
6		7	A	Portsmouth	D	0-0	0-0	14		10,567
7		14	H	Watford	L	0-1	0-1	16		8741
8		18	H	Port Vale	W	3-1	3-0	—	Byrne, Meade, Robinson	5790
9		21	A	Derby Co	L	1-3	0-1	16	Meade	12,004
10		28	H	Bristol R	W	3-1	1-1	12	Codner 2, Byrne	6392
11	Oct	5	A	Sunderland	L	2-4	2-1	14	Byrne, Robinson	15,119
12		12	H	Ipswich T	D	2-2	0-1	15	Byrne, Chivers	9010
13		19	A	Charlton Ath	L	0-2	0-2	18		5598
14		26	H	Swindon T	L	0-2	0-1	19		7370
15		30	H	Leicester C	L	1-2	0-1	—	Codner	6424
16	Nov	2	A	Blackburn R	L	0-1	0-0	20		9877
17		6	H	Grimsby T	W	3-0	3-0	—	Meade 2, Gall	4420
18		9	H	Middlesbrough	D	1-1	1-0	20	Gall	8270
19		16	A	Cambridge U	D	0-0	0-0	17		7625
20		23	A	Oxford U	L	1-3	0-1	19	Gall	4563
21		30	H	Plymouth Arg	W	1-0	0-0	18	O'Reilly	6713
22	Dec	7	A	Southend U	L	1-2	0-1	22	Wade	6303
23		14	H	Newcastle U	D	2-2	1-2	20	O'Reilly, Farrington	7658
24		21	H	Millwall	L	3-4	0-1	21	Gall 2, Chapman	7598
25		26	A	Leicester C	L	1-2	0-1	23	Gallacher	16,767
26		28	A	Wolverhampton W	L	0-2	0-2	23		13,606
27	Jan	1	H	Bristol C	D	0-0	0-0	23		7555
28		11	H	Barnsley	W	3-1	2-0	23	Robinson, Wade, Chapman	6107
29		17	A	Tranmere R	D	1-1	0-0	—	Meade	7179
30	Feb	1	H	Charlton Ath	L	1-2	1-1	22	Walker	8870
31		8	A	Swindon T	L	1-2	1-0	23	Gall	9127
32		15	H	Oxford U	L	1-2	1-2	24	Robinson	6096
33		22	A	Plymouth Arg	D	1-1	0-1	24	Gall	5259
34		29	H	Southend U	W	3-2	1-1	24	Meade, Codner, Munday	8271
35	Mar	7	A	Newcastle U	W	1-0	0-0	20	Gall	24,597
36		10	A	Grimsby T	W	1-0	0-0	—	Walker	4583
37		14	H	Blackburn R	L	0-3	0-2	20		10,845
38		21	A	Middlesbrough	L	0-4	0-2	23		13,054
39		28	H	Cambridge U	D	1-1	0-0	23	Gall	7702
40		31	A	Watford	W	1-0	0-0	—	Meade	7589
41	Apr	11	A	Port Vale	L	1-2	0-0	23	Gall	6441
42		15	H	Derby Co	L	1-2	0-1	—	Gall	8159
43		20	A	Bristol R	L	1-4	0-2	24	Gall	6092
44		25	H	Sunderland	D	2-2	2-2	24	Gall, Codner	9851
45		29	H	Portsmouth	W	2-1	1-0	—	Robinson, Meade	11,647
46	May	2	A	Ipswich T	L	1-3	1-2	23	Meade	26,803

Final League Position: 23

GOALSCORERS

League (56): Gall 13, Meade 9, Codner 6, Robinson 6, Byrne 5, O'Reilly 3, Wade 3, Barham 2 (1 pen), Chapman 2, Walker 2, Bissett 1, Chivers 1, Farrington 1, Gallacher 1, Munday 1.
Rumbelows Cup (5): Byrne 2, Codner 1, Meade 1, Robinson 1.
FA Cup (6): Chapman 2 (1 pens), Meade 2, Gall 1, Walker 1.

Digweed	Crumplin	Chapman	Wilkins	Chivers	O'Reilly	Iovan	Byrne	Wade	Codner	Walker	Bissett	Robinson	Barham	Meade	Beeney	Farrington	Briley	Clarkson	Gall	Gallacher	Sommer	McCarthy	Munday	O'Dowd	Funnell	Match No.
1	2	3	4	5	6	7†	8	9	10*	11	12	14														1
1	2	3	4	5	6	7*	8	9†	10	11	12	14														2
1	12	3	4	2	6		8	9*	10	11†	5	14	7													3
1		3	4	2	6		8		10		5	11	7	9												4
	2*	3	4	1	6		8		10		5	11	7	9	12											5
	2	3	4	5	6		8		10			11	7	9	1											6
		3†	4	2	6		8		10		5	11	7	9*	1	12	14									7
		3	4	2*	6		8		10		5	11	7	9	1	12										8
		3	4	2	6		8†		10		5	11*	7	9	1	14	12									9
	2	3	4*		6		8		10			11	7	9	1	12										10
	2	3		5	6		8†		10			11	7	9*	1	14	4	12								11
	2	3	4	5	6		8		10			11	7	9	1											12
	2	3		5			8		10		6	11	7	9	1		4									13
	2	3		5					10		6†	11	7*	12	1	8	4	14	9							14
	2	3	14	5	6				10			11*	7	12	1	8	4†		9							15
	2		4	5	6				10	11	12		7*		1	8			9	3						16
	2			5	6				10			11	7		1	8	4*	12	9	3						17
	2			5	6				10			11	7*		1	8	4	12	9	3						18
	2			5		7			10			11				8	4		9	3	1	6				19
	2			5	6				10			11	7		1	8	4		9	3						20
	2		14	5	6				10			11	7		1	8*	4†	12	9	3						21
	2	12		5	6		8		10			11	7		1		4		9*	3						22
	2		4	5	6				10			11	7		1	8			9	3						23
	2		4	5	6				10			11	7		1	8			9	3						24
	2		4	5	6				10			11	7	12	1	8*			9	3						25
	2		4	5	6†				10			11	7	12	1	8*	14		9	3						26
	2		4	5					10	11	6		7	12	1	8*			9	3						27
	2		4		6				10			11	7	8	1				9	3		5				28
	2		4		6				10*		12	11	7	8	1				9	3		5				29
	2		4	14	6			9*	10	11†	12		7	8	1					3		5				30
1	2		4		6				10			11	7	8					9	3		5				31
1	2		4		6				10		12	11†	7	8*			14		9	3		5				32
1			4		6				10			11	7	8					9	3		5	2			33
1			4		6				10			11	7	8					9	3		5	2			34
1			4		6				10		12	11	7	8*					9	3		5	2			35
1			4	12	6				10			11	7	8*					9	3		5	2			36
1			4*	12	6				10			11	7†	8			14		9	3		5	2			37
1			4		6				10			11	7	8					9*	3		5	2	12		38
1		7	4		6				10			11		8*			12		9	3		5	2			39
1		7	4		6				10			11		8					9	3		5	2			40
1		11	4		6				10				7	8					9	3		5	2			41
1			4		6				10			11	7	8					9	3		5	2			42
1		11	4		6				10				7	8*			12		9	3		5	2			43
1			4		6				10			11	7	8					9	3		5	2			44
1			4		6				10			11	7	8					9	3		5	2			45
1	12		4		6				10			11	7*	8†					9	3		5	2		14	46
20	27	35	24	36	28	4	13	7	44	23	11	34	22	35	24	8	11	4	30	31	1	20	14	—	—	
+2s	+2s	+2s	+2s					+1s				+2s	+2s	+2s	+5s	+5s	+6s	+4s	+9s	+1s				+1s	+1s	

Rumbelows Cup	Second Round	Brentford (a)	1-4
		(h)	4-2
FA Cup	Third Round	Crawley (h)	5-0
	Fourth Round	Bolton W (a)	1-2

BRIGHTON & HOVE ALBION

Player and Position	Ht	Wt	Date	Birth Place	Source	Clubs	League App	Gls
Goalkeepers								
Mark Beeney	6 4	13 00	30 12 67	Pembury		Gillingham	2	—
						Maidstone U	50	—
						Aldershot (loan)	7	—
						Brighton & HA	27	—
Perry Digweed	6 0	11 04	26 10 59	London	Apprentice	Fulham	15	—
						Brighton & HA	175	—
						WBA (loan)	—	—
						Charlton Ath (loan)	—	—
						Newcastle U (loan)	—	—
						Chelsea (loan)	3	—
Defenders								
Nicky Bissett	6 2	12 10	5 4 64	Fulham	Barnet	Brighton & HA	61	7
Russel Bromage*	5 11	11 05	9 11 59	Stoke	Apprentice	Port Vale	347	13
						Oldham Ath (loan)	2	—
						Bristol C	46	1
						Brighton & HA	1	—
						Maidstone U (loan)	3	—
Ian Chapman	5 8	11 05	31 5 70	Brighton		Brighton & HA	126	2
Gary Chivers	5 11	11 05	15 5 60	Stockwell	Apprentice	Chelsea	133	4
						Swansea C	10	—
						QPR	60	—
						Watford	14	—
						Brighton & HA	174	13
Bernard Gallacher	5 8	11 02	22 3 67	Johnstone	Apprentice	Aston Villa	57	—
						Blackburn R (loan)	4	—
						Brighton & HA	31	1
Stefan Iovan*	6 1		23 8 60	Bucharest	Steaua	Brighton & HA	6	—
Paul McCarthy	6 0	13 06	4 8 71	Cork	Trainee	Brighton & HA	44	—
Stuart Munday	5 11	11 00	28 9 72	London	Trainee	Brighton & HA	14	1
Greg O'Dowd*	5 10	10 00	16 3 73	Dublin	Trainee	Brighton & HA	1	—
Gary O'Reilly	5 11	12 00	21 3 61	Isleworth	Amateur	Tottenham H	45	—
						Brighton & HA	79	3
						Crystal Palace	70	2
						Birmingham C (loan)	1	—
						Brighton & HA	28	3
Wayne Stemp*	5 11	11 02	9 9 70	Epsom	Trainee	Brighton & HA	4	—
Midfield								
Mark Barham*	5 7	11 00	12 7 62	Folkestone	Apprentice	Norwich C	177	23
						Huddersfield T	27	1
						Middlesbrough	4	—
						WBA	4	—
						Brighton & HA	73	8
Les Briley*	5 6	11 00	2 10 56	Lambeth	Apprentice	Chelsea	—	—
						Hereford U	61	2
						Wimbledon	61	2
						Aldershot	157	3
						Millwall	227	13
						Brighton & HA	15	—
John Crumplin	5 8	11 10	26 5 67	Bath	Bognor	Brighton & HA	143	4
Derek McGrath‡	5 5	10 01	21 1 72	Dublin	Trainee	Brighton & HA	6	—
John Robinson	5 10	11 05	29 8 71	Rhodesia	Trainee	Brighton & HA	56	6
Dean Wilkins	5 8	11 08	12 7 62	Hillingdon	Apprentice	QPR	6	—
						Brighton & HA	2	—
						Orient (loan)	10	—
						Zwolle	—	—
						Brighton & HA	205	17

BRIGHTON & HOVE ALBION

Foundation: After barely two seasons in existence, a professional club named Brighton United, consisting mostly of Scotsmen, was forced to disband in 1900. The club's manager John Jackson determined to keep the professional game alive in the town and initiated the movement which led to the formation of Brighton & Hove Rangers that same year.

First Football League game: 28 August, 1920, Division 3, v Southend U (a), L 0-2 – Hayes; Woodhouse, Little; Hall, Comber, Bentley; Longstaff, Ritchie, Doran, Rodgerson, March.

Did you know: In 1921–22 Brighton's Irish international Jack Doran scored hat-tricks away and at home to Exeter City on successive Wednesdays with Brighton winning 3-0 and 3-1. These were the club's first hat-tricks in the League.

Managers (and Secretary-managers)
John Jackson 1901–05, Frank Scott-Walford 1905–08, John Robson 1908–14, Charles Webb 1919–47, Tommy Cook 1947, Don Welsh 1947–51, Billy Lane 1951–61, George Curtis 1961–63, Archie Macaulay 1963–68, Fred Goodwin 1968–70, Pat Saward 1970–73, Brian Clough 1973–74, Peter Taylor 1974–76, Alan Mullery 1976–81, Mike Bailey 1981–82, Jimmy Melia 1982–83, Chris Catlin 1983–86, Alan Mullery 1986–87, Barry Lloyd January 1987–.

Player and Position	Ht	Wt	Birth Date	Birth Place	Source	Clubs	League App	League Gls
Forwards								
David Clarkson	5 9	10 00	1 2 68	Preston	Sunshine GC	Brighton & HA	13	—
Robert Codner	5 11	11 05	23 1 65	Walthamstow	Dagenham	Leicester C	—	—
						Barnet	—	—
						Brighton & HA	160	24
Mark Farrington	5 10	11 12	15 6 65	Liverpool	Apprentice	Everton	—	—
						Norwich C	14	2
						Cambridge U (loan)	10	1
						Cardiff C	31	3
						Feyenoord	—	—
						Brighton & HA	28	2
Simon Funnell§			8 8 74	Brighton	Trainee	Brighton & HA	1	—
Mark Gall	5 10	12 00	14 5 63	Brixton	Greenwich Bor	Maidstone U	85	31
						Brighton & HA	31	13
Raphael Meade*	5 10	11 09	22 11 62	Islington	Apprentice	Arsenal	41	14
						Sporting Lisbon	—	—
						Dundee U	11	4
						Luton T	4	—
						Ipswich T	1	—
						Odense	—	—
						Plymouth Arg	5	—
						Brighton & HA	40	9
Peter Reed *			27 10 72	Brighton	Trainee	Brighton & HA	—	—
David Savage*	5 11	10 04	30 7 73	Dublin	Kilkenny C	Brighton & HA	—	—
Bryan Wade*	5 8	11 05	25 6 63	Bath	Trowbridge T	Swindon T	60	19
						Swansea C	36	5
						Haverfordwest	—	—
						Brighton & HA	18	9
Clive Walker	5 8	11 04	26 5 57	Oxford	Apprentice	Chelsea	198	60
						Sunderland	50	10
						QPR	21	1
						Fulham	109	29
						Brighton & HA	68	5

Trainees
Barrett, Sean M; Funnell, Simon P; Logan, William P; Moulding, Matthew A; Myall, Stuart T; Oliva, Umberto; Pryce-Jones, Liam; Reid, Philip C; Rogers, Sean T; Simmonds, Daniel B; Tuck, Stuart G; Williams, Jamie P; Wosahlo, Bradley E.

Associated Schoolboys
Andrews, Phillip D; Kember, Paul M. J; Smith, Daniel K; Taylor, Paul D; Whitehouse, Timothy J.

Associated Schoolboys who have accepted the club's offer of a Traineeship/Contract
Fox, Mark S; Yorke-Johnson, Ross.

BRISTOL CITY 1991–92   *Back row (left to right):* Andy Patterson, Louie Donowa, Chris Giles, Gerald Harrison, Deion Vernon, Dave Rennie, Gary Campbell, Graham Smith, Wayne Allison, Martin Scott, Andy May.
Centre row: Tony Fawthrop (Chief Scout), Junior Bent, Matt Bryant, Rob Edwards, Keith Welch, Steve Weaver, Andy Leaning, Ronnie Sinclair, Nicky Morgan, Bob Taylor, Mark Aizlewood, Buster Footman (Physiotherapist), Alan Crawford.
Front row: Micky Mellon, Andy Llewellyn, John Bailey, Jimmy Lumsden (Manager), Gary Shelton, Tony Taylor (Assistant Manager), Dave Smith, Jason Watkins, Steve Clifford.

Division 1   **BRISTOL CITY**

Ashton Gate, Bristol BS3 2EJ. Telephone Bristol (0272) 632812 (5 lines). Commercial Dept: 0272 633836. Clubcall: 0898 121176.

Ground capacity: 23,636.

Record attendance: 43,335 v Preston NE, FA Cup 5th rd, 16 February 1935.

Record receipts: £97,777.50 v Chelsea, FA Cup 4th round, 27 January 1990.

Pitch measurements: 115yd × 75yd.

Chairman: L. J. Kew.

Vice-chairman: W. I. Williams.

Directors: O. W. Newland, P. Manning, M. Fricker, K. Sage, D. Coller.

Commercial Manager: John Cox.

Manager: Denis Smith. *Assistant Manager:* Russell Osman. *Physio:* Buster Footman. *Football Secretary:* Miss Jean Harrison. *Commercial Manager:* John Cox.

Year Formed: 1894. Turned Professional: 1897. Ltd Co.: 1897. BCFC (1982) PLC.

Former Grounds: 1894, St John's Lane; 1904, Ashton Gate.

Former Names: Bristol South End 1894–97.

Club Nickname: 'Robins'.

Record League Victory: 9-0 v Aldershot, Division 3 (S), 28 December 1946 – Eddols; Morgan, Fox; Peacock, Roberts, Jones (1); Chilcott, Thomas, Clark (4 incl. 1p), Cyril Williams (1), Hargreaves (3).

Record Cup Victory: 11-0 v Chichester C, FA Cup, 1st rd, 5 November 1960 – Cook; Collinson, Thresher; Connor, Alan Williams, Etheridge; Tait (1), Bobby Williams (1), Atyeo (5), Adrian Williams (3), Derrick. (1 og).

Record Defeat: 0-9 v Coventry C, Division 3 (S), 28 April 1934.

Most League Points (2 for a win): 70, Division 3 (S), 1954–55.

Most League points (3 for a win): 91, Division 3, 1989–90.

Most League Goals: 104, Division 3 (S), 1926–27.

Highest League Scorer in Season: Don Clark, 36, Division 3 (S), 1946–47.

Most League Goals in Total Aggregate: John Atyeo, 314, 1951–66.

Most Capped Player: Billy Wedlock, 26, England.

Most League Appearances: John Atyeo, 597, 1951–66.

Record Transfer Fee Received: £600,000 from Norwich C for Rob Newman, June 1991.

Record Transfer Fee Paid: £250,000 to Celtic for Dariusz Dziekanowski, January 1992.

Football League Record: 1901 Elected to Division 2; 1906–11 Division 1; 1911–22 Division 2; 1922–23 Division 3 (S); 1923–24 Division 2; 1924–27 Division 3 (S); 1927–32 Division 2; 1932–55 Division 3 (S); 1955–60 Division 2; 1960–65 Division 3; 1965–76 Division 2; 1976–80 Division 1; 1980–81 Division 2; 1981–82 Division 3; 1982–84 Division 4; 1984–90 Division 3; 1990–92 Division 2; 1992– Division 1.

Honours: Football League: Division 1 – Runners-up 1906–07; Division 2 – Champions 1905–06; Runners-up 1975–76; Division 3 (S) – Champions 1922–23, 1926–27, 1954–55; Runners-up 1937–38; Division 3 – Runners-up 1964–65, 1989–90. *FA Cup:* Runners-up 1909. *Football League Cup:* Semi-final 1970–71, 1988–89. *Welsh Cup:* Winners 1934. *Anglo-Scottish Cup:* Winners 1977–78. *Freight Rover Trophy:* Winners 1985–86; Runners-up 1986–87.

Colours: Red shirts, white shorts, red and white stockings. **Change colours:** Purple shirts, green shorts, white stockings with purple top.

BRISTOL CITY 1991–92 LEAGUE RECORD

Match No.	Date		Venue	Opponents	Result		H/T Score	Lg. Pos.	Goalscorers	Attendance
1	Aug	17	A	Southend U	D	1-1	0-1	—	Taylor	6720
2		20	H	Brighton & HA	W	2-1	1-0	—	Scott, Bryant	11,299
3		24	H	Blackburn R	W	1-0	1-0	2	Allison	11,317
4		31	A	Port Vale	D	1-1	0-1	4	Morgan	7057
5	Sep	4	H	Bristol R	W	1-0	0-0	—	Allison	20,183
6		7	A	Leicester C	L	1-2	1-2	5	Morgan	17,815
7		14	H	Tranmere R	D	2-2	2-1	5	Allison, Shelton	11,235
8		17	H	Millwall	D	2-2	1-2	—	Bryant, Scott (pen)	10,862
9		21	A	Ipswich T	L	2-4	1-1	10	Allison, Smith	9692
10		28	H	Portsmouth	L	0-2	0-2	14		9830
11	Oct	5	A	Derby Co	L	1-4	0-1	18	Edwards	11,880
12		12	H	Watford	W	1-0	1-0	11	Connor	7882
13		19	A	Barnsley	W	2-1	1-0	8	May, Shelton	6566
14		26	H	Newcastle U	D	1-1	0-1	9	Taylor	8613
15	Nov	2	A	Cambridge U	D	0-0	0-0	9		4810
16		5	H	Plymouth Arg	W	2-0	2-0	—	Morgan, Allison	7735
17		9	H	Sunderland	W	1-0	1-0	9	Allison	10,570
18		16	A	Oxford U	D	1-1	0-0	10	Allison	5780
19		23	A	Middlesbrough	L	1-3	1-2	11	Taylor	12,928
20		30	H	Charlton Ath	L	0-2	0-1	11		9123
21	Dec	7	A	Grimsby T	L	1-3	1-1	12	Rennie	4866
22		21	H	Bristol R	L	2-3	1-2	14	Rennie, Bent	6306
23		26	H	Swindon T	D	1-1	0-1	16	Taylor	14,636
24		28	H	Port Vale	W	3-0	2-0	12	Allison, Osman, Bent	9235
25	Jan	1	A	Brighton & HA	D	0-0	0-0	13		7555
26		11	A	Blackburn R	L	0-4	0-3	14		12,964
27		18	A	Southend U	D	2-2	0-1	14	Dziekanowski, Gavin	9883
28	Feb	1	H	Barnsley	L	0-2	0-0	16		9508
29		4	A	Swindon T	L	0-2	0-0	—		9627
30		8	A	Newcastle U	L	0-3	0-0	18		29,263
31		22	A	Charlton Ath	L	1-2	1-0	21	Shelton	5900
32		29	H	Grimsby T	D	1-1	1-0	20	Aizlewood	8992
33	Mar	7	A	Wolverhampton W	D	1-1	1-1	22	Osman	12,542
34		10	A	Plymouth Arg	L	0-1	0-0	—		9734
35		14	H	Cambridge U	L	1-2	1-0	23	Scott	9579
36		17	H	Wolverhampton W	W	2-0	0-0	—	Dziekanowski 2	11,623
37		21	A	Sunderland	W	3-1	3-0	20	Cole, Allison 2	18,933
38		28	H	Oxford U	D	1-1	0-0	20	Dziekanowski	12,402
39		31	A	Tranmere R	D	2-2	0-0	—	Cole, Rosenior	5797
40	Apr	4	H	Leicester C	W	2-1	1-1	17	Rosenior, Cole	13,020
41		7	H	Middlesbrough	D	1-1	0-1	—	Cole	12,814
42		11	A	Millwall	W	3-2	0-1	16	Rosenior 2, Cole	6989
43		18	H	Ipswich T	W	2-1	1-0	17	Rosenior, Cole	16,941
44		20	A	Portsmouth	L	0-1	0-1	17		17,151
45		25	H	Derby Co	L	1-2	1-1	17	Atteveld	16,648
46	May	2	A	Watford	L	2-5	1-1	17	Cole 2	10,582

Final League Position: 17

GOALSCORERS

League (55): Allison 10, Cole 8, Rosenior 5, Dziekanowski 4, Taylor 4, Morgan 3, Scott 3 (1 pen), Shelton 3, Bent 2, Bryant 2, Osman 2, Rennie 2, Aizlewood 1, Atteveld 1, Connor 1, Edwards 1, Gavin 1, May 1, Smith 1.
Rumbelows Cup (5): Morgan 2, Smith 2, Allison 1.
FA Cup (5): Dziekanowski 2, Bent 1, May 1, own goal 1.

Welch	Llewellyn	Scott	May	Bryant	Aizlewood	Shelton	Rennie	Allison	Taylor	Smith	Morgan	Bent	Edwards	Harrison	Caesar	Connor	Leaning	Osman	Gavin	Dziekanowski	Mellon	McIntyre	Cole	Rosenior	Atteveld	Match No.
1	2	3	4	5	6	7	8	9	10	11																1
1	2	3	4	5	6	7	8	9	10	11																2
1	2	3	4	5	6	7	8	9	10*	11	12															3
1	2	3	4	5	6	7	8	9	10*	11	12															4
1	2*	3	4	5	6	7	8	9		11	10	12														5
1		3	2	5	6		8	9		11	10	7*	4		12											6
1		3	2	5	6*	7	8	9		11	10	12	4													7
1		3	2	5		7	8	9	12	11	10*		4†		14	6										8
1	2	3	4	5		7	8	9		11					6	10										9
1	2	3	4	5		7†	8	9		11	10		14		6*	12										10
1	2	3	4*	5	6		8	9		11		12	7			10										11
	2	3	4				8	9	12	11	10*		14		5	7†	1	6								12
	2	3	4			7	8	9	12		10*				5	11	1	6								13
	2	3	4			7	8	12	9	14	10*				5	11	1	6†								14
	2	3		5	6	7	8	10	9						4	11	1									15
	2	3	4	5	6	7	8	9		11	10						1									16
	2†	3	4	5	6	7	8	9		11	10*					12	1	14								17
	2	3	4	5	6	7	8	9	12	11						10*	1									18
	2*	3	4	5		7	8	9	12	11			14			10†	1	6								19
	2	3	12	5		7	8†	9	10	11			14			4*	1	6								20
	2	3	4	5			8	9	10				7		6		1	11								21
	2*	3	4	5	6		8	9	10			12					1	7	11							22
	2	3	4	5	6		8	9	10								1	7	11							23
	2	3*	4†	5	6		8	9	10			12	14				1	7	11							24
	2	3	4	5	6		8*	9	10			12					1	7	11							25
		3	2	5	6		8*	9	10†			14	12		7		1	4	11							26
		3	7	5	6			9	12		8*	2					1	4	11	10						27
	2	3	4	5	10			9*	7								1	6	11	8	12					28
	2	3	4	5	10	12		9*	7								1	6		8	11					29
	2	3	4*	5		12	8	9	7								1	6	11	10						30
1		3	4	5	6	8†		9				2	12							10	14					31
1		3	4	5	6			9				10	7	8						2	11					32
1	2	3	4	5						10		12	8					6	7	9*14		11†				33
1	2	3	4	5						10	9*	12	8					6	11		7					34
1	2*	3	11	5	4					10		12	8					6	7†		14		9			35
1	2	3	11	5	4					10			8*					6	7		12		9			36
1	2	3	11	5	4					10*			14					6	7	8†			9	12		37
1	2	3	11	5	4					10								6*	7†	8			9	12	14	38
1	2	3	11	5	4					10*			14					6	7	8			9†	12		39
1	2	3	11	5	4					12			14					6	7	8†			9	10*		40
1	2*	3†11		5	4					12								6	7	8			9	10	14	41
1	2	3	11	5	4					12								6†	7	8*			9	10	14	42
1		3	11	5	4													6	7	8			9	10	2	43
1		3	11	5	4					12								6	7*	8			9	10	2	44
1	2	3	11	5	4†					10			14					6*12	7	8			9		7	45
	7†	3	11	5	4					10			14				1	6		8*12			9		2	46
26	37	46	44	43	34	18	27	37	13	17	15	7	12	—	9	9	20	30	12	16	12	1	12	5	4	
+1s			1s				6s	5s	1s	4s	10s8s	4s	1s		2s			1s	2s	1s	4s			3s	3s	

Rumbelows Cup — Second Round — Bristol R (a) 3-1 / (h) 2-4

FA Cup — Third Round — Wimbledon (h) 1-1 / (a) 1-0
Fourth Round — Leicester C (a) 2-1
Fifth Round — Nottingham F (a) 1-4

BRISTOL CITY

Player and Position	Ht	Wt	Birth Date	Birth Place	Source	Clubs	League App	Gls
Goalkeepers								
Andy Leaning	6 1	13 07	18 5 62	York	Rowntree M	York C	69	—
						Sheffield U	21	—
						Bristol C	74	—
Steve Weaver*	5 11	10 02	5 5 72	Bristol	Trainee	Bristol C	—	—
Keith Welch	6 0	12 00	3 10 68	Bolton	Trainee	Bolton W	—	—
						Rochdale	205	—
						Bristol C	26	—
Defenders								
John Bailey‡	5 8	11 03	1 4 57	Liverpool	Apprentice	Blackburn R	120	1
						Everton	171	3
						Newcastle U	40	—
						Bristol C	80	1
Matthew Bryant	6 1	12 11	21 9 70	Bristol	Trainee	Bristol C	65	3
						Walsall (loan)	13	—
Gus Caesar (To Airdrie January 1992)	6 0	12 00	5 3 66	London	Apprentice	Arsenal	44	—
						QPR (loan)	5	—
						Cambridge U	—	—
						Bristol C	10	—
Robert Edwards	6 0	11 06	1 7 73	Kendal		Carlisle U	48	5
						Bristol C	20	1
Chris Honor (To Airdrie Aug 1991)	5 9	10 09	5 6 68	Bristol	Apprentice	Bristol C	60	1
						Torquay U (loan)	3	—
						Hereford U (loan)	3	—
						Swansea C (loan)	2	—
Andy Llewellyn	5 7	11 12	26 2 66	Bristol	Apprentice	Bristol C	274	3
Russell Osman	6 0	11 10	14 2 59	Repton	Apprentice	Ipswich T	294	17
						Leicester C	108	8
						Southampton	96	6
						Bristol C	31	2
Andy Paterson			5 5 72	Glasgow		Bristol C	—	—
Martin Scott	5 8	9 10	7 1 68	Sheffield	Apprentice	Rotherham U	94	3
						Nottingham F (loan)	—	—
						Bristol C	73	4
Midfield								
Mark Aizlewood	6 0	12 08	1 10 59	Newport	Apprentice	Newport Co	38	1
						Luton T	98	3
						Charlton Ath	152	9
						Leeds U	70	3
						Bradford C	39	1
						Bristol C	76	3
Ray Atteveld	5 10	12 00	8 9 66	Amsterdam	Haarlem	Everton	51	1
						West Ham U (loan)	1	—
						Bristol C	7	1
Chris Giles *			26 2 73	Leeds	Trainee	Bristol C	—	—
Gerry Harrison	5 10	12 02	15 4 72	Lambeth	Trainee	Watford	9	—
						Bristol C	4	—
						Cardiff C (loan)	10	1
Andy May	5 8	11 00	26 2 64	Bury	Apprentice	Manchester C	150	8
						Huddersfield T	114	5
						Bolton W (loan)	10	2
						Bristol C	90	4
Michael Mellon	5 8	11 03	18 3 72	Paisley	Trainee	Bristol C	25	—
Gary Shelton	5 7	11 03	21 3 58	Nottingham	Apprentice	Walsall	24	—
						Aston Villa	24	7
						Notts Co (loan)	8	—
						Sheffield W	198	18
						Oxford U	65	1
						Bristol C	105	20
Jason Watkins*	5 08	10 08	27 9 72	Kent	Trainee	Bristol C	—	—
Forwards								
Wayne Allison	6 1	12 06	16 10 68	Huddersfield		Halifax T	84	23
						Watford	7	—
						Bristol C	80	16
Junior Bent	5 5	10 06	1 3 70	Huddersfield	Trainee	Huddersfield T	36	6
						Burnley (loan)	9	3
						Bristol C	38	4
						Stoke C (loan)	1	—
Gary Campbell	6 0	11 08	25 8 72	Glasgow	Trainee	Bristol C	—	—
Steve Clifford			13 7 73	Telford	Trainee	Bristol C	—	—

BRISTOL CITY

Foundation: The name Bristol City came into being in 1897 when the Bristol South End club, formed three years earlier, decided to adopt professionalism and apply for admission to the Southern League after competing in the Western League. The historic meeting was held at The Albert Hall, Bedminster. Bristol City employed Sam Hollis from Woolwich Arsenal as manager and gave him £40 to buy players. In 1901 they merged with Bedminster, another leading Bristol club.

First Football League game: 7 September, 1901, Division 2, v Blackpool (a) W 2-0 – Moles; Tuft, Davies; Jones, McLean, Chambers; Bradbury, Connor, Boucher, O'Brien (2), Flynn.

Did you know: When City were first promoted from the Second Division in 1905–06, it was the only campaign in which as many as three of their players scored 20 or more League goals in a season – William Maxwell 25, Walter Bennett and Sammy Gilligan 20 each.

Managers (and Secretary-managers)
Sam Hollis 1897–99, Bob Campbell 1899–1901, Sam Hollis 1901–05, Harry Thickett 1905–10, Sam Hollis 1911–13, George Hedley 1913–15, Jack Hamilton 1915–19, Joe Palmer 1919–21, Alex Raisbeck 1921–29, Joe Bradshaw 1929–32, Bob Hewison 1932–49 (under suspension 1938–39), Bob Wright 1949–50, Pat Beasley 1950–58, Peter Doherty 1958–60, Fred Ford 1960–67, Alan Dicks 1967–80, Bobby Houghton 1980–82, Roy Hodgson 1982, Terry Cooper 1982–88 (Director from 1983), Joe Jordan 1988–90, Jimmy Lumsden 1990–92, Denis Smith March 1992–.

Player and Position	Ht	Wt	Birth Date	Birth Place	Source	Clubs	League App	League Gls
Terry Connor	5 9	11 08	9 11 62	Leeds	Apprentice	Leeds U	96	19
						Brighton & HA	156	51
						Portsmouth	48	12
						Swansea	33	5
						Bristol C	—	—
						Bristol C	—	—
						Bristol C	11	1
Jacki Dziekanowski	6 1	12 13	30 9 62	Warsaw	Legia Warsaw	Celtic	49	10
						Bristol C	34	8
Mark Gavin	5 8	10 07	10 12 63	Bailleston	Apprentice	Leeds U	30	3
						Hartlepool U (loan)	7	—
						Carlisle U	13	1
						Bolton W	49	3
						Rochdale	23	6
						Hearts	9	—
						Bristol C	69	6
						Watford	13	—
						Bristol C	14	1
Jim McIntyre	5 11	11 05	24 5 72	Dumbarton	Duntocher B	Bristol C	1	—
Nicky Morgan	5 10	12 08	30 10 59	East Ham	Apprentice	West Ham U	21	2
						Portsmouth	95	32
						Stoke C	88	21
						Bristol C	70	20
Leroy Rosenior	6 1	11 10	24 3 64	London	School	Fulham	54	16
						QPR	38	7
						Fulham	34	20
						West Ham U	53	15
						Fulham (loan)	11	3
						Charlton Ath (loan)	3	—
						Bristol C	8	5
Deion Vernon	5 11	11 07	7 3 73	Bristol	Trainee	Bristol C	—	—

Trainees
Benton, Stephen; Bessell, Wayne A; Durbin, Gary J; Fowler, Jason K. G; Hicks, Nathan J; Hogg, Andrew K; Kennedy, Paul; Limna, James A; Lumsden, Jamie; Mark, Jonathan; Milsom, Paul J; Skidmore, Robert J; Steadman, Matthew; Wyatt, Michael J.

Associated Schoolboys
Barclay, Dominic A; Barnes, John P; Bendon, Jody; Carey, Louis A; Carree, Nicholas W; Dallimore, Ian V; Farrow, Marcus W; Gitsham, Scott; Haines, Daniel C; Hewitt, Richard D; Horne, Stuart; Huggins, Dean; Jacobs, Kristen; Lewis, Kristian C; Parrott, Lee; Peebles, Ross; Pettitt, David M; Ponfield, Stuart; Richards, Mark D; Rudge, Nicholas S; Simmonds, Dean; Warner, Phillip G; Williams, Simon K.

Associated Schoolboys who have accepted the club's offer of a Traineeship/Contract
Donaldson, Michael I; Licata, Guiseppe; Westlake, Andrew E.

114

BRISTOL ROVERS 1991–92   *Back row (left to right):* Marcus Stewart, Ian Hazel, Billy Clark, Ian Willmott, Marcus Browning, Devon White, David Mehew, Lee Maddison.
Centre row: Dennis Rofe (Chief Coach), Roy Dolling (Physiotherapist), Andy Reece, Brian Parkin, Bob Bloomer, Gavin Kelly, David Wilson, Ray Kendall (Kit Manager), Martin
Steve Yates, Richard Evans.
Dobson (Manager).
Front row: Phil Purnell, Adrian Boothroyd, Carl Saunders, Geoff Twentyman, Tony Pounder, Ian Alexander, Lee Archer, Paul Chenoweth.

Division 1   **BRISTOL ROVERS**

Twerton Park, Twerton, Bath. Telephone: 0272 352508. Training ground: 0272 861743. Match day ticket office: 0225 312327. Offices: 199 Two Mile Road, Kingswood, Bristol BS15 1AZ. (0272) 352303. Pirates Hotline 0898 338345.

Ground capacity: 9464.

Record attendance: 9464 v Liverpool, FA Cup 4th rd, 8 February 1992 (Twerton Park). 38,472 v Preston NE, FA Cup 4th rd, 30 January 1960.

Record receipts: £62,480 v Liverpool, FA Cup 4th rd, 8 February 1992.

Pitch measurements: 110yd × 75yd.

President: Marquis of Worcester.

Vice-Presidents: Dr W. T. Cussen, A. I. Seager, H. E. L. Brown, R. Redmond.

Chairman: D. H. A. Dunford.

Vice-chairman: G. M. H. Dunford.

Directors: R. Craig, V. Stokes (managing director in charge of administration), R. Andrews.

Manager: Dennis Rofe. *Coach:* Des Bulpin. *Physio:* Roy Dolling. *Youth team coach:* Tony Gill. *Commercial Manager:* A. Wood. *Secretary:* R. C. Twyford. *Assistant:* I. M. Wilson. Office Manager: Mrs Angela Mann.

Year Formed: 1883. Turned Professional: 1897. Ltd Co.: 1896.

Former Grounds: Purdown, Three Acres, Ashley Hill, Rudgeway, Eastville.

Former Names: 1883, Black Arabs; 1884, Eastville Rovers; 1897, Bristol Eastville Rovers; 1898, Bristol Rovers.

Club Nickname: 'Pirates'.

Record League Victory: 7-0 v Brighton & HA, Division 3 (S), 29 November 1952 – Hoyle; Bamford, Geoff Fox; Pitt, Warren, Sampson; McIlvenny, Roost (2), Lambden (1), Bradford (1), Peterbridge (2). (1 og). 7-0 v Swansea T, Division 2, 2 October 1954 – Radford; Bamford, Watkins; Pitt, Muir, Anderson; Petherbridge, Bradford (2), Meyer, Roost (1), Hooper (2). (2 ogs). 7-0 v Shrewsbury T, Division 3, 21 March 1964 – Hall; Hillard, Gwyn Jones; Oldfield, Stone (1), Mabbutt; Jarman (2), Brown (1), Biggs (1p), Hamilton, Bobby Jones (2).

Record Cup Victory: 6-0 v Merthyr Tydfil, FA Cup, 1st rd, 14 November 1987 – Martyn; Alexander (Dryden), Tanner, Hibbitt, Twentyman, Jones, Holloway, Meacham (1), White (2), Penrice (3) (Reece), Purnell.

Record Defeat: 0-12 v Luton T, Division 3 (S), 13 April 1936.

Most League Points (2 for a win): 64, Division 3 (S), 1952–53.

Most League points (3 for a win): 93, Division 3, 1989–90.

Most League Goals: 92, Division 3 (S), 1952–53.

Highest League Scorer in Season: Geoff Bradford, 33, Division 3 (S), 1952–53.

Most League Goals in Total Aggregate: Geoff Bradford, 245, 1949–64.

Most Capped Player: Neil Slatter, 10 (22), Wales.

Most League Appearances: Stuart Taylor, 545, 1966–80.

Record Transfer Fee Received: £1,000,000 from Crystal Palace for Nigel Martyn, November 1989.

Record Transfer Fee Paid: £130,000 to Fulham for Justin Skinner, August 1991.

Football League Record: 1920 Original Member of Division 3; 1921–53 Division 3 (S); 1953–62 Division 2; 1962–74 Division 3; 1974–81 Division 2; 1981–90 Division 3; 1990–92 Division 2; 1992– Division 1.

Honours: Football League: Division 2 best season: 6th, 1955–56, 1958–59; Division 3 (S) – Champions 1952–53; Division 3 – Champions 1989–90; Runners-up 1973–74. *FA Cup:* best season: 6th rd, 1950–51, 1957–58. *Football League Cup:* best season: 5th rd, 1970–71, 1971–72.

Colours: Blue and white quartered shirts, white shorts, blue stockings with two white rings on top. **Change colours:** Yellow shirts, blue shorts, yellow stockings.

BRISTOL ROVERS 1991-92 LEAGUE RECORD

Match No.	Date		Venue	Opponents	Result		H/T Score	Lg. Pos.	Goalscorers	Atten-dance
1	Aug	17	H	Ipswich T	D	3-3	1-1	—	Stewart, White 2	6444
2		23	A	Tranmere R	D	2-2	1-1	—	Stewart 2 (1 pen)	10,150
3		31	H	Newcastle U	L	1-2	0-1	20	Skinner	6334
4	Sep	4	A	Bristol C	L	0-1	0-0	—		20,183
5		7	H	Grimsby T	L	2-3	0-1	22	White, Evans	4641
6		14	A	Southend U	L	0-2	0-0	23		4670
7		17	A	Swindon T	L	0-1	0-1	23		11,391
8		21	H	Oxford U	W	2-1	0-0	24	Alexander, Cross	4854
9		28	A	Brighton & HA	L	1-3	1-1	24	Saunders	6392
10	Oct	5	H	Middlesbrough	W	2-1	0-1	21	Reece, Twentyman	4936
11		12	A	Charlton Ath	L	0-1	0-0	23		5685
12		19	H	Plymouth Arg	D	0-0	0-0	23		5049
13		26	A	Sunderland	D	1-1	1-1	22	Reece	14,746
14	Nov	2	H	Port Vale	D	3-3	2-1	24	Saunders 2, Skinner	3565
15		5	A	Wolverhampton W	W	3-2	1-1	—	Reece, Pounder, Saunders	8536
16		9	A	Barnsley	W	1-0	0-0	22	Reece	6688
17		16	H	Watford	D	1-1	1-1	22	Saunders	5064
18		20	A	Leicester C	D	1-1	0-1	—	Mehew	10,095
19		23	A	Derby Co	L	2-3	2-1	22	Cross, Mehew	6513
20		30	A	Millwall	W	1-0	1-0	21	Mehew	7824
21	Dec	7	H	Cambridge U	D	2-2	2-1	20	Mehew, White	5280
22		14	A	Blackburn R	L	0-3	0-3	22		12,295
23		21	H	Bristol C	W	3-2	2-1	18	White, Pounder, Saunders	6306
24		26	A	Portsmouth	L	0-2	0-1	19		10,710
25		28	A	Newcastle U	L	1-2	1-0	21	White	19,329
26	Jan	1	H	Leicester C	D	1-1	1-1	21	Saunders	6673
27		11	H	Tranmere R	W	1-0	0-0	18	Stewart	7138
28		18	A	Ipswich T	L	0-1	0-0	20		10,435
29		29	H	Portsmouth	W	1-0	1-0	—	White	5330
30	Feb	1	A	Plymouth Arg	D	0-0	0-0	15		6631
31		8	H	Sunderland	W	2-1	0-0	15	Saunders 2 (1 pen)	6318
32		15	A	Derby Co	L	0-1	0-0	15		11,154
33		22	H	Millwall	W	3-2	1-1	14	White, Mehew, Barber (og)	5747
34		28	A	Cambridge U	L	1-6	1-1	—	Heaney (og)	6164
35	Mar	7	H	Blackburn R	W	3-0	2-0	15	Mehew 2, White	6313
36		11	A	Wolverhampton W	D	1-1	0-0	—	White	6968
37		14	A	Port Vale	W	1-0	1-0	14	Saunders	5861
38		21	H	Barnsley	D	0-0	0-0	15		5665
39		28	A	Watford	L	0-1	0-0	16		7496
40	Apr	1	H	Southend U	W	4-1	0-1	—	Mehew, Stewart, Skinner, Taylor	5375
41		4	A	Grimsby T	W	1-0	1-0	12	Taylor	4859
42		12	H	Swindon T	D	1-1	0-0	—	Clark	6905
43		18	A	Oxford U	D	2-2	0-2	15	Taylor, Pounder	6891
44		20	H	Brighton & HA	W	4-1	2-0	12	Pounder, Taylor 3	6092
45		25	A	Middlesbrough	L	1-2	1-0	13	Taylor	14,057
46	May	2	H	Charlton Ath	W	1-0	0-0	13	Mehew	7630

Final League Position: 13

GOALSCORERS

League (60): Saunders 10 (1 pen), White 10, Mehew 9, Taylor 7, Stewart 5 (1 pen), Pounder 4, Reece 4, Skinner 3, Cross 2, Alexander 1, Clark 1, Evans 1, Twentyman 1, own goals 2.
Rumbelows Cup (5): Mehew 2, White 2, own goal 1.
FA Cup (7): Saunders 6, Alexander 1.

Parkin	Alexander	Twentyman	Yates	Mehew	Boothroyd	Evans	Reece	White	Stewart	Pounder	Purnell	Clark	Willmott	Wilson	Skinner	Archer	Saunders	Cross	Browning	Jones	Kelly	Moore	Maddison	Bloomer	Taylor G.	Hopkins	Taylor J.	Match No.
1	2	3	4	5	6	7*	8	9	10	11	12																	1
1			4	5*	2		8	9	10	11	12	3	6	7														2
1		3	4	5†	2		8	9	10	11	12		6	7*	14													3
1		3	4		2		8	9	10	11		5		7*	6	12												4
1	2	3	4	5	6*		8	9	10	11†					7	14	12											5
1	2	3	4		14		8	9	10	7*		5†	11	12	6													6
1	2	3	4					9		11		5		7*	6		10	8	12									7
1	2	3	4	7				9*		11		5				14	10	8	12	6†								8
1	2	3	4	7*				9		11		5			6		10	8	12									9
1	2	3	4	7			8	9		11					6		10*	5	12									10
1	2	3	4	7			8	9		11	12				6*			5	10									11
1	2	3	4	7			8	9*		11	12				6			5	10									12
1	2	3	4	7			8	9	12	11					6			5	10*									13
1		3	4	7*	2		8	9		11	12				6		10	5										14
1	2	3	4	7			8	9		11					6		10	5										15
1	2	3	4	7			8	9		11					6		10	5										16
1	2	3	4	7			8	9	12	11*					6		10	5										17
1	2	3	4	7			8	9	12	11					6		10*	5										18
1	2	3	4	7*			8	9	12	11†		14			6		10	5										19
1	2	3	4	7*			8	9		11	12				6		10	5										20
	2*	3	4	7			8	9		11	12				6		10	5			1							21
	2	3	4	7†	14		8	9	12	11*					6		10	5			1							22
	2	3	4	7			8	9		11					6		10	5			1							23
1	2	3	4	7†	14		8	9	12	11*					6		10	5										24
1	2	3	4	7			8	9	12	11					6		10	5*										25
1	2	3	4	7			8	9		11					6		10	5										26
1	2		4				8			11	12				6		10	7	9*			3		5				27
1	2		4				8			11†	12				6		10	7	9			3		5*	14			28
1	2		4	7			8	9*	12	11		5			6†		10		14			3						29
1	2		4	7			8	9		11					6		10					3		5				30
1	2			7†	14		8	9	12	11*		4			6		10	5				3						31
1	2			7			8	9	12	11		4			6		10*	5				3						32
1	2			7			8	9	12	11*		4			6		10	5				3						33
1	2			7†			8	9	12	11*		4			6		10	5	14							3		34
1	2			7			8	9		11		4			6		10	5								3		35
1	2			7			8	9	12	11*		4			6		10	5								3		36
1	2			7*			8	9		11		4			6		10	5					12			3		37
1	2			7*				9	12	11		4			6		10	8†	14					5		3		38
1	2		4	7			8		12	11*		3			6				14				5†				9	39
1	2		4	7			8		10*	11		3			6		12						5				9	40
1	2		4	7			8		10*	11†		3			6		12						5	14			9	41
1	2		4	7†			8		12	11*		3			6		10						5	14			9	42
1	2		4	7			8		10	11		3			6*								5	12			9	43
1	2		4	7			8		10†	11		3			6				14				5*	12			9	44
1	2		4	7			8		10*	11†		3			6				14				5				9	45
1	2		4	7			8		10	11		3			6								5				9	46
43	41	25	39	37	8	2	42	35	17	38	5	22	2	3	41	3	31	31	5	1	3	7	8	4	1	4	8	
				+5s					+16s	+2s	+7s	+2s			+1s	+2s	+5s	+1s	+6s				+2s	+5s		+2s		

Rumbelows Cup	Second Round	Bristol C (h)	1-3
		(a)	4-2
	Third Round	Nottingham F (a)	0-2
FA Cup	Third Round	Plymouth Arg (h)	5-0
	Fourth Round	Liverpool (h)	1-1
		(a)	1-2

BRISTOL ROVERS

Player and Position	Ht	Wt	Birth Date	Birth Place	Source	Clubs	League App	Gls
Goalkeepers								
Gavin Kelly	6 0	12 13	29 9 68	Beverley		Hull C	11	—
						Bristol R (loan)	—	—
						Bristol R	10	—
Brian Parkin	6 3	13 00	12 10 65	Birkenhead	Local	Oldham Ath	6	—
						Crewe Alex (loan)	12	—
						Crewe Alex	86	—
						Crystal Palace (loan)	—	—
						Crystal Palace	20	—
						Bristol R	112	—
Defenders								
Bob Bloomer*	5 10	11 06	21 6 66	Sheffield		Chesterfield	141	15
						Bristol R	22	—
Adrian Boothroyd	5 8	10 12	8 2 77	Bradford	Trainee	Huddersfield T	10	—
						Bristol R	16	—
Billy Clark	6 0	12 03	19 5 67	Christchurch	Local	Bournemouth	4	—
						Bristol R	80	3
Jeff Hopkins	6 1	11 11	14 4 64	Swansea	Apprentice	Fulham	219	4
						Crystal Palace	70	2
						Bristol R	6	—
						Plymouth Arg (loan)	8	—
Vaughan Jones	5 8	11 11	2 9 59	Tonyrefail	Apprentice	Bristol R	101	3
						Newport Co	68	4
						Cardiff C	11	—
						Bristol R	268	9
Lee Maddison	5 11	11 00	5 10 72	Bristol	Trainee	Bristol R	10	—
Gareth Taylor	6 02	12 05	25 2 73	Weston Super Mare	Trainee	Southampton	—	—
						Bristol R	1	—
Geoff Twentyman	6 1	13 02	10 3 59	Liverpool	Chorley	Preston NE	98	4
						Bristol R	244	6
Ian Willmott‡	5 10	12 06	10 7 68	Bristol	Weston Super Mare	Bristol R	22	—
Steven Yates	5 11	12 06	29 1 70	Bristol	Trainee	Bristol R	152	—
Midfield								
Ian Alexander	5 8	10 07	26 1 63	Glasgow	Leicester Juv	Rotherham U	11	—
						Pezoporikos	—	—
						Motherwell	24	2
						Morton	7	1
						Bristol R	232	5
Lee Archer	5 6	9 04	6 11 72	Bristol	Trainee	Bristol R	5	—
Paul Chenoweth	5 4	8 0	5 2 73	Bristol	Trainee	Southampton	—	—
						Bristol R	—	—
						Bristol R	—	—
Steve Cross	5 10	11 05	22 12 59	Wolverhampton	Apprentice	Shrewsbury T	262	34
						Derby Co	73	3
						Bristol R	32	2
Andy Reece	5 11	12 04	5 9 62	Shrewsbury	Willenhall	Bristol R	213	15
Justin Skinner	6 0	11 03	30 1 69	London	Apprentice	Fulham	135	23
						Bristol R	42	3
David Wilson	5 9	10 10	20 3 69	Burnley	Apprentice	Manchester U	4	—
						Charlton Ath (loan)	7	2
						Lincoln C (loan)	3	—
						Bristol R	3	—
Forwards								
Marcus Browning	5 11	12 00	22 4 71	Bristol	Trainee	Bristol R	12	—
Richard Evans	5 11	11 07	12 4 68	Ebbw Vale	Weymouth	Bristol R	2	1

BRISTOL ROVERS

Foundation: Bristol Rovers were formed at a meeting in Stapleton Road, Eastville, in 1883. However, they first went under the name of the Black Arabs (wearing black shirts). Changing their name to Eastville Rovers in their second season, they won the Gloucestershire Senior Cup in 1888–89. Original members of the Bristol & District League in 1892, this eventually became the Western League and Eastville Rovers adopted professionalism in 1897.

First Football League game: 28 August, 1920, Division 3, v Millwall (a) L 0-2 – Stansfield; Bethune, Panes; Boxley, Kenny, Steele; Chance, Bird, Sims, Bell, Palmer.

Did you know: When drawn away to RA Portsmouth in the FA Cup in November 1896, Bristol Rovers decided that their chances were so poor that they scratched from the competition. RA Portsmouth were FA Amateur Cup finalists that year and one of the strongest sides in the south of England.

Managers (and Secretary-managers)
Alfred Homer 1899–1920 (continued as secretary to 1928), Ben Hall 1920–21, Andy Wilson 1921–26, Joe Palmer 1926–29, Dave McLean 1929–30, Albert Prince-Cox 1930–36, Percy Smith 1936–37, Brough Fletcher 1938–49, Bert Tann 1950–68 (continued as GM to 1972), Fred Ford 1968–69, Bill Dodgin Snr 1969–72, Don Megson 1972–77, Bobby Campbell 1978–79, Harold Jarman 1979–80, Terry Cooper 1980–81, Bobby Gould 1981–83, David Williams 1983–85, Bobby Gould 1985–87, Gerry Francis 1987–91, Martin Dobson 1991–92, Dennis Rofe January 1992–.

Player and Position	Ht	Wt	Date	Birth Place	Source	Clubs	League App	Gls
Michael Knop*			29 12 71	Northwich	Trainee	Leeds U	—	—
						Bristol R	—	—
David Mehew	5 11	11 07	29 10 67	Camberley		Leeds U	—	—
						Bristol R	198	60
Paul Nixon‡	5 10	11 03	23 09 63	Seaham	New Zealand	Bristol R	44	6
Tony Pounder	5 8	11 00	11 3 66	Yeovil	Weymouth	Bristol R	85	7
Philip Purnell	5 8	10 02	16 9 64	Bristol	Mangotsfield	Bristol R	153	22
						Swansea C (loan)	5	1
Carl Saunders	5 8	10 12	25 11 64	Marston Green	Local	Stoke C	164	23
						Bristol R	94	31
Marcus Stewart	5 10	10 03	7 11 72	Bristol	Trainee	Bristol R	33	5
John Taylor	6 2	11 12	24 10 64	Norwich	Local	Colchester U	—	—
						Sudbury	—	—
						Cambridge U	160	46
						Bristol R	8	7

Trainees
Bennett, Anthony P; Crossey, Scott; Elliott, Dean M; Gurney, Andrew R; Impey, Scott; Paul, Martin L; Smith, Ian S; Stewart, Andrew W; Thomas, Spencer P; Tovey, Paul W.

**Non-Contract
Stevens, Mark.

Associated Schoolboys
French, Jonathan; Hamer, Rhys A; Harris, Paul; Long, Christopher C; Parkinson, Matthew S; Rogers, Stuart.

Associated Schoolboys who have accepted the club's offer of a Traineeship/Contract
Harrington, Mark P; Micciche, Marco.

**Non-Contract Players who are retained must be re-signed before they are eligible to play in League matches.

BURNLEY 1991–92 *Back row (left to right):* Andy Farrell, Mike Conroy, David Williams, Chris Pearce, Ian Walsh, Paul France, Roger Eli.
Centre row: Paul McKay, John Francis, Steve Harper, Danny Sonner, Steve Davis, Ian Measham, Jason Hardy, John Deary.
Front row: Joe Jakub, Graham Lancashire, Peter Mumby, David Hamilton, John Pender, Ian Bray, Neil Howarth, Mark Monington.

Division 2   **BURNLEY**

Turf Moor, Burnley BB10 4BX. Telephone Burnley (0282) 27777. Clubcall: 0898 121153.

Ground capacity: 20,912.

Record attendance: 54,775 v Huddersfield T, FA Cup 3rd rd, 23 February 1924.

Record receipts: £63,988 v Sheffield W, FA Cup 6th rd, 12 March 1983.

Pitch measurements: 115yd × 73yd.

Chairman: F. J. Teasdale.

Vice-chairman: Dr R. D. Iven MRCS (Eng), LRCP (Lond), MRCGP.

Directors: B. Dearing LLB, B. Rothwell JP, C. Holt, R. Blakeborough.

Manager: Jimmy Mullen. *Secretary:* Mark Blackbourne. *Youth Team Coach:* Harry Wilson. *Commercial Manager:* Cynthia Haworth. *Physio:* Jimmy Holland. *Year Formed:* 1882. Turned Professional: 1883. Ltd Co.: 1897. *Former Grounds:* 1881, Calder Vale; 1882, Turf Moor. *Former Names:* 1881–82, Burnley Rovers. *Club Nickname:* 'The Clarets'.

Record League Victory: 9-0 v Darwen, Division 1; 9 January 1892 – Hillman; Walker, McFettridge, Lang, Matthew, Keenan, Nicol (3), Bowes, Espie (1), McLardie (3), Hill (2).

Record Cup Victory: 9-0 v Crystal Palace, FA Cup, 2nd rd (replay) 10 February 1909 – Dawson; Barron, McLean; Cretney (2), Leake, Moffat; Morley, Ogden, Smith (3), Abbott (2), Smethams (1). 9-0 v New Brighton, FA Cup, 4th rd, 26 January 1957 – Blacklaw; Angus, Winton; Seith, Adamson, Miller; Newlands (1), McIlroy (3), Lawson (3), Cheesebrough (1), Pilkington (1). 9-0 v Penrith FA Cup, 1st rd, 17 November 1984 – Hansbury; Miller, Hampton, Phelan, Overson (Kennedy), Hird (3 incl. 1p), Grewcock (1), Powell (2), Taylor (3), Biggins, Hutchison.

Record Defeat: 0-10 v Aston Villa, Division 1, 29 August 1925 and v Sheffield U, Division 1, 19 January 1929.

Most League Points (2 for a win): 62, Division 2, 1972–73.

Most League points (3 for a win): 83, Division 4, 1991–92.

Most League Goals: 102, Division 1, 1960–61.

Highest League Scorer in Season: George Beel, 35, Division 1, 1927–28.

Most League Goals in Total Aggregate: George Beel, 178, 1923–32.

Most Capped Player: Jimmy McIlroy, 51 (55), Northern Ireland.

Most League Appearances: Jerry Dawson, 522, 1907–28.

Record Transfer Fee Received: £300,000 from Everton for Martin Dobson, August 1974, and from Derby Co for Leighton James, November 1975.

Record Transfer Fee Paid: £165,000 to QPR for Leighton James, September 1978.

Football League Record: 1888 Original Member of the Football League; 1897–98 Division 2; 1898–1900 Division 1; 1900–13 Division 2; 1913–30 Division 1; 1930–47 Division 2; 1947–71 Division 1; 1971–73 Division 2; 1973–76 Division 1; 1976–80 Division 2; 1980–82 Division 3; 1982–83 Division 2; 1983–85 Division 3; 1985–92 Division 4; 1992– Division 2.

Honours: Football League: Division 1 – Champions 1920–21, 1959–60; Runners-up 1919–20, 1961–62; Division 2 – Champions 1897–98, 1972–73; Runners-up 1912–13, 1946–47; Division 3 – Champions 1981–82; Division 4 – Champions 19 Record 30 consecutive 91–92; Division 1 games without defeat 1920–21. *FA Cup:* Winners 1913–14; Runners-up 1946–47, 1961–62. *Football League Cup:* semi-final 1960–61, 1968–69, 1982–83. *Anglo Scottish Cup:* Winners 1978–79. *Sherpa Van Trophy:* Runners-up 1988. **European Competitions:** *European Cup:* 1960–61. *European Fairs Cup:* 1966–67.

Colours: Claret shirts with sky blue sleeves, white shorts and stockings. **Change colours:** All white with claret facings.

BURNLEY 1991–92 LEAGUE RECORD

Match No.	Date		Venue	Opponents	Result		H/T Score	Lg. Pos.	Goalscorers	Attendance
1	Aug	17	A	Rotherham U	L	1-2	1-0	—	Conroy	6042
2		31	A	Doncaster R	W	4-1	1-1	3	Conroy 2 (1 pen), Harper, Yates	2940
3	Sep	3	H	Chesterfield	W	3-0	1-0	—	Eli 3	6647
4		7	H	Crewe Alex	D	1-1	0-0	2	Francis	9657
5		14	A	Hereford U	L	0-2	0-1	8		4400
6		21	H	Rochdale	L	0-1	0-0	10		8633
7		28	A	Scarborough	L	1-3	1-2	11	Lancashire	2596
8	Oct	5	H	Carlisle U	W	2-0	1-0	11	Pender, Lancashire	6157
9		12	A	Wrexham	W	6-2	4-2	8	Lancashire 3, Harper, Davis, Eli	3181
10		19	H	Walsall	W	2-0	2-0	7	Davis (pen), Lancashire	7289
11		26	A	Lincoln C	W	3-0	1-0	7	Francis, Conroy (pen), Lancashire	3235
12	Nov	2	A	Halifax T	W	2-0	0-0	3	Deary, Farrell	4491
13		5	H	York C	W	3-1	2-1	—	Conroy, Deary, Lancashire	7389
14		9	H	Mansfield T	W	3-2	1-1	3	Conroy (pen), Davis, Pender	11,848
15		23	A	Maidstone U	W	1-0	1-0	3	Conroy (pen)	2375
16		30	A	Northampton T	W	2-1	1-0	2	Conroy 2	4020
17	Dec	14	H	Scunthorpe U	D	1-1	1-0	2	Farrell	8419
18		26	H	Rotherham U	L	1-2	0-0	1	Francis	13,812
19		28	H	Doncaster R	W	2-1	2-0	1	Conroy, Eli	9605
20	Jan	1	A	Chesterfield	W	2-0	2-0	1	Deary, Francis	7789
21		11	A	Blackpool	L	2-5	0-2	2	Conroy, Francis	8007
22		18	H	Gillingham	W	4-1	1-1	1	Conroy 3, Randall	8908
23	Feb	1	A	Walsall	D	2-2	0-1	1	Eli, Conroy	5287
24		8	H	Lincoln C	W	1-0	1-0	1	Conroy	9748
25		11	H	Northampton T	W	5-0	1-0	—	Deary, Eli, Conroy, Harper, Francis	8825
26		15	A	Scunthorpe U	D	2-2	0-2	1	Conroy (pen), Davis	5303
27		22	H	Blackpool	D	1-1	1-1	1	Eli	18,183
28		29	A	Cardiff C	W	2-0	0-0	1	Randall, Conroy	16,030
29	Mar	3	A	Gillingham	L	0-3	0-1	—		3729
30		7	H	Barnet	W	3-0	1-0	1	Davis, Barnett (og), Deary	12,018
31		14	H	Halifax T	W	1-0	1-0	3	Pender	10,903
32		21	A	Mansfield T	W	1-0	1-0	2	Conroy	8336
33		24	A	Barnet	D	0-0	0-0	—		4881
34		28	H	Maidstone U	W	2-1	0-0	1	Davis, Eli	10,986
35		31	H	Hereford U	W	2-0	2-0	—	Monington, Conroy	10,578
36	Apr	4	A	Crewe Alex	L	0-1	0-0	1		5530
37		20	H	Scarborough	D	1-1	1-1	1	Eli	12,312
38		22	H	Cardiff C	W	3-1	1-1	—	Painter, Farrell, Conroy	12,408
39		25	A	Carlisle U	D	1-1	1-1	1	Francis	10,000
40		28	A	York C	W	2-1	0-1	—	Deary, Francis	7620
41	May	2	H	Wrexham	L	1-2	1-0	1	Conroy	21,216
42		5	A	Rochdale	W	3-1	2-1	—	Measham, Conroy, Painter	8175

Final League Position: 1

GOALSCORERS

League (79): Conroy 24 (5 pens), Eli 10, Francis 8, Lancashire 8, Davis 6 (1 pen), Deary 6, Farrell 3, Harper 3, Pender 3, Painter 2, Randall 2, Measham 1, Monington 1, Yates 1, own goals 1.
Rumbelows Cup (3): Conroy 1, Davis 1, own goal 1.
FA Cup (8): Harper 3, Eli 2, Conroy 1, Davis 1, Lancashire 1.

Pearce	Measham	Jakub	Deary	Pender	Monington	Farrell	Davis	Francis	Conroy	Harper	Hardy	Lancashire	Marriott	France	Bray	Yates	Eli	Hamilton	Sonner	Mumby	Randall	Kendall	Walker	Painter	Williams	McKenzie	Match No.
1	2	3	4	5	6	7	8	9†10		11*12		14															1
			8	5	6		4	9	10	14			1	2*	3†	7	11	12									2
			8	5	6		4	9	10	3			1			11	7	2									3
		8*	5		6	12	4	9	10	3			1			11	7	2									4
	12		5		6	11	4	9	10	3			1		14	8†	7	2*									5
	11	8	5		6	2		9	10		4		1		3*	7†12		14									6
	2	10	8	5	14	6	4			3			9*	1		12	11		7†								7
	2	10*	8	5		6	4			7			9†	1		3	12	11	14								8
		10	8	5	12	6	4			7			9*	1	2	3	11										9
		10	8	5		6	4	12		7			9	1	2	3*	11										10
	2	3	8	5		6	4	9	10	7						12	11*										11
		3	8	5		6	4	9	10	7			12	1	2		11*										12
		3	8	5		6	4	9	10*	7			11	1	2			12									13
		3	8	5		6	4	9*10		7			11	1	2		12										14
	2	3	8	5		6	4	9	10	7			1				11										15
	2	3	8			6	4	9	10	7			12	1		5	11*										16
1	2	3	8†	5		6	4	9	10	7			12			14	11*										17
1	2	3	8	5		6†	4	9	10	7			11*				12				14						18
1	2	3	8	5		6	4	9	10				12			14	11*				7†						19
	2	3	8	5		6	4	9	10*				12				11				7	1					20
	2	3	8	5		6	4	9	10	7*							11				12	1					21
1	2	3	8	5		6*	4	9	10	7			11†			14					12						22
1	2	3	8	5		6†	4	9	10	14			12				11*				7						23
1	2	3	8	5		6	4	9	10	7			12				11*										24
1	2	3	8	5		6†	4	9	10	7			12				11*				14						25
1	2	3	8	5		6*	4	9	10	7							11				12						26
	2	3	8	5		6*	4	9	10	7†			14				11				12	1					27
	2	3	8			5	4	9	10	7			12				11*				6	1					28
	2	3	8			5	4	9	10	7*			12			14	11				6†	1					29
	2	3	8	5		6	4*	9	10	7							11				12	1					30
	2	3	8	5	12		4		9	10	7*		11								6	1					31
		3	8	5		2	4	9	10	7							11				6	1					32
1		3	8	5		2	4	9	10	7			12				11*				6						33
1		3	8	5		2	4	9*10		7†						14	12				6			11			34
1		3		5	6	2	4		10				12				8	11*			7			9			35
1		3	8	5	6	2	4		10*				12				7	11						9			36
1	2	3	8	5		6	4	9	10	12							11*							7			37
	2	3	8	5		6	4	9	10	12							11*							7	1		38
	2	3	8	5		6	4	9	10	11*							7							1	12		39
	2	3	8	5		6	4	9	10	11*							7							1	12		40
	2	3	8	5	12	6†	4	9	10				14				7							1	11*		41
	2	3	8	5			4	9	10	11			6											7*	1	12	42
14	27	38	40	39	8 +1s	38 +4s +1s	40	36 +1s	38	31 +4s	2 +1s	9 +16s	15	6 +1s	5 +8s	9 +4s	29 +1s	3 +3s	—	1	11 +7s	2	6	9	5	1 +3s	

Rumbelows Cup First Round Wigan Ath (a) 1-3
                                               (h) 2-3

FA Cup First Round Doncaster R (h) 1-1
                                               (a) 3-1
                Second Round Rotherham U (h) 2-0
                Third Round Derby Co (h) 2-2
                                               (a) 0-2

BURNLEY

Player and Position	Ht	Wt	Date	Birth Place	Source	Clubs	League App	Gls
Goalkeepers								
Chris Pearce*	6 0	11 04	7 8 61	Newport	Apprentice	Wolverhampton W	—	—
						Blackburn R	—	—
						Rochdale (loan)	5	—
						Barnsley (loan)	—	—
						Rochdale	36	—
						Port Vale	48	—
						Wrexham	25	—
						Burnley	181	—
Nicky Walker On loan from Aberdeen						Burnley	6	—
Ian Walsh*	5 11	11 02	16 8 73	Southport	Trainee	Everton	—	—
						Burnley	—	—
David Williams	6 0	12 00	18 9 68	Liverpool	Trainee	Oldham Ath	—	—
						Burnley	22	—
						Rochdale (loan)	7	—
Defenders								
Ian Bray*	5 8	11 05	6 12 62	Neath	Apprentice	Hereford U	108	4
						Huddersfield T	89	1
						Burnley	17	—
Steve Davis	6 2	12 08	30 10 68	Hexham	Trainee	Southampton	6	—
						Burnley (loan)	9	—
						Notts Co (loan)	2	—
						Burnley	40	6
Roger Eli	5 10	12 00	11 9 65	Bradford	Apprentice	Leeds U	2	—
						Wolverhampton W	18	—
						Cambridge U	—	—
						Crewe Alex	27	1
						York C	4	1
						Bury	2	—
						Burnley	88	20
Paul France*	6 1	11 08	10 9 68	Huddersfield	Trainee	Huddersfield T	11	—
						Cobh Ramblers (loan)	—	—
						Bristol C	—	—
						Burnley	8	—
Graham Lawrie‡	5 8	10 12	4 9 71	Aberdeen	Keith	Burnley	—	—
Paul McKay	5 8	10 05	28 1 71	Banbury	Trainee	Burnley	12	—
Ian Measham	5 11	11 08	14 12 64	Barnsley	Apprentice	Huddersfield T	17	—
						Lincoln C (loan)	6	—
						Rochdale (loan)	12	—
						Cambridge U	46	—
						Burnley	137	2
John Pender	6 0	12 07	19 11 63	Luton	Apprentice	Wolverhampton W	117	3
						Charlton Ath	41	—
						Bristol C	83	3
						Burnley	79	3
Midfield								
John Deary	5 10	11 11	18 10 62	Ormskirk	Apprentice	Blackpool	303	43
						Burnley	124	15
Andy Farrell	5 11	11 00	7 10 65	Colchester	School	Colchester U	105	5
						Burnley	193	14
David Hamilton*	5 6	10 00	7 11 60	South Shields	Apprentice	Sunderland	—	—
						Blackburn R	114	7
						Cardiff C (loan)	10	—
						Wigan Ath	103	7
						Chester C	28	—
						Burnley	15	—
Jason Hardy*	5 8	10 00	14 12 69	Burnley	Trainee	Burnley	43	1
						Halifax T (loan)	4	—

BURNLEY

Foundation: The majority of those responsible for the formation of the Burnley club in 1881 were from the defunct rugby club Burnley Rovers. Indeed, they continued to play rugby for a year before changing to soccer and dropping "Rovers" from their name. The changes were decided at a meeting held in May 1882 at the Bull Hotel.

First Football League game: 8 September, 1888, Football League, v PNE (a), L 2-5 – Smith; Lang, Bury, Abrams, Friel, Keenan, Brady, Tait, Poland (1), Gallocher (1), Yates.

Did you know: In winning promotion to the First Division in 1972–73, Burnley called on only 17 players, a club record. No less than six were ever-present – Alan Stevenson, Keith Newton, Colin Waldron, Jimmy Thomson, Frank Casper and Leighton James.

Managers (and Secretary-managers)
Arthur F. Sutcliffe 1893–96*, Harry Bradshaw 1896–99*, Ernest Mangall 1899–1903*, Spen Whittaker 1903–10, R. H. Wadge 1910*, John Haworth 1910–24, Albert Pickles 1925–32, Tom Bromilow 1932–35, Alf Boland 1935–39*, Cliff Britton 1945–48, Frank Hill 1948–54, Allan Brown 1954–57, Billy Dougall 1957–58, Harry Potts 1958–70 (GM to 1972), Jimmy Adamson 1970–76, Joe Brown 1976–77, Harry Potts 1977–79, Brian Miller 1979–83, John Bond 1983–84, John Benson 1984–85, Martin Buchan 1985, Tommy Cavanagh 1985–86, Brian Miller 1986–89, Frank Casper 1989–91, Jimmy Mullen October 1991–.

Neil Howarth			15 11 71	Farnworth	Trainee	Burnley	1	—
Joe Jakub	5 6	9 06	7 12 56	Falkirk	Apprentice	Burnley	42	—
						Bury	265	27
						AZ 67	—	—
						Chester C	42	1
						Burnley	131	8
Paul McKenzie	5 09	11 10	4 10 69	Aberdeen	Peterhead	Burnley	4	—
Mark Monington	5 8	11 00	21 10 70	Bilsthorpe	School	Burnley	33	2
Robert Painter	5 11	11 00	26 1 71	Ince	Trainee	Chester C	84	8
						Maidstone U	30	5
						Burnley	9	2
Adrian Randall	5 11	11 00	10 11 68	Amesbury	Apprentice	Bournemouth	3	—
						Aldershot	107	12
						Burnley	18	2
Brian Welch	5 08	11 11	17 7 73	South Shields	Hebburn	Burnley	—	—
Forwards								
Mike Conroy	6 0	11 00	31 12 65	Glasgow	Apprentice	Coventry C	—	—
						Clydebank	114	38
						St Mirren	10	1
						Reading	80	7
						Burnley	38	24
John Francis	5 8	11 02	21 11 63	Dewsbury	Emley	Sheffield U	42	6
						Burnley	101	26
Steve Harper	5 10	11 05	3 2 69	Stoke	Trainee	Port Vale	28	2
						Preston NE	77	10
						Burnley	35	3
Graham Lancashire			19 10 72	Blackpool	Trainee	Burnley	26	8
Peter Mumby*	5 9	11 05	22 2 69	Bradford	Trainee	Leeds U	6	—
						Shamrock R (loan)	—	—
						Burnley	46	9
Danny Sonner			9 1 72	Wigan	Wigan Ath	Burnley	5	—
Mark Yates	5 11	11 09	24 1 70	Birmingham	Trainee	Birmingham C	54	6
						Burnley	17	1

Trainees
Anderson, Stuart P; Bowes, David; Brass, Christopher P; Dowell, Wayne A; King, Andrew R; Lawson, Andrew P; Livesey, David; Livingstone, Richard; Murray, Paul G; Parry, Christopher M; Peake, Warren C; Rahman, Jamalur; Ritchie, Murrey J; Robinson, Lee A; Vaughan, Paul; Wallace, Simon P; Weller, Paul.

Associated Schoolboys
Arthur, Paul M; Atkinson, Paul; Binningsley, David; Blakeston, Scott; McCluskey, Anthony; Mullin, John; Palmer, Carl E; Robinson, Lee J; Smith, Ian P; Stubbs, Jason E.

Associated Schoolboys who have accepted the club's offer of a Traineeship/Contract
Taylor, Matthew J.

126

BURY 1991–92   *Back row (left to right):* Pat Bradley, Ian Stevens, Darren Wilson, Michael Pollitt, Colin Greenall, Kevin Hulme.
Centre row: Jack Chapman (Assistant Manager), David Lee, Nigel Smith, Gary Kelly, Paul Robertson, Liam Robinson, Mandy Johnson (Physiotherapist).
Front row: Ronnie Mauge, Phil Parkinson, Peter Valentine, Mike Walsh (Manager), Alan Knill, Mark Kearney, Roger Stanislaus.

Division 3 **BURY**

Gigg Lane, Bury B19 9HR. Telephone 061-764 4881. Commercial Dept. 061-705 2144. Clubcall: 0898 121197. Community Programme: 061-797 5423. Social Club: 061-764 6771. Fax No: 061-764-5521

Ground capacity: 8337.

Record attendance: 35,000 v Bolton W, FA Cup 3rd rd, 9 January 1960.

Record receipts: £37,000 v Bolton W, Division 3 play-off, 19 May 1991.

Pitch measurements: 112yd × 72yd.

President.

Chief Executive/Chairman: T. Robinson.

Vice-chairman: Canon J. R. Smith MA.

Directors: C. H. Eaves, I. Pickup, J. Smith, A. Noonan, F. Mason.

Manager: Mike Walsh. *Assistant Manager:* Jack Chapman. *Physio:* Mandy Johnson. *Assistant secretary:* S. Atkinson. *Commercial Manager:* Neville Neville.

Year Formed: 1885. Turned Professional: 1885. Ltd Co.: 1897.

Club Nickname: 'Shakers'.

Club Sponsors: MacPherson Paints

Record League Victory: 8-0 v Tranmere R, Division 3, 10 January 1970 – Forrest; Tinney, Saile; Anderson, Turner, McDermott; Hince (1), Arrowsmith (1), Jones (4), Kerr (1), Grundy. (1 og).

Record Cup Victory: 12-1 v Stockton, FA Cup, 1st rd (replay), 2 February 1897 – Montgomery; Darroch, Barbour; Hendry (1), Clegg, Ross (1); Wylie (3), Pangbourn, Millar (4), Henderson (2), Plant. (1 og).

Record Defeat: 0-10 v Blackburn R, FA Cup, preliminary round, 1 October 1887 and v West Ham U, Milk Cup, 2nd rd, 2nd leg, 25 October 1983.

Most League Points (2 for a win): 68, Division 3, 1960–61.

Most League points (3 for a win): 84, Division 4, 1984–85.

Most League Goals: 108, Division 3, 1960–61.

Highest League Scorer in Season: Craig Madden, 35, Division 4, 1981–82.

Most League Goals in Total Aggregate: Craig Madden, 129, 1978–86.

Most Capped Player: Bill Gorman, 11 (13), Eire and (4), Northern Ireland.

Most League Appearances: Norman Bullock, 506, 1920–35.

Record Transfer Fee Received: £250,000 from Sheffield U for Jamie Hoyland, July 1990.

Record Transfer Fee Paid: £175,000 to Shrewsbury T for John McGinlay, July 1990.

Football League Record: 1894 Elected to Division 2; 1895–1912 Division 1; 1912–24 Division 2; 1924–29 Division 1; 1929–57 Division 2; 1957–61 Division 3; 1961–67 Division 2; 1967–68 Division 3; 1968–69 Division 2; 1969–71 Division 3; 1971–74 Division 4; 1974–80 Division 3; 1980–85 Division 4; 1985–Division 3.

Honours: Football League: Division 1 best season: 4th, 1925–26; Division 2 – Champions 1894–95; Runners-up 1923–24; Division 3 – Champions 1960–61; Runners-up 1967–68. *FA Cup:* Winners 1900, 1903. *Football League Cup:* Semi-final 1963.

Colours: White shirts, navy blue shorts, navy stockings. **Change colours:** Red shirts, white shorts, red stockings.

BURY 1991–92 LEAGUE RECORD

Match No.	Date		Venue	Opponents	Result		H/T Score	Lg. Pos.	Goalscorers	Attendance
1	Aug	17	A	Birmingham C	L	2-3	1-2	—	Lee (pen), Robinson	9033
2		24	H	Shrewsbury T	D	0-0	0-0	19		2373
3		31	A	Reading	L	2-3	0-1	22	Valentine, Smith	2886
4	Sep	3	H	Peterborough U	W	3-0	2-0	—	Robinson, Robinson (og), Stevens	2240
5		7	A	Hull C	W	1-0	1-0	9	Stevens	3679
6		14	H	Huddersfield T	D	4-4	4-1	10	Robinson, Greenall, Stevens, Smith	4409
7		17	H	Fulham	W	3-1	2-1	—	Valentine, Greenall, Robinson	2248
8		21	A	Stockport Co	L	0-2	0-0	9		5083
9		28	H	Hartlepool U	D	1-1	1-0	10	Greenall	2600
10	Oct	5	A	Darlington	W	2-0	1-0	7	Stevens 2	3006
11		12	H	Preston NE	L	2-3	2-1	10	Robinson, Greenall	4265
12		19	A	Exeter C	L	2-5	0-3	15	Robinson 2 (2 pen)	3904
13		26	H	Brentford	L	0-3	0-2	17		2280
14	Nov	2	A	WBA	D	1-1	1-0	17	Stevens	8439
15		5	H	Stoke C	L	1-3	1-1	—	Stevens	3245
16		9	H	Bolton W	D	1-1	0-1	19	Robinson	5886
17		22	A	Wigan Ath	L	0-2	0-1	—		2268
18		30	H	Bournemouth	L	0-1	0-1	21		1886
19	Dec	21	A	Shrewsbury T	D	1-1	1-1	21	Robinson	2573
20		26	H	Reading	L	0-1	0-0	22		2333
21		28	H	Birmingham C	W	1-0	0-0	20	Smith	4254
22	Jan	1	A	Peterborough U	D	0-0	0-0	21		5567
23		4	A	Bradford C	D	1-1	0-1	21	Stevens	6354
24		11	H	Swansea C	W	1-0	0-0	20	Wilson D	2161
25		18	A	Torquay U	W	2-0	1-0	15	Stevens, Stanislaus	2625
26	Feb	8	A	Brentford	W	3-0	2-0	18	Stanislaus, Hulme, Stevens	6789
27		11	A	Bournemouth	L	0-4	0-1	—		3558
28		15	H	Leyton Orient	W	4-2	3-0	16	Stevens 3, Hulme	2120
29		22	A	Swansea C	L	1-2	1-0	17	Greenall (pen)	2787
30		25	H	Chester C	L	1-2	1-2	—	Stanislaus	2283
31		29	H	Bradford C	L	0-1	0-0	19		2983
32	Mar	3	H	Torquay U	D	0-0	0-0	—		1663
33		7	A	Chester C	L	1-3	1-1	22	Valentine	1228
34		11	A	Stoke C	W	2-1	0-0	—	Stevens 2	12,385
35		14	H	WBA	D	1-1	1-1	19	Kearney	3810
36		21	A	Bolton W	L	1-2	0-1	21	Hulme	7619
37		24	A	Leyton Orient	L	0-4	0-1	—		3074
38		28	H	Wigan Ath	L	1-4	0-1	22	Lyons	2618
39		31	A	Huddersfield T	L	0-3	0-2	—		5890
40	Apr	4	H	Hull C	W	3-2	2-0	21	Lyons 2, Robinson	2245
41		11	A	Fulham	L	2-4	0-3	21	Hulme, Knill	4060
42		14	H	Exeter C	W	3-1	2-1	—	Lyons, Wilson I, Stevens	1756
43		18	H	Stockport Co	D	0-0	0-0	21		4726
44		20	A	Hartlepool U	D	0-0	0-0	21		2503
45		25	H	Darlington	W	1-0	0-0	21	Stevens	2351
46	May	2	A	Preston NE	L	0-2	0-1	21		6932

Final League Position: 21

GOALSCORERS

League (55): Stevens 17, Robinson 10 (2 pens), Greenall 5 (1 pen), Hulme 4, Lyons 4, Smith 3, Stanislaus 3, Valentine 3, Kearney 1, Knill 1, Lee 1 (1 pen), Wilson D 1, Wilson I 1, own goals 1.
Rumbelows Cup (2): Mauge 1, Stanislaus 1.
FA Cup (0).

Kelly	Wilson D	Stanislaus	Robinson	Valentine	Greenall	Lee	Hulme	Stevens	Parkinson	Kearney	Smith	Wilson I	Mauge	Knill	Jones	Anderson	Robertson	Cullen	Hughes	Fitcroft	Lyons	Match No.
1	2	3	4	5	6	7	8*	9	10	11	12											1
1	2	3	4	5	6	7	8	9*	10	11		12										2
1	2	3	8	5	6		14	9†	10	4	7	11*	12									3
1	2	3	8	5	6			9	10	4	7	11										4
1	2	3	8	5	6		12	9	10	4	7*	11†	14									5
1	2	3	8	5	6			9	10	4	7	11*	12									6
1	2	3	8	5	6		12	9*	14	4	7	11†	10									7
1	2	3	8	5	6		12	9†	14	10		11*	4	7								8
1	2	3	8	5	6			9*	10	4	7	11†		14	12							9
1	2	3	8	5	6			9	10	4	7*	11		12								10
1	2	3	8	5	6			9	10	4	7	11*		12								11
1		3	8	5*	6			9	14	4	7	11	10†	12	2							12
1	2	3†	8	5	6		10	9*	14	4	7	11		12								13
1	2		8	5	6			9		4	7	11						3	10			14
1	2		8	5	6			9	12	4	7	11*						3	10			15
1			8	5	6			9†		4	7	11*		2	14			3	10	12		16
1		3	8	5	2		12	9	4		7	14		6†					10*	11		17
1	14	3	8	5	2		12	9*	4	10	7	11†		6								18
1		3	8	5	2			9	4	10	7			6		11						19
1	3	12	8	5	2			9	4	10	7			6†	14	11*						20
1	3	11	8	5	2			9	4	10	7			6								21
1	3	11	8*	5	2			9	4	10	7			6	12							22
1	3	11*	8	5	2			9	4	10	7			6	12							23
1	3	11	8*	5	2		12	9	4	10	7			6								24
1	3	11	8*	5	2		12	9	4		7		10†	6	14							25
1	3	11	8	5	2		7	9	10					6					4			26
1	3†	11	8	5	2		7	9	4	10			14	6*					12			27
1	3	11	8†	5	2		7	9	4*	10			14	6					12			28
1	3*	11	8	5	2		7	9	10†	12	4	14		6								29
1	3	11	12		2		7	9	10*	8	4	5		6								30
1	3	11	8		2		7	9	10		4			6					5			31
1	12	11	8	5	2		7	9	10		4			6				3*				32
1		11		5	2		7	9	10	8				6				3	4			33
1		11		5	2		7	9	10	8				6				3	4			34
1		11		5	2		7	9	10	8*				6				3	4	12		35
1		11*	12	5	2		7	9	10	8			14	6				3†	4			36
1	3*	11	8	5	2			9	10†	7			14	6	12			4				37
1	2	3	8					9	10	7*			4	6	12				5		11	38
1	2*	3	8					9	10	7			4	6	12				5		11	39
1		3	8				7*	9	10	12			4	6			2		5		11	40
1		3	8†				7	9	14	10*		12	4	6			2		5		11	41
1			8					9	10		3	11	4	6			2		5		7	42
1	12	14	8					9*	10†		3	11	4	6			2		5		7	43
1	12		8	5				9	10		3		4	6			2			11*	7	44
1	12		8†	5			14	9	10		3	11*	4	6			2				7	45
1	12		8	5			14	9	10		3*	11	4	6			2				7†	46
46	30	36	38	38	37	2	21	44	26	43	30	21	15	33	—	3	5	4	13	12	9	
	+	+	+	+			+	+	+		+	+	+	+	+	+			+	+		
	2s	4s	3s	1s			9s	1s	6s		4s	3s	7s	2s	9s	2s			4s	1s		

Rumbelows Cup	First Round	Hartlepool U (a)	0-1
		(h)	2-2
FA Cup	First Round	Bradford C (h)	0-1

BURY

Player and Position	Ht	Wt	Birth Date	Birth Place	Source	Clubs	League App	Gls
Goalkeepers								
Gary Kelly	5 10	12 03	3 8 66	Fulwood	Apprentice	Newcastle U	53	—
						Blackpool (loan)	5	—
						Bury	130	—
Michael Pollitt	6 3	13 03	29 2 72	Farnworth	Trainee	Manchester U	—	—
						Oldham Ath (loan)	—	—
						Bury	—	—
						Lincoln C (loan)	—	—
Defenders								
Lee Anderson	5 09	11 03	4 10 73	Bury	Trainee	Bury	5	—
Ian Hughes	5 10	10 09	2 8 74	Bury	Trainee	Bury	17	—
Mark Kearney	5 10	11 00	12 6 62	Ormskirk	Marine	Everton	—	—
						Mansfield T	250	29
						Bury (loan)	13	1
						Bury	52	1
Alan Knill	6 2	10 09	8 10 64	Slough	Apprentice	Southampton	—	—
						Halifax T	118	6
						Swansea C	89	3
						Bury	98	3
Paul Robertson	5 7	11 06	5 2 72	Stockport	York C	Stockport Co	10	—
						Bury	5	—
Roger Stanislaus	5 9	12 11	2 11 68	Hammersmith	Trainee	Arsenal	—	—
						Brentford	111	4
						Bury	84	5
Peter Valentine	5 10	12 00	16 4 63	Huddersfield	Apprentice	Huddersfield T	19	1
						Bolton W	68	1
						Bury	283	13
Mick Walsh‡	6 0	12 00	20 6 56	Manchester		Bolton W	177	4
						Everton	20	—
						Norwich C (loan)	5	—
						Burnley (loan)	3	—
						Ft Lauderdale	—	—
						Manchester C	4	—
						Blackpool	153	5
						Bury	—	—
Darren Wilson	5 11	13 00	30 9 71	Manchester		Manchester C	—	—
						Bury	32	1
Midfield								
Pat Bradley‡	5 10	12 03	27 4 72	Sydney	Trainee	Bury	1	—
Philip Parkinson	5 10	10 11	1 12 67	Chorley	Apprentice	Southampton	—	—
						Bury	145	5
Nigel Smith*	5 7	10 04	21 12 69	Leeds	Leeds U	Burnley	13	—
						Bury	34	3
Ian Wilson*	5 7	10 10	27 3 58	Aberdeen	Elgin C	Leicester C	285	17
						Everton	34	1
						Besiktas	—	—
						Derby Co	11	—
						Bury	24	1
Forwards								
Kevin Hulme	5 10	11 09	2 12 67	Farnworth	Radcliffe Bor	Bury	78	12
						Chester C (loan)	4	—
David Jones	6 3	14 04	3 7 64	Harrow		Chelsea	—	—
						Bury	1	—
						Leyton Orient	2	—
						Burnley	4	—
						Ipswich T	—	—
						Doncaster R	40	14
						Bury	9	—

BURY

Foundation: A meeting at the Waggon & Horses Hotel, attended largely by members of Bury Wesleyans and Bury Unitarians football clubs, decided to form a new Bury club. This was officially formed at a subsequent gathering at the Old White Horse Hotel, Fleet Street, Bury on April 24, 1885.

First Football League game: 1 September, 1894, Division 2, v Manchester C (h) W 4-2 – Lowe; Gillespie, Davies; White, Clegg, Ross; Wylie, Barbour (2), Millar (1), Ostler (1), Plant.

Did you know: In their two FA Cup-winning seasons, 1899–1900 and 1902–03, Bury played a total of 13 cup-ties (including replays) scoring 27 goals and conceding just five. Indeed only Sheffield United and Nottingham Forest were able to score against them.

Managers (and Secretary-managers)
T. Hargreaves 1887*, H. S. Hamer 1887–1907*, Archie Montgomery 1907–15, William Cameron 1919–23, James Hunter Thompson 1923–27, Percy Smith 1927–30, Arthur Paine 1930–34, Norman Bullock 1934–38, Jim Porter 1944 45, Norman Bullock 1945–49, John McNeil 1950–53, Dave Russell 1953–61, Bob Stokoe 1961–65, Bert Head 1965–66, Les Shannon 1966–69, Jack Marshall 1969, Les Hart 1970, Tommy McAnearney 1970–72, Alan Brown 1972–73, Bobby Smith 1973–77, Bob Stokoe 1977–78, David Hatton 1978–79, Dave Connor 1979–80, Jim Iley 1980–84; Martin Dobson 1984–89, Sam Ellis 1989–90, Mike Walsh December 1990–.

Player and Position	Ht	Wt	Date	Birth Place	Source	Clubs	League App	Gls
Darren Lyons†			9 11 66	Manchester	Ashton U	Bury	10	4
Ron Mauge	5 10	11 00	10 3 69	Islington	Trainee	Charlton Ath	—	—
						Fulham	50	2
						Bury	51	6
						Manchester C (loan)	—	—
Liam Robinson	5 6	11 04	29 12 65	Bradford	School	Nottingham F	—	—
						Huddersfield T	21	2
						Tranmere R (loan)	4	3
						Bury	248	83
Ian Stevens	5 9	12 00	21 10 66	Malta		Preston NE	11	2
						Stockport Co	2	—
						Lancaster C	—	—
						Bolton W	47	7
						Bury	45	17

Trainees
Calderbank, Darren P; Emmett, Darren; Greenhalgh, Lawrence L; Heaney, David R; Morris, Paul I; Thornley, James D; Wilkinson, Lee.

**Non-Contract
Bennett, Michael; Craven, Peter A; Lyons, Darren P; Pacey, Jon S; Winter, Julian.

Associated Schoolboys
Berry, Damian J; Booth, Gary M; Brown, Stuart I; George, Lee J; Nuttall, Mark; Palfrey, Ian A; Rawlinson, Craig A; Steele, Winfield J. J; Stevens, Richard A; Williams, Anthony M.

Associated Schoolboys who have accepted the club's offer of a Traineeship/Contract
Adams, Daniel B; Byrne, Steven A; Higgens, Saul J; Wallace, Richard E; Williamson, Paul J.

**Non-Contract Players who are retained must be re-signed before they are eligible to play in League matches.

CAMBRIDGE UNITED 1991–92 *Back row (left to right)*: Michael Cheetham, Gary Clayton, Steve Claridge, Richard Wilkins, Jim Carstairs, Gus Caesar, Danny O'Shea, Colin Bailie, David Robinson.

Centre row: Neville Proctor (Chief Scout), Graham Scarff (First Team Coach), Liam Daish, Phil Chapple, John Vaughan, Mark Sale, Jon Sheffield, Dion Dublin, John Taylor, Peter Prince (Physiotherapist), Neil Lanham (Technical Adviser).

Front row: Andy Fensome, Lee Philpott, Fergus O'Donoghue, Chris Leadbitter, Gary Peters (Assistant Manager), John Beck (Manager), Gary Johnson (Youth Manager), Matthew Proctor, Daniel Stalley, Tony Dennis, Alan Kimble.

Division 1   CAMBRIDGE UNITED

Abbey Stadium, Newmarket Rd, Cambridge. Telephone Teversham (0223) 241237. Clubcall: 0898 121141.

Ground capacity: 10,100.

Record attendance: 14,000 v Chelsea, Friendly, 1 May 1970.

Record receipts: £86,308 v Manchester U, Rumbelows Cup 2nd rd 2nd leg, 9 October 1991.

Pitch measurements: 110yd × 74yd.

President: D. A. Ruston.

Chairman: R. H. Smart.

Vice-chairman: D. A. Ruston.

Directors: G. Harwood, J. Howard, R. Hunt, G. Lowe, R. Smith.

Team Manager: John Beck. *Assistant Manager:* Gary Peters. *Physio:* Ken Steggles. *First team coach:* Graham Scarff. *Secretary:* Steve Greenall. *Commercial Manager:* John Holmes. *Stadium Manager:* Ian Darler. *Youth manager:* Gary Johnson.

Year Formed: 1919. Turned Professional: 1946. Ltd Co.: 1948.

Former Names: Abbey United until 1949.

Club Nickname: 'United'.

Record League Victory: 6-0 v Darlington, Division 4, 18 September 1971 – Roberts; Thompson, Akers, Guild, Eades, Foote, Collins (1p), Horrey, Hollett, Greenhalgh (4), Phillips. (1 og). 6-0 v Hartlepool, Division 4, 11 February 1989 – Vaughan; Beck, Kimble, Turner, Chapple (1), Daish, Clayton, Holmes, Taylor (3 incl. 1p), Bull (1), Leadbitter (1).

Record Cup Victory: 5-1 v Bristol C, FA Cup, 5th rd, second replay, 27 February 1990 – Vaughan; Fensome, Kimble, Bailie (O'Shea), Chapple, Daish, Cheetham (Robinson), Leadbitter (1), Dublin (2), Taylor (1), Philpott (1).

Record Defeat: 0-6 v Aldershot, Division 3, 13 April 1974 and v Darlington, Division 4, 28 September 1974 and v Chelsea, Division 2, 15 January 1983.

Most League Points (2 for a win): 65, Division 4, 1976–77.

Most League points (3 for a win): 86, Division 3, 1990–91.

Most League Goals: 87, Division 4, 1976–77.

Highest League Scorer in Season: David Crown, 24, Division 4, 1985–86.

Most League Goals in Total Aggregate: Alan Biley, 74, 1975–80.

Most Capped Player: Tom Finney, 7 (15), Northern Ireland.

Most League Appearances: Steve Spriggs, 416, 1975–87.

Record Transfer Fee Received: £350,000 from Derby Co for Alan Biley, January 1980–.

Record Transfer Fee Paid: £150,000 to Shrewsbury T for Mick Heathcote, September 1991.

Football League Record: 1970 Elected to Division 4; 1973–74 Division 3; 1974–77 Division 4; 1977–78 Division 3; 1978–84 Division 2; 1984–85 Division 3; 1985–90 Division 4; 1990–91 Division 3; 1991–92 Division 2; 1992– Division 1.

Honours: Football League: Division 2 best season: 5th, 1991–92; Division 3 – Champions 1990–91; Runners-up 1977–78; Division 4 – Champions 1976–77. *FA Cup:* best season: 6th rd, 1989–90, 1990–91. *Football League Cup:* 4th rd, 1980–81.

Colours: Yellow shirts, black shorts, black and yellow stockings. **Change colours:** All sky blue with amber and black trim.

CAMBRIDGE UNITED 1991–92 LEAGUE RECORD

Match No.	Date		Venue	Opponents	Result		H/T Score	Lg. Pos.	Goalscorers	Atten-dance
1	Aug	17	A	Grimsby T	W	4-3	1-1	—	Dublin, Taylor, Wilkins, O'Shea	7657
2		24	H	Swindon T	W	3-2	1-1	3	Philpott 2, Summerbee (og)	6232
3		31	A	Watford	W	3-1	1-0	2	Philpott, Claridge, Cheetham	8902
4	Sep	3	H	Southend U	L	0-1	0-0	—		6412
5		7	A	Millwall	W	2-1	1-1	4	Cheetham, Rowett	8332
6		13	H	Derby Co	D	0-0	0-0	—		7293
7		17	H	Wolverhampton W	W	2-1	2-0	—	Taylor, Wilkins	6552
8		21	A	Portsmouth	L	0-3	0-2	4		7801
9		29	H	Leicester C	W	5-1	2-0	—	Dublin 2, Claridge 2, Heathcote	7052
10	Oct	5	A	Port Vale	L	0-1	0-0	4		5991
11		12	H	Sunderland	W	3-0	2-0	3	Dublin, Wilkins, Dennis	7857
12		18	A	Tranmere R	W	2-1	2-0	—	Dublin, Claridge	7625
13		26	H	Barnsley	W	2-1	0-0	2	Claridge, Dublin	5534
14	Nov	2	H	Bristol C	D	0-0	0-0	3		4810
15		6	A	Newcastle U	D	1-1	0-0	—	Claridge	13,077
16		9	A	Ipswich T	W	2-1	1-0	1	Rowett, Claridge	20,586
17		16	H	Brighton & HA	D	0-0	0-0	1		7625
18		23	A	Charlton Ath	W	2-1	2-0	1	Taylor, Dublin	6350
19		30	H	Oxford U	D	1-1	0-0	1	Dublin	6496
20	Dec	7	A	Bristol R	D	2-2	1-2	1	Dublin, Taylor	5280
21		22	A	Southend U	D	1-1	1-1	—	Philpott	9353
22		26	H	Plymouth Arg	D	1-1	0-0	2	Dublin	7105
23		29	H	Watford	L	0-1	0-0	—		8439
24	Jan	1	A	Blackburn R	L	1-2	0-0	5	Chapple	15,001
25		11	A	Swindon T	W	2-0	0-0	4	Heaney, Dublin	10,878
26		18	H	Grimsby T	L	0-1	0-1	6		6092
27		31	H	Tranmere R	D	0-0	0-0	—		5491
28	Feb	8	A	Barnsley	D	0-0	0-0	7		6196
29		11	A	Plymouth Arg	W	1-0	0-0	—	Cheetham	4290
30		15	H	Charlton Ath	W	1-0	0-0	3	Dennis	6472
31		22	A	Oxford U	L	0-1	0-1	4		5605
32		25	H	Blackburn R	W	2-1	2-0	—	Chapple, May (og)	7857
33		28	H	Bristol R	W	6-1	1-1	—	Fensome (pen), Dublin 2, Leadbitter, Heaney, Taylor	6164
34	Mar	7	A	Middlesbrough	D	1-1	0-0	3	Dublin	14,686
35		10	H	Newcastle U	L	0-2	0-2	—		8254
36		14	A	Bristol C	W	2-1	0-1	3	Heathcote, Norbury	9579
37		17	H	Middlesbrough	D	0-0	0-0	—		7318
38		21	H	Ipswich T	D	1-1	0-0	2	Heathcote	9766
39		28	A	Brighton & HA	D	1-1	0-0	3	Heathcote	7702
40	Apr	1	D	Derby Co	D	0-0	0-0	—		15,353
41		4	H	Millwall	W	1-0	0-0	2	Dublin	6385
42		11	A	Wolverhampton W	L	1-2	0-0	2	Norbury	11,188
43		17	H	Portsmouth	D	2-2	1-0	—	Claridge, Wilkins	9492
44		21	A	Leicester C	L	1-2	0-1	—	Claridge	21,894
45		25	H	Port Vale	W	4-2	0-1	5	Heathcote, Claridge (pen), Chapple, Philpott	7559
46	May	2	A	Sunderland	D	2-2	1-2	5	Claridge 2	19,042

Final League Position: 5

GOALSCORERS

League (65): Dublin 15, Claridge 12 (1 pen), Heathcote 5, Philpott 5, Taylor 5, Wilkins 4, Chapple 3, Cheetham 3, Dennis 2, Heaney 2, Norbury 2, Rowett 2, Fensome 1 (1 pen), Leadbitter 1, O'Shea 1, own goals 2.
Rumbelows Cup (5): Claridge 2, Dublin 2, Taylor 1.
FA Cup (2): Dublin 2.

Vaughan	Fensome	Kimble	Bailie	Clayton	O'Shea	Cheetham	Wilkins	Dublin	Taylor	Philpott	Dennis	Claridge	Leadbitter	Chapple	Rowett	Heathcote	Daish	Sheffield	Heaney	Norbury	Raynor	White	Match No.
1	2	3	4*	5	6	7	8	9	10	11	12												1
1	2	3	4*	5	6	7	8	9	10†11		12	14											2
1	2	3	4	5	6	7	8*	9	10†11			14	12										3
1	2	3	4	5	6	7		9	10	11†	8*14	12											4
1	2	3	4	5		7			10†11		8	9	12	6	14*								5
1	2	3	4	5		7			10	11	8	9		6									6
1	2	3	4	5		7	8		10	11		9		6									7
1	2	3	4	5†		7	8	12	10	11*14		9		6									8
1	2	3				7	8	9*12	11			4	10	6		5							9
1	2	3	14			7*	8	9	12	11		4†10		6		5							10
1	2	3	14	5			8	9	7†11			4	10*12			6							11
1	2	3		5			8	9	7	11		4	10			6							12
	2	3	12	5			8	9	7	11		4*10†14				6	1						13
1	2	3	8	5			9	7	11	4	10					6							14
1	2	3	8	14	5†		9	7	11*	4	10	12				6							15
1	2	3	8	5			9	12	11	4	10†					7*14	6						16
1	2	3	8	5	14	12	9		11†	4	10					7*	6						17
1	2	3	8			7*11	9	10		4			6	12	5								18
1	2	3	8			7	11	9	10*12	4			6		5								19
1	2	3	8*	14	7	12	9	10	11	4†			6		5								20
1	2	3	4	5		8	9	10	11*	7		12	6										21
1	2	3	4*	5		8	9	10	11	7		6	12										22
1	2	3	4	5		8	9	10	11			6	7										23
1	2	3	4	5		8	9*10	11	12			6	7†14										24
1	2	3	12				4	9	10†11	7	8*	5		6	14								25
1	2	3	4				8	9	10	11		5	7*	6	12								26
1	2	3				10	8†9	12	11*	4	14	7	5	6									27
1	2	3	4*	5	7	10	9	11	8			6	12										28
	2	3	5	7*10†	9	11	4	8		14	6	1	12										29
	2	3	12	5	9	11	4	10†	8*		6	1	7	14									30
	2	3	5	9†11	4	10	8*		12	6	1	7	14										31
	2	3	8	9	12	4	10†	5	7*	6	1	11	14										32
	2	3	8	9	12	4†10*14	5	7	6	1	11												33
2*	3	12	8	9	10	4	7†5	6	1	11	14												34
3	4	2	9	10	8	5	7*	6	1	11	12												35
3	4†2*	9	8	10	11	5	14	6	1	7	12												36
3	8	9	14	4	10*11	5	2	6†1	7	12													37
3	8	9	14	4	10*11	5	2	6	1	7†12													38
3	7*	8	9	4	11	5	2	6	1	10	12												39
3	6	7†8	9	4	11	5	2	1	10*12	14													40
1	3	6	9	12	11	4	8	5	2	14	7†10*												41
1	3	6	7	8	9*	4	12	11†5	2	10	14												42
1	3	6	11*	8	9	12†	4	10	14	5	2	7											43
1	3*	6	8	9	11	4	10	12	5	2	7												44
1		6	8	9*	11	4	10	3	5	2	12	7											45
1	3	6	8	12	11	4	10	5	2	9*	7												46

33 34 45 23 9 30 21 30 40 27 29 36 25 14 29 10 17 22 13 9 4 5 1
+ + + + + + + + + + + + + + + +
5s 2s 1s 1s 2s 3s 8s 2s 4s 4s 11s 3s 5s 4s 10s3s 1s

Rumbelows Cup	First Round	Reading (h)	1-0
		(a)	3-0
	Second Round	Manchester U (a)	0-3
		(h)	1-1
FA Cup	Third Round	Coventry C (a)	1-1
		(h)	1-0
	Fourth Round	Swindon T (h)	0-3

CAMBRIDGE UNITED

Player and Position	Ht	Wt	Birth Date	Birth Place	Source	Clubs	League App	Gls
Goalkeepers								
Jon Sheffield	5 11	11 07	1 2 69	Bedworth		Norwich C	1	—
						Aldershot (loan)	26	—
						Ipswich T (loan)	—	—
						Cambridge U (loan)	2	—
						Cambridge U	13	—
						Sheffield U (loan)	—	—
John Vaughan	5 10	13 01	26 6 64	Isleworth	Apprentice	West Ham U	—	—
						Charlton Ath (loan)	6	—
						West Ham U	—	—
						Bristol R (loan)	6	—
						Wrexham (loan)	4	—
						Bristol C (loan)	2	—
						Fulham	44	—
						Bristol C (loan)	3	—
						Cambridge U	151	—
Defenders								
Colin Bailie	5 11	10 11	31 3 64	Belfast	Apprentice	Swindon T	107	4
						Reading	84	1
						Cambridge U	119	3
Phil Chapple	6 2	12 07	26 11 66	Norwich	Apprentice	Norwich C	—	—
						Cambridge U	169	17
Liam Daish	6 2	13 05	23 9 68	Portsmouth	Apprentice	Portsmouth	1	—
						Cambridge U	105	2
Andy Fensome	5 8	11 02	18 2 69	Northampton	Trainee	Norwich C	—	—
						Newcastle U (loan)	—	—
						Cambridge U	94	1
Mike Heathcote	6 2	12 05	10 9 65	Durham		Middlesbrough	—	—
						Spennymoor U	—	—
						Sunderland	9	—
						Halifax T (loan)	7	1
						York C (loan)	3	—
						Shrewsbury T	44	6
						Cambridge U	22	5
Alan Kimble	5 8	11 00	6 8 66	Poole		Charlton Ath	6	—
						Exeter C (loan)	1	—
						Cambridge U	253	20
Fergus O'Donohue‡			7 10 69	Cork	Cork C	Cambridge U	—	—
Danny O'Shea	6 0	12 08	26 3 63	Kennington	Apprentice	Arsenal	6	—
						Charlton Ath (loan)	9	—
						Exeter C	45	2
						Southend U	118	12
						Cambridge U	97	1
Jamie Smeeth			7 9 74	Hackney		Cambridge U	—	—
Daniel Stalley‡	5 10		20 4 73	Cambridge	Cambridge C	Cambridge U	—	—
Midfield								
Michael Cheetham	5 11	11 05	30 6 67	Amsterdam	Army	Ipswich T	4	—
						Cambridge U	102	20
Gary Clayton	5 11	12 08	2 2 63	Sheffield	Apprentice Burton Albion	Rotherham U	—	—
						Doncaster R	35	5
						Cambridge U	118	7
						Peterborough (loan)	4	—
John Fowler			27 10 74	Preston	Trainee	Cambridge U	—	—
Lee Philpott	5 9	10 06	21 2 70	Barnet	Trainee	Peterborough U	4	—
						Cambridge U	118	15
Matthew Proctor‡			4 10 72	Bury St Edmunds	Trainee	Cambridge U	—	—
Richard Wilkins	6 0	12 00	28 5 65	London	Haverhill R	Colchester U	152	22
						Cambridge U	73	7

CAMBRIDGE UNITED

Foundation: The football revival in Cambridge began soon after World War II when the Abbey United club (formed 1919) decided to turn professional and in 1949 changed their name to Cambridge United. They were competing in the United Counties League before graduating to the Eastern Counties League in 1951 and the Southern League in 1958.

First Football League game: 15 August, 1970, Division 4, v Lincoln C (h) D 1-1 – Roberts; Thompson, Meldrum (1), Slack, Eades, Hardy, Leggett, Cassidy, Lindsey, McKinven, Harris.

Did you know: John Collins scored from the penalty spot in four consecutive League games in September–October 1972 aand in each case it was United's only goal of the game.

Managers (and Secretary-managers)
Bill Whittaker 1949–55, Gerald Williams 1955, Bert Johnson 1955–59, Bill Craig 1959–60, Alan Moore 1960–63, Roy Kirk 1964–66, Bill Leivers 1967–74, Ron Atkinson 1974–78, John Docherty 1978–83, John Ryan 1984–85, Ken Shellito 1985, Chris Turner 1985–90, John Beck January 1990–.

Player and Position	Ht	Wt	Birth Date	Birth Place	Source	Clubs	League App	Gls
Forwards								
Steve Claridge	5 11	11 08	10 4 66	Portsmouth	Fareham	Bournemouth	7	1
						Weymouth	—	—
						Crystal Palace	—	—
						Aldershot	62	19
						Cambridge U	79	28
Tony Dennis	5 7	10 02	1 12 63	Eton	Slough	Cambridge U	95	9
Dion Dublin	6 0	12 04	22 4 69	Leicester		Norwich C	—	—
						Cambridge U	156	52
Chris Leadbitter	5 9	10 07	17 10 67	Middlesbrough	Apprentice	Grimsby T	—	—
						Hereford U	36	1
						Cambridge U	138	12
Mike Norbury			22 1 69	Kemsworth	Ossett	Scarborough	—	—
						Bridlington T	—	—
						Cambridge U	28	4
Philip Parkhill			22 2 74	Harrogate		Cambridge U	—	—
Paul Raynor	6 0	11 04	29 4 66	Nottingham	Apprentice	Nottingham F	3	—
						Bristol R (loan)	8	—
						Huddersfield T	50	9
						Swansea C	191	27
						Wrexham (loan)	6	—
						Cambridge U	8	—
David Robinson	5 11		27 9 71	Ely	Trainee	Cambridge U	—	—
Gary Rowett	6 00	12 10	6 3 74	Bromsgrove	Trainee	Cambridge U	13	2
Devon White	6 3	14 00	2 3 64	Nottingham	Arnold T	Lincoln C	29	4
						Boston U	—	—
						Bristol R	202	53
						Cambridge U	2	—

Trainees
Burgess, Christopher; Gibbens, Neil; Goddard, Wayne L; Granville, Daniel P; Kilbane, Farrell N; Nyamah, Kofi.
**Non-Contract
Patmore, Warren J.
Associated Schoolboys
Collard, Allan; Gutzmore, Leon; Harradine, Robert; Hawes, Mark; Kyd, Michael R; Shorley, Guy; Stock, Russell J.
**Non-Contract Players who are retained must be re-signed before they are eligible to play in League matches.

CARDIFF CITY 1991–92 *Back row (left to right):* Lee Baddeley, Gareth Abraham, Chris Pike.
Centre row: Jimmy Goodfellow, Harry Parsons, Pat Heard, Damon Searle, Cameron Toshack, Gavin Ward, Roger Hansbury, Alan Lewis, Jason Perry, Mark Jones, Gavin Tait (Development Officer).
Front row: Jamie Unsworth, Nathan Blake, Tony Clemo (Chairman), Roger Gibbins, Eddie May (Team Coach), Cohen Griffith, Robin Semark.

Division 3   **CARDIFF CITY**

Ninian Park, Cardiff CF1 8SX. Telephone Cardiff (0222) 398636. Newsline (0898) 888603. Fax No: (0222) 341148.

Ground capacity: 18,000.

Record attendance: 61,566, Wales v England, 14 October 1961. Club record: 57,893 v Arsenal, Division 1, 22 April 1953.

Record receipts: £50,517.75 v QPR, FA Cup, 3rd rd, 6 January 1990.

Pitch measurements: 114yd × 78yd.

Directors: D. Henderson.

First team coach: Eddie May. *Commercial Manager:* Keith Butler. *Physio:* Jimmy Goodfellow.

Year Formed: 1899. Turned Professional: 1910. Ltd Co.: 1910.

Former Grounds: Riverside, Sophia Gardens, Old Park and Fir Gardens. Moved to Ninian Park, 1910.

Former Names: 1899–1902, Riverside; 1902–08, Riverside Albion; 1908, Cardiff City.

Club Nickname: 'Bluebirds'.

Record League Victory: 9-2 v Thames, Division 3 (S), 6 February 1932 – Farquharson; E. L. Morris, Roberts; Galbraith, Harris, Ronan; Emmerson (1), Keating (1), Jones (1), McCambridge (1), Robbins (5).

Record Cup Victory: 8-0 v Enfield, FA Cup, 1st rd, 28 November 1931 – Farquharson; Smith, Roberts; Harris (1), Galbraith, Ronan; Emmerson (2), Keating (3); O'Neill (2), Robbins, McCambridge.

Record Defeat: 2-11 v Sheffield U, Division 1, 1 January 1926.

Most League Points (2 for a win): 66, Division 3 (S), 1946–47.

Most League points (3 for a win): 86, Division 3, 1982–83.

Most League Goals: 93, Division 3 (S), 1946–47.

Highest League Scorer in Season: Stan Richards, 30, Division 3 (S), 1946–47.

Most League Goals in Total Aggregate: Len Davies, 128, 1920–31.

Most Capped Player: Alf Sherwood, 39 (41), Wales.

Most League Appearances: Phil Dwyer, 471, 1972–85.

Record Transfer Fee Received: £215,000 from Portsmouth for Jimmy Gilligan, October 1989.

Record Transfer Fee Paid: £180,000 to San Jose Earthquakes for Godfrey Ingram, September 1982.

Football League Record: 1920 Elected to Division 2; 1921 –29 Division 1; 1929–31 Division 2; 1931–47 Division 3 (S); 1947–52 Division 2; 1952–57 Division 1; 1957–60 Division 2; 1960–62 Division 1; 1962–75 Division 2; 1975–76 Division 3; 1976–82 Division 2; 1982–83 Division 3; 1983–85 Division 2; 1985–86 Division 3; 1986–88 Division 4; 1988–90 Division 3; 1990–92 Division 4; 1992– Division 3.

Honours: Football League: Division 1 – Runners-up 1923–24; Division 2 – Runners-up 1920–21, 1951–52, 1959–60; Division 3 (S) – Champions 1946–47; Division 3 – Runners-up 1975–76, 1982–83; Division 4 – Runners-up 1987–88. *FA Cup:* Winners 1926–27 (only occasion the Cup has been won by a club outside England); Runners-up 1925. *Football League Cup:* Semi-final 1965–66. *Welsh Cup:* Winners 20 times. *Charity Shield:* 1927. **European Competitions:** *European Cup-Winners' Cup:* 1964–65, 1965–66, 1967–68, 1968–69, 1969–70, 1970–71, 1971–72, 1973–74, 1974–75, 1976–77, 1977–78, 1988–89.

Colours: All blue **Change colours:** Red shirts, white shorts, red stockings.

CARDIFF CITY 1991–92 LEAGUE RECORD

Match No.	Date		Venue	Opponents		Result	H/T Score	Lg. Pos.	Goalscorers	Atten-dance
1	Aug	17	H	Lincoln C	L	1-2	0-2	—	Pike (pen)	5137
2		24	A	Crewe Alex	D	1-1	1-0	16	Dale	3799
3		31	H	Carlisle U	W	1-0	0-0	11	Jones (pen)	4096
4	Sep	4	A	Maidstone U	D	1-1	1-1	—	Dale	1019
5		7	H	Rochdale	L	1-2	0-1	15	Pike	4029
6		14	A	Blackpool	D	1-1	1-1	15	Davies (og)	3931
7		17	A	Halifax T	D	1-1	1-0	—	Dale	1041
8		21	H	Scarborough	W	2-1	1-1	12	Heard, Dale	3227
9		28	A	Barnet	L	1-3	1-2	14	Dale	4000
10	Oct	5	H	Wrexham	W	5-0	2-0	12	Dale, Blake, Pike 3	3652
11		19	A	Mansfield T	L	0-3	0-1	12		3180
12		26	H	Doncaster R	W	2-1	1-1	12	Pike 2 (2 pen)	2491
13	Nov	2	H	Scunthorpe U	D	2-2	0-0	12	Dale, Pike	2356
14		5	A	Gillingham	D	0-0	0-0	—		2641
15		23	H	Northampton T	W	3-2	1-1	10	Gibbins, Dale 2	2922
16		30	H	Rotherham U	W	1-0	1-0	10	Dale	3551
17	Dec	14	A	York C	W	3-1	1-1	7	Pike, Dale 2	1904
18		26	A	Lincoln C	D	0-0	0-0	9		3162
19		28	A	Carlisle U	D	2-2	0-0	9	Pike (pen), Ramsey	3080
20	Jan	1	H	Maidstone U	L	0-5	0-1	9		8023
21		11	H	Hereford U	W	1-0	0-0	9	Dale	5305
22		18	A	Walsall	D	0-0	0-0	9		3654
23		25	H	Chesterfield	W	4-0	2-0	8	Pike 2, Dale, Blake	5131
24		31	H	Mansfield T	W	3-2	2-1	—	Blake, Pike (pen), Newton	8201
25	Feb	8	A	Doncaster R	W	2-1	1-1	7	Dale, Douglas (og)	2094
26		11	A	Rotherham U	W	2-1	1-0	—	Newton, Blake	3827
27		15	H	York C	W	3-0	0-0	5	Pike 2 (1 pen), Dale	8067
28		22	A	Hereford U	D	2-2	0-1	5	Ramsey, Harrison	5691
29		29	H	Burnley	L	0-2	0-0	7		16,030
30	Mar	3	A	Walsall	W	2-1	0-1	—	Dale, Searle	7517
31		7	A	Chesterfield	D	2-2	0-2	6	Newton, Dale	3803
32		10	H	Gillingham	L	2-3	2-1	—	Griffith, Dale	8521
33		14	A	Scunthorpe U	L	0-1	0-0	8		2766
34		28	A	Northampton T	D	0-0	0-0	7		2678
35		31	H	Blackpool	D	1-1	1-1	—	Burgess (og)	8430
36	Apr	4	A	Rochdale	L	0-2	0-1	9		2651
37		11	H	Halifax T	W	4-0	1-0	9	Ramsey (pen), Dale 2, Pike	5261
38		14	A	Scarborough	D	2-2	0-1	—	Pike 2	935
39		20	H	Barnet	W	3-1	2-0	9	Pike (pen), Dale, Newton	7720
40		22	A	Burnley	L	1-3	1-1	—	Blake	12,408
41		25	A	Wrexham	W	3-0	2-0	9	Pike 2, Gill	4002
42		28	H	Crewe Alex	D	1-1	1-0	—	Blake	10,523

Final League Position: 9

GOALSCORERS

League (66): Dale 22, Pike 21 (7 pens), Blake 6, Newton 4, Ramsey 3 (1 pen), Gibbins 1, Gill 1, Griffith 1, Harrison 1, Heard 1, Jones 1 (1 pen), Searle 1, own goals 3.
Rumbelows Cup (4): Gibbins 1, Jones 1 (1 pen), Millar 1, Searle 1.
FA Cup (1): Pike 1.

Hansbury	Jones	Searle	Gibbins	Abraham	Lewis	Semark	Matthews	Griffith	Pike	Heard	Baddeley	Perry	Millar	Dale	Ramsey	Blake	Ward	Toshack	Unsworth	Marriott	Williams	Gorman	Newton	Harrison	Gill	Bellamy	Walsh	Match No.
1	2	3	4	5*	6	7	8	9	10	11	12																	1
1	2	3	4	5	14		8†	7*	12			6	9	10	11													2
1	2	3	4	5				7*	8			6	9	10	11	12												3
1	2	3	4	5			12	14	8			6	9	10*	11	7†												4
1	2	3	4*	5			12	14	8			6	9	10	11	7†												5
	2	3	4	5	8		12	7				6	9	10*	11		1											6
	2	3	4	5†	8		12	7*	14			6	9	10	11		1											7
	2	3	4	5					8	9*	11†	6		10		7	1		12		14							8
	2	3	4				12		8	11	5	6		10	7*	9	1											9
	2	3	4*				12		8	9	5	6		10†	7	11	1		14									10
		3	4	5†		2			8	9	12	6		10	7*	11	1		14									11
		3	4	5		7			8	9		6		10		11	1		2									12
1	2	3	4				12		8	9	5*	6		10	7	11												13
1		3	4	5	8	2	12		9*			6		10	7	11												14
1		3	4		6	2	12		8	9*	5			10	7	11												15
		3	4		6	2	12		8	9*	5			10	7	11	1											16
		3	4			2	12		8	9*	7	6		10			1				5	11						17
		3	4			2			8	9	11*	6		10	7	12	1				5							18
		3	4			2			8	9		6		10	7	11	1				5							19
		3	4			2*			8	9	12	6		10	7	11	1				5							20
	2	3	4	6*	14	12†			8	9				10	7	11	1				5							21
		3	4						8	9	6	5		10	7	11	1					2						22
		3	4						8	9		5		10	7	12	1					2	6	11*				23
		3	4							9		5*	12	10	7	11	1					2	6	8				24
		3	4		14		12			9*		5		10	7	11	1					2	6	8†				25
		3	4				12			9*		5		10	7	11	1					2	6	8				26
		3	4	5						9		2		10	7	11	1						6	8				27
		3	4	5†			12			9*		2		10	7	11	1				14		6	8				28
		3	4				12			9	5	2		10	7	11*	1				14		6	8†				29
		3	4*						11	9	5	2		10	7		1				12		6	8				30
		3	4				12		11	9	5*	2		10	7		1						6	8				31
		3	4	5*	14		12		11†	9		2		10	7		1						6	8				32
1		3	4			2	12			9*	5	6		10	7†						14	11		8				33
1		3	4			2	12			9				10	7								6	8		5	11*	34
1		3	4		14	2	12		11*	9				10	7								6	8†		5		35
1		3*	4			2	12		8	9				10	7	11							6			5		36
1		3	4				12			9*		6		10	7	11						2†		8	14	5		37
1	2*	3	4				12			9		6		10	7†	11								8	14	5		38
1	12	3			14	2†			8	9*		6		10	7	11									4	5		39
1		3				2			8	9		6		10	7	11									4	5		40
1		3	4*		6	2	12		8	9				10	7†	11									14	5		41
1		3	4		6	2	12		8	9*				10	7	11										5		42
18	13	42	41	13	8	4	12	26	36	7	14	35	8	41	39	27	24	—	1	—	5	7	18	10	3	9	1	
+1s				+2s	+4s	+2s	+3s	+11s	+4s	+1s	+4s	+1s	+7s						+4s		+1s	+2s	+1s	+4s		+3s		

Rumbelows Cup	First Round	Bournemouth (h)	3-2
		(a)	1-4
FA Cup	First Round	Swansea C (a)	1-2

CARDIFF CITY

Player and Position	Ht	Wt	Date	Birth Place	Source	Clubs	League App	Gls
Goalkeepers								
Roger Hansbury*	5 11	12 00	26 1 55	Barnsley	Apprentice	Norwich C	78	—
						Bolton W (loan)	—	—
						Cambridge U (loan)	11	—
						Orient (loan)	—	—
						Eastern Ath	—	—
						Burnley	83	—
						Cambridge U	37	—
						Birmingham C	57	—
						Sheffield U (loan)	5	—
						Wolverhampton W (loan)	3	—
						Colchester U (loan)	4	—
						Cardiff C	99	—
Gavin Ward	6 2	12 12	30 6 70	Sutton Coldfield		Shrewsbury T	—	—
						WBA	—	—
						Cardiff C	27	—
Defenders								
Gareth Abraham	6 4	12 11	13 2 69	Merthyr Tydfil	Trainee	Cardiff C	87	4
Lee Baddeley	6 01	12 10	12 7 74	Cardiff		Cardiff C	20	—
Nathan Blake	5 10	12 00	27 1 72	Newport	Trainee	Cardiff C	77	10
Andrew Gorman§	5 11	13 03	13 9 74	Cardiff	Trainee	Cardiff C	11	—
Pat Heard*	5 9	11 05	17 3 60	Hull	Apprentice	Everton	11	—
						Aston Villa	24	2
						Sheffield W	25	3
						Newcastle U	34	2
						Middlesbrough	25	2
						Hull C	80	5
						Rotherham U	44	7
						Cardiff C	46	4
Alan Lewis	6 2	12 10	31 5 71	Pontypridd	Trainee	Cardiff C	50	—
Neil Matthews‡	6 0	11 07	3 12 67	Manchester	Apprentice	Blackpool	76	1
						Cardiff C	52	1
Jason Perry	5 11	10 04	2 4 70	Newport		Cardiff C	119	—
Damon Searle	5 11	10 05	26 10 71	Cardiff	Trainee	Cardiff C	77	1
John Williams	6 1	13 12	3 10 60	Liverpool	Amateur	Tranmere R	173	13
						Port Vale	50	2
						Bournemouth	117	9
						Wigan Ath (loan)	4	—
						Cardiff C	5	—
Midfield								
Roger Gibbins	5 10	11 09	6 9 55	Enfield	Apprentice	Tottenham H	—	—
						Oxford U	19	2
						Norwich C	48	12
						N England	—	—
						Cambridge U	100	12
						CardiffC	139	17
						Swansea C	35	6
						Newport Co	79	9
						Torquay U	33	5
						Newport Co	—	—
						Cardiff C	134	7
Gary Gill	5 10	11 09	28 11 64	Middlesbrough	Apprentice	Middlesbrough	77	2
						Hull C (loan)	1	—
						Darlington	56	9
						Cardiff C	6	1
Mark Jones*	5 8	9 12	26 9 61	Berinsfield	Apprentice	Oxford U	129	7
						Swindon T	40	9
						Cardiff C	36	2

CARDIFF CITY

Foundation: Credit for the establishment of a first class professional football club in such a rugby stronghold as Cardiff, is due to members of the Riverside club formed in 1899 out of a cricket club of that name. Cardiff became a city in 1905 and in 1908 the local FA granted Riverside permission to call themselves Cardiff City.

First Football League game: 28 August, 1920, Division 2, v Stockport C (a) W 5-2 – Kneeshaw; Brittain, Leyton; Keenor (1), Smith, Hardy; Grimshaw (1), Gill (2), Cashmore, West, Evans (1).

Did you know: Welsh international Billy Rees scored most goals for Cardiff City in senior World War Two games – a total of 74 including 33 in 1944–45. After the war he helped City into the Second Division before going to Spurs.

Managers (and Secretary-managers)
Davy McDougall 1910–11, Fred Stewart 1911–33, Bartley Wilson 1933–34, B. Watts-Jones 1934–37, Bill Jennings 1937–39, Cyril Spiers 1939–46, Billy McCandless 1946–48, Cyril Spiers 1948–54, Trevor Morris 1954–58, Bill Jones 1958–62, George Swindin 1962–64, Jimmy Scoular 1964–73, Frank O'Farrell 1973–74, Jimmy Andrews 1974–78, Richie Morgan 1978–82, Len Ashurst 1982–84, Jimmy Goodfellow 1984, Alan Durban 1984–86, Frank Burrows 1986–89, Len Ashurst 1989–91.

Player and Position	Ht	Wt	Birth Date	Birth Place	Source	Clubs	League App	Gls
Paul Ramsey	5 11	13 00	3 9 62	Derry	Apprentice	Leicester C	290	13
						Cardiff C	39	3
Robin Semark*	5 7	9 09	5 9 72	Portsmouth	Trainee	Cardiff C	6	—
Jamie Unsworth*			1 5 73	Bury	Trainee	Cardiff C	4	—
Forwards								
Anthony Bird§	5 10	11 09	1 9 74	Cardiff	Trainee	Cardiff C	—	—
Carl Dale	6 0	12 00	29 4 66	Colwyn Bay	Bangor C	Chester C	116	41
						Cardiff C	41	22
Cohen Griffith	5 10	10 08	26 12 62	Georgetown	Kettering T	Cardiff C	120	19
Paul Marriott §			26 9 73	Liverpool	Trainee	Cardiff C	1	—
Paul Millar	6 2	12 07	16 1 66	Belfast	Portadown	Port Vale	40	5
						Hereford U (loan)	5	2
						Cardiff C	15	—
Chris Pike	6 2	12 07	19 10 61	Cardiff	Barry T	Fulham	42	4
						Cardiff C (loan)	6	2
						Cardiff C	120	53
Cameron Toshack†	6 2	12 00	7 3 70	Cardiff	Trainee	Swansea C	—	—
						Bristol C	—	—
						Cardiff C	5	—
Alan Walsh*	6 0	11 00	9 12 56	Darlington	Horden CW	Middlesbrough	3	—
						Darlington	251	90
						Bristol C	218	77
						Walsall	—	—
						Glenavon	—	—
						Shrewsbury T	4	—
						Southampton	—	—
						Cardiff C	1	—

Trainees
Bird, Anthony; Callaway, Nilsson A. D; Crocker, Mathew; Donovan, Jason M; Dore, Craig A; Gorman, Andrew D; Hainsworth, Darren J; Jones, Nathan J; Marriott, Paul W; Parsons, Andrew K; Popham, Philip H; Sime, Leighton R; Speake, Jason W.

Associated Schoolboys
Haslam, Christopher; James, Philip; Jenkins, Daniel J; Jones, Ian; Jones, Mark; Keepin, Andrew W; Tobutt, Richard; Toole, Andrew.

Associated Schoolboys who have accepted the club's offer of a Traineeship/Contract
Bartley, Kevin D; Evans, Terry; Graham, Ben; Street, Daniel C; Walker, Lee; Young, Scott.

CARLISLE UNITED 1991–92 *Back row (left to right):* Mike Graham, John Deakin, Ian Dalziel, Dean Walling, Richard Sendall, Jeff Thorpe, Darren Edmondson.
Centre row: Tony Fyfe, David Miller, Jason Priestley, Ian Taylor, Kelham O'Hanlon, Simon Jeffels, John Holliday.
Front row: Peter Hampton (Assistant Manager/Physiotherapist), Derek Walsh, Paul Proudlock, Aidan McCaffery (Manager), Mick Bennett, Lee Armstrong, David Wilkes (Youth Team Coach).

Division 3 **CARLISLE UNITED**

Brunton Park, Carlisle CA1 1LL. Telephone Carlisle (0228) 26237. Commercial Dept: (0228) 24014.

Ground capacity: 18,506.

Record attendance: 27,500 v Birmingham C, FA Cup 3rd rd, 5 January 1957 and v Middlesbrough, FA Cup 5th rd, 7 February 1970.

Record receipts: £75,988.50 v Liverpool, FA Cup 3rd 7 January 1989.

Pitch measurements: 117yd × 78yd.

President: J. C. Monkhouse.

Vice-presidents: J. Johnstone JP, T. L. Sibson, Dr T. Gardner MB, CHB.

Chairman: H. A. Jenkins.

Vice-chairman: J. R. Sheffield.

Directors: R. S. Liddell, T. A. Bingley, C. J. Vasey, J. B. Lloyd, A. Liddell, A. Hodgkinson.

Team Manager: Aidan McCaffery.

Assistant Manager: Peter Hampton. *Physio:* Peter Hampton. *Commercial Manager:* Jim Thoburn. *Club Secretary:* Miss Alison Moore.

Year Formed: 1903. Ltd Co.: 1921.

Former Grounds: 1903–5, Milholme Bank; 1905–9, Devonshire Park; 1909– Brunton Park.

Former Names: Shaddonate United.

Club Nickname: 'Cumbrians' or 'The Blues'.

Record League Victory: 8-0 v Hartlepools U, Division 3 (N), 1 September 1928 – Prout; Smiles, Cook; Robinson (1) Ross, Pigg; Agar (1), Hutchison (1), McConnell (4), Ward (1), Watson. 8-0 v Scunthorpe United, Division 3 (N), 25 December 1952 – MacLaren; Hill, Scott; Stokoe, Twentyman, Waters; Harrison (1), Whitehouse (5), Ashman (2), Duffett, Bond.

Record Cup Victory: 6-1 v Billingham Synthonia, FA Cup, 1st rd, 17 November 1956 – Fairley; Hill, Kenny; Johnston, Waters, Thompson; Mooney, Broadis (1), Ackerman (2), Garvie (3), Bond.

Record Defeat: 1-11 v Hull C, Division 3 (N), 14 January 1939.

Most League Points (2 for a win): 62, Division 3 (N), 1950–51.

Most League points (3 for a win): 80, Division 3, 1981–82.

Most League Goals: 113, Division 4, 1963–64.

Highest League Scorer in Season: Jimmy McConnell, 42, Division 3 (N), 1928–29.

Most League Goals in Total Aggregate: Jimmy McConnell, 126, 1928–32.

Most Capped Player: Eric Welsh, 4, Northern Ireland.

Most League Appearances: Alan Ross, 466, 1963–79.

Record Transfer Fee Received: £275,000 from Vancouver Whitecaps for Peter Beardsley, April 1981.

Record Transfer Fee Paid: £120,000 to York C for Gordon Staniforth, October 1979.

Football League Record: 1928 Elected to Division 3 (N); 1958–62 Division 4; 1962–63 Division 3; 1963–64 Division 4; 1964–65 Division 3; 1965–74 Division 2; 1974–75 Division 1; 1975–77 Division 2; 1977–82 Division 3; 1982–86 Division 2; 1986–87 Division 3; 1987–92 Division 4; 1992– Division 3.

Honours: Football League: Division 1 best season: 22nd, 1974–75; Promoted from Division 2 (3rd) 1973–74; Division 3 – Champions 1964–65; Runners-up 1981–82; Division 4 – Runners-up 1963–64. *FA Cup:* 6th rd 1974–75. *Football League Cup:* Semi-final 1969–70.

Colours: Blue shirts, white shorts, blue stockings. **Change colours:** All yellow.

CARLISLE UNITED 1991–92 LEAGUE RECORD

Match No.	Date		Venue	Opponents	Result		H/T Score	Lg. Pos.	Goalscorers	Atten- dance
1	Aug	17	A	Doncaster R	W	3-0	1-0	—	Sendall, Fyfe, Proudlock	2639
2		24	H	Blackpool	L	1-2	1-2	7	Walling	4369
3		31	A	Cardiff C	L	0-1	0-0	14		4096
4	Sep	3	H	Rotherham U	L	1-3	1-1	—	Barnsley (pen)	2346
5		14	H	Lincoln C	L	0-2	0-2	19		2149
6		17	H	Mansfield T	L	1-2	0-0	—	Edmondson	1803
7		21	A	Northampton T	D	2-2	1-1	20	Watson 2	2656
8		28	H	Walsall	D	3-3	1-0	22	Fyfe 2, Barnsley (pen)	2148
9	Oct	5	A	Burnley	L	0-2	0-1	22		6157
10		12	H	Scunthorpe U	D	0-0	0-0	22		1988
11		19	A	Wrexham	L	0-3	0-1	22		1266
12		26	H	Crewe Alex	W	2-1	0-0	20	Watson, Fyfe	1905
13	Nov	2	H	Gillingham	D	0-0	0-0	21		1672
14		5	A	Barnet	L	2-4	1-0	—	Bodley (og), Fyfe (pen)	2983
15		9	A	Scarborough	D	2-2	0-2	21	Thorpe, Graham	1501
16		23	H	Hereford U	W	1-0	0-0	20	Walling	2032
17		30	H	Maidstone U	W	3-0	2-0	17	Watson 2, Barnsley (pen)	2146
18	Dec	21	A	Blackpool	L	0-1	0-0	20		3440
19		26	H	Doncaster R	W	1-0	1-0	17	Jeffels	3174
20		28	H	Cardiff C	D	2-2	0-0	17	Watson, Jeffels	3080
21	Jan	1	A	Rotherham U	L	0-1	0-0	18		4850
22		4	A	Chesterfield	D	0-0	0-0	17		2892
23		11	H	Rochdale	D	0-0	0-0	17		2494
24		18	A	York C	L	0-2	0-0	20		1953
25		25	H	Halifax T	D	1-1	0-1	18	Watson (pen)	2091
26	Feb	7	A	Crewe Alex	L	1-2	1-1	—	Watson	3232
27		12	A	Maidstone U	L	1-5	0-3	—	Watson	944
28		22	A	Rochdale	L	1-3	1-2	21	Watson	1691
29		29	H	Chesterfield	L	1-2	0-2	21	Edmondson	2038
30	Mar	3	H	York C	D	1-1	1-1	—	Watson	1681
31		6	A	Halifax T	L	2-3	1-0	—	Walling, Watson	1015
32		10	H	Barnet	L	1-3	0-2	—	Holmes M	1888
33		14	A	Gillingham	W	2-1	1-0	21	Holmes M, Watson	2789
34		21	H	Scarborough	D	2-2	0-0	21	Walling, Holmes M	1813
35		24	H	Wrexham	L	0-1	0-0	—		1826
36		28	A	Hereford U	L	0-1	0-1	21		1810
37	Apr	1	A	Lincoln C	L	0-1	0-0	—		2118
38		11	A	Mansfield T	L	1-2	1-0	21	Walling	3085
39		18	H	Northampton T	W	2-1	1-0	21	Watson, Holmes M	1935
40		21	A	Walsall	D	0-0	0-0	—		2406
41		25	H	Burnley	D	1-1	0-1	21	Thomas	10,000
42	May	2	A	Scunthorpe U	L	0-4	0-2	22		3851

Final League Position: 22

GOALSCORERS

League (41): Watson 14 (1 pen), Fyfe 5 (1 pen), Walling 5, Holmes M 4, Barnsley 3 (3 pens), Edmondson 2, Jeffels 2, Graham 1, Proudlock 1, Sendall 1, Thomas 1, Thorpe 1, own goals 1.
Rumbelows Cup (2): Barnsley 2.
FA Cup (4): Barnsley 2 (2 pens), Fyfe 1, Watson 1.

O'Hanlon	Armstrong	Barnsley	Miller	Jeffels	Graham	Thomas	Sendall	Walling	Fyfe	Proudlock	Thorpe	Wilkes	Edmondson	Potts	Deakin	Bennett	Nevin	Watson	Gallimore	Lowery	Holliday	Walsh	Gorman	Cranston	Freeman	Holmes M	Prins	Match No.
1	2	3	4	5	6	7†	8*	9	10	11	12	14																1
1		3	4	5	6	7		9	10†	8	11*	14		2	12													2
1	14	3	4	5	6	7		9*	10	8	12			2		11†												3
1		3	4	5	6	7		10		8	9*	12		2		11												4
1	14	3	4	5	6	7				8	9	11†	12	10*	2													5
1	12	2*	4	5	6	7				8	11	10			3			9										6
1	2		4	5	6	7		9		11	12	10*			3			8										7
1	2		4	5	6	7*		12	9	11	10				3			8										8
1	2		4	5	6	7*		12	9†	11	10							8	3	14								9
1	2		4	5	6	7		9	10	12								11*	3	8								10
1	2		4		6	7		9	10	12					3			11*		8	5							11
1			4		7			9	10				6					11	3	8	5							12
1			4		7			9*	10	12			6					11	3	8	5							13
1			4		7			9	10	12			6					11	3	8	5*							14
1			2	7	4*12			10	9	14			6					11	3	8	5†							15
1	5		4		2	7		8	10	9	11*		6					12	3									16
1	6		4	5	2	7*		8	10	9								11	3									17
1	6		4	5	2			8	10	9			3					11			7							18
1	6		4	5	2			8	10	9			3					11			7							19
1	6*		4	5	2			8		9			3				12	11			7	10						20
1			4	5	2			8		9			3		6			11			7	10						21
1			4	5	2	6		8		9			3					11			7	10						22
1	2		4	5		6		8		9	11							10			7	3						23
1			4	5	2	6		8		9	10	7	11*					8				3	12					24
1	14			5	2	7		9	10	11			6†					8			4	12	3*					25
1	2			4	7			9	10*12	11†			6				14	8		5			3					26
1	2		5	4	7			9	10†12	11			6*				14	8					3					27
1				2	8			12	10*	7†11			6				14	9		5			3	4				28
1	6*			5	2	8		10		11			7				12	9	3					4				29
1	6			5	2	12		10*		11			7				9	8	3					4				30
1	6			2	9			10		11			7					8	3		5			4				31
1	6			2	9			10		11			7					8	3		5			4				32
1	6			2	9			10			11		7					8	3		5			4				33
1	6	14		2	9			10		11	12		7†					8	3		5*			4				34
1	6		4	5	2†			10*12		7	11							9	3		14			8				35
1	6			5	2	4		10			12	11						9	3		7*			8				36
1	2	6		5				8	14	10†12	11							9		4*	3			7				37
1	2*	6				12	8		4	10		11†						9		5	3			7		14		38
1		6		4	8			10						5	3		12	9		2				7	11*			39
1		6		4*	8			10	11					5	12			9		3	2			7				40
1	14	6			8			10				3†		4	12			9		5	2			7	11*			41
1	14	6			8			9				3†		4	11		12			5	2			7	10*			42
42	8 +6s	28	25 +1s	26	37 +1s	35 +2s	1	33 +4s	25 +1s	26 +8s	23 +5s	1 +3s	26 +1s	3 +3s	3	5	2 +2s	34 +6s	16 +1s	6	16 +1s	14	5 +2s	—	4	15	3 +1s	

Rumbelows Cup   First Round   Rochdale (a)   1-5
                                           (h)   1-1
FA Cup   First Round   Crewe Alex (h)   1-1
                                         (a)   3-5

CARLISLE UNITED

Player and Position	Ht	Wt	Birth Date	Birth Place	Source	Clubs	League App	Gls
Goalkeepers								
Kelham O'Hanlon	6 1	13 03	16 5 62	Saltburn	Apprentice	Middlesbrough	87	—
						Rotherham U	248	—
						Carlisle U	42	—
Jason Priestley*	5 11	12 02	25 10 70	Leeds	Trainee	Carlisle U	22	—
						Hartlepool U (loan)	16	—
						Scarborough (loan)	10	—
Defenders								
Lee Armstrong*			19 10 72	Workington	Trainee	Carlisle U	20	—
Andy Barnsley	6 0	11 11	9 6 62	Sheffield	Denaby U	Rotherham U	28	—
						Sheffield U	77	1
						Rotherham U	83	3
						Carlisle U	28	3
Ian Dalziel	5 8	11 10	24 10 62	South Shields	Apprentice	Derby Co	22	4
						Hereford U	150	8
						Carlisle U	79	2
Darren Edmondson	6 0	12 02	4 11 71	Coniston	Trainee	Carlisle U	58	2
Mike Graham*	5 9	11 07	24 2 59	Lancaster	Apprentice	Bolton W	46	—
						Swindon T	141	1
						Mansfield T	133	1
						Carlisle U	138	3
John Holliday	6 4	11 00	13 3 70	Penrith		Carlisle U	17	—
Simon Jeffels‡	6 1	11 08	18 1 66	Barnsley	Apprentice	Barnsley	42	—
						Preston NE (loan)	1	—
						Carlisle U	76	5
Craig Potts§			25 2 74	Carlisle	Trainee	Carlisle U	6	—
Midfield								
Nick Cranston*			20 10 72	Carlisle	Trainee	Carlisle U	2	—
John Deakin‡	5 8	10 08	29 6 66	Sheffield	Barnsley	Doncaster R	23	—
						Apprentice	—	—
						Grimsby T	—	—
						Shepshed C	—	—
						Birmingham C	7	—
						Carlisle U	3	—
Paul Gorman‡	5 10	11 08	6 8 63	Dublin	Apprentice	Arsenal	6	—
						Birmingham C	6	—
						Carlisle U	148	7
						Shelbourne (loan)	—	—
						Shrewsbury T	64	1
						Carlisle U	5	—
Tony Lowery‡	5 9	11 01	6 7 61	Wallsend	Ashington	WBA	1	—
						Walsall (loan)	6	1
						Mansfield T	252	19
						Walsall (loan)	6	—
						Carlisle U	7	—
Jason Prins§			1 11 74	Wisbech	Trainee	Carlisle U	4	—
Gwyn Thomas*	5 7	11 05	26 9 57	Swansea	Apprentice	Leeds U	89	3
						Barnsley	201	17
						Hull C	22	—
						Carlisle U	37	1
Jeffrey Thorpe	5 10	12 08	17 11 72	Whitehaven	Trainee	Carlisle U	28	1
Derek Walsh	5 7	11 05	24 10 67	Hamilton	Apprentice	Everton	1	—
						Hamilton A	2	—
						Carlisle U	97	6
David Wilkes†	5 8	10 02	10 3 64	Barnsley	Apprentice	Barnsley	17	2
						Halifax (loan)	4	—
						Hong Kong H	—	—
						Stockport Co	8	—
						Hong Kong H	—	—
						Carlisle U	5	—

CARLISLE UNITED

Foundation: Carlisle United came into being in 1903 through the amalgamation of Shaddongate United and Carlisle Red Rose. The new club was admitted to the Second Division of the Lancashire Combination in 1905–06, winning promotion the following season.

First Football League game: 25 August, 1928, Division 3 (N), v Accrington S (a) W 3-2 – Prout; Coulthard, Cook; Harrison, Ross, Pigg; Agar, Hutchison, McConnell (1), Ward (1), Watson. (1 o.g).

Did you know: Club record goalscorer Jimmy McConnell scored four hat-tricks for United in his initial Football League season of 1928–29. He netted a total of 15 hat-tricks, including four four's in the League, before moving to Crewe in 1932.

Managers (and Secretary-managers)
H. Kirkbride 1904–05*, McCumiskey 1905–06*, J. Houston 1906–08*, Bert Stansfield 1908–10, J. Houston 1910–12, D. Graham 1912–13, George Bristow 1913–30, Billy Hampson 1930–33, Bill Clarke 1933–35, Robert Kelly 1935–36, Fred Westgarth 1936–38, David Taylor 1938–40, Howard Harkness 1940–45, Bill Clark 1945–46*, Ivor Broadis 1946–49, Bill Shankly 1949–51, Fred Emery 1951–58, Andy Beattie 1958–60, Ivor Powell 1960–63, Alan Ashman 1963–67, Tim Ward 1967–68, Bob Stokoe 1968–70, Ian MacFarlane 1970–72, Alan Ashman 1972–75, Dick Young 1975–76, Bobby Moncur 1976–80, Martin Harvey 1980, Bob Stokoe 1980–85, Bryan "Pop" Robson 1985, Bob Stokoe 1985–86, Harry Gregg 1986–87, Cliff Middlemass 1987–91, Aidan McCaffery April 1991–.

Player and Position	Ht	Wt	Birth Date	Birth Place	Source	Clubs	League App	League Gls
Forwards								
Tony Fyfe*	6 2	12 00	23 2 62	Carlisle		Carlisle U	74	17
						Scarborough (loan)	6	1
						Halifax T	16	—
						Carlisle	16	3
Eric Gates‡	5 6	10 08	28 6 55	Ferryhill	Apprentice	Ipswich T	296	73
						Sunderland	181	43
						Carlisle U	38	8
Micky Holmes	5 8	10 12	9 9 65	Blackpool		Bradford C	5	—
						Burnley	—	—
						Wolverhampton W	83	13
						Huddersfield T	7	—
						Cambridge U	11	—
						Rochdale	54	7
						Torquay U	40	3
						Carlisle U	15	4
Paul Nevin*	6 00	12 00	23 6 64	London		Carlisle U	8	—
Paul Proudlock	5 10	11 00	25 10 65	Hartlepool		Hartlepool U	15	—
						Middlesbrough	5	1
						Carlisle U	129	17
Richard Sendall	5 10	11 06	10 7 67	Stamford	Apprentice	Watford	—	—
						Blackpool	11	—
						Carlisle U	74	13
						Cardiff C (loan)	4	—
Dean Walling	6 0	11 00	17 4 69	Leeds	Trainee	Leeds U	—	—
						Rochdale	65	8
						Guiseley	—	—
						Carlisle U	74	10
Andy Watson	5 9	11 12	1 4 67	Leeds	Harrogate T	Halifax T	83	15
						Swansea	14	1
						Carlisle U	35	14

Trainees
Brown, Paul B; Caig, Antony; Fleming, William J; Grainger, Christopher; McKenzie, Michael F; Nugent, Richard; Potts, Craig; Prins, Jason.

Associated Schoolboys
Armstrong, Gavin; Bird, Shane L; Doswell, Lee A; Fryer, Andrew; Holt, Steven; Jansen, Matthew B; Murray, Paul; Scott, Alan; Varty, John W; Wightman, Mark R.

Associated Schoolboys who have accepted the club's offer of a Traineeship/Contract
Cleeland, Marc; Delap, Rory J; Gray, Alan M; Prokas, Richard; Wilson, Graeme J.

CHARLTON ATHLETIC 1991–92   *Back row (left to right):* Scott Minto, Darren Pitcher, Simon Webster, Tommy Caton, Robert Lee, Colin Walsh.
Centre row: Stuart Balmer, Steve Brown, Carl Leaburn, Bob Bolder, Mike Salmon, Alex Dyer, Anthony Barness, John Bumstead.
Front row: Dean Dye, Paul Gorman, Paul Bacon, Alan Curbishley (First Team Coach), Andy Peake, Steve Gritt (First Team Coach), Kim Grant, Mark Tivey, Andy Salako.

Division 1   **CHARLTON ATHLETIC**

The Valley, Floyd Road, Charlton, London SE7 8BL. Telephone 081-293-4567. Fax No: 081-293-5143. Clubcall (0891) 121146.

Ground capacity: 12,300.

Record attendance: 75,031 v Aston Villa, FA Cup 5th rd, 12 February 1938 (at The Valley).

Record receipts: £114,618.70 v Liverpool (at Selhurst Park), Division 1, 23 January 1988.

President: R. D. Collins.

Chairman: R. N. Alwen.

Vice-chairman: M. J. Norris.

Directors: R. D. Collins, R. A. Murray, M. A. Simons, M. Stevens, D. G.Ufton.

General Manager: Arnie Warren.

Assistant General Manager: Jonathan Fuller. *Commercial Manager:* Andy Bryant. *Stadium Manager:* Roy King. *Publications manager:* Steve Dixon. *Player-coaches:* Alan Curbishley and Steve Gritt. *Physio:* Jimmy Hendry. *Secretary:* Chris Parkes. *Reserve team manager:* Keith Peacock. *Youth team manager:* John Cartwright. *Youth development officer:* Jimmy Hampson.

Year Formed: 1905. Turned Professional: 1920. Ltd Co.: 1919.

Former Grounds: 1906, Siemens Meadow; 1907, Woolwich Common; 1909, Pound Park; 1913, Horn Lane; 1919, The Valley; 1923, Catford (The Mount); 1924, The Valley; 1985 Selhurst Park; 1991 Upton Park; 1992 The Valley.

Club Nickname: 'Addicks', 'Robins' or 'Valiants'.

Record League Victory: 8-1 v Middlesbrough, Division 1, 12 September 1953 – Bartram; Campbell, Ellis; Fenton, Ufton, Hammond; Hurst (2), O'Linn (2), Leary (1), Firmani (3), Kiernan.

Record Cup Victory: 7-0 v Burton A, FA Cup, 3rd rd, 7 January 1956 – Bartram; Campbell, Townsend; Hewie, Ufton, Hammond; Hurst (1), Gauld (1), Leary (3), White, Kiernan (2).

Record Defeat: 1-11 v Aston Villa, Division 2, 14 November 1959.

Most League Points (2 for a win): 61, Division 3 (S), 1934–35.

Most League points (3 for a win): 77, Division 2, 1985–86.

Most League Goals: 107, Division 2, 1957–58.

Highest League Scorer in Season: Ralph Allen, 32, Division 3 (S), 1934–35.

Most League Goals in Total Aggregate: Stuart Leary, 153, 1951–62.

Most Capped Player: John Hewie, 19, Scotland.

Most League Appearances: Sam Bartram, 582, 1934–56.

Record Transfer Fee Received: £650,000 from Crystal Palace for Mike Flanagan, August 1979.

Record Transfer Fee Paid: £600,000 to Chelsea for Joe McLaughlin, August 1989.

Football League Record: 1921 Elected to Division 3 (S); 1929–33 Division 2; 1933–35 Division 3 (S); 1935–36 Division 2; 1936–57 Division 1; 1957–72 Division 2; 1972–75 Division 3; 1975–80 Division 2; 1980–81 Division 3; 1981–86; Division 2; 1986–90 Division 1; 1990–92 Division 2; 1992– Division 1.

Honours: Football League: Division 1 – Runners-up 1936–37; Division 2 – Runners-up 1935–36, 1985–86; Division 3 (S) – Champions 1928–29, 1934–35; Promoted from Division 3 (3rd) 1974–75, 1980–81. *FA Cup:* Winners 1947; Runners-up 1946. *Football League Cup:* best season: 4th rd, 1962–63, 1964–65, 1978–79, 1986–87. *Full Members' Cup:* Runners-up 1987.

Colours: Red shirts, white shorts, red stockings. **Change colours:** Blue shirts, black shorts, black stockings.

152

CHARLTON ATHLETIC 1991–92 LEAGUE RECORD

Match No.	Date		Venue	Opponents	Result		H/T Score	Lg. Pos.	Goalscorers	Attendance
1	Aug	18	H	Newcastle U	W	2-1	0-0	—	Lee, Leaburn	9322
2		24	A	Wolverhampton W	D	1-1	1-1	8	Lee	16,309
3	Sep	1	H	Derby Co	L	0-2	0-0	—		6602
4		3	A	Tranmere R	D	2-2	0-1	—	Webster, Lee	7609
5		7	A	Plymouth Arg	W	2-0	0-0	12	Pitcher (pen), Nelson	5602
6		14	H	Portsmouth	W	3-0	2-0	7	Nelson, Lee 2	5707
7		17	H	Sunderland	L	1-4	1-1	—	Webster	5807
8		21	A	Watford	L	0-2	0-2	14		8459
9		28	H	Port Vale	W	2-0	1-0	9	Nelson, Leaburn	4049
10	Oct	5	A	Leicester C	W	2-0	0-0	7	Nelson, James (og)	11,467
11		12	H	Bristol R	W	1-0	0-0	5	Leaburn	5685
12		19	H	Brighton & HA	W	2-0	2-0	5	Nelson, Walsh	5598
13		23	A	Oxford U	W	2-1	0-0	—	Pitcher, Lee	4069
14		26	A	Southend U	D	1-1	0-1	3	Leaburn	7320
15		30	H	Ipswich T	D	1-1	1-1	—	Gatting	6939
16	Nov	2	A	Grimsby T	L	0-1	0-1	4		4743
17		6	H	Swindon T	D	0-0	0-0	—		5398
18		9	H	Blackburn R	L	0-2	0-1	4		711.:
19		16	A	Middlesbrough	L	0-2	0-0	7		13,093
20		23	H	Cambridge U	L	1-2	0-2	10	Gorman	6350
21		30	A	Bristol C	W	2-0	1-0	9	Pardew, Gorman	9123
22	Dec	7	H	Barnsley	D	1-1	0-0	9	Pardew (pen)	4581
23		26	A	Ipswich T	L	0-2	0-1	10		13,826
24		28	H	Derby Co	W	2-1	1-0	10	Leaburn, Nelson	14,367
25	Jan	8	H	Oxford U	D	2-2	0-2	—	Leaburn, Lee	4101
26		15	H	Wolverhampton W	L	0-2	0-1	—		5703
27		18	A	Newcastle U	W	4-3	1-3	8	Barness, Walsh 2, O'Brien (og)	15,663
28	Feb	1	A	Brighton & HA	W	2-1	1-1	8	Gorman, Lee	8870
29		8	H	Southend U	W	2-0	0-0	9	Webster, Leaburn	9724
30		15	A	Cambridge U	L	0-1	0-0	9		6472
31		22	H	Bristol C	W	2-1	0-1	8	Walsh, Webster	5900
32		26	A	Millwall	L	0-1	0-1	—		12,882
33		29	A	Barnsley	L	0-1	0-0	10		6050
34	Mar	3	H	Grimsby T	L	1-3	0-3	—	Leaburn	3658
35		7	H	Millwall	W	1-0	0-0	7	Hendry	8177
36		10	A	Swindon T	W	2-1	1-0	—	Leaburn, Webster	7196
37		21	A	Blackburn R	W	2-0	0-0	5	Lee, Leaburn	14,844
38		28	H	Middlesbrough	D	0-0	0-0	6		8250
39		31	A	Portsmouth	W	2-1	0-0	—	Leaburn, Whyte	14,539
40	Apr	4	A	Plymouth Arg	D	0-0	0-0	4		6787
41		11	A	Sunderland	W	2-1	0-0	6	Lee, Minto	21,326
42		18	H	Watford	D	1-1	0-1	6	Lee	7477
43		21	A	Port Vale	D	1-1	0-0	—	Gritt	8461
44		25	A	Leicester C	W	2-0	2-0	6	Lee, Whyte	15,357
45		28	H	Tranmere R	L	0-1	0-1	—		7645
46	May	2	A	Bristol R	L	0-1	0-0	7		7630

Final League Position: 7

GOALSCORERS

League (54): Lee 12, Leaburn 11, Nelson 6, Webster 5, Walsh 4, Gorman 3, Pardew 2 (1 pen), Pitcher 2 (1 pen), Whyte 2, Barness 1, Gatting 1, Gritt 1, Hendry 1, Minto 1, own goals 2.
Rumbelows Cup (5): Leaburn 2, Minto 1, Peake 1, Walsh 1.
FA Cup (4): Gatting 2, Grant 1, Leaburn 1.

Bolder	Pitcher	Minto	Peake	Gritt	Gatting	Lee	Bumstead	Leaburn	Nelson	Walsh	Webster	Bacon	Dyer	Barness	Brown	Gorman	Grant	Balmer	Pardew	Rosenior	Wilder	Curbishley	Darlington	Tivey	Hendry	Whyte	Match No.
1	2	3	4	5	6	7	8	9	10	11																	1
1	2	3	4		6	7		9	10	11	5	8															2
1	2	3	4		6	7		9	10	11	5	8*	12														3
1	2	3	4		6	7		9	10	11	5	8															4
1	2	3	4	14	6	7		9	10*	11	5	8†	12														5
1	2	3†	4	14	6	7		9	10	11*	5	8	12														6
1	2		4	3†	6	7		9	10	11*	5	8	12	14													7
1	2		4		6	7		9†	10	11	5	8*	12	3	14												8
1	2	3	4		6	7†	8	9	10	11*	5	14	12														9
1	2		4		6		8		10*		5	7	11	3		9	12										10
1	2	3	4		6	7	8	9	10		5	11															11
1	2	3	4		6	7	8	9	10	11	5*		12														12
1	2	3	4		6	7	8	9	10	11	5																13
1	2	3	4		6	7	8	9	10	11	5																14
1	2	3	4		6	7	8	9	10	11	5																15
1	2	3	4		6	7	8	9	10*	11	5		12														16
1	2	3	4		6	7	8	9	10*	11	5		12														17
1	2	3	4			7	8	9	10	11	5		12	6*													18
1	2	3	4			7	8	9	10*	11	5		12				6										19
1	2	3	4			7	8	9			5		11*	14†		10		6	12								20
1	2	3			6	7	8	12		11	5					10*			4	9							21
1	2	3			6	7	8			11	5					10			4	9							22
1	4	3†			6	7	8	12	10	11	5							14		9*	2						23
1	2				6	7	8	9	10	11	5			3					4								24
1	2				6	7	8*	9	10	11	5			3			12		4								25
1	2				6	7		9	10	11	5			3			12	5	4			8*					26
1	2	11†	14	6		8		9	10	11†	5	7*		3			12		4				12				27
1	2	11†	14	6	7	8			10		5			3		9*			4				12				28
1	2		14	6	7	8†	9	10	11*		5			3		12			4								29
1	2	14			6	7	8†	9	10*	11	5			3		12			4								30
1	2				6	7	8*	9	10	11	5			3		12			4								31
1	2		8					9	10	11	5*	12		3				6	4			7†	14				32
1	2		8	6				9	10	11	5	7*		3					4						12		33
1	2		6*			8†	9	10	11		5	14		3			12		4						7		34
1	2	3				8	9	10	11		5	7*							6	4					12		35
1	2	3				7	8	9	10*	11†	5		14						6	4					12		36
1	2†	3		14		7	8	9	10*	11	5								6	4					12		37
1	2	3				7	8	9	10	11	5								6	4							38
1	2	3				7	8	9	10*	11	5								6	4						12	39
1	2	3				7*	8	9		11	5		12						6	4					10		40
1	2	3		14	12	7	8	9†		11*	5		4						6						10		41
1	2	3				7	8		9	11	5								6	4					10		42
1	2	3		12			8	9*	10	11	5								6	4						7	43
1	2	3		12	14	7*	8		10	11†	5								6	4						9	44
1	2	3		12			7	8†		10*	11	5		14					6	4						9	45
1	2						7	8		10	11	5		3					6	4						9	46
46	46	32	20	4	30	39	36	37	41	42	44	11	3	16	—	5	—	16	23	3	2	1	1	—	1	7	
		+			+	+			+			+	+	+	+	+	+	+	+			+	+	+	+	+	
		1s			10s	2s			2s			3s	10s	6s	1s	3s	4s	2s	1s			1s	1s	4s	1s		

Rumbelows Cup	First Round	Fulham (h)	4-2
		(a)	1-1
	Second Round	Norwich C (h)	0-2
		(a)	0-3
FA Cup	Third Round	Barnet (h)	3-1
	Fourth Round	Sheffield U (h)	0-0
		(a)	1-3

CHARLTON ATHLETIC

Player and Position	Ht	Wt	Birth Date	Birth Place	Source	Clubs	League App	Gls
Goalkeepers								
Bob Bolder	6 3	14 06	2 10 58	Dover	Dover	Sheffield W	196	—
						Liverpool	—	—
						Sunderland	22	—
						Luton T (loan)	—	—
						Charlton Ath	222	—
Lee Harrison	6 2	12 02	12 9 71	Billericay	Trainee	Charlton Ath	—	—
						Fulham (loan)	—	—
						Gillingham (loan)	2	—
Mike Salmon	6 2	13 00	14 7 64	Leyland	Local	Blackburn R	1	—
						Chester C (loan)	16	—
						Stockport Co	118	—
						Bolton W	26	—
						Wrexham (loan)	17	—
						Wrexham	83	—
						Charlton Ath	7	—
Defenders								
Paul Bacon	5 9	10 04	20 12 70	London	Trainee	Charlton Ath	15	—
Stuart Balmer	6 1	12 04	20 6 69	Falkirk	Celtic	Charlton Ath	42	—
Anthony Barness	5 10	10 12	25 3 72	London	Trainee	Charlton Ath	22	1
Steve Brown			13 5 72	Brighton	Trainee	Charlton Ath	1	—
Tommy Caton	6 2	13 00	6 10 62	Liverpool	Apprentice	Manchester C	165	8
						Arsenal	81	2
						Oxford U	53	3
						Charlton Ath	57	5
Steve Gatting	5 11	11 11	29 5 59	Park Royal	Apprentice	Arsenal	58	5
						Brighton & HA	316	19
						Charlton Ath	32	1
Steve Gritt	5 9	10 10	31 10 57	Bournemouth	Apprentice	Bournemouth	6	3
						Charlton Ath	347	24
						Walsall	20	1
						Charlton Ath	26	1
Scott Minto	5 10	10 00	6 8 71	Cheshire	Trainee	Charlton Ath	102	4
Darren Pitcher	5 9	12 02	12 10 69	London	Trainee	Charlton Ath	90	5
						Galway U (loan)	—	—
Mark Reid‡	5 8	11 05	15 9 61	Kilwinning	Celtic BC	Celtic	124	5
						Charlton Ath	211	15
Andy Salako*			8 11 72	Nigeria	Trainee	Charlton Ath	1	—
Simon Webster	6 0	11 07	20 1 64	Earl Shilton	Apprentice	Tottenham H	3	—
						Exeter C (loan)	26	—
						Norwich C (loan)	—	—
						Huddersfield T	118	4
						Sheffield U	37	3
						Charlton Ath	128	10
Midfield								
John Bumstead	5 7	10 05	27 11 58	Rotherhithe	Apprentice	Chelsea	339	38
						Charlton Ath	36	—
Alan Curbishley	5 11	11 10	8 11 57	Forest Gate	Apprentice	West Ham U	85	5
						Birmingham C	130	11
						Aston Villa	36	1
						Charlton Ath	63	6
						Brighton & HA	116	13
						Charlton Ath	26	—
Jermaine Darlington§			11 4 74	London	Trainee	Charlton Ath	2	—
The Vinh Nguyen	5 08	10 10	25 10 73	Vietnam	Trainee	Charlton Ath	—	—
Alan Pardew	5 10	11 00	18 7 61	Wimbledon	Yeovil	Crystal Palace	128	8
						Charlton Ath	24	2

CHARLTON ATHLETIC

Foundation: Although formed in 1905 by members of such clubs as East Street Mission, Blundell Mission, and Charlton Reds, Charlton Athletic did not really make their presence felt until adopting professionalism and joining the Southern League in 1920. Before that, they had played in such competitions as the Lewisham, Southern Suburban and London Leagues.

First Football League game: 27 August, 1921, Division 3 (S), v Exeter C (h) W 1-0 – Hughes; Mitchell, Goodman; Dowling (1), Hampson, Dunn; Castle, Bailey, Halse, Green, Wilson.

Did you know: As Football League championship runners-up, Charlton were invited to replace Italy in the game against France in Paris and won 5-2. This was in April 1937.

Managers (and Secretary-managers)
Walter Rayner 1920–25, Alex MacFarlane 1925–28, Albert Lindon 1928, Alex MacFarlane 1928–32, Albert Lindon 1932–33, Jimmy Seed 1933–56, Jimmy Trotter 1956–61, Frank Hill 1961–65, Bob Stokoe 1965–67, Eddie Firmani 1967–70, Theo Foley 1970–74, Andy Nelson 1974–80, Mike Bailey 1980–81, Alan Mullery 1981–82, Ken Craggs 1982, Lennie Lawrence 1982–91, Steve Gritt/Alan Curbishley July 1991–.

Player and Position	Ht	Wt	Birth Date	Birth Place	Source	Clubs	League App	Gls
Colin Walsh	5 9	10 11	22 7 62	Hamilton	Apprentice	Nottingham F	139	32
						Charlton Ath	131	15
						Peterborough U (loan)	5	1
						Middlesborough (loan)	13	1
Daniel Wareham‡	5 10	10 08	29 12 72	Kent	Trainee	Charlton Ath	—	—
Forwards								
Alex Dyer	5 11	11 12	14 11 65	West Ham	Apprentice	Watford	—	—
						Blackpool	108	19
						Hull C	60	14
						Crystal Palace	17	2
						Charlton Ath	48	2
Paul Gorman	5 9	12 02	18 9 68	Macclesfield	Trainee Fisher Ath	Doncaster R	16	2
						Charlton Ath	16	5
Kim Grant	5 10	10 12	25 9 72	Ghana	Trainee	Charlton Ath	16	2
Carl Leaburn	6 3	12 12	30 3 69	Lewisham	Apprentice	Charlton Ath	119	15
						Northampton T (loan)	9	—
Robert Lee	5 8	10 12	1 2 66	West Ham	ABTA	Charlton Ath	291	58
Garry Nelson	5 10	11 04	16 1 61	Southend	Amateur	Southend U	129	17
						Swindon T	79	7
						Plymouth Arg	74	20
						Brighton & HA	144	47
						Notts Co (loan)	2	—
						Charlton Ath	41	6
Mark Tivey*	5 9	10 00	10 2 71	London	Trainee	Charlton Ath	1	—

Trainees
Antoine, Ricky B; Appiah, Sam K; Bakes, Sean; Darlington, Jermaine C; Embery, John A; Gray, Andrew J; Gray, Darren A; Hodgson, Paul; Linger, Paul H; Mills, Daniel R; Newton, Shaun O; Primus, Linvoy S; Rufus, Richard R; Short, Marlon; Sturgess, Paul C.

Associated Schoolboys
Burt, Leslie; Clark, Scott A; Frampton, Stephen G; Hodges, Lee L; Kyte, Jamie R; Larkin, Andrew K; Lee, Dean J; Mahoney, Barry J; Melville-Brown, Luke S. W; Morley, Darren R; Notley, Jay; Stuart, Jamie C; Tindall, Jason.

Associated Schoolboys who have accepted the club's offer of a Traineeship/Contract
Jackson, James T; Lawson, John W.

CHELSEA 1991–92 *Back row (left to right):* Graham Stuart, Gareth Hall, Damian Matthew, Kevin Hitchcock, Steve Clarke, Graeme Le Saux, Kevin McAllister.
Centre row: Eddie Niedzwiecki, Bob Ward, David Lee, Kerry Dixon, Paul Elliott, Dave Beasant, Kenneth Monkou, Erland Johnsen, Alan Dickens, Gwyn Williams, Dave Collyer.
Front row: Jason Cundy, Dennis Wise, Gordon Durie, Ian Porterfield, Andy Townsend, Tom Boyd, Kevin Wilson.

FA Premier

CHELSEA

Stamford Bridge, London SW6. Telephone 071-385 5545. Club-call: 0898 121159. Ticket News and Promotions: 0898 121011. Ticket credit card service: 071-386-7799. Fax No: 071 381 4831

Ground capacity: 36,965 (28,000 covered).

Record attendance: 82,905 v Arsenal, Division 1, 12 October 1935.

Record receipts: £315,000 v Sunderland, FA Cup 6th rd, 9 March, 1992.

Pitch measurements: 110yd × 72yd.

President: G. M. Thomson.

Chairman: K. W. Bates.

Vice-chairman.

Directors: C. Hutchinson (Managing), Y. S. Todd, S. S. Tollman.

Team Manager: Ian Porterfield.

Assistant Manager: Gwyn Williams. *First team coach:* Don Howe. *Physio:* Bob Ward. *Reserve Team Manager:* Eddie Niedzwiecki. *Company Secretary/Director:* Yvonne Todd. *Match Secretary:* Keith Lacy. *Commercial Manager:* John Shaw.

Year Formed: 1905. Turned Professional: 1905. Ltd Co.: 1905.

Club Nickname: 'The Blues'.

Record League Victory: 9-2 v Glossop N E, Division 2, 1 September 1906 – Byrne; Walton, Miller; Key (1), McRoberts, Henderson; Moran, McDermott (1), Hilsdon (5), Copeland (1); Kirwan (1).

Record Cup Victory: 13-0 v Jeunesse Hautcharage, ECWC, 1st rd 2nd leg, 29 September 1971 – Bonetti; Boyle, Harris (1), Hollins (1p), Webb (1), Hinton, Cooke, Baldwin (3), Osgood (5), Hudson (1), Houseman (1).

Record Defeat: 1-8 v Wolverhampton W, Division 1, 26 September 1953.

Most League Points (2 for a win): 57, Division 2, 1906–07.

Most League points (3 for a win): 99, Division 2, 1988–89.

Most League Goals: 98, Division 1, 1960–61.

Highest League Scorer in Season: Jimmy Greaves, 41, 1960–61.

Most League Goals in Total Aggregate: Bobby Tambling, 164, 1958–70.

Most Capped Player: Ray Wilkins, 24 (84), England.

Most League Appearances: Ron Harris, 655, 1962–80.

Record Transfer Fee Received: £2,200,000 from Tottenham H for Gordon Durie, July 1991.

Record Transfer Fee Paid: £1,600,000 to Wimbledon for Dennis Wise, July 1990.

Football League Record: 1905 Elected to Division 2; 1907–10 Division 1; 1910–12 Division 2; 1912–24 Division 1; 1924–30 Division 2; 1930–62 Division 1; 1962–63 Division 2; 1963–75 Division 1; 1975–77 Division 2; 1977–79 Division 1; 1979–84 Division 2; 1984–88 Division 1; 1988–89 Division 2; 1989–92 Division 1; 1992– FA Premier League.

Honours: Football League: Division 1 – Champions 1954–55; Division 2 – Champions 1983–84, 1988–89; Runners-up 1906–7, 1911–12, 1929–30, 1962–63, 1976–77. *FA Cup:* Winners 1970; Runners-up 1914–15, 1966–67. *Football League Cup:* Winners 1964–65; Runners-up 1971–72. *Full Members' Cup:* Winners 1985–86. *Zenith Data Systems Cup:* Winners 1989–90. **European Competitions:** *European Fairs Cup:* 1958–60, 1965–66, 1968–69; *European Cup-Winners' Cup:* 1970–71 (winners), 1971–72.

Colours: Royal blue shirts and shorts, white stockings. **Change colours:** White shirts with red stripe, black shorts, black stockings.

CHELSEA 1991–92 LEAGUE RECORD

Match No.	Date		Venue	Opponents	Result		H/T Score	Lg. Pos.	Goalscorers	Atten-dance
1	Aug	17	H	Wimbledon	D	2-2	1-1	—	Elliott, Allon	22,574
2		21	A	Oldham Ath	L	0-3	0-2	—		14,997
3		24	A	Tottenham H	W	3-1	2-0	12	Dixon, Wilson, Townsend	34,645
4		28	H	Notts Co	D	2-2	0-1	—	Elliott, Allon	15,847
5		31	H	Luton T	W	4-1	3-0	7	Le Saux, Townsend, Dixon, Wise	17,457
6	Sep	3	A	Sheffield U	W	1-0	0-0	—	Wise	17,400
7		7	A	West Ham U	D	1-1	0-0	5	Dixon	18,875
8		14	H	Leeds U	L	0-1	0-0	9		23,439
9		18	H	Aston Villa	W	2-0	1-0	—	Jones, Townsend	17,182
10		21	A	QPR	D	2-2	0-1	5	Townsend, Wise	19,579
11		28	H	Everton	D	2-2	0-1	5	Wilson, Wise	19,038
12	Oct	5	A	Arsenal	L	2-3	2-1	6	Le Saux, Wilson	42,074
13		19	H	Liverpool	D	2-2	1-1	9	Jones, Myers	30,230
14		26	A	Crystal Palace	D	0-0	0-0	10		21,841
15	Nov	2	A	Coventry C	W	1-0	1-0	8	Le Saux	11,343
16		16	H	Norwich C	L	0-3	0-2	10		15,755
17		23	A	Southampton	L	0-1	0-1	12		14,933
18		30	H	Nottingham F	W	1-0	0-0	11	Dixon	19,420
19	Dec	7	A	Sheffield W	L	0-3	0-0	11		27,383
20		15	H	Manchester U	L	1-3	0-1	—	Allen C	23,120
21		21	H	Oldham Ath	W	4-2	3-1	9	Wise (pen), Allen C 2, Elliott	13,136
22		26	A	Notts Co	L	0-2	0-1	11		11,933
23		28	A	Luton T	L	0-2	0-2	12		10,738
24	Jan	1	H	Manchester C	D	1-1	0-0	14	Allen C	18,196
25		11	H	Tottenham H	W	2-0	1-0	12	Allen C, Wise	28,628
26		18	A	Wimbledon	W	2-1	1-0	8	Townsend, Allen C	8413
27	Feb	1	A	Liverpool	W	2-1	1-1	6	Jones, Wise	38,681
28		8	H	Crystal Palace	D	1-1	0-1	7	Cascarino	17,810
29		12	H	Southampton	D	1-1	0-0	—	Townsend	7148
30		22	A	Nottingham F	D	1-1	0-1	8	Allen C	24,095
31		26	A	Manchester U	D	1-1	0-0	—	Donaghy (og)	44,872
32		29	H	Sheffield W	L	0-3	0-3	7		17,538
33	Mar	11	A	Norwich C	W	1-0	0-0	—	Dixon	13,413
34		14	H	Coventry C	L	0-1	0-0	9		10,962
35		21	H	Sheffield U	L	1-2	0-1	11	Cundy	11,247
36		28	A	Manchester C	D	0-0	0-0	12		23,633
37	Apr	4	H	West Ham U	W	2-1	1-1	9	Wise, Cascarino	20,684
38		11	A	Leeds U	L	0-3	0-0	12		31,363
39		18	H	QPR	W	2-1	1-0	11	Clarke, Wise (pen)	18,952
40		20	A	Aston Villa	L	1-3	0-0	11	Sinclair	19,269
41		25	H	Arsenal	D	1-1	0-0	11	Wise	26,003
42	May	2	A	Everton	L	1-2	0-1	14	Newton	20,163

Final League Position: 14

GOALSCORERS

League (50): Wise 10 (2 pens), Allen C 7, Townsend 6, Dixon 5, Elliott 3, Jones 3, Le Saux 3, Wilson 3, Allon 2, Cascarino 2, Clarke 1, Cundy 1, Myers 1, Newton 1, Sinclair 1, own goals 1.
Rumbelows Cup (2): Townsend 1, Wise 1.
FA Cup (6): Allen 2, Wise 2, Jones 1, Stuart 1.

Beasant	Clarke	Boyd	Townsend	Elliott	Monkou	Le Saux	Hall	Dixon	Wilson	Wise	Dickens	Allon	Sinclair	Hitchcock	Johnsen	Myers	Jones	Matthew	Pearce	Cundy	Stuart	Lee	Allen C	Burley	Cascarino	Gilkes	Barnard	Newton	Match No.
1	2	3	4	5	6	7	8*	9	10†	11	12	14																	1
1	2	3	4	5	6	7		9	12	11	8*	14	10†																2
	2	3	4	5		7		9	10	11	8			1	6														3
	2	3	4	5		7*		9	10	11	8†	12		1	6	14													4
	2	3	8	5	6	7		9	10*	11	12			1			4												5
	2	3	8	5	6	7		9	10	11				1			4												6
	2	3	8	5	6	7		9	10*	11	12			1			4												7
	2	3†	8	5	6	7		9	10*	11	14	12		1			4												8
1	2	3	8	5	6	7		9		11	12	10*					4												9
1	2	3*	8	5	6	7		9	10	11	12						4												10
1	2	3	8	5	6	7		9	10	11							4												11
	2	3*	8	5	6	7		9	10	11	12			1			4												12
	2	3*	8	5	6	7			10				9†	1		11	4	12	14										13
	2	3	8	5		7*		9	10					1			4	12		6	11								14
1	2	3		5		7		9	10	11							4	8		6									15
1	2			5	6	7		9	10	11						3*	4	8†	14		12								16
	2			5	6	7		9	10	11	8	12		1			4					3*							17
	2	3	8	5	6	7		9		11				1			4						10						18
	2	3	8	5	6	7*		9		11†				1			4				12		10	14					19
	2	3*	8	5	6	7		9		11				1			4				12		10						20
1	2		8	5	6	3		9		11							4				7		10						21
1	2	14	8	5	6†	3		9	12	11							4				7*		10						22
	2*	3	8	5	6	7		9		11	14						4†				12		10						23
1		3	8	5		7*	2	9		11							4			6	12		10						24
			8	5		3	2	9	12	11				1			4†			6	7*		10	14					25
		3	8	5			2	9		11				1			4			6	7		10						26
		3	8	5		7	2			11				1			4			6	9		10						27
			8	5		3*	7†	2		11			14	1			4			6	12		10		9				28
			8		5	7†				14		4		1	6	3					11*		10	2	9	12			29
			5				2	12	14	11	8			1		3				6	7*		10	4†	9				30
			8	5		7*	2	12		11				1	3	4				6	9		10						31
			8	5			7	2	12	11†				1	3					6	14		10	4	9*				32
1	2		8			6	7	9				3					4				5	11			10				33
1	2		8	5*	6	7		9†	14			3					4				11	12	10						34
1	2			5		12		9*	14			3†				14	4			6	7	10	8						35
1	2			6	7					11				5	3	4					9				8	10			36
1	2		5	6	7					11					3	4*					9				8	10	12		37
1	2†	8	5	6	7*	14				11					3	4					9			,	10	12			38
1	2	8	5*	6	7	9				11			3			4					10					12			39
1	2†		8		6	7	9			11				3	14	4*	12				10				5				40
1			8		6†	3	14	9		11			2		5		4	12			7*				10				41
1			8		6	3†		9		11			2		5		4	12			7*				10			14	42
21	31	22	35	35	31	39	9	32	15	37	6	2	8	21	6	9	35	2	—	12	20	1	15	6	11	—	1	—	
	+1s						+1s	+1s	+3s	+7s	+1s	+4s	+9s			+1s	+2s			+5s	+2s		+7s		+1s	+2s	+1s +3s	+1s	

Rumbelows Cup — Second Round — Tranmere R (h) — 1-1
(a) — 1-3

FA Cup — Third Round — Hull C (a) — 2-0
Fourth Round — Everton (h) — 1-0
Fifth Round — Sheffield U (h) — 1-0
Sixth Round — Sunderland (h) — 1-1
(a) — 1-2

CHELSEA

Player and Position	Ht	Wt	Birth Date	Birth Place	Source	Clubs	League App	League Gls
Goalkeepers								
Dave Beasant	6 4	13 00	20 3 59	Willesden	Edgware T	Wimbledon	340	—
						Newcastle U	20	—
						Chelsea	116	—
Ian Chatfield	5 10	10 10	10 11 72	Redhill	Trainee	Chelsea	—	—
Kevin Hitchcock	6 1	12 02	5 10 62	Custom House	Barking	Nottingham F	—	—
						Mansfield T (loan)	14	—
						Mansfield T	168	—
						Chelsea	35	—
						Northampton T (loan)	17	—
Defenders								
Darren Barnard	5 9	11 00	30 11 71	Rinteln	Workingham	Chelsea	4	—
Tom Boyd (To Celtic February 1992)	5 11	11 04	24 11 65	Glasgow	S Form	Motherwell	252	6
						Chelsea	23	—
Steve Clarke	5 9	11 02	29 8 63	Saltcoats	Beith Jnrs	St Mirren	151	6
						Chelsea	163	6
Jason Cundy	6 1	13 10	12 11 69	Wimbledon	Trainee	Chelsea	41	2
						Tottenham H (loan)	10	—
Paul Elliott	6 2	11 11	18 3 64	London	Apprentice	Charlton Ath	63	1
						Luton T	66	4
						Aston Villa	57	7
						Bari	—	—
						Celtic	54	2
						Chelsea	70	6
Gareth Hall	5 8	10 07	20 3 69	Croydon		Chelsea	83	1
Erland Johnsen	6 0	12 10	5 4 67	Fredrikstad	Bayern Munich	Chelsea	31	—
Graeme Le Saux	6 0	12 00	17 10 68	Jersey		Chelsea	76	8
David Lee	6 3	14 00	26 11 69	Kingswood	Trainee	Chelsea	72	6
						Reading (loan)	5	5
						Plymouth Arg (loan)	9	1
Kenneth Monkou	6 0	12 09	29 11 64	Surinam	Feyenoord	Chelsea	94	2
Ian Pearce	6 01	12 00	7 5 74	Bury St Edmunds	School	Chelsea	3	—
Frank Sinclair	5 8	11 02	3 12 71	Lambeth	Trainee	Chelsea	12	1
						WBA (loan)	6	1
Midfield								
Craig Burley	6 1	11 07	24 9 71	Ayr	Trainee	Chelsea	9	—
Alan Dickens	5 11	12 01	3 9 64	Plaistow	Apprentice	West Ham U	192	23
						Chelsea	48	1
Vinny Jones	5 11	11 10	5 1 65	Watford	Wealdstone	Wimbledon	77	9
						Leeds U	46	5
						Sheffield U	33	2
						Chelsea	35	3
Damien Matthew	5 11	10 10	23 9 70	Islington	Trainee	Chelsea	17	—
Andy Myers	5 08	9 10	3 11 73	Hounslow	Trainee	Chelsea	14	1
Andy Townsend	5 11	12 07	23 7 63	Maidstone	Weymouth	Southampton	83	5
						Norwich C	71	8
						Chelsea	69	8
Dennis Wise	5 6	9 05	15 12 66	Kensington		Wimbledon	135	27
						Chelsea	71	20
Forwards								
Joe Allon	5 11	11 02	12 11 66	Gateshead		Newcastle U	9	2
						Swansea C	34	11
						Hartlepool U	112	50
						Chelsea	11	2
						Port Vale (loan)	6	—

CHELSEA

Foundation: Chelsea may never have existed but for the fact that Fulham rejected an offer to rent the Stamford Bridge ground from Mr. H. A. Mears who had owned it since 1904. Fortunately he was determined to develop it as a football stadium rather than sell it to the Great Western Railway and got together with Frederick Parker, who persuaded Mears of the financial advantages of developing a major sporting venue. Chelsea FC was formed in 1905, and when admission to the Southern League was denied, they immediately gained admission to the Second Division of the Football League.

First Football League game: 2 September, 1905, Division 2, v Stockport C (a) L 0-1 – Foulke; Mackie, McEwan; Key, Harris, Miller; Moran, J. T. Robertson, Copeland, Windridge, Kirwan.

Did you know: Chelsea was the first Football League club to produce a 16-page magazine-type programme selling at 6d (2½p) in December 1948. In February 1966 they were also the first club to publish full-colour pictures in the programme. This was for their game with AC Milan.

Managers (and Secretary-managers)
John Tait Robertson 1905–07, David Calderhead 1907–33, A. Leslie Knighton 1933–39, Billy Birrell 1939–52, Ted Drake 1952–61, Tommy Docherty 1962–67, Dave Sexton 1967–74, Ron Suart 1974–75, Eddie McCreadie 1975–77, Ken Shellito 1977–78, Danny Blanchflower 1978–79, Geoff Hurst 1979–81, John Neal 1981–85 (Director to 1986), John Hollins 1985–88, Bobby Campbell 1988–91, Ian Porterfield June 1991–.

Player and Position	Ht	Wt	Birth Date	Birth Place	Source	Clubs	League App	League Gls
Tony Cascarino	6 2	11 10	1 9 62	St Paul's Cray	Crockenhill	Gillingham	219	78
						Millwall	105	42
						Aston Villa	46	11
						Celtic	—	—
						Chelsea	11	2
Kerry Dixon	6 0	13 00	24 7 61	Luton	Apprentice Dunstable	Tottenham H	—	—
						Reading	116	51
						Chelsea	335	147
Kevin McAllister (To Falkirk Aug 1991)	5 5	11 00	8 11 62	Falkirk		Falkirk	64	18
						Chelsea	106	7
						Falkirk (loan)	6	3
Eddie Newton	5 11	11 02	13 12 71	Hammersmith	Trainee	Chelsea	1	1
						Cardiff C (loan)	19	4
Graham Stuart	5 8	11 06	24 10 70	Tooting	Trainee	Chelsea	48	5

Trainees
Colgan, Nicholas V; Davies, Jeremy M; Goddard, Ryan N. J; Izzet, Mustafa K; Martin, Steven M; McLennan, Jason D; Metcalfe, Christian W; Norman, Craig T; Rowe, Ezekiel B; Scott, Barry; Shipperley, Neil J; Skiverton, Terence J.

Associated Schoolboys
Baker, Joseph P. J; Carney, John L; Carroll, Lee G; Collins, Kevin J; Dennis, Daniel G; Duberry, Michael W; Ellis, Clinton; Fewings, Neil L; Ho, Wai K; Hughes, Andrew J; Keadell, Mark P; Kent, Mathew J; Lazic, Vladimir; McCann, Christian; Mendes, Hillyard A; Nicholls, Mark; Parsons, John; Pritchard, Justin; Rouse, Mark; Stewart, Damien; Thomas, Rhodri O; Wright, Robert A.

Associated Schoolboys who have accepted the club's offer of a Traineeship/Contract
Bowder, Stanley R; Christie, Terry W; Hughes, John P; Sakala, Landilani; Yates, Paul S.

162

CHESTER CITY 1991–92 *Back row (left to right)*: David Pugh, Barry Butler, Graham Abel, Billy Stewart, Barry Siddall, Chris Lightfoot, Spencer Whelan, Garry Bennett, Joe Hinnigan (Physiotherapist).
Front row: Arthur Albiston, Paul McGuinness, Brian Croft, Harry McNally (Manager), R Crofts (Chairman), Graham Barrow (Assistant Manager), Roger Preece, Eddie Bishop.

Division 2   **CHESTER CITY**

The Deva Stadium, Bumpers Lane, Chester. Telephone Chester (0244) 371376, 371809. Cityline (Ticket and Travel Information) (0244) 373829.

Ground capacity: 6000.

Record attendance: 20,500 v Chelsea, FA Cup 3rd rd (replay), 16 January, 1952.

Record receipts: £30,609 v Sheffield W, FA Cup 4th rd, 31 January 1987.

Pitch measurements: 115yd × 75yd.

Club Patron: Duke of Westminster.

President: Reg Rowlands.

Chairman: R. H. Crofts.

Directors: P. Russell, W. D. MacDonald, N. A. MacLennon, H. McNally.

Team Manager: Harry McNally.

Assistant Manager: Graham Barrow.

Secretary: R. A. Allan.

Physio: Joe Hinnigan.

Commercial Manager: Miss A. Walker.

Year Formed: 1884. Turned Professional: 1902. Ltd Co.: 1909.

Former Grounds: Faulkner Street; Old Showground; 1904, Whipcord Lane; 1906, Sealand Road; 1990 Moss Rose Ground, Macclesfield; 1992 The Stadium, Bumpers Lane.

Former Names: Chester until 1983.

Club Nickname: 'Blues'.

Record League Victory: 12-0 v York C, Division 3 (N), 1 February 1936 – Middleton; Common, Hall; Wharton, Wilson, Howarth; Horsman (2), Hughes, Wrightson (4), Cresswell (2), Sargeant (4).

Record Cup Victory: 6-1 v Darlington, FA Cup, 1st rd, 25 November 1933 – Burke; Bennett, Little; Pitcairn, Skitt, Duckworth; Armes (3), Whittam, Mantle (2), Cresswell (1), McLachlan.

Record Defeat: 2-11 v Oldham Ath, Division 3 (N), 19 January 1952.

Most League Points (2 for a win): 56, Division 3 (N), 1946–47 and Division 4, 1964–65.

Most League points (3 for a win): 84, Division 4, 1985–86.

Most League Goals: 119, Division 4, 1964–65.

Highest League Scorer in Season: Dick Yates, 36, Division 3 (N), 1946–47.

Most League Goals in Total Aggregate: Gary Talbot, 83, 1963–67 and 1968–70.

Most Capped Player: Bill Lewis, 7 (30), Wales.

Most League Appearances: Ray Gill, 408, 1951–62.

Record Transfer Fee Received: £300,000 from Liverpool for Ian Rush, May 1980.

Record Transfer Fee Paid: £94,000 to Barnsley for Stuart Rimmer, August 1991.

Football League Record: 1931 Elected Division 3 (N); 1958–75 Division 4; 1975–82 Division 3; 1982–86 Division 4; 1986–92 Division 3; 1992– Division 2.

Honours: Football League: Division 3 best season: 5th, 1977–78; Division 3 (N) – Runners-up 1935–36; Division 4 – Runners-up 1985–86. *FA Cup:* best season: 5th rd, 1976–77, 1979– 80. *Football League Cup:* Semi-final 1974–75. *Welsh Cup:* Winners 1908, 1933, 1947. *Debenhams Cup:* Winners 1977.

Colours: Royal blue shirts, white shorts, blue stockings, white trim. **Change colours:** Gold shirts, black shorts, black stockings.

CHESTER CITY 1991–92 LEAGUE RECORD

Match No.	Date		Venue	Opponents	Result		H/T Score	Lg. Pos.	Goalscorers	Attendance
1	Aug	17	H	Fulham	W	2-0	1-0	—	Lightfoot, Bennett	1444
2		23	A	Wigan Ath	L	1-2	1-0	—	Rimmer	2637
3		31	H	Swansea C	W	2-0	0-0	7	Abel, Morton	1162
4	Sep	4	A	Huddersfield T	L	0-2	0-1	—		5321
5		7	H	Bournemouth	L	0-1	0-0	14		1117
6		14	A	Bradford C	D	1-1	0-0	14	Bishop	4843
7		17	A	Birmingham C	L	2-3	2-2	—	Bishop, Rimmer	8154
8		21	H	WBA	L	1-2	1-1	20	Barrow	3895
9		28	A	Torquay U	L	2-3	1-2	21	Bishop, Rimmer	2062
10	Oct	5	H	Stoke C	D	0-0	0-0	21		4212
11		12	A	Leyton Orient	L	0-1	0-1	21		4049
12		18	A	Stockport Co	W	4-0	1-0	—	Bennett 3, Rimmer	4838
13		26	H	Bolton W	L	0-1	0-0	20		1867
14	Nov	2	H	Preston NE	W	3-2	1-0	19	Rimmer 2, Bishop	1219
15		5	A	Peterborough U	L	0-2	0-2	—		2810
16		9	A	Hull C	L	0-1	0-1	21		4305
17		23	H	Reading	D	2-2	1-1	22	Rimmer, Abel	1124
18		30	A	Exeter C	D	0-0	0-0	23		3235
19	Dec	14	H	Shrewsbury T	L	1-4	1-1	24	Morton	1016
20		26	A	Swansea C	L	0-3	0-2	24		4098
21		28	A	Fulham	D	2-2	0-0	24	Abel (pen), Lightfoot	3708
22	Jan	1	H	Huddersfield T	D	0-0	0-0	24		3504
23		4	H	Darlington	L	2-5	2-2	24	Comstive, Tait (og)	1020
24		11	A	Hartlepool U	L	0-1	0-0	24		3088
25		18	H	Brentford	D	1-1	0-1	24	Butler	1447
26	Feb	8	A	Bolton W	D	0-0	0-0	24		6609
27		11	H	Exeter C	W	5-2	3-1	—	Butler 2, Rimmer, Abel (pen), Comstive	871
28		15	A	Shrewsbury T	D	2-2	2-1	24	Rimmer, Lightfoot	2807
29		18	H	Wigan Ath	W	1-0	0-0	—	Rimmer	1065
30		22	H	Hartlepool U	W	2-0	2-0	22	Butler 2	1072
31		25	A	Bury	W	2-1	2-1	—	Lightfoot, Bennett	2283
32		29	A	Darlington	D	1-1	0-0	20	Rimmer	2579
33	Mar	3	A	Brentford	L	0-2	0-1	—		6869
34		7	H	Bury	W	3-1	1-1	20	Bennett 2, Abel	1228
35		10	H	Peterborough U	L	2-4	1-1	—	Butler, Abel (pen)	1063
36		14	A	Preston NE	W	3-0	2-0	18	Rimmer, Bennett 2	3909
37		21	A	Hull C	D	1-1	1-0	20	Comstive	1269
38		24	H	Stockport Co	W	3-2	1-0	—	Abel 2 (1 pen), Bennett	3747
39		28	A	Reading	D	0-0	0-0	19		2813
40		31	H	Bradford C	D	0-0	0-0	—		1149
41	Apr	3	A	Bournemouth	L	0-2	0-1	—		5974
42		11	H	Birmingham C	L	0-1	0-0	20		4895
43		18	A	WBA	D	1-1	0-0	19	Abel (pen)	10,137
44		20	H	Torquay U	W	2-0	1-0	19	Rimmer, Lightfoot	1317
45		25	A	Stoke C	W	1-0	0-0	18	Bennett	18,474
46	May	2	H	Leyton Orient	W	1-0	0-0	18	Barrow	2008

Final League Position: 18

GOALSCORERS

League (56): Rimmer 13, Bennett 11, Abel 9 (5 pens), Butler 6, Lightfoot 5, Bishop 4, Comstive 3, Barrow 2, Morton 2, own goals 1.
Rumbelows Cup (5): Bennett 2, Rimmer 2, Barrow 1.
FA Cup (1): Barrow 1.

Siddall	Whelan	Albiston	Butler	Abel	Lightfoot	Bishop	Barrow	Rimmer	Bennett	Pugh	McGuinness	Croft	Stewart	Morton	Preece	Allen	Comstive	Nolan	Match No.
1	2	3	4*	5	6	7	8	9	10	11	12								1
1	2	3	4	5	6	7	8	9	10	11*	12								2
	2	3	4	5	6	7	8	9	10†	11*	12		1	14					3
	2	3	4*	5	6	7	8	9	12	14		11	1	10†					4
	2	3	4†	5	6	7	8	9	12	14		11	1	10*					5
	2	3	4	5	6	7	8	9	10*	11			1	12					6
	2	3	4	5	6	7	8	9	10*		12	11	1						7
		3	4	5	6	7	8	9	10		2	11	1						8
		3	8	5	6	7	9*	10	4	2			1	11	12				9
	6	3	12	5*	7	8	10	4	2	11			1	9					10
	2	3	6	5	7	9	10	4	8	11*			1	12					11
	2	3		5	6	7	8	9	10	4		11	1						12
	2†	3	14	5	6	7	8	9	10*	4		11	1	12					13
	2	3	14	5	6	7	8	9	10*	4†		11	1	12					14
	2	3	4†	5*	6	7	8	9	12	11			1	10	14				15
	2	3		5	6	7	8	9		11			1	10*	4	12			16
1	2	3	4	5	6	7	8	9	10*	11		12							17
	2	3	14	5	6	7	8	9	10†	11*			1	12			4		18
	2	3	12	5	6	7	8		10	11*			1	9			4		19
1	2	3	11*	5	6	7†	8	9	10			12	14				4		20
	2	3		5	6	8	9	10	11*				1	12	7		4		21
	2	3		5	6	8	9		10			12	1	7*	11		4		22
	3†	2		5	6	8	9		10	14		12	1	7*	11		4		23
				5	6	8	9	11	3			12	1	10*	2		4	7	24
		9	5	6	8	10	7	3	11*				1	12	2		4		25
		3	9	5	6	8	10	7*	11			12	1		2		4		26
		3	9	5	6	8	10	7	11				1		2		4		27
	14	3	9	5†	6	8	10	7*	11			12	1		2		4		28
	5	3	9†		6	8	10	7*	11			12	1	14	2		4		29
	5	3	9	6	8	10	7	4					1	11	2				30
	5	3	9*	12	6	8	10	7	11				1		2		4		31
	5*	3	9	12	6	8	10	7†	11			14	1		2		4		32
	5	3	9	12	6*	8	10	7†	11				1	14	2		4		33
	5*	3	9†	12	6	8	10	7	11				1	14	2		4		34
		3	9†	5	6	8	10	7	11*			12	1	14	2		4		35
	2	3	9	5	6		10	7	11				1	12	8*		4		36
1	2	3	9	5	6		10	11	7*					12	8		4		37
	2*	3	9	5	6		10	7	11				1	12	8		4		38
1		3	9*	5	6	8	10	7	11			12			2		4		39
1	14	3	9*	5	6	8†	10	7	11			12			2		4		40
1		3	9*	5	6	8	10	7	11			12			2		4		41
1		3	9*	5	6	8	10	7†	11			14		12	2		4		42
	2	3	9	5	6		10	7	11			12	1		8*		4		43
		3	9	5	6	8*	10	7	11				1	12	2		4		44
		3	9	5	6	8	10	7	11				1		2		4*		45
		3	9	5	6	7†	8	10	11			12	1	14	2		4*		46
9	30	44	36	40	44	21	40	44	40	33	3	18	37	12	26	—	28	1	
	+2s		+5s +4s									+2s +2s +4s +14s				+22s3s	+1s		

Rumbelows Cup

Rumbelows Cup	First Round	Lincoln C (h)	1-0
		(a)	3-4
	Second Round	Manchester C (a)	1-3
		(at Stockport) (h)	0-3
FA Cup	First Round	Guiseley (h)	1-0
	Second Round	Crewe Alex (a)	0-2

CHESTER CITY

Player and Position	Ht	Wt	Birth Date	Birth Place	Source	Clubs	League App	Gls
Goalkeepers								
Barry Siddall*	6 1	14 02	12 9 54	Ellesmere Port	Apprentice	Bolton W	137	—
						Sunderland	167	—
						Darlington (loan)	8	—
						Port Vale	81	—
						Blackpool (loan)	7	—
						Stoke City	20	—
						Tranmere R (loan)	12	—
						Manchester C (loan)	6	—
						Blackpool	110	—
						Stockport Co	21	—
						Hartlepool U	11	—
						WBA	—	—
						Carlisle U	24	—
						Chester C	9	—
Billy Stewart	5 11	11 07	1 1 65	Liverpool	Apprentice	Liverpool	—	—
						Wigan Ath	14	—
						Chester C	223	—
Defenders								
Graham Abel	6 2	13 00	17 9 60	Runcorn	Runcorn	Chester C	263	28
Arthur Albiston‡	5 7	11 05	14 7 57	Edinburgh	Apprentice	Manchester U	379	6
						WBA	43	2
						Dundee	10	—
						Chesterfield	3	1
						Chester C	44	—
Barry Butler	6 2	13 00	4 6 62	Farnworth	Atherton T	Chester C	237	15
Joe Hinnigan	6 0	12 00	3 12 55	Liverpool	S Liverpool	Wigan Ath	66	10
						Sunderland	63	4
						Preston NE	52	8
						Gillingham	103	7
						Wrexham	29	1
						Chester C	54	2
Spencer Whelan	6 1	11 13	17 9 71	Liverpool	Liverpool	Chester C	43	—
Midfield								
Andrew Allen§			4 9 74	Liverpool	Trainee	Chester C	1	—
Graham Barrow	6 2	13 07	13 6 54	Chorley	Altrincham	Wigan Ath	179	36
						Chester C	202	15
Eddie Bishop	5 8	11 07	28 11 62	Liverpool	Runcorn	Tranmere R	76	19
						Chester C	40	11
						Crewe Alex (loan)	3	—
Paul Comstive	6 1	12 07	25 11 61	Southport	Amateur	Blackburn R	6	—
						Rochdale (loan)	9	2
						Wigan Ath	35	2
						Wrexham	99	8
						Burnley	82	17
						Bolton W	49	3
						Chester C	28	3
Chris Lightfoot	5 11	11 00	1 4 70	Wimwick	Trainee	Chester C	173	16
Paul McGuinness*	5 7	11 05	2 3 66	Manchester	Local	Manchester U	—	—
						Crewe Alex	13	—
						Manchester U	—	—
						Brighton & HA (loan)	—	—
						Chester C	14	—
David Nolan‡			24 2 68	Liverpool	Bromborough Pool	Chester C	1	—
Roger Preece	5 9	10 12	9 6 69	Much Wenlock	Apprentice	Coventry C	—	—
						Wrexham	110	12
						Chester C	64	—
David Pugh	5 10	11 02	19 9 64	Liverpool	Runcorn	Chester C	107	6

CHESTER CITY

Foundation: All students of soccer history have read about the medieval games of football in Chester, but the present club was not formed until 1884 through the amalgamation of King's School Old Boys with Chester Rovers. For many years Chester were overshadowed in Cheshire by Northwich Victoria and Crewe Alexandra who had both won the Senior Cup several times before Chester's first success in 1894–95.

First Football League game: 2 September, 1931, Division 3 (N), v Wrexham (a) D 1-1 – Johnson; Herod, Jones; Keeley, Skitt, Reilly; Thompson, Ranson, Jennings (1), Cresswell, Hedley.

Did you know: In 1933–34 Chester figured in one of the most remarkable turnabouts in Football League history. In November they beat Rochdale 7-1 at home, but in March they lost 6-0 away to the same club.

Managers (and Secretary-managers)
Charlie Hewitt 1930–36, Alex Raisbeck 1936–38, Frank Brown 1938–53, Louis Page 1953–56, John Harris 1956–59, Stan Pearson 1959–61, Bill Lambton 1962–63, Peter Hauser 1963–68, Ken Roberts 1968–76, Alan Oakes 1976–82, Cliff Sear 1982, John Sainty 1982–83, John McGrath 1984, Harry McNally June 1985–.

Player and Position	Ht	Wt	Birth Date	Birth Place	Source	Clubs	League App	Gls
Forwards								
Gary Bennett	6 1	12 06	20 9 63	Liverpool		Wigan Ath	20	3
						Chester C	126	36
						Southend U	42	6
						Chester C	80	15
Brian Croft	5 9	10 10	27 9 67	Chester		Chester C	59	3
						Cambridge U	17	2
						Chester C	114	3
Neil Morton	5 10	11 00	21 12 68	Congleton	Trainee Northwich Vic	Crewe Alex Chester C	31 68	1 9
Stuart Rimmer	5 7	9 04	12 10 64	Southport	Apprentice	Everton	3	—
						Chester C	114	67
						Watford	10	1
						Notts Co	4	2
						Walsall	88	31
						Barnsley	15	1
						Chester C	44	13

Trainees
Allen, Andrew; Barthorpe, Darren J; Brooks, Philip; Limbert, Mark; Lord, Jeremy J; O'Hara, Paul J.

Associated Schoolboys
Atkinson, Eric J; Bayliss, David A; Dixon, Neil; Evans, Thomas P; Hillman, Mark; Holden, Richard G; Ingman, David J; Jeanrenaud, Paul; Kopanski, Alan; Lewis, Ian P; Millar, Scott G; Moss, Steven J; Noon, Philip B; Pemberton, Michael A; Roberts, Daniel L; Roberts, Joel H; Stevenson, Keith D; Sweeney, Roy J; Turner, David J; White, David J; Wilson, Nicky K.

CHESTERFIELD 1991–92 *Back row (left to right):* Iain Dunn, Dave Waller, Chris Benjamin, Steve Williams, Jamie Hewitt, Lee Francis, Dave Caldwell.
Centre row: Tony Brien, Sean Dyche, Mark Golding, Paul McGugan, Andy Morris, Mick Leonard, Lee Turnbull, Lee Rogers.
Front row: Neil Grayson, Paul Lemon, Steve Hetzke (Coach), Chris McMenemy (Manager), Dave Rushbury (Physiotherapist/Assistant Manager), Bryn Gunn, John Cooke.

Division 3   **CHESTERFIELD**

Recreation Ground, Chesterfield S40 4SX. Telephone Chesterfield (0246) 209765. Commercial Dept: (0246) 231535.

Ground capacity: 11,638.

Record attendance: 30,968 v Newcastle U, Division 2, 7 April 1939.

Record receipts: £32,410 v Sheffield U, Division 3, 25 March 1989.

Pitch measurements: 112yd × 72yd.

President: His Grace the Duke of Devonshire MC, DL, JP.

Vice-president: P. C. J. T. Kirkman.

Chairman: J. N. Lea.

Vice-chairman: B. W. Hubbard.

Associate Directors: J. A. Plant, R. F. Pepper.

Team Manager: Chris McMenemy.

Physio: Dave Rushbury.

Assistant Manager: Chris McMenemy.

Secretary: Nicola Hodgson.

Commercial Manager: Jim Brown.

Year Formed: 1866. Turned Professional: 1891. Ltd Co.: 1871.

Club Nickname: 'Blues' or 'Spireites'.

Record League Victory: 10-0 v Glossop, Division 2, 17 January 1903 – Clutterbuck; Thorpe, Lerper; Haig, Banner, Thacker; Tomlinson (2), Newton (1), Milward (3), Munday (2), Steel (2).

Record Cup Victory: 5-0 v Wath Ath (away), FA Cup, 1st rd, 28 November 1925 – Birch; Saxby, Dennis; Wass, Abbott, Thompson; Fisher (1), Roseboom (1), Cookson (2), Whitfield (1), Hopkinson.

Record Defeat: 0-10 v Gillingham, Division 3, 5 September 1987.

Most League Points (2 for a win): 64, Division 4, 1969–70.

Most League points (3 for a win): 91, Division 4, 1984–85.

Most League Goals: 102, Division 3 (N), 1930–31.

Highest League Scorer in Season: Jimmy Cookson, 44, Division 3 (N), 1925–26.

Most League Goals in Total Aggregate: Ernie Moss, 161, 1969–76, 1979–81 and 1984–86.

Most Capped Player: Walter McMillen, 4 (7), Northern Ireland.

Most League Appearances: Dave Blakey, 613, 1948–67.

Record Transfer Fee Received: £200,000 from Wolverhampton W for Alan Birch, August 1981.

Record Transfer Fee Paid: £150,000 to Carlisle U for Phil Bonnyman, March 1980.

Football League Record: 1899 Elected to Division 2; 1909 failed re-election; 1921–31 Division 3 (N); 1931–33 Division 2; 1933–36 Division 3 (N); 1936–51 Division 2; 1951–58 Division 3 (N); 1958–61 Division 3; 1961–70 Division 4; 1970–83 Division 3; 1983–85 Division 4; 1985–89 Division 3; 1989–92 Division 4; 1992– Division 3.

Honours: Football League: Division 2 best season: 4th, 1946–47; Division 3 (N) – Champions 1930–31, 1935–36; Runners-up 1933–34; Division 4 – Champions 1969–70, 1984–85. *FA Cup:* best season: 5th rd, 1932–33, 1937–38, 1949–50. *Football League Cup:* best season: 4th rd, 1964–65. *Anglo-Scottish Cup:* Winners 1980–81.

Colours: Blue shirts, white shorts, white stockings. **Change colours:** Yellow shirts, green shorts, yellow stockings.

CHESTERFIELD 1991–92 LEAGUE RECORD

Match No.	Date		Venue	Opponents	Result		H/T Score	Lg. Pos.	Goalscorers	Atten-dance
1	Aug	17	H	Maidstone U	W	3-0	1-0	—	Williams, Hewitt 2	3462
2		31	H	Mansfield T	L	0-2	0-1	16		4740
3	Sep	3	A	Burnley	L	0-3	0-1	—		6647
4		7	A	York C	W	1-0	1-0	14	Lancaster	2382
5		14	H	Scunthorpe U	L	0-1	0-0	16		3338
6		17	H	Walsall	L	0-1	0-0	—		2690
7		21	A	Lincoln C	W	2-1	2-0	13	Dyche, Cooke	2896
8	Oct	5	A	Gillingham	W	1-0	1-0	9	Cooke	2835
9		12	H	Rotherham U	D	1-1	1-0	10	Turnbull	6133
10		15	H	Northampton T	D	1-1	1-0	—	Cooke	2426
11		19	A	Halifax T	L	0-2	0-0	11		1506
12		26	H	Hereford U	W	2-0	1-0	9	Hewitt, Hawke	2949
13	Nov	2	A	Rochdale	D	3-3	1-2	9	Turnbull 2 (1 pen), McGugan	1852
14		9	H	Blackpool	D	1-1	0-0	11	Francis	4917
15		23	A	Wrexham	W	1-0	1-0	8	Turnbull	1636
16		30	A	Barnet	W	2-1	1-0	7	Cooke, Lancaster	3725
17	Dec	21	H	Northampton T	L	1-2	1-0	10	Williams	3048
18		26	A	Maidstone U	W	1-0	1-0	10	Cooke	1325
19		28	A	Mansfield T	L	1-2	0-2	10	Turnbull (pen)	6503
20	Jan	1	H	Burnley	L	0-2	0-2	10		7789
21		4	H	Carlisle U	D	0-0	0-0	11		2892
22		18	H	Doncaster R	D	0-0	0-0	10		3372
23		25	A	Cardiff C	L	0-4	0-2	11		5131
24	Feb	8	A	Hereford U	L	0-1	0-1	14		2315
25		11	H	Barnet	W	3-2	1-1	—	Lemon, Norris 2	3076
26		15	H	Crewe Alex	L	1-3	1-0	13	Turnbull	3172
27		22	H	Scarborough	W	1-0	0-0	11	Norris	2749
28		29	A	Carlisle U	W	2-1	2-0	10	Dunn, Norris	2038
29	Mar	3	A	Doncaster R	W	1-0	1-0	—	McGugan	2385
30		7	A	Cardiff C	D	2-2	2-0	10	Norris, Dyche	3803
31		14	H	Rochdale	L	0-1	0-1	11		3231
32		17	A	Scarborough	L	2-3	2-2	—	Norris, Turnbull (pen)	1302
33		21	A	Blackpool	L	1-3	1-3	12	Norris	4447
34		24	H	Crewe Alex	W	2-1	0-1	—	Dyche, Lancaster	2534
35		28	H	Wrexham	D	1-1	0-1	11	McGugan	2961
36		31	A	Scunthorpe U	L	0-2	0-1	—		2224
37	Apr	4	H	York C	L	1-3	1-2	13	Lancaster	2461
38		7	H	Halifax T	W	4-0	0-0	—	Lancaster 2, Norris, Morris	1802
39		11	A	Walsall	D	2-2	1-1	11	Norris, Lemon	2472
40		18	H	Lincoln C	L	1-5	1-0	12	Cooke	2748
41		25	H	Gillingham	D	3-3	1-1	13	Norris, Lancaster, Cooke (pen)	2109
42	May	2	A	Rotherham U	D	1-1	0-1	13	Morris	8852

Final League Position: 13

GOALSCORERS

League (49): Norris 10, Cooke 7 (1 pen), Lancaster 7, Turnbull 7 (3 pens), Dyche 3, Hewitt 3, McGugan 3, Lemon 2, Morris 2, Williams 2, Dunn 1, Francis 1, Hawke 1.
Rumbelows Cup (1): Lancaster 1.
FA Cup (1): Cooke 1.

Leonard	Dyche	Williams	Rogers	Brien	McGugan	Gunn	Hewitt	Morris	Caldwell	Grayson	Benjamin	Turnbull	Lancaster	Evans	Francis	Cooke	Dunn	Goldring	Hawke	Hebberd	Lemon	Norris	Whitehead	Match No.
1	2	3	4	5	6	7	8	9	10*	11	12													1
1	2	3	4†	5	6	7			12	10*		8	9	11	14									2
1	2	3		5	6	7			11*10				9	12	4	8								3
1	2	3		5	6	7			10†14				9*12		4	8	11							4
	2	3		5	6	7			10*12	14			9		4	8	11†	1						5
1	2	3		5	6	7			10 12	14			9†		4	8	11*							6
1	2	3		5	6	7	11		10*				9	12	4	8								7
1	2	3		5	6		11				12	7	9		4	8			10*					8
1	2	3		5	6		11					7	9		4	8			10					9
1	2	3		5		6	11				12	7	9		4	8			10*					10
1	2	3		5		6	11		14	12		7	9		4	8*			10†					11
1	2	3		5	6		11					7	9		4	8			10					12
1	2	3		5	6		11					7	9		4	8			10					13
1	2	3†		5	6		11		14			7	9*		4	8			10 12					14
1	2	3 14		5	6		11		9*			7†			4	8	12		10					15
1	2	3	7	5	6		11		9*				10		4	8	12							16
1	2	3*	7	5	6		11		14			9	10†		4	8	12							17
1	2	3		5	6		11		12	9*		7	10		4	8								18
1	2	3		5	6		11		9			7	10		4	8*			12					19
1	2	3†14		5	6		11					7	10*		4	8	12		9					20
1	2		3	5	6		11*		9			7	14		4	8†12			10					21
	2		3		6		11	12				7*			4	8		1	10	5	9			22
	2		3	12	6		11					7	14		4*	8†		1	10	5	9			23
1	2	12		3	6		11	8*				7			4				10	5	9			24
1	2	3		5	6		11					9			4				10	7	8			25
1	2	3		5	6		11					9			4	12			10	7*	8			26
1	2	3		5	6		11					9			4		7		10		8			27
1	2	3	12	5	6		11					9			4		7*		10		8			28
1	2	3	12	5	6		11					9			4		7		10*		8			29
1	2	3	10	5	6		11					9			4	12	7*				8			30
1	2	3	14	5	6†		11					9			4	12	7*		10		8			31
1	2	3*	6	5			11					9			4	7			10	12	8			32
1	2		3	5	6		11						9		4				10	7	8			33
1	2		3	5	6		11						9		4				10	7	8			34
1	2	4*	3	5	6		11					9			12				10	7	8			35
1	2		3*	5	6		11					9			12	4			10	7	8			36
1	2			5	6		11					9			3	4			10	7*	8	12		37
1	2			5	6*			3	14			9†			4	11			10	12	8	7		38
	2			5				3	12			9*			4	11		1	10	6	8	7		39
	2			5				3	12			14	9*		4	11		1	10	6†	8	7		40
	2	3		5	6		11	9	10*12			7						1	4†		8	14		41
	2			5	6		3	9		11					4	7		1	10		8			42

```
35  42  30  13  40  37   9  37   4   5   9   —  26  27   1  37  29   8   7  22  13  21   3
     +   +       +       +                   +   +   +   +   +   +   +   +   +       +   +           +
    1s  5s  1s              4s  4s  6s  4s  1s  2s  4s  2s  4s  5s              2s  2s          2s
```

Rumbelows Cup   First Round   Stoke C (a)   0-1

                                           (h)   1-2

FA Cup   First Round   Darlington (a)   1-2

CHESTERFIELD

Player and Position	Ht	Wt	Birth Date	Place	Source	Clubs	League App	Gls
Goalkeepers								
Mark Goldring	6 2	13 00	17 9 72	Southampton	Trainee	Chesterfield	7	—
Mick Leonard	6 1	12 04	9 5 59	Carshalton	Epsom & Ewell	Halifax T	69	—
						Notts Co	204	—
						Chesterfield	127	—
						Halifax T (loan)	3	—
Defenders								
Tony Brien	6 0	12 00	10 2 69	Dublin	Apprentice	Leicester C	16	1
						Chesterfield	156	7
Lee Francis*	5 10	10 11	24 10 69	Walthamstow	Trainee	Arsenal	—	—
						Chesterfield (loan)	2	—
						Chesterfield	68	2
Neil Grayson*			1 1 64	York	Rowntree M	Doncaster R	129	6
						York C	1	—
						Chesterfield	15	—
Bryn Gunn*	6 2	13 07	21 8 58	Kettering	Apprentice	Nottingham F	131	1
						Shrewsbury T (loan)	9	—
						Walsall (loan)	6	—
						Mansfield T (loan)	5	—
						Peterborough U	131	14
						Chesterfield	91	10
Jamie Hewitt*	5 10	10 08	17 5 68	Chesterfield	School	Chesterfield	249	14
Paul McGugan	6 3	13 07	17 7 64	Glasgow	Eastercraigs	Celtic	47	2
						Barnsley	49	2
						Chesterfield	59	4
Lee Rogers	5 10	12 00	21 10 66	Doncaster	Doncaster R	Chesterfield	187	—
Midfield								
Sean Dyche	6 0	12 04	28 6 71	Kettering	Trainee	Nottingham F	—	—
						Chesterfield	92	7
Trevor Hebberd	6 0	11 04	19 6 58	Winchester	Apprentice	Southampton	97	7
						Bolton W (loan)	6	—
						Leicester C (loan)	4	1
						Oxford U	260	37
						Derby Co	81	10
						Portsmouth	—	—
						Chesterfield	24	—
Scott Whitehead§			20 4 74	Doncaster	Trainee	Chesterfield	5	—
Steven Williams	5 11	11 06	18 7 70	Mansfield		Mansfield T	11	—
						Chesterfield	67	7
Forwards								
Chris Benjamin*	5 11	13 00	5 12 72	Sheffield	Trainee	Chesterfield	15	1
Dave Caldwell*	5 10	10 08	31 7 60	Aberdeen	Inverness Caley	Mansfield T	157	57
						Carlisle U (loan)	4	—
						Swindon T (loan)	5	—
						Chesterfield	68	17
						Torquay U	24	4
						Overpelt	—	—
						Torquay U	17	6
						Overpelt	—	—
						Chesterfield	32	4
John Cooke*	5 8	11 00	25 4 62	Salford	Apprentice	Sunderland	55	4
						Carlisle U (loan)	6	2
						Sheffield W	—	—
						Carlisle U	106	11
						Stockport Co	58	7
						Chesterfield	53	8
Iain Dunn*	5 10	11 07	1 4 70	Derwent	School	York C	77	11
						Chesterfield	13	1

CHESTERFIELD

Foundation: Chesterfield are fourth only to Stoke, Notts County and Nottingham Forest in age for they can trace their existence as far back as 1866, although it is fair to say that they were somewhat casual in the first few years of their history playing only a few friendlies a year. However, their rules of 1871 are still in existence showing an annual membership of 2s (10p), but it was not until 1891 that they won a trophy (the Barnes Cup) and followed this a year later by winning the Sheffield Cup, Barnes Cup and the Derbyshire Junior Cup.

First Football League game: 2 September, 1899, Division 2, v Sheffield W (a) L 1-5 – Hancock; Pilgrim, Fletcher; Ballantyne, Bell, Downie; Morley, Thacker, Gooing, Munday (1), Geary.

Did you know: Six different goalscorers for the same side in a Football League game is sufficiently rare to be worthy of special mention and Chesterfield had this number on their score sheet when they beat Stockport County 8-1 in the Second Division in April 1902. The names included an 'own goal' and Herbert Munday with a hat-trick.

Managers (and Secretary-managers)
E. Russell Timmeus 1891–95*, Gilbert Gillies 1895–1901, E. F. Hind 1901–02, Jack Hoskin 1902–06, W. Furness 1906–07, George Swift 1907–10, G. H. Jones 1911–13, R. L. Weston 1913–17, T. Callaghan 1919, J. J. Caffrey 1920–22, Harry Hadley 1922, Harry Parkes 1922–27, Alec Campbell 1927, Ted Davison 1927–32, Bill Harvey 1932–38, Norman Bullock 1938–45, Bob Brocklebank 1945–48, Bobby Marshall 1948–52, Ted Davison 1952–58, Duggie Livingstone 1958–62, Tony McShane 1962–67, Jimmy McGuigan 1967–73, Joe Shaw 1973–76, Arthur Cox 1976–80, Frank Barlow 1980–83, John Duncan 1983–87, Kevin Randall 1987–88, Paul Hart 1988–91, Chris McMenemy April 1991–.

Player and Position	Ht	Wt	Birth Date	Place	Source	Clubs	League App	Gls
Gary Evans*			20 12 68	Balby	Thorne Colliery	Chesterfield	5	—
Dave Lancaster	6 3	14 00	8 9 61	Preston	Colne Dynamoes	Blackpool	8	1
						Chesterfield (loan)	12	4
						Chesterfield	29	7
Paul Lemon	5 10	11 07	3 6 66	Middlesbrough	Apprentice	Sunderland	107	15
						Carlisle U (loan)	2	—
						Walsall (loan)	2	—
						Reading (loan)	3	—
						Chesterfield	54	4
Andy Morris	6 5	15 07	17 11 67	Sheffield		Rotherham U	7	—
						Chesterfield	118	19
						Exeter C (loan)	7	2
Steve Norris	5 9	10 08	22 9 61	Coventry	Telford	Scarborough	45	13
						Notts Co (loan)	1	—
						Carlisle U	29	5
						Halifax T	57	37
						Chesterfield	21	10
Lee Turnbull	6 0	11 09	27 9 67	Teesside	Local	Middlesbrough	16	4
						Aston Villa	—	—
						Doncaster R	123	21
						Chesterfield	46	16
Dave Waller‡	5 10	10 00	20 12 63	Urmston	Local	Crewe Alex	168	55
						Shrewsbury T	11	3
						Chesterfield	119	53

Trainees
Bell, Scott A; Cooper, Damian R. W; Harper, Marcus J; Jones, Mark D; Meylan, Martin P; Smith, Paul; Whitehead, Scott A.

Associated Schoolboys
Beswick, David; Cambell, Daniel M; Clarke, Robert I; Evans, Lee J; Goodwin, Robert; Hamilton, Michael J; Hickton, Grant C; Holmes, Warren; Houghton, Darren C; Otter, Nicholas A; Paddick, Carl; Pearson, Michael R; Pick, Ashley C; Pilgrim, David J; Probert, James A; Smith, Mark; Tomlinson, Ronald J; Walker, Daniel K; Wilcockson, Andrew.

COLCHESTER UNITED 1991–92   *Back row (left to right):* David Martin, Mike Masters, Shaun Elliott.
Centre row: Ian Phillips (Assistant Coach), Steve Foley (Youth Team/Assistant Coach), Paul Roberts, Paul Newell, Tony English, Scott Barrett, Martin Grainger, Roy McDonough (Player/Coach), Chris Toulson (Physiotherapist).
Front row: Gary Bennett, Nicky Smith, Eamonn Collins, Steve McGavin, Jason Cook, Steve Restarick, Warren Donald, Mark Kinsella.

Division 3   **COLCHESTER UNITED**

Layer Road Ground, Colchester. Telephone (0206) 574042. Commercial dept: (0206) 574042.

Ground capacity: 7223.

Record attendance: 19,072 v Reading, FA Cup 1st rd, 27 November 1948.

Record receipts: £26,330 v Barrow, GM Vauxhall Conference, 2 May 1992.

Pitch measurements: 110yd × 71yd.

Patron: Councillor P. Spendlove.

Chairman: J. Bowdidge.

Directors: H. Carson, J. Worsp, P. Heard, R. Jackson.

Player-coach: Roy McDonough.

Assistant coach: Steve Foley/Ian Phillips.

Physio: Ray Cole.

Club administrator: Sue Smith.

Commercial manager: Marie Partner.

Lottery Manager: Jackie McDonough.

Programme Editor: Hal Mason.

Year Formed: 1937. Turned Professional: 1937. Ltd Co.: 1937.

Club Nickname: 'The U's'.

Record League Victory: 9-1 v Bradford C, Division 4, 30 December 1961 – Ames; Millar, Fowler; Harris, Abrey, Ron Hunt; Foster, Bobby Hunt (4), King (4), Hill (1), Wright.

Record Cup Victory: 7-1 v Yeovil (away), FA Cup, 2nd rd (replay), 11 December 1958 – Ames; Fisher, Fowler; Parker, Milligan, Hammond; Williams (1), McLeod (2), Langman (4), Evans, Wright.

Record Defeat: 0-8 v Leyton Orient, Division 4, 15 October 1989.

Most League Points (2 for a win): 60, Division 4, 1973–74.

Most League points (3 for a win): 81, Division 4, 1982–83.

Most League Goals: 104, Division 4, 1961–62.

Highest League Scorer in Season: Bobby Hunt, 37, Division 4, 1961–62.

Most League Goals in Total Aggregate: Martyn King, 131, 1959–65.

Most Capped Player: None.

Most League Appearances: Micky Cook, 613, 1969–84.

Record Transfer Fee Received: £90,000 from Gillingham for Trevor Lee, January 1981.

Record Transfer Fee Paid: £40,000 to Lokeren for Dale Tempest, August 1987.

Football League Record: 1950 Elected to Division 3 (S); 1958–61 Division 3; 1961–62 Division 4; 1962–65 Division 4; 1965–66 Division 4; 1966–68 Division 3; 1968–74 Division 4; 1974–76 Division 3; 1976–77; 1977–81 Division 3; 1981–90 Division 4; l990–92 GM Vauxhall Conference; 1992– Division 3.

Honours: Football League: Division 3 (S) best season: 3rd, 1956–57; Division 4 – Runners-up 1961–62. *FA Cup* best season: 1970–71, 6th rd (record for a Fourth Division club shared with Oxford United and Bradford City). *Football League Cup*: best season 5th rd 1974–75. *FA Trophy winners 1991–92*.

Colours: Royal blue and white striped shirts, royal blue shorts with white side panel, royal blue stockings with white hoops. **Change Colours**: Red shirts, black shorts, black stockings.

COLCHESTER UNITED

Player and Position	Ht	Wt	Birth Date	Birth Place	Source	Clubs	League App	Gls
Goalkeepers								
Scott Barrett	6 0	12 11	2 4 63	Ilkeston	Amateur	Wolverhampton W	30	—
						Stoke C	51	—
						Colchester U (loan)	13	—
						Stockport Co (loan)	10	—
						Colchester U	—	—
Defenders								
James Goodwin			20 7 74	Colchester	Trainee	Colchester U	—	—
Julian Hazell			25 9 73	Luton	Trainee	Colchester U	—	—
Paul Roberts	5 09	11 13	27 4 62	London	Apprentice	Millwall	146	—
						Brentford	62	—
						Swindon T	27	—
						Southend U	38	—
						Aldershot	39	—
						Exeter C	3	—
						Southend U	54	—
						Fisher Ath	—	—
Midfield								
Gary Bennett	5 07	9 13	13 11 70	Enfield	Trainee	Colchester U	45	5
Eamonn Collins	5 06	8 13	22 10 65	Dublin	Apprentice	Blackpool	—	—
						Southampton	3	—
						Portsmouth	5	—
						Exeter C (loan)	9	—
						Gillingham (loan)	—	—
						Colchester U	39	2
Jason Cook*	5 7	10 06	29 12 69	Edmonton	Trainee	Tottenham H	—	—
						Southend U	30	1
						Colchester U	—	—
Warren Donald	5 07	10 01	7 10 64	Uxbridge	Apprentice	West Ham U	2	—
						Northampton T (loan)	11	2
						Northampton T	177	11
						Colchester U	—	—
Shaun Elliott‡	6 0	11 10	26 1 58	Haltwhistle	Apprentice	Sunderland	321	12
						Norwich C	31	2
						Blackpool	67	—
						Colchester U	—	—
Tony English	6 00	11 00	10 10 66	Luton		Colchester U	222	35
Mark Kinsella	5 09	11 00	12 8 72	Dublin	Home Farm	Colchester U	6	—
Nick Smith	5 08	10 00	28 1 69	Berkley		Southend U	60	6
						Colchester U	—	—
Forwards								
Paul Abrahams			31 10 73	Colchester	Trainee	Colchester U	—	—
Martin Grainger	5 11	11 13	23 8 72	Enfield	Trainee	Colchester U	7	2
Roy McDonough‡	6 1	11 11	16 10 58	Solihull	Apprentice	Birmingham C	2	1
						Walsall	82	15
						Chelsea	—	—
						Colchester U	93	24
						Southend U	22	4
						Exeter C	20	1
						Cambridge U	32	5
						Southend U	186	30
						Colchester U	—	—
Steve McGavin			24 1 69	North Walsham	Trainee	Ipswich T	—	—
						Sudbury T	—	—
						Colchester U	—	—
Steve Restarick			28 11 71	London	Trainee	Colchester U	1	—

COLCHESTER UNITED

Foundation: Colchester United was formed in 1937 when a number of enthusiasts of the much older Colchester Town club decided to establish a professional concern as a limited liability company. The new club continued at Layer Road which had been the amateur club's home since 1909.

First Football League game: 19 August, 1950. Division 3 (S), v Gillingham (a) D 0-0 – Wright; Kettle, Allen; Bearryman, Stewart, Elder; Jones, Curry, Turner, McKim, Church.

Did you know: After beating Accrington Stanley 3-2 on 2 September 1961 and 4-0 on 13 January 1962, the Lancashire club subsequently withdrew from the League. Colchester lost their place on top of Division 4 and never regained it, though they were promoted.

Managers (and Secretary-managers)
Ted Fenton 1946–48, Jimmy Allen 1948–53, Jack Butler 1953–55, Benny Fenton 1955–63, Neil Franklin 1963–68, Dick Graham 1968–72, Jim Smith 1972–75, Bobby Roberts 1975–82, Allan Hunter 1982–83, Cyril Lea 1983–86, Mike Walker 1986–87, Roger Brown 1987–88, Jock Wallace 1989, Mick Mills 1990, Ian Atkins 1990–91, Roy McDonough 1991–.

Player and Position	Ht	Wt	Birth Date	Place	Source	Clubs	League App	Gls
Ian Stewart	5 7	11 09	10 9 61	Belfast	Juniors	QPR	67	2
						Millwall (loan)	11	3
						Newcastle U	42	3
						Portsmouth	1	—
						Brentford (loan)	7	—
						Aldershot	101	—
						Colchester U	—	—

COVENTRY CITY 1991–92 *Back row (left to right):* Michael Gynn, Stewart Robson, Trevor Peake, Robert Rosario, Andy Pearce, Peter Billing, Peter Ndlovu, Craig Middleton.
Centre row: George Dalton (Physiotherapist), Brian Borrows, Lee Hurst, Steve Ogrizovic, Paul Edwards, Lloyd McGrath, Brian Eastick (Reserve Team Coach), Mick Mills (Assistant Manager).
Front row: Kenny Sansom, Ray Woods, Kevin Drinkell, Terry Butcher (Player/Manager), David Smith, Dean Emerson, Kevin Gallacher.

FA Premier

COVENTRY CITY

Highfield Road Stadium, King Richard Street, Coventry CV2 4FW. Telephone General Enquiries: (0203) 223535. Ticket office: (0203) 225545. Pools and Lotteries: (0203) 257755. Club Shop: (0203) 257707. Telex No: 312132, answer back code COV AFC. Fax No: 0203 630318

Ground capacity: 25,311.

Record attendance: 51,455 v Wolverhampton W, Division 2, 29 April 1967.

Record receipts: £177,271. 55 v Nottingham F, Littlewoods Cup Semi-final 2nd leg, 25 February 1990.

Pitch measurements: 110yd × 75yd.

Life President: Derrick H. Robbins.

Chairman: P. D. H. Robins.

Vice-chairman: B. A. Richardson.

Directors: M. F. French FCA, J. F. W. Reason, A. M. Jepson.

Managing Director: G. W. Curtis.

Secretary: Graham Hover.

Team-manager: Bobby Gould.

Assistant Manager: Phil Neal. *Physio:* George Dalton. *Commercial Manager:* Arthur Pepper.

Year Formed: 1883. Turned Professional: 1893. Ltd Co.: 1907.

Former Grounds: Binley Road, 1883–87; Stoke Road, 1887–99; Highfield Road, 1899–.

Former Names: 1883–98, Singers FC; 1898, Coventry City FC.

Club Nickname: 'Sky Blues'.

Record League Victory: 9-0 v Bristol C, Division 3 (S), 28 April 1934 – Pearson; Brown, Bisby; Perry, Davidson, Frith; White (2), Lauderdale, Bourton (5), Jones (2), Lake.

Record Cup Victory: 7-0 v Scunthorpe U, FA Cup, 1st rd, 24 November 1934 – Pearson; Brown, Bisby; Mason, Davidson, Boileau; Birtley (2), Lauderdale (2), Bourton (1), Jones (1), Liddle (1).

Record Defeat: 2-10 v Norwich C, Division 3 (S), 15 March 1930.

Most League Points (2 for a win): 60, Division 4, 1958–59 and Division 3, 1963–64.

Most League points (3 for a win): 63, Division 1, 1986–87.

Most League Goals: 108, Division 3 (S), 1931–32.

Highest League Scorer in Season: Clarrie Bourton, 49, Division 3 (S), 1931–32.

Most League Goals in Total Aggregate: Clarrie Bourton, 171, 1931–37.

Most Capped Player: Dave Clements, 21 (48), Northern Ireland and Ronnie Rees, 21 (39), Wales.

Most League Appearances: George Curtis, 486, 1956–70.

Record Transfer Fee Received: £1,250,000 from Nottingham F for Ian Wallace, July 1980.

Record Transfer Fee Paid: £900,000 to Dundee U for Kevin Gallacher, January 1990.

Football League Record: 1919 Elected to Division 2; 1925–26 Division 3 (N); 1926–36 Division 3 (S); 1936–52 Division 2; 1952–58 Division 3 (S); 1958–59 Division 4; 1959–64 Division 3; 1964–67 Division 2; 1967–92 Division 1; 1992– FA Premier League.

Honours: Football League: Division 1 best season: 6th, 1969–70; Division 2 – Champions 1966–67; Division 3 – Champions 1963–64; Division 3 (S) – Champions 1935–36; Runners-up 1933–34; Division 4 – Runners-up 1958–59. *FA Cup:* Winners 1986–87. *Football League Cup:* best season: Semi-final 1980–81, 1989–90. **European Competitions:** *European Fairs Cup:* 1970–71.

Colours: All sky blue. **Change colours:** All red.

COVENTRY CITY 1991–92 LEAGUE RECORD

Match No.	Date		Venue	Opponents	Result	H/T Score	Lg. Pos.	Goalscorers	Atten-dance
1	Aug	17	H	Manchester C	L	0-1	0-1	—	18,013
2		21	H	Luton T	W	5-0	3-0	—	Gallacher 2, Rosario, Smith, Furlong	10,084
3		24	A	QPR	D	1-1	0-0	6	Gynn	9393
4		28	H	Sheffield U	W	3-1	3-1	—	Smith (pen), Furlong, Rosario	12,601
5		31	H	Wimbledon	L	0-1	0-1	8		9469
6	Sep	3	A	Oldham Ath	L	1-2	0-1	—	Furlong	12,996
7		7	A	Arsenal	W	2-1	1-0	6	Dixon (og), Ndlovu	28,142
8		14	H	Notts Co	W	1-0	0-0	4	Furlong	10,685
9		18	H	Leeds U	D	0-0	0-0	—		15,488
10		21	A	Everton	L	0-3	0-1	8		20,542
11		28	H	Aston Villa	W	1-0	1-0	6	Ndlovu	17,851
12	Oct	5	A	West Ham U	W	1-0	0-0	5	Gallacher	21,817
13		19	H	Crystal Palace	L	1-2	0-1	6	Gynn (pen)	10,591
14		26	A	Liverpool	L	0-1	0-1	9		33,339
15	Nov	2	H	Chelsea	L	0-1	0-1	10		11,343
16		16	A	Nottingham F	L	0-1	0-1	14		21,154
17		23	A	Norwich C	L	2-3	1-0	14	Gallacher 2	12,056
18		30	H	Southampton	W	2-0	1-0	13	Gallacher, Pearce	8585
19	Dec	7	A	Manchester U	L	0-4	0-3	15		42,549
20		20	A	Luton T	L	0-1	0-0	—		7533
21		26	A	Sheffield U	W	3-0	0-0	14	Robson, Flynn, Billing	19,638
22		28	A	Wimbledon	D	1-1	1-0	13	Robson	3270
23	Jan	1	H	Tottenham H	L	1-2	1-1	15	Rosario	19,639
24		11	H	QPR	D	2-2	1-0	16	Gallacher, Rosario	11,999
25		18	A	Manchester C	L	0-1	0-0	16		23,005
26	Feb	1	A	Crystal Palace	W	1-0	1-0	15	Smith	13,818
27		8	H	Liverpool	D	0-0	0-0	17		21,540
28		22	A	Southampton	D	0-0	0-0	17		13,719
29		29	H	Manchester U	D	0-0	0-0	17		23,967
30	Mar	4	H	Norwich C	D	0-0	0-0	—		8549
31		7	A	Sheffield W	D	1-1	0-0	15	Gallacher	23,959
32		11	H	Nottingham F	L	0-2	0-2	—		11,158
33		14	A	Chelsea	W	1-0	0-0	16	Robson	10,962
34		21	H	Oldham Ath	D	1-1	1-1	16	Pearce	12,840
35		28	H	Tottenham H	L	3-4	1-3	17	Flynn, Smith, McGrath	22,744
36	Apr	4	H	Arsenal	L	0-1	0-1	19		14,133
37		8	H	Sheffield W	D	0-0	0-0	—		13,293
38		11	A	Notts Co	L	0-1	0-0	19		6655
39		18	H	Everton	L	0-1	0-0	19		14,669
40		20	A	Leeds U	L	0-2	0-0	19		26,582
41		25	H	West Ham U	W	1-0	1-0	19	Gynn	15,392
42	May	2	A	Aston Villa	L	0-2	0-2	19		31,984

Final League Position: 19

GOALSCORERS

League (35): Gallacher 8, Furlong 4, Rosario 4, Smith 4 (1 pen), Gynn 3 (1 pen), Robson 3, Flynn 2, Ndlovu 2, Pearce 2, Billing 1, McGrath 1, own goals 1.
Rumbelows Cup (6): Gallacher 2, Rosario 2, Furlong 1, McGrath 1.
FA Cup (1): Borrows 1 (1 pen).

Ogrizovic	Borrows	McGrath	Robson	Pearce	Peake	Woods	Gynn	Rosario	Gallacher	Smith	Furlong	Edwards	Atherton	Billing	Ndlovu	Drinkell	Emerson	Greenman	Booty	Hurst	Middleton	Sansom	Flynn	Heald	Sealey	Match No.
1	2	3	4	5	6	7	8	9	10	11*	12															1
1	2	3	4	5	6	7	8	9	10*	11	12															2
1		2	4	5		7	8†	9*		11	10	3	6	12	14											3
1	2	8	4	5		7		9		11†	10	3*	6	12	14											4
1	2	7	4	5				9*	10	11	8	3	6	12												5
1	2	8	4	5		7		9		11*	10	3	6	12												6
1	2	8	4	5		7†		9	10	11*		3	6	12	14											7
1	2	7	4	5			8†	9	10	11*		3	6	12	14											8
1	2	7	4	5			8	9	10*	11		3	6	12												9
1	2	7	4	5			8*	9		11	10	3†	6	12	14											10
1	2	7		5			8	9	10	11	12	3*	6				4									11
1	2	7	4	5			8	9†	10	11*	12	3	6		14											12
1	2	7	4	5			8	9	10	11†	12	3	6*		14											13
1	2*	3	4	5		7†	8	9	10	11	12		6		14											14
1		8	4	5		7*		9	10	11			6	12				2		3						15
1	2	12	4	5		7	8	9*	10				6	11						3						16
1		7	4*	5			8	9	10	11	12		6					2		3						17
1	2	7		5			8*	9	10	11			6	12			4			3						18
1	2	7		5				9†	10	11*			6	12	14	8	4			3						19
1	2	7		5				9	10	11	12		6			8*	4			3						20
1	2	7	4					9*	10	11	12		6				5					3	8			21
1	2	7	4					9*	10	11	12		6				5					3	8			22
1	2	7	4	5				9	10	11*	12		6									3	8			23
1	2	7	4	5				9	10	11*			6								12	3	8			24
1	2†		4	5			8*	9	10	11	12		6		14							3	7			25
1			4					9	10	11			6			8	5		2			3	7			26
1	2		4					9	10	11			6				5			8		3	7			27
1	2		4					9	10	11	12		6				5			8		3	7*			28
1	2		4	5				9	10	11			6							8		3	7			29
1	2	14	4	5				9*	10	11	12		6							8†		3	7			30
1	2	8	4	5				9	10	11			6									3	7			31
1	2	8	4	5				9†	10*	11	12		6		14							3	7			32
1	2	8*	4†	5				9	10	11	12		6		14							3	7			33
	2	10	4	5				9		11*	12		6			8						3	7	1		34
	2	8		5				9	10	11	12		6				4					3*	7	1		35
	2	8†	4	5				9	10	11	12		6		14							3	7*		1	36
	2	7	4	5			8	9	10*	11†	12		6									3	14		1	37
1	2	7	4	5			8	9*	10		12		6									3	11			38
1	2	10†	4	5			8	9*		11	12		6		14							3	7			39
1	2	11	4	5			8	9*	10†		12		6		14							3	7			40
1	12	2	4				8	9	10	11			6				5					3*	7			41
1	2	3	4				8	9*	10	11†	12		6		14		5						7			42
38	**34**	**38**	**37**	**36**	**2**	**9**	**21**	**26**	**33**	**23**	**27**	**4**	**35**	**17**	**9**	**2**	**10**	**4**	**2**	**8**	**1**	**21**	**21**	**2**	**2**	

Substitute appearances: +1s +2s · +2s +3s · +1s +10s1s · +5s +14s2s +11s · +1s +2s · +1s

Rumbelows Cup	Second Round	Rochdale (h)		4-0
		(a)		0-1
	Third Round	Arsenal (h)		1-0
	Fourth Round	Tottenham H (h)		1-2
FA Cup	Third Round	Cambridge U (h)		1-1
		(a)		0-1

COVENTRY CITY

Player and Position	Ht	Wt	Birth Date	Birth Place	Source	Clubs	League App	Gls
Goalkeepers								
Clive Baker*	5 9	11 00	14 3 59	N Walsham	Amateur	Norwich C	14	—
						Barnsley	291	—
						Coventry C	—	—
Steve Ogrizovic	6 5	15 00	12 9 57	Mansfield	ONRYC	Chesterfield	16	—
						Liverpool	4	—
						Shrewsbury T	84	—
						Coventry C	316	1
Defenders								
Peter Atherton	5 11	12 03	6 4 70	Orrell	Trainee	Wigan Ath	149	1
						Coventry C	35	—
Peter Billing	6 2	12 07	24 10 64	Liverpool	S Liverpool	Everton	1	—
						Crewe Alex	88	1
						Coventry C	55	1
Martyn Booty	5 8	12 01	30 5 71	Kirby Muxloe	Trainee	Coventry C	3	—
Brian Borrows	5 10	10 12	20 12 60	Liverpool	Amateur	Everton	27	—
						Bolton W	95	—
						Coventry C	263	9
Dave Busst	6 01	12 10	30 6 67	Birmingham	Moor Green	Coventry C	—	—
Terry Butcher†	6 4	14 0	28 12 58	Singapore	Amateur	Ipswich T	271	16
						Rangers	127	9
						Coventry C	6	—
Paul Edwards	5 11	11 00	25 12 63	Birkenhead	Altrincham	Crewe Alex	86	6
						Coventry C	36	—
Alun French*			1 11 72	Coventry	Trainee	Coventry C	—	—
Chris Greenman	5 10	11 06	22 12 68	Bristol	School	Coventry C	4	—
Lee Middleton*	5 9	11 09	10 9 70	Nuneaton	Trainee	Coventry C	2	—
Andrew Pearce	6 4	13 00	20 4 66	Bradford	Halesowen	Coventry C	47	3
Kenny Sansom	5 6	11 08	26 9 58	Camberwell	Apprentice	Crystal Palace	172	3
						Arsenal	314	6
						Newcastle U	20	—
						QPR	36	—
						Coventry C	30	—
Midfield								
Jason Bickley*			19 10 72	Coventry	Trainee	Coventry C	—	—
Dean Emerson*	5 10	11 07	27 12 62	Salford	Local	Stockport Co	156	7
						Rotherham U	55	8
						Coventry C	114	—
Terry Fleming	5 09	11 00	5 1 73	Marston Green	Trainee	Coventry C	—	—
Sean Flynn	5 08	11 08	13 3 68	Birmingham	Halesowen	Coventry C	22	2
Mick Gynn	5 5	10 10	19 8 61	Peterborough	Apprentice	Peterborough U	156	33
						Coventry C	221	30
Lee Hurst	6 0	11 09	21 9 70	Nuneaton	Trainee	Coventry C	14	—
Lloyd McGrath	5 9	10 06	24 2 65	Birmingham	Apprentice	Coventry C	178	4
Stewart Robson	5 11	11 13	6 11 64	Billericay	Apprentice	Arsenal	151	16
						West Ham U	69	4
						Coventry C (loan)	4	—
						Coventry C	37	3
David Smith	5 8	10 02	29 3 68	Gloucester		Coventry C	148	18
Karl Wilson	5 9	10 12	19 11 73	Dublin		Coventry C	—	—
Forwards								
Warren Bufton*			3 11 72	Johannesburg	Trainee	Coventry C	—	—

COVENTRY CITY

Foundation: Workers at Singer's cycle factory formed a club in 1883. The first success of Singers' FC was to win the Birmingham. Junior Cup in 1891 and this led in 1894 to their election to the Birmingham and District League. Four years later they changed their name to Coventry City and joined the Southern League in 1908.

First Football League game: 30 August, 1919, Division 2, v Tottenham H (h) L 0-5 – Lindon; Roberts, Chaplin, Allan, Hawley, Clarke, Sheldon, Mercer, Sambrooke, Lowes, Gibson.

Did you know: Centre-half George Mason captained Coventry City on and off over a spell of 17 seasons 1935–52, being regular skipper in 13 consecutive seasons.

Managers (and Secretary-managers)
Harry Buckle 1909–10, Robert Wallace 1910–13*, Frank Scott-Walford 1913–15, William Clayton 1917–19, Harry Pollitt 1919–20, Albert Evans 1920–24, Jimmy Kerr 1925–28, James McIntyre 1928–31, Harry Storer 1931–45, Dick Bayliss 1945–47, Billy Frith 1947–48, Harry Storer 1948–53, Jack Fairbrother 1953–54, Charlie Elliott 1954–55, Jesse Carver 1955–56, Harry Warren 1956–57, Billy Frith 1957–61, Jimmy Hill 1961–67, Noel Cantwell 1967–72, Bob Dennison 1972–81 (became GM), Dave Sexton 1981–83, Bobby Gould 1983–84, Don Mackay 1985–86, George Curtis 1986–87 (became MD), John Sillett 1987–90, Terry Butcher 1990–92, Don Howe 1992, Bobby Gould July 1992–.

Player and Position	Ht	Wt	Birth Date	Birth Place	Source	Clubs	League App	Gls
Kevin Drinkell	5 11	12 06	18 8 60	Grimsby	Apprentice	Grimsby T	270	89
						Norwich C	121	50
						Rangers	36	12
						Coventry C	41	5
						Birmingham C (loan)	5	2
Paul Furlong	6 0	11 08	1 10 68	Wood Green	Enfield	Coventry C	37	4
Kevin Gallacher	5 7	9 11	23 11 66	Clydebank	Duntocher BC	Dundee U	131	27
						Coventry C	80	22
Matthew Jenkins‡	5 7	10 07	6 6 72	Leamington Spa	Trainee	Coventry C	—	—
Craig Middleton	5 9	11 00	10 9 70	Nuneaton	Trainee	Coventry C	2	—
Peter Ndlovu	5 8		25 2 73	Zimbabwe	Bulawayo H	Coventry C	23	2
Robert Rosario	6 3	12 01	4 3 66	Hammersmith	Hillingdon Bor	Norwich C	126	18
						Wolverhampton W (loan)	2	1
						Coventry C	31	4
Tony Sheridan	6 00	11 08	21 10 74	Dublin		Coventry C	—	—
Ray Woods	5 11	11 00	7 6 65	Birkenhead	Apprentice Colne D	Tranmere R	7	2
						Wigan Ath	28	3
						Coventry C	21	1

Trainees
Carmichael, David; Carr, Gerard J; Coleman, Daniel J; Crews, Barry W; Davies, Martin L; Hepburn, Graham; McNeil, Richard L; Melrose, Craig J; O'Brien, Paul W; O'Toole, Gavin F; Smith, Ricky; Stephenson, Michael J; Williams, Stephen D; Woods, Darragh W; Young, Scott C.

Associated Schoolboys
Brown, Andrew; Christie, Iyseden; Field, Marc I; Handford, Paul M; Hyndman, Craig N; Robinson, Mark T; Williams, James D; Willis, Adam P; Wood, Simon.

Associated Schoolboys who have accepted the club's offer of a Traineeship/Contract
Barnwell, Jamie; Blake, Timothy A; Chadwick, Luke D; Cleland, Jamie A; Jones, Richard J; Keelings, Tommy L; Rogers, Lee.

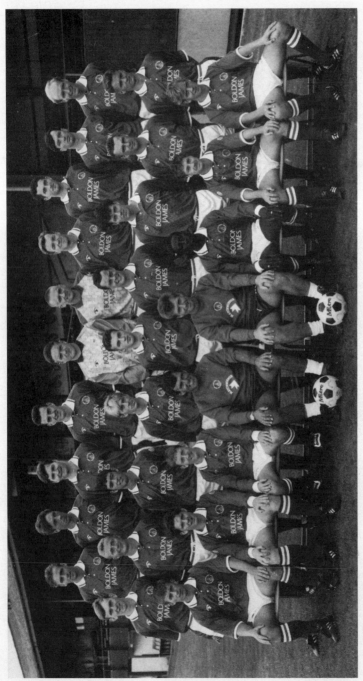

CREWE ALEXANDRA 1991–92 *Back row (left to right):* Dave McKearney, Mark Gardiner, Neil Sorvel, Neil Rutherford, Mark Gardiner, Neil Sorvel, Craig Hignett, Justin Wall, Jason Smart, Michael Jackson, Rob Edwards, Martin Disley.
Centre row: Ian Rutherford, Mark Gardiner, Neil Sorvel, Craig Hignett, Justin Wall, Jason Smart, Michael Jackson, Rob Edwards, Martin Disley, Curran, Aidan Murphy, Ron Futcher.
Front row: Steve Walters, Colin Rose, Steve Garvey, Dario Gradi (Manager), Kenny Swain (Assistant Manager), Gus Wilson, Tony Naylor, Rob Jones.
(Photo by courtesy of Steve Finch L.R.P.S.)

Division 3   CREWE ALEXANDRA

Football Ground, Gresty Rd, Crewe. Telephone Crewe (0270) 213014. (0270) 55657.

Ground capacity: 7200.

Record attendance: 20,000 v Tottenham H, FA Cup 4th rd, 30 January 1960.

Record receipts: £41,093 v Liverpool, FA Cup 3rd rd, 6 January 1992.

Pitch measurements: 112yd × 74yd.

President: N. Rowlinson.

Chairman: J. Bowler.

Vice-chairman: J. McMillan.

Directors: K. Potts, D. Rowlinson, R. Clayton, N. Hassall, E. Westman, J. R. Holmes.

Manager: Dario Gradi.

Coach/Assistant Manager: Kenny Swain.

Secretary/Commercial Manager: Mrs Gill Palin.

Year Formed: 1877. Turned Professional: 1893. Ltd Co.: 1892.

Club Nickname: 'Railwaymen'.

Record League Victory: 8-0 v Rotherham U, Division 3 (N), 1 October 1932 – Foster; Pringle, Dawson; Ward, Keenor (1), Turner (1); Gillespie, Swindells (1), McConnell (2), Deacon (2), Weale (1).

Record Cup Victory: 5-0 v Druids, FA Cup, 1st rd, 15 October 1887 – Hickton; Conde, Cope; Bayman, Halfpenny, Osborne (1); Pearson, Payne (1), Price (1), Tinsley, Ellis. (2 scorers unknown.).

Record Defeat: 2-13 v Tottenham H, FA Cup 4th rd replay, 3 February 1960.

Most League Points (2 for a win): 59, Division 4, 1962–63.

Most League points (3 for a win): 78, Division 4, 1988–89.

Most League Goals: 95, Division 3 (N), 1931–32.

Highest League Scorer in Season: Terry Harkin, 35, Division 4, 1964–65.

Most League Goals in Total Aggregate: Bert Swindells, 126, 1928–37.

Most Capped Player: Bill Lewis, 12 (30), Wales.

Most League Appearances: Tommy Lowry, 436, 1966–78.

Record Transfer Fee Received: £600,000 from Liverpool for Rob Jones, October 1991.

Record Transfer Fee Paid: £80,000 to Barnsley for Darren Foreman, March 1990.

Football League Record: 1892 Original Member of Division 2; 1896 Failed re-election; 1921 Re-entered Division 3 (N); 1958–63 Division 4; 1963–64 Division 3; 1964–68 Division 4; 1968–69 Division 3; 1969–89 Division 4; 1989–91 Division 3; 1991–92 Division 4; 1992– Division 3.

Honours: Football League: Division 2 best season: 10th, 1892–93. *FA Cup:* best season: semi-final 1888. *Football League Cup:* best season: 3rd rd, 1974–75, 1975–76, 1978–79.

Colours: Red shirts, white shorts, red stockings. **Change colours:** Blue shirts, white shorts, blue stockings.

CREWE ALEXANDRA 1991–92 LEAGUE RECORD

Match No.	Date		Venue	Opponents	Result		H/T Score	Lg. Pos.	Goalscorers	Attendance
1	Aug	17	A	Barnet	W	7-4	3-2	—	Naylor, Futcher, Edwards R 3, Hignett 2 (1 pen)	5090
2		24	H	Cardiff C	D	1-1	0-1	5	Murphy	3799
3		31	A	Rotherham U	W	2-1	1-1	2	Naylor, Edwards R	4362
4	Sep	7	A	Burnley	D	1-1	0-0	1	Hamilton (og)	9657
5		13	H	Mansfield T	L	1-2	1-2	—	Naylor	4667
6		17	H	Northampton T	D	1-1	1-1	—	Naylor	3597
7		21	A	Scunthorpe U	L	0-1	0-1	9		3021
8		28	H	Gillingham	W	2-1	1-0	6	Evans, McKearney	3126
9	Oct	5	A	Doncaster R	W	3-1	1-0	6	Evans 2, Walters	1779
10		11	H	Walsall	L	0-1	0-1	—		4749
11		19	H	Scarborough	D	3-3	2-0	8	McKearney, Hignett, Clarkson	2696
12		26	A	Carlisle U	L	1-2	0-0	10	Edwards R	1905
13	Nov	5	H	Maidstone U	D	1-1	1-1	—	Hignett	2476
14		9	H	Wrexham	W	2-1	2-0	10	Gardiner 2	3596
15		23	A	Blackpool	W	2-0	1-0	7	Carr 2	4534
16		30	H	Hereford U	W	4-2	3-0	5	Naylor, Futcher, Hignett 2 (1 pen)	2990
17	Dec	26	A	Barnet	W	3-0	2-0	8	Hignett (pen), Edwards R, Naylor	4736
18		28	H	Rotherham U	L	0-1	0-1	8		4490
19	Jan	11	H	Lincoln C	W	1-0	0-0	8	Walters	3060
20		18	A	Rochdale	L	0-1	0-1	8		2965
21	Feb	7	A	Carlisle U	W	2-1	1-1	—	Naylor, Hignett	3232
22		12	A	Hereford U	W	2-1	1-1	—	Futcher, Gardiner	2181
23		15	H	Chesterfield	W	3-1	0-1	7	Gardiner, Naylor, Walters	3172
24		18	A	Scarborough	L	1-2	1-0	—	Carr	1352
25		22	A	Lincoln C	D	2-2	1-2	7	Naylor, Hignett (pen)	2261
26		25	H	York C	W	1-0	1-0	—	Naylor	3327
27		28	H	Halifax T	W	3-2	2-1	—	Evans, Clarkson, Naylor	3514
28	Mar	3	H	Rochdale	D	1-1	0-0	—	Clarkson	3870
29		7	A	York C	D	1-1	1-1	5	Naylor	2208
30		11	A	Maidstone U	L	0-2	0-1	—		1174
31		21	A	Wrexham	L	0-1	0-0	8		3899
32		24	A	Chesterfield	L	1-2	1-0	—	Clarkson	2534
33		28	H	Blackpool	W	1-0	0-0	8	Naylor	4913
34		31	A	Mansfield T	L	3-4	0-3	—	Clarkson 2, McKearney	3108
35	Apr	4	H	Burnley	W	1-0	0-0	8	Gardiner	5530
36		11	A	Northampton T	W	1-0	0-0	7	Hignett	3300
37		14	A	Halifax T	L	1-2	1-0	—	McKearney	1022
38		18	H	Scunthorpe U	D	1-1	0-0	8	Hignett	3313
39		20	A	Gillingham	W	1-0	0-0	8	Naylor	2928
40		24	H	Doncaster R	W	1-0	1-0	—	Futcher	3639
41		28	A	Cardiff C	D	1-1	0-1	—	Macauley	10,523
42	May	2	A	Walsall	W	3-2	3-0	6	Hignett 2, Naylor	4995

Final League Position: 6

GOALSCORERS

League (66): Naylor 15, Hignett 13 (4 pens), Clarkson 6, Edwards R 6, Gardiner 5, Evans 4, Futcher 4, McKearney 4, Carr 3, Walters 3, Macauley 1, Murphy 1, own goals 1.
Rumbelows Cup (12): Naylor 3, Callaghan 2, Evans 2, Futcher 2, Edwards R 1, Gardiner 1, Hignett 1.
FA Cup (8): Naylor 3, Hignett 2, Barnsley 1 (o pens), Gardiner 1, Walters 1.

Greygoose	Wilson	Jones R	Smart	Callaghan	Walters	Hignett	Naylor	Futcher	Gardiner	Edwards R	Murphy	Garvey	Carr	Jasper	Rose	McPhillips	Evans	McKearney	Rutherford	Downes	Payne	Sorvel	Clarkson	Noble	Swain	Jackson	Disley	Whitehurst	Match No.
1	2	3	4	5	6*	7	8	9†10	11	12	14																		1
1	2	3		5	6	7	8†	9*10	11	12	14	4																	2
1	2	3		5†	6*	7	8	9	10	11		14	4	12															3
1	2	3	4	5	6		8	9	10*11†12	7			14																4
1	2	3	4	5	6		8	9†10	11	12	7*			14															5
1	2	3*		5	6	9	8*	10	11	12	7	4																	6
1	2	3		5	6	9	8*		10	11	7†		4	14		12													7
1	2	3		5	6			12	10	11			4			8†	9*	7	14										8
1	2			5	6				10	11			4			8	9	3		7*12									9
1	2			5	6			12	10	11			4			8†	9*	3		14	7								10
1		2		5	6	7			10	11			4				9	3			12		8*						11
1	2			5	6	7			10	11			4			8*	9	3					12						12
	2			5			7		10	12			4			8*	9					14	6	11†	1	3			13
1	2			5	6	7			10	12			4				9	3				8	11*						14
1	2	3			6	7	8	9*10	11†		4		12									14				5			15
1	2			5	6	7	8*	9†10	11		4	12						3					14						16
1	2			5	6	7	8	10	11*		4	9†						3				12	14						17
1	2			5	6	7* 8		11			4	14	9†			3						12	10						18
1	2			5	6	7	8*	10	11		4	12					3					9					14†		19
1	2			5	12	7† 8	14	4	10*	3			6	11							9								20
1	2			5†	6	8	12	10	14	4	3		11								9*								21
1	2			5	6	7	8	9	10	11*	4	3					12												22
1	2			5	6	7	8*	9	10	11†	4	3						14	12										23
1	2			5	6	7	8	9*10	11	4	3											12							24
1	2			5		7	8	9	10	11*12	4	3										6†14							25
1	2			5		7	8	9	10†11	4	12	3									6	14							26
	2	5			8		10	12			7*	4	6		9†	3						14	11	1					27
	2	5		12	8	10		7	4	6		9*	3									11							28
	2	5	7	10	8	6	4	12	11*	3		9	1																29
	2	5	14	7	10	8	12	6†	4	11*	3		9	1															30
	2	5		6	7	8	11†	4	12	3		9	1																31
1	2	5	4	6	7	8	12	10	3		9																		32
1	2	11*	6†	7	8	10	4	3		9																12			33
1	2	11*	7	8	10	4	3		9																12				34
1	2	6	7	8	10	4	11	9																					35
1	2	11	6*	7	8	10†	4	14	9	12																			36
1	2	10	6	7	8	4	5	11	9																				37
1	2	8	6	7	12	4	11																						38
1	2	6	7	8	9†10	12	11	4*	14																				39
	2	11	6	7	8	9*10	4																1				12		40
	2	11*	6	7	8	9†10	14	4	12												12	1							41
	2	14	11	6	7	8†9*10	4	12	1												12	1							42

33	41	8	10	36	34	32	34	18	37	22	1	8	33	3	2	5	13	30	—	1	3	5	18	7	1	1	—	4	
+	+	+	+			+	+	+	+	+	+	+	+	+	+	+	+	+		+	+	+	+				+	+	
1s	1s	1s	1s			3s	1s	6s	6s	3s	3s	4s	3s	1s	4s	1s	1s	1s		3s	4s	10s					1s	6s	

Edwards P—Match No. 28(1) 29(1); Bishop—Match No. 31(10) 32(11*) 34(6†); Kelly—Match No. 31(14*); Macauley—Match No. 33(5) 34(5) 35(5) 36(5) 38(5) 39(5) 40(5) 41(5) 42(5); Smith—Match No. 33(14) 34(14) 35(3) 36(3) 37(3) 38(3*) 39(3) 40(3) 41(3) 42(3).

Rumbelows Cup	First Round	Doncaster R (h)	5-2
		(a)	4-2
	Second Round	Newcastle U (h)	3-4
		(a)	0-1
FA Cup	First Round	Carlisle U (a)	1-1
		(h)	5-3
	Second Round	Chester C (h)	2-0
	Third Round	Liverpool (h)	0-4

CREWE ALEXANDRA

Player and Position	Ht	Wt	Birth Date	Place	Source	Clubs	League App	Gls
Goalkeepers								
Paul Edwards*	5 11	11 08	22 2 65	Liverpool	St Helens T	Crewe Alex	29	—
Dean Greygoose	5 11	11 05	18 12 64	Thetford	Apprentice	Cambridge U	26	—
						Orient (loan)	—	—
						Lincoln C (loan)	6	—
						Orient	1	—
						Crystal Palace	—	—
						Crewe Alex	175	—
Daniel Noble†	5 11	12 09	2 9 70	Hull	Trainee	Stoke C	3	—
						Crewe Alex	7	—
Defenders								
Aaron Callaghan	5 11	11 02	8 10 66	Dublin	Apprentice	Stoke C	7	—
						Crewe Alex (loan)	8	—
						Oldham Ath	16	2
						Crewe Alex	158	6
Darren Carr	6 0	12 07	4 9 68	Bristol		Bristol R	30	—
						Newport Co	9	—
						Sheffield U	13	1
						Crewe Alex	72	3
Chris Downes†	5 10	10 08	17 1 69	Sheffield	Trainee	Sheffield U	2	—
						Scarborough (loan)	2	—
						Stockport Co	11	1
						Crewe Alex	2	—
Mike Jackson§			4 12 73	West Cheshire	Trainee	Crewe Alex	1	—
Neil Lennon	5 9	11 06	25 6 71	Lurgan	Trainee	Manchester C	1	—
						Crewe Alex	34	3
David McKearney	5 10	11 02	20 6 68	Crosby		Bolton W	—	—
						Crewe Alex	79	6
Steve Macauley	6 1	12 00	4 3 69	Lytham	Fleetwood	Crewe Alex	9	1
Jason Smart	6 0	12 00	15 2 69	Rochdale	Trainee	Rochdale	117	4
						Crewe Alex	89	2
Shaun Smith	5 10	11 00	9 4 71	Leeds	Trainee	Halifax T	7	—
						Crewe Alex	10	—
Neil Sorvel	5 11		2 3 73	Widnes	Trainee	Crewe Alex	9	—
Kenny Swain†	5 9	11 07	28 1 52	Birkenhead	Wycombe W	Chelsea C	119	26
						Aston Villa	148	2
						Nottingham F	112	2
						Portsmouth	113	
						WBA (loan)	7	1
						Crewe Alex	126	1
Justin Wall†	5 10		3 2 73	Stockport	Trainee	Crewe Alex	—	—
Gus Wilson			11 4 63	Manchester	Runcorn	Crewe Alex	41	—
Midfield								
Richard Annon			4 12 68	Leeds	Guiseley	Crewe Alex	—	—
Martin Disley			24 6 71	Ormskirk		Crewe Alex	2	—
Craig Hignett	5 10	10 08	12 1 70	Whiston		Crewe Alex	107	34
Dale Jasper*	6 0	11 07	14 1 64	Croydon	Apprentice	Chelsea	10	—
						Brighton & HA	49	6
						Crewe Alex	111	2
Paul Kelly*	5 8	11 07	6 3 71	Urmston	Trainee	Manchester C	—	—
						Crewe Alex	1	—
Aidan Murphy*	5 10	10 10	17 9 67	Manchester	Apprentice	Manchester U	—	—
						Lincoln C (loan)	2	—
						Oldham Ath (loan)	—	—
						Crewe Alex	113	13
Colin Rose†	5 8	10 09	22 1 72	Winsford	Trainee	Crewe Alex	22	1
Steve Walters	5 10	11 08	9 1 72	Plymouth	Trainee	Crewe Alex	92	5
Forwards								
Phil Clarkson	5 10	10 08	13 11 68	Hambleton	Fleetwood	Crewe Alex	28	6
Robert Edwards	5 8	11 07	23 2 70	Manchester	Trainee	Crewe Alex	71	18
Stewart Evans	6 4	11 05	15 11 60	Maltby	Apprentice	Rotherham U	—	—
						Gainsborough T	—	—
						Sheffield U	—	—
						Wimbledon	175	50
						WBA	14	1
						Plymouth Arg	45	10
						Rotherham U	65	14
						Torquay U (loan)	15	5
						Crewe Alex	17	4

CREWE ALEXANDRA

Foundation: Crewe Alexandra played cricket and probably rugby before they decided to form a football club in 1877. Whether they took the name "Alexandra" from a pub where they held their meetings, or whether it was after Princess Alexandra, is a matter of conjecture. Crewe's first trophy was the Crewe and District Cup in 1887 and it is worth noting that they reached the semi-finals of the FA Cup the following year.

First Football League game: 3 September, 1892, Division 2, v Burton Swifts (a) L 1-7 – Hickton; Moore, Cope; Linnell, Johnson, Osborne; Bennett, Pearson (1), Bailey, Barnett, Roberts.

Did you know: Crewe were the last amateur side to reach the semi-finals of the FA Cup when they were beaten 4-0 by Preston North End in February 1888.

Managers (and Secretary-managers)
W. C. McNeill 1892–94*, J. G. Hall 1895–96*, R. Roberts* (1st team sec.) 1897, J. B. Bromerley 1898–1911* (continued as Hon. Sec. to 1925), Tom Bailey 1925–38, George Lillicrop 1938–44, Frank Hill 1944–48, Arthur Turner 1948–51, Harry Catterick 1951–53, Ralph Ward 1953–55, Maurice Lindley 1955–58, Harry Ware 1958–60, Jimmy McGuigan 1960–64, Ernie Tagg 1964–71 (continued as secretary to 1972), Dennis Viollet 1971, Jimmy Melia 1972–73, Ernie Tagg 1974, Harry Gregg 1975–78, Warwick Rimmer 1978–79, Tony Waddington 1979–81, Arfon Griffiths 1981–82, Peter Morris 1982–83, Dario Gradi June 1983–.

Player and Position	Ht	Wt	Birth Date	Birth Place	Source	Clubs	League App	Gls
Paul Fishenden‡	6 0	10 12	2 8 63	Hillingdon	Local	Wimbledon	75	25
						Fulham (loan)	3	—
						Millwall (loan)	3	—
						Orient (loan)	4	—
						Crewe Alex	81	25
Ron Futcher*	6 0	12 10	25 9 56	Chester	Apprentice	Chester	4	—
						Luton T	120	40
						Manchester C	17	7
						Barnsley	19	6
						Oldham Ath	65	30
						Bradford C	42	18
						Port Vale	52	20
						Burnley	57	25
						Crewe Alex	21	4
Mark Gardiner	5 10	10 07	25 12 66	Cirencester	Apprentice	Swindon T	10	1
						Torquay U	49	4
						Crewe Alex	135	31
Steve Garvey			22 11 73	Tameside	Trainee	Crewe Alex	12	—
Andrew Gunn‡	6 0	12 01	2 2 71	Barking	Trainee	Watford	—	—
						Crewe Alex	4	—
Terry McPhillips‡	5 10	11 00	1 1 68	Manchester	Trainee	Liverpool	—	—
						Halifax T	93	28
						Northampton T (loan)	1	—
						Crewe Alex	6	—
Tony Naylor	5 8	10 08	29 3 67	Manchester	Droylsden	Crewe Alex	50	16
Ian Rutherford†	5 10		24 12 72	Hitchin	Trainee	Luton T	—	—
						Crewe Alex	2	—

Trainees
Adebola, Dele; Byrne, Christopher; Duffy, Christopher J; Frawley, Andrew; Hughes, Anthony B; Jackson, Michael J; Keen, Ryan H; Maloney, Michael P; Meeson, Christopher; Rushton, Paul; Stephenson, Ashlyn R; Tierney, Francis; Watson, Melvin M; Whalley, Gareth; Williams, Carwyn; Woodward, Andrew S.

**Non-Contract
Mayfield, Alex; McPhillips, Terence; Rutherford, Ian.

Associated Schoolboys
Aimes, David; Bell, Christopher G; Brown, Scott; Byrne, Liam S; Carroll, Kevin T; Challoner, Darren; Corcoran, Matthew L; Edwards, Gareth J; Ellis, Duncan J; Humphray, Darren J; Hyland, Mark J; Keen, Anthony M; Murphy, Daniel B; Murray, Thomas O; Oakes, Andrew M; Parker, Justin N; Pope, Steven A; Riley, Andrew S; Simpson, Wesley L; Smith, Matthew; Staley, Benjamin L; Street, Kevin; Wiggins, Nikolas.

Associated Schoolboys who have accepted the club's offer of a Traineeship/Contract
Ceraolo, Mark; Chapman, Iain A; Fraser, Stuart A; Hawtin, Dale C; Ouslem, Joseph A; Rivers, Mark A.

**Non-Contract Players who are retained must be re-signed before they are eligible to play in League matches.

CRYSTAL PALACE 1991–92 *Back row (left to right):* Ricky Newman, Jeff Hopkins, Garry Thompson, Martin Chester, Tony Witter, Chris Coleman, Alan Pardew, Gareth Southgate, Dean Gordon.

Centre row: Alan Smith (Assistant Manager), Wally Downes (Coach), Spike Hill (Kit Manager), Paul Bodin, Paul Brazier, Rudi Hedman, Stan Collymore, Jimmy Glass, Nigel Martyn, Andy Woodman, Perry Suckling, Andy Thorn, John Salako, Torje Eike (Physio), David West (Physio), Dave Garland (Youth Team Coach).

Front row: Jamie Moralee, Eddie McGoldrick, John Humphrey, Simon Rodger, Mark Bright, Geoff Thomas (Captain), Steve Coppell (Manager), Andy Gray, Ian Wright, Eric Young, Simon Osborn, Richard Shaw, David Whyte.

FA Premier CRYSTAL PALACE

Selhurst Park, London SE25 6PU. Telephone 081-653 4462. Lottery Office: 081-771 9502. Souvenir Shop: 081-6535 584, Fax: 081-771 5311. Clubline: 0898 400333. Palace Ticket Line: 0898 400333. Palace Publications: 081-771 8299. Fax No: 081-653 6312

Ground capacity: 29,949.

Record attendance: 51,482 v Burnley, Division 2, 11 May 1979.

Record receipts: £292,000 v Manchester U, Division 1, 30 November 1991.

Pitch measurements: 110yd × 74yd.

Commercial Manager: Graham Drew.

Chairman: R. G. Noades.

Directors: R. Anderson, B. Coleman OBE, A. S. C. De Souza, G. Geraghty, S. Hume-Kendall, M. E. Lee, P. H. N. Norman.

Team Manager: Steve Coppell. *Assistant Manager:* Alan Smith. *Coaches:* Wally Downes and Steve Harrison. *Physio:* David West. *Company Secretary:* Doug Miller. *Club Secretary:* Mike Hurst. *Assistant Secretary:* Terry Byfield. *Marketing Manager:* Tony Willis.

Year Formed: 1905. Turned Professional: 1905. Ltd Co.: 1905.

Former Grounds: 1905, Crystal Palace; 1915, Herne Hill; 1918, The Nest; 1924, Selhurst Park. *Club Nickname:* 'The Eagles'. *Club Sponsors:* Tulip Computers

Record League Victory: 9-0 v Barrow, Division 4, 10 October 1959 – Rouse; Long, Noakes; Truett, Evans, McNichol; Gavin (1), Summersby (4 incl. 1p), Sexton, Byrne (2), Colfar (2).

Record Cup Victory: 8-0 v Southend U, Rumbelows League Cup, 2nd rd (1st leg), 25 September 1990 – Martyn; Humphrey (Thompson (1)), Shaw, Pardew, Young, Thorn, McGoldrick, Thomas, Bright (3), Wright (3), Barber (Hodges (1)).

Record Defeat: 0-9 v Liverpool, Division 1, 12 September 1990.

Most League Points (2 for a win): 64, Division 4, 1960–61.

Most League points (3 for a win): 81, Division 2, 1988–89.

Most League Goals: 110, Division 4, 1960–61.

Highest League Scorer in Season: Peter Simpson, 46, Division 3 (S), 1930–31.

Most League Goals in Total Aggregate: Peter Simpson, 154, 1930–36.

Most Capped Player: Paddy Mulligan, 14 (50), Eire; Ian Walsh, 14 (18), Wales; Peter Nicholas, 14 (73) Wales.

Most League Appearances: Jim Cannon, 571, 1973–88.

Record Transfer Fee Received: £2,500,000 from Arsenal for Ian Wright, September 1991.

Record Transfer Fee Paid: £1,800,000 to Sunderland for Marco Gabbiadini, September 1991.

Football League Record: 1920 Original Members of Division 3; 1921–25 Division 2; 1925–58 Division 3 (S); 1958–61 Division 4; 1961–64 Division 3; 1964–69 Division 2; 1969–73 Division 1; 1973–74 Division 2; 1974–77 Division 3; 1977–79 Division 2; 1979–81 Division 1; 1981–89 Division 2; 1989–92 Division 1; 1992– FA Premier League.

Honours: Football League: Division 1 best season: 3rd 1990–91; Division 2 – Champions 1978–79; Runners-up 1968–69; Division 3 – Runners-up 1963–64; Division 3 (S) – Champions 1920–21; Runners-up 1928–29, 1930–31, 1938–39; Division 4 – Runners-up 1960–61. *FA Cup:* best season: Runners-up 1989–90. *Football League Cup:* best season: 5th rd, 1968–69, 1970–71, 1991–92. *Zenith Data Systems Cup:* Winners: 1991.

Colours: Red and blue shirts, red shorts, red stockings. **Change colours:** Yellow shirts, light blue shorts, white stockings.

CRYSTAL PALACE 1991–92 LEAGUE RECORD

Match No.	Date		Venue	Opponents	Result		H/T Score	Lg. Pos.	Goalscorers	Atten-dance
1	Aug	24	A	Manchester C	L	2-3	1-2	22	Thomas, Bright	28,023
2		27	H	Wimbledon	W	3-2	2-1	—	Bright, Gray (pen), Wright	16,736
3		31	H	Sheffield U	W	2-1	0-0	14	Thomas, Wright	15,507
4	Sep	4	A	Aston Villa	W	1-0	1-0	—	Wright	20,740
5		7	A	Everton	D	2-2	1-0	9	Gray (pen), Bright	21,065
6		14	H	Arsenal	L	1-4	0-1	13	Bright	24,228
7		17	H	West Ham U	L	2-3	1-0	—	Salako, Wright	21,363
8		21	A	Oldham Ath	W	3-2	1-1	12	Salako, Wright, Bright	13,391
9		28	H	QPR	D	2-2	0-1	12	Bright, Collymore	15,372
10	Oct	1	H	Leeds U	W	1-0	0-0	—	Bright	18,298
11		5	A	Sheffield W	L	1-4	1-3	8	Bright	26,230
12		19	A	Coventry C	W	2-1	1-0	7	Bright, Gabbiadini	10,591
13		26	H	Chelsea	D	0-0	0-0	7		21,841
14	Nov	2	A	Liverpool	W	2-1	0-1	7	Gabbiadini, Thomas	34,231
15		16	H	Southampton	W	1-0	0-0	5	Thomas	15,861
16		23	A	Nottingham F	L	1-5	0-2	5	Thomas	22,387
17		30	H	Manchester U	L	1-3	1-1	6	Mortimer	29,017
18	Dec	7	A	Norwich C	D	3-3	1-1	8	Newman (og), McGoldrick, Osborn	12,667
19		22	H	Tottenham H	L	1-2	0-2	—	Fenwick (og)	22,491
20		26	A	Wimbledon	D	1-1	0-0	10	Gabbiadini	15,009
21		28	A	Sheffield U	D	1-1	0-1	11	Gabbiadini	17,969
22	Jan	1	H	Notts Co	W	1-0	1-0	10	Gabbiadini	14,202
23		11	H	Manchester C	D	1-1	1-0	8	Bright	14,766
24		18	A	Leeds U	D	1-1	1-1	9	Thomas	27,717
25	Feb	1	H	Coventry C	L	0-1	0-1	9		13,818
26		8	A	Chelsea	D	1-1	1-0	10	Whyte	17,810
27		16	A	Tottenham H	W	1-0	0-0	—	McGoldrick	19,834
28		22	A	Manchester U	L	0-2	0-1	9		46,347
29		25	H	Luton T	D	1-1	1-0	—	Bright	12,109
30		29	H	Norwich C	L	3-4	2-4	11	Osborn, Bright 2	14,201
31	Mar	3	H	Nottingham F	D	0-0	0-0	—		12,608
32		7	A	Luton T	D	1-1	1-0	—	McGoldrick	8591
33		11	A	Southampton	L	0-1	0-1	—		12,926
34		14	H	Liverpool	W	1-0	1-0	10	Young	23,680
35		21	H	Aston Villa	D	0-0	0-0	10		15,368
36		28	A	Notts Co	W	3-2	1-2	7	Coleman, Bright, Mortimer	7674
37	Apr	4	H	Everton	W	2-0	0-0	7	Coleman, Bright (pen)	14,338
38		11	A	Arsenal	L	1-4	1-3	8	Coleman	36,016
39		18	H	Oldham Ath	D	0-0	0-0	10		12,267
40		20	A	West Ham U	W	2-0	1-0	10	Bright, Coleman	17,710
41		25	H	Sheffield W	D	1-1	0-1	10	Bright	21,573
42	May	2	A	QPR	L	0-1	0-1	10		14,903

Final League Position: 10

GOALSCORERS

League (53): Bright 17 (1 pen), Thomas 6, Gabbiadini 5, Wright 5, Coleman 4, McGoldrick 3, Gray 2 (2 pens), Mortimer 2, Osborn 2, Salako 2, Collymore 1, Whyte 1, Young 1, own goals 2.
Rumbelows Cup (15): Bright 4, Gray 4 (2 pens), Thorn 2, Collymore 1, Gabbiadini 1, Thomas 1, Walker 1 (o pens), Whyte 1.
FA Cup (0).

Martyn	Humphrey	Bodin	Gray	Shaw	Sinnott	Salako	Thomas	Bright	Wright	McGoldrick	Pardew	Thorn	Suckling	Southgate	Young	Collymore	Osborn	Gabbiadini	Rodger	Mortimer	Coleman	Gordon	Whyte	Moralee	Hedman	Sullivan	Barnes	Match No.
1	2	3*	4	5	6	7	8	9	10	11	12																	1
1	2	12	4	3*	5	7	8	9	10	11				6														2
1	2		4	3	5	7	8	9	10	11				6														3
1	2		4	3	5	7	8	9	10	11				6														4
1	2		4	3	5	7	8	9	10*	11	12			6														5
	2†		4	3	5	7	8*	9	10	11	12	6	1			14												6
	2		4	3		7		9	10	11*	8	6	1				5	12										7
	2	3	4		6	7		9	10	11		8	1				5											8
1	2	3	4		6	10		9		11	7		14			5†12			8*									9
1			4	3	11*	8	9					6		2	5	12	7	10										10
1			4	3		8	9		14			6		2	5	12	7*10†11											11
1			4	12	3	8	9		11			6		2	5		10	7*										12
1			4	3		8	9		11			6		2	5		10*	7	12									13
1	6	4†		3		8	9		11	14				2	5		10	12	7*									14
1	6		4	3†		8	9		11					2	5	12	10		7*14									15
1	3		4			8	9		11			6		2	5		10	7										16
1	14		4			8†	9		11			6		2	5	12	10	7*	3									17
1			4				9		11			6		2	5	8	10*12	7	3									18
1	6		4				9		11					2		8	10	7	5	3*12								19
1	6		4	3			9		11					2		8	10	7	5*	12								20
1	2		4	3			9		11					5		8	10	7	6									21
1	2		4	3		8	9		11					5			10	7	6									22
1	2		4	3		8	9		11*			6		5			10	7			12							23
1	2		4	3		8	9		11			6		5			10*	7			12							24
1	2		4†	3		8	9		11			6		5		12		7		10*14								25
1	2			3		8	9		11			6		5			4	7		10								26
1	2			3		8	9		11			6		5			4	7		10								27
1	2			3		8	9		11			6		5			4	7		10								28
1	2			3†		8	9		11			6	12	5			4	7	14	10*								29
1	2		3			8*	9		11			6	12	5			4	7	14	10†								30
1	2		3				9		11			6	8	5			4*	7	12	10								31
1	2		3†14				9		11			6	8	5				7	4*10	12								32
1	2		3				9		11			6	8	5	14			7	12	10*	4†							33
1	2		3				9		11			6	8	5				7	4	10								34
1	2		3				9					6	8	5	11			7	4	10								35
1	2		3			8	9					6	4	5	11*			7	12	10								36
1	2		3			8	9					6	4	5	11*			7†12	10				14					37
1	2		3			8	9					6	4	5	11*			7	10				12					38
1	2		3			8	9		11			6	4*	5	14			7†10					12					39
1	2		3			8	9		11			6	4	5					10	7*	12							40
1	2		3			8	9		11			6	4	5					10*	7†	12	14						41
	2		3			8	9		11			6	4						7†	5	12		10			1	14*	42
38	36	3	25	9	35	10	30	42	8	36	3	33	3	26	30	4	13	15	20	17	14	2	7	2	—	1	—	
	+1s		+1s		+1s	+1s							+5s		+4s	+8s	+1s		+2s	+4s	+4s	+2s	+4s	+4s	+3s		+1s	

Rumbelows Cup	Second Round	Hartlepool U (a)	1-1
		(h)	6-1
	Third Round	Birmingham C (a)	1-1
		(h)	1-1
		(h)	2-1
	Fourth Round	Swindon T (a)	1-0
	Fifth Round	Nottingham F (h)	1-1
		(a)	2-4
FA Cup	Third Round	Leicester C (a)	0-1

CRYSTAL PALACE

Player and Position	Ht	Wt	Birth Date	Place	Source	Clubs	League App	Gls
Goalkeepers								
James Glass	6 01	11 10	1 8 73	Epsom	Trainee	Crystal Palace	—	—
Nigel Martyn	6 2	14 00	11 8 66	St Austell	St Blazey	Bristol R	101	—
						Crystal Palace	101	—
Perry Suckling†	6 1	11 02	12 10 65	Leyton	Apprentice	Coventry C	27	—
						Manchester C	39	—
						Crystal Palace	59	—
						West Ham U (loan)	6	—
						Brentford (loan)	8	—
Andrew Woodman	6 1	12 04	11 8 71	Denmark Hill	Trainee	Crystal Palace	—	—
Defenders								
Chris Coleman	6 2	12 10	10 6 70	Swansea	Apprentice	Swansea C	160	2
						Crystal Palace	18	4
Dean Gordon	6 00	11 05	10 2 73	Croydon	Trainee	Crystal Palace	4	—
Rudi Hedman†	6 3	12 00	16 11 64	London	Local	Colchester U	176	10
						Crystal Palace	21	—
						Leyton Orient (loan)	5	—
John Humphrey	5 10	11 01	31 1 61	Paddington	Apprentice	Wolverhampton W	149	3
						Charlton Ath	194	3
						Crystal Palace	75	1
Simon Rodger	5 9	11 07	3 10 71	Shoreham	Trainee	Crystal Palace	22	—
Richard Shaw	5 9	11 08	11 9 68	Brentford	Apprentice	Crystal Palace	84	1
						Hull C (loan)	4	—
Lee Sinnott	6 1	12 07	12 7 65	Aldridge	Apprentice	Walsall	40	2
						Watford	78	2
						Bradford C	173	6
						Crystal Palace	36	—
Gareth Southgate	5 10	11 12	3 9 70	Watford	Trainee	Crystal Palace	31	—
Andy Thorn	6 0	11 05	12 11 66	Carshalton	Apprentice	Wimbledon	107	2
						Newcastle U	36	2
						Crystal Palace	84	2
Eric Young	6 2	13 00	25 3 60	Singapore	Slough T	Brighton & HA	126	10
						Wimbledon	99	9
						Crystal Palace	64	4
Midfield								
Robert Bowry			19 5 71	London	Trainee	Crystal Palace	—	—
Martin Chester*	5 08	10 01	23 8 72	Farnborough	Whyteleafe	Crystal Palace	—	—
Andy Gray	5 11	13 03	22 2 64	Lambeth	Dulwich H	Crystal Palace	98	27
						Aston Villa	37	4
						QPR	11	2
						Crystal Palace	90	12
						Tottenham H (loan)	14	1
Eddie McGoldrick	5 10	12 00	30 4 65	London	Nuneaton	Northampton T	107	9
						Crystal Palace	105	3
Paul Mortimer	5 11	11 03	8 5 68	London	Fulham	Charlton Ath	113	17
						Aston Villa	12	1
						Crystal Palace	21	2
Ricky Newman	5 10	11 00	5 8 70	Guildford		Crystal Palace	—	—
						Maidstone U (loan)	10	1
Simon Osborn	5 10	11 04	19 1 72	New Addington	Trainee	Crystal Palace	18	2
Geoff Thomas	5 10	10 07	5 8 64	Manchester	Local	Rochdale	11	1
						Crewe Alex	125	20
						Crystal Palace	166	24
Forwards								
Andy Barnes	5 11	12 06	31 3 67	Croydon	Sutton U	Crystal Palace	1	—
Paul Brazier*			8 11 72	Bromley	Trainee	Crystal Palace	—	—

CRYSTAL PALACE

Foundation: There was a Crystal Palace club as early as 1861 but the present organisation was born in 1905 after the formation of a club by the company that controlled the Crystal Palace (the building that is), had been rejected by the FA who did not like the idea of the Cup Final hosts running their own club. A separate company had to be formed and they had their home on the old Cup Final ground until 1915.

First Football League game: 28 August, 1920, Division 3, v Merthyr T (a) L 1-2 – Alderson; Little, Rhodes; McCracken, Jones, Feebury; Bateman, Conner, Smith, Milligan (1), Whibley.

Did you know: Crystal Palace played three goalless draws with First Division Notts County in the FA Cup second round in 1923–24 before winning 2-1 at Villa Park.

Managers (and Secretary-managers)
John T. Robson 1905–07, Edmund Goodman 1907–25 (had been secretary since 1905 and afterwards continued in this position to 1933). Alec Maley 1925–27, Fred Maven 1927–30, Jack Tresadern 1930–35, Tom Bromilow 1935–36, R. S. Moyes 1936, Tom Bromilow 1936–39, George Irwin 1939–47, Jack Butler 1947–49, Ronnie Rooke 1949–50, Charlie Slade and Fred Dawes (joint managers) 1950–51, Laurie Scott 1951–54, Cyril Spiers 1954–58, George Smith 1958–60, Arthur Rowe 1960–62, Dick Graham 1962–66, Bert Head 1966–72 (continued as GM to 1973), Malcolm Allison 1973–76, Terry Venables 1976–80, Ernie Walley 1980, Malcolm Allison 1980–81, Dario Gradi 1981, Steve Kember 1981–82, Alan Mullery 1982–84, Steve Coppell June 1984–.

Player and Position	Ht	Wt	Birth Date	Birth Place	Source	Clubs	League App	Gls
Mark Bright	6 0	11 00	6 2 62	Stoke	Leek T	Port Vale	29	10
						Leicester C	42	6
						Crystal Palace	222	91
Stan Collymore	6 4	13 01	22 1 71	Stone	Stafford R	Crystal Palace	18	1
Jamie Moralee	6 1	11 01	2 12 71	Wandsworth	Trainee	Crystal Palace	6	—
John Salako	5 9	11 00	11 2 69	Nigeria	Trainee	Crystal Palace	125	10
						Swansea C (loan)	13	3
David Whyte	5 9	10 06	20 4 71	Greenwich		Crystal Palace	11	1
						Charlton Ath (loan)	8	2

Trainees
Clark, Timothy J; Cornish, Steven G; Cutler, Scott S; Daly, Sean F; Finnan, Anthony O; Halpin, Mark; Holman, Mark B; McCall, Stuart M; McPherson, Andrew; Ndah, George E; Oliva, Umberto; Rollinson, Simon A; Sparrow, Paul; Stokoe, Paul D; Tomlin, Darren M; Vincent, Jamie R; Watts, Grant S; Williams, David.

**Non-Contract
Suckling, Perry J.

Associated Schoolboys
Bell, Stuart J; Freeman, Andrew; Harris, Jason A; Monger, Adam J; Quinn, Robert J; Robertson, Simon; Sherling, William; Wareing, Paul A; White, Craig.

Associated Schoolboys who have accepted the club's offer of a Traineeship/Contract
Little, Glen; Roberts, Christopher.

**Non-Contract Players who are retained must be re-signed before they are eligible to play in League matches.

DARLINGTON 1991-92 *Back row (left to right):* Gary Coatsworth, Kevan Smith, Jim Willis, Mike Trotter, John Borthwick.
Centre row: Lee Tucker, Gary Gill, Lee Ellison, Matthew Coddington, Mark Prudhoe, Adrian Swan, Drew Coverdale, David Cork, Mark Sunley, Ron Lamprell (Physio).
Front row: Mike Tait, Mitch Cook, Steve Mardenborough, Barrie Geldart (Chief Scout), Ray Hankin (Youth Team Coach), Frank Gray (Manager), Tony McAndrew (Assistant
Manager), Andy Toman, Les McJannet, Anthony Isaacs.

Division 3   **DARLINGTON**

Feethams Ground, Darlington. Telephone Darlington (0325) 465097 (three lines).

Ground capacity: 9968.

Record attendance: 21,023 v Bolton W, League Cup 3rd rd, 14 November 1960.

Record receipts: £32,300 v Rochdale, Division 4, 11 May 1991.

Pitch measurements: 110yd × 74yd.

President: J. L. T. Moore.

Chairman: R. Corden.

Vice-chairman: A. Noble.

Directors: J. Brockbank, R. Tonks.

Manager: Billy McEwan.

Chief Executive: T. D. Hughes.

Secretary: Brian Anderson.

Physio: Nigel Carnell.

Year Formed: 1883. Turned Professional: 1908. Ltd Co.: 1891.

Club Nickname: 'The Quakers'.

Record League Victory: 9-2 v Lincoln C, Division 3 (N), 7 January 1928 – Archibald; Brooks, Mellen; Kelly, Waugh, McKinnell; Cochrane (1), Gregg (1), Ruddy (3), Lees (3), McGiffen (1).

Record Cup Victory: 7-2 v Evenwood T, FA Cup, 1st rd, 17 November 1956 – Ward; Devlin, Henderson; Bell (1p), Greener, Furphy; Forster (1), Morton (3), Tulip (2), Davis, Moran.

Record Defeat: 0-10 v Doncaster R, Division 4, 25 January 1964.

Most League Points (2 for a win): 59, Division 4, 1965–66.

Most League points (3 for a win): 85, Division 4, 1984–85.

Most League Goals: 108, Division 3 (N), 1929–30.

Highest League Scorer in Season: David Brown, 39, Division 3 (N), 1924–25.

Most League Goals in Total Aggregate: Alan Walsh, 90, 1978–84.

Most Capped Player: None.

Most League Appearances: Ron Greener, 442, 1955–68.

Record Transfer Fee Received: £200,000 from Leicester C for Jim Willis, December 1991.

Record Transfer Fee Paid: £95,000 to Motherwell for Nick Cusack, January 1992.

Football League Record: 1921 Original Member Division 3 (N); 1925–27 Division 2; 1927–58 Division 3 (N); 1958–66 Division 4; 1966–67 Division 3; 1967–85 Division 4; 1985–87 Division 3; 1987–89 Division 4; 1989–90 GM Vauxhall Conference; 1990–91 Division 4; 1991– Division 3.

Honours: Football League: Division 2 best season: 15th, 1925–26; Division 3 (N) – Champions 1924–25; Runners-up 1921–22; Division 4 Champions 1990–91 – Runners-up 1965–66. *FA Cup:* best season: 3rd rd, 1910–11, 5th rd, 1957–58. *Football League Cup:* best season: 5th rd, 1967–68. GM Vauxhall Conference Champions 1989–90.

Colours: Black and white. **Change colours:** All pale blue.

98

DARLINGTON 1991–92 LEAGUE RECORD

Match No.	Date		Venue	Opponents	Result		H/T Score	Lg. Pos.	Goalscorers	Attendance
1	Aug	17	A	Bournemouth	W	2-1	0-0	—	Watson (og), Willis	6210
2		24	H	WBA	L	0-1	0-0	13		5658
3		31	A	Birmingham C	L	0-1	0-1	15		8768
4	Sep	3	H	Bolton W	W	3-2	3-0	—	Willis, Cook, Coatsworth	3384
5		7	H	Stoke C	L	0-1	0-0	17		4230
6		14	A	Leyton Orient	L	1-2	0-0	20	Toman	3962
7		21	H	Brentford	L	1-2	1-2	21	Cook	3900
8		28	A	Wigan Ath	W	2-1	1-0	19	Cook, Borthwick	2034
9	Oct	5	H	Bury	L	0-2	0-1	20		3006
10		12	A	Exeter C	L	1-4	1-2	20	Ellison (pen)	3548
11		19	H	Shrewsbury T	D	3-3	0-2	21	Ellison 2 (1 pen), Hamilton	2188
12		26	A	Hull C	L	2-5	2-1	22	Ellison, Norton (og)	3514
13	Nov	2	H	Hartlepool U	W	4-0	3-0	22	Ellison 2, MacPhail (og), McCarrison	5041
14		5	A	Reading	D	2-2	0-0	—	Hamilton, Toman	2808
15		9	A	Preston NE	L	1-2	0-0	22	Cork	4643
16		23	H	Peterborough U	L	1-2	1-0	24	Smith	2815
17		30	H	Fulham	W	3-1	1-0	20	Ellison 2, McCarrison	2655
18	Dec	14	A	Huddersfield T	L	1-2	0-1	21	Pickering	5677
19		22	A	WBA	L	1-3	0-2	—	Ellison (pen)	13,261
20		26	H	Birmingham C	D	1-1	1-0	21	Gill	4421
21		28	H	Bournemouth	D	0-0	0-0	22		3172
22	Jan	1	A	Bolton W	L	0-2	0-0	23		5841
23		4	A	Chester C	W	5-2	2-2	22	Pickering, Mardenborough 2, Ellison, Borthwick	1020
24		11	H	Torquay U	W	3-2	3-1	22	Toman 2, Mardenborough	2493
25		18	A	Stockport Co	L	0-2	0-0	22		4186
26		28	A	Swansea C	L	2-4	1-3	—	Dewhurst, Cusack	2743
27	Feb	1	A	Shrewsbury T	W	2-0	1-0	20	Mardenborough 2	2675
28		8	H	Hull C	L	0-1	0-0	21		3636
29		11	A	Fulham	L	0-4	0-1	—		2988
30		15	H	Huddersfield T	L	1-3	1-1	22	Pickering	3120
31		22	A	Torquay U	L	0-3	0-2	24		2415
32		29	H	Chester C	D	1-1	0-0	24	Pickering	2579
33	Mar	3	H	Stockport Co	L	1-3	1-1	—	Cusack	2384
34		7	A	Bradford C	W	1-0	1-0	24	O'Shaughnessy	5579
35		10	H	Reading	L	2-4	0-1	—	Borthwick, Cusack	2388
36		14	A	Hartlepool U	L	0-2	0-2	24		4442
37		21	H	Preston NE	L	0-2	0-0	24		2270
38		28	A	Peterborough U	D	1-1	1-1	24	Cusack	5218
39		31	H	Leyton Orient	L	0-1	0-0	—		1704
40	Apr	3	A	Stoke C	L	0-3	0-2	—		13,579
41		7	H	Bradford C	L	1-3	1-2	—	Mardenborough	1946
42		11	H	Swansea C	D	1-1	0-1	24	Cork	1507
43		17	A	Brentford	L	1-4	0-3	—	Cork	8383
44		20	H	Wigan Ath	L	0-1	0-1	24		1223
45		25	A	Bury	L	0-1	0-0	24		2351
46	May	2	H	Exeter C	W	5-2	2-1	24	Cusack 2, Pickering, Borthwick 2	1573

Final League Position: 24

GOALSCORERS

League (56): Ellison 10 (3 pens), Cusack 6, Mardenborough 6, Borthwick 5, Pickering 5, Toman 4, Cook 3, Cork 3, Hamilton 2, McCarrison 2, Willis 2, Coatsworth 1, Dewhurst 1, Gill 1, O'Shaughnessy 1, Smith 1, own goals 3.
Rumbelows Cup (1): Cook 1.
FA Cup (3): Ellison 1 (1 pen), Smith 1, Toman 1.

Prudhoe	McJannet	Gray	Willis	Smith	Gill	Cook	Toman	Borthwick	Cork	Tait	Coatsworth	Mardenborough	Trotter	Ellison	Clark	Hamilton	Tucker	Coverdale	Pickering	McCarrison	Gregan	Sunley	Dewhurst	Gaughan	O'Shaughnessy	Cusack	Isaacs	Hinchley	Match No.
1	2	3	4	5	6	7	8	9	10	11*	12																		1
1	2	3*	4	5	6	7	8	9	10		11	12																	2
1	12			4	5		3	8	9	10	11	2	7	6*															3
1		3*	4	5			7	8	9	12	11	2	10	6															4
1		3*	4	5			7	8	9†	12	11	2	10	6	14														5
1		3†	4	5	11		7	8	9*	12		2	14	6	10														6
1			4	5*	6	3	8	9		11		12		10	2	7													7
1			4		6	3	8*14	10	11		5	12		9†	2	7													8
1			4		6	3	8	14	10†11	5				9*	2	7	12												9
1			4	5	6	3	8		10*11					9	2	7	12												10
1			4	5	6		8	10		11*				9	2	7	12	3											11
1	4			5	6		8	10	11*		2	12		9		7		3											12
1	2			5	6	3	8		11					9		7		4	10										13
1	2			5	6	3	8	12	14	11				9*		7†		4	10										14
1	2			5	6†	3	8	12	14	11				9*		7		4	10										15
1	2			5*		3†	8	12	6	11	14			9		7		4	10										16
1	2	4		5		3	8	12		11	7			9*		6			10										17
1	2			5		3	8*	9		11	12			10	7			6	4										18
1				5			3	8†12	14				10	9				7*	6		4	2	11						19
1				5		7	3	8	12				10	9*				6			4	2	11						20
1				5	7		8	3					10	9				6			4	2	11						21
1				5	7*		8	12	3				10	9				6			4	2	11						22
1				5	7		8	12	3				10*	9				6			4	2	11						23
1				5	7	14	8	12	3				10*	9†				6			4	2	11						24
1				5	7	6	8	12	3				10	9*							4	2	11						25
1				5		8		3	10	12			6	4*				11	2		7	9							26
1				5		8		3	7	10			4					11	2		6	9							27
1				5		8	14	3	7†	10*	12		4					11	2		6	9							28
1				5		8		3		10			8	4				11	2		6	9	7						29
1	3			5	7		8		11				10					4			2	6	9						30
1	2			5*12		3	8	14	11				10†					4			7	6	9						31
1	2			5		3	8		6	10								11			7	4	9						32
1	2			5		3	8†12	10*	6									14	11		7	4	9						33
1	2			5		3	8	10										14	11		7	4	9		6				34
1	2			5		3	8	12	10									14	7†11			4	9		6*				35
1	2			5		3	8	12	10									14	11		4†		7*	6	9				36
1	2						3	8	10									11	5*	4		7	6	9	12				37
1							8	10	6		12								3		5	4	7		9	11*	2		38
1							8	12	10	6			11†						3		5	4	7		9	14	2*		39
1							8†10	11	6*										3		5*	4	7	6	9	12	2		40
1							8	10		11									3		5*	4	7	6	9	12	2		41
1	2			5			8†12	10	6				11					14	3				7	4*	9				42
1	2			5			8	10	6				11						3				7	4	9				43
1	2			5			8	10					11						3		4		7		9	6			44
1				5				10	4				11*					12	3		6	2	8		9	7†			45
1				5				12	10†4	7								3	11		6	2*	8		9	14			46

46 19 6 12 39 19 26 43 11 22 34 9 21 5 25 5 11 — 10 29 5 17 15 11 20 15 21 4 6
 + + + + + + + + +
 1s 1s 1s 18s8s 1s 8s 2s 5s 4s 5s

Reed—Match No. 40(12); Shaw—Match No. 45(14).

Rumbelows Cup	First Round	Huddersfield T (h)	1-0
		(a)	0-4
FA Cup	First Round	Chesterfield (h)	2-1
	Second Round	Hartlepool U (h)	1-2

DARLINGTON

Player and Position	Ht	Wt	Birth Date	Birth Place	Source	Clubs	League App	Gls
Goalkeepers								
Matt Coddington*	6 1	11 05	17 9 69	Lytham St Annes	Trainee	Middlesbrough	—	—
						Bury (loan)	—	—
						Halifax T (loan)	—	—
						Darlington	—	—
Mark Prudhoe	6 0	12 12	8 11 63	Washington	Apprentice	Sunderland	7	—
						Hartlepool U (loan)	3	—
						Birmingham C	1	—
						Walsall	26	—
						Doncaster R (loan)	5	—
						Sheffield W (loan)	—	—
						Grimsby T (loan)	8	—
						Hartlepool U (loan)	13	—
						Bristol C (loan)	3	—
						Carlisle U	34	—
						Darlington	104	—
Adrian Shaw			31 7 73	Middlesbrough		Darlington	—	—
Defenders								
Drew Coverdale*	5 11	10 06	20 9 69	Teesside	Trainee	Middlesbrough	—	—
						Darlington	30	3
Allan Evans‡	6 1	12 13	12 10 56	Dunfermline	Dunfermline U	Dunfermline Ath	98	14
						Aston Villa	380	51
						Leicester C	14	—
						Darlington	1	—
Frank Gray‡	5 10	11 10	27 10 54	Glasgow	Apprentice	Leeds U	193	17
						Nottingham F	81	5
						Leeds U	142	10
						Sunderland	146	8
						Darlington	49	7
Sean Gregan			29 3 74	Cleveland	Trainee	Darlington	17	—
Gary Hinchley	6 0	12 00	14 11 68	Guisborough		Darlington	14	—
						Guisborough	—	—
						Darlington	6	—
Les McJannet*	5 8	10 04	2 8 61	Cumnock	Matlock T	Scarborough	34	—
						Darlington	85	5
Steve O'Shaughnessy	6 2	13 00	13 10 67	Wrexham		Leeds U	—	—
						Bradford C	1	—
						Rochdale	109	16
						Exeter C	3	—
						Shrewsbury T	—	—
						Darlington	15	1
Adam Reed§			18 2 75	Bishop Auckland	Trainee	Darlington	1	—
Kevan Smith	6 3	12 02	13 12 59	Yarm	Stockton	Darlington	245	11
						Rotherham U	59	4
						Coventry C	6	—
						York C	31	5
						Darlington	85	5
Mark Sunley			13 10 71	Stockton		Middlesbrough	—	—
						Darlington	15	—
Midfield								
Steven Gaughan	5 11	11 02	14 4 70	Doncaster	Trainee	Doncaster R	67	3
						Sunderland	—	—
						Darlington	20	—
Anthony Isaacs			8 4 73	Middlesbrough	Trainee	Darlington	9	—
Steve Mardenborough	5 8	11 00	11 9 64	Birmingham	Apprentice	Coventry C	—	—
						Wolverhampton W	9	1
						Cambridge U (loan)	6	—
						Swansea C	36	7
						Newport Co	64	11
						Cardiff C	32	1
						Hereford U	27	—
						Darlington	64	7
Nick Pickering	6 0	12 02	4 8 63	Newcastle	Apprentice	Sunderland	179	18
						Coventry C	78	9
						Derby Co	45	3
						Darlington	29	5
Simon Shaw§			21 9 73	Teeside	Trainee	Darlington	1	—
Mick Tait*	5 11	12 05	30 9 56	Wallsend	Apprentice	Oxford U	64	23
						Carlisle U	106	20
						Hull C	33	3
						Portsmouth	240	30
						Reading	99	9
						Darlington	79	2

DARLINGTON

Foundation: A football club was formed in Darlington as early as 1861 but the present club began in 1883 and reached the final of the Durham Senior Cup in their first season, losing to Sunderland in a replay after complaining that they had suffered from intimidation in the first. The following season Darlington won this trophy and for many years were one of the leading amateur clubs in their area.

First Football League game: 27 August, 1921, Division 3 (N), v Halifax T (h) W 2-0 – Ward; Greaves, Barbour; Dickson (1), Sutcliffe, Malcolm; Dolphin, Hooper (1), Edmunds, Wolstenholme, Winship.

Did you know: Famous winger Mark Hooper and his brother Bill partnered each other in many League games for Darlington, but only once did they both score. That was in a 4-0 win over Rotherham County on 11 October 1924 in Division 3 (N).

Managers (and Secretary-managers)
Tom McIntosh 1902–11, W. L. Lane 1911–12*, Dick Jackson 1912–19, Jack English 1919–28, Jack Fairless 1928–33, George Collins 1933–36, George Brown 1936–38, Jackie Carr 1938–42, Jack Surtees 1942, Jack English 1945–46, Bill Forrest 1946–50, George Irwin 1950–52, Bob Gurney 1952–57, Dick Duckworth 1957–60, Eddie Carr 1960–64, Lol Morgan 1964–66, Jimmy Greenhalgh 1966–68, Ray Yeoman 1968–70, Len Richley 1970–71, Frank Brennan 1971, Ken Hale 1971–72, Allan Jones 1972, Ralph Brand 1972–73, Dick Conner 1973–74, Billy Horner 1974–76, Peter Madden 1976–78, Len Walker 1978–79, Billy Elliott 1979–83, Cyril Knowles 1983–87, Dave Booth 1987–89, Brian Little 1989–1991, Frank Gray 1991–92, Ray Hankin 1992, Billy McEwan July 1992–.

Player and Position	Ht	Wt	Birth Date	Birth Place	Source	Clubs	League App	Gls
Andy Toman	5 10	11 09	7 3 62	Northallerton	Bishop Auckland	Lincoln C	24	4
						Hartlepool U	112	28
						Darlington	86	9
Forwards								
John Borthwick*	6 0	10 12	24 3 64	Hartlepool		Hartlepool U	117	15
						Darlington	75	15
David Cork*	5 9	11 08	28 10 62	Doncaster	Apprentice	Arsenal	7	1
						Huddersfield T	110	25
						WBA (loan)	4	—
						Scunthorpe U	15	—
						Darlington	64	11
Nicky Cusack	6 0	11 13	24 12 65	Rotherham	Alvechurch	Leicester C	16	1
						Peterborough U	44	10
						Motherwell	77	17
						Darlington	42	12
Tony Ellison			13 1 73	Bishop Auckland	Trainee	Darlington	40	13
Dugald McCarrison On loan from Celtic						Darlington	5	2
Lee Tucker*			14 9 71	Middlesbrough	Trainee	Middlesbrough	—	—
						Darlington	5	—

Trainees
Bean, Michael; Cooper, Paul; Cooper, Richard P; Filer, Simon; Jenkins, Paul; Ravenhall, Vincent; Reed, Adam M; Robinson, Carl; Scollett, Matthew; Shaw, Simon R.

Associated Schoolboys
Christie, Ross; Fielding, Charles M; Key, Daniel C; Malsbury, Gary; Robinson, Dustin; Trees, Steven R.

Associated Schoolboys who have accepted the club's offer of a Traineeship/Contract
Blake, Robert J; Carter, Stuart; Casey, Mark; Hack, Benjamin, C; Middleton, James; Scott, Ryan; Theakston, Justin.

DERBY COUNTY 1991–92 *Back row (left to right):* Phil Gee, Ted McMinn, Michael Forsyth, Andy Comyn, Peter Shilton, Ian Ormondroyd, Martin Taylor, Justin Phillips, Simon Coleman, Paul Williams, Jason Kavanagh. *Front row:* Dean Sturridge, Steve Round, Jon Davidson, Steve Hayward, Geraint Williams, Gary Micklewhite, Mark Clarke, Steve Taylor, Martyn Chalk.

Division 1   **DERBY COUNTY**

Baseball Ground, Shaftesbury Crescent, Derby DE3 8NB. Telephone Derby (0332) 40105. Ramtique Sports Shop: (0332) 292081. Clubcall: 0898 121187.

Ground capacity: 23,000 (14,000 seats).

Record attendance: 41,826 v Tottenham H, Division 1, 20 September 1969.

Record receipts: £146,651 v Aston Villa, FA Cup 4th rd, 5 February 1992.

Pitch measurements: 110yd × 75yd.

Chairman: B. E. Fearn. *Vice-chairman:* L. V. Pickering. *Managing Director. Associate Directors:* A. S. Webb, P. Gadsby.

Directors: C. M. McKerrow, W. Hart, J. N. Kirkland, A. Cox, M. Mills, S. P. Adams.

Manager: Arthur Cox. *Assistant Manager:* Roy McFarland. *Physio:* Gordon Guthrie. *General manager/secretary:* Michael Dunford. *Marketing Manager:* C. Tunnicliffe (Tel. 0332 40105).

Year Formed: 1884. Turned Professional: 1884. Ltd Co.: 1896.

Former Grounds: 1884–95, Racecourse Ground; 1895, Baseball Ground.

Club Nickname: 'The Rams'.

Record League Victory: 9-0 v Wolverhampton W, Division 1, 10 January 1891 – Bunyan; Archie Goodall, Roberts; Walker, Chalmers, Roulston (1); Bakewell, McLachlan, Johnny Goodall (1), Holmes (2), McMillan (5). 9-0 v Sheffield W, Division 1, 21 January 1899 – Fryer; Methven, Staley; Cox, Archie Goodall, May; Oakden (1), Bloomer (6), Boag, McDonald (1), Allen. (1 og).

Record Cup Victory: 12-0 v Finn Harps, UEFA Cup, 1st rd 1st leg, 15 September 1976 – Moseley; Thomas, Nish, Rioch (1), McFarland, Todd (King), Macken, Gemmill, Hector (5), George (3), James (3).

Record Defeat: 2-11 v Everton, FA Cup 1st rd, 1889–90.

Most League Points (2 for a win): 63, Division 2, 1968–69 and Division 3 (N), 1955–56 and 1956–57.

Most League points (3 for a win): 84, Division 3, 1985–86 and Division 3, 1986–87.

Most League Goals: 111, Division 3 (N), 1956–57.

Highest League Scorer in Season: Jack Bowers, 37, Division 1, 1930–31 and Ray Straw, 37 Division 3 (N), 1956–57.

Most League Goals in Total Aggregate: Steve Bloomer, 292, 1892–1906 and 1910–14.

Most Capped Player: Peter Shilton, 34 (125), England.

Most League Appearances: Kevin Hector, 486, 1966–78 and 1980–82.

Record Transfer Fee Received: £2,900,000 from Liverpool for Dean Saunders, July 1991.

Record Transfer Fee Paid: £1,300,000 to Leicester C for Paul Kitson, March 1992 and to Notts Co for Tommy Johnson, March 1992.

Football League Record: 1888 Founder Member of the Football League; 1907–12 Division 2; 1912–14 Division 1; 1914–15 Division 2; 1915–21 Division 1; 1921–26 Division 2; 1926–53 Division 1; 1953–55 Division 2; 1955–57 Division 3 (N); 1957–69 Division 2; 1969–80 Division 1; 1980–84 Division 2; 1984–86 Division 3; 1986–87 Division 2; 1987–91 Division 1; 1991–92 Division 2; 1992– Division 1.

Honours: Football League: Division 1 – Champions 1971–72, 1974–75; Runners-up 1895–96, 1929–30, 1935–36; Division 2 – Champions 1911–12, 1914–15, 1968–69, 1986–87; Runners-up 1925–26; Division 3 (N) Champions 1956–57; Runners-up 1955–56. *FA Cup:* Winners 1945–46; Runners-up 1897–98, 1898–99, 1902–03. *Football League Cup:* Semifinal 1967–68. *Texaco Cup:* 1971–72. **European Competitions:** *European Cup:* 1972–73, 1975–76; *UEFA Cup:* 1974–75, 1976–77.

Colours: White shirts with black collar and red flash on sleeve, black shorts with red flash on one side, white stockings, black turnover. **Change colours:** Yellow shirts with blue and red sleeves, blue shorts, yellow stockings.

DERBY COUNTY 1991–92 LEAGUE RECORD

Match No.	Date		Venue	Opponents		Result	H/T Score	Lg. Pos.	Goalscorers	Atten-dance
1	Aug	17	A	Sunderland	D	1-1	0-0	—	Harford	20,509
2		21	H	Middlesbrough	W	2-0	0-0	—	Comyn, Harford	12,805
3		24	H	Southend U	L	1-2	0-2	7	Williams P	12,284
4	Sep	1	A	Charlton Ath	W	2-0	0-0	—	Williams P, Harford	6602
5		4	H	Blackburn R	L	0-2	0-1	—		12,078
6		7	H	Barnsley	D	1-1	1-0	11	Williams P	10,559
7		13	A	Cambridge U	D	0-0	0-0	—		7293
8		18	A	Oxford U	L	0-2	0-0	—		4319
9		21	H	Brighton & HA	W	3-1	1-0	11	Davison, Patterson, Williams P (pen)	12,004
10		28	A	Newcastle U	D	2-2	1-1	13	Davison, Ormondroyd	17,581
11	Oct	5	H	Bristol C	W	4-1	1-0	8	Aizlewood (og), Micklewhite, Davison 2	11,880
12		12	A	Swindon T	W	2-1	1-0	6	Williams P, Gee	11,883
13		19	H	Portsmouth	W	2-0	0-0	6	McMinn, Williams P	13,190
14		26	A	Millwall	W	2-1	1-1	6	Davison, Ormondroyd	7660
15	Nov	2	H	Tranmere R	L	0-1	0-1	7		11,501
16		6	A	Port Vale	L	0-1	0-0	—		8589
17		9	A	Wolverhampton W	W	3-2	1-1	6	Davison, Ormondroyd, Bennett (og)	15,672
18		16	A	Ipswich T	W	1-0	0-0	3	Davison	12,493
19		23	A	Bristol R	W	3-2	1-2	3	Patterson, Williams P (pen), Davison	6513
20		30	H	Leicester C	L	1-2	0-2	3	Ormondroyd	19,306
21	Dec	7	A	Watford	W	2-1	1-0	4	Ormondroyd 2	8302
22		26	H	Grimsby T	D	0-0	0-0	5		16,392
23		28	H	Charlton Ath	L	1-2	0-1	8	Ormondroyd	14,367
24	Jan	1	A	Middlesbrough	D	1-1	0-1	8	Chalk	16,288
25		11	A	Southend U	L	0-1	0-1	9		8295
26		18	H	Sunderland	L	1-2	0-2	11	Williams G	15,384
27	Feb	1	A	Portsmouth	W	1-0	0-0	11	Gabbiadini	12,008
28		8	H	Millwall	L	0-2	0-0	11		12,773
29		11	A	Blackburn R	L	0-2	0-0	—		15,350
30		15	H	Bristol R	W	1-0	0-0	10	Coleman	11,154
31		22	A	Leicester C	W	2-1	1-0	9	Ormondroyd, Simpson	18,148
32		29	H	Watford	W	3-1	2-0	6	Williams P 3 (1 pen)	14,052
33	Mar	7	A	Plymouth Arg	D	1-1	1-1	6	Simpson	8864
34		11	H	Port Vale	W	3-1	1-1	—	Williams G, Simpson, Gabbiadini	14,983
35		14	A	Tranmere R	L	3-4	1-1	5	Kitson, Coleman, Simpson	10,386
36		21	H	Wolverhampton W	L	1-2	1-0	9	Kitson	21,024
37		24	H	Plymouth Arg	W	2-0	1-0	—	Johnson T, McMinn	13,799
38		28	A	Ipswich T	L	1-2	0-2	8	Simpson	15,305
39	Apr	1	A	Cambridge U	D	0-0	0-0	—		15,353
40		4	A	Barnsley	W	3-0	2-0	5	Simpson, Forsyth, Williams P (pen)	10,121
41		7	A	Grimsby T	W	1-0	1-0	—	Gabbiadini	7040
42		11	H	Oxford U	D	2-2	1-1	5	Simpson, Williams P (pen)	15,555
43		15	A	Brighton & HA	W	2-1	1-0	—	Gabbiadini 2	8159
44		20	H	Newcastle U	W	4-1	2-0	3	Williams P (pen), Kitson, Ramage 2	21,363
45		25	A	Bristol C	W	2-1	1-1	3	Gabbiadini, Micklewhite	16,648
46	May	2	H	Swindon T	W	2-1	1-0	3	Kitson, Johnson T	22,608

Final League Position: 3

GOALSCORERS

League (69): Williams P 13 (6 pens), Davison 8, Ormondroyd 8, Simpson 7, Gabbiadini 6, Kitson 4, Harford 3, Coleman 2, Johnson T 2, McMinn 2, Micklewhite 2, Patterson 2, Ramage 2, Williams G 2, Chalk 1, Comyn 1, Forsyth 1, Gee 1, own goals 2.
Rumbelows Cup (3): Forsyth 1, Gee 1, Williams P 1 (1 pen).
FA Cup (7): Gee 2, Williams P 2, Chalk 1, Comyn 1, Ormondroyd 1.

Shilton	Sage	Forsyth	Williams G	Coleman	Comyn	Micklewhite	Gee	Harford	Williams P	McMinn	Cross	Pickering	Taylor	Hayward	Ramage	Patterson	Stallard	Ormondroyd	Davison	Kavanagh	Chalk	Davidson	Sturridge	Gabbiadini	Simpson	Round	Kitson	Johnson T	Match No.
1	2	3	4	5	6	7	8*	9	10	11	12																		1
1	2	3	4	5	6	7	8	9	10	11																			2
1	2	3	4	5	6	7	8*	9	10	11		12																	3
	2	3	4	5	6	7	8	9	10	11*	12		1																4
1	2	3	4	5	6	7†	8*	9	10	11	12			14															5
1	2	3	4	5	6	7	8	9	10	11*	12																		6
1	2	3	4	5	6	7	8		10	11				12	9*														7
1	2	3	4	5	6	7	8†		10*	11				9	12	14													8
1	2	3	4	5	6	7*			10	11					12			8	9										9
1	2*	3	4	5	6	7			10	11					12			8	9										10
1	2	3	4	5	6	7			10	11								8	9										11
1		3	4	5	6	7	9		10	11						2		8											12
1	2	3	4	5	6	7	9		10	11								8											13
1	2	3	4	5	6	7			10	11								8	9										14
1	2	3	4	5	6	7	11*		10						12			8	9										15
1	2	3	4	5	6	7	11		10									8	9										16
1	2	3	4	5	6	7	11		10									8	9										17
1	2*	3	4	5	6	7			10	11								8	9										18
1		3*	4		6	7	12		10	11				5†		2		8	9	14									19
1			4	5	6	7			10	11						2		8	9		3								20
1		3	4	5	6	7	9		10	11						2		8											21
1		3	4	5	6	7	9*		10	11						2		8			12								22
1		3	4	5	6	7†	9*		10	11						2		8			14	12							23
1		3	4	5	6				10	11						2	9	8			7								24
1		3†	4	5	6										12	2	9	8		14	7	10	11*						25
1		3	4	5	6	7*	9		10	11								8		2	12								26
1		3	4	5	6				10	11								8		2	7			9					27
1		3	4	5	6		12		10	11								8		2	7*			9					28
1		3	4	5	6	7			10	11								8		2				9					29
1		3	4	5	6	7	12		10	11								8		2				9*					30
1		3	4	5	6				10	7								8		2				9	11				31
1		3	4	5	6				10	7								8		2				9	11				32
			4	5	6		12		10	7*			1					8		2				9	11	3			33
			4	5	6	7			10				1							2				9	11	3	8		34
		3	4	5	6				10				1							2				9	11		8	7	35
		3	4	5	6				10	12			1							2				9	11*		8	7	36
		3	4	5	6				10*	12										2				9	11		8	7	37
		3	4	5	6				10											2				9	11		8	7	38
		3	4	5	6				10											2				9	11		8	7	39
		3		5	6			4	10*											2				9	11	12	8	7	40
		3		5	6			4	10											2				9	11		8	7	41
		3		5	6			4	10											2				9	11		8	7	42
		3		5	6	8		4	10											2				9	11			7	43
		3			6		4	5	10											2				9	11		8	7	44
		3			6	12	4	5	10											2				9	11		8*	7	45
		3		5	6	12		4	10											2				9*	11		8	7	46
31	17	43	39	43	46	28 +4s	17 +2s	6	41	35 +2s	— +4s	— +1s	5 +4s	3	7	8	2	25 +4s	10 +1s	22 +3s	4 +3s	1	1	20	16	2 +1s	12	12	

Sutton—Match No. 37(1) 38(1) 39(1) 40(1) 41(1) 42(1) 43(1) 44(1) 45(1) 46(1).

Rumbelows Cup	Second Round	Ipswich T (h)	0-0
		(a)	2-0
	Third Round	Oldham Ath (a)	1-2
FA Cup	Third Round	Burnley (a)	2-2
		(h)	2-0
	Fourth Round	Aston Villa (h)	3-4

DERBY COUNTY

Player and Position	Ht	Wt	Birth Date	Birth Place	Source	Clubs	League App	League Gls
Goalkeepers								
Simon Dunne	6 01	12 08	9 9 73	Dublin		Derby Co	—	—
Steve Sutton	6 1	13 07	16 4 61	Hartington	Apprentice	Nottingham F	199	—
						Mansfield T (loan)	8	—
						Derby Co (loan)	14	—
						Coventry C (loan)	1	—
						Luton T (loan)	14	—
						Derby Co	10	—
Martin Taylor	5 11	12 04	9 12 66	Tamworth	Mile Oak R	Derby Co	15	—
						Carlisle U (loan)	10	—
						Scunthorpe U (loan)	8	—
Defenders								
Robert Briscoe*	5 8	10 13	4 9 69	Derby	Trainee	Derby Co	13	1
Simon Coleman	6 0	10 08	13 3 68	Worksop		Mansfield T	96	7
						Middlesbrough	55	2
						Derby Co	43	2
Andy Comyn	6 1	12 00	2 8 68	Manchester	Alvechurch	Aston Villa	15	—
						Derby Co	46	1
Jonathan Davidson	5 8	11 11	1 3 70	Cheadle	Trainee	Derby Co	12	—
Mike Forsyth	5 11	12 02	20 3 66	Liverpool	Apprentice	WBA	29	—
						Derby Co	234	5
Shane Nicholson	5 10	11 06	3 6 70	Newark	Trainee	Lincoln C	133	6
						Derby Co	—	—
Mark Patterson	5 10	11 05	13 9 68	Leeds	Trainee	Carlisle U	22	—
						Derby Co	33	3
Justin Phillips	6 3	14 07	17 12 71	Derby	Trainee	Derby Co	3	1
Steve Round	5 10	11 00	9 11 70	Buxton	Trainee	Derby Co	3	—
Mel Sage	5 8	10 04	24 3 64	Gillingham	Apprentice	Gillingham	132	5
						Derby Co	140	4
Midfield								
Tommy Curtis	5 08	11 04	1 3 73	Exeter	School	Derby Co	—	—
Steve Hayward	5 10	11 07	8 9 71	Walsall	Trainee	Derby Co	11	—
Jason Kavanagh	5 9	11 00	23 11 71	Birmingham	Birmingham C Schoolboys	Derby Co	36	—
Colin Loss*	5 11	11 04	15 8 73	Brentwood	Trainee	Norwich C	—	—
Ted McMinn	6 0	12 11	28 9 62	Castle Douglas	Glenafton Ath	Queen of South	62	5
						Rangers	63	4
						Seville	—	—
						Derby Co	104	7
Gary Micklewhite	5 7	10 04	21 3 61	Southwark	Apprentice	Manchester U		
						QPR	106	11
						Derby Co	234	31
Steve Taylor	5 8	10 04	10 1 70	Holbrook	Trainee	Derby Co	—	—
Peter Weston	5 7	10 12	13 2 74	Stoke	Trainee	Derby Co	—	—
Geraint Williams	5 7	10 06	5 1 62	Treorchy	Apprentice	Bristol R	141	8
						Derby Co	277	9
Paul Williams	5 11	12 00	26 3 71	Burton	Trainee	Derby Co	70	18
						Lincoln C (loan)	3	—
Forwards								
Martyn Chalk	5 6	10 00	30 8 69	Louth	Louth U	Derby Co	7	1
Mark Clarke	5 09	11 02	22 11 72	Birmingham	Trainee	Derby Co	—	—
Marco Gabbiadini	5 10	11 02	20 1 68	Nottingham	Apprentice	York C	60	14
						Sunderland	157	74
						Crystal Palace	15	5
						Derby Co	20	6

DERBY COUNTY

Foundation: Derby County was formed by members of the Derbyshire County Cricket Club in 1884, when football was booming in the area and the cricketers thought that a football club would help boost finances for the summer game. To begin with, they sported the cricket club's colours of amber, chocolate and pale blue, and went into the game at the top immediately entering the FA Cup.

First Football League game: 8 September, 1888, Football League, v Bolton W (a) W 6-3 – Marshall; Latham, Ferguson, Williamson; Monks, W. Roulstone; Bakewell (2), Cooper (2), Higgins, H. Plackett, L. Plackett (2).

Did you know: In 1904–05 Derby County made a club record start to their League season by winning their first five games and conceding only one goal in the process. This was in the First Division.

Managers (and Secretary-managers)
Harry Newbould 1896–1906, Jimmy Methven 1906–22, Cecil Potter 1922–25, George Jobey 1925–41, Ted Magner 1944–46, Stuart McMillan 1946–53, Jack Barker 1953–55, Harry Storer 1955–62, Tim Ward 1962–67, Brian Clough 1967–73, Dave Mackay 1973–76, Colin Murphy 1977, Tommy Docherty 1977–79, Colin Addison 1979–82, Johnny Newman 1982, Peter Taylor 1982–84, Roy McFarland 1984, Arthur Cox May 1984–.

Player and Position	Ht	Wt	Birth Date	Birth Place	Source	Clubs	League App	Gls
Tommy Johnson	5 10	10 00	15 1 71	Newcastle	Trainee	Notts Co	118	47
						Derby Co	12	2
Paul Kitson	5 11	10 12	9 1 71	Co Durham	Trainee	Leicester C	50	6
						Derby Co	12	4
Craig Ramage	5 9	11 08	30 3 70	Derby	Trainee	Derby Co	36	4
						Wigan Ath (loan)	10	2
Paul Simpson	5 6	11 11	26 7 66	Carlisle	Apprentice	Manchester C	118	18
						Oxford U	144	43
						Derby Co	16	7
Kris Sleeuwenhoek†	5 7	10 00	2 10 71	Oldham	Wolves Schoolboys	Derby Co	—	—
Mark Stallard	6 00	12 05	24 10 74	Derby	Trainee	Derby Co	3	—
Robert Straw	5 9	11 08	4 11 70	Derby	Trainee	Derby Co	—	—
Dean Sturridge	5 07	10 10	27 7 73	Birmingham	Trainee	Derby Co	1	—

Trainees
Allen, Craig C; Anderson, Wayne S; Blount, Mark; Carsley, Lee K; Cooper, Kevin L; Dakin, Simon M; Darkes, Craig J; Geddis, Stewart R; Magill, Luke; McKeever, Nigel R; Moore, Michael T; Thomson, Jon M; Wood, Mark A.

**Non-Contract
Sleeuwenhoek, Kris; Wilson, Kevin P.

Associated Schoolboys
Ashbee, Ian; Brocklehurst, Lynley; Devey, Wayne; Filik, Robert P; Flindall, Andrew M; Giles, Damon P; Joseph, Marc; Marshall, Andrew J; McGann, Thomas; McHugh, Edward T; Rafferty, Brian; Richards, David; Rutter, James.

Associated Schoolboys who have accepted the club's offer of a Traineeship/Contract
Davies, William; Green, Mathew R; Johnson, Brian A; Matthews, Martin; Sutton, Wayne F; Warren, Matthew T. J; Wrack, Darren; Wright, Nicholas J.

**Non-Contract Players who are retained must be re-signed before they are eligible to play in League matches.

DONCASTER ROVERS 1991–92 *Back row (left to right):* Dave Blakey (General Manager), Eric Brailsford (Physiotherapist), Colin Douglas, Andy Holmes, David Jones, Paul Crichton, Mark Samways, John Muir, Brendan Ormsby, Lee Boyle, Jim Golze (Youth Team Coach).
Centre row: Shane Reddish, Kevin Noteman, Rufus Brevett, Max Nicholson, Steve Beaglehole (Assistant Manager), Billy Bremner (Manager), Lee Turnbull, David Harle, Eddie Gormley, Grant Morrow.
Front row: Chris Redhead, Mark Rankine, Mark Place, Vince Brockie, Steve Adams, John Stiles.

Division 3   **DONCASTER ROVERS**

Belle Vue Ground, Doncaster. Telephone Doncaster (0302) 539441.

Ground capacity: 7794.

Record attendance: 37,149 v Hull C, Division 3 (N), 2 October 1948.

Record receipts: £22,000 v QPR, FA Cup 3rd rd, 5 January 1985.

Pitch measurements: 110yd × 76yd.

Chairman: J. J. Burke.

Vice-chairman: K. Chappell.

Directors: J. Ryan, M. J. H. Collett, W. Turner.

Manager: Steve Beaglehole.

Commercial Manager: Bill Turner. *Secretary:* Mrs K. J. Oldale. *Physio:* Eric Brailsford. *Youth Team Coach:* Jim Golze.

Doncaster Rovers Football Club Ltd.

(Founded 1879)

Year Formed: 1879. Turned Professional: 1885. Ltd Co.: 1905 and 1920.

Former Grounds: 1880–1916, Intake Ground; 1920–22, Benetthorpe Ground; 1922, Low Pasture, Belle Vue.

Club Nickname: 'Rovers'.

Record League Victory: 10-0 v Darlington, Division 4, 25 January 1964 – Potter; Raine, Meadows; Windross (1), White, Ripley (2); Robinson, Book (2), Hale (4), Jeffrey, Broadbent (1).

Record Cup Victory: 7-0 v Blyth Spartans, FA Cup, 1st rd, 27 November 1937 – Imrie; Shaw, Rodgers; McFarlane, Bycroft, Cyril Smith; Burton (1), Kilourhy (4), Morgan (2), Malam, Dutton.

Record Defeat: 0-12 v Small Heath, Division 2, 11 April 1903.

Most League Points (2 for a win): 72, Division 3 (N), 1946–47.

Most League points (3 for a win): 85, Division 4, 1983–84.

Most League Goals: 123, Division 3 (N), 1946–47.

Highest League Scorer in Season: Clarrie Jordan, 42, Division 3 (N), 1946–47.

Most League Goals in Total Aggregate: Tom Keetley, 180, 1923–29.

Most Capped Player: Len Graham, 14, Northern Ireland.

Most League Appearances: Fred Emery, 417, 1925–36.

Record Transfer Fee Received: £200,000 from Leeds U for Ian Snodin, May 1985.

Record Transfer Fee Paid: £60,000 to Stirling Albion for John Philliben, March 1984.

Football League Record: 1901 Elected to Division 2; 1903 Failed re-election; 1904 Re-elected; 1905 Failed re-election; 1923 Re-elected to Division 3 (N); 1935–37 Division 2; 1937–47 Division 3 (N); 1947–48 Division 2; 1948–50 Division 3 (N); 1950–58 Division 2; 1958–59 Division 3; 1959–66 Division 4; 1966–67 Division 3; 1967–69 Division 4; 1969–71 Division 3; 1971–81 Division 4; 1981–83 Division 3; 1983–84 Division 4; 1984–88 Division 3; 1988–92 Division 4; 1992– Division 3.

Honours: Football League: Division 2 best season: 7th, 1901–02; Division 3 (N) Champions 1934–35, 1946–47, 1949–50; Runners-up 1937–38, 1938–39; Division 4 – Champions 1965–66, 1968–69; Runners-up 1983–84. Promoted 1980–81 (3rd). *FA Cup:* best season: 5th rd, 1951–52, 1953–54, 1954–55, 1955–56. *Football League Cup:* best season: 5th rd, 1975–76.

Colours: All red. **Change colours:** All green.

DONCASTER ROVERS 1991–92 LEAGUE RECORD

Match No.	Date		Venue	Opponents	Result		H/T Score	Lg. Pos.	Goalscorers	Atten- dance
1	Aug	17	H	Carlisle U	L	0-3	0-1	—		2639
2		24	A	Scunthorpe U	L	2-3	1-2	22	Kerr, Tynan	3505
3		31	H	Burnley	L	1-4	1-1	22	Noteman	2940
4	Sep	3	A	Northampton T	L	1-3	0-1	—	Noteman	2702
5		7	H	Wrexham	W	3-1	1-0	19	Noteman 2, Rankine	1474
6		14	A	Barnet	L	0-1	0-1	22		3762
7		18	A	Scarborough	L	0-1	0-1	—		1506
8		20	H	Blackpool	L	0-2	0-2	—		2428
9		28	A	Rochdale	D	1-1	0-1	23	Milner (og)	2653
10	Oct	5	H	Crewe Alex	L	1-3	0-1	23	Rankine	1779
11		12	A	Maidstone U	D	2-2	1-0	23	Rankine, McKenzie	1255
12		19	H	Gillingham	D	1-1	0-0	23	Limber	1468
13		26	A	Cardiff C	L	1-2	1-1	23	Gormley	2491
14	Nov	2	A	Mansfield T	D	2-2	2-0	23	Harle, Noteman	4180
15		6	A	Rotherham U	D	1-1	0-0	—	Gormley	3507
16		8	H	York C	L	0-1	0-1	—		2144
17		30	H	Lincoln C	L	1-5	0-3	23	Ormsby	1999
18	Dec	20	H	Scunthorpe U	L	1-2	1-1	—	Gormley	1825
19		26	A	Carlisle U	L	0-1	0-1	23		3174
20		28	A	Burnley	L	1-2	0-2	23	Noteman	9605
21	Jan	1	H	Northampton T	L	0-3	0-1	23		1973
22		4	A	Walsall	W	3-1	2-0	23	Muir, Gormley, Noteman	3444
23		11	H	Halifax T	L	0-2	0-0	23		2067
24		18	A	Chesterfield	D	0-0	0-0	23		3372
25	Feb	1	A	Gillingham	L	1-2	0-1	23	Ormsby	2366
26		8	H	Cardiff C	L	1-2	1-1	23	Noteman	2094
27		12	A	Lincoln C	L	0-2	0-1	—		2011
28		18	H	Hereford U	W	2-0	2-0	—	Noteman, Gormley	1270
29		22	A	Halifax T	D	0-0	0-0	22		1285
30		29	H	Walsall	L	0-1	0-0	22		1919
31	Mar	3	H	Chesterfield	L	0-1	0-1	—		2385
32		7	A	Hereford U	W	1-0	1-0	22	Noteman	1974
33		10	A	Rotherham U	L	1-3	0-0	—	Jeffrey	4883
34		14	H	Mansfield T	L	0-1	0-0	22		2846
35		21	A	York C	D	1-1	0-0	22	Jeffrey	2122
36		31	H	Barnet	W	1-0	1-0	—	Jeffrey	1247
37	Apr	3	A	Wrexham	W	2-1	2-1	—	Nicholson, Reddish	2769
38		11	H	Scarborough	W	3-2	2-0	22	Worboys, Jeffrey, Nicholson	1638
39		14	A	Blackpool	L	0-1	0-0	—		4353
40		20	H	Rochdale	W	2-0	1-0	22	Worboys, Jeffrey	2255
41		24	A	Crewe Alex	L	0-1	0-1	—		3639
42	May	2	H	Maidstone U	W	3-0	1-0	21	Reddish, Ormsby (pen), Jeffrey	1680

Final League Position: 21

GOALSCORERS

League (40): Noteman 10, Jeffrey 6, Gormley 5, Ormsby 3 (1 pen), Rankine 3, Nicholson 2, Reddish 2, Worboys 2, Harle 1, Kerr 1, Limber 1, McKenzie 1, Muir 1, Tynan 1, own goals 1.
Rumbelows Cup (4): Whitehurst 2, Cullen 1, Noteman 1.
FA Cup (2): Rankine 1, Whitehurst 1.

Samways	Rankine	Limber	Cullen	Ormsby	Crosby	Reddish	Muir	Tynan	Whitehurst	Gormley	Bennett	Kerr	Ashurst	Douglas	Noteman	Crichton	Boyle	Harle	Morrow	Rowe	Gallagher	McKenzie	Stiles	Raven	Nicholson	Stevenson	Penny	Worboys	Match No.
1	2	3	4	5*	6	7	8	9	10	11	12																		1
1	2		8	5		7*12	9	10		11		3	4		6														2
	2		8	5		7*	9	12	10	11		3	4		6	1													3
	2		8	5		7	9*12	10		11		3	4		6	1													4
	2		8*	5		12	9	10		11		3	4		6	1		7											5
	2		8†	5		12	9*	10		11		3	4		6	1		7	12	14									6
	2		8	5		12	9*14	10		11†		3	4		6	1		7		14									7
	2		8	5		12	9*10			11		3	4		6	1		7											8
	2		8	5		12	9*	10		11		3	4		6	1		7											9
1	2		8	5*		12	9	10		11		3	4		6			7											10
	10	3		5						11			4	2	6	1		7		8					9				11
	10	3		5		14				11	12		4	2	6	1		7				12	8†		9*				12
1	10	3		5						11	12		4	2	6			7				12	8		9*				13
1	10	3		5						11			4	2	6			7					8		9				14
1	10	3		5						11			4*	2	6			7					8†	14	9				15
1	10	3		5						11	12		4	2†	6			7*				12	8	14	9				16
1	9	3		5						11	12		4	2†	6				7*	10		12	8	14					17
1	9	3	6*	5						11	12		4	2					7	10†		12	8	14					18
1	9	3		5		14				11	12		4	2	6				7†	10*		12	8						19
1	9	3		5						11	12		4	2	6				7	10		12	8*						20
1	9	3		5						11	12		4	2	6				7*	10		12	8†	14					21
1	9	3		5						11			4	2	6				7	10			8						22
1	9	3		5						11	12		4	2	6				7*	10		12	8						23
1	9	3		5						11			4	2	6				7	10			8						24
1		3		5						11	12		4	2	6				7	10		12	8*		9				25
1				5						11	12		4	2	6				7	10	3†	12	8	14	9*				26
1				5		14				11	12		4	2	6†				7	10		12	8		9*				27
1				5						11	12		4	2	6				7	10		12	8		9				28
1				5						11	12		4	2	6				7†	10*		12	8	14	9				29
1				5						11			4	2	6				7*	10			8		9				30
1				5						11	12		4	2	6				7	10*		12	8		9				31
1				5						11			4	2	6				7				8		9				32
1				5						11	12		4	2	6*				7			12	8	14	9†				33
1				5						11	12		4	2	6				7			12	8		9*				34
1				5						11	12		4	2	6			6	7*			12	8		9				35
				5	14					11	12		4	2†	6	1				8		12			9			7*	36
				5	4					11				2	6*	1				8		12			9			7	37
				5						11			4	2	6	1				8		12			9			7*	38
				5						11			4	2	6	1				8					9		7		39
				5	14					11			4	2	6	1				8		12			9†			7*	40
				5	12					11			4	2	6	1				8					9*		7		41
				5	4					11				2	6	1				8			7		9				42
26	24	12	7	35	15	15	14	5	9	37	3	7	37	33	34	16	2	13	19	18	2	7	9	7	21	1	1	6	
			+		+	+	+	+							+					+	+	+			+			+	
			1s		7s	2s	6s	6s							2s					1s	1s	7s	10s 1s			3s			1s	

Prindiville—Match No. 27(3) 28(3*) 29(3) 30(3) 31(3) 32(3) 33(3) 34(3) 35(3) 36(3) 37(3) 38(3) 39(3) 40(3) 41(3) 42(3); Morris—Match No. 30(12); Jeffrey—Match No. 32(10) 33(10) 34(10) 35(10) 36(10) 37(10) 38(10) 39(10) 40(10) 41(10) 42(10).

Rumbelows Cup	First Round	Crewe Alex (a)	2-5
		(h)	2-4
FA Cup	First Round	Burnley (a)	1-1
		(h)	1-2

DONCASTER ROVERS

Player and Position	Ht	Wt	Birth Date	Birth Place	Source	Clubs	League App	League Gls
Goalkeepers								
Paul Crichton	6 1	12 05	3 10 68	Pontefract	Apprentice	Nottingham F	—	—
						Notts Co (loan)	5	—
						Darlington (loan)	5	—
						Peterborough U (loan)	4	—
						Darlington (loan)	3	—
						Swindon T (loan)	4	—
						Rotherham U (loan)	6	—
						Torquay U (loan)	13	—
						Peterborough U	47	—
						Doncaster R	36	—
Mark Samways	6 0	11 12	11 11 68	Doncaster	Trainee	Doncaster R	121	—
						Leeds U (loan)	—	—
						Scunthorpe U (loan)	8	—
Defenders								
Jack Ashurst*	6 0	12 04	12 10 54	Renton	Apprentice	Sunderland	140	4
						Blackpool	53	3
						Carlisle U	194	2
						Leeds U	89	1
						Doncaster R	73	1
						Bridlington	—	—
						Doncaster R	66	1
Lee Boyle*			22 1 72	North Shields	Ipswich T	Doncaster R	3	
Andy Crosby			3 3 73	Rotherham	Trainee	Leeds U	—	—
						Doncaster R	44	—
Jon Cullen			10 1 73	Durham	Trainee	Doncaster R	9	—
Colin Douglas	6 1	11 00	9 9 62	Hurtford	Celtic BC	Celtic	—	—
						Doncaster R	212	48
						Rotherham U	83	4
						Doncaster R	171	4
Brendan Ormsby*	5 11	11 09	1 10 60	Birmingham	Apprentice	Aston Villa	117	4
						Leeds U	46	5
						Shrewsbury T (loan)	1	—
						Doncaster R	78	8
Chris Penny†			16 2 73	Rochford	Brigg T	Doncaster R	1	—
Steve Prindiville†	5 9	11 04	26 12 68	Harlow	Apprentice	Leicester C	1	—
						Chesterfield	43	1
						Mansfield T	28	—
						Doncaster R	16	—
Shane Reddish	5 10	11 10	5 5 71	Bolsover	Mansfield T	Doncaster R	29	2
Mark Roe*			31 10 71	Sheffield	Trainee	Doncaster R	—	—
Midfield								
Eddie Gormley	5 7	10 07	23 10 68	Dublin	Bray W	Tottenham H	—	—
						Chesterfield (loan)	4	—
						Motherwell (loan)	—	—
						Shrewsbury T (loan)	—	—
						Doncaster R	77	10
David Harle*	5 9	10 07	15 8 63	Denaby	Apprentice	Doncaster R	61	3
						Exeter C	43	6
						Doncaster R	83	17
						Leeds U	3	—
						Bristol C (loan)	8	—
						Bristol C	15	2
						Scunthorpe U	89	10
						Peterborough U	22	2
						Doncaster R	45	3
Chris Redhead*	5 8	9 12	19 9 71	Newcastle	Trainee	Doncaster R	—	—
Brian Rowe			24 10 71	Sunderland	Trainee	Doncaster R	29	—

DONCASTER ROVERS

Foundation: In 1879 Mr. Albert Jenkins got together a team to play a game against the Yorkshire Institution for the Deaf. The players stuck together as Doncaster Rovers joining the Midland Alliance in 1889 and the Midland Counties League in 1891.

First Football League game: 7 September, 1901, Division 2, v Burslem Port Vale (h) D 3-3 – Eggett; Simpson, Layton; Longden, Jones, Wright; Langham, Murphy, Price, Goodson (2), Bailey (1).

Did you know: After leading 3-1 at home to Hartlepools United on 5 December 1931, Doncaster were unbeaten at home in a run of 33 League games before going down 2-0 to Stockport County on 4 September 1933. This sequence was made up of 23 wins and ten draws.

Managers (and Secretary-managers)
Arthur Porter 1920–21*, Harry Tufnell 1921–22, Arthur Porter 1922–23, Dick Ray 1923–27, David Menzies 1928–36, Fred Emery 1936–40, Bill Marsden 1944– 46, Jackie Bestall 1946–49, Peter Doherty 1949–58, Jack Hodgson and Sid Bycroft (joint managers) 1958, Jack Crayston 1958–59 (continued as Sec-Man to 1961), Jackie Bestall (TM) 1959–60, Norman Curtis 1960–61, Danny Malloy 1961–62, Oscar Hold 1962–64, Bill Leivers 1964–66, Keith Kettleborough 1966–67, George Raynor 1967–68, Lawrie McMenemy 1968–71, Maurice Setters 1971–74, Stan Anderson 1975–78, Billy Bremner 1978–85, Dave Cusack 1985–87, Dave Mackay 1987–89, Billy Bremner July 1989–.

John Stiles*	5 9	10 12	6	5 64	Manchester	Vancouver W	Leeds U	65	2
							Doncaster R	89	2
							Rochdale (loan)	4	—
Forwards									
Craig Bennett			29	8 73	Doncaster	Trainee	Doncaster R	7	—
Simon Holland§			26	3 73	Sunderland	Trainee	Doncaster R	1	—
Roger McKenzie*			27	1 73	Sheffield	Trainee	Doncaster R	17	1
Neil Morris †			3	5 70	Sheffield	Trainee	Doncaster R	1	—
Grant Morrow	5 10	11 07	4	10 70	Glasgow	Rowntree M	Doncaster R	41	3
Max Nicholson*			3	10 71	Leeds	Trainee	Doncaster R	27	2
Tommy Tynan	5 10	12 09	17	11 55	Liverpool	Apprentice	Liverpool	—	—
							Swansea C (loan)	6	2
							Sheffield W	91	31
							Lincoln C	9	1
							Newport Co	183	66
							Plymouth Arg	80	43
							Rotherham U	32	13
							Plymouth Arg (loan)	9	10
							Plymouth Arg	173	74
							Torquay U	35	13
							Doncaster R	11	1
Billy Whitehurst‡	6 0	13 00	10	6 59	Thurnscoe	Mexborough	Hull C	193	47
							Newcastle U	28	7
							Oxford U	40	4
							Reading	17	8
							Sunderland	17	3
							Hull C	36	5
							Sheffield U	22	2
							Stoke C (loan)	3	—
							Doncaster R	22	1
							Crewe Alex (loan)	10	—

Trainees
Armstrong, Stephen; Burton, Arron L; Edmunds, Christopher J; Holland, Simon L. D; Roberts, Jamie S; Soar, Mark; Sykes, Paul R; Thew, Lee; Wasilewski, Steven C.

**Non-Contract
Prindiville, Steven A.

Associated Schoolboys
Bell, Lynden; Buxton, Nick G; Cairns, Luke; Clarke, Paul R; Clegg, Christopher G; Dacre, Gary J; Fairclough, David E; Harmer, Russell; Long, James; McMillan, Jamie; Nixon, Russell S; Oliver, Jonathon; Perkins, Sean P; Ring, Gerard; Severn, Kevin A. G.

Associated Schoolboys who have accepted the club's offer of a Traineeship/Contract
Grant, Leon A; Maxfield, Scott; Robinson, Antony.

**Non-Contract Players who are retained must be re-signed before they are eligible to play in League matches.

EVERTON 1991–92 *Back row (left to right):* Andy Hinchcliffe, Eddie Youds, Neville Southall, Martin Keown, Gerry Payton, Dave Watson, Alan Harper.
Centre row: Les Helm (Physiotherapist), Jimmy Gabriel (Reserve Team Coach), Raymond Atteveld, Robert Warzycha, Neil McDonald, Mike Newell, John Ebbrell, Peter Beagrie, Pat Nevin, Colin Harvey (First Team Coach).
Front row: Kevin Sheedy, Ian Snodin, Mark Ward, Howard Kendall (Manager), Kevin Ratcliffe, Tony Cottee, Peter Beardsley.

FA Premier

EVERTON

Goodison Park, Liverpool L4 4EL. Telephone 051-521 2020. Match ticket information: 051-523 6642. Match information: 0898 121599. Clubcall 0898 121199. Dial-a-seat service: 051-525 1231. Ticket office 051-523-6666.

Ground capacity: 38,500 (35,235 seats).

Record attendance: 78,299 v Liverpool, Division 1, 18 September 1948.

Record receipts: £207,780 v Liverpool, FA Cup, 5th rd, 21 February 1988.

Pitch measurements: 112yd × 78yd.

Chairman: Dr. D. M. Marsh.

Directors: A. W. Waterworth, K. M. Tamlin, D. A. B. Newton, W. Kenright, Sir Philip Carter, CBE, Sir Desmond Pitcher.

Manager: Howard Kendall. ***Assistant Manager:*** Colin Harvey.

Physio: Les Helm. ***Coach. Reserve Team Coach:*** Jimmy Gabriel. ***Chief Executive & Secretary:*** Jim Greenwood. ***Marketing Manager:*** Derek Johnston. ***Promotions manager:*** Colum Whelan.

Year Formed: 1878. Turned Professional: 1885. Ltd Co.: 1892.

Former Grounds: 1878, Stanley Park; 1882, Priory Road; 1884, Anfield Road; 1892, Goodison Park.

Former Names: St Domingo FC, 1878–79.

Club Nickname: 'The Toffees'.

Record League Victory: 9-1 v Manchester C, Division 1, 3 September 1906 – Scott; Balmer, Crelley; Booth, Taylor (1), Abbott (1); Sharp, Bolton (1), Young (4), Settle (2), George Wilson. 9-1 v Plymouth Arg, Division 2, 27 December 1930 – Coggins; Williams, Cresswell; McPherson, Griffiths, Thomson; Critchley, Dunn, Dean (4), Johnson (1), Stein (4).

Record Cup Victory: 11-2 v Derby Co, FA Cup, 1st rd, 18 January 1890 – Smalley; Hannah, Doyle; Kirkwood (3), Holt, Parry; Latta, Brady (3), Geary (2), Chadwick, Millward (3).

Record Defeat: 4-10 v Tottenham H, Division 1, 11 October 1958.

Most League Points (2 for a win): 66, Division 1, 1969–70.

Most League points (3 for a win): 90, Division 1, 1984–85.

Most League Goals: 121, Division 2, 1930–31.

Highest League Scorer in Season: William Ralph 'Dixie' Dean, 60, Division 1, 1927–28 (All-time League record).

Most League Goals in Total Aggregate: William Ralph 'Dixie' Dean, 349, 1925–37.

Most Capped Player: Neville Southall, 61, Wales.

Most League Appearances: Ted Sagar, 465, 1929–53.

Record Transfer Fee Received: £2,750,000 from Barcelona for Gary Lineker, July 1986.

Record Transfer Fee Paid: £2,000,000 to West Ham U for Tony Cottee, July 1988.

Football League Record: 1888 Founder Member of the Football League; 1930–31 Division 2; 1931–51 Division 1; 1951–54 Division 2; 1954–92 Division 1; 1992– FA Premier League.

Honours: *Football League: Division 1* – Champions 1890–91, 1914–15, 1927–28, 1931–32, 1938–39, 1962–63, 1969–70, 1984–85, 1986–87; Runners-up 1889–90, 1894–95, 1901–02, 1904–05, 1908–09, 1911–12, 1985–86; *Division 2* Champions 1930–31; Runners-up 1953–54. *FA Cup:* Winners 1906, 1933, 1966, 1984; Runners-up 1893, 1897, 1907, 1968, 1985, 1986, 1989. *Football League Cup:* Runners-up 1976–77, 1983–84. *League Super Cup:* Runners-up 1986. *Simod Cup:* Runners-up 1989. *Zenith Data Systems Cup:* Runners-up 1991. **European Competitions:** *European Cup:* 1963–64, 1970–71. *European Cup-Winners' Cup:* 1966–67, 1984–85 (winners). *European Fairs Cup:* 1962–63, 1964–65, 1965–66. *UEFA Cup:* 1975–76, 1978–79, 1979–80.

Colours: Royal blue shirts with white collar and white trim on sleeve, white shorts with blue trim, blue stockings. **Change colours:** Yellow and blue.

EVERTON 1991–92 LEAGUE RECORD

Match No.	Date		Venue	Opponents		Result	H/T Score	Lg. Pos.	Goalscorers	Attendance
1	Aug	17	A	Nottingham F	L	1-2	1-0	—	Pearce (og)	24,422
2		20	H	Arsenal	W	3-1	1-0	—	Ward 2, Cottee	31,200
3		24	H	Manchester U	D	0-0	0-0	9		36,085
4		28	A	Sheffield W	L	1-2	0-0		Watson	28,690
5		31	A	Liverpool	L	1-3	0-2	18	Newell	39,072
6	Sep	3	H	Norwich C	D	1-1	0-0	—	Ward	19,197
7		7	H	Crystal Palace	D	2-2	0-1	18	Warzycha, Beardsley	21,065
8		14	A	Sheffield U	L	1-2	1-0	19	Beardsley	19,817
9		17	A	Manchester C	W	1-0	0-0	—	Beardsley	27,509
10		21	H	Coventry C	W	3-0	1-0	14	Beardsley 3 (1 pen)	20,542
11		28	A	Chelsea	D	2-2	1-0	14	Ebbrell, Beardsley	19,038
12	Oct	5	H	Tottenham H	W	3-1	3-1	10	Cottee 3 (1 pen)	29,505
13		19	H	Aston Villa	L	0-2	0-1	14		27,688
14		26	A	QPR	L	1-3	0-2	15	Cottee	10,002
15	Nov	2	A	Luton T	W	1-0	0-0	12	Warzycha	8022
16		16	H	Wimbledon	W	2-0	1-0	9	Cottee (pen), Watson	18,762
17		23	H	Notts Co	W	1-0	1-0	9	Cottee	24,230
18		30	A	Leeds U	L	0-1	0-0	10		30,043
19	Dec	7	H	West Ham U	W	4-0	3-0	7	Cottee, Beagrie, Beardsley, Johnston	21,563
20		14	A	Oldham Ath	D	2-2	1-1	7	Sheedy, Nevin	14,955
21		21	A	Arsenal	L	2-4	2-3	8	Warzycha, Johnston	29,684
22		26	H	Sheffield W	L	0-1	0-0	9		30,788
23		28	H	Liverpool	D	1-1	0-1	10	Johnston	37,681
24	Jan	1	A	Southampton	W	2-1	1-0	9	Ward, Beardsley	16,546
25		11	A	Manchester U	L	0-1	0-0	9		46,619
26		19	H	Nottingham F	D	1-1	0-1	—	Watson	17,717
27	Feb	2	A	Aston Villa	D	0-0	0-0	—		17,451
28		8	H	QPR	D	0-0	0-0	9		18,212
29		23	H	Leeds U	D	1-1	0-0	—	Jackson	19,248
30		29	A	West Ham U	W	2-0	1-0	9	Johnston, Ablett	20,976
31	Mar	7	A	Oldham Ath	W	2-1	1-1	7	Beardsley 2	21,014
32		10	A	Wimbledon	D	0-0	0-0	—		3569
33		14	H	Luton T	D	1-1	0-1	7	Johnston	16,707
34		17	A	Notts Co	D	0-0	0-0	—		7480
35		21	H	Norwich C	L	3-4	2-1	8	Johnston 2, Beardsley	11,900
36	Apr	1	H	Southampton	L	0-1	0-1	—		15,201
37		4	A	Crystal Palace	L	0-2	0-0	13		14,338
38		11	H	Sheffield U	L	0-2	0-1	16		18,285
39		18	A	Coventry C	W	1-0	0-0	13	Beagrie	14,669
40		20	H	Manchester C	L	1-2	1-2	15	Nevin	21,101
41		25	A	Tottenham H	D	3-3	0-3	15	Beardsley 2, Unsworth	34,630
42	May	2	H	Chelsea	W	2-1	1-0	12	Beardsley (pen), Beagrie	20,163

Final League Position: 12

GOALSCORERS

League (52): Beardsley 15 (2 pens), Cottee 8 (2 pens), Johnston 7, Ward 4, Beagrie 3, Warzycha 3, Watson 3, Nevin 2, Ablett 1, Ebbrell 1, Jackson 1, Newell 1, Sheedy 1, Unsworth 1, own goals 1.
Rumbelows Cup (8): Beardsley 3, Beagrie 2, Atteveld 1, Cottee 1, Newell 1.
FA Cup (1): Beardsley 1.

Southall	Harper	Ebbrell	Ratcliffe	Watson	Keown	Warzycha	Sheedy	Beardsley	Cottee	Ward	McDonald	Nevin	Newell	Hinchcliffe	Atteveld	Jackson	Beagrie	Johnston	Ablett	Barlow	Jenkins	Unsworth	Match No.
1	2	3	4	5	6	7†	8	9	10	11*12		14											1
1	2	3	4	5	6	7	8	9	10	11*	12												2
1	2	3	4	5	6	7*	8	9	10†11		12	14											3
1	2	3	4	5	6	7*	8	9	10†11	12		14											4
1	2	3	12	5	6*14	11	8	10†	7	4		9											5
1	2	6	4	5		7	10	8	11			9	3										6
1	2†	3	4	5	6	7*10	8		11	12		9	14										7
1		4		5	6	7	10	8	12	11*		9		3	2								8
1		4		5	6	7*10	8		11	12		9		3	2								9
1		4		5	6	7	10*	8	11	12		9		3	2								10
1		4		5	6	7*10	8	12	11			9		3	2								11
1	2	4	3	5	6	7	10†	8	9	11*	12		14										12
1	10	4	3*	5	6	7	11†	8	9		12		14		2								13
1		4		5	6	7*10	8	9	11†	12	3		14		2								14
1		4		5	6	14	8	12	7*	9	3	10		2†11									15
1	10	4		5	6		8	9	7		3					2	11						16
1	14	4		5	6	12	8	10	7		3					2	11*	9†					17
1	3	4		5	6	12	8	10	7*			9				2	11						18
1		4		5	6	12	8	10	7*		3					2	11	9					19
1	12	4		5	6	7†10*	8		14		3					2	11	9					20
1	3	4		5		7	10*	8	12		14				2	6	11†	9					21
1	3	4		5	6	7*	8	10	11							2	12	9					22
1	3	4		5	6	7*	8	10	12							2	11	9					23
1	3	4		5	6	7*	8	10	12		14					2	11†	9					24
1	3	4		5	6	7†	8	12	10		14					2	11*	9					25
1	10	4		5	6	7*	8	12	11							2†14		9	3				26
1		4		5	6	12	8*10	11	7							2		9	3				27
1	10*	4		5	6	12	8		7		14					2	11	9†	3				28
1		4		5	6	7†	8	10*11			14					2	12	9	3				29
1	14	4		5	6		8	10†	7		11					2*12		9	3				30
1	10	4		5	6*		8		7		11					2	12	9	3				31
1	14	4		5	6	10†	8		7		11					2	12	9*	3				32
1	10	4		5	6	12	8		7		14					2†11		9*	3				33
1	10	4		5†	6	12	8		7		11*					2	14	9	3				34
1	10	4			6	7	8		11					5		2		9	3*12				35
1	3	4			6	7*	8	12	10							2	11	9	5				36
1	3	4			6	7*	8		10							2	11	9	5	12			37
1	2	4			6*		8	10†	7	14						5	11	9	3	12			38
1	10			5	6		8		4	7						2	11	9*	3	12			39
1	3	4			6	12	8		10	7*						2†11			5	9		14	40
1	4		2				8		10	7						6	11		5	9	3*12		41
1	4†				6	12	8		10	7						2	11		5	9*14	3		42
42	29	39	8	35	39	26	16	42	17	37	1	7	8	15	8	30	20	21	17	3	1	1	
	+4s	+1s			+11s				+7s			+4s	10s5s	3s	5s		+7s		+4s	2s	1s		

Rumbelows Cup	Second Round	Watford (h)		1-0
		(a)		2-1
	Third Round	Wolverhampton W (h)		4-1
	Fourth Round	Leeds U (h)		1-4
FA Cup	Third Round	Southend U (h)		1-0
	Fourth Round	Chelsea (a)		0-1

EVERTON

Player and Position	Ht	Wt	Date	Birth Place	Source	Clubs	League App	Gls
Goalkeepers								
Jason Kearton	6 1	11 10	9 7 69	Ipswich (Australia)	Brisbane Lions	Everton	—	—
						Stoke C (loan)	16	—
						Blackpool (loan)	15	—
Gerry Peyton	6 2	13 09	20 5 56	Birmingham	Atherstone T	Burnley	30	—
						Fulham	345	—
						Southend U (loan)	10	—
						Bournemouth	202	—
						Everton	—	—
						Bolton W (loan)	1	—
						Norwich C (loan)	—	—
Neville Southall	6 1	12 01	16 9 58	Llandudno	Winsford	Bury	39	—
						Everton	371	—
						Port Vale (loan)	9	—
Defenders								
Gary Ablett	6 0	11 04	19 11 65	Liverpool	Apprentice	Liverpool	109	1
						Derby Co (loan)	6	—
						Hull C (loan)	5	—
						Everton	17	1
Andy Hinchcliffe	5 10	12 10	5 2 69	Manchester	Apprentice	Manchester C	112	8
						Everton	39	1
Matthew Jackson	6 1	12 12	19 10 71	Leeds	School	Luton T	9	—
						Preston NE (loan)	4	—
						Everton	30	1
Iain Jenkins	5 9	11 06	24 11 72	Prescot	Trainee	Everton	4	—
Martin Keown	6 1	12 04	24 7 66	Oxford	Apprentice	Arsenal	22	—
						Brighton & HA (loan)	23	1
						Aston Villa	112	3
						Everton	83	—
Neil Moore	6 1	12 01	21 9 72	Liverpool	Trainee	Everton	—	—
John O'Neil‡	6 1	13 07	14 11 72	Liverpool	Trainee	Everton	—	—
Kevin Ratcliffe*	5 11	12 07	12 11 60	Mancot	Apprentice	Everton	359	2
David Unsworth§	5 11	12 01	16 10 73	Preston	Trainee	Everton	2	1
Dave Watson	6 0	11 12	20 11 61	Liverpool	Amateur	Liverpool	—	—
						Norwich C	212	11
						Everton	200	17
David Wilson*	5 9	11 04	27 10 72	Liverpool	Trainee	Everton	—	—
Midfield								
John Ebbrell	5 7	9 12	1 10 69	Bromborough	FA School	Everton	96	4
David Gouldstone‡	5 8	11 05	19 12 72	Wirral	Trainee	Everton	—	—
Alan Harper	5 8	10 09	1 11 60	Liverpool	Apprentice	Liverpool	—	—
						Everton	127	4
						Sheffield W	35	—
						Manchester C	50	1
						Everton	33	—
Stuart McCall (To Rangers Aug 1991)	5 6	10 01	10 6 64	Leeds	Apprentice	Bradford C	238	37
						Everton	103	6
Michael McDonough‡	5 7	11 09	15 9 72	Ormskirk	Trainee	Everton	—	—
Ian Snodin	5 7	8 12	15 8 63	Rotherham	Apprentice	Doncaster R	188	25
						Leeds U	51	6
						Everton	96	2
Mark Ward	5 6	9 12	10 10 62	Prescot	Apprentice	Everton	—	—
						Northwich V	—	—
						Oldham Ath	84	12
						West Ham U	165	12
						Manchester C	55	14
						Everton	37	4

EVERTON

Foundation: St. Domingo Church Sunday School formed a football club in 1878 which played at Stanley Park. Enthusiasm was so great that in November 1879 they decided to expand membership and changed the name to Everton playing in black shirts with a white sash and nicknamed the "Black Watch". After wearing several other colours, royal blue was adopted in 1901.

First Football League game: 8 September, 1888, Football League, v Accrington (h) W 2-1 – Smalley; Dick, Ross; Holt, Jones, Dobson; Fleming (2), Waugh, Lewis, E. Chadwick, Farmer.

Did you know: Everton was the first Football League club to provide Scotland with two players for the international against England. Jack Robertson and John Bell appeared in the side beaten 3-1 at Celtic Park in April 1898.

Managers (and Secretary-managers)
W. E. Barclay 1888–89*, Dick Molyneux 1889–1901*, William C. Cuff 1901–18*, W. J. Sawyer 1918–19*, Thomas H. McIntosh 1919–35*, Theo Kelly 1936–48, Cliff Britton 1948–56, Ian Buchan 1956–58, Johnny Carey 1958–61, Harry Catterick 1961–73, Billy Bingham 1973–77, Gordon Lee 1977–81, Howard Kendall 1981–87, Colin Harvey 1987–90, Howard Kendall November 1990–.

Norman Whiteside‡	6 0	12 08	7	5 65	Belfast	Apprentice	Manchester U	206	47
							Everton	29	9

Forwards

Stuart Barlow	5 10	11 00	16	7 68	Liverpool		Everton	9	—
							Rotherham U (loan)	1	—
Peter Beagrie	5 8	9 10	28	11 65	Middlesbrough	Local	Middlesbrough	33	2
							Sheffield U	84	11
							Stoke C	54	7
							Everton	63	5
							Sunderland (loan)	5	1
Peter Beardsley	5 8	11 07	18	1 61	Newcastle	Wallsend BC	Carlisle U	102	22
							Vancouver W	—	—
							Manchester U	—	—
							Vancouver W	—	—
							Newcastle U	147	61
							Liverpool	131	46
							Everton	42	15
Tony Cottee	5 8	11 04	11	7 65	West Ham	Apprentice	West Ham U	212	92
							Everton	116	44
Mo Johnston	5 9	10 06	30	4 63	Glasgow	Milton Battlefield	Partick T	85	41
							Watford	38	23
							Celtic	99	52
							Nantes	—	—
							Rangers	65	26
							Everton	42	14
Pat Nevin	5 6	10 00	6	9 63	Glasgow	Gartcosh U	Clyde	73	17
							Chelsea	193	36
							Everton	109	16
							Tranmere R (loan)	8	—
Phil Quinlan			17	4 71	Madrid	Trainee	Everton	—	—
							Huddersfield T (loan)	8	2
Robert Warzycha			20	6 63	Poland	Gornik Zabrze	Everton	45	5

Trainees
Carridge, John J; Doolan, John; Grant, Anthony J; Jones, Terence P; Kenny, William; Langton, Edward P; Norris, Barry; Powell, Mark A; Priest, Christopher; Reeves, Stephen T; Renforth, Glenn L; Ruffer, Carl J; Sharrock, Mark; Tait, Paul; Unsworth, David G; Williams, Lee J; Woods, Kenneth.

Associated Schoolboys
Adair, Daniel A; Arnison, Paul S; Barton, Jonathan; Brennan, Jonathon W; Brown, Paul R; Cumberbatch, Grant; Donnachie, John; Dreslin, John C; Hennigan, Gerard J; Hussin, Edward W; King, Peter J; Leeming, Daniel J; Lowes, Trevor; McCann, Gavin P; McChrystal, Colin R; McHugh, Bartholomew; Plant, Marc D; Price, Gregory T; Price, Roy J; Roscoe, Christopher J; Ross, Leo K; Singleton, Benjamin P; Speare, James P. V; Weathers, Andrew W; Woods, Matthew J; Wright, Christopher L.

Associated Schoolboys who have accepted the club's offer of a Traineeship/Contract
Emery, Richard; Holcroft, Peter I; McMahon, Alan D; Price, Christopher; Roberts, Sean M; Smith, Alex P; Smith, Dean A.

220

EXETER CITY 1991–92 *Back row (left to right):* Jon Brown, Kevin Maloy, David Cole, Kevin Miller, Scott Daniels.
Third row: Mike Davenport (Physiotherapist), Gordon Hobson, Gary Marshall, Steve D'Shaughnessy, David Cooper, Chris O'Donnell, Tony Frankland, Graham Waters, Mike Radford (Youth Development Officer).
Second row: Scott Hiley, Steve Moran, Mark Cooper, Alan Ball (Manager), Steve Williams (Assistant Manager), Darren Rowbotham, Tom Kelly.
Front row: Glen Sprod, Mark Brown, Neil Fairchild, Zak Locke, Craig Taylor, Toby Redwood.

Division 2 **EXETER CITY**

St James Park, Exeter EX4 6PX. Telephone Exeter (0392) 54073.

Ground capacity: 8960.

Record attendance: 20,984 v Sunderland, FA Cup 6th rd (replay), 4 March 1931.

Record receipts: £32,007 v Newcastle U, FA Cup 5th rd replay, 18 February 1981.

Pitch measurements: 114yd × 73yd.

President: W. C. Hill.

Directors: L. G. Vallance, A. W. Gooch, S. Dawe, G. Vece, C. Hill, A. R. Trump.

Manager: Alan Ball.

Coach/Assistant Manager: Steve Williams.

Physio: M. Davenport.

Secretary: M. A. Holladay.

Company Secretary: A. R. Trump.

Commercial Manager: Mike Lewis.

Year Formed: 1904. Turned Professional: 1908. Ltd Co.: 1908.

Club Nickname: 'The Grecians'.

Record League Victory: 8-1 v Coventry C, Division 3 (S), 4 December 1926 – Bailey; Pollard, Charlton; Pullen, Pool, Garrett; Purcell (2), McDevitt, Blackmore (2), Dent (2), Compton (2). 8-1 v Aldershot, Division 3 (S), 4 May 1935 – Chesters; Gray, Miller; Risdon, Webb, Angus; Jack Scott (1), Wrightson (1), Poulter (3), McArthur (1), Dryden (1). (1 og).

Record Cup Victory: 9-1 v Aberdare, FA Cup 1st rd, 26 November 1927 – Holland; Pollard, Charlton; Phoenix, Pool, Gee; Purcell (2), McDevitt, Dent (4), Vaughan (2), Compton (1).

Record Defeat: 0-9 v Notts Co, Division 3 (S), 16 October 1948 and v Northampton T, Division 3 (S), 12 April 1958.

Most League Points (2 for a win): 62, Division 4, 1976–77.

Most League points (3 for a win): 89, Division 4, 1989–90.

Most League Goals: 88, Division 3 (S), 1932–33.

Highest League Scorer in Season: Fred Whitlow, 33, Division 3 (S), 1932–33.

Most League Goals in Total Aggregate: Tony Kellow, 129, 1976–78, 1980–83, 1985–88.

Most Capped Player: Dermot Curtis, 1 (17), Eire.

Most League Appearances: Arnold Mitchell, 495, 1952–66.

Record Transfer Fee Received: £500,000 from Glasgow Rangers for Chris Vinnicombe, November 1989.

Record Transfer Fee Paid: £65,000 to Blackpool for Tony Kellow, March 1980.

Football League Record: 1920 Elected Division 3; 1921–58 Division 3 (S); 1958–64 Division 4; 1964–66 Division 3; 1966–77 Division 4; 1977–84 Division 3; 1984–90 Division 4; 1990–92 Division 3; 1992– Division 2.

Honours: Football League: Division 3 best season: 8th, 1979–80; Division 3 (S) – Runners-up 1932–33; Division 4 – Champions 1989–90; Runners-up 1976–77. *FA Cup:* best season: 6th rd replay, 1931. *Football League Cup:* never beyond 4th rd. *Division 3 (S) Cup:* Winners 1934.

Colours: Red and white striped shirts, black shorts, white stockings. **Change colours:** Navy blue shirts, yellow shorts.

EXETER CITY 1991-92 LEAGUE RECORD

Match No.	Date		Venue	Opponents		Result	H/T Score	Lg. Pos.	Goalscorers	Attendance
1	Aug	17	A	WBA	L	3-6	1-2	—	Cooper, Moran, Marshall	12,892
2		24	H	Brentford	L	1-2	0-2	24	Moran	3518
3		31	A	Shrewsbury T	L	1-6	1-3	24	Rowbotham	2912
4	Sep	4	H	Torquay U	W	1-0	0-0	—	Kelly	5772
5		7	A	Huddersfield T	D	0-0	0-0	22		5758
6		14	H	Hartlepool U	D	1-1	0-0	22	Daniels	2906
7		17	H	Stockport Co	W	2-1	2-1	—	Knowles (og), Whiston	3033
8		21	A	Peterborough U	D	1-1	0-1	18	Wimbleton	4249
9		28	H	Reading	W	2-1	0-0	14	Daniels 2	3383
10	Oct	5	A	Hull C	W	2-1	0-1	12	Chapman, Moran	3143
11		12	H	Darlington	W	4-1	2-1	8	Moran 4	3548
12		19	H	Bury	W	5-2	3-0	5	Kelly 2 (1 pen), Chapman 2, Moran	3904
13		26	A	Wigan Ath	L	1-4	1-1	8	Hilaire	1761
14	Nov	2	A	Leyton Orient	L	0-1	0-0	9		3038
15		6	H	Bradford C	W	1-0	0-0	—	Gardner (og)	2625
16		9	H	Stoke C	D	0-0	0-0	6		5309
17		23	A	Birmingham C	L	0-1	0-0	9		11,319
18		30	H	Chester C	D	0-0	0-0	9		3235
19	Dec	14	A	Swansea C	L	0-1	0-1	11		2848
20		22	A	Brentford	L	0-3	0-2	—		7226
21		26	H	Shrewsbury T	W	1-0	0-0	11	Hiley	3857
22		28	H	WBA	D	1-1	0-0	11	Moran (pen)	5830
23	Jan	1	A	Torquay U	L	0-1	0-0	13		5696
24		11	H	Bolton W	D	2-2	1-1	14	Moran 2	3336
25		18	A	Preston NE	W	3-1	2-0	13	Robson, Wimbleton, Hilaire	3585
26		25	H	Fulham	D	1-1	1-0	12	Moran (pen)	4002
27	Feb	8	H	Wigan Ath	L	0-1	0-0	16		3036
28		11	A	Chester C	L	2-5	1-3	—	Moran, Wimbleton	871
29		15	H	Swansea C	W	2-1	2-0	14	Moran, Thompstone	2360
30		22	A	Bolton W	W	2-1	1-1	13	Kelly, Wimbleton	5631
31		29	H	Bournemouth	L	0-3	0-1	14		4538
32	Mar	3	A	Preston NE	W	4-1	2-1	—	Hilaire 2, Moran 2	2214
33		7	A	Fulham	D	0-0	0-0	12		3957
34		10	A	Bradford C	D	1-1	0-0	—	Whiston	4170
35		14	H	Leyton Orient	W	2-0	0-0	13	Morris, Marshall	3070
36		21	A	Stoke C	L	2-5	1-3	14	Whiston, Thompstone	13,634
37		24	A	Bournemouth	L	0-1	0-1	—		4959
38		28	H	Birmingham C	W	2-1	1-1	13	Moran 2 (1 pen)	5479
39		31	A	Hartlepool U	L	1-3	0-1	—	Morris	2222
40	Apr	4	H	Huddersfield T	L	0-1	0-0	14		3047
41		10	A	Stockport Co	L	1-4	1-1	—	Hodge	4546
42		14	A	Bury	L	1-3	1-2	—	Marshall	1756
43		18	H	Peterborough U	D	2-2	1-1	15	Kelly (pen), Thompstone	3057
44		20	A	Reading	L	0-1	0-1	17		3325
45		25	H	Hull C	L	0-3	0-0	20		2772
46	May	2	A	Darlington	L	2-5	1-2	20	Moran, Chapman	1573

Final League Position: 20

GOALSCORERS

League (57): Moran 19 (3 pens), Kelly 5 (2 pens), Chapman 4, Hilaire 4, Wimbleton 4, Daniels 3, Marshall 3, Thompstone 3, Whiston 3, Morris 2, Cooper 1, Hiley 1, Hodge 1, Robson 1, Rowbotham 1, own goals 2.
Rumbelows Cup (0).
FA Cup (3): Brown 1, Marshall 1, Moran 1.

Maloy	Hiley	Brown	Williams	Daniels	O'Donnell	Rowbotham	Cooper	Moran	Kelly	Marshall	Hobson	O'Shaughnessy	Miller	O'Doherty	Waters	Cole	Redwood	Wimbleton	Chapman	Cook	Whiston	Dolan	Hodge	Hilaire	Harris	Damerell	Humphrey	Edwards	Match No.
1	2	3	4	5	6	7	8	9	10	11																			1
1	2	3	4	5	6†	7	8	9	10	11*	12	14																	2
	2	12	4†		6	7	8	9	3	10			1		5	11*	14												3
	2	8	4		6	7†		9	10	11		14	1		5	12	3*												4
	2	3	4	5		7*		9	10	12		6	1					8	11										5
	2	11	4	5		7*							1					8	10	3	6	9	12						6
	2		4	5						11			1					8	10	3	6	9		7					7
	2		4	5					12	11			1					8	10	3	6	9*		7*					8
	2		4	5					12	11			1					8	10	3	6	9*		7†	14				9
	2		4	5					12	11			1					8	10	3	6	9*		7					10
	2		4	5				9		11			1					8	10	3	6			7					11
	2		4	5				9		11			1					8	10	3	6			7					12
	2	12	4	5				9†		11*			1					8	10	3	6		14	7					13
	2		4	5				9		11			1					8*	10	3	6		12	7					14
	2		4	5				9		11			1					8	10*	3	6		12	7					15
	2	3	4	5				9		11			1					8	10†		6	14	12	7*					16
	2	8	4	5				9†		11			1						10*	3	6	14	12	7					17
	2	10		5					12				1				14	8	11†	3	6		9	7*	4				18
	2	8	4†	5				9	12				1				14		10*	3	6			7	11				19
	2	11		5		7							1					8		3	6		12		4*		9	10	20
	2	11	4	5				9	7				1					8		3	6		12					10*	21
	2	11	4	5				9	7				1					8		3	6							10	22
	2		4	5				9	7†				1				14	8		3	6		12					10	23
	2		4	5				9	7				1					8		3	6		12					10*	24
	2		4	5				9	10				1					8			6			7					25
	2		4					9	7				1					8		3	6		12						26
			4						7				1					8	12	3			10						27
			4	5				9	12				1			2			3				8†	7*					28
	2		4	5				9					1					8	3†	6		11*		7					29
	2		4	5				9	10				1					8			6		12	7*					30
		6	4	5				9*	10				1					8		3			12	7					31
		6	4	5				9	10	11			1					8		3				7					32
	2		4	5					10	11			1					8		3	6			7					33
	2			5					10	11			1					8		3	6			7*	4				34
	2			5					10	7			1					8		3	6		11		4				35
	2		4†	5					10	12			1					8		3	6		11						36
	2	11	4*	5					10				1					8		3	6		7						37
	2	7	4	5				9	12				1					8*		3	6		11						38
	2		4	5				9	10	12			1					8†		3	6		11						39
	2		4	5				9	10	12			1					8*		3	6		11						40
	2		4	5				9	10	12			1							3	6*		11	8					41
	2		4					9*	10	12			1							3	6		11	8		5			42
	2		4	5					10	11			1							3	6		7	8					43
	2	6	4	5					10†				1						11	3			7	8*	14				44
1	2	8	4†	5*					10	14								11		3	6		7	12					45
1	2*		4	5				9	10									8	14	3	6		7	12					46
4	33	33	36	43	2	5	3	31	32	17	—	1	42	2	1	—	1	35	17	38	36	5	16	24	5	1	2	4	

Substitute appearances: +2s (Daniels); +3s +11s +1s +2s (Moran/Kelly/Marshall); +1s +2s (Miller/O'Doherty); +1s +3s (Wimbleton/Chapman); +2s +7s +9s +1s (Cook/Whiston/Hodge/Hilaire)

Cooper D—Match No. 23(11*) 25(3) 26(10) 27(6) 28(6) 29(14) 30(3) 31(2) 32(2) 34(12) 36(14) 42(5) 44(12); Robson—Match No. 24(11) 25(11) 26(11*) 27(11*) 28(11) 29(12) 30(11) 31(11); Thompstone—Match No. 26(5) 27(9) 28(10) 29(10) 36(7) 37(9) 38(10) 39(7*) 40(7†) 41(7) 42(7†) 43(9) 44(9) 45(9) 46(11†); Tonge—Match No. 27(2) 28(14) 42(14); Masefield—Match No. 27(5); Morris—Match No. 33(9) 34(9) 35(9) 36(9*) 37(12) 39(14) 40(14).

Rumbelows Cup	First Round	Birmingham C (h)	0-1
		(a)	0-4
FA Cup	First Round	Colchester U (a)	0-0
		(h)	0-0
		Exeter won 4-2 on penalties	
	Second Round	Swansea C (h)	0-0
		(a)	2-1
	Third Round	Portsmouth (h)	1-2

EXETER CITY

Goalkeepers

Kevin Maloy	6 1	12 00	12 11 66	Aldershot	Taunton T	Exeter C	4	—
Kevin Miller	6 1	12 10	15 3 69	Falmouth	Newquay	Exeter C	119	—

Defenders

Jon Brown	5 10	11 03	8 9 66	Barnsley	Denaby U	Exeter C	64	—
David Cole‡	6 0	11 10	28 9 62	Barnsley		Sunderland	—	—
						Swansea C	8	—
						Swindon T	69	3
						Torquay U	110	6
						Rochdale	84	7
						Exeter C	2	—
Andy Cook	5 9	10 12	10 8 69	Romsey	Apprentice	Southampton	16	1
						Exeter C	38	—
David Cooper	6 00	12 00	7 3 73	Welwyn	Trainee	Luton T	—	—
						Exeter C	13	—
Tony Frankland*	6 1	10 07	11 10 72	Greenwich		Exeter C	7	—
Tom Kelly	5 10	11 10	28 3 64	Bellshill	Hibernian	Hartlepool U	15	—
						Torquay U	120	—
						York C	35	2
						Exeter C	66	8
Paul Masefield‡	5 11	12 08	21 10 70	Birmingham	Trainee	Birmingham C	—	—
						Preston NE	—	—
						Exeter C	1	—
Chris O'Donnell‡	5 9	12 00	26 5 68	Newcastle	Apprentice	Ipswich T	14	—
						Northampton T (loan)	1	—
						Leeds U	1	—
						Exeter C	2	—
Toby Redwood§			7 10 73	Newton Abbot	Trainee	Exeter C	1	—
Alan Tonge†	5 8	11 11	25 2 72	Bury	Trainee	Manchester U	—	—
						Exeter C	3	—

Midfield

Gary Chapman	5 10	12 00	1 5 64	Leeds		Bradford C	5	—
						Notts Co	25	4
						Mansfield T (loan)	6	—
						Exeter C	20	4
Scott Daniels	6 1	11 09	22 11 69	Benfleet	Trainee	Colchester U	73	—
						Exeter C	86	6
Andy Harris	5 10	12 02	17 11 70	Birmingham	Trainee	Birmingham C	1	—
						Exeter C	6	—
						Oxford U (loan)	1	—
Scott Hiley	5 9	10 07	27 9 68	Plymouth	Trainee	Exeter C	177	9
Steve Neville‡	5 9	11 00	18 9 57	Walthamstow	Apprentice	Southampton	5	1
						Exeter C	93	22
						Sheffield U	49	6
						Exeter C (loan)	33	17
						Exeter C	59	10
						Bristol C	134	40
						Exeter C	120	39
Ian Thompstone	6 0	11 03	17 1 71	Manchester	Trainee	Manchester C	1	1
						Oldham Ath	—	—
						Exeter C	15	3
Graham Waters*	5 8	11 02	5 11 71	St Austell	Trainee	Oxford U	—	—
						Exeter C	2	—
Peter Whiston	6 0	11 06	4 1 68	Widnes		Plymouth Arg	10	—
						Torquay U (loan)	8	1
						Torquay U	32	—
						Exeter C	36	3
Steve Williams	5 11	10 11	12 7 58	London	Apprentice	Southampton	278	18
						Arsenal	95	4
						Luton T	40	1
						Exeter C	36	—
Paul Wimbleton*	5 8	10 06	13 11 64	Havant	Apprentice	Portsmouth	10	—
						Cardiff C	119	17
						Bristol C	16	2
						Shrewsbury T	34	1
						Maidstone U (loan)	2	1
						Exeter C	36	4

EXETER CITY

Foundation: Exeter City was formed in 1904 by the amalgamation of St. Sidwell's United and Exeter United. The club first played in the East Devon League and then the Plymouth & District League. After an exhibition match between West Bromwich Albion and Woolwich Arsenal was held to test interest as Exeter was then a rugby stronghold, Exeter City decided at a meeting at the Red Lion Hotel to turn professional in 1908.

First Football League game: 28 August, 1920, Division 3, v Brentford (h) W 3-0 – Pym; Coleburne, Feebury (1p); Crawshaw, Carrick, Mitton; Appleton, Makin, Wright (1), Vowles (1), Dockray.

Did you know: City's first professional, Jack Banks, made his debut for them in a Plymouth & District League game against Millbrook Rangers at St James' Park on 14 December 1907. However the game was abandoned 20 minutes after the interval when for the third time that afternoon the ball burst and there were no more available.

Managers (and Secretary-managers)
Arthur Chadwick 1910–22, Fred Mavin 1923–27, Dave Wilson 1928–29, Billy McDevitt 1929–35, Jack English 1935–39, George Roughton 1945–52, Norman Kirkman 1952–53, Norman Dodgin 1953–57, Bill Thompson 1957–58, Frank Broome 1958–60, Glen Wilson 1960–62, Cyril Spiers 1962–63, Jack Edwards 1963–65, Ellis Stuttard 1965–66, Jock Basford 1966–67, Frank Broome 1967–69, Johnny Newman 1969–76, Bobby Saxton 1977–79, Brian Godfrey 1979–83, Gerry Francis 1983–84, Jim Iley 1984–85, Colin Appleton 1985–87, Terry Cooper 1988–91, Alan Ball August 1991–.

Forwards

Name	ft	st lb		DOB	Birthplace	Signed from	Club	Apps	Gls
Mark Damerell†	5 9	11 00	31	7 65	Plymouth	St Blazey	Plymouth Arg	6	—
							Exeter C	1	—
Eamonn Dolan	5 10	12 03	20	9 67	Dagenham	Apprentice	West Ham U	15	3
							Bristol C (loan)	3	—
							Birmingham C	12	1
							Exeter C	7	—
Vince Hilaire*	5 6	10 00	10	10 59	Forest Hill	Apprentice	Crystal Palace	255	29
							Luton T	6	—
							Portsmouth	146	26
							Leeds U	44	6
							Stoke C (loan)	5	1
							Charlton Ath (loan)	—	—
							Stoke C	10	2
							Exeter C	33	4
John Hodge	5 06	10 00	1	4 69	Ormskirk	Falmouth	Exeter C	23	1
Gary Marshall	5 11	10 10	20	4 64	Bristol	Shepton Mallet	Bristol C	68	7
							Torquay U (loan)	7	1
							Carlisle U	21	2
							Scunthorpe U	41	3
							Exeter C	60	6
Steve Moran	5 8	11 00	10	1 61	Croydon	Amateur	Southampton	180	78
							Leicester C	43	14
							Reading	116	30
							Exeter C	34	19
Trevor Morgan‡	6 1	13 01	30	9 56	Forest Gate	Leytonstone	Bournemouth	53	13
							Mansfield T	12	6
							Bournemouth	88	33
							Bristol C	32	8
							Exeter C	30	9
							Bristol R	55	24
							Bristol C	19	8
							Bolton W	77	17
							Colchester U	32	12
							Exeter C	17	3

Trainees
Allen, Stephen J. A; Brown, Mark J; Redwood, Toby R. B; Taylor, Craig.

**Non-Contract
Sprod, Glenn A; Tonge, Alan J.

Associated Schoolboys
Beavis, Ian J; Green, Brendan S; Grylls, Casey B. H. V; Hines, Christopher J; Littley, James M; McConnell, Barry; Medlin, Nicholas R. M; Murch, Stephen; Page, Mark J; Parsons, Timothy J; Rodwell, Andrew; Rollason, Andrew; Smith, Jason L.

**Non-Contract Players who are retained must be re-signed before they are eligible to play in League matches.

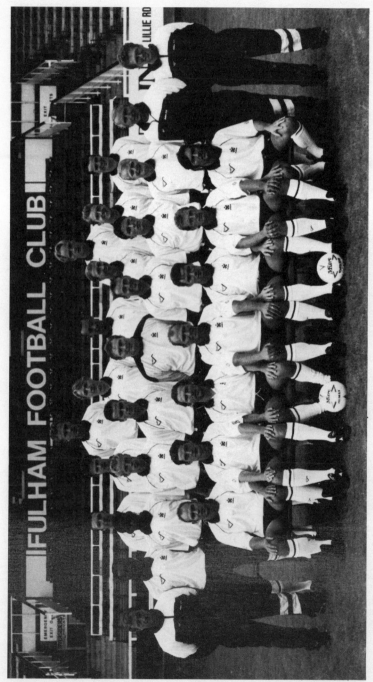

FULHAM 1991–92 *Back row (left to right):* Danny O'Connor, Julian Hails, Glen Thomas, Stacey North, John Finch, Graham Baker, Kelly Haag, Gary Cobb, Gary Brazil.
Centre row: Ray Lewington (First Team Coach), Stephen Rocastle, Udo Onwere, Mark Tucker, Steve Milton, Jim Stannard, Martin Pike, Martin Ferney, Simon Morgan, Alan Dicks (Manager), Kevin Thomas (Physiotherapist).
Front row: John Marshall, Justin Skinner, Peter Scott, Gavin Nebbeling, Mark Newson, Jeff Eckhardt, Mark Kelly.

Division 2 — **FULHAM**

Craven Cottage, Stevenage Rd, Fulham, London SW6. Telephone 071-736 6561. Commercial Office: 071-736 4634. Clubcall: 0898 121198.

Ground capacity: 16,815.

Record attendance: 49,335 v Millwall, Division 2, 8 October 1938.

Record receipts: £80,247 v Chelsea, Division 2, 8 October 1983.

Pitch measurements: 110yd × 75yd.

Chairman: Jimmy Hill.

Directors: W. F. Muddyman (Vice-chairman), C. A. Swain, A. Muddyman, T. Wilson, D. E. Shrimpton.

Manager: Don Mackay.

Assistant Manager: Ray Lewington. *Physio:* Chris Smith. *Commercial/Community Manager:* Tom Enefer. *Youth Team Coach:* Terry Bullivant. *Club Secretary:* Mrs Janice O'Doherty. *Commercial Manager:* David Gore.

Year Formed: 1879. Turned Professional: 1898. Ltd Co.: 1903 ‹bi›Reformed: ‹r›1987.

Former Grounds: 1879 Star Road, Fulham; c.1883 Eel Brook Common, 1884 Lillie Road; 1885 Putney Lower Common; 1886 Ranelagh House, Fulham; 1888 Barn Elms, Castelnau; 1889 Purser's Cross (Roskell's Field), Parsons Green Lane; 1891 Eel Brook Common; 1891 Half Moon, Putney; 1895 Captain James Field, West Brompton; 1896 Craven Cottage.

Former Names: 1879–88, Fulham St Andrew's. *Club Nickname:* 'Cottagers'.

Record League Victory: 10-1 v Ipswich T, Division 1, 26 December 1963 – Macedo; Cohen, Langley; Mullery (1), Keetch, Robson (1); Key, Cook (1), Leggat (4), Haynes, Howfield (3).

Record Cup Victory: 6-0 v Wimbledon (away), FA Cup, 1st rd (replay), 3 December 1930 – Iceton; Gibbon, Lilley; Oliver, Dudley, Barrett; Temple, Hammond (1), Watkins (1), Gibbons (2), Penn (2). 6-0 v Bury, FA Cup, 3rd rd, 7 January 1938 – Turner; Bacuzzi, Keeping; Evans, Dennison, Tompkins; Higgins, Worsley, Rooke (6), O'Callaghan, Arnold.

Record Defeat: 0-10 v Liverpool, League Cup 2nd rd, 1st leg, 23 September 1986.

Most League Points (2 for a win): 60, Division 2, 1958–59 and Division 3, 1970–71.

Most League points (3 for a win): 78, Division 3, 1981–82.

Most League Goals: 111, Division 3 (S), 1931–32.

Highest League Scorer in Season: Frank Newton, 43, Division 3 (S), 1931–32.

Most League Goals in Total Aggregate: Gordon Davies, 159, 1978–84, 1986–91.

Most Capped Player: Johnny Haynes, 56, England.

Most League Appearances: Johnny Haynes, 594, 1952–70.

Record Transfer Fee Received: £333,333 from Liverpool for Richard Money, May 1980.

Record Transfer Fee Paid: £150,000 to Orient for Peter Kitchen, February 1979, and to Brighton & HA for Teddy Maybank, December 1979.

Football League Record: 1907 Elected to Division 2; 1928–32 Division 3 (S); 1932–49 Division 2; 1949–52 Division 1; 1952–59 Division 2; 1959–68 Division 1; 1968–69 Division 2; 1969–71 Division 3; 1971–80 Division 2; 1980–82 Division 3; 1982–86 Division 2; 1986–92 Division 3; 1992– Division 2.

Honours: Football League: Division 1 best season: 10th, 1959–60; Division 2 – Champions 1948–49; Runners-up 1958–59; Division 3 (S) – Champions 1931–32; Division 3 – Runners-up 1970–71. *FA Cup:* Runners-up 1974–75. *Football League Cup:* best season: 5th rd, 1967–68, 1970–71.

Colours: White shirts red and black trim, black shorts, white stockings red and black trim.
Change colours: All red.

FULHAM 1991–92 LEAGUE RECORD

Match No.	Date		Venue	Opponents	Result	H/T Score	Lg. Pos.	Goalscorers	Atten- dance
1	Aug	17	A	Chester C	L 0-2	0-1	—		1444
2		24	H	Birmingham C	L 0-1	0-1	22		4762
3		31	A	Torquay U	W 1-0	0-0	18	Onwere	3299
4	Sep	3	H	WBA	D 0-0	0-0	—		4523
5		7	H	Swansea C	W 3-0	1-0	10	Pike 2, Brazil	3426
6		14	A	Stoke C	D 2-2	0-1	11	Cole, Newson	10,567
7		17	A	Bury	L 1-3	1-2	—	Thomas	2248
8		21	H	Leyton Orient	W 2-1	1-1	12	Eckhardt, Haag	4934
9		27	A	Bournemouth	D 0-0	0-0	—		6450
10	Oct	5	H	Brentford	L 0-1	0-1	15		7710
11		12	A	Bradford C	W 4-3	3-1	13	Newson, Onwere, Brazil, Haag	5143
12		19	A	Bolton W	W 3-0	1-0	8	Brazil 2, Cole	5152
13		26	H	Preston NE	W 1-0	1-0	7	Morgan	4022
14	Nov	2	H	Hull C	D 0-0	0-0	6		3365
15		6	A	Huddersfield T	L 1-3	1-1	—	Onwere	5064
16		9	A	Hartlepool U	L 0-2	0-0	12		2999
17		23	H	Stockport Co	L 1-2	0-0	13	Cole	3680
18		30	A	Darlington	L 1-3	0-1	15	Brazil	2655
19	Dec	21	A	Birmingham C	L 1-3	0-1	16	Brazil	8877
20		26	H	Torquay U	W 2-1	2-1	16	Farrell, Morgan	4186
21		28	H	Chester C	D 2-2	0-0	17	Thomas, Scott	3708
22	Jan	1	A	WBA	W 3-2	2-1	15	Farrell 3	16,442
23		11	A	Peterborough U	L 1-4	0-1	15	Newson (pen)	4975
24		18	H	Shrewsbury T	L 0-1	0-0	16		3440
25		25	A	Exeter C	D 1-1	0-1	15	Brazil	4002
26		28	H	Wigan Ath	D 1-1	0-1	—	Morgan	2466
27	Feb	1	H	Bolton W	D 1-1	1-0	16	Kelly M	3804
28		8	A	Preston NE	W 2-1	2-0	15	Brazil, Farrell	3878
29		11	H	Darlington	W 4-0	1-0	—	Brazil 2, Farrell, Eckhardt	2988
30		15	A	Reading	W 2-0	0-0	12	Eckhardt, Farrell	4388
31		22	H	Peterborough U	L 0-1	0-1	12		5233
32		28	A	Wigan Ath	W 2-0	1-0	—	Eckhardt, Farrell	2202
33	Mar	3	A	Shrewsbury T	D 0-0	0-0	—		2137
34		7	H	Exeter C	D 0-0	0-0	10		3957
35		10	H	Huddersfield T	W 1-0	0-0	—	Eckhardt	3134
36		14	A	Hull C	D 0-0	0-0	11		3742
37		20	H	Hartlepool U	W 1-0	1-0	—	Haag	4359
38		27	A	Stockport Co	L 0-2	0-1	—		4654
39		31	H	Stoke C	D 1-1	1-0	—	Haag	5779
40	Apr	4	A	Swansea C	D 2-2	0-1	11	Hails, Eckhardt	3307
41		7	H	Reading	W 1-0	0-0	—	Eckhardt	3499
42		11	H	Bury	W 4-2	3-0	10	Brazil 2 (1 pen), Thomas, Haag	4060
43		18	A	Leyton Orient	W 1-0	0-0	10	Farrell	7094
44		20	H	Bournemouth	W 2-0	0-0	7	Brazil (pen), Farrell	7619
45		26	A	Brentford	L 0-4	0-4	—		12,071
46	May	2	H	Bradford C	W 2-1	2-1	9	Brazil, Haag	8671

Final League Position: 9

GOALSCORERS

League (57): Brazil 14 (2 pens), Farrell 10, Eckhardt 7, Haag 6, Cole 3, Morgan 3, Newson 3 (1 pen), Onwere 3, Thomas 3, Pike 2, Hails 1, Kelly M 1, Scott 1.
Rumbelows Cup (3): Brazil 2 (2 pens), Browne 1.
FA Cup (0).

Stannard	Marshall	Pike	Newson	Eckhardt	Thomas	Scott	Onwere	Haag	Brazil	Morgan	Milton	Cobb	Baker	Georgiou	Browne	Cole	Kelly M	Nebbeling	Finch	Farrell	Byrne	Hails	Kelly P	Tucker	Match No.
1	2	3	4	5	6	7	8†	9*	10	11	12	14													1
1	2	3		5	6	7	8*	9†	10	11		4	12	14											2
1	2	3	4	5	6	14	8		10			12	7	9*	11†										3
1	2	3	4	5	6	11	8*	9	10			12	7												4
1	2	3	4	5	6†	11	8	12	10	14		7*				9									5
1	2	3	4	5	6	11	8		10			12				9	7*								6
1	2	3	4	5	6	11	8		10			12				9	7*								7
1	2	3	4	5	6	11	8	12	10			7*				9									8
1	2	3	4	5	6	11	8		10	12		7*				9									9
1	2	3	4	5	6	11	8	12	10			7*				9									10
1	2	3	4	5	6	11	8	12	10	7						9*									11
1	2	3	4	5	6	11	8		10	7						9									12
1	2	3	4	5	6	11	8†	12	10	7				14		9*									13
1	2	3	4		6	11	8	12	10	7						9	5*								14
1	2	3	4		6	11	8		10	7		12				9		5*							15
1	2	3	4		6	11	8	5	10	7		12				9*									16
1	2		4	5	6	11	8*		10	7		12				9		3							17
1	2	3	4*	5	6	11	8	9	10	7									12						18
1	8	3†	2		4		6	11*	14	12	10	7					5			9					19
1	2*	3	4	5	6	11	12		10	7							8			9					20
1	2	3	4	5	6	11			10	7							8			9					21
1	8	3	2	4	6	11	12		10	7							5*			9					22
1	8†	3	2	4*	6	11	12	14	10	7							5			9					23
1	2	3		5*	6		8†	12	10	7							4			9	11	14			24
1	2	3			8	6			10	5							4			9		7	11		25
1	2	3		5†	6	14		12	10	7							4			9*		11	8		26
1	2	3		5	6	4		12	10	7							11			9*		8			27
1	2	3		5	6	4		12	10	7							11†			9*		8	14		28
1	2	3		5	6	4		12	10	7							11			9*		8†14			29
1	2	3		5	6	4			10	7							11			9		8			30
1	2	3		5	6	4		12	10	7							11*			9		8			31
1	2	3	8		6	4		12	10								11	5		9		7*			32
1	2	3	8		6	4		12	10								11	5		9*		7			33
1	2	3	8		6	4		11	10	7								5		9*		12			34
1	2	3	8		6	4		11	10	7								5		9					35
1	2	3	8		6	12		11	10	7								5		9			4*		36
1	4	3	7		6			11	10								8	5		9					37
1	2	3	7†		6	14		11	10	4							8	5*		9		12			38
1	4	3	7		6			11	10	2							8	5		9					39
1	4	3	7		6			11	10	2							8	5		9*		12			40
1	4	3	7		6		9	11	10	2							8*	5				12			41
1†		3	7		6	11	9	12	10	2							8	5					4*	14	42
1		3	5	7	6	4	11	12	10	2										9*		8			43
1		3			6	7	8	11	10	2								5		9		4			44
1		3	14	7	6	4*		11	10	2†							12	5		9		8			45
1		3	2	7	6	4		11*	10								12	5		9		8			46
46	41	45	25	43	45	37	19	18	46	34	—	4	3	1	1	13	19	16	5	25	5	11	3	1	
			+			+	+	+		+		+	+	+	+		+	+				+	+		
			1s			2s	8s	16s		2s		1s	7s	1s	3s		2s	1s				7s	1s		

Rumbelows Cup First Round Charlton Ath (a) 2-4
(h) 1-1
FA Cup First Round Hayes (h) 0-2

FULHAM

Player and Position	Ht	Wt	Date	Birth Place	Source	Clubs	League App	Gls
Goalkeepers								
David Coles‡	5 10	12 00	15 6 64	Wandsworth	Apprentice	Birmingham C	—	—
						Mansfield T	3	—
						Aldershot	120	—
						Newport Co (loan)	14	—
						HJK Helsinki	—	—
						Crystal Palace	—	—
						Brighton & HA	1	—
						Aldershot	30	—
						Fulham	—	—
Jim Stannard	6 0	13 06	6 10 62	London	Local	Fulham	41	—
						Charlton Ath (loan)	1	—
						Southend U (loan)	17	—
						Southend U	92	—
						Fulham	223	1
Defenders								
Jeff Eckhardt	5 11	11 06	7 10 65	Sheffield		Sheffield U	74	2
						Fulham	184	14
Martin Ferney	5 11	12 04	8 11 71	Lambeth	Trainee	Fulham	14	—
John Finch*	6 1	11 12	5 7 66	Lambeth	Dorking	Fulham	7	—
Simon Morgan	5 11	12 07	5 9 66	Birmingham		Leicester C	160	3
						Fulham	68	3
Gavin Nebbeling	6 0	12 04	15 5 63	Johannesburg	Arcadia S	Crystal Palace	151	8
						Northampton T (loan)	11	—
						Fulham	58	—
						Hereford U (loan)	3	—
Mark Newson	5 10	12 06	7 12 60	Stepney	Apprentice	Charlton Ath	—	—
						Maidstone U	—	—
						Bournemouth	177	23
						Fulham	73	4
Stacey North	6 2	12 06	25 11 64	Luton	Apprentice	Luton T	25	—
						Wolverhampton W (loan)	3	—
						WBA	98	—
						Fulham	38	—
Martin Pike	5 9	11 04	21 10 64	South Shields	Apprentice	WBA	—	—
						Peterborough U	126	8
						Sheffield U	129	5
						Tranmere R (loan)	2	—
						Bolton W (loan)	5	1
						Fulham	111	7
Steve Rocastle*			8 11 71	Lewisham	Norwich C	Fulham	—	—
Glen Thomas	6 0	11 06	6 10 67	London	Apprentice	Fulham	164	6
Mark Tucker	5 11	11 07	27 4 72	Woking	Trainee	Fulham	2	—
Midfield								
Graham Baker*	5 9	10 08	3 12 58	Southampton	Apprentice	Southampton	113	22
						Manchester C	117	19
						Southampton	60	9
						Aldershot (loan)	7	2
						Fulham	10	1
Corey Browne*			2 7 70	Enfield		Fulham	1	—
Gary Cobb	5 8	11 05	6 8 68	Luton	Apprentice	Luton T	9	—
						Northampton T (loan)	1	—
						Swansea C (loan)	5	—
						Fulham	22	—
Sean Farrell	6 1	12 08	28 2 69	Watford	Apprentice	Luton T	25	1
						Colchester U (loan)	9	1
						Northampton T (loan)	4	1
						Fulham	25	10

FULHAM

Foundation: Churchgoers were responsible for the foundation of Fulham, which first saw the light of day as Fulham St. Andrew's Church Sunday School FC in 1879. They won the West London Amateur Cup in 1887 and the championship of the West London League in its initial season of 1892–93. The name Fulham had been adopted in 1888.

First Football League game: 3 September, 1907, Division 2, v Hull C (h) L 0-1 – Skene; Ross, Lindsay; Collins, Morrison, Goldie; Dalrymple, Freeman, Bevan, Hubbard, Threlfall.

Did you know: Fulham's strongest finish to any Football League season was in 1948–49 when they were runners-up in the Second Division. They were unbeaten in their last eight matches with Arthur Rowley scoring in each of the last seven.

Managers (and Secretary-managers)
Harry Bradshaw 1904–09, Phil Kelso 1909–24, Andy Ducat 1924–26, Joe Bradshaw 1926–29, Ned Liddell 1929–31, Jim MacIntyre 1931–34, Jim Hogan 1934–35, Jack Peart 1935–48, Frank Osborne 1948–64 (was secretary-manager or GM for most of this period), Bill Dodgin Snr 1949–53, Duggie Livingstone 1956–58, Bedford Jezzard 1958–64 (GM for last two months), Vic Buckingham 1965–68, Bobby Robson 1968, Bill Dodgin Jnr 1969–72, Alec Stock 1972–76, Bobby Campbell 1976–80, Malcolm Macdonald 1980–84, Ray Harford 1984–86, Ray Lewington 1986–90, Alan Dicks 1990–91, Don Mackay December 1991–.

Player and Position	Ht	Wt	Birth Date	Place	Source	Clubs	League App	Gls
Mark Kelly	5 8	10 06	7 10 66	Blackpool		Shrewsbury T	—	—
						Cardiff C	105	2
						Fulham	39	1
Paul Kelly§	5 07	10 13	24 2 74	London	Trainee	Fulham	3	—
Ray Lewington*	5 6	11 08	7 9 56	Lambeth	Apprentice	Chelsea	85	4
						Vancouver W	—	—
						Wimbledon (loan)	23	—
						Fulham	174	20
						Sheffield U	36	—
						Fulham	60	1
John Marshall	5 10	11 04	18 8 64	Surrey	Apprentice	Fulham	306	23
Daniel O'Connor*			13 12 72	Barking	Trainee	Fulham	—	—
Udo Onwere	6 0	11 03	9 11 71	Hammersmith	Trainee	Fulham	34	4
Peter Scott*	5 8	10 10	1 10 63	London	Apprentice	Fulham	277	27
Forwards								
Gary Brazil	5 11	9 13	19 9 62	Tunbridge Wells	Apprentice	Crystal Palace	—	—
						Sheffield U	62	9
						Port Vale (loan)	6	3
						Preston NE	166	58
						Mansfield T (loan)	—	—
						Newcastle U	23	2
						Fulham	88	18
George Georgiou*			19 8 72	St Pancras	Wembley T	Fulham	4	—
Kelly Haag	6 0	12 03	6 10 70	Enfield	Trainee	Brentford	5	—
						Fulham	57	9
Julian Hails			20 11 67	Lincoln		Fulham	18	1
Steve Milton‡	6 0	12 07	13 4 63	London	Apprentice	West Ham U	—	—
					Whyteleafe	Fulham	58	9

Trainees
Armitage, James A; Brodrick, Darren; Hendricks, Alan W; Hurdle, Agustus A. J; Jamfy, Kwabena; Jupp, Duncan A; Kelly, Paul L. M; Lewis, Karl J; Lewis, Leon J; Munoz, Mark S; Murphy, Gary J; Omogbehin, Collin L; Richards, Jonathan I; Rudgely, Simon P. D; Sheldrick, Paul C; Sugrue, James S; Whitaker, Andrew T; Wright, Stuart J.

Associated Schoolboys
Abbott, Stuart R. C; Bartley, Carl; Bascombe, Roland; Dafedjaiye, Matthew; Fenner, James H; Fernley, David J; Flynn, Paul; Hutchins, Lee D; Johns, Jason; McMahon, James; Miles, Nick; Pittman, Neal L; Probets, Clayton; Ray, Kevin P; Smith, David P; Whitty, Colm; Williams, Carl.

Associated Schoolboys who have accepted the club's offer of a Traineeship/Contract
Andrews, Nicholas; Girdler, Stuart; Hawkins, Benjamin J; Haworth, Robert J; Mison, Michael; Omigie, David P; Power, James S; Power, Raymond O.

GILLINGHAM 1991–92 *Back row (left to right):* Malcolm Machin (Youth Team Trainer), Steve Lovell, Austin Berkley, Karl Elsey, Richard Carpenter, Andy Arnott, Paul Clark, Tim O'Shea, George Shipley (Youth Team Manager).

Centre row: Ron Hillyard (Assistant Manager), Lee Palmer, Tony Butler, Paul Hague, Harvey Lim, Peter Beadle, Shane Rufer, Alan Walker, Javed Mughal (Physiotherapist).

Front row: Joe Dunne, Mark Dempsey, Paul Burke, Damien Richardson (Manager), Eliot Martin, Tony Eeles, Mark O'Connor.

Division 3   **GILLINGHAM**

Priestfield Stadium, Gillingham. Telephone Medway (0634) 851854/8576828. Commercial Office: 851462.

Ground capacity: 10,412.

Record attendance: 23,002 v QPR, FA Cup 3rd rd 10 January 1948.

Record receipts: £49,377 v Swindon T, play-offs, 22 May 1987.

Pitch measurements: 114yd × 75yd.

President: J. W. Leech.

Vice-presidents: G. B. Goodere, G. V. W. Lukehurst.

Chairman: B. R. Baker.

Managing Director: A. Smith.

Vice-chairman: Rt. Hon. Earl Henry Sondes.

Directors: P. H. Giles FCA, M. G. Lukehurst, T. Carney.

Manager: Damien Richardson. *Assistant Manager:* Ron Hillyard. *Player Coach:* Ron Hillyard. *Physio:* Javed Mughal. *Company Secretary/Chief Executive:* Barry Bright. *Commercial Manager:* Bill Williams.

Year Formed: 1893. Turned Professional: 1894. Ltd Co.: 1893.

Former Names: New Brompton, 1893–1913.

Club Nickname: 'The Gills'.

Record League Victory: 10-0 v Chesterfield, Division 3, 5 September 1987 – Kite; Haylock, Pearce, Shipley (2) (Lillis), West, Greenall (1), Pritchard (2), Shearer (2), Lovell, Elsey (2), David Smith (1).

Record Cup Victory: 10-1 v Gorleston, FA Cup, 1st rd, 16 November 1957 – Brodie; Parry, Hannaway; Riggs, Boswell, Laing; Payne, Fletcher (2), Saunders (5), Morgan (1), Clark (2).

Record Defeat: 1-9 v Bristol R, Southern League, 4 September 1907.

Most League Points (2 for a win): 62, Division 4, 1973–74.

Most League points (3 for a win): 83, Division 3, 1984–85.

Most League Goals: 90, Division 4, 1973–74.

Highest League Scorer in Season: Ernie Morgan, 31, Division 3 (S), 1954–55 and Brian Yeo, 31, Division 4, 1973–74.

Most League Goals in Total Aggregate: Brian Yeo, 135, 1963–75.

Most Capped Player: Tony Cascarino, 3 (38), Republic of Ireland.

Most League Appearances: John Simpson, 571, 1957–72.

Record Transfer Fee Received: £300,000 from Tottenham H for Peter Beadle, June 1992.

Record Transfer Fee Paid: £102,500 to Tottenham H for Mark Cooper, October 1987.

Football League Record: 1920 Original Member of Division 3; 1921 Division 3 (S); 1938 Failed re-election; Southern League 1938–44; Kent League 1944–46; Southern League 1946–50; 1950 Re-elected to Division 3 (S); 1958–64 Division 4; 1964–71 Division 3; 1971–74 Division 4; 1974–89 Division 3; 1989–92 Division 4; 1992– Division 3.

Honours: Football League: Division 3 best season: 4th, 1978–79, 1984–85; Division 4 – Champions 1963–64; Runners-up 1973–74. *FA Cup:* best season: 5th rd, 1969–70. *Football League Cup:* best season: 4th rd, 1964.

Colours: Royal blue shirts, royal blue shorts, black stockings. **Change colours:** Black and white striped shirts, black shorts, black stockings.

GILLINGHAM 1991–92 LEAGUE RECORD

Match No.	Date		Venue	Opponents	Result	H/T Score	Lg. Pos.	Goalscorers	Attendance
1	Aug	17	H	Scunthorpe U	W 4-0	1-0	—	Elsey, Crown, O'Connor, Beadle	3480
2		24	A	York C	D 1-1	0-1	4	Crown	2324
3	Sep	4	A	Hereford U	L 0-2	0-1	—		2544
4		7	H	Scarborough	W 2-0	0-0	10	Arnott, Lovell	3375
5		14	A	Wrexham	L 1-2	1-2	11	Elsey	1642
6		17	A	Blackpool	L 0-2	0-1	—		3035
7		21	H	Barnet	D 3-3	2-2	15	Eeles, Crown 2	4864
8		28	A	Crewe Alex	L 1-2	0-1	16	Trusson (pen)	3126
9	Oct	5	H	Chesterfield	L 0-1	0-1	19		2835
10		12	A	Halifax T	W 3-0	1-0	13	Crown 2, Beadle	1435
11		19	A	Doncaster R	D 1-1	0-0	14	Lovell	1468
12		26	H	Northampton T	W 3-1	0-0	13	Crown 3	2544
13	Nov	2	A	Carlisle U	D 0-0	0-0	13		1672
14		5	H	Cardiff C	D 0-0	0-0	—		2641
15		9	H	Maidstone U	D 1-1	0-0	13	O'Connor	6716
16		23	A	Mansfield T	L 3-4	2-2	14	Lovell, Crown, Arnott	3287
17	Dec	14	A	Rotherham U	D 1-1	1-0	13	Crown	3137
18		21	H	York C	D 1-1	0-0	13	Crown	2711
19		26	A	Scunthorpe U	L 0-2	0-1	15		3883
20	Jan	1	H	Hereford U	W 2-1	2-1	15	Lovell, Smith	3392
21		4	A	Lincoln C	L 0-1	0-0	15		2169
22		11	H	Walsall	W 4-0	4-0	12	Crown 3, Elsey	2715
23		18	A	Burnley	L 1-4	1-1	14	Walker	8908
24	Feb	1	H	Doncaster R	W 2-1	1-0	13	Smith, O'Connor	2366
25		8	A	Northampton T	D 0-0	0-0	11		3007
26		15	H	Rotherham U	W 5-1	4-1	10	Lovell 3, Dempsey, Crown	2486
27		22	A	Walsall	W 1-0	1-0	10	Dempsey	2987
28		29	H	Lincoln C	L 1-3	1-1	11	Lovell	3160
29	Mar	3	H	Burnley	W 3-0	1-0	—	Crown, Beadle, Lovell	3729
30		7	A	Rochdale	L 1-2	0-0	12	Crown	1941
31		10	A	Cardiff C	W 3-2	1-2	—	Green 2, Crown	8521
32		14	H	Carlisle U	L 1-2	0-1	10	Crown	2789
33		17	H	Rochdale	D 0-0	0-0	—		2300
34		21	H	Maidstone U	D 1-1	0-1	10	Lovell	3264
35		28	H	Mansfield T	W 2-0	2-0	10	Lovell, Beadle	2682
36		31	H	Wrexham	W 2-1	2-0	—	Lovell (pen), Green	3078
37	Apr	4	A	Scarborough	L 1-2	0-0	10	Crown	1174
38		11	A	Blackpool	W 3-2	1-1	10	Lovell, Crown, Beadle	3684
39		18	A	Barnet	L 0-2	0-1	10		4049
40		20	H	Crewe Alex	L 0-1	0-0	11		2928
41		25	A	Chesterfield	D 3-3	1-1	11	Thomas, Lovell, Green	2109
42	May	2	H	Halifax T	W 2-0	0-0	11	Lovell 2 (1 pen)	2413

Final League Position: 11

GOALSCORERS

League (63): Crown 22, Lovell 16 (2 pens), Beadle 5, Green 4, Elsey 3, O'Connor 3, Arnott 2, Dempsey 2, Smith 2, Eeles 1, Thomas 1, Trusson 1 (1 pen), Walker 1.
Rumbelows Cup (4): Beadle 2, Lovell 1, Walker 1.
FA Cup (4): Walker 3, Smith 1.

Lim	O'Shea	Palmer	Elsey	Walker	Butler	Clark	Lovell	Crown	O'Connor	Eeles	Beadle	Trusson	Martin	Clarke	Arnott	Dempsey	Carpenter	Branagan	Smith	Polston	Osborne	Berkley	Dunne	Green	Thomas	Harrison	Match No.
1	2	3	4†	5	6	7	8	9*	10	11	12	14															1
1	2		4	5	6	7	8*	9	10	11†	12	14	3														2
1	2	3	4†	5	6	7	8	9	10*	11	12	14															3
1	2	3	4†	5		7	8		10	11	9*	14			6	12											4
1	2		4†	5		7	8		10	11	9	3*			6	12	14										5
1	2		4	5		7	8	12	10*	11	9†		3		6		14										6
1	2		4	5		7	12	8	10	11	9*		3†		6		14										7
1	2		3†	5		7	12	8	10*	11	9		4		6		14										8
1	2		3	5		7	10	8		11	12		4*		6	9†	14										9
	2		3	5		7	10	8		11	4		9*	6		12		1									10
1	2*		3	5		7	10	8		11	4		9	6		12											11
1	2		3	5		7	10	8		11	6*	9				12			4								12
1	2		3	5		7	10	8		11*	6	9				12			4								13
1	2		3	5		7	10	8		11	6*	9†			14	12			4								14
1	2		3*	5		7	10	8		11	12				6	9			4								15
1	2	3*	5†			7	10	8		11	12				6	9			4		14						16
1	2			5		7	10	8		11	12					9*			4		3		6				17
1	2		3	5		7	10	8		11	12	14				9*			4		6†						18
1	2		3*	5		7	10	8		11†	9	14				6			4								19
1	2					7	10	8		11	9*		3	5	6	12			4†		14						20
1	2	12	14			7	10	8†		11	9*		3	5	6				4								21
1	2	9	5†			7	10	8		11			3		6*	14			4		12						22
1	2	9	5†			7	10	8*		11			3		6	14			4		12						23
1	2	14	8†	5		7	10			11	9*		3		6	12			4								24
1	2		8	5		7	10			11	9*		3		6	12			4								25
1	2	14	8	5		7	10	9*		11			3		6†	12			4								26
1	2	14	8	5†		7	10	9		11	12		3			6							4*				27
1	2	14	8†	5		7	10	9		11*	12		3			6			4								28
1	2	12		5		7	10	9		11	8		3			6*			4								29
1	2	12		5		7	10	9		11	8		3*			6			4								30
1		3		5		7	10	9		11	8					6			4*				12	2			31
1		3†		5		7	10	9		11	14					4					8*		12	2			32
1				5		7	10	9			12		3			6			4		8*			2	11		33
1		12		5		7	10	9			8		3			6			4				11*	2			34
1				5		7	10	9			8		3			12					6*			2	11		35
1				5		7	10	9	4		8		3			6								2	11		36
1				5		7	10	9	4		8		3*			12							6	2	11		37
1				5		7	10	9	4		8		3			6								2	11		38
1				5		7	10	9	4		8		3*			12					6			2	11		39
1				5		7	10	9†	4		8		3			12					6		14	2	11*		40
				5		7	10	9	4		3					6*			8		12			2	11	1	41
				5		7	10	9	4		8†		3			12					6		14	2	11*	1	42
39	30	5	25	39	5	42	40	35	38	14	25	6	22	9	7	18	2	1	26	1	4	—	7	12	8	2	

Substitute appearances: Palmer +6s, Elsey +2s, Walker +1s; +2s +1s +1s +3s +8s +4s; +2s +12s +12s +1s; +1s +1s +3s +4s

Rumbelows Cup	First Round	Portsmouth (a)			1-2
		(h)			3-4
FA Cup	First Round	Brentford (a)			3-3
		(h)			1-3

GILLINGHAM

Player and Position	Ht	Wt	Date	Birth Place	Source	Clubs	League App	Gls
Goalkeepers								
Harvey Lim	6 0	13 07	30 8 67	Halesworth	Apprentice	Norwich C	—	—
						Plymouth Arg (loan)	—	—
						Gillingham	82	—
Defenders								
Tony Butler	6 1	11 07	28 9 72	Stockport	Trainee	Gillingham	11	—
Brian Clarke	6 3	13 08	10 10 68	Eastbourne	School	Gillingham	44	—
Richard Green*	6 0	11 08	22 11 67	Wolverhampton		Shrewsbury T	125	5
						Swindon T	—	—
						Gillingham	12	4
Paul Hague	6 2	12 06	16 9 72	Durham	Trainee	Gillingham	7	—
Mark Leahy			22 1 73	Tenterden	Ashford T	Gillingham	—	—
Eliot Martin	5 8	10 06	27 9 72	Plumstead	Trainee	Gillingham	22	—
Lee Palmer	6 0	12 04	19 9 70	Gillingham	Trainee	Gillingham	72	4
Alan Walker	6 1	12 07	17 12 59	Mossley	Telford U	Lincoln C	75	4
						Millwall	92	8
						Gillingham	151	7
Midfield								
Austin Berkley*	5 9	10 10	28 1 73	Dartford	Trainee	Gillingham	3	—
Richard Carpenter	5 11	12 00	30 9 72	Sheppey	Trainee	Gillingham	12	1
Paul Clark	5 10	12 12	14 9 58	Benfleet	Apprentice	Southend U	33	1
						Brighton & HA	79	9
						Reading (loan)	2	—
						Southend U	276	3
						Gillingham	42	—
Mark Dempsey	5 7	10 09	10 12 72	Dublin	Trainee	Gillingham	32	2
Joe Dunne	5 9	11 00	25 5 73	Dublin	Trainee	Gillingham	37	—
Tony Eeles	5 7	9 12	15 11 70	Chatham	Trainee	Gillingham	59	3
Karl Elsey‡	5 10	12 00	20 11 58	Swansea	Pembroke B	QPR	7	—
						Newport Co	123	15
						Cardiff C	59	5
						Gillingham	128	13
						Reading	44	3
						Maidstone U	72	5
						Gillingham	27	3
Michael Harle‡	6 0	12 00	31 10 72	Lewisham	Trainee	Gillingham	2	—
Neil Smith	5 7	11 10	30 9 71	London	Trainee	Tottenham H	—	—
						Gillingham	26	2
Mike Trusson‡	5 10	12 04	26 5 59	Northolt	Apprentice	Plymouth Arg	73	15
						Stoke C (loan)	—	—
						Sheffield U	126	31
						Rotherham U	124	19
						Brighton & HA	37	2
						Gillingham	74	7
Forwards								
Andrew Arnott	6 1	12 06	18 10 73	Chatham	Trainee	Gillingham	19	2
Peter Beadle	6 0	11 12	13 5 72	London	Trainee	Gillingham	67	14
Paul Burke‡	5 6	10 00	8 8 72	Camberwell	Trainee	Gillingham	—	—
David Crown	5 10	11 04	16 2 58	Enfield	Walthamstow	Brentford	46	8
						Portsmouth	28	2
						Exeter C (loan)	7	3
						Reading	88	15
						Cambridge U	106	45
						Southend U	113	61
						Gillingham	66	33

GILLINGHAM

Foundation: The success of the pioneering Royal Engineers of Chatham excited the interest of the residents of the Medway Towns and led to the formation of many clubs including Excelsior. After winning the Kent Junior Cup and the Chatham District League in 1893, Excelsior decided to go for bigger things and it was at a meeting in the Napier Arms, Brompton, in 1893 that New Brompton FC came into being as a professional concern, securing the use of a ground in Priestfield Road.

First Football League game: 28 August, 1920, Division 3, v Southampton (h) D 1-1 – Branfield; Robertson, Sissons; Battiste, Baxter, Wigmore; Holt, Hall, Gilbey (1), Roe, Gore.

Did you know: Irishman Damien Richardson scored his first goal for the Gills against Mansfield Town on 11 November 1972 and reached his century of League and Cup goals against the same opponents on 8 March 1980.

Managers (and Secretary-managers)
W. Ironside Groombridge 1896–1906* (previously financial secretary), Steve Smith 1906–08, W. I. Groombridge 1908–19*, George Collins 1919–20, John McMillan 1920–23, Harry Curtis 1923–26, Albert Hoskins 1926–29, Dick Hendrie 1929–31, Fred Maven 1932–37, Alan Ure 1937–38, Bill Harvey 1938–39, Archie Clark 1939–57, Harry Barratt 1957–62, Freddie Cox 1962–65, Basil Hayward 1966–71, Andy Nelson 1971–74, Len Ashurst 1974–75, Gerry Summers 1975–81, Keith Peacock 1981–87, Paul Taylor 1987–88, Keith Burkinshaw 1988–89, Damien Richardson May 1989–.

Player and Position	Ht	Wt	Birth Date	Birth Place	Source	Clubs	League App	Gls
Steve Lovell	5 9	12 03	16 7 60	Swansea	Apprentice	Crystal Palace	74	3
						Stockport Co (loan)	12	—
						Millwall	146	44
						Swansea C (loan)	2	1
						Gillingham	220	91
Mark O'Connor	5 7	10 02	10 3 63	Rochdale	Apprentice	QPR	3	—
						Exeter C (loan)	38	1
						Bristol R	80	10
						Bournemouth	128	12
						Gillingham	95	7
Lawrence Osborne	5 10	11 07	20 10 67	London	Apprentice	Arsenal	—	—
						Newport Co	15	—
						Redbridge F	—	—
						Maidstone U	54	8
						Gillingham	5	—

Trainees
Agutter, Andrew J; Aston, Wayne D; Cropper, Nicholas M; Ealham, Lee P; Giemza, Stefan; Golden, Paul T; Harrison, Stuart J; Hunt, Kevin; Newman, Terry R; Russell, Steven J; Smale, Justin P; Tekell, Lee D; Trott, Robin F; Watson, Paul J; Wren, Nicholas J.

Associated Schoolboys
Bernini, Scott; Birchley, Warren J; Brooks, James; Carcary, Murray J; Clifford, Kevin D; Connelly, Paul; Corbyn, Richard; Crowley, Robert T; Dean, Sam; Dolan, Paul R; Gardner, Lee D; Ghaemmaghami, Shervin; Kearns, Andrew S; Lander, Daniel M; Massey, Simon; Prior, Jason; Ralph, Matthew; Stevens, Justin G; Williams, Kevin J; Wilson, Paul A. F.

Associated Schoolboys who have accepted the club's offer of a Traineeship/Contract
Christou, Christopher B; Hake, Kevin S; Maxted, Daniel R; Smith, Gary J; Verrall, Damon F.

GRIMSBY TOWN 1991-92 *Back row (left to right):* Peter Jellett (Physiotherapist), Steve Sherwood, Gary Birtles, Murray Jones, Ian Baraclough, Ian Knight, Mark Lever, John Cockerill, Neil Woods, Paul Futcher, Paul Agnew, Paul Reece, Richard O'Kelly (Youth Coach).
Front row: Dave Gilbert, John McDermott, Tony Rees, Kevin Jobling, Shaun Cunnington, Alan Buckley (Manager), Arthur Mann (Reserve Team Manager), Chris Hargreaves, Mark Smith, Jim Dobbin, Tommy Watson, Gary Childs.

Division 1   **GRIMSBY TOWN**

Blundell Park, Cleethorpes, South Humberside DN35 7PY. Telephone Cleethorpes (0472) 697111. Clubcall: 0898 121576. Fax No: 0472 693665

Ground capacity: 17,526.

Record attendance: 31,651 v Wolverhampton W, FA Cup 5th rd, 20 February 1937.

Record receipts: £96,636 v Tottenham H, Rumbelows Cup 3rd rd, 29 October 1991.

Pitch measurements: 111yd × 74yd.

Presidents: T. J. Lindley, T. Wilkinson.

Chairman: P. W. Furneaux.

Vice-chairman: W. H. Carr.

Directors: P. W. Furneaux (Chairman), T. Aspinall, G. W. Duffield, G. Lamming, J. Mager.

Manager: Alan Buckley. *Assistant Manager:* Arthur Mann. *Company Secretary:* I. Fleming. *Commercial Manager:* A. Richardson. *Physio:* Peter Jellett. *Youth team coach:* Richard O'Kelly. *Lottery Manager:* T. Harvey.

Year Formed: 1878. Turned Professional: 1890. Ltd Co.: 1890.

Former Grounds: Clee Park; Abbey Park. *Former Names:* Grimsby Pelham. *Club Nickname:* 'The Mariners'.

Record League Victory: 9-2 v Darwen, Division 2, 15 April 1899 – Bagshaw; Lockie, Nidd; Griffiths, Bell (1), Nelmes; Jenkinson (3), Richards (1), Cockshutt (3), Robinson, Chadburn (1).

Record Cup Victory: 8-0 v Darlington, FA Cup, 2nd rd, 21 November 1885 – G. Atkinson; J. H. Taylor, H. Taylor; Hall, Kimpson, Hopewell; H. Atkinson (1), Garnham, Seal (3), Sharman, Monument (4).

Record Defeat: 1-9 v Arsenal, Division 1, 28 January 1931.

Most League Points (2 for a win): 68, Division 3 (N), 1955–56.

Most League points (3 for a win): 83, Division 3, 1990–91.

Most League Goals: 103, Division 2, 1933–34.

Highest League Scorer in Season: Pat Glover, 42, Division 2, 1933–34.

Most League Goals in Total Aggregate: Pat Glover, 182, 1930–39.

Most Capped Player: Pat Glover, 7, Wales.

Most League Appearances: Keith Jobling, 448, 1953–69.

Record Transfer Fee Received: £500,000 from QPR for Andy Tillson, December 1990.

Record Transfer Fee Paid: £110,000 to Watford for Jimmy Gilligan, July 1985.

Football League Record: 1892 Original Member Division 2; 1901–03 Division 1; 1903 Division 2; 1910 Failed re-election; 1911 re-elected Division 2; 1920–21 Division 3; 1921–26 Division 3 (N); 1926–29 Division 2; 1929–32 Division 1; 1932–34 Division 2; 1934–48 Division 1; 1948–51 Division 2; 1951–56 Division 3 (N); 1956–59 Division 2; 1959–62 Division 3; 1962–64 Division 2; 1964–68 Division 3; 1968–72 Division 4; 1972–77 Division 3; 1977–79 Division 4; 1979–80 Division 3; 1980–87 Division 2; 1987–88 Division 3; 1988–90 Division 4; 1990–91 Division 3; 1991–92 Division 2; 1992– Division 1.

Honours: Football League: Division 1 best season: 5th, 1934–35; Division 2 – Champions 1900–01, 1933–34; Runners-up 1928–29; Division 3 (N) – Champions 1925–26, 1955–56; Runners-up 1951–52; Division 3 – Champions 1979–80; Runners-up 1961–62; Division 4 – Champions 1971–72; Runners-up 1978–79; 1989–90. *FA Cup:* Semi-finals, 1936, 1939. *Football League Cup:* best season: 5th rd, 1979–80, 1984–85. *League Group Cup:* Winners 1981–82.

Colours: Black and white vertical striped shirts, black shorts with red triangular panel on side, white stockings with red band on turnover. **Change colours:** All yellow.

GRIMSBY TOWN 1991–92 LEAGUE RECORD

Match No.	Date		Venue	Opponents		Result	H/T Score	Lg. Pos.	Goalscorers	Attendance
1	Aug	17	H	Cambridge U	L	3-4	1-1	—	Watson, Rees 2	7657
2		24	A	Oxford U	W	2-1	2-1	13	Cockerill, McDermott	4511
3		31	H	Tranmere R	D	2-2	0-1	14	Woods 2	7018
4	Sep	4	A	Leicester C	L	0-2	0-1	—		16,242
5		7	A	Bristol R	W	3-2	1-0	16	Jobling, Jones, Gilbert	4641
6		14	H	Plymouth Arg	W	2-1	1-0	11	Jobling, Jones	5432
7		17	H	Portsmouth	D	1-1	1-0	—	Woods	5348
8		21	A	Sunderland	W	2-1	1-0	8	Dobbin, Cunnington	16,535
9		28	H	Ipswich T	L	1-2	1-1	11	Gilbert	6621
10	Oct	5	A	Watford	L	0-2	0-2	15		6930
11		12	H	Port Vale	L	1-2	1-1	18	Childs	8218
12		19	H	Middlesbrough	W	1-0	0-0	13	Woods	10,265
13		26	A	Blackburn R	L	1-2	1-1	13	Childs	11,096
14	Nov	2	H	Charlton Ath	W	1-0	1-0	12	Childs	4743
15		6	A	Brighton & HA	L	0-3	0-3	—		4420
16		9	A	Newcastle U	L	0-2	0-2	16		16,959
17		23	H	Millwall	D	1-1	0-0	18	Cunnington	5701
18		26	A	Wolverhampton W	L	1-2	0-1	—	Dobbin	9378
19		30	A	Swindon T	D	1-1	1-1	22	Dobbin	8397
20	Dec	7	H	Bristol C	W	3-1	1-1	16	Woods, Jones, Smith	4866
21		14	A	Barnsley	L	1-4	0-2	19	Smith	6856
22		26	A	Derby Co	D	0-0	0-0	20		16,392
23		28	A	Tranmere R	D	1-1	0-1	20	Ford	7900
24	Jan	1	H	Wolverhampton W	L	0-2	0-1	22		9158
25		11	H	Oxford U	W	1-0	1-0	20	Rees	5117
26		18	A	Cambridge U	W	1-0	1-0	16	Dobbin	6092
27	Feb	8	H	Blackburn R	L	2-3	1-3	19	Mendonca, Cunnington	10,014
28		15	A	Millwall	D	1-1	1-1	18	Rees	6807
29		18	H	Southend U	W	3-2	1-0	—	Smith, Cunnington, Dobbin	5337
30		22	H	Swindon T	D	0-0	0-0	16		6817
31		29	A	Bristol C	D	1-1	0-1	17	Woods	8992
32	Mar	3	A	Charlton Ath	W	3-1	3-0	—	Smith, Barness (og), Rees	3658
33		7	H	Barnsley	L	0-1	0-1	17		6913
34		10	H	Brighton & HA	L	0-1	0-0	—		4583
35		17	H	Leicester C	L	0-1	0-0	—		6377
36		21	H	Newcastle U	D	1-1	1-1	18	Cunnington	11,613
37		28	A	Southend U	L	1-3	1-2	19	Woods	4591
38		31	A	Plymouth Arg	W	2-1	1-0	—	Mendonca, Woods	6274
39	Apr	4	H	Bristol R	L	0-1	0-1	18		4859
40		7	H	Derby Co	L	0-1	0-1	—		7040
41		11	A	Portsmouth	L	0-2	0-1	18		10,576
42		18	H	Sunderland	W	2-0	0-0	18	Dobbin, Mendonca	8864
43		21	A	Ipswich T	D	0-0	0-0	—		22,393
44		25	H	Watford	L	0-1	0-1	19		6483
45		28	A	Middlesbrough	L	0-2	0-2	—		18,570
46	May	2	A	Port Vale	W	1-0	1-0	19	Watson	8678

Final League Position: 19

GOALSCORERS

League (47): Woods 8, Dobbin 6, Cunnington 5, Rees 5, Smith 4, Childs 3, Jones 3, Mendonca 3, Gilbert 2, Jobling 2, Watson 2, Cockerill 1, Ford 1, McDermott 1, own goals 1.
Rumbelows Cup (5): Birtles 1, Dobbin 1, Gilbert 1 (1 pen), Jones 1, Rees 1.
FA Cup (1): Cunnington 1.

Sherwood	McDermott	Jobling	Futcher	Lever	Dobbin	Watson	Gilbert	Rees	Smith	Woods	Jones	Agnew	Cockerill	Birtles	North	Childs	Cunnington	Hargreaves	Reece	Ford	Rodger	Mendonca	Knight	Match No.
1	2	3	4	5	6†	7	8	9	10*	11	12	14												1
1	2	3	4	5	6	7	8		14	11†	9*	10	12											2
1	2	3	4	5	6	7†	8		14	11	9*	10†	12											3
1	2	3	4	5	6	7	8		14	11	9*	10†	12											4
1	2	3	4	5	6	7†	8		14	11	9*	10	12											5
1	2	3	4	5	6	7†	8		14	11*	9	10		12										6
1	2	3	4	5	6		8		12	11	9	10				7*								7
1	2		4	5			8	9	10	11		3		12		7*	6							8
1	2		4*	5			8		10	11	9†	3	14	12		7	6							9
1	2		4	5			8	9	10†	11	12	3	14			7*	6							10
1	2*		4	5			8	9	10†	11	12	3	14			7	6							11
1	2	3	4	5			8	9	10	11						7	6							12
1	2	3	4	5			8	9	10†	11	12		14			7*	6							13
1	2		4	5	14		8*	9	12	11	10†	3				7	6							14
1	2		4	5			8*	9	10	11	12	3				7	6							15
1	2*		4	5			8	9	10	11	12	3				7	6							16
		3	4	5			8	9	10	11*	12					7	6		1	2				17
		3	4	5			8	9	10	11	12					7	6*		1	2				18
		3	4	5	6		8*	9	10	11	12					7			1	2				19
		3	4	5	6		8	9	10*	11	12					7			1	2				20
		3	4†	5			8	9	10	11	12	14				7*	6		1	2				21
	2	3	4	5			8	9	10	11							6		1	7				22
	2	3	4	5	6		8	9	10	11	12								1*	7				23
1	2	3	4†	5	6		8	9	10*	11	12		14							7				24
	2	3		5	6		8	9*			12					7			1	11	4	10		25
	2	3		5	6		8	9			12					7			1	11	4	10*		26
	2†	3		5			8	9		11	12					7*	6		1	14	4	10		27
	2	3		5			8*	9	10	11	12					7	6		1	14	4			28
	2	3		5			8*	9	10	11	12					7†	6		1	14	4			29
	2	3		5			8	9	10*	11	12					7	6		1		4			30
	2	3		5			8	9	10	11†	12	14				7*	6		1				4	31
	2	3		5			8	9	10	11*	12					7	6		1				4	32
	2	3		5*			8	9	10	11	12					7	6		1				4	33
	2	3		5			8	9	10	11	12					7*	6		1	14			4†	34
	2	3		5†			8	9*	10	11	12					7	6		1	14	4			35
	2	3	4	5			8*	9		11	12						6		1	7		10		36
1	2	3	4*	5			8	9†		11	12	14					6			7		10		37
1	2	3		5			8	9		11							6			7	4	10		38
1	2	3†	14	5			8	9*		11	12						6			7	4	10		39
1	2	3		5			8†	9	12	11							6	14		7*	4	10		40
	2	3		5			8	9*	12	11							6	14	1	7	4	10†		41
	2	3		5			8	9		11	12					7*	6		1		4	10		42
	2	3		5		7	8	9		11							6		1		4	10		43
	2	3		5		7	8*	9		11†	12						6	14	1		4	10		44
	2	3		5		7	8	9*		11	12						6		1		4	10		45
	2	3		5		7	8	9*		11	12						6		1		4	10		46
21	39	35	29	35	32	13	41	22	28	30	14	20	8	3	—	29	33	2	25	17	16	10	4	
		+1s		+1s		+4s		+1s	+12s	+7s	+14s	+4s	+2s	+5s	+1s		+8s			+5s				

Rumbelows Cup	First Round	Rotherham U (a)	3-1
		(h)	1-0
	Second Round	Aston Villa (h)	0-0
		(a)	1-1
	Third Round	Tottenham H (h)	0-3
FA Cup	First Round	Blackpool (a)	1-2

GRIMSBY TOWN

Player and Position	Ht	Wt	Birth Date	Birth Place	Source	Clubs	League App	League Gls
Goalkeepers								
Paul Reece	5 11	12 07	16 7 68	Nottingham	Kettering	Grimsby T	54	—
Steve Sherwood	6 4	14 07	10 12 53	Selby	Apprentice	Chelsea	16	—
						Brighton & HA (loan)	—	—
						Millwall (loan)	1	—
						Brentford (loan)	62	—
						Watford	211	1
						Grimsby T	176	—
Defenders								
Paul Agnew	5 9	10 04	15 8 65	Lisburn	Cliftonville	Grimsby T	185	3
Paul Futcher	6 0	12 03	25 9 56	Chester	Apprentice	Chester	20	—
						Luton T	131	1
						Manchester C	37	—
						Oldham Ath	98	1
						Derby Co	35	—
						Barnsley	230	—
						Halifax T	15	—
						Grimsby T	51	—
Ian Knight*	6 2	12 04	26 10 66	Hartlepool	Apprentice	Barnsley	—	—
						Sheffield W	21	—
						Scunthorpe U (loan)	2	—
						Grimsby T	21	2
Mark Lever	6 3	12 05	29 3 70	Beverley	Trainee	Grimsby T	152	6
John McDermott	5 7	10 07	3 2 69	Middlesbrough		Grimsby T	200	2
Graham Rodger	6 2	11 11	1 4 67	Glasgow	Apprentice	Wolverhampton W	1	—
						Coventry C	36	2
						Luton T	28	2
						Grimsby T	16	—
Midfield								
Gary Childs	5 7	10 08	19 4 64	Birmingham	Apprentice	WBA	3	—
						Walsall	131	17
						Birmingham C	55	2
						Grimsby T	98	12
John Cockerill	6 0	12 07	12 7 61	Cleethorpes	Stafford R	Grimsby T	107	19
Gary Croft§			17 2 74	Burton-on-Trent	Trainee	Grimsby T	1	—
Shaun Cunnington	5 8	10 04	4 1 66	Bourne	Amateur	Wrexham	199	12
						Grimsby T	182	13
Jim Dobbin	5 10	10 06	17 9 63	Dunfermline	Whitburn BC	Celtic	2	—
						Motherwell (loan)	2	—
						Doncaster R	64	13
						Barnsley	129	12
						Grimsby T	32	6
Kevin Jobling	5 9	10 13	1 1 68	Sunderland	Apprentice	Leicester C	9	—
						Grimsby T	161	8
Tommy Watson	5 8	10 10	29 9 69	Liverpool	Trainee	Grimsby T	114	16
Forwards								
Ian Baraclough	6 1	11 02	4 12 70	Leicester	Trainee	Leicester C	—	—
						Wigan Ath (loan)	9	2
						Grimsby T (loan)	4	—
						Grimsby T	—	—
Garry Birtles*	6 0	12 00	27 7 56	Nottingham	Long Eaton U	Nottingham F	87	32
						Manchester U	58	11
						Nottingham F	125	38
						Notts Co	63	9
						Grimsby T	69	9
Tony Ford	5 9	12 08	14 5 59	Grimsby	Apprentice	Grimsby T	354	54
						Sunderland (loan)	9	1
						Stoke C	112	13
						WBA	114	14
						Grimsby T	22	1

GRIMSBY TOWN

Foundation: Grimsby Pelham FC as they were first known, came into being at a meeting held at the Wellington Arms in September 1878. Pelham is the family name of big landowners in the area, the Earls of Yarborough. The receipts for their first game amounted to 6s. 9d. (approx. 39p). After a year, the club name was changed to Grimsby Town.

First Football League game: 3 September, 1892, Division 2, v Northwich Victoria (h) W 2-1 – Whitehouse; Lundie, T. Frith; C. Frith, Walker, Murrell; Higgins, Henderson, Brayshaw, Riddoch (2), Ackroyd.

Did you know: Grimsby beat Sunderland 4-0 and 6-0 in successive seasons at Blundell Park (1935–36 and 1936–37) with Pat Glover scoring three and five goals respectively. Indeed Glover scored in all four games against Sunderland in these two seasons totalling ten goals.

Managers (and Secretary-managers)
H. N. Hickson 1902–20*, Haydn Price 1920, George Fraser 1921–24, Wilf Gillow 1924–32, Frank Womack 1932–36, Charles Spencer 1937–51, Bill Shankly 1951–53, Billy Walsh 1954–55, Allenby Chilton 1955–59, Tim Ward 1960–62, Tom Johnston 1962–64, Jimmy McGuigan 1964–67, Don McEvoy 1967–68, Bill Harvey 1968–69, Bobby Kennedy 1969–71, Lawrie McMenemy 1971–73, Ron Ashman 1973–75, Tom Casey 1975–76, Johnny Newman 1976–79, George Kerr 1979–82, David Booth 1982–85, Mike Lyons 1985–87, Bobby Roberts 1987–88, Alan Buckley June 1988–.

David Gilbert	5 4	10 04	22	6 63	Lincoln	Apprentice	Lincoln C	30	1
							Boston U	—	—
							Scunthorpe U	1	—
							Northampton T	120	21
							Grimsby T	141	27
Chris Hargreaves	5 10	10 13	12	5 72	Cleethorpes	Trainee	Grimsby T	47	5
Murray Jones	6 4	14 00	7	10 64	Bexley	Carshalton	Crystal Palace	—	—
							Bristol C	—	—
							Doncaster R (loan)	5	—
							Exeter C	20	3
							Grimsby T	28	3
Marc North‡	5 10	11 00	25	9 66	Ware	Apprentice	Luton T	18	3
							Lincoln C (loan)	4	—
							Scunthorpe U (loan)	5	2
							Birmingham C (loan)	5	1
							Grimsby T	67	17
							Leicester C	71	9
							Grimsby T	1	—
Tony Rees	5 9	11 13	1	8 64	Merthyr Tydfil	Apprentice	Aston Villa	—	—
							Birmingham C	95	12
							Peterborough U (loan)	5	2
							Shrewsbury T (loan)	2	—
							Barnsley	31	3
							Grimsby T	94	28
Mark Smith	5 11	11 05	19	12 61	Sheffield	Gainsborough Tr	Scunthorpe U	1	—
							Kettering	—	—
							Rochdale	27	7
							Huddersfield T	96	11
							Grimsby T	51	4
Neil Woods	6 1	12 12	30	7 66	York	Apprentice	Doncaster R	65	16
							Rangers	3	—
							Ipswich T	27	5
							Bradford C	14	2
							Grimsby T	81	20

Trainees
Burns, Stuart I; Connelly, Martin J; Croft, Gary; Dunlop, Simon A; Gowshall, Joby; Handyside, Peter D; Harriott, Kevin A; Hunter, Christopher H; Maddison, Craig; Madigan, Terrence G; Talbot, Kyle.

Associated Schoolboys
Allen, Dean; Bacon, Daniel J; Broni, Kevin; Cox, Jonathan D; Hamnett, John C; Mundell, Andrew A; Petchey, Stuart; Rushby, Mathew S; Wilkinson, David A.

Associated Schoolboys who have accepted the club's offer of a Traineeship/Contract
Barratt, Mark A; Lambert, Darren K; Martin, Paul A; Neil, James D.

244

HALIFAX TOWN 1991-92 *Back row (left to right):* Paul Donnelly, Mark Ellis, Tony Gregory, Neil Griffiths, Ian Hutchinson, Jamie Paterson.
Centre row: Steve Norris, Tommy Graham, Nick Richardson, Jon Gould, Nick Brown, Steve Richards, Chris Lucketti, Billy Barr.
Front row: Kevin Megson, Greg Abbott, Alan Kamara, Brian Taylor (Assistant Manager), Jim McCalliog (Manager), Ian Juryeff, Graham Cooper, Dave Evans.

Division 3   **HALIFAX TOWN**

Shay Ground, Halifax HX1 2YS. Offices: 7 Clare Road, Halifax HX1 2HX. Telephone Halifax (0422) 353423/366593. Ground: 0422 361582 (Match day only). Fax No: (0422) 349487

Ground capacity: 8049.

Record attendance: 36,885 v Tottenham H, FA Cup 5th rd, 15 February 1953.

Record receipts: £27,000 v Manchester U, League Cup, 2nd rd, 1st leg, 26 September 1990.

Pitch measurements: 110yd × 70yd.

President: John S. Crowther.

Vice-president: F. Hinchliffe.

Chairman: S. J. Brown.

Vice-chairman: D. C. Greenwood.

Director: B. J. Boulton.

Manager: John McGrath.

Assistant Manager: Oshor Williams.

Physio: Mike Rathbone.

General Manager/Secretary: Bev. Fielding.

Commercial Manager.

Lottery Manager: R. Barr.

Year Formed: 1911. Turned Professional: 1911. Ltd Co.: 1911.

Former Grounds: Sandhall and Exley.

Club Nickname: 'The Shaymen'.

Record League Victory: 6-0 v Bradford PA, Division 3 (N), 3 December 1955 – Johnson; Griffiths, Ferguson; Watson, Harris, Bell; Hampson (2), Baker (3), Watkinson (1), Capel, Lonsdale. 6-0 v Doncaster R, Division 4, 2 November 1976 – Gennoe; Trainer, Loska (Bradley), McGill, Dunleavy (1), Phelan, Hoy (2), Carroll (1), Bullock (1), Lawson (1), Johnston.

Record Cup Victory: 7-0 v Bishop Auckland, FA Cup 2nd rd (replay), 10 January 1967 – White; Russell, Bodell; Smith, Holt, Jeff Lee; Taylor (2), Hutchison (2), Parks (2), Atkins (1), McCarthy.

Record Defeat: 0-13 v Stockport Co, Division 3 (N), 6 January, 1934.

Most League Points (2 for a win): 57, Division 4, 1968–69.

Most League points (3 for a win): 60, Division 4, 1982–83.

Most League Goals: 83, Division 3 (N), 1957–58.

Highest League Scorer in Season: Albert Valentine. 34, Division 3 (N), 1934–35.

Most League Goals in Total Aggregate: Ernest Dixon, 129, 1922–30.

Most Capped Player: None.

Most League Appearances: John Pickering, 367, 1965–74.

Record Transfer Fee Received: £250,000 from Watford for Wayne Allison, July 1989.

Record Transfer Fee Paid: £50,000 to Hereford U for Ian Juryeff, September 1990.

Football League Record: 1921 Original Member of Division 3 (N); 1958–63 Division 3; 1963–69 Division 4; 1969–76 Division 3; 1976–92 Division 4; 1992– Division 3.

Honours: Football League: Division 3 best season: 3rd, 1970–71; Division 3 (N) – Runners-up 1934–35; Division 4 – Runners-up 1968–69. *FA Cup:* best season; 5th rd, 1932–33, 1952–53. *Football League Cup:* best season: 4th rd, 1964.

Colours: Royal blue shirts, white shorts, royal blue stockings. **Change colours:** All red.

246

HALIFAX TOWN 1991-92 LEAGUE RECORD

Match No.	Date		Venue	Opponents		Result	H/T Score	Lg. Pos.	Goalscorers	Attendance
1	Aug	17	H	Northampton T	L	0-1	0-0	—		1834
2		24	A	Maidstone U	W	1-0	0-0	10	Juryeff	1216
3		30	H	York C	D	0-0	0-0	—		2167
4	Sep	7	A	Walsall	L	0-3	0-1	18		2981
5		13	H	Rotherham U	L	0-4	0-0	—		2653
6		17	H	Cardiff C	D	1-1	0-1	—	Bradley	1041
7		27	H	Mansfield T	L	1-3	0-1	—	Norris	2026
8	Oct	5	A	Lincoln C	D	0-0	0-0	18		2092
9		12	H	Gillingham	L	0-3	0-1	20		1435
10		19	H	Chesterfield	W	2-0	0-0	17	Norris 2 (1 pen)	1506
11		26	A	Rochdale	L	0-1	0-0	16		2323
12	Nov	2	H	Burnley	L	0-2	0-0	19		4491
13		6	A	Hereford U	W	2-0	1-0	—	Juryeff, Norris	2207
14		9	A	Barnet	L	0-3	0-1	19		4837
15		22	H	Scarborough	W	1-0	1-0	—	Richardson	1395
16		30	A	Blackpool	L	0-3	0-3	18		3118
17	Dec	13	H	Wrexham	W	4-3	1-1	—	Patterson, Richardson 2, Juryeff	881
18		21	H	Maidstone U	D	1-1	0-1	15	Cooper	1040
19		26	A	Northampton T	L	0-4	0-4	16		3147
20		28	A	York C	D	1-1	0-0	16	Wilson	2396
21	Jan	11	A	Doncaster R	W	2-0	0-0	16	Norris, Hutchinson	2067
22		18	H	Scunthorpe U	L	1-4	0-1	17	Patterson	1232
23		25	A	Carlisle U	D	1-1	1-0	16	Richardson	2091
24	Feb	8	H	Rochdale	D	1-1	1-0	16	Cooper	2213
25		12	H	Blackpool	L	1-2	0-2	—	Barr (pen)	2158
26		15	A	Wrexham	L	0-2	0-0	19		2076
27		22	H	Doncaster R	D	0-0	0-0	19		1285
28		28	A	Crewe Alex	L	2-3	1-2	—	Wilson, Richardson	3514
29	Mar	3	A	Scunthorpe U	L	0-1	0-0	—		2448
30		6	H	Carlisle U	W	3-2	0-1	—	Bradley, Cooper, Wilson	1015
31		11	H	Hereford U	L	0-2	0-0	—		918
32		14	A	Burnley	L	0-1	0-0	20		10,903
33		21	H	Barnet	W	3-1	0-0	20	Richardson 2, Wilson (pen)	1756
34		28	A	Scarborough	L	0-3	0-3	20		1363
35		31	A	Rotherham U	L	0-1	0-0	—		4517
36	Apr	3	H	Walsall	W	1-0	1-0	—	Wilson	1006
37		7	A	Chesterfield	L	0-4	0-0	—		1802
38		11	A	Cardiff C	L	0-4	0-1	20		5261
39		14	H	Crewe Alex	W	2-1	0-1	—	Barr 2	1022
40		21	A	Mansfield T	L	2-3	0-1	—	Juryeff, Abbott	3936
41		25	H	Lincoln C	L	1-4	1-1	20	Richardson	1296
42	May	2	A	Gillingham	L	0-2	0-0	20		2413

Final League Position: 20

GOALSCORERS

League (34): Richardson 8, Norris 5 (1 pen), Wilson 5 (1 pen), Juryeff 4, Barr 3 (1 pen), Cooper 3, Bradley 2, Patterson 2, Abbott 1, Hutchinson 1.
Rumbelows Cup (6): Barr 2, Cooper 1, Juryeff 1, Norris 1 (1 pen), Richardson 1.
FA Cup (2): Hildersley 1, Richardson 1.

Gould	Evans	Kamara	Abbott	Richards	Graham	Megson	Cooper	Juryeff	Richardson	Patterson	Barr	Norris	Bradley	Matthews	Lucketti	Bracey	Ellis	Lewis	Hildersley	Wilson	Hutchinson	Gregory	Hardy	Donovan	Brown	German	Longley	Griffiths	Match No.
1	2	3	4	5	6	7	8	9	10	11																			1
1	2	3	4	5	6		11	9	10		7	8																	2
1	2	3	4	5	6		11	9	10		7	8																	3
1	2	3	4	5	12	14	11*	9	10		7†	8	6																4
1	2	3	4*	5	12	14	11	9	10	7†		8	6																5
1		3	4	5				9	10	11	7	2	8	6															6
1		3	12	5	4*				10	11	7†	2	8	6	9	14													7
1	4	3	11*	5					10		7	2	8	6	9	12													8
1	4†	3	11	5					10*	14	7	2	8	6	9	12													9
	4	3		5	10			9	7			2	8		6	1		11											10
	4	3	12†	5	10			9	7*			2	8		14	1		11	6										11
	4	3		5	7			9	10			2	8		6	1		11											12
	4	3*		5	7			9	10			2	8		12	1		11	6										13
	4			5	7*			9	10			2	8		3	1		11	6	12									14
14		7		5				9	10			2	8	3†	4	1		11*	6	12									15
14		7†		5				9	10	12		2	8*	3	4	1			6	11									16
		7		5				9	10	14	11*	2	8†	3	4	1			12	6									17
		7					8	9	10			2	5		4	1		6	11	3									18
11	12	7	14				8	9	10			2*	5†		4	1		6		3									19
11*		7					8	9	10			2	5		4	1		6	12	3									20
		7					8	9	10			2	5		4	1		6	11	3									21
14		7					8	9	10	12		2†	5*		4	1		6	11	3									22
	6	7		5			8	9	10		11*	2			4	1				3		12							23
	6	7		5			8	9	10			2			4	1				3	11*	12							24
	6	7†	14	5			8	9	10			2			4	1				3	11*	12							25
	6	7*		5			8†	9	10			2			4	1			14	3		12	11						26
	6			5			8	9	10			2			4				11	3				7	1				27
	6			5			8	9*	10			2†	14		4	1			11	3		12	7						28
	6	12		5			8	9*	10			2			4	1			11	3			7						29
	6			5			8	9	10			2			4	1			11	3			7						30
	6			5			8	9	10		4	2				1			11	3			7						31
	6	10				12	8	9				2	5		4	1			11	3		7*							32
12	6	10					8	9				2*	5		4	1			11	3		7							33
7	6	10					8	9				2	5		4	1			11	3									34
7	6	10					8	9				2	5		4	1			11	3									35
12	6	10	2				8	9	11				5		4	1				3		7*							36
7	6	10	2				8	9	11				5		4	1				3									37
7	6	10	2				8	9	11				5		4	1				3									38
7	6	10	2				8	12					5		4	1			11	3		9*							39
	6	10	2				8	9			7*		5		4	1			11	3							12		40
5	6	10	2				8	9							4	1			11	3						7*		12	41
5	6	10	2				8	9	11*						4	1				3						7	12		42
9	26	34	24	24	12	8	19	37	41	13	34	17	25	3	31	32	6	11	14	23	4	5	—	6	1	2	1	—	
+5s	+1s	+4s	+1s	+2s	+2s	+3s			+2s	+1s			+1s		+5s	+1s				+4s		+1s	+4s			+1s	+2s		

Rumbelows Cup First Round Tranmere R (h) 3-4
                                                                (a) 3-4
FA Cup First Round Witton (a) 1-1
                                                                (h) 1-2

HALIFAX TOWN

Player and Position	Ht	Wt	Birth Date	Birth Place	Source	Clubs	League App	League Gls
Goalkeepers								
Lee Bracey	6 1	12 08	11 9 68	Ashford	Trainee	West Ham U	—	—
						Swansea C	99	—
						Halifax T	32	—
Nicky Brown			25 1 73	Northampton	Trainee	Norwich C	—	—
						Halifax T	1	—
Defenders								
Billy Barr	5 11	11 07	21 1 69	Halifax	Trainee	Halifax T	168	10
Russell Bradley	6 0	12 05	28 3 66	Birmingham		Nottingham F	—	—
						Hereford U (loan)	12	1
						Hereford U	77	3
						Halifax T	26	2
Brian Butler‡	5 6	10 08	4 7 66	Salford	Apprentice	Blackpool	74	5
						Stockport Co	32	2
						Halifax T	56	4
David Evans	5 11	12 05	20 5 58	West Bromwich	Apprentice	Aston Villa	2	—
						Halifax T	218	9
						Bradford C	223	3
						Halifax T	73	1
Ian Hutchinson*	5 8	11 05	7 11 72	Teeside	Trainee	Halifax T	8	1
Alan Kamara	5 9	10 12	15 7 58	Sheffield	Kiveton Park	York C	10	—
						Darlington	134	1
						Burton Alb	—	—
						Scarborough	159	2
						Halifax T	35	—
Chris Lucketti			28 9 71	Littleborough	Trainee	Rochdale	1	—
						Stockport Co	—	—
						Halifax T	36	—
Steve Richards‡	6 0	12 00	24 10 61	Dundee	Apprentice	Hull C	58	2
						Gainsborough T	—	—
						York C	7	—
						Lincoln C	21	—
						Cambridge U	4	2
						Scarborough	164	13
						Halifax T	25	—
Paul Wilson	5 10	10 12	2 8 68	Bradford	Trainee	Huddersfield T	15	—
						Norwich C	—	—
						Northampton T	140	6
						Halifax T	23	5
Midfield								
Greg Abbott	5 9	10 07	14 12 63	Coventry	Apprentice	Coventry C	—	—
						Bradford C	281	38
						Halifax T	28	1
Graham Ccoper*	5 10	10 09	18 11 65	Huddersfield	Local	Huddersfield T	74	13
						Wrexham	63	16
						York C (loan)	2	—
						Halifax T	39	4
Paul Donnelly‡	5 8	10 00	23 12 71	Liverpool	Trainee	Halifax T	13	—
David German§			16 10 73	Sheffield	Sheffield W	Halifax T	4	—
Tommy Graham‡	5 9	11 09	31 3 58	Glasgow	Arthurlie	Aston Villa	—	—
						Barnsley	38	13
						Halifax T	71	17
						Doncaster R	11	2
						Scunthorpe U	109	21
						Scarborough	111	11
						Halifax T	58	4
Tony Gregory*	5 8	10 10	21 3 68	Doncaster	Apprentice	Sheffield W	18	1
						Halifax T	17	1

HALIFAX TOWN

Foundation: The idea of a soccer club in a Rugby League stronghold was first mooted by a Mr. A. E. Muir who soon interested Joe McClelland (who became secretary-manager of the new club) and Dr. A. H. Muir their first chairman. Following correspondence in *The Halifax Evening Courier* the club was formed at a meeting at the Saddle Hotel in May 1911.

First Football League game: 27 August, 1921, Division 3 (N), v Darlington (a) L 0-2 – Haldane; Hawley, Mackrill; Hall, Wellock, Challinor; Pinkey, Hetherington, Woods, Dent, Phipps.

Did you know: Halifax Town's most prolific goalscorer, Yorkshireman Ernest Dixon actually topped their League score-sheet in no less than seven consecutive seasons 1922–29. He joined Huddersfield Town in September 1929 but moved to Nelson the following month.

Managers (and Secretary-managers)
A. M. Ricketts 1911–12*, Joe McClelland 1912–30, Alec Raisbeck 1930–36, Jimmy Thomson 1936–47, Jack Breedon 1947–50, William Wootton 1951–52, Gerald Henry 1952–54, Willie Watson 1954–56, Billy Burnikell 1956, Harry Hooper 1957–62, Willie Watson 1964–66, Vic Metcalfe 1966–67, Alan Ball Snr 1967–70, George Kirby 1970–71, Ray Henderson 1971–72, George Mulhall 1972–74, Johnny Quinn 1974–76, Alan Ball Snr 1976–77, Jimmy Lawson 1977–78, George Kirby 1978–81, Mick Bullock 1981–84, Mick Jones 1984–86, Bill Ayre 1986–90, Jim McCalliog 1990–91, John McGrath October 1991–.

Player and Position	Ht	Wt	Date	Birth Place	Source	Clubs	League App	Gls
Neil Griffiths	6 0	12 03	4 9 72	Halifax	Trainee	Halifax T	3	—
Scott Longley§			16 7 73	Wakefield	Trainee	Halifax T	1	—
Jamie Patterson	5 5	9 07	26 4 73	Dumfries	Trainee	Halifax T	21	3
Nick Richardson	6 0	12 07	11 4 67	Halifax	Local	Halifax T	101	17
Forwards								
Mark Ellis‡	5 9	10 09	6 1 62	Bradford	Trinity Ath	Bradford C	218	30
						Halifax T	37	4
Ron Hildersley	5 4	9 02	6 4 65	Fife	Apprentice	Manchester C	1	—
						Chester (loan)	9	—
						Chester C	9	—
						Rochdale	16	—
						Preston NE	58	3
						Cambridge U (loan)	9	3
						Blackburn R	30	4
						Wigan Ath	4	—
						Halifax T	18	—
Ian Juryeff	5 11	12 00	24 11 62	Gosport	Apprentice	Southampton	2	—
						Mansfield T (loan)	12	5
						Reading (loan)	7	1
						Leyton Orient	111	44
						Ipswich T (loan)	2	—
						Halifax T	17	7
						Hereford U	28	4
						Halifax T	71	13
Kevin Megson	5 11	11 00	1 7 71	Halifax	Trainee	Bradford C	27	—
						Halifax T	15	—

Trainees
Armstrong, Leighton J; Blackwell, Danyel; German, David; Gray, Ryan P; Hook, Steven J; Issacs, Michael D; Longley, Scott E; Lynch, Christopher J; Niblo, Johnathan W; Radio, Leano; Shaw, Peter A; Warnes, Andrew M; Yates, Sean A.

Associated Schoolboys
Billington, Paul A; Brooks, Bryan P; Calland, Matthew W; Curran, James A. D; Hamer, Adam; King, Stephen J; Leatherbarrow, Nathan J; Mucci, Carlo; Pearson, Andrew; Siddle, Paul A; Spencer, James A.

HARTLEPOOL UNITED 1991–92 *Back row (left to right)*: Keith Nobbs, Paul Dalton, Ian McGuckin, Steve Tupling.
Centre row: Eddie Kyle (Youth Team Coach), Andy Davies, John Tinkler, John MacPhail, Martin Hodge, Ian Bennyworth, Nicky Southall, Mark Nesbitt, Gary Henderson (Physiotherapist).
Front row: Ricardo Gabbiadini, Paul Olsson, Brian Honour, David McCreery (Assistant Manager), Paul Baker, Alan Murray (Manager), Rob McKinnon, Mick Smith, Steven Fletcher.

Division 2   **HARTLEPOOL UNITED**

HUFC
1 9 0 8
HARTLEPOOL UNITED
FOOTBALL CLUB LTD
VICTORIA GROUND
HARTLEPOOL
CLEVELAND TS24 8BZ
TEL: 0429-272584
FAX: 0429-863007

The Victoria Ground, Clarence Road, Hartlepool. Telephone Hartlepool (0429) 272584. Fax No: 0429 863007

Ground capacity: 9020.

Record attendance: 17,426 v Manchester U, FA Cup 3rd rd, 5 January 1957.

Record receipts: £42,300 v Tottenham H, Rumbelows Cup, 2nd rd 2nd leg, 9 October 1990.

Pitch measurements: 110yd × 75yd.

President: E. Leadbitter.

Chairman: G. Gibson.

Vice-chairman: A. Bamford.

Directors: D. Dukes, A. Elliott.

Manager: Alan Murray.

Assistant Manager: Dave McCreery.

Assistant secretary: Miss L. Charlton.

Physio: Gary Henderson.

Year Formed: 1908. Turned Professional: 1908. Ltd Co.: 1908.

Former Names: Hartlepools United until 1968; Hartlepool until 1977.

Club Nickname: 'The Pool'.

Record League Victory: 10-1 v Barrow, Division 4, 4 April 1959 – Oakley; Cameron, Waugh; Johnson, Moore, Anderson; Scott (1), Langland (1), Smith (3), Clark (2), Luke (2). (1 og).

Record Cup Victory: 6-0 v North Shields, FA Cup, 1st rd, 30 November 1946 – Heywood; Brown, Gregory; Spelman, Lambert, Jones; Price, Scott (2), Sloan (4), Moses, McMahon.

Record Defeat: 1-10 v Wrexham, Division 4, 3 March 1962.

Most League Points (2 for a win): 60, Division 4, 1967–68.

Most League points (3 for a win): 82, Division 4, 1990–91.

Most League Goals: 90, Division 3 (N), 1956–57.

Highest League Scorer in Season: William Robinson, 28, Division 3 (N), 1927–28.

Most League Goals in Total Aggregate: Ken Johnson, 98, 1949–64.

Most Capped Player: Ambrose Fogarty, 1 (11), Eire.

Most League Appearances: Wattie Moore, 447, 1948–64.

Record Transfer Fee Received: £300,000 from Chelsea for Joe Allon, August 1991.

Record Transfer Fee Paid: £60,000 to Barnsley for Andy Saville, March 1992.

Football League Record: 1921 Original Member of Division 3 (N); 1958–68 Division 4; 1968–69 Division 3; 1969–91 Division 4; 1991–92 Division 3; 1992– Division 2.

Honours: Football League: Division 3 best season: 11th, 1991–92; Division 3 (N) – Runners-up 1956–57. *FA Cup:* best season: 4th rd, 1954–55, 1977–78, 1988–89. *Football League Cup:* best season: 4th rd, 1974–75.

Colours: Sky blue, navy blue and white squared shirts, navy blue shorts, sky blue stockings.
Change colours: All yellow.

HARTLEPOOL UNITED 1991–92 LEAGUE RECORD

Match No.	Date		Venue	Opponents	Result		H/T Score	Lg. Pos.	Goalscorers	Attendance
1	Aug	17	A	Torquay U	L	1-3	0-2	—	Baker	4163
2		24	H	Reading	W	2-0	1-0	10	Baker, Olsson	2858
3		31	A	Bradford C	D	1-1	0-0	10	Rush	5872
4	Sep	3	H	Brentford	W	1-0	0-0	—	Gabbiadini	3660
5		7	H	Leyton Orient	L	2-3	1-1	11	Dalton, Rush	3581
6		14	A	Exeter C	D	1-1	0-0	13	Baker (pen)	2906
7		17	A	Stoke C	L	2-3	0-2	—	Baker, Olsson	9394
8		21	H	Birmingham C	W	1-0	1-0	12	Baker	4643
9		28	A	Bury	D	1-1	0-1	12	Gabbiadini	2600
10	Oct	5	H	Wigan Ath	W	4-3	3-1	11	Honour, Dalton 2, McKinnon	3047
11		12	A	Bournemouth	L	0-2	0-1	14		4817
12		19	H	Hull C	L	2-3	1-2	16	Southall 2	2868
13		26	A	Peterborough U	L	2-3	0-2	18	Bennyworth, Honour	3385
14	Nov	2	A	Darlington	L	0-4	0-3	18		5041
15		5	H	WBA	D	0-0	0-0	—		2810
16		9	H	Fulham	W	2-0	0-0	17	Honour, Morgan (og)	2999
17		23	A	Shrewsbury T	W	4-1	3-0	14	Olsson 2, Dalton, Baker	2368
18		30	H	Huddersfield T	D	0-0	0-0	14		4017
19	Dec	14	A	Preston NE	W	4-1	2-0	14	Baker 2, Dalton, Johnson	5032
20		20	A	Reading	W	1-0	0-0	—	Baker	2535
21		26	H	Bradford C	W	1-0	1-0	7	Baker	5412
22		28	H	Torquay U	D	1-1	1-1	8	Johnson	3812
23	Jan	1	A	Brentford	L	0-1	0-0	9		7103
24		11	H	Chester C	W	1-0	0-0	7	Honour	3088
25		18	A	Bolton W	D	2-2	1-0	7	Olsson, Kelly (og)	6129
26	Feb	1	A	Hull C	W	2-0	1-0	7	Dalton, Baker	3483
27		8	H	Peterborough U	L	0-1	0-0	8		2481
28		11	A	Huddersfield T	L	0-1	0-1	—		5559
29		15	H	Preston NE	W	2-0	0-0	8	Peake, Baker	2140
30		18	H	Stockport Co	L	0-1	0-0	—		2473
31		22	A	Chester C	L	0-2	0-2	10		1072
32		29	A	Swansea C	L	0-1	0-0	11		2669
33	Mar	3	H	Bolton W	L	0-4	0-3	—		2244
34		6	A	Stockport Co	W	1-0	0-0	—	Baker	4473
35		11	A	WBA	W	2-1	1-0	—	Dalton 2 (1 pen)	10,307
36		14	H	Darlington	W	2-0	2-0	9	Smith (og), Dalton	4442
37		20	A	Fulham	L	0-1	0-1	—		4359
38		28	H	Shrewsbury T	W	4-2	2-1	10	Thomas, Dalton, Fletcher, Johnrose (pen)	2515
39		31	H	Exeter C	W	3-1	1-0	—	Dalton 2, Southall	2222
40	Apr	4	A	Leyton Orient	L	0-4	0-1	10		4245
41		11	H	Stoke C	D	1-1	1-1	11	Olsson	4360
42		18	A	Birmingham C	L	1-2	0-0	11	Fletcher	13,698
43		20	H	Bury	D	0-0	0-0	11		2503
44		24	A	Wigan Ath	D	1-1	0-0	—	MacPhail	2002
45		28	A	Swansea C	D	1-1	1-1	—	Dalton	2167
46	May	2	H	Bournemouth	W	1-0	0-0	11	Johnrose	2612

Final League Position: 11

GOALSCORERS

League (57): Baker 13 (1 pen), Dalton 13 (1 pen), Olsson 6, Honour 4, Southall 3, Fletcher 2, Gabbiadini 2, Johnrose 2 (1 pen), Johnson 2, Rush 2, Bennyworth 1, MacPhail 1, McKinnon 1, Peake 1, Thomas 1, own goals 3.
Rumbelows Cup (5): Baker 1, Fletcher 1, Gabbiadini 1, Honour 1, Tinkler 1.
FA Cup (6): Baker 2 (1 pen), Dalton 1, Honour 1, Johnson 1, Tinkler 1.

Hodge	Nesbitt	McKinnon	McCreery	Nobbs	Bennyworth	Rush	Olsson	Baker	Honour	Dalton	MacPhail	Tinkler	Fletcher	Gabbiadini	Tupling	Smith M	Southall	Johnson	Smith A	Cross	Peake	Johnrose	Davies	McGuckin	Saville	Thomas	Jones	Match No.
1	2*	3	4	5	6	7	8	9	10	11	12																	1
1		3	4*	2	6	7	8	9	10	11	5	12																2
1		3	4*	2	6	7	8	9	10	11	5	12																3
1		3		2	6	7	8		10	11	5	4	9*	12														4
1		3		2	6	7	8		10	11	5	4	9*	12														5
1		3		2		7	8	9	10	11	5	4																6
1		3	12	2	6	7†	8	9	10*	11	5	4			14													7
1		3		2	6	7	8	9	10	11	5	4																8
1		3	7*	2	6		8	9	10	11	5	4	12															9
1		3		2	6		8	9	10	11	5	4*	14			7†	12											10
1		3		2			8*	9	10	11	5	4	12		6	7												11
1		3		2			8	9	10	11	5	4			6	7												12
1		3	4	2	6		8	9	10	11	5		12			7*												13
1		3	14	2	6†		8		10	11	5	4	12			7*	9											14
1		3	4*	2			8		10	11	5		7	9	6	12												15
1		3	4*	2			8		10	11	5		7	9	6	12												16
1		3		2			8	9	10	11	5	4			6		12	7*										17
1		3		2†			8	9	10	11	5	4			6	14	12	7*										18
1		3	4				8	9	10	11	5				6		2	7										19
1		3	4*	2			8	9	10	11	5		12		6			7										20
1		3	4	2			8	9	10		5				6		11	7										21
1		3	4*	2			8	9	10	11	5		12		6			7										22
1		3	4	2			8	9	10	11	5		12		6			7*										23
1			4*	2			8	9	10	11	5		12		6				7	3								24
1				2			8	9	10	11*	5	4	12		6				7	3								25
1				2			8	9	10	11	5	4	12		6				7*	3								26
1			4*	2			8	9	10	11	5		12	14	6				7†	3								27
1				2			8	9	10	11	5	4	12		6				7*	3								28
1				2			8	9	10	11	5	4			6					3	7							29
1				2			8	9	10	11	5	4	12		6					3	7*							30
1				2			8	9	10	11	5	4	14	12	6*					3	7†							31
1				2			8	9	10		5	4	12		6					3	7	11*						32
1			12	2			8	9	10		5	4			6					3*	7	11						33
1				2			8	9	10	11	5	4	12	14	6*					3†	7							34
1				2			8		10	11	5	4								3	7	9	6					35
1				2			8		10	11		4								3		9	6	5	7			36
1			6	2			8		10	11		4					7			3		9	12	5*				37
1			6	2			8		10	11		4	12							3		9		5		7*		38
1			6	2*			8		10	11		4	12							3		9		5		7		39
1			6	2			8		10	11		4	12							3		9		5		7*		40
			6	2			8		10	11		4					7*			3		9		5		12	1	41
			6	2			8		10	11		4					7*			3		9		5		12	1	42
			6	2			8		10	11	5	4								3		9				7	1	43
			6	2			8		10	11	5	4	12							3		9				7*	1	44
			6	2			8		10	11	5	4					7			3		9					1	45
			6	2*			8		10	11	5	4					12			3		9				7	1	46
40	1	23	27	41	12	8	46	29	40	43	40	31	14	1	17	7	13	7	4	21	5	15	2	7	1	5	6	
			+3s										+1s	+8s	+4s	+8s	+4s	+1s	+9s	+1s		+1s		+1s		+2s		

Rumbelows Cup

	First Round	Bury (h)	1-0
		(a)	2-2
	Second Round	Crystal Palace (h)	1-1
		(a)	1-6
FA Cup	First Round	Shrewsbury T (h)	3-2
	Second Round	Darlington (a)	2-1
	Third Round	Ipswich T (a)	1-1
		(h)	0-2

HARTLEPOOL UNITED

Player and Position	Ht	Wt	Birth Date	Birth Place	Source	Clubs	League App	Gls
Goalkeepers								
Martin Hodge	6 2	13 07	4 2 59	Southport	Apprentice	Plymouth Arg	43	—
						Everton	25	—
						Preston NE (loan)	44	—
						Oldham Ath (loan)	4	—
						Gillingham (loan)	4	—
						Sheffield W	197	—
						Leicester C	75	—
						Hartlepool U	40	—
Steven Jones			31 1 74	Teesside	Trainee	Hartlepool U	6	—
Defenders								
Paul Cross	5 7	9 06	31 10 65	Barnsley	Apprentice	Barnsley	118	—
						Hartlepool U	21	—
						Preston NE (loan)	5	—
Andy Davies*	6 0	11 06	6 6 72	Wolverhampton	Trainee	Torquay U	13	—
						Hartlepool U	7	—
Scott Garrett			9 1 74	Gateshead	Trainee	Hartlepool U	—	—
Tommy McGuckin	6 02	12 02	24 4 73	Middlesbrough	Trainee	Hartlepool U	7	—
Rob McKinnon (To Motherwell Jan 1992)	5 11	11 01	31 7 66	Glasgow	Rutherglen G	Newcastle U	1	—
						Hartlepool U	247	7
						Manchester U (loan)	—	—
John MacPhail	6 0	12 03	7 12 55	Dundee	St Columba's	Dundee	68	—
						Sheffield U	135	7
						York C	142	24
						Bristol C	26	1
						Sunderland	130	22
						Hartlepool U	83	2
Keith Nobbs	5 10	11 10	19 9 61	Bishop Auckland	Apprentice	Middlesbrough	1	—
						Halifax T	87	1
						Bishop Auckland	—	—
						Hartlepool U	253	1
Mick Smith*	6 1	11 09	28 10 58	Sunderland	Lambton St BC	Lincoln C	25	—
						Wimbledon	205	14
						Aldershot (loan)	7	—
						Seaham Red	—	—
						Hartlepool U	55	6
Midfield								
Paul Dalton	5 11	11 07	25 4 67	Middlesbrough	Brandon U	Manchester U	—	—
						Hartlepool U	151	37
Brian Honour	5 7	12 05	16 2 64	Horden	Apprentice Peterlee	Darlington	74	4
						Peterlee	—	—
						Hartlepool U	264	19
Lenny Johnrose	5 11	12 00	29 11 69	Preston	Trainee	Blackburn R	42	11
						Hartlepool U	15	2
						Preston NE (loan)	3	1
David McCreery*	5 6	10 7	16 9 57	Belfast	Apprentice	Manchester U	87	7
						QPR	57	4
						Tulsa R	—	—
						Newcastle U	243	2
						Hearts	29	—
						Hartlepool U	60	—
Mark Nesbitt*			11 1 72	Doncaster R	Trainee	Middlesbrough	—	—
						Hartlepool U	2	—
Paul Olsson	5 8	10 11	24 12 65	Hull	Apprentice	Hull C	—	—
						Exeter C (loan)	8	—
						Exeter C	35	2
						Scarborough	48	5
						Hartlepool U	100	9
John Tinkler*	5 8	11 07	24 8 68	Trimdon		Hartlepool U	170	7

HARTLEPOOL UNITED

Foundation: The inspiration for the launching of Hartlepool United was the West Hartlepool club which won the FA Amateur Cup in 1904–05. They had been in existence since 1881 and their Cup success led in 1908 to the formation of the new professional concern which first joined the North-Eastern League. In those days they were Hartlepools United and won the Durham Senior Cup in their first two seasons.

First Football League game: 27 August, 1921, Division 3 (N), v Wrexham (a) W 2-0 – Gill; Thomas, Crilly; Dougherty, Hopkins, Short; Kessler, Mulholland (1), Lister (1), Robertson, Donald.

Did you know: Albert Mundy's record of scoring for Aldershot at Hartlepools in only six seconds is well known, but Doug Cooper scored for Hartlepool against Aldershot in only 20 seconds in November 1960.

Managers (and Secretary-managers)
Alfred Priest 1908–12, Percy Humphreys 1912–13, Jack Manners 1913–20, Cecil Potter 1920–22, David Gordon 1922–24, Jack Manners 1924–27, Bill Norman 1927–31, Jack Carr 1932–35 (had been player-coach since 1931), Jimmy Hamilton 1935–43, Fred Westgarth 1943–57, Ray Middleton 1957–59, Bill Robinson 1959–62, Allenby Chilton 1962–63, Bob Gurney 1963–64, Alvan Williams 1964–65, Geoff Twentyman 1965, Brian Clough 1965–67, Angus McLean 1967–70, John Simpson 1970–71, Len Ashurst 1971–74, Ken Hale 1974–76, Billy Horner 1976–83, Johnny Duncan 1983, Mike Docherty 1983, Billy Horner 1984–86, John Bird 1986–88, Bobby Moncur 1988–89, Cyril Knowles 1989–91, Alan Murray May 1991–.

Player and Position	Ht	Wt	Birth Date	Birth Place	Source	Clubs	League App	Gls
Steve Tupling*	6 0	12 08	11 7 64	Wensleydale	Apprentice	Middlesbrough	—	—
						Carlisle U (loan)	1	—
						Darlington	111	8
						Newport Co	33	2
						Cardiff C	5	—
						Torquay U (loan)	3	—
						Exeter C (loan)	9	1
						Hartlepool U	89	3
Forwards								
Paul Baker	6 1	12 10	5 1 63	Newcastle	Bishop Auckland	Southampton	—	—
						Carlisle U	71	11
						Hartlepool U	197	67
Steve Fletcher			26 6 72	Hartlepool	Trainee	Hartlepool U	32	4
Andrew Saville	6 0	12 00	12 12 64	Hull	Local	Hull C	100	18
						Walsall	38	5
						Barnsley	82	21
						Hartlepool U	1	—
Nicky Southall			28 1 72	Teeside		Hartlepool U	22	3
John Thomas*	5 8	11 03	5 8 58	Wednesbury		Everton	—	—
						Tranmere R (loan)	11	2
						Halifax T (loan)	5	—
						Bolton W	22	6
						Chester	44	20
						Lincoln C	67	20
						Preston NE	78	38
						Bolton W	73	31
						WBA	18	1
						Preston NE	27	6
						Hartlepool U	7	1
Paul Thompson	5 11	11 10	17 4 73	Newcastle	Trainee	Hartlepool U	—	—

Trainees
Chew, Paul; Hutchinson, Robert A; Leahy, Mark; Lester, Jason M; Lowery, Paul A; Potter, Steven; Skedd, Anthony S; Strike, Anthony P; Walton, Charles A; Watson, Mark A.

Associated Schoolboys
McBeth, Simon.

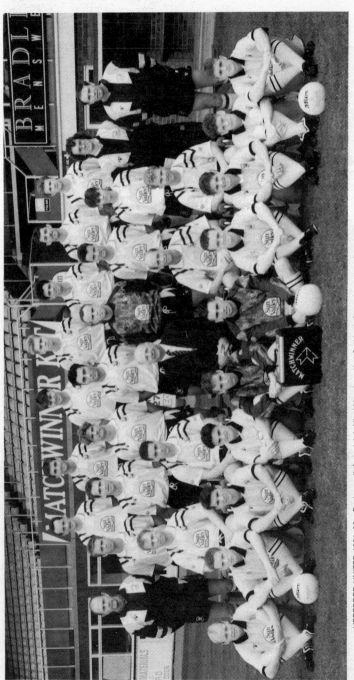

HEREFORD UNITED 1991–92 *Back row (left to right)*: Nigel Vaughan, Karl Goddard, Steve Lowndes, Russell Bradley, Steve Devine, Mel Pejic, Harry Caffrey.
Centre row: Peter Isaac (Coach), Richard Jones, Jon Narbett, Peter Heritage, Paul Robinson, Tony Elliott, Steve McIntyre, Chris Fry, Colin Taylor (Physiotherapist), John Layton (Youth Officer).
Front row: Alan Hall, Andy Theodosiou, John Sillett (Manager), Greg Downs (Player/Coach), Simon Brain.
Sitting on the floor (all YTS): Shane Jones, Gareth Davies, Stephen McElroy, Paul Parker, Andrew Watkins, Sean Seaward, Paul Burton, Mark Davies, Paul Eversham, Adrian Mooney.

Division 3   **HEREFORD UNITED**

Edgar Street, Hereford. Telephone Hereford (0432) 276666.
Commercial Dept: (0432) 273155.

Ground capacity: 13,777.

Record attendance: 18,114 v Sheffield W, FA Cup 3rd rd, 4 January 1958.

Record receipts: £72,840 v Manchester U, FA Cup 4th rd, 28 January 1990.

Pitch measurements: 111yd × 74yd.

Chairman: P. S. Hill FRICS.

Vice-chairman: M. B. Roberts.

Directors: D. H. Vaughan, A. J. Phillips, G. C. E. Hales, H. A. R. Cotterell, J. W. T. Duggan.

Manager: Greg Downs.

Assistant Manager.

Physio: Colin Taylor.

Secretary: David Vaughan.

Commercial Manager: Paul Roberts.

Year Formed: 1924. Turned Professional: 1924. Ltd Co.: 1939.

Club Nickname: 'United'.

Record League Victory: 6-0 v Burnley (away), Division 4, 24 January 1987 – Rose; Rodgerson, Devine, Halliday, Pejic, Dalziel, Harvey (1p), Wells, Phillips (3), Kearns (2), Spooner.

Record Cup Victory: 6-1 v QPR, FA Cup, 2nd rd, 7 December 1957 – Sewell; Tomkins, Wade; Masters, Niblett, Horton (2p); Reg Bowen (1), Clayton (1), Fidler, Williams (1), Cyril Beech (1).

Record Defeat: 0-6 v Rotherham U, Division 4, 29 April 1989.

Most League Points (2 for a win): 63, Division 3, 1975–76.

Most League points (3 for a win): 77, Division 4, 1984–85.

Most League Goals: 86, Division 3, 1975–76.

Highest League Scorer in Season: Dixie McNeil, 35, 1975–76.

Most League Goals in Total Aggregate: Stewart Phillips, 93, 1980–88, 1990–91.

Most Capped Player: Brian Evans, 1 (7), Wales.

Most League Appearances: Mel Pejic, 412, 1980–92.

Record Transfer Fee Received: £200,000 from QPR for Darren Peacock, December 1990.

Record Transfer Fee Paid: £50,000 to Halifax T for Ian Juryeff, December 1989.

Football League Record: 1972 Elected to Division 4; 1973–76 Division 3; 1976–77 Division 2; 1977–78 Division 3; 1978–92 Division 4; 1992– Division 3.

Honours: Football League: Division 2 best season: 22nd, 1976–77; Division 3 – Champions 1975–76; Division 4 – Runners-up 1972–73. *FA Cup:* best season: 4th rd, 1971–72, 1976–77, 1981–82, 1989–90. *Football League Cup:* best season: 3rd rd, 1974–75. *Welsh Cup:* Winners, 1990.

Colours: White shirts, black shorts, white stockings. **Change colours:** All red.

258

HEREFORD UNITED 1991–92 LEAGUE RECORD

Match No.	Date		Venue	Opponents	Result		H/T Score	Lg. Pos.	Goalscorers	Attendance
1	Aug	17	A	Wrexham	W	1-0	1-0	—	Brain	3225
2		24	H	Scarborough	W	4-1	4-1	2	Theodosiou, Narbett 3 (2 pen)	2600
3		31	A	Barnet	L	0-1	0-0	4		2860
4	Sep	4	H	Gillingham	W	2-0	1-0	—	Heritage, Narbett (pen)	2544
5		7	A	Rotherham U	D	0-0	0-0	4		3778
6		14	A	Burnley	W	2-0	1-0	2	Lowndes, Heritage	4400
7		17	H	York C	W	2-1	2-0	—	Brain, Heritage	3540
8		21	A	Walsall	L	0-3	0-2	4		4509
9		28	H	Lincoln C	W	3-0	3-0	3	Heritage, Narbett, Lowndes	2801
10	Oct	5	A	Scunthorpe U	D	1-1	0-0	3	Martin (og)	2384
11		26	A	Chesterfield	L	0-2	0-1	4		2949
12	Nov	2	A	Maidstone U	L	2-3	2-1	4	Lowndes, Downs (pen)	846
13		6	H	Halifax T	L	0-2	0-1	—		2207
14		9	H	Rochdale	D	1-1	1-0	8	Brain	2959
15		23	A	Carlisle U	L	0-1	0-0	11		2032
16		30	A	Crewe Alex	L	2-4	0-3	11	Russell, Vaughan	2990
17	Dec	26	H	Wrexham	W	3-1	1-0	11	Fry, Brain, Narbett	3542
18		28	H	Barnet	D	2-2	2-1	11	Heritage, Pejic	4654
19	Jan	1	A	Gillingham	L	1-2	1-2	14	Caffery	3392
20		11	A	Cardiff C	L	0-1	0-0	15		5305
21		18	H	Blackpool	L	1-2	1-1	15	Narbett (pen)	3008
22	Feb	8	H	Chesterfield	W	1-0	1-0	15	Brain	2315
23		12	A	Crewe Alex	L	1-1	1-1	—	Heritage	2181
24		15	A	Mansfield T	D	1-1	1-1	15	Heritage	2550
25		18	A	Doncaster R	L	0-2	0-2	—		1270
26		22	H	Cardiff C	D	2-2	1-0	15	Brain, Fry	5691
27		25	H	Mansfield T	L	0-1	0-1	—		2122
28		29	A	Northampton T	W	1-0	1-0	15	Downs	2428
29	Mar	3	A	Blackpool	L	0-2	0-0	—		3560
30		7	H	Doncaster R	L	0-1	0-1	16		1974
31		11	A	Halifax T	W	2-0	0-0	—	Narbett (pen), Brain	918
32		14	H	Maidstone U	D	2-2	0-1	15	Brain, Titterton	1910
33		21	A	Rochdale	L	1-3	0-1	17	Jones R	2122
34		28	H	Carlisle U	W	1-0	1-0	16	Heritage	1810
35		31	A	Burnley	L	0-2	0-2	—		10,578
36	Apr	4	H	Rotherham U	W	1-0	0-0	16	Fry	1868
37		7	A	Scarborough	D	1-1	0-0	—	Brain	1008
38		11	A	York C	L	0-1	0-1	15		1614
39		18	H	Walsall	L	1-2	1-1	16	Caffery	2291
40		20	A	Lincoln C	L	0-3	0-1	16		2358
41		25	H	Scunthorpe U	L	1-2	1-1	16	Devine	1587
42		28	H	Northampton T	L	1-2	0-2	—	Brain	1297

Final League Position: 17

GOALSCORERS

League (44): Brain 10, Heritage 8, Narbett 8 (5 pens), Fry 3, Lowndes 3, Caffery 2, Downs 2 (1 pen), Devine 1, Jones R 1, Pejic 1, Russell 1, Theodosiou 1, Titterton 1, Vaughan 1, own goals 1.
Rumbelows Cup (2): Narbett 1 (1 pen), Theodosiou 1.
FA Cup (8): Brain 4, Fry 1, Heritage 1, Lowndes 1, Narbett 1.

Elliott	Vaughan	Downs	Theodosiou	Devine	Lowndes	Hall	Heritage	Brain	Robinson	Caffery	Fry	Bradley	Narbett	Pejic	Titterton	Goddard	Jones S	Jennings	Wade	Judge	McIntyre	Russell	Morah	Nebbeling	Jones R	Culpin	Davies	Burton	Match No.
1	2	3	4	5	6	7	8	9	10	11*	12																		1
1		3	4		6	7	12	9	10	8			2	5*11															2
1	11	3	4	12	6	7*10		9					2	5	8														3
1		3	4	12	6	7	10	9					2	5*11	8														4
1		3	4	5	6	7	10	9					2	11	8														5
1		3	4	5	6	7	10	9					2	11	8														6
1		3	4	5	6	7	10	9*	12				2	11	8														7
1		3	4	5*	6		10	9	12				2	11	8	7†14													8
1		3	4	5	6		10	9					2	11	8	7													9
1		3	4	5		10	9	6	2*				11	8	7	12													10
1		3	4	5	6	12	10	9		2			11	8†	7*	14													11
1		3	4	5†	6	7*10	12	9	11				2	14		8													12
		3†	4	5	6	12	10	9	14	11			2*	7		8	1												13
		5	3	4		6	11	10	8				7				1		2	9									14
10*		3	4	5†12	7	9				2			6				11	1		8	14								15
10			5	3	7	4	8†			2			6*12				11	1		9	14								16
6	3			7		9	8			2			10	5	12				1	11				4*					17
6*	3			7		9	8			11			10	5	12				1	2				4					18
1		3		5	7	9*	8		6	11			10				12			2				4					19
		3	4	5		7	9	8					2	10		6				11	1								20
1	14	3†	4	5	7	6	9	8*					2	10		12				11				6					21
1		3	4	5	7	11*10		9		12									8		2				6				22
1		3	4	5	6*			9	8		7	12							11		2				10				23
1		3	4	5			9	8		11	7		6						2						10				24
1		3†	4	5	12	14	9	8		11	7*		6						2						10				25
		3	4	5	11		10	9			7		8						2						6				26
		3	4	5	11	12	10	9			7*		8						14	2†	1				6				27
	12	3		5	7*		9	8	10				6		11				4	1	2						7†		28
		3		5		14	9	8*10			12		6		11				4	1	2						7†		29
		3	8	5		7*		9					6		11	10†	4	1	2					12	14				30
		3	4	5			10	9			7		8	6			2	1							11				31
		3	4	5			10	9			7		8	6			2	1							11				32
		3*		5	12		10	9		14	7†		8	6			2	1	4						11				33
		3	4	5	2		10	9		12	7		8	6				1							11*				34
		3	4	5	2		10	9*14	12		7		8	6				1							11†				35
		3	4	5	11		10	9			7		8	6			2	1											36
		3	4	5	11		10	9			7		8	6				1							2				37
	12	3*	4†	5	11		10	9	14		7		8	6				1							2				38
		3		5	2		10	9		11	7		8	6				1					12		4*				39
	12	3	4				10	9	14	11*	7†		8	6				1	2				5						40
	3			5			10	9		11			8			7		1	2*				6			4	12		41
		3	4	5			9	10			7		8	6		11		1				2							42
18	8	40	33	35	29	15	38	40	7	12	33	3	33	15	20	—	3	9	10	24	12	3	—	3	14	1	4	—	
+4s			+2s	+3s	+5s	+1s	+1s	+4s	+5s	+4s					+5s	+1s	+2s	+2s			+2s			+2s	+2s	+1s		+1s	

Rumbelows Cup First Round Torquay U (a) 0-2
  (h) 2-1
FA Cup First Round Atherstone (a) 0-0
  (h) 3-0
Second Round Aylesbury (a) 3-2
Third Round Woking (a) 0-0
  (h) 2-1
Fourth Round Nottingham F (a) 0-2

HEREFORD UNITED

Player and Position	Ht	Wt	Birth Date	Birth Place	Source	Clubs	League App	Gls
Goalkeepers								
Tony Elliott*	6 0	12 12	30 11 69	Nuneaton		Birmingham C	—	—
						Hereford U	75	—
Alan Judge	5 11	11 06	15 5 60	Kingsbury	Amateur	Luton T	11	—
						Reading (loan)	33	—
						Reading	44	—
						Oxford U	80	—
						Lincoln C (loan)	2	—
						Cardiff C (loan)	8	—
						Hereford U	24	—
George Wood‡	6 3	14 00	26 9 52	Douglas	East Stirling	East Stirling	44	1
						Blackpool	117	—
						Everton	103	—
						Arsenal	60	—
						Crystal Palace	192	—
						Cardiff C	67	—
						Blackpool (loan)	15	—
						Hereford U	41	—
Defenders								
Gareth Davies			11 12 73	Hereford	Trainee	Hereford U	4	—
Steve Devine	5 9	10 07	11 12 64	Strabane	Apprentice	Wolverhampton W	—	—
						Derby Co	11	—
						Stockport Co	2	—
						Hereford U	245	4
Greg Downs	5 9	10 07	13 12 58	Carlton	Apprentice	Norwich C	169	7
						Torquay U (loan)	1	1
						Coventry C	146	4
						Birmingham C	17	—
						Hereford U	40	2
Karl Goddard*	5 9	10 10	29 12 67	Leeds	Apprentice	Manchester U	—	—
						Bradford C	73	—
						Exeter C (loan)	1	—
						Colchester U (loan)	16	1
						Hereford U	9	1
Steve McIntyre	6 01	12 00	15 5 66	Ayr	Trainee	Ayr U	127	6
						Hereford U	12	—
Andy Theodosiou	6 0	12 10	30 10 70	Stoke Newington	Tottenham H	Norwich C	—	—
						Hereford U	33	1
David Titterton	5 11	12 09	25 9 71	Hatton	Trainee	Coventry C	2	—
						Hereford U	25	1
Midfield								
Henry Caffery	5 8	10 00	15 2 66	Paisley	Trainee	Clydebank	41	3
						Hereford U	34	4
Derek Hall	5 8	11 02	5 1 65	Manchester	Apprentice	Coventry C	1	—
						Torquay U (loan)	10	2
						Torquay U	45	4
						Swindon T	10	—
						Southend U	123	15
						Halifax T	49	4
						Hereford U	20	—
Richard Jones	5 11	11 01	26 4 69	Pontypool		Newport Co	41	1
						Hereford U	113	6
Shane Jones*	5 9	10 02	8 11 72	Tredegar	Trainee	Hereford U	38	—
Jon Narbett	5 10	10 08	21 11 68	Birmingham	Apprentice	Shrewsbury T	26	3
						Hereford U	149	31
						Leicester C (loan)	—	—
Nigel Vaughan*	5 5	8 10	20 5 59	Caerleon	Apprentice	Newport Co	224	32
						Cardiff C	149	42
						Reading (loan)	5	1
						Wolverhampton W	93	10
						Hereford U	13	1

HEREFORD UNITED

Foundation: A number of local teams amalgamated in 1924 under the chairmanship of Dr. E. W. Maples to form Hereford United and joined the Birmingham Combination. They graduated to the Birmingham League four years later.

First Football League game: 12 August, 1972, Division 4, v Colchester U (a) L 0-1 – Potter; Mallender, Naylor; Jones, McLaughlin, Tucker; Slattery, Hollett, Owen, Radford, Wallace.

Did you know: When they joined the Football League in 1972, Hereford United lost only one of their first 25 home League games.

Managers (and Secretary-managers)
Eric Keen 1939, George Tranter 1948–49, Alex Massie 1952, George Tranter 1953–55, Joe Wade 1956–62, Ray Daniels 1962–63, Bob Dennison 1963–67, John Charles 1967–71, Colin Addison 1971–74, John Sillett 1974–78, Mike Bailey 1978–79, Frank Lord 1979–82, Tommy Hughes 1982–83, Johnny Newman 1983–87, Ian Bowyer 1987–90, Colin Addison 1990–91, John Sillett 1991–92, Greg Downs May 1992–.

Player and Position	Ht	Wt	Birth Date	Birth Place	Source	Clubs	League App	League Gls
Meashach Wade			23 1 73	Bermuda	Pembroke	Hereford U	10	—
Forwards								
Simon Brain	5 6	10 08	31 3 66	Evesham	Cheltenham T	Hereford U	63	18
Paul Burton*	5 9	10 01	6 8 73	Hereford		Hereford U	5	1
Paul Culpin†	5 10	11 10	8 2 62	Kirby Muxloe		Leicester C	—	—
						Nuneaton	—	—
						Coventry C	9	2
						Northampton T	63	23
						Peterborough U	47	14
						Hereford U	2	—
Chris Fry	5 9	9 06	23 10 69	Cardiff	Trainee	Cardiff C	55	1
						Hereford U	37	3
Peter Heritage*	6 1	13 00	8 11 60	Bexhill	Hythe T	Gillingham	57	11
						Hereford U	57	9
Jedd Jennings			15 10 71	Bermuda	Pembroke	Hereford U	11	—
Steve Lowndes*	5 10	10 13	17 6 60	Cwmbran	Amateur	Newport Co	208	39
						Millwall	96	16
						Barnsley	116	20
						Hereford U	49	4
Paul Robinson	6 4	14 07	21 2 71	Nottingham	Notts Co, Bury	Scarborough	20	3
						Plymouth Arg	11	3
						Hereford U	11	—

Trainees
Davis, Mark J; Eversham, Paul J; Harris, Leigh J; Heathcock, Adrian N; Parker, Paul A; Watkins, Andrew J; Watkins, Christopher W.

HUDDERSFIELD TOWN 1991–92 *Back row (left to right)*: Chris Marsden, Iwan Roberts, Mark Wright, Graham Mitchell, Lee Martin, Tim Clarke, Simon Trevitt, Ken O'Doherty, Jon Dyson, Iffy Onuora.

Centre row: Gary Haylock, David Campbell, Keiron O'Regan, John Donovan, Kevin Donovan, John Kelly, Neil Parsley, Peter Jackson, Chris Billy, Dudley Lewis, Keith Edwards, Simon Ireland.

Front row: Wayne Jones (Physiotherapist), Matthew Johnson, Robert Wilson, Simon Charlton, Eoin Hand (Manager), Ian Ross (Assistant Manager), Brian Byrne, Gary Barnett, George Mulhall (Youth Team Manager).

Division 2   **HUDDERSFIELD TOWN**

© 1973

Leeds Rd, Huddersfield HD1 6PE. Telephone (0484) 420335. Lottery office: (0484) 425045. Recorded Information: (0898) 121635.

Ground capacity: 17,010.

Record attendance: 67,037 v Arsenal, FA Cup 6th rd, 27 February 1932.

Record receipts: £52,607 v Newcastle U, Division 2, 7 May, 1984.

Pitch measurements: 115yd × 75yd.

Chairman: K. S. Longbottom.

Vice-chairman: D. G. Headey.

Directors: C. Hodgkinson, J. B. Buckley, F. L. Thewlis, G. A. Leslie.

Associate directors: T. S. Fisher, T. J. Cherry.

Manager: Ian Ross. *Assistant Manager. Coach:* George Mulhall. *Secretary:* C. D. Patzelt. *Commercial Manager:* Tony Flynn. *Chief Executive:* Paul Fletcher. *Physio:* Wayne Jones.

Year Formed: 1908. Turned Professional: 1908. Ltd Co.: 1908.

Club Nickname: 'The Terriers'.

Record League Victory: 10-1 v Blackpool, Division 1, 13 December 1930 – Turner; Goodall, Spencer; Redfern, Wilson, Campbell; Bob Kelly (1), McLean (4), Robson (3), Davies (1), Smailes (1).

Record Cup Victory: 7-1 v Chesterfield (away), FA Cup, 3rd rd, 12 January 1929 – Turvey; Goodall, Wadsworth; Evans, Wilson, Naylor: Jackson (1), Kelly, Brown (3), Cumming (2), Smith. (1 og).

Record Defeat: 1-10 v Manchester C, Division 2, 7 November 1987.

Most League Points (2 for a win): 66, Division 4, 1979–80.

Most League points (3 for a win): 82, Division 3, 1982–83.

Most League Goals: 101, Division 4, 1979–80.

Highest League Scorer in Season: Sam Taylor, 35, Division 2, 1919–20; George Brown, 35, Division 1, 1925–26.

Most League Goals in Total Aggregate: George Brown, 142, 1921–29 and Jimmy Glazzard, 142, 1946–56.

Most Capped Player: Jimmy Nicholson, 31 (41), Northern Ireland.

Most League Appearances: Billy Smith, 520, 1914–34.

Record Transfer Fee Received: £250,000 from Reading for Craig Maskell, July 1990.

Record Transfer Fee Paid: £275,000 to Watford for Iwan Roberts, August 1990.

Football League Record: 1910 Elected to Division 2; 1920–52 Division 1; 1952–53 Division 2; 1953–56 Division 1; 1956–70 Division 2; 1970–72 Division 1; 1972–73 Division 2; 1973–75 Division 3; 1975–80 Division 4; 1980–83 Division 3; 1983–88 Division 2; 1988–92 Division 3; 1992– Division 2.

Honours: Football League: Division 1 – Champions 1923–24, 1924–25, 1925–26; Runners up 1926–27, 1927–28, 1933–34; Division 2 – Champions 1969–70; Runners-up 1919–20, 1952–53; Division 4 – Champions 1979–80. *FA Cup:* Winners 1922; Runners-up 1920, 1928, 1930, 1938. *Football League Cup:* Semi-final, 1967–68.

Colours: Blue and white striped shirts, white shorts, white stockings. **Change colours:** Red/black hooped shirts, black shorts, black stockings.

HUDDERSFIELD TOWN 1991–92 LEAGUE RECORD

Match No.	Date		Venue	Opponents	Result		H/T Score	Lg. Pos.	Goalscorers	Atten- dance
1	Aug	17	A	Bolton W	D	1-1	1-0	—	Marsden	7606
2		25	H	Bradford C	W	1-0	1-0	—	O'Regan	9234
3		31	A	Brentford	W	3-2	1-1	—	O'Regan (pen), Roberts, Starbuck	5459
4	Sep	4	H	Chester C	W	2-0	1-0	—	Onuora, Barnett	5321
5		7	H	Exeter C	D	0-0	0-0	3		5758
6		14	A	Bury	D	4-4	1-4	4	Roberts 2, Starbuck 2	4409
7		17	A	Wigan Ath	W	3-1	2-1	—	Starbuck 2, Roberts	3531
8		21	H	Bournemouth	D	0-0	0-0	4		6802
9		28	A	Leyton Orient	L	0-1	0-1	5		3741
10	Oct	5	H	Swansea C	W	1-0	0-0	5	Roberts	5578
11		12	A	Torquay U	W	1-0	0-0	4	Barnett	2936
12		19	A	Preston NE	L	0-1	0-0	4		6866
13		25	H	Stockport Co	L	0-1	0-0	—		9229
14	Nov	2	A	Stoke C	W	2-0	2-0	4	Roberts 2	10,116
15		6	H	Fulham	W	3-1	1-1	—	O'Regan, Starbuck, Jackson	5064
16		9	H	Birmingham C	W	3-2	1-0	3	Roberts 2, Onuora	11,688
17		23	A	WBA	L	1-2	1-2	4	Roberts	14,029
18		30	A	Hartlepool U	D	0-0	0-0	4		4017
19	Dec	14	H	Darlington	W	2-1	1-0	4	Starbuck (pen), Roberts	5677
20		22	A	Bradford C	D	1-1	1-0	—	Roberts	10,050
21		26	H	Brentford	W	2-1	1-0	4	Roberts, O'Regan	10,605
22		28	H	Bolton W	W	1-0	1-0	4	Roberts	11,884
23	Jan	1	A	Chester C	D	0-0	0-0	4		3504
24		11	A	Reading	L	0-1	0-0	4		4732
25		18	H	Peterborough U	D	0-0	0-0	5		8763
26		25	A	Shrewsbury T	D	1-1	0-1	5	Onuora	3688
27	Feb	1	H	Preston NE	L	1-2	1-0	5	Roberts	6700
28		7	A	Stockport Co	D	0-0	0-0	—		7519
29		11	H	Hartlepool U	W	1-0	1-0	—	Roberts	5559
30		15	A	Darlington	W	3-1	1-1	4	Onuora 2, Starbuck (pen)	3120
31		22	H	Reading	L	1-2	0-1	5	Roberts	6259
32		25	H	Hull C	D	1-1	0-0	—	Roberts	6003
33		29	A	Hull C	L	0-1	0-1	4		5310
34	Mar	3	A	Peterborough U	L	0-2	0-1	—		6257
35		7	H	Shrewsbury T	W	2-1	1-1	4	Onuora, Roberts	4674
36		10	A	Fulham	L	0-1	0-0	—		3134
37		14	H	Stoke C	L	1-2	0-2	7	Starbuck (pen)	10,156
38		21	A	Birmingham C	L	0-2	0-1	8		12,482
39		28	H	WBA	W	3-0	1-0	8	Starbuck, Billy, Strodder (og)	7428
40		31	H	Bury	W	3-0	2-0	—	Starbuck, Billy, Roberts	5890
41	Apr	4	A	Exeter C	W	1-0	0-0	6	Roberts	3047
42		11	H	Wigan Ath	W	3-1	2-0	5	Roberts, Trevitt, Starbuck	7058
43		14	A	Bournemouth	D	1-1	0-1	—	Roberts	7655
44		20	H	Leyton Orient	W	1-0	1-0	5	Onuora	10,011
45		25	A	Swansea C	W	1-0	1-0	4	Roberts	3964
46	May	2	H	Torquay U	W	4-0	2-0	3	Starbuck 2, Onuora, Barnett	7961

Final League Position: 3

GOALSCORERS

League (59): Roberts 24, Starbuck 14 (3 pens), Onuora 8, O'Regan 4 (1 pen), Barnett 3, Billy 2, Jackson 1, Marsden 1, Trevitt 1, own goals 1.
Rumbelows Cup (11): Roberts 3, Starbuck 3, Barnett 2, Onuora 2, Charlton 1.
FA Cup (9): Roberts 3, Donovan 2, Onuora 2, O'Regan 1, Stapleton 1.

Clarke	Trevitt	Charlton	Marsden	Mitchell	Jackson	O'Regan	Onuora	Roberts	Haylock	Barnett	Starbuck	Donovan	Ireland	Wright	Parsley	Stapleton	Kelly	Walsh	O'Doherty	Callaghan	McNab	Martin	Billy	Campbell	Booth	Butler	Match No.
1	2	3	4	5	6	7	8	9	10	11																	1
1	2	3	4	5	6	7	8	9		11	10																2
1	2	3	4	5	6	7	8	9		11	10																3
1	2	3	4	5	6	7	8	9		11	10																4
1	2	3	4	5	6	7	8*	9		11	10	12															5
1	2	3†	4	5	6	7		9		11	10	8*	12	14													6
1		3	4	5	6	7		9		11	10	8			2												7
1	2	3	4	5	6	7	12	9		11	10	8*															8
1	2	3	4	5	6	7	8	9		11*	10	12															9
1	2	3	4	5	6	7	8	9		11*	10	12															10
1	2	3	4	5	6	7	8	9		11	10																11
1	2	3	4	5	6	7	8*	9		11	10	12															12
1	2	3	4	5	6	7	8*	9		11	10	12															13
1	2	3	4	5	6	7		9		11	10						8										14
1	2	3	4	5	6	7		9		11	10						8										15
1	2	3	4	5	6	7	12	9		11	10*						8										16
1	2	3		5	6	7	10	9		11		12					8	4*									17
1	2	3		5	6	7	10	9		11		12				4	8*										18
1	2	3		5	6	7	8	9		11	10*	12	4														19
1	2			5	6	7	8	9		11	10*		3				4	12									20
1	2	3		5	6	7	8	9		11	10						4										21
1	2	3		5	6	7	8	9		11	10						4										22
1	2	3		5	6	7	8	9*		11†	10		12				4	14									23
1	2	3		5	6	7	8	9			10*	11					4	12									24
1	2	3		5		7	8	9			10	11					4*	12	6								25
1	2	3		5	6	7	12	9			10*	11					4			8							26
1	2†	3		5	6	7	10	9				12		11*			14			8	4						27
		3		5	6	7	11	9				10			2		8*			4	1		12				28
		3		5*	6	7	11	9				10	12		2		8			4	1						29
		3			6	7	11	9				10			2		8			4	1			5			30
		3			6	7†	11	9				10	12	14	2		8*			4	1			5			31
	2	3			6		11	9				10	12				7			8*	4	1		5			32
	2	3		5	6	14	11	9				10	12				7†			8*	4	1					33
	2	3		5	6	7	11	9*		8	10	12									4	1					34
1	2	3		5	6	7	11	9		8	10										4						35
1	2	3		5	6	7	11	9		8*	10										4			12			36
1	2	3		5	6	7	11	9			10									8*	4			12			37
1	2	3		5	6	7†	11	9					4				10*			8	14		12				38
1	2	3	4	5	6		11	9			10												7			8	39
1	2	3	4*	5	6	12	11	9			10												7			8	40
1	2	3	4	5	6			9		11	10												7			8	41
1	2	3	4	5	6		11	9		12	10												7*			8	42
1	2	3	4	5	6		11	9			10												7			8	43
1	2	3	4	5	6		11	9		12	10*												7			8	44
1	2	3	4	5	6		11	9		12	10												7*			8	45
1	2	3		5	6	7	11	9		12	10†						4						8*	14			46
39	41	45	23	43	45	37	38	46	1	27	42	4	3	4	5	5	13	—	1	8	11	7	8	3	—	7	
											+	+	+	+	+	+	+		+	+				+	+		
											2s	3s	4s	2s	6s	6s	4s		1s	4s				2s	3s		

HUDDERSFIELD TOWN

Player and Position	Ht	Wt	Birth Date	Place	Source	Clubs	League App	Gls
Goalkeepers								
Tim Clarke	6 3	13 07	19 9 68	Stourbridge	Halesowen	Coventry C	—	—
						Huddersfield T	39	—
Lee Martin*	5 11	11 08	9 9 68	Huddersfield	Trainee	Huddersfield T	54	—
Defenders								
David Campbell*			13 9 69	Dublin	Bohemians	Huddersfield T	4	—
Simon Charlton	5 7	10 11	25 10 71	Huddersfield	Trainee	Huddersfield T	78	—
Jon Dyson			18 12 71	Mirfield	School	Huddersfield T	—	—
Peter Jackson	6 1	12 06	6 4 61	Bradford	Apprentice	Bradford C	278	24
						Newcastle U	60	3
						Bradford C	58	5
						Huddersfield T	83	2
Matthew Johnson*	5 7	9 10	17 3 73	Huddersfield	Trainee	Huddersfield T	—	—
Graham Mitchell	6 0	11 05	16 2 68	Shipley	Apprentice	Huddersfield T	206	2
Ken O'Doherty*	6 0	12 00	30 3 63	Dublin	UCD	Crystal Palace	42	—
						Huddersfield T	65	1
						Exeter C (loan)	2	—
Neil Parsley	5 10	10 11	25 4 66	Liverpool	Witton Alb	Leeds U	—	—
						Chester C (loan)	6	—
						Huddersfield T	13	—
						Doncaster R (loan)	3	—
Simon Trevitt	5 11	11 02	20 12 67	Dewsbury	Apprentice	Huddersfield T	173	2
Mark Wright	5 9	10 08	29 1 70	Manchester	Trainee	Everton	1	—
						Blackpool (loan)	3	—
						Huddersfield T (loan)	10	1
						Huddersfield T	8	—
Midfield								
John Kelly	5 10	10 09	20 10 60	Bebbington	Cammellaird	Tranmere R	64	9
						Preston NE	130	27
						Chester C	85	17
						Swindon T	7	1
						Oldham Ath	52	6
						Walsall	39	1
						Huddersfield T (loan)	10	—
						Huddersfield T	18	—
Chris Marsden	5 11	10 12	3 1 69	Sheffield	Trainee	Sheffield U	16	1
						Huddersfield T	112	9
Kieran O'Regan	5 9	10 08	9 11 63	Cork	Tranmore Ath	Brighton & HA	86	2
						Swindon T	26	1
						Huddersfield T	158	20
Forwards								
Gary Barnett	5 6	9 13	11 3 63	Stratford	Apprentice	Coventry C	—	—
						Oxford U	45	9
						Wimbledon (loan)	5	1
						Fulham (loan)	2	1
						Fulham	180	30
						Huddersfield T	84	7
Chris Billy	5 11	11 08	2 1 73	Huddersfield	Trainee	Huddersfield T	10	2
Andy Booth§	6 00	10 08	6 12 73	Huddersfield	Trainee	Huddersfield T	3	—
Brian Byrne*			23 3 72	Dublin	Trainee	Huddersfield T	—	—
						Shelbourne (loan)	—	—
Kevin Donovan	5 7	10 10	17 12 71	Halifax	Trainee	Huddersfield T	17	1
						Halifax T (loan)	6	—

HUDDERSFIELD TOWN

Foundation: A meeting, attended largely by members of the Huddersfield & District FA, was held at the Imperial Hotel in 1906 to discuss the feasibility of establishing a football club in this rugby stronghold. However, it was not until a man with both the enthusiasm and the money to back the scheme came on the scene, that real progress was made. This benefactor was Mr. Hilton Crowther and it was at a meeting at the Albert Hotel in 1908, that the club formally came into existence with a capital of £2,000 and joined the North-Eastern League.

First Football League game: 3 September, 1910, Division 2, v Bradford PA (a) W 1-0 – Mutch; Taylor, Morris; Beaton, Hall, Bartlett; Blackburn, Wood, Hamilton (1), McCubbin, Jee.

Did you know: In 1923–24 when most League sides played the same opponents on successive Saturdays, Charlie Wilson netted a hat-trick against Arsenal in a 3-1 win at Highbury and followed this with another hat-trick in a 6-1 victory over the Gunners at Huddersfield.

Managers (and Secretary-managers)
Fred Walker 1908–10, Richard Pudan 1910–12, Arthur Fairclough 1912–19, Ambrose Langley 1919–21, Herbert Chapman 1921–25, Cecil Potter 1925–26, Jack Chaplin 1926–29, Clem Stephenson 1929–42, David Steele 1943–47, George Stephenson 1947–52, Andy Beattie 1952–56, Bill Shankly 1956–59 Eddie Boot 1960–64 Tom Johnston 1964–68, Ian Greaves 1968–74, Bobby Collins 1974–75, Tom Johnston 1975–77 (GM), 1977–78, Mike Buxton 1978–86, Steve Smith 1986–87, Malcolm Macdonald 1987–88, Eoin Hand 1988–92, Ian Ross January 1992–.

Player and Position	Ht	Wt	Birth Date	Birth Place	Source	Clubs	League App	Gls
Keith Edwards‡	5 8	10 03	16 7 57	Stockton		Sheffield U	70	29
						Hull C	132	57
						Sheffield U	191	114
						Leeds U	38	6
						Aberdeen	9	2
						Hull C	55	29
						Stockport Co	27	10
						Huddersfield T (loan)	10	4
						Huddersfield T	18	4
						Plymouth Arg (loan)	3	1
Gary Haylock‡	6 0	11 12	31 12 70	Bradford	Trainee	Huddersfield T	13	4
						Shelbourne (loan)	—	—
Simon Ireland			23 11 71	Barnstaple	School	Huddersfield T	15	—
						Wrexham (loan)	5	—
Iffy Onuora	5 10	11 10	28 7 67	Glasgow		Huddersfield T	104	18
Iwan Roberts	6 3	12 05	26 6 68	Banour		Watford	63	9
						Huddersfield T	90	37
Philip Starbuck	5 10	10 13	24 11 68	Nottingham	Apprentice	Nottingham F	36	2
						Birmingham C (loan)	3	—
						Hereford U (loan)	6	—
						Blackburn R (loan)	6	1
						Huddersfield T	44	14

Trainees
Booth, Andrew D; Brennan, Anthony; Collins, Simon; Dysart, John; Forrest, Marc S; McKenzie, Wayne; Mooney, Thomas; Payne, Stephen J; Rowe, Rodney C; Thompson, Paul; Whitehead, Scot; Wood, Sean P. A.

**Non-Contract
Gledhill, Richard.

Associated Schoolboys
Aspinall, Brendan J; Booth, Martin; Bullock, Richard M; Collins, Sam J; Cramp, Richard J; Crompton, Glen S; Crowther, Mathew J; Crowther, Paul; Eastwood, Stephen; Garside, Liam; Hart, Andrew C; Heddon, Matthew P; Illingworth, Jeremy M; Keighley, James H; Lawson, Ian J; Lumb, Gavin J; Mitchell, David P; Moorhouse, Robert J; Mullany, James; Rayne, Dean E; Stokes, Andrew J; Stott, Michael J; Sykes, James A; Thompson, Andrew J; Wood, Michael J; Wood, Nicholas I.

Associated Schoolboys who have accepted the club's offer of a Traineeship/Contract
Baldry, Simon; Donaldson, Stephen; Midwood, Michael A; Taylor, Craig L.

**Non-Contract Players who are retained must be re-signed before they are eligible to play in League matches.

HULL CITY 1991–92 *Back row (left to right):* Paul Waites, Lee Warren, Leigh Jenkinson, Neil Buckley, Alan Fettis, Peter Swan, Nicky Brown, Leigh Palin, Andy Payton.
Middle row: Mark Boughen, Lee Said, Ross Thompson, Bernard Ellison (Chief Scout), Wayne Jacobs, David Mail, Herry Ngata, Malcolm Shotton (Youth Team Coach), Roger Greenwood, Gary Hobson, David Walmsley, Jeff Radcliffe (Physiotherapist), Neil Allison, Keith Morrow, Paul Welburn.
Front row (seated): Ken De Mange, Mark Calvert, Graeme Atkinson, Jeff Lee (Assistant Manager), Terry Dolan (Manager), Russ Wilcox, Paul Hunter, Stuart Young.
Front row: Steve Wilson, Matthew Hopkin, Mark Willingham, Simon Knight, Steve Fisher, Adam Lowthorpe, Mark Gallagher, Steve Mulligan, Dean Stowe, Nicky Houghton, Mark Shirtliff.

Division 2   **HULL CITY**

Boothferry Park, Hull HU4 6EU. Telephone Hull (0482) 51119. Commercial Manager (0482) 566050. Club shop: 0482 28297. Football in the Community Office: 0482 56808. Fax No: 0482 565752

Ground capacity: 17.528.

Record attendance: 55,019 v Manchester U, FA Cup 6th rd, 26 February 1949.

Record receipts: £79,604 v Liverpool FA Cup, 5th rd, 18 February 1989.

Pitch measurements: 115yd × 75yd.

President: T. C. Waite FIMI, MIRTE.

Honorary Vice-president: D. Robinson, H. Bermitz, J. Johnson BA, DPA.

Vice-presidents: R. Beercock, K. Davis, N. Howe, R. Booth, A. Fetiveau, W. Law.

Chairman: M. W. Fish FCA.

Vice-chairman: R. M. Chetham.

Directors: G. H. C. Needler MA, FCA, M. G. ST, Quinton BA, MBA, T. C. Waite FIMI, MIRTE.

Manager: Terry Dolan. *Assistant Manager:* Jeff Lee. *Physio:* Jeff Radcliffe, MCSP, SRP. *Secretary:* Tom Wilson. *Commercial Manager:* Simon Cawkill. *Stadium Manager:* John Cooper. *Ticket Office/Gate Manager:* Wilf Rogerson. *Hon. Medical Officers:* G. Hoyle, MBCHB, FRCS, Dr. B. Kell, MBBS.

Year Formed: 1904. Turned Professional: 1905. Ltd Co.: 1905.

Former Grounds: 1904, Boulevard Ground (Hull RFC); 1905, Anlaby Road (Hull CC); 1944/5 Boulevard Ground; 1946, Boothferry Park.

Club Nickname: 'The Tigers'.

Record League Victory: 11-1 v Carlisle U, Division 3 (N), 14 January 1939 – Ellis; Woodhead, Dowen; Robinson (1), Blyth, Hardy; Hubbard (2), Richardson (2), Dickinson (2), Davies (2), Cunliffe (2).

Record Cup Victory: 8-2 v Stalybridge Celtic (away), FA Cup, 1st rd, 26 November 1932 – Maddison; Goldsmith, Woodhead; Gardner, Hill (1), Denby; Forward (1), Duncan, McNaughton (1), Wainscoat (4), Sargeant (1).

Record Defeat: 0-8 v Wolverhampton W, Division 2, 4 November 1911.

Most League Points (2 for a win): 69, Division 3, 1965–66.

Most League points (3 for a win): 90, Division 4, 1982–83.

Most League Goals: 109, Division 3, 1965–66.

Highest League Scorer in Season: Bill McNaughton, 39, Division 3 (N), 1932–33.

Most League Goals in Total Aggregate: Chris Chilton, 195, 1960–71.

Most Capped Player: Terry Neill, 15 (59), Northern Ireland.

Most League Appearances: Andy Davidson, 520, 1952–67.

Record Transfer Fee Received: £750,000 from Middlesbrough for Andy Payton, November 1991.

Record Transfer Fee Paid: £200,000 to Leeds U for Peter Swan, March 1989.

Football League Record: 1905 Elected to Division 2; 1930–33 Division 3 (N); 1933–36 Division 2; 1936–49 Division 3 (N); 1949–56 Division 2; 1956–58 Division 3 (N); 1958–59 Division 3; 1959–60 Division 2; 1960–66 Division 3; 1966–78 Division 2; 1978–81 Division 3; 1981–83 Division 4; 1983–85 Division 3; 1985–91 Division 2; 1991–92 Division 3; 1992– Division 2.

Honours: Football League: Division 2 best season: 3rd, 1909–10; Division 3 (N) – Champions 1932–33, 1948–49; Division 3 – Champions 1965–66; Runners-up 1958–59; Division 4 – Runners-up 1982–83. *FA Cup:* best season: Semi-final, 1930. *Football League Cup:* best season: 4th, 1973–74, 1975–76, 1977–78. *Associate Members' Cup:* Runners-up 1984.

Colours: Black and amber striped shirts, black shorts, amber stockings. **Change colours:** Green and white shirts, white shorts, green stockings.

HULL CITY 1991–92 LEAGUE RECORD

Match No.	Date		Venue	Opponents	Result		H/T Score	Lg. Pos.	Goalscorers	Atten- dance
1	Aug	17	A	Reading	W	1-0	0-0	—	Jenkinson	4639
2		24	H	Peterborough U	L	1-2	0-0	11	Payton	4806
3		31	A	Bournemouth	D	0-0	0-0	13		5015
4	Sep	3	H	Birmingham C	L	1-2	0-0	—	Palin	4801
5		7	H	Bury	L	0-1	0-1	21		3679
6		14	A	Wigan Ath	W	1-0	1-0	16	Young	2445
7		17	A	Brentford	L	1-4	0-4	—	Jenkinson (pen)	4586
8		21	H	Torquay U	W	4-1	2-1	14	Young, Walmsley 2, Norton	3093
9		28	A	WBA	L	0-1	0-0	16		11,932
10	Oct	5	H	Exeter C	L	1-2	1-0	18	Jenkinson	3143
11		11	A	Swansea C	D	0-0	0-0	—		2725
12		19	A	Hartlepool U	W	3-2	2-1	17	Payton 2, Calvert	2868
13		26	H	Darlington	W	5-2	1-2	12	Payton 2, Stoker 2, Windass	3514
14	Nov	2	A	Fulham	D	0-0	0-0	14		3365
15		5	H	Shrewsbury T	W	4-0	3-0		Payton, Norton, Windass, Warren	5025
16		9	H	Chester C	W	1-0	1-0	8	Payton	4305
17		23	A	Leyton Orient	L	0-1	0-1	10		3510
18		30	H	Preston NE	D	2-2	1-0	10	Brown, Walmsley	4280
19	Dec	14	A	Bolton W	L	0-1	0-0	12		5273
20		20	A	Peterborough U	L	0-3	0-2	—		7904
21		26	H	Bournemouth	L	0-1	0-0	15		4741
22		28	H	Reading	L	0-1	0-1	18		3661
23	Jan	1	A	Birmingham C	D	2-2	1-1	17	France 2	12,983
24		11	A	Stockport Co	L	0-2	0-0	18		3982
25		18	A	Bradford C	L	1-2	0-0	20	Mail	6369
26		25	H	Stoke C	L	0-1	0-1	21		4996
27	Feb	1	H	Hartlepool U	L	0-2	0-1	22		3483
28		8	A	Darlington	W	1-0	0-0	20	Windass	3636
29		11	A	Preston NE	L	1-3	1-1	—	Wilcox	2932
30		22	A	Stockport Co	D	1-1	0-0	23	Wilcox	4490
31		25	A	Huddersfield T	D	1-1	0-0	—	Atkinson	6003
32		29	H	Huddersfield T	W	1-0	1-0	22	Kelly	5310
33	Mar	3	H	Bradford C	D	0-0	0-0	—		4224
34		7	A	Stoke C	W	3-2	1-0	19	Jenkinson 2, Atkinson	13,563
35		10	A	Shrewsbury T	W	3-2	2-0	—	Wilcox, Atkinson, Jenkinson	1956
36		14	H	Fulham	D	0-0	0-0	17		3742
37		21	A	Chester C	D	1-1	0-1	17	Windass	1269
38		28	H	Leyton Orient	W	1-0	0-0	17	Atkinson	3802
39		31	A	Wigan Ath	D	1-1	0-1	—	Atkinson	3385
40	Apr	4	A	Bury	L	2-3	0-2	18	France, Windass	2245
41		11	H	Brentford	L	0-3	0-1	19		3770
42		14	A	Torquay U	L	1-2	1-0	—	Windass	2339
43		20	H	WBA	W	1-0	1-0	20	Jenkinson	4815
44		25	A	Exeter C	W	3-0	0-0	19	Atkinson, France, Jenkinson	2772
45		29	H	Bolton W	W	2-0	1-0	—	Wilcox, Matthews	3997
46	May	2	H	Swansea C	W	3-0	1-0	14	Atkinson 2, Matthews	4070

Final League Position: 14

GOALSCORERS

League (54): Atkinson 8, Jenkinson 8 (1 pen), Payton 7, Windass 6, France 4, Wilcox 4, Walmsley 3, Matthews 2, Norton 2, Stoker 2, Young 2, Brown 1, Calvert 1, Kelly 1, Mail 1, Palin 1, Warren 1.
Rumbelows Cup (3): Jenkinson 1, Payton 1, Young 1.
FA Cup (2): Hunter 1, Wilcox 1.

Fettis	Mail	Jacobs	Wilcox	Buckley	Calvert	Matthews	Payton	Hunter	Norton	Jenkinson	Hobson	Walmsley	Palin	Warren	Allison	Ngata	Brown	Atkinson	Stoker	Young	Wilson	Windass	Shotton	France	Pearson	Kelly	Hockaday	Match No.
1	2	3	4	5	6	7*	8	9†	10	11	12	14																1
1	2	3	4	5	6*		8	9	10	11	12	7																2
1		3	4				8	9*	7	11	6			10	2	5	12											3
1		3	4				8	9*	7	11	6			10	2	5	12											4
1	4*	3					9†	7	11	6	12	10		5	8	2	14											5
1		3	4*12		14				10	11	5						8†	2	7	6	9							6
1	3*	4†	5						10	11	12	14					8	2	7	6	9							7
1			4		14				10	11	6*	7	12	5			2	3	8	9†								8
1	6	12							10	11	5	7*		4			2	3	8	9								9
	6	12							10	11	5	14		4			7†	2	3*	8	9	1						10
1	5	3			6		8		10	11				4			12	7†	9*			2	14					11
1	5	3			7	12	8		10	11			14	4*					9†			2	6					12
1	14	3	5		4†	8		9*10		11	12							7				2	6					13
1	4	3	5				8		10	11							9*	7	12			2	6					14
1	4	3	5				8		10	11			14				9†	7*12				2	6					15
1	4†	3	5				8		10	11			14				9*	7	12			2	6					16
1	4	3	5	9					10	11			14				8	12	7†			2*	6					17
1	4	3	5			12			10	11							8	9	7*			2	6					18
1	4	3	5				8		10	11				7	2*		9		12				6					19
1	4	3	5				8		10	11				7			9					2	6					20
1	4	3	5			12		9	10	11			8†	7								2	6*14					21
1	4†	3	5			8*		14	10	11				7				12				2	6	9				22
1		3	5				8		10	11				7			4*12					2	6	9				23
1		3					8	10*	4	11	5			7				12				2	6	9				24
1	4	3	5				8		2	11				7								10	6	9				25
1	4	3*	5						2	11				7			8					10	6	12	9			26
1			5						2	11			3	7			4					10	6*12	9			8	27
1	4		5†					7		11*			14		3		6					10	12	9	8		2	28
1	4		5*							11†				7			6	3		14		10	12	9	8		2	29
1	4		5											7			6	3	11			10		9	8		2	30
1	4		5											7		14	6	3	11	12		10		8†	9		2*	31
1	4		5											7			6	3	11			10		9	8		2	32
1	4		5											7	12		6	3	11*			10		9	8		2	33
1	4		5											7			6	3	8			10		9			2	34
1	4		5											7			6	3	8	12		10		9			2*	35
1	4		5											7			6	3	8			10		9			2	36
	4		5											7			6	3*	8		1	10	12	9			2	37
1	4		5			10†14								7			6	3	8				12	9*			2	38
1	4		5					12						7			6	3	8			10		9			2*	39
1	4*		5					12		11†				7	2		6	3	8			14	10	9				40
1	4		5					12		11				7		3	6	2†	8			14	10	9*				41
	4		5						2	11				7		3	6		8*	12	1	10		9				42
1	4		5			2*				14				7	11		6	3	8	12		10		9†				43
1	4		5			2				14					11		6	12	3	8		7	10*	9†				44
1	4*		5			2		12						7	11		6	3	8			10		9				45
1			5			2		9		7	11			3			6	4	8			10						46
43	36	23	40	4	7	10	10	11	45	41	15	4	13	26	5	7	25	22	19	7	3	31	16	10	15	6	12	
	+1s	+2s			+1s	+4s	+6s	+4s			+1s		+1s	+5s	+5s	+2s	+4s	+3s	+5s	+8s				+1s	+1s		+7s	

Rumbelows Cup

	First Round	Blackburn R (a)	1-1
		(h)	1-0
	Second Round	QPR (h)	0-3
		(a)	1-5
FA Cup	First Round	Morecambe (a)	1-0
	Second Round	Blackpool (a)	1-0
	Third Round	Chelsea (h)	0-2

HULL CITY

Player and Position	Ht	Wt	Birth Date	Birth Place	Source	Clubs	League App	Gls
Goalkeepers								
David Cleminshaw	6 1	12 09	1 11 70	South Cave	Trainee	Hull C	—	—
Alan Fettis	6 01	11 04	1 2 71	Newtownards	Newtonards	Hull C	43	—
Steve Wilson§	5 10	10 07	24 4 74	Hull	Trainee	Hull C	5	—
Defenders								
Neil Allison§	6 02	11 10	20 10 73	Hull	Trainee	Hull C	8	—
Nicky Brown*	6 0	12 03	16 10 66	Hull	Local	Hull C	86	3
Neil Buckley*	6 2	13 06	25 9 68	Hull	Trainee	Hull C	60	3
						Burnley (loan)	5	—
Gary Hobson	6 02	12 10	12 11 72	North Ferriby	Trainee	Hull C	20	—
David Hockaday	5 10	10 09	9 11 57	Billingham	Amateur	Blackpool	147	24
						Swindon T	245	6
						Hull C	47	1
Wayne Jacobs	5 9	10 02	3 2 69	Sheffield	Apprentice	Sheffield W	6	—
						Hull C	129	4
David Mail	5 11	11 12	12 9 62	Bristol	Apprentice	Aston Villa	—	—
						Blackburn R	206	4
						Hull C	73	2
David Norton	5 7	11 03	3 3 65	Cannock	Apprentice	Aston Villa	44	2
						Notts Co	27	1
						Rochdale (loan)	9	—
						Hull C (loan)	15	—
						Hull C	45	2
Malcolm Shotton*	6 3	13 12	16 2 57	Newcastle	Apprentice	Leicester C	—	—
						Nuneaton Bor		
						Oxford U	263	12
						Portsmouth	10	—
						Huddersfield T	16	1
						Barnsley	66	6
						Hull C	59	2
Paul Waites*	5 10	12 08	24 1 71	Hull	Trainee	Hull C	11	—
Russell Wilcox	6 0	11 10	25 3 64	Hemsworth	Apprentice	Doncaster R	1	—
						Cambridge U	—	—
						Frickley	—	—
						Northampton T	138	9
						Hull C	71	5
Dean Windass	5 09	12 03	1 4 69	Hull	Trainee	Hull C	32	6
Midfield								
Graeme Atkinson	5 10	10 02	11 11 71	Hull	Trainee	Hull C	54	9
Mark Calvert	5 9	11 05	11 9 70	Newcastle	Trainee	Hull C	23	1
Ken De Mange*	5 9	11 10	3 9 64	Dublin	Home Farm	Liverpool	—	—
						Scunthorpe U (loan)	3	2
						Leeds U	15	1
						Hull C	68	2
Roger Greenwood*			31 8 73	Barnsley	Trainee	Hull C	—	—
Mike Matthews	5 8	11 03	25 9 60	Hull	Apprentice	Wolverhampton W	76	7
						Scunthorpe U	58	5
						Halifax T	99	8
						Scarborough	7	1
						Stockport Co	35	3
						Scarborough	66	3
						Hull C	16	2
Herry Ngata†			24 8 71	New Zealand		Hull C	25	—

HULL CITY

Foundation: The enthusiasts who formed Hull City in 1904 were brave men indeed. More than that they were audacious for they immediately put the club on the map in this Rugby League fortress by obtaining a three-year agreement with the Hull Rugby League club to rent their ground! They had obtained quite a number of conversions to the dribbling code, before the Rugby League forbade the use of any of their club grounds by Association Football clubs. By that time, Hull City were well away having entered the FA Cup in their initial season and the Football League, Second Division after only a year.

First Football League game: 2 September, 1905, Division 2, v Barnsley (h) W 4-1 – Spendiff; Langley, Jones; Martin, Robinson, Gordon (2); Rushton, Spence (1), Wilson (1), Howe, Raisbeck.

Did you know: David Mercer scored six goals for Hull City against Sheffield United on 4 January 1919. No wonder United paid what was then a record fee of £4,500 for this player in December 1920.

Managers (and Secretary-managers)
James Ramster 1904–05*, Ambrose Langley 1905–13, Harry Chapman 1913–14, Fred Stringer 1914–16, David Menzies 1916–21, Percy Lewis 1921–23, Bill McCracken 1923–31, Haydn Green 1931–34, John Hill 1934–36, David Menzies 1936, Ernest Blackburn 1936–46, Major Frank Buckley 1946–48, Raich Carter 1948–51, Bob Jackson 1952–55, Bob Brocklebank 1955–61, Cliff Britton 1961–70 (continued as GM to 1971), Terry Neill 1970–74, John Kaye 1974–77, Bobby Collins 1977–78, Ken Houghton 1978–79, Mike Smith 1979–82, Bobby Brown 1982, Colin Appleton 1982–84, Brian Horton 1984–88, Eddie Gray 1988–89, Colin Appleton 1989, Stan Ternent 1989–91, Terry Dolan February 1991–.

Player and Position	Ht	Wt	Birth Date	Birth Place	Source	Clubs	League App	League Gls
Leigh Palin	5 9	10 03	12 9 65	Worcester	Apprentice	Aston Villa	—	—
						Shrewsbury T (loan)	2	—
						Nottingham F	—	—
						Bradford C	71	10
						Stoke C	19	3
						Hull C	57	7
						Rochdale (loan)	3	—
Gareth Stoker	5 09	10 03	22 2 73	Bishop Auckland	Trainee	Leeds U	—	—
						Hull C	24	2
Lee Warren	6 0	11 13	28 2 69	Manchester	Trainee	Leeds U	—	—
						Rochdale	31	1
						Hull C	84	1
						Lincoln C (loan)	3	1
Forwards								
Darren France	6 00	14 02	8 8 67	Hull	N.Ferriby	Hull C	17	4
Paul Hunter	6 0	12 09	30 8 68	Kirkcaldy	Leven Royal Colts	East Fife	164	56
						Hull C	42	5
Leigh Jenkinson	6 0	12 02	9 7 69	Thorne	Trainee	Hull C	104	9
						Rotherham U (loan)	7	—
Ian McParland‡	5 8	10 08	4 10 61	Edinburgh	Ormiston Pr	Notts Co	221	69
						Hull C	47	7
						Walsall (loan)	11	6
David Walmsley*			23 11 72	Hull	Trainee	Hull C	10	4
Stuart Young	5 11	12 00	16 12 72	Hull	Trainee	Arsenal	—	—
						Hull C	15	2

Trainees
Allison, Neil J; Boughen, Mark R; Fisher, Steven L; Gallagher, Mark; Hopkin, Matthew C; Houghton, Nicholas N; Knight, Simon; Lowthorpe, Andrew; Morrow, Keith P; Mulligan, Stephen T; Noonan, Lee; Said, Lee S; Shirtliffe, Mark A; Stowe, Dean D; Thompson, Ross M; Welburn, Paul A; Willingham, Mark J; Wilson, Stephen L.

Associated Schoolboys
Armstrong, Gary; Clegg, Michael J; Gray, Andrew; Hoyle, David; Hunnaball, Richard L; Junk, Robert S; Knight, Paul M; Robinson, Ryan; Scott, Gary; Skewis, Darren A; Tyas, Rodger; Watson, Phillip; White, Paul.

Associated Schoolboys who have accepted the club's offer of a Traineeship/Contract
Burke, Neil; Cass, Jamie M; Edeson, Matthew K; Kirk, Wayne K; Mitchell, Alexander S; Stead, Nathan D.

IPSWICH TOWN 1991–92 *Back row (left to right):* Glenn Pennyfather, Steve Greaves, David Lowe, Tony Humes, Neil Thompson, Gavin Johnson, David Gregory, Neil Gregory, David Hill.
Centre row: Simon Milton, Steve Palmer, Jason Dozzell, Phil Whelan, Craig Forrest, Phil Parkes, Brian Gayle, Gary Thompson, Lee Honeywood, Simon Betts.
Front row: Romeo Zondervan, Mick Stockwell, Paul Goddard, David Linighan, Frank Yallop, Chris Kiwomya, Steve Whitton.

FA Premier

IPSWICH TOWN

Portman Road, Ipswich, Suffolk IP1 2DA. Telephone Ipswich (0473) 219211 (4 lines). Sales & Marketing Dept: (0473) 212202.

Ground capacity: 23,000.

Record attendance: 38,010 v Leeds U, FA Cup 6th rd, 8 March 1975.

Record receipts: £105,950 v AZ 67 Alkmaar, UEFA Cup Final 1st leg, 6 May 1981.

Pitch measurements: 112yd × 70yd.

Chairman: J. Kerr MBE.

President: P. M. Cobbold.

Vice-president: J. M. Sangster.

Directors: H. R. Smith, K. H. Brightwell, J. Kerridge, D. Sheepshanks, P. M. Cobbold.

Manager: John Lyall. *Assistant Manager:* Charlie Woods. *First Team Coach:* Mick McGiven. *Reserve Coach:* Bryan Klug. *Physio:* D. Bingham. *Youth Team Coach:* Peter Trevivian. *Secretary:* David C. Rose. *Commercial Manager:* Mike Noye.

Year Formed: 1878. Turned Professional: 1936. Ltd Co.: 1936.

Club Nickname: 'Blues' or 'Town'.

Record League Victory: 7-0 v Portsmouth, Division 2, 7 November 1964 – Thorburn; Smith, McNeil; Baxter, Bolton, Thompson; Broadfoot (1), Hegan (2), Baker (1), Leadbetter, Brogan (3). 7-0 v Southampton, Division 1, 2 February 1974 – Sivell; Burley, Mills (1), Morris, Hunter, Beattie (1), Hamilton (2), Viljoen, Johnson, Whymark (2), Lambert (1) (Woods). 7-0 v WBA, Division 1, 6 November 1976 – Sivell; Burley, Mills, Talbot, Hunter, Beattie (1), Osborne, Wark (1), Mariner (1) (Bertschin), Whymark (4), Woods.

Record Cup Victory: 10-0 v Floriana, European Cup, Prel. rd, 25 September 1962 – Bailey; Malcolm, Compton; Baxter, Laurel, Elsworthy (1); Stephenson, Moran (2), Crawford (5), Phillips (2), Blackwood.

Record Defeat: 1-10 v Fulham, Division 1, 26 December 1963.

Most League Points (2 for a win): 64, Division 3 (S), 1953–54 and 1955–56.

Most League points (3 for a win): 84. Division 2, 1991–92.

Most League Goals: 106, Division 3 (S), 1955–56.

Highest League Scorer in Season: Ted Phillips, 41, Division 3 (S), 1956–57.

Most League Goals in Total Aggregate: Ray Crawford, 203, 1958–63 and 1966–69.

Most Capped Player: Allan Hunter, 47 (53), Northern Ireland.

Most League Appearances: Mick Mills, 591, 1966–82.

Record Transfer Fee Received: £800,000 from Sheffield United for Brian Gayle, September 1991.

Record Transfer Fee Paid: £650,000 to Derby Co for Geraint Williams, July 1992.

Football League Record: 1938 Elected to Division 3 (S); 1954–55 Division 2; 1955–57 Division 3 (S); 1957–61 Division 2; 1961–64 Division 1; 1964–68 Division 2; 1968–86 Division 1; 1986–92 Division 2; 1992– FA Premier League.

Honours: Football League: Division 1 – Champions 1961–62; Runners-up 1980–81, 1981–82; Division 2 – Champions 1960–61, 1967–68, 1991–92; Division 3 (S) – Champions 1953–54, 1956–57. *FA Cup:* Winners 1977–78. *Football League Cup:* best season: Semi-final 1981–82, 1984–85, *Texaco Cup:* 1972–73. **European Competitions:** *European Cup:* 1962–63. *European Cup-Winners' Cup:* 1978–79. *UEFA Cup:* 1973–74, 1974–75, 1975–76, 1977–78, 1979–80, 1980–81 (winners), 1981–82, 1982–83.

Colours: Blue shirts, white shorts, blue stockings. **Change colours:** White shirts, blue shorts.

IPSWICH TOWN 1991–92 LEAGUE RECORD

Match No.	Date		Venue	Opponents	Result		H/T Score	Lg. Pos.	Goalscorers	Atten- dance
1	Aug	17	A	Bristol R	D	3-3	1-1	—	Dozzell, Goddard, Stockwell	6444
2		20	H	Port Vale	W	2-1	1-0	—	Kiwomya, Thompson (pen)	8937
3		24	H	Middlesbrough	W	2-1	0-0	1	Dozzell, Goddard	9822
4		31	A	Blackburn R	W	2-1	1-0	1	Kiwomya, Goddard	8898
5	Sep	3	H	Swindon T	L	1-4	1-2	—	Kiwomya	11,002
6		7	H	Southend U	W	1-0	0-0	3	Thompson (pen)	12,732
7		14	A	Barnsley	L	0-1	0-0	4		6786
8		17	A	Newcastle U	D	1-1	1-0	—	Kiwomya	16,336
9		21	H	Bristol C	W	4-2	1-1	2	Thompson, Linighan, Kiwomya, Goddard	9692
10		28	A	Grimsby T	W	2-1	1-1	2	Lowe, Johnson	6621
11	Oct	5	H	Oxford U	W	2-1	2-0	2	Milton, Whitton	9932
12		12	A	Brighton & HA	D	2-2	1-0	2	Milton, Dozzell	9010
13		19	H	Millwall	D	0-0	0-0	3		11,175
14		26	A	Portsmouth	D	1-1	1-1	5	Milton	8007
15		30	A	Charlton Ath	D	1-1	1-1	—	Whitton	6939
16	Nov	2	A	Leicester C	D	2-2	0-0	5	Wark, Johnson	11,331
17		5	H	Sunderland	L	0-1	0-1	—		9768
18		9	H	Cambridge U	L	1-2	0-1	7	Stockwell	20,586
19		16	A	Derby Co	L	0-1	0-0	9		12,493
20		23	A	Wolverhampton W	W	2-1	0-1	6	Linighan, Dozzell	11,915
21		30	H	Tranmere R	W	4-0	2-0	5	Milton, Thompson, Linighan, Wark (pen)	11,072
22	Dec	7	A	Plymouth Arg	L	0-1	0-1	6		4986
23		20	A	Swindon T	D	0-0	0-0	—		7404
24		26	H	Charlton Ath	W	2-0	1-0	6	Kiwomya 2	13,826
25		28	H	Blackburn R	W	2-1	0-1	3	Johnson, Dozzell	17,675
26	Jan	1	A	Port Vale	W	2-1	1-0	2	Kiwomya 2	8075
27		11	A	Middlesbrough	L	0-1	0-0	5		15,104
28		18	H	Bristol R	W	1-0	0-0	3	Milton	10,435
29	Feb	1	A	Millwall	W	3-2	1-0	3	Dozzell, Thompson, Kiwomya	8847
30		8	H	Portsmouth	W	5-2	3-1	2	Dozzell 2, Kiwomya 2, Awford (og)	13,494
31		21	A	Tranmere R	W	1-0	0-0	—	Milton	9161
32		29	H	Plymouth Arg	W	2-0	0-0	2	Kiwomya, Whitton	12,852
33	Mar	7	A	Watford	W	1-0	0-0	2	Whitton	9199
34		14	H	Leicester C	D	0-0	0-0	2		16,174
35		17	H	Watford	L	1-2	0-0	—	Dozzell	12,484
36		21	A	Cambridge U	D	1-1	0-0	3	Milton	9766
37		28	H	Derby Co	W	2-1	2-0	1	Dozzell 2	15,305
38		31	H	Barnsley	W	2-0	1-0	—	Kiwomya 2	14,148
39	Apr	4	A	Southend U	W	2-1	0-0	1	Whelan, Thompson	10,003
40		7	A	Wolverhampton W	W	2-1	0-0	—	Whelan, Whitton (pen)	17,379
41		11	H	Newcastle U	W	3-2	1-2	1	Whitton (pen), Wark, Kiwomya	20,673
42		14	A	Sunderland	L	0-3	0-0	—		22,131
43		18	A	Bristol C	L	1-2	0-1	1	Whitton (pen)	16,941
44		21	H	Grimsby T	D	0-0	0-0	—		22,393
45		25	A	Oxford U	D	1-1	1-1	1	Johnson	10,525
46	May	2	H	Brighton & HA	W	3-1	2-1	1	Whitton 2 (1 pen), Johnson	26,803

Final League Position: 1

GOALSCORERS

League (70): Kiwomya 16, Dozzell 11, Whitton 9 (4 pens), Milton 7, Thompson 6 (2 pens), Johnson 5, Goddard 4, Linighan 3, Wark 3 (1 pen), Stockwell 2, Whelan 2, Lowe 1, own goals 1.
Rumbelows Cup (0).
FA Cup (8): Dozzell 4, Johnson 1, Kiwomya 1, Milton 1, Whitton 1.

Forrest	Yallop	Thompson	Zondervan	Gayle	Humes	Stockwell	Goddard	Johnson	Dozzell	Kiwomya	Lowe	Whitton	Linighan	Milton	Wark	Gregory	Edmonds	Moncur	Youds	Palmer	Pennyfather	Whelan	Match No.
1	2	3	4	5	6	7	8*	9	10	11	12												1
1	12	3	7	5	6	4*	8	2	10	11		9											2
1	12	3	7	5		4*	8	2	10	11†14		9	6										3
1		3	7	5		4	8	2	10	11		9	6										4
1	14	3	7†	5		4	8	2	10	11	12	9*	6										5
1		3	7	5		4	8*	2	10	11	12	9	6										6
1		3	7	5		4	8	2*	10	11	12	9	6										7
1	12	3	7	5*		4	8	2	10	11		9	6										8
1	5	3	7			4*	8	2†	10	11	12	9	6	14									9
1	5	3	8			4*		2	10	11	7	9	6	12									10
1	5	3	8			4				11	7	9	6	10	2								11
1		3		5		4			10	11*	7	9	6	8	2	12							12
1	2	3	8			4			10		7	9	6	11*	5		12						13
1	2	3*	8			4		12	10		7†	9	6	11	5		14						14
1	2	3				4			10	11	7	9	6	8	5								15
1	2	3				4		12	10	11	7*	9	6	8	5								16
1	2*	3				4		12	10	11		9	6	7†	5		14			8			17
1	12	3				4		2	10	11		9*	6	7	5					8			18
1	12	3				4			10	11	7	9	6		5					8	2*		19
1		3				4	8	2	10	11		9	6	7	5								20
1		3				4		2	10	11	12	9*	6	7	5					8			21
1	12	3				4		2	10	11		9	6	7	5					8*			22
1		3				4		2	10	11		9	6	7	5					8			23
1		3				4		2	10	11		9	6	7	5					8			24
1		3				4		2	10	11*	12	9	6	7	5					8			25
1		3				4		2	10	11		9	6	7	5					8			26
1	12	3				4		2	10	11		9	6	7	5					8*	3		27
1		3	12			4		2	10	11		9	6	7	5					8*			28
1		3	12			4		2	10	11		9	6	7	5*					8			29
1		3				4		2	10	11		9	6	7	5					8			30
1		3				4	12	2	10	11*		9	6	7	5					8			31
1		3	14			4	12	2†	10*	11		9	6	7	5					8			32
1		3				4		2	10	11		9	6	7	5					8			33
1		3				4	12	2	10	11		9	6	7	5					8*			34
1		3*				4	12	2	10	11		9	6	7	5					8			35
1		3	2			4	8		10	11		9	6	7	5								36
1		3	2			4	8	12	10	11		9	6	7*	5								37
1		3	2			4	8	12	10	11		9†	6*	7	5					14			38
1		3	2			4	8*	12	10	11		9		7†	5					14		6	39
1		3	2			4	8†	12	10	11		9		7*	5					14		6	40
1		3	2			4	8†	12	10	11		9		7†	5					14		6	41
1		3	2			4	8		10	11		9	6	7*						12			42
1		3	2			4†	8	14	10	11		9		7	5*					12		6	43
1		3	2*			4	8	14	10	11		9		7†	5					12		6	44
1		3	2			4	8		10	11		9	6	7	5								45
1		3	2†			4*	8	14	10	11		9		7	5					12		6	46
46	9	45	25	5	5	46	19	33	45	43	7	43	36	31	36	—	—	5	1	16	2	8	
			+8s	+3s			+5s	+9s				+7s		+3s	+1s	+1s	+2s	+1s		+7s	+1s		

Rumbelows Cup	Second Round	Derby Co (a)		0-0
		(h)		0-2
FA Cup	Third Round	Hartlepool U (h)		1-1
		(a)		2-0
	Fourth Round	Bournemouth (h)		3-0
	Fifth Round	Liverpool (h)		0-0
		(a)		2-3

IPSWICH TOWN

Player and Position	Ht	Wt	Date	Birth Place	Source	Clubs	League App	Gls
Goalkeepers								
Ron Fearon	6 0	11 12	19 11 60	Romford	Apprentice	QPR	—	—
						Reading	61	—
						Sutton	—	—
						Ipswich T	28	—
						Brighton & HA (loan)	7	—
						Leyton Orient	—	—
						Ipswich T	—	—
Craig Forrest	6 4	12 03	20 9 67	Vancouver	Apprentice	Ipswich T	162	—
						Colchester U (loan)	11	—
Phil Parkes*	6 3	15 01	8 8 50	Sedgeley	Amateur	Walsall	52	—
						QPR	344	—
						West Ham U	344	—
						Ipswich T	3	—
Jason Winters	6 0	11 08	15 9 71	Oatham	Trainee	Chelsea	—	—
						Ipswich T	—	—
Defenders								
Simon Betts*	5 8	10 01	3 3 73	Middlesbrough	Trainee	Ipswich T	—	—
Jason Dozzell	6 2	12 04	9 12 67	Ipswich	School	Ipswich T	291	45
Lee Honeywood	5 8	10 10	3 8 71	Chelmsford	Trainee	Ipswich T	—	—
Gavin Johnson	6 0	11 01	10 10 70	Ipswich	Trainee	Ipswich T	59	5
David Linighan	6 2	10 12	9 1 65	Hartlepool	Local	Hartlepool U	91	5
						Leeds U (loan)	—	—
						Derby Co	—	—
						Shrewsbury T	65	1
						Ipswich T	163	8
Neil Thompson	6 0	13 07	2 10 63	Beverley	Apprentice	Nottingham F	—	—
						Hull C	31	—
						Scarborough	87	15
						Ipswich T	128	15
Phil Whelan	6 4	14 01	7 8 72	Stockport		Ipswich T	8	2
Frank Yallop	5 11	11 03	4 4 64	Watford	Apprentice	Ipswich T	255	4
Edward Youds	6 0	11 00	3 5 70	Liverpool	Trainee	Everton	8	—
						Cardiff C (loan)	1	—
						Wrexham (loan)	20	2
						Ipswich T	1	—
Midfield								
Andy Bernal	5 10	12 05	16 7 66	Canberra		Ipswich T	9	—
Darren Edmonds*	5 9	11 06	12 4 71	Watford	Trainee	Leeds U	—	—
						Ipswich T	2	—
Steve Greaves*	5 10	11 11	17 1 70	London	Trainee	Fulham	1	—
						Waterford (loan)	—	—
						Brighton & HA (loan)	—	—
						Preston NE	2	—
						Ipswich T	—	—
David Gregory	5 10	11 03	23 1 70	Sudbury	Trainee	Ipswich T	28	1
Simon Milton	5 9	11 09	23 8 63	London	Bury St Edmunds	Ipswich T	149	34
						Exeter C (loan)	2	3
						Torquay U (loan)	4	1
Steve Palmer	6 1	12 07	31 3 68	Brighton	Cambridge Univ	Ipswich T	51	1
Glenn Pennyfather	5 8	10 10	11 2 63	Billericay	Apprentice	Southend U	238	36
						Crystal Palace	34	1
						Ipswich T	11	1
Ian Redford (To St Johnstone Aug 1991)	5 10	11 08	5 4 60	Dundee	Errol R	Dundee	85	34
						Rangers	172	23
						Dundee U	101	20
						Ipswich T	68	8

IPSWICH TOWN

Foundation: Considering that Ipswich Town only reached the Football League in 1938, many people outside of East Anglia may be surprised to learn that this club was formed at a meeting held in the Town Hall as far back as 1878 when Mr. T. C. Cobbold, MP, was voted president. Originally it was the Ipswich Association FC to distinguish it from the older Ipswich Football Club which played rugby. These two amalgamated in 1888 and the handling game was dropped in 1893.

First Football League game: 27 August, 1938, Division 3 (S), v Southend U (h) W 4-2 – Burns; Dale, Parry; Perrett, Fillingham, McLuckie; Williams, Davies (1), Jones (2), Alsop (1), Little.

Did you know: During their first Football League season in 1938–39 their Portman Road ground was so badly flooded that it was impossible to gain access by normal means. Their Third Division game with Reading on 28 January was postponed and the team received their wages at the local police station.

Managers (and Secretary-managers)
Mick O'Brien 1936–37, Scott Duncan 1937–55 (continued as secretary), Alf Ramsey 1955–63, Jackie Milburn 1963–64, Bill McGarry 1964–68, Bobby Robson 1969–82, Bobby Ferguson 1982–87, Johnny Duncan 1987–90, John Lyall May 1990–.

Player and Position	Ht	Wt	Birth Date	Birth Place	Source	Clubs	League App	Gls
Mike Stockwell	5 6	10 02	14 2 65	Chelmsford	Apprentice	Ipswich T	219	15
John Wark†	5 10	11 07	4 8 57	Glasgow	Apprentice	Ipswich T	296	94
						Liverpool	70	28
						Ipswich T	89	23
						Middlesbrough	32	2
						Ipswich T	37	3
Romeo Zondervan	5 9	10 02	4 3 59	Surinam	Den Haag	Twente Enschede	—	—
						WBA	84	5
						Ipswich T	274	13
Forwards								
Paul Goddard	5 8	12 00	12 10 59	Harlington	Apprentice	QPR	70	23
						West Ham U	170	54
						Newcastle U	61	19
						Derby Co	49	15
						Millwall	20	1
						Ipswich T	43	10
Chris Kiwomya	5 10	10 05	2 12 69	Huddersfield		Ipswich T	135	33
David Lowe	5 11	11 00	30 8 65	Liverpool	Apprentice	Wigan Ath	188	40
						Ipswich T	134	37
						Port Vale (loan)	9	2
Gary Thompson	6 0	11 04	7 9 72	Ipswich		Ipswich T	—	—
Steve Whitton	6 0	12 07	4 12 60	East Ham	Apprentice	Coventry C	74	21
						West Ham U	39	6
						Birmingham C (loan)	8	2
						Birmingham C	95	28
						Sheffield W	32	4
						Ipswich T	96	20

Trainees
Connell, Graham; Cook, Adam; Cotterell, Leo S; Devine, Declan P; Durrant, Lee R; Eason, Jeremy J; Harrison, Gary D; Morgan, Philip J; Pearn, Steven; Pirie, David W; Powley, Darren L. W; Ryland, Richard; Shaw, Marcus; Smedley, Martin; Smith, Kevin L; Tanner, Adam D; Theodorou, Theodoros.

**Non-Contract
Gregory, Neil R; Wark, John.

Associated Schoolboys
Abbott, Daniel A; Bell, Leon C; Byrne, Stephen; Coates, Scott L; Eaton, Daniel J; Ellis, Kevin E; Graham, Stephen; Hood, Paul; Miller, Marc P; Morin, Gareth N; Naylor, Richard A; Portrey, Simon D; Pryke, Damian A; Ross, John E. G; Travers, Benjamin; Woolsey, Jeffrey A.

Associated Schoolboys who have accepted the club's offer of a Traineeship/Contract
Dolby, Gavin P; Mansfield, Graham P; Mortley, Peter R; Norfolk, Lee R; Scowcroft, James B; Vaughan, Anthony J; Weston, Kenneth; Weston, Matthew.

**Non-Contract Players who are retained must be re-signed before they are eligible to play in League matches.

LEEDS UNITED 1991–92 *Back row (left to right)*: Bobby Davison, Chris Whyte, Gary McAllister, John Lukic, Mervyn Day, Peter Haddock, Lee Chapman, Rod Wallace. *Centre row*: Alan Sutton (Physiotherapist), Ray Wallace, Steve Hodge, Chris Fairclough, John McClelland, Mike Whitlow, Mel Sterland, Mick Hennigan (Coach). *Front row*: David Batty, Gary Speed, Imre Varadi, Howard Wilkinson (Manager), Gordon Strachan, Tony Dorigo. Chris Kamara. (Photo © LUAFC).

FA Premier

LEEDS UNITED

Elland Road, Leeds LS11 0ES. Telephone Leeds (0532) 716037 (4 lines). Ticket Office: 710710. Clubcall: 0898 12 11 81. Fax No: 706560

Ground capacity: 30,900.

Record attendance: 57,892 v Sunderland, FA Cup 5th rd (replay), 15 March 1967.

Record receipts: £291,549 v Manchester U, Rumbelows Cup semi-final 2nd leg, 24 February 1991.

Pitch measurements: 117yd × 76yd.

President: The Right Hon The Earl of Harewood LLD.

Chairman: L. Silver OBE.

Vice-chairman: P. J. Gilman.

Deputy Chairman: J. W. G. Marjason.

Managing Director: W. J. Fotherby.

Directors: R. Barker MCIT, MBIM, Coun. M. J. Bedford, E. Carlile, Coun. M. Feldman, G. M. Holmes BSC (ECON), Coun. A. Hudson, R. P. Ridsdale, K. Woolmer.

Manager: Howard Wilkinson. *Assistant Manager:* Mike Hennigan. *Company Secretary:* N. Pleasants. *Coaches:* Mike Hennigan, Peter Gunby, Paul Hart. *Physio:* Alan Sutton.

Commercial Manager: Bob Baldwin.

Year Formed: 1919, as Leeds United after disbandment (by FA order) of Leeds City (formed in 1904). Turned Professional: 1920. Ltd Co.: 1920.

Club Nickname: 'United'.

Record League Victory: 8-0 v Leicester C, Division 1, 7 April 1934 – Moore; George Milburn, Jack Milburn; Edwards, Hart, Copping; Mahon (2), Firth (2), Duggan (2), Furness (2), Cochrane.

Record Cup Victory: 10-0 v Lyn (Oslo), European Cup, 1st rd 1st leg, 17 September 1969 – Sprake; Reaney, Cooper, Bremner (2), Charlton, Hunter, Madeley, Clarke (2), Jones (3), Giles (2) (Bates), O'Grady (1).

Record Defeat: 1-8 v Stoke C, Division 1, 27 August 1934.

Most League Points (2 for a win): 67, Division 1, 1968–69.

Most League points (3 for a win): 85, Division 2, 1989–90.

Most League Goals: 98, Division 2, 1927–28.

Highest League Scorer in Season: John Charles, 42, Division 2, 1953–54.

Most League Goals in Total Aggregate: Peter Lorimer, 168, 1965–79 and 1983–86.

Most Capped Player: Billy Bremner, 54, Scotland.

Most League Appearances: Jack Charlton, 629, 1953–73.

Record Transfer Fee Received: £825,000 from Everton for Ian Snodin, January 1987.

Record Transfer Fee Paid: £1,700,000 to Southampton for Rodney and Ray Wallace, July 1991.

Football League Record: 1920 Elected to Division 2; 1924–27 Division 1; 1927–28 Division 2; 1928–31 Division 1; 1931–32 Division 2; 1932–47 Division 1; 1947–56 Division 2; 1956–60 Division 1; 1960–64 Division 2; 1964–82 Division 1; 1982–90 Division 2; 1990–92 Division 1; 1992– FA Premier League.

Honours: Football League: Division 1 – Champions 1968–69, 1973–74, 1991–92; Runners-up 1964–65, 1965–66, 1969–70, 1970–71, 1971–72; Division 2 – Champions 1923–24, 1963–64, 1989–90; Runners-up 1927–28, 1931–32, 1955–56. *FA Cup:* Winners 1972; Runners-up 1965, 1970, 1973. *Football League Cup:* Winners 1967–68. **European Competitions:** *European Cup:* 1969–70, 1974–75 (runners-up). *European Cup-Winners' Cup:* 1972–73 (runners-up). *European Fairs Cup:* 1965–66, 1966–67 (runners-up), 1967–68 (winners), 1968–69, 1970–71 (winners). *UEFA Cup:* 1971–72, 1973–74, 1979–80.

Colours: All white. **Change colours:** Blue with yellow trim.

LEEDS UNITED 1991–92 LEAGUE RECORD

Match No.	Date		Venue	Opponents	Result		H/T Score	Lg. Pos.	Goalscorers	Atten-dance
1	Aug	20	H	Nottingham F	W	1-0	1-0	—	McAllister	29,457
2		24	H	Sheffield W	D	1-1	0-0	10	Hodge	30,260
3		28	A	Southampton	W	4-0	1-0	—	Speed 2, Strachan 2 (2 pen)	15,847
4		31	A	Manchester U	D	1-1	1-0	6	Chapman	43,778
5	Sep	3	H	Arsenal	D	2-2	0-1	—	Strachan (pen), Chapman	29,396
6		7	H	Manchester C	W	3-0	2-0	4	Dorigo, Batty, Strachan (pen)	29,986
7		14	A	Chelsea	W	1-0	0-0	2	Shutt	23,439
8		18	A	Coventry C	D	0-0	0-0	—		15,488
9		21	H	Liverpool	W	1-0	1-0	2	Hodge	32,917
10		28	A	Norwich C	D	2-2	0-0	2	Dorigo, Speed	15,828
11	Oct	1	A	Crystal Palace	L	0-1	0-0	—		18,298
12		5	H	Sheffield U	W	4-3	3-0	2	Hodge 2, Sterland 2 (1 pen)	28,362
13		19	A	Notts Co	W	4-2	2-1	2	Chapman, Hodge, Whyte, McAllister	12,964
14		26	H	Oldham Ath	W	1-0	0-0	1	Kilcline (og)	28,199
15	Nov	2	A	Wimbledon	D	0-0	0-0	2		7025
16		16	H	QPR	W	2-0	0-0	1	Sterland, Wallace Rod	27,087
17		24	A	Aston Villa	W	4-1	1-0	—	Wallace Rod, Sterland, Chapman 2	23,666
18		30	H	Everton	W	1-0	0-0	1	Wallace Rod	30,043
19	Dec	7	A	Luton T	W	2-0	0-0	1	Wallace Rod, Speed	11,550
20		14	H	Tottenham H	D	1-1	1-1	1	Speed	31,404
21		22	A	Nottingham F	D	0-0	0-0	—		27,170
22		26	H	Southampton	D	3-3	2-0	2	Hodge 2, Speed	29,053
23		29	H	Manchester U	D	1-1	0-0	1	Sterland (pen)	32,638
24	Jan	1	A	West Ham U	W	3-1	2-1	1	Chapman 2, McAllister	21,766
25		12	A	Sheffield W	W	6-1	3-1	—	Chapman 3, Dorigo, Whitlow, Wallace Rod	32,228
26		18	H	Crystal Palace	D	1-1	1-1	1	Fairclough	27,717
27	Feb	1	H	Notts Co	W	3-0	1-0	1	Sterland, Batty, Wallace Rod	27,224
28		8	A	Oldham Ath	L	0-2	0-1	2		18,409
29		23	A	Everton	D	1-1	0-0	—	Keown (og)	19,248
30		29	H	Luton T	W	2-0	0-0	2	Cantona, Chapman	28,231
31	Mar	3	H	Aston Villa	D	0-0	0-0	—		28,896
32		7	A	Tottenham H	W	3-1	1-0	1	Wallace Rod, Newsome, McAllister	27,622
33		11	A	QPR	L	1-4	1-1	—	Speed	14,641
34		14	H	Wimbledon	W	5-1	3-0	1	Chapman 3, Wallace Rod, Cantona	26,760
35		22	A	Arsenal	D	1-1	0-0	—	Chapman	27,844
36		28	H	West Ham U	D	0-0	0-0	1		31,101
37	Apr	4	A	Manchester C	L	0-4	0-2	2		30,239
38		11	A	Chelsea	W	3-0	0-0	1	Wallace Rod, Chapman, Cantona	31,363
39		18	A	Liverpool	D	0-0	0-0	2		37,186
40		20	H	Coventry C	W	2-0	0-0	1	Fairclough, McAllister (pen)	26,582
41		26	A	Sheffield U	W	3-2	1-1	—	Wallace Rod, Newsome, Gayle (og)	32,000
42	May	2	H	Norwich C	W	1-0	1-0	1	Wallace Rod	32,673

Final League Position: 1

GOALSCORERS

League (74): Chapman 16, Wallace Rod 11, Hodge 7, Speed 7, Sterland 6 (2 pens), McAllister 5 (1 pen), Strachan 4 (4 pens), Cantona 3, Dorigo 3, Batty 2, Fairclough 2, Newsome 2, Shutt 1, Whitlow 1, Whyte 1, own goals 3.
Rumbelows Cup (11): Chapman 4, Speed 3, Wallace Rod 2, Shutt 1, Sterland 1 (1 pen).
FA Cup (0).

Lukic	McClelland	Dorigo	Batty	Fairclough	Whyte	Strachan	Wallace Rod	Chapman	McAllister	Speed	Hodge	Sterland	Wetherall	Shutt	Varadi	Whitlow	Kamara	Newsome	Kelly	Davison	Cantona	Agana	Match No.
1	2	3	4	5	6	7	8	9	10	11													1
1	2†	3	4	5	6	7	8	9	10	11*	12		14										2
1	2	3	4	5†	6	7	8	9	10*	11	12	2											3
1	5	3	4		6	7	8	9	10*	11	12	2											4
1	5	3†	4		6	7	8	9	10	11	12	2*	14										5
1	5	3	4		6	7	8*	9	10	11	12	2											6
1	5	3	4		6	7*		9	10	11	12	2		8									7
1	5	3	4		6	7		9	10	11	12	2		8*									8
1	5	3	4		6	7	8	9	10	11*	12	2											9
1	5	3	4		6	7*	8†	9	10	11	12	2	14										10
1	5	3	4		6	7*	8	9	10†	11	12	2	14										11
1	5	3	4	12	6	7		9	10†	11		2*	14	8									12
1		3	4	5	6	7		9*	10	11	12†	2	14	8									13
1		3	4	5	6	7*	8	9	10	11†	12	2	14										14
1		3	4	5	6	7	8*	9	10	11	12	2											15
1		3	4	5	6	7	8	9	10	11*	12	2											16
1	11	3	4	5	6	7	8	9	10			2											17
1	14	3	4	5	6	7	8	9	10	11*	12†	2											18
1		3	4	5	6	7	8	9	10	11		2											19
1	5	3	4		6	7	8	9	10	11		2											20
1	5	3	4		6	7*	8	9	10	11	12	2											21
1	5	3	4		6	7	8	9	10	11		2											22
1		3	4*	5	6	7	8	9	10	11	12	2											23
1		3	4	5	6	7	8	9	10	11		2											24
1		3	4†	5	6	7*	8	9	10	11	12	2	14										25
1		3	4	5	6	7	8	9*	10†	11		2						12			14		26
1		3	4	5	6	7†	8	9	10	11		2*						12			14		27
1		3	4	5	6	7	8	9†	10	11		2*						12			14		28
1		3	4	5	6	7	8*		10	11		2						12			9		29
1		3*	4	5	6	7	8†	9	10	11		2									12	14	30
1	14		4	5†	6	7		9	10	11		2				3		12			8*		31
1			4	5	6	7	8	9	10	11		2†				3*		14			12		32
1			4	5	6	7	8	9	10*	11		2				3					12		33
1			4	5	6	7*	8	9	10	11		2				3					12		34
1		3	4	5	6	7	8	9	10	11		2											35
1		3	4	5	6	7	8*	9	10	11		2									12		36
1		3	4	5	6	7	8	9	10	11		2											37
1		3	4	5	6	7	8*	9	10	11		2†						14			12		38
1		3	4	5	6	7*	8	9	10	11		2									12		39
1		3	4	5	6	7†	8*	9	10	11		2						14			12		40
1		3	4	5	6	7†	8	9	10*	11		2						14			12		41
1		3	4	5	6	7*	8	9†	10	11		2						12			14		42

Appearances / substitute totals:

```
42 16 38 40 30 41 35 34 38 41 41 12 29  —  6  2  3  —  7  —  —  6  1
      +           +        +              +     +  +  +  +  +  +  +  +  +  +
      2s          1s       1s             1s    11s 2s 1s 8s 1s 7s 2s 3s 2s 2s 9s 1s
```

	Round	Opponent	Result
Rumbelows Cup	Second Round	Scunthorpe U (a)	0-0
		(h)	3-0
	Third Round	Tranmere R (h)	3-1
	Fourth Round	Everton (a)	4-1
	Fifth Round	Manchester U (h)	1-3
FA Cup	Third Round	Manchester U (h)	0-1

LEEDS UNITED

Goalkeepers

Name	Ht	Wt	Date of birth	Birthplace	Source	Club	Apps	Gls
Scott Cousin			31 1 75	Leeds	Trainee	Leeds U	—	—
Mervyn Day	6 2	15 01	26 6 55	Chelmsford	Apprentice	West Ham U	194	—
						Orient	170	—
						Aston Villa	30	—
						Leeds U	225	—
						Coventry C (loan)	—	—
						Luton T (loan)	4	—
						Sheffield U (loan)	1	—
John Lukic	6 4	13 07	11 12 60	Chesterfield	Apprentice	Leeds U	146	—
						Arsenal	223	—
						Leeds U	80	—
Tony O'Dowd*			6 7 70	Dublin	Shelbourne	Leeds U	—	—
						Kilkerry (loan)	—	—

Defenders

Name	Ht	Wt	Date of birth	Birthplace	Source	Club	Apps	Gls
Jim Beglin‡	5 11	11 00	29 7 63	Dublin	Shamrock R	Liverpool	64	2
						Leeds U	19	—
						Plymouth Arg (loan)	5	—
						Blackburn R (loan)	6	—
Len Curtis*			2 1 73	Dublin		Leeds U	—	—
Tony Dorigo	5 10	10 00	31 12 65	Melbourne	Apprentice	Aston Villa	111	1
						Chelsea	146	11
						Leeds U	38	3
Chris Fairclough	5 11	11 02	12 4 64	Nottingham	Apprentice	Nottingham F	107	1
						Tottenham H	60	5
						Leeds U	118	14
Peter Haddock	5 11	11 05	9 12 61	Newcastle	Apprentice	Newcastle U	57	—
						Burnley (loan)	7	—
						Leeds U	118	1
Dylan Kerr	5 11	12 05	14 1 67	Valetta	Arcadia Shepherds	Leeds U	8	—
						Doncaster R (loan)	7	1
						Blackpool (loan)	13	1
John McClelland*	6 2	13 05	7 12 55	Belfast	Portadown	Cardiff C	4	1
						Bangor	—	—
						Mansfield	125	8
						Rangers	96	4
						Watford	184	3
						Leeds U	24	—
						Watford (loan)	1	—
						Notts Co (loan)	6	—
Jon Newsome	6 2	13 11	6 9 70	Sheffield	Trainee	Sheffield W	7	—
						Leeds U	10	2
Steven Nicholson‡			20 10 71	Leeds	Trainee	Leeds U	—	—
Mel Sterland	5 10	12 10	1 1 61	Sheffield	Apprentice	Sheffield W	279	37
						Rangers	9	3
						Leeds U	111	16
Ray Wallace	5 6	10 02	2 10 69	Lewisham	Trainee	Southampton	35	—
						Leeds U	—	—
David Wetherall	6 3	12 00	14 3 71	Sheffield	School	Sheffield W	—	—
						Leeds U	1	—
Chris Whyte	6 1	11 10	2 9 61	London	Amateur	Arsenal	90	8
						Crystal Palace (loan)	13	—
						Los Angeles	—	—
						WBA	84	7
						Leeds U	79	4

Midfield

Name	Ht	Wt	Date of birth	Birthplace	Source	Club	Apps	Gls
David Batty	5 7	10 07	2 12 68	Leeds	Trainee	Leeds U	172	3
Steve Hodge	5 7	9 12	25 10 62	Nottingham	Apprentice	Nottingham F	123	30
						Aston Villa	53	12
						Tottenham H	45	7
						Nottingham F	82	20
						Leeds U	23	7
Gary McAllister	5 10	9 06	25 12 64	Motherwell	Fir Park BC	Motherwell	59	6
						Leicester C	201	47
						Leeds U	80	7
Gary Speed	5 9	10 06	8 9 69	Hawarden	Trainee	Leeds U	105	17
Gordon Strachan	5 6	10 03	9 2 57	Edinburgh		Dundee	60	13
						Aberdeen	183	55
						Manchester U	160	33
						Leeds U	127	30

LEEDS UNITED

Foundation: Immediately the Leeds City club (founded in 1904) was wound up by the FA in October 1919, following allegations of illegal payments to players, a meeting was called by a Leeds solicitor, Mr. Alf Masser, at which Leeds United was formed. They joined the Midland League playing their first game in that competition in November 1919. It was in this same month that the new club had discussions with the directors of a virtually bankrupt Huddersfield Town who wanted to move to Leeds in an amalgamation. But Huddersfield survived even that crisis.

First Football League game: 28 August, 1920, Division 2, v Port Vale (a) L 0-2 – Down; Duffield, Tillotson; Musgrove, Baker, Walton; Mason, Goldthorpe, Thompson, Lyon, Best.

Did you know: In 1926–27 United's Scottish international centre-forward Tom Jennings scored three hat-tricks (3-4-4) in consecutive games. Around this spell he netted 19 goals in nine successive First Division games.

Managers (and Secretary-managers)
Dick Ray 1919–20, Arthur Fairclough 1920–27, Dick Ray 1927–35, Bill Hampson 1935–47, Willis Edwards 1947–48, Major Frank Buckley 1948–53, Raich Carter 1953–58, Bill Lambton 1958–59, Jack Taylor 1959–61, Don Revie 1961–74, Brian Clough 1974, Jimmy Armfield 1974–78, Jock Stein 1978, Jimmy Adamson 1978–80, Allan Clarke 1980–82, Eddie Gray 1982–85, Billy Bremner 1985–88, Howard Wilkinson October 1988–.

Name	ft in	wt	Birth date	Birthplace	Signed from	Club	Apps	Gls
Mark Tinkler			24 10 74	Bishop Auckland	Trainee	Leeds U	—	—
Russell Wigley			9 1 72	Cardiff	Trainee	Leeds U	—	—
Forwards								
Eric Cantona	5 10	11 12	24 5 66	Paris	Nimes	Leeds U	15	3
Lee Chapman	6 3	13 00	5 12 59	Lincoln	Amateur	Stoke C	99	34
						Plymouth Arg (loan)	4	—
						Arsenal	23	4
						Sunderland	15	3
						Sheffield W	149	63
						Niort	—	—
						Nottingham F	48	15
						Leeds U	97	49
Bob Davison	5 8	11 08	17 7 59	South Shields	Seaham CW	Huddersfield T	2	—
						Halifax T	63	29
						Derby Co	206	83
						Leeds U	91	31
						Derby Co (loan)	10	8
						Sheffield U (loan)	11	4
Damian Henderson			12 5 73	Leeds	Trainee	Leeds U	—	—
Garry Kelly			9 7 74	Drogheda	Home Farm	Leeds U	2	
Steven Mulrain*			23 10 72	Lambeth	Trainee	Leeds U	—	—
Ryan Nicholls			10 5 73	Cardiff	Trainee	Leeds U	—	—
Patrick O'Connell			7 10 73	Dublin	Trainee	Leeds U	—	—
Carl Shutt	5 10	11 10	10 10 61	Sheffield	Spalding U	Sheffield W	40	16
						Bristol C	46	10
						Leeds U	65	17
Imre Varadi	5 8	11 01	8 7 59	Paddington	Letchworth GC	Sheffield U	10	4
						Everton	26	6
						Newcastle U	81	39
						Sheffield W	76	33
						WBA	32	9
						Manchester C	65	26
						Sheffield W	22	3
						Leeds U	22	4
						Luton T (loan)	6	1
Rodney Wallace	5 7	10 01	2 10 69	Lewisham	Trainee	Southampton	128	45
						Leeds U	34	11

Trainees
Atkinson, Richard; Ball, Stephen; Billy, Marlon; Byrne, Alexander; Couzens, Andrew J; Daly, Kevin; Flear, Christopher R; Gallagher, John; Hepworth, Richard; Hill, Stephen; O'Hara, Gary J; Oliver, Simon; Philpott, Marcus; Tobin, Steven; Whelan, Noel.

Associated Schoolboys
Blunt, Jason J; Brookman, Gareth E; Brown, Matthew; Cotterrall, Nathan P; Cross, Graham; Davies, Lawrence; Fawell, Nicholas; Fidler, Richard M; Flanagan, Matthew J; Flower, Carl D; Holmes, Damian L; Jackson, Mark G; Kirby, Philip; McDonald, Philip J; Noble, John R; Owen, Alun H; Pitt, Robert R; Shepherd, Paul; Sullivan, Christopher J; Thomson, Jamie; Wake, Alex D; Ward, Richard A; Webb, Paul A.

Associated Schoolboys who have accepted the club's offer of a Traineeship/Contract
Bowman, Robert A; Connor, David M; Ford, Mark S; Hoyle, Michael S; Littlewood, Martin; Lynam, Gary M; Smithard, Mathew P; Symons, Paul.

LEICESTER CITY 1991-92 *Back row (left to right):* Des Linton, Colin Gordon, Steve Walsh, Tony James, Carl Muggleton, Kevin Poole, Russell Hoult, Paul Fitzpatrick, Richard Smith, Jason Peake.
Centre row: Ali Mauchlen, Andy Jeffrey, Colin Gibson, Paul Reid, Gary Mills, Ian Baraclough, Paul Ramsey, David Oldfield, Ricky Hill, Scott Oakes.
Front row: Nicky Platnauer, Kevin Russell, Tommy Wright, Paul Kitson, Allan Evans (Coach), Brian Little (Manager), John Gregory (Coach), Steven Holden, David Kelly, Ashley Ward, Rob Johnson.

Division 1   **LEICESTER CITY**

City Stadium, Filbert St, Leicester LE2 7FL. Telephone Leicester (0533) 555000. Marketing: 0533 854000. Ticket line: 0898 12 10 28. Clubcall: 0898 121185.

Ground capacity: 22,181.

Record attendance: 47,298 v Tottenham H, FA Cup 5th rd, 18 February 1928.

Record receipts: £179,912 v Nottingham F, Zenith Data Systems Cup, 12 February 1992.

Pitch measurements: 112yd × 75yd.

President: K. R. Brigstock.

Chairman: Martin George.

Vice-Chairman: T. Smeaton.

Directors: J. M. Elsom FCA, R. W. Parker, J. E. Sharp, T. W. Shipman, W. K. Shooter FCA.

Manager: Brian Little.

Coaches: Allan Evans, John Gregory. *Secretary:* Alan Bennet. *Youth Coach:* Steve Hunt. *Physio:* Mark Geeson. *PRO:* Alan Birchenall. *Director of Marketing:* Barrie Pierpoint.

Year Formed: 1884.

Former Grounds: 1884, Victoria Park; 1887, Belgrave Road; 1888, Victoria Park; 1891, Filbert Street.

Former Names: 1884–1919, Leicester Fosse.

Club Nickname: 'Fiberts' or 'Foxes'.

Record League Victory: 10-0 v Portsmouth, Division 1, 20 October 1928 – McLaren; Black, Brown; Findlay, Carr, Watson; Adcock, Hine (3), Chandler (6), Lochhead, Barry (1).

Record Cup Victory: 8-1 v Coventry C (away), League Cup, 5th rd, 1 December 1964 – Banks; Sjoberg, Norman (2); Roberts, King, McDerment; Hodgson (2), Cross, Goodfellow, Gibson (1), Stringfellow (2). (1 og).

Record Defeat: 0-12 (as Leicester Fosse) v Nottingham F, Division 1, 21 April 1909.

Most League Points (2 for a win): 61, Division 2, 1956–57.

Most League points (3 for a win): 77, Division 2, 1991–92.

Most League Goals: 109, Division 2, 1956–57.

Highest League Scorer in Season: Arthur Rowley, 44, Division 2, 1956–57.

Most League Goals in Total Aggregate: Arthur Chandler, 259, 1923–35.

Most Capped Player: Gordon Banks, 37 (73), England.

Most League Appearances: Adam Black, 528, 1920–35.

Record Transfer Fee Received: £1,350,000 from Derby Co for Paul Kitson, March 1992.

Record Transfer Fee Paid: £500,000 to Everton for Wayne Clarke, July 1989.

Football League Record: 1894 Elected to Division 2; 1908–09 Division 1; 1909–25 Division 2; 1925–35 Division 1; 1935–37 Division 2; 1937–39 Division 1; 1946–54 Division 2; 1954–55 Division 2; 1955–57 Division 2; 1957–69 Division 1; 1969–71 Division 2; 1971–78 Division 1; 1978–80 Division 2; 1980–81 Division 1; 1981–83 Division 2; 1983–87 Division 1; 1987–92 Division 2; 1992– Division 1.

Honours: Football League: Division 1 – Runners-up 1928–29; Division 2 – Champions 1924–25, 1936–37, 1953–54, 1956–57, 1970–71, 1979–80; Runners-up 1907–08. *FA Cup:* Runners-up 1949, 1961, 1963, 1969. *Football League Cup:* Winners 1964; Runners-up 1965. **European Competitions:** *European Cup-Winners' Cup:* 1961–62.

Colours: Blue shirts, white shorts, white stockings. **Change colours:** Red shirts, black shorts, black stockings.

LEICESTER CITY 1991–92 LEAGUE RECORD

Match No.	Date		Venue	Opponents	Result		H/T Score	Lg. Pos.	Goalscorers	Atten-dance
1	Aug	17	A	Swindon T	D	0-0	0-0	—		12,426
2		24	H	Plymouth Arg	W	2-0	1-0	6	Gibson, Kitson	11,852
3		31	A	Southend U	W	2-1	0-0	5	Wright, Walsh	6944
4	Sep	4	H	Grimsby T	W	2-0	1-0	—	Fitzpatrick, Gibson	16,242
5		7	H	Bristol C	W	2-1	2-1	2	Gibson, Fitzpatrick	17,815
6		14	A	Middlesbrough	L	0-3	0-0	3		16,633
7		17	A	Barnsley	L	1-3	1-1	—	Kelly	9318
8		21	H	Blackburn R	W	3-0	2-0	3	Walsh, Kitson, Gordon	13,287
9		29	A	Cambridge U	L	1-5	0-2	—	Gordon	7052
10	Oct	5	H	Charlton Ath	L	0-2	0-0	9		11,467
11		12	A	Newcastle U	L	0-2	0-0	12		16,966
12		19	H	Wolverhampton W	W	3-0	2-0	7	Gordon 2, Wright	14,428
13		26	A	Oxford U	W	2-1	1-0	7	Wright, Thompson	5206
14		30	A	Brighton & HA	W	2-1	1-0	—	Walsh, Kitson	6424
15	Nov	2	H	Ipswich T	D	2-2	0-0	6	Kitson, Oldfield	11,331
16		5	A	Portsmouth	L	0-1	0-1	—		7147
17		9	A	Watford	W	1-0	1-0	5	Kitson	9271
18		20	H	Bristol R	D	1-1	1-0	—	Wright	10,095
19		23	A	Port Vale	L	0-1	0-1	7		11,405
20		30	A	Derby Co	W	2-1	2-0	6	Fitzpatrick, Walsh	19,306
21	Dec	7	H	Millwall	D	1-1	0-0	7	Gordon	12,127
22		14	A	Sunderland	L	0-1	0-0	7		15,094
23		26	H	Brighton & HA	W	2-1	1-0	7	Mauchlen, Thompson	16,767
24		28	H	Southend U	W	2-0	0-0	6	Oldfield, Smith	15,635
25	Jan	1	A	Bristol R	D	1-1	1-1	6	Oldfield	6673
26		11	A	Plymouth Arg	D	2-2	0-2	7	Turner (og), Thompson	5846
27		18	H	Swindon T	W	3-1	1-0	5	Fitzpatrick, Wright 2	14,226
28	Feb	1	A	Wolverhampton W	L	0-1	0-1	6		18,574
29		8	H	Oxford U	W	2-1	1-0	6	Kitson, Wright	12,178
30		15	A	Port Vale	W	2-1	1-1	4	Russell 2	8084
31		22	H	Derby Co	L	1-2	0-1	5	Mills (pen)	18,148
32		29	A	Millwall	L	0-2	0-2	7		7562
33	Mar	11	H	Portsmouth	D	2-2	0-1	—	Mills, Russell	14,207
34		14	A	Ipswich T	D	0-0	0-0	9		16,174
35		17	A	Grimsby T	W	1-0	0-0	—	Wright	6377
36		21	H	Watford	L	1-2	0-2	7	Walsh	14,519
37		27	A	Tranmere R	W	2-1	0-1	—	Ormondroyd, Gee	9061
38	Apr	1	H	Middlesbrough	W	2-1	1-0	—	Mills, Wright	19,352
39		4	A	Bristol C	L	1-2	0-1	6	Oldfield	13,020
40		8	H	Sunderland	W	3-2	3-2	—	Wright, Mills 2 (1 pen)	16,533
41		11	A	Barnsley	W	3-1	0-1	3	Walsh, Mills (pen), Wright	14,438
42		15	H	Tranmere R	W	1-0	0-0	—	Russell	18,555
43		18	A	Blackburn R	W	1-0	0-0	2	Russell	18,075
44		21	H	Cambridge U	W	2-1	1-0	—	Wright, Gee	21,894
45		25	A	Charlton Ath	L	0-2	0-2	2		15,357
46	May	2	H	Newcastle U	L	1-2	0-1	4	Walsh	21,861

Final League Position: 4

GOALSCORERS

League (62): Wright 12, Walsh 7, Kitson 6, Mills 6 (3 pens), Gordon 5, Russell 5, Fitzpatrick 4, Oldfield 4, Gibson 3, Thompson 3, Gee 2, Kelly 1, Mauchlen 1, Ormondroyd 1, Smith 1, own goals 1.
Rumbelows Cup (5): Kitson 2, Kelly 1, Mills 1, Walsh 1.
FA Cup (2): Kitson 1, Smith 1.

Poole	Mills	Platnauer	Fitzpatrick	Smith	James	Gibson	Reid P	Ward	Kelly	Kitson	Wright	Oldfield	Walsh	Russell	Gordon	Linton	Mauchlen	Oakes	Thompson	Coatsworth	Muggleton	Willis	Trotter	Holden	Ormondroyd	Gee	Grayson	Hill	Match No.
1	2	3	4	5	6	7	8	9†	10	11*	12	14																	1
1	2	3	4		6		8	14	10†	11	9*	7	5		12														2
1	2	3†	4*14		6		8		10	11	9	7	5		12														3
1	2	3	4		6		8		10	11	9	7	5																4
1	2	3	4		6		8		10	11†	9*	7	5	14	12														5
1	2	3*	4		6		8†		10	11	9	7	5	14				12											6
1	2	3	4*				8	12	10	11	9	7	5																7
1	2	3			6		8	12	10	11	9†	7	5		4*		14												8
1	2	3	12		6		8*		10	11	9	7†	5		4		14												9
1	2	3	4*		6		8	12	10		9	7	5				11												10
1	2			4	6	8		11*	10	12	9	7	5						3										11
1	2		14	4	6†	3		12		10	9	7	5		11*				8										12
1	2	6	4			3			10		9	7	5		11		8*		12										13
1	2	6	4			3			10		9*	7	5		11		12		8										14
1	2	6	4			3			10		9	7	5		11				8										15
1	2	6*	4			3†			10		9	7	5		11		12		8	14									16
1	2	6	4			3			10		9	7	5		11		12		8*										17
1	2	6	4			3*		14	10		9	7	5		11†		12		8										18
1	2	3	6		4				9	10		7	5		11				8										19
1	2	3			6			12	10			7	5		9		11		8*	4									20
1	2	3	6		14				10*12			7	5		9		11		8	4†									21
1	2	3*	6		4			12	10†	8		7	5		9		11		14										22
1	2	12	4			3			10	11*		7	5		9		6		8										23
1	2	9	4			3			10	11		7	5				6		8										24
	2	12	4			3				11		7	5		9†		6		8			1	10*14						25
	2		4			3			11		9	7	5		6				8			1	10						26
	2	6	4			3			11		9	7	5						8			1	10*12						27
1	2	12	4			3	14		11		9	7†	5		10*				8		6								28
1	2	3	4						11		9	7	5	12			10		8*		6								29
1	2	3	4						11		9	7*		8	6		10		12		5								30
1	2	14	4					3†	11		9			8	12		10		7		5				6*				31
1	2		6					3	12		11	9		5	8		10*		7		4								32
1	2	3	4								9		5	8				6	7						10	11			33
1	2	3	4								9		5	8					7						10	11	6		34
1	2	3	4*								9		5	8					7		12				10	11	6		35
1	2	3									9	12	5	8					7	4*					10	11	6		36
1	2	3									9		8	5					7						10	11	6	4	37
1	2	14									9*	8	5	12					7						10	11	6	4	38
1	2										9	8	5	12					7*						10	11	6	4	39
1	2*										9	8	5	12					7						10	11	6	4	40
1	2	3									9	8	5						7						10	11	6	4	41
1	2	3									9	8†	5	14	12				7						10*	11	6	4	42
1	2	3									9	8	5	12					7						10	11*	6	4	43
1	2	3†									9	8	5	12					7						10	11*	6	4	44
1	2	14									9	8*	5	12					7						10	11†	6	4	45
	2	3				14					9	8	5	12					7			1			10*11†	6	4		46
42	46	26	21	23	12	17	10	2	12	29	42	39	43	7	18	—	14	1	31	2	4	9	—	1	14	14	13	10	
		+3s	+5s	+2s	+1s			+2s	+8s		+1s	+2s	+2s		+13s	+3s	+1s		+6s		+3s		+1s		+1s	+2s			

Whitlow—Match No. 38(3†) 39(3) 40(3) 44(14) 45(3).

Rumbelows Cup	First Round	Maidstone U (h)	3-0
		(a)	1-0
	Second Round	Arsenal (h)	1-1
		(a)	0-2
FA Cup	Third Round	Crystal Palace (h)	1-0
	Fourth Round	Bristol C (h)	1-2

LEICESTER CITY

Player and Position	Ht	Wt	Birth Date	Birth Place	Source	Clubs	League App	Gls
Goalkeepers								
Russell Hoult	6 4	13 02	22 11 72	Leicester	Trainee	Leicester C	—	—
						Lincoln C (loan)	2	—
						Blackpool (loan)	—	—
Carl Muggleton	6 1	11 13	13 9 68	Leicester	Apprentice	Leicester C	29	—
						Chesterfield (loan)	17	—
						Blackpool (loan)	2	—
						Hartlepool U (loan)	8	—
						Stockport Co (loan)	4	—
						Liverpool (loan)	—	—
Kevin Poole	5 10	11 10	21 7 63	Bromsgrove	Apprentice	Aston Villa	28	—
						Northampton T (loan)	3	—
						Middlesbrough	34	—
						Hartlepool U (loan)	12	—
						Leicester C	42	—
Defenders								
Ian Blyth			21 10 74	Coventry	Trainee	Leicester C	—	—
Gary Coatsworth	6 1	11 06	7 10 68	Sunderland		Barnsley	6	—
						Darlington	22	2
						Leicester C	3	—
Colin Gibson	5 8	10 08	6 4 60	Bridport	Apprentice	Aston Villa	185	10
						Manchester U	79	9
						Port Vale (loan)	6	2
						Leicester C	35	4
Tony James	6 3	14 00	27 6 67	Sheffield	Gainsborough T	Lincoln C	29	—
						Leicester C	82	10
Andy Jeffrey‡	5 10	11 00	15 1 72	Bellshill	Trainee	Leicester C	—	—
Nicky Platnauer	5 10	12 12	10 6 61	Leicester	Bedford T	Bristol R	24	7
						Coventry C	44	6
						Birmingham C	28	2
						Reading (loan)	7	—
						Cardiff C	115	6
						Notts Co	57	1
						Leicester C	29	—
Richard Smith	6 0	12 00	3 10 70	Leicester	Trainee	Leicester C	33	1
						Cambridge U (loan)	4	—
Michael Trotter	6 3	12 02	27 10 69	Hartlepool	Trainee	Middlesbrough	—	—
						Doncaster R (loan)	3	—
						Darlington	29	2
						Leicester C	2	—
Steve Walsh	6 3	14 00	3 11 64	Fulwood	Local	Wigan Ath	126	4
						Leicester C	195	22
Jimmy Willis	6 2	12 04	12 7 68	Liverpool	Blackburn R	Halifax T	—	—
						Stockport Co	10	—
						Darlington	90	6
						Leicester C	10	—
						Bradford C (loan)	9	1
Midfield								
Paul Fitzpatrick	6 4	11 10	5 10 65	Liverpool	Local	Tranmere R	—	—
						Liverpool	—	—
						Preston NE	—	—
						Bolton W	14	—
						Bristol C	44	7
						Carlisle U	109	4
						Preston NE (loan)	2	—
						Leicester C	26	4
Simon Grayson	5 11	10 11	16 12 69	Ripon	Trainee	Leeds U	2	—
						Leicester C	13	—
Ricky Hill‡	5 11	13 00	5 3 59	London	Apprentice	Luton T	436	54
						Leicester C	26	—
Ally Mauchlen	5 7	10 05	29 6 60	Kilwinning	Irvine Meadow	Kilmarnock	120	10
						Motherwell	76	4
						Leicester C	239	11
						Leeds U (loan)	—	—
Gary Mills	5 8	11 05	11 11 61	Northampton	Apprentice	Nottingham F	58	8
						Derby Co	18	1
						Nottingham F	79	4
						Notts Co	75	8
						Leicester C	133	15
Jason Peake*	5 9	11 05	29 9 71	Leicester	Trainee	Leicester C	8	1
						Hartlepool U (loan)	4	1
Steve Thompson	5 11	11 10	2 11 64	Oldham	Apprentice	Bolton W	335	49
						Luton T	5	—
						Leicester C	34	3

LEICESTER CITY

Foundation: In 1884 a number of young footballers who were mostly old boys of Wyggeston School, held a meeting at a house on the Roman Fosse Way and formed Leicester Fosse FC. They collected 9d (less than 4p) towards the cost of a ball, plus the same amount for membership. Their first professional, Harry Webb from Stafford Rangers, was signed in 1888 for 2s 6d (12p) per week, plus travelling expenses.

First Football League game: 1 September, 1894, Division 2, v Grimsby T (a) L 3-4 – Thraves; Smith, Bailey; Seymour, Brown, Henrys; Hill, Hughes, McArthur (1), Skea (2), Priestman.

Did you know: In 1924–25 City not only had the Second Division's highest goalscorer in Arthur Chandler with 32 goals, but the second highest in Johnny Duncan with 30. They won promotion that season.

Managers (and Secretary-managers)
William Clark 1896–97, George Johnson 1898–1907*, James Blessington 1907–09, Andy Aitken 1909–11, J. W. Bartlett 1912–14, Peter Hodge 1919–26, William Orr 1926–32, Peter Hodge 1932–34, Andy Lochhead 1934–36, Frank Womack 1936–39, Tom Bromilow 1939–45, Tom Mather 1945–46, Johnny Duncan 1946–49, Norman Bullock 1949–55, David Halliday 1955–58, Matt Gillies 1959–68, Frank O'Farrell 1968–71, Jimmy Bloomfield 1971–77, Frank McLintock 1977–78, Jock Wallace 1978–82, Gordon Milne 1982–86, Bryan Hamilton 1986–87, David Pleat 1987–91, Brian Little May 1991–.

Name				Birthplace	Previous club	Club	Apps	Goals
Mike Whitlow	5 11	12 01	13 1 68	Northwich	Witton Alb	Leeds U	77	4
						Leicester C	5	—
Darren Williams	5 10	10 05	15 12 68	Birmingham	Trainee	Leicester C	10	2
						Lincoln C (loan)	9	—
						Chesterfield (loan)	5	1
Forwards								
Phil Gee	5 9	10 04	19 12 64	Pelsall	Gresley R	Derby Co	124	26
						Leicester C	14	2
Colin Gordon	6 1	12 12	17 1 63	Stourbridge	Oldbury U	Swindon T	72	33
						Wimbledon	3	—
						Gillingham (loan)	4	2
						Reading	24	9
						Bristol C (loan)	8	4
						Fulham	17	2
						Birmingham C	26	3
						Hereford U (loan)	6	—
						Walsall (loan)	6	1
						Bristol R (loan)	4	—
						Leicester C	21	5
Steven Holden	6 0	11 13	4 9 72	Luton	Trainee	Leicester C	—	—
David Oldfield	6 0	12 02	30 5 68	Perth, Aust	Apprentice	Luton T	29	4
						Manchester C	26	6
						Leicester C	103	16
Ian Ormondroyd	6 4	13 07	22 9 64	Bradford	Thackley	Bradford C	87	20
						Oldham Ath (loan)	10	1
						Aston Villa	56	6
						Derby Co	25	8
						Leicester C	14	1
Paul Reid	5 5	10 02	19 1 68	Warley	Apprentice	Leicester C	162	21
						Bradford C (loan)	7	—
Kevin Russell	5 8	10 10	6 12 66	Portsmouth	Apprentice	Brighton & HA	—	—
						Portsmouth	4	1
						Wrexham	84	43
						Leicester C	43	10
						Peterborough U (loan)	7	3
						Cardiff C (loan)	3	—
						Hereford U (loan)	3	1
						Stoke C (loan)	5	1
Ashley Ward	6 1	11 07	24 11 70	Middleton	Trainee	Manchester C	1	—
						Wrexham (loan)	4	2
						Leicester C	10	—
Tommy Wright	5 7	9 10	10 1 66	Fife	Apprentice	Leeds U	81	24
						Oldham Ath	112	23
						Leicester C	129	22

Trainees
Bedded, Mathew J; Bunting, Nathan J; Byrne, Thomas A; Cameron, Darren J; Clines, Jaimes R; Crane, Adrian P; Eustace, Scott D; Foley, Dean; Gallagher, Gordon P; Grace, Gary I; Haughton, Warren A; Joachim, Julian K; Kane, Liam B. D; Lewis, Neil A; Mogg, Lewis R; Newcombe, Simon; Thompson, Ian T; Thorpe, Anthony.

Associated Schoolboys
Clarke, Stuart D; Dalby, Craig A; Doherty, James W; Hallam, Craig D; Heskey, Emile; James, Scott; Johnson, Colin; Kerr, Matthew; King, Darryl J; Lee, Christian; Oram, Kevin F; Purcell, Darren; Quincey, Lee P.

Associated Schoolboys who have accepted the club's offer of a Traineeship/Contract
Maisey, Neil K; Warmer, Timothy V.

LEYTON ORIENT 1991–92 *Back row (left to right):* Adrian Whitbread, Mark Cooper, Paul Heald, Paul Newell, Kevin Nugent, Warren Hackett.
Centre row: Bernie Dixson (Chief Scout), Ricky Otto, Wayne Burnett, Chris Bart-Williams, Terry Howard, Keith Day, Chris Zoricich, Greg Berry, Steve Castle, Bill Songhurst (Physiotherapist).
Front row: Andy Sayer, Kevin Hales, Lee Harvey, Peter Eustace (Team Manager), Frank Clark (Managing Director), Danny Carter, Kenny Achampong, Kevin Dickenson.

Division 2   **LEYTON ORIENT**

Leyton Stadium, Brisbane Road, Leyton, London E10 5NE. Telephone 081-539 2223/4. Community scheme: 081 558 7595. Clubcall: 0898 121150.

Ground capacity: 18,869 (7171 seats).

Record attendance: 34,345 v West Ham U, FA Cup 4th rd, 25 January 1964.

Record receipts: £87,867.92 v West Ham U, FA Cup 3rd rd, 10 January 1987.

Pitch measurements: 110yd × 80yd.

Chairman: T. Wood OBE.

Managing Director: Frank Clark.

Directors: A. Pincus, D. L. Weinrabe, H. Linney, M. Pears.

Team manager: Peter Eustace. *Physio:* Bill Songhurst. *Secretary:* Miss Carol Stokes. *Asst. Sec:* Mrs Sue Tilling. *Commercial Manager:* Frank Woolf.

Year Formed: 1881. Turned Professional: 1903. Ltd Co.: 1906.

Former Grounds: Glyn Road, 1884–96; Whittles Athletic Ground, 1896–1900; Millfields Road, 1900–30; Lea Bridge Road, 1930–37.

Former Names: 1881–86, Glyn Cricket and Football Club; 1886–88, Eagle Football Club; 1888–98, Orient Football Club; 1898–1946, Clapton Orient; 1946–66, Leyton Orient; 1966–87, Orient.

Club Nickname: 'The O's'.

Record League Victory: 8-0 v Crystal Palace, Division 3 (S), 12 November 1955 – Welton; Lee, Earl; Blizzard, Aldous, McKnight; White (1), Facey (3), Burgess (2), Heckman, Hartburn (2). 8-0 v Rochdale, Division 4, 20 October 1987 – Wells; Howard, Dickenson, Smalley, Day, Hull, Hales, Castle (Sussex) Shinners, Godfrey (Harvey), Comfort. 8-0 v Colchester U, Division 4, 15 October 1988 – Wells; Howard, Dickenson, Hales (1p), Day (1). Sitton (1), Baker (1), Ward, Hull (3). Juryeff, Comfort (1).

Record Cup Victory: 9-2 v Chester, League Cup, 3rd rd, 15 October 1962 – Robertson; Charlton, Taylor; Gibbs, Bishop, Lea; Deeley (1), Waites (3), Dunmore (2), Graham (3), Wedge.

Record Defeat: 0-8 v Aston Villa, FA Cup 4th rd, 30 January 1929.

Most League Points (2 for a win): 66, Division 3 (S), 1955–56.

Most League points (3 for a win): 75, Division 4, 1988–89.

Most League Goals: 106, Division 3 (S), 1955–56.

Highest League Scorer in Season: Tom Johnston, 35, Division 2, 1957–58.

Most League Goals in Total Aggregate: Tom Johnston, 121, 1956–58, 1959–61.

Most Capped Player: John Chiedozie, 8 (10), Nigeria.

Most League Appearances: Peter Allen, 432, 1965–78.

Record Transfer Fee Received: £600,000 from Notts Co for John Chiedozie, August 1981.

Record Transfer Fee Paid: £175,000 to Wigan Ath for Paul Beesley, October 1989.

Football League Record: 1905 Elected to Division 2; 1929–56 Division 3 (S); 1956–62 Division 2; 1962–63 Division 1; 1963–66 Division 2; 1966–70 Division 3; 1970–82 Division 2; 1982–85 Division 3; 1985–89 Division 4; 1989–92 Division 3; 1992– Division 2.

Honours: Football League: Division 1 best season: 22nd, 1962–63; Division 2 – Runners-up 1961–62; Division 3 – Champions 1969–70; Division 3 (S) – Champions 1955–56; Runners-up 1954–55. *FA Cup:* Semi-final 1977–78. *Football League Cup:* best season: 5th rd, 1963.

Colours: Red shirts with black and white bars, white shorts, red stockings. **Change colours:** White shirts with black and blue bars, blue shorts, blue stockings.

LEYTON ORIENT 1991–92 LEAGUE RECORD

Match No.	Date		Venue	Opponents	Result		H/T Score	Lg. Pos.	Goalscorers	Attendance
1	Aug	17	A	Brentford	L	3-4	1-1	—	Nugent 2, Sayer	6156
2		24	H	Stockport Co	D	3-3	2-2	17	Sayer, Nugent 2	3650
3		31	A	Bolton W	L	0-1	0-0	21		5058
4	Sep	3	H	Bradford C	D	1-1	1-0	—	Sayer	3435
5		7	A	Hartlepool U	W	3-2	1-1	19	Otto, Castle, Carter	3581
6		14	H	Darlington	W	2-1	0-0	12	Otto 2	3962
7		17	H	Preston NE	D	0-0	0-0	—		3296
8		21	A	Fulham	L	1-2	1-1	17	Nugent	4934
9		28	H	Huddersfield T	W	1-0	1-0	11	Day	3741
10	Oct	5	A	Peterborough U	W	2-0	1-0	9	Nugent 2	4291
11		12	H	Chester C	W	1-0	1-0	7	Jones	4049
12		19	H	Bournemouth	D	1-1	0-1	7	Castle	3878
13		26	A	Stoke C	L	0-2	0-1	10		9555
14	Nov	2	H	Exeter C	W	1-0	0-0	7	Castle	3038
15		5	A	Swansea C	D	2-2	2-2	—	Otto, Howard	2081
16		9	A	Torquay U	L	0-1	0-1	10		2388
17		23	H	Hull C	W	1-0	1-0	7	Howard	3510
18		30	A	Wigan Ath	D	1-1	0-1	8	Berry	2066
19	Dec	20	A	Stockport Co	L	0-1	0-0	—		2745
20		26	H	Bolton W	W	2-1	0-1	9	Cooper 2	4896
21		28	H	Brentford	W	4-2	2-2	7	Berry 2, Castle, Jones	7333
22	Jan	1	A	Bradford C	D	1-1	1-1	8	Castle	6810
23		11	A	Birmingham C	D	2-2	1-0	9	Nugent, Castle	10,445
24		18	H	WBA	D	1-1	1-1	9	Jones	6329
25		28	H	Shrewsbury T	W	2-0	1-0	—	Castle, Achampong	3197
26	Feb	1	A	Bournemouth	W	1-0	1-0	7	Nugent	6544
27		8	H	Stoke C	L	0-1	0-1	7		9153
28		11	A	Wigan Ath	W	3-1	0-1	—	Berry, Whitbread, Jones	3142
29		15	A	Bury	L	2-4	0-3	7	Taylor, Carter	2120
30		22	H	Birmingham C	D	0-0	0-0	7		5995
31		29	A	Shrewsbury T	W	1-0	1-0	7	Howard	2873
32	Mar	3	A	WBA	W	3-1	3-0	—	Howard, Berry, Nugent	11,165
33		7	H	Reading	D	1-1	1-1	8	Nugent	4436
34		10	H	Swansea C	L	1-2	0-1	—	Castle	3328
35		14	A	Exeter C	L	0-2	0-0	8		3070
36		21	H	Torquay U	W	2-0	0-0	7	Otto, Nugent	3636
37		24	H	Bury	W	4-0	1-0	—	Berry 3, Wilder	3074
38		28	A	Hull C	L	0-1	0-0	7		3802
39		31	A	Darlington	W	1-0	0-0	—	Cooper	1704
40	Apr	4	H	Hartlepool U	W	4-0	1-0	5	Cooper, Achampong, Jones, Castle	4245
41		11	A	Preston NE	L	1-2	0-0	8	Castle	3926
42		18	H	Fulham	L	0-1	0-0	8		7094
43		20	A	Huddersfield T	L	0-1	0-1	9		10,011
44		25	H	Peterborough U	L	1-2	1-0	10	Cooper	5996
45		29	A	Reading	L	2-3	0-1	—	Okai, Cooper	2690
46	May	2	A	Chester C	L	0-1	0-0	10		2008

Final League Position: 10

GOALSCORERS

League (62): Nugent 12, Castle 10, Berry 8, Cooper 6, Jones 5, Otto 5, Howard 4, Sayer 3, Achampong 2, Carter 2, Day 1, Okai 1, Taylor 1, Whitbread 1, Wilder 1.
Rumbelows Cup (6): Nugent 3, Berry 1, Burnett 1, Sayer 1.
FA Cup (9): Berry 2, Nugent 2, Castle 1 (1 pen), Cooper 1, Day 1, Harvey 1, Howard 1.

Heald	Howard	Dickenson	Whitbread	Day	Bart-Williams	Berry	Burnett	Nugent	Sayer	Otto	Carter	Zorich	Castle	Newell	Harvey	Hackett	Jones	Achampong	Turner	Hales	Cooper	Roeder	Taylor	Wilder	Hendon	Okai	Cobb	Tomlinson	Match No.
1	2	3	4†	5	6	7*	8	9	10	11	12	14																	1
1	2	3		5	6	7*	8	9	10	11			4	12															2
	2*	3		5	12	6	14	8†	9	10	11		4	7	1														3
	2	3		5	6	7	12	9	10	11			4	8*	1														4
	2	3		5†	14	6	7	9	10*	11	12		4	8	1														5
	2	3	4	5	6†	12	14	9	10	11			7*	8	1														6
	2	3	4	5	6	12		9	10*	11			7	8	1														7
	2		4	5	6	11	8	9	10*				7	14	1	3	12†												8
	2	3	4	5	6		8	9	10	11*			7		1		12												9
	2		4	5	6*		8	9	10	11†		14	7		1	3	12												10
	2		4	5	6		8	9	10	11			7*		1	3	12												11
	2		4	5	6	7*	8	9	10	11†		14			1	3	12												12
	2		4	5	6*	7	8	9	10	11						3	12		1										13
	2		4		6		8	9	10	11*	12	14	7†	5		3			1										14
	2		4		6		8	9	10	11	12		7*	5		3			1										15
	2		4	5	6		8	9	10	11	12	14	7*			3†			1										16
	2		4	5	6		8	9	10	11			7			3	12	9*	1										17
	2		4	5	6		8†	9	10	11	12	14	7			3		9*	1										18
	2		4	5	6*		8	9	10	11	12		7			3			1										19
	2		4	5	6*		8	9	10	11	12		7			3			1										20
	2		4†	5	6		8	9	10*	11	12	14	7			3			1										21
	2		4†	5	6*		8	9	10	11	12	14	7			3			1										22
	2		4*	5	6		8	9†	10	11	12	14	7			3			1										23
	2		4	5	6		8	9	10	11	12		7*			3			1										24
	2		4	5	6	7	8†	9*	10	11		14				3	12		1										25
	2		4	5	6	7	8	9*	10	11†		14				3	12		1										26
	2†		4	5	6	7*	8	9	10	11						3	12		1										27
	2		4	5	6		8	9	10*	11		14	7†			3	12		1										28
	2		4	5*	6	7	8	9	10	11		14				3†	12		1										29
	2		4	5	6	7*	8		10	11	12	14				3†		9	1										30
	2		4	5	6		8		10	11	12	14	7†					9*	1					3					31
	2		4	5	6		8		10	11	12	14	7†					9*	1					3					32
	2		4	5	6	7	8		10	11	12							9*	1					3					33
	2		4	5	6	7		9	10	11†	12	14	8*						1					3					34
	2		4	5	6	7		9	10	11†	12	14	8						1					3*					35
	2		4	5	6	7		9	10	11*	12		8						1					3					36
	2		4	5	6	7†	8		10*	11	12	14						9	1					3					37
	2		4	5	6	7†	8		10*	11	12	14						9	1					3					38
	2		4	5	6		8		10	11			7					9	1					3					39
	2		4	5	6	7	8		10*	11†		14					12	9	1		5	10		3					40
	2		4	5†	6	7	8		10*	11		14					12	9	1		5	10	14	3					41
	2		4	5*	6	7	8		10	11							12	9	1		5	10		3					42
	2	10	4	5	6	7*	8			11†		14					12	9	1		5		14	3	4				43
	2		4	5	6	7*	8		10	11	12						12	9	1			10	7	3	4				44
	2		4	5	6	7	8		10	11*	12						12	9	1		5	10	7	3					45
	2		4†	5	6	7*	8		10	11							12	9	1					3	4†				46

Totals:

	2	45	8	43	31	15	30	33	36	8	23	15	19	35	10	5	22	20	20	34	6	11	6	6	16	5	1	1	—

Substitute appearances: Day +2s; Berry +6s, Burnett +3s; Sayer +1s, Otto +9s, Carter +5s, Zorich +3s, Castle +2s; Hackett +8s; Achampong +10s, Hales +4s; Cooper +4s, Roeder +7s, Taylor +2s, Wilder +5s; Okai +1s; Tomlinson +1s.

Warren—Match No. 46(14).

Rumbelows Cup	First Round	Northampton T (h)	5-0
		(a)	0-2
	Second Round	Sheffield W (h)	0-0
		(a)	1-4
FA Cup	First Round	Welling (h)	2-1
	Second Round	WBA (h)	2-1
	Third Round	Oldham Ath (a)	1-1
		(h)	4-2
	Fourth Round	Portsmouth (a)	0-2

LEYTON ORIENT

Player and Position	Ht	Wt	Date	Birth Place	Source	Clubs	League App	Gls
Goalkeepers								
Paul Heald	6 2	12 05	20 8 68	Wath on Dean	Trainee	Sheffield U	—	—
						Leyton Orient	105	—
						Coventry C (loan)	2	—
Paul Newell	6 1	11 05	23 2 69	Greenwich	Trainee	Southend U	15	—
						Leyton Orient	18	—
Chris Turner	6 0	12 04	15 9 58	Sheffield	Apprentice	Sheffield W	91	—
						Lincoln C (loan)	5	—
						Sunderland	195	—
						Manchester U	64	—
						Sheffield W	75	—
						Leeds U (loan)	2	—
						Leyton Orient	34	—
Defenders								
Adam Baker‡			1 6 72	Newham	Trainee	Leyton Orient	—	—
Keith Day	6 1	11 00	29 11 62	Grays	Aveley	Colchester U	113	12
						Leyton Orient	182	8
Kevin Dickenson*	5 6	10 06	24 2 62	London	Apprentice	Tottenham H	—	—
						Charlton Ath	75	1
						Leyton Orient	192	3
Warren Hackett			16 12 71	Newham	Tottenham H	Leyton Orient	26	—
Kevin Hales	5 7	10 04	13 1 61	Dartford	Apprentice	Chelsea	20	2
						Leyton Orient	271	22
Lee Harvey	5 11	11 07	21 12 66	Harlow	Local	Leyton Orient	163	19
Terry Howard	6 1	11 07	26 2 66	Stepney	Amateur	Chelsea	6	—
						Crystal Palace (loan)	4	—
						Chester C (loan)	2	—
						Leyton Orient	235	23
Mark O'Neill			4 10 72	Dublin	Trainee	Leyton Orient	—	—
Glenn Roeder‡	6 0	12 13	13 12 55	Woodford	Apprentice	Orient	115	4
						QPR	157	17
						Notts Co (loan)	4	—
						Newcastle U	193	8
						Watford	78	2
						Leyton Orient	8	—
Adrian Whitbread	6 2	11 13	22 10 71	Epping	Trainee	Leyton Orient	89	1
Midfield								
Wayne Burnett			4 9 71	Lambeth	Trainee	Leyton Orient	40	—
Steve Castle	5 11	12 05	17 5 56	Ilford	Apprentice	Leyton Orient	243	55
Brett Patience			12 10 73	London	Trainee	Leyton Orient	—	—
Keith Sharman	6 2	12 00	6 11 71	London	Trainee	Leyton Orient	—	—
Gerry Solomon‡			16 11 68	London	Hendon	Leyton Orient	—	—
Chris Zoricich	5 11	11 10	3 5 69	New Zealand		Leyton Orient	50	—
Forwards								
Kenny Achampong	5 9	10 10	26 6 66	London	Apprentice	Fulham	81	15
						West Ham U (loan)	—	—
						Charlton Ath	10	—
						Leyton Orient	58	6
Greg Berry	5 11	12 00	5 3 71	Essex	East Thurrock	Leyton Orient	80	14
Danny Carter	5 11	11 12	29 6 69	Hackney	Billericay	Leyton Orient	94	12
Paul Cobb			13 12 72	Thurrock	Purfleet	Leyton Orient	5	—
Mark Cooper	6 1	13 00	5 4 67	Watford	Apprentice	Cambridge U	71	17
						Tottenham H	—	—
						Shrewsbury T (loan)	6	2
						Gillingham	49	11
						Leyton Orient	93	30

LEYTON ORIENT

Foundation: There is some doubt about the foundation of Leyton Orient, and, indeed, some confusion with clubs like Leyton and Clapton over their early history. As regards the foundation, the most favoured version is that Leyton Orient was formed originally by members of Homerton Theological College who established Glyn Cricket Club in 1881 and then carried on through the following winter playing football. Eventually many employees of the Orient Shipping Line became involved and so the name Orient was chosen in 1888.

First Football League game: 2 September, 1905, Division 2, v Leicester Fosse (a) L 1-2 – Butler; Holmes, Codling; Lamberton, Boden, Boyle; Kingaby (1), Wootten, Leigh, Evenson, Bourne.

Did you know: Goalkeeper Arthur Wood enjoyed a remarkable run of 235 consecutive League and Cup appearances for the Orient from September 1921 to December 1926. He then missed the game at Blackpool in which Orient were beaten 6-0.

Managers (and Secretary-managers)
Sam Omerod 1905–06, Ike Ivenson 1906, Billy Holmes 1907–22, Peter Proudfoot 1922–29, Arthur Grimsdell 1929–30, Peter Proudfoot 1930–31, Jimmy Seed 1931–33, David Pratt 1933–34, Peter Proudfoot 1935–39, Tom Halsey 1939, Billy Wright 1939–45, Billy Hall 1945, Billy Wright 1945–46, Charlie Hewitt 1946–48, Neil McBain 1948–49, Alec Stock 1949–56, 1956–58, 1958–59, Johnny Carey 1961–63, Benny Fenton 1963–64, Dave Sexton 1965, Dick Graham 1966–68, Jimmy Bloomfield 1968–71, George Petchey 1971–77, Jimmy Bloomfield 1977–81, Paul Went 1981, Ken Knighton 1981, Frank Clark 1982–91 (MD), Peter Eustace 1991–.

Player and Position	Ht	Wt	Birth Date	Birth Place	Source	Clubs	League App	League Gls
Andy Jones	5 11	13 06	9 1 63	Wrexham	Rhyl	Port Vale	90	49
						Charlton Ath	66	15
						Port Vale (loan)	17	3
						Bristol C (loan)	4	1
						Bournemouth	40	8
						Leyton Orient	30	5
Steve Okai§			3 12 73	Ghana	School	Leyton Orient	1	1
Ricky Otto			9 11 67	London	Dartford	Leyton Orient	33	5
Andy Sayer*	5 9	10 12	6 6 66	Brent	Apprentice	Wimbledon	58	15
						Cambridge U (loan)	5	—
						Fulham	53	15
						Leyton Orient	30	6
						Sheffield U (loan)	3	—
Robert Taylor	6 0	11 07	30 4 71	Norwich	Trainee	Norwich C	—	—
						Leyton Orient (loan)	3	1
						Birmingham C	—	—
						Leyton Orient	11	1
Michael Tomlinson			15 9 72	Lambeth	Trainee	Leyton Orient	2	1
Mark Warren§			12 11 74	Clapton	Trainee	Leyton Orient	1	—

Trainees
Beckett, Nathan J; Brunning, John J; Cooper, Paul; Denny, Neil R; Fowler, Lee P; Gamble, Bradley D; Lakin, Barry; McCarthy, John I; McDermott, Dean P; Ramage, Andrew W; Rolls, George E; Stephenson, Andrew J; Sweetman, Nicholas E; Thompson, David C; Warren, Mark W.

**Non-Contract
Welsh, Alexander.

Associated Schoolboys
Gilby, Frank S; Howard, Anthony; Loomes, Jody D; Martin, Gary D; Pipal, Joseph; Purse, Darren J; Rayment, Stuart; Skinner, Keith R; Trott, Ian J.

Associated Schoolboys who have accepted the club's offer of a Traineeship/Contract
Bird, Robert J; Collinson, David J; Ludden, Dominic J. R; Okai, Stephen P; Wedlock, Grant.

**Non-Contract Players who are retained must be re-signed before they are eligible to play in League matches.

LINCOLN CITY 1991–92 *Back row (left to right):* Paul Dobson, Paul Ward, Neil Smith, Grant Brown, David Puttnam, Shane Nicholson, Dean West. *Centre row:* Ian Bowling, Kevin Finney, Tony Lormor, Sean Dunphy, Keith Alexander (Youth Team Coach), Jason Lee, Matt Carmichael, Matt Dickins. *Front row:* Paul Smith, Graham Bressington, Colin Clarke (Assistant Manager), Steve Thompson (Manager), Neil McDiarmid (Physiotherapist), John Schofield, David Clarke.

Division 3   LINCOLN CITY

Sincil Bank, Lincoln LN5 8LD. Telephone Lincoln (0522) 522224 and 510263. Executive Club: (0522) 532634. Fax No: (0522) 520564

Ground capacity: 11,500.

Record attendance: 23,196 v Derby Co, League Cup 4th rd, 15 November 1967.

Record receipts: £34,843.30 v Tottenham H, Milk Cup 2nd rd, 26 October 1983.

Pitch measurements: 110yd × 75yd.

Hon. Life Presidents: V. C. Withers, D. W. L. Bocock.

President: H. Dove. *Chairman:* K. J. Reames. *Vice-chairman:* M. B. Pryor.

Directors: G. R. Davey (Managing), R. Staples, H. C. Sills.

Hon. Consultant Surgeon: Mr Brian Smith. *Hon. Club Doctor:* Nick Huntley. *Secretary:* G. R. Davey. *Manager:* Steve Thompson. *Physio:* Neil McDiarmid GRAD DIP (Phys), MCSP, SRP.

Year Formed: 1883. Turned Professional: 1892. Ltd Co.: 1892.

Former Grounds: 1883, John O'Gaunt's; 1894, Sincil Bank.

Club Nickname: 'The Red Imps'.

Record League Victory: 11-1 v Crewe Alex, Division 3 (N), 29 September 1951 – Jones; Green (1p), Varney; Wright, Emery, Grummett (1); Troops (1), Garvey, Graver (6), Whittle (1), Johnson (1).

Record Cup Victory: 8-1 v Bromley, FA Cup, 2nd rd, 10 December 1938 – McPhail; Hartshorne, Corbett; Bean, Leach, Whyte (1); Hancock, Wilson (1), Ponting (3), Deacon (1), Clare (2).

Record Defeat: 3-11 v Manchester C, Division 2, 23 March 1895.

Most League Points (2 for a win): 74, Division 4, 1975–76.

Most League points (3 for a win): 77, Division 3, 1981–82.

Most League Goals: 121, Division 3 (N), 1951–52.

Highest League Scorer in Season: Allan Hall, 42, Division 3 (N), 1931–32.

Most League Goals in Total Aggregate: Andy Graver, 144, 1950–55 and 1958–61.

Most Capped Player: David Pugh, 3 (7), Wales and George Moulson, 3, Eire.

Most League Appearances: Tony Emery, 402, 1946–59.

Record Transfer Fee Received: £250,000 plus increments from Blackburn R for Matt Dickins, March 1992.

Record Transfer Fee Paid: £60,000 to Southampton for Gordon Hobson, September 1988, £60,000 to Sheffield U for Alan Roberts, October 1989, and £60,000 to Leicester C for Grant Brown, January 1990.

Football League Record: 1892 Founder member of Division 2. Remained in Division 2 until 1920 when they failed re-election but also missed seasons 1908–09 and 1911–12 when not re-elected. 1921–32 Division 3 (N); 1932–34 Division 2; 1934–48 Division 3 (N); 1948–49 Division 2; 1949–52 Division 3 (N); 1952–61 Division 2; 1961–62 Division 3; 1962–76 Division 4; 1976–79 Division 3; 1979–81 Division 4; 1981–86 Division 3; 1986–87 Division 4; 1987–88 GM Vauxhall Conference; 1988–92 Division 4; 1992– Division 3.

Honours: Football League: Divison 2 best season: 5th, 1901–02; Division 3 (N) – Champions 1931–32, 1947–48, 1951–52; Runners-up 1927–28, 1930–31, 1936–37; Division 4 – Champions 1975–76; Runners-up 1980–81. *FA Cup:* best season: 1st rd of Second Series (5th rd equivalent), 1886–87, 2nd rd (5th rd equivalent), 1889–90, 1901–02. *Football League Cup:* best season: 4th rd, 1967–68. GM Vauxhall Conference Champions – 1987–88.

Colours: Red and white striped shirts, black shorts, red stockings with white trim. **Change colours:** All blue.

LINCOLN CITY 1991–92 LEAGUE RECORD

Match No.	Date		Venue	Opponents	Result		H/T Score	Lg. Pos.	Goalscorers	Atten-dance
1	Aug	17	A	Cardiff C	W	2-1	2-0	—	Carmichael (pen), Dobson	5137
2		24	H	Rotherham U	L	0-2	0-0	11		4134
3		31	A	Rochdale	L	0-1	0-1	18		2086
4	Sep	4	H	Barnet	L	0-6	0-2	—		3067
5		14	A	Carlisle U	W	2-0	2-0	17	Lee 2	2149
6		17	A	Maidstone U	W	2-0	1-0	—	Smith P, Puttnam	1113
7		21	H	Chesterfield	L	1-2	0-2	14	Dobson	2896
8		28	A	Hereford U	L	0-3	0-3	15		2801
9	Oct	5	H	Halifax T	D	0-0	0-0	16		2092
10		13	A	Blackpool	L	0-3	0-1	—		5086
11		19	A	York C	D	1-1	0-0	19	Smith P	1893
12		26	H	Burnley	L	0-3	0-1	19		3235
13	Nov	5	A	Walsall	D	0-0	0-0	—		2555
14		9	A	Northampton T	L	0-1	0-0	20		2575
15		23	H	Scunthorpe U	W	4-2	1-1	17	Finney, Lormor 3	3078
16		30	A	Doncaster R	W	5-1	3-0	16	Lormor, Puttnam, Finney, Lee, Carmichael	1999
17	Dec	17	H	Scarborough	L	0-2	0-2	—		1752
18		21	A	Rotherham U	D	1-1	1-0	18	West G	3293
19		26	H	Cardiff C	D	0-0	0-0	19		3162
20		28	H	Rochdale	L	0-3	0-3	19		2916
21	Jan	1	A	Barnet	L	0-1	0-1	20		3739
22		4	H	Gillingham	W	1-0	0-0	16	Dobson	2169
23		11	A	Crewe Alex	L	0-1	0-0	18		3060
24		18	H	Wrexham	D	0-0	0-0	18		2213
25	Feb	8	H	Burnley	L	0-1	0-1	20		9748
26		12	H	Doncaster R	W	2-0	1-0	—	Lee, Dobson	2011
27		15	A	Scarborough	D	1-1	1-0	18	Smith P	1614
28		22	H	Crewe Alex	D	2-2	2-1	18	Lormor, Lee	2261
29		29	A	Gillingham	W	3-1	1-1	17	Puttnam, Kabia 2	3160
30	Mar	3	A	Wrexham	D	1-1	0-0	—	Puttnam	2716
31		7	H	Mansfield T	W	2-0	1-0	15	Nicholson, Lormor	4387
32		11	H	Walsall	W	1-0	0-0	—	Puttnam	2021
33		18	H	York C	D	0-0	0-0	—		1875
34		21	H	Northampton T	L	1-2	0-2	14	Brown	2486
35		24	A	Mansfield T	D	0-0	0-0	—		3064
36		28	A	Scunthorpe U	W	2-0	1-0	14	Schofield, West D	3297
37	Apr	1	H	Carlisle U	W	1-0	0-0	—	West D	2118
38		11	H	Maidstone U	W	1-0	1-0	12	Carmichael	2241
39		18	A	Chesterfield	W	5-1	0-1	11	Lormor, Dunphy, Puttnam, Carmichael (pen), Kabia	2748
40		20	H	Hereford U	W	3-0	1-0	10	West D, Carmichael, Lee	2358
41		25	A	Halifax T	W	4-1	1-1	10	Lormor 2, Abbbott (og), Alexander	1296
42	May	2	H	Blackpool	W	2-0	1-0	10	Carmichael 2 (2 pen)	7884

Final League Position: 10

GOALSCORERS

League (50): Lormor 9, Carmichael 7 (4 pens), Lee 6, Puttnam 6, Dobson 4, Kabia 3, Smith P 3, West D 3, Finney 2, Alexander 1, Brown 1, Dunphy 1, Nicholson 1, Schofield 1, West G 1, own goals 1.
Rumbelows Cup (4): Schofield 2, Dobson 1, Ward 1.
FA Cup (1): Lee 1.

Dickins	Smith P	Clarke	West D	Carmichael	Brown	Finney	Ward	Lee	Dobson	Puttnam	Alexander	West G	Nicholson	Hoult	Schofield	Bowling	Costello	Smith N	Lormor	Dye	Bressington	Kabia	Dixon	Dunphy	Chapman	Match No.
1	2	3	4	5	6	7	8	9	10*	11	12															1
1	2	3†	4*		6	7	8	9	10	11	12	5	14													2
	4	12	14	5	6	2†	8		9*	10	11		3	1	7											3
	2	4	6	12		8	9		10*	11		5	3	1	7											4
	2	6	4	5	10	8*	9			3		7	1		11	12										5
	2	8*	4	5	6	10		9†		12	14	3		7	1	11										6
	2	4	5	6	8†		9	12	11			3		7	1	10*	14									7
	2	8	4*	5	6		9	10	12			3		7	1	11										8
1	14	2	4	6†	8	9	12	11*		5		3			7	10										9
1	4	12	2	6	8	9	11*			5		3			7	10										10
1	2	5	6	4	8	9*	11	12				3			7	10										11
1	2	4	6	8	9	11			5			3			7	10*12										12
1	2	3	14	6	4	8	9*	10	11†	5				7	12											13
1	2	3	6	4	8	12	9*11		5					7	10											14
1	11	12	2*	6	4	8	9		5	3				7	10											15
1	2	3	6	4	8*	9	11		5					7	10 12											16
1	2	3	14	12	6	4†	8	9	11	5*			7	10												17
1	2	3	14	12	6	4	8	9	11*	5			7	10												18
1	2	3	6	4	8	9*	11	12	5			7	10													19
1	2	3	14	6	4*	8	9	11	12	5†			7	10												20
1	2	3	4	5	6	8			11	12	9		7	10*												21
1	2	3†14	5	6	8		12	9	11*	4		7	10													22
1	2	3*	4	5	6	8		12	11	9		7	10													23
1	2	3	4†	5	6	8	14	12	11	9		7	10*													24
	2	3	12	5†	6	8	9*	11	14	4				7	1			10								25
	2	4	5	6	8*	9	12	11†			3			7	1			10	14							26
	2	3	5	6	8	9	12	11					7	1			10*	4								27
	2	3	12	5	6	9†	11	8					7	1			10	4*14								28
	2	3	4	5*	6	11	12	8†					7	1			10		9	14						29
	2	3	4*	5	6	8	11	12					7	1			10		9							30
	2	3*	5	6	8	9	11	4					7	1			10		12							31
	2	3	5	6	8*	9	11	14	4				7†	1			10		12							32
	2	12	5	6	8*	9	11	3					7	1			10		4							33
1	3	12	2	6	9	11	5*	4					7				10		8							34
1	2	3	12	5	6	9	11	4					7				10		8*							35
	2	3*12	5	6	9	11	4						7	1			10		8							36
	2	4	5	6	12	9	11	3					7	1			10*		8							37
	2	4	5	7		9†	11	12	3					1			10		8*14	6						38
	2	3†	4	6	9*		11	12					7	1			10		8		5	14				39
	2	3	4	6	8*	9	11						7	1			10		12		5					40
	2	3	4	6	8*	9†	11	14					7	1			10		12		5					41
	2	3	4	6	8*12	9	11						7	1			10†14				5					42
20	39	27	19	36	37	21	28	33	4	37	5	14	28	2	39	20	3	—	33	—	2	10	—	5	—	

Substitute appearances (+):
Smith P 1s · Clarke 13s4s · West D 2s · Carmichael 1s · Brown 2s · Finney 7s · Ward 2s · Lee 10s4s · Dobson 1s · Schofield 1s · Costello 2s · Smith N 2s · Lormor 1s · Bressington 5s · Kabia 3s · Dunphy 1s

Rumbelows Cup	First Round	Chester C (a)	0-1
		(h)	4-3
FA Cup	First Round	Stockport Co (a)	1-3

LINCOLN CITY

Player and Position	Ht	Wt	Date	Birth Place	Source	Clubs	League App	Gls
Goalkeepers								
Ian Bowling	6 3	14 08	27 7 65	Sheffield	Gainsborough T	Lincoln C	44	—
						Hartlepool U (loan)	1	—
Defenders								
Grant Brown	6 0	11 12	19 11 69	Sunderland	Trainee	Leicester C	14	—
						Lincoln C	103	4
Paul Casey‡	5 8	10 06	6 10 61	Rinteln	Apprentice	Sheffield U	25	1
						Boston U	—	—
						Lincoln C	49	4
Darren Chapman§			15 11 74	Lincoln	Trainee	Lincoln C	1	—
Sean Dunphy	6 3	13 05	5 11 70	Rotherham	Trainee	Barnsley	6	—
						Lincoln C	5	1
Stephen Stoutt‡	5 8	11 06	5 4 64	Halifax	Local	Huddersfield T	6	—
						Wolverhampton W	94	5
						Grimsby T	3	1
						Lincoln C	46	1
Steve Thompson‡	6 1	14 04	28 7 55	Sheffield	Boston U	Lincoln C	154	8
						Charlton Ath	95	—
						Leicester C	—	—
						Sheffield U	20	1
						Lincoln C	27	—
Dean West			5 12 72	Wakefield	Leeds U	Lincoln C	33	4
Gary West	6 2	12 07	25 8 64	Scunthorpe	Apprentice	Sheffield U	75	1
						Lincoln C	83	4
						Gillingham	52	3
						Port Vale	17	1
						Lincoln C (loan)	3	—
						Gillingham (loan)	1	—
						Lincoln C	18	1
Midfield								
Graham Bressington	6 0	12 06	8 7 66	Eton	Wycombe W	Lincoln C	113	3
David Clarke*	5 10	11 00	3 12 64	Nottingham	Apprentice	Notts Co	123	7
						Lincoln C	109	6
Kevin Finney	6 0	12 00	19 10 69	Newcastle-U-Lyme	Apprentice	Port Vale	37	1
						Lincoln C	23	2
Jon Schofield	5 11	11 03	16 5 65	Barnsley	Gainsborough T	Lincoln C	139	8
Neil Smith‡	5 10	10 12	10 2 70	Warley	Trainee	Shrewsbury T	1	—
						Redditch	—	—
						Lincoln C	17	—
Paul Ward	5 11	12 05	15 9 63	Bedlington	Apprentice	Chelsea		
						Middlesbrough	76	1
						Darlington	124	9
						Leyton Orient	31	1
						Scunthorpe U	55	6
						Lincoln C	38	—
Forwards								
Keith Alexander†	6 4	13 06	14 11 58	Nottingham	Barnet	Grimsby T	83	26
						Stockport Co	11	—
						Lincoln C	38	4
Matt Carmichael	6 2	11 07	13 5 64	Singapore	Army	Lincoln C	92	14
Ben Dixon§			16 9 74	Lincoln	Trainee	Lincoln C	3	—

LINCOLN CITY

Foundation: Although there was a Lincoln club as far back as 1861, the present organisation was formed in 1883 winning the Lincolnshire Senior Cup in only their fourth season. They were Founder members of the Midland League in 1889 and that competition's first champions.

First Football League game: 3 September, 1892, Division 2, v Sheffield U (a) L 2-4 – W. Gresham; Coulton, Neill; Shaw, Mettam, Moore; Smallman, Irving (1), Cameron (1), Kelly, J. Gresham.

Did you know: When Lincoln City topped Division Four by a margin of six points in 1975–76 they had suffered only four defeats (all away from home) and only Newport County had scored as many as three goals against them all season.

Managers (and Secretary-managers)
David Calderhead 1900–07, John Henry Strawson 1907–14 (had been secretary), George Fraser 1919–21, David Calderhead Jnr. 1921–24, Horace Henshall 1924–27, Harry Parkes 1927–36, Joe McClelland 1936–46, Bill Anderson 1946–65 (GM to 1966), Roy Chapman 1965–66, Ron Gray 1966–70, Bert Loxley 1970–71, David Herd 1971–72, Graham Taylor 1972–77, George Kerr 1977–78, Willie Bell 1977–78, Colin Murphy 1978–85, John Pickering 1985, George Kerr 1985–87, Peter Daniel 1987, Colin Murphy 1987–90, Allan Clarke 1990, Steve Thompson November 1990–.

Player and Position	Ht	Wt	Birth Date	Birth Place	Source	Clubs	League App	Gls
Paul Dobson	5 9	10 06	17 12 62	Hartlepool	Amateur	Newcastle U	—	—
						Hartlepool U	31	8
						Horden	—	—
						Hartlepool U	80	24
						Torquay U	77	38
						Doncaster R	24	10
						Scarborough	61	22
						Halifax T (loan)	1	1
						Hereford U (loan)	6	1
						Lincoln C	21	5
Dean Dyet	5 9	11 00	14 3 69	Lincoln	Lincoln C	Charlton Ath	—	—
						Lincoln C	—	—
Jason Kabia			28 5 69	Sutton in Ashfield	Oakham U	Lincoln C	15	3
Jason Lee	6 3	13 08	9 5 71	London	Trainee	Charlton Ath	1	—
						Stockport Co (loan)	2	—
						Lincoln C	52	9
Tony Lormor	6 1	12 03	29 10 70	Ashington	Trainee	Newcastle U	8	3
						Norwich C (loan)	—	—
						Lincoln C	90	29
David Puttnam	5 10	11 09	3 2 67	Leicester	Leicester U	Leicester C	7	—
						Lincoln C	105	13
Keith Scott‡	6 3	12 00	10 6 67	London	Leicester U	Lincoln C	16	2
Paul Smith	5 11	10 09	9 11 64	Rotherham	Apprentice	Sheffield U	36	1
						Stockport Co (loan)	7	5
						Port Vale	44	7
						Lincoln C	146	24

Trainees
Barker, Adrian; Carbon, Matthew P; Chapman, Darren; Charles, Richard; Diamond, Stuart; Dixon, Ben; Donnelly, Stuart; Hackett, Lee; Hunt, Mark A; Parkinson, Steven; Whittle, Simon.

**Non-Contract
Alexander, Keith.

Associated Schoolboys
Brown, Michael A; Foster, Jonathan; Fraser, Gregory A.

Associated Schoolboys who have accepted the club's offer of a Traineeship/Contract
Morgan, James; Rawlinson, Christopher; Spencer, Robin; Williams, Steven.

**Non-Contract Players who are retained must be re-signed before they are eligible to play in League matches.

LIVERPOOL 1991–92 *Back row (left to right)*: Steve Staunton, Glenn Hysen, Nicky Tanner, Mike Hooper, Gary Gillespie, Bruce Grobbelaar, Mark Wright, Gary Ablett, Jan Molby.
Centre row: Roy Evans (First Team Trainer), Michael Marsh, Steve McManaman, Barry Venison, Ian Rush, Jimmy Carter, Ronnie Rosenthal, David Speedie, Ronnie Moran (First Team Coach), Phil Boersma (First Team Trainer).
Front row: Dean Saunders, Ray Houghton, John Barnes, Steve Nicol, Graeme Souness (Manager), Ronnie Whelan, Steve McMahon, Peter Beardsley, David Burrows.
(Picture by Harry Ormesher)

FA Premier

LIVERPOOL

Anfield Road, Liverpool 4. Telephone 051-263 2361. Clubcall: 0898 121184. Ticket and Match Information: 051-260 9999 (24-hour service) or 051-260 8680 (office hours) or 0898 121584 for Ticket Call.

Ground capacity: 44,931.

Record attendance: 61,905 v Wolverhampton W, FA Cup 4th rd, 2 February 1952.

Record receipts: £342,000 v Genoa, UEFA Cup, 4th rd 2nd leg, 18 March 1992.

Pitch measurements: 110yd × 75yd.

Chairman: D. R. Moores.

Vice-chairman: S. T. Moss JP, DL.

Directors: Sir J. W. Smith CBE, JP, DL, HON. LLD, S. C. Reakes JP, J. T. Cross, G. A. Ensor LLB, N. White FSCA, T. D. Smith.

Vice-presidents: C. J. Hill, H. E. Roberts, W. D. Corkish FCA, R. Paisley OBE, HON MSC.

Team Manager: Graeme Souness. *Coach:* Ron Moran. *Chief Executive/General Secretary:* Peter Robinson. *Commercial Manager:* K. Addison.

Year Formed: 1892. Turned Professional: 1892. Ltd Co.: 1892.

Club Nickname: 'Reds' or 'Pool'.

Record League Victory: 10-1 v Rotherham T, Division 2, 18 February 1896 – Storer; Goldie, Wilkie; McCarthy, McQueen, Holmes; McVean (3), Ross (2), Allan (4), Becton (1), Bradshaw.

Record Cup Victory: 11-0 v Stromsgodset Drammen, ECWC 1st rd 1st leg, 17 September 1974 – Clemence; Smith (1), Lindsay (1p), Thompson (2), Cormack (1), Hughes (1), Boersma (2), Hall, Heighway (1), Kennedy (1), Callaghan (1).

Record Defeat: 1-9 v Birmingham C, Division 2, 11 December 1954.

Most League Points (2 for a win): 68, Division 1, 1978–79.

Most League points (3 for a win): 90, Division 1, 1987–88.

Most League Goals: 106, Division 2, 1895–96.

Highest League Scorer in Season: Roger Hunt, 41, Division 2, 1961–62.

Most League Goals in Total Aggregate: Roger Hunt, 245, 1959–69.

Most Capped Player: Emlyn Hughes, 59 (62), England.

Most League Appearances: Ian Callaghan, 640, 1960–78.

Record Transfer Fee Received: £3,200,000 from Juventus for Ian Rush, June 1986.

Record Transfer Fee Paid: £2,900,000 to Derby Co for Dean Saunders, July 1991.

Football League Record: 1893 Elected to Division 2; 1894–95 Division 1; 1895–96 Division 2; 1896–1904 Division 1; 1904–05 Division 2; 1905–54 Division 1; 1954–62 Division 2; 1962–92 Division 1; 1992– FA Premier League.

Honours: Football League: Division 1 – Champions 1900–01, 1905–06, 1921–22, 1922–23, 1946–47, 1963–64, 1965–66, 1972–73, 1975–76, 1976–77, 1978–79, 1979–80, 1981–82, 1982–83, 1983–84, 1985–86, 1987–88, 1989–90 (Liverpool have a record number of 18 league Championship wins); Runners-up 1898–99, 1909–10, 1968–69, 1973–74, 1974–75, 1977–78, 1984–85, 1986–87, 1988–89, 1990–91; Division 2 – Champions 1893–94, 1895–96, 1904–05, 1961–62. *FA Cup:* Winners 1965, 1974, 1986, 1989, 1992; Runners-up 1914, 1950, 1971, 1977, 1988; *Football League Cup:* Winners 1981, 1982, 1983, 1984; Runners-up 1977–78, 1986–87 *League Super Cup:* Winners 1985–86. **European Competitions:** *European Cup:* 1964–65, 1966–67, 1973–74, 1976–77 (winners), 1977–78 (winners), 1978–79, 1979–80, 1980–81 (winners), 1981–82, 1982–83, 1983–84 (winners), 1984–85 (runners-up); *European Cup Winners Cup:* 1965–66 (runners-up), 1971–72, 1974–75; *European Fairs Cup:* 1967–68, 1968–69, 1969–70, 1970–71; *UEFA Cup:* 1972–73 (winners), 1975–76 (winners), 1991–92; *Super Cup:* 1977 (winners), 1978, 1984; *World Club Championship:* 1981 (runners-up).

Colours: All red with white markings. **Change colours:** Racing green with white markings.

LIVERPOOL 1991–92 LEAGUE RECORD

Match No.	Date		Venue	Opponents	Result		H/T Score	Lg. Pos.	Goalscorers	Atten-dance
1	Aug	17	H	Oldham Ath	W	2-1	0-1	—	Houghton, Barnes	38,841
2		21	A	Manchester C	L	1-2	0-1	—	McManaman	37,322
3		24	A	Luton T	D	0-0	0-0	11		11,132
4		27	H	QPR	W	1-0	0-0	—	Saunders	32,700
5		31	H	Everton	W	3-1	2-0	2	Burrows, Saunders, Houghton	39,072
6	Sep	7	A	Notts Co	W	2-1	0-1	2	Rosenthal, Walters (pen)	16,051
7		14	H	Aston Villa	D	1-1	1-1	3	Walters (pen)	38,400
8		21	A	Leeds U	L	0-1	0-1	9		32,917
9		28	H	Sheffield W	D	1-1	1-0	9	Houghton	37,071
10	Oct	6	A	Manchester U	D	0-0	0-0	—		44,997
11		19	A	Chelsea	D	2-2	1-1	10	McManaman, Elliott (og)	30,230
12		26	H	Coventry C	W	1-0	1-0	8	Houghton	33,339
13	Nov	2	H	Crystal Palace	L	1-2	1-0	9	Hysen	34,231
14		17	A	West Ham U	D	0-0	0-0	—		23,569
15		23	A	Wimbledon	D	0-0	0-0	11		13,373
16		30	H	Norwich C	W	2-1	2-1	9	Molby, Houghton	34,881
17	Dec	7	A	Southampton	D	1-1	0-0	10	Redknapp	10,053
18		13	H	Nottingham F	W	2-0	1-0	8	McMahon, Molby	35,285
19		18	A	Tottenham H	W	2-1	1-1	—	Saunders, Houghton	27,434
20		20	H	Manchester C	D	2-2	1-0	4	Saunders, Nicol	36,743
21		26	A	QPR	D	0-0	0-0	5		21,693
22		28	A	Everton	D	1-1	1-0	6	Tanner	37,681
23	Jan	1	H	Sheffield U	W	2-1	0-1	5	Houghton, Saunders	35,993
24		11	A	Luton T	W	2-1	0-1	3	McManaman, Saunders	35,095
25		18	A	Oldham Ath	W	3-2	2-1	3	McManaman, Saunders, Thomas	18,952
26		29	H	Arsenal	W	2-0	1-0	—	Molby (pen), Houghton	33,753
27	Feb	1	H	Chelsea	L	1-2	1-1	3	Rosenthal	38,681
28		8	A	Coventry C	D	0-0	0-0	3		21,540
29		22	A	Norwich C	L	0-3	0-0	5		20,411
30		29	H	Southampton	D	0-0	0-0	5		34,449
31	Mar	11	H	West Ham U	W	1-0	1-0	—	Saunders	30,821
32		14	A	Crystal Palace	L	0-1	0-1	5		23,680
33		21	H	Tottenham H	W	2-1	0-0	4	Saunders 2	36,968
34		28	A	Sheffield U	L	0-2	0-1	4		26,943
35		31	H	Notts Co	W	4-0	2-0	—	Thomas, McManaman, Rush, Venison	25,457
36	Apr	8	A	Wimbledon	L	2-3	2-1	—	Thomas, Rosenthal	26,134
37		11	A	Aston Villa	L	0-1	0-0	5		35,755
38		18	H	Leeds U	D	0-0	0-0	6		37,186
39		20	A	Arsenal	L	0-4	0-3	6		38,517
40		22	A	Nottingham F	D	1-1	1-1	—	Rush	23,787
41		26	H	Manchester U	W	2-0	1-0	—	Rush, Walters	38,669
42	May	2	A	Sheffield W	D	0-0	0-0	6		34,861

Final League Position: 6

GOALSCORERS

League (47): Saunders 10, Houghton 8, McManaman 5, Molby 3 (1 pen), Rosenthal 3, Rush 3, Thomas 3, Walters 3 (2 pens), Barnes 1, Burrows 1, Hysen 1, McMahon 1, Nicol 1, Redknapp 1, Tanner 1, Venison 1, own goals 1.
Rumbelows Cup (11): McManaman 3, Rush 3, Saunders 2, Walters 2, Houghton 1.
FA Cup (14): Barnes 3 (l pens), McManaman 3, Saunders 2, Thomas 2, Houghton 1, Molby 1, Rush 1, Whelan 1.

Grobbelaar	Ablett	Burrows	Nicol	Whelan	Wright	Saunders	Houghton	McManaman	Barnes	McMahon	Walters	Marsh	Tanner	Rosenthal	Harkness	Rush	Hooper	Jones R	Hysen	Molby	Redknapp	Thomas	Venison	Kozma	Hutchison	Match No.
1	2	3	4	5	6	7	8	9	10	11*	12															1
1	2	3	4	5	6†	7	8	9	10*	11	12	14														2
1	2	3	4	5†		7	8	9		11	10*	14	6	12												3
1		3	4			7	8	9		11	10*	5	2	12	6											4
1	2	3	4	5†		7	8	9		11	10*	14	6	12												5
1	2	3	4			7	8	9			10	5	6	12	11*											6
1	2	3	4			7*	8	9			10	5	6	11†	14	12										7
1	2	3	4			7	8	11			10*	5	6†	12	14	9										8
1	14	3	4			7	8	10		11	12	5*	6†		2	9										9
	2	3	4			7*	8	12		11	10	14	6			9		1	5†							10
1		3	4			7	8	5		11	10		6			9		2								11
1		3				7*	8			11	10		6	12	14	9		2	4	5†						12
1	10	3				7	8			11			6	12		9		2	4	5*						13
1		3	4				7			11	10	8	6			9		2		5						14
1	10	3	4			7				11		8	6	9*		2		12	5							15
1	2	3	4	5		7	8	9		11*	12	6							10							16
1		3	4	5		7	8	9		11		6		2†				14	10*	12						17
1		3	4	5		7	8	9		11		6		2					10							18
1		3	4	5		7	8	9		11†		14	6	2					10*	12						19
1		3	4	5		7	8	9†		11*	12	14	6	2					10							20
1	3*		4	5		7	8			9		6		2					10	11	12					21
1	3		4	5*		7	8	12		9		6		2					10	11						22
1	3		4	5		7	8	12		9*		6		2					10	11						23
1			4	5		7	8	9	10			6	12	2					3*	11						24
1			4	5		7	8	9	10*		12	6	3	2						11						25
1			4	5		7	8			9	12	6	3	2					10	11*						26
1	3			5†		7	8	11		9*	12	6	4	2					10	14						27
1	3			5		7	8	11		9*	4	6†	12	14	2				10							28
1			5			7†	8	11		14	4	12	3	9			2		10					6*		29
1	3	4	5			7		11*		6		12		2†	10	9			14	8						30
1		4		6		7	8†	11	10*	14	12		2					5	9	3						31
1		4	6					10		7*	11	12	2		14	5†	9	3	8							32
1	3	4	14			7		12	10	8*	6		9	2		5†	11									33
1	3	4	5			8	7			12		9	2	10		11*	6									34
1	3	5				7*		8	6			9†	2	10	11	4	12	14								35
1		5				7	8		9	12	4	6*	2	10	11	3										36
1		4	5			7	8		9†	12	6		2*	10	11	3	14									37
1	3	4				7	8	10		12		9	2	5	11*	6										38
	4					7†	8	10	12	11	3		9	1	2*	5			6	14						39
	4					8		10	11	7	3	2	9	1		5			6							40
	3					6	7	8	10	12	4†		9*	1	2	5			11	14						41
	3	4	5†	6		8		10*		7	12	2	9	1		11				14						42

37	13	30	34	9	21	36	36	26	12	15	18	19	32	7	7	16	5	28	3	25	5	16	9	3	—	
				+			+	+			+	+		+	+		+			+	+	+	+	+	+	
				1s			1s	4s			7s	15s		13s	4s		2s			2s	1s	1s	1s	4s	2s 3s	

Rumbelows Cup	Second Round	Stoke C (h)	2-2
		(a)	3-2
	Third Round	Port Vale (h)	2-2
		(a)	4-1
	Fourth Round	Peterborough U (a)	0-1
FA Cup	Third Round	Crewe Alex (a)	4-0
	Fourth Round	Bristol R (a)	1-1
		(h)	2-1
	Fifth Round	Ipswich T (a)	0-0
		(h)	3-2
	Sixth Round	Aston Villa (h)	1-0
	Semi-Final	Portsmouth (at Highbury)	1-1
		(at Villa Park)	0-0; Liverpool won 3-1 on penalties
	Final	Sunderland (at Wembley)	2-0

LIVERPOOL

Player and Position	Ht	Wt	Birth Date	Birth Place	Source	Clubs	League App	League Gls
Goalkeepers								
Bruce Grobbelaar	6 1	13 00	6 10 57	Durban	Vancouver W	Crewe Alex	24	1
						Vancouver W	—	—
						Liverpool	406	—
Michael Hooper	6 2	13 05	10 2 64	Bristol	Local	Bristol C	1	—
						Wrexham (loan)	20	—
						Wrexham	14	—
						Liverpool	42	—
						Leicester C (loan)	14	—
Defenders								
David Burrows	5 8	11 00	25 10 68	Dudley	Apprentice	WBA	46	1
						Liverpool	112	1
David Collins*	6 1	12 10	30 10 71	Dublin	Trainee	Liverpool		
						Wigan Ath (loan)	9	—
Gary Gillespie (To Celtic Aug 1991)	6 2	12 07	5 7 60	Stirling	School	Falkirk	22	—
						Coventry C	172	6
						Liverpool	156	14
Steve Hollis*	5 10	11 06	22 8 72	Liverpool	Trainee	Liverpool	—	—
Glenn Hysen (To GAIS Goth'g May 1992)	6 1	12 08	30 10 59	Gothenburg	Fiorentina	Liverpool	72	2
Barry Jones*	6 0	12 00	30 6 70	Liverpool	Prescot T	Liverpool	—	—
Rob Jones	5 11	11 00	5 11 71	Wrexham	Trainee	Crewe Alex	75	2
						Liverpool	28	—
Rodney McAree	5 07	10 02	19 8 74	Dungannon	Trainee	Liverpool	—	—
Steve Nicol	5 10	12 00	11 12 61	Irvine	Ayr U BC	Ayr U	70	7
						Liverpool	276	35
Michael Thomas	5 10	12 04	24 8 67	Lambeth	Apprentice	Arsenal	163	24
						Portsmouth (loan)	3	—
						Liverpool	17	3
Barry Venison	5 10	11 09	16 8 64	Consett	Apprentice	Sunderland	173	2
						Liverpool	110	1
Tom White	5 08	11 08	6 11 74	Auckland NZ		Liverpool	—	—
Mark Wright	6 3	12 01	1 8 63	Dorchester	Amateur	Oxford U	10	—
						Southampton	170	7
						Derby Co	144	10
						Liverpool	21	—
Midfield								
Warren Godfrey*	5 11	11 02	31 3 72	Liverpool	Trainee	Liverpool	—	—
Steve Harkness	5 9	10 11	27 8 71	Carlisle	Trainee	Carlisle U	13	—
						Liverpool	11	—
Ray Houghton	5 8	11 04	9 1 62	Glasgow	Amateur	West Ham U	1	—
						Fulham	129	16
						Oxford U	83	10
						Liverpool	153	28
Craig Johnston	5 8	10 13	8 12 60	Johannesburg	Sydney C	Middlesbrough	64	16
						Liverpool	190	30
Marc Kenny	5 11	11 00	17 9 73	Dublin	Trainee	Liverpool	—	—
Istvan Kozma	6 0	11 13	3 12 64	Paszto	Bordeaux	Dunfermline Ath	90	8
						Liverpool	10	—
Kevin Lampkin*	5 10	11 08	20 12 72	Liverpool	Trainee	Liverpool	—	—
Jan Molby	6 1	14 07	4 7 63	Denmark	Ajax	Liverpool	183	37
Scott Paterson	5 11	12 00	13 5 72	Aberdeen	Cove Rangers	Liverpool	—	—
Jamie Redknapp	5 11	11 08	25 6 73	Barton-on-Sea	Trainee	Bournemouth	13	—
						Liverpool	6	1
Jamie Robinson*	6 1	12 03	26 2 72	Liverpool	Trainee	Liverpool	—	—

LIVERPOOL

Foundation: But for a dispute between Everton FC and their landlord at Anfield in 1892, there may never have been a Liverpool club. This dispute persuaded the majority of Evertonians to quit Anfield for Goodison Park, leaving the landlord, Mr. John Houlding, to form a new club. He originally tried to retain the name "Everton" but when this failed, he founded Liverpool Association FC on 15 March, 1892.

First Football League game: 2 September, 1893, Division 2, v Middlesbrough (a) W 2-0 – McOwen; Hannah, McLean; Henderson, McQue (1), McBride; Gordon, McVean (1), M. McQueen, Stott, H. McQueen.

Did you know: In 1967–68 Liverpool fielded an unchanged side for their first 12 League games and made only one change in their first 17. The original team was: Lawrence;, Lawler, Byrne, Smith, Yeats, Hughes, Callaghan, Hunt, Hateley, St John, Thompson.

Managers (and Secretary-managers)
W. E. Barclay 1892–96, Tom Watson 1896–1915, David Ashworth 1920–22, Matt McQueen 1923–28, George Patterson 1928–36 (continued as secretary), George Kay 1936–51, Don Welsh 1951–56, Phil Taylor 1956–59, Bill Shankly 1959–74, Bob Paisley 1974–83, Joe Fagan 1983–85, Kenny Dalglish 1985–91, Graeme Souness April 1991–.

Nick Tanner	6 1	13 10	24	5 65	Bristol	Mangotsfield	Bristol R	107	3
							Liverpool	36	1
							Norwich C (loan)	6	—
							Swindon T (loan)	7	—
Ronnie Whelan	5 9	10 13	25	9 61	Dublin	Home Farm	Liverpool	322	44
Forwards									
John Barnes	5 11	12 00	7	11 63	Jamaica	Sudbury Court	Watford	233	65
							Liverpool	152	62
Tony Cousins	5 9	11 10	25	8 69	Dublin	Dundalk	Liverpool	—	—
Robbie Fowler	5 09	11 08	9	4 75	Liverpool	Trainee	Liverpool	—	—
Don Hutchison	6 2	11 04	9	5 71	Gateshead	Trainee	Hartlepool U	24	2
							Liverpool	3	—
Lee Jones	5 7	9 11	29	5 73	Wrexham	Trainee	Wrexham	39	10
							Liverpool	—	—
Steve McManaman	5 11	10 02	11	2 72	Liverpool	School	Liverpool	32	5
Mike Marsh	5 8	10 14	21	7 69	Liverpool	Kirkby T	Liverpool	39	—
Russell Payne*	5 10	11 08	8	7 70	Wigan	Skelmersdale	Liverpool	—	—
							Crewe Alex (loan)	6	—
Ronny Rosenthal	5 10	11 12	11	10 63	Haifa	Standard Liege	Luton T	—	—
							Liverpool	44	15
Ian Rush	6 0	12 06	20	10 61	St Asaph	Apprentice	Chester	34	14
							Liverpool	224	139
							Juventus	29	7
							Liverpool	115	44
Dean Saunders	5 8	10 06	21	6 64	Swansea	Apprentice	Swansea C	49	12
							Cardiff C (loan)	4	—
							Brighton & HA	72	21
							Oxford U	59	22
							Derby Co	106	42
							Liverpool	36	10
Mark Walters	5 9	11 05	12	1 61	Birmingham	Apprentice	Aston Villa	181	39
							Rangers	106	32
							Liverpool	50	6

Trainees
Brydon, Lee; Charnock, Philip A; Dennis, Wayne A; Embleton, Daniel C; Fallon, Sean P. F; Fox, Michael J; Gelling, Stuart; Holcroft, Robert J; Jones, Stuart J; Matteo, Dominic; Matthews, Anthony; Neal, Ashley J; Nestor, Terry; O'Donnell, Paul G; Scott, John A; Stalker, Mark E; Walsh, Stephen J; Whittaker, Stuart.

Associated Schoolboys
Brenchley, Scott A; Brunskill, Iain R; Carragher, James L; Clegg, David L; Cooling, Michael J; Harris, Andrew D. D; Joyce, Paul C; Kinney, Westley M; Livingstone, Maurice A; Lyonette, Paul M; Morris, Stephen; Murphy, John J; Quinn, Stuart; Stannard, John F; Vanzyl, John E; Walker, Robert F.

Associated Schoolboys who have accepted the club's offer of a Traineeship/Contract
Frodsham, Ian T; Li, Christian; Snape, Paul F.

LUTON TOWN 1991–92 *Back row (left to right):* Julian James, Darren Salton, Graham Rodger, Andy Petterson, Alec Chamberlain, Sean Farrell, Des Linton, John Dreyer. *Centre row:* Mick Harford, Trevor Peake, Darron McDonough, Marvin Johnson, Kurt Nogan, Richard Harvey, Chris Kamara. *Front row:* Colin Murphy (Assistant Manager), Brian Stein, Scott Oakes, Ceri Hughes, Paul Telfer, Jason Rees, Mark Pembridge, David Preece, David Pleat (Manager). (Apex Photography)

Division 1   LUTON TOWN

Kenilworth Road Stadium, 1 Maple Rd, Luton, Beds. LU4 8AW.
Telephone Offices: Luton (0582) 411622; Credit Hotline (0582)
30748 (24 hrs); Banqueting: (0582) 411526. Special Loupe
system for deaf and blind in our handicapped ares. Soccer
Line, 0839 664466 for latest news and views about Luton Town,
44p per min. peak, 33p per min. off peak.

Ground capacity: 13,449.

Record attendance: 30,069 v Blackpool, FA Cup 6th rd replay,
4 March 1959.

Record receipts: £77,000 v Oxford U, Littlewoods Cup semi-
final, 28 February 1988.

Pitch measurements: 110yd × 72yd.

President: E. Pearson.

Chairman: R. J. Smith. *Managing Director:* D. A. Kohler.

Secretary: J. K. Smylie.

Directors: P. Collins, E. S. Pearson, H. Richardson, N. Terry.

Commercial Manager: Andy King/Wendy Grzybowska.

Manager: David Pleat. *Reserve team coach:* John Moore. *Youth team coach:* Terry Westley.
Physio: B. Owen.

Year Formed: 1885. Turned Professional: 1890. Ltd Co.: 1897.

Former Grounds: 1885, Excelsior, Dallow Lane; 1897, Dunstable Road; 1905, Kenilworth
Road.

Club Nickname: 'The Hatters'.

Record League Victory: 12-0 v Bristol R, Division 3 (S), 13 April 1936 – Dolman; Mackey,
Smith; Finlayson, Nelson, Godfrey; Rich, Martin (1), Payne (10), Roberts (1), Stephenson.

Record Cup Victory: 9-0 v Clapton, FA Cup, 1st rd (replay after abandoned game), 30
November 1927 – Abbott; Kingham, Graham; Black, Rennie, Fraser; Pointon, Yardley
(4), Reid (2), Woods (1), Dennis (2).

Record Defeat: 0-9 v Small Heath, Division 2, 12 November 1898.

Most League Points (2 for a win): 66, Division 4, 1967–68.

Most League points (3 for a win): 88, Division 2, 1981–82.

Most League Goals: 103, Division 3 (S), 1936–37.

Highest League Scorer in Season: Joe Payne, 55, Division 3 (S), 1936–37.

Most League Goals in Total Aggregate: Gordon Turner, 243, 1949–64.

Most Capped Player: Mal Donaghy, 58 (76), Northern Ireland.

Most League Appearances: Bob Morton, 494, 1948–64.

Record Transfer Fee Received: £1,500,000 from Nottingham F for Kingsley Black, August
1991.

Record Transfer Fee Paid: £850,000 to Odense for Lars Elstrup, August 1989.

Football League Record: 1897 Elected to Division 2; 1900 Failed re-election; 1920 Division
3; 1921 Division 3 (S); 1937–55 Division 2; 1955–60 Division 1; 1960–63 Division 2; 1963–
65 Division 3; 1965–68 Division 4; 1968–70 Division 3; 1970–74 Division 2; 1974–75
Division 1; 1975–82 Division 2; 1982– Division 1.

Honours: Football League: Division 1 best season: 7th, 1986–87; Division 2 – Champions
1981–82; Runners-up 1954–55, 1973–74; Division 3 – Runners-up 1969–70; Division 4 –
Champions 1967–68; Division 3 (S) – Champions 1936–37; Runners-up 1935–36. *FA Cup:*
Runners-up 1959. *Football League Cup:* Winners 1987–88; Runners-up 1988–89. *Simod
Cup:* Runners-up 1988.

Colours: White shirts, blue shorts, white stockings. **Change colours:** Blue shirts, white
shorts, blue stockings.

LUTON TOWN 1991–92 LEAGUE RECORD

Match No.	Date		Venue	Opponents	Result		H/T Score	Lg. Pos.	Goalscorers	Atten- dance
1	Aug	17	A	West Ham U	D	0-0	0-0	—		25,079
2		21	A	Coventry C	L	0-5	0-3	—		10,084
3		24	H	Liverpool	D	0-0	0-0	19		11,132
4		27	A	Arsenal	L	0-2	0-1	—		25,898
5		31	A	Chelsea	L	1-4	0-3	22	Gray	17,457
6	Sep	4	H	Southampton	W	2-1	2-1	—	Gray, Harvey	8055
7		7	A	Wimbledon	L	0-3	0-1	20		3231
8		14	H	Oldham Ath	W	2-1	0-0	17	Harford 2	9005
9		17	H	QPR	L	0-1	0-0	—		9985
10		21	A	Manchester U	L	0-5	0-1	21		46,491
11		28	H	Notts Co	D	1-1	0-0	20	Gray	7629
12	Oct	5	A	Aston Villa	L	0-4	0-1	21		18,722
13		19	H	Sheffield W	D	2-2	1-1	21	Harford, Nogan	9401
14		26	A	Norwich C	L	0-1	0-1	21		10,541
15	Nov	2	H	Everton	L	0-1	0-0	21		8022
16		16	A	Tottenham H	L	1-4	1-0	21	Harford	27,543
17		23	H	Manchester C	D	2-2	1-0	22	Harford, Dreyer	10,031
18		30	A	Sheffield U	D	1-1	0-0	22	Telfer	21,804
19	Dec	7	H	Leeds U	L	0-2	0-0	22		11,550
20		20	H	Coventry C	W	1-0	0-0	—	Harford	7533
21		26	H	Arsenal	W	1-0	0-0	22	Harford	12,655
22		28	H	Chelsea	W	2-0	2-0	20	Harvey, Dreyer (pen)	10,738
23	Jan	1	A	Nottingham F	D	1-1	1-0	19	Pembridge	23,809
24		11	A	Liverpool	L	1-2	1-0	20	Tanner (og)	35,095
25		18	H	West Ham U	L	0-1	0-0	22		11,088
26	Feb	1	A	Sheffield W	L	2-3	2-1	22	Preece, Oakes	22,291
27		8	H	Norwich C	W	2-0	0-0	21	Preece, Harford	8554
28		15	A	Manchester C	L	0-4	0-1	21		22,137
29		22	H	Sheffield U	W	2-1	2-1	20	Stein, Harford	9003
30		25	A	Crystal Palace	D	1-1	0-1	—	Pembridge (pen)	12,109
31		29	A	Leeds U	L	0-2	0-0	20		28,231
32	Mar	7	H	Crystal Palace	D	1-1	0-1	19	Oakes	8591
33		11	H	Tottenham H	D	0-0	0-0	—		11,494
34		14	A	Everton	D	1-1	1-0	19	Stein	16,707
35		21	A	Southampton	L	1-2	1-0	20	Pembridge	15,315
36	Apr	4	H	Wimbledon	W	2-1	1-1	20	Varadi, Preece	7754
37		11	A	Oldham Ath	L	1-5	1-2	20	Harford	13,210
38		14	H	Nottingham F	W	2-1	2-1	—	Harford, James J	8014
39		18	H	Manchester U	D	1-1	0-1	20	Harford	13,410
40		20	A	QPR	L	1-2	0-0	20	Pembridge (pen)	10,749
41		25	H	Aston Villa	W	2-0	1-0	20	Stein, Pembridge	11,178
42	May	2	A	Notts Co	L	1-2	1-1	20	James J	11,380

Final League Position: 20

GOALSCORERS

League (38): Harford 12, Pembridge 5 (2 pens), Gray 3, Preece 3, Stein 3, Dreyer 2 (1 pen), Harvey 2, James J 2, Oakes 2, Nogan 1, Telfer 1, Varadi 1, own goals 1.
Rumbelows Cup (4): Gray 3, Nogan 1.
FA Cup (0).

Chamberlain	Beaumont	Harvey	McDonough	Rodger	Dreyer	Farrell	Preece	Stein	Pembridge	Black	Gray	Peake	Jackson	Nogan	Glover	Holsgrove	Telfer	Harford	Thompson	Hughes	James J	Rees	Oakes	Linton	Kamara	Sutton	Campbell	Salton	Match No.
1	2	3	4	5	6	7*	8	9	10	11	12																		1
1	2	3	4	5	6	7	8	9*	10	11	12																		2
1	2	3	4	5	6		8	9	10	11	7																		3
1	2*		4†	5	3	14	8	9	10	11	7	6	12																4
1	2*		4	5	3		8	9	10	11†	7	6		12	14														5
1	12	3	4	5	6		8	11	10			7		2*	14	9†													6
1		3	4†	5	6		8	9	10		7		2	12	14		11*												7
1		3	4†	5	6	7	8*	9	10				2	12	14		11												8
1		3	4	5	6	7	8*	9	10				2	12	14		11†												9
1		3	4	5	6	7	8†	9	10				2*	12	14		11												10
1		3	4†	5	6	7	8	9*	10				2	12	14		11												11
1		3	4		5†		8	9	10		12	6	2		14		11*						7						12
1	3†				5		8		10			6			14		11*	9		12	2		7		4				13
1	12	3			5		8		10			6†			14		11	9			2		7*		4				14
1		3			5		8		10†		12	6			14		11	9			2*		7		4				15
1		3			5		8		10			6					11	9		12	2*		7		4				16
1		3			5		8		10			6					11	9		12	2*		7		4				17
		3			5		8		10			6					12	9*			2		7	11	4	1			18
		3			5		8†		10			6					12	9		14	2*		7	11	4	1			19
		3			5		8		10			6					12	9			2		7	11*	4	1			20
		3			5		8*		10			6					11	9		12	2		7		4	1			21
		3			5		8†		10			6					11*	9		12	2		7		4	1	14		22
		3			5		8*		10			6					11†	9		12	2		7		4	1	14		23
		3			5		8		10			6					11*	9		12	2		7		4	1			24
		3			5		8		10			6					11	9†		12	2		7*		4	1	14		25
		3			5		8*		10			6					11	9		12	2		7		4	1			26
		3			5		8		10			6					11	9		12	2		7		4*	1			27
		3			5		8		10			6					11	9		12	2*		7†		4	1	14		28
		3			5		8†		10			6					11*	9		12	2		7		4	1	14		29
		3			5		8†		10			6					11	9		12	2		7*		4	1	14		30
		3			5		8*		10			6					11	9		12	2		7†		4	1	14		31
		3			5		8*		10			6					11	9		12	2		7		4				32
		3			5		8		10			6					11	9			2		7		4				33
		3			5		8†		10			6					11	9		12	2		7*		4		14		34
		3			5		8†		10			6					11	9		12	2*		7		4				35
1		3			5		8		10			6					11	9			2				4				36
1	3†				5		8		10			6					11*	9		12	2				4	14			37
1		3			5		8†		10			6					11	9		12	2				4	14			38
1		3			5		8*		10			6					11	9		12	2				4	14			39
1	3†				5		8		10			6					11	9		12	2				4	14			40
1					5		8		10			6					11	9			2		7*		4			3	41
1					5		8		10			6					11	9		12	2		7		4*	14		3†	42
24	6 +3s	31 +1s	9	11 +1s	42	3 +1s	34 +4s	32 +7s	42	4	9 +5s	38	7	6 +2s	1 +8s	1	17 +3s	29	5	6 +12s	28	3 +2s	15 +6s	2 +1s	28	14	4 +7s	2 +1s	

Day—Match No. 32(1) 33(1) 34(1) 35(1); Williams—Match No. 35(14); Varadi—Match No. 36(7) 37(7) 38(7*) 39(7†) 40(7*) 41(12).

Rumbelows Cup	Second Round	Birmingham C (h)	2-2
		(a)	2-3
FA Cup	Third Round	Sheffield U (a)	0-4

LUTON TOWN

Player and Position	Ht	Wt	Birth Date	Birth Place	Source	Clubs	League App	Gls
Goalkeepers								
Alec Chamberlain	6 2	13 00	20 6 64	March	Ramsey T	Ipswich T	—	—
						Colchester U	184	—
						Everton	—	—
						Tranmere R (loan)	15	—
						Luton T	106	—
Andy Petterson	6 1	14 04	26 9 69	Freemantle		Luton T	—	—
						Swindon T (loan)	—	—
						Ipswich T (loan)	—	—
Jurgen Sommer	6 04	15 12	27 2 64	New York	Trainee	Luton T	—	—
						Brighton & HA (loan)	1	—
Defenders								
Tim Allpress	6 0	12 00	27 1 71	Hitchin	Trainee	Luton T	1	—
						Preston NE (loan)	7	—
Dave Beaumont (To Hibs Oct 1991)	5 10	11 05	10 12 63	Edinburgh	'S' Form	Dundee U	89	3
						Luton T	76	—
Jamie Campbell	6 1	11 03	21 10 72	Birmingham	Trainee	Luton T	11	—
John Dreyer	6 0	11 10	11 6 63	Alnwick	Wallingford T	Oxford U	60	2
						Torquay U (loan)	5	—
						Fulham (loan)	12	2
						Luton T	136	8
Ken Gillard	5 9	11 08	30 4 72	Dublin	Trainee	Luton T	—	—
David Greene	6 02	13 05	26 10 73	Luton	Trainee	Luton T	—	—
Richard Harvey	5 9	11 10	17 4 69	Letchworth	Apprentice	Luton T	104	2
Marvin Johnson	5 11	11 06	29 10 68	Wembley	Apprentice	Luton T	63	—
Des Linton	6 1	11 13	5 9 71	Birmingham	Trainee	Leicester C	11	—
						Luton T	3	—
Trevor Peake	6 0	12 09	6 7 57	Nuneaton	Nuneaton Bor	Lincoln C	171	7
						Coventry C	278	6
						Luton T	38	—
Mark Pembridge	5 7	11 01	29 11 70	Merthyr	Trainee	Luton T	60	6
Darren Salton	6 1	12 01	16 3 72	Edinburgh	Trainee	Luton T	3	—
Kevin Shanley‡	5 11	11 11	8 9 70	Ireland	Trainee	Luton T	—	—
Midfield								
Ceri Hughes	5 9	11 06	26 2 71	Pontypridd	Trainee	Luton T	36	1
Julian James	5 10	11 11	22 3 70	Tring	Trainee	Luton T	69	4
						Preston NE (loan)	6	—
Chris Kamara	6 1	12 00	25 12 57	Middlesbrough	Apprentice	Portsmouth	63	7
						Swindon T	147	21
						Portsmouth	11	—
						Brentford	152	28
						Swindon T	87	6
						Stoke C	60	5
						Leeds U	20	1
						Luton T	28	—
Michael O'Brien*	5 10	11 04	28 11 70	Dublin	Trainee	Luton T	—	—
Scott Oakes	5 10	9 12	5 8 72	Leicester	Trainee	Leicester C	3	—
						Luton T	21	2
David Preece	5 5	10 00	28 5 63	Bridgnorth	Apprentice	Walsall	111	5
						Luton T	222	9
Jason Rees	5 5	9 08	22 12 69	Pontpridd	Trainee	Luton T	40	—
Paul Telfer	5 9	10 02	21 10 71	Edinburgh	Trainee	Luton T	21	1
Aaron Tighe‡	5 9	10 09	11 7 69	Banbury	Apprentice	Luton T	—	—
						Leicester C (loan)	—	—

LUTON TOWN

Foundation: Formed by an amalgamation of two leading local clubs, Wanderers and Excelsior a works team, at a meeting in Luton Town Hall in April 1885. The Wanderers had three months earlier changed their name to Luton Town Wanderers and did not take too kindly to the formation of another Town club but were talked around at this meeting. Wanderers had already appeared in the FA Cup and the new club entered in its inaugural season.

First Football League game: 4 September, 1897, Division 2, v Leicester Fosse (a) D 1-1 – Williams; McCartney, McEwen; Davies, Stewart, Docherty; Gallacher, Coupar, Birch, McInnes, Ekins (1).

Did you know: Joe Payne was not the only prolific goalscorer to move from Luton to Chelsea. Another whose career was largely swallowed up by the Second World War was local discovery Hugh Billington. He scored two goals when making his League debut in November 1938 and had registered four hat-tricks before the war interrupted the League programme. Afterwards he added another three trebles before his transfer to Chelsea in 1948.

Managers (and Secretary-managers)
Charlie Green 1901–28*, George Thomson 1925, John McCartney 1927–29, George Kay 1929–31, Harold Wightman 1931–35, Ted Liddell 1936–38, Neil McBain 1938–39, George Martin 1939–47, Dally Duncan 1947–58, Syd Owen 1959–60, Sam Bartram 1960–62, Bill Harvey 1962–64, George Martin 1965–66, Allan Brown 1966–68, Alec Stock 1968–72, Harry Haslam 1972–78, David Pleat 1978–86, John Moore 1986–87, Ray Harford 1987–89, Jim Ryan 1900–91, David Pleat June 1991–.

Player and Position	Ht	Wt	Birth Date	Birth Place	Source	Clubs	League App	Gls
Forwards								
Lars Elstrup‡	5 11	11 11	24 3 63	Roby, Denmark	OB Odense	Luton T	60	19
David Gormley‡	5 6	10 09	5 8 72	Dublin		Luton T	—	—
Philip Gray	5 10	11 07	2 10 68	Belfast	Apprentice	Tottenham H	9	—
						Barnsley (loan)	3	—
						Fulham (loan)	3	—
						Luton T	14	3
Mick Harford	6 2	12 09	12 2 59	Sunderland	Lambton St BC	Lincoln C	115	41
						Newcastle U	19	4
						Bristol C	30	11
						Birmingham C	92	25
						Luton T	139	57
						Derby Co	58	15
						Luton T	29	12
Paul Holsgrove‡	6 1	12 00	26 8 69	Wellington	Trainee	Aldershot	3	—
						Wimbledon (loan)	—	—
						WBA (loan)	—	—
						Wokingham	—	—
						Luton T	2	—
Kurt Nogan	5 10	11 01	9 9 70	Cardiff	Trainee	Luton T	33	3
Brian Stein*	5 10	11 08	19 10 57	South Africa	Edgware T	Luton T	388	128
						Caen	—	—
						Annecy	—	—
						Luton T	39	3
Martin Williams	5 09	11 12	12 7 73	Luton	Trainee	Luton T	1	—

Trainees
Brittain, Vincent J; Elliott, Andrew; Goodfellow, Scott; Hancock, Paul J; Hartson, John; Holtham, Matthew D; Murray, Paul A; Newman, Paul S; Philip, Richard W; Rogers, Lee; Ryan, Neil; Skelton, Aaron M; Sutton, Robert A.

Associated Schoolboys
Garnish, James F; Goodridge, Steven J; Hartwig, Scott; Hayter, Robert A; Issott, Gary D; Johnson, Simon K; McLaren, Paul A; Mumford, Peter M; Palmer, Stephen; Smith, Gary M; Thomas, David W; Watkins, Neil S.

Associated Schoolboys who have accepted the club's offer of a Traineeship/Contract
Campbell, Lee A; Draper, Andrew J; Jukes, Andrew; McDonagh, Patrick; Simpson, Gary J; Woolgar, Matthew.

316

MAIDSTONE UNITED 1991–92 *Back row (left to right):* Ken Steggles (Physiotherapist), Paul Rumble, Mark Smalley, Jesse Roast, Liburd Henry, Nicky Johns, Darren Oxbrow, Iain Hesford, Steve Cuggy, Bradley Sandeman, Neil Ellis, Tony Sorrell, Clive Walker (Assistant Manager). *Front row:* Darren Davis, Jason Lillis, Alan Tutton, Paul Haylock, Graham Carr (Manager), Les Thompson, Mark Gall, Robbie Painter, Lawrence Osborne.

Division 3 — **MAIDSTONE UNITED**

Ground: Watling Street, Dartford, Kent DA2 6EN. Club office: 1, Bower Terrace, Maidstone ME16 8RY. Telephone (0622) 754403. Ticket office: 0622 756700. Ground (match day only, three hours before kick-off): 0322 288371.

Ground capacity: 5250.

Record attendance: (at The Stadium, London Road, Maidstone): 10,591 v Charlton Ath., FA Cup 3rd rd replay, 15 January 1979.

Pitch measurements: 110yd × 75yd.

Manager: Clive Walker.

Coach: Dave Madden.

Directors: J. C. Thompson (Chairman), G. Pearson, D. Berry, Dr M. J. Frank (Club Doctor), R. J. Gilbert.

Secretary: M. K. Mercer.

Physio: F. D. Brooks.

Commercial Manager: M. Ling.

Year Formed: 1897.

Club Nickname: 'Stones'.

Former Leagues: East Kent, Thames & Medway Combination, Kent, Corinthian, Athenian, Isthmian, Southern, GM Vauxhall Conference

Record League Victory: 6-1 v Scunthorpe U, Division 4, 15 September 1990 – Beeney; Roast, Rumble (1), Berry, Golley, Madden (Henry), Pritchard, Osborne, Charlery (2), Butler (2), Sorrell (1).

Record Defeat: 2-6 v Fulham, Autoglass Trophy, 23 October 1991.

Most League points (3 for a win): 73, Division 4, 1989–90.

Most League Goals: 77, Division 4, 1989–90.

Highest League Scorer in Season: Steve Butler, 21, Division 4, 1989–90.

Most League Goals in Total Aggregate: Steve Butler, 41, Division 4, 1989–91.

Most Capped Player: None.

Most League Appearances: Darren Oxbrow, 85, 1989–92, Mark Gall, 85, 1989–91.

Record Transfer Fee Received: £300,000 from Wimbledon for Warren Barton, June 1990.

Record Transfer Fee Paid: £40,000 to Watford for Liburd Henry, July 1990.

Football League Record: 1989 Promoted to Division 4; 1992– Division 3.

Honours: Football League: best season: 5th, Division 4 to reach play-offs, 1989–90. *FA Cup:* Never past 3rd rd. *Football League Cup:* Never past 1st rd.

Colours: Gold shirts, black shorts, black stockings with gold trim. **Change colours:** Blue and white shirts, white shorts, blue stockings.

MAIDSTONE UNITED 1991–92 LEAGUE RECORD

Match No.	Date		Venue	Opponents	Result		H/T Score	Lg. Pos.	Goalscorers	Atten- dance
1	Aug	17	A	Chesterfield	L	0-3	0-1	—		3462
2		24	H	Halifax T	L	0-1	0-0	23		1216
3	Sep	4	H	Cardiff C	D	1-1	1-1	—	Cuggy (pen)	1019
4		7	A	Scunthorpe U	L	0-2	0-0	23		2738
5		14	H	Walsall	W	2-1	2-1	21	Donegal, Osborne	1139
6		17	H	Lincoln C	L	0-2	0-1	—		1113
7		21	A	Rotherham U	D	3-3	1-1	22	Osborne, Henry, Gall	3870
8		28	H	York C	W	1-0	1-0	20	Nethercott	1037
9	Oct	5	A	Mansfield T	L	0-2	0-1	21		3207
10		12	H	Doncaster R	D	2-2	0-1	21	Gall, Osborne	1255
11		19	H	Rochdale	D	1-1	1-0	20	Sandeman	1016
12	Nov	2	H	Hereford U	W	3-2	1-2	16	Stebbing, Richards, Hesford	846
13		5	A	Crewe Alex	D	1-1	1-1	—	Richards	2476
14		9	A	Gillingham	D	1-1	0-0	18	Osborne	6716
15		23	H	Burnley	L	0-1	0-1	21		2375
16		30	A	Carlisle U	L	0-3	0-2	21		2146
17	Dec	21	A	Halifax T	D	1-1	1-0	21	Painter	1040
18		26	H	Chesterfield	L	0-1	0-1	21		1325
19	Jan	1	A	Cardiff C	W	5-0	1-0	21	Henry (pen), Painter, Stebbing, Sandeman, Smalley	8023
20		4	H	Blackpool	D	0-0	0-0	21		1774
21		8	H	Barnet	D	1-1	1-0	—	Davis	1988
22		11	A	Wrexham	D	0-0	0-0	21		3167
23		18	H	Northampton T	D	1-1	0-0	21	Henry	1364
24	Feb	12	H	Carlisle U	W	5-1	3-0	—	Sandeman 3, Henry, Lillis	944
25		15	A	Barnet	L	2-3	0-2	20	Painter, Davis	2871
26		22	A	Wrexham	L	2-4	1-2	20	Lillis, Stebbing	1491
27		29	A	Blackpool	D	1-1	1-1	20	Lillis	4136
28	Mar	3	A	Northampton T	L	0-1	0-0	—		1677
29		7	H	Scarborough	W	2-1	0-0	20	Smalley, Painter	1019
30		11	H	Crewe Alex	W	2-0	1-0	—	Henry, Painter	1174
31		14	A	Hereford U	D	2-2	1-0	18	Haylock, Henry	1910
32		21	H	Gillingham	D	1-1	1-0	19	Henry	3264
33		28	A	Burnley	L	1-2	0-0	18	Newman	10,986
34		31	A	Walsall	D	1-1	1-1	—	Oxbrow	2045
35	Apr	4	H	Scunthorpe U	L	0-1	0-0	18		1237
36		7	A	Rochdale	W	2-1	0-1	—	Sandeman, Lillis	2248
37		11	A	Lincoln C	L	0-1	0-1	18		2241
38		18	H	Rotherham U	D	0-0	0-0	18		1744
39		20	A	York C	D	1-1	0-1	18	Sandeman	1638
40		25	H	Mansfield T	D	0-0	0-0	18		1602
41		29	A	Scarborough	L	0-2	0-0	—		939
42	May	2	A	Doncaster R	L	0-3	0-1	18		1680

Final League Position: 18

GOALSCORERS

League (45): Henry 7 (1 pen), Sandeman 7, Painter 5, Lillis 4, Osborne 4, Stebbing 3, Davis 2, Gall 2, Richards 2, Smalley 2, Cuggy 1 (1 pen), Donegal 1, Haylock 1, Hesford 1, Nethercott 1, Newman 1, Oxbrow 1.
Rumbelows Cup (0).
FA Cup (2): Henry 1, Thompson 1.

Hesford	Haylock	Rumble	Oxbrow	Davis	Osborne	Gall	Painter	Henry	Sandeman	Ellis	Lillis	Cuggy	Thompson	Donegal	Smalley	Nethercott	Stebbing	Richards	Owers	Tutton	Breen	Rutter	Newman	Hazel	Sinclair	Match No.
1	2	3	4	5	6	7	8	9	10*	11†	12	14														1
1	2	11	4	5	6	7†	8		10*		12	14	3	9												2
1	14		4	5†	6	12	8	11	10*		7		3	9		2										3
1	2†	11*			6		8	7	10		12	14	3	9*	6	5										4
1	4			14		2	10	12	8†		7		3	9*	6	5	11									5
1	4†					2	10*	12	8		7	14	3	9	6	5	11									6
1	12	2			6		10	8	9		7		3*		4	5	11									7
1		2			6		10	8	9*		7	12	3		4	5	11									8
1		2			6*		10	8†	9	7	12	14	3		4	5	11									9
1				5	4*	10	7	9	12	2	11		3		6		8									10
1	4		5			10	7	11			2		3		6		8	9								11
1	4		5			10	12	11			2		3		6		8	9	7*							12
1	4		5			10	7	11			2		3		6		8	9								13
1	4		5			10	7	11			2		3		6		8	9								14
1	4		5			10	7	11			2	9*12	3		6		8									15
1	4		5			10†	7*	11			2	12	3	9	14	6	8									16
1	2		5		6		7	11	9	10			3		4		8									17
1	2		5		6		7	11*	9	10			3	12	4		8									18
1	2		5		6		7	11	9	10			3		4		8									19
1	2		5		6		7*	11	9	10			3		4		8			12						20
1	2†		5		6		7	11*	9	10	14		3	12	4		8									21
1	2		6				7	11	9	10			3	12	4		8				5*					22
1	2		6				7	11	9	10			3		4		8				5					23
1	2		6					11	9	10	7		3		4		8				5					24
1	2		6				12	11	9	10*	7		3		4		8				5					25
1	2		6*				12	11	9	10†	7		3	14	4		8				5					26
1	2		6					11	9	10	7*		3	14†	4		8			12	5					27
1	2		6				7	11*	9	12			3		4		8				5		10			28
1	2		6					11	9	10	7		3		4		8				5					29
1	2		6					11*	9†	10	7		3	12	4		8				5		14			30
1	2		6					11*		10	7		3	12	4		8				5		9			31
1	2		6					11	9	10	7		3		4		8				5					32
1	2		6					11	9	10	7		12		4		8				5		3*			33
1	2		6					11*	9	10	7		12		4		8				5		3			34
1			6					12	9	10	7		3	14	4		8				5		2†	11*		35
1	2		6					11	9	10	7		3		4		8				5					36
1	2*		6						9	10	7		3		4		8†			14	5		11	12		37
1			6*						9	10	7		3	2	4		8				5		11	12		38
1									9	10	7		3	6*	4		8	12			5		11	2		39
1								11	9	10	7		3		4		8				5		6	2		40
1	5		6†						9	10	7*		3	12	4		8			14			11	2		41
1	8							11	9	10	7		3	6*	4						5			2		42
42	31 +1s	3 +2s	31	20	16	7	27 +3s	36 +3s	35 +1s	22 +2s	21 +6s	1 +2s	38 +12s	9	33 +5s	13 +1s	37	4	1	— +4s	19	—	9 +1s	6 +1s	1 +2s	

Rumbelows Cup   First Round   Leicester C (a)   0-3
                                                   (h)   0-1
FA Cup   First Round   Sutton (h)   1-0
               Second Round Kettering (h)   1-2

MAIDSTONE UNITED

Player and Position	Ht	Wt	Date	Birth Place	Source	Clubs	League App	Gls
Goalkeepers								
Iain Hesford	6 2	13 12	4 3 60	Zambia	Apprentice	Blackpool	202	—
						Sheffield W	—	—
						Fulham (loan)	3	—
						Notts Co (loan)	10	—
						Sunderland	97	—
						Hull C	91	—
						Maidstone U	42	1
Nicky Johns*	6 2	11 05	8 6 57	Bristol	Minehead	Millwall	50	—
						Tampa Bay R	—	—
						Sheffield U (loan)	1	—
						Charlton Ath	288	—
						QPR	10	—
						Maidstone U	42	—
Defenders								
Gary Breen	6 01	12 07	12 12 73	London		Maidstone U	19	—
Darren Davis	6 0	11 00	5 2 67	Sutton Ashfield	Apprentice	Notts Co	92	1
						Lincoln C	102	4
						Maidstone U	31	2
Paul Haylock	5 8	11 00	24 3 63	Lowestoft	Apprentice	Norwich C	155	3
						Gillingham	152	—
						Maidstone U	48	1
Darren Oxbrow	6 1	12 06	1 9 69	Ipswich	Trainee	Ipswich T	—	—
						Maidstone U	85	2
Jesse Roast*	6 1	12 07	16 3 64	Barking	Barking	Maidstone U	32	—
Paul Rumble‡	5 11	11 05	14 3 69	Hemel Hempstead	Trainee	Watford	—	—
						Scunthorpe U (loan)	8	1
						Maidstone U	55	3
Mark Smalley	5 11	11 06	2 1 65	Newark	Apprentice	Nottingham F	3	—
						Birmingham C (loan)	7	—
						Bristol R (loan)	10	—
						Leyton Orient	64	4
						Mansfield T	49	2
						Maidstone U	34	2
Gary Stebbing	5 9	11 00	11 8 65	Croydon	Apprentice	Crystal Palace	102	3
						Southend U (loan)	5	—
						KV Ostend	—	—
						Maidstone U	76	4
Midfield								
Mark Golley‡	6 1	13 00	28 10 62	Beckenham	Sutton U	Maidstone U	81	3
Ian Hazel†	5 10	10 04	1 12 67	London	Apprentice	Wimbledon	7	—
						Bristol R (loan)	3	—
						Bristol R	14	—
						Maidstone U	8	—
David Madden*	6 0	11 03	6 1 63	London	Apprentice	Southampton	—	—
						Bournemouth (loan)	5	—
						Arsenal	2	—
						Charlton Ath	20	1
						Reading	9	1
						Crystal Palace	27	5
						Birmingham C (loan)	5	1
						Maidstone U	10	—
Adrian Owers*	5 8	10 02	26 2 65	Danbury	Apprentice	Southend U	27	—
						Chelmsford C		—
						Brighton & HA	40	4
						Gillingham (loan)	10	—
						Maidstone U	1	—
Bradley Sandeman	5 10	10 08	24 2 70	Northampton	Trainee	Northampton T	58	3
						Maidstone U	57	8

MAIDSTONE UNITED

Foundation: Formed by a group of local businessmen in 1897, the club played in the East Kent League, Thames and Medway Combination and back to the Kent League up to 1939. At the end of the war, the club reformed in 1946 playing as amateurs in the Corinthian, Athenian and Isthmian Leagues. Re-adopted professionalism when joining the Southern League in 1971.

First Football League game: 19 August, 1989, Division 4, v Peterborough U (a) L 0-1 – Beeney; Barton (Stebbing), Cooper, Berry, Golley, Pearce, Lillis (Charlery), Elsey, Sorrell, Butler, Gall.

Did you know: One of United's finest games was when they were still in the Southern League and held Second Division Charlton Athletic to a 1-1 draw in the FA Cup third round on 9 January 1979. They lost the replay 3-1.

Managers (and Secretary-managers)
Keith Spurgeon 1971, Bobby Houghton 1971–72, Ernie Morgan 1972–73, Robin Stepney 1973–75, Terry Adlington 1975–77, Barry Watling 1977–81, Bill Williams 1980–85, Barry Fry 1985–86, Bill Williams 1981–84, Barry Fry 1985–86, Bill Williams 1986–87, John Still 1987–89, Keith Peacock 1989–91, Graham Carr 1991, Clive Walker January 1992–.

Player and Position	Ht	Wt	Birth Date	Birth Place	Source	Clubs	League App	Gls
Tony Sorrell	5 10	12 04	17 10 66	Bromchurch	Bishops Stortford	Maidstone U	55	8
Alan Tutton*			23 2 73	Bexley		Maidstone U	4	—
Forwards								
Steve Cuggy	5 11	11 10	18 3 71	Wallsend	Blyth Spartans	Maidstone U	13	1
Glen Donegal	6 2	12 08	20 6 69	Northampton	Trainee	Northampton T	20	3
						Aylesbury	—	—
						Maidstone U	28	2
Neil Ellis	6 0	12 00	30 4 69	Bebington	Bangor C	Chester C	21	1
						Maidstone U	28	—
Liburd Henry	5 11	11 00	29 8 67	Dominica	Ley'st/Ilford	Watford	10	1
						Halifax T (loan)	5	—
						Maidstone U	67	9
Jason Lillis	5 11	11 10	1 10 69	Chatham	Trainee	Gillingham	29	3
						Maidstone U	75	18
						Carlisle U (loan)	4	1
Steve Rutter†			24 7 68	Kent	Trainee	Maidstone U	1	—
Robert Sinclair§			9 4 74	Greenwich	Trainee	Maidstone U	1	—
Les Thompson	5 10	11 00	23 9 68	Cleethorpes		Hull C	35	4
						Scarborough (loan)	3	1
						Maidstone U	38	—

Trainees
Adlington, Thomas; Chaplin, Matthew J; Davies, Andrew I; Heath, Dean M; Johnston, Daniel E; Mas, Bartolme W. P; Mearns, John F; Older, Christian M; Porter, Graham A; Sinclair, Robert A; Wilson-Head, Robert S.

**Non-Contract
Donker, Richmond; Hazel, Ian; Whitfield, John S.

Associated Schoolboys
Britt, James J; Carr, Russell E; Everitt, James; Planck, Thomas E; Stillman, James J.

**Non-Contract Players who are retained must be re-signed before they are eligible to play in League matches.

322

MANCHESTER CITY 1991–92 *Back row (left to right):* Neil Pointon, David White, Paul Lake, Niall Quinn, Colin Hendry, Mark Brennan. *Centre row:* Roy Bailey (Medical Trainer), Tony Book (First Team Coach), Clive Allen, Andy Hill, Tony Coton, Martyn Margetson, Gary Megson, Wayne Clarke, Sam Ellis (Assistant Manager). *Front row:* Adrian Heath, Ian Brightwell, Steve Redmond, Peter Reid (Player/Manager), Keith Curle, Jason Beckford, Michael Sheron. (Picture courtesy of the Manchester Evening News)

FA Premier   **MANCHESTER CITY**

Maine Road, Moss Side, Manchester M14 7WN. Telephone 061-226 1191/2. Ticket Office: 061-226 2224. Development Office: 061-226 3143. Clubcall: 0898 121191. Ticketcall: 0898 121591.

Ground capacity: 39,359.

Record attendance: 84,569 v Stoke C, FA Cup 6th rd, 3 March 1934 (British record for any game outside London or Glasgow).

Record receipts: £469,419, Manchester U v Oldham Ath, FA Cup semi-final, 8 April 1990.

Pitch measurements: 117yd × 77yd.

Chairman: P. J. Swales. *Vice-charman:* F. Pye. *Directors:* I. L. G. Niven, C. B. Muir OBE, M. T. Horwich, W. C. Adams, A. Thomas, G. Doyle, W. A. Miles, B. Turnbull, J. Greibach. *Secretary:* Bernard Halford. *Commercial Manager:* P. Critchley. *General Manager:* Jimmy Frizzell. *Player-manager:* Peter Reid. *Assistant Manager:* Sam Ellis.

Year Formed: 1887 as Ardwick FC; 1894 as Manchester City. Turned Professional: 1887 as Ardwick FC. Ltd Co.: 1894.

Former Grounds: 1880–81, Clowes Street; 1881–82, Kirkmanshulme Cricket Ground; 1882–84, Queens Road; 1884–87, Pink Bank Lane; 1887–1923, Hyde Road (1894–1923, as City); 1923, Maine Road.

Former Names: 1887–94, Ardwick FC (formed through the amalgamation of West Gorton and Gorton Athletic, the latter having been formed in 1880).

Club Nickname: 'Blues' or 'The Citizens'.

Record League Victory: 10-1 v Huddersfield T, Division 2, 7 November 1987 – Nixon; Gidman, Hinchcliffe, Clements, Lake, Redmond, White (3), Stewart (3), Adcock (3), McNab (1), Simpson.

Record Cup Victory: 10-1 v Swindon T, FA Cup, 4th rd, 29 January 1930 – Barber; Felton, McCloy; Barrass, Cowan, Heinemann; Toseland, Marshall (5), Tait (3), Johnson (1), Brook (1).

Record Defeat: 1-9 v Everton, Division 1, 3 September 1906.

Most League Points (2 for a win): 62, Division 2, 1946–47.

Most League points (3 for a win): 82, Division 2, 1988–89.

Most League Goals: 108, Division 2, 1926–27.

Highest League Scorer in Season: Tommy Johnson, 38, Division 1, 1928–29.

Most League Goals in Total Aggregate: Tommy Johnson, 158, 1919–30.

Most Capped Player: Colin Bell, 48, England.

Most League Appearances: Alan Oakes, 565, 1959–76.

Record Transfer Fee Received: £1,700,000 from Tottenham H for Paul Stewart, June 1988.

Record Transfer Fee Paid: £2,500,000 to Wimbledon for Keith Curle, August 1991.

Football League Record: 1892 Ardwick elected founder member of Division 2; 1894 Newly-formed Manchester C elected to Division 2; Division 1 1899–1902, 1903–09, 1910–26, 1928–38, 1947–50, 1951–63, 1966–83, 1985–87, 1989–92; Division 2 1902–03, 1909–10, 1926–28, 1938–47, 1950–51, 1963–66, 1983–85, 1987–89; 1992– FA Premier League.

Honours: Football League: Division 1 – Champions 1936–37, 1967–68; Runners-up 1903–04, 1920–21, 1976–77; Division 2 – Champions 1898–99, 1902–03, 1909–10, 1927–28, 1946–47, 1965–66; Runners-up 1895–96, 1950–51, 1987–88. *FA Cup:* Winners 1904, 1934, 1956, 1969; Runners-up 1926, 1933, 1955, 1981. *Football League Cup:* Winners 1970, 1976; Runners-up 1973–74. **European Competitions:** *European Cup:* 1968–69. *European Cup-Winners' Cup:* 1969–70 (winners), 1970–71. *UEFA Cup:* 1972–73, 1976–77, 1977–78, 1978–79.

Colours: Sky blue shirts, dark blue collar, white shorts, navy blue stockings. **Change colours:** Purple shirt with candy-stripe, purple shorts, purple stockings with white top.

MANCHESTER CITY 1991–92 LEAGUE RECORD

Match No.	Date		Venue	Opponents	Result		H/T Score	Lg. Pos.	Goalscorers	Attendance
1	Aug	17	A	Coventry C	W	1-0	1-0	—	Quinn	18,013
2		21	H	Liverpool	W	2-1	1-0	—	White 2	37,322
3		24	H	Crystal Palace	W	3-2	2-1	1	Brennan 2 (2 pen), White	28,023
4		28	A	Norwich C	D	0-0	0-0	—		15,376
5		31	A	Arsenal	L	1-2	1-0	3	Brightwell I	35,009
6	Sep	4	H	Nottingham F	W	2-1	1-0	—	Quinn, Hill	29,146
7		7	A	Leeds U	L	0-3	0-2	3		29,986
8		14	H	Sheffield W	L	0-1	0-0	7		29,453
9		17	H	Everton	L	0-1	0-0	—		27,509
10		21	A	West Ham U	W	2-1	0-0	6	Redmond (pen), Hendry	25,588
11		28	H	Oldham Ath	L	1-2	1-0	8	White	31,271
12	Oct	6	A	Notts Co	W	3-1	0-0	—	Sheron, Allen C 2 (1 pen)	11,878
13		19	A	Tottenham H	W	1-0	0-0	3	Quinn	30,502
14		26	H	Sheffield U	W	3-2	2-2	3	Sheron, Quinn, Hughes	25,495
15	Nov	2	A	Southampton	W	3-0	1-0	3	Quinn, Sheron, Gittens (og)	13,933
16		16	H	Manchester U	D	0-0	0-0	3		38,180
17		23	A	Luton T	D	2-2	0-1	3	Curle, Quinn	10,031
18		30	H	Wimbledon	D	0-0	0-0	3		22,429
19	Dec	7	A	Aston Villa	L	1-3	0-2	4	White	26,265
20		14	H	QPR	D	2-2	2-0	4	White, Curle	21,437
21		20	A	Liverpool	D	2-2	0-1	5	White 2	36,743
22		26	H	Norwich C	W	2-1	2-1	4	Quinn, White	28,164
23		28	H	Arsenal	W	1-0	0-0	4	White	32,325
24	Jan	1	A	Chelsea	D	1-1	0-0	4	Sheron	18,196
25		11	A	Crystal Palace	D	1-1	0-1	4	Curle (pen)	14,766
26		18	H	Coventry C	W	1-0	0-0	4	White	23,005
27	Feb	1	H	Tottenham H	W	1-0	1-0	4	White	30,123
28		8	A	Sheffield U	L	2-4	1-3	5	Curle (pen), Hill	26,562
29		15	H	Luton T	W	4-0	1-0	3	White 2, Hill, Heath	22,137
30		22	A	Wimbledon	L	1-2	0-2	3	Sheron	5802
31		29	H	Aston Villa	W	2-0	1-0	3	Quinn, White	28,268
32	Mar	7	A	QPR	L	0-4	0-2	4		10,779
33		15	H	Southampton	L	0-1	0-1	—		24,265
34		21	A	Nottingham F	L	0-2	0-0	5		24,115
35		28	H	Chelsea	D	0-0	0-0	6		23,633
36	Apr	4	H	Leeds U	W	4-0	2-0	6	Hill, Sheron, Quinn, Brennan	30,239
37		7	A	Manchester U	D	1-1	0-1	—	Curle (pen)	46,781
38		11	A	Sheffield W	L	0-2	0-0	6		32,138
39		18	H	West Ham U	W	2-0	1-0	5	Pointon, Clarke W	25,601
40		20	A	Everton	W	2-1	2-1	5	Quinn 2	21,101
41		25	H	Notts Co	W	2-0	1-0	5	Simpson, Quinn	23,426
42	May	2	A	Oldham Ath	W	5-2	2-1	5	Mike, White 3, Sheron	18,588

Final League Position: 5

GOALSCORERS

League (61): White 18, Quinn 12, Sheron 7, Curle 5 (3 pens), Hill 4, Brennan 3 (2 pens), Allen C 2 (1 pen), Brightwell I 1, Clarke W 1, Heath 1, Hendry 1, Hughes 1, Mike 1, Pointon 1, Redmond 1 (1 pen), Simpson 1, own goals 1.
Rumbelows Cup (10): White 3, Heath 2, Quinn 2, Allen 1, Brennan 1, Sheron 1.
FA Cup (1): Reid 1.

Margetson	Hill	Pointon	Reid	Curle	Redmond	White	Brightwell I	Quinn	Megson	Brennan	Heath	Coton	Hendry	Hughes	Sheron	Dibble	Allen C	Hoekman	Quigley	McMahon	Brightwell D	Simpson	Clarke W	Vonk	Mike	Match No.
1	2	3	4*	5	6	7	8	9	10	11	12															1
	2	3	4*	5	6	7	8	9	10	11	12	1														2
	2	3	4	5	6†	7	8	9	10*	11	12	1	14													3
	2	3	4	5	6	7	8		10	11	9	1														4
	2	3	4*	5	6	7	8	9	10	11†	12	1	14													5
	2	3	4	5	6	7	8	9	10	11		1														6
	2	3	4	5	6	7	8	9	10	11*	12	1														7
	2	3	4	5	6	7	8	9	10	11*	12	1														8
	2†	3	4*	5	6	7		9	10		8	1	14	11	12											9
	2	3		5	6	7	4	9	10		8	1	12	11*												10
	2†	3		5*	6	7	4	9	10		8		12	11	14	1										11
		3	4		6	7		9	10	2†	8	1	11*	5	12	14										12
	2	3	4	5	6			9	10		8	1		11	7											13
	2	3	4	5	6			9	10		8	1		11	7											14
	2	3	4	5	6			9*	10		8	1	12	11	7											15
	2	3	4†	5	6	7*		9	10		8	1	14	11	12											16
1	2	3	4	5	6	7*		9	10		8			11	12											17
	2†	3	4*	5	6	7		9	10		8	1	14	11	12											18
	2	3	4	5	6	7		9	10		8	1		11*	12											19
	2	3	4	5	6	7		9	10		8	1		11												20
		3	4	5	6	7	2	9	10		8	1		11												21
		3	4	5	6	7	2	9	12		8	1		11						10*						22
	2*	3	4	5	6	7		9	10		8	1		11						12						23
		3	4†	5	6	7	2	9	10		8*	1		11	14					12						24
		3	4*	5	6	7	2	9	10		8	1		11†	14					12						25
	2	3*	4	5	6	7	8	9				1		11						10		12				26
	2	3	4*	5	6	7	8	9				1		11						10		12				27
	2	3	4	5	6†	7	8	9				1		11*	14					10		12				28
	2	3	4*	5	6	7	8	9				1		11†	14					10		12				29
	2	3	4	5	6*	7	8†	9				1		11	14					10		12				30
	2	3	4	5	6	7	8	9			12	1		11*						10						31
	2	3	4	5	6	7	8*	9				1		11	12					10						32
	2	3	4*	5	6†	7	8	9				1		11	14					10		12				33
1	2	3	4*	5†	6	7	8	9						11						10		12		14		34
	2	3	4*	5	6	7	8	9				1		11						10		12				35
	2	3	4	5	6	7	8	9*				1		11						10		12				36
	2	3	4*	5	6	7	8†	9				1		11						10		12		14		37
	2	3	4†	5	6	7	8	9				1		11						10*		12		14		38
	2*	3	4	5	6	7	8	9				1		11						10		12				39
		3	4†	5	6	7	8*	9				1		11						10		12		14		40
	2	3	4	5		7	8	9				1		11										6	10	41
	2	3	4	5		7	8	9				1		11										6	10	42
3	36	39	29	40	31	39	36	35	18	13	20	37	—	24	20	2	—	—	—	18	3	9	—	8	2	
			+2s		+4s		+4s		+8s		+6s		+9s			+3s	1s	5s		+1s	2s	5s	1s			

Rumbelows Cup	Second Round	Chester C (h)	3-1
		(a at Stockport)	3-0
	Third Round	QPR (h)	0-0
		(a)	3-1
	Fourth Round	Middlesbrough (a)	1-2
FA Cup	Third Round	Middlesbrough (a)	1-2

MANCHESTER CITY

Goalkeepers

Name	Ht	Wt	Born	Birthplace	Source	Club	Apps	Gls
Tony Coton	6 1	11 08	19 5 61	Tamworth	Mile Oak	Birmingham C	94	—
						Hereford U (loan)	—	—
						Watford	233	—
						Manchester C	72	—
Andy Dibble	6 2	13 07	8 5 65	Cwmbran	Apprentice	Cardiff C	62	—
						Luton T	30	—
						Sunderland (loan)	12	—
						Huddersfield T (loan)	5	—
						Manchester C	74	—
						Aberdeen (loan)	5	—
						Middlesbrough (loan)	19	—
						Bolton W (loan)	13	—
						WBA (loan)	9	—
Martyn Margetson	6 0	13 10	8 9 71	West Glamorgan	Trainee	Manchester C	5	—

Defenders

Name	Ht	Wt	Born	Birthplace	Source	Club	Apps	Gls
Keith Curle	6 0	11 09	14 11 63	Bristol	Bristol	Bristol R	32	4
						Torquay U	16	5
						Bristol C	121	1
						Reading	40	—
						Wimbledon	93	3
						Manchester C	40	5
Andy Hill	5 11	12 00	20 1 65	Maltby	Apprentice	Manchester U	—	—
						Bury	264	10
						Manchester C	44	5
Nicky Limber	5 09	11 01	23 1 74	Doncaster	Trainee	Doncaster R	13	1
						Manchester C	—	—
Mark Peters*	5 11	10 10	6 7 72	St Asaph	Trainee	Manchester C	—	—
Neil Pointon	5 10	11 00	28 11 64	Warsop Vale	Apprentice	Scunthorpe U	159	2
						Everton	102	5
						Manchester C	74	2
Steve Redmond	5 11	12 13	2 11 67	Liverpool	Apprentice	Manchester C	235	7
Michael Vonk	6 03	13 03	28 10 68	Alkmaar	SVV Dordrecht	Manchester C	9	—

Midfield

Name	Ht	Wt	Born	Birthplace	Source	Club	Apps	Gls
Mark Brennan	5 10	10 13	4 10 65	Rossendale	Apprentice	Ipswich T	168	19
						Middlesbrough	65	6
						Manchester C	29	6
David Brightwell	6 1	13 05	7 1 71	Lutterworth		Manchester C	4	—
						Chester C (loan)	6	—
Ian Brightwell	5 10	11 07	9 4 68	Lutterworth	Trainee	Manchester C	176	15
Gary Flitcroft	5 11	11 08	6 11 72	Bolton	Trainee	Manchester C	—	—
						Bury (loan)	12	—
Sean Harkin			3 12 73	Birmingham	Trainee	Manchester C	—	—
Michael Hughes	5 6	10 08	2 8 71	Larne	Carrick R	Manchester C	26	1
David Kerr	5 11	11 00	6 9 74	Dumfries	Trainee	Manchester C	—	—
Paul Lake	6 0	12 02	28 10 68	Manchester	Trainee	Manchester C	108	7
Steve Lomas			18 1 74	Hanover	Trainee	Manchester C	—	—
Steve McMahon	5 9	11 08	20 8 61	Liverpool	Apprentice	Everton	100	11
						Aston Villa	75	7
						Liverpool	203	29
						Manchester C	18	—
Gary Megson	5 10	11 06	2 5 59	Manchester	Apprentice	Plymouth Arg	78	10
						Everton	22	2
						Sheffield W	123	13
						Nottingham F	—	—
						Newcastle U	24	1
						Sheffield W	110	12
						Manchester C	82	2
Phil Owen			11 1 75	Bangor	Trainee	Manchester C	—	—
Mike Quigley	5 6	9 04	2 10 70	Manchester	Trainee	Manchester C	5	—

MANCHESTER CITY

Foundation: Manchester City was formed as a Limited Company in 1894 after their predecessors Ardwick had been forced into bankruptcy. However, many historians like to trace the club's lineage as far back as 1880 when St. Mark's Church, West Gorton added a football section to their cricket club. They amalgamated with Gorton Athletic in 1884 as Gorton FC. Because of a change of ground they became Ardwick in 1887.

First Football League game: 3 September, 1892, Division 2, v Bootle (h) W 7-0 – Douglas; McVickers, Robson; Middleton, Russell, Hopkins; Davies (3), Morris (2), Angus (1), Weir (1), Milarvie.

Did you know: One of City's most prolific scorers was Jim Currier who may be unknown to many of the club's fans because he was only "guesting" from Bolton Wanderers during World War Two. However, in 1940–41 he scored 47 League and Cup goals including five in successive games against Rochdale beaten 9-1 and 6-1.

Managers (and Secretary-managers)
Joshua Parlby 1893–95*, Sam Omerod 1895–1902, Tom Maley 1902–06, Harry Newbould 1906–12, Ernest Magnall 1912–24, David Ashworth 1924–25, Peter Hodge 1926–32, Wilf Wild 1932–46 (continued as secretary to 1950), Sam Cowan 1946–47, John "Jock" Thomson 1947–50, Leslie McDowall 1950–63, George Poyser 1963–65, Joe Mercer 1965–71 (continued as GM to 1972), Malcolm Allison 1972–73, Johnny Hart 1973, Ron Saunders 1973–74, Tony Book 1974–79, Malcolm Allison 1979–80, John Bond 1980–83, John Benson 1983, Billy McNeill 1983–86, Jimmy Frizzell 1986–87 (continued as GM), Mel Machin 1987–89, Howard Kendall 1990, Peter Reid November 1990–.

Peter Reid	5 8	10 07	20 6 56	Huyton	Apprentice	Bolton W	225	23
						Everton	159	8
						QPR	29	1
						Manchester C	79	1
Fitzroy Simpson	5 8	10 07	26 2 70	Trowbridge	Trainee	Swindon T	105	9
						Manchester C	11	1
Garry Sliney	5 10	12 03	2 9 73	Dublin		Manchester C	—	—
Michael Wallace	5 8	10 02	5 10 70	Farnworth	Trainee	Manchester C	—	—
Forwards								
Wayne Clarke*	6 0	11 08	28 2 61	Wolverhampton	Apprentice	Wolverhampton W	148	30
						Birmingham C	92	38
						Everton	57	18
						Leicester C	11	1
						Manchester C	21	2
						Shrewsbury T (loan)	7	6
						Stoke C (loan)	9	3
						Wolverhampton W (loan)	1	—
Adie Mike§			16 11 73	Manchester	Trainee	Manchester C	2	1
Niall Quinn	6 4	12 04	6 10 66	Dublin	Eire Youth	Arsenal	67	14
						Manchester C	82	36
Mike Sheron	5 9	11 03	11 1 72	Liverpool	Trainee	Manchester C	29	7
						Bury (loan)	5	1
Scott Thomas	5 09	10 08	30 10 74	Bury	Trainee	Manchester C	—	—
David White	6 1	12 09	30 10 67	Manchester		Manchester C	227	62

Trainees
Beirne, Michael A; Bibby, Richard C; Edghill, Richard A; Foster, John C; Foster, Matthew R; Ingram, Rae; Lewis, Ian R; Lydiate, Joseph L; McDowell, Stephen A; McHugh, Darren R; McLean, Joseph; Mike, Adrian R; Riches, Nevin; Sharpe, John J.

**Non-Contract
Bell, Stephen J; Whitley, James.

Associated Schoolboys
Brennan, Steven J; Brown, Michael R; Creighton, Mark G; Crooks, Lee R; Davis, Leon; Evans, Gareth J; Gibbons, Gavin; Greenacre, Christopher M; Hawtin, Mark A; Kielty, Gerrard T; McDonnell, John M; Morgan, Matthew A; Morley, David T; Rothwell, Neil A; Samuel, Gavin; Sandbach, Steven B; Seymour, Andrew; Smith, Ian R; Tucker, Adrian J; Williams, Scott M.

Associated Schoolboys who have accepted the club's offer of a Traineeship/Contract
Beech, Christopher; Harkin, Joseph; Roe, David; Turner, David E; Walker, David A.

**Non-Contract Players who are retained must be re-signed before they are eligible to play in League matches.

328

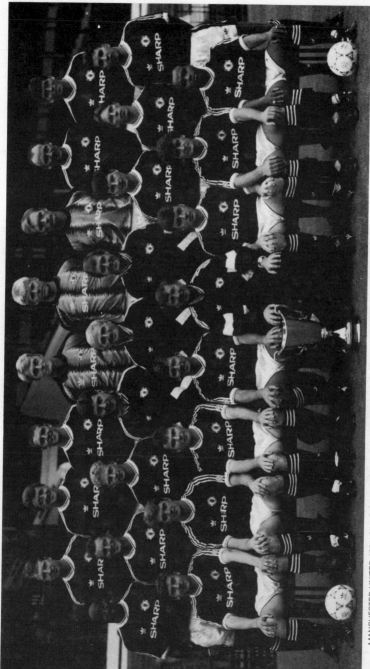

MANCHESTER UNITED 1991–92 *Back row (left to right):* Lee Martin, Steve Bruce, Lee Sharpe, Gary Walsh, Peter Schmeichel, Jim Leighton, Mike Phelan, Neil Webb.
Centre row: Paul Ince, Clayton Blackmore, Mark Robins, Brian Kidd (Assistant Manager), Jim McGregor (Physiotherapist), Norman Davies (Kit Manager), Denis Irwin, Russell Beardsmore, Darren Ferguson.
Front row: Andrei Kanchelskis, Gary Pallister, Brian McClair, Bryan Robson, Alex Ferguson (Manager), Mal Donaghy, Mark Hughes, Danny Wallace.

FA Premier   **MANCHESTER UNITED**

Old Trafford, Manchester M16 0RA. Telephone 061-872 1661.
Ticket and Match Information: 061-872 0199. Membership
enquiries: 061-872 5208. Souvenir shop: 061-872 3398.
Ground capacity: 34,031.
Record attendance: 76,962 Wolverhampton W v Grimsby T,
FA Cup semi-final. 25 March 1939. Club record: 70,504 v
Aston Villa, Division 1, 27 December 1920.
Record receipts: £432,345.80 v Legia Warsaw, European Cup-
Winners Cup semi-final 2nd leg, 24 April 1991.
Pitch measurements: 116yd × 76yd.
President: Sir Matt Busby CBE, KCSG.
Vice-presidents: J. A. Gibson, W. A. Young, J. G. Gulliver, R. L. Edwards.
Chairman/Chief Executive: C. M. Edwards.
Directors: J. M. Edelson, R. Charlton CBE, E. M. Watkins LL.M, A. M. Midani, N.
Burrows, R. L. Olive, M. Knighton.
Manager: Alex Feguson. *Assistant manager:* Brian Kidd.
Coaches: Jim Ryan, Bryan 'Pop' Robson.
Secretary: Kenneth Merrett. *Commercial Manager:* D. A. McGregor. *Physio:* Jim McGre-
gor.
Year Formed: 1878 as Newton Heath LYR; 1902, Manchester United. Turned Professional:
1885. Ltd Co.: 1907.
Former Grounds: 1880–93, North Road, Monsall Road; 1893, Bank Street; 1910, Old
Trafford (played at Maine Road 1941–49).
Former Names: Newton Heath, 1880–1902. *Club Nickname:* 'Red Devils'.
Record League Victory: 10-1 v Wolverhampton W, Division 2, 15 October 1892 – Warner;
Mitchell, Clements; Perrins, Stewart (3), Erentz; Farman (1), Hood (1), Donaldson (3),
Carson (1), Hendry (1).
Record Cup Victory: 10-0 v RSC Anderlecht, European Cup, Prel. rd (2nd leg), 26
September 1956 – Wood; Foulkes, Byrne; Colman, Jones, Edwards; Berry (1), Whelan
(2), Taylor (3), Viollet (4), Pegg.
Record Defeat: 0-7 v Blackburn R, Division 1, 10 April 1926 and v Aston Villa, Division
1, 27 December 1930 and v Wolverhampton W. Division 2, 26 December 1931.
Most League Points (2 for a win): 64, Division 1, 1956–57.
Most League points (3 for a win): 81, Division 1, 1987–88.
Most League Goals: 103, Division 1, 1956–57 and 1958–59.
Highest League Scorer in Season: Dennis Viollet, 32, 1959–60.
Most League Goals in Total Aggregate: Bobby Charlton, 199, 1956–73.
Most Capped Player: Bobby Charlton, 106, England.
Most League Appearances: Bobby Charlton, 606, 1956–73.
Record Transfer Fee Received: £1,800,000 from Barcelona for Mark Hughes, August 1986.
Record Transfer Fee Paid: £2,300,000 to Middlesbrough for Gary Pallister, August 1989.
Football League Record: 1892 Newton Heath elected to Division 1; 1894–1906 Division 2;
1906–22 Division 1; 1922–25 Division 2; 1925–31 Division 1; 1931–36 Division 2; 1936–37
Division 1; 1937–38 Division 2; 1938–74 Division 1; 1974–75 Division 2; 1975–92 Division
1; 1992– FA Premier League.
Honours: Football League: Division 1 – Champions 1907–8, 1910–11, 1951–52, 1955–56,
1956–57, 1964–65, 1966–67; runners-up 1946–47, 1947–48, 1948–49, 1950–51, 1958–59,
1963–64, 1967–68, 1979–80, 1987–88, 1991–92. *Division 2* – Champions 1935–36, 1974–75;
runners-up 1896–97, 1905–06, 1924–25, 1937–38. *FA Cup:* Winners 1909, 1948, 1963, 1977,
1983, 1985, 1990; Runners-up 1957, 1958, 1976, 1979. *Football League Cup:* Winners 1991–
92, 1982–83 (Runners-up), 1990–91 (Runners-up). **European Competitions:** *European Cup:*
1956–57 (s-f), 1957–58 (s-f), 1965–66 (s-f), 1967–68 (winners), 1968–69 (s-f). *European
Cup-Winners' Cup:* 1963–64, 1977–78, 1983–84, 1990–91 (winners), 1991–92. *European
Fairs Cup:* 1964–65. *UEFA Cup:* 1976–77, 1980–81, 1982–83, 1984–85.
Colours: Red shirts, white shorts, black stockings. **Change colours:** Royal blue shirts, royal
blue shorts, royal blue stockings.

MANCHESTER UNITED 1991–92 LEAGUE RECORD

Match No.	Date		Venue	Opponents	Result		H/T Score	Lg. Pos.	Goalscorers	Atten- dance
1	Aug	17	H	Notts Co	W	2-0	1-0	—	Hughes, Robson	46,278
2		21	A	Aston Villa	W	1-0	1-0	—	Bruce (pen)	39,995
3		24	A	Everton	D	0-0	0-0	2		36,085
4		28	H	Oldham Ath	W	1-0	0-0	—	McClair	42,078
5		31	A	Leeds U	D	1-1	0-1	1	Robson	43,778
6	Sep	3	A	Wimbledon	W	2-1	2-0	—	Blackmore, Pallister	13,824
7		7	H	Norwich C	W	3-0	3-0	1	Irwin, McClair, Giggs	44,946
8		14	A	Southampton	W	1-0	0-0	1	Hughes	19,264
9		21	H	Luton T	W	5-0	1-0	1	Ince, Bruce (pen), McClair 2, Hughes	46,491
10		28	A	Tottenham H	W	2-1	1-1	1	Hughes, Robson	35,087
11	Oct	6	H	Liverpool	D	0-0	0-0	—		44,997
12		19	H	Arsenal	D	1-1	1-1	1	Bruce	46,594
13		26	A	Sheffield W	L	2-3	2-1	2	McClair 2	38,260
14	Nov	2	H	Sheffield U	W	2-0	1-0	1	Beesley (og), Kanchelskis	42,942
15		16	A	Manchester C	D	0-0	0-0	2		38,180
16		23	H	West Ham U	W	2-1	2-0	1	Giggs, Robson	47,185
17		30	A	Crystal Palace	W	3-1	1-1	2	Webb, McClair, Kanchelskis	29,017
18	Dec	7	H	Coventry C	W	4-0	3-0	2	Bruce, Webb, McClair, Hughes	42,549
19		15	A	Chelsea	W	3-1	1-0	—	Irwin, McClair, Bruce (pen)	23,120
20		26	A	Oldham Ath	W	6-3	2-0	1	Irwin 2, Kanchelskis, McClair 2, Giggs	18,947
21		29	A	Leeds U	D	1-1	0-0	—	Webb	32,638
22	Jan	1	H	QPR	L	1-4	0-2	2	McClair	38,554
23		11	H	Everton	W	1-0	0-0	1	Kanchelskis	46,619
24		18	A	Notts Co	D	1-1	0-1	2	Blackmore (pen)	21,055
25		22	H	Aston Villa	W	1-0	0-0	—	Hughes	45,022
26	Feb	1	A	Arsenal	D	1-1	1-1	2	McClair	41,703
27		8	H	Sheffield W	D	1-1	1-1	1	McClair	47,074
28		22	H	Crystal Palace	W	2-0	1-0	1	Hughes 2	46,347
29		26	H	Chelsea	D	1-1	0-0	—	Hughes	44,872
30		29	A	Coventry C	D	0-0	0-0	1		23,967
31	Mar	14	A	Sheffield U	W	2-1	0-1	2	McClair, Blackmore	30,183
32		18	A	Nottingham F	L	0-1	0-0	—		28,062
33		21	H	Wimbledon	D	0-0	0-0	2		45,428
34		28	A	QPR	D	0-0	0-0	2		22,603
35		31	A	Norwich C	W	3-1	1-0	—	Ince 2, McClair	17,489
36	Apr	7	H	Manchester C	D	1-1	1-0	—	Giggs	46,781
37		16	H	Southampton	W	1-0	0-0	—	Kanchelskis	43,972
38		18	A	Luton T	D	1-1	1-0	1	Sharpe	13,410
39		20	H	Nottingham F	L	1-2	1-1	2	McClair	47,576
40		22	A	West Ham U	L	0-1	0-0	—		24,197
41		26	A	Liverpool	L	0-2	0-1	—		38,669
42	May	2	H	Tottenham H	W	3-1	1-0	2	McClair, Hughes 2	44,595

Final League Position: 2

GOALSCORERS

League (63): McClair 18, Hughes 11, Bruce 5 (3 pens), Kanchelskis 5, Giggs 4, Irwin 4, Robson 4, Blackmore 3 (1 pen), Ince 3, Webb 3, Pallister 1, Sharpe 1, own goals 1.
Rumbelows Cup (15): McClair 4, Giggs 3, Kanchelskis 2, Robins 2, Blackmore 1, Bruce 1, Robson 1, Sharpe 1.
FA Cup (3): Hughes 1, Kanchelskis 1, McClair 1.

Schmeichel	Irwin	Blackmore	Bruce	Ferguson	Parker	Robson	Ince	McClair	Hughes	Kanchelskis	Pallister	Giggs	Donaghy	Webb	Phelan	Martin	Robins	Sharpe	Walsh	Match No.
1	2	3	4	5†	6	7	8*	9	10	11	12	14								1
1	2	3	4		6	7	8	9	10	11				5						2
1	2†	3*	4		6	7	8	9	10	14	11			5	12					3
1	3	12	4	14	2	7	8*	9	10		6	11		5†						4
1	3	11	4†		2	7	8*	9	10		6	12		5	14					5
1	12	11	4		2	7		9	10		6		3	8	5*					6
1	3	12	4		2	7		9	10	8*	6	11		5†	14					7
1	3		4			7	12	9	10	8*	6	11		5	2					8
1	3	9*	4			7	8	12	10		6	11		5	2					9
1	3	12	4			7	8	9	10	5*	6	11			2					10
1	3	5	4			7	8†	9	10	12	6	11	14		2*					11
1	3	2	4			7	8	9	10	12	6	11		5*						12
1	3	10	4*		2	7		9	8		6	11		5	12					13
1	3		4		2	12	8	9	7*	14	11†	6		5			10			14
1	3	8	4		2	7	12	9	10		6	11		5*						15
1	3	12	4		2*	7		9	10	8	6	11		5						16
1	3*	12	4		2	7		9	10	8	6	11		5						17
1	3	12	4		2*		8	9	10	7	6	11		5						18
1	3	12	4		2		8	9	10	7	6	11*		5						19
1	3*	12	4		2	7†	8	9	10	11	6		14	5						20
1	3*		4		2		8	9	10	7†	6	11	14	5	12					21
1	3		4		2		8	9	10		6	12		5	7*			11		22
1	3*		4		2		8	9	10	7	6	11	12	5						23
1	3	12	4*		2		8	9	10	7	6	11†		5	14					24
1	3		4			7	8	9	10	11	6		2	5						25
1	3		4			7	8*	9	10	11	6	12	2	5						26
1	3						8	9	10	11	6	2*	4	5†	14			12		27
1	3	14				7	8	9	10	11*	6		4	5†	2			12		28
	3	12	14			7†	8	9	10	11*	6		4	5	2				1	29
	3	12	2				8	9	10	7*	6	11	4	5					1	30
1	3	12	4*		2	7	8	9		11	6			5				10		31
1	3	2	4				8	9	10*	12	6		14	5†	7			11		32
1	3	2	4				8	9	10	7	6	11		5*				12		33
1	3		4			7		9	10	8*	6	11	2	5				12		34
1	3	12	4			7*	8	9	10		6			5	2			11		35
1	3	5*	4				8	9	10	12	6	7			2			11		36
1	3		4		2		8*	9	10	7	6	11	12	5						37
1	3	14	4		2†			9	10*	12	6	7	8	5				11		38
1	3	2	4					9	12	7	6	10	14	8*	5			11†		39
1	2	8*	4	14				9	10	12	6	7	3†	5				11		40
1	2		4			7	8	9	10	5	6*	11	3					12		41
1	3		4		2		8*	9	10	7	11	6		5				12		42
40	37	19	37	2	24	26	31	41	38	28	37	32	16	29	14	—	1	8	2	

```
  +  +      +   +   +   +   +   +   +   +   +   +   +   +
  1s 14s    2s  2s  1s  2s  1s  1s  6s  3s  6s  4s  2s  4s  1s  1s  6s
```

Rumbelows Cup	Second Round	Cambridge U (h)		3-0	
		(a)		1-1	
	Third Round	Portsmouth (h)		3-1	
	Fourth Round	Oldham Ath (h)		2-0	
	Fifth Round	Leeds U (a)		3-1	
	Semi-Final	Middlesbrough (a)		0-0	
		(h)		2-1	
	Final	Nottingham F (at Wembley)		1-0	
FA Cup	Third Round	Leeds U (a)		1-0	
	Fourth Round	Southampton (a)		0-0	
		(h)		2-2; lost 4-2 on penalties	

MANCHESTER UNITED

Player and Position	Ht	Wt	Birth Date	Birth Place	Source	Clubs	League App	Gls
Goalkeepers								
Jim Leighton (To Dundee Feb 1992)	6 1	12 08	24 7 58	Johnstone	Dalry T	Aberdeen	300	—
						Manchester U	73	—
						Arsenal (loan)	—	—
						Reading (loan)	8	—
Peter Schmeichel	6 4	14 00	18 11 63	Gladsake	Brondby	Manchester U	40	—
Gary Walsh	6 1	12 12	21 3 68	Wigan		Manchester U	37	—
						Airdrie (loan)	3	—
Ian Wilkinson	5 11		2 7 73	Warrington	Trainee	Manchester U	—	—
Defenders								
Derek Brazil	6 0	12 00	14 12 68	Dublin	Rivermount BC	Manchester U	2	—
						Oldham Ath (loan)	1	—
						Swansea C (loan)	12	1
Steve Bruce	6 0	12 06	31 12 60	Newcastle	Apprentice	Gillingham	205	29
						Norwich C	141	14
						Manchester U	161	25
Brian Carey	6 3	11 13	31 5 68	Cork	Cork C	Manchester U	—	—
						Wrexham (loan)	3	—
						Wrexham (loan)	13	1
Mal Donaghy	5 10	12 07	13 9 57	Belfast	Larne	Luton T	410	16
						Manchester U	89	—
						Luton T (loan)	5	—
Dennis Irwin	5 7	9 07	31 10 65	Cork	Apprentice	Leeds U	72	1
						Oldham Ath	167	4
						Manchester U	72	4
Sean McAuley‡	5 10	10 11	23 6 72	Sheffield	Trainee	Manchester U	—	—
Lee Martin	5 11	11 05	5 2 68	Hyde		Manchester U	72	1
Gary Pallister	6 4	13 00	30 6 65	Ramsgate	Billingham	Middlesbrough	156	5
						Darlington (loan)	7	—
						Manchester U	111	4
Neil Whitworth	6 2	12 06	12 4 72	Ince		Wigan Ath	2	—
						Manchester U	1	—
						Preston NE (loan)	6	—
						Barnsley (loan)	11	—
Midfield								
Russell Beardsmore	5 6	8 10	28 9 68	Wigan	Apprentice	Manchester U	56	4
						Blackburn R (loan)	2	—
Clayton Blackmore	5 9	11 03	23 9 64	Neath	Apprentice	Manchester U	172	19
Adrian Doherty	5 8	10 06	10 6 73	Strabane	School	Manchester U	—	—
Darren Ferguson	5 10	10 04	9 2 72	Glasgow	Trainee	Manchester U	9	—
Mark Gordon*	5 8		29 8 73	Salford	Trainee	Manchester U	—	—
Paul Ince	5 11	11 06	21 10 67	Ilford	Trainee	West Ham U	72	7
						Manchester U	90	6
Craig Lawton	5 7	10 03	5 1 72	Mancot	Trainee	Manchester U	—	—
Paul Parker	5 7	10 09	4 4 64	Essex	Apprentice	Fulham	153	2
						QPR	125	1
						Manchester U	26	—
Mike Phelan	5 11	12 03	24 9 62	Nelson	Apprentice	Burnley	168	9
						Norwich C	156	9
						Manchester U	89	2
Bryan Robson	5 11	11 12	11 1 57	Chester-Le-Street	Apprentice	WBA	197	39
						Manchester U	316	72
Lee Sharpe	5 11	11 04	27 5 71	Birmingham	Trainee	Torquay U	14	3
						Manchester U	77	4
Paul Sixsmith*	5 10	10 12	22 9 71	Bolton	Trainee	Manchester U	—	—
Peter Smyth*	5 6		25 6 73	Belfast	Trainee	Manchester U	—	—

MANCHESTER UNITED

Foundation: Manchester United was formed as comparatively recently as 1902 after their predecessors, Newton Heath, went bankrupt. However, it is usual to give the date of the club's foundation as 1878 when employees of the Lancashire and Yorkshire Railway Company formed Newton Heath L and YR. Cricket and Football Club. They won the Manchester Cup in 1886 and as Newton Heath FC were admitted to the Second Division in 1892.

First Football League game: 3 September, 1892, Division 1, v Blackburn R (a) L 3-4 – Warner; Clements, Brown; Perrins, Stewart, Erentz; Farman (1), Coupar (1), Donaldson (1), Carson, Mathieson.

Did you know: The nearest United came to equalling their record of 14 League wins in a row in 1904–05 in Division Two, was at the start of 1985–86 when they won their first ten First Division games.

Managers (and Secretary-managers)
Ernest Magnall 1900–12, John Robson 1914–21, John Chapman 1921–26, Clarence Hildrith 1926–27, Herbert Bamlett 1927–31, Walter Crickmer 1931–32, Scott Duncan 1932–37, Jimmy Porter 1938–44, Walter Crickmer 1944–45*, Matt Busby 1945–69 (continued as GM then Director), Wilf McGuinness 1969–70, Frank O'Farrell 1971–72, Tommy Docherty 1972–77, Dave Sexton 1977–81, Ron Atkinson 1981–86, Alex Ferguson November 1986–.

Player and Position	Ht	Wt	Birth Date	Birth Place	Source	Clubs	League App	Gls
Kieran Toal	5 8	11 01	14 12 71	Manchester	Trainee	Manchester U	—	—
Neil Webb	6 1	13 02	30 7 63	Reading	Apprentice	Reading	72	22
						Portsmouth	123	34
						Nottingham F	146	47
						Manchester U	74	8
Paul Wratten‡	5 7	9 13	29 11 70	Middlesbrough	Trainee	Manchester U	2	—
Forwards								
Ryan Giggs	5 11	9 09	29 11 73	Cardiff	School	Manchester U	40	5
Mark Hughes	5 8	12 05	1 11 63	Wrexham	Apprentice	Manchester U	89	37
						Barcelona	—	—
						Manchester U	145	48
Andrei Kanchelskis	5 10	12 04	23 1 69	Kirovograd	Donetsk	Manchester U	35	5
Brian McClair	5 9	12 02	8 12 63	Airdrie	Apprentice	Aston Villa	—	—
						Motherwell	39	15
						Celtic	145	99
						Manchester U	193	70
Colin McKee			22 8 73	Glasgow	Trainee	Manchester U	—	—
Giuliano Maiorana	5 9	11 08	18 4 69	Cambridge	Histon	Manchester U	7	—
Mark Robins	5 7	10 01	22 12 69	Ashton-under-Lyme	Apprentice	Manchester U	48	11
Danny Wallace	5 4	10 06	21 1 64	London	Apprentice	Southampton	255	64
						Manchester U	45	6

Trainees
Beckham, David R. J; Brown, Karl D; Burke, Raphael E; Butt, Nicholas; Casper, Christopher M; Davies, Simon I; Dean, Craig; Gillespie, Keith R; Gough, Paul; Neville, Gary A; Noone, Andrew C; O'Kane, John A; Rawlinson, Mark D; Riley, Steven; Roberts, Joseph E; Savage, Robert W; Scholes, Paul; Switzer, George; Taylor, Leonard A; Telford, Colin L; Thornley, Benjamin L.

Associated Schoolboys
Badoo, Mark O; Christopher, Anton; Duncan, Andrew; Eadie, Craig S; Eyre, Richard P; Gardner, David S; Gibson, Paul R; Hall, Stephen; Heckingbottom, Paul; Hudson, Vincent J; Lyons, Paul; Marsh, Neil D; Maxon, Heath R; McGlinchey, Brian; Murdock, Colin J; Mustoe, Neil; Neville, Philip J; O'Donnell, Gerard; Parkin, Daniel J; Smith, Thomas E; Trees, Robert V; Twiss, Michael J; Wallwork, Ronald.

Associated Schoolboys who have accepted the club's offer of a Traineeship/Contract
Appleton, Michael A; Barnes, Lee M; Cooke, Terence J; Flash, Richard G; Hart, Ian M; Irving, Richard J; Johnson, David A; McDonald, Robert F; Mitten, Paul J; Monaghan, Matthew S; Pilkington, Kevin W; Ryan, Mark; Twynham, Gary S; Westwood, Ashley M; Whittam, Philip R.

334

MANSFIELD TOWN 1991–92 *Back row (left to right):* Martin Clark, Steve Wilkinson, Jason Pearcey, Greg Fee, Andy Beasley, Phil Stant, Gary Ford. *Centre row:* Kevin Randall (Youth Team Coach), Ian Stringfellow, Kevin Gray, Steve Spooner, Paul Holland, Nicky Roddis, Gary Castledine, Dennis Pettitt (Club Physiotherapist), John Newman (Chief Scout). *Front row:* Chris Withe, Malcolm Murray, Steve Charles, George Foster (Player/Manager), Bill Dearden (Assistant Manager), Paul Fleming, Wayne Davidson, Peter Morgan.

Division 2   **MANSFIELD TOWN**

Field Mill Ground, Quarry Lane, Mansfield. Telephone Mansfield (0623) 23567. Commercial Office: 0623 658070. Fax No: 0623 25014

Ground capacity: 10,468.

Record attendance: 24,467 v Nottingham F, FA Cup 3rd rd, 10 January 1953.

Record receipts: £46,915 v Sheffield W, FA Cup 3rd rd, 5 January 1991.

Pitch measurements: 115yd × 72yd.

Chairman: J. W. Pratt.

Directors: G. Hall (Managing), J. A. Brown.

Player-manager: George Foster. *Assistant Manager/Coach:* Bill Dearden. *Physio:* Dennis Pettitt.

Community Scheme Organiser: D. Bentley Tel: 0623 25197.

Secretary: J. D. Eaton.

Commercial Manager: J. Slater.

Year Formed: 1910. Turned Professional: 1910. Ltd Co.: 1921.

Former Names: Mansfield Wesleyans 1891–1910.

Club Nickname: 'The Stags'.

Record League Victory: 9-2 v Rotherham U, Division 3 (N), 27 December 1932 – Wilson; Anthony, England; Davies, S. Robinson, Slack; Prior, Broom, Readman (3), Hoyland (3), Bowater (3).

Record Cup Victory: 8-0 v Scarborough (away), FA Cup, 1st rd, 22 November 1952 – Bramley; Chessell, Bradley; Field, Plummer, Lewis; Scott, Fox (3), Marron (2), Sid Watson (1), Adam (2).

Record Defeat: 1-8 v Walsall, Division 3 (N), 19 January 1933.

Most League Points (2 for a win): 68, Division 4, 1974–75.

Most League points (3 for a win): 81, Division 4, 1985–86.

Most League Goals: 108, Division 4, 1962–63.

Highest League Scorer in Season: Ted Harston, 55, Division 3 (N), 1936–37.

Most League Goals in Total Aggregate: Harry Johnson, 104, 1931–36.

Most Capped Player: John McClelland, 6 (53), Northern Ireland.

Most League Appearances: Rod Arnold, 440, 1970–83.

Record Transfer Fee Received: £500,000 from Middlesbrough for Simon Coleman, September 1989.

Record Transfer Fee Paid: £80,000 to Leicester C for Steve Wilkinson, September 1989.

Football League Record: 1931 Elected to Division 3 (S); 1932–37 Division 3 (N); 1937–47 Division 3 (S); 1947–58 Division 3 (N); 1958–60 Division 3; 1960–63 Division 4; 1963–72 Division 3; 1972–75 Division 4; 1975–77 Division 3; 1977–78 Division 2; 1978–80 Division 3; 1980–86 Division 4; 1986–91 Division 3; 1991–92 Division 4; 1992– Division 2.

Honours: Football League: Division 2 best season: 21st, 1977–78; Division 3 – Champions 1976–77; Division 4 – Champions 1974–75; Division 3 (N) – Runners-up 1950–51. *FA Cup:* best season: 6th rd, 1968–69. *Football League Cup:* best season: 5th rd, 1975–76. *Freight Rover Trophy:* Winners 1986–87.

Colours: Amber shirts with blue trim, blue shorts, amber stockings. **Change colours:** Green shirt, white shorts, white stockings.

MANSFIELD TOWN 1991–92 LEAGUE RECORD

Match No.	Date		Venue	Opponents	Result		H/T Score	Lg. Pos.	Goalscorers	Atten- dance
1	Aug	17	A	Scarborough	D	0-0	0-0	—		2343
2		24	H	Barnet	L	1-2	1-2	17	Charles (pen)	2668
3		31	A	Chesterfield	W	2-0	1-0	9	Ford, Holland	4740
4	Sep	3	H	Wrexham	W	3-0	0-0	—	Stringfellow, Wilkinson 2	1965
5		7	H	Blackpool	D	1-1	1-0	8	Wilkinson	2629
6		13	A	Crewe Alex	W	2-1	2-1	8	Stant, Charles (pen)	4667
7		17	A	Carlisle U	W	2-1	0-0	—	Stant, Charles	1803
8		27	A	Halifax T	W	3-1	1-0	—	Stant, Fee, Wilkinson	2026
9	Oct	5	H	Maidstone U	W	2-0	1-0	2	Wilkinson, Stant	3207
10		12	A	Rochdale	W	2-0	0-0	1	Holland, Stant	3871
11		19	A	Cardiff C	W	3-0	1-0	1	Fee, Wilkinson, Charles	3180
12		26	A	Scunthorpe U	W	4-1	1-0	1	Wilkinson 2, Charles (pen), Stant	3610
13	Nov	2	H	Doncaster R	D	2-2	0-2	1	Stant 2	4180
14		5	A	Northampton T	W	2-1	1-1	—	Angus (og), Fee	2181
15		9	A	Burnley	L	2-3	1-1	2	Wilkinson 2	11,848
16		23	H	Gillingham	W	4-3	2-2	1	Stant 2, Withe, Holland	3287
17		30	H	Walsall	W	3-1	2-0	1	Stant 2, Ford	3398
18	Dec	21	A	Barnet	L	0-2	0-1	2		4209
19		26	H	Scarborough	L	1-2	0-0	2	Clarke N	4012
20		28	H	Chesterfield	W	2-1	2-0	2	Stant, Holland	6503
21	Jan	1	A	Wrexham	L	2-3	1-2	3	Wilkinson 2	2442
22		4	A	York C	W	2-1	2-0	2	Holland, Wilkinson	2660
23		18	A	Rotherham U	D	1-1	1-0	2	McLoughlin	6454
24		31	A	Cardiff C	L	2-3	1-2	—	McLoughlin, Stant	8201
25	Feb	8	H	Scunthorpe U	L	1-3	0-2	4	Spooner	3496
26		11	A	Walsall	D	3-3	1-0	—	O'Hara (og), Fairclough, Stant	2963
27		15	H	Hereford U	D	1-1	1-1	4	Spooner	2550
28		25	H	Hereford U	W	1-0	1-0	—	McLoughlin	2122
29		29	H	York C	W	5-2	3-1	3	Tutill (og), Fee, Fairclough, Stant 2	3290
30	Mar	3	H	Rotherham U	W	1-0	0-0	—	Stant	5713
31		7	A	Lincoln C	L	0-2	0-1	3		4387
32		10	A	Northampton T	W	2-0	1-0	—	Stant, Ford	2852
33		14	A	Doncaster R	W	1-0	0-0	2	Ford	2846
34		21	H	Burnley	L	0-1	0-1	3		8336
35		24	H	Lincoln C	D	0-0	0-0	—		3064
36		28	A	Gillingham	L	0-2	0-2	3		2682
37		31	H	Crewe Alex	W	4-3	3-0	—	Wilkinson, Stant 2, Fairclough	3108
38	Apr	4	A	Blackpool	L	1-2	1-1	3	Stant	6055
39		11	H	Carlisle U	W	2-1	0-1	3	Holland, Charles (pen)	3085
40		21	H	Halifax T	W	3-2	1-0	—	Stant 3	3936
41		25	A	Maidstone U	D	0-0	0-0	3		1602
42	May	2	H	Rochdale	W	2-1	0-0	3	Stringfellow, Stant	5671

Final League Position: 3

GOALSCORERS

League (75): Stant 26, Wilkinson 14, Charles 6 (4 pens), Holland 6, Fee 4, Ford 4, Fairclough 3, McLoughlin 3, Spooner 2, Stringfellow 2, Clarke N 1, Withe 1, own goals 3.
Rumbelows Cup (2): Gray 1, Spooner 1.
FA Cup (0).

Beasley	Fleming	Withe	Spooner	Fee	Gray	Ford	Holland	Stant	Wilkinson	Charles	Foster	Stringfellow	Murray	Carr	Pearcey	Fairclough	Kite	Clarke N	Clark	McLoughlin	Castledine	Noteman	Match No.
1	2	3	4	5	6	7	8	9	10	11													1
1	2	3	4		6	7	8†	9*	10	11	5	12	14										2
1	2	3	4	5		7	8	9	10	11	6												3
1	2	3	4	5		7	8		10	11	6	9											4
1	2	3	4	5		7	8	12	10	11	6	9*											5
1	2	3	4	5		7	8	9*	10	11	6	12											6
1	2	3	4	5		7	8	9	10	11	6												7
1	2	3*	4	5	12	7	8	9	10	11	6												8
1	2		4	5		7	8	9	10	11	6			3									9
	2		4	5		7	8	9	10	11	6			3	1								10
	2		4	5		7	8	9	10	11	6			3	1								11
	2		4	5		7	8	9	10	11	6			3	1								12
	2		4	5		7	8	9	10	11*	6			3	1	12							13
	2		4	5		7	8	9	10	11	6			3	1								14
	2		4	5		7	8	9	10	11	6			3	1								15
	2	3	4	5		7	8	9	10	11	6						1						16
	2	3	4		5	7	8*	9	10	11	6					12	1						17
	2		4			7*	8	9	10	11	6			3		12	1	5					18
	2*						8	9	10	11	6	7		3		4	1	5	12				19
			4	5		7	8	9	10	11	6			3		2	1						20
			4	5	14	7	8	9*	10	11†	6	12		3		2	1						21
	2		4		5	7	8	9	10	11*	6			3		12	1						22
	2		4		5	7	8	9		11*	6			3		12	1			10			23
	2		4		5	7	8	9		11*	3			6		12	1			10			24
	2†		4		5	7		9		11	6	12		3*		8	1		14	10			25
	2		4	5		7		9		11				3		8	1	6		10			26
	2		4	5		7	8	9		11					1	3		6		10			27
	2		4	5		7	8			11		9			1	3		6		10			28
	2		4	5	14	7	8	9		11		12			1	3		6†		10*			29
	2		4	5		7	8	9		11		12			1	3		6		10*			30
	2		4	5	14	7	8	9		11		12			1	3†		6		10*			31
	2		4*	5		7	8	9		11		10			1	3		6			12		32
	2			5		7	8	9		11		10*			1	3		6			12	4	33
	2			5	14	7		9	10*	11					1	3		6	4	12	8†		34
	2			5		7		9	10	11					1	3		6	4	8			35
	2			5		7	8	9*	10	11					1	3		6			12	4	36
	2			5	14	7	8*	9	10	11†					1	3		6	7		12	4	37
	2*			5	12		8	9	10					3	1	11		6	7			4	38
	2			5	12	7	8	9	10†	3			14		1			6*	4		11		39
	2*			5	6	7	8	9	10	3			14		1			4			12	11†	40
				5	6	7	8	9	10†	3			14	2	1			12			4	11*	41
				5	6	7	8	9		3	10			2	1						11	4	42
9	38	10	31	33	11	39	38	39	30	40	24	7	—	20	22	18	11	16	7	10	3	6	
		+1s	+7s		+1s							+10s	+1s					+7s		+2s	+2s	+4s	

Rumbelows Cup First Round Blackpool (h) 0-3
(a) 2-4
FA Cup First Round Preston NE (h) 0-1

MANSFIELD TOWN

Player and Position	Ht	Wt	Birth Date	Birth Place	Source	Clubs	League App	League Gls
Goalkeepers								
Andy Beasley	6 2	12 01	5 2 64	Sedgley	Apprentice	Luton T	—	—
						Mansfield T	94	—
						Gillingham (loan)	—	—
						Peterborough U (loan)	7	—
						Scarborough (loan)	4	—
Jason Pearcey	6 1	13 05	23 7 71	Leamington Spa	Trainee	Mansfield T	32	—
Defenders								
Cliff Carr*	5 5	10 04	19 6 64	London	Apprentice	Fulham	145	14
						Stoke C	124	1
						Mansfield T	20	—
Nicky Clarke	5 11	12 00	20 8 67	Walsall	Apprentice	Wolverhampton W	82	1
						Mansfield T	16	1
Wayne Fairclough	5 10	9 12	27 4 68	Nottingham	Apprentice	Notts Co	71	—
						Mansfield T	79	9
Greg Fee	6 1	12 00	24 6 64	Halifax		Bradford C	7	—
						Boston U		—
						Sheffield W	26	—
						Preston NE (loan)	15	—
						Northampton T (loan)	1	—
						Leyton Orient (loan)	5	—
						Mansfield T	44	4
Paul Fleming	5 7	10 00	6 9 67	Halifax		Halifax T	139	1
						Mansfield T	38	—
George Foster	5 10	11 02	26 9 56	Plymouth	Apprentice	Plymouth Arg	212	6
						Torquay U (loan)	6	3
						Exeter C (loan)	28	—
						Derby Co	30	—
						Mansfield T	363	—
Malcolm Murray (To Partick T 1991)	5 11	11 02	26 7 64	Buckie	Buckie T	Hearts	27	—
						Hull C	11	—
						Mansfield T	59	—
Chris Withe	5 10	11 03	25 9 62	Liverpool	Apprentice	Newcastle U	2	—
						Bradford C	143	2
						Notts Co	80	3
						Bury	31	1
						Chester C (loan)	2	—
						Mansfield T (loan)	11	—
						Mansfield T	20	1
Midfield								
Steve Chambers‡	5 10	10 10	20 7 68	Worksop	Apprentice	Sheffield W	—	—
						Mansfield T	57	—
Steve Charles	5 9	10 07	10 5 60	Sheffield	Sheffield Univ	Sheffield U	123	10
						Wrexham	113	37
						Mansfield T	214	36
Martin Clark	5 9	10 11	13 10 68	Uddington	Hamilton A	Clyde	51	2
						Nottingham F	—	—
						Falkirk (loan)	3	1
						Mansfield T (loan)	14	1
						Mansfield T	33	—
Gary Ford	5 8	11 10	8 2 61	York	Apprentice	York C	366	52
						Leicester C	16	2
						Port Vale	75	12
						Walsall (loan)	13	2
						Mansfield T	51	5
Kevin Gray	6 0	13 00	7 1 72	Sheffield	Trainee	Mansfield T	66	1
Paul Holland	5 11	12 04	8 7 73	Lincoln	School	Mansfield T	39	6

MANSFIELD TOWN

Foundation: Many records give the date of Mansfield Town's formation as 1905. But the present club did not come into being until 1910 when the Mansfield Wesleyans (formed 1891) and playing in the Notts and District League, decided to spread their wings and changed their name to Mansfield Town, joining the new Central Alliance in 1911.

First Football League game: 29 August, 1931, Division 3 (S), v Swindon T (h) W 3-2 – Wilson; Clifford, England; Wake, Davis, Blackburn; Gilhespy, Readman (1), Johnson, Broom (2), Baxter.

Did you know: Mansfield's record goalscorer Ted Harston scored a hat-trick when making his debut for them against Southport, 19 October 1935, following his transfer from Bristol City.

Managers (and Secretary-managers)
John Baynes 1922–25, Ted Davison 1926–28, Jack Hickling 1928–33, Henry Martin 1933–35, Charlie Bell 1935, Harold Wightman 1936, Harold Parkes 1936–38, Jack Poole 1938–44, Lloyd Barke 1944–45, Roy Goodall 1945–49, Freddie Steele 1949–51, George Jobey 1952–53, Stan Mercer 1953–55, Charlie Mitten 1956–58, Sam Weaver 1958–60, Raich Carter 1960–63, Tommy Cummings 1963–67, Tommy Eggleston 1967–70, Jock Basford 1970–71, Danny Williams 1971–74, Dave Smith 1974–76, Peter Morris 1976–78, Billy Bingham 1978–79, Mick Jones 1979–81, Stuart Boam 1981–83, Ian Greaves 1983–89, George Foster February 1989–.

Nick Roddis			18	2 73	Rotherham	Trainee	Nottingham F	—	—
							Mansfield T	—	—
Steve Spooner	5 10	12 00	25	1 61	Sutton	Apprentice	Derby Co	8	—
							Halifax T	72	13
							Chesterfield	93	14
							Hereford U	84	19
							York C	72	11
							Rotherham U	19	1
							Mansfield T	43	2

Forwards

Gary Castledine			27	3 70	Dumfries		Mansfield T	7	—
Wayne Davidson	5 9	11 00	7	12 68	Wallsend		Mansfield T	—	—
Paul McLoughlin	5 10	10 07	23	12 63	Bristol	Bristol C	Cardiff C	49	4
							Gisborne C	—	—
							Hereford U	74	14
							Wolverhampton W	28	4
							Mansfield T	12	3
							Walsall (loan)	10	5
							York C (loan)	1	—
Kevin Noteman	5 10	10 09	15	10 69	Preston	Trainee	Leeds U	1	—
							Doncaster R	106	20
							Mansfield T	6	—
Phil Stant	6 1	12 07	13	10 62	Bolton	Camberley Army	Reading	4	2
							Hereford U	89	38
							Notts Co	22	6
							Blackpool (loan)	12	5
							Lincoln C (loan)	4	—
							Huddersfield T (loan)	5	1
							Fulham	19	5
							Mansfield T	40	26
Ian Stringfellow	5 9	10 02	8	5 69	Nottingham	Apprentice	Mansfield T	123	20
Steve Wilkinson	6 0	10 12	1	9 68	Lincoln	Apprentice	Leicester C	9	1
							Rochdale (loan)	—	—
							Crewe Alex (loan)	5	2
							Mansfield T	106	40

Trainees
Cann, Scott; Crookes, Dominic; Doughty, Stephen; Foster, Stephen; Johnson, Carl; Jordan, Jonathan P; Langton, Mark; Mowbray, Scott G; Perkins, Christopher P; Smith, Dean; Timons, Christopher; Ward, Darren; Wilson, Kevin.

Associated Schoolboys
Clarke, Darrell J; Musson, Robert J; Peach, Anthony R; Stark, Wayne R; Storer, David J; Wragg, Doyan W; Wright, Darren.

Associated Schoolboys who have accepted the club's offer of a Traineeship/Contract
Kerry, Christopher B; Marrows, Dean; Morgan, James K.

MIDDLESBROUGH 1991–92 *Back row (left to right):* Jimmy Phillips, Nicky Mohan, Paul Wilkinson, Alan Kernaghan, Willie Falconer, Robbie Mustoe, Gary Hamilton. *Centre row:* Tommy Johnson (Physiotherapist), Ian Arnold, Curtis Fleming, Steve Pears, Ian Ironside, Stuart Ripley, Owen McGee, Ray Train (Reserve Team Coach). *Seated:* Gary Parkinson, Mark Proctor, Lennie Lawrence (Manager), Tony Mowbray, John Pickering (Assistant Manager), Bernie Slaven, John Hendrie.

FA Premier   **MIDDLESBROUGH**

Ayresome Park, Middlesbrough, Cleveland TS1 4PB. Telephone Middlesbrough (0642) 819659/815996. Commercial Dept. (0642) 826664. Clubcall: 0898 121181. Fax No: 0642 820244

Ground capacity: 26,101.

Record attendance: 53,596 v Newcastle U, Division 1, 27 December 1979.

Record receipts: £178,977 v Manchester U, Rumbelows Cup semi-final 1st leg, 4 March 1992.

Pitch measurements: 114yd × 74yd.

Chairman: M. C. Henderson.

Directors: G. Fordy, S. Gibson, R. Corbidge.

Chief Executive/Secretary: Keith Lamb.

Manager: Lennie Lawrence. *Coach:* John Pickering. *Physio:* Mike Nile. *Youth Development Officer:* Ron Bone. *Marketing Manager:* Mitch Hatfield. *Press & PRO:* Clive Armitage.

Year Formed: 1876. Turned Professional: 1889; became amateur 1892, and professional again, 1899. Ltd Co.: 1892.

Former Grounds: 1877, Old Archery Ground, Linhorpe Road; 1903, Ayresome Park.

Club Nickname: 'The Boro'.

Record League Victory: 9-0 v Brighton & HA, Division 2, 23 August 1958 – Taylor; Bilcliff, Robinson; Harris (2 pens), Phillips, Walley; Day, McLean, Clough (5), Peacock (2), Holliday.

Record Cup Victory: 9-3 v Goole T, FA Cup, 1st rd, 9 January 1915 – Williamson; Haworth, Weir; Davidson, Cook, Malcolm; Wilson, Carr (3), Elliott (3), Tinsley (3), Davies.

Record Defeat: 0-9 v Blackburn R, Division 2, 6 November 1954.

Most League Points (2 for a win): 65, Division 2, 1973–74.

Most League points (3 for a win): 94, Division 3, 1986–87.

Most League Goals: 122, Division 2, 1926–27.

Highest League Scorer in Season: George Camsell, 59, Division 2, 1926–27 (Second Division record).

Most League Goals in Total Aggregate: George Camsell, 326, 1925–39.

Most Capped Player: Wilf Mannion, 26, England.

Most League Appearances: Tim Williamson, 563, 1902–23.

Record Transfer Fee Received: £2,300,000 from Manchester United for Gary Pallister, August 1989.

Record Transfer Fee Paid: £750,000 to Hull C for Andy Payton, November 1991.

Football League Record: 1899 Elected to Division 2; 1902–24 Division 1; 1924–27 Division 2; 1927–28 Division 1; 1928–29 Division 2; 1929–54 Division 1; 1954–66 Division 2; 1966–67 Division 3; 1967–74 Division 2; 1974–82 Division 1; 1982–86 Division 2; 1986–87 Division 3; 1987–88 Division 2; 1988–89 Division 1; 1989–92 Division 2; 1992– FA Premier League.

Honours: Football League: Division 1 best season: 3rd, 1913–14. Division 2 – Champions 1926–27, 1928–29, 1973–74; Runners-up 1901–02, 1991–92. Division 3 – Runners-up 1966–67, 1986–87. *FA Cup:* best season: 6th rd, 1935–36, 1946–47, 1969–70, 1974–75, 1976–77, 1977–78; old last eight 1900–01, 1903–04. *Football League Cup:* Semi-final 1975–76, 1991–92. *Amateur Cup:* Winners 1895, 1898, *Anglo-Scottish Cup:* Winners 1975–76.

Colours: Red shirts, white shorts, red stockings. **Change colours:** All sky blue.

MIDDLESBROUGH 1991–92 LEAGUE RECORD

Match No.	Date		Venue	Opponents		Result	H/T Score	Lg. Pos.	Goalscorers	Atten- dance
1	Aug	17	H	Millwall	W	1-0	1-0	—	Mustoe	16,234
2		21	A	Derby Co	L	0-2	0-0	—		12,805
3		24	A	Ipswich T	L	1-2	0-0	17	Wilkinson	9822
4		27	H	Newcastle U	W	3-0	1-0	—	Wilkinson, Proctor, Falconer	16,970
5		31	H	Portsmouth	W	2-0	0-0	3	Falconer, Slaven	12,320
6	Sep	4	A	Oxford U	W	2-1	0-0	—	Slaven 2	4229
7		7	A	Watford	W	2-1	2-0	1	Wilkinson, Falconer	8715
8		14	H	Leicester C	W	3-0	0-0	1	Slaven, Wilkinson 2	16,633
9		17	H	Tranmere R	W	1-0	0-0	—	Falconer	16,550
10		21	A	Plymouth Arg	D	1-1	0-1	1	Wilkinson	5280
11		28	H	Sunderland	W	2-1	2-0	1	Slaven, Wilkinson	19,424
12	Oct	5	A	Bristol R	L	1-2	1-0	1	Yates (og)	4936
13		12	H	Wolverhampton W	D	0-0	0-0	1		15,253
14		19	A	Grimsby T	L	0-1	0-0	1		10,265
15		26	H	Port Vale	W	1-0	1-0	1	Kernaghan	11,403
16	Nov	2	H	Southend U	D	1-1	0-1	1	Ripley	9664
17		5	A	Barnsley	L	1-2	0-2	—	Slaven	6525
18		9	A	Brighton & HA	D	1-1	0-1	2	Slaven (pen)	8270
19		16	H	Charlton Ath	W	2-0	0-0	2	Mohan, Slaven	13,093
20		23	H	Bristol C	W	3-1	2-1	2	Payton, Slaven 2	12,928
21		30	A	Blackburn R	L	1-2	1-1	2	Slaven (pen)	15,541
22	Dec	7	H	Swindon T	D	2-2	1-0	2	Wilkinson, Slaven	13,300
23		26	A	Newcastle U	W	1-0	0-0	3	Wilkinson	26,563
24		28	A	Portsmouth	L	0-4	0-3	4		12,324
25	Jan	1	H	Derby Co	D	1-1	1-0	4	Mohan	16,288
26		11	H	Ipswich T	W	1-0	0-0	3	Payton	15,104
27		18	A	Millwall	L	0-2	0-1	4		8125
28	Feb	8	A	Port Vale	W	2-1	1-0	5	Hendrie, Mustoe	7019
29		22	H	Blackburn R	D	0-0	0-0	7		19,353
30		29	A	Swindon T	W	1-0	0-0	5	Kernaghan	10,379
31	Mar	7	H	Cambridge U	D	1-1	0-0	4	Wilkinson	14,686
32		14	A	Southend U	W	1-0	0-0	4	Slaven (pen)	7272
33		17	A	Cambridge U	D	0-0	0-0	—		7318
34		21	H	Brighton & HA	W	4-0	2-0	4	Slaven 3 (1 pen), Hendrie	13,054
35		28	A	Charlton Ath	D	0-0	0-0	4		8250
36	Apr	1	A	Leicester C	L	1-2	0-1	—	Pollock	19,352
37		4	H	Watford	L	1-2	0-0	7	Wilkinson	13,669
38		7	A	Bristol C	D	1-1	1-0	—	Hendrie	12,814
39		10	A	Tranmere R	W	2-1	1-0	—	Proctor, Phillips	8842
40		13	H	Barnsley	L	0-1	0-0	—		12,743
41		15	H	Oxford U	W	2-1	0-0	—	Ripley, Payton	11,928
42		18	H	Plymouth Arg	W	2-1	1-1	3	Ripley, Falconer	15,086
43		20	A	Sunderland	L	0-1	0-1	4		25,093
44		25	H	Bristol R	W	2-1	0-1	4	Wilkinson 2	14,057
45		28	H	Grimsby T	W	2-0	2-0	—	Phillips (pen), Wilkinson	18,570
46	May	2	A	Wolverhampton W	W	2-1	0-0	2	Gittens, Wilkinson	19,123

Final League Position: 2

GOALSCORERS

League (58): Slaven 16 (4 pens), Wilkinson 15, Falconer 5, Hendrie 3, Payton 3, Ripley 3, Kernaghan 2, Mohan 2, Mustoe 2, Phillips 2 (1 pen), Proctor 2, Gittens 1, Pollock 1, own goals 1.
Rumbelows Cup (8): Wilkinson 3, Hendrie 1, Mustoe 1, Parkinson 1 (1 pen), Ripley 1, Slaven 1.
FA Cup (7): Wilkinson 4, Kernaghan 2, Hendrie 1.

FA Cup				
	Third Round	Manchester C (h)	2-1	
	Fourth Round	Sheffield W (a)	2-1	
	Fifth Round	Portsmouth (a)	1-1	
		(h)	2-4	

Pears	Parkinson	Phillips	Mowbray	Kernaghan	Falconer	Mustoe	Proctor	Wilkinson	Ripley	Hendrie	Slaven	Fleming	Shannon	Hewitt	Pollock	Arnold	Marwood	Young	Mohan	Payton	Peake	Gittens	Ironside	Match No.
1	2	3	4	5	6	7	8	9	10	11														1
1	2	3	4	5	6	7*	8	9	10	11	12													2
1	2†	3	4	5	6	7	8*	9	10	11	12	14												3
1	2	3	4	5	6	7	8	9	10	11														4
1	2	3	4	5	6	7*	8	9	10	11	12													5
1	2	3	4	5	6	7	8	9	10*	11	12													6
1	2	3	4	5	6	10	8	9		11	7													7
1	2	3	4	5	6	10*	8	9	12	11	7													8
1	2	3	4	5	6	12	8	9	10	11*	7													9
1	2†	3	4	5	6	12	8*	9	10	11	7	14												10
1	2	3	4	5		6	8	9	10	11	7													11
1	2	3	4	5		6†	8	9	10	11	7*	12	14											12
1	2	3	4	5		6	8	9	10†		7	12			11*	14								13
1	2	3	4	5		6	8	9			7	10			11									14
1	2	3	4	5		6	8*	9		11	7	12			10									15
1	2†	3	4	5		6		9	10*	11	7	12			8	14								16
1	2*	3	4	5		6	8	9	10	11	7	12												17
1		3		4	6	14		9	10	11	12	2			8†		7*		5					18
1		3		4	6		8	9	10*	11	7	2			12				5					19
1		3		4	6		8	9		11	7	2			12				5	10*				20
1	14	3		4	6*		8	9		11	7	2†			12				5	10				21
1		3		4	6		8	9	10		7	2			11*				5	12				22
1		3		4	6		8	9			7	2			11*				5	12	10			23
1	14	3		4	6	12		9			7	2*			10†				5	8	11			24
1	2	3		4	6*		11†	9	10		7		14						5	12	8			25
1	2	3		4	6			9	11	10*	7				8				5	12				26
1	2	3		4	6	12		9	11	10	7†								5	8*	14			27
1	2	3		4	6	12		9	11	10	7*								5	8				28
1	2	3			6*	12		9	11	10†	14								5	8	7	4		29
1		3		4	6			9	11		7	2			10				5	8				30
1	2†	3		4		12		9	11	10	7				8*				5		6	14		31
1		3		4		11		9	10		7	2			8				5		6			32
1		3		4		11		9	10		7	2			8*				5		6	12		33
1		3		4		11		9*	10†		7	2		14	8				5	12	6			34
1		4		3		8		9	11*	10	7	2							5	12	6			35
1		4		3		14		9	11*	10	7	2			8†				5	12	6			36
1		4		3		14		9	11	10	7*	2			8				5†	12	6			37
1		3		4		11		9	10	12	7	2			8*				5		6			38
1		3		4†		8	7	9	11*	10		2							5	12	6	14		39
1	14	3		4		7		9	11	10	12	2†			8*				5		6			40
1		3				8	14	9	11	10*	7	2							5	12	6†	4		41
1	14	3			6	8		9	11*		7†	2		12					5	10		4		42
1		3				8	7†	9	11	10	12	2							5*	14	6	4		43
1		3				8		9	11*	12	7	2			14				5	10	6†	4		44
1		3				8		9	11		7	2			6				5	10		4		45
1		3				8		9	11†	10	7*	2			6				5	12	14	4	1	46
45	23	43	17	38	25	28	27	46	36	38	28	23	—	—	21	—	3	—	27	8	20	9	1	
	+4s					+2s	+9s		+3s		+10s	+5s	+1s	+2s	+5s	+1s			+1s	+11s	+3s	+3s		

Rumbelows Cup

	Second Round	Bournemouth (h)	1-1
		(a)	2-1
	Third Round	Barnsley (h)	1-0
	Fourth Round	Manchester C (h)	2-1
	Fifth Round	Peterborough U (a)	0-0
		(h)	1-0
	Semi-Final	Manchester U (h)	0-0
		(a)	1-2

MIDDLESBROUGH

Player and Position	Ht	Wt	Birth Date	Birth Place	Source	Clubs	League App	Gls
Goalkeepers								
Andrew Collett	5 11	12 00	28 10 73	Middlesbrough	Trainee	Middlesbrough	—	—
Ian Ironside	6 2	13 00	8 3 64	Sheffield	Apprentice	Barnsley	—	—
						N Ferriby U	—	—
						Scarborough	88	—
						Middlesbrough	1	—
						Scarborough (loan)	7	—
Stephen Pears	6 0	12 11	22 1 62	Brandon	Apprentice	Manchester U	4	—
						Middlesbrough (loan)	12	—
						Middlesbrough	250	—
Defenders								
Lee Crosby‡			23 1 72	Hartlepool	Trainee	Middlesbrough	—	—
Willie Falconer	6 1	12 10	5 4 66	Aberdeen	Lewis Utd	Aberdeen	77	13
						Watford	98	12
						Middlesbrough	25	5
Curtis Fleming	5 10	11 10	8 10 68	Manchester	St Patrick's	Swindon T	—	—
						Middlesbrough	28	—
Philip Gilchrist	6 0	11 12	25 8 73	Stockton	Trainee	Nottingham F	—	—
						Middlesbrough	—	—
Nicky Mohan	6 2	12 00	6 10 70	Middlesbrough	Trainee	Middlesbrough	55	2
Tony Mowbray (To Celtic Nov 1991)	6 1	12 02	22 11 63	Saltburn	Apprentice	Middlesbrough	348	25
Gary Parkinson	5 10	11 11	10 1 68	Middlesbrough	Amateur	Everton	—	—
						Middlesbrough	198	5
Jim Phillips	6 0	12 07	8 2 66	Bolton	Apprentice	Bolton W	108	2
						Rangers	25	—
						Oxford U	79	8
						Middlesbrough	99	4
Andrew Todd	5 10	10 11	21 9 74	Derby	Trainee	Middlesbrough	—	—
Midfield								
Gary Hamilton‡	5 8	11 02	27 12 65	Glasgow	Apprentice	Middlesbrough	229	25
						Darlington (loan)	11	2
Graham Kavanagh	5 10		3 12 73	Dublin	Home Farm	Middlesbrough	—	—
Robert Lake			13 10 71	Stockton	Trainee	Middlesbrough	—	—
Alan Moore	5 10	11 00	25 11 74	Dublin	Rivermount	Middlesbrough	—	—
Robbie Mustoe	5 10	10 08	28 8 68	Oxford		Oxford U	91	10
						Middlesbrough	71	6
Andy Payton	5 9	10 06	23 10 66	Burnley		Hull C	144	55
						Middlesbrough	19	3
Andy Peake	5 10	12 00	1 11 61	Market Harborough	Apprentice	Leicester C	147	13
						Grimsby T	39	4
						Charlton Ath	177	5
						Middlesbrough	23	—
Jamie Pollock			16 2 74	Stockton	Trainee	Middlesbrough	27	1
Mark Proctor	5 10	12 08	30 1 61	Middlesbrough	Apprentice	Middlesbrough	109	12
						Nottingham F	64	5
						Sunderland (loan)	5	—
						Sunderland	112	19
						Sheffield W	59	4
						Middlesbrough	109	6
Martin Russell‡	5 9	10 05	27 4 67	Dublin	Apprentice	Manchester U	—	—
						Birmingham C (loan)	5	—
						Leicester C	20	—
						Norwich C (loan)	—	—
						Scarborough	51	9
						Middlesbrough	11	2
Rab Shannon On loan from Dundee						Middlesbrough	1	—

MIDDLESBROUGH

Foundation: The story of how the idea of a Middlesbrough football club was first mooted at a tripe supper at the Corporation Hotel in 1875 is well known locally. But the club was formally established at a meeting in the Talbot Hotel the following year and is one of the oldest clubs in the North East.

First Football League game: 2 September, 1899, Division 2, v Lincoln C (a) L 0-3 – Smith; Shaw, Ramsey; Allport, McNally, McCracken; Wanless, Longstaffe, Gettins, Page, Pugh.

Did you know: While playing for Middlesbrough Brian Clough scored 5,3,2,1,1 in consecutive League games against Brighton, the club he managed in 1973-74.

Managers (and Secretary-managers)
John Robson 1899–1905, Alex Massie 1905–06, Andy Aitken 1906–09, J. Gunter 1908–10*, Andy Walker 1910–11, Tom McIntosh 1911–19, James Howie 1920–23, Herbert Bamlett 1923–26, Peter McWilliam 1927–34, Wilf Gillow 1934–44, David Jack 1944–52, Walter Rowley 1952–54, Bob Dennison 1954–63, Raich Carter 1963–66, Stan Anderson 1966–73, Jack Charlton 1973–77, John Neal 1977–81, Bobby Murdoch 1981–82, Malcolm Allison 1982–84, Willie Maddren 1984–86, Bruce Rioch 1986–90, Colin Todd 1990–91, Lennie Lawrence July 1991–.

Forwards

Name				Birthplace	Signed	Club	Apps	Gls
Ian Arnold*			4 7 72	Durham City	Trainee	Middlesbrough	3	—
Ian Baird (To Hearts July 1991)	6 0	12 09	1 4 64	Southampton	Apprentice	Southampton	17	3
						Cardiff C (loan)	12	6
						Southampton	5	2
						Newcastle U (loan)	5	1
						Leeds U	85	33
						Portsmouth	20	1
						Leeds U	77	17
						Middlesbrough	63	19
Paul Hanford*			4 1 72	Middlesbrough	Trainee	Middlesbrough	—	—
John Hendrie	5 7	11 04	24 10 63	Lennoxtown	Apprentice	Coventry C	21	2
						Hereford U (loan)	6	—
						Bradford C	173	46
						Newcastle U	34	4
						Leeds U	27	5
						Middlesbrough	79	6
John Hewitt On loan from Celtic						Middlesbrough	2	—
Alan Kernaghan	6 2	12 12	25 4 67	Otley	Apprentice	Middlesbrough	184	13
						Charlton Ath (loan)	13	—
Nicholas Peverell	5 11	11 10	28 4 73	Middlesbrough	Trainee	Middlesbrough	—	—
Stuart Ripley	5 11	12 06	20 11 67	Middlesbrough	Apprentice	Middlesbrough	249	26
						Bolton W (loan)	5	1
Bernie Slaven	5 11	10 10	13 11 60	Paisley		Morton	22	1
						Airdrie	2	—
						Q of the S	2	—
						Albion R	42	27
						Middlesbrough	289	114
Paul Wilkinson	6 0	11 00	30 10 64	Louth	Apprentice	Grimsby T	71	27
						Everton	31	7
						Nottingham F	34	5
						Watford	134	52
						Middlesbrough	46	15
Michael Young	5 11	12 00	15 4 73	Newcastle	Trainee	Middlesbrough	1	—

Trainees
Barron, Michael J; Illman, Neil D; Lee, Anthony S; Maddick, Kevin A; McDowell, Roddy; Oliver, Michael; Roberts, Ben J; Taylor, Mark S.

**Non-Contract
Bell, Steven; Cole, Anthony R.

Associated Schoolboys
Cummings, Peter; Devers, Peter; Dixon, Steven K; Dolan, Lee P; Harrison, Paul; Hood, James W; Lee, Nigel P; Mills, Andrew D; Richardson, Paul; Skingsley, Ross A; Summerbell, Mark; Ward, Richard T.

Associated Schoolboys who have accepted the club's offer of a Traineeship/Contract
Dwyer, Paul J; Johnson, Ian; McGargle, Stephen; Norton, Paul; Stamp, Philip L.

**Non-Contract Players who are retained must be re-signed before they are eligible to play in League matches.

346

MILLWALL 1991-92 *Back row (left to right):* Alan McLeary, Keith Stevens, Chris Armstrong, John McGlashan, David Thompson, John Humphrey, Mick McCarthy. *Centre row:* Steve Harrison, John McGinlay, Jon Goodman, Mark Falco, Aidan Davison, Brian Horne, Ken Cunningham, Paul Stephenson, Alex Rae, Peter Melville (Physiotherapist). *Front row:* John Colquhoun, Paul Kerr, Ian Bogie, Bruce Rioch (Manager), Phil Barber, Ian McNeill (Assistant Manager), Colin Cooper, Ian Dawes, Malcolm Allen.

Division 1   MILLWALL

The Den, Cold Blow Lane, London SE14 5RH. Telephone 071-639 3143, Commercial Dept: 071-639 4590. Credit Card Bookings 071-277 6877. Club Shop 071-358 0181.

Ground capacity: 19,922.

Record attendance: 48,672 v Derby Co, FA Cup 5th rd, 20 February 1937.

Record receipts: £106,839 v West Ham U, Division 2, 10 November 1990.

Pitch measurements: 112yd × 74yd.

President: Lord Mellish.

Chairman: R. I. Burr. *Vice-chairman:* P. W. Mead. *Directors:* J. D. Burnige, B. E. Mitchell, P. M. Mead, D. Sullivan. *Chief Executive Secretary:* G. I. S. Hortop. *Manager:* Mick McCarthy. *Assistant Manager:* Ian McNeill. *Coach. Commercial Director:* Mike Ryan. *Commercial Manager:* W. W. Neil. *Physio:* Peter Melville. *Chief Scout:* Allen Batsford.

Year Formed: 1885. Turned Professional: 1893. Ltd Co.: 1894.

Former Grounds: 1885, Glengall Road, Millwall; 1886, Back of 'Lord Nelson'; 1890, East Ferry Road; 1901, North Greenwich; 1910, The Den.

Former Names: 1885, Millwall Rovers; 1889, Millwall Athletic.

Club Nickname: 'The Lions'.

Record League Victory: 9-1 v Torquay U, Division 3 (S), 29 August 1927 – Lansdale; Tilling, Hill; Amos, Bryant (3), Graham; Chance, Hawkins (3), Landells (1), Phillips (2), Black. 9-1 v Coventry C, Division 3 (S), 19 November 1927 – Lansdale; Fort, Hill; Amos, Collins (1), Graham; Chance, Landells (4), Cock (2), Phillips (2), Black.

Record Cup Victory: 7-0 v Gateshead, FA Cup, 2nd rd, 12 December 1936 – Yuill; Ted Smith, Inns; Brolly, Hancock, Forsyth; Thomas (1), Mangnall (1), Ken Burditt (2), McCartney (2), Thorogood (1).

Record Defeat: 1-9 v Aston Villa, FA Cup 4th rd, 28 January 1946.

Most League Points (2 for a win): 65, Division 3 (S), 1927–28 and Division 3, 1965–66.

Most League points (3 for a win): 90, Division 3, 1984–85.

Most League Goals: 127, Division 3 (S), 1927–28.

Highest League Scorer in Season: Richard Parker, 37, Division 3 (S), 1926–27.

Most League Goals in Total Aggregate: Teddy Sheringham, 93, 1984–91.

Most Capped Player: Eamonn Dunphy, 22 (23), Eire.

Most League Appearances: Barry Kitchener, 523, 1967–82.

Record Transfer Fee Received: £2,000,000 from Nottingham F for Teddy Sheringham, July 1991.

Record Transfer Fee Paid: £800,000 to Derby Co for Paul Goddard, December 1989.

Football League Record: 1920 Original Members of Division 3; 1921 Division 3 (S); 1928–34 Division 2; 1934–38 Division 3 (S); 1938–48 Division 2; 1948–58 Division 3 (S); 1958–62 Division 4; 1962–64 Division 3; 1964–65 Division 4; 1965–66 Division 3; 1966–75 Division 2; 1975–76 Division 3; 1976–79 Division 2; 1979–85 Division 3; 1985–88 Division 2; 1988–90 Division 1; 1990–92 Division 2; 1992– Division 1.

Honours: Football League: Division 2 – Champions 1987–88; Division 3 (S) – Champions 1927–28, 1937–38; Runners-up 1952–53; Division 3 – Runners–up 1965–66, 1984–85; Division 4 – Champions 1961–62; Runners–up 1964–65. *FA Cup:* Semi-final 1900, 1903, 1937 (first Division 3 side to reach semi-final). *Football League Cup:* best season: 5th rd, 1973–74, 1976–77. *Football League Trophy:* Winners 1982–83.

Colours: Blue shirts, white shorts, blue stockings. **Change colours:** Yellow shirts, black shorts, black stockings.

MILLWALL 1991–92 LEAGUE RECORD

Match No.	Date		Venue	Opponents	Result	H/T Score	Lg. Pos.	Goalscorers	Attendance
1	Aug	17	A	Middlesbrough	L 0-1	0-1	—		16,234
2		24	H	Sunderland	W 4-1	3-1	12	Barber 2, Falco, Kerr	10,016
3		31	A	Plymouth Arg	L 2-3	1-2	19	Rae, Burrows (og)	5369
4	Sep	4	H	Brighton & HA	L 1-2	1-1	—	Falco	9266
5		7	H	Cambridge U	L 1-2	1-1	21	Kerr (pen)	8332
6		14	A	Oxford U	D 2-2	2-1	22	Colquhoun, Rae	4622
7		17	A	Bristol C	D 2-2	2-1	—	McCarthy, Colquhoun	10,862
8		21	H	Newcastle U	W 2-1	1-1	19	Kerr 2	9156
9		28	A	Barnsley	W 2-0	1-0	16	Rae 2	6544
10	Oct	5	H	Blackburn R	L 1-3	0-1	19	Cooper	8026
11		12	A	Southend U	W 3-2	2-1	16	Rae, Stephenson, Colquhoun	7266
12		19	A	Ipswich T	D 0-0	0-0	15		11,175
13		26	H	Derby Co	L 1-2	1-1	18	Kerr	7660
14		29	A	Watford	W 2-0	0-0	—	Rae, Kerr	7366
15	Nov	2	H	Portsmouth	D 1-1	1-0	13	Armstrong	6060
16		5	A	Tranmere R	L 1-2	0-1	—	Kerr (pen)	6108
17		9	A	Port Vale	W 2-0	0-0	13	Falco 2	8944
18		16	H	Wolverhampton W	W 2-1	2-1	12	Barber, McGinlay	9469
19		23	A	Grimsby T	D 1-1	0-0	12	McGinlay	5701
20		30	H	Bristol R	L 0-1	0-1	13		7824
21	Dec	7	A	Leicester C	D 1-1	0-0	13	Kerr	12,127
22		21	A	Brighton & HA	W 4-3	1-0	11	McGinlay 2, Kerr (pen), Verveer	7598
23		26	H	Watford	L 0-4	0-2	13		9237
24		28	H	Plymouth Arg	W 2-1	1-1	11	McCarthy, McGinlay	6980
25	Jan	1	A	Swindon T	L 1-3	0-3	12	McGinlay	9746
26		11	A	Sunderland	L 2-6	1-1	13	Rae, Kerr	16,533
27		18	H	Middlesbrough	W 2-0	1-0	13	McGinlay, Rae	8125
28	Feb	1	H	Ipswich T	L 2-3	0-1	13	Rae, Kerr (pen)	8847
29		8	A	Derby Co	W 2-0	0-0	13	McGinlay, Rae	12,773
30		15	H	Grimsby T	D 1-1	1-1	13	Rae	6807
31		22	A	Bristol R	L 2-3	1-1	13	Goodman, Armstrong	5747
32		26	H	Charlton Ath	W 1-0	1-0	—	Kerr (pen)	12,882
33		29	H	Leicester C	W 2-0	2-0	11	Cooper, Goodman	7562
34	Mar	7	A	Charlton Ath	L 0-1	0-0	11		8177
35		11	H	Tranmere R	L 0-3	0-2	—		6456
36		14	A	Portsmouth	L 1-6	0-3	15	Verveer	14,944
37		21	H	Port Vale	W 1-0	0-0	12	Allen	6148
38		28	A	Wolverhampton W	D 0-0	0-0	14		11,880
39	Apr	1	H	Oxford U	W 2-1	0-1	—	Stephenson, Goodman	5850
40		4	A	Cambridge U	L 0-1	0-0	14		6385
41		8	H	Swindon T	D 1-1	1-1	—	Allen	6722
42		11	H	Bristol C	L 2-3	1-0	15	Barber, Atteveld (og)	6989
43		18	A	Newcastle U	W 1-0	0-0	13	Allen	23,821
44		22	H	Barnsley	D 1-1	1-1	—	Allen (pen)	5703
45		25	A	Blackburn R	L 1-2	0-0	16	Armstrong	12,820
46	May	2	H	Southend U	W 2-0	0-0	15	Armstrong, Allen	7574

Final League Position: 15

GOALSCORERS

League (64): Kerr 12 (5 pens), Rae 11, McGinlay 8, Allen 5 (1 pen), Armstrong 4, Barber 4, Falco 4, Colquhoun 3, Goodman 3, Cooper 2, McCarthy 2, Stephenson 2, Verveer 2, own goals 2.
Rumbelows Cup (3): Armstrong 1, Colquhoun 1, Stephenson 1.
FA Cup (5): Rae 2, Kerr 1, Thompson 1, Verveer 1.

Davison	Dawes	Cooper	McGlashan	Thompson	Wood	Kerr	Colquhoun	Falco	Rae	Barber	Armstrong	Bogie	McLeary	Stephenson	Cunningham	McCarthy	Stevens	Branagan	Goodman	McGinlay	Verveer	Allen	Roberts	Keller	Match No.
1	2	3	4	5	6	7*	8	9	10†	11	12	14													1
1	2	3	4	5		7*	8†	9	10	11	12	14	6												2
1	2	3	4	5	12	7	8	9	10	11			6*												3
1	2	3	4†	5		7	8	9	10	11*	12	14	6												4
1		3	5†		2	7	8	9		11*10	4		6	12	14										5
1	2	3			6	7	8			12	4*			11†		5	14								6
1	2	3			6	7	8	9*10		12	4			11		5									7
1	2	3			6	7	8	9*10		12	4			11†		5	14								8
1	2	3			6	7	8	9*10		12	4			11		5									9
1	2	3	6			7	8	9	10		4			11		5									10
1		3	6			7	8	9	10	12	4			11*		5	2								11
1		3	5			7	8	9*10		12	14	4	6	11†		2									12
1*		3	5			7	8	9	10	11	4		6		12	2									13
		3	5			7	8	9	10	11	4		6*				2	1	12						14
		3	5			7	8	9*10		11	4		6				2	1	12						15
		3	5			7	8		10	11	4*	9	6				2	1		12					16
		3*	5			7	8	9	10	11	4		6		12		2	1							17
	3		5			4*	8	9†10		11	14		6		12		2	1		7					18
	3		5			4*	8†		10	11	14	9	6	2	12		1			7					19
	3		5			4		10*11		8	9	6	12	2			1			7					20
	3		5			4		10	11	12	9	6	8	2			1			7*					21
	3		5			4		10	11		9	6	8	2			1			7	9				22
	3		5			4		10	11*14	12	6	8		2			1			7†	9				23
	3					4	11				9	6	7	2	5		1			10	8				24
	3					4*	11	14	12		9	6	7	2	5	1				10†	8				25
1	3					4	11	12	6*		9		7	2	5					10	8				26
1	3	2					12	11*	6		9	4	7		5					10	8				27
1	3	2	5				12	11*	6		9†	4	7		14					10	8				28
1	3	2	5			9	7	6						4		11	10	8							29
1	2	3	5				7	6		12		9		4		11*10	8								30
1	2	3*14†					7	6	9	12	5			4		11	10	8							31
1	2	3				9	7	6*		12	5			4		11	10	8							32
1	2	3	6			9	7			12	5			4		11	10*	8							33
1	2	3	6			9	7			12	5			4		11	10*	8							34
1	2	3	6			9*	7		12		4	5				11	10	8							35
1		3	6			9†	7	11	14		4*	5		2		10		8	12						36
1	3	5					10†11	12		6	7	2		4	8*			14	9						37
1	3		14				10	11		6†	7*	2		4	8	12	5	9							38
1	3	6					10	11			7	2		4	8		5	9							39
1	3	6	10				11†				7	2		4	8*12		5	9	14						40
1	3	6					11				7	2		4	8		5	9	10						41
1	3	6†14					11				7	2		4	8*12		5	9	10						42
1		6	14				10†11				7*	3		4	8	12	5	9	2						43
1	3	6	14				11†				7*	2		4	8	12	5	9	10						44
1	3	6		12			10†11	8			7	2*		4			5	9	14						45
	3	6		12			10	8			7	2	4*				5	9	11	1					46
33	36	36	5	29	6	32	27	19	36	26	8	20	28	26	15	14	24	12	15	19	24	10	5	1	
				+	+	+	+		+	+	+	+		+	+	+	+		+	+	+	+	+		
				3s	4s	1s	2s		2s	2s	3s	17s5s		2s	2s	3s	3s		2s	6s	1s	1s	2s		

Rumbelows Cup	Second Round	Swindon T (h)	2-2
		(a)	1-3
FA Cup	Third Round	Huddersfield T (a)	4-0
	Fourth Round	Norwich C (a)	1-2

MILLWALL

Player and Position	Ht	Wt	Birth Date	Birth Place	Source	Clubs	League App	League Gls
Goalkeepers								
Keith Branagan	6 1	13 02	10 7 66	Fulham		Cambridge U	110	—
						Millwall	46	—
						Brentford (loan)	2	—
						Gillingham (loan)	1	—
						Fulham (loan)	—	—
Aidan Davison	6 1	13 02	11 5 68	Sedgefield	Billingham Syn	Notts Co	1	—
						Leyton Orient (loan)	—	—
						Bury	—	—
						Chester C (loan)	—	—
						Blackpool (loan)	—	—
						Millwall	33	—
						Derby Co (loan)	3	4
John Donegan	6 0	13 01	19 5 71	Cork	Kilkenny	Millwall	—	—
Carl Emberson	6 1	12 11	13 7 73	Epsom	Trainee	Millwall	—	—
Brian Horne	5 11	13 13	5 10 67	Billericay	Apprentice	Millwall	163	—
						Watford (loan)	—	—
Kasey Keller	5 11	11 13	29 11 69	Washington	Portland Univ	Millwall	1	—
Defenders								
Colin Cooper	5 10	10 00	28 2 67	Durham		Middlesbrough	188	6
						Millwall	36	2
Ken Cunningham	5 11	11 02	28 6 71	Dublin		Millwall	45	—
Ian Dawes	5 7	11 11	22 2 63	Croyden	Apprentice	QPR	229	3
						Millwall	144	5
Mark Foran	6 4	13 12	30 10 73	Aldershot	Trainee	Millwall	—	—
Brian Lee	5 11	11 00	24 9 73	Greenwich	Trainee	Millwall	—	—
Mick McCarthy	6 2	12 12	7 2 59	Barnsley	Apprentice	Barnsley	272	7
						Manchester C	140	2
						Celtic	48	—
						Lyon	—	—
						Millwall	35	2
Alan McLeary	5 11	10 08	6 10 64	London	Apprentice	Millwall	301	5
David Thompson	6 3	12 07	20 11 68	N'humberland	Trainee	Millwall	97	6
Midfield								
Phil Barber	5 11	12 06	10 6 65	Tring	Aylesbury U	Crystal Palace	234	35
						Millwall	29	4
Ian Bogie	5 7	10 02	6 12 67	Newcastle	Apprentice	Newcastle U	14	—
						Preston NE	79	12
						Millwall	25	—
Paul Kerr	5 8	11 04	9 6 64	Portsmouth	Apprentice	Aston Villa	24	3
						Middlesbrough	125	13
						Millwall	44	14
Paul Manning	5 06	10 03	21 1 74	Lewisham	Trainee	Millwall	—	—
Andy Roberts	5 10	12 08	20 3 74	Dartford	Trainee	Millwall	7	—
Keith Stevens	6 0	12 05	21 6 64	Merton	Apprentice	Millwall	315	4
Peter Terry†	6 1	11 00	11 9 72	Edmonton	Trainee	Aldershot	1	—
						Millwall	—	—
Forwards								
Malcolm Allen	5 8	10 06	21 3 67	Deiniolen	Apprentice	Watford	39	5
						Aston Villa (loan)	4	—
						Norwich C	35	8
						Millwall	40	14
Chris Armstrong	6 0	11 00	19 6 71	Newcastle	Local	Wrexham	60	13
						Millwall	25	4

MILLWALL

Foundation: Formed in 1885 as Millwall Rovers by employees of Morton & Co, a iam and marmalade factory in West Ferry Road. The founders were predominantly Scotsmen. Their first headquarters was the The Islanders pub in Tooke Street, Millwall. Their first trophy was the East End Cup in 1887.

First Football League game: 28 August, 1920, Division 3, v Bristol R (h) W 2-0 – Lansdale; Fort, Hodge; Voisey (1), Riddell, McAlpine; Waterall, Travers, Broad (1), Sutherland, Dempsey.

Did you know: Millwall was the first Third Division club to have one of their players capped for England. That was their captain Jack Fort right-back against Belgium in May 1921.

Managers (and Secretary-managers)
Fred Kidd 1893–99, Edward Stopher 1899–1900, George Saunders 1900–11, Herbert Lipsham 1911–18, Robert Hunter 1918–33, Bill McCracken 1933–36, Charlie Hewitt 1936–40, Bill Voisey 1940–44, Jack Cock 1944–48, Charlie Hewitt 1948–56, Ron Gray 1956–57, Jimmy Seed 1958–59, Reg Smith 1959–61, Ron Gray 1961–63, Billy Gray 1963–66, Benny Fenton 1966–74, Gordon Jago 1974–77, George Petchey 1978–80, Peter Anderson 1980–82, George Graham 1982–86, John Docherty 1986–90, Bob Pearson 1990, Bruce Rioch 1990–92, Mick McCarthy March 1992–.

Player and Position	Ht	Wt	Date	Birth Place	Source	Clubs	League App	Gls
John Colquhoun	5 7	10 00	14 7 63	Stirling	Grangemouth Inter	Stirling Alb	104	45
						Celtic	32	4
						Hearts	231	54
						Millwall	27	3
Sean Devine	5 10	12 00	6 9 72	Lewisham	Trainee	Millwall	—	—
Tony Dolby	5 10	11 12	16 6 74	Greenwich	Trainee	Millwall	—	—
Mark Falco	6 0	12 00	22 10 60	Hackney	Apprentice	Tottenham H	174	67
						Chelsea (loan)	3	—
						Watford	33	14
						Rangers	14	5
						QPR	87	27
						Millwall	21	4
Jon Goodman	5 11	12 10	2 6 71	Walthamstow	Bromley	Millwall	40	8
John Humphrey	5 11	12 09	2 7 69	Guildford	Leatherhead	Millwall	—	—
						Exeter C (loan)	2	—
John McGinlay	5 9	11 06	8 4 64	Inverness	Elgin C	Shrewsbury T	60	27
						Bury	25	9
						Millwall	27	8
John McGlashan	6 1	12 00	3 6 67	Dundee	Dundee Violet	Montrose	68	11
						Millwall	16	—
Alex Rae	5 9	11 00	30 9 69	Glasgow	Bishopbriggs	Falkirk	83	20
						Millwall	77	21
Paul Stephenson	5 10	10 09	2 1 68	Newcastle	Apprentice	Newcastle U	61	1
						Millwall	93	6
Etienne Verveer	5 11	11 12	22 9 67	Surinam	Chur	Millwall	25	2

Trainees
Beard, Mark; Bedford, Roy D; Chapman, Daniel G; Knight, Glen J; McArthur, Frank P; Middleton, Matthew J; Owen, Daniel; Pitcher, Geoffrey; Smith, Brett R.

**Non-Contract
Kennedy, Mark.

Associated Schoolboys
Coomansingh, Darren; Du Chasse, Colin D; Dunn, Stacy; Edwards, Scott; Felton, Andrew S; Godbold, Marc; Hatcher, Kevin T; Johnson, Steven L; Kelly, Steven; Morey, Robert B; O'Neil, Phil; Smith, David M. J; Sole, Salvatore; Thatcher, Ben D; Watkinson, Russell; Wood, Darren; Woolterton, Toby.

Associated Schoolboys who have accepted the club's offer of a Traineeship/Contract
Francis, Dean; Gordon, Neville; Irving, Paul R; Morgan, Vaughan A.

**Non-Contract Players who are retained must be re-signed before they are eligible to play in League matches.

NEWCASTLE UNITED 1991–92 *Back row (left to right):* David Roche, Lee Makel, Andy Hunt, David Robinson, Robbie Elliott, Anthony Cole, Scott Sloan, Matthew Appleby, Alan Neilson, Tommy Heron, Alan Thompson, John Watson.
Centre row: Tony Galvin (First Team Coach), Colin Suggett (Junior Team Coach), Tommy Wright, John Anderson, Bjorn Kristensen, Lee Clark, Steve Howey, Steve Watson, Darren Bradshaw, Liam O'Brien, Pavel Srnicek, Derek Fazackerley (Reserve Team Coach), Chris Guthrie (Kit Man), Derek Wright (Physiotherapist).
Front row: Ray Ranson, Franz Carr, Kevin Brock, Mick Quinn, Ossie Ardiles (Manager), Kevin Scott, Mark Stimson, Gavin Peacock, John Gallacher, Archie Gourlay.

Division 1   **NEWCASTLE UNITED**

St James' Park, Newcastle-upon-Tyne NE1 4ST. Telephone 091-232 8361. Promotions/Commercial Manager: 091-232 2285. Ticket Office Hotline: 091-2611571. Club Shop: 091-2616357. Club Shop Answering Service: 091-232 4080. Football in the Community Scheme: 091-261 9715. Harveys Restaurant: 091-222 1860. Clubcall: 0898 121190 Clubcall Ticket Line: 0898 121590. Fax No: 091-232 9875

Ground capacity: 30,348.

Record attendance: 68,386 v Chelsea, Division 1, 3 Sept 1930.

Record receipts: £157,153 v Sunderland, Division 2 play-off, semi-final, 16 May 1990.

Pitch measurements: 115yd × 75yd.

President: Stan Seymour.

Chairman: Sir John Hall. *Vice-chairman:* Peter G. Mallinger.

Directors: D. S. Hall, W. F. Shepherd.

Manager: Kevin Keegan. *Assistant Manager:* Terry McDermott. *Coaches:* Derek Fazackerley and Colin Suggett. *Physio:* Derek Wright. *General Manager/Secretary:* R. Cushing.

Assistant Secretary: K. Slater. *Commercial Manager:* G. McDonnell.

Year Formed: 1881. Turned Professional: 1889. Ltd Co.: 1890.

Former Grounds: South Byker, 1881; Chillingham Road, Heaton, 1886 to 1892.

Former Names: Stanley 1881; Newcastle East End 1882–1892.

Club Nickname: 'Magpies'.

Record League Victory: 13-0 v Newport Co, Division 2, 5 October 1946 – Garbutt; Cowell, Graham; Harvey, Brennan, Wright; Milburn (2), Bentley (1), Wayman (4), Shackleton (6), Pearson.

Record Cup Victory: 9-0 v Southport (at Hillsborough) FA Cup, 4th rd, 1 February 1932 – McInroy; Nelson, Fairhurst; McKenzie, Davidson, Weaver (1); Boyd (1), Jimmy Richardson (3), Cape (2), McMenemy (1), Lang (1).

Record Defeat: 0-9 v Burton Wanderers, Division 2, 15 April 1895.

Most League Points (2 for a win): 57, Division 2, 1964–65.

Most League points (3 for a win): 80, Division 2, 1983–84 and Division 2, 1989–90.

Most League Goals: 98, Division 1, 1951–52.

Highest League Scorer in Season: Hughie Gallacher, 36, Division 1, 1926–27.

Most League Goals in Total Aggregate: Jackie Milburn, 178, 1946–57.

Most Capped Player: Alf McMichael, 40, Northern Ireland.

Most League Appearances: Jim Lawrence, 432, 1904–22.

Record Transfer Fee Received: £2,000,000 from Tottenham H for Paul Gascoigne, July 1988.

Record Transfer Fee Paid: £850,000 to Wimbledon for Dave Beasant, June 1988 and £850,000 to Wimbledon for Andy Thorn, August 1988.

Football League Record: 1893 Elected to Division 2; 1898–1934 Division 1; 1934–48 Division 2; 1948–61 Division 1; 1961–65 Division 2; 1965–78 Division 1; 1978–84 Division 2; 1984–89 Division 1; 1989–92 Division 2; 1992– Division 1.

Honours: Football League: Division 1 – Champions 1904–05, 1906–07, 1908–09, 1926–27; Division 2 – Champions 1964–65; Runners-up 1897–98, 1947–48. *FA Cup:* Winners 1910, 1924, 1932, 1951, 1952, 1955; Runners-up 1905, 1906, 1908, 1911, 1974. *Football League Cup:* Runners-up 1975–76. *Texaco Cup:* Winners 1973–74, 1974–75. **European Competitions:** *European Fairs Cup:* 1968–69 (winners), 1969–70, 1970–71 *UEFA Cup:* 1977–78. *Anglo-Italian Cup:* Winners 1973.

Colours: Black and white striped shirts, black shorts, black stockings. **Change colours:** Canary shirts, green shorts, canary stockings.

NEWCASTLE UNITED 1991–92 LEAGUE RECORD

Match No.	Date	Venue	Opponents	Result	H/T Score	Lg. Pos.	Goalscorers	Attendance
1	Aug 18	A	Charlton Ath	L	1-2	0-0	—	Carr	9322
2	24	H	Watford	D	2-2	1-1	19	Hunt, Clark	22,440
3	27	A	Middlesbrough	L	0-3	0-1	—		16,970
4	31	A	Bristol R	W	2-1	1-0	18	O'Brien, Quinn	6334
5	Sep 4	H	Plymouth Arg	D	2-2	0-1	—	Carr, Quinn	19,543
6	7	A	Tranmere R	L	2-3	2-1	19	O'Brien, Clark	11,465
7	14	H	Wolverhampton W	L	1-2	0-0	20	Madden (og)	20,195
8	17	H	Ipswich T	D	1-1	0-1	—	Quinn (pen)	16,336
9	21	A	Millwall	L	1-2	1-1	22	Neilson	9156
10	28	H	Derby Co	D	2-2	0-1	23	Hunt, Quinn	17,581
11	Oct 5	A	Portsmouth	L	1-3	0-2	24	Quinn	10,175
12	12	H	Leicester C	W	2-0	0-0	22	Hunt, Clark	16,966
13	19	A	Oxford U	W	4-3	2-1	21	Hunt, Peacock 3	16,454
14	26	A	Bristol C	D	1-1	1-0	20	Clark	8613
15	Nov 2	A	Swindon T	L	1-2	0-1	21	Peacock	10,731
16	6	H	Cambridge U	D	1-1	0-0	—	Hunt	13,077
17	9	H	Grimsby T	W	2-0	2-0	21	Hunt, Howey	16,959
18	17	A	Sunderland	D	1-1	0-1	—	O'Brien	29,224
19	20	H	Southend U	W	3-2	3-1	—	Peacock 2 (1 pen), Hunt	14,740
20	23	H	Blackburn R	D	0-0	0-0	16		23,639
21	30	A	Barnsley	L	0-3	0-3	17		9648
22	Dec 7	H	Port Vale	D	2-2	1-1	17	Makel, Peacock (pen)	18,162
23	14	A	Brighton & HA	D	2-2	2-1	18	Peacock, Kelly	7658
24	20	A	Plymouth Arg	L	0-2	0-1	—		5048
25	26	H	Middlesbrough	L	0-1	0-0	21		26,563
26	28	H	Bristol R	W	2-1	0-1	18	Brock, Kelly	19,329
27	Jan 1	A	Southend U	L	0-4	0-2	20		9458
28	11	A	Watford	D	2-2	1-2	22	Kelly, Hunt	9811
29	18	H	Charlton Ath	L	3-4	3-1	23	Clark, Hunt, Brock	15,663
30	Feb 1	A	Oxford U	L	2-5	0-1	23	Scott, Peacock (pen)	5872
31	8	H	Bristol C	W	3-0	0-0	22	Kelly 2, O'Brien	29,263
32	15	A	Blackburn R	L	1-3	1-1	22	Kelly	19,511
33	22	H	Barnsley	D	1-1	0-0	22	Kelly	27,670
34	29	A	Port Vale	W	1-0	1-0	19	Watson S	10,321
35	Mar 7	H	Brighton & HA	L	0-1	0-0	21		24,597
36	10	A	Cambridge U	W	2-0	2-0	—	Peacock, Kelly	8254
37	14	H	Swindon T	W	3-1	1-0	18	Kelly, Peacock, Quinn	23,138
38	21	A	Grimsby T	D	1-1	1-1	19	Sheedy	11,613
39	29	H	Sunderland	W	1-0	1-0	—	Kelly	30,306
40	31	A	Wolverhampton W	L	2-6	1-3	—	Quinn, Peacock	14,480
41	Apr 4	H	Tranmere R	L	2-3	1-2	19	Brock 2	21,125
42	11	A	Ipswich T	L	2-3	2-1	19	Peacock 2	20,673
43	18	H	Millwall	L	0-1	0-0	21		23,821
44	20	A	Derby Co	L	1-4	0-2	22	Peacock	21,363
45	25	H	Portsmouth	W	1-0	0-0	20	Kelly	25,989
46	May 2	A	Leicester C	W	2-1	1-0	20	Peacock, Walsh (og)	21,861

Final League Position: 20

GOALSCORERS

League (66): Peacock 16 (3 pens), Kelly 11, Hunt 9, Quinn 7 (1 pen), Clark 5, Brock 4, O'Brien 4, Carr 2, Howey 1, Makel 1, Neilson 1, Scott 1, Sheedy 1, Watson S 1, own goals 2.
Rumbelows Cup (5): Peacock 3, Howey 1, Hunt 1.
FA Cup (2): Hunt 2.

Smicek	Watson S	Elliott	O'Brien	Scott	Bradshaw	Clark	Peacock	Quinn	Carr	Brock	Roche	Robinson	Hunt	Neilson	Makel	Stimson	Howey	Walker	Appleby	Maguire	Wright	Thompson	Bodin	Kelly	Wilson	Ranson	Kilcline	Sheedy	Match No.
1	2†	3	4	5	6	7	8	9	10	11*12	14																		1
1	2	3	4	5	6	7	8	9	10				11																2
1	12	3	4†	5	6	7	8	9	10	14			11*	2															3
1		3	4	5	6	7	8	9	10				11*	2	12														4
1		3	4	5	6	7	8†	9	10				11*	2	12		14												5
1	2	3	4	5	6	7	8	9	10	11*12																			6
1		3	4	5	6	7	2	9	10	8			11																7
1			4	5	6	7	2	9	10*	8	12		11†			3	14												8
1			4	5	6	7	8	9					11	12	2	3		10*											9
1		3	4	5	6†	7	8	9					11	14	12	2		10*											10
1			4	5	6	7	8	9	12				11†	10*	2	3	14												11
1			4	5		7				11†12	9*		10	2		3	14		6										12
			4	5		7	8			11	12		10*	2		3	9		6		1								13
			4	5		7	8*			11	12		10	2†	14	3	9		6		1								14
			4	5	2	7	8			11			10*			3	9		6		1	12							15
			4	5	2*	7	8		10	11			14			3†	9		6		1	12							16
	12		4	5			8		10*	2			11			3	9		6		1	7							17
	12		4	5	2*		8			7			11	14		3	9		6		1	10†							18
	2		4	5	14		8			12	7		10*			3†	9		6		1	11							19
	2	3	4	5			8			12	7		10				9		6		1	11*							20
	2		4	5	14		8			12	7		10			3	9		6†		1	11*							21
			4	5			8			11	2		10	7		3			6		1			9					22
	12		4*	5			8			11	2		10	7		3			6		1			9					23
	12			5	2*		8			11	4		10	7†	14	3			6		1			9					24
	2			5			8		12	11	4*		10	7†	14	3			6		1			9					25
	2			5		7	8			11			10*			3	12		6		1		4	9					26
	2			5		7	8			12	11		10			3			6		1		4	9*					27
	2		4	5		7	8			10	12					3*			6		1	11		9					28
	2		4	5		7	8			11			14	10†		3	12		6		1			9*					29
			4	5		7	8			11			10†	2		3*	12	14	6		1			9					30
	7		4	5			8			11	12					3			6		1			9		2		10*	31
	7		4	5			8		10		12		11			3			6		1			9		2*			32
	2		4				8		10*		12		11	14		3			6		1			9			5	7†	33
	7		4		6		8		12	10*			11	2		3					1			9			5		34
	7*		4		6		8			11	12			2		3					1			9			5	10	35
	2		4		6	7	8			11											1		3	9			5	10	36
	2		4		6	7	8			11							12				1		3*	9			5	10	37
	2				6	7	8			11						3					1			9	12		5	10	38
	2		4		6	7	8			11						3					1			9			5	10	39
	2		4		6	7	8			11						3					1			9			5*	10	40
1	2				6	7	8		12	11						3					1		5	9				10	41
			4		6	7*	8		12	11						3					1		5	9		2†		10	42
			4		6	7*	8		12	11						3					1			9			5	10	43
	2		4		6	7*	8			11						3	12				1			9			5	10	44
			4		6	7	8		12	11*						3					1			9		2	5	10	45
			4		6	7	8		12	11*						3†					1			9		2	5	10	46
13	23	9	40	44	17	25	46	18	12	31	18	—	21	16	5	23	13	2	16	3	33	12	6	25	2	5	12	13	
	+5s				+2s	+4s		+4s	+3s	+4s	+8s	+3s	+6s		+4s	+1s	+8s		+2s			+2s			+1s				

McDonough—Match No. 38(4*) 30(12) 41(4*); Kristensen—Match No. 42(14) 43(2†); Garland—Match No. 43(14) 46(14).

Rumbelows Cup	Second Round	Crewe Alex (a)	4-3
		(h)	1-0
	Third Round	Peterborough U (a)	0-1
FA Cup	Third Round	Bournemouth (a)	0-0
		(h)	2-2; lost 4-3 on penalties

NEWCASTLE UNITED

Goalkeepers

Name					Birthplace		Club		
Pavel Srnicek	6 2	14 9	10	3 68	Ostrava	Banik Ostrava	Newcastle U	20	—
Tommy Wright	6 1	13 05	29	8 63	Belfast	Linfield	Newcastle U	56	—
							Hull C (loan)	6	—

Defenders

Name					Birthplace		Club		
Matthew Appleby	5 10	11 02	16	4 72	Middlesbrough	Trainee	Newcastle U	19	—
Darren Bradshaw*	5 10	11 03	19	3 67	Sheffield	Matlock T	Chesterfield	18	—
							York C	59	3
							Newcastle U	38	—
Tony Cole‡	6 0	11 04	18	9 72	Gateshead	School	Newcastle U	—	—
Robbie Elliott	5 10	10 13	25	12 73	Newcastle	Trainee	Newcastle U	15	—
Brian Kilcline	6 2	12 00	7	5 62	Nottingham	Apprentice	Notts Co	158	9
							Coventry C	173	28
							Oldham Ath	8	—
							Newcastle U	12	—
Bjorn Kristensen	6 1	12 05	10	10 63	Malling	Aarhus	Newcastle U	80	4
Philip Mason	5 6	10 07	3	12 71	Consett	Trainee	Newcastle U	—	—
Alan Neilson	5 11	11 07	26	9 72	Wegburg	Trainee	Newcastle U	19	1
Michael Parkinson‡	5 7	11 04	8	6 71	Sunderland	Trainee	Newcastle U	—	—
Ray Ranson	5 9	11 12	12	6 60	St Helens	Apprentice	Manchester C	183	1
							Birmingham C	137	—
							Newcastle U	80	1
David Roche	5 11	12 01	13	12 70	Newcastle	Trainee	Newcastle U	36	—
Kevin Scott	6 2	11 06	17	12 66	Easington		Newcastle U	164	6
Mark Stimson	5 11	11 00	27	12 67	Plaistow		Tottenham H	2	—
							Leyton Orient (loan)	10	—
							Gillingham (loan)	18	—
							Newcastle U	84	2
Steve Watson	6 0	12 07	1	4 74	North Shields	Trainee	Newcastle U	52	1

Midfield

Name					Birthplace		Club		
Roy Aitken (To St Mirren Aug 1991)	6 0	12 00	24	11 58	Irvine	Celtic BC	Celtic	483	40
							Newcastle U	54	1
Billy Askew‡	5 5	10 10	2	10 59	Lumley	Apprentice	Middlesbrough	12	—
							Blackburn R (loan)	—	—
							Hull C	253	19
							Newcastle U	6	—
							Shrewsbury T (loan)	5	—
Kevin Brock	5 9	10 12	9	9 62	Middleton Stoney	Apprentice	Oxford U	246	26
							QPR	40	2
							Newcastle U	138	13
Lee Clark	5 7	11 07	27	10 72	Wallsend	Trainee	Newcastle U	48	7
Peter Garland	5 9	12 00	20	1 71	Croydon	Trainee	Tottenham H	1	—
							Newcastle U	2	—
Archie Gourlay‡	5 8	10 00	29	6 69	Greenock		Morton	2	—
							Newcastle U	3	—
							Morton (loan)	4	—
Tom Heron‡	5 9	11 01	31	3 73	Wallsend	Trainee	Newcastle U	—	—
Darron McDonough	5 11	12 06	7	11 62	Antwerp	Apprentice	Oldham Ath	183	14
							Luton T	105	5
							Newcastle U	3	—
Lee Makel	5 10	9 10	11	1 73	Sunderland	Trainee	Newcastle U	12	1
Liam O'Brien	6 1	13 03	5	9 64	Dublin	Shamrock R	Manchester U	31	2
							Newcastle U	112	13
Gavin Peacock	5 7	11 00	18	11 67	Kent		QPR	17	1
							Gillingham	70	11
							Bournemouth	56	8
							Newcastle U	73	23
Kevin Sheedy	5 9	10 11	21	10 59	Builth Wells	Apprentice	Hereford U	51	4
							Liverpool	3	—
							Everton	274	67
							Newcastle U	13	1

NEWCASTLE UNITED

Foundation: It stemmed from a newly formed club called Stanley in 1881. In October 1882 they changed their name to Newcastle East End to avoid confusion with Stanley in Co. Durham. Shortly afterwards another club Rosewood merged with them. Newcastle West End had been formed in August 1882 and they played on a ground which is now St. James' Park. In 1889, West End went out of existence after a bad run and the remaining committee men invited East End to move to St. James' Park. They accepted and at a meeting in Bath Lane Hall in 1892, changed their name to Newcastle United.

First Football League game: 2 September, 1893, Division 2, v Royal Arsenal (a) D 2-2 – Ramsay; Jeffery, Miller; Crielly, Graham, McKane; Bowman, Crate (1), Thompson, Sorley (1), Wallace. Graham and not Crate scored according to some reports.

Did you know: United's FA Cup-winning side of 1910 included nine internationals. The side was Lawrence; McCracken, Carr, Veitch, Low, McWilliam, Rutherford, Howie, Shepherd, Higgins, Wilson. At the time only Lawrence and Low had not been capped but they received this honour in the following season.

Managers (and Secretary-managers)
Frank Watt 1895–32 (continued as secretary to 1932), Andy Cunningham 1930–35, Tom Mather 1935–39, Stan Seymour 1939–47 (Hon-manager), George Martin 1947–50, Stan Seymour 1950–54 (Hon-manager), Duggie Livingstone 1954–56, Stan Seymour (Hon-manager 1956–58), Charlie Mitten 1958–61, Norman Smith 1961–62, Joe Harvey 1962–75, Gordon Lee 1975–77, Richard Dinnis 1977, Bill McGarry 1977–80, Arthur Cox 1980–84, Jack Charlton 1984, Willie McFaul 1985–88, Jim Smith 1988–91, Ossie Ardiles 1991–92, Kevin Keegan February 1992–.

Neil Simpson (To Motherwell October 1991)	5 10	11 06	15 11 61	London	Middlefield W	Aberdeen Newcastle U	206 4	19 —
Alan Thompson	6 0	12 05	22 12 73	Newcastle	Trainee	Newcastle U	14	—
John Watson	5 9	10 10	14 4 74	South Shields	Trainee	Newcastle U	1	—
Forwards								
Franz Carr	5 7	10 12	24 9 66	Preston	Apprentice	Blackburn R Nottingham F Sheffield W (loan) West Ham U (loan) Newcastle U	— 131 12 3 15	— 17 — — 2
John Gallacher	5 10	10 08	26 1 69	Glasgow		Falkirk Newcastle U	18 29	5 6
Steve Howey	6 1	10 09	26 10 71	Sunderland	Trainee	Newcastle U	33	1
Andy Hunt	6 0	11 07	9 6 70	Thurrock	Kettering T	Newcastle U	43	11
David Kelly	5 11	10 10	25 11 65	Birmingham	Alvechurch	Walsall West Ham U Leicester C Newcastle U	147 41 66 25	63 7 22 11
Alan Lamb‡	5 10	11 12	30 10 70	Gateshead		Nottingham F Hereford U (loan) Hartlepool U Newcastle U	— 10 14 —	— 2 — —
Mick Quinn	5 9	13 00	2 5 62	Liverpool	Apprentice	Derby Co Wigan Ath Stockport Co Oldham Ath Portsmouth Newcastle U	— 69 63 80 121 110	— 19 39 34 54 57
Scott Sloan (To Falkirk Oct 1991)	5 10	11 06	14 12 67	Wallsend	Ponteland	Berwick R Newcastle U	61 16	20 1

Trainees
Alderson, Richard; Anderson, Daniel L; Armstrong, Alun; Christie, Gary S; Cornish, Darren; Dinning, Tony; Finley, Robin; Geddes, Paul A; Greenwood, Thomas P; Kirkham, Peter J; Lewis, Stephen; Milner, John F; Morton, Graeme F; Walton, Simon S.

Associated Schoolboys
Aiston, Sam J; Baldwin, Shaun T; McAlindon, Gareth E; McGivern, Joseph C; Pepper, Graham A; Pouton, Alan; Rushworth, John.

Associated Schoolboys who have accepted the club's offer of a Traineeship/Contract
Appleby, Richard D; Murray, Nathan A; Stokoe, Graham L.

NORTHAMPTON TOWN 1991–92 *Back row (left to right):* Michael Bell, David Scope, Sean Parker, Jason Burnham, Greg Campbell, Kevin Wilkin, Tony Adcock, Paul Wilson.
Centre row: Dennis Casey (Physiotherapist), David Johnson, Steve Terry, Terry Angus, Peter Gleasure, Steve Brown, Darren Wood, Irvin Gernon, Billy Best (Youth Team Manager).
Front row: Theo Foley (Manager), Trevor Quow, Stuart Beavon, Phil Chard, Adrian Thorpe, Bobby Barnes, Joe Kiernan (Assistant Manager). (Photo by Pete Norton)

Division 3   **NORTHAMPTON TOWN**

County Ground, Abington Avenue, Northampton NN1 4PS. Telephone Northampton (0604) 234100. Commercial Dept: (0604) 234100. Information Line: 0898 700275.

Ground capacity: 11,907.

Record attendance: 24,523 v Fulham, Division 1, 23 April 1966.

Record receipts: £47,292.40 v Coventry C, FA Cup 3rd rd, 6 January 1990.

Pitch measurements: 112yd × 75yd.

Chairman: B. J. Ward.

Company Secretary: Philip Mark Hough.

Manager: Phil Chard.

Assistant Manager.

Physio.

Commercial Manager: Philip Mark Hough.

Youth team coach.

Year Formed: 1897. Turned Professional: 1901. Ltd Co.: 1901.

Club Nickname: 'The Cobblers'.

Record League Victory: 10-0 v Walsall, Division 3 (S), 5 November 1927 – Hammond; Watson, Jeffs; Allen, Brett, Odell; Daley, Smith (3), Loasby (3), Hoten (1), Wells (3).

Record Cup Victory: 10-0 v Sutton T, Prem. rd 7 December 1907 – Cooch; Prennan, Lloyd Davies, Tirrell (1), McCartney, Hickleton, Badenock (3), Platt (3), Lowe (1), Chapman (2), McDiarmid.

Record Defeat: 0-11 v Southampton, Southern League, 28 December 1901.

Most League Points (2 for a win): 68, Division 4, 1975–76.

Most League points (3 for a win): 99, Division 4, 1986–87.

Most League Goals: 109, Division 3, 1962–63 and Division 3 (S), 1952–53.

Highest League Scorer in Season: Cliff Holton, 36, Division 3, 1961–62.

Most League Goals in Total Aggregate: Jack English, 135, 1947–60.

Most Capped Player: E. Lloyd Davies, 12 (16), Wales.

Most League Appearances: Tommy Fowler, 521, 1946–61.

Record Transfer Fee Received: £265,000 from Watford for Richard Hill, July 1987.

Record Transfer Fee Paid: £85,000 to Manchester C for Tony Adcock, January 1988.

Football League Record: 1920 Original Member of Division 3; 1921 Division 3 (S); 1958–61 Division 4; 1961–63 Division 3; 1963–65 Division 2; 1965–66 Division 1; 1966–67 Division 2; 1967–69 Division 3; 1969–76 Division 4; 1976–77 Division 3; 1977–87 Division 4; 1987–90 Division 3; 1990–92 Division 4; 1992– Division 3.

Honours: Football League: Division 1 best season: 21st, 1965–66; Division 2 – Runners-up 1964–65; Division 3 – Champions 1962–63; Division 3 (S) – Runners-up 1927–28, 1949–50; Division 4 – Champions 1986–87; Runners-up 1975–76. *FA Cup:* best season: 5th rd, 1933–34, 1949–50, 1969–70. *Football League Cup:* best season: 5th rd, 1964–65, 1966–67.

Colours: White shirts, claret sleeves, claret shorts, claret stockings.
Change colours: Yellow shirts, claret trim, claret shorts, claret stockings.

NORTHAMPTON TOWN 1991–92 LEAGUE RECORD

Match No.	Date		Venue	Opponents	Result		H/T Score	Lg. Pos.	Goalscorers	Atten-dance
1	Aug	17	A	Halifax T	W	1-0	0-0	—	Chard	1834
2		30	A	Wrexham	D	2-2	1-1	—	Angus, Thorpe	2196
3	Sep	3	H	Doncaster R	W	3-1	1-0	—	Ormsby (og), Thorpe	2702
4		7	H	Barnet	D	1-1	1-0	9	Barnes	4339
5		14	A	Rochdale	L	0-1	0-0	10		2631
6		17	A	Crewe Alex	D	1-1	1-1	—	Farrell (pen)	3597
7		21	H	Carlisle U	D	2-2	1-1	11	Wilson, Barnes	2656
8	Oct	5	H	Blackpool	D	1-1	0-1	13	Barnes	3355
9		12	A	Scarborough	L	1-2	0-0	14	Adcock	2023
10		15	H	Chesterfield	D	1-1	0-1	—	Adcock	2426
11		19	H	Scunthorpe U	L	0-1	0-1	15		2575
12		26	A	Gillingham	L	1-3	0-0	15	Campbell	2544
13	Nov	2	A	Rotherham U	L	0-1	0-0	18		3146
14		5	H	Mansfield T	L	1-2	1-1	—	Adcock	2181
15		9	H	Lincoln C	W	1-0	0-0	17	Adcock	2575
16		23	A	Cardiff C	L	2-3	1-1	19	Burnham 2	2922
17		30	H	Burnley	L	1-2	0-1	20	Campbell	4020
18	Dec	7	H	Scarborough	W	3-2	0-0	—	Barnes, Adcock, Bell	1815
19		21	A	Chesterfield	W	2-1	0-1	16	McClean, Terry	3048
20		26	H	Halifax T	W	4-0	4-0	14	Adcock 2, Chard, Barnes	3147
21		28	H	Wrexham	D	1-1	1-0	14	Angus	3209
22	Jan	1	A	Doncaster R	W	3-0	1-0	13	Chard, Campbell, Scope	1973
23		11	H	York C	D	2-2	2-2	13	Terry, Barnes	3355
24		18	A	Maidstone U	D	1-1	0-0	12	Terry	1364
25		28	A	Walsall	W	2-1	2-1	—	Beavon 2	2399
26	Feb	8	H	Gillingham	D	0-0	0-0	10		3007
27		11	A	Burnley	L	0-5	0-1	—		8825
28		15	A	Walsall	L	0-1	0-1	11		2480
29		22	A	York C	D	0-0	0-0	12		2044
30		29	H	Hereford U	L	0-1	0-1	13		2428
31	Mar	3	H	Maidstone U	W	1-0	0-0	—	Brown	1677
32		10	A	Mansfield T	L	0-2	0-1	—		2852
33		14	H	Rotherham U	L	1-2	0-2	12	Brown	2561
34		21	A	Lincoln C	W	2-1	2-0	11	Bell, Beavon (pen)	2486
35		28	H	Cardiff C	D	0-0	0-0	15		2678
36		31	H	Rochdale	D	2-2	1-1	—	McClean 2	2010
37	Apr	4	A	Barnet	L	0-3	0-1	15		2816
38		11	H	Crewe Alex	L	0-1	0-0	16		3300
39		14	A	Scunthorpe U	L	0-3	0-2	—		2286
40		18	A	Carlisle U	L	1-2	0-1	17	Benton	1935
41		25	A	Blackpool	L	0-1	0-0	17		5915
42	·	28	A	Hereford U	W	2-1	2-0	—	Bell 2	1297

Final League Position: 16

GOALSCORERS

League (46): Adcock 7, Barnes 6, Bell 4, Beavon 3 (1 pen), Brown 3, Campbell 3, Chard 3, McClean 3, Terry 3, Angus 2, Burnham 2, Thorpe 2, Benton 1, Farrell 1 (1 pen), Scope 1, Wilson 1, own goals 1.
Rumbelows Cup (2): Barnes 2.
FA Cup (2): Adcock 1, Chard 1.

Beresford	Chard	Wilson	Terry	Angus	Brown	Burnham	Quow	Adcock	Bell	Gernon	Campbell	Barnes	Thorpe	Johnson	Farrell	Scope	Beavon	Wood	McClean	Richardson	Kiernan	Parker	Edwards	Colkin	Parsons	Aldridge	Bulzis	Benton	Match No.
1	2	3	4	5	6	7	8	9	10*	11	12																		1
1	2		4	5	6	7	8		3	9	10	11																	2
1	2	9	4	5	6	7	8		3*		10	11	12																3
1	2	3	4	5	6	7	8	12	9		10	11*																	4
1	2	3	4	5	6	7†	8	12	9		10	11*	14																5
1	2	3	4	5	6	12	8		9		10	11†	14*	7															6
1	2	3	4	5	6	12	8*	11†	9		10			7	14														7
1	2	3	4		6	5	8	12	9		10		14	7*	11†														8
1	2	3	4	5	6		7	11*	9	12	10						8												9
1	2	12		5	6	3		11	9		10						7*		8										10
1	2	3	4	5	6		8*	11	9		10					12	7												11
1	2	3*	4	5	6†	14	8	11	12	9	10						7												12
1	2	3	4*	5	12	14	8	11		9	10						7	6†											13
1	2	3	4*	5	12	6	8	11	14	9	10†						7												14
1	2	3		5	4	6	8	11		9		12	7*	10															15
	2*			5	14		6	12	11	10†	4	7			3		8		9	1									16
	2	14		5			6	12	11	10	4*	7			3		8		9†	1									17
	2	3		5	12		6*	4	11	10		14	8				7		9†	1									18
	2		3	5	10†		6	4	11*		12	8	14				7		9	1									19
	2		3	5	10		6	4	11		12	8					7		9*	1									20
	2		3	5	10		6*	4	11		12	8					7		9	1									21
	2*		3	5			6	4	12		11	8	10	14			7		9†	1									22
	2		3	5	10		6	4	9*		11	8	12				7			1									23
	2*		3	5	10		6	4†		14	12	8	9				7		11	1									24
			3	5	10		6	4		2	12	8	9*				7		11	1									25
			3	5			6	4	8	2	9		10				7		11	1									26
			3	5			6	4*	8	2	9		10				7		11	1	12								27
			3	5			6		8†	2							7		11	1	12	4*	9	14					28
			3	5	10		6		12	2		9	4				7		11	1			8*						29
			3	5	10		6	4†	8*		11		9				7			1	12	14			2				30
			3	5	10		6		8		11		9				7			1		4			2				31
			3	5	10		6		8	9							7		11	1		4			2				32
				5	10		6	14	8†	9	12				3*		7		11	1		4			2				33
			3	5	10		6		8	9	12						7		11	1		4*			2				34
			3	5	10		6		8	9			12				7		11	1		4*			2				35
			3	5	10		6		8	9		4					7		11	1					2				36
	11†		3	5	10		6		8								7			1	9	4			2*	12	14		37
	11		3	5	10		6		8								7			1	9				2	12		4*	38
			3		10		6		8								7			1	9	4*	5	2	14	11†	12		39
	11		3		10†		6		8								7			1	9	5*		2	14	12		4	40
	11*		3				5		8								7			1	9	4			2	10		6	41
	11		3				5		8								7			1	9	4			2	10		6	42
15	29	14	37	37	31	36	24	14	23	27	12	18	11	9	4	1	33	1	19	27	6	5	7	2	13	2	1	4	
		+2s				+4s	+4s	+3s				+7s	+1s	+10s	+1s	+6s			+4s			+3s	+1s		+1s	+3s	+3s	+1s	

Adams—Match No. 41(12).

Rumbelows Cup	First Round	Leyton Orient (a)		0-5
		(h)		2-0
FA Cup	First Round	Crawley (a)		2-4

NORTHAMPTON TOWN

Player and Position	Ht	Wt	Birth Date	Birth Place	Source	Clubs	League App	League Gls
Goalkeepers								
Peter Gleasure†	5 11	12 13	8 10 60	Luton	Apprentice	Millwall	55	—
						Northampton T (loan)	11	—
						Northampton T	333	—
						Gillingham (loan)	3	—
Barry Richardson	6 0	12 00	5 8 69	Willington Key	Trainee	Sunderland	—	—
						Scunthorpe U	—	—
						Scarborough	30	—
						Northampton T	27	—
Defenders								
Terry Angus			14 1 66	Coventry	VS Rugby	Northampton T	79	4
James Benton§			9 4 75	Wexford	Trainee	Northampton T	5	1
Lee Colkin§			15 7 74	Nuneaton	Trainee	Northampton T	3	—
Irving Gernon‡	6 2	12 01	30 12 62	Birmingham	Apprentice	Ipswich T	76	—
						Northampton T (loan)	9	—
						Gillingham	35	1
						Reading	25	—
						Northampton T	48	1
David Johnson‡	5 10	11 02	10 3 67	Northampton	Irthling-borough D	Northampton T	47	—
Sean Parker			23 8 73	Newcastle	Trainee	Northampton T	6	—
Mark Parsons§			24 2 75	Luton	Trainee	Northampton T	13	—
Steve Terry	6 1	13 03	14 6 62	Clapton	Apprentice	Watford	160	14
						Hull C	62	4
						Northampton T	100	11
Darren Wood‡	6 1	12 08	22 10 68	Derby	Trainee	Chesterfield	67	3
						Reading	32	2
						Northampton T	4	1
Midfield								
Craig Adams§			9 11 74	Northampton	Trainee	Northampton T	1	—
Stuart Beavon	5 6	10 04	30 11 58	Wolverhampton	Apprentice	Tottenham H	4	—
						Notts Co (loan)	6	—
						Reading	396	44
						Northampton T	74	13
Michael Bell			15 11 71	Newcastle	Trainee	Northampton T	64	4
Riccardo Bulzis§			22 11 74	Bedford	Trainee	Northampton T	4	—
Philip Chard	5 8	11 03	16 10 60	Corby	Nottingham F	Peterborough U	172	18
						Northampton T	115	27
						Wolverhampton W	34	5
						Northampton T	101	12
Daniel Kiernan§			16 12 73	Northampton	Trainee	Northampton T	9	—
Trevor Quow‡	5 7	10 12	28 9 60	Peterborough	Apprentice	Peterborough U	203	17
						Gillingham	79	3
						Northampton T	88	2
Forwards								
Martin Aldridge§			6 12 74	Northampton	Trainee	Northampton T	5	—
Steve Brown	5 9	10 12	6 7 66	Northampton	Irthling-borough D	Northampton T	96	6
Jason Burnham			8 5 73	Mansfield	Trainee	Northampton T	40	2
Greg Campbell‡	5 11	11 05	13 7 65	Portsmouth	Apprentice	West Ham U	5	—
						Brighton & HA (loan)	2	—
						Plymouth Arg	35	6
						Northampton T	47	7

NORTHAMPTON TOWN

Foundation: Formed in 1897 by school teachers connected with the Northampton and District Elementary Schools' Association, they survived a financial crisis at the end of their first year when they were £675 in the red and became members of the Midland League – a fast move indeed for a new club. They achieved Southern League membership in 1901.

First Football League game: 28 August, 1920, Division 3, v Grimsby T (a) L 0-2 – Thorpe; Sproston, Hewison; Jobey, Tomkins, Pease; Whitworth, Lockett, Thomas, Freeman, MacKechnie.

Did you know: In the next home game after scoring a club League record of five against Crystal Palace in 1928–29 Ralph Hoten scored four in a 6-1 win over Torquay United.

Managers (and Secretary-managers)
Arthur Jones 1897–1907*, Herbert Chapman 1907–12, Walter Bull 1912–13, Fred Lessons 1913–19, Bob Hewison 1920–25, Jack Tresadern 1925–30, Jack English 1931–35, Syd Puddefoot 1935–37, Warney Cresswell 1937–39, Tom Smith 1939–49, Bob Dennison 1949–54, Dave Smith 1954–59, David Bowen 1959–67, Tony Marchi 1967–68, Ron Flowers 1968–69, Dave Bowen 1969–72 (continued as GM and secretary to 1985 when joined the board), Billy Baxter 1972–73, Bill Dodgin Jnr 1973–76, Pat Crerand 1976–77, Bill Dodgin Jnr 1977, John Petts 1977–78, Mike Keen 1978–79, Clive Walker 1979–80, Bill Dodgin Jnr 1980–82, Clive Walker 1982–84, Tony Barton 1984–85, Graham Carr 1985–90, Theo Foley 1990–92, Phil Chard April 1992– .

Player and Position	Ht	Wt	Birth Date	Birth Place	Source	Clubs	League App	Gls
Dean Edwards†	5 11	11 07	25 2 62	Wolverhampton	Apprentice Telford U	Shrewsbury T	13	1
						Wolverhampton W	31	9
						Exeter C	54	17
						Torquay U	109	26
						Stockport Co	—	—
						Torquay U	7	—
						Exeter C	4	—
						Northampton T	7	—
Christian McClean‡	6 4	14 00	17 10 63	Colchester	Clacton	Bristol R	51	6
						Swansea C	4	—
						Northampton T	19	3
David Scope‡	5 8	10 12	10 5 67	Newcastle	Blyth Sp	Northampton T	19	1
Adrian Thorpe‡	5 6	11 00	20 11 63	Chesterfield	Heanor T	Bradford C	17	1
						Tranmere R (loan)	5	3
						Notts Co	59	9
						Walsall	27	1
						Northampton T	52	6
Kevin Wilkin‡			1 10 67	Cambridge	Cambridge C	Northampton T	9	2

Trainees
Adams, Craig J; Aldridge, Martin J; Benton, James; Bulzis, Riccardo; Colkin, Lee; Kiernan, Daniel J; Lamb, Paul D; Parsons, Mark C; Reed, Nigel J; Underwood, Simon S; Waring, James M.

Associated Schoolboys
Bingham, Matthew J; Knight, Stuart A; Pigg, Darren W; Stancombe, Simon R; Tero, Mark J; Willis, Ian.

NORWICH CITY 1991–92 *Back row (left to right):* Robert Fleck, David Phillips, Daryl Sutch, John Polston, Dale Gordon, Ian Culverhouse, Mark Bowen.
Centre row: Mike Walker (Reserve Team Manager), Chris Sutton, Tim Sheppard (Physiotherapist), Tim Wooding, Darren Beckford, Colin Woodthorpe, Mark Walton, Tim Sherwood, Bryan Gunn, Rob Newman, Ian Butterworth, Ruel Fox, Keith Webb (Youth Team Manager), Ian Crook, David Williams (Assistant Manager).
Front row: Jason Minett, Jeremy Goss, Henrik Mortensen, Lee Power, Dave Stringer (Manager), Steve Ball, Paul Blades, David Smith, Robert Ullathorne.

FA Premier

NORWICH CITY

Carrow Road, Norwich NR1 1JE. Telephone Norwich (0603) 612131. Box Office: (0603) 761661. Clubcall: 0898 121144. Match Information Line: 0898 121514.

Ground capacity: 20,319.

Record attendance: 43,984 v Leicester C, FA Cup 6th rd, 30 March 1963.

Record receipts: £173,570 v Nottingham F, FA Cup 6th rd, 9 March 1991.

Pitch measurements: 114yd × 74yd.

President: G. C. Watling.

Chairman: Robert T. Chase JP.

NORWICH CITY FC

Vice-chairman: J. A. Jones.

Directors: B. W. Lockwood, G. A. Paterson, A. Scholes DMS, IPFA, D. Stringer.

Manager: Mike Walker.

Assistant Manager: John Deehan.

Reserve Team Coach: John Faulkner. *Commercial Manager:* Ray Cossey. *Physio:* Tim Sheppard MCSP, SRP.

Secretary: A. R. W. Neville.

Year Formed: 1902. Turned Professional: 1905. Ltd Co.: 1905.

Former Grounds: 1902, Newmarket Road; 1908–35, The Nest, Rosary Road.

Club Nickname: 'The Canaries'.

Record League Victory: 10-2 v Coventry C, Division 3 (S), 15 March 1930 – Jarvie; Hannah, Graham; Brown, O'Brien, Lochhead (1); Porter (1), Anderson, Hunt (5), Scott (2), Slicer (1).

Record Cup Victory: 8-0 v Sutton U, FA Cup, 4th rd, 28 January 1989 – Gunn; Culverhouse, Bowen, Butterworth, Linighan, Townsend (Crook), Gordon, Fleck (3), Allen (4), Phelan, Putney (1).

Record Defeat: 2-10 v Swindon T, Southern League, 5 September 1908.

Most League Points (2 for a win): 64, Division 3 (S), 1950–51.

Most League points (3 for a win): 84, Division 2, 1985–86.

Most League Goals: 99, Division 3 (S), 1952–53.

Highest League Scorer in Season: Ralph Hunt, 31. Division 3 (S), 1955–56.

Most League Goals in Total Aggregate: Johnny Gavin, 122, 1945–54, 1955–58.

Most Capped Player: Martin O'Neill, 18 (64), Northern Ireland.

Most League Appearances: Ron Ashman, 592, 1947–64.

Record Transfer Fee Received: £1,200,000 from Arsenal for Andy Linighan, July 1990 and from Chelsea for Andy Townsend, July 1990.

Record Transfer Fee Paid: £925,000 to Port Vale for Darren Beckford, June 1991.

Football League Record: 1920 Original Member of Division 3; 1921 Division 3 (S): 1934–39 Division 2; 1946–58 Division 3 (S); 1958–60 Division 3; 1960–72 Division 2; 1972–74 Division 1; 1974–75 Division 2; 1975–81 Division 1; 1981–82 Division 2; 1982–85 Division 1; 1985–86 Division 2; 1986–92 Division 1; 1992– FA Premier League.

Honours: Football League: Division 1 best season: 4th, 1988–89; Division 2 – Champions 1971–72, 1985–86. Division 3 (S) – Champions 1933–34; Division 3 – Runners-up 1959–60. *FA Cup:* Semi-finals 1959, 1989, 1992. *Football League Cup:* Winners 1962, 1985; Runners-up 1973, 1975.

Colours: Yellow shirts green trim, green shorts yellow trim, yellow stockings. **Change colours:** All white with blackcurrant trim.

NORWICH CITY 1991–92 LEAGUE RECORD

Match No.	Date		Venue	Opponents	Result		H/T Score	Lg. Pos.	Goalscorers	Atten-dance
1	Aug	17	H	Sheffield U	D	2-2	0-1	—	Fleck 2	16,380
2		21	A	QPR	W	2-0	1-0	—	Gordon, Newman	10,726
3		24	A	Oldham Ath	D	2-2	1-2	5	Crook, Newman	13,548
4		28	H	Manchester C	D	0-0	0-0	—		15,376
5		31	H	Tottenham H	L	0-1	0-1	15		19,460
6	Sep	3	A	Everton	D	1-1	0-0	—	Phillips	19,197
7		7	A	Manchester U	L	0-3	0-3	16		44,946
8		14	H	West Ham U	W	2-1	2-1	14	Fox, Gordon	15,348
9		18	H	Sheffield W	W	1-0	1-0	—	Fleck (pen)	12,503
10		21	A	Notts Co	D	2-2	0-1	10	Ullathorne, Bowen (pen)	9488
11		28	H	Leeds U	D	2-2	0-0	10	Gordon 2	15,828
12	Oct	5	A	Wimbledon	L	1-3	0-1	15	Beckford	3531
13		19	A	Southampton	D	0-0	0-0	15		12,516
14		26	H	Luton T	W	1-0	1-0	11	Newman	10,541
15	Nov	2	A	Nottingham F	D	0-0	0-0	11		13,014
16		16	A	Chelsea	W	3-0	2-0	8	Fleck 2, Bowen	15,755
17		23	H	Coventry C	W	3-2	0-1	8	Bowen, Fleck, Sutton	12,056
18		30	A	Liverpool	L	1-2	1-2	8	Beckford	34,881
19	Dec	7	A	Crystal Palace	D	3-3	1-1	9	Thorn (og), Beckford, Newman	12,667
20		21	H	QPR	L	0-1	0-0	11		11,436
21		26	A	Manchester C	L	1-2	1-2	13	Newman	28,164
22		28	A	Tottenham H	L	0-3	0-1	14		27,969
23	Jan	1	A	Aston Villa	W	2-1	0-0	12	Fleck (pen), Ullathorne	15,318
24		11	H	Oldham Ath	L	1-2	1-1	14	Beckford	10,986
25		18	A	Sheffield U	L	0-1	0-0	14		17,549
26	Feb	1	H	Southampton	W	2-1	0-0	12	Ullathorne, Fleck	10,660
27		8	A	Luton T	L	0-2	0-0	16		8554
28		11	A	Arsenal	D	1-1	0-0	—	Fox	22,352
29		22	H	Liverpool	W	3-0	0-0	10	Woodthorpe, Fleck 2	20,411
30		29	A	Crystal Palace	W	4-3	4-2	10	Sutton, Newman, Polston, Goss	14,201
31	Mar	4	A	Coventry C	D	0-0	0-0	—		8549
32		11	H	Chelsea	L	0-1	0-0	—		13,413
33		14	A	Nottingham F	L	0-2	0-2	14		20,721
34		21	H	Everton	W	4-3	1-2	13	Beckford 3, Newman	11,900
35		28	A	Aston Villa	L	0-1	0-0	14		16,985
36		31	A	Manchester U	L	1-3	0-1	—	Power	17,489
37	Apr	8	H	Arsenal	L	1-3	0-1	—	Butterworth	12,971
38		11	A	West Ham U	L	0-4	0-2	17		16,896
39		18	H	Notts Co	L	0-1	0-0	18		12,100
40		20	A	Sheffield W	L	0-2	0-2	18		27,362
41		25	H	Wimbledon	D	1-1	1-0	18	Fleck	11,061
42	May	2	A	Leeds U	L	0-1	0-1	18		32,673

Final League Position: 18

GOALSCORERS
League (47): Fleck 11 (2 pens), Beckford 7, Newman 7, Gordon 4, Bowen 3 (1 pen), Ullathorne 3, Fox 2, Sutton 2, Butterworth 1, Crook 1, Goss 1, Phillips 1, Polston 1, Power 1, Woodthorpe 1, own goals 1.
Rumbelows Cup (12): Fleck 6, Beckford 3, Fox 1, Gordon 1, Newman 1.
FA Cup (8): Sutton 3, Fleck 2 (1 pen), Bowen 1, Newman 1, Phillips 1.

Gunn	Culverhouse	Bowen	Butterworth	Blades	Crook	Gordon	Fleck	Newman	Beckford	Phillips	Fox	Goss	Ullathorne	Ball	Sherwood	Sutton	Polston	Woodthorpe	Sutch	Walton	Power	Smith	Johnson	Match No.
1	2	3	4	5	6	7	8	9	10*	11	12													1
1	2	3	4	5	6	7	8	9	10*	11	12													2
1	2	3	4	5	6	7	8	9	10	11														3
1	2	3	4	5	6	7	8	9	10*	11	12													4
1	2*	3	4	5	6	7	8	9	10	11	12													5
1	2	3	4	5	6	7	8	9	10*	11	12													6
1	2	3	4	5	6	7	8	9	10*	11†	12	14												7
1	2	3	4	5	6	7	8	9				10		12		11*								8
1		3	4	5	6	7	8	9				2	10	12		11*								9
1		3	4	5	6	7*	8	9			12	2	10			11†	14							10
1		3	4	5	6	7	8	9				2	10			11								11
1		3	4	5	6*	7	8	9				2	10	12		11								12
1		3	4	5		7*	8	9			12	2	10	6		11								13
1		3	4	5		7	8	9			12	2	10	6		11*								14
1		3	4	5		7	8	9		11		2	10	6										15
1		3	4	5			8	9		11		2	6		7	10								16
1		3	4	5	12		8	9		11†		2	6		7	10*	14							17
1		3	4*	5			8	9		11		2	6		7	10	12							18
1		3		5			8	9		11		2	12	6	7*	10	4							19
1		3		5			8	9		11		2	12	6	7	10*	4							20
1		3		5			8	9		11*		2	12	6	7†	10	4	14						21
1		3		5			8	9			12	2	11	6		10	4	7*						22
1		3		5			8	9			10	2	7	6	11		4*	12						23
1		3		5	6		8	9			10*	2	7		11		4	12						24
1*		3			10		8	9			12	6	11		4	5	2	7						25
		3			10*		8	9		7		2	12	6	11	4	5			1				26
	2	3	4		10		8	9*		11		7	6				5	12		1				27
	2		4				8	9		11		7	6			10	5	3		1				28
	2		4				8	9		11		7	6			10	5	3		1				29
	2		4				8	9		11		7	6			10	5	3		1				30
	2		4		12			9		11		7*	6		14	10†	5	3	8	1				31
	2		4				8	9		11		7	6			12	5	3	10*	1				32
	2	12	4				8	9		11*		7	6			10	5	3		1				33
	2	3†	4				8	9		11		7	6			10	5*	12	14	1				34
	2	3	4					9		11		7	6			10	5		8	1				35
	2	3	4				8*	9		11†		7	6			10	14	5		1	12			36
	2	3	4					9	10			7	6		11	12	5		8*	1				37
	2		4					9	10			7	6			12†	5	3	14	1	8*		11	38
	2		4				8	9	10			7	6		11		5	3		1				39
	2		4				8	9	10*			7	6				5	3		1	12		11	40
	2	3	4				8	9	10*	11		7	6				5	12		1				41
	2		4				8	9		11		7	6			12	5	3*		1			10	42
25	21	35	31	26	20	15	35	41	25	34	27	29	20	—	7	16	16	12	5	17	2	1	2	
	+1s			+1s		+1s				+5s		+10s	4s		+2s	+5s	3s	3s	4s		+2s			

Rumbelows Cup	Second Round	Charlton Ath (a)	2-0	
		(h)	3-0	
	Third Round	Brentford (h)	4-1	
	Fourth Round	West Ham U (h)	2-1	
	Fifth Round	Tottenham H (a)	1-2	
FA Cup	Third Round	Barnsley (h)	1-0	
	Fourth Round	Millwall (h)	2-1	
	Fifth Round	Notts Co (h)	3-0	
	Sixth Round	Southampton (a)	0-0	
		(h)	2-1	
	Semi-Final	Sunderland (at Hillsborough)	0-1	

NORWICH CITY

Player and Position	Ht	Wt	Birth Date	Birth Place	Source	Clubs	League App	Gls
Goalkeepers								
Bryan Gunn	6 2	13 13	22 12 63	Thurso	Invergordon BC	Aberdeen	15	—
						Norwich C	200	—
Mark Walton	6 2	13 13	1 6 69	Merthyr	Swansea C	Luton T	—	—
						Colchester U	40	—
						Norwich C	22	—
Defenders								
Paul Blades	6 0	10 12	5 1 65	Peterborough	Apprentice	Derby Co	166	1
						Norwich C	47	—
Mark Bowen	5 8	11 13	7 12 63	Neath	Apprentice	Tottenham H	17	2
						Norwich C	170	14
Ian Butterworth	6 1	12 10	25 1 64	Nantwich	Apprentice	Coventry C	90	—
						Nottingham F	27	—
						Norwich C	184	3
Ian Culverhouse	5 10	11 02	22 9 64	B Stortford	Apprentice	Tottenham H	2	—
						Norwich C	213	—
Rob Newman	6 2	12 00	13 12 63	London	Apprentice	Bristol C	394	52
						Norwich C	41	7
Adrian Pennock	6 0	12 04	27 3 71	Ipswich	Trainee	Norwich C	1	—
John Polston	5 11	11 00	10 6 68	London	Apprentice	Tottenham H	24	1
						Norwich C	46	5
Robert Ullathorne	5 7	10 07	11 10 71	Wakefield	Trainee	Norwich C	22	3
Tim Wooding	6 0	12 00	5 7 73	Wellingborough	Trainee	Norwich C	—	—
Colin Woodthorpe	5 11	11 08	13 1 69	Ellesmere Pt	Apprentice	Chester C	155	6
						Norwich C	16	1
Midfield								
Steve Ball*	6 0	12 01	2 9 69	Colchester	Trainee	Arsenal	—	—
						Colchester U	4	—
						Norwich C	2	—
Ian Crook	5 8	10 06	18 1 63	Romford	Apprentice	Tottenham H	20	1
						Norwich C	170	11
Dale Gordon (To Rangers November 1991)	5 10	11 08	9 1 67	Gt Yarmouth	Apprentice	Norwich C	206	31
Jeremy Goss	5 9	10 09	11 5 65	Cyprus	Amateur	Norwich C	88	4
Andrew Johnson	5 11	11 06	2 5 74	Bristol	Trainee	Norwich C	2	—
Jason Minett	5 10	10 02	2 8 71	Peterborough	Trainee	Norwich C	2	—
David Phillips	5 10	11 02	29 7 63	Wegberg	Apprentice	Plymouth Arg	73	15
						Manchester C	81	13
						Coventry C	100	8
						Norwich C	110	9
David Smith	5 9	11 12	26 12 70	Liverpool	Trainee	Norwich C	5	—
Daryl Sutch	6 0	12 00	11 9 71	Lowestoft	Trainee	Norwich C	13	—
Forwards								
Darren Beckford	6 1	11 01	12 5 67	Manchester	Apprentice	Manchester C	11	—
						Bury (loan)	12	5
						Port Vale (loan)	11	4
						Port Vale	167	68
						Norwich C	30	7
Dean Coney‡	6 0	13 04	18 9 63	Dagenham	Apprentice	Fulham	211	56
						QPR	48	7
						Norwich C	17	1
Robert Fleck	5 8	11 08	11 8 65	Glasgow	Possil Y M	Partick Th	2	1
						Rangers	85	29
						Norwich C	143	40
Ruel Fox	5 6	10 00	14 1 68	Ipswich	Apprentice	Norwich C	113	11

NORWICH CITY

Foundation: Formed in 1902, largely through the initiative of two local schoolmasters who called a meeting at the Criterion Cafe, they were shocked by an FA Commission which in 1904 declared the club professional and ejected them from the FA Amateur Cup. However, this only served to strengthen their determination. New officials were appointed and a professional club established at a meeting in the Agricultural Hall in March 1905.

First Football League game: 28 August, 1920, Division 3, v Plymouth A (a) D 1-1 – Skermer; Gray, Gadsden; Wilkinson, Addy, Martin; Laxton, Kidger, Parker, Whitham (1), Dobson.

Did you know: When Norwich beat Brighton 18-0 in the wartime South Regional League on Christmas Day 1940, ten of the goals were scored in the first half with top scorer Fred Chadwick ("guesting" from Ipswich Town) getting six. Brighton were short of players and made up the number on arrival at the ground.

Managers (and Secretary-managers)
John Bowman 1905–07, James McEwen 1907–08, Arthur Turner 1909–10, Bert Stansfield 1910–15, Major Frank Buckley 1919–20, Charles O'Hagan 1920–21, Albert Gosnell 1921–26, Bert Stansfield 1926, Cecil Potter 1926–29, James Kerr 1929–33, Tom Parker 1933–37, Bob Young 1937–39, Jimmy Jewell 1939, Bob Young 1939–45, Cyril Spiers 1946–47, Duggie Lochhead 1945–50, Norman Low 1950–55, Tom Parker 1955–57, Archie Macaulay 1957–61, Willie Reid 1961–62, George Swindin 1962, Ron Ashman 1962–66, Lol Morgan 1966–69, Ron Saunders 1969–73, John Bond 1973–80, Ken Brown 1980–87, Dave Stringer December 1987–92, Mike Walker June 1992–.

Player and Position	Ht	Wt	Birth Date	Birth Place	Source	Clubs	League App	Gls
Henrik Mortensen	5 10	11 07	12 2 68	Odder, Denmark	Aarhus	Norwich C	18	—
Lee Power	5 11	11 02	30 6 72	Lewisham	Trainee	Norwich C	21	4
Chris Sutton	6 2	11 12	10 3 73	Nottingham	Trainee	Norwich C	23	2

Trainees
Akinbiyi, Adeola P; Brace, Deryn P. J; Bugg, Philip E; Burrows, Peter M; Collins, Sean C; Cureton, Jamie; Eadie, Darren M; Ewins, Scott R; Marshall, Andrew J; Mortimer, Philip D; Roberts, Glyn S; Snowling, Scott; Weston, Gary W.

Associated Schoolboys
Baines, Wesley; Carus, Joshua M. E; Cobbold, Christopher S; Crowfoot, Darren L; Dibble, Anthony J; Herd, Stuart A; Jones, Owen R; Morgan, Christian W; Nicholls, Ryan J; Prior, Adam G; Shore, James A; Spiteri, Denis; Storey, Neil M; Woodman, Clayton K.

Associated Schoolboys who have accepted the club's offer of a Traineeship/Contract
Carey, Shaun P; Gibb, Alistair S; Harrington, Justin D; Kreft, Stacey J; Liffen, Neil J; Mellon, Richard C; Oldbury, Marcus J; Ruse, Barry O; Wright, Jonathan.

**Non-Contract Players who are retained must be re-signed before they are eligible to play in League matches.

NOTTINGHAM FOREST 1991–92 *Back row (left to right):* Garry Parker, Roy Keane, Tommy Gaynor, Brian Rice, Terry Wilson, Des Walker, Scot Gemmill, Nigel Jemson. *Centre row:* Ron Fenton (Assistant Manager), Liam O'Kane (Coach), Brian Laws, Carl Tiler, Stephen Sutton, Stephen Chettle, Mark Crossley, Teddy Sheringham, Alan Mahood, Graham Lyas (Physiotherapist), Archie Gemmill (Coach). *Front row:* Nigel Clough, Lee Glover, Gary Charles, Brian Clough (Manager), Stuart Pearce, Ian Woan, Gary Crosby.

FA Premier

NOTTINGHAM FOREST

City Ground, Nottingham NG2 5FJ. Telephone Nottingham (0602) 822202. Information Desk: 821122. Commercial Manager 820444.

Ground capacity: 31,920 (15,114 seats).

Record attendance: 49,946 v Manchester U, Division 1, 28 October 1967.

Record receipts: £222,954 v Wolverhampton W, FA Cup.

Pitch measurements: 115yd × 78yd.

Chairman: M. Roworth.

Joint Vice-chairmen: J. F. Hickling/I. I. Korn.

Directors: G. E. Macpherson JP, F. Reacher, J. M. Smith, C. Wootton, Dr. G. W. Waterhouse.

Manager: Brian Clough OBE, MA. *Assistant Manager:* Ron Fenton. *Secretary:* P. White. *Commercial Manager:* Dave Pullan. *Coach:* Liam O'Kane. *Physio:* G. Lyas.

Year Formed: 1865. Turned Professional: 1889. Ltd Co.: 1982.

Former Grounds: 1865, Forest Racecourse; 1879, The Meadows; 1880, Trent Bridge Cricket Ground; 1882, Parkside, Lenton; 1885, Gregory, Lenton; 1890, Town Ground; 1898, City Ground.

Club Nickname: 'Reds'.

Record League Victory: 12-0 v Leicester Fosse, Division 1, 12 April 1909 – Iremonger; Dudley, Maltby; Hughes (1), Needham, Armstrong; Hooper (3), Marrison, West (3), Morris (2), Spouncer (3 incl. 1p).

Record Cup Victory: 14-0 v Clapton (away), FA Cup, 1st rd, 17 January 1891 – Brown; Earp, Scott; A. Smith, Russell, Jeacock; McCallum (2), 'Tich' Smith (1), Higgins (5), Lindley (4), Shaw (2).

Record Defeat: 1-9 v Blackburn R, Division 2, 10 April 1937.

Most League Points (2 for a win): 70, Division 3 (S), 1950–51.

Most League points (3 for a win): 74, Division 1, 1983–84.

Most League Goals: 110, Division 3 (S), 1950–51.

Highest League Scorer in Season: Wally Ardron, 36, Division 3 (S), 1950–51.

Most League Goals in Total Aggregate: Grenville Morris, 199, 1898–1913.

Most Capped Player: Martin O'Neill, 36 (64), Northern Ireland.

Most League Appearances: Bob McKinlay, 614, 1951–70.

Record Transfer Fee Received: £1,500,000 from Manchester U for Neil Webb, August 1989.

Record Transfer Fee Paid: £2,000,000 to Millwall for Teddy Sheringham, July 1991.

Football League Record: 1892 Elected to Division 1; 1906–07 Division 2; 1907–11 Division 1; 1911–22 Division 2; 1922–25 Division 1; 1925–49 Division 2; 1949–51 Division 3 (S); 1951–57 Division 2; 1957–72 Division 1; 1972–77 Division 2; 1977–92 Division 1; 1992– FA Premier League.

Honours: Football League: Division 1 – Champions 1977–78; Runners-up 1966–67, 1978–79; Division 2 – Champions 1906–07, 1921–22; Runners-up 1956–57; Division 3 (S) – Champions 1950–51. *FA Cup:* Winners 1898, 1959; Runners-up 1991. *Anglo-Scottish Cup:* Winners 1976–77; *Football League Cup:* Winners 1977–78, 1978–79, 1988–89, 1989–90; Runners-up 1979–80, 1991–92. *Simod Cup:* Winners 1989. *Zenith Data Systems Cup:* 1991–92. *European Competitions: Fairs Cup:* 1961–62, 1967–68. *European Cup:* 1978–79 (winners), 1979–80 (winners), 1980–81. *Super Cup:* 1979–80 (winners), 1980–81 (runners-up). *World Club Championship:* 1980–81 (runners-up). *UEFA Cup:* 1983–84, 1984–85.

Colours: Red shirts, white shorts, red stockings. **Change colours:** White shirts, black shorts, white stockings.

NOTTINGHAM FOREST 1991–92 LEAGUE RECORD

Match No.	Date		Venue	Opponents	Result		H/T Score	Lg. Pos.	Goalscorers	Attendance
1	Aug	17	H	Everton	W	2-1	0-1	—	Clough, Jemson	24,422
2		20	A	Leeds U	L	0-1	0-1	—		29,457
3		24	A	Notts Co	W	4-0	0-0	3	Crosby, Charles, Sheringham, Keane	21,044
4		28	H	Tottenham H	L	1-3	1-1	—	Clough	24,018
5		31	H	Oldham Ath	W	3-1	2-0	4	Gemmill, Keane, Pearce	23,244
6	Sep	4	A	Manchester C	L	1-2	0-1	—	Sheringham	29,146
7		7	A	Sheffield W	L	1-2	0-1	13	Crosby	31,289
8		14	H	Wimbledon	W	4-2	2-1	8	Keane 2, Black, Elkins (og)	19,707
9		21	A	Aston Villa	L	1-3	1-0	13	Teale (og)	28,506
10		28	H	West Ham U	D	2-2	1-2	13	Woan, Sheringham	25,613
11	Oct	5	A	QPR	W	2-0	1-0	9	Sheringham 2	13,508
12		19	A	Sheffield U	L	2-4	1-2	12	Parker, Chettle	23,080
13		26	H	Southampton	L	1-3	0-1	14	Black	20,026
14	Nov	2	A	Norwich C	D	0-0	0-0	17		13,014
15		16	H	Coventry C	W	1-0	1-0	13	Sheringham	21,154
16		23	H	Crystal Palace	W	5-1	2-0	10	Sheringham 2 (1 pen), Pearce, Gemmill, Woan	22,387
17		30	A	Chelsea	L	0-1	0-0	12		19,420
18	Dec	8	H	Arsenal	W	3-2	1-0	—	Woan, Sheringham, Gemmill	22,095
19		13	A	Liverpool	L	0-2	0-1	11		35,285
20		22	H	Leeds U	D	0-0	0-0	—		27,170
21		26	A	Tottenham H	W	2-1	1-0	8	Clough, Pearce	31,079
22		28	A	Oldham Ath	L	1-2	1-1	9	Pearce	16,496
23	Jan	1	H	Luton T	D	1-1	0-1	11	Walker	23,809
24		11	H	Notts Co	D	1-1	1-0	11	Black	30,168
25		19	A	Everton	D	1-1	1-0	—	Gemmill	17,717
26	Feb	1	H	Sheffield U	L	2-5	1-3	14	Keane, Pearce (pen)	22,412
27		22	H	Chelsea	D	1-1	1-0	15	Sheringham	24,095
28	Mar	3	A	Crystal Palace	D	0-0	0-0	—		12,608
29		11	A	Coventry C	W	2-0	2-0	—	Smith (og), Sheringham	11,158
30		14	H	Norwich C	W	2-0	2-0	13	Keane, Gemmill	20,721
31		18	H	Manchester U	W	1-0	0-0	—	Clough	28,062
32		21	H	Manchester C	W	2-0	0-0	7	Crosby, Keane	24,115
33		31	A	Arsenal	D	3-3	2-1	—	Woan, Clough, Keane	27,036
34	Apr	2	A	Wimbledon	L	0-3	0-2	—		3542
35		4	H	Sheffield W	L	0-2	0-2	10		26,105
36		8	A	Southampton	W	1-0	0-0	—	Tiler	14,905
37		14	A	Luton T	L	1-2	1-2	—	Black	8014
38		18	A	Aston Villa	W	2-0	1-0	8	Gemmill, Sheringham	22,800
39		20	H	Manchester U	W	2-1	1-1	8	Woan, Gemmill	47,576
40		22	H	Liverpool	D	1-1	1-1	—	Sheringham (pen)	23,787
41		25	H	QPR	D	1-1	0-0	7	Gemmill	22,228
42	May	2	A	West Ham U	L	0-3	0-0	8		20,629

Final League Position: 8

GOALSCORERS

League (60): Sheringham 13 (2 pens), Gemmill 8, Keane 8, Clough 5, Pearce 5 (1 pen), Woan 5, Black 4, Crosby 3, Charles 1, Chettle 1, Jemson 1, Parker 1, Tiler 1, Walker 1, own goals 3.
Rumbelows Cup (20): Sheringham 5, Keane 4, Gaynor 3, Black 2, Gemmill 2, Glover 2, Clough 1, Pearce 1.
FA Cup (7): Clough 2, Pearce 2, Sheringham 2 (1 pen), Llewellyn 1 (o pens).

Crossley	Charles	Pearce	Walker	Tiler	Keane	Crosby	Gemmill	Clough	Sheringham	Jemson	Chettle	Laws	Black	Williams	Parker	Gaynor	Woan	Wassall	Glover	Marriott	Orlygsson	Kaminsky	Wilson	Stone	Match No.
1	2	3	4*	5	6	7	8	9	10	11	12														1
1	2	3		5	6	7	8	9	10	11		4													2
1	2	3		5	6	7	8	9	10	11*		4	12												3
1	2	3		5	6	7	8	9	10	11		4													4
1	2	3		5	6	7	8	9	10	11		4													5
1	2	3		5	6	7	8	9	10	11*		4	12												6
1	2	3		5	6	7	8	9	10			4		11											7
1	2			5	6	7	8	9	10			4		11	3										8
1	2			5	6	7	8*	9†	10			4	14	11	3	12									9
1	2	3	12	5	6						10	4		7		8	9*	11							10
1	2	3	4	5	6	7					10	12		11		8	9*								11
1	2	3	4	5	6*	7					10	12		11†		8	9	14							12
1		3	4*	5		7	8	9			2	12	11	10			6								13
1	2	3	4		6	7	8		10		5			11			9								14
1	2	3	4		6	7	8		10		5			11			9								15
1	2	3	4		6†	7*	8	12	10		5			11		14	9								16
1	2	3	4		6*		8	9	10		5			11			12		7						17
1	2	3	4	5	6	7	8	9	10								11								18
1	2	3	4	12	6	7	8	9	10*		5						11								19
1	2	3	4	5	6		8	9	10					7*			11		12						20
1	2	3	4	5	6*		8	9	10					7			11		12						21
1	2	3	4	5	6		8	9	10*					7			11		12						22
1	2	3	4	5	6	7	8	9	10								11								23
1	2*	3	4	5†	6	12	8		10					7			11	14	9						24
1		3	4		6		8		10		12		2	7			11	5*	9						25
1		3	4	5	6	12	8	9					2	7*			11		10						26
1		3	4		6	7	8	9	10				2				11		5						27
1	2	3	4	5	6		8	9	10								7		11						28
1	2	3	4		6	7	8	9	10								5		11						29
1	2	3	4	5	6	7	8	9	10								11								30
	2	3	4		6	7	8	9	10								11		5	1					31
	2*	3	4		6	7	8	9	10			12					11		5	1					32
	2		4		6		8	9	10				3	7			11		5	1					33
	2†		4	14	6		8	9					3*	12		7	11	5	10	1					34
			4	5	6	7	8	9					2		3		11		10	1					35
			4*	11	6	7	8	9	10				2		3		5		12	1					36
1			4*		6	7	8	9	10					11	3		5				2	12			37
1					6	5	8	9	10				2	7	3		11		4						38
1			4		6	5	8	9	10				2		3		11		7						39
1			4		6	5	8	9	10				2		3		11		7						40
1			4		6	5	8	9	10				2		3		11		12					7*	41
1			4			5	8	9	10				2	7	3		11*		12		6†			14	42
36	30	30	32	24	39	31	39	33	39	6	17	10	25	9	5	3	20	10	12	6	5	—	1	—	
	+1s		+2s			+2s		+1s				+5s	+5s				+1s	+1s	+4s	+4s	+1s		+1s		

Rumbelows Cup			
	Second Round	Bolton W (h)	4-0
		(a)	5-2
	Third Round	Bristol R (h)	2-0
	Fourth Round	Southampton (h)	0-0
		(a)	1-0
	Fifth Round	Crystal Palace (a)	1-1
		(h)	4-2
	Semi-Final	Tottenham H (a)	1-1
		(a)	2-1
	Final	Manchester U (at Wembley)	0-1
FA Cup	Third Round	Wolverhampton W (h)	1-0
	Fourth Round	Hereford U (h)	2-0
	Fifth Round	Bristol C (h)	4-1
	Sixth Round	Portsmouth (a)	0-1

NOTTINGHAM FOREST

Goalkeepers

Name			Birth date	Birthplace	Source	Club	Apps	Gls
Mark Crossley	6 0	13 09	16 6 69	Barnsley		Nottingham F	84	—
						Manchester U (loan)	—	—
Christian Davies	6 01	12 09	18 11 74	Essex	Trainee	Nottingham F	—	—
Leigh Hawkes‡	6 0	11 13	30 11 73	Romford	Trainee	Nottingham F	—	—
Andrew Marriott	6 0	12 07	11 10 70	Nottingham	Trainee	Arsenal		
						Nottingham F	6	—
						WBA (loan)	3	—
						Blackburn R (loan)	2	—
						Colchester U (loan)	10	—
						Burnley (loan)	·15	—
Mark Smith	6 1	13 09	2 1 73	Birmingham	Trainee	Nottingham F	—	—

Defenders

Name			Birth date	Birthplace	Source	Club	Apps	Gls
Craig Boardman	6 0	11 08	30 11 70	Barnsley	Trainee	Nottingham F	—	—
Gary Bowyer	6 0	12 13	22 6 71	Manchester		Hereford U	14	2
						Nottingham F	—	—
Ray Byrne	6 1	11 02	4 7 72	Newry	Newry	Nottingham F	—	—
Stuart Cash*	5 11	11 10	5 9 65	Tipton	Halesowen	Nottingham F	—	—
						Rotherham U (loan)	8	1
						Brentford (loan)	11	—
						Shrewsbury T (loan)	8	1
Gary Charles	5 9	10 13	13 4 70	London		Nottingham F	42	1
						Leicester C (loan)	8	—
Steve Chettle	6 1	12 00	27 9 68	Nottingham	Apprentice	Nottingham F	139	6
Martin Fancutt‡	5 8	10 08	15 10 73	Derby	Trainee	Nottingham F	—	—
Cuan Forrest			26 3 74	Zimbabwe	Trainee	Nottingham F	—	—
Chris Hope	6 0	11 01	14 11 72	Sheffield	Darlington	Nottingham F	—	—
Ian Kilford	5 10	10 05	6 10 73	Bristol	Trainee	Nottingham F	—	—
Brian Laws	5 10	11 05	14 10 61	Wallsend	Apprentice	Burnley	125	12
						Huddersfield T	56	1
						Middlesbrough	107	12
						Nottingham F	107	4
Barrett Noble‡	5 9	10 07	6 2 74	Sheffield	Trainee	Nottingham F	—	
Stuart Pearce	5 10	12 09	24 4 62	Shepherds Bush	Wealdstone	Coventry C	51	4
						Nottingham F	236	39
Carl Tiler	6 2	13 00	11 2 70	Sheffield	Trainee	Barnsley	71	3
						Nottingham F	26	1
Des Walker	5 11	11 03	26 11 65	Hackney	Apprentice	Nottingham F	264	1
Vance Warner	5 11	11 05	3 9 74	Leeds	Trainee	Nottingham F	—	
Darren Wassall	5 11	11 09	27 6 68	Edgbaston		Nottingham F	27	—
						Hereford U (loan)	5	—
						Bury (loan)	7	1
Brett Williams	5 10	11 11	19 3 68	Dudley	Apprentice	Nottingham F	34	—
						Stockport Co (loan)	2	—
						Northampton T (loan)	4	—
						Hereford U (loan)	14	—
						Oxford U (loan)	7	—
Dale Wright	6 00	12 05	21 12 74	Middlesbrough	Trainee	Nottingham F	—	—

Midfield

Name			Birth date	Birthplace	Source	Club	Apps	Gls
Kingsley Black	5 8	10 11	22 6 68	Luton	School	Luton T	127	26
						Nottingham F	25	4
Gary Crosby	5 7	9 11	8 5 64	Sleaford	Lincoln U	Lincoln C	7	—
						Grantham	—	—
						Nottingham F	123	11
Scot Gemmill	5 10	10 01	2 1 71	Paisley	School	Nottingham F	43	8
Neil Glasser	5 09	11 03	17 10 74	Johannesbury	Trainee	Nottingham F	—	—
Stephen Howe	5 7	10 04	6 11 73	Annitsford	Trainee	Nottingham F	—	—
Roy Keane	5 10	11 03	10 8 71	Cork	Cobh Ramblers	Nottingham F	74	16
Anthony Loughlan*	6 0	12 03	19 1 70	Surrey	Leicester U	Nottingham F	2	1

Foundation: One of the oldest football clubs in the world, Nottingham Forest was formed at a meeting in the Clinton Arms in 1865. Known originally as the Forest Football Club, the game which first drew the founders together was "shinney" a form of hockey. When they determined to change to football in 1865, one of their first moves was to buy a set of red caps to wear on the field.

First Football League game: 3 September, 1892, Division 2, v Everton (a) D 2-2 – Brown; Earp, Scott; Hamilton, A. Smith, McCracken; McCallum, W. Smith, Higgins (2), Pike, McInnes.

Did you know: Grenville Morris created a club record in 1902–03 by scoring in eight consecutive League games for the Forest. Dave "Boy" Martin equalled the run of games in 1936–37 but his total of ten goals was one short of Morris.

Managers (and Secretary-managers)
Harry Radford 1889–97*, Harry Haslam 1897–1909*, Fred Earp 1909–12*, Bob Masters 1912–25*, John Baynes 1925–29*, Stan Hardy 1930–31*, Noel Watson 1931–36*, Harold Wightman 1936–39, Billy Walker 1939–60, Andy Beattie 1960–63, John Carey 1963–68, Matt Gillies 1969–72, Dave Mackay 1972–73, Allan Brown 1973–75, Brian Clough January 1975–.

Name	Ht	Wt	Birthdate	Birthplace	From	Club	Apps	Gls
Alan Mahood (To Morton March 1992)	5 8	9 12	26 3 73	Kilwinning	Bonnyton Th	Morton	8	—
						Nottingham F	—	—
Thorvaldur Orlygsson	5 11	10 08	2 8 66	Odense	Akureyri	Nottingham F	17	1
Brian Rice (To Falkirk Aug 1991)	6 0	11 10	11 10 63	Glasgow	Whitburn Central	Hibernian	84	11
						Nottingham F	91	9
						Grimsby T (loan)	4	—
						WBA (loan)	3	—
						Stoke C (loan)	18	—
Steven Stone	5 9	11 03	20 8 71	Gateshead	Trainee	Nottingham F	1	—
Mark Telford‡			17 12 71	South Shields	Trainee	Notts Co	—	—
						Nottingham F	—	—
Terry Wilson	6 0	10 10	8 2 69	Broxburn	Apprentice	Nottingham F	100	9
						Newcastle U (loan)	2	—
Ian Woan	5 10	11 09	14 12 67	Wirral	Runcorn	Nottingham F	33	8
Forwards								
Darren Barry‡	5 10	11 08	5 3 73	Cork	Trainee	Nottingham F	—	—
Steven Bell‡	5 11	11 09	4 12 73	Middlesbrough	Trainee	Nottingham F	—	—
Nigel Clough	5 9	11 04	19 3 66	Sunderland	AC Hunters	Nottingham F	269	91
Tommy Gaynor	6 1	13 02	29 1 63	Limerick	Limerick	Doncaster R	33	7
						Nottingham F	57	10
						Newcastle U (loan)	4	1
Lee Glover	5 10	12 01	24 4 70	Kettering	Trainee	Nottingham F	44	4
						Leicester C (loan)	5	—
						Barnsley (loan)	8	—
						Luton T (loan)	1	—
Jason Kaminsky			3 12 73	Leicester	Trainee	Nottingham F	1	—
Paul McGregor	5 10	10 04	17 12 74	Liverpool	Trainee	Nottingham F	—	—
Dale Pearce‡	5 11	10 11	6 10 73	Newcastle	Trainee	Nottingham F	—	—
Teddy Sheringham	5 8	12 04	2 4 66	Highams Park	Apprentice	Millwall	220	93
						Aldershot (loan)	5	—
						Nottingham F	39	13
Luke Yates‡	5 6	11 01	19 3 74	Sandwell	Trainee	Nottingham F	—	—

Trainees
Armstrong, Craig; Hellewell, Craig; Marshall, Lee; Mitchell, Andrew J.

Associated Schoolboys
Bibby, David; Blair, Matthew C; Chivers, David; Clifford, Mark; Cowling, Lee; Gilmore, Craig; Inwood, Dale; Mendum, Craig; Morgan, Ian; Orr, Stephen; Poole, Darren; Priest, Christen; Thom, Stuart P; Turner, Darren; Waddley, Kevin; Walley, Mark; Watkins, Darren; Wood, Matthew; Woolford, Stephen; Ziccardi, Mariano.

Associated Schoolboys who have accepted the club's offer of a Traineeship/Contract
Guinan, Stephen; Haywood, Paul; Hinshelwood, Danny; Hughes, Luke; Rookyard, Carl; Smith, Richard; Stratford, Lee; Walker, Justin.

376

NOTTS COUNTY 1991–92 *Back row (left to right):* Mick Jones (Assistant Manager), Paul Harding, Richard Dryden, Charlie Palmer, Dean Yates, Steve Cherry, Kevin Blackwell, Craig Short, Alan Paris, Dave Regis, Don O'Riordan, Dave Wilson (Physiotherapist).
Front row: Phil Robinson, Chris Short, Tommy Johnson, Phil Turner, Derek Pavis (Chairman), Neil Warnock (Manager), Mark Draper, Kevin Bartlett, Dean Thomas, Gary Chapman.

Division 1 **NOTTS COUNTY**

County Ground, Meadow Lane, Nottingham NG2 3HJ. Telephone Nottingham (0602) 861155. Ticket office: (0602) 850632. Clubcall: 0898 121101. Football in the Community: 863656. County '75: 864718. Supporters Club: 866802.
Ground capacity: 19,196.
Record attendance: 47,310 v York C, FA Cup 6th rd, 12 March 1955.
Record receipts: £124,539 v Manchester C, FA Cup 6th rd, l6 February 1991.
Pitch measurements: 114yd × 74yd.
Chairman: D. C. Pavis.
Vice-chairman: J. Mounteney.
Directors: W. A. Hopcroft, P. Jackson, D. Ward, F. Sherwood.
Team Manager: Neil Warnock.
Commerical Manager: Miss S. Shaw.
Coach: Mick Jones.
Chief Executive: N. E. Hook MCIM, AMLD.
Physio: David Wilson BA, MCSP, DIPTP, GRAD DIP PHYS SRP.
Year Formed: 1862 *(see Foundation).* Turned Professional: 1885. Ltd Co.: 1888.
Former Grounds: 1862, The Park; 1864, The Meadows; 1877, Beeston Cricket Ground; 1880, Castle Ground; 1883, Trent Bridge; 1910, Meadow Lane.
Club Nickname: 'Magpies'.
Record League Victory: 11-1 v Newport C, Division 3 (S), 15 January 1949 – Smith; Southwell, Purvis; Gannon, Baxter, Adamson; Houghton (1), Sewell (4), Lawton (4), Pimbley, Johnston (2).
Record Cup Victory: 15-0 v Rotherham T (at Trent Bridge), FA Cup, 1st rd, 24 October 1885 – Sherwin; Snook, H. T. Moore; Dobson (1), Emmett (1), Chapman; Gunn (1), Albert Moore (2), Jackson (3), Daft (2), Cursham (4). (1 og).
Record Defeat: 1-9 v Blackburn R, Division 1, 16 November, 1889 and v Aston Villa, Division 1, 29 September, 1888 and v Portsmouth, Division 2, 9 April, 1927.
Most League Points (2 for a win): 69, Division 4, 1970–71.
Most League points (3 for a win): 87, Division 3, 1989–90.
Most League Goals: 107, Division 4, 1959–60.
Highest League Scorer in Season: Tom Keetley, 39, Division 3 (S), 1930–31.
Most League Goals in Total Aggregate: Les Bradd, 124, 1967–78.
Most Capped Player: Harry Cursham, 8, England and Martin O'Neill, 8 (64), Northern Ireland.
Most League Appearances: Albert Iremonger, 564, 1904–26.
Record Transfer Fee Received: £1,300,000 from Derby Co for Tommy Johnson, March 1992.
Transfer Fee Paid: £750,000 to Sheffield U for Tony Agana, November 1991.
Football League Record: 1888 Founder Member of the Football League; 1893–97 Division 2; 1897–1913 Division 1; 1913–14 Division 2; 1914–20 Division 1; 1920–23 Division 2; 1923–26 Division 1; 1926–30 Division 2; 1930–31 Division 3 (S); 1931–35 Division 2; 1935–50 Division 3 (S); 1950–58 Division 2; 1958–59 Division 3; 1959–60 Division 4; 1960–64 Division 3; 1964–71 Division 4; 1971–73 Division 3; 1973–81 Division 2; 1981–84 Division 1; 1984–85 Division 2; 1985–90 Division 3; 1990–91 Division 2; 1991– Division 1.
Honours: Football League: Division 1 best season: 3rd, 1890–91, 1900–01; Division 2 – Champions 1896–97, 1913–14, 1922–23; Runners-up 1894–95, 1980–81; Division 3 (S) – Champions 1930–31, 1949–50; Runners-up 1936–37; Division 3 – Runners-up 1972-73; Division 4 – Champions 1970–71; Runners-up 1959–60. *FA Cup:* Winners 1893–94; Runners-up 1890–91. *Football League Cup:* best season: 5th rd, 1963–64, 1972–73, 1975–76.
Colours: Black and white broad striped shirts, amber sleeve and neck trim, black shorts with white side flash, black stockings with white and amber trim. **Change colours:** Purple shirts, white shorts, purple stockings.

NOTTS COUNTY 1991–92 LEAGUE RECORD

Match No.	Date		Venue	Opponents	Result		H/T Score	Lg. Pos.	Goalscorers	Attendance
1	Aug	17	A	Manchester U	L	0-2	0-1	—		46,278
2		20	H	Southampton	W	1-0	1-0	—	Yates	9613
3		24	H	Nottingham F	L	0-4	0-0	15		21,044
4		28	A	Chelsea	D	2-2	1-0	—	Johnson T, Bartlett	15,847
5		31	A	West Ham U	W	2-0	0-0	13	Bartlett 2	20,093
6	Sep	3	H	Sheffield W	W	2-1	1-1	—	Johnson T 2 (1 pen)	12,297
7		7	H	Liverpool	L	1-2	1-0	12	Johnson T	16,051
8		14	A	Coventry C	L	0-1	0-0	15		10,685
9		17	A	Sheffield U	W	3-1	0-0	—	Bartlett 2, Rideout	19,375
10		21	H	Norwich C	D	2-2	1-0	11	Rideout, Bowen (og)	9488
11		28	A	Luton T	D	1-1	0-0	11	Johnson T (pen)	7629
12	Oct	6	H	Manchester C	L	1-3	0-0	—	Thomas	11,878
13		19	H	Leeds U	L	2-4	1-2	17	Lund, Johnson T	12,964
14		26	A	Arsenal	L	0-2	0-0	19		30,011
15	Nov	2	A	Oldham Ath	W	2-0	2-0	15	Rideout, Johnson T	7634
16		16	A	Aston Villa	L	0-1	0-1	17		23,020
17		23	A	Everton	L	0-1	0-1	18		24,230
18		30	H	QPR	L	0-1	0-0	18		7901
19	Dec	7	A	Tottenham H	L	1-2	1-1	19	Short Craig	23,364
20		20	A	Southampton	D	1-1	0-1	—	Slawson	11,054
21		26	H	Chelsea	W	2-0	1-0	18	Yates, Johnson T	11,933
22		28	H	West Ham U	W	3-0	0-0	18	Turner, Harding, Agana	11,163
23	Jan	1	A	Crystal Palace	L	0-1	0-1	18		14,202
24		11	A	Nottingham F	D	1-1	0-1	18	Dryden	30,168
25		18	H	Manchester U	D	1-1	1-0	18	Johnson T (pen)	21,055
26	Feb	1	A	Leeds U	L	0-3	0-1	19		27,224
27		8	H	Arsenal	L	0-1	0-1	19		11,221
28		22	A	QPR	D	1-1	0-0	19	Bartlett	8300
29		25	H	Wimbledon	D	1-1	1-0	—	Short Craig	6198
30	Mar	7	A	Wimbledon	L	0-2	0-1	20		4196
31		10	H	Aston Villa	D	0-0	0-0	—		8389
32		14	A	Oldham Ath	L	3-4	1-3	21	Draper, Williams, Lund	12,125
33		17	H	Everton	D	0-0	0-0	—		7480
34		21	A	Sheffield W	L	0-1	0-0	21		23,910
35		28	H	Crystal Palace	L	2-3	2-1	21	Short Craig, Wilson	7674
36		31	A	Liverpool	L	0-4	0-2	—		25,457
37	Apr	7	H	Tottenham H	L	0-2	0-1	—		9205
38		11	H	Coventry C	W	1-0	0-0	21	Sansom (og)	6655
39		18	A	Norwich C	W	1-0	0-0	21	Matthews	12,100
40		20	H	Sheffield U	L	1-3	1-1	21	Bartlett	12,605
41		25	A	Manchester C	L	0-2	0-1	21		23,426
42	May	2	H	Luton T	W	2-1	1-1	21	Matthews 2	11,380

Final League Position: 21

GOALSCORERS

League (40): Johnson T 9 (3 pens), Bartlett 7, Matthews 3, Rideout 3, Short Craig 3, Lund 2, Yates 2, Agana 1, Draper 1, Dryden 1, Harding 1, Slawson 1, Thomas 1, Turner 1, Williams 1, Wilson 1, own goals 2.
Rumbelows Cup (4): Bartlett 2, Johnson T 2 (1 pen).
FA Cup (4): Draper 1, Johnson T 1, Lund 1, Turner 1.

Cherry	Palmer	Paris	Short Craig	Yates	O'Riordan	Thomas	Turner	Regis	Draper	Johnson T	Bartlett	Short Chris	Harding	Dryden	Rideout	Lund	Johnson M	Agana	Slawson	Wells	Williams	McClelland	Wilson	Farina	Robinson	Devlin	Matthews	Cox	Match No.
1	2	3	4	5	6*	7	8	9	10	11†12	14																		1
1	2	3	4	5		7	8	9	10	11			6																2
1	2†	3	4	5		7	8	9	10	11	12	14	6*																3
1	2	3	4	5		7		9†12		11*10	14		6	8															4
1	2	3	4	5		7	12	9*		6	11	10		8															5
1	2	3	4	5		7	8			6	11	10*		12	9														6
1	2	3	4	5		7	8	12		6	11	10*			9														7
1	2†	3*	4	5		7	8	12		6	11	10	14		9														8
1		3	4	5		7				6	11	10	2	8	9														9
1	12	3	4	5		7	14			6†11*10			2	8	9														10
1	8	3	4	5		7	14			12	11	10†	2*	6	9														11
1	2	3	4	5		7	14	12		8	11	10*		6†	9														12
1	2	3	4†	5		7		8	12	6	11	10				14	9*												13
1	2	3		5†		7	8			6	11*12			14	10			9	4										14
1	2†	3	4			7	14			6	11	10*		8	5	9	12												15
1	2	3	4	5		7				6	11			8	9		10												16
1	2	3	4	5†		7	12			6	11*	14		8	9		10												17
1	2	14	4			7	12			6	11*		5†	8	3	9	10												18
1	2	3	4			7	8			12	11*		5	6	9		10												19
1	2	3	4	5		7	8			11			6	9			10*12												20
1	2	3	4	5		7	8			11			6	9			10												21
1	2	3	4	5		7	8			11†			6	9		12	10*14												22
1	2	3	4	5		7*	8			11			6	9†		12	10 14												23
1	2	3	4			7	8			11†12			6	9	5		10*14												24
1	2	3	4			7	8			6	11	10	5	9															25
1	2	3	4			7	8			6	11*10			5†		9		12 14											26
1	2	3	4			7†	8			6	11*10		5	9		12		14											27
1	2		4			7				11	10		5	6	3	9		8											28
1	2		4			7				11*10			5	6	3	12	9	8											29
1	2					10*				6	11	12	5	8	3	14	9†			7		4							30
1	2					8				6	11*10		5	9†	3	14	12			7		4							31
1	2	4	11			8†				6		10	14	3		9	12			7	5*								32
1	2	4	12			8*				6		10 5		3		9	12			7	11								33
1	2	4	5			7*				6		10†8 14		3		9	12			11									34
1	2	4	5			8				6				3	9*		12			7	11†10 14								35
1	2	4	5			8				6†		12		3	9					7		10 14 11*							36
1	2	4				12				6		5 8 3		9†		14				7*	10 11								37
1	2	4				12				6		10	8* 3		5					7	11		9†14						38
1	2	4				9				6		10†12 8 3		5						7*	11		14						39
1	2	4				9				6		10 8 3		5						7*	11		12						40
1	2					6				10†		8 3	4 5 9							7	11*		12 14						41
1	2	4				3				6		5 8		9						7	11*		12 10						42

Totals: 42 40 26 38 24 1 34 22 5 32 31 24 20 25 28 9 10 5 11 3 — 14 6 8 1 1 1 1 —

+ + + + + + + + + + + + + + + +

1s 1s 1s 2s 7s 4s 3s 5s 7s 4s 1s 2s 3s 2s 10s 1s 1s 2s 1s 4s 1s

Rumbelows Cup	Second Round	Port Vale (a)	1-2
		(h)	3-2
FA Cup	Third Round	Wigan Ath (h)	2-0
	Fourth Round	Blackburn R (h)	2-1
	Fifth Round	Norwich C (a)	0-3

NOTTS COUNTY

Player and Position	Ht	Wt	Birth Date	Birth Place	Source	Clubs	League App	League Gls
Goalkeepers								
Kevin Blackwell	5 11	12 10	21 12 58	Luton	Boston U	Barnet	—	—
						Scarborough	44	—
						Notts Co	—	—
Steve Cherry	5 11	11 00	5 8 60	Nottingham	Apprentice	Derby Co	77	—
						Port Vale (loan)	4	—
						Walsall	71	—
						Plymouth Arg	73	—
						Chesterfield (loan)	10	—
						Notts Co	152	—
Paul Dolan	6 4	13 05	16 4 66	Ottawa	Vancouver W	Notts Co	—	—
James Walker			9 7 73	Mansfield	Trainee	Notts Co	—	—
Defenders								
Lee Barrow*			1 5 73	Belper	Trainee	Notts Co	—	—
Paul Coxt	5 11	11 12	1 1 72	Nottingham	Trainee	Notts Co	1	—
Richard Dryden	6 0	11 02	14 6 69	Stroud		Bristol R	13	—
						Exeter C	92	13
						Manchester C (loan)	—	—
						Notts Co	29	1
Steven Hodder*	5 9	11 03	18 10 71	Sheffield	Nottingham F	Notts Co	—	—
Michael Johnson	5 11	11 06	7 7 73	Nottingham	Trainee	Notts Co	5	—
Don O'Riordan	6 0	11 12	14 5 57	Dublin	Apprentice	Derby Co	6	1
						Doncaster R (loan)	2	—
						Tulsa	—	—
						Preston NE	158	8
						Carlisle U	84	18
						Middlesbrough	41	2
						Grimsby T	86	14
						Notts Co	92	4
						Mansfield T (loan)	6	—
Charlie Palmer	5 11	12 03	10 7 63	Aylesbury	Apprentice	Watford	10	1
						Derby Co	51	2
						Hull C	70	1
						Notts Co	129	6
Alan Paris	5 11	10 12	15 8 64	Slough	Slough T	Watford	—	—
						Peterborough U	137	2
						Leicester C	88	3
						Notts Co	42	1
Chris Short	5 10	12 02	9 5 70	Munster		Scarborough	43	1
						Manchester U (loan)	—	—
						Notts Co	42	1
Craig Short	6 0	11 04	25 6 68	Bridlington	Pickering T	Scarborough	63	7
						Notts Co	125	5
Dean Thomas	5 9	11 08	19 12 61	Bedworth	Nuneaton Bor	Wimbledon	57	8
						Dusseldorf	—	—
						Northampton T	74	11
						Notts Co	90	5
Anthony Thompson*			1 7 72	Mansfield	Trainee	Notts Co	—	—
Richard Walker			9 11 71	Derby	Trainee	Notts Co	—	—
Dean Yates	6 1	10 04	26 10 67	Leicester	Apprentice	Notts Co	292	33
Midfield								
Steve Aldridge*			4 9 71	Basford		Notts Co	—	—
Shaun Browne*			3 11 71	Nottingham	Nottingham F	Notts Co	—	—
Mark Draper	5 10	10 00	11 11 70	Derbyshire	Trainee	Notts Co	134	16
Paul Harding	5 10	12 05	6 3 64	Mitcham	Barnet	Notts Co	53	1
Gary Patterson			27 11 72	Newcastle	Trainee	Notts Co	—	—
Philip Robinson	5 9	10 10	6 1 67	Stafford	Apprentice	Aston Villa	3	1
						Wolverhampton W	71	8
						Notts Co	66	5
						Birmingham C (loan)	9	1
Eddie Snook	5 7	10 01	18 10 68	Washington	Apprentice	Notts Co	—	—
Phil Turner	5 8	10 13	12 2 62	Sheffield	Apprentice	Lincoln C	241	19
						Grimsby T	62	8
						Leicester C	24	2
						Notts Co	127	10
Mark Wells			15 10 71	Leicester	Trainee	Notts Co	1	—

NOTTS COUNTY

Foundation: For many years the foundation date of the Football League's oldest club was given as 1862 and the club celebrated its centenary in 1962. However, the researches of Keith Warsop have since shown that the club was on a very haphazard basis at that time, playing little more than practice matches. The meeting which put it on a firm footing was held at the George IV Hotel in December 1864, when they became known as the Notts Football Club.

First Football League game: 15 September, 1888, Football League, v Everton (a) L 1-2 – Holland; Guttridge, McLean; Brown, Warburton, Shelton; Hodder, Harker, Jardine, Moore (1), Wardle.

Did you know: Notts County scored a total of 33 goals against Newport County in five consecutive home League games – 1948–49 11-1, 1949–50 7-0, 1958–59 1-1, 1960–61 6-0 and 1961–62 8-1. This is a record of its kind.

Managers (and Secretary-managers)
Edwin Browne 1883–93*, Tom Featherstone 1893*, Tom Harris 1893–1913*, Albert Fisher 1913–27, Horace Henshall 1927–34, Charlie Jones 1934–35, David Pratt 1935, Percy Smith 1935–36, Jimmy McMullan 1936–37, Harry Parkes 1938–39, Tony Towers 1939–42, Frank Womack 1942–43, Major Frank Buckley 1944–46, Arthur Stollery 1946–49, Eric Houghton 1949–53, George Poyser 1953–57, Tommy Lawton 1957–58, Frank Hill 1958–61, Tim Coleman 1961–63, Eddie Lowe 1963–65, Tim Coleman 1965–66, Jack Burkitt 1966–67, Andy Beattie (GM 1967), Billy Gray 1967–68, Jimmy Sirrel 1969–75, Ron Fenton 1975–77, Jimmy Sirrel 1978–82 (continued as GM to 1984), Howard Wilkinson 1982–83, Larry Lloyd 1983–84, Richie Barker 1984–85, Jimmy Sirrel 1985–87, John Barnwell 1987–88, Neil Warnock January 1989–.

Andy Williams	6 0	11 09	29 7 62	Birmingham	Solihull	Coventry C	9	—
						Rotherham U	87	13
						Leeds U	46	3
						Port Vale (loan)	5	—
						Notts Co	15	1
Forwards								
Tony Agana	5 11	12 02	2 10 63	London	Weymouth	Watford	15	1
						Sheffield U	118	42
						Notts Co	13	1
						Leeds U (loan)	2	—
Kevin Bartlett	5 9	10 12	12 10 62	Portsmouth	Apprentice	Portsmouth	3	—
						Fareham	—	—
						Cardiff C	82	25
						WBA	37	10
						Notts Co	83	28
John Brough*			8 1 73	Ilkeston	Trainee	Notts Co	—	—
Paul Devlin	5 08	10 10	14 4 72	Birmingham	Stafford R	Notts Co	2	—
Frank Farina†	5 09	11 00	5 9 64	Australia	Bari	Notts Co	3	—
Craig Finch‡			21 12 71	Burton-on-Trent	Trainee	Notts Co	—	—
Gary Lund	5 11	11 00	13 9 64	Grimsby	School	Grimsby T	60	24
						Lincoln C	44	13
						Notts Co	151	42
Rob Matthews†	5 11	11 06	14 10 70	Slough	Trainee	Notts Co	5	3
Paul Rideout (To Rangers January 1992)	5 11	12 01	14 8 64	Bournemouth	Apprentice	Swindon T	95	38
						Aston Villa	54	19
						Bari	99	23
						Southampton	75	19
						Swindon T (Loan)	9	1
						Notts Co	11	3
Steve Slawson	6 01	12 02	13 11 72	Nottingham	Trainee	Notts Co	13	1
Kevin Wilson	5 7	10 10	18 4 61	Banbury	Banbury U	Derby Co	122	30
						Ipswich T	98	34
						Chelsea	152	42
						Notts Co	8	1
Gavin Worboys			14 7 74	Doncaster	Trainee	Doncaster R	7	2
						Notts Co	—	—

Trainees
Armeni, Christopher C; Blatherwick, Steven S; Galloway, Michael A; Hill, Philip W; Horseman, Brian G; Malpass, Jody; Muir, James M; Rogers, Kevin A; Saunders, Darren D; Sherlock, Paul G; Simpson, Michael; Smith, Paul A; Ward, Richard; Wells, Iain D.

Associated Schoolboys
Barke, Christopher P; Brearley, Richard; Burke, Anthony G; Chadbourne, Martyn; Clark, Andrew D; Eaton, Jamie; Evans, Dion M; Fitzgerald, Louis; Folwell, John A; Gare, Darren; George, Alex; Gregory, Daniel J; Gregory, Ross; Hope, John E; Hunt, James M; Marston, Marvin A; Spray, Gary R; Warner, David M; Wilkes, Timothy C.

Associated Schoolboys who have accepted the club's offer of a Traineeship/Contract
Dodson, Matthew J; Gallagher, Thomas D; Henry, Alvin M; King, Jon; Lawley, Edward W. H; Ludlow, Lee; Marshall, Daniel J; Needham, Ben; Ridgeway, Ian D; Rigby, Malcolm R.

382

OLDHAM ATHLETIC 1991–92 *Back row (left to right):* Andy Kenton, Greg Wilson, Rob Miller, Andy Holden, Richard Jobson, John Keeley, Jon Hallworth, Paul Gerrard, Brian Kilcline, Ian Thompstone, Mike Fillery, Chris Makin.

Centre row: Bill Urmson (Coach), Jim Cassell (Chief Scout), Paul Moulden, Willie Donachie (Player Coach), Frank Bunn, Paul Bernard, Andy Ritchie, Andy Barlow, Rick Holden, Wayne Heseltine, David Currie, Neil Adams, Ronnie Evans (Kit Manager), Ian Liversedge (Physiotherapist).

Front row: Nick Henry, Paul Kane, Ian Marshall, Roger Palmer, Joe Royle (Manager), Earl Barrett, Graeme Sharp, Mike Milligan, Neil Redfearn.

FA Premier **OLDHAM ATHLETIC**

Boundary Park, Oldham. Telephone 061-624 4972. Commercial Dept: 061-652 0966. Ticket call: 0898 121582. Clubcall: 0898 121142.

Ground capacity: 16,839 (seats 11,295, standing 5544).

Record attendance: 47,671 v Sheffield W, FA Cup 4th rd. 25 January 1930.

Record receipts: £110,637 v Liverpool, Division 1, 18 January 1992.

Pitch measurements: 110yd × 74yd.

President: R. Schofield.

Chairman & Chief Executive: I. H. Stott.

Vice-chairman: D. A. Brierley.

Directors: G. T. Butterworth, R. Adams, D. R. Taylor, P. Chadwick, J. Slevin, N. Holden.

Manager: Joe Royle.

Secretary: Terry Cale. *Commercial Manager:* Alan Hardy. *Player-coach:* Willie Donachie. *Coaches:* Billy Urmson, Andy Holden. *Physio:* Ian Liversedge.

Year Formed: 1895. Turned Professional: 1899. Ltd Co.: 1906.

Former Grounds: Sheepfoot Lane; 1905, Boundary Park.

Former Names: 1895, Pine Villa; 1899, Oldham Athletic.

Club Nickname: 'The Latics'.

Record League Victory: 11-0 v Southport, Division 4, 26 December 1962 – Hollands; Branagan, Marshall; McCall, Williams, Scott; Ledger (1), Johnstone, Lister (6), Colquhoun (1), Whitaker (3).

Record Cup Victory: 10-1 v Lytham, FA Cup, 1st rd, 28 November 1925 – Gray; Wynne, Grundy; Adlam, Heaton, Naylor (1), Douglas, Pynegar (2), Ormston (2), Barnes (3), Watson (2).

Record Defeat: 4-13 v Tranmere R, Division 3 (N), 26 December 1935.

Most League Points (2 for a win): 62, Division 3, 1973–74.

Most League points (3 for a win): 88, Division 2, 1990–91.

Most League Goals: 95, Division 4, 1962–63.

Highest League Scorer in Season: Tom Davis, 33, Division 3 (N), 1936–37.

Most League Goals in Total Aggregate: Roger Palmer, 141, 1980–92.

Most Capped Player: Albert Gray, 9 (24), Wales.

Most League Appearances: Ian Wood, 525, 1966–80.

Record Transfer Fee Received: £1,700,000 from Aston Villa for Earl Barrett, February 1992.

Record Transfer Fee Paid: £700,000 to Aston Villa for Ian Olney, June 1992.

Football League Record: 1907 Elected to Division 2; 1910–23 Division 1; 1923–35 Division 2; 1935–53 Division 3 (N); 1953–54 Division 2; 1954–58 Division 3 (N); 1958–63 Division 4; 1963–69 Division 3; 1969–71 Division 4; 1971–74 Division 3; 1974–91 Division 2; 1991–92 Division 1; 1992– FA Premier League.

Honours: Football League: Division 1 – Runners-up 1914–15; Division 2 – Champions 1990–91; Runners-up 1909–10; Division 3 (N) – Champions 1952–53; Division 3 – Champions 1973–74; Division 4 – Runners-up 1962–63. *FA Cup:* Semi-final 1913, 1989–90*Football League Cup:* Runners-up 1990.

Colours: All blue with red piping. **Change colours:** Red and white shirts, white shorts, white stockings.

OLDHAM ATHLETIC 1991–92 LEAGUE RECORD

Match No.	Date		Venue	Opponents	Result		H/T Score	Lg. Pos.	Goalscorers	Attendance
1	Aug	17	A	Liverpool	L	1-2	1-0	—	Barrett	38,841
2		21	H	Chelsea	W	3-0	2-0	—	Marshall, Holden, Currie	14,997
3		24	H	Norwich C	D	2-2	2-1	7	Marshall, Barrett	13,548
4		28	A	Manchester U	L	0-1	0-0	—		42,078
5		31	A	Nottingham F	L	1-3	0-2	17	Marshall	23,244
6	Sep	3	H	Coventry C	W	2-1	1-0	—	Adams, Henry	12,996
7		7	H	Sheffield U	W	2-1	2-0	11	Snodin, Marshall	15,064
8		14	A	Luton T	L	1-2	0-0	12	Marshall	9005
9		21	H	Crystal Palace	L	2-3	1-1	17	Marshall, Holden	13,391
10		28	A	Manchester C	W	2-1	0-1	15	Sharp 2	31,271
11	Oct	5	H	Southampton	D	1-1	0-1	17	Henry	13,133
12		19	H	West Ham U	D	2-2	2-1	16	McDonald, Breacker (og)	14,365
13		26	A	Leeds U	L	0-1	0-0	16		28,199
14	Nov	2	A	Notts Co	L	0-2	0-2	18		7634
15		16	H	Arsenal	D	1-1	0-0	18	Barlow	15,681
16		23	A	QPR	W	3-1	3-1	15	Henry, Palmer, Sharp	8947
17		30	H	Aston Villa	W	3-2	1-1	14	Sharp 2 (1 pen), Palmer	15,370
18	Dec	7	A	Wimbledon	L	1-2	0-1	16	Marshall (pen)	4011
19		14	H	Everton	D	2-2	1-1	14	Palmer, Milligan	14,955
20		21	A	Chelsea	L	2-4	1-3	15	Marshall 2	13,136
21		26	H	Manchester U	L	3-6	0-2	17	Sharp, Milligan, Bernard	18,947
22		28	H	Nottingham F	W	2-1	1-1	16	Sharp, Bernard	16,496
23	Jan	1	A	Sheffield W	D	1-1	0-0	16	Adams	32,679
24		11	A	Norwich C	W	2-1	1-1	15	Holden, Bernard	10,986
25		18	H	Liverpool	L	2-3	1-2	15	Adams, Bernard	18,952
26		25	A	Tottenham H	D	0-0	0-0	14		20,843
27	Feb	1	H	West Ham U	L	0-1	0-1	16		19,012
28		8	A	Leeds U	W	2-0	1-0	12	Bernard, Barlow	18,409
29		15	H	QPR	W	2-1	1-0	9	Holden, Jobson	13,092
30		22	A	Aston Villa	L	0-1	0-0	11		20,509
31		29	H	Wimbledon	L	0-1	0-1	13		12,166
32	Mar	7	A	Everton	L	1-2	1-1	14	Fleming	21,014
33		10	A	Arsenal	L	1-2	0-1	—	Ritchie	22,096
34		14	H	Notts Co	W	4-3	3-1	15	Ritchie 2, Holden, Marshall	12,125
35		21	A	Coventry C	D	1-1	1-1	15	Henry	12,840
36		28	H	Sheffield W	W	3-0	1-0	13	Sharp, Jobson, Adams	15,897
37	Apr	4	A	Sheffield U	L	0-2	0-1	15		19,843
38		11	H	Luton T	W	5-1	2-1	15	Sharp 4, Milligan	13,210
39		18	A	Crystal Palace	D	0-0	0-0	15		12,267
40		20	H	Tottenham H	W	1-0	1-0	12	Henry	15,443
41		25	A	Southampton	L	0-1	0-0	15		15,857
42	May	2	H	Manchester C	L	2-5	1-2	17	Henry, Moulden	18,588

Final League Position: 17

GOALSCORERS

League (63): Sharp 12 (1 pen), Marshall 10 (1 pen), Henry 6, Bernard 5, Holden 5, Adams 4, Milligan 3, Palmer 3, Ritchie 3, Barlow 2, Barrett 2, Jobson 2, Currie 1, Fleming 1, McDonald 1, Moulden 1, Snodin 1, own goals 1.
Rumbelows Cup (11): Ritchie 4, Sharp 2, Henry 1, Holden 1, Jobson 1, Milligan 1, Palmer 1.
FA Cup (3): Adams 1, Palmer 1, Sharp 1.

Hallworth	Halle	Snodin	Henry	Barrett	Jobson	Bernard	Marshall	Sharp	Milligan	Holden	Currie	Kane	Adams	Fleming	Kilcline	Ritchie	Barlow	McDonald	Palmer	Moulden	Keeley	Match No.
1	2	3	4	5	6	7†	8	9	10	11*12			14									1
1	2	3*	4	5	6		8	9	10	11	12		7									2
1	2	3	4	5	6†		8	9	10	11	12		7*	14								3
1		3	4	5				9	10	11	8	12	7	2	6*							4
1	2	3	4	5		7*	8	9	10	11			12	6								5
1	2	3	4	5			8	9	10	11			7	6								6
1	2	3†	4	5			8	9	10	11			7*	14	6	12						7
1	2		4	5			8*	9	10	11			7	3	6	12						8
1	7†	3*	4	5			8	9	10	11			14	2	6	12						9
1			4	5	2	12	8	9	10	11			14	3	6†	7*						10
1			4	5	6	12	8	9	10	11				2*			3		7			11
1			4	5	6		8	9	10	11				2			3		7			12
1		2	4		6		8	9	10	11				2*			3		7	12		13
1		2	4		6		8	9	10	11			14	5†			3		7*12			14
1			4	5	6		8	9	10	11*			12	2			3		7			15
1			4	5	6		8	9	10	12				2*		11	3		7			16
1			4	5	6		8	9	10	12				2		11*	3		7			17
1			4	5	6		8	9	10	11				2		12	3*		7			18
1			4	5	6		8	9	10	11				2			3		7			19
1			4	5	6		8	9	10	12				2*		11	3		7			20
1			4	5	6	14	8	9	10	12				2*		11†	3		7			21
1	2		4	5	6	3	8	9	10	11			7									22
1	2*		4	5	6		8	9		11			7				3	10	12			23
1			4	5	6	3	8	9		11			7	2				10				24
1		3	4	5	6		8	9	10	11			7	2*			12					25
1		2	4	5			8	9	10	11			7				3					26
1		2	4	5	6		8	9	10†	11*			7	14			3		12			27
1		2	4	5	6		8	9		11			7				3	10				28
1		2	4	5	6		8	9		11			7				3	10				29
1			4	5	6		8	9	12	11*			7	2			3	10				30
1			4	5	6	7	8	9	12	11*				2			3	10				31
1			4	5	6			9	10	11				2		12	3	8	7*			32
1			4	5	6			9	10	11			7	2		12	3	8*				33
1			4	5	6			9	10	11			7	2			3	8*	12			34
1			4	5	6			9	10	11			7	2			3	8*	12			35
1			4	5	6		8	9	10	11*			7	2		12	3					36
1			4	5	6		10†	9		11			7	2			3	8*14	12			37
1			4	5	6		14	9	10	11			7†	2			3	8*	12			38
1			4	5	6		8	9	10	11			7	2			3					39
1			4	5	6		8	9	10	11			7	2			3					40
1			4	5	6		8	9	10	11				2			3	12	7*			41
			4	5*	6		8	9	10	11			7	2			3†12			14	1	42
41	10	8	42	29	36	16	41	42	36	38	1	1	21	28	8	7	28	14	14	—	1	
						+5s							+4s	+3s	+3s	+5s	+4s	+7s	+3s	+7s	+2s	

Rumbelows Cup	Second Round	Torquay U (h)		7-1
		(a)		2-0
	Third Round	Derby Co (h)		2-1
	Fourth Round	Manchester U (a)		0-2
FA Cup	Third Round	Leyton Orient (h)		1-1
		(a)		2-4

OLDHAM ATHLETIC

Player and Position	Ht	Wt	Birth Date	Birth Place	Source	Clubs	League App	League Gls
Goalkeepers								
Paul Gerrard			22 1 73	Heywood	Trainee	Oldham Ath	—	—
Jon Hallworth	6 2	12 10	26 10 65	Stockport	School	Ipswich T	45	—
						Swindon T (loan)	—	—
						Bristol R (loan)	2	—
						Fulham (loan)	—	—
						Oldham Ath	118	—
John Keeley	6 1	14 02	27 7 61	Plaistow	Apprentice	Southend U	54	—
						Chelmsford	—	—
						Brighton & HA	138	—
						Oldham Ath	1	—
						Oxford U (loan)	6	—
						Reading (loan)	6	—
Defenders								
Andy Barlow	5 9	11 01	24 11 65	Oldham		Oldham Ath	247	5
Willie Donachie	5 9	11 03	5 10 51	Glasgow	Juniors	Manchester C	351	2
						Portland T	—	—
						Norwich C	11	—
						Portland T	—	—
						Burnley	60	3
						Oldham Ath	169	3
Gunnar Halle	5 11	11 02	11 8 65	Oslo	Lillestrom	Oldham Ath	27	—
Marvin Harriott			20 4 74	Dulwich	Trainee	West Ham U	—	—
						Oldham Ath	—	—
Wayne Heseltine*	5 9	11 06	3 12 69	Bradford	Trainee	Manchester U	—	—
						Oldham Ath	1	—
Andy Holden	6 1	13 00	14 9 62	Flint	Rhyl	Chester C	100	17
						Wigan Ath	49	4
						Oldham Ath	21	4
Richard Jobson	6 1	12 02	9 5 63	Hull	Burton A	Watford	28	4
						Hull C	221	17
						Oldham Ath	80	3
Neil McDonald	5 11	11 04	2 11 65	Newcastle	Wallsend BC	Newcastle U	180	24
						Everton	90	4
						Oldham Ath	17	1
Ian Marshall	6 1	12 12	20 3 66	Liverpool	Apprentice	Everton	15	1
						Oldham Ath	143	34
Robert Miller			3 11 72	Manchester	Trainee	Oldham Ath	—	—
Midfield								
Paul Bernard	5 11	11 08	30 12 72	Edinburgh	Trainee	Oldham Ath	23	6
Mike Fillery*	5 11	13 00	17 9 60	Mitcham	Apprentice	Chelsea	161	32
						QPR	97	9
						Portsmouth	64	6
						Oldham Ath	2	—
						Millwall (loan)	1	—
						Torquay U (loan)	4	—
Craig Fleming	6 0	11 07	6 10 71	Calder	Trainee	Halifax T	57	—
						Oldham Ath	32	1
Nick Henry	5 6	9 08	21 2 69	Liverpool	Trainee	Oldham Ath	149	10
Paul Kane (To Aberdeen Nov 1991)	5 8	9 09	20 6 65	Edinburgh	Salvesen BC	Hibernian	247	33
						Oldham Ath	21	—
Chris Makin			8 5 73	Manchester	Trainee	Oldham Ath	—	—
Mike Milligan	5 8	11 00	20 2 67	Manchester	Apprentice	Oldham Ath	162	17
						Everton	17	1
						Oldham Ath	36	3
Gregory Wilson			11 11 72	Ashton-u-Lyne	Trainee	Oldham Ath	—	—

OLDHAM ATHLETIC

Foundation: It was in 1895 that John Garland, the landlord of the Featherstall and Junction Hotel, decided to form a football club. As Pine Villa they played in the Oldham Junior League. In 1899 the local professional club Oldham County, went out of existence and one of the liquidators persuaded Pine Villa to take over their ground at Sheepfoot Lane and change their name to Oldham Athletic.

First Football League game: 9 September, 1907, Division 2, v Stoke (a) W 3-1 – Hewitson; Hodson, Hamilton; Fay, Walders, Wilson; Ward, W. Dodds (1), Newton (1), Hancock, Swarbrick (1).

Did you know: The Scottish team beaten 1-0 at Stamford Bridge in April 1913 included two players from Oldham Athletic – Dave Wilson and Joe Donnachie.

Managers (and Secretary-managers)
David Ashworth 1906–14, Herbert Bamlett 1914–21, Charlie Roberts 1921–22, David Ashworth 1923–24, Bob Mellor 1924–27, Andy Wilson 1927–32, Jimmy McMullan 1933–34, Bob Mellor 1934–45 (continued as secretary to 1953), Frank Womack 1945–47, Billy Wootton 1947–50, George Hardwick 1950–56, Ted Goodier 1956–58, Norman Dodgin 1958–60, Jack Rowley 1960–63, Les McDowall 1963–65, Gordon Hurst 1965–66, Jimmy McIlroy 1966–68, Jack Rowley 1968–69, Jimmy Frizzell 1970–82, Joe Royle July 1982–.

Player and Position	Ht	Wt	Date	Birth Place	Source	Clubs	League App	Gls
Forwards								
Neil Adams	5 8	10 08	23 11 65	Stoke	Local	Stoke C	32	4
						Everton	20	—
						Oldham Ath (loan)	9	—
						Oldham Ath	84	14
Frankie Bunn	5 11	10 06	6 11 62	Birmingham	Apprentice	Luton T	59	9
						Hull C	95	23
						Oldham Ath	78	26
Rick Holden	5 11	12 07	9 9 64	Skipton		Burnley	1	—
						Halifax T	67	12
						Watford	42	8
						Oldham Ath	129	19
Andrew Kenton*			7 4 73	Crosby	Trainee	Oldham Ath	—	—
Paul Moulden	5 10	11 00	6 9 67	Farnworth	Apprentice	Manchester C	64	18
						Bournemouth	32	13
						Oldham Ath	34	4
Roger Palmer	5 10	11 00	30 1 59	Manchester	Apprentice	Manchester C	31	9
						Oldham Ath	441	141
Andy Ritchie	5 9	11 11	28 11 60	Manchester	Apprentice	Manchester U	33	13
						Brighton & HA	89	23
						Leeds U	136	40
						Oldham Ath	150	66
Graeme Sharp	6 1	11 08	16 10 60	Glasgow	Eastercraigs	Dumbarton	40	17
						Everton	322	111
						Oldham Ath	42	12
Neil Tolson	6 01	10 07	25 10 73	Wordley	Trainee	Walsall	9	1
						Oldham Ath	—	—

Trainees
Everingham, Nicholas P; Eyre, John R; Graham, Richard E; Gray, Ian J; Hall, David T; Hoolickin, Anthony P; Lane, Steven; Lockley, Richard J; Mayo, Jonathan P; Price, Stephen J; Rickers, Paul S.

Associated Schoolboys
Allott, Mark S; Beresford, David; Darnbrough, Lee; Ferguson, Richard; Graham, Alan A; Hall, Mark; Hill, Phillip A; Hughes, Andrew J; Johnson, Adrian; Kay, Simon P; Levendis, Andrew; Meehan, Andrew T; Quinn, Dean S; Richardson, Lloyd M; Smith, Howard; Smith, Matthew C; Street, John P; Swinnerton, David C; Thorp, Matthew C; Walker, Ian S.

Associated Schoolboys who have accepted the club's offer of a Traineeship/Contract
Adams, Christian; Berry, Matthew; Boden, Liam T; Booth, Matthew J; Feltham, Paul D; Frost, John A; Hilton, Robert C; Knapman, Stephen C; Pemberton, Martin C; Serrant, Carl; Speak, Matthew I; Woods, Andrew N.

388

OXFORD UNITED 1991–92 *Back row (left to right):* Matthew Keeble, Paul Simpson, Garry Smart, John Durnin, Paul Byrne, Stuart Fisher, Joey Beauchamp, Matthew McDonnell, Paul Evans, Les Robinson, Paul Harwood.
Centre row: Maurice Evans (General Manager), John Clinkard (Physiotherapist), Darren Jackson, Ceri Evans, Ken Veysey, Andrew Melville, Paul Kee, Jon Muttock, Chris Allen, David Moss (Coach), Steve McClaren (Youth Coach).
Front row: Mark Stein, Mickey Lewis, Michael Ford, Jimmy Magilton, Brian Horton (Manager), Steve Foster, Lee Nogan, David Penney, Les Phillips.

Division 1   **OXFORD UNITED**

Manor Ground, Headington, Oxford. Telephone Oxford (0865) 61503. Supporters Club: (0865) 63063. Clubcall (information) 0898 121029. Clubcall (match commentary) 0898 121172. Fax No: (0865) 741820

Ground capacity: 11,071.

Record attendance: 22,750 v Preston NE, FA Cup 6th rd, 29 February 1964.

Record receipts: £71,304 v Aston Villa, Milk Cup semi-final, 12 March 1986.

Pitch measurements: 110yd × 75yd.

President: The Duke of Marlborough.

Chairman: P. D. McGeough.

Managing Director: K. A. Cox.

Directors: D. M. Clitheroe, P. L. Lowe, T. J. Midgley (Environmental director).s.

Manager: Brian Horton. *Coach:* David Moss. *Physio:* John Clinkard. *Secretary:* Mick Brown. *Marketing manager:* Ross Fenton.

Year Formed: 1893. Turned Professional: 1949. Ltd Co.: 1949.

Former Grounds: 1893–94 Headington Quarry; 1894–98 Wootten's Field; 1898–1902 Sandy Lane Ground; 1902–09 Britannia Field; 1909–10 Sandy Lane; 1910–14 Quarry Recreation Ground; 1914–22 Sandy Lane; 1922–25 The Paddock Manor Road; 1925–Manor Ground.

Former Names: 1893, Headington; 1894, Headington United; 1960, Oxford United.

Club Nickname: 'The U's'.

Record League Victory: 7-0 v Barrow, Division 4, 19 December 1964 – Fearnley; Beavon, Quartermann; Ron Atkinson (1), Kyle, Jones; Morris, Booth (3), Willey (1), Graham Atkinson (1), Harrington (1).

Record Cup Victory: 6-0 v Gillingham, League Cup, 2nd rd (1st leg), 24 September 1986 – Judge; Langan, Trewick, Phillips (Brock), Briggs, Shotton, Houghton (1), Aldridge (4 incl. 1p), Charles (Leworthy), Hebberd, Slatter. (1 og).

Record Defeat: 0-6 v Liverpool, Division 1, 22 March 1986.

Most League Points (2 for a win): 61, Division 4, 1964–65.

Most League points (3 for a win): 95, Division 3, 1983–84.

Most League Goals: 91, Division 3, 1983–84.

Highest League Scorer in Season: John Aldridge, 30, Division 2, 1984–85.

Most League Goals in Total Aggregate: Graham Atkinson, 77, 1962–73.

Most Capped Player: Ray Houghton, 12 (46), Eire and Neil Slatter, 12 (22), Wales.

Most League Appearances: John Shuker, 478, 1962–77.

Record Transfer Fee Received: £1,190,000 from Derby Co for Dean Saunders, October 1988.

Record Transfer Fee Paid: £285,000 to Gillingham for Colin Greenall, February 1988.

Football League Record: 1962 Elected to Division 4; 1965–68 Division 3; 1968–76 Division 2; 1976–84 Division 3; 1984–85 Division 2; 1985–88 Division 1; 1988–92 Division 2; 1992– Division 1.

Honours: Football League: Division 1 best season: 18th, 1985–86, 1986–87; Division 2 – Champions 1984–85; Division 3 – Champions 1967–68, 1983–84; Division 4 – Promoted 1964–65 (4th). *FA Cup:* best season: 6th rd, 1963–64 (record for 4th Division club). *Football League Cup:* Winners 1985–86.

Colours: Gold, navy blue trim, navy blue shorts, navy stockings. **Change colours:** All red.

OXFORD UNITED 1991–92 LEAGUE RECORD

Match No.	Date		Venue	Opponents	Result		H/T Score	Lg. Pos.	Goalscorers	Attendance
1	Aug	17	A	Port Vale	L	1-2	1-0	—	Magilton	6984
2		24	H	Grimsby T	L	1-2	1-2	23	Magilton	4511
3		31	A	Sunderland	L	0-2	0-1	24		16,151
4	Sep	4	H	Middlesbrough	L	1-2	0-0	—	Nogan	4229
5		7	A	Wolverhampton W	L	1-3	0-3	24	Nogan	12,549
6		14	H	Millwall	D	2-2	1-2	24	Aylott, Melville	4622
7		18	H	Derby Co	W	2-0	0-0	—	Aylott, Penney	4319
8		21	A	Bristol R	L	1-2	0-0	24	Penney	4854
9		28	H	Plymouth Arg	W	3-2	1-0	22	Nogan, Simpson, Penney	3726
10	Oct	5	A	Ipswich T	L	1-2	0-2	23	Magilton	9932
11		12	H	Tranmere R	W	1-0	0-0	21	Aylott	5760
12		19	A	Newcastle U	L	3-4	1-2	22	Durnin, Ford, Lewis	16,454
13		23	H	Charlton Ath	L	1-2	0-0	—	Magilton	4069
14		26	H	Leicester C	L	1-2	0-1	23	Simpson	5206
15		30	A	Southend U	W	3-2	3-1	—	Stein, Simpson 2	4873
16	Nov	2	H	Barnsley	L	0-1	0-1	22		3419
17		6	A	Watford	L	0-2	0-1	—		4785
18		9	A	Portsmouth	L	1-2	0-1	23	Magilton	7557
19		16	H	Bristol C	D	1-1	0-0	24	Simpson	5780
20		23	H	Brighton & HA	W	3-1	1-0	24	Simpson, Magilton, Nogan	4563
21		30	A	Cambridge U	D	1-1	0-0	23	Nogan	6496
22	Dec	7	H	Blackburn R	L	1-3	0-2	24	Melville	5924
23		26	H	Southend U	L	0-1	0-0	24		5601
24		28	H	Sunderland	W	3-0	0-0	24	Durnin, Aylott, Beauchamp	6140
25	Jan	8	A	Charlton Ath	D	2-2	2-0	—	Durnin, Beauchamp	4101
26		11	A	Grimsby T	L	0-1	0-1	24		5117
27		18	H	Port Vale	D	2-2	1-1	24	Beauchamp, Lewis	4199
28		28	A	Swindon T	L	1-2	0-1	—	Magilton	8926
29	Feb	1	H	Newcastle U	W	5-2	1-0	24	Foster 2, Durnin, Simpson, Aylott	5872
30		8	A	Leicester C	L	1-2	0-1	24	Melville	12,178
31		15	A	Brighton & HA	W	2-1	2-1	23	Simpson 2	6096
32		22	H	Cambridge U	W	1-0	1-0	23	Melville	5605
33		29	A	Blackburn R	D	1-1	1-1	23	Durnin	13,917
34	Mar	7	H	Swindon T	W	5-3	3-2	19	Durnin 2, Magilton (pen), Beauchamp 2	7795
35		11	A	Watford	D	0-0	0-0	—		5808
36		14	A	Barnsley	L	0-1	0-0	22		5436
37		21	H	Portsmouth	W	2-1	0-0	22	Beauchamp, Aylott	8432
38		28	A	Bristol C	D	1-1	0-0	21	Bannister	12,402
39	Apr	1	A	Millwall	L	1-2	0-0	—	Allen	5850
40		4	H	Wolverhampton W	W	1-0	0-0	20	Penney	7165
41		11	A	Derby Co	D	2-2	1-1	20	Magilton (pen), Lewis	15,555
42		15	A	Middlesbrough	L	1-2	0-0	—	Magilton	11,928
43		18	H	Bristol R	D	2-2	2-0	20	Magilton, Lewis	6891
44		20	A	Plymouth Arg	L	1-3	1-2	21	Bannister	9735
45		25	H	Ipswich T	D	1-1	1-1	22	Magilton	10,525
46	May	2	A	Tranmere R	W	2-1	0-0	21	Durnin, Beauchamp	9173

Final League Position: 21

GOALSCORERS

League (66): Magilton 12 (2 pens), Simpson 9, Durnin 8, Beauchamp 7, Aylott 6, Nogan 5, Lewis 4, Melville 4, Penney 4, Bannister 2, Foster 2, Allen 1, Ford 1, Stein 1.
Rumbelows Cup (0).
FA Cup (5): Beauchamp 1, Magilton 1 (1 pen), Penney 1, Simpson 1, Vickers 1 (o pens).

Veysey	Robinson	Ford	Jackson	Foster	Melville	Magilton	Stein	Nogan	Penney	Simpson	Durnin	Byrne	Evans	Phillips	Lewis	Smart	Kee	Aylott	Beauchamp	Harris	Druce	Keeley	McClaren	Wanless	Allen	Williams	Bannister	Match No.
1	2	3	4	5	6	7	8	9	10*	11	12																	1
1	2	3		5	6	7	8*	4	10	11†	9	12	14															2
1	2	3		5		7	8*	9	10	11	12		6	4														3
1	2	3		5	6	7		9		11	10			4	8													4
1	2*	3		5	6	7		9	12	11	10			4	8†	14												5
	2			5	6	7			10	12	11			4	8*	3	1	9										6
	2			5	6	7			10	8	11			4		3	1	9										7
	2			5	6	7			10	8	11*	12		4		3	1	9										8
1	2			5	6	7			10	8	11			4*		3		9	12									9
1	2			5	6	7			10	8*	11				4	3		9	12									10
1	2			5	6	7			10	11	8				4	3		9										11
1		2		5	6	7			10	11	8				4	3		9										12
1		2		5	6	7		12	10*	11	8				4	3		9										13
	2			5	6	7	8		10	12					4	3	1	9		11*								14
	2			5	6	7	8*		10	11					4	3	1	9	12									15
	2			5	6	7	8†		10*	11			14		4	3	1	9	12									16
	2			5	6	7			10	11	8				4	3		9				1						17
	2			5	6	7			10	11	12				4	3		9				1	8*					18
	2			5	6	7			10	11					4	3		9				1	8					19
	2			5	6	7			10*	11	12				4	3		9				1	8					20
	2			5	6	7			10	11	12				4	3		9*				1	8					21
	2				6	7			10	11	12		5		4	3		9*	14			1	8†					22
1	2				6	7				11	10		5		4	3		9	8									23
1	2				6	7				11	10		5		4	3		9	8									24
1	2				6	7				11	10		5		4	3		9	8									25
1	2				6	7				11	10		5		4	3		9	8*						12			26
1	2†				6	7			14	11	10*		5		4	3		9	8						12			27
1		14			6	7		2		11	10*		5		4	3†		9	8						12			28
1		3	2		6	7				11	10		5		4			9	8									29
1	2		3		6					11	10		5		4				8				7		12	9*		30
1	2	3			6	7				11	10		5		4			9	8									31
1		3			6	7					10		5		4	2		9	8					11				32
1					6	7					10		5		4	2		9	8					11	3			33
1					6	7			12		10		5		4	2		9*	8					11	3			34
1					6	7			12		10		5		4	2		9*	8					11	3			35
1					6	7			12		10		5		4	2		9	8					11*	3			36
1					6	7					10		5		4	2		9	8					11*	3	12		37
1					6	7				11	10*		5		4	2		9	8						3	12		38
1					6	7			10*			14	5		4	2		9	8					11†	3	12		39
1					6	7			3		10		5		4	2			8					11		9		40
1					6	7			3		10		5		4	2			8					11		9		41
1					6	7			3		10		5		4	2			8					11		9		42
1					6	7			3		10*		5		4	2		12	8					11		9		43
1					6	7			3		12		5		4	2		9	8					11*			10	44
1					6	7			3		9		5		4	2	1	12	8					11*			10	45
	3				6	7					10		5		4	2	1	9	8					11				46
32	**27**	**9**	**4**	**22**	**45**	**44**	**6**	**22**	**17**	**30**	**28**	**—**	**27**	**7**	**40**	**38**	**8**	**35**	**24**	**1**	**—**	**6**	**4**	**3**	**13**	**7**	**7**	
		+1s			+1s				+6s	+1s	+9s	+1s	+2s		+1s			+2s	+3s				+2s		+3s	+1s	+3s	

Rumbelows Cup	Second Round	Portsmouth (a)	0-0
		(h)	0-1
FA Cup	Third Round	Tranmere R (h)	3-1
	Fourth Round	Sunderland (h)	2-3

OXFORD UNITED

Player and Position	Ht	Wt	Birth Date	Birth Place	Source	Clubs	League App	League Gls
Goalkeepers								
Paul Kee	6 3	12 12	8 11 69	Belfast	Ards	Oxford U	42	—
Ken Veysey	5 11	11 08	8 6 67	Hackney		Torquay U	72	—
						Oxford U	57	—
Defenders								
Ceri Evans	6 1	14 02	2 10 63	Christchurch	Otaga Univ	Oxford U	75	3
Paul Evans*	5 7	11 01	16 3 72	Shrewsbury	Trainee	Oxford U	—	—
Stuart Fisher*	5 11	11 06	21 3 73	Oxford	Trainee	Oxford U	—	—
Mike Ford	5 11	12 05	9 2 66	Bristol		Leicester C	—	—
						Devizes	—	—
						Cardiff C	145	13
						Oxford U	78	5
Steve Foster*	6 0	14 00	24 9 57	Portsmouth	Apprentice	Portsmouth	109	6
						Brighton HA	172	6
						Aston Villa	15	3
						Luton T	163	11
						Oxford U	95	9
Paul Harwood*	5 7	10 08	12 1 73	Oxford	Trainee	Oxford U	—	—
Darren Jackson	6 1	12 08	24 9 71	Bristol	Trainee	Oxford U	11	—
Andy Melville	6 1	12 06	29 11 68	Swansea	School	Swansea C	175	22
						Oxford U	91	7
Jon Muttock*	6 2	13 00	23 12 71	Oxford	Trainee	Oxford U	1	—
Gary Smart	5 9	11 03	29 4 64	Totnes	Wokingham	Oxford U	111	—
Midfield								
Paul Byrne‡	5 9	11 06	30 6 72	Dublin	Trainee	Oxford U	6	—
Mickey Lewis	5 8	12 07	15 2 65	Birmingham	School	WBA	24	—
						Derby Co	43	1
						Oxford U	155	6
Steve McClaren	5 7	9 08	3 5 61	Fulford	Apprentice	Hull C	178	16
						Derby Co	25	—
						Lincoln C (loan)	8	—
						Bristol C	61	2
						Oxford U	33	—
Jim Magilton	5 10	12 07	6 5 69	Belfast	Apprentice	Liverpool	—	—
						Oxford U	81	18
Les Phillips	5 8	10 06	7 1 63	London	Apprentice	Birmingham C	44	3
						Oxford U	168	9
Les Robinson	5 8	11 05	1 3 67	Mansfield		Mansfield T	15	—
						Stockport Co	67	3
						Doncaster R	82	12
						Oxford U	71	—
Paul Wanless	6 01	13 04	14 12 73	Oxford	Trainee	Oxford U	6	—
Forwards								
Chris Allen	5 11	12 02	18 11 72	Oxford	Trainee	Oxford U	14	1
Trevor Aylott*	6 1	14 00	26 11 57	London	Apprentice	Chelsea	29	2
						QPR (loan)	—	—
						Barnsley	96	26
						Millwall	32	5
						Luton T	32	10
						Crystal Palace	53	12
						Barnsley (loan)	9	—
						Bournemouth	147	27
						Birmingham C	27	—
						Oxford U	37	6
Joey Beauchamp	5 11	11 03	13 3 71	Oxford	Trainee	Oxford U	35	7
						Swansea C (loan)	5	2

OXFORD UNITED

Foundation: There had been an Oxford United club around the time of World War I but only in the Oxfordshire Thursday League and there is no connection with the modern club which began as Headington in 1893, adding "United" a year later. Playing first on Quarry Fields and subsequently Wootten's Fields, they owe much to a Dr. Hitchings for their early development.

First Football League game: 18 August, 1962, Division 4, v Barrow (a) L 2-3 – Medlock; Beavon, Quartermain; R. Atkinson, Kyle, Jones; Knight, G. Atkinson (1), Houghton (1), Cornwell, Colfar.

Did you know: Oxford United failed to score in only six out of 64 League and Cup games in 1983–84 when 15 of their players appeared on the scoresheet.

Managers (and Secretary-managers)
Harry Thompson 1949–58 (Player Manager 1949–51), Arthur Turner 1959–69 (continued as GM to 1972), Ron Saunders 1969, Gerry Summers 1969–75, Mick Brown 1975–79, Bill Asprey 1979–80, Ian Greaves 1980–82, Jim Smith 1982–85, Maurice Evans 1985–88, Mark Lawrenson 1988, Brian Horton October 1988–.

Player and Position	Ht	Wt	Date	Birth Place	Source	Clubs	League App	Gls
Mark Druce	5 11	11 11	3 3 74	Oxford	Trainee	Oxford U	2	—
John Durnin	5 10	11 10	18 8 65	Liverpool	Waterloo Dock	Liverpool	—	—
						WBA (loan)	5	2
						Oxford U	124	33
Matthew Keeble	5 5	9 12	8 9 72	Chipping Norton	Trainee	Oxford U	—	—
Matt McDonnell	5 10	10 10	10 4 71	Reading	Trainee	Oxford U	—	—
David Penney	5 8	10 07	17 8 64	Wakefield	Pontefract	Derby Co	19	—
						Oxford U	61	7
						Swansea C (loan)	12	3

Trainees
Bayliss, Gary J; Caine, Michael F; Conneely, Michael; Didcock, Tristan; Ford, Robert J; Girolami, Adriano U; Holmes, Keith N; Maisey, Darren; Morrissey, Terence; Mutchell, Robert D; Stevens, Greg R; Tavinor, Stephen J; Wallbridge, Andrew J; Wild, Robert P.

Associated Schoolboys
Bastable, Gary J; Byles, Paul J; Gardner, John W; Goodwin, Richard; Gordon, Ian P; Hammond, Paul J; Keane, Paul; Lyford, Neil R; Mann, Alan S; McGregor, Christian N; Moodey, Jonathan J; Smith, Lee J; Wells, Nicholas K; Whitehead, Mathew B; Wilsdon, Christian J.

Associated Schoolboys who have accepted the club's offer of a Traineeship/Contract
Border, Benjamin J; Forinton, Howard L; Godfrey, Russell L; Goodall, Grant S; Greig, Neil J; Maciak, Jason; Watts, Darren W.

PETERBOROUGH UNITED 1991–92 *Back row (left to right):* Mick Halsall, Garry Kimble, Garry Butterworth, Fred Barber, Ken Charley, Micky Turner, Paul Culpin, Neil Pope.

Centre row: Bill Harvey (Club Physiotherapist), Peter Costello, Chris Swailes, David Robinson, Ian Bennett, Steve Welsh, Pat Gavin, Hamish Curtis, Chris White, Keith Oakes (Team Physiotherapist).

Front row: Marcus Ebdon, Ian McInerney, Worrell Sterling, Lil Fuccillo (Team Coach), Chris Turner (Manager), Gerry McElhinney (Youth Team Manager), Noel Luke, David Riley, Gary Cooper.

Division 1 **PETERBOROUGH UNITED**

London Road Ground, Peterborough PE2 8AL. Telephone Peterborough (0733) 63947. Fax No: 0733 557210

Ground capacity: 15,414.

Record attendance: 30,096 v Swansea T, FA Cup 5th rd, 20 February 1965.

Record receipts: £51,315 v Brighton & HA, 5th rd, 15 February 1986.

Pitch measurements: 112yd × 75yd.

President: C. W. Swift OBE.

Chairman: J. F. Devaney.

Vice-chairman: M. C. Lewis.

Directors: M. G. Cook, FCA, A. Devaney (Miss), J. T. Dykes, A. Palkovich, P. Sagar.

Chief Executive/Company Secretary: M. B. Devaney (Mrs).

Manager: Chris Turner.

Assistant Manager: Lil Fuccillo.

Managing Director/Secretary: Arnold V. Blades.

Physio: Keith Oakes.

Commercial Manager: M. Vincent.

Year Formed: 1934. Turned Professional: 1934. Ltd Co.: 1934.

Club Nickname: 'The Posh'.

Record League Victory: 8-1 v Oldham Ath, Division 4, 26 November 1969 – Drewery; Potts, Noble; Conmy, Wile, Wright; Moss (1), Price (3), Hall (4), Halliday, Robson.

Record Cup Victory: 6-0 v Redditch, FA Cup, 1st rd (replay), 22 November 1971 – Drewery; Carmichael, Brookes; Oakes, Turner, Wright; Conmy, Price (1), Hall (2), Barker (2), Robson (1).

Record Defeat: 1-8 v Northampton T, FA Cup 2nd rd (2nd replay), 18 December 1946.

Most League Points (2 for a win): 66, Division 4, 1960–61.

Most League points (3 for a win): 82, Division 4, 1981–82.

Most League Goals: 134, Division 4, 1960–61.

Highest League Scorer in Season: Terry Bly, 52, Division 4, 1960–61.

Most League Goals in Total Aggregate: Jim Hall, 122, 1967–75.

Most Capped Player: Tony Millington, 8 (21), Wales.

Most League Appearances: Tommy Robson, 482, 1968–81.

Record Transfer Fee Received: £110,000 from Blackpool for Bob Doyle, July 1979.

Record Transfer Fee Paid: £100,000 to Halifax T for David Robinson, July 1989.

Football League Record: 1960 Elected to Division 4; 1961–68 Division 3, when they were demoted for financial irregularities; 1968–74 Division 4; 1974–79 Division 3; 1979–91 Division 4; 1991–92 Division 3; 1992– Division 1.

Honours: Football League: Division 3 best season: promotion through play-offs 1991–92; Division 4 – Champions 1960–61, 1973–74. *FA Cup:* best season: 6th rd, 1965. *Football League Cup:* Semi-final 1966.

Colours: Royal blue shirts, white shorts, blue stockings **Change colours:** Green shirts, white shorts, green stockings.

PETERBOROUGH UNITED 1991–92 LEAGUE RECORD

Match No.	Date		Venue	Opponents	Result		H/T Score	Lg. Pos.	Goalscorers	Attendance
1	Aug	17	H	Preston NE	W	1-0	0-0	—	Riley	6036
2		24	A	Hull C	W	2-1	0-0	4	Kimble, McInerney	4806
3		31	H	Stoke C	D	1-1	1-1	6	Kimble	7174
4	Sep	3	A	Bury	L	0-3	0-2	—		2240
5		7	H	Wigan Ath	D	0-0	0-0	8		4488
6		14	A	Birmingham C	D	1-1	0-0	9	Hicks (og)	9408
7		17	A	WBA	L	0-4	0-2	—		10,037
8		21	H	Exeter C	D	1-1	1-0	16	Halsall (pen)	4249
9		28	A	Swansea C	L	0-1	0-0	18		2685
10	Oct	5	H	Leyton Orient	L	0-2	0-1	19		4291
11		12	A	Brentford	L	1-2	0-1	19	Culpin	7705
12		19	A	Reading	D	1-1	1-0	20	Charlery	2954
13		26	H	Hartlepool U	W	3-2	2-0	19	Riley 2, Charlery	3385
14	Nov	2	A	Shrewsbury T	L	0-2	0-0	21		1866
15		5	H	Chester C	W	2-0	2-0	—	Charlery 2	2810
16		9	H	Bradford C	W	2-1	1-0	14	Riley, Sterling	9224
17		23	A	Darlington	W	2-1	0-1	12	Riley, Charlery	2815
18		30	H	Torquay U	D	1-1	0-0	12	Culpin	4007
19	Dec	14	A	Stockport Co	L	0-3	0-1	15		2768
20		20	H	Hull C	W	3-0	2-0	—	Robinson D, Riley, Charlery	7904
21		26	A	Stoke C	D	3-3	2-2	12	Robinson D, Halsall, Sterling	14,732
22		28	A	Preston NE	D	1-1	1-0	12	Charlery	5200
23	Jan	1	H	Bury	D	0-0	0-0	12		5567
24		11	H	Fulham	W	4-1	1-0	11	Ebdon (pen), Adcock 2, Sterling	4975
25		18	A	Huddersfield T	D	0-0	0-0	12		8763
26	Feb	1	H	Reading	W	5-3	2-2	10	Lee (og), Halsall 2, Kimble, Charlery	3792
27		8	A	Hartlepool U	W	1-0	0-0	9	Charlery	2481
28		15	H	Stockport Co	W	3-2	1-1	9	Adcock 2, Cooper G (pen)	5301
29		22	A	Fulham	W	1-0	1-0	8	Adcock	5233
30		29	H	Bolton W	W	1-0	0-0	8	Adcock	6270
31	Mar	3	H	Huddersfield T	W	2-0	1-0	—	Riley, Barnes	6257
32		7	A	Bournemouth	W	2-1	1-1	6	Barnes, Riley	5379
33		10	A	Chester C	W	4-2	1-1	—	Cooper G 2 (1 pen), Adcock, Barnes	1063
34		14	H	Shrewsbury T	W	1-0	0-0	3	Halsall	7377
35		21	A	Bradford C	L	1-2	0-2	5	Riley	6896
36		24	A	Bolton W	L	1-2	1-2	—	Charlery	5421
37		28	H	Darlington	D	1-1	1-1	6	Robinson D	5218
38		31	H	Birmingham C	L	2-3	1-1	—	Barnes 2	12,081
39	Apr	3	A	Wigan Ath	L	0-3	0-1	—		2485
40		8	H	Bournemouth	W	2-0	2-0	—	Charlery, Cooper G (pen)	4910
41		11	H	WBA	D	0-0	0-0	7		9040
42		18	A	Exeter C	D	2-2	1-1	7	Charlery, Butterworth	3057
43		21	A	Swansea C	W	3-1	1-0	—	Charlery, Kimble, Sterling	5526
44		25	A	Leyton Orient	W	2-1	0-1	6	Charlery, Ebdon	5996
45		28	A	Torquay U	D	2-2	1-1	—	Charlery 2 (1 pen)	1934
46	May	2	H	Brentford	L	0-1	0-1	6		14,539

Final League Position: 6

GOALSCORERS

League (65): Charlery 16 (1 pen), Riley 9, Adcock 7, Barnes 5, Halsall 5 (1 pen), Cooper G 4 (3 pens), Kimble 4, Sterling 4, Robinson D 3, Culpin 2, Ebdon 2 (1 pen), Butterworth 1, McInerney 1, own goals 2.
Rumbelows Cup (11): Gavin 4, Charlery 2, Kimble 2, Halsall 1, Riley 1, Sterling 1.
FA Cup (7): Cooper G 2 (1 pens), Charlery 1, Culpin 1, Halsall 1, Riley 1, Sterling 1.

Barber	White	Butterworth	Halsall	Robinson D	Welsh	Sterling	Ebdon	Gavin	Riley	Kimble	Luke	McInerney	Cooper G	Charley	Costello	Culpin	Johnson	Howarth	Robinson R	Adcock	Barnes	Cooper S	Salman	Bennett	Match No.
1	2	3	4	5	6	7*	8	9†	10	11	12	14													1
1	2	3	4	5	6		8	9	10*	11	7	12													2
1	2	3	4	5	6	14	8	9	10*	11†	7	12													3
1	2	3	4	5	6	14	8†	9	10*	11	7	12													4
1		3	4	5	6	7				11	2	10	8	9*	12										5
1		3	4	5	6	7		9		11	2	10	8												6
1	14	3	4	5	6			9		11†	2	10*	8	12											7
1		3	4	5	6	7	14	9		11*	2	12	8†	10											8
1		3	4	5	6	7		9*		11	2	12	8	10											9
1		3	4	5	6	7	14	9		11	2	12	8†	10*											10
1	2	3	4	5	6	7	14	9*		11			8†	10	12										11
1	2		4		6	7		9*		11			8	10	12	3	5								12
1	2		4		6	7		9		11			8	10		3	5								13
1	8†	14	4	5	6	7*		9		11	2			10	12	3									14
1	14		4	5	6	7		9		11†	2		8*	10	12	3									15
1	11		4	5	6	7		9			2		8	10		3									16
1			4	5	6	7		9		11			8	10		3									17
1			4	5	6	7		9		11*	2		8	10	12	3									18
1			4	5	6	7		9*		11	2		8	10	12	3†			14						19
1			4	5	6	7	12	9		11	2		8*	10		3									20
1			4	5	6	7		9		11*	2		8	10	12	3†			14						21
1			4	5	6	7		9		11*	2		8	10		3			12						22
1			4	5	6	7	8	9*		11	2			10				3	12						23
1	12		4	5	6	7	8			11*	2			10				3	9						24
1			4	5	6	7	8			11	2			10				3	9						25
1			4	5	6	7	12			11*	2		8	10				3	9						26
1			4	5	6	7				11	2		8	10				3	9						27
1			4	5	6	7	12				2		8	10				3	9	11*					28
1			4	5	6	7					2		8	10				3	9	11					29
1			4	5	6	7			10		2		8					3	9	11					30
1			4	5	6	7			10		2		8					3	9	11					31
1			4	5	6	7			10		2		8					3	9	11					32
1			4	5	6	7			10		2		8					3	9	11					33
1	14		4	5	6	7			10*		2		8		12			3†	9	11					34
1			4	5	6	7	12				2		8	10				3	9	11*					35
1	14		4	5	6	7	12				2		8†	10				3	9	11*					36
1			4	5	6	7					2		8	10				3	9	11*	12				37
1			4	5	6	7					2		8		12			3	9	11	10*				38
1			4	5		7					2		8		12			3	9	11*	10	6			39
			4	5	6	7	14				2		8	10†				3	9*	11			12	1	40
			4	5	6	7	14				2		8	10				3	9*	11†			12	1	41
			4	5	6	7	8	14			2			10	12			3	9*	11†				1	42
			4		6	7	8			11	2			10			5	3	9*				12	1	43
			4	5		7	8			11*	2			10			6	3	9				12	1	44
			4	5		7	8			11	2			10			6	3	9*				12	1	45
			4	5		7	8			11*	2			10			6	3	9				12	1	46

```
39  7 14 45 43 42 43 12  8 23 30 42  3 33 33  —  — 11  6 24 23 15  2  1  7
 +  +                 +  +  +  +           +  +        +  +  +           +
1s 5s              2s 3s 3s 5s         1s 7s      4s 1s 7s     1s 3s 1s     7s
```

Rumbelows Cup	First Round	Aldershot (h)	3-1
		(a)	2-1
	Second Round	Wimbledon (a)	2-1
		(h)	2-2
	Third Round	Newcastle U (h)	1-0
	Fourth Round	Liverpool (h)	1-0
	Fifth Round	Middlesbrough (h)	0-0
		(a)	0-1
FA Cup	First Round	Harlow (h)	7-0
	Second Round	Reading (h)	0-0
		(a)	0-1

PETERBOROUGH UNITED
Goalkeepers

Name	Ht	Wt	Born	Birthplace	Source	Club	Apps	Gls
Fred Barber	5 11	11 07	28 8 63	Ferryhill	Apprentice	Darlington	135	—
						Everton	—	—
						Walsall	153	—
						Peterborough U (loan)	6	—
						Chester C (loan)	8	—
						Blackpool (loan)	2	—
						Peterborough U	39	—
Ian Bennett†	6 0		10 10 70	Worksop	Trainee	Newcastle U	—	—
						Peterborough U	14	—

Defenders

Name	Ht	Wt	Born	Birthplace	Source	Club	Apps	Gls
Paul Hill‡			28 1 73	Nottingham	Trainee	Peterborough U	1	—
Lee Howarth‡	6 01	12 06	3 1 68	Bolton	Chorley	Peterborough U	7	—
Peter Johnson‡	5 9	11 00	5 10 58	Harrogate	Apprentice	Middlesbrough	43	—
						Newcastle U	16	—
						Bristol C (loan)	20	—
						Doncaster R	12	—
						Darlington	89	2
						Crewe Alex	8	—
						Exeter C	5	—
						Southend U	126	3
						Gillingham	69	2
						Peterborough U	11	—
David Robinson	6 0	12 03	14 1 65	Cleveland	Billingham	Hartlepool U	66	1
						Halifax T	72	1
						Peterborough U	94	9
Ronnie Robinson	5 9	11 00	22 10 66	Sunderland	Vaux Breweries	Ipswich T	—	—
						Leeds U	27	—
						Doncaster R	78	5
						WBA	1	—
						Rotherham U	86	2
						Peterborough U	27	—
Chris Swailes‡	6 1	12 11	19 10 70	Gateshead	Trainee	Ipswich T	—	—
						Peterborough U	—	—
Steve Welsh	6 0	12 03	19 4 68	Glasgow	Army	Cambridge U	1	—
						Peterborough U	42	—
Chris White†	5 11	11 10	11 12 70	Chatham	Trainee	Portsmouth	—	—
						Peterborough U	8	—

Midfield

Name	Ht	Wt	Born	Birthplace	Source	Club	Apps	Gls
Garry Butterworth†	5 8	10 11	8 9 69	Peterborough	Trainee	Peterborough U	124	4
Gary Cooper	5 8	11 03	20 11 65	Edgware	Fisher Ath	Maidstone U	60	7
						Peterborough U	39	5
Marcus Ebdon†	5 9	11 00	17 10 70	Pontypool	Trainee	Everton	—	—
						Peterborough U	15	2
Mick Halsall	5 10	11 04	21 7 61	Bootle	Apprentice	Liverpool	—	—
						Birmingham C	36	3
						Carlisle U	92	11
						Grimsby T	12	—
						Peterborough U	223	26
Noel Luke	5 11	10 11	28 12 64	Birmingham	School	WBA	9	1
						Mansfield T	50	9
						Peterborough U	249	27
Micky Turner†	5 10	12 07	15 10 71	Cuckfield	Trainee	Portsmouth	—	—
						Peterborough U	—	—

Forwards

Name	Ht	Wt	Born	Birthplace	Source	Club	Apps	Gls
Tony Adcock	5 10	12 04	27 2 63	Bethnal Green	Apprentice	Colchester U	210	98
						Manchester C	15	5
						Northampton T	72	30
						Bradford C	38	6
						Northampton T	35	10
						Peterborough U	24	7

PETERBOROUGH UNITED

Foundation: The old Peterborough & Fletton club, founded in 1923, was suspended by the FA during season 1932–33 and disbanded. Local enthusiasts determined to carry on and in 1934 a new professional club Peterborough United was formed and entered the Midland League the following year.

First Football League game: 20 August 1960, Division 4, v Wrexham (h) W 3-0 – Walls; Stafford, Walker; Rayner, Rigby, Norris; Halls, Emery (1), Bly (1), Smith, McNamee (1).

Did you know: In their record-breaking 1960–61 season Peterborough United were prevented from scoring at home by only one side, Stockport County, who won 1-0. Yet United beat them 6-0 at Stockport.

Managers (and Secretary-managers)
Jock Porter 1934–36, Fred Taylor 1936–37, Vic Poulter 1937–38, Sam Madden 1938–48, Jack Blood 1948–50, Bob Gurney 1950–52, Jack Fairbrother 1952–54, George Swindin 1954–58, Jimmy Hagan 1958–62, Jack Fairbrother 1962–64, Gordon Clark 1964–67, Norman Rigby 1967–69, Jim Iley 1969–72, Noel Cantwell 1972–77, John Barnwell 1977–78, Billy Hails 1978–79, Peter Morris 1979–82, Martin Wilkinson 1982–83, John Wile 1983–86, Noel Cantwell 1986–88 (continued as GM), Mick Jones 1988–89, Mark Lawrenson 1989–90, Chris Turner January 1991–.

Bobby Barnes	5 7	10 05	17 12 62	Kingston	Apprentice	West Ham U	43	5
						Scunthorpe U (loan)	6	—
						Aldershot	49	26
						Swindon T	45	13
						Bournemouth	14	—
						Northampton T	99	37
						Peterborough U	15	5
Ken Charlery	6 1	12 07	28 11 64	Stepney	Fisher Ath	Maidstone U	59	11
						Peterborough U	78	32
Peter Costello	6 0	11 07	31 10 69	Halifax	Trainee	Bradford C	20	2
						Rochdale	34	10
						Peterborough U	6	—
						Lincoln C (loan)	3	—
Pat Gavin†	6 0	12 00	5 6 67	Hammersmith	Hanwell T	Gillingham	13	7
						Leicester C	3	—
						Gillingham (loan)	34	1
						Peterborough U	22	5
Garry Kimble*	5 8	11 00	6 8 66	Poole		Charlton Ath	9	1
						Exeter C (loan)	1	—
						Cambridge U	41	2
						Doncaster R	65	1
						Fulham	3	—
						Maidstone U	—	—
						Gillingham	48	1
						Peterborough U	30	4
Ian McInerney†			1 9 72	Limerick	Trainee	Peterborough U	10	1
David Riley†	5 7	10 10	8 12 60	Northampton	Keyworth U	Nottingham F	12	2
						Darlington (loan)	6	2
						Peterborough U (loan)	12	2
						Port Vale	76	11
						Peterborough U	84	21
Worrell Sterling	5 8	10 08	8 6 65	Bethnal Green	Apprentice	Watford	94	14
						Peterborough U	149	21

Trainees
Allen, Daniel J; Brown, Paul J; Collins, David J; Dawson, James P; Denniss, Clive; Hyatt, Lee C; Judge, Kevin A; Matthews, Michael; Murray, Marc; O'Connor, Jason J; Oliver, Thomas A; Shooter, Ian; Simpson, Craig G; Wilson, Simon R.

**Non-Contract
Bennett, Ian M; Edbon, Marcus; Gavin, Patrick J; Turner, Michael G; White, Christopher J.

**Non-Contract Players who are retained must be re-signed before they are eligible to play in League matches.

PLYMOUTH ARGYLE 1991–92 *Back row (left to right):* Eamonn Salmon (Physiotherapist), Paul Maxwell, Ryan Cross, Michael Evans, Nicky Marker, Robbie Turner, Morrys Scott, Adrian Burrows, Steve Morgan, Andy Morrison, Peter Distin (Youth Development Officer).

Centre row: Alan Gillett (Assistant Team Manager), Danis Salman, Mark Quamina, Mark Fiore, Mark Damerell, Steve Morris, Rhys Wilmot, Dave Walters, Adam King, Kenny Brown, Darren Garner, Owen Pickard, Gordon Nisbet (Youth Team Manager).

Front row: Tony Spearing, Andy Clement, Paul Adcock, Kevin Hodges, David Kemp (Team Manager), Martin Barlow, Jason Rowbotham, Marc Edworthy, Mark Clode.

Division 2   **PLYMOUTH ARGYLE**

Home Park, Plymouth, Devon P12 3DQ. Telephone Plymouth (0752) 562561-2-3. Marketing Department: 0752 569597. Lottery Shop: 561041. Pilgrim Shop: 0752 558292.

Ground capacity: 19,700.

Record attendance: 43,596 v Aston Villa, Division 2, 10 October 1936.

Record receipts: £96,989.57 v Derby Co, FA Cup 6th rd, 10 March 1984.

Pitch measurements: 112yd × 75yd.

President: S. J. Rendell.

Chairman: D. McCauley.

Directors: P. Bloom, G. Jasper, D. Angilley, I. Jones.

Player-manager: Peter Shilton.

Assistant manager: John McGovern.

Chief Executive: Liz Baker.

Commercial Manager: R. Bond.

Year Formed: 1886. Turned Professional: 1903. Ltd Co.: 1903.

Former Names: 1886–1903, Argyle Athletic Club.

Club Nickname: 'The Pilgrims'.

Record League Victory: 8-1 v Millwall, Division 2, 16 January 1932 – Harper; Roberts, Titmuss; Mackay, Pullan, Reed; Grozier, Bowden (2), Vidler (3), Leslie (1), Black (1). (1 og).

Record Cup Victory: 6-0 v Corby T, FA Cup, 3rd rd, 22 January 1966 – Leiper; Book, Baird; Williams, Nelson, Newman; Jones (1), Jackson (1), Bickle (3), Piper (1), Jennings.

Record Defeat: 0-9 v Stoke C, Division 2, 17 December 1960.

Most League Points (2 for a win): 68, Division 3 (S), 1929–30.

Most League points (3 for a win): 87, Division 3, 1985–86.

Most League Goals: 107, Division 3 (S), 1925–26 and 1951–52.

Highest League Scorer in Season: Jack Cock, 32, Division 3 (S), 1925–26.

Most League Goals in Total Aggregate: Sammy Black, 180, 1924–38.

Most Capped Player: Moses Russell, 20 (23), Wales.

Most League Appearances: Kevin Hodges, 529, 1978–92.

Record Transfer Fee Received: £250,000 from Everton for Gary Megson, February 1980 and £250,000 from Bradford C for Sean McCarthy, July 1990.

Record Transfer Fee Paid: £200,000 to Hartlepool U for Paul Dalton, May 1992.

Football League Record: 1920 Original Member of Division 3; 1921–30 Division 3 (S); 1930–50 Division 2; 1950–52 Division 3 (S); 1952–56 Division 2; 1956–58 Division 3 (S); 1958–59 Division 3; 1959–68 Division 2; 1968–75 Division 3; 1975–77 Division 2; 1977–86 Division 3; 1986– Division 2.

Honours: Football League: Division 2 best season: 4th, 1931–32, 1952–53; Division 3 (S) – Champions 1929–30, 1951–52; Runners-up 1921–22, 1922–23, 1923–24, 1924–25, 1925–26, 1926–27 (record of six consecutive years); Division 3 – Champions 1958–59; Runners-up 1974–75, 1985–86. *FA Cup:* best season: semi-final 1983–84. *Football League Cup:* Semi-final 1965, 1974.

Colours: Green and white striped shirts, black shorts, black stockings. **Change colours:** All white.

PLYMOUTH ARGYLE 1991–92 LEAGUE RECORD

Match No.	Date		Venue	Opponents		Result	H/T Score	Lg. Pos.	Goalscorers	Attendance
1	Aug	17	H	Barnsley	W	2-1	1-0	—	Marshall, Turner	6352
2		24	A	Leicester C	L	0-2	0-1	15		11,852
3		31	A	Millwall	W	3-2	2-1	7	Marshall, Burrows, Wood (og)	5369
4	Sep	4	A	Newcastle U	D	2-2	1-0	—	Salman, Marshall	19,543
5		7	H	Charlton Ath	L	0-2	0-0	17		5602
6		14	A	Grimsby T	L	1-2	0-1	19	Burrows	5432
7		17	A	Southend U	L	1-2	0-1	—	Marshall	4585
8		21	H	Middlesbrough	D	1-1	1-0	20	Burrows	5280
9		28	A	Oxford U	L	2-3	0-1	20	Fiore, Barlow	3726
10	Oct	5	H	Swindon T	L	0-4	0-2	22		6208
11		12	A	Blackburn R	L	2-5	0-2	24	Marshall, Barlow	10,830
12		19	A	Bristol R	D	0-0	0-0	24		5049
13		26	H	Watford	L	0-1	0-1	24		4090
14	Nov	2	H	Wolverhampton W	W	1-0	1-0	23	Marshall	4200
15		5	A	Bristol C	L	0-2	0-2	—		7735
16		8	A	Tranmere R	L	0-1	0-0	—		7490
17		16	H	Port Vale	W	1-0	0-0	23	Marshall	4363
18		23	H	Sunderland	W	1-0	0-0	23	Fiore	6007
19		30	A	Brighton & HA	L	0-1	0-0	24		6713
20	Dec	7	H	Ipswich T	W	1-0	1-0	23	Fiore	4986
21		20	H	Newcastle U	W	2-0	1-0	—	Regis, Barlow	5048
22		26	A	Cambridge U	D	1-1	0-0	22	Turner (pen)	7105
23		28	A	Millwall	L	1-2	1-1	22	Morgan	6980
24	Jan	1	H	Portsmouth	W	3-2	2-1	19	Turner, Morrison, Marshall	8887
25		11	H	Leicester C	D	2-2	2-0	21	Witter, Fiore	5846
26		18	A	Barnsley	W	3-1	3-0	18	Marshall 3	5322
27	Feb	1	H	Bristol R	D	0-0	0-0	19		6631
28		4	A	Portsmouth	L	1-4	0-2	—	Regis	10,467
29		8	A	Watford	L	0-1	0-0	21		7260
30		11	H	Cambridge U	L	0-1	0-0	—		4290
31		22	H	Brighton & HA	D	1-1	1-0	20	Smith	5259
32		29	A	Ipswich T	L	0-2	0-0	22		12,852
33	Mar	7	H	Derby Co	D	1-1	1-1	23	Morrison	8864
34		10	H	Bristol C	W	1-0	0-0	—	Marshall	9734
35		14	A	Wolverhampton W	L	0-1	0-0	21		11,556
36		21	H	Tranmere R	W	1-0	0-0	21	Morgan	7447
37		24	A	Derby Co	L	0-2	0-1	—		13,799
38		28	A	Port Vale	L	0-1	0-1	22		5310
39		31	H	Grimsby T	L	1-2	0-1	—	McCall	6274
40	Apr	4	A	Charlton Ath	D	0-0	0-0	23		6787
41		11	H	Southend U	L	0-2	0-1	24		7060
42		16	A	Sunderland	W	1-0	0-0	—	Marshall	28,813
43		18	A	Middlesbrough	L	1-2	1-1	22	Marshall	15,086
44		20	H	Oxford U	W	3-1	2-1	20	Morrison, Marker, Lee	9735
45		25	A	Swindon T	L	0-1	0-1	21		10,463
46	May	2	H	Blackburn R	L	1-3	1-2	22	Smith	17,459

Final League Position: 22

GOALSCORERS

League (42): Marshall 14, Fiore 4, Barlow 3, Burrows 3, Morrison 3, Turner 3 (1 pen), Morgan 2, Regis 2, Smith 2, Lee 1, Marker 1, McCall 1, Salman 1, Witter 1, own goals 1.
Rumbelows Cup (3): Barlow 1, Morrison 1, Turner 1.
FA Cup (0).

Wilmot	Salman	Spearing	Marker	Cross	Morgan	Barlow	Marshall	Turner	Morrison	Fiore	Clement	Quamina	Burrows	Evans	Scott	Edworthy	Walter	Damerell	Hopkins	Hodges K	Garner	Regis	Jones	Meaker	Smith	Witter	Van Rossum	Nugent	Match No.
1	2	3	4	5	6	7	8	9	10	11*	12																		1
1	2	3	4	5	6	12	8	9	10	14	11†	7*																	2
1		3	4		6	7	8	9	10†	2				5	11*	12	14												3
1*12		3	4		6	7	8	9	10	2				5	11														4
		3*	4		6	7	8	9	10	2				5	11†12	14		1											5
	2	3	4		6	7	8		10	12	14			5	9†11*			1											6
	2	3	4		6	7	8		10	11				5	9			1											7
	2	3	4		6	7	8		10	11*12				5	9			1											8
		3	4		6	7	8	9	11	2	10			5				1											9
1	2	3*	4		6	7	8	9	11	10				5	12														10
1	2		4	10*	6	7	8	9	11†3	12				5	14														11
1	2		4	11	6	7	8	9	10*	3				5	12														12
1	2		4	11	6	7*	8		10	3	9			5					12										13
1	2		4	11	6		8		10	3	12	9†14							5		7*								14
1	2		4	11†	6	14	8		10	3		9*12							7	5									15
1	2		4		6	7	8		10	3	11								5			9							16
1	2		4		6	7*	8	11	10	3	12								5†		9	14							17
1		2	4		6		8	11	10	3									5		9	7							18
1		2	4		6	12	8	11	10*	3									5		9	7							19
1		2	4		6		8	11	12	10	3								5*		9	7							20
1	3	2	4		6	12	8	11	5	10											9	7*							21
1	3	2	4		6	7*	8	11	5	10	14										9	12†							22
1	3	2	4		6	7†	8	11	5	10*14						12					9								23
1	3	2	4		6	7	8	11	5	10*						12					9								24
1	12	2			6	7	8	11	5	10*	3										9			4					25
1	10	2	4		6		8	11	5	12	3										9*				7				26
1	10	2	4		6	7	8	11	5*		3										9				12				27
1	10	2	4		6		8	11	3*									5		12	9				7				28
1	10	2	4				8	11	6	12				5						7*	9	3							29
1	3	2	4		6		8	11	7	10*										12	9					5			30
1	2		4		6	7	10	11	8	3				5							9								31
1		2	4		6	12				11†	3		14					7	8*	9			10			5			32
1	2	3	6						11	10	5	4†							14	8*	9			12	7				33
1	2	3	6						11	10	5							7	8	9					4				34
1	2	3	6						11	10†	5	8						14	7*12		9				4				35
1		3	6						11	7	10	5							2		9				8	4			36
1		3	6						11	7	10†	5	8*						2		9				12	4	14		37
1		3	5						11	7†10*								2		14	12	6	9						38
1		5			3				10				4						2			11	6	9					39
		5			3				10			4	12		6				2				9	11					40
		5			3				10			4	12		6				2*		9		11†						41
		5	2		3				10			4		9					7			11							42
			2		3				10				6	5	9				7			11							43
		5	2		3				10*			4		9					7			11							44
		5	2		3†					4	10			9				14	7*12			11							45
		5	2		3				10*	4	12			9†					7			11					14		46
34	26	30	44	12	45	23	44	25	29	25	20	4	14	11	3	7	5	—	8	11	8	21	—	4	14	3	9	2	
		+			+					+	+	+	+	+	+	+	+		+		+	+	+	+		+		+	
		2s			5s					1s	7s	6s	1s	1s	2s	3s	8s		1s		3s	2s	3s	1s		4s		2s	

Lee—Match No. 38(4), 39(7), 40(7), 41(7), 42(6), 43(4), 44(6), 45(6), 46(6); McCall—Match No. 38(8), 39(8), 40(8*), 41(8), 42(8), 43(8), 44(8), 45(8), 46(8); Shilton—Match No. 40(1), 41(1), 42(1), 43(1), 44(1), 45(1), 46(1); Pickard—Match No. 41(14), 44(12).

Rumbelows Cup	First Round	Shrewsbury T (a)		1-1
		(h)		2-2
FA Cup	Third Round	Bristol R (a)		0-5

PLYMOUTH ARGYLE

Player and Position	Ht	Wt	Birth Date	Birth Place	Source	Clubs	League App	League Gls
Goalkeepers								
Steve Morris*	5 11	11 06	28 7 66	Tredegar	Merthyr T	Plymouth Arg	—	—
Peter Shilton†	6 0	14 00	18 9 49	Leicester	Apprentice	Leicester C	286	1
						Stoke C	110	—
						Nottingham F	202	—
						Southampton	188	—
						Derby Co	175	—
						Plymouth Arg	7	—
David Walter*	6 3	13 03	3 9 64	Barnstable	Bideford T	Exeter C	44	—
						Plymouth Arg (loan)	—	—
						Plymouth Arg	15	—
Rhys Wilmot	6 1	12 00	21 2 62	Newport	Apprentice	Arsenal	8	—
						Hereford U (loan)	9	—
						Orient (loan)	46	—
						Swansea C (loan)	16	—
						Plymouth Arg (loan)	17	—
						Plymouth Arg	116	—
Defenders								
Adrian Burrows	5 11	11 12	16 1 59	Sutton	Local	Mansfield T	78	5
						Northampton T	88	4
						Plymouth Arg	235	13
						Southend U (loan)	6	—
Andy Clement*	5 8	11 00	12 11 67	Cardiff	Apprentice	Wimbledon	26	—
						Bristol R (loan)	6	—
						Newport Co (loan)	5	1
						Woking	—	—
						Plymouth Arg	42	—
Ryan Cross	5 11	11 00	11 10 72	Plymouth	Trainee	Plymouth Arg	19	—
Steve McCall	5 11	11 03	15 10 60	Carlisle	Apprentice	Ipswich T	257	7
						Sheffield W	29	2
						Carlisle U (loan)	6	—
						Plymouth Arg	9	1
Nick Marker	6 1	13 00	3 5 65	Exeter	Apprentice	Exeter C	202	3
						Plymouth Arg	195	11
Paul Maxwell*	5 11	11 00	15 7 73	Plymouth	Trainee	Plymouth Arg	—	—
Steve Morgan	5 11	13 00	19 9 68	Oldham	Apprentice	Blackpool	144	10
						Plymouth Arg	85	5
Andy Morrison	5 11	12 00	30 7 70	Inverness	Trainee	Plymouth Arg	84	6
Jason Rowbotham‡	5 9	11 00	3 1 69	Cardiff	Trainee	Plymouth Arg	9	—
Danis Salman*	5 10	11 08	12 3 60	Cyprus	Apprentice	Brentford	325	8
						Millwall	93	4
						Plymouth Arg	74	4
						Peterborough U (loan)	1	—
Tony Spearing	5 9	10 12	7 10 64	Romford	Apprentice	Norwich C	69	—
						Stoke C (loan)	9	—
						Oxford U (loan)	5	—
						Leicester C	73	1
						Plymouth Arg	30	—
Erik Van Rossum*			27 3 63	Nijmegen	Twente	Plymouth Arg	9	—
Midfield								
Mark Clode	5 6	9 06	24 2 73	Plymouth	Trainee	Plymouth Arg	—	—
Mark Edworthy	5 7	9 08	24 12 72	Barnstable	Trainee	Plymouth Arg	15	—
Mark Fiore	5 10	11 10	18 11 69	Southwark	Trainee	Wimbledon	1	—
						Plymouth Arg	82	8
Darren Garner	5 6	11 01	10 12 71	Plymouth	Trainee	Plymouth Arg	17	1
Kevin Hodges	5 8	10 00	12 6 60	Bridport	Apprentice	Plymouth Arg	526	81
						Torquay U (loan)	3	—
Mark Quamina*	5 10	11 07	25 11 69	St Helier	Trainee	Wimbledon	1	—
						Plymouth Arg	5	—

PLYMOUTH ARGYLE

Foundation: The Plymouth Argyle Association Football Club developed out of the Argyle Athletic club which was formed in 1886 at a meeting in Argyle Terrace, Mutley. Plymouth was a rugby stronghold, but servicemen brought soccer to the town and it spread quickly. At first Argyle Athletic Club played both soccer and rugby in colours of green and black. The rugby section was eventually disbanded, and after a number of exhibition games had satisfied the locals of the feasibility of running a professional club, Plymouth Argyle was formed in 1903.

First Football League game: 28 August 1920, Division 3, v Norwich C (h) D 1–1 – Craig; Russell, Atterbury; Logan, Dickinson, Forbes; Kirkpatrick, Jack, Bowler, Heeps (1), Dixon.

Did you know: When Argyle finished Division 3 (S) runners-up six times in a row in the 1920s it was suggested that they did not want promotion (only the top team gained went up those days). However, their finish of a draw followed by five successive victories in one of those seasons (1926–27) is still a club record.

Managers (and Secretary-managers)
Frank Brettell 1903–05, Bob Jack 1905–06, Bill Fullerton 1906-07, Bob Jack 1910–38, Jack Tresadern 1938–47, Jimmy Rae 1948–55, Jack Rowley 1955–60, Neil Dougall 1961, Ellis Stuttard 1961–63, Andy Beattie 1963–64, Malcolm Allison 1964–65, Derek Ufton 1965–68, Billy Bingham 1968–70, Ellis Stuttard 1970–72, Tony Waiters 1972–77, Mike Kelly 1977–78, Malcolm Allison 1978–79, Bobby Saxton 1979–81, Bobby Moncur 1981–83, Johnny Hore 1983–84, Dave Smith 1984–88, Ken Brown 1988–90, David Kemp 1990–92, Peter Shilton March 1992–.

Player and Position	Ht	Wt	Birth Date	Birth Place	Source	Clubs	League App	Gls
Forwards								
Paul Adcock	5 8	10 02	2 5 72	Ilminster	Trainee	Plymouth Arg	12	—
Martin Barlow	5 7	10 03	25 6 71	Barnstable	Trainee	Plymouth Arg	60	4
Mike Evans	6 0	11 02	1 1 73	Plymouth	Trainee	Plymouth Arg	17	—
Stephen Jones§			11 3 74	Plymouth	Trainee	Plymouth Arg	1	—
Dwight Marshall	5 11	11 08	3 10 65	Jamaica	Grays Ath	Plymouth Arg	44	14
Kevin Nugent	6 1	12 04	10 4 69	Edmonton	Trainee	Leyton Orient	94	20
						Cork C (loan)	—	—
						Plymouth Arg	4	—
Owen Pickard*	5 10	11 03	18 11 69	Barnstaple	Trainee	Plymouth Arg	16	1
Dave Regis	6 3	13 00	3 6 64	Paddington	Barnet	Notts Co	47	15
						Plymouth Arg	24	2
Morrys Scott*	6 3	12 06	17 12 70	Swansea	Trainee	Cardiff C	9	—
						Colchester U	—	—
						Southend U	—	—
						Plymouth Arg	6	—
David Smith	6 0	11 00	25 6 61	Sidcup	Welling U	Gillingham	104	10
						Bristol C	97	10
						Plymouth Arg	18	2
Rob Turner	6 3	14 01	18 9 66	Easington	Apprentice	Huddersfield T	1	—
						Cardiff C	39	8
						Hartlepool U (loan)	7	1
						Bristol R	26	2
						Wimbledon	10	—
						Bristol C	52	12
						Plymouth Arg	64	17

Trainees
Balfour, Dax; Bull, Leighton J; Crocker, Marcus A; Draper, Ryan J; Jones, Gerrard; Jones, Stephen A; Richardson, Harry S; Roberts, Kevan P; Sullivan, Martyn G; Widger, Andrew; Wotton, Garry L.

**Non-Contract
Shilton, Peter L.

Associated Schoolboys
Dawe, Simon; Fallon, Christopher; Garland, Philip L; Hobbs, Peter C; King, Simon; Lockyer, Adam J; Longden, Matthew; Nicholls, Keir C; Sammels, David H. J; Sullivan, Craig D; Thomas, Christopher M; Thompson, Mark R.

Associated Schoolboys who have accepted the club's offer of a Traineeship/Contract
Hutchinson, James; Morgan, James A; Rutkowski, Yan M; Twiddy, Christopher.

**Non-Contract Players who are retained must be re-signed before they are eligible to play in League matches.

PORTSMOUTH 1991–92 *Back row (left to right):* Mark Chamberlain, Lee Russell, Guy Whittingham, Colin Clarke, Alan Gough, Shaun Gough, Darrell Powell, Warren Aspinall, Ray Daniel.

Centre row: Gordon Neave, Darren Anderton, Chris Burns, Graham Hogg, Alan Knight, Andy Gosney, Guy Butters, Kit Symons, Gary Stevens, Neil Sillett.

Front row: Warren Neill, Steve Wigley, Kenny Black, Andy Awford, Gavin Maguire, Graham Paddon, Jim Smith, Martin Kuhl, John Beresford, Stuart Doling, Micky Ross, Shaun Murray.

Division 1   **PORTSMOUTH**

Fratton Park, Frogmore Rd, Portsmouth PO4 8RA. Telephone Portsmouth (0705) 731204. Commercial Dept: (0705) 827111. Ticket Office: (0705) 750825. Lottery Office: (0705) 825016. Clubcall: 0898 338383.

Ground capacity: 26,352.

Record attendance: 51,385 v Derby Co, FA Cup 6th rd, 26 February 1949.

Record receipts: £208,000 Nottingham F, FA Cup 6th rd, 7 March 1992.

Pitch measurements: 116yd × 73yd.

Chairman: J. A. Gregory.

Vice-chairman: D. K. Deacon.

Directors: M. H. Gregory, J. P. R. Prevost FCA, D. Deacon, B. Henson, P. Britten.

Team Manager: Jim Smith.

Coach: Graham Paddon.

Club Secretary: P. Weld.

Marketing Manager: Julie Baker.

Physio: N. Sillett.

Youth Team Coach: K. Todd.

Year Formed: 1898. Turned Professional: 1898. Ltd Co.: 1898.

Club Nickname: 'Pompey'.

Record League Victory: 9-1 v Notts Co, Division 2, 9 April 1927 – McPhail; Clifford, Ted Smith; Reg Davies (1), Foxall, Moffat; Forward (1), Mackie (2), Haines (3), Watson, Cook (2).

Record Cup Victory: 7-0 v Stockport Co, FA Cup, 3rd rd, 8 January 1949 – Butler; Rookes, Ferrier; Scoular, Flewin, Dickinson; Harris (3), Barlow, Clarke (2), Phillips (2), Froggatt.

Record Defeat: 0-10 v Leicester C, Division 1, 20 October 1928.

Most League Points (2 for a win): 65, Division 3, 1961–62.

Most League points (3 for a win): 91, Division 3, 1982–83.

Most League Goals: 91, Division 4, 1979–80.

Highest League Scorer in Season: Billy Haines, 40, Division 2, 1926–27.

Most League Goals in Total Aggregate: Peter Harris, 194, 1946–60.

Most Capped Player: Jimmy Dickinson, 48, England.

Most League Appearances: Jimmy Dickinson, 764, 1946–65.

Record Transfer Fee Received: £2,000,000 from Tottenham H for Darren Anderton, May 1992.

Record Transfer Fee Paid: £450,000 to QPR for Colin Clarke, June 1990.

Football League Record: 1920 Original Member of Division 3; 1921 Division 3 (S); 1924–27 Division 2; 1927–59 Division 1; 1959–61 Division 2; 1961–62 Division 3; 1962–76 Division 2; 1976–78 Division 3; 1978–80 Division 4; 1980–83 Division 3; 1983–87 Division 2; 1987–88 Division 1; 1988–92 Division 2; 1992– Division 1.

Honours: Football League: Division 1 – Champions 1948–49, 1949–50; Division 2 – Runners-up 1926–27, 1986–87; Division 3 (S) – Champions 1923–24; Division 3 – Champions 1961–62, 1982–83. *FA Cup:* Winners 1939; Runners-up 1929, 1934. *Football League Cup:* best season: 5th rd, 1960–61, 1985–86.

Colours: Blue shirts, white shorts, red stockings. **Change colours:** Red shirts, black shorts, red stockings.

PORTSMOUTH 1991–92 LEAGUE RECORD

Match No.	Date		Venue	Opponents		Result	H/T Score	Lg. Pos.	Goalscorers	Attendance
1	Aug	17	A	Blackburn R	D	1-1	0-0	—	Anderton	11,118
2		24	H	Port Vale	W	1-0	1-0	10	Clarke	8083
3		31	A	Middlesbrough	L	0-2	0-0	16		12,320
4	Sep	3	H	Sunderland	W	1-0	0-0	—	Burns	9621
5		7	H	Brighton & HA	D	0-0	0-0	13		10,567
6		14	A	Charlton Ath	L	0-3	0-2	17		5707
7		17	A	Grimsby T	D	1-1	0-1	—	Wigley	5348
8		21	H	Cambridge U	W	3-0	2-0	12	Wigley, Burns, Kimble (og)	7801
9		28	A	Bristol C	W	2-0	2-0	7	Beresford 2 (1 pen)	9830
10	Oct	5	H	Newcastle U	W	3-1	2-0	5	Beresford (pen), Stimson (og), Clarke	10,175
11		12	A	Barnsley	L	0-2	0-1	9		6579
12		19	A	Derby Co	L	0-2	0-0	12		13,190
13		26	H	Ipswich T	D	1-1	1-1	12	Burns	8007
14	Nov	2	A	Millwall	D	1-1	0-1	11	Anderton	6060
15		5	H	Leicester C	W	1-0	1-0	—	Whittingham	7147
16		9	H	Oxford U	W	2-1	1-0	11	Butters 2	7557
17		16	A	Swindon T	W	3-2	0-0	6	Whittingham, Anderton, Powell	10,738
18		23	A	Watford	L	1-2	0-1	9	Doling	8135
19		30	H	Wolverhampton W	W	1-0	1-0	10	Burns	11,101
20	Dec	14	H	Southend U	D	1-1	1-1	10	Anderton	9006
21		21	A	Sunderland	L	0-1	0-1	10		14,432
22		26	H	Bristol R	W	2-0	1-0	8	Cross (og), Burns	10,710
23		28	H	Middlesbrough	W	4-0	3-0	7	Whittingham, Powell, Beresford (pen), Kuhl	12,324
24	Jan	1	A	Plymouth Arg	L	2-3	1-2	9	Powell, Chamberlain	8887
25		11	A	Port Vale	W	2-0	2-0	6	Powell, Anderton	5925
26		18	H	Blackburn R	D	2-2	0-1	7	Beresford, Whittingham	20,106
27		29	A	Bristol R	L	0-1	0-1	—		5330
28	Feb	1	H	Derby Co	L	0-1	0-0	7		12,008
29		4	H	Plymouth Arg	W	4-1	2-0	—	Powell, Whittingham 2, Marker (og)	10,467
30		8	A	Ipswich T	L	2-5	1-3	8	Anderton, Powell	13,494
31		22	A	Wolverhampton W	D	0-0	0-0	10		15,770
32		29	H	Tranmere R	W	2-0	2-0	8	Burns, McLoughlin	16,644
33	Mar	11	A	Leicester C	D	2-2	1-0	—	Burns, Clarke	14,207
34		14	H	Millwall	W	6-1	3-0	7	Kuhl, Whittingham 3, McLoughlin, Burns	14,944
35		17	A	Southend U	W	3-2	2-2	—	Whittingham, Clarke, Aspinall	6832
36		21	A	Oxford U	L	1-2	0-0	6	Anderton	8432
37		28	H	Swindon T	D	1-1	0-0	7	Beresford (pen)	16,007
38		31	H	Charlton Ath	L	1-2	0-0	—	Minto (og)	14,539
39	Apr	7	A	Tranmere R	L	0-2	0-1	—		6692
40		11	H	Grimsby T	W	2-0	1-0	8	Doling, Aspinall	10,576
41		17	A	Cambridge U	D	2-2	0-1	—	Kuhl, Aspinall	9492
42		20	H	Bristol C	W	1-0	1-0	9	Wigley	17,151
43		22	H	Watford	D	0-0	0-0	—		14,417
44		25	A	Newcastle U	L	0-1	0-0	9		25,989
45		29	A	Brighton & HA	L	1-2	0-1	—	Aspinall	11,647
46	May	2	H	Barnsley	W	2-0	0-0	7	Symons, Whittingham	11,169

Final League Position: 7

GOALSCORERS

League (65): Whittingham 11, Burns 8, Anderton 7, Beresford 6 (4 pens), Powell 6, Aspinall 4, Clarke 4, Kuhl 3, Wigley 3, Butters 2, Doling 2, McLoughlin 2, Chamberlain 1, Symons 1, own goals 5.
Rumbelows Cup (8): Beresford 2 (1 pen), Anderton 1, Aspinall 1, Burns 1, Butters 1, Clarke 1, Kuhl 1.
FA Cup (11): Anderton 5, Clarke 2, Whittingham 2, Aspinall 1, McLoughlin 1.

Rumbelows Cup	First Round	Gillingham (h)	2-1
		(a)	4-3
	Second Round	Oxford U (h)	0-0
		(a)	1-0

Knight	Awford	Beresford	Burns	Symons	Butters	Anderton	Kuhl	Clarke	Whittingham	Powell	Chamberlain	Russell	Doling	Aspinall	Wigley	Murray	Neill	Hebberd	Ross	Gosney	Daniel	Hendon	McLoughlin	McFarlane	Match No.
1	2	3	4	5	6	7	8	9	10*	11†	12	14													1
1	2	3	4	5	6	7	8	9		11	12		10*												2
1	2	3	4	5	6	7	8	9		11	10†	14*	12												3
1	2	3	4	5	6	7	8	9	10	11															4
1	2	3	4	5	6†	7	8	9	10	11*		14		12											5
1	2	3*	4	5		7	8	9	10†	11		6	14	12											6
1	2	3	14	5		7	8		10†			6	4*	9	12	11									7
1	2		4	5	6		8	9*	12			3		10	11		7								8
1	2	3	4	5	6	11		9*	12		8			10			7								9
1	2	3	4	5	6	11		9†	12		8*			10			7	14							10
1	2	3	4	5	6	11†	8	9	12			14					7	10*							11
1	2*	3	4†	5	6	11	8	9	10		12						7	14							12
1	2	3	4	5	6	11	8†	9	10*		12						7	14							13
1	2	3*	4	5	6	11	8	9	12		10†						7	14							14
1	2		4	5	6	11	8	9	12			3		10*			7	14†							15
1	2		4	5	6	11*	8	9	10†			3		12			7	14							16
	2	10†	4	5	6	11	8	9	14			3*		12			7			1					17
1	2	3	4	5	6	11	8	14	9		10†			12			7*								18
1	2	3	4	5	6	11	8		9		12			10*			7								19
1	2	3	4†	5	6	11	8	9	12			14		10*			7								20
1	2	3	4*	5	6	11	8		9†			14		10	12		7								21
1	2	3	4	5	6	11	8		9*			14		10†	12		7								22
1	2	3	4	5		11	8		9*		6			10†	12		7						14		23
1	2	3	4†	5	6	11*	8	9	10			12		14			7								24
1	2	3	12	5	6	11*	8	9†	4					10	14		7								25
1	2	3	9*	5	6	11	8		12	4				10†	14		7								26
1	2	3	9	5	6*	11	8		10	4				14			7†						12		27
1	2	3	10*	5	6	11	8		14	4				9†			7						12		28
1		3	10	5	6	11	8	9		4							7					2			29
1	2	3	10	5	6*	11	8	9	12	4							7†						14		30
1	2	3	14		6	11	8	9*	12	4†							7						10		31
1	2	3	6	5		11*	8	9	12	4†				14			7						10		32
1	2	3	6	5	7*	11	8	9	12	4†				14			7						10		33
1	2	3	6	5		11	8*	9†	10			14		12			7						4		34
1	2	3	6	5			8	9	10	11*				12			7						4		35
1	2	3†	6	5		11	8	9	10*			14		12			7						4		36
1	2	3	6†	5		11	8*	9	10			14		12			7						4		37
1	2†	3	6	5		11		9	10			14		8*	12		7						4		38
1	2	3†	6	5		11	8	9	10			14		12			7						4*		39
1	2		6	5		12	8	9	10*	11†		4			14		7				3				40
1	2		6*	5		11	8	9†			12			10	14		7				3		4		41
1	2*		12	5			8	9				6		10	11†		7				3		4	14	42
1	2		6	5		11	8†	9*				10		14	12		7				3		4		43
1	2		6	5		11*	8	9						10†	12		7				3		4	14	44
1	2		6	5		12	8	9*	10			4		14	11		7				3†				45
1	2†		6	5		14	8	9	10	11*				12			7				3		4		46
45	45	35	42	46	32	40	41	19	30	26	10	7	7	9	8	2	38	1	—	1	7	1	14	—	

Substitute appearances (+):

```
                +  +  +        +  +  +    +   +   +       +  +      +  +      +  +     +
                4s 1s 2s       5s 5s 10s  6s 2s  6s      15s15s    3s 3s     1s 3s    2s
```

PORTSMOUTH

Player and Position	Ht	Wt	Date	Birth Place	Source	Clubs	League App	Gls
Goalkeepers								
Andy Gosney	6 4	13 05	8 11 63	Southampton	Apprentice	Portsmouth	48	—
						York C (loan)	5	—
Alan Gough*	5 10	12 01	10 3 71	Watford	Shelbourne	Portsmouth	—	—
						Fulham (loan)	—	—
Alan Knight	6 1	13 02	3 7 61	Ballham	Apprentice	Portsmouth	446	—
Defenders								
Andy Awford	5 9	11 09	14 7 72	Worcester	Trainee	Portsmouth	63	—
Guy Butters	6 3	13 00	30 10 69	Hillingdon	Trainee	Tottenham H	35	1
						Southend U (loan)	16	3
						Portsmouth	56	2
Shaun Gale	6 0	11 06	8 10 69	Reading	Trainee	Portsmouth	3	—
Graeme Hogg (To Hearts Aug 1991)	6 1	12 12	17 6 64	Aberdeen	Apprentice	Manchester U	83	1
						WBA (loan)	7	—
						Portsmouth	100	2
Gavin Maguire	5 10	11 08	24 11 67	Hammersmith	Apprentice	QPR	40	—
						Portsmouth	70	—
						Newcastle U (loan)	3	—
Warren Neill	5 8	11 10	21 11 62	Acton	Apprentice	QPR	181	3
						Portsmouth	148	—
Gary Stevens	6 0	12 00	30 3 62	Hillingdon	Apprentice	Brighton & HA	133	2
						Tottenham H	147	6
						Portsmouth	52	3
Kit Symons	6 1	11 09	5 3 71	Basingstoke	Trainee	Portsmouth	50	1
Midfield								
John Beresford	5 5	10 04	4 9 66	Sheffield	Apprentice	Manchester C	—	—
						Barnsley	88	5
						Portsmouth	107	8
Kenny Black (To Airdrie Sept 1991)	5 9	12 01	29 11 63	Stenhousemuir	Linlithgow Rose	Rangers	22	1
						Motherwell	17	—
						Hearts	178	15
						Portsmouth	62	3
Chris Burns	6 00	12 00	9 11 67	Manchester	Cheltenham T	Portsmouth	46	8
Mark Chamberlain	5 8	10 07	19 11 61	Stoke	Apprentice	Port Vale	96	17
						Stoke C	112	17
						Sheffield W	66	8
						Portsmouth	107	15
Ray Daniel	5 10	11 00	10 12 64	Luton	Apprentice	Luton T	22	4
						Gillingham (loan)	5	—
						Hull C	58	3
						Cardiff C	56	1
						Portsmouth	22	—
Stuart Doling	5 6	10 06	28 10 72	Newport, IOW	Trainee	Portsmouth	13	2
Martin Kuhl	5 11	11 13	10 1 65	Frimley	Apprentice	Birmingham C	111	5
						Sheffield U	38	4
						Watford	4	—
						Portsmouth	154	26
Alan McLoughlin	5 8	10 00	20 4 67	Manchester	Local	Manchester U	—	—
						Swindon T	9	—
						Torquay U	24	4
						Swindon T	97	19
						Southampton	24	1
						Aston Villa (loan)	—	—
						Portsmouth	14	2
Lee Russell	5 11	11 04	3 9 69	Southampton	Trainee	Portsmouth	33	1
Lee Tierling‡			25 10 72	Wegberg	Trainee	Portsmouth	—	—

PORTSMOUTH

Foundation: At a meeting held in his High Street, Portsmouth offices in 1898, solicitor Alderman J. E. Pink and five other business and professional men agreed to buy some ground close to Goldsmith Avenue for £4,950 which they developed into Fratton Park in record breaking time. A team of professionals was signed up by manager Frank Brettell and entry to the Southern League obtained for the new club's September 1899 kick-off.

First Football League game: 28 August, 1920, Division 3, v Swansea T (h) W 3-0 – Robson; Probert, Potts; Abbott, Harwood, Turner; Thompson, Stringfellow (1), Reid (1), James (1), Beedie.

Did you know: Portsmouth included eight internationals in five of their Southern League games in 1902–03 – Albert Houlker, Daniel Cunliffe, Steve Smith, Fred Wheldon, Arthur Chadwick (England); Matt Reilly (Ireland); Bob Marshall and Sandy Brown (Scotland).

Managers (and Secretary-managers)
Frank Brettell 1898–1901, Bob Blyth 1901–04, Richard Bonney 1905–08, Bob Brown 1911–20, John McCartney 1920–27, Jack Tinn 1927–47, Bob Jackson 1947–52, Eddie Lever 1952–58, Freddie Cox 1958–61, George Smith 1961–70, Ron Tindall 1970–73 (GM to 1974), John Mortimore 1973–74, Ian St. John 1974–77, Jimmy Dickinson 1977–79, Frank Burrows 1979–82, Bobby Campbell 1982–84, Alan Ball 1984–89, John Gregory 1989–90, Frank Burrows 1990–1991, Jim Smith May 1991–.

Forwards

Name	Ht	Wt	Born	Birthplace	Source	Club	Apps	Gls
Darren Anderton	6 0	11 07	3 3 72	Southampton	Trainee	Portsmouth	62	7
Warren Aspinall	5 9	12 05	13 9 67	Wigan	Apprentice	Wigan Ath	51	22
						Everton	7	—
						Aston Villa	44	14
						Portsmouth	100	19
Colin Clarke	5 11	12 10	30 10 62	Newry	Apprentice	Ipswich T	—	—
						Peterborough U	82	18
						Gillingham (loan)	8	1
						Tranmere R	45	22
						Bournemouth	46	26
						Southampton	82	36
						Bournemouth (loan)	4	2
						QPR	46	11
						Portsmouth	66	17
Simon Guthrie†			24 6 72	Newcastle	Trainee	Sunderland	—	—
						Portsmouth	—	—
Mark Kelly	5 8	9 10	27 11 69	Sutton		Portsmouth	49	2
						Tottenham H (loan)	—	—
Andy McFarlane†	6 03	13 10	30 11 66	Wolverhampton	Cradley T	Portsmouth	2	—
Shaun Murray	5 8	11 02	7 2 70	Newcastle	Trainee	Tottenham H	—	—
						Portsmouth	27	1
Darryl Powell	6 0	12 03	15 11 71	London	Trainee	Portsmouth	47	6
Mike Ross	5 6	9 13	2 9 71	Southampton	Trainee	Portsmouth	4	—
Guy Whittingham	5 10	11 12	10 11 64	Evesham	Yeovil,Army	Portsmouth	114	46
Steve Wigley	5 9	10 05	15 10 61	Ashton	Curzon Ashton	Nottingham F	82	2
						Sheffield U	28	1
						Birmingham C	87	4
						Portsmouth	120	12

Trainees
Askham, Paul N; Birmingham, Michael J; Bromige, Glyn J; Burton, Nicholas J; Green, Barry J; O'Brien, Simon; Ogburn, Mark; Owen, Christian P; Pearson, Dylan; Price, Benjamin; Sutton, Graham W; Watts, Christian J; Wiseman, Simon L; Young, Roy E.

**Non-Contract
McFarlane, Andrew A.

Associated Schoolboys
Ahmet, Jason J; Anstey, Craig D; Brown, Lee P; Burden, Steven L; Burton, Deon J; Coe, Douglas G; Crotty, Anthony M; Dines, Stephen; Fitches, Ben; Gilbert, Greig F; Headington, Marcus J; Hooker, Kevin L; Lewis, David J; Osborne, Steven A; Page, Christopher M; Sanger, Jon D; Sherrington, James D; Spake, Daniel; Steeves, Jamie S; Stephenson, Lawrence M; Thompson, Mark; Woodley, Simon P.

Associated Schoolboys who have accepted the club's offer of a Traineeship/Contract
Cunningham, Aaron M; Gardner, Christopher D; Hussey, Matthew R; Igoe, Samuel G; Mosedale, Anthony J; Rowe, David J; Stewart, Paul T.

**Non-Contract Players who are retained must be re-signed before they are eligible to play in League matches.

PORT VALE 1991–92 *Back row (left to right)*: Martin Foyle, Simon Mills, Robin Van Der Laan, Neil Aspin, Tim Parkin, Ryan Kidd, Nico Jalink, Paul West, Dean Glover, Darren Hughes.

Centre row: John Rudge (Manager), Jim Joyce (Physiotherapist), Alan Webb, Trevor Wood, Mark Grew, John Jeffers, Bobby Downes (Youth Coach), Mike Peijic (Coach).

Front row: Kevin Kent, Dave Rushton, Ray Walker, Andy Porter, Brian Mills, Ian Banks. (Picture courtesy of Staffordshire Sentinel Newspapers)

Division 2

PORT VALE

Vale Park, Burslem, Stoke-on-Trent. Telephone Stoke-on-Trent (0782) 814134. Commercial Dept/Club Shop: (0782) 835524. Clubcall: 0898 121636. Fax No: 834981

Ground capacity: 20,992.

Record attendance: 50,000 v Aston Villa, FA Cup 5th rd, 20 February 1960.

Record receipts: £170,022 v Liverpool, Rumbelows Cup 3rd rd replay, 20 November 1991.

Pitch measurements: 116yd × 76yd.

President: J. Burgess.

Chairman: W. T. Bell TECH ENG, MIMI.

Vice-chairman: A. Belfield.

Directors: I. McPherson, N. C. Tizley. *Consultant:* P. Haynes.

Manager: John Rudge. *Secretary:* Eddie Harrison. *Commercial Manager:* Margaret Moran-Smith. *Coach:* Bobby Downes. *Physio:* J. Joyce MCSP, SRP, GRAD.DIP (Phys). *Medical Officer:* Dr. G. Gardner MB, ChB. *Stadium manager:* F. W. Lodey. *Groundsman:* R. Fairbanks. *Community scheme officer:* I. Miller.

Year Formed: 1876. Turned Professional: 1885. Ltd Co.: 1911.

Former Grounds: 1876, Limekin Lane, Longport; 1881, Westport; 1884, Moorland Road, Burslem; 1886, Athletic Ground, Cobridge; 1913, Recreation Ground, Hanley; 1950, Vale Park.

Former Names: Burslem Port Vale; became Port Vale, 1913.

Club Nickname: 'Valiants'.

Record League Victory: 9-1 v Chesterfield, Division 2, 24 September 1932 – Leckie; Shenton, Poyser; Sherlock, Round, Jones; McGrath, Mills, Littlewood (6), Kirkham (2), Morton (1).

Record Cup Victory: 7-1 v Irthlingborough (away), FA Cup, 1st rd, 12 January 1907 – Matthews; Dunn, Hamilton; Eardley, Baddeley, Holyhead; Carter, Dodds (2), Beats, Mountford (2), Coxon (3).

Record Defeat: 0-10 v Sheffield U, Division 2, 10 December 1892 and v Notts Co, Division 2, 26 February 1895.

Most League Points (2 for a win): 69, Division 3 (N), 1953–54.

Most League points (3 for a win): 88, Division 4, 1982–83.

Most League Goals: 110, Division 4, 1958–59.

Highest League Scorer in Season: Wilf Kirkham 38, Division 2, 1926–27.

Most League Goals in Total Aggregate: Wilf Kirkham, 154, 1923–29, 1931–33.

Most Capped Player: Sammy Morgan, 7 (18), Northern Ireland.

Most League Appearances: Roy Sproson, 761, 1950–72.

Record Transfer Fee Received: £925,000 from Norwich C for Darren Beckford, June 1991.

Record Transfer Fee Paid: £375,000 from Oxford U for Martin Foyle, June 1991.

Football League Record: 1892 Original Member of Division 2, Failed re-election in 1896; Re-elected 1898; Resigned 1907; Returned in Oct, 1919, when they took over the fixtures of Leeds City; 1929–30 Division 3 (N); 1930–36 Division 2; 1936–38 Division 3 (N); 1938–52 Division 3 (S); 1952–54 Division 3 (N); 1954–57 Division 2; 1957–58 Division 3 (S); 1958–59 Division 4; 1959–65 Division 3; 1965–70 Division 4; 1970–78 Division 3; 1978–83 Division 4; 1983–84 Division 3; 1984–86 Division 4; 1986–89 Division 3; 1989– Division 2.

Honours: Football League: Division 2 best season: 5th, 1930–31; Division 3 (N) – Champions 1929–30, 1953–54; Runners-up 1952–53; Division 4 – Champions 1958–59; Promoted 1969–70 (4th). *FA Cup:* Semi-final 1954, when in Division 3. *Football League Cup:* never past 3rd rd.

Colours: White shirts, black shorts, black and white stockings. **Change colours:** Light blue shirts, white shorts, blue and white stockings.

PORT VALE 1991–92 LEAGUE RECORD

Match No.	Date		Venue	Opponents	Result		H/T Score	Lg. Pos.	Goalscorers	Attendance
1	Aug	17	H	Oxford U	W	2-1	0-1	—	Foyle 2	6984
2		20	A	Ipswich T	L	1-2	0-1	—	Walker (pen)	8937
3		24	A	Portsmouth	L	0-1	0-1	14		8083
4		27	H	Barnsley	D	0-0	0-0	—		6229
5		31	H	Bristol C	D	1-1	1-0	10	Mills S	7057
6	Sep	3	A	Wolverhampton W	W	2-0	0-0	—	Houchen 2	16,115
7		7	H	Swindon T	D	2-2	0-0	7	Foyle 2	7168
8		14	A	Blackburn R	L	0-1	0-1	13		10,225
9		18	A	Brighton & HA	L	1-3	0-3	—	Houchen	5790
10		21	H	Southend U	D	0-0	0-0	18		5988
11		28	A	Charlton Ath	L	0-2	0-1	19		4049
12	Oct	5	H	Cambridge U	W	1-0	0-0	17	Porter	5991
13		12	A	Grimsby T	W	2-1	1-1	10	Mills S, Beckford	8218
14		19	H	Sunderland	D	3-3	1-0	14	Swan, Foyle, Van der Laan	7525
15		26	A	Middlesbrough	L	0-1	0-1	14		11,403
16	Nov	2	A	Bristol R	D	3-3	1-2	17	Foyle 2, Van der Laan	3565
17		6	H	Derby Co	W	1-0	0-0	—	Jalink	8589
18		9	H	Millwall	L	0-2	0-0	15		8944
19		16	A	Plymouth Arg	L	0-1	0-0	15		4363
20		23	A	Leicester C	W	1-0	1-0	14	Jeffers	11,405
21		30	H	Watford	W	2-1	0-0	12	Foyle, Van der Laan	5777
22	Dec	7	A	Newcastle U	D	2-2	1-1	11	Hughes, Glover (pen)	18,162
23		13	H	Tranmere R	D	1-1	1-1	—	West	6426
24		21	H	Wolverhampton W	D	1-1	0-1	12	Van der Laan	8480
25		26	A	Barnsley	D	0-0	0-0	11		8843
26		28	A	Bristol C	L	0-3	0-2	14		9235
27	Jan	1	H	Ipswich T	L	1-2	0-1	17	Hughes	8075
28		11	H	Portsmouth	L	0-2	0-2	17		5925
29		18	A	Oxford U	D	2-2	1-1	19	Houchen, Swan	4199
30	Feb	1	A	Sunderland	D	1-1	1-1	18	Foyle	19,488
31		8	H	Middlesbrough	L	1-2	0-1	20	Kernaghan (og)	7019
32		15	A	Leicester C	L	1-2	1-1	20	Foyle	8084
33		22	A	Watford	D	0-0	0-0	19		6602
34		29	H	Newcastle U	L	0-1	0-1	21		10,321
35	Mar	6	A	Tranmere R	L	1-2	0-0	—	Jeffers	8471
36		11	A	Derby Co	L	1-3	1-1	—	Jeffers	14,983
37		14	H	Bristol R	L	0-1	0-1	24		5861
38		21	A	Millwall	L	0-1	0-0	24		6148
39		28	H	Plymouth Arg	W	1-0	1-0	24	Walker (pen)	5310
40		31	H	Blackburn R	W	2-0	1-0	—	Van der Laan, Foyle	10,384
41	Apr	4	A	Swindon T	L	0-1	0-1	24		8014
42		11	H	Brighton & HA	W	2-1	0-0	22	Swan, Lowe	6441
43		15	A	Southend U	D	0-0	0-0	—		4462
44		21	H	Charlton Ath	D	1-1	0-0	—	Mills B	8461
45		25	A	Cambridge U	L	2-4	1-0	23	Mills B, Lowe	7559
46	May	2	H	Grimsby T	L	0-1	0-1	24		8678

Final League Position: 24

GOALSCORERS

League (42): Foyle 11, Van der Laan 5, Houchen 4, Jeffers 3, Swan 3, Hughes 2, Lowe 2, Mills B 2, Mills S 2, Walker 2 (2 pens), Beckford 1, Glover 1 (1 pen), Jalink 1, Porter 1, West 1, own goals 1.
Rumbelows Cup (7): Foyle 4, Houchen 1, Mills B 1, Van der Laan 1.
FA Cup (0).

Grew	Mills S	Hughes	Walker	Aspin	Glover	Jalink	Van der Laan	Houchen	Foyle	Kent	Swan	Mills B	Jeffers	Porter	Webb	Beckford	Parkin	West	Williams	Cross	Allon	Lowe	Kidd	Match No.
1	2	3	4	5	6	7	8	9	10	11														1
1	2	3	4	5	6	7	8	9	10	11*	12													2
1	2	3	4	5	6	7	8	9†	10	11*	12	14												3
1	2	3	4	5	6	7*	8	9	10		11		12											4
1	2	3	4	5	6		8	9*	10		11	12		7										5
1	2	3	4	5	6		8	9	10		11			7										6
1	2	3	4	5	6		8	9*	10	14	12	11		7†										7
1	2	3	4	5	6	14	8	9*	10		12	11†		7										8
1		3*	4	5	6	7	8	9	10		12		2	11										9
1	2	3	4	5†	6	7*	8	9	10		12	14	11											10
1			4*		6	12	8		10	11	5	9	3	7†	2	14								11
1	2	3			6		8		10	11*	5	9	12	4	7									12
1	2	3	11		6		8	9*	10		5		12	4	7									13
1	2	3	11		6		8		10		5	9	12	4	7*									14
1	2	3		5	6		8		10		9	7	4	11										15
1	2	3		5	6	7	8		10		9		11	4										16
1	2	3		5	6	7	8		10		9		11	4										17
1	2	3		5	6	7	8		10*14		9		11	4†	12									18
1	2	3		5	6	7	8*		10	14	12	11	4†	9										19
1		3		5	6	7	8		10	14	12	11	4	2†					9*					20
1		3		5	6	7	8		10		12	11	4*	2					9					21
1	2	3		5	6	7	8		12 10			11	4						9*					22
1	2	3		5	6	7	8		10		11		9	4										23
1	2	3		5	6	7	8		10		12	11		9*					4					24
1	2	3		5	6	7	8		12 10			9*	11						4					25
1	2	3		5	6	7	8	10†	9*12		11	14							4					26
1	2	3		5	6	7*	8	9	10		12	11							4					27
1	2	3		5	6	12	8	9	10		7	11*	14	4†										28
1	2	3	4		6		8	9	10	11	5		12	7*										29
1	2	3	4		6	12	8	9*	10		5		11	7										30
1	2	3	4		6	12	8		10	14	5	9†11		7*										31
1		3	4	2	6		8	9	10	7	5		11*							12				32
1		3	4		6	9	8		10	7	5		11	2										33
1		3	4	2	6	12		9†10		7	5		11	8*						14				34
1		3	4	2	6	12			10		5		11	8					7	9*				35
1		3	4	2	6*12†		8		10		5		11	7					9	14				36
1		3	4	2	6		8		10	7	9						5		11*12					37
1			4	2	6		8		10	12	9		3	7					5*	11†14				38
1		3	4	2	6		8		10		11		5			9*12						7		39
1		3	4	2	6		8		10		5	12	11			9*						7		40
1 12		3	4	2	6		8		10	11	5					9*						7		41
1 14		3	4	2	6		8			5	10*12	11				9†						7		42
1	2	3	4	5	6		8		10*	9	12	11										7		43
1	2	3*	4	5	6		8		10		9	11		12								7		44
1	2		4		6		8		10		5	9*	11		12							7	3	45
1	2	4	3		6		8	12	10	14	5	9*	11†									7		46
46	31	42	26	42	46	20	43	18	43	13	27	13	27	30	3	4	4	5	5	7	2	8	1	

+2s (leftmost); Van der Laan +8s; Foyle +3s; Swan +10s; Mills B +6s; Jeffers +8s; Porter +6s; Webb +2s; Parkin +1s; West +3s; Cross +1s; Allon +4s; Lowe +1s

Rumbelows Cup — Second Round — Notts Co (h) — 2-1
(a) — 2-3
Third Round — Liverpool (a) — 2-2
(h) — 1-4

FA Cup — Third Round — Sunderland (a) — 0-3

PORT VALE

Player and Position	Ht	Wt	Birth Date	Place	Source	Clubs	League App	Gls
Goalkeepers								
Mark Grew*	5 11	12 08	15 2 58	Bilston	Amateur	WBA	33	—
						Wigan Ath (loan)	4	—
						Notts Co (loan)	—	—
						Leicester C	5	—
						Oldham Ath (loan)	5	—
						Ipswich T	6	—
						Fulham (loan)	4	—
						WBA (loan)	1	—
						Derby Co (loan)	—	—
						Port Vale	184	—
						Blackburn R (loan)	13	—
Trevor Wood	6 0	12 06	3 11 68	Jersey	Apprentice	Brighton & HA	—	—
						Port Vale	37	—
Defenders								
Neil Aspin	6 0	12 03	12 4 65	Gateshead	Apprentice	Leeds U	207	5
						Port Vale	125	1
Dean Glover	5 10	11 11	29 12 63	Birmingham	Apprentice	Aston Villa	28	—
						Sheffield U (loan)	5	—
						Middlesbrough	50	5
						Port Vale	153	6
Darren Hughes	5 11	10 11	6 10 65	Prescot	Apprentice	Everton	3	—
						Shrewsbury T	37	1
						Brighton & HA	26	2
						Port Vale	184	4
Ryan Kidd*	6 0	11 07	6 10 71	Heywood	Trainee	Port Vale	1	—
Tim Parkin*	6 2	13 03	31 12 57	Penrith	Apprentice	Blackburn R	13	—
						Malmo	—	—
						Bristol R	206	12
						Almondsbury G	—	—
						Swindon T	110	6
						Port Vale	48	1
						Shrewsbury T (loan)	5	—
Alan Webb	5 10	12 00	1 1 63	Wellington	Apprentice	WBA	24	—
						Lincoln C (loan)	11	—
						Port Vale	190	2
Paul West*	5 11	11 00	22 6 70		Alcester T	Port Vale	—	—
Midfield								
Ian Banks*	5 8	9 00	1 10 72	Stone	Trainee	Port Vale	—	—
Nico Jalink‡	5 10	11 00	22 6 64	Rotterdam	RKC Waalwijk	Port Vale	28	1
Simon Mills	5 8	11 04	16 8 64	Sheffield	Apprentice	Sheffield W	5	—
						York C	99	5
						Port Vale	181	8
Andy Porter	5 9	11 02	17 9 68	Manchester	Trainee	Port Vale	129	3
David Rushton*	5 09	10 02	3 5 73	Stoke	Trainee	Port Vale	—	—
Peter Swan	6 0	11 12	28 9 66	Leeds	Local	Leeds U	49	11
						Hull C	80	24
						Port Vale	33	3
Ray Walker	5 10	12 00	6 7 81	North Shields	Apprentice	Aston Villa	23	—
						Port Vale (loan)	15	1
						Port Vale	241	23
Forwards								
Chris Boswell*	6 2	13 01	21 10 72	Tittensor	Trainee	Port Vale	—	—
Nicky Cross	5 9	11 04	7 2 61	Birmingham	Apprentice	WBA	105	15
						Walsall	109	45
						Leicester C	58	15
						Port Vale	69	15

PORT VALE

Foundation: Formed in 1876 as Port Vale, adopting the prefix 'Burslem' in 1884 upon moving to that part of the city. It was dropped in 1911.

First Football League game: 3 September 1892, Division 2, v Small Heath (a) L 1-5 – Frail; Clutton, Elson; Farrington, McCrindle, Delves; Walker, Scarratt, Bliss (1), Jones. (Only 10 men).

Did you know: Two early Port Vale players, Tom Kirkham and Jim Mason, subsequently became top-class referees, officiating at the FA Cup Final and internationals.

Managers (and Secretary-managers)
Sam Gleaves 1896–1905*, Tom Clare 1905–11, A. S. Walker 1911–12, H. Myatt 1912–14, Tom Holford 1919–24 (continued as trainer), Joe Schofield 1924–30, Tom Morgan 1930–32, Tom Holford 1932–35, Warney Cresswell 1936–37, Tom Morgan 1937–38, Billy Frith 1945–46, Gordon Hodgson 1946–51, Ivor Powell 1951, Freddie Steele 1951–57, Norman Low 1957–62, Freddie Steele 1962–65, Jackie Mudie 1965–67, Sir Stanley Matthews (GM) 1965–68, Gordon Lee 1968–74, Roy Sproson 1974–77, Colin Harper 1977, Bobby Smith 1977–78, Dennis Butler 1978–79, Alan Bloor 1979, John McGrath 1980–83, John Rudge December 1983–.

Player and Position	Ht	Wt	Birth Date	Birth Place	Source	Clubs	League App	Gls
Martin Foyle	5 10	11 02	2 5 63	Salisbury	Amateur	Southampton	12	1
						Blackburn R (loan)	—	—
						Aldershot	98	35
						Oxford U	126	36
						Port Vale	43	11
Michael Harrison	6 1		19 1 73	Cannock	Trainee	Port Vale	—	—
Keith Houchen	6 2	12 08	25 7 60	Middlesbrough	Chesterfield	Hartlepool U	170	65
						Orient	76	20
						York C	67	19
						Scunthorpe U	9	3
						Coventry C	54	7
						Hibernian	57	11
						Port Vale	42	8
John Jeffers	5 10	11 10	5 10 68	Liverpool	Trainee	Liverpool	—	—
						Port Vale	119	6
Kevin Kent	5 11	11 00	19 3 65	Stoke	Apprentice	WBA	2	—
						Newport Co	33	1
						Mansfield T	229	36
						Port Vale	34	—
Gary McKinstry*	5 9	10 08	7 1 72	Banbridge	Portadown	Port Vale	—	—
Brian Mills	5 9	10 10	26 12 71	Stone	Trainee	Port Vale	23	4
Robin Van der Laan	5 11	12 05	5 9 68	Schiedam	Wageningen	Port Vale	61	9

Trainees
Allum, Christopher D; Blake, Martin G; Brown, Christopher E; Burbridge, Nigel J; Byrne, Paul T; Carvell, Matthew J; Dyas, Mark W; Gillard, Christopher N.T; Heron, Derek J; Hickey, Benjamin J; Lovatt, Gregory; McCarthy, Anthony M; Mitchell, Richard D; Mountford, Wayne; Palmer, Shane M; Parris, Mark A; Royall, Adam; Shea, Gareth D; Stirk, Mark A.

Associated Schoolboys
Burton, Matthew; Patrick, Matthew; Talbot, David A.

Associated Schoolboys who have accepted the club's offer of a Traineeship/Contract
Corden, Simon W; Hughes, Simon D; Johnson, Mark; Ormiston, Christopher J; Sheard, Timothy S.

PRESTON NORTH END 1991–92 *Front row:* Neil Williams, Gary Swann, John Thomas, Graham Shaw, Les Chapman (Manager), Warren Joyce, Stephen Senior, David Thompson, Martin James.

Centre row: Roy Tunks (First Team Coach), Jeff Wrightson, Bob Atkins, Ronnie Jepson, Adrian Hughes, Alan Kelly, Simon Farnworth, George Berry, Matthew Lambert, Mike Flynn, Nigel Greenwood, Walter Joyce (Coach).

Back row (left to right): Adam Siddall, Lee Ashcroft, David Burrow, David Christie, David Eaves, Craig Moylon, Lee Cartwright, Jason Kerfoot.

Division 2   **PRESTON NORTH END**

Deepdale, Preston PR1 6RU. Telephone Preston (0772) 795919. Answerphone (0772) 709170. Pitch Hire: (0772) 705468. Community Office: (0772) 704275.

Ground capacity: 16,500.

Record attendance: 42,684 v Arsenal, Division 1, 23 April 1938.

Record receipts: £68,650 v Sheffield W, FA Cup 3rd rd, 4 January 1992.

Pitch measurements: 110yd × 71yd. (Artificial surface.).

President: Tom Finney OBE, JP.

Vice President: T. C. Nicholson JP, FCIOB.

Chairman: K. W. Leeming.

Vice-chairman: M. J. Woodhouse.

Directors: J. T. Garratt, E. Griffith BVSC, MRCVS (Company Secretary), D. Shaw, J. E. Starkie LL.B. (Lond), M. J. Woodhouse (Jnr).Wignall, J. T. Worden.

Manager: Les Chapman. *Coach:* Walter Joyce. *Physio:* Mark Leather MCSP, SRP. *Secretary:* D. J. Allan. *Chief Executive:* Paul Agnew.

Year Formed: 1881. Turned Professional: 1885. Ltd Co.: 1893.

Club Nickname: 'The Lilywhites' or 'North End'.

Record League Victory: 10-0 v Stoke, Division 1, 14 September 1889 – Trainer; Howarth, Holmes; Kelso, Russell (1), Graham; Gordon, Jimmy Ross (2), Nick Ross (3), Thomson (2), Drummond (2).

Record Cup Victory: 26-0 v Hyde, FA Cup, 1st rd, 15 October 1887 – Addision; Howarth, Nick Ross; Russell (1), Thomson (5), Graham (1); Gordon (5), Jimmy Ross (8), John Goodall (1), Dewhurst (3), Drummond (2).

Record Defeat: 0-7 v Blackpool, Division 1, 1 May 1948.

Most League Points (2 for a win): 61, Division 3, 1970–71.

Most League points (3 for a win): 90, Division 4, 1986–87.

Most League Goals: 100, Division 2, 1927–28 and Division 1, 1957–58.

Highest League Scorer in Season: Ted Harper, 37, Division 2, 1932–33.

Most League Goals in Total Aggregate: Tom Finney, 187, 1946–60.

Most Capped Player: Tom Finney, 76, England.

Most League Appearances: Alan Kelly, 447, 1961–75.

Record Transfer Fee Received: £765,000 from Manchester C for Michael Robinson, June 1979.

Record Transfer Fee Paid: £125,000 to Norwich C for Mike Flynn, December 1989.

Football League Record: 1888 Founder Member of League; 1901–04 Division 2; 1904–12 Division 1; 1912–13 Division 2; 1913–14 Division 1; 1914–15 Division 2; 1919–25 Division 1; 1925–34 Division 2; 1934–49 Division 1; 1949–51 Division 2; 1951–61 Division 1; 1961–70 Division 2; 1970–71 Division 3; 1971–74 Division 2; 1974–78 Division 3; 1978–81 Division 2; 1981–85 Division 3; 1985–87 Division 4; 1987–92 Division 3; 1992– Division 2.

Honours: Football League: Division 1 – Champions 1888–89 (first champions), 1889–90; Runners-up 1890–91, 1891–92, 1892–93, 1905–06, 1952–53, 1957–58; Division 2 – Champions 1903–04, 1912–13, 1950–51; Runners-up 1914–15, 1933–34; Division 3 – Champions 1970–71; Division 4 – Runners-up 1986–87. *FA Cup:* Winners 1889, 1938; Runners-up 1888, 1922, 1937, 1954, 1964. *Double Performed:* 1888–89. *Football League Cup:* best season: 4th rd, 1963, 1966, 1972, 1981.

Colours: White shirts, navy blue shorts, navy blue stockings. **Change colours:** All yellow.

PRESTON NORTH END 1991–92 LEAGUE RECORD

Match No.	Date		Venue	Opponents	Result		H/T Score	Lg. Pos.	Goalscorers	Atten- dance
1	Aug	17	A	Peterborough U	L	0-1	0-0	—		6036
2		24	H	Torquay U	W	3-0	1-0	7	Shaw, Ashcroft, Greenwood	3654
3		30	A	Stockport Co	L	0-2	0-2	—		5405
4	Sep	3	H	Bournemouth	D	2-2	0-1	—	James M, Greenwood	3170
5		7	H	Bradford C	D	1-1	0-0	18	Joyce (pen)	4160
6		14	A	Swansea C	D	2-2	1-1	18	Shaw 2	3170
7		17	A	Leyton Orient	D	0-0	0-0	—		3296
8		21	H	Stoke C	D	2-2	1-1	19	Jepson, Swann	6345
9		28	A	Birmingham C	L	1-3	1-1	20	Shaw	8760
10	Oct	1	H	WBA	W	2-0	0-0	—	Swann, Senior	5293
11		12	A	Bury	W	3-2	1-2	15	Ashcroft, Greenwood, Shaw	4265
12		19	H	Huddersfield T	W	1-0	0-0	11	James M	6866
13		26	A	Fulham	L	0-1	0-1	13		4022
14	Nov	2	A	Chester C	L	2-3	0-1	15	Shaw, Swann	1219
15		5	H	Wigan Ath	W	3-0	2-0	—	Swann, Joyce 2 (1 pen)	3657
16		9	H	Darlington	W	2-1	0-0	9	Thomas, Shaw	4643
17		23	A	Bolton W	L	0-1	0-0	11		7033
18		30	A	Hull C	D	2-2	0-1	11	Thomas, Shaw	4280
19	Dec	14	H	Hartlepool U	L	1-4	0-2	14	Ashcroft	5032
20		20	A	Torquay U	L	0-1	0-1	—		2183
21		26	H	Stockport Co	W	3-2	2-1	13	Swann, Shaw (pen), James M	6782
22		28	H	Peterborough U	D	1-1	0-1	13	Cartwright	5200
23	Jan	1	A	Bournemouth	L	0-1	0-1	16		5508
24		11	A	Shrewsbury T	L	0-2	0-0	16		3154
25		18	H	Exeter C	L	1-3	0-2	18	Lambert	3585
26		25	A	Brentford	L	0-1	0-1	19		7559
27	Feb	1	A	Huddersfield T	W	2-1	0-0	17	Shaw, Cartwright	6700
28		8	H	Fulham	L	1-2	0-2	19	Johnrose	3878
29		11	H	Hull C	W	3-1	1-1	—	Williams, Jepson 2	2932
30		15	A	Hartlepool U	L	0-2	0-0	18		2140
31		22	H	Shrewsbury T	D	2-2	0-0	18	James M, Wrightson	3342
32		29	A	Reading	D	2-2	0-2	18	Lambert, Shaw	3390
33	Mar	3	A	Exeter C	L	1-4	1-2	—	Ashcroft	2214
34		7	H	Brentford	W	3-2	2-2	17	Shaw, Thompson, Ashcroft	3548
35		10	A	Wigan Ath	L	0-3	0-1	—		3364
36		14	A	Chester C	L	0-3	0-2	22		3909
37		21	A	Darlington	W	2-0	0-0	22	Jepson 2	2270
38		28	H	Bolton W	W	2-1	1-0	20	Joyce (pen), Flynn	7327
39		31	H	Swansea C	D	1-1	1-0	—	Greenall	3367
40	Apr	4	A	Bradford C	D	1-1	0-1	19	Shaw	6044
41		11	H	Leyton Orient	W	2-1	0-0	18	Flynn, Howard (og)	3926
42		14	H	Reading	D	1-1	1-0	—	Cartwright	3203
43		18	A	Stoke C	L	1-2	1-1	18	Thompson	16,151
44		21	A	Birmingham C	W	3-2	2-0	—	Cartwright, Flynn, Shaw	7738
45		25	A	WBA	L	0-3	0-1	17		11,318
46	May	2	H	Bury	W	2-0	1-0	17	Joyce, Finney	6932

Final League Position: 17

GOALSCORERS

League (61): Shaw 14 (1 pen), Ashcroft 5, Jepson 5, Joyce 5 (3 pens), Swann 5, Cartwright 4, James M 4, Flynn 3, Greenwood 3, Lambert 2, Thomas 2, Thompson 2, Finney 1, Greenall 1, Johnrose 1, Senior 1, Williams 1, Wrightson 1, own goals 1.
Rumbelows Cup (6): Joyce 2 (1 pen), Swann 2, Shaw 1, Wrightson 1.
FA Cup (6): Flynn 1, Greenwood 1, Senior 1, Shaw 1, Swann 1, Thomas 1.

Farnworth	Senior	Swann	Wrightson	Flynn	Berry	Thompson	Joyce	Jepson	Shaw	James M	Williams	Ashcroft	Greenwood	Lambert	Kelly	James J	Cartwright	Cross	Thomas	Allpress	Hughes	Kerfoot	Ainsworth	Whitworth	Finney	Johnrose	Greenall	Christie	Match No.
1	2	3	4	5	6	7	8	9	10	11																			1
1	2	4	6	5			8	9*	10	3	7	11	12																2
1	2	8*	6	5	7				9	10	3	12	14	11	4†														3
	2	8	3	5	6	7*	4	9	10	11				12	1														4
	2	4	3	5	6*		8	9	10	11	12	7			1														5
	2	4	3	5			12		9	10	11	7			1		6	8*											6
	2	11	6	5			12	8	9	10†	3	7*			1		4	14											7
	2	4	3	5			12	8	9	10	11	7*			1		6												8
	2	4	7	5				8	9	10*	11				1		6	3	12										9
	2	4	7	5				8	10	11			9		1		6	3											10
	2†	4	7	5			12	8	10		14	11	9		1		6	3*											11
	2	4	6	5			12	8	10	11		7	9*		1			3											12
	2	4	6	5			12	8	10		14	7			1		11	3†	9*										13
	2*	4	3	5				9	8	10	11†	14	7		1		12		6										14
		4	3	5				9	8	10	11	2	7		1				6										15
	2	4*	3	5				9†	8	10	11	14	7		1		12		6										16
	2	4	3†	5					8*	10	11	14	7	12	1			9	6										17
	2	4	3	5						10	11	7		12	1		8	9*	6										18
	2	4	3	5						10		7	11*	14	1		8	9	6†	12									19
	2		3	5						10		7	11	6*	1		8	9	12	4									20
	2	4	3	5*						10	11	7	9		1		8		12	6									21
	2	4	3	5						10	11	7	9*		1		8	12	6										22
	2	4	3	5			12		10†			7			1		8	9	11*	6	14								23
1	2	4	3	5					10*			7					8	9		6	12	11							24
1	2	4	3*						10†			7		12			8	9		6	11	5	14						25
1	2	4					12	11			7	10	3				8			6		5		9*					26
1	2†	4		3					10*	11		7	9	14			8			6		12	5						27
1	2	11	3	5					10		12	7*	9				8			4†			6		14				28
1	2		4	5			9*	10		11		7					3	8					6		12				29
1	2		4	5				10		11		7	9				3	8					6						30
	2		4	5		9	10	3	11			7			1		8			6									31
	2	14	4	5			9	10	11			7*	12		3	1	8			6†									32
	2	8	6	5		14		9†	10	11	12	7			3*	1	4												33
1	2		3	5			9*	8		10	11	12	7				4		6										34
1	2		3	5			9	8		10	11	7		12			4*		6										35
1			3	5			9	8	12	10	11	2*	7				4		6										36
1		6		5		11	8	9	10	3	2	7					4												37
1				5		11	8	9	10	3	2	7					4							12			6		38
1				5		11	8	9	10*	3	2	7					4							12			6		39
1	7*			5		11	8	9	10	3	2						4							12			6		40
1				5		11	8	9	10	3	2	7*					4										6	12	41
1		5		5		11	8	9	10	3	2	7					4										6		42
1				5		11	8	9*	10	3	2	7					4										6	12	43
1				5		11	8	9	10	3	2	7					4										6		44
1	12			5		11*	8	9†	10	3	2	7					4							14			6		45
1				5		11	8	9*	10	3	2	7					4								12		6		46
23	35 + 1s	28 + 1s	36	43	4	18 + 7s	28 + 1s	23 + 1s	45 + 1s	36	17 + 9s	35 + 3s	16 + 4s	7 + 4s	23	6 + 2s	31	5 + 3s	8 + 2s	7 + 1s	14 + 3s	— + 3s	2 + 2s	6 + 2s	—	1	9 + 2s	—	

Rumbelows Cup	First Round	Scarborough (h) — 5-4
		(a) — 1-3
FA Cup	First Round	Mansfield T (a) — 1-0
	Second Round	Witton (h) — 5-1
	Third Round	Sheffield W (h) — 0-2

PRESTON NORTH END

Player and Position	Ht	Wt	Birth Date	Birth Place	Source	Clubs	League App	Gls
Goalkeepers								
Simon Farnworth	6 0	11 10	28 10 63	Chorley	Apprentice	Bolton W	113	—
						Stockport Co (loan)	10	—
						Tranmere R (loan)	7	—
						Bury	105	—
						Preston NE	46	—
Alan Kelly	6 2	12 05	11 8 68	Preston		Preston NE	142	—
Defenders								
Bob Atkins*	6 0	12 02	16 10 62	Leicester	Local	Sheffield U	40	3
						Preston NE	—	—
Mike Bennett†	5 7	10 00	24 12 62	Bolton	Apprentice	Bolton W	65	1
						Wolverhampton W	6	—
						Cambridge U	76	—
						Bradford C	—	—
						Preston NE	86	1
						Carlisle U	17	—
						Preston NE	—	—
David Burrow*	5 10	11 07	14 10 72	Preston	Trainee	Preston NE	—	—
Mike Flynn	6 0	11 00	23 2 69	Oldham	Trainee	Oldham Ath	40	1
						Norwich C	—	—
						Preston NE	101	5
Colin Greenall	5 10	11 06	30 12 63	Billinge	Apprentice	Blackpool	183	9
						Gillingham	62	4
						Oxford U	67	2
						Bury (loan)	3	—
						Bury	68	5
						Preston NE	9	1
Adrian Hughes*	6 2	12 12	19 12 70	Billinge	Trainee	Preston NE	100	3
Matthew Lambert‡	6 0	12 06	28 9 71	Morecambe	Trainee	Preston NE	16	2
Craig Moylon	5 10		16 10 72	Munster	Trainee	Preston NE	—	—
Steve Senior*	5 8	11 04	15 5 64	Sheffield	Apprentice	York C	168	6
						Darlington (loan)	5	—
						Northampton T	4	—
						Wigan Ath	109	3
						Preston NE	73	3
Adam Siddall*	5 5		12 5 73	Manchester	Trainee	Preston NE	—	—
Jeff Wrightson*	5 11	11 00	18 5 68	Newcastle	Apprentice	Newcastle U	4	—
						Preston NE	166	4
Midfield								
Lee Cartwright	5 8	10 06	19 9 72	Rossendale	Trainee	Preston NE	47	5
David Eaves	5 11	11 07	13 2 73	Blackpool	Trainee	Preston NE	3	—
David Flitcroft	5 11	12 03	14 1 74	Bolton	Trainee	Preston NE	—	—
Martin James	5 10	11 07	18 5 71	Formby	Trainee	Preston NE	73	6
Warren Joyce	5 9	11 11	20 1 65	Oldham	Local	Bolton W	184	17
						Preston NE	177	34
Gary Swann‡	5 9	11 02	11 4 62	York	Apprentice	Hull C	186	9
						Preston NE	199	37
David Thompson*	5 11	12 04	27 5 62	Manchester	Local	Rochdale	155	13
						Manchester U (loan)	—	—
						Notts Co	55	8
						Wigan Ath	108	14
						Preston NE	46	4
Neil Williams*	5 11	11 04	23 10 64	Waltham Abbey	Apprentice	Watford	—	—
						Hull C	91	10
						Preston NE	121	6

PRESTON NORTH END

Foundation: North End Cricket and Rugby Club which was formed in 1863, indulged in most sports before taking up soccer in about 1879. In 1881 they decided to stick to football to the exclusion of other sports and even a 16-0 drubbing by Blackburn Rovers in an invitation game at Deepdale, a few weeks after taking this decision, did not deter them for they immediately became affiliated to the Lancashire FA.

First Football League game: 8 September 1888, Football League, v Burnley (h) W 5-2 – Trainer; Haworth, Holmes; Robertson, W. Graham, J. Graham; Gordon (1), Ross (2), Goodall, Dewhurst (2), Drummond.

Did you know: Johnny Goodall was the first player ever to score hat-tricks in successive Football League games when he helped Preston to beat Wolves 5-2 and Notts County 7-0 in October – November 1888.

Managers (and Secretary-managers)
Charlie Parker 1906–15, Vincent Hayes 1919–23, Jim Lawrence 1923–25, Frank Richards 1925-27, Alex Gibson 1927–31, Lincoln Hayes 1931–32 (run by committee 1932–36), Tommy Muirhead 1936–37 (run by committee 1937–49), Will Scott 1949–53, Scot Symon 1953–54, Frank Hill 1954–56, Cliff Britton 1956–61, Jimmy Milne 1961–68, Bobby Seith 1968–70, Alan Ball Sr 1970–73, Bobby Charlton 1973–75, Harry Catterick 1975–77, Nobby Stiles 1977–81, Tommy Docherty 1981, Gordon Lee 1981–83, Alan Kelly 1983–85, Tommy Booth 1985–86, Brian Kidd 1986, John McGrath 1986–90, Les Chapman May 1990–.

Player and Position	Ht	Wt	Birth Date	Birth Place	Source	Clubs	League App	Gls
Forwards								
Gareth Ainsworth‡	5 09	11 09	10 5 73	Blackburn	Trainee	Blackburn R	—	—
						Preston NE	5	—
Lee Ashcroft	5 10	11 00	7 9 72	Preston	Trainee	Preston NE	52	6
David Christie	6 1		26 2 73	Salford	Trainee	Preston NE	2	—
Stephen Finney	5 10	12 00	31 10 73	Hexham	Trainee	Preston NE	2	1
Nigel Greenwood‡	5 11	12 00	27 11 66	Preston	Apprentice	Preston NE	45	14
						Bury	110	25
						Preston NE	30	4
Tony Hancock†	6 1	12 12	31 1 67	Manchester	Stockport Georgians	Stockport Co	22	5
						Burnley	17	—
						Preston NE	—	—
Ronnie Jepson	6 1	13 02	12 5 63	Stoke	Nantwich	Port Vale	22	—
						Peterborough U (loan)	18	5
						Preston NE	38	8
Jason Kerfoot	5 8	10 10	17 4 73	Preston	Trainee	Preston NE	4	—
Graham Shaw	5 8	10 01	7 6 67	Newcastle	Apprentice	Stoke C	99	18
						Preston NE	121	29

Trainees
Allardyce, Craig S; Bagnall, John A; Burton, Simon P; Close, Jamie T; Critchley, Adam D; England, Kieran J; Hall, Andrew B; Heavey, Paul A; Hindle, Paul J; Ilse, Thomas W. S; McCullough, Gary; O'Connor, Kerry; Raywood, Matthew; Rimmer, Christopher E; Schofield, Christopher; Sheridan, Brian J; Williams, Christopher J.

**Non-Contract
Knights, Paul C; Nixon, Craig G.

Associated Schoolboys
Alder, Joseph; Andrews, Brett P; Arnold, Lee; Bolton, Michael R. D; Booker, Geoffrey S; Borland, John R; Borwick, Christopher S; Boustead, Steven G; Calligan, John K; Garratt, Leroy; Ginocchio, Mark; Haworth, Robert A; Hayton, Kyle; Kilbane, Kevin D; Lucas, David A; McKenna, Paul S; McMenemy, Paul J; Neilson, Christopher; Poole, David; Price, James R; Roberts, Gary P; Spencer, Neil D; Stanley, Ian; Stewart, Simon D. S; Taylor, Thomas P; Woods, Daniel M; Wright, James C.

Associated Schoolboys who have accepted the club's offer of a Traineeship/Contract
Banks, Andrew M; Brandes, Christopher M; Farragher, Kieran T; Holland, Christopher J; Linford, Paul R; Parkinson, Christopher; Parkinson, Stuart G; Squires, James A.

**Non-Contract Players who are retained must be re-signed before they are eligible to play in League matches.

QUEENS PARK RANGERS 1991–92 *Back row (left to right):* Dennis Bailey, Les Ferdinand, Roy Wegerle, Michael Meaker, Mark Falco, Jan Stejskal, Alan McDonald, Peter Caldwell, Darren Peacock, Paul Vowles, Karl Ready, Dominic Iorfa.

Centre row: Des Bulpin (Youth Team Manager), Ron Berry (Kit Manager), Frank Sibley (First Team Coach), Paul Bromage, David McEnroe, Maurice Doyle, Bradley Allen, Tony Roberts, Andy Tillson, Brian Law, Alan McCarthy, Andrew Impey, Roger Cross (Reserve Team Manager), Brian Morris (Physiotherapist), Les Boyle (Youth Team Trainer).

Front row: Ray Wilkins, David Bardsley, Rufus Brevett, Andy Sinton, Clive Wilson, Gerry Francis (Manager), Paul Parker, Simon Barker, Danny Maddix, Justin Channing, Robert Herrera.

FA Premier   **QUEENS PARK RANGERS**

South Africa Road, W12 7PA. Telephone 081-743 0262. Box Office: 081-749 5744. Supporters Club: 081-749 6771. Club Shop: 081-749 6862. Marketing: 081-740 8737.

Ground capacity: 23,480 (23,000 covered).

Record attendance: 35,353 v Leeds U, Division 1, 27 April 1974.

Record receipts: £180,963 v Manchester U, Division 1, 28 March 1992.

Pitch measurements: 112yd × 72yd.

Chairman: R. C. Thompson.

Directors: (Corporate): R. B. Copus (Club): P. D. Ellis, A. Ingham, A. Ellis.

Manager: Gerry Francis. *Assistant Coach:* Frank Sibley. *Secretary:* Miss S. F. Marson. *Marketing Executive:* Lynne Davie. *Reserve Team Coach:* Roger Cross. *Physio:* Brian Morris.

Year Formed: 1885 *(see Foundation).* Turned Professional: 1898. Ltd Co.: 1899.

Former Grounds: 1885 *(see Foundation),* Welford's Fields; 1888–99; London Scottish Ground, Brondesbury, Home Farm, Kensal Rise Green, Gun Club Wormwood Scrubs, Kilburn Cricket Ground; 1899, Kensal Rise Athletic Ground; 1901, Latimer Road, Notting Hill; 1904, Agricultural Society, Park Royal; 1907, Park Royal Ground; 1917, Loftus Road; 1931, White City; 1933, Loftus Road; 1962, White City; 1963, Loftus Road.

Former Names: 1885–87, St Jude's.

Club Nickname: 'Rangers' or 'Rs'.

Record League Victory: 9-2 v Tranmere R, Division 3, 3 December 1960 – Drinkwater; Woods, Ingham; Keen, Rutter, Angell; Lazarus (2), Bedford (2), Evans (2), Andrews (1), Clark (2).

Record Cup Victory: 8-1 v Bristol R (away), FA Cup, 1st rd, 27 November 1937 – Gilfillan; Smith, Jefferson; Lowe, James, March; Cape, Mallett, Cheetham (3), Fitzgerald (3), Bott (2). 8-1 v Crewe Alex, Milk Cup, 1st rd, 3 October 1983 – Hucker; Neill, Dawes, Waddock (1), McDonald (1), Fenwick, Micklewhite (1), Stewart (1), Allen (1), Stainrod (3), Gregory.

Record Defeat: 1-8 v Mansfield T, Division 3, 15 March 1965 and v Manchester U, Division 1, 19 March 1969.

Most League Points (2 for a win): 67, Division 3, 1966–67.

Most League points (3 for a win): 85, Division 2, 1982–83.

Most League Goals: 111, Division 3, 1961–62.

Highest League Scorer in Season: George Goddard, 37, Division 3 (S), 1929–30.

Most League Goals in Total Aggregate: George Goddard, 172, 1926–34.

Most Capped Player: Don Givens, 26 (56), Eire.

Most League Appearances: Tony Ingham, 519, 1950–63.

Record Transfer Fee Received: £1,300,000 from Arsenal for David Seaman, May 1990.

Record Transfer Fee Paid: £1,000,000 to Luton T for Roy Wegerle, December 1989.

Football League Record: 1920 Original Member of Division 3; 1921 Division 3 (S); 1948–52 Division 2; 1952–58 Division 3 (S); 1958–67 Division 3; 1967–68 Division 2; 1968–69 Division 1; 1969–73 Division 2; 1973–79 Division 1; 1979–83 Division 2; 1983–92 Division 1; 1992– FA Premier League.

Honours: Football League: Division 1 – Runners-up 1975–76; Division 2 – Champions 1982–83; Runners-up 1967–68, 1972–73; Division 3 (S) – Champions 1947–48; Runners-up 1946–47; Division 3 – Champions 1966–67. *FA Cup:* Runners-up 1982. *Football League Cup:* Winners 1966–67; Runners-up 1985–86. (In 1966–67 won Division 3 and Football League Cup.) **European Competition:** *UEFA Cup:* 1976–77, 1984–85.

Colours: Blue and white hooped shirts, white shorts, white stockings. **Change colours:** Red and black hooped shirts, black shorts, black stockings with 4 red bands at top.

426

QUEENS PARK RANGERS 1991–92 LEAGUE RECORD

Match No.	Date		Venue	Opponents	Result		H/T Score	Lg. Pos.	Goalscorers	Atten- dance
1	Aug	17	A	Arsenal	D	1-1	1-0	—	Bailey	38,099
2		21	H	Norwich C	L	0-2	0-1	—		10,726
3		24	H	Coventry C	D	1-1	0-0	17	Wegerle	9393
4		27	A	Liverpool	L	0-1	0-0	—		32,700
5		31	A	Sheffield W	L	1-4	0-3	21	Bailey	25,022
6	Sep	4	H	West Ham U	D	0-0	0-0	21		16,616
7		7	H	Southampton	D	2-2	0-1	21	Barker, Thompson	9237
8		14	A	Tottenham H	L	0-2	0-0	22		30,059
9		17	A	Luton T	W	1-0	0-0	—	Barker	9985
10		21	H	Chelsea	D	2-2	1-0	20	Wilson, Peacock	19,579
11		28	A	Crystal Palace	D	2-2	1-0	19	Barker, Wegerle (pen)	15,372
12	Oct	5	H	Nottingham F	L	0-2	0-1	19		13,508
13		19	A	Wimbledon	W	1-0	0-0	19	Bailey	4630
14		26	H	Everton	W	3-1	2-0	18	Bailey, Barker 2	10,002
15	Nov	2	A	Aston Villa	L	0-1	0-1	19		10,642
16		16	A	Leeds U	L	0-2	0-0	19		27,087
17		23	H	Oldham Ath	L	1-3	1-3	21	Ferdinand	8947
18		30	A	Notts Co	W	1-0	0-0	19	Ferdinand	7901
19	Dec	7	H	Sheffield U	W	1-0	0-0	17	Wegerle	10,106
20		14	A	Manchester C	D	2-2	0-2	17	Wegerle, Bailey	21,437
21		21	A	Norwich C	W	1-0	0-0	13	Bailey	11,436
22		26	H	Liverpool	D	0-0	0-0	15		21,693
23		28	H	Sheffield W	D	1-1	1-0	15	Wilkins	12,990
24	Jan	1	A	Manchester U	W	4-1	2-0	13	Sinton, Bailey 3	38,554
25		11	A	Coventry C	D	2-2	0-1	13	Penrice 2	11,999
26		18	H	Arsenal	D	0-0	0-0	13		20,497
27	Feb	1	H	Wimbledon	D	1-1	1-0	13	Penrice	9194
28		8	A	Everton	D	0-0	0-0	13		18,212
29		15	A	Oldham Ath	L	1-2	0-1	14	Wegerle	13,092
30		22	H	Notts Co	D	1-1	0-0	14	Ferdinand	8300
31		29	A	Sheffield U	D	0-0	0-0	14		17,958
32	Mar	7	H	Manchester C	W	4-0	2-0	13	Ferdinand 2, Wilson (pen), Barker	10,779
33		11	H	Leeds U	W	4-1	1-1	—	Ferdinand, Allen, Sinton, Wilson (pen)	14,641
34		14	A	Aston Villa	W	1-0	0-0	8	Ferdinand	19,630
35		21	A	West Ham U	D	2-2	0-1	9	Allen 2	20,401
36		28	H	Manchester U	D	0-0	0-0	9		22,603
37	Apr	4	A	Southampton	L	1-2	0-1	11	Ferdinand	15,205
38		11	H	Tottenham H	L	1-2	1-0	14	Sinton	20,678
39		18	A	Chelsea	L	1-2	0-1	16	Allen	18,952
40		20	H	Luton T	W	2-1	0-0	14	Ferdinand 2	10,749
41		25	A	Nottingham F	D	1-1	0-0	14	Allen	22,228
42	May	2	H	Crystal Palace	W	1-0	1-0	11	Humphrey (og)	14,903

Final League Position: 11

GOALSCORERS

League (48): Ferdinand 10, Bailey 9, Barker 6, Allen 5, Wegerle 5 (1 pen), Penrice 3, Sinton 3, Wilson 3 (2 pens), Peacock 1, Thompson 1, Wilkins 1, own goals 1.
Rumbelows Cup (9): Thompson 3, Bailey 2, Barker 2, Bardsley 1, Penrice 1.
FA Cup (0).

Stejskal	Bardsley	Brevett	Wilkins	Peacock	Maddix	Bailey	Barker	Ferdinand	Wegerle	Sinton	Holloway	Thompson	Wilson	Allen	McDonald	Roberts	Tillson	Iorfa	Walsh	Penrice	McCarthy	Impey	Ready	Meaker	Match No.
1	2	3	4*	5	6	7	8	9	10	11	12														1
1	2	3		5	6	7*	8	9	10	11			4	12											2
1	2	14		5	6	7	8	9*	10	11			4	12	3†										3
1	2			5	6	7	8	9*	10	11			4	12	3										4
1	2			5	6	7	8	9	10	11*			4	12	3										5
1	2	3		5	6	7	8	12	10				4*	9	11										6
1	2	3		5	6*	7	8		10		12		4	9	11										7
	2†	3			6		8		10*	11	14	9	7	12	5	1	4								8
1	2	3†			6	12	8			11	14	9	7		5		4			10*					9
1	2	3			6		8			11	4	9	7		5					10					10
1	2	3			6	12	8		10*	11	4	9	7		5										11
1	2	3*			6	12	8	9	10	11	4		7		5										12
1	2			5	6	10	8			11	7	9	3		4										13
1	2			5	6	10	8			11	7	9	3		4										14
1	2			5	6	10	8			11	7	9	3		4*					12					15
1	2	12		5	6		8	14		11	7	9†	3		4*					10					16
1	2		4	5	6	7*	8	9		11	12		3							10					17
1	2		4	5			8	9		11			3		6					10		7			18
1	2		4	5			8		10	11	12		3		6					9*		7			19
1	2		4	5			8	14	10	11	12		3*		6					9		7†			20
1	2		4	5			8	9	10	11	7		3		6										21
1	2		4	5			8	9	10	11	7		3		6										22
1	2		4	5			8	9*	10	11	7	12	3		6										23
1	2		4	5			8	9	10	11	7		3		6										24
1	2		4	5			8	9	10*		7		3		6					12		11			25
1	2		4	5			8	9*	12	11	7		3		6					10					26
1			4	5			8*	9	12	11	7		3							10		2			27
1	2†		4	5			8	9*	12	11	7		3		6		14			10					28
1	2		4	5			8*		10	11	7		3		6					9				12	29
1	2		4	5			8	9		11			3		6					10		7			30
1	2		7	5			8	9		11			3		6					10		4			31
1	2		7	5		12	8	9		11			3		6					10*		4			32
1	2		4	5		12		9		11*	7		3		6					10		8			33
1	2		7	5			8	9		11			3		6					10		4			34
1	2		7	5		12	8	9		11			3		6					10*		4			35
1	2		7	5			8	9		11			3		6					10		4			36
1	2			5		7	8	9		11*			3		6					10	12	4			37
1	2		7	5			8	9*		11			3		6					10	12	4			38
1	2		7	5			8	9		11			3		6					12	4*	10			39
1	2		7	5			8	9		11			3		6					10*	12	4			40
1	2		7	5	6		8	9*		11			3							10	12	4			41
1	2		7	5		12	8	9*		11			3		6					10		4			42
41	41	6 +1s	26 +1s	39	19 +5s	19 +3s	31 +2s	21 +3s	18	38 +6s	34 +5s	10	40 +1s	10 +1s	27	1	9 +1s	—	2	13 +1s	3	13 +6s	1	— +1s	

Rumbelows Cup	Second Round	Hull C (a)	3-0
		(h)	5-1
	Third Round	Manchester C (a)	0-0
		(h)	1-3
FA Cup	Third Round	Southampton (a)	0-2

QUEENS PARK RANGERS

Goalkeepers

Name	Ht	Wt	D M Y	Birthplace	Source	Club	Apps	Gls
Peter Caldwell			5 6 72	Dorchester	Trainee	QPR	—	—
Tony Roberts	6 0	12 00	4 8 69	Bangor	Trainee	QPR	19	—
Jan Stejskal	6 3	12 00	15 1 62	Czechoslovakia	Sparta	QPR	67	—

Defenders

Name	Ht	Wt	D M Y	Birthplace	Source	Club	Apps	Gls
David Bardsley	5 10	10 06	11 9 64	Manchester	Apprentice	Blackpool	45	—
						Watford	100	7
						Oxford U	74	7
						QPR	110	1
Rufus Brevett	5 8	11 00	24 9 69	Derby	Trainee	Derby Co	—	—
						Doncaster R	109	3
						QPR	17	—
Justin Channing	5 10	11 03	19 11 68	Reading	Apprentice	QPR	53	4
Darren Finlay	5 04	10 00	19 12 73	Belfast	Trainee	QPR	—	—
Stephen Gallen	6 00	12 00	21 11 73	London	Trainee	QPR	—	—
Roberto Herrera	5 7	10 06	12 6 70	Torbay	Trainee	QPR	6	—
						Torquay U (loan)	11	—
Brian Law	6 2	11 10	1 1 70	Merthyr	Apprentice	QPR	20	—
Alan McCarthy	5 11	12 10	11 1 72	London	Trainee	QPR	5	—
Alan McDonald	6 2	12 07	12 10 63	Belfast	Apprentice	QPR	247	8
						Charlton Ath (loan)	9	—
Danny Maddix	5 11	11 00	11 10 67	Ashford	Apprentice	Tottenham H	—	—
						Southend U (loan)	2	—
						QPR	125	6
Darren Peacock	6 2	12 06	3 2 68	Bristol	Apprentice	Newport Co	28	—
						Hereford U	59	4
						QPR	58	1
Karl Ready	6 1	12 00	14 8 72	Neath	Apprentice	QPR	1	—
Andy Tillson	6 2	12 07	30 6 66	Huntingdon	Kettering	Grimsby T	105	5
						QPR	29	2
Paul Vowels‡			26 8 71	Neath	Trainee	QPR	—	—
Tony Witter	6 1	12 07	12 8 65	London	Grays Ath	Crystal Palace	—	—
						QPR	—	—
						Millwall (loan)	—	—
						Plymouth Arg (loan)	3	1

Midfield

Name	Ht	Wt	D M Y	Birthplace	Source	Club	Apps	Gls
Simon Barker	5 9	11 00	4 11 64	Farnworth	Apprentice	Blackburn R	182	35
						QPR	122	11
Ray Bromage‡			30 9 72	Neath	Trainee	QPR	—	—
Ian Holloway	5 7	9 12	12 3 63	Kingswood	Apprentice	Bristol R	111	14
						Wimbledon	19	2
						Brentford (loan)	13	2
						Brentford	16	—
						Torquay U (loan)	5	—
						Bristol R	179	26
						QPR	40	—
David McEnroe	5 8	10 10	19 8 72	Dublin	Trainee	QPR	—	—
David Macciochi*			14 9 72	Harlow	Trainee	QPR	—	—
Mike Meaker	5 11	11 05	18 8 71	Greenford	Trainee	QPR	9	—
						Plymouth Arg (loan)	4	—
Michael Rutherford‡	5 9	11 10	6 6 72	Sidcup	Trainee	QPR	2	—
Andy Sinton	5 7	10 07	19 3 66	Newcastle	Apprentice	Cambridge U	93	13
						Brentford	149	28
						QPR	124	15
Gary Waddock	5 9	12 07	17 3 62	Kingsbury	Apprentice	QPR	203	8
						Charleroi	—	—
						Millwall	58	2
						QPR	—	—
						Swindon T (loan)	6	—
Ray Wilkins	5 8	11 02	14 9 56	Hillingdon	Apprentice	Chelsea	179	30
						Manchester U	160	7
						AC Milan	73	2
						Paris St Germain	—	—
						Rangers	70	2
						QPR	88	4

QUEENS PARK RANGERS

Foundation: There is an element of doubt about the date of the foundation of this club, but it is believed that in either 1885 or 1886 it was formed through the amalgamation of Christchurch Rangers and St. Jude's Institute FC. The leading light was George Wodehouse, whose family maintained a connection with the club until comparatively recent times. Most of the players came from the Queen's Park district so this name was adopted after a year as St. Jude's Institute.

First Football League game: 28 August, 1920, Division 3, v Watford (h) L 1-2 – Price; Blackman, Wingrove; McGovern, Grant, O'Brien; Faulkner, Birch (1), Smith, Gregory, Middlemiss.

Did you know: Rangers' list of managers includes a sequence of an Irishman, Scotsman, Welshman and an Englishman, namely Mick O'Brien, Billy Birrell, Ted Vizard and Dave Mangnall.

Managers (and Secretary-managers)
James Cowan 1906–13, James Howie 1913–20, Ted Liddell 1920–24, Will Wood 1924–25 (had been secretary since 1903), Bob Hewison 1925–30, John Bowman 1930–31, Archie Mitchell 1931–33, Mick O'Brien 1933–35, Billy Birrell 1935–39, Ted Vizard 1939–44, Dave Mangnall 1944–52, Jack Taylor 1952–59, Alec Stock 1959–65 (GM to 1968), Jimmy Andrews 1965, Bill Dodgin Jnr 1968, Tommy Docherty 1968, Les Allen 1969–70, Gordon Jago 1971–74, Dave Sexton 1974–77, Frank Sibley 1977–78, Steve Burtenshaw 1978–79, Tommy Docherty 1979–80, Terry Venables 1980–84, Gordon Jago 1984, Alan Mullery 1984, Frank Sibley 1984–85, Jim Smith 1985–88, Trevor Francis 1988–90, Don Howe 1990–91, Gerry Francis June 1991–.

Clive Wilson	5 7	10 00	13 11 61	Manchester	Local	Manchester C	98	9
						Chester C (loan)	21	2
						Manchester C (loan)	11	—
						Chelsea	81	5
						QPR	53	4
Forwards								
Bradley Allen	5 7	10 00	13 9 71	Harold Wood	Schoolboys	QPR	22	7
Dennis Bailey	6 0	11 01	13 11 65	Lambeth	Farnborough	Crystal Palace	5	1
						Bristol R (loan)	17	9
						Birmingham C	75	23
						Bristol R (loan)	6	1
						QPR	24	9
Maurice Doyle	5 8	10 07	17 10 69	Ellesmere Port	Trainee	Crewe Alex	8	2
						QPR	—	—
						Crewe Alex (loan)	7	2
						Wolverhampton W (loan)	—	—
Les Ferdinand	5 11	13 05	18 12 66	London	Hayes	QPR	53	20
						Brentford (loan)	3	—
						Besiktas (loan)	—	—
Doug Freedman	5 09	11 00	21 1 74	Glasgow	Trainee	QPR	—	—
Andrew Impey	5 8	10 06	13 9 71	Hammersmith	Yeading	QPR	13	—
Dominic Iorfa (To Galatasaray Jan 1992)	6 1	12 12	1 10 68	Lagos	Antwerp	QPR	8	—
Gary Penrice	5 7	10 00	23 3 64	Bristol	Mangotsfield	Bristol R	188	54
						Watford	43	18
						Aston Villa	20	1
						QPR	19	3
Garry Thompson	6 1	14 00	7 10 59	Birmingham	Apprentice	Coventry C	134	38
						WBA	91	39
						Sheffield W	36	7
						Aston Villa	60	17
						Watford	34	8
						Crystal Palace	20	3
						QPR	15	1

Trainees
Bircham, Stephen; Bryan, Marvin L; Davey, Joseph L; Dichio, Daniele S. E; Dickinson, Steven D; Duong, Vinh T; Graham, Mark R; Jackson, Stephen; Magill, Robert D; McCardle, Martin; Millard, Martyn L. D; Peacock, John S; Pratt, Benjamin K; Wilkinson, Gary R.

**Non-Contract
Francis, Gerald C. J.

Associated Schoolboys
Brazier, Matthew R; Cook, Anthony M; Cooper, Paul; Harris, Jonathan; Hodges, Kevin; Holman, Lee C; Hurst, Richard A; Marsden, David J; McCarthy, Billy; Monteath, Jonathan; Morrish, Luke; Nuttall, Steven R; Plummer, Christopher S; Power, Graeme R; Sharpe, Robert L; Waring, Ian A; White, Dene; Wilson, Ross E.

Associated Schoolboys who have accepted the club's offer of a Traineeship/Contract
Challis, Trevor M; Cross, John R; Gallen, Kevin A; Goodwin, Lee; Goodwin, Paul A.

**Non-Contract Players who are retained must be re-signed before they are eligible to play in League matches.

READING 1991–92 *Back row (left to right):* Craig Maskell, Brendan Rodgers, Mark Holzman, Scott Taylor, Stuart Lovell, Chris Seymour, David Leworthy.
Centre row: Colin Lee (Coach), Nathan Fealey, Floyd Streete, Adrian Williams, Danny Honey, Steve Francis, Trevor Senior, Keith McPherson, Neale Cooper, John Haselden (Physiotherapist).
Front row: Michael Gilkes, Kevin Dillon, Linden Jones, Mark McGhee (Player/Manager), Danny Bailey, Mick Gooding, Steve Richardson.

Division 2   **READING**

Elm Park, Norfolk Road, Reading. Telephone Reading (0734) 507878.

Ground capacity: 13,200.

Record attendance: 33,042 v Brentford, FA Cup 5th rd, 19 February 1927.

Record receipts: £70,693.79 v Arsenal, FA Cup 3rd rd, 10 January 1987.

Pitch measurements: 112yd × 77yd.

Life President: J. H. Brooks.

Chairman: John Madejski.

Managing Director: M. J. Lewis.

Directors: G. Denton.

Manager: Mark McGhee. *Coach:* Colin Lee. *Youth Development officer:* Colin Clark. *Physio:* John Haselden. *Commercial Manager:* Kevin Girdler. *Secretary:* Jayne E. Hill.

Year Formed: 1871. Turned Professional: 1895. Ltd Co.: 1895.

Former Grounds: 1871, Reading Recreation; Reading Cricket Ground; 1882, Coley Park; 1889, Caversham Cricket Ground; 1896, Elm Park.

Club Nickname: 'The Royals'.

Record League Victory: 10-2 v Crystal Palace, Division 3 (S), 4 September 1946 – Groves; Glidden, Gulliver; McKenna, Ratcliffe, Young; Chitty, Maurice Edelston (3), McPhee (4), Barney (1), Deverell (2).

Record Cup Victory: 6-0 v Leyton, FA Cup, 2nd rd, 12 December 1925 – Duckworth; Eggo, McConnell; Wilson, Messer, Evans; Smith (2), Braithwaite (1), Davey (1), Tinsley, Robson (2).

Record Defeat: 0-18 v Preston NE, FA Cup 1st rd, 1893–94.

Most League Points (2 for a win): 65, Division 4, 1978–79.

Most League points (3 for a win): 94, Division 3, 1985–86.

Most League Goals: 112, Division 3 (S), 1951–52.

Highest League Scorer in Season: Ronnie Blackman, 39, Division 3 (S), 1951–52.

Most League Goals in Total Aggregate: Ronnie Blackman, 156, 1947–54.

Most Capped Player: Billy McConnell, 8, Northern Ireland.

Most League Appearances: Martin Hicks, 500, 1978–91.

Record Transfer Fee Received: £325,000 from Watford for Trevor Senior, July 1987.

Record Transfer Fee Paid: £250,000 to Leicester C for Steve Moran, November 1987 and £250,000 to Huddersfield T for Craig Maskell, August 1990.

Football League Record: 1920 Original Member of Division 3; 1921–26 Division 3 (S); 1926–31 Division 2; 1931–58 Division 3 (S); 1958–71 Division 3; 1971–76 Division 4; 1976–77 Division 3; 1977–79 Division 4; 1979–83 Division 3; 1983–84 Division 4; 1984–86 Division 3; 1986–88 Division 2; 1988–92 Division 3; 1992– Division 2.

Honours: Football League: Division 2 best season: 13th, 1986–87; Division 3 – Champions 1985–86. Division 3 (S) – Champions 1925–26; Runners-up 1931–32, 1934–35, 1948–49, 1951–52; Division 4 – Champions 1978–79. *FA Cup:* Semi-final 1927. *Football League Cup:* best season: 4th rd, 1965, 1966, 1978. *Simod Cup:* Winners 1987–88.

Colours: Navy and white hooped shirts, navy blue shorts, navy blue stockings. **Change colours:** Yellow and navy blue hooped shirts, yellow shorts, yellow stockings.

READING 1991–92 LEAGUE RECORD

Match No.	Date		Venue	Opponents		Result	H/T Score	Lg. Pos.	Goalscorers	Attendance
1	Aug	17	H	Hull C	L	0-1	0-0	—		4639
2		24	A	Hartlepool U	L	0-2	0-1	23		2858
3		31	H	Bury	W	3-2	1-0	16	Senior, McPherson, McGhee	2886
4	Sep	3	A	Swansea C	W	2-1	0-0	—	Byrne, Senior	3206
5		7	H	Birmingham C	D	1-1	1-1	12	Byrne	6649
6		14	A	Brentford	L	0-1	0-0	17		5775
7		17	A	Torquay U	W	2-1	1-0	—	Senior, Holzman	2591
8		21	H	Bradford C	L	1-2	1-1	15	Gooding	3765
9		28	A	Exeter C	L	1-2	0-0	17	Lovell	3383
10	Oct	5	H	Bournemouth	D	0-0	0-0	17		4033
11		11	A	Wigan Ath	D	1-1	0-0	—	Cockram	1817
12		19	H	Peterborough U	D	1-1	0-1	18	Dillon (pen)	2954
13		26	A	Shrewsbury T	W	2-1	0-0	16	Dillon, Taylor	2398
14	Nov	2	A	Bolton W	D	1-1	0-0	16	Gooding	3632
15		5	H	Darlington	D	2-2	0-0	—	Maskell, Williams	2808
16		9	H	WBA	L	1-2	0-1	18	Taylor	5826
17		23	A	Chester C	D	2-2	1-1	17	Maskell 2 (1 pen)	1124
18		30	H	Stockport Co	D	1-1	1-1	18	Maskell	3511
19	Dec	20	H	Hartlepool U	L	0-1	0-0	—		2535
20		26	A	Bury	W	1-0	0-0	17	Maskell	2333
21		28	A	Hull C	W	1-0	1-0	15	Senior	3661
22	Jan	1	H	Swansea C	W	1-0	0-0	14	Senior	5083
23		11	H	Huddersfield T	W	1-0	0-0	13	Senior	4732
24		18	A	Stoke C	L	0-3	0-1	14		10,835
25	Feb	1	A	Peterborough U	L	3-5	2-2	14	Richardson, Lee, Maskell (pen)	3792
26		8	H	Shrewsbury T	W	2-1	1-0	13	Lee, Senior	3303
27		11	A	Stockport Co	L	0-1	0-0	—		3720
28		15	H	Fulham	L	0-2	0-0	17		4388
29		22	A	Huddersfield T	W	2-1	1-0	16	Lee, Williams	6259
30		29	H	Preston NE	D	2-2	2-0	16	Lee 2	3390
31	Mar	4	H	Stoke C	L	3-4	2-2	—	Lovell, Williams, Gooding	4362
32		7	A	Leyton Orient	D	1-1	1-1	16	Maskell	4436
33		10	A	Darlington	W	4-2	1-0	—	Maskell 3, Cork (og)	2388
34		14	H	Bolton W	W	1-0	1-0	14	Brown P (og)	3515
35		21	A	WBA	L	0-2	0-2	15		10,707
36		28	A	Chester C	D	0-0	0-0	15		2813
37	Apr	1	H	Brentford	D	0-0	0-0	—		5660
38		4	A	Birmingham C	L	0-2	0-2	17		12,229
39		7	A	Fulham	L	0-1	0-0	—		3499
40		11	H	Torquay U	W	6-1	4-1	16	Dillon, Lovell, Barkus, McGhee, Maskell 2	3111
41		14	A	Preston NE	D	1-1	0-1	—	Maskell	3203
42		18	A	Bradford C	L	0-1	0-0	16		5492
43		20	H	Exeter C	W	1-0	1-0	15	McGhee	3325
44		25	A	Bournemouth	L	2-3	1-1	15	Watson (og), Williams	6486
45		29	H	Leyton Orient	W	3-2	1-0	—	Maskell 2, McGhee	2690
46	May	2	H	Wigan Ath	W	3-2	0-2	12	Maskell (pen), McGhee, Lovell	2748

Final League Position: 12

GOALSCORERS

League (59): Maskell 16 (3 pens), Senior 7, Lee 5, McGhee 5, Lovell 4, Williams 4, Dillon 3 (1 pen), Gooding 3, Byrne 2, Taylor 2, Barkus 1, Cockram 1, Holzman 1, McPherson 1, Richardson 1, own goals 3.
Rumbelows Cup (0).
FA Cup (6): Lovell 2, Williams 2, Gooding 1, Taylor 1.

Francis	Jones	Richardson	McPherson	Cooper	Williams	Holzman	Dillon	McGhee	Leworthy	Gilkes	Senior	Gooding	Byrne	Maskell	Bailey	Streete	Lovell	Taylor	Cockram	Morrow	Leighton	Britton	Archibald	Gray	Lee	Fealey	Keeley	Giamattei	Match No.
1	2	3	4	5	6	7†	8	9*	10	11	12	14																	1
1	2		4	5*	6	14	8		10	11†	9	3	7	12															2
1		3	4		2		8		10	11	9			7*		5	6	12											3
1		3	4	5	2		10			11*	9	8	7			12	6												4
1	2	3	4	5	14		10*	12	11	9	8	7†					6												5
1	2	3	4	5		10	8		12	11*	9		7				6												6
1	2	3	4	5	14	11	10*			9	8†	7	12				6												7
1	2	3	4		14		8		10	11†	9*	5	7	12			6												8
1		3	4	14	6	2	8		10*	9	5			11†			12	7											9
1		3	4	8	6	2				9	5			11			10	7											10
1		3†	4	8*	6	2	11	12		9	5						10	7	14										11
1			4		6	2	8	10		3	12	11				5	9*	7											12
1			4		6	2	8	9*		11	12	5					10	3	7										13
1	2		4		6		8	9		11	5						10	7		3									14
1	2†		4		6	7		9	12	11	5	10*				8	14			3									15
1	2		4		6	12		9	10*	11	5					7	8			3									16
1	2		4	7	6	3		9*		8	5					10	12	11											17
		3	4		5			9†		11	7		10			6	8*	2	12		1		14						18
		3	4		5					11	7		10	8	6	9*	2				1		12						19
	2	3	4		5					11	7		10	8	6	9					1								20
	2	3	4		5				14	9	7		10*	8	6	12	11†				1								21
	2	3	4*		5					11	9	7	10	8	6		12				1								22
	2				5	3				11	9	7		8	6	4					1		10						23
	2				5	3				11†	9	7		8	6	10*	4	12			1		14						24
	2	3	4					10†		9	14		8	12		7	11				1			5	6*				25
	2		4					9					10	8	6	7	3	11						5		1			26
	2	3	4					9			7		10	8*	6		12							5		1			27
	2	3	4	5				9		11			10	8*	6		7									1	12		28
	2	3	4					9		11			10	8	6		7							5		1			29
	2	3	4					9		12	11		10	8	6		7*							5		1			30
	2	3	4					9		7	12		5	10	8	6	11*									1			31
1	2	3	4					9		7	12		5	10		6	11*	14											32
1	2	3	4					9		7	12		5	10		6	11†	14											33
1	2	3	4					9		7	12		5	10	8	6	11*												34
1	2	3	4					9		7	12		5	10	8†		11*	14											35
1		3	4					9		7	12	14	5	10*		6	2†												36
1		3	4					5		7	12		9	2		10	11	6											37
1	2*	3	4					9		7	8†		5	10	11	6	12												38
1	14	3	4					5†		7	12		2	10	11	6													39
1		3	4					5†		8	9		2	12		6	11	14											40
1	2	3	4					8		9			5	7		6	11	12											41
1	2	3	4	5				8		9			7			6	11											12†	42
1	2	3	4	5				8		9			7	6			11												43
1		3	4	5				8		9		2	7	6†			11												44
1	2		4	5				8		9		3	7			12	11												45
1*	2		4	5				8		9		10	3			7	12	11											46
32	28	38	44	6	40	11	29	23	3	19	20	39	7	29	23	34	16	22	2	3	8	—	1	—	5	1	6	—	
	+		+		+		+	+	+	+		+	+			+	+		+	+	+				+		+		
1s		1s		5s		9s	3s	1s	5s	1s		5s	1s			8s	7s	4s			2s				1s		2s		

Seymour—Match No. 32(8†) 33(8*) 35(6) 42(14); Robinson—Match No. 36(8) 37(8*) 39(8*) 40(10) 41(10*) 42(10*) 43(10) 44(10*); Barkus—Match No. 36(11) 38(14) 39(9) 40(7*) 44(12) 45(10*); Bass—Match No. 44(14) 45(6) 46(6).

Rumbelows Cup	First Round	Cambridge U (a)	0-1
		(h)	0-3
FA Cup	First Round	Slough (a)	3-3
		(h)	2-1
	Second Round	Peterborough U (a)	0-0
		(h)	1-0
	Third Round	Bolton W (a)	0-2

READING

Goalkeepers

Name				Born	Source	Club	Apps	Gls
Steve Francis	5 11	11 05	29 5 64	Billericay	Apprentice	Chelsea	71	—
						Reading	182	—
Daniel Honey	6 02	13 00	2 4 73	Ascot	Trainee	Reading	—	—

Defenders

Name				Born	Source	Club	Apps	Gls
David Bass§			29 11 74	Frimley	Trainee	Reading	3	—
Neale Cooper (To Dunfermline Ath Nov 1991)	6 1	12 07	24 11 63	India	Trainee	Aberdeen	132	6
						Aston Villa	20	—
						Rangers	17	1
						Reading	14	—
Andrew Gray§			25 10 73	Southampton	Trainee	Reading	1	—
Mark Holzman	5 06	10 00	21 2 73	Reading	Trainee	Reading	16	1
Linden Jones*	5 6	10 08	5 3 61	Tredegar	Apprentice	Cardiff C	145	2
						Newport Co	142	5
						Reading	152	8
Keith McPherson	5 11	10 11	11 9 63	Greenwich	Apprentice	West Ham U	1	—
						Cambridge U (loan)	11	1
						Northampton T	182	8
						Reading	90	4
Steve Richardson	5 5	10 03	11 2 62	Slough	Apprentice	Southampton	—	—
						Reading	365	3
Brendan Rodgers*	5 06	10 03	26 1 73	Larne	Trainee	Reading	—	—
Chris Seymour*	5 10	11 00	14 9 71	Reading	Trainee	Reading	13	—
Floyd Streete*	5 11	14 00	5 5 59	Jamaica	Rivet S	Cambridge U	125	19
						Utrecht	—	—
						Derby Co	35	—
						Wolverhampton W	159	6
						Reading	38	—
Adrian Williams	5 10	11 00	16 8 71	Reading	Trainee	Reading	71	6

Midfield

Name				Born	Source	Club	Apps	Gls
Danny Bailey	5 7	12 07	21 5 64	London	Apprentice	Bournemouth	2	—
						Torquay U	1	—
						Wealdstone		
						Exeter C	64	2
						Reading	50	2
Allan Cockram†	5 8	10 08	8 10 63	Kensington	Local	Tottenham H	2	—
						Bristol R	1	—
						St Albans	—	—
						Brentford	90	14
						Brighton & HA	—	—
						Reading	6	1
Kevin Dillon	6 0	12 07	18 12 59	Sunderland	Apprentice	Birmingham C	186	15
						Portsmouth	215	45
						Newcastle U	62	—
						Reading	29	3
Aaron Giamattei§			11 10 73	Reading	Trainee	Reading	2	—
Mick Gooding	5 7	10 08	12 4 59	Newcastle	B Auckland	Rotherham U	102	10
						Chesterfield	12	—
						Rotherham U	156	33
						Peterborough U	47	21
						Wolverhampton W	44	4
						Reading	111	13
Stuart Lovell	5 10	10 06	9 1 72	Sydney	Trainee	Reading	54	6
Scott Taylor	5 9	11 00	28 11 70	Portsmouth	Trainee	Reading	93	5

Forwards

Name				Born	Source	Club	Apps	Gls
Steve Archibald‡	5 10	11 02	27 9 56	Glasgow	Fernhill Ath	Clyde	65	7
						Aberdeen	76	29
						Tottenham H	131	58
						Barcelona	—	—
						Blackburn R	20	6
						Hibernian	44	15
						St Mirren	16	2
						Reading	2	—

READING

Foundation: Reading was formed as far back as 1871 at a public meeting held at the Bridge Street Rooms. They first entered the FA Cup as early as 1877 when they amalgamated with the Reading Hornets. The club was further strengthened in 1889 when Earley FC joined them. They were the first winners of the Berks and Bucks Cup in 1878–79.

First Football League game: 28 August 1920, Division 3, v Newport C (a) W 1-0 – Crawford; Smith, Horler; Christie, Mavin, Getgood; Spence, Weston, Yarnell, Bailey (1), Andrews.

Did you know: Reading beat Burslem Port Vale 2-1 when the Potteries side were the first professional outfit to pay them a visit on 27 December 1892. The visitors goals were scored by Billy Beats who became Reading's trainer 22 years later.

Managers (and Secretary-managers)
Thomas Sefton 1897–1901*, James Sharp 1901–02, Harry Matthews 1902–20, Harry Marshall 1920–22, Arthur Chadwick 1923–25, H. S. Bray 1925–26 (secretary only since 1922 and 26–35), Andrew Wylie 1926–31, Joe Smith 1931–35, Billy Butler 1935–39, John Cochrane 1939, Joe Edelston 1939–47, Ted Drake 1947–52, Jack Smith 1952–55, Harry Johnston 1955–63, Roy Bentley 1963–69, Jack Mansell 1969–71, Charlie Hurley 1972–77, Maurice Evans 1977–84, Ian Branfoot 1984–89, Ian Porterfield 1989–91, Mark McGhee May 1991–.

Lea Barkus§			7 12 74	Reading	Trainee	Reading	6	1
Nathan Fealey*	6 00	12 02	12 3 73	Aldershot	Trainee	Reading	1	—
Michael Gilkes	5 8	10 02	20 7 65	Hackney		Reading	200	20
						Chelsea (loan)	1	—
						Southampton (loan)	6	—
David Leworthy‡	5 9	12 00	22 10 62	Portsmouth	Apprentice	Portsmouth	1	—
						Fareham T	—	—
						Tottenham H	11	3
						Oxford U	37	8
						Shrewsbury T (loan)	6	3
						Reading	44	7
Mark McGhee†	5 10	12 00	25 5 57	Glasgow	Apprentice	Bristol C	—	—
						Morton	64	37
						Newcastle U	28	5
						Aberdeen	164	63
						Hamburg	30	7
						Celtic	88	27
						Newcastle U	67	24
						Reading	32	5
Craig Maskell	5 10	11 04	10 4 68	Aldershot	Apprentice	Southampton	6	1
						Swindon T (loan)	—	—
						Huddersfield T	87	43
						Reading	72	26
David Robinson	6 0	13 02	27 11 69	Newcastle	Trainee	Newcastle U	8	—
						Peterborough U (loan)	7	3
						Reading	8	—
Trevor Senior*	6 1	12 08	28 11 61	Dorchester	Dorchester T	Portsmouth	11	2
						Aldershot (loan)	10	7
						Reading	164	102
						Watford	24	1
						Middlesbrough	10	2
						Reading	137	52

Trainees
Barkus, Lea P; Bass, David; Edgar, Nicholas F; Ferguson, Gary; Gardiner, Dudley J; Giamattei, Aaron P; Gray, Andrew; Humphries, Steven P; Kent, Aron R; McCance, Daren; McGuigan, Gareth J; Minor, David J; Mukabaa, Anthony G; Silvey, Paul S; Timothy, David.

**Non-Contract
Kemp, Graham; McGhee, Mark.

Associated Schoolboys
Allen, Johnathan T; Caswell, James R; Curran, James M; Green, David J; Hands, Andrew P; Jenkins, Steven D; Jupp, Peter R; Murphy, Michael J; Simpson, Derek F; Stowell, Mathew D; Topham, Neil R; Wilkinson, Robert H.

Associated Schoolboys who have accepted the club's offer of a Traineeship/Contract
Brown, Philip R; Champion, Marc G; Holzman, Gary R; Montgomery, Noel T; Thorpe, Michael S.

**Non-Contract Players who are retained must be re-signed before they are eligible to play in League matches.

436

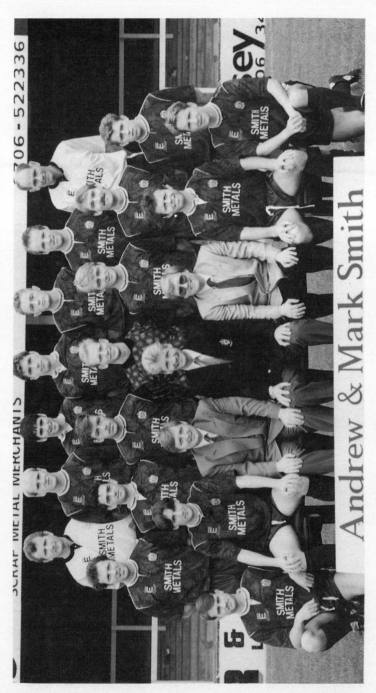

ROCHDALE 1991–92   *Back row (left to right):* Mick Docherty (Assistant Manager), Jimmy Graham, Paul Herring, Zac Hughes, Andy Milner, John Halpin, Jimmy Robson (Youth Development Officer).
Centre row: John Ryan, Steve Whitehall, Paul Butler, Gareth Gray, Alan Reeves, Tony Brown, Vince Chapman.
Front row: Phil Lockett, Steve Morgan, Andrew Smith (Sponsor), Dave Sutton (Manager), Mark Smith (Sponsor), Steve Doyle, Andy Flounders.

Division 3 — **ROCHDALE**

Spotland, Willbutts Lane, Rochdale OL11 5DA. Telephone Rochdale (0706) 44648. Fax No: 0706 48466

Ground capacity: 10,735.

Record attendance: 24,231 v Notts Co, FA Cup 2nd rd, 10 December 1949.

Record receipts: £46,000 v Burnley, Division 4, 5 May 1992.

Pitch measurements: 113yd × 75yd.

President: Mrs L. Stoney.

Chairman: D. F. Kilpatrick.

Vice-chairman: G. Morris.

Directors: T. Butterworth, C. Dunphy, L. Hilton, G. R. Brierley, J. Marsh, P. M. Mace, M.CH, FRCS.

Manager: Dave Sutton.

Secretary: Mrs Anne Pettifor.

Assistant Manager: Mick Docherty.

Coach: Jimmy Robson.

Commercial Manager: S. Walmsley.

Advertising & Sponsorship Manager: L. Duckworth.

Physio: P. Stock.

Coach: J. Lee.

Year Formed: 1907. Turned Professional: 1907. Ltd Co.: 1910.

Club Nickname: 'The Dale'.

Record League Victory: 8-1 v Chesterfield, Division 3 (N), 18 December 1926 – Hill; Brown, Ward; Hillhouse, Parkes, Braidwood; Hughes, Bertram, Whitehurst (5), Schofield (2), Martin (1).

Record Cup Victory: 8-2 v Crook T, FA Cup, 1st rd, 26 November 1927 – Moody; Hopkins, Ward; Braidwood, Parkes, Barker; Tompkinson, Clennell (3), Whitehurst (4), Hall, Martin (1).

Record Defeat: 0-8 v Wrexham, Division 3 (N), 28 December 1929, 0-8 v Leyton Orient, Division 4, 20 October 1987, and 1-9 v Tranmere R, Division 3 (N), 25 December 1931.

Most League Points (2 for a win): 65, Division 4, 1978–79.

Most League points (3 for a win): 67, Division 4, 1991–92.

Most League Goals: 105, Division 3 (N), 1926–27.

Highest League Scorer in Season: Albert Whitehurst, 44, Division 3 (N), 1926–27.

Most League Goals in Total Aggregate: Reg Jenkins, 119, 1964–73.

Most Capped Player: None.

Most League Appearances: Graham Smith, 317, 1966–74.

Record Transfer Fee Received: £200,000 from Bristol C for Keith Welch, July 1991.

Record Transfer Fee Paid: £80,000 to Scunthorpe U for Andy Flounders, August 1991.

Football League Record: 1921 Elected to Division 3 (N); 1958–59 Division 3; 1959–69 Division 4; 1969–74 Division 3; 1974–92 Division 4; 1992– Division 3.

Honours: Football League: Division 3 best season: 9th, 1969–70; Division 3 (N) – Runners-up 1923–24, 1926–27. *FA Cup:* best season: 5th rd, 1989–90. *Football League Cup:* Runners-up 1962 (record for 4th Division club).

Colours: Blue/white trim. **Change colours** Yellow and black.

438

ROCHDALE 1991–92 LEAGUE RECORD

Match No.	Date		Venue	Opponents	Result		H/T Score	Lg. Pos.	Goalscorers	Atten-dance
1	Aug	17	H	York C	D	1-1	0-1	—	Tutill (og)	2247
2		31	H	Lincoln C	W	1-0	1-0	10	Flounders (pen)	2086
3	Sep	3	A	Walsall	W	3-1	2-0	—	Flounders 2 (1 pen), Milner	3111
4		7	A	Cardiff C	W	2-1	1-0	7	Ryan, Reeves	4029
5		14	H	Northampton T	W	1-0	0-0	4	Milner	2631
6		17	H	Rotherham U	D	1-1	1-0	—	Whitehall	4043
7		21	A	Burnley	W	1-0	0-0	3	Milner	8633
8		28	H	Doncaster R	D	1-1	1-0	4	Bowden	2653
9	Oct	12	H	Mansfield T	L	0-2	0-0	6		3871
10		19	A	Maidstone U	D	1-1	0-0	5	Brown M	1016
11		26	A	Halifax T	W	1-0	1-0	6	Flounders	2323
12	Nov	2	H	Chesterfield	D	3-3	2-1	6	Flounders, Halpin, Kinsey	1852
13		5	A	Scunthorpe U	L	2-6	0-3	—	Bowden 2	2331
14		9	A	Hereford U	D	1-1	0-1	6	Judge (og)	2959
15		23	H	Barnet	W	1-0	1-0	6	Bowden	3033
16		30	A	Scarborough	L	2-3	0-1	8	Flounders, Milner	1643
17	Dec	14	H	Blackpool	W	4-2	2-1	5	Flounders, Milner, Whitehall 2	2892
18		26	A	York C	W	1-0	0-0	7	Flounders	2745
19		28	A	Lincoln C	W	3-0	3-0	7	Whitehall, Milner, Flounders	2916
20	Jan	1	H	Walsall	D	1-1	0-1	6	Flounders (pen)	3001
21		11	A	Carlisle U	D	0-0	0-0	6		2494
22		18	H	Crewe Alex	W	1-0	1-0	6	Flounders	2965
23	Feb	8	A	Halifax T	D	1-1	0-0	8	Flounders	2213
24		11	H	Scarborough	D	2-2	0-2	—	Flounders (pen), Reeves	2069
25		15	A	Blackpool	L	0-3	0-3	9		4632
26		22	H	Carlisle U	W	3-1	2-1	8	Milner, Bowden, Whitehall	1691
27		29	A	Wrexham	L	1-2	0-0	9	Whitehall	3458
28	Mar	3	A	Crewe Alex	D	1-1	0-0	—	Flounders	3870
29		7	H	Gillingham	W	2-1	0-1	9	Flounders, Milner	1941
30		10	H	Scunthorpe U	W	2-0	1-0	—	Milner, Lister (og)	2036
31		14	H	Chesterfield	W	1-0	1-0	6	Whitehall	3231
32		17	A	Gillingham	D	0-0	0-0	—		2300
33		21	H	Hereford U	W	3-1	1-0	6	Payne, Whitehall, Flounders (pen)	2122
34		28	A	Barnet	L	0-3	0-2	5		3099
35		31	A	Northampton T	D	2-2	1-1	—	Cowdrill, Bowden	2010
36	Apr	4	A	Cardiff C	W	2-0	1-0	5	Reeves, Milner	2651
37		7	H	Maidstone U	L	1-2	1-0	—	Flounders	2248
38		11	A	Rotherham U	L	0-2	0-1	5		5086
39		20	A	Doncaster R	L	0-2	0-1	7		2255
40		22	H	Wrexham	W	2-1	1-0	—	Parker, Leonard	1945
41	May	2	A	Mansfield T	L	1-2	0-0	8	Payne	5671
42		5	H	Burnley	L	1-3	1-2	—	Ryan	8175

Final League Position: 8

GOALSCORERS

League (57): Flounders 17 (5 pens), Milner 10, Whitehall 8, Bowden 6, Reeves 3, Payne 2, Ryan 2, Brown M 1, Cowdrill 1, Halpin 1, Kinsey 1, Leonard 1, Parker 1, own goals 3.
Rumbelows Cup (7): Milner 3, Ryan 2, Whitehall 2.
FA Cup (4): Flounders 1, Halpin 1, Jones 1, Milner 1.

Dearden	Whitehall	Ryan	Brown T	Reeves	Jones	Graham	Doyle	Flounders	Milner	Halpin	Morgan	Butler	Payne	Williams	Hilditch	Bowden	Gray	Brown M	Palin	Kinsey	Rose	Kilner	Cowdrill	Parker	Stiles	Leonard	Match No.
1	2†	3	4	5	6	7	8	9	10*	11	12	14															1
1	2	3	4	5	6	7	8	9*	10†	11	12		14														2
	2	3	4	5	6	7	8	9	10*		12			11	1												3
	2	3	4	5	6	7	8	9	10*		12			11	1												4
	2*	3	4	5	6	7		9	10		12			11	1												5
	2*	3	4	5	6	7		9	10					11	1	12											6
	2	3	4	5	6	7		9			12			11*	1	10											7
	2*	3	4	5	6	7†	8	9	11		12				1	14	10										8
11†			4	5	6*	7	8	9	14	3			10			12	1	2									9
10			4	5	6	3*	8	9	14	11		12				7†	1	2									10
14	3*	4	5			7	8	9		6						12	1	2	10	11†							11
14	3	4	5			7	8	9*		6						12	1	2	10†	11							12
	3	4	5	14	7†	8	9			6						12	1	2	10	11*							13
10	3	4	5	6	7		9	12	11*							8	1	2									14
		4	5	6*	3†	8	9	12	11				7			10		2		14	1						15
	3	4				8	9	7	11			5	6			10		2			1						16
14	7	4				3	9†	8	11*			5	6			10		2		12	1						17
14	7	4*				3	8	9	11	12		5†	6			10		2			1						18
10	7*	4				3	5	9	8	11		12	6					2			1						19
10	7	4				3		9	8	11†12		5	6*					2		14	1						20
12		4				3	7	9*	8	11		5	6			10		2			1						21
12		4				3	7	9	8*11			5	6			10		2			1						22
		4				3	7	9	8	12		5	6			10*		2			1	11					23
		4	14			3	7	9	8	12		5	6			10		2†			1	11*					24
12	14	4	2				8	9		11†		5	6			10					1		7*	3			25
11	14	4	2				8	9		7*12		5	6†			10					1			3			26
11	14	4	2				8	9		7*12		5†	6			10					1			3			27
	11	4	5				8	9		7			2	6		10					1			3			28
12	11	4	5				8	9*	7			14	2	6†		10					1			3			29
12	11	4	5				8	9†	7			14	2	6*		10					1			3			30
7*11		4	5				8	9				6	12	2		10					1			3			31
7†11		4	5	14			8	9				6*12	2								1			3	10		32
7		4	5				11*	8†	9			12	10	2	6						1			3	14		33
11		5						9		12			2	6		10					1		3	4	7*	8	34
	11	4	2					9				12	5	6		10					1		3		7*	8	35
12	11	4	5				9	7				2†	6			10					1		3	14		8*	36
12	11	4	5	2			9	7					6			10*					1		3			8	37
12	11		5	2			9	7					6			10*	4†				1		3	14		8	38
12	7	4	5	14			9	8	11*				6			10					1		3†			2	39
	7	4	5	3			9	8		14		2*	6†			12					1			11		10	40
	7	4	5	3			9†	8		14		2*	6			12					1			11		10	41
12	7	4	5				9	8					6*					2			1			11		10	42
2	20	29	40	33	12	29	27	42	28	22	1	22	32	6	—	25	6	18	3	3	28	3	15	5	2	9	

```
        +  +        +  +  +            +  +  +  +  +      +  +          +            +  +
      14s3s        1s 1s 2s          5s 9s 11s3s 2s    2s 6s        3s          1s 2s
```

Rumbelows Cup	First Round	Carlisle U (h)	5-1
		(a)	1-1
	Second Round	Coventry C (a)	0-4
		(h)	1-0
FA Cup	First Round	Gretna (a)	0-0
		(h)	3-1
	Second Round	Huddersfield T (h)	1-2

ROCHDALE

Goalkeepers

Name	Ht	Wt	DOB	Birthplace	From	Club	Apps	Gls
Gareth Gray*	6 0	11 02	24 2 70	Longridge	Darwen	Bolton W	—	—
						Rochdale	6	—
Kevin Rose	6 1	13 06	23 11 60	Evesham	Ledbury T	Lincoln C	—	—
						Ledbury T	—	—
						Hereford U	268	—
						Bolton W	10	—
						Halifax T (loan)	—	—
						Carlisle U (loan)	11	—
						Rochdale (loan)	3	—
						Rochdale	28	—

Defenders

Name	Ht	Wt	DOB	Birthplace	From	Club	Apps	Gls
Malcolm Brown*	6 2	12 06	13 12 56	Salford	Apprentice	Bury	11	—
						Huddersfield T	256	16
						Newcastle U	39	—
						Huddersfield T	96	1
						Rochdale	11	—
						Stockport Co	71	3
						Rochdale	18	1
Tony Brown	6 2	12 07	17 9 58	Bradford	Thackley	Leeds U	24	1
						Doncaster (loan)	14	—
						Doncaster R	73	2
						Scunthorpe U	54	2
						Rochdale	109	—
Paul Butler	6 2	13 00	2 11 72	Bradford	Trainee	Rochdale	27	—
Vincent Chapman	5 9	11 00	5 12 67	Newcastle	Tow Law T	Huddersfield T	6	—
						York C (loan)	—	—
						Rochdale	24	1
Barry Cowdrill*	5 11	11 04	3 1 57	Birmingham	Sutton Coldfield	WBA	131	—
						Rotherham U (loan)	2	—
						Bolton W	119	4
						Rochdale	15	1
Zac Hughes‡	5 11	11 12	6 6 71	Bentley, Australia	Trainee	Rochdale	2	—
Alex Jones (To Motherwell Jan 1992)	6 2	12 08	27 11 64	Blackburn	Apprentice	Oldham Ath	9	—
						Stockport Co (loan)	3	—
						Preston NE	101	3
						Carlisle U	62	4
						Rochdale	13	—
Alan Reeves	6 0	12 00	19 11 67	Birkenhead		Norwich C	—	—
						Gillingham (loan)	18	—
						Chester C	40	2
						Rochdale	34	3
John Ryan	5 10	11 07	18 2 62	Oldham	Apprentice	Oldham Ath	77	8
						Newcastle U	28	1
						Sheffield W	8	1
						Oldham Ath	23	—
						Mansfield T	62	1
						Chesterfield	82	6
						Rochdale	32	2

Midfield

Name	Ht	Wt	DOB	Birthplace	From	Club	Apps	Gls
John Bowden	6 0	11 07	21 1 63	Stockport	Local	Oldham Ath	82	5
						Port Vale	70	7
						Wrexham	142	17
						Rochdale	31	6
Steve Doyle	5 9	11 09	2 6 58	Port Talbot	Apprentice	Preston NE	197	8
						Huddersfield T	161	6
						Sunderland	100	2
						Hull C	47	2
						Rochdale	58	—
Jimmy Graham	5 11	11 00	15 11 68	Glasgow	Trainee	Bradford C	7	—
						Rochdale (loan)	11	—
						Rochdale	59	1
John Halpin*	5 10	11 07	15 11 61	Broxburn	Celtic BC	Celtic	7	—
						Sunderland (loan)	—	—
						Carlisle U	153	17
						Rochdale	31	1

ROCHDALE

Foundation: Considering the love of rugby in their area, it is not surprising that Rochdale had difficulty in establishing an Association Football club. The earlier Rochdale Town club formed in 1900 went out of existence in 1907 when the present club was immediately established and joined the Manchester League, before graduating to the Lancashire Combination in 1908.

First Football League game: 27 August 1921, Division 3 (N), v Accrington Stanley (h) W 6-3 – Crabtree; Nuttall, Sheehan; Hill, Farrer, Yarwood; Hoad, Sandiford, Dennison (2), Owens (3), Carney (1).

Did you know: In one of the finest goalscoring spells in Rochdale's history in 1926–27, Albert Whitehurst scored in ten out of 11 successive League games, totalling 21 goals including five against Chesterfield.

Managers (and Secretary-managers)
Billy Bradshaw 1920 (run by committee 1920–22), Tom Wilson 1922–23, Jack Peart 1923–30, Will Cameron 1930–31, Herbert Hopkinson 1932–34, Billy Smith 1934–35, Ernest Nixon 1935–37, Sam Jennings 1937–38, Ted Goodier 1938–52, Jack Warner 1952–53, Harry Catterick 1953–58, Jack Marshall 1958–60, Tony Collins 1960–68, Bob Stokoe 1967–68, Len Richley 1968–70, Dick Conner 1970–73, Walter Joyce 1973–76, Brian Green 1976–77, Mike Ferguson 1977–78, Doug Collins 1979, Bob Stokoe 1979–80, Peter Madden 1980–83, Jimmy Greenhoff 1983–84, Vic Halom 1984–86, Eddie Gray 1986–88, Danny Bergara 1988–89, Terry Dolan 1989–91, Dave Sutton February 1991–.

Paul Herring*	5 11	11 03	1 7 73	Hyde	Trainee	Rochdale	1	—
Phil Lockett*	5 9	11 02	6 9 72	Stockton	Trainee	Rochdale	3	—
Steve Morgan*	5 9	11 05	28 12 70	Wrexham	Trainee	Oldham Ath	2	—
						Wrexham (loan)	7	1
						Rochdale	23	3
Carl Parker	6 00	12 00	25 3 71	Burnley	Rossendale	Rochdale	6	1
Mark Payne	5 9	11 09	3 8 60	Cheltenham		Stockport Co	87	16
						Rochdale	34	2
Forwards								
Jason Anders§	5 10	10 06	13 3 74	Rochdale	Trainee	Rochdale	2	—
Antony Colleton§	5 8	10 06	17 1 74	Manchester	Trainee	Rochdale	1	—
Andy Flounders	5 11	11 06	13 12 63	Hull	Apprentice	Hull C	159	54
						Scunthorpe U	196	87
						Rochdale	42	17
Mark Hilditch‡	6 0	12 01	20 8 60	Royton	Amateur	Rochdale	197	40
						Tranmere R	49	12
						Wigan Ath	103	26
						Rochdale	16	2
Steve Kinsey†	5 07	10 00	2 1 63	Manchester	Apprentice	Manchester C	101	8
						Chester	3	1
						Chesterfield	3	—
						Minnesota	—	—
						Rochdale	6	1
Mark Leonard	5 11	11 10	27 9 62	St Helens	Witton A	Everton	—	—
						Tranmere R (loan)	7	—
						Crewe Alex	54	15
						Stockport Co	73	24
						Bradford C	157	29
						Rochdale	9	1
Andy Milner	5 11	11 07	10 2 67	Kendal	Netherfield	Manchester C	—	—
						Rochdale	84	19
Steve Whitehall	5 09	10 11	8 12 66	Bromborough	Southport	Rochdale	34	8

Trainees
Anders, Jason S; Beever, Anthony M; Brown, Richard A; Clayton, Michael; Colleton, Anthony; Gregory, Andrew E; Grimbaldeston, David A; Milligan, Stephen J. F; Murray, William A; Newsham, Paul J; Tate, Keith N; Thackra, James; Wilkinson, Adam.

Associated Schoolboys
Chadwick, Gavin R. D; Lenegan, Neil R; Yale, Lee D.

Associated Schoolboys who have accepted the club's offer of a Traineeship/Contract
McCartney, William; McCormick, Matthew P.

442

ROTHERHAM UNITED 1991–92   *Back row (left to right):* Julian Watts, Nigel Johnson, Stuart Ford, Stewart Evans, Bill Mercer, Nicky Law, Shaun Goater.
Centre row: Billy Russell (Youth Team Coach), Des Hazel, Ronnie Robinson, John Breckin (Assistant Manager), Neil Richardson, Albert Pickering, Ian Bailey (Physiotherapist).
Front row: Ian Hathaway, Simon Thompson, Chris Hutchings, Phil Henson (Manager), Shaun Goodwin, Dean Barrick, Andy Taylor.

Division 2 **ROTHERHAM UNITED**

Millmoor Ground, Rotherham. Telephone Rotherham (0709) 562434.

Ground capacity: 13,791.

Record attendance: 25,000 v Sheffield U, Division 2, 13 December 1952 and v Sheffield W, Division 2, 26 January 1952.

Record receipts: £44,091 v Manchester U, Littlewoods Cup, 2nd rd 1st leg, 28 September 1989.

Pitch measurements: 115yd × 75yd.

President: Sir J. Layden.

Chairman: K. F. Booth.

Directors: R. Hull (Vice-chairman), C. A. Luckock, J. A. Webb.

Manager: Phil Henson. *Assistant Manager:* John Breckin. *Physio:* Ian Bailey. *Secretary:* N. Darnill. *Commercial Manager:* D. Nicholls.

Year Formed: 1884. Turned Professional: 1905. Ltd Co.: 1920.

Former Grounds: Red House Ground; 1907, Millmoor.

Former Names: 1884, Thornhill United; 1905, Rotherham County; 1925, amalgamated with Rotherham Town under Rotherham United.

Club Nickname: 'The Merry Millers'.

Record League Victory: 8-0 v Oldham Ath, Division 3 (N), 26 May 1947 – Warnes; Selkirk, Ibbotson; Edwards, Horace Williams, Danny Williams; Wilson (2), Shaw (1), Ardron (3), Guest (1), Hainsworth (1).

Record Cup Victory: 6-0 v Spennymoor U, FA Cup, 2nd rd, 17 December 1977 – McAlister; Forrest, Breckin, Womble, Stancliffe, Green, Finney, Phillips (3), Gwyther (2) (Smith), Goodfellow, Crawford (1). 6-0 v Wolverhampton W, FA Cup, 1st rd, 16 November 1985 – O'Hanlon; Forrest, Dungworth, Gooding (1), Smith (1), Pickering, Birch (2), Emerson, Tynan (1), Simmons (1), Pugh.

Record Defeat: 1-11 v Bradford C, Division 3 (N), 25 August 1928.

Most League Points (2 for a win): 71, Division 3 (N), 1950–51.

Most League points (3 for a win): 82, Division 4, 1988–89.

Most League Goals: 114, Division 3 (N), 1946–47.

Highest League Scorer in Season: Wally Ardron, 38, Division 3 (N), 1946–47.

Most League Goals in Total Aggregate: Gladstone Guest, 130, 1946–56.

Most Capped Player: Harold Millership, 6, Wales.

Most League Appearances: Danny Williams, 459, 1946–62.

Record Transfer Fee Received: £200,000 from Bristol C for Martin Scott, December 1990.

Record Transfer Fee Paid: £100,000 to Cardiff C for Ronnie Moore, August 1980.

Football League Record: 1893 Rotherham Town elected to Division 2; 1896 Failed re-election; 1919 Rotherham County elected to Division 2; 1923–51 Division 3 (N); 1951–68 Division 2; 1968–73 Division 3; 1973–75 Division 4; 1975–81 Division 3; 1981–83 Division 2; 1983–88 Division 3; 1988–89 Division 4; 1989–91 Division 3; 1991–92 Division 4; 1992– Division 2.

Honours: Football League: Division 2 best season: 3rd, 1954–55 (equal points with champions and runners-up); Division 3 – Champions 1980–81; Division 3 (N) – Champions 1950–51; Runners-up 1946–47, 1947–48, 1948–49; Division 4 – Champions 1988–89; Runners-up 1991–92. *FA Cup:* best season: 5th rd, 1953, 1968. *Football League Cup:* Runners-up 1961.

Colours: Red shirts, white shorts, red stockings. **Change colours:** White shirts with black collar, black shorts with red and white trim, black stockings with red and white tops.

ROTHERHAM UNITED 1991–92 LEAGUE RECORD

Match No.	Date		Venue	Opponents	Result		H/T Score	Lg. Pos.	Goalscorers	Attendance
1	Aug	17	H	Burnley	W	2-1	0-1	—	Johnson, Cunningham	6042
2		24	A	Lincoln C	W	2-0	0-0	3	Cunningham, Robinson R	4134
3		31	H	Crewe Alex	L	1-2	1-1	5	Johnson	4362
4	Sep	3	A	Carlisle U	W	3-1	1-1	—	Goodwin, Richardson, Page	2346
5		7	H	Hereford U	D	0-0	0-0	6		3778
6		13	A	Halifax T	W	4-0	0-0	—	Cunningham, Goater, Hutchings, Wilson	2653
7		17	A	Rochdale	D	1-1	0-1	—	Hutchings (pen)	4043
8		21	H	Maidstone U	D	3-3	1-1	5	Hazel, Page 2	3870
9		28	A	Blackpool	L	0-3	0-1	7		5356
10	Oct	12	A	Chesterfield	D	1-1	0-1	9	Cunningham	6133
11		25	H	York C	W	4-0	1-0	—	Page, Hutchings, Cunningham 2	4676
12	Nov	2	H	Northampton T	W	1-0	0-0	4	Cunningham	3146
13		6	A	Doncaster R	D	1-1	0-0	—	Wilson	3507
14		9	A	Scunthorpe U	L	0-1	0-0	5		4175
15		22	H	Walsall	W	2-1	1-0	—	Cunningham, Watts	4192
16		30	A	Cardiff C	L	0-1	0-1	6		3551
17	Dec	14	H	Gillingham	D	1-1	0-1	6	Cunningham	3137
18		21	H	Lincoln C	D	1-1	0-1	6	Cunningham	3293
19		26	A	Burnley	W	2-1	0-0	6	Cunningham, Page	13,812
20		28	A	Crewe Alex	W	1-0	1-0	6	Hazel	4490
21	Jan	1	H	Carlisle U	W	1-0	0-0	5	Page	4850
22		4	H	Scarborough	L	0-2	0-0	5		4497
23		11	A	Barnet	W	5-2	3-0	5	Todd, Page 3, Goodwin	3552
24		18	H	Mansfield T	D	1-1	0-1	5	Hazel	6454
25	Feb	8	A	York C	D	1-1	1-0	5	Todd	3526
26		11	H	Cardiff C	L	1-2	0-1	—	Hazel	3827
27		15	A	Gillingham	L	1-5	1-4	6	Goater	2486
28		22	H	Barnet	W	3-0	1-0	6	Hutchings, Page, Cunningham	3841
29		29	A	Scarborough	W	3-0	0-0	5	Richardson, Hazel, Page	2604
30	Mar	3	A	Mansfield T	L	0-1	0-0	—		5713
31		7	H	Wrexham	W	3-0	0-0	4	Cunningham 2, Howard	3562
32		10	H	Doncaster R	W	3-1	0-0	—	Howard, Cunningham 2	4883
33		14	A	Northampton T	W	2-1	2-0	4	Barrick, Goodwin	2561
34		21	H	Scunthorpe U	W	5-0	2-0	4	Goater 3, Goodwin, Howard	4528
35		28	A	Walsall	W	2-0	0-0	4	Hazel, Goater	3524
36		31	H	Halifax T	W	1-0	0-0	—	Wilson	4517
37	Apr	4	A	Hereford U	L	0-1	0-0	4		1868
38		11	H	Rochdale	W	2-0	1-0	4	Goater, Goodwin	5086
39		18	A	Maidstone U	D	0-0	0-0	3		1744
40		20	H	Blackpool	W	2-0	1-0	2	Hazel, Cunningham	8992
41		28	A	Wrexham	W	3-0	1-0	—	Goater 2, Hazel	3477
42	May	2	H	Chesterfield	D	1-1	1-0	2	Cunningham	8852

Final League Position: 2

GOALSCORERS

League (70): Cunningham 18, Page 11, Goater 9, Hazel 8, Goodwin 5, Hutchings 4 (1 pen), Howard 3, Wilson 3, Johnson 2, Richardson 2, Todd 2, Barrick 1, Robinson R 1, Watts 1.
Rumbelows Cup (1): Robinson 1.
FA Cup (4): Page 2, Cunningham 1, Goodwin 1.

Mercer	Hutchings	Robinson R	Richardson	Johnson	Law	Goodwin	Barrick	Cunningham	Page	Hazel	Goater	Watts	Hathaway	Ford	Taylor	Todd	Wilson	Pickering	McKnight	Snodin	Howard	Russell	Match No.
1	2	3	4	5	6	7	8	9	10	11													1
1	2	3	4	5	6	7	8	9	10	11													2
1	2	3	4	5	6	7	8	9	10	11													3
1	2	3	4	5	6	7†	8	9	10	11*	12	14											4
1	2	3	4*	5	6		8	9	10		11	12	7										5
	2			5	6		8	9	10	11*	12			1	3	4	7						6
	2				6		8	9	10	11		5		1	3		7	4					7
	2				6	7*	8	9	10	11	12	5		1	3	4							8
	2				6	7	8	9	10	11		5		1	3	4							9
1*	3				6	7		9	10	11	12	5				4	8	2					10
	3			5	6	7*12		9	10	11						4	8	2	1				11
	3			5	6	7		9	10	11						4	8	2	1				12
	3				6	7	12		10	11	9	5				4*	8	2	1				13
1	3				6	7	8	9	10	11	4	5						2					14
1	3				6	7	8	9	10	11		5				4		2					15
1	3			5	6	7	8	9	10*	11	12					4		2					16
1	3			5	6	7	8*	9	10†12	11		14				4		2					17
1	3			5	6	7		9	10	11		8				4		2					18
1	3			5	6	7	8	9	10	11						4		2					19
1	3			5	6	7	8	9	10	11						4		2					20
1	3			5*	6	7	8	9	10	11		12				4		2					21
1	3			5	6	7	8	9	10*	11	12					4		2					22
1	3			5	6	7	8	9	10	11						4		2					23
1	3			5	6	7	8*	9	10	11	12					4		2					24
1	3			5	6	7	8	9	10	11						4*12		2					25
1	3			5	6	7	8*	9	10	11		12				4		2					26
1	3			5	6	7*	8	9		11	10	12				4		2					27
1	3	8		5	6	7		9	10	11						4		2					28
1	3	8		5	6	7		9	10	11						4		2					29
1		8		5	6	7		9	10	11						4		2		3			30
1	3			5	6	7		9	10*	11						4		2		8		12	31
1	3			5	6	7		9		11						4		2		8	10		32
1	3	4		5	6	7	8	9*		11†		14				12		2			10		33
1	3	8		5	6	7	11				9	14				4*12		2†			10		34
1	3	8		5	6	7*11				12	9					4		2			10		35
1	3†	8*		5	6	7	11			12	9	14				4					10	2	36
1	3	8*		5	6	7	11			12	9					4					10	2	37
1	3	4		5	6	7	8			11	9										10	2	38
1	3	4		5	6	7	8	12		11	9*										10	2	39
1	3	4		5	6	7	8	12	14	11	9										10†	2*	40
1	3	4		5	6	7	8	9		11	10				2								41
1	3	4		5	6	7	8	9	12	11	10*				2								42
35	41	5	18	35	42	39	32	34	29	34	17	7	2	4	6	23	11	27	3	3	9	6	
						+	+	+	+	+	+	+						+			+		
						2s	2s	2s	4s	7s	3s	6s						3s			1s		

Rumbelows Cup	First Round	Grimsby T (h)	1-3
		(a)	0-1
FA Cup	First Round	Scunthorpe U (a)	1-1
		(h)	3-3
		Rotherham won 7-6 on penalties	
	Second Round	Burnley (a)	0-2

ROTHERHAM UNITED

Player and Position	Ht	Wt	Date	Birth Place	Source	Clubs	League App	Gls
Goalkeepers								
Stuart Ford*	5 11	11 13	20 7 71	Sheffield	Trainee	Rotherham U	5	—
						Scarborough (loan)	6	—
Billy Mercer	6 1	11 00	22 5 69	Liverpool	Trainee	Liverpool	—	—
						Rotherham U	50	—
Defenders								
Mark Hodges	6 0	11 00	24 10 71	Sheffield	Trainee	Rotherham U	4	—
Nigel Johnson	6 2	12 08	23 6 64	Rotherham	Apprentice	Rotherham U	54	1
						Nottingham F (loan)	—	—
						Rotherham U	35	—
						Manchester C	4	—
						Rotherham U	144	7
Nicky Law	6 0	13 05	8 9 61	Greenwich	Apprentice	Arsenal	—	—
						Barnsley	114	1
						Blackpool	66	1
						Plymouth Arg	38	5
						Notts Co	47	4
						Scarborough (loan)	12	—
						Rotherham U	74	2
Ally Pickering	5 9	10 08	22 6 67	Manchester	Buxton	Rotherham U	38	—
Neil Richardson	5 10	10 08	3 6 68	Sunderland		Rotherham U	36	4
Michael Ridenton	6 00	11 11	23 8 68	New Zealand	Mount Wellington	Rotherham U	—	—
Billy Russell	5 10	11 04	14 9 59	Glasgow	Apprentice	Everton	—	—
						Celtic	—	—
						Doncaster R	244	15
						Scunthorpe U	117	7
						Rotherham U	104	2
Andy Taylor	5 08	11 00	19 1 73	Rotherham	Trainee	Rotherham U	6	—
Midfield								
Dean Barrick	5 9	11 04	30 9 69	Hemsworth	Trainee	Sheffield W	11	2
						Rotherham U	53	3
Shaun Goodwin	5 7	8 10	14 6 69	Rotherham	Trainee	Rotherham U	155	18
Chris Hutchings	5 10	11 00	5 7 57	Winchester	Harrow Bor	Chelsea	87	3
						Brighton & HA	153	4
						Huddersfield T	110	10
						Walsall	40	—
						Rotherham U	41	4
Jason Rockett			26 9 69	London		Rotherham U	—	—
Glynn Snodin (To Hearts March 1992)	5 6	9 05	14 2 60	Rotherham	Apprentice	Doncaster R	309	61
						Sheffield W	59	1
						Leeds U	94	10
						Rotherham U	3	—
						Oldham Ath (loan)	8	1
Mark Todd	5 7	10 00	4 12 67	Belfast	Trainee	Manchester U	—	—
						Sheffield U	70	5
						Wolverhampton W (loan)	7	—
						Rotherham U	23	2
Robert Wilson*	5 10	11 11	5 6 61	Kensington	Apprentice	Fulham	175	34
						Millwall	28	12
						Luton T	24	1
						Fulham	47	4
						Huddersfield T	57	8
						Rotherham U	14	3

ROTHERHAM UNITED

Foundation: This club traces its history back to the formation of Thornhill United in 1878 (reformed 1884). They changed their name to Rotherham County in 1905. Confusion exists because of the existence of the Rotherham Town club (founded c. 1885) and in the Football League as early as 1893 but this club was not the one previously mentioned. The Town amalgamated with Rotherham County to form Rotherham United in 1925.

First Football League game: 2 September 1893, Division 2, Rotherham T v Lincoln C (a) D 1-1 – McKay; Thickett, Watson; Barr, Brown, Broadhead; Longden, Cutts, Leatherbarrow, McCormick, Pickering. (1 og). 30 August 1919, Division 2, Rotherham C v Nottingham F (h) W 2-0 – Branston; Alton, Baines; Bailey, Coe, Stanton; Lee (1), Cawley (1), Glennon, Lees, Lamb.

Did you know: In 1950–51 Rotherham fielded four players named Williams who were unrelated – Horace, Bobby, Danny and Ken.

Managers (and Secretary-managers)
Billy Heald 1925–29 (secretary only for long spell), Stanley Davies 1929–30, Billy Heald 1930–33, Reg Freeman 1934–52, Andy Smailes 1952–58, Tom Johnston 1958–62, Danny Williams 1962–65, Jack Mansell 1965–67, Tommy Docherty 1967–68, Jimmy McAnearney 1968–73, Jimmy McGuigan 1973–79, Ian Porterfield 1979–81, Emlyn Hughes 1981–83, George Kerr 1983–85, Norman Hunter 1985–87, Dave Cusack 1987–88, Billy McEwan 1988–91, Phil Henson January 1991–.

Player and Position	Ht	Wt	Birth Date	Birth Place	Source	Clubs	League App	Gls
Forwards								
Tony Cunningham	6 2	13 10	12 11 57	Jamaica	Stourbridge	Lincoln C	123	32
						Barnsley	42	11
						Sheffield W	28	5
						Manchester C	18	1
						Newcastle U	47	4
						Blackpool	71	17
						Bury	58	17
						Bolton W	9	4
						Rotherham U	36	18
Shaun Goater	6 2	12 10	25 2 70	Bermuda		Manchester U	—	—
						Rotherham U	58	13
Ian Hathaway	5 8	10 06	22 8 68	Worsley	Bedworth U	Mansfield T	44	2
						Rotherham U	21	1
Desmond Hazel	5 10	10 04	15 7 67	Bradford	Apprentice	Sheffield W	6	—
						Grimsby T (loan)	9	2
						Rotherham U	152	19
Jonathan Howard	5 10	11 07	7 10 71	Sheffield	Trainee	Rotherham U	11	3
Don Page	5 10	11 04	18 1 64	Manchester	Runcorn	Wigan Ath	74	15
						Rotherham U	31	11

Trainees
Anson, Simon D; Bennett, Paul S; Breckin, Ian; Bunting, James R. S; Clarke, Matthew J; Dolby, Christopher J; Gleeson, Stephen K; Hall, Jason; Hardwick, Matthew J; Hinshelwood, Shane; Hurst, Paul M; Ingram, Richard; Jarvis, Steven M; Lawlor, Shane M; Smith, Scott D; Tesh, John A; Varney, Paul.

Associated Schoolboys
Ayrton, Matthew R; Britton, Martin B; Cooper, Mark; Curry, Kevin J; Garlick, Richard P; Hempsey, Scott A; Heppenstall, Michael; Hogg, Stuart S; Hopson, Gavin J; Melbourne, Andrew M; Portman, Robert D; Riley, Matthew M; Surtees, Mathew D; Thomas, Steven M; Usher, Colin; Wake, Ryan; Webster, Paul A; Wellwood, Howard R.

Associated Schoolboys who have accepted the club's offer of a Traineeship/Contract
Handbury, Lee A; Hilton, Christopher; Hoe, Michael J.

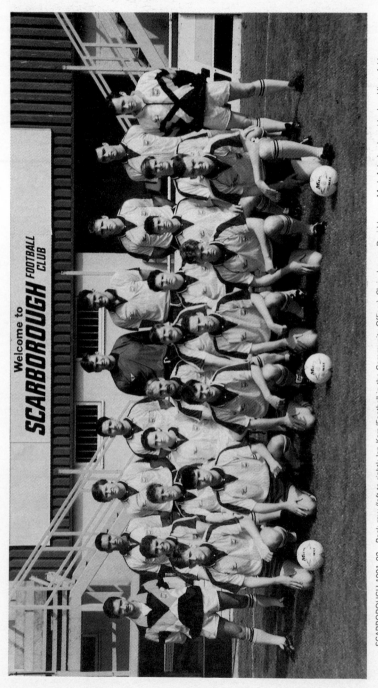

SCARBOROUGH 1991–92 *Back row (left to right):* Ian Kerr (Football in the Community Officer), Chris James, David Logan, Mark Ash, Ian Ironside, Lee Hirst, Adrian Meyer, Andrew Fletcher, Andrew Davidson (Club Doctor).

Centre row: John Moore, Tony Halliday, Steve Carter, Ray McHale (Manager), Phil Chambers (Youth Team Coach), Tommy Mooney, John Ashdjian, Darren Foreman.

Front row: Paul Mudd, Jon Rocca, Chris Lee, Gary Himsworth, David Holmes, Andrew Mockler.

Division 3 **SCARBOROUGH**

The McCain Stadium, Seamer Road, Scarborough YO12 4HF.
Telephone (0723) 375094.

Ground capacity: 7176.

Record attendance: 11,130 v Luton T, FA Cup 3rd rd, 8 January 1938. Football League: 7314 v Wolverhampton W, Division 4, 15 August 1987.

Record receipts: £19,754 v Wolverhampton W, Division 4, 15 August 1987.

Pitch measurements: 120yd × 75yd.

President and Chief Executive: J. Birley.

Chairman: G. Richmond.

Directors: M. Bramham, B. Connolly, J. Fawcett, A. Jenkinson, A. D. Mollon.

Manager: Ray McHale.

Assistant Manager: Phil Chambers.

Secretary: K. E. Sheppard MISM, MLIA.

Administrator: Miss H. Crinnion.

Assistant Secretary: Miss S. B. Wright.

Commercial Manager: Shirley Nettleton.

Physio: K. Warner.

Year Formed: 1879. Turned Professional: 1926. Ltd Co.: 1933.

Former Grounds: 1879–87, Scarborough Cricket Ground; 1887–98, Recreation Ground; 1898–Athletic Ground.

Club Nickname: 'The Boro'.

Record League Victory: 4-0 v Bolton W, Division 4, 29 August 1987 – Blackwell; McJannet, Thompson, Bennyworth (Walker), Richards (1) (Cook), Kendall, Hamill (1), Moss, McHale, Mell (1), Graham. (1 og). 4-0 v Newport C, Division 4, 12 April 1988 – Ironside; McJannet, Thompson, Kamara, Richards (1), Short (1), Adams (Cook 1), Brook, Outhart (1), Russell, Graham.

Record Cup Victory: 6-0 v Rhyl Ath, FA Cup, 1st rd, 29 November 1930 – Turner; Severn, Belton; Maskell, Robinson, Wallis; Small (1), Rand (2), Palfreman (2), A. D. Hill (1), Mickman.

Record Defeat: 1-16 v Southbank, Northern League, 15 November 1919.

Most League points (3 for a win): 77, Division 4, 1988–89.

Most League Goals: 69, Division 4, 1990–91.

Highest League Scorer in Season: George Oghani, 14, Division 4, 1990–91.

Most League Goals in Total Aggregate: Paul Dobson, 22, 1989–91.

Most Capped Player: None.

Most League Appearances: Steve Richards, 164, 1987–91.

Record Transfer Fee Received: £240,000 from Notts Co for Chris Short, September 1990.

Record Transfer Fee Paid: £102,000 to Leicester C for Martin Russell, March 1989.

Football League Record: Promoted to Division 4 1987; 1992– Division 3.

Honours: Football League: Division 4 best season: 5th, 1988–89. *FA Cup:* best season: 3rd rd, 1931, 1938, 1976, 1978. *Football League Cup:* best season: 3rd rd, 1989.

Colours: Red shirts, white shorts, red stockings. **Change colours:** Yellow shirts, blue shorts, yellow stockings.

SCARBOROUGH 1991–92 LEAGUE RECORD

Match No.	Date	Venue	Opponents	Result	H/T Score	Lg. Pos.	Goalscorers	Attendance
1	Aug 17	H	Mansfield T	D	0-0	0-0	—	2343
2	24	A	Hereford U	L	1-4	1-4	19	Lowndes (og)	2600
3	31	H	Walsall	L	2-3	1-2	21	Mooney, Ashdjian	2022
4	Sep 3	A	Scunthorpe U	D	1-1	0-1	—	Mudd	3185
5	7	A	Gillingham	L	0-2	0-0	21		3375
6	18	H	Doncaster R	W	1-0	1-0	—	Meyer	1506
7	21	A	Cardiff C	L	1-2	1-1	21	Ashdjian	3227
8	28	H	Burnley	W	3-1	2-1	18	Meyer, Mooney, Ashdjian	2596
9	Oct 5	A	York C	L	1-4	1-3	20	Ashdjian	2971
10	12	H	Northampton T	W	2-1	0-0	15	Mockler (pen), Lee	2023
11	19	A	Crewe Alex	D	3-3	0-2	16	Jules, Meyer, Mooney	2696
12	26	H	Barnet	L	0-4	0-2	17		1942
13	Nov 2	A	Blackpool	D	1-1	1-1	17	Meyer	3057
14	5	H	Wrexham	W	4-1	0-1	—	Sertori (og), Ashdjian, Jules 2	1164
15	9	H	Carlisle U	D	2-2	2-0	15	Fletcher, Mockler (pen)	1501
16	22	A	Halifax T	L	0-1	0-1	—		1395
17	30	H	Rochdale	W	3-2	1-0	15	Himsworth, Fletcher 2	1643
18	Dec 7	A	Northampton T	L	2-3	0-0	—	Foreman, Ashdjian	1815
19	17	A	Lincoln C	W	2-0	2-0	—	Mockler (pen), Mooney	1752
20	26	A	Mansfield T	W	2-1	0-0	13	Thompson, Ashdjian	4012
21	28	A	Walsall	D	0-0	0-0	13		3488
22	Jan 1	H	Scunthorpe U	W	4-1	1-1	11	Fletcher, Mooney 2, Foreman	2237
23	4	A	Rotherham U	W	2-0	0-0	9	Law (og), Thompson	4497
24	Feb 8	A	Barnet	L	1-5	0-2	12	Jules	2851
25	11	A	Rochdale	D	2-2	2-0	—	Brown (og), Mooney	2069
26	15	H	Lincoln C	D	1-1	0-1	14	Meyer	1614
27	18	H	Crewe Alex	W	2-1	0-1	—	Mockler (pen), Moore	1352
28	22	A	Chesterfield	L	0-1	0-0	13		2749
29	29	H	Rotherham U	L	0-3	0-0	14		2604
30	Mar 7	A	Maidstone U	L	1-2	0-0	14	Jules	1019
31	10	A	Wrexham	L	0-2	0-1	—		2044
32	14	H	Blackpool	L	1-2	1-2	17	Price	1965
33	17	H	Chesterfield	W	3-2	2-2	—	Holmes, Himsworth (pen), Ashdjian	1302
34	21	A	Carlisle U	D	2-2	0-0	15	Jules 2	1813
35	28	H	Halifax T	W	3-0	3-0	12	Marshall, Mooney, Thompson	1363
36	Apr 4	H	Gillingham	W	2-1	0-0	11	Himsworth (pen), Jules	1174
37	7	H	Hereford U	D	1-1	0-0	—	Hirst	1008
38	11	A	Doncaster R	L	2-3	0-2	13	Curran, Fletcher	1638
39	14	A	Cardiff C	D	2-2	1-0	—	Gabbiadini, Curran	935
40	20	A	Burnley	D	1-1	1-1	12	Hirst	12,312
41	25	H	York C	W	1-0	0-0	12	Ashdjian	2108
42	29	H	Maidstone U	W	2-0	0-0	—	Lee, Himsworth	939

Final League Position: 12

GOALSCORERS

League (64): Ashdjian 9, Jules 8, Mooney 8, Fletcher 5, Meyer 5, Himsworth 4 (2 pens), Mockler 4 (4 pens), Thompson 3, Curran 2, Foreman 2, Hirst 2, Lee 2, Gabbiadini 1, Holmes 1, Marshall 1, Moore 1, Mudd 1, Price 1, own goals 4.
Rumbelows Cup (10): Mooney 3, Foreman 2 (1 pen), Ashdjian 1, Himsworth 1, Hirst 1, Jules 1, Mockler 1 (1 pen).
FA Cup (0).

Priestley	James	Mudd	Mockler	Hirst	Meyer	Ashdjian	Lee	Mooney	Foreman	Himsworth	Moore	Jules	Carter	Logan	Ash	Reed	Hughes	Fletcher	Holmes	Thompson	Hewitt	Taylor	Ironside	Rocca	Swales	Price	Manderson	Curran	Match No.
1	2	3	4	5	6	7†	8	9	10*	11	12	14																	1
1	2	3	12	5*	6		4	9	10	11		8	14	7†															2
1	2	5	8*		6	7	4	9	12	11†	10	14			3														3
1	14	7		5	6†	12	4	9*	10	11		8			3	2													4
1	5	7			6		4	9	10	11		8			3	2													5
1	2	7	8	5	6		4	9	10	11					3														6
1	2	8*	5		6	7	4	9	10	11		14			3	12†													7
1		8	5		6	10	4	9*	12	11			14		3	2	7†												8
1		8	5		6	10	4	9	12	11					3*	2	7												9
	2	8*	5		6	10	4	9	12						3		7	1											10
	2†	8	5		6	11	4	9	10			12		14	3		7*	1											11
		8	5		6	10†	4	9		11*				7	3	2	14	1		12									12
		3	8	5	6	12	4	9		11					2		7*	1		10									13
		3	8	5	6	7	4	9†		11				14	2			1		10*	12								14
		3	8	5	6	7*	4	9		11				14	2			1		10†	12								15
	2	3	8	5	6		4	9	12	11				14			7†	1		10*									16
	2	3	8	5	6		4	9*	12	11				14			7†	1		10									17
	2*	3	8	5	6	14	4	9	12	11							7†	1		10									18
	2	3	8*	5	6	12	4	9		11							7	1		10									19
		5	6			7	4	9*	12	11		8		14	3	2		1		10†									20
		5	6			7	4	9	12	11†		8		14	3	2		1		10*									21
		5	6			7†	4	9	12	11		8		14	3	2		1		10*									22
		5	6			14	4	9†	12	11		8			3	2	7	1		10*									23
		5	6			14	4	9	12	11		8			3	2†	7	1		10*									24
		5	12		6		4	9†		11*		8		14	3		7	1		10									25
		5	12		6		4	9		11		8			3	2	7*	1		10									26
		5	11		6	14	4	9	12			8†			3	2	7	1		10*									27
		5	6			14	4	9	12	11†		8			3	2	7	1		10*									28
		5	12		6	14	4	9*		11		8			3	2†	7	1		10									29
			11	5†	6		4	9				8		14	3	2	12			10*			1						30
		5	6			12	4†	9*		11		8		14					7	10			1	2	3				31
		5	6			14	4	9	12	11									7	10*			1	2†	3	8			32
		5	6			14	4	9	12	11									7	10			1	2†	3	8*			33
		5	6			7†	4	9	12	11		8		14		2				10			1		3*				34
		3		5		7	4	9*	12	11						2							1					6	35
		3		5		7	4	9†	12	11		8											1					6	36
		3		5		7	4	9*	12	11		8																6	37
		3		5		7	4	9†	12	11		8																6	38
		3		5		7	4	9†	12	11		8		14														6	39
		3		5		7*	4	9	12	11		8		14														6	40
		3		5		7	4	9	12	11†		8		14														6	41
		3		5		7	4	9	12	11		8								10*								6	42
9	12	36	20	30	30	18	41	40	12	33	3	30	2	21	16	5	17	14	3	22	2	1	7	3	4	2	—	8	
		+1s		+4s		+14s						+12s	+3s	+4s	+11s	+1s	+3s	+1s		+7s						+1s	+1s		

McGee—Match No. 35(8) 36(2) 37(2) 38(2) 39(2) 40(2) 41(2) 42(2); Marshall—Match No. 35(10†) 36(10*) 37(10†) 38(10*); Gabbiadini—Match No. 35(14) 36(14) 37(14) 38(14) 39(10*) 40(10†) 41(10*); Ford—Match No. 37(1) 38(1) 39(1) 40(1) 41(1) 42(1).

Rumbelows Cup	First Round	Preston NE (a)		4-5
		(h)		3-1
	Second Round	Southampton (h)		1-3
		(a)		2-2
FA Cup	First Round	Wigan Ath (h)		0-2

SCARBOROUGH

Player and Position	Ht	Wt	Birth Date	Birth Place	Source	Clubs	League App	Gls
Goalkeepers								
Stephen Hewitt‡			17 4 73	Hull	Trainee	Scarborough	2	—
Philip Hughes‡	5 11	12 07	19 11 64	Manchester	Apprentice	Manchester U	—	—
						Leeds U	6	—
						Bury	80	—
						Wigan Ath	99	—
						Scarborough	17	—
Ian Taylor‡	6 1	12 00	25 11 67	Doncaster	Bridlington T	Carlisle U	—	—
						Scarborough	1	—
Defenders								
Mark Ash‡	5 9	11 04	22 1 68	Sheffield	Apprentice	Rotherham U	20	—
						Scarborough	39	—
Ian Bennyworth†	6 0	12 07	15 1 62	Hull	Apprentice	Hull C	1	—
						Scarborough	89	3
						Nuneaton Bor	—	—
						Hartlepool U	82	3
						Scarborough	—	—
Chris Curran†	6 1	12 06	6 1 71	Manchester	Trainee	Crewe Alex	5	—
						Scarborough	8	2
Lee Hirst	6 2	12 07	26 1 69	Sheffield		Scarborough	72	4
Chris James‡			16 1 69	Sheffield	Matlock	Scarborough	13	—
David Logan‡	5 9	10 11	5 12 63	Middlesbrough	Whitby	Mansfield T	67	1
						Northampton T	41	1
						Halifax T	3	—
						Stockport Co	60	4
						Scarborough	55	1
Owen McGee†	5 7	10 07	20 4 70	Teesside	Trainee	Middlesbrough	21	1
						Leicester C	—	—
						Scarborough	8	—
Adrian Meyer	6 0	14 00	22 9 70	Bristol	Trainee	Scarborough	65	8
Paul Mudd	5 8	11 02	13 11 70	Hull	Trainee	Hull C	1	—
						Scarborough	60	2
Jon Rocca‡			4 11 70	Sheffield	Trainee	Scarborough	3	—
Steve Swales§			26 12 73	Whitby	Trainee	Scarborough	4	—
Midfield								
Chris Lee	5 10	11 07	18 6 71	Halifax	Trainee	Bradford C	—	—
						Rochdale	26	2
						Scarborough	50	2
David Manderson§			18 10 73	Glasgow	Trainee	Scarborough	1	—
Andrew Mockler	5 11	11 13	18 11 70	Stockton	Trainee	Arsenal	—	—
						Scarborough	58	9
Simon Thompson	5 8	10 08	27 2 70	Sheffield	Trainee	Rotherham U	28	—
						Scarborough	23	3
Forwards								
John Ashdjian			13 9 72	Hackney	Trainee	Northampton T	—	—
						Scarborough	64	18
Steve Carter	5 8	12 00	13 4 72	Sunderland	Manchester U	Scarborough	37	3
Paul Eshelby‡	5 9	11 00	29 5 70	Sheffield		Exeter C	19	1
						Scarborough	3	—
Andy Fletcher‡	6 0	13 00	12 8 71	Cleveland	Trainee	Middlesbrough	—	—
						Scarborough	27	6
Darren Foreman	5 10	10 08	12 2 68	Southampton		Barnsley	47	8
						Crewe Alex	23	4
						Scarborough	38	7

SCARBOROUGH

Foundation: Scarborough came into being as early as 1879 when they were formed by members of the town's cricket club and went under the name of Scarborough Cricketers' FC with home games played on the North Marine Road Cricket Ground.

First Football League game: 15 August 1987, Division 4, v Wolverhampton W (h) D 2-2 – Blackwell; McJannet, Thompson, Bennyworth, Richards, Kendall, Hamill, Moss, McHale (1), Mell (1), Graham.

Did you know: As a Midland League side in the 1930s Scarborough three times beat Football League clubs in the FA Cup – Lincoln City 6-4 in 1930–31, York City 3-1 (a) in 1932–33 and Darlington 2-0 (a) in 1937–38.

Managers (and Secretary-managers)
B. Chapman 1945–47*, George Hall 1946–47, Harold Taylor 1947–48, Frank Taylor 1948–50, A. C. Bell (Director & Hon. TM) 1950–53, Reg Halton 1953–54, Charles Robson (Hon. TM) 1954–57, George Higgins 1957–58, Andy Smailes 1959–61, Eddie Brown 1961–64, Albert Franks 1964–65, Stuart Myers 1965–66, Graham Shaw 1968–69, Colin Appleton 1969–73, Ken Houghton 1974–75, Colin Appleton 1975–81, Jimmy McAnearney 1981–82, John Cottam 1982–84, Harry Dunn 1984–86, Neil Warnock 1986–88, Colin Morris 1989, Ray McHale November 1989–.

Player and Position	Ht	Wt	Birth Date	Birth Place	Source	Clubs	League App	Gls
Ricardo Gabbiadini‡	6 0	13 05	11 3 70	Newport	Trainee	York C	1	—
						Sunderland	1	—
						Blackpool (loan)	5	3
						Brighton & HA (loan)	1	—
						Grimsby T (loan)	3	1
						Crewe Alex (loan)	2	—
						Hartlepool U	14	2
						Scarborough	7	1
Gary Himsworth	5 7	9 08	19 12 69	Appleton	Trainee	York C	88	8
						Scarborough	59	5
David Holmes‡			22 11 71	Derby	Trainee	Scarborough	9	1
Mark Jules	5 9		5 9 71	Bradford	Trainee	Bradford C	—	—
						Scarborough	41	8
Tommy Mooney	5 10	12 05	11 8 71	Teesside North	Trainee	Aston Villa	—	—
						Scarborough	67	21
John Moore‡	6 0	11 11	1 10 66	Consett	Apprentice	Sunderland	16	1
						St Patricks Ath (loan)	—	—
						Newport Co (loan)	2	—
						Darlington (loan)	2	1
						Mansfield T (loan)	5	1
						Rochdale (loan)	10	2
						Hull C	14	1
						Sheffield U (loan)	5	—
						Utrecht	—	—
						Shrewsbury T	8	1
						Crewe Alex	1	—
						Scarborough	7	1
Mark Price§			15 10 73	Keighley	Trainee	Scarborough	3	1

Trainees
Batten, Ian G; Brooks, Duncan G; Cawthorn, Paul J; Clarke, Simon J; Harper, Lee J; Henson, Steven W; Jarman, Matthew J; Kingham, Mark A; Manderson, David A; Pratt, Jeremy M; Price, Mark A. R. J; Robinson, Neal B; Swales, Stephen C; Tomlinson, Sean; Watt, Craig R; Wignall, Adrian; Williams, David J.

**Non-Contract
Curran, Christopher P; McGee, Owen E.

**Non-Contract Players who are retained must be re-signed before they are eligible to play in League matches.

454

SCUNTHORPE UNITED 1991–92 *Back row (left to right)*: Phil McLoughlin (Physiotherapist), Dean Martin, Graham Alexander, Andy Stevenson, Gary Hyde, Mark Lillis, Paul Musselwhite, Steve Lister, Stuart Hicks, Glenn Humphries, Ian Hamilton, Joe Joyce, David Cowling.
Front row: Tony Daws, Mark Hine, Sam Goodacre, David Moore, Bill Green (Manager), John Buckley, Andy Godfrey, Paul Longden.

Division 3 **SCUNTHORPE UNITED**

Glanford Park, Scunthorpe, South Humberside. Telephone Scunthorpe (0724) 848077. Fax No: 0724 857986.

Ground capacity: 9200.

Record attendance: Old Showground: 23,935 v Portsmouth, FA Cup 4th rd, 30 January 1954. Glanford Park: 8775 v Rotherham U, Division 4, 1 May 1989.

Record receipts: £44,481 v Leeds U, Rumbelows Cup 2nd rd 1st leg, 24 September 1991.

Pitch measurements: 111yd × 73yd.

President: Sir Reginald Sheffield, Bt.

Vice-presidents: I. T. Botham, G. Johnson, A. Harvey, G. J. Alston, R. Ashman.

Chairman: T. E. Belton.

Vice-chairman: D. M. Fletton.

Directors: R. Garton, J. B. Borrill, C. Plumtree, J. Hayes.

Manager: Bill Green. *Assistant Manager:* D. Moore. *Youth Development Officer:* D. Moore. *Physio:* Phil McLoughlin. *Chief Executive Secretary:* A. D. Rowing. *Commercial Manager:* A. D. Rowing.

Year Formed: 1899. Turned Professional: 1912. Ltd Co.: 1912.

Former Grounds: Old Showground to 1988.

Former Names: Amalgamated with Brumby Hall: North Lindsey United to become Scunthorpe & Lindsey United, 1910; dropped '& Lindsey' in 1958.

Club Nickname: 'The Iron'.

Record League Victory: 8-1 v Luton T, Division 3, 24 April 1965 – Sidebottom; Horstead, Hemstead; Smith, Neale, Lindsey; Bramley (1), Scott, Thomas (5), Mahy (1), Wilson (1).

Record Cup Victory: 9-0 v Boston U, FA Cup, 1st rd, 21 November 1953 – Malan; Hubbard, Brownsword; Sharpe, White, Bushby; Mosby (1), Haigh (3), Whitfield (2), Gregory (1), Mervyn Jones (2).

Record Defeat: 0-8 v Carlisle U, Division 3 (N), 25 December 1952.

Most League Points (2 for a win): 66, Division 3 (N), 1956–57, 1957–58.

Most League points (3 for a win): 83, Division 4, 1982–83.

Most League Goals: 88, Division 3 (N), 1957–58.

Highest League Scorer in Season: Barrie Thomas, 31, Division 2, 1961–62.

Most League Goals in Total Aggregate: Steve Cammack, 110, 1979–81, 1981–86.

Most Capped Player: None.

Most League Appearances: Jack Brownsword, 595, 1950–65.

Record Transfer Fee Received: £350,000 from Aston Villa for Neil Cox, February 1991.

Record Transfer Fee Paid: £55,000 to Bristol City for Glenn Humphries, March 1991.

Football League Record: 1950 Elected to Division 3 (N); 1958–64 Division 2; 1964–68 Division 3; 1968–72 Division 4; 1972–73 Division 3; 1973–83 Division 4; 1983–84 Division 3; 1984–92 Division 4; 1992– Division 3.

Honours: Football League: Division 2 best season: 4th, 1961–62; Division 3 (N) – Champions 1957–58. *FA Cup:* best season: 5th rd, 1957–58, 1969–70. *Football League Cup:* never past 3rd rd.

Colours: Sky blue shirts with two claret rings on sleeves, white collar, white shorts with claret stripe, white stockings with claret and blue bar. **Change colours**: White shirts with claret brush stroke, claret shorts with sky blue stripe, sky blue stockings with claret and white bar.

SCUNTHORPE UNITED 1991–92 LEAGUE RECORD

Match No.	Date		Venue	Opponents	Result		H/T Score	Lg. Pos.	Goalscorers	Attendance
1	Aug	17	A	Gillingham	L	0-4	0-1	—		3480
2		24	H	Doncaster R	W	3-2	2-1	13	Helliwell, Alexander, Daws	3505
3		31	A	Blackpool	L	1-2	1-1	19	Buckley	3273
4	Sep	3	H	Scarborough	D	1-1	1-0	—	Joyce	3185
5		7	H	Maidstone U	W	2-0	0-0	12	Hill, Daws	2738
6		14	A	Chesterfield	W	1-0	0-0	9	Humphries	3338
7		17	A	Barnet	L	2-3	1-1	—	Humphries, White	3094
8		21	H	Crewe Alex	W	1-0	1-0	8	Hamilton	3021
9		28	A	Wrexham	L	0-4	0-2	9		1635
10	Oct	5	H	Hereford U	D	1-1	0-0	10	Daws (pen)	2384
11		12	A	Carlisle U	D	0-0	0-0	11		1988
12		19	A	Northampton T	W	1-0	1-0	10	Helliwell	2575
13		26	H	Mansfield T	L	1-4	0-1	11	Daws	3610
14	Nov	2	A	Cardiff C	D	2-2	0-0	11	Hill, Pike (og)	2356
15		5	H	Rochdale	W	6-2	3-0	—	Hamilton, Brown T (og), Lister, Helliwell, Alexander, Hill	2331
16		9	H	Rotherham U	W	1-0	0-0	7	Daws	4175
17		23	A	Lincoln C	L	2-4	1-1	17	Martin, Alexander	3078
18		30	H	York C	W	1-0	0-0	9	Hamilton	2887
19	Dec	14	A	Burnley	D	1-1	0-1	9	Pender (og)	8419
20		20	A	Doncaster R	W	2-1	1-1	—	Humphries, Alexander	1825
21		26	H	Gillingham	W	2-0	1-0	5	White, Martin	3883
22		28	H	Blackpool	W	2-1	1-1	5	White 2	4271
23	Jan	1	A	Scarborough	L	1-4	1-1	7	White	2237
24		18	A	Halifax T	W	4-1	1-0	7	White 3, Hamilton	1232
25		25	H	Walsall	D	1-1	1-0	6	White	3165
26	Feb	8	A	Mansfield T	W	3-1	2-0	6	Alexander, Hamilton (pen), White	3496
27		11	A	York C	L	0-3	0-2	—		2255
28		15	H	Burnley	D	2-2	2-0	8	Helliwell, White	5303
29	Mar	3	H	Halifax T	W	1-0	0-0	—	Buckley	2448
30		7	A	Walsall	L	1-2	0-1	8	Buckley	2722
31		10	A	Rochdale	L	0-2	0-1	—		2036
32		14	H	Cardiff C	W	1-0	0-0	9	Buckley	2766
33		21	A	Rotherham U	L	0-5	0-2	9		4528
34		28	H	Lincoln C	L	0-2	0-1	9		3297
35		31	H	Chesterfield	W	2-0	1-0	—	Helliwell, Hamilton (pen)	2224
36	Apr	4	A	Maidstone U	W	1-0	0-0	7	Hamilton	1237
37		11	H	Barnet	D	1-1	0-1	8	Hamilton (pen)	3361
38		14	H	Northampton T	W	3-0	2-0	—	Hill, Buckley, Daws	2286
39		18	A	Crewe Alex	D	1-1	0-0	7	Helliwell	3313
40		20	H	Wrexham	W	3-1	0-0	6	Joyce, Hamilton (pen), Buckley	2900
41		25	A	Hereford U	W	2-1	1-1	5	Helliwell 2	1587
42	May	2	H	Carlisle U	W	4-0	2-0	5	Elliott, Daws, Hill, Helliwell	3851

Final League Position: 5

GOALSCORERS

League (64): White 11, Hamilton 9 (4 pens), Helliwell 9, Daws 7 (1 pen), Buckley 6, Alexander 5, Hill 5, Humphries 3, Joyce 2, Martin 2, Elliott 1, Lister 1, own goals 3.
Rumbelows Cup (3): Alexander 1, Helliwell 1, Humphries 1.
FA Cup (4): Helliwell 2, Daws 1, White 1.

Batch	Joyce	Longden	Hine	Hicks	Humphries	Alexander	Hamilton	Daws	Buckley	Helliwell	Martin	Musselwhite	Lister	Hyde	Hill	White	Stevenson	Whitehead	Marples	Samways	Elliott	Match No.
1	2	3	4	5	6	7	8	9	10*	11	12											1
	2	3	4	5	6	7	8	9	10	11			1									2
	2	3		5	6	7†	8	9	10	11		4*	1		12	14						3
	2	3	4	5	6	7	8	9	10	11			1									4
	2	3	4†	5	6	7*	8	9		11			1	14	12	10						5
	2	3		5*	6	7	8	9		11		4	1		12	10						6
	2	3			6	7	8	9		11*		4	1		5	10	12					7
	2	3			6	7	8	9				4	1		5	12	10	11*				8
	2	3	14		6	7†	8	9	12	11		4	1		5	10*						9
	2	3	8		6†	7	12	9		11		4*	1		5	10	14					10
	2	3			6	7	8	9*	12	11		4	1		5	10						11
	2	3			6	7	8	9		11		4	1		5	10						12
	2	3		5		7	8	9		11		4	1			10	6					13
	2	3		5		7	8*	9	12	11		4	1		6	10						14
	2	3		5		7	8	9		11		4	1		6	10						15
	2	3		5		7	8	9		11		4			6	10						16
	2	3		5		7	8	9		11		4	1		6	10						17
	2	3		5		7	8	9		11		4			6	10	1					18
	2	3		5		7	8	9		11		4			6*	10	12	1				19
	2	3		5	6	7†	8	9*		11		4			14	10	12	1				20
	2	3		5	6	7	8	9		11		4				10		1				21
	2	3		5	6	7*	8	9		11		4			12	10		1				22
	2	3		5	6	7†	8	9*	14	11		4			12	10		1				23
	2			5	6	7	8	9		11		4			3	10		1				24
	2	3		5	6	7	8			11		4				10		9	1			25
	2	3		5	6	7	8			11		4	1			10		9				26
	2	3	12	5	6†	7	8			11		4	1		14	10*		9				27
	2	3	12	5	6*	7	8	14		11		4				10		9†	1			28
	2	3		5		7	8		12	11		4	1		6	10		9*				29
	2	3		5†		7	8		12	11		4	1		6	10	14	9*				30
	2	3		5		7*	8	9		11		4	1		6	10	12					31
	2	3	14	5		7*	8	9†		11		4	1		6	10	12					32
	2	3	14	5		7	8	9*		11		4	1		6	10†	12					33
	2†		14	5	6	7*	8	9		11		4	1		3	10	12					34
	2				6	7	8		10	11		4			3			9		1	5	35
	2	3			6	7	8		10	11		4						9		1	5	36
	2	3			6	7*	8		12	11		4				10		9		1	5	37
	2	3			6	7*	8	9	12	11		4				10				1	5	38
	2	3			6	7	8	9	10	11		4								1	5	39
	2	3			6	7	8		10	11		4						9		1	5	40
	2	3			6	7	8	9	12	11		4				10*				1	5	41
	2	3			6	7	8	9	10	11		4								1	5	42
1	40	40	7	21	32	30	41	32	26	38	36	24	16	1	36	15	1	8	1	8	8	
	+1s	+3s				+6s		+4s	+2s	+1s	+1s				+3s	+7s	+1s	+7s	+1s			

Rumbelows Cup	First Round	Wrexham (a)	0-1
		(h)	3-0
	Second Round	Leeds U (h)	0-0
		(a)	0-3
FA Cup	First Round	Rotherham U (h)	1-1
		(a)	3-3
		lost 7-6 on penalties	

SCUNTHORPE UNITED

Player and Position	Ht	Wt	Birth Date	Birth Place	Source	Clubs	League App	Gls
Goalkeepers								
Nigel Batch †	6 0	12 07	9 11 57	Huddersfield	Trainee	Derby Co	—	—
						Grimsby T	348	—
						Lincoln C	—	—
						Darlington	30	—
						Stockport Co (loan)	12	—
						Scunthorpe U	2	—
Paul Musselwhite	6 2	12 07	22 12 68	Portsmouth	Portsmouth	Scunthorpe U	132	
Defenders								
Graham Alexander	5 10	11 00	10 10 71	Coventry	Trainee	Scunthorpe U	37	5
Stuart Hicks	6 1	12 06	30 5 67	Peterborough	Apprentice	Peterborough U	—	—
						Wisbech	—	—
						Colchester U	64	—
						Scunthorpe U	67	1
Glenn Humphries	6 0	12 00	11 8 64	Hull	Apprentice	Doncaster R	180	8
						Lincoln C (loan)	9	—
						Bristol C	85	—
						Scunthorpe U	42	4
Joe Joyce	5 9	10 05	18 3 61	Consett	Amateur	Barnsley	334	4
						Scunthorpe U	61	2
Steve Lister‡	6 1	11 00	18 11 61	Doncaster	Apprentice	Doncaster R	237	30
						Scunthorpe U	182	30
						York C (loan)	4	1
Paul Longden	5 9	11 00	28 9 62	Wakefield	Apprentice	Barnsley	5	—
						Scunthorpe U	348	—
Midfield								
David Cowling†	5 7	11 04	27 11 58	Doncaster	Apprentice	Mansfield T	—	—
						Huddersfield T	340	43
						Scunthorpe U (loan)	1	—
						Reading	10	1
						Scunthorpe U	89	5
Allan Evans‡	5 9	11 04	19 4 73	Coventry	Trainee	Scunthorpe U	—	—
Ian Hamilton	5 9	11 03	14 12 67	Stevenage	Apprentice	Southampton	—	—
						Cambridge U	24	1
						Scunthorpe U	145	18
David Hill	5 9	10 03	6 6 66	Nottingham	Local	Scunthorpe U	140	10
						Ipswich T	61	—
						Scunthorpe U (loan)	9	1
						Scunthorpe U	37	5
Mark Hine	5 8	9 11	18 5 64	Middlesbrough	Local	Grimsby T	22	1
						Darlington	128	8
						Peterborough U	55	8
						Scunthorpe U	22	2
Gary Hyde‡	6 0	9 07	28 12 69	Wolverhampton	Trainee	Darlington	38	3
						Leicester C	—	—
						Scunthorpe U	8	—
Dean Martin	5 10	10 02	9 9 67	Halifax	Local	Halifax T	153	7
						Scunthorpe U	37	2
Andy Stevenson	6 0	12 03	29 9 67	Scunthorpe	School	Scunthorpe U	78	1
						Doncaster R (loan)	1	—
Forwards								
John Buckley	5 9	10 07	10 5 62	Glasgow	Queen's Park	Doncaster R	84	11
						Leeds U	10	1
						Leicester C (loan)	5	—
						Doncaster R (loan)	6	—
						Rotherham U	105	13
						Partick T	26	5
						Scunthorpe U	28	6

SCUNTHORPE UNITED

Foundation: The year of foundation for Scunthorpe United has often been quoted as 1910, but the club can trace its history back to 1899 when Brumby Hall FC, who played on the Old Showground, consolidated their position by amalgamating with some other clubs and changing their name to Scunthorpe United. The year 1910 was when that club amalgamated with North Lindsey United as Scunthorpe and Lindsey United. The link is Mr. W. T. Lockwood whose chairmanship covers both years.

First Football League game: 19 August, 1950, Division 3 (N), v Shrewsbury T (h) D 0-0 – Thompson; Barker, Brownsword; Allen, Taylor, McCormick; Mosby, Payne, Gorin, Rees, Boyes.

Did you know: In FA Cup-ties in the 1950s Scunthorpe, then in Division 3 (N), beat one First Division side (Newcastle United) and held two others (Sunderland and Portsmouth) to draws, all away from home.

Managers (and Secretary-managers)
Harry Allcock 1915–53*, Tom Crilly 1936–37, Bernard Harper 1946–48, Leslie Jones 1950–51, Bill Corkhill 1952–56, Ron Suart 1956–58, Tony McShane 1959, Bill Lambton 1959, Frank Soo 1959–60, Dick Duckworth 1960–64, Fred Goodwin 1964–66, Ron Ashman 1967–73, Ron Bradley 1973–74, Dick Rooks 1974–76, Ron Ashman 1976–81, John Duncan 1981–83, Allan Clarke 1983–84, Frank Barlow 1984–87, Mick Buxton 1987–91, Bill Green February 1991–.

Player and Position	Ht	Wt	Birth Date	Birth Place	Source	Clubs	League App	Gls
Tony Daws	5 9	10 02	10 9 66	Sheffield		Notts Co	8	1
						Sheffield U	11	3
						Scunthorpe U	159	59
Andy Godfrey‡	5 9	11 04	6 10 72	Gainsborough	Trainee	Scunthorpe U	—	—
Sam Goodacre	5 10	11 00	1 12 70	Sheffield	School	Sheffield W	—	—
						Scunthorpe U	—	—
Ian Helliwell	6 3	13 12	7 12 62	Rotherham	Matlock T	York C	160	40
						Scunthorpe U	39	9
Ian Miller‡	5 8	11 12	13 5 55	Perth		Bury	15	—
						Nottingham F	—	—
						Doncaster R	124	14
						Swindon T	127	9
						Blackburn R	268	16
						Port Vale	21	1
						Scunthorpe U	12	—
Jonathan Stanger‡			20 1 73	Blackburn	Trainee	Manchester U	—	—
						Scunthorpe U	—	—
Jason White	6 00	12 09	19 10 71	Meriden	Trainee	Derby Co	—	—
						Scunthorpe U	22	11

Trainees
Collom, Delme G; Ellender, Paul; Hall, James M; McCullagh, Paul A; McNeil, James W; Pickford, Richard M; Raspin, William R; Ryan, Tim J.

**Non-Contract
Moore, David.

Associated Schoolboys
Ellis, Lee D.

**Non-Contract Players who are retained must be re-signed before they are eligible to play in League matches.

SHEFFIELD UNITED 1991–92 *Back row (left to right)*: Ian Bryson, Michael Lake, Vinnie Jones, Brian Deane, Phil Kite, Bob Booker, Paul Beesley, Jamie Hoyland, Glyn Hodges.
Centre row: Derek French (Physiotherapist), Chris Wilder, Carl Bradshaw, John Pemberton, Simon Tracey, Colin Hill, Tony Agana, John Gannon, Geoff Taylor (Coach).
Front row: Brian Marwood, Dane Whitehouse, Richard Lucas, Dave Bassett (Team Manager), Clive Mendonca, Mitchum Ward, Tom Cowan.

FA Premier

SHEFFIELD UNITED

Bramall Lane Ground, Sheffield S2 4SU. Telephone Sheffield (0742) 738955. Bladesline (recorded message): 0898 888650.

Ground capacity: 32,000 (22,000 seats).

Record attendance: 68,287 v Leeds U, FA Cup 5th rd, 15 February 1936.

Record receipts: £178,124 v Tottenham H, Rumbelows Cup 4th rd, 27 November 1990.

Pitch measurements: 110yd × 72yd.

President: R. Wragg M.INST.BM.

Chairman: P. G. Woolhouse.

Managing Director: D. Dooley.

Directors: D. Dooley, A. H. Laver, M. A. Wragg, R. Wragg.

Team Manager: Dave Bassett. *Team Coach:* Geoff Taylor. *Youth Coach:* Keith Mincher. *Assistant Manager. Physio:* Derek French. *Secretary:* D. Capper AFA. *Commercial Manager:* Andy R. Daykin. *Youth Development Officer:* John Dungworth. *Community Programme Organiser:* Tony Currie, Tel: 769314.

Year Formed: 1889. Turned Professional: 1889. Ltd Co.: 1899.

Club Nickname: 'The Blades'.

Record League Victory: 10-0 v Burslem Port Vale, Division 2, 10 December 1892 – Howlett; Witham, Lilley; Howell, Hendry, Needham; Drummond (1), Wallace (1), Hammond (4), Davies (2), Watson (2).

Record Cup Victory: 5-0 v Newcastle U (away), FA Cup, 1st rd, 10 January 1914 – Gough; Cook, English; Brelsford, Howley, Sturgess; Simmons (2), Gillespie (1), Kitchen (1), Fazackerley, Revill (1). 5-0 v Corinthians, FA Cup, 1st rd, 10 January 1925 – Sutcliffe; Cook, Milton; Longworth, King, Green; Partridge, Boyle (1), Johnson 4), Gillespie, Tunstall. 5-0 v Barrow, FA Cup, 3rd rd, 7 January 1956 – Burgin; Coldwell, Mason; Fountain, Johnson, Iley; Hawksworth (1), Hoyland (2), Howitt, Wragg (1), Grainger (1).

Record Defeat: 0-13 v Bolton W, FA Cup 2nd rd, 1 February 1890.

Most League Points (2 for a win): 60, Division 2, 1952–53.

Most League points (3 for a win): 96, Division 4, 1981–82.

Most League Goals: 102, Division 1, 1925–26.

Highest League Scorer in Season: Jimmy Dunne, 41, Division 1, 1930–31.

Most League Goals in Total Aggregate: Harry Johnson, 205, 1919–30.

Most Capped Player: Billy Gillespie, 25, Northern Ireland.

Most League Appearances: Joe Shaw, 629, 1948–66.

Record Transfer Fee Received: £400,000 from Leeds U for Alex Sabella, May 1980.

Record Transfer Fee Paid: £650,000 to Leeds U for Vinny Jones, September 1990.

Football League Record: 1892 Elected to Division 2; 1893–1934 Division 1; 1934–39 Division 2; 1946–49 Division 1; 1949–53 Division 2; 1953–56 Division 1; 1956–61 Division 2; 1961–68 Division 1; 1968–71 Division 2; 1971–76 Division 1; 1976–79 Division 2; 1979–81 Division 3; 1981–82 Division 4; 1982–84 Division 3; 1984–88 Division 2; 1988–89 Division 3; 1989–90 Division 2; 1990–92 Division 1; 1992– FA Premier League.

Honours: Football League: Division 1 – Champions 1897–98; Runners-up 1896–97, 1899–1900; Division 2 – Champions 1952–53; Runners-up 1892–93, 1938–39, 1960–61, 1970–71, 1989–90; Division 4 – Champions 1981–82. *FA Cup:* Winners 1899, 1902, 1915, 1925; Runners-up 1901, 1936. *Football League Cup:* best season: 5th rd, 1961–62, 1966–67, 1971–72.

Colours: Colours: Narrow red and white striped shirts with thin black stripe, black shorts, black stockings with red and white trim. **Change colours:** Yellow shirts, red shorts, red stockings.

SHEFFIELD UNITED 1991–92 LEAGUE RECORD

Match No.	Date		Venue	Opponents	Result	H/T Score	Lg. Pos.	Goalscorers	Attendance
1	Aug	17	A	Norwich C	D 2-2	1-0	—	Deane, Hill	16,380
2		20	H	West Ham U	D 1-1	0-0	—	Beesley	21,463
3		24	H	Southampton	L 0-2	0-1	16		18,029
4		28	A	Coventry C	L 1-3	1-3	—	Bryson	12,601
5		31	A	Crystal Palace	L 1-2	0-0	20	Hodges	15,507
6	Sep	3	H	Chelsea	L 0-1	0-0	—		17,400
7		7	A	Oldham Ath	L 1-2	0-2	22	Deane	15,064
8		14	H	Everton	W 2-1	0-1	20	Hoyland, Bryson	19,817
9		17	H	Notts Co	L 1-3	0-0	—	Agana	19,375
10		21	A	Arsenal	L 2-5	0-4	24	Agana, Mendonca	30,244
11		28	H	Wimbledon	D 0-0	0-0	22		16,062
12	Oct	5	A	Leeds U	L 3-4	0-3	22	Hoyland, Agana, Bradshaw	28,362
13		19	H	Nottingham F	W 4-2	2-1	22	Whitehouse, Agana, Bryson, Hoyland	23,080
14		26	A	Manchester C	L 2-3	2-2	22	Gayle 2	25,495
15	Nov	2	A	Manchester U	L 0-2	0-1	22		42,942
16		17	H	Sheffield W	W 2-0	1-0	—	Whitehouse, Deane	31,832
17		23	A	Tottenham H	W 1-0	0-0	20	Gage	28,168
18		30	H	Luton T	D 1-1	0-0	20	Bryson	21,804
19	Dec	7	A	QPR	L 0-1	0-0	21		10,106
20		14	H	Aston Villa	W 2-0	1-0	19	Ward, McGrath (og)	18,401
21		21	A	West Ham U	D 1-1	0-0	19	Deane	19,287
22		26	H	Coventry C	L 0-3	0-0	20		19,638
23		28	H	Crystal Palace	D 1-1	1-0	19	Hoyland	17,969
24	Jan	1	A	Liverpool	L 1-2	1-0	20	Deane	35,993
25		11	A	Southampton	W 4-2	1-1	19	Ward, Lake 2, Marwood	13,689
26		18	H	Norwich C	W 1-0	0-0	19	Bryson	17,549
27	Feb	1	A	Nottingham F	W 5-2	3-1	17	Lake, Gannon, Bryson, Bradshaw, Deane	22,412
28		8	H	Manchester C	W 4-2	3-1	15	Lake, Gayle, Deane, Whitehouse	26,562
29		22	A	Luton T	L 1-2	1-2	18	Bryson	9003
30		29	H	QPR	D 0-0	0-0	18		17,958
31	Mar	11	A	Sheffield W	W 3-1	2-0	—	Whitehouse, Davison 2	40,327
32		14	H	Manchester U	L 1-2	1-0	17	Deane	30,183
33		21	A	Chelsea	W 2-1	1-0	17	Whitehouse 2	11,247
34		28	H	Liverpool	W 2-0	1-0	15	Deane 2	26,943
35		31	A	Aston Villa	D 1-1	0-0	—	Gage	15,745
36	Apr	4	H	Oldham Ath	W 2-0	1-0	12	Whitehouse, Bryson	19,843
37		11	A	Everton	W 2-0	1-0	10	Bryson, Cork	18,285
38		14	H	Tottenham H	W 2-0	2-0	—	Deane 2	21,526
39		18	H	Arsenal	D 1-1	1-0	7	Davison	25,034
40		20	A	Notts Co	W 3-1	1-1	7	Beesley, Hodges, Davison	12,605
41		26	A	Leeds U	L 2-3	1-1	—	Cork, Chapman (og)	32,000
42	May	2	A	Wimbledon	L 0-3	0-3	9		8768

Final League Position: 9

GOALSCORERS

League (65): Deane 12, Bryson 9, Whitehouse 7, Agana 4, Davison 4, Hoyland 4, Lake 4, Gayle 3, Beesley 2, Bradshaw 2, Cork 2, Gage 2, Hodges 2, Ward 2, Gannon 1, Hill 1, Marwood 1, Mendonca 1, own goals 2.
Rumbelows Cup (3): Deane 2, Hoyland 1.
FA Cup (7): Deane 2, Bradshaw 1, Gayle 1, Hodges 1, Lake 1, Whitehouse 1.

Tracey	Pemberton	Cowan	Jones	Beesley	Hill	Hoyland	Whitehouse	Agana	Deane	Bryson	Booker	Hodges	Wilder	Wood	Littlejohn	Mendonca	Hartfield	Duffield	Lucas	Barnes	Lake	Gayle	Kite	Gannon	Bradshaw	Gage	Peel	Ward	Match No.
1	2	3	4	5	6	7	8*	9	10	11	12																		1
1	2	3	4	5	6	7	14	9	10*	12	8	11†																	2
1		3	4	5	6	12	11†	9*		7	10		2	8	14														3
1	2	3*	4	5	6	7	14	9		11	10				8†		12												4
1	2	3		12	6	5				7	4	10			14	11†	9	8*											5
1	2	3		12	6	5				7	4	10			8*	9†	11	14											6
1	2				6	5	8*	9	10†	7	4	11					3	14	12										7
1				5	6	8		9		7	14	11	2		12	4				3†	10*								8
1	10*				6	8	9			7	4†	11	2		12					3	14	5							9
1	6†	8	3	10*						7	14	11	2		12							5		4					10
	2	3			6			9	8*	7	14	11			10†					12		5	1	4					11
		3			6			9	8	7	12	10				2*				11†		5	1	4	14				12
	2	3			6			9*	8	11		7†			12					14		5	1	4	10				13
	2	3			6			9	8	11*		7			12					14		5	1	4	10†				14
1	2	3			6			9	8	11		7								12		5		4	10*				15
1	2	3			6			9	8	11		10										5		4	7				16
1	2*				6			9†	8	11	12	10										5		4	7	3		14	17
1	2				6			9	8	11	12	10									14	5		4*	7†	3			18
1	2†				6			9	8*	11	12	10									14	5		4	7	3			19
1		3			6			9	8	11		10										5		4	7	2			20
1		3			6			9	8	11	7*	10			12							5		4		2			21
1		3			6			9	8	11	7	10								12		5		4*		2			22
1		3			6			9	8	11†	7*	10			14					12		5		4		2			23
1		3	14		6			9†	8	7	12	10				11*						5		4		2			24
1		3*		5	6			9		11		10			14						8			4		2		7†	25
1		3			6			14		11†		10									8	5		4		2		7*	26
1					6			9*	10	11	12									3	8	5		4	7	2			27
1					6			9	10	11	7*									3	8	5		4		2			28
1					6†	14		12	10	7		9*								3		5		4	11	2			29
1					6				10	11										3	8*	5		4	7	2		12	30
1					6				10	11*	12									3		5		4	7	2			31
1	14				6				10*	11										3		5		4	7	2†			32
1					6	14			10	11†										3		5		4	7*	2			33
					6				10†	11	12									3		5		4		2		14	34
					6				10	11†										3	14	5		4		2		7*	35
					6			7	10	11	14									3		5		4		2*			36
					6			7	10	11										3		5		4		2			37
					6			7†	10	11	12									3		5		4	14	2			38
	2				6			7*	10†	11	12									3		5		4	14				39
	2	3			6			7	10	11†	12											5		4*					40
	2				6			7	10	11	12	14								3		5		4*	11				41
	2	3			6			7	10	14												5		4	11*				42
29	19	20	4	38	11	23	25	13	30	29	8	22	4	3	5	4	6	—	—	15	8	33	4	32	15	22	—	4	
	+	+	+	+	+			+	+	+		+			+	+	+	+	+		+				+		+	+	
	1s	2s	4s	3s	9s			5s	4s	4s		1s			2s	6s	1s	2s	1s		10s				3s		1s	2s	

Marwood—Match No. 25(12) 26(12) 28(12) 30(9) 40(14); Rogers—Match No. 29(8) 31(8) 32(8) 33(8) 34(8) 35(8) 36(8) 37(8) 38(8) 39(8) 40(8) 41(8) 42(8); Davison—Match No. 31(9†) 32(12) 33(12) 34(7*) 35(12) 36(12) 37(12) 38(9*) 39(9) 40(9) 42(9†); Cork—Match No. 31(14) 32(9) 33(9) 34(9) 35(9) 36(9†) 37(9*) 41(9†); Rees—Match No. 34(1) 35(1) 36(1) 37(1) 38(1) 39(1) 40(1) 41(1); Day—Match No. 42(1); Reed—Match No. 42(12).

Rumbelows Cup	Second Round	Wigan Ath (a)	2-2
		(h)	1-0
FA Cup	Third Round	West Ham U (h)	0-2
	Third Round	Luton T (h)	4-0
	Fourth Round	Charlton Ath (a)	0-0
		(h)	3-1
	Fifth Round	Chelsea (a)	0-1

SHEFFIELD UNITED

Goalkeepers

Name	Ht	Wt	Born	Birthplace	Source	Club	Apps	Gls
Phil Kite	6 1	14 07	26 10 62	Bristol	Apprentice	Bristol R	96	—
						Tottenham H (loan)	—	—
						Southampton	4	—
						Middlesbrough (loan)	2	—
						Gillingham	70	—
						Bournemouth	7	—
						Sheffield U	11	—
						Mansfield T (loan)	12	—
Mel Rees	6 2	12 12	25 1 67	Cardiff	Trainee	Cardiff C	31	—
						Watford	3	—
						Crewe Alex (loan)	6	—
						Southampton (loan)	—	—
						Leyton Orient (loan)	9	—
						WBA	18	—
						Norwich C (loan)	—	—
						Sheffield U	8	—
Simon Tracey	6 0	13 00	9 12 67	Woolwich	Apprentice	Wimbledon	1	—
						Sheffield U	113	—

Defenders

Name	Ht	Wt	Born	Birthplace	Source	Club	Apps	Gls
David Barnes	5 10	11 01	16 11 61	London	Apprentice	Coventry C	9	—
						Ipswich T	17	—
						Wolverhampton W	88	4
						Aldershot	69	1
						Sheffield U	67	1
Paul Beesley	6 1	11 05	21 7 65	Wigan		Wigan Ath	155	3
						Leyton Orient	32	1
						Sheffield U	77	3
Tom Cowan	5 8	10 08	28 8 69	Bellshill	Netherdale BC	Clyde	16	2
						Rangers	12	—
						Sheffield U	40	—
Ashley Fickling			15 11 72	Sheffield	Trainee	Sheffield U	—	—
Kevin Gage	5 9	11 02	21 4 64	Chiswick	Apprentice	Wimbledon	168	15
						Aston Villa	115	8
						Sheffield U	22	2
Brian Gayle	6 1	12 07	6 3 65	London		Wimbledon	83	3
						Manchester C	55	3
						Ipswich T	58	4
						Sheffield U	33	3
Charles Hartfield	6 0	12 00	4 9 71	London	Trainee	Arsenal	—	—
						Sheffield U	7	—
Colin Hill	5 11	12 02	12 11 63	Hillingdon	Apprentice	Arsenal	46	1
						Brighton & HA (loan)	—	—
						Maritimo	—	—
						Colchester U	69	—
						Sheffield U	82	1
						Leicester C (loan)	10	—
John Pemberton	5 11	12 03	11 11 64	Oldham	Chadderton	Rochdale	1	—
						Crewe Alex	121	1
						Crystal Palace	78	2
						Sheffield U	41	—
Cliff Powell‡	6 0	12 00	21 2 68	Watford	Apprentice	Watford	—	—
						Hereford U (loan)	7	—
						Sheffield U	10	—
						Doncaster R (loan)	4	—
						Cardiff C (loan)	1	—
Brian Smith‡	5 9	11 02	27 10 66	Sheffield	Local	Sheffield U	84	—
						Scunthorpe U (loan)	6	1
David Walton	6 02	13 04	10 4 73	Bedlingham	Trainee	Sheffield U	—	—
Mitch Ward	5 8	10 07	18 6 71	Sheffield	Trainee	Sheffield U	10	2
						Crewe Alex (loan)	4	1
Chris Wilder	5 10	10 08	23 9 67	Wortley	Apprentice	Southampton	—	—
						Sheffield U	93	1
						Walsall (loan)	4	—
						Charlton Ath (loan)	1	—
						Charlton Ath (loan)	2	—
						Leyton Orient (loan)	16	1

Midfield

Name	Ht	Wt	Born	Birthplace	Source	Club	Apps	Gls
Ian Bryson	5 11	11 11	26 11 62	Kilmarnock		Kilmarnock	215	40
						Sheffield U	139	33
John Gannon	5 8	10 10	18 12 66	Wimbledon	Apprentice	Wimbledon	16	2
						Crewe Alex (loan)	15	—
						Sheffield U (loan)	16	1
						Sheffield U	93	4
Jamie Hoyland	6 0	12 08	23 1 66	Sheffield	Apprentice	Manchester C	2	—
						Bury	172	35
						Sheffield U	47	4
Michael Lake	6 1	13 07	16 11 66	Manchester	Macclesfield T	Sheffield U	29	4
Richard Lucas	5 10	11 04	22 9 70	Sheffield	Trainee	Sheffield U	10	—

SHEFFIELD UNITED

Foundation: In March 1889, Yorkshire County Cricket Club formed Sheffield United six days after an FA Cup semi-final between Preston North End and West Bromwich Albion had finally convinced Charles Stokes, a member of the cricket club, that the formation of a professional football club would prove successful at Bramall Lane. The United's first secretary, Mr. J. B. Wostinholm was also secretary of the cricket club.

First Football League game: 3 September 1892, Division 2, v Lincoln C (h) W 4-2 – Lilley; Witham, Cain; Howell, Hendry, Needham (1); Wallace, Dobson, Hammond (3), Davies, Drummond.

Did you know: When United enjoyed their record away League victory 10-0 at Burslem Port Vale in December 1892, they were four goals ahead after only six minutes. It was their first away League win of the season.

Managers (and Secretary-managers)
J. B. Wostinholm 1889–1899*, John Nicholson 1899–1932, Ted Davison 1932–52, Reg Freeman 1952–55, Joe Mercer 1955–58, Johnny Harris 1959–68 (continued as GM to 1970), Arthur Rowley 1968–69, Johnny Harris (GM resumed TM duties) 1969–73, Ken Furphy 1973–75, Jimmy Sirrel 1975–77, Harry Haslam 1978–81, Martin Peters 1981, Ian Porterfield 1981–86, Billy McEwan 1986–88, Dave Bassett January 1988–.

Name	Ht ft	Ht st lb	Day	Mth Yr	Birthplace	Signed from	Club	Apps	Gls
Brian Marwood	5 7	11 06	5	2 60	Seaham Harbour	Apprentice	Hull C	158	51
							Sheffield W	128	27
							Arsenal	52	16
							Sheffield U	22	3
							Middlesbrough (loan)	3	—
Paul Rogers	6 00	11 13	21	3 65	Portsmouth	Sutton U	Sheffield U	13	—
Dane Whitehouse	5 8	10 12	14	10 70	Sheffield	Trainee	Sheffield U	55	8
Julian Winter‡	6 0	11 02	6	9 65	Huddersfield	Local	Huddersfield T	93	5
							Scunthorpe U (loan)	4	—
							Sheffield U	—	—
Forwards									
Carl Bradshaw	6 0	11 00	2	10 68	Sheffield	Apprentice	Sheffield W	32	4
							Barnsley (loan)	6	1
							Manchester C	5	—
							Sheffield U	75	6
Alan Cork	6 0	12 00	4	3 59	Derby	Amateur	Derby Co	—	—
							Lincoln C (loan)	5	—
							Wimbledon	430	145
							Sheffield U	8	2
Brian Deane	6 3	12 07	7	2 68	Leeds	Apprentice	Doncaster R	66	12
							Sheffield U	156	68
Peter Duffield	5 6	10 07	4	2 69	Middlesbrough		Middlesbrough	—	—
							Sheffield U	58	14
							Halifax T (loan)	12	6
							Rotherham U (loan)	17	4
Glyn Hodges	6 0	12 03	30	4 63	Streatham	Apprentice	Wimbledon	232	49
							Newcastle U	7	—
							Watford	86	15
							Crystal Palace	7	—
							Sheffield U	38	6
Adrian Littlejohn	5 10	10 04	26	9 70	Wolverhampton	WBA	Walsall	44	1
							Sheffield U	7	—
Clive Mendonca	5 10	11 07	9	9 68	Tullington	Apprentice	Sheffield U	13	4
							Doncaster R (loan)	2	—
							Rotherham U	84	27
							Sheffield U	10	1
							Grimsby T (loan)	10	3
Nathan Peel	6 1	12 07	17	5 72	Blackburn	Trainee	Preston NE	10	1
							Sheffield U	1	—
John Reed	5 6	8 11	27	8 72	Rotherham	Trainee	Sheffield U	1	—
							Scarborough (loan)	14	5
							Scarborough (loan)	6	—

Trainees
Anthony, Graham J; Battersby, Tony; Brocklehurst, David; Butterfield, Timothy; Cherrill, Matthew G; Cope, Steven; Dickerson, Ian; Evans, James D; Foreman, Matthew; Godwin, Jon B; Kent, Shane; Myhill, Craig; Reaney, Andrew; Roberts, Dean E; Stammers, Christopher A; Thomson, Martin; Wainwright, Danny; Wainwright, Lee.

Associated Schoolboys
Andison, Gary P; Collins, Eric; Crump, Andrew J; Dickman, Lewis L; Ellis, Lee A; Evans, Thomas R; Fowell, Keith M; Henderson, Dean; Hill, Matthew D; Hobson, Daniel D; Holt, Craig; Laidlaw, James R; Metcalf, Ian R; Oxer, Richard; Pearson, Gary; Powell, Craig I; Quinn, Wayne R; Rixon, James; Sampey, Mark P; Simpson, Andrew J; Taylor, James A; Vine, Darren M; Ward, Timothy M. J; Wood, Paul J; Wright, John D.

Associated Schoolboys who have accepted the club's offer of a Traineeship/Contract
Innes, Lee M; Kennedy, Steven; Letts, Simon C; McGovern, Craig P; Pearson, Gregg; Tee, Jason K; Zivkovic, Barry L.

SHEFFIELD WEDNESDAY 1991–92 *Back row (left to right):* Richie Barker (Assistant Manager), Phil King, Steve McCall, Peter Shirtliff, Viv Anderson, Kevin Pressman, Carlton Palmer, Chris Turner, Paul Warhurst, Nigel Worthington, Darren Wood, Gordon Watson, Alan Smith (Physiotherapist). *Front row:* Roland Nilsson, Paul Williams, John Harkes, David Hirst, Trevor Francis (Manager), Nigel Pearson, Danny Wilson, Steve MacKenzie, John Sheridan.

FA Premier   **SHEFFIELD WEDNESDAY**

Hillsborough, Sheffield, S6 1SW. Telephone Sheffield (0742) 343122. Box Office: Sheffield 337233. Clubcall: 0898 121186.

Ground capacity: 41,237.

Record attendance: 72,841 v Manchester C, FA Cup 5th rd, 17 February 1934.

Record receipts: £533,918 Sunderland v Norwich C, FA Cup semi-final, 5 April 1992.

Pitch measurements: 115yd × 75yd.

Chairman: D. G. Richards.

Vice-chairman: K. T. Addy.

Directors: C. Woodward, E. Barron, G. K. Hulley, R. M. Grierson FCA, J. Ashton MP.

Manager: Trevor Francis. *Assistant Manager:* Richie Barker. *Physio:* A. Smith. *Secretary:* G. H. Mackrell FCCA. *Commercial Manager:* R. Gorrill (Tel. 0742 337235).

Year Formed: 1867 (fifth oldest League club). Turned Professional: 1887. Ltd Co.: 1899.

Former Grounds: 1867, Highfield; 1869, Myrtle Road; 1877, Sheaf House; 1887, Olive Grove; 1899, Owlerton (since 1912 known as Hillsborough). Some games were played at Endcliffe in the 1880s. Until 1895 Bramall Lane was used for some games.

Former Names: The Wednesday until 1929.

Club Nickname: 'The Owls'.

Record League Victory: 9-1 v Birmingham, Division 1, 13 December 1930 – Brown; Walker, Blenkinsop; Strange, Leach, Wilson; Hooper (3), Seed (2), Ball (2), Burgess (1), Rimmer (1).

Record Cup Victory: 12-0 v Halliwell, FA Cup, 1st rd, 17 January 1891 – Smith; Thompson, Brayshaw; Harry Brandon (1), Betts, Cawley (2); Winterbottom, Mumford (2), Bob Brandon (1), Woolhouse (5), Ingram (1).

Record Defeat: 0-10 v Aston Villa, Division 1, 5 October 1912.

Most League Points (2 for a win): 62, Division 2, 1958–59.

Most League points (3 for a win): 88, Division 2, 1983–84.

Most League Goals: 106, Division 2, 1958–59.

Highest League Scorer in Season: Derek Dooley, 46, Division 2, 1951–52.

Most League Goals in Total Aggregate: Andy Wilson, 199, 1900–20.

Most Capped Player: Nigel Worthington, 37, Northern Ireland.

Most League Appearances: Andy Wilson, 502, 1900–20.

Record Transfer Fee Received: £1,750,000 from Real Sociedad for Dalian Atkinson, July 1990.

Record Transfer Fee Paid: £1,200,000 to Rangers for Chris Woods, August 1991.

Football League Record: 1892 Elected to Division 1; 1899–1900 Division 2; 1900–20 Division 1; 1920–26 Division 2; 1926–37 Division 1; 1937–50 Division 2; 1950–51 Division 1; 1951–52 Division 2; 1952–55 Division 1; 1955–56 Division 2; 1956–58 Division 1; 1958–59 Division 2; 1959–70 Division 1; 1970–75 Division 2; 1975–80 Division 3; 1980–84 Division 2; 1984–90 Division 1; 1990–91 Division 2; 1991–92 Division 1; 1992– FA Premier League.

Honours: Football League: Division 1 – Champions 1902–03, 1903–04, 1928–29, 1929–30; Runners-up 1960–61; Division 2 – Champions 1899–1900, 1925–26, 1951–52, 1955–56, 1958–59; Runners-up 1949–50, 1983–84. *FA Cup:* Winners 1896, 1907, 1935; Runners-up 1890, 1966. *Football League Cup:* Winners 1990–91. **European Competitions:** *Fairs Cup:* 1961–62, 1963–64.

Colours: Blue and white striped shirts, black shorts, black stockings. **Change colours:** Yellow and black shirts, black shorts, yellow stockings.

SHEFFIELD WEDNESDAY 1991–92 LEAGUE RECORD

Match No.	Date		Venue	Opponents	Result		H/T Score	Lg. Pos.	Goalscorers	Atten- dance
1	Aug	17	H	Aston Villa	L	2-3	2-1	—	Hirst, Wilson	36,749
2		24	A	Leeds U	D	1-1	0-0	20	Hirst	30,260
3		28	H	Everton	W	2-1	0-0	—	Wilson, Anderson	28,690
4		31	H	QPR	W	4-1	3-0	9	Palmer 3, Sheridan	25,022
5	Sep	3	A	Notts Co	L	1-2	1-1	—	Pearson	12,297
6		7	H	Nottingham F	W	2-1	1-0	8	Williams, Francis	31,289
7		14	A	Manchester C	W	1-0	0-0	5	Williams	29,453
8		18	A	Norwich C	L	0-1	0-1	—		12,503
9		21	H	Southampton	W	2-0	1-0	4	Williams, Worthington	27,291
10		28	A	Liverpool	D	1-1	0-0	4	Harkes	37,071
11	Oct	2	A	Wimbledon	L	1-2	0-0	—	Pearson	3121
12		5	H	Crystal Palace	W	4-1	3-1	4	Worthington, Hirst 2, Palmer	26,230
13		19	A	Luton T	D	2-2	1-1	5	Hirst, Sheridan	9401
14		26	H	Manchester U	W	3-2	1-2	5	Hirst, Jemson 2	38,260
15	Nov	2	H	Tottenham H	D	0-0	0-0	4		31,573
16		17	A	Sheffield U	L	0-2	0-1	—		31,832
17		23	H	Arsenal	D	1-1	1-0	7	Hirst	32,174
18		30	A	West Ham U	W	2-1	1-0	4	Harkes, Jemson	24,116
19	Dec	7	H	Chelsea	W	3-0	0-0	3	Hirst 2, Williams	27,383
20		21	H	Wimbledon	W	2-0	0-0	3	Sheridan 2 (1 pen)	20,574
21		26	A	Everton	W	1-0	0-0	3	Hirst	30,788
22		28	A	QPR	D	1-1	0-1	3	Hirst	12,990
23	Jan	1	H	Oldham Ath	D	1-1	0-0	3	Sharp (og)	32,679
24		12	H	Leeds U	L	1-6	1-3	—	Sheridan	32,228
25		18	A	Aston Villa	W	1-0	0-0	5	Jemson	28,036
26	Feb	1	H	Luton T	W	3-2	1-2	5	Hirst, Williams, Harkes	22,291
27		8	A	Manchester U	D	1-1	1-1	4	Hirst	47,074
28		15	H	Arsenal	L	1-7	1-1	4	Worthington	26,805
29		22	H	West Ham U	W	2-1	0-1	4	Palmer, Anderson	26,150
30		29	A	Chelsea	W	3-0	3-0	4	Wilson, Worthington, Williams	17,538
31	Mar	7	H	Coventry C	D	1-1	0-0	3	Anderson	23,959
32		11	H	Sheffield U	L	1-3	0-2	—	King	40,327
33		14	A	Tottenham H	W	2-0	0-0	3	Hirst, Williams	23,027
34		21	H	Notts Co	W	1-0	0-0	3	Hirst	23,910
35		28	A	Oldham Ath	L	0-3	0-1	3		15,897
36	Apr	4	A	Nottingham F	W	2-0	2-0	3	Williams, Hirst	26,105
37		8	A	Coventry C	D	0-0	0-0	—		13,293
38		11	H	Manchester C	W	2-0	0-0	3	Hirst, Worthington	32,138
39		18	A	Southampton	W	1-0	0-0	3	Hirst	17,715
40		20	H	Norwich C	W	2-0	2-0	3	Nilsson, Sheridan	27,362
41		25	A	Crystal Palace	D	1-1	1-0	3	Williams	21,573
42	May	2	H	Liverpool	D	0-0	0-0	3		34,861

Final League Position: 3

GOALSCORERS

League (62): Hirst 18, Williams 9, Sheridan 6 (1 pen), Palmer 5, Worthington 5, Jemson 4, Anderson 3, Harkes 3, Wilson 3, Pearson 2, Francis 1, King 1, Nilsson 1, own goals 1.
Rumbelows Cup (5): Francis 2, Anderson 1, Hirst 1, Williams 1.
FA Cup (3): Bart-Williams 1, Hirst 1, Sheridan 1.

Woods	Nilsson	King	Palmer	Pearson	Warhurst	Wilson	Sheridan	Hirst	Williams	Worthington	Harkes	Francis	Anderson	MacKenzie	Watson	Hyde	Jemson	Bart-Williams	Pressman	Shirtliff	Johnson	Match No.
1	2	3	4	5	6	7	8*	9	10†	11	12	14										1
1	2	3	4	5	6	7	8	9†	10*	11			14	12								2
1	2	3	4	5		7	8	9	10†	11		14	6	12*								3
1	2	3	4	5		7	8	9†	10	11*		14	6	12								4
1		3	4	6	5	7	8	9†	10*	11		14	2	12								5
1	2	3	4	6	5	7	8		10	11*			14	12		9†						6
1	2	3	4	6	5	7			10	11				12		9*	8					7
1	2	3	4	6	5	7			10	11	14					9*	8†	12				8
1	2	3	4	6*	5	7			10	11			8	14	12	9†						9
1	2	3	4	6	5	7			10	11			8	12		9*						10
1	2	3†	4	6	5	7			10	11			8	12	14	9*						11
1	2	3	4	6	5	7		9*	10	11			12			8						12
1	2	3	4	6		7†	8	9	10	11*			5	14	12							13
1	2	3	4	5		7	8	9†	10	11*	14		6	12								14
1	2	3*	4	5		7†	8	9	10	11	14		6	12								15
1	2	3	4	5		7†	8	9	10	11*	14		6	12								16
1	2†	3	4	5	6		8	9	12		7				14	10*	11					17
1		3	4*	5	6		8	9		11			2	12		10	7					18
	2	3	4	5	6†		8	9	12	11			14			10*	7		1			19
1	2	3	4	5	6		8	9*	12	11						10	7					20
1	2	3	4	5	6	14	8†	9	12	11						10*	7					21
1	2	3	4	5	6		8	9	10†	11			14	12			7*					22
1		3	4		6		8†	9*	12	11			2	14		10	7			5		23
1	2	3	4	5†			8		12	11*	14		6		7	10	9					24
1	2*	3	4			7				11	12		6			8	10			5	9	25
1	2	3	4	6	5			9	10	11*	7		12			8						26
1	2	3	4	6	5	7		9	12	11†	14					8		10*				27
1	2	3	4*	6		7		9	12	11	14		5			8†		10				28
1	2		4			7		9	12	3	11		5			8†	14	6			10*	29
1	2	3	4	14		7		9	10*	11			5			8†		6			12	30
1	2	3	4	14		7		9	10	11*			5				12	6			8†	31
1	2	3	4	11†		7*		9	10	14			5			8	12	6				32
1	2		4	5	3	7		9*	10	11						8†	12	14			6	33
1	2		4	5	3	7†		9	10	11	14					12		8*			6	34
1	2	12	4	5	3*	7		9	10	11	14						8†				6	35
1	2	3	4	5		7	8*	9	10	11	12							6				36
1	2	3	4	5		7	8	9	10†	11	12	14						6*				37
1	2	3	4	5	6	7	8*	9	10†	11	12	14										38
1	2	3	4	5	6	7	8	9*	10†	11	14	12										39
1	2	3	4	5	6	7	8*		10	11	12	14									9†	40
1	2	3	4	5		7	8	9*	10	11	12							6				41
1	2	3	4	5	6	7	8*	9	10†	11	12							14				42

Apps (starts): 41 39 38 42 31 31 35 24 33 31 31 34 14 —15 — 4 9 11 12 1 12 5

Sub appearances: +1s (Palmer) · +2s (Wilson) +1s (Sheridan) · +9s (Harkes) · +15s (Anderson) +20s (MacKenzie) +7s (Watson) +3s (Hyde) · +4s (Jemson) +9s (Bart-Williams) +3s (Pressman) · +1s (Johnson)

Rumbelows Cup	Second Round	Leyton Orient (a)	0-0
		(h)	4-1
	Third Round	Southampton (h)	1-1
		(a)	0-1
FA Cup	Third Round	Preston NE (a)	2-0
	Fourth Round	Middlesbrough (h)	1-2

SHEFFIELD WEDNESDAY

Player and Position	Ht	Wt	Birth Date	Birth Place	Source	Clubs	League App	Gls
Goalkeepers								
Marlon Beresford	6 1	10 11	2 9 69	Lincoln	Trainee	Sheffield W	—	—
						Bury (loan)	1	—
						Ipswich T (loan)	—	—
						Northampton T (loan)	13	—
						Crewe Alex (loan)	3	—
						Northampton T (loan)	15	—
Lance Key			13 5 68	Kettering	Histon	Sheffield W	—	—
						York C (loan)	—	—
Kevin Pressman	6 1	13 00	6 11 67	Fareham	Apprentice	Sheffield W	59	—
						Stoke C (loan)	4	—
Chris Woods	6 2	12 08	14 11 59	Boston	Apprentice	Nottingham F	—	—
						QPR	63	—
						Norwich C (loan)	10	—
						Norwich C	206	—
						Rangers	173	—
						Sheffield W	41	—
Defenders								
Viv Anderson	6 0	11 01	29 8 56	Nottingham	Apprentice	Nottingham F	328	15
						Arsenal	120	9
						Manchester U	54	2
						Sheffield W	44	5
Paul Burton*			8 11 72	Barnsley	Trainee	Sheffield W	—	—
Scott Cam*	5 9	10 00	3 5 70	Sheffield	Trainee	Sheffield W	—	—
Phil King	5 10	12 00	28 12 67	Bristol		Exeter C	27	—
						Torquay U	24	3
						Swindon T	116	4
						Sheffield W	107	1
Roland Nilsson	6 0	11 06	27 11 63	Helsingborg	Gothenburg	Sheffield W	81	1
Carlton Palmer	5 10	11 00	5 12 65	West Bromwich	Trainee	WBA	121	4
						Sheffield W	134	8
Nigel Pearson	6 1	13 07	21 8 63	Nottingham	Heanor T	Shrewsbury T	153	5
						Sheffield W	159	13
Peter Shirtliff	6 2	13 04	6 4 61	Barnsley	Apprentice	Sheffield W	188	4
						Charlton Ath	103	7
						Sheffield W	84	4
Shaun Sowden‡			25 3 68	Blackburn	Histon	Sheffield W	—	—
Paul Warhurst	6 1	14 00	26 9 69	Stockport	Trainee	Manchester C	—	—
						Oldham Ath	67	2
						Sheffield W	33	—
Julian Watts	6 3	12 01	17 3 71	Sheffield		Rotherham U	20	1
						Sheffield W	—	—
Darren Wood*	5 10	11 08	9 6 64	Scarborough	Apprentice	Middlesbrough	101	6
						Chelsea	144	3
						Sheffield W	11	—
Nigel Worthington	5 10	12 06	4 11 61	Ballymena	Ballymena U	Notts Co	67	4
						Sheffield W	267	10
Midfield								
Chris Bart-Williams	5 11	11 10	16 6 74	Freetown	Trainee	Leyton Orient	36	2
						Sheffield W	15	—
Leroy Chambers			25 10 72	Sheffield	Trainee	Sheffield W	—	—
John Harkes	5 10	11 10	8 3 67	New Jersey	USSF	Sheffield W	52	5
Graham Hyde	5 7	11 07	10 11 70	Doncaster	Trainee	Sheffield W	13	—
Ryan Jones			23 7 73	Sheffield	Trainee	Sheffield W	—	—
John Sheridan	5 9	10 08	1 10 64	Stretford	Local	Leeds U	230	47
						Nottingham F	—	—
						Sheffield W	97	18

SHEFFIELD WEDNESDAY

Foundation: Sheffield, being one of the principal centres of early Association Football, this club was formed as long ago as 1867 by the Sheffield Wednesday Cricket Club (formed 1825) and their colours from the start were blue and white. The inaugural meeting was held at the Adelphi Hotel and the original committee included Charles Stokes who was subsequently a founder member of Sheffield United.

First Football League game: 3 September, 1892, Division 1, v Notts C (a) W 1-0 – Allan; T. Brandon (1), Mumford; Hall, Betts, H. Brandon; Spiksley, Brady, Davis, R. N. Brown, Dunlop.

Did you know: Wednesday's finest outside-right, Mark Hooper, played throughout their consecutive League championship-winning seasons of 1928–29 and 1929–30 without missing a single game, League or Cup. Indeed around this time he made 174 consecutive First Division appearances.

Managers (and Secretary-managers)
Arthur Dickinson 1891–1920*, Robert Brown 1920–33, Billy Walker 1933–37, Jimmy McMullan 1937–42, Eric Taylor 1942–58 (continued as GM to 1974), Harry Catterick 1958–61, Vic Buckingham 1961–64, Alan Brown 1964–68, Jack Marshall 1968–69, Danny Williams 1969–71, Derek Dooley 1971–73, Steve Burtenshaw 1974–75, Len Ashurst 1975–77, Jackie Charlton 1977–83, Howard Wilkinson 1983–88, Peter Eustace 1988–89, Ron Atkinson 1989–91, Trevor Francis June 1991–.

Mike Williams	5 8	10 06	21 11 69	Bradford	Maltby	Sheffield W	—	—
Danny Wilson	5 6	11 04	1 1 60	Wigan	Wigan Ath	Bury	90	8
						Chesterfield	100	13
						Nottingham F	10	1
						Scunthorpe U (loan)	6	3
						Brighton & HA	135	33
						Luton T	110	24
						Sheffield W	72	9
Forwards								
Trevor Francis†	5 10	11 07	19 4 54	Plymouth	Apprentice	Birmingham C	280	118
						Nottingham F	70	28
						Manchester C	26	12
						Sampdoria	68	17
						Atalanta	21	1
						Rangers	18	—
						QPR	32	12
						Sheffield W	70	5
David Hirst	5 11	12 05	7 12 67	Barnsley	Apprentice	Barnsley	28	9
						Sheffield W	189	72
Nigel Jemson	5 10	11 10	10 8 69	Preston	Trainee	Preston NE	32	8
						Nottingham F	48	13
						Bolton W (loan)	5	—
						Preston NE (loan)	9	2
						Sheffield W	20	4
David Johnson	6 2	13 08	29 10 70	Rother Valley	Trainee	Sheffield W	6	—
						Hartlepool U (loan)	7	2
Nick Robinson*			10 5 73	Basingstoke	Trainee	Sheffield W	—	—
Gordon Watson	6 0	12 00	20 3 71	Kent	Trainee	Charlton Ath	31	7
						Sheffield W	9	—
Paul Williams	5 7	10 03	16 8 65	London	Woodford T	Charlton Ath	82	23
						Brentford (loan)	7	3
						Sheffield W	86	24

Trainees
Baird, Carl A; Curzon, Richard E; Dean, Simon J; Flint, Jonathan A; Frank, Ian D; Holmes, Darren P; Linighan, Brian; Linighan, John; Parker, Scott; Robinson, Paul; Rodgers, Neil; Rowntree, Michael C; Simpson, Ronald K; Stewart, Simon A; Wright, Jeremy H.

Associated Schoolboys
Bailey, Gavin J; Barker, Richard I; Brown, Steven M; Cadet, Ryan L; Dey, Brendon S; Gallagher, Richard; Harrison, Andrew J; Ludlam, Craig; McVeigh, Michael B; Milley, Christopher; Pass, Steven D; Scargill, Jonathan M; Sharman, Samuel J; Sykes, Paul K; Thorpe, Steven M; Waring, Phillip; Woods, Stuart M.

Associated Schoolboys who have accepted the club's offer of a Traineeship/Contract
Burkill, Matthew J; Burrows, Marc L; Carter, Simon; Faulkner, David P; Guest, Mark A; Jacks, Daniel M.

SHREWSBURY TOWN 1991 *Back row (left to right):* Mark Blake, Dean Spink, Graeme Worsley, Michael Heathcote, Steve Perks, Tony Kelly, Ken Hughes, Neil Lyne, Kevin Summerfield, Paul Gorman, Tom Lynch.
Front row: Paul Wimbleton, Michael Brown, Darren Ryan, Pat O'Toole, Sean Parrish, Carl Griffiths, Robert Hopkins.

Division 3   **SHREWSBURY TOWN**

Gay Meadow, Shrewsbury. Telephone Shrewsbury (0743) 360111. Commercial Dept: 56316. Clubcall: 0898 121194.

Ground capacity: 15,000.

Record attendance: 18,917 v Walsall, Division 3, 26 April 1961.

Record receipts: £36,240 v Ipswich T, FA Cup 5th rd, 13 February 1982.

Pitch measurements: 116yd × 76yd.

President.

Vice-president: Dr J. Millard Bryson.

Chairman: K. R. Woodhouse.

Directors: F. C. G. Fry, R. Bailey (vice-chairman), M. J. Starkey, G. W. Nelson, W. H. Richards.

Manager: John Bond. *Commercial Manager:* M. Thomas. *Physio:* Malcolm Musgrove. *Coach:* Fred Davies. *Secretary:* M. J. Starkey.

Year Formed: 1886. Turned Professional: 1905 (approx). Ltd Co.: 1936.

Former Grounds: Old Shrewsbury Racecourse.

Club Nickname: 'Town' or 'Shrews'.

Record League Victory: 7-0 v Swindon T, Division 3 (S), 6 May 1955 – McBride; Bannister, Keech; Wallace, Maloney, Candlin; Price, O'Donnell (1), Weigh (4), Russell, McCue (2).

Record Cup Victory: 7-1 v Banbury Spencer, FA Cup, 1st rd, 4 November 1961 – Gibson; Walters, Skeech; Wallace, Pountney, Harley; Kenning (2), Pragg, Starkey (1), Rowley (2), McLaughlin (2).

Record Defeat: 1-8 v Norwich C, Division 3 (S), 1952–53 and v Coventry C, Division 3, 22 October 1963.

Most League Points (2 for a win): 62, Division 4, 1974–75.

Most League points (3 for a win): 65, Division 2, 1984–85.

Most League Goals: 101, Division 4, 1958–59.

Highest League Scorer in Season: Arthur Rowley, 38, Division 4, 1958–59.

Most League Goals in Total Aggregate: Arthur Rowley, 152, 1958–65 (thus completing his League record of 434 goals).

Most Capped Player: Jimmy McLaughlin, 5 (12), Northern Ireland and Bernard McNally, 5, Northern Ireland.

Most League Appearances: Colin Griffin, 406, 1975–89.

Record Transfer Fee Received: £385,000 from WBA for Bernard McNally, July 1989.

Record Transfer Fee Paid: £100,000 to Aldershot for John Dungworth, November 1979 and £100,000 to Southampton for Mark Blake, August 1990.

Football League Record: 1950 Elected to Division 3 (N); 1951–58 Division 3 (S); 1958–59 Division 4; 1959–74 Division 3; 1974–75 Division 4; 1975–79 Division 3; 1979–89 Division 2; 1989– Division 3.

Honours: Football League: Division 2 best season: 8th, 1983–84, 1984–85; Division 3 – Champions 1978–79; Division 4 – Runners-up 1974–5. *FA Cup:* best season: 6th rd, 1978–79, 1981–82. *Football League Cup:* Semi-final 1961. *Welsh Cup:* Winners 1891, 1938, 1977, 1979, 1984, 1985; Runners-up 1931, 1948, 1980.

Colours: Amber/blue trim shirts, blue trim, blue shorts, amber stockings, blue trim. **Change colours:** Red shirts, white shorts, red stockings.

SHREWSBURY TOWN 1991–92 LEAGUE RECORD

Match No.	Date	Venue	Opponents	Result	H/T Score	Lg. Pos.	Goalscorers	Attendance
1	Aug 18	H	Wigan Ath	W 1-0	0-0	—	Carr	3834
2	24	A	Bury	D 0-0	0-0	6		2373
3	31	H	Exeter C	W 6-1	3-1	3	Hopkins, Henry 2 (1 pen), Summerfield, Lynch, Lyne	2912
4	Sep 4	A	Stoke C	L 0-1	0-0	—		10,182
5	7	H	Brentford	W 1-0	0-0	4	Lyne	3193
6	14	A	Torquay U	W 2-1	1-1	3	Summerfield, Henry (pen)	2811
7	17	A	Bournemouth	L 0-1	0-0	—		4454
8	21	H	Swansea C	D 0-0	0-0	6		3427
9	28	A	Bradford C	L 0-3	0-0	7		5324
10	Oct 5	H	Birmingham C	D 1-1	0-1	8	Henry	7035
11	12	A	WBA	L 0-2	0-1	12		12,457
12	19	A	Darlington	D 3-3	2-0	13	Griffiths 2, Henry	2188
13	26	H	Reading	L 1-2	0-0	14	Griffiths	2398
14	Nov 2	H	Peterborough U	W 2-0	0-0	12	Griffiths, Cash	1866
15	5	A	Hull C	L 0-4	0-3	—		5025
16	23	H	Hartlepool U	L 1-4	0-3	18	Donaldson	2368
17	26	A	Stockport Co	W 4-1	2-0	—	Bennett 2, Summerfield, Lyne	3650
18	30	H	Bolton W	L 1-3	1-1	16	Smith	3937
19	Dec 14	A	Chester C	W 4-1	1-1	13	MacKenzie, Lightfoot (og), Griffiths 2	1016
20	21	H	Bury	D 1-1	1-1	11	Worsley	2573
21	26	A	Exeter C	L 1-1	0-0	14		3857
22	28	A	Wigan Ath	D 1-1	1-1	14	Summerfield	2276
23	Jan 1	H	Stoke C	W 1-0	1-0	11	Summerfield	8557
24	11	H	Preston NE	W 2-0	0-0	10	Griffiths, Hopkins	3154
25	18	A	Fulham	W 1-0	0-0	10	Lyne	3440
26	25	H	Huddersfield T	D 1-1	1-0	8	Lyne	3688
27	28	A	Leyton Orient	L 0-2	0-1	—		3197
28	Feb 1	H	Darlington	L 0-2	0-1	11		2675
29	8	A	Reading	L 1-2	0-1	11	Spink	3303
30	11	A	Bolton W	L 0-1	0-1	—		5276
31	15	H	Chester C	D 2-2	1-2	13	Summerfield, Taylor	2807
32	22	A	Preston NE	D 2-2	0-0	14	Harmon 2	3342
33	29	H	Leyton Orient	L 0-1	0-1	15		2873
34	Mar 3	H	Fulham	D 0-0	0-0	—		2137
35	7	A	Huddersfield T	L 1-2	1-1	15	Summerfield	4674
36	10	H	Hull C	L 2-3	0-2	—	Griffiths, Lyne	1956
37	14	A	Peterborough U	L 0-1	0-0	20		7377
38	20	H	Stockport Co	L 0-1	0-1	—		3186
39	28	A	Hartlepool U	L 2-4	1-2	21	Lynch, Bremner	2515
40	31	H	Torquay U	D 2-2	2-0	—	McKeown, Lyne	2172
41	Apr 4	A	Brentford	L 0-2	0-1	22		5561
42	11	A	Bournemouth	L 1-2	1-0	22	Lyne	2586
43	17	A	Swansea C	W 2-1	0-1	—	Taylor, Hopkins	3429
44	21	H	Bradford C	W 3-2	2-0	—	Bremner, Henry 2	2707
45	25	A	Birmingham C	L 0-1	0-1	22		19,868
46	May 2	H	WBA	L 1-3	0-3	22	Donaldson	7442

Final League Position: 22

GOALSCORERS

League (53): Griffiths 8, Lyne 8, Henry 7 (2 pens), Summerfield 7, Hopkins 3, Bennett 2, Bremner 2, Donaldson 2, Harmon 2, Lynch 2, Taylor 2, Carr 1, Cash 1, MacKenzie 1, McKeown 1, Smith 1, Spink 1, Worsley 1, own goals 1.
Rumbelows Cup (7): Summerfield 4, Lyne 2, Carr 1.
FA Cup (2): Lyne 1, Smith 1.

Hughes	Gorman	Lynch	Henry	Heathcote	Blake	Smith	Summerfield	Spink	Carr	Lyne	Griffiths	Hopkins	O'Toole	Cash	Taylor	Parkin	Worsley	Perks	Ryan	Donaldson	Bennett	Evans P	MacKenzie	Clark	Walsh	Paskin	Harmon	McKeown	Match No.
1	2	3	4	5	6	7*	8	9	10	11	12																		1
1	2	3	4	5	6	7	8	9*		11	12	10																	2
1	2	3	4	5†	6	7*	8	9		11	12	10	14																3
1	2	3	4	5	6	7	8	9*		11		10	12																4
1	2	3	4	5	6	7†	8	12		11	9*	14	10																5
1	2	5	4		6	7	8			11*	12	9			3	10													6
1	2	12	4		5	7	8			11	9*	14	10		3		6†												7
1	2		4		5		8	9		11		10			3		6	7											8
1	2	11	4†		5	7	8	9			12		14		3*		6	10											9
1	2	11	4		6	7	8	12		9					3*	10	5												10
1	11		4		6	7†	8	12		9			14		3*	10	5	2											11
1		3	4		6	7	8			9	11				10		5	2											12
		3	4		6	7*	8			9	11	5	12		10		2	1											13
14		3	4		6		8	12		9	11*	5					7	2	1	10†									14
2†		3*	4		6		8	12		9	11	5					7	1		10							14		15
	2	5	4		6	7*	8	12		9			14		3†			1		10	11								16
	2	3	4		6	11†	8	5		9					10			1		12	7*		14						17
	2	3	4		6	7†	8	5		9*			14		11		10	1		12									18
		3	4		6	7*	8	5		9	11						2	1		12			10						19
		3	4		6	12	8*	5		9	11						2	1					10	7					20
		3	4		6		8	5		9*	11	7						1		12			10	2					21
		3	4		6	7*	8	5		14	12	11†					2	1		9			10						22
		3†	4		6		8	5		11	9*	12					2	1		7			10	14					23
			4		6	14	8	5		11†	9	12					2	1		7*			10	3					24
			4		6		8	5		11	9	7					2	1					10	3					25
	12		4		6		8	5		11	9	7			10*		2	1						3					26
	12		4		6		8	5		11*	9	7†			10		2	1		14				3					27
		3	4		6		8	5		11	9*				10†		2	1		14			12		7				28
					6		8	5		11†	9	7	12		10		2	1		14				3	4*				29
					6		8	5		11	9	7*	4		10		2	1		12				3					30
		3	4*		6		8	5		11	12				10			1		7				2	9				31
1		3	4		6		8	5		7*	11				10					9†12				2			14		32
1		3	4		6†		8	5		7*	12	11	14							9				2			10		33
		3	4				8	5		11	12	10		6			7	1		9*				2					34
		3	4				8	5		11	12	9			10*		7	1						2				6	35
		3	4				8	5		11	9	10					7*	1						2			12	6	36
1		3	4†			7*	8	5		10	9		14		11									2			12	6	37
1		3†	4			7	8*	5		10			14		11					9				2			12	6	38
1		3	4				8			10			12				7						11	2*				6	39
1		3	4*				8	5		10	14		12				7†						11	2				6	40
1		3*	10				8	5		11							7			12				2				6	41
1		3			6		8	5		11	10		12				7							2				4*	42
1		3*			6		8	5		11	10		12				7						4	2					43
1					6	12	8	5		11	10		3				7*						4	2					44
1		3			6	12	8	5		11	10†		14				7						4	2*					45
		3			6		8	5		11							7†			9			10	4	2*				46
23	14	37	39	5	39	19	44	34	1	43	20	18	13	8	29	5	23	22	2	9	2	1	13	21	2	1	1	8	
	+1s	+3s	+1s				+3s		+6s		+1s	+7s	+9s	+14s			+2s			+10s	+1s			+2s		+4s			

Williams MS—Match No. 39(5) 41(4) 46(12); Bremner—Match No. 39(9) 40(9) 41(9) 42(9) 43(9) 44(9) 45(9); Barton—Match No. 46(1); Williams M—Match No. 46(14).

Rumbelows Cup	First Round	Plymouth Arg (h)	1-1
		(a)	2-2
	Second Round	Wolverhampton W (a)	1-6
		(h)	3-1
FA Cup	First Round	Hartlepool U (a)	2-3

SHREWSBURY TOWN

Player and Position	Ht	Wt	Date	Birth Place	Source	Clubs	League App	Gls
Goalkeepers								
Michael Barton§			23 9 73	Gainsborough	Trainee	Shrewsbury T	1	—
Scott Cooksey‡			24 6 72	Birmingham	Derby Co	Shrewsbury T	—	—
Ken Hughes*	6 0	11 08	9 1 66	Barmouth		Crystal Palace	—	—
						Shrewsbury T	74	—
Steve Perks*	6 0	12 02	19 4 63	Shrewsbury	Apprentice	Shrewsbury T	243	—
Defenders								
Mark Blake	6 0	12 04	19 12 67	Portsmouth	Apprentice	Southampton	18	2
						Colchester U (loan)	4	1
						Shrewsbury T (loan)	10	—
						Shrewsbury T	85	2
Howard Clark	5 11	11 01	19 9 68	Coventry	Apprentice	Coventry C	20	1
						Shrewsbury T	23	—
						Darlington (loan)	5	—
Sean Parrish*	5 9	10 00	14 3 72	Wrexham	Trainee	Shrewsbury T	3	—
Mark Taylor	5 10	11 00	22 2 66	Walsall	Local	Walsall	113	4
						Sheffield W	9	—
						Shrewsbury T (loan)	19	2
						Shrewsbury T	29	2
Mark Williams†	6 00	13 00	28 9 70	Cheshire	Newtown	Shrewsbury T	3	—
Graeme Worsley	5 10	11 02	4 1 69	Liverpool	Bootle	Shrewsbury T	77	2
Midfield								
Paul Evans§	5 06	10 08	1 9 74	Oswestry	Trainee	Shrewsbury T	2	—
Tony Henry*	5 11	12 11	26 11 57	Newcastle	Apprentice	Manchester C	79	6
						Bolton W	70	22
						Oldham Ath	190	25
						Stoke C	62	11
						Mazda	—	—
						Shrewsbury T	80	14
Robert Hopkins	5 7	10 05	25 10 61	Birmingham	Apprentice	Aston Villa	3	1
						Birmingham C	123	21
						Manchester C	7	1
						WBA	83	11
						Birmingham C	50	9
						Shrewsbury T	27	3
Tommy Lynch	6 0	12 06	10 10 64	Limerick	Limerick	Sunderland	4	—
						Shrewsbury T	101	4
Steve MacKenzie	5 11	12 05	23 11 61	Romford	Apprentice	Crystal Palace	—	—
						Manchester C	58	8
						WBA	148	23
						Charlton Ath	100	7
						Sheffield W	15	2
						Shrewsbury T	13	1
Patrick O'Toole	5 7	11 00	2 1 65	Dublin	Shelbourne	Leicester C	—	—
						Exeter C (loan)	6	—
						Shrewsbury T	38	—
Darren Ryan*			3 7 72	Oswestry	Trainee	Shrewsbury T	4	—
Mark A Smith	5 9	10 04	16 12 64	Bellshill	St Mirren BC	Queen's Park	82	7
						Celtic	6	1
						Dunfermline Ath	53	6
						Stoke C (loan)	2	—
						Nottingham F	—	—
						Mansfield T (loan)	7	—
						Shrewsbury T	22	1

SHREWSBURY TOWN

Foundation: Shrewsbury School having provided a number of the early England and Wales internationals it is not surprising that there was a Town club as early as 1876 which won the Birmingham Senior Cup in 1879. However, the present Shrewsbury Town club was formed in 1886 and won the Welsh FA Cup as early as 1891.

First Football League game: 19 August, 1950, Division 3 (N), v Scunthorpe U (a) D 0-0 – Eggleston; Fisher, Lewis; Wheatley, Depear, Robinson; Griffin, Hope, Jackson, Brown, Barker.

Did you know: When Arthur Rowley broke the British first-class goalscoring record with his 411th League goal at 8.14 pm on 26 September 1962 with a right-foot shot against Millwall, the game was held up as fans invaded the pitch to congratulate him. He had equalled the record at Millwall nine days earlier.

Managers (and Secretary-managers)
W. Adams 1905–12*, A. Weston 1912–34*, Jack Roscamp 1934–35, Sam Ramsey 1935–36, Ted Bousted 1936–40, Leslie Knighton 1945–49, Harry Chapman 1949–50, Sammy Crooks 1950–54, Walter Rowley 1955–57, Harry Potts 1957–58, Johnny Spuhler 1958, Arthur Rowley 1958–68, Harry Gregg 1968–72, Maurice Evans 1972–73, Alan Durban 1974–78, Richie Barker 1978, Graham Turner 1978–84, Chic Bates 1984–87, Ian McNeill 1987–90, Asa Hartford 1990–91, John Bond January 1991–.

Player and Position	Ht	Wt	Birth Date	Birth Place	Source	Clubs	League App	Gls
Kevin Summerfield	5 11	11 00	7 1 59	Walsall	Apprentice	WBA	9	4
						Birmingham C	5	1
						Walsall	54	17
						Cardiff C	10	1
						Plymouth Arg	139	26
						Exeter C (loan)	4	—
						Shrewsbury T	76	12
Forwards								
Kevin Bremner On loan from Dundee						Shrewsbury T	7	2
O'Neill Donaldson	6 00	11 04	24 11 69	Birmingham	Hinckley Ath	Shrewsbury T	19	2
Carl Griffiths	5 9	10 06	15 7 71	Oswestry	Trainee	Shrewsbury T	92	22
Darren Harmon	5 05	9 12	30 1 73	Northampton	Trainee	Notts Co	—	—
						Shrewsbury T	10	4
Neil Lyne	6 1	12 04	4 4 70	Leicester	Leicester U	Nottingham F	—	—
						Walsall (loan)	7	—
						Shrewsbury T (loan)	16	6
						Shrewsbury T	44	8
Dean Spink	5 11	13 08	22 1 67	Birmingham	Halesowen T	Aston Villa	—	—
						Scarborough (loan)	3	2
						Bury (loan)	6	1
						Shrewsbury T	96	12
Billy Weir‡	5 5	9 12	11 4 68	Baillieston	Bailieston J	Shrewsbury T	17	1
Mark Williams§			10 12 73	Bangor	Trainee	Shrewsbury T	1	—

Trainees
Atkinson, Neil C; Barton, Michael G; Brown, Romilly L; Davies, Ashley J; Evans, Jason S; Evans, Paul S; Forster, Nicholas J; Hanmer, Gareth C; Hodgin, Christopher J; Jenkins, Sam B; Pitman, Jason A; Seabury, Kevin; Steer, James A; Taylor, Steven D; Thelwell, Kevin D; Williams, Mark; Yates, Jason J.
**Non-Contract
Williams, Mark S.
Associated Schoolboys
Ayton, Paul K; Cadman, Robert J; Caudwell, Scott A; Connor, Leighton T; Edwards, John C. A; Finney, John D; Holgate, Christopher; Martin, Lee; Smith, Colin; Wheeler, Ryan; Woods, David; Woods, Simon.
**Non-Contract Players who are retained must be re-signed before they are eligible to play in League matches.

478

SOUTHAMPTON 1991–92 *Back row (left to right):* Jason Dodd, Andy Cook, Alexsey Cherednik, Jon Gittens, Sergei Gotsmanov.
Third row: Steve Roast, Nicky Banger, Francis Benali, Neil Maddison, Tommy Widdrington, Matthew Bound, David Hughes, Jeff Kenna, Paul Tisdale.
Second row: Alan McLoughlin, Matthew Le Tissier, Steve Davis, Ian Andrews, Paul Moody, Tim Flowers, Neil Ruddock, Richard Hall, Paul Rideout, Lee Powell.
Front row: Lew Chatterley (First Team Coach), Micky Adams, Russell Osman, Glenn Cockerill, Ian Branfoot (Manager), Kevin Moore, Barry Horne, Alan Shearer, Don Taylor (Physiotherapist).

FA Premier   **SOUTHAMPTON**

The Dell, Milton Road, Southampton SO9 4XX. Telephone Southampton (0703) 220505. Ticket enquiries: (0703) 228575.

Ground capacity: 21,900.

Record attendance: 31,044 v Manchester U, Division 1, 8 October 1969.

Record receipts: £156,493 v Norwich C, FA Cup 6th rd, 7 March 1992.

Pitch measurements: 110yd × 72yd.

Chairman: F. G. L. Askham FCA.

Vice-Chairman: K. St. J. Wiseman.

Directors: E. T. Bates, I. L. Gordon, B. H. D. Hunt, M. R. Richards FCA.

President: J. Corbett.

Manager: Ian Branfoot. Assistant Manager: John Mortimore. *Coach:* Lew Chatterley. *Physio:* Don Taylor. *Secretary:* Brian Truscott. *Commercial Manager:* Bob Russell.

Year Formed: 1885. Turned Professional: 1894. Ltd Co.: 1897.

Former Grounds: 1885, Antelope Ground; 1897, County Cricket Ground; 1898, The Dell.

Former Names: Southampton St Mary's until 1885.

Club Nickname: 'The Saints'.

Record League Victory: 9-3 v Wolverhampton W, Division 2, 18 September 1965 – Godfrey; Jones, Williams; Walker, Knapp, Huxford; Paine (2), O'Brien (1), Melia, Chivers (4), Sydenham (2).

Record Cup Victory: 7-1 v Ipswich T, FA Cup, 3rd rd, 7 January 1961 – Reynolds; Davies, Traynor; Conner, Page, Huxford; Paine (1), O'Brien (3 incl. 1p), Reeves, Mulgrew (2), Penk (1).

Record Defeat: 0-8 v Tottenham H, Division 2, 28 March 1936 and v Everton, Division 1, 20 November 1971.

Most League Points (2 for a win): 61, Division 3 (S), 1921–22 and Division 3, 1959–60.

Most League points (3 for a win): 77, Division 1, 1983–84.

Most League Goals: 112, Division 3 (S), 1957–58.

Highest League Scorer in Season: Derek Reeves, 39, Division 3, 1959–60.

Most League Goals in Total Aggregate: Mike Channon, 185, 1966–77, 1979–82.

Most Capped Player: Peter Shilton, 49 (125), England.

Most League Appearances: Terry Paine, 713, 1956–74.

Record Transfer Fee Received: £1,700,000 from Leeds U for Rodney and Ray Wallace, July 1991.

Record Transfer Fee Paid: £1,000,000 to Swindon T for Alan McLoughlin, December 1990.

Football League Record: 1920 Original Member of Division 3; 1921 Division 3 (S); 1922–53 Division 2; 1953–58 Division 3 (S); 1958–60 Division 3; 1960–66 Division 2; 1966–74 Division 1; 1974–78 Division 2; 1978–92 Division 1; 1992– FA Premier League.

Honours: Football League: Division 1 – Runners-up 1983–84; Division 2 – Runners-up 1965–66, 1977–78; Division 3 (S) – Champions 1921–22; Runners-up 1920–21; Division 3 – Champions 1959–60. *FA Cup:* Winners 1975–76; Runners-up 1900, 1902. *Football League Cup:* Runners-up 1978–79. **European Competitions:** *European Fairs Cup:* 1969–70. *UEFA Cup:* 1971–72, 1981–82, 1982–83, 1984–85. *European Cup-Winners' Cup:* 1976–77. *Zenith Data Systems Cup:–* Runners-up 1991–92.

Colours: Red and white striped shirts, black shorts, white stockings, red trim. **Change colours:** Blue shirts, white shorts, blue stockings, red/white trim.

SOUTHAMPTON 1991–92 LEAGUE RECORD

Match No.	Date		Venue	Opponents	Result		H/T Score	Lg. Pos.	Goalscorers	Attendance
1	Aug	17	H	Tottenham H	L	2-3	1-1	—	Shearer, Hall	18,581
2		20	A	Notts Co	L	0-1	0-1	—		9613
3		24	A	Sheffield U	W	2-0	1-0	13	Shearer, Le Tissier	18,029
4		28	H	Leeds U	L	0-4	0-1	—		15,847
5		31	H	Aston Villa	D	1-1	1-1	19	Shearer	16,161
6	Sep	4	A	Luton T	L	1-2	1-2	—	Le Tissier (pen)	8055
7		7	A	QPR	D	2-2	1-0	19	Shearer, Dowie	9237
8		14	H	Manchester U	L	0-1	0-0	21		19,264
9		18	H	Wimbledon	W	1-0	0-0	—	Cockerill	11,280
10		21	A	Sheffield W	L	0-2	0-1	19		27,291
11		28	H	Arsenal	L	0-4	0-1	21		18,050
12	Oct	5	A	Oldham Ath	D	1-1	1-0	20	Shearer	13,133
13		19	H	Norwich C	D	0-0	0-0	20		12,516
14		26	A	Nottingham F	W	3-1	1-0	20	Le Tissier 2 (1 pen), Shearer	20,026
15	Nov	2	H	Manchester C	L	0-3	0-1	20		13,933
16		16	A	Crystal Palace	L	0-1	0-0	20		15,861
17		23	H	Chelsea	W	1-0	1-0	19	Shearer	14,933
18		30	A	Coventry C	L	0-2	0-1	21		8585
19	Dec	7	H	Liverpool	D	1-1	0-0	20	Shearer	10,053
20		20	H	Notts Co	D	1-1	1-0	—	Dowie	11,054
21		26	A	Leeds U	D	3-3	0-2	21	Dowie 2, Shearer	29,053
22		28	A	Aston Villa	L	1-2	0-1	22	Shearer	23,094
23	Jan	1	H	Everton	L	1-2	0-1	22	Adams	16,546
24		11	H	Sheffield U	L	2-4	1-1	22	Le Tissier, Hall	13,689
25		18	A	Tottenham H	W	2-1	1-0	21	Adams, Dowie	23,191
26	Feb	1	A	Norwich C	L	1-2	0-0	21	Cockerill	10,660
27		12	A	Chelsea	D	1-1	0-0	—	Horne	7148
28		22	H	Coventry C	D	0-0	0-0	22		13,719
29		29	A	Liverpool	D	0-0	0-0	22		34,449
30	Mar	3	H	West Ham U	W	1-0	0-0	—	Dowie	14,548
31		11	H	Crystal Palace	W	1-0	0-0	—	Le Tissier	12,926
32		15	A	Manchester C	W	1-0	1-0	—	Dowie	24,265
33		21	H	Luton T	W	2-1	0-1	18	Shearer, Dowie	15,315
34	Apr	1	A	Everton	W	1-0	1-0	—	Cockerill	15,201
35		4	H	QPR	W	2-1	1-0	17	Dowie, Shearer (pen)	15,205
36		8	H	Nottingham F	L	1-2	0-0	—		14,905
37		14	A	West Ham U	W	1-0	0-0	—	Adams	18,298
38		16	A	Manchester U	L	0-1	0-0	—		43,972
39		18	H	Sheffield W	L	0-1	0-0	17		17,715
40		20	A	Wimbledon	W	1-0	1-0	17	Hall	4025
41		25	H	Oldham Ath	W	1-0	0-0	13	Shearer	15,857
42	May	2	A	Arsenal	L	1-5	0-0	16	Cockerill	37,702

Final League Position: 16

GOALSCORERS

League (39): Shearer 13 (1 pen), Dowie 9, Le Tissier 6 (2 pens), Cockerill 4, Adams 3, Hall 3, Horne 1.
Rumbelows Cup (6): Shearer 3, Cockerill 2, Le Tissier 1.
FA Cup (10): Hall 2, Horne 2, Shearer 2, Gray 1, Le Tissier 1, Ruddock 1, Wood 1.

Flowers	Dodd	Osman	Horne	Hall	Ruddock	Le Tissier	Cockerill	Shearer	Rideout	Adams	Moody	McLoughlin	Lee	Banger	Benali	Dowie	Hurlock	Gittens	Andrews	Gray	Wood	Moore	Kenna	Gilkes	Powell	Maddison	Widdrington	Bound	Match No.
1	2	3	4	5	6	7	8	9	10*	11	12																		1
1	2	3*	4	5	6	7	8	9	10	11		12																	2
1	2	3	4	5	6	7	8	9	10	11																			3
1	2	3	4	5	6	7*	8	9	10†	11	14		12																4
1	2		4	5	6	7†	8	9		3		10*	11	12	14														5
1	2		4	5	6	7	8	9		3			11*	12	10														6
1	2		4	5	6	7*	8	9		3			11	12	10														7
1	2	6†	4	5		7	8	9		3			12		10	11*	14												8
1	2	4*			6	7†	8	9		3			11	14	10	12	5												9
	2		4	14	6†	12	8	9				11		7	3*	10	5		1										10
1	2		4	5	6	7	8	9					11		10*	12				3									11
1	2		4	5	6		8	9				11		7		10				3									12
1	2				6	11	8	9		3				7*	12	4				10	5								13
1	2				6	11	8	9		3				7		4				10	5								14
1	2		10		6	11	8	9		3				7		4	12			5*									15
1	2		10		6	11	8	9		3				12		4*	7			5									16
1	2		10	5		7	8	9		3						4	6			11									17
1	2		10		6*	7	8	9		3				12		4	5			11									18
1	2		7		6		8	9		3*				12	14	10†	5			4	11								19
1	2				6	7*	8	9		3				12		10	4			11	5								20
1			7				8	9		3						10	4	5		11	2	6							21
1	2		4	14			8	9		3				12		10		5		11*	6	7†							22
1	14				6	7	8	9		3					12	10	4†	5*		11	2								23
1	2		4	5		7	8*	9		3				12		10	11			6									24
1			4	5		7*		9		3			12			11	10	8		6		2							25
1			4*	5	6	7	12	9		3						11†	10	8		14		2							26
1			4	5	6	7	8	9		3						11	10*	12				2							27
1	14		4	5	6	7							11†			3	12	8		10*		2							28
1	2		4		6	7	8	9		3						10	11						5						29
1	2		4		6	7	8	9		3						10	11						5						30
1	2		4		6	7		9		3						10	8						5	11					31
1	2		4		6		8	9		3		7*				10	11						5	12					32
1			4*		6		8	9		3						10	11						5		2	7	12		33
1			12		6		8			3						10	11						5		2	7	4*	9	34
1			12		6		8	9		3						10	11						5*		2	7†	14	4	35
1					6		8*	9	4	3						10	11						5		2	7	12		36
1			4		6	7	8	9		3						11	10*						5		2		12		37
1			4	14	6†	7		9		3						11	12						5		2		10	8*	38
1				5		7	8*	9		3†						11	10	4				6			2	14	12		39
1			4	5		7*	8	9		3						11	12	10				6			2				40
1			7					9		3					10*	11	4					6	5†		2	12	8	14	41
1			4	5		7	8	9		3						11	12	10				6†	14		2*				42
41	26	5	34	21	30	31	36	41	4	34	2	—	11	—	19	25	27	9	1	10	15	14	4	1	4	2	—		

+ 2s 5s 1s 1s 2s 2s 8s 4s 3s 5s 2s 2s 2s 1s 2s 3s 2s 1s 1s

Rumbelows Cup	Second Round	Scarborough (a)	3-1
		(h)	2-2
	Third Round	Sheffield W (a)	1-1
	Fourth Round	Nottingham F (a)	0-0
		(h)	0-1
FA Cup	Third Round	QPR (h)	2-0
	Fourth Round	Manchester U (h)	0-0
		(a)	2-2
		Southampton won 4-2 on penalties	
	Fifth Round	Bolton W (a)	2-2
		(h)	3-2
	Sixth Round	Norwich C (h)	0-0
		(a)	1-2

SOUTHAMPTON

Player and Position	Ht	Wt	Date	Birth Place	Source	Clubs	League App	Gls
Goalkeepers								
Ian Andrews	6 2	12 02	1 12 64	Nottingham	Apprentice	Leicester C	126	—
						Swindon T (loan)	1	—
						Celtic	5	—
						Leeds U (loan)	1	—
						Southampton	5	—
Tim Flowers	6 2	13 04	3 2 67	Kenilworth	Apprentice	Wolverhampton W	63	—
						Southampton (loan)	—	—
						Southampton	138	—
						Swindon T (loan)	2	—
						Swindon T (loan)	5	—
Defenders								
Mick Adams	5 7	10 10	8 11 61	Sheffield	Apprentice	Gillingham	92	5
						Coventry C	90	9
						Leeds U	73	2
						Southampton	87	3
Francis Benali	5 9	11 01	30 12 68	Southampton	Apprentice	Southampton	68	—
Matthew Bound	6 2	14 00	9 11 72	Trowbridge	Trainee	Southampton	1	—
Aleksey Cherednik	5 9	11 07	12 12 60	USSR	Dnepr	Southampton	23	—
Jason Dodd	5 10	11 10	2 11 70	Bath		Southampton	69	—
Jon Gittens	5 11	12 06	22 1 64	Moseley	Paget R	Southampton	18	—
						Swindon T	126	6
						Southampton	19	—
						Middlesbrough (loan)	12	—
Richard Hall	6 1	13 00	14 3 72	Ipswich	Trainee	Scunthorpe U	22	3
						Southampton	27	3
Jeff Kenna	5 11	11 09	27 8 70	Dublin	Trainee	Southampton	16	—
						Wigan Ath (loan)	—	—
Kevin Moore	5 11	12 02	29 4 58	Grimsby	Local	Grimsby T	400	27
						Oldham Ath	13	1
						Southampton	116	8
						Bristol R (loan)	7	—
Stephen Roast	5 6	9 04	19 9 72	London	Trainee	Southampton	—	—
Neil Ruddock	6 2	12 06	9 5 68	London	Apprentice	Millwall		
						Tottenham H	9	—
						Millwall	2	1
						Southampton	107	9
Steve Wood	6 0	11 09	2 2 63	Bracknell	Apprentice	Reading	219	9
						Millwall	110	—
						Southampton	15	—
Midfield								
Glenn Cockerill	6 0	12 04	26 8 59	Grimsby	Louth U	Lincoln C	71	10
						Swindon T	26	1
						Lincoln C	115	25
						Sheffield U	62	10
						Southampton	250	32
Stuart Gray	5 10	11 05	19 4 60	Withernsea	Local	Nottingham F	49	3
						Bolton W (loan)	10	—
						Barnsley	120	23
						Aston Villa	106	9
						Southampton	12	—
Barry Horne	5 10	11 06	18 5 62	St Asaph	Rhyl	Wrexham	136	17
						Portsmouth	70	7
						Southampton	112	6
David Hughes	5 9	10 10	30 12 72	St Albans	Trainee	Southampton	—	—
Terry Hurlock	5 9	13 02	22 9 58	Hackney	Leytonstone	Reading	29	18
						Millwall	104	8
						Rangers	—	—
						Southampton	29	—

SOUTHAMPTON

Foundation: Formed largely by players from the Deanery FC, which had been established by school teachers in 1880. Most of the founders were connected with the young men's association of St. Mary's Church. At the inaugural meeting held in November 1885 the club was named Southampton St. Mary's and the church's curate was elected president.

First Football League game: 28 August 1920, Division 3, v Gillingham (a) D 1-1 – Allen; Parker, Titmuss; Shelley, Campbell, Turner; Barratt, Dominy (1), Rawlings, Moore, Foxall.

Did you know: In season 1936–37 Southampton often fielded a forward line that included players from four different countries – J.L. Summers and Arthur Holt (England), Willie Boyd (Scotland), Jimmy Dunne (Ireland) and Fred Smallwood (Wales).

Managers (and Secretary-managers)
Cecil Knight 1894–95*, Charles Robson 1895–97, E. Arnfield 1897–1911* (continued as secretary), George Swift 1911–12, E. Arnfield 1912–19, Jimmy McIntyre 1919–24, Arthur Chadwick 1925–31, George Kay 1931–36, George Gross 1936–37, Tom Parker 1937–43, J. R. Sarjantson stepped down from the board to act as secretary-manager 1943–47 with the next two listed being team managers during this period), Arthur Dominy 1943–46, Bill Dodgin Snr 1946–49, Sid Cann 1949–51, George Roughton 1952–55, Ted Bates 1955–73, Lawrie McMenemy 1973–85, Chris Nicholl 1985–91, Ian Branfoot June 1991–.

Player and Position	Ht	Wt	Birth Date	Birth Place	Source	Clubs	League App	Gls
Dave Lee	5 8	10 02	5 11 67	Manchester	Schools	Bury	208	35
						Southampton	19	—
Neil Maddison	5 9	11 08	2 10 69	Darlington	Trainee	Southampton	17	2
Paul Tisdale	5 8	10 12	14 1 73	Malta	Trainee	Southampton	—	—
Tommy Widdrington	5 8	11 01	21 11 71	Newcastle	Trainee	Southampton	3	—
						Wigan Ath (loan)	6	—
Forwards								
Nicky Banger	5 8	10 06	25 2 71	Southampton	Trainee	Southampton	10	—
Iain Dowie	6 0	13 03	9 1 65	Hatfield	Hendon	Luton T	66	16
						Fulham (loan)	5	1
						West Ham U	12	4
						Southampton	30	9
Sergei Gotsmanov (To Halle Sept 1991)	5 8	11 01	17 3 59	USSR	Dynamo Minsk	Brighton & HA	16	4
						Southampton	8	—
Danny Hoekman‡			21 9 64	Nijmegen	Den Haag	Manchester C	1	—
						Southampton	—	—
Matthew Le Tissier	6 0	11 06	14 10 68	Guernsey	Vale Recreation	Southampton	173	60
Callum MacDonald	5 08	10 10	21 9 73	Stirling	Trainee	Southampton	—	—
Paul Moody	6 3	13 12	13 6 67	Waterlooville	Waterlooville	Southampton	4	—
Lee Powell	5 5	8 10	2 6 73	Newport	Trainee	Southampton	4	—
Alan Shearer	5 11	11 03	13 8 70	Newcastle	Trainee	Southampton	118	23

Trainees
Bartlett, Neal; Cleeve, Anthony G; Frost, Neil; McKilligan, Neil; Meara, Russell; Murphy, Kevin; Robinson, Matthew R; Savage, Ian; Selby, Neil S; Shiers, Benjamin D; Thomas, Martin R; Thorne, Kevin M; Whitman, Nathan; Winstanley, James.

**Non-Contract
Pickering, Christopher.

Associated Schoolboys
Basham, Steven; Carbery, Thomas; Care, Simon J; Carr, Neil; Cole, James; Conaty, Steven; Coxon, Jordan D; Everest, Anthony D; Flaharen, Darryl J; Griffiths, Paul; Gulliver, Ross; Harris, Stephen P; Hayward, Daniel; Jansen, Nicholas J; Joseph, Urias; Liney, Andrew; Miles, Darren L; Phillips, Sam; Pickersgill, Gavin; Spedding, Duncan; Totten, Alexander; Warburton, Nicholas M; Waters, Jamie S; Williams, Andrew P; Woodfield, Jamie P.

Associated Schoolboys who have accepted the club's offer of a Traineeship/Contract
Allen, Peter; Doherty, Kevin T; Harper, Paul; Hopper, Neil; McNally, Aron A; Rowe, Richard M.
**Non-Contract Players who are retained must be re-signed before they are eligible to play in League matches.

SOUTHEND UNITED 1991–92 *Back row (left to right):* Dean Austin, Ian Benjamin, Brett Angell, Andy Sussex, Spencer Prior, Pat Scully, Andy Edwards, Paul Smith.
Centre row: David Webb (Manager), Kevin Lock (Team Coach), Steve Tilson, John Cornwell, David Martin, Paul Sansome, Tony Parks, Christian Hyslop, Steven Heffer, Danny Greaves (Youth Team Coach), Alan Raw (Physiotherapist).
Front row: Adam Locke, Spencer Barham, Mark Hall, Andy Ansah, Jason Cook, Chris Powell, Peter Butler, Kevin O'Callaghan.

Division 1 SOUTHEND UNITED

Roots Hall Football Ground, Victoria Avenue, Southend-on-Sea SS2 6NQ. Telephone Southend (0702) 340707. Commercial Dept: (0702) 332113. Soccerline: 0839 664444. Ticket office: 0702 435602. Shop: 0702 435067. Infoline: 0839 664443.

Ground capacity: 14,428.

Record attendance: 31,090 v Liverpool FA Cup 3rd rd, 10 January 1979.

Record receipts: £36,599 v Liverpool, FA Cup 3rd rd, 10 January 1979.

Pitch measurements: 110yd × 74yd.

President: N. J. Woodcock.

Chairman: V. T. Jobson. *Vice-chairman:* J. W. Adams. *Secretary:* J. W. Adams.

Directors: J. Bridge, J. N. Foster, D. M. Markscheffel, R. J. Osborne (Company Secretary), F. Van Wezel.

Associate Directors: R. F. Moore OBE, W. E. Parsons.

Manager: Colin Murphy. *Coaches:* Kevin Lock, Danny Greaves. *Commercial manager/director:* J. W. Adams. *Treatment of Injury Officer:* Alan Raw. *Stadium Manager:* R. Davy Jnr.

Year Formed: 1906. Turned Professional: 1906. Ltd Co.: 1919.

Former Grounds: 1906, Roots Hall, Prittlewell; 1920, Kursaal; 1934, Southend Stadium; 1955, Roots Hall Football Ground.

Club Nickname: 'The Blues' or 'The Shrimpers'.

Record League Victory: 9-2 v Newport Co, Division 3 (S), 5 September 1936 – McKenzie; Nelson, Everest (1); Deacon, Turner, Carr; Bolan, Lane (1), Goddard (4), Dickinson (2), Oswald (1).

Record Cup Victory: 10-1 v Golders Green, FA Cup, 1st rd, 24 November 1934 – Moore; Morfitt, Kelly; Mackay, Joe Wilson, Carr (1); Lane (1), Johnson (5), Cheesmuir (2), Deacon (1), Oswald. 10-1 v Brentwood, FA Cup, 2nd rd, 7 December 1968 – Roberts; Bentley, Birks; McMillan (1) Beesley, Kurila; Clayton, Chisnall, Moore (4), Best (5), Hamilton. 10-1 v Aldershot, Leyland Daf Cup, Pr rd, 6 November 1990 – Sansome; Austin, Powell, Cornwell, Prior (1), Tilson (3), Cawley, Butler, Ansah (1), Benjamin (1), Angell (1).

Record Defeat: 1-11, v Northampton T, Southern League, 30 December 1909.

Most League Points (2 for a win): 67, Division 4, 1980–81.

Most League points (3 for a win): 85, Division 3, 1990–91.

Most League Goals: 92, Division 3 (S), 1950–51.

Highest League Scorer in Season: Jim Shankly, 31, 1928–29 and Sammy McCrory, 1957–58, both in Division 3 (S).

Most League Goals in Total Aggregate: Roy Hollis, 122, 1953–60.

Most Capped Player: George Mackenzie, 9, Eire.

Most League Appearances: Sandy Anderson, 451, 1950–63.

Record Transfer Fee Received: £150,000 from Crystal Palace for Glenn Pennyfather, November 1987, £150,000 from Wolverhampton W for Shane Westley, June 1989 and £150,000 from Tottenham H for Justin Edinburgh, July 1990.

Record Transfer Fee Paid: £175,000 to Brentford for Keith Jones, October 1991.

Football League Record: 1920 Original Member of Division 3; 1921–58 Division 3 (S); 1958–66 Division 3; 1966–72 Division 4; 1972–76 Division 3; 1976–78 Division 4; 1978–80 Division 3; 1980–81 Division 4; 1981–84 Division 3; 1984–87 Division 4; 1987–89 Division 3; 1989–90 Division 4; 1990–91 Division 3; 1991–92 Division 2; 1992– Division 1.

Honours: Football League: Best season: 12th, Division 2, 1991–92. Division 3 Runners-up – 1990–91; Division 4 – Champions 1980–81; Runners-up 1971–72, 1977–78. *FA Cup:* best season: old 3rd rd, 1920–21, 5th rd, 1925–26, 1951–52, 1975–76. *Football League Cup:* never past 3rd rd.

Colours: Blue shirts, yellow trim, yellow shorts, blue trim, blue stockings. **Change colours:** All yellow.

486

SOUTHEND UNITED 1991–92 LEAGUE RECORD

Match No.	Date		Venue	Opponents		Result	H/T Score	Lg. Pos.	Goalscorers	Attendance
1	Aug	17	H	Bristol C	D	1-1	1-0	—	Benjamin	6720
2		24	A	Derby Co	W	2-1	2-0	9	Sussex, Angell	12,284
3		31	H	Leicester C	L	1-2	0-0	15	Martin	6944
4	Sep	3	A	Cambridge U	W	1-0	0-0	—	Benjamin	6412
5		7	A	Ipswich T	L	0-1	0-0	15		12,732
6		14	H	Bristol R	W	2-0	0-0	10	Ansah, Angell	4670
7		17	H	Plymouth Arg	W	2-1	1-0	—	Angell, Benjamin	4585
8		21	A	Port Vale	D	0-0	0-0	7		5988
9		28	H	Wolverhampton W	L	0-2	0-0	10		8368
10	Oct	4	A	Tranmere R	D	1-1	1-0	—	Angell	7358
11		12	H	Millwall	L	2-3	1-2	14	Sussex, Tilson	7266
12		19	A	Watford	W	2-1	1-0	11	Sussex, Dublin (og)	6862
13		26	H	Charlton Ath	D	1-1	1-0	11	Austin (pen)	7320
14		30	H	Oxford U	L	2-3	1-3	—	Angell, Tilson	4873
15	Nov	2	A	Middlesbrough	D	1-1	1-0	10	Angell	9664
16		5	H	Blackburn R	W	3-0	1-0	—	Angell 2, Benjamin	4860
17		9	H	Swindon T	W	3-2	1-0	10	Angell 2, Tilson	7709
18		20	A	Newcastle U	L	2-3	1-3	—	Angell, Tilson	14,740
19		23	H	Barnsley	W	2-1	0-0	8	Angell, Tilson	5060
20		30	A	Sunderland	W	2-1	1-1	8	Angell, Scully	13,575
21	Dec	7	H	Brighton & HA	W	2-1	1-0	5	Ansah, Tilson	6303
22		14	A	Portsmouth	D	1-1	1-1	5	Scully	9006
23		22	H	Cambridge U	D	1-1	1-1	—	Benjamin	9353
24		26	A	Oxford U	W	1-0	0-0	4	Angell	5601
25		28	A	Leicester C	L	0-2	0-0	5		15,635
26	Jan	1	H	Newcastle U	W	4-0	2-0	3	Angell 2, Jones, Ansah	9458
27		11	H	Derby Co	W	1-0	1-0	2	Ansah	8295
28		18	A	Bristol C	D	2-2	1-0	2	Angell, Ansah	9883
29	Feb	1	H	Watford	W	1-0	0-0	2	Benjamin	7581
30		8	A	Charlton Ath	L	0-2	0-0	3		9724
31		15	A	Barnsley	L	0-1	0-0	5		5328
32		18	A	Grimsby T	L	2-3	0-1	—	Austin, Ansah	5337
33		22	H	Sunderland	W	2-0	2-0	3	Angell, Jones	7473
34		29	A	Brighton & HA	L	2-3	1-1	4	Benjamin, Angell	8271
35	Mar	10	A	Blackburn R	D	2-2	2-1	—	Ansah, Angell	14,404
36		14	H	Middlesbrough	L	0-1	0-0	8		7272
37		17	H	Portsmouth	L	2-3	2-2	—	Tilson, Jones	6832
38		21	A	Swindon T	L	1-3	1-1	10	Ansah	8628
39		28	H	Grimsby T	W	3-1	2-1	9	Angell, Scully, Ansah	4591
40	Apr	1	A	Bristol R	L	1-4	1-0	—	Jones	5375
41		4	H	Ipswich T	L	1-2	0-0	10	Prior	10,003
42		11	A	Plymouth Arg	W	2-0	1-0	10	Marker (og), Benjamin	7060
43		15	H	Port Vale	D	0-0	0-0	—		4462
44		20	A	Wolverhampton W	L	1-3	1-1	11	Benjamin	10,953
45		25	H	Tranmere R	D	1-1	1-0	11	Jones	4761
46	May	2	A	Millwall	L	0-2	0-0	12		7574

Final League Position: 12

GOALSCORERS

League (63): Angell 21, Ansah 9, Benjamin 9, Tilson 7, Jones 5, Scully 3, Sussex 3, Austin 2 (1 pen), Martin 1, Prior 1, own goals 2.
Rumbelows Cup (1): Angell 1.
FA Cup (0).

Sansome	Austin	Powell	Martin	Edwards	Prior	Ansah	Sussex	O'Callaghan	Benjamin	Angell	Tilson	Scully	Locke	Cornwell	Hall	Jones	Hyslop	Butler	Royce	Match No.
1	2	3	4	5	6	7	8	9*	10	11	12									1
1	2	3	4	5	6	7	8		10	11	9									2
1	2	3	4	12	6	7			10	11	9	5*		8						3
1	2	3	4		6	7			10	11	9	5		8						4
1	2	3	4†		6	7	12	14	10	11	9*	5		8						5
1	2	3			6	7	4		10	11	9	5		8						6
1	2	3			6	7	4		10	11	9	5		8						7
1	2	3			6	7*	4		10	11	9	5		8	12					8
1	2	3			6		4		10	11	9	5	12	8	7*					9
1	2	3			6		4		10	11	9	5	7	8						10
1	2	3			6	7	4		10	11	9	5		8						11
1	2	3			6	7	11*		10	12	9	5		8		4				12
1	2	3			6	7			10	11*	9	5	12	8		4				13
1	2	3			6	7			10	11*	9	5		8	12	4				14
1	2	3			6	7			10	11	9	5		8		4				15
1	2	3			6	7*			10	11	9	5	12	8		4				16
1	2	3		6		7			10	11	9	5		8		4				17
1	2	3			6	7		12	10*	11	9	5		8		4				18
1	2				6	7			10	11	9	5		8		4	3			19
1	2	3			6	7			10	11	9	5		8		4				20
1	2	3			6	7			10	11	9	5		8		4				21
1	2	3			6	7			10	11	9	5		8		4				22
1	2	3			6	7			10	11	9	5		8		4				23
1	2	3			6	7			10	11	9	5		8		4				24
1	2	3			6	7			10†	11	9*	5	12	8		4		14		25
1	2	3			6	7			10	11	9	5		8		4*		12		26
1	2	3			6	7			10	11	9	5		8		4*		12		27
1	2	3			6	7			10	11	9	5		8		4				28
1	2	3	14		6†	7*			10	11	9	5		8	12	4				29
1	2	3		6		7	12	14	10*		9†	5		8	11	4				30
1	2	3		6		7		14	10		9†	5	12	8	11*	4				31
1	2	3		6		7	11		10		9	5		8		4				32
1	2	3			6	7*			10	11	9	5		8		4		12		33
1	2	3			6	7			10	11	9	5		8		4				34
1	2	3			6	7			10	11	9	5		8		4				35
1	2	3			6				10	11	9	5	7	8		4				36
1	2				6				10	11	9	5	7*	8		4	3	12		37
1	2	3			6	7			10	11	9	5		8		4				38
	2	3			6	7			10	11	9	5		8		4			1	39
1	2	3			6	7			10	11	9	5		8		4				40
1	2	3			6	7		12	10*	11	9	5		8		4				41
1	2	3			6	7			10	11	9	5		8		4				42
1	2	3			6	7			10	11	9	5		8		4				43
1	2	3			6			14	9	10	11†	12	5	7*	8	4				44
1	2	3			6	7			10	11	9	5		8		4				45
1		3	2		6	7		10	12	11	9*	5		8		4				46
45	45	44	5 +2s	7	42	40	12 +3s	2 +6s	45	42	44 +1s	44 +2s	5	43 +5s	1	33 +2s	2 +1s	4 +5s	1	

Rumbelows Cup   First Round   Watford (a)   0-2
                                                             (h)   1-1

FA Cup   Third Round   Everton (a)   0-1

SOUTHEND UNITED

Player and Position	Ht	Wt	Date	Birth Place	Source	Clubs	League App	Gls
Goalkeepers								
John Cheesewright‡	6 0	11 05	12 1 73	Hornchurch	Tottenham H	Southend U	—	—
Simon Royce	6 00	12 00	9 9 71	London	Heybridge S	Southend U	1	—
Paul Sansome	6 0	12 00	6 10 61	N Addington	Apprentice	Crystal Palace	—	—
						Millwall	156	—
						Southend U	187	—
Defenders								
Dean Austin	6 0	12 04	26 4 70	Hemel Hempstead	St Albans	Southend U	96	2
Spencer Barham*	5 9	10 05	14 8 72	Essex	Trainee	Charlton Ath	—	—
						Southend U	—	—
Christian Hyslop	5 11	11 10	14 6 72	Watford	Trainee	Southend U	13	—
Chris Powell	5 8	11 00	8 9 69	Lambeth	Trainee	Crystal Palace	3	—
						Aldershot (loan)	11	—
						Southend U	89	1
Spencer Prior	6 3	12 10	22 4 71	Rochford	Trainee	Southend U	90	3
Pat Scully	6 1	12 07	23 6 70	Dublin	Trainee	Arsenal	—	—
						Preston NE (loan)	13	1
						Northampton T (loan)	15	—
						Southend U	65	3
Midfield								
Peter Butler	5 9	11 01	27 8 66	Halifax	Apprentice	Huddersfield T	5	—
						Cambridge U (loan)	14	1
						Bury	11	—
						Cambridge U	55	9
						Southend U	142	9
						Huddersfield T (loan)	7	—
John Cornwell	6 0	12 00	13 10 64	Bethnal Green	Apprentice	Orient	202	35
						Newcastle U	33	1
						Swindon T	25	—
						Southend U	62	2
Andy Edwards	6 2	12 06	17 9 71	Epping	Trainee	Southend U	20	1
Keith Jones	5 9	10 11	14 10 65	Dulwich	Apprentice	Chelsea	52	7
						Brentford	169	13
						Southend U	34	5
Adam Locke	5 10	11 10	20 8 70	Croydon	Trainee	Crystal Palace	—	—
						Southend U	38	4
David Martin	6 1	11 08	25 4 63	East Ham	Apprentice	Millwall	140	6
						Wimbledon	35	3
						Southend U	5	1
Paul Smith	5 11	12 00	18 9 71	London	Trainee	Southend U	12	1
Steve Tilson	5 11	11 10	27 7 66	Essex	Burnham	Southend U	116	17
Forwards								
Brett Angell	6 1	12 03	20 8 68	Marlborough		Portsmouth	—	—
						Cheltenham T	—	—
						Derby Co	—	—
						Stockport Co	70	28
						Southend U	85	36
Andy Ansah	5 10	11 01	19 3 69	Lewisham		Crystal Palace	—	—
						Brentford	8	2
						Southend U	87	19

SOUTHEND UNITED

Foundation: The leading club in Southend around the turn of the century was Southend Athletic, but they were an amateur concern. Southend United was a more ambitious professional club when they were founded in 1906, employing Bob Jack as secretary-manager and immediately joining the Second Division of the Southern League.

First Football League game: 28 August 1920, Division 3, v Brighton & HA (a) W 2-0 – Capper; Reid, Newton; Wileman, Henderson, Martin; Nicholls, Nuttall, Fairclough (2), Myers, Dorsett.

Did you know: Jimmy Shankly scored a club record seven League hat-tricks for Southend between 1928 and 1931, including five goals in a 6-0 win over Merthyr Town on 1 March 1930. He was a member of the famous footballing Shankly family which included Bill the former Liverpool manager.

Managers (and Secretary-managers)
Bob Jack 1906–10, George Molyneux 1910–11, O. M. Howard 1911–12, Joe Bradshaw 1912–19, Ned Liddell 1919–20, Tom Mather 1920–21, Ted Birnie 1921–34, David Jack 1934–40, Harry Warren 1946–56, Eddie Perry 1956–60, Frank Broome 1960, Ted Fenton 1961–65, Alvan Williams 1965–67, Ernie Shepherd 1967–69, Geoff Hudson 1969–70, Arthur Rowley 1970–76, Dave Smith 1976–83, Peter Morris 1983–84, Bobby Moore 1984–86, Dave Webb 1986–87, Dick Bate 1987, Paul Clark 1987–88, Dave Webb (GM) December 1988–92, Colin Murphy May 1992–.

Player and Position	Ht	Wt	Birth Date	Birth Place	Source	Clubs	League App	Gls
Ian Benjamin	5 11	12 00	11 12 61	Nottingham	Apprentice	Sheffield U	5	3
						WBA	2	—
						Notts Co	—	—
						Peterborough U	80	14
						Northampton T	150	59
						Cambridge U	25	2
						Chester C	22	2
						Exeter C	32	4
						Southend U	106	26
Francisco Cagigao	5 09	12 00	10 11 69	London	Arsenal	Barcelona	—	—
						Southend U	—	—
Mark Hall	5 7	11 07	13 1 73	London	Trainee	Tottenham H	—	—
						Southend U	6	—
Steven Heffer			11 1 73	Southend	West Ham U	Southend U	—	—
Kevin O'Callaghan	5 8	11 04	19 10 61	London	Apprentice	Millwall	20	3
						Ipswich T	115	3
						Portsmouth	87	16
						Millwall	76	14
						Southend U	8	—
Andy Sussex	6 0	11 06	23 11 64	Enfield	Apprentice	Leyton Orient	144	17
						Crewe Alex	102	24
						Southend U	15	3
						Exeter C (loan)	—	—

Trainees
Ashenden, Scott; Baxter, Scott A; Brown, Stephen R; Capleton, Melvin D. R; Davidson, Craig L; Gonzaque, Michael G; Grayburn, Gavin; Hoddle, Mark D; Holman, Matthias T; Ives, Spencer B; Jones, Antony; Jones, Michael; Jones, Shane N; Rowbury, Neil P; Sains, Daniel B; Southon, Jamie P; Thake, Ben.

**Non-Contract
Grayburn, Marlon S; Jones, James H.

**Non-Contract Players who are retained must be re-signed before they are eligible to play in League matches.

490

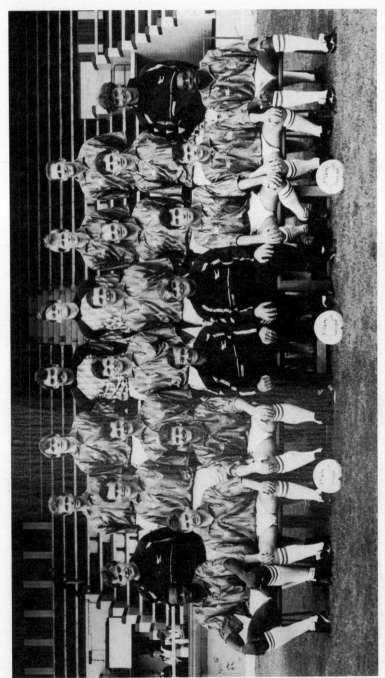

STOCKPORT COUNTY 1991–92 *Back row (left to right):* Bill Williams, Malcolm Brown, David Redfern, Phil Church, Paul Wheeler, Neil Matthews.
Centre row: Dave Jones (Youth Team Manager), Peter Ward, Chris Beaumont, James Gannon, Alan Finley, Andy Kilner, Tony Barras, Rodger Wylde (Physiotherapist).
Front row: Kevin Francis, Darren Knowles, Andy Thorpe, Danny Bergara (Manager), John Sainty (Assistant Manager), David Frain, Lee Todd, Paul Williams.

Division 2   **STOCKPORT COUNTY**

Edgeley Park, Hardcastle Road, Stockport, Cheshire SK3 9DD. Telephone 061-480 8888. Information line: 0898 121930. Lottery office: 061 480 1247. Clubcall: 0898 121638. Promotions Office: 061-480 8117. Fax No: 061 480 0230.

Ground capacity: 8520.

Record attendance: 27,833 v Liverpool, FA Cup 5th rd, 11 February 1950.

Record receipts: £41,560 v Burnley, Autoglass Trophy, 15 April 1992.

Pitch measurements: 110yd × 71yd.

Hon Vice-presidents: Mike Yarwood OBE, Freddie Pye, Andrew Barlow, Peter Snape MP.

Chairman: B. Elwood. *Vice-chairman:* G. White.

Directors: M. Baker, B. Taylor, M. H. Rains, R. McCadden, V. Snell.

Chief Executive: Dave Coxon.

Secretary: John Simpson.

Manager: Danny Bergara. *Assistant. Manager:* John Sainty. *Physio:* Rodger Wylde. *Assistant Secretary:* Andrea Welborn. *Commercial manager:* John Rutter. *General Manager. Programme Editor:* Steve Bellis.

Year Formed: 1883. Turned Professional: 1891. Ltd Co.: 1908.

Former Grounds: 1883 Heaton Norris Recreation Ground; 1884 Heaton Norris Wanderers Cricket Ground; 1885 Chorlton's Farm, Chorlton's Lane; 1886 Heaton Norris Cricket Ground; 1887 Wilkes' Field, Belmont Street; 1889 Nursery Inn, Green Lane; 1902 Edgeley Park.

Former Names: Heaton Norris Rovers, 1883–88; Heaton Norris, 1888–90.

Club Nicknames: 'County' or 'Hatters'.

Record League Victory: 13-0 v Halifax T, Division 3 (N), 6 January 1934 – McGann; Vincent (1p), Jenkinson; Robinson, Stevens, Len Jones; Foulkes (1), Hill (3), Lythgoe (2), Stevenson (2), Downes (4).

Record Cup Victory: 6-2 v West Auckland T (away), FA Cup, 1st rd, 14 November 1959 – Lea; Betts (1), Webb; Murray, Hodder, Porteous; Wilson (1), Holland, Guy (2), Ritchie (1), Davock (1).

Record Defeat: 1-8 v Chesterfield, Division 2, 19 April 1902.

Most League Points (2 for a win): 64, Division 4, 1966–67.

Most League points (3 for a win): 82, Division 4, 1990–91.

Most League Goals: 115, Division 3 (N), 1933–34.

Highest League Scorer in Season: Alf Lythgoe, 46, Division 3 (N), 1933–34.

Most League Goals in Total Aggregate: Jack Connor, 132, 1951–56.

Most Capped Player: Harry Hardy, 1, England.

Most League Appearances: Andy Thorpe, 489, 1978–86, 1988–92.

Record Transfer Fee Received: £80,000 from Manchester C for Stuart Lee, September 1979.

Record Transfer Fee Paid: £50,000 to Rochdale for David Frain, July 1989 and £50,000 to Hull C for Keith Edwards, September 1989.

Football League Record: 1900 Elected to Division 2; 1904 Failed re-election; 1905–21 Division 2; 1921–22 Division 3 (N); 1922–26 Division 2; 1926–37 Division 3 (N); 1937–38 Division 2; 1938–58 Division 3 (N); 1958–59 Division 3; 1959–67 Division 4; 1967–70 Division 3; 1970–91 Division 4; 1991–92 Division 3; 1992– Division 2.

Honours: Football League: Division 2 best season: 10th, 1905–06; Division 3 (N) – Champions 1921–22, 1936–37; Runners-up 1928–29, 1929-30; Division 4 – Champions 1966–67; Runners-up 1990–91. *FA Cup:* best season: 5th rd, 1935, 1950. *Football League Cup:* best season: 4th rd, 1972–73. *Autoglass Trophy:* Runners-up 1991–92.

Colours: Blue with red and white flecked shirts, royal blue shorts, white stockings. **Change colours:** All red.

STOCKPORT COUNTY 1991–92 LEAGUE RECORD

Match No.	Date		Venue	Opponents	Result		H/T Score	Lg. Pos.	Goalscorers	Atten- dance
1	Aug	17	H	Swansea C	W	5-0	2-0	—	Kilner 2 (2 pen), Williams B, Francis, Frain	4241
2		24	A	Leyton Orient	D	3-3	2-2	5	Williams B, Beaumont, Barras	3650
3		30	H	Preston NE	W	2-0	2-0	—	Barras, Gannon	5405
4	Sep	3	A	Wigan Ath	W	3-1	0-1	—	Williams P, Wheeler, Francis	3567
5		6	H	Torquay U	W	2-1	1-0	—	Wheeler, Gannon	5618
6		14	A	WBA	L	0-1	0-0	2		11,845
7		17	A	Exeter C	L	1-2	1-2	—	Francis	3033
8		21	H	Bury	W	2-0	0-0	3	Francis, Gannon	5083
9		28	A	Stoke C	D	2-2	0-2	4	Lillis, Francis	12,954
10	Oct	5	H	Bradford C	W	4-1	2-1	3	Paskin, Francis, Kilner, Mitchell (og)	5825
11		12	A	Birmingham C	L	0-3	0-2	5		12,634
12		18	H	Chester C	L	0-4	0-1	—		4838
13		25	A	Huddersfield T	W	1-0	0-0	—	Gannon	9229
14	Nov	1	A	Bournemouth	L	0-1	0-0	—		4649
15		5	H	Bolton W	D	2-2	1-2	—	Frain (pen), Matthews	4860
16		23	A	Fulham	W	2-1	0-0	6	Francis, Beaumont	3680
17		26	A	Shrewsbury T	L	1-4	0-2	—	Lillis	3650
18		30	A	Reading	D	1-1	1-1	6	Wheeler	3511
19	Dec	14	H	Peterborough U	W	3-0	1-0	6	Francis, Frain, Gannon (pen)	2768
20		20	H	Leyton Orient	W	1-0	0-0	—	Francis	2745
21		26	A	Preston NE	L	2-3	1-2	6	Flynn (og), Gannon	6782
22		28	A	Swansea C	L	1-2	1-1	6	Preece	4353
23	Jan	1	H	Wigan Ath	D	3-3	2-2	6	Preece, Francis, Gannon (pen)	4149
24		4	H	Brentford	W	2-1	0-1	6	Gannon, Francis	4421
25		11	A	Hull C	W	2-0	0-0	5	Preece, Francis	3982
26		18	A	Darlington	W	2-0	0-0	4	Ward, Preece	4186
27	Feb	7	H	Huddersfield T	D	0-0	0-0	—		7519
28		11	H	Reading	W	1-0	0-0	—	Finley	3720
29		15	A	Peterborough U	L	2-3	1-1	6	Barras (pen), Preece	5301
30		18	A	Hartlepool U	W	1-0	0-0	—	Francis	2473
31		22	H	Hull C	D	1-1	0-0	4	Wheeler	4490
32		29	A	Brentford	L	1-2	1-2	6	Preece	7484
33	Mar	3	A	Darlington	W	3-1	1-1	—	Preece 3	2384
34		6	H	Hartlepool U	L	0-1	0-0	—		4473
35		10	A	Bolton W	D	0-0	0-0	—		7635
36		13	H	Bournemouth	W	5-0	3-0	—	Gannon 2 (1 pen), Preece, Francis, Barras	3576
37		20	A	Shrewsbury T	W	1-0	1-0	—	Wheeler	3186
38		24	A	Chester C	L	2-3	0-1	—	Gannon, Preece	3747
39		27	H	Fulham	W	2-0	1-0	—	Gannon, Thomas (og)	4654
40		31	H	WBA	W	3-0	1-0	—	Barras, Frain, Preece	6090
41	Apr	4	A	Torquay U	L	0-2	0-1	3		2693
42		10	H	Exeter C	W	4-1	1-1	—	Gannon 3 (1 pen), Preece	4546
43		18	A	Bury	D	0-0	0-0	4		4726
44		20	A	Stoke C	D	0-0	0-0	4		8129
45		25	A	Bradford C	L	0-1	0-0	5		7099
46	May	2	H	Birmingham C	W	2-0	2-0	5	Gannon, Francis	7840

Final League Position: 5

GOALSCORERS

League (75): Gannon 16 (4 pens), Francis 15, Preece 13, Barras 5 (1 pen), Wheeler 5, Frain 4 (1 pen), Kilner 3 (2 pens), Beaumont 2, Lillis 2, Williams B 2, Finley 1, Matthews 1, Paskin 1, Ward 1, Williams P 1, own goals 3.
Rumbelows Cup (2): Francis 1, Wheeler 1.
FA Cup (3): Francis 1, Gannon 1, Ward 1 (o pens).

Redfern	Thorpe	Williams P	Frain	Barras	Williams B	Gannon	Ward	Francis	Beaumont	Kilner	Matthews	Knowles	Wheeler	Moore	Paskin	Edwards	Lillis	Finley	Todd	Carstairs	Preece	Muir	Loram	Miller	Match No.
1	2	3	4	5	6	7*	8	9	10	11	12														1
1	2	3	4	5	6	7	8	9†	10*			11	12	14											2
1	2	3	4	5	6	7	8	9	10*	11	12														3
1	6	3	4	5		7	8	9		11		2	10												4
1	6	3	4*	5		7	8			11	9	2	10	12											5
1	6	3	4	5		7	8*	9		11†	12	2	10		14										6
1	8	3	4	5	6	7		9		11†	12	2*	10		14										7
	2	3	12	5	6	7	4	9		11		10*				8	1								8
	4	3		5	6	7	10	9		12		2				8	1	11*							9
	4	3		5	6	7	10	9		11		2				8*	1	12							10
	4	3		5	6	7	10	9*	8†	11		2				1	12	14							11
	4	3†	14	5	6	7	10		8*	11	12					1	9	2							12
			4	5	6	7	10		8	11*	12	2				1	9			3					13
	2	12	4	5	6	7	10		8	11						1	9*			3					14
	2		4	5	6	7	10		8	11						1	9	12		3*					15
	2				6	7	10	9	8			4				1	11		5	3					16
	2				6	7	10	9	8		12	4*				1	11		5	3					17
	2		4	5		7	10	9	8	11*	12					1		6		3					18
	14		4	5†		7	8	9	10	11*	12	2				1		6		3					19
			4	5		7	8	9	10	11		2				1		6		3					20
			4	5		7	8*	9	10	11		2				1		6		3	12				21
			4	5	12	7		9	10			2				1		6*	11	3	8				22
	6*		4	5		7	8	9	10		12	2				1				3	11				23
			4	5	6	7	8	9	10			2				1				3	11				24
			4	5	6	7	8	9	10			2				1				3	11				25
			4	5	6	7	8	9	10			2				1				3	11				26
			4	5	6	7*	8	9	10			2				1			12	3	11				27
			4	5	6		8	9	10			2				1			7	3	11				28
			4	5	6		8	9	10			2				1			7	3	11				29
			4	5	6	7	8	9	10			2				1				3	11				30
			4	5	6	7*	8	9	10			2	12			1				3	11				31
	7		4	5	6		8		10			2*	9			1				3	11	12			32
					6	7	8	9*	10		12	2				1		4	5	3	11				33
					6	7	8	9*	10		12	2	14			1		4†	5	3	11				34
			4	5	6	7	8	9*	10		12	2				1				3	11				35
			4	5		7	8	9*	10†		12	2				1		6	14	3	11				36
			4*	5		7	8	9	14		12	2†				1		6	10	3	11				37
			4	5	14	7	8	9*			12	2				1		6	10†	3	11				38
			4	5	6	7	8		10		12	2				1				3	11	9*			39
			4	5	6	7	8	9*	10			2				1				3	11	12			40
			4	5	6	7	8		10*			2				1				3	11†	9	12	14	41
			4*	5	6	7	8	9	10			2				1				3	11	12			42
			4	5	6	7	8	9	10			2				1				3	11				43
			4	5	6	7	8	9	10			2				1			12	3†	11*			14	44
			4	5	6	7	8		10	11*		2				1		12		3			9†	14	45
			4	5	6	7	8	9	10		12	2*				1				3	11				46

Totals (appearances):

Redfern	Thorpe	Williams P	Frain	Barras	Williams B	Gannon	Ward	Francis	Beaumont	Kilner	Matthews	Knowles	Wheeler	Moore	Paskin	Edwards	Lillis	Finley	Todd	Carstairs	Preece	Muir	Loram	Miller
7	33	12	37	42	33	43	44	34	33	13	4	28	13	—	3	39	9	15	17	20	23	3	1	—

Substitute appearances: + 1s (Thorpe), + 1s (Williams P), + 2s (Frain), + 2s (Williams B), + 1s (Gannon), + 1s (Ward), + 5s (Francis), + 5s (Beaumont), + 3s (Kilner), + 9s (Matthews), + 1s (Knowles), + 2s (Wheeler), + 2s, + 3s, + 2s, + 2s, + 1s, + 3s, + 3s

Rumbelows Cup	First Round	Bradford C (h)	1-1
		(a)	1-3
FA Cup	First Round	Lincoln C (h)	3-1
	Second Round	Wigan Ath (a)	0-2

STOCKPORT COUNTY

Player and Position	Ht	Wt	Birth Date	Birth Place	Source	Clubs	League App	League Gls
Goalkeepers								
Phil Church‡			5 12 72	Bridgend	Trainee	Norwich C	—	—
						Stockport Co	—	—
Paul Cooper‡	5 11	13 10	21 12 53	Brierley Hill	Apprentice	Birmingham C	17	—
						Ipswich T	447	—
						Leicester C	56	—
						Manchester C	15	—
						Stockport Co	22	—
Neil Edwards	5 8	11 02	5 12 70	Aberdare	Trainee	Leeds U	—	—
						Huddersfield T (loan)	—	—
						Stockport Co	39	—
David Redfern	6 2	13 08	8 11 62	Sheffield	School	Sheffield W	—	—
						Doncaster R (loan)	—	—
						Rochdale (loan)	19	—
						Rochdale	68	—
						Gainsborough T	—	—
						Stockport Co	42	—
Defenders								
Tony Barras	6 0	12 03	29 3 71	Teesside	Trainee	Hartlepool U	12	—
						Stockport Co	82	5
Jim Carstairs	6 0	12 05	29 1 71	Fife	Trainee	Arsenal	—	—
						Brentford (loan)	8	—
						Cambridge U	—	—
						Stockport Co	20	—
Alan Finley	6 3	14 03	10 12 67	Liverpool	Marine	Shrewsbury T	63	2
						Stockport Co	37	4
Jim Gannon	6 2	12 06	7 9 68	London	Dundalk	Sheffield U	—	—
						Halifax T (loan)	2	—
						Stockport Co	91	23
David Miller	5 11	11 02	8 1 64	Burnley	Apprentice	Burnley	32	3
						Crewe Alex (loan)	3	—
						Colne Dyn	—	—
						Tranmere R	29	1
						Preston NE	58	2
						Burnley (loan)	4	—
						Carlisle U	109	7
						Stockport Co	3	—
Andy Thorpe*	5 11	12 00	15 9 60	Stockport	Amateur	Stockport Co	314	3
						Tranmere R	53	—
						Stockport Co	175	—
Bill Williams	6 1	12 11	7 10 60	Rochdale	Local	Rochdale	95	2
						Stockport Co	104	1
						Manchester C	1	—
						Stockport Co	118	5
Midfield								
David Frain	5 8	10 05	11 10 62	Sheffield	Rowlinson YC	Sheffield U	44	5
						Rochdale	42	12
						Stockport Co	111	9
Darren Knowles	5 6	10 01	8 10 70	Sheffield	Trainee	Sheffield U	—	—
						Stockport Co	52	—
Mark Lillis*	6 0	13 06	17 1 60	Manchester	Local	Huddersfield T	206	56
						Manchester C	39	11
						Derby Co	15	1
						Aston Villa	31	4
						Scunthorpe U	68	23
						Stockport Co	11	2
Richard Scanlon*			11 9 71	Southport	Trainee	Liverpool	—	—
						Stockport Co	—	—

STOCKPORT COUNTY

Foundation: Formed at a meeting held at Wellington Road South by members of Wycliffe Congregational Chapel in 1883, they called themselves Heaton Norris Rovers until changing to Stockport County in 1890, a year before joining the Football Combination.

First Football League game: 1 September 1900, Division 2, v Leicester Fosse (a) D 2-2 – Moores; Earp, Wainwright; Pickford, Limond, Harvey; Stansfield, Smith (1), Patterson, Foster, Betteley (1).

Did you know: On 28 August 1948 County were 3-0 down at Crewe in a Division 3 (N) game when Len Barker (who was making his debut) scored a hat-trick to force a 3-3 draw.

Managers (and Secretary-managers)
Fred Stewart 1894–1911, Harry Lewis 1911–14, David Ashworth 1914–19, Albert Williams 1919–24, Fred Scotchbrook 1924–26, Lincoln Hyde 1926–31, Andrew Wilson 1932–33, Fred Westgarth 1934–36, Bob Kelly 1936–38, George Hunt 1938–39, Bob Marshall 1939–49, Andy Beattie 1949–52, Dick Duckworth 1952–56, Billy Moir 1956–60, Reg Flewin 1960–63, Trevor Porteous 1963–65, Bert Trautmann (GM) 1965–66, Eddie Quigley (TM) 1965–66, Jimmy Meadows 1966–69, Wally Galbraith 1969–70, Matt Woods 1970–71, Brian Doyle 1972–74, Jimmy Meadows 1974–75, Roy Chapman 1975–76, Eddie Quigley 1976–77, Alan Thompson 1977–78, Mike Summerbee 1978–79, Jimmy McGuigan 1979–82, Eric Webster 1982–85, Colin Murphy 1985, Les Chapman 1985–86, Jimmy Melia 1986, Colin Murphy 1986–87, Asa Hartford 1987–89, Danny Bergara April 1989–.

Forwards

Name						Club	Apps	Gls
Chris Beaumont	5 11	11 07	5 12 65	Sheffield	Denaby	Rochdale	34	7
						Stockport Co	101	22
Kevin Francis	6 7	15 08	6 12 67	Moseley	Mile Oak Rovers	Derby Co	10	—
						Stockport Co	48	20
Andy Kilner*			11 10 66	Bolton	Apprentice	Burnley	5	—
						Stockport Co	42	14
						Rochdale (loan)	3	—
Neil Matthews	5 11	12 00	19 9 66	Grimsby	Apprentice	Grimsby T	11	1
						Scunthorpe U (loan)	1	—
						Halifax T (loan)	9	2
						Bolton W (loan)	1	—
						Halifax T	105	29
						Stockport Co	38	15
						Halifax T (loan)	3	—
Chris Moore			4 11 72	Derby	Trainee	Stockport Co	1	—
John Muir	6 2	14 06	26 4 63	Sedgley	Dudley T	Doncaster R	76	18
						Stockport Co	4	—
Andy Preece	6 1	12 00	27 3 67	Evesham		Northampton T	1	—
						Worcester C	—	—
						Wrexham	51	7
						Stockport Co	25	13
Lee Todd	5 5	10 03	7 3 72	Hartlepool	Hartlepool U	Stockport Co	33	—
Peter Ward	6 0	11 10	15 10 64	Co Durham	Chester-le-Street	Huddersfield T	37	2
						Rochdale	84	10
						Stockport Co	44	1
Paul Wheeler	5 11	11 03	3 1 65	Caerphilly	Apprentice	Bristol R	—	—
						Aberaman	—	—
						Cardiff C	101	10
						Hull C	5	—
						Hereford U	54	12
						Stockport Co	22	5
Paul Williams	5 6	10 07	11 9 69	Leicester	Trainee	Leicester C	—	—
						Stockport Co	44	3
Jason Withe‡			16 8 71	Liverpool	WBA	Burnley	—	—
						Crewe Alex	—	—
						Stockport Co	—	—

Trainees
Holmes, Carl S; Leigh, Malcolm; Miller, Peter D; Nelson, Michael J; O'Hearns, Stephen.
**Non-Contract
Connelly, Sean P.
**Non-Contract Players who are retained must be re-signed before they are eligible to play in League matches.

496

STOKE CITY

STOKE CITY 1991–92 *Back row (left to right):* Wayne Biggins, Noel Blake, Tony Gallimore, Lee Sandford, Peter Fox, Carl Beeston, Ian Cranson.
Centre row: Les Parton (Youth Development Officer), Peter Henderson (Coach), Mick Kennedy, Mark Devlin, David Kevan, Tony Kelly, Tony Ellis, John Butler, Paul Barnes, Richard Gray (Physiotherapist), Tony Lacey (Youth Coach).
Front row: Lee Fowler, Ian Scott, Lou Macari (Manager), Harry Cartlidge (Managing Director of Ansells), Chic Bates (Assistant Manager), Paul Ware, Darren Boughey.

Division 2 **STOKE CITY**

Victoria Ground, Stoke-on-Trent. Telephone Stoke-on-Trent (0782) 413511. Commercial Dept: (0782) 45840. Soccerline Information: 0898 700278. City Chatline: 0898 888654. Stoke City Souvenir Shop 0782 747078.

Ground capacity: 25,084.

Record attendance: 51,380 v Arsenal, Division 1, 29 March 1937.

Record receipts: £109,000 v Liverpool, Rumbelows Cup 2nd rd 2nd leg, 9 October 1991.

Pitch measurements: 116yd × 75yd.

President: Sir Stanley Matthews CBE.

Vice-president: J. A. M. Humphries.

Chairman: P. Coates. *Vice-chairman:* K. A. Humphreys. *Directors:* P. J. Wright, R. D. Kenyon. *Associate Director:* Tony Waddington. *Manager:* Lou Macari. *Assistant manager:* Chic Bates. *Physio:* Richard Gray. *Secretary:* M. J. Potts. *Sales & Marketing Manager:* M. J. Cullerton.

Year Formed: 1863 *(see Foundation).* Turned Professional: 1885. Ltd Co.: 1908.

Former Grounds: 1875, Sweeting's Field; 1878, Victoria Ground (previously known as the Athletic Club Ground).

Club Nickname: 'The Potters'.

Record League Victory: 10-3 v WBA, Division 1, 4 February 1937 – Doug Westland; Brigham, Harbot; Tutin, Turner (1p), Kirton; Matthews, Antonio (2), Freddie Steele (5), Jimmy Westland, Johnson (2).

Record Cup Victory: 7-1 v Burnley, FA Cup, 2nd rd (replay), 20 February 1896 – Clawley; Clare, Eccles; Turner, Grewe, Robertson; Willie Maxwell, Dickson, A. Maxwell (3), Hyslop (4), Schofield.

Record Defeat: 0-10 v Preston NE, Division 1, 14 September 1889.

Most League Points (2 for a win): 63, Division 3 (N), 1926–27.

Most League points (3 for a win): 77, Division 3, 1991–92.

Most League Goals: 92, Division 3 (N), 1926–27.

Highest League Scorer in Season: Freddie Steele, 33, Division 1, 1936–37.

Most League Goals in Total Aggregate: Freddie Steele, 142, 1934–49.

Most Capped Player: Gordon Banks, 36 (73), England.

Most League Appearances: Eric Skeels, 506, 1958–76.

Record Transfer Fee Received: £750,000 from Everton for Peter Beagrie, October 1989.

Record Transfer Fee Paid: £480,000 to Sheffield W for Ian Cranson, July 1989.

Football League Record: 1888 Founder Member of Football League; 1890 Not re-elected; 1891 Re-elected; relegated in 1907, and after one year in Division 2, resigned for financial reasons; 1919 re-elected to Division 2; 1922–23 Division 1; 1923–26 Division 2; 1926–27 Division 3 (N); 1927–33 Division 2; 1933–53 Division 1; 1953–63 Division 2; 1963–77 Division 1; 1977–79 Division 2; 1979–85 Division 1; 1985–90 Division 2; 1990–92 Division 3; 1992– Division 2.

Honours: Football League: Division 1 best season: 4th, 1935–36, 1946–47; Division 2 – Champions 1932–33, 1962–63; Runners-up 1921–22; Promoted 1978–79 (3rd); Division 3 (N) – Champions 1926–27. *FA Cup:* Semi-finals 1899, 1971, 1972. *Football League Cup:* Winners 1971–72. *Autoglass Trophy:* Winners 1992. **European Competitions:** *UEFA Cup:* 1972–73, 1974–75.

Colours: Red and white striped shirts, white shorts, red stockings. **Change colours:** Purple shirts, purple shorts, purple stockings with yellow and white trim.

STOKE CITY 1991–92 LEAGUE RECORD

Match No.	Date		Venue	Opponents	Result		H/T Score	Lg. Pos.	Goalscorers	Attendance
1	Aug	17	A	Bradford C	L	0-1	0-1	—		7556
2		24	H	Bournemouth	D	1-1	1-1	20	Biggins (pen)	10,011
3		31	A	Peterborough U	D	1-1	1-1	20	Biggins	7174
4	Sep	4	H	Shrewsbury T	W	1-0	0-0	—	Biggins	10,182
5		7	A	Darlington	W	1-0	0-0	7	Ellis	4230
6		14	H	Fulham	D	2-2	1-0	7	Biggins, Cranson	10,567
7		17	H	Hartlepool U	W	3-2	2-0	—	Biggins 2, Butler	9394
8		21	A	Preston NE	D	2-2	1-1	8	Biggins 2	6345
9		28	H	Stockport Co	D	2-2	2-0	8	Biggins 2 (1 pen)	12,954
10	Oct	5	A	Chester C	D	0-0	0-0	10		4212
11		12	H	Bolton W	W	2-0	1-0	6	Biggins, Scott	12,420
12		19	A	Swansea C	L	1-2	0-2	9	Ellis	3363
13		26	H	Leyton Orient	W	2-0	1-0	6	Biggins, Cranson	9555
14	Nov	2	H	Huddersfield T	L	0-2	0-2	8		10,116
15		5	A	Bury	W	3-1	1-1	—	Ellis 2, Overson	3245
16		9	A	Exeter C	D	0-0	0-0	5		5309
17		23	H	Torquay U	W	3-0	2-0	5	Biggins, Stein 2	9124
18		30	A	WBA	D	2-2	1-1	5	Overson 2	17,207
19	Dec	14	H	Wigan Ath	W	3-0	2-0	5	Stein, Kelly, Biggins	8419
20		21	A	Bournemouth	W	2-1	1-1	4	Biggins, Kelly	5436
21		26	H	Peterborough U	D	3-3	2-2	5	Kevan, Stein, Biggins	14,732
22		28	H	Bradford C	D	0-0	0-0	5		12,208
23	Jan	1	A	Shrewsbury T	L	0-1	0-1	5		8557
24		4	H	Birmingham C	W	2-1	0-0	5	Ware, Biggins	18,914
25		11	A	Brentford	L	0-2	0-1	6		9004
26		18	H	Reading	W	3-0	1-0	6	Jones (og), Butler, Stein	10,835
27		25	A	Hull C	W	1-0	1-0	4	Russell	4996
28	Feb	1	H	Swansea C	W	2-1	1-0	3	Ware, Beeston	11,299
29		8	A	Leyton Orient	W	1-0	1-0	2	Beeston	9153
30		12	H	WBA	W	1-0	1-0	—	Stein	23,645
31		15	A	Wigan Ath	L	0-1	0-1	2		5695
32		22	H	Brentford	W	2-1	1-0	1	Butler, Stein	16,417
33		29	A	Birmingham C	D	1-1	0-1	1	Barnes	22,162
34	Mar	4	A	Reading	W	4-3	2-2	—	Stein, Foley, Ware, McPherson (og)	4362
35		7	H	Hull C	L	2-3	0-1	1	Barnes, Stein	13,563
36		11	H	Bury	L	1-2	0-0	1	Barnes	12,385
37		14	A	Huddersfield T	W	2-1	2-0	1	Biggins, Stein	10,156
38		21	H	Exeter C	W	5-2	3-1	1	Biggins, Stein, Beeston, Grimes, Steele	13,634
39		28	A	Torquay U	L	0-1	0-1	1		3260
40		31	A	Fulham	D	1-1	0-1	—	Stein	5779
41	Apr	3	H	Darlington	W	3-0	2-0	—	Biggins 2 (1 pen), Stein	13,579
42		11	A	Hartlepool U	D	1-1	1-1	1	Stein	4360
43		18	H	Preston NE	W	2-1	1-1	2	Stein, Biggins (pen)	16,151
44		20	A	Stockport Co	D	0-0	0-0	2		8129
45		25	H	Chester C	L	0-1	0-0	2		18,474
46	May	2	A	Bolton W	L	1-3	1-0	4	Stein	10,000

Final League Position: 4

GOALSCORERS

League (69): Biggins 22 (4 pens), Stein 16, Ellis 4, Barnes 3, Beeston 3, Butler 3, Overson 3, Ware 3, Cranson 2, Kelly 2, Foley 1, Grimes 1, Kevan 1, Russell 1, Scott 1, Steele 1, own goals 2.
Rumbelows Cup (7): Biggins 2 (l pens), Kelly 2, Beeston 1, Cranson 1, Ellis 1.
FA Cup (1): Beeston 1.

Kearton	Butler	Cranson	Blake	Fowler	Kevan	Gallimore	Beeston	Kelly	Biggins	Sandford	Ellis	Scott	Overson	Kennedy	Stein	Ware	Sinclair	Barnes	Russell	Foley	Grimes	Rennie	Steele	Wright	Pressman	Bent	Heath	Match No.
1	2	3	4	5*	6	7	8	9	10	11	12																	1
1	2	7	5	11	4		8	12	10	3*	9				6													2
1		7	5	11	4		8	9*	10		12		3	2	6													3
1		7	5	11	4		8	9*	10		12		3	2	6													4
1	2	7	5	11	4		8	12†	10*	3	9	14			6													5
1	2	7	5	11†	4		8	12	10*	3	9			14	6													6
1	2	7	5*	12	4				10	3		11	8	6	9													7
1	2	7		11	4		8		10	3			5	6	9													8
1	2	7		11			8		10	3		4	5	6	9													9
1	2	7	11				8		10	3		4	5	6	9													10
1	2	7		11	4*		8		10	3		12	5	6	9													11
1	2	7		11*	4		8		10	3	9	12	5		6													12
1	2	7		11	4		8		10	3	9		5		6													13
1	2	7		11	4		8	12	10	3	9*		5		6													14
1	2	7		11*	4		8		10	3	9		5		6	12												15
1	2	7		11	4		8		10	3			5	6	9													16
		7		11	4		8		10†	3	12	14	5	2	6	9*	1											17
	3	7			4		8		10	6	12		5	2	9	11*	1											18
	3	7			4		8		10	6			5	2	9	11	1											19
	3	7			4		8		10	6			5	2	9	11	1											20
	3	7			4		8		10	6*	12		5	2	9	11	1											21
	3	7			4		8		10	6	12		5	2	9	11*	1											22
	3	7			4		8		10	6			5	2	9	11	1											23
	3	7			4		8		10	6			5	2	9		1		11									24
	3	7			4*		8		10	6	12		5	2	9		1		11									25
	3*	7			4		8		10	6			5		9		1		11	2	12							26
	3	7	5		4*		8		10	6					9		1		11	2	12							27
		7	5*		4		8		10†	6	14		3		9		1		11	2	12							28
	3	7			4		8		10	6			5		9*	11	1			2	12							29
	3	7			4		8		10	6			5		9	11	1			2								30
	3	7			4		8		10	6			5		9		1			2	12		11*					31
	3	7			4		8		10	6			5		9		1			2			11					32
	3	7			4		8		10	6			5		9		1			2	12		11*					33
	3	7			4				10	6			5		9*		1			2	12		11			8		34
	3*	7			4		8		10	6			5		9	8	1			2			11					35
	3				4	12	8		10	6	12		5		9		1			2			11*		1			36
	3	7			4		8		10	6			5		9					2			11		1			37
	3	7			4†		8		10	6*	12	14	5		9					2			11		1			38
	3	7			4				10	6	12	14	5		9	11*				2					1		8†	39
	3	7			4		8		10	6			5		9		1			2							11	40
	3	7			4				10	6			5		9		1			2						8	11	41
	3	7	5		4		8		10*	6	12				9		1			2							11	42
	3	14			4		8		10	6	12		5†	2	9		1						7				11*	43
	3	5			4		8		10	6				2	9	11	1						7					44
	3	5			4		8		10	6	12			2	9	11*	1						7†				14	45
	3	5			4		8		10	6				2	9	11	1						7					46
16	42	41	12	15	43	2	42	10	41	37	9	6	34	19	36	22	26	3	5	20	4	1	7	3	4	1	5	
			+1s	+1s			+1s	+1s	+3s		+1s	+6s	+3s	+1s	+1s	+2s			+10s	+6s							+1s	

Rumbelows Cup   First Round   Chesterfield (h)   1-0
   (a)   2-1
   Second Round   Liverpool (a)   2-2
   (h)   2-3
FA Cup   First Round   Telford (h)   0-0
   (a)   1-2

STOKE CITY

Player and Position	Ht	Wt	Date	Birth Place	Source	Clubs	League App	Gls
Goalkeepers								
Peter Fox	5 11	12 10	5 7 57	Scunthorpe	Apprentice	Sheffield W	49	—
						West Ham U (loan)	—	—
						Barnsley (loan)	1	—
						Stoke C	399	—
Ron Sinclair	5 10	11 09	19 11 64	Stirling	Apprentice	Nottingham F	—	—
						Wrexham (loan)	11	—
						Sheffield U (loan)	—	—
						Leeds U (loan)	—	—
						Derby Co (loan)	—	—
						Leeds U	8	—
						Halifax T (loan)	14	—
						Bristol C	44	—
						Walsall (loan)	11	—
						Stoke C	26	—
Defenders								
Noel Blake*	6 0	13 05	12 1 62	Kingston, Jamaica	Sutton C T	Walsall	—	—
						Aston Villa	4	—
						Shrewsbury T (loan)	6	—
						Birmingham C	76	5
						Portsmouth	144	10
						Leeds U	51	4
						Stoke C	75	3
						Bradford C (loan)	6	—
Robert Brunton			5 9 73	Dublin	Belvedere	Stoke C	—	—
John Butler	5 11	11 07	7 2 62	Liverpool	Prescot Cables	Wigan Ath	245	15
						Stoke C	142	6
Ian Cranson	5 11	12 04	2 7 64	Easington	Apprentice	Ipswich T	131	5
						Sheffield W	30	—
						Stoke C	67	4
Lee Fowler	5 7	11 11	26 1 69	Nottingham	Trainee	Stoke C	32	—
Ashley Grimes	5 11	11 11	2 8 57	Dublin	Bohemians	Manchester U	90	10
						Coventry C	32	1
						Luton T	87	3
						Osasuna	—	—
						Stoke C	20	2
Vince Overson	6 0	13 00	15 5 62	Kettering	Apprentice	Burnley	211	6
						Birmingham C	182	3
						Stoke C	35	3
Paul Rennie	5 9	11 07	26 10 71	Nantwich	Trainee	Crewe Alex	2	—
						Stoke C	5	—
Lee Sandford	6 1	12 02	22 4 68	Basingstoke	Apprentice	Portsmouth	72	1
						Stoke C	93	4
Ian Wright	5 11	12 02	10 3 72	Lichfield	Trainee	Stoke C	5	—
Midfield								
Paul Baines†			15 1 72	Tamworth	Trainee	Stoke C	2	—
Carl Beeston	5 9	10 03	30 6 67	Stoke	Apprentice	Stoke C	159	9
John Berks‡	5 7	10 11	17 3 73	Stoke	Trainee	Stoke C	—	—
Darren Boughey†	5 9	10 13	30 11 70	Stoke	Trainee	Stoke C	7	—
						Wigan Ath (loan)	2	2
						Exeter C (loan)	8	1
David Bright†			5 9 72	Bathavon	School	Stoke C	—	—
Mark Devlin	5 9	11 03	18 1 73	Irvine	Trainee	Stoke C	21	2
Stephen Farrell*			8 3 73	Kilmarnock	Trainee	Stoke C	2	—
Steve Foley	5 7	10 12	4 10 62	Liverpool	Apprentice	Liverpool	—	—
						Fulham (loan)	3	—
						Grimsby T	31	2
						Sheffield U	66	14
						Swindon T	151	23
						Stoke C	20	1
Tony Gallimore	5 10	11 10	21 2 72	Crewe	Trainee	Stoke C	11	—
						Carlisle U (loan)	16	—
Tony Kelly*	5 9	10 12	14 2 66	Meridan	St Albans C	Stoke C	51	5
						Hull C (loan)	6	1
Mick Kennedy*	5 10	10 06	9 4 61	Salford	Apprentice	Halifax T	76	4
						Huddersfield T	81	9
						Middlesbrough	68	5
						Portsmouth	129	4
						Bradford C	45	2
						Leicester C	9	—
						Luton T	32	—
						Stoke C	52	3
David Kevan	5 8	9 10	31 8 68	Wigtown	Apprentice	Notts Co	89	3
						Cardiff C (loan)	7	—
						Stoke C	65	1
						Maidstone U (loan)	3	—

STOKE CITY

Foundation: The date of the formation of this club has long been in doubt. The year 1863 was claimed, but more recent research by Wade Martin has uncovered nothing earlier than 1868, when a couple of Old Carthusians, who were apprentices at the local works of the old North Staffordshire Railway Company, met with some others from that works, to form Stoke Ramblers. It should also be noted that the old Stoke club went bankrupt in 1908 when a new club was formed.

First Football League game: 8 September 1888, Football League, v WBA (h) L 0-2 – Rowley; Clare, Underwood; Ramsey, Shutt, Smith; Sayer, McSkimming, Staton, Edge, Tunnicliffe.

Did you know: In 1931–32 when Stoke finished third in Division Two they fielded the same team for 16 consecutive weeks – a club record. The line-up was Lewis; McGrory, Beachill, Robertson, Turner, Sellars, Liddle, Bussey, Mawson, Sale, Archibald.

Managers (and secretary-managers)
Tom Slaney 1874–83*, Walter Cox 1883–84*, Harry Lockett 1884–90, Joseph Bradshaw 1890–92, Arthur Reeves 1892–95, William Rowley 1895–97, H. D. Austerberry 1897–1908, A. J. Barker 1908–14, Peter Hodge 1914–15, Joe Schofield 1915–19, Arthur Shallcross 1919–23, John "Jock" Rutherford 1923, Tom Mather 1923–35, Bob McGrory 1935–52, Frank Taylor 1952–60, Tony Waddington 1960–77, George Eastham 1977–78, Alan A'Court 1978, Alan Durban 1978–81, Richie Barker 1981–83, Bill Asprey 1984–85, Mick Mills 1985–89, Alan Ball 1989–91, Lou Macari May 1991–.

Player and Position	Ht	Wt	Birth Date	Birth Place	Source	Clubs	League App	Gls
Keith Long	5 09	10 00	14 11 73	Dublin	St Josephs Boys	Stoke C	—	—
Chris Male	5 9	11 09	16 6 72	Portsmouth		Stoke C	—	—
Danny Martin†	5 10	10 07	15 3 73	Tamworth	Trainee	Stoke C	—	—
Ian Scott*	5 9	11 04	20 9 67	Radcliffe	Apprentice	Manchester C	24	3
						Stoke C	30	2
						Crewe Alex (loan)	12	1
Paul Ware	5 8	11 02	7 11 70	Congleton	Trainee	Stoke C	86	6
Forwards								
Paul Barnes	5 10	10 02	16 11 67	Leicester	Apprentice	Notts Co	53	14
						Stoke C	24	3
						Chesterfield (loan)	1	—
Wayne Biggins	5 11	11 00	20 11 61	Sheffield	Apprentice	Lincoln C	8	1
						Kings Lynn	—	—
						Burnley	78	29
						Norwich C	79	16
						Manchester C	32	9
						Stoke C	114	44
Tony Ellis	5 11	11 00	20 10 64	Salford	Northwich V	Oldham Ath	8	—
						Preston NE	86	26
						Stoke C	77	19
Adrian Heath*	5 6	10 01	11 1 61	Stoke	Apprentice	Stoke C	95	16
						Everton	226	71
						Espanol	—	—
						Aston Villa	9	—
						Manchester C	75	4
						Stoke C	6	—
Michael Macari†			4 2 73	Kilwinning	Trainee	West Ham U	—	—
						Stoke C	—	—
Jason Percival			20 9 73	Nuneaton	Trainee	Stoke C	—	—
Mark Reid			17 10 73	Dublin	Belvedere	Stoke C	—	—
Mark Stein	5 3	9 02	28 1 66	Capetown, SA		Luton T	54	19
						Aldershot (loan)	2	1
						QPR	33	4
						Oxford U	82	18
						Stoke C	36	16

Trainees
Davies, Stephen M; Green, Anthony J; Jennings, Gareth J; Jones, Marcus L; Jukes, Paul W; Lacey, John P; Lovelock, Owen J; McLeish, Alexander P; Mills, Andrew J; Moseley, Christopher K; Mulligan, James; Potts, Adrian H; Robinson, Jason L; Stokes, Lee F; Sutton, Stuart A; Wileman, Matthew L; Winstone, Simon J.

**Non-Contract
Macari, Michael.

Associated Schoolboys
Allerton, Daniel J; Ayres, Timothy; Barratt, Richard J; Birch, Mark; Callan, Aidan J; Coker, Jonathan P; Coyne, Kevin; Field, Lee; Hawkes, Marc J; Hope, Mathew P; Jackson, Christopher; Woodvine, Andrew T.

Associated Schoolboys who have accepted the club's offer of a Traineeship/Contract
Blair, Scott; Hassall, Steven K; Long, Ian G.

**Non-Contract Players who are retained must be re-signed before they are eligible to play in League matches.

502

SUNDERLAND 1991–92 *Back row (left to right):* Tony Cullen, Anthony Smith, Simon Guthrie, Peter Davenport, Thomas Hauser, Ian Sampson, Richard Ord, Brian Mooney, Gordon Armstrong, David Wales.
Centre row: Viv Busby (Chief Coach), Steve Smelt (Physiotherapist), Paul Moore, John Kay, Colin Pascoe, Steve Gaughan, Tim Carter, Tony Norman, Paul Williams, Gary Bennett, Gary Owers, Martin Gray, Jim Morrow (Youth Development Officer), Denis Smith (Manager).
Front row: Malcolm Crosby (Reserve Team Coach), Keiron Brady, David Rush, Marco Gabbiadini, Paul Hardyman, Kevin Ball, Paul Bracewell, Brian Atkinson, Warren Hawke, Wayne Walls, Jonathan Trigg, Steven Brodie, Roger Jones (Youth Team Coach).

Division 1   **SUNDERLAND**

Roker Park Ground, Sunderland. Telephone Sunderland 091-514 0332. Commercial Dept: 091-567 2275. Fax No: 091 514 5854

Ground capacity: 31,887.

Record attendance: 75,118 v Derby Co, FA Cup 6th rd replay, 8 March 1933.

Record receipts: £186,000 v Tottenham H, Division 1, 28 August 1990.

Pitch measurements: 113yd × 74yd.

Chairman: R. S. Murray FCCA.

Deputy chairman: G. S. Wood.

Directors: J. G. Wood, J. R. Featherstone, G. Davidson.

Manager: Malcolm Crosby. *General Manager/Secretary:* G. Davidson FCA. *Chief Coach:* Bobby Ferguson. *Reserve team coach:* Roger Jones. *Physio:* Steve Smelt. *Youth development officer:* J. Morrow. *Youth team coach:* Jonathan Trigg. *Commercial Manager:* Alec King.

Year Formed: 1879. Turned Professional: 1886. Ltd Co.: 1906.

Former Grounds: 1879, Blue House Field, Hendon; 1882, Groves Field, Ashbrooke; 1883, Horatio Street; 1884, Abbs Field, Fulwell; 1886, Newcastle Road; 1898, Roker Park.

Former Names: 1879–80, Sunderland and District Teacher's AFC.

Club Nickname: 'Rokermen'.

Record League Victory: 9-1 v Newcastle U, Division 1, 5 December 1908 – Roose; Forster, Melton; Daykin, Thomson, Low; Mordue, Hogg (4), Brown, Holley (3), Bridgett (2).

Record Cup Victory: 11-1 v Fairfield, FA Cup, 1st rd, 2 February 1895 – Doig; McNeill, Johnston; Dunlop, McCreadie (1), Wilson; Gillespie (1), Millar (5), Campbell, Hannah (3), Scott (1).

Record Defeat: 0-8 v West Ham U, Division 1, 19 October 1968 and v Watford, Division 1, 25 September 1982.

Most League Points (2 for a win): 61, Division 2, 1963–64.

Most League points (3 for a win): 93, Division 3, 1987–88.

Most League Goals: 109, Division 1, 1935–36.

Highest League Scorer in Season: Dave Halliday, 43, Division 1, 1928–29.

Most League Goals in Total Aggregate: Charlie Buchan, 209, 1911–25.

Most Capped Player: Martin Harvey, 34, Northern Ireland.

Most League Appearances: Jim Montgomery, 537, 1962–77.

Record Transfer Fee Received: £1,500,000 from Crystal Palace for Marco Gabbiadini, September 1991.

Record Transfer Fee Paid: £900,000 to WBA for Don Goodman, December 1991.

Football League Record: 1890 Elected to Division 1; 1958–64 Division 2; 1964–70 Division 1; 1970–76 Division 2; 1976–77 Division 1; 1977–80 Division 2; 1980–85 Division 1; 1985–87 Division 2; 1987–88 Division 3; 1988–90 Division 2; 1990–91 Division 1; 1991–92 Division 2; 1992– Division 1.

Honours: Football League: Division 1 – Champions 1891–92, 1892–93, 1894–95, 1901–02, 1912–13, 1935–36; Runners-up 1893–94; 1897–98, 1900–01, 1922–23, 1934–35; Division 2 – Champions 1975–76; Runners-up 1963–64, 1979–80; Division 3 – Champions 1987–88. *FA Cup:* Winners 1937, 1973; Runners-up 1913, 1992; *Football League Cup:* Runners-up 1984–85. **European Competitions:** *Cup-winners Cup:* 1973–74.

Colours: Red and white striped shirts, black shorts, red stockings, white turnover. **Change colours:** White shirts, blue and green sleeves, navy blue shorts, white stockings, navy blue trim.

SUNDERLAND 1991–92 LEAGUE RECORD

Match No.	Date		Venue	Opponents		Result	H/T Score	Lg. Pos.	Goalscorers	Attendance
1	Aug	17	H	Derby Co	D	1-1	0-0	—	Armstrong	20,509
2		20	A	Barnsley	W	3-0	2-0	—	Owers, Armstrong, Pascoe	12,454
3		24	A	Millwall	L	1-4	1-3	11	Owers (pen)	10,016
4		31	H	Oxford U	W	2-0	1-0	6	Gabbiadini, Armstrong	16,151
5	Sep	3	A	Portsmouth	L	0-1	0-0	—		9621
6		7	H	Blackburn R	D	1-1	1-1	10	Atkinson	17,043
7		14	A	Swindon T	L	3-5	0-3	15	Owers, Gabbiadini, Armstrong	11,417
8		17	A	Charlton Ath	W	4-1	1-1	—	Owers (pen), Gabbiadini 3	5807
9		21	H	Grimsby T	L	1-2	0-1	13	Pascoe	16,535
10		28	A	Middlesbrough	L	1-2	0-2	17	Brady	19,424
11	Oct	5	H	Brighton & HA	W	4-2	1-2	13	Beagrie, Rush 2, Armstrong	15,119
12		12	A	Cambridge U	L	0-3	0-2	17		7857
13		19	A	Port Vale	D	3-3	0-1	17	Brady 2, Ball	7525
14		26	H	Bristol R	D	1-1	1-1	16	Bennett	14,746
15	Nov	2	H	Watford	W	3-1	2-0	15	Byrne 2, Armstrong	12,790
16		5	A	Ipswich T	W	1-0	1-0	—	Armstrong	9768
17		9	A	Bristol C	L	0-1	0-1	14		10,570
18		17	H	Newcastle U	D	1-1	1-0	—	Davenport	29,224
19		23	A	Plymouth Arg	L	0-1	0-0	15		6007
20		30	H	Southend U	L	1-2	1-1	15	Byrne	13,575
21	Dec	7	A	Wolverhampton W	L	0-1	0-0	19		11,922
22		14	H	Leicester C	W	1-0	0-0	16	Goodman	15,094
23		21	H	Portsmouth	W	1-0	1-0	13	Awford (og)	14,432
24		26	A	Tranmere R	L	0-1	0-1	14		13,658
25		28	A	Oxford U	L	0-3	0-0	17		6140
26	Jan	1	H	Barnsley	W	2-0	1-0	15	Armstrong, Goodman	16,107
27		11	H	Millwall	W	6-2	1-1	11	Hardyman, Byrne, Goodman 3, Davenport	16,533
28		18	A	Derby Co	W	2-1	2-0	12	Goodman, Byrne	15,384
29	Feb	1	H	Port Vale	D	1-1	1-1	12	Armstrong	19,488
30		8	A	Bristol R	L	1-2	0-0	12	Byrne	6318
31		11	H	Tranmere R	D	1-1	1-0	—	Hardyman	18,060
32		22	A	Southend U	L	0-2	0-2	12		7473
33		29	H	Wolverhampton W	W	1-0	1-0	13	Byrne (pen)	20,106
34	Mar	14	A	Watford	L	0-1	0-1	16		8091
35		21	H	Bristol C	L	1-3	0-3	17	Atkinson	18,933
36		29	A	Newcastle U	L	0-1	0-1	—		30,306
37	Apr	8	H	Leicester C	L	2-3	2-3	—	Bennett, Goodman	16,533
38		11	H	Charlton Ath	L	1-2	0-0	21	Bennett	21,326
39		14	H	Ipswich T	W	3-0	0-0	—	Goodman 2, Rush	22,131
40		16	H	Plymouth Arg	L	0-1	0-0	—		28,813
41		18	A	Grimsby T	L	0-2	0-0	19		8864
42		20	H	Middlesbrough	W	1-0	1-0	18	Davenport	25,093
43		25	A	Brighton & HA	D	2-2	2-2	18	Goodman, Rogan	9851
44		27	H	Swindon T	D	0-0	0-0	—		16,716
45		29	A	Blackburn R	D	2-2	0-1	—	Armstrong, Davenport	15,079
46	May	2	H	Cambridge U	D	2-2	2-1	18	Goodman, Rush	19,042

Final League Position: 18

GOALSCORERS

League (61): Goodman 11, Armstrong 10, Byrne 7 (1 pen), Gabbiadini 5, Davenport 4, Owers 4 (2 pens), Rush 4, Bennett 3, Brady 3, Atkinson 2, Hardyman 2, Pascoe 2, Ball 1, Beagrie 1, Rogan 1, own goals 1.
Rumbelows Cup (1): Hauser 1.
FA Cup (14): Byrne 7, Atkinson 2, Davenport 2, Armstrong 1, Hardyman 1, Rush 1.

Rumbelows Cup	Second Round	Huddersfield T (h)	1-2
		(a)	0-4

Norman	Williams	Hardyman	Bennett	Ord	Owers	Bracewell	Atkinson	Armstrong	Gabbiadini	Pascoe	Hauser	Sampson	Kay	Ball	Davenport	Agboola	Rush	Beagrie	Brady	Rogan	Cullen	Byrne	Russell	Goodman	Mooney	Carter	Hawke	Smith A	Match No.
1	2	3	4	5	6	7	8	9	10	11																			1
1	2	3	4	5	6	7	8	9	10	12	11*																		2
1	2	3	4	5†	6	7	8*	9	10	12	11	14																	3
1		3	4		6	7	8	9	10		11*		2	5	12														4
1		3	4		6	7	8	9	10	12	11*		2	5															5
1			4		6	7	8*	9	10	12	11		2	5		3													6
1		3	4		6	7	8†	9	10*	11		14	2	5	12														7
1		3	4		6	7		9	10	11			2	5	8														8
1		3	4		6	7		9	10*	11		12	2	5	8														9
1		3	4		7	6*		9					2	5	8		10	11	12										10
1					6	7		9				4	2	5	8		10	11		3									11
1	10†				6	7		9				4	2	5	14			11	12	3	8*								12
1			4		6	7		9					2	5	10*		12	11	8	3									13
1			4†		7	6		9	12			14	2	5				11	8*	3		10							14
1			4			7	12	9		11			2	5	6*		8†			3		10		14					15
1			4			7		9		11			2	5	6		8			3		10							16
1			4		12	7†		9		11			2	5	6		8*			3		10		14					17
1			4		12	7		9		11		14	2	5	6*		8†			3		10							18
1			4		12	7		9		11*			2	5	6		8			3		10†		14					19
1			4		11	7		9		12		14	2	5	6†					3		10		8*					20
1	14		4		11	7		9					2	5	6†		12			3		10		8*					21
1			4		6	7		9		12			2	5	11*					3		10		8					22
1	11		4		6	7		9		12			2	5	10*					3				8					23
1	9†	10*	4		6	7				14	12		2	5	11					3				8					24
1	14		4		6*	7		9					2	5	12			11		3†		10		8					25
1		3	4		6	7	11	9					2	5								10		8					26
1			4	5	6*	7	11	9					2		12					3		10		8					27
1			4	5		7	11†	9					2	14	6*		12			3		10		8					28
1			4	5		7	11	9†					2	14	6*		12			3		10		8					29
1			4	5	14	7*	11	9					2		12		6†			3		10		8					30
1			4	5			11	9			7		2		6					3		10		8					31
1	12			5		7	11	9					2	4	6*					3		10		8					32
1				5		7	11	9				4	2		12		6*		14	3†		10		8					33
1	14			5		7	11†	9					2	4	8*		6			3		10		12					34
1			5*			7	11	9					2	4	8		6†			3		10		12	14				35
1				5		7	11	9					2	4	8*		6			3		10			12	1			36
1			4	5			11	9					2		8		6*			3		10			7	12			37
1			4	5			11	9					2		8*		6		12	3		10			7				38
1			4	5		14	11	9					2		12		6			3		10		8*	7				39
1			4	5†		14	11	9					2		12		6			3		10*		8	7				40
1			4	5	14	7	11	9					2		12		6*			3		10		8†					41
1	12	3	4			7	11	9*					2		6							10†	5	8	14				42
1	12		4		6	7	11*	9†					2							3	14	10	5	8					43
1			12	5	6	7	11					4*	2		9†					3		10		8	14				44
1			4	5	6*		11	9					2	5								10		8	7†		14	3	45
		3	4		6		11	9															5	8	7	1	10	2	46
44	4 +3s	29 +3s	38 +1s	5 +1s	24 +6s	39	29 +1s	40	9	12 +8s	5 +7s	7 +1s	41	31 +2s	25 +11s	1	20 +5s	5	4 +4s	33	1	27	1 +3s	20 +2s	6 +3s	2	2 +2s	2	

Gray—Match No. 45(12).

FA Cup			
	Third Round	Port Vale (h)	3-0
	Fourth Round	Oxford U (a)	3-2
	Fifth Round	West Ham U (h)	1-1
		(a)	3-2
	Sixth Round	Chelsea (a)	1-1
		(h)	2-1
	Semi-Final	Norwich C (at Hillsborough)	1-0
	Final	Liverpool (at Wembley)	0-2

506

SUNDERLAND

Player and Position	Ht	Wt	Birth Date	Birth Place	Source	Clubs	League App	League Gls
Goalkeepers								
Tim Carter	6 1	12 00	5 10 67	Bristol	Apprentice	Bristol R	47	—
						Newport Co (loan)	1	—
						Sunderland	24	—
						Carlisle U (loan)	4	—
						Bristol C (loan)	3	—
						Birmingham C (loan)	2	—
Tony Norman	6 2	12 08	24 2 58	Mancot	Amateur	Burnley	—	—
						Hull C	372	—
						Sunderland	133	—
Defenders								
Kevin Ball	5 9	11 06	12 11 64	Hastings	Amateur	Coventry C	—	—
						Portsmouth	105	4
						Sunderland	66	4
Gary Bennett	6 1	12 01	4 12 61	Manchester	Amateur	Manchester C	—	—
						Cardiff C	87	11
						Sunderland	296	23
Paul Hardyman	5 8	11 04	11 3 64	Portsmouth	Fareham	Portsmouth	117	3
						Sunderland	106	9
John Kay	5 10	11 06	29 1 64	Sunderland	Apprentice	Arsenal	14	—
						Wimbledon	63	2
						Middlesbrough (loan)	8	—
						Sunderland	160	—
Richard Ord	6 2	12 08	3 3 70	Easington	Trainee	Sunderland	69	2
						York C (loan)	3	—
Ian Patterson	6 02	13 00	4 4 73	Chatham	Trainee	Sunderland	—	—
Anton Rogan	5 11	12 06	25 3 66	Belfast	Distillery	Celtic	127	4
						Sunderland	66	2
Ian Sampson	6 2	12 08	14 11 68	Wakefield	Goole T	Sunderland	8	—
Anthony Smith			22 11 68	Sunderland	Trainee	Sunderland	11	—
						Hartlepool U (loan)	8	—
Jonathan Trigg*	5 8	10 06	8 5 71	Jersey	Trainee	Sunderland	—	—
Wayne Walls			23 7 72	Sunderland	Trainee	Sunderland	—	—
Paul Williams	6 0	12 02	25 9 70	Liverpool	Trainee	Sunderland	10	—
						Swansea C (loan)	12	—
Midfield								
Gordon Armstrong	6 0	11 02	15 7 67	Newcastle	Apprentice	Sunderland	262	44
Paul Bracewell	5 8	10 09	19 7 62	Stoke	Apprentice	Stoke C	129	5
						Sunderland	38	4
						Everton	95	7
						Sunderland	113	2
Martin Gray	5 9	10 11	17 8 71	Stockton	Trainee	Sunderland	1	—
						Aldershot (loan)	5	—
Brian Mooney	5 11	11 02	2 2 66	Dublin	Home Farm	Liverpool	—	—
						Wrexham (loan)	9	—
						Preston NE	128	20
						Sheffield W (loan)	—	—
						Sunderland	15	—
Gary Owers	5 10	11 10	3 10 68	Newcastle	Apprentice	Sunderland	186	21
David Wales*	5 9		24 8 72	Sunderland	Trainee	Sunderland	—	—
Forwards								
Brian Atkinson	5 10	12 00	19 1 71	Darlington	Trainee	Sunderland	52	2
Kieron Brady	5 9	11 13	17 9 71	Glasgow	Trainee	Sunderland	33	7
Stephen Brodie	5 10		14 1 73	Sunderland	Trainee	Sunderland	—	—

SUNDERLAND

Foundation: A Scottish schoolmaster named James Allan, working at Hendon Boarding School, took the initiative in the foundation of Sunderland in 1879 when they were formed as The Sunderland and District Teachers' Association FC at a meeting in the Adults School, Norfolk Street. Because of financial difficulties, they quickly allowed members from outside the teaching profession and so became Sunderland AFC in October 1880.

First Football League game: 13 September, 1890, Football League, v Burnley (h) L 2-3 – Kirtley; Porteous, Oliver; Wilson, Auld, Gibson; Spence (1), Miller, Campbell (1), Scott, D. Hannah.

Did you know: Sunderland had no English manager for over 60 years before Alan Brown was first appointed to the job in 1957.

Managers (and Secretary-managers)
Tom Watson 1888–96, Bob Campbell 1896–99, Alex Mackie 1899–1905, Bob Kyle 1905–28, Johnny Cochrane 1928–39, Bill Murray 1939–57, Alan Brown 1957–64, George Hardwick 1964–65, Ian McColl 1965–68, Alan Brown 1968–72, Bob Stokoe 1972–76, Jimmy Adamson 1976–78, Ken Knighton 1979–81, Alan Durban 1981–84, Len Ashurst 1984–85, Lawrie McMenemy 1985–87, Denis Smith 1987–91, Malcolm Crosby April 1992–.

Player and Position	Ht	Wt	Birth Date	Birth Place	Source	Clubs	League App	League Gls
John Byrne	6 0	12 04	1 2 61	Manchester	Apprentice	York C	175	55
						QPR	126	30
						Le Havre	—	—
						Brighton & HA	51	14
						Sunderland	27	7
Tony Cullen*	5 6	11 07	30 9 69	Newcastle		Sunderland	29	—
						Carlisle U (loan)	2	1
						Rotherham U (loan)	3	1
						Bury (loan)	4	—
Peter Davenport	5 11	11 03	24 3 61	Birkenhead	Amateur Cammel Laird	Everton	—	—
						Nottingham F	118	54
						Manchester U	92	22
						Middlesbrough	59	7
						Sunderland	65	11
Donald Goodman	5 10	11 00	9 5 66	Leeds		Bradford C	70	14
						WBA	158	60
						Sunderland	22	11
Thomas Hauser	6 3	12 06	10 4 65	West Germany	Berne OB	Sunderland	53	9
Warren Hawke	5 10	10 11	20 9 70	Durham	Trainee	Sunderland	23	1
						Chesterfield (loan)	8	2
Paul Moore*	5 8		22 2 73	Sunderland	Trainee	Sunderland	—	—
Colin Pascoe	5 9	10 00	9 4 65	Bridgend	Apprentice	Swansea C	174	39
						Sunderland	126	22
David Rush	5 11	10 10	15 5 71	Sunderland	Trainee	Sunderland	36	6
						Hartlepool U (loan)	8	2
Craig Russell§			4 2 74	South Shields	Trainee	Sunderland	4	—

Trainees
Carr, David A; Cronin, Gareth; Ferry, David L; Gray, Michael; Harwood, Paul; Jeffrey, Paul E; McGee, Dean; Musgrave, Sean; Robinson, Anthony; Russell, Craig S; Smith, Martin.

Associated Schoolboys
Berrisford, Adrian C; Coultard, David; Forster, Lee C; Hails, Stuart A; Lawson, Ian D; Mavin, Simon; Mawson, David; Pickering, Steven; Scothern, Andrew; Smith, Stephen; Stoddart, Neil.

Associated Schoolboys who have accepted the club's offer of a Traineeship/Contract
Beary, Daniel M; Carmichael, Barry; Gate, Paul W; Manners, Andrew C; Piggott, Craig; Preece, David; Waldock, John A.

508

SWANSEA CITY 1991–92 *Back row (left to right):* Ron Walton (Youth Team Coach), Jason Bowen, Paul Raynor, Steve McMahon, Mark Harris, Chris McClean, Keith Walker, Jimmy Gilligan, John Cornforth, Ken Davey (Physiotherapist).

Centre row: Frank Burrows (Manager), Paul Chalmers, Simon Davey, David Hough, Mark Kendall, James Heeps, Lee Bracey, Stephen Jenkins, Marc Coates, Mark Davies, Bobby Smith (Assistant Manager).

Front row: Alan Davies, Steve Thornber, Russell Coughlin, Doug Sharpe (Chairman), Terry Connor, Mal Griffiths (Director), Andrew Legg, Gary Henshaw, Shaun Chapple.

Division 2   **SWANSEA CITY**

Vetch Field, Swansea SA1 3SU. Telephone Swansea (0792) 474114. Club shop: 33, William St, Swansea SA1 3QS. 0792 462584. Fax No: (0792) 646120

Ground capacity: 16,540.

Record attendance: 32,796 v Arsenal, FA Cup 4th rd, 17 February 1968.

Record receipts: £36,477.42 v Liverpool, Division 1, 18 September 1982.

Pitch measurements: 112yd × 74yd.

Secretary: George Taylor.

Chairman: D. J. Sharpe.

Directors: D. G. Hammond FCA, MBIM (Vice-chairman), M. Griffiths.

Chief Executive: Robin Sharpe.

Team Manager: Frank Burrows. *Assistant Manager:* Bobby Smith. *Youth Team Manager:* Ron Walton. *Physio:* Ken Davey. *Commercial and Marketing Manager. Programme Editor:* Major Reg Pike.

Year Formed: 1912. Turned Professional: 1912. Ltd Co.: 1912.

Former Names: Swansea Town until February 1970.

Club Nickname: 'The Swans'.

Record League Victory: 8-0 v Hartlepool U, Division 4, 1 April 1978 – Barber; Evans, Bartley, Lally (1) (Morris), May, Bruton, Kevin Moore, Robbie James (3 incl. 1p), Curtis (3), Toshack (1), Chappell.

Record Cup Victory: 12-0 v Sliema W (Malta), ECWC 1st rd 1st leg, 15 September 1982 – Davies; Marustik, Hadziabdic (1), Irwin (1), Kennedy, Rajkovic (1), Loveridge (2) (Leighton James), Robbie James, Charles (2), Stevenson (1), Latchford (1) (Walsh (3)).

Record Defeat: 0-8 v Liverpool, FA Cup 3rd rd, 9 January 1990.

Most League Points (2 for a win): 62, Division 3 (S), 1948–49.

Most League points (3 for a win): 70, Division 4, 1987–88.

Most League Goals: 90, Division 2, 1956–57.

Highest League Scorer in Season: Cyril Pearce, 35, Division 2, 1931–32.

Most League Goals in Total Aggregate: Ivor Allchurch, 166, 1949–58, 1965–68.

Most Capped Player: Ivor Allchurch, 42 (68), Wales.

Most League Appearances: Wilfred Milne, 585, 1919–37.

Record Transfer Fee Received: £370,000 from Leeds U for Alan Curtis, May 1979.

Record Transfer Fee Paid: £340,000 to Liverpool for Colin Irwin, August 1981.

Football League Record: 1920 Original Member of Division 3; 1921–25 Division 3 (S); 1925–47 Division 2; 1947–49 Division 3 (S); 1949–65 Division 2; 1965–67 Division 3; 1967–70 Division 4; 1970–73 Division 3; 1973–78 Division 4; 1978–79 Division 3; 1979–81 Division 2; 1981–83 Division 1; 1983–84 Division 2; 1984–86 Division 3; 1986–88 Division 4; 1988–92 Division 3; 1992– Division 2.

Honours: Football League: Division 1 best season: 6th, 1981–82; Division 2 – Promoted 1980–81 (3rd); Division 3 (S) – Champions 1924–25, 1948–49; Division 3 – Promoted 1978–79 (3rd); Division 4 – Promoted 1969–70 (3rd), 1977–78 (3rd). *FA Cup:* Semi-finals 1926, 1964. *Football League Cup:* best season: 4th rd, 1964–65, 1976–77. *Welsh Cup:* Winners 9 times; Runners-up 8 times. **European Competitions:** *European Cup-Winners Cup:* 1961–62, 1966–67, 1981–82, 1982–83, 1983–84, 1991–92.

Colours: White shirts, white shorts, black stockings. **Change colours:** All yellow.

SWANSEA CITY 1991–92 LEAGUE RECORD

Match No.	Date		Venue	Opponents		Result	H/T Score	Lg. Pos.	Goalscorers	Attendance
1	Aug	17	A	Stockport Co	L	0-5	0-2	—		4241
2		24	H	Bolton W	D	1-1	1-1	20	Connor	3578
3		31	A	Chester C	L	0-2	0-0	23		1162
4	Sep	3	H	Reading	L	1-2	0-0	—	Williams	3206
5		7	A	Fulham	L	0-3	0-1	24		3426
6		14	H	Preston NE	D	2-2	1-1	24	Flynn (og), Raynor	3170
7		21	A	Shrewsbury T	D	0-0	0-0	24		3427
8		28	H	Peterborough U	W	1-0	0-0	24	Legg	2685
9	Oct	5	A	Huddersfield T	L	0-1	0-0	24		5578
10		11	H	Hull C	D	0-0	0-0	—		2725
11		19	H	Stoke C	W	2-1	2-0	22	Harris, Davies A	3363
12		26	A	Torquay U	L	0-1	0-0	23		1908
13	Nov	1	A	Wigan Ath	L	0-1	0-0	—		2092
14		5	H	Leyton Orient	D	2-2	2-2	—	Coughlin, Beauchamp	2081
15		8	H	Bournemouth	W	3-1	1-0	—	Brazil, Walker, Williams	2698
16		23	A	Bradford C	W	6-4	4-1	21	Williams 3, Beauchamp, Legg, Gilligan	5728
17		30	A	Brentford	L	2-3	2-0	22	Williams, Legg	6669
18	Dec	14	H	Exeter C	W	1-0	1-0	19	Williams	2848
19		26	H	Chester C	W	3-0	2-0	18	Gilligan 3	4098
20		28	H	Stockport Co	W	2-1	1-1	16	Purnell, Gilligan	4353
21	Jan	1	A	Reading	L	0-1	0-0	18		5083
22		11	A	Bury	L	0-1	0-0	19		2161
23		18	H	Birmingham C	L	0-2	0-1	21		4147
24		25	A	WBA	W	3-2	0-2	17	Thornber 3	10,395
25		28	H	Darlington	W	4-2	3-1	—	Williams 2, Legg, Chapple	2743
26	Feb	1	A	Stoke C	L	1-2	0-1	15	Gilligan	11,299
27		8	H	Torquay U	W	1-0	1-0	14	Gilligan	3418
28		11	A	Brentford	D	1-1	0-1	—	Legg	3582
29		15	A	Exeter C	L	1-2	0-2	15	Harris	2360
30		22	H	Bury	W	2-1	0-1	15	Raynor, Legg	2787
31		29	A	Hartlepool U	W	1-0	0-0	12	Thornber	2669
32	Mar	3	A	Birmingham C	D	1-1	0-1	—	Williams	9475
33		6	H	WBA	D	0-0	0-0	—		5629
34		10	A	Leyton Orient	W	2-1	1-0	—	Chalmers, Legg	3328
35		14	H	Wigan Ath	W	3-0	0-0	12	Legg, Johnson (og), Chalmers	3726
36		20	A	Bournemouth	L	0-3	0-2	—		4385
37		28	H	Bradford C	D	2-2	2-1	14	Chalmers 2	3748
38		31	A	Preston NE	D	1-1	0-1	—	Chalmers	3367
39	Apr	4	H	Fulham	D	2-2	1-0	13	Chalmers 2	3307
40		7	A	Bolton W	D	0-0	0-0	—		3535
41		11	A	Darlington	D	1-1	1-0	13	Williams	1507
42		17	H	Shrewsbury T	L	1-2	1-0	—	Harris	3429
43		21	A	Peterborough U	L	1-3	0-1	—	Legg	5526
44		25	H	Huddersfield T	L	0-1	0-1	16		3964
45		28	A	Hartlepool U	D	1-1	1-1	—	Chapple	2167
46	May	2	A	Hull C	L	0-3	0-1	19		4070

Final League Position: 19

GOALSCORERS

League (55): Williams 11, Legg 9, Chalmers 7, Gilligan 7, Thornber 4, Harris 3, Beauchamp 2, Chapple 2, Raynor 2, Brazil 1, Connor 1, Coughlin 1, Davies A 1, Purnell 1, Walker 1, own goals 2.
Rumbelows Cup (5): Thornber 2, Chalmers 1, Chapple 1, Gilligan 1.
FA Cup (3): Gilligan 1, Harris 1, Walker 1.

Bracey	Jenkins	Thornber	Coughlin	Harris	Hough	Raynor	Comforth	Davies A	Connor	Legg	Chalmers	McClean	Williams	Ford	Kendall	Freestone	Chapple	Brazil	Gilligan	Davey	Freeman	Bowen	Beauchamp	Walker	Agboola	Purnell	Wallace Ray	Hodgson	Match No.
1	2	3	4*	5	6	7	8	9	10	11	12																		1
1	2	3		5	6	9*	8		10	11	12	4	7†	14															2
1	2	3		5	6	14	8*		10	11	12	9†	7	4															3
	2	3*	8	5	6				10	11	12	9	7	4	1														4
	2	3	4	5	6	12			10	11†		9*	7	8		1	14												5
	2	3*	4	5		9		14	10	11			7†	8		1		6	12										6
	2	3	4*	5					10	11	12		8	7		1		6	9										7
	2	3	4	5					10	11	12		7*	8		1		6	9										8
	2		4	5			8		10	11	12			7		1	3	6	9*										9
	2		4*	5			8	14	10	11	12			7†		1	3	6	9										10
	2		4	5			8		10	11				7		1	3	6	9										11
	2		4	5			8*		10	11	12			7		1	3	6	9										12
	2	14	4	5		12				11			8†	7*		1	3	6	9		10								13
	2		4	5						11			8	7		1	3	6	9				10						14
	2		4	5						11			8	7		1	3*	6	9				10	12					15
	2	14	4*	5						11			8	7†		1		6	9				10	12	3				16
	2	14		5						11	12		8*	7		1		6	9				10†	4	3				17
	2		12	5						11			8	7		1		6	9					4	3	10*			18
	2	14	12	5						11			8	7*		1		6†	9					4	3	10			19
	2			5						11			8	7		1		6	9					4	3	10			20
	2	14	12	5						11			8†	7*		1		6	9					4	3	10			21
	2	12		5			8			11			14	7		1		6*	9					4	3	10†			22
	2		12	5			8			11				7		1		6	9					4	3	10*			23
	2	12		5			8*			11			14	7		1		6	9					4	3	10†			24
	2			5			8			11				7		1		6	9					4	3	10			25
	2	12		5			8			11				7		1		6*	9					4	3	10			26
	2			5			8			11				7		1		6	9					4	3	10			27
	2			5			8			11				7		1		6	9					4	3	10			28
	2†	14		5			8			11				7		1		6	9		12			4	3	10*			29
	2			5			8			11				7		1		6	9					4	3	10			30
	2*			5			8			11				12		1		6	9	7				4	3	10*			31
	2*			5			8			11				7		1		6	9		12			4	3	10			32
	2			5			8			11				7		1		6	9*	12	10			4	3				33
	2			5			8			11*				7		1		6	9		10	12		4	3				34
	2			5			8			11				7		1		6	9		10			4	3				35
	2*	12		5			8†			11				7		1		6	9		10	14		4	3				36
		12		5			8			11				7		1		6	9†		10			4	3		2	14	37
				5			8			11				7		1	3		9		10	12		4	6		2		38
	2	12		5			8*			11				7		1	3		9		10	14		4	6†				39
	2			5			8			11				7		1	3*		9		10	12		4	6				40
	2			5			8			11				7		1	3		9†	12	10	14		4	6*				41
	2			5			8			11				7		1	3		9		10			4	6				42
	2			5			8*			11				7		1	3		9		10	14		4	6†			12	43
				5			8			11				7		1	3†		9*		10	14		4	6			12	44
	2			5			8			11				7		1	3		9		10			4	6				45
	2*			5			8†			11				7		1	3		9		10	12		4	6				46
3	31	26	32	44	5	18	17	6	6	46	14	4	36	42	1	42	17	12	24	3	8	5	5	30	20	5	2	1	
		+3s	+7s	+1s		+8s		+2s					+7s			+3s	+2s		+4s		+1s	+2s	+4s	+6s	+2s	+1s		+2s	

Davies M—Match No. 44(2); Barnhouse Match No. 46(14).

Rumbelows Cup	First Round	Walsall (h)		2-2
		(a)		1-0
	Second Round	Tottenham H (h)		1-0
		(a)		1-5
FA Cup	First Round	Cardiff C (h)		2-1
	Second Round	Exeter C (a)		0-0
		(h)		1-2

SWANSEA CITY

Goalkeepers

							Apps	Goals
Roger Freestone	6 2	12 03	19 8 68	Newport		Newport Co	13	—
						Chelsea	42	—
						Swansea C (loan)	14	—
						Hereford U (loan)	8	—
						Swansea C	42	—
Jimmy Heeps			16 5 71	Luton	Trainee	Swansea C	1	—
Mark Kendall	6 0	12 04	20 9 58	Blackwood	Apprentice	Tottenham H	29	—
						Chesterfield (loan)	9	—
						Newport Co	272	—
						Wolverhampton W	147	—
						Swansea C	12	—
						Burnley (loan)	2	—

Defenders

							Apps	Goals
Reuben Agboola	5 9	11 02	30 5 62	London	Apprentice	Southampton	90	—
						Sunderland	140	—
						Charlton Ath (loan)	1	—
						Port Vale (loan)	9	—
						Swansea C	21	—
Mark Davies*	5 11	11 08	9 8 72	Swansea	Trainee	Swansea C	1	—
Mark Harris	6 1	13 00	15 7 63	Reading	Wokingham	Crystal Palace	2	—
						Burnley (loan)	4	—
						Swansea C	126	6
Steven McMahon	6 04	14 03	22 4 70	Glasgow	Ferguslie	Swansea C	—	—
Paul Miller‡	6 1	12 02	11 10 59	London	Apprentice	Tottenham H	208	7
						Charlton Ath	42	2
						Watford	20	1
						Bournemouth	47	1
						Brentford (loan)	3	—
						Swansea C	12	—
Des Trick*	6 0	12 00	7 11 69	Swansea	Trainee	Swansea C	29	—

Midfield

							Apps	Goals
David Barnhouse§			19 3 75	Swansea	Trainee	Swansea C	1	—
Jason Bowen			24 8 72	Merthyr	Trainee	Swansea C	14	—
Shaun Chapple	5 11	12 03	14 2 73	Swansea	Trainee	Swansea C	21	2
John Cornforth	6 1	11 05	7 10 67	Whitley Bay	Apprentice	Sunderland	32	2
						Doncaster R (loan)	7	3
						Shrewsbury T (loan)	3	—
						Lincoln C (loan)	9	1
						Swansea C	17	—
Russell Coughlin	5 8	11 08	15 2 60	Swansea	Apprentice	Manchester C	—	—
						Blackburn R	24	—
						Carlisle U	130	13
						Plymouth Arg	131	18
						Blackpool	102	8
						Shrewsbury T (loan)	5	—
						Swansea C	62	1
Alan Davies (Deceased)	5 8	11 04	5 12 61	Manchester	Apprentice	Manchester U	7	—
						Newcastle U	21	1
						Charlton Ath (loan)	1	—
						Carlisle U (loan)	4	1
						Swansea C	84	8
						Bradford C	26	1
						Swansea C	43	4
Jonathan Ford	6 01	13 01	12 4 68	Birmingham	Cradley	Swansea C	44	—
Gary Henshaw‡	5 9	11 08	18 2 65	Leeds	Apprentice	Grimsby T	50	9
						Bolton W	70	4
						Rochdale (loan)	9	1
						Swansea C	—	—
David Hough	5 11	11 02	20 2 66	Crewe	Apprentice	Swansea C	227	9
Andy Legg	5 8	10 07	28 7 66	Neath	Briton Ferry	Swansea C	163	26
Steve Thornber*	5 10	11 02	11 10 65	Dewsbury	Local	Halifax T	104	4
						Swansea C	117	5

SWANSEA CITY

Foundation: The earliest Association Football in Wales was played in the Northern part of the country and no international took place in the South until 1894, when a local paper still thought it necessary to publish an outline of the rules and an illustration of the pitch markings. There had been an earlier Swansea club, but this has no connection with Swansea Town (now City) formed at a public meeting in June 1912.

First Football League game: 28 August 1920, Division 3, v Portsmouth (a) L 0-3 – Crumley; Robson, Evans; Smith, Holdsworth, Williams; Hole, I. Jones, Edmundson, Rigsby, Spottiswood.

Did you know: At the end of season 1931–32 Swansea had to meet Wrexham in a Welsh Cup Final replay. They chose to play on a Friday, the day before their last Second Division game of the season against Bury. Nine of the same players appeared in both games which they won by the same score – 2-0.

Managers (and Secretary-managers)
Walter Whittaker 1912–14, William Bartlett 1914–15, Joe Bradshaw 1919–26, Jimmy Thomson 1927–31, Neil Harris 1934–39, Haydn Green 1939–47, Bill McCandless 1947–55, Ron Burgess 1955–58, Trevor Morris 1958–65, Glyn Davies 1965–66, Billy Lucas 1967–69, Roy Bentley 1969–72, Harry Gregg 1972–75, Harry Griffiths 1975–78, John Toshack 1978–83 (resigned October re-appointed in December) 1983–84, Colin Appleton 1984, John Bond 1984–85, Tommy Hutchison 1985–86, Terry Yorath 1986–89, Ian Evans 1989–90, Terry Yorath 1990–91, Frank Burrows March 1991–.

Keith Walker	6 0	11 09	17	4 66	Edinburgh	ICI Juveniles	Stirling Alb	91	17
							St Mirren	43	6
							Swansea C	69	1
John Williams	6 02	12 04	11	5 68	Birmingham	Cradley	Swansea C	39	11
Forwards									
Paul Chalmers	5 10	10 03	31	10 63	Glasgow	Eastercraigs	Celtic	4	1
							Bradford C (loan)	2	—
							St Mirren	101	23
							Swansea C	58	13
Marc Coates*	5 09	10 09	10	10 72	Swansea	Trainee	Swansea C	—	—
Simon Davey*	5 10	11 02	1	10 70	Swansea	Trainee	Swansea C	49	4
Clive Freeman*	5	12 12	12	9 62	Leeds		Doncaster R	—	—
							Bridlington	—	—
							Swansea C	14	—
							Carlisle U (loan)	4	—
Jimmy Gilligan	6 2	11 07	24	1 64	Hammersmith	Apprentice	Watford	27	6
							Lincoln C (loan)	3	—
							Grimsby T	25	4
							Swindon T	17	5
							Lincoln C	11	1
							Newport Co (loan)	5	1
							Cardiff C	99	35
							Portsmouth	32	5
							Swansea C	62	23
David Hodgson‡	5 9	12 02	1	11 60	Gateshead	Amateur	Middlesbrough	125	16
							Liverpool	28	4
							Sunderland	40	5
							Norwich C	6	2
							Middlesbrough (loan)	2	—
							Jerez	—	—
							Sheffield W	11	1
							Metz	—	—
							Swansea C	6	—
Steve Jenkins			16	7 72	Merthyr	Trainee	Swansea C	35	—

Trainees
Barnhouse, David J; Bishop, Matthew; Coates, Jonathan S; Denham, Martin A; Elsey, Kristian G; Moran, Lee; Power, Christian J; Twose, Geraint C; West, Martyn S; Williams, Steven S.

Associated Schoolboys
Florid, Pieir; Jenkins, David M.

514

SWINDON TOWN 1991–92 *Back row (left to right):* Colin Calderwood, Adrian Viveash, Richard Green, Fraser Digby, Shaun Taylor, Nicky Hammond, David Mitchell, Nestor Lorenzo, Steve White.
Centre row: John Trollope (Youth Team Manager), Nicky Summerbee, Darren Hall, Paul Trollope, Edwin Murray, Fitzroy Simpson, Shaun Close, Steve Foley, Martin Ling, Andy Rowland (Reserve Team Manager).
Front row: Kevin Morris (Physiotherapist), Paul Hunt, David Bennett, Ross Maclaren, Duncan Shearer, Glenn Hoddle (Manager), John Gorman (Assistant Manager), Tom Jones, David Kerslake, Micky Hazard, Eddie Buckley (Kit Manager).

Division 1   **SWINDON TOWN**

County Ground, Swindon, Wiltshire SN1 2ED. Telephone Swindon (0793) 430430. Clubcall: 0898 121640. Fax No: 0793 536170

Ground capacity: 16,432.

Record attendance: 32,000 v Arsenal, FA Cup 3rd rd, 15 January 1972.

Record receipts: £101,221 v Aston Villa, FA Cup 5th rd, 16 February 1992.

Pitch measurements: 114yd × 72yd.

President: C. J. Green.

Chairman: R. V. Hardman.

Vice-chairman: J. M. Spearman.

Directors: P. T. Archer, Sir Seton Willis Bt., C. J. Puffett, J. R. Hunt (Associate). *Chief Executive:* Peter Day.

SWINDON TOWN FC

Manager: Glenn Hoddle. *Assistant Manager:* John Gorman. *Coach:* Andy Rowland. *Physio:* Kevin Morris. *Secretary:* Jon Pollard. *Youth Team Manager:* John Trollope. *Marketing Managerr:* Mike Sullivan.

Year Formed: 1881 *(see Foundation).* Turned Professional: 1894. Ltd Co.: 1894.

Former Grounds: 1881–96, The Croft.

Club Nickname: 'Robins'.

Record League Victory: 9-1 v Luton T, Division 3 (S), 28 August 1920 – Nash; Kay, Macconachie; Langford, Hawley, Wareing; Jefferson (1), Fleming (4), Rogers, Batty (2), Davies (1). (1 og).

Record Cup Victory: 10-1 v Farnham U Breweries (away), FA Cup, 1st rd (replay), 28 November 1925 – Nash; Dickenson, Weston, Archer, Bew, Adey; Denyer (2), Wall (1), Richardson (4), Johnson (3), Davies.

Record Defeat: 1-10 v Manchester C, FA Cup 4th rd (replay), 25 January 1930. 1-10 v Kettering, Southern League, 28 December 1901.

Most League Points (2 for a win): 64, Division 3, 1968–69.

Most League points (3 for a win): 102, Division 4, 1985–86 (League record).

Most League Goals: 100, Division 3 (S), 1926–27.

Highest League Scorer in Season: Harry Morris, 47, Division 3 (S), 1926–27.

Most League Goals in Total Aggregate: Harry Morris, 216, 1926–33.

Most Capped Player: Rod Thomas, 30 (50), Wales.

Most League Appearances: John Trollope, 770, 1960–80.

Record Transfer Fee Received: £1,000,000 from Southampton for Alan McLoughlin, December 1990.

Record Transfer Fee Paid: £250,000 to Huddersfield T for Duncan Shearer, June 1988.

Football League Record: 1920 Original Member of Division 3; 1921–58 Division 3 (S); 1958–63 Division 3; 1963–65 Division 2; 1965–69 Division 3; 1969–74 Division 2; 1974–82 Division 3; 1982–86 Division 4; 1986–87 Division 3; 1987–92 Division 2; 1992– Division 1.

Honours: Football League: Division 2 best season; 4th, 1989–90; Division 3 – Runners-up 1962–63, 1968–69; Division 4 – Champions 1985–86 (with record 102 points). *FA Cup:* Semi-finals 1910, 1912. *Football League Cup:* Winners 1968–69. *Anglo-Italian Cup:* Winners 1970.

Colours: Red shirts, red shorts, red stockings. **Change colours**: White and green shirts, blue shorts, blue stockings.

SWINDON TOWN 1991–92 LEAGUE RECORD

Match No.	Date		Venue	Opponents	Result		H/T Score	Lg. Pos.	Goalscorers	Atten- dance
1	Aug	17	H	Leicester C	D	0-0	0-0	—		12,426
2		24	A	Cambridge U	L	2-3	1-1	20	Shearer, Hazard (pen)	6232
3		31	H	Barnsley	W	3-1	0-1	11	White, Ling, Shearer	7449
4	Sep	3	A	Ipswich T	W	4-1	2-1	—	White, Calderwood, Taylor, Hazard	11,002
5		7	A	Port Vale	D	2-2	0-0	8	White, MacLaren	7168
6		14	H	Sunderland	W	5-3	3-0	6	White, Simpson, Hazard 2 (1 pen), Shearer	11,417
7		17	H	Bristol R	W	1-0	1-0	—	Jones	11,391
8		21	A	Wolverhampton W	L	1-2	0-1	5	White	15,219
9		28	H	Watford	W	3-1	2-0	3	Shearer, Simpson, Taylor	8863
10	Oct	5	A	Plymouth Arg	W	4-0	2-0	3	Shearer 4	6208
11		12	H	Derby Co	L	1-2	0-1	4	Hazard (pen)	11,883
12		19	H	Blackburn R	W	2-1	0-0	4	White, Calderwood	10,717
13		26	A	Brighton & HA	W	2-0	1-0	4	Shearer 2	7370
14	Nov	2	H	Newcastle U	W	2-1	1-0	2	Calderwood, White	10,731
15		6	A	Charlton Ath	D	0-0	0-0	—		5398
16		9	A	Southend U	L	2-3	0-1	3	White, Shearer	7709
17		16	H	Portsmouth	L	2-3	0-0	4	White 2	10,738
18		22	A	Tranmere R	D	0-0	0-0	—		9585
19		30	H	Grimsby T	D	1-1	1-1	7	Simpson	8397
20	Dec	7	A	Middlesbrough	D	2-2	0-1	8	Simpson, Shearer	13,300
21		20	H	Ipswich T	D	0-0	0-0	—		7404
22		26	A	Bristol C	D	1-1	1-0	9	Shearer	14,636
23		28	A	Barnsley	D	1-1	1-0	9	Shearer	8357
24	Jan	1	H	Millwall	W	3-1	3-0	7	Shearer 2, Ling	9746
25		11	H	Cambridge U	L	0-2	0-0	8		10,878
26		18	A	Leicester C	L	1-3	0-1	9	Bodin	14,226
27		28	H	Oxford U	W	2-1	1-0	—	Kerslake, Shearer	8926
28	Feb	1	A	Blackburn R	L	1-2	1-0	9	Mitchell	14,887
29		4	H	Bristol C	W	2-0	0-0	—	Jones, Shearer	9627
30		8	H	Brighton & HA	W	2-1	0-1	4	Calderwood 2	9127
31		22	A	Grimsby T	D	0-0	0-0	6		6817
32		29	H	Middlesbrough	L	0-1	0-0	9		10,379
33	Mar	7	A	Oxford U	L	3-5	2-3	10	Close, Mitchell 2	7795
34		10	H	Charlton Ath	L	1-2	0-1	—	Shearer	7196
35		14	A	Newcastle U	L	1-3	0-1	10	Mitchell	23,138
36		17	H	Tranmere R	W	2-0	1-0	—	Shearer 2	6780
37		21	A	Southend U	W	3-1	1-1	8	Shearer, Bodin (pen), Mitchell	8628
38		28	A	Portsmouth	D	1-1	0-0	10	Jones	16,007
39	Apr	4	H	Port Vale	W	1-0	1-0	8	Jones	8014
40		8	A	Millwall	D	1-1	1-1	—	Gibson	6722
41		12	A	Bristol R	D	1-1	0-0	—	Taylor	6905
42		18	H	Wolverhampton W	W	1-0	1-0	8	Ling	10,863
43		20	A	Watford	D	0-0	0-0	8		9911
44		25	H	Plymouth Arg	W	1-0	1-0	8	Taylor	10,463
45		27	A	Sunderland	D	0-0	0-0	—		16,716
46	May	2	A	Derby Co	L	1-2	0-1	8	Hazard	22,608

Final League Position: 8

GOALSCORERS

League (69): Shearer 22, White 10, Hazard 6 (3 pens), Calderwood 5, Mitchell 5, Jones 4, Simpson 4, Taylor 4, Ling 3, Bodin 2 (1 pen), Close 1, Gibson 1, Kerslake 1, MacLaren 1.
Rumbelows Cup (13): Shearer 6, White 3, Hazard 1, Mitchell 1, Summerbee 1, Taylor 1.
FA Cup (7): Shearer 4, Mitchell 2, Calderwood 1.

Digby	Kerslake	Summerbee	Hoddle	Calderwood	Taylor	Hazard	Shearer	Simpson	MacLaren	Mitchell	White	Foley	Jones	Ling	Viveash	Lorenzo	Hammond	Close	Bodin	Waddock	Gibson	Moncur	Match No.
1	2	3†	4	5	6	7	8	9	10	11*	12	14											1
1		3	4	5	6	7	8	9	10*	11†			2	12	14								2
1			4	5	6	7†	8	9	10		11		2	14	3*	12							3
1			4	5	6	7	8	9	10		11*		2	12	3								4
			4	5	6	7*	8	9	10		11		2	12	3		1						5
			4	5	6	7	8	9	10		11		2		3		1						6
		3	4	5	6	7	8	9	10		11		2				1						7
		3	4	5	6	7*	8	9	10		11		2				1	12					8
	12	3	4	5	6	7*	8	9	10		11		2				1						9
1	2	3	4*	5	6	7	8	9	10		11		12										10
1	2			5	6	7	8	9*	10		11	12	4			3†		14					11
	2	3		5	6	7	8	9	10		11		4				1						12
	2	3		5	6	7	8	9	10		11		4				1						13
	2	3		5	6	7	8	9	10		11		4				1						14
	2	3		5	6	7*	8	9	10		11†	12	4				1	14					15
	2*	3		5	6	7	8	9	10		11	12	4				1						16
	2	3		5		7	8	9	10		11		4		6		1						17
	2			5		7	8	9	10		11	3	4		6		1						18
	2	12		5		7	8	9	10		11	3	4*		6		1						19
	2	3		5		7	8	9	10		11		4		6		1						20
	2	12		5	6	7	8†	9	10	14	11		4*		3		1						21
	2	12		5	6	7*	8	9	10	14	11†	3	4				1						22
	2			5	6	7	8	9	10	12	11*	3	4				1						23
	2			5	6	7	8	9	10		11	3	4				1						24
	2	14		5	6	7	8	9*	10	12	11	3	4†				1						25
1	2	12		5	6	7	8	9	10		11		4*						3				26
1	2			5	6	7	8	9	10		11	12	4*						3				27
1	2	12		5	6	7	8†		10*	11		9	4					14	3				28
	2			5	6	7	8		10	11		9	4				1		3				29
	2			5	6	7	8	12	10	11		9	4				1		3*				30
	2	12		5	6	7	8	9	10*	11			4				1		3				31
	2†	12		5	6	7*	8	9	10	11			4				1	14	3				32
	2	7*	10	5	6		8			11			4			12	1	9	3				33
	2	7	10	5	6		8						4*	12	11		1	9	3				34
1	2		10	5	6	7	8			11		12	4*			9			3				35
1	2	9	10	5	6	7	8			11			4						3				36
1	2		10	5	6	7	8			11			4						3	9			37
1	2	12	10*	5	6	7				11			4						3	9	8		38
1	2			5	6	7				11			4			10			3	9*	8	12	39
1	2	12		5	6	7				11			4			10			3		8	9*	40
1	2		10	5	6	7				11			4			9			3		8		41
1	2		10	5	6	7				11			4*			9			3		8	12	42
1	2		10	5	6	7				11			4			9		12	3		8*		43
1	2		10	5	6	7				11*			4†			9		12	3	14	8		44
1	2	14		5	6	7				11						9†		12	3	4	8*		45
1	2		10	5	6	7				11*						9		8	3	4		12	46
21	38	16	22	46	42	44	37	29	32	24	21	5	37	17	9	2	25	4	21	5	8	1	

```
21 38 16 22 46 42 44 37 29 32 24 21  5 37 17  9  2 25  4 21  5  8  1
    +  +                    +            +  +  +  +  +  +        +        +  +  +
   1s 11s                  1s          3s 2s 4s 4s 1s 2s       8s       1s 1s 2s
```

Rumbelows Cup	First Round	WBA (h)	2-0
		(a)	2-2
	Second Round	Millwall (a)	2-2
		(h)	3-1
	Third Round	Huddersfield T (a)	4-1
	Fourth Round	Crystal Palace (h)	0-1
FA Cup	Third Round	Watford (h)	3-2
	Fourth Round	Cambridge U (a)	3-0
	Fifth Round	Aston Villa (h)	1-2

SWINDON TOWN

Player and Position	Ht	Wt	Birth Date	Birth Place	Source	Clubs	League App	League Gls
Goalkeepers								
Fraser Digby	6 1	12 12	23 4 67	Sheffield	Apprentice	Manchester U	—	—
						Oldham Ath (loan)	—	—
						Swindon T (loan)	—	—
						Swindon T	223	—
Nicky Hammond	6 0	11 13	7 9 67	Hornchurch	Apprentice	Arsenal	—	—
						Bristol R (loan)	3	—
						Peterborough U (loan)	—	—
						Aberdeen (loan)	—	—
						Swindon T	34	—
Defenders								
Colin Calderwood	6 0	11 09	20 1 65	Stranraer	Amateur	Mansfield T	100	1
						Swindon T	284	18
Darren Hall	5 10	11 06	3 1 73	Grays	Trainee	Swindon T	—	—
Glenn Hoddle	6 0	11 06	27 10 57	Hayes	Apprentice	Tottenham H	377	88
						Monaco		
						Chelsea	—	—
						Swindon T	22	—
Nestor Lorenzo	5 10	12 08	28 2 66	Argentina	Bari	Swindon T	24	2
Ross MacLaren	5 10	12 12	14 4 62	Edinburgh	Rangers	Shrewsbury T	161	18
						Derby Co	122	4
						Swindon T	160	9
John Moncur	5 7	9 10	22 9 66	Stepney	Apprentice	Tottenham H	21	1
						Doncaster R (loan)	4	—
						Cambridge U (loan)	4	—
						Portsmouth (loan)	7	—
						Brentford (loan)	5	1
						Ipswich T (loan)	6	—
						Nottingham F (loan)	—	—
						Swindon T	3	—
Lee Spalding‡	5 9	11 00	21 8 72	Swindon	Trainee	Swindon T	—	—
Shaun Taylor	6 1	13 00	26 3 63	Plymouth	Bideford	Exeter C	200	16
						Swindon T	42	4
Adrian Viveash	6 1	11 12	30 9 69	Swindon	Trainee	Swindon T	35	1
Midfield								
Paul Bodin	6 0	12 01	13 9 64	Cardiff	Chelsea	Newport Co	—	—
						Cardiff C	57	3
						Bath C	—	—
						Newport Co	6	1
						Swindon T	93	9
						Crystal Palace	9	—
						Swindon T	21	2
						Newcastle U (loan)	6	—
Micky Hazard	5 7	10 05	5 2 60	Sunderland	Apprentice	Tottenham H	91	13
						Chelsea	81	9
						Portsmouth	8	1
						Swindon T	78	14
Tommy Jones	5 10	11 07	7 10 64	Aldershot	Weymouth	Aberdeen	28	3
						Swindon T	168	12
David Kerslake	5 8	11 04	19 6 66	London	Apprentice	QPR	58	6
						Swindon T	104	1
Martin Ling	5 7	9 12	15 7 66	West Ham	Apprentice	Exeter C	116	14
						Swindon T	2	—
						Southend U	138	31
						Mansfield T (loan)	3	—
						Swindon T (loan)	1	—
						Swindon T	21	3

SWINDON TOWN

Foundation: It is generally accepted that Swindon Town came into being in 1881, although there is no firm evidence that the club's founder, Rev. William Pitt, captain of the Spartans (an offshoot of a cricket club) changed his club's name to Swindon Town before 1883, when the Spartans amalgamated with St. Mark's Young Men's Friendly Society.

First Football League game: 28 August 1920, Division 3, v Luton T (h) W 9-1 – Nash; Kay, Macconachie; Langford, Hawley, Wareing; Jefferson (1), Fleming (4), Rogers, Batty (2), Davies (1). (1 og).

Did you know: In a Division 3 (S) game at home to Bournemouth on 2 January 1926, Swindon were 2-0 down after only ten minutes but then went on to win 8-2 with Frank "Swerver" Richardson scoring four.

Managers (and Secretary-managers)
Sam Allen 1902–33, Ted Vizard 1933–39, Neil Harris 1939–41, Louis Page 1945–53, Maurice Lindley 1953–55, Bert Head 1956–65, Danny Williams 1965–69, Fred Ford 1969–71, Dave Mackay 1971–72, Les Allen 1972–74, Danny Williams 1974–78, Bobby Smith 1978–80, John Trollope 1980–83, Ken Beamish 1983–84, Lou Macari 1984–89, Ossie Ardiles 1989–91, Glenn Hoddle April 1991–.

Player and Position	Ht	Wt	Birth Date	Birth Place	Source	Clubs	League App	Gls
Edwin Murray	5 11	11 07	31 8 73	Redbridge	Trainee	Swindon T	1	—
Paul Trollope*	6 0	12 02	3 6 72	Swindon	Trainee	Swindon T	—	—
						Torquay U (loan)	10	—
Forwards								
Dave Bennett	5 9	10 07	11 7 59	Manchester	Amateur	Manchester C	52	9
						Cardiff C	77	18
						Coventry C	172	25
						Sheffield W	28	—
						Swindon T	1	—
						Shrewsbury T (loan)	2	2
Shaun Close	5 8	10 01	8 9 66	Islington	Trainee	Tottenham H	9	—
						Bournemouth	39	8
						Swindon T	37	1
Paul Hunt	5 5	10 02	8 10 71	Swindon	Trainee	Swindon T	6	—
David Mitchell	6 1	11 08	13 6 62	Scotland	Feyenoord	Chelsea	7	—
						Newcastle U (loan)	2	1
						Swindon T	27	5
Nick Summerbee	5 11	11 08	26 8 71	Altrincham	Trainee	Swindon T	35	—
Steve White	5 11	11 04	2 1 59	Chipping Sodbury	Mangotsfield U	Bristol R	50	20
						Luton T	72	25
						Charlton Ath	29	12
						Lincoln C (loan)	3	—
						Luton T (loan)	4	—
						Bristol R	101	24
						Swindon T	204	76

Trainees
Fishlock, Murray E; French, Robert J. D; Lane, Steven J; Luwero, Stephen; O'Sullivan, Wayne S. J; O'Driscoll, Mark A; Phillips, Kevin M; Phillips, Marcus S; Thomson, Andrew J; Williams, Barry J.

Associated Schoolboys
Bates, Andrew P; Gee, David G; Harvey, Iain D; Holloway, Jonathan S; Horgan, Gary A; Jay, Christopher R; Jordon, Mark J; King, Mark D; Little, Paul D; Medcroft, Scott J; Mifsud, Justin A; Miles, Wayne; Mills, Carl L; Taylor, Clive A; Thorne, Gary R.

Associated Schoolboys who have accepted the club's offer of a Traineeship/Contract
Grey, Kerry C; McPhee, Norman B; Philips, James A; Reeves, Stephen J; Worrall, Benjamin J.

TORQUAY UNITED 1991–92   *Back row (left to right):* Wayne Dobbins, Paul Smith, Chris Myers, Gareth Howells, Ian Gandy, Paul Holmes, Mark Loram.
Centre row: John James (Chief Scout), Matthew Elliott, Andy Rowland, Mark Dobie, David Hodges, Alex Crook, Chris Curran, Arron Davis, Darran Rowbotham, Paul Compton (Y.T. Officer).
Front row: Sean Joyce, Neil Sang, John Uzzell, Mike Bateson (Chairman), Wes Saunders, Paul Hall, Scott Colcombe, Micky Holmes.

Division 3   **TORQUAY UNITED**

Plainmoor Ground, Torquay, Devon TQ1 3PS. Telephone Torquay (0803) 328666/7. Clubcall: 0898 121641. Fax No: 0803 323976

Ground capacity: 6057.

Record attendance: 21,908 v Huddersfield T, FA Cup 4th rd, 29 January 1955.

Record receipts: £26,205 v Exeter C, Division 3, 1 January 1992.

Pitch measurements: 110yd × 71yd.

President: A. J. Boyce.

Chairman/Managing Director: M. Bateson.

Directors: M. Beer, I. Hayman, W. Rogers, D. Turner, D. Wilson, M. Benney, Mrs S. Bateson.

Team Manager: Paul Compton.

Assistant Manager: Justin Fashanu.

Physio: Norman Medhurst.

Company Secretary: C. Olney. *Lottery Administrators:* C. Munslow and A. Sandford. *Commercial manager:* D. Turner.

Year Formed: 1898. Turned Professional: 1921. Ltd Co.: 1921.

Former Grounds: 1898, Teignmouth Road; 1901, Torquay Recreation Ground; 1905, Cricket Field Road; 1907–10, Torquay Cricket Ground.

Former Names: 1910, Torquay Town; 1921, Torquay United.

Club Nickname: 'The Gulls'.

Record League Victory: 9-0 v Swindon T, Division 3 (S), 8 March 1952 – George Webber; Topping, Ralph Calland; Brown, Eric Webber, Towers; Shaw (1), Marchant (1), Northcott (2), Collins (3), Edds (2).

Record Cup Victory: 7-1 v Northampton T, FA Cup, 1st rd, 14 November 1959 – Gill; Penford, Downs; Bettany, George Northcott, Rawson; Baxter, Cox, Tommy Northcott (1), Bond (3), Pym (3).

Record Defeat: 2-10 v Fulham, Division 3 (S), 7 September 1931 and v Luton T, Division 3 (S), 2 September 1933.

Most League Points (2 for a win): 60, Division 4, 1959–60.

Most League points (3 for a win): 77, Division 4, 1987–88.

Most League Goals: 89, Division 3 (S), 1956–57.

Highest League Scorer in Season: Sammy Collins, 40, Division 3 (S), 1955–56.

Most League Goals in Total Aggregate: Sammy Collins, 204, 1948–58.

Most Capped Player: None.

Most League Appearances: Dennis Lewis, 443, 1947–59.

Record Transfer Fee Received: £125,000 from Manchester U for Lee Sharpe, May 1988.

Record Transfer Fee Paid: £60,000 to Dundee for Wes Saunders, July 1990.

Football League Record: 1927 Elected to Division 3 (S); 1958–60 Division 4; 1960–62 Division 3; 1962–66 Division 4; 1966–72 Division 3; 1972–91 Division 4; 1991– Division 3.

Honours: Football League: Division 3 best season: 4th, 1967–68; Division 3 (S) – Runners-up 1956–57; Division 4 – Promoted 1959–60 (3rd), 1965–66 (3rd), 1990–91 (Play-offs). *FA Cup:* best season: 4th rd, 1949, 1955, 1971, 1983, 1990. *Football League Cup:* never past 3rd rd. *Sherpa Van Trophy:* Runners-up 1989.

Colours: Yellow and white striped shirts, navy shorts, navy stockings. **Change colours:** Blue shirts, white shorts, blue stockings.

TORQUAY UNITED 1991–92 LEAGUE RECORD

Match No.	Date		Venue	Opponents	Result		H/T Score	Lg. Pos.	Goalscorers	Attendance
1	Aug	17	H	Hartlepool U	W	3-1	2-0	—	Elliott, Rowland, Loram (pen)	4163
2		24	A	Preston NE	L	0-3	0-1	14		3654
3		31	H	Fulham	L	0-1	0-1	17		3299
4	Sep	4	A	Exeter C	L	0-1	0-0	—		5772
5		6	A	Stockport Co	L	1-2	0-1	—	Elliott	5618
6		14	H	Shrewsbury T	L	1-2	1-1	23	Rowbotham	2811
7		17	H	Reading	L	1-2	0-1	—	Darby	2591
8		21	A	Hull C	L	1-4	1-2	23	Rowbotham (pen)	3093
9		28	H	Chester C	W	3-2	2-1	23	Holmes M, Darby, Elliott	2062
10	Oct	5	A	Bolton W	L	0-1	0-1	23		5092
11		12	H	Huddersfield T	L	0-1	0-0	24		2936
12		19	A	Bradford C	L	0-2	0-0	24		4543
13		26	H	Swansea C	W	1-0	0-0	24	Elliott	1908
14	Nov	2	A	Birmingham C	L	0-3	0-1	24		9478
15		6	H	Bournemouth	W	1-0	0-0	—	Holmes P	1884
16		9	H	Leyton Orient	W	1-0	1-0	20	Whitbread (og)	2388
17		23	A	Stoke C	L	0-3	0-2	23		9124
18		30	A	Peterborough U	D	1-1	0-0	24	Elliott	4007
19	Dec	14	H	Brentford	D	1-1	0-1	23	Rowbotham (pen)	2475
20		20	H	Preston NE	W	1-0	1-0	—	Loram (pen)	2183
21		26	A	Fulham	L	1-2	1-2	20	Hall	4186
22		28	A	Hartlepool U	D	1-1	1-1	21	Loram (pen)	3812
23	Jan	1	H	Exeter C	W	1-0	0-0	20	Fashanu	5696
24		4	H	WBA	W	1-0	0-0	17	Fashanu	4159
25		11	A	Darlington	L	2-3	1-3	17	Dobbins, Joyce	2493
26		18	H	Bury	L	0-2	0-1	19		2625
27	Feb	1	H	Bradford C	D	1-1	1-0	21	Fashanu (pen)	2243
28		8	A	Swansea C	L	0-1	0-1	22		3418
29		15	A	Brentford	L	2-3	0-1	23	Saunders, Loram	6079
30		22	H	Darlington	W	3-0	2-0	21	Fashanu 2, Loram	2415
31		29	A	WBA	L	0-1	0-0	22		11,669
32	Mar	3	A	Bury	D	0-0	0-0	—		1663
33		7	H	Wigan Ath	L	0-1	0-0	23		2198
34		10	A	Bournemouth	L	1-2	0-2	—	Fashanu	4083
35		21	A	Leyton Orient	L	0-2	0-0	23		3636
36		24	H	Birmingham C	L	1-2	1-0	—	Myers	2446
37		28	H	Stoke C	W	1-0	1-0	23	Dobie	3260
38		31	A	Shrewsbury T	D	2-2	0-2	—	Myers, Dobie	2172
39	Apr	4	H	Stockport Co	W	2-0	1-0	23	Fashanu, Saunders	2693
40		7	A	Wigan Ath	D	0-0	0-0	—		1970
41		11	A	Reading	L	1-6	1-4	23	Myers	3111
42		14	H	Hull C	W	2-1	0-1	—	Myers, Fashanu	2339
43		20	A	Chester C	L	0-2	0-1	23		1317
44		25	A	Bolton W	W	2-0	1-0	23	Fashanu (pen), Moore	2178
45		28	H	Peterborough U	D	2-2	1-1	—	Fashanu (pen), Saunders	1934
46	May	2	A	Huddersfield T	L	0-4	0-2	23		7961

Final League Position: 23

GOALSCORERS

League (42): Fashanu 10 (3 pens), Elliott 5, Loram 5 (3 pens), Myers 4, Rowbotham 3 (2 pens), Saunders 3, Darby 2, Dobie 2, Dobbins 1, Hall 1, Holmes M 1, Holmes P 1, Joyce 1, Moore 1, Rowland 1, own goals 1.
Rumbelows Cup (4): Elliott 2, Hodges 1, Loram 1 (1 pen).
FA Cup (7): Loram 3, Hall 2, Colcombe 1, Holmes M 1.

Howells	Myers	Loram	Whiston	Elliott	Holmes M	Hodges D	Colcombe	Rowland	Dobie	Dobbins	Hall	Joyce	Uzzell	Holmes P	Sang	Rowbotham	Curran	McNichol	Darby	Lange	Fillery	Compton	Edwards	Lloyd	Fashanu	Davis	Hodges K	Saunders	Match No.
1	2	3	4	5	6	7	8	9	10	11																			1
1	2	3	4	5	6	7	8*	9	10	11†	12	14																	2
1	2	3		5	6	12		9	10*	11	7		4	8															3
1	2	3	7	5	6			9	12	11*		10	4	8															4
1	2		3	5	6*			9	10	8		7	4	11	12														5
1	2	4*		5	6		12†	10	8	9			3	11		7	14												6
1	2	3		5	6				10			9	4*	11†	12	·7			8	14									7
				5	6	9	11		10	2		8*	3		12	7†			4	14	1								8
1		10		5	6		8*			11	12					7	2		9		3	4							9
1	12	10		5	6		8			11						7*	2		9		3	4							10
1	3	10		5	6		12			8			2			7			9*		11	4							11
1	3	9		5	6	14				8			12	2		7†					11*	4	10						12
1	11	3		5						8		9		2	6	7						4	10						13
1	12			5			11*			8		9		2†	6	7	3		14			4	10						14
1		11		5	6					8		9	3	2		7						4	10						15
1		11		5	6					8		9	3	2		7			12			4	10*						16
1	14	11		5	6	12				8		9	3†	2		7						4*	10						17
1	4*	11		5	6			12		8		9	3	2		7							10						18
1		10		5	6		11		12	8		9	3*	2		7						4							19
1		10		5			11			7*	8	12		3	6		2								4	9			20
1		10		5			11			7	8			3	6		2*		12						4	9			21
1	3	10		5			11			7*	8	12		2	6										4	9			22
1	3	10		5			11			7	8	12		2	6*			5							4	9			23
1	3						11*			7	8			2	6			5	12						4	9	10		24
1	3	12		5			11			7	8	14		2	9†		6								4		10*		25
1	4	10		5			11*			7	8			2			6		12							9	3		26
1		11		5			12				8			2	14		6†		10						4	9	3*	7	27
1	11	3		5						8				2			6		10*						4	9	7	12	28
1	2	11		5	6		10*			12														8	9	3	7	4	29
1	2	11			6		10					7	8				2							5	9	3		4	30
1	2	11		5			10					7	8	6											3	9		4	31
1	2	11		5			10					7	8	6											3	9		4	32
1	2	11		5			10					7	8	6											3	9		4	33
1	6	11		5*			10†					7	8	2	14		12						3		9			4	34
		10	9	5			12					7	8	2			6						4*						35
	10	9					11					7	8	2			6											4	36
1	10						14	9				7	8	2			5		6†							12		4	37
1	10						14	9				7†	8*	2	12		5		6							3		4	38
1	10†							9				5	8	2					6					7	2*			4	39
	10						12	9				5	8	2					6					7	2*			4	40
	6							10				9	14	12	8*				2				5	7				4	41
	10							9				5	8	2					6*					7	12			4	42
	10							9	12			5	8	2										7				4	43
	10							12	9			5*	8	2										7				4	44
	10							9*				5	8	2					12					7				4	45
1	10							9				7†	8	2			6							12				4	46

Totals:

Howells	Myers	Loram	Whiston	Elliott	Holmes M	Hodges D	Colcombe	Rowland	Dobie	Dobbins	Hall	Joyce	Uzzell	Holmes P	Sang	Rowbotham	Curran	McNichol	Darby	Lange	Fillery	Compton	Edwards	Lloyd	Fashanu	Davis	Hodges K	Saunders
38	36	30	4	33	18	3	21	5	18	18	34	29	10	36	8	14	15	2	6	1	4	19	7	13	21	9	3	17
+3s	+1s					+3s	+7s	+2s	+2s	+3s	+4s	+6s		+6s			+2s		+8s						+3s	+1s		

Lowe—Match No. 35(1) 40(1) 41(1) 42(1) 43(1) 44(1) 45(1); Herrera—Match No. 35(3) 36(3) 37(3*) 39(3) 40(3) 41(3) 42(3) 43(3) 44(3) 45(3) 46(3*); Franklin—Match No. 35(11†) 46(14); Moore—Match No. 36(5) 43(6) 44(6) 45(6) 46(5); Trollope—Match No. 37(11) 38(11) 39(11) 40(11) 41(11†) 42(11) 43(11*) 44(11) 45(11) 46(11); Smith—Match No. 39(12); Bennellick—Match No. 39(14).

Rumbelows Cup	First Round	Hereford U	(h)	2-0
			(a)	1-2
	Second Round	Oldham Ath	(a)	1-7
			(h)	0-2
FA Cup	First Round	Birmingham C	(h)	3-0
	Second Round	Farnborough	(h)	1-1
			(a)	3-4

TORQUAY UNITED

Player and Position	Ht	Wt	Birth Date	Birth Place	Source	Clubs	League App	League Gls
Goalkeepers								
Ian Gandy‡			28 4 73	Worcester	Trainee	Liverpool Torquay U	— —	— —
Gareth Howells*	6 1	12 08	13 6 70	Guildford	Trainee	Tottenham H Swindon T (loan) Leyton Orient (loan) Torquay U	— — — 83	— — — —
Matthew Lowe§			28 2 74	West Midlands	Trainee	Torquay U	7	—
Defenders								
Paul Compton†	6 02	14 05	6 6 61	Stroud	Trowbridge T	Bournemouth Aldershot Torquay U	64 13 100	— — 4
Alex Crook‡			28 11 72	Torquay	Trainee	Torquay U	—	—
Chris Curran	5 11	11 09	17 9 71	Birmingham	Trainee	Torquay U	31	—
Arron Davis			11 2 72	Essex	Trainee	Torquay U	12	—
Matthew Elliott	6 3	13 06	1 11 68	Surrey	Epsom & Ewell	Charlton Ath Torquay U Scunthorpe U (loan)	— 124 8	— 15 1
Paul Holmes	5 10	11 00	18 2 68	Sheffield	Apprentice	Doncaster R Torquay U	47 138	1 4
Philip Lloyd*	5 11	11 11	26 12 64	Hemsworth	Apprentice	Middlesbrough Barnsley Darlington Torquay U	— — 127 170	— — 3 7
Jim McNichol‡	6 0	12 10	9 6 58	Glasgow	Apprentice	Ipswich T Luton T Brentford Exeter C Torquay U Exeter C Torquay U	— 15 155 87 124 42 2	— — 22 10 13 8 —
Wes Saunders	6 0	11 11	23 2 63	Sunderland	School	Newcastle U Bradford C (loan) Carlisle U Dundee Torquay U	79 4 97 50 73	— — 11 2 9
John Uzzell*	5 10	11 03	31 3 59	Plymouth	Apprentice	Plymouth Arg Torquay U	302 92	6 2
Midfield								
Ian Bastow	5 8	9 02	12 8 71	Torquay	Trainee	Torquay U	11	—
James Bennellick§			19 9 74	Torquay	Trainee	Torquay U	1	—
Scott Colcombe	5 6	10 00	15 12 71	West Bromwich	Trainee	WBA Torquay U	— 28	— —
Wayne Dobbins*	5 7	10 08	30 8 68	Bromsgrove	Apprentice	WBA Torquay U	45 21	— 1
David Hodges‡	5 9	10 02	17 1 70	Hereford		Mansfield T Torquay U	85 16	7 —
Sean Joyce	5 8	10 05	15 2 67	Doncaster		Doncaster R Exeter C (loan) Torquay U	41 1 131	2 — 12
Chris Myers	5 11	11 03	1 4 69	Yeovil	Trainee	Torquay U	77	6
Neil Sang	5 9	10 07	23 5 72	Liverpool	Trainee	Everton Torquay U	— 14	— —
Forwards								
Duane Darby§			17 10 73	West Midlands	Trainee	Torquay U	14	2

TORQUAY UNITED

Foundation: The idea of establishing a Torquay club was agreed by olboys of Torquay College and Torbay College, while sitting in Princess Gardens listening to the band. A proper meeting was subsequently held at Tor Abbey Hotel at which officers were elected. This was in 1898 and the club's first competition was the Eastern League (later known as the East Devon League).

First Football League game: 27 August 1927, Division 3(S), v Exeter C (h) D 1-1 – Millsom; Cook, Smith; Wellock, Wragg, Connor, Mackey, Turner (1), Jones, McGovern, Thomson.

Did you know: In 1969–70 United created a League record by drawing eight consecutive Third Division games.

Managers (and Secretary-managers)
Percy Mackrill 1927–29, A. H. Hoskins 1929*, Frank Womack 1929–32, Frank Brown 1932–38, Alf Steward 1938–40, Billy Butler 1945–46, Jack Butler 1946–47, John McNeil 1947–50, Bob John 1950, Alex Massie 1950–51, Eric Webber 1951–65, Frank O'Farrell 1965–68, Alan Brown 1969–71, Jack Edwards 1971–73, Malcolm Musgrove 1973–76, Mike Green 1977–81, Frank O'Farrell 1981–82 (continued as GM to 1983), Bruch Rioch 1982–84, Dave Webb 1984–85, John Sims 1985, Stuart Morgan 1985–87, Cyril Knowles 1987–89, Dave Smith 1989–91, John Impey 1991–92, Ivan Golac 1992. Paul Compton May 1992–.

Player and Position	Ht	Wt	Birth Date	Birth Place	Source	Clubs	League App	Gls
Mark Dobie*			8 11 63	Carlisle	Gretna	Cambridge U	—	—
						Torquay U	20	2
Justin Fashanu	6 1	13 01	19 2 61	Kensington	Apprentice	Norwich C	90	35
						Nottingham F	32	3
						Southampton (loan)	9	3
						Notts Co	64	20
						Brighton & HA	16	2
						Edmonton	—	—
						Manchester C	2	—
						West Ham U	2	—
						Leyton Orient	5	—
						Newcastle U	—	—
						Toronto	—	—
						Torquay U	42	20
Jeff Franklin§			8 12 73	London	Trainee	Torquay U	2	—
Paul Hall	5 9	10 02	3 7 72	Manchester	Trainee	Torquay U	65	1
Mark Loram	6 0	12 00	13 8 67	Paignton	Brixham	Torquay U	52	8
						QPR (loan)	—	—
						QPR	—	—
						Torquay U (loan)	13	4
						Torquay U	196	36
						Stockport Co (loan)	4	—
Darren Moore§			22 4 74	West Midlands	Trainee	Torquay U	5	1
Andy Rowland‡	6 2	13 10	1 10 65	Taunton		Southampton	—	—
						Torquay U	16	1
Paul Smith*	5 8	9 09	5 10 67	London	Apprentice	Arsenal	—	—
						Brentford	17	1
						Bristol R	16	1
						Torquay U	74	12

Trainees
Anbany, Simon J; Bennellick, James A; Darby, Duane A; Franklin, Jeffrey T; Gardiner, Matthew; Ginter, Anthony P; Gordon, Andrew N; Hardy, Paul A; Lowe, Matthew I; Manton, Neil R; Moore, Darren M; O'Connor, Christopher J; Poblocki, Dean W; Stamps, Scott.

**Non-Contract
Compton, Paul D.

Associated Schoolboys
Baker, Kevin C; Head, Kevin; Nickson, Adam; Nickson, Carl; Setter, Lee T.

Associated Schoolboys who have accepted the club's offer of a Traineeship/Contract
Maloney, Shaun M; White, Richard; Winteridge, Graham J.

**Non-Contract Players who are retained must be re-signed before they are eligible to play in League matches.

TOTTENHAM HOTSPUR 1991–92 *Back row (left to right):* John Moncur, Andy Polston, Gudni Bergsson, Erik Thorstvedt, Mitchell Thomas, Ian Walker, David Tuttle, Steve Sedgley, Justin Edinburgh.

Centre row: Doug Livermore (Assistant Manager), Philip Gray, Brian Statham, Pat Van den Hauwe, Vinny Samways, David Howells, Paul Moran, Navim, John Hendry, Ray Clemence (Reserve Team Manager/Goalkeeping Coach).

Front row: Paul Walsh, Mark Robson, Paul Stewart, Terry Fenwick, Peter Shreeves (Team Manager), Gary Mabbutt, Gary Lineker, Paul Gascoigne, Paul Allen.

FA Premier

TOTTENHAM HOTSPUR

748 High Rd, Tottenham, London N17 0AP. Telephone 081-808 6666. Commercial Dept: 081-808 0281. Recorded information: 0898 100515. Additional recorded information: 081 880 3377.; Dial-a-seat: 081-808 3030. Spurs Line: 0898 100500. Fax No: 081-801 4230

Ground capacity: 32,786.

Record attendance: 75,038 v Sunderland, FA Cup 6th rd, 5 March 1938.

Record receipts: £336,702 v Manchester U, Division 1, 28 September 1991.

Pitch measurements: 110yd × 73yd.

Vice-president: F. P. Sinclair. *Chairman:* A. G. Berry. *Vice-chairman:* D. A. Alexiou. *Holding Company:* Tottenham Hotspur plc. *Chief Executive:* T. F. Venables. *Chairman:* A. Sugar. *Vice-chairman:* N. Solomon. *First Team Coach:* Doug Livermore. *Assistant first team coach:* Ray Clemence. *Physios:* John Sheridan and Dave Butler. *Chief Scout:* Ted Buxton. *Secretary:* Peter Barnes. *Commercial Manager:* Mike Rollo. *PRO:* John Fennelly.

Year Formed: 1882. Turned Professional: 1895. Ltd Co.: 1898.

Former Grounds: 1882, Tottenham Marshes; 1885, Northumberland Park; 1898, White Hart Lane.

Former Names: 1882–85, Hotspur Football Club.

Club Nickname: 'Spurs'.

Record League Victory: 9-0 v Bristol R, Division 2, 22 October 1977 – Daines; Naylor, Holmes, Hoddle (1), McAllister, Perryman, Pratt, McNab, Moores (3), Lee (4), Taylor (1).

Record Cup Victory: 13-2 v Crewe Alex, FA Cup, 4th rd (replay), 3 February 1960 – Brown; Hills, Henry; Blanchflower, Norman, Mackay; White, Harmer (1), Smith (4), Allen (5), Jones (3 incl. 1p).

Record Defeat: 0-7 v Liverpool, Division 1, 2 September 1978.

Most League Points (2 for a win): 70, Division 2, 1919–20.

Most League points (3 for a win): 77, Division 1, 1984–85.

Most League Goals: 115, Division 1, 1960-61.

Highest League Scorer in Season: Jimmy Greaves, 37, Division 1, 1962–63.

Most League Goals in Total Aggregate: Jimmy Greaves, 220, 1961–70.

Most Capped Player: Pat Jennings, 74 (119), Northern Ireland.

Most League Appearances: Steve Perryman, 655, 1969–86.

Record Transfer Fee Received: £5,500,000 from Lazio for Paul Gascoigne, May 1992.

Record Transfer Fee Paid: £2,200,000 to Chelsea for Gordon Durie, August 1991.

Football League Record: 1908 Elected to Division 2; 1909–15 Division 1; 1919–20 Division 2; 1920–28 Division 1; 1928–33 Division 2; 1933–35 Division 1; 1935–50 Division 2; 1950–77 Division 1; 1977–78 Division 2; 1978–92 Division 1; 1992– FA Premier League.

Honours: Football League: Division 1 – Champions 1950–51, 1960–61; Runners-up 1921–22, 1951–52, 1956–57, 1962–63; Division 2 – Champions 1919–20, 1949–50; Runners-up 1908–09, 1932–33; Promoted 1977–78 (3rd). *FA Cup:* Winners 1901 (as non-League club), 1921, 1961, 1962, 1967, 1981, 1982, 1991 (8 wins stands as the record); Runners-up 1986–87. *Football League Cup:* Winners 1970–71, 1972–73; Runners-up 1981–82. **European Competitions:** *European Cup:* 1961–62. *European Cup-Winners' Cup:* 1962–63 (winners), 1963–64, 1967–68, 1981–82 (runners-up), 1982–83, 1991–92. *UEFA Cup:* 1971–72 (winners), 1972–73, 1973–74 (runners-up), 1983–84 (winners), 1984–85.

Colours: White shirts, navy blue shorts, navy stockings with white turnover. **Change colours:** All yellow or all sky blue.

TOTTENHAM HOTSPUR 1991–92 LEAGUE RECORD

Match No.	Date		Venue	Opponents	Result		H/T Score	Lg. Pos.	Goalscorers	Atten-dance
1	Aug	17	A	Southampton	W	3-2	1-1	—	Lineker 2, Durie	18,581
2		24	H	Chelsea	L	1-3	0-2	14	Lineker	34,645
3		28	A	Nottingham F	W	3-1	1-1	—	Lineker, Durie, Bergsson	24,018
4		31	A	Norwich C	W	1-0	1-0	5	Lineker	19,460
5	Sep	7	A	Aston Villa	D	0-0	0-0	10		33,096
6		14	H	QPR	W	2-0	0-0	6	Lineker 2	30,059
7		21	A	Wimbledon	W	5-3	3-1	3	Lineker 4 (1 pen), Samways	11,927
8		28	H	Manchester U	L	1-2	1-1	7	Durie	35,087
9	Oct	5	A	Everton	L	1-3	1-3	11	Lineker	29,505
10		19	H	Manchester C	L	0-1	0-0	13		30,502
11		26	A	West Ham U	L	1-2	1-2	13	Lineker	23,946
12	Nov	2	A	Sheffield W	D	0-0	0-0	16		31,573
13		16	H	Luton T	W	4-1	0-1	11	Houghton 2, Lineker 2	27,543
14		23	H	Sheffield U	L	0-1	0-0	13		28,168
15	Dec	1	A	Arsenal	L	0-2	0-0	—		38,892
16		7	H	Notts Co	W	2-1	1-1	13	Walsh, Mabbutt	23,364
17		14	A	Leeds U	D	1-1	1-1	13	Howells	31,404
18		18	H	Liverpool	L	1-2	1-1	—	Walsh	27,434
19		22	A	Crystal Palace	W	2-1	2-0	—	Walsh, Lineker	22,491
20		26	H	Nottingham F	L	1-2	0-1	12	Stewart	31,079
21		28	H	Norwich C	W	3-0	1-0	8	Allen, Lineker, Nayim	27,969
22	Jan	1	A	Coventry C	W	2-1	1-1	8	Lineker, Stewart	19,639
23		11	A	Chelsea	L	0-2	0-1	10		28,628
24		18	A	Southampton	L	1-2	0-1	11	Mabbutt	23,191
25		25	H	Oldham Ath	D	0-0	0-0	10		20,843
26	Feb	1	A	Manchester C	L	0-1	0-1	10		30,123
27		16	H	Crystal Palace	L	0-1	0-0	—		19,834
28		22	H	Arsenal	D	1-1	0-0	13	Stewart	33,124
29	Mar	7	H	Leeds U	L	1-3	0-1	17	Allen	27,622
30		11	A	Luton T	D	0-0	0-0	—		11,494
31		14	H	Sheffield W	L	0-2	0-0	18		23,027
32		21	A	Liverpool	L	1-2	0-0	19	Stewart	36,968
33		28	H	Coventry C	W	4-3	3-1	18	Durie 3, Lineker	22,744
34	Apr	1	H	West Ham U	W	3-0	1-0	—	Lineker 3 (1 pen)	31,809
35		4	H	Aston Villa	L	2-5	2-2	18	Lineker, Teale (og)	26,370
36		7	A	Notts Co	W	2-0	1-0	—	Lineker 2	9205
37		11	A	QPR	W	2-1	0-1	13	Gray, Durie	20,678
38		14	A	Sheffield U	L	0-2	0-2	—		21,526
39		18	H	Wimbledon	W	3-2	2-1	12	Lineker 2, Hendry	23,934
40		20	A	Oldham Ath	L	0-1	0-1	13		15,443
41		25	H	Everton	D	3-3	3-0	12	Allen, Minton, Stewart	34,630
42	May	2	A	Manchester U	L	1-3	0-1	15	Lineker	44,595

Final League Position: 15

GOALSCORERS

League (58): Lineker 28 (2 pens), Durie 7, Stewart 5, Allen 3, Walsh 3, Houghton 2, Mabbutt 2, Bergsson 1, Gray 1, Hendry 1, Howells 1, Minton 1, Nayim 1, Samways 1, own goals 1.
Rumbelows Cup (14): Lineker 5 (2 pens), Allen 2, Durie 2, Howells 1, Samways 1, Stewart 1, Walsh 1, own goals 1.
FA Cup (0).

Thorstvedt	Fenwick	Van Den Hauwe	Sedgley	Howells	Mabbutt	Stewart	Durie	Samways	Lineker	Allen	Nayim	Bergsson	Walker	Hendry	Hendon	Tuttle	Houghton	Edinburgh	Walsh	Gray	Cundy	Minton	Match No.
1	2	3	4	5*	6	7	8	9	10	11†	12	14											1
1	2*	3		5	6	7	8	9	10	11	4	12											2
	2	3		5	6		8†	9	10	11*	4	12	1	14									3
	2	3		5	6	7	8	9	10		4	11	1										4
	2	3		5	6	7	8	9	10		4	11	1										5
	2	3	14	5*	6	7	8	9†	10	12	4	11	1										6
		3		5	6	7	8	9	10	11*	4	2†	1					12					7
		3	12		6	7	8	9	10	11	4*	2†	1			5		14					8
1		3	12		6	7	8	9†	10	11	4*	2				14		5					9
1		3*	7	12	6		8	9	10	11	4†	5						2	14				10
1		3*		5	6		8	9	10	11	4†	12						14	2				11
1		3	4*	5	6	7	8		10†	11	9	12						2	14				12
1		3	4	5†	6			9	10	11*	12	7						14	2	8			13
1		3	12	5*	6		8	9	10		4†	7						14	2	11			14
1	2	3		5	6	7	8	9*		11	12	4							10				15
1	2	3	14	5†	6	7	8	9*		11	12	4							10				16
1	2	3	14	5	6	7	8†	9*		11	12	4							10				17
1	2	3		5*	6	7		9	10	11	12	4							8				18
1	2		14	5	6	7		9	10*	11	12	4						3†	8				19
1	2	3	14	5	6	7		9*	10	11	12	4†							8				20
1	2	3	4		6	7		9	10	11		5						12	8*				21
1	2	3	4	5	6	7		9†	10	11	12							14	8*				22
1	2	3	4	5*	6	7†		9	10	11								14	12	8			23
	3†		4		6	7	8	9*	10	11		14	1					12	2	5			24
	3		4		6	7	8		10	11		5*	1					12	2	9			25
	3		4	5*		7	8	9†	10	11	14	6	1						2	12			26
1	2	3	4	5†	6	7	8	9*	10	11		14						12					27
1	2	3	4	5	6	7	8	9*	10	11								12					28
1	2	3†	4	5	6	7	8		10*	11		14						12	9				29
1	2		4	5	6	7	8			11	12							3	10*	9			30
1	2*		4	5†	6	7	8			11	12	14						3	10	9			31
1	2	10	4	5*	6	7	8			11								3	12	9			32
1	2		14		6	7	8	9	10†	11								3	12	4*	5		33
	2†		14		6	7	8	9	10	11			1					3	12	4*	5		34
	2		14		6	7	8	9	10	11			1			2		3	12	4	5		35
	2		14		6	7		9	10*	11	12		1					3	8†	4	5		36
	2		14		6†	7	8	9*	10	11			1					3	12	4	5		37
	14	2			6	7	8†	9*	10	11	12		1					3		4	5		38
	2		14		6	7		9	10	11	12		1					3	8*	4†	5		39
	2*		14		6	7		9	10	11	12		1					3	8†	4	5		40
	2		14		6	7	8		10	11			1					3	12	4*	5	9†	41
	2		12		6	7	8		10	11			1					3		4	5	9*	42
24	22	35	21	27	40	38	31	26	35	38	22	17	18	1	—	2	—	22	17	14	10	2	

Substitute appearances: Thorstvedt +1s; Van Den Hauwe +13s; Sedgley +4s; Samways +1s; Nayim +1s; Bergsson +9s; Walker +11s; Tuttle +4s; Houghton +2s; Edinburgh +10s; Walsh +1s; Gray +12s.

Rumbelows Cup	Second Round	Swansea C (a)		0-1
		(h)		5-1
	Third Round	Grimsby T (a)		3-0
	Fourth Round	Coventry C (a)		2-1
	Fifth Round	Norwich C (h)		2-1
	Semi-Final	Nottingham F (a)		1-1
		(h)		1-2
FA Cup	Third Round	Aston Villa (a)		0-0
		(h)		0-1

TOTTENHAM HOTSPUR

Player and Position	Ht	Wt	Birth Date	Birth Place	Source	Clubs	League App	League Gls
Goalkeepers								
Kevin Dearden	5 11	12 08	8 3 70	Luton	Trainee	Tottenham H	—	—
						Cambridge U (loan)	15	—
						Hartlepool U (loan)	10	—
						Oxford U (loan)	—	—
						Swindon T (loan)	1	—
						Peterborough U (loan)	7	—
						Hull C (loan)	3	—
						Rochdale (loan)	2	—
						Birmingham C (loan)	12	—
Erik Thorstvedt	6 3	14 04	28 10 62	Stavanger	IFK Gothenburg	Tottenham H	113	—
Ian Walker	6 1	11 09	31 10 71	Watford	Trainee	Tottenham H	19	—
						Oxford U (loan)	2	—
						Ipswich T (loan)	—	—
Defenders								
Gudni Bergsson	5 10	10 07	21 7 65	Iceland	Valur	Tottenham H	66	2
David Culverhouse			9 4 73	Harlow	Trainee	Tottenham H	—	—
Justin Edinburgh	5 9	11 06	18 12 69	Brentwood	Trainee	Southend U	37	—
						Tottenham H (loan)	—	—
						Tottenham H	39	1
Terry Fenwick	5 11	11 01	17 11 59	Camden, Co. Durham	Apprentice	Crystal Palace	70	—
						QPR	256	33
						Tottenham H	88	8
						Leicester C (loan)	8	1
Ian Hendon	6 0	12 10	5 12 71	Ilford	Trainee	Tottenham H	4	—
						Portsmouth (loan)	4	—
						Leyton Orient (loan)	6	—
Gary Mabbutt	5 9	10 10	23 8 61	Bristol	Apprentice	Bristol R	131	10
						Tottenham H	339	25
David McDonald	5 10	11 00	2 1 71	Dublin	Trainee	Tottenham H	—	—
						Gillingham (loan)	10	—
Andrew Marlowe			25 9 73	Birmingham	Trainee	Tottenham H	—	—
Stuart Nethercott	5 9	12 04	21 3 73	Chadwell Heath	Trainee	Tottenham H	—	—
						Maidstone U (loan)	13	1
						Barnet (loan)	3	—
Andy Polston*	5 10	11 00	26 7 70	Walthamstow	Trainee	Tottenham H	1	—
						Cambridge U (loan)	3	—
						Gillingham (loan)	3	—
Steve Sedgley	6 1	12 06	26 5 68	Enfield	Apprentice	Coventry C	84	3
						Tottenham H	100	—
David Tuttle	6 1	12 10	6 2 72	Reading	Trainee	Tottenham H	8	—
Pat Van Den Hauwe	6 0	10 08	16 12 60	Dendermonde	Apprentice	Birmingham C	123	1
						Everton	135	2
						Tottenham H	98	—
Neil Young	5 8	11 03	31 8 73	Harlow	Trainee	Tottenham H	—	—
Midfield								
Paul Allen	5 7	10 10	28 8 62	Aveley	Apprentice	West Ham U	152	6
						Tottenham H	253	20
Nick Barmby	5 06	11 04	11 2 74	Hull	Trainee	Tottenham H	—	—
Darren Caskey			21 8 74	Basildon	Trainee	Tottenham H	—	—
Matthew Edwards‡	5 10	9 08	15 6 71	Hammersmith	Trainee	Tottenham H	—	—
						Reading (loan)	8	—
Paul Gascoigne	5 10	11 07	27 5 67	Gateshead	Apprentice	Newcastle U	92	21
						Tottenham H	92	19
Scott Houghton	5 5	11 06	22 10 71	Hitchin	Trainee	Tottenham H	10	2
						Ipswich T (loan)	8	1
Greg Howell‡	5 9	11 02	26 3 73	Swindon	Trainee	Tottenham H	—	—
Nayim	5 8	11 04	5 11 66	Ceuta	Barcelona	Tottenham H	94	8
Vinny Samways	5 8	9 00	27 10 68	Bethnal Green	Apprentice	Tottenham H	120	8
Kevin Smith‡	5 9	12 00	25 12 71	Kent	Trainee	Tottenham H	—	—
Andrew Turner			23 3 75	Woolwich	Trainee	Tottenham H	—	—
Kevin Watson			3 1 74	Hackney	Trainee	Tottenham H	—	—
Forwards								
Gordon Durie	6 0	12 00	6 12 65	Paisley	Hill O'Beath	East Fife	81	26
						Hibernian	47	14
						Chelsea	123	51
						Tottenham H	31	7
Ian Gilzean*	6 1	12 08	10 12 69	Enfield	Trainee	Tottenham H	—	—
John Hendry	5 11	10 00	6 1 70	Glasgow	Hillington YC	Dundee	2	—
						Forfar Ath (loan)	10	6
						Tottenham H	9	3
						Charlton Ath (loan)	5	1

TOTTENHAM HOTSPUR

Foundation: The Hotspur Football Club was formed from an older cricket club in 1882. Most of the founders were old boys St. John's Presbyterian School and Tottenham Grammar School. The Casey brothers were well to the fore as the family provided the club's first goalposts (painted blue and white) and their first ball. They soon adopted the local YMCA as their meeting place, but after a couple of moves settled at the Red House, which is still their headquarters, although now known simply as 748 High Road.

First Football League game: 1 September, 1908, Division 2, v Wolverhampton W (h) W 3-0 – Hewitson; Coquet, Burton; Morris (1), Steel (D), Darnell; Walton, Woodward (2), Macfarlane, R. Steel, Middlemiss.

Did you know: Frank Osborne scored a hat-trick for Spurs in each of three consecutive First Division games in October and November 1925.

Managers (and Secretary-managers)
Frank Brettell 1898–99, John Cameron 1899–1906, Fred Kirkham 1907–08, Peter McWilliam 1912–27, Billy Minter 1927–29, Percy Smith 1930–35, Jack Tresadern 1935–38, Peter McWilliam 1938–42, Arthur Turner 1942–46, Joe Hulme 1946–49, Arthur Rowe 1949–55, Jimmy Anderson 1955–58, Bill Nicholson 1958–74, Terry Neill 1974–76, Keith Burkinshaw 1976–84, Peter Shreeves 1984–86, David Pleat 1986–87, Terry Venables 1987–91, Peter Shreeves 1991–92.

Player and Position	Ht	Wt	Birth Date	Birth Place	Source	Clubs	League App	Gls
Lee Hodges			4 9 73	Epping	Trainee	Tottenham H	—	—
David Howells	5 11	11 01	15 12 67	Guildford	Trainee	Tottenham H	134	14
Gary Lineker	5 11	12 02	30 11 60	Leicester	Apprentice	Leicester C	194	95
						Everton	41	30
						Barcelona	99	44
						Tottenham H	105	67
Paul Mahorn			13 8 73	Whipps Cross	Trainee	Tottenham H	—	—
Jeffrey Minton			28 12 73	Hackney	Trainee	Tottenham H	2	1
Ollie Morah	5 11	13 05	3 9 72	Islington	Trainee	Tottenham H	—	—
						Hereford U (loan)	2	—
Paul Moran	5 10	11 00	22 5 68	Enfield	Trainee	Tottenham H	28	2
						Portsmouth (loan)	3	—
						Leicester C (loan)	10	1
						Newcastle U (loan)	1	—
						Southend U	1	—
Anthony Potts	5 8	11 09	24 10 72	Erith	Trainee	Tottenham H	—	—
Mark Robson*	5 7	10 05	22 5 69	Newham	Trainee	Exeter C	26	7
						Tottenham H	8	—
						Reading (loan)	7	—
						Watford (loan)	1	—
						Plymouth Arg (loan)	7	—
						Exeter C (loan)	8	1
Paul Stewart	5 11	11 10	7 10 64	Manchester	Apprentice	Blackpool	201	56
						Manchester C	51	26
						Tottenham H	131	28
Paul Walsh	5 7	10 08	1 10 62	Plumstead	Apprentice	Charlton Ath	87	24
						Luton T	80	24
						Liverpool	77	25
						Tottenham H	128	19
						QPR (loan)	2	—

Trainees
Binks, Spencer C; Campbell, Sulzeer J; Day, Christopher N; Deanus, Del; Grogan, Darren M; Heath, Michael; Hill, Daniel R. L; Jordan, Kevin; Kinnear, Colin B. T; Landon, Christopher S; McDougald, David E. J; Reynolds, Christopher C; Robinson, Stephen; Wood, Dean B.

Associated Schoolboys
Allen, Robert P; Arber, Mark A; Archer, Paul L. J; Callcut, Dean E; Carlisle, Jason A; Fortune, Quinton; Gain, Peter T; Gallagher, Stuart; Hughes, Richard; Janney, Mark; Lapidge, Lee; Laycock, Wayne D; Outram, Ross P; Payne, Ian N; Pook, Andrew; Shave, Arran L; Spencer, Simon D; Williams, Richard I; Wormull, Simon J.

Associated Schoolboys who have accepted the club's offer of a Traineeship/Contract
Anderson, Ijah M; Clapham, James R; Foot, Daniel F; Haynes, Junior L. A; Hudson, William G; Knott, Gareth R; Le Bihan, Neil E. R; Quy, Andrew J; Reynolds, Andrew; Simpson, Robert A; Slade, Steven A; Townley, Leon.

532

TRANMERE ROVERS 1991–92 *Back row (left to right):* Graham Branch, Mike Foster, Ged Brannan, John McGreal, Ian Nolan, Kenny Irons, John Morrissey, Tony Thomas.
Centre row: Warwick Rimmer (Youth Development Officer), Ray Mathias (Reserves Manager), Steve Vickers, Jim Steel, Shaun Garnett, Chris Malkin, Eric Nixon, Paul Collings, Dave Higgins, Dave Martindale, Ronnie Moore (Coach), Kenny Jones (Trainer), Norman Wilson (Secretary).
Front row: Jim Harvey, Steve Cooper, Mark Hughes, John King (Manager), Ian Muir, Steve Mungall, John Aldridge, Neil McNab.

Division 1   **TRANMERE ROVERS**

Prenton Park, Prenton Road West, Birkenhead. Telephone 051-608 3677. Commercial/Cashline 051-608 0371. Valley Road Training Centre: 051-652 2578. Shop: 051-608 0438.

Ground capacity: 17,500.

Record attendance: 24,424 v Stoke C, FA Cup 4th rd, 5 February 1972.

Record receipts: £70,077 v Liverpool, 8 August 1992.

Pitch measurements: 112yd × 71 yd.

President: H. B. Thomas.

Chairman: P. R. Johnson.

Vice-chairman and Chief Executive: F. D. Corfe.

Directors: A. J. Adams BDS, G. E. H. Jones LLB, F. J. Williams, J. J. Holsgrove FCA, G. A. Higham MSC TECH LRSC, M INST PI.

Secretary: Norman Wilson FAAI.

Manager: John King. *Trainer:* Kenny Jones. *Youth Development Manager:* Warwick Rimmer. *Coach:* Ronnie Moore. *Physio:* Alec McLellan.

Commercial Manager: Nigel Coates.

Development Manager: Nobby Abbott.

Year Formed: 1885. Turned Professional: 1912. Ltd Co.: 1920.

Former Grounds: 1884, Steeles Field; 1887, Ravenshaws Field/Old Prenton Park; 1912, Prenton Park.

Former Names: Belmont AFC, 1884–85.

Club Nickname: 'The Rovers'.

Record League Victory: 13-4 v Oldham Ath, Division 3 (N), 26 December 1935 – Gray; Platt, Fairhurst; McLaren, Newton, Spencer; Eden, MacDonald (1), Bell (9), Woodward (2), Urmson (1).

Record Cup Victory: 9-0 v AP Leamington, FA Cup, 1st rd, 24 November 1979 – Johnson; Mathias, Flood (Mungall), Bramhall, Edwards, Evans (2), O'Neil (2 incl. 1p), Parry, Peplow, Lumby (3), Beamish (1). (1 og).

Record Defeat: 1-9 v Tottenham H, FA Cup 3rd rd (replay), 14 January 1953.

Most League Points (2 for a win): 60, Division 4, 1964–65.

Most League points (3 for a win): 80, Division 4, 1988–89 and Division 3, 1989–90.

Most League Goals: 111, Division 3 (N), 1930–31.

Highest League Scorer in Season: Bunny Bell, 35, Division 3 (N), 1933–34.

Most League Goals in Total Aggregate: Ian Muir, 123, 1985–92.

Most Capped Player: John Aldridge, 8(47), Republic of Ireland.

Most League Appearances: Harold Bell, 595, 1946–64 (incl. League record 401 consecutive appearances).

Record Transfer Fee Received: £120,000 from Cardiff C for Ronnie Moore, February 1979.

Record Transfer Fee Paid: £250,000 to Real Sociedad for John Aldridge, July 1991.

Football League Record: 1921 Original Member of Division 3 (N): 1938–39 Division 2; 1946–58 Division 3 (N); 1958–61 Division 3; 1961–67 Division 4; 1967–75 Division 3; 1975–76 Division 4; 1976–79 Division 3; 1979–89 Division 4; 1989–91 Division 3; 1991–92 Division 2; 1992– Division 1.

Honours: Football League Division 2 best season: 14th, 1991–92; Division 3 (N) – Champions 1937–38; Promotion to 3rd Division: 1966–67, 1975–76; Division 4 – Runners-up 1988–89. *FA Cup:* best season: 5th rd, 1967–68. *Football League Cup:* best season: 4th rd, 1961, 1982, 1989, 1990. *Welsh Cup:* Winners 1935; Runners-up 1934. *Leyland Daf Cup:* Winners 1990; Runners-up 1991.

Colours: All white. **Change colours:** Claret/sky blue shirts, sky blue shorts and stockings.

TRANMERE ROVERS 1991–92 LEAGUE RECORD

Match No.	Date		Venue	Opponents	Result	H/T Score	Lg. Pos.	Goalscorers	Atten-dance
1	Aug	17	A	Brighton & HA	W 2-0	2-0	—	Aldridge 2	9679
2		23	H	Bristol R	D 2-2	1-1	—	Aldridge (pen), Steel	10,150
3		31	A	Grimsby T	D 2-2	1-0	9	Aldridge, Thomas	7018
4	Sep	3	H	Charlton Ath	D 2-2	1-0	—	Malkin, Hughes	7609
5		7	H	Newcastle U	W 3-2	1-2	6	Malkin, Thomas, Vickers	11,465
6		14	A	Bristol C	D 2-2	1-2	9	Brannan, Irons	11,235
7		17	A	Middlesbrough	L 0-1	0-0	—		16,550
8		21	H	Barnsley	W 2-1	1-0	9	Aldridge, Higgins	8482
9		28	A	Blackburn R	D 0-0	0-0	8		11,449
10	Oct	4	H	Southend U	D 1-1	0-1	—	Steel	7358
11		12	H	Oxford U	L 0-1	0-0	13		5760
12		18	H	Cambridge U	L 1-2	0-2	—	Aldridge	7625
13		26	A	Wolverhampton W	D 1-1	0-1	15	Steel	12,266
14	Nov	2	A	Derby Co	W 1-0	1-0	14	Aldridge	11,501
15		5	H	Millwall	W 2-1	1-0	—	Irons, Aldridge (pen)	6108
16		8	H	Plymouth Arg	W 1-0	0-0	—	Aldridge (pen)	7490
17		22	H	Swindon T	D 0-0	0-0	—		9585
18		30	A	Ipswich T	L 0-4	0-2	14		11,072
19	Dec	13	A	Port Vale	D 1-1	1-1	—	Cooper S	6426
20		26	H	Sunderland	W 1-0	1-0	12	Irons	13,658
21		28	H	Grimsby T	D 1-1	1-0	13	Aldridge	7900
22	Jan	1	A	Watford	D 0-0	0-0	14		9892
23		11	A	Bristol R	L 0-1	0-0	16		7138
24		17	H	Brighton & HA	D 1-1	0-0	—	Muir	7179
25		24	H	Watford	D 1-1	0-0	—	Morrissey	6187
26		31	A	Cambridge U	D 0-0	0-0	—		5491
27	Feb	8	A	Wolverhampton W	W 4-2	2-2	14	Aldridge (pen), Malkin, Morrissey 2	11,371
28		11	A	Sunderland	D 1-1	0-1	—	Aldridge	18,060
29		21	H	Ipswich T	L 0-1	0-0	—		9161
30		29	A	Portsmouth	L 0-2	0-2	16		16,644
31	Mar	6	H	Port Vale	W 2-0	1-0	—	Harvey, Aldridge	8471
32		11	A	Millwall	W 3-0	2-0	—	Morrissey, Aldridge 2	6456
33		14	H	Derby Co	W 4-3	1-1	12	Aldridge 3 (1 pen), Irons	10,386
34		17	A	Swindon T	L 0-2	0-1	—		6780
35		21	A	Plymouth Arg	L 0-1	0-0	13		7447
36		27	H	Leicester C	L 1-2	1-0	—	Muir	9061
37		31	H	Bristol C	D 2-2	0-0	—	Nolan, Steel	5797
38	Apr	4	A	Newcastle U	W 3-2	2-1	15	Aldridge 2, Morrissey	21,125
39		7	H	Portsmouth	W 2-0	1-0	—	Irons, Thomas	6692
40		10	H	Middlesbrough	L 1-2	0-1	—	Muir	8842
41		15	A	Leicester C	L 0-1	0-0	—		18,555
42		18	A	Barnsley	D 1-1	1-1	14	Muir	5811
43		20	H	Blackburn R	D 2-2	1-1	14	Muir, Irons	13,705
44		25	A	Southend U	D 1-1	0-1	15	Irons	4761
45		28	A	Charlton Ath	W 1-0	1-0	—	Aldridge	7645
46	May	2	H	Oxford U	L 1-2	0-0	14	Aldridge	9173

Final League Position: 14

GOALSCORERS

League (56): Aldridge 22 (5 pens), Irons 7, Morrissey 5, Muir 5, Steel 4, Malkin 3, Thomas 3, Brannan 1, Cooper S 1, Harvey 1, Higgins 1, Hughes 1, Nolan 1, Vickers 1.
Rumbelows Cup (13): Aldridge 8 (2 pens), Steel 3, Irons 1, Malkin 1.
FA Cup (7): Aldridge 3, Irons 2, Malkin 1, Morrissey 1.

Nixon	Higgins	Brannan	Irons	Hughes	Garnett	Morrissey	Aldridge	Steel	Martindale	Thomas	Malkin	McNab	Vickers	Harvey	Cooper S	Mungall	Branch	Nolan	Muir	Nevin	McGreal	Match No.
1	2	3†	4	5	6	7*	8	9	10	11	12	14										1
1	2	3	4	5	6	7	8	9	10	11												2
1	2	3	4*	5	6	7	8		10	11	9	12										3
1	2	3	4	5		7†	8		10*	11	9		6	12	14							4
1	2	3	4*	5		7†	8		10	11	9	12	6	14								5
1	2	3	4			7†	8		10	11	9	12	6	14*	5							6
1	2	3	4*	5†		7	8		10	11	9	12	6	14								7
1	2	3	4	5		7	8	12	10	11	9*		6									8
1	2	3	4†	5		7*	8	9	10	11	12	14	6									9
1	2	3*	4	5			8	9	10	7	12		6			11						10
1	2	3	4*	5		7†	8	9	10	14	12		6			11						11
1		3	4	5	2	7	8	9	12	10	6*					11						12
1		3	4	5		7	8	9	10	12	6					11*	2					13
1		3	4	5		7	8	10	9		6					11	2					14
1	2	3*	4	5		7	8	10	9		6		12			11						15
1	2	3	4	5		7	8	10	9*		6		12			11						16
1	2		4	5		7	8	12	10	9*	6	14		3†		11						17
1	2	3	4	5†		7	8	9	10*	12	6	14				11						18
1	2	3*	4	5		7	8			9	6	12	10			11						19
1	2		4	5		7	8			6	9	10	3			11						20
1	2		4	5*		7	8	12		6	9	10	3			11						21
1	2		4	5		7	8	12		6	9	10*	3			11						22
1	2		4	5*		7		9	10	3	6	8				11	12					23
1	2		4†	5*		7		9	10	14	6	8	3			11	12					24
1			4	5	2	7		9	8	11	6		3			10						25
1			4	5	2	7	8	10	11	9	6		3									26
1			5	2*	7	8	10	11	9	6	4		3			12						27
1	2		5			7*	8	10	11	9	6		3			4	12					28
1	2		4	5*		7	8	9†	11	12	6	14				3	10					29
1	2		4	5†			8	11	9*	6	10	7	14			3	12					30
1	2		4			7	8	9	11	6	5		3			12	10*					31
1	2		4			7	8	11	6	5			3			10	9					32
1	2		4			7	8	11	6	5			3			10	9					33
1	2				7	8	12	4†	11	6	5	14	3			10*	9					34
1	2		4		7	8	11	6	5				3			10	9					35
1	2		4		7	8	12	11	6	5			3			10*	9					36
1	2		4		7*	8	9	11	12	6	5		3			10						37
1	2		4*		7	8	9	12	11	6	5		3			10						38
1	2		4		7	8	9	11	10	6	5		3									39
1			4	2	7	8	9*14	11	10	6	5†		3			12						40
1			4	5	2*	8	12	7	11	9	6		3			10						41
1			4	5		8	7*	9	6	11	2	12	3			10						42
1			4*	5	7	8	3	11	12	6	9	2				10						43
1			4	7*	8	9	11	12	6	2	3	10	5									44
1			4		8	9	11	7	6	2	3	10	5									45
1			4		8	9	11	7*	6	2	12	3	10	5								46
46	33	18	43	33	8	40	43	16	29	30	23	3	43	19	4	17	—	34	13	8	3	

Substitute appearances: Steel +5s, Martindale +2s, Malkin +12s, McNab +9s, Harvey +5s, Cooper S +5s, Mungall +1s, Branch +4s, Muir +7s.

Rumbelows Cup	First Round	Halifax T (a)	4-3
		(h)	4-3
	Second Round	Chelsea (a)	1-1
		(h)	3-1
	Third Round	Leeds U (a)	1-3
FA Cup	First Round	Runcorn (a)	3-0
	Second Round	York C (a)	1-1
		(h)	2-1
	Third Round	Oxford U (a)	1-3

TRANMERE ROVERS

Player and Position	Ht	Wt	Date	Birth Place	Source	Clubs	League App	Gls
Goalkeepers								
Paul Collings*	6 2	12 00	30 9 68	Liverpool		Tranmere R	4	—
Eric Nixon	6 2	14 03	4 10 62	Manchester	Curzon Ashton	Manchester C	58	—
						Wolverhampton W (loan)	16	—
							3	—
						Bradford C (loan)	4	—
						Southampton (loan)	16	—
						Carlisle U (loan)	8	—
						Tranmere R (loan)	180	—
						Tranmere R		
Defenders								
Ged Brannan	6 0	13 03	15 1 72	Liverpool	Trainee	Tranmere R	36	2
Daniel Coyne			27 8 73	St Asaph	Trainee	Tranmere R	—	—
Anthony Draper			29 11 73	Liverpool	Trainee	Tranmere R	—	—
Mike Foster	5 9	11 06	24 9 73	Portmadoc		Tranmere R	—	—
Dave Higgins	6 0	11 00	19 8 61	Liverpool	Eagle	Tranmere R	28	—
						Caernarfon	—	—
						Tranmere R	187	6
Mark Hughes	6 1	12 10	3 2 62	Morriston	Apprentice	Bristol R	74	3
						Torquay U (loan)	9	1
						Swansea C	12	—
						Bristol C	22	—
						Tranmere R	247	9
John McGreal	5 11	10 08	2 6 72	Birkenhead	Trainee	Tranmere R	3	—
Steve Mungall	5 8	11 02	22 5 58	Bellshill		Motherwell	20	—
						Tranmere R	433	9
Ian Nolan	6 0	11 10	8 7 70	Liverpool	Marine	Tranmere R	34	1
Tony Thomas	5 11	12 05	12 7 71	Liverpool	Trainee	Tranmere R	114	10
Steven Vickers	6 2	12 00	13 10 67	B Auckland	Spennymoor U	Tranmere R	258	11
Midfield								
Shaun Garnett	6 2	11 00	22 11 69	Wallasey	Trainee	Tranmere R	29	1
Jimmy Harvey*	5 9	11 04	2 5 58	Lurgan	Glenavon	Arsenal	3	—
						Hereford U (loan)	11	—
						Hereford U	267	39
						Bristol C	3	—
						Wrexham (loan)	6	—
						Tranmere R	184	18
Neil McNab	5 7	11 00	4 6 57	Greenock		Morton	14	—
						Tottenham H	72	3
						Bolton W	35	4
						Brighton & HA	103	4
						Leeds U (loan)	5	—
						Portsmouth (loan)	—	—
						Manchester C	221	16
						Tranmere R	74	4
						Huddersfield T (loan)	11	—
Dave Martindale	5 11	11 10	9 4 64	Liverpool	Apprentice	Liverpool	—	—
						Caernarfon	—	—
						Tranmere R	127	7
Forwards								
Michael Smith			28 9 73	Liverpool	Trainee	Tranmere R	—	—
John Aldridge	5 11	11 10	18 9 58	Liverpool	South Liverpool	Newport Co	170	69
						Oxford U	114	72
						Liverpool	83	50
						Tranmere R	43	22
Graham Branch	6 2		12 2 72	Liverpool	Heswall Ath	Tranmere R	4	—

TRANMERE ROVERS

Foundation: Formed in 1884 as Belmont they adopted their present title the following year and eventually joined their first league, the West Lancashire League in 1889–90, the same year as their first success in the Wirral Challenge Cup. The club almost folded in 1899–1900 when all the players left en bloc to join a rival club, but they survived the crisis and went from strength to strength winning the 'Combination' title in 1907–08 and the Lancashire Combination in 1913–14. They joined the Football League in 1920 from the Central League.

First Football League game: 27 August 1921, Division 3 (N), v Crewe Alex (h) W 4-1 – Bradshaw; Grainger, Stuart (1); Campbell, Milnes (1), Heslop; Moreton, Groves (1), Hyam, Ford (1), Hughes.

Did you know: In the first 13 seasons after World War Two, Tranmere fielded only three different goalkeepers in Football League games – George Payne, Harold Lloyd and Albert Harris.

Managers (and Secretary-managers)
Bert Cooke 1912–35, Jackie Carr 1935–36, Jim Knowles 1936–39, Bill Ridding 1939–45, Ernie Blackburn 1946–55, Noel Kelly 1955–57, Peter Farrell 1957–60, Walter Galbraith 1961, Dave Russell 1961–69, Jackie Wright 1969–72, Ron Yeats 1972–75, John King 1975–80, Bryan Hamilton 1980–85, Frank Worthington 1985–87, Ronnie Moore 1987, John King April 1987–.

Player and Position	Ht	Wt	Date	Birth Place	Source	Clubs	League App	Gls
Steve Cooper	5 11	10 12	22 6 64	Birmingham		Birmingham C	—	—
						Halifax (loan)	7	1
						Mansfield T (loan)	—	—
						Newport Co	38	11
						Plymouth Arg	73	15
						Barnsley	77	13
						Tranmere R	26	3
						Peterborough U (loan)	9	—
Kenny Irons	5 9	11 00	4 11 70	Liverpool	Trainee	Tranmere R	78	13
Chris Malkin	6 0	10 12	4 6 67	Bebington	Overpool	Tranmere R	125	29
Alan Morgan			2 11 73	Aberystwyth	Trainee	Tranmere R	—	—
John Morrissey	5 8	11 04	8 3 65	Liverpool	Apprentice	Everton	1	—
						Wolverhampton W	10	1
						Tranmere R	258	38
Ian Muir	5 7	10 10	5 5 63	Coventry	Apprentice	QPR	2	2
						Burnley (loan)	2	1
						Birmingham C	1	—
						Brighton & HA	4	—
						Swindon T (loan)	2	—
						Tranmere R	268	123
Jim Steel	6 3	14 00	4 12 59	Dumfries	Apprentice	Oldham Ath	108	24
						Wigan Ath (loan)	2	2
						Wrexham (loan)	9	6
						Port Vale	28	6
						Wrexham	164	51
						Tranmere R	174	29

Trainees
Edwards, Michael; Evans, John D; Hardy, Neil J. P; Hill, Christopher; Johnson, Philip; Jones, Gary S; Jones, Martin W; Kenworthy, Jonathan P; McCullach, Edward; Moore, Darren E; Richardson, Marcus A; Smith, Paul.

Associated Schoolboys
Bradley, Carl M; Burns, Brian; Cooke, Ian; Davies, Philip A; Exton, Peter; Griffiths, Steven; Hammond, John E; Hazlehurst, Ian J; Lepts, Damien A.

Associated Schoolboys who have accepted the club's offer of a Traineeship/Contract
Allen, Gavin; Rogers, David R.

WALSALL 1991–92 *Back row (left to right):* Tony Grealish (Player-coach), Chris Marsh, Kevin MacDonald, Colin Methven, Mark Gayle, Martin Goldsmith, Fred Barber, Mick Cecere, Steve O'Hara, Martin Lane, Tom Bradley (Physiotherapist).
Front row: Robbie Jackson, Charlie Ntamark, Rod McDonald, Kenny Hibbitt (Manager), Dean Smith, Russell Musker, Wayne Williams.

Division 3   **WALSALL**

Bescot Staum, Bescot Cresent, Walsall ES1 4SA. Telephone Walsall (0922) 22791. Commercial Dept: (0922) 30696. Clubcall: 0898 121104.

Ground capacity: 10,400.

Record attendance: 10,628 B International, England v Switzerland, 20 May 1991.

Record receipts: £50,926.50 v Watford, FA Cup 5th rd, 2nd replay, 2 March 1987 (at Fellows Park); £42,401 v Aston Villa, Friendly, 18 August 1990.

Pitch measurements: 113yd × 73yd.

Chairman: J. W. Bonser. *Managing Director:* R. Dox.

Directors: M. N. Lloyd, K. H. Morrall, T. F. Hargreaves, K. R. Whalley, C. Welch.

Manager: Kenny Hibbitt. *General Manager:* Paul Taylor. *Physio:* T. Bradley. *Secretary/Commercial Manager:* Roy Whalley.

Year Formed: 1888. Turned Professional: 1888. Ltd Co.: 1921.

Former Grounds: Fellows Park to 1990.

Former Names: Walsall Swifts (founded 1877) and Walsall Town (founded 1879) amalgamated in 1888 and were known as Walsall Town Swifts until 1895.

Club Nickname: 'The Saddlers'.

Record League Victory: 10-0 v Darwen, Division 2, 4 March 1899 – Tennent; E. Peers (1), Davies; Hickinbotham, Jenkyns, Taggart; Dean (3), Vail (2), Aston (4), Martin, Griffin.

Record Cup Victory: 6-1 v Leytonstone (away), FA Cup, 1st rd, 30 November 1946 – Lewis; Netley, Skidmore; Crutchley, Foulkes, Newman; Maund (1), Talbot, Darby (1), Wilshaw (2), Davies (2). 6-1 v Margate, FA Cup, 1st rd (replay), 24 November 1955 – Davies; Haddington, Vinall; Dorman, McPherson, Crook; Morris, Walsh (3), Richards (2), McLaren (1), Moore.

Record Defeat: 0-12 v Small Heath, 17 December 1892 and v Darwen, 26 December 1896, both Division 2.

Most League Points (2 for a win): 65, Division 4, 1959–60.

Most League points (3 for a win): 82, Division 3, 1987–88.

Most League Goals: 102, Division 4, 1959–60.

Highest League Scorer in Season: Gilbert Alsop, 40, Division 3 (N), 1933–34 and 1934–35.

Most League Goals in Total Aggregate: Tony Richards, 184, 1954–63, and Colin Taylor, 184, 1958–63, 1964–68, 1969–73.

Most Capped Player: Mick Kearns, 15 (18), Eire.

Most League Appearances: Colin Harrison, 467, 1964–82.

Record Transfer Fee Received: £600,000 from West Ham U for David Kelly, July 1988.

Record Transfer Fee Paid: £175,000 to Birmingham C for Alan Buckley, June 1979.

Football League Record: 1892 Elected to Division 2; 1895 Failed re-election; 1896–1901 Division 2; 1901 Failed re-election; 1921 Original Member of Division 3 (N); 1927–31 Division 3 (S); 1931–36 Division 3 (N); 1936–58 Division 3 (S); 1958–60 Division 4; 1960–61 Division 3; 1961–63 Division 2; 1963–79 Division 3; 1979–80 Division 4; 1980–88 Division 3; 1988–89 Division 2; 1989–90 Division 3; 1990–92 Division 4; 1992– Division 3.

Honours: Football League: Division 2 best season: 6th, 1898–99; Division 3 – Runners-up 1960–61; Division 4 – Champions 1959–60; Runners-up 1979–80. *FA Cup:* best season: 5th rd, 1939, 1975, 1978, and last 16 1888–89. *Football League Cup:* Semi-final 1983–84.

Colours: Red shirts, white shorts, red stockings. **Change colours:** All yellow.

WALSALL 1991–92 LEAGUE RECORD

Match No.	Date		Venue	Opponents		Result	H/T Score	Lg. Pos.	Goalscorers	Atten-dance
1	Aug	17	A	Blackpool	L	0-3	0-1	—		4141
2		24	H	Wrexham	D	0-0	0-0	20		3307
3		31	A	Scarborough	W	3-2	2-1	13	McDonald 2, Cecere	2022
4	Sep	3	H	Rochdale	L	1-3	0-2	—	McDonald	3111
5		7	H	Halifax T	W	3-0	1-0	11	MacDonald, McLoughlin, McDonald	2981
6		14	A	Maidstone U	L	1-2	1-2	13	Methven	1139
7		17	A	Chesterfield	W	1-0	0-0	—	McLoughlin	2690
8		21	H	Hereford U	W	3-0	2-0	7	Marsh, Anderson, McLoughlin	4509
9		28	A	Carlisle U	D	3-3	0-1	8	McDonald, Anderson, McLoughlin	2148
10	Oct	5	H	Barnet	W	2-0	2-0	7	Methven, McDonald	4981
11		11	A	Crewe Alex	W	1-0	1-0	—	McDonald	4749
12		19	A	Burnley	L	0-2	0-2	6		7289
13	Nov	2	A	York C	L	0-2	0-0	8		1605
14		5	H	Lincoln C	D	0-0	0-0	—		2555
15		22	A	Rotherham U	L	1-2	0-1	—	McDonald	4192
16		30	A	Mansfield T	L	1-3	0-2	12	McDonald	3398
17	Dec	20	A	Wrexham	L	1-2	0-1	—	Cecere	2571
18		26	H	Blackpool	W	4-2	2-0	12	McDonald 3, MacDonald	4675
19		28	H	Scarborough	D	0-0	0-0	12		3488
20	Jan	1	A	Rochdale	D	1-1	1-0	12	McDonald	3001
21		4	H	Doncaster R	L	1-3	0-2	12	O'Hara	3444
22		11	A	Gillingham	L	0-4	0-4	12		2715
23		18	H	Cardiff C	D	0-0	0-0	13		3654
24		25	A	Scunthorpe U	D	1-1	0-1	12	Ntamark	3165
25		28	H	Northampton T	L	1-2	1-2	—	Cecere	2399
26	Feb	1	H	Burnley	D	2-2	1-0	14	Cecere, O'Hara	5287
27		11	A	Mansfield T	D	3-3	0-1	—	Cecere 2, Ntamark	2963
28		15	A	Northampton T	W	1-0	1-0	12	McDonald	2480
29		22	H	Gillingham	L	0-1	0-1	14		2987
30		29	A	Doncaster R	W	1-0	0-0	12	Samways (og)	1919
31	Mar	3	A	Cardiff C	L	1-2	1-0	—	Perry (og)	7517
32		7	H	Scunthorpe U	W	2-1	1-0	13	Edwards, Cecere	2722
33		11	A	Lincoln C	L	0-1	0-0	—		2021
34		14	H	York C	D	1-1	1-1	13	Tolson	2541
35		28	H	Rotherham U	L	0-2	0-0	17		3524
36		31	H	Maidstone U	D	1-1	1-1	—	Ntamark	2045
37	Apr	3	A	Halifax T	L	0-1	0-1	—		1006
38		11	H	Chesterfield	D	2-2	1-1	17	McDonald 2	2472
39		18	H	Hereford U	W	2-1	1-1	15	McDonald, Cecere	2291
40		21	H	Carlisle U	D	0-0	0-0	—		2406
41		25	A	Barnet	W	1-0	1-0	14	MacDonald	3207
42	May	2	H	Crewe Alex	L	2-3	0-3	15	McDonald, O'Hara	4995

Final League Position: 15

GOALSCORERS

League (48): McDonald 18, Cecere 8, McLoughlin 4, MacDonald 3, Ntamark 3, O'Hara 3, Anderson 2, Methven 2, Edwards 1, Marsh 1, Tolson 1, own goals 2.
Rumbelows Cup (2): MacDonald 1 (1 pen), Ntamark 1.
FA Cup (1): Tolson 1.

Gayle	Williams	Statham	Methven	Musker	Smith	MacDonald	Ntamark	Jackson	Cecere	McDonald	Marsh	Lane	Anderson	Grealish	O'Hara	Sinclair	Hobson	McLoughlin	Walsh	Essers	McKnight	Tolson	Edwards	Winter	Brown	Robinson	May	Chine	*Match No.*
1	2	3	4	5	6	7	8	9†	10*	11	12	14																	1
1	2	3	4	5*	6	7	8	14	10	11	12		9†																2
1	2		4		6	7	8*		10	11		5	3	9	12														3
1	2	3	4	5	6	7	8		10	11			9																4
	2	3	4		6	7	8			11	10					1	5	9											5
	2	3	4			7	8			11	12			10*	6	1	5	9											6
	2	3	4			7	8			11	10		12		6	1	5*	9											7
	2	3	4			7	8			11	10		5		6	1		9											8
	2	3*	4			7	8		12	11	10		5		6	1		9											9
	2	3	4				8		12	11†	10		5	14	6	1		9*	7										10
	2	3	4				8			11	10		5		6	1		9	7										11
	2	3*	4				8		12	11	10		5		6	1		9	7										12
	2	3	4			7			12	11	10	14		8†	6	1		9	5*										13
	2	3	4			7	8		12	11	10		5		6	1				9*									14
	2		4			7	8		9†	11	10	3	5	12	6*						1	14							15
	2		4			7	8	9	12	11	10*	3	5		6						1								16
	2		4			7	8	9*	10	11	3		5		6						1		12						17
	2		4			7*	8	9†	10	11	3	14	5		6						1		12						18
	2		4				8	9			3	10*	5		6						1		7	11	12				19
	2		4				8	9		11	10	3	5		6						1		7						20
	2		4				8	9*	10	11†		3	5		6						1		7	12	14				21
	2	3†	4				8		10	11			5		6						1	12	7*	9	14				22
1	2		4				8		10	11	9		5		6								7†	12	3	14*			23
1	2		4				8		10	11	9		5*		6								12	7	3				24
1	2†		4				8		10	11	9		5		6							14	12	7*	3				25
1	2		4*				8		10	11	9		5		6							14	12	7†	3				26
1	2		4				8		10	11	9		5		6									7	3				27
1	2	3	4				8		10	11	9		5		6									7					28
1	2	3	4				8		10	11*	9		5		6							12		7					29
1	2	3	4				8		10		9		5		6							11*	12	7					30
1	2	3	4				8		10		9	12			6							11†	5	7*			14		31
1	2	3	4				8		10	11	9				6								5	7*			12		32
1	2	3	4				8		10	11	9				6							12	5	7*					33
1	2	3	4				8		10	11*	9				6							7	5	12					34
1	2	3	4				8	12	10	11					6								5	7*				9	35
1	2	3	4		5†		8		10	11*	9				14								6				12	7	36
1	2	3	4				8		10*	12	9				6								5				11	7	37
1	2	3	4			5*	8		10	11	9				6								12					7	38
1	2	3	4		6	5	8*		10	11	9				7								12						39
1	2	3	4		6	5	8		10*	11	9				7†								12					14	40
1	2	3	4		6	5	8		10	11	9												7						41
1	2	3	4			5	8		10	11	9				7										6				42
24	42	29	42	3	9	20	41	7 + 2s	29 + 6s	38 + 1s	34 + 3s	6 + 4s	25 + 1s	3 + 2s	35 + 2s	10	3	9	4	1	8	3 + 6s	13 + 9s	13 + 3s	6 + 3s	— + 1s	1 + 3s	4 + 1s	

Rumbelows Cup	First Round	Swansea C (a)	2-2
		(h)	0-1
FA Cup	First Round	Yeovil (a)	1-1
		(h)	0-1

WALSALL

Goalkeepers

Name	Ht	Wt	DOB	Birthplace	Source	Club	Apps	Gls
Mark Gayle	6 0	12 00	21 10 69	Bromsgrove	Trainee	Leicester C	—	—
						Blackpool	—	—
						Walsall	24	—
Allen McKnight‡	6 1	13 07	27 1 64	Antrim	Distillery	Celtic	12	—
						Albion R (loan)	36	—
						West Ham U	23	—
						Stockport Co	—	—
						Rotherham U	3	—
						Walsall	8	—

Defenders

Name	Ht	Wt	DOB	Birthplace	Source	Club	Apps	Gls
Richard Brown§	5 10	10 13	25 12 73	Sutton Coldfield	Trainee	Walsall	9	—
Richard Knight	5 09	10 13	31 8 74	Burton	Trainee	Walsall	—	—
Martin Lane*	5 9	11 04	12 4 61	Altrincham	Amateur	Manchester U	—	—
						Chester C	175	3
						Coventry C	3	—
						Wrexham (loan)	6	—
						Chester C	99	—
						Walsall	10	—
Colin Methven	6 2	12 07	10 12 55	Kirkcaldy	Leven Royals	East Fife	144	14
						Wigan Ath	296	21
						Blackpool	173	11
						Carlisle U (loan)	12	—
						Walsall	74	3
Dean Smith	6 0	12 01	19 3 71	West Bromwich	Trainee	Walsall	64	—
Derek Statham	5 5	11 05	24 3 59	Wolverhampton	Apprentice	WBA	299	8
						Southampton	64	2
						Stoke C	41	1
						Walsall	29	—
Wayne Williams	5 11	11 09	17 11 63	Telford	Apprentice	Shrewsbury T	221	7
						Northampton T	55	1
						Walsall	42	—

Midfield

Name	Ht	Wt	DOB	Birthplace	Source	Club	Apps	Gls
Colin Anderson‡	5 9	10 07	26 4 62	Newcastle	Apprentice	Burnley	6	—
						Torquay U	109	11
						QPR (loan)	—	—
						WBA	140	10
						Walsall	26	2
David Edwards	5 10	10 08	13 1 74	Bridgnorth	Trainee	Walsall	22	1
Tony Grealish‡	5 7	11 08	21 9 56	Paddington	Apprentice	Orient	171	10
						Luton T	78	2
						Brighton & HA	100	6
						WBA	65	5
						Manchester C	11	—
						Rotherham U	110	6
						Walsall	36	1
Kevin MacDonald	6 1	12 06	22 12 60	Inverness	Inverness Caley	Leicester C	138	8
						Liverpool	40	1
						Leicester C (loan)	3	—
						Rangers (loan)	3	—
						Coventry C	31	—
						Cardiff C (loan)	8	—
						Walsall	20	3
Russell Musker‡	5 8	11 03	10 7 62	Liverpool	Apprentice	Bristol C	46	1
						Exeter C (loan)	6	—
						Gillingham	64	7
						Torquay U	66	1
						Walsall	3	—
Charlie Ntamark	5 8	11 12	22 7 64	Cameroon		Walsall	83	6
Steve O'Hara	6 1	12 02	21 1 71	Bellshill	Trainee	Walsall	75	3

Foundation: Two of the leading clubs around Walsall in the 1880s were Walsall Swifts (formed 1877) and Walsall Town (formed 1879). The Swifts were winners of the Birmingham Senior Cup in 1881, while the Town reached the 4th round (5th round modern equivalent) of the FA Cup in 1883. These clubs amalgamated as Walsall Town Swifts in 1888, becoming simply Walsall in 1895.

First Football League game: 3 September 1892, Division 2, v Darwen (h) L 1-2 – Hawkins; Withington, Pinches; Robinson, Whitrick, Forsyth; Marshall, Holmes, Turner, Gray (1), Pangbourn.

Did you know: Centre-forward Gilbert Alsop scored a total of 13 goals in five consecutive games in 1934–35, including five in a 6-1 win away to Carlisle United.

Managers (and Secretary-managers)
H. Smallwood 1888–91*, A. G. Burton 1891–93, J. H. Robinson 1893–95, C. H. Ailso 1895–96*, A. E. Parsloe 1896–97*, L. Ford 1897–98*, G. Hughes 1898–99*, L. Ford 1899–1901*, J. E. Shutt 1908–13*, Haydn Price 1914–20, Joe Burchell 1920–26, David Ashworth 1926–27, Jack Torrance 1927–28, James Kerr 1928–29, S. Scholey 1929–30, Peter O'Rourke 1930–32, G. W. Slade 1932–34, Andy Wilson 1934–37, Tommy Lowes 1937–44, Harry Hibbs 1944–51, Tony McPhee 1951, Brough Fletcher 1952–53, Major Frank Buckley 1953–55, John Love 1955–57, Billy Moore 1957–64, Alf Wood 1964, Reg Shaw 1964–68, Dick Graham 1968, Ron Lewin 1968–69, Billy Moore 1969–72, John Smith 1972–73, Doug Fraser 1973–77, Dave Mackay 1977–78, Alan Ashman 1978, Frank Sibley 1979, Alan Buckley 1979–86, Neil Martin (joint manager with Buckley) 1981–82, Tommy Coakley 1986–88, John Barnwell 1989–90, Kenny Hibbitt May 1990–.

Name			Date	Birthplace	Source	Clubs	Apps	Gls
Martin Singleton‡	5 10	11 00	2 8 63	Banbury	Apprentice	Coventry C	23	1
						Bradford C	71	3
						WBA	19	1
						Northampton T	50	4
						Walsall	28	1
Steve Winter	5 07	10 03	26 10 73	Bristol	Trainee	Walsall	16	—
Forwards								
Michele Cecere	6 0	11 04	4 1 68	Chester	Apprentice	Oldham Ath	52	8
						Huddersfield T	54	8
						Stockport Co (loan)	1	—
						Walsall	67	14
Athuman Chine	5 08	10 05	12 3 67	Dar Es Salaam		Walsall	5	—
Pierre Essers†			20 2 59	Holland		Walsall	1	—
Martin Goldsmith	6 0	11 11	4 11 69	Walsall	Trainee	Walsall	7	2
						Larne (loan)	—	—
Gordon Hobson‡	5 9	10 07	27 11 57	Sheffield	Sheffield RGRS	Lincoln C	272	73
						Grimsby T	52	18
						Southampton	33	8
						Lincoln C	61	22
						Exeter C	38	7
						Walsall	3	—
Robbie Jackson	5 08	11 03	9 2 73	Altrincham	Manchester C	Walsall	10	2
Rod McDonald			20 3 67	London	Colne Dynamoes	Walsall	75	23
Chris Marsh	5 10	12 11	14 1 70	Dudley	Trainee	Walsall	85	3
Leroy May	6 01	11 07	12 8 69	Wolverhampton	Tividale	Walsall	4	—
Simon Robinson†			6 4 65	West Bromwich	Mansfield T	Blackpool	—	—
						Walsall	1	—

Trainees
Brown, Richard C; Butler, Martin N; Carrington, Mark; Demerios, Christakis A; Donovan, John D; Hodgson, Craig B; Instone, Wayne A; McManus, Steven; Norman, Karl M; Norris, Jonathan D; Read, Paul J; Richardson, Jason P; Rose, Brett J; Ryder, Stuart H; Turner, Emlyn A; Vaughan, Stephen A.

**Non-Contract
Heyes, Darren L; Robinson, Simon W.

Associated Schoolboys
Adams, Daniel; Ashfield, Robert S; Bray, Darren N; Derry, Leighton W; Hingley, Philip W; Hubble, Robin; Mathews, Stuart J; Phillips, Wayne S; Rollo, James; Simcox, Robert S; Smith, Christopher G; Webb, Neal; Webb, Neil.

Associated Schoolboys who have accepted the club's offer of a Traineeship/Contract
Blackwood, Ian C; Gardner, Richard R; Jones, John T; Parker, Paul J; Pickett, James A; Thomas, Mathew.

**Non-Contract Players who are retained must be re-signed before they are eligible to play in League matches.

WATFORD 1991–92 *Back row (left to right)*: Stuart Murdoch (Reserve Team Manager), Alex Inglethorpe, Julian Alsford, Barry Ashby, Steve Butler, Andy Kennedy, Jason Soloman, Jason Drysdale, Mark Gavin, Gary Williams.

Centre row: Kenny Jackett (Youth Team Coach), Darren Bazeley, Alan Devonshire, Luther Blissett, Simon Sheppard, David James, Keith Waugh, David Holdsworth, Eddie Denton, Joe Gallen, Billy Hails (Physiotherapist), Ken Brooks (Kit Manager).

Front row: James Meara, Gary Porter, Keith Dublin, Nigel Gibbs, Peter Nicholas, Peter Taylor (Assistant Manager), Steve Perryman (Manager), Joe McLaughlin, Trevor Putney, Andy Hessenthaler, Rod Thomas, David Byrne.

Division 1 **WATFORD**

Vicarage Road Stadium, Watford WD1 8ER. Telephone Watford (0923) 230933. Hornet Hotline 24-hour club news service: 0898 338 338. Ticket office: 220393. Club shop: 220847. Junior Hornets Club: 253836. Marketing: 225761. Catering: 221457.

Ground capacity: 26,996.

Record attendance: 34,099 v Manchester U, FA Cup 4th rd (replay), 3 February 1969.

Record receipts: £104,347 v Liverpool, FA Cup 6th rd (replay). 17 March 1986.

Pitch measurements: 115yd × 75yd.

Life President: Elton John.

Chairman: J. Petchey. *Vice-chairman:* G. A. Smith.

Directors: E. John, G. S. Lawson Rogers, C. D. Lissack, Dr. S. R. Timperley PHD, M. Winwood.

Chief Executive: Eddie Plumley FAAI.

Team Manager: Steve Perryman MBE. *Assistant Manager:* Peter Taylor. *Reserve team coach:* Stuart Murdoch. *Youth team coach:* Kenny Jackett. *Physio:* Billy Hails. *Commercial Manager:* Allan Robson ACIS. *Public Relations Manager:* Ed Coan.

Year Formed: 1891 *(see Foundation)*. Turned Professional: 1897. Ltd Co.: 1909.

Former Grounds: 1899, Cassio Road; 1922, Vicarage Road.

Former Names: West Herts.

Club Nickname: 'The Hornets'.

Record League Victory: 8-0 v Sunderland, Division 1, 25 September 1982 – Sherwood; Rice, Rostron, Taylor, Terry, Bolton, Callaghan (2), Blissett (4), Jenkins (2), Jackett, Barnes.

Record Cup Victory: 10-1 v Lowestoft T, FA Cup, 1st rd, 27 November 1926 – Yates; Prior, Fletcher (1); F. Smith, 'Bert' Smith, Strain; Stephenson, Warner (3), Edmonds (2), Swan (2), Daniels (1). (1 og).

Record Defeat: 0-11 v Southampton, Southern League, 13 December 1902.

Most League Points (2 for a win): 71, Division 4, 1977–78.

Most League points (3 for a win): 80, Division 2, 1981–82.

Most League Goals: 92, Division 4, 1959–60.

Highest League Scorer in Season: Cliff Holton, 42, Division 4, 1959–60.

Most League Goals in Total Aggregate: Luther Blissett, 158, 1976–83, 1984–88, 1991–.

Most Capped Player: John Barnes, 31 (67), England and Kenny Jackett, 31, Wales.

Most League Appearances: Luther Blissett, 415, 1976–83, 1984–88, 1991–.

Record Transfer Fee Received: £1,000,000 from AC Milan for Luther Blissett, July 1983 and £1,000,000 from Manchester C for Tony Coton, July 1990.

Record Transfer Fee Paid: £550,000 to AC Milan for Luther Blissett, August 1984.

Football League Record: 1920 Original Member of Division 3; 1921–58 Division 3 (S); 1958–60 Division 4; 1960–69 Division 3; 1969–72 Division 2; 1972–75 Division 3; 1975–78 Division 4; 1978–79 Division 3; 1979–82 Division 2; 1982–88 Division 1; 1988–92 Division 2; 1992– Division 1.

Honours: Football League: Division 1 – Runners-up 1982–83; Division 2 – Runners-up 1981–82; Division 3 – Champions 1968–69; Runners-up 1978–79; Division 4 – Champions 1977–78; Promoted 1959–60 (4th). *FA Cup:* Runners-up 1984. *Football League Cup:* Semi-final 1978–79. **European Competitions:** *UEFA Cup:* 1983–84.

Colours: Yellow shirts (black/red striped band), red shorts, yellow trim, red stockings (yellow/black tops). **Change colours:** White shirts (light blue/navy chessboard pattern), navy blue shorts with light blue trim, navy blue stockings (light blue tops).

WATFORD 1991–92 LEAGUE RECORD

Match No.	Date		Venue	Opponents		Result	H/T Score	Lg. Pos.	Goalscorers	Attendance
1	Aug	17	H	Wolverhampton W	L	0-2	0-0	—		13,547
2		24	A	Newcastle U	D	2-2	1-1	22	Nicholas, Blissett	22,440
3		31	H	Cambridge U	L	1-3	0-1	22	Blissett	8902
4	Sep	3	A	Barnsley	W	3-0	1-0	—	Bazeley, Blissett, Kennedy	6500
5		7	H	Middlesbrough	L	1-2	0-2	20	McLaughlin	8715
6		14	A	Brighton & HA	W	1-0	1-0	18	Butler	8741
7		17	A	Blackburn R	L	0-1	0-1	—		9452
8		21	H	Charlton Ath	W	2-0	2-0	17	Butler, Blissett	8459
9		28	A	Swindon T	L	1-3	0-2	18	Porter	8863
10	Oct	5	H	Grimsby T	W	2-0	2-0	16	Hessenthaler, Putney	6930
11		12	A	Bristol C	L	0-1	0-1	20		7882
12		19	A	Southend U	L	1-2	0-1	20	Porter (pen)	6862
13		26	A	Plymouth Arg	W	1-0	1-0	17	Bazeley	4090
14		29	H	Millwall	L	0-2	0-0	—		7366
15	Nov	2	A	Sunderland	L	1-3	0-2	19	Porter	12,790
16		6	H	Oxford U	W	2-0	1-0	—	Porter (pen), Bazeley	4785
17		9	H	Leicester C	L	0-1	0-1	19		9271
18		16	A	Bristol R	D	1-1	1-1	16	Blissett	5064
19		23	H	Portsmouth	W	2-1	1-0	16	Blissett 2	8135
20		30	A	Port Vale	L	1-2	0-0	16	Porter	5777
21	Dec	7	H	Derby Co	L	1-2	0-1	21	Blissett	8302
22		22	H	Barnsley	D	1-1	0-1	—	Nogan	7522
23		26	A	Millwall	W	4-0	2-0	17	Porter, Butler 2, Drysdale	9237
24		29	A	Cambridge U	W	1-0	0-0	—	Butler	8439
25	Jan	1	H	Tranmere R	D	0-0	0-0	16		9892
26		11	H	Newcastle U	D	2-2	2-1	15	Holdsworth, Porter (pen)	9811
27		18	A	Wolverhampton W	L	0-3	0-0	17		14,175
28		24	A	Tranmere R	D	1-1	0-0	—	Butler	6187
29	Feb	1	A	Southend U	L	0-1	0-0	17		7581
30		8	H	Plymouth Arg	W	1-0	0-0	16	Blissett	7260
31		22	H	Port Vale	D	0-0	0-0	18		6602
32		29	A	Derby Co	L	1-3	0-2	18	Nogan	14,052
33	Mar	7	H	Ipswich T	L	0-1	0-0	18		9199
34		11	A	Oxford U	D	0-0	0-0	—		5808
35		14	H	Sunderland	W	1-0	1-0	19	Porter (pen)	8091
36		17	H	Ipswich T	W	2-1	0-0	—	Drysdale 2	12,484
37		21	A	Leicester C	W	2-1	2-0	16	Butler, Nogan	14,519
38		28	H	Bristol R	W	1-0	0-0	13	Drysdale (pen)	7496
39		31	H	Brighton & HA	L	0-1	0-0	—		7589
40	Apr	4	A	Middlesbrough	W	2-1	0-0	13	Holdsworth, Butler	13,669
41		11	H	Blackburn R	W	2-1	1-1	12	Bazeley 2	10,522
42		18	A	Charlton Ath	D	1-1	1-0	12	Nogan	7477
43		20	H	Swindon T	D	0-0	0-0	13		9911
44		22	A	Portsmouth	D	0-0	0-0	—		14,417
45		25	A	Grimsby T	W	1-0	1-0	12	Nogan	6483
46	May	2	H	Bristol C	W	5-2	1-1	10	Drysdale, Bazeley, Putney, Blissett, Gibbs	10,582

Final League Position: 10

GOALSCORERS

League (51): Blissett 10, Butler 8, Porter 8 (4 pens), Bazeley 6, Drysdale 5 (1 pen), Nogan 5, Holdsworth 2, Putney 2, Gibbs 1, Hessenthaler 1, Kennedy 1, McLaughlin 1, Nicholas 1.
Rumbelows Cup (4): Bazeley 1, Blissett 1, Kennedy 1, Porter 1.
FA Cup (2): Blissett 2.

James	Gibbs	Morrow	Dublin	McLaughlin	Putney	Thomas	Porter	Butler	Kennedy	Nicholas	Blissett	Ashby	Bazeley	Soloman	Hessenthaler	Drysdale	Devonshire	Holdsworth	Nogan	Johnson	Waugh	Lavin	Inglethorpe	Match No.
1	2	3	4	5	6	7†	8	9	10*11	12	14													1
1	2	3	4	5	6		12	8	9	11	10†	7*14												2
1	2	3	4		6		10	9	8*11	7	5†12	14												3
1	2	3	4	5	6		10	12	8	11	7*	9†14												4
1	2	3†	4	5	6		10	12	8*11	7	9	14												5
1	2	3	4	5	6		10†	8	12	11	7*	9	14											6
1	2	3*	4	5	6†		10	9	12	11	7	14	8											7
1	2		4	5			10	9	12	11	8	14	6†	3	7*									8
1	2		4	5	12		10	9		11	8	6*14	7	3†										9
1	2		4	5	6		10	9		11	8		7	3										10
1	2		4	5	6		10	9		11	8†	12	7*	3	14									11
1	2	12	4	5	6		10	9*		11	8	7	3											12
1	2		4	5	6		10	12		11	8*	7	3	9										13
1	2		4	5	6*		10	12		11	8	7	3	9										14
1	2		4	5	6		10	12		11	8	7	3*	9										15
1	2		4	5	6		10	9*		11	8	12	7	3										16
1			4	5*	6†		10	9		11	8	12	3	7	14	2								17
1			4				12	10	9*		8	6	11	2	7	3		5						18
1			4				12	10*14		11	9	6	8†	2	7	3		5						19
1	2		4		12		10			11	9	6	8*		7	3		5						20
1	2		4				10	12		11*	9	6†	8	14	7	3		5						21
1	2		4				10			11	9		12	6*	7	3		5	8					22
1	2		4	14			10	9		11†		12	6	7	3		5	8*						23
1	2		4				10	8		12	9*	6		7	3		5		11					24
1	2		4		6		10*	8		11†	9	12		7	3		5		14					25
	2		4		6		10	14		11*	9†	12		7	3		5	8	1					26
	2		4	6	11		10*12			9				7	3		5	8	1					27
	2		4*	6	11		10	12		9				7	3		5	8	1					28
1	2†		4	6	11		10	12		9	14			7	3		5	8*						29
1	2		4	6	11		10*12			9				7	3		5	8						30
1	2		4	6	11		10	12		5*	9		14	7	3†			8						31
1	2		4	6	11†		12	10		9			14	7	3*		5	8						32
1	2		4				10	11		9	6			7	3		5	8						33
1	2		4				10	12		9*	6		11	7	3		5	8						34
1	2		4				10†12			9*	6		11	7	3		5	8	14					35
1	2		4				10			9	6	12	11	7	3		5	8*						36
1	2		4				10			6	9		11	7	3		5	8						37
1	2		4	14			10*	12		6	9†11			7	3		5	8						38
1	−2		4	14			10			6*	9	11†		7	3		5	8	12					39
1	2		4	14			10	12		6	9*11			7	3†		5	8						40
1	2		4	14			10	12		6	9†11			7	3		5	8*						41
1	2		4	14			10*	12		6	9†11			7	3		5	8						42
1	2		4	14			10*			6	9†11			7	3		5	8	12					43
1	2		4		6		12	10		9	11*			7	3		5	8						44
1	2		4	11†			12	10		14	6	9*		7	3		5	8						45
1	2		4	11			12	10*		14	6†	9		7	3		5	8						46

Totals: 43 43 7 46 22 26 1 34 28 4 25 34 18 25 19 35 36 — 33 23 1 3 — —

Sub appearances: Gibbs +1s; Putney +2s; Thomas +4s; Porter +10s; Butler +15s; Kennedy +3s; Blissett +8s; Ashby +3s; Bazeley +9s; Soloman +10s; Drysdale +1s; Devonshire +1s; Nogan +1s; Waugh +1s; Lavin +2s

Rumbelows Cup	First Round	Southend U (h)	2-0
		(a)	1-1
	Second Round	Everton (a)	0-1
		(h)	1-2
FA Cup	Third Round	Swindon T (a)	2-3

WATFORD

Player and Position	Ht	Wt	Date	Birth Place	Source	Clubs	League App	Gls
Goalkeepers								
David James	6 4	14 07	1 8 70	Welwyn	Trainee	Watford	89	—
Simon Sheppard	6 04	14 03	7 8 73	Clevedon	Trainee	Watford	—	—
Keith Waugh	6 1	13 00	27 10 56	Sunderland	Apprentice	Sunderland	—	—
						Peterborough U	195	—
						Sheffield U	99	—
						Cambridge U (loan)	4	—
						Bristol C (loan)	3	—
						Bristol C	167	—
						Coventry C	1	—
						Watford	3	—
Defenders								
Julian Alsford			24 12 72	Poole		Watford	—	—
Barry Ashby	6 2	12 03	21 11 70	London	Trainee	Watford	62	1
Jason Drysdale	5 10	10 07	17 11 70	Bristol	Trainee	Watford	87	5
Keith Dublin	5 11	11 09	29 1 66	Wycombe	Apprentice	Chelsea	51	—
						Brighton & HA	132	5
						Watford	89	5
Nigel Gibbs	5 7	10 02	20 11 65	St Albans	Apprentice	Watford	264	3
David Holdsworth	5 11	11 04	8 11 68	London	Trainee	Watford	125	8
Joe McLaughlin	6 1	12 00	2 6 60	Greenock	School	Morton	134	3
						Chelsea	220	5
						Charlton Ath	31	—
						Watford	46	2
Danny Nwaokolo			11 10 73	London	Trainee	Watford	—	—
Jason Soloman	6 1	11 09	6 10 70	Welwyn	Trainee	Watford	37	—
Midfield								
Edward Denton*	5 10	11 03	18 5 70	Oxford	Trainee	Oxford U	2	—
						Watford	2	—
Alan Devonshire*	5 11	11 00	13 4 56	London	Southall & Ealing	West Ham U	358	29
						Watford	25	1
Richard Johnson			27 4 74	Australia	Trainee	Watford	2	—
Gerard Lavin			5 2 74	Corby	Trainee	Watford	1	—
Jim Meara	5 07	10 06	7 10 72	London	Trainee	Watford	—	—
Peter Nicholas	5 8	11 08	10 11 59	Newport	Apprentice	Crystal Palace	127	7
						Arsenal	60	1
						Crystal Palace	47	7
						Luton T	102	1
						Aberdeen	39	3
						Chelsea	80	2
						Watford	40	1
Gary Porter	5 5	9 10	6 3 66	Sunderland	Apprentice	Watford	248	34
Trevor Putney	5 7	10 11	11 2 61	Harold Hill	Brentwood W	Ipswich T	103	8
						Norwich C	82	9
						Middlesbrough	48	1
						Watford	28	2
Forwards								
Darren Bazeley	5 10	10 09	5 10 72	Northampton	Trainee	Watford	42	6
Luther Blissett	5 11	12 00	1 2 58	Jamaica		Watford	246	95
						AC Milan	30	5
						Watford	127	44
						Bournemouth	121	56
						Watford	42	10
Steve Butler	6 2	11 01	27 1 62	Birmingham	Army	Brentford	21	3
						Maidstone U	76	41
						Watford	53	9

WATFORD

Foundation: Tracing this club's foundation proves difficult. Nowadays it is suggested that Watford was formed as Watford Rovers in 1891. Another version is that Watford Rovers were not forerunners of the present club whose history began in 1898 with the amalgamation of West Herts and Watford St. Mary's.

First Football League game: 28 August 1920, Division 3, v QPR (a) W 2-1 – Williams; Horseman, F. Gregory; Bacon, Toone, Wilkinson; Bassett, Ronald (1), Hoddinott, White (1), Waterall.

Did you know: In February 1948 Watford signed five players from Leicester City in one of the biggest wholesale transfer deals in Football League history. They were John Osborne, Tom Hartley, Tom Eggleston, Joe Calvert and Dennis Cheney.

Managers (and Secretary-managers)
John Goodall 1903–10, Harry Kent 1910–26, Fred Pagnam 1926–29, Neil McBain 1929–37, Bill Findlay 1938–47, Jack Bray 1947–48, Eddie Hapgood 1948–50, Ron Gray 1950–51, Haydn Green 1951–52, Len Goulden 1952–55 (GM to 1956), Johnny Paton 1955–56, Neil McBain 1956–59, Ron Burgess 1959–63, Bill McGarry 1963–64, Ken Furphy 1964–71, George Kirby 1971–73, Mike Keen 1973–77, Graham Taylor 1977–87, Dave Bassett 1987–88, Steve Harrison 1988–90, Colin Lee 1990, Steve Perryman November 1990–.

Player and Position	Ht	Wt	Birth Date	Birth Place	Source	Clubs	League App	Gls
David Byrne	5 8	11 00	5 3 61	London	Kingstonian	Gillingham	23	3
						Millwall	63	6
						Cambridge U (loan)	4	—
						Blackburn R (loan)	4	—
						Plymouth Arg	45	2
						Bristol R (loan)	2	—
						Watford	17	2
						Reading (loan)	7	2
						Fulham (loan)	5	—
Joe Gallen	5 11	11 08	2 9 72	Hammersmith	Trainee	Watford	—	—
Andy Hessenthaler	5 07	11 00	17 8 65	Gravesend	Redbridge F	Watford	35	1
Alex Inglethorpe	5 10	11 07	14 11 71	Epsom	School	Watford	3	—
Andy Kennedy	6 1	12 00	8 10 64	Stirling	Sauchie Ath	Rangers	15	3
						Birmingham C	76	18
						Sheffield U (loan)	9	1
						Blackburn R	59	23
						Watford	25	4
						Bolton W (loan)	1	—
Lee Nogan	5 10	11 00	21 5 69	Cardiff	Apprentice	Oxford U	64	10
						Brentford (loan)	11	2
						Southend U (loan)	6	1
						Watford	23	5
Rod Thomas	5 6	10 03	10 10 70	London	Trainee	Watford	83	9
						Gillingham (loan)	8	1

Trainees
Adams, Daniel J; Boachie, Nana; Dyer, Bruce A; Liburd, Marc E; McIntosh, Craig; Merritt, Justin; Page, Robert J; Slinn, Kevin P; White, John S.

Associated Schoolboys
Allen, Mark J; Buoy, Nicholas; Calderhead, Robert; Campbell, Paul I; Connolly, David; Easton, Clint; Fitzgerald, Gary; Marshall, Robert; Morrissey, Robert E; Ross, Jamie M; Sargent, David G; Smallridge, Adam; Williams, Nicholas B.

Associated Schoolboys who have accepted the club's offer of a Traineeship/Contract
Birch, Terry; Gould, Darran; Hutchins, Neil; Parkin, Steven C; Simpson, Colin R; Vier, Matthew P; Walters, Scott.

550

WEST BROMWICH ALBION 1991–92   *Back row (left to right):* Kirk Hammond, Darren Rogers, Daryl Burgess, Marc Sinfield, Colin West, Gary Strodder, Mel Rees, Paul Williams, Paul Raven, Gary Piggott, Adrian Foster, Kwame Ampadu, Les Palmer.
Third row: Dave Matthews (Kit Manager), Barry Wyle (Assistant Physiotherapist), Alex Grace, Matthew Nelson, Darren Bailey, Lyndon Price, Roy Hunter, Justin Howse, Craig Shakespeare, Graham Roberts, Gary Hackett, Dave Pritchard, Stuart Bowen, Ian Cockerill (Psychologist), Cyril Lea (Youth Team Manager).
Second row: Gary Bannister, Tony Ford, Gary Robson, Graham Harbey, Darren Bradley, Stuart Pearson (Assistant Manager), Bobby Gould (Manager), Norman Bodell (Coach), Steve Parkin, Winston White, Bernard McNally, Simeon Hodson, Don Goodman.
Front row: Stacey Caldicott, Paul Tate, Stephen Hewitt, Richard Harris, Scott Darton, John Macgowan (Physiotherapist), Phillip Maxwell, Danny Hicks, Tony Annan, Damian Coll, Barry Duncan, James McCue.

Division 2   **WEST BROMWICH ALBION**

The Hawthorns, West Bromwich B71 4LF. Telephone 021-525 8888 (all Depts). Fax No: 021-553 6634

Ground capacity: 31,700 (10,865 seats).

Record attendance: 64,815 v Arsenal, FA Cup 6th rd, 6 March 1937.

Record receipts: £161,632.50 v Aston Villa, FA Cup 5th rd, 17 February 1990.

Pitch measurements: 115yd × 75yd.

President: Sir F. A. Millichip. *Vice-president:* J. S. Lucas.

Chairman: T. J. Summers.

Directors: J. W. Brandrick, M. C. McGinnity, A. B. Hale, C. M. Stapleton, J. G. Silk.

Manager: Ossie Ardiles. *Assistant Manager:* Keith Burkinshaw. *Coaches:* Dennis Mortimer and Cyril Lea. *Physio:* Danny Thomas. *Secretary:* Dr J. J. Evans BA, PHD. (Wales). *Club Statistician:* Tony Matthews. *Commercial Manager:* Alan Stevenson.

Year Formed: 1879. Turned Professional: 1885. Ltd Co.: 1892.

Former Grounds: 1879, Coopers Hill; 1879, Dartmouth Park; 1881, Bunns Field, Walsall Street; 1882, Four Acres (Dartmouth Cricket Club); 1885, Stoney Lane; 1900, The Hawthorns.

Former Names: 1879–81, West Bromwich Strollers.

Club Nicknames: 'Throstles', 'Baggies', 'Albion'.

Record League Victory: 12-0 v Darwen, Division 1, 4 April 1892 – Reader; Horton, McCulloch; Reynolds (2), Perry, Groves; Bassett (3), McLeod, Nicholls (1), Pearson (4), Geddes (1). (1 og).

Record Cup Victory: 10-1 v Chatham (away), FA Cup, 3rd rd, 2 March 1889 – Roberts; Horton, Green; Timmins (1), Charles Perry, Horton; Bassett (2), Perry (1), Bayliss (2), Pearson, Wilson (3). (1 og).

Record Defeat: 3-10 v Stoke C, Division 1, 4 February 1937.

Most League Points (2 for a win): 60, Division 1, 1919–20.

Most League points (3 for a win): 72, Division 2, 1988–89.

Most League Goals: 105, Division 2, 1929–30.

Highest League Scorer in Season: William 'Ginger' Richardson, 39, Division 1, 1935–36.

Most League Goals in Total Aggregate: Tony Brown, 218, 1963–79.

Most Capped Player: Stuart Williams, 33 (43), Wales.

Most League Appearances: Tony Brown, 574, 1963–80.

Record Transfer Fee Received: £1,500,000 from Manchester U for Bryan Robson, October 1981.

Record Transfer Fee Paid: £748,000 to Manchester C for Peter Barnes, July 1979.

Football League Record: 1888 Founder Member of Football League; 1901–02 Division 2; 1902–04 Division 1; 1904–11 Division 2; 1911–27 Division 1; 1927–31 Division 2; 1931–38 Division 1; 1938–49 Division 2; 1949–73 Division 1; 1973–76 Division 2; 1976–86 Division 1; 1986–91 Division 2; 1991–92 Division 3; 1992– Division 2.

Honours: Football League: Division 1 – Champions 1919–20; Runners-up 1924–25, 1953–54; Division 2 – Champions 1901–02, 1910–11; Runners-up 1930–31, 1948–49; Promoted to Division 1 1975–76 (3rd). *FA Cup:* Winners 1888, 1892, 1931, 1954, 1968; Runners-up 1886, 1887, 1895, 1912, 1935. *Football League Cup:* Winners 1965–66; Runners-up 1966–67, 1969–70. **European Competitions:** *European Cup-Winners' Cup:* 1968–69; *European Fairs Cup:* 1966–67; *UEFA Cup:* 1978–79, 1979–80, 1981–82.

Colours: Navy blue and white striped shirts, white shorts, blue and white stockings. **Change colours:** Red and yellow striped shirts, red shorts.

WEST BROMWICH ALBION 1991–92 LEAGUE RECORD

Match No.	Date	Venue	Opponents	Result	H/T Score	Lg. Pos.	Goalscorers	Atten-dance
1	Aug 17	H	Exeter C	W 6-3	2-1	—	Shakespeare 2 (2 pen), Goodman 2, Foster, Williams	12,892
2	24	A	Darlington	W 1-0	0-0	1	Goodman	5658
3	31	H	Wigan Ath	D 1-1	1-1	4	McNally	12,053
4	Sep 3	A	Fulham	D 0-0	0-0	—		4523
5	7	A	Bolton W	L 0-3	0-1	6		7980
6	14	H	Stockport Co	W 1-0	0-0	6	Williams	11,845
7	17	H	Peterborough U	W 4-0	2-0	—	Robson 2, Williams, Bowen	10,037
8	21	A	Chester C	W 2-1	1-1	1	Robson, Burgess	3895
9	28	H	Hull C	W 1-0	0-0	1	Burgess	11,932
10	Oct 1	H	Preston NE	L 0-2	0-0	—		5293
11	12	H	Shrewsbury T	W 2-0	1-0	3	Goodman, West	12,457
12	19	A	Brentford	W 2-1	1-0	1	Ampadu, Goodman	8575
13	26	A	Birmingham C	L 0-1	0-0	3		26,168
14	Nov 2	H	Bury	D 1-1	0-1	3	Robson	8439
15	5	A	Hartlepool U	D 0-0	0-0	—		2810
16	9	A	Reading	W 2-1	1-0	4	Robson, Goodman	5826
17	23	H	Huddersfield T	W 2-1	2-1	3	Robson, Harbey	14,029
18	30	H	Stoke C	D 2-2	1-1	3	Shakespeare, Goodman	17,207
19	Dec 14	A	Bradford C	D 1-1	0-1	3	Bradley	7195
20	22	H	Darlington	W 3-1	2-0	—	Strodder, Sinclair, Fereday	13,261
21	26	A	Wigan Ath	W 1-0	0-0	3	Shakespeare (pen)	5068
22	28	A	Exeter C	D 1-1	0-0	1	Shakespeare (pen)	5830
23	Jan 1	H	Fulham	L 2-3	1-2	3	Robson, Shakespeare (pen)	16,442
24	4	A	Torquay U	L 0-1	0-0	4		4159
25	11	H	Bournemouth	W 4-0	1-0	2	Robson, Bannister 2, Williams	10,932
26	18	A	Leyton Orient	D 1-1	1-1	3	Bradley	6329
27	25	H	Swansea C	L 2-3	2-0	3	Roberts 2 (1 pen)	10,395
28	Feb 1	H	Brentford	W 2-0	2-0	2	Taylor, Fereday	15,984
29	8	A	Birmingham C	W 3-0	2-0	1	Robson, Taylor 2	27,508
30	12	A	Stoke C	L 0-1	0-1	—		23,645
31	15	H	Bradford C	D 1-1	1-1	3	Shakespeare	12,607
32	22	A	Bournemouth	L 1-2	0-1	3	Taylor	7721
33	29	H	Torquay U	W 1-0	0-0	3	Hunter	11,669
34	Mar 3	H	Leyton Orient	L 1-3	0-3	—	Bannister	11,165
35	6	A	Swansea C	D 0-0	0-0	—		5629
36	11	H	Hartlepool U	L 1-2	0-1	—	Williams	10,307
37	14	A	Bury	D 1-1	1-1	5	Taylor	3810
38	21	H	Reading	W 2-0	2-0	3	Strodder, Raven	10,707
39	28	A	Huddersfield T	L 0-3	0-1	4		7428
40	31	A	Stockport Co	L 0-3	0-1	—		6090
41	Apr 4	H	Bolton W	D 2-2	1-1	8	Ampadu, Taylor	10,287
42	11	A	Peterborough U	D 0-0	0-0	9		9040
43	18	H	Chester C	D 1-1	0-1	9	Rogers	10,137
44	20	A	Hull C	L 0-1	0-1	10		4815
45	25	H	Preston NE	W 3-0	1-0	8	Taylor, Ampadu, West	11,318
46	May 2	A	Shrewsbury T	W 3-1	3-0	7	Strodder, Shakespeare, Taylor	7442

Final League Position: 7

GOALSCORERS

League (64): Robson 9, Shakespeare 8 (5 pens), Taylor 8, Goodman 7, Williams 5, Ampadu 3, Bannister 3, Strodder 3, Bradley 2, Burgess 2, Fereday 2, Roberts 2 (1 pen), West 2, Bowen 1, Foster 1, Harbey 1, Hunter 1, McNally 1, Raven 1, Rogers 1, Sinclair 1.
Rumbelows Cup (2): Goodman 1, Shakespeare 1 (1 pen).
FA Cup (7): Shakespeare 2 (1 pens), Goodman 1, McNally 1, Robson 1, Strodder 1, Williams 1.

Miller	Bradley	Harbey	Ford	Strodder	Burgess	Bannister	Goodman	Foster	Shakespeare	Ampadu	Williams	McNally	Piggott	Hodson	Naylor	Parkin	Robson	Bowen	Pritchard	Palmer	Hackett	West	White	Rogers	Sinclair	Fereday	Roberts	Taylor	Match No.
1	2	3	4	5	6	7	8*	9	10	11†	12	14																	1
1	2	3	4	5	6		8		10	11	12	7	9*																2
1	2	3	4	5		8		12	10	11	9*	7		6															3
	2	3	4	5	6	8		11*	10	12	9	7†			1	14													4
		3	4	5	6			9	10	11	12	7	8*		1	2													5
		3	4	5	6	7*			10		12			2	1	8	9	11†	14										6
		3	4	5	6				10†		7			2	1	8	9	11*		12	14								7
	14	3	4	5	6				10		7		12	2†	1	8	9	11*											8
		3	4	5	6		7		10		12			2	1	8	9*	11†	14										9
		3	4	5	6				10		8*			2	1	7	9	11	12										10
		3	4	5	6		8†		10		14			2	1	7		11*	12			9							11
	7	3	4	5	6*		8		10	11		12		2	1							9							12
	6	3	4	5			8		10	11*	12	7		2	1							9							13
	14	3	4	5	6		8		10					2	1		12	11†	7			9*							14
	7	3	4	5	6	12	8		10	11*				2	1		9												15
	4†	3		5	6	12	8		10			7		2	1		9*				14		11						16
	4	3		5	6		8		10		12	7		2	1		9*						11						17
	4	3		5†	6		8		10		12	7			1	2	9						11*	14					18
	4	3		5					10	12	8	7		6	1		9								2	11*			19
	4	3		5	6	12			10		8	7			1		9								2	11*			20
	4*	3		5	6			14	10	12	8	7			1		9†								2	11			21
	4	3		5				9*	10	12	8	7		6	1								11†	14	2				22
	4	3		5†					10	12	8	7*			1		9						11	6	2	14			23
	4	3				9*			10	12	8	7		11†	1									6	2	14	5		24
	4	3		5	6	8			10*	11†	12			2	1		9						14			7			25
	4	3		5	6	8								2	1		9				11					7	10		26
	4	3		5	6	8†			12		14			2	1		9				11					7*	10		27
	4	3			6				5		14	12		2	1		9*				11					7	10	8†	28
	4	3			6				5			12		2	1		9				11					7*	10	8	29
	4	3			6	12			5					2*	1		9				11					7	10	8	30
	4†	3			6			12	5					2	1		9				11*			14		7	10	8	31
	4	3			6			12	5					2†	1		9	11*						14		7	10	8	32
	4	3			6				5		12						9						11*			7	10†	8	33
	4	3*			6	9			5		12	11†														7	10	8	34
	4	3			6	9			5			'11					7										10	8	35
	4	3		5	6	9			14		12	11*					7									2†	10	8	36
		3		4	6				5		9												10					8	37
	4	3		5	6				10		12												7					8	38
	4	3		5	6				10		12						14						7*					8	39
		3		5	6				10	11*	12			2†			9				7							8	40
	4	3		5	6				10	11	9										7					12		8	41
	4	3		5	6				10	11	9				1		12				7*					2		8	42
	4	3		5					10	11*	9				1		6				7†	12		14		2		8	43
	4	3		5					10	11†	9*				1		6				7	12		14		2		8	44
	4†	3		5						11			12		1		10				7	9		6		2		8*	45
		3		5					4	11			9		1		10				7			6		2		8	46
3	35 + 2s	46	15	37	36	11 + 4s	11	4 + 4s	42 + 2s	15 + 6s	16 + 18s	17 + 4s	3 + 2s	25	34	8 + 1s	29 + 3s	8	1 + 4s	— + 1s	13 + 2s	5 + 2s	9 + 1s	4 + 6s	6	19 + 3s	12	19	

Dibble—Match No. 33(1) 34(1) 35(1) 36(1) 37(1) 38(1) 39(1) 40(1) 41(1*); Raven—Match No. 33(2) 34(2) 35(2) 37(2) 38(2) 39(2) 40(14); Hunter—Match No. 33(14) 34(14) 38(14) 40(4) 41(2) 45(14); Cartwright—Match No. 37(7) 38(9†) 39(9†); Heggs—Match No. 37(11) 38(11*) 39(11).

Rumbelows Cup	First Round	Swindon T (a)	0-2
		(h)	2-2
FA Cup	First Round	Marlow (h)	6-0
	Second Round	Leyton Orient (a)	1-2

WEST BROMWICH ALBION

Player and Position	Ht	Wt	Birth Date	Birth Place	Source	Clubs	League App	Gls
Goalkeepers								
Jonathan Gould	6 1	12 07	18 7 68	London	Derby Co	Halifax T	33	—
						WBA	—	—
Stuart Naylor	6 4	12 10	6 12 62	Wetherby	Yorkshire A	Lincoln C	49	—
						Peterborough U (loan)	8	—
						Crewe Alex (loan)	55	—
						WBA	234	—
Defenders								
Stewart Bowen*	5 7		12 12 72	West Bromwich	Trainee	WBA	8	1
Daryl Burgess	5 11	12 03	20 4 71	Birmingham	Trainee	WBA	95	2
Graham Harbey	5 8	10 08	29 8 64	Chesterfield	Apprentice	Derby Co	40	1
						Ipswich T	59	1
						WBA	97	2
Simeon Hodson	5 9	10 02	5 3 66	Lincoln	Apprentice	Notts Co	27	—
						Charlton Ath	5	—
						Lincoln C	56	—
						Newport Co	34	1
						WBA	81	—
Steve Parkin*	5 6	10 07	7 11 65	Mansfield	Apprentice	Stoke C	113	5
						WBA	48	2
Lyndon Price*	5 10		13 5 73	Birmingham	Trainee	WBA	—	—
Paul Raven	6 0	12 03	28 7 70	Salisbury	Schools	Doncaster R	52	4
						WBA	30	1
						Doncaster R (loan)	8	—
Graham Roberts*	5 11	13 10	3 7 59	Southampton	School	Southampton	—	—
						Bournemouth	—	—
						Sholing S	—	—
						Portsmouth	—	—
						Dorchester T	—	—
						Weymouth	—	—
						Tottenham H	209	23
						Rangers	55	3
						Chelsea	70	18
						WBA	39	6
Darren Rogers*	5 10	11 04	9 4 71	Birmingham	Trainee	WBA	14	1
Gary Strodder	6 1	11 04	1 4 65	Leeds	Apprentice	Lincoln C	132	6
						West Ham U	65	2
						WBA	71	4
Paul Williams	6 2	12 09	8 9 63	Sheffield	Nuneaton	Preston NE	1	—
						Newport Co	26	3
						Sheffield U	8	—
						Hartlepool U	8	—
						Stockport	24	14
						WBA	44	5
Midfield								
Darren Bradley	5 10	11 04	24 11 65	Birmingham	Apprentice	Aston Villa	20	—
						WBA	172	6
Stacy Coldicott	5 11	11 02	29 4 74	Worcester	Trainee	WBA	—	—
Wayne Fereday	5 9	11 00	16 6 63	Warley	Apprentice	QPR	197	21
						Newcastle U	33	—
						Bournemouth	23	—
						WBA	22	2
Jonathan Hanson*			10 1 73	Bloxwich	Leicester U	WBA	—	—
Carl Heggs	6 00	11 08	11 10 70	Leicester	Leicester U	WBA	3	—
Roy Hunter	5 09	11 00	29 10 73	Saltburn	Trainee	WBA	6	1
Bernard McNally	5 7	10 11	17 2 63	Shrewsbury	Apprentice	Shrewsbury T	282	23
						WBA	87	7
David Pritchard*	5 9	11 05	27 5 72	Wolverhampton	Trainee	WBA	5	—
Gary Robson	5 5	10 10	6 7 65	Co Durham	Apprentice	WBA	196	26
Craig Shakespeare	5 10	11 05	26 10 63	Birmingham	Apprentice	Walsall	284	45
						Sheffield W	17	—
						WBA	98	10

WEST BROMWICH ALBION

Foundation: There is a well known story that when employees of Salter's Spring Works in West Bromwich decided to form a football club in 1879, they had to send someone to the nearby Association Football stronghold of Wednesbury to purchase a football. A weekly subscription of 2d (less than 1p) was imposed and the name of the new club was West Bromwich Strollers.

First Football League game: 8 September 1888, Football League, v Stoke (a) W 2-0 – Roberts; J. Horton, Green; E. Horton, Perry, Bayliss; Bassett, Woodhall (1), Hendry, Pearson, Wilson (1).

Did you know: With William "Ginger" Richardson dominating the list of Albion's goalscoring feats, the fact that Harold "Popeye" Jones actually scored more goals in a single season is sometimes overlooked. This is because it was a wartime season, 1939–40, when he scored 50 first-team goals including six hat-tricks.

Managers (and Secretary-managers)
Louis Ford 1890–92*, Henry Jackson 1892–94*, Edward Stephenson 1894–95*, Clement Keys 1895–96*, Frank Heaven 1896–1902*, Fred Everiss 1902–48, Jack Smith 1948–52, Jesse Carver 1952, Vic Buckingham 1953–59, Gordon Clark 1959–61, Archie Macaulay 1961–63, Jimmy Hagan 1963–67, Alan Ashman 1967–71, Don Howe 1971–75, Johnny Giles 1975–77, Ronnie Allen 1977, Ron Atkinson 1978–81, Ronnie Allen 1981–82, Ron Wylie 1982–84, Johnny Giles 1984–85, Ron Saunders 1986–87, Ron Atkinson 1987–88, Brian Talbot 1988–91, Bobby Gould 1991–92, Ossie Ardiles May 1992–.

Forwards

Kwame Ampadu	5 10	10 13	20 11 70	Bradford	Trainee	Arsenal	2	—
						Plymouth Arg (loan)	6	1
						WBA (loan)	7	1
						WBA	21	3
Gary Bannister	5 8	11 01	22 7 60	Warrington	Apprentice	Coventry C	22	3
						Sheffield W	118	55
						QPR	136	56
						Coventry C	43	11
						WBA	72	18
						Oxford U (loan)	10	2
Neil Cartwright	5 9	10 13	20 2 71	Stourbridge	Trainee	WBA	11	—
Adrian Foster*	5 9	11 00	20 7 71	Kidderminster	Trainee	WBA	27	2
Gary Hackett	5 8	10 13	11 10 62	Stourbridge	Bromsgrove R	Shrewsbury T	150	17
						Aberdeen	15	—
						Stoke C	73	7
						WBA	34	2
Les Palmer*	5 10	10 10	5 9 71	Birmingham	Trainee	WBA	8	1
Gary Piggott	5 11	12 02	1 4 69	Warley	Dudley T	WBA	5	—
Bob Taylor	5 10	11 02	3 2 67	Horden	Horden CW	Leeds U	42	9
						Bristol C	106	50
						WBA	19	8
Colin West*	6 2	13 11	13 11 62	Wallsend	Apprentice	Sunderland	102	21
						Watford	45	20
						Rangers	10	2
						Sheffield W	45	8
						WBA	73	22
						Port Vale (loan)	—	—
Winston White	5 10	10 12	26 10 58	Leicester	Apprentice	Leicester C	12	1
						Hereford U	175	21
						Chesterfield	1	—
						Port Vale	1	—
						Stockport Co	4	—
						Bury	125	11
						Rochdale (loan)	4	—
						Colchester U	65	8
						Burnley	104	14
						WBA	16	1

Trainees
Annan, Tony; Coll, Damien M; Darton, Scott R; Grace, Alexander; Hammond, Kirk; Harris, Richard J; Hewitt, Steven J; Hicks, Daniel; Howse, Justin J; Maxwell, Phillip; McCue, James G; Nelson, Matthew J; Sinfield, Marc R; Tate, Paul D; Treacy, John P.

Associated Schoolboys
Ashmore, Graham R; Atkinson, Peter; Beagan, Neil T; Berry, Craig S; Costigan, Glyn B; Cresswell, Mark A; Cutler, Neil A; Dew, Robert A; Gee, Craig P; Green, Jason K; Hardiker, Paul J; Hurst, John C; Schofield, Paul B; Taylor, Stuart G; Torre, Stephen R; Turner, Brendon; Turner, Stuart.

Associated Schoolboys who have accepted the club's offer of a Traineeship/Contract
Harnett, David R; Harris, Lee P; Love, Brett A; Marshall, Daniel P; Owen, Darren L; Skitt, Craig.

WEST HAM UNITED 1991–92 *Back row (left to right)*: Tony Gale, Colin Foster, Trevor Morley, Ludek Miklosko, Alvin Martin, Matthew Rush, Martin Allen. *Centre row*: Mike Small, Tim Breacker, George Parris, Frank McAvennie, Leroy Rosenior, Simon Livett. *Front row*: Kevin Keen, Chris Hughton, Julian Dicks, Ian Bishop, Mitchell Thomas, Steve Potts, Stuart Slater.

Division 1   **WEST HAM UNITED**

Boleyn Ground, Green Street, Upton Park, London E13. Telephone 081-472 2740. General: 081-472 5756. Commercial: 081-475 0555. Hammer Line: 081-472 3322. Dial-a-seat: 081-472 2422. Football in the Community: 0898 121165 Clubcall.

Ground capacity: 22,503.

Record attendance: 42,322 v Tottenham H, Division 1, 17 October 1970.

Record receipts: £146,074 v Tottenham H, League Cup 5th rd, 27 January 1987.

Pitch measurements: 112yd × 72yd.

Chairman: T. W. Brown FCIS, ATII, FCCA.

Vice-chairman: M. W. Cearns ACIB.

Directors: L. C. Cearns, W. F. Cearns, C. J. Warner, P. J. Storrie (managing).

Manager: Billy Bonds MBE. *Assistant manager:* Harry Redknapp. *Physio:* John Green BSC (Hons), MCSP, SRP.

Secretary: T. M. Finn. *Commercial Manager:* Brian Blower.

Year Formed: 1895. Turned Professional: 1900. Ltd Co.: 1900.

Former Grounds: Memorial Recreation Ground, Canning Town: 1904 Boleyn Ground.

Former Names: Thames Ironworks FC, 1895–1900.

Club Nickname: 'The Hammers'.

Record League Victory: 8-0 v Rotherham U, Division 2, 8 March 1958 – Gregory; Bond, Wright; Malcolm, Brown, Lansdowne; Grice, Smith (2), Keeble (2), Dick (4), Musgrove. 8-0 v Sunderland, Division 1, 19 October 1968 – Ferguson; Bonds, Charles; Peters, Stephenson, Moore (1); Redknapp, Boyce, Brooking (1), Hurst (6), Sissons.

Record Cup Victory: 10-0 v Bury, League Cup, 2nd rd (2nd leg), 25 October 1983 – Parkes; Stewart (1), Walford, Bonds (Orr), Martin (1), Devonshire (2), Allen, Cottee (4), Swindlehurst, Brooking (2), Pike.

Record Defeat: 2-8 v Blackburn R, Division 1, 26 December 1963.

Most League Points (2 for a win): 66, Division 2, 1980–81.

Most League points (3 for a win): 87, Division 2, 1990–91.

Most League Goals: 101, Division 2, 1957–58.

Highest League Scorer in Season: Vic Watson, 41, Division 1, 1929–30.

Most League Goals in Total Aggregate: Vic Watson, 306, 1920–35.

Most Capped Player: Bobby Moore, 108, England.

Most League Appearances: Billy Bonds, 663, 1967–88.

Record Transfer Fee Received: £2,000,000 from Everton for Tony Cottee, July 1988.

Record Transfer Fee Paid: £1,250,000 to Celtic for Frank McAvennie, March 1989.

Football League Record: 1919 Elected to Division 2; 1923–32 Division 1; 1932–58 Division 2; 1958–78 Division 1; 1978–81 Division 2; 1981–89 Division 1; 1989–91 Division 2; 1991–Division 1.

Honours: Football League: Division 1 best season: 3rd, 1985–86; Division 2 – Champions 1957–58, 1980–81; Runners-up 1922–23, 1990–91. *FA Cup:* Winners 1964, 1975, 1980; Runners-up 1922–23. *Football League Cup:* Runners-up 1966, 1981. **European Competitions:** *European Cup-Winners' Cup:* 1964–65 (winners), 1965–66, 1975–76 (runners-up), 1980–81.

Colours: Claret and blue shirts, white shorts, white stockings. **Change colours:** White shirts, blue shorts, blue stockings.

WEST HAM UNITED 1991–92 LEAGUE RECORD

Match No.	Date		Venue	Opponents		Result	H/T Score	Lg. Pos.	Goalscorers	Atten- dance
1	Aug	17	H	Luton T	D	0-0	0-0	—		25,079
2		20	A	Sheffield U	D	1-1	0-0	—	Small	21,463
3		24	A	Wimbledon	L	0-2	0-1	18		10,081
4		28	H	Aston Villa	W	3-1	0-0	—	Small, Rosenior, Brown	23,644
5		31	H	Notts Co	L	0-2	0-0	16		20,093
6	Sep	4	A	QPR	D	0-0	0-0	—		16,616
7		7	H	Chelsea	D	1-1	0-0	17	Small	18,875
8		14	A	Norwich C	L	1-2	1-2	18	Small	15,348
9		17	A	Crystal Palace	W	3-2	0-1	—	Thomas, Morley, Small	21,363
10		21	H	Manchester C	L	1-2	0-0	18	Brown	25,588
11		28	A	Nottingham F	D	2-2	2-1	18	Small 2 (1 pen)	25,613
12	Oct	5	H	Coventry C	L	0-1	0-0	18		21,817
13		19	A	Oldham Ath	D	2-2	1-2	18	Small, McAvennie	14,365
14		26	H	Tottenham H	W	2-1	2-1	17	Small, Thomas	23,946
15	Nov	2	A	Arsenal	W	1-0	0-0	14	Small	33,539
16		17	H	Liverpool	D	0-0	0-0	—		23,569
17		23	A	Manchester U	L	1-2	0-2	17	McAvennie	47,185
18		30	H	Sheffield W	L	1-2	0-1	17	Breacker	24,116
19	Dec	7	A	Everton	L	0-4	0-3	18		21,563
20		21	H	Sheffield U	D	1-1	0-0	18	Dicks (pen)	19,287
21		26	A	Aston Villa	L	1-3	0-2	19	McAvennie	31,959
22		28	A	Notts Co	L	0-3	0-0	21		11,163
23	Jan	1	H	Leeds U	L	1-3	1-2	21	Dicks (pen)	21,766
24		11	H	Wimbledon	D	1-1	0-0	21	Morley	18,485
25		18	A	Luton T	W	1-0	0-0	20	Small	11,088
26	Feb	1	H	Oldham Ath	W	1-0	1-0	20	Thomas	19,012
27		22	A	Sheffield W	L	1-2	1-0	21	Small	26,150
28		29	H	Everton	L	0-2	0-1	21		20,976
29	Mar	3	A	Southampton	L	0-1	0-0	—		14,548
30		11	A	Liverpool	L	0-1	0-1	—		30,821
31		14	H	Arsenal	L	0-2	0-1	22		22,640
32		21	H	QPR	D	2-2	1-0	22	Small, Breacker	20,401
33		28	H	Leeds U	D	0-0	0-0	22		31,101
34	Apr	1	A	Tottenham H	L	0-3	0-1	—		31,809
35		4	A	Chelsea	L	1-2	1-1	22	Allen C	20,684
36		11	H	Norwich C	W	4-0	2-0	22	Rush 2, Dicks (pen), Bishop	16,896
37		14	A	Southampton	L	0-1	0-0	—		18,298
38		18	A	Manchester C	L	0-2	0-1	22		25,601
39		20	H	Crystal Palace	L	0-2	0-1	22		17,710
40		22	H	Manchester U	W	1-0	0-0	—	Brown	24,197
41		25	A	Coventry C	L	0-1	0-1	22		15,392
42	May	2	H	Nottingham F	W	3-0	0-0	22	McAvennie 3	20,629

Final League Position: 22

GOALSCORERS

League (37): Small 13 (1 pen), McAvennie 6, Brown 3, Dicks 3 (3 pens), Thomas 3, Breacker 2, Morley 2, Rush 2, Allen C 1, Bishop 1, Rosenior 1.
Rumbelows Cup (8): Small 4 (1 pen), Keen 1, McAvennie 1, Morley 1, Parris 1.
FA Cup (8): Allen 2, Dicks 2, Morley 2, Foster 1, Small 1.

Miklosko	Brown	Thomas	Breacker	Foster	Parris	Bishop	Slater	Small	Rosenior	Allen M	Keen	Morley	Rush	Parks	Hughton	Potts	Gale	McAvennie	Dicks	Atteveld	Allen C	Martin A	Clarke	Martin D	Match No.
1	2	3	4	5	6	7*	8	9	10	11	12														1
1	2	3	4	5	6	7	8	9	10†	11*	12	14													2
1	2	3	4	5	6	7	8*	9	10	11†	14	12													3
1	2	3	4	5	6	7	8	9	10	11*		12													4
	2	3	4	5	6	7	8	9	10*	12	11†			1		14									5
	2	3	4	5	6	7	8	9†	12	11*	14			1		10									6
1	2	3	4	5	6	7	8	9		11						10									7
1	2	3	4	5	6†	7	8	9	12	11*	14					10									8
1	2	3	4	5	6	7	8	9		11						10									9
1	2	3	4	5	6	7	8	9	12	11*						10									10
1		3	2	5	6	7	8	9*	12	11						10	4								11
1	5	3†	2		6	7	8	9		14	12	11*				10	4								12
1		3	2		6	7	8†	9		14	10	11*				5	4	12							13
1		3	2		6	7	11	9		12	10*					5	4	8							14
1		3	2		6	7	11	9			10					5	4	8							15
1		3	2		6	7	11	9			10					5	4	8							16
1		3	2		6	7	11	9		12	10*					5	4	8							17
1		3	2		6	7	11	9		12	10*					5	4	8							18
1		3	2		6*	7	11	9		10	12					5	4	8							19
1	2				6	7	11	9*		10	12					5	4	8	3						20
1			2		6	7	11	9*		10	12					5	4	8	3						21
1			2		6	7	11	9		10						5	4	8	3						22
1	6	2				7	11	9*		10	12					5	4	8	3						23
1	9	6*	2	5	7	11	14			10†	12						4	8	3						24
1	9	6	2	5	7	11*	14			12	10						4	8†	3						25
	9	6	2	5		11	12		7	10*				1			4	8	3						26
12		6				7	11	9	10	8*				1			4		3	6					27
	8	6	2†	5		7	11*	9	10	12	14			1			4		3						28
	8	6†		5		7	11	9	10	12	14			1		2	4*		3						29
1	2	6*				7	11	9	10	8	12					5	4		3						30
1	2			5	14	7	11	9	10†	6	12						4	8*	3						31
1	2	12	14	5		7*	11	9	10	6†							4	8	3						32
1	2	8	4	5		7	11*	9	10†							6	14	12	3						33
1	2†	8	6*	5		7	11	9	14							10	4	12	3						34
1	2	9		5		7				11*	12					6	4	8	3		10				35
1		6	2			7	11	9*	12	8							4		3		10	5			36
1			2			7	11	9	12	6	8*						4		3		10	5			37
1			2			7	11	9*	6	10							4	8	3			5	12		38
1	12	6	2*			7	11		8	9							4		3		10	5			39
1	10	6				7	11	9	8							2	4		3			5			40
1	10†	6				7*	11	9	8	12						2	4		3			5	14		41
1		6*				7	11	9	8							2	4	12	3			5		10	42
36	25	34	33	24	20	41	41	37	5	14	20	13	3	6	—	34	24	16	23	1	4	7	—	1	

Substitute appearances:
Brown +2s, Thomas +1s, Breacker +1s; Parris +1s; Rosenior +3s, Allen M +4s, Keen +5s, Morley +9s, Rush +11s, Parks +7s; Potts +1s; Gale +1s, McAvennie +4s; Clarke +1s, Martin D +1s

Rumbelows Cup	Second Round	Bradford C (a)		1-1
		(h)		4-0
	Third Round	Sheffield U (a)		2-0
	Fourth Round	Norwich C (a)		1-2
FA Cup	Third Round	Farnborough (a at West Ham)		1-1
		(h)		1-0
	Fourth Round	Wrexham (h)		2-2
		(a)		1-0
	Fifth Round	Sunderland (a)		1-1
		(h)		2-3

WEST HAM UNITED

Player and Position	Ht	Wt	Birth Date	Birth Place	Source	Clubs	League App	League Gls
Goalkeepers								
Steven Banks	5 11	11 04	9 2 72	Hillingdon	Trainee	West Ham U	—	—
Ludek Miklosko	6 5	14 00	9 12 61	Ostrava	Banik Ostrava	West Ham U	100	—
Tony Parks	5 11	10 08	26 1 63	Hackney	Apprentice	Tottenham H	37	—
						Oxford U (loan)	5	—
						Gillingham (loan)	2	—
						Brentford	71	—
						QPR (loan)	—	—
						Fulham	2	—
						Southend U	—	—
						West Ham U	6	—
Defenders								
Tim Breacker	6 0	12 06	2 7 65	Bicester		Luton T	210	3
						West Ham U	58	3
Kenny Brown	5 8	11 06	11 7 67	Barking	Apprentice	Norwich C	25	—
						Plymouth Arg	126	4
						West Ham U	27	3
Julian Dicks	5 7	10 08	8 8 68	Bristol	Apprentice	Birmingham C	89	1
						West Ham U	118	18
Colin Foster	6 4	13 10	16 7 64	Chislehurst	Apprentice	Orient	174	10
						Nottingham F	72	5
						West Ham U	82	4
Tony Gale	6 1	13 10	19 11 59	London	Apprentice	Fulham	277	19
						West Ham U	245	4
Kevin Horlock	6 00	12 00	1 11 72	Plumstead	Trainee	West Ham U	—	—
Paul Marquis	6 01	12 00	29 8 72	Enfield	Trainee	West Ham U	—	—
Alvin Martin*	6 1	13 03	29 7 58	Bootle	Apprentice	West Ham U	401	24
John Padington*	5 08	10 05	29 9 72	Redbridge	Trainee	West Ham U	—	—
George Parris	5 9	12 00	11 9 64	Ilford	Apprentice	West Ham U	223	12
Steven Potts	5 7	10 04	7 5 67	Hartford, USA	Apprentice	West Ham U	149	1
Mitchell Thomas	6 02	12 00	2 10 64	Luton	Apprentice	Luton T	107	1
						Tottenham H	157	6
						West Ham U	35	3
Midfield								
Martin Allen	5 10	11 00	14 8 65	Reading	School	QPR	136	16
						West Ham U	98	12
Ian Bishop	5 9	10 06	29 5 65	Liverpool	Apprentice	Everton	1	—
						Crewe Alex (loan)	4	—
						Carlisle U	132	14
						Bournemouth	44	2
						Manchester U	19	2
						West Ham U	98	7
Kevin Keen	5 6	9 08	25 2 67	Amersham	Apprentice	West Ham U	173	14
Simon Livett*	5 10	12 02	8 1 69	Newham	YTS	West Ham U	1	—
Matthew Rush	5 11	12 10	6 8 71	Dalston	Trainee	West Ham U	15	2
Forwards								
Clive Allen	5 10	12 03	20 5 61	London	Apprentice	QPR	49	32
						Arsenal		
						Crystal Palace	25	9
						QPR	87	40
						Tottenham H	105	60
						Bordeaux	—	—
						Manchester C	53	16
						Chelsea	16	7
						West Ham U	4	1
Simon Clarke	5 11	11 02	23 9 71	Chelmsford	Trainee	West Ham U	2	—

WEST HAM UNITED

Foundation: Thames Ironworks FC was formed by employees of this shipbuilding yard in 1895 and entered the FA Cup in their initial season at Chatham and the London League in their second. Short of funds, the club was wound up in June 1900 and relaunched a month later as West Ham United. Connection with the Ironworks was not finally broken until four years later.

First Football League game: 30 August 1919, Division 2, v Lincoln City (h) D 1-1 – Hufton; Cope, Lee; Lane, Fenwick, McCrae; D. Smith, Moyes (1), Puddefoot, Morris, Bradshaw.

Did you know: The Hammers must be the kind of club that attracts loyalty, for they have had four players each of whom have had more than 20 years on their books – Jim Barrett 1923–45, Dick Walker 1933–57, Ernie Gregory 1939–60 and Billy Bonds 1967–89.

Managers (and Secretary-managers)
Syd King 1902–32, Charlie Paynter 1932–50, Ted Fenton 1950–61, Ron Greenwood 1961–74 (continued as GM to 1977), John Lyall 1974–89, Lou Macari 1989–90, Billy Bonds February 1990–.

Player and Position	Ht	Wt	Birth Date	Place	Source	Clubs	League App	Gls
Frank McAvennie*	5 9	11 00	22 11 59	Glasgow	Johnstone B	St Mirren	135	50
						West Ham U	85	33
						Celtic	55	27
						West Ham U	68	16
Dean Martin			31 8 72	London	Fisher Ath	West Ham U	2	—
Trevor Morley	5 11	12 01	20 3 62	Nottingham	Nuneaton	Northampton T	107	39
						Manchester C	72	18
						West Ham U	81	24
John Purdie			28 12 72	Newham	Trainee	West Ham U	—	—
Stuart Slater	5 9	10 04	27 3 69	Sudbury	Apprentice	West Ham U	141	11
Mike Small	6 0	13 05	2 3 62	Birmingham		Luton T	3	—
						Peterborough U (loan)	4	1
						PAOK Salonika	—	—
						Brighton & HA	39	15
						West Ham U	40	13

Trainees
Basham, Michael; Canham, Scott W; Clarke, Anthony R; Comerford, Anthony; Currie, Darren P; Holland, Matthew R; Johnson, Roy J; Knight, Jason G; Lowe, John; Miller, Simon R; Reeve, Mark E; Richards, Tony S; Small, Keith P; Waters, Gary J; White, David T; Williamson, Daniel A.

**Non-Contract
Whitmarch, Paul.

Associated Schoolboys
Blaney, Steven D; Browne, Anthony; Clements, Mathew C; Farrell, Kevin J; Foley, Westley A; John, Jerome L; Josceyline, Wayne; Lockwood, Mathew D; Maeer, Darren J; Moore, Scott; Oakley, Warren N; Omoyimni, Emmanuel; Potter, Andrew B; Richardson, Stuart J; Shipp, Daniel A.

Associated Schoolboys who have accepted the club's offer of a Traineeship/Contract
Bates, Jonathon P; Geraghty, Jason W; Rose, Christopher A; Victory, Jamie C.

**Non-Contract Players who are retained must be re-signed before they are eligible to play in League matches.

WIGAN ATHLETIC 1991–92   *Back row (left to right):* Niel Leyland, Ian Hartley, Kevin Langley, Darren Patterson, Nigel Adkins, Phil Daley, Gary Worthington, Tony Pennock, Lee Hackett.

Centre row: Mick Lyons, Dave Philpotts, Andy Pilling, Bryan Griffiths, Jimmy Carberry, Don Page, Allen Tankard, Alan Johnson, Peter Atherton, Joe Parkinson, Steve Appleton, Gary Powell, David Crompton, Alex Cribley.

Front row: Paul Gray, Phil Jones, Neill Rimmer, Bryan Hamilton, Jeremy Smith, Barry Edwardson, Steve Nugent.

Kneeling: Damian Kelly, Simon Gallagher, Anthony Harrison, Andrew Roberts, Tyrone Grimes, Matthew Brooks, Paul Johanson, Carl Greenwood, Steve O'Brien, John Robertson, Martin Peoples.

Division 2   **WIGAN ATHLETIC**

Springfield Park, Wigan. Telephone Wigan (0942) 44433. Commercial Dept: (0942) 43067. Latics Line: 0898 338308.

Ground capacity: 11,434.

Record attendance: 27,500 v Hereford U, 12 December 1953.

Record receipts: £40,577 v Leeds U, FA Cup 6th rd, 15 March 1987.

Pitch measurements: 114yd × 72yd.

President: T. Hitchen.

Chairman: W. Kenyon.

Directors: J. A. Bennett, J. D. Fillingham, S. Jackson, R. Pearce, P. F. Spencer, B. Jeffrey.

Chief Executive: Bryan Hamilton.

Vice-president: J. H. Farrimond.

Secretary: W. Kenyon.

Commercial Manager: B. Eccles.

Manager: Bryan Hamilton.

First team coach: David Philpotts.

Physio: Alex Cribley.

Safety officer: D. Stott.

Groundsman: D. Pinch.

Year Formed: 1932.

Club Nickname: 'The Latics'.

Record League Victory: 7-2 v Scunthorpe U (away), Division 4, 12 March 1982 – Tunks; McMahon, Glenn, Wignall, Cribley, Methven (1), O'Keefe, Barrow (1), Bradd (3), Houghton (2), Evans.

Record Cup Victory: 6-0 v Carlisle U (away), FA Cup, 1st rd, 24 November 1934 – Caunce; Robinson, Talbot; Paterson, Watson, Tufnell; Armes (2), Robson (1), Roberts (2), Felton, Scott (1).

Record Defeat: 1-6 v Bristol R, Division 3, 3 March 1990.

Most League Points (2 for a win): 55, Division 4, 1978–79 and 1979–80.

Most League points (3 for a win): 91, Division 4, 1981–82.

Most League Goals: 80, Division 4, 1981–82.

Highest League Scorer in Season: Warren Aspinall, 21, Division 3, 1985–86.

Most League Goals in Total Aggregate: Peter Houghton, 62, 1978–84.

Most Capped Player: None.

Most League Appearances: Colin Methven, 296, 1979–86.

Record Transfer Fee Received: £329,000 from Coventry C for Peter Atherton, August 1991.

Record Transfer Fee Paid: £65,000 to Everton for Eamon O'Keefe, January 1982.

Football League Record: 1978 Elected to Division 4; 1982–92 Division 3; 1992– Division 2.

Honours: Football League: Best season in Division 3: 4th, 1985–86, 1986–87; Division 4 – Promoted (3rd) 1981–82. *FA Cup:* 4th rd 1979–80, 1985–86. *Football League Cup:* best season: 4th rd, 1981–82. *Freight Rover Trophy:* Winners 1984–85.

Colours: Blue shirts red and white trim, blue shorts with red and white trim, blue stockings.
Change colours: Red shirts with blue and white trim, red shorts with blue and white trim, red stockings.

WIGAN ATHLETIC 1991–92 LEAGUE RECORD

Match No.	Date		Venue	Opponents	Result	H/T Score	Lg. Pos.	Goalscorers	Attendance
1	Aug	18	A	Shrewsbury T	L 0-1	0-0	—		3834
2		23	H	Chester C	W 2-1	0-1	—	Worthington 2	2637
3		31	A	WBA	D 1-1	1-1	11	Worthington	12,053
4	Sep	3	H	Stockport Co	L 1-3	1-0	—	Powell	3567
5		7	A	Peterborough U	D 0-0	0-0	20		4488
6		14	H	Hull C	L 0-1	0-1	21		2445
7		17	H	Huddersfield T	L 1-3	1-2	—	Powell	3531
8		21	A	Bolton W	D 1-1	1-0	22	Kelly (og)	6923
9		28	H	Darlington	L 1-2	0-1	22	Powell	2034
10	Oct	5	A	Hartlepool U	L 3-4	1-3	22	Powell, Daley 2	3047
11		11	H	Reading	D 1-1	0-0	—	Griffiths	1817
12		19	A	Birmingham C	D 3-3	2-1	23	Jones, Daley 2	9662
13		26	H	Exeter C	W 4-1	1-1	21	Johnson, Powell, Connelly, Daley	1761
14	Nov	1	H	Swansea C	W 1-0	0-0	—	Johnson	2092
15		5	A	Preston NE	L 0-3	0-2	—		3657
16		9	A	Brentford	L 0-4	0-1	23		6675
17		22	H	Bury	W 2-0	1-0	—	Worthington, Griffiths	2268
18		30	H	Leyton Orient	D 1-1	1-0	19	Powell	2066
19	Dec	14	A	Stoke C	L 0-3	0-2	20		8419
20		26	H	WBA	L 0-1	0-0	23		5068
21		28	H	Shrewsbury T	D 1-1	1-1	23	Daley	2276
22	Jan	1	A	Stockport Co	D 3-3	2-2	22	Connelly, Daley 2	4149
23		11	H	Bradford C	W 2-1	2-1	23	Langley, Daley	2548
24		18	A	Bournemouth	L 0-3	0-0	23		4338
25		28	A	Fulham	D 1-1	1-0	—	Taylor	2466
26	Feb	8	A	Exeter C	W 1-0	0-0	23	Griffiths	3036
27		11	A	Leyton Orient	L 1-3	1-0	—	Taylor	3142
28		15	H	Stoke C	W 1-0	1-0	20	Griffiths (pen)	5695
29		18	A	Chester C	L 0-1	0-0	—		1065
30		22	A	Bradford C	D 1-1	0-0	20	Worthington	5621
31		28	H	Fulham	L 0-2	0-1	—		2202
32	Mar	3	H	Bournemouth	W 2-0	1-0	—	Johnson, Worthington (pen)	1790
33		7	A	Torquay U	W 1-0	0-0	21	Daley	2198
34		10	H	Preston NE	W 3-0	1-0	—	Worthington 2, Daley	3364
35		14	A	Swansea C	L 0-3	0-0	21		3726
36		20	H	Brentford	W 2-1	1-0	—	Pilling, Parkinson	2371
37		28	A	Bury	W 4-1	1-0	18	Worthington (pen), Parkinson, Daley, Powell	2618
38		31	A	Hull C	D 1-1	1-0	—	Worthington	3385
39	Apr	3	H	Peterborough U	W 3-0	1-0	—	Johnson, Langley, Worthington	2485
40		7	H	Torquay U	D 0-0	0-0	—		1970
41		11	A	Huddersfield T	L 1-3	0-2	17	Daley	7058
42		18	H	Bolton W	D 1-1	1-0	17	Worthington	3557
43		20	A	Darlington	W 1-0	1-0	16	Worthington	1223
44		24	H	Hartlepool U	D 1-1	0-0	—	Daley	2002
45		28	H	Birmingham C	W 3-0	2-0	—	Worthington 2, Pilling	5950
46	May	2	A	Reading	L 2-3	2-0	15	Patterson, Parkinson	2748

Final League Position: 15

GOALSCORERS

League (58): Worthington 15 (2 pens), Daley 14, Powell 7, Griffiths 4 (1 pen), Johnson 4, Parkinson 3, Connelly 2, Langley 2, Pilling 2, Taylor 2, Jones 1, Patterson 1, own goals 1.
Rumbelows Cup (8): Patterson 3, Worthington 2, Griffiths 1 (1 pen), Jones 1, Rimmer 1.
FA Cup (4): Griffiths 1, Pilling 1, Powell 1, Worthington 1.

Adkins	Appleton	Parkinson	Atherton	Patterson	Langley	Powell	Rimmer	Daley	Worthington	Griffiths	Jones	Gray	Johnson	Tankard	Pilling	Carberry	Smith	Widdrington	Nugent	Smyth	Connelly	Williams	Edwardson	Sharratt	Collins	Taylor	Skipper	Doolan	Match No.
1	2*	3	4	5	6	7	8	9	10	11†	12	14																	1
1	12	2		5	6*	7	8	9	10	11†	3	14	4																2
1				5	6	9	8		10	11*	2		4	3	7		12												3
1				5	6	9	8		10	11*	2		4	3	7			12											4
1				5	6†	9	8		10	11	2	14	4	3	7*		12												5
1				5	6	7	8		10	11*	2	9†	4	3			12	14											6
1				5		7	8		10		6		4	3	14	11*	12	2	9†										7
1					9	6	7	8	10	11*	2		4	3			12	5											8
1					2	6	7	8†	9	10*11			4	3	12			5	14										9
1		2		5	6	7		9		11		10*	4	3			12	8											10
1					6	7		9		11			4	3			12	5	10*	2	8								11
1	12				6	7		9		11†10			4	3*					2	8	5	14							12
1		2			6	7		9		11	10		4	3					12	8	5*								13
1		2			6	7		9	14	11†10*			4	3					12	8	5								14
1		2		5	6	7		9	11*		10†		4	3		14			12	8									15
1		2		10*	6	7		9	14	11			4	3					12	8†	5								16
1		2		5	6	7			10	11	4			3	9*				12	8									17
1		2		5	6	7			10	11	4	12	3	9*						8									18
1		2		5	6	7†		14	10*11		4	12	3	9						8									19
1		2		5	6	14		9	10*11†		4	12	3	7						8									20
1		2		5	6	14*		9	10	11	7†	4	3							8				12					21
1		2		5	6			9	10	11	7	4	3							8									22
1		2		5	6	10†		9		11	7*	4	3	12										14	8				23
1		2		5	6	10*		9	14	11†	7	4	3	12											8				24
1	12	2		5	6			9	14	11	7	4	3												8*10†				25
1		2		5	6			9	12	11	7	4	3												8	10*			26
1		2		5	6			9	12	11	7	4	3												8	10*			27
1		2		5†	6			9	12	11*	7	4	3												8	10	14		28
1		2			6			9	11		7	4	3	12											8*10		5		29
1		2			6			9	11		7	4	3												8	10	5		30
1		2			14	6		9	11†		7	4	3								12				8	10*	5		31
1		2		11	6*14			9	10		7	4	3	8†							12				5				32
1		2		11	6	12		9	10*		7	4	3	8											5				33
1		2		11	6	12		9	10		7	4	3	8*											5				34
1		2		11	6	12		9	10*		7	4	3	8	14										5†				35
1	5	2		11	6	12		9	10		7	4	3	8*															36
1	5†	2		11	6*12			9	10		7	4	3	8											14				37
1	14	2		11	6	12		9	10		7*	4	3	8†											5				38
1	14	2		11	6			9	10*12		7	4	3	8†											5				39
1		2		11	6			9	10		7	4	3	8											5				40
1		2		11	6	12		9	10*		7	4	3	8											5				41
1		2		11	6	12		9	10*		7	4	3	8											5				42
1		2		11	6			9	10		7	4	3	8											5				43
1		2		11	6	8*		9	10	12	7†	4	3	14											5				44
1		2		11	6			9	10			4	3	8											5		7		45
1		2		11	6†12			9	10	5		4	3	8*											14		7		46
46	4	36	1	39	45	22	9	37	34	26	40	2	41	44	21	1	—	5	2	2	12	4	—	—	9	7	15	2	

+5s (Patterson)   +1s (Langley)   +12s (Powell)   +1s (Daley) +7s (Worthington) +2s (Griffiths) +1s (Jones) +3s (Johnson) +3s (Tankard)   +6s (Pilling) +4s (Carberry) +6s (Widdrington) +1s (Nugent)   +6s (Connelly)   +1s (Collins) +4s (Taylor)   +3s (Skipper)

Rumbelows Cup	First Round	Burnley (h)		3-1
		(a)		3-2
	Second Round	Sheffield U (h)		2-2
		(a)		0-1
FA Cup	First Round	Scarborough (a)		2-0
	Second Round	Stockport Co (h)		2-0
	Third Round	Notts Co (a)		0-2

WIGAN ATHLETIC

Player and Position	Ht	Wt	Birth Date	Birth Place	Source	Clubs	League App	League Gls
Goalkeepers								
Nigel Adkins	5 11	12 07	11 3 65	Birkenhead	Apprentice	Tranmere R	86	—
						Wigan Ath	117	—
Giuseppe Paladino‡			29 8 65	Whiston	St Helens	Wigan Ath	7	—
Tony Pennock	5 11	10 09	10 4 71	Swansea	School	Stockport Co	—	—
						Wigan Ath (loan)	2	—
						Wigan Ath	—	—
Defenders								
Steve Appleton	5 11	10 09	27 7 73	Liverpool	Trainee	Wigan Ath	19	—
John Doolan	5 10	10 12	10 11 68	Liverpool	Knowsley U	Wigan Ath	2	—
Barry Edwardson§			4 11 72	Billinge	Trainee	Wigan Ath	1	—
Darren Patterson	6 1	12 00	15 10 69	Belfast	Trainee	WBA	—	—
						Wigan Ath	97	6
Peter Skipper†	5 11	12 05	11 4 58	Hull	Local	Hull C	23	2
						Scunthorpe U (loan)	1	—
						Darlington	91	4
						Hull C	265	17
						Oldham Ath	27	1
						Walsall	81	2
						Wrexham	4	—
						Wigan Ath	18	—
John Smyth‡	5 10	11 00	28 4 70	Dundalk	Dundalk	Liverpool	—	—
						Burnley	—	—
						Wigan Ath	8	—
Allen Tankard	5 10	11 07	21 5 69	Fleet	Apprentice	Southampton	5	—
						Wigan Ath	168	3
Midfield								
James Carberry‡	5 10	11 02	13 10 60	Liverpool	Trainee	Everton	—	—
						Wigan Ath	65	6
Alan Johnson	5 11	11 12	19 2 71	Ince	Trainee	Wigan Ath	128	11
Philip Jones	5 8	10 09	1 12 69	Liverpool	Trainee	Everton	1	—
						Blackpool (loan)	6	—
						Wigan Ath	61	2
Kevin Langley	6 1	10 03	24 5 64	St Helens	Apprentice	Wigan Ath	160	6
						Everton	16	2
						Manchester C (loan)	9	—
						Manchester C	—	—
						Chester C (loan)	9	—
						Birmingham C	76	2
						Wigan Ath	84	4
Joe Parkinson	5 11	12 02	11 6 71	Eccles	Trainee	Wigan Ath	106	6
Andy Pilling	5 10	11 04	30 6 69	Wigan		Preston NE	1	—
						Wigan Ath	125	16
Neill Rimmer	5 6	10 03	13 11 67	Liverpool	Apprentice	Everton	1	—
						Ipswich T	22	3
						Wigan Ath	106	6
Forwards								
Phil Daley	6 2	12 09	12 4 67	Walton	Newton	Wigan Ath	112	30
Paul Gray	5 9	11 08	28 1 70	Portsmouth	Trainee	Luton T	7	1
						Wigan Ath	5	—
Bryan Griffiths	5 9	11 00	26 1 65	Prescot	St Helens T	Wigan Ath	145	31
Steve Nugent			7 5 73	Wigan	Trainee	Wigan Ath	4	—
Gary Powell	5 10	10 02	2 4 69	Holylake	Trainee	Everton	—	—
						Lincoln C (loan)	11	—
						Scunthorpe U (loan)	4	1
						Wigan Ath (loan)	14	4
						Wigan Ath	34	7

WIGAN ATHLETIC

Foundation: Following the demise of Wigan Borough and their resignation from the Football League in 1931, a public meeting was called in Wigan at the Queen's Hall in May 1932 at which a new club Wigan Athletic, was founded in the hope of carrying on in the Football League. With this in mind, they bought Springfield Park for £2250, but failed to gain admission to the Football League until 46 years later.

First Football League game: 19 August 1978, Division 4, v Hereford U (a) D 0-0 – Brown; Hinnigan, Gore, Gillibrand, Ward, Davids, Corrigan, Purdie, Houghton, Wilkie, Wright.

Did you know: In 1934–35 Wigan Athletic became the first non-league club to register a 6-1 FA Cup victory on the ground of a Football League club by winning at Carlisle.

Managers (and Secretary-managers)
Charlie Spencer 1932–37, Jimmy Milne 1946–47, Bob Pryde 1949–52, Ted Goodier 1952–54, Walter Crook 1954–55, Ron Suart 1955–56, Billy Cooke 1956, Sam Barkas 1957, Trevor Hitchen 1957–58, Malcolm Barrass 1958–59, Jimmy Shirley 1959, Pat Murphy 1959–60, Allenby Chilton 1960, Johnny Ball 1961–63, Allan Brown 1963–66, Alf Craig 1966–67, Harry Leyland 1967–68, Alan Saunders 1968, Ian McNeill 1968–70, Gordon Milne 1970–72, Les Rigby 1972–74, Brian Tiler 1974–76, Ian McNeill 1976–81, Larry Lloyd 1981–83, Harry McNally 1983–85, Bryan Hamilton 1985–86, Ray Mathias 1986–89, Bryan Hamilton March 1989–.

Player and Position	Ht	Wt	Birth Date	Birth Place	Source	Clubs	League App	Gls
Chris Sharratt	5 07	11 04	13 8 70	West Kirby	Stalybridge C	Wigan Ath	4	—
Jeremy Smith*	5 10	11 00	10 7 71	Leeds	Goole	Wigan Ath	6	—
Gary Worthington	5 10	10 05	10 11 66	Cleethorpes	Apprentice	Manchester U	—	—
						Huddersfield T	—	—
						Darlington	40	15
						Wrexham	72	18
						Wigan Ath	53	20

Trainees
Brooks, Matthew L; Gallagher, Andrew N; Gallagher, Simon K; Greenwood, Carl; Grimes, Tyrone C; Hackett, Lee C; Harrison, Anthony; Hartley, Ian M; Kelly, Damian P; Leyland, Neil T; O'Brien, Stephen J; Peoples, Martin P; Roberts, Andrew T; Robertson, John N.

**Non-Contract
Skipper, Peter D.

Associated Schoolboys
Dowds, Scott K; Maguire, Gareth A; McAteer, Michael; Millet, Michael P; Moss, Ian D; Newton, Steven J; O'Hara, Terence; Purnell, Daniel S; Scott, Anthony; Tyrrell, Kevin M; Weston, Steven M.

Associated Schoolboys who have accepted the club's offer of a Traineeship/Contract
Dixon, Stephen; Ogden, Neil; Saint, Darren; Strong, Greg.

**Non-Contract Players who are retained must be re-signed before they are eligible to play in League matches.

WIMBLEDON 1991-92   *Back row (left to right):* Joe Dillon, Neal Ardley, Chris Perry, Dean Blackwell, Paul Miller, Hans Segers, Steve Allen, Neil Sullivan, Stewart Castledine, Aidan Newhouse, Brian McAllister, Warren Barton, Ron Suart.
Centre row: Syd Neal, Carlton Fairweather, John Scales, Robbie Earle, Lawrie Sanchez, Steve Anthrobus, Scott Fitzgerald, John Fashanu, Alan Cork, Roger Joseph, Detzi Kruszynski, Mickey Bennett, Roger Smith.
Front row: Terry Burton, Andy Clarke, Gerald Dobbs, Paul McGee, Terry Gibson, Peter Withe, Gary Elkins, Vaughan Ryan, Justin Skinner, Terry Phelan, Joe Kinnear.

FA Premier

WIMBLEDON

Selhurst Park, South Norwood, London E5. Telephone: 081-771 2233.

Ground capacity: 29,949.

Record attendance: 18,000 v HMS Victory, FA Amateur Cup 3rd rd, 1934–35 (at Plough Lane).

Record receipts: £122,846 v Crystal Palace, Division 1, 26 December 1991.

Pitch measurements: 110yd × 74yd.

President: Rt Hon Lord Michael Havers of Bury St Edmunds.

Chairman: S. G. Reed.

Vice-chairman: J. Lelliott.

Managing Director: S. Hammam.

Directors: P. Cork, P. R. Cooper, N. N. Hammam.

Chief Executive: David Barnard.

Manager: Joe Kinnear.

Assistant manager: Terry Burton.

Physio: Steve Allen.

Secretary: Adrian Cook.

Commercial Manager: Reg Davis.

Year Formed: 1889. Turned Professional: 1964. Ltd Co.: 1964.

Former Names: Wimbledon Old Centrals, 1899–1905.

Club Nickname: 'The Dons'.

Record League Victory: 6-0 v Newport C, Division 3, 3 September 1983 – Beasant; Peters, Winterburn, Galliers, Morris, Hatter, Evans (2), Ketteridge (1), Cork (3 incl. 1p), Downes, Hodges (Driver).

Record Cup Victory: 7-2 v Windsor & Eton, FA Cup, 1st rd, 22 November 1980 – Beasant; Jones, Armstrong, Galliers, Mick Smith (2), Cunningham (1), Ketteridge, Hodges, Leslie, Cork (1), Hubbick (3).

Record Defeat: 0-8 v Everton, League Cup 2nd rd, 29 August 1978.

Most League Points (2 for a win): 61, Division 4, 1978–79.

Most League points (3 for a win): 98, Division 4, 1982–83.

Most League Goals: 97, Division 3, 1983–84.

Highest League Scorer in Season: Alan Cork, 29, 1983–84.

Most League Goals in Total Aggregate: Alan Cork, 145, 1977–92.

Most Capped Player: Glyn Hodges 5 (16), Wales.

Most League Appearances: Alan Cork, 430, 1977–92.

Record Transfer Fee Received: £2,500,000 from Manchester C for Keith Curle, August 1991.

Record Transfer Fee Paid: £775,000 to Port Vale for Robbie Earle, July 1991.

Football League Record: 1977 Elected to Division 4; 1979–80 Division 3; 1980–81 Division 4; 1981–82 Division 3; 1982–83 Division 4; 1983–84 Division 3; 1984–86 Division 2; 1986–92 Division 1; 1992– FA Premier League.

Honours: Football League: Division 1 best season: 6th, 1986–87; Division 3 – Runners-up 1983–84; Division 4 – Champions 1982–83. *FA Cup:* Winners 1987–88. *Football League Cup:* best season: 4th rd, 1979–80, 1983–84, 1988–89. *League Group Cup:* Runners-up 1981–82.

Colours: Blue shirts yellow trim, blue shorts yellow trim, blue stockings yellow trim.
Change colours: White shirts, black shorts, white stockings.

WIMBLEDON 1991–92 LEAGUE RECORD

Match No.	Date		Venue	Opponents		Result	H/T Score	Lg. Pos.	Goalscorers	Attendance
1	Aug	17	A	Chelsea	D	2-2	1-1	—	Fashanu, Earle	22,574
2		24	H	West Ham U	W	2-0	1-0	8	Earle, Fashanu	10,081
3		27	A	Crystal Palace	L	2-3	1-2	—	Fashanu, Earle	16,736
4		31	H	Coventry C	W	1-0	1-0	10	Cork	9469
5	Sep	3	H	Manchester U	L	1-2	0-2	—	Fashanu	13,824
6		7	H	Luton T	W	3-0	1-0	7	Clarke, Ryan 2	3231
7		14	A	Nottingham F	L	2-4	1-2	11	McGee, Fashanu (pen)	19,707
8		18	A	Southampton	L	0-1	0-0	—		11,280
9		21	H	Tottenham H	L	3-5	1-3	16	Fashanu (pen), Cork, Bennett	11,927
10		28	A	Sheffield U	D	0-0	0-0	17		16,062
11	Oct	2	H	Sheffield W	W	2-1	0-0	—	Blackwell, Newhouse	3121
12		5	H	Norwich C	W	3-1	1-0	7	Fitzgerald, Fashanu, Clarke	3531
13		19	H	QPR	L	0-1	0-0	11		4630
14		26	A	Aston Villa	L	1-2	0-2	12	Fashanu	16,928
15	Nov	2	H	Leeds U	D	0-0	0-0	13		7025
16		16	A	Everton	L	0-2	0-1	15		18,762
17		23	H	Liverpool	D	0-0	0-0	16		13,373
18		30	A	Manchester C	D	0-0	0-0	16		22,429
19	Dec	7	A	Oldham Ath	W	2-1	1-0	14	Earle 2	4011
20		21	A	Sheffield W	L	0-2	0-0	16		20,574
21		26	H	Crystal Palace	D	1-1	0-0	16	Barton	15,009
22		28	H	Coventry C	D	1-1	0-1	17	Earle	3270
23	Jan	1	A	Arsenal	D	1-1	1-0	17	Miller	26,839
24		11	A	West Ham U	D	1-1	0-0	17	Sanchez	18,485
25		18	H	Chelsea	L	1-2	0-1	17	Earle	8413
26	Feb	1	A	QPR	D	1-1	0-1	18	Fashanu (pen)	9194
27		8	H	Aston Villa	W	2-0	1-0	18	Fashanu, Phelan	5534
28		22	H	Manchester C	W	2-1	2-0	16	Fashanu, Earle	5802
29		25	A	Notts Co	D	1-1	0-1	—	Fashanu (pen)	6198
30		29	A	Oldham Ath	W	1-0	1-0	12	McGee	12,166
31	Mar	7	H	Notts Co	W	2-0	1-0	11	Fashanu, Earle	4196
32		10	H	Everton	D	0-0	0-0	—		3569
33		14	A	Leeds U	L	1-5	0-3	12	Miller	26,760
34		21	A	Manchester U	D	0-0	0-0	14		45,428
35		28	H	Arsenal	L	1-3	0-2	16	Earle	11,299
36	Apr	2	H	Nottingham F	W	3-0	2-0	—	Earle, Fashanu 2	3542
37		4	A	Luton T	L	1-2	1-1	14	Fashanu	7754
38		8	A	Liverpool	W	3-2	1-2	—	Sanchez, Clarke, Fashanu (pen)	26,134
39		18	A	Tottenham H	L	2-3	1-2	14	Sanchez, Earle	23,934
40		20	H	Southampton	L	0-1	0-1	16		4025
41		25	H	Norwich C	D	1-1	0-1	17	Elkins	11,061
42	May	2	H	Sheffield U	W	3-0	3-0	13	Fashanu, Earle 2	8768

Final League Position: 13

GOALSCORERS

League (53): Fashanu 18 (5 pens), Earle 14, Clarke 3, Sanchez 3, Cork 2, McGee 2, Miller 2, Ryan 2, Barton 1, Bennett 1, Blackwell 1, Elkins 1, Fitzgerald 1, Newhouse 1, Phelan 1.
Rumbelows Cup (3): Clarke 1, Fashanu 1 (1 pen), McGee 1.
FA Cup (1): Fashanu 1.

Player appearance grid (League season):

Segers	Joseph	Phelan	Barton	Scales	Fitzgerald	Clarke	Earle	Fashanu	Ryan	Fairweather	Cork	Elkins	Newhouse	Ardley	McGee	Gibson	Kruszynski	Bennett	Blackwell	Anthrobus	Miller	Sanchez	McAllister	Hayes	Dobbs	Sullivan	Castledine	Match No.
1	2	3	4	5	6*	7	8	9	10	11	12																	1
1	2	3	4	5	6	7*	8	9	10	11†12		14																2
1	2	3	4	5	6†12		8	9*10	11		7	14																3
1	2	3	4*	5	6	12	8	9†10	11		7	14																4
1	2	3	4	5	6†12		9	10	11	8*	7	14																5
1	2	3	4	5	6	7	10	11*	9†	8	14	12																6
1	2		4	5	6	14	8	9			12	3		11	7*10†													7
1	2		4	5	6	7	8	9	10		12	3*14		11†														8
1	2	3	4	5	6*14		8	9	10		12			11†		7												9
1	2	3	4*	5	6	14	8	9	10	11						7†12												10
1	2	3	4	5	6	14	8		10*	11		9				7†12												11
1	2	3	4	5	6	14	8	9				11	10*			7†12												12
1	2*	3	4	10	6	11	8	9			12					7	5											13
1		3	4	10			8	9	6		12	5		2	11	7*												14
1		3	4	5	6		8	9				2		7	10					11								15
1	14	3	4	5	6	12	8	9				2		7†	10					11*								16
1	2	3	4	5	6	12	8				9*			7	10					11								17
1	2	3	4	5	6		8	9			12			7*	10					11								18
1	2	3	4	5	6		8	9				7			10					11								19
1	2	3	4	5	6		8	9				7	12							11*10								20
1	2	3	4	5	6		8	9				7	12							11	10*							21
1	2	3	4	5	6		8	9				7	12							11	10*							22
1	2†	3	4	5	6	12	8	9	14			7*								11	10							23
1		3	4	5	6	12	8	9				7*		2						11		10						24
1			4	5	6	11	8	9	2												7	10	3					25
1		3	4	5		12	8	9	6		2										7*10	11						26
1		3	4	5		12	8	9	14		2			11*							7	10†	6					27
1		3	4	5			8	9	10		2			11							7		6					28
1	2†	3	4	5		12	8	9	14					10	11						7		6*					29
1		3	4	5	6	12	8	9*14						11†							7	10						30
1		3	4	5	6	12	8	9*			2*			11							7	10						31
1		3	4	5	6	2	8	9						11*							7	10	12					32
1		3	4	5	6	12	8	9*						11							7	10	2					33
1		3	4	5	6	12	8				9*	2	11								7	10						34
1		3	4	5	6	11	8	9	12			2*									7	10						35
1	3†	4	5	6	12	8	9	2													7	10	14		11*			36
1		3	4	5	6	12	8	9	2												7	10*			11			37
1		3	4	5	12	2	8	9			11										7	10	6*					38
1	6*	3	4	5	12	2	8	9			11†										7	10		14				39
	11	3	4	5		2	8	9			12										7*10	6				1		40
1	2		4	5*10	11	8	9				3										7	6					12	41
1	2		4		5	11†	8	9			3										7	10*	6		14		12	42
41	25	37	42	41	34 +2s	13 +21s	40	38	16	6 +5s	12 +7s	15 +3s	5 +7s	7 +1s	15 +1s	7	1	5	1	10 +3s	22	16	9 +1s	1 +1s	2 +2s	1	— +2s	

+1s under Segers

Rumbelows Cup   Second Round   Peterborough U (h)   1-2
                                                              (a)   2-2
FA Cup   Third Round   Bristol C (a)   1-1
                                                            (h)   0-1

WIMBLEDON

Player and Position	Ht	Wt	Birth Date	Birth Place	Source	Clubs	League App	Gls
Goalkeepers								
Hans Segers	5 11	12 07	30 10 61	Eindhoven	PSV Eindhoven	Nottingham F	58	—
						Stoke C (loan)	1	—
						Sheffield U (loan)	10	—
						Dunfermline Ath (loan)	4	—
						Wimbledon	149	—
Neil Sullivan	6 0	12 01	24 2 70	Sutton	Trainee	Wimbledon	2	—
Defenders								
Warren Barton	6 0	11 00	19 3 69	London	Leytonstone/ Ilford	Maidstone U	42	—
						Wimbledon	79	4
Dean Blackwell	6 1	12 10	5 12 69	London	Trainee	Wimbledon	42	1
						Plymouth Arg (loan)	7	—
Gerald Dobbs	5 8	11 07	24 1 71	London	Trainee	Wimbledon	4	—
Gary Elkins	5 8	10 10	4 5 66	Wallingford	Apprentice	Fulham	104	2
						Exeter C (loan)	5	—
						Wimbledon	28	1
Scott Fitzgerald	6 0	12 02	13 8 69	London	Trainee	Wimbledon	37	1
Roger Joseph	5 11	11 13	24 12 65	Paddington	Juniors	Brentford	104	2
						Wimbledon	114	—
Brian McAllister	5 11	12 05	30 11 70	Glasgow	Trainee	Wimbledon	13	—
						Plymouth Arg (loan)	8	—
Chris Perry	5 09	11 01	26 4 73	London	Trainee	Wimbledon	—	—
Terry Phelan	5 8	10 00	16 3 67	Manchester		Leeds U	14	—
						Swansea C	45	—
						Wimbledon	159	1
John Scales	6 0	12 02	4 7 66	Harrogate		Leeds U	—	—
						Bristol R	72	2
						Wimbledon	168	10
Justin Skinner	5 07	11 00	17 9 72	London	Trainee	Wimbledon	—	—
Midfield								
Neil Ardley			1 9 72	Epsom	Trainee	Wimbledon	9	—
Michael Bennett	5 10	11 11	27 7 69	London	Apprentice	Charlton Ath	35	2
						Wimbledon	18	2
Stewart Castledine	6 00	12 00	22 1 73	London	Trainee	Wimbledon	2	—
Robbie Earle	5 9	10 10	27 1 65	Newcastle, Staffs	Amateur	Stoke C	—	—
						Port Vale	294	77
						Wimbledon	40	14
Detsi Kruszynski	6 0	12 12	14 10 61	Divschav	Homburg	Wimbledon	71	4
						Brentford (loan)	8	—
Jamie McCarthy	5 10	11 07	14 8 73	London	Trainee	Wimbledon	—	—
Paul McGee	5 6	9 10	17 5 68	Dublin	Bohemians	Colchester U	3	—
						Wimbledon	57	9
Aiden Newhouse	6 0	12 00	23 5 72	Wallasey	Trainee	Chester C	44	6
						Wimbledon	22	2
Vaughan Ryan	5 8	10 12	2 9 68	Westminster		Wimbledon	82	3
						Sheffield U (loan)	3	—
Lawrie Sanchez	5 11	11 07	22 10 59	Lambeth	Amateur	Reading	262	28
						Wimbledon	228	27
Steve Talboys	5 11	11 10	18 9 66	Bristol	Gloucester C	Wimbledon	—	—
Forwards								
Steve Anthrobus	6 2	12 13	10 11 68	Lewisham		Millwall	21	4
						Southend U (loan)	—	—
						Wimbledon	23	—
Andy Clarke	5 10	11 07	22 7 67	London	Barnet	Wimbledon	46	6

WIMBLEDON

Foundation: Old boys from Central School formed this club as Wimbledon Old Centrals in 1889. Their earliest successes were in the Clapham League before switching to the Southern Suburban League in 1902.

First Football League game: 20 August 1978, Division 4, v Halifax T (h) D 3-3 – Guy; Bryant (1), Galvin, Donaldson, Aitken, Davies, Galliers, Smith, Connell (1), Holmes, Leslie (1).

Did you know: The Wimbledon non-league side which created the biggest sensation was arguably the one that beat First Division Burnley 1-0 at Turf Moor in the FA Cup third round in January 1975. The team was Guy; Stockley, Bryant, Donaldson, Edwards, Cooke, Rice, Bassett, Mahon, Somers, Connell. England amateur international Mick Mahon scored the goal.

Managers (and Secretary-managers)
Les Henley 1955–71, Mike Everitt 1971–73, Dick Graham 1973–74, Allen Batsford 1974–78, Dario Gradi 1978–81, Dave Bassett 1981–87, Bobby Gould 1987–90, Ray Harford 1990–91, Peter Withe 1991, Joe Kinnear January 1992–.

Player and Position	Ht	Wt	Birth Date	Birth Place	Source	Clubs	League App	Gls
Steve Cotterill	6 1	12 05	20 7 64	Cheltenham	Burton Albion	Wimbledon	10	3
Carlton Fairweather	5 11	11 00	22 9 61	London	Tooting	Wimbledon	138	26
John Fashanu	6 1	11 12	18 9 62	Kensington	Amateur	Cambridge U	—	—
						Norwich C	7	1
						C Palace (loan)	1	—
						Lincoln C	36	10
						Millwall	50	12
						Wimbledon	211	90
Terry Gibson	5 5	10 00	23 12 62	Walthamstow	Apprentice	Tottenham H	18	4
						Coventry C	98	43
						Manchester U	23	1
						Wimbledon	78	21
						Swindon T	9	1
Martin Hayes On loan from Celtic						Wimbledon	2	—
Paul Miller	6 0	11 00	31 1 68	Bisley	Trainee	Wimbledon	61	9
						Newport Co (loan)	6	2
						Bristol C (loan)	3	—

Trainees
Alexander, Timothy M; Allen, Leighton G; Bullen, Michael; Cable, Marc B; Fairbairn, Neil; Fear, Peter S; Jennings, Paul; Laker, Barry J; Lingley, Peter C; Marchant, Giles R; Mosley, David; Orriss, Craig J; Payne, Grant; Rootes, Michael; Swift, Kieron; Taylor, Geoffrey J; Thomas, Mark L.

Associated Schoolboys
Archer, Jay; Board, Kevin J. F; Bower, Mathew; Bowers, Omari C; Bray, Dean M; Cobb, Simon P; Cort, Carl E. R; Courtney, Lee; Evell, Jason J; Griffiths, Leonard W; Hodges, Daniel W; Jones, David G; Jones, Lee; Laidlaw, Iain L; Owusu, Clement; Piper, Leonard H; Williams, Lee M.

Associated Schoolboys who have accepted the club's offer of a Traineeship/Contract
Brooker, Daniel P; Cunningham, Jason; Di'Rubbo, Franco; Fell, Gavin A.

574

WOLVERHAMPTON WANDERERS 1991–92 *Back row (left to right):* Paul Cook, Mark Venus, Robert Hindmarch, Mike Stowell, Shane Westley, Paul Jones, Gary Bellamy, John Paskin, Nicky Clarke.
Third row: Steve Bull, Andy Mutch, Robbie Dennison, Tom Bennett, Colin Taylor, Paul McLoughlin, Tim Steele, Kevin Ashley, Mark Burke.
Second row: Andy Thompson, Keith Downing, Garry Pendrey (Coach), Chris Evans (Youth Team Coach), Graham Turner (Manager), Paul Darby (Physiotherapist), Brian Roberts, Paul Birch.
Front row: Stuart Leeding, Andrew Harnett, Andrew Kelly, Warren Jones, Mark Turner, Darren Smith.

Division 1 **WOLVERHAMPTON WANDERERS**

Molineux Grounds, Wolverhampton WV1 4QR. Telephone Admin office: Wolverhampton (0902) 712181; lottery shop: (0902) 27524. Commercial Office: (0902) 23166. Ticket office: 0902 25899. Fax No: 071 436

Ground capacity: 25,000.

Record attendance: 61,315 v Liverpool, FA Cup 5th rd, 11 February 1939.

Record receipts: £110,623 v Sheffield W, FA Cup 3rd rd, 6 January 1990.

Pitch measurements: 116yd × 74yd.

President: Sir Jack Hayward. *Chairman:* Jonathan Hayward. *Directors:* Billy Wright, John Harris, Nic Stones. *Team Manager:* Graham Turner. *Coaches:* Gary Pendrey and Chris Evans. *Physio:* Paul Darby. *Secretary:* Keith Pearson ACIS. *Commercial Manager:* Keith Butler.

Year Formed: 1877 *(see Foundation).* Turned Professional: 1888. Ltd Co.: 1982.

Former Grounds: 1877, Goldthorn Hill; 1884, Dudley Road; 1889, Molineux.

Former Names: 1880, St Luke's, Blakenhall combined with The Wanderers to become Wolverhampton Wanderers (1923) Ltd until 1982.

Club Nickname: 'Wolves'.

Record League Victory: 10-1 v Leicester C, Division 1, 15 April 1938 – Sidlow; Morris, Dowen; Galley, Cullis, Gardiner; Maguire (1), Horace Wright, Westcott (4), Jones (1), Dorsett (4).

Record Cup Victory: 14-0 v Cresswell's Brewery, FA Cup, 2nd rd, 13 November 1886 – I. Griffiths; Baugh, Mason; Pearson, Allen (1), Lowder; Hunter (4), Knight (2), Brodie (4), B. Griffiths (2), Wood. Plus one goal 'scrambled through'.

Record Defeat: 1-10 v Newton Heath, Division 1, 15 October 1892.

Most League Points (2 for a win): 64, Division 1, 1957–58.

Most League points (3 for a win): 92, Division 4, 1988–89.

Most League Goals: 115, Division 2, 1931–32.

Highest League Scorer in Season: Dennis Westcott, 38, Division 1, 1946–47.

Most League Goals in Total Aggregate: Bill Hartill, 164, 1928–35.

Most Capped Player: Billy Wright, 105, England (70 consecutive).

Most League Appearances: Derek Parkin, 501, 1967–82.

Record Transfer Fee Received: £1,150,000 from Manchester C for Steve Daley, September 1979.

Record Transfer Fee Paid: £1,175,000 to Aston Villa for Andy Gray, September 1979.

Football League Record: 1888 Founder Member of *Football League:* 1906–23 Division 2; 1923–24 Division 3 (N); 1924–32 Division 2; 1932–65 Division 1; 1965–67 Division 2; 1967–76 Division 1; 1976–77 Division 2; 1977–82 Division 1; 1982–83 Division 2; 1983–84 Division 1; 1984–85 Division 2; 1985–86 Division 3; 1986–88 Division 4; 1988–89 Division 3; 1989–92 Division 2; 1992– Division 1.

Honours: Football League: Division 1 – Champions 1953–54, 1957–58, 1958–59; Runners-up 1937–38, 1938–39, 1949–50, 1954–55, 1959–60; Division 2 – Champions 1931–32, 1976–77; Runners-up 1966–67, 1982–83; Division 3 (N) – Champions 1923–24; Division 3 – Champions 1988–89; Division 4 – Champions 1987–88. *FA Cup:* Winners 1893, 1908, 1949, 1960; Runners-up 1889, 1896, 1921, 1939. *Football League Cup:* Winners 1973–74, 1979–80. *Texaco Cup:* 1970–71. *Sherpa Van Trophy:* Winners 1988. **European Competitions:** *European Cup:* 1958–59, 1959–60. *European Cup-Winners Cup:* 1960–61. *UEFA Cup:* 1971–72 (runners-up), 1973–74, 1974–75, 1980–81.

Colours: Gold shirts, black shorts, gold stockings. **Change colours:** All sky blue.

WOLVERHAMPTON WANDERERS 1991–92 LEAGUE RECORD

Match No.	Date		Venue	Opponents	Result		H/T Score	Lg. Pos.	Goalscorers	Atten- dance
1	Aug	17	A	Watford	W	2-0	0-0	—	Mutch, Bull	13,547
2		24	H	Charlton Ath	D	1-1	1-1	5	Bull	16,309
3		31	A	Brighton & HA	D	3-3	2-2	8	Mutch 2, Bull	10,621
4	Sep	3	H	Port Vale	L	0-2	0-0	—		16,115
5		7	H	Oxford U	W	3-1	3-0	9	Dennison, Bull, Steele	12,549
6		14	A	Newcastle U	W	2-1	0-0	8	Steele, Bull	20,195
7		17	A	Cambridge U	L	1-2	0-2	—	Bull	6552
8		21	H	Swindon T	W	2-1	1-0	6	Steele, Bull	15,219
9		28	A	Southend U	W	2-0	0-0	4	Birch, Ashley	8368
10	Oct	5	A	Barnsley	L	1-2	1-0	6	Cook	14,082
11		12	A	Middlesbrough	D	0-0	0-0	8		15,253
12		19	A	Leicester C	L	0-3	0-2	10		14,428
13		26	H	Tranmere R	D	1-1	1-0	10	Birch	12,266
14	Nov	2	A	Plymouth Arg	L	0-1	0-0	16		4200
15		5	H	Bristol R	L	2-3	1-1	—	Bull 2	8536
16		9	H	Derby Co	L	2-3	1-1	18	Coleman (og), Cook (pen)	15,672
17		16	A	Millwall	L	1-2	1-2	20	Cook (pen)	9469
18		23	H	Ipswich T	L	1-2	1-0	21	Birch	11,915
19		26	H	Grimsby T	W	2-1	1-0	—	Madden, Birch	9378
20		30	A	Portsmouth	L	0-1	0-1	20		11,101
21	Dec	7	H	Sunderland	W	1-0	0-0	15	Cook	11,922
22		21	A	Port Vale	D	1-1	1-0	17	Bull	8480
23		26	A	Blackburn R	D	0-0	0-0	18		18,277
24		28	H	Brighton & HA	W	2-0	2-0	15	Burke, Mutch	13,606
25	Jan	1	A	Grimsby T	W	2-0	1-0	11	Birch, Cook	9158
26		15	A	Charlton Ath	W	2-0	1-0	—	Bull, Bennett	5703
27		18	H	Watford	W	3-0	0-0	10	Cook, Bull, Holdsworth (og)	14,175
28	Feb	1	H	Leicester C	W	1-0	1-0	10	Bull	18,574
29		8	A	Tranmere R	L	3-4	2-2	10	Cook, Bull, Burke	11,371
30		22	A	Portsmouth	D	0-0	0-0	11		15,770
31		29	A	Sunderland	L	0-1	0-1	12		20,106
32	Mar	7	H	Bristol C	D	1-1	1-1	12	Bull	12,542
33		11	A	Bristol R	D	1-1	0-0	—	Bull	6968
34		14	H	Plymouth Arg	W	1-0	0-0	11	Venus	11,556
35		17	A	Bristol C	L	0-2	0-0	—		11,623
36		21	A	Derby Co	W	2-1	0-1	11	Birch (pen), Bull	21,024
37		28	H	Millwall	D	0-0	0-0	11		11,880
38		31	H	Newcastle U	W	6-2	3-1	—	Mutch 3, Bennett, Cook, Bull	14,480
39	Apr	4	A	Oxford U	L	0-1	0-0	11		7165
40		7	A	Ipswich T	L	1-2	0-0	—	Mutch	17,379
41		11	A	Cambridge U	W	2-1	0-0	11	Rankine, Mutch	11,188
42		14	A	Blackburn R	W	2-1	0-1	—	Bull, Birch	14,114
43		18	A	Swindon T	L	0-1	0-1	10		10,863
44		20	A	Southend U	W	3-1	1-1	10	Bull, Mountfield, Birch	10,953
45		26	A	Barnsley	L	0-2	0-1	10		7244
46	May	2	H	Middlesbrough	L	1-2	0-0	11	Mutch	19,123

Final League Position: 11

GOALSCORERS

League (61): Bull 20, Mutch 10, Birch 8 (1 pen), Cook 8 (2 pens), Steele 3, Bennett 2, Burke 2, Ashley 1, Dennison 1, Madden 1, Mountfield 1, Rankine 1, Venus 1, own goals 2.
Rumbelows Cup (8): Bull 3, Birch 2, Steele 2, Burke 1.
FA Cup (0).

Stowell	Ashley	Venus	Bennett	Madden	Downing	Birch	Cook	Bull	Mutch	Dennison	Steele	Bellamy	Burke	Clarke W	Paskin	Thompson	Taylor	McLoughlin	Mountfield	Clarke N	Rankine	Kelly	Match No.
1	2	3	4	5	6	7	8	9	10	11													1
1	2	3	4	5	6	7*	8	9	10	11	12												2
1	2	3	4	5	6	7	8	9	10	11													3
1	2	3	4	5	6	7	8	9	10	11*	12												4
1	2*	3	4	5	6		8	9	10	11	12	7											5
1	2	3	4	5	6*		8	9	10	11	12		7										6
1	2	3	4	5	6		8	9	10	11*	12		7										7
1	2	3	4	5	6	11	8	9		7*	12	10											8
1	2	3	4	5	6	7	8	9	12		11		10*										9
1	2	3	4	5	6*	7	8	9	12	10			11										10
1	2	3	4	5		7	8*	9	12	6						10	11						11
1	2*	3	4	5	6	7		9	10†	12	8				14	11							12
1	2	3	4	5	6	7		9	10*	11	8					12							13
1	2	3	4	5	6	7	8		11*	10							12	9					14
1	2†	3	4	5	6	7		9	11*	12	14	8						10					15
1	2	3	4	5	6	7	11	9	10										8				16
1	2	3	4	5	6*	7	11	9	10	12									8				17
1	2	3	4*		6	7	11	9	10	12									8	5			18
1	2	3	4	5	6	7	8	9	10										11				19
1	2	3	4*	5		7	8		10	6	12					14			9	11†			20
1	2	3	4	5		7	8		10	11*	12					6†	14		9				21
1	2	3	4	5		7	8	9	10							11			6				22
1	2	3	4*	5		7	8	9	10		12					11			6				23
1	2	3		5		7	8	9	10				4			11			6				24
1	2	3	14	5		7*	8	9	10	12			4†			11			6				25
1	2	3	4	5		7	8	9	10							11			6				26
1	2	3	4	5		7	8	9	10*							11			6				27
1	2	3	4	5		7	8*	9				10				11			6		12		28
1	2	3	4	5		7	8*	9		12		10				11			6				29
1	2*	3	4			7	8	9	14	12			10†			11			5	6			30
1		3	4		6	7	8	9	10	12						11*			5		14		31
1	2	3	4		6*	7	8	9	10	11†	12								5		14		32
1	2	3	4	11	6	7	8	9	10*										5		12		33
1	2	3	4		6	7	8	9								11			5		10		34
1	2	3	4		6	7	8	9	12							11*			5		10		35
1	2*	3	4		6	7	8	9	10	12			11						6		5		36
1		3	4		6	7	8	9	10	12	14		11†						2		5*		37
1	2*	3	4	5	11	7	8	9	10										6			12	38
1	2	3	4*	5	11	7	8	9†	10										6		14	12	39
1	2	3		5	11	7	8	9	10										6		4		40
1	2	3		5	11	7	8	9	10										6		4		41
1	2	3		5	11	7	8	9	10										6		4		42
1	2*	3		5	11	7	8	9	10	12									6		4		43
1	2	3		5	11	7	8	9	10				4						6				44
1	2	3		5	11	7*	8	9	10	14			4†						6			12	45
1	2	3		5	11*	7	8	9	10	12			4						6				46

Totals:

Stowell	Ashley	Venus	Bennett	Madden	Downing	Birch	Cook	Bull	Mutch	Dennison	Steele	Bellamy	Burke	Clarke W	Paskin	Thompson	Taylor	McLoughlin	Mountfield	Clarke N	Rankine	Kelly
46	44	46	37	43	30	43	43	43	35	12	10	1	13	1	1	15	1	3	28	1	10	—

Substitute appearances: Venus +1s; Downing +2s; Birch +2s; Dennison +2s; Steele +10s; Bellamy +7s; Burke +3s; Clarke W +5s; Thompson +1s; Taylor +2s; McLoughlin +2s; Rankine +5s; Kelly +3s

Rumbelows Cup	Second Round	Shrewsbury T (h)	6-1
		(a)	1-3
	Third Round	Everton (a)	1-4
FA Cup	Third Round	Nottingham F (a)	0-1

WOLVERHAMPTON WANDERERS

Goalkeepers

Name	Ht	Wt	DOB	Birthplace	Source	Clubs	Apps	Gls
Paul Jones			18 4 67	Chirk	Shrewsbury T	Bridgnorth	—	—
						Kidderminster H	—	—
						Wolverhampton W	—	—
Tony Lange*	6 0	12 09	10 12 64	London	Apprentice	Charlton Ath	12	—
						Aldershot (loan)	7	—
						Aldershot	125	—
						Wolverhampton W	8	—
						Aldershot (loan)	2	—
						Torquay U (loan)	1	—
						Portsmouth (loan)	—	—
Mike Stowell	6 2	11 10	19 4 65	Preston	Leyland Motors	Preston NE	—	—
						Everton	—	—
						Chester C (loan)	14	—
						York C (loan)	6	—
						Manchester C (loan)	14	—
						Port Vale (loan)	7	—
						Wolverhampton W	7	—
						(loan)	2	—
						Preston NE (loan)	85	—
						Wolverhampton W		

Defenders

Name	Ht	Wt	DOB	Birthplace	Source	Clubs	Apps	Gls
Kevin Ashley	5 7	10 04	31 12 68	Birmingham	Apprentice	Birmingham C	57	1
						Wolverhampton W	60	1
Gary Bellamy	6 2	11 05	4 7 62	Worksop	Apprentice	Chesterfield	184	7
						Wolverhampton W	136	9
						Cardiff C (loan)	9	—
Tom Bennett	5 11	11 08	12 12 69	Falkirk	Trainee	Aston Villa	—	—
						Wolverhampton W	96	2
Rob Hindmarch	6 1	13 4	27 4 61	Stannington	Apprentice	Sunderland	115	2
						Portsmouth (loan)	2	—
						Derby Co	164	9
						Wolverhampton W	40	2
Warren Jones*	5 09	9 13	12 9 72	Chester	Trainee	Wolverhampton W	—	—
Andrew Kelly*	5 09	11 00	2 10 72	Wolverhampton	Trainee	Wolverhampton W	—	—
Stuart Leeding*	5 8	9 10	6 1 72	Wolverhampton	Trainee	Wolverhampton W	—	—
Lawrie Madden	5 11	13 01	28 9 55	London	Amateur Manchester Univ	Arsenal	—	—
						Mansfield T	10	—
						Charlton Ath	113	7
						Millwall	47	2
						Sheffield W	212	2
						Leicester C (loan)	3	—
						Wolverhampton W	43	1
Derek Mountfield	6 1	12 07	2 11 62	Liverpool	Apprentice	Tranmere R	26	1
						Everton	106	19
						Aston Villa	90	9
						Wolverhampton W	28	1
Brian Roberts*	5 8	11 07	6 11 55	Manchester	Apprentice	Coventry C	215	1
						Hereford U (loan)	5	—
						Birmingham C	187	—
						Wolverhampton W	21	—
Darren Simkin	6 00	12 00	24 3 70	Walsall	Blakenhall	Wolverhampton W	—	—
Mark Venus	6 0	11 08	6 4 67	Hartlepool		Hartlepool U	4	—
						Leicester C	61	1
						Wolverhampton W	135	3
Shane Westley	6 2	12 10	16 6 65	Canterbury	Apprentice	Charlton Ath	8	—
						Southend U	144	10
						Norwich C (loan)	—	—
						Wolverhampton W	42	1

Midfield

Name	Ht	Wt	DOB	Birthplace	Source	Clubs	Apps	Gls
Paul Birch	5 6	10 09	20 11 62	West Bromwich	Apprentice	Aston Villa	173	16
						Wolverhampton W	65	10

WOLVERHAMPTON WANDERERS

Foundation: Another club where precise details of information are confused, due in part to the existence of an earlier Wolverhampton club which played rugby. However, it is now considered likely that it came into being in 1879 when players from St. Luke's (founded 1877) and Goldthorn (founded 1876) broke away to form Wolverhampton Wanderers Association FC.

First Football League game: 8 September 1888, Football League, v Aston Villa (h) D 1–1 – Baynton; Baugh, Mason; Fletcher, Allen, Lowder; Hunter, Cooper, Anderson, White, Cannon. Scorer (Cox og).

Did you know: Wolves provided the England half-back line in four consecutive internationals in May and June 1958 – Eddie Clamp, Billy Wright and Bill Slater. All four games against USSR (2), Brazil and Austria were drawn.

Managers (and Secretary-managers)
George Worrall 1877–85*, John Addenbrooke 1885–1922, George Jobey 1922–24, Albert Hoskins 1924–26 (had been secretary since 1922), Fred Scotchbrook 1926–27, Major Frank Buckley 1927–44, Ted Vizard 1944–48, Stan Cullis 1948–64, Andy Beattie 1964–65, Ronnie Allen 1966–68, Bill McGarry 1968–76, Sammy Chung 1976–78, John Barnwell 1978–81, Ian Greaves 1982, Graham Hawkins 1982–84, Tommy Docherty 1984–85, Bill McGarry 1985, Sammy Chapman 1985–86, Brian Little 1986, Graham Turner October 1986–.

Paul Cook	5 11	10 10	22 2 67	Liverpool		Wigan Ath	83	14
						Norwich C	6	—
						Wolverhampton W	113	16
Robert Dennison	5 7	11 00	30 4 63	Banbridge	Glenavon	WBA	16	1
						Wolverhampton W	206	28
Keith Downing	5 8	11 00	23 7 65	Oldbury	Mile Oak	Notts Co	23	1
						Wolverhampton W	160	6
Jim Kelly	5 7	11 10	14 2 73	Liverpool	Trainee	Wrexham	22	—
						Wolverhampton W	3	—
Mark Rankine	5 10	11 01	30 9 69	Doncaster	Trainee	Doncaster R	165	20
						Wolverhampton W	15	1
Andy Thompson	5 4	10 06	9 11 67	Carnock	Apprentice	WBA	24	1
						Wolverhampton W	211	23
Mark Turner	6 01	11 01	4 10 72	Bebbington	Paget R	Wolverhampton W	—	—
Forwards								
Steve Bull	5 11	11 04	28 3 65	Tipton	Apprentice	WBA	4	2
						Wolverhampton W	247	155
Mark Burke	5 10	11 08	12 2 69	Solihull	Apprentice	Aston Villa	7	—
						Middlesbrough	57	6
						Darlington (loan)	5	1
						Ipswich T (loan)	—	—
						Wolverhampton W	24	2
Andrew Harnett*	6 00	12 02	30 8 73	Bromsgrove	Trainee	Wolverhampton W	—	—
Andy Mutch	5 10	11 00	28 12 63	Liverpool	Southport	Wolverhampton W	250	88
Darren Roberts			12 10 69	Birmingham	Burton Alb	Wolverhampton W	—	—
Darren Smith*	5 11	12 00	29 4 70	Nottingham	Burton Alb	Wolverhampton W	—	—
Tim Steele	5 9	11 00	1 2 67	Coventry	Apprentice	Shrewsbury T	61	5
						Wolverhampton W	71	7
						Stoke C (loan)	7	1
Colin Taylor	6 0	12 07	25 12 71	Liverpool	Trainee	Wolverhampton W	18	2
						Wigan Ath (loan)	7	2

Trainees
Bowers, Kevin T; Bradbury, Shaun D; Clarke, Matthew L; Collier, Daniel J; Davies, Mark; De Bont, Andrew C; Goode, Mark G; Howard, Jonathan M; Humphrey, Paul B; Jackson, Grant S; Owen, John G; Owen, Steve; Piearce, Stephen; Scandrett, Raymond P; Shaw, Darren R; Smith, James J. A; Smith, Jason J; Voice, Scott H; Walker, Steven J; Warmer, Garry P.

Associated Schoolboys
Biddle, Steven J; Brodie, Craig K; Bytheway, Matthew; Davis, Paul; Edwards, Neil P; Holmes, Martin L; Hughes, David O; Mahon, Gavin; McCabe, Richard; Owen, Adrian J; Ponting, Matthew A; Povey, Neil; Robyns, Gethin; Warr, John R; Westley, Paul D; Wilson, Christopher J.

Associated Schoolboys who have accepted the club's offer of a Traineeship/Contract
Barnett, Jason; Dale, David A; Graham, Iain; Hanbury, Jay P; Innes, Michael P; Macbeth, Andrew M.

WREXHAM 1991–92   *Back row (left to right)*: Lee Jones, Mike Williams, Andy Preece, Alex Goss, Mark Morris, Vince O'Keefe, Mark Sertori, Chris Armstrong, Nigel Beaumont, James Kelly.

Centre row: Cliff Sear (Youth Team Coach), David Rhodes (Vice-Chairman), Steve Watkin, Wayne Phillips, Sean Reck, Karl Connolly, Barry Williams (Deputy Chairman), Gino Paletta (Director), Kevin Reeves (Assistant Manager).

Front row: Steve Wade (Physio), Ian Griffiths, Joey Murray, Gareth Owen, Brian Flynn (Manager), Pryce Griffiths (Chairman), Joey Jones (Player/Coach), Andy Thackeray, Steve Weaver, Phil Hardy, Mike Rigg (Community Scheme Organiser).

Division 3   WREXHAM

Racecourse Ground, Mold Road, Wrexham. Telephone Wrexham (0978) 262129. Commercial Dept: (0978) 352536. Clubcall: 0898 121642. Fax No: (0978) 357821. Football in the community (0978) 358545.

Ground capacity: 17,500.

Record attendance: 34,445 v Manchester U, FA Cup 4th rd, 26 January 1957.

Record receipts: £126,012 v West Ham U, FA Cup 4th rd, 4 February 1992.

Pitch measurements: 111 yd × 71 yd.

President: G. Mytton. *Chairman:* W. P. Griffiths. *Managing Director:* D. L. Rhodes.

Directors: C. Griffiths, S. Mackreth, G. Palletta, B. Williams (vice-chairman).

Manager: Brian Flynn. *Assistant Manager:* Kevin Reeves. *Secretary:* D. L. Rhodes. *Player-coach:* Joey Jones. *Commercial Manager:* P. Stokes. *Physio:* Steve Wade.

Year Formed: 1873 (oldest club in Wales). Turned Professional: 1912. Ltd Co.: 1912.

Former Grounds: Acton Park.

Club Nickname: 'Robins'.

Record League Victory: 10-1 v Hartlepools, Division 4, 3 March 1962 – Keelan; Peter Jones, McGavan; Tecwyn Jones, Fox, Ken Barnes; Ron Barnes (3), Bennion (1), Davies (3), Ambler (3), Ron Roberts.

Record Cup Victory: 6-0 v Gateshead, FA Cup, 1st rd, 20 November 1976 – Lloyd; Evans, Whittle, Davis, Roberts, Thomas (Hill), Shinton (3 incl. 1p), Sutton, Ashcroft (2), Lee (1), Griffiths. 6-0 v Charlton Ath, FA Cup, 3rd rd, 5 January 1980 – Davies; Darracott, Kenworthy, Davis, Jones (Hill), Fox, Vinter (3), Sutton, Edwards (1), McNeil (2), Carrodus.

Record Defeat: 0-9 v Brentford, Division 3, 15 October 1963.

Most League Points (2 for a win): 61, Division 4, 1969–70 and Division 3, 1977–78.

Most League points (3 for a win): 71, Division 4, 1988–89.

Most League Goals: 106, Division 3 (N), 1932–33.

Highest League Scorer in Season: Tom Bamford, 44, Division 3 (N), 1933–34.

Most League Goals in Total Aggregate: Tom Bamford, 175, 1928–34.

Most Capped Player: Dai Davies, 28 (51), Wales.

Most League Appearances: Arfon Griffiths, 592, 1959–61, 1962–79.

Record Transfer Fee Received: £300,000 from Manchester U for Mickey Thomas, November 1978, from Manchester C for Bobby Shinton, July 1979 and from Liverpool for Lee Jones, March 1992.

Record Transfer Fee Paid: £210,000 to Liverpool for Joey Jones, October 1978.

Football League Record: 1921 Original Member of Division 3 (N); 1958–60 Division 3; 1960–62 Division 4; 1962–64 Division 3; 1964–70 Division 4; 1970–78 Division 3; 1978–82 Division 2; 1982–83 Division 3; 1983–92 Division 4; 1992– Division 3.

Honours: Football League: Division 2 best season: 15th, 1978–79; Division 3 – Champions 1977–78; Division 3 (N) – Runners-up 1932–33; Division 4 – Runners-up 1969–70. *FA Cup:* best season: 6th rd, 1973–74, 1977–78. *Football League Cup:* best season: 5th rd, 1961, 1978. *Welsh Cup:* Winners 21 times. Runners-up 19 times. Record number of victories and appearances in finals. **European Competition:** *European Cup-Winners' Cup:* 1972–73, 1975–76, 1978–79, 1979–80, 1984–85, 1986–87, 1990–91.

Colours: Red shirts, white shorts, red stockings. **Change colours:** White shirts, red shorts, white stockings.

WREXHAM 1991–92 LEAGUE RECORD

Match No.	Date		Venue	Opponents		Result	H/T Score	Lg. Pos.	Goalscorers	Attendance
1	Aug	17	H	Hereford U	L	0-1	0-1	—		3225
2		24	A	Walsall	D	0-0	0-0	18		3307
3		30	H	Northampton T	D	2-2	1-1	—	Connolly, Bowden (pen)	2196
4	Sep	3	A	Mansfield T	L	0-3	0-0	—		1965
5		7	A	Doncaster R	L	1-3	0-1	22	Phillips S	1474
6		14	H	Gillingham	W	2-1	2-1	18	Bowden 2 (1 pen)	1642
7		21	A	York C	D	2-2	2-1	19	Owen, Watkin	1816
8		28	H	Scunthorpe U	W	4-0	2-0	13	Watkin 2, Davies, Humphries (og)	1635
9	Oct	5	A	Cardiff C	L	0-5	0-2	15		3652
10		12	H	Burnley	L	2-6	2-4	18	Davies, Preece	3181
11		19	H	Carlisle U	W	3-0	1-0	13	Watkin, Preece, Thomas	1266
12	Nov	2	H	Barnet	W	1-0	1-0	14	Watkin	1886
13		5	A	Scarborough	L	1-4	1-0	—	Watkin	1164
14		9	A	Crewe Alex	L	1-2	0-2	16	Owen	3596
15		19	A	Blackpool	L	0-4	0-2	—		2842
16		23	H	Chesterfield	L	0-1	0-1	18		1636
17	Dec	13	A	Halifax T	L	3-4	1-1	—	Connolly 2, Davies	881
18		20	H	Walsall	W	2-1	1-0	—	Connolly, Watkin	2571
19		26	A	Hereford U	L	1-3	0-1	20	Davies	3542
20		28	A	Northampton T	D	1-1	0-1	20	Phillips W	3209
21	Jan	1	H	Mansfield T	W	3-2	2-1	16	Thackeray, Owen, Connolly	2442
22		11	H	Maidstone U	D	0-0	0-0	19		3167
23		18	A	Lincoln C	D	0-0	0-0	19		2213
24	Feb	8	H	Blackpool	D	1-1	1-1	18	Phillips W	4053
25		15	H	Halifax T	W	2-0	0-0	17	Jones L, Owen	2076
26		22	A	Maidstone U	W	4-2	2-1	16	Jones L 2, Thackeray, Owen	1491
27		29	H	Rochdale	W	2-1	0-0	16	Jones L, Thackeray	3458
28	Mar	3	H	Lincoln C	D	1-1	0-0	—	Jones L	2716
29		7	A	Rotherham U	L	0-3	0-0	17		3562
30		10	A	Scarborough	W	2-0	1-0	—	Paskin, Carey	2044
31		14	A	Barnet	L	0-2	0-0	16		2917
32		21	H	Crewe Alex	W	1-0	0-0	16	Owen	3899
33		24	A	Carlisle U	W	1-0	0-0	16	Gallimore (og)	1826
34		28	A	Chesterfield	D	1-1	1-0	13	Phillips W	2961
35		31	A	Gillingham	L	1-2	0-2	—	Connolly	3078
36	Apr	3	H	Doncaster R	L	1-2	1-2	—	Connolly	2769
37		18	H	York C	W	2-1	0-0	14	Connolly, Paskin	2261
38		20	A	Scunthorpe U	L	1-3	0-0	14	Longden (og)	2900
39		22	A	Rochdale	L	1-2	0-1	—	Watkin	1945
40		25	H	Cardiff C	L	0-3	0-2	15		4002
41		28	H	Rotherham U	L	0-3	0-1	—		3477
42	May	2	A	Burnley	W	2-1	0-1	14	Paskin, Owen	21,216

Final League Position: 14

GOALSCORERS

League (52): Connolly 8, Watkin 8, Owen 7, Jones L 5, Davies 4, Bowden 3 (2 pens), Paskin 3, Phillips W 3, Thackeray 3, Preece 2, Carey 1, Phillips S 1, Thomas 1, own goals 3.
Rumbelows Cup (1): Thackeray 1.
FA Cup (10): Watkin 5, Thomas 2, Connolly 1, Jones L 1, Phillips W 1.

O'Keefe	Thackeray	Hardy	Sertori	Thomas	Jones J	Bowden	Phillips W	Connolly	Jones L	Davies	Owen	Preece	Skipper	Durkan	Phillips S	Griffiths	Beaumont	Kelly	Watkin	Marshall	Morris	Cross	Carey	Lunt	Pejic	Flynn	Paskin	Jones K	Match No.
1	2	3	4	5	6	7	8*	9	10	11	12																		1
1	2	3	4	5	6	7		9	10	8	12	11*																	2
1	2	3	4	5	6	7		9	10	8		11																	3
1	2	3	4	5*		7	11	9	10†	8			6	12	14														4
1	2	3	4†	5		7	12	8	10	6*	9	11				14													5
1	2	3		5		7	4	9	10	8	11		6																6
1	2	3		5	6		9*	7†		8	12					11	4	10	14										7
1	2	3		5	6					7		8	11				4	10	9										8
1	2	3		5	6				12	7*	8	11					4	10	9										9
1	2	3		5	6				12	7*	8	11					4	10	9										10
	2	3		5	6	7				8		11					4	9	10		1								11
	2	3	6	5		9				7		8	11				4		10		1								12
	2	3	6	5		9		12		7		8	11*				4		10		1								13
	2	3		5	6		14	12		7*	8						4	11	10		1	9†							14
	2†	3	7	5	6			9	12	14	8						4	11*	10		1								15
	2	3	8	5†	6*		14	12		7		11					4	9	10		1								16
1	2	3	6	5			10	9*		7	8						4	11				12							17
1	2	3	6	5			9			7	8						4	11	10										18
1	2	3	6	5			14	9	12	7	8†						11*	10					4						19
1	2	3	6	5			11	9*		7	8							10					4		12				20
1	2	3	6	5			11	9		7	8							10					4						21
1	2	3	6	5			11	9	12	7	8†							10*					4		14				22
1	2	3	6	5			11	9		7								10					4		8				23
1	2	3	6	5			11	9	12	7*								10					4		8				24
1	2	3	6	5			11	9	12		14						10*						4		7	8†			25
1	2	3	6				11	9	10		8												4		5	7			26
1	2	3	6				11	9	10		8												4		5	7			27
1	2	3	6				11	9	10		8												4		5*	7	12		28
1	2	3	6				11	9	10		8									5		4				7			29
1	2	3	6				11	9	10		8						12		4						5*	7			30
1	2	3	6				11	9†			8							12		4					5*	7			31
1	2	3	6				11	9			8							10							5*	7			32
1	2	3	6				11	9			8							10							5*	7†			33
1	2	3	6				11	9*			8							10								7*			34
1	2	3	6				11	9			8															7*			35
1	2	3	6				12	9			8															7*14			36
1	2	3	6				11	9			8						12									7			37
1	2	3	6				11	9			8						12		14							7			38
	2	3*	6				11	9			8						10			1						7			39
	2	3	6				11	9			8						10			1						7			40
1	2	3	6	4			11*	9			8						10					7					12		41
1	2	3	6	10†			11*	9			8						4										12		42
34	42	42	36	26	11	6	28	33	11	21	33	9	2	—	1	3	13	9	24	3	8	3	13	—	6	6	14	—	
+2s	+3s	+10s	+1s	+3s	+1s			+2s	+1s		+3s	+1s		+1s			+1s		+4s				+3s		+1s	+1s	+3s	+1s	

Ireland—Match No. 31(10) 32(12) 33(14) 35(12) 36(11†); Jones D—Match No 31(14); Lewis—Match No. 32(4) 33(4) 34(4) 35(4) 36(4) 37(4*) 38(4†) 39(4) 42(14); Taylor—Match No. 33(12) 34(12) 35(10) 36(10) 37(10) 38(10*) 39(12) 40(4) 42(7); Humes—Match No. 34(5) 35(5) 36(5) 37(5) 38(5) 39(5) 40(5) 42(5); Knight—Match No. 41(5).

Rumbelows Cup	First Round	Scunthorpe U (h)	1-0
		(a)	0-3
FA Cup	First Round	Winsford (h)	5-2
	Second Round	Telford (h)	1-0
	Third Round	Arsenal (h)	2-1
	Fourth Round	West Ham U (a)	2-2
		(h)	0-1

WREXHAM

Player and Position	Ht	Wt	Date	Birth Place	Source	Clubs	League App	Gls
Goalkeepers								
Mark Morris	5 11	12 00	1 8 68	Chester		Wrexham	63	—
Vince O'Keefe*	6 2	13 00	2 4 57	Coleshill	Local	Birmingham C	—	—
						Peterborough U (loan)	—	—
						Walsall	—	—
						AP Leamington	53	—
						Exeter C	108	—
						Torquay U	68	—
						Blackburn R	2	—
						Bury (loan)	7	—
						Blackpool (loan)	83	—
						Wrexham		
Defenders								
Nigel Beaumont*	6 1	12 07	11 2 67	Pontefract		Bradford C	2	—
						Wrexham	115	4
Phil Hardy			9 4 73	Chester		Wrexham	75	—
Tony Humes	5 11	10 10	19 3 66	Blyth	Apprentice	Ipswich T	120	10
						Wrexham	8	—
Joey Jones*	5 10	11 07	4 3 55	Llandudno	Amateur	Wrexham	98	2
						Liverpool	72	3
						Wrexham	146	6
						Chelsea	78	2
						Huddersfield T	68	3
						Wrexham	132	11
Craig Knight§			24 10 73	Wrexham	Trainee	Wrexham	1	—
Dudley Lewis*	5 10	10 09	17 11 62	Swansea	Apprentice	Swansea C	230	2
						Huddersfield T	34	—
						Halifax T (loan)	11	—
						Wrexham	9	—
Mel Pejic	5 9	10 08	27 4 59	Chesterton	Local	Stoke C	1	—
						Hereford U	413	14
						Wrexham	7	—
Wayne Phillips	5 10	11 00	15 12 70	Bangor	Trainee	Wrexham	63	3
Mark Sertori	6 3	12 00	1 9 67	Manchester		Stockport Co	4	—
						Lincoln C	50	9
						Wrexham	83	2
Mike Williams‡	5 10	10 12	6 2 65	Mancot	Apprentice	Chester C	34	4
						Wrexham	178	3
Midfield								
Brian Flynn*	5 4	12 00	12 10 55	Pt Talbot	Limerick	Burnley	120	8
						Leeds U	154	11
						Burnley (loan)	2	—
						Burnley	80	11
						Cardiff C	32	—
						Doncaster R	27	—
						Limerick	—	—
						Bury	19	—
						Doncaster R	24	1
						Wrexham	98	5
Ian Griffiths‡	5 6	10 02	17 4 60	Birkenhead	Amateur	Tranmere R	116	5
						Rochdale	42	5
						Port Vale	12	—
						Wigan Ath	82	7
						Bolton W	—	—
						Wigan Ath	11	—
						Wrexham	14	—
Kevin Jones§			16 2 74	Wrexham	Trainee	Wrexham	1	—
Robert Lunt§	5 7	10 10	11 12 73	Widnes	Trainee	Wrexham	9	—
Joey Murray‡	5 8	10 11	5 11 71	Liverpool	Liverpool	Wrexham	11	—
Gareth Owen	5 9	11 04	21 10 71	Chester	Trainee	Wrexham	76	9
Sean Reck‡	5 10	12 07	5 5 67	Oxford	Apprentice	Oxford U	14	—
						Newport Co (loan)	15	—
						Reading (loan)	1	—
						Wrexham	45	2

WREXHAM

Foundation: The oldest club still in existence in Wales, Wrexham was founded in 1873 by a group of local businessmen initially to play a 17-a-side game against the Provincial Insurance team. By 1875 their team formation was reduced to 11 men and a year later they were among the founders of the Welsh FA.

First Football League game: 27 August 1921, Division 3 (N), v Hartlepools U (h) L 0-2 – Godding; Ellis, Simpson; Matthias, Foster, Griffiths; Burton, Goode, Cotton, Edwards, Lloyd.

Did you know: Centre-forward Bernard Evans scored within 25 seconds in his Football League debut for Wrexham on Bradford City's ground in September 1954.

Managers (and Secretary-managers)
Ted Robinson 1912–25* (continued as secretary to 1930), Charlie Hewitt 1925–29, Jack Baynes 1929–31, Ernest Blackburn 1932–36, Jimmy Logan 1937–38, Arthur Cowell 1938, Tom Morgan 1938–40, Tom Williams 1940–49, Les McDowall 1949–50, Peter Jackson 1951–54, Cliff Lloyd 1954–57, John Love 1957–59, Billy Morris 1960–61, Ken Barnes 1961–65, Billy Morris 1965, Jack Rowley 1966–67, Alvan Williams 1967–68, John Neal 1968–77, Arfon Griffiths 1977–81, Mel Sutton 1981–82, Bobby Roberts 1982–85, Dixie McNeil 1985–89, Brian Flynn November 1989–.

Name	Ht	Wt	Date	Birthplace	From	Club	Apps	Gls
Andy Thackeray	5 9	11 00	13 2 68	Huddersfield		Manchester C	—	—
						Huddersfield T	2	—
						Newport Co	54	4
						Wrexham	152	14
Mickey Thomas	5 6	10 07	7 7 54	Mochdre	Amateur	Wrexham	230	33
						Manchester U	90	11
						Everton	10	—
						Brighton & HA	20	—
						Stoke C	57	14
						Chelsea	44	9
						WBA	20	—
						Derby Co (loan)	9	—
						Wichita W	—	—
						Shrewsbury T	40	1
						Leeds U	3	—
						Stoke C (loan)	5	—
						Stoke C	38	7
						Wrexham	26	1

Forwards

Name	Ht	Wt	Date	Birthplace	From	Club	Apps	Gls
Karl Connolly			9 2 70	Prescot	Napoli (Liverpool)	Wrexham	36	8
Jonathan Cross§			2 3 75	Wallasey	Trainee	Wrexham	6	—
Gordon Davies‡	5 7	10 12	3 8 55	Merthyr	Merthyr T	Fulham	247	113
						Chelsea	13	6
						Manchester C	31	9
						Fulham	147	45
						Wrexham	22	4
Kieron Durkan§			1 12 73	Chester	Trainee	Wrexham	1	—
David Jones*	5 9	11 04	6 5 71	Wrexham	Trainee	Aston Villa	—	—
						Wrexham	1	—
John Paskin	5 10	11 10	1 2 62	Capetown	Seiko	WBA	25	5
						Wolverhampton W	34	3
						Stockport Co (loan)	5	1
						Birmingham C (loan)	10	3
						Shrewsbury T (loan)	1	—
						Wrexham	34	6
Mark Taylor	5 7	10 00	20 11 64	Hartlepool	Local	Hartlepool U	47	4
						Crewe Alex (loan)	3	—
						Blackpool	119	43
						Cardiff C (loan)	6	3
						Wrexham	9	—
Steve Watkin	5 10	11 00	16 6 71	Wrexham	School	Wrexham	37	9

Trainees
Brammer, David; Burke, Damian P. W; Coulthard, Christopher; Cross, Jonathan N; Douglas, Iain S; Durkan, Kieron J; Jones, Kevin R; Knight, Craig; Laughton, Richard J; Lunt, Robert J; Myddleton, Phillip J; Oldfield, Damon M; Pugh, Stephen; Roden, Damian J; Sadler, Philip A; Smith, Mark A; Williams, Scott J.

Associated Schoolboys
Acott, Lee; Clays, Warren M; Cody, Michael D; Davey, Richard W; Davies, Stephen; Edwards, Arwel R; Futcher, Stephen A; McGregor, Mark D. T; Rawlins, Richard; Roberts, Ryland; Williams, Gavin P.

Associated Schoolboys who have accepted the club's offer of a Traineeship/Contract
Barnes, Richard I; Hughes, Bryan; Jones, Scott L; Morgan, Steven J; Pritchard, Andrew; Roberts, Paul; Williams, Christopher.

YORK CITY 1991–92   *Back row (left to right):* Alan Little (Coach), Paul Atkin, Ray Warburton, Paul Stancliffe, Chris Marples, Dean Kiely, Ian Helliwell, Steve Tutill, Ian Blackstone, Jeff Miller (Physiotherapist).
Front row: Nigel Pepper, Glenn Naylor, Andy Curtis, Steve Bushell, Tony Barratt, John Bird (Manager), Shaun Reid, Tony Canham, John McCarthy, Andy McMillan, Wayne Hall.

Division 3   **YORK CITY**

Bootham Crescent, York. Telephone York (0904) 624447.

Ground capacity: 12,760.

Record attendance: 28,123 v Huddersfield T, FA Cup 6th rd, 5 March 1938.

Record receipts: £38,054 v Liverpool, FA Cup 5th rd, 15 February 1986.

Pitch measurements: 115yd × 75yd.

Chairman: D. M. Craig OBE, JP, BSC, FICE, FIMUNE, FCI ARB, M CONS E.

Directors: B. A. Houghton, C. Webb, E. B. Swallow, J. E. H. Quickfall FCA.

Manager: John Ward.

Assistant Manager: Alan Little.

Secretary: Keith Usher.

Commercial Manager: Mrs Sheila Smith.

Physio: Jeff Miller.

Hon. Orthopaedic Surgeon: Mr Peter De Boer MA, FRCS.

Medical Officer: Dr. R. Porter.

Year Formed: 1922. Turned Professional: 1922. Ltd Co.: 1922.

Former Grounds: 1922, Fulfordgate; 1932, Bootham Crescent.

Club Nickname: 'Minstermen'.

Record League Victory: 9-1 v Southport, Division 3 (N), 2 February 1957 – Forgan; Phillips, Howe; Brown (1), Cairney, Mollatt; Hill, Bottom (4 incl. 1p), Wilkinson (2), Wragg (1), Fenton (1).

Record Cup Victory: 6-0 v South Shields (away), FA Cup, 1st rd, 16 November 1968 – Widdowson; Baker (1p), Richardson; Carr, Jackson, Burrows; Taylor, Ross (3), Mac-Dougall (2), Hodgson, Boyer.

Record Defeat: 0-12 v Chester, Division 3 (N), 1 February 1936.

Most League Points (2 for a win): 62, Division 4, 1964–65.

Most League points (3 for a win): 101, Division 4, 1983–84.

Most League Goals: 96, Division 4, 1983–84.

Highest League Scorer in Season: Bill Fenton, 31, Division 3 (N), 1951–52; Arthur Bottom, 31, Division 3 (N), 1954–55 and 1955–56.

Most League Goals in Total Aggregate: Norman Wilkinson, 125, 1954–66.

Most Capped Player: Peter Scott, 7 (10), Northern Ireland.

Most League Appearances: Barry Jackson, 481, 1958–70.

Record Transfer Fee Received: £100,000 from Carlisle U for Gordon Staniforth, October 1979, and from QPR for John Byrne, October 1985.

Record Transfer Fee Paid: £50,000 to Aldershot for Dale Banton, November 1984.

Football League Record: 1929 Elected to Division 3 (N); 1958–59 Division 4; 1959–60 Division 3; 1960–65 Division 4; 1965–66 Division 3; 1966–71 Division 4; 1971–74 Division 3; 1974–76 Division 2; 1976–77 Division 3; 1977–84 Division 4; 1984–88 Division 3; 1988–92 Division 4; 1992– Division 3.

Honours: Football League: Division 2 best season: 15th, 1974–75; Division 3 – Promoted 1973–74 (3rd); Division 4 – Champions 1983–84. *FA Cup:* Semi-finals 1955, when in Division 3. *Football League Cup:* best season: 5th rd, 1962.

Colours: Red shirts, blue shorts, red stockings. **Change colours:** White shirts, red shorts, blue stockings.

YORK CITY 1991–92 LEAGUE RECORD

Match No.	Date		Venue	Opponents	Result	H/T Score	Lg. Pos.	Goalscorers	Attendance
1	Aug	17	A	Rochdale	D	1-1	1-0	—	Naylor	2247
2		24	H	Gillingham	D	1-1	1-0	14	Naylor	2324
3		30	A	Halifax T	D	0-0	0-0	—		2167
4	Sep	3	H	Blackpool	W	1-0	0-0	—	McCarthy	2686
5		7	H	Chesterfield	L	0-1	0-1	13		2382
6		17	A	Hereford U	L	1-2	0-2	—	Stancliffe	3540
7		21	H	Wrexham	D	2-2	1-2	18	Naylor, Canham	1816
8		28	A	Maidstone U	L	0-1	0-1	21		1037
9	Oct	5	H	Scarborough	W	4-1	3-1	14	Canham, Naylor, Tutill, McCarthy	2971
10		12	A	Barnet	L	0-2	0-0	17		4474
11		19	A	Lincoln C	D	1-1	0-0	18	McCarthy	1893
12		25	A	Rotherham U	L	0-4	0-1	—		4676
13	Nov	2	H	Walsall	W	2-0	0-0	15	Reid, Hall	1605
14		5	A	Burnley	L	1-3	1-2	—	McCarthy	7389
15		8	H	Doncaster R	W	1-0	1-0	—	Canham	2144
16		30	A	Scunthorpe U	L	0-1	0-0	14		2887
17	Dec	14	H	Cardiff C	L	1-3	1-1	15	Canham	1904
18		21	A	Gillingham	D	1-1	0-0	17	Barratt	2711
19		26	H	Rochdale	L	0-1	0-0	18		2745
20		28	H	Halifax T	D	1-1	0-0	18	Hall	2396
21	Jan	1	A	Blackpool	L	1-3	0-2	19	Pepper	3534
22		4	H	Mansfield T	L	1-2	0-0	20	McCarthy	2660
23		11	A	Northampton T	D	2-2	2-2	20	Pepper, Canham	3355
24		18	H	Carlisle U	W	2-0	0-0	16	Barratt 2	1953
25	Feb	8	H	Rotherham U	D	1-1	0-1	17	Hall	3526
26		11	H	Scunthorpe U	W	3-0	2-0	—	Blackstone, Pepper 2 (1 pen)	2255
27		15	A	Cardiff C	L	0-3	0-1	16		8067
28		22	H	Northampton T	D	0-0	0-0	17		2044
29		25	A	Crewe Alex	L	0-1	0-1	—		3327
30		29	A	Mansfield T	L	2-5	1-3	18	McCarthy, Atkin	3290
31	Mar	3	H	Carlisle U	D	1-1	1-1	—	Blackstone	1681
32		7	H	Crewe Alex	D	1-1	1-1	18	McMillan	2208
33		14	A	Walsall	D	1-1	1-1	19	Blackstone	2541
34		18	A	Lincoln C	D	0-0	0-0	—		1875
35		21	H	Doncaster R	D	1-1	0-0	18	Blackstone	2127
36	Apr	4	A	Chesterfield	W	3-1	2-1	19	Blackstone, Naylor 2	2461
37		11	H	Hereford U	W	1-0	1-0	19	Blackstone	1614
38		18	A	Wrexham	L	1-2	0-0	19	Naylor	2261
39		20	H	Maidstone U	D	1-1	1-0	19	Naylor	1638
40		25	A	Scarborough	L	0-1	0-0	19		2108
41		28	H	Burnley	L	1-2	1-0	—	Blackstone	7620
42	May	2	H	Barnet	L	1-4	0-0	19	Blackstone	2643

Final League Position: 19

GOALSCORERS

League (42): Blackstone 8, Naylor 8, McCarthy 6, Canham 5, Pepper 4 (1 pen), Barratt 3, Hall 3, Atkin 1, McMillan 1, Reid 1, Stancliffe 1, Tutill 1.
Rumbelows Cup (3): Blackstone 1, Canham 1, McCarthy 1.
FA Cup (4): Blackstone 2, Hall 1, McCarthy 1.

Kiely	McMillan	Crosby	Reid	Tutill	Stancliffe	Pepper	McCarthy	Blackstone	Naylor	Canham	Marples	Atkin	Osborne	Hall	Barratt	Warburton	Curtis	Gosney	McLoughlin	Tilley	Bushell	Shepstone	Match No.
1	2	3	4	5	6	7	8	9	10	11													1
	2	3	4	5	6	7	8	9	10	11	1												2
	2	3	4	5		7	8	9			1	6	10	11*	12								3
	2	3	4	5		7	8			11	1		9	10		6							4
	2	3	4	5		7	8		12	11	1		9*	10		6							5
	2	3	4	5	6	7	8			11	1		9*	12	10								6
	2		4	5		7	8	9		11	1	6	12	3	10*								7
			4	5		7	8	10*		11	1	6	9	3	2	12							8
	2		4	5		7	8	10*		11	1	6	12	3	9								9
	2		4	5	6†	7	8	10		11	1	14	12	3	9*								10
	2		4	5		7	8		12	11		6	9*	3	14	10†		1					11
	2		4	5		7	8		12	11		6		3	10*	9		1					12
	2	3	4	5		7	8	9				6		10	11			1					13
	2	3	4	5		7	8	9*		11		6		10	12			1					14
	2	3	4	5		7	8	9		11*		6		10	12			1					15
	2	3	4	5		7	8	9		11	1	6		10									16
	2	3	4	5		7	8	9	12	11	1	6		10*									17
	2	3	4	5		7	8			11	1	6		10	9								18
	2	3*	4			7	8		12	11	1	6		10	9	5							19
	2	3	4			7	8		12	11	1	6		10	9*	5							20
	2	3*	4			7	8		12	11	1	6		10	9	5							21
	2	3	4	5		7	8	9		11	1			10	6								22
1	2	3	4	5		7	8			11†	12	10		6						9*		14	23
1	2	3	4	5			8			11		6		10			7			9			24
1	2	3	4†	5	14		8		12	11		6		10					7*	9			25
1	2	3		5		7	8			11		6		10	12					9*	4		26
1	2	3		5	14	7	8			11		6†		10	12					9*	4		27
1	2	3		5	6	7	8			11*	12			10						9	4		28
1	2	3		5	6	7	8			11	12			10						9*	4		29
1	2	3		5	6†	7	8			11			9*	10	12					14	4		30
1	2	3		5	6	7	8			11		9		10							4		31
1	2		4	5†			8		10	11	12	6		3	14					7*		9	32
1	2		4	5		7	8	9		11		6		3			12			10*			33
1	2		4	5		7	8	9		11		6		3			12			10*			34
1	2		4†	5*		7	8	9		11		6		3			12			10		14	35
1	2			5	6		8	9		11				3			7			10	4		36
1	2			5	6		8	9		11				3	12		7			10*	4		37
1	2			5	6		8	9		11				3	12		7			10*	4		38
1	2			5	6	12	8	9		11				3			7			10	4*		39
1	2			5	6		8	9		11				3	12		7			10*	4		40
1	2			5	6		8	9		11				3			7			10	4		41
1	2			5	6	12	8	9*		11				3			7			10†	4	14	42
21	41	25	28	39	16 +2s	33 +2s	42	26 +4s	14 +7s	28 +3s	16	29 +4s	6 +3s	36 +1s	15 +6s	7 +2s	4 +3s	5	1	13 +2s	15 +1s	2	

Rumbelows Cup	First Round	Bolton W (a)	2-2
		(h)	1-2
FA Cup	First Round	Bridlington (a)	2-1
	Second Round	Tranmere R (h)	1-1
		(a)	1-2

YORK CITY

Player and Position	Ht	Wt	Date	Birth Place	Source	Clubs	League App	Gls
Goalkeepers								
Dean Kiely	5 11	11 08	10 10 70	Manchester	WBA	Coventry C	—	—
						Ipswich T (loan)	—	—
						York C	38	—
Chris Marples	5 11	11 12	3 8 64	Chesterfield		Chesterfield	84	—
						Stockport Co	57	—
						York C	136	—
						Scunthorpe U (loan)	1	—
Defenders								
Paul Atkin	6 0	12 04	3 9 69	Nottingham	Trainee	Notts Co	—	—
						Bury	21	1
						York C	33	1
Tony Barratt	5 8	10 02	18 10 65	Salford	Billingham T	Grimsby T	22	—
						Hartlepool U	98	4
						York C	108	8
Phil Crosby	5 9	10 08	9 11 62	Leeds	Apprentice	Grimsby T	39	1
						Rotherham U	183	2
						Peterborough U	87	—
						York C	25	—
Andy McMillan	5 10	10 13	22 6 68	South Africa		York C	135	2
Mark Ogley‡	5 10	11 02	10 3 67	Barnsley	Apprentice	Barnsley	19	—
						Aldershot (loan)	8	—
						Carlisle U	33	1
						Aldershot	62	—
						York C	—	—
Paul Stancliffe	6 2	12 13	5 5 58	Sheffield	Apprentice	Rotherham U	285	8
						Sheffield U	278	12
						Rotherham U (loan)	5	—
						Wolverhampton W	17	—
						York C	18	1
Steve Tutill	6 0	11 10	1 10 69	Derwent	Trainee	York C	166	2
Ray Warburton	6 0	11 05	7 10 67	Rotherham	Apprentice	Rotherham U	4	—
						York C	74	6
Midfield								
Steve Bushell	5 7	10 05	28 12 72	Manchester	Trainee	York C	31	—
Andy Curtis*	5 10	11 07	2 12 72	Doncaster	Trainee	York C	12	—
Wayne Hall	5 8	10 04	25 10 68	Rotherham	Darlington	York C	112	7
Nigel Pepper	5 10	10 03	25 4 68	Rotherham	Apprentice	Rotherham U	45	1
						York C	74	7
Shaun Reid*	5 8	11 08	13 10 65	Huyton	Local	Rochdale	133	4
						Preston NE (loan)	3	—
						York C	106	7
Forwards								
Ian Blackstone	6 0	13 02	7 8 64	Harrogate	Harrogate	York C	58	14
Tony Canham	5 8	10 07	8 6 60	Leeds	Harrogate R	York C	247	48
Jonathan McCarthy	5 9	11 05	18 8 70	Middlesbrough		Hartlepool U	1	—
						Shepshed	—	—
						York C	69	8
Glenn Naylor	5 9	11 10	11 8 72	York	Trainee	York C	42	13
Steve Osborne‡	5 10	11 11	3 3 69	Middlesbrough	South Bank	Peterborough U	60	7
						York C	9	—
Darren Tilley			15 3 67	Bristol	Yate T	York C	15	—

YORK CITY

Foundation: Although there was a York City club formed in 1903 by a soccer enthusiast from Darlington, this has no connection with the modern club because it went out of existence during World War I. Unlike many others of that period who restarted in 1919, York City did not re-form until 1922 and the tendency now is to ignore the modern club's pre-1922 existence.

First Football League game: 31 August 1929, Division 3 (N), v Wigan Borough (a) W 2-0 – Farmery; Archibald, Johnson; Beck, Davis, Thompson; Evans, Gardner, Cowie (1), Smailes, Stockhill (1).

Did you know: After holding Newcastle United to a 1-1 draw at St James' Park in the FA Cup third round in 1929–30 (York's initial League season) nearly 13,000 packed their ground at Fulfordgate for the replay with the gates being locked 1½ hours before kick-off. York were beaten 2-1.

Managers (and Secretary-managers)
Bill Sherrington 1924–60 (was secretary for most of this time but virtually secretary-manager for a long pre-war spell), John Collier 1929–36, Tom Mitchell 1936–50, Dick Duckworth 1950–52, Charlie Spencer 1952–53, Jimmy McCormick 1953–54, Sam Bartram 1956–60, Tom Lockie 1960–67, Joe Shaw 1967–68, Tom Johnston 1968–75, Wilf McGuinness 1975–77, Charlie Wright 1977–80, Barry Lyons 1980–81, Denis Smith 1982–87, Bobby Saxton 1987–88, John Bird 1988–91, John Ward November 1991–.

Trainees
Barker, Paul D; Dickinson, Jason K; Dooley, Eammon G; Ellis, Robert J; Gosling, Michael J; Hall, Craig; Henry, Craig L; Jordan, Scott D; Markwick, Brett A; Maynard, Andrew G; Mennell, Nicholas; Murty, Graeme S; Smith, Andrew; Tomlinson, Lea R.

Associated Schoolboys
Barlow, Stephen M; Cresswell, Richard P. W; Groome, Jonathan; Haddon, Steven; Hall, Philip D; Jones, Simon D; Masson, Jonathan P; Minett, Alex J. R; Nellies, Murray; O'Hara, Daniel; Pickering, Ian; Ranson, David; Robinson, Wesley K; Shephard, Lewis M; Tate, Christopher; Walker, Adam D; Watkinson, Mark; Williams, Darren.

Associated Schoolboys who have accepted the club's offer of a Traineeship/Contract
Davison, Jamie; Medworth, Lee; Mockler, Paul F; Roberts, Steven; Simpson, Elliott; Warrington, Andrew.

Blackburn players continued from page 71

Player and Position	Ht	Wt	Birth Date	Birth Place	Source	Clubs	League App	Gls
Forwards								
Mike Newell	6 0	11 00	27 1 65	Liverpool	Amateur	Liverpool	—	—
						Crewe Alex	3	—
						Wigan Ath	72	25
						Luton T	63	18
						Leicester C	81	21
						Everton	68	15
						Blackburn R	20	6
Duncan Shearer	5 10	10 09	28 8 62	Fort William	Inverness Clach	Chelsea	2	1
						Huddersfield T	83	38
						Swindon T	159	78
						Blackburn R	6	1
Craig Skinner	5 10	11 00	21 10 70	Bury	Trainee	Blackburn R	16	—
David Speedie	5 7	11 00	20 2 60	Glenrothes	Amateur	Barnsley	23	—
						Darlington	88	21
						Chelsea	162	47
						Coventry C	122	31
						Liverpool	12	6
						Blackburn R	36	23
Gary Tallon	5 10	11 02	5 9 73	Drogheda	Trainee	Blackburn R	—	—
Peter Thorne	6 00	12 10	21 6 73	Manchester	Trainee	Blackburn R	—	—
Roy Wegerle	5 8	10 02	19 3 64	South Africa	Tampa Bay R	Chelsea	23	3
						Swindon T (loan)	7	1
						Luton T	45	10
						QPR	75	29
						Blackburn R	12	2
Jason Wilcox	5 10	11 06	15 7 71	Bolton	Trainee	Blackburn R	57	4

END OF SEASON PLAY-OFFS 1991–92

The Football League's decision to implement a series of play-offs for promotion—and initially also relegation—coincided with the increase in attendances during the regular schedule of League games. The 1991–92 season proved no exception and crowds at Wembley for the finals of the three divisions involved again showed the interest aroused.

In the Fourth Division, Blackpool found themselves faced with a penalty shoot-out as in 1990–91. This time they won through at the expense of Scunthorpe United after the match finished at 1-1 following extra time.

The previous year Dave Bamber's failure from the penalty spot had ended Blackpool's hopes against Torquay United. Now he was able to feel sympathy for Scunthorpe players Graham Alexander and Jason White when they were literally put on the spot. Bamber had put Blackpool in front after 40 minutes, Tony Daws equalising seven minutes after the interval. Eventually Blackpool won 4-3 on penalties.

The Third Division epic nearly required extra time but Peterborough United managed to edge out Stockport County during 90 minutes in an exciting finale. Ken Charlery scored for Posh after 51 minutes with a header which hit the crossbar and bounced down. Was it over the line? Stockport came back strongly and with three minutes remaining, Kevin Francis equalised having had an earlier effort ruled out for offside. But Peterborough were not finished and Charlery raced through, shook off a defender and calmly lobbed the ball over the advancing Neil Edwards in the last minute.

The near 58,000 aggregate for these two finals was eclipsed by the Second Division affair between Blackburn Rovers and Leicester City. The 68,147 crowd was more than watched England and Brazil the previous weekend. Blackburn ended a 26-year exile out of the First Division, the year that England won the World Cup. The only goal came from a penalty conceded by Steve Walsh on David Speedie in the dying seconds of the first half. Mike Newell converted the kick. He had another opportunity from the spot six minutes from the final whistle, but this time Carl Muggleton in the Leicester goal saved the shot.

Blackburn's £6 million investment in players to achieve promotion under Kenny Dalglish was thus rewarded. The club has every reason to be grateful for the financial assistance rendered by chairman Jack Walker.

PLAY-OFFS
Semi-finals, First Leg
10 MAY

DIVISION 2

Blackburn R (2) 4 *(Sellars, Newell, Speedie 2)*
Derby Co (2) 2 *(Gabbiadini, Johnson)*   19,677
Blackburn R: Mimms; May, Wright, Cowans, Moran (Richardson), Hendry, Price, Atkins, Speedie (Shearer), Newell, Sellars.
Derby Co: Sutton; Kavanagh, Forsyth, McMinn (Micklewhite), Coleman, Comyn, Johnson, Kitson, Gabbiadini, Williams P, Simpson.

Cambridge U (0) 1 *(O'Shea)*
Leicester C (1) 1 *(Russell)*   9225
Cambridge U: Vaughan; Heathcote, Kimble, Dennis (Raynor), Chapple, O'Shea, Cheetham, Wilkins, Dublin, Claridge, Philpott (Norbury).
Leicester C: Muggleton; Mills, Whitlow, Hill, Walsh, James, Thompson, Grayson, Wright, Ormondroyd, Russell.

DIVISION 3

Stockport Co (1) 1 *(Ward)*
Stoke C (0) 0   7537
Stockport Co: Edwards; Knowles (Wheeler), Todd, Frain, Barras, Williams B, Gannon, Ward, Francis, Beaumont, Preece.

Stoke C: Sinclair; Fowler, Butler, Kevan, Blake, Sandford, Cranson, Beeston, Stein, Biggins, Grimes.

DIVISION 4

Barnet (1) 1 *(Carter)*
Blackpool (0) 0   5629
Barnet: Pape; Poole, Cooper, Bodley, Howell, Horton, Hunt, Carter, Bull, Hoddle, Showler (Willis).
Blackpool: McIlhargey; Burgess, Cook, Groves, Gouck (Rodwell), Gore, Davies (Murphy), Horner, Bamber, Sinclair, Eyres.

Crewe Alex (2) 2 *(Hignett, Naylor)*
Scunthorpe U (2) 2 *(Helliwell 2)*   6083
Crewe Alex: Noble; Wilson, Smith, McKearney, Macauley, Walters, Hignett, Naylor, Futcher (Clarkson), Gardiner, Callaghan.
Scunthorpe U: Samways; Joyce, Longden, Hill, Elliott, Humphries, Martin, Hamilton, Daws, Buckley (Alexander), Helliwell.

11 MAY

DIVISION 3

Peterborough U (0) 2 *(Charlery, Halsall)*
Huddersfield T (1) 2 *(Onuora, Robinson D (og))*   11,751
Peterborough U: Barber; Luke, Robinson R, Halsall, Robinson D, Howarth, Sterling, Ebdon, Adcock, Charlery, Edwards (Cooper S).
Huddersfield T: Clarke; Trevitt, Charlton, Kelly, Mitchell, Jackson, O'Regan, Billy, Roberts, Starbuck, Onuora.

Semi-finals, Second Leg
13 MAY

DIVISION 2

Derby Co (1) 2 *(Comyn, McMinn)*
Blackburn R (0) 1 *(Moran)*   22,920
Derby Co: Sutton; Kavanagh, Forsyth, McMinn, Coleman, Comyn, Johnson, Kitson, Gabbiadini, Williams P, Simpson.
Blackburn R: Mimms; May, Wright, Cowans, Moran, Hendry, Richardson, Atkins, Speedie, Newell, Sellars.

Leicester C (2) 5 *(Wright 2, Thompson, Russell, Ormondroyd)*
Cambridge U (0) 0   21,024
Leicester C: Muggleton; Mills, Whitlow (Oldfield), Hill, Walsh, James, Thompson, Grayson, Wright, Ormondroyd, Russell.
Cambridge U: Vaughan; Heathcote, Kimble, Dennis, Chapple, O'Shea (Norbury), Cheetham, Wilkins, Dublin, Claridge, Philpott.

DIVISION 3

Stoke C (0) 1 *(Stein)*
Stockport Co (1) 1 *(Beaumont)*   16,170
Stoke C: Sinclair; Foley, Butler, Kevan (Heath), Blake (Kelly), Sandford, Cranson, Fowler, Stein, Biggins, Grimes.
Stockport Co: Edwards; Knowles, Todd, Frain, Barras, Williams B, Gannon, Ward, Francis, Beaumont, Preece (Wheeler).

DIVISION 4

Blackpool (1) 2 *(Groves, Garner (pen))*
Barnet (0) 0 7588

Blackpool: McIlhargey; Burgess, Cook, Groves, Davies, Gore, Rodwell, Horner, Bamber, Garner, Eyres.
Barnet: Pape; Poole, Cooper, Bodley, Howell, Horton, Hunt (Willis), Carter, Bull, Hoddle (Payne), Showler.

Scunthorpe U (0) 2 *(Martin, Hamilton)*
Crewe Alex (0) 0 7938

Scunthorpe U: Samways; Joyce, Longden, Hill, Elliott, Humphries, Martin, Hamilton, Daws, Buckley, Helliwell.
Crewe Alex: Edwards; Wilson, Smith, McKearney, Macauley, Murphy (Evans), Hignett, Naylor, Clarkson, Gardiner, Callaghan.

DIVISION 3
14 MAY

Huddersfield T (1) 1 *(Starbuck)*
Peterborough U (0) 2 *(Sterling, Cooper S)* 16,167

Huddersfield T: Clarke; Trevitt, Charlton, Kelly, Mitchell, Jackson, O'Regan, Billy (Barnett), Roberts, Starbuck, Onuora.
Peterborough U: Barber; Luke, Robinson R, Halsall, Robinson D, Welsh, Sterling (Cooper S), Ebdon, Adcock, Charlery, Barnes.

Finals (at Wembley)
23 MAY

DIVISION 4

Blackpool (1) 1 *(Bamber)*
Scunthorpe U (0) 1 *(Daws)* 22,741

Blackpool: McIlhargey; Burgess, Cook, Groves, Davies (Murphy), Gore, Rodwell, Horner (Sinclair), Bamber, Garner, Eyres.
Scunthorpe U: Samways; Joyce, Longden, Hill, Elliott, Humphries, Martin, Hamilton, Daws (White), Buckley (Alexander), Helliwell.
aet; Blackpool won 4–3 on penalties.

24 MAY
DIVISION 3

Peterborough U (0) 2 *(Charlery 2)*
Stockport Co (0) 1 *(Francis)* 35,087

Peterborough U: Barber; Luke, Robinson R, Halsall, Robinson D, Welsh (Howarth), Sterling, Ebdon, Adcock, Charlery, Barnes.
Stockport Co: Edwards; Knowles, Todd, Frain, Barras, Williams B, Gannon, Ward (Wheeler), Francis, Beaumont, Preece.

25 MAY
DIVISION 2

Blackburn R (1) 1 *(Newell (pen))*
Leicester C (0) 0 68,147

Blackburn R: Mimms; May, Wright, Cowans, Moran, Hendry, Price, Atkins, Speedie, Newell, Sellars (Richardson).
Leicester C: Muggleton; Mills, Whitlow, Hill, Walsh, James (Gee), Thompson, Grayson, Wright, Ormondroyd, Russell.

Mike Newell scores from the penalty spot for Blackburn Rovers, beating Carl Muggleton in the Leicester goal during the Second Division play-off final at Wembley. (Colorsport)

BARCLAYS LEAGUE FINAL TABLES 1991–92

DIVISION 1

		P	Home W	D	L	Goals F	A	Away W	D	L	Goals F	A	Pts	GD
1	Leeds U	42	13	8	0	38	13	9	8	4	36	24	82	+37
2	Manchester U	42	12	7	2	34	13	9	8	4	29	20	78	+30
3	Sheffield W	42	13	5	3	39	24	8	7	6	23	25	75	+13
4	Arsenal	42	12	7	2	51	22	7	8	6	30	24	72	+35
5	Manchester C	42	13	4	4	32	14	7	6	8	29	34	70	+13
6	Liverpool	42	13	5	3	34	17	3	11	7	13	23	64	+7
7	Aston Villa	42	13	3	5	31	16	4	4	11	17	28	60	+4
8	Nottingham F	42	10	7	4	36	27	6	4	11	24	31	59	+2
9	Sheffield U	42	9	6	6	29	23	7	3	11	36	40	57	+2
10	Crystal Palace	42	7	8	6	24	25	7	7	7	29	36	57	−8
11	QPR	42	6	10	5	25	21	6	8	7	23	26	54	+1
12	Everton	42	8	8	5	28	19	5	6	10	24	32	53	+1
13	Wimbledon	42	10	5	6	32	20	3	9	9	21	33	53	0
14	Chelsea	42	7	8	6	31	30	6	6	9	19	30	53	−10
15	Tottenham H	42	7	3	11	33	35	8	4	9	25	28	52	−5
16	Southampton	42	7	5	9	17	28	7	5	9	22	27	52	−16
17	Oldham Ath	42	11	5	5	46	36	3	4	14	17	31	51	−4
18	Norwich C	42	8	6	7	29	28	3	6	12	18	35	45	−16
19	Coventry C	42	6	7	8	18	15	5	4	12	17	29	44	−9
20	Luton T	42	10	7	4	25	17	0	5	16	13	54	42	−33
21	Notts Co	42	7	5	9	24	29	3	5	13	16	33	40	−22
22	West Ham U	42	6	6	9	22	24	3	5	13	15	35	38	−22

DIVISION 2

		P	Home W	D	L	Goals F	A	Away W	D	L	Goals F	A	Pts	GD
1	Ipswich T	46	16	3	4	42	22	8	9	6	28	28	84	+20
2	Middlesbrough	46	15	6	2	37	13	8	5	10	21	28	80	+17
3	Derby Co	46	11	4	8	35	24	12	5	6	34	27	78	+18
4	Leicester C	46	14	4	5	41	24	9	4	10	21	31	77	+7
5	Cambridge U	46	10	9	4	34	19	9	8	6	31	28	74	+18
6	Blackburn R	46	14	5	4	41	21	7	6	10	29	32	74	+17
7	Charlton Ath	46	9	7	7	25	23	11	4	8	29	25	71	+6
8	Swindon T	46	15	3	5	38	22	3	12	8	31	33	69	+14
9	Portsmouth	46	15	6	2	41	12	4	6	13	24	39	69	+14
10	Watford	46	9	5	9	25	23	9	6	8	26	25	65	+3
11	Wolverhampton W	46	11	6	6	36	24	7	4	12	25	30	64	+7
12	Southend U	46	11	5	7	37	26	6	6	11	26	37	62	0
13	Bristol R	46	11	9	3	43	29	5	5	13	17	34	62	−3
14	Tranmere R	46	9	9	5	37	32	5	10	8	19	24	61	0
15	Millwall	46	10	4	9	32	32	7	6	10	32	39	61	−7
16	Barnsley	46	11	4	8	27	25	5	5	11	19	32	59	−11
17	Bristol C	46	10	8	5	30	24	3	7	13	25	47	54	−16
18	Sunderland	46	10	8	5	36	23	4	3	16	25	42	53	−4
19	Grimsby T	46	7	5	11	25	28	7	6	10	22	34	53	−15
20	Newcastle U	46	9	6	8	38	30	4	5	14	28	54	52	−18
21	Oxford U	46	10	6	7	39	30	3	5	15	27	43	50	−7
22	Plymouth Arg	46	11	5	7	26	26	2	4	17	16	38	48	−22
23	Brighton & HA	46	7	7	9	36	37	5	4	14	20	40	47	−21
24	Port Vale	46	7	8	8	23	25	3	7	13	19	34	45	−17

DIVISION 3

		P	W	Home D	L	Goals F	A	W	Away D	L	Goals F	A	Pts	GD
1	Brentford	46	17	2	4	55	29	8	5	10	26	26	82	+26
2	Birmingham C	46	15	6	2	42	22	8	6	9	27	30	81	+17
3	Huddersfield T	46	15	4	4	36	15	7	8	8	23	23	78	+21
4	Stoke C	46	14	5	4	45	24	7	9	7	24	25	77	+20
5	Stockport Co	46	15	5	3	47	19	7	5	11	28	32	76	+24
6	Peterborough U	46	13	7	3	38	20	7	7	9	27	38	74	+7
7	WBA	46	12	6	5	45	25	7	8	8	19	24	71	+15
8	Bournemouth	46	13	4	6	33	18	7	7	9	19	30	71	+4
9	Fulham	46	11	7	5	29	16	8	6	9	28	37	70	+4
10	Leyton Orient	46	12	7	4	36	18	6	4	13	26	34	65	+10
11	Hartlepool U	46	12	5	6	30	21	6	6	11	27	36	65	0
12	Reading	46	9	8	6	33	27	7	5	11	26	35	61	−3
13	Bolton W	46	10	9	4	26	19	4	8	11	31	37	59	+1
14	Hull C	46	9	4	10	28	23	7	7	9	26	31	59	0
15	Wigan Ath	46	11	6	6	33	21	4	8	11	25	43	59	−6
16	Bradford C	46	8	10	5	36	30	5	9	9	26	31	58	+1
17	Preston NE	46	12	7	4	42	32	3	5	15	19	40	57	−11
18	Chester C	46	10	6	7	34	29	4	8	11	22	30	56	−3
19	Swansea C	46	10	9	4	35	24	4	5	14	20	41	56	−10
20	Exeter C	46	11	7	5	34	25	3	4	16	23	55	53	−23
21	Bury	46	8	7	8	31	31	5	5	13	24	43	51	−19
22	Shrewsbury T	46	7	7	9	30	31	5	4	14	23	37	47	−15
23	Torquay U	46	13	3	7	29	19	0	5	18	13	49	47	−26
24	Darlington	46	5	5	13	31	39	5	2	16	25	51	37	−34

DIVISION 4

		P	W	Home D	L	Goals F	A	W	Away D	L	Goals F	A	Pts	GD
1	Burnley	42	14	4	3	42	16	11	4	6	37	27	83	+36
2	Rotherham U	42	12	6	3	38	16	10	5	6	32	21	77	+33
3	Mansfield T	42	13	4	4	43	26	10	4	7	32	27	77	+22
4	Blackpool	42	17	3	1	48	13	5	7	9	23	32	76	+26
5	Scunthorpe U	42	14	5	2	39	18	7	4	10	25	41	72	+5
6	Crewe Alex	42	12	6	3	33	20	8	4	9	33	31	70	+15
7	Barnet	42	16	1	4	48	23	5	5	11	33	38	69	+20
8	Rochdale	42	12	6	3	34	22	6	7	8	23	31	67	+4
9	Cardiff C	42	13	3	5	42	26	4	12	5	24	27	66	+13
10	Lincoln C	42	9	5	7	21	24	8	6	7	29	20	62	+6
11	Gillingham	42	12	5	4	41	19	3	7	11	22	34	57	+10
12	Scarborough	42	12	5	4	39	28	3	7	11	25	40	57	−4
13	Chesterfield	42	6	7	8	26	28	8	4	9	23	33	53	−12
14	Wrexham	42	11	4	6	31	26	3	5	13	21	47	51	−21
15	Walsall	42	5	10	6	28	26	7	3	11	20	32	49	−10
16	Northampton T	42	5	9	7	25	23	6	4	11	21	34	46	−11
17	Hereford U	42	9	4	8	31	24	3	4	14	13	33	44	−13
18	Maidstone U	42	6	9	6	24	22	2	9	10	21	34	42	−11
19	York C	42	6	9	6	26	23	2	7	12	16	35	40	−16
20	Halifax T	42	7	5	9	23	35	3	3	15	11	40	38	−41
21	Doncaster R	42	6	2	13	21	35	3	6	12	19	30	35	−25
22	Carlisle U	42	5	9	7	24	27	2	4	15	17	40	34	−26

Aldershot's record expunged from the table.

ALL-TIME FOOTBALL LEAGUE TABLES
1888–1992

	P	W	D	L	Goals F	A
Aberdare Athletic	252	78	59	115	334	413
Accrington Stanley*	1542	544	298	700	2441	2954
Aldershot[1]	2346	789	605	952	3217	3632
Arsenal	3524	1537	870	1117	5845	4727
Ashington	328	109	71	148	489	650
Aston Villa	3660	1557	825	1278	6247	5456
Barnet	42	21	6	15	81	61
Barnsley	3504	1272	886	1346	4995	5276
Barrow	1924	624	414	886	2606	3349
Birmingham City	3578	1340	866	1372	5296	5274
Blackburn Rovers	3700	1442	890	1368	5812	5671
Blackpool	3468	1289	855	1324	5090	5132
Bolton Wanderers	3706	1442	863	1401	5605	5416
Bootle	22	8	3	11	49	63
AFC Bournemouth	2770	1046	724	1000	3845	3731
Bradford (Park Avenue)	2190	837	476	877	3516	3582
Bradford City	3376	1252	864	1260	4907	4846
Brentford	2882	1110	719	1053	4236	4092
Brighton & Hove Albion	2838	1137	709	992	4249	3920
Bristol City	3372	1314	847	1211	4939	4713
Bristol Rovers	2834	1066	714	1054	4241	4223
Burnley	3702	1451	874	1377	5628	5551
Burton United[2]	484	147	80	257	657	994
Burton Wanderers	90	42	13	35	167	146
Bury	3622	1358	847	1417	5377	5421
Cambridge United	988	356	272	360	1282	1330
Cardiff City	2762	1000	691	1071	3829	4160
Carlisle United	2490	900	591	999	3612	3893
Charlton Athletic	2702	976	671	1055	4016	4274
Chelsea	3146	1211	821	1114	4762	4641
Chester City	2432	853	615	964	3454	3612
Chesterfield	3194	1235	752	1207	4663	4529
Colchester United	1838	675	485	678	2647	2679
Coventry City	2806	1025	712	1069	4105	4141
Crewe Alexandra	2950	987	696	1267	4056	4842
Crystal Palace	2796	1030	746	1020	3973	3985
Darlington	2798	957	667	1174	4026	4540
Darwen	232	75	27	130	401	619
Derby County	3668	1454	870	1344	5874	5528
Doncaster Rovers	2834	1018	699	1117	4025	4362
Durham City	286	95	54	137	394	529
Everton	3648	1537	884	1227	6018	5201
Exeter City	2895	987	738	1170	3991	4455
Fulham	3116	1155	765	1196	4650	4608
Gainsborough Trinity	564	175	118	271	718	1029
Gateshead	1466	559	361	546	2292	2335
Gillingham	2682	940	699	1043	3591	3931
Glossop North End	618	197	136	285	829	1026
Grimsby Town	3630	1411	798	1421	5449	5529
Halifax Town	2842	906	734	1202	3649	4484
Hartlepool United	2844	955	630	1259	3833	4731
Hereford United	912	298	255	359	1098	1200
Huddersfield Town	3020	1174	774	1072	4380	4096
Hull City	3232	1244	841	1147	4775	4496
Ipswich Town	2016	831	489	696	3063	2815
Leeds United[3]	3124	1284	786	1054	4761	4288
Leicester City	3528	1313	884	1331	5445	5540
Leyton Orient	3232	1087	825	1320	4160	4731
Lincoln City	3514	1284	819	1411	5292	5544
Liverpool	3524	1650	851	1023	6071	4527
Loughborough Town	158	34	20	104	170	410
Luton Town	2842	1101	704	1037	4452	4186
Maidstone United	134	43	37	54	188	188
Manchester City	3558	1463	850	1245	5929	5314
Manchester United	3556	1568	872	1116	5956	4841
Mansfield Town	2426	894	619	913	3648	3621

	P	W	D	L	Goals F	A
Merthyr Town	420	115	106	199	524	779
Middlesbrough	3374	1287	805	1282	5188	5025
Middlesbrough Ironopolis	28	8	4	16	37	72
Millwall	2822	1114	732	976	4135	3839
Nelson	412	154	73	185	668	796
New Brighton	884	287	187	410	1191	1527
New Brighton Tower	102	48	24	30	194	148
Newcastle United	3544	1443	815	1286	5661	5174
Newport County	2672	888	625	1159	3700	4557
Northampton Town	2878	1119	659	1100	4433	4318
Northwich Victoria	50	12	5	33	72	156
Norwich City	2756	1012	736	1008	3988	4026
Nottingham Forest	3560	1338	879	1343	5275	5225
Notts County	3744	1402	907	1435	5505	5608
Oldham Athletic	3180	1191	799	1190	4671	4714
Oxford United	1330	454	387	489	1708	1747
Peterborough United	1472	584	414	474	2195	1923
Plymouth Argyle	2832	1096	725	1011	4288	4010
Portsmouth	2776	1028	718	1030	4141	4129
Port Vale[4]	3344	1188	865	1291	4595	4863
Preston North End	3726	1431	923	1372	5629	5409
Queen's Park Rangers	2776	1105	699	972	4176	3843
Reading	2892	1158	710	1024	4439	4129
Rochdale	2840	936	709	1195	3870	4553
Rotherham United[5]	2946	1111	676	1159	4425	4598
Scarborough	226	87	62	77	306	297
Scunthorpe United	1903	678	530	695	2625	2687
Sheffield United	3588	1443	849	1296	5677	5385
Sheffield Wednesday	3584	1422	880	1282	5557	5234
Shrewsbury Town	1898	662	515	721	2610	2709
Southampton	2744	1066	704	974	4247	4005
Southend United	2898	1101	705	1092	4274	4228
Southport	2200	723	568	909	2961	3488
Stalybridge Celtic	76	33	11	32	104	110
Stockport County	3448	1267	822	1359	4877	5060
Stoke City	3392	1223	829	1340	4715	4974
Sunderland	3630	1489	870	1271	5925	5336
Swansea City	2818	1035	671	1112	4076	4353
Swindon Town	2868	1089	744	1035	4286	4135
Thames	84	20	17	47	107	202
Torquay United	2604	921	658	1025	3641	4014
Tottenham Hotspur	3024	1275	735	1014	5065	4292
Tranmere Rovers	2844	1086	677	1081	4327	4227
Walsall	3076	1074	739	1263	4546	4883
Watford	2848	1073	729	1046	4130	4003
West Bromwich Albion	3680	1440	890	1350	5844	5530
West Ham United	2774	1060	678	1036	4304	4195
Wigan Athletic	644	262	173	209	903	806
Wigan Borough[6]	412	145	94	173	635	706
Wimbledon	644	265	181	198	961	840
Wolverhampton W	3690	1504	824	1362	4155	5669
Workington	1194	385	310	499	1525	1810
Wrexham	2824	1060	687	1077	4260	4186
York City	2504	878	620	1006	3672	3824

The above figures do not include games played at the start of season 1939–40 before the competition was abandoned because of the outbreak of World War II, nor do they include the old end-of-season Test matches or the modern Play-offs.

* Includes the original club known simply as Accrington but none of the games played during season 1961–62 when they resigned from the League.

[1] Games played 1991–92 expunged from the record.

[2] Includes Burton Swifts who amalgamated with Burton Wanderers to form Burton United in 1901.

[3] Includes Leeds City and the eight games played 1919–20.

[4] Includes only 34 games played 1919–20 when took over from Leeds City.

[5] Including Rotherham County who amalgamated with Rotherham Town to form Rotherham United in 1925.

[6] Games played in season 1931–32 prior to their resignation on 26 October were expunged from the record and therefore not included in these figures.

FOOTBALL LEAGUE 1888–89 to 1991–92

FOOTBALL LEAGUE

	First	Pts	Second	Pts	Third	Pts
1888–89a	Preston NE	40	Aston Villa	29	Wolverhampton W	28
1889–90a	Preston NE	33	Everton	31	Blackburn R	27
1890–91a	Everton	29	Preston NE	27	Notts Co	26
1891–92b	Sunderland	42	Preston NE	37	Bolton W	36

FIRST DIVISION

Maximum points: a 44; *b* 52; *c* 60; *d* 68; *e* 76; *f* 84; *g* 126; *h* 120; *k* 114.

	First	Pts	Second	Pts	Third	Pts
1892–93c	Sunderland	48	Preston NE	37	Everton	36
1893–94c	Aston Villa	44	Sunderland	38	Derby Co	36
1894–95c	Sunderland	47	Everton	42	Aston Villa	39
1895–96c	Aston Villa	45	Derby Co	41	Everton	39
1896–97c	Aston Villa	47	Sheffield U*	36	Derby Co	36
1897–98c	Sheffield U	42	Sunderland	37	Wolverhampton W*	35
1898–99d	Aston Villa	45	Liverpool	43	Burnley	39
1899–1900d	Aston Villa	50	Sheffield U	48	Sunderland	41
1900–01d	Liverpool	45	Sunderland	43	Notts Co	40
1901–02d	Sunderland	44	Everton	41	Newcastle U	37
1902–03d	The Wednesday	42	Aston Villa*	41	Sunderland	41
1903–04d	The Wednesday	47	Manchester C	44	Everton	43
1904–05d	Newcastle U	48	Everton	47	Manchester C	46
1905–06e	Liverpool	51	Preston NE	47	The Wednesday	44
1906–07e	Newcastle U	51	Bristol C	48	Everton*	45
1907–08e	Manchester U	52	Aston Villa*	43	Manchester C	43
1908–09e	Newcastle U	53	Everton	46	Sunderland	44
1909–10e	Aston Villa	53	Liverpool	48	Blackburn R*	45
1910–11e	Manchester U	52	Aston Villa	51	Sunderland*	45
1911–12e	Blackburn R	49	Everton	46	Newcastle U	44
1912–13e	Sunderland	54	Aston Villa	50	Sheffield W	49
1913–14e	Blackburn R	51	Aston Villa	44	Middlesbrough*	43
1914–15e	Everton	46	Oldham Ath	45	Blackburn R*	43
1919–20f	WBA	60	Burnley	51	Chelsea	49
1920–21f	Burnley	59	Manchester C	54	Bolton W	52
1921–22f	Liverpool	57	Tottenham H	51	Burnley	49
1922–23f	Liverpool	60	Sunderland	54	Huddersfield T	53
1923–24f	Huddersfield T*	57	Cardiff C	57	Sunderland	53
1924–25f	Huddersfield T	58	WBA	56	Bolton W	55
1925–26f	Huddersfield T	57	Arsenal	52	Sunderland	48
1926–27f	Newcastle U	56	Huddersfield T	51	Sunderland	49
1927–28f	Everton	53	Huddersfield T	51	Leicester C	48
1928–29f	Sheffield W	52	Leicester C	51	Aston Villa	50
1929–30f	Sheffield W	60	Derby Co	50	Manchester C*	47
1930–31f	Arsenal	66	Aston Villa	59	Sheffield W	52
1931–32f	Everton	56	Arsenal	54	Sheffield W	50
1932–33f	Arsenal	58	Aston Villa	54	Sheffield W	51
1933–34f	Arsenal	59	Huddersfield T	56	Tottenham H	49
1934–35f	Arsenal	58	Sunderland	54	Sheffield W	49
1935–36f	Sunderland	56	Derby Co*	48	Huddersfield T	48
1936–37f	Manchester C	57	Charlton Ath	54	Arsenal	52
1937–38f	Arsenal	52	Wolverhampton W	51	Preston NE	49
1938–39f	Everton	59	Wolverhampton W	55	Charlton Ath	50
1946–47f	Liverpool	57	Manchester U*	56	Wolverhampton W	56
1947–48f	Arsenal	59	Manchester U*	52	Burnley	52
1948–49f	Portsmouth	58	Manchester U*	53	Derby Co	53
1949–50f	Portsmouth*	53	Wolverhampton W	53	Sunderland	52
1950–51f	Tottenham H	60	Manchester U	56	Blackpool	50
1951–52f	Manchester U	57	Tottenham H*	53	Arsenal	53
1952–53f	Arsenal*	54	Preston NE	54	Wolverhampton W	51
1953–54f	Wolverhampton W	57	WBA	53	Huddersfield T	51
1954–55f	Chelsea	52	Wolverhampton W*	48	Portsmouth*	48
1955–56f	Manchester U	60	Blackpool*	49	Wolverhampton W	49
1956–57f	Manchester U	64	Tottenham H*	56	Preston NE	56
1957–58f	Wolverhampton W	64	Preston NE	59	Tottenham H	51
1958–59f	Wolverhampton W	61	Manchester U	55	Arsenal*	50
1959–60f	Burnley	55	Wolverhampton W	54	Tottenham H	53
1960–61f	Tottenham H	66	Sheffield W	58	Wolverhampton W	57
1961–62f	Ipswich T	56	Burnley	53	Tottenham H	52
1962–63f	Everton	61	Tottenham H	55	Burnley	54
1963–64f	Liverpool	57	Manchester U	53	Everton	52
1964–65f	Manchester U*	61	Leeds U	61	Chelsea	56
1965–66f	Liverpool	61	Leeds U*	55	Burnley	55
1966–67f	Manchester U	60	Nottingham F*	56	Tottenham H	56

* *Won or placed on goal average.*

	First	Pts	Second	Pts	Third	Pts
1967–68f	Manchester C	58	Manchester U	56	Liverpool	55
1968–69f	Leeds U	67	Liverpool	61	Everton	57
1969–70f	Everton	66	Leeds U	57	Chelsea	55
1970–71f	Arsenal	65	Leeds U	64	Tottenham H*	52
1971–72f	Derby Co	58	Leeds U*	57	Liverpool*	57
1972–73f	Liverpool	60	Arsenal	57	Leeds U	53
1973–74f	Leeds U	62	Liverpool	57	Derby Co	48
1974–75f	Derby Co	53	Liverpool*	51	Ipswich T	57
1975–76f	Liverpool	60	QPR	59	Manchester U	56
1976–77f	Liverpool	57	Manchester C	56	Ipswich T	52
1977–78f	Nottingham F	64	Liverpool	57	Everton	55
1978–79f	Liverpool	68	Nottingham F	60	WBA	59
1979–80f	Liverpool	60	Manchester U	58	Ipswich T	53
1980–81f	Aston Villa	60	Ipswich T	56	Arsenal	53
1981–82g	Liverpool	87	Ipswich T	83	Manchester U	78
1982–83g	Liverpool	82	Watford	71	Manchester U	70
1983–84g	Liverpool	80	Southampton	77	Nottingham F*	74
1984–85g	Everton	90	Liverpool*	77	Tottenham H	77
1985–86g	Liverpool	88	Everton	86	West Ham U	84
1986–87g	Everton	86	Liverpool	77	Tottenham H	71
1987–88h	Liverpool	90	Manchester U	81	Nottingham F	73
1988–89k	Arsenal*	76	Liverpool	76	Nottingham F	64
1989–90k	Liverpool	79	Aston Villa	70	Tottenham H	63
1990–91k	Arsenal†	83	Liverpool	76	Crystal Palace	69
1991–92g	Leeds U	82	Manchester U	78	Sheffield W	75

No official competition during 1915–19 and 1939–46.
† *2 pts deducted.*

SECOND DIVISION
Maximum points: a 44; *b* 56; *c* 60; *d* 68; *e* 76; *f* 84; *g* 126; *h* 132; *k* 138.

	First	Pts	Second	Pts	Third	Pts
1892–93a	Small Heath	36	Sheffield U	35	Darwen	30
1893–94b	Liverpool	50	Small Heath	42	Notts Co	39
1894–95c	Bury	48	Notts Co	39	Newton Heath*	38
1895–96c	Liverpool*	46	Manchester C	46	Grimsby T*	42
1896–97c	Notts Co	42	Newton Heath	39	Grimsby T	38
1897–98c	Burnley	48	Newcastle U	45	Manchester C	39
1898–99d	Manchester C	52	Glossop NE	46	Leicester Fosse	45
1899–1900d	The Wednesday	54	Bolton W	52	Small Heath	46
1900–01d	Grimsby T	49	Small Heath	48	Burnley	44
1901–02d	WBA	55	Middlesbrough	51	Preston NE*	42
1902–03d	Manchester C	54	Small Heath	51	Woolwich A	48
1903–04d	Preston NE	50	Woolwich A	49	Manchester U	48
1904–05d	Liverpool	58	Bolton W	56	Manchester U	53
1905–06e	Bristol C	66	Manchester U	62	Chelsea	53
1906–07e	Nottingham F	60	Chelsea	57	Leicester Fosse	48
1907–08e	Bradford C	54	Leicester Fosse	52	Oldham Ath	50
1908–09e	Bolton W	52	Tottenham H*	51	WBA	51
1909–10e	Manchester C	54	Oldham Ath*	53	Hull C*	53
1910–11e	WBA	53	Bolton W	51	Chelsea	49
1911–12e	Derby Co*	54	Chelsea	54	Burnley	52
1912–13e	Preston NE	53	Burnley	50	Birmingham	46
1913–14e	Notts Co	53	Bradford PA*	49	Woolwich A	49
1914–15e	Derby Co	53	Preston NE	50	Barnsley	47
1919–20f	Tottenham H	70	Huddersfield T	64	Birmingham	56
1920–21f	Birmingham*	58	Cardiff C	58	Bristol C	51
1921–22f	Nottingham F	56	Stoke C*	52	Barnsley	52
1922–23f	Notts Co	53	West Ham U*	51	Leicester C	51
1923–24f	Leeds U	54	Bury*	51	Derby Co	51
1924–25f	Leicester C	59	Manchester U	57	Derby Co	55
1925–26f	Sheffield W	60	Derby Co	57	Chelsea	52
1926–27f	Middlesbrough	62	Portsmouth*	54	Manchester C	54
1927–28f	Manchester C	59	Leeds U	57	Chelsea	54
1928–29f	Middlesbrough	55	Grimsby T	53	Bradford*	48
1929–30f	Blackpool	58	Chelsea	55	Oldham Ath	53
1930–31f	Everton	61	WBA	54	Tottenham H	51
1931–32f	Wolverhampton W	56	Leeds U	54	Stoke C	52
1932–33f	Stoke C	56	Tottenham H	55	Fulham	50
1933–34f	Grimsby T	59	Preston NE	52	Bolton W*	51
1934–35f	Brentford	61	Bolton W*	56	West Ham U	56
1935–36f	Manchester U	56	Charlton Ath	55	Sheffield U*	52
1936–37f	Leicester C	56	Blackpool	55	Bury	52
1937–38f	Aston Villa	57	Manchester U*	53	Sheffield U	53
1938–39f	Blackburn R	55	Sheffield U	54	Sheffield W	53
1946–47f	Manchester C	62	Burnley	58	Birmingham C	55
1947–48f	Birmingham C	59	Newcastle U	56	Southampton	52
1948–49f	Fulham	57	WBA	56	Southampton	55
1949–50f	Tottenham H	61	Sheffield W*	52	Sheffield U*	52

* *Won or placed on goal average/goal difference.*

	First	Pts	Second	Pts	Third	Pts
1950–51f	Preston NE	57	Manchester C	52	Cardiff C	50
1951–52f	Sheffield W	53	Cardiff C*	51	Birmingham C	51
1952–53f	Sheffield U	60	Huddersfield T	58	Luton T	52
1953–54f	Leicester C*	56	Everton	56	Blackburn R	55
1954–55f	Birmingham C*	54	Luton T*	54	Rotherham U	54
1955–56f	Sheffield W	55	Leeds U	52	Liverpool*	48
1956–57f	Leicester C	61	Nottingham F	54	Liverpool	53
1957–58f	West Ham U	57	Blackburn R	56	Charlton Ath	55
1958–59f	Sheffield W	62	Fulham	60	Sheffield U*	53
1959–60f	Aston Villa	59	Cardiff C	58	Liverpool*	50
1960–61f	Ipswich T	59	Sheffield U	58	Liverpool	52
1961–62f	Liverpool	62	Leyton O	54	Sunderland	53
1962–63f	Stoke C	53	Chelsea*	52	Sunderland	52
1963–64f	Leeds U	63	Sunderland	61	Preston NE	56
1964–65f	Newcastle U	57	Northampton T	56	Bolton W	50
1965–66f	Manchester C	59	Southampton	54	Coventry C	53
1966–67f	Coventry C	59	Wolverhampton W	58	Carlisle U	52
1967–68f	Ipswich T	59	QPR*	58	Blackpool	58
1968–69f	Derby Co	63	Crystal Palace	56	Charlton Ath	50
1969–70f	Huddersfield T	60	Blackpool	53	Leicester C	51
1970–71f	Leicester C	59	Sheffield U	56	Cardiff C*	53
1971–72f	Norwich C	57	Birmingham C	56	Millwall	55
1972–73f	Burnley	62	QPR	61	Aston Villa	50
1973–74f	Middlesbrough	65	Luton T	50	Carlisle U	49
1974–75f	Manchester U	61	Aston Villa	58	Norwich C	53
1975–76f	Sunderland	56	Bristol C*	53	WBA	53
1976–77f	Wolverhampton W	57	Chelsea	55	Nottingham F	52
1977–78f	Bolton W	58	Southampton	57	Tottenham H*	56
1978–79f	Crystal Palace	57	Brighton*	56	Stoke C	56
1979–80f	Leicester C	55	Sunderland	54	Birmingham C*	53
1980–81f	West Ham U	66	Notts Co	53	Swansea C	50
1981–82g	Luton T	88	Watford	80	Norwich C	71
1982–83g	QPR	85	Wolverhampton W	75	Leicester C	70
1983–84g	Chelsea*	88	Sheffield W	88	Newcastle U	80
1984–85g	Oxford U	84	Birmingham C	82	Manchester C	74
1985–86g	Norwich C	84	Charlton Ath	77	Wimbledon	76
1986–87g	Derby Co	84	Portsmouth	78	Oldham Ath††	75
1987–88h	Millwall	82	Aston Villa*	78	Middlesbrough	78
1988–89k	Chelsea	99	Manchester C	82	Crystal Palace	81
1989–90k	Leeds U*	85	Sheffield U	85	Newcastle U††	80
1990–91k	Oldham Ath	88	West Ham U	87	Sheffield W	82
1991–92k	Ipswich T	84	Middlesbrough	80	Derby Co	78

No competition during 1915–19 and 1939–46.
††Not promoted after play-offs.

THIRD DIVISION

Maximum points: 92; 138 from 1981–82.

		Pts		Pts		Pts
1958–59	Plymouth Arg	62	Hull C	61	Brentford*	57
1959–60	Southampton	61	Norwich C	59	Shrewsbury T*	52
1960–61	Bury	68	Walsall	62	QPR	60
1961–62	Portsmouth	65	Grimsby T	62	Bournemouth*	59
1962–63	Northampton T	62	Swindon T	58	Port Vale	54
1963–64	Coventry C*	60	Crystal Palace	60	Watford	58
1964–65	Carlisle U	60	Bristol C*	59	Mansfield T	59
1965–66	Hull C	69	Millwall	65	QPR	57
1966–67	QPR	67	Middlesbrough	55	Watford	54
1967–68	Oxford U	57	Bury	56	Shrewsbury T	55
1968–69	Watford*	64	Swindon T	64	Luton T	61
1969–70	Orient	62	Luton T	60	Bristol R	56
1970–71	Preston NE	61	Fulham	60	Halifax T	56
1971–72	Aston Villa	70	Brighton	65	Bournemouth*	62
1972–73	Bolton W	61	Notts Co	57	Blackburn R	55
1973–74	Oldham Ath	62	Bristol R*	61	York C	61
1974–75	Blackburn R	60	Plymouth Arg	59	Charlton Ath	55
1975–76	Hereford U	63	Cardiff C	57	Millwall	56
1976–77	Mansfield T	64	Brighton & HA	61	Crystal Palace*	59
1977–78	Wrexham	61	Cambridge U	58	Preston NE*	56
1978–79	Shrewsbury T	61	Watford*	60	Swansea C	60
1979–80	Grimsby T	62	Blackburn R	59	Sheffield W	58
1980–81	Rotherham U	61	Barnsley*	59	Charlton Ath	59
1981–82	Burnley*	80	Carlisle U	80	Fulham	78
1982–83	Portsmouth	91	Cardiff C	86	Huddersfield T	82
1983–84	Oxford U	95	Wimbledon	87	Sheffield U*	83
1984–85	Bradford C	94	Millwall	90	Hull C	87
1985–86	Reading	94	Plymouth Arg	87	Derby Co	84
1986–87	Bournemouth	97	Middlesbrough	94	Swindon T	87
1987–88	Sunderland	93	Brighton & HA	84	Walsall	82
1988–89	Wolverhampton W	92	Sheffield U	84	Port Vale	84
1989–90	Bristol R	93	Bristol C	91	Notts Co	87
1990–91	Cambridge U	86	Southend U	85	Grimsby T*	83
1991–92	Brentford	82	Birmingham C	81	Huddersfield T	78

* Won or placed on goal average/goal difference.

FOURTH DIVISION
Maximum points: 92; 138 from 1981–82.

	First	Pts	Second	Pts	Third	Pts	Fourth	Pts
1958–59	Port Vale	64	Coventry C*	60	York C	60	Shrewsbury T	58
1959–60	Walsall	65	Notts Co*	60	Torquay U	60	Watford	57
1960–61	Peterborough U	66	Crystal Palace	64	Northampton T*	60	Bradford PA	60
1961–62†	Millwall	56	Colchester U	55	Wrexham	53	Carlisle U	52
1962–63	Brentford	62	Oldham Ath*	59	Crewe Alex	59	Mansfield T*	57
1963–64	Gillingham*	60	Carlisle U	60	Workington T	59	Exeter C	58
1964–65	Brighton	63	Millwall*	62	York C	62	Oxford U	61
1965–66	Doncaster R*	59	Darlington	59	Torquay U	58	Colchester U*	56
1966–67	Stockport Co	64	Southport*	59	Barrow	59	Tranmere R	58
1967–68	Luton T	66	Barnsley	61	Hartlepool U	60	Crewe Alex	58
1968–69	Doncaster R	59	Halifax T	57	Rochdale*	56	Bradford C	56
1969–70	Chesterfield	64	Wrexham	61	Swansea C	60	Port Vale	59
1970–71	Notts Co	69	Bournemouth	60	Oldham Ath	59	York C	56
1971–72	Grimsby T	63	Southend U	60	Brentford	59	Scunthorpe U	57
1972–73	Southport	62	Hereford U	58	Cambridge U	57	Aldershot*	56
1973–74	Peterborough U	65	Gillingham	62	Colchester U	60	Bury	59
1974–75	Mansfield T	68	Shrewsbury T	62	Rotherham U	59	Chester*	57
1975–76	Lincoln C	74	Northampton T	68	Reading	60	Tranmere R	58
1976–77	Cambridge U	65	Exeter C	62	Colchester U*	59	Bradford C	59
1977–78	Watford	71	Southend U	60	Swansea C*	56	Brentford	56
1978–79	Reading	65	Grimsby T*	61	Wimbledon*	61	Barnsley	61
1979–80	Huddersfield T	66	Walsall	64	Newport Co	61	Portsmouth*	60
1980–81	Southend U	67	Lincoln C	65	Doncaster R	56	Wimbledon	55
1981–82	Sheffield U	96	Bradford C*	91	Wigan Ath	91	AFC Bournemouth	88
1982–83	Wimbledon	98	Hull C	90	Port Vale	88	Scunthorpe U	83
1983–84	York C	101	Doncaster R	85	Reading*	82	Bristol C	82
1984–85	Chesterfield	91	Blackpool	86	Darlington	85	Bury	84
1985–86	Swindon T	102	Chester C	84	Mansfield T	81	Port Vale	79
1986–87	Northampton T	99	Preston NE	90	Southend U	80	Wolverhampton W††	79
1987–88	Wolverhampton W	90	Cardiff C	85	Bolton W	78	Scunthorpe U††	77
1988–89	Rotherham U	82	Tranmere R	80	Crewe Alex	78	Scunthorpe U††	77
1989–90	Exeter C	89	Grimsby T	79	Southend U	75	Stockport Co††	74
1990–91	Darlington	83	Stockport Co*	82	Hartlepool U	82	Peterborough U	80
1991–92†*	Burnley	80	Rotherham U*	77	Mansfield T	77	Blackpool	76

†*Maximum points:* 88 owing to Accrington Stanley's resignation.   ††*Not promoted after play-offs.*
†* *Maximum points:* 126 owing to Aldershot being expelled.

THIRD DIVISION—SOUTH (1920–1958)
Maximum points: a 84; b 92.

1920–21a	Crystal Palace	59	Southampton	54	QPR	53
1921–22a	Southampton*	61	Plymouth Arg	61	Portsmouth	53
1922–23a	Bristol C	59	Plymouth Arg*	53	Swansea T	53
1923–24a	Portsmouth	59	Plymouth Arg	55	Millwall	54
1924–25a	Swansea T	57	Plymouth Arg	56	Bristol C	53
1925–26a	Reading	57	Plymouth Arg	56	Millwall	53
1926–27a	Bristol C	62	Plymouth Arg	60	Millwall	56
1927–28a	Millwall	65	Northampton T	55	Plymouth Arg	53
1928–29a	Charlton Ath*	54	Crystal Palace	54	Northampton T*	52
1929–30a	Plymouth Arg	68	Brentford	61	QPR	51
1930–31a	Notts Co	59	Crystal Palace	51	Brentford	50
1931–32a	Fulham	57	Reading	55	Southend U	53
1932–33a	Brentford	62	Exeter C	58	Norwich C	57
1933–34a	Norwich C	61	Coventry C*	54	Reading*	54
1934–35a	Charlton Ath	61	Reading	53	Coventry C	51
1935–36a	Coventry C	57	Luton T	56	Reading	54
1936–37a	Luton T	58	Notts Co	56	Brighton	53
1937–38a	Millwall	56	Bristol C	55	QPR*	53
1938–39a	Newport Co	55	Crystal Palace	52	Brighton	49
1939–46	Competition cancelled owing to war.					
1946–47a	Cardiff C	66	QPR	57	Bristol C	51
1947–48a	QPR	61	Bournemouth	57	Walsall	51
1948–49a	Swansea T	62	Reading	55	Bournemouth	52
1949–50a	Notts Co	58	Northampton T*	51	Southend U	51
1950–51b	Nottingham F	70	Norwich C	64	Reading*	57
1951–52b	Plymouth Arg	66	Reading*	61	Norwich C	61
1952–53b	Bristol R	64	Millwall*	62	Northampton T	62
1953–54b	Ipswich T	64	Brighton	61	Bristol C	56
1954–55b	Bristol C	70	Leyton O	61	Southampton	59
1955–56b	Leyton O	66	Brighton	65	Ipswich T	64
1956–57b	Ipswich T*	59	Torquay U	59	Colchester U	58
1957–58b	Brighton	60	Brentford*	58	Plymouth Arg	58

* *Won or placed on goal average.*

THIRD DIVISION—NORTH (1921–1958)

Maximum points: a 76; b 84; c 80; d 92.

	First	Pts	Second	Pts	Third	Pts
1921–22a	Stockport Co	56	Darlington*	50	Grimsby T	50
1922–23a	Nelson	51	Bradford PA	47	Walsall	46
1923–24b	Wolverhampton W	63	Rochdale	62	Chesterfield	54
1924–25b	Darlington	58	Nelson*	53	New Brighton	53
1925–26b	Grimsby T	61	Bradford PA	60	Rochdale	59
1926–27b	Stoke C	63	Rochdale	58	Bradford PA	55
1927–28b	Bradford PA	63	Lincoln C	55	Stockport Co	54
1928–29g	Bradford C	63	Stockport Co	62	Wrexham	52
1929–30b	Port Vale	67	Stockport Co	63	Darlington*	50
1930–31b	Chesterfield	58	Lincoln C	57	Wrexham*	54
1931–32c	Lincoln C*	57	Gateshead	57	Chester	50
1932–33b	Hull C	59	Wrexham	57	Stockport Co	54
1933–34b	Barnsley	62	Chesterfield	61	Stockport Co	59
1934–35b	Doncaster R	57	Halifax T	55	Chester	54
1935–36b	Chesterfield	60	Chester*	55	Tranmere R	55
1936–37b	Stockport Co	60	Lincoln C	57	Chester	53
1937–38b	Tranmere R	56	Doncaster R	54	Hull C	53
1938–39b	Barnsley	67	Doncaster R	56	Bradford C	52
1939–46	Competition cancelled owing to war.					
1946–47b	Doncaster R	72	Rotherham U	64	Chester	56
1947–48b	Lincoln C	60	Rotherham U	59	Wrexham	50
1948–49b	Hull C	65	Rotherham U	62	Doncaster R	50
1949–50b	Doncaster R	55	Gateshead	53	Rochdale*	51
1950–51d	Rotherham U	71	Mansfield T	64	Carlisle U	62
1951–52d	Lincoln C	69	Grimsby T	66	Stockport Co	59
1952–53d	Oldham Ath	59	Port Vale	58	Wrexham	56
1953–54d	Port Vale	69	Barnsley	58	Scunthorpe U	57
1954–55d	Barnsley	65	Accrington S	61	Scunthorpe U*	58
1955–56d	Grimsby T	68	Derby Co	63	Accrington S	59
1956–57d	Derby Co	63	Hartlepool U	59	Accrington S*	58
1957–58d	Scunthorpe U	66	Accrington S	59	Bradford C	57

* Won or placed on goal average.

PROMOTED AFTER PLAY-OFFS
(Not accounted for in previous section)

1986–87	Aldershot to Division 3.
1987–88	Swansea C to Division 3.
1988–89	Leyton O to Division 3.
1989–90	Cambridge U to Division 3; Sunderland to Division 1.
1990–91	Notts Co to Division 1; Tranmere R to Division 2; Torquay U to Division 3.
1991–92	Blackburn R to Division 1; Peterborough U to Division 2 (Divisions to be FA Premier League and First Division for 1992–93).

LEAGUE TITLE WINS

LEAGUE DIVISION 1 – Liverpool 18, Arsenal 10, Everton 9, Manchester U 7, Aston Villa 7, Sunderland 6, Newcastle U 4, Sheffield W 4, Huddersfield T 3, Leeds U 3, Wolverhampton W 3, Blackburn R 2, Portsmouth 2, Preston NE 2, Burnley 2, Manchester C 2, Tottenham H 2, Derby Co 2, Chelsea, Sheffield U, WBA, Ipswich T, Nottingham F 1 each.

LEAGUE DIVISION 2 – Leicester C 6, Manchester C 6, Sheffield W 5, Birmingham C (one as Small Heath) 4, Derby Co 4, Liverpool 4, Ipswich T 3, Leeds U 3, Notts Co 3, Preston NE 3, Middlesbrough 3, Grimsby T 2, Norwich C 2, Nottingham F 2, Tottenham H 2, WBA 2, Aston Villa 2, Stoke C 2, Burnley 2, Chelsea 2, Manchester U 2, West Ham U 2, Wolverhampton W 2, Bolton W 2, Huddersfield T, Bristol C, Brentford, Bury, Bradford C, Everton, Fulham, Sheffield U, Newcastle U, Coventry C, Blackpool, Blackburn R, Sunderland, Crystal Palace, Luton T, QPR, Oxford U, Millwall, Oldham Ath 1 each.

LEAGUE DIVISION 3 – Portsmouth 2, Oxford U 2, Plymouth Arg, Southampton, Bury, Northampton T, Coventry C, Carlisle U, Hull C, QPR, Watford, Leyton O, Preston NE, Aston Villa, Bolton W, Oldham Ath, Blackburn R, Hereford U, Mansfield T, Wrexham, Shrewsbury T, Grimsby T, Rotherham U, Burnley, Bradford C, Bournemouth, Reading, Sunderland, Wolverhampton W, Bristol R, Cambridge U, Brentford 1 each.

LEAGUE DIVISION 4 – Chesterfield 2, Doncaster R 2, Peterborough U 2, Port Vale, Walsall, Millwall, Brentford, Gillingham, Brighton, Stockport Co, Luton T, Notts Co, Grimsby T, Southport, Mansfield T, Lincoln C, Cambridge U, Watford, Reading, Huddersfield T, Southend U, Sheffield U, Wimbledon, York C, Swindon T, Northampton T, Wolverhampton W, Rotherham U, Exeter C, Darlington, Burnley 1 each.

To 1957–58

DIVISION 3 (South) – Bristol C 3; Charlton Ath, Ipswich T, Millwall, Notts Co, Plymouth Arg, Swansea T 2 each; Brentford, Bristol R, Cardiff C, Crystal Palace, Coventry C, Fulham, Leyton O, Luton T, Newport Co, Nottingham F, Norwich C, Portsmouth, QPR, Reading, Southampton, Brighton 1 each.

DIVISION 3 (North) – Barnsley, Doncaster R, Lincoln C 3 each; Chesterfield, Grimsby T, Hull C, Port Vale, Stockport Co 2 each; Bradford PA, Bradford C, Darlington, Derby Co, Nelson, Oldham Ath, Rotherham U, Scunthorpe U, Stoke C, Tranmere R, Wolverhampton W 1 each.

RELEGATED CLUBS

1891–92 League extended. Newton Heath, Sheffield W and Nottingham F admitted. *Second Division formed* including Darwen.

1892–93 In Test matches, Sheffield U and Darwen won promotion in place of Notts Co and Accrington S.

1893–94 In Tests, Liverpool and Small Heath won promotion. Newton Heath and Darwen relegated.

1894–95 After Tests, Bury promoted, Liverpool relegated.

1895–96 After Tests, Liverpool promoted, Small Heath relegated.

1896–97 After Tests, Notts Co promoted, Burnley relegated.

1897–98 Test system abolished after success of Stoke C and Burnley. League extended. Blackburn R and Newcastle U elected to First Division. *Automatic promotion and relegation introduced.*

DIVISION 1 TO DIVISION 2

1898–99 Bolton W and Sheffield W
1899–1900 Burnley and Glossop
1900–01 Preston NE and WBA
1901–02 Small Heath and Manchester C
1902–03 Grimsby T and Bolton W
1903–04 Liverpool and WBA
1904–05 League extended. Bury and Notts Co, two bottom clubs in First Division, re-elected.
1905–06 Nottingham F and Wolverhampton W
1906–07 Derby Co and Stoke C
1907–08 Bolton W and Birmingham C
1908–09 Manchester C and Leicester Fosse
1909–10 Bolton W and Chelsea
1910–11 Bristol C and Nottingham F
1911–12 Preston NE and Bury
1912–13 Notts Co and Woolwich Arsenal
1913–14 Preston NE and Derby Co
1914–15 Tottenham H and Chelsea*
1919–20 Notts Co and Sheffield W
1920–21 Derby Co and Bradford PA
1921–22 Bradford C and Manchester U
1922–23 Stoke C and Oldham Ath
1923–24 Chelsea and Middlesbrough
1924–25 Preston NE and Nottingham F
1925–26 Manchester C and Notts Co
1926–27 Leeds U and WBA
1927–28 Tottenham H and Middlesbrough
1928–29 Bury and Cardiff C
1929–30 Burnley and Everton
1930–31 Leeds U and Manchester U
1931–32 Grimsby T and West Ham U
1932–33 Bolton W and Blackpool
1933–34 Newcastle U and Sheffield U
1934–35 Leicester C and Tottenham H
1935–36 Aston Villa and Blackburn R
1936–37 Manchester U and Sheffield W
1937–38 Manchester C and WBA
1938–39 Birmingham C and Leicester C
1946–47 Brentford and Leeds U
1947–48 Blackburn R and Grimsby T
1948–49 Preston NE and Sheffield U
1949–50 Manchester C and Birmingham C

1950–51 Sheffield W and Everton
1951–52 Huddersfield and Fulham
1952–53 Stoke C and Derby Co
1953–54 Middlesbrough and Liverpool
1954–55 Leicester C and Sheffield W
1955–56 Huddersfield and Sheffield U
1956–57 Charlton Ath and Cardiff C
1957–58 Sheffield W and Sunderland
1958–59 Portsmouth and Aston Villa
1959–60 Luton T and Leeds U
1960–61 Preston NE and Newcastle U
1961–62 Chelsea and Cardiff C
1962–63 Manchester C and Leyton O
1963–64 Bolton W and Ipswich T
1964–65 Wolverhampton W and Birmingham C
1965–66 Northampton T and Blackburn R
1966–67 Aston Villa and Blackpool
1967–68 Fulham and Sheffield U
1968–69 Leicester C and QPR
1969–70 Sunderland and Sheffield W
1970–71 Burnley and Blackpool
1971–72 Huddersfield T and Nottingham F
1972–73 Crystal Palace and WBA
1973–74 Southampton, Manchester U, Norwich C
1974–75 Luton T, Chelsea, Carlisle U
1975–76 Wolverhampton W, Burnley, Sheffield U
1976–77 Sunderland, Stoke C, Tottenham H
1977–78 West Ham U, Newcastle U, Leicester C
1978–79 QPR, Birmingham C, Chelsea
1979–80 Bristol C, Derby Co, Bolton W
1980–81 Norwich C, Leicester C, Crystal Palace
1981–82 Leeds U, Wolverhampton W, Middlesbrough
1982–83 Manchester C, Swansea C, Brighton & HA
1983–84 Birmingham C, Notts Co, Wolverhampton W
1984–85 Norwich C, Sunderland, Stoke C
1985–86 Ipswich T, Birmingham C, WBA
1986–87 Leicester C, Manchester C, Aston Villa
1987–88 Chelsea**, Portsmouth, Watford, Oxford U
1988–89 Middlesbrough, West Ham U, Newcastle U
1989–90 Sheffield W, Charlton Ath, Millwall
1990–91 Sunderland and Derby Co
1991–92 Luton T, Notts Co and West Ham U

* *Subsequently re-elected to Division 1 when League was extended after the War.*
** *Relegated after play-offs.*

DIVISION 2 TO DIVISION 3

1920–21 Stockport Co
1921–22 Bradford and Bristol C
1922–23 Rotherham C and Wolverhampton W
1923–24 Nelson and Bristol C
1924–25 Crystal Palace and Coventry C
1925–26 Stoke C and Stockport Co
1926–27 Darlington and Bradford C
1927–28 Fulham and South Shields
1928–29 Port Vale and Clapton O
1929–30 Hull C and Notts Co
1930–31 Reading and Cardiff C
1931–32 Barnsley and Bristol C
1932–33 Chesterfield and Charlton Ath
1933–34 Millwall and Lincoln C
1934–35 Oldham Ath and Notts Co
1935–36 Port Vale and Hull C
1936–37 Doncaster R and Bradford C

1937–38 Barnsley and Stockport Co
1938–39 Norwich C and Tranmere R
1946–47 Swansea T and Newport Co
1947–48 Doncaster R and Millwall
1948–49 Nottingham F and Lincoln C
1949–50 Plymouth Arg and Bradford
1950–51 Grimsby T and Chesterfield
1951–52 Coventry C and QPR
1952–53 Southampton and Barnsley
1953–54 Brentford and Oldham Ath
1954–55 Ipswich T and Derby Co
1955–56 Plymouth Arg and Hull C
1956–57 Port Vale and Bury
1957–58 Doncaster R and Notts Co
1958–59 Barnsley and Grimsby T
1959–60 Bristol C and Hull C
1960–61 Lincoln C and Portsmouth

1961–62 Brighton & HA and Bristol R
1962–63 Walsall and Luton T
1963–64 Grimsby T and Scunthorpe U
1964–65 Swindon T and Swansea T
1965–66 Middlesbrough and Leyton O
1966–67 Northampton T and Bury
1967–68 Plymouth Arg and Rotherham U
1968–69 Fulham and Bury
1969–70 Preston NE and Aston Villa
1970–71 Blackburn R and Bolton W
1971–72 Charlton Ath and Watford
1972–73 Huddersfield T and Brighton & HA
1973–74 Crystal Palace, Preston NE, Swindon T
1974–75 Millwall, Cardiff C, Sheffield W
1975–76 Oxford U, York C. Portsmouth
1976–77 Carlisle U, Plymouth Arg, Hereford U

1977–78 Blackpool, Mansfield T, Hull C
1978–79 Sheffield U, Millwall, Blackburn R
1979–80 Fulham, Burnley, Charlton Ath
1980–81 Preston NE, Bristol C, Bristol R
1981–82 Cardiff C, Wrexham, Orient
1982–83 Rotherham U, Burnley, Bolton W
1983–84 Derby Co, Swansea C, Cambridge U
1984–85 Notts Co, Cardiff C, Wolverhampton W
1985–86 Carlisle U, Middlesbrough, Fulham
1986–87 Sunderland**, Grimsby T, Brighton & HA
1987–88 Huddersfield T, Reading, Sheffield U**
1988–89 Shrewsbury T, Birmingham C, Walsall
1989–90 Bournemouth, Bradford, Stoke C
1990–91 WBA and Hull C
1991–92 Plymouth Arg, Brighton & HA, Port Vale

DIVISION 3 TO DIVISION 4

1958–59 Rochdale, Notts Co, Doncaster R, Stockport
1959–60 Accrington S, Wrexham, Mansfield T, York C
1960–61 Chesterfield, Colchester U, Bradford C, Tranmere R
1961–62 Newport Co, Brentford, Lincoln C, Torquay U
1962–63 Bradford PA, Brighton, Carlisle U, Halifax T
1963–64 Millwall, Crewe Alex, Wrexham, Notts Co
1964–65 Luton T, Port Vale, Colchester U, Barnsley
1965–66 Southend U, Exeter C, Brentford, York C
1966–67 Doncaster R, Workington, Darlington, Swansea T
1967–68 Scunthorpe U, Colchester U, Grimsby T, Peterborough U (demoted)
1968–69 Oldham Ath, Crewe Alex, Hartlepool, Northampton
1969–70 Bournemouth, Southport, Barrow, Stockport Co
1970–71 Reading, Bury, Doncaster R, Gillingham
1971–72 Mansfield T, Barnsley, Torquay U, Bradford C
1972–73 Rotherham U, Brentford, Swansea C, Scunthorpe U
1973–74 Cambridge U, Shrewsbury T, Southport, Rochdale

1974–75 AFC Bournemouth, Tranmere R, Watford, Huddersfield T
1975–76 Aldershot, Colchester U, Southend U, Halifax T
1976–77 Reading, Northampton T, Grimsby T, York C
1977–78 Port Vale, Bradford C, Hereford U, Portsmouth
1978–79 Peterborough U, Walsall, Tranmere R, Lincoln C
1979–80 Bury, Southend U, Mansfield T, Wimbledon
1980–81 Sheffield U, Colchester U, Blackpool, Hull C
1981–82 Wimbledon, Swindon T, Bristol C, Chester
1982–83 Reading, Wrexham, Doncaster R, Chesterfield
1983–84 Scunthorpe U, Southend U, Port Vale, Exeter C
1984–85 Burnley, Orient, Preston NE, Cambridge U
1985–86 Lincoln C, Cardiff C, Wolverhampton W, Swansea C
1986–87 Bolton W**, Carlisle U, Darlington, Newport Co,
1987–88 Doncaster R, York C, Grimbsy T, Rotherham U**
1988–89 Southend U, Chesterfield, Gillingham, Aldershot
1989–90 Cardiff C, Northampton T, Blackpool, Walsall
1990–91 Crewe Alex, Rotherham U, Mansfield T
1991–92 Bury, Shrewsbury T, Torquay U, Darlington

**Relegated after play-offs.*

APPLICATIONS FOR RE-ELECTION
FOURTH DIVISION

Eleven: Hartlepool U.
Seven: Crewe Alex.
Six: Barrow (lost League place to Hereford U 1972), Halifax T, Rochdale, Southport (lost League place to Wigan Ath 1978), York C.
Five: Chester C, Darlington, Lincoln C, Stockport Co, Workington (lost League place to Wimbledon 1977).
Four: Bradford PA (lost League place to Cambridge U 1970), Newport Co, Northampton T.
Three: Doncaster R, Hereford U.
Two: Bradford C, Exeter C, Oldham Ath; Scunthorpe U; Torquay U.
One: Aldershot, Colchester U, Gateshead (lost League place to Peterborough U 1960), Grimsby T, Swansea C, Tranmere R, Wrexham, Blackpool, Cambridge U, Preston NE.
Accrington S resigned and Oxford U were elected 1962.
Port Vale were forced to re-apply following expulsion in 1968.

THIRD DIVISIONS NORTH & SOUTH

Seven: Walsall.
Six: Exeter C, Halifax T, Newport Co.
Five: Accrington S, Barrow, Gillingham, New Brighton, Southport.
Four: Rochdale, Norwich C.
Three: Crystal Palace, Crewe Alex, Darlingon, Hartlepool U, Merthyr T, Swindon T.
Two: Aberdare Ath, Aldershot, Ashington, Bournemouth, Brentford, Chester, Colchester U, Durham C, Millwall, Nelson, QPR, Rotherham U, Southend U, Tranmere R, Watford, Workington.
One: Bradford C, Bradford PA, Brighton, Bristol R, Cardiff C, Carlisle U, Charlton Ath, Gateshead, Grimsby T, Mansfield T, Shrewsbury T, Torquay U, York C.

LEAGUE STATUS FROM 1986–87

RELEGATED FROM LEAGUE	PROMOTED TO LEAGUE
1986–87 Lincoln C	Scarborough
1987–88 Newport Co	Lincoln C
1988–89 Darlington	Maidstone U
1989–90 Colchester U	Darlington
1990–91 —	Barnet
1991–92 —	Colchester U

LEADING GOALSCORERS 1991–92

	League	FA Cup	Rumbelows League Cup	Other Cups	Total
DIVISION 1					
Ian Wright *(Arsenal) (Including 5 for Crystal Palace)*	29	0	2	0	31
Gary Lineker *(Tottenham H)*	28	0	5	2	35
Brian McClair *(Manchester U)*	18	1	4	2	25
David White *(Manchester C)*	18	0	3	0	21
David Hirst *(Sheffield W)*	18	1	1	1	21
John Fashanu *(Wimbledon)*	18	1	1	0	20
Mark Bright *(Crystal Palace)*	17	0	4	1	22
Lee Chapman *(Leeds U)*	16	0	4	0	20
Peter Beardsley *(Everton)*	15	1	3	1	20
Robert Fleck *(Norwich C)*	11	2	6	0	19
Mick Harford *(Luton T) (Including 3 for Derby Co)*	15	0	0	0	15
Robbie Earle *(Wimbledon)*	14	0	0	1	15
Teddy Sheringham *(Nottingham F)*	13	2	5	2	22
Alan Shearer *(Southampton)*	13	2	3	3	21
Mike Small *(West Ham U)*	13	1	4	0	18
Kevin Campbell *(Arsenal)*	13	0	0	1	14
Alan Smith *(Arsenal)*	12	1	4	0	17
Graeme Sharp *(Oldham Ath)*	12	1	2	0	15
Paul Merson *(Arsenal)*	12	0	1	0	13
DIVISION 2					
Duncan Shearer *(Blackburn R) (Including 32 for Swindon T)*	23	4	6	0	33
David Speedie *(Blackburn R)*	23	1	0	2	26
John Aldridge *(Tranmere R)*	22	3	8	7	40
Brett Angell *(Southend U)*	21	0	1	1	23
Steve Bull *(Wolverhampton W)*	20	0	3	0	23
Don Goodman *(Sunderland) (Including 9 for WBA)*	18	1	1	0	20
Gavin Peacock *(Newcastle U)*	16	1	3	2	22
Marco Gabbiadini *(Derby Co) (Including 5 for Sunderland, 7 for Crystal Palace)*	16	0	1	2	19
Paul Simpson *(Derby Co) (Including 12 for Oxford U)*	16	1	0	2	19
Chris Kiwomya *(Ipswich T)*	16	1	0	2	19
Bernie Slaven *(Middlesbrough)*	16	0	1	1	18
Paul Wilkinson *(Middlesbrough)*	15	4	3	2	24
Dion Dublin *(Cambridge U)*	15	1	3	0	19
Mark Gall *(Brighton & HA) (Including 3 for Maidstone U)*	15	1	0	1	17
Dwight Marshall *(Plymouth Arg)*	14	0	0	1	15
DIVISION 3					
Dean Holdsworth *(Brentford)*	24	4	6	4	38
Iwan Roberts *(Huddersfield T)*	24	3	3	4	34
Wayne Biggins *(Stoke C)*	22	0	2	4	28
Jimmy Quinn *(Bournemouth)*	19	2	2	1	24
Steve Moran *(Exeter C)*	19	1	0	1	21
Mark Stein *(Stoke C) (Including 1 for Oxford U)*	17	0	0	6	23
Nigel Gleghorn *(Birmingham C)*	17	0	5	0	22
Gary Blissett *(Brentford)*	17	1	0	0	18
Ian Stevens *(Bury)*	17	0	0	1	18
Ken Charlery *(Peterborough U)*	16	1	2	7	26
Jim Gannon *(Stockport Co)*	16	1	0	4	21
Kevin Francis *(Stockport Co)*	15	1	1	9	26
Andy Walker *(Bolton W)*	15	3	0	0	18
Gary Worthington *(Wigan Ath)*	15	1	2	0	18
DIVISION 4					
Dave Bamber *(Blackpool)*	26	1	6	2	35
Phil Stant *(Mansfield T)*	26	0	0	0	26
Mike Conroy *(Burnley)*	24	1	2	2	29
Carl Dale *(Cardiff C)*	22	0	0	2	24
Dave Crown *(Gillingham)*	22	0	0	1	23
Chris Pike *(Cardiff C)*	21	1	0	1	23
Gary Bull *(Barnet)*	20	2	2	2	26
Tony Cunningham *(Rotherham U)*	18	1	0	0	19
Rod McDonald *(Walsall)*	18	0	0	0	18
Andy Flounders *(Rochdale)*	17	1	0	0	18
Steve Lovell *(Gillingham)*	16	0	1	0	17
Tony Naylor *(Crewe Alex)*	15	3	3	2	23
Steve Norris *(Chesterfield) (Including 5 for Halifax T)*	15	1	0	0	16
Craig Hignett *(Crewe Alex)*	13	2	1	3	19

NB. Other Cups: European Cup, Cup-Winners' Cup, UEFA Cup, Zenith Data Systems Cup and Autoglass Trophy plus play-offs.

FA CHARITY SHIELD WINNERS 1908–91

1908	Manchester U v QPR	4-0 after 1-1 draw
1909	Newcastle U v Northampton T	2-0
1910	Brighton v Aston Villa	1-0
1911	Manchester U v Swindon T	8-4
1912	Blackburn R v QPR	2-1
1913	Professionals v Amateurs	7-2
1919	WBA v Tottenham H	2-0
1920	Tottenham H v Burnley	2-0
1921	Huddersfield T v Liverpool	1-0
1922	Not played	
1923	Professionals v Amateurs	2-0
1924	Professionals v Amateurs	3-1
1925	Amateurs v Professionals	6-1
1926	Amateurs v Professionals	6-3
1927	Cardiff C v Corinthians	2-1
1928	Everton v Blackburn R	2-1
1929	Professionals v Amateurs	3-0
1930	Arsenal v Sheffield W	2-1
1931	Arsenal v WBA	1-0
1932	Everton v Newcastle U	5-3
1933	Arsenal v Everton	3-0
1934	Arsenal v Manchester C	4-0
1935	Sheffield W v Arsenal	1-0
1936	Sunderland v Arsenal	2-1
1937	Manchester C v Sunderland	2-0
1938	Arsenal v Preston NE	2-1
1948	Arsenal v Manchester U	4-3
1949	Portsmouth v Wolverhampton W	1-1*
1950	World Cup Team v Canadian Touring Team	4-2
1951	Tottenham H v Newcastle U	2-1
1952	Manchester U v Newcastle U	4-2
1953	Arsenal v Blackpool	3-1
1954	Wolverhampton W v WBA	4-4*
1955	Chelsea v Newcastle U	3-0

1956	Manchester U v Manchester C	1-0
1957	Manchester U v Aston Villa	4-0
1958	Bolton W v Wolverhampton W	4-1
1959	Wolverhampton W v Nottingham F	3-1
1960	Burnley v Wolverhampton W	2-2*
1961	Tottenham H v FA XI	3-2
1962	Tottenham H v Ipswich T	5-1
1963	Everton v Manchester U	4-0
1964	Liverpool v West Ham U	2-2*
1965	Manchester U v Liverpool	2-2*
1966	Liverpool v Everton	1-0
1967	Manchester U v Tottenham H	3-3*
1968	Manchester C v WBA	6-1
1969	Leeds U v Manchester C	2-1
1970	Everton v Chelsea	2-1
1971	Leicester C v Liverpool	1-0
1972	Manchester C v Aston Villa	1-0
1973	Burnley v Manchester C	1-0
1974	Liverpool† v Leeds U	1-1
1975	Derby Co v West Ham U	2-0
1976	Liverpool v Southampton	1-0
1977	Liverpool v Manchester U	0-0*
1978	Nottingham F v Ipswich T	5-0
1979	Liverpool v Arsenal	3-1
1980	Liverpool v West Ham U	1-0
1981	Aston Villa v Tottenham H	2-2*
1982	Liverpool v Tottenham H	1-0
1983	Manchester U v Liverpool	2-0
1984	Everton v Liverpool	1-0
1985	Everton v Manchester U	2-0
1986	Everton v Liverpool	1-1*
1987	Everton v Coventry C	1-0
1988	Liverpool v Wimbledon	2-1
1989	Liverpool v Arsenal	1-0
1990	Liverpool v Manchester U	1-1*

Each club retained shield for six months.   † *Won on penalties.*

FA CHARITY SHIELD 1991

Arsenal (0) 0, Tottenham H (0) 0
At Wembley, 10 August 1991, attendance 65,483

Arsenal: Seaman; Dixon, Winterburn, Hillier, O'Leary, Adams, Rocastle (Thomas), Davis, Smith, Merson, Campbell (Cole).

Tottenham H: Thorstvedt; Fenwick, Van Den Hauwe, Sedgley, Howells, Mabbutt, Stewart, Nayim, Samways, Lineker, Allen.

Referee: T. Holbrook (Staffs).

FOOTBALL LEAGUE REPRESENTATIVE GAME

4 March (in Caserta)

Italian Second Division (2) 2 *(Gelsi, Bresciani)*

Football League Second Division (1) 1 *(Kitson)*   5000

Italian League: Aglialatela; Franchini, Tramezzani, Ziliani (Rosa), Petruzzi, Nunziata, Bresciani (Bosi), Rocco (Carbone), Ferrante (Poggi), Gelsi, Ganz.
Football League: Mimms (Nixon); Kerslake, Drysdale, Coleman (Hoddle), Calderwood, Smith, Kerr, Williams P, Dziekanowski (Cook), Kitson (Goodman), Bull.

TRANSFERS 1991–92

	From	To	Fee
May 1991			
28 Cook, Mitchell	Halifax Town	Darlington	Free
31 Smalley, Mark A.	Mansfield Town	Maidstone United	Free
30 Tiler, Carl	Barnsley	Nottingham Forest	£1,400,000
June 1991			
25 Agnew, Stephen M.	Barnsley	Blackburn Rovers	£700,000
14 Beckford, Darren R.	Port Vale	Norwich City	£925,000
27 Boyd, Thomas	Motherwell	Chelsea	£800,000
13 Carr, Franz A.	Nottingham Forest	Newcastle United	£250,000
6 Dorigo, Anthony R.	Chelsea	Leeds United	£1,300,000
25 Foyle, Martin J.	Oxford United	Port Vale	£375,000
24 Jones, Alexander	Carlisle United	Rochdale	£17,500
14 Manuel, William A. J.	Gillingham	Brentford	£60,000
11 Newsome, Jon	Sheffield Wednesday	Leeds United	(Combined fee) £250,000*
28 Payne, Mark C.	Stockport County	Rochdale	Exchange
5 Pennock, Anthony	Stockport County	Wigan Athletic	Free
18 Robinson, Paul J.	Plymouth Argyle	Hereford United	Free
7 Wallace, Rodney S.	Southampton	Leeds United	£1,600,000
6 Ward, Peter	Rochdale	Stockport County	Exchange + £35,000
3 Wilson, Darren A.	Manchester City	Bury	Free
July 1991			
22 Abbott, Gregory S.	Bradford City	Halifax Town	£25,000
2 Bailey, Dennis	Birmingham City	Queens Park Rangers	£175,000
31 Baird, Ian J.	Middlesbrough	Heart of Midlothian	£350,000
2 Barber, Philip A.	Crystal Palace	Millwall	£100,000
24 Bartram, Vincent L.	Wolverhampton Wanderers	AFC Bournemouth	£65,000
24 Bishop, Darren C.	Bury	Barnsley	£50,000
22 Butler, Lee S.	Aston Villa	Barnsley	£165,000
19 Cascarino, Tony G.	Aston Villa	Celtic	£1,100,000
22 Clarke, Timothy J.	Coventry City	Huddersfield Town	£15,000
19 Cascarino, Anthony G.	Aston Villa	Celtic	£1,100,000
16 Conroy, Michael K.	Reading	Burnley	£35,000
25 Cooper, Colin T.	Middlesbrough	Millwall	£300,000
26 Davis, Steven P.	Burnley	Barnsley	£180,000
5 Dobbin, James	Barnsley	Grimsby Town	£200,000
16 Dobbins, Wayne L.	West Bromwich Albion	Torquay United	£30,000
19 Earle, Robert	Port Vale	Wimbledon	£775,000
17 Elliott, Paul	Celtic	Chelsea	£1,400,000
5 Ellis, Neil J.	Chester City	Maidstone United	£10,000
4 Fitzpatrick, Paul J.	Carlisle United	Leicester City	£40,000
4 Fleming, Paul	Halifax Town	Mansfield Town	£10,000
25 Hodge, Stephen B	Nottingham Forest	Leeds United	£900,000
15 Jones, Murray L.	Exeter City	Grimsby Town	£75,000
5 Ling, Martin	Southend United	Swindon Town	£15,000
11 Lyne, Neil G.F.	Nottingham Forest	Shrewsbury Town	Nominal
17 Milligan, Michael J.	Everton	Oldham Athletic	£600,000
26 Mitchell, David S.	Chelsea	Swindon Town	£30,000
31 Morris, Mark J.	Sheffield United	AFC Bournemouth	£95,000
24 Mortimer, Paul H.	Charlton Athletic	Aston Villa	£350,000
15 Newman, Robert N.	Bristol City	Norwich City	£600,000
25 O'Shaughnessy, Stephen	Rochdale	Exeter City	£10,000
8 Pearson, John S.	Leeds United	Barnsley	£135,000
1 Peyton, Gerald J.	AFC Bournemouth	Everton	£80,000
30 Poole, Kevin	Middlesbrough	Leicester City	£40,000
29 Richards, Stephen C.	Scarborough	Halifax Town	£40,000
1 Ryan, John B.	Chesterfield	Rochdale	Free
31 Sale, Mark D.	Stoke City	Cambridge United	Nominal
5 Saunders, Dean N	Derby County	Liverpool	£2,900,000
17 Sharp, Graeme M.	Everton	Oldham Athletic	£500,000
3 Sheffield, Jonathan	Norwich City	Cambridge United	Free
1 Shepherd, Anthony	Carlisle United	Motherwell	£35,000
23 Sheringham, Edward P.	Millwall	Nottingham Forest	£2,000,000
1 Spearing, Anthony	Leicester City	Plymouth Argyle	Free
4 Sussex, Andy	Crewe Alexandra	Southend United	£100,000
26 Taylor, Shaun	Exeter City	Swindon Town	£200,000
25 Teale, Shaun	AFC Bournemouth	Aston Villa	£300,000
30 Ward, Ashley S.	Manchester City	Leicester City	£80,000
17 Warhurst, Paul	Oldham Athletic	Sheffield Wednesday	£750,000
8 Wallace, Raymond G.	Southampton	Leeds United	£100,000
25 Welch, Keith	Rochdale	Bristol City	£200,000
15 Wetherall, David	Sheffield Wednesday	Leeds United	(Combined fee) £250,000*
15 Wright, Mark	Derby County	Liverpool	£2,200,000
August 1991			
23 Aitken, Robert S.	Newcastle United	St Mirren	£150,000
14 Allon, Joseph B.	Hartlepool United	Chelsea	£200,000
16 Armstrong, Christopher P.	Wrexham	Millwall	£50,000
23 Atherton, Peter	Wigan Athletic	Coventry City	£329,000
15 Barber, Frederick	Walsall	Peterborough United	£25,000

	From	To	Fee
16 Bogie, Ian	Preston North End	Millwall	£145,000
5 Beardsley, Peter	Liverpool	Everton	£1,000,000
14 Blissett, Luther L.	AFC Bournemouth	Watford	£40,000
22 Brown, Malcolm	Stockport County	Rochdale	Not disclosed
15 Brown, Michael A.	Shrewsbury Town	Bolton Wanderers	£100,000
6 Buckley, John W.	Partick Thistle	Scunthorpe United	£40,000
15 Coleman, Simon	Middlesbrough	Derby County	£300,000
17 Colquhoun, John	Heart of Midlothian	Millwall	£400,000
8 Comyn, Andrew J.	Aston Villa	Derby County	£200,000
2 Cornforth, John M.	Sunderland	Swansea City	£50,000
1 Cowan, Thomas	Rangers	Sheffield United	£350,000
5 Crosby, Phil	Peterborough United	York City	Free
14 Cunningham, Anthony E.	Bolton Wanderers	Rotherham United	£50,000
14 Curle, Keith	Wimbledon	Manchester City	£2,500,000
17 Davis, Stephen M.	Southampton	Burnley	£60,000
14 Dobie, Mark W. G.	Cambridge United	Torquay United	£10,000
30 Donowa, Brian L.	Bristol City	Birmingham City	£60,000
9 Dryden, Richard	Exeter City	Notts County	£250,000
16 Durie, Gordon S.	Chelsea	Tottenham Hotspur	£2,200,000
16 Falco, Mark P.	Queens Park Rangers	Millwall	£175,000
16 Falconer, William H.	Watford	Middlesbrough	Exchange
15 Fleming, Craig	Halifax Town	Oldham Athletic	£80,000
16 Fleming, Curtis	St Patricks	Middlesbrough	£50,000
15 Gillespie, Gary T.	Liverpool	Celtic	£925,000
8 Graham, Deiniol W. T.	Manchester United	Barnsley	£50,000
16 Gray, Phillip	Tottenham Hotspur	Luton Town	£275,000
12 Harper, Alan	Manchester City	Everton	£1,300,000**
16 Helliwell, Ian	York City	Scunthorpe United	£80,000
16 Hogan, Thomas E.	Cobh Ramblers	Birmingham City	Nominal
23 Hogg, Graeme J.	Portsmouth	Heart of Midlothian	£200,000
11 Holloway, Ian S.	Bristol Rovers	Queens Park Rangers	£230,000
14 Honor, Christian	Bristol City	Airdrieonians	£20,000
15 Houchen, Keith M.	Hibernian	Port Vale	£100,000
15 Ironside, Ian	Scarborough	Middlesbrough	£80,000
30 Jones, Vincent P.	Sheffield United	Chelsea	£575,000
9 Kamara, Alan	Scarborough	Halifax Town	£5,000
15 Kelly, Anthony G.	Shrewsbury Town	Bolton Wanderers	£100,000
1 Kilcline, Brian	Coventry City	Oldham Athletic	£400,000
27 Lancaster, David	Blackpool	Chesterfield	£70,000
27 Lee, David	Bury	Southampton	£350,000
13 McAllister, Kevin	Chelsea	Falkirk	£225,000
15 McCall, Stuart	Everton	Rangers	£1,200,000
16 Mardon, Paul J.	Bristol City	Birmingham City	£65,000
1 Mendonca, Clive P.	Rotherham United	Sheffield United	£110,000
21 Millar, Paul	Port Vale	Cardiff City	£60,000
12 Munro, Stuart	Rangers	Blackburn Rovers	£350,000
16 Nelson, Garry P.	Brighton & Hove Albion	Charlton Athletic	£50,000
16 Norton, David W.	Notts County	Hull City	£80,000
5 O'Hanlon, Kelham G.	Rotherham United	Carlisle United	£25,000
29 Overson, Vincent D.	Birmingham City	Stoke City	£55,000
16 Page, Donald R.	Wigan Athletic	Rotherham United	Not disclosed
16 Painter, Peter R.	Chester City	Maidstone United	£30,000
8 Parker, Paul A.	Queens Park Rangers	Manchester United	£2,000,000
27 Peake, Trevor	Coventry City	Luton Town	£100,000
1 Peel, Nathan J.	Preston North End	Sheffield United	£50,000
1 Putney, Trevor A.	Middlesbrough	Watford	Exchange
16 Quamina, Mark E.	Wimbledon	Plymouth Argyle	Free
5 Quinn, James M.	West Ham United	AFC Bournemouth	£40,000
23 Ramsey, Paul	Leicester City	Cardiff City	£100,000
9 Rice, Brian	Nottingham Forest	Falkirk	£65,000
11 Rimmer, Stuart A.	Barnsley	Chester City	£150,000
8 Sinnott, Lee	Bradford City	Crystal Palace	£300,000
27 Skinner, Justin	Fulham	Bristol Rovers	£130,000
16 Small, Michael A.	Brighton & Hove Albion	West Ham United	£400,000
16 Speedie, David R.	Liverpool	Blackburn Rovers	£400,000
1 Stant, Philip R.	Fulham	Mansfield Town	£50,000
17 Starbuck, Phillip M.	Nottingham Forest	Huddersfield Town	Not disclosed
7 Staunton, Stephen	Liverpool	Aston Villa	£1,100,000
16 Swan, Peter H.	Hull City	Port Vale	£300,000
7 Thomas, Mitchell A.	Tottenham Hotspur	West Ham United	£500,000
19 Thompson, Gary L.	Crystal Palace	Queens Park Rangers	£225,000*
13 Thompson, Steven J.	Bolton Wanderers	Luton Town	£180,000
13 Walters, Mark E.	Rangers	Liverpool	£1,250,000
12 Ward, Mark W.	Manchester City	Everton	£1,300,000**
16 West, Gary	Port Vale	Lincoln City	£25,000
16 Wilkinson, Paul	Watford	Middlesbrough	£550,000
6 Williams, Gareth	Aston Villa	Barnsley	£200,000
19 Witter, Anthony J.	Crystal Palace	Queens Park Rangers	£225,000*
15 Woods, Christopher C. E.	Rangers	Sheffield Wednesday	£1,200,000
30 Yates, Mark J.	Birmingham City	Burnley	£40,000

Temporary Transfers

	From	To	
15 Beresford, Marlon	Sheffield Wednesday	Northampton Town	
2 Brown, Kenneth J.	Plymouth Argyle	West Ham United	

	From	To	Fee
23 Byrne, Brian	Huddersfield Town	Shelbourne	
21 Byrne, David S.	Watford	Reading	
19 Dale, Carl	Chester City	Cardiff City	
27 Hoult, Russell	Leicester City	Lincoln City	
13 Keaton, Jason	Everton	Stoke City	
22 Kerr, Dylan	Leeds United	Doncaster Rovers	
29 Marriott, Andrew	Nottingham Forest	Burnley	
15 Miller, Alan	Arsenal	West Bromwich Albion	
14 Morrow, Stephen	Arsenal	Watford	
29 O'Doherty, Kenneth B.	Huddersfield Town	Exeter City	
15 Priestley, Jason A.	Carlisle United	Scarborough	
15 Rush, David	Sunderland	Hartlepool United	
13 Smith, Mark A.	Nottingham Forest	Shrewsbury Town	

September 1991

	From	To	Fee
2 Black, Kingsley	Luton Town	Nottingham Forest	£1,500,000
18 Bowden, Jon L.	Wrexham	Rochdale	£10,000
6 Bradley, Russell	Hereford United	Halifax Town	£45,000
3 Brown, Kenneth J.	Plymouth Argyle	West Ham United	£175,000
6 Caesar, Gus C.	Cambridge United	Bristol City	Free
5 Chapman, Gary A.	Notts County	Exeter City	£10,000
13 Cook, Andrew C.	Southampton	Exeter City	£50,000
21 Connor, Terence F.	Swansea City	Bristol City	£190,000
5 Cooper, Mark N.	Exeter City	Birmingham City	Exchange
12 Cross, Stephen C.	Derby County	Bristol Rovers	£40,000
5 Currie, David N.	Oldham Athletic	Barnsley	£250,000
3 Dale, Carl	Chester City	Cardiff City	£100,000
6 Dolan, Eamonn J.	Birmingham City	Exeter City	Exchange
3 Dowie, Iain	West Ham United	Southampton	£500,000
19 Evans, Stewart J.	Rotherham United	Crewe Alexandra	£10,000
25 Freestone, Roger	Chelsea	Swansea City	£50,000
17 Gayle, Brian W.	Ipswich Town	Sheffield United	£700,000
23 Gray, Stuart	Aston Villa	Southampton	£200,000
12 Harford, Michael G.	Derby County	Luton Town	£325,000
12 Heathcote, Michael	Shrewsbury Town	Cambridge United	£150,000
4 Hill, David M.	Ipswich Town	Scunthorpe United	£30,000
9 Hurlock, Terry A.	Rangers	Southampton	£400,000
17 Jemson, Nigel B.	Nottingham Forest	Sheffield Wednesday	£800,000
16 Rideout, Paul D.	Southampton	Notts County	£250,000
13 Rowbotham, Darren	Exeter City	Torquay United	£25,000
20 Smith, Mark A.	Nottingham Forest	Shrewsbury Town	£25,000
13 Taylor, Robert M.	Sheffield Wednesday	Shrewsbury Town	£70,000
12 Titterton, David S. J.	Coventry City	Hereford United	£8,000
13 Whiston, Peter M.	Torquay United	Exeter City	£25,000
6 Wimbleton, Paul P.	Shrewsbury Town	Exeter City	Free
24 Wright, Ian E.	Crystal Palace	Arsenal	£2,500,000

Temporary Transfers

	From	To
12 Aylott, Trevor K. C.	Birmingham City	Oxford United
26 Beagrie, Peter	Everton	Sunderland
26 Beckford, Jason N.	Manchester City	Port Vale
11 Berry, George F.	Preston North End	Aldershot
12 Brazil, Derek M.	Manchester United	Swansea City
9 Byrne, Brian	Shelbourne	Huddersfield Town (Tr. back)
12 Cash, Stuart	Nottingham Forest	Shrewsbury Town
19 Clark, Howard W.	Coventry City	Darlington
26 Clarke, Wayne	Manchester City	Wolverhampton Wanderers
5 Cole, Andrew A.	Arsenal	Fulham
12 Costello, Peter	Peterborough United	Lincoln City
26 Cross, Paul	Barnsley	Preston North End
19 Davison, Robert	Leeds United	Derby County
6 Dibble, Andrew G.	Manchester City	Bolton Wanderers
27 Dibble, Andrew G.	Bolton Wanderers	Manchester City (Tr. back)
19 Dickinson, Stephen	Bradford City	Blackpool
3 Edwards, Neil R.	Leeds United	Stockport County
13 Farrell, Sean	Luton Town	Northampton Town
26 Fillery, Michael	Oldham Athletic	Torquay United
5 Freestone, Roger	Chelsea	Swansea City
2 Glover, Edward I.	Nottingham Forest	Luton Town
19 Hamilton, Gary J.	Middlesbrough	Darlington
26 Hawke, Warren R.	Sunderland	Chesterfield
23 Hayes, Martin	Celtic	Coventry City
27 Hewitt, John	Celtic	Middlesbrough
12 James, Julian C.	Luton Town	Preston North End
12 Lange, Anthony S.	Wolverhampton Wanderers	Torquay United
30 McLoughlin, Alan F.	Southampton	Aston Villa
5 McLoughlin, Paul B.	Wolverhampton Wanderers	Walsall
25 Matthews, Neil	Stockport County	Halifax Town
26 Marshall, Colin	Barnsley	Wrexham
26 Mauge, Ronald C.	Bury	Manchester City
5 Nethercott, Stuart	Tottenham Hotspur	Maidstone United
19 Ormondroyd, Ian	Aston Villa	Derby County
19 Parkin, Timothy J.	Port Vale	Shrewsbury Town
11 Paskin, William J.	Wolverhampton Wanderers	Stockport County

610

	From	To	Fee
5 Redfearn, Neil D.	Oldham Athletic	Barnsley	
26 Reed, John P.	Sheffield United	Scarborough	
27 Rush, David	Hartlepool United	Sunderland (Tr. back)	
18 Shannon, Robert	Dundee	Middlesbrough	
5 Sinclair, Ronald	Bristol City	Walsall	
15 Stein, Mark E. S.	Oxford United	Stoke City	
11 Todd, Mark	Sheffield United	Rotherham United	
20 Walker, Andrew	Celtic	Newcastle United	
16 Walsh, Paul	Tottenham Hotspur	Queens Park Rangers	
19 Watson, Andrew A.	Swansea City	Carlisle United	
12 Widdrington, Thomas	Southampton	Wigan Athletic	
2 Williams, David P.	Burnley	Rochdale	

October 1991

	From	To	Fee
4 Aylott, Trevor K. C.	Birmingham City	Oxford United	Free
17 Beaumont, David	Luton Town	Hibernian	£110,000
23 Byrne, John F.	Brighton & Hove Albion	Sunderland	£225,000
8 Carter, James W. C.	Liverpool	Arsenal	£500,000
31 Coatsworth, Gary	Darlington	Leicester City	£15,000
2 Edwards, Neil R.	Leeds United	Stockport County	£5,000
1 Gabbiadini, Marco	Sunderland	Crystal Palace	£1,800,000
24 Gall, Mark I.	Maidstone United	Brighton & Hove Albion	£45,000
18 Jackson, Matthew A.	Luton Town	Everton	£600,000
1 Jones, Andrew M.	AFC Bournemouth	Leyton Orient	£90,000
21 Jones, Keith A.	Brentford	Southend United	£175,000
4 Jones, Robert M.	Crewe Alexandra	Liverpool	£300,000
22 Linton, Desmond	Leicester City	Luton Town	Exchange
1 McDonald, Neil	Everton	Oldham Athletic	£500,000
18 Mortimer, Paul H.	Aston Villa	Crystal Palace	£500,000
22 Oakes, Scott J.	Leicester City	Luton Town	Exchange
29 Penrice, Gary	Aston Villa	Queens Park Rangers	£625,000
10 Redfearn, Neil D.	Oldham Athletic	Barnsley	£180,000
4 Rogan, Anthony G. P.	Celtic	Sunderland	£350,000
22 Thompson, Stephen J.	Luton Town	Leicester City	Exchange
9 Wood, Stephen	Millwall	Southampton	£400,000
25 Wright, Alan	Blackpool	Blackburn Rovers	£400,000

Temporary Transfers

	From	To
30 Allpress, Timothy J.	Luton Town	Preston North End
30 Beauchamp, Joseph D.	Oxford United	Swansea City
17 Bracey, Lee M. I.	Swansea City	Halifax Town
1 Branagan, Keith	Millwall	Gillingham
28 Branagan, Keith	Gillingham	Millwall (Tr. back)
9 Connelly, Dean	Barnsley	Wigan Athletic
31 Cullen, Anthony	Sunderland	Bury
4 Dibble, Andrew G.	Manchester City	Bolton Wanderers
10 Drinkell, Kevin	Coventry City	Birmingham City
3 Gallimore, Anthony	Stoke City	Carlisle United
17 Gosney, Andrew	Portsmouth	York City
3 Gray, Brian	Birmingham City	Shelbourne
17 Harris, Andrew	Birmingham City	Oxford United
31 Haylock, Garry	Huddersfield Town	Shelbourne
24 Hopkins, Jeffrey	Crystal Palace	Plymouth Argyle
17 James, Julian	Preston North End	Luton Town (Tr. back)
31 Johnson, David A.	Sheffield Wednesday	Hartlepool United
24 Kennedy, Andrew J.	Watford	Bolton Wanderers
11 Key, Lance	Sheffield Wednesday	York City
15 Kinnaird, Paul	St Mirren	Leyton Orient
24 Lewis, Dudley K.	Huddersfield Town	Halifax Town
31 McCarrison, Dugald	Celtic	Darlington
10 Maguire, Gavin	Portsmouth	Newcastle United
18 Marwood, Brian	Sheffield United	Middlesbrough
24 Matthews, Neil	Halifax Town	Stockport Co (Tr. back)
25 Maxwell, Alastair	Motherwell	Liverpool
24 Moncur, John F.	Tottenham Hotspur	Ipswich Town
30 Morrow, Stephen	Arsenal	Reading
10 Osman, Russell	Southampton	Bristol City
24 Palin, Leigh	Hull City	Rochdale
3 Payne, Russell	Liverpool	Crewe Alexandra
17 Richards, Carroll L.	Blackpool	Maidstone United
3 Rutherford, Mark	Birmingham City	Shelbourne
17 Smith, Neil J.	Tottenham Hotspur	Gillingham
11 Suckling, Perry	Crystal Palace	Brentford
25 Turner, Christopher R.	Sheffield Wednesday	Leyton Orient
17 Walker, Andrew F.	Celtic	Newcastle United (Tr. back)
17 Williams, William J.	AFC Bournemouth	Wigan Athletic
3 Wood, Paul A.	Sheffield United	AFC Bournemouth

November 1991

	From	To	Fee
12 Agana, Patrick A.	Sheffield United	Notts County	£750,000
8 Agboola, Reuben	Sunderland	Swansea City	Free
21 Bart-Williams, Christopher G.	Leyton Orient	Sheffield Wednesday	£275,000
22 Booker, Robert	Sheffield United	Brentford	Free
27 Comstive, Paul	Bolton Wanderers	Chester City	£10,000

		From	To	Fee
29	Cooper, Neale	Reading	Dunfermline Athletic	Nominal
28	Cowans, Gordon S.	Aston Villa	Blackburn Rovers	£200,000
21	Ford, Tony	West Bromwich Albion	Grimsby Town	£50,000
8	Gordon, Dale A.	Norwich City	Rangers	£1,200,000
28	Harris, Andrew	Birmingham City	Exeter City	Free
8	Hendry, Edward C. J.	Manchester City	Blackburn Rovers	£700,000
20	Johnston, Maurice T.	Rangers	Everton	£1,500,000
1	Kamara, Christopher	Leeds United	Luton Town	£150,000
22	Kane, Paul	Oldham Athletic	Aberdeen	£350,000
8	Mowbray, Anthony M.	Middlesbrough	Celtic	£1,000,000
15	Newell, Michael C.	Everton	Blackburn Rovers	£1,100,000
15	Osman, Russell	Southampton	Bristol City	£60,000
21	Pardew, Alan	Crystal Palace	Charlton Athletic	Free
29	Parker, Garry S.	Nottingham Forest	Aston Villa	£650,000
8	Payton, Andrew P.	Hull City	Middlesbrough	£750,000
7	Regis, David	Notts County	Plymouth Argyle	£200,000
28	Peake, Andrew M.	Charlton Athletic	Middlesbrough	£150,000
8	Sloan, Scott	Newcastle United	Falkirk	£50,000
25	Smith, Neil J.	Tottenham Hotspur	Gillingham	£40,000
7	Stein, Mark E. S.	Oxford United	Stoke City	£100,000
27	Tallon, Gary T.	Drogheda United	Blackburn Rovers	Nominal
1	Todd, Mark	Sheffield United	Rotherham United	£35,000
21	Turner, Christopher R.	Sheffield Wednesday	Leyton Orient	£75,000
1	Watson, Andrew A.	Swansea City	Carlisle United	£30,000
7	Wood, Paul A.	Sheffield United	AFC Bournemouth	£40,000
15	Youds, Edward P.	Everton	Ipswich Town	£250,000

Temporary Transfers

21	Bennett, David	Swindon Town	Shrewsbury Town
28	Britton, Gerard J.	Celtic	Reading
1	Carstairs, James W.	Cambridge United	Stockport County
21	Carter, Timothy D.	Sunderland	Birmingham City
15	Gage, Kevin	Aston Villa	Sheffield United
15	Gosney, Andrew R.	York City	Portsmouth (Tr. back)
18	Harrison, Lee	Charlton Athletic	Fulham
22	Hewitt, John	Middlesbrough	Celtic (Tr back)
5	Keeley, John H.	Oldham Athletic	Oxford United
26	Kennedy, Andrew J.	Bolton Wanderers	Watford (Tr. back)
21	Kite, Philip D.	Sheffield United	Mansfield Town
29	Leighton, James	Manchester United	Reading
1	Livingstone, Glen	Aston Villa	Omagh Town
1	Mcinerney, Ian	Peterborough United	Derry City
4	McLoughlin, Paul B.	Walsall	Wolverhampton Wanderers (Tr. back)
20	Meaker, Michael	Queens Park Rangers	Plymouth Argyle
20	Morah, Olisa H.	Tottenham Hotspur	Hereford United
29	Morrow, Stephen	Reading	Arsenal (Tr. back)
7	Mountfield, Derek	Aston Villa	Wolverhampton Wanderers
6	Narbett, Jonathan V.	Hereford United	Leicester City
21	Paskin, John	Wolverhampton Wanderers	Birmingham City
18	Polston, Andrew	Tottenham Hotspur	Gillingham
27	Raven, Paul	West Bromwich Albion	Doncaster Rovers
23	Reed, John	Scarborough	Sheffield United (Tr. back)
21	Rose, Kevin	Bolton Wanderers	Rochdale
28	Rosenior, Leroy	West Ham United	Charlton Athletic
7	Russell, Kevin J.	Leicester City	Hereford United
21	Sinclair, Ronald	Bristol City	Stoke City
13	Sommer, Juergen P.	Luton Town	Brighton & Hove Albion
20	Statham, Brian	Tottenham Hotspur	AFC Bournemouth
28	Sutton, Steven	Nottingham Forest	Luton Town
1	West, Colin	West Bromwich Albion	Port Vale
29	Whitehead, Philip M.	Barnsley	Scunthorpe United
28	Wilder, Christopher J.	Sheffield United	Charlton Athletic
21	Will, James	Arsenal	Sheffield United
12	Witter, Tony	Queens Park Rangers	Millwall

December 1991

6	Allen, Clive D.	Manchester City	Chelsea	£250,000
5	Clarke, Nicholas J.	Wolverhampton Wanderers	Mansfield Town	£25,000
6	Gavin, Mark W.	Watford	Bristol City	£60,000
6	Goodman, Donald R.	West Bromwich Albion	Sunderland	£900,000
4	Kelly, David T.	Leicester City	Newcastle United	£250,000
24	McMahon, Steve	Liverpool	Manchester City	£900,000
9	Nogan, Lee M.	Oxford United	Watford	£275,000
18	Ormondroyd, Ian	Aston Villa	Derby County	£350,000
12	Osborne, Lawrence W.	Maidstone United	Gillingham	£40,000
18	Preece, Andrew	Wrexham	Stockport County	£10,000
12	Randall, Adrian J.	Aldershot	Burnley	£40,000
6	Rose, Kevin P.	Bolton Wanderers	Rochdale	Nominal
19	Smith, David A.	Bristol City	Plymouth Argyle	£200,000
16	Thomas, Michael L.	Arsenal	Liverpool	£1,500,000
24	Thompson, Simon	Rotherham United	Scarborough	Nominal
20	Trotter, Michael	Darlington	Leicester City	£200,000
20	Willis, James A.	Darlington	Leicester City	£200,000
19	Wilson, Paul A.	Northampton Town	Halifax Town	Nominal

612

	From	To	Fee
13 Sheffield, Jonathan	Cambridge United	Sheffield United	
21 Sinclair, Frank M.	West Bromwich Albion	Chelsea (Tr. back)	
6 Smith, Anthony	Sunderland	Hartlepool United	
16 Smith, Jeremy	Wigan Athletic	Derry City	
16 Statham, Brian	Tottenham Hotspur	Brentford	
30 Stevenson, Andrew J.	Scunthorpe United	Doncaster Rovers	
22 Taylor, Colin	Wolverhampton Wanderers	Wigan Athletic	
9 Walker, Andrew	Celtic	Bolton Wanderers	
9 Witter, Anthony J.	Queens Park Rangers	Plymouth Argyle	
15 Whitehurst, William	Doncaster Rovers	Crewe Alexandra	
16 Whitworth, Neil A.	Manchester United	Preston North End	
11 Williams, Andrew	Port Vale	Leeds United (Tr. back)	
30 Wilson, Terry	Nottingham Forest	Newcastle United	

February 1992

	From	To	Fee
7 Adcock, Anthony C.	Northampton Town	Peterborough United	(Combined fee) £70,000*
7 Barnes, David O.	Northampton Town	Peterborough United	(Combined fee) £70,000*
25 Barrett, Earl D.	Oldham Athletic	Aston Villa	£1,700,000
6 Boyd, Thomas	Chelsea	Celtic	Exchange
19 Carstairs, James	Cambridge United	Stockport County	Nominal
7 Cascarino, Anthony G.	Celtic	Chelsea	Exchange
14 Fereday, Wayne	AFC Bournemouth	West Bromwich Albion	£60,000
28 Foley, Steven	Swindon Town	Stoke City	£50,000
21 Gage, Kevin W.	Aston Villa	Sheffield United	£150,000
21 Harmon, Darren	Notts County	Shrewsbury Town	Free
21 Holmes, Michael	Torquay United	Carlisle United	£15,000
28 Johnrose, Leonard	Blackburn Rovers	Hartlepool United	£50,000
21 Kelly, James	Wrexham	Wolverhampton Wanderers	Exchange
28 Kelly, Paul A.	Manchester City	Crewe Alexandra	Nominal
8 Kozma, Istvan	Dunfermline Athletic	Liverpool	£300,000
7 Leighton, James	Manchester United	Dundee	£200,000
3 Mountfield, Derek	Aston Villa	Wolverhampton Wanderers	£150,000
28 Muir, Johnny G.	Doncaster Rovers	Stockport County	Not disclosed
26 Norris, Stephen M.	Halifax Town	Chesterfield	£33,000
28 O'Neill, Alan	Cobh Ramblers	Birmingham City	£15,000
21 Paskin, William J.	Wolverhampton Wanderers	Wrexham	Exchange
7 Price, Christopher J.	Aston Villa	Blackburn Rovers	£150,000
13 Rodger, Graham	Luton Town	Grimsby Town	£135,000
28 Sherwood, Timothy A.	Norwich City	Blackburn Rovers	£500,000
20 Simpson, Paul D.	Oxford United	Derby County	£500,000
28 Statham, Brian	Tottenham Hotspur	Brentford	£70,000
11 Walker, Andrew F.	Celtic	Bolton Wanderers	£160,000

Temporary Transfers

	From	To
27 Agana, Patrick A.	Notts County	Leeds United
27 Allon, Joseph B.	Chelsea	Port Vale
7 Atteveld, Raymond	Everton	West Ham United
27 Blake, Noel	Stoke City	Bradford City
6 Branagan, Keith	Millwall	Fulham
13 Cowdrill, Barry J.	Bolton Wanderers	Rochdale
21 Dewhurst, Robert	Darlington	Blackburn Rovers (Tr. back)
27 Dibble, Andrew G.	Manchester City	West Bromwich Albion
13 Donovan, Kevin	Huddersfield Town	Halifax Town
26 Gallimore, Anthony	Stoke City	Carlisle United
19 Gittens, Jon	Southampton	Middlesbrough
27 Gray, Andrew A.	Crystal Palace	Tottenham Hotspur
22 Hayes, Martin	Celtic	Wimbledon
27 Hendry, John	Tottenham Hotspur	Charlton Athletic
21 Hogan, Thomas E.	Birmingham City	Cobh Ramblers
6 Keeley, John	Oldham Athletic	Reading
19 Kilcline, Brian	Oldham Athletic	Newcastle United
14 Kite, Phillip	Mansfield Town	Sheffield United (Tr. back)
6 Leighton, James	Reading	Manchester United (Tr. back)
17 McLoughlin, Alan F.	Southampton	Portsmouth
14 Marples, Christopher	York City	Scunthorpe United
18 Moncur, John F.	Tottenham Hotspur	Nottingham Forest
27 Moore, Kevin	Bristol Rovers	Southampton (Tr. back)
13 Nethercott, Stuart	Tottenham Hotspur	Barnet
28 Newman, Richard	Crystal Palace	Maidstone United
13 Paskin, William J.	Wolverhampton Wanderers	Shrewsbury Town
20 Paskin, William J.	Shrewsbury Town	Wolverhampton Wanderers (Tr. back)
13 Peake, Jason W.	Leicester City	Hartlepool United
21 Peyton, Gerard J.	Everton	Bolton Wanderers
20 Rennie, David	Bristol City	Birmingham City
12 Sherwood, Timothy A.	Norwich City	Blackburn Rovers
20 Steele, Timothy L.	Wolverhampton Wanderers	Stoke City
21 Walker, Joseph N.	Heart of Midlothian	Burnley
20 Whitworth, Neil A.	Manchester United	Barnsley
27 Wilder, Christopher J.	Sheffield United	Leyton Orient
4 Williams, Andrew	Leeds United	Notts County
27 Williams, Brett	Nottingham Forest	Oxford United

March 1992

	From	To	Fee
27 Allen, Clive D.	Chelsea	West Ham United	£275,000
26 Atteveld, Raymond	Everton	Bristol City	£250,000

	From	To	Fee
26 Cook, Mitchell C.	Darlington	Blackpool	Nominal
9 Cork, Alan G.	Wimbledon	Sheffield United	Free
27 Cowdrill, Barry J.	Bolton Wanderers	Rochdale	Nominal
26 Curran, Christopher	Crewe Alexandra	Scarborough	Nominal
27 Dickins, Matthew J.	Lincoln City	Blackburn Rovers	£250,000
6 Duxbury, Michael	Blackburn Rovers	Bradford City	Free
24 Garland, Peter J.	Tottenham Hotspur	Newcastle United	£35,000
11 Gee, Phillip	Derby County	Leicester City	Exchange*
13 Grayson, Simon N.	Leeds United	Leicester City	£50,000
27 Greenall, Colin	Bury	Preston North End	£50,000
27 Heath, Adrian P.	Manchester City	Stoke City	£50,000
2 Hughton, Christopher W.G.	West Ham United	Brentford	Nominal
27 Humes, Anthony	Ipswich Town	Wrexham	£40,000
23 Johnson, Thomas	Notts County	Derby County	£1,300,000
12 Jones, Phillip L.	Wrexham	Liverpool	£300,000
20 Kilcline, Brian	Oldham Athletic	Newcastle United	£300,000
11 Kitson, Paul	Leicester City	Derby County	£800,000*
27 Leonard, Mark	Bradford City	Rochdale	Nominal
19 Lydiate, Jason L.	Manchester United	Bolton Wanderers	Free
26 McCall, Stephen H.	Sheffield Wednesday	Plymouth Argyle	Nominal
20 McDonough, Darron K.	Luton Town	Newcastle United	£90,000
27 McLoughlin, Alan F.	Southampton	Portsmouth	£400,000
23 Mahood, Alan S.	Nottingham Forest	Morton	Nominal
31 Miller, David	Carlisle United	Stockport County	£25,000
30 Moncur, John	Tottenham Hotspur	Swindon Town	£80,000
27 Noteman, Kevin S.	Doncaster Rovers	Mansfield Town	£25,000
23 Nugent, Kevin	Leyton Orient	Plymouth Argyle	£200,000
11 Ormondroyd, Ian	Derby County	Leicester City	Exchange
27 Painter, Peter R.	Maidstone United	Burnley	£25,000
10 Raynor, Paul J.	Swansea City	Cambridge United	Free
26 Rees, Melvyn	West Bromwich Albion	Sheffield United	£25,000
20 Reid, Wesley	Bradford City	Airdrieonians	£70,000
19 Rennie, David	Bristol City	Birmingham City	£120,000
20 Robinson, Ronald	Rotherham United	Peterborough United	Free
26 Sale, Mark	Cambridge United	Birmingham City	Nominal
13 Saville, Andrew V.	Barnsley	Hartlepool United	£60,000
27 Shearer, Duncan	Swindon Town	Blackburn Rovers	£800,000
6 Simpson, Fitzroy	Swindon Town	Manchester City	£500,000
6 Sutton, Stephen J.	Nottingham Forest	Derby County	£300,000
28 Taylor, John P.	Cambridge United	Bristol Rovers	Exchange**
24 Taylor, Peter M.	Blackpool	Wrexham	£30,000
24 Tolson, Neil	Walsall	Oldham Athletic	£150,000
13 Watts, Julian	Rotherham United	Sheffield Wednesday	£80,000
6 Wegerle, Roy C.	Queens Park Rangers	Blackburn Rovers	£1,200,000
28 White, Devan W.	Bristol Rovers	Cambridge United	Exchange + £100,000**
27 Whitlow, Michael	Leeds United	Leicester City	£250,000
27 Williams, Andrew	Leeds United	Notts County	£115,000
27 Wilson, Kevin J.	Chelsea	Notts County	£225,000

* £1,300,000 deal + swap.

Temporary Transfers

19 Bannister, Gary	West Bromwich Albion	Oxford United	
18 Bellamy, Gary	Wolverhampton Wanderers	Cardiff City	
26 Bent, Junior A.	Bristol City	Stoke City	
19 Bishop, Edwards M.	Chester City	Crewe Alexandra	
27 Bremner, Kevin	Dundee	Shrewsbury Town	
24 Butler, Peter J. F.	Southend United	Huddersfield Town	
4 Callaghan, Nigel	Huddersfield Town	Aston Villa (Tr. back)	
26 Charnley, James	St Mirren	Bolton Wanderers	
12 Cole, Andrew A.	Arsenal	Bristol City	
26 Cooper, Stephen B.	Tranmere Rovers	Peterborough United	
26 Cundy, Jason V.	Chelsea	Tottenham Hotspur	
6 Davison, Robert	Leeds United	Sheffield United	
5 Day, Mervyn R.	Leeds United	Luton Town	
19 Dearden, Kevin C.	Tottenham Hotspur	Birmingham City	
26 Elliott, Matthew S.	Torquay United	Scunthorpe United	
5 Flitcroft, Garry W.	Manchester City	Bury	
26 Ford, Stuart	Rotherham United	Scarborough	
26 Gibson, Terrence B.	Wimbledon	Swindon Town	
4 Gilkes, Michael E.	Reading	Southampton	
26 Gough, Alan T.	Portsmouth	Fulham	
6 Green, Richard E.	Swindon Town	Gillingham	
24 Harrison, Lee D.	Charlton Athletic	Gillingham	
13 Harrison, Gerald	Cardiff City	Bristol City (Tr. back)	
10 Heald, Paul A.	Leyton Orient	Coventry City	
26 Hendon, Ian M.	Tottenham Hotspur	Leyton Orient	
17 Herrerra, Roberto	Queens Park Rangers	Torquay United	
26 Hill, Colin F.	Sheffield United	Leicester City	
26 Horne, Brian	Millwall	Watford	
25 Hoult, Russell	Leicester City	Blackpool	
11 Ireland, Simon P.	Huddersfield Town	Wrexham	
5 Ironside, Ian	Middlesbrough	Scarborough	
5 Jeffrey, Michael R.	Bolton Wanderers	Doncaster Rovers	

Continued on Page 28

The things they said . . .

Anonymous First Division chairman, after the clubs voting for a breakaway premier league had been accused of greed:
"What's wrong with greed?" June 1991.

Vicenzo Matarasse, Bari chief, to David Platt:
"You're better than Paul Gascoigne. That's why I paid £5¼ million for you." July 1991.

Steve Coppell, Crystal Palace manager, on the proposed 'super league':
". . . the worst thing to have happened to football for a long time . . . The big clubs will get richer, leaving a situation like the one in Scotland, where only three teams have a realistic chance of winning anything." 1 August 1991.

Jim Farry, Scottish FA secretary, after 16 players had been sent off in the first week of the season:
"The main reason is the total ignorance of so-called professional players. They obviously don't know the laws of the game." 17 August 1991.

David Hay, St Mirren manager, on the same subject:
"Referees are following rules made by men who don't pay to watch football. Those rules are ruining the game for those who do. I appreciate they are trying to make the game more entertaining . . . but is it working?" 17 August 1991.

Terry Butcher, Coventry manager, after his side lost 1-0 at home to Wimbledon:
"I'd like to apologize to all the fans who paid good money to watch that. If people are subjected to that kind of garbage every Saturday, the crowds will be down to 200. If that game is the future of British football, I want no part of it." 31 August 1991.

Mike Bateson, Torquay chairman:
"I deplore the practice of sacking managers willy-nilly, despite the fact that two have been sacked in the 18 months I've been here." October 1991.

Graham Taylor, England manager, arguing for a reduction in size of the new Premier League, after finding 12 injured players in his squad for the European Championship qualifying match against Turkey:
"I don't think I would be doing my job if I did not make the point that we cannot carry on hammering our best players like this." 7 October 1991.

Sir Alf Ramsey, on England's 1-0 victory over Turkey at Wembley:
". . . performance was regrettable and a total misunderstanding in that it involved a team that could not possibly play together. It was a selection mistake by the manager, even allowing for the problems and the players who were unfit beforehand."

Bobby Charlton, on the same match:
"There was simply no cohesion in that England performance. There was no adventure and no one like Paul Gascoigne who was inventive."

Steve Coppell, joining the growing band of managers concerned with the increased workload on the leading players:
"We are treating top quality athletes like shire horses." 31 October 1991.

Jimmy Greaves, commenting on a refereeing decision during a televised Rumbelows Cup tie:
"I don't know what's going on out there, but whatever it is it's diabolical." October 1991.

Don Howe's tribute to Bryan Robson on his retirement from international football:
"He had a terrific inner drive and an inner desire to win. He always wanted to win more than anyone else. And he wanted to do that, not to grab a headline, but for his team and country." November 1991.

Gordon Taylor, PFA chief executive, on Sir John Quinton and Rick Parry, the new Premier League's chairman and chief executive designate, respectively:
"It's quite clear that football isn't safe in their hands." 15 December 1991.

Ken Bates, Chelsea chairman, in his programme notes:
"At a time when he complains of too many League games, I see he is planning more friendly matches at international level. When Graham Taylor pays the players' wages, he can call the tune." 15 December 1991.

Mike Bateson, Torquay chairman, after the FA took no further action against Brentford's Gary Blissett for the challenge that left Torquay's John Uzzell with a badly smashed cheekbone:
"We are spending enormous time and money to try to make football the family game that it was. To allow this to happen on the pitch, I know certain areas where it might have caused a riot. The FA are allowing hooliganism on the pitch to go unpunished." 20 January 1992.

Nat Lofthouse, on Third Division Bolton before their fourth round Cup tie:
"We're a First Division club in every sense of the word." 24 January 1992.

Sir John Hall, Newcastle chairman, on his manager's status:
"Let's kill off once and for all the rumours that Ossie's job is on the line. If he leaves this club, it will be of his own volition." 2 February 1992.

Kevin Keegan, after being presented to the Press by Sir John Hall as Newcastle's new manager:
"This is the only job in the world that I would ever have taken." 5 February 1992.

Sir John Hall, after sacking Ardiles:
"I feel absolutely dreadful about what has happened. . . . When I said those words, I meant each and every one of them."

Samesh Kumar, Birmingham chairman, after crowd disturbances during the match with Stoke led to a 20-minute interruption:
"There were some scandalous decisions by the referee and you can understand supporters being incited, but we don't condone violence. There has been no trouble here for 18 months." 29 February 1992.

Graeme Souness, Liverpool manager, after their physical game with Southampton:
"The referee was a disgrace. If that is the standard of refereeing, then English football has no future." 29 February 1992.

Kenny Hibbitt, Walsall manager, on the match referee after Chris Marsh was sent off against Cardiff:
"It was handbag stuff. If you start sending players off for scratching at each other, then you might as well send a team out wearing skirts." 8 March 1992.

Joseph S. Blatter, FIFA General Secretary, writing in FIFA News:
"In North America . . . the professional referee has long been a way of life. So he should be in football, the world's premier sport." March 1992.

Gerry Francis, QPR manager, after his side went 17 games with only one defeat:
"We are so high in the table, our noses are bleeding." 15 March 1992.

Brian Clough, on hearing the Liverpool manager was going in for heart surgery:
"My heart goes out to Graeme Souness." April 1992.

Barry Fry, Barnet manager, twice a heart-attack victim:
"If you think Liverpool is a danger to your health, try managing Barnet."

Michael Parkinson, *Daily Telegraph* feature writer, on the Souness/*Sun* affair:
"*It is difficult to imagine the new polished image of soccer they keep talking about when the manager of one of our most respected teams is pictured on the front page of a tabloid paper eating his girlfriend. . . . What he did was so crass, so insensitive and so plain bloody silly that he must still have been under the influence of the anaesthetic when the pictures were taken.*" 20 April 1992.

David Pleat, Luton manager, on his club's orange away strip:
"*It's a bloody stupid colour. I think one of the directors' wives must have chosen it.*" April 1992.

Kop choir to Manchester United team, whose title hopes had just disappeared at Anfield:
"*Always look on the bright side of life.*" May 1992.

***Sunderland Greats* book, in the biography of one of the old Roker heroes:**
"*Constructed entirely from pre-cast concrete, Charlie Hurley is without doubt the greatest human being to have ever lived. . . . He often played when fatally injured with his head missing.*"

Trevor Summers, new West Brom chairman, on the sacking of the manager:
"*If Bobby Gould is honest, he knew he had to win something this season, because he didn't have a hope of staying if he didn't. His style of play at times was not what the fans wanted.*" 5 May 1992.

David Hill, Sky TV head of sport, on the new £304m deal with the FA Premier League:
"*The biggest advance in TV football since the invention of the camera.*" May 1992.

Alex Ferguson, Manchester United manager, on the same subject:
"*The most ludicrous and backward step football has taken for a long time.*"

Rick Parry, the FA Premier League chief executive, on ITV's attempt to block the Sky deal:
"*We're not going to have a Premier League at this rate, with me in court all the time.*"

Gary Lineker:
"*I'm not as nice as all that. In fact I swore only last week.*"

Terry Venables, on seeing Paul Gascoigne finally sign for Lazio:
"*It's like watching your mother-in-law drive over a cliff in your new car.*"

Rod Stewart, rock star and stalwart Scottish fan, on the birth of his daughter:
"*It's like seeing Scotland score a goal. You never get used to it.*"

Mr Ellemann-Jensen, the Danish Foreign Minister, after Denmark, fresh from their referendum opting out of the Maastricht Treaty, won the European Championships by beating Germany 2-0 in the final:
"*If you can't join them, beat them.*" 26 June 1992.

Peter Schmeichel, the Danish goalkeeper, and John Jensen (7) combine to prevent Germany scoring in the 1992 European Championship Final. Denmark won 2-0. (Colorsport)

LEAGUE ATTENDANCES SINCE 1946–47

Season	Matches	Total	Div. 1	Div. 2	Div. 3 (S)	Div. 3 (N)
1946–47	1848	35,604,606	15,005,316	11,071,572	5,664,004	3,863,714
1947–48	1848	40,259,130	16,732,341	12,286,350	6,653,610	4,586,829
1948–49	1848	41,271,414	17,914,667	11,353,237	6,998,429	5,005,081
1949–50	1848	40,517,865	17,278,625	11,694,158	7,104,155	4,440,927
1950–51	2028	39,584,967	16,679,454	10,780,580	7,367,884	4,757,109
1951–52	2028	39,015,866	16,110,322	11,066,189	6,958,927	4,880,428
1952–53	2028	37,149,966	16,050,278	9,686,654	6,704,299	4,708,735
1953–54	2028	36,174,590	16,154,915	9,510,053	6,311,508	4,198,114
1954–55	2028	34,133,103	15,087,221	8,988,794	5,996,017	4,051,071
1955–56	2028	33,150,809	14,108,961	9,080,002	5,692,479	4,269,367
1956–57	2028	32,744,405	13,803,037	8,718,162	5,622,189	4,601,017
1957–58	2028	33,562,208	14,468,652	8,663,712	6,097,183	4,332,661
					Div. 3	Div. 4
1958–59	2028	33,610,985	14,727,691	8,641,997	5,946,600	4,276,697
1959–60	2028	32,538,611	14,391,227	8,399,627	5,739,707	4,008,050
1960–61	2028	28,619,754	12,926,948	7,033,936	4,784,256	3,874,614
1961–62	2015	27,979,902	12,061,194	7,453,089	5,199,106	3,266,513
1962–63	2028	28,885,852	12,490,239	7,792,770	5,341,362	3,261,481
1963–64	2028	28,535,022	12,486,626	7,594,158	5,419,157	3,035,081
1964–65	2028	27,641,168	12,708,752	6,984,104	4,436,245	3,512,067
1965–66	2028	27,206,980	12,480,644	6,914,757	4,779,150	3,032,429
1966–67	2028	28,902,596	14,242,957	7,253,819	4,421,172	2,984,648
1967–68	2028	30,107,298	15,289,410	7,450,410	4,013,087	3,354,391
1968–69	2028	29,382,172	14,584,851	7,382,390	4,339,656	3,075,275
1969–70	2028	29,600,972	14,868,754	7,581,728	4,223,761	2,926,729
1970–71	2028	28,194,146	13,954,337	7,098,265	4,377,213	2,764,331
1971–72	2028	28,700,729	14,484,603	6,769,308	4,697,392	2,749,426
1972–73	2028	25,448,642	13,998,154	5,631,730	3,737,252	2,081,506
1973–74	2027	24,982,203	13,070,991	6,326,108	3,421,624	2,163,480
1974–75	2028	25,577,977	12,613,178	6,955,970	4,086,145	1,992,684
1975–76	2028	24,896,053	13,089,861	5,798,405	3,948,449	2,059,338
1976–77	2028	26,182,800	13,647,585	6,250,597	4,152,218	2,132,400
1977–78	2028	25,392,872	13,255,677	6,474,763	3,332,042	2,330,390
1978–79	2028	24,540,627	12,704,549	6,153,223	3,374,558	2,308,297
1979–80	2028	24,623,975	12,163,002	6,112,025	3,999,328	2,349,620
1980–81	2028	21,907,569	11,392,894	5,175,442	3,637,854	1,701,379
1981–82	2028	20,006,961	10,420,793	4,750,463	2,836,915	1,998,790
1982–83	2028	18,766,158	9,295,613	4,974,937	2,943,568	1,552,040
1983–84	2028	18,358,631	8,711,448	5,359,757	2,729,942	1,557,484
1984–85	2028	17,849,835	9,761,404	4,030,823	2,667,008	1,390,600
1985–86	2028	16,488,577	9,037,854	3,551,968	2,490,481	1,408,274
1986–87	2028	17,379,218	9,144,676	4,168,131	2,350,970	1,715,441
1987–88	2030	17,959,732	8,094,571	5,341,599	2,751,275	1,772,287
1988–89	2036	18,464,192	7,809,993	5,887,805	3,035,327	1,791,067
1989–90	2036	19,445,442	7,883,039	6,867,674	2,803,551	1,891,178
1990–91	2036	19,508,202	8,618,709	6,285,068	2,835,759	1,768,666
1991–92	2064*	20,487,273	9,989,160	5,809,787	2,993,352	1,694,974

This is the first time since the war that attendances have risen for six consecutive seasons.

*Figures include matches played by Aldershot.

BARCLAYS LEAGUE ATTENDANCES 1991–92

	TOTAL ATTENDANCES	AVERAGE ATTENDANCES
TOTAL	20,487,273	9926
DIVISION 1	9,989,160	21,622
DIVISION 2	5,809,787	10,525
DIVISION 3	2,993,352	5423
DIVISION 4	1,694,974	3404

(Division 4 figures include matches played by Aldershot)

DIVISION ONE STATISTICS

	Average gate			Season 1991/92	
	1990/91	1991/92	+/−%	Highest	Lowest
Arsenal	36,864	31,905	−13.5	42,073	22,096
Aston Villa	25,663	24,818	−3.3	39,995	15,745
Chelsea	20,738	18,684	−9.9	30,230	7,148
Coventry City	13,794	13,876	+0.6	23,962	8,454
Crystal Palace	19,660	17,618	−10.4	29,017	12,109
Everton	25,028	23,148	−7.5	37,681	14,783
Leeds United	28,946	29,459	+1.8	33,020	26,220
Liverpool	36,038	34,799	−3.4	39,072	25,457
Luton Town	10,274	9,715	−5.4	13,410	7,533
Manchester City	27,874	27,690	−0.7	38,180	21,437
Manchester United	43,218	44,984	+4.1	47,576	38,554
Norwich City	15,468	13,858	−10.4	20,411	10,514
Nottingham Forest	22,137	23,721	+7.2	30,168	19,707
Notts County	8,164	10,987	+34.6	21,055	6,198
Oldham Athletic	13,247	15,087	+13.9	18,952	12,125
Queens Park Rangers	13,524	13,592	+0.5	22,603	8,495
Sheffield United	21,461	22,097	+3.0	31,832	16,062
Sheffield Wednesday	26,605	29,560	+11.1	40,327	20,574
Southampton	15,413	14,070	−8.7	18,581	8,658
Tottenham Hotspur	30,632	27,761	−9.4	35,087	19,834
West Ham United	22,551	21,342	−5.4	25,678	16,896
Wimbledon	7,631	6,905	−9.5	15,009	3,121

DIVISION TWO STATISTICS

	Average gate			Season 1991/92	
	1990/91	1991/92	+/−%	Highest	Lowest
Barnsley	8,937	7,508	−16.0	13,337	5,328
Blackburn Rovers	8,126	13,251	+63.1	19,511	8,898
Brighton & Hove Albion	8,386	8,002	−4.6	11,647	4,420
Bristol City	13,495	11,479	−14.9	20,183	7,735
Bristol Rovers	5,929	5,850	−1.3	7,622	3,547
Cambridge United	5,503	7,078	+28.6	9,741	4,810
Charlton Athletic	6,548	6,786	+3.6	15,357	3,658
Derby County	16,257	14,664	−9.8	22,608	10,559
Grimsby Town	7,237	6,921	−4.4	11,613	4,583
Ipswich Town	11,772	14,274	+21.3	26,467	8,646
Leicester City	11,546	15,202	+31.7	21,894	10,950
Middlesbrough	17,023	14,703	−13.6	19,424	9,685
Millwall	10,846	7,921	−27.0	12,882	5,703
Newcastle United	16,834	21,148	+25.6	30,261	13,136
Oxford United	5,780	5,671	−1.9	10,528	3,420
Plymouth Argyle	6,851	6,739	−1.6	17,459	4,090
Portsmouth	9,689	11,789	+21.7	20,133	7,147
Port Vale	8,092	7,382	−8.8	10,384	5,310
Southend United	6,174	6,733	+9.1	10,003	4,462
Sunderland	22,577	18,390	−18.5	29,224	12,790
Swindon Town	9,805	10,009	+2.1	13,238	7,261
Tranmere Rovers	6,740	8,845	+31.2	13,705	5,797
Watford	9,576	8,511	−11.1	13,547	4,785
Wolverhampton Wanderers	15,837	13,743	−13.2	19,123	8,536

DIVISION THREE STATISTICS

	Average gate			Season 1991/92	
	1990/91	*1991/92*	*+/−%*	*Highest*	*Lowest*
AFC Bournemouth	6,017	5,471	−9.1	7,721	3,558
Birmingham City	7,030	12,400	+76.4	27,508	8,154
Bolton Wanderers	7,277	6,030	−17.1	10,000	3,535
Bradford City	6,644	6,115	−8.0	10,050	4,170
Brentford	6,144	7,156	+16.5	12,071	4,586
Bury	3,572	2,901	−18.8	5,886	1,663
Chester City	1,564	1,857	+18.7	4,895	871
Darlington	4,021	2,904	−27.8	5,658	1,223
Exeter City	4,243	3,627	−14.5	5,830	2,214
Fulham	4,057	4,492	+10.7	8,671	2,465
Hartlepool United	3,180	3,201	+0.7	5,413	2,140
Huddersfield Town	5,351	7,540	+40.9	11,884	4,674
Hull City	6,165	4,115	−33.3	5,310	3,093
Leyton Orient	4,194	4,460	+6.3	7,347	2,795
Peterborough United	5,211	6,279	+20.5	14,539	2,810
Preston North End	5,214	4,722	−9.4	7,740	2,932
Reading	4,079	3,841	−5.8	6,649	2,535
Shrewsbury Town	3,442	3,456	+0.4	8,557	1,866
Stockport County	3,562	4,896	+37.5	8,129	2,745
Stoke City	11,565	13,007	+12.5	23,626	8,527
Swansea City	3,665	3,367	−8.1	5,629	2,081
Torquay United	2,986	2,734	−8.4	5,696	1,884
West Bromwich Albion	11,993	12,711	+6.0	26,168	8,439
Wigan Athletic	2,889	2,862	−0.9	5,950	1,787

DIVISION FOUR STATISTICS

	Average gate			Season 1991/92	
	1990/91	*1991/92*	*+/−%*	*Highest*	*Lowest*
Barnet	2,918	3,643	+24.8	5,090	2,038
Blackpool	4,059	4,335	+6.8	8,007	2,842
Burnley	7,882	10,521	+33.5	21,218	5,876
Cardiff City	2,946	6,195	+110.3	16,030	2,356
Carlisle United	3,006	2,554	−15.0	9,051	1,672
Chesterfield	3,712	3,439	−7.4	7,789	1,802
Crewe Alexandra	3,748	3,733	−0.4	5,530	2,476
Doncaster Rovers	2,831	2,058	−27.3	3,507	1,247
Gillingham	3,523	3,135	−11.0	6,717	2,322
Halifax Town	1,699	1,633	−3.9	4,291	881
Hereford United	2,599	2,735	+5.2	5,744	1,294
Lincoln City	2,967	2,822	−4.9	7,884	1,737
Maidstone United	1,854	1,429	−22.9	3,264	842
Mansfield Town	2,683	3,803	+41.7	8,333	1,966
Northampton Town	3,710	2,789	−24.8	4,344	1,784
Rochdale	2,238	2,784	+24.4	8,175	1,691
Rotherham United	4,600	4,750	+3.3	8,930	3,137
Scarborough	1,597	1,677	+5.0	2,604	935
Scunthorpe United	3,114	3,189	+2.4	5,303	2,224
Walsall	4,149	3,367	−18.8	5,287	2,045
Wrexham	1,885	2,605	+38.4	4,053	1,266
York City	2,516	2,506	−0.4	7,620	1,605

*The above figures include games played by Aldershot before termination of their League membership.

LEAGUE CUP FINALISTS 1961–92

Played as a two-leg final until 1966. All subsequent finals at Wembley.

Year	Winners	Runners-up	Score
1961	Aston Villa	Rotherham U	0-2, 3-0 (aet)
1962	Norwich C	Rochdale	3-0, 1-0
1963	Birmingham C	Aston Villa	3-1, 0-0
1964	Leicester C	Stoke C	1-1, 3-2
1965	Chelsea	Leicester C	3-2, 0-0
1966	WBA	West Ham U	1-2, 4-1
1967	QPR	WBA	3-2
1968	Leeds U	Arsenal	1-0
1969	Swindon T	Arsenal	3-1 (aet)
1970	Manchester C	WBA	2-1 (aet)
1971	Tottenham H	Aston Villa	2-0
1972	Stoke C	Chelsea	2-1
1973	Tottenham H	Norwich C	1-0
1974	Wolverhampton W	Manchester C	2-1
1975	Aston Villa	Norwich C	1-0
1976	Manchester C	Newcastle U	2-1
1977	Aston Villa	Everton	0-0, 1-1 (aet), 3-2 (aet)
1978	Nottingham F	Liverpool	0-0 (aet), 1-0
1979	Nottingham F	Southampton	3-2
1980	Wolverhampton W	Nottingham F	1-0
1981	Liverpool	West Ham U	1-1 (aet), 2-1

MILK CUP

Year	Winners	Runners-up	Score
1982	Liverpool	Tottenham H	3-1 (aet)
1983	Liverpool	Manchester U	2-1 (aet)
1984	Liverpool	Everton	0-0 (aet), 1-0
1985	Norwich C	Sunderland	1-0
1986	Oxford U	QPR	3-0

LITTLEWOODS CUP

Year	Winners	Runners-up	Score
1987	Arsenal	Liverpool	2-1
1988	Luton T	Arsenal	3-2
1989	Nottingham F	Luton T	3-1
1990	Nottingham F	Oldham Ath	1-0

RUMBELOWS LEAGUE CUP

Year	Winners	Runners-up	Score
1991	Sheffield W	Manchester U	1-0
1992	Manchester U	Nottingham F	1-0

LEAGUE CUP WINS
Liverpool 4, Nottingham F 4, Aston Villa 3, Manchester C 2, Norwich C 2, Tottenham H 2, Wolverhampton W 2, Arsenal 1, Birmingham C 1, Chelsea 1, Leeds U 1, Leicester C 1, Luton T 1, Manchester U 1, Oxford U 1, QPR 1, Sheffield W 1, Stoke C 1, Swindon T 1, WBA 1.

APPEARANCES IN FINALS
Liverpool 6, Nottingham F 6, Aston Villa 5, Arsenal 4, Norwich C 4, Manchester C 3, Manchester U 3, Tottenham H 3, WBA 3, Chelsea 2, Everton 2, Leicester C 2, Luton T 2, QPR 2, Stoke C 2, West Ham U 2, Wolverhampton W 2, Birmingham C 1, Leeds U 1, Newcastle U 1, Oldham U 1, Oxford U 1, Rochdale 1, Rotherham U 1, Sheffield W 1, Southampton 1, Sunderland 1, Swindon T 1.

APPEARANCES IN SEMI-FINALS
Aston Villa 8, Liverpool 8, Tottenham H 8, West Ham U 7, Arsenal 6, Manchester U 6, Nottingham F 6, Chelsea 5, Manchester C 5, Norwich C 5, Leeds U 4, WBA 4, Burnley 3, Everton 3, QPR 3, Wolverhampton W 3, Birmingham C 2, Bristol C 2, Coventry C 2, Ipswich T 2, Leicester C 2, Luton T 2, Middlesbrough 2, Oxford U 2, Plymouth Arg 2, Southampton 2, Stoke C 2, Sunderland 2, Swindon T 2, Blackburn R 1, Blackpool 1, Bolton W 1, Bury 1, Cardiff C 1, Carlisle U 1, Chester C 1, Derby Co 1, Huddersfield T 1, Newcastle U 1, Oldham Ath 1, Peterborough U 1, Rochdale 1, Rotherham U 1, Sheffield W 1, Shrewsbury T 1, Walsall 1, Watford 1.

LEAGUE CUP FINALISTS 1961–91

1960–61 ROTHERHAM UNITED Ironside; Perry, Morgan, Lambert, Madden, Waterhouse, Webster, Weston, Houghton, Kirkman, Bambridge. *Scorers:* Webster, Kirkman.

2–0 ASTON VILLA Sims; Lynn, Lee, Crowe, Dugdale, Deakin, McEwan, Thomson, Brown, Wylie, McParland.
ASTON VILLA Sidebottom; Neal, Lee, Crowe, Dugdale, Deakin, McEwan, O'Neill, McParland, Thomson, Burrows. *Scorers:* O'Neill, Burrows, McParland.

3–0 ROTHERHAM UNITED Ironside; Perry, Morgan, Lambert, Madden, Waterhouse, Webster, Weston,
aet Houghton, Kirkman, Bambridge. **Aston Villa won on aggregate 3–2.**

1961–62 ROCHDALE Burgin; Milburn, Winton, Bodell, Aspden, Thompson, Wragg, Hepton, Bimpson, Cairns, Whitaker.

0–3 NORWICH CITY Kennon; McCrohan, Ashman, Burton, Butler, Mullett, Mannion, Lythgoe, Scott, Hill, Punton. *Scorers:* Lythgoe 2, Punton.
NORWICH CITY Kennon; McCrohan, Ashman, Burton, Butler, Mullett, Mannion, Lythgoe, Scott, Hill, Punton. *Scorer:* Hill.

1–0 ROCHDALE Burgin; Milburn, Winton, Bodell, Aspden, Thompson, Whyke, Richardson, Bimpson, Cairns, Whitaker. **Norwich City won on aggregate 4–0.**

1962–63 BIRMINGHAM CITY Schofield; Lynn, Green, Hennessey, Smith, Beard, Hellawell, Bloomfield, Harris, Leek, Auld. *Scorers:* Leek 2, Bloomfield.

3–1 ASTON VILLA Sims; Fraser, Aitken, Crowe, Sleeuwenhoek, Lee, Baker, Graham, Thomson, Wylie, Burrows. *Scorer:* Thomson.
ASTON VILLA Chatterley took the place of Sleeuwenhoek.

0–0 BIRMINGHAM CITY No change in team. **Birmingham City won on aggregate 3–1.**

1963–64 STOKE CITY Leslie; Asprey, Allen, Palmer, Kinnell, Skeels, Dobing, Viollet, Ritchie, McIlroy, Bebbington. *Scorer:* Bebbington.

1–1 LEICESTER CITY Banks; Sjoberg, Appleton, Dougan, King, Cross, Riley, Heath, Keyworth, Gibson, Stringfellow. *Scorer:* Gibson.
LEICESTER CITY Banks; Sjoberg, Norman, Cross, King, Appleton, Riley, Gibson, Keyworth, Sweenie, Stringfellow. *Scorers:* Stringfellow, Gibson, Riley.

3–2 STOKE CITY Irvine; Asprey, Allen, Palmer, Kinnell, Skeels, Dobing, Viollet, Ritchie, McIlroy, Bebbington. *Scorers:* Viollet, Kinnell. **Leicester City won on aggregate 4–3.**

1964–65 CHELSEA Bonetti; Hinton, Harris, Hollins, Young, Boyle, Murray, Graham, McCreadie, Venables, Tambling. *Scorers:* Tambling, Venables (pen), McCreadie.

3–2 LEICESTER CITY Banks; Sjoberg, Norman, Chalmers, King, Appleton, Hodgson, Cross, Goodfellow, Gibson, Sweenie. *Scorers:* Appleton, Goodfellow.
LEICESTER CITY Banks; Walker, Norman, Roberts, Sjoberg, Appleton, Hodgson, Cross, Goodfellow, Gibson, Stringfellow.

0–0 CHELSEA Bonetti; Hinton, McCreadie, Harris, Mortimore, Upton, Murray, Boyle, Bridges, Venables, Tambling. **Chelsea won on aggregate 3–2.**

1965–66 WEST HAM UNITED Standen; Burnett, Burkett, Peters, Brown, Moore, Brabrook, Boyce, Byrne, Hurst, Dear. *Scorers:* Moore, Byrne.

2–1 WEST BROMWICH ALBION Potter; Cram, Fairfax, Fraser, Campbell, Williams, Brown, Astle, Kaye, Lovett, Clark. *Scorer:* Astle.
WEST BROMWICH ALBION Potter; Cram, Fairfax, Fraser, Campbell, Williams, Brown, Astle, Kaye, Hope, Clark. *Scorers:* Kaye, Brown, Clark, Williams.

4–1 WEST HAM UNITED Standen; Burnett, Peters, Bovington, Brown, Moore, Brabrook, Boyce, Byrne, Hurst, Sissons. *Scorer:* Peters. **West Bromwich Albion won on aggregate 5–3.**

1966–67 QUEEN'S PARK RANGERS Springett; Hazell, Langley, Sibley, Hunt, Keen, Lazarus, Sanderson, Allen, Marsh, Morgan R. *Scorers:* Morgan R, Marsh, Lazarus.

3–2 WEST BROMWICH ALBION Sheppard; Cram, Williams, Collard, Clarke D, Fraser, Brown, Astle, Kaye, Hope, Clark C. *Scorer:* C Clark 2.

1967–68 LEEDS UNITED Sprake; Reaney, Cooper, Bremner, Charlton, Hunter, Greenhoff, Lorimer, Madeley, Giles, Gray (Belfitt). *Scorer:* Cooper.

1–0 ARSENAL Furnell; Storey, McNab, McLintock, Simpson, Ure, Radford, Jenkins, Graham, Sammels, Armstrong.

1968–69 SWINDON TOWN Downsborough; Thomas, Trollope, Butler, Burrows, Harland, Heath, Smart, Smith, Noble (Penman), Rogers. *Scorers:* Smart, Rogers 2.

3–1 ARSENAL Wilson; Storey, McNab, McLintock, Ure, Simpson (Graham), Radford, Sammels, Court, Gould, Armstrong. *Scorer:* Gould.

1969–70 MANCHESTER CITY Corrigan; Book, Mann, Doyle, Booth, Oakes, Heslop, Bell, Summerbee (Bowyer), Lee, Pardoe. *Scorers:* Doyle, Pardoe.

2–1 WEST BROMWICH ALBION Osborne; Fraser, Wilson, Brown, Talbut, Kaye, Cantello, Suggett, Astle, Hartford (Krzywicki), Hope. *Scorer:* Astle.

1970–71 TOTTENHAM HOTSPUR Jennings; Kinnear, Knowles, Mullery, Collins, Beal, Gilzean, Perryman, Chivers, Peters, Neighbour. *Scorer:* Chivers 2.

2–0 ASTON VILLA Dunn; Bradley, Aitken, Godfrey, Turnbull, Tiler, McMahon, Rioch, Lochhead, Hamilton, Anderson.

622

1971–72 STOKE CITY Banks; Marsh, Pejic, Bernard, Smith, Bloor, Conroy, Greenhoff (Mahoney), Ritchie, Dobing, Eastham. *Scorers:* Conroy, Eastham.

2–1 CHELSEA Bonetti; Mulligan (Baldwin), Harris, Hollins, Dempsey, Webb, Cooke, Osgood, Hudson, Houseman. *Scorer:* Osgood.

1972–73 TOTTENHAM HOTSPUR Jennings; Kinnear, Knowles, Pratt (Coates), England, Beal, Gilzean, Perryman, Chivers, Peters, Pearce. *Scorer:* Coates.

1–0 NORWICH CITY Keelan; Payne, Butler, Stringer, Forbes, Briggs, Livermore, Blair (Howard), Cross, Paddon, Anderson.

1973–74 WOLVERHAMPTON WANDERERS Pierce; Palmer, Parkin, Bailey, Munro, McAlle, Sunderland, Hibbitt, Richards, Dougan, Wagstaffe (Powell). *Scorers:* Hibbitt, Richards.

2–1 MANCHESTER CITY MacRae; Pardoe, Donachie, Doyle, Booth, Towers, Summerbee, Bell, Lee, Law, Marsh. *Scorer:* Bell.

1974–75 ASTON VILLA Cumbes; Robson, Aitken, Ross, Nicholl, McDonald, Graydon, Little, Leonard, Hamilton, Carrodus. *Scorer:* Graydon.

1–0 NORWICH CITY Keelan; Machin, Sullivan, Morris, Forbes, Stringer, Miller, MacDougall, Boyer, Suggett, Powell.

1975–76 MANCHESTER CITY Corrigan; Keegan, Donachie, Doyle, Watson, Oakes, Barnes, Booth, Royle, Hartford, Tueart. *Scorers:* Barnes, Tueart.

2–1 NEWCASTLE UNITED Mahoney; Nattrass, Kennedy, Barrowclough, Keeley, Howard, Burns, Cassidy, Macdonald, Gowling, Craig. *Scorer:* Gowling.

1976–77 ASTON VILLA Burridge; Gidman, Robson, Phillips, Nicholl, Mortimer, Deehan, Little, Gray, Cropley, Carrodus.

0–0 EVERTON Lawson; Jones, Darracott, Lyons, McNaught, King, Hamilton, Dobson, Latchford, McKenzie, Goodlass.   *First replay (at Hillsborough)*

R: 1–1 ASTON VILLA Burridge; Gidman, Robson, Phillips, Nicholl, Mortimer, Deehan, Little, Gray, Cowans,
aet Carrodus. *Scorer:* Kenyon og.

EVERTON Lawson; Bernard, Darracott, Lyons, McNaught, King, Hamilton (Pearson), Kenyon, Latchford, McKenzie, Goodlass. *Scorer:* Latchford.   *Second replay (at Old Trafford, Manchester)*

R: 3–2 ASTON VILLA Burridge; Gidman (Smith), Robson, Phillips, Nicholl, Mortimer, Graydon, Little, Deehan,
aet Cropley, Cowans. *Scorers:* Little 2, Nicholl.

EVERTON Lawson; Robinson, Darracott, Lyons, McNaught, King, Hamilton, Dobson, Latchford, Pearson (Seargeant), Goodlass. *Scorers:* Latchford, Lyons.

1977–78 NOTTINGHAM FOREST Woods; Anderson, Clark, McGovern (O'Hare), Lloyd, Burns, O'Neill, Bowyer, Withe, Woodcock, Robertson.

0–0 LIVERPOOL Clemence; Neal, Smith, Thompson, Kennedy (Fairclough), Hughes, Dalglish, Case,
aet Heighway, McDermott, Callaghan.   *Replay (at Old Trafford, Manchester)*

R: 1–0 NOTTINGHAM FOREST Woods; Anderson, Clark, O'Hare, Lloyd, Burns, O'Neill, Bowyer, Withe, Woodcock, Robertson. *Scorer:* Robertson (pen).

LIVERPOOL Clemence; Neal, Smith, Thompson, Kennedy, Hughes, Dalglish, Case (Fairclough), Heighway, McDermott, Callaghan.

1978–79 NOTTINGHAM FOREST Shilton; Barrett, Clark, McGovern, Lloyd, Needham, O'Neill, Gemmill, Birtles, Woodcock, Robertson. *Scorers:* Birtles 2, Woodcock.

3–2 SOUTHAMPTON Gennoe; Golac, Peach, Williams, Nicholl, Waldron, Ball, Boyer, Hayes (Sealy), Holmes, Curran. *Scorers:* Peach, Holmes.

1979–80 WOLVERHAMPTON WANDERERS Bradshaw; Palmer, Parkin, Daniel, Berry, Hughes, Carr, Hibbitt, Gray, Richards, Eves. *Scorer:* Gray.

1–0 NOTTINGHAM FOREST Shilton; Anderson, Gray, McGovern, Needham, Burns, O'Neill, Bowyer, Birtles, Francis, Robertson.

1980–81 LIVERPOOL Clemence; Neal, Kennedy A, Irwin, Kennedy R, Hansen, Dalglish, Lee, Heighway (Case), McDermott, Souness. *Scorer:* Kennedy A.

1–1 WEST HAM UNITED Parkes; Stewart, Lampard, Bonds, Martin, Devonshire, Neighbour, Goddard,
aet (Pearson), Cross, Brooking, Pike. *Scorer:* Stewart (pen).   *Replay (at Villa Park)*

R: 2–1 LIVERPOOL Clemence; Neal, Kennedy A, Thompson, Kennedy R, Hansen, Dalglish, Lee, Rush, McDermott, Case. *Scorers:* Dalglish, Hansen.

WEST HAM UNITED Parkes; Stewart, Lampard, Bonds, Martin, Devonshire, Neighbour, Goddard, Cross, Brooking, Pike (Pearson). *Scorer:* Goddard.

1981–82 LIVERPOOL Grobbelaar; Neal, Kennedy, Thompson A, Whelan, Lawrenson, Dalglish, Lee, Rush, McDermott (Johnson), Souness. *Scorers:* Whelan 2, Rush.

3–1 TOTTENHAM HOTSPUR Clemence; Hughton, Miller, Price, Hazard (Villa), Perryman, Ardiles,
aet Archibald, Galvin, Hoddle, Crooks. *Scorer:* Archibald.

1982–83 LIVERPOOL Grobbelaar; Neal, Kennedy, Lawrenson, Whelan, Hansen, Dalglish, Lee, Rush, Johnston (Fairclough), Souness. *Scorers:* Kennedy, Whelan.

2–1 MANCHESTER UNITED Bailey; Duxbury, Albiston, Moses, Moran (Macari), McQueen, Wilkins,
aet Muhren, Stapleton, Whiteside, Coppell. *Scorer:* Whiteside.

1983–84 LIVERPOOL Grobbelaar; Neal, Kennedy, Lawrenson, Whelan, Hansen, Dalglish, Lee, Rush, Johnston (Robinson), Souness.

0–0 EVERTON Southall; Stevens, Bailey, Ratcliffe, Mountfield, Reid, Irvine, Heath, Sharp, Richardson,
aet Sheedy (Harper).

R: **1–0** LIVERPOOL   Grobbelaar; Neal, Kennedy, Lawrenson, Whelan, Hansen, Dalglish, Lee, Rush, Johnston, Souness. *Scorer:* Souness.

EVERTON   Southall; Stevens, Bailey, Ratcliffe, Mountfield, Reid, Irvine (King), Heath, Sharp, Richardson, Harper.   *Replay (at Maine Road, Manchester)*

1984–85 NORWICH CITY   Woods; Haylock, Van Wyk, Bruce, Mendham, Watson, Barham, Channon, Deehan, Hartford, Donowa. *Scorer:* Chisholm (og).

1–0 SUNDERLAND   Turner; Venison, Pickering, Bennett, Chisholm, Corner (Gayle), Daniel, Wallace, Hodgson, Berry, Walker.

1985–86 OXFORD UNITED   Judge; Langan, Trewick, Phillips, Briggs, Shotton, Houghton, Aldridge, Charles, Hebberd, Brock. *Scorers:* Hebberd, Houghton, Charles.

3–0 QUEEN'S PARK RANGERS   Barron; McDonald, Dawes, Neill, Wicks, Fenwick, Allen (Rosenoir), James, Bannister, Byrne, Robinson.

1986–87 ARSENAL   Lukic; Anderson, Sansom, Williams, O'Leary, Adams, Rocastle, Davis, Quinn (Groves), Nicholas, Hayes (Thomas). *Scorer:* Nicholas 2.

2–1 LIVERPOOL   Grobbelaar; Gillespie, Venison, Spackman, Whelan, Hansen, Walsh (Dalglish), Johnston, Rush, Molby, McMahon (Wark). *Scorer:* Rush.

1987–88 LUTON TOWN   Dibble; Breacker, Johnson, Hill, Foster, Donaghy, Wilson, Stein B, Harford (Stein M), Preece (Grimes). *Scorers:* Stein B 2, Wilson.

3–2 ARSENAL   Lukic; Winterburn, Sansom, Thomas, Caesar, Adams, Rocastle, Davis, Smith, Groves (Hayes), Richardson. *Scorers:* Hayes, Smith.

1988–89 NOTTINGHAM FOREST   Sutton; Laws, Pearce, Walker, Wilson, Hodge, Gaynor, Webb, Clough, Chapman, Parker. *Scorers:* Clough 2 (1 pen), Webb.

3–1 LUTON TOWN   Sealey; Breacker, Grimes (McDonough), Preece, Foster, Beaumont, Wilson, Wegerle, Harford, Hill, Black. *Scorer:* Harford.

1989–90 NOTTINGHAM FOREST   Sutton; Laws, Pearce, Walker, Chettle, Hodge, Crosby, Parker, Clough, Jemson, Carr. *Scorer:* Jemson.

1–0 OLDHAM ATHLETIC   Rhodes; Irwin, Barlow, Henry, Barrett, Warhurst, Adams, Ritchie, Bunn (Palmer), Milligan, Holden R.

1990–91 SHEFFIELD WEDNESDAY   Turner; Nilsson, King, Harkes (Madden), Shirtliff, Pearson, Wilson, Sheridan, Hirst, Williams, Worthington. *Scorer:* Sheridan.

1–0 MANCHESTER UNITED   Sealey; Irwin, Blackmore, Bruce, Webb (Phelan), Pallister, Robson, Ince, McClair, Hughes, Sharpe.

Manchester United's Andrei Kanchelskis (left) prepares to cross the ball with Nottingham Forest full-back Brett Williams attempting to block the kick. United won the 1992 Rumbelows Cup Final 1–0 with a goal from Brian McClair. (Colorsport)

RUMBELOWS CUP 1991–92

FIRST ROUND, FIRST LEG
20 AUG

Barnet (2) 5 *(Evans 2, Carter, Bull 2)*
Brentford (2) 5 *(Cadette 2, Godfrey, Holdsworth 2)* 2416
Barnet: Berryman; Blackford, Naylor, Horton (Lynch), Howell, Johnson, Poole, Carter, Bull, Evans, Hoddle.
Brentford: Bayes; Ratcliffe (Gayle), Manuel, Bates, Evans, Buckle, Jones, Godfrey, Holdsworth, Cadette (Blissett), Smillie.

Blackburn R (1) 1 *(Buckley (og))*
Hull C (0) 1 *(Payton)* 6308
Blackburn R: Mimms; Atkins, Sulley, Reid, Moran, Dobson, Irvine, Agnew, Speedie, Garner, Shepstone (Gayle).
Hull C: Fettis; Mail, Jacobs, Wilcox, Buckley, Calvert, Hobson, Payton, Hunter, Norton, Jenkinson.

Bolton W (1) 2 *(Philliskirk, Darby)*
York C (0) 2 *(McCarthy, Blackstone)* 3017
Bolton W: Rose; Brown P, Cowdrill, Kelly, Seagraves, Stubbs, Storer, Comstive (Burke), Reeves, Philliskirk, Darby.
York C: Marples; McMillan, Crosby, Reid, Tutill, Stancliffe (Atkin), McCarthy, Pepper, Blackstone, Naylor (Hall), Canham.

Chester C (0) 1 *(Barrow)*
Lincoln C (0) 0 1018
Chester C: Siddall; Whelan, Albiston, Butler (McGuinness), Abel, Lightfoot, Bishop, Barrow, Rimmer, Bennett, Pugh (Croft).
Lincoln C: Dickins; Smith (Nicholson), Clarke, West D, West G, Carmichael, Finney, Ward, Lee, Dobson (Alexander), Puttnam.

Crewe Alex (3) 5 *(Edwards, Gardiner, Naylor 2, Callaghan)*
Doncaster R (1) 2 *(Whitehurst 2)* 2900
Crewe Alex: Greygoose; Wilson, Jones, Carr, Callaghan, Walters, Hignett (Murphy), Naylor (Garvey), Futcher, Gardiner, Edwards.
Doncaster R: Samways; Rankine, Noteman, Cullen, Jones, Boyle, Reddish, Muir, Tynan (Rowe), Whitehurst, Bennett.

Darlington (1) 1 *(Cook)*
Huddersfield T (0) 0 3140
Darlington: Prudhoe; McJannet, Gray (Mardenborough), Willis, Smith, Gill, Cook, Toman, Borthwick, Cork, Coatsworth.
Huddersfield T: Clarke; Trevitt, Charlton, Marsden, Mitchell, Jackson, O'Regan, Onuora, Roberts, Starbuck, Barnett (Donovan).

Halifax T (3) 3 *(Norris (pen), Richardson, Juryeff)*
Tranmere R (2) 4 *(Irons, Aldridge 3 (1 pen))* 1910
Halifax T: Gould; Barr, Kamara, Abbott, Richards, Graham, Megson (Patterson), Norris, Juryeff, Richardson, Cooper.
Tranmere R: Nixon; Higgins, Brannan, Irons, Hughes, Garnett, Morrissey, Aldridge, Steel (Malkin), Martindale, Thomas.

Hartlepool U (1) 1 *(Baker)*
Bury (0) 0 2833
Hartlepool U: Hodge; Nobbs, McKinnon, McCreery (Tinkler), MacPhail, Bennyworth, Gabbiadini, Olsson, Baker, Honour, Dalton.

Bury: Kelly; Wilson D, Stanislaus, Robinson, Valentine, Greenall, Lee, Smith (Mauge), Stevens (Hulme), Parkinson, Kearney.

Leyton Orient (3) 5 *(Burnett, Nugent 2, Sayer, Berry)*
Northampton T (0) 0 2954
Leyton Orient: Heald; Howard, Dickenson, Zoricich, Day, Bart-Williams, Berry (Carter), Burnett, Nugent, Sayer, Otto.
Northampton T: Gleasure; Chard, Wilson (Johnson), Terry, Angus, Brown, Burnham (Campbell), Quow, Bell, Adcock, Gernon.

Mansfield T (0) 0
Blackpool (2) 3 *(Bamber 2, Charles (og))* 2124
Mansfield T: Beasley; Fleming, Withe, Spooner, Fee, Gray, Ford, Holland, Stant, Wilkinson (Stringfellow), Charles.
Blackpool: McIlhargey; Davies, Wright, Groves, Stoneman, Gore, Rodwell, Gouck, Bamber, Garner, Eyres.

Peterborough U (1) 3 *(Gavin 3)*
Aldershot (0) 1 *(Bertschin)* 2731
Peterborough U: Barber; White, Butterworth, Halsall, Robinson D, Welsh, Luke, Ebdon, Riley, Gavin, Kimble.
Aldershot: Granville; Brown, Cooper, Burvill (Puckett), Flower, Whitlock, Rees, Henry, Bertschin, Ogley, Stewart (Heath).

Portsmouth (1) 2 *(Clarke, Kuhl)*
Gillingham (0) 1 *(Beadle)* 4801
Portsmouth: Knight; Awford, Beresford, Burns, Symons, Butters, Anderton, Kuhl, Clarke, Whittingham (Chamberlain), Powell.
Gillingham: Lim; O'Shea, Martin, Elsey, Walker, Butler, Clark, Lovell, Crown (Beadle), O'Connor, Eeles (Trusson).

Preston NE (2) 5 *(Wrightson, Swann 2, Shaw, Joyce (pen))*
Scarborough (2) 4 *(Ashdjian, Mooney, Hirst, Foreman)* 2683
Preston NE: Farnworth; Senior, Swann, Wrightson, Flynn, Berry, Thompson, Joyce, Jepson, Shaw, James.
Scarborough: Priestley; James, Mudd, Lee, Hirst, Meyer, Ashdjian (Jules), Mockler (Moore), Mooney, Foreman, Himsworth.

Rochdale (2) 5 *(Milner 2, Ryan, Whitehall 2)*
Carlisle U (1) 1 *(Barnsley)* 1650
Rochdale: Gray; Whitehall, Ryan, Brown T, Reeves, Jones, Graham, Doyle, Flounders, Milner, Halpin.
Carlisle U: O'Hanlon; Armstrong, Barnsley, Miller, Jeffels, Graham, Thomas, Thorpe (Wilkes), Walling, Fyfe, Proudlock.

Rotherham U (0) 1 *(Robinson)*
Grimsby T (2) 3 *(Dobbin, Jones, Rees)* 3839
Rotherham U: Mercer; Hutchings, Robinson, Richardson, Johnson, Law, Goodwin, Barrick (Goater), Cunningham, Page, Hazel.
Grimsby T: Sherwood; McDermott, Agnew (Jones), Futcher, Lever (Birtles), Dobbin, Watson, Gilbert, Rees, Jobling, Woods.

Shrewsbury T (1) 1 *(Summerfield)*
Plymouth Arg (0) 1 *(Morrison)* 2152
Shrewsbury T: Hughes; Gorman, Lynch, Henry, Heathcote, Blake, Smith, Summerfield, Spink, Hopkins, Lyne.

Plymouth Arg: Wilmot; Salman, Spearing, Marker, Cross, Morgan, Barlow, Marshall, Turner, Morrison, Fiore (Clement).

Stockport Co (0) 1 *(Wheeler)*
Bradford C (1) 1 *(Tinnion (pen))* 3834
Stockport Co: Redfern; Thorpe (Knowles), Williams P, Frain, Barras, Williams B, Gannon (Wheeler), Ward, Francis, Beaumont, Lewis.
Bradford C: Tomlinson; Mitchell, Dowson, James, Oliver, Gardner, Babb, Duxbury L, Torpey, Tinnion, Stewart.

Swansea C (1) 2 *(Thornber, Chalmers)*
Walsall (0) 2 *(Ntamark, MacDonald (pen))* 2029
Swansea C: Bracey; Jenkins, Thornber, McClean, Harris, Hough, Davies (Chalmers), Cornforth, Raynor (Coughlin), Connor, Legg.
Walsall: Gayle; Williams, Statham, Methven, Musker, Smith, MacDonald, Ntamark, Lane, Cecere (Marsh), McDonald.

Swindon T (2) 2 *(Mitchell, Hazard)*
WBA (0) 0 6611
Swindon T: Digby; Foley (Jones), Summerbee, Hoddle, Calderwood, Taylor, Hazard, Shearer, Simpson, MacLaren, Mitchell (White).
WBA: Naylor; Bradley, Harbey, Ford, Strodder, Burgess, Bannister, Goodman, Foster (McNally), Shakespeare, Ampadu (Williams).

Torquay U (1) 2 *(Elliott, Loram (pen))*
Hereford U (0) 0 2410
Torquay U: Howells; Myers, Loram, Whiston, Elliott, Holmes M, Hodges, Colcombe, Rowland, Dobie, Dobbins.
Hereford U: Elliott; Vaughan (Fry), Downs, Theodosiou, Devine, Lowndes, Hall, Heritage, Brain, Robinson, Narbett.

Watford (2) 2 *(Blissett, Porter)*
Southend U (0) 0 6231
Watford: James; Gibbs, Soloman, Dublin, McLaughlin, Putney, Blissett, Kennedy (Thomas), Butler, Porter, Nicholas.
Southend U: Sansome; Austin, Powell, Martin, Edwards, Prior, Ansah, Sussex, O'Callaghan (Tillson), Benjamin, Angell.

Wigan Ath (1) 3 *(Patterson, Griffiths (pen), Worthington)*
Burnley (1) 1 *(Conroy)* 2826
Wigan Ath: Adkins; Parkinson, Jones, Atherton, Patterson, Langley, Powell, Rimmer, Daley, Worthington (Gray), Griffiths.
Burnley: Pearce; Measham, Bray, Davis, Pender, Monington, Eli (Harper), Deary, Francis, Conroy, Jakub (Farrell).

Wrexham (0) 1 *(Thackeray)*
Scunthorpe U (0) 0 1621
Wrexham: O'Keefe; Thackeray, Hardy, Sertori, Thomas, Jones J, Bowden, Davies, Connolly, Jones L, Preece.
Scunthorpe U: Musselwhite; Joyce, Longden, Hine, Hicks, Humphries, Alexander (Lister), Hamilton, Daws, Buckley, Helliwell.

21 AUG

Cambridge U (0) 1 *(Claridge)*
Reading (0) 0 3701
Cambridge U: Vaughan; Fensome, Kimble, Bailie, Clayton, O'Shea, Cheetham, Wilkins, Dublin, Taylor, Philpott (Claridge).

Reading: Francis; Jones, Richardson, McPherson, Cooper, Williams, Holzman, Dillon, Gooding, Leworthy, Gilkes (McGhee).

Cardiff C (1) 3 *(Millar, Gibbins, Searle)*
Bournemouth (1) 2 *(Morrell, Cooke)* 3439
Cardiff C: Hansbury; Jones, Searle, Gibbins, Abraham, Perry, Griffith (Pike), Matthews, Millar, Dale, Heard (Lewis).
Bournemouth: Bartram; Baker, Morrell, Morris, Watson, O'Driscoll, Rowland (Cooke), Jones, Quinn, Case, Holmes.

Charlton Ath (2) 4 *(Leaburn, Minto, Walsh, Peake)*
Fulham (0) 2 *(Brazil 2 (2 pens)) at West Ham* 3027
Charlton Ath: Bolder; Pitcher, Minto, Peake, Gritt, Gatting, Lee, Bacon, Leaburn, Nelson, Walsh (Salako).
Fulham: Stannard; Marshall, Pike (Cobb), Newson, Eckhardt, Thomas, Scott, Onwere, Haag (Milton), Brazil, Morgan.

Exeter C (0) 0
Birmingham C (1) 1 *(Rodgerson)* 4071
Exeter C: Malloy; Hiley, Brown, Williams, Daniels, O'Donnell, Rowbotham (Hobson), Cooper, Moran, Kelly, Marshall.
Birmingham C: Thomas; Clarkson, Frain, Yates, Hicks, Mardon, Rodgerson, Dolan, Peer, Gleghorn, Sturridge (Okenla).

Leicester C (1) 3 *(Kitson, Kelly, Mills)*
Maidstone U (0) 0 9610
Leicester C: Poole; Mills, Platnauer, Fitzpatrick, Walsh, James, Gibson, Reid (Oldfield), Ward (Wright), Kelly, Kitson.
Maidstone U: Hesford; Haylock, Thompson, Oxbrow, Davis, Osborne, Gall (Cuggy), Painter, Donegal (Lillis), Sandeman, Rumble.

Stoke C (1) 1 *(Ellis)*
Chesterfield (0) 0 7815
Stoke C: Fox; Butler, Cranson, Kevan, Blake, Sandford, Ellis, Beeston, Kelly, Biggins (Barnes), Fowler.
Chesterfield: Leonard; Dyche, Williams, Rogers, Brien, McGugan, Gunn, Hewitt (Cooke), Morris, Benjamin (Evans), Grayson.

FIRST ROUND, SECOND LEG
27 AUG

Aldershot (0) 1 *(Puckett)*
Peterborough U (1) 2 *(Gavin, Halsall)* 1601
Aldershot: Granville; Brown, Cooper, Talbot (Hopkins), Flower, Whitlock, Rees, Puckett, Bertschin, Henry, Stewart (Heath).
Peterborough U: Barber; White, Butterworth, Halsall, Robinson D, Welsh, Luke, Ebdon, Gavin, Riley (McInerney), Kimble.
Peterborough U won 5–2 on aggregate.

Birmingham C (2) 4 *(Hicks, Yates, Peer, Gleghorn)*
Exeter C (0) 0 6177
Birmingham C: Thomas; Clarkson, Frain, Yates, Hicks, Mardon, Rodgerson, Dolan (Aylott), Peer, Gleghorn, Sturridge (Okenla).
Exeter C: Miller; Hiley, Brown, Williams, Cole, Daniels, Rowbotham, O'Shaughnessy (Marshall), Moran, Cooper, Kelly.
Birmingham C won 5–0 on aggregate.

Blackpool (1) 4 *(Bamber 3, Groves)*
Mansfield T (1) 2 *(Gray, Spooner)*   2155
Blackpool: McIlhargey; Davies, Wright, Groves (Richards), Stoneman, Gore, Rodwell, Gouck, Bamber, Garner, Eyres.
Mansfield T: Pearcey; Fleming, Withe, Spooner, Foster, Gray (Stringfellow), Ford, Holland, Stant, Wilkinson, Charles.
Blackpool won 7–2 on aggregate.

Bournemouth (1) 4 *(Jones 2, Quinn, Watson)*
Cardiff C (1) 1 *(Jones (pen))*   4489
Bournemouth: Bartram; Baker, Morrell, Morris, Watson, O'Driscoll, Bond, Jones, Quinn, Case, Holmes.
Cardiff C: Hansbury; Jones, Searle, Gibbins, Abraham, Perry, Griffith (Pike). Heard, Millar, Dale, Ramsey.
Bournemouth won 6–4 on aggregate.

Brentford (3) 3 *(Holdsworth, Godfrey, Evans)*
Barnet (0) 1 *(Carter)*   5583
Brentford: Benstead; Peters (Line), Manuel, Bates, Evans, Buckle, Jones, Godfrey, Holdsworth, Blissett, Smillie.
Barnet: Phillips; Blackford, Naylor, Bodley, Hoddle (Johnson), Willis, Poole, Carter, Bull, Lowe (Lynch), Showler.
Brentford won 8–6 on aggregate.

Burnley (0) 2 *(Patterson (og), Davis)*
Wigan Ath (0) 3 *(Patterson, Rimmer, Jones)*   3876
Burnley: Pearce; France, Bray (Farrell), Davis, Pender, Monington, Eli, Deary, Francis, Conroy, Hamilton (Harper).
Wigan Ath: Adkins; Parkinson (Appleton), Tankard, Johnson, Patterson, Langley, Jones, Rimmer, Daley (Gray), Worthington, Griffiths.
Wigan Ath won 6–3 on aggregate.

Bury (0) 2 *(Stanislaus, Mauge)*
Hartlepool U (0) 2 *(Gabbiadini, Fletcher)*   1917
Bury: Kelly; Wilson D, Stanislaus, Kearney, Valentine, Greenall, Smith, Parkinson (Mauge), Hulme, Robinson, Wilson I.
Hartlepool U: Hodge; Nobbs, McKinnon, McCreery (Tinkler), Baker, Bennyworth, Tupling, Olsson, Gabbiadini (Fletcher), Honour, Dalton.
Hartlepool U won 3–2 on aggregate.

Carlisle U (0) 1 *(Barnsley)*
Rochdale (0) 1 *(Ryan)*   1572
Carlisle U: O'Hanlon; Edmondson, Barnsley, Miller, Jeffels, Graham (Deakin), Thomas, Proudlock, Walling, Fyfe, Thorpe (Wilkes).
Rochdale: Gray; Whitehall, Ryan, Brown T, Reeves, Jones, Graham, Doyle, Flounders, Brown M, Halpin (Milner).
Rochdale won 6–2 on aggregate.

Chesterfield (0) 1 *(Lancaster)*
Stoke C (1) 2 *(Kelly, Beeston)*   5391
Chesterfield: Leonard; Dyche, Williams, Rogers, Brien, McGugan, Gunn, Cooke (Turnbull), Lancaster, Grayson, Morris (Evans).
Stoke C: Fox; Butler, Fowler, Cranson, Blake, Kennedy, Kevan, Beeston, Kelly (Barnes), Higgins, Scott (Ellis).
Stoke C won 3–1 on aggregate.

Doncaster R (1) 2 *(Cullen, Noteman)*
Crewe Alex (0) 4 *(Futcher 2, Naylor, Hignett)*   1376
Doncaster R: Crichton; Rankine, Gormley (Muir), Ashurst, Ormsby, Douglas, Bennett (Rowe), Cullen, Tynan, Whitehurst, Noteman.

Crewe Alex: Greygoose; Wilson, Jones, Carr, Callaghan (Smart), Murphy (Jasper), Hignett, Naylor, Futcher, Gardiner, Edwards.
Crewe Alex won 9–4 on aggregate.

Fulham (1) 1 *(Browne)*
Charlton Ath (1) 1 *(Leaburn)*   3563
Fulham: Stannard; Marshall, Pike, Browne, Eckhardt, Thomas, Baker (Kelly), Onwere, Georgiou, Brazil, Morgan.
Charlton Ath: Bolder; Pitcher, Minto, Peake, Webster, Gatting, Lee, Bacon, Leaburn (Grant), Nelson, Walsh (Gritt).
Charlton Ath won 5–3 on aggregate.

Gillingham (1) 3 *(Lovell, Walker, Beadle)*   5114
Portsmouth (2) 4 *(Anderton, Beresford (pen), Butters, Aspinall)*
Gillingham: Lim; O'Shea, Palmer, Elsey (Trusson), Walker, Butler, Clark, Lovell, Crown, O'Connor (Beadle), Eeles.
Portsmouth: Knight; Awford, Beresford, Burns, Symons, Butters, Anderton, Doling (Aspinall), Clarke, Chamberlain, Powell.
Portsmouth won 6–4 on aggregate.

Grimsby T (1) 1 *(Birtles)*
Rotherham U (0) 0   3637
Grimsby T: Sherwood; McDermott, Jobling, Futcher, Lever, Dobbin, Watson, Gilbert (Hargreaves), Birtles (Smith), Cockerill, Woods.
Rotherham U: Mercer; Hutchings, Robinson, Richardson, Johnson, Law, Goodwin, Barrick, Cunningham, Page (Goater), Hazel.
Grimsby T won 4–1 on aggregate.

Hull C (0) 1 *(Jenkinson)*
Blackburn R (0) 0   3227
Hull C: Fettis; Warren, Jacobs, Wilcox, Allison, Hobson, Norton, Payton, Hunter, Palin, Jenkinson.
Blackburn R: Mimms; Atkins, Sulley, Reid, Moran, Dobson, May, Agnew (Richardson), Speedie, Garner, Livingstone (Gayle).
Hull C won 2–1 on aggregate.

Plymouth Arg (1) 2 *(Barlow, Turner)*
Shrewsbury T (0) 2 *(Summerfield, Carr)*   3580
Plymouth Arg: Wilmot; Salman (Clement), Spearing, Marker, Cross, Morgan, Barlow, Marshall, Turner, Morrison, Fiore (Scott).
Shrewsbury T: Hughes; Gorman, Lynch, Henry, Heathcote, Blake (Carr), Smith, Summerfield, Spink, Hopkins (Griffiths), Lyne.
aet; Shrewsbury T won on away goals.

Scunthorpe U (0) 3 *(Humphries, Alexander, Helliwell)*
Wrexham (0) 0   2125
Scunthorpe U: Musselwhite; Joyce, Longden, Hine, Hicks, Humphries, Alexander, Hamilton, Daws, Buckley (Hyde), Helliwell.
Wrexham: O'Keefe; Thackeray, Hardy, Sertori, Thomas, Jones J (Preece), Bowden, Owen, Connolly, Jones L, Davies.
Scunthorpe U won 3–1 on aggregate.

Tranmere R (1) 4 *(Aldridge 2, Steel 2)*
Halifax T (2) 3 *(Barr 2, Cooper)*   4285
Tranmere R: Nixon; Higgins, Brannan, Irons, Hughes, Garnett (McNab), Morrissey, Aldridge, Steel, Martindale, Thomas.
Halifax T: Gould; Evans, Kamara, Abbott, Richards, Graham, Barr, Norris, Juryeff, Richardson, Cooper (Megson).
Tranmere R won 8–6 on aggregate.

Walsall (0) 0
Swansea C (1) 1 *(Thornber)* 2812
Walsall: Gayle; Williams, Statham, Methven, Lane (Marsh), Smith, MacDonald, Ntamark, Jackson, Cecere, McDonald.
Swansea C: Bracey; Jenkins, Thornber, Ford, Harris, Hough, Williams (Raynor), Cornforth, McClean, Connor, Legg.
Swansea C won 3–2 on aggregate.

York C (1) 1 *(Canham)*
Bolton W (1) 2 *(Darby, Patterson)* 2757
York C: Marples; McMillan, Crosby, Reid, Atkin, Hall, Pepper, McCarthy, Blackstone, Osborne, Canham (Curtis).
Bolton W: Rose; Brown P, Burke, Kelly, Seagraves, Stubbs, Storer (Winstanley), Fisher (Patterson), Reeves, Philliskirk, Darby.
Bolton W won 4–3 on aggregate.

28 AUG
Bradford C (1) 3 *(Duxbury L 2 (1 pen), Stuart)*
Stockport Co (0) 1 *(Francis)* 3806
Bradford C: Tomlinson; Mitchell, Dowson, James, Oliver, Gardner, Babb, Duxbury L, Torpey, Tinnion, Stuart.
Stockport Co: Redfern; Thorpe, Williams P, Frain (Wheeler), Barras, Williams B, Gannon, Ward, Francis, Beaumont, Matthews.
aet; Bradford C won 4–2 on aggregate.

Hereford U (1) 2 *(Narbett (pen), Theodosiou)*
Torquay U (1) 1 *(Elliott)* 2333
Hereford U: Elliott; Lowndes, Downs, Theodosiou, Bradley, Hall, Caffrey (Pejic), Narbett, Brain (Robinson), Heritage, Fry.
Torquay U: Howells; Myers, Loram, Whiston, Elliott, Holmes M, Hodges (Sang), Hall, Rowland, Dobie, Dobbins.
Torquay U won 3–2 on aggregate.

Huddersfield T (1) 4 *(Roberts, Starbuck 2, Onuora)*
Darlington (0) 0 3907
Huddersfield T: Clarke; Trevitt, Charlton, Marsden, Mitchell, Jackson, O'Regan, Onuora, Roberts, Starbuck, Barnett.
Darlington: Prudhoe; McJannet, Gray (Mardenborough), Willis, Smith, Gill, Cook, Toman, Borthwick, Cork, Tait.
Huddersfield T won 4–1 on aggregate.

Lincoln C (1) 4 *(Schofield 2, Dobson, Ward)*
Chester C (1) 3 *(Bennett, Rimmer 2)* 2170
Lincoln C: Hoult; Finney, Nicholson, West D (Dobson), West G (Clarke), Carmichael, Schofield, Ward, Lee, Alexander, Puttnam.
Chester C: Stewart; Whelan, Albiston, Butler (McGuinness), Abel, Lightfoot, Bishop, Barrow, Rimmer, Bennett, Pugh.
aet; Chester C won on away goals.

Maidstone U (0) 0
Leicester C (0) 1 *(Kitson)* 1638
Maidstone U: Hesford; Haylock, Thompson, Oxbrow, Davies, Osborne, Cuggy (Gall), Painter, Donegal, Lillis, Ellis.
Leicester C: Poole; Mills, Platnauer, Fitzpatrick, Walsh, James, Oldfield, Gibson (Russell), Wright, Kelly, Kitson (Ward).
Leicester C won 4–0 on aggregate.

Reading (0) 0
Cambridge U (2) 3 *(Taylor, Dublin, Claridge)* 3578
Reading: Francis; Jones, Richardson, McPherson, Cooper, Williams (Gilkes), Dillon, Holzman, McGhee, Leworthy (Senior), Gooding.
Cambridge U: Vaughan; Fensome, Kimble, Bailie (Dennis), Clayton, O'Shea, Cheetham, Wilkins, Dublin (Claridge), Taylor, Philpott.
Cambridge U won 4–0 on aggregate.

Scarborough (0) 3 *(Foreman (pen), Jules, Mooney)*
Preston NE (1) 1 *(Joyce)* 2035
Scarborough: Priestley; James, Logan, Lee, Mudd, Meyer, Carter (Jules), Moore, Mooney, Foreman (Ashdjian), Himsworth.
Preston NE: Farnworth; Senior (Thompson), James, Swann, Flynn, Wrightson, Williams (Berry), Joyce, Jepson, Shaw, Ashcroft.
aet; Scarborough won 7–6 on aggregate.

Southend U (1) 1 *(Angell)*
Watford (1) 1 *(Kennedy)* 3802
Southend U: Sansome; Austin, Powell, Martin, Scully, Prior, Locke, Sussex, Tilson, Benjamin (Ansah), Angell.
Watford: James; Gibbs, Soloman, Dublin, McLaughlin, Putney, Blissett, Kennedy, Butler, Porter, Nicholas.
Watford won 3–1 on aggregate.

WBA (1) 2 *(Goodman, Shakespeare (pen))*
Swindon T (0) 2 *(Shearer 2)* 8522
WBA: Naylor; Bradley, Harbey, Ford, Strodder, Burgess (Foster), McNally, Goodman (Bannister), Williams, Shakespeare, Ampadu.
Swindon T: Digby; Jones, Viveash, Hoddle, Calderwood, Taylor, Hazard, Shearer, White, MacLaren, Simpson.
Swindon T won 4–2 on aggregate.

10 SEPT
Northampton T (1) 2 *(Barnes 2)*
Leyton Orient (0) 0 1437
Northampton T: Richardson; Chard, Wilson, Terry, Angus, Brown, Burnham, Quow, Gernon, Barnes, Thorpe.
Leyton Orient: Newell; Howard, Dickenson, Whitbread, Zoricich, Bart-Williams, Carter, Castle, Nugent, Sayer, Otto (Burnett).
Leyton Orient won 5–2 on aggregate.

SECOND ROUND, FIRST LEG
24 SEPT
Blackpool (0) 1 *(Bamber)*
Barnsley (0) 0 4123
Blackpool: McIlhargey; Davies, Wright, Groves, Briggs, Gore, Rodwell, Horner, Bamber, Sinclair (Garner), Eyres.
Barnsley: Butler; Robinson, Fleming, Banks, Smith, Taggart, O'Connell, Redfearn, Rammell, Graham (Saville), Archdeacon.

Bradford C (1) 1 *(Leonard)*
West Ham U (1) 1 *(Small)* 7034
Bradford C: Tomlinson; Mitchell, Dowson, James, Leonard, Gardner, Babb, Duxbury L, Torpey, Tinnion, Reid.
West Ham U: Miklosko; Brown, Parris, Thomas, Foster, Breacker, Bishop, Slater, Small, Potts, Morley (Gale).

Brentford (3) 4 *(Godfrey, Cadette, Holdsworth 2)*
Brighton & HA (0) 1 *(Robinson)*   4927
Brentford: Benstead; Bates, Manuel, Millen, Evans, Rostron, Gayle (Peters), Godfrey, Holdsworth, Cadette (Blissett), Smillie.
Brighton & HA: Beeney; Chivers, Chapman, Wilkins, Bissett, O'Reilly, Barham, Byrne, Meade (Farrington), Codner, Robinson.

Crewe Alex (3) 3 *(Evans 2, Callaghan)*
Newcastle U (2) 4 *(Hunt, Peacock 3)*   4251
Crewe Alex: Greygoose; Wilson, Jones, Carr, Callaghan, Walters, Garvey (McKearney), McPhillips, Evans, Gardiner, Edwards.
Newcastle U: Srnicek; Neilson, Elliott, O'Brien, Scott, Bradshaw, Clark, Peacock, Quinn, Hunt (Howey), Roche (Appleby).

Everton (0) 1 *(Beardsley)*
Watford (0) 0   8264
Everton: Southall; Atteveld, Hinchcliffe, Keown, Watson, Ebbrell, Nevin, Beardsley, Newell, Sheedy, Ward (Cottee).
Watford: James; Gibbs, Soloman, Dublin, McLaughlin, Putney, Hessenthaler, Blissett (Butler), Bazeley, Porter, Nicholas.

Hull C (0) 0
QPR (1) 3 *(Barker 2, Thompson)*   4979
Hull C: Fettis; Brown, Atkinson, Wilcox, Allison, Hobson, Walmsley, Payton (Calvert), Stoker, Norton, Jenkinson.
QPR: Stejskal; Bardsley, Peacock, Holloway, McDonald, Maddix, Wilson, Barker, Thompson, Wegerle (Ferdinand), Sinton (Herrera).

Leyton Orient (0) 0
Sheffield W (0) 0   6231
Leyton Orient: Newell; Howard, Achampong (Zoricich), Whitbread, Day, Bart-Williams, Carter, Hackett, Nugent, Burnett, Otto.
Sheffield W: Woods; Nilsson, King, Wood, Warhurst, Anderson, Wilson, Harkes, Jemson, Watson, Worthington.

Middlesbrough (0) 1 *(Wilkinson)*
Bournemouth (0) 1 *(Lawrence)*   10,577
Middlesbrough: Pears; Parkinson, Phillips, Mowbray, Kernaghan, Falconer (Mustoe), Slaven, Proctor, Wilkinson, Ripley, Hendrie.
Bournemouth: Bartram; Bond, Rowland, Morris, Watson, O'Driscoll, Cooke (Lawrence), Mundee, Quinn, Case, Holmes (Fereday).

Oldham Ath (1) 7 *(Ritchie 4, Sharp, Henry, Milligan)*
Torquay U (0) 1 *(Hodges)*   7250
Oldham Ath: Hallworth; Halle (Fleming), Snodin (Bernard), Henry, Barrett, Kilcline, Kane, Ritchie, Sharp, Milligan, Holden.
Torquay U: Howells; Curran, Loram, Uzzell, Elliott, Holmes M (Sang), Dobbins, Hall, Darby, Hodges, Colcombe.

Portsmouth (0) 0
Oxford U (0) 0   4682
Portsmouth: Knight; Awford, Beresford, Burns, Symons, Butters, Neill, Kuhl (Anderton), Clarke, Wigley, Murray.
Oxford U: Kee; Robinson, Smart, Phillips, Foster, Melville, Magilton, Penney, Lewis, Nogan, Simpson.

Port Vale (1) 2 *(Foyle, Mills B)*
Notts Co (0) 1 *(Johnson)*   4722
Port Vale: Grew; Mills S, Hughes, Walker, Swan, Glover, Porter, Van der Laan, Houchen (Mills B), Foyle, Kent.
Notts Co: Cherry; Short Chris, Paris, Short Craig, Yates, Harding, Thomas, Dryden, Rideout, Bartlett (Turner), Johnson.

Scarborough (1) 1 *(Mooney)*
Southampton (2) 3 *(Shearer 2, Cockerill)*   2303
Scarborough: Priestley; James, Logan, Lee, Hirst, Meyer, Ashdjian, Mockler, Mooney, Foreman (Fletcher), Himsworth (Jules).
Southampton: Flowers; Dodd, Gray, Horne, Hall, Ruddock, Le Tissier, Cockerill, Shearer, Dowie, Adams.

Scunthorpe U (0) 0
Leeds U (0) 0   8392
Scunthorpe U: Musselwhite; Joyce, Longden, Martin, Lister, Humphries, Alexander, Hamilton, Daws, Hill, Helliwell.
Leeds U: Lukic; Sterland, Dorigo, Batty, McClelland, Whyte, Strachan (Shutt), Hodge, Chapman, McAllister, Speed.

Sunderland (0) 1 *(Hauser)*
Huddersfield T (1) 2 *(Charlton, Starbuck)*   8161
Sunderland: Norman; Kay, Hardyman, Bennett, Ball, Owers, Bracewell, Davenport, Armstrong, Hauser (Ord), Pascoe (Atkinson).
Huddersfield T: Clarke; Trevitt, Charlton, Marsden, Mitchell, Jackson, O'Regan, Onuora, Roberts, Starbuck, Barnett.

Wigan Ath (2) 2 *(Worthington, Patterson)*
Sheffield U (1) 2 *(Deane 2)*   3647
Wigan Ath: Adkins; Jones (Pilling), Tankard, Johnson, Widdrington, Langley, Powell, Rimmer, Patterson, Worthington, Griffiths.
Sheffield U: Kite; Wilder, Hartfield, Gannon, Gayle, Hill, Bryson (Hoyland), Lake, Agana, Deane (Mendonca), Whitehouse.

Wimbledon (1) 1 *(McGee)*
Peterborough U (2) 2 *(Charlery, Sterling)*   2081
Wimbledon: Segers; Joseph, Phelan, Barton, Fitzgerald (Cork), Bennett, Scales, Earle, Fashanu, Ryan, McGee (Clarke).
Peterborough U: Barber; Luke, Butterworth, Halsall, Robinson D, Welsh, Sterling, Cooper G, Gavin, Charlery (Riley), Kimble.

Wolverhampton W (4) 6 *(Birch 2, Burke, Bull 2, Steele)*
Shrewsbury T (1) 1 *(Summerfield)*   12,229
Wolverhampton W: Stowell; Ashley, Venus, Bennett, Madden, Downing, Steele, Cook, Bull, Burke, Birch.
Shrewsbury T: Hughes; Gorman, Cash, Henry, Blake, Taylor, Smith, Summerfield, Spink (Hopkins), Parkin, Lyne.

25 SEPT

Bristol R (1) 1 *(Llewellyn (og))*
Bristol C (2) 3 *(Morgan, Smith, Allison)*   5155
Bristol R: Parkin; Alexander, Twentyman, Yates, Clark, Archer, Boothroyd, Cross, White, Saunders, Stewart (Browning).
Bristol C: Welch; Llewellyn, Scott, May, Bryant, Caesar, Shelton (Edwards), Rennie, Allison, Morgan, Smith.

Charlton Ath (0) 0
Norwich C (1) 2 *(Gordon, Newman)* 2886
Charlton Ath: Bolder; Pitcher, Barness, Peake, Webster, Gatting, Lee, Bacon, Leaburn, Nelson, Dyer (Grant).
Norwich C: Gunn; Phillips (Woodthorpe), Bowen, Butterworth, Blades, Crook, Gordon, Fleck (Beckford), Newman, Fox, Ullathorne.

Chelsea (0) 1 *(Townsend)*
Tranmere R (0) 1 *(Aldridge)* 11,311
Chelsea: Beasant; Clarke, Boyd, Jones, Elliott (Allon), Monkou, Le Saux, Townsend, Dixon, Wilson, Wise.
Tranmere R: Nixon; Higgins, Brannan, Irons, Hughes, Vickers, Morrissey, Aldridge, Steel, Martindale, Thomas.

Coventry C (2) 4 *(Rosario 2, Gallacher, McGrath)*
Rochdale (0) 0 5982
Coventry C: Ogrizovic; Borrows, Billing, Emerson, Pearce, Edwards, McGrath, Ndlovu, Rosario (Hurst), Gallacher, Furlong.
Rochdale: Williams; Payne, Reeves, Ryan, Brown T, Jones, Graham, Doyle, Flounders (Butler), Milner (Whitehall), Halpin.

Derby Co (0) 0
Ipswich T (0) 0 10,215
Derby Co: Shilton; Sage, Forsyth, Williams G, Coleman, Comyn, Micklewhite (Patterson), Ormondroyd, Gee (Hayward), Williams P, McMinn.
Ipswich T: Forrest; Johnson, Thompson, Stockwell, Yallop, Linighan, Zondervan, Goddard, Whitton, Dozzell, Kiwomya.

Grimsby T (0) 0
Aston Villa (0) 0 13,835
Grimsby T: Sherwood; McDermott, Agnew (Smith), Futcher, Lever, Cunnington, Childs, Gilbert, Jones (Rees), Dobbin, Woods.
Aston Villa: Spink; Kubicki, Staunton, Teale, McGrath, Richardson, Yorke, Blake, Regis, Cowans, Mortimer.

Hartlepool U (0) 1 *(Honour)*
Crystal Palace (1) 1 *(Bright)* 6697
Hartlepool U: Hodge; Nobbs, McKinnon, Tinkler, MacPhail, Bennyworth, Gabbiadini (McCreery), Olsson, Baker, Honour, Dalton.
Crystal Palace: Martyn; Humphrey, Bodin, Gray, Young, Sinnott, Osborn, Pardew, Bright, Salako, McGoldrick.

Leicester C (0) 1 *(Walsh)*
Arsenal (1) 1 *(Wright)* 20,679
Leicester C: Poole; Mills, Platnauer, Gordon (Mauchlen), Walsh, James, Oldfield, Gibson, Wright, Kelly, Kitson.
Arsenal: Seaman; Dixon, Thomas, Campbell, Linighan (O'Leary), Adams, Rocastle, Davis, Wright, Merson, Groves.

Liverpool (1) 2 *(Rush 2)*
Stoke C (1) 2 *(Cranson, Kelly)* 18,389
Liverpool: Grobbelaar; Ablett, Burrows, Nicol, Marsh, Tanner, Saunders (Rosenthal), McManaman, Rush, Walters, McMahon.
Stoke C: Fox; Butler, Sandford, Scott, Overson, Kennedy, Cranson, Beeston, Ellis (Kelly), Biggins, Fowler.

Luton T (0) 2 *(Gray, Nogan)*
Birmingham C (1) 2 *(Rodgerson, Gleghorn)* 6315
Luton T: Chamberlain; Jackson, Dreyer, Telfer, Rodger, Beaumont, Preece, Stein (Nogan), Gray (Salton), Pembridge, Thompson.
Birmingham C: Thomas; Clarkson, Matthewson, Donowa, Hicks, Mardon, Rodgerson, Frain, Peer, Gleghorn, Sturridge.

Manchester C (0) 3 *(White 2, Quinn)*
Chester C (0) 1 *(Bennett)* 10,987
Manchester C: Coton; Hill, Pointon, Brightwell I, Curle, Redmond, White, Heath, Quinn, Megson, Hughes.
Chester C: Stewart; McGuinness, Albiston, Pugh, Abel, Lightfoot, Bishop (Butler), Barrow, Rimmer, Bennett, Croft (Morton).

Manchester U (1) 3 *(Giggs, McClair, Bruce)*
Cambridge U (0) 0 30,934
Manchester U: Walsh; Phelan, Irwin, Bruce, Webb (Giggs), Pallister, Robson, Ince, McClair, Hughes, Blackmore.
Cambridge U: Vaughan; Fensome (Clayton), Kimble, Bailie, Chapple, O'Shea, Cheetham, Wilkins, Dublin (Claridge), Taylor, Philpott.

Millwall (1) 2 *(Stephenson, Armstrong)*
Swindon T (2) 2 *(White 2)* 6048
Millwall: Davison; Dawes, Cooper, Stevens, McCarthy, Wood, Kerr, Colquhoun, Armstrong (Falco), Rae, Stephenson.
Swindon T: Hammond; Jones, Summerbee, Hoddle, Calderwood, Taylor, Hazard, Shearer (Viveash), Simpson, McLaren, White.

Nottingham F (2) 4 *(Keane, Gaynor 2, Black)*
Bolton W (0) 0 19,936
Nottingham F: Crossley; Charles (Laws), Pearce, Chettle, Tiler, Keane (Boardman), Black, Parker, Gaynor, Sheringham, Woan.
Bolton W: Rose; Brown P, Burke, Kelly, Came, Stubbs, Green (Storer), Patterson, Reeves, Philliskirk (Jeffrey), Darby.

Swansea C (0) 1 *(Gilligan)*
Tottenham H (0) 0 11,416
Swansea C: Freestone; Jenkins, Thornber, Coughlin, Harris, Brazil, Williams, Ford, Gilligan, Raynor, Legg.
Tottenham H: Walker; Hendon, Van Den Hauwe (Moncur), Nayim, Sedgley, Mabbutt, Stewart, Durie (Hendry), Samways, Howells, Allen.

SECOND ROUND, SECOND LEG
8 OCT

Arsenal (0) 2 *(Wright, Merson)*
Leicester C (0) 0 28,580
Arsenal: Seaman; Dixon, Winterburn, Thomas, Pates, Adams, Rocastle, Wright (Groves), Smith, Merson, Campbell.
Leicester C: Poole; Mills, Mauchlen (Platnauer), Smith, Walsh, James, Oldfield, Gibson, Wright, Kelly, Ward.
Arsenal won 3–1 on aggregate.

Barnsley (1) 2 *(O'Connell, Pearson)*
Blackpool (0) 0 6315
Barnsley: Butler; Robinson, Archdeacon, Fleming, Saville (Graham), Taggart, O'Connell, Redfearn, Pearson, Currie, Rammell (Bishop).
Blackpool: McIlhargey; Davies, Wright, Groves, Briggs, Gore, Rodwell (Taylor), Horner, Bamber, Sinclair, Eyres.
aet; Barnsley won 2–1 on aggregate.

Birmingham C (1) 3 *(Peer, Gleghorn 2)*
Luton T (0) 2 *(Gray 2)* 13,252
Birmingham C: Thomas; Clarkson, Matthewson, Donowa, Hicks, Mardon, Rodgerson, Frain, Peer, Gleghorn, Sturridge.
Luton T: Chamberlain; Jackson, Harvey, Thompson (Nogan), Beaumont, Peake, Telfer, Gray, Harford (Stein), Pembridge, Preece.
Birmingham C won 5–4 on aggregate.

Bolton W (2) 2 *(Darby, Kelly)* 5469
Nottingham F (3) 5 *(Sheringham, Keane 2, Gaynor, Black)*
Bolton W: Rose; Brown P, Burke, Kelly, Came, Stubbs, Storer, Patterson, Reeves, Green, Darby.
Nottingham F: Crossley; Charles (Chettle), Pearce, Walker, Tiler, Keane, Crosby, Parker (Gemmill), Gaynor, Sheringham, Black.
Nottingham F won 9–2 on aggregate.

Bournemouth (0) 1 *(Quinn)*
Middlesbrough (1) 2 *(Hendrie, Parkinson (pen))* 5528
Bournemouth: Bartram; Bond, Rowland, Morris, Watson, O'Driscoll, Cooke (Fereday), Wood, Quinn, McGorry (Mundee), Holmes.
Middlesbrough: Pears; Parkinson, Phillips, Mowbray, Kernaghan, Mustoe, Shannon (Pollock), Proctor, Wilkinson, Ripley (Slaven), Hendrie.
aet; Middlesbrough won 3–2 on aggregate.

Bristol C (1) 2 *(Morgan, Smith)*
Bristol R (1) 4 *(White 2, Mehew 2)* 9880
Bristol C: Welch; Llewellyn, Scott, Harrison (Taylor), Bryant (Bent), Aizlewood, Edwards, Rennie, Allison, Morgan, Smith.
Bristol R: Parkin; Alexander (Clark), Twentyman, Yates, Cross, Skinner, Mehew (Purnell), Reece, White, Browning, Pounder.
aet; Bristol R won on away goals.

Chester C (0) 0 *at Stockport*
Manchester C (1) 3 *(Allen, Sheron, Brennan)* 4146
Chester C: Stewart; McGuinness, Albiston, Pugh, Lightfoot, Whelan, Bishop, Barrow, Morton (Butler), Bennett, Croft.
Manchester C: Coton; Hill, Pointon, Brightwell I, Brennan, Redmond, Sheron, Heath, Allen, Megson (Hoekman), Hughes.
Manchester C won 6–1 on aggregate.

Crystal Palace (2) 6 *(Bright 2, Gabbiadini, Thorn, Gray (pen), Collymore)*
Hartlepool U (0) 1 *(Tinkler)* 9153
Crystal Palace: Martyn; Southgate (Gordon), Sinnott, Gray, Young, Thorn, Collymore, Thomas, Bright, Gabbiadini, McGoldrick.
Hartlepool U: Hodge; Nobbs, McKinnon, Tinkler, Mac-Phail, Bennyworth (Fletcher), Gabbiadini (Tupling), Olsson, Baker, Honour, Dalton.
Crystal Palace won 7–2 on aggregate.

Ipswich T (0) 0
Derby Co (2) 2 *(Gee, Williams P (pen))* 8982
Ipswich T: Forrest; Wark, Thompson, Stockwell, Yallop, Linighan, Lowe, Zondervan, Whitton, Milton (Gregory), Kiwomya.
Derby Co: Shilton; Patterson, Forsyth, Williams G, Coleman, Comyn, Micklewhite, Ormondroyd, Gee, Williams P, McMinn.
Derby Co won 2–0 on aggregate.

Leeds U (0) 3 *(Sterland (pen), Chapman, Speed)*
Scunthorpe U (0) 0 14,558
Leeds U: Lukic; Sterland, Dorigo, Batty, McClelland, Whyte, Hodge, Shutt (Kelly), Chapman, Williams (Fairclough), Speed.
Scunthorpe U: Musselwhite; Joyce, Longden, Martin (Alexander), Lister, Stevenson, Buckley (Hine), Hamilton, Daws, Hill, Helliwell.
Leeds U won 3–0 on aggregate.

Peterborough U (1) 2 *(Kimble, Riley)*
Wimbledon (0) 2 *(Clarke, Fashanu (pen))* 5939
Peterborough U: Barber; Luke, Butterworth, Halsall, Robinson D, Welsh, Sterling, Cooper G, Riley, Charlery (Ebdon), Kimble (Gavin).
Wimbledon: Segers; Joseph, Phelan, Barton (Cork), Scales, Fitzgerald, Elkins (Bennett), Earle, Fashanu, Blackwell, Clarke.
Peterborough U won 4–3 on aggregate.

Rochdale (0) 1 *(Milner)*
Coventry C (0) 0 2288
Rochdale: Gray; Brown M, Ryan (Payne), Brown T, Reeves, Jones, Graham, Doyle, Flounders, Milner, Butler (Whitehall).
Coventry C: Baker; Borrows, Edwards, Robson (Emerson), Pearce, Billing, McGrath, Gynn, Furlong (Rosario), Gallacher, Ndlovu.
Coventry C won 4–1 on aggregate.

Sheffield U (0) 1 *(Hoyland)*
Wigan Ath (0) 0 6608
Sheffield U: Kite; Frickling, Cowan, Gannon, Gayle, Beesley, Bryson (Ward), Hoyland, Agana, Bradshaw, Whitehouse (Lake).
Wigan Ath: Adkins; Appleton, Tankard, Johnson, Patterson (Smyth), Langley, Powell, Widdrington, Daley, Gray (Smith), Griffiths.
Sheffield U won 3–2 on aggregate.

Shrewsbury T (1) 3 *(Summerfield, Lyne 2)*
Wolverhampton W (1) 1 *(Steele)* 5784
Shrewsbury T: Perks; Worsley (Hopkins), Cash, Henry, Lynch, Blake, Smith, Summerfield, Lyne, Taylor, Spink (Parkin).
Wolverhampton W: Stowell; Ashley, Venus, Bennett, Madden, Bellamy, Birch, Cook, Bradbury, Steele, Thompson.
Wolverhampton W won 7–4 on aggregate.

Swindon T (0) 3 *(Shearer 2, White)*
Millwall (1) 1 *(Colquhoun)* 7137
Swindon T: Digby; Jones, Summerbee, Kerslake, Calderwood, Taylor, Hazard, Shearer, Simpson, MacLaren, White.
Millwall: Davison; Dawes, Cooper, Bogie, McCarthy, Thompson, Kerr, Colquhoun, Falco (Armstrong), Rae, Stephenson (Goodman).
Swindon T won 5–3 on aggregate.

Tranmere R (1) 3 *(Steel, Aldridge (pen), Malkin)*
Chelsea (0) 1 *(Wise)* 11,165
Tranmere R: Nixon; Higgins, Brannan, Irons (Malkin), Hughes, Vickers, Morrissey, Aldridge, Steel, Martindale (McNab), Mungall.
Chelsea: Hitchcock; Clarke, Boyd, Matthew, Elliott, Monkou, Le Saux, Townsend, Dixon (Allon) (Myers), Wilson, Wise.
aet; Tranmere R won 4–2 on aggregate.

Watford (0) 1 *(Bazeley)*
Everton (0) 2 *(Newell, Beardsley)* 11,561
Watford: James; Gibbs, Drysdale, Dublin, McLaughlin, Putney, Hessenthaler (Bazeley), Blissett, Butler, Porter, Nicholas.
Everton: Southall; Harper, Ratcliffe, Ebbrell, Watson, Keown (Atteveld), Warzycha (Newell), Beardsley, Cottee, Sheedy, Nevin.
Everton won 3–1 on aggregate.

9 OCT

Aston Villa (0) 1 *(Teale)*

Grimsby T (0) 1 *(Gilbert (pen))*   15,338

Aston Villa: Spink; Kubicki, Staunton, Teale, McGrath, Richardson, Yorke, Regis, Atkinson, Cowans, Mortimer (Olney).
Grimsby T: Sherwood; McDermott, Smith, Futcher, Lever, Cunnington, Childs, Gilbert, Rees (Jones), Dobbin, Woods.
aet; Grimsby T won on away goals.

Brighton & HA (3) 4 *(Byrne 2, Codner, Meade)*

Brentford (1) 2 *(Cadette, Holdsworth)*   4502

Brighton & HA: Beeney; Crumplin, Chapman, Wilkins, Chivers, O'Reilly, Barham, Byrne, Meade (Farrington), Codner, Robinson.
Brentford: Bayes; Bates, Manuel (Holdsworth), Ratcliffe, Evans, Rostron, Jones, Godfrey, Gayle, Cadette (Peters), Smillie.
aet; Brentford won 6–5 on aggregate.

Cambridge U (0) 1 *(Dublin)*

Manchester U (1) 1 *(McClair)*   9248

Cambridge U: Vaughan; Fensome, Kimble, Dennis, O'Shea, Daish, Rowett (Bailie), Wilkins, Dublin, Claridge, Philpott.
Manchester U: Wilkinson; Donaghy, Irwin, Bruce, Blackmore, Pallister (Robins), Robson, Ince, McClair, Hughes, Martin (Giggs).
Manchester U won 4–1 on aggregate.

Huddersfield T (0) 4 *(Onuora, Roberts 2, Barnett)*

Sunderland (0) 0   11,177

Huddersfield T: Clarke; Trevitt, Charlton, Marsden, Mitchell, Jackson, O'Regan, Onuora, Roberts, Starbuck, Barnett.
Sunderland: Norman; Kay, Rogan, Sampson, Ball, Owers, Bracewell, Davenport (Brady), Armstrong, Rush (Cullen), Hardyman.
Huddersfield T won 6–1 on aggregate.

Newcastle U (0) 1 *(Howey)*

Crewe Alex (0) 0   9197

Newcastle U: Srnicek; Neilson, Stimson, O'Brien, Scott, Appleby, Clark, Peacock, Walker (Howey), Hunt, Carr.
Crewe Alex: Greygoose; Wilson, Downes, Carr, Callaghan (Rose), McKearney, Payne (Futcher), McPhillips, Evans, Gardiner, Edwards.
Newcastle U won 5–3 on aggregate.

Norwich C (2) 3 *(Fleck 2, Beckford)*

Charlton Ath (0) 0   5507

Norwich C: Gunn; Goss, Bowen (Woodthorpe), Butterworth, Blades, Fleck (Ball), Gordon, Beckford, Newman, Fox, Ullathorne.
Charlton Ath: Bolder; Pitcher, Barness, Peake, Webster, Gatting, Bacon (Gorman), Salako, Grant, Minto, Dyer.
Norwich C won 5–0 on aggregate.

Notts Co (0) 3 *(Bartlett 2, Johnson (pen))*

Port Vale (1) 2 *(Foyle, Houchen)*   4419

Notts Co: Cherry; Palmer, Paris, Short Craig, Yates, Draper (Dryden), Thomas, Turner; Rideout, Bartlett, Johnson (Regis).
Port Vale: Grew; Mills S, Hughes, Porter, Swan, Glover, Kerr (Mills B), Van der Laan, Houchen, Foyle, Jeffers (Kidd).
aet; Port Vale won on away goals.

Oxford U (0) 0

Portsmouth (1) 1 *(Burns)*   4114

Oxford U: Veysey; Robinson, Smart, Lewis (Wanless), Foster, Melville, Magilton, Evans (Beauchamp), Durnin, Nogan, Simpson.
Portsmouth: Knight; Awford, Beresford, Hurns, Symons, Butters, Neill, Kuhl, Clarke, Wigley, Chamberlain (Powell).
Portsmouth won 1–0 on aggregate.

QPR (3) 5 *(Bardsley, Thompson 2, Bailey 2)*

Hull C (1) 1 *(Young)*   5251

QPR: Stejskal; Bardsley, Wilson, Tillson, Peacock, Maddix (Ready), Holloway, Barker, Thompson, Bailey, Sinton (Impey).
Hull C: Wilson; Windass, Jacobs, Warren, Mail, Hobson (Atkinson), De Mange (Walmsley), Stoker, Young, Norton, Jenkinson.
QPR won 8–1 on aggregate.

Sheffield W (0) 4 *(Anderson, Williams, Francis 2)*

Leyton Orient (1) 1 *(Nugent)*   14,398

Sheffield W: Woods; Anderson, King, Palmer, Warhurst, Pearson, Wilson, Hyde (Wood), Hirst (Francis), Williams, Worthington.
Leyton Orient: Newell; Howard, Burnett (Harvey), Whitbread, Day, Bart-Williams, Carter, Castle, Nugent, Hackett, Achampong.
Sheffield W won 4–1 on aggregate.

Southampton (2) 2 *(Le Tissier, Cockerill)*

Scarborough (0) 2 *(Himsworth, Mockler (pen))*   4036

Southampton: Flowers; Dodd, Gray, Horne (Dowie), Hall, Ruddock, Le Tissier, Cockerill, Shearer, Hurlock, Adams.
Scarborough: Hughes; James, Logan, Lee, Hirst, Meyer, Reed (Himsworth), Mockler, Mooney, Ashdjian, Jules (Foreman).
Southampton won 5–3 on aggregate.

Stoke C (0) 2 *(Biggins 2 (1 pen))*

Liverpool (1) 3 *(McManaman, Saunders, Walters)* 22,335

Stoke C: Fox; Butler, Sandford, Scott, Overson, Kennedy, Cranson (Kevan), Beeston, Kelly (Wright), Biggins, Fowler.
Liverpool: Hooper; Harkness, Burrows, Nicol, McManaman, Tanner, Saunders, Houghton, Rush, Walters, McMahon.
Liverpool won 5–4 on aggregate.

Torquay U (0) 0

Oldham Ath (1) 2 *(Jobson, Holden)*   1955

Torquay U: Lowe; Holmes P, Myers, Compton, Elliott, Holmes M, Loram, Joyce, Rowland (Darby), Hodges, Colcombe (Dobbins).
Oldham Ath: Hallworth; Fleming, Barlow, Henry, Barrett, Jobson, Kane, Marshall, Sharp, Milligan, Holden.
Oldham Ath won 9–1 on aggregate.

Tottenham H (1) 5 *(Allen, Lineker (pen), Brazil (og), Stewart, Samways)*

Swansea C (0) 1 *(Chapple)*   20,198

Tottenham H: Thorstvedt; Bergsson, Sedgley, Nayim, Tuttle (Houghton), Mabbutt, Stewart, Durie, Samways, Lineker, Allen.
Swansea C: Freestone; Jenkins, Ford, Coughlin (Chapple), Harris, Brazil, Davey (Williams), Davies, Gilligan, Raynor, Legg.
Tottenham H won 5–2 on aggregate.

West Ham U (2) 4 *(Keen, Morley, Parris, Small)*

Bradford C (0) 0   17,232

West Ham U: Miklosko; Breacker, Thomas, Gale, Foster, Parris, Bishop, Small (McAvennie), Keen, Morley.
Bradford C: Tomlinson; Mitchell, Dowson, James, Oliver, Gardner, Babb, Duxbury L, Torpey (Leonard), Tinnion, Morgan (McCarthy).
West Ham U won 5–1 on aggregate.

THIRD ROUND
29 OCT

Birmingham C (0) 1 *(Sturridge)*
Crystal Palace (0) 1 *(Gray)*   17,270
Birmingham C: Thomas; Clarkson, Matthewson, Peer, Hicks, Mardon, Okenla (Jones), Frain, Donowa, Gleghorn, Sturridge.
Crystal Palace: Martyn; Southgate, Sinnott, Gray, Young, Thorn (Humphrey), Rodger, Thomas, Bright, Gabbiadini, McGoldrick.

Grimsby T (0) 0
Tottenham H (1) 3 *(Howells, Lineker, Durie)*   17,017
Grimsby T: Sherwood; McDermott, Jobling (Smith), Futcher (Watson), Lever, Cunnington, Childs, Rees, Cockerill, Gilbert, Woods.
Tottenham H: Thorstvedt; Edinburgh, Van Den Hauwe, Howells (Bergsson), Sedgley, Mabbutt, Stewart, Durie, Samways, Lineker, Allen (Walsh).

Huddersfield T (0) 1 *(Barnett)*
Swindon T (2) 4 *(Shearer 2, Summerbee, Taylor)* 10,088
Huddersfield T: Clarke; Trevitt, Charlton, Marsden, Mitchell, Jackson, O'Regan, Onuora (Stapleton), Roberts, Starbuck, Barnett.
Swindon T: Hammond; Kerslake, Summerbee, Jones, Calderwood, Taylor, Hazard, Shearer, Simpson, MacLaren, White (Foley).

Leeds U (0) 3 *(Chapman 2, Shutt)*
Tranmere R (0) 1 *(Aldridge)*   18,266
Leeds U: Lukic; Sterland, Dorigo, Hodge (Kamara), Fairclough, Whyte, Strachan, Shutt, Chapman, McAllister, Wallace (Williams).
Tranmere R: Nixon; Steel (Harvey), Brannan, Irons (Cooper); Hughes, Vickers, Morrissey, Aldridge, Malkin, Martindale, Mungall.

Liverpool (1) 2 *(McManaman, Rush)*
Port Vale (1) 2 *(Van der Laan, Foyle)*   21,553
Liverpool: Grobbelaar; Harkness, Burrows, Hysen, Molby (Marsh), Tanner, Saunders, McManaman (Rosenthal), Rush, Walters, McMahon.
Port Vale: Grew; Mills S, Hughes, Porter, Aspin, Glover, Jalink, Van der Laan (Kidd), Swan, Foyle, Jeffers.

Manchester C (0) 0
QPR (0) 0   15,512
Manchester C: Coton; Hill, Pointon, Reid, Curle, Redmond, Sheron (Hoekman), Heath (Hendry), Quinn, Brightwell I, Hughes.
QPR: Stejskal; Bardsley, Wilson, Tillson, Peacock, Maddix, Holloway, Barker, Thompson, Bailey, Sinton.

Middlesbrough (1) 1 *(Wilkinson)*
Barnsley (0) 0   9381
Middlesbrough: Pears; Parkinson, Phillips, Mowbray, Kernaghan, Mustoe, Slaven, Pollock, Wilkinson, Marwood (Fleming), Hendrie.
Barnsley: Butler; Robinson, Archdeacon, Fleming (Bullimore), Smith, Taggart, O'Connell, Redfearn, Williams, Currie (Graham), Rammell.

Oldham Ath (0) 2 *(Palmer, Sharp)*
Derby Co (1) 1 *(Forsyth)*   11,219
Oldham Ath: Hallworth; Barrett, Barlow, Bernard (Adams), Kilcline (Palmer), Jobson, McDonald, Marshall, Sharp, Milligan, Holden.
Derby Co: Shilton; Sage, Forsyth, Williams G, Coleman, Comyn, Micklewhite, Ormondroyd, Gee (Hayward), Williams P, McMinn.

Peterborough U (0) 1 *(Charlery)*
Newcastle U (0) 0   10,382
Peterborough U: Barber; Luke, Johnson, Halsall, Robinson D, Welsh, Sterling, Cooper G, Riley (Butterworth), Charlery, Kimble (Culpin).
Newcastle U: Wright; Bradshaw, Stimson, O'Brien, Scott, Appleby, Clark, Makel (Gourlay), Howey, Hunt (Fashanu), Roche.

Sheffield U (0) 0
West Ham U (1) 2 *(McAvennie, Small (pen))*   11,144
Sheffield U: Kite; Pemberton, Cowan, Gannon, Gayle, Beesley, Bryson (Mendonca), Hoyland, Agana, Bradshaw (Lake), Whitehouse.
West Ham U: Miklosko; Breacker, Thomas, Gale (Allen), Potts, Parris, Bishop, McAvennie, Small, Keen, Slater.

30 OCT

Coventry C (1) 1 *(Gallacher)*
Arsenal (0) 0   15,337
Coventry C: Ogrizovic; Booty, Hurst, Robson, Pearce, Billing, Woods, McGrath, Furlong, Gallacher, Smith.
Arsenal: Seaman; Dixon, Winterburn, Davis, Pates (Linighan), Adams, Rocastle, Wright, Smith, Merson, Limpar (Groves).

Everton (2) 4 *(Beagrie 2, Cottee, Beardsley)*
Wolverhampton W (1) 1 *(Bull)*   19,065
Everton: Southall; .Atteveld, Hinchcliffe, Ebbrell, Watson, Keown, Nevin (Warzycha), Beardsley, Cottee (Youds), Newell, Beagrie.
Wolverhampton W: Stowell; Ashley, Venus, Bennett, Madden, Downing, Birch, Steele, Bull, Mutch, Dennison.

Manchester U (0) 3 *(Robins 2, Robson)*
Portsmouth (0) 1 *(Beresford)*   29,543
Manchester U: Schmeichel; Parker, Irwin (Robins), Bruce, Webb, Pallister (Robson), Donaghy, Kanchelskis, McClair, Blackmore, Giggs.
Portsmouth: Knight; Awford, Beresford, Burns, Symons, Butters, Neill, Kuhl, Clarke (Whittingham), Chamberlain (Aspinall), Anderton.

Norwich C (0) 4 *(Fox, Fleck, Beckford 2)*
Brentford (0) 1 *(Manuel)*   7394
Norwich C: Gunn; Phillips, Bowen, Butterworth, Blades (Polston), Goss (Ball), Gordon, Fleck, Newman, Fox, Beckford.
Brentford: Bayes; Bates, Manuel, Millen, Evans, Ratcliffe (Rostron), Godfrey (Buckle), Gayle, Holdsworth, Blissett, Smillie.

Nottingham F (1) 2 *(Glover, Gemmill)*
Bristol R (0) 0   17,529
Nottingham F: Crossley; Charles, Pearce, Walker, Chettle, Gemmill, Crosby, Parker, Sheringham (Woan), Glover, Black.
Bristol R: Parkin; Alexander, Twentyman, Yates, Cross, Skinner, Mehew (Purnell), Reece, White, Saunders, Pounder.

Sheffield W (1) 1 *(Hirst)*
Southampton (0) 1 *(Shearer)*   17,627
Sheffield W: Woods; Nilsson, King, Palmer, Harkes, Anderson, Wilson, Sheridan, Hirst, Williams (Jemson), Worthington.
Southampton: Flowers; Dodd, Adams, Hurlock, Hall (Dowie), Ruddock, Gittens, Cockerill, Shearer, Gray (Horne), Le Tissier.

THIRD ROUND REPLAYS
19 NOV
Crystal Palace (0) 1 *(Thomas)*
Birmingham C (0) 1 *(Gleghorn) aet*   10,698
Crystal Palace: Martyn; Southgate, Humphrey, Gray, Young, Thorn (Coleman), Rodger (Collymore), Thomas, Bright, Gabbiadini, McGoldrick.
Birmingham C: Thomas; Clarkson, Frain, Peer, Matthewson, Mardon, Rodgerson, Tait (Fox), Donowa, Gleghorn, Sturridge (Okenla).

20 NOV
Port Vale (1) 1 *(Foyle)*
Liverpool (3) 4 *(McManaman, Walters, Houghton, Saunders)*
Port Vale: Grew; Mills S, Hughes, Porter (Mills B), Aspin, Glover, Jalink, Van der Laan, Swan, Foyle, Jeffers.
Liverpool: Grobbelaar; Hysen, Burrows, Marsh, Molby, Tanner, Saunders, Houghton (Rosenthal), McManaman, Walters (Ablett), McMahon.

QPR (1) 1 *(Penrice)*
Manchester C (1) 3 *(Heath 2, Quinn)*   11,033
QPR: Stejskal; Bardsley, Brevett, Wilkins, Peacock, Maddix, Bailey, Barker, Ferdinand, Penrice, Wilson.
Manchester C: Coton; Hill, Pointon, Megson, Curle, Redmond, White, Heath, Quinn, Brightwell I, Hughes.

Southampton (0) 1 *(Horne)*
Sheffield W (0) 0   10,801
Southampton: Flowers; Dodd, Adams, Hurlock, Hall, Gittens, Le Tissier, Cockerill, Shearer, Horne, Moore.
Sheffield W: Woods; Nilsson, King, Palmer, Anderson, Pearson, Wilson, Sheridan, Hirst, Williams, Harkes (Jemson).

3 DEC
THIRD ROUND SECOND REPLAY
Crystal Palace (2) 2 *(Gray (pen), Thorn)*
Birmingham C (1) 1 *(Peer)*   11,384
Crystal Palace: Martyn; Southgate, Coleman, Gray, Young, Thorn, Rodger, Osborn, Bright, Gabbiadini (Collymore), McGoldrick.
Birmingham C: Carter; Clarkson, Frain, Peer, Matthewson, Mardon, Rodgerson, Tait (Hicks), Donowa, Gleghorn, Sturridge (Paskin).

FOURTH ROUND
Middlesbrough (0) 2 *(Mustoe, Wilkinson)*
Manchester C (0) 1 *(White)*   17,286
Middlesbrough: Pears; Fleming, Phillips, Kernaghan, Mohan, Mustoe, Slaven, Proctor, Wilkinson, Ripley, Pollock.
Manchester C: Coton; Hill, Pointon, Brennan (Allen), Curle, Redmond, White, Heath, Quinn, Brightwell I, Hughes (Sheron).

Peterborough U (1) 1 *(Kimble)*
Liverpool (0) 0   14,114
Peterborough U: Barber; Luke, Johnson, Halsall, Robinson D, Welsh, Sterling, Cooper G, Riley, Charlery, Kimble.
Liverpool: Grobbelaar; Ablett (Harkness), Burrows, Nicol, Wright, Tanner, Saunders, Houghton, McManaman, Molby, Marsh.

4 DEC
Coventry C (0) 1 *(Furlong)*
Tottenham H (1) 2 *(Allen, Durie)*   20,095
Coventry C: Ogrizovic; Borrows, Hurst, Emerson, Pearce, Billing, McGrath, Middleton, Rosario, Gallacher, Furlong.
Tottenham H: Thorstvedt; Fenwick, Van Den Hauwe, Bergsson, Howells, Mabbutt, Stewart, Durie, Samways (Sedgley), Walsh (Nayim), Allen.

Everton (1) 1 *(Atteveld)*
Leeds U (2) 4 *(Speed, Chapman, Wallace 2)*   25,467
Everton: Southall; Ebbrell, Hinchcliffe, Ratcliffe (Harper), Watson, Keown, Ward, Beardsley, Johnston, Cottee (Beagrie), Atteveld.
Leeds U: Lukic; Sterland, Dorigo, Batty, Fairclough, Whyte, Strachan (Hodge), Wallace, Chapman, McAllister, Speed.

Manchester U (2) 2 *(McClair, Kanchelskis)*
Oldham Ath (0) 0   38,550
Manchester U: Schmeichel; Parker, Irwin, Bruce, Webb, Pallister, Robson (Ince), Kanchelskis, McClair, Hughes, Giggs (Blackmore).
Oldham Ath: Hallworth; McDonald (Holden), Barlow, Hendry, Barrett, Jobson, Palmer, Marshall, Sharp, Milligan, Fleming.

Norwich C (0) 2 *(Fleck 2 (1 pen))*
West Ham U (0) 1 *(Small)*   16,325
Norwich C: Gunn; Phillips, Bowen, Sutton, Blades (Crook), Goss, Ullathorne, Fleck, Newman, Sherwood, Beckford (Fox).
West Ham U: Miklosko; Breacker, Thomas, Gale, Potts, Parris, Bishop, McAvennie, Small, Allen, Slater.

Nottingham F (0) 0
Southampton (0) 0   17,939
Nottingham F: Crossley; Charles, Pearce, Walker, Chettle (Tiler), Wassall, Crosby, Gemmill, Clough, Sheringham, Woan.
Southampton: Flowers; Dodd, Adams, Hurlock (Hall), Gittens, Ruddock, Le Tissier (Dowie), Cockerill, Shearer, Horne, Gray.

17 DEC
Swindon T (0) 0
Crystal Palace (1) 1 *(Gray)*   10,044
Swindon T: Hammond; Kerslake, Viveash (Jones), Foley (Close), Calderwood, Taylor, Hazard, Shearer, Simpson, MacLaren, White.
Crystal Palace: Martyn; Southgate, Coleman, Gray, Young, Thorn, Rodger, Osborn (Humphrey), Bright, Gabbiadini (Whyte), McGoldrick.

FOURTH ROUND REPLAY
Southampton (0) 0
Nottingham F (1) 1 *(Gemmill)*   10,861
Southampton: Flowers; Dodd, Adams, Horne, Moore (Banger), Ruddock, Gittens, Cockerill, Shearer, Gray (McLoughlin), Le Tissier.
Nottingham F: Crossley; Charles (Wassall), Pearce, Walker (Glover), Tiler, Keane, Black, Gemmill, Clough, Sheringham, Woan.

FIFTH ROUND

8 JAN

Crystal Palace (0) 1 *(Walker (og))*

Nottingham F (0) 1 *(Clough)*   14,941

Crystal Palace: Martyn; Humphrey, Sinnott, Gray, Young, Thorn, Rodger (Whyte), Thomas, Bright, Gabbiadini, McGoldrick.
Nottingham F: Crossley; Charles, Pearce, Walker, Tiler, Keane, Crosby, Gemmill, Clough, Sheringham (Glover), Black.

Leeds U (1) 1 *(Speed)*

Manchester U (1) 3 *(Blackmore, Kanchelskis, Giggs)*
                                                       28,886

Leeds U: Lukic; Sterland, Dorigo (McClelland), Batty, Fairclough, Whyte, Strachan, Wallace, Chapman (Hodge), McAllister, Speed.
Manchester U; Schmeichel; Parker, Blackmore, Bruce, Webb, Pallister, Kanchelskis (Sharpe), Ince, McClair, Hughes, Giggs (Donaghy).

Peterborough U (0) 0

Middlesbrough (0) 0   15,302

Peterborough U: Barber; Luke, Johnson, Halsall, Robinson D, Welsh, Sterling, Cooper G, Riley (Culpin), Charlery, Kimble.
Middlesbrough: Pears; Parkinson, Phillips, Kernaghan, Mohan, Mustoe, Slaven, Hendrie, Wilkinson, Pollock, Ripley.

Tottenham H (0) 2 *(Walsh, Lineker)*

Norwich C (1) 1 *(Fleck)*   29,471

Tottenham H: Thorstvedt; Fenwick (Bergsson), Van Den Hauwe, Sedgley, Nayim, Mabbutt, Stewart, Walsh, Samways (Houghton), Lineker, Allen.
Norwich C: Gunn; Phillips, Bowen, Sutton, Blades, Goss, Fox, Fleck, Newman, Crook (Beckford), Ullathorne.

FIFTH ROUND REPLAYS

5 FEB

Nottingham F (3) 4 *(Sheringham 3, Pearce)*

Crystal Palace (1) 2 *(Bright, Whyte)*   18,918

Nottingham F: Crossley; Laws, Pearce, Walker, Tiler, Keane, Crosby, Gemmill, Clough, Sheringham, Black.
Crystal Palace: Martyn; Humphrey, Sinnott, Osborn, Southgate, Thorn, Rodger, Thomas (Coleman), Bright, Whyte, McGoldrick.

12 FEB

Middlesbrough (0) 1 *(Ripley)*

Peterborough U (0) 0   21,973

Middlesbrough: Pears; Parkinson, Phillips, Kernaghan, Mohan, Mustoe, Proctor, Pollock, Wilkinson, Hendrie, Ripley.
Peterborough U: Barber; Luke, Curtis, Halsall, Robinson D, Welsh, Sterling, Cooper G, Gavin, Charlery, Kimble (Costello).

SEMI-FINALS, FIRST LEG

9 FEB

Nottingham F (0) 1 *(Sheringham)*

Tottenham H (1) 1 *(Lineker (pen))*   21,402

Nottingham F: Crossley; Laws, Pearce, Walker, Wassall, Keane, Crosby, Gemmill, Clough, Sheringham, Black.
Tottenham H: Thorstvedt; Fenwick, Van Den Hauwe, Sedgley, Howells, Bergsson, Stewart, Durie, Samways (Nayim), Lineker (Edinburgh), Allen.

4 MAR

Middlesbrough (0) 0

Manchester U (0) 0   25,572

Middlesbrough: Pears; Parkinson, Phillips, Mohan, Mustoe (Proctor), Slaven, Pollock, Wilkinson, Hendrie, Ripley.
Manchester U: Schmeichel; Parker, Irwin, Donaghy (Phelan), Webb, Pallister, Robson, Ince (Sharpe), McClair, Hughes, Giggs.

SEMI-FINALS, SECOND LEG

1 MAR

Tottenham H (1) 1 *(Lineker)*

Nottingham F (1) 2 *(Glover, Keane) aet*   28,216

Tottenham H: Thorstvedt; Fenwick (Edinburgh), Van Den Hauwe, Sedgley, Howells, Mabbutt, Stewart, Durie, Nayim (Samways), Lineker, Allen.
Nottingham F: Crossley; Laws, Pearce, Walker, Wassall, Keane, Crosby, Gemmill, Clough, Sheringham, Glover.

11 MAR

Manchester U (1) 2 *(Sharpe, Giggs)*

Middlesbrough (0) 1 *(Slaven) aet*   45,875

Manchester U: Schmeichel; Parker, Irwin, Bruce, Webb, Pallister, Robson, Ince, McClair, Sharpe (Robins), Giggs.
Middlesbrough: Pears; Fleming, Phillips, Kernaghan, Mohan, Mustoe (Proctor), Slaven, Pollock, Wilkinson, Hendrie, Ripley (Falconer).

FINAL at Wembley

12 APR

Manchester U (1) 1 *(McClair)*

Nottingham F (0) 0   76,810

Manchester U: Schmeichel; Parker, Irwin, Bruce, Pallister, Kanchelskis (Sharpe), Ince, McClair, Hughes, Giggs.
Nottingham F: Marriott; Charles (Laws), Williams, Walker, Wassall, Keane, Crosby, Gemmill, Clough, Sheringham, Black.
Referee: G. Courtney (Spennymoor).

LEAGUE CUP ATTENDANCES

Totals	Season	Attendances	Games	Average
	1960/61	1,204,580	112	10,755
	1961/62	1,030,534	104	9,909
	1962/63	1,029,893	102	10,097
	1963/64	945,265	104	9,089
	1964/65	962,802	98	9,825
	1965/66	1,205,876	106	11,376
	1966/67	1,394,553	118	11,818
	1967/68	1,671,326	110	15,194
	1968/69	2,064,647	118	17,497
	1969/70	2,299,819	122	18,851
	1970/71	2,035,315	116	17,546
	1971/72	2,397,154	123	19,489
	1972/73	1,935,474	120	16,129
	1973/74	1,722,629	132	13,050
	1974/75	1,901,094	127	14,969
	1975/76	1,841,735	140	13,155
	1976/77	2,236,636	147	15,215
	1977/78	2,038,295	148	13,772
	1978/79	1,825,643	139	13,134
	1979/80	2,322,866	169	13,745
	1980/81	2,051,576	161	12,743
	1981/82	1,880,682	161	11,681
	1982/83	1,679,756	160	10,498
	1983/84	1,900,491	168	11,312
	1984/85	1,876,429	167	11,236
	1985/86	1,579,916	163	9,693
	1986/87	1,531,498	157	9,755
	1987/88	1,539,253	158	9,742
	1988/89	1,552,780	162	9,585
	1989/90	1,836,916	168	10,934
	1990/91	1,675,496	159	10,538
	1991/92	1,622,337	164	9,892

636

THE FOOTBALL TRUST
Helping the game

During the past year, the Football Trust has received over £32m to support the game at all levels. The Government annually contributes some £20m from the 1990 Budget concession on pool betting duty, and a further £12m is donated by the pools companies Littlewoods, Vernons and Zetters from their Spotting-the-Ball competition.

The Trust's prime responsibility is to assess the professional game to fund capital works in line with the recommendations of the Taylor Report. Trust grants have been awarded to English and Scottish League clubs for major projects such as relocation schemes, new stands and seating and roofing initiatives. Last season the following awards were made:

		£
Aberdeen	New Beach End Stand	1,900,000
Arsenal	Redevelopment of the North Bank	2,000,000
Aston Villa	Cover and Seating in Trinity Road	107,650
	New Witton Lane Stand	1,700,000
Barnsley	New East Stand	1,000,000
Blackburn Rovers	New Darwen End Stand	1,000,000
Cardiff City	Redevelopment of Ninian Park	500,000
Chelsea	Redevelopment of the North Stand	1,850,000
Chester City	New Stadium	500,000
Crystal Palace	Cover and Seating the Members' End	432,100
Ipswich Town	New North and South Stands	217,700
Manchester City	Redevelopment of the Platt Lane Stand	2,000,000
Manchester United	New Stretford End Stand	1,400,000
Montrose	New Stand	330,000
Motherwell	New South Stand	1,100,000
Northampton Town	New Stadium	500,000
Norwich City	Seating the Barclay Stand	2,000,000
Nottingham Forest	New Bridgford End Stand	1,900,000
Notts County	Redevelopment of Meadow Lane	2,000,000
Oldham Athletic	New Rochdale Road End Stand	1,095,850
Port Vale	New Hamil Road Stand	520,000
Preston North End	Seating in the Pavilion Stand	6,600
Rochdale	New Main Stand	400,000
Sheffield United	Seating in the Spion Kop Corner	465,000
Sheffield Wednesday	New South Stand	960,000
Stirling Albion	New Stadium	500,000
Swindon Town	Seating in the North Stand	210,000
Torquay United	New Ellacombe End Stand	300,000
Tranmere Rovers	New Stand at the Bebington Kop End	1,000,000
Walsall	Seating in the William Sharp Stand	21,700
West Bromwich Albion	Seating and Cover at the Smethwick End	400,000
Wolves	Waterloo Road Stand	1,250,000

The Trust also awards grants to enable clubs to pursue important safety work and facility improvements. Initiatives include facilities for people with disabilities, family enclosures, new toilets, and anti-hooligan measures such as closed circuit television, stewarding and transport improvements. Last season, the Trust offered over £7.7m towards improving the safety and comfort of supporters throughout England and Scotland, bringing the Trust's total support for safety and improvement work to some £62.6m. A further £2.5m was awarded in grant aid to assist clubs with policing and stewarding costs, and £600,000 towards the installation and upgrading of CCTV at 32 English and Scottish League grounds.

The remainder of the Trust's income is allocated to projects for the general benefit of the game in the pyramid and at grass roots level. Grants have been made towards essential safety work at non-League clubs and for pitch and dressing room improvements. The Trust has also continued to support the dual use of educational facilities, artificial floodlight pitches, hard surface play areas, charitable playing fields' organizations, youth and community groups and the supply of kit to junior teams.

JEWSON'S FAMILY INVOLVEMENT

Advertising and sponsorship go hand in hand with top sport these days and Association Football is no exception. One of the big deals which helped clubs throughout the Football League last season was the Jewson deal worth more than £2.5m, spread over three years.

The Norwich based builders' merchants chain paid out £350,000 in each of the first two years to a total of 57 League clubs for improvements to family and disabled fans' enclosures and facilities. It was broken down to five awards of £20,000 each season to five First Division clubs, six of £15,000 for Division Two and eight £10,000 grants to clubs in both Divisions Three and Four.

The projects included diverse schemes like Aldershot's renovating the family room, to Birmingham's improving the Junior Blues room to providing a crèche and family-area seating at York. The total cost of all the projects undertaken by Football League clubs in the first two years of the scheme amounted to some £4.5m.

Of the bigger ventures Bradford embarked on a two-tier stand which accommodates nearly 2,000 family spectators, so fathers can keep an eye on their children and still watch the game. A similar redevelopment was carried out by Welsh club Cardiff City. The scheme certainly goes a long way to help reburnish the game's image at top level and makes it more convivial for folk of all ages to watch.

And to further improve the participation of families in football, Jewson ran a parallel scheme, in conjunction with national Sunday newspaper *The People*, whereby fans could nominate their clubs for an extra award.

Bobby Moore, captain of England's World Cup winning team in 1966 was a key member of the judging committee which decided the top two clubs in each of the four divisions and the overall winner.

Sunderland took the top prize of £30,000 in 1992 with Aston Villa (Div 1), Brentford (Div 3) and Walsall (Div 4) each collecting £15,000; Leeds, Newcastle, Leyton Orient and Scunthorpe all collected £1,000 as runners-up in their respective divisions.

Factors considered by the judging committee included facilities, team involvement with the fans, innovations and community relations. The awards could be spent by the winners in any way they liked — even towards signing a player if necessary!

In the 1992–93 season the awards will be restricted to Divisions One, Two and Three as it is considered the new Premier League will be funded from other sources and is outside the Football League with whom the deal was struck by Jewsons.

Obviously the deal benefits both the clubs and the sponsors. Not only do the teams such as those in the lower divisions pick up extra income, but they also can obtain the materials at discounted prices. On the other side of the coin, Jewsons gain name exposure at the League's stadia as well as word-of-mouth publicity. No doubt other such schemes to benefit the game will be forthcoming . . . and the more the merrier.

TREVOR WILLIAMSON

ZENITH DATA SYSTEMS CUP 1991-92

FIRST ROUND
1 OCT
Grimsby T (1) 1 *(Rees)*
Wolverhampton W (0) 0   1593
Grimsby T: Sherwood; McDermott, Smith, Futcher, Lever, Cunnington, Childs, Gilbert, Rees (Jones), Dobbin, Woods.
Wolverhampton W: Stowell; Ashley, Venus, Bennett, Madden, Downing, Birch, Cook, Bull, Dennison (Burke), Bellamy.

Port Vale (1) 1 *(Foyle)*
Blackburn R (0) 0   2355
Port Vale: Grew; Webb (Kidd), Hughes, Mills S, Swan, Glover, Porter, Van der Laan, Mills B, Foyle, Kent.
Blackburn R: Mimms; Brown (Reid), Dobson, Richardson, Hill, May, Skinner, Garner, Gayle (Irvine), Johnrose, Wilcox.

Tranmere R (2) 6 *(McNab, Aldridge 3 (1 pen), Steel, Martindale)*
Newcastle U (2) 6 *(Quinn 3 (1 pen), Peacock 2, Clark)*
                                                             4056
Tranmere R: Nixon; Higgins, Brannan (Mungall), Irons, Hughes, Vickers (Branch), Malkin, Aldridge, Steel, Martindale, McNab.
Newcastle U: Srnicek; Neilson, Elliott, O'Brien, Scott, Bradshaw, Clark, Peacock, Quinn, Hunt, Brock (Roche).
aet; Tranmere R won 3-2 on penalties.

Plymouth Arg (1) 1 *(Turner)*
Portsmouth (0) 0   2303
Plymouth Arg: Walter; Clement, Spearing, Marker, Burrows, Morgan, Barlow, Marshall, Turner, Quamina, Fiore.
Portsmouth: Gosney; Maguire, Russell, Burns, Symons, Butters, Neill, Chamberlain (Ross), Powell, Murray (Doling), Anderton.

Swindon T (0) 3 *(White 2, MacLaren)*
Oxford U (0) 3 *(Simpson 2, Melville)*   5868
Swindon T: Digby; Jones, Summerbee (Hoddle), Kerslake, Calderwood, Taylor, Ling (Close), Shearer, Simpson, MacLaren, White.
Oxford U: Veysey; Robinson, Beauchamp (Allen), Lewis, Evans, Melville, Magilton, Penney, Aylott, Nogan (Smart), Simpson.
aet; Swindon T won 4-3 on penalties.

SECOND ROUND
Everton (1) 3 *(Newell, Watson, Cottee)*
Oldham Ath (1) 2 *(Holden, Milligan)*   4588
Everton: Southall; Harper, Hinchcliffe, Ebbrell, Watson, Youds, Nevin, Beardsley, Newell (Atteveld), Cottee, Sheedy.
Oldham Ath: Keeley; Fleming (Bernard), Barlow, Henry, Barrett, Jobson, Kane, Ritchie (Marshall), Sharp, Milligan, Holden.

2 OCT
FIRST ROUND
Leicester C (3) 4 *(Wright 2, Kelly, Walsh)*
Barnsley (0) 3 *(Archdeacon, Currie, Saville) aet*   3995
Leicester C: Poole; Mills, Oakes (Ward), Fitzpatrick, Walsh, Linton, Oldfield, Gibson, Wright, Kelly, Mauchlen (Reid).

Barnsley: Butler; Robinson, Fleming, Bishop (Archdeacon), Saville, Taggart, O'Connell (Williams), Redfearn, Pearson, Currie, Rammell.

Bristol R (1) 1 *(Pounder)*
Ipswich T (1) 3 *(Dozzell, Lowe 2)*   1490
Bristol R: Parkin; Alexander, Twentyman, Yates, Cross, Skinner, Evans (Browning), Reece, White (Stewart), Saunders, Pounder.
Ipswich T: Forrest; Whelan, Thompson, Zondervan, Yallop, Wark, Lowe, Gregory, Whitton, Dozzell, Milton.

Cambridge U (1) 1 *(Taylor)*
Charlton Ath (1) 1 *(Gorman)*   3168
Cambridge U: Sheffield; Fensome, Kimble, Leadbitter (Dennis), Heathcote, Daish, Cheetham, Wilkins, Dublin, Claridge, Taylor.
Charlton Ath: Bolder; Pitcher, Barness, Peake, Webster, Gatting, Bumstead, Bacon (Salako), Gorman (Grant), Nelson, Dyer.
aet; Cambridge U won 4-2 on penalties.

Watford (0) 0
Southend U (1) 1 *(Sussex)*   1700
Watford: James; Gibbs (Blissett), Morrow, Dublin, McLaughlin (Soloman), Putney, Hessenthaler, Bazeley, Butler, Porter, Nicholas.
Southend U: Sansome; Austin, Powell, Sussex, Scully, Prior, Locke, Cornwell, Tilson, Benjamin, Cagigao.

22 OCT
SECOND ROUND
Leeds U (0) 1 *(Wallace Rod)*
Nottingham F (2) 3 *(Crosby, Sheringham 2 (1 pen))* 6145
Leeds U: Lukic; Sterland (Wallace Rod), Dorigo, Batty, Fairclough, Whyte, Newsome (Grayson), Shutt, Snodin, Kamara, Speed.
Nottingham F: Crossley; Chettle, Pearce, Walker, Tiler, Wassall, Crosby, Gemmill, Sheringham (Gaynor), Black, Parker (Laws).

Middlesbrough (0) 4 *(Wilkinson 2, Phillips, Slaven)*
Derby Co (2) 2 *(Micklewhite, Stallard) aet*   6385
Middlesbrough: Pears; Parkinson (Fleming), Phillips, Mowbray, Kernaghan, Mustoe, Slaven, Proctor, Wilkinson, Pollock (Arnold), Marwood.
Derby Co: Taylor; Patterson, Forsyth, Hayward, Coleman, Comyn, Micklewhite, Stallard (Chalk), Gee, Williams P (Davidson), McMinn.

Sheffield U (0) 3 *(Whitehouse 2, Gayle)*
Notts Co (1) 3 *(Draper, Bartlett, Slawson)*   3291
Sheffield U: Kite; Pemberton, Cowan, Gannon, Gayle, Beesley (Lake), Bryson (Mendonca), Hoyland, Littlejohn, Bradshaw, Whitehouse.
Notts Co: Cherry; Palmer, Paris, Johnson M, Yates, Draper, Dryden, Harding, Regis (Slawson), Bartlett (Wells), Johnson T.
aet; Notts Co won 2-1 on penalties.

Tranmere R (2) 5 *(Aldridge 3, Martindale, Steel)*
Grimsby T (1) 1 *(Vickers (og))*   4053
Tranmere R: Nixon; Higgins, Brannan, Irons, Hughes, Vickers, Morrissey, Aldridge, Steel, Martindale, Mungall (Harvey).
Grimsby T: Sherwood; McDermott, Jobling (Smith), Futcher, Lever (Birtles), Cunnington, Childs, Gilbert, Rees, Watson, Woods.

Bristol C (1) 1 *(Taylor)*
Southampton (0) 2 *(Shearer, Le Tissier)* 5672
Bristol C: Leaning; Llewellyn, Scott, Rennie, Caesar, Bryant, Shelton (Aizlewood), May, Allison, Taylor, Connor.
Southampton: Flowers; Dodd, Adams, Hurlock, Wood, Ruddock, Lee, Cockerill, Shearer, Gray, Le Tissier.

Crystal Palace (0) 4 *(McGoldrick, Bright, Thomas, Gray)*
Southend U (1) 2 *(Jones, Angell)* aet 7185
Crystal Palace: Martyn; Southgate, Sinnott, Gray, Young, Thorn, Mortimer, Thomas, Bright (Gordon), Gabbiadini (Osborn), McGoldrick.
Southend U: Sansome; Austin, Powell, Jones, Scully, Prior, Ansah, Cornwell, Tilson, Benjamin (Locke), Angell.

Ipswich T (0) 1 *(Lowe)*
Luton T (0) 1 *(Telfer)* 5750
Ipswich T: Forrest; Yallop (Edmonds), Thompson, Stockwell, Wark (Palmer), Linighan, Lowe, Zondervan, Whitton, Dozzell, Milton.
Luton T: Chamberlain; Telfer, Allpress, Hughes, Salton, Rodger, Williams (Rees), James, Harford (Campbell), Nogan, Pembridge.
aet; Ipswich T won 2–1 on penalties.

Plymouth Arg (2) 4 *(Fiore, Marker, Evans, Marshall)*
Millwall (0) 0 2022
Plymouth Arg: Wilmot; Salman, Clement, Marker, Evans, Morgan, Barlow (Hodges), Marshall, Turner, Fiore, Cross.
Millwall: Davison; Stevens, Cooper, Bogie, McLeary, Thompson, Kerr (Barber), Colquhoun, Falco, Rae, Stephenson (Armstrong).

West Ham U (1) 2 *(Parris, McAvennie)*
Cambridge U (0) 1 *(Rowett)* 7812
West Ham U: Miklosko; Breacker, Hughton, Gale, Potts, Parris, Bishop, McAvennie, Small, Keen, Allen.
Cambridge U: Sheffield; Clayton, Kimble, Dennis, O'Shea, Daish, Rowett (Fensome), Wilkins, Dublin, Taylor (Leadbitter), Philpott.

23 OCT

Coventry C (0) 0
Aston Villa (1) 2 *(Olney, Yorke)* 6447
Coventry C: Ogrizovic; Borrows, Edwards, Robson, Pearce, Butcher, McGrath, Greenman (Emerson), Rosario (Ndlovu), Gallacher, Furlong.
Aston Villa: Sealey; Price, Small, Teale, Ehiogu, Richardson (Cowans), Daley, Blake, Olney, McLoughlin, Yorke.

Leicester C (0) 4 *(Wright 2, Kitson, Gordon)*
Port Vale (0) 0 4853
Leicester C: Poole; Mills, Gibson, Smith, Walsh, Fitzpatrick, Oldfield, Mauchlen, Wright, Kitson, Gordon.
Port Vale: Grew; Mills S, Hughes, Porter, Swan (Mills B), Glover (Parkin), Rushton, Jalink, Jeffers, Foyle, Aspin.

Sheffield W (1) 3 *(Hirst, Hyde, Jemson)*
Manchester C (1) 2 *(Hendry 2)* 7951
Sheffield W: Woods; Nilsson, King, Palmer, Anderson, Wood, Harkes (Wilson), Hyde, Hirst, Williams, Worthington (Jemson).
Manchester C: Margetson; Quigley (Mauge), Pointon, Hendry, Curle, Redmond, Sheron, Heath, Brennan, Brightwell I, Hughes.

Brighton & HA (2) 3 *(Barham, Robinson, Chivers)*
Wimbledon (1) 2 *(Scales, Earle)* 2796
Brighton & HA: Beeney; Crumplin, Chapman, Briley, Chivers, Bissett, Barham, Farrington, Meade, Codner, Robinson.
Wimbledon: Segers; Ryan, Phelan, Barton, Elkins, Fitzgerald, Gibson (Cork), Earle, Fashanu, Scales, McGee (Bennett).

Chelsea (0) 1 *(Jones)*
Swindon T (0) 0 5784
Chelsea: Hitchcock; Clarke, Boyd, Jones, Elliott, Cundy, Le Saux, Burley, Allon (Pearce), Wilson, Myers.
Swindon T: Hammond; Kerslake, Summerbee, Jones, Calderwood, Taylor, Hazard, Shearer, Simpson, MacLaren, White.

Norwich C (1) 1 *(Beckford)*
QPR (1) 2 *(Sinton, Impey)* 4436
Norwich C: Gunn; Phillips, Bowen, Butterworth, Blades (Woodthorpe), Goss, Gordon, Beckford, Newman, Fox, Mortensen.
QPR: Stejskal; Bardsley, Wilson, Tillson, Peacock, Maddix, Holloway, Barker, Thompson, Bailey, Sinton (Impey).

QUARTER-FINALS
19 NOV
Aston Villa (0) 0
Nottingham F (1) 2 *(Pearce, Woan)* 7858
Aston Villa: Sealey; Kubicki (Carruthers), Small, Teale, Nielsen, Richardson, Daley, Atkinson, Olney (Beinlich), Blake, Cox.
Nottingham F: Crossley; Charles, Pearce, Walker, Chettle, Keane (Wassall), Crosby, Gemmill, Glover, Sheringham, Woan (Clough).

26 NOV
Middlesbrough (0) 0
Tranmere R (0) 1 *(Aldridge)* 6592
Middlesbrough: Pears; Fleming, Phillips, Kernaghan, Mohan, Mustoe, Slaven, Proctor, Wilkinson, Ripley, Pollock (Young).
Tranmere R: Nixon; Higgins, Brannan, Irons, Hughes, Vickers, Morrissey, Aldridge, Steel, Martindale, Nolan (Harvey).

Notts Co (0) 1 *(Harding)*
Sheffield W (0) 0 4118
Notts Co: Cherry; Palmer, Dryden, Short Craig, Short Chris, O'Riordan (Turner), Thomas, Harding, Rideout, Agana, Johnson T.
Sheffield W: Woods; Anderson, King (Watson), Palmer, Warhurst, Pearson, Harkes, Wilson (Bart-Williams), Jemson, Williams.

Chelsea (1) 2 *(Jones, Allon)*
Ipswich T (1) 2 *(Kiwomya 2)* 6325
Chelsea: Hitchcock; Clarke, Boyd (Allon), Jones, Elliott, Monkou, Le Saux, Dickens, Dixon, Wilson (Stuart), Wise.
Ipswich T: Forrest; Johnson, Thompson, Stockwell, Wark, Linighan, Palmer, Goddard (Yallop), Milton, Dozzell (Lowe), Kiwomya.
aet; Chelsea won 4–3 on penalties.

Plymouth Arg (0) 0
Southampton (0) 1 *(Le Tissier)* 5578
Plymouth Arg: Wilmot; Spearing, Clement, Marker, Hopkins, Morgan, Meaker (Barlow), Marshall, Scott, Fiore, Turner.

640

Southampton: Flowers; Dodd, Adams, Hurlock, Ruddock, Gittens, Le Tissier, Cockerill, Shearer, Horne, Wood.

QPR (0) 2 *(Bardsley, Wilkins)*
Crystal Palace (2) 3 *(Thomas, Gabbiadini, Young)* 4492
QPR: Roberts; Bardsley, Wilson, Wilkins, Peacock, McDonald, Channing (Impey), Barker (Holloway), Ferdinand, Penrice, Sinton.
Crystal Palace: Martyn; Southgate (Humphrey), Coleman, Gray, Young, Thorn, Mortimer, Thomas, Bright, Gabbiadini (Osborn), McGoldrick.

West Ham U (2) *(McAvennie 2)*
Brighton & HA (0) 0 8146
West Ham U: Miklosko; Breacker, Thomas, Gale, Potts, Parris, Bishop, McAvennie, Small, Keen, Slater.
Brighton & HA: Beeney; Crumplin (Walker), Gallagher, Briley, Chivers, O'Reilly, Iovan, Meade, Gall, Codner, Farrington.

27 NOV
Leicester C (2) 2 *(Oldfield, Thompson)*
Everton (0) 1 *(Beardsley)* 13,242
Leicester C: Poole; Mills, Platnauer, Smith (Coatsworth), Walsh, Fitzpatrick, Oldfield, Thompson (Reid), Gordon, Kitson, Mauchlen.
Everton: Southall; Jackson (Atteveld), Hinchcliffe, Harper, Watson, Keown, Warzycha (Beagrie), Beardsley, Johnston, Cottee, Ward.

SEMI-FINALS
NORTHERN SECTION
10 DEC
Tranmere R (0) 0
Nottingham F (1) 2 *(Keane 2)* 8034
Tranmere R: Nixon; Higgins, Brannan, Irons, Hughes (Harvey), Vickers, Morrissey, Aldridge, McNab, Cooper, Nolan.
Nottingham F: Crossley; Charles, Pearce, Walker (Wassall), Chettle, Keane (Black), Crosby, Gemmill, Clough, Sheringham, Woan.

SOUTHERN SECTION
Crystal Palace (0) 0
Chelsea (1) 1 *(Dixon)* 8416
Crystal Palace: Martyn; Southgate (Rodger), Coleman (Whyte), Gray, Young, Thorn, Mortimer, Osborn, Bright, Gabbiadini, McGoldrick.
Chelsea: Hitchcock; Clark, Boyd, Jones, Elliott, Monkou, Le Saux, Townsend, Dixon, Allon, Wise.

7 JAN
Southampton (0) 2 *(Shearer, Le Tissier (pen))*
West Ham U (1) 1 *(Bishop)* 6861
Southampton: Flowers; Dodd, Adams, Horne, Hall, Wood, Le Tissier, Hurlock, Shearer, Dowie, Banger (Lee).
West Ham U: Miklosko; Breacker, Dicks, Gale, Foster, Thomas, Bishop, McAvennie, Brown, Keen (Morley), Slater.

NORTHERN SECTION
8 JAN
Notts Co (1) 1 *(Short Chris)*
Leicester C (0) 2 *(Wright, Fitzpatrick) aet* 11,559
Notts Co: Cherry; Palmer, Paris, Short Craig, Yates, Short Chris (Draper), Rideout, Turner, Harding (Slawson), Agana, Johnson T.
Leicester C: Muggleton; Mills, Reid, Smith, Walsh, Mauchlen (Gordon), Oldfield (Fitzpatrick), Thompson, Wright, Willis, Kitson.

SOUTHERN SECTION FINAL, First Leg
21 JAN
Southampton (1) 2 *(Shearer, Hurlock)*
Chelsea (0) 0 8726
Southampton: Flowers; Kenna, Adams, Horne, Hall, Wood, Le Tissier, Hurlock, Shearer, Dowie, Benali.
Chelsea: Hitchcock; Hall, Boyd, Jones, Elliott, Monkou, Stuart (Le Saux), Townsend, Dixon, Allon, Wise.

SOUTHERN SECTION FINAL, Second Leg
29 JAN
Chelsea (1) 1 *(Wise (pen))*
Southampton (2) 3 *(Le Tissier 3 (1 pen))* 9781
Chelsea: Hitchcock; Burley, Boyd, Jones, Elliott (Wilson), Cundy, Le Saux, Townsend, Stuart, Allon, Wise (Gilkes).
Southampton: Flowers; Kenna, Adams, Horne, Hall, Ruddock, Le Tissier, Hurlock, Shearer, Dowie, Benali.
Southampton won 5–1 on aggregate.

NORTHERN SECTION FINAL, First Leg
12 FEB
Leicester C (0) 1 *(Gordon)*
Nottingham F (0) 1 *(Gemmill)* 19,537
Leicester C: Poole; Mills, Platnauer, Smith, Walsh, Gordon (Thompson), Oldfield, Russell, Wright, Mauchlen, Kitson.
Nottingham F: Crossley; Laws, Glover, Walker, Wassall, Keane, Crosby, Gemmill, Clough, Sheringham, Black.

NORTHERN SECTION FINAL, Second Leg
26 FEB
Nottingham F (1) 2 *(Crosby, Wassall)*
Leicester C (0) 0 21,562
Nottingham F: Crossley; Laws, Pearce, Walker, Wassall, Keane, Crosby (Glover), Gemmill, Clough, Sheringham, Black (Charles).
Leicester C: Poole; Mills, Reid, Smith (Willis), Walsh, Gordon (Fitzpatrick), Thompson, Russell, Wright, Mauchlen, Kitson.
Nottingham F won 3–1 on aggregate.

FINAL (at Wembley)
29 MAR
Nottingham F (2) 3 *(Gemmill 2, Black)*
Southampton (0) 2 *(Le Tissier, Moore) aet* 67,688
Nottingham F: Marriott; Charles, Pearce (Chettle), Walker, Wassall, Keane, Crosby, Gemmill, Clough, Sheringham, Black.
Southampton: Flowers; Kenna, Benali, Horne, Moore, Ruddock, Le Tissier, Cockerill, Shearer, Dowie, Hurlock.
Referee: K. Hackett (Sheffield).

AUTOGLASS TROPHY 1991–92

Rotherham U and Chesterfield given byes to First Round

PRELIMINARY ROUND
15 OCT

Wrexham (0) 1 *(Preece)*
Mansfield T (0) 0   627
Wrexham: Morris; Thackeray, Hardy, Beaumont, Thomas, Jones J, Phillips, Owen, Kelly, Watkin, Preece.
Mansfield T: Pearcey; Fleming, Carr, Spooner, Fee, Foster, Ford, Holland, Stant, Wilkinson, Charles.

22 OCT

Aldershot (0) 0
Brentford (1) 2 *(Sealy 2)*   1348
Aldershot: Granville; Brown, Cooper, Hopkins (Terry), Flower, Ogley, Rees, Puckett (Halbert), Henry, Randall, Heath.
Brentford: Suckling; Bates, Manuel, Millen, Ratcliffe, Rostron, Buckle, Gayle, Sealy (Holdsworth), Blissett (Peters), Smillie.

Blackpool (1) 1 *(Rodwell)*
Burnley (3) 3 *(Francis, Eli 2)*   2805
Blackpool: McIlhargey; Davis (Brook), Wright, Groves, Briggs, Gore, Rodwell, Horner (Taylor), Bamber, Sinclair, Eyres.
Burnley: Marriott; Measham, Jakub, Davis, Pender, Farrell, Harper, Deary, Lancashire (Conroy), Eli, Francis.

Bournemouth (2) 3 *(Wood 2, McGorry)*
Swansea C (0) 0   1814
Bournemouth: Bartram; O'Driscoll, Rowland, Morris, Mundee, McCorry, Cooke, Wood, Quinn (Fereday), Case, Holmes (Mitchell).
Swansea C: Freestone; Jenkins, Ford, Chapple, Harris, Brazil, Freeman (Bowen), Davies, Gilligan, Raynor, Legg.

Darlington (2) 2 *(Willis, Ellison (pen))*
Crewe Alex (0) 2 *(Hignett, McPhillips)*   1095
Darlington: Prudhoe; Coatsworth, Coverdale, Willis, Smith (Sunley), Trotter, Hamilton, Toman, Ellison, Borthwick, Tucker.
Crewe Alex: Greygoose; Wilson, McKearney, Carr, Callaghan, Sorvel, Hignett, McPhillips, Evans, Gardiner, Edwards.

Hull C (2) 2 *(Matthews, Windass)*
Bradford C (1) 1 *(Tinnion)*   1218
Hull C: Fettis; Windass, Jacobs, Matthews, Mail, Shotton, Calvert (Stoker), Payton, Walmsley (Wilcox), Norton, Jenkinson.
Bradford C: Tomlinson; Mitchell (McCarthy), Dowson, James, Oliver (Stuart), Gardner, Babb, Duxbury L, Torpey, Tinnion, Reid.

Leyton Orient (1) 1 *(Otto)*
Reading (0) 0   1052
Leyton Orient: Newell; Howard, Hackett, Whitbread, Day, Bart-Williams, Achampong, Jones, Nugent, Castle, Otto (Harvey).
Reading: Francis; Holzman, Streete, McPherson, Gooding, Williams, Taylor (Lovell), Dillon, Senior, McGhee, Gilkes.

Peterborough U (0) 2 *(Charlery, Howarth)*
Wrexham (0) 0   1085
Peterborough U: Barber; White, Butterworth, Halsall, Howarth, Welsh, Sterling, Cooper G, Riley (Gavin), Charlery, Kimble.

Wrexham: Morris; Thackeray, Hardy, Beaumont, Marshall (Davies), Jones J, Phillips (Sertori), Owen, Kelly, Jones L, Preece.

Rochdale (0) 1 *(Whitehall)*
Preston NE (0) 1 *(Joyce)*   1255
Rochdale: Gray; Brown M, Harpin, Brown T, Reeves, Jones, Bowden, Doyle, Flounders, Whitehall, Milner (Hilditch).
Preston NE: Kelly; Senior, Cross, Swann, Flynn, Wrightson, Ashcroft, Joyce, Thomas, Shaw, James (Thompson).

Scunthorpe U (0) 1 *(Hamilton)*
Bury (1) 3 *(Stevens, Hulme, Wilson)*   1122
Scunthorpe U: Musselwhite; Joyce, Longden, Martin (Hyde), Lister, Humphries (Alexander), Buckley, Hamilton, Daws, Hill, Helliwell.
Bury: Kelly; Anderson (Wilson D), Stanislaus, Kearney, Hughes, Greenall, Smith, Robinson (Hulme), Stevens, Parkinson, Wilson I.

Walsall (0) 0
Stoke C (0) 2 *(Sandford 2)*   3578
Walsall: Sinclair; Williams, Statham, O'Hara, Methven, Marsh, Anderson (Jackson), Ntamark, Walsh, Cecere, McDonald.
Stoke C: Kearton; Butler, Cranson, Fowler, Overson, Sandford, Kevan (Ware), Beeston, Scott, Biggins, Ellis.

Wigan Ath (0) 0
Huddersfield T (1) 1 *(Roberts)*   1214
Wigan Ath: Adkins; Smyth, Tankard, Johnson, Appleton (Pilling), Langley, Powell, Connolly (Carberry), Daley, Jones, Griffiths.
Huddersfield T: Clarke; Trevitt, Charlton, Marsden, Mitchell, Jackson, O'Regan, Donovan, Roberts, Starbuck, Barnett.

WBA (2) 4 *(Rogers, West, Shakespeare, Ampadu)*
Shrewsbury T (0) 0   6997
WBA: Naylor; Hodson, Harvey, Ford, Rogers, Bradley, McNally, Goodman (Robson), West, Shakespeare (Williams); Ampadu.
Shrewsbury T: Perks; Worsley, Cash (Smith), Henry, Lynch, Blake, Hopkins, Summerfield, Lyne, Taylor, Griffiths (Gorman).

York C (0) 1 *(McCarthy)*
Carlisle U (1) 1 *(Fyfe)*   957
York C: Gosney; McMillan, Hall, Reid, Tutill, Atkin, Pepper, McCarthy, Naylor, Barratt, Canham.
Carlisle U: O'Hanlon; Edmondson, Thorpe, Miller, Holliday, Jeffels, Thomas, Lowery (Armstrong), Walling, Fyfe, Proudlock.

23 OCT

Exeter C (2) 2 *(Whiston, Moran)*
Torquay U (1) 1 *(Edwards)*   2957
Exeter C: Miller; Hiley, Cook, Hodge (Marshall), Dennis, Whiston, Hilaire, Wimbleton, Moran, Chapman, Kelly.
Torquay U: Howells; Holmes P, Loram, Compton, Elliott, Sang, Rowbotham, Hall, Joyce, Edwards, Myers.

Maidstone U (1) 2 *(Gall, Owers)*
Fulham (2) 6 *(Brazil 3, Pike, Haag 2)*   937
Maidstone U: Hesford; Sandeman (Owers), Thompson (Painter), Haylock, Oxbrow, Nethercott, Gall, Stebbing, Richards, Osborne, Henry.
Fulham: Stannard; Cobb, Pike, Newson, Kelly, Thomas, Morgan (Nebbeling), Onwere, Cole, Brazil (Haag), Scott.

19 NOV

Barnet (1) 3 *(Carter, Willis, Evans)*
Aldershot (0) 0   1313
Barnet: Phillips; Poole, Naylor, Bodley, Howell (Evans),
Willis, Wilson, Carter, Bull, Lowe (Horton), Showler.
Aldershot: Granville; Brown, McDonald, Henry, Ogley,
Berry (Heath), Rees, Phillips, Bertschin, Randall
(Puckett), Hopkins.

Bradford C (2) 3 *(Torpey 2, McCarthy)*
Hartlepool U (2) 3 *(Tinkler, Baker, Fletcher)*   1562
Bradford C: Evans; Mitchell, Dowson, James, Richards,
Babb, McCarthy, Duxbury L, Torpey, Tinnion, Reid.
Hartlepool U: Hodge; Nobbs, McKinnon, Tinkler, Smith,
Tupling, Southall (Fletcher), Olsson, Baker, Honour,
Dalton.

Burnley (2) 2*(Francis, Eli)*
Doncaster R (0) 0   2590
Burnley: Marriott; Measham, Jakub, Davis, Pender,
Farrell, Harper, Deary, Francis (Yates), Conroy
(Lancashire), Eli.
Doncaster R: Samways; Rowe, Boyle, Crosby, Ormsby,
Douglas, Harle, Gormley (Tynan), Rankine, McKenzie
(Limber), Noteman.

Bury (2) 2 *(Lewis (og), Robinson)*
Halifax T (1) 2 *(Cooper 2)*   788
Bury: Kelly; Greenall, Stanislaus, Hughes, Valentine,
Knill, Smith, Robinson, Jones (Stevens), Parkinson,
Cullen.
Halifax T: Gould; Barr, Richards (Hildersley), Lucketti,
Lewis, Bradley, Richardson, Abbott, Ellis, Juryeff,
Cooper (Evans).

Carlisle U (3) 4 *(Thorpe, Fyfe, Walling 2)*
Stockport Co (0) 0   894
Carlisle U: O'Hanlon; Armstrong, Bennett, Miller, Jeffels
(Barnsley), Edmondson, Thomas, Walling, Proudlock,
Fyfe, Thorpe.
Stockport Co: Edwards; Thorpe, Williams P (Todd),
Frain, Barras, Williams B, Gannon, Beaumont, Francis,
Ward, Lillis (Kilner).

Crewe Alex (1) 2 *(Edwards R 2)*
Chester C (0) 1 *(Lightfoot)*   1779
Crewe Alex: Greygoose; Wilson, McKearney, Carr,
Jackson, Walters, Hignett, Naylor (Disley), Jasper,
Futcher (Evans), Edwards R.
Chester C: Siddall; Whelan, Albiston, Butler, Abel,
Lightfoot, Bishop, Barrow, Rimmer, Morton (Bennett),
Croft.

Huddersfield T (0) 1 *(Roberts)*
Scarborough (0) 1 *(Jules)*   1134
Huddersfield T: Clarke; Trevitt, Charlton, Donovan,
Mitchell, Jackson, O'Regan, Stapleton, Roberts, Onuora,
Barnett (Ireland).
Scarborough: Hughes; James, Mudd, Lee, Hirst, Meyer,
Carter (Himsworth), Mockler, Mooney, Fletcher
(Holmes), Jules.

Preston NE (1) 2 *(Thomas, Joyce)*
Bolton W (0) 1 *(Reeves)*   2709
Preston NE: Kelly; Senior, Wrightson, Swann, Flynn,
Allpress, Ashcroft, Joyce, Thomas, Shaw, James.
Bolton W: Dibble; Brown P, Burke, Kelly, Came,
Winstanley, Brown M, Green (Cowdrill), Reeves, Storer,
Darby.

Shrewsbury T (0) 1 *(Griffiths)*
Lincoln C (0) 0   615
Shrewsbury T: Perks; Gorman, O'Toole, Worsley, Lynch,
Blake, Smith, Summerfield, Lyne, Taylor (Spink),
Griffiths.
Lincoln C: Dickins; Puttnam, Nicholson, Finney, West
(Clarke), Brown, Schofield, Ward (Carmichael), Lee,
Lormor, Alexander.

Torquay U (0) 0
Hereford U (1) 1 *(Russell)*   2134
Torquay U: Howells; Holmes P, Uzzell, Compton, Elliott,
Holmes M, Rowbotham (Darby), Hall, Joyce, Edwards,
Loram.
Hereford U: Judge; Pejic, Downs, Theodosiou, Devine,
Wade, Hall, Russell, Heritage, Fry, Vaughan.

Swansea C (0) 0
Cardiff C (0) 0   2955
Swansea C: Freestone; Jenkins, Agboola (Davies),
Thornber, Harris, Brazil, Williams, Chapple, Gilligan,
Beauchamp, Legg.
Cardiff C: Hansbury; Matthews, Searle, Gibbins (Millar),
Baddeley, Perry (Gorman), Ramsey, Lewis, Pike, Dale,
Blake.

20 NOV

Fulham (1) 2 *(Morgan, Cole)*
Gillingham (0) 0   1108
Fulham: Harrison; Cobb, Pike, Newson, Nebbeling,
Finch, Morgan, Onwere, Cole, Brazil (Haag), Kelly P
(Kelly M).
Gillingham: Lim; Polston, Martin, Smith, Clarke,
Dempsey (Berkley), Clark, Carpenter, Arnott (Butler),
Lovell, Eeles.

Reading (0) 0
Northampton T (2) 2 *(Adcock, McClean)*   1151
Reading: Francis; Richardson, Holzman, McPherson,
Gooding, Seymour (Cockram), Streete, Lovell, McGhee,
Maskell (Leworthy), Taylor.
Northampton T: Richardson; Chard, Johnson, Gernon,
Angus, Burnham, Campbell (Quow), Beavon, McClean,
Bell, Adcock.

3 DEC

Northampton T (1) 1 *(Chard)*
Leyton Orient 2 *(Richardson (og), Berry)*   1193
Northampton T: Richardson; Chard, Johnson (Brown),
Quow, Angus, Burnham, Beavon, Campbell, McClean,
Bell (Wilson), Adcock.
Leyton Orient: Turner; Howard, Hackett, Whitbread,
Day, Burnett, Hales, Castle (Harvey), Jones, Nugent,
Berry.

4 DEC

Lincoln C (0) 1 *(West G)*
WBA (0) 2 *(Williams, Robson)*   1861
Lincoln C: Dickins; Smith, Clarke, Finney (West D),
West G, Carmichael, Schofield, Ward, Lee, Lormor,
Puttnam.
WBA: Naylor; Hobson, Harbey, Bradley, Strodder,
Burgess, McNally, Williams, Robson, Shakespeare,
White (Bannister).

10 DEC

Bolton W (0) 4 *(Reeves 3, Philliskirk)*
Rochdale (0) 1 *(Milner)*   1507
Bolton W: Felgate; Brown P, Burke, Kelly, Seagraves,
Came, Brown M, Green, Reeves, Philliskirk, Darby.
Rochdale: Rose; Brown M, Graham, Brown T, Butler,
Payne, Ryan, Milner, Flounders, Bowden, Halpin.

Cardiff C (3) 3 *(Pike, Dale 2)*
Bournemouth (2) 3 *(Mundee, Ekoku, Quinn)*   1337
Cardiff: Ward; Matthews, Searle, Gibbins, Baddeley,
Perry, Seamark (Lewis), Griffith, Pike, Dale, Blake.
Bournemouth: Bartram; Mundee, Rowland, Morris,
Statham, O'Driscoll, Ekoku (Fereday), McGorry, Quinn,
Cooke, Holmes.

Gillingham (2) 4 *(Smith 2, Crown, Haylock (og))*
Maidstone U (0) 2 *(Ellis, Osborne)* 2300
Gillingham: Dalton; O'Shea, Polston, Smith, Walker, Dempsey (Berkley), Clark, Crown, Eeles, Lovell, O'Connor.
Maidstone U: Hesford; Sandeman, Thompson, Haylock, Davis (Painter), Oxbrow, Henry, Stebbing, Ellis, Osborne, Smalley.

17 DEC

Brentford (1) 3 *(Luscombe, Holdsworth 2 (1 pen))*
Barnet (1) 6 *(Carter 3, Bull 2, Poole)* 1871
Brentford: Benstead; Bates, Peters, Gayle, Evans, Buckle, Luscombe, Godfrey, Holdsworth, Blissett, Smillie (Ratcliffe).
Barnet: Pape; Poole, Naylor, Bodley, Cawley (Willis), Horton (Hunt), Wilson, Carter, Bull, Hoddle, Showler.

Doncaster R (0) 2 *(Rankine, Limber)*
Blackpool (0) 2 *(Rodwell, Bamber)* 613
Doncaster R: Samways; Douglas, Limber, Ashurst, Crosby, Cullen, Morrow, Gormley, Rankine, McKenzie (Nicholson), Noteman.
Blackpool: McIlhargey; Davies (Taylor), Stoneman, Groves, Hedworth, Gore, Rodwell, Gouck, Bamber, Sinclair, Garner (Bonner).

18 DEC

Stoke C (2) 3 *(Barnes, Stein (pen), Ware)*
Birmingham C (1) 1 *(Tait)* 5932
Stoke C: Fox; Ware, Butler (Rennie), Kevan, Overson, Sandford, Cranson, Beeston, Stein, Barnes, Kelly.
Birmingham C: Cheeseright; Clarkson, Frain, Peer, Hicks, Mardon, Rodgerson, Tait, Atkins (Okenla), Gleghorn, Cooper.

7 JAN

Birmingham C (0) 0
Walsall (0) 1 *(Ntamark)* 5239
Birmingham C: Miller; Clarkson, Frain, Cooper, Hicks, Matthewson, Rodgerson, Peer, Beckford, Gleghorn, Okenla (Hogan).
Walsall: McKnight; Williams, Statham (Brown), Methven, Anderson, O'Hara, Edwards, Ntamark, Tolson (Grealish), Cecere, Winter.

Chester C (2) 2 *(Morton, Bennett)*
Darlington (0) 1 *(Gill)* 416
Chester C: Stewart; Preece, Nolan (Butler), Comstive, Abel, Lightfoot, Bennett, Barrow, Rimmer, Morton, Croft.
Darlington: Prudhoe; Sunley, Pickering, Gregan, Smith, Cork (Coverdale), Gill, Toman, Ellison, Borthwick, Dewhurst.

Halifax T (0) 0
Scunthorpe U (0) 2 *(White, Alexander)* 646
Halifax T: Gould; Barr, Hutchinson, Lucketti, Bradley, Lewis, Abbott, Kamara, Juryeff (Griffiths), Richardson, Hildersley (Donnelly).
Scunthorpe U: Whitehead; Joyce, Longden, Martin, Hicks, Lister, Alexander, Hamilton, Daws, Hyde, White.

Hartlepool U (2) 2 *(Dalton, Baker)*
Hull C (0) 0 1550
Hartlepool U: Hodge; Nobbs, Smith A, Tinkler, MacPhail, Tupling, Southall, Olsson, Baker, Fletcher, Dalton.
Hull C: Fettis; Windass, Jacobs, Mail, Palin, Shotton, Hockaday (Young), Matthews, France, Norton, Jenkinson.

Hereford U (1) 2 *(Brain 2)*
Exeter C (0) 1 *(Marshall)* 1564
Hereford U: Judge; Wade, Theodosiou, Heritage, Devine, Vaughan (Burton), Hall, Narbett, Titterton, Robinson (Jones S), Brain.
Exeter C: Miller; Hiley, Cook, Brown, Daniels, Whiston, Wimbleton, Robson, Marshall, Moran, Chapman (Hodge).

Stockport Co (2) 3 *(Gannon 3 (1 pen))*
York C (0) 0 1397
Stockport Co: Edwards; Thorpe, Knowles, Frain, Barras, Holmes, Gannon, Lillis, Francis, Beaumont (Carstairs), Moore (Kilner).
York C: Kiely; McMillan, Crosby, Reid, Tutill, Warburton, Barratt, McCarthy, Blackstone (Naylor), Hall, Canham.

8 JAN

Scarborough (0) 1 *(Meyer)*
Wigan Ath (0) 1 *(Sharratt)* 636
Scarborough: Hewitt; Ash, Hirst (Ashdjian), Lee, Meyer, Mudd, Jules, Himsworth, Mooney, Foreman (Fletcher), Thompson.
Wigan Ath: Adkins; Parkinson, Tankard, Johnson, Patterson, Langley, Jones, Connelly, Daley, Worthington (Sharratt), Griffiths.

14 JAN

Mansfield T (2) 2 *(Stant 2)* 1771
Peterborough U (1) 1 *(Sterling) abandoned 69 mins; fog*

FIRST ROUND

Barnet (2) 3 *(Johnson (og), Carter, Murphy)*
Northampton T (1) 2 *(Thorpe 2)* 1422
Barnet: Phillips; Poole, Horton (Murphy), Bodley, Nugent, Cooper, Hunt, Carter, Bull, Lowe, Showler (Hoddle).
Northampton T: Richardson; Johnson (Gernon), Terry, Angus, Quow, Burnham (Bell), Beavon, Barnes, Thorpe, Brown, Campbell.

Bury (0) 2 *(Greenall, Hulme)*
Chesterfield (0) 1 *(Cooke)* 1036
Bury: Kelly; Greenall, Wilson D, Parkinson, Valentine, Knill (Mauge), Smith, Robinson, Stevens, Kearney (Hulme), Stanislaus.
Chesterfield: Goldring; Dyche, Rogers, Francis, Lemon, McGugan, Turnbull (Gunn), Cooke, Grayson (Evans), Hebberd, Lancaster.

Carlisle U (0) 1 *(Watson)*
Stockport Co (3) 3 *(Francis 3)* 1243
Carlisle U: O'Hanlon; Armstrong (Fyfe), Graham, Miller, Jeffels, Thomas (Cranston), Walsh, Watson, Walling, Proudlock, Thorpe.
Stockport Co: Edwards; Knowles, Todd, Frain, Barras, Williams B, Gannon, Ward, Francis, Lillis, Wheeler.

Crewe Alex (1) 2 *(Edwards R, Hignett)*
Bolton W (0) 0 2155
Crewe Alex: Greygoose; Wilson, McKearney, Carr, Callaghan, Sorvel, Hignett, McPhillips (Gardiner), Clarkson, Jasper, Edwards R.
Bolton W: Felgate; Stubbs, Burke, Kelly, Seagraves, Came, Green (Storer), Patterson (Spooner), Walker, Philliskirk, Darby.

Fulham (1) 2 *(Marshall, Morgan)*
Gillingham (0) 0   1483
Fulham: Stannard; Marshall, Pike, Newson (Finch),
Eckhardt, Thomas, Morgan, Onwere (Haag), Farrell,
Brazil, Scott.
Gillingham: Lim; O'Shea, Martin, Smith, Clarke,
Dempsey (Arnott), Clark, Lovell, Elsey (Berkley),
Crown, O'Connor.

Huddersfield T (1) *(Roberts)*
Blackpool (0) *abandoned half-time; fog*   1319

Preston NE (1) 2 *(Thomas, Ainsworth)*
Hull C (1) 3 *(Windass, Palin, Pearson) aet*   2152
Preston NE: Farnworth; Senior, Wrightson, Swann, Flynn
(Finney), Hughes (Lambert), Ashcroft, Cartwright,
Thomas, Shaw, Ainsworth.
Hull C: Fettis; Norton, Jacobs, Mail, Allison, Hobson,
Palin, Matthews (Calvert), Pearson, Windass, Jenkinson.

Rotherham U (2) 2 *(Goodwin, Page)*
Chester C (0) 0 *abandoned 66 mins; fog*   1489

Stoke C (1) 3 *(Biggins 2 (1 pen), Stein)*
Cardiff C (0) 0   4551
Stoke C: Fox; Kennedy, Grimes (Barnes), Kevan,
Overson, Sandford, Cranson, Beeston, Stein, Biggins,
Kelly (Ellis).
Cardiff C: Ward; Jones (Unsworth), Searle, Gibbins,
Baddeley, Lewis, Ramsey, Griffith, Pike, Dale (Toshack),
Blake.

WBA (0) 0
Exeter C (1) 1 *(Robson)*   6034
WBA: Naylor; Hodson, Harbey, Bradley, Strodder,
Burgess, White, Bannister, Robson, Parkin (Williams),
Hackett (Cartwright).
Exeter C: Miller; Brown, Cooper, Wimbleton, Daniels,
Whiston, Marshall, Hilaire, Moran (Sprod), Hodge
(Waters), Robson.

21 JAN

Burnley (0) 0
Scarborough (0) 0 *abandoned 90 mins; frost*   3812

Hartlepool U (1) 2 *(Honour, Tinkler)*
Scunthorpe U (1) 1 *(Hamilton)*   1351
Hartlepool U: Hodge; Nobbs, Smith A, Tinkler,
MacPhail, Tupling, Fletcher, Olsson, Baker (Southall),
Honour, Dalton, Smith M.
Scunthorpe U: Whitehead; Joyce, Hill, Martin, Hicks,
Humphries, Alexander, Hamilton, Hyde (Buckley),
White, Helliwell.

Hereford U (0) 0
Walsall (0) 1 *(Marsh) aet*   1503
Hereford U: Elliott; McIntyre, Downs, Theodosiou,
Devine, Hall, Wade, Lowndes, Fry (Titterton), Brain,
Heritage.
Walsall: Gayle; Williams, Brown, Methven, Anderson,
O'Hara, Winter, Ntamark, Marsh, Cecere (Tolson),
McDonald.

Huddersfield T (1) 1 *(Roberts)*
Blackpool (1) 1 *(Garner)*   1585
Huddersfield T: Clarke; Trevitt, Charlton, Donovan
(Kelly), Mitchell, O'Doherty, O'Regan, Onuora
(Wright), Roberts, Starbuck, Ireland.
Blackpool: McIlhargey; Davies (Horner), Kerr, Groves,
Briggs, Gore, Rodwell, Gouck (Sinclair), Bamber,
Garner, Eyres.
aet; Huddersfield T won 3–1 on penalties.

Leyton Orient (2) 3 *(Otto, Nugent, Day)*
Brentford (0) 2 *(Holdsworth 2)*   1861
Leyton Orient: Turner; Howard, Hackett, Burnett, Day,
Roeder, Hales, Castle (Achampong), Jones (Cooper),
Nugent, Otto.
Brentford: Benstead; Godfrey, Manuel (Buckle), Millen,
Evans, Ratcliffe, Luscombe, Finnigan, Holdsworth,
Blissett (Gayle), Smillie.

Rotherham U (2) 3 *(Wilson, Page, Goater)*
Chester C (0) 0   2543
Rotherham U: Mercer; Pickering, Hutchings, Todd,
Johnson, Law, Wilson, Barrick, Cunningham (Goater),
Page (Barlow), Hazel.
Chester C: Stewart; Preece, Pugh, Comstive, Abel,
Lightfoot, Bennett (Morton), Barrow, Butler, Rimmer,
Croft.

4 FEB

PRELIMINARY ROUND

Mansfield T (0) 0
Peterborough U (2) 3 *(Foster (og), Gavin, Sterling)* 2578
Mansfield T: Kite; Fleming, Carr, Spooner, Gray, Foster
(Clarke), Ford, Fairclough, Stant, McLoughlin, Charles.
Peterborough U: Barber; Luke, Robinson R, Halsall,
Robinson D, Welsh, Sterling, Cooper G, Gavin, Charlery
(Costello), Kimble.

FIRST ROUND

Burnley (0) 3 *(Conroy, Deary, Eli)*
Scarborough (0) 1 *(Jules)*   2956
Burnley: Pearce; Measham, Jakub, Davis, Pender,
Farrell, Harper, Deary, Francis, Conroy, Eli.
Scarborough: Hughes; Ash, Logan, Lee, Mudd, Meyer,
Jules, Himsworth, Mooney, Fletcher (Foreman),
Thompson (Ashdjian).

QUARTER-FINALS

Northern Section

Bury (1) 1 *(Knill)*
Huddersfield T (0) 2 *(Onuora, Roberts)*   1786
Bury: Kelly; Wilson D (Anderson), Greenall, Valentine,
Knill, Stanislaus, Hughes, Robinson, Stevens, Smith,
Wilson I (Hulme).
Huddersfield T: Martin; Parsley, Charlton (Wright),
Kelly, Mitchell, Jackson, Callaghan, O'Regan, Roberts,
Onuora, Starbuck.

Crewe Alex (0) 1 *(Naylor)*
Hull C (0) 0   2348
Crewe Alex: Greygoose; Wilson, McKearney, Carr,
Callaghan, Walters, Hignett, Naylor, Whitehurst,
Gardiner (Edwards R), Sorvel.
Hull C: Fettis; Hockaday, Atkinson (Mail), Warren,
Wilcox, Hobson, Young (Hunter), Norton, Pearson,
Windass, Jenkinson.

Stockport Co (1) 3 *(Francis 3)*
Hartlepool U (0) 0   2255
Stockport Co: Edwards; Knowles, Todd, Frain, Barras,
Williams B, Gannon, Ward, Francis, Beaumont, Wheeler
(Finley).
Hartlepool U: Hodge; Nobbs, Southall, Tinkler,
MacPhail, Tupling, Thompson (Gabbiadini), Olsson,
Baker, Honour, Dalton.

Southern Section

Barnet (0) 0
Leyton Orient (1) 1 *(Jones)* 2969

Barnet: Pape; Poole, Naylor, Bodley (Willis), Nugent, Horton, Wilson (Hunt), Carter, Bull, Lowe, Showler.
Leyton Orient: Turner; Howard, Hackett, Burnett, Day, Whitbread, Carter, Achampong, Jones, Nugent, Berry.

5 FEB

Stoke C (3) 3 *(Ware, Beeston, Stein)*
Walsall (0) 1 *(Marsh)* 7381

Stoke C: Fox; Ware (Ellis), Butler, Kevan, Overson, Sandford (Blake), Cranson, Beeston, Stein, Foley, Barnes.
Walsall: Gayle; Williams, Brown, Lane, Anderson (Tolson), O'Hara, Winter (Edwards), Ntamark, Marsh, Cecere, McDonald.

18 FEB

FIRST ROUND

Bournemouth (0) 1 *(Case)*
Wrexham (0) 2 *(Jones L 2)* 2279

Bournemouth: Bartram; Mundee, Rowland, Mitchell, Morrell, O'Driscoll, Cooke, Wood, Ekoku, Case, Holmes.
Wrexham: O'Keefe; Thackeray, Hardy, Carey, Flynn (Watkin), Sertori, Durkan, Owen, Connolly, Jones L, Phillips.

Peterborough U (0) 1 *(Costello)*
Shrewsbury T (0) 0 2049

Peterborough U: Barber; Luke, Robinson R, Halsall, Robinson D, Welsh, Sterling (Costello), Cooper G, Gavin, Charlery, Ebdon (Butterworth).
Shrewsbury T: Perks; Lynch, Clark, O'Toole, Spink, Blake, Hopkins, Summerfield, Donaldson, Taylor, Griffiths (Ryan).

QUARTER-FINALS

Northern Section

Rotherham U (0) 1 *(Hazel)*
Burnley (0) 1 *(Francis)* 2578

Rotherham U: Mercer; Pickering, Hutchings, Wilson (Hathaway), Johnson, Law, Richardson, Barrick, Cunningham, Goater (Page), Hazel.
Burnley: Pearce; Measham, Jakub, Davis, Pender, Farrell, Harper, Deary, Francis, Conroy, Eli (Lancashire).
aet; Burnley won 4–2 on penalties.

25 FEB

Southern Section

Fulham (0) 0
Wrexham (0) 2 *(Paskin, Phillips)* 2236

Fulham: Stannard; Finch (Haag), Pike, Scott, Eckhardt, Thomas, Morgan, Hails, Farrell, Brazil, Kelly M (Kelly P).
Wrexham: O'Keefe; Thackeray, Hardy, Carey, Durkan, Sertori, Paskin, Owen, Connolly, Jones L, Phillips.

Peterborough U (0) 1 *(Charlery)*
Exeter C (0) 0 2321

Peterborough U: Barber; Luke, Robinson R, Halsall, Robinson D, Welsh, McInerney, Cooper G, Costello (Butterworth), Charlery, Kimble (Riley).
Exeter C: Miller; Brown, Cooper, Williams (Hodge), Daniels, Whiston, Hilaire, Wimbleton, Moran, Kelly, Robson.

SEMI-FINALS

17 MAR

Northern Section

Burnley (2) 2 *(Conroy (pen), Eli)*
Huddersfield T (0) 0 10,775

Burnley: Walker; Measham, Jakub, Monington, Pender, Farrell, Harper (Lancashire), Deary, Francis, Conroy, Eli.
Huddersfield T: Clarke; Trevitt, Charlton, McNab (Starbuck), Mitchell, Jackson, O'Regan (Kelly), Donovan, Roberts, Wright, Onuora.

Crewe Alex (0) 1 *(McKearney)*
Stockport Co (2) 2 *(Ward, Wheeler)* 5594

Crewe Alex: Noble; Wilson, McKearney, Carr, Smart, Walters, Garvey, Naylor, Evans, Sorvel (Hignett), Rose (McPhillips).
Stockport Co: Edwards; Thorpe, Carstairs, Frain, Barras, Finley, Gannon, Ward, Francis, Todd, Wheeler.

Southern Section

Leyton Orient (0) 0
Stoke C (1) 1 *(Stein)* 3792

Leyton Orient: Turner; Howard, Wilder, Burnett (Taylor), Day, Whitbread, Carter (Jones), Zoricich, Otto, Nugent, Berry.
Stoke C: Pressman; Foley, Butler, Kevan, Overson, Sandford, Cranson, Beeston, Stein, Biggins, Ware.

Peterborough U (2) 3 *(Riley, Charlery, Costello)*
Wrexham (0) 1 *(Connolly)* 3929

Peterborough U: Barber; Luke, Butterworth, Halsall, Robinson D, Welsh, Sterling, Cooper G (Howarth), Riley, Charlery, Costello.
Wrexham: O'Keefe; Thackeray, Hardy, Carey, Flynn, Sertori, Paskin, Owen, Connolly, Watkin (Cross), Phillips.

SECTION FINALS

Southern First Leg

Stoke C (2) 3 *(Biggins 2, Sandford)* 14,355
Peterborough U (1) 3 *(Halsall, Charlery, Overson (og))*

Stoke C: Pressman; Kevan, Butler, Foley, Overson (Grimes), Sandford, Cranson, Beeston, Stein, Biggins, Heath.
Peterborough U: Bennett; Salman (Ebdon), Robinson R, Halsall, Robinson D, Welsh, Sterling, Cooper G, Riley, Charlery, Edwards (Cooper S).

Northern First Leg

7 APR

Burnley (0) 0
Stockport Co (1) 1 *(Francis)* 13,259

Burnley: Pearce; Farrell, Jakub, Davis, Pender, Monington, Yates, Deary, Lancashire, Bray (McKenzie), Eli.
Stockport Co: Edwards; Thorpe, Carstairs, Frain, Barras, Williams B, Gannon, Ward, Francis, Knowles, Wheeler.

15 APR

Northern Second Leg

Stockport Co (1) 2 *(Francis, Gannon)*
Burnley (1) 1 *(Pender)* 8260

Stockport Co: Edwards; Thorpe, Carstairs, Frain, Barras, Williams B, Gannon, Ward, Francis, Beaumont, Wheeler.
Burnley: Pearce; Farrell, Jakub, Davis, Pender, Yates, Harper (McKenzie), Deary, Francis, Conroy, Eli (Monington).

Southern Second Leg

Peterborough U (0) 0

Stoke C (0) 1 *(Ware)* 12,214

Peterborough U: Bennett; Luke, Robinson R, Halsall, Robinson D, Welsh, Sterling, Cooper G, Riley, Charlery, Edwards (Cooper S).
Stoke C: Fox; Kevan, Butler, Foley, Blake, Sandford, Cranson (Grimes), Beeston, Stein, Ware, Heath.

FINAL (at Wembley)

16 MAY

Stoke C (0) 1 *(Stein)*

Stockport Co (0) 0 48,339

Stoke C: Fox; Butler, Kevan, Cranson, Overson, Sandford, Kelly, Foley, Stein, Biggins, Heath.
Stockport Co: Edwards; Knowles, Todd, Frain (Thorpe), Barras, Williams B, Gannon, Ward, Francis, Beaumont, Wheeler (Williams P).
Referee: R. Hart (Darlington).

FULL MEMBERS' CUP

Totals	Season	Attendances	Games	Average
	1985/86	180,401	28	6,443
	1986/87	218,506	35	6,243
	1987/88	291,763	39	7,481
	1988/89	297,917	39	7,639
	1989/90	381,010	38	10,027
	1990/91	307,150	40	7,679
	1991/92	330,723	42	7,874

1985/86 to 1986/87 – Full Members Cup; 1987/88 to 1988/89 – Simod Cup; 1989/90 to 1991/92 – Zenith Data Systems Cup

ASSOCIATE MEMBERS' CUP

Totals	Season	Attendances	Games	Average
	1983/84	135,813	51	2,663
	1984/85	210,279	75	2,804
	1985/86	212,114	67	3,166
	1986/87	279,594	81	3,452
	1987/88	359,787	82	4,388
	1988/89	320,775	81	3,960
	1989/90	276,787	83	3,335
	1990/91	286,351	84	3,409
	1991/92	267,264	78	3,426

1983/84 – Associate Members' Cup; 1984/85 to 1986/87 – Freight Rover Trophy; 1987/88 to 1988/89 – Sherpa Van Trophy; 1989/90 to 1990/91 – Leyland DAF Cup; 1991/92 Autoglass Trophy.

FA CUP FINALS 1872–1992

1872 and 1874–92	Kennington Oval	1911	Replay at Old Trafford
1873	Lillie Bridge	1912	Replay at Bramall Lane
1886	Replay at Derby		
1893	Fallowfield, Manchester	1915	Old Trafford, Manchester
1894	Everton	1920–22	Stamford Bridge
1895–1914	Crystal Palace	1923 to date	Wembley
1901	Replay at Bolton	1970	Replay at Old Trafford
1910	Replay at Everton	1981	Replay at Wembley

Year	Winners	Runners-up	Score
1872	The Wanderers	Royal Engineers	1-0
1873	The Wanderers	Oxford University	2-0
1874	Oxford University	Royal Engineers	2-0
1875	Royal Engineers	Old Etonians	2-0 (after 1-1 draw aet)
1876	The Wanderers	Old Etonians	3-0 (after 1-1 draw aet)
1877	The Wanderers	Oxford University	2-1 (aet)
1878	The Wanderers*	Royal Engineers	3-1
1879	Old Etonians	Clapham R	1-0
1880	Clapham R	Oxford University	1-0
1881	Old Carthusians	Old Etonians	3-0
1882	Old Etonians	Blackburn R	1-0
1883	Blackburn Olympic	Old Etonians	2-1 (aet)
1884	Blackburn R	Queen's Park, Glasgow	2-1
1885	Blackburn R	Queen's Park, Glasgow	2-0
1886	Blackburn R†	WBA	2-0 (after 0-0 draw)
1887	Aston Villa	WBA	2-0
1888	WBA	Preston NE	2-1
1889	Preston NE	Wolverhampton W	3-0
1890	Blackburn R	Sheffield W	6-1
1891	Blackburn R	Notts Co	3-1
1892	WBA	Aston Villa	3-0
1893	Wolverhampton W	Everton	1-0
1894	Notts Co	Bolton W	4-1
1895	Aston Villa	WBA	1-0
1896	Sheffield W	Wolverhampton W	2-1
1897	Aston Villa	Everton	3-2
1898	Nottingham F	Derby Co	3-1
1899	Sheffield U	Derby Co	4-1
1900	Bury	Southampton	4-0
1901	Tottenham H	Sheffield U	3-1 (after 2-2 draw)
1902	Sheffield U	Southampton	2-1 (after 1-1 draw)
1903	Bury	Derby Co	6-0
1904	Manchester C	Bolton W	1-0
1905	Aston Villa	Newcastle U	2-0
1906	Everton	Newcastle U	1-0
1907	Sheffield W	Everton	2-1
1908	Wolverhampton W	Newcastle U	3-1
1909	Manchester U	Bristol C	1-0
1910	Newcastle U	Barnsley	2-0 (after 1-1 draw)
1911	Bradford C	Newcastle U	1-0 (after 0-0 draw)
1912	Barnsley	WBA	1-0 (aet, after 0-0 draw)
1913	Aston Villa	Sunderland	1-0
1914	Burnley	Liverpool	1-0
1915	Sheffield U	Chelsea	3-0
1920	Aston Villa	Huddersfield T	1-0 (aet)
1921	Tottenham H	Wolverhampton W	1-0
1922	Huddersfield T	Preston NE	1-0
1923	Bolton W	West Ham U	2-0
1924	Newcastle U	Aston Villa	2-0
1925	Sheffield U	Cardiff C	1-0
1926	Bolton W	Manchester C	1-0
1927	Cardiff C	Arsenal	1-0
1928	Blackburn R	Huddersfield T	3-1
1929	Bolton W	Portsmouth	2-0
1930	Arsenal	Huddersfield T	2-0
1931	WBA	Birmingham	2-1
1932	Newcastle U	Arsenal	2-1
1933	Everton	Manchester C	3-0
1934	Manchester C	Portsmouth	2-1
1935	Sheffield W	WBA	4-2
1936	Arsenal	Sheffield U	1-0
1937	Sunderland	Preston NE	3-1
1938	Preston NE	Huddersfield T	1-0 (aet)
1939	Portsmouth	Wolverhampton W	4-1
1946	Derby Co	Charlton Ath	4-1 (aet)
1947	Charlton Ath	Burnley	1-0 (aet)
1948	Manchester U	Blackpool	4-2
1949	Wolverhampton W	Leicester C	3-1
1950	Arsenal	Liverpool	2-0
1951	Newcastle U	Blackpool	2-0
1952	Newcastle U	Arsenal	1-0

Year	Winners	Runners-up	Score
1953	Blackpool	Bolton W	4-3
1954	WBA	Preston NE	3-2
1955	Newcastle U	Manchester C	3-1
1956	Manchester C	Birmingham C	3-1
1957	Aston Villa	Manchester U	2-1
1958	Bolton W	Manchester U	2-0
1959	Nottingham F	Luton T	2-1
1960	Wolverhampton W	Blackburn R	3-0
1961	Tottenham H	Leicester C	2-0
1962	Tottenham H	Burnley	3-1
1963	Manchester U	Leicester C	3-1
1964	West Ham U	Preston NE	3-2
1965	Liverpool	Leeds U	2-1 (aet)
1966	Everton	Sheffield W	3-2
1967	Tottenham H	Chelsea	2-1
1968	WBA	Everton	1-0 (aet)
1969	Manchester C	Leicester C	1-0
1970	Chelsea	Leeds U	2-1 (aet)
	(after 2-2 draw, after extra time, at Wembley)		
1971	Arsenal	Liverpool	2-1 (aet)
1972	Leeds U	Arsenal	1-0
1973	Sunderland	Leeds U	1-0
1974	Liverpool	Newcastle U	3-0
1975	West Ham U	Fulham	2-0
1976	Southampton	Manchester U	1-0
1977	Manchester U	Liverpool	2-1
1978	Ipswich T	Arsenal	1-0
1979	Arsenal	Manchester U	3-2
1980	West Ham U	Arsenal	1-0
1981	Tottenham H	Manchester C	3-2
	(after 1-1 draw, after extra time, at Wembley)		
1982	Tottenham H	QPR	1-0
	(after 1-1 draw, after extra time, at Wembley)		
1983	Manchester U	Brighton & HA	4-0
	(after 2-2 draw, after extra time, at Wembley)		
1984	Everton	Watford	2-0
1985	Manchester U	Everton	1-0 (aet)
1986	Liverpool	Everton	3-1
1987	Coventry C	Tottenham H	3-2 (aet)
1988	Wimbledon	Liverpool	1-0
1989	Liverpool	Everton	3-2 (aet)
1990	Manchester U	Crystal Palace	1-0
	(after 3-3 draw, after extra time, at Wembley)		
1991	Tottenham H	Nottingham F	2-1 (aet)
1992	Liverpool	Sunderland	2-0

* *Won outright, but restored to the Football Association.*

† *A special trophy was awarded for third consecutive win.*

FA CUP WINS

Tottenham H 8, Aston Villa 7, Manchester U 7, Blackburn R 6, Newcastle U 6, Arsenal 5, Liverpool 5, The Wanderers 5, WBA 5, Bolton 4, Everton 4, Manchester C 4, Sheffield U 4, Wolverhampton W 4, Sheffield W 3, West Ham U 3, Bury 2, Nottingham F 2, Old Etonians 2, Preston NE 2, Sunderland 2, Barnsley 1, Blackburn Olympic 1, Blackpool 1, Bradford C 1, Burnley 1, Cardiff C 1, Charlton Ath 1, Chelsea 1, Clapham R 1, Coventry C 1, Derby Co 1, Huddersfield T 1, Ipswich T 1, Leeds U 1, Notts Co 1, Old Carthusians 1, Oxford University 1, Portsmouth 1, Royal Engineers 1, Southampton 1, Wimbledon 1.

APPEARANCES IN FINALS

Arsenal 11, Everton 11, Manchester U 11, Newcastle U 11, Liverpool 10, WBA 10, Aston Villa 9, Tottenham H 9, Blackburn R 8, Manchester C 8, Wolverhampton W 8, Bolton W 7, Preston NE 7, Old Etonians 6, Sheffield U 6, Huddersfield T 5, *The Wanderers 5, Sheffield W 5, Derby Co 4, Leeds U 4, Leicester C 4, Oxford University 4, Royal Engineers 4, Sunderland 4, West Ham U 4, Blackpool 3, Burnley 3, Chelsea 3, Nottingham F 3, Portsmouth 3, Southampton 3, Barnsley 2, Birmingham C 2, *Bury 2, Cardiff C 2, Charlton Ath 2, Clapham R 2, Notts Co 2, Queen's Park (Glasgow) 2, *Blackburn Olympic 1, *Bradford C 1, Brighton & HA 1, Bristol C 1, Coventry C 1, Crystal Palace 1, Fulham 1, *Ipswich T 1, Luton T 1, *Old Carthusians 1, QPR 1, Watford 1, *Wimbledon 1.

* *Denotes undefeated.*

APPEARANCES IN SEMI-FINALS

Everton 22, Liverpool 19, WBA 19, Manchester U 18, Arsenal 17, Aston Villa 17, Blackburn R 16, Sheffield W 15, Derby Co 13, Newcastle U 13, Tottenham H 13, Wolverhampton W 13, Bolton W 12, Nottingham F 12, Sunderland 11, Southampton 10, Preston NE 10, Manchester C 10, Sheffield U 10, Chelsea 10, Birmingham C 9, Southampton 9, Burnley 8, Leeds U 8, Huddersfield T 7, Leicester C 7, Old Etonians 6, Oxford University 6, West Ham U 6, The Wanderers 5, Notts Co 5, Fulham 5, Portsmouth 5, Queen's Park (Glasgow) 4, Royal Engineers 4, Blackpool 3, Cardiff C 3, Clapham R 3, Ipswich T 3, Luton T 3, Millwall 3, Norwich C 3, Old Carthusians 3, Stoke C 3, The Swifts 3, Watford 3, Barnsley 2, Blackburn Olympic 2, Bristol C 2, Bury 2, Charlton Ath 2, Crystal Palace (professional club) 2, Grimsby T 2, Oldham Ath 2, Swansea C 2, Swindon T 2, Bradford C 1, Brighton & HA 1, Cambridge University 1, Coventry C 1, Crewe Alex 1, Crystal Palace (amateur club) 1, Darwen 1, Derby Junction 1, Glasgow R 1, Hull C 1, Marlow 1, Old Harrovians 1, Orient 1, Plymouth Arg 1, Port Vale 1, QPR 1, Reading 1, Shropshire W 1, Wimbledon 1, York C 1.

FA CUP FINALISTS 1872–1991

R: replay; aet: after extra time.

1871–72 THE WANDERERS R. de C. Welch; C. W. Alcock, M. P. Betts, A. G. Bonsor, E. E. Bowen, W. P. Crake, T. C. Hooman, E. Lubbock, A. C. Thompson, R. W. S. Vidal, C. H. R. Wollaston. (In alphabetical order.) *Scorer:* 'A. H. Chequer' (M. P. Betts).

1–0 ROYAL ENGINEERS Capt. Marindin; Capt. Merriman, Lieut. Addison; Lieut. Creswell, Lieut. Mitchell, Lieut. Renny-Tailyour; Lieut. Rich, Lieut. Goodwyn, Lieut. Muirhead, Lieut. Cotter, Lieut. Bogle.

1872–73 THE WANDERERS E. E. Bowen; C. M. Thompson, R. de C. Welch; Hon. A. F. Kinnaird, L. S. Howell, C. H. R. Wollaston; J. R. Sturgiss, Rev. H. H. Stewart, W. S. Kenyon-Slaney, R. K. Kingsford, A. G. Bonsor. *Scorers:* Kinnaird, Wollaston.

2–0 OXFORD UNIVERSITY A. Kirke-Smith; A. J. Leach, C. C. Mackarness; F. H. Birley; C. J. Longman, F. B. Chappell-Maddison; H. B. Cixon, W. B. Paton, R. W. S. Vidal, W. E. Sumner, C. J. Ottaway.

1873–74 OXFORD UNIVERSITY C. E. B. Neapean; C. C. Mackarness, F. H. Birley; F. T. Green, R. W. S. Vidal, C. J. Ottaway; R. H. Benson, F. J. Patton, W. S. Rawson, F. B. Chappell-Maddison, Rev. A. H. Johnson. *Scorers:* Mackarness, Patton.

2–0 ROYAL ENGINEERS Capt. Merriman; Major Marindin, Lieut. G. W. Addison; Lieut. G. C. Onslow, Lieut. H. G. Oliver, Lieut. T. Digby; Lieut. H. W. Renny-Tailyour, Lieut. H. E. Rawson, Lieut. J. E. Blackman, Lieut. A. K. Wood, Lieut. P. G. von Donop.

1874–75 ROYAL ENGINEERS Capt. Merriman; Lieut. G. H. Sim, Lieut. G. C. Onslow; Lieut. R. M. Ruck, Lieut. P. G. von Donop, Lieut. C. K. Wood; Lieut. H. E. Rawson, Lieut. R. H. Stafford, Capt. H. W. Renny-Tailyour, Lieut. Mein, Lieut. C. Wingfield Stratford. *Scorers:* (First match) Renny-Tailyour; (Second match) Renny-Tailyour, Stafford.

1–1 OLD ETONIANS Capt. E. H. Drummond-Moray; M. Farrer, E. Lubbock; F. H. Wilson, Hon. A. F. **aet** Kinnaird, J. H. Stronge; F. J. Patton, C. E. Farmer, A. G. Bonsor, A. Lubbock, T. Hammond. (C. J. **R:2–0** Ottaway, W. S. Kenyon-Slaney, R. H. Benson and A. G. Thompson took part in the first match in place of A. Lubbock, T. Hammond, M. Farrer and Capt. E. H. Drummond-Moray.) *Scorer:* Bonsor.

1875–76 THE WANDERERS W. D. O. Greig; A. Stratford, W. Lindsay; F. B. C. Maddison, F. H. Birley, C. H. R. Wollaston; H. Heron, F. Heron, J. H. Edwards, J. Kenrick, T. Hughes. *Scorers:* (First match) Edwards; (Second match) Wollaston, Hughes 2.

1–1 OLD ETONIANS Q. Hogg; E. Lubbock, Hon. E. Lyttelton; M. G. Faner, Hon. A. F. Kinnaird, J. H. **aet** Stronge; W. S. Kenyon-Slaney, Hon. A. Lyttelton, J. R. Sturgis, A. G. Bonsor, H. P. Allene. (C. Meysey, **R:3–0** A. C. Thompson and J. E. C. Welldon took part in the first match in place of J. H. Stronge, M. G. Faner and E. Lubbock.) *Scorer:* Bonsor.

1876–77 THE WANDERERS Hon. A. F. Kinnaird; W. Lindsay, A. Stratford; F. H. Birley, C. A. Denton, F. T. Green; H. Heron, T. Hughes, J. Kenrick, H. Wace, C. H. R. Wollaston. *Scorers:* Heron, Kenrick.

2–1 OXFORD UNIVERSITY E. H. Allington; J. Bain, O. R. Dunnell; J. H. Savory, A. H. Todd, E. W. **aet** Waddington; P. H. Fernandez, A. F. Hills, H. S. Otter, E. H. Parry, W. S. Rawson. *Scorer:* Kinnaird (og).

1877–78 THE WANDERERS J. Kirkpatrick; A. Stratford, W. Lindsay; Hon. A. F. Kinnaird, F. T. Green, C. H. R. Wollaston; H. Heron, J. G. Wylie, H. Wace, C. A. Denton, J. Kenrick. *Scorers:* Kenrick 2, opponent own goal.

3–1 ROYAL ENGINEERS L. B. Friend; J. H. Cowan, W. J. Morris; C. B. Mayne, F. C. Heath, C. E. Haynes; M. Lindsay, R. B. Hedley, F. G. Bond, H. H. Barnet, O. E. Ruck. *Scorer:* unknown.

1878–79 OLD ETONIANS J. P. Hawtrey; E. Christian, L. Bury; Hon. A. F. Kinnaird, E. Lubbock, C. J. Clerke; N. Pares, H. C. Goodhart, H. Whitfield, J. B. T. Chevallier, H. Beaufoy. *Scorer:* Clerke.

1–0 CLAPHAM ROVERS R. H. Birkett; R. A. Ogilvie, E. Field; N. C. Bailey, J. F. M. Prinsep, F. L. Rawson; A. J. Stanley, S. W. Scott, H. S. Bevington, E. F. Growse, C. Keith-Falconer.

1879–80 CLAPHAM ROVERS R. H. Birkett; R. A. Ogilvie, E. Field; A. Weston, N. C. Bailey, H. Brougham; A. J. Stanley, F. Barry, F. J. Sparks, C. A. Lloyd-Jones, E. A. Ram. *Scorer:* Lloyd-Jones.

1–0 OXFORD UNIVERSITY P. C. Parr; C. W. Wilson, C. J. S. King; F. A. H. Phillips, B. Rogers, R. T. Heygate; G. B. Childs, J. Eyre, F. D. Crowdy, E. H. Hill, J. B. Lubbock.

1880–81 OLD CARTHUSIANS L. F. Gillett; W. H. Norris, E. G. Colvin; J. F. M. Prinsep, A. J. Vintcent, W. E. Hansell; L. M. Richards, W. R. Page, E. G. Wyngard, E. H. Parry, A. H. Todd. *Scorers:* Wyngard, Parry, Todd.

3–0 OLD ETONIANS J. F. P. Rawlinson; C. W. Foley, C. H. French; Hon. A. F. Kinnaird, R. B. Farrer, J. B. T. Chevallier; W. J. Anderson, H. C. Goodhart, R. H. Macaulay, H. Whitfield, P. C. Novelli.

1881–82 OLD ETONIANS J. F. P. Rawlinson; T. H. French, P. J. de Paravicini; Hon. A. F. Kinnaird, C. W. Foley, P. C. Novelli; A. T. R. Dunn, R. H. Macaulay, H. C. Goodhart, W. J. Anderson, J. B. T. Chevallier. *Scorer:* Anderson.

1–0 BLACKBURN ROVERS R. Howarth; H. McIntyre, F. Suter; H. Sharples, F. W. Hargreaves, J. Duckworth; J. Douglas, T. Strachan, J. Brown, G. Avery, J. Hargreaves.

1882–83 BLACKBURN OLYMPIC T. Hacking; J. T. Ward, S. A. Warburton; T. Gibson, W. Astley, J. Hunter; T. Dewhurst, A. Matthews, G. Wilson, J. Costley, J. Yates. *Scorers:* Costley, Matthews.

2–1 OLD ETONIANS J. F. P. Rawlinson; T. H. French, P. J. de Paravicini; Hon. A. F. Kinnaird, C. W. **aet** Foley, J. B. T. Chevallier; W. J. Anderson, R. H. Macaulay, H. C. Goodhart, A. T. B. Dunn, H. W. Bainbridge. *Scorer:* Goodhart.

1883–84 BLACKBURN ROVERS H. J. Arthur; J. Beverley, F. Suter; H. McIntyre, J. Hargreaves, J. H. Forrest; J. M. Lofthouse, J. Douglas, J. Sowerbutts, J. Inglis, J. Brown. *Scorers:* Brown, Forrest.

2–1 QUEEN'S PARK G. Gillespie; W. Arnott, J. MacDonald; C. Campbell, J. J. Gow, W. Anderson; W. W. Watt, Dr Smith, W. Harrower, D. S. Allan, R. M. Christie. *Scorer:* Christie.

1884–85 BLACKBURN ROVERS H. J. Arthur; R. G. Turner, F. Suter; H. McIntyre, G. Haworth, J. H. Forrest; J. M. Lofthouse, J. Douglas, J. Brown, H. E. Fecitt, J. Sowerbutts. *Scorers:* Forrest, Brown.

2–0 QUEEN'S PARK G. Gillespie; W. Arnott, W. Macleod; C. Campbell, J. MacDonald, A. Hamilton; W. Anderson, W. Sellar, W. Gray, N. McWhannel, D. S. Allan.

1885–86 BLACKBURN ROVERS H. J. Arthur; Turner, Suter; Douglas, Forrest, McIntyre; Walton, Strachan, Brown, Fecitt, J. Sowerbutts. (Heyes played in the first match at the Oval, but Walton took his place in the **0–0** replay.) *Scorers:* Brown, Sowerbutts.

*R:*2-0 WEST BROMWICH ALBION   Roberts; H. Green, H. Bell; Horton, Perry, Timmins; Woodhall, T. Green, Bayliss, Loach, G. Bell.

1886–87 ASTON VILLA   Warner; Coulton, Simmonds; Yates, Dawson, Burton; Davis, Brown, Hunter, Vaughton, Hodgetts. *Scorers:* Hunter, Hodgetts.

2-0 WEST BROMWICH ALBION   Roberts; H. Green, Aldridge; Horton, Perry, Timmins; Woodhall, T. Green, Bayliss, Paddock, Pearson.

1887–88 WEST BROMWICH ALBION   Roberts; Aldridge, Green; Horton, Perry, Timmins; Bassett, Woodhall, Bayliss, Wilson, Pearson. *Scorers:* Woodhall, Bayliss.

2-1 PRESTON NORTH END   Dr R. H. Mills-Roberts; Howarth, N. J. Ross; Holmes, Russell, Graham; Gordon, J. Ross, J. Goodall, F. Dewhurst, Drummond. *Scorer:* Goodall.

1888–89 PRESTON NORTH END   Dr R. H. Mills-Roberts; Howarth, Holmes; Drummond, Russell, Graham; Gordon, Ross, J. Goodall, F. Dewhurst, Thompson. *Scorers:* Dewhurst, Ross, Thompson.

3-0 WOLVERHAMPTON WANDERERS   Baynton; Baugh, Mason; Fletcher, Allen, Lowder; Hunter, Wykes, Broodie, Wood, Knight.

1889–90 BLACKBURN ROVERS   J. K. Horne; Southworth (Jas.), Forbes; Barton, Dewar, Forrest; Lofthouse, Campbell, Southworth (John), Walton, Townley. *Scorers:* Dewar, Southworth (John), Lofthouse, Townley 3.

6-1 SHEFFIELD WEDNESDAY   Smith (J.); Brayshaw, H. Morley; Dungworth, Betts, Waller; Ingram, Woodhouse, Bennett, Mumford, Cawley. *Scorer:* Bennett.

1890–91 BLACKBURN ROVERS   Pennington; Brandon, J. Forbes; Barton, Dewar, Forrest; Lofthouse, Walton, Southworth (John), Hall, Townley. *Scorers:* Dewar, Southworth, Townley.

3-1 NOTTS COUNTY   Thraves; Ferguson, Hendry; H. Osborne, Calderhead, Shelton; A. McGregor, McInnes, Oswald, Locker, H. B. Daft. *Scorer:* Oswald.

1891–92 WEST BROMWICH ALBION   Reader; Nicholson, McCulloch; Reynolds, Perry, Groves; Bassett, McLeod, Nicholls, Pearson, Geddes. *Scorers:* Geddes, Nicholls, Reynolds.

3-0 ASTON VILLA   Warner; Evans, Cox; H. Devey, Cowan, Baird; Athersmith, J. Devey, Dickson, Campbell, Hodgetts.

1892–93 WOLVERHAMPTON WANDERERS   Rose; Baugh, Swift; Malpass, Allen, Kinsey; R. Topham, Wykes, Butcher, Wood, Griffin. *Scorer:* Allen.

1-0 EVERTON   Williams; Howarth, Kelso; Stewart, Holt, Boyle; Latta, Gordon, Maxwell, Chadwick, Milward.

1893–94 NOTTS COUNTY   Toone; Harper, Hendry; Bramley, Calderhead, A. Shelton; Watson, Donnelly, Logan, Bruce, H. B. Daft. *Scorers:* Watson, Logan 3.

4-1 BOLTON WANDERERS   Sutcliffe; Somerville, Jones; Gardiner, Paton, Hughes; Dickinson, Wilson, Tannahill, Bentley, Cassidy. *Scorer:* Cassidy.

1894–95 ASTON VILLA   Wilkes; Spencer, Welford; Reynolds, Cowan (Jas.), Russell; Athersmith, Chatt, J. Devey, Hodgetts, S. Smith. *Scorer:* Devey.

1-0 WEST BROMWICH ALBION   Reader; Williams, Horton; Taggart, Higgins, T. Perry; Bassett, McLeod, Richards, Hutchinson, Banks.

1895–96 SHEFFIELD WEDNESDAY   Massey; Earp, Langley; H. Brandon, Crawshaw, Petrie; Brash, Brady, L. Bell, Davis, Spiksley. *Scorer:* Spiksley 2.

2-1 WOLVERHAMPTON WANDERERS   Tennant; Baugh, Dunn; Owen, Malpass, Griffiths; Tonks, Henderson, Beats, Wood, Black. *Scorer:* Black.

1896–97 ASTON VILLA   Whitehouse; Spencer, Evans; Reynolds, Cowan (Jas.), Crabtree; Athersmith, J. Devey, Campbell, Wheldon, Cowan (John). *Scorers:* Campbell, Wheldon, Crabtree.

3-2 EVERTON   Menham; Meecham, Storrier; Boyle, Holt, Stewart; Taylor, Bell, Hartley, Chadwick, Milward. *Scorers:* Boyle, Bell.

1897–98 NOTTINGHAM FOREST   Allsop; Richie, Scott; Forman (Frank), McPherson, Wragg; McInnes, Richards, Benbow, Capes, Spouncer. *Scorers:* Capes 2, McPherson.

3-1 DERBY COUNTY   Fryer; Methven, Leiper; Cox, A. Goodall, Turner; J. Goodall, Bloomer. Boag, Stevenson, McQueen. *Scorer:* Bloomer.

1898–99 SHEFFIELD UNITED   Foulke; Thickett, Boyle; Johnson, Morren, Needham; Bennett, Beers, Hedley, Almond, Priest. *Scorers:* Bennett, Beers, Almond, Priest.

4-1 DERBY COUNTY   Fryer; Methven, Staley; Cox, Paterson, May; Arkesden, Bloomer, Boag, McDonald, Allen. *Scorer:* Boag.

1899– BURY   Thompson; Darrock, Davidson; Pray, Leeming, Ross; Richards, Wood, McLuckie, Sagar, Plant.
1900 *Scorers:* McLuckie 2, Wood, Plant.

4-0 SOUTHAMPTON   Robinson; Meehan, Durber; Meston, Chadwick, Petrie; Turner, Yates, Farrell, Wood, Milward.

1900–01 TOTTENHAM HOTSPUR   Clawley; Erentz, Tait; Norris, Hughes, Jones; Smith, Cameron, Brown, Copeland, Kirwan. *Scorers:* (First match) Brown 2; (Second match) Cameron, Smith, Brown.

2-2 SHEFFIELD UNITED   Foulke; Thickett, Boyle; Johnson, Morren, Needham; Bennett, Field, Hedley, *R:*3-1 Priest, Lipsham. *Scorers:* (First match) Bennett, Priest; (Second match) Priest.

1901–02 SHEFFIELD UNITED   Foulke; Thickett, Boyle; Needham, Wilkinson, Johnson; Barnes, Common, Hedley, Priest, Lipsham. (Bennett was injured in the first match and Barnes took his place in the replay.) *Scorers:* (First match) Common; (Second match) Hedley, Barnes.

1-1 SOUTHAMPTON   Robinson; C. B. Fry, Molyneux; Meston, Bowman, Lee; A. Turner, Wood, Brown, *R:*2-1 Chadwick, J. Turner. *Scorers:* (First match) Wood; (Second match) Brown.

1902–03 BURY   Monteith; Lindsey, McEwen; Johnson, Thorpe, Ross; Richards, Wood, Sagar, Leeming, Plant. *Scorers:* Ross, Sagar, Leeming 2, Wood, Plant.

6-0 DERBY COUNTY   Fryer; Methven, Morris; Warren, A. Goodall, May; Warrington, York, Boag, Richards, Davis.

1903–04 MANCHESTER CITY   Hillman; McMahon, Burgess; Frost, Hynds, S. B. Ashworth; Meredith, Livingstone, Gillespie, A. Turnbull, Booth. *Scorer:* Meredith.

1-0 BOLTON WANDERERS   D. Davies; Brown, Struthers; Clifford, Greenhaigh, Freebairn; Stokes, Marsh, Yenson, White, Taylor.

1904–05 ASTON VILLA   George; Spencer, Miles; Pearson, Leake, Windmill; Brawn, Garratty, Hampton, Bache, Hall. *Scorer:* Hampton 2.

2-0 NEWCASTLE UNTED   Lawrence; McCombie, Carr; Gardner, Aitken, McWilliam; Rutherford, Howie, Appleyard, Veitch, Gosnell.

1905–06 EVERTON Scott; W. Balmer, Crelly; Makepeace, Taylor, Abbott; Sharp, Bolton, Young, Settle, H. P. Hardman. *Scorer:* Young.

1-0 NEWCASTLE UNITED Lawrence; McCombie, Carr; Gardner, Aitken, McWilliam; Rutherford, Howie, Veitch, Orr, Gosnell.

1906–07 SHEFFIELD WEDNESDAY Lyall; Layton, Burton; Brittleton, Crawshaw, Bartlett; Chapman, Bradshaw, Wilson, Stewart, Simpson. *Scorers:* Stewart, Simpson.

2-1 EVERTON Scott; W. Balmer, R. Balmer; Makepeace, Taylor, Abbott; Sharp, Bolton, Young, Settle, H. P. Hardman. *Scorer:* Sharp.

1907–08 WOLVERHAMPTON WANDERERS Lunn; Jones, Collins; Rev. K. R. G. Hunt, Wooldridge, Bishop; Harrison, Shelton, Hedley, Radford, Pedley. *Scorers:* Hunt, Hedley, Harrison.

3-1 NEWCASTLE UNITED Lawrence; McCracken, Pudan; Gardner, Veitch, McWilliam; Rutherford, Howie, Appleyard, Speedie, Wilson. *Scorer:* Howie.

1908–09 MANCHESTER UNITED Moger; Stacey, Hayes; Duckworth, Roberts, Bell; Meredith, Halse, J. Turnbull, A. Turnbull, Wall. *Scorer:* A. Turnbull.

1-0 BRISTOL CITY Clay; Annan, Cottle; Hanlin, Wedlock, Spear; Staniforth, Hardy, Gilligan, Burton, Hilton.

1909–10 NEWCASTLE UNITED Lawrence; McCracken, Carr; Veitch, Low, McWilliam; Rutherford, Howie, Shepherd, Higgins, Wilson. (Whitson was injured in the first match and Carr took his place in the replay.) *Scorers:* (First match) Rutherford; (Second match) Shepherd 2 (1 pen.)

1-1 BARNSLEY Mearns; Downs, Ness; Glendinning, Boyle, Utley; Bartrop, Gadsby, Lillycrop, Tuffnell,
R:2-0 Forman. *Scorer:* (First match) Tuffnell.

1910–11 BRADFORD CITY Mellors; Campbell, Taylor; Robinson, Torrance, McDonald; Logan, Spiers, O'Rourke, Devine, Thompson. (Gildea played centre-half in the first match.) *Scorer:* Spiers.

0-0 NEWCASTLE UNITED Lawrence; McCracken, Whitson; Veitch, Low, Willis; Rutherford, Jobey,
R:1-0 Stewart, Higgins, Wilson.

1911–12 BARNSLEY Cooper; Downs, Taylor; Glendinning, Bratley, Utley; Bartrop, Tuffnell, Lillycrop, Travers,
0-0 Moore. *Scorer:* Tuffnell.
R:1-0 WEST BROMWICH ALBION Pearson; Cook, Pennington; Baddeley, Buck, McNeal; Jephcott, Wright,
aet Pailor, Bowser, Shearman.

1912–13 ASTON VILLA Hardy; Lyons, Weston; Barber, Harrop, Leach; Wallace, Halse, Hampton, C. Stephenson, Bache. *Scorer:* Barber.

1-0 SUNDERLAND Butler; Gladwin, Ness; Cuggy, Thompson, Low; Mordue, Buchan, Richardson, Holley, Martin.

1913–14 BURNLEY Sewell; Bamford, Taylor; Halley, Boyle, Watson; Nesbit, Lindley, Freeman, Hodgson, Mosscrop. *Scorer:* Freeman.

1-0 LIVERPOOL Campbell; Longworth, Pursell; Fairfoul, Ferguson, McKinlay; Sheldon, Metcalf, Miller, Lacey, Nicholl.

1914–15 SHEFFIELD UNITED Gough; Cook, English; Sturgess, Brelsford, Utley; Simmons, Fazackerley, Kitchen, Masterman, Evans. *Scorers:* Simmons, Fazackerley, Kitchen.

3-0 CHELSEA Molyneux; Bettridge, Harrow; Taylor, Logan, Walker; Ford, Halse, Thompson, Croal, McNeil.

1919–20 ASTON VILLA Hardy; Smart, Weston; Ducat, Barson, Moss; Wallace, Kirton, Walker, C. Stephenson, Dorrell. *Scorer:* Kirton.

1-0 HUDDERSFIELD TOWN Mutch; Wood, Bullock; Slade, Wilson, Watson; Richardson, Mann, Taylor,
aet Swan, Islip.

1920–21 TOTTENHAM HOTSPUR Hunter; Clay, McDonald; Smith, Walters, Grimsdell; Banks, Seed, Cantrell, Bliss, Dimmock. *Scorer:* Dimmock.

1-0 WOLVERHAMPTON WANDERERS George; Woodward, Marshall; Gregory, Hodnet, Riley; Lea, Burrill, Edmonds, Potts, Brooks.

1921–22 HUDDERSFIELD TOWN Mutch; Wood, Wadsworth; Slade, Wilson, Watson; Richardson, Mann, Islip, Stephenson, W. H. Smith. *Scorer:* Smith (pen).

1-0 PRESTON NORTH END J. F. Mitchell; Hamilton, Doolan; Duxbury, McCall, Williamson; Rawlings, Jefferis, Roberts, Woodhouse, Quinn.

1922–23 BOLTON WANDERERS Pym; Haworth, Finney; Nuttall, Seddon, Jennings; Butler, Jack, J. R. Smith, J. Smith, Vizard. *Scorers:* Jack, J. R. Smith.

2-0 WEST HAM UNITED Hufton; Henderson, Young; Bishop, Kay, Tresadern, Richards, Brown, V. Watson, Moore, Ruffell.

1923–24 NEWCASTLE UNITED Bradley; Hampson, Hudspeth; Mooney, Spencer, Gibson; Low, Cowan, Harris, McDonald, Seymour. *Scorers:* Harris, Seymour.

2-0 ASTON VILLA Jackson; Smart, Mort; Moss, Dr V. E. Milne. Blackburn; York, Kirton, Capewell, Walker, Dorrell.

1924–25 SHEFFIELD UNITED Sutcliffe; Cook, Milton; Pantling, King, Green; Mercer, Boyle, Johnson, Gillespie, Tunstall. *Scorer:* Tunstall.

1-0 CARDIFF CITY Farquharson; Nelson, Blair; Wake, Keenor, Hardy; W. Davies, Gill, Nicholson, Beadles, J. Evans.

1925–26 BOLTON WANDERERS Pym; Haworth, Greenhalgh; Nuttall, Seddon, Jennings; Butler, Jack, J. R. Smith, J. Smith, Vizard. *Scorer:* Jack.

1-0 MANCHESTER CITY Goodchild; Cookson, McCloy; Pringle, Cowan, McMullan; Austin, Browell, Roberts, Johnson, Hicks.

1926–27 CARDIFF CITY Farquharson; Nelson, Watson; Keenor, Sloan, Hardy; Curtis, Irving, Ferguson, I. Davies, McLachlan. *Scorer:* Ferguson.

1-0 ARSENAL Lewis; Parker, Kennedy; Baker. Butler, John; Hulme, Buchan, Brain, Blyth, Hoar.

1927–28 BLACKBURN ROVERS Crawford; Hutton, Jones; Healless, Rankin, Campbell; Thornewell, Puddefoot, Roscamp, McLean, Rigby. *Scorers:* Roscamp 2, McLean.

3-1 HUDDERSFIELD TOWN Mercer; Goodall, Barkas; Redfern, Wilson, Steele; A. Jackson, Kelly, Brown, Stephenson, W. H. Smith. *Scorer:* Jackson.

1928–29 BOLTON WANDERERS Pym; Haworth, Finney; Kean, Seddon, Nuttall; Butler, McClelland, Blackmore, Gibson, W. Cook. *Scorers:* Butler, Blackmore.

2-0 PORTSMOUTH Gilfillan; Mackie, Bell; Nichol, McIlwaine, Thackeray; Forward, J. Smith, Weddle. Watson, F. Cook.

1929–30 ARSENAL Preedy; Parker, Hapgood; Baker, Seddon, John; Hulme, Jack, Lambert, James, Bastin. *Scorers:* James, Lambert.
2-0 HUDDERSFIELD TOWN Turner; Goodall, Spence; Naylor, Wilson, Campbell; A. Jackson, Kelly, Davies, Raw, W. H. Smith.
1930–31 WEST BROMWICH ALBION Pearson; Shaw, Trentham; Magee, W. Richardson, Edwards; Glidden, Carter, W. G. Richardson, Sandford, Wood. *Scorer:* W. G. Richardson 2.
2-1 BIRMINGHAM Hibbs; Liddell, Barkas; Cringan, Morrall, Leslie; Briggs, Crosbie, Bradford, Gregg, Curtis. *Scorer:* Bradford.
1931–32 NEWCASTLE UNITED McInroy; Nelson, Fairhurst; McKenzie, Davidson, Weaver; Boyd, Richardson, Allen, McMenemy, Lang. *Scorer:* Allen 2.
2-1 ARSENAL Moss; Parker, Hapgood; C. Jones, Roberts, Male; Hulme, Jack, Lambert, Bastin, John. *Scorer:* John.
1932–33 EVERTON Sagar; Cook, Cresswell; Britton, White, Thomson; Geldard, Dunn, Dean, Johnson, Stein. *Scorers:* Stein, Dean, Dunn.
3-0 MANCHESTER CITY Langford; Cann, Dale; Busby, Cowan, Bray; Toseland, Marshall, Herd, McMullan, Brook.
1933–34 MANCHESTER CITY Swift; Barnett, Dale; Busby, Cowan, Bray; Toseland, Marshall, Tilson, Herd, Brook. *Scorer:* Tilson 2.
2-1 PORTSMOUTH Gilfillan; Mackie, W. Smith; Nichol, Allen, Thackeray; Worrall, J. Smith, Weddle, Easson, Rutherford. *Scorer:* Rutherford.
1934–35 SHEFFIELD WEDNESDAY Brown; Nibloe, Catlin; Sharp, Millership, Burrows; Hooper, Surtees, Palethorpe, Starling, Rimmer. *Scorers:* Rimmer 2, Palethorpe, Hooper.
4-2 WEST BROMWICH ALBION Pearson; Shaw, Trentham; Murphy, W. Richardson, Edwards; Glidden, Carter, W. G. Richardson, Sandford, Boyes. *Scorers:* Boyes, Sandford.
1935–36 ARSENAL Wilson; Male, Hapgood; Crayston, Roberts, Copping; Hulme, Bowden, Drake, James, Bastin. *Scorer:* Drake.
1-0 SHEFFIELD UNITED Smith; Hooper, Wilkinson; Jackson, Johnson, McPherson; Barton, Barclay, Dodds, Pickering, Williams.
1936–37 SUNDERLAND Mapson; Gorman, Hall; Thomson, Johnson, McNab; Duns, Carter, Gurney, Gallacher, Burbanks. *Scorers:* Gurney, Carter, Burbanks.
3-1 PRESTON NORTH END Burns; Gallimore, A. Beattie; Shankly, Tremelling, Milne; Dougal, Beresford, F. O'Donnell, Fagan, H. O'Donnell. *Scorer:* F. O'Donnell.
1937–38 PRESTON NORTH END Holdcroft; Gallimore, A. Beattie; Shankly, Smith, Batey; Watmough, Mutch, Maxwell, R. Beattie, H. O'Donnell. *Scorer:* Mutch (pen).
1-0 HUDDERSFIELD TOWN Hesford; Craig, Mountford; Willingham, Young, Boot; Hulme, Isaac,
aet McFadyen, Barclay, Beasley.
1938–39 PORTSMOUTH Walker; Morgan, Rochford; Guthrie, Rowe, Wharton; Worrall, McAlinden, Anderson, Barlow, Parker. *Scorers:* Parker 2, Barlow, Anderson.
4-1 WOLVERHAMPTON WANDERERS Scott; Morris, Taylor; Galley, Cullis, Gardiner; Burton, McIntosh, Westcott, Dorsett, Maguire. *Scorer:* Dorsett.
1945–46 DERBY COUNTY Woodley; Nicholas, Howe; Bullions, Leuty, Musson; Harrison, Carter, Stamps, Doherty, Duncan. *Scorers:* H. Turner (og), Doherty, Stamps 2.
4-1 CHARLTON ATHLETIC Bartram; Phipps, Shreeve; H. Turner, Oakes, Johnson; Fell, Brown, A. A.
aet Turner, Welsh, Duffy. *Scorer:* H. Turner.
1946–47 CHARLTON ATHLETIC Bartram; Croker, Shreeve; Johnson, Phipps. Whittaker; Hurst, Dawson, W. Robinson, Welsh, Duffy. *Scorer:* Duffy.
1-0 BURNLEY Strong; Woodruff, Mather; Attwell, Brown, Bray; Chew, Morris, Harrison, Potts, F. P.
aet Kippax.
1947–48 MANCHESTER UNITED Crompton; Carey, Aston; Anderson, Chilton, Cockburn; Delaney, Morris, Rowley, Pearson, Mitten. *Scorers:* Rowley 2, Pearson, Anderson.
4-2 BLACKPOOL Robinson; Shimwell, Crosland; Johnston, Hayward, Kelly; Matthews, Munro, Mortensen, Dick, Rickett. *Scorers:* Shimwell (pen), Mortensen.
1948–49 WOLVERHAMPTON WANDERERS Williams; Pritchard, Springthorpe; W. Crook, Shorthouse, Wright; Hancock, Smyth, Pye, Dunn, Mullen. *Scorers:* Pye 2, Smyth.
3-1 LEICESTER CITY Bradley; Jelly, Scott; W. Harrison, Plummer, King; Griffiths, Lee, J. Harrison, Chisholm, Adam. *Scorer:* Griffiths.
1949–50 ARSENAL Swindin; Scott, Barnes; Forbes, L. Compton, Mercer; Cox, Logie, Goring, Lewis, D. Compton. *Scorer:* Lewis 2.
2-0 LIVERPOOL Sidlow; Lambert, Spicer; Taylor, Hughes, Jones; Payne, Baron, Stubbins, Fagan, Liddell.
1950–51 NEWCASTLE UNITED Fairbrother; Cowell, Corbett; Harvey, Brennan, Crowe; Walker, Taylor, Milburn, G. Robledo, Mitchell. *Scorer:* Milburn 2.
2-0 BLACKPOOL Farm; Shimwell, Garrett; Johnston, Hayward, Kelly; Matthews, Mudie, Mortensen; W. J. Slater, Perry.
1951–52 NEWCASTLE UNITED Simpson; Cowell, McMichael; Harvey, Brennan, E. Robledo; Walker, Foulkes, Milburn, G. Robledo, Mitchell. *Scorer:* G. Robledo.
1-0 ARSENAL Swindin; Barnes, L. Smith; Forbes, Daniel, Mercer; Cox, Logie, Holton, Lishman, Roper.
1952–53 BLACKPOOL Farm; Shimwell, Garrett; Fenton, Johnston, Robinson; Matthews, Taylor, Mortensen, Mudie, Perry. *Scorers:* Mortensen 3, Perry.
4-3 BOLTON WANDERERS Hanson; Ball, R. Banks; Wheeler, Barass, Bell; Holden, Moir, Lofthouse. Hassall, Langton. *Scorers:* Lofthouse, Moir, Bell.
1953–54 WEST BROMWICH ALBION Sanders; Kennedy, Millard; Dudley, Dugdale, Barlow; Griffin, Ryan, Allen, Nicholls, Lee. *Scorers:* Allen 2 (1 pen), Griffin.
3-2 PRESTON NORTH END Thompson; Cunningham, Walton; Docherty, Marston, Forbes; Finney, Foster, Wayman, Baxter, Morrison. *Scorers:* Morrison, Wayman.
1954–55 NEWCASTLE UNITED Simpson; Cowell, Batty; Scoular, Stokoe, Casey; White, Milburn, Keeble, Hannah, Mitchell. *Scorers:* Milburn, Mitchell, Hannah.
3-1 MANCHESTER CITY Trautmann; Meadows, Little; Barnes, Ewing, Paul; Spurdle, Hayes, Revie, Johnstone, Fagan. *Scorer:* Johnstone.

1955–56 MANCHESTER CITY   Trautmann; Leivers, Little; Barnes, Ewing, Paul; Johnstone, Hayes, Revie, Dyson, Clarke. *Scorers:* Hayes, Dyson, Johnstone.

3-1 BIRMINGHAM CITY   Merrick; Hall, Green; Newman, Smith, Boyd; Astall, Kinsey, Brown, Murphy, Govan. *Scorer:* Kinsey.

1956–57 ASTON VILLA   Sims; Lynn, Aldis; Crowther, Dugdale, Saward; Smith, Sewell, Myerscough, Dixon, McParland. *Scorer:* McParland 2.

2-1 MANCHESTER UNITED   Wood; Foulkes, Byrne; Colman, J. Blanchflower, Edwards; Berry, Whelan, T. Taylor, R. Charlton, Pegg. *Scorer:* Taylor.

1957–58 BOLTON WANDERERS   Hopkinson; Hartle, Banks; Hennin, Higgins, Edwards; Birch, Stevens, Lofthouse, Parry, Holden. *Scorer:* Lofthouse 2.

2-0 MANCHESTER UNITED   Gregg; Foulkes, Greaves; Goodwin, Cope, Crowther; Dawson, E. Taylor, R. Charlton, Viollet, Webster.

1958–59 NOTTINGHAM FOREST   Thomson; Whare, McDonald; Whitefoot, McKinlay, Burkitt; Dwight, Quigley, Wilson, Gray, Imlach. *Scorers:* Dwight, Wilson.

2-1 LUTON TOWN   Baynham; McNally, Hawkes; Groves, Owen, Pacey; Bingham, Brown, Morton, Cummins, Gregory. *Scorer:* Pacey.

1959–60 WOLVERHAMPTON WANDERERS   Finlayson; Showell, Harris; Clamp, Slater, Flowers; Deeley, Stobart, Murray, Broadbent, Horne. *Scorers:* McGrath (og), Deeley 2.

3-0 BLACKBURN ROVERS   Leyland; Bray, Whelan; Clayton, Woods, McGrath; Bimpson, Dobing, Dougan, Douglas, McLeod.

1960–61 TOTTENHAM HOTSPUR   Brown; Baker, Henry; D. Blanchflower, Norman, Mackay; Jones, White, Smith, Allen, Dyson. *Scorers:* Smith, Dyson.

2-0 LEICESTER CITY   Banks; Chalmers, Norman; McLintock, King, Appleton; Riley, Walsh, McIlmoyle, Keyworth, Cheesebrough.

1961–62 TOTTENHAM HOTSPUR   Brown; Baker, Henry; D. Blanchflower, Norman, Mackay; Medwin, White, Smith, Greaves, Jones. *Scorers:* Greaves, Smith, Blanchflower (pen).

3-1 BURNLEY   Blacklaw; Angus, Elder; Adamson, Cummings, Miller; Connelly, McIlroy, Pointer, Robson, Harris. *Scorer:* Robson.

1962–63 MANCHESTER UNITED   Gaskell; Dunne, Cantwell; Crerand, Foulkes, Setters; Giles, Quixall, Herd, Law, R. Charlton. *Scorers:* Herd 2, Law.

3-1 LEICESTER CITY   Banks; Sjoberg, Norman; McLintock, King, Appleton; Riley, Cross, Keyworth, Gibson, Stringfellow. *Scorer:* Keyworth.

1963–64 WEST HAM UNITED   Standen; Bond, Burkett; Bovington, Brown, Moore; Brabrook, Boyce, Byrne, Hurst, Sissons. *Scorers:* Sissons, Hurst, Boyce.

3-2 PRESTON NORTH END   Kelly; Ross, Smith; Lawton, Singleton, Kendall; Wilson, Ashworth, Dawson, Spavin, Holden. *Scorers:* Holden, Dawson.

1964–65 LIVERPOOL   Lawrence; Lawler, Byrne; Strong, Yeats, Stevenson; Callaghan, Hunt, St John, Smith, Thompson. *Scorers:* Hunt, St John.

2-1 LEEDS UNITED   Sprake; Reaney, Bell; Bremner, J. Charlton, Hunter; Giles, Storrie, Peacock, Collins, **aet** Johanneson. *Scorer:* Bremner.

1965–66 EVERTON   West; Wright, Wilson; Gabriel, Labone, Harris; Scott, Trebilcock, Young, Harvey, Temple. *Scorers:* Trebilcock 2, Temple.

3-2 SHEFFIELD WEDNESDAY   Springett; Smith, Megson; Eustace, Ellis, Young; Pugh, Fantham, McCalliog, Ford, Quinn. *Scorers:* McCalliog, Ford.

1966–67 TOTTENHAM HOTSPUR   Jennings; Kinnear, Knowles; Mullery, England, Mackay; Robertson, Greaves, Gilzean, Venables, Saul. *Scorers:* Robertson, Saul.

2-1 CHELSEA   Bonetti; A. Harris, McCreadie; Hollins, Hinton, R. Harris; Cooke, Baldwin, Hateley, Tambling, Boyle. *Scorer:* Tambling.

1967–68 WEST BROMWICH ALBION   Osborne; Fraser, Williams; Brown, Talbut, Kaye (Clarke); Lovett, Collard, Astle, Hope, Clark. *Scorer:* Astle.

1-0 EVERTON   West; Wright, Wilson; Kendall, Labone, Harvey; Husband, Ball, Royle, Hurst, **aet** Morrissey.

1968–69 MANCHESTER CITY   Dowd; Book, Pardoe; Doyle, Booth, Oakes; Summerbee, Bell, Lee, Young, Coleman. *Scorer:* Young.

1-0 LEICESTER CITY   Shilton; Rodrigues, Nish; Roberts, Woollett, Cross; Fern, Gibson, Lochhead, Clarke, Glover (Manley).

1969–70 CHELSEA   Bonetti; Webb, McCreadie; Hollins, Dempsey, R. Harris (Hinton); Baldwin, Houseman, Osgood, Hutchinson, Cooke. *Scorers:* Houseman, Hutchinson.

2-2 LEEDS UNITED   Sprake; Madeley, Cooper; Bremner, J. Charlton, Hunter; Lorimer, Clarke, Jones, Giles, **aet** E. Gray. *Scorers:* Charlton, Jones.

Replay (at Old Trafford, Manchester)

R:2-1 CHELSEA   Bonetti; R. Harris, McCreadie; Hollins, Dempsey, Webb; Baldwin, Cooke, Osgood (Hinton), **aet** Hutchinson, Houseman. *Scorers:* Osgood, Webb.

LEEDS UNITED   Harvey; Madeley, Cooper; Bremner, J. Charlton, Hunter; Lorimer, Clarke, Jones, Giles, E. Gray. *Scorer:* Jones.

1970–71 ARSENAL   Wilson; Rice, McNab; Storey (Kelly), McLintock, Simpson; Armstrong, Graham, Radford, Kennedy, George. *Scorers:* Kelly, George.

2-1 LIVERPOOL   Clemence; Lawler, Lindsay; Smith, Lloyd, Hughes; Callaghan, Evans (Thompson), Heigh**aet** way, Toshack, Hall. *Scorer:* Heighway.

1971–72 LEEDS UNITED   Harvey; Reaney, Madeley; Bremner, J. Charlton, Hunter; Lorimer, Clarke, Jones, Giles, E. Gray. *Scorer:* Clarke.

1-0 ARSENAL   Barnett; Rice, McNab; Storey, McLintock, Simpson; Armstrong, Ball, George, Radford (Kennedy), Graham.

1972–73 SUNDERLAND   Montgomery; Malone, Guthrie; Horswill, Watson, Pitt; Kerr, Hughes, Halom, Porterfield, Tueart. *Scorer:* Porterfield.

1-0 LEEDS UNITED   Harvey; Reaney, Cherry; Bremner, Madeley, Hunter; Lorimer, Clarke, Jones, Giles, E. Gray (Yorath).

1973–74 LIVERPOOL   Clemence; Smith, Lindsay, Thompson, Cormack, Hughes, Keegan, Hall, Heighway,

Toshack, Callaghan. *Scorers:* Keegan 2, Heighway.

3-0 NEWCASTLE UNITED McFaul; Clark, Kennedy, McDermott, Howard, Moncur, Smith (Gibb), Cassidy, Macdonald, Tudor, Hibbitt.

1974–75 WEST HAM UNITED Day; McDowell, T. Taylor, Lock, Lampard, Bonds, Paddon, Brooking, Jennings, A. Taylor, Holland. *Scorer:* A. Taylor 2.

2-0 FULHAM Mellor; Cutbush, Lacy, Moore, Fraser, Mullery, Conway, Slough, Mitchell, Busby, Barrett.

1975–76 SOUTHAMPTON Turner; Rodrigues, Peach, Holmes, Blyth, Steele, Gilchrist, Channon, Osgood, McCalliog, Stokes. *Scorer:* Stokes.

1-0 MANCHESTER UNITED Stepney; Forsyth, Houston, Daly, Greenhoff, Buchan, Coppell, McIlroy, Pearson, Macari, Hill (McCreery).

1976–77 MANCHESTER UNITED Stepney; Nicholl, Albiston, McIlroy, B. Greenhoff, Buchan, Coppell, J. Greenhoff, Pearson, Macari, Hill (McCreery). *Scorers:* Pearson, J. Greenhoff.

2-1 LIVERPOOL Clemence; Neal, Jones, Smith, Kennedy, Hughes, Keegan, Case, Heighway, Johnson (Callaghan), McDermott. *Scorer:* Case.

1977–78 IPSWICH TOWN Cooper; Burley, Mills, Osborne (Lambert), Hunter, Beattie, Talbot, Wark, Mariner, Geddis, Woods. *Scorer:* Osborne.

1-0 ARSENAL Jennings; Rice, Nelson, Price, Young, O'Leary, Brady (Rix), Hudson, Macdonald, Stapleton, Sunderland.

1978–79 ARSENAL Jennings; Rice, Nelson, Talbot, O'Leary, Young, Brady, Sunderland, Stapleton, Price (Walford), Rix. *Scorers:* Talbot, Stapleton, Sunderland.

3-2 MANCHESTER UNITED Bailey; Nicholl, Albiston, McIlroy, McQueen. Buchan, Coppell, J. Greenhoff, Jordan, Macari, Thomas. *Scorers:* McQueen, McIlroy.

1979–80 WEST HAM UNITED Parkes; Stewart, Lampard, Bonds, Martin, Devonshire, Allen, Pearson, Cross, Brooking, Pike. *Scorer:* Brooking.

1-0 ARSENAL Jennings; Rice, Devine (Nelson), Talbot, O'Leary, Young, Brady, Sunderland, Stapleton, Price, Rix

1980–81 TOTTENHAM HOTSPUR Aleksic; Hughton, Miller, Roberts, Perryman, Villa (Brooke), Ardiles, Archibald, Galvin, Hoddle, Crooks. *Scorer:* Hutchison (og).

1-1 MANCHESTER CITY Corrigan; Ranson, McDonald, Reid, Power, Caton, Bennett, Gow, MacKenzie, **aet** Hutchison (Henry), Reeves. *Scorer:* Hutchison.

R:3-2 TOTTENHAM HOTSPUR Aleksic; Hughton, Miller, Roberts, Perryman, Villa, Ardiles, Archibald, Galvin, Hoddle, Crooks. *Scorers:* Villa 2, Crooks.

MANCHESTER CITY Corrigan; Ranson, McDonald (Tueart), Caton, Reid, Gow, Power, MacKenzie, Reeves, Bennett, Hutchison. *Scorers:* MacKenzie, Reeves (pen).

1981–82 TOTTENHAM HOTSPUR Clemence; Hughton, Miller, Price, Hazard (Brooke), Perryman, Roberts, Archibald, Galvin, Hoddle, Crooks. *Scorer:* Hoddle.

1-1 QPR Hucker; Fenwick, Gillard, Waddock, Hazell, Roeder, Currie, Flanagan, Allen (Micklewhite), Stain- **aet** rod, Gregory. *Scorer:* Fenwick.

R:1-0 TOTTENHAM HOTSPUR Clemence; Hughton, Miller, Price, Hazard (Brooke), Perryman, Roberts, Archibald, Galvin, Hoddle, Crooks. *Scorer:* Hoddle (pen).

QPR Hucker; Fenwick, Gillard, Waddock, Hazell, Neill, Currie, Flanagan, Micklewhite (Burke), Stainrod, Gregory.

1982–83 MANCHESTER UNITED Bailey; Duxbury, Moran, McQueen, Albiston, Davies, Wilkins, Robson, Muhren, Stapleton, Whiteside. *Scorers:* Stapleton, Wilkins.

2-2 BRIGHTON & HOVE ALBION Moseley; Ramsey (Ryan), Stevens, Gatting, Pearce, Smillie, Case, **aet** Grealish, Howlett, Robinson, Smith. *Scorers:* Smith, Stevens.

R:4-0 MANCHESTER UNITED Bailey; Duxbury, Albiston, Wilkins, Moran, McQueen, Robson, Muhren, Stapleton, Whiteside, Davies. *Scorers:* Robson 2, Whiteside, Muhren (pen).

BRIGHTON & HOVE ALBION Moseley; Gatting, Pearce, Grealish, Foster, Stevens, Case, Howlett, Robinson, Smith, Smillie.

1983–84 EVERTON Southall; Stevens, Bailey, Ratcliffe, Mountfield, Reid, Steven, Heath, Sharp, Gray, Richardson. *Scorers:* Sharp, Gray.

2-0 WATFORD Sherwood; Bardsley, Price (Atkinson), Taylor, Terry, Sinnott, Callaghan, Johnston, Reilly, Jackett, Barnes.

1984–85 MANCHESTER UNITED Bailey; Gidman, Albiston (Duxbury), Whiteside, McGrath, Moran, Robson, Strachan, Hughes, Stapleton, Olsen. *Scorer:* Whiteside.

1-0 EVERTON Southall; Stevens, Van den Hauwe, Ratcliffe, Mountfield, Reid, Steven, Gray, Sharp, Brace- **aet** well, Sheedy.

1985–86 LIVERPOOL Grobbelaar; Lawrenson, Beglin, Nicol, Whelan, Hansen, Dalglish, Johnston, Rush, Molby, MacDonald. *Scorers:* Rush 2, Johnston.

3-1 EVERTON Mimms; Stevens (Heath), Van Den Hauwe, Ratcliffe, Mountfield, Reid, Steven, Lineker, Sharp, Bracewell, Sheedy. *Scorer:* Lineker.

1986–87 COVENTRY CITY Ogrizovic; Phillips, Downs, McGrath, Kilcline (Rodger), Peake, Bennett, Gynn, Regis, Houchen, Pickering. *Scorers:* Bennett, Houchen, Mabbutt (og).

3-2 TOTTENHAM HOTSPUR Clemence; Hughton (Claesen), M. Thomas, Hodge, Gough. Mabbutt, C. **aet** Allen, P. Allen, Waddle, Hoddle, Ardiles (Stevens). *Scorers:* C. Allen, Kilcline (og).

1987–88 WIMBLEDON Beasant; Goodyear, Phelan, Jones, Young, Thorn, Gibson (Scales), Cork (Cunningham), Fashanu, Sanchez, Wise. *Scorer:* Sanchez.

1-0 LIVERPOOL Grobbelaar; Gillespie, Ablett, Nicol, Spackman (Molby), Hansen, Beardsley, Aldridge (Johnston), Houghton, Barnes, McMahon.

1988–89 LIVERPOOL Grobbelaar; Ablett, Staunton (Venison), Nicol, Whelan, Hansen, Beardsley, Aldridge (Rush), Houghton, Barnes, McMahon. *Scorers:* Aldridge, Rush 2.

3-2 EVERTON Southall; McDonald, Van Den Hauwe, Ratcliffe, Watson, Bracewell (McCall), Nevin, Steven, **aet** Sharp, Cottee, Sheedy (Wilson). *Scorer:* McCall 2.

1989–90 MANCHESTER UNITED Leighton; Ince, Martin (Blackmore), Bruce, Phelan, Pallister (Robins), Robson, Webb, McClair, Hughes, Wallace. *Scorers:* Robson, Hughes 2.

3-3 CRYSTAL PALACE Martyn; Pemberton, Shaw, Gray (Madden), O'Reilly, Thorn, Barber (Wright), **aet** Thomas, Bright, Salako, Pardew. *Scorers:* O'Reilly, Wright 2.

R:1–0 MANCHESTER UNITED Sealey; Ince, Martin, Bruce, Phelan, Pallister, Robson, Webb, McClair, Hughes, Wallace, *Scorer:* Martin.

CRYSTAL PALACE Martyn; Pemberton, Shaw, Gray, O'Reilly, Thorn, Barber (Wright), Thomas, Bright, Salako (Madden), Pardew.

1990–91 TOTTENHAM HOTSPUR Thorstvedt; Edinburgh, Van Den Hauwe, Sedgley, Howells, Mabbutt, Stewart, **2-1** Gascoigne (Nayim), Samways (Walsh), Lineker, Allen. *Scorers:* Stewart, Walker (og). **aet** NOTTINGHAM FOREST Crossley; Charles, Pearce, Walker, Chettle, Keane, Crosby, Parker, Clough, Glover (Laws), Woan (Hodge). *Scorer:* Pearce.

Ian Rush and Michael Thomas celebrate as Liverpool's goalscorers in the 1992 FA Cup Final against Sunderland. Rush took his total of final goals to five, a record in the competition at this stage. (Allsport)

FA CUP 1991–92

PRELIMINARY AND QUALIFYING ROUNDS

Preliminary Round

Brandon United v Shotton Comrades	7-1
Darwen v Hebburn	1-1, 1-2
Esh Winning v Netherfield	1-3
Alnwick Town v Chester-le-Street Town	4-3
Consett v Willington	5-0
Clitheroe v Langley Park	4-4, 1-1, 0-1
(*1st replay at Clitheroe*) (*2nd replay at Consett*)	
Bridlington Town v Evenwood Town	5-1
Ashington v Crook Town	3-1
Prudhoe East End v Bedlington Terriers	0-2
Garforth Town v Whickham	4-1
Darlington CB v Horden CW	3-2
Spennymoor United v Easington Colliery	1-0
Stockton v Billingham Town	2-4
Great Harwood Town v Eccleshill United	6-0
Durham City v South Bank	4-0
Penrith v Ferryhill Athletic	1-0
Washington v Shildon	1-3
(*at Shildon*)	
Blackpool (wren) Rovers v Thackley	3-2
West Auckland Town v Denaby United	3-5
Seaham Red Star v Peterlee Newtown	3-2
Sheffield v Congleton Town	2-0
Burscough v Leyland DAF	
(*walkover for Burscough*)	
Irlam Town v Curzon Ashton	0-0, 1-4
Knowsley United v Atherton LR	5-1
Prescot AFC v Chadderton	3-2
Newtown v Glossop	4-2
Liversedge v Maine Road	3-1
Salford City v Warrington Town	0-0, 0-1
Ashton United v Rhyl	0-0, 0-1
Radcliffe Borough v Nantwich Town	0-1
Newcastle Town v Ossett Albion	2-0
Harworth CI v Maltby MW	2-1
Lancaster City v Winsford United	1-5
Armthorpe Welfare v Vauxhall GM	1-1, 2-1
Worksop Town v Brigg Town	3-1
Ossett Town v North Ferriby United	2-0
Rossendale United v Heanor Town	2-4
Arnold Town v Belper Town	0-2
(*at Belper Town*)	
Grantham Town v Ilkeston Town	1-5
Eastwood Town v Farsley Celtic	2-4
St Helens Town v Borrowash Victoria	1-3
Holbeach United v Hinckley Athletic	2-3
Rocester v Oakham United	1-3
Dudley Town v Lincoln United	1-4
Sandwell Borough v Alfreton Town	1-2
Boston v Harrogate Town	2-3
Irthlingborough Diamonds v Wednesfield	2-2, 3-3, 1-2
Tamworth v Lye Town	2-2, 3-1
Oldbury United v Blakenall	1-2
Solihull Borough v Spalding United	1-0
Hinckley v Bridgnorth Town	2-4
Racing Club Warwick v Rushall Olympic	2-1
Stourbridge v Long Buckby	1-0
Hinckley Town v Boldmere St Michaels	3-1
Willenhall Town v Wellingborough Town	6-1
Hednesford Town v Northampton Spencer	1-1, 1-1, 1-0
Stamford Town v Paget Rangers	2-1
Walsall Wood v Raunds Town	1-1, 1-3
Banbury United v Stratford Town	4-1
Highgate United v Chasetown	0-3
Malvern Town v Halesowen Harriers	3-2
Tring Town v Hemel Hempstead	0-3
Chalfont St Peter v Flackwell Heath	2-0
Evesham United v Rothwell Town	3-1
Rushden Town v Friar Lane OB	3-2
Edgware Town v Southall	4-0

Waltham Abbey v Stevenage Borough	0-1
Desborough Town v Vauxhall Motors	
(*walkover for Desborough Town*)	
Braintree Town v Bury Town	2-1
Mirrlees Blackstone v Great Yarmouth Town	2-1
Aveley v Felixstowe Town	2-0
Barton Rovers v Bourne Town	3-4
Wisbech Town v Burnham Ramblers	4-3
Collier Row v Saffron Walden Town	2-2, 3-2
Leyton-Wingate v Eynesbury Rovers	6-0
Hitchin Town v Tiptree United	1-1, 0-1
Purfleet v Gorleston	3-1
Kings Lynn v Haverhill Rovers	5-2
March Town United v Histon	1-1, 1-2
Walthamstow Pennant v Langford	3-2
Arlesey Town v Clapton	0-1
Sudbury Town v Barking	2-2, 2-2, 2-1
Letchworth Garden City v Potton United	1-1, 0-2
Haringey Borough v Watton United	5-0
East Thurrock United v Royston Town	1-0
Canvey Island v Harwich & Parkeston	0-2
Rainham Town v Lowestoft Town	0-1
(*at Lowestoft Town*)	
Barkingside v Baldock Town	1-1, 0-5
Ware v Milton Keynes Borough	5-1
Ford United v Hornchurch	2-1
Halstead Town v Hoddesdon Town	3-2
Basildon United v Brimsdown Rovers	0-1
Wolverton v Uxbridge	1-0
Witham Town v Welwyn Garden City	3-1
Newmarket Town v Biggleswade Town	1-1, 2-2, 0-1
Leighton Town v Kingsbury Town	3-2
Croydon v Darenth Heathside	3-0
(*at Darenth Heathside*)	
Yeading v Rayners Lane	8-0
Cheshunt v Tilbury	0-3
Burnham v Feltham & Hounslow Borough	1-1, 4-0
(*1st match at Windsor & Eton*)	
Beckenham Town v Wingate & Finchley	1-0
Egham Town v Wembley	0-1
Dulwich Hamlet v Harefield United	2-1
Hertford Town v Northwood	3-2
Horsham YMCA v Erith & Belvedere	1-2
Shoreham v Sheppey United	0-3
Molesey v Ringmer	4-0
Corinthian v Merstham	6-0
Chertsey Town v Worthing	2-2, 1-4
Chichester City v Chipstead	1-3
Faversham Town v Eastbourne Town	0-0, 4-0
(*replay at Eastbourne United*)	
Whyteleafe v Ashford Town	2-0
Tunbridge Wells v Burgess Hill Town	0-2
Canterbury City v Arundel	1-0
Leatherhead v Corinthian Casuals	3-1
Cove v Slade Green	2-1
Chatham Town v Steyning Town	1-3
Lewes v Three Bridges	4-3
Metropolitan Police v Hastings Town	2-4
Tooting & Mitcham United v Redhill	2-0
Whitstable Town v Eastbourne United	0-1
Hampton v Haywards Heath Town	3-0
Hythe Town v Croydon Athletic	4-4, 1-2
Langney Sports v Southwick	0-1
Lancing v Wick	4-1
Epsom & Ewell v Walton & Hersham	1-5
Oakwood v Havant Town	0-3
Newbury Town v Horndean	1-0
Selsey v Malden Vale	2-1
Bracknell Town v Portfield	2-2, 1-2
Buckingham Town v Abingdon United	1-0
Sholing Sports v Maidenhead United	0-6

Totton AFC v Lymington AFC	2-2, 2-3
Horsham v Hungerford Town	2-1
Bournemouth v Abingdon Town	1-2
Calne Town v Westbury United	1-2
Fareham Town v Thatcham Town	1-5
Thame United v Eastleigh	1-1, 2-0
Chard Town v Witney Town	1-2
Cwmbran Town v Paulton Rovers	1-0
Glastonbury v Keynsham Town	1-0
Gosport Borough v Clevedon Town	1-3
Barry Town v Ton Pentre	3-1
Radstock Town v Devizes Town	0-2
Bridgend Town v Chippenham Town	2-0
Yate Town v Bristol Manor Farm	4-1
Frome Town v Exmouth Town	3-1
Shortwood United v Weston-super-Mare	3-0
Melksham Town v Welton Rovers	1-1, 2-1
Dawlish Town v Maesteg Park	1-2
St Blazey v Minehead	0-3
Clandown v Ilfracombe Town	1-3
Torrington v Barnstaple Town	3-1
Bideford v Falmouth Town	2-3

First Qualifying Round

Workington v Gateshead	0-1
Alnwick Town v Brandon United	1-1, 1-0
Netherfield v Billingham Synthonia	3-2
Newcastle Blue Star v Hebburn	5-1
Annfield Plain v North Shields	0-4
Ashington v Consett	0-4
Bridlington Town v Blyth Spartans	3-2
Northallerton Town v Langley Park	1-0
Cleator Moor Celtic v Gretna	0-7
Spennymoor United v Bedlington Terriers	0-1
Darlington CB v Murton	1-3
Whitby Town v Garforth Town	0-1
Dunston FB v Guisborough Town	1-0
Penrith v Billingham Town	4-2
Durham City v Tow Law Town	1-0
Morecambe v Great Harwood Town	1-0
Norton & Stockton Ancients v Guiseley	0-4
Seaham Red Star v Shildon	3-0, 1-2
(*match ordered to be replayed*)	
Denaby United v Harrogate RA	1-0
Fleetwood Town v Blackpool (wren) Rovers	3-2
Prescot AFC v Accrington Stanley	0-5
Knowsley United v Sheffield	2-0
Curzon Ashton v Bangor City	1-1, 2-1
Buxton v Burscough	4-2
Caernarfon Town v Colwyn Bay	1-1, 1-2
Rhyl v Newtown	1-0
Warrington Town v Hyde United	1-0
Marine v Liversedge	4-0
Flixton v Mossley	1-1, 1-2
Winsford United v Nantwich Town	3-0
Harworth CI v Droylsden	0-1
Bootle v Newcastle Town	2-1
Eastwood Hanley v Northwich Victoria	2-1
Heanor Town v Armthorpe Welfare	0-2
Ossett Town v Southport	0-1
Stalybridge Celtic v Worksop Town	4-0
Skelmersdale United v Macclesfield Town	0-4
Borrowash Victoria v Belper Town	2-0
Farsley Celtic v Emley	0-1
Horwich RMI v Ilkeston Town	1-0
Harrogate Town v Frickley Athletic	2-2, 3-3, 2-3
(*1st replay at Harrogate Town FC*)	
Alfreton Town v Hinckley Athletic	1-0
Lincoln United v Gainsborough Trinity	3-1
Goole Town v Oakham United	0-1
Bridgnorth Town v Matlock Town	1-2
Solihull Borough v Wednesfield	3-0
Blakenall v Boston United	1-2
Moor Green v Tamworth	0-3
West Midlands Police v Burton Albion	0-1
Willenhall Town v Racing Club Warwick	2-1
Hinckley Town v Leicester United	2-0
Shepshed Albion v Stourbridge	2-0
Chasetown v Bilston Town	0-0, 1-0

Banbury United v Hednesford Town	2-1
Raunds Town v Gresley Rovers	1-1, 0-2
VS Rugby v Stamford Town	2-0
APV Peterborough City v Alvechurch	0-0, 2-3
Evesham United v Malvern Town	2-4
Chalfont St Peter v Nuneaton Borough	0-4
Corby Town v Hemel Hempstead	1-0
Bedworth United v Bromsgrove Rovers	0-2
Desborough Town v Rushden Town	2-4
Stevenage Borough v Sutton Coldfield Town	0-2
Redditch United v Edgware Town	5-1
Wisbech Town v Kettering Town	0-3
Bourne Town v Braintree Town	0-3
Aveley v Heybridge Swifts	0-2
Bishops Stortford v Mirrlees Blackstone	1-1, 0-2
Kings Lynn v Cambridge City	3-3, 2-1
Purfleet v Collier Row	2-2, 1-0
Tiptree United v Dagenham	0-2
Harlow Town v Leyton-Wingate	4-1
(*at Ware FC*)	
Clacton Town v Billericay Town	1-2
Sudbury Town v Histon	1-0
Clapton v Chelmsford City	1-5
Enfield v Walthamstow Pennant	4-0
Lowestoft Town v Boreham Wood	2-1
Harwich & Parkeston v Potton United	2-1
East Thurrock United v Grays Athletic	1-1, 1-2
Redbridge Forest v Haringey Borough	5-0
Stowmarket Town v Hendon	1-4
Halstead Town v Baldock Town	2-3
Ford United v Wivenhoe Town	3-1
Dartford v Ware	5-1
Thetford Town v St Albans City	0-2
Biggleswade Town v Brimsdown Rovers	1-2
Witham Town v Wealdstone	1-3
Chesham United v Wolverton	2-0
Berkhamsted Town v Harrow Borough	3-2
Tilbury v Leighton Town	1-1, 0-1
Yeading v Ruislip Manor	3-1
Slough Town v Croydon	2-2, 3-0
Hertford Town v Staines Town	2-0
Dulwich Hamlet v Burnham	1-0
Wembley v Windsor & Eton	1-0
Fisher Athletic v Beckenham Town	4-0
Banstead Athletic v Wokingham Town	1-2
Corinthian v Erith & Belvedere	1-3
Molesey v Crawley Town	1-5
Hailsham Town v Sheppey United	1-1, 1-4
Whitehawk v Bromley	0-2
Whyteleafe v Worthing	1-2
Faversham Town v Carshalton Athletic	3-2
Dover Athletic v Chipstead	6-0
Steyning Town v Bognor Regis Town	0-1
Cove v Burgess Hill Town	1-1, 0-4
Leatherhead v Dorking	1-2
Gravesend & Northfleet v Canterbury City	2-1
Herne Bay v Kingstonian	0-2
Eastbourne United v Lewes	1-4
Tooting & Mitcham United v Margate	2-1
Peacehaven & Telscombe v Hastings Town	2-1
Walton & Hersham v Littlehampton Town	1-1, 1-2
Lancing v Hampton	1-3
Southwick v Sittingbourne	1-3
Tonbridge v Croydon Athletic	2-1
Camberley Town v Marlow	1-3
Portfield v Havant Town	1-2
Selsey v Andover	2-1
Romsey Town v Newbury Town	2-1
Pagham v Basingstoke Town	1-3
Horsham v Buckingham Town	1-0
Lymington AFC v Bashley	2-4
Newport (IW) v Maidenhead United	0-3
Swanage Town & Herston v Waterlooville	1-1, 0-2
Thame United v Abingdon Town	2-0
Thatcham Town v Salisbury	1-1, 0-3
Poole Town v Westbury United	3-1
Brockenhurst v Dorchester Town	1-2
Clevedon Town v Witney Town	2-2, 0-1
Glastonbury v Trowbridge Town	0-4

Mangotsfield United v Cwmbran Town	4-2
Wimborne Town v Weymouth	1-2
Yate Town v Barry Town	0-3
Bridgend Town v Cheltenham Town	3-3, 0-5
Taunton Town v Devizes Town	2-0
Stroud v Bath City	1-3
Maesteg Park v Frome Town	4-0
Melksham Town v Worcester City	1-8
Gloucester City v Shortwood United	4-1
St Austell v Liskeard Athletic	2-3
Falmouth Town v Minehead	2-0
Torrington v Tiverton Town	2-2, 2-3
Saltash United v Ilfracombe Town	6-0

Second Qualifying Round

Gateshead v Alnwick Town	6-0
Netherfield v Newcastle Blue Star	2-1
North Shields v Consett	3-1
Bridlington Town v Northallerton Town	4-0
Gretna v Bedlington Terriers	3-1
Murton v Garforth Town	3-1
Dunston FB v Penrith	2-2, 6-6, 1-2
Durham City v Morecambe	1-4
Guiseley v Shildon	5-1
Denaby United v Fleetwood Town	1-0
Accrington Stanley v Knowsley United	2-2, 1-2
Curzon Ashton v Buxton	1-0
Colwyn Bay v Rhyl	2-0
Warrington Town v Marine	0-0, 0-1
Mossley v Winsford United	1-1, 0-6
Droylsden v Bootle	1-1, 3-1
Eastwood Hanley v Armthorpe Welfare	3-2
Southport v Stalybridge Celtic	1-2
Macclesfield Town v Borrowash Victoria	1-2
Emley v Horwich RMI	4-2
Frickley Athletic v Alfreton Town	4-1
Lincoln United v Oakham United	2-0
Matlock Town v Solihull Borough	2-1
Boston United v Tamworth	1-1, 0-1
Burton Albion v Willenhall Town	4-1
Hinckley Town v Shepshed Albion	3-3, 2-3
Chasetown v Banbury United	1-1, 2-1
Gresley Rovers v VS Rugby	3-3, 0-3
Alvechurch v Malvern Town	3-0
Nuneaton Borough v Corby Town	2-2, 0-1
Bromsgrove Rovers v Rushden Town	1-0
Sutton Coldfield Town v Redditch United	1-3
Kettering Town v Braintree Town	3-1
Heybridge Swifts v Mirrlees Blackstone	1-1, 1-0
Kings Lynn v Purfleet	4-2
Tiptree United v Harlow Town	0-6
Billericay Town v Sudbury Town	3-1
Chelmsford City v Enfield	1-1, 1-2
Lowestoft Town v Harwich & Parkeston	1-0
Grays Athletic v Redbridge Forest	3-1
Hendon v Baldock Town	1-2
Ford United v Dartford	0-1
St Albans City v Brimsdown Rovers	1-1, 0-2
Wealdstone v Chesham United	2-4
Berkhamsted Town v Leighton Town	2-0
Yeading v Slough Town	0-0, 0-1
Hertford Town v Dulwich Hamlet	2-1
Windsor & Eton v Fisher Athletic	3-2
Wokingham Town v Erith & Belvedere	1-2
Crawley Town v Sheppey United	2-0
Bromley v Worthing	3-1
Faversham Town v Dover Athletic	0-0, 1-2
Bognor Regis Town v Burgess Hill Town	1-2
Dorking v Gravesend & Northfleet	3-4
Kingstonian v Lewes	3-2
Tooting & Mitcham Utd v Peacehaven & Telscombe	2-0
Littlehampton Town v Hampton	1-3
Sittingbourne v Tonbridge	1-2
Marlow v Havant Town	2-1
Selsey v Romsey Town	1-6
Basingstoke Town v Horsham	1-1, 1-2
Bashley v Maidenhead United	1-1, 0-1
Waterlooville v Thame United	3-3, 2-3

Salisbury v Poole Town	2-0
Dorchester Town v Witney Town	3-2
Trowbridge Town v Mangotsfield United	3-0
Weymouth v Barry Town	1-1, 3-2
Cheltenham Town v Taunton Town	8-0
Bath City v Maesteg Park	5-2
Worcester City v Gloucester City	2-1
Liskeard Athletic v Falmouth Town	5-1
Tiverton Town v Saltash United	0-0, 2-1

Third Qualifying Round

Gateshead v Netherfield	0-0, 3-0
North Shields v Bridlington Town	0-2
Gretna v Murton	3-0
Penrith v Morecambe	0-3
Guiseley v Denaby United	1-1, 2-1
Knowsley United v Curzon Ashton	2-0
Colwyn Bay v Marine	4-3
Winsford United v Droylsden	3-2
Eastwood Hanley v Stalybridge Celtic	1-2
Borrowash Victoria v Emley	0-3
Frickley Athletic v Lincoln United	0-0, 2-3
Matlock Town v Tamworth	0-2
Burton Albion v Shepshed Albion	3-2
Chasetown v VS Rugby	0-0, 0-3
Alvechurch v Corby Town	2-0
Bromsgrove Rovers v Redditch United	2-0
Kettering Town v Heybridge Swifts	3-0
Kings Lynn v Harlow Town	2-3
Billericay Town v Enfield	1-3
Lowestoft Town v Grays Athletic	1-2
Baldock Town v Dartford	2-2, 2-1
Brimsdown Rovers v Chesham United	2-2, 1-2
Berkhamsted Town v Slough Town	1-4
Hertford Town v Windsor & Eton	1-2
Erith & Belvedere v Crawley Town	1-2
Bromley v Dover Athletic	0-3
Burgess Hill Town v Gravesend & Northfleet	0-1
Kingstonian v Tooting & Mitcham United	0-0, 3-2
Hampton v Tonbridge	2-2, 0-3
Marlow v Romsey Town	2-0
Horsham v Maidenhead United	1-1, 1-0
Thame United v Salisbury	0-4
Dorchester Town v Trowbridge Town	1-0
Weymouth v Cheltenham Town	4-0
Bath City v Worcester City	1-2
Liskeard Athletic v Tiverton Town	1-3

Fourth Qualifying Round

Whitley Bay v Witton Albion	1-4
Guiseley v Bishop Auckland	2-1
Runcorn v Gateshead	1-0
Barrow v Bridlington Town	0-1
Telford United v Knowsley United	1-0
Colwyn Bay v Morecambe	0-2
Chorley v Emley	2-2, 1-1, 0-1
Leek Town v Lincoln United	0-2
Gretna v Stalybridge Celtic	3-2
Winsford United v Altrincham	3-2
Welling United v Alvechurch	5-1
Colchester United v Burton Albion	5-0
Kettering Town v Stafford Rangers	0-0, 2-0
Gravesend & Northfleet v Harlow Town	1-1, 0-1
Grays Athletic v Atherstone United	0-2
Enfield v VS Rugby	2-1
Tamworth v Bromsgrove Rovers	0-1
Baldock Town v Halesowen Town	1-1, 0-1
Aylesbury United v Chesham United	1-1, 3-1
Tiverton Town v Dover Athletic	1-0
Merthyr Tydfil v Windsor & Eton	1-1, 0-1
Tonbridge v Yeovil Town	1-2
Worcester City v Marlow	1-2
Salisbury v Farnborough Town	1-7
Horsham v Crawley Town	0-0, 0-3
Slough Town v Kingstonian	2-1
Weymouth v Sutton United	1-1, 0-3
Hayes v Dorchester Town	1-0

COMPETITION PROPER

FIRST ROUND
15 NOV
Fulham (0) 0
Hayes (0) 2 *(Day, Stephen)* 6404
Fulham: Stannard; Marshall, Pike, Newson, Cobb, Thomas, Morgan, Onwere, Haag, Brazil, Scott.
Hayes: O'Reilly; Kelly, Keen, Hayward, Leather, Cox, Day, Marshall, Seabrook (Clarke), Stephen, Dixon (Pope).

16 NOV
Aldershot (0) 0
Enfield (0) 1 *(Brush)* 2384
Aldershot: Granville; Brown, McDonald, Henry, Flower, Berry, Rees, Puckett, Bertschin, Randall, Heath (Phillips).
Enfield: McCutcheon; Keen N (Smart), Mason, Keen M, Pearce, Brush, Mosely, Kane, Manderson, Robinson (Vance), Westley.

Atherstone U (0) 0
Hereford U (0) 0 2588
Atherstone U: Sharkey; Everitt, Upton, Randle, Jackson, Redgate, Olner, Green, Tolley, Brain, Williams.
Hereford U: Judge; Fry, Downs, Theodosiou, Devine, Lowndes, Hall, Brain (Robinson), Heritage, Vaughan, McIntyre.

Barnet (2) 5 *(Bull, Naylor, Carter, Evans, Showler)*
Tiverton T (0) 0 3964
Barnet: Phillips; Poole (Horton), Naylor (Evans), Bodley, Howell, Willis, Wilson, Carter, Bull, Lowe, Showler.
Tiverton T: Nott; Stuart, Greening, Rogers (Annunziata), Short, Steele, Scott, Smith, Jones (Charlesworth), Down, Saunders.

Blackpool (1) 2 *(Groves, Bamber)*
Grimsby T (0) 1 *(Cunnington)* 4074
Blackpool: McIlhargey; Burgess, Stoneman, Groves, Briggs, Gore, Rodwell, Horner, Bamber, Sinclair, Eyres.
Grimsby T: Sherwood; Jobling, Agnew, Watson, Birtles (Jones) (Hargreaves), Cunnington, Childs, Smith, Rees, Cockerill, Woods.

Bournemouth (0) 3 *(Bond, Mundee 2 (2 pens))*
Bromsgrove R (1) 1 *(O'Meara (pen))* 4301
Bournemouth: Bartram; Bond, Rowland, Fereday (McGorry), O'Driscoll, Cooke, Mundee, Wood, Quinn, Case, Holmes.
Bromsgrove R: Cooksey; Skelding, Brighton, Richardson, O'Meara, O'Connor, Daly, Stott, Hanks (Cunningham), Crisp, Cooper.

Bridlington T (0) 1 *(Stevenson)*
York C (0) 2 *(Blackstone 2)* 1650
Bridlington T: Ingham; Brentano, Smith, Noteman, Warburton, Stevenson, Sellers, Harvey, Norbury, Radford, Hopkinson.
York C: Marples; McMillan, Crosby, Reid, Tutill, Atkin, Pepper, McCarthy, Blackstone, Hall, Barratt.

Burnley (0) 1 *(Davis)*
Doncaster R (0) 1 *(Rankine)* 7076
Burnley: Pearce; France, Jakub, Davis, Pender, Farrell, Harper, Deary, Francis, Conroy, Lancashire (Eli).
Doncaster R: Samways; Rowe, Boyle, Crosby, Ormsby, Douglas, Harle, Gormley, Rankine, Whitehurst, Noteman.

Bury (0) 0
Bradford C (0) 1 *(Tinnion)* 3805
Bury: Kelly; Greenall, Stanislaus, Parkinson, Valentine, Knill, Smith, Robinson, Stevens, Jones (Hulme), Wilson I.
Bradford C: Tomlinson; Morgan, Dowson, James, Gardner, Babb, McCarthy, Duxbury, Torpey, Tinnion, Reid.

Carlisle U (0) 1 *(Watson)*
Crewe Alex (1) 1 *(Hignett)* 3106
Carlisle U: O'Hanlon; Graham, Thorpe, Miller, Jeffels, Edmondson, Thomas, Lowery (Walling), Proudlock, Fyfe, Watson (Armstrong).
Crewe Alex: Greygoose; Wilson, McKearney, Carr, Callaghan, Sorvel (Futcher), Hignett, Naylor (Payne), Evans, Gardiner, Edwards.

Chester C (1) 1 *(Barrow)*
Guiseley (0) 0 1851
Chester C: Siddall; Whelan, Albiston, Butler, Abel, Lightfoot, Bishop, Barrow, Rimmer, Bennett (Morton), Croft.
Guiseley: Masted; Atkinson, Hogarth, Tetley, Adams, McKenzie (Wilkinson), Roberts A, Colville (Noteman), Elliott, Waites, Roberts W.

Colchester U (0) 0
Exeter C (0) 0 4965
Colchester U: Barrett; Donald, Cook, Kinsella, English, Elliott, Collins, Bennett, McDonough, McGavin, Smith (Grainger).
Exeter C: Miller; Hiley, Cook, Williams, Daniels, Whiston, Hilaire, Brown, Moran, Chapman, Kelly.

Crawley T (2) 4 *(Cant, Hulme, Whittington 2)*
Northampton T (2) 2 *(Chard, Adcock)* 3370
Crawley T: Winterton; Webber, Powell, Wickens, Vessey, Cant, Tonner, Hulme, Venables, Whittington, Gallagher.
Northampton T: Richardson; Chard, Wilson, Angus (Gernon), Terry, Burnham (Campbell), Brown, Quow, McClean, Barnes, Adcock.

Darlington (1) 2 *(Ellison (pen), Smith)*
Chesterfield (1) 1 *(Cooke)* 3628
Darlington: Prudhoe; McJannet, Cook, Pickering, Smith, Trotter, Cork, Toman, Ellison, McCarrison, Tait.
Chesterfield: Goldring; Dyche, Williams, Francis, Brien, McGugan, Turnbull, Cooke, Grayson, Hebberd, Hewitt.

Gretna (0) 0
Rochdale (0) 0 2037
Gretna: Leeming; Mulholland, McCartney, Wilson J, O'Hagan, Goodrick, Armstrong, Carruthers, Pickford, Nelson, Moat.
Rochdale: Gray; Brown M, Graham, Brown T, Reeves, Jones, Ryan, Bowden, Flounders (Milner), Whitehall (Kinsey), Halpin.

Halesowen T (2) 2 *(Flynn, Hazelwood)*
Farnborough T (2) 2 *(Hobson, Broome)* 1866
Halesowen T: Rowe; Whittingham, Edwards, Smith, Bowles, Bradley (Goodall), Hazelwood, Flynn, Bennett, Shilvock, Harrison.
Farnborough T: Power; Stemp, Baker, Broome, Bye, Wigmore, Holmes, Doherty (Horton), Hobson, Reid, Rogers (Fleming).

Hartlepool U (1) 3 *(Tinkler, Johnson, Baker (pen))*
Shrewsbury T (1) 2 *(Lyne, Smith)* 2864
Hartlepool U: Hodge; Nobbs, McKinnon, Tinkler, MacPhail (Southall), Tupling, Johnson, Olsson, Baker, Honour, Dalton.
Shrewsbury T: Perks; Gorman, O'Toole, Worsley, Lynch, Blake, Smith, Summerfield, Lyne (Spink), Taylor, Griffiths.

Huddersfield T (3) 7 *(O'Regan, Donovan 2, Stapleton, Roberts 2, Onuora)*
Lincoln U (0) 0 6763
Huddersfield T: Clarke; Trevitt, Charlton, Donovan, Mitchell, Doherty, O'Regan, Stapleton (Wright), Roberts, Onuora, Barnett (Ireland).
Lincoln U: Waby; North, Dye, Crombie, Ward P, Park (Hinchcliffe), Brown P, Barker, Goddard, Ward W (Brown S), Carter.

Kettering T (0) 1 *(Christie)*
Wycombe W (0) 1 *(Carroll)* 3317
Kettering T: Shoemake; Huxford, Jones, Nicol, Price, Slack, Graham, Brown, Christie, Bancroft (Cotton), Hill.
Wycombe W: Hyde; Cousins, Stapleton, Crossley, Creaser, Smith, Hutchinson, Deakin, Carroll, Scott, Guppy.

Kidderminster H (0) 0
Aylesbury U (0) 1 *(Davies)* 1773
Kidderminster H: Green; Benton, McGrath, Weir, Barnett, Wolsey, Joseph, Howell (Davies), Whitehouse, Lilwall, Humphreys.
Aylesbury U: Garner; Day, Ashby, Benning, Hutter, Wright, Mason, Davies, Hercules, Collins, Robinson.

Leyton Orient (0) 2 *(Howard, Cooper)*
Welling U (1) 1 *(Berry)* 4695
Leyton Orient: Turner; Howard, Hackett, Whitbread, Day, Hales (Burnett), Achampong, Castle, Jones, Cooper, Otto (Berry).
Welling U: Barron; Hone, Clemence, Browne, Ransom, Berry, White, Francis, Abbott, Robbins, Reynolds.

Maidstone U (1) 1 *(Thompson)*
Sutton U (0) 0 2008
Maidstone U: Hesford; Sandeman (Smalley), Thompson, Haylock, Oxbrow, Davis, Painter, Stebbing, Cuggy (Lillis), Osborne, Henry.
Sutton U: McCann; Dawson, Gates (Dack), Golley, Priddle, Hemsley, Rogers, Beeks, Smith, Griffiths (Feltham), Scott.

Mansfield T (1) 1 *(Wilkinson)*
Preston NE (1) 1 *(Shaw) abandoned after 32 mins—fog*

Morecambe (0) 0
Hull C (1) 1 *(Wilcox)* 2853
Morecambe: Allison; Tomlinson, Armstrong, Parillon, Miller, Lodge, Brown, Dullagan (Holden), Coleman, MacMahon (McMahon), Cain.
Hull C: Fettis; Warren, Jacobs, Mail, Wilcox, Shotton, Stoker (Atkinson), Ngata, Windass, Norton, Jenkinson.

Peterborough U (6) 7 *(Cooper 2 (1 pen), Riley, Sterling, Halsall, Charlery, Culpin)*
Harlow T (0) 0 4341
Peterborough U: Barber; Luke, Johnson, Halsall, Robinson D, Welsh, Sterling (Butterworth), Cooper G, Riley (Culpin), Charlery, Kimble.
Harlow T: Mallett; Armstrong, Burns, Gleeson, Durant, Emmanuel, St Hilaire (Porter), Battram, McLean, Margerrison (Cottington), Head.

Runcorn (0) 0
Tranmere R (1) 3 *(Irons, Aldridge 2) at Tranmere* 6588
Runcorn: Paladino; Byrne, Mullen, Carroll, Hill, Redman (Imrie), Brabin, Harold, Shaughnessy, Saunders, Withers (Hawtin).
Tranmere R: Nixon; Higgins, Brannan, Irons, Hughes (Harvey), Vickers, Morrissey, Aldridge, Malkin (Cooper), Martindale, Nolan.

Scarborough (0) 0
Wigan Ath (1) 2 *(Pilling, Worthington)* 1889
Scarborough: Hughes; Ash, Mudd, Lee, Hirst, Meyer, Ashdjian (Himsworth), Mockler, Mooney, Fletcher (Holmes), Jules.
Wigan Ath: Adkins; Parkinson, Tankard, Johnson, Patterson, Langley, Powell, Connelly, Daley (Pilling) (Smyth), Worthington, Griffiths.

Scunthorpe U (0) 1 *(Helliwell)*
Rotherham U (1) 1 *(Cunningham)* 4511
Scunthorpe U: Musselwhite; Alexander, Longden, Martin (Hyde), Humphries, Lister, Buckley (White), Hamilton, Daws, Hill, Helliwell.
Rotherham U: Mercer; Pickering, Hutchings, Goater, Watts, Law, Goodwin, Barrick, Cunningham, Page, Hazel.

Slough T (1) 3 *(Pluckrose, Fielder, McKinnon)*
Reading (0) 3 *(Williams, Gooding, Taylor)* 3990
Slough T: Bunting; Stacey, Pluckrose, Knight, Anderson, Donnellan, Fielder, McKinnon, Joseph, Thompson, Mallinson.
Reading: Francis; Richardson, Holzman, McPherson, Gooding, Williams, Streete, Dillon, McGhee, Maskell, Taylor.

Stockport Co (0) 3 *(Gannon, Ward (og), Francis)*
Lincoln C (0) 1 *(Lee)* 3864
Stockport Co: Edwards; Thorpe, Williams P, Frain, Barras, Williams B, Gannon, Beaumont, Francis, Ward, Kilner.
Lincoln C: Dickins; West D (Lee), Clarke (Carmichael), Finney, West G, Brown, Schofield, Ward, Puttnam, Lormor, Alexander.

Stoke C (0) 0
Telford U (0) 0 9974
Stoke C: Fox; Butler (Ellis), Sandford, Kevan, Overson, Kennedy, Cranson, Beeston, Stein, Biggins, Fowler.
Telford U: Acton; Humphreys, Brindley, Dyson, Nelson, Whittington, Myers, Grainger, Benbow, Langford, Parrish.

Swansea C (1) 2 *(Gilligan, Harris)*
Cardiff C (1) 1 *(Pike)* 9315
Swansea C: Freestone; Jenkins, Agboola, Coughlin, Harris, Walker, Williams, Thornber, Gilligan, Bowen, Legg.
Cardiff C: Hansbury; Matthews, Searle, Gibbins, Baddeley, Perry, Ramsey, Griffith (Millar), Pike, Dale, Blake.

Torquay U (2) 3 *(Loram, Hall 2)*
Birmingham C (0) 0 4123
Torquay U: Howells; Holmes P, Uzzell, Compton, Elliott, Holmes M, Rowbotham, Hall, Joyce, Edwards, Loram.
Birmingham C: Thomas; Clarkson, Matthewson, Cooper, Hicks (Peer), Mardon, Rodgerson, Frain, Donowa, Gleghorn, Sturridge.

WBA (3) 6 *(Strodder, Goodman, Shakespeare 2 (1 pen), McNally, Robson)*

Marlow (0) 0   11,082

WBA: Naylor; Ford, Harbey, Bradley (Williams), Strodder, Burgess, McNally, Goodman, Robson (Rogers), Shakespeare, White.

Marlow: Ellis; Franks, Poole (George), Stone (Hooper), Hubbick, West, Lay, Regan, Watkins, Hannigan, Caesar.

Windsor & Eton (1) 1 *(Gilman)*

Woking (0) 1 *(Baron) abandoned after 69 mins—fog*

Witton Albion (1) 1 *(Thomas)*

Halifax T (0) 1 *(Hildersley)*   2002

Witton Albion: Zelem; Stewart, Coathup, McNeilis, Connor Jim, Anderson, Thomas, Hooton, Lutkevitch (Dyson), Grimshaw, Connor Joe.

Halifax T: Gould; Barr, Bradley, Evans, Richards, Lewis, Abbott (Hildersley), Norris, Juryeff, Richardson, Ellis.

Wrexham (1) 5 *(Connolly, Watkin 3, Thomas)*

Winsford U (1) 2 *(Esdail)*   2933

Wrexham: Morris; Thackeray, Hardy, Beaumont, Thomas, Jones J, Sertori, Owen, Connolly, Watkin, Kelly.

Winsford U: Mayfield; Lloyd, Whitney, Edey, Taylor (Neatis), Esdail, Grant (Hall), Thomas, Cameron, Blackwood, Sheridan.

Yeovil T (0) 1 *(Wilson)*

Walsall (0) 1 *(Tolson)*   4635

Yeovil T: Hervin; Harrower, Rowbotham, Shail, Rutter (Cooper), Batty, McDermott, Wallace, Wilson, Spencer, Conning.

Walsall: McKnight; Williams, Lane, Methven, Anderson, O'Hara, MacDonald, Ntamark, Jackson (Musker), Marsh, Cecere (Tolson).

17 NOV

Emley (0) 0   9035

Bolton W (1) 3 *(Reeves 2, Philliskirk) at Huddersfield*

Emley: Dennis; Bramle, Smith, Wright, Codd, Farrar, Burrows, Broadbent (Wilson), Duke, Cooper, Joyce (Green).

Bolton W: Felgate; Brown P, Burke, Kelly, Seagraves, Winstanley, Brown M (Stubbs), Green (Storer), Reeves, Philliskirk, Darby.

18 NOV

Brentford (2) 3 *(Holdsworth 2, Blissett)*

Gillingham (1) 3 *(Walker 2, Smith)*   5830

Brentford: Bayes; Bates, Manuel, Millen, Evans, Ratcliffe, Godfrey, Gayle, Holdsworth, Blissett (Sealy), Smillie.

Gillingham: Lim; O'Shea, Elsey, Smith (Eeles), Walker, Dempsey, Clark, Crown, Beadle (Arnott), Lovell, O'Connor.

26 NOV

Windsor & Eton (2) 2 *(Gilman 2)*

Woking (1) 4 *(Milton, Mitchell, Biggins, Friel)*   2534

Windsor & Eton: Mitchell; Parkins, Walters, White, Richards, Woods, Williams, Bates, Evans, Gilman, Franks (Reynolds).

Woking: Batty; Mitchell, Cowler, Pratt, Baron, Wye S, Brown, Biggins, Milton, Friel, Collier.

FIRST ROUND REPLAYS

Crewe Alex (2) 5 *(Walters, Naylor 2, Gardiner, Barnsley (og))*

Carlisle U (0) 3 *(Barnsley 2 (2 pens), Fyfe) aet*   3270

Crewe Alex: Greygoose; Wilson, McKearney, Carr, Jackson, Walters, Hignett, Naylor, Futcher (Evans), Gardiner, Edwards.

Carlisle U: O'Hanlon; Graham, Barnsley, Miller, Jeffels, Edmondson (Bennett), Thomas, Walling, Proudlock, Fyfe, Watson.

Farnborough T (0) 4 *(Read 3, Coombs (pen))*

Halesowen T (0) 0   1673

Farnborough T: Power; Stemp, Baker, Broome, Fleming, Wigmore, Rogers, Hobson (Holmes), Coombs, Read (Doherty), Horton.

Halesowen T: Rowe; Whittingham, Edwards (Attwood), Smith, Bowles, Bradley, Hazlewood, Flynn, Bennett, Shilvock (Laker), Harrison.

Gillingham (0) 1 *(Walker)*

Brentford (1) 3 *(Holdsworth 2, Sealy)*   7328

Gillingham: Lim; O'Shea, Elsey (Eeles), Smith, Walker, Dempsey, Clark, Crown, Arnott (Beadle), Lovell, O'Connor.

Brentford: Bayes; Bates, Manuel, Millen, Evans, Ratcliffe (Buckle), Godfrey, Sealy, Holdsworth, Blissett, Smillie.

Hereford U (1) 3 *(Lowndes, Brain 2)*

Atherstone U (0) 0   3479

Hereford U: Judge; Wade, Pejic, Theodosiou, Devine, Hall, Vaughan, Lowndes, Fry, Brain, Heritage.

Atherstone U: Starkey; Everitt, Upton, Randle, Jackson, Redgate, Olner, Green, Tolley, Brain (Wilson), Williams (Shelton).

Rotherham U (1) 3 *(Page 2, Goodwin)*

Scunthorpe U (0) 3 *(Helliwell, Daws, White)*   4829

Rotherham U: Mercer; Pickering, Hutchings, Todd, Watts, Law, Goodwin, Barrick, Cunningham, Page, Hazel (Goater).

Scunthorpe U: Musselwhite; Alexander, Longden, Martin (Hine), Humphries, Lister, Buckley (White), Hamilton, Daws, Hill, Helliwell.

aet; Rotherham U won 7–6 on penalties.

Telford U (1) 2 *(Benbow 2)*

Stoke C (0) 1 *(Beeston)*   4052

Telford U: Acton; Humphreys, Brindley, Dyson, Nelson, Whittington, Myers, Grainger, Benbow, Langford, Parrish.

Stoke C: Fox; Ware, Sandford (Blake), Kevan, Overson, Kennedy, Cranson, Beeston, Stein, Biggins, Scott (Ellis).

27 NOV

FIRST ROUND

Mansfield T (0) 0

Preston NE (0) 1 *(Thomas)*   7509

Mansfield T: Pearcey; Fleming, Withe, Spooner, Gray, Foster, Ford, Holland, Stant, Wilkinson, Charles.

Preston NE: Kelly; Senior, Wrightson, Swann, Flynn, Allpress, Ashcroft, Cartwright, Thomas, Shaw, James.

FIRST ROUND REPLAYS

Doncaster R (1) 1 *(Whitehurst)*

Burnley (1) 3 *(Harper 2, Eli)*   4207

Doncaster R: Samways; Reddish (Cullen), Rowe, Crosby, Ormsby, Douglas, Harle, Gormley (Nicholson), Rankine, Whitehurst, Noteman.

Burnley: Pearce; Measham, Jakub, Davis, Pender (Yates), Farrell, Harper, Deary, Francis, Conroy, Eli.

Exeter C (0) 0
Colchester U (0) 0 4066
Exeter C: Miller; Brown, Cook, Williams, Daniels, Whiston, Hilaire (Redwood), Wimbleton (Cole), Marshall, Kelly, Chapman.
Colchester U: Barrett; Donald, Cook, Kinsella, English, Goodwin (Grainger), Collins, Bennett (Restarick), McDonough, McGavin, Smith.
aet; Exeter C won 4–2 on penalties.

Halifax T (0) 1 *(Richardson)*
Witton Albion (0) 2 *(Thomas, Grimshaw) aet* 2172
Halifax T: Gould; Barr, Bradley, Lucketti, Richards, Evans, Abbott, Norris, Juryeff, Richardson, Ellis (Hildersley).
Witton Albion: Zelem; Coathup, Hooton, McNeilis, Connor Jim, Anderson (Hill), Thomas, Cuddy, Lutkevitch (Alford), Grimshaw, Connor Joe.

Reading (2) 2 *(Williams, Lovell)*
Slough T (0) 1 *(Joseph)* 6363
Reading: Honey; Richardson, Holzman (Seymour), McPherson, Gooding, Williams, Streete, Taylor, Lovell, Maskell, Gilkes.
Slough T: Bunting; Whitby, Pluckrose, Hill, Anderson, Donnellan (Stanley), Fielder, Dell, Joseph, Thompson, Mallinson.

Rochdale (3) 3 *(Jones, Milner, Flounders)*
Gretna (0) 1 *(Carruthers)* 4300
Rochdale: Gray; Brown M, Kinsey (Butler), Brown T, Jones, Payne, Milner, Doyle, Flounders (Whitehall), Bowden, Halpin.
Gretna: Leeming; Mulholland, McCartney, Wilson J, O'Hagan, Goodrick, Armstrong, Carruthers, Pickford, Nelson, Moat.

Walsall (0) 0
Yeovil T (0) 1 *(Cooper) aet* 3869
Walsall: McKnight; Williams, Lane, Methven, Anderson, O'Hara, McDonald, Ntamark, Jackson (Cecere), Marsh, MacDonald.
Yeovil T: Hervin; Harrower, Batty, Shail, Rutter, McDermott, Carroll (Cooper), Wallace, Wilson, Spencer, Conning.

Wycombe W (0) 0
Kettering T (0) 2 *(Brown, Graham)* 5299
Wycombe W: Hyde; Cousins, Stapleton, Crossley, Creaser, Smith (Hutchinson), Carroll, Deakin, West, Scott, Guppy.
Kettering T: Bastock; Huxford, Jones, Nicol, Price, Slack, Graham, Brown, Christie, Bancroft, Hill.

SECOND ROUND
7 DEC

Aylesbury U (1) 2 *(Hercules 2)*
Hereford U (2) 3 *(Fry, Heritage, Brain)* 3200
Aylesbury U: Garner; Tomlinson, Ashby, Benning, Hutter, Wright (Cassidy), Mason, Davies, Hercules, Collins, Robinson.
Hereford U: Judge; Fry, Downs, Theodosiou, Devine, Pejic, Hall, Brain, Heritage, Narbett, Lowndes.

Blackpool (0) 0
Hull C (0) 1 *(Hunter)* 4554
Blackpool: McIlhargey; Davies (Garner), Stoneman, Groves, Murphy, Hedworth, Rodwell, Bonner, Bamber, Sinclair (Howard), Taylor.
Hull C: Fettis (Stoker); Warren, Jacobs, Mail, Wilcox, Shotton, Palin, Walmsley (Hunter), Brown, Norton, Jenkinson.

Bolton W (2) 3 *(Burke, Reeves, Philliskirk (pen))*
Bradford C (0) 1 *(Tinnion)* 7129
Bolton W: Felgate; Brown P, Burke, Kelly, Seagraves, Stubbs (Came), Brown M, Green, Reeves, Philliskirk, Darby.
Bradford C: Tomlinson; Mitchell, Richards (Stuart), James, Leonard, Babb, McCarthy, Duxbury, Torpey, Tinnion, Jewell.

Bournemouth (0) 2 *(Quinn 2)*
Brentford (0) 1 *(Bates)* 6538
Bournemouth: Bartram; Bond, Rowland, Morris, Mundee, O'Driscoll, Ekoku, Wood (McGorry), Quinn, Case, Holmes (Cooke).
Brentford: Benstead; Bates, Manuel (Gayle), Millen, Evans, Ratcliffe, Sealy, Buckle, Holdsworth, Blissett (Godfrey), Smillie.

Burnley (0) 2 *(Conroy, Lancashire)*
Rotherham U (0) 0 9775
Burnley: Pearce; Measham, Jakub, Davis, Pender, Farrell, Harper, Deary, Francis, Conroy, Eli (Lancashire).
Rotherham U: Mercer; Pickering, Hutchings, Todd, Johnson, Law, Goodwin, Barrick (Goater), Cunningham, Page, Hazel.

Crewe Alex (0) 2 *(Hignett, Naylor)*
Chester C (0) 0 5299
Crewe Alex: Greygoose; Wilson, McKearney, Carr, Callaghan, Walters, Hignett, Naylor, Futcher (Evans), Gardiner, Edwards (Jasper).
Chester C: Stewart; Whelan, Albiston, Comstive, Abel, Lightfoot, Bishop, Barrow, Rimmer (Morton), Bennett, Butler.

Enfield (0) 1 *(Robinson)*
Barnet (1) 4 *(Bull, Carter 3)* 5120
Enfield: McCutcheon; Smart, Mason, Keen, Pearce (Manderson), Brush, Mosely, Kane, Warmington, Robinson, Westley.
Barnet: Pape; Poole (Blackford), Naylor (Murphy), Bodley, Howell, Horton, Wilson, Carter, Bull, Lowe, Showler.

Exeter C (0) 0
Swansea C (0) 0 4186
Exeter C: Miller; Hiley, Cook, Williams, Daniels, Whiston, Hilaire (Marshall), Wimbleton (Brown), Moran, Harris, Chapman.
Swansea C: Freestone; Ford, Agboola, Walker, Harris, Chapple, Williams, Coughlin, Gilligan, Bowen, Legg.

Hayes (0) 0
Crawley T (1) 2 *(Hulme 2)* 4203
Hayes: O'Reilly; Keen, Kelly, Hayward, Leather, Cox, Day, Marshall, Seabrook, Pope (Clarke), Stephen.
Crawley T: Winterton; Webber, Powell, Wickens, Vessey, Cant, Towner (Davies), Hulme, Venables, Whittington, Gallagher.

Maidstone U (1) 1 *(Henry)*
Kettering T (1) 2 *(Brown, Oxbrow (og))* 2750
Maidstone U: Hesford; Sandeman, Thompson, Haylock, Oxbrow, Davis, Smalley, Stebbing, Donegal (Painter), Osborne, Henry.
Kettering T: Bastock; Huxford, Jones, Nicol, Price, Slack, Graham, Brown, Christie, Bancroft, Hill.

Peterborough U (0) 0
Reading (0) 0 5328
Peterborough U: Barber; Luke, Johnson, Halsall, Robinson D, Welsh, Sterling, Cooper G, Riley (Culpin), Charlery, Kimble.
Reading: Leighton; Taylor, Richardson, McPherson, Williams, Streete, Gooding, Bailey, Lovell (Britton), Maskell, Gilkes.

Preston NE (3) 5 *(Shaw, Swann, Senior, Flynn, Greenwood)*
Witton Albion (0) 1 *(Thomas)* 6736
Preston NE: Kelly; Senior, Wrightson, Swann, Flynn, Allpress, Ashcroft, Cartwright, Thomas, Shaw, James (Greenwood).
Witton Albion: Mason; Coathup (Stewart), Hooton, McNeilis, Connor Jim, Anderson, Thomas, Cuddy (McCluskie), Lutkevitch, Grimshaw, Connor Joe.

Rochdale (1) 1 *(Halpin)*
Huddersfield T (0) 2 *(Roberts, Onuora)* 5776
Rochdale: Rose; Brown M, Graham, Brown T, Doyle (Butler), Payne, Ryan, Milner, Flounders, Bowden, Halpin (Whitehall).
Huddersfield T: Clarke; Trevitt, Charlton, Wright, Mitchell, Jackson, O'Regan, Starbuck (Stapleton), Roberts, Onuora, Barnett.

Torquay U (0) 1 *(Loram)*
Farnborough T (1) 1 *(Read)* 2725
Torquay U: Howells; Holmes P, Uzzell, Myers, Elliott, Hodges, Rowbotham (Colcombe), Hall, Joyce, Edwards (Derby), Loram.
Farnborough T: Power; Stemp, Baker, Broome, Bye, Wigmore, Rogers, Fleming, Coney, Read, Horton.

Wigan Ath (1) 2 *(Griffiths, Powell)*
Stockport Co (0) 0 4168
Wigan Ath: Adkins; Parkinson, Tankard, Jones, Patterson, Langley, Powell, Connolly (Johnson), Pilling, Worthington (Daley), Griffiths.
Stockport Co: Edwards; Williams P, Todd, Frain, Finley, Barras, Gannon, Beaumont, Francis, Ward, Wheeler (Kilner).

Woking (1) 3 *(Friel 3)*
Yeovil T (0) 0 4500
Woking: Batty; Mitchell, Cowler, Pratt, Baron, Wye S, Brown, Parr, Milton, Friel, Collier.
Yeovil T: Hervin; Harrower, Batty, Shail, Rutter, Carroll (Henderson), McDermott, Wallace, Wilson, Spencer, Conning (Pritcher).

Wrexham (0) 1 *(Watkin)*
Telford U (0) 0 3897
Wrexham: O'Keefe; Thackeray, Hardy, Beaumont, Thomas, Sertori, Connolly, Owen, Jones L, Watkin, Kelly.
Telford U: Acton; Humphreys, Brindley, Dyson, Nelson, Whittington, Myers, Grainger, Benbow, Langford, Parrish.

York C (0) 1 *(Hall)*
Tranmere R (1) 1 *(Morrissey)* 4646
York C: Marples; McMillan, Crosby, Reid, Tutill, Atkin, Pepper, McCarthy, Blackstone (Naylor), Hall, Canham.
Tranmere R: Nixon; Higgins, Brannan, Irons, Hughes, Vickers, Morrissey, Aldridge, McNab, Cooper, Nolan.

9 DEC
Leyton Orient (1) 2 *(Berry 2)*
WBA (0) 1 *(Williams)* 6189
Leyton Orient: Turner; Howard, Hackett, Whitbread, Day, Harvey, Achampong, Castle, Jones (Cooper), Nugent, Berry.
WBA: Naylor; Hodson, Harbey, Bradley, Strodder, Burgess, McNally, Williams, Robson (Bannister), Shakespeare, White.

17 DEC
Darlington (0) 1 *(Toman)*
Hartlepool U (2) 2 *(Dalton, Honour)* 5509
Darlington: Prudhoe; McJannet, Cook, Gregan (Borthwick), Smith, Pickering, Hamilton, Toman, Ellison, Mardenborough, Tait.
Hartlepool U: Hodge; Nobbs, McKinnon, McCreery, MacPhail, Tupling, Johnson, Olsson, Baker, Honour, Dalton.

SECOND ROUND REPLAYS
Farnborough T (2) 4 *(Coney, Read, Doherty, Broome)*
Torquay U (0) 3 *(Holmes M, Loram, Colcombe)* 2285
Farnborough T: Power; Stemp, Baker, Broome, Bye, Wigmore, Doherty, Holmes, Coney, Read, Horton (Fleming).
Torquay U: Howells; Holmes P, Dobbins, Compton, Elliott, Holmes M, Rowbotham, Hall, Joyce (Derby), Loram, Colcombe.

Reading (0) 1 *(Lovell)*
Peterborough U (0) 0 4373
Reading: Leighton; Taylor, Richardson, McPherson, Williams, Streete, Gooding, Bailey, Britton (Lovell), Maskell, Gilkes.
Peterborough U: Barber; Luke, Johnson, Halsall, Robinson D, Welsh, Sterling, Cooper (Ebdon), Riley, Charlery, Kimble (Culpin).

Swansea C (0) 1 *(Walker)*
Exeter C (1) 2 *(Brown, Marshall)* 3159
Swansea C: Freestone; Ford, Agboola, Walker, Harris (Jenkins), Chapple, Williams, Coughlin, Gilligan, Bowen (Raynor), Legg.
Exeter C: Miller; Hiley, Cook, Williams (Harris), Daniels, Whiston, Marshall, Wimbleton, Moran, Brown, Hilaire.

Tranmere R (1) 2 *(Aldridge, Irons)*
York C (0) 1 *(McCarthy)* 5546
Tranmere R: Collings; Higgins, Mungall, Irons, Hughes (Martindale), Vickers, Morrissey, Aldridge, Harvey, Cooper (Steel), Nolan.
York C: Marples; McMillan, Crosby, Reid, Tutill, Atkin, Pepper, McCarthy, Blackstone, Hall, Canham.

THIRD ROUND
4 JAN
Blackburn R (1) 4 *(Speedie, Newell 2, Cowans)*
Kettering T (0) 1 *(Brown)* 13,821
Blackburn R: Mimms; Brown, Wright, Cowans, Hill, Moran, Skinner, Atkins, Newell, Speedie (Garner), Sellars (Reid).

Kettering T: Bastock; Huxford (Waller), Jones, Nicol, Price, Slack, Keast, Brown, Christie, Bancroft (Graham), Hill.

Bolton W (0) 2 *(Philliskirk 2)*
Reading (0) 0   7301
Bolton W: Felgate; Stubbs, Burke, Kelly, Seagraves, Came, Green, Patterson, Jeffrey, Philliskirk, Fisher.
Reading: Leighton; Jones, Richardson, McPherson, Williams, Streete, Gooding, Bailey (Lovell), Senior, Maskell (Cockram), Gilkes.

Bournemouth (0) 0
Newcastle U (0) 0   10,651
Bournemouth: Bartram; Bond, Rowland, Morris, Mundee, O'Driscoll, Brooks, Wood, Quinn (Crooke) (Holmes), Case, Ekoku.
Newcastle U: Wright; Watson, Bradshaw, O'Brien, Scott, Appleby, Clarke, Peacock, Kelly, Hunt (Howey), Brock.

Brighton & HA (3) 5 *(Gall, Walker, Chapman 2 (1 pen), Meade)*
Crawley T (0) 0   18,031
Brighton & HA: Beeney; Crumplin, Gallacher, Chapman, Chivers, Bissett, Robinson (Wilkins), Meade, Gall (Wade), Clarkson, Walker.
Crawley T: Winterton; Webber, Powell, Wickens (Davis), Vessey, Cant, Venables, Hulme, Searle, Whittington (Towner), Gallagher.

Bristol C (0) 1 *(Barton (og))*
Wimbledon (1) 1 *(Fashanu)*   12,679
Bristol C: Leaning; Llewellyn (Bent), Scott, May, Bryant, Aizlewood, Osman, Rennie, Allison, Taylor, Gavin.
Wimbledon: Segers; McGee, Phelan, Barton, Scales, Fitzgerald, Newhouse, Earle, Fashanu, Sanchez, Anthrobus.

Burnley (1) 2 *(Harper, Eli)*
Derby Co (1) 2 *(Chalk, Comyn)*   18,772
Burnley: Kendall; Measham, Jakub, Davis, Pender, Farrell, Harper, Deary, Francis (Lancashire), Conroy, Eli.
Derby Co: Shilton; Patterson, Forsyth, Williams G, Coleman, Comyn, Chalk, Ormondroyd, Stallard, Williams P, McMinn.

Coventry C (0) 1 *(Borrows (pen))*
Cambridge U (1) 1 *(Dublin)*   11,428
Coventry C: Ogrizovic; Borrows, Sansom, Robson, Pearce, Billing, McGrath, Booty (Furlong), Rosario, Gallacher, Smith.
Cambridge U: Vaughan; Fensome, Kimble, Bailie, Chapple, O'Shea, Rowett (Heathcote) (Dennis), Wilkins, Dublin, Taylor, Philpott.

Everton (1) 1 *(Beardsley)*
Southend U (0) 0   22,606
Everton: Southall; Jackson, Harper (Cottee), Ebbrell, Watson, Keown, Warzycha (Nevin), Beardsley, Johnston, Ward, Beagrie.
Southend U: Sansome; Austin, Powell, Jones, Scully, Prior, Ansah, Cornwell, Tilson, Benjamin, Angell.

Exeter C (0) 1 *(Moran)*
Portsmouth (1) 2 *(Whittingham, Aspinall)*   6755
Exeter C: Miller; Hiley, Cook, Williams, Daniels, Whiston, Marshall, Wimbleton, Moran, Brown, Cooper.
Portsmouth: Knight; Awford, Beresford, Powell, Symons, Butters, Neill, Kuhl, Whittingham (Wigley), Chamberlain (Aspinall), Anderton.

Farnborough T (0) 1 *(Coney (pen))*
West Ham U (0) 1 *(Dicks) at West Ham*   23,449
Farnborough T: Power; Stemp, Baker (Horton), Broome, Bye, Wigmore, Doherty (Rogers), Holmes, Coney, Read, Fleming.
West Ham U: Miklosko; Breacker, Dicks, Gale, Potts (Morley), Thomas, Bishop, McAvennie, Small, Keen, Slater.

Huddersfield T (0) 0
Millwall (4) 4 *(Thompson, Verveer, Rae 2)*   10,879
Huddersfield T: Clarke; Trevitt, Wright, Kelly (Walsh), Mitchell, Jackson, O'Regan, Onuora, Roberts, Starbuck, Barnett.
Millwall: Davison; Cunningham, Dawes, Thompson, McCarthy, Rae, Stephenson, Verveer, Bogie, McGinlay, Kerr (Armstrong).

Hull C (0) 0
Chelsea (1) 2 *(Jones, Wise)*   13,580
Hull C: Fettis; Young (Hobson), Jacobs, Stoker (Hockaday), Wilcox, Shotton, Palin, Matthews, France, Norton, Jenkinson.
Chelsea: Hitchcock; Hall, Boyd, Jones, Elliott, Cundy, Stuart, Townsend, Dixon, Allen, Wise.

Ipswich T (0) 1 *(Dozzell)*
Hartlepool U (1) 1 *(Baker)*   12,502
Ipswich T: Forrest; Johnson, Thompson, Stockwell (Yallop), Wark, Linighan, Milton, Palmer (Pennyfather), Whitton, Dozzell, Kiwomya.
Hartlepool U: Hodge; Nobbs, McKinnon, McCreery, MacPhail, Tupling, Southall, Olsson, Baker, Tinkler (Fletcher), Dalton.

Leicester C (0) 1 *(Smith)*
Crystal Palace (0) 0   19,613
Leicester C: Muggleton; Mills, Reid, Smith, Walsh, Mauchlen, Oldfield, Thompson, Gordon, Willis (Kitson), Wright.
Crystal Palace: Martyn; Humphrey, Sinnott, Gray, Young, Thorn, Mortimer, Thomas, Bright, Gabbiadini (Rodger), McGoldrick.

Middlesbrough (0) 2 *(Kernaghan, Wilkinson)*
Manchester C (1) 1 *(Reid)*   21,174
Middlesbrough: Pears; Parkinson, Phillips, Kernaghan, Mohan, Mustoe (Hendrie), Slaven (Payton), Pollock, Wilkinson, Peake, Ripley.
Manchester C: Coton; Brightwell I (Sheron), Pointon, Reid, Curle, Redmond, White, Heath, Quinn, McMahon (Megson), Hughes.

Norwich C (0) 1 *(Fleck (pen))*
Barnsley (0) 0   12,189
Norwich C: Gunn; Phillips, Bowen, Sutton, Blades (Polston), Goss, Fox, Fleck, Newman, Beckford (Crook), Ullathorne.
Barnsley: Butler; Fleming, Bishop, Bullimore, Smith (Currie) (Saville), Williams, Robinson, Redfearn, O'Connell, Rammell, Archdeacon.

Nottingham F (0) 1 *(Clough)*
Wolverhampton W (0) 0   27,068
Nottingham F: Crossley; Charles, Pearce, Walker, Tiler, Keane, Crosby, Gemmill, Clough, Sheringham, Black.
Wolverhampton W: Stowell; Ashley, Venus, Burke (Dennison), Madden, Bennett, Birch, Cook, Bull, Mutch, Thompson.

Oldham Ath (0) 1 *(Sharp)*
Leyton Orient (1) 1 *(Day)* 10,764
Oldham Ath: Hallworth; Fleming, Bernard, Henry, Barrett, Jobson, Adams, Marshall, Sharp, Palmer, Holden.
Leyton Orient: Turner; Howard, Hackett, Burnett, Day, Whitbread, Achampong (Hales), Castle, Cooper (Jones), Nugent, Berry.

Oxford U (2) 3 *(Beauchamp, Magilton (pen), Vickers (og))*
Tranmere R (0) 1 *(Malkin)* 6027
Oxford U: Veysey; Smart, Jackson, Lewis, Evans, Melville, Magilton, Beauchamp, Aylott, Durnin, Simpson.
Tranmere R: Nixon; Higgins, Mungall (McNab), Irons, Hughes, Vickers, Morrissey, Aldridge, Harvey, Cooper (Malkin), Nolan.

Preston NE (0) 0
Sheffield W (0) 2 *(Sheridan, Bart-Williams)* 14,337
Preston NE: Farnworth; Senior, Wrightson, Swann, Flynn, Hughes, Ashcroft, Cartwright, Thomas, Shaw, Joyce (Kerfoot).
Sheffield W: Woods; Nilsson, King, Palmer, Anderson, Harkes (Wilson), Bart-Williams, Sheridan (Hyde), Watson, Jemson, Worthington.

Sheffield U (1) 4 *(Hodges, Deane, Lake, Whitehouse)*
Luton T (0) 0 12,201
Sheffield U: Tracey; Lake, Cowan, Gannon, Hill, Beesley, Ward (Bryson), Hoyland (Gage), Hodges, Deane, Whitehouse.
Luton T: Chamberlain; James (Campbell), Harvey, Kamara, Dreyer, Peake, Telfer, Stein, Oakes, Pembridge, Preece.

Southampton (2) 2 *(Wood, Le Tissier)*
QPR (0) 0 13,710
Southampton: Flowers; Dodd, Adams, Horne, Hall, Wood, Le Tissier, Hurlock, Shearer, Dowie, Gray.
QPR: Stejskal; Bardsley, Wilson, Wilkins, Peacock, McDonald, Holloway (Penrice), Barker, Bailey, Wegerle, Sinton.

Sunderland (2) 3 *(Atkinson, Davenport, Byrne)*
Port Vale (0) 0 15,564
Sunderland: Norman; Kay, Rogan, Bennett, Hardyman, Owers (Sampson), Bracewell, Davenport, Armstrong, Byrne, Atkinson (Brady).
Port Vale: Grew; Mills S, Hughes, Porter, Aspin, Glover, Jalink (Webb), Van der Laan, Houchen, Foyle, Jeffers (Mills B).

Swindon T (2) 3 *(Shearer 2, Mitchell)*
Watford (1) 2 *(Blissett 2)* 10,133
Swindon T: Hammond; Kerslake, Jones, Ling, Calderwood, Taylor, Hazard, Shearer, Simpson (Summerbee), MacLaren, Mitchell.
Watford: James; Gibbs, Drysdale, Dublin, Holdsworth, Putney, Hessenthaler, Butler, Blissett, Porter, Nicholas (Bazeley).

Woking (0) 0
Hereford U (0) 0 4500
Woking: Batty; Mitchell, Cowler, Pratt, Baron, Wye S, Brown, Biggins, Milton, Friel, Collier.
Hereford U: Judge; Fry, Downs, Nebbeling, Devine, Vaughan (Titterton), Hall, Jones, Heritage, Narbett, Wade.

Wrexham (0) 2 *(Thomas, Watkin)*
Arsenal (1) 1 *(Smith)* 13,342
Wrexham: O'Keefe; Thackeray, Hardy, Carey, Thomas, Sertori, Davies, Owen, Connolly, Watkin, Phillips.
Arsenal: Seaman; Dixon, Winterburn, Hillier, O'Leary, Adams, Rocastle, Campbell, Smith, Merson, Carter (Groves).

5 JAN
Aston Villa (0) 0
Tottenham H (0) 0 29,316
Aston Villa: Sealey; Kubicki, Staunton (Ehiogu), Teale, McGrath, Richardson, Daley, Blake, Regis, Parker, Yorke.
Tottenham H: Thorstvedt; Fenwick, Van Den Hauwe, Sedgley, Howells, Mabbutt, Stewart, Walsh, Samways, Lineker, Allen.

Bristol R (2) 5 *(Alexander, Saunders 4)*
Plymouth Arg (0) 0 6767
Bristol R: Parkin; Alexander, Twentyman (Pounder), Yates, Maddison, Skinner, Cross, Reece, Browning, Saunders, Stewart.
Plymouth Arg: Wilmot; Spearing, Salman (Edworthy), Burrows, Morrison, Morgan, Barlow, Marshall, Regis, Fiore, Turner.

Charlton Ath (1) 3 *(Gatting, Leaburn, Grant)*
Barnet (1) 1 *(Carter)* 9618
Charlton Ath: Bolder; Pitcher, Barness, Bacon (Gritt), Webster, Gatting, Lee, Bumstead, Leaburn, Nelson (Grant), Walsh.
Barnet: Pape; Poole, Naylor (Murphy), Bodley, Howell, Horton, Wilson, Carter, Bull, Lowe (Willis), Cooper.

Notts Co (0) 2 *(Johnson T, Turner)*
Wigan Ath (0) 0 5913
Notts Co: Cherry; Palmer, Paris, Short Craig, Yates, Short Chris, Rideout, Turner, Harding (Lund), Agana (Slawson), Johnson T.
Wigan Ath: Adkins; Parkinson, Tankard, Johnson, Patterson, Langley, Jones, Connelly, Daley, Worthington, Griffiths (Powell).

6 JAN
Crewe Alex (0) 0
Liverpool (3) 4 *(McManaman, Barnes 3 (1 pen))* 7457
Crewe Alex: Greygoose; Wilson, McKearney, Carr (Sorvel), Callaghan, Walters, Hignett, Naylor, Jasper (Rose), Gardiner, Edwards.
Liverpool: Grobbelaar; Jones R, Molby, Nicol, Wright, Tanner, Saunders, Houghton (Marsh), McManaman, Barnes, Thomas.

THIRD ROUND REPLAYS
14 JAN
Cambridge U (0) 1 *(Dublin)*
Coventry C (0) 0 9864
Cambridge U: Vaughan; Fensome, Kimble, Dennis, Chapple (Heathcote), Daish, Rowett, Wilkins, Dublin, Taylor, Philpott.
Coventry C: Ogrizovic; Borrows, Sansom, Booty (Woods), Pearce, Billing, McGrath, Gynn, Rosario, Furlong, Hurst.

Derby Co (2) 2 *(Gee, Patterson)*
Burnley (0) 0 *abandoned after 76 mins—fog*

Hereford U (1) 2 *(Narbett, Brain)*
Woking (0) 1 *(Pratt) aet*   8679
Hereford U: Elliott; Wade, Downs, Theodosiou, Devine, Hall, Narbett, Lowndes, Fry (Titterton), Brain, Heritage.
Woking: Batty; Mitchell, Cowler, Pratt, Baron, Wye S, Brown (Parr), Biggins, Milton, Friel, Collier (Wye L).

Newcastle U (0)
Bournemouth (0) *abandoned after 17 mins—fog*

Tottenham H (0) 0
Aston Villa (1) 1 *(Yorke)*   25,462
Tottenham H: Thorstvedt; Fenwick (Bergsson), Van Den Hauwe, Sedgley, Walsh, Mabbutt, Stewart, Durie (Nayim), Samways, Lineker, Allen.
Aston Villa: Sealey; Kubicki, Staunton, Teale, McGrath, Richardson, Daley, Smith, Regis, Parker, Yorke.

West Ham U (0) 1 *(Morley)*
Farnborough T (0) 0   23,869
West Ham U: Miklosko; Breacker, Dicks, Gale, Foster, Thomas, Bishop, McAvennie, Brown, Morley, Slater.
Farnborough T: Power; Stemp, Baker (Rogers), Broome, Bye, Wigmore, Doherty, Holmes, Coney, Read, Fleming.

Wimbledon (0) 0
Bristol C (1) 1 *(May)*   3747
Wimbledon: Segers; McGee, Phelan, Barton, Scales, Fitzgerald, Newhouse, Earle, Fashanu, Sanchez, Anthrobus (Clarke).
Bristol C: Leaning; Caesar, Scott, Osman, Bryant, Aizlewood, Bent (Taylor), May, Morgan, Edwards, Gavin.

THIRD ROUND
15 JAN
Leeds U (0) 0
Manchester U (1) 1 *(Hughes)*   31,819
Leeds U: Lukic; Sterland, Dorigo, Hodge (Davison), Fairclough, Whyte, Williams (Whitlow), Wallace, Chapman, McAllister, Speed.
Manchester U: Schmeichel; Parker, Irwin, Bruce, Webb, Pallister, Kanchelskis, Ince, McClair, Hughes, Giggs.

THIRD ROUND REPLAYS
Hartlepool U (0) 0
Ipswich T (1) 2 *(Dozzell, Milton)*   8500
Hartlepool U: Hodge; Nobbs, Tinkler, McCreery (Southall), MacPhail, Tupling, Fletcher, Olsson, Baker, Honour, Dalton.
Ipswich T: Forrest; Johnson, Thompson, Stockwell, Wark, Linighan, Milton, Palmer, Whitton, Dozzell, Kiwomya.

Leyton Orient (0) 4 *(Harvey, Nugent 2, Castle (pen))*
Oldham Ath (1) 2 *(Adams, Palmer)*   10,056
Leyton Orient: Turner; Howard, Hackett, Burnett, Day, Whitbread, Harvey (Taylor), Castle, Jones, Nugent, Berry.
Oldham Ath: Hallworth; Fleming, Bernard, Henry, Barrett, Jobson, Adams, Marshall, Sharp, Palmer, Holden.

22 JAN
Newcastle U (1) 2 *(Hunt 2)*
Bournemouth (0) 2 *(Wood, Bond)*   25,954
Newcastle U: Wright; Watson, Thompson, O'Brien, Scott, Appleby, Clark, Peacock, Roche (Howey), Hunt, Brock.

Bournemouth: Bartram; Bond, Rowland, Morris, Mundee, O'Driscoll, Holmes (Brooks), Wood, Quinn, Case (Cooke), Ekoku.
aet; Bournemouth won 4–3 on penalties.

25 JAN
Derby Co (0) 2 *(Williams P, Ormondroyd)*
Burnley (0) 0   18,374
Derby Co: Shilton; Kavanagh, Forsyth, Williams G, Coleman, Comyn, Chalk, Ormondroyd, Gee, Williams P, McMinn.
Burnley: Pearce; Measham, Jakub, Davis, Pender, Farrell, Harper (Eli), Deary, Francis, Conroy, Lancashire (Yates).

FOURTH ROUND
Bolton W (0) 2 *(Walker, Philliskirk (pen))*
Brighton & HA (0) 1 *(Meade)*   12,635
Bolton W: Felgate; Stubbs, Burke, Kelly, Seagraves, Came, Green (Reeves), Patterson, Walker, Philliskirk, Darby.
Brighton & HA: Beeney; Crumplin, Gallacher, Chapman, McCarthy, Bissett, Robinson, Meade, Wade, Clarkson (Codner), Walker.

Cambridge U (0) 0
Swindon T (1) 3 *(Calderwood, Shearer 2)*   7428
Cambridge U: Vaughan; Fensome, Kimble, Bailie, Chapple, Daish, Cheetham, Wilkins, Dublin (Dennis), Taylor, Heaney (Rowett).
Swindon T: Digby; Kerslake, Bodin, Ling, Calderwood, Taylor, Hazard, Shearer, Simpson, MacLaren, Mitchell.

Leicester C (0) 1 *(Kitson)*
Bristol C (1) 2 *(Bent, Dziekanowski)*   19,313
Leicester C: Muggleton; Mills, Reid, Smith, Walsh, Fitzpatrick (Ward), Oldfield, Thompson, Wright, Willis, Kitson.
Bristol C: Leaning; Llewellyn, Scott, May, Bryant, Osman, Bent, Dziekanowski, Morgan (Allison), Aizlewood, Gavin.

Portsmouth (0) 2 *(Anderton 2)*
Leyton Orient (0) 0   16,138
Portsmouth: Knight; Awford, Beresford, Powell (Wigley), Symons, Butters, Neill, Kuhl, Whittingham, Burns, Anderton.
Leyton Orient: Turner; Howard, Hackett, Burnett, Day, Whitbread, Roeder, Castle, Jones (Cooper), Nugent, Otto (Achampong).

West Ham U (1) 2 *(Dicks, Morley)*
Wrexham (0) 2 *(Phillips, Jones L)*   24,712
West Ham U: Miklosko; Breacker, Dicks, Potts, Foster, Thomas, Keen, McAvennie (Small), Brown, Morley, Slater.
Wrexham: O'Keefe; Thackeray, Hardy, Carey, Thomas, Sertori, Davies, Owen, Connolly (Jones L), Watkin, Phillips.

26 JAN
Charlton Ath (0) 0
Sheffield U (0) 0   11,982
Charlton Ath: Bolder; Pitcher, Barness, Pardew, Webster, Gatting, Lee, Bumstead, Leaburn, Nelson, Walsh (Grant).
Sheffield U: Tracey; Hill, Barnes, Gannon, Gayle, Beesley, Hodges (Gage), Lake, Bryson, Deane, Whitehouse (Marwood).

Chelsea (0) 1 *(Allen)*
Everton (0) 0   21,152
Chelsea: Hitchcock; Hall (Stuart), Boyd, Jones, Elliott, Cundy, Le Saux, Townsend, Dixon, Allen, Wise.

Everton: Southall; Jackson, Ablett, Ebbrell, Watson, Keown, Nevin (Warzycha), Beardsley, Cottee, Ward, Beagrie.

Nottingham F (1) 2 *(Pearce, Sheringham)*
Hereford U (0) 0   24,259
Nottingham F: Crossley; Charles (Crosby), Pearce, Walker, Wassall, Keane, Black, Gemmill, Glover, Sheringham, Woan.

Hereford U: Elliott; McIntyre, Downs, Theodosiou, Devine, Lowndes, Hall, Brain, Heritage, Vaughan (Fry), Wade.

27 JAN

Southampton (0) 0
Manchester U (0) 0   19,506
Southampton: Flowers; Kenna, Adams, Horne, Hall, Ruddock, Le Tissier, Hurlock, Shearer, Dowie (Cockerill), Benali.

Manchester U: Schmeichel; Parker, Irwin, Donaghy, Webb, Pallister, Robson, Ince, McClair, Hughes, Blackmore (Giggs).

4 FEB

Notts Co (1) 2 *(Lund, Draper)*
Blackburn R (0) 1 *(Newell)*   12,173
Notts Co: Cherry; Palmer, Paris, Short Craig, Dryden, Draper, Thomas, Turner, Lund (Slawson), Bartlett, Johnson T.

Blackburn R: Mimms; Brown, Wright, Cowans, Hill, Moran, Reid (Hendry), Atkins, Speedie, Newell, Sellars (Garner).

Sheffield W (1) 1 *(Hirst)*
Middlesbrough (1) 2 *(Hendrie, Wilkinson)*   29,772
Sheffield W: Woods; Nilsson, King, Palmer, Warhurst, Pearson, Harkes, Hyde, Hirst, Williams (Anderson), Worthington (Francis).

Middlesbrough: Pears; Parkinson, Phillips, Kernaghan, Mohan, Mustoe, Pollock (Proctor), Peake, Wilkinson, Hendrie, Ripley (Payton).

FOURTH ROUND REPLAY

Wrexham (0) 0
West Ham U (1) 1 *(Foster)*   17,995
Wrexham: O'Keefe; Thackeray, Hardy, Carey, Thomas, Sertori, Davies (Jones L), Owen, Connolly, Watkin, Phillips.

West Ham U: Parks; Breacker, Dicks, Potts, Foster, Thomas, Keen, McAvennie (Martin), Brown, Small (Morley), Slater.

FOURTH ROUND

5 FEB

Bristol R (0) 1 *(Saunders)*
Liverpool (1) 1 *(Saunders)*   9464
Bristol R: Parkin; Alexander, Clark, Yates, Cross, Mehew, Skinner, Reece, White, Saunders, Pounder.

Liverpool: Grobbelaar; Jones R, Wright, Tanner, Burrows, Marsh, Houghton, Molby, Walters, McManaman, Saunders.

Derby Co (2) 3 *(Gee 2, Williams P)*
Aston Villa (4) 4 *(Yorke 3, Parker)*   22,452
Derby Co: Shilton; Kavanagh (Davidson), Forsyth, Williams G, Coleman, Comyn, Chalk (Stallard), Ormondroyd, Gee, Williams P, McMinn.

Aston Villa: Sealey; Kubicki, Small, Teale, McGrath, Richardson, Daley, Yorke, Regis, Parker, Froggatt (Carruthers).

Ipswich T (2) 3 *(Dozzell, Whitton, Kiwomya)*
Bournemouth (0) 0   17,193
Ipswich T: Forrest; Johnson, Thompson, Stockwell, Wark, Linighan, Milton, Palmer, Whitton, Dozzell, Kiwomya.

Bournemouth: Bartram; Bond, Rowland, Morris, Mundee, O'Driscoll, Brooks (Morrell), Wood, Quinn, Case, Ekoku (Holmes).

Norwich C (1) 2 *(Bowen, Fleck)*
Millwall (0) 1 *(Kerr)*   16,500
Norwich C: Walton; Phillips, Bowen, Sutton, Polston, Goss, Beckford, Fleck, Newman, Crook, Ullathorne.

Millwall: Davison; Cooper, Dawes, Stevens, Thompson, Rae, Colquhoun, Verveer, Kerr, McGinlay, Falco (Goodman).

Oxford U (0) 2 *(Simpson, Penney)*
Sunderland (2) 3 *(Byrne, Hardyman, Atkinson)*   9968
Oxford U: Veysey; Foster, Jackson, Lewis, Evans, Melville, Penney, Beauchamp (Allen), Aylott, Durnin (Robinson), Simpson.

Sunderland: Norman; Kay, Rogan, Bennett, Hardyman, Davenport, Bracewell, Rush, Ball, Byrne (Pascoe), Atkinson.

FOURTH ROUND REPLAYS

Manchester U (1) 2 *(Kanchelskis, McClair)*
Southampton (2) 2 *(Gray, Shearer)*   33,414
Manchester U: Schmeichel; Parker, Irwin, Donaghy (Sharpe), Webb, Pallister, Robson, Ince, McClair, Giggs, Kanchelskis (Hughes).

Southampton: Flowers; Kenna, Adams, Horne, Hall, Ruddock, Le Tissier, Cockerill, Shearer, Gray (Maddison), Benali.
aet; Southampton won 4–2 on penalties.

Sheffield U (3) 3 *(Deane, Gayle, Bradshaw)*
Charlton Ath (0) 1 *(Gatting)*   15,779
Sheffield U: Tracey; Gage, Barnes, Gannon, Gayle, Beesley (Hill), Bradshaw (Whitehouse), Lake, Bryson, Deane, Hodges.

Charlton Ath: Bolder; Pitcher, Barness, Pardew, Webster, Gatting, Lee (Gorman), Bumstead (Minto), Leaburn, Nelson, Walsh.

11 FEB

Liverpool (0) 2 *(McManaman, Saunders)*
Bristol R (1) 1 *(Saunders)*   30,142
Liverpool: Grobbelaar; Jones R, Burrows, Nicol, Wright, Marsh, Saunders, Houghton, Rosenthal (Rush), Redknapp, McManaman.

Bristol R: Parkin; Alexander, Clark, Yates, Cross (Boothroyd), Mehew, Skinner, Reece, White, Saunders, Pounder (Stewart).

FIFTH ROUND

15 FEB

Chelsea (1) 1 *(Stuart)*
Sheffield U (0) 0   34,447
Chelsea: Hitchcock; Hall, Myers, Jones (Wilson), Elliott, Cundy, Le Saux, Townsend, Cascarino, Allen (Dixon), Stuart.

Sheffield U: Kite; Gage, Barnes, Gannon, Gayle, Beesley, Bradshaw, Lake (Hill), Bryson (Hodges), Deane, Whitehouse.

Norwich C (2) 3 *(Sutton 2, Phillips)*
Notts Co (0) 0   14,511
Norwich C: Walton; Culverhouse, Woodthorpe, Butterworth, Polston, Goss, Fox, Fleck, Newman, Sutton, Phillips.
Notts Co: Cherry; Palmer, Paris, Short Craig, Short Chris, Draper, Thomas, Turner, Harding (Johnson T), Bartlett, Agana (Dryden).

Nottingham F (1) 4 *(Llewellyn (og), Clough, Pearce, Sheringham (pen))*
Bristol C (0) 1 *(Dziekanowski)*   24,615
Nottingham F: Crossley; Laws, Pearce, Walker, Wassall, Keane, Crosby, Gemmill, Clough (Glover), Sheringham (Charles), Black.
Bristol C: Leaning; Llewellyn, Scott, Aizlewood, Bryant, Osman, Bent, Shelton, Allison, Dziekanowski, Edwards.

Portsmouth (0) 1 *(Whittingham)*
Middlesbrough (0) 1 *(Kernaghan)*   18,138
Portsmouth: Knight; Awford, Beresford, Powell, Symons, Murray (Chamberlain), Neill, Kuhl, Whittingham, Burns, Anderton.
Middlesbrough: Pears; Parkinson, Phillips, Kernaghan, Mohan, Mustoe, Pollock (Proctor), Peake, Wilkinson, Hendrie (Payton), Ripley.

Sunderland (0) 1 *(Byrne)*
West Ham U (0) 1 *(Small)*   25,475
Sunderland: Norman; Kay, Rogan, Bennett (Pascoe), Hardyman, Davenport, Bracewell, Ball, Armstrong, Byrne, Atkinson.
West Ham U: Parks; Breacker, Dicks, Potts, Foster, Atteveld, Keen, Brown, Small, Allen, Slater.

16 FEB
Bolton W (0) 2 *(Walker, Green)*
Southampton (2) 2 *(Hall 2)*   20,136
Bolton W: Felgate; Spooner, Burke, Kelly, Seagraves, Came, Brown (Green), Patterson (Reeves), Walker, Philliskirk, Darby.
Southampton: Flowers; Kenna, Adams (Lee), Horne, Hall, Ruddock, Le Tissier, Cockerill, Shearer, Gray, Benali.

Ipswich T (0) 0
Liverpool (0) 0   26,140
Ipswich T: Forrest; Johnson, Thompson, Stockwell, Wark, Linighan, Milton, Palmer, Whitton, Dozzell, Kiwomya.
Liverpool: Grobbelaar; Jones R, Burrows, Nicol, Wright, Marsh, Saunders, Houghton, Rush, Redknapp (Kozma), McManaman.

Swindon T (0) 1 *(Mitchell)*
Aston Villa (1) 2 *(Yorke, Froggatt)*   16,402
Swindon T: Hammond; Kerslake, Bodin, Ling, Calderwood, Taylor, Hazard, Shearer, Jones (Sampson), MacLaren, Mitchell.
Aston Villa: Sealey; Kubicki, Staunton, Teale, McGrath, Richardson, Daley, Yorke (Small), Regis, Parker, Froggatt.

FIFTH ROUND REPLAYS
26 FEB
Liverpool (1) 3 *(Houghton, Molby, McManaman)*
Ipswich T (0) 2 *(Johnson, Dozzell) aet*   27,355
Liverpool: Grobbelaar; Jones R, Harkness (Kozma), Nicol, Wright, Marsh, Saunders, Houghton, Walters (Rosenthal), Molby, McManaman.

Ipswich T: Forrest; Johnson, Thompson, Stockwell, Wark (Zondervan), Linighan, Milton, Palmer (Goddard), Whitton, Dozzell, Kiwomya.

Middlesbrough (2) 2 *(Wilkinson 2)*
Portsmouth (2) 4 *(Clarke 2, Anderton 2)*   19,479
Middlesbrough: Pears; Parkinson, Phillips, Pollock, Mohan, Mustoe, Peake, Payton (Slaven), Wilkinson, Hendrie, Ripley.
Portsmouth: Knight; Awford, Beresford, Powell, Symons, Butters, Neill, Kuhl, Clarke, Burns (Aspinall), Anderton.

Southampton (1) 3 *(Shearer, Horne 2)*
Bolton W (1) 2 *(Walker, Darby) aet*   18,009
Southampton: Flowers; Dodd, Benali, Horne, Hall, Ruddock, Le Tissier, Cockerill, Shearer, Gray (Moody), Hurlock.
Bolton W: Felgate; Spooner, Burke, Kelly, Seagraves, Came, Green (Reeves), Patterson (Stubbs), Walker, Philliskirk, Darby.

West Ham U (1) 2 *(Allen 2)*
Sunderland (2) 3 *(Byrne 2, Rush)*   25,830
West Ham U: Parks; Breacker, Dicks, Potts, Foster, Atteveld (Morley), Bishop, Keen, Small, Allen, Slater.
Sunderland: Norman; Kay, Rogan, Rush, Hardyman, Davenport (Brady), Bracewell, Ball, Armstrong, Byrne, Atkinson.

SIXTH ROUND
7 MAR
Portsmouth (1) 1 *(McLoughlin)*
Nottingham F (0) 0   25,402
Portsmouth: Knight; Awford, Beresford, Powell (Aspinall), Symons, Burns, Neill, Kuhl, Clarke (Whittingham), McLoughlin, Anderton.
Nottingham F: Crossley; Laws, Pearce, Walker, Wassall, Keane, Crosby, Gemmill, Clough, Sheringham (Chettle), Glover.

Southampton (0) 0
Norwich C (0) 0   20,088
Southampton: Flowers; Dodd, Benali, Horne, Moore, Ruddock, Le Tissier, Cockerill, Shearer, Dowie, Hurlock.
Norwich C: Walton; Culverhouse, Woodthorpe, Butterworth, Polston, Goss, Fox, Fleck, Newman, Sutton, Phillips.

8 MAR
Liverpool (0) 1 *(Thomas)*
Aston Villa (0) 0   29,109
Liverpool: Grobbelaar; Jones R, Venison, Nicol, Whelan, Wright, Saunders, Houghton, Thomas (Molby), Barnes, McManaman (Rosenthal).
Aston Villa: Spink; Blake (Kubicki), Staunton, Teale, McGrath, Richardson, Daley, Parker, Regis, Atkinson, Yorke (Froggatt).

9 MAR
Chelsea (1) 1 *(Allen)*
Sunderland (0) 1 *(Byrne)*   33,948
Chelsea: Hitchcock; Hall, Myers, Wilson, Elliott, Cundy, Stuart, Townsend, Dixon, Allen, Wise.
Sunderland: Norman; Kay, Rogan, Bennett (Sampson), Hardyman, Rush, Bracewell, Davenport, Armstrong, Byrne, Atkinson (Brady).

SIXTH ROUND REPLAYS
18 MAR

Norwich C (0) 2 *(Newman, Sutton)*
Southampton (1) 1 *(Ruddock) aet*   21,017

Norwich C: Walton; Culverhouse, Woodthorpe (Crook), Butterworth, Polston, Goss, Fox, Fleck (Beckford), Newman, Sutton, Bowen.

Southampton: Flowers; Dodd (Kenna), Benali, Horne, Moore, Ruddock, Le Tissier, Cockerill, Shearer, Dowie, Hurlock.

Sunderland (1) 2 *(Davenport, Armstrong)*
Chelsea (0) 1 *(Wise)*   26,039

Sunderland: Norman; Kay, Rogan, Ball, Hardyman (Ord), Rush, Bracewell, Davenport, Armstrong, Byrne, Atkinson.

Chelsea: Beasant; Clarke, Sinclair, Jones, Elliott, Cundy (Allen), Le Saux (Stuart), Townsend, Dixon, Cascarino, Wise.

SEMI-FINALS
5 APR

Liverpool (0) 1 *(Whelan)*
Portsmouth (0) 1 *(Anderton) aet at Highbury*   41,869

Liverpool: Grobbelaar; Jones R, Burrows (Venison), Nicol, Whelan, Wright, McManaman, Houghton (Marsh), Rush, Barnes, Thomas.

Portsmouth: Knight; Awford, Beresford, McLoughlin (Whittingham), Symons, Burns, Neill, Kuhl, Chamberlain (Aspinall), Clarke, Anderton.

Sunderland (1) 1 *(Byrne)*
Norwich C (0) 0 *at Hillsborough*   40,102

Sunderland: Norman; Kay, Rogan, Ball (Bennett), Hardyman, Bracewell, Davenport, Rush, Armstrong, Byrne, Atkinson.

Norwich C: Walton; Culverhouse, Woodthorpe, Butterworth, Polston, Goss, Fox, Fleck, Newman, Sutton (Sutch), Bowen.

SEMI-FINAL REPLAY
13 APR

Portsmouth (0) 0
Liverpool (0) 0 *at Villa Park*   40,077

Portsmouth: Knight; Awford, Beresford, McLoughlin (Aspinall), Daniel, Neill, Symons, Burns, Kuhl, Clarke (Whittingham), Anderton.

Liverpool: Grobbelaar; Jones R (Walters), Burrows, Nicol, Whelan (Venison), Wright, Saunders, Molby, Rush, Barnes, Thomas.

aet; Liverpool won 3–1 on penalties.

FINAL at Wembley
9 MAY

Liverpool (0) 2 *(Thomas, Rush)*
Sunderland (0) 0   79,544

Liverpool: Grobbelaar; Jones R, Burrows, Nicol, Molby, Wright, Saunders, Houghton, Rush, McManaman, Thomas.

Sunderland: Norman; Owers, Ball, Bennett, Rogan, Rush (Hardyman), Bracewell, Davenport, Armstrong, Byrne, Atkinson (Hawke).

Referee: P. Don (Middlesex).

Anton Rogan (left) and Gary Owers attempt to dispossess Liverpool striker Dean Saunders in the 1992 FA Cup Final. (Allsport)

THE SCOTTISH SEASON 1991–92

This was a season with some good and some bad and a fair amount pretty indifferent. Which would you like first?

It has to be said that we did not do well in the European club events. Celtic were the only team of the four to make any headway at all, and they were comprehensively defeated in the next round. Rangers again met strong opposition, but one hopes that they may soon find their feet amongst the elite; both Rangers and Motherwell went out on the 'away goals' rule, but Aberdeen lost both legs of their match. It was a sad chapter in foreign competition.

It was not long before the Skol Cup was under way. This popular competition, with the certainty of a result in every game, usually throws up a few surprises. In the early stages Brechin only just succumbed to St Mirren after penalties, while Raith Rovers disposed of Motherwell in no uncertain manner; Ayr beat St Johnstone, and Airdrie enjoyed a well-deserved victory at Pittodrie. They went on to put out Celtic – after penalties – and were only just stopped from reaching the final by a late penalty for Dunfermline. The Pars met Hibs in the final at Hampden, and the Edinburgh side were much the better on the occasion and thus clinched their place in Europe for next season.

The Scottish Cup saw a determined sally by the Highland League clubs. Champions Ross County went out in the second round having travelled about as far as footballers can in this country for a game: they had to cross the Tweed into England where they lost in a high-scoring game. Peterhead were within a few minutes of defeating Cowdenbeath, but they lost the replay convincingly. It was left to Caledonian and Huntly to carry the flag into the third round, where they disposed of the Second Division leaders at the time, Dumbarton and Clyde. Huntly enjoyed a home tie against Airdrie and it was one of the events of the season: although eventually the Broomfield team proved too strong, Huntly went down with flying colours. Caley went one better: two goals down to St Johnstone in Inverness, they staged a wonderful fight back, and the draw gave them the chance of a replay at McDiarmid Park. There the Premier Division team won easily in the end, but the game had fired the imagination of the North, and the A9 was full that evening. Aberdeen again lost at Pittodrie, in the third round, having drawn Rangers. It was a close game, and it is always a pity to see the giants at each other in such an early round. The quarter-finals should have led to semi-finals amongst the four teams topping the league at the time but it did not quite work out that way: Airdrie, having a memorable season in the cups, took out Hibs, and followed that by defeating Hearts in the semis after – it must be said – one very dreary game and a less drab replay. Meantime Rangers had disposed of Celtic in the other semi-final. It was an appalling night, and called for a good deal of character from the players. Ten-man Rangers were that keen to win, and they did. It was not Celtic's night: they hit the woodwork several times, but the goal that did come was from Ally McCoist. So to the final, always a great occasion, and one which both teams savoured. Rangers, without Cup success for a long spell, were not to be denied; but Airdrie went at it hard, and if the 2-1 scoreline flattered them, their effort was certainly rewarded.

The Premier Division had its interest. It was fairly soon obvious that there were the usual 'top half' and 'bottom half'. The Old Firm, the New Firm and the two Edinburgh teams occupied the upper part, and were soon away from the others. After that it was almost a double competition in one. At the top Hearts played tremendously well and held top spot into the New Year. Then Rangers drew ominously ahead, and there was no catching them. Celtic put a solid string of results together late on to overtake Hearts. Second position in the table was important, for it meant a passport to the European games; and both teams were out of the Cup. On the final league day, Celtic needed only a draw with their vastly superior goal difference, but they lost to Hibs while Hearts made no mistake against Falkirk. Hearts deserved the position after an excellent showing throughout the long programme, but Celtic must have been sick at heart to have stumbled after their fine run and when on the brink of success. However, their dismay was not to be long-lived, for soon they learnt that, because of the expansion in countries wishing to enter teams, Scotland was to have another entry to the UEFA Cup. Celtic breathed a sigh of relief, and we all hope that they can take advantage of their luck. Hibs, after a fine start, fell back but a strong finish saw them above Aberdeen. The Dons lost faith in themselves and did not have a good season. The new manager has a task ahead of him, but, with a bevy of good youngsters available and a solid backing of experience, he can hope to challenge for the top again, particularly if he can avoid the crippling injury list which the club sustained this season. Dundee United were enigmatic, and too often playing below their obvious capacity. They too have a fine squad of home-bred young players, and, with a gain in experience, the team's time must come again soon. They finished in fourth place in the league, but still deserved the report 'could do better'.

So much for the top end; what of the rest? Newcomers Falkirk and Airdrie, many experts' choice for the immediate drop, surprised many if not themselves and were soon comfortably placed above Dunfermline and St Mirren. The Pars had a poor league season and never quite came to terms with themselves. The new management team found matters beyond them, and early on they were destined for the First Division where they may hope to regroup and soon return to the top stream. The Buddies also looked doomed, but while they held on to hope for a long time, they ultimately failed to avoid the eleventh place. The other four teams shuffled around close to each other, but it was Airdrie who in the end took seventh place and thus added to their cups laurels.

In the First Division, Dundee made the pace for most of the season. For some time, Kilmarnock and Raith Rovers were in the hunt, but during the last weeks it became a race of three teams for the two places. Dundee were the best placed always, but Partick Thistle and Hamilton Academical fought it out till the end, and finally Partick just pipped Hamilton on goal difference while Dundee took the championship flag. At the bottom end of the table, Forfar never recovered from an abysmal start and they occupied the foot of the table for very nearly the whole season. Montrose dropped to eleventh, and despite their efforts, they could not catch the others, of whom Meadowbank were the nearest and most vulnerable.

The Second Division, too, had an exciting climax. Clyde were in the early lead, but they fell away after Christmas, and while East Fife hovered in the promotion area for a time, they managed to lose several games when it really mattered, and it was left to Dumbarton to forge to the front, with Cowdenbeath never far away; meantime Alloa had a splendid run, and swept up the table. Dumbarton secured their promotion a couple of games out, but on the final afternoon, Alloa played Cowdenbeath in a decider for the second promotion place. In front of a crowd of over 5000, there was one of those no-scoring draws which is full of excitement and interest. It was enough to confirm Cowdenbeath's return to the First Division.

There can be no doubt about which was the best team in Scotland: Rangers were well ahead of the rest, and they took the long season in their stride with their large playing squad which could cope with the temporary absence of two or three players. Although they lost the odd game, they were not often at a disadvantage, and their steady defence and inventive midfield gave their forwards ample opportunity. In Ally McCoist and Mark Hateley they had a partnership which took full advantage of the situation, and the former's quickness to take a chance made him the first Scot to win the coveted Golden Boot – a real boost to player, club and country, and a very popular award to a man who contrives to pass on his enjoyment of the game wherever he goes. Rangers yearn for European success, and perhaps they now have the team and the experience to make a serious challenge.

There has been a good deal of dissatisfaction, particularly amongst the upper echelon of clubs, with the forty-four game league. Again there are talks of breakaways and reorganizations. One cannot but have sympathy for those clubs who attract nearly all the paying public to their games and yet command only a small part of the league's voting power. The tail continues to wag the dog, and it is high time that there was a sensible and if possible unbiased assessment of the present day needs of football – not forgetting the fans. It would be good to see an end to the closed shop of the league teams, and the introduction, possibly, of some new blood, with teams having to fight to retain their places at the foot of the Second Division. But there seems little hope of such an assessment being made, certainly with any effect.

Before the international season switched to Sweden the Under-21s had a magnificent attack on the European stronghold, and were within a whisker of reaching the final.

ALAN ELLIOTT

ABERDEEN
Premier Division

Year Formed: 1903. *Ground & Address:* Pittodrie Stadium, Pittodrie St, Aberdeen AB21QH. *Telephone:* 0224 632328.
Ground Capacity: total: 21,779. seated: All. *Size of Pitch:* 110yd × 72yd.
Chairman: Richard M. Donald. *Secretary:* Ian J. Taggart. *Commercial Manager:* Dave Johnston.
Manager: Willie Miller. *Assist. Manager:* Drew Jarvie. *Physio:* David Wylie. *Coach:* Neil Cooper.
Managers since 1975: Ally MacLeod; Billy McNeill; Alex Ferguson; Ian Porterfield; Alex Smith and Jocky Scott; Willie
Miller. *Club Nickname(s):* The Dons. *Previous Grounds:* None.
Record Attendance: 45,061 v Hearts, Scottish Cup 4th rd; 13 Mar, 1954.
Record Transfer Fee received: £970,000 for David Robertson to Rangers (July 1991).
Record Transfer Fee paid: £650,000 for Hans Gillhaus from PSV Eindhoven, November 1989.
Record Victory: 13-0 v Peterhead, Scottish Cup; 9 Feb, 1923.
Record Defeat: 0-8 v Celtic, Division I; 30 Jan, 1965.
Most Capped Players: Alex McLeish, 76, Scotland.
Most League Appearances: 556: Willie Miller, 1973–90.

ABERDEEN 1991–92 LEAGUE RECORD

Match No.	Date		Venue	Opponents	Result		H/T Score	Lg. Pos.	Goalscorers	Atten- dance
1	Aug	10	A	Airdrieonians	W	2-1	0-1	—	Irvine, Gillhaus	6337
2		14	A	Falkirk	W	1-0	0-0	—	Booth	8462
3		17	H	Dunfermline Ath	W	3-1	1-0	2	Bett, Grant, Jess	13,849
4		24	H	Celtic	W	1-0	1-0	1	Gillhaus	20,503
5		31	A	Dundee U	D	0-0	0-0	1		11,961
6	Sept	7	H	St Johnstone	L	1-2	1-0	4	Van de Ven	12,071
7		14	A	Motherwell	W	1-0	1-0	4	Gillhaus	6452
8		21	H	Hibernian	D	1-1	1-0	4	Grant	11,850
9		28	A	Rangers	W	2-0	0-0	2	Jess, Grant	36,330
10	Oct	5	H	St Mirren	W	4-1	2-0	1	Ten Caat, Grant, Irvine, Mason	10,154
11		9	A	Hearts	L	0-1	0-1	—		15,569
12		12	H	Airdrieonians	W	3-1	1-0	3	Ten Caat, Jess 2	8998
13		19	A	Dunfermline Ath	D	0-0	0-0	3		5157
14		26	A	St Johnstone	W	3-1	1-1	3	Van de Ven, Jess, Mason	5682
15		30	H	Motherwell	W	3-1	0-0	—	Winnie, Mason, Gillhaus	9092
16	Nov	2	H	Dundee U	L	0-1	0-1	3		13,728
17		9	A	Celtic	L	1-2	1-1	4	Jess	36,837
18		16	A	St Mirren	W	1-0	0-0	3	McIntyre (og)	3634
19		20	H	Hearts	L	0-2	0-1	—		15,338
20		23	A	Hibernian	L	0-1	0-0	4		8942
21		30	H	Falkirk	D	1-1	0-1	5	Gillhaus (pen)	10,614
22	Dec	4	H	Rangers	L	2-3	1-2	—	Ten Caat, Irvine	20,081
23		7	A	Airdrieonians	L	0-2	0-1	6		3071
24		14	A	St Johnstone	W	4-1	1-1	5	Jess, Grant, Booth, Roddie	9292
25		28	H	Celtic	D	2-2	2-0	5	Ten Caat, Jess	20,422
26	Jan	1	A	Dundee U	L	0-4	0-0	—		7777
27		4	H	St Mirren	D	0-0	0-0	6		8774
28		11	A	Hearts	W	4-0	1-0	6	Jess 2, Booth, Mason	16,291
29		14	A	Motherwell	D	3-3	1-2	—	Kane, Jess, Roddie	5221
30		18	A	Falkirk	D	2-2	0-2	5	Mason, Booth	5122
31	Feb	1	H	Dunfermline Ath	D	1-1	0-0	5	Jess	7549
32		8	H	Hibernian	L	0-1	0-0	5		9568
33		25	A	Rangers	D	0-0	0-0	—		38,513
34		29	A	St Mirren	W	2-0	2-0	5	Mason, Smith	3853
35	Mar	14	A	Celtic	L	0-1	0-0	6		29,380
36		18	H	Hearts	W	2-0	1-0	—	Ten Caat, Mason	10,581
37		21	H	Dundee U	L	0-2	0-1	5		10,350
38		28	H	Airdrieonians	W	1-0	0-0	5	Irvine	6805
39	Apr	4	A	Dunfermline Ath	D	0-0	0-0	5		3033
40		8	A	St Johnstone	D	0-0	0-0	—		4524
41		11	H	Motherwell	W	2-0	2-0	4	Grant, Kane	6902
42		18	A	Hibernian	D	1-1	0-0	4	Paatelainen	6777
43		25	H	Falkirk	D	1-1	0-1	5	Booth	6461
44	May	2	H	Rangers	L	0-2	0-1	6		16,580

Final League Position: 6

League (55): Jess 12, Mason 7, Grant 6, Booth 5, Gillhaus 5 (1 pen), Ten Caat 5, Irvine 4, Kane 2, Roddie 2, Van de
Ven 2, Bett 1, Paatelainen 1, Smith 1, Winnie 1, own goal 1. *Scottish Cup* (0). *Skol Cup* (4): Booth 1, Grant 1, Van
de Ven 1, Winnie 1.

Most League Goals in Season (Individual): 38: Benny Yorston, Division I; 1929–30.
Most Goals Overall (Individual): 199: Joe Harper.

Honours
League Champions: Division I 1954–55. Premier Division 1979–80, 1983–84, 1984–85; *Runners-up:* Division I 1910–11, 1936–37, 1955–56, 1970–71, 1971–72. Premier Division 1977–78, 1980–81, 1981–82, 1988–89, 1989–90, 1990–91.
Scottish Cup Winners: 1947, 1970, 1982, 1983, 1984, 1986, 1990; *Runners-up:* 1937, 1953, 1954, 1959, 1967, 1978.
League Cup Winners: 1955–56, 1976–77, 1985–86, 1989–90; *Runners-up:* 1946–47, 1978–79, 1979–80, 1987–88, 1988–89.
Drybrough Cup Winners: 1971, 1980.
European: *European Cup* 12 matches (1980–81, 1984–85, 1985–86); *Cup Winners Cup Winners:* 1982–83. Semi-finals 1983–84. 35 matches (1967–68, 1970–71, 1978–79, 1982–83, 1983–84, 1986–87, 1990–91; *UEFA Cup* 34 matches (*Fairs Cup:* 1968–69. *UEFA Cup:* 1971–72, 1972–73, 1973–74, 1977–78, 1979–80, 1981–82, 1987–88, 1988–89, 1989–90, 1991–92).
Club colours: Shirt, Shorts, Stockings: Red with white trim.

Snelders, T	Wright, S	Connor, R	Grant, B	Irvine, B	McKimmie, S	Van de Ven, P	Bett, J	Jess, E	Ten Caat, T	Gillhaus, H	Winnie, D	Booth, S	Watson, Gregg	Van der Ark, W	Cameron, I	Mason, P	Watson, Graham	Gibson, A	Roddie, A	Smith, G	Kane, P	Watt, M	McLeish, A	Ferguson, G	Humphries, M	Paatelainen, M	Match No.
1	2	3	4	5	6	7	8	9†	10*	11	12	14															1
1	2	10	4	5	6	7†	8		14	11	3	9*	12														2
1	2	10	4	5	6	12	8		14	11	3	9*	7†														3
1	2		4	5	6	7	8	9*	10†	11	3	14	12														4
1	2	10	4*	5	6	12	8	9†		11	3	14	7														5
1	2*	10	4	5	6	12	8	9		11	3	14	7†														6
1	2	3	4	5	6	12	8	9	10*	11		14	7†														7
1	2		4	5	6	7	8	9	10*	11	3†	14	12														8
1	2	3		4	5	6	7†	8	10	11*		9	12		14												9
1	2	3		4	5†	6	7	8	10	11		9*	12		14												10
1	2	3		4	5	6	7*	8	10	11		9†	12		14												11
1	2	3		4†	5	6	7	8	10	11		9*	12			14											12
1	2	3		4*		6	8	9†	10	11		14	5		12	7											13
1			2	5	6	4	8	9*	10	11†	3	14	12		7												14
1			2	5	6	4*	8	9†	10	11	3	14	12		7												15
1			2	5	6	9	8		10	11†	3	14	4		12	7*											16
1				5	7	4*	8	9	10	11	3		6	12		2†	14										17
1				5	6	4	8	9	10†	11*	3	12	2		14												18
1				5	6	4	8	9†	10	11	3	12	2			7*	14										19
1				5	6	7	8	9	10	11	3		2		12							4*					20
				5	6	7	8	9	10†	11	3		2		12	14			4*			1					21
1					6	7*	8	9	10†	11	3		2		14	12			4			5					22
1		4			6	7	8	9	10†	11*	3		2		14	12						5					23
1	4*	5				7	8	9†	10	11	3		14			6	2				12						24
1		4	6		2	7	8	9†	10	12	3		14								11*	5					25
1		4	6			7	8	9	10†	11	3*	14	2								12	5					26
1		4	6		2	7	8	9†	10	11	3	14										5					27
1		4†	6		2	7	8	9	10	11	3	14	12									5*					28
1	6	4		5	2	7*	8	9†	10	11	3	14									12						29
1	6	4		5	2	7	8	9*	10	11	3	12															30
1	6	4		5	2	7		9*	10	11	3	8	12†							14							31
1	6	4		5	2	7		9	10†	11	3	8								14							32
1	6	4		5	2	7†	8		10	11	3	8								14							33
	6	4		5	2	7*	8	9	10	11	3		12									1					34
1	6	4		5	2	7	8	9	10†	11	3		14														35
1	6	4		5	2	7	8	9†	10	11	3		14														36
1	6	4		5	2	7	8	9†	10	11*	3		12								14						37
1		4		5	2	7	8	9	10	6	3	11															38
1	6	4			2	7*	8	9	10		3	11	12							5							39
1	6	4		5	2	7	8	9	10†		3	11	14														40
1	6	4		5	2	7*	8	9	10†	11	3		12								14						41
1	6	4		5	2	7	8	9†	12	11	3		10*		14												42
1	6	4		5	2	7†	8	9	10*	11	3				14	12											43
1	6	4		5	2	7†		9	12	11*	3	8			14	10											44
42	23	11	33	41	39	20	38	33	28	24	27	21	4	7	4	28	4	2	1	15	22	2	7	0	2	6	
			+3s				+6s	+2s	+5s	+1s	+12s	+6s				+11s	+2s	+3s		+5s	+3s		+9s	+1s	+3s	+4s	

AIRDRIEONIANS — Premier Division

Year Formed: 1878. *Ground & Address:* Broomfield Park, Gartlea Rd, Airdrie M16 9JL. *Telephone:* 0236 62067.
Ground Capacity: 10,250. seated: 1350. *Size of Pitch:* 112yd × 67yd.
Chairman and Secretary: George W. Peat CA. *Commercial Manager:* David McParland.
Manager: Alex MacDonald. *Assistant Manager:* Ian Bird. *Physio:* Harrison Stevenson. *Coach:* Joe Craig.
Managers since 1975: I. McMillan; J. Stewart; R. Watson; W. Munro; A. MacLeod; D. Whiteford; G. McQueen; J.
Bone. *Club Nickname(s):* The Diamonds or The Waysiders. *Previous Grounds:* Mavisbank.
Record Attendance: 24,000 v Hearts, Scottish Cup; 8 Mar, 1952.
Record Transfer Fee received: £200,000 for Sandy Clark to West Ham U, May 1982.
Record Transfer Fee paid: £175,000 for Owen Coyle from Clydebank, February 1990.
Record Victory: 15-1 v Dundee Wanderers, Division II; 1 Dec, 1894.

AIRDRIEONIANS 1991–92 LEAGUE RECORD

Match No.	Date		Venue	Opponents	Result	H/T Score	Lg. Pos.	Goalscorers	Attendance
1	Aug	10	H	Aberdeen	L 1-2	1-0	—	Lawrence	6337
2		13	H	Hearts	L 2-3	1-2	—	Conn, Lawrence (pen)	6326
3		17	A	St Mirren	W 2-1	0-0	7	Lawrence, Coyle	3927
4		24	H	Motherwell	L 0-1	0-0	8		5066
5		31	A	Falkirk	L 2-3	1-2	9	Watson, Coyle	4955
6	Sept	7	H	Hibernian	L 0-1	0-0	10		5621
7		14	A	Dunfermline Ath	W 2-1	2-1	10	Stewart, Watson	4515
8		21	A	Celtic	L 1-3	1-1	10	Black	17,552
9		28	H	St Johnstone	L 1-2	1-0	10	Balfour	3153
10	Oct	5	H	Rangers	L 0-4	0-3	10		11,101
11		8	A	Dundee U	D 0-0	0-0	—		5763
12		12	A	Aberdeen	L 1-3	0-1	11	Gray	8998
13		19	H	St Mirren	W 4-1	1-0	10	Boyle, Coyle, Watson, Kirkwood	2590
14		26	H	Dundee U	L 1-3	0-1	10	Black (pen)	1954
15	Nov	2	A	Falkirk	D 0-0	0-0	10		4338
16		5	A	Hibernian	D 2-2	1-1	—	Kirkwood 2 (2 pens)	6622
17		9	A	Motherwell	W 2-1	1-0	10	Watson, Balfour	5509
18		12	H	Dunfermline Ath	W 3-1	2-1	10	Coyle 2, Smith A	1975
19		16	A	Rangers	L 0-4	0-1	10		36,934
20		23	H	Celtic	L 0-3	0-0	10		10,102
21		30	A	Hearts	L 0-1	0-0	10		12,073
22	Dec	4	A	St Johnstone	L 0-1	0-1	—		3582
23		7	A	Aberdeen	W 2-0	1-0	10	Coyle 2	3071
24		14	H	Hibernian	L 0-3	0-0	10		3784
25		28	H	Motherwell	W 2-0	0-0	10	Coyle, Lawrence	4723
26	Jan	1	A	Falkirk	W 3-0	1-0	—	Kirkwood 2 (1 pen), Smith A	5446
27		4	A	Rangers	D 0-0	0-0	10		12,276
28		11	A	Dundee U	L 1-2	0-0	10	Kirkwood	6056
29		15	A	Dunfermline Ath	D 0-0	0-0	—		3429
30		18	H	Hearts	W 2-1	2-0	10	Lawrence 2	5930
31	Feb	1	A	St Mirren	L 1-4	0-2	10	Kirkwood	3435
32		8	A	Celtic	L 0-2	0-1	10		18,845
33		22	H	St Johnstone	L 0-3	0-1	10		2921
34		29	A	Rangers	L 0-5	0-2	10		40,568
35	Mar	14	A	Motherwell	W 3-0	1-0	10	Jack, Conn, Boyle	5065
36		17	H	Dundee U	W 1-0	1-0	—	Kirkwood	2533
37		21	H	Falkirk	D 2-2	0-2	10	Coyle 2	4214
38		28	A	Aberdeen	L 0-1	0-0	10		6805
39	Apr	7	A	Hibernian	W 2-0	1-0	—	Conn, Lawrence	3254
40		11	A	Dunfermline Ath	W 3-2	0-2	10	Boyle, Conn, Kirkwood (pen)	1912
41		18	H	Celtic	D 0-0	0-0	10		8296
42		21	H	St Mirren	D 1-1	0-0	—	Smith A	2031
43		25	A	Hearts	D 2-2	1-1	8	Conn, Coyle	5310
44	May	2	A	St Johnstone	D 1-1	0-0	7	Smith A	3699

Final League Position: 7

League (50): Coyle 11, Kirkwood 9 (4 pens), Lawrence 7 (1 pen), Conn 5, Smith A 4, Watson 4, Boyle 3, Balfour 2,
Black 2 (1 pen), Gray 1, Jack 1, Stewart 1. *Scottish Cup* (9): Smith A 5, Black 1, Boyle 1, Conn 1, Coyle 1. *Skol
Cup* (4): Coyle 2, Crainie 1 (pen), Watson 1.

Record Defeat; 1-11 v Hibernian, Division I; 24 Oct, 1959.
Most Capped Player: Jimmy Crapnell, 9, Scotland.
Most League Appearances: 523: Paul Jonquin, 1962–79.
Most League Goals in Season (Individual): 52, Hugh Baird, Division II, 1954–55. *Most Goals Overall (Individual):* —.

Honours
League Champions: Division II 1902–03, 1954–55, 1973–74; *Runners-up:* Division I 1922–23, 1923–24, 1924–25, 1925–26.
First Division 1979–80, 1989–90, 1990–91. Division II 1900–01, 1946–47, 1949–50, 1965–66.
Scottish Cup Winners: 1924; *Runners-up:* 1975, 1992. *Scottish Spring Cup Winners:* 1976.
League Cup semi-finalists: 1991–92.
Club colours: Shirt: White with Red diamond. Shorts: White. Stockings: Red.

McKnight, A	Kidd, W	Jack, P	Sandison, J	Honor, C	Conn, S	Lawrence, A	Balfour, E	Stewart, A	Coyle, O	Kirkwood, D	Smith, J	Abercromby, M	Martin, J	Crainie, D	McPhee, I	Watson, J	Butler, J	Boyle, J	Harvey, G	Black, K	Smith, A	Gray, S	McKenna, A	McCulloch, W	Caesar, A	Reid, W	Match No.
1	2	3	4	5	6	7	8	9	10	11																	1
1	2	3	4	5	6	9	8	7	10	11																	2
	2	3†	4		6	9	8	7	10	11*	5		1	12	14												3
	2	3†	4	8	6	9	7	11	10			14	1			5											4
	2	11*	4	6	10	7	8	3	9				1			5	12										5
	2	11*	4	6		7	8	3	9†12				1			5	10	14									6
	2		4	6	14	7	8	3	9*12				1			5†	10	11									7
	2	12	4	6	5†10		8	3	9*14				1				7	11									8
	2		4	6		10†	8	3	9				1		12		7*	11	5	14							9
	2		4	6			8	3	9	14			1			5*	7†12	11	10								10
	2		4	6			8	3	10				1			5†	7	11	9	14							11
	2		4	5		8*	3	10	6				1			14	7	11	9†12								12
	2		4	6	5†		8	3	9	10			1			14	7	11									13
	2		4	5		9	8	3	10†	6			1			12	7*	11	14								14
	2		4	5		10	8	3		6			1			9	7	11									15
			4	5	10*	7	3	9	6				1			12	2	11	8								16
	2	3	4		6		8		10	11†		1	12	5		7		9		14*							17
	2		4	5		9	8	3	10				1			12	7	11	6*		1						18
	2	12	4†	5		9	8	3	10	12			1				7*	11	6								19
	2†		4		6	5	8	3	10	12			1	14		11	7		9*								20
	7		4	6	5		8	3	10	2			1			9†		11	14								21
	2	12	4	5			8	3	9	6			1			10*	7	11									22
	2		4	5			8	3	11	10			1				7		6	9							23
	2	8*	4	3†	5	14			11	10			1			12		7	6	9							24
	2		4	5		11		3	10	8			1				7		6	9							25
	2	12	4	5		11		3	10†	8*			1			14	7		6	9							26
	2		4	5		11*14		3	10	8†			1			12	7		6	9							27
	2	14	4	5			8	3	11	10			1				7		6	9†							28
	2		4	5		14	8	3	10	11			1				7		6	9†							29
	2		4	5		9	8	3	10	11			1				7		6								30
	14		4	5		9	8	3	10†11				1				7		6						2		31
	14		4	5		10*	8	3	12	11†			1				7		6	9					2		32
			4	5		10	8†	3	12	11			1			14	7*		6	9					2		33
			4	5		10	8	3	11				1				7		6	9					2		34
	2	11	4	5	10*		8	3	9	12			1				7		6								35
	2		4	10	12		8	3	9	11*			1				7		6							5	36
	2		4	10*12			8	3	9	11			1				7		6							5	37
		2	4				8	3	10	11		14	1				7		6	9†					5*12		38
		2	4	5*	9	14	8	3	10	12			1				7		11†					6		39
		3	4	5	11*	8		10	14	9†			1				7		12				2	6		40
			4	5	11†	9*	8	3	10				1				7		6	14				2	12	41
			4	5		9†	8	3*10	12				1				7		6	14				2	11	42
			4	2†10			8	3	12	7			1				14		6	9*				5	11	43
	2		4		6	9*	8	3	10	11†			1				14		12					5	7	44
2	32	17	40	30	26	26	40	41	40	27	1	1	41	0	0	10	1	36	0	33	22	0	0	1	12	5	
		+			+	+	+							+	+		+	+		+	+	+	+		+		
		7s			1s	5s	1s							3s	9s		3s	3s		1s	12s	1s	2s		6s 2s 2s		2s

ALBION ROVERS   Second Division

Year Formed: 1882. *Ground & Address:* Cliftonhill Stadium, Main St, Coatbridge ML5 3RB. *Telephone:* 0236 432350.
Ground Capacity: total: 1238. seated: 538. *Size of Pitch:* 110yd × 70yd.   *Chairman:* Jack McGoogan. *Secretary:* D.
Forrester C.A. *Commercial Manager:* Jacqueline Crawford.   *Manager:* Michael Oliver. *Assistant Manager:* A. Rose.
Physio: Jim Maitland. Coach: —.   *Managers since 1975:* G. Caldwell; S. Goodwin; H. Hood; J. Baker; D. Whiteford;
M. Ferguson; W. Wilson; B. Rooney; A. Ritchie; T. Gemmell; D. Provan.   *Club Nickname(s):* The Wee Rovers.
Previous Grounds: Cowheath Park, Meadow Park, Whifflet.   *Record Attendance:* 27,381 v Rangers, Scottish Cup
2nd rd; 8 Feb, 1936.   *Record Transfer Fee received:* £40,000 from Motherwell for Bruce Cleland.   *Record Transfer
Fee paid:* £7000 for Gerry McTeague to Stirling Albion, September 1989.   *Record Victory:* 12-0 v Airdriehill, Scottish

ALBION ROVERS 1991–92 LEAGUE RECORD

Match No.	Date		Venue	Opponents	Result		H/T Score	Lg. Pos.	Goalscorers	Atten- dance
1	Aug	10	H	Arbroath	L	0-1	0-0	—		250
2		17	H	Alloa	W	2-1	0-0	8	McAnenay, McTeague	265
3		24	H	Queen of the S	D	1-1	1-1	7	Clark (pen)	270
4		31	A	Dumbarton	L	3-4	1-2	10	Stalker, Edgar 2	586
5	Sept	7	A	Cowdenbeath	L	0-1	0-1	13		254
6		14	H	Stranraer	W	2-1	1-1	8	Ferguson, Henderson	221
7		17	H	East Stirling	D	1-1	1-0	—	Thomson	291
8		23	A	Queen's Park	D	1-1	0-0	—	Cadden	329
9		28	H	Brechin C	L	0-3	0-2	10		216
10	Oct	5	A	Berwick R	L	1-3	0-2	12	Clark	305
11		12	H	Clyde	D	2-2	2-0	12	Henderson 2	491
12		19	A	East Fife	L	2-3	0-2	14	Moore 2	537
13		26	H	Stenhousemuir	D	1-1	1-1	13	Ferguson	202
14	Nov	2	A	Arbroath	L	1-2	1-1	14	Edgar	360
15		9	A	Alloa	L	0-1	0-0	14		391
16		16	A	Queen of the S	W	4-2	3-1	13	McCoy, McKeown, Clark, Anderson	530
17		23	H	Cowdenbeath	L	0-4	0-2	14		288
18		30	A	Stranraer	W	2-1	0-1	13	McCoy 2	466
19	Dec	14	A	Stenhousemuir	D	1-1	0-0	12	Clark (pen)	329
20		26	H	Dumbarton	L	0-3	0-1	—		650
21		28	A	East Stirling	L	1-2	0-1	13	McCoy	363
22	Jan	4	H	Queen's Park	D	1-1	1-1	13	Clark	284
23		11	H	Berwick R	L	1-2	1-2	13	McCoy	218
24		18	A	Brechin C	W	2-1	0-0	13	Paterson (og), Jackson	328
25	Feb	1	H	East Fife	L	0-1	0-0	13		333
26		4	A	Clyde	L	2-6	1-1	—	McCoy 2	376
27		8	A	Queen of the S	L	0-3	0-1	14		624
28		15	H	Dumbarton	D	1-1	1-0	14	Moore	335
29		24	H	East Stirling	L	1-3	1-2	—	McCoy	142
30		29	A	Berwick R	D	1-1	0-0	14	Moore	325
31	Mar	10	H	Alloa	L	1-3	1-1	—	Anderson	213
32		14	A	Arbroath	D	1-1	1-0	14	McKenzie	397
33		21	H	Queen's Park	L	3-4	1-0	14	Hendry, McCoy, Quinton	214
34		28	A	East Fife	L	1-3	0-1	14	Moore	705
35	Apr	4	H	Cowdenbeath	L	1-2	0-0	14	McCoy	273
36		11	A	Stenhousemuir	L	0-4	0-0	14		309
37		18	H	Brechin C	L	1-2	0-2	14	McCoy	202
38		25	A	Stranraer	L	0-2	0-2	14		397
39	May	2	H	Clyde	L	0-2	0-2	14		378

Final League Position: 14

League (42): McCoy 11, Clark 5 (2 pens), Moore 5, Edgar 3, Henderson 3, Anderson 2, Ferguson 2, Cadden 1, Hendry
1, Jackson 1, McAnenay 1, McKenzie 1, McKeown 1, McTeague 1, Quinton 1, Stalker 1, Thomson 1, own goal 1.
Scottish Cup (0).   *Skol Cup* (4): McAnenay 2, Stalker 1, Watson 1.   *B & Q Cup* (5): Archer 1, Cadden 1, Ferguson
1, Henderson 1, Troup 1.

Continued from foot of p. 677.
Match No. 30(14) 33(8) 34(5*) 35(12) 36(12) 39(14); Riley D—Match No. 31(8*); Hendry A—Match No. 33(11†) 34(11)
35(11) 37(11†) 38(11) 39(11); Jackson D—Match No. 34(1) 35(1) 36(1); Bulloch S—Match No. 34(10); Meechan J—
Match No. 36(11*); Hinchcliffe C—Match No. 39(1).

Cup; 3 Sept, 1887. *Record Defeat:* 0-9 v St. Johnstone, League Cup, 9 March 1946. *Most Capped Player:* Jock White, 1 (2), Scotland. *Most League Appearances:* 399, Murdy Walls, 1921–36. *Most League Goals in Season (Individual):* 41: Jim Renwick, Division II; 1932–33. *Most Goals Overall (Individual):* 105: Bunty Weir, 1928–31.

Honours
League Champions: Division II 1933–34, Second Division 1988–89; *Runners-up:* Division II 1913–14, 1937–38, 1947–48.
Scottish Cup Runners-up: 1920. *League Cup:* —.
Club colours: Shirt: Yellow with red trim. Shorts: Red with yellow stripes. Stockings: Yellow.

McCulloch, R	Millar, G	McKeown, D	Edgar, D	McTeague, G	Clark, R	McAnenay, M	Cadden, S	Ferguson, W	Stalker, I	Miller, J	Watson, E	Troup, W	Cougan, C	Walsh, R	Henderson, J	Connelly, S	Maxwell, D	Thomson, R	Archer, S	Moore, S	Easton, S	Cranmer, C	Cousin, J	Pryce, J	Green, J	McLafferty, M	McConnachie, R	Anderson, R	Match No.
1	2	3	4	5	6	7	8	9*10	11†12	14																			1
1	2	3	8*	5	6	7		9	11	14	4	10†12																	2
1	2	10	12	5	6	7	8	9	11	3†	4*14																		3
1	2	3	12	5	6		9	4	14	8†10		11*	7																4
1		3	8*	5	6	7	4	9	11	10†		12			2	14													5
		3	12	5	6		4	9	8*	11		10†			2	14	1	7											6
		3	8*	5	6		4	9		10†		12	14		2	7	1	11											7
				5	6		4	9*		10		3	12		2	7	1		8†11	14									8
				5	6		8	9†	10*		12				2	14	1		4	11	7	3							9
				5	6		8	7	10*			12			2	9†	1		4	11	14	3							10
		3		5	6		8	11†		10	12				2	9	1		7	4*			14						11
		3		5	6		8	9			12				2		1		7*11		10†		4		14				12
		3			6		8	11*			12	14			2				9		7	5	4†10	1					13
	3	2			6		11								4				9		7				8	10	1	5	14
		3			6		7	14							2				8†	12	5					11*	1	4	15
		8			6										2†				7*12	4		3			14		1	5	16
		8			6			14							2				4†12		7	3*					1	5	17
		3			6										2				9*	7†					12	14	1	5	18
	2				6		7					3							9*	4					12		1	5	19
2*	3				6		7					4†							9	14	5				12		1		20
					6		7												9	14	4*	5			12		1		21
14					6		7	12											9†	4	5						1		22
6					6		7												9	4	11†	5					1		23
12	3				6		8	9				14							7						10†		1		24
8	3				6		7	9*																5	12		1		25
14	3				6		8†12																	5			1		26
4	3				6														7	8	14					11*	1	5†	27
	3				6		7												11								1	5	28
	3				6		7*												4†								1	5	29
8	3				6														7						12		1	5	30
4	3				6														7						14		1	5	31
8	3				6														7						14		1	5	32
	3				6														7*								1	5	33
4	3				6														8						6	14			34
4†	3				6		8																	5		14			35
4	3				6		8	14																5					36
8	3				6		7																			14	1	5	37
8†	3				6		7																				1	5	38
2	4						7	9											6						8	12			39

Totals: 5 18 32 5 12 36 5 28 16 6 8 2 8 1 14 4 7 1 15 17 12 12 1 7 5 19 4 15
Substitute appearances: +3s +3s +5s 1s 4s 1s 6s 5s +3s +3s 4s 1s +3s 12s

McCoy G—Match No. 15(9) 16(10) 17(10) 18(10) 19(10) 20(10) 21(10) 22(10) 23(10) 25(10†) 26 (10) 27(10) 28(10) 29(10) 31(10†) 32(10†) 33(10) 35(10) 36(10) 37(10) 38(10) 39(10*); Horne J—Match No. 15(10) 16(9) 17(11) 18(8) 19(8) 20(8) 21(11) 22(11*) 23(14) 25(14) 27(12) 28(12) 29(14) 30(10†) 31(12) 32(12) 33(12) 34(7) 35(7*) 36(7) 38(12); Gallagher B—Match No. 16(11) 17(9) 18(11) 19(11) 20(11) 21(8) 22(8) 23(8) 28(8*) 29(9) 30(9*); Gallagher J—Match No. 18(4) 21(3) 22(3) 23(3*) 24(11) 25(11) 26(11) 27(9) 28(14) 29(11) 30(11) 31(11) 32(11*) 33(14) 34(12) 38(14) 39(31); Kelly J—Match No. 20(12) 21(2†) 23(12) 24(4*) 25(4) 26(4) 27(2) 28(4†) 29(12) 30(2) 31(2) 32(2) 33(2) 37(2) 38(2) 39(5); Jackson S—Match No. 22(2) 23(2) 24(2) 25(2) 26(2) 28(2) 29(2) 30(4) 32(4) 33(4) 34(2) 35(2) 36(2) 37(4) 38(4); McBride M—Match No. 26(7*); McKenzie T—Match No. 26(9) 28(9) 29(8) 31(9) 32(9) 33(9) 34(9†) 35(9) 36(9†) 37(9) 38(9*); Quinton I—

Continued on p. 676.

ALLOA

Second Division

Year Formed: 1883. *Ground & Address:* Recreation Park, Clackmannan Rd, Alloa FK10 1RR. *Telephone:* 0259 722695.
Ground Capacity: total: 4111. seated: 424. *Size of Pitch:* 110yd × 75yd.
Chairman: Pat Lawlor. *Secretary:* E. G. Cameron. *Commercial Manager:* William McKie.
Manager: Hugh McCann. *Assistant Manager and Coach:* Lindsay Muir. *Physio:* Norrie Gray.
Managers since 1975: H. Wilson; A Totten; W. Garner; J. Thomson; D. Sullivan; G. Abel; B. Little.
Club Nickname(s): The Wasps. *Previous Grounds:* None.
Record Attendance: 13,000 v Dunfermline Athletic, Scottish Cup 3rd rd replay; 26 Feb, 1939.
Record Transfer Fee received: £30,000 for Martin Nelson to Hamilton A (1988).
Record Transfer Fee paid: —.

ALLOA 1991–92 LEAGUE RECORD

Match No.	Date		Venue	Opponents	Result	H/T Score	Lg. Pos.	Goalscorers	Attendance
1	Aug	10	A	Brechin C	W 2-0	1-0	—	McCallum 2	426
2		17	A	Albion R	L 1-2	0-0	5	Newbigging	265
3		24	A	Clyde	L 0-2	0-1	10		598
4		31	A	Queen's Park	L 1-2	0-1	12	Newbigging	443
5	Sept	7	A	Queen of the S	W 3-1	1-1	8	McCallum, Moffat 2	527
6		14	A	East Fife	D 0-0	0-0	7		583
7		17	A	Berwick R	W 1-0	0-0	—	Smith	361
8		21	A	Stenhousemuir	L 0-4	0-2	8		406
9		28	A	Arbroath	D 2-2	0-1	9	Wilcox 2	497
10	Oct	5	H	Dumbarton	L 1-2	1-1	10	Hendry M	667
11		12	A	Cowdenbeath	D 1-1	1-0	10	Hendry M	333
12		19	H	East Stirling	L 0-1	0-1	10		377
13		26	A	Stranraer	L 0-1	0-0	12		370
14	Nov	5	H	Brechin C	W 1-0	0-0	—	Smith	270
15		9	H	Albion R	W 1-0	0-0	9	Newbigging	391
16		16	H	Clyde	W 4-2	2-1	9	Newbigging (pen), Smith, McCulloch, Moffat	598
17		23	H	Queen of the S	W 3-1	2-0	9	McAvoy, Hendry M, Newbigging	479
18		30	H	East Fife	D 0-0	0-0	8		671
19	Dec	14	H	Stranraer	W 3-1	1-0	5	Hendry M, Ramsay 2	432
20		28	H	Berwick R	W 2-1	2-0	5	Hendry M, Moffat	553
21	Jan	1	A	Stenhousemuir	D 1-1	0-1	—	McAvoy	493
22		11	A	Dumbarton	D 2-2	2-0	6	Newbigging, McCulloch	914
23		18	A	Arbroath	D 0-0	0-0	5		403
24		25	H	Queen's Park	W 1-0	1-0	5	Hendry M	576
25	Feb	1	A	East Stirling	L 1-2	1-0	7	Henry S	438
26		8	H	Brechin C	W 6-1	3-1	6	Lee, Wilcox, Hendry M, Newbigging (pen), Smith 2	428
27		15	A	Berwick R	W 1-0	0-0	5	McAvoy	337
28		25	H	Cowdenbeath	W 4-2	3-1	—	Hendry M 2, Gibson, Henry S	535
29		29	H	Stranraer	D 0-0	0-0	4		489
30	Mar	3	H	Stenhousemuir	W 1-0	1-0	—	Henry S	470
31		10	A	Albion R	W 3-1	1-1	—	Romaines, Ramsay, Newbigging	213
32		14	H	Queen's Park	W 2-1	0-0	3	Hendry M, Newbigging (pen)	675
33		21	A	Dumbarton	D 1-1	0-0	3	Newbigging (pen)	656
34		28	H	Queen of the S	W 3-1	0-0	3	Gibson, Smith 2	765
35	Apr	4	A	Clyde	W 1-0	0-0	3	Hendry M	582
36		11	H	East Stirling	W 1-0	1-0	3	Moffat	608
37		18	A	Arbroath	W 3-1	0-1	2	Wilcox, McCormick, Hendry M	569
38		25	H	East Fife	L 1-2	0-1	3	Moffat	1281
39	May	2	H	Cowdenbeath	D 0-0	0-0	3		5050

Final League Position: 3

League (58): Hendry M 12, Newbigging 10 (4 pens), Smith 7, Moffat 6, Wilcox 4, Henry S 3, McAvoy 3, McCallum 3, Ramsay 3, Gibson 2, McCulloch 2, Lee 1, McCormick 1, Romaines 1. *Scottish Cup* (7): McAvoy 2, Moffat 2, Newbigging 2 (1 pen), Hendry M 1. *Skol Cup* (1): McCallum 1. *B & Q Cup* (1): Henry S 1.

Record Victory: 9-2 v Forfar Ath, Division II; 18 Mar, 1933.
Record Defeat: 0-12 v Patrick T, Scottish Cup 3rd rd, 24 Oct 1885.
Most Capped Player: Jock Hepburn, 1, Scotland.
Most League Appearances: —.
Most League Goals in Season (Individual): 49: William 'Wee' Crilley, Division II; 1921–22.
Most Goals Overall (Individual): —.

Honours
League Champions: Division II 1921–22; *Runners-up:* Division II 1938–39. Second Division 1976–77, 1981–82, 1984–85, 1988–89.
Scottish Cup: —.   *League Cup:* —.
Club colours: Shirt: Gold with black trim. Shorts: Black. Stockings: Gold.

Butter, J	Newbigging, W	Lee, R	Wilcox, D	McCulloch, K	Campbell, C	McCallum, M	Romaines, S	Smith, S	Bennett, N	Gibson, J	Moffat, B	Irvine, J	Ramsay, S	Black, I	McAvoy, N	Henry, S	Hendry, M	Thomson, J	Campbell, K	Binnie, N	Conroy, J	McCormick, S	Match No.
1	2	3	4	5	6	7†	8	9	10	11*	12	14											1
1	2	3	4*	5	6	7	8	9	10	11†	12	14											2
1	2	3	4	5†	6	7			10	11		9	8*	12	14								3
1	2	3	4†	5	6	7				11*		9	14	8	12	10							4
1	2	3†	14	5	6	7		9		11		8	12	4	10*								5
1	2	3	4	5	6	10		9*		11		7	8†	12	14								6
1	2	3	4	5	6		8*	9	14	11	12		7†	10									7
1	2	3	4	5	6	10	8	7*	14	9		11†	12										8
1	2	3	4	5	6	7*	8		11†	9	12	10	14										9
1	2	3	4	5	6	10			11*			7	8	12	9								10
1	2		4	5			8	14	3	11*	7	10		12	6†	9							11
1	2		4	5	12		8	6	3	11†	7*10		14		9								12
1			4	5	6*		8	7	10	12	14		3	9†	2	11							13
1	2	3		5	6		4	9		7*		8	12	11	10								14
1	2	3		5	6		4	9	12			8	7*11	10									15
1	2	3	14	5	6		4	9		7*12	8	11†	10										16
1	2	3	12	5	6		4*	9	14	7†	8	11	10										17
1	2	3		5	6		4	9†	12	7	14	8	11*	10									18
1	2	3		5	6		4	9		7†14	8	11	10										19
1	2	3		5	6		4	9*	14	7	8	12	11	10†									20
1	2	3		5	6		4	9		7*	8	12	11	10									21
	2	3	14	5	6	12	4	9		8	11	7*10†				1							22
1	2	3	5		6		4	9*		7	14	11	12	10†	8								23
1	2		5		6		4	9		12	14	11	7†10	8	3*								24
1	2	3	5		6		4	9		12	14	7*10†	8	11									25
1	2	3	5				4	9		11	7*12	8	10	6									26
1	2	3	5		6		4	9		7			11†	8	10	14							27
1	2	3	5		6		4	9		11	12		8	14	7*10†								28
1	2	3	5		6		4	9†		12			8	11	7*10	14							29
1	2	3	5		6		4	9		11†12			8	14	7	10*							30
1	2	3	5		6		4	9		11†12			8	14	7*10								31
1	2	3	5		6		4	9*		11†12			8	14	7	10							32
1	2	3		5	6		4	9		11†12			8	14	7*10								33
1	2	3		5	6		4	9		11	10		8†	14	7*				12				34
1	2	3		5	6		4	9		11	7		8†	14	10*				12				35
1		3		5	6		4	9		11†	7		8	14	10*	2			12				36
1		3	14	5*	6		4	9		11	7		8	2†	10				12				37
1		3	8*	5	6		4	9		11	7		2		10				12				38
1	2	3		5	6		4†	9		11	7		8	14	10*				12				39
38	35	35	23	29	36	8	35	34	10	20	24	3	28	1	19	12	29	6	3	1	0	0	

+ 5s (Wilcox); + 2s (McCallum); + + + + 1s 2s 3s 14s 11s (Romaines–Moffat); + + + 10s 11s 3s (Ramsay–McAvoy); + + 1s 1s (Hendry–Thomson); + + 1s 5s (Conroy–McCormick)

ARBROATH   Second Division

Year Formed: 1878. *Ground & Address:* Gayfield Park, Arbroath DD11 1QB. *Telephone:* 0241 72157.
Ground Capacity; 7,000. *seated:* 896. *Size of Pitch:* 115yd × 71 yd.
President: James King. *Secretary:* Andrew Warrington. *Commercial Manager:* David Kean.
Manager: Mike Lawson. *Assistant Manager:* Jim Holmes. *Physio:* William Shearer. *Coach:* —.
Managers since 1975: A. Henderson; I. J. Stewart; G. Fleming; J. Bone; J Young; W. Borthwick.
Club Nickname(s): The Red Lichties. *Previous Grounds:* None.
Record Attendance: 13,510 v Rangers, Scottish Cup 3rd rd; 23 Feb, 1952.
Record Transfer Fee received: £50,000 for Mark McWalter to St Mirren (June 1987).
Record Transfer Fee paid: £20,000 for Douglas Robb from Montrose (1981).

ARBROATH 1991–92 LEAGUE RECORD

Match No.	Date		Venue	Opponents	Result		H/T Score	Lg. Pos.	Goalscorers	Atten-dance
1	Aug	10	A	Albion R	W	1-0	0-0	—	Holmes W	250
2		17	H	Stranraer	W	1-0	1-0	2	McKenna	257
3		24	A	Berwick R	D	0-0	0-0	2		392
4		31	H	Cowdenbeath	W	2-1	0-1	2	McKenna, Sorbie	449
5	Sept	7	H	East Stirling	D	3-3	1-2	2	McKenna 2, Roberts	460
6		14	A	Clyde	D	1-1	0-0	2	Roberts	560
7		17	A	Dumbarton	L	1-2	1-2	—	Farnan	777
8		21	H	Brechin C	W	3-2	1-2	3	Sorbie 2, McKenna	664
9		28	A	Alloa	D	2-2	1-0	4	Morton, McKenna	497
10	Oct	5	A	East Fife	D	2-2	1-0	4	Carlin, Sorbie	652
11		12	H	Queen of the S	L	2-3	2-1	4	Sorbie, Boyd	490
12		19	A	Stenhousemuir	L	1-2	0-1	7	McNaughton	322
13		26	H	Queen's Park	D	2-2	0-1	6	McKenna 2	267
14	Nov	2	H	Albion R	W	2-1	1-1	5	McKenna, Sorbie	360
15		9	H	Stranraer	L	0-2	0-1	7		483
16		16	H	Berwick R	D	1-1	0-0	7	McNaughton	368
17		23	A	East Stirling	D	1-1	0-1	7	McKenna	265
18		30	H	Clyde	D	0-0	0-0	6		556
19	Dec	14	A	Queen's Park	L	0-1	0-0	8		384
20		28	H	Dumbarton	W	1-0	0-0	7	McNaughton	667
21	Jan	1	A	Brechin C	D	1-1	0-0	—	Brown (og)	1081
22		11	H	East Fife	D	0-0	0-0	7		820
23		18	A	Alloa	D	0-0	0-0	7		403
24		25	A	Queen of the S	W	2-0	1-0	7	Sorbie, McNaughton	653
25	Feb	1	H	Stenhousemuir	W	2-0	0-0	5	Holmes W, Adam	435
26		8	H	Clyde	W	3-0	1-0	5	Adam, McNaughton, Sorbie	795
27		15	A	Stranraer	L	0-1	0-0	6		395
28		18	A	Cowdenbeath	L	1-3	0-3	—	Watt (og)	313
29		22	H	Queen's Park	W	2-1	1-1	5	McLean (og), Morton	480
30		29	A	East Stirling	W	5-0	3-0	5	Morton 2, Sorbie 2, Farnan	274
31	Mar	7	A	East Fife	L	1-3	1-2	6	Sorbie	772
32		14	H	Albion R	D	1-1	0-1	6	Adam	397
33		21	A	Stenhousemuir	L	0-1	0-0	6		329
34		28	H	Cowdenbeath	W	1-0	0-0	6	Sorbie	645
35	Apr	4	A	Brechin C	L	0-1	0-1	6		544
36		11	H	Queen of the S	L	0-3	0-1	6		332
37		18	H	Alloa	L	1-3	1-0	7	McNaughton	569
38		25	A	Berwick R	L	2-3	1-2	7	McNaughton, Tosh	71
39	May	2	A	Dumbarton	D	1-1	0-1	7	Holmes W	2104

Final League Position: 7

League (49): Sorbie 12, McKenna 10, McNaughton 7, Morton 4, Adam 3, Holmes W 3, Farnan 2, Roberts 2, Boyd 1, Carlin 1, Tosh 1, own goals 3. *Scottish Cup* (2): Adam 1, McNaughton 1. *Skol Cup* (0). *B & Q Cup* (2): Holmes W 1, Hunter 1.

Record Victory: 36-0 v Bon Accord, Scottish Cup 1st rd; 12 Sep, 1885.
Record Defeat: 0-8 v Kilmarnock, Division II; 3 Jan, 1949.
Most Capped Player: Ned Doig, 2 (5), Scotland.
Most League Appearances: 445: Tom Cargill, 1966–81.
Most League Goals in Season (Individual): 45: Dave Easson, Division II; 1958–59.
Most Goals Overall (Individual): 120: Jimmy Jack; 1966–71.

Honours
League Champions Runners-up: Division II 1934–35, 1958–59, 1967–68, 1971–72.
Scottish Cup: —.
League Cup: —.
Club colours: Shirt: Maroon with white neck & cuffs. Shorts: White. Stockings: Maroon with white hoop tops.

Balfour, D	Hamilton, J	Farnan, C	Mitchell, B	Sneddon, H	Morton, J	Joyce, B	Brown, S	McKenna, A	Sorbie, S	Holmes, W	Smith, R	Gallagher, J	Carlin, G	Florence, S	Martin, C	Roberts, P	Hunter, M	Tosh, P	Harkness, M	McNaughton, B	Boyd, W	Strachan, A	Adam, C	Tindal, K	Smith, Richard	Gray, B	Match No.
1	2	3	4	5	6	7	8	9*	10	11	12																1
1	2	3	4			14	8	9	10	7*12	11†	5	6														2
1	2	3	6			14	8	9*	10	7†12	11	5	4														3
1	2	3*	4			14	8†	9	10	12		11	5		6	7											4
1	2	3*	4				8	9	10			11	5		6	7†12		14									5
1	2	3	4	5	8	14		9	10	11					6	7†											6
1	2	3	4	5	8	14		9	10	12	11†				6	7*											7
1	2	3	4	5*12	8			9	10	14	11†				6	7											8
1	2	3	4		8	14		9	10	11*		5			6	7†12											9
1	2	3	4		12		8*	9	10	11		5		14	6	7†											10
	2	3*	4†	12				9	10	11		5	6	14					1	7	8						11
	2	3	4*11	12				9†	10	14		5	6						1	7	8						12
	2	3	4	12				9	10	11*		5	6						1	7	8						13
	2	3	4		8			9	10	11		5	6						1	7							14
	2	3	4	11				9	10	7		5†	6*						1	8	14	12					15
	2	3	4	11*				9	10	7†14			6						1	8	5	12					16
	2	3	4					9	10	7			6						1	8	5	11					17
	2	3	4					9†	10	14			6						1	8	5	7	11				18
	2	3	4					14	10	12			6	9*					1	8	5	7†11					19
	2	3	4					9	10	12			6	14					1	8†	5	7*11					20
	2	3	4					9†	10				6	14					1	8	5	7	11				21
	2	3	4					9†	10	12			6	14					1	8	5	7*11					22
	2	10	4		8			9*			12				3				1		5	11	6	7			23
			4	14	8			9†	10	7*12					3				1		5	11	6	2			24
12		3						9	10†	7			4	6					1	5	11	8		2*			25
	2	3			12			9†					4	14					1	6	5	11*	8	10			26
	2	3			12			9	10	7*			4						1	6	5	11	8	6			27
	2	3		14				9†			12		4						1	10*		11	8	7			28
	2	6		5		7*		14	10		12			9†	3				1		4	11	8				29
	2	10		5		7		14			12		6		3				1	9*	4	11	8†				30
	2	10		5		7					12		6		3			14	1	9*	4	11†	8				31
	2	6				7†			10						3	5		14	1		4	11	8			9	32
	2	8		5			14		10		12		6		3	7†			1		4	11				9*	33
	2	11	4	5				9*	10†14				6		3				1	12			8	7			34
	2	11	4	5				9	10	14	12		6		3*				1	8				7†			35
	2	8	4	5		7†		9			12		6	14	3				1			11	10*				36
	2	6	4					9	14	11	12				3				1	10*	5		8	7†			37
	2	6*		5		7	8†	9		11	12				3				1		4		10		14		38
1	2	6		5		7†	8	9		11	12				3						4		10*		14		39
11	36	37	32	12	15	4	4	25	36	15	2	8	11	11	33	7	0	3	28	24	25	16	21	11	2	0	

Substitute appearances: 1s; 1s; 12s4s; 7s; 10s11s; 2s; 3s 2s 6s; 1s 1s 2s; 1s; 2s.

AYR UNITED   First Division

Year Formed: 1910. *Ground & Address:* Somerset Park, Tryfield Place, Ayr KA8 9NB. *Telephone:* 0292 263435.
Ground Capacity: total: 15,870. seated: 1593. *Size of Pitch:* 111yd × 72yd.
Chairman: Robert A. Loudon. *Secretary:* David Quayle. *Commercial Manager:* Mike James.
Manager: George Burley. *Assistant Manager:* David Wells. *Physio:* Robert Pender. *Coach:* David Wells.
Managers since 1975: Alex Stuart; Ally MacLeod; Willie McLean; George Caldwell; Ally MacLeod.
Club Nickname(s): The Honest Men. *Previous Grounds:* None.
Record Attendance: 25,225 v Rangers, Division I; 13 Sept, 1969.
Record Transfer Fee received: £300,000 for Steven Nicol to Liverpool (Oct 1981).
Record Transfer Fee paid: £50,000 for Peter Weir from St Mirren, June 1990.
Record Victory: 11-1 v Dumbarton, League Cup; 13 Aug, 1952.

AYR UNITED 1991–92 LEAGUE RECORD

Match No.	Date		Venue	Opponents	Result	H/T Score	Lg. Pos.	Goalscorers	Attendance
1	Aug	10	A	Forfar Ath	W 3-2	2-1	—	Fraser, Shaw, Smith	824
2		13	A	Montrose	W 3-1	0-0	—	Bryce 2 (1 pen), Fraser	976
3		17	H	Clydebank	W 3-0	1-0	1	Bryce (pen), Shaw 2	2685
4		24	H	Raith R	W 1-0	0-0	2	Smith	3270
5		31	A	Kilmarnock	D 1-1	0-0	2	Agnew	8380
6	Sept	7	A	Partick T	L 1-3	0-2	2	Graham	3971
7		14	A	Dundee	L 1-3	1-1	4	Auld	3410
8		21	H	Meadowbank T	W 7-0	3-0	4	Graham, McAllister, George, Shaw 2, Agnew, McLean	1605
9		28	A	Morton	W 4-3	1-1	3	Fraser, Shaw, McLean, McAllister	2601
10	Oct	5	H	Stirling Albion	L 1-2	0-1	3	Graham	2505
11		9	A	Hamilton A	L 1-3	0-2	—	Bryce	1839
12		12	H	Forfar Ath	W 4-0	2-0	4	Bryce, Graham 2, Shaw	1782
13		19	A	Clydebank	L 2-3	1-0	5	Smith, Shaw	1100
14		26	A	Partick T	L 0-3	0-2	6		2170
15		29	H	Dundee	W 4-1	3-0	—	Agnew, Smith 2, Shaw	2414
16	Nov	2	H	Kilmarnock	L 0-3	0-3	6		6064
17		9	H	Raith R	D 0-0	0-0	6		1441
18		16	A	Stirling Albion	D 0-0	0-0	6		978
19		19	H	Hamilton A	L 0-2	0-1	—		2216
20		23	A	Meadowbank T	D 1-1	1-0	7	Bryce	440
21		26	A	Forfar Ath	W 1-0	0-0	—	Bryce	530
22		30	H	Montrose	W 2-0	0-0	5	Shaw (pen), Graham	1898
23	Dec	3	H	Morton	W 3-2	0-1	—	Walker, Graham 2	2221
24		14	H	Partick T	L 0-2	0-0	6		2791
25		28	H	Raith R	D 1-1	0-0	6	Walker	2257
26	Jan	1	A	Kilmarnock	D 1-1	0-0	—	Agnew	8211
27		4	H	Stirling Albion	L 1-2	0-2	6	Traynor	2217
28		7	A	Dundee	D 1-1	1-1	—	Agnew	2502
29		11	A	Hamilton A	L 1-2	0-1	6	Bryce	1530
30		18	A	Montrose	D 0-0	0-0	7		718
31	Feb	1	H	Clydebank	W 3-1	2-1	7	Traynor 3	1918
32		8	H	Meadowbank T	D 0-0	0-0	6		1742
33		15	A	Partick T	L 1-4	0-1	7	Bryce	2771
34		29	A	Stirling Albion	W 2-1	0-1	7	McTurk, Walker	790
35	Mar	7	H	Hamilton A	W 2-0	1-0	6	Graham 2	2004
36		14	A	Raith R	W 4-2	3-1	6	Graham 3, Walker	1473
37		17	A	Morton	L 0-2	0-1	—		1175
38		21	H	Kilmarnock	L 0-2	0-0	7		5530
39		28	H	Forfar Ath	W 1-0	1-0	7	McLean	1311
40	Apr	4	A	Clydebank	L 0-1	0-1	7		677
41		11	H	Dundee	D 0-0	0-0	7		2418
42		18	A	Meadowbank T	W 1-0	0-0	7	Graham	367
43		25	H	Montrose	D 0-0	0-0	7		1249
44	May	2	H	Morton	W 1-0	1-0	6	Walker	1595

Final League Position: 6

League (63): Graham 14, Shaw 10 (1 pen), Bryce 9 (2 pens), Agnew 5, Smith 5, Walker 5, Traynor 4, Fraser 3, McLean 3, McAllister 2, Auld 1, George 1, McTurk 1. *Scottish Cup* (2): George 1, Graham 1. *Scottish Cup* (6): Shaw 3, Graham 2, Bryce 1 (pen). *B & Q Cup* (9): Smith 3, Graham 2, Auld 1, Fraser 1, McLean 1, Shaw 1.

Record Defeat: 0-9 in Division I v Rangers (1929); v Hearts (1931); v Third Lanark (1954).
Most Capped Player: Jim Nisbet, 3, Scotland.
Most League Appearances: 371: Ian McAllister, 1977–90.
Most League Goals in Season (Individual): 66: Jimmy Smith, 1927–28.
Most Goals Overall (Individual): —.

Honours
League Champions: Division II 1911–12, 1912–13, 1927–8, 1936–37, 1958–59, 1965–66. Second Division 1987–88;
Runners-up: Division II 1910–11, 1955–56, 1968–69.
Scottish Cup: —. *League Cup:* —.
Club colours: Shirt: White with broad black chest panel and pinstripe. Shorts: Black. Stockings: White with black diamond tops.

Duncan, C	Burley, G	Agnew, G	Furphy, W	Auld, S	McAllister, I	Fraser, A	Bryce, T	Graham, A	George, D	Shaw, G	Smith, M	McLean, P	Kennedy, D	Purdie, D	Walker, T	McTurk, A	Hood, G	Gardner, L	Evans, S	Brown, R	Traynor, J	Howard, N	Weir, P	Archibald, S	McVie, G	Robertson, M	Match No.
1	2	3	4	5	6	7	8	9	10	11*12																	1
1	2	3	4	5		7	8	9	10	11		6															2
1	2	3	4	5		7*	8	9	10	12		11	6														3
1		3	4	5		7*	8	9	10	11	12	6	2														4
1	2	3	4	5			8	9	10	11*12		6	7														5
1	2†	3	4	5	14		8	9	10	12	11*	6	7														6
		3		5	6	7	8	9	10	11*		4	2	1	12												7
		3	4	5	6	14	8	9	10†12			7	2	1		11*											8
		3	4	5	6	11*	8	9	10	12		7	2	1													9
1		3	4	5	14	7	8	9	10	11*12		6†	2														10
		3	4	5		7†	8*	9	10	11		6	2	1		12	14										11
		3	4	5			8	9	10	12	11*	7	2	1		6											12
1		3	4	14			8	9	10	12	11*	6	2			5†	7										13
1		3	4	5		8*	9	10	12	11		2				7	6										14
1		3	4	5		8*	9	10	12	11		2				7	6										15
1		3	4	5		8	9		10	11		2				7	6										16
1		3	4	5		8	9	6	10*11			2†			12		7	14									17
1		3	4			8	9	10	12	7		6				11*			2	5							18
1		3	4			8	9		12		7*					11†14		6	2	5							19
1		3	4			8	9	10	12	11		7						6*	2	5							20
1*		3	4			8			9	10		6			12		7		2	5	11						21
		3	4			8	9		12			6	1	10			7		2	5	11*						22
		3†	4			8	9		12		6	14	1	10			7		2	5	11*						23
		3	4	14		8	9		12		7*	6	1	10					2	5	11†						24
		3	4			8*		6	9	12	7	2	1	10					5		11						25
		3	4†	5			9	8	12		7	6	1	10				14	2		11*						26
		3	4	5*			9	8	12		7†	6	1	10				14	2		11						27
		3	4	6		8†	9*11		12			7	1	10					2	5	14						28
		3	4	6†		8	9	11	12			7	1	10					2*	5	14						29
			4			8	9	11	12		7*	6	1	10				3	2	5							30
	2	3	4			8†	9	11	12			6	1	10*					7	5	14						31
	2	3	4	5		8*	9	11	12			6	1	10†14					7								32
	2	3		5		14	9	11	12		7†	6	1		8				4		10*						33
		3	4*			8	9		14		6	2	1	12†11		7			10	5							34
		3				8	9		12		6	2	1	10	11*		7		4	5							35
		3				8	9		11		6	2	1	10			7		5				4				36
		3				8	9		11		6*12		1	10	14		7†		2	5			4				37
			4			8	9	6	11		12	3	1	10*			7		2	5							38
			4			8	9	6		14	7	3	1	10	11†				2	5							39
			4			8	9*	6	11		7	3	1	10	12				2	5							40
	2		4			12	9	8			7	3	1	10	11*				6	5							41
			4				9	6*		12	7	2	1	10	11	14	8			5†			3				42
			4			11		6	9		7*14			12	10		8		2	5				3†	1		43
			4			11		6		12	7	14	1	9	10		8*		2	5				3†			44
16	9	36	39	22	4	8	39	40	34	16	11	29	38	27	20	11	2	16	6	0	26	21	7	1	5	1	

+	+	+	+					+	+	+	+				+	+	+		+	+			+
1s	3s	1s	2s					24s	8s	1s	4s				4s	5s	3s		2s	1s			3s

BERWICK RANGERS   Second Division

Year Formed: 1881. *Ground & Address:* Shielfield Park, Tweedmouth, Berwick-upon-Tweed TD15 2EF. *Telephone:*
0289 307424.   *Ground Capacity:* total: 5235. seated: 1475. *Size of Pitch:* 112yd × 76yd.
Chairman: D. E. Cochrane. *Vice-chairman:* D. McLean. *Chief Executive:* Alan Bowes. *Secretary:* Mrs Carole Fletcher.
Commercial Manager: —.
Manager: John Andersen. *Assistant Manager:* J. McNamara. *Physio:* Gordon Roberts. *Coach:* R. Johnson, I. Oliver.
Managers since 1975: H. Melrose; G. Haig; D. Smith; F. Connor; J. McSherry; E Tait; J. Thomson; J. Jefferies.
Club Nickname(s): The Borderers. *Previous Grounds:* Bull Stot Close, Pier Field, Meadow Field, Union Park, Old
Shielfield.
Record Attendance: 13,365 v Rangers, Scottish Cup 1st rd; 28 Jan, 1967.

BERWICK RANGERS 1991–92 LEAGUE RECORD

Match No.	Date		Venue	Opponents	Result	H/T Score	Lg. Pos.	Goalscorers	Atten- dance
1	Aug	10	H	Stenhousemuir	L	0-1	0-0	—	490
2		17	A	Dumbarton	D	1-1	0-0	12	Tait	524
3		24	H	Arbroath	D	0-0	0-0	11		392
4		31	A	Queen of the S	W	3-0	2-0	5	Bickmore 2, Todd	576
5	Sept	7	H	Brechin C	D	1-1	1-0	5	Todd	378
6		10	A	Clyde	L	0-2	0-0			547
7		14	A	East Stirling	L	1-4	1-1	9	Ross (pen)	296
8		17	H	Alloa	L	0-1	0-0	—		361
9		28	A	Cowdenbeath	L	0-2	0-2	14		307
10	Oct	5	H	Albion R	W	3-1	2-0	11	Ross, Todd, Leitch	305
11		12	A	Queen's Park	L	2-3	1-1	13	Scally, McGovern	303
12		19	H	Stranraer	D	0-0	0-0	13		255
13		26	H	East Fife	L	1-2	0-1	14	Todd	260
14	Nov	2	A	Stenhousemuir	W	2-0	1-0	10	Bickmore, Ross	264
15		9	H	Dumbarton	D	2-2	2-2	12	Thorpe, Bickmore	305
16		16	A	Arbroath	D	1-1	0-0	10	Bickmore	368
17		23	A	Brechin C	D	2-2	0-2	10	Ross, Thorpe	398
18	Dec	14	A	East Fife	L	1-3	0-1	13	Ross	677
19		21	H	Queen of the S	D	1-1	1-1	12	Graham	259
20		28	A	Alloa	L	1-2	0-2	12	Ross	553
21	Jan	1	H	Clyde	W	2-1	0-0	—	Bickmore, Thorpe	334
22		11	A	Albion R	W	2-1	2-1	12	Todd, Cass	218
23		18	H	Cowdenbeath	L	1-3	1-0	12	Thorpe	346
24	Feb	1	A	Stranraer	D	2-2	2-1	12	Thorpe, O'Donnell	436
25		8	A	East Stirling	W	4-0	2-0	11	Todd, Bickmore 2, Graham	312
26		15	H	Alloa	L	0-1	0-0	12		337
27		18	H	East Stirling	W	1-0	0-0	—	Todd	355
28		25	H	Queen's Park	L	1-3	1-0	—	Graham (pen)	390
29		29	H	Albion R	D	1-1	0-0	12	Thorpe	325
30	Mar	3	A	Clyde	W	1-0	1-0	—	Bickmore	411
31		7	A	Brechin C	D	2-2	1-0	10	Tait, Todd	324
32		14	H	Stranraer	L	1-2	1-1	10	Tait	270
33		21	A	Cowdenbeath	L	1-4	1-1	11	Tait	657
34		28	H	Dumbarton	L	1-5	0-4	11	Tait	174
35	Apr	4	H	Stenhousemuir	L	0-1	0-1	13		114
36		11	A	Queen's Park	L	1-4	0-2	13	Thorpe	337
37		18	A	Queen of the S	W	3-0	2-0	13	Bickmore 2, Bell (og)	598
38		25	H	Arbroath	W	3-2	2-1	11	Bickmore, Tait, Davidson (pen)	71
39	May	2	H	East Fife	L	1-4	0-1	12	Davidson	150

Final League Position: 12

League (50): Bickmore 12, Todd 8, Thorpe 7, Ross 6 (1 pen), Tait 6, Graham 3 (1 pen), Davidson 2 (1 pen), Cass 1,
Leitch 1, McGovern 1, O'Donnell 1, Scally 1, own goal 1.   *Scottish Cup* (7): Bickmore 2, Neil 2, Graham 1, Locke 1,
Todd 1.   *Skol Cup* (0).   *B & Q Cup* (4): Ross 2, Thorpe 1, Todd 1.

Record Transfer Fee received: —.   *Record Transfer Fee paid:* —.
Record Victory: 8-1 v Forfar Ath, Division II; 25 Dec, 1965: v Vale of Leithen, Scottish Cup; Dec, 1966.
Record Defeat: 1-9 v Hamilton A, First Division; 9 Aug, 1980.
Most Capped Player: —.
Most League Appearances: 435: Eric Tait, 1970–87.
Most League Goals in Season (Individual): 38: Ken Bowron, Division II; 1963–64.
Most Goals Overall (Individual): 115: Eric Tait, 1970–87.

Honours
League Champions: Second Division 1978–79.
Scottish Cup: —.
League Cup: Semi-final 1963–64.
Club colours: Shirt: Black and gold stripes. Shorts: Black, gold trim. Stockings: Gold and black.

Neilson, D	McLaren, P	O'Donnell, J	Garner, W	Wilson, W	Leitch, G	Neil, M	Thorpe, B	Todd, K	Ross, A	Tait, G	Bickmore, S	Graham, T	Marshall, B	Sneddon, M	McGovern, J	Callachan, R	Davidson, G	Cass, M	Scally, D	Clinging, I	Egan, J	Locke, S	Malcolm, D	Wojtowycz, M	Irvine, M	Purves, S	Rae, R	Match No.
1	2	3	4	5	6	7	8†	9	10*11	12	14																	1
1	2	3†	4	6	8*14			9	10	7	11		5	12														2
1	2	3	4	5	6	7		9	8		10		11†		14													3
1	2	3	4	5†11				9*12		10			8		7	6	14											4
1	2	3†	4	5	11			9	12		10		8		7*	6	14											5
1	2	3	6*	5	8			9	7		10†			14		4	11	12										6
1	2†	3	6	5	8			9	10					14		4	11	12	7*									7
1	2	3		5	6			9	10				12	14		4	8*	7	11†									8
1	2†	3		5	6	11		9	10					14		4	8	7										9
		3	4	5	11		8	10	9					6		2		7		1								10
	14	3		4	8	11	9	10					12	6*	2	5	7†		1									11
1	12	3		5	7		8	9	10							2	6	11*			4							12
1	12			4	5	7		8	9	10*			11†			2	6	14			3							13
1		3	6	5	8		7	9	12	11*10						2	14				4†							14
1	12	3		5	7		8	9	11		10			6*		4	2											15
1	12	3		5	7		8	9	11		10			6*		4	2											16
1	12	3		5	7		8	9	11		10		14	6†		4*	2											17
1	2†	3	4	5	7		8	10	9				11	14			6											18
		3	5			6	8	9†10			14	11			12	2		7*		1	4							19
		3	5	6†	7	8	9	10		11	14					2				1	4							20
1		3	4	5		11	8	9		10				12	6	2	7*											21
1			4	5		7	8	9		10	11					2	6				3							22
1			5		6	7	8	9		10	11					14	4	2				3†						23
1		3	5	6	11	7	8	9		10							4	2										24
1		3	4*	5	6		8	9†		12	10	11			14		2	7										25
1		3		5	6†	4	8	9		14	10	11					2	7										26
		3		5		6	8	9		12	10*11†			7	14	2	4			1								27
		3		5		6	8	9		12	10	11*		7†14		2	4			1								28
		3	4	5		6	8	9		14	10	11†		12		2	7*			1								29
		3	4	5			8	9		11	10	12		6	7*	2				1								30
		3	4	5		7	8	9*		11	10	12		6		2				1								31
		3	4	5		6	8	9		11	10			7		2				1								32
1		14		5	2	7*	8	9		11†10	6			12		4					3							33
1		3	4	5*14		10†	9			8		11		6	7	2					12							34
1		3	5				9		10		11			8		2						4	6	7*12				35
1		3	5*	6		8	9		10		11			7		4							12	14	2†			36
1		3		7*		5	9		8	10	11			6	4†						12				2	14		37
1		3	5				8		11	10				7	9	2	6*				4†			12	14		38
1		3	5		7		8		9	10				6	11	4	2											39
29	10	35	27	32	27	14	31	37	17	13	27	13	1	15	12	34	22	6	2	10	9	1	1	1	2	0		
+6s	+1s		+1s	+1s			+3s	+5s	+2s	+5s			+3s	+9s	+5s		+3s	+3s			+2s	+1s	+1s		+2s	+2s		

BRECHIN CITY Second Division

Year Formed: 1906. *Ground & Address:* Glebe Park, Trinity Rd, Brechin, Angus DD9 6BJ. *Telephone:* 0356 622856.
Ground Capacity: total: 3900. seated: 1518. *Size of Pitch:* 110yd × 67yd.
Chairman: Hugh Campbell Adamson. *Secretary:* George C. Johnston. *Commercial Manager:* —.
Manager: John Ritchie. *Assistant Manager:* John Young. *Physio:* Jack Sunter. *Coach:* —.
Managers since 1975: Charlie Dunn; Ian Stewart; Doug Houston; Ian Fleming.
Club Nickname(s): The City. *Previous Grounds:* Nursery Park.
Record Attendance: 8122 v Aberdeen, Scottish Cup 3rd rd; 3 Feb, 1973.
Record Transfer Fee received: £46,000 for Ken Eadie to Falkirk (1986).
Record Transfer Fee paid: £15,000 for Gerry Lesslie from Dundee U.

BRECHIN CITY 1991–92 LEAGUE RECORD

Match No.	Date		Venue	Opponents	Result	Score	H/T	Lg. Pos.	Goalscorers	Atten- dance
1	Aug	10	H	Alloa	L	0-2	0-1	—		426
2		17	A	Stenhousemuir	W	2-0	0-0	8	Brown, Ritchie	362
3		24	H	East Fife	D	4-4	1-1	6	Thomson N, Ritchie, Hutt, Conway	568
4		31	A	East Stirling	D	3-3	0-3	7	Ritchie, Conway, Lees	205
5	Sept	7	A	Berwick R	D	1-1	0-1	7	Conway	378
6		14	H	Dumbarton	L	0-4	0-3	10		491
7		17	H	Clyde	W	1-0	0-0	—	Ritchie (pen)	542
8		21	A	Arbroath	L	2-3	2-1	9	Lees, Brown	664
9		28	A	Albion R	W	3-0	2-0	8	Thomson S, Lees 2	216
10	Oct	5	H	Cowdenbeath	L	0-1	0-0	8		430
11		12	A	Stranraer	W	3-1	3-0	7	McKillop, Brand, Ritchie	496
12		19	A	Queen's Park	W	2-0	0-0	5	Thomson S, Lorimer	340
13		26	H	Queen of the S	W	7-1	2-0	5	Thomson S, Nicolson, Ritchie 2, Brand 3	350
14	Nov	5	A	Alloa	L	0-1	0-0	—		270
15		9	H	Stenhousemuir	W	1-0	1-0	4	Brown	366
16		16	A	East Fife	L	1-2	1-2	5	Nicolson	667
17		23	H	Berwick R	D	2-2	2-0	6	Ritchie 2	398
18		30	A	Dumbarton	L	0-3	0-1	7		670
19	Dec	14	A	Queen of the S	L	2-4	2-1	9	Ritchie, Lorimer	597
20		28	A	Clyde	D	0-0	0-0	9		472
21	Jan	1	H	Arbroath	D	1-1	0-0	—	Ross	1081
22		7	H	East Stirling	D	0-0	0-0	—		376
23		18	H	Albion R	L	1-2	0-0	9	Ross	328
24	Feb	1	A	Queen's Park	W	1-0	0-0	9	Ross	347
25		4	H	Stranraer	W	2-1	1-1	—	Ross, Scott	350
26		8	A	Alloa	L	1-6	1-3	9	Lees	428
27		12	A	Cowdenbeath	L	1-2	0-2	—	Lees	318
28		15	H	Queen of the S	D	1-1	1-1	9	Paterson	426
29		25	A	Dumbarton	W	3-1	0-0	—	Ritchie 2, Miller	390
30		29	H	Clyde	L	1-2	0-0	8	Ross	466
31	Mar	7	H	Berwick R	D	2-2	0-1	8	Brand 2	324
32		14	A	East Stirling	D	0-0	0-0	9		163
33		21	H	East Fife	L	0-1	0-0	9		476
34		28	A	Stranraer	D	1-1	0-1	9	Lees	450
35	Apr	4	H	Arbroath	W	1-0	1-0	8	Ross	544
36		11	A	Cowdenbeath	L	1-2	0-2	8	Ross (pen)	569
37		18	A	Albion R	W	2-1	0-0	8	Paterson, Brand	202
38		25	H	Queen's Park	W	1-0	1-0	8	Lees	373
39	May	2	H	Stenhousemuir	D	0-0	0-0	8		324

Final League Position: 8

League (54): Ritchie 12 (1 pen), Lees 8, Brand 7, Ross 7 (1 pen), Brown 3, Conway 3, Thomson S 3, Lorimer 2, Nicolson 2, Paterson 2, Hutt 1, McKillop 1, Miller 1, Scott 1, Thomson N 1. *Scottish Cup* (1): Ritchie. *Skol Cup* (3): Ritchie 2 (1 pen), Pryde 1. *B & Q Cup* (2): Ritchie 2.

Record Victory: 12-1 v Thornhill, Scottish Cup 1st rd; 28 Jan, 1926 .
Record Defeat: 0-10 v Airdrieonians, Albion R and Cowdenbeath, all in Division II; 1937–38.
Most Capped Player: —.
Most League Appearances: 459: David Watt, 1975–89.
Most League Goals in Season (Individual): 26: W. McIntosh, Division II; 1959–60.
Most Goals Overall (Individual): 131: Ian Campbell.

Honours
League Champions: Second Division 1982–83. C Division 1953–54. Second Division Champions 1989–90. *Runners-up:* —.
Scottish Cup: —.
League Cup: —.
Club colours: Shirt, Shorts, Stockings: Red with white trimmings.

Ainslie, C	Baillie, R	Conway, F	Brown, R	Nicolson, K	Hutt, G	Thomson, S	Paterson, I G	Ritchie, P	Scott, D	Lees, G	Thomson, N	Brand, I	Pryde, I	Dow, R	Allan, R	McKillop, A	Clark, J	Traynor, R	Lawrie, D	Lorimer, R	Garden, S	Hill, H	Fisher, D	Wardell, S	Gibson, J	Miller, M	Ross, A	Cairney, H	Match No.
1	2	3	4*	5	6	7	8	9	10	11†	12	14																	1
1	2	3	4	5	6	7	12	9	10*			8	14	11†															2
1		3	4	5	6	7		9	10			8	14	11†	2														3
	2	3		5	6	7	12	9	10	11	8*					1	4												4
	2	3		5	6*	7	12	9	10			8		11†		1			4	14									5
	2*	3	4		6	7	14	9	10		12	8†		11	5	1													6
	2	3	4		6	7	8	9	10	11†					5	1	14												7
	2	3	4		6	7	8	9	10	11					5	1													8
	2*	3	4		6	7	12	9†	10	11		8		14	5	1													9
	2	3	4		6*	7†	8	9	10	11	12	14			5	1													10
	2	3	4		6	7		9	10	11					5	1				8									11
	2	3	4		6	7		9	10	11*	12				5†	1				8		14							12
	2	3	4	5		7	8*	9	10	11						1				6†	12	14							13
	2*	3	4	5		7		9	10	11	12					1				6	8†	14							14
	2*	3	4	5	6	7	8	9	10	11						1					12								15
	2†	3	4	5	6	7*		9	10	11	12					1					8	14							16
	2	3	4	5*			8	9	10	11						1				6	12	7							17
	2		4		6			9	10	11	12				5	1				3	8	7*							18
	2	3	4		6			9	10	11		14			5	1				8		7†							19
	2		4			7		9	10	11					5	1				6					3		8		20
	2		4			7		9	10†						5	1				6		14			3		8	11	21
	2		4		6	7*		9		14					5	1				10	8	12			3†			11	22
	2		4		6		8	9			12				5	1				7	14	11*			3†		10		23
	2	3	4						10	11*					5	1				6	8	7†			12		14	9	24
	2	3	4						10	11					5	1				6*	8	7†			12		14	9	25
	2†	3	4						10	11					5	1				6	8	7*			12		14	9	26
		3	4		6				10	11					2*	1				12	8	7†			14		9	5	27
		3	4		6					11		14			5*	1				10	8	7†			12		9	2	28
			4		6	7		9*			12	14			5	1				3	8	10†		11			2		29
			4		6*	7					12				5	1				3	8			11		10	9	2	30
	2		4		6	7				11					5	1					8	12			3	10*	9		31
	2		4		6	7				11*						1					8				3	10	9	5	32
	2†		4		6	7				11*		14				1					8	12			3	10	9	5	33
			4		6	7										1				10	8	14			3		9	5	34
			4		6	7										1				10	8*	12	14		3		9	5	35
			4			7										1				3	8	14	6			10	9	5	36
			4		6	7				11†						1				3	8	12	14			10	9*	5	37
			4		6	7				11*						1				3	8	12				10	9	5	38
			4		6	7				11*						1				3	8	12				10	9	5	39
3	24	19	37	16	15	11	16	24	28	29	19	15	2	6	26	19	1	1	4	23	5	14	5	5	9	12	19	13	
			+1s		+2s		+8s		+3s	+4s	+11s		+2s			+2s					+6s	+8s	+4s			+5s			

Hutchison, W—Match No. 32(12); McLaren, P—Match No. 34(2) 35(2) 36(2) 37(2) 38(2) 39(2); Heggie, A—Match No. 34(11†) 35(11†) 35(11†).

CELTIC
Premier Division

Year Formed: 1888. *Ground & Address:* Celtic Park, 95 Kerrydale St, Glasgow G40 3RE. *Telephone:* 041 556 2611. *Ground Capacity:* total: 51,709. *Seated:* 9000. *Size of Pitch:* 115yd × 75yd. *Chairman:* J. Kevin Kelly. *Chief Executive:* Terry Cassidy. *Financial Consultant:* —. *Secretary:* Chris D. White, CA. *Commercial Manager:* Rodney Turner. *Manager:* Liam Brady. *Assistant Manager:* Tommy Craig. *Physio:* Brian Scott. *First team coach:* Mick Martin. *Reserve team coach:* Bobby Lennox. *Managers since 1975:* Jock Stein; Billy McNeill; David Hay; Billy McNeill. *Club Nickname(s):* The Bhoys. *Previous Grounds:* None. *Record Attendance:* 92,000 v Rangers, Division I; 1 Jan, 1938. *Record Transfer Fee received:* £1,400,000 for Paul Elliott to Chelsea, July 1991. *Record Transfer Fee paid:* £1,100,000 for Tony Cascarino from Aston Villa, July 1991. *Record Victory:* 11-0 v Dundee, Division I; 26 Oct, 1895. *Record Defeat:* 0-8 v Motherwell, Division I; 30 Apr, 1937. *Most Capped Player:* Danny McGrain, 62, Scotland. *Most League Appearances:* 486: Billy McNeill, 1957–75. *Most League Goals in Season (Individual):* 50: James McGrory, Division I; 1935–36. *Most Goals Overall (Individual):* 397: James McGrory; 1922–39.

Final League Position: 3

CELTIC 1991–92 LEAGUE RECORD

Match No.	Date		Venue	Opponents	Result		H/T Score	Lg. Pos.	Goalscorers	Atten-dance
1	Aug	10	A	Dundee U	W	4-3	3-1	—	Nicholas, Coyne, Collins 2	16,731
2		13	A	Dunfermline Ath	W	3-1	1-1	—	Nicholas 2, Coyne	13,794
3		17	H	Falkirk	W	4-1	3-0	1	Gillespie, Coyne 2, Collins	32,469
4		24	A	Aberdeen	L	0-1	0-1	5		20,503
5		31	H	Rangers	L	0-2	0-1	5		50,756
6	Sept	7	H	St Mirren	D	0-0	0-0	5		21,323
7		14	A	St Johnstone	L	0-1	0-1	6		9993
8		21	H	Airdrieonians	W	3-1	1-1	5	Miller, Galloway, Nicholas (pen)	17,552
9		28	A	Hibernian	D	1-1	1-0	5	Nicholas	18,021
10	Oct	5	H	Hearts	W	3-1	2-1	5	McNally, Nicholas (pen), Cascarino	33,621
11		8	A	Motherwell	W	2-0	1-0	—	Coyne, Nicholas	13,283
12		12	H	Dundee U	W	4-1	2-0	5	Nicholas 2, Coyne, Galloway	28,281
13		19	A	Falkirk	L	3-4	1-3	5	Collins, McStay 2	11,008
14		26	A	St Mirren	W	5-0	1-0	4	McStay, Coyne 2, Creaney, O'Neil	10,473
15		30	H	St Johnstone	W	4-0	2-0	—	Nicholas 2 (1 pen), Collins, Coyne	18,854
16	Nov	2	A	Rangers	D	1-1	0-0	4	Cascarino	37,387
17		9	H	Aberdeen	W	2-1	1-1	3	Nicholas, Creaney	36,837
18		16	A	Hearts	L	1-3	1-0	4	Coyne	22,666
19		20	H	Motherwell	D	2-2	2-2	—	Nicholas 2	16,350
20		23	A	Airdrieonians	W	3-0	0-0	3	Cascarino, Coyne, Creaney	10,102
21		30	H	Dunfermline Ath	W	1-0	1-0	3	Coyne	20,744
22	Dec	4	H	Hibernian	D	0-0	0-0	—		22,340
23		7	A	Dundee U	D	1-1	1-0	3	Morris	11,585
24		14	H	St Mirren	W	4-0	1-0	3	Collins, Creaney 2, Lambert (og)	16,825
25		28	A	Aberdeen	D	2-2	0-2	3	Mowbray, Cascarino	20,422
26	Jan	1	H	Rangers	L	1-3	0-1	—	Mowbray	51,381
27		4	H	Hearts	L	1-2	0-0	4	Collins	30,415
28		8	A	St Johnstone	W	4-2	1-0	3	McStay, Gillespie, Coyne, Collins	9283
29		11	A	Motherwell	D	0-0	0-0	3		12,115
30		18	A	Dunfermline Ath	W	1-0	1-0	3	Coyne	9863
31	Feb	1	H	Falkirk	W	2-0	0-0	3	Coyne, McStay	16,927
32		8	H	Airdrieonians	W	2-0	1-0	3	Creaney 2	18,845
33		22	A	Hibernian	W	2-0	2-0	3	Creaney, Nicholas	16,756
34		29	A	Hearts	W	2-1	2-0	3	Creaney 2	20,863
35	Mar	14	H	Aberdeen	W	1-0	0-0	3	Collins	29,380
36		17	H	Motherwell	W	4-1	2-1	—	Nicholas, McStay, Creaney, Miller	15,582
37		21	A	Rangers	W	2-0	1-0	3	Nicholas, Creaney	42,160
38		28	H	Dundee U	W	3-1	1-0	3	Creaney, Nicholas, Whyte	22,522
39	Apr	4	A	Falkirk	W	3-0	1-0	2	Creaney, Nicholas, Collins	8842
40		8	A	St Mirren	D	1-1	0-1	—	Boyd	7316
41		11	H	St Johnstone	W	3-2	1-0	2	Fulton, Nicholas 2	13,237
42		18	A	Airdrieonians	D	0-0	0-0	2		8296
43		25	H	Dunfermline Ath	W	2-0	1-0	2	McStay, Collins	12,699
44	May	2	H	Hibernian	L	1-2	0-1	3	Fulton	25,532

League (88): Nicholas 21 (3 pens), Coyne 15, Creaney 14, Collins 11, McStay 7, Cascarino 4, Fulton 2, Galloway 2, Gillespie 2, Miller 2, Mowbray 2, Boyd 1, McNally 1, Morris 1, O'Neil 1, Whyte 1, own goal 1. *Scottish Cup* (11): Creaney 6, Coyne 4, Collins 1. *Skol Cup* (7): Creaney 3, Nicholas 2, Fulton 1, Miller 1.

Honours
League Champions: (35 times) Division I 1892–93, 1893–94, 1895–96, 1897–98, 1904–05, 1905–06, 1906–07, 1907–08, 1908–09, 1909–10, 1913–14, 1914–15, 1915–16, 1916–17, 1918–19, 1921–22, 1925–26, 1935–36, 1937–38, 1953–54, 1965–66, 1966–67, 1967–68, 1968–69, 1969–70, 1970–71, 1971–72, 1972–73, 1973–74. Premier Division 1976–77, 1978–79, 1980–81, 1981–82, 1985–86, 1987–88; *Runners-up:* 21 times.
Scottish Cup Winners: (27 times) 1892, 1899, 1900, 1904, 1907, 1908, 1911, 1912, 1914, 1923, 1925, 1927, 1931, 1933, 1937, 1951, 1954, 1965, 1967, 1969, 1971, 1972, 1974, 1975, 1977, 1980, 1985, 1988, 1989; *Runners-up:* 16 times.
League Cup Winners: (9 times) 1956–57, 1957–58, 1965–66, 1966–67, 1967–68, 1968–69, 1969–70, 1974–75, 1982–83; *Runners-up:* 9 times.
European: *European Cup Winners:* 1966–67. 78 matches (1966–67 winners, 1967–68, 1968–69, 1969–70 runners-up, 1970–71, 1971–72 semi-finals, 1972–73, 1973–74 semi-finals, 1974–75, 1977–78, 1979–80, 1981–82, 1982–83, 1986–87, 1988–89); *Cup Winners Cup:* 35 matches (1963–64 semi-finals, 1965–66 semi-finals, 1975–76, 1980–81, 1984–85, 1985–86, 1989–90); *UEFA Cup:* 20 matches (*Fairs Cup:* 1962–63, 1964–65. *UEFA Cup:* 1976–77, 1983–84, 1987–88, 1991–92).
Club colours: Shirt: Green and white hoops. Shorts: White. Stockings: White.

Bonner, P	Morris, C	Rogan, A	Grant, P	Whyte, D	Wdowczyk, D	Fulton, S	Coyne, T	Cascarino, A	Nicholas, C	Collins, J	Creaney, G	Galloway, M	Gillespie, G	O'Neil, B	McNally, M	Miller, J	Walker, A	Dziekanowski, D	McStay, P	Smith, B	Mowbray, T	Marshall, G	Boyd, T	Match No.
1	2	3	4	5	6	7†	8	9*	10	11	12	14												1
1	2	3	4	5	6†	7	8*	9	10	11	12	14												2
1	2*	3	4†	5		7	8	9	10	11	12			6	14									3
1	2	3†	4	5	14	7	8		10*	11	9	12		6										4
1	2	3	4	5		7†	8*	9	10	11	12	14		6										5
1		5		3	8			10†12		9	4	6	11	2	7*	14								6
1		4	14	3	8†		10	12	11	9*	5	6		2	7									7
1	2	4	5	3	8†	9	10	11			6			14	7									8
1	2	4	6	3	8†	9	12	10*11		5				14	7									9
1		4	5	3		9	12	10*11†		8		6	14	2	7									10
1		4	3	14		9	10†11			5	6	8		2	7*	12								11
1	14	3				9	12	10*11		5	6†	4		2	7				8					12
1	2	3				9	12†10	11		5*	4	6	7						8	14				13
1	2	4	5	3	14	9	10*		12		11	6	7†						8					14
1	12		6	3		9	14	10*11		5		4	2		7†				8					15
1	12		6	3		9	14	10*11		5		4	2		7†				8					16
1	3*					9	14	10*11	12	4	6	7	2						8	5				17
1				14		9	12	10	11*	4†	3	6	7	2					8	5				18
1	4*	3				9	14	10†		12	5	6	11	2	7				8					19
14		4	5	3		9	10			12	11	6		2†	7*				8		1			20
		4	5	3		9	7†10		14	11	6			2					8		1			21
14		5	3*			9	7	10	12	11	6†	4		2					8		1			22
6		5		3*	9†	7	10	11		4	2	12							8	14	1			23
3		4	5			9	7*10†11		14	2	6	12							8		1			24
2		4	6		14	9	12	10†11		7*	3								8	5	1			25
2	4†	6		14		9*10	11	12	7		3								8	5	1			26
2	4	6		14		9*10	11	12	7		3								8	5†	1			27
2		5		3†14	9		11	10		6	4		7						8		1			28
2		5	3	14	9*12		11	10		6	4		7†						8		1			29
2		5	3		9		11	10		6	4		7						8		1			30
2		5		14	9		12	11	10*	3	6	4	7†						8		1			31
2†		5		7	9*		12	11	10	6		4		14					8		1	3		32
2		5		12		10†11	9	14		6	4		7*						8		1	3		33
2		5		7†	9*		12	11	10	6	4								8	14	1	3		34
2				4*	9		11	10		6	12	8	7							5	1	3		35
				11	12		10	14	9*	2	6	4†	7						8	5	1	3		36
2		6			12		10*11	9	14	4			7†						8	5	1	3		37
	8	6		3†11	12		10		9*	7	4								2	5	1	14		38
2		6		14	12		10	11	9*	7	4†								8	5	1	3		39
2		6		14	12		10*11	9		7	4†								8	5	1	3		40
2		6		4†			10	11	9	14									8	5	1	3		41
2		6		12			10	11*	9	7	4								8	5	1	3		42
2		6†		4	12		10	11	9	14			7*						8	5	1	3		43
2		6		4	12		10	11	9				5		7*				8		1	3		44
19	29	5	20	38	18	18	32	13	32	36	21	26	24	25	22	23	0	31	1	14	25	12		
+		+	+	+	+	+	+	+	+	+			+	+	+	+	+		+	+		+		
3s		2s	2s	1s	12s7s		11s5s	2s	11s8s				3s	3s	3s	1s	1s		2s	1s		1s		

CLYDE

Second Division

Year Formed: 1878. *Ground & Address:* Douglas Park, Douglas Park Lane, Hamilton M13 0DF. *Telephone:* (Mon–Fri: 041 248 7953), (Match Days Only): 0698 286103.
Ground Capacity: total: 9168. seated: 1595. *Size of Pitch:* 110yd × 70yd.
Chairman: John F. McBeth F.R.I.C.S. *Secretary:* John D. Taylor. *Commercial Manager:* John Donnelly.
Manager: Alex Smith. *Assistant Manager:* John Cushley. *Physio:* J. Watson. *Coach:* —.
Managers since 1975: S. Anderson; C. Brown; J. Clark.
Club Nickname(s): The Bully Wee. *Previous Grounds:* None.
Record Attendance: 52,000 v Rangers, Division I; 21 Nov, 1908.
Record Transfer Fee received: £95,000 for Pat Nevin to Chelsea (July 1983).
Record Transfer Fee paid: £14,000 for Harry Hood from Sunderland (1966).

CLYDE 1991–92 LEAGUE RECORD

Match No.	Date		Venue	Opponents	Result		H/T Score	Lg. Pos.	Goalscorers	Attendance
1	Aug	10	H	East Fife	W	1-0	1-0	—	Morrison	629
2		17	A	Queen of the S	W	2-1	0-1	1	Clarke, Morrison	766
3		24	H	Alloa	W	2-0	1-0	1	Morrison, Scott	598
4		31	A	Stenhousemuir	W	2-1	1-1	1	McCoy, Morrison	586
5	Sept	7	A	Dumbarton	D	0-0	0-0	1		1029
6		10	H	Berwick R	W	2-0	0-0	—	McAulay 2	547
7		14	H	Arbroath	D	1-1	0-0	1	Tennant	560
8		17	A	Brechin C	L	0-1	0-0	—		542
9		28	A	Stranraer	L	0-2	0-0	3		770
10	Oct	5	H	Queen's Park	W	3-1	1-1	3	Thompson D, Clarke, Wilson	554
11		12	A	Albion R	D	2-2	0-2	3	Thompson D, Morrison	491
12		19	H	Cowdenbeath	W	4-0	0-0	2	Thompson D 2, Ronald 2	532
13		26	H	East Stirling	W	2-1	0-1	1	Clarke, Mallan	378
14	Nov	2	A	East Fife	W	2-1	2-0	1	McCoy, Clarke	848
15		16	A	Alloa	L	2-4	1-2	2	Scott, Thomson J	598
16		23	H	Dumbarton	L	0-1	0-0	3		834
17		30	A	Arbroath	D	0-0	0-0	3		556
18	Dec	7	H	Queen of the S	L	2-3	1-3	3	Thomson J, Wilson	538
19		14	A	East Stirling	L	1-2	1-0	3	Watson	383
20		28	H	Brechin C	D	0-0	0-0	3		472
21	Jan	1	A	Berwick R	L	1-2	0-0	—	Clarke	334
22		11	A	Queen's Park	W	1-0	0-0	4	Thompson D	883
23		18	H	Stranraer	W	4-2	2-0	4	Thompson D 2 (1 pen), McGarvey 2	418
24		21	H	Stenhousemuir	D	0-0	0-0	—		423
25	Feb	1	A	Cowdenbeath	W	3-0	2-0	2	Clarke, Thompson D 2	546
26		4	H	Albion R	W	6-2	1-1	—	Morrison (pen), McGarvey 2, Mallan, Thompson D 2	376
27		8	A	Arbroath	L	0-3	0-1	2		795
28		15	H	East Fife	W	4-0	2-0	2	McGarvey, Thompson D 2, Morrison	610
29		29	A	Brechin C	W	2-1	0-0	3	Mallan, Thompson D	466
30	Mar	3	H	Berwick R	L	0-1	0-1	—		411
31		14	A	Cowdenbeath	L	1-3	0-0	5	Speirs	764
32		17	H	Queen of the S	W	2-1	0-0	—	Mallan, Thompson D	434
33		21	H	Stranraer	D	1-1	1-1	5	Clarke	466
34		28	A	Queen's Park	L	0-1	0-1	5		769
35	Apr	4	H	Alloa	L	0-1	0-0	5		582
36		11	A	Dumbarton	L	1-2	0-1	5	Archibald	1001
37		18	H	Stenhousemuir	W	4-0	0-0	5	McGarvey, Quinn 2, Mallan	351
38		25	A	East Stirling	L	1-2	1-2	5	Archibald	382
39	May	2	A	Albion R	W	2-0	2-0	5	Wilson, Thompson D	378

Final League Position: 5

League (61): Thompson D 16 (1 pen), Clarke 7, Morrison 7 (1 pen), McGarvey 6, Mallan 5, Wilson 3, Archibald 2, McAulay 2, McCoy 2, Quinn 2, Ronald 2, Scott 2, Thomson J 2, Speirs 1, Tennant 1, Watson 1. *Scottish Cup* (3): Morrison 1 Scott 1, Wilson 1. *Skol Cup* (0). *B & Q Cup* (0).

Record Victory: 11-1 v Cowdenbeath, Division II; 6 Oct, 1951.
Record Defeat: 0-11 v Dumbarton, Scottish Cup 4th rd, 22 Nov, 1879; v Rangers, Scottish Cup 4th rd, 13 Nov, 1880.
Most Capped Player: Tommy Ring, 12, Scotland.
Most League Appearances: 428: Brian Ahern.
Most League Goals in Season (Individual): 32: Bill Boyd, 1932–33.
Most Goals Overall (Individual): —.

Honours
League Champions: Division II 1904–05, 1951–52, 1956–57, 1961–62, 1972–73. Second Division 1977–78, 1981–82;
Runners-up: Division II 1903–04, 1905–06, 1925–26, 1963–64.
Scottish Cup Winners: 1939, 1955, 1958; *Runners-up:* 1910, 1912, 1949.
League Cup: —.
Club colours: Shirt: White with red and black trim. Shorts: Black. Stockings: White.

Stevenson, H	Knox, K	Tennant, S	Morrison, S	Speirs, C	Thomson, J	Thompson, D	Wilson, K	Scott, M	McCoy, G	Clarke, S	Wylde, G	McAulay, J	McVie, G	Mallan, S	Ronald, P	McFarlane, R	O'Hara, F	MacIver, S	Gaughan, M	Ross, S	Watson, E	Tierney, P	Wylde, G	Morrison, S	McGarvey, F	Haggerty, N	Howie, S	Burke, P	Match No.
1	2	3	4	5	6*	7	8	9†	10	11	12	14																	1
1	2	3	4	5		7		12	10†	8	11			6	9*	14													2
1	2	3	4	5		7*	8	9†	12	10	11	14		6															3
1	2	3	4	5			8*	9†	10		11	7		14	12	6													4
1	2	3	4		5		8			9*	11	7		12	10	6													5
1	2	3	4		5		8			10	11	7		14		6	9†												6
1	2	3	4		5		8			9	11	7*		12	10	6													7
1	2	3	4		5		8			9	11	7†		12	10*	6	14												8
1	2	3	4*	5	6	7	8	12		11				10					9										9
	2	3	4		5	7	8	12	10	11†			14			6			9*	1									10
	2	3	14		5	7	8	12		4	11†				10	6			9*	1									11
1	2	3	11		5	7	8	9*			4			12	10	6													12
1	2	3	11	14	5	7†	8	9*			4			12	10	6													13
1	2	3	11†	14	5			9*	10	4		7		12	8	6													14
1	2	3	8	14	5		4	9*					7	11†	10	6							12						15
1	2	3			5		9	11*		10	7			8	6								12				4		16
1	2	3	12		5	7		11†		10	14			8	6								9*				4		17
1	2	3	12		5	7	10	14		11*				8†	6								9				4		18
1	8	3	12		5	7	9	14		10*				6					2				4	11†					19
1	2	3		5		7	12	9		8				4	6										10	11*			20
1	2	3		5*	10	7	12			8				4†	6							11	14		9				21
1	2	3		5		7	8	4							6		11†					14		12	9	10*			22
1	2	3		5		7	4	11†		6	8*					10						14		12	9				23
1	2	3		5		7	8	11†		6	4*					10						14		12	9				24
	2	3†		5		7		4*	6		11	8					14						12	9		1	10		25
	2*			5		7	14		6		11	8	10†				12					4	9		1	3		26
				5	12	7	10		6		11	8				2	14					4*	9		1	3†		27
				5	4	7	10		6		11	8	3		2*							12	9		1			28
	2	3	5	14		7	10	4†	6		11	8										12	9*		1			29
	2	3	5			7	10	4	6		11	8*										12	9		1			30
10	3†		5	14		7		9			11	8	2												1			31
4			5	8		7	10*	9	6		11	2†					14		12			1	3						32
10	3*		5	8		7	4	6		11	12	2			14	9†						1						33
3			5	10		7	12	4	6		11*	8	2									1						34
2	3*		5	7		9	4	10	12	6												1						35
3			5	7	11	4	6		14	10*	2			12		1												36
3			5	7	10	4	11	2	6		8†		14	9*		1												37
2	3		5	7	11	4†	9	8*	6						12		1											38
3			5	7†	10	8	4*	6						12	9	1												39

Totals: 22 35 34 14 23 23 31 29 12 4 28 29 10 2 14 25 28 4 6 3 2 6 1 1 4 12 1 15 4
Substitutes: +4s +3s +3s +3s +7s +1s +1s +4s +9s +4s +1s +1s +4s +6s +12s

Archibald S—Match No. 34(9†) 35(8) 36(8) 38(10); Roberts P—Match No. 34(14); Quinn K—Match No. 35(11) 36(9†) 37(12) 38(14) 39(11); Malone P—Match No. 39(14).

CLYDEBANK   First Division

Year Formed: 1965. *Ground & Address:* Kilbowie Park, Arran Place, Clydebank G81 2PB. *Telephone:* 041 952 2887.
Ground Capacity: total: 9950. seated: All. *Size of Pitch:* 110yd × 68yd.
Chairman: C. A. Steedman. *Secretary:* I. C. Steedman. *Commercial Manager:* David Curwood.
Manager: J. S. Steedman. *Managing Director:* J. S. Steedman. *Physio:* John Jolly. *Coach:* Jim Fallon.
Managers since 1975: William Munro; J. S. Steedman.
Club Nickname(s): The Bankies. *Previous Grounds:* None.
Record Attendance: 14,900 v Hibernian, Scottish Cup 1st rd; 10 Feb, 1965.
Record Transfer Fee received: £175,000 for Owen Coyle from Airdrieonians, February 1990.
Record Transfer Fee paid: £50,000 for Gerry McCabe from Clyde.

CLYDEBANK 1991–92 LEAGUE RECORD

Match No.	Date		Venue	Opponents	Result		H/T Score	Lg. Pos.	Goalscorers	Attendance
1	Aug	10	H	Dundee	L	1-2	0-0	—	Templeton (pen)	1466
2		13	H	Raith R	L	0-2	0-2	—		791
3		17	A	Ayr U	L	0-3	0-1	12		2685
4		24	H	Montrose	W	4-1	1-1	10	Eadie 2, Rowe, Harvey	667
5		31	A	Morton	W	7-1	2-1	6	Eadie 3 (2 pens), Henry, Wright, Rowe, Traynor	1855
6	Sept	7	H	Kilmarnock	D	1-1	0-1	7	Eadie	2249
7		14	A	Forfar Ath	L	1-2	0-0	9	Wright	612
8		21	A	Hamilton A	D	0-0	0-0	7		1299
9		28	H	Stirling Albion	L	0-1	0-1	8		846
10	Oct	5	H	Meadowbank T	D	1-1	1-0	7	Eadie	615
11		8	A	Partick T	W	3-0	1-0	—	Rowe, Eadie 2	2751
12		12	A	Dundee	L	0-4	0-2	8		2314
13		19	H	Ayr U	W	3-2	0-1	8	Harvey, Henry, Eadie	1100
14		26	A	Kilmarnock	L	1-2	0-1	8	John Dickson	2231
15		29	H	Forfar Ath	D	3-3	1-2	—	John Dickson, Eadie 2	537
16	Nov	2	H	Morton	W	3-1	3-0	8	Wright, McIntosh, Henry	1242
17		9	A	Montrose	W	3-1	0-1	8	John Dickson, Rowe 2	620
18		16	A	Meadowbank T	D	1-1	1-0	8	John Dickson	277
19		19	H	Partick T	D	0-0	0-0	—		1984
20		23	H	Hamilton A	D	1-1	1-0	8	McIntosh	1031
21		30	A	Raith R	L	0-4	0-3	8		1195
22	Dec	3	A	Stirling Albion	L	0-3	0-1	—		712
23		7	H	Dundee	D	2-2	2-1	8	Mair, Henry	1329
24		14	H	Kilmarnock	L	0-3	0-2	8		2184
25		28	H	Montrose	W	4-2	2-2	8	Mair, McIntosh 2, Henry	648
26	Jan	4	H	Meadowbank T	D	1-1	0-0	9	Henry	724
27		7	A	Forfar Ath	W	3-1	1-1	—	McIntosh, Eadie 2	400
28		11	A	Partick T	L	1-2	1-1	9	Eadie	2908
29		14	A	Morton	L	0-5	0-1	—		1440
30		18	A	Raith R	D	1-1	0-0	9	Eadie	756
31	Feb	1	A	Ayr U	L	1-3	1-2	9	Eadie	1918
32		8	A	Hamilton A	W	3-2	2-1	9	Harvey, Eadie, King	1468
33		26	H	Stirling Albion	W	2-1	0-1	—	Wright, Eadie	623
34		29	A	Meadowbank T	L	0-2	0-0	9		300
35	Mar	10	A	Partick T	L	0-2	0-2	—		2164
36		14	A	Montrose	D	2-2	1-0	9	Flannigan, Eadie	524
37		21	H	Morton	L	2-3	0-3	9	Eadie, Harvey	1047
38		28	A	Dundee	L	0-3	0-2	9		3545
39	Apr	4	H	Ayr U	W	1-0	1-0	9	Henry	677
40		7	A	Kilmarnock	L	0-1	0-0	—		2094
41		11	H	Forfar Ath	W	2-0	1-0	9	Whyte (og), Henry	449
42		18	H	Hamilton A	L	1-3	0-2	9	Eadie	1137
43		25	A	Raith R	D	0-0	0-0	9		939
44	May	2	A	Stirling Albion	L	0-2	0-2	9		1121

Final League Position: 9

League (59): Eadie 22 (2 pens), Henry 8, McIntosh 5, Rowe 5, John Dickson 4, Harvey 4, Wright 4, Mair 2, Flannigan 1, King 1, Templeton 1 (pen), Traynor 1, own goal 1. *Scottish Cup* (4): Eadie 2, Harvey 1, Henry 1. *Skol Cup* (0). *B & Q Cup* (5): John Dickson 2, Eadie 1, Henry 1, McIntosh 1.

Record Vicory: 8-1 Arbroath, First Division; 3 Jan 1977.
Record Defeat: 1-9 v Gala Fairydean, Scottish Cup qual. rd; 15 Sept, 1965.
Most Capped Player: —.
Most League Appearances: 620: Jim Fallon; 1968–86.
Most League Goals in Season (Individual): 28: Blair Millar, First Division; 1978–79.
Most Goals Overall (Individual) : 84, Blair Millar, 1977–83.

Honours
League Champions: Second Division 1975–76; *Runners-up:* First Division 1976–77, 1984–85.
Scottish Cup: Semi-finalists 1990.   *League Cup:* —.
Club colours: Shirt: Red, black and white fleck design. Shorts: White. Stockings: Red with black tops.

Spence, W	Traynor, J	Crawford, J	Smith, B	Sweeney, S	Wright, B	Harvey, P	Lansdowne, A	Kelly, P	Dickson, John	Mair, G	Maher, J	Templeton, H	Rowe, G	Rossiter, B	Eadie, K	McIntosh, M	Henry, J	King, T	Dickson, Joe	Duncanson, J	Curry, T	Goldie, P	Gallacher, J	Woods, S	Flannigan, C	Sermanni, P	Match No.
1	2	3	4	5	6	7	8	9	10†	11		14															1
1	2	3		5	6	7	8†	9		11	4	10*	12	14													2
1	2	3		5	6	7				11	4	14	10*	8†	9	12											3
1	12	3		5	6	8			14	11	4	10*	2		9	7†											4
1	2	3		5	6	7				11	4		8	9	10												5
1	2	3		5	6	7			14	11	4		8†	9	10												6
1	2	3		5	6	7				11	4		8*	9	12	10											7
1	2	3		5	6	7	14			11	4			9	10†	8											8
1	2	3		5	6	7	14			11	4			9	10	8†											9
1	2	3			6	7	14	8*	11†	4		12	9	5	10												10
1	12	3			6	7	14	11	4		2*		9	8	10†												11
1		3		5	6	7		14	11	4	2†		9	8	10												12
1	2	3			6	7		11		4		9	5	10	8												13
1	2	3			6	7		11		4		9	5	10	8												14
1	12	3		5	6	7†	14	11		4		9	2	10	8*												15
1	2	12		5	6*	7		11		4		9	3	10	8												16
1				5	6	7		11	14	4		2	9	3	10†	8*12											17
1				5	6	7		10	11	4		8*	9	3		12	2										18
1				5	6	7		10	11	4			9	3	14	8†	2										19
1				5	6*	7		10	11	4		8†	9	3	14	12	2										20
1			5*			7		10†11		4		8	9	3	14	12	2	6									21
1	6					7	8	14	11	4		5†	9	3	10	2											22
1	3				6	7		14	11	4		8	9	5	10†	2											23
1		3			6	7	12	14	9*11†	4		8		5	10	2											24
1	3				8	7			11	4			9	6	10	2	5										25
1	3				8	7		14	11†	4		5	9	6	10	2											26
1	3				8	7		14	11	4		5	9	6	10†	2											27
1	3				8	7		14	11	4		5	9	6	10†12	2*											28
1		3			8	7		14	11†	4		5	9		10	2*	6	12									29
1					8	7	3	11		4		5	9		10		6	2									30
1	3				6	7	8	11		4		2	9	5	10												31
	3				8	7*12	14		4		2	9	6	10†11			5	1									32
	3				6	7	11*	12	4		10	9	5	8			2	1									33
	3				6	7	12	14	11*	4		10†	9	5	8			2	1								34
	3				6	7	14*10†11		4		2	9	5	8			12	1									35
	3				6	7		11	4		2	9		8			5	1	10								36
1	3				6	7		14	4		12	9	5	11†	8*			2	10								37
1	3	4			6†	7	14	11		5	9			8			12	2*	10								38
1	3	4				8				5	2	9		7		6			10	11							39
1	3	4			14	8				5	2	9		7		6†			10	11							40
	3	4				8				5	2	9		7	14	6			10†11								41
1	3	4			14	8		12		5	2*	9		7		6			10	11†							42
	3	4*			12	14	8	9		11	2			7		6		5	1	10†							43
	3	4				8	9	10†	5		2			7	11	6			1							14	44
37	12	35	10	18	36	38	11	7	14	28	38	2	30	7	39	25	32	16	12	9	1	8	2	5	8	4	
+3s	+1s		+1s	+3s	+3s	+9s	+10s	+3s	+1s	+2s	+3s	+1s			+2s	+3s	+5s	+1s		+1s	+2s					+1s	

COWDENBEATH First Division

Year Formed: 1881. *Ground & Address:* Central Park, Cowdenbeath KY4 9EY. *Telephone:* 0383 511205.
Ground Capacity: total: 4778. seated: 1072. *Size of Pitch:* 110yd × 70yd.
Chairman: Gordon McDougall. *Secretary:* J. Ronald Fairbairn. *Commercial Manager:* James Colvin.
Manager: —. *Assistant Manager:* —. *Physio:* James Reekie. *Coach:* John Brownlie.
Managers since 1975: D. McLindon; F. Connor; P. Wilson; A Rolland; H. Wilson; W. McCulloch; J. Clark; J. Craig;
R. Campbell; J. Blackley; J. Brownlie.
Club Nickname(s): Cowden. *Previous Grounds:* North End Park, Cowdenbeath.
Record Attendance: 25,586 v Rangers, League Cup quarter final; 21 Sept, 1949.
Record Transfer Fee received: £12,000 for Roddy Grant from St. Johnstone, Oct 1988.
Record Transfer Fee paid: —.

COWDENBEATH 1991–92 LEAGUE RECORD

Match No.	Date		Venue	Opponents	Result	H/T Score	Lg. Pos.	Goalscorers	Atten- dance
1	Aug	10	H	Queen of the S	L	0-1	0-0	—	332
2		17	A	East Stirling	W	3-2	2-1	7	Robertson A, Malone (pen), Lamont P	319
3		24	H	Stenhousemuir	W	2-0	1-0	3	Wright, Lamont P	305
4		31	A	Arbroath	L	1-2	1-0	6	Robertson A	449
5	Sept	7	H	Albion R	W	1-0	1-0	4	Irving	254
6		14	A	Queen's Park	W	3-2	1-0	4	Malone, Buckley, Irving	422
7		17	A	Stranraer	D	2-2	0-2	—	Syme, Lamont P	569
8		21	H	East Fife	D	3-3	3-2	4	Syme, Lamont P, Wright	603
9		28	H	Berwick R	W	2-0	2-0	2	Buckley, Archibald	307
10	Oct	5	A	Brechin C	W	1-0	0-0	2	Syme	430
11		12	H	Alloa	D	1-1	0-1	2	Buckley	333
12		19	A	Clyde	L	0-4	0-0	3		532
13		26	H	Dumbarton	W	2-1	2-1	3	Lamont P 2	309
14	Nov	2	A	Queen of the S	D	3-3	0-2	3	Scott, Lamont P 2	514
15		9	H	East Stirling	W	3-2	2-2	3	Lamont P 2, Malone	225
16		16	A	Stenhousemuir	D	3-3	0-1	3	Malone (pen), Fraser, Syme	374
17		23	A	Albion R	W	4-0	2-0	2	Scott, Buckley 3	288
18		30	H	Queen's Park	L	0-2	0-1	2		365
19	Dec	14	A	Dumbarton	D	0-0	0-0	2		964
20		28	H	Stranraer	W	2-0	1-0	2	Malone (pen), Scott	321
21	Jan	1	A	East Fife	L	0-1	0-1	—		1259
22		18	A	Berwick R	W	3-1	0-1	2	Douglas, Buckley 2	346
23	Feb	1	H	Clyde	L	0-3	0-2	4		546
24		8	A	Stenhousemuir	W	4-2	1-1	4	Buckley 2, Lamont P 2	366
25		12	H	Brechin C	W	2-1	2-0	—	Syme, Buckley	318
26		15	H	East Stirling	W	4-0	2-0	3	Irving, Buckley 2, Malone	309
27		18	H	Arbroath	W	3-1	3-0	—	Malone, Wright, Irving	313
28		22	A	Stranraer	L	0-1	0-0	2		467
29		25	A	Alloa	L	2-4	1-3	—	Buckley, McMahon	535
30		29	A	East Fife	W	3-1	2-0	2	Buckley 2, McGovern	909
31	Mar	7	A	Queen's Park	W	2-1	2-0	1	Buckley, Fraser	603
32		14	H	Clyde	W	3-1	0-0	1	Lamont P 3	764
33		21	H	Berwick R	W	4-1	1-1	1	Buckley 2, Robertson A, Irvine	657
34		28	A	Arbroath	L	0-1	0-0	1		645
35	Apr	4	A	Albion R	W	2-1	0-0	1	Archibald, Lamont P	273
36		11	H	Brechin C	W	2-1	2-0	1	Buckley, Lamont P	569
37		18	A	Dumbarton	L	1-2	0-1	3	Wright	1807
38		25	H	Queen of the S	W	3-1	1-1	2	Buckley, Malone, Lamont P (pen)	782
39	May	2	A	Alloa	D	0-0	0-0	2		5050

Final League Position: 2

League (74): Buckley 21, Lamont P 18 (1 pen), Malone 8 (3 pens), Syme 5, Irving A 4, Wright 4, Robertson A 3, Scott 3, Archibald 2, Fraser 2, Douglas 1, Irvine N 1, McGovern 1, McMahon 1. *Scottish Cup* (8): Lamont P 3, Malone 2 (1 pen), Archibald 1, Irving A 1, own goal, 1. *Skol Cup* (1): Robertson A 1. *B & Q Cup* (2): Fraser 1, Robertson A 1.

Record Victory: 12-0 v Johnstone, Scottish Cup 1st rd; 21 Jan, 1928.
Record Defeat: 1-11 v Clyde, Division II; 6 Oct, 1951.
Most Capped Player: Jim Paterson, 3, Scotland.
Most League Appearances: —.
Most League Goals in Season (Individual): 40: Willie Devlin, Division II; 1925–26.
Most Goals Overall (Individual): —.

Honours

League Champions: Division II 1913–14, 1914–15, 1938–39; *Runners-up:* Division II 1921–22, 1923–24, 1969–70. Second Division 1991–92.
Scottish Cup: —.
League Cup: —.
Club colours: Shirt: Royal blue shadow vertical stripe with white chest band. Shorts: White with blue side stripe. Stockings: Royal blue.

Robertson, C	Fraser, S	Robertson, A	Bennett, W	Archibald, E	Irvine, N	Wright, J	Malone, G	Lamont, P	Irving, A	Scott, C	Syme, W	Johnston, P	Lamont, W	Watt, D	Douglas, H	Buckley, G	Ferguson, S	McGovern, D	O'Hanlon, S	McMahon, B	Hamill, K	Match No.
1	2	3	4	5	6	7	8	9	10	11												1
	12	3		5	6	7†	8*	9	10	11	14			1	2	4						2
	12	11	3*	5	6	7	8	9			14			1	2	4†		10				3
1	12	11	3*	5	6	7	8†	9							2	4		10		14		4
	14	3		5	6†	7	8	9*	10	11				1	2	4		12				5
	14	3		5	6	7	8	9*	10	11				1	2	4†		12				6
	12	3		5	6	7	8*	9		11†	14			1	2	4		10				7
		3		5	6	7	8*	9	10		14			1	2	4		11†		12		8
	12	3		5	6	7	8	9	10					1	2	4*		11				9
	12	3		5	6*	7	8	9†	10		14			1	2	4		11				10
		3		5		7	8	9	10*		12		6†	1	2	4		11		14		11
	4	3		5		7	8	9	10	11*	12			1	2			6				12
	4	3		5			8	9		11†	14			1	2	10	7	6				13
	4	3*		5			8	9		11	14			1	2	10	7†	6		12		14
	4	3		5			8	9		11	14			1	2	10	7†	6				15
	4	3		5			8	9		11*	12			1	2	10	7	6				16
1	4†	3		5			8	9		11	14		12		2	10	7*	6				17
	4†	3		5			8	9		11	14		12		2	10	7*	6	1			18
	12	3	4	5			8	9		11*	7				2	10		6	1			19
		3	4	5			8	9	7†	11	14		12		2	10		6*	1			20
		3	4	5			8	9*	7†	11	12		14		2	10		6	1			21
		3	4	5	7*		8	9		11†	12		14		2	10		6	1			22
		3	4	5	7†		8	9		11					2	10		6	1	14		23
	14	3	4	5	7		8	9	12	11					2†	10*		6	1			24
		3	4	5	7		8	9	12	11				1	2	10*		6				25
	3		4	5	7		8	9*		11†	14			1	2	10		6		12		26
	3		4*	5	7		8	9		11†	14			1	2	10		6		12		27
	3	10	4	5	7*		8†	9		11	12		14	1	2	10		6				28
	3*	11	4	5	7			9†			14			1	2	10		6		12	8	29
	8	3	4	5	7			9		11*				1	2	10		6		12		30
	8	3	4	5	7†		12	9		11*				1	2	10	14	6				31
	8	3	4	7*				9	12	11				1	2	10	5	6				32
	8	3	4	7*				9	12	11†				1	2	10	5	6	14			33
	8	3	4	7*				9	12	11				1	2	10	5	6				34
	2	3	6	4	7			9		14						5	10†	11*	8		12	35
	8	3	4	5	7			9†	14		12			1	2	10		6		11*		36
		3		5	4	7	8	9	12						2	10		6	1	11*		37
		3		5	4	7	8	9	11†						2	10		6	1	14		38
		3		5	4	7	8	9*		11	12				2	10		6	1			39
3	19	37	3	36	31	26	31	36	14	15	20	0	26	37	14	33	7	28	0	10	1	2

+
10s · 1s · 1s 16s 1s · 12s 3s · 4s 2s 4s 1s 1s · 4s 2s

DUMBARTON

First Division

Year Formed: 1872. *Ground & Address:* Boghead Park, Miller St, Dumbarton G82 2JA. *Telephone:* 0389 62569/67864.
Ground Capacity: total: 10,700. seated: 700. *Size of Pitch:* 110yd × 75yd.
Chairman: A. Hagen. *Secretary:* Alistair Paton. *Company Secretary:* Robert Dawson.
Manager: Billy Lamont. *Assistant Manager:* Billy Simpson. *Physio:* Bobby McCallum. *Coaches:* Jim Chapman, Donald McNeil.
Managers since 1975: A. Wright; D. Wilson; S. Fallon; W. Lamont; D. Wilson; D. Whiteford; A. Totten; M. Clougherty; R. Auld; J. George.
Club Nickname(s): The Sons. *Previous Grounds:* Broadmeadow, Ropework Lane.
Record Attendance: 18,000 v Raith Rovers, Scottish Cup; 2 Mar, 1957.
Record Transfer Fee received: £125,000 for Graeme Sharp to Everton (March 1982).

DUMBARTON 1991–92 LEAGUE RECORD

Match No.	Date		Venue	Opponents	Result	H/T Score	Lg. Pos.	Goalscorers	Atten- dance
1	Aug	10	A	Queen's Park	W 3-0	0-0	—	Gibson, Gilmour, Meechan	657
2		17	H	Berwick R	D 1-1	0-0	3	McQuade	524
3		24	A	Stranraer	L 1-2	1-1	4	Martin	630
4		31	H	Albion R	W 4-3	2-1	3	Meechan, Gilmour 2 (1 pen), MacIver	586
5	Sept	7	A	Clyde	D 0-0	0-0	3		1029
6		14	A	Brechin C	W 4-0	3-0	3	McConville, Gibson, Gilmour, McQuade	491
7		17	H	Arbroath	W 2-1	2-1	—	Gilmour, McQuade	777
8		21	A	East Stirling	W 2-1	0-1	1	Meechan 2	355
9		28	H	East Fife	L 1-2	0-1	1	Gilmour	753
10	Oct	5	A	Alloa	W 2-1	1-1	1	Willock, McQuade	667
11		12	H	Stenhousemuir	W 1-0	1-0	1	Willock	607
12		19	A	Queen of the S	W 4-2	2-1	1	McQuade, Gilmour, Meechan, McConville	893
13		26	A	Cowdenbeath	L 1-2	1-2	2	McQuade	309
14	Nov	2	H	Queen's Park	W 3-1	1-1	2	Gilmour 2, Gibson	557
15		9	A	Berwick R	D 2-2	2-2	1	Gilmour (pen), Meechan	305
16		16	H	Stranraer	W 1-0	0-0	1	Gibson	631
17		23	A	Clyde	W 1-0	0-0	1	Gibson	834
18		30	H	Brechin C	W 3-0	1-0	1	McQuade, Gibson, Gilmour (pen)	670
19	Dec	4	A	Cowdenbeath	D 0-0	0-0	1		964
20		26	A	Albion R	W 3-0	1-0	1	Melvin, Willock 2	650
21		28	A	Arbroath	L 0-1	0-0	1		667
22	Jan	11	H	Alloa	D 2-2	0-2	1	Gilmour, Willock	914
23		14	H	East Stirling	D 1-1	1-0	—	Gilmour (pen)	787
24		18	A	East Fife	D 2-2	0-2	1	Gibson, Gilmour (pen)	1220
25	Feb	1	H	Queen of the S	W 3-1	2-1	1	Meechan, Gilmour 2 (1 pen)	627
26		4	A	Stenhousemuir	L 0-1	0-0	—		426
27		8	H	Stranraer	D 0-0	0-0	1		621
28		15	A	Albion R	D 1-1	0-1	1	Willock	335
29		25	H	Brechin C	L 1-3	1-2	—	Gilmour (pen)	390
30		29	A	Queen's Park	D 0-0	0-0	1		589
31	Mar	14	A	Queen of the S	W 2-1	0-1	2	Gibson, Willock	583
32		17	H	East Stirling	L 0-1	0-0	—		584
33		21	H	Alloa	D 1-1	0-0	2	McConville	656
34		28	A	Berwick R	W 5-1	4-0	2	Marsland, McQuade 3, Meechan	174
35	Apr	4	A	East Fife	W 2-0	1-0	2	McQuade, Gibson	1166
36		11	H	Clyde	W 2-1	1-0	2	Meechan, Gilmour	1001
37		18	A	Cowdenbeath	W 2-1	1-0	1	McQuade 2	1807
38		25	H	Stenhousemuir	W 1-0	1-0	1	Martin	1022
39	May	2	H	Arbroath	D 1-1	1-0	1	Gilmour	2104

Final League Position: 1

League (65): Gilmour 19 (7 pens), McQuade 13, Gibson 9, Meechan 9, Willock 7, McConville 3, Martin 2, MacIver 1, Marsland 1, Melvin 1. *Scottish Cup* (4): Boyd 1, Dempsey 1, Gilmour 1 (pen), McQuade 1. *Skol Cup* (2): Gibson 2. *B & Q Cup* (1): Gibson 1.

Record Transfer Fee paid: £50,000 for Charlie Gibson from Stirling Albion 1989.
Record Victory: 13-1 v Kirkintilloch Cl. 1st Rd; 1 Sept, 1888.
Record defeat; 1-11 v Albion Rovers, Division II; 30 Jan, 1926: v Ayr United, League Cup; 13 Aug, 1952.
Most Capped Player: John Lindsay, 8, Scotland; James McAulay, 8, Scotland.
Most League Appearances: 297: Andy Jardine, 1957-67.
Most Goals in Season (Individual): 38: Kenny Wilson, Division II; 1971-72.
Most Goals Overall (Individual): 169: Hughie Gallacher, 1954-62 (including C Division 1954-55).

Honours
League Champions: Division I 1890-91 (shared with Rangers), 1891-92. Division II 1910-11, 1971-72. Second Division 1991-92; *Runners-up:* First Division 1983-84. Division II 1907-08.
Scottish Cup Winners: 1883; *Runners-up:* 1881, 1882, 1887, 1891, 1897.   *League Cup:* —.
Club colours: Shirt: Gold. Shorts: Gold. Stockings: Gold and black.

McFarlane, I	Marsland, J	Boyd, J	Melvin, M	Martin, P	Gow, S	McQuade, J	Dempsey, J	Gibson, C	Meechan, J	Gilmour, J	Foster, A	Millar, S	McNair, C	McCracken, D	MacIver, S	McGarvey, M	McConville, R	Willock, A	Hughes, J	Cowell, J	Edgar, D	Nelson, M	Carson, T	Match No.
1	2	3*	4	5	6	7†	8	9	10	11	12	14												1
1	2	3	4	5	6	7	8*	9	10	11			12											2
1	2	3	4	5		7	8	9	10			11*		6	12									3
1	2†		4	5	6	7	8	9	10	11	3*			12	14									4
1	2	3	4	5	6	7		9*	10	11				12	14		8†							5
1	14		3	5	2	7		9†	4*	11	12			6		10	8							6
1		10†	3	5	2*	7	4		9	12	11			6		14	8							7
1		3	4	5	2	7	6	9	8	11							10							8
1		3	4	5	2	7	6	9*	8	11					12		10							9
1	3	14	4	5	2†	12	6	9	8	11							10	7*						10
1	2	3	6	5		7	4	9	8	11						12	10*							11
1	14	3	2	5	4	7	6	9	8†	11							10*	12						12
1	4	3	2	5	6	7	8*	9	10†	11							12		14					13
1	14	3	6	5	2	7*	4	9	8	11							10†		12					14
1		3	4	5	2	7	6	9†	8	11		12					10*		14					15
1		3	4	5	2	7	6	9	8	11							10*		12					16
1	14	3	4	5	2	7	6	9	8	11*						12	10†							17
1	2	3	4	5		7	6	9	8†	12						14	11*	10						18
1		3	6	5	2	7	4*	9	8	11†					12	14	10							19
1	5	3	4		2		6	9	8	11†							10*	7	12	14				20
1		3	4	5	2		6	9	8								10	7	12	11*				21
1	4†	3	6	5	2	7	8*	9		11							10		12	14				22
1	8	3	4	5	2	7	6	9†		11							10*		12	14				23
1	4	3	6	5	2	7	8	9*		11							10		12					24
1	4	3	6	5	2		10	9	8	11								7*	12					25
1	4	3*	6	5	2		10	9†	8	11		14						7	12					26
1	6	3	4	5	2			9	8	11							10	7*	12					27
1	4	3	6	5	2		14	9†	8	11							10	7*	12					28
1	4	3	6	5	2	9	12		8	11						14		7†				10*		29
1	4	3	6	5	2	7	10		12	11						8*	9†		14					30
1	4	3	6†	5	2	7	10	9	14	11								12		8*				31
1	4	3		5	2	7	10	9†	6	11							12		14	8*				32
1	3	14	4	5	2	7	10†	9*	6	11							8		12					33
	6	3	4	5	2	7		9	8	11*						14	10†		12				1	34
	6	3	4	5	2	7		9	8	11*							10†		12			14	1	35
	4	3	6	5	2	7		9*	8	11							10		12				1	36
	2	3	4	5		7†		9	8	11						14	10		12			6*	1	37
	2	3	4	5		7		9	8	11							10*		12			6	1	38
	4	3	6	5	2	7		9*	8	11									12			10	1	39
33	29	34	38	38	34	32	28	37	33	36	1	1	0	3	0	3	21	12	3	1	0	6	6	
	+4s	+2s				+1s	+2s			+3s	+1s	+4s	+1s	+1s	+3s	+3s	+5s	+3s	+18s	+3s	+7s	+1s	+2s	

DUNDEE   Premier Division

Year Formed: 1893. *Ground & Address:* Dens Park, Sandeman St, Dundee DD3 7JY. *Telephone:* 0382 826104. *Ground Capacity:* 20,136. seated: 11,516. *Size of Pitch:* 115yd × 77yd. *Chairman:* Ron Dixon. *Secretary:* Robert Swinton. *Marketing manager:* Derek Souter. *Manager:* Simon Stainrod. *Assistant Manager:* Jim Duffy. *Coach:* —. *Managers since 1975:* David White; Tommy Gemmell; Donald Mackay; Archie Knox; Jocky Scott; Dave Smith; Gordon Wallace; Iain Munro. *Club Nickname(s):* The Dark Blues or The Dee. *Previous Grounds:* Carolina Port 1893–98. *Record Attendance:* 43,024 v Rangers, Scottish Cup; 1953. *Record Transfer Fee received:* £500,000 for Tommy Coyne to Celtic, March 1989. *Record Transfer Fee paid:* £200,000 for Jim Leighton, February 1992. *Record Victory:* 10-0 Division II v Alloa; 9 Mar, 1947 and v Dunfermline Ath; 22 Mar, 1947. *Record Defeat:* 0-11 v Celtic, Division I; 26 Oct, 1895. *Most Capped Player:* Alex Hamilton, 24, Scotland. *Most League Appearances:* 341: Doug Cowie 1945–61. *Most*

DUNDEE 1991–92 LEAGUE RECORD

Match No.	Date		Venue	Opponents	Result		H/T Score	Lg. Pos.	Goalscorers	Atten- dance
1	Aug	10	A	Clydebank	W	2-1	0-0	—	Craig, Campbell D	1466
2		13	A	Forfar Ath	W	4-2	1-1	—	McQuillan, Craig, Dodds 2	2458
3		17	H	Meadowbank T	W	3-1	2-1	2	Dodds 2, Craig	2860
4		24	H	Hamilton A	W	4-1	3-0	1	Jamieson, Bremner, Dodds, Craig	2751
5		31	H	Raith R	W	1-0	0-0	1	Craig	3122
6	Sept	7	A	Morton	L	0-3	0-2	1		2036
7		14	H	Ayr U	W	3-1	1-1	1	West 2, Dodds	3410
8		21	H	Kilmarnock	W	2-1	1-1	1	Campbell S (pen), Jamieson	3786
9		28	A	Montrose	W	2-1	0-0	1	Jamieson, Campbell S (pen)	2228
10	Oct	5	H	Partick T	L	1-2	0-1	2	Beedie	4799
11		8	A	Stirling Albion	D	1-1	1-1	—	McMartin	1380
12		12	H	Clydebank	W	4-0	2-0	1	Chisholm, Dodds, Bremner, Campbell D (pen)	2314
13		19	A	Meadowbank T	W	2-1	1-0	1	Bremner, Dodds	747
14		26	H	Morton	L	0-1	0-0	2		1965
15		29	A	Ayr U	L	1-4	0-3	—	Dodds	2414
16	Nov	2	H	Raith R	D	1-1	1-1	2	Dodds	2397
17		9	A	Hamilton A	W	3-1	3-0	1	Gallagher 2, Dodds	1866
18		16	A	Partick T	W	6-2	3-2	1	Gallagher 3, Bremner 2, McQuillan	5042
19		19	H	Stirling Albion	D	0-0	0-0	—		2719
20		23	A	Kilmarnock	W	2-1	1-1	1	Chisholm, McCall	7137
21		30	H	Forfar Ath	W	4-0	1-0	1	McCall, Gallagher 2, Jamieson	2976
22	Dec	3	H	Montrose	W	1-0	1-0	—	Beedie	2779
23		7	A	Clydebank	D	2-2	1-2	1	Bremner, Campbell S	1329
24		14	A	Morton	D	0-0	0-0	1		1567
25		28	H	Hamilton A	L	1-2	1-2	1	Gallagher	4595
26	Jan	1	A	Raith R	L	0-1	0-0	—		3976
27		4	H	Partick T	W	1-0	0-0	1	Chisholm	4544
28		7	H	Ayr U	D	1-1	1-1	—	McCall	2502
29		11	A	Stirling Albion	D	1-1	0-0	1	Craig	2273
30		18	A	Forfar Ath	W	3-0	3-0	1	Beedie, Craig, West	2218
31	Feb	1	H	Meadowbank T	W	2-1	2-0	1	Dodds 2 (1 pen)	3038
32		8	H	Kilmarnock	D	1-1	0-1	1	Gallagher	5990
33		22	A	Montrose	W	3-2	1-0	1	Chisholm, Beedie, McCall	2363
34		29	A	Partick T	L	0-2	0-1	1		8437
35	Mar	7	H	Stirling Albion	W	5-0	3-0	1	Dodds, McCall 2, Stainrod, Gallagher	3190
36		14	A	Hamilton A	D	1-1	1-0	1	Dodds	2830
37		21	H	Raith R	W	3-2	1-1	1	McCall 2, Dodds	4452
38		28	H	Clydebank	W	3-0	2-0	1	Chisholm, Stainrod, Dodds	3545
39	Apr	4	A	Meadowbank T	D	0-0	0-0	1		1221
40		7	A	Morton	D	2-2	2-1	—	Dodds 2 (1 pen)	4452
41		11	A	Ayr U	D	0-0	0-0	1		2418
42		18	A	Kilmarnock	L	0-2	0-1	1		4933
43		25	H	Forfar Ath	W	3-1	0-0	1	McQuillan, Ritchie, McCall	5227
44	May	2	A	Montrose	L	1-2	0-0	1	Gallagher	6878

Final League Position: 1

League (80): Dodds 19 (2 pens), Gallagher 11, McCall 9, Craig 7, Bremner 6, Chisholm 5, Beedie 4, Jamieson 4, Campbell S 3 (2 pens), McQuillan 3, West 3, Campbell D 2 (1 pen), Stainrod 2, McMartin 1, Ritchie 1. *Scottish Cup* (2): Dinnie 1, McMartin 1. *Skol Cup* (2): Craig 2. *B & Q Cup* (0).

League Goals in Season (Individual): 38: Dave Halliday, Division I; 1923–24. *Most Goals Overall (individual):* 113: Alan Gilzean.

Honours
League Champions: Division I 1961–62. First Division 1978–79, 1991–92. Division II 1946–47; *Runners-up:* Division I 1902–03, 1906–07, 1908–09, 1948–49, 1980–81.
Scottish Cup Winners: 1910; *Runners-up:* 1925, 1952, 1964.
League Cup Winners: 1951–52, 1952–53, 1973–74; *Runners-up:* 1967–68, 1980–81.
European: European Cup: 1962–63 (semi-final). *Cup Winners' Cup:* 1964–65.
UEFA Cup: (*Fairs Cup* 1967–68 semi-final), 1971–72, 1973–74, 1974–75.
Club colours: Shirt: Dark blue with red and white trim. Shorts: White. Stockings: Blue and White.

Mathers, P	McMartin, G	Campbell, S	Forbes, G	McQuillan, J	Craib, M	Campbell, D	Craig, A	Bremner, K	Dodds, W	Beedie, S	McLeod, G	Dow, A	Fraser, C	Jamieson, W	Chisholm, G	Dinnie, A	West, C	Shannon, R	McCall, I	Gallagher, E	Forsyth, S	Frail, S	Leighton, J	Stainrod, S	Ritchie, P	Christie, M	Match No.
1	2	3	4	5	6	7	8	9	10	11																	1
1		3	5	2	6	7	8	9	10	11			4														2
1	12	3	5	2	6	7	8	9	10	11*			4														3
1	14	3		2	6	7†	8	9	10	11			4*	5	12												4
1		3		2	6	7	8	9	10	11			4	5													5
1	14	3		2	6	7†	8	9	10	11			4*	5	12												6
1	9	3			6	14	8		10†	11				5	4	2	7										7
1	9	3		2	6		8		10	11				5	4		7										8
1	9	3		2	6	14	8		10	11†				5	4	12	7*										9
1	8*	3		2	6		9†		10	11			14	5	4	12	7										10
1	9†	3		2	6	7		14	10	11*	8			5	4	12											11
1	12			2	6	7		9†	10	11*	8		14	5	4	3											12
1	12	3			6	7†		9	10	11			14	5	4	2*			8								13
1	14	3		2			7	9	10	11	8†			5	4				6								14
1	14	3		2			7	9	10	11	8†			5	4				6								15
1	7†			2	14		8	9†	10	11			6	5	4	14		3									16
1		3		2	4		8	9†	10	11	14		6	5	4		7										17
1		3		2			7		10	11			6†	5	4	14			8	9							18
1		3		2	6			12	10	11				5	4	7			8*	9							19
1		3		2	6*		14	12	10	11				5	4	7†			8	9							20
1		3		2	6		14	12	10	11†				5	4	7			8	9*							21
1		3†		2	6		7	12	10	11			14	5	4				8*	9							22
1		3		2			14	7	8	11			6	5†	4				10	9							23
1		3		2			7	12	10	11†			6	5	4	14			8	9*							24
1				2			7*	12	10	11	14		6†	5	4	3			8	9							25
1		3		2					10	11†			6	5	4	7	12		8*	9	14						26
1		3		2					12	11			6	5	4	7	8†		10*	9	14						27
1		3		2				12	10	11†			6	5	4	7	14		8	9*							28
1				2			7		10	11	3		6	5	4				8	9							29
1					6		9†		10	11	3			5	4		7		8			2	14				30
1				2	6		9*		10		3			5	4		7†		11	12	14	8					31
	7			2	6*		8†		10					5	4	3			11	12	14		1	9			32
	6			2					10	7				5	4	3			11	9			1	8			33
	6			2					10	7	11			5	4	3†			14				1	8	9		34
	6			2			8		10	7†14					4	3			11	12	5		1	9*			35
	6			2			8		10	7					4	3			11		5		1	9			36
	6			2			8		10	7					4	3			11†14		5		1	9*	12		37
	8			2					10†	7				5	4	3			11	14	6		1	9*	12		38
	8			2					10	7				5	4	3			11		6		1	9*	12		39
	14			2					10	7				5	4	3			11	12	6	8†	1	9*			40
	8	3			14				10	7†				5	4	2			11		6		1	9			41
	8*	3							10					5	4	2			11	12	6		1	9	7		42
		3			7				10†	8*				5	4	2			11	12	6		1	14	9		43
		3*			7				10	8				5	4	2			11	12	6		1	14	9†		44
31	17	29	3	39	19	12	23	15	42	40	12	0	12	38	37	24	7	4	26	13	11	2	13	11	3	1	
	+8s	+1s		+1s		+3s	+2s	+9s	+3s	+4s					+2s	+5s	+2s		+1s	+9s	+4s	+1s		+2s	+3s		

DUNDEE UNITED Premier Division

Year Formed: 1909 (1923). *Ground & Address:* Tannadice Park, Tannadice St, Dundee DD3 7JW. *Telephone:* 0382 833166. *Ground Capacity:* (new stand building) total: 20,862. seated: 2562. *Size of Pitch:* 110 × 74yd. *Chairman:* James Y. McLean. *Company Secretary:* Miss Priti Trivedi. *Commercial Manager:* James Connor. *Manager:* James Y. McLean. *Physio:* John Sharp. *Coach:* Paul Sturrock. *Managers since 1975:* J. McLean. *Club Nickname(s):* The Terrors. *Previous Grounds:* None. *Record Attendance:* 28,000 v Barcelona, Fairs Cup; 16 Nov, 1966. *Record Transfer Fee received:* £900,000 for Kevin Gallacher to Coventry C (Jan 1990). *Record Transfer Fee paid:* £350,000 for Michael O'Neill from Newcastle U, August 1989; Victor Ferreyra from San Lorenzo, Sept 1991. *Record Victory:* 14-0 v Nithsdale Wanderers, Scottish Cup 1st rd; 17 Jan, 1931. *Record Defeat:* 1-12 v Motherwell, Division II; 23 Jan, 1954. *Most Capped Player:* Maurice Malpas, 49, Scotland. *Most League Appearances:* 578, Dave Narey; 1973–92. *Most Appearances in European Matches:* 75, Dave Narey (record for Scottish player). *Most League Goals in Season (Individual):* 41: John Coyle, Division II; 1955–56. *Most Goals Overall (Individual):* 158: Peter McKay.

DUNDEE UNITED 1991–92 LEAGUE RECORD

Match No.	Date		Venue	Opponents	Result	H/T Score	Lg. Pos.	Goalscorers	Atten-dance
1	Aug	10	H	Celtic	L	3-4	1-3	—	O'Neill M 2 (1 pen), Ferguson	16,731
2		13	H	St Mirren	W	4-1	3-0	—	O'Neill M (pen), McKinley, Jackson 2 (1 pen)	5771
3		17	A	St Johnstone	D	1-1	1-1	6	Jackson	7700
4		24	A	Hibernian	L	0-1	0-0	7		9862
5		31	H	Aberdeen	D	0-0	0-0	7		11,961
6	Sept	7	H	Dunfermline Ath	W	3-0	1-0	6	Bowman, Van der Hoorn, Ferguson	5680
7		14	A	Rangers	D	1-1	0-1	5	Ferguson	36,347
8		21	A	Hearts	D	1-1	1-0	6	Ferguson	11,746
9		28	A	Motherwell	D	2-2	2-1	6	Malpas (pen), Bollan	6844
10	Oct	5	A	Falkirk	W	4-0	1-0	6	Ferguson, Ferreyra 2, Paatelainen	5155
11		8	H	Airdrieonians	D	0-0	0-0	—		5763
12		12	A	Celtic	L	1-4	0-2	7	O'Neill M	28,281
13		19	A	St Johnstone	L	1-2	1-0	7	French	6202
14		26	A	Airdrieonians	W	3-1	1-0	6	Ferguson, Clark, Paatelainen	1954
15		29	H	Rangers	W	3-2	1-1	—	McKinnon, Jackson (pen), Ferguson	15,041
16	Nov	2	A	Aberdeen	W	1-0	1-0	6	McInally	13,728
17		6	A	Dunfermline Ath	W	2-1	1-0	—	Jackson, Bowman	3528
18		9	H	Hibernian	D	1-1	1-0	5	McKinnon	8812
19		16	H	Falkirk	W	2-1	1-0	5	Ferreyra, Whittaker (og)	7290
20		23	H	Hearts	L	0-1	0-0	6		12,796
21		30	A	St Mirren	D	1-1	0-0	6	Cleland	3375
22	Dec	3	A	Motherwell	D	1-1	1-0	—	Jackson	4023
23		7	H	Celtic	D	1-1	0-1	5	Welsh	11,585
24		14	H	Dunfermline Ath	D	0-0	0-0	6		4782
25		21	A	Rangers	L	0-2	0-1	6		41,448
26		28	A	Hibernian	L	2-3	1-0	6	Paatelainen, Malpas	7688
27	Jan	1	H	Aberdeen	W	4-0	0-0	—	Ferguson, Paatelainen, Jackson 2	7777
28		4	A	Falkirk	W	3-1	1-0	5	McKinnon, Jackson 2	5163
29		11	H	Airdrieonians	W	2-1	0-0	5	Ferreyra, Jackson	6056
30		18	H	St Mirren	L	1-3	0-2	6	McInally	4933
31	Feb	1	A	St Johnstone	D	1-1	1-1	6	Ferguson	6364
32		8	A	Hearts	L	0-1	0-0	6		10,516
33		22	H	Motherwell	D	2-2	0-1	6	Cleland, Ferguson	4746
34		29	H	Falkirk	W	2-1	2-0	6	Paatelainen 2	5592
35	Mar	7	A	Dunfermline Ath	W	1-0	0-0	5	McKinnon	3042
36		14	H	Hibernian	W	1-0	1-0	4	Cleland	5588
37		17	A	Airdrieonians	L	0-1	0-1	—		2533
38		21	A	Aberdeen	W	2-0	1-0	4	Ferguson, McInally	10,350
39		28	A	Celtic	L	1-3	0-1	4	Ferguson	22,522
40	Apr	4	H	St Johnstone	W	2-1	1-1	4	Cleland, Bowman	5553
41		11	H	Rangers	L	1-2	0-0	5	McInally	11,713
42		18	H	Hearts	W	2-0	1-0	5	Malpas, Ferguson	6711
43		25	A	St Mirren	W	1-0	1-0	4	Ferguson	1431
44	May	2	A	Motherwell	W	2-1	1-0	4	Johnson, Ferguson	3151

Final League Position: 4

League (66): Ferguson 15, Jackson 11 (2 pens), Paatelainen 6, Cleland 4, Ferreyra 4, McInally 4, McKinnon 4, O'Neill M 4 (2 pens), Bowman 3, Malpas 3 (1 pen), Bollan 1, Clark 1, French 1, Johnson 1, McKinley 1, van der Hoorn 1, Welsh 1, own goal 1. *Scottish Cup* (7): Ferguson 2, Ferreyra 1, Malpas 1, O'Neil J 1, Paatelainen 1, own goal 1. *Skol Cup* (5): Paatelainen 2, Clark 1, French 1, O'Neill M 1.

Honours
League Champions: Premier Division 1982–83. Division II 1924–25, 1928–29; *Runners-up:* Division II 1930–31, 1959–60.
Scottish Cup Runners-up: 1974, 1981, 1985, 1987, 1988, 1991.
League Cup Winners: 1979–80, 1980–81; *Runners-up:* 1981–82, 1984–85.
Summer Cup Runners-up: 1964–65.   *Scottish War Cup Runners-up:* 1939–40.
European: *European Cup:* 8 matches 1983–84 (semi-finals), 1988–89; *Cup Winners Cup:* 4 matches 1974–75; *UEFA Cup Runners-up:* 1986–87. 78 matches (*Fairs Cup:* 1966–67, 1969–70, 1970–71. *UEFA Cup:* 1971–72, 1975–76, 1977–78, 1978–79, 1979–80, 1980–81, 1981–82, 1982–83, 1984–85, 1985–86, 1986–87, 1987–88, 1989–90, 1990–91).
Club colours: Tangerine jersey, black shorts. Change colours: all white.

Main, A	Cleland, A	Malpas, M	Bowman, D	Muller, J	McKinlay, W	O'Neil, J	O'Neill, M	French, H	Preston, A	Ferguson, D	Dailly, C	Paatelainen, M	Van der Kamp, G	Narey, D	Jackson, D	Clark, J	McLaren, A	Van der Hoorn, F	Bollan, G	Connolly, P	McInally, J	Ferreyra, Y	Welsh, B	McKinnon, R	Johnson, G	Pochettino, JL	Match No.
1	2	3	4	5	6	7	8	9†10	11			14															1
12	3	2	5	4	7*	8		11	9			14	1	6	10†												2
7	3	2	5	4		8				9*		14	1	6†10	11	12											3
2*	3	4	5	8		11†12				9			1	10	6	14	7										4
1	6†	3	4	12	8			14	9					10		2	7*	5	11								5
1		3	4		8		9			10*		14		6		2	7†	5	11	12							6
1		3	4		8					10		9†14		6		2		5	11		7						7
1		3	4		8		9†			10		14		6		2		5	11		7						8
1		3	12		8					10		14		6		2	7*	5	11		4	9†					9
	3	4	8	7						10*		14	1	6				5	12		11	9†					10
12	3	4	8	7						10	14		1	6				5	11		2*	9†					11
2	3	4	8		9*					10		14	1	6				5	11†12		7						12
	3	4	8	14	10†					12	11		1	6		2	7*	5			9						13
	3	4	8							10	9*12		1		2			5		7			6	11			14
	3	4	8	14						10			1	6	9†	2		5		7				11			15
	3	4	8							10		12	1	6	9	2		5		7				11*			16
	3	4	8							10		12	1	6	9*	2		5		7				11			17
14	3	4†	8							10			1	6	9*	2		5		7	12			11			18
12	3	4	8*							10			1		6	2	14	5		7	9†			11			19
	3	4								10		12	1	6	8	2		5		7*	9			11			20
14	3	4†								8		1	6	10	2	12		5		7	9			11*			21
	3	4	8							10		12	1	6	2			5		7	9*			11			22
	3	14	8							10			1	7	2	12		5		4	9*	6	11†				23
4	3		8							11			1	6	10†	2	7	5		9*12			14				24
8	3	4								10			1	6	14	2	11	5		7	9†						25
8	3	4				10*14	7						1	6	9	2	12	5						11†			26
8	3	4								10	11		1		9	2	7*	5		6				12			27
8	3	4								10	11		1		9	2		5		6				7			28
8	3	4								10	11		1		9	2		5		6	14			7†			29
8	3	4									11		1		9	2		5	14	6	10			7†			30
8	3	4	7							10	14		1		9†	2		5		6				11			31
14	3	4	7							10	11		1	6		2		5		8†	9						32
2	3	4	7							9			1					6	11	10			5	8			33
1	2	3	4							10	11†			9	14			5		12		7*	6	8			34
1	2	3	4							10	11			9*14				5				7†	6	12	8		35
1	2	3	4							10	11				14			5		12		7†	6	9	8*		36
1	2	3	4							10	11			12	14			5				7	6	9*	8†		37
1	2	3		12						10	11			9				5			4	7*	6		8		38
1	2	3	14	11						10				9				5			4*	7†	6	12	8		39
1	2	3	11							10								5			4	7*	6	9	8	12	40
1	2*	3	11							10				6	14			5			4	7†12	9	8			41
1	10	3		11						9				6		2		5			4	7*			8	12	42
1	10	3	12	11						9	7†			6	14	2		5			4				8*		43
1	14	3	10	11						12	7*			6	9	2		5			4				8†		44
17	24	44	37	4	22	11	5	5	2	37	5	15	27	24	24	31	7	41	8	1	32	20	10	21	10	0	
+7s			+4s	+1s		+1s	+3s	+1s		+1s	+3s	+15s		+4s	+4s	+6s		+2s	+4s		+3s	+1s	+4s		+2s		

DUNFERMLINE ATHLETIC First Division

Year Formed: 1885. *Ground & Address:* East End Park, Halbeath Rd, Dunfermline KY12 7RB. *Telephone:* 0383 724295. *Ground Capacity:* total: 18,340. seated: 4020. *Size of Pitch:* 114yd × 72yd. *Chairman:* C. R. Woodrow. *Secretary:* Henry W. Melrose. *Commercial Manager:* Audrey Kelly. *Manager:* Jocky Scott. *Assistant Manager:* Gordon Wallace. *Physio:* Philip Yeates, M.C.S.P. *Managers since 1975:* G. Miller; H. Melrose; P. Stanton; T. Forsyth; J. Leishman; I. Munro. *Club Nickname(s):* The Pars. *Previous Grounds:* None. *Record Attendance:* 27,816 v Celtic, Division I; 30 April, 1968. *Record Transfer Fee received:* £200,000 for Ian McCall to Rangers (Aug 1987). *Record Transfer Fee paid:* £540,000 for Istvan Kozma from Bordeaux, September 1989. *Record Victory:* 11-2 v Stenhousemuir, Division II; 27 Sept, 1930. *Record Defeat:* 1-11 v Hibernian, Scottish Cup, 3rd rd replay, 26 Oct, 1889. *Most Capped*

DUNFERMLINE ATHLETIC 1991–92 LEAGUE RECORD

Match No.	Date		Venue	Opponents		Result	H/T Score	Lg. Pos.	Goalscorers	Attendance
1	Aug	10	H	Hearts	L	1-2	0-1	—	Farningham	10,736
2		13	H	Celtic	L	1-3	1-1	—	McCall	13,794
3		17	A	Aberdeen	L	0-3	0-1	11		13,849
4		24	A	Rangers	L	0-4	0-2	12		35,559
5		31	H	St Johnstone	D	0-0	0-0	12		5536
6	Sept	7	A	Dundee U	L	0-3	0-1	12		5680
7		14	H	Airdrieonians	L	1-2	1-2	12	McCathie	4515
8		21	A	Motherwell	L	0-3	0-1	12		4541
9		28	H	St Mirren	L	1-4	1-1	12	Moyes	4428
10	Oct	5	A	Hibernian	L	0-3	0-2	12		7602
11		8	H	Falkirk	L	0-4	0-3	—		5454
12		12	A	Hearts	L	0-1	0-0	12		9002
13		19	H	Aberdeen	D	0-0	0-0	12		5157
14	Nov	2	A	St Johnstone	L	2-3	1-1	12	Leitch, Robertson	4509
15		6	H	Dundee U	L	1-2	0-1	—	McWilliams	3528
16		9	H	Rangers	L	0-5	0-2	12		13,351
17		12	A	Airdrieonians	L	1-3	1-2	—	Moyes	1,975
18		16	H	Hibernian	L	1-2	0-1	12	Leitch	6001
19		20	A	Falkirk	W	1-0	1-0	—	Moyes	4500
20		23	H	Motherwell	D	0-0	0-0	12		4679
21		30	A	Celtic	L	0-1	0-1	12		20,744
22	Dec	4	A	St Mirren	D	0-0	0-0	—		2866
23		7	H	Hearts	L	0-2	0-2	12		8774
24		14	A	Dundee U	D	0-0	0-0	12		4782
25		28	A	Rangers	L	1-2	0-0	12	O'Boyle	41,328
26	Jan	1	H	St Johnstone	L	0-3	0-0	—		6570
27		4	A	Hibernian	L	0-5	0-1	12		7644
28		11	H	Falkirk	W	1-0	1-0	12	Leitch	5237
29		15	A	Airdrieonians	D	0-0	0-0	—		3429
30		18	H	Celtic	L	0-1	0-1	12		9863
31	Feb	1	A	Aberdeen	D	1-1	0-0	12	McParland	7549
32		8	A	Motherwell	W	2-1	2-1	12	McParland, French	6375
33		22	H	St Mirren	D	0-0	0-0	12		3389
34		29	H	Hibernian	D	0-0	0-0	12		4960
35	Mar	7	H	Dundee U	L	0-1	0-0	12		3042
36		11	A	Falkirk	L	0-2	0-1	—		2810
37		14	H	Rangers	L	1-3	0-3	12	Leitch	12,274
38		21	A	St Johnstone	L	0-1	0-0	12		3156
39		28	H	Hearts	L	0-1	0-0	12		7488
40	Apr	4	A	Aberdeen	D	0-0	0-0	12		3033
41		11	A	Airdrieonians	L	2-3	2-0	12	McWilliams, Moyes	1912
42		18	H	Motherwell	W	3-1	1-0	12	French, Sinclair, McWilliams	2310
43		25	A	Celtic	L	0-2	0-1	12		12,699
44	May	2	A	St Mirren	L	1-3	0-2	12	Moyes	1077

Final League Position: 12

League (22): Moyes 5, Leitch 4, McWilliams 3, French 2, McParland 2, Farningham 1, McCall 1, McCathie 1, O'Boyle 1, Robertson 1, Sinclair 1. *Scottish Cup* (4): Cunnington 1, Davies 1, French 1, McParland 1. *Skol Cup* (9): Leitch 2, O'Boyle 2, Kozma 1, McParland 1, McWilliams 1 (pen), Moyes 1, Robertson 1.

Player: Andy Wilson, 6 (12), Scotland. *Most League Appearances:* 360: Bobby Robertson; 1977–88. *Most League Goals in Season (Individual):* 55: Bobby Skinner, Division II; 1925–26. *Most Goals Overall (Individual):* 154: Charles Dickson.

Honours
League Champions: First Division 1988–89. Division II 1925–26. Second Division 1985–86; *Runners-up:* First Division 1986–87. Division II 1912–13, 1933–34, 1954–55, 1957–58, 1972–73. Second Division 1978–79.
Scottish Cup Winners: 1961, 1968; *Runners-up:* 1965.
League Cup Runners-up: 1949–50.
European: *European Cup:* —. *Cup Winners Cup:* 1961–62, 1968–69 (semi-finals). *UEFA Cup:* 1962–63, 1964–65, 1965–66, 1966–67, 1969–70 *(Fairs Cup)*.
Club colours: Shirt: Broad black and white vertical stripes. Shorts: Black. Stockings: Black with red diamond tops.

Rhodes, A	Wilson, T	Cunnington, E	McCathie, N	Moyes, D	Irons, D	Davies, W	Farningham, R	McParland, I	McCall, I	Kozma, I	Haro, M	O'Boyle, G	Leitch, S	McWilliams, D	Williamson, A	Robertson, C	Gallagher, E	Drizic, M	Sharp, R	Sinclair, C	Kelly, N	French, H	Bowes, M	Reilly, J	Shannon, R	Cooper, N	Laing, D	Grant, A	Match No.
1	2*	3	4	5	6†	7	8	9	10	11	12	14																	1
1	2	3	4	5	12	7	8	9*	10†	11			6	14															2
1		3	4	5		7*	2	8	10	11	6	9†	12	14															3
1	2	3	4	5		7	6	8*10	11		9	12																	4
1	2	3	4	5		7		8*	11		9	12			6	10†14													5
1	2†	3	4		7			11	14	8	12				6	10*	9												6
1	2	3	4			7†		14	10	11		9	8		6		5												7
1	2*	3	4			7†		9	10	12		11	8		14				6										8
1		2	4	5	12			10	7	6†		11*	9		8				3	14									9
1	2	3	4	5	12			9	10†	7			14		8				6			11*							10
1	2	3	4	5	12				10*					7		8	9		6			14	11†						11
1	2		4	5			8					12	10	7*	6	9			6			11							12
1	2	10	4	5								8			9	7	6		3			11							13
1	2	6*	4	5					10						9	7			3	11†		8	12	14					14
1	2*		4	5							12		14	10	7	8			3	11†		9			6				15
1		3	4	5			8						11	10	7	6						9			2				16
1	2†		4	5							12		7*	11	10	6			3			9	14	8					17
1			4	5						11		8	10		7	6			3			9			2				18
1		6	4	5						11		8	10†	7		6			3			9	14		2				19
1		6	4	5		7				11		8†							3	14		9	10		2				20
1	2	6		5						12		11	8	10					3			9			7*	4			21
1	11*		4	5		8				7		12		10					3			9			2	6			22
1			4	5						12		11*	14	10†		8			3	7		9			2	6			23
1	11		4	5			7†			12		10			8*				3	14		9			2	6			24
1	11		4	5						12		14		10	7	8†			3			9*			2	6			25
1	11†		4	5									10	7	12	8			3	14		9			2	6*			26
1	6		4	5						12		11*			7	8†			3	10		9	14		2				27
1	11		4	5									10	7	8				3			9			2	6			28
1	11		4	5								14	10†	7	8				3			9			2	6			29
1	3†11		4	5								14	7	10	8							9			2	6*			30
1	3		4	5		7		12		11		10*										9	2		8	6			31
1	3		4			7		10							5						11	9	2		8	6			32
1			4				11	10†				14	7	5	12	3						9	2*		8	6			33
1			4				11					10	7	5	8	3*						9	12		2	6			34
1	12		4	5			11	14				10	7*	3	8†							9			2	6			35
1	3		4	5		7						10									11†	9	2		8	6	14		36
1			4	5			11					10			8					7	9	2		3	6				37
1	11†			5					4			10			8					14	7	9	2*		3	6			38
1	11	12		5			14		4			10			8						7†	9	2		3	6*			39
1	11		4	5			8					10			6				3		7	9	2						40
1	11	5†					8*					10	7		4				3	14		9	2			6	12		41
1	10							5					7		4					11		9	2		3†	6	14		42
1	10	12		5									7		4					11		9	2		3	6*14			43
1	3	4	5				14					12	10		7	6				8†	9	2*							44
44	16	35	38	39	1	22	4	11	9	18	7	12	29	21	6	31	3	1	25	10	8	31	12	1	27	21	0	0	
	+1s	+2s			+1s	+11s		+5s		+5s	+3s	+4s	+4s	+3s	+1s				+7s			+2s	+4s		+3s	+1s			

McAllister, P—Match No. 30(12) 38(12) 42(8) 43(8†).

EAST FIFE   Second Division

Year Formed: 1903. *Ground & Address:* Bayview Park, Methil Fife KY8 3AG. *Telephone:* 0333 26323. *Fax:* 26376.
Ground Capacity: total: 5147. seated: 600. *Size of Pitch:* 110yd × 71yd.
Chairman: James Baxter. *Secretary:* William McPhee. *Commercial Manager:* James Bonthrone.
Manager: Gavin Murray. *Assistant Manager:* William Brown. *Physio:* Bud Porteous. *Coach:* David Gorman.
Managers since 1975: Frank Christie; Roy Barry; David Clarke.
Club Nickname(s): The Fifers. *Previous Grounds:* None.
Record Attendance: 22,515 v Raith Rovers, Division I; 2 Jan, 1950.
Record Transfer Fee received: £150,000 for Paul Hunter from Hull C, March 1990.
Record Transfer Fee paid: £70,000 for John Sludden from Kilmarnock, July 1991.

EAST FIFE 1991–92 LEAGUE RECORD

Match No.	Date		Venue	Opponents		Result	H/T Score	Lg. Pos.	Goalscorers	Atten- dance
1	Aug	10	A	Clyde	L	0-1	0-1	—		629
2		17	H	Queen's Park	W	2-0	1-0	6	Sludden, Herd	624
3		24	A	Brechin C	D	4-4	1-1	5	McBride, Brown I, Sludden, Spence	568
4		31	H	Stranraer	W	2-1	1-0	4	Beaton, Scott	596
5	Sept	7	A	Stenhousemuir	L	1-2	1-0	6	Sludden	500
6		14	H	Alloa	D	0-0	0-0	6		583
7		17	H	Queen of the S	W	4-1	2-0	—	Sludden 2, Beaton, McBride	612
8		21	A	Cowdenbeath	D	3-3	2-3	5	Sludden 2, McBride	603
9		28	A	Dumbarton	W	2-1	1-0	5	Sludden, Scott	753
10	Oct	5	H	Arbroath	D	2-2	0-1	5	Hayton, McKenna (og)	652
11		12	A	East Stirling	L	1-4	1-2	5	Sludden 2	399
12		19	H	Albion R	W	3-2	2-0	4	Scott, McBride, Sludden	537
13		26	A	Berwick R	W	2-1	1-0	4	Sludden, Beaton	260
14	Nov	2	H	Clyde	L	1-2	0-2	4	Wilson	848
15		9	A	Queen's Park	L	0-1	0-1	6		512
16		16	H	Brechin C	W	2-1	2-1	4	Beaton, Hope	667
17		23	H	Stenhousemuir	D	4-4	1-1	4	Hope, Sludden 2, Beaton	657
18		30	A	Alloa	D	0-0	0-0	4		671
19	Dec	14	H	Berwick R	W	3-1	1-0	4	Beaton (pen), Scott 2	677
20		28	A	Queen of the S	L	1-3	0-1	—	Brown W	971
21	Jan	1	H	Cowdenbeath	W	1-0	1-0	—	McBride	1259
22		8	A	Stranraer	W	2-0	1-0	—	Brown W, Sludden	528
23		11	A	Arbroath	D	0-0	0-0	2		820
24		18	A	Dumbarton	D	2-2	2-0	3	Hope, Brown W	1220
25	Feb	1	A	Albion R	W	1-0	0-0	3	Scott	333
26		4	H	East Stirling	D	2-2	0-0	—	Hayton, Beaton	774
27		8	H	Queen's Park	D	2-2	0-0	3	Sludden, Hayton	839
28		15	A	Clyde	L	0-4	0-2	4		610
29		22	H	Queen of the S	W	5-1	3-1	4	Sludden, Scott 2, Brown W, McBride	720
30		29	A	Cowdenbeath	L	1-3	0-2	6	McBride	909
31	Mar	7	H	Arbroath	W	3-1	2-1	5	Scott 2, Sludden	772
32		14	A	Stenhousemuir	W	2-1	1-0	4	Beaton (pen), Hayton	460
33		21	A	Brechin C	W	1-0	0-0	4	Scott	476
34		28	H	Albion R	W	3-1	1-0	4	Scott 2, McCracken	705
35	Apr	4	H	Dumbarton	L	0-2	0-1	4		1166
36		11	A	Stranraer	W	2-1	1-1	4	Sludden, Beaton (pen)	457
37		18	A	East Stirling	D	1-1	1-1	4	Scott	714
38		25	A	Alloa	W	2-1	1-0	4	Sludden, Scott	1281
39	May	2	A	Berwick R	W	4-1	1-0	4	McBride, Sludden, Brown W, Scott	150

Final League Position: 4

League (72): Sludden 21, Scott 16, Beaton 9 (3 pens), McBride 8, Brown W 5, Hayton 4, Hope 3, Brown I 1, Herd 1, McCracken 1, Spence 1, Wilson 1, own goal 1. *Scottish Cup* (11): Beaton 4, Skelligan 3, Sludden 2, Brown W 1, Scott 1. *Skol Cup* (2): Hope 2. *B & Q Cup* (6): Sludden 2, Hayton 1, Scott 1, Spence 1, Wilson 1.

Record Victory: 13-2 v Edinburgh City, Division II; 11 Dec, 1937.
Record Defeat: 0-9 v Hearts, Division I; 5 Oct, 1957.
Most Capped Player: George Aitken, 5 (8), Scotland.
Most League Appearances: 517: David Clarke, 1968–86.
Most League Goals in Season (Individual): 41: Jock Wood, Division II; 1926–27 and Henry Morris, Division II; 1947–48.
Most Goals Overall (Individual): 196: George Dewar (149 in League).

Honours
League Champions: Division II 1947–48; *Runners-up:* Division II 1929–30, 1970–71. Second Division 1983–84.
Scottish Cup Winners: 1938; *Runners-up:* 1927, 1950.
League Cup Winners: 1947–48, 1949–50, 1953–54.
Club colours: Shirt: Black and gold stripes. Shorts: Black with gold flashes. Stockings: Black with gold and white tops.

Charles, R	Taylor, PH	Spence, T	Herd, W	Beaton, D	Burns, W	McBride, J	Wilson, S	Scott, R	Sludden, J	Hope, D	Brown, I	Hamilton, R	Hall, A	Moffat, J	Prior, S	Rogerson, S	Brown, W	Hayton, G	Bell, G	Allan, G	Cowell, J	Smith, P	Skelligan, R	Speirs, A	McCracken, D	Callaghan, T	Blyth, A	Match No.
1	2*	3	4	5	6	7	8	9	10	11	12																	1
1		3†	4	5	6	7	8	9	10	11		2	14															2
1	12	3	4	5	6*	7	8	9	10	11†14	2																	3
	2	3	4	5	6	7	8	9	10*11	12				1														4
1	2	3	4	5	6	7	8	9	10	11*12																		5
1	2	3	4†	5	6	7			9*10	11	12					8	14											6
1	2	3		5	6	7	4	12	10*11	9†						8		14										7
	2	3	12	5	6	7	4*	9	10	11				1		8												8
1		3		5	6	7	4	9†10	11							8		14	2									9
1		3		5	6	7	4	9	10							8		14	2	11†								10
1	14			5	6	7	4	9	10							8		12	2	3†11*								11
1	14	3		5	6	7	4	9*10	11†							8		12			2							12
1	6	3		5		7	4	12	10	11*						8		9			2							13
1	3			5	6	7	4	12	10	11*						8		9			2							14
1	2			5	6	7	4	9†10	12	14						8		11*			3							15
1	2			5	6	8	4	14	10	11	9†							12			7*	3						16
1	2*			5	6	8	4		10	11	9†				12			14			7	3						17
1		3	4	5	6	7		9	10										11	2	8							18
1	2	3		5	6	7	8	9	10†11*									12					4	14				19
1	2	3		5	6	7	8	9	10*11									12					4†14					20
1		3	4	5	6	7		11	10									9					2†14		8			21
1	2	3	4	5		7		9	10	11								6							8			22
1	2	3	4	5		7		9†10*11									6	14						12	8			23
1	2	3	4†	5		7			10	11								6	9*					14	12	8		24
1	2†	3	14	5		7	4	9	10	11								6							8			25
1		3	2	5		7†	4	9	10	11*								6	12					14	8			26
1	2	3	4	5		7		9	10	14								6†12						11*	8			27
1	2†	3	4	5		7	14	9*10	11									6	12						8			28
1		3	2	5	6*	7	12	9	10	11								4†						14	8			29
1		2		5	6	7	12	9	10	11†								4			3			14	8*			30
1	2	3		5	6	7	4	9	10									8		12				11*				31
1	2	3		5	6	7	4	9	10*									8	12					11				32
1	2	3		5	6	7*	4	9	10									8	12					11				33
1	2	3		5	6	7*	8	9	10	4									12					11†14				34
1	2	3		5	6	7	8*	9†10	12														11	14	4			35
1	2	3		5	6†12	14		9	10	4														11*	8	7		36
1	2	3		5	6*11		8	9	10	4†														14	12	7		37
1	2*	3†		5	6	11	8	9	10	4											14				12	7		38
1	2	3			6†11		8	9	10	4							7							12	5*		14	39
37	28	33	16	38	31	38	28	33	39	29	3	2	0	2	10	0	14	4	3	2	4	9	3	7	12	4	0	
	+		+		+	+	+		+	+					+	+	+	+		+			+	+	+		+	
	3s		2s		1s	4s	4s		3s	6s					1s	1s	1s	3s		13s			1s	3s	8s		1s	

EAST STIRLINGSHIRE   Second Division

Year Formed: 1880. *Ground & Address:* Firs Park, Firs St, Falkirk FK2 7AY. *Telephone:* 0324 23583.
Ground Capacity: total: 1880. seated: 200. *Size of Pitch:* 112yd × 72yd.
Chairman: William Laird. *Secretary:* Marshall Paterson. *Commercial Manager:* I. McFarlane.
Manager: Dom Sullivan. *Assistant Manager:* Bobby McCulley. *Physio:* S. McMillan. *Coach:* —.
Managers since 1975: I. Ure; D. McLinden; W. P. Lamont; M. Ferguson; W. Little; D. Whiteford; D. Lawson; J. D. Connell, A. Mackin.
Club Nickname(s): The Shire. *Previous Grounds:* Burnhouse, Randyford Park, Merchiston Park, New Kilbowie Park.
Record Attendance: 12,000 v Partick T, Scottish Cup 3rd rd; 19 Feb 1921.
Record Transfer Fee received: £35,000 for Jim Docherty to Chelsea (1978).
Record Transfer Fee paid: £2000 for John Workman from Stranraer, Oct 1989.

EAST STIRLINGSHIRE 1991–92 LEAGUE RECORD

Match No.	Date	Venue	Opponents	Result	H/T Score	Lg. Pos.	Goalscorers	Attendance
1	Aug 10	A	Stranraer	W 5-3	2-0	—	Lytwyn 2 (1 pen), Ross, Diver 2	590
2	17	H	Cowdenbeath	L 2-3	1-2	4	McKinnon, Lytwyn	319
3	24	A	Queen's Park	L 2-4	1-0	9	Lytwyn 2	455
4	31	H	Brechin C	D 3-3	3-0	9	Diver, McKinnon, Lytwyn	205
5	Sept 7	A	Arbroath	D 3-3	2-1	9	Lytwyn, McConville, McKinnon	460
6	14	H	Berwick R	W 4-1	1-1	5	McNally 2, Barclay, Crawford	296
7	17	A	Albion R	D 1-1	0-1	—	McTeague (og)	291
8	21	H	Dumbarton	L 1-2	1-0	6	Diver	355
9	28	H	Stenhousemuir	W 2-1	0-0	6	McKinnon, McConville	338
10	Oct 5	A	Queen of the S	L 1-5	0-1	7	Ross	460
11	12	H	East Fife	W 4-2	2-1	6	McNally, McConville, Diver 2	399
12	19	A	Alloa	W 1-0	1-0	6	Diver	377
13	26	A	Clyde	L 1-2	1-0	8	Thomson J (og)	378
14	Nov 2	H	Stranraer	D 2-2	1-0	8	Diver, Crawford	193
15	9	A	Cowdenbeath	L 2-3	2-2	8	Diver 2	225
16	16	H	Queen's Park	W 2-1	1-1	8	Lytwyn, Crawford	324
17	23	H	Arbroath	D 1-1	1-0	8	Lytwyn	265
18	Dec 14	A	Clyde	W 2-1	0-1	6	Speirs (pen), Barclay	383
19	28	H	Albion R	W 2-1	1-0	6	Diver, Cranmer (og)	363
20	Jan 7	A	Brechin C	D 0-0	0-0	—		376
21	11	H	Queen of the S	W 2-1	0-1	5	Diver 2	245
22	14	A	Dumbarton	D 1-1	0-1	—	Lytwyn	787
23	18	A	Stenhousemuir	L 1-2	0-1	6	McKinnon	385
24	Feb 1	H	Alloa	W 2-1	0-1	6	Diver, Workman	438
25	4	A	East Fife	D 2-2	0-0	—	McKinnon, Speirs	774
26	8	H	Berwick R	L 0-4	0-2	7		312
27	15	A	Cowdenbeath	L 0-4	0-2	7		309
28	18	A	Berwick R	L 0-1	0-0	—		355
29	24	A	Albion R	W 3-1	2-1	—	McConville, Friar, Diver	142
30	29	H	Arbroath	L 0-5	0-3	7		274
31	Mar 14	H	Brechin C	D 0-0	0-0	8		163
32	17	A	Dumbarton	W 1-0	0-0	—	Diver	584
33	21	A	Queen of the S	W 3-2	3-1	7	McKinnon, Diver, Lytwyn	408
34	28	A	Stenhousemuir	L 0-3	0-2	7		364
35	Apr 4	H	Stranraer	W 1-0	0-0	7	Friar	170
36	11	A	Alloa	L 0-1	0-1	7		608
37	18	A	East Fife	D 1-1	1-1	6	McKinnon	714
38	25	H	Clyde	W 2-1	2-1	6	McKinnon, Rooney	382
39	May 2	A	Queen's Park	D 1-1	0-0	6	Diver	397

Final League Position: 6

League (61): Diver 18, Lytwyn 11 (1 pen), McKinnon 9, McConville 4, Crawford 3, McNally 3, Barclay 2, Friar 2, Ross 2, Spiers 2 (1 pen), Rooney 1, Workman 1, own goals 3.   *Scottish Cup* (0).   *Skol Cup* (2): Diver 1, Lytwyn 1.   *B & Q Cup* (2): McKinnon 1, Ross 1.

Record Victory: 11-2 v Vale of Bannock, Scottish Cup 2nd rd; 22 Sept, 1888.
Record Defeat: 1-12 v Dundee United, Division II; 13 Apr, 1936.
Most Capped Player: Humphrey Jones, 5 (14), Wales.
Most League Appearances: 431: Gordon Simpson, 1968–80.
Most League Goals in Season (Individual): 36: Malcolm Morrison, Division II; 1938–39.
Most Goals Overall (Individual): —.

Honours
League Champions: Division II 1931–32; *Runners-up:* Division II 1962–63. Second Division 1979–80.
Scottish Cup: —.
League Cup: —.
Club colours: Shirt: Black and white hoops. Shorts: Black. Stockings: Black.

Watson, G	Gardiner, F	Russell, G	McAleer, E	Brannigan, K	Ross, B	McKinnon, C	Rooney, J	Diver, D	Kennedy, H	Lytwyn, C	Griffen, J	Barclay, S	Lawson, O	McNally, J	Thomson, S	Craig, D	McConville, A	Mitchell, B	Crawford, P	Watson, T	Houston, P	Walker, D	Workman, J	Speirs, G	Ferguson, S	McMillan, C	Friar, P	Roberts, P	Match No.
1	2	3	4	5	6	7	8	9	10	11†		14																	1
	2	3	4	5	6	7	8	9	10	11*	12	1																	2
1	2	3	4	5	6	7	8	9		11			10*	12															3
1	2	3	4	5	6†	10	7	9		11*				12	14	8													4
1	2		4	5	6*	10	7†	9		11				12	14	3	8												5
1			4				8†	3		11*	14			9	10	7	5	6	2	12									6
1			4		12		7*	3	9	11	10†				6	5	8		2	14									7
1	2		4		6		3	10				14		9†	7	5	8	11											8
1	2	3			6	7	4	9		11*				12	8	5	10												9
1	2	3			6	8	4	9		11†		14		12	7*	5	10												10
1	2	3				8	4	9		11					6	5	10				7								11
1	2	3				8	4	9		11†						5	10		14		7	6							12
1	2	3		14		8	4	9		11*						5	10				7	6†	12						13
1	2		4			8		9		11†	3				10	5			14		7	6							14
1	2		4			10		9		11	3				8*	5			12		7	6							15
1	2	3	10*			8	4	9		11					9	5	12				7	6							16
1	2	3				8	4	9		11					9	5	10				7	6†							17
1	8	2						9		11†	14				7	5	10						4	3		6			18
1	2	8	10					9†			14					5		11			7		4	3		6			19
1	2	8						9			12	10*		14		5		11			7†		4	3		6			20
1	2	8						9				10		14		5		11			7†		4	3		6			21
1	2	7						9		11*					8	5	10		12				4	3		6			22
1	2	7						9		11†	14				8	5	10		12				4	3		6*			23
1	2†	7		14				9		11					8	5	6						4	3		10			24
1		7		8*				9			14	11†		12	2	5	10						4	3		6			25
1		7		8				9	5	11†				12	2		10*		14				4	3		6			26
1			6			7	12	9			14				8	5	10				4†			3*	11	2			27
1		7						9	3	12					8	5	14		10*	11†	4			6		2			28
1		7						9		10*					8	5	11		12		4			6		2	3		29
1		7						9		10*	14				8	5	11		7†	12	4			6		2	3		30
1		7						9					1		8	5	11*		14		4			6	12	2	3	10†	31
1		7						9		10			1		8	5					4			6	11	2	3		32
1		7						9		11			1		8	5					4			6	10	2	3		33
1		7		14				9		11				12	8*	5					4			6	10†	2	3		34
1		8	4					9		11*					10†	5	6		12		7		14			2	3		35
1	12	8	4					9		11*					7†	5	6		14		10					2	3		36
1	2	7	6					9		11					8*	5					4		12				3	10	37
1		7	6					9		10†					8	5	14				4			11		2	3		38
1	12		6*			7		9		10					8	5					4		14		11†	2	3		39
35	4	21 +2s	16	5 +2s	13	37 +3s	19	35	11 +2s	19 +1s	0 +1s	12 +11s	4	6 +6s	27 +5s	34	24 +3s	2	5 +5s	13 +6s	28	1 +5s	10	19	4 +2s	13	11	1	

FALKIRK   Premier Division

Year Formed: 1876. *Ground & Address:* Brockville Park, Hope St, Falkirk FK1 5AX. *Telephone:* 0324 24121/32487.
Fax: 10324 612418.   *Ground Capacity:* total: 13,800. seated: 2661. *Size of Pitch:* 110yd × 70yd.
Chairman: —. *Secretary:* George Deans. *Commercial Manager:* Jim Hendry.
Manager: Jim Jefferies. *Assistant Manager:* Billy Brown. *Physio:* Joe Cross. *Coach:* Willie Wilson.
Managers since 1975: J. Prentice; G. Miller; W. Little; J. Hagart; A. Totten; G. Abel; W. Lamont; D. Clarke; J. Duffy.
Club Nickname(s): The Bairns. *Previous Grounds:* Randyford; Blinkbonny Grounds; Hope Street.
Record Attendance: 23,100 v Celtic, Scottish Cup 3rd rd; 21 Feb, 1953.
Record Transfer Fee received: £270,000 for Gordon Marshall to Celtic, Aug 1991.
Record Transfer Fee paid: £225,000 to Chelsea for Kevin McAllister, Aug 1991.
Record Victory: 12-1 v Laurieston, Scottish Cup 2nd rd; 23 Mar, 1893.

FALKIRK 1991–92 LEAGUE RECORD

Match No.	Date		Venue	Opponents	Result	H/T Score	Lg. Pos.	Goalscorers	Attendance
1	Aug	10	H	Motherwell	D 1-1	1-0	—	Stainrod	5543
2		14	H	Aberdeen	L 0-1	0-0	—		8462
3		17	A	Celtic	L 1-4	0-3	9	Baptie	32,469
4		24	A	St Mirren	D 0-0	0-0	9		5112
5		31	H	Airdrieonians	W 3-2	2-1	8	McAllister 2, May	4955
6	Sept	7	H	Rangers	L 0-2	0-1	8		12,848
7		14	A	Hibernian	D 2-2	1-1	9	May, Baptie	8800
8		21	A	St Johnstone	W 3-2	3-1	8	McAllister, May, Stainrod	6106
9		28	H	Hearts	L 1-2	1-2	9	McAllister	8339
10	Oct	5	H	Dundee U	L 0-4	0-1	9		5155
11		8	A	Dunfermline Ath	W 4-0	3-0	—	Cody, May, Godfrey, McAllister	5454
12		12	A	Motherwell	L 2-4	1-1	8	Baptie, May	5991
13		19	H	Celtic	W 4-3	3-1	8	Grant (og), May, Stainrod, Duffy	11,008
14		26	A	Rangers	D 1-1	1-0	8	Godfrey	36,441
15	Nov	2	A	Airdrieonians	D 0-0	0-0	8		4338
16		9	H	St Mirren	W 3-0	1-0	8	Baptie, McAllister, Stainrod	4235
17		12	H	Hibernian	W 3-2	2-1	—	McAllister, May 2	5572
18		16	A	Dundee U	L 1-2	0-1	8	McAllister	7290
19		20	H	Dunfermline Ath	L 0-1	0-1	—		4500
20		23	A	St Johnstone	L 2-3	0-0	9	Stainrod, Rice (pen)	4915
21		30	A	Aberdeen	D 1-1	1-0	8	Duffy	10,614
22	Dec	4	A	Hearts	D 1-1	1-0	—	Sloan	11,742
23		7	H	Motherwell	L 0-1	0-1	9		4900
24		14	H	Rangers	L 1-3	0-2	9	Sloan	11,801
25		21	A	Hibernian	W 1-0	0-0	8	Taylor	6942
26		28	A	St Mirren	W 1-0	1-0	7	Hughes	4961
27	Jan	1	H	Airdrieonians	L 0-3	0-1	—		5446
28		4	A	Dundee U	L 1-3	0-1	8	Hughes	4975
29		11	A	Dunfermline Ath	L 0-1	0-1	9		5237
30		18	H	Aberdeen	D 2-2	2-0	9	Grant (og), Cadette	5122
31	Feb	1	A	Celtic	L 0-2	0-0	9		16,927
32		8	A	St Johnstone	D 1-1	1-0	9	McAllister	5418
33		29	A	Dundee U	L 1-2	0-2	9	May	5592
34	Mar	4	H	Hearts	L 1-2	0-2	—	Smith	6002
35		11	H	Dunfermline Ath	W 2-0	1-0	—	Cadette, McGivern	2810
36		14	H	St Mirren	W 1-0	1-0	9	Sloan	4133
37		21	A	Airdrieonians	D 2-2	2-0	9	McGivern, Cadette	4214
38		28	A	Motherwell	W 1-0	0-0	9	McGivern	4395
39	Apr	4	H	Celtic	L 0-3	0-1	9		8842
40		7	A	Rangers	L 1-4	1-2	9	Sloan	36,832
41		11	H	Hibernian	L 2-3	1-3	9	Smith, Baptie	3943
42		18	H	St Johnstone	W 2-0	2-0	8	Baptie 2	3703
43		25	A	Aberdeen	D 1-1	1-0	7	McQueen	6461
44	May	2	H	Hearts	L 0-2	0-1	9		7348

Final League Position: 9

League (54): McAllister 9, May 9, Baptie 7, Stainrod 5, Sloan 4, Cadette 3, McGivern 3, Duffy 2, Godfrey 2, Hughes 2, Smith 2, Cody 1, McQueen 1, Rice 1 (pen), Taylor 1, own goals 2.   *Scottish Cup* (3): Sloan 2, McGivern 1.   *Skol Cup* (3): McAllister 2, Taylor 1.

Record Defeat: 1-11 v Airdrieonians, Division I; 28 Apr. 1951.
Most Capped Player: Alex Parker, 14 (15), Scotland.
Most League Appearances: (post-war): John Markie, 349.
Most League Goals in Season (Individual): 43: Evelyn Morrison, Division I; 1928-29.
Most Goals Overall (Individual): Dougie Moran, 86.

Honours
League Champions: Division II 1935-36, 1969-70, 1974-75. First division 1990-91. Second Division 1979-80; *Runners-up:* Division I 1907-08, 1909-10. First Division 1985-86. Division II 1904-05, 1951-52, 1960-61.
Scottish Cup Winners: 1913, 1957.   *League Cup Runners-up:* 1947-48.
Club colours: Shirt: Dark blue with white flashings. Shorts: White. Stockings: Red.

Westwater, I	Duffy, N	McQueen, T	Hughes, J	Godfrey, P	Rice, B	McGivern, S	Taylor, A	May, E	Stainrod, S	Smith, P	Baptie, C	Cody, S	McAllister, K	Taggart, C	Oliver, N	Lennox, G	McKenzie, S	Whittaker, B	Mooney, M	Sloan, S	McDougall, G	Hamilton, G	Cadette, R	Johnston, F	Rutherford, P	Simpson, M	Match No.
1	2	3	4	5	6	7	8	9	10	11																	1
1	2	3	4	5	6	7†	8	12	10	11	14		9*														2
1	2	3	4	5	6	12	8	9*	10†	11	14		7														3
1	2	3	4	5	6*	9	8	12		11	10		7														4
1	2	3	4	5	6*	9	8	12	10	11			7														5
1	2*	3	4		14	9	8	6	10†	11	5		12		7												6
1	2	3	4	5			8	6	10	11	9		7														7
1	2	3	4			9†	8	6*	10	11	5		12		7	14											8
1	2	3	4			9*	8	6	10	11	5		12		7												9
1	2	3	4			6†	8*	9	10	11	5		7		12	14											10
1		3	4	5				9	10	11	6	8†	7		14	2											11
1		3	4	5				9	10	11	6	8*	7		12	2											12
1	6	3	4	5			8		10	11	9†		7		2	14											13
1	6	3		5			8		10	11	9†		7		2	14					4						14
1	6	3		5*		12	8		10		9		7		14	2		11			4†						15
1			4			14	9	6	10		5		7*		2	12		11		3	8†						16
1	2		4			9		6	10		5		7					11		3	8						17
1	2		4			9†	8		10	14	5		7		3			11			6*		12				18
1			4			12	9	10	11		5		7		2			6*		3	8						19
1	2		4		11		8†	7	10	9	5		14		3	12		6*									20
1	2		4		6†		8*	9		11	5		7		3	12		14		10							21
1	2		4		6*		8†	9		11	5		7		3	12		14		10							22
1			4		3*	14	8	6	10	11	5		7		2	12		9†									23
1	2		4		12		8	6	10	11	5		7		3*			9									24
1	6	3	4		11†		8	9			5		7		2	14				10							25
1	6	3	4		11	14	8	9†			5		7*		2	12				10							26
1	6	3	4	14	11†	9	8*				5		7		2	12				10							27
	8	3	4	6		12			10		5		7		2†11*					9	1	14					28
1	6	3	4		11*		12†				5		7	14	2	8				10			9				29
1	6	3	4		11	8*					5		7	12	2					10			9				30
1	6	3		5		9*			11	4	7				2	8				10			12				31
1	6	3		5		12	8†		11	4	7				2	14				10			9*				32
1	2		4			8	6		11*	5	7		3							10†			12	9	14		33
1	6		4			8		10		11	5		7†		2								9	3	14		34
1	4		5			8		6†		11			7		2					10			9	3	14		35
1	4		5			8				11			7		2	6				10			9	3			36
1	4		5			8†				11	12		7		2	6				10			9	3*14			37
1	4		5			8	10						7		2	6				12			9	3	11*		38
1	4		5			8†	10						7		2	6				12			9	3	11*14		39
1	4		5	6		8*		11			12		7		2					10			9	3			40
1*		3	5				6		11	10	7		14		2	12					4		9		8†		41
			5			8†	9		11	10	7				2	6		14			1	4		3			42
	4	3	5			8	9		11	10	7				2†	6						1		14			43
	4*	3	5			8	9		11	10	7				2	6†						1	12	14			44
40	39	26	38	15	14	23	21	33	22	31	34	2	42	0	34	15	0	6	0	20	4	2	11	10	2	0	
	+1s	+2s	+7s	+1s	+3s	+1s	+1s	+4s	+3s				+8s	+1s	+10s2s			+4s	+3s		+1s	+3s	+2s	+4s	+1s		

FORFAR ATHLETIC   Second Division

Year Formed: 1885. *Ground & Address:* Station Park, Carseview Road, Forfar. *Telephone:* 0307 63576.
Ground Capacity: total: 8359. seated: 711. *Size of Pitch:* 115yd × 69yd.
Chairman: George Enston. *Secretary:* David McGregor. *Commercial Manager:* —.
Manager: Tommy Campbell. *Assistant Manager:* —. *Physio:* Andy Bell. *Coach:* John Smith.
Managers since 1975: Jerry Kerr; Archie Knox; Alex Rae; Doug Houston; Henry Hall; Bobby Glennie; Paul Hegarty.
Club Nickname(s): Sky Blues. *Previous Grounds:* None.
Record Attendance: 10,780 v Rangers, Scottish Cup 2nd rd; 2 Feb, 1970.
Record Transfer Fee received: £57,000 for Craig Brewster to Raith R, July 1991.
Record Transfer Fee paid: £50,000 for Ian McPhee from Aidrieonians, 1991.

FORFAR ATHLETIC 1991–92 LEAGUE RECORD

Match No.	Date		Venue	Opponents	Result		H/T Score	Lg. Pos.	Goalscorers	Attendance
1	Aug	10	H	Ayr U	L	2-3	1-2	—	Paton, Adam	824
2		13	H	Dundee	L	2-4	1-1	—	Hegarty, Johnston	2458
3		17	A	Raith R	L	0-2	0-2	11		1175
4		24	H	Morton	L	1-4	0-1	12	Adam	752
5		31	H	Montrose	L	1-2	0-0	12	Mearns	748
6	Sept	7	A	Hamilton A	L	0-4	0-3	12		1177
7		14	H	Clydebank	W	2-1	0-0	12	Pryde, Paton	612
8		21	A	Stirling Albion	W	3-1	1-1	11	Pryde, Adam (pen), Paton	432
9		28	H	Partick T	L	0-3	0-1	12		1525
10	Oct	5	H	Kilmarnock	L	0-1	0-0	12		1099
11		9	A	Meadowbank T	D	0-0	0-0	—		175
12		12	A	Ayr U	L	0-4	0-2	12		1782
13		19	H	Raith R	L	0-1	0-0	12		599
14		26	A	Hamilton A	D	0-0	0-0	12		394
15		29	A	Clydebank	D	3-3	2-1	—	McAulay, Winter, Pryde	537
16	Nov	2	H	Montrose	D	2-2	0-2	12	Winter 2	623
17		9	A	Morton	W	3-1	0-1	12	Petrie 3	1349
18		16	A	Kilmarnock	L	2-4	0-3	12	Winter 2	3560
19		19	H	Meadowbank T	D	0-0	0-0	—		467
20		23	H	Stirling Albion	D	1-1	0-1	12	McAulay	593
21		26	A	Ayr U	L	0-1	0-0			530
22		30	A	Dundee	L	0-4	0-1	12		2976
23	Dec	3	A	Partick T	D	1-1	1-0	—	Campbell	1501
24		14	A	Hamilton A	L	1-2	0-1	12	Campbell	1200
25		28	H	Morton	L	1-5	1-0	12	Campbell	628
26	Jan	1	A	Montrose	L	1-2	1-1	—	Petrie	937
27		4	H	Kilmarnock	D	0-0	0-0	12		1185
28		7	H	Clydebank	L	1-3	1-1	—	Whyte	400
29		11	A	Meadowbank T	L	0-2	0-1	12		201
30		18	H	Dundee	L	0-3	0-3	12		2218
31	Feb	1	A	Raith R	L	0-2	0-0	12		1242
32		8	A	Stirling Albion	L	1-4	0-2	12	Price	658
33		22	A	Partick T	D	0-0	0-0	12		1155
34		29	A	Kilmarnock	L	0-2	0-0	12		3076
35	Mar	7	H	Meadowbank T	W	1-0	0-0	12	Winter	334
36		14	A	Morton	D	1-1	0-1	12	Petrie	1061
37		21	A	Montrose	W	2-0	1-0	12	McKenna, Winter (pen)	666
38		28	A	Ayr U	L	0-1	0-1	12		1311
39	Apr	4	H	Raith R	L	1-2	0-2	12	Winter (pen)	609
40		7	H	Hamilton A	L	1-3	0-1	—	Petrie	510
41		11	A	Clydebank	L	0-2	0-1	12	—	449
42		18	H	Stirling Albion	D	1-1	0-0	12	Petrie	424
43		25	A	Dundee	L	1-3	0-0	12	Whyte	5227
44	May	2	A	Partick T	D	0-0	0-0	12		9959

Final League Position: 12

League (36): Winter 8 (2 pens), Petrie 7, Adam 3 (1 pen), Campbell 3, Paton 3, Pryde 3, McAulay 2, Whyte 2, Hegarty 1, Johnston 1, McKenna 1, Mearns 1, Price 1. *Scottish Cup* (1): Brazil 1. *Skol Cup* (0). *B & Q Cup* (2): Whyte 2.

Record Victory: 14-1 v Lindertis, Scottish Cup 1st rd; 1 Sept 1988.
Record Defeat: 2-12 v King's Park, Division II; 2 Jan, 1930.
Most Capped Player: —.
Most League Appearances: 376: Alex Brash, 1974–86.
Most League Goals in Season (Individual): 45: Dave Kilgour, Division II; 1929–30.
Most Goals Overall (Individual): 124, John Clark.

Honours
League Champions: Second Division 1983–84. C Division 1948–49.
Scottish Cup: Semi-finals 1982.
League Cup: Semi-finals 1977–78.
Club colours: Shirt: Sky blue. Shorts: Navy. Stockings: Sky blue.

Thomson, S	Morris, R	Winter, G	Hegarty, P	Adam, C	Holt, J	Paton, P	Brazil, A	Whyte, G	McAulay, A	Petrie, S	Campbell, A	Johnston, C	Hamill, A	Peters, S	Paterson, I	Mearns, G	Pryde, I	Smith, P	Dolan, S	Hutton, G	MacKinnon, D	McKenna, I	McPhee, I	Price, G	Ramsey, A	Byrne, J	Glass, S	Match No.
1	2	3	4	5	6	7	8	9	10*	11	12																	1
1	2	3	4	5	6	7†	8	9	10*	11	12	14																2
1	2	10	5		6		8	9			11†	14	7*	3	4	12												3
1	6*	12	4	5	8	10		9		11			14	3	2	7†												4
1	4	10†	5		8*	2	9						14	3	6	7	11	12										5
1	4	6		2			14	9		8	12	7*	11			3	5†											6
1	6	14	4	5	8	7	9*			11			3			12	10†				2							7
1	6		4	5	8	7	9			11*			3			12	10				2							8
1	6	14	4	5	8	7†	9			11*			3				10				2	12						9
1	8	3		5	2	7	9*			14	12	10	11†								4	6						10
1	4	3†		5	2	8	9*14	11		7			10			12						6						11
1	6			5	2	7				10	12		8			9					4	11*	3					12
1	8			2	7*		10	12	11		14	6				9†		5			4		3					13
1	8	11		5	2		12	14	7*		6		9†			10					4		3					14
1		10		5			11	8	9	7	6		2								4		3					15
1	8	10		5	2		11	9		7†	6		14								4		3					16
1	8	10		5	2	7	14	9		6†			11*								4		3	12				17
1	8†10			5	2	7*	11		12	6			14								4		3	9				18
1	8†10			5	2		12	11		14	3		6	7							4			9*				19
1		10		5	2†	8	11*14	9		6			7								4		3	12				20
1		10		5	2	4		11	14	8	7†	6				12							3	9*				21
1		10		5	14	2†	7	11*	9	8			6	12							4							22
1	8	10†		5		2	7		11*	3			14			6					4	12		9				23
1	8	10		5		2	6		11	3		14	7†								4	12		9*				24
1	8	10		5		2		7†	9*	3			14								4	12	6	11				25
1	8	10*		5		6		11	7	3			14								2	12	4	9†				26
1	8	3		5		4	11	6*	9				7								2	10		12				27
1	8	6*		5		4	11	14	9	3			7†								2	10		12				28
1	4	12		5			11	9		7†	6		14								2	8*	3	10				29
1	4	10		5		6	11	14	9	7			2								8†	3*12						30
1	3	12		5	6	4	11	10*	9	7			14				2				8†							31
1	4	6	7	5	11†		9			3		8	10			14	2*				12							32
1	2	10		4	5	12	9	11*		3		6	7			8												33
1	2	10	4†	5	12		9			3			7*			8						11	6	14				34
1	2	10		5	12	9				3			11		14						7		8†	6*	4			35
1	2	10		5	12	9	14			3			11								7		8†	6*	4			36
1	2	10	8*	5		9	12			3			11								7	6†14		4				37
1	2	10	8	5		9				3			14	11							7*	12		4	6†			38
1	8	6			14	5	10	9		3			7								2	11			4†			39
1	8	6			4	5	10*	9		3			7	12							2	11						40
1	2	10*	8		6	5		11		3			12	7			14	9†						4				41
1	3*10			5		12	9		11	6			7†		14						2	8		4				42
1	5	6			2		9	8†11		3			14	10								7		4				43
1	2	5				3	11	12	10				14	4		7	9†				8					6*		44
44	40	36	8	9	36	18	22	38	12	36	7	7	39	3	2	11	27	0	2	2	27	18	16	11	3	9	1	
		+5s				+1s	+3s			+13s	+5s	+5s	+7s				+4s	+6s	+8s	+1s	+3s	+1s	+1s	+5s		+8s	+1s	

HAMILTON ACADEMICAL First Division

Year Formed: 1874–75. *Ground & Address:* Douglas Park, Douglas Park Lane, Hamilton M13 0DF. *Telephone:* 0698 286103. *Ground Capacity:* total: 6550. seated: 1610. *Size of Pitch:* 110yd × 70yd.
Chairman: George J. Fulston. *Secretary:* Scott Struthers. *Commercial Manager:* George Miller.
Manager: —. *Assistant Manager:* Willie McLean. *Physio:* Frank Ness. *Coach:* Colin Miller.
Managers since 1975: J. Eric Smith; Dave McParland; John Blackley; Bertie Auld; John Lambie; Jim Dempsey, John Lambie; Billy McLaren. *Club Nickname(s):* The Accies. *Previous Grounds:* Bent Farm, South Avenue, South Haugh.
Record Attendance: 28,690 v Hearts, Scottish Cup 3rd tie; 3 Mar, 1937.
Record Transfer Fee received: £110,000 for Willie Jamieson to Dundee, January 1990.
Record Transfer Fee paid: £60,000 for Paul Martin from Kilmarnock, 1988.

HAMILTON ACADEMICAL 1991–92 LEAGUE RECORD

Match No.	Date		Venue	Opponents	Result		H/T Score	Lg. Pos.	Goalscorers	Attendance
1	Aug	10	A	Montrose	D	2-2	2-2	—	Hillcoat, Clark	885
2		13	A	Kilmarnock	W	2-1	2-1	—	McCluskey, Clark	4347
3		17	H	Morton	D	1-1	0-0	5	McCluskey	1805
4		24	A	Dundee	L	1-4	0-3	6	Smith	2751
5		31	H	Partick T	D	1-1	0-1	5	Harris (pen)	2722
6	Sept	7	H	Forfar Ath	W	4-0	3-0	5	Harris (pen), McCluskey, Smith 2	1177
7		14	A	Stirling Albion	W	1-0	1-0	5	Smith	996
8		21	H	Clydebank	D	0-0	0-0	5		1299
9		28	A	Meadowbank T	D	3-3	2-0	5	McCluskey, Harris, McKee	320
10	Oct	5	A	Raith R	W	3-1	2-1	4	Reid, McCluskey 2	1007
11		9	H	Ayr U	W	3-1	2-0	—	Smith 2, Napier	1839
12		12	H	Montrose	W	2-0	1-0	3	McCluskey, Smith	1104
13		19	A	Morton	L	0-1	0-0	3		1723
14		26	A	Forfar Ath	D	0-0	0-0	4		394
15		30	H	Stirling Albion	W	3-1	0-1	—	Smith, Clark, Cramb	1309
16	Nov	2	A	Partick T	D	1-1	0-0	3	Smith	2760
17		9	H	Dundee	L	1-3	0-3	3	McCluskey	1866
18		16	H	Raith R	W	4-1	1-0	2	Clark, Harris, Reid, McCluskey	1433
19		19	A	Ayr U	W	2-0	1-0	—	Clark 2	2216
20		23	A	Clydebank	D	1-1	0-1	2	Harris (pen)	1031
21		30	H	Kilmarnock	D	2-2	0-1	2	McCluskey, Weir	3893
22	Dec	4	H	Meadowbank T	W	3-1	0-1	—	Reid, Harris, McDonald (pen)	1372
23		14	H	Forfar Ath	W	2-1	1-0	2	McCluskey, Clark	1200
24		17	A	Montrose	W	3-1	1-0	—	Clark, Harris 2 (1 pen)	505
25		28	A	Dundee	W	2-1	2-1	2	McDonald, Clark	4595
26	Jan	1	H	Partick T	L	0-2	0-1	—		2852
27		4	A	Raith R	L	1-2	0-0	2	Clark	2299
28		8	A	Stirling Albion	L	0-3	0-1	—		845
29		11	H	Ayr U	W	2-1	1-0	2	Clark, McCluskey	1530
30		18	A	Kilmarnock	W	2-0	0-0	2	Clark 2	4662
31	Feb	1	H	Morton	D	0-0	0-0	2		1921
32		8	H	Clydebank	L	2-3	1-2	3	McGuigan, Miller	1468
33		22	A	Meadowbank T	W	2-1	2-0	3	Millen, Clark	464
34		29	H	Raith R	W	1-0	1-0	3	Napier	1885
35	Mar	7	A	Ayr U	L	0-2	0-1	3		2004
36		14	A	Dundee	D	1-1	0-1	3	McDonald	2830
37		21	A	Partick T	D	0-0	0-0	3		6079
38		28	H	Montrose	W	4-1	2-0	3	McAnenay, McDonald, Smith 2	1206
39	Apr	4	A	Morton	D	1-1	0-0	3	Smith	1428
40		7	A	Forfar Ath	W	3-1	1-0	—	Ward 2, Smith	510
41		11	H	Stirling Albion	W	1-0	1-0	3	McDonald (pen)	1638
42		18	A	Clydebank	W	3-1	2-0	3	Ward 3	1137
43		25	H	Kilmarnock	L	0-1	0-1	3		3449
44	May	2	A	Meadowbank T	W	2-0	1-0	3	Reid, Hillcoat	1687

Final League Position: 3

League (72): Clark 14, Smith 13, McCluskey 12, Harris 8 (4 pens), McDonald 5 (2 pens), Ward 5, Reid 4, Hillcoat 2, Napier 2, Cramb 1, McAnenay 1, McGuigan 1, McKee 1, Millen 1, Miller 1, Weir 1. *Scottish Cup* (0). *Skol Cup* (2): Burns H 1, Clark 1. *B & Q Cup* (13): McCluskey 3, Smith 3, Napier 2, Harris 1, Millen 1, Miller 1, Reid 1, Weir 1.

Record Victory: 11-1 v Chryston, Lanarkshire Cup; 28 Nov, 1885.
Record Defeat: 1-11 v Hibernian, Division I; 6 Nov, 1965.
Most Capped Player: Colin Miller, 5, (16) Canada.
Most League Appearances: 447: Rikki Ferguson, 1974–88.
Most League Goals in Season (Individual): 34: David Wilson, Division I; 1936–37.
Most Goals Overall (Individual): 246: David Wilson, 1928–39.

Honours
League Champions: First Division 1985–86, 1987–88. Division II 1903–04; *Runners-up:* Division II 1952–53, 1964–65.
Scottish Cup Runners-up: 1911, 1935.   *League Cup:* Semi-finalists three times.
Club colours: Shirt: Red and white hoops. Shorts: White. Stockings: White.

Ferguson, A	McKee, K	Miller, C	Millen, A	Hillcoat, C	Napier, C	Clark, G	Burns, H	McCluskey, G	Reid, W	McDonald, P	Moore, S	Harris, C	Weir, J	Smith, T	Cramb, C	McAnenay, M	Stark, W	McKenzie, P	McGuigan, R	McLean, S	Monaghan, M	McCulloch, R	Ward, K	Match No.
1	2	3	4	5	6	7	8	9	10	11														1
1	2	3		4	5	10	8	9	6	11	14	7†												2
1	2	3		4	6	10	8*	9	12	11		7	5											3
1	2	3		6†	5	9	8		10	11	12	7*	4	14										4
1	2	3	4	6†10			8*	9		11		12	5	7	14									5
1	2*	3	4		6		12	9†	8	11		7	5	10	14									6
1	2	3	4	14	6*		12	9	8	11		7†	5	10										7
1	2	3	4		12		8	9	6	11	14	7*	5	10†										8
1	2	3	4		12		8*	9	6	11		7	5	10†		14								9
1	2	3	4		6			9	8	11		7	5	10										10
1	2	3	4		8			9		11*		7	5	10			12	6						11
1	2	3	4	11†			9	8				7	5	10		14		6						12
1	2	3	4				9	8†				7	5	10*	12	14	11	6						13
1	2	3	4				9*					7	5	10	8	12	11	6						14
1	2†	3	4		12							7	5	10	9	11*		6	8	14				15
1*	2	3	4		9			8				7	5	10	14		12	6†11						16
	2	3	4		11		9	8	14			7	5	10*			12	6†		1				17
	2	3	4		10†		9	8	11			7	5			14		6		1				18
	2	3	4		10		9†	8	11			7	5					6		1				19
	2	3	4		10		9	8	11			7	5				12	6*		1				20
	2	3	4		10*		9	8	11			7	5				12	6		1				21
	2	3	4		10		9	8	11			7*	5				12	6		1				22
	2	3	4		8		9*	6	11			7		10			12	5		1				23
	2	3	4	14	8*		9	6	12			7		10†	11		5			1				24
	2		4	6	10			8	11			7	5	9			3			1				25
	2†	3	4	14	12		9	8	11			7	5	10*			6			1				26
		3	4	2	14	10	9†	8	11			7	5				12	6*		1				27
	2†	3	4	6	9	12		8	11			7	5	14		10*				1				28
	2	3		4	7	9*	12	8	11			5						6	10		1			29
	2	3	4	6	7	9		8	11			5						10			1			30
		3	4	2	7*10	9		11				5	12			8	6			1				31
		3		2	7	8	9†		12	5	10	14	6	4						1*				32
		3	4	2	6	10	9					5					7	8		1		11		33
		3	4	2	6	10	9		12			5					7	8*		1		11		34
		3	4	2	8	10	9†		12			7*	5	14			6			1		11		35
		3	4	2		14	9†	8	11			5	10				6			1		7		36
		3	4	2	12			8	11			5	10†14	9		6			1		7*			37
		3	4	2		12		8	11			5	10†14	9†		6			1		7			38
		3	4	2		12		8	11			5	10	9*		6	14		1		7†			39
	2	3	4	7	12			8	11			14	5	10*			6†		1		9			40
	2	3	4	7	12			8	11			5	10				6		1		9*			41
	2	3	4	7	10*			8	11			12	5				6		1		9			42
	2*	3	4	7			12	8	11			14	5	10			6†		1		9			43
	2	3	4	7	10*		12	8	11†			5	14				6		1		9			44
16	34	43	39	24	18	24	7	29	34	34	0	27	40	25	2	4	6	29	9	0	13	15	12	

Substitute appearances: +3s +4s +8s +2s +3s +1s +4s +3s +5s   +4s +10s +4s +8s   +1s +1s

HEART OF MIDLOTHIAN Premier Division

Year Formed: 1874. *Ground & Address:* Tynecastle Park, Gorgie Rd, Edinburgh EH11 2NL. *Telephone:* 031 337 6132. *Ground Capacity:* total: 25,177. seated: 11,987. *Size of Pitch:* 110yd × 74yd. *Chairman:* A. Wallace Mercer. *Secretary:* L. W. Porteous. *Commercial Manager:* Charles Burnett. *Manager:* Joe Jordan. *Assistant Manager:* Frank Connor. *Physio:* Alan Rae. *Coach:* Sandy Clark. *Managers since 1975:* J. Hagart; W. Ormond; R. Moncur; T. Ford; A. MacDonald; A. MacDonald & W. Jardine; A. MacDonald. *Club Nickname(s):* Hearts. *Previous Grounds:* The Meadows 1874, Powderhall 1878, Old Tynecastle 1881, (Tynecastle Park, 1886). *Record Attendance:* 53,396 v Rangers, Scottish Cup 3rd rd; 13 Feb, 1932. *Record Transfer Fee received:* £700,000 for John Robertson to Newcastle U (April 1988). *Record Transfer Fee paid:* £750,000 for Dave McPherson from Rangers (Dec 1988). *Record Victory:* 21-0 v Anchor, EFA Cup 1880. *Record Defeat:* 1-8 v Vale of Leithen, Scottish Cup, 1888. *Most Capped Player:* Bobby

HEART OF MIDLOTHIAN 1991–92 LEAGUE RECORD

Match No.	Date		Venue	Opponents	Result		H/T Score	Lg. Pos.	Goalscorers	Atten- dance
1	Aug	10	A	Dunfermline Ath	W	2-1	1-0	—	Crabbe, Robertson	10,736
2		13	A	Airdrieonians	W	3-2	2-1	—	Robertson 2 (1 pen), Baird	6326
3		17	H	Rangers	W	1-0	1-0	3	Crabbe	22,534
4		24	A	St Johnstone	W	1-0	1-0	2	Levein	7516
5		31	H	Hibernian	D	0-0	0-0	2		22,208
6	Sept	7	H	Motherwell	W	2-0	0-0	1	Crabbe, Baird	9003
7		14	A	St Mirren	W	3-2	1-1	1	Millar, McPherson, Crabbe	5836
8		21	H	Dundee U	D	1-1	0-1	1	McKinlay	11,746
9		28	A	Falkirk	W	2-1	2-1	1	Crabbe, Millar	8339
10	Oct	5	A	Celtic	L	1-3	1-2	2	Robertson	33,621
11		9	H	Aberdeen	W	1-0	1-0	—	Crabbe	15,569
12		12	H	Dunfermline Ath	W	1-0	0-0	1	McLaren	9002
13		19	A	Rangers	L	0-2	0-1	2		36,481
14		26	A	Motherwell	W	1-0	1-0	2	Ferguson I	5417
15		30	H	St Mirren	D	0-0	0-0			8683
16	Nov	2	A	Hibernian	D	1-1	1-1	1	Robertson	19,831
17		9	H	St Johnstone	W	2-1	0-0	1	Baird, Hogg	10,222
18		16	H	Celtic	W	3-1	0-1	1	Wright, Levein, Crabbe	22,666
19		20	A	Aberdeen	W	2-0	1-0	—	Baird, Robertson	15,338
20		23	A	Dundee U	W	1-0	0-0	1	Robertson	12,796
21		30	H	Airdrieonians	W	1-0	0-0	1	Crabbe (pen)	12,073
22	Dec	4	H	Falkirk	D	1-1	0-1	—	Crabbe	11,742
23		7	A	Dunfermline Ath	W	2-0	2-0	1	Millar, Crabbe (pen)	8774
24		14	H	Motherwell	W	3-1	3-1	1	Crabbe (pen), Baird, Millar	10,006
25		21	A	St Mirren	W	1-0	0-0	1	Millar	5216
26		28	A	St Johnstone	W	5-0	1-0	1	Baird, Robertson 2, Crabbe 2	10,064
27	Jan	1	H	Hibernian	D	1-1	0-0	—	Ferguson I	20,358
28		4	A	Celtic	W	2-1	0-0	1	Crabbe, Millar	30,417
29		11	H	Aberdeen	L	0-4	0-1	2		16,291
30		18	A	Airdrieonians	L	1-2	0-2	2	Robertson	5930
31	Feb	1	H	Rangers	L	0-1	0-1	2		24,356
32		8	H	Dundee U	W	1-0	0-0	2	Bannon	10,516
33		29	H	Celtic	L	1-2	0-2	2	Robertson (pen)	20,863
34	Mar	4	A	Falkirk	W	2-1	2-0	—	Mackay, Ferguson D	6002
35		14	H	St Johnstone	W	2-0	1-0	2	McKinlay, Millar	8799
36		18	A	Aberdeen	L	0-2	0-1	—		10,581
37		21	A	Hibernian	W	2-1	1-0	2	Hunter (og), Ferguson I	14,429
38		28	H	Dunfermline Ath	W	1-0	0-0	2	Robertson	7488
39	Apr	7	A	Motherwell	W	1-0	1-0	—	Robertson	4502
40		11	H	St Mirren	D	0-0	0-0	3		6200
41		18	A	Dundee U	L	0-2	0-1	3		6711
42		25	H	Airdrieonians	D	2-2	1-1	3	Crabbe, McPherson	5310
43		28	A	Rangers	D	1-1	0-0	—	Robertson (pen)	36,129
44	May	2	H	Falkirk	W	2-0	1-0	2	Bannon, Ferguson I	7348

Final League Position: 2

League (60): Crabbe 15 (3 pens), Robertson 14 (3 pens), Millar 7, Baird 6, Ferguson I 4, Bannon 2, Levein 2, McKinlay 2, McPherson 2, Ferguson D 1, Hogg 1, Mackay 1, McLaren 1, Wright 1, own goal 1. *Scottish Cup* (9): Robertson 4 (1 pen), Crabbe 1, Ferguson I 1, Hogg 1, Mackay 1, McLaren 1. *Skol Cup* (5): Baird 2, Crabbe 2, Robertson 1 (pen).

Walker, 29, Scotland.   *Most League Appearances:* 406, Henry Smith, 1981–92.   *Most League Goals in Season (Individual):* 44: Barney Battles.   *Most Goals Overall (Individual):* 206: Jimmy Wardhaugh, 1946–59.

Honours
League Champions: Division I 1894–95, 1896–97, 1957–58, 1959–60. First Division 1979–80; *Runners–up:* Division I 1893–94, 1898–99, 1903–04, 1905–06, 1914–15, 1937–38, 1953–54, 1956–57, 1958–59, 1964–65. Premier Division 1985–86, 1987–88, 1991–92. First Division 1977–78, 1982–83.
Scottish Cup Winners: 1891, 1896, 1901, 1906, 1956; *Runners–up:* 1903, 1907, 1968, 1976, 1986.
League Cup Winners: 1954–55, 1958–59, 1959–60, 1962–63; *Runners–up:* 1961–62.
European: *European Cup* 4 matches (1958–59, 1960–61). *Cup Winners Cup* 4 matches (1976–77). *UEFA Cup:* 28 matches. (*Fairs Cup:* 1961–62, 1963–64, 1965–66. *UEFA Cup:* 1984–85, 1986–87, 1988–89, 1990–91).
Club colours: Shirt: Maroon. Shorts: White. Stockings: Maroon with white tops.

Smith, H	McLaren, A	McKinlay, T	Levein, C	Mackay, G	McPherson, D	Crabbe, S	Ferguson, D	Baird, I	Millar, J	Robertson, J	Foster, W	Bannon, E	Wright, G	Hogg, G	Harrison, T	Penney, S	Ferguson, I	Snodin, G	Match No.
1	2	3	4	5	6	7†	8	9*	10	11		12	14						1
1	2		4	5	6	7	8	9*	10	11		12	3						2
1	2	4		5	6	7*	8	9	10	11		12	3						3
1		3	4	5	6	7†	8	9	10	11			2			14			4
1	2	3	4	5	6	7*	8	9	10	11		12							5
1		3	4	5*	6	7	8†	9	10	11			14	2		12			6
1		3	4	5	6	7*	8	9	10	11			2			12			7
1		3	4	5	6	7	8		10	11			2				9		8
1		3	4	5	6	7	8		10	11			2	12			9*		9
1	2	3	4	5	6†	7	8	9*	10	11			14					12	10
1	2	3	4	5	6	7	8	9*	10	11								12	11
1	2	3	4	5	6	7	8	9	10	11*								12	12
1	2	3	4	5	6	7*	8	9	10	11								12	13
1	2	3	4	5	6	7	8		10	11†			14				9		14
1	2	3	4†	5	6	7*	8		10	11			14				12	9	15
1	2			5	6	7†	8	9	10	11			4	3				14	16
1	2			5	6	7	8	9					4	3			10		17
1	2	3	4	5	6	7	8†	9*	10	11			14					12	18
1	2	3	4	5	6	7		9*	10	11†		8	14					12	19
1	2	3	4	5	6	7†		9	10	11*		8	14					12	20
1	2	3	4		6	7		9*	10	11	5	8						12	21
1	2	3*	4	5	6	7		9	10	11		8†	14					12	22
1	2	3	4	5	6	7		9	10	11*		8						12	23
1	2	3	4†	5	6	7*		9	10	11		8	14					12	24
1	2	3		5	6	7	14	9	10	11*		8†	4					12	25
1	2	3	4	5	6	7	8	9*	10	11								12	26
1	2	3	4†	5	6	7*	8	9	10	11			14					12	27
1	2	3	4	5†	6	7*	8	9	10	11			14					12	28
1	2	3	4	5	6	7	8	9	10	11									29
1	2	3	4	5†	6	7*	8	9	10	11			14					12	30
1	2	3	4	12	6	7	8		10	11				5*			9		31
1	2	3	4	14	6	12	8		10	11			9*	5				7†	32
1	2	3		5	6	7*	8	9	10	11			4					12	33
1	2	3		4	6		8	9	10	11†		12	14	5			7*		34
1	2†	3		5	6		8		10	11		12	9*	4			7	14	35
1	2	3	4	5	6	7*	8		10	11†			14				9	12	36
1	2	3	4	5*	6	12	8			11		7	10				9		37
1	2	3	4	5	6	12	8	14		11		7*	10†				9		38
1		14	4	5	6	7	8			11		10†	2				9	3	39
1	2	3†		5*	6	7	8		10	11		12	4				9	14	40
1	2		4	5	6	7	8		10			9	12	11*				3	41
1	2		4	5	6	7	8	9*	10			11	12					3	42
1	2	14	4	5	6		8	9*	10	11		7					12	3†	43
1	2	3	4	5	6	12	8		10	11*		7					9		44

```
44 38 37 36 41 44 37 37 30 40 42  1 10 15 13  0  3 12  4
    +         +          +  +          +  +  +  +  +  +  +  +
    2s        2s         4s 1s         1s 6s 3s 9s 5s 1s 6s 18s3s
```

HIBERNIAN   Premier Division

Year formed: 1875. *Ground & Address:* Easter Road Stadium, Albion Rd, Edinburgh EH7 5QG. *Telephone:* 031 661 2159. *Ground Capacity:* total: 22,260. seated: 6670. *Size of Pitch:* 112yd × 74yd. *Chairman:* Douglas Cromb. *Managing Director:* —. *Secretary:* Cecil F. Graham, F.A.A.I., M.Inst. C.M. *Commercial Manager:* Kenneth McLean. *Manager:* Alex Miller. *Assistant Manager:* Murdo MacLeod. *Physio:* Stewart Collie. *Coach:* Andy Watson. *Manager since:* Eddie Turnbull; Willie Ormond; Bertie Auld; Pat Stanton; John Blackley. *Club Nickname(s):* Hibees. *Previous Grounds:* Meadows 1875–78, Powderhall 1878–79, Mayfield 1875–80, First Easter Road 1880–92, Second Easter Road 1892–. *Record Attendance:* 65,860 v Hearts, Division I; 2 Jan, 1950. *Record Transfer Fee received:* £1,000,000 for Andy Goram to Rangers (June 1991). *Record Transfer Fee paid:* £450,000 for Keith Wright from Dundee. *Record Victory:* 22-1 v 42nd Highlanders; 3 Sept, 1881. *Record Defeat:* 0-10 v Rangers; 24 Dec, 1898. *Most Capped Player:*

HIBERNIAN 1991–92 LEAGUE RECORD

Match No.	Date		Venue	Opponents	Result	H/T Score	Lg. Pos.	Goalscorers	Attendance
1	Aug	10	H	St Mirren	W 4-1	2-0	—	Weir 2, McGinlay 2	8271
2		13	A	St Johnstone	W 2-1	0-0	—	McIntyre (pen), Hamilton	9236
3		17	A	Motherwell	D 1-1	1-1	4	Wright	8018
4		24	H	Dundee U	W 1-0	0-0	3	Weir	9862
5		31	A	Hearts	D 0-0	0-0	4		22,208
6	Sept	7	A	Airdrieonians	W 1-0	0-0	4	Weir	5621
7		14	H	Falkirk	D 2-2	1-1	3	McGraw, Weir	8800
8		21	A	Aberdeen	D 1-1	0-1	3	Weir	11,850
9		28	H	Celtic	D 1-1	0-1	4	McGinlay	18,021
10	Oct	5	H	Dunfermline Ath	W 3-0	2-0	4	Hunter, Wright, McGinlay	7602
11		8	A	Rangers	L 2-4	1-0	—	Weir, McGinlay	35,364
12		12	A	St Mirren	W 1-0	1-0	4	McIntyre	4572
13		19	H	Motherwell	D 0-0	0-0	4		7141
14	Nov	2	H	Hearts	D 1-1	1-1	5	Wright	19,831
15		5	H	Airdrieonians	D 2-2	1-1	—	Wright, McIntyre (pen)	6622
16		9	A	Dundee U	D 1-1	0-1	6	Hunter	8812
17		12	A	Falkirk	L 2-3	1-2	—	McGinlay 2	5512
18		16	H	Dunfermline Ath	W 2-1	1-0	6	McGinlay, Wright	6001
19		19	H	Rangers	L 0-3	0-0	—		16,833
20		23	H	Aberdeen	W 1-0	0-0	5	Lennon	8942
21		30	A	St Johnstone	W 1-0	0-0	4	McIntyre	6717
22	Dec	4	A	Celtic	D 0-0	0-0	—		22,340
23		7	H	St Mirren	D 0-0	0-0	4		6943
24		14	A	Airdrieonians	W 3-0	0-0	4	Weir, Hamilton, Evans	3784
25		21	H	Falkirk	L 0-1	0-0	4		6942
26		28	H	Dundee U	W 3-2	0-1	4	Evans 2, Wright	7688
27	Jan	1	A	Hearts	D 1-1	0-0	—	McIntyre	20,358
28		4	H	Dunfermline Ath	W 5-0	1-0	3	Wright 3, Weir, Evans	7644
29		11	A	Rangers	L 0-2	0-1	4		40,616
30		18	H	St Johnstone	L 0-1	0-0	4		7107
31	Feb	1	A	Motherwell	D 1-1	0-0	4	Tortolano	6105
32		8	A	Aberdeen	W 1-0	0-0	4	Weir	9568
33		22	H	Celtic	L 0-2	0-2	4		16,756
34		29	A	Dunfermline Ath	D 0-0	0-0	4		4960
35	Mar	10	H	Rangers	L 1-3	0-2	—	Evans	13,387
36		4	A	Dundee U	L 0-1	0-1	5		5588
37		21	H	Hearts	L 1-2	0-1	6	Weir	14,429
38		28	A	St Mirren	W 1-0	1-0	6	Evans	1918
39	Apr	4	A	Motherwell	D 0-0	0-0	6		4423
40		7	H	Airdrieonians	L 0-2	0-1	—		3254
41		11	A	Falkirk	W 3-2	3-1	6	Hamilton, Donald, McIntyre	3943
42		18	H	Aberdeen	D 1-1	0-0	6	Donald	6777
43		25	A	St Johnstone	D 1-1	0-0	6	Donald	3895
44	May	2	A	Celtic	W 2-1	1-0	5	Whyte (og), McGinlay	25,532

Final League Position: 5

League (53): Weir 11, McGinlay 9, Wright 9, Evans 6, McIntyre 6 (2 pens), Donald 3, Hamilton 3, Hunter 2, Lennon 1, McGraw 1, Tortolano 1, own goal 1. *Scottish Cup* (7): Wright 3 (1 pen), Evans 1, McGinlay 1, McIntyre 1, Weir 1. *Skol Cup* (11): Wright 5, McGinlay 2, McIntyre 2 (1 pen), Evans 1, MacLeod 1.

Lawrie Reilly, 38, Scotland. *Most League Appearances:* 446: Arthur Duncan. *Most League Goals in Season (Individual):* 42: Joe Baker. *Most Goals Overall (Individual):* 364: Gordon Smith.

Honours
League Champions: Division I 1902–03, 1947–48, 1950–51, 1951–52. First Division 1980–81. Division II 1893–94, 1894–95, 1932–33; *Runners-up:* Division I 1896–97, 1946–47, 1949–50, 1952–53, 1973–74.
Scottish Cup Winners: 1887, 1902; *Runners-up:* 1896, 1914, 1923, 1924, 1947, 1958, 1972, 1979.
League Cup Winners: 1972–73, 1991–92; *Runners-up:* 1950–51, 1968–69, 1974–75.
European: *European Cup* 6 matches (1955–56 semi-finals). *Cup Winners Cup* 6 matches (1972–73). *UEFA Cup* 54 matches (*Fairs Cup:* 1960–61 semi-finals, 1961–62, 1962–63, 1965–66, 1967–68, 1968–69, 1970–71. *UEFA Cup:* 1973–74, 1974–75, 1975–76, 1976–77, 1978–79).
Club colours: Shirt: Green with white sleeves. Shorts: White. Stockings: Green with white trim.

Burridge, J	Miller, W	Mitchell, G	Orr, N	McIntyre, T	MacLeod, M	Weir, M	Hamilton, B	Wright, K	McGraw, M	McGinlay, P	Evans, G	Lennon, D	Milne, C	Raynes, S	Hunter, G	Fellenger, D	Tortolano, J	Beaumont, D	Sneddon, A	Findlay, W	Bailey, L	Nicholls, D	Reid, C	Farrell, D	Tweed, S	Love, G	Donald, G	Match No.
1	2	3*	4	5	6	7†	8	9	10	11	12	14																1
1	2		4	5		7	8	9	10	6	11†	3	14															2
1	2*	3	7	5	12	8	9	10†	11	14			4		6													3
1	2	3		5	6	7	14	9	12	11	10*	8†			4													4
1		3	2	5	6	7†	8	9	12	11	10*	14			4													5
1		3	14	5	6	7†	8	9	10*	11	12	2			4													6
1	2	3		5	6*	7	8	9	10	11	12				4													7
1	14	3	2	5	6	7†	8	9	10*	11	12				4													8
1	2	3	14	5	6†	7	8	9	12	11	10*				4													9
1		3	2	5	6†	7	8	9	10*	11	12				4	14												10
1		3†	2	5	6	7	8	9		11	10				4	14												11
1		3	2	5		7	8	9		11	10				6	4												12
1	2	3	12	5		7	8	9		11	10				4	6*												13
1	2	3		5	6	7	8	9		11	10							4										14
1	2	3*	12	5	6		8†	9		11	10				4	7		14										15
1			8†	5	6			9		11	10*	14			4	12	7	2	3									16
1	2	3†	7*		6		8	9		11	10				4	14	5	12										17
1				5	6*		8	9		11	12	7			4	10*	8	2										18
1				5	6*		8	9		11	12	7†			4	10	2	3	14									19
1	2			5†			8	9		11	12				6	3	4	14		7*	10							20
1	2			5		7	8	9	10	11					4	3						6						21
1	2			5		7		9	10*	11	14	12			4	3	8					6†						22
1	2			5		7		9	10†	11	14	12			4	3	8					6*						23
	2			5		7*	8	9	10†	11	14	12			4	3	6						1					24
	2			5		7	8	9	12	11	10*	14			4	3	6†						1					25
	2			5		7	8	9	10*	11	12				6	3			4				1					26
	2			5		7*	8	9		11	12				6	3	10						1	4				27
	2			5†		7	8	9	12	11	10				6	3	14		4*				1					28
	2	12				7	8	9		11	10*				6	3	5						1	4				29
1	2							9	12	11	10	7*			6	3	4	5	8									30
1	2	3	14	5		7	8	9		11	10†				6	4												31
1		3	2	5	6†	7	8	9		11	14				4	10												32
1		3	2		6	7	8	9		11	10*				4	12	5											33
1	2	3	4	5	6		8	9	10*	11	12					7												34
1		3	2	5	6		8	9	14	11	10				4	7†												35
1	2	3	7	5	6†		8	9			10				4	11						14						36
	2	3		5		7	8	9	12	11	10				4	6*							1					37
1		3	2		12			9	10	11	7		4†			6		8				14	5					38
1			4		12			9†	14	11	10		2			6	5	7	8							3*		39
1	2		7				8			11	10		4			6	3	5*	9								12	40
	2	12	5*			7	8		14	11	10					6	3		4				1				9†	41
1	2	3		5	6		8			11	10†					6			9*			14					12	42
	2	3	14	5	6	7	8*			11	10†							12					1	4			9	43
1	2	3	4	5†	6	7	8	9		11	12											14					10*	44
35	29	26	21	37	22	30	37	40	14	43	26	3	7	0	37	4	22	17	3	8	1	5	9	3	1	1	3	
		+	+	+	+	+				+	+	+	+		+	+	+	+	+	+			+			+		
		1s	1s	7s	1s	3s				10s	15s	8s	1s		1s	2s	3s	4s	2s	1s			3s			2s		

KILMARNOCK   First Division

Year Formed: 1869. *Ground & Address:* Rugby Park, Kilmarnock KA1 2DP. *Telephone:* 0563 25184.
Ground Capacity: total: 12,991. seated: 3141. *Size of Pitch:* 115yd × 75yd.
Chairman: Robert Fleeting. *Secretary:* Kevin Collins. *Commercial Manager:* Dennis Martin.
Manager: Tommy Burns. *General Manager:* Jim Fleeting. *Assistant Manager:* Billy Stark. *Physio:* Hugh Allan. *Coach:* —.
Managers since 1975: W. Fernie; D. Sneddon; J. Clunie; E. Morrison; J. Fleeting. *Club Nickname(s):* Killie. *Previous Grounds:* Rugby Park (Dundonald Rd); The Grange; Holm Quarry; Present ground since 1899.
Record Attendance: 35,995 v Rangers, Scottish Cup; 10 March, 1962.
Record Transfer Fee received: £120,000 for Davie Provan to Celtic, 1978.
Record Transfer Fee Paid: £100,000 for Bobby Williamson from Rotherham United (Nov 1990).
Record Victory: 11-1 v Paisley Academical, Scottish Cup; 18 Jan, 1930 (15-0 v Lanemark, Ayrshire Cup; 15 Nov, 1890).
Record Defeat: 1-9 v Celtic, Division I; 13 Aug, 1938.
Most Capped Player: Joe Nibloe, 11, Scotland.

KILMARNOCK 1991–92 LEAGUE RECORD

Match No.	Date		Venue	Opponents	Result	H/T Score	Lg. Pos.	Goalscorers	Attendance
1	Aug	10	H	Stirling Albion	D 0-0	0-0	—		4416
2		13	H	Hamilton A	L 1-2	1-2	—	McSkimming	4347
3		17	A	Partick T	L 0-1	0-0	10		5248
4		24	A	Meadowbank T	W 3-2	1-2	7	Williamson 2 (1 pen), Mitchell	1222
5		31	H	Ayr U	D 1-1	0-0	9	Montgomerie	8380
6	Sept	7	A	Clydebank	D 1-1	1-0	9	Campbell	2249
7		14	H	Montrose	D 0-0	0-0	6		3478
8		21	A	Dundee	L 1-2	1-1	8	Williamson	3786
9		28	H	Raith R	W 1-0	1-0	6	Campbell	3385
10	Oct	5	A	Forfar Ath	W 1-0	0-0	6	Mitchell	1099
11		8	H	Morton	W 1-0	1-0	—	Campbell	3677
12		12	A	Stirling Albion	W 3-0	2-0	6	Mitchell, MacPherson, Williamson	1947
13		19	H	Partick T	L 2-3	2-1	6	Williamson, Campbell	4962
14		26	H	Clydebank	W 2-1	1-0	5	Burns T, Campbell	2231
15		29	A	Montrose	D 2-2	1-2	—	Jack, Mitchell	901
16	Nov	2	A	Ayr U	W 3-0	3-0	5	Burns T, Mitchell, Williamson	6064
17		9	H	Meadowbank T	W 1-0	0-0	4	MacPherson	3828
18		16	H	Forfar Ath	W 4-2	3-0	5	Jack 2, Mitchell 2	3560
19		19	A	Morton	W 1-0	0-0	—	Jack	2637
20		23	H	Dundee	L 1-2	1-1	4	Mitchell	7137
21		30	A	Hamilton A	D 2-2	1-0	3	Burns H, Williamson	3893
22	Dec	3	A	Raith R	D 1-1	0-1	—	Williamson	2280
23		7	H	Stirling Albion	W 2-0	0-0	3	Williamson, Burns H	3790
24		14	A	Clydebank	W 3-0	2-0	3	Burns H, Mitchell, Campbell	2184
25		28	A	Meadowbank T	L 0-1	0-0	3		1690
26	Jan	1	A	Ayr U	D 1-1	0-0	—	Campbell	8211
27		4	A	Forfar Ath	D 0-0	0-0	4		1185
28		7	H	Montrose	W 5-1	3-1	—	Campbell 2, Black (pen), Jack, Dorman (og)	3183
29		11	H	Morton	L 0-1	0-0	3		4988
30		18	H	Hamilton A	L 0-2	0-0	5		4662
31	Feb	1	A	Partick T	L 1-2	0-0	5	Black	4873
32		8	A	Dundee	D 1-1	1-0	5	Jack	5990
33		26	H	Raith R	W 1-0	0-0	—	MacPherson	3657
34		29	H	Forfar Ath	W 2-0	0-0	4	Burns H, Campbell	3076
35	Mar	14	H	Meadowbank T	W 2-1	0-1	4	Tait, Jack	2884
36		21	A	Ayr U	W 2-0	0-0	4	Tait, Burns T	5530
37		24	A	Morton	D 0-0	0-0	—		3015
38		28	A	Stirling Albion	L 0-1	0-1	4		1984
39	Apr	4	H	Partick T	L 1-3	0-2	5	Black (pen)	5640
40		7	H	Clydebank	W 1-0	0-0	—	Mitchell	2094
41		11	A	Montrose	W 1-0	0-0	4	McGachie (og)	793
42		18	H	Dundee	W 2-0	1-0	4	Jamieson (og), Tait	4933
43		25	A	Hamilton A	W 1-0	1-0	4	Jack	3449
44	May	2	A	Raith R	D 1-1	0-1	4	Porteous	1960

Final League Position: 4

League (59): Campbell 10, Mitchell 10, Williamson 9 (1 pen), Jack 8, Byrns H 4, Black 3 (2 pens), Burns T 3, MacPherson 3, Tait 3, McSkimming 1, Montgomerie 1, Porteous 1, own goals 3. *Scottish Cup* (2): Burns H 1, Mitchell. *Skol Cup* (2): Campbell 1, McSkimming 1. *B & Q Cup* (1): Burns H 1.

Most League Appearances: 481: Alan Robertson, 1972–88.
Most League Goals in Season (Individual): 34: Harry 'Peerie' Cunningham 1927–28 and Andy Kerr 1960–61.
Most Goals Overall (Individual): 148: W. Culley; 1912–23.

Honours
League Champions: Division I 1964–65. Division II 1897–98, 1898–99; *Runners-up:* Division I 1959–60, 1960–61, 1962–63, 1963–64. First Division 1975–76, 1978–79, 1981–82. Division II 1953–54, 1973–74, Second Division 1989–90.
Scottish Cup Winners: 1920, 1929; *Runners-up:* 1898, 1932, 1938, 1957, 1960.
League Cup Runners-up: 1952–53, 1960–61, 1962–63.
European: *European Cup* 1965–66. *Cup Winners Cup:* —. *UEFA Cup Fairs Cup:* 1964–65, 1966–67 (semi-finals), 1969–70, 1970–71.
Club colours: Shirt: Blue and white vertical stripes. Shorts: Blue. Stockings: Blue.

Geddes, R	MacPherson, A	Reilly, M	Flexney, P	Burgess, S	Tait, T	Stark, W	Jack, R	Williamson, R	Burns, T	McSkimming, S	Porteous, I	Montgomerie, R	McStay, W	Mitchell, A	Campbell, C	McQuilter, R	Elliott, D	Callaghan, T	Brayshaw, A	Burns, H	Jenkins, E	Skilling, M	Paterson, C	Black, T	Graham, A	Stephen, R	Clark, C	Reid, D	Match No.
1	2	3	4	5	6	7*	8	9	10	11†12	14																		1
1	2	3	5		6		8	9	10	11			4	7															2
1	12	3	5		6		8*	9	10	11		2	4	7															3
1	2	3	5		6*		12	9	10	11		14	4	7	8†														4
1	2	3	5		6			9	10	11		4†14		7	8														5
1	2	3	5		6*		14	9	10	11†	7	4			8	12													6
1	2	3†	5				12	9	10	11	6	4		7*	8		14												7
1	2		5				8	9	10	3	12	6		7	11*			4†14											8
1	2	12	5		4		14	9	10	3				7	11†			6*	8										9
1	2		5				8	9	10	3†12	6			7	11*			4		14									10
1	2		5				10*	9	6		8	3		7	11				4	12									11
1	2	12	5					9	10	3		4		7	11			6*	8										12
1	2	12	5		4			9	10	3	14			7	11†			6*	8										13
1	2		5		4			9	10	3	14			7	11†	12	6*		8										14
1	2	12	4				10	9	6	3*				7	11				8	5									15
1	2		4		14		10	9	6		3			7	11†				8	5									16
1	2		4				10	9	6	14				7	11†				8	5	3								17
1	2		4*		12		10	9†	6	14				7	11				8	5	3								18
1	2						10	9	6			4		7	11				8	5	3								19
1	2						10†	9	6	14		4		7	11				8	5	3								20
	2		4				10*	9	6†12	14				7	11				8	5	3	1						21
			4				9	14	6*11	12	3			7	10				8	5	2†	1						22
	2		4				10†	9		11	6			7	14				8	5	3	1						23
	2		4				9		11	6				7	10				8	5	3	1						24
	2						14	9	11*12	6	4			7	10†				8	5	3	1						25
	2		4					9	6	11*	12			7	10				8	5	3	1						26
	2	11	4				14	9	6					7	10†				8	5	3	1						27
1	2	11	4				14	9†	6*		8			7	10				12	5	3							28
	2	11†	4				9		6		8			7	10				14	5	3	1						29
	2		4*		12		14	9		11	6			7	10				8†	5	3	1						30
	2							9	6	14		4	12	7	10				8	5*	3	1	11†					31
1	2				10		9		6			4	12	7	11		14*		8	5†	3							32
1	2	3			5		9	10†	6		14	4		7	11				8									33
1	2				5		9		6		14	4	12	7	11†				8		3			10*				34
1	2				6		14		10			4		11	9				8	5	3					7†		35
1	2				10		11		6	14	8†	4	12	7	9*					5	3							36
1	2				10		11		6		8†	4		7	9				14	5	3							37
1	2				10		11†14		6		8*	4		7	9					12	5	3						38
1	2				10		14	9	6			4		7	11†				8	5	3							39
	8						9†10		6	11		4		7					2	5	3	1						40
1	8	3					9	10	6	11		4		7					2	5								41
1	10	3			14		9		6	11†	8	4		7					2	5								42
1	8	3			12		9		6	11†	7*	4	2	10	14					5								43
1	8†	3			11		9	12			7	4	2	10*14					6	5								44
33	42	15	27	1	18	1	27	33	40	23	16	26	5	42	35	0	0	6	0	29	0	28	23	11	1	1	1		
	+	+		+			+	+		+	+	+	+	+			+		+		+	+	+	+	+				
	1s	4s		5s			10s3s			7s	9s	4s	4s				3s		1s		2s	1s	1s	3s	2s	1s			

Roberts M—Match No. 40(14).

MEADOWBANK THISTLE   First Division

Year Formed: 1974. *Ground & Address:* Meadowbank Stadium, London Rd, Edinburgh EH7 6AE. *Telephone:* 031 661
5351.   *Ground Capacity:* total: 16,500. seated: 16,500. Main stand only used 7,500.   *Size of Pitch:* 105yd × 72yd.
Chairman: John P. Blacklaw. *Secretary:* William L. Mill. *Directors:* W. P. Hunter, M. M. Morrison. *Commercial
Manager:* W. P. Hunter.
Manager: Donald Park. *Assistant Manager:* George Mackie. *Club Doctor:* Dr. M. M. Morrison. *Physio:* Arthur Duncan.
Coach: Graeme Armstrong.
Managers since 1975: John Bain; Alec Ness; Willie MacFarlane; Terry Christie.
Club Nickname(s): Thistle; Wee Jags. *Previous Grounds:* None.
Record Attendance: 4000 v Albion Rovers, League Cup 1st rd; 9 Sept, 1974.
Record Transfer Fee received: £115,000 for John Inglis to St Johnstone (1990).

MEADOWBANK THISTLE 1991–92 LEAGUE RECORD

Match No.	Date		Venue	Opponents	Result		H/T Score	Lg. Pos.	Goalscorers	Atten- dance
1	Aug	10	H	Raith R	W	2-0	2-0	—	Young, Little	703
2		13	H	Partick T	L	0-1	0-0	—		1135
3		17	A	Dundee	L	1-3	1-2	7	Logan	2860
4		24	H	Kilmarnock	L	2-3	2-1	8	Young, Irvine (pen)	1222
5		31	A	Stirling Albion	W	3-2	1-2	8	Logan, Little, Irvine	640
6	Sept	7	A	Montrose	D	2-2	1-0	8	Irvine, McNaughton	601
7		14	H	Morton	L	0-1	0-1	10		505
8		21	A	Ayr U	L	0-7	0-3	10		1605
9		28	H	Hamilton A	D	3-3	0-2	10	Irvine 2, Sprott	320
10	Oct	5	A	Clydebank	D	1-1	0-1	10	Nicol	615
11		9	H	Forfar Ath	D	0-0	0-0	—		175
12		12	A	Raith R	D	1-1	1-0	9	Logan	766
13		19	H	Dundee	L	1-2	0-1	10	Kane	747
14		26	H	Montrose	D	0-0	0-0	10		188
15		29	A	Morton	L	1-2	0-1	—	Logan	1043
16	Nov	2	H	Stirling Albion	L	0-1	0-1	10		257
17		9	A	Kilmarnock	L	0-1	0-0	10		3828
18		16	H	Clydebank	D	1-1	0-1	10	Logan	277
19		19	A	Forfar Ath	D	0-0	0-0	—		467
20		23	H	Ayr U	D	1-1	0-1	10	Roseburgh (pen)	440
21		30	A	Partick T	W	2-0	1-0	9	Roseburgh, Grant	2468
22	Dec	4	A	Hamilton A	L	1-3	1-0	—	Roseburgh (pen)	1372
23		7	A	Raith R	L	0-1	0-0	10		549
24		14	A	Montrose	D	2-2	0-2	10	Roseburgh 2	525
25		28	H	Kilmarnock	W	1-0	0-0	10	Williamson	1690
26	Jan	1	A	Stirling Albion	D	0-0	0-0	—		768
27		4	A	Clydebank	D	1-1	0-0	10	Perry	724
28		11	H	Forfar Ath	W	2-0	1-0	10	Kane, Perry	201
29		18	H	Partick T	D	0-0	0-0	10		887
30	Feb	1	A	Dundee	L	1-2	0-2	10	Perry	3038
31		8	A	Ayr U	D	0-0	0-0	10		1742
32		12	H	Morton	L	1-2	0-2	—	Kane	352
33		22	H	Hamilton A	L	1-2	0-2	10	Kane	464
34		29	H	Clydebank	W	2-0	0-0	10	Roseburgh, Coughlin	300
35	Mar	7	A	Forfar Ath	L	0-1	0-0	10		334
36		14	A	Kilmarnock	L	1-2	1-0	10	Christie	2884
37		2	H	Stirling Albion	D	0-0	0-0	10		351
38		28	A	Raith R	L	0-3	0-1	10		885
39	Apr	4	H	Dundee	D	0-0	0-0	10		1221
40		8	H	Montrose	L	0-1	0-0	—		286
41		11	A	Morton	L	1-3	0-0	10	Graham	1026
42		18	H	Ayr U	L	0-1	0-0	10		367
43		25	A	Partick T	W	2-1	1-1	10	Roseburgh 2	6656
44	May	2	A	Hamilton A	L	0-2	0-1	10		1687

Final League Position: 10

League (37): Roseburgh 8 (2 pens), Irvine 5 (1 pen), Logan 5, Kane 4, Perry 3, Little 2, Young 2, Christie 1, Coughlin
1, Graham 1, Grant 1, McNaughton 1, Nicol 1, Sprott 1, Williamson 1.   *Scottish Cup* (6): Little 2, Perry 2, Roseburgh
1, Williamson 1.   *Skol Cup* (0).   *B & Q Cup* (1): Logan 1.

Record Transfer Fee Paid: £28,000 for Victor Kasule from Albion Rovers (1987).
Record Victory: 6-0 v Raith R, Second Division; 9 Nov, 1985.
Record Defeat: 0-8 v Hamilton A, Division II; 14 Dec, 1974.
Most Capped Player: —.
Most League Appearances: 446: Walter Boyd, 1979–89.
Most League Goals In Season (Individual): 21: John McGachie, 1986–87. *(Team):* 69; Second Division, 1986–87.
Most Goals Overall (Individual): 63: Adrian Sprott, 1980–85.

Honours
League Champions: Second Division 1986–87; *Runners-up:* Second Division 1982–83. First Division 1987–88.
Scottish Cup: —.   *League Cup:* Semi-finals 1984–85.
Club colours: Shirt: Amber with black trim. Shorts: Black. Stockings: Amber.

McQueen, J	Nicol, A	Banks, A	Armstrong, G	Williamson, S	Roseburgh, D	Kane, K	Young, J	Little, I	Coughlin, J	Irvine, W	Boyd, W	McNaughton, B	Grant, D	Christie, M	Logan, S	Sprott, A	McNeill, W	Neil, C	Ryrie, B	Murray, M	Perry, J	Scott, S	Graham, T	Duthie, M	Hutchinson, M	Cormack, P	Match No.
1	2	3	4	5	6*	7	8	9†10	11	12			14														1
1	2	3	4			7	8	9	6†11				14	5	10												2
1	2	3	4	12	8	9†	6	11					14	5	10*	7											3
1	2	3	4			8	9	6	11	14			5	10†	7												4
1	6	3	4	12	8*	9	2	11	5	10			7														5
1	12	6*	3	4	8	9†	2	11					14	5	10	7											6
1	2	12	3	11	8	9	4	6†					14	5	10*	7											7
1	2	3	4	12	8	9†	6	11*14					5	10	7												8
1	2	6	3	4	11	9†	8*12						5	10	7	14											9
1	2	6	3	4	11†8	5	12						10	7	14	9*											10
1	2	6*	3	4	11	8	5	12					10	7	14	9†											11
1	2	6	3	4	14	9	5						10	7	11	8†											12
1	2	3	4	6	14	12	9†	5*					10	7	11	8											13
1	2	3	4	6	12	8*	14						5	10	7	11	9†										14
1	2	3	4	6	12	9*	14						5	10†	7	11	8										15
1	2†12	3	4	6	10	9	8*						5		7	11				14							16
1	12	3	4	6	11	9	8						5	10*	7	2											17
1	2	8	3	4	6	12	9	14					5	10*	7†11												18
1	2	8	3	4	6	12	9†	14					5	10	7*11												19
1	2	8	3	4	6	12	9						5	10	11		7*										20
1	2	3	4	6	8	9							5	10	7†11	14											21
1	2	8	3	4	6	7	9						5	10*	11	12											22
1	2	8	3	4	6	7*	9						5	10	11	12											23
1	2*	8	3	4	6	7	9	12					5†10	11							14						24
1	2	8	3	4	6		9	7					5	10	11												25
1	2	8	3	4	6	9*	7						5	10	11						12						26
1	2	8	3	4	6	14	9*	7					5†10	11							12						27
1		8	3	4	6	11		7					5	10							9	2					28
1		8	3	4	6	11	7†	5	14				10	12							9	2*					29
1	2	8	3	4	6	11	12	7*					5†10	14							9						30
1	2		3	4	6								5	10	11	14					9†						31
1		8	3	4	6	14	9	2					5*10	11†12							7						32
1	2	8	3		6	11	9	4					5		10						7						33
1	2	8	3	4	6	11	9	5	10				12								7*						34
1	2	8	3	4	6	11	9	5	7†				10*										12	14			35
1	2	8	3	4	6	11	5*12	10					14								9†		7				36
1	2	8	3	4	6	11	9	5	10				7														37
1	2	3	4	5	6	11*	9†	12	10	8			7										14				38
1	2†	8	3	4	11	9	6	7	5	10													14				39
1		8	3	4	11	7*	9	2	10†	5			6	12									14				40
1		3	4	5	11†14	8	6	12	9	10			7*									2					41
1		3	4	5	6	12	7*10	8	9†	11												2	14				42
1	6	3	5	10	11†	8	4												7		9	2	14				43
1	6	3	5	10	8	4	12												7*		9	2	11†14				44
44	33	32	44	42	30	26	13	37	30	16	0	0	31	34	18	24	7	1	2	1	11	2	4	1	1	0	
	+	+			+	+	+	+	+	+			+	+			+		+		+		+	+	+	+	
	1s	3s			12s3s	1s	1s	12s3s	5s				3s	10s			1s		4s		2s		3s	1s	1s		

MONTROSE   Second Division

Year Formed: 1879. *Ground & Address:* Links Park, Wellington St, Montrose DD10 8QD. *Telephone:* 0674 73200.
Ground Capacity: total: 6500. seated: 268. *Size of Pitch:* 113yd × 70yd.
Chairman: Bryan Keith. *Secretary:* Malcolm J. Watters. *Commercial Manager:* Allan Paul.
Manager: Jim Leishman. *Assistant Manager:* Cammy Fraser. *Physio:* David Rankine. *Coach:* Les Barr.
Managers since 1975: A. Stuart; K. Cameron; R. Livingstone; S. Murray; D. D'Arcy; I. Stewart; C. McLelland; D.
Rougvie. *Club Nickname(s):* The Gable Endies. *Previous Grounds:* None.
Record Attendance: 8983 v Dundee, Scottish Cup 3rd rd; 17 Mar, 1973.
Record Transfer Fee received: £50,000 for Gary Murray to Hibernian (Dec 1980).
Record Transfer Fee paid: £17,500 for Jim Smith from Airdrieonians (Feb 1992).

MONTROSE 1991–92 LEAGUE RECORD

Match No.	Date		Venue	Opponents	Result	H/T Score	Lg. Pos.	Goalscorers	Attendance
1	Aug	10	H	Hamilton A	D 2-2	2-2	—	Allan, Robertson	885
2		13	H	Ayr U	L 1-3	0-0	—	King	976
3		17	A	Stirling Albion	D 2-2	0-1	9	Den Bieman, Allan (pen)	938
4		24	A	Clydebank	L 1-4	1-1	11	King	667
5		31	H	Forfar Ath	W 2-1	0-0	10	King, Wolecki	748
6	Sept	7	H	Meadowbank T	D 2-2	0-1	10	King, Maver	601
7		14	A	Kilmarnock	D 0-0	0-0	7		3478
8		21	A	Partick T	L 0-1	0-0	9		2405
9		28	H	Dundee	L 1-2	0-0	9	Mackay	2228
10	Oct	5	A	Morton	D 1-1	0-1	8	Den Bieman	1250
11		8	H	Raith R	L 0-3	0-2	—		683
12		12	A	Hamilton A	L 0-2	0-1	11		1104
13		19	H	Stirling Albion	W 4-1	0-1	9	McGachie 3, Den Bieman	557
14		26	H	Meadowbank T	D 0-0	0-0	9		188
15		29	H	Kilmarnock	D 2-2	2-1	—	McGachie, Kerr	901
16	Nov	2	A	Forfar Ath	D 2-2	2-0	9	McGachie, Kerr (pen)	623
17		9	H	Clydebank	L 1-3	1-0	9	Den Bieman	620
18		16	H	Morton	D 1-1	0-0	9	Allan (pen)	674
19		19	A	Raith R	L 1-2	0-0	—	McGachie	812
20		23	H	Partick T	L 0-2	0-0	9		1204
21		30	A	Ayr U	L 0-2	0-0	11		1898
22	Dec	3	A	Dundee	L 0-1	0-1	—		2779
23		14	H	Meadowbank T	D 2-2	2-0	11	Maver, McGachie	525
24		17	H	Hamilton A	L 1-3	0-1	—	King	505
25		28	A	Clydebank	L 2-4	2-2	11	King, Mackay	648
26	Jan	1	H	Forfar Ath	W 2-1	1-1	—	Maver, Mackay	937
27		4	A	Morton	D 2-2	0-2	11	Mackay 2	1312
28		7	A	Kilmarnock	L 1-5	1-3	—	Mackay	3183
29		11	H	Raith R	D 2-2	0-2	11	Den Bieman, Mackay	1200
30		18	H	Ayr U	D 0-0	0-0	11		718
31	Feb	1	A	Stirling Albion	L 1-4	0-2	11	Mackay	729
32		8	A	Partick T	L 0-3	0-0	11		2503
33		22	H	Dundee	L 2-3	0-1	11	Fotheringham, McGachie	2363
34		29	H	Morton	D 1-1	1-0	11	Craib	756
35	Mar	7	A	Raith R	L 0-5	0-2	11		1090
36		14	H	Clydebank	D 2-2	0-1	11	Allan, McGachie	524
37		21	A	Forfar Ath	L 0-2	0-1	11		666
38		28	A	Hamilton A	L 1-4	0-2	11	Robertson	1206
39	Apr	4	H	Stirling Albion	D 0-0	0-0	11		569
40		8	A	Meadowbank T	W 1-0	0-0	—	Smith	286
41		11	H	Kilmarnock	L 0-1	0-0	11		793
42		18	H	Partick T	L 0-1	0-1	11		1999
43		25	A	Ayr U	D 0-0	0-0	11		1249
44	May	2	A	Dundee	W 2-1	0-0	11	Maver, Den Bieman	6878

Final League Position: 11

League (45): McGachie 9, Mackay 8, Den Bieman 6, King 6, Allan 4 (2 pens), Maver 4, Kerr 2 (1 pen), Robertson 2,
Craib 1, Fotheringham 1, Smith 1, Wolecki 1. *Scottish Cup* (0). *Skol Cup* (2): Rougvie 1, Wolecki 1. *B & Q Cup*
(8): King 3, Den Bieman 1, Kerr 1, McGachie 1, Maver 1, Rougvie 1.

Record Victory: 12-0 v Vale of Leithen, Scottish Cup 2nd rd; 4 Jan, 1975.
Record Defeat: 0-13 v Aberdeen; 17 Mar, 1951.
Most Capped Player: Alexander Keillor, 2 (6), Scotland.
Most League Appearances: —.
Most League Goals in Season (Individual): 28: Brian Third, Division II; 1972–73.
Most Goals Overall (Individual): —.

Honours
League Champions: Second Division 1984–85; *Runners–up:* 1990–91.
Scottish Cup: Quarter-finals 1973, 1976.   *League Cup:* Semi-finals 1975–76.
Club colours: Shirt: Blue with white pin stripe. Shorts: White. Stockings: Red.

Larter, D	Morrison, B	Fleming, J	Robertson, I	Mackay, H	Thomson, M	Maver, G	Allan, M	Wolecki, E	King, S	Den Bieman, I	Lyons, A	Fotheringham, J	Dornan, A	Kerr, B	Rougvie, D	Dolan, A	Chalmers, C	McGachie, J	McCarron, F	Craib, S	Fraser, C	Smith, J	Forbes, G	Callaghan, W	Locke, A	Masson, P	Houghton, G	Match No.
1	2	3	4	5	6	7*	8	9	10	11†12	14																	1
1	2	3	4	5			8	9†10	11	7*12	6	14																2
1	2	3	4	7			8†	9	10	11	14	6		5														3
1	2	3	4			7	8†	9	10	11	14	6		5														4
1	2	3	4			7	8†	9	11	12		6	14	5	10*													5
1	2	3	4			7	8†	9*10	11		14	6	12	5														6
1	2	3	4*			7	14	9	10	11		6	8†	5		12												7
1	2	3				7	8	9†10	11		14	6		5		4												8
1	2	3	4	12		7*	8†	9	10	11		6	14	5														9
1	2	3	12	8†	5	7	14	9	4	11		6			10*													10
1	2	3				7	14	9*		11		6	8†	5		10	12											11
1	2	3*				7	12	14	10	11		6		5		8	9†	4										12
1	2		4			7*	8		3	11		12	6	10			14	9	5†									13
1	2	10				7	8		3	11*		12		4			6	9	5									14
1	2	10				7	8*		3	11		12		4			6	9	5									15
1	2	10				7	8		3	11*		12		4			6	9	5									16
1	4	3				7	8*		10	11		12		6	5		2	9										17
1	4	3		12		7*	8		10	11				6	5		2	9										18
1	4†	3		12		7	8	14	10	11			6*	5			2	9										19
1	4			10		7	8*12		3	11				6	5		2	9										20
1	4			12		7	8	14		3†11				6	5		2*	9		10								21
1	4	3				7	8	12	10	11†		14		6	5		2	9*										22
1	4	3		12		7	8			11		14		6	5		2*	9†		10								23
1	2	3		14		7	12		5	11		8	6	4				9†		10*								24
1	4	3		8*		7†12		10	11		14	5	6			2	9											25
1	2	3		8		7			11			6	4				9	5	10									26
1		3		8		7			11†		14	6	4			2	9	5	10									27
1	2	3		8*		7	12		11			14	6	4†			2	9	5	10								28
1	4†	3		8		7			11			14	6				2	9	5	10								29
1	2	3	4	9		7			11			8	6						5	10								30
1	2	3	4	8		7†14			11			9	6						5	10								31
1	2	12	3	8†			7		10	11			6*				9		14	4	5							32
1		3	2	9			8†		5	7		11	6				10		14	4								33
1		3	2						10	7			6				8	11	4		5	9						34
1	2	3				7			10	8			6†				9	14	4	5		11						35
1	2	3				7†	8		6	14					11		9			4	5		10					36
1		3	2			7*	8			14		12			10		9†			4	6	5	11					37
	2	12	3			7	8*		4			14			11		9			6	5	10†	1					38
1	2		3			7	10*			14			8†				6	9	12	5	4	11						39
1	2		4			7	8			12					10*		9	14		6	5†11			3				40
1	2		4			7	8†		3								9	14		5	6	11		10*12				41
1	2	3	4			7	8			11								10		5	6	9						42
1	2		3			7	14			11								6	8†	5	4	9				10		43
1	2	3	4			7†12			10					14				11	8*	5	6	9						44

43 40 35 23 14   2 39 28 11 30 37   1   4 24 18 17   7 16 28 11 13   8 11   9 11   1   2   1
 + + +   + +   + +   +   + + +   +   +
 2s 1s 6s   10s5s   5s 1s 19s   4s   1s 2s 1s   6s   1s

MORTON   First Division

Year Formed: 1874. *Ground & Address:* Cappielow Park, Sinclair St, Greenock. *Telephone:* 0475 23511.
Ground Capacity: total: 14,250. seated: 5150. *Size of Pitch:* 110yd × 71yd.
Chairman: John Wilson. *Secretary:* Mrs Jane Rankin. *Commercial Manager:* Iain Baxter.
Manager: Allan McGraw. *Assistant Manager:* John McMaster. *Physio:* John Tierney. *Coach:* Billy Osborne.
Managers since 1975: Joe Gilroy; Benny Rooney; Alex Miller; Tommy McLean; Willie McLean.
Club Nickname(s): The Ton. *Previous Grounds:* Grant Street 1874, Garvel Park 1875, Cappielow Park 1879, Ladyburn
Park 1882, (Cappielow Park 1883). *Record Attendance:* 23,000 v Celtic; 1922. *Record Transfer Fee received:* £350,000
for Neil Orr to West Ham U. *Record Transfer Fee paid:* £35,000 for Roddy MacDonald from Hearts.
Record Victory: 11-0 v Carfin Shamrock Scottish Cup 1st rd; 13 Nov, 1886.

MORTON 1991–92 LEAGUE RECORD

Match No.	Date		Venue	Opponents	Result		H/T Score	Lg. Pos.	Goalscorers	Atten- dance
1	Aug	10	H	Partick T	W	2-1	1-0	—	Mathie, Gahagan	3340
2		13	H	Stirling Albion	W	2-1	0-1	—	Doak 2	1549
3		17	A	Hamilton A	D	1-1	0-0	3	Doak	1805
4		24	A	Forfar Ath	W	4-1	1-0	3	Mathie 2, Alexander, Gahagan	752
5		31	H	Clydebank	L	1-7	1-2	4	McInnes	1855
6	Sept	7	H	Dundee	W	3-0	2-0	4	Collins, Rafferty, Mathie	2036
7		14	A	Meadowbank T	W	1-0	1-0	3	McInnes	505
8		21	A	Raith R	D	1-1	0-0	3	Mathie	1219
9		28	H	Ayr U	L	3-4	1-1	4	Mathie, Furphy (og), McArthur	2601
10	Oct	5	H	Montrose	D	1-1	1-0	5	McInnes (pen)	1250
11		8	A	Kilmarnock	L	0-1	0-1	—		3677
12		12	H	Partick T	W	4-3	3-1	5	Doak, Alexander, McInnes, Mathie	3256
13		19	H	Hamilton A	W	1-0	0-0	4	McArthur	1723
14		26	A	Dundee	W	1-0	0-0	3	Lilley	1965
15		29	H	Meadowbank T	W	2-1	1-0	—	Doak, Lilley	1043
16	Nov	2	A	Clydebank	L	1-3	0-3	4	Pickering	1242
17		9	H	Forfar Ath	L	1-3	1-0	5	McInnes	1349
18		16	A	Montrose	D	1-1	0-0	5	Mathie (pen)	674
19		19	H	Kilmarnock	L	0-1	0-0	—		2637
20		23	H	Raith R	L	0-2	0-1	6		1280
21		30	A	Stirling Albion	L	1-2	1-1	7	Alexander	826
22	Dec	3	A	Ayr U	L	2-3	1-0	—	Mathie, Deeney	2221
23		7	H	Partick T	L	0-1	0-0	7		2194
24		14	A	Dundee	D	0-0	0-0	7		1567
25		28	A	Forfar Ath	W	5-1	0-1	7	Doak, Mathie 2, Rafferty, McInnes	628
26	Jan	4	H	Montrose	D	2-2	2-0	7	Alexander 2	1312
27		11	A	Kilmarnock	W	1-0	0-0	7	Mathie	4988
28		14	H	Clydebank	W	5-0	1-0	—	Alexander, McInnes, Mathie 2 (1 pen), Tolmie	1440
29		18	H	Stirling Albion	W	2-0	0-0	6	Doak, Mathie	1635
30	Feb	1	A	Hamilton A	D	0-0	0-0	6		1921
31		8	A	Raith R	L	0-2	0-2	7		1703
32		12	A	Meadowbank T	W	2-1	2-0	—	Doak, Alexander	352
33		29	A	Montrose	D	1-1	0-1	6	Alexander	756
34	Mar	14	A	Forfar Ath	D	1-1	1-0	7	Alexander	1061
35		17	H	Ayr U	W	2-0	1-0	—	Tolmie, Hopkin	1175
36		21	A	Clydebank	W	3-2	3-0	6	Hopkin, Tolmie, Doak	1047
37		24	H	Kilmarnock	D	0-0	0-0	—		3015
38		28	H	Partick T	L	0-1	0-1	6		4367
39	Apr	4	H	Hamilton A	D	1-1	0-0	6	Mathie	1428
40		7	A	Dundee	D	2-2	1-2	—	Mathie, Rafferty	4452
41		11	H	Meadowbank T	W	3-1	0-0	6	Lilley, Hopkin, McArthur	1026
42		18	A	Raith R	L	0-1	0-1	6		1432
43		25	A	Stirling Albion	L	3-4	2-2	6	Johnstone, Alexander, Mathie	686
44	May	2	A	Ayr U	L	0-1	0-1	7		1595

Final League Position: 7

League (66): Mathie 18 (2 pens), Alexander 10. Doak 9, McInnes 7 (1 pen), Hopkin 3, Lilley 3, McArthur 3, Rafferty
3, Tolmie 3, Gahagan 2, Collins 1, Deeney 1, Johnstone 1, Pickering 1, own goal 1. *Scottish Cup* (9): Alexander 3,
Mathie 3 (2 pens), Hopkin 1, McArthur 1, Rafferty 1. *Skol Cup* (2): McInnes 1, Ogg 1. *B & Q Cup* (4): Mathie 2,
Doak 1, McArthur 1.

Record Defeat: 1-10 v Port Glasgow Ath, Division II; 5 May, 1894 and v St Bernards, Division II; 14 Oct, 1933.
Most Capped Player: Jimmy Cowan, 25, Scotland.
Most League Appearances: 358: David Hayes, 1969–84.
Most League Goals in Season (Individual): 58: Allan McGraw, Division II; 1963–64.
Most Goals Overall (Individual): —.

Honours
League Champions: First Division 1977–78, 1983–84, 1986–87. Division II 1949–50, 1963–64, 1966–67.
Scottish Cup Winners: 1922; Runners-up: 1948. *League Cup Runners-up:* 1963–64.
European: *European Cup* —. *Cup Winners Cup* —. *UEFA Cup (Fairs):* 1968–69.
Club colours: Shirt: Blue and white hoops. Shorts: White. Stockings: Blue.

Wylie, D	Pickering, M	Ogg, G	Rafferty, S	Doak, M	Hunter, J	Mathie, A	Collins, D	Alexander, R	Fowler, J	Gahagan, J	McInnes, D	McGoldrick, K	Deeney, M	McDonald, I	Boag, J	McArthur, S	Hopkin, D	Lilley, D	MacCabe, D	Kelly, G	Brown, C	Johnstone, D	Tolmie, J	Mahood, A	Graham, P	Match No.
1	2*	3	4	5	6	7	8	9	10	11	12															1
1	2*	3	4	5	6	7	8	9	10		12	14	11†													2
1	2		4	5	6†	7	8	9	3	11*	10		14	12												3
1	2	3	4	5		7	11	9*			12		10	14	8	6†										4
1	2†	3	4	5		7	11	9			12		10	14	8*	6										5
1	3		4*	5		7	2			11	10			9†	12	6	8	14								6
1	3		4	5		7	2	9		11*	10			14	12†	6	8									7
1	3		4	5		7	2	9			10			14		6	8	11†								8
1	3		4	5		7	2	9			10			14		6	8	11†								9
1	3		4	5		7	2	9			10*			14	12	6	8	11†								10
1		3	4*	5		7	2	9			10			12	11	6	8†14									11
1	3	12	5			7	2	9			10			4	6	8†14	11*									12
1	9	3	12	5		7	2				10			4*	6	8	14	11†								13
1	3	12	5			7	2				10			4	6	8	11†	9*14								14
1	3		4	5		7	2				10			12	6	8†11*	9	14								15
1	3	12	5			7	2				10			4	6*	8	11†	9	14							16
1	3		4†	5		7	2		11		10			8*		12		9	14	6						17
1	3	5	4			7	2	9	12		10			8*	6	11										18
1	3		4*	5		7	2	9			10			12	6	8†		14			11					19
1	3		4	5		7	2	9			10			8†	6*12			14			11					20
1	3	12	5			7	2	9†14			10			4*			11			8	6					21
1	3		4	5		7	2		11†		10		14		8			9			6					22
1	3		4	5		7†	2				10		11		8		14	9			6					23
1	3*		4	5		7	2				10		11	6	8		14	9†		12						24
1		3	4	5		7	2				10		11		8					6		9				25
1		3	4	5		7	2	9			10	14			8†		12					6	11*			26
1	3	14	4	5		7	2	9			10				8							6	11†			27
1	3		4	5		7	2	9			10				8		14					6	11†			28
1	3		4	5		7	2	9			10†				8					14		6	11			29
1	3		4	5		7	2	9			12				8					10*		6	11			30
1	3†		4	5		7	2	9			10*				8		14			12		6	11			31
1	3			5		7*	2	9	14	11	10			6	8†		12		4							32
1	3		4	5		7	2	9			11†10			6	8*		14		12							33
1	3		4	5		7	2	9						8*10†14			12					6	11			34
1	3		4	5		7	2	9			10				8	14						6	11†			35
1	3		4	5		7	2	9			10				8*14		12					6	11†			36
1	3		4	5		7	2				10				8	9†14						6	11			37
1	3		4	5		7	2				10				8	12	9*					6	11			38
1	3		4	5		7	2				10		14	8	9†							6	11			39
1	3	6	4	5		7	2				10			8	9							11†14				40
1	3		4	5			2	9			10		14	8†11							6		7			41
1	3	14	4*	5			2	9			10†			6	8	11	12						7			42
	3	12	5			7	2	9			10			8	11*14						6		4†	1		43
	3	4†	5			7	2	9	14		12			11*	8						6		10	1		44
42	34	17	37	43	3	42	44	30	5	6	38	1	4	11	19	29	17	13	4	2	5	18	14	4	2	
		+	+								+		+	+	+	+	+				+		+		+	
		2s	6s								4s		2s	4s	6s	5s	6s				4s		4s		12s8s	
																					6s				1s	

MOTHERWELL Premier Division

Year Formed: 1886. *Ground & Address:* Fir Park, Motherwell ML1 2QN. *Telephone:* 0698 61437/8/9.
Ground Capacity: total: 15,500. seated: 6500. *Size of Pitch:* 110yd × 75yd.
Chairman: John C. Chapman. *Secretary:* Alan C. Dick. *Commercial Manager:* John Swinburne.
Manager: Tommy McLean. *Assistant Manager:* Tom Forsyth. *Physio:* Bobby Holmes. *Coach:* Cameron Murray.
Managers since 1975: Ian St John; Willie McLean; Rodger Hynd; Ally MacLeod; David Hay; Jock Wallace; Bobby
Watson. *Club Nickname(s):* The'Well. *Previous Grounds:* Roman Road, Dalziel Park.
Record Attendance: 35,632 v Rangers, Scottish Cup 4th rd replay; 12 Mar, 1952.
Record Transfer Fee received: £375,000 for Andy Walker to Celtic (Aug 1987).
Record Transfer Fee paid: £110,000 for Iain Ferguson from Hearts (Dec 1990).
Record Victory: 12-1 v Dundee U, Division II; 23 Jan, 1954.

MOTHERWELL 1991–92 LEAGUE RECORD

Match No.	Date		Venue	Opponents		Result	H/T Score	Lg. Pos.	Goalscorers	Attendance
1	Aug	10	A	Falkirk	D	1-1	0-1	—	Nijholt (pen)	5543
2		13	A	Rangers	L	0-2	0-1	—		35,321
3		17	H	Hibernian	D	1-1	1-1	8	McCart	8018
4		24	A	Airdrieonians	W	1-0	0-0	6	Nijholt (pen)	5066
5		31	H	St Mirren	W	1-0	0-0	6	Nijholt (pen)	5749
6	Sept	7	A	Hearts	L	0-2	0-0	7		9003
7		14	H	Aberdeen	L	0-1	0-1	7		6452
8		21	H	Dunfermline Ath	W	3-0	1-0	7	Philliben, Dolan, Russell	4541
9		28	A	Dundee U	D	2-2	1-2	7	Angus, Dolan	6844
10	Oct	5	A	St Johnstone	W	1-0	0-0	7	Griffin	5014
11		8	H	Celtic	L	0-2	0-1	—		13,283
12		12	H	Falkirk	W	4-2	1-1	6	O'Donnell, Cusack 2, Kirk	5991
13		19	A	Hibernian	D	0-0	0-0	6		7141
14		26	H	Hearts	L	0-1	0-1	7		5417
15		30	A	Aberdeen	L	1-3	0-0	—	Arnott	9092
16	Nov	2	A	St Mirren	W	2-1	1-0	7	Manley (og), Fridge (og)	2689
17		9	H	Airdrieonians	L	1-2	0-1	7	Cooper (pen)	5509
18		16	H	St Johnstone	D	1-1	0-0	7	Russell	4570
19		20	A	Celtic	D	2-2	2-2	—	Arnott 2	16,350
20		23	A	Dunfermline Ath	D	0-0	0-0	7		4679
21		30	H	Rangers	L	0-2	0-0	7		15,350
22	Dec	3	H	Dundee U	D	1-1	0-1	—	Kirk	4023
23		7	A	Falkirk	W	1-0	1-0	7	Arnott	4900
24		14	A	Hearts	L	1-3	1-3	7	McCart	10,006
25		28	A	Airdrieonians	L	0-2	0-0	8		4723
26	Jan	1	H	St Mirren	W	3-0	1-0	—	Nijholt, Cooper, Kirk	4380
27		4	A	St Johnstone	D	0-0	0-0	7		4965
28		11	H	Celtic	D	0-0	0-0	7		12,115
29		4	H	Aberdeen	D	3-3	2-1	—	Kirk, Nijholt, O'Donnell	5221
30		18	A	Rangers	L	0-2	0-1	7		38,127
31	Feb	1	H	Hibernian	D	1-1	0-0	7	Angus	6105
32		8	H	Dunfermline Ath	L	1-2	1-2	8	Arnott	6375
33		22	A	Dundee U	D	2-2	1-0	8	Kirk, O'Donnell	4746
34		29	A	St Johnstone	W	3-1	1-0	7	Kirk, Cooper, McKinnon	4373
35	Mar	14	H	Airdrieonians	L	0-3	0-1	7		5065
36		17	A	Celtic	L	1-4	1-2	—	Arnott	15,582
37		21	A	St Mirren	W	2-1	1-1	7	Jones, O'Donnell	2112
38		28	H	Falkirk	L	0-1	0-0	7		4395
39	Apr	4	A	Hibernian	D	0-0	0-0	7		4423
40		7	H	Hearts	L	0-1	0-1	—		4502
41		11	A	Aberdeen	L	0-2	0-2	7		6902
42		18	A	Dunfermline Ath	L	1-3	0-1	7	Arnott	2310
43		23	H	Rangers	L	1-2	1-1	—	Arnott	12,515
44	May	2	H	Dundee U	L	1-2	0-1	10	Angus	3151

Final League Position: 10

League (43): Arnott 8, Kirk 6, Nijholt 5 (3 pens), O'Donnell 4, Angus 3, Cooper 3 (1 pen), Cusack 2, Dolan 2, McCart 2, Russell 2, Griffin 1, Jones 1, McKinnon 1, Philliben 1, own goals 2. *Scottish Cup* (6): Arnott 1, Ferguson 1, Kirk 1, Martin 1, Nijholt 1 (pen), O'Donnell 1. *Skol Cup* (1): Kirk 1.

Record Defeat: 0-8 v Aberdeen, Premier Division; 26 Mar, 1979.
Most Capped Player: George Stevenson, 12, Scotland.
Most League Appearances: 626: Bobby Ferrier, 1918–37.
Most League Goals in Season (Individual): 52: Willie McFadyen, Division I; 1931–32.
Most Goals Overall (Individual): 283: Hugh Ferguson, 1916–25.

Honours
League Champions: Division I 1931–32. First Division 1981–82, 1984–85. Division II 1953–54, 1968–69; *Runners-up:* Division I 1926–27, 1929–30, 1932–33, 1933–34. Division II 1894–95, 1902–03.
Scottish Cup: 1952, 1991; *Runners-up:* 1931, 1933, 1939, 1951.
League Cup: 1950–51; *Runners-up:* 1954–55. *Scottish Summer Cup:* 1944, 1965.
Club colours: Shirt: Amber with claret trimmings. Shorts: Claret. Stockings: Amber.

Thomson, W	Griffin, J	Nijholt, L	Maaskant, R	Philliben, J	McCart, C	Arnott, D	O'Donnell, P	Kirk, S	Angus, I	Cooper, D	Ferguson, I	Shepherd, A	McLeod, J	Verheul, B	Dolan, J	McGrillen, P	Dykstra, S	Simpson, N	Russell, R	Cusack, N	Gardner, J	Martin, B	McKinnon, R	Jones, A	Bryce, S	Gourlay, A	Match No.
1	2	3	4	5	6	7*	8	9	10	11	12																1
1	2	3	4	5	6		8	14	10	11	12		7*					9†									2
1	2	3		5*	6		8	7	10	11	9†	12			4	14											3
	8	3	5	2	6		10	7		11	9*	12					1	4									4
1	8	3	5	2†	6		10	7	12	11	9		14		4*												5
1	4	3	5	2*	6		8	7	10	11	12				9												6
1	2	3		5	6		8	12	10	11*			14	7	4*			9									7
1	2*	3		5	6		8	10		11	7†				4	14		12	9								8
1	2	3		5	6		10		11*	12		7			4	8		14	9†								9
1	2†	3			6		8	7		11*	14				5	4		12	9	10							10
1		3		5	6		8	10*		11	14	12			2	4		7†	9								11
1	2	3		5	6	7†	8	10		11	14				12	4*		9									12
1	2	3*		5	6	7†	10	12		11	14				8	4		9									13
1	2			5*	6	7	10	8		11	12				3	4		9									14
1		3		5	6	7	8†	10		11					2	4		9	14								15
1	2	3†	14		6	7	8	10*	11	12					5	4		9									16
1		3		5	6		8	10		11		7			2†	14		4	9								17
1	2	3		5		7	8	12		11	14				4			10†	9		6*						18
1	2	3		5†	6	7	10			11					4*	12		9	14								19
1	2	3		5†		7	10	14		11					4			9			6	8					20
1	2	3	4	5			10			11	9					14			7		6†	8					21
1	2	3		5*	6	7	10	9		11					4			12				8					22
1		3		5	6	7	10	12		11					2			8	9*	4							23
1		3		5†	6	7	10	8			14				4			9		11		2					24
1		3		5†	6	7	10	8	11*		14				4			12		9		2					25
1	2*	3		5		7	10	8		11					4			9†	12	14		6					26
1		3		5		7*	10	12	6	11					8			4	9†	14		2					27
1	2			5		7	10	9	8	11					4							6	3				28
1	2			5†		7	10	9	8	11	14				4							6	3				29
1	2†			5		7	10	9		11*	14				4				8	12		6	3				30
1	2				6	7	10	9	8	11	12				4*								3	5			31
1	2		4*			7	10	8	6†	11	9							12		14			3	5			32
1	2						10	9	8	11	7†		14		4							6	3	5			33
1	2						10	9	8*	11	7†				4	14		12				6	3	5			34
1	2					7	10	9	12	11	8†				4	14						6	3	5*			35
1	2							9	10	8	14				4	11†		12	7*			6	3	5			36
1	2							9	10	12	8	11			4†	14*			7			6	3	5			37
1	2								10	12	8	9			4*	11			7†			6	3	5	14		38
1					6		10	7	8	12	11*				2	14				9		4	3	5†			39
1					6		10	7	8*	11					2	14		12				4	3	5	9†		40
1	2				6	7	12	10		11	8†				4						9*		3	5	14		41
1	2							9	10	8†	11				4*			12	7			6	3	5	14		42
1	2			5	6			9	10	8	11					14		12†	7*			4	3				43
1	2		12		6			9	10	8						11		14	7*			4†	3	5			44
43	22	39	12	30	22	26	42	28	23	38	9	1	9	1	28	5	1	20	7	17	6	25	16	12	2	0	
		+2s				+10s	+2s	+1s	+11s	+4s	+5s		+2s		+4s	+11s		+1s		+9s		+6s		+3s	+1s		

PARTICK THISTLE   Premier Division

Year Formed: 1876. *Ground & Address:* Firhill Park, 90 Firhill Rd, Glasgow G20 7AL. *Telephone:* 041 945 4811.
Ground Capacity: total: 13,376. seated: 2906. *Size of Pitch:* 110yd × 74yd.
Chairman: James Oliver. *Company Secretary:* Robert Reid. *Secretary:* Robert Reid. *General Commercial Manager:* Jez
Mozey. *Manager:* John Lambie. *Assistant Manager:* Gerry Collins. *Physio:* John Hart. *Coach:* Ian Jardine.
Managers since 1975: R. Auld; P. Cormack; B. Rooney; R. Auld; D. Johnstone; W. Lamont; S. Clark.
Club Nickname(s): The Jags. *Previous Grounds:* Jordanvale Park; Muirpark; Inchview; Meadowside Park.
Record Attendance: 49,838 v Rangers, Division I; 18 Feb, 1922. *Record Transfer Fee received:* £200,000 for Mo
Johnston to Watford. *Record Transfer Fee paid:* £85,000 for Andy Murdoch from Celtic, Feb 1991.
Record Victory: 16-0 v Royal Albert, Scottish Cup 1st rd; 17 Jan, 1931.
Record Defeat: 0-10 v Queen's Park, Scottish Cup; 3 Dec, 1881.

PARTICK THISTLE 1991–92 LEAGUE RECORD

Match No.	Date	Venue	Opponents	Result	H/T Score	Lg. Pos.	Goalscorers	Atten- dance
1	Aug 10	A	Morton	L	1-2	0-1	—	Rae	3340
2	13	A	Meadowbank T	W	1-0	0-0	—	McGlashan	1135
3	17	H	Kilmarnock	W	1-0	0-0	6	McGlashan	5248
4	24	H	Stirling Albion	W	1-0	0-0	4	English	3341
5	31	A	Hamilton A	D	1-1	1-0	3	English	2722
6	Sept 7	A	Ayr U	W	3-1	2-0	3	Shaw 2, Duffy (pen)	3971
7	14	H	Raith R	W	5-0	3-0	2	Farningham 3, McGlashan, English	3224
8	21	H	Montrose	W	1-0	0-0	2	Shaw	2405
9	28	A	Forfar Ath	W	3-0	1-0	2	McGlashan, Adam (og), Farningham	1525
10	Oct 5	A	Dundee	W	2-1	1-0	1	English, McGlashan	4799
11	8	H	Clydebank	L	0-3	0-1	—		2751
12	12	H	Morton	L	3-4	1-3	2	Tierney, Farningham, McGlashan (pen)	3256
13	19	A	Kilmarnock	W	3-2	1-2	2	Irons, Law, Shaw	4962
14	26	H	Ayr U	W	3-0	2-0	1	McGlashan 2 (1 pen), Law	2170
15	29	A	Raith R	L	0-1	0-0	—		2027
16	Nov 2	H	Hamilton A	D	1-1	0-0	1	Johnston	2760
17	9	A	Stirling Albion	D	1-1	0-1	2	Kennedy	2064
18	16	H	Dundee	L	2-6	2-3	4	McGlashan, Johnston	5042
19	19	A	Clydebank	D	0-0	0-0	—		1984
20	23	A	Montrose	W	2-0	0-0	3	Shaw, Morrison (og)	1204
21	30	H	Meadowbank T	L	0-2	0-1	4		2468
22	Dec 3	H	Forfar Ath	D	1-1	0-1	—	English	1501
23	7	A	Morton	W	1-0	0-0	4	Irons	2194
24	14	A	Ayr U	W	2-0	0-0	4	Irons, Rae	2791
25	21	H	Raith R	L	0-1	0-1	4		2333
26	28	H	Stirling Albion	L	0-1	0-1	4		2718
27	Jan 1	A	Hamilton A	W	2-0	1-0	—	Irons, McGlashan	2852
28	4	A	Dundee	L	0-1	0-0	5		4544
29	11	H	Clydebank	W	2-1	1-1	4	Duffy, Irons	2908
30	18	A	Meadowbank T	D	0-0	0-0	3		887
31	Feb 1	H	Kilmarnock	W	2-1	0-0	3	Irons, Shaw	4873
32	8	H	Montrose	W	3-0	0-0	2	McGlashan 2, Kinnaird	2503
33	15	H	Ayr U	W	4-1	1-0	2	Shaw, Farningham, McGlashan, Irons	2771
34	22	A	Forfar Ath	D	0-0	0-0	2		1155
35	29	H	Dundee	W	2-0	1-0	2	Shaw, McGlashan	8437
36	Mar 10	A	Clydebank	W	2-0	2-0	—	Farningham, Kinnaird	2164
37	14	A	Stirling Albion	D	1-1	0-0	2	McGlashan	2107
38	21	H	Hamilton A	D	0-0	0-0	2		6079
39	28	H	Morton	W	1-0	1-0	2	McGlashan	4367
40	Apr 4	A	Kilmarnock	W	3-1	2-0	2	Irons, Rae, Shaw	5640
41	11	A	Raith R	D	0-0	0-0	2		3514
42	18	A	Montrose	W	1-0	1-0	2	McGlashan	1999
43	25	H	Meadowbank T	L	1-2	1-1	2	McGlashan	6656
44	May 2	H	Forfar Ath	D	0-0	0-0	2		9959

Final League Position: 2

League (62): McGlashan 18 (4 pens), Shaw 9, Irons 8, Farningham 7, English 5, Rae 3, Duffy 2 (1 pen), Johnston 2,
Kinnaird 2, Law 2, Kennedy 1, Tierney 1, own goals 2. *Scottish Cup* (0). *Skol Cup* (2): McGlashan 1, own goal 1.
B & Q Cup (4): McGlashan 2, Rae 1, Shaw 1.

Most Capped Player: Alan Rough, 51 (53), Scotland.
Most League Appearances: 410: Alan Rough, 1969–82.
Most League Goals in Season (Individual): 41: Alec Hair, Division I; 1926–27.
Most Goals Overall (Individual): —.

Honours
League Champions: First Division 1975–76. Division II 1896–97, 1899–1900, 1970–71; *Runners-up:* Division II 1901–02.
Scottish Cup Winners: 1921; *Runners-up:* 1930.
League Cup Winners: 1971–72; *Runners-up:* 1953–54, 1956–57, 1958–59.
European: *European Cup* —. *Cup Winners Cup* —. *UEFA Cup* 6 matches (*Fairs Cup:* 1963–64. *UEFA Cup:* 1972–73).
Club colours: Shirts: Amber with red shoulders and sleeves. Shorts: Red with amber stripe. Stockings: Red.

Murdoch, A	Robertson, G	McLaughlin, P	Duffy, J	Rae, G	Johnston, S	Shaw, G	Bell, D	McGlashan, C	McWalter, M	English, I	Roche, D	Law, R	Tierney, G	Magee, K	Irons, D	Farningham, R	McGovern, P	Friar, P	Kennedy, A	Harvie, S	Lowrie, R	Flood, J	Murray, M	Kinnaird, P	Annand, E	Nelson, C	McVicar, D	Peebles, G	Match No.
1	2	3	4	5	6	7	8	9	10	11*12																			1
1	2	3	4	5	6	7		9		11*		10†	8	12	14														2
1	2*	3	4	5	6	7	12	9	10†				8	14		11													3
1	2	3	4	5	6	7		9	10†14				8	12		11*													4
1	2	3	4	5	6*	7†		9	14	10				12		11	8												5
1	2*	3	4	5	6	7		9	10†				14	12		11	8												6
1	2	3	4	5	6*	7		9					11†	12		10	8												7
1	2	3	4	5	6*	7		9					11†			10	8	14											8
1	2	3	4	5	6	7		9					11†			10	8	14											9
1	2	3	4*	5	6	7	14	9		11†		12				10	8												10
1	2	3		5	6	7		9		11		4				10	8												11
1		3		5	6	7	12	9		11		4				10*	8		2										12
1		3	14	10	7	8†		9					2	5		11	4		6										13
1	2	3			8†	7*10		9			12		4	5		11			6	14									14
1	2*	3			10	7		9			12		4	5		11	8		6										15
	2†	3	14		10	7		9			12		4	5		11*	8		6	1									16
1	2	3			10	7		9					4	5		11	8		6										17
1			4	12	10	7		9					2	5*		11	8		6	3†		14							18
1	14	3	4	5†10*	7			9					2			12	8		6	11									19
1	12	3	4	5		7		9					2			10	8		6	11*									20
1	12	3	4	5		7		9					2			10	8	14	6†11*										21
1	2	14	4	5		7	12		10				6†			11	8	9*					3						22
1	2		4	5		7		9		11			6			10	8*		12				3						23
1	2	14	4	5		7†	8*	9		11						10		12	6				3						24
1	2		4	5		7	8	9		11						10			6*	12			3						25
1	2*	3	4	5		12	8†	9		14						10			11	7	6								26
1	7	3	4	5		12	8	9								6							10*	2		11			27
1	6	3	4	5		7*	8	9					12			10								2		11			28
1	8	3	4	5				9		14						6	7						10†	2		11			29
1	8	3	4	5		12		9								6	7						10	2		11*			30
1		3	4	5		7	12	9								6							10	8	2	11*			31
1		3	4	5		7*		9					6			14	10	8†						2	11	12			32
1		3	4	5		7	9†			14			6			12	10*	8						2	11				33
	3†14		4	5		7*		9		12			6			10	8						2	11	1				34
	6		4	5		7		9		12						10	8						2	11*	1		3		35
	6		4	5		7		9		12						10	8						2	11*	1		3		36
	6		4	5		7		9						14		10	8						2	11†	1		3		37
	6*		4	5		7		9				12		14		10	8						2	11†	1		3		38
	11		4	5		7		9*		12			6			10	8						2		1		3		39
		3	4	5†		7		9					6			10	8						2		1	11	14		40
	11		4			7		9*		12		6	5			10	8						2		1		3		41
		3	4			7		9				6	5			10	8						2		1	11			42
	3†14		4	5		7		9		12				10*	14	6	8						2	11	1	3	10†		43
	8*		4	5	14	7		9	12				6										2	11	1	3	10†		44
32	33	30	37	36	19	40	8	43	5	12	1	25	9	0	40	33	1	1	9	7	1	4	23	13	0	11	10	1	
+	+	+	+	+	+	+	+	+	+	+		+	+	+	+		+			+			+	+			+		
3s	3s	1s	2s	1s	3s	4s	1s	2s	14s	1s		6s	4s	6s	1s		4s			2s			2s			1s		1s	

QUEEN OF THE SOUTH Second Division

Year Formed: 1919. *Ground & Address:* Palmerston Park,Terregles St, Dumfries DG2 9BA. *Telephone:* 0387 54853.
Ground Capacity: total: 6750. seated: 1300. *Size of Pitch:* 112yd × 72yd.
Chairman: W. J. Harkness C.B.E. *Secretary:* Mrs Doreen Alcorn. *Commercial Manager:* W. J. Harkness.
Manager: —. *Assistant Manager:* —. *Physio:* Mrs. M. Hamilton. *Coach:* —.
Managers since 1975: M. Jackson; G. Herd; A. Busby; R. Clark; M. Jackson; D. Wilson; W. McLaren; A. MacLeod.
Club Nickname(s): The Doonhamers. *Previous Grounds:* None.
Record Attendance: 24,500 v Hearts, Scottish Cup 3rd rd; 23 Feb, 1952.
Record Transfer Fee received: £100,000 for K. McMinn to Rangers, 1985.
Record Transfer Fee paid: —.
Record Victory: 11-1 v Stranraer, Scottish Cup 1st rd; 16 Jan, 1932.

QUEEN OF THE SOUTH 1991–92 LEAGUE RECORD

Match No.	Date	Venue	Opponents	Result	H/T Score	Lg. Pos.	Goalscorers	Attendance
1	Aug 10	A	Cowdenbeath	W 1-0	0-0	—	McGuire J	332
2	17	H	Clyde	L 1-2	1-0	8	Thomson A	766
3	24	A	Albion R	D 1-1	1-1	8	Gordon	270
4	31	H	Berwick R	L 0-3	0-2	11		576
5	Sept 7	H	Alloa	L 1-3	1-1	14	Thomson I	527
6	14	H	Stenhousemuir	W 2-1	1-1	11	Thomson A 2	502
7	17	H	East Fife	L 1-4	0-2	—	Moffat	612
8	21	H	Stranraer	L 0-2	0-0	14		659
9	28	A	Queen's Park	W 4-1	2-0	12	McGuire J 2, Thomson I, Thomson A	444
10	Oct 5	H	East Stirling	W 5-1	1-0	9	Thomson A 3, McGuire J 2	460
11	12	A	Arbroath	W 3-2	1-2	9	Thomson A, McGhie, Thomson I (pen)	490
12	19	H	Dumbarton	L 2-4	1-2	9	Thomson A, Templeton	893
13	26	A	Brechin C	L 1-7	0-2	9	Templeton	350
14	Nov 2	H	Cowdenbeath	D 3-3	2-0	9	McGuire J, McFarlane, Thomson I	514
15	16	H	Albion R	L 2-4	1-3	12	Thomson I, Templeton	530
16	23	A	Alloa	L 1-3	0-2	12	Gordon	479
17	30	A	Stenhousemuir	W 3-1	1-1	11	Thomson A, Thomson I 2	413
18	Dec 7	A	Clyde	W 3-2	3-1	10	McGuire J, Thomson A, Thomson I	538
19	14	H	Brechin C	W 4-2	1-2	10	Thomson A 2, McGuire J 2	597
20	21	A	Berwick R	D 1-1	1-1	9	Templeton	259
21	28	H	East Fife	W 3-1	1-0	8	Templeton, Bell, Thomson A	971
22	Jan 1	A	Stranraer	W 2-0	2-0	—	McGuire J, Thomson A	750
23	11	A	East Stirling	L 1-2	1-0	8	McGuire J	245
24	18	A	Queen's Park	D 2-2	1-0	8	Thomson A, McGhie	735
25	25	H	Arbroath	L 0-2	0-1	8		653
26	Feb 1	A	Dumbarton	L 1-3	1-2	8	Hetherington	627
27	8	H	Albion R	W 3-0	1-0	8	Thomson A 2, McGuire J	624
28	15	A	Brechin C	D 1-1	1-1	8	Smyth	426
29	22	A	East Fife	L 1-5	1-3	9	McKeown	720
30	29	H	Stenhousemuir	L 1-3	1-2	10	Thomson A	506
31	Mar 14	H	Dumbarton	L 1-2	1-0	11	Robertson	583
32	17	A	Clyde	L 1-2	0-0	—	Thomson I	434
33	21	H	East Stirling	L 2-3	1-3	12	Thomson A, Robertson	408
34	28	A	Alloa	L 1-3	0-0	12	Campbell (og)	765
35	Apr 4	H	Queen's Park	W 5-3	2-2	11	McKeown, Templeton, McGuire J, Bell, Thomson A	465
36	11	A	Arbroath	W 3-0	1-0	11	Thomson A 3	332
37	18	H	Berwick R	L 0-3	0-2	11		598
38	25	A	Cowdenbeath	L 1-3	1-1	12	Templeton	782
39	May 2	A	Stranraer	W 3-1	1-0	11	Thomson A 2, Thomson I	547

Final League Position: 11

League (71): Thomson A 26, McGuire J 13, Thomson I 10 (1 pen), Templeton 7, Bell 2, Gordon 2, McGhie 2, McKeown 2, Robertson 2, Hetherington 1, McFarlane 1, Moffat 1, Smyth 1, own goal 1. *Scottish Cup* (1): Thomson A 1. *Skol Cup* (0). *B & Q Cup* (12): Thomson A 6, McGuire J 4, Robertson 1, own goal 1.

Record Defeat: 2-10 v Dundee, Division I; 1 Dec, 1962.
Most Capped Player: Billy Houliston, 3, Scotland.
Most League Appearances: 619: Allan Ball; 1962–83.
Most League Goals in Season (Individual): 33: Jimmy Gray, Division II; 1927–28.
Most Goals Overall (Individual): —.

Honours
League Champions: Division II 1950–51; *Runners-up:* Division II 1932–33, 1961–62, 1974–75. Second Division 1980–81, 1985–86.
Scottish Cup: —.
League Cup: —.
Club colours: Shirt: Royal blue. Shorts: White. Stockings: Royal blue with white tops.

Davidson, A	Campbell, K	Smyth, D	Mills, D	Hetherington, K	McKeown, B	McGuire, J	Thomson, I	Thomson, A	Gordon, S	Bell, A	Sim, W	Robertson, J	McGhie, W	Moffat, I	McGuire, D	Leslie, S	Fraser, G	McFarlane, A	Thomson, M	Templeton, H	Gillespie, A	Match No.
1	2	3	4	5†	6	7	8	9	10	11		14										1
1	2	6	5	4		7†	8	9	10			11	3	14								2
1	2	6	5	4		11	9	10	3	12	8				7*							3
1	2†	6*	5	4		12	11	9	10	3	14	8			7							4
1	2				8	11	9		6		4	5	10	3	7							5
1		5		4	11		9	10	8	6		2	7	3								6
1		5		4	11		9	10	3	6		2	12	7†	8*14							7
			4	2	11		9	10	6			5	14	8†				3	1	7		8
			8	6	9	2	10		4	11	5							3	1	7		9
1				9	8	10	2	11	4		5							6	3	7		10
1				10	6	9	2	8	4	11	5							3		7		11
1				10	4	9	2	8		11	5	6*	12					3		7		12
1				10	6	9	2	8*	4	11	5	14	12					3†		7		13
1		14		10*	6	9	2	8	4	11	5†	12						3		7		14
1		5		10	6	9†	2	8	4	11		14						3		7		15
		5		10	8	9	2		11	6								3	1	7	4	16
		5		10	6	9	2	8		11								3	1	7	4	17
		5		10	6	9	2	8		11								3	1	7	4	18
		5*		10	6	9	2	8†		11	12	14						3	1	7	4	19
		5		10	6	9	2	8		11								3	1	7	4	20
		5		10	6	9	2	8		11								3	1	7	4	21
		5		10		9	2	8	3	11	6			7				1		4		22
		5		10	6	9	11	8	14		2	7		3†	1					4		23
			4	10	11	9		8*	6		2	14	12	3	1	7†	5					24
		5		10	6	9	2	8		11		14						3	1	7†	4	25
			6	4	10	8	9	2			11†14	12		3	1	7*	5					26
			6	4	10	8	9	2			11			3	1	7	5					27
	3		4	10	6	9	2		11		8				1	7	5					28
	3	14	4†		9	2	6	11		10	7	8		1		5						29
1	5*	4		10		9	6	8†	11	2	14	12	3		7							30
1		5		4	10	8	9	2	11	6	7*	12	3									31
1			4	10	8	9	2	11	6	7			3					5				32
1	2*10			6	9	8	12	11	4	14		3				7†	5					33
1			4	10	8†	9	6	3	11	2	14					7	5					34
1			4	10	6	9	8	3	11	2						7	5					35
1			4	10	6	9	8	3	11	2	14					7†	5					36
1	2		10	6	9	8*	3	4	11	12						7	5					37
1	5		10	3	9	6†	4	11	2	8	14					7						38
1	5		10	6	9	2	3	11	4	8						7						39
23	4	9	8	17	16	36	34	39	36	31	13	27	27	1	17	2	3	23	16	27	20	
	+1s		+1s			+1s						+3s	+2s	+1s	+5s	+8s	+1s			+7s	+2s	

QUEEN'S PARK Second Division

Year Formed: 1867. *Ground & Address:* Hampden Park, Mount Florida, Glasgow G42 9BA. *Telephone:* 041 632 1275.
Ground Capacity: total: 48,643. seated: 16,160. *Size of Pitch:* 115yd × 75yd.
President: Martin B. Smith. *Chairman:* —. *Secretary:* James C. Rutherford. *Commercial Manager:* —. *Physio:* R. C. Findlay. *Coach:* Edward Hunter.
Coaches since 1975: D. McParland, J. Gilroy.
Club Nickname(s): The Spiders. *Previous Grounds:* 1st Hampden (Titwood Park), 2nd Hampden, 3rd Hampden.
Record Attendance: 95,772 v Rangers, Scottish Cup; 18 Jan, 1930.
Record for ground: 149,547, Scotland v England, 1937.
Record Transfer Fee received: —.
Record Transfer Fee paid: —.
Record Victory: 16-0 v St Peters, Scottish Cup 1st rd; 29 Aug, 1885.

QUEEN'S PARK 1991–92 LEAGUE RECORD

Match No.	Date		Venue	Opponents	Result		H/T Score	Lg. Pos.	Goalscorers	Atten- dance
1	Aug	10	H	Dumbarton	L	0-3	0-0	—		657
2		17	A	East Fife	L	0-2	0-1	14		624
3		24	H	East Stirling	W	4-2	0-1	13	Mackay 2, O'Neill, McEntegart	455
4		31	H	Alloa	W	2-1	1-0	8	MacColl, McEntegart	443
5	Sept	7	A	Stranraer	L	1-2	1-1	11	McFadyen James	583
6		14	A	Cowdenbeath	L	2-3	0-1	13	O'Neill, O'Brien	422
7		17	A	Stenhousemuir	W	3-1	2-0	—	McFadyen James, McCormick 2	391
8		23	H	Albion R	W	1-0	1-0	—	Caven	329
9		28	H	Queen of the S	L	1-4	0-2	11	O'Neill	444
10	Oct	5	A	Clyde	L	1-3	1-1	13	O'Brien	554
11		12	H	Berwick R	W	3-2	1-1	11	McCormick, McFadyen Joe, Jackson	303
12		19	A	Brechin C	L	0-2	0-0	11		340
13		26	A	Arbroath	D	2-2	1-0	10	Elder, O'Neill (pen)	267
14	Nov	2	A	Dumbarton	L	1-3	1-1	11	Rodden	557
15		9	H	East Fife	W	1-0	1-0	11	O'Neill	512
16		16	A	East Stirling	L	1-2	1-1	11	Caven	324
17		23	H	Stranraer	L	0-1	0-0	11		470
18		30	A	Cowdenbeath	W	2-0	1-0	10	McCormick 2	365
19	Dec	14	H	Arbroath	W	1-0	0-0	11	McCormick	384
20		28	H	Stenhousemuir	W	2-1	2-0	11	O'Neill, O'Brien	432
21	Jan	4	A	Albion R	D	1-1	1-1	11	McCormick	284
22		11	H	Clyde	L	0-1	0-0	11		883
23		18	A	Queen of the S	D	2-2	0-1	11	Mackay, McCormick	735
24		25	A	Alloa	L	0-1	0-1	11		576
25	Feb	1	H	Brechin C	L	0-1	0-0	11		347
26		8	A	East Fife	D	2-2	0-0	12	McCormick, O'Brien	839
27		15	A	Stenhousemuir	W	2-0	2-0	11	Rodden, McCormick	363
28		22	A	Arbroath	L	1-2	1-1	12	McCormick	480
29		25	A	Berwick R	W	3-1	0-1	—	Rodden 2, McLean	390
30		29	H	Dumbarton	D	0-0	0-0	11		589
31	Mar	7	A	Cowdenbeath	L	1-2	0-2	12	Rodden	603
32		14	A	Alloa	L	1-2	0-1	12	Jack	675
33		21	A	Albion R	W	4-3	0-1	10	McCormick 2, Caven, Stevenson	214
34		28	H	Clyde	W	1-0	1-0	10	Jackson	769
35	Apr	4	A	Queen of the S	L	3-5	2-2	10	O'Brien, Rodden, Flannigan	465
36		11	H	Berwick R	W	4-1	2-0	10	McCormick 2, Caven 2	337
37		18	H	Stranraer	W	5-2	4-1	9	McCormick 2, Caven, McEntegart, Jackson	474
38		25	A	Brechin C	L	0-1	0-1	10		373
39	May	2	H	East Stirling	D	1-1	0-0	9	McEntegart	397

Final League Position: 9

League (59): McCormick 17, Caven 6, O'Neill 6 (1 pen), Rodden 6, O'Brien 5, McEntegart 4, Jackson 3, Mackay 3, McFadyen James 2, Elder 1, Flannigan 1, Jack 1, MacColl 1, McFadyen Joe 1, McLean 1, Stevenson 1. *Scottish Cup* (0). *Skol Cup* (4): Mackay 2, Mackenzie 2. *B & Q Cup* (1): O'Brien 1.

Record Defeat: 0-9 v Motherwell, Division I; 26 Apr, 1930.
Most Capped Player: Walter Arnott, 14, Scotland.
Most League Appearances: 473: J. B. McAlpine.
Most League Goals in Season (Individual): 30: William Martin, Division I; 1937–38.
Most Goals Overall (Individual): 163: J. B. McAlpine.

Honours
League Champions: Division II 1922–23. B Division 1955–56. Second Division 1980–81.
Scottish Cup Winners: 1874, 1875, 1876, 1880, 1881, 1882, 1884, 1886, 1890, 1893; *Runners-up:* 1892, 1900.
League Cup: —.
FA Cup runners-up: 1884, 1885.
Club colours: Shirt: White and black hoops. Shorts: White. Stockings: White with black hoops.

Houston, J	Callan, D	MacColl, A	Elder, G	Mackay, M	McEntegart, S	Jack, S	O'Brien, J	Jackson, D	Mackenzie, K	McCormick, S	Greig, D	McFadyen, James	Moonie, J	Stevenson, C	Caven, R	O'Neill, J	McArthur, P	Chalmers, J	McFadyen, Joe	McKeever, R	Orr, G	Rodden, J	Flannigan, M	Graham, D	Orr, J	McLean, S	Match No.
1	2*	3	4	5	6	7	8	9	10†	11	12	14															1
		3	4	5	6	7	9†	14	10*	11	12		1	2	8												2
		3†	4	5	6	7*	9	10	12	11			1	2	8	14											3
		3	4	5	6	7	9	10		11†	12		1	2	8*	14											4
	2	3	4	5	6	7	9	10†		11			1		8	14											5
	2	3†	4	5	6	7	9	10*		11	12		1	14	8												6
	2	3	4	6	5	8	9	10		11†		14	1		7												7
	2	3	4	14	6	5	8	10	9†	11*			1		7	12											8
	2†	3	4	7	6	5	8	14		11			1		10	9											9
	2	3	4	6	5	8	14	10	9†	7	12	11*	1														10
	2	3†	4	5	6	8	9	10	14		12				7	11*		1									11
	2		4	5	6†	8*	14	10	9		12			3	7	11		1									12
	2		4	5	6	8	9*	10			12			3	7	11		1									13
	2		4	5	6	8		10						3†	7			1	9*		11	12	14				14
			4	5*	6	8		10			12				7	11†		1				9	14	3	2		15
			4	5†	6	8		10			14				7	11	12	1	9*					3	2		16
			4	5	6	8		10			12				7	11*		1						9	3	2	17
			4	5	6†	8		10		11				3	7			1			6		14	9		2	18
			4	5		8		10			12			3	7			1			6		11*	9		2	19
			4	5	6	8	14	10			12			3	7			1				10	11*	9		2†	20
			4	5	6	8		14		11				3	7			1				10		9†	3	2	21
			4	5	6*	8	14			11	12			3	7			1			6	10		9†		2	22
	2	3*	4	5†	6	8				11	12				7			1				10	14	9			23
			4	5	6†	8		14		11					7			1				10		9	3	2	24
			4	5	6†	8		14		11	12				7			1				10*	11	9	3	2	25
			4	5		8				11	12			3	7			1			6	10*	11	9		2	26
			4	5	6	8					12			3	7			1			6	10	11*	9		2	27
			4	5	6	8	14			11					7†			1			6	10		9	3	2	28
			4	5	6	8				11	12				7			1			6	10*		9	3	2	29
			4	5		8				11					7			1			6	10		9	3	2	30
			4	5	6	8	14			11	12				7†			1			6	10		9	3*	2	31
			4	5	6	8	14			11†	12				7			1			6	10		9	3	2*	32
			4	5	6	8				11*	12			3	7			1			6	10		9	3	2	33
			4	5	6	8	14			11*	12				7			1			6	10		9†	3	2	34
			4	5	6	8	14			11*	12				7			1			6	10		9†	3	2	35
			4	5	6	8				11*	12			3	7			1			6	10		9		2	36
			4	6	5	8*				11	12			3	7			1			6	10		9		2	37
			4	6	5	8†	14			11				3	7			1			6	10		9		2	38
			4	6	5	8				11	12			3	7			1			6	10		9		2	39
1	8	13	34	25	23	37	30	22	13	31	0	6	9	17	35	12	2	29	3	0	13	21	6	18	11	10	
		+			+	+	+	+	+	+	+		+	+	+	+		+			+	+	+	+	+	+	
		1s			2s	3s	2s	1s	7s	1s	1s		2s	3s	2s			13s	3s		4s	1s	3s		8s	1s	

RAITH ROVERS
First Division

Year Formed: 1883. *Ground & Address:* Stark's Park, Pratt St, Kirkcaldy KY1 1SA. *Telephone:* 0592 263514.
Ground Capacity: total: 8500. seated: 3040. *Size of Pitch:* 113yd × 67yd.
Chairman: P. J. Campsie. *Secretary:* P. J. Campsie. *Commercial Manager:* P. Rodger.
Manager: James Nicholl. *Assistant Manager and Coach:* Martin Harvey. *Physio:* Gerry Docherty. *Reserve Coach:* Joe
Samall. *Managers since 1975:* R. Paton; A. Matthew; W. McLean; G. Wallace; R. Wilson; F. Connor.
Club Nickname(s): Rovers. *Previous Grounds:* Robbie's Park.
Record Attendance: 31,306 v Hearts, Scottish Cup 2nd rd; 7 Feb, 1953.
Record Transfer Fee received: £110,000 for Paul Sweeney to Newcastle U (March 1989).
Record Transfer Fee paid: £70,000 for Kenny Macdonald from Airdrieonians (Oct 1989).
Record Victory: 10-1 v Coldstream, Scottish Cup 2nd rd; 13 Feb, 1954.

RAITH ROVERS 1991–92 LEAGUE RECORD

Match No.	Date		Venue	Opponents	Result		H/T Score	Lg. Pos.	Goalscorers	Attendance
1	Aug	10	A	Meadowbank T	L	0-2	0-2	—		703
2		13	A	Clydebank	W	2-0	2-0	—	Brewster, Dalziel	791
3		17	H	Forfar Ath	W	2-0	2-0	4	Williamson, Ferguson	1175
4		24	A	Ayr U	L	0-1	0-0	5		3270
5		31	H	Dundee	L	0-1	0-0	7		3122
6	Sept	7	H	Stirling Albion	W	1-0	1-0	6	MacKenzie	1252
7		14	A	Partick T	L	0-5	0-3	8		3224
8		21	H	Morton	D	1-1	0-0	6	MacKenzie	1219
9		28	A	Kilmarnock	L	0-1	0-1	7		3385
10	Oct	5	H	Hamilton A	L	1-3	1-2	9	Dalziel	1007
11		8	A	Montrose	W	3-0	2-0	—	MacLeod, Dalziel, Strang	683
12		12	H	Meadowbank T	D	1-1	0-1	7	Brewster	766
13		19	A	Forfar Ath	W	1-0	0-0	7	Brewster	599
14		26	A	Stirling Albion	W	3-1	2-0	7	Dalziel 3	600
15		29	H	Partick T	W	1-0	0-0	—	Strang	2027
16	Nov	2	A	Dundee	D	1-1	1-1	7	Brewster	2397
17		9	H	Ayr U	D	0-0	0-0	7		1441
18		16	A	Hamilton A	L	1-4	0-1	7	Dalziel	1433
19		19	H	Montrose	W	2-1	0-0	—	Dalziel (pen), Brewster	812
20		23	A	Morton	W	2-0	1-0	5	Dalziel, Brewster	1280
21		30	H	Clydebank	W	4-0	3-0	6	Dalziel 3, Brewster	1195
22	Dec	3	H	Kilmarnock	D	1-1	1-0	—	McStay	2280
23		7	A	Meadowbank T	W	1-0	0-0	5	Dalziel	549
24		14	H	Stirling Albion	L	1-2	1-0	5	Sinclair	1199
25		21	A	Partick T	W	1-0	1-0	5	Brewster	2333
26		28	A	Ayr U	D	1-1	0-0	5	Dunleavy	2257
27	Jan	1	H	Dundee	W	1-0	0-0	—	Dalziel	3976
28		4	A	Hamilton A	W	2-1	0-0	3	Brewster, Hetherston	2299
29		11	A	Montrose	D	2-2	2-0	5	Strang, McStay	1200
30		18	A	Clydebank	D	1-1	0-0	4	Dalziel	756
31	Feb	1	H	Forfar Ath	W	2-0	0-0	4	McKenna (og), Dalziel	1242
32		8	H	Morton	W	2-0	2-0	4	Dalziel 2	1703
33		26	A	Kilmarnock	L	0-1	0-0	—		3657
34		29	A	Hamilton A	L	0-1	0-1	5		1885
35	Mar	7	H	Montrose	W	5-0	2-0	4	Dalziel 2, Nicholl, Brewster 2	1090
36		14	H	Ayr U	L	2-4	1-3	5	Nelson 2	1473
37		21	A	Dundee	L	2-3	1-1	5	Chisholm (og), Williamson	4452
38		28	H	Meadowbank T	W	3-0	1-0	5	Dalziel 3	885
39	Apr	4	A	Forfar Ath	W	2-1	2-0	4	Brewster, Dalziel	609
40		7	A	Stirling Albion	W	2-1	2-0	—	Dalziel, Nelson	786
41		11	H	Partick T	D	0-0	0-0	5		3514
42		18	A	Morton	W	1-0	1-0	5	Dalziel	1432
43		25	H	Clydebank	D	0-0	0-0	5		939
44	May	2	H	Kilmarnock	D	1-1	1-0	5	MacKenzie	1960

Final League Position: 5

League (59): Dalziel 26 (1 pen), Brewster 12, MacKenzie 3, Nelson 3, Strang 3, McStay 2, Williamson 2, Dunleavy 1,
Ferguson 1, Hetherston 1, MacLeod 1, Nicholl 1, Sinclair 1, own goals 2. *Scottish Cup* (0). *Skol Cup* (5): Brewster
2, MacKenzie 2, Nelson. *B & Q Cup* (5): Dalziel 5 (1 pen).

Record Defeat: 2-11 v Morton, Division II; 18 Mar, 1936.
Most Capped Player: Dave Morris, 6, Scotland.
Most League Appearances: 430: Willie McNaught.
Most League Goals in Season (Individual): 38: Norman Haywood, Division II; 1937–38.
Most Goals Overall (Individual): 105: Ernie Copland (League).

Honours
League Champions: Division II 1907–08, 1909–10 (shared), 1937–38, 1948–49; Runners-up: Division II 1908–09, 1926–27, 1966–67. Second Division 1975–76, 1977–78, 1986–87.
Scottish Runners-up: 1913.   League Cup Runners-up: 1948–49.
Club colours: Shirt: Navy blue, white trim. Shorts: White. Stockings: Red.

Arthur, G	MacLeod, I	McGeachie, G	Coyle, R	Dennis, S	Sinclair, D	Ferguson, I	Dalziel, G	Quinn, S	Brewster, C	Nelson, M	Burn, P	Williamson, T	Nicholl, J	MacKenzie, A	McStay, J	Young, D	Raeside, R	Dunleavy, D	Strang, S	Hetherston, P	Dair, J	Match No.
1	2	3	4	5	6	7	8	9†	10	11		14										1
1	3	6		5	4	9	8		10	11		7	2									2
1	3*	6	12	5	4	9	8		10	11		7	2									3
1	3†	6		5	4	9	14		10	11		7	2	8								4
1	3	6		5	4	9*	12		10	11		7	2	8								5
1	3*	6		5	4	12	8		10	11		7		9†	2	14						6
1	3	6		5	4*		8		10	11	12	7		9	2							7
1	3	6		5		7	8		10†	4	11			9	2	14						8
1	3	6	4	5			8		11	10		7†	2	9		14						9
1	3	6*	12	5	14		8		10	11†	4	7	2	9								10
1	3		4	5			8*		10	11	12				2		6		7	9		11
1	3		4	5					10	11	12			8	2*	14	6		7	9†		12
1	3	5*	4				12		8	10	11†		7		2		6	14		9		13
1	3		4	5			8		10*	11			7		2		6	12		9		14
1	3		4	5		7	8		10	11*					2†	14	6	12		9		15
1	3		4	5			8		10	11			7		2		6			9		16
1	3		4	5			8		10*	11			7†	14	2		6	12		9		17
1	3		4	5			8		10				7		2	12	6			9*	11	18
1	3	5	4				8*		10				7	9	2		6	12		11		19
1	3	6	4	5			8		10				7	9	2					11		20
1	3	6	4	5			8		10*	11				9	2			12		7		21
1	3	6*	4	5			8		10	11				9	2			12		7		22
1	3		4	5	14		8*		10†	11				9	2		6	12		7		23
1	3	5	4				8			11				9	2*		6	12	10	7		24
1	3	5	6	5			8		10	11				4	2			7		9		25
1	3		4	5			8		10	11				6	2			7		9		26
1	3		4	5			8		10	11		14		6	2			7		9†		27
1	3	4*	5				9		10	11	12	14		6	2			7†		8		28
1	3	5							10	11	7	4		2	12	6			9*	8		29
1	3		4	5			8		10	11		7		6	2					9		30
1	3		4	5			8		10		12	7	9	2	6*					11		31
1	3		4	5			8		10†	11	14	9	2	6					7			32
1	3	6	4	5			8		12	11		7*	9	2					10			33
1	3	6	4	5			8		12	11*		7	9	2					10			34
1	3	6	4	5			8		10	12		7*	9	2					11			35
1	3	6*	4	5	12		8		10	11		7		2					9			36
1	3*	4	5	6			8		10	12		14	7	9†	2				11			37
1	3	5	6				8		10	11	7	4	12		2*				9†	14		38
1	3	5	6				8		10*	11	7	4	12		2				9			39
1	3	5	6				8		10	11	7*	4	12		2				9			40
1	3	5	6				8		10*	11	12	4	9†	2					7	14		41
1	3	5	6				8		10	11		4	9	2					7			42
1	3	5	6				8*		10	11	4†	9	2		12				7	14		43
1	3	5	6				8		10	11*	4†	9	2		12				7	14		44
44	44	18	27	42	19	7	38	1	40	32	11	18	32	18	34	4	12	6	6	31	0	
		+2s		+3s	+2s	+1s	+1s	+2s	+2s	+4s	+7s		+4s			+5s	+1s	+5s	+7s		+4s	

RANGERS

Premier Division

Year Formed: 1873. *Ground & Address:* Ibrox Stadium, Edminston Drive, Glasgow G51 2XD. *Telephone:* 041 427 8500. *Ground Capacity:* total: 44,500. seated: 36,500. *Size of Pitch:* 115yd × 75yd. *Chairman:* David Murray. *Secretary:* R. C. Ogilvie. *Commercial Manager:* Bob Reilly. *Manager:* Walter Smith. *Assistant Manager:* Archie Knox. *Physio:* Bill Collins. *Coach:* Davie Dodds. *Reserve team coaches:* John McGregor, Billy Kirkwood. *Managers since 1975:* Jock Wallace; John Greig; Jock Wallace; Graeme Souness. *Club Nickname(s):* The Gers. *Previous Grounds:* Burnbank, Kinning Park. *Record Attendance:* 118,567 v Celtic, Division I; 2 Jan, 1939. *Record Transfer Fee received:* £5,500,000 for Trevor Steven to Marseille (Aug 1991). *Record Transfer Fee paid:* £2,000,000 for Alexei Mikhailichenko from Sampdoria, June 1991. *Record Victory:* 14-2 v Blairgowrie, Scottish Cup 1st rd; 20 Jan, 1934. *Record Defeat:* 2-10 v Airdrieonians, 1886. *Most Capped Player:* George Young, 53, Scotland. *Most League Appearances:* 496: John Greig, 1962–78. *Most League Goals in Season (Individual):* 44: Sam English, Division I; 1931–32. *Most Goals Overall (Individual):* 233: Bob McPhail; 1927–39.

Honours
League Champions: (42 times) Division I 1890–91 (shared), 1898–99, 1899–1900, 1900–01, 1901–02, 1910–11, 1911–12,

---

RANGERS 1991–92 LEAGUE RECORD

Match No.	Date	Venue	Opponents	Result	H/T Score	Lg. Pos.	Goalscorers	Attendance
1	Aug 10	H	St Johnstone	W 6-0	2-0	—	Johnston 2 (2 pens), Hateley 3, Ferguson	35,104
2	13	H	Motherwell	W 2-0	1-0	—	Maaskant (og), Steven	35,321
3	17	A	Hearts	L 0-1	0-1	5		22,534
4	24	H	Dunfermline Ath	W 4-0	2-0	4	Huistra, Johnston, Spencer, McCoist	35,559
5	31	A	Celtic	W 2-0	1-0	3	Hateley 2	50,756
6	Sept 7	A	Falkirk	W 2-0	1-0	2	Nisbet, Huistra	12,848
7	14	H	Dundee U	D 1-1	1-0	2	McCoist	36,347
8	21	A	St Mirren	W 2-1	1-1	2	Huistra, Nisbet	14,503
9	28	H	Aberdeen	L 0-2	0-0	3		36,330
10	Oct 5	A	Airdrieonians	W 4-0	3-0	3	Nisbet, Johnston, McCoist 2	11,101
11	8	H	Hibernian	W 4-2	0-1	—	McCoist 2, Tortolano (og), Huistra	35,364
12	12	A	St Johnstone	W 3-2	2-0	2	McCoist 2, Nisbet	10,322
13	19	H	Hearts	W 2-0	1-0	1	McCoist, Mikhailichenko	36,481
14	26	H	Falkirk	D 1-1	0-1	1	Johnston	36,441
15	29	A	Dundee U	L 2-3	1-1	—	McCoist 2 (1 pen)	15,041
16	Nov 2	H	Celtic	D 1-1	0-0	2	McCoist	37,387
17	9	A	Dunfermline Ath	W 5-0	2-0	2	Gough, Gordon 2, Hateley, McCoist	13,351
18	16	A	Airdrieonians	W 4-0	1-0	2	Robertson D, Hateley 2, McCoist	36,934
19	19	A	Hibernian	W 3-0	0-0	—	McCoist 2, Hateley	16,833
20	23	H	St Mirren	L 0-1	0-1	2		36,272
21	30	A	Motherwell	W 2-0	0-0	2	Gordon, Gough	15,350
22	Dec 4	A	Aberdeen	W 3-2	2-1	2	Hateley 2, McCoist	20,081
23	7	H	St Johnstone	W 3-1	1-0	2	Mikhailichenko, Brown, Hateley	35,784
24	14	A	Falkirk	W 3-1	2-0	2	McCoist, Hateley, McCall	11,801
25	21	H	Dundee U	W 2-0	1-0	2	McCoist 2	41,448
26	28	H	Dunfermline Ath	W 2-1	0-0	2	Stevens, Gordon	41,328
27	Jan 1	A	Celtic	W 3-1	1-0	—	McCoist, Hateley (pen), Brown	51,789
28	4	A	Airdrieonians	D 0-0	0-0	2		12,276
29	11	H	Hibernian	W 2-0	1-0	1	Gordon, McCoist	40,616
30	18	H	Motherwell	W 2-0	1-0	1	McCoist, Mikhailichenko	38,127
31	Feb 1	A	Hearts	W 1-0	0-0	1	McCoist	24,356
32	8	A	St Mirren	W 2-1	2-1	1	McCoist, Mikhailichenko	16,521
33	25	H	Aberdeen	D 0-0	0-0	—		38,513
34	29	H	Airdrieonians	W 5-0	2-0	1	Brown, Hateley 3 (2 pens), Rideout	40,568
35	Mar 10	A	Hibernian	W 3-1	2-0	—	McCoist, Hateley 2	13,387
36	14	A	Dunfermline Ath	W 3-1	3-0	1	Mikhailichenko 2, Nisbet	12,274
37	21	H	Celtic	L 0-2	0-1	1		42,160
38	28	A	St Johnstone	W 2-1	1-0	1	Hateley 2	9,697
39	Apr 7	H	Falkirk	W 4-1	2-1	—	McCoist 3, Mikhailichenko	36,832
40	11	A	Dundee U	W 2-1	0-0	1	Mikhailichenko, Brown	11,713
41	18	A	St Mirren	W 4-0	1-0	1	McCoist 2, Stevens, Huistra	40,362
42	23	A	Motherwell	W 2-1	1-1	—	Mikhailichenko 2	12,515
43	28	H	Hearts	D 1-1	0-0	—	McCoist	36,129
44	May 2	A	Aberdeen	W 2-0	1-0	1	McCoist 2	16,580

Final League Position: 1

League (101): McCoist 34 (1 pen), Hateley 21 (3 pens), Mikhailichenko 10, Gordon 5, Huistra 5, Johnston 5 (2 pens), Nisbet 5, Brown 4, Gough 2, Stevens 2, Ferguson 1, McCall 1, Rideout 1, Robertson D 1, Spencer 1, Steven 1, own goals 2. *Scottish Cup* (9): McCoist 4, Hateley 2, Mikhailichenko 2, Gough 1. *Skol Cup* (9): Johnston 5, Durrant 1, McCoist 1, Robertson D 1, Spackman 1.

1912–13, 1917–18, 1919–20, 1920–21, 1922–23, 1923–24, 1924–25, 1926–27, 1927–28, 1928–29, 1929–30, 1930–31, 1932–33, 1933–34, 1934–35, 1936–37, 1938–39, 1946–47, 1948–49, 1949–50, 1952–53, 1955–56, 1956–57, 1958–59, 1960–61, 1962–63, 1963–64, 1974–75. Premier Division 1975–76, 1977–78, 1986–87, 1988–89, 1989–90, 1990–91, 1991–92; *Runners-up:* 23 times.
Scottish Cup Winners: (25 times) 1894, 1897, 1898, 1903, 1928, 1930, 1932, 1934, 1935, 1936, 1948, 1949, 1950, 1953, 1960, 1962, 1963, 1964, 1966, 1973, 1976, 1978, 1979, 1981, 1992; *Runners-up:* 15 times.
League Cup Winners: (17 times) 1946–47, 1948–49, 1960–61, 1961–62, 1963–64, 1964–65, 1970–71, 1975–76, 1977–78, 1978–79, 1981–82, 1983–84, 1984–85, 1986–87, 1987–88, 1988–89, 1990–91; *Runners-up:* 7 times.
European: *European Cup:* 59 matches (1956–57, 1957–58, 1959–60 semi-finals, 1961–62, 1963–64, 1964–65, 1975–76, 1976–77, 1978–79, 1987–88, 1989–90). *Cup Winners Cup Winners:* 1971–72. 50 matches (1960–61 runners-up, 1962–63, 1966–67 runners-up, 1969–70, 1971–72 winners, 1973–74, 1977–78, 1979–80, 198 1–82, 1983–84).
UEFA Cup: 38 matches (*Fairs Cup:* 1967–68, 1968–69 semi-finals, 1970–71. *UEFA Cup:* 1982–83, 1984–85, 1985–86, 1986–87, 1988–89).
Club colours: Shirt: Royal blue with red and white trim. Shorts: White. Stockings: Red.

Goram, A	Stevens, G	Robertson, D	Gough, R	Spackman, N	Nisbet, S	Steven, T	Ferguson, I	Hateley, M	Johnston, M	Huistra, P	Robertson, A	Spencer, J	McCall, S	Durrant, I	McCoist, A	Mikhailichenko, A	Kuznetsov, O	Brown, J	Vinnicombe, C	McSwegan, G	McGregor, J	Morrow, J	Gordon, D	Rideout, P	Pressley, S	Robertson, L	Match No.
1	2	3	4	5	6	7	8*	9	10	11	12																1
1	2	3	4	5	6	7	8	9	10	11																	2
1	2	3	4	5	6		8	9	10	11†			14	7													3
1	2	3	4	5	6		12	9*		11			8	7	10†	14											4
1	2	3	4	5	6		8	9	10	11					7												5
1	2	3	4	5	6		8	9		11		12			7	10*											6
1	2	3		5	6		8	9		11		12		7	10*		4										7
1	2	3	4	5	6			9	10	11				7	8												8
1	2	3		5	6			9*	10			14	8	12	7	11†	4										9
1	2	3		5	6				10	11*	12		8	7	9		4										10
1	2	3		5	6				10	11	7*	14	8	12	9		4†										11
1	2	3		5	6					11†		8	10		9	14	4						7				12
1	2	3	4	5	6				10	11			8		9								7				13
1	2	3	4	5	6		12		10	11*		14	8		9								7†				14
1	2	3		5	6				10	11*		12	8	7†	9	14	4										15
1	2	3	4	5	6				10	11			8†	7	9	14											16
1	2	3	4	5	6†				10	11			8		9	14							7				17
1	2	3	4	5					10	11			8		9†	14		6					7				18
1	2	3	4	5					10	11			8		9			6					7				19
1	2	3	4	5					10	11†			8		9	14		6					7				20
1	2*	3	4	5					10				8	12	9	11		6					7				21
1	2	3	4	5					10				8	12	9	11*		6					7				22
1	2	3	4	5					10			14	8	12	9	11*		6					7†				23
1	2	3	4	5					10				8		9	11		6					7				24
1	2	3	4	5					10			14	8	12	9	11		6*					7†				25
1	2*	3	4	5					10				8	12	9	11		6					7				26
1	2	3	4	5					10			14	8*	12	9	11†		6					7				27
1	2	3	4	5					10				8		9	11		6					7				28
1	2	3	4	5					10				8		9	11		6					7				29
1	2	3	4	5			12		10*				8		9	11		6					7				30
1	2	3	4	5					10				8		9	11		6	14				7†				31
1	2	3	4	5					10				8		9	11		6					7				32
1	2	3	4	5			8		10	11				14	9			6					7†				33
1	2	3	4	5†			8		10*	11			12	14	9			6					7				34
1	2		4	5			12		10	11			8		9			6					7*				35
1	2	3	4	5			12		10	11			8*	7	9			6									36
1	2	3	4	5			12		10				8	7†	9	11*	14	6									37
1	2	3	4	5					10	11†		7	8*		9	14								12			38
1	2		4	5					10*	11			8		9	14		6				3	12	7†			39
1	2	3	4	5			12		10*	11			8		9†	14		6						7			40
1	2		4	5					10	14			8		9	11		6				3		7†			41
1	2*	3		5					10			7	8		9	11	4	6						12			42
1		3		5					10	11*		14	8	12	9		2	6†					4			7	43
1	2	3	4						10	11			8		9			6			5			7			44
44	43	42	33	42	20	2	12	29	10	25	3	4	35	9	37	24	16	18	1	0	1	3	23	7	0	1	
+4s	+1s	+1s	+7s	+3s	+4s	+1s			+4s	+1s			+3s	+2s		+7s	+1s	+4s					+4s	+1s			

ST JOHNSTONE　　　　Premier Division

Year Formed: 1884. *Ground & Address:* McDiarmid Park, Crieff Road, Perth PH1 2SJ. *Telephone:* 0738 26961. *Clubcall:*
0898 121559. *Ground Capacity:* total: 10,721. seated: all. *Size of Pitch:* 115yd × 75yd.
Chairman: G. S. Brown. *Secretary and General Manager:* John Litster.　*Commercial Manager* —.
Manager: Alex Totten. *Assistant Manager:* Bert Paton. *Physio:* J. Peacock. *Coaches:* T. Campbell, R. Stewart.
Managers since 1975: J. Stewart, J. Storrie; A. Stuart; A. Rennie; I. Gibson.
Club Nickname(s): Saints. *Previous Grounds:* Recreation Grounds, Muirton Park.
Record Attendance: (McDiarmid Park): 10,504 v Rangers, Premier Division; 20 Oct, 1990.
Record Transfer Fee received: £400,000 for Ally McCoist to Sunderland (1982).
Record Transfer Fee paid: £285,000 for Paul Wright from Hibernian (Aug 1991).
Record Victory: 9-0 v Albion R, League Cup; 9 March, 1946.
Record Defeat: 1-10 v Third Lanark, Scottish Cup; 24 January, 1903.

ST JOHNSTONE 1991–92 LEAGUE RECORD

Match No.	Date		Venue	Opponents		Result	H/T Score	Lg. Pos.	Goalscorers	Attendance
1	Aug	10	A	Rangers	L	0-6	0-2	—		35,104
2		13	A	Hibernian	L	1-2	0-0	—	Ward	9236
3		17	H	Dundee U	D	1-1	1-1	10	Grant	7700
4		24	H	Hearts	L	0-1	0-1	11		7516
5		31	H	Dunfermline Ath	D	0-0	0-0	10		5536
6	Sept	7	A	Aberdeen	W	2-1	0-1	9	Redford, Curran	12,071
7		14	H	Celtic	W	1-0	1-0	8	Wright	9993
8		21	H	Falkirk	L	2-3	1-3	9	Treanor (pen), Moore	6106
9		28	A	Airdrieonians	W	2-1	0-1	8	Turner 2	3153
10	Oct	5	A	Motherwell	L	0-1	0-0	8		5014
11		9	A	St Mirren	D	1-1	0-1	—	Wright	3122
12		12	H	Rangers	L	2-3	0-2	9	Curran, Wright	10,322
13		19	A	Dundee U	W	2-1	0-1	9	Treanor (pen), Wright	6202
14		26	A	Aberdeen	L	1-3	1-1	9	Curran	5682
15		30	A	Celtic	L	0-4	0-2	—		18,854
16	Nov	2	H	Dunfermline Ath	W	3-2	1-1	9	Wright, Bingham, Curran	4509
17		9	A	Hearts	L	1-2	0-0	9	Curran	10,222
18		16	A	Motherwell	D	1-1	0-0	9	Wright	4570
19		20	H	St Mirren	W	1-0	0-0	—	Stewart (pen)	5808
20		23	A	Falkirk	W	3-2	0-0	8	Redford, Stewart (pen), Maskrey	4915
21		30	H	Hibernian	L	0-1	0-0	9		6717
22	Dec	4	H	Airdrieonians	W	1-0	1-0	—	Wright	3582
23		7	A	Rangers	L	1-3	0-1	8	Arkins	35,784
24		14	A	Aberdeen	L	1-4	1-1	8	Stewart (pen)	9292
25		28	H	Hearts	L	0-5	0-1	9		10,064
26	Jan	1	A	Dunfermline Ath	W	3-0	0-0	—	Baltacha, Arkins, Curran	6570
27		4	A	Motherwell	D	0-0	0-0	9		4965
28		8	H	Celtic	L	2-4	0-1	—	Arkins, Wright	9283
29		11	A	St Mirren	W	5-1	4-1	8	Wright, Curran 2, Arkins, Elliot (og)	2994
30		18	A	Hibernian	W	1-0	0-0	8	Arkins	7107
31	Feb	1	H	Dundee U	D	1-1	1-1	8	Wright	6364
32		8	H	Falkirk	D	1-1	0-1	7	Wright	5418
33		22	A	Airdrieonians	W	3-0	1-0	7	Wright 2, Maskrey	2921
34		29	A	Motherwell	L	1-3	0-1	8	Grant	4373
35	Mar	7	H	St Mirren	L	1-2	1-1	8	Wright	3404
36		14	A	Hearts	L	0-2	0-1	8		8799
37		21	H	Dunfermline Ath	W	1-0	0-0	8	Turner	3156
38		28	H	Rangers	L	1-2	0-1	8	Wright	9697
39	Apr	4	A	Dundee U	L	1-2	1-1	8	Wright	5553
40		8	H	Aberdeen	D	0-0	0-0	—		4524
41		11	A	Celtic	L	2-3	0-1	8	Redford, Cherry	13,237
42		18	A	Falkirk	L	0-2	0-2	8		3703
43		25	H	Hibernian	D	1-1	0-0	9	Wright	3895
44	May	2	H	Airdrieonians	D	1-1	0-0	8	Wright	3699

Final League Position: 8

League (52): Wright 18, Curran 8, Arkins 5, Redford 3, Stewart 3 (3 pens), Turner 3, Grant 2, Maskrey 2, Treanor 2
(2 pens), Baltacha 1, Bingham 1, Cherry 1, Moore 1, Ward 1, own goal 1.　*Scottish Cup* (7): Moore 3, Wright 3,
McGinnis 1.　*Skol Cup* (2): Redford 1, Ward 1.

Most Capped Player: Sandy McLaren, 5, Scotland.
Most League Appearances: 298: Drew Rutherford.
Most League Goals in Season (Individual): 36: Jimmy Benson, Division II; 1931–32.
Most Goals Overall (Individual): 14: John Brogan, 1977–83.

Honours
League Champions: First Division 1982–83, 1989–90. Division II 1923–24, 1959–60, 1962–63; *Runners-up:* Division II 1931–32. Second Division 1987–88.
Scottish Cup: Semi-finals 1934, 1968, 1991.
League Cup Runners-up: 1969.
European: *European Cup* —. *Cup Winners Cup* —. *UEFA Cup:* 1971–72.
Club colours: Shirt: Royal blue with white trim. Shorts: White. Stockings: Royal blue, white trim.

Hamilton, L	Treanor, M	Baltacha, S	Redford, I	Inglis, J	Turner, T	Moore, A	Davies, J	Wright, P	Grant, R	Curran, H	McVicar, D	Ward, K	Stewart, R	Barron, D	McGinnis, G	Maskrey, S	Bingham, D	Cherry, P	Dunne, L	Deas, P	Arkins, V	Kennedy, S	Match No.
1	2	3	4	5	6	7	8	9	10*	11†	12	14											1
1	2	3	4		8	7	6	9	10	11†			14	5									2
1	2	3	4	5	11	7	8	9	10†	12			14	6*									3
1	2	3	4	5	11	7†	8	9	10	12			14										4
1	2	3	10†		8		6	9		11		12			4	5	7*14						5
1	2	3	10	5	8		6	9†		11		14	12		4	7*							6
1	2	3	10	5	8		9*14			11†				4	7			6	12				7
1	2	3	10	5	8	14	12	9		11†				4	7			6*					8
1	12	3	10	5	8	7	6†	9	14	11			2*	4									9
1	2	3†11	5	8	7	6	9	10					14	4									10
1	2	3	11	5	8	7*	6	9	10†	12	14			4									11
1	2	3	10	5*	8	7	6	9		12	14		11	4†									12
1	2		10†	8		6	9	14	11	3			4	7									13
1	2		10	5	8		6	9	14	11	3		4	7†									14
1	2	3	10	5		6	9	8†11	4*14						7	12							15
1	2		5		8	9	14	10	7†	4		6*	11	12	3								16
1	4		5		8	9	14	10	7	2		6	11†	3									17
1	3		5	7†	8	9	10	14	2	6	11*	12	4										18
1	3		5	7	8	9	10*	14	2	6	11†	12	4										19
1	12	3	10	5	7	8	9†	11*	2	14	6	4											20
1	3	10	5	7	6	9	11*	2	14	8	4†12												21
1	3	5	8	6	9	14	11	2	4	7	10†												22
1	3	5	8	7†	9	11	2	4	14	6	10												23
1	12	3	5*	8	14	7†	9	11	2	4	6	10											24
1	6	5†	8	7*12	11	2	9	4	14	3	10												25
2	3	7	10	11	5	8	4	6	9	1													26
1	2†	3	7	14	10	11	5	8	4	6	9												27
1	2	3*	12	7	14	10	11	5	8	4	6†	9											28
1	2	5	8*	7	9	11	4	6	12	3	10												29
1	2	5	8	7	9	11	12	4	6*	3	10												30
1	5	8	7	6	9	11	2	4	3	10													31
1	11†	5	8	7	6	9	2	14	4	3	10												32
1	2	5	12	7*	9	8	11	4	6	14	3	10†											33
1	2	5	8	14	4	10†	3	7	9	11	6												34
1	5	7	8	9	11†	2	6	14	10	4	3												35
1	2	3	10*	5	12	7	8†	9	11	6	14	4											36
1	2	3	5	7	12	9	8	11	6*	14	4	10†											37
1	2	3	6†	5	7	8	9	10	11	12	4*	14											38
1	2	3	6*	5	7	8	9†10	11	4	12	14												39
1	2	3	6	5	7	8	9	10*11†	14	4	12												40
1	2	3	6	5	7	8	9	11	10†	4	14												41
1	2	3	6*	5	7	8	9	10†11	4	12	14												42
1	2	3	5	8	9	12	11†	14	6	7	4	10*											43
1	2	3	5	8	9	10*11	6	14	4	7†	12												44
43	31	30	28	39	31	18	37	39	17	36	3	2	17	1	28	12	7	24	9	17	14	1	
+	+		+	+	+	+	+	+	+	+			+		+	+	+		+	+	+		
2s	1s		1s	2s	3s	3s	2s	8s	3s	1s			10s		3s	1s	12s2s		8s	1s	7s		

ST MIRREN   First Division

Year Formed: 1877. *Ground & Address:* St Mirren Park, Love St, Paisley PA3 2EJ. *Telephone:* 041 889 2558/041 840
1337. *Ground Capacity:* total: 12,450. seated: 5974 covered, 460 uncovered. *Size of Pitch:* 112yd × 73yd.
Chairman: Alan W. Marshall. *Secretary:* A. R. Craig. *Commercial Manager:* Jack Copland.
Manager: Jimmy Bone. *Assistant Manager:* Gordon Smith. *Physio:* Andrew Binning. *Coach:* —.
Managers since 1975: Alex Ferguson; Jim Clunie; Rikki MacFarlane; Alex Miller; Alex Smith; Tony Fitzpatrick; David
Hay. *Club Nickname(s):* The Buddies. *Previous Grounds:* Short Roods 1877–79, Thistle Park Greenhill 1879–83,
Westmarch 1883–94.
Record Attendance: 47,438 v Celtic, League Cup, 20 Aug, 1949.
Record Transfer Fee received: £850,000 for Ian Ferguson to Rangers (1988).
Record Transfer Fee paid: £400,000 for Thomas Stickroth from Bayer Uerdingen, 1990.
Record Victory: 15-0 v Glasgow University, Scottish Cup 1st rd; 30 Jan, 1960.
Record Defeat: 0-9 v Rangers, Division I; 4 Dec, 1897.

ST MIRREN 1991–92 LEAGUE RECORD

Match No.	Date		Venue	Opponents		Result	H/T Score	Lg. Pos.	Goalscorers	Atten- dance
1	Aug	10	A	Hibernian	L	1-4	0-2	—	Irvine	8271
2		13	A	Dundee U	L	1-4	0-3	—	Lambert	5771
3		17	H	Airdrieonians	L	1-2	0-0	12	Black (pen)	3927
4		24	H	Falkirk	D	0-0	0-0	10		5112
5		31	A	Motherwell	L	0-1	0-0	11		5749
6	Sept	7	A	Celtic	D	0-0	0-0	11		21,323
7		14	H	Hearts	L	2-3	1-1	11	Irvine, Charnley	5836
8		21	H	Rangers	L	1-2	1-1	11	Martin	14,503
9		28	A	Dunfermline Ath	W	4-1	1-1	11	Irvine, Charnley, Lambert, Broddle	4428
10	Oct	5	A	Aberdeen	L	1-4	0-2	11	Charnley	10,154
11		9	H	St Johnstone	D	1-1	1-0	—	Torfason	3122
12		12	H	Hibernian	L	0-1	0-1	10		4572
13		19	A	Airdrieonians	L	1-4	0-1	11	Martin	2590
14		26	H	Celtic	L	0-5	0-1	11		10,473
15		30	A	Hearts	D	0-0	0-0	—		8683
16	Nov	2	H	Motherwell	L	1-2	0-1	11	Torfason	2689
17		9	H	Falkirk	L	0-3	0-1	11		4235
18		16	H	Aberdeen	L	0-1	0-0	11		3634
19		20	A	St Johnstone	L	0-1	0-0	—		5808
20		23	A	Rangers	W	1-0	1-0	11	McGowne	36,272
21		30	H	Dundee U	D	1-1	0-0	11	Elliot	3375
22	Dec	4	H	Dunfermline Ath	D	0-0	0-0	—		2866
23		7	H	Hibernian	D	0-0	0-0	11		6943
24		14	A	Celtic	L	0-4	0-0	11		16,825
25		21	H	Hearts	L	0-1	0-0	11		5216
26		28	H	Falkirk	L	0-1	0-1	11		4961
27	Jan	1	A	Motherwell	L	0-3	0-1	—		4380
28		4	A	Aberdeen	D	0-0	0-0	11		8774
29		11	H	St Johnstone	L	1-5	1-4	11	Broddle	2994
30		18	A	Dundee U	W	3-1	2-0	11	Torfason 2, Charnley	4933
31	Feb	1	H	Airdrieonians	W	4-1	2-0	11	Torfason 3, Hewitt	3435
32		8	H	Rangers	L	1-2	1-2	11	Torfason	16,521
33		22	A	Dunfermline Ath	D	0-0	0-0	11		3389
34		29	A	Aberdeen	L	0-2	0-2	11		3853
35	Mar	7	A	St Johnstone	W	2-1	1-1	11	McDowall, Aitken	3404
36		14	A	Falkirk	L	0-1	0-1	11		4133
37		21	H	Motherwell	L	1-2	1-1	11	Hewitt	2112
38		28	H	Hibernian	L	0-1	0-1	11		1918
39	Apr	8	H	Celtic	D	1-1	1-0	—	Hewitt	7316
40		11	A	Hearts	D	0-0	0-0	11		6200
41		18	A	Rangers	L	0-4	0-1	11		40,362
42		21	A	Airdrieonians	D	1-1	0-0	—	McDowall	2031
43		25	H	Dundee U	L	0-1	0-1	11		1431
44	May	2	H	Dunfermline Ath	W	3-1	2-0	11	Lavety 2, Stickroth	1077

Final League Position: 11

League (33): Torfason 8, Charnley 4, Hewitt 3, Irvine 3, Broddle 2, Lambert 2, Lavety 2, McDowall 2, Martin 2, Aitken
1, Black 1 (pen), Elliot 1, McGowne 1, Stickroth 1. *Scottish Cup* (0). *Skol Cup* (4): Kinnaird 1, Lambert 1, McWhirter
1, own goal 1.

Most Capped Player: Godmundor Torfason, 29, Iceland.
Most League Appearances: 351: Tony Fitzpatrick, 1973–88.
Most League Goals in Season (Individual): 45: Dunky Walker, Division I; 1921–22.
Most Goals Overall (Individual): 221: David McCrae, 1923–34.

Honours
League Champions: First Division 1976–77. Division II 1967–68; *Runners-up:* 1935–36.
Scottish Cup Winners: 1926, 1959, 1987; *Runners-up:* 1908, 1934, 1962.
League Cup Runners-up: 1955–56.
Victory Cup: 1919–20. *Summer Cup:* 1943–44. *Anglo-Scottish Cup:* 1979–80.
European: *European Cup* —. *Cup Winners Cup:* 1987–88. *UEFA Cup:* 1980–81, 1983–84, 1985–86.
Club colours: Shirt: Black and white vertical stripes. Shorts: White with black side panel. Stockings: White with black hoop. Change colours: All red.

Money, C	Wishart, F	Reid, M	McWhirter, N	Baillie, A	Martin, B	McIntyre, P	Lambert, P	Kinnaird, P	Charnley, J	Elliot, D	McGowne, K	Irvine, A	McDonald, A	Fridge, L	Dawson, R	Black, T	McDowall, K	Aitken, R	McGill, D	Manley, R	Torfason, G	Broddie, J	Fullarton, J	Lavety, B	McEwan, A	Beattie, J	Stickroth, T	Hewitt, J	Match No.
1	2	3	4	5	6	7	8	9†10	11			14																	1
1	2	3	4	5	6	7	8*12		10	11		9†14																	2
			5	4	7	10	12		6	11†14		9		1	2	3	8*												3
1		2*	5	8†	7	10	6	11		9	14	12		3	4														4
	12		5	8	7†10	6*14	2	9		1	3	4	11																5
	14		5	8	7	10*	11†	2	9	1	3	4	12	6															6
			5	8	12	10	11	2	9	1	3	4	6*	7															7
	3		5	7†8		14	2	9	1	4	6	10	11																8
	3		5	7	10	2	9†	1	12	4	14	6*8	11																9
	3		5	7	10	2*	9†	1	12	4	14	6	8	11															10
		2	5	7	10	14	1	3	8	4	6	9†11																	11
1	2	5	8	7	10†14	11	4	6	9	3																			12
1†	2	5	4	7	10	14	3	8	6	9	11																		13
		5	4	7	11†2	9	1	8*	6	10	3	12	14																14
		5	2	7	10	12	8	1	3	4†	14	6	9	11															15
		5†	2	7	9	1	3	10	4	14	6	8	11																16
		5†	2	7*	11	8	1	10	4	12	6	9	3	14															17
1		5†	8	7	14	2	9	10	4	11	6	3																	18
1		5	12	7	11*	2	9	8†4	14	6	10															3			19
1		8	7	5*14	2	9	12	4	10†	6	11															3			20
1		8	7*	5	11	2	9†	12	4	14	6	10															3			21
1		8*	7	5	11	2	9†	14	4	6	12	10															3			22
1		8†12		5	11	2	9†	14	4	6	7*10																3			23
1		8*12		5	11	2†	9	14	4	6	7	10															3			24
1		8		5	11	2	9†14	4	6*	7	10														3	12			25
1		8†		5	11	6	9	2*	12	4	7	10														3	14		26
1	11*	12		8	5	9	2			4	14	6									10					3	7†		27
1	11	4	7	5†8	2	14			12	6	10														3	9*		28
1	11	2*	8	5†7	12	9			14	4	6	10														3			29
1	8		12	14	11	2	6	5	4	9*10	3	7†																	30
			7*8†	12		2	1	5	4	6	9	11											3	14	10				31
			7*8		12	2	1	14	4	6	9	11											3	5†10					32
1		5	8		14	6	2†		4	9	11											3	7*10						33
1		5	8	7†	6	2*		4	9	11											3	12	10						34
1	2		12	8	11*	6		5	4	9	3											7	10						35
1	3*		12	2	8		4	6	9	11												5	7	10†					36
1	14		8	11†	2	5	4	6	12	3											7	10							37
1	6		8	2		5	4	6	3	7	10*																		38
1	2		8	4	5†	14	6	9	11	3	7	10																	39
1	2	14	8	11†	4	6	9	5	3	7	10*																		40
1	5	2	8	4	6	9	11	14	3†	7	10																		41
1	2†3	10		14	7	8	4	6	9	5	11																		42
1	2*14	8		12	7	5†4	6	11	9	3	10																		43
1	14	5		6†	2	4	9	11	10	7	8																		44

30	9	11	9	17	17	20	36	1	23	21	31	25	0	14	5	9	19	34	3	32	27	35	0	3	0	24	13	14	
	+	+	+		+	+	+		+	+	+	+		+	+		+			+	+			+	+	+		+	
	4s	2s	1s		3s	4s	2s		3s	7s	5s	3s		3s	3s		2s			10s	10s			2s	1s	2s		1s 4s	

Kinsey S—Match No. 33(12) 34(14) 36(14) 37(9*) 38(12) 40(12); Baker M—Match No. 44(3).

STENHOUSEMUIR Second Division

Year Formed: 1884. *Ground & Address:* Ochilview Park, Gladstone Rd, Stenhousemuir FK5 5QL. *Telephone:* 0324 562992. *Ground Capacity:* total: 3480. seated: 340. *Size of Pitch:* 113yd × 78yd. *Chairman:* Greig Thomson. *Secretary:* A. T. Bulloch. *Commercial Manager:* Greig Thomson. *(Vice-Chairman)* *Manager:* Dennis Lawson. *Assistant Manager:* David Connell. *Physio:* Lee Campbell. *Coach:* David Connell. *Managers since 1975:* H. Glasgow; J. Black; A. Rose; W. Henderson; A. Rennie; J. Meakin. *Club Nickname(s):* The Warriors. *Previous Grounds:* Tryst Ground 1884–86, Goschen Park 1886–90. *Record Attendance:* 12,500 v East Fife, Scottish Cup 4th rd; 11 Mar, 1950. *Record Transfer Fee received:* £30,000 for David Beaton to Falkirk (June 1989). *Record Transfer Fee paid:* £7000 to Meadowbank Th

STENHOUSEMUIR 1991–92 LEAGUE RECORD

Match No.	Date		Venue	Opponents	Result		H/T Score	Lg. Pos.	Goalscorers	Atten-dance
1	Aug	10	A	Berwick R	W	1-0	0-0	—	Bainbridge	490
2		17	H	Brechin C	L	0-2	0-0	11		362
3		24	A	Cowdenbeath	L	0-2	0-1	14		305
4		31	H	Clyde	L	1-2	1-1	14	Speirs (pen)	586
5	Sept	7	H	East Fife	W	2-1	0-1	12	Girasoli, Donald	500
6		14	A	Queen of the S	L	1-2	1-1	14	Speirs	502
7		17	H	Queen's Park	L	1-3	0-2	—	Girasoli	391
8		21	H	Alloa	W	4-0	2-0	12	Girasoli, McCormick, Wilson, Conroy	406
9		28	A	East Stirling	L	1-2	0-0	13	McCormick	338
10	Oct	5	H	Stranraer	L	0-1	0-0	14		320
11		12	A	Dumbarton	L	0-1	0-1	14		607
12		19	H	Arbroath	W	2-1	1-0	12	Bainbridge, Donald	322
13		26	A	Albion R	D	1-1	1-1	11	Bainbridge	202
14	Nov	2	H	Berwick R	L	0-2	0-1	12		264
15		9	A	Brechin C	L	0-1	0-1	13		366
16		16	H	Cowdenbeath	D	3-3	1-0	14	Clouston, McCormick, Donald	374
17		23	A	East Fife	D	4-4	1-1	13	Speirs, Donald, McCormick, Quinton	657
18		30	H	Queen of the S	L	1-3	1-1	14	Mathieson	413
19	Dec	14	A	Albion R	D	1-1	0-0	14	Mathieson	329
20		28	A	Queen's Park	L	1-2	0-2	14	Prior	432
21	Jan	1	H	Alloa	D	1-1	1-0	—	Nelson	493
22		11	A	Stranraer	L	2-3	1-1	14	McLafferty, Kemp	449
23		18	A	East Stirling	W	2-1	1-0	14	Anderson, McLafferty	385
24		21	A	Clyde	D	0-0	0-0	—		423
25	Feb	1	A	Arbroath	L	0-2	0-0	14		435
26		4	H	Dumbarton	W	1-0	0-0	—	Cairney	426
27		8	H	Cowdenbeath	L	2-4	1-1	13	Anderson, Mathieson	366
28		15	H	Queen's Park	L	0-2	0-2	13		363
29		29	A	Queen of the S	W	3-1	2-1	13	Fisher, Haddon, Prior	506
30	Mar	3	A	Alloa	L	0-1	0-1	—		470
31		11	A	Stranraer	D	1-1	0-1	14	Conroy	410
32		14	H	East Fife	L	1-2	0-1	13	Conroy	460
33		21	H	Arbroath	W	1-0	0-0	13	Mathieson	329
34		28	A	East Stirling	W	3-0	2-0	13	Mathieson, McCallum 2	364
35	Apr	4	A	Berwick R	W	1-0	1-0	12	McCallum	114
36		11	A	Albion R	W	4-0	0-0	12	McCallum 2, Mathieson, Girasoli	309
37		18	A	Clyde	L	0-4	0-0	12		351
38		25	H	Dumbarton	L	0-1	0-1	13		1022
39	May	2	A	Brechin C	D	0-0	0-0	13		324

Final League Position: 13

League (46): Mathieson 6, McCallum 5, Donald 4, Girasoli 4, McCormick 4, Bainbridge 3, Conroy 3, Speirs 3 (1 pen), Anderson 2, McLafferty 2, Prior 2, Cairney 1, Clouston 1, Fisher 1, Haddon 1, Kemp 1, Nelson 1, Quinton 1, Wilson 1. *Scottish Cup* (1): McLafferty 1. *Skol Cup* (2): Bainbridge 1, McCormick 1. *B & Q Cup* (3): Bainbridge 1, Conroy 1, Speirs 1.

for Lee Bullen (Nov 1990). *Record Victory:* 9-2 v Dundee U, Division II; 19 Apr, 1937. *Record Defeat:* 2-11 v Dunfermline Ath, Division II; 27 Sept, 1930. *Most Capped Player:* —. *Most League Appearances:* 298: Harry Cairney. *Most League Goals in Season (Individual):* 32, Robert Taylor, Division II; 1925–26. *Most Goals Overall (Individual):* —.

Honours
League Champions: —. *Scottish Cup:* Semi-finals 1902–03. *League Cup:* Quarter-finals 1947–48, 1960–61, 1975–76.
Club colours: Shirt: Maroon with white pinstripe. Shorts: White. Stockings: Maroon with three white hoops.

Kelly, C	Aitken, N	Hallford, E	Cairney, H	Tracey, K	Gardiner, J	Bell, A	Clouston, B	McCormick, S	Walker, C	Donald, G	Bainbridge, S	Mann, G	McAvoy, M	Speirs, A	Quinton, I	Wilson, C	Anderson, P	Girasoli, C	Barnstaple, K	Ferguson, N	Bullen, L	Conroy, J	Anderson, R	Murdoch, S	Fallon, M	Mathieson, M	Kemp, B	Nelson, M	Match No.
1	2	3	4	5	6	7*	8	9	10	11	12																		1
1	2	3	4	5			8*	9†11	12	14		6		7	10														2
1	2	3	4	5	14		8	11†	9	7*	12	10		6															3
1		3	8	5	2		9		10†12	11	7	6		4*14															4
		3	8	5	2		9	12	14	11†	6	7		4	10*	1													5
14		3	6	5	2		9		12	11	10*	8†		4	7	1													6
	2	3	4		8		9		7*	12		11			5	14	6	10†											7
	2	3	6	5†	8		9*		10	12				7	4	11	1			14									8
	2	3	6		8		9		10	14				7†	4	11*	1			12	5								9
	2	3	4	5	8				14	7*	12			6	9†	1		11	10										10
	2	3	4	14	7			9†			10*	6	12	5		1		11		8									11
	2	3		5	8		9		12	7*		6	14	4		1		11†		10									12
	2	3		5	7		9		14	10		6	8	4		1		11†											13
	2*	3		5	7		9		12	10		6	14	4		1		11†								8			14
		3			8		9		10	7†	12	4		5		1		14								6		2	15
	2*	3			8		10		7	14		11†	6	5		1		12		9						9		4	16
	2	3			7		10		8*			11	4	5		1		12		9						9		6	17
1	14	3			7				8			11	6	5	10*			12		9						9		2	18
1		3			6				14					4				7†		9						9		2	19
1	2†	3								14		10		6												4			20
1	2		8		9					11		6														3	4		21
1	2		4	5	9				8	6								11*								3	12		22
1			4	5	2		9	14		6								11†								3			23
1			4	5	2		9	12		6								11*								3			24
1			2	6	4		9	14		6								11†								3			25
1			2	5			8	9		3															11	6			26
1			2	5			8	9		6								12								11	3*		27
1					4		9	14		6								12								8	3*		28
1	2				4		9			6																7*	3		29
1	2				4		9*			6								12								7	3		30
1	2				7		9			6								12								8	3		31
1	2				4		9			6	14							12								10†	3		32
1	2				7					12																9	3		33
1	2				7					14																9	3		34
1	2				7†					14																9	3		35
1	2				7					12																9	3		36
1	2	12			4					8*																9	3		37
1	2				7*					6	12																3		38
1	2				7†					3	14															9			39
26	27	20	18	17	1		1	36	26	3	11	6	0	1	9	16	2	30	7	13	1	1	10	1	1	18	20	7	

Substitute appearances: Kelly +2s; Tracey +2s; Gardiner +1s; Donald +1s; Bainbridge +12s; Mann +6s; McAvoy +2s; Quinton +3s; Wilson +3s; Girasoli +9s; Anderson, R +11s; Nelson +1s.

Hutchinson T—Match No. 15(11*) 18(4†); Prior S—Match No. 19(5) 20(5) 21(5) 25(5) 26(4) 27(4) 28(5) 29(5) 30(5) 31(5) 32(5) 33(5) 34(5) 35(5) 36(5) 37(5) 38(5) 39(5); Barr R—Match No. 19(8) 20(8) 22(7) 23(7) 24(7) 25(7) 26(7) 27(7†) 28(7†) 29(8) 30(8) 31(4*) 32(7*) 33(4) 34(4) 35(4) 36(4) 37(6) 38(4) 39(4); Guthrie F—Match No. 19(10); McLafferty W—Match No. 19(11) 20(9) 21(10) 22(10) 23(8) 24(8) 25(8) 29(12) 31(11) 32(8) 33(8) 34(8) 35(8) 36(8) 38(8) 39(8); Livingstone J—Match No. 20(7); McKenzie, T—Match No. 20(11); Hulme M—Match No. 21(7); Fisher J—Match No. 23(10) 24(10) 25(10) 26(10) 27(10) 28(10) 29(10) 30(10) 31(10) 32(11) 33(6) 34(6) 35(6) 36(6) 37(11) 38(11) 39(6); Robertson M—Match No. 27(14) 28(2) 29(14) 30(14); Haddon L—Match No. 28(11) 29(11†) 30(11†) 34(12) 35(12) 36(11*) 37(7) 38(10) 39(11); McCallum M—Match No. 33(10) 34(10*) 35(10) 36(10) 37(10) 38(9) 39(10); Irvine J—Match No. 33(11*) 34(11†) 35(11*).

STIRLING ALBION First Division

Year Formed: 1945. *Ground & Address:* The club is moving from Annfield by 1 July 1992 and will be in their new stadium in January 1993. Home games wil be played at Stenhousemuir for the first part of the season.
Chairman: Peter McKenzie. *Secretary:* Duncan McCallum. *Commercial Manager:* —.
Manager: John Brogan. *Assistant Managers:* Tom O'Neill, Jimmy Sinclair. *Physio:* George Cameron. *Coach:* Jim McSherry. *Managers since 1975:* A. Smith; G. Peebles; J. Fleeting.
Club Nickname(s): The Binos. *Previous Grounds:* None.
Record Attendance: 26,400 v Celtic, Scottish Cup 4th rd; 14 Mar, 1959.
Record Transfer Fee received: £70,000 for John Philliben to Doncaster R (Mar 1984).
Record Transfer Fee paid: £17,000 for Douglas Lawrie from Airdrieonians, December 1989.

STIRLING ALBION 1991–92 LEAGUE RECORD

Match No.	Date		Venue	Opponents		Result	H/T Score	Lg. Pos.	Goalscorers	Atten- dance
1	Aug	10	A	Kilmarnock	D	0-0	0-0	—		4416
2		13	A	Morton	L	1-2	1-0	—	Hendry	1549
3		17	H	Montrose	D	2-2	1-0	7	Hendry 2	938
4		24	A	Partick T	L	0-1	0-0	9		3341
5		31	H	Meadowbank T	L	2-3	2-1	11	Mitchell (pen), Lawrie	640
6	Sept	7	A	Raith R	L	0-1	0-1	11		1252
7		14	H	Hamilton A	L	0-1	0-1	11		996
8		21	H	Forfar Ath	L	1-3	1-1	12	Moore (pen)	432
9		28	A	Clydebank	W	1-0	1-0	11	Moore	846
10	Oct	5	A	Ayr U	W	2-1	1-0	11	McInnes, Moore	2505
11		8	H	Dundee	D	1-1	1-1	—	McInnes	1380
12		12	H	Kilmarnock	L	0-3	0-2	10		1947
13		19	A	Montrose	L	1-4	1-0	11	Watters	557
14		26	H	Raith R	L	1-3	0-2	11	Armstrong	600
15		30	A	Hamilton A	L	1-3	1-0	—	Reilly	1309
16	Nov	2	A	Meadowbank T	W	1-0	1-0	11	McInnes	257
17		9	H	Partick T	D	1-1	1-0	11	Lloyd	2064
18		16	H	Ayr U	D	0-0	0-0	11		978
19		19	A	Dundee	D	0-0	0-0	—		2719
20		23	A	Forfar Ath	D	1-1	1-0	11	Lloyd	593
21		30	H	Morton	W	2-1	1-1	10	Lawrie, Armstrong	826
22	Dec	3	H	Clydebank	W	3-0	1-0	—	Watters 2, Reilly	712
23		7	A	Kilmarnock	L	0-2	0-0	9		3790
24		14	A	Raith R	W	2-1	0-1	9	Watters 2	1199
25		28	A	Partick T	W	1-0	1-0	9	Watters	2718
26	Jan	1	H	Meadowbank T	D	0-0	0-0	—		768
27		4	A	Ayr U	W	2-1	2-0	8	Armstrong, Reilly	2217
28		8	H	Hamilton A	W	3-0	1-0	—	Watters 3	845
29		11	H	Dundee	D	1-1	0-0	8	Pew	2273
30		18	A	Morton	L	0-2	0-0	8		1635
31	Feb	1	H	Montrose	W	4-1	2-0	8	Armstrong, Mitchell (pen), Watters, Shanks	729
32		8	H	Forfar Ath	W	4-1	2-0	8	Moore, Watters 2, Pew	658
33		26	A	Clydebank	L	1-2	1-0	—	Watters	623
34		29	A	Ayr U	L	1-2	1-0	8	Moore	790
35	Mar	7	A	Dundee	L	0-5	0-3	8		3190
36		14	H	Partick T	D	1-1	0-0	8	Watters	2107
37		21	A	Meadowbank T	D	0-0	0-0	8		351
38		28	H	Kilmarnock	W	1-0	1-0	8	Watters	1984
39	Apr	4	A	Montrose	D	0-0	0-0	8		569
40		7	H	Raith R	L	1-2	0-2	—	Reilly	786
41		11	A	Hamilton A	L	0-1	0-1	8		1638
42		18	A	Forfar Ath	D	1-1	0-0	8	Mitchell (pen)	424
43		25	H	Morton	W	4-3	2-2	8	Lawrie, Watters, McInnes, Moore	686
44	May	2	H	Clydebank	W	2-0	2-0	8	Watters, Moore	1121

Final League Position: 8

League (50): Watters 17, Moore 7 (1 pen), Armstrong 4, McInnes 4, Reilly 4, Hendry 3, Lawrie 3, Mitchell 3 (3 pens), Lloyd 2, Pew 2, Shanks 1. *Scottish Cup* (1): Reilly. *Skol Cup* (0). *B & Q Cup* (3): Moore 1, Reilly 1, Watters 1.

Record Victory: 20-0 v Selkirk, Scottish Cup, 1st rd; 8 Dec, 1984.
Record Defeat: 0-9 v Dundee U, Division I; 30 Dec, 1967.
Most Capped Player: —.
Most League Appearances: 504: Matt McPhee, 1967–81.
Most League Goals in Season (Individual): 29: Joe Hughes, Division II; 1969–70.
Most Goals Overall (Individual): 129: Billy Steele, 1971–83.

Honours
League Champions: Division II 1952–53, 1957–58, 1960–61, 1964–65. Second Division 1976–77, 1990–91; *Runners-up:* Division II 1948–49, 1950–51.
Scottish Cup —. *League Cup* —.
Club colours: Shirt: Red with white sleeves. Shorts: White. Stockings: White.

McGeown, M	Mitchell, C	Hay, G	Shanks, D	Lawrie, D	Kerr, J	Reid, J	McInnes, I	Hendry, M	Robertson, S	Docherty, R	Conway, M	McCormack, J	Moore, V	Armstrong, P	Watters, W	Lloyd, D	Pew, D	O'Neill, T	Brogan, J	Picken, J	Docherty, A	Reilly, R	Watson, P	Smith, J	Match No.
1	2	3	4	5	6	7*	8	9†	10	11	12	14													1
1	2	3		5	6	7	4	9*	10	11	12	14	8†												2
1	2	3	4	5	6	7	10	9†		11	12		8*	14											3
1	2		4	5	6	14	7	9	12	11			8*	3	10†										4
1	2		4	5	6	7		9†	10	11	14	3	8												5
1			4	5	3			9	10	11		6	2	8		7									6
1	2		4		7†	12		9	10	11		6	3	5	8*	14									7
1	2					4†	8	10	11	6		5	3	7	9	14									8
	2			5	6	7		10	11†	8	3*	14	9		4			1		12					9
1	2			5	6	4	10	11	8	14	9†	3				12						7*			10
1	2			5	6	7	10	11	4	8		3		9											11
1	2	12		5	6	7	10	11	4†	8	14		3*	9											12
1	2			5	6	4	12	10	8	9			11*	7	3										13
1	2			5	6	12	10	11	3	8†	14	7	9*			4									14
1	2			6	12	4	10	11†	5	8*	3	7		14	9										15
1	2	3*	4	5	6	14	7	11	10	12		8	9†												16
1	2		4	5	6	10		3	8	14	7	9									11†				17
1	2		4	5	6	12	10	3	8	7*	9			14	11†										18
1	2		4	5	6	12	10	14	3	8	11†	9*				7									19
1	2		4†	5	6	12	10	14	3	8	11	9*				7									20
1	2		4	5	6	10		3	8	11*	9	14				7†									21
1	2			5	6	14	4	10	12	3*	8	11	9			7†									22
1	2			5	6	14	4*	10	12	3	8	11	9†			7									23
1	2		4	5	6	12	10	14	3*	8†	11	9				7									24
1	2		4	5	6	14	8	10	3	11	9†					7									25
1	2		4	5	6	7	8	10	3†	14	11	9													26
1	2		4	5	6	14	8	10		11	9		3			7†									27
1	2		4	5	6	14	8	10	3	12	11*	9				7†									28
1	2		4	5	6	7†	8	10	3	12	11*	9	14												29
1	2	3	4	5	6	7†	8	10*		12	11	9	14												30
1	2	3	4	5	6	14	8	10*		12	11	9†	7												31
1	2†		4	5	6	11*	10	14		8	3	9	12			7									32
1	2	3	4	5	6	10		14	8	11†	9	12										7*			33
1	2	6	4†	5		11*	10	14		8	3	9				12						7			34
1	2	3*	4	5	6	10†	12	14		8	11	9										7			35
1			4	5	6	8		10	2			11†	9									12	7*	3	14	36
1	14		4	5	6	8†		10	2*			11	9									12	7	3		37
1	2		4	5	6	8		10				11	9										7	3		38
1	2	14	4†	5	6	11		10*		8			9									12	7	3		39
1	2	5	14		6	12		10*		8	11†		9									4	7	3		40
1	2	14	4†	5	6	8		10		12	11*		9										7	3		41
1	2	14	4†	5	6	8		10		12	11*		9									7†		3		42
1	2		4	5	6	8		10		12	11*		9										7	3		43
1	2		4	5	6	10		11		8*			9		14							12	7†	3		44
43	41	10	32	40	40	7	40	8	25	23	7	18	27	29	35	9	2	5	0	1	2	30	10	0	
+	+	+			+		+	+	+	+	+	+	+	+	+	+		+			+		+		
1s	3s	2s			13s3s		5s	5s	6s	2s	10s3s	3s	1s	6s				1s			9s		1s		

STRANRAER
Second Division

Year Formed: 1870. *Ground & Address:* Stair Park, London Rd, Stranraer DG9 8BS. *Telephone:* 0776 3271.
Ground Capacity: total: 5000. seated: 700. *Size of Pitch:* 110 × 70yd.
Chairman: T. Rice. *Secretary:* Graham Rodgers. *Commercial Manager:* —.
Manager: —. *Assistant Manager:* —. *Physio:* —. *Coach:* John McNiven.
Managers since 1975: J. Hughes; N. Hood; G. Hamilton; D. Sneddon; J. Clark; R. Clark; A. McAnespie.
Club Nickname(s): The Blues. *Previous Grounds:* None.
Record Attendance: 6500 v Rangers, Scottish Cup 1st rd; 24 Jan, 1948.
Record Transfer Fee received: — .
Record Transfer Fee paid: £15,000 for Colin Harkness from Kilmarnock, August 1989.

STRANRAER 1991–92 LEAGUE RECORD

Match No.	Date		Venue	Opponents	Result	H/T Score	Lg. Pos.	Goalscorers	Atten-dance
1	Aug	10	H	East Stirling	L	3-5	0-2	—	Cook, Harkness 2 (1 pen)	590
2		17	A	Arbroath	L	0-1	0-1	13		257
3		24	H	Dumbarton	W	2-1	1-1	12	Henderson, Sloan	630
4		31	A	East Fife	L	1-2	0-1	13	Sloan	596
5	Sept	7	H	Queen's Park	W	2-1	1-1	10	Grant 2	583
6		14	A	Albion R	L	1-2	1-1	12	Sloan	221
7		17	H	Cowdenbeath	D	2-2	2-0	—	Cook, Ewing	569
8		21	A	Queen of the S	W	2-0	0-0	7	Sloan 2	659
9		28	H	Clyde	W	2-0	0-0	7	Ewing, Henderson	770
10	Oct	5	A	Stenhousemuir	W	1-0	0-0	6	Gallagher	320
11		12	H	Brechin C	L	1-3	0-3	8	Harkness	496
12		19	A	Berwick R	D	0-0	0-0	8		255
13		26	H	Alloa	W	1-0	0-0	7	Geraghty	370
14	Nov	2	A	East Stirling	D	2-2	0-1	7	Cook, Spittal	193
15		9	H	Arbroath	W	2-0	1-0	5	McNiven, Sloan	483
16		16	A	Dumbarton	L	0-1	0-0	6		631
17		23	A	Queen's Park	W	1-0	0-0	5	O'Brien (og)	470
18		30	A	Albion R	L	1-2	1-0	5	Sloan	466
19	Dec	14	H	Alloa	L	1-3	0-1	7	Cook	432
20		28	A	Cowdenbeath	L	0-2	0-1	10		321
21	Jan	1	H	Queen of the S	L	0-2	0-2	—		750
22		8	H	East Fife	L	0-2	0-1	—		528
23		11	H	Stenhousemuir	W	3-2	1-1	10	Grant, Sloan 2	449
24		18	A	Clyde	L	2-4	0-2	10	Sloan, Henderson	418
25	Feb	1	H	Berwick R	D	2-2	1-2	10	Henderson, Gallagher	436
26		4	A	Brechin C	L	1-2	1-1	—	Henderson	350
27		8	A	Dumbarton	D	0-0	0-0	10		621
28		15	H	Arbroath	W	1-0	0-0	10	Grant	395
29		22	H	Cowdenbeath	W	1-0	0-0	8	Grant	467
30		29	A	Alloa	D	0-0	0-0	9		489
31	Mar	11	H	Stenhousemuir	D	1-1	1-0	—	Henderson	410
32		14	A	Berwick R	W	2-1	1-1	7	Sloan, McDowall	270
33		21	A	Clyde	D	1-1	1-1	8	Henderson	466
34		28	H	Brechin C	D	1-1	1-0	8	Sloan	450
35	Apr	4	A	East Stirling	L	0-1	0-0	9		170
36		11	H	East Fife	L	1-2	1-1	9	Sloan	457
37		18	A	Queen's Park	L	2-5	1-4	10	Ewing, Cook	474
38		25	H	Albion R	W	2-0	2-0	9	Sloan, Harkness	397
39	May	2	H	Queen of the S	L	1-3	0-1	10	Ewing	547

Final League Position: 10

League (46): Sloan 14, Henderson 7, Cook 5, Grant 5, Ewing 4, Harkness 4 (1 pen), Gallagher 2, Geraghty 1, McDowall 1, McNiven 1, Spittal 1, own goal 1. *Scottish Cup* (7): Harkness 3, Sloan 3, Gallagher 1. *Skol Cup* (0). *B & Q Cup* (5): Cook 1, Gallagher 1, Harkness 1, Henderson 1, McCann 1.

Record Victory: 7-0 Brechin C, Division II; 6 Feb, 1965.
Record Defeat: 1-11 v Queen of the South, Scottish Cup 1st rd; 16 Jan, 1932.
Most Capped Player: —.
Most League Appearances: 256: Dan McDonald.
Most League Goals in Season (Individual): 27: Derek Frye, Second Division; 1977–78.
Most Goals Overall (Individual): —.

Honours
League Champions: —.
Scottish Cup: —.
League Cup: —.
Club colours: Shirt: Royal blue with amber chest band. Shorts: Royal blue. Stockings: Royal blue.

Duffy, B	Hughes, J	Love, J	Spittal, I	Gallagher, A	McCann, J	Ewing, A	Grant, A	Harkness, C	Scott, R	Henderson, D	Cook, D	Duncan, G	Shirkie, S	Sloan, T	Geraghty, M	Lowe, L	Elliot, D	McNiven, J	Walker, D	McDowall, P	Holland, B	Brannigan, K	Evans, S	Match No.
1	2	3	4	5	6*	7†	8	9	10	11	12	14												1
1	3	12	4		2	7	10	9		11	8†	6	5*	14										2
1	2	3*	6	5	4	14	8†	12		11	9	10		7										3
1	2	3†	4	5	10	12	8			11	9	6*		7	14									4
1	3	10	4	5	2		8			11	9	6		7										5
1	3	10	4	5	2		8			11	9†	6		7	14									6
1	3		4		11		8	9†			10	6	5*	7	14	2	12							7
1	3	12	5		2	7	11	9		10*	4	6		8										8
1	3	12	4		2	10	8	9†		11	14	6	5*	7										9
1	2	3	4	5	10	8*	12			11	9†	6		7	14									10
1	2	3*	4	5	12	10	8			11	9	6†		7	14									11
1	3		6		10			9		11	12	8	5	7*	2			4						12
1	2	3	6				8	9		10	12		5	7*		11		4						13
1	2	3	12	6		7	8	9*		10	14		5			11		4†						14
1	3	11	2	6		7		9*		10†	12	8	14					4				5		15
	3	11	6		2	7	14	9		10	12	8	5*					4†	1					16
1	3	10	6		2			9†		11	12	8		7*	14			4				5		17
1	3	10	6		2	7†		9		11*	14	12		8				4				5		18
1	3	10	6		2*	12		9†		11	14	8		7				4				5		19
1	2	10	4				8	9*		11†	12	6		7	14						3	5		20
1	2	3	6		10	12		9		11	14	8		7†				4*				5		21
1	3	10			2†	12	8	9		11		6	14	7				4*				5		22
1	2	10					8	9		11		6	14	7†				4		3		5		23
1	2	10				8		9		11	14		5†	7				4		3			6	24
1	2		6				8	9*		11	12	10		7				4		3		5		25
1	2		6				8	9		11	12	10		7*				4		3		5		26
1	2	10	4				8	9		11		6		7						3		5		27
1	2	14	4	10			8	9		11		6†		7						3		5		28
1	2	14	4	10			8	9		11		6†		7						3		5		29
1		14	4	6	2		8*	9†		11	12			7						3		5	10	30
1			4	6	2		8	9		11				7						3		5	10	31
1	2	12	4	6			8†	9		11	14			7						3		5	10*	32
1	2	14	4	6			8	9		11*	12			7†						3		5	10	33
1	2		4	6			8	9		11*	12			7						3		5	10	34
1	2	14	4				8	9		11†	12	10		7*						3		5	6	35
1	3	11	2		10		8	9			12	14		7*				4				5	6†	36
	2	3	4	6			8*	9		11	12		14	7					1			5†	10	37
	2	3	6	4				9		11*	10		12	7					1			5	8	38
1	2	3	6	4	10		8	9		11*	12			7								5		39
36	36	21	27	22	25	19	28	20	1	32	16	27	12	35	2	2	0	19	2	14	3	21	9	
+	+			+	+	+	+			+	+	+			+	+	+	+	+					
8s	1s			1s	5s	3s	9s			1s	10s	4s			1s	11s	1s	1s	3s					

B & Q SCOTTISH LEAGUE FINAL TABLES

PREMIER DIVISION

	P	W	Home D	L	Goals F	A	W	Away D	L	Goals F	A	GD	Pts
Rangers	44	14	5	3	50	14	19	1	2	51	17	+70	72
Hearts	44	12	7	3	26	15	15	2	5	34	22	+23	63
Celtic	44	15	3	4	47	20	11	7	4	41	22	+46	62
Dundee U	44	10	7	5	37	25	9	6	7	29	25	+16	51
Hibernian	44	7	8	7	28	25	9	9	4	25	20	+8	49
Aberdeen	44	9	6	7	32	23	8	8	6	23	19	+13	48
Airdrieonians	44	7	5	10	25	33	6	5	11	25	37	−20	36
St Johnstone	44	5	7	10	21	32	8	3	11	31	41	−21	36
Falkirk	44	7	2	13	29	41	5	9	8	25	32	−19	35
Motherwell	44	5	6	11	25	29	5	8	9	18	32	−18	34
St Mirren	44	2	5	15	18	36	4	7	11	15	37	−40	24
Dunfermline Ath	44	2	7	13	11	35	2	3	17	11	45	−58	18

FIRST DIVISION

	P	W	Home D	L	Goals F	A	W	Away D	L	Goals F	A	GD	Pts
Dundee	44	13	5	4	46	20	10	7	5	34	28	+32	58
Partick T	44	11	4	7	33	24	12	7	3	19	12	+26	57
Hamilton A	44	12	6	4	39	21	10	7	5	33	27	+24	57
Kilmarnock	44	12	4	6	31	20	9	8	5	28	17	+22	54
Raith R	44	11	7	4	33	16	10	4	8	26	26	+17	53
Ayr U	44	11	4	7	35	21	7	7	8	28	34	+8	47
Morton	44	9	6	7	32	28	8	6	8	34	31	+7	46
Stirling Albion	44	8	7	7	35	29	6	6	10	15	28	−7	41
Clydebank	44	7	8	7	33	33	5	4	13	26	44	−18	36
Meadowbank T	44	4	8	10	17	20	3	8	11	20	39	−22	30
Montrose	44	3	10	9	28	38	2	7	13	17	47	−40	27
Forfar Ath	44	3	7	12	18	38	2	5	15	18	47	−49	22

SECOND DIVISION

	P	W	Home D	L	Goals F	A	W	Away D	L	Goals F	A	GD	Pts
Dumbarton	39	9	8	3	29	20	11	4	4	36	17	+28	52
Cowdenbeath	39	14	2	3	40	20	8	5	7	34	32	+22	51
Alloa	39	13	4	3	34	15	7	6	6	24	23	+20	50
East Fife	39	10	7	2	42	26	9	4	7	30	31	+15	49
Clyde	39	11	4	4	38	15	7	3	10	23	28	+18	43
East Stirling	39	10	4	5	32	33	5	7	8	29	37	−9	41
Arbroath	39	9	7	3	29	23	3	7	10	20	25	+1	38
Brechin C	39	7	7	6	27	24	6	5	8	27	31	−1	38
Queen's Park	39	10	3	7	31	26	4	4	11	28	37	−4	35
Stranraer	39	9	4	7	29	29	4	5	10	17	27	−10	35
Queen of the S	39	6	2	11	37	44	8	3	9	34	42	−15	33
Berwick R	39	4	6	10	20	32	6	5	8	30	33	−15	31
Stenhousemuir	39	7	3	9	27	28	4	5	11	19	29	−11	30
Albion R	39	2	6	12	19	39	3	4	12	23	42	−39	20

SCOTTISH LEAGUE 1890–91 to 1991–92

*On goal average/difference.   †Held jointly after indecisive play-off.   ‡Won on deciding match.
††Held jointly.   ¶Two points deducted for fielding ineligible player.
Competition suspended 1940–45 during war.   ‡‡Two points deducted for registration irregularities.

PREMIER DIVISION

Maximum points: 72

	First	Pts	Second	Pts	Third	Pts
1975–76	Rangers	54	Celtic	48	Hibernian	43
1976–77	Celtic	55	Rangers	46	Aberdeen	43
1977–78	Rangers	55	Aberdeen	53	Dundee U	40
1978–79	Celtic	48	Rangers	45	Dundee U	44
1979–80	Aberdeen	48	Celtic	47	St Mirren	42
1980–81	Celtic	56	Aberdeen	49	Rangers*	44
1981–82	Celtic	55	Aberdeen	53	Rangers	43
1982–83	Dundee U	56	Celtic*	55	Aberdeen	55
1983–84	Aberdeen	57	Celtic	50	Dundee U	47
1984–85	Aberdeen	59	Celtic	52	Dundee U	47
1985–86	Celtic*	50	Hearts	50	Dundee U	47

Maximum points: 88

	First	Pts	Second	Pts	Third	Pts
1986–87	Rangers	69	Celtic	63	Dundee U	60
1987–88	Celtic	72	Hearts	62	Rangers	60

Maximum points: 72

	First	Pts	Second	Pts	Third	Pts
1988–89	Rangers	56	Aberdeen	50	Celtic	46
1989–90	Rangers	51	Aberdeen*	44	Hearts	44
1990–91	Rangers	55	Aberdeen	53	Celtic*	41

Maximum points: 88

	First	Pts	Second	Pts	Third	Pts
1991–92	Rangers	72	Hearts	63	Celtic	62

FIRST DIVISION

Maximum points: 52

	First	Pts	Second	Pts	Third	Pts
1975–76	Partick T	41	Kilmarnock	35	Montrose	30

Maximum points: 78

	First	Pts	Second	Pts	Third	Pts
1976–77	St Mirren	62	Clydebank	58	Dundee	51
1977–78	Morton*	58	Hearts	58	Dundee	57
1978–79	Dundee	55	Kilmarnock*	54	Clydebank	54
1979–80	Hearts	53	Airdrieonians	51	Ayr U	44
1980–81	Hibernian	57	Dundee	52	St Johnstone	51
1981–82	Motherwell	61	Kilmarnock	51	Hearts	50
1982–83	St Johnstone	55	Hearts	54	Clydebank	50
1983–84	Morton	54	Dumbarton	51	Partick T	46
1984–85	Motherwell	50	Clydebank	48	Falkirk	45
1985–86	Hamilton A	56	Falkirk	45	Kilmarnock	44

Maximum points: 88

	First	Pts	Second	Pts	Third	Pts
1986–87	Morton	57	Dunfermline Ath	56	Dumbarton	53
1987–88	Hamilton A	56	Meadowbank T	52	Clydebank	49

Maximum points: 78

	First	Pts	Second	Pts	Third	Pts
1988–89	Dunfermline Ath	54	Falkirk	52	Clydebank	48
1989–90	St Johnstone	58	Airdrieonians	54	Clydebank	44
1990–91	Falkirk	54	Airdrieonians	53	Dundee	52

Maximum points: 88

	First	Pts	Second	Pts	Third	Pts
1991–92	Dundee	58	Partick T*	57	Hamilton A	57

SECOND DIVISION

Maximum points: 52

	First	Pts	Second	Pts	Third	Pts
1975–77	Clydebank*	40	Raith R	40	Alloa	35

Maximum points: 78

	First	Pts	Second	Pts	Third	Pts
1976–77	Stirling A	55	Alloa	51	Dunfermline Ath	50
1977–78	Clyde*	53	Raith R	53	Dunfermline Ath	48
1978–79	Berwick R	54	Dunfermline Ath	52	Falkirk	50
1979–80	Falkirk	50	East Stirling	49	Forfar Ath	46
1980–81	Queen's Park	50	Queen of the S	46	Cowdenbeath	45
1981–82	Clyde	59	Alloa*	50	Arbroath	50
1982–83	Brechin C	55	Meadowbank T	54	Arbroath	49
1983–84	Forfar Ath	63	East Fife	47	Berwick R	43
1984–85	Montrose	53	Alloa	50	Dunfermline Ath	49
1985–86	Dunfermline Ath	57	Queen of the S	55	Meadowbank T	49
1986–87	Meadowbank T	55	Raith R*	52	Stirling A	52
1987–88	Ayr U	61	St Johnstone	59	Queen's Park	51
1988–89	Albion R	50	Alloa	45	Brechin C	43
1989–90	Brechin C	49	Kilmarnock	48	Stirling A	47
1990–91	Stirling A	54	Montrose	46	Cowdenbeath	45

Maximum points: 88

| 1991–92 | Dumbarton | 52 | Cowdenbeath | 51 | Alloa | 50 |

FIRST DIVISION to 1974–75

Maximum points: a 36; b 44; c 40; d 52; e 60; f 68; g 76; h 84.

	First	Pts	Second	Pts	Third	Pts
1890–91a††	Dumbarton	29	Rangers	29	Celtic	24
1891–92b	Dumbarton	37	Celtic	35	Hearts	30
1892–93a	Celtic	29	Rangers	28	St Mirren	23
1893–94a	Celtic	29	Hearts	26	St Bernard's	22
1894–95a	Hearts	31	Celtic	26	Rangers	21
1895–96a	Celtic	30	Rangers	26	Hibernian	24
1896–97a	Hearts	28	Hibernian	26	Rangers	25
1897–98a	Celtic	33	Rangers	29	Hibernian	22
1898–99a	Rangers	36	Hearts	26	Celtic	24
1899–1900a	Rangers	32	Celtic	25	Hibernian	24
1900–01c	Rangers	35	Celtic	29	Hibernian	25
1901–02a	Rangers	28	Celtic	26	Hearts	22
1902–03b	Hibernian	37	Dundee	31	Rangers	29
1903–04d	Third Lanark	43	Hearts	39	Rangers*	38
1904–05d	Celtic‡	41	Rangers	41	Third Lanark	35
1905–06e	Celtic	49	Hearts	43	Airdrieonians	38
1906–07f	Celtic	55	Dundee	48	Rangers	45
1907–08f	Celtic	55	Falkirk	51	Rangers	50
1908–09f	Celtic	51	Dundee	50	Clyde	48
1909–10f	Celtic	54	Falkirk	52	Rangers	46
1910–11f	Rangers	52	Aberdeen	48	Falkirk	44
1911–12f	Rangers	51	Celtic	45	Clyde	42
1912–13f	Rangers	53	Celtic	49	Hearts*	41
1913–14g	Celtic	65	Rangers	59	Hearts*	54
1914–15g	Celtic	65	Hearts	61	Rangers	50
1915–16g	Celtic	67	Rangers	56	Morton	51
1916–17g	Celtic	64	Morton	54	Rangers	53
1917–18f	Rangers	56	Celtic	55	Kilmarnock	43
1918–19f	Celtic	58	Rangers	57	Morton	47
1919–20h	Rangers	71	Celtic	68	Motherwell	57
1920–21h	Rangers	76	Celtic	66	Hearts	56
1921–22h	Celtic	67	Rangers	66	Raith R	56
1922–23g	Rangers	55	Airdrieonians	50	Celtic	46
1923–24g	Rangers	59	Airdrieonians	50	Celtic	41
1924–25g	Rangers	60	Airdrieonians	57	Hibernian	52
1925–26g	Celtic	58	Airdrieonians*	50	Hearts	50
1926–27g	Rangers	56	Motherwell	51	Celtic	49
1927–28g	Rangers	60	Celtic*	55	Motherwell	55
1928–29g	Rangers	67	Celtic	51	Motherwell	50
1929–30g	Rangers	60	Motherwell	55	Aberdeen	53
1930–31g	Rangers	60	Celtic	58	Motherwell	56
1931–32g	Motherwell	66	Rangers	61	Celtic	48
1932–33g	Rangers	62	Motherwell	59	Hearts	50
1933–34g	Rangers	66	Motherwell	62	Celtic	47
1934–35g	Rangers	55	Celtic	52	Hearts	50
1935–36g	Celtic	66	Rangers*	61	Aberdeen	61
1936–37g	Rangers	61	Aberdeen	54	Celtic	52
1937–38g	Celtic	61	Hearts	58	Rangers	49
1938–39g	Rangers	59	Celtic	48	Aberdeen	46
1946–47e	Rangers	46	Hibernian	44	Aberdeen	39
1947–48e	Hibernian	48	Rangers	46	Partick T	36
1948–49e	Rangers	46	Dundee	45	Hibernian	39
1949–50e	Rangers	50	Hibernian	49	Hearts	43
1950–51e	Hibernian	48	Rangers*	38	Dundee	38
1951–52e	Hibernian	45	Rangers	41	East Fife	37
1952–53e	Rangers*	43	Hibernian	43	East Fife	39
1953–54e	Celtic	43	Hearts	38	Partick T	35
1954–55e	Aberdeen	49	Celtic	46	Rangers	41
1955–56f	Rangers	52	Aberdeen	46	Hearts*	45
1956–57f	Rangers	55	Hearts	53	Kilmarnock	42
1957–58f	Hearts	62	Rangers	49	Celtic	46
1958–59f	Rangers	50	Hearts	48	Motherwell	44
1959–60f	Hearts	54	Kilmarnock	50	Rangers*	42
1960–61f	Rangers	51	Kilmarnock	50	Third Lanark	42
1961–62f	Dundee	54	Rangers	51	Celtic	46
1962–63f	Rangers	57	Kilmarnock	48	Partick T	46

	First	Pts	Second	Pts	Third	Pts
1963–64f	Rangers	55	Kilmarnock	49	Celtic*	47
1964–65f	Kilmarnock*	50	Hearts	50	Dunfermline Ath	49
1965–66f	Celtic	57	Rangers	55	Kilmarnock	45
1966–67f	Celtic	58	Rangers	55	Clyde	46
1967–68f	Celtic	63	Rangers	61	Hibernian	45
1968–69f	Celtic	54	Rangers	49	Dunfermline Ath	45
1969–70f	Celtic	57	Rangers	45	Hibernian	44
1970–71f	Celtic	56	Aberdeen	54	St Johnstone	44
1971–72f	Celtic	60	Aberdeen	50	Rangers	44
1972–73f	Celtic	57	Rangers	56	Hibernian	45
1973–74f	Celtic	53	Hibernian	49	Rangers	48
1974–75f	Rangers	56	Hibernian	49	Celtic	45

SECOND DIVISION to 1974–75

Maximum points: a 76; b 72; c 68; d 52; e 60; f 36; g 44; h 52.

	First		Second		Third	
1893–94f	Hibernian	29	Cowlairs	27	Clyde	24
1894–95f	Hibernian	30	Motherwell	22	Port Glasgow	20
1895–96f	Abercorn	27	Leith Ath	23	Renton	21
1896–97f	Partick T	31	Leith Ath	27	Kilmarnock	21
1897–98f	Kilmarnock	29	Port Glasgow	25	Morton	22
1898–99f	Kilmarnock	32	Leith Ath	27	Port Glasgow	25
1899–1900f	Partick T	29	Morton	26	Port Glasgow	20
1900–01f	St Bernard's	26	Airdrieonians	23	Abercorn	21
1901–02g	Port Glasgow	32	Partick T	31	Motherwell	26
1902–03g	Airdrieonians	35	Motherwell	28	Ayr U	27
1903–04g	Hamilton A	37	Clyde	29	Ayr U	28
1904–05g	Clyde	32	Falkirk	28	Hamilton A	27
1905–06g	Leith Ath	34	Clyde	31	Albion R	27
1906–07g	St Bernard's	32	Vale of Leven*	27	Arthurlie	27
1907–08g	Raith R	30	Dumbarton	‡‡27	Ayr U	27
1908–09g	Abercorn	31	Raith R*	28	Vale of Leven	28
1909–10g‡	Leith Ath	33	Raith R	33	St Bernard's	27
1910–11g	Dumbarton	31	Ayr U	27	Albion R	25
1911–12g	Ayr U	35	Abercorn	30	Dumbarton	27
1912–13h	Ayr U	34	Dunfermline Ath	33	East Stirling	32
1913–14g	Cowdenbeath	31	Albion R	27	Dunfermline Ath	26
1914–15h	Cowdenbeath*	37	St Bernard's*	37	Leith Ath	37
1921–22a	Alloa	60	Cowdenbeath	47	Armadale	45
1922–23a	Queen's Park	57	Clydebank	¶50	St Johnstone	¶45
1923–24a	St Johnstone	56	Cowdenbeath	55	Bathgate	44
1924–25a	Dundee U	50	Clydebank	48	Clyde	47
1925–26a	Dunfermline Ath	59	Clyde	53	Ayr U	52
1926–27a	Bo'ness	56	Raith R	49	Clydebank	45
1927–28a	Ayr U	54	Third Lanark	45	King's Park	44
1928–29b	Dundee U	51	Morton	50	Arbroath	47
1929–30a	Leith Ath*	57	East Fife	57	Albion R	54
1930–31a	Third Lanark	61	Dundee U	50	Dunfermline Ath	47
1931–32a	East Stirling*	55	St Johnstone	55	Raith Rovers*	46
1932–33c	Hibernian	54	Queen of the S	49	Dunfermline Ath	47
1933–34c	Albion R	45	Dunfermline Ath*	44	Arbroath	44
1934–35c	Third Lanark	52	Arbroath	50	St Bernard's	47
1935–36c	Falkirk	59	St Mirren	52	Morton	48
1936–37c	Ayr U	54	Morton	51	St Bernard's	48
1937–38c	Raith R	59	Albion R	48	Airdrieonians	47
1938–39c	Cowdenbeath	60	Alloa*	48	East Fife	48
1946–47d	Dundee	45	Airdrieonians	42	East Fife	31
1947–48e	East Fife	53	Albion R	42	Hamilton A	40
1948–49e	Raith R*	42	Stirling Albion	42	Airdrieonians*	41
1949–50e	Morton	47	Airdrieonians	44	St Johnstone*	36
1950–51e	Queen of the S*	45	Stirling Albion	45	Ayr U	36
1951–52e	Clyde	44	Falkirk	43	Ayr U	39
1952–53e	Stirling Albion	44	Hamilton A	43	Queen's Park	37
1953–54e	Motherwell	45	Kilmarnock	42	Third Lanark*	36
1954–55e	Airdrieonians	46	Dunfermline Ath	42	Hamilton A	39
1955–56b	Queen's Park	54	Ayr U	51	St Johnstone	49
1956–57b	Clyde	64	Third Lanark	51	Cowdenbeath	45
1957–58b	Stirling Albion	55	Dunfermline Ath	53	Arbroath	47
1958–59b	Ayr U	60	Arbroath	51	Stenhousemuir	40
1959–60b	St Johnstone	53	Dundee U	50	Queen of the S	49
1960–61b	Stirling Albion	55	Falkirk	54	Stenhousemuir	50
1961–62b	Clyde	54	Queen of the S	53	Morton	44

	First	Pts		Second	Pts		Third	Pts
1962–63b	St Johnstone	55		East Stirling	49		Morton	48
1963–64b	Morton	67		Clyde	53		Arbroath	46
1964–65b	Stirling Albion	59		Hamilton A	50		Queen of the S	45
1965–66b	Ayr U	53		Airdrieonians	50		Queen of the S	49
1966–67b	Morton	69		Raith R	58		Arbroath	57
1967–68b	St Mirren	62		Arbroath	53		East Fife	40
1968–69b	Motherwell	64		Ayr U	53		East Fife*	47
1969–70b	Falkirk	56		Cowenbeath	55		Queen of the S	50
1970–71b	Partick T	56		East Fife	51		Arbroath	46
1971–72b	Dumbarton*	52		Arbroath	52		Stirling Albion	50
1972–73b	Clyde	56		Dumfermline Ath	52		Raith R*	47
1973–74b	Airdrieonians	60		Kilmarnock	59		Hamilton A	55
1974–75a	Falkirk	54		Queen of the S	53		Montrose	53

Elected to First Division: 1894 Clyde; 1897 Partick T; 1899 Kilmarnock; 1900 Partick T; 1902 Partick T; 1903 Airdrieonians; 1905 Falkirk, Aberdeen and Hamilton A; 1906 Clyde; 1910 Raith R; 1913 Ayr U.

RELEGATED FROM PREMIER DIVISION

1975–76 Dundee, St Johnstone
1976–77 Hearts, Kilmarnock
1977–78 Ayr U, Clydebank
1978–79 Hearts, Motherwell
1979–80 Dundee, Hibernian
1980–81 Kilmarnock, Hearts
1981–82 Partick T, Airdrieonians
1982–83 Morton, Kilmarnock
1983–84 St Johnstone, Motherwell
1984–85 Dumbarton, Morton
1985–86 *No relegation due to League reorganization*
1986–87 Clydebank, Hamilton A
1987–88 Falkirk, Dunfermline Ath, Morton
1988–89 Hamilton A
1989–90 Dundee
1990–91 None
1991–92 St Mirren, Dunfermline Ath

RELEGATED FROM DIVISION 1

1975–76 Dunfermline Ath, Clyde
1976–77 Raith R, Falkirk
1977–78 Alloa Ath, East Fife
1978–79 Montrose, Queen of the S
1979–80 Arbroath, Clyde
1980–81 Stirling A, Berwick R
1981–82 East Stirling, Queen of the S
1982–83 Dunfermline Ath, Queen's Park
1983–84 Raith R, Alloa
1984–85 Meadowbank T, St Johnstone
1985–86 Ayr U, Alloa
1986–87 Brechin C, Montrose
1987–88 East Fife, Dumbarton
1988–89 Kilmarnock, Queen of the S
1989–90 Albion R, Alloa
1990–91 Clyde, Brechin C
1991–92 Montrose, Forfar Ath

RELEGATED FROM DIVISION 1 (TO 1973–74)

1921–22 *Queen's Park, Dumbarton, Clydebank
1922–23 Albion R, Alloa
1923–24 Clyde, Clydebank
1924–25 Third Lanark, Ayr U
1925–26 Raith R, Clydebank
1926–27 Morton, Dundee U
1927–28 Dunfermline Ath, Bo'ness
1928–29 Third Lanark, Raith R
1929–30 St Johnstone, Dundee U
1930–31 Hibernian, East Fife
1931–32 Dundee U, Leith Ath
1932–33 Morton, East Stirling
1933–34 Third Lanark, Cowdenbeath
1934–35 St Mirren, Falkirk
1935–36 Airdrieonians, Ayr U
1936–37 Dunfermline Ath, Albion R
1937–38 Dundee, Morton
1938–39 Queen's Park, Raith R
1946–47 Kilmarnock, Hamilton A
1947–48 Airdrieonians, Queen's Park
1948–49 Morton, Albion R
1949–50 Queen of the S, Stirling Albion
1950–51 Clyde, Falkirk

1951–52 Morton, Stirling Albion
1952–53 Motherwell, Third Lanark
1953–54 Airdrieonians, Hamilton A
1954–55 No clubs relegated
1955–56 Stirling Albion, Clyde
1956–57 Dunfermline Ath, Ayr U
1957–58 East Fife, Queen's Park
1958–59 Queen of the S, Falkirk
1959–60 Arbroath, Stirling Albion
1960–61 Ayr U, Clyde
1961–62 St Johnstone, Stirling Albion
1962–63 Clyde, Raith R
1963–64 Queen of the S, East Stirling
1964–65 Airdrieonians, Third Lanark
1965–66 Morton, Hamilton A
1966–67 St Mirren, Ayr U
1967–68 Motherwell, Stirling Albion
1968–69 Falkirk, Arbroath
1969–70 Raith R, Partick T
1970–71 St Mirren, Cowdenbeath
1971–72 Clyde, Dunfermline Ath
1972–73 Kilmarnock, Airdrieonians
1973–74 East Fife, Falkirk

*Season 1921–22 only 1 club promoted, 3 clubs relegated.

The Scottish Football League was reconstructed into three divisions at the end of the 1974–75 season, so the usual relegation statistics do not apply. Further reorganization took place at the end of the 1985–86 season. From 1986–87, the Premier and First Division had 12 teams each. The Second Division remains at 14. From 1988–89, the Premier Division contained 10 teams, and the First Division 14 teams but in 1991–92 the Premier and First Division reverted to 12.

Scottish League championship wins: Rangers 42, Celtic 35, Aberdeen 4, Hearts 4, Hibernian 4, Dumbarton 2, Dundee 1, Dundee United 1, Kilmarnock 1, Motherwell 1, Third Lanark 1.

SCOTTISH LEAGUE SKOL CUP FINALS 1946–92

Season	Winners	Runners-up	Score
1946–47	Rangers	Aberdeen	4-0
1947–48	East Fife	Falkirk	4-1 after 0-0 draw
1948–49	Rangers	Raith R	2-0
1949–50	East Fife	Dunfermline Ath	3-0
1950–51	Motherwell	Hibernian	3-0
1951–52	Dundee	Rangers	3-2
1952–53	Dundee	Kilmarnock	2-0
1953–54	East Fife	Partick T	3-2
1954–55	Hearts	Motherwell	4-2
1955–56	Aberdeen	St Mirren	2-1
1956–57	Celtic	Partick T	3-0 after 0-0 draw
1957–58	Celtic	Rangers	7-1
1958–59	Hearts	Partick T	5-1
1959–60	Hearts	Third Lanark	2-1
1960–61	Rangers	Kilmarnock	2-0
1961–62	Rangers	Hearts	3-1 after 1-1 draw
1962–63	Hearts	Kilmarnock	1-0
1963–64	Rangers	Morton	5-0
1964–65	Rangers	Celtic	2-1
1965–66	Celtic	Rangers	2-1
1966–67	Celtic	Rangers	1-0
1967–68	Celtic	Dundee	5-3
1968–69	Celtic	Hibernian	6-2
1969–70	Celtic	St Johnstone	1-0
1970–71	Rangers	Celtic	1-0
1971–72	Partick T	Celtic	4-1
1972–73	Hibernian	Celtic	2-1
1973–74	Dundee	Celtic	1-0
1974–75	Celtic	Hibernian	6-3
1975–76	Rangers	Celtic	1-0
1976–77	Aberdeen	Celtic	2-1
1977–78	Rangers	Celtic	2-1
1978–79	Rangers	Aberdeen	2-1
1979–80	Dundee U	Aberdeen	3-0 after 0-0 draw
1980–81	Dundee U	Dundee	3-0
1981–82	Rangers	Dundee U	2-1
1982–83	Celtic	Rangers	2-1
1983–84	Rangers	Celtic	3-2
1984–85	Rangers	Dundee U	1-0
1985–86	Aberdeen	Hibernian	3-0
1986–87	Rangers	Celtic	2-1
1987–88	Rangers	Aberdeen	3-3
		(Rangers won 5-3 on penalties)	
1988–89	Rangers	Aberdeen	3-2
1989–90	Aberdeen	Rangers	2-1
1990–91	Rangers	Celtic	2-1
1991–92	Hibernian	Dunfermline Ath	2-0

SCOTTISH LEAGUE CUP WINS

Rangers 17, Celtic 9, Hearts 4, Aberdeen 4, Dundee 3, East Fife 3, Dundee U 2, Hibernian 2, Motherwell 1, Partick T 1.

APPEARANCES IN FINALS

Rangers 23, Celtic 20, Aberdeen 9, Hibernian 6, Dundee 5, Hearts 5, Dundee U 4, Partick T 4, East Fife 3, Kilmarnock 3, Dunfermline Ath 2, Motherwell 2, Falkirk 1, Morton 1, Raith R 1, St Johnstone 1, St Mirren 1, Third Lanark 1.

SKOL CUP 1991-92

FIRST ROUND

13 AUG

Alloa (0) 0 *(at Ochilview Park, Stenhousemuir)*
Stranraer (0) 0 *aet*   445
Alloa: Butter; Newbigging, Lee R, Wilcox, McCulloch, Campbell, McCallum, Romaines, Smith (Irvine), Bennett, Gibson (Moffat).
Stranraer: Duffy; McCann, Hughes, Spittal, Shirkie, Duncan, Grant, Cook, Harkness, Scott (Ewing), Henderson.
(Stranraer won 8-7 on penalties)

East Fife (1) 2 *(Hope 2)*
East Stirling (1) 2 *(Lytwyn, Diver) aet*   802
East Fife: Charles; Taylor PH, Spence, Herd, Beaton, Burns, McBride, Wilson, Scott (Brown I), Sludden, Hope.
East Stirling: Watson; Gardiner, Russell, McAleer, Brannigan, Ross, McKinnon, Rooney, Diver, Kennedy, Lytwyn (Barclay).
(East Stirling won 4-2 on penalties)

Queen of the S (0) 0
Albion R (2) 4 *(Stalker, McAnenay 2, Watson)*   841
Queen of the S: Davidson; Campbell (McGhie), Smyth, Mills, Hetherington, Sim (Robertson), McGuire, Thomson I, Thomson A, Gordon, Bell.
Albion R: McCulloch; Millar G, Troup, Cadden, McTeague, Clark, Bowman, Edgar (Cougan), Ferguson (Watson), McKeown, McAnenay.

Queen's Park (2) 4 *(Mackenzie 2, Mackay 2)*
Stenhousemuir (0) 2 *(McCormick, Bainbridge)*   677
Queen's Park: Houston; Stevenson, MacColl, Elder, Mackay, McEntegart, Jack, O'Brien, Rodden (Jackson), Mackenzie, McCormick (James McFadyen).
Stenhousemuir: Kelly; Aitken, Hallford, Cairney, Tracey, Gardiner, Bell (Speirs), Clouston, McCormick, Walker (Bainbridge), Donald.

14 AUG

Berwick R (0) 0
Dumbarton (0) 1 *(Gibson)*   501
Berwick R: Neilson; McLaren, O'Donnell, Garner, Wilson, Neil, Graham (Tait), Leitch, Todd, Bickmore, Sneddon.
Dumbarton: McFarlane; Marsland, Boyd, Melvin, Martin, Gow, McQuade, Dempsey, Gibson, Meechan, Gilmour.

21 AUG

Cowdenbeath (1) 1 *(Robertson)*
Arbroath (0) 0   438
[replay; Cowdenbeath won 5-1 on Aug 14 but included an ineligible player]
Cowdenbeath: Lamont W; Watt, Bennett (Syme), Douglas, Archibald, Irvine, Wright, Malone, Lamont P, Irving (Buckley), Robertson A.
Arbroath: Balfour; Hamilton, Florence, Farnan, Carlin, Sneddon (Tindal), Brown (Tosh), Mitchell, Smith, Sorbie, Gallagher.

SECOND ROUND

20 AUG

Brechin C (2) 3 *(Pryde, Ritchie, 2 [1 pen])*   723
St Mirren (1) 3 *(Hutt [og], Kinnaird, McWhirter) aet*
Brechin C: Ainslie; Baillie, Conway, Brown, Nicolson, Hutt (Brand), Thomson S, Thomson N, Ritchie, Scott, Pryde (Paterson).
St Mirren: Money; Dawson, Black, McWhirter, Martin, McGowne, Wishart (Kinnaird), McIntyre, Irvine (McEwan), Lambert, Elliot.
(St Mirren won 5-4 on penalties)

Dumbarton (0) 1 *(Gibson)*
Airdrieonians (0) 2 *(Crainie [pen], Coyle) aet*   3000
Dumbarton: McFarlane; Marsland, Boyd, Melvin, Gow, Dempsey, McQuade, McNair, Gibson, Meechan, Gilmour.
Airdrieonians: Martin; Kidd, Jack (McPhee), Sandison, Smith, Conn, Stewart, Balfour, Lawrence, Coyle, Kirkwood (Crainie).

Dundee U (0) 3 *(Paatelainen, O'Neill M, Clark)*
Montrose (0) 2 *(Wolecki, Rougvie)*   4256
Dundee U: Van der Kamp; Cleland, Malpas, McKinlay, Clark, Bowman, Van der Hoorn, O'Neill M (Muller), Paatelainen, Jackson, Preston (McLaren).
Montrose: Larter; Morrison, Fleming, Robertson, Rougvie, Dornan, Lyons (Kerr), Allan (Fotheringham), Wolecki, King, Den Bieman.

Dunfermline Ath (2) 4 *(Moyes, O'Boyle, Leitch, McParland)*
Alloa (0) 1 *(McCallum)*   3185
Dunfermline Ath: Rhodes; Wilson, Cunnington, McCathie, Moyes, Haro (Leitch), Davies, McParland, O'Boyle, McCall, Kozma (Sinclair).
Alloa: Butter; Newbigging, Lee R, Ramsay, McCulloch, Campbell, McCallum, Romaines (Black), Irvine (Moffat), Bennett, Gibson.

Falkirk (1) 3 *(McAllister 2, Taylor)*
East Stirling (0) 0   2767
Falkirk: Westwater; Duffy, McQueen, Hughes, Godfrey, Rice, McAllister, Taylor, McGivern (Baptie), Stainrod (May), Smith.
East Stirling: Watson G; Gardner, Russell, McAleer, Brannigan, Ross, McKinnon, Rooney, Lytwyn (Barclay), Kennedy (McNally), Diver.

Hamilton A (0) 2 *(Burns, Clark)*
Forfar Ath (0) 0 *aet*   1267
Hamilton A: Ferguson; McKee, Miller, Napier, Weir, Reid, Harris, Burns, McCluskey (Hillcoat), Clark, McDonald.
Forfar Ath: Thomson; Brazil, Hamill, Morris, Hegarty, Peters (Lorimer), Paterson (Campbell), Holt, Whyte, Winter, Petrie.

Hearts (3) 3 *(Crabbe 2, Baird)*
Clydebank (0) 0   7867
Hearts: Smith; McLaren (Foster), McKinlay, Levein, Mackay, McPherson, Crabbe, Ferguson D (Wright), Baird, Millar, Robertson.
Clydebank: Spence; Traynor, Crawford, Maher, Rowe, Wright, Harvey, Lansdowne, Eadie, John Dickson, Mair.

Partick T (1) 2 *(Watson [og], McGlashan)*
Albion R (0) 0 2457
Partick T: Murdoch; Robertson, McLaughlin, Duffy, Rae, Johnston, Shaw, Annand, McGlashan, Law, Irons.
Albion R: McCulloch; Millar G, Troup (Cougan), Cadden (Edgar), McTeague, Clark, McAnenay, Stalker, Ferguson, McKeown, Watson.

Raith R (1) 4 *(MacKenzie, Nelson, Brewster 2)*
Motherwell (0) 1 *(Kirk)* 3204
Raith R: Arthur; Nicholl, MacLeod, Sinclair, Dennis, McGeachie, Williamson, MacKenzie, Ferguson, Brewster, Nelson.
Motherwell: Dykstra; Griffin, Angus, Dolan, Nijholt, McCart, Russell (Ferguson), O'Donnell, Cusack, Kirk, Cooper.

Rangers (3) 6 *(Durrant, Johnston 4, Spackman)*
Queen's Park (0) 0 32,230
Rangers: Goram; Stevens, Robertson D, Spackman, Nisbet, McCall (Robertson A), Johnston, Spencer, Durrant, Huistra (McCoist).
Queen's Park: Moonie; Stevenson, MacColl, Elder, Mackay, McEntegart (Jackson), Jack, Caven, O'Brien, Mackenzie, McCormick (O'Neill).

Stirling Albion (0) 0
Hibernian (2) 3 *(McIntyre, Evans, Wright)* 3342
Stirling Albion: McGeown; Mitchell, Watson, Shanks (Pew), Lawrie, Kerr, McInnes, Moore (Conway), Hendry, Robertson, Docherty.
Hibernian: Burridge; Miller, Mitchell, Hunter, McIntyre (Hamilton), MacLeod, Weir, Milne (McGraw), Wright, Evans, McGinlay.

21 AUG

Clyde (0) 0 2107
Aberdeen (1) 4 *(Grant, Van de Ven, Winnie, Booth)*
Clyde: Stevenson; Knox, Tennant, Morrison (McCoy), Speirs, McVie, Thompson D, Wilson, Scott (McAuley), Clarke, Wylde.
Aberdeen: Snelders; Wright, Winnie, Grant, Irvine, McKimmie, Van de Ven, Bett (Gregg Watson), Van der Ark, Jess (Booth), Gillhaus.

Dundee (2) 2 *(Craig 2)* 3084
Ayr U (0) 4 *(Bryce [pen], Shaw 2, Graham) aet*
Dundee: Mathers; McQuillan, Campbell S, Fraser, Jamieson (Chisholm), Craib, Campbell D, Craig, Bremner, Dodds, Beedie.
Ayr U: Duncan; Burley, Agnew, Furphy, Auld, McLean, Fraser (Shaw), Bryce, Graham, George, Smith.

Meadowbank T (0) 0
St Johnstone (1) 2 *(Redford, Ward)* 1223
Meadowbank T: McQueen; Nicol, Armstrong, Williamson, Grant, Neil (Boyd), Logan, Young (Kane), Little, Christie, Irvine.
St Johnstone: Hamilton; Treanor, Baltacha, Redford, McGinnis, Dunne, Moore, Davies (Turner), Wright, Curran, Ward (Grant).

Morton (1) 2 *(McInnes, Ogg)*
Celtic (4) 4 *(Nicholas 2, Creaney 2)* 9518
Morton: Wylie; Pickering, Ogg, Rafferty, Doak, Collins, Mathie, Fowler (McDonald), Alexander, McInnes, Gahagan (McGoldrick).
Celtic: Bonner; Morris, Rogan, Grant, Whyte (Galloway), Gillespie, Fulton, Coyne, Creaney, Nicholas, Collins (Miller).

26 AUG

Cowdenbeath (0) 0
Kilmarnock (0) 1 *(Wright [og])* 1561
Cowdenbeath: Lamont W; Watt, Robertson A, Fraser, Archibald, Irvine, Wright, Malone, Lamont P, Buckley, Johnston (Syme).
Kilmarnock: Geddes; MacPherson, Reilly, McStay, Flexney, Tait, Mitchell, Campbell (Jack), Williamson, Burns T, McSkimming.

THIRD ROUND

27 AUG

Ayr U (2) 2 *(Shaw, Graham)*
St Johnstone (0) 0 5176
Ayr U: Duncan; Kennedy, Agnew, Furphy, Auld, McLean, Smith (Walker), Bryce (McAllister), Graham, George, Shaw.
St Johnstone: Hamilton; Treanor (Davies), Baltacha, McGinnis, Inglis, Redford, Moore, Turner, Wright, Curran, Ward (Grant).

Celtic (1) 3 *(Miller, Creaney, Fulton)*
Raith R (1) 1 *(MacKenzie)* 21,081
Celtic: Bonner; Morris, Wdowczyk, Grant, Whyte, Gillespie, Fulton, Coyne (Walker), Creaney (McNally), Galloway, Miller.
Raith R: Arthur; Nichol (Burn), MacLeod, Sinclair, Dennis, McGeachie, Williamson (Dalziel), MacKenzie, Ferguson, Brewster, Nelson.

Dundee U (1) 1 *(French)*
Falkirk (0) 0 6737
Dundee U: Main; Clarke, Malpas, Bowman, Van der Hoorn, Narey, McLaren, McKinlay, French, Paatelainen, Bollan.
Falkirk: Westwater; Duffy, McQueen, Hughes, Baptie, Rice (Oliver), McAllister, Taylor (Mooney), McGivern, May, Smith.

28 AUG

Aberdeen (0) 0
Airdrieonians (0) 1 *(Watson)* 13,000
Aberdeen: Snelders; Wright, Winnie, Grant, Irvine, McKimmie, Van de Ven, Bett, Van der Ark (Jess), Cameron (Booth), Gillhaus.
Airdrieonians: Martin; Kidd (Kirkwood), Stewart, Sandison, Watson (Boyle), Honor, Lawrence, Balfour, Coyle, Conn, Jack.

Dunfermline Ath (1) 1 *(Leitch)*
St Mirren (0) 1 *(Lambert) aet* 3867
Dunfermline Ath: Rhodes; Wilson, Cunnington, McCathie, Moyes, Williamson, Davies, McParland (McWilliams), Leitch, McCall (Gallagher), Kozma.
St Mirren: Fridge; Wishart (McGowne), Black, Aitken, Baillie, Charnley, McIntyre, Martin, Irvine (McGill), Lambert, Elliot.
(Dunfermline Ath won 3-2 on penalties)

Hamilton A (0) 0
Hearts (0) 2 *(Robertson [pen], Baird)* 4000
Hamilton A: Ferguson; McKee (Moore), Miller, Millen, Weir, Reid, Harris (Clark), Burns, Smith, Napier, McDonald.
Hearts: Smith; Hogg, McKinlay, Levein, Mackay, McPherson, Crabbe, Ferguson D, Baird, Millar (Harrison), Robertson (Foster).

Kilmarnock (1) 2 *(Campbell, McSkimming)*
Hibernian (1) 3 *(MacLeod, McGinlay, Wright)* 6507
Kilmarnock: Geddes; MacPherson, Reilly, McStay (Jack), Flexney, Tait, Mitchell, Campbell, Williamson, Porteous, McSkimming.
Hibernian: Burridge; Miller, Mitchell, Hunter, Orr, MacLeod, Weir (Hamilton), Milne, Wright, McGraw (Fellenger), McGinlay.

Partick T (0) 0
Rangers (1) 2 *(Johnston, Robertson D)*   12,587
Partick T: Murdoch; Robertson, McLaughlin, Duffy, Rae, Johnston, Shaw, Farningham, McGlashan, McWalter (English), Irons.
Rangers: Goram; Stevens (Ferguson), Robertson D, Gough, Spackman, Nisbet, McCall, Spencer, Johnston, Durrant (McCoist), Huistra.

QUARTER-FINALS

3 SEPT

Airdrieonians (0) 0
Celtic (0) 0 *aet*   10,200
Airdrieonians: Martin; Kidd, Stewart, Sandison, Watson, Honor, Lawrence, Balfour, Coyle (Kirkwood), Conn (Jack), Boyle.
Celtic: Bonner; Morris, Rogan, Galloway, Whyte, Wdowczyk, Miller, Fulton (O'Neil), Nicholas (Creaney), Cascarino, Collins.
(Airdrieonians won 4-2 on penalties)

Ayr U (0) 0
Hibernian (1) 2 *(McGinlay, Wright)*   8730
Ayr U: Duncan; Burley, Agnew, Furphy, Auld, McLean, Smith, Bryce, Graham, George, Shaw (Walker).
Hibernian: Burridge; Miller, Mitchell, Hunter, McIntyre, MacLeod (Orr), Weir (Evans), Hamilton, Wright, McGraw, McGinlay.

Dunfermline Ath (2) 3 *(O'Boyle, Robertson, Kozma)*
Dundee U (0) 1 *(Paatelainen)*   7220
Dunfermline Ath: Rhodes; Wilson, Cunnington, McCathie, Moyes, Williamson, Davies, O'Boyle, Leitch, Robertson (Gallagher), Kozma.
Dundee U: Main; Clark, Malpas, Bowman, Van der Hoorn, Narey, McLaren, McKinley (Ferguson), French (O'Neill M), Paatelainen, Bollan.

4 SEPT

Hearts (0) 0
Rangers (1) 1 *(McCoist)*   22,878
Hearts: Smith; Hogg, McKinlay, Levein, Mackay, McPherson, Crabbe, Ferguson D, Baird, Millar, Robertson (Penney).
Rangers: Goram; Stevens, Robertson D, Gough, Spackman, Nisbet, McCall, Ferguson, Hateley, Johnston, McCoist (Huistra).

SEMI-FINALS

24 SEPT *at Tynecastle Park*

Dunfermline Ath (0) 1 *(McWilliams [pen])*
Airdrieonians (1) 1 *(Coyle) aet*   10,662
Dunfermline Ath: Rhodes; Cunnington, Sharp (Wilson), McCathie, Moyes, Haro, McWilliams, Robertson, McParland (Davies), McCall, Leitch.
Airdrieonians: Martin; Kidd, Stewart, Sandison, Watson, Honor, Conn (Jack) (Kirkwood), Balfour, Coyle, Lawrence, Black.
(Dunfermline Ath won 3-2 on penalties)

25 SEPT *at Hampden Park*

Rangers (0) 0
Hibernian (1) 1 *(Wright)*   40,901
Rangers: Goram; Stevens, Robertson D, Brown, Spackman, Nisbet, McCall, Durrant, Hateley, Johnston, Huistra (McCoist).
Hibernian: Burridge; Miller, Mitchell, Hunter, McIntyre, MacLeod, Weir, Hamilton, Wright, McGraw (Evans), McGinlay.

FINAL

27 OCT *at Hampden Park*

Hibernian (0) 2 *(McIntyre [pen], Wright)*
Dunfermline Ath (0) 0   40,377
Hibernian: Burridge; Miller, Mitchell, Hunter, McIntyre, MacLeod, Weir, Hamilton, Wright, Evans, McGinlay.
Dunfermline Ath: Rhodes; Wilson, Sharp (Cunnington), McCathie, Moyes, Robertson, McWilliams, Kozma, Leitch, Davies, Sinclair (McCall).
Referee: B McGinlay (Balfron).

SCOTTISH CUP FINALS 1874–1992

Year	Winners	Runners-up	Score
1874	Queen's Park	Clydesdale	2-0
1875	Queen's Park	Renton	3-0
1876	Queen's Park	Third Lanark	2-0 after 1-1 draw
1877	Vale of Leven	Rangers	3-2 after 0-0 and 1-1 draws
1878	Vale of Leven	Third Lanark	1-0
1879	Vale of Leven*	Rangers	
1880	Queen's Park	Thornlibank	3-0
1881	Queen's Park†	Dumbarton	3-1
1882	Queen's Park	Dumbarton	4-1 after 2-2 draw
1883	Dumbarton	Vale of Leven	2-1 after 2-2 draw
1884	Queen's Park‡	Vale of Leven	
1885	Renton	Vale of Leven	3-1 after 0-0 draw
1886	Queen's Park	Renton	3-1
1887	Hibernian	Dumbarton	2-1
1888	Renton	Cambuslang	6-1
1889	Third Lanark§	Celtic	2-1
1890	Queen's Park	Vale of Leven	2-1 after 1-1 draw
1891	Hearts	Dumbarton	1-0
1892	Celtic¶	Queen's Park	5-1
1893	Queen's Park	Celtic	2-1
1894	Rangers	Celtic	3-1
1895	St Bernard's	Renton	2-1
1896	Hearts	Hibernian	3-1
1897	Rangers	Dumbarton	5-1
1898	Rangers	Kilmarnock	2-0
1899	Celtic	Rangers	2-0
1900	Celtic	Queen's Park	4-3
1901	Hearts	Celtic	4-3
1902	Hibernian	Celtic	1-0
1903	Rangers	Hearts	2-0 after 1-1 and 0-0 draws
1904	Celtic	Rangers	3-2
1905	Third Lanark	Rangers	3-1 after 0-0 draw
1906	Hearts	Third Lanark	1-0
1907	Celtic	Hearts	3-0
1908	Celtic	St Mirren	5-1
1909	●●		
1910	Dundee	Clyde	2-1 after 2-2 and 0-0 draws
1911	Celtic	Hamilton A	2-0 after 0-0 draw
1912	Celtic	Clyde	2-0
1913	Falkirk	Raith R	2-0
1914	Celtic	Hibernian	4-1 after 0-0 draw
1920	Kilmarnock	Albion R	3-2
1921	Partick T	Rangers	1-0
1922	Morton	Rangers	1-0
1923	Celtic	Hibernian	1-0
1924	Airdrieonians	Hibernian	2-0
1925	Celtic	Dundee	2-1
1926	St Mirren	Celtic	2-0
1927	Celtic	East Fife	3-1
1928	Rangers	Celtic	4-0
1929	Kilmarnock	Rangers	2-0
1930	Rangers	Partick T	2-1 after 0-0 draw
1931	Celtic	Motherwell	4-2 after 2-2 draw
1932	Rangers	Kilmarnock	3-0 after 1-1 draw
1933	Celtic	Motherwell	1-0
1934	Rangers	St Mirren	5-0
1935	Rangers	Hamilton A	2-1
1936	Rangers	Third Lanark	1-0
1937	Celtic	Aberdeen	2-1
1938	East Fife	Kilmarnock	4-2 after 1-1 draw
1939	Clyde	Motherwell	4-0
1947	Aberdeen	Hibernian	2-1
1948	Rangers	Morton	1-0 after 1-1 draw
1949	Rangers	Clyde	4-1
1950	Rangers	East Fife	3-0
1951	Celtic	Motherwell	1-0
1952	Motherwell	Dundee	4-0
1953	Rangers	Aberdeen	1-0 after 1-1 draw
1954	Celtic	Aberdeen	2-1
1955	Clyde	Celtic	1-0 after 1-1 draw
1956	Hearts	Celtic	3-1
1957	Falkirk	Kilmarnock	2-1 after 1-1 draw
1958	Clyde	Hibernian	1-0
1959	St Mirren	Aberdeen	3-1
1960	Rangers	Kilmarnock	2-0
1961	Dunfermline Ath	Celtic	2-0 after 0-0 draw
1962	Rangers	St Mirren	2-0
1963	Rangers	Celtic	3-0 after 1-1 draw
1964	Rangers	Dundee	3-1

Year	Winners	Runners-up	Score
1965	Celtic	Dunfermline Ath	3-2
1966	Rangers	Celtic	1-0 after 0-0 draw
1967	Celtic	Aberdeen	2-0
1968	Dunfermline Ath	Hearts	3-1
1969	Celtic	Rangers	4-0
1970	Aberdeen	Celtic	3-1
1971	Celtic	Rangers	2-1 after 1-1 draw
1972	Celtic	Hibernian	6-1
1973	Rangers	Celtic	3-2
1974	Celtic	Dundee U	3-0
1975	Celtic	Airdrieonians	3-1
1976	Rangers	Hearts	3-1
1977	Celtic	Rangers	1-0
1978	Rangers	Aberdeen	2-1
1979	Rangers	Hibernian	3-2 after 0-0 and 0-0 draws
1980	Celtic	Rangers	1-0
1981	Rangers	Dundee U	4-1 after 0-0 draw
1982	Aberdeen	Rangers	4-1 (aet)
1983	Aberdeen	Rangers	1-0 (aet)
1984	Aberdeen	Celtic	2-1 (aet)
1985	Celtic	Dundee U	2-1
1986	Aberdeen	Hearts	3-0
1987	St Mirren	Dundee U	1-0 (aet)
1988	Celtic	Dundee U	2-1
1989	Celtic	Rangers	1-0
1990	Aberdeen	Celtic	0-0 (aet)
		(Aberdeen won 9-8 on penalties)	
1991	Motherwell	Dundee U	4-3 (aet)
1992	Rangers	Airdrieonians	2-1

*Vale of Leven awarded cup, Rangers failing to appear for replay after 1-1 draw.
†After Dumbarton protested the first game, which Queen's Park won 2-1.
‡Queen's Park awarded cup, Vale of Leven failing to appear.
§Replay by order of Scottish FA because of playing conditions in first match, won 3-0 by Third Lanark.
¶After mutually protested game which Celtic won 1-0.
●●Owing to riot, the cup was withheld after two drawn games – Celtic 2-1 , Rangers 2-1.

SCOTTISH CUP WINS

Celtic 29, Rangers 25, Queen's Park 10, Aberdeen 7, Hearts 5, Clyde 3, St Mirren 3, Vale of Leven 3, Dunfermline Ath 2, Falkirk 2, Hibernian 2, Kilmarnock 2, Motherwell 2, Renton 2, Third Lanark 2, Airdrieonians 1, Dumbarton 1, Dundee 1, East Fife 1, Morton 1, Partick T 1, St Bernard's 1.

APPEARANCES IN FINAL

Celtic 46, Rangers 41, Aberdeen 13, Queen's Park 12, Hearts 10, Hibernian 10, Kilmarnock 7, Vale of Leven 7, Clyde 6, Dumbarton 6, Dundee U 6, Motherwell 6, St Mirren 6, Third Lanark 6, Renton 5, Dundee 4, Airdrieonians 3, Dunfermline Ath 3, East Fife 3, Falkirk 2, Hamilton A 2, Morton 2, Partick T 2, Albion R 1, Cambuslang 1, Clydesdale 1, Raith R 1, St Bernard's 1, Thornlibank 1.

Rangers players Iain Durrant, Gary Stevens, Steve McCall and Nigel Spackman celebrate a League and Cup double.
(Allsport)

SCOTTISH CUP 1991–92

FIRST ROUND
7 DEC

Albion R (0) 0
Arbroath (1) 2 (*Adam, McNaughton*)   264
Albion R: McLafferty; Walsh, Archer, Pryce, Anderson, Clark, Cadden, Horne, Gallagher B, McCoy (Ferguson), Moore (Green).
Arbroath: Harkness; Hamilton, Farnan, Mitchell, Boyd, Martin, Strachan, McNaughton, McKenna, Sorbie (Ray Smith), Adam (Holmes W).

Alloa (3) 7 (*Newbigging 2 (1 pen), Hendry, Moffat 2, McAvoy 2*)
Hawick Royal Albert (0) 1 (*Stavert*)   541
Alloa: Butter; Newbigging, Lee R, Romaines, McCulloch, Campbell C, Moffat, Ramsay, Smith, Hendry (Irvine), McAvoy (Gibson).
Hawick Royal Albert: Lindsay S; Page D, McDonald, Stewart, Page S, Stoddart, Halfpenny, Wallace, Scott, Brown (Waldie), Stavert (Lindsay G).

East Fife (2) 6 (*Skelligan 2, Scott, Beaton 3*)
Queen's Park (0) 0   791
East Fife: Charles; Taylor, Spence, Skelligan, Beaton, Burns, McBride, Wilson, Scott, Sludden (Herd), Hope (Brown W).
Queen's Park: Chalmers; Orr J, Stevenson, Elder, Jack, Jackson, Caven, Graham, O'Brien, Rodden (Joe McFadyen), McCormick (James McFadyen).

East Stirling (0) 0
Dumbarton (2) 2 (*McQuade, Boyd*)   339
East Stirling: Watson G; Russell, Workman, McAleer (McNally), Craig, Houston, Watson T, McKinnon, Crawford, McConville, Lytwyn (Barclay).
Dumbarton: McFarlane; Gow, Boyd, Melvin, Martin, Dempsey, McQuade, Meechan, Gibson, McConville (Wilcock), Gilmour (Hughes).

Vale of Leithen (1) 1 (*Thorpe*)
Stranraer (1) 2 (*Harkness 2*)   250
Vale of Leithen: McDermott; Taylor, McTighe, Bird, McNaughton, Lynch, Thorpe, Mitchell, Hogarth, Gray (Cormack), Selkirk (Brown).
Stranraer: Holland; McCann, Hughes, McNiven, Brannigan, Spittal, Ewing, Sloan, Harkness, Love (Cook), Henderson (Duncan).

14 DEC

Gala Fairydean (1) 2 (*Thorburn, Ainslie*)
Ross County (1) 2 (*Grant, Duff*)   650
Gala Fairydean: Ramage; Hendry, McGarry, Wilson, Anderson W, Notman, Ainslie, Collins (Knox), Thorburn, Loughran, Lothian.
Ross County: Ure; Somerville, Campbell, Williamson, Bellshaw, Robertson, Ferries, Grant (Ross), Duff, Connelly, Wilson (MacPherson).

FIRST ROUND REPLAYS

16 DEC

Ross County (3) 3 (*Connelly 2 (1 pen), Robertson*)
Gala Fairydean (0) 0   1940
Ross County: Ure; Somerville (MacPherson), Campbell, Williamson, MacLeod, Robertson, Ferries, Grant (Ross), Duff, Connelly, Wilson.
Gala Fairydean: O'Brien; Hendry, McGarry, Wilson, Anderson W, Notman, Collins, Ainslie (Knox), Thorburn, Loughran, Lothian (Smith).

SECOND ROUND
4 JAN

Alloa (0) 0
Dumbarton (0) 2 (*Gilmour (pen), Dempsey*)   1134
Alloa: Butter; Newbigging, Lee R, Romaines, McCulloch, Campbell C, Irvine, Ramsay, Smith, Hendry, McAvoy (Bennett).
Dumbarton: McFarlane; Gow, Boyd, Marsland, Martin, Melvin, Hughes, Dempsey, Gibson, McConville (Willock), Gilmour (Edgar).

Berwick R (3) 7 (*Bickmore 2, Neil 2, Graham, Lock, Todd*)
Ross County (2) 4 (*Grant, MacLeod, Wilson, Connelly*)
                                                          600
Berwick R: Neilson; Davidson, O'Donnell, Locke, Wilson, Callachan, Neil, Thorpe, Todd, Bickmore, Graham.
Ross County: Ure; Somerville, Campbell, MacLeod, Bellshaw, Robertson, Ferries, Grant, Duff, Connelly, Wilson.

Brechin C (0) 0
East Fife (0) 0   1003
Brechin C: Allan; Baillie, Gibson, Brown, McKillop, Lorimer, Lees, Hill, Ritchie, Scott (Thomson), Brand (Wardell).
East Fife: Charles; Herd, Spence, Skelligan, Beaton, Burns, McBride, McCracken, Scott, Sludden (Hope), Speirs (Hayton).

Huntly (0) 4 (*Walker K, Dunsire 2, McGinlay*)
Civil Service Strollers (2) 2 (*Lynch, Smith*)
                                                          700
Huntly: Gardiner; Walker K, Girling, Walker C, Murphy, Dunsire, De Barros, Copland, Thomson, McGinlay, Selbie.
Civil Service Strollers: Wilson; Finn, Hemmingway, Rutherford, Triplett, Todd, Davies, Burns, Smith, Chambers, Lynch.

Peterhead (1) 1 (Brown)
Cowdenbeath (0) 1 (*Fraser (og)*)   650
Peterhead: Tait; Watson, Fraser, Burke, Sievwright, Morland, Brebner, Cheyne, McKenzie, Brown, McIntosh.
Cowdenbeath: O'Hanlon; Watt, Robertson A, Irvine, Archibald, McGovern, Syme, Malone, Lamont P, Buckley, Scott.

Stenhousemuir (1) 1 (*McLafferty*)
Caledonian (0) 4 (*Hercher, Urquhart, Christie, Polwarth*)
                                                          1500
Stenhousemuir: Kelly; Aitken, Kemp, Cairney, Prior, Anderson P, Barr, Nelson, McCormick, McLafferty, Quinton (Mann).
Caledonian: McRitchie; Davidson, Mann, Hercher, Taylor, Andrew, Macdonald, Lisle, Urquhart, Christie (Mitchell), Robertson (Polwarth).

Stranraer (2) 4 (*Gallagher, Sloan 2, Harkness*)
Queen of the S (0) 1 (*Thomson A*)   1250
Stranraer: Duffy; McCann, Hughes, Duncan, Brannigan, Shirkie, Sloan, Grant, Cook, Gallagher (Ewing), Henderson (Harkness).
Queen of the S: Thomson M; Gordon, Sim, Gillespie, Hetherington, Thomson I, Templeton, Bell, Thomson A, McGuire J (McGhie), Robertson (McGuire D).

14 JAN

Clyde (1) 2 (*Wilson, Scott*)

Arbroath (0) 0   600

Clyde: Stevenson; Knox, Tennant, Clarke (Tierney), Speirs, McFarlane (Morrison), Thompson D, Wilson, McGarvey, Wylde, Scott.
Arbroath: Harkness; Hamilton, Tindal, Mitchell, Boyd, Martin, Strachan (Tosh), McNaughton, McKenna, Sorbie (Holmes W), Adam.

SECOND ROUND REPLAYS

11 JAN

Cowdenbeath (4) 6 (*Lamont P 3, Malone (pen), Archibald, Irving*)

Peterhead (0) 1 (*McKenzie*)   566

Cowdenbeath: O'Hanlon; Watt, Robertson A, Irvine, Archibald (Douglas), McGovern, Wright (Irving), Malone, Lamont P, Buckley, Scott.
Peterhead: Tait; Watson, Fraser, Burke (Loch), Sievwright, Morland, Brebner, Cheyne (Bain), McKenzie, Brown, McIntosh.

14 JAN

East Fife (1) 3 (*Brown W, Sludden, Skelligan*)

Brechin C (1) 1 (*Ritchie*)   1277

East Fife: Charles; Taylor, Spence, Herd (Skelligan), Beaton, Brown W, McBride, McCracken, Hayton, Sludden, Hope (Speirs).
Brechin C: Allan; Baillie, Gibson, Brown, McKillop, Lorimer, Lees (Paterson), Hill, Ritchie, Scott, Brand.

THIRD ROUND

22 JAN

Aberdeen (0) 0

Rangers (1) 1 (*McCoist*)   23,000

Aberdeen: Snelders; McKimmie, Winnie (Roddie), Grant, Irvine, Wright, Mason, Bett, Booth (Kane), Jess, Gillhaus.
Rangers: Goram; Stevens, Robertson D, Gough, Spackman, Brown, Gordon, McCall, McCoist, Ferguson, (Huistra), Mikhailichenko.

25 JAN

Airdrieonians (0) 2 (*Smith, Boyle*)

Stranraer (0) 1 (*Sloan*)   3000

Airdrieonians: Martin; Kidd, Stewart, Sandison, Honor, Black, Boyle, Balfour (Smith A), Lawrence, Coyle, Kirkwood.
Stranraer: Duffy; Hughes, McDowall, McCann, Brannigan, Spittal, Sloan, Duncan, Grant, Gallagher (Cook), Henderson.

Ayr U (0) 1 (*George*)

Motherwell (0) 1 (*Martin*)   7894

Ayr U: Purdie; Burley, Agnew, Furphy, Howard, Kennedy (Shaw), Traynor, Bryce, Graham, Walker, George.
Motherwell: Thomson; Nijholt, McKinnon, Dolan, Philliben, Martin, Arnott (Ferguson), Angus, Kirk, O'Donnell, Cooper.

Caledonian (1) 3 (*Christie, Urquhart, Hercher*)

Clyde (1) 1 (*Morrison*)   3500

Caldonian: McRitchie; Davidson, Mann, Hercher, Taylor, Andrew, Mitchell, Lisle, Urquhart (Macdonald), Christie, Robertson (Polwarth).
Clyde: Stevenson; Knox, Tennant, Wilson, Speirs, Wylde, Thompson D, Morrison (Mallan), McGarvey, Burke, McIver (Thomson J).

Celtic (3) 6 (*Creaney 3, Coyne 3*)

Montrose (0) 0   18,579

Celtic: Marshall; Morris, Wdowczyk (Cascarino), O'Neil, Whyte, Gillespie (Galloway), Miller, McStay, Coyne, Creaney, Collins.
Montrose: Larter; Chalmers, Fleming (Allan), Robertson, McCarron, Dornan, Maver, Morrison, Fotheringham (Mackay), Craib, Den Dieman.

Clydebank (1) 3 (*Harvey, Eadie, Henry*)

Cowdenbeath (1) 1 (*Malone*)   1019

Clydebank: Spence; Rowe, Duncanson, Maher, McIntosh, Wright, Harvey, Lansdowne, Eadie, Henry, Kelly (John Dickson).
Cowdenbeath: O'Hanlon; Watt, Robertson A, Fraser, Archibald, McGovern, Wright, Malone, Lamont P, Buckley, Syme (Ferguson).

Dumbarton (0) 0

Huntly (0) 2 (*McGinlay 2*)   1755

Dumbarton: McFarlane; Gow, Boyd, Marsland, Martin, Melvin, Meechan, Dempsey, Gibson, Cowell (Edgar), Gilmour.
Huntly: Gardiner; Walker K, Girling, Walker C, Murphy, Dunsire, De Barros, Copland (Stewart), Thomson (Barbour), McGinlay, Selbie.

Forfar Ath (0) 0

Dunfermline Ath (0) 0   2100

Forfar Ath: Thomson; MacKinnon, Winter (Paton), Brazil, Holt, Morris, Pryde, McKenna, Petrie, McAulay, Whyte.
Dunfermline Ath: Rhodes; Shannon, Cunnington, McCathie, Moyes, Robertson (Davies), McWilliams, Kozma, French, Leitch, Sinclair (McParland).

Hamilton A (0) 0

Falkirk (0) 1 (*Sloan*)   4261

Hamilton A: McCulloch; McKee (Smith), Miller, Millen, Weir, Hillcoat, Napier, Reid (McCluskey), Clark, McGuigan, McDonald.
Falkirk: Westwater; Oliver, McQueen, Hughes, Godfrey, Duffy, McAllister, Taylor, Cadette (McGivern), Sloan, Cody (Mooney).

Hibernian (1) 2 (*Wright 2 (1 pen)*)

Partick T (0) 0   11,988

Hibernian: Burridge; Miller, Mitchell, Tortolano, Beaumont, Hunter, Weir, Hamilton, Wright, Evans, McGinlay.
Partick T: Murdoch; Murray, McLaughlin, Duffy, Rae, Irons, Shaw, Farningham, Flood (McGlashan), Robertson, Law.

Meadowbank T (0) 1 (*Williamson*)

Kilmarnock (0) 1 (*Mitchell*)   2301

Meadowbank T: McQueen; Nicol, Armstrong, Williamson, Grant, Roseburgh, Coughlin, Banks, Little, Christie, Kane.
Kilmarnock: Graham; MacPherson, Black, Montgomerie, Tait, Burns T, Mitchell, Burns H, Williamson, Campbell, Elliott (McSkimming).

Morton (1) 4 (*Mathie 2 (1 pen), Rafferty, Alexander*)

East Fife (2) 2 (*Beaton, Sludden*)   2476

Morton: Wylie; Collins, Pickering, Rafferty, Doak, Johnstone, Mathie, McArthur, Alexander, McInnes (Brown), Tolmie.
East Fife: Charles; Taylor, Spence, Wilson (Herd), Beaton, Brown W, McBride, McCracken, Scott, Sludden, Hope.

Raith R (0) 0
St Johnstone (0) 2 (*Wright, Moore*)   7166
Raith R: Arthur; McStay, MacLeod (Strang), Coyle, Dennis, Raeside (Williamson), Nicholl, Dalziel, MacKenzie, Brewster, Hetherston.
St Johnstone: Hamilton; McGinnis, Deas, Cherry, Inglis, Davies (Stewart), Moore (Grant), Turner, Wright, Arkins, Curran.

St Mirren (0) 0
Hearts (0) 0   8952
St Mirren: Money; McGowne, Beattie, Aitken, McDowall (Lambert), Manley, McIntyre, Broddle, Torfason, Charnley, Elliot (Stickroth).
Hearts: Smith; McLaren, McKinlay, Levein, Wright, McPherson, Crabbe, Ferguson D, Baird, Millar, Robertson (Ferguson I).

26 JAN
Dundee U (4) 6 (*Malpas, Ferguson 2, Ferreyra, O'Neil J, Garner (og)*)
Berwick R (0) 0   6207
Dundee U: Van der Kamp; Clark, Malpas, Bowman, Van der Hoorn, McInally, O'Neil J, Jackson (Bollan), Ferreyra, Ferguson (Connolly), Paatelainen.
Berwick R: Neilson; Cass, O'Donnell, Davidson, Garner, Leitch (Graham), Callachan (McGovern), Thorpe, Todd, Neil, Bickmore.

3 FEB
Dundee (0) 1 (*Dinnie*)
Stirling Albion (0) 1 (*Reilly*)   3851
Dundee: Mathers; McQuillan, Dinnie, Chisholm, Forsyth, McLeod (Bremner), Frail (McMartin), Craig, Gallagher, Dodds, McCall.
Stirling Albion: McGeown; Mitchell, Hay, Shanks (Pew), Lawrie, Kerr, Reilly (Moore), McInnes, Watters, Robertson, Armstrong.

THIRD ROUND REPLAYS
4 FEB
Kilmarnock (0) 1 (*Burns T*)
Meadowbank T (1) 1 (*Little*)   4680
Kilmarnock: Geddes; MacPherson, Black, Montgomerie, Tait, Burns T, Mitchell, Burns H, Williamson (Roberts), Campbell, Callaghan (McStay).
Meadowbank T: McQueen; Nicol, Armstrong, Williamson, Grant, Roseburgh, Coughlin, Little, Perry (McNeill), Christie, Kane (Irvine).
aet; Meadowbank T won 4-3 on penalties.

Motherwell (4) 4 (*Nijholt (pen), Arnott, Kirk, Ferguson*)
Ayr U (0) 1 (*Graham*)   6507
Motherwell: Thomson; Nijholt, McKinnon, Dolan, Philliben, Angus, Arnott, Kirk (Simpson), Ferguson, O'Donnell, Cooper (Gardner).
Ayr U: Purdie; Burley, Agnew, Furphy, Howard (Weir), Kennedy, Traynor, Bryce, Graham, Smith (Shaw), George.

5 FEB
Dunfermline Ath (0) 3 (*Cunnington, French, McParland*)
Forfar Ath (0) 1 (*Brazil*)   3113
Dunfermline Ath: Rhodes; Bowes, Sharp (Sinclair), McCathie, Moyes, Cooper, Davies, Shannon, French, McParland (Laing), Cunnington.
Forfar Ath: Thomson; MacKinnon, Morris, Brazil, Holt, Hamill, Pryde, McKenna (Winter), Petrie, Paton, Whyte (Price).

Hearts (0) 3 (*Robertson 3 (1 pen)*)
St Mirren (0) 0   12,130
Hearts: Smith; McLaren, McKinlay, Levein, Wright, McPherson, Ferguson I, Ferguson D (Crabbe), Baird (Bannon), Millar, Robertson.
St Mirren: Fridge; McGowne, Beattie, Aitken, McDowall, Manley (Elliott), McIntyre (Stickroth), Lambert, Torfason, Charnley, Broddle.

Stirling Albion (0) 0 *at McDiarmid Park*
Dundee (1) 1 (*McMartin*)   3418
Stirling Albion: McGeown; Mitchell, Hay, Shanks (Moore), Lawrie, Kerr, Reilly (Pew), McInnes, Watters, Robertson, Armstrong.
Dundee: Mathers; McQuillan, Dinnie, Chisholm, Forsyth, Fraser, McMartin, Craig, Gallagher, Dodds, McCall.

FOURTH ROUND
11 FEB
Celtic (1) 2 (*Creaney, Coyne*)
Dundee U (1) 1 (*Paatelainen*)   26,224
Celtic: Marshall; Morris, Galloway, O'Neil, Whyte, Gillespie (Fulton), Miller, McStay, Coyne, Creaney (Nicholas), Collins.
Dundee U: Van der Kamp; Clark, Malpas, Bowman, Van der Hoorn, O'Neil J (McKinnon), McInally, Cleland, Jackson (Ferreyra), Ferguson, Paatelainen.

15 FEB
Caledonian (0) 2 (*Hercher (pen), Polwarth*)
St Johnstone (1) 2 (*Moore 2*)   5500
Caledonian: McRitchie; Mann, McAllister, Hercher, Taylor, Andrew, Mitchell (Macdonald), Lisle, Urquhart (Polwarth), Christie, Robertson.
St Johnstone: Hamilton; McGinnis, Deas, Cherry, Inglis, Davies, Moore (Maskrey), Turner (Treanor), Wright, Arkins, Curran.

Clydebank (0) 1 (*Eadie*)
Hibernian (2) 5 (*McGinlay, Weir, McIntyre, Wright, Evans*)   7350
Clydebank: Gallacher; Rowe (Kelly), Crawford, Maher, Goldie (Smith), McIntosh, Harvey, Wright, Eadie, Henry, King.
Hibernian: Burridge; Orr, Mitchell, Hunter, McIntyre, MacLeod, Weir, Hamilton, Wright, Evans, McGinlay.

Dunfermline Ath (1) 1 (*Davies*)
Hearts (1) 2 (*Hogg, Crabbe*)   12,822
Dunfermline Ath: Rhodes; Bowes, Williamson, McCathie, Moyes, Cooper, Davies, Shannon, French, McParland (Leitch), Cunnington (McWilliams).
Hearts: Smith; McLaren, McKinlay, Hogg, Mackay (Wright), McPherson, Ferguson I, Ferguson D, Bannon (Crabbe), Millar, Robertson.

Falkirk (0) 0
Dundee (0) 0   7517
Falkirk: Westwater; Oliver, McQueen, Baptie, Godfrey (May), Duffy, McAllister, Taylor, Cadette, Sloan (McGivern), Smith.
Dundee: Leighton; McQuillan, Dinnie, Chisholm, Jamieson, Forsyth, McMartin, McCall, Gallagher, Dodds, Beedie (Craig).

Huntly (0) 1 (*Dunsire*)
Airdrieonians (0) 3 (*Smith 3*)   3300
Huntly: Gardiner; Walker K, Girling, Walker C, Murphy, Dunsire, De Barros (Stewart), Copland, Thomson, McGinlay, Selbie (Barbour).
Airdrieonians: Martin; Jack, Stewart, Honor, Caesar, Black, Boyle, Balfour, Smith, Coyle, Lawrence (Kirkwood).

Morton (1) 2 (*McArthur, Alexander*)
Meadowbank T (0) 2 (*Perry, Little*) 2755
Morton: Wylie; Collins, Pickering, Rafferty, Doak, Boag, Mathie, McArthur, Alexander, McInnes (Brown), Gahagan (Lilley).
Meadowbank T: McQueen; Nicol, Armstrong, Sprott (McNeill), Coughlin, Roseburgh, Perry, Banks, Little (Grant), Christie, Kane.

Rangers (0) 2 (*Mikhailichenko 2*)
Motherwell (1) 1 (*O'Donnell*) 38,444
Rangers: Goram; Stevens, Robertson D, Gough, Spackman, Brown, Gordon (McSwegan), Ferguson, McCoist, Rideout, Mikhailichenko.
Motherwell: Thomson; Nijholt, McKinnon, Simpson (Dolan), Jones, Martin, Arnott, Angus, Kirk (Ferguson), O'Donnell, Cooper.

FOURTH ROUND REPLAYS

24 FEB

Dundee (0) 0
Falkirk (0) 1 (*Sloan*) 7722
Dundee: Leighton; McQuillan, Dinnie (McLeod), Chisholm, Jamieson (Craig), Forsyth, Beedie, McMartin, Gallagher, Dodds, McCall.
Falkirk: Westwater; Oliver, McQueen (Johnston), May, Baptie, Duffy, McAllister, Taylor, McGivern, Sloan, Smith.

26 FEB

Meadowbank T (2) 2 (*Roseburgh, Perry*)
Morton (0) 3 (*Mathie (pen), Hopkin, Alexander*) 1642
Meadowbank T: McQueen; Nicol, Armstrong, Williamson, Coughlin, Roseburgh, Perry, Banks, Little, McNeill (Grant), Kane.
Morton: Wylie; Collins, Pickering (McArthur), Rafferty, Doak, Boag, Mathie, Brown, Alexander, Hopkin (Lilley), Tolmie.

St Johnstone (1) 3 (*McGinnis, Wright 2*)
Caledonian (0) 0 9693
St Johnstone: Hamilton; Traynor, Deas, Stewart, Inglis, McGinnis, Moore, Turner (Maskrey), Wright, Grant, Curran (Davies).
Caledonian: McRitchie; Davidson, McAllister, Hercher, Taylor, Mann, Mitchell, Lisle, Urquhart (Macdonald), Christie, Robertson (Polwarth).

QUARTER-FINALS

3 MAR

St Johnstone (0) 0
Rangers (2) 3 (*McCoist, Gough, Hateley*) 10,107
St Johnstone: Hamilton; Treanor (Stewart), Deas, McGinnis, Inglis, Dunne, Moore, Turner, Wright, Arkins (Grant), Curran.
Rangers: Goram; Stevens, Robertson D, Gough, Spackman, Brown, Gordon, Ferguson, McCoist, Hateley, Huistra.

7 MAR

Celtic (2) 3 (*Creaney 2, Collins*)
Morton (0) 0 28,016
Celtic: Marshall; Morris, Boyd, Fulton, Mowbray, Whyte, Miller (Galloway), McStay, Coyne, Creaney (Nicholas), Collins.
Morton: Wylie; Collins, Ogg, Rafferty, Doak, Johnstone, Mathie, McArthur, Alexander, Hopkin (Brown), Tolmie (Lilley).

Hibernian (0) 0
Airdrieonians (0) 2 (*Coyle, Conn*) 11,000
Hibernian: Burridge; Miller, Mitchell, Hunter, McIntyre, MacLeod, Weir (Findlay) (Orr), Hamilton, Wright, Evans, McGinlay.
Airdrieonians: Martin; Kidd, Stewart, Sandison, Honor, Black, Boyle, Balfour, Lawrence (Coyle), Conn, Jack (Kirkwood).

8 MAR

Hearts (2) 3 (*Ferguson I, Robertson, Mackay*)
Falkirk (1) 1 (*McGivern*) 11,227
Hearts: Smith; McLaren, McKinlay, Wright, Mackay, McPherson, Ferguson I, Ferguson D, Bannon, Millar, Robertson.
Falkirk: Westwater; Duffy, Oliver, Hughes, Baptie, May, McAllister, Taylor (Johnston), McGivern (Cadette), Sloan, Smith.

SEMI-FINALS

31 MAR *at Hampden Park*

Celtic (0) 0
Rangers (1) 1 (*McCoist*) 45,191
Celtic: Marshall; Morris, Boyd, O'Neil (Galloway), Mowbray, Whyte, Miller, McStay, Creaney, Nicholas (Coyne), Collins.
Rangers: Goram; Stevens, Robertson D, Gough, Spackman, Brown, Gordon (Rideout), McCall, McCoist, Durrant, Huistra.

4 APR *at Hampden Park*

Airdrieonians (0) 0
Hearts (0) 0 27,310
Airdrieonians: Martin; Kidd, Stewart, Sandison, Honor, Black, Boyle, Balfour, Coyle, Lawrence (Jack), Kirkwood (Conn).
Hearts: Smith; McLaren, McKinlay, Levein, Mackay, McPherson, Bannon (Crabbe), Ferguson D, Ferguson I, Wright, Robertson.

SEMI-FINAL REPLAY

14 APR *at Hampden Park*

Airdrieonians (1) 1 (*Black*)
Hearts (0) 1 (*McLaren*) 11,163
Airdrieonians: Martin; Kidd, Stewart, Sandison, Honor, Black, Boyle, Balfour, Lawrence (Caesar), Coyle, Kirkwood (Conn).
Hearts: Smith; McLaren, Snodin, Levein, Bannon (Wright), McPherson, Crabbe, Ferguson D, Ferguson I, Wright, Robertson.
aet; Airdrieonians won 4-2 on penalties.

FINAL

9 MAY *at Hampden Park*

Rangers (2) 2 (*Hateley, McCoist*)
Airdrieonians (0) 1 (*Smith*) 44,045
Rangers: Goram; Stevens, Robertson D, Gough, Spackman, Brown, Durrant (Gordon), McCall, McCoist, Hateley, Mikhailichenko.
Airdrieonians: Martin; Kidd, Stewart, Honor, Caesar, Jack, Boyle, Balfour, Lawrence (Smith), Coyle, Kirkwood (Reid).
Referee: D. Hope (Linburn).

B & Q CUP 1991-92

FIRST ROUND

1 OCT

Berwick R (2) 3 *(Ross 2, Todd)*
East Stirling (1) 2 *(McKinnon, Ross)*   215
Berwick R: Egan; Davidson, Leitch, Garner, Wilson, McGovern, Scally, Thorpe, Ross, Todd (Cass), Callachan.
East Stirling: Watson G; Kennedy, McAleer, Rooney, Craig, Ross, Thomson (Barclay), McKinnon, Diver, McConville, Lytwyn.

Brechin C (1) 2 *(Ritchie 2)*   350
Albion R (0) 4 *(Archer, Troup, Ferguson, Henderson)*
Brechin C: Allan; Conway, Paterson (Brand), Brown, McKillop, Nicolson, Thomson N (Hutt), Lees, Ritchie, Scott, Thomson S.
Albion R: Connelly; Pryce (Cadden), Cousin, Archer, McTeague, Clark, Ferguson, Miller J, Henderson, Troup, Moore.

Clydebank (2) 4 *(McIntosh, Henry, Eadie, John Dickson)*
Clyde (0) 0   577
Clydebank: Spence; Traynor, Crawford, Maher, McIntosh, Wright, Harvey, John Dickson, Eadie, Henry, Mair.
Clyde: Ross; Knox, Tennant, Clarke, Speirs, McFarlane, Thompson D, Wilson, MacIver, Wylde (Morrison), Scott.

Cowdenbeath (2) 2 *(Fraser, Robertson)*
Partick T (1) 3 *(Shaw, Rae, McGlashan) aet*   833
Cowdenbeath: Lamont W; Watt (Buckley), Robertson A, Fraser, Archibald, Irvine, Wright, Malone, Lamont P, Syme, Scott (McGovern).
Partick T: Murdoch; Robertson, Harvie, Duffy, Rae, Johnston, Shaw, Law (Bell), McGlashan, Irons, McGovern (English).

Dundee (0) 0
Ayr U (2) 2 *(Smith, Fraser)*   2058
Dundee: Carson; Dinnie, Campbell S, Chisholm, McQuillan, Fraser, Craib, Craig (McLeod), Campbell D, Dodds, McMartin.
Ayr U: Purdie; Kennedy, Agnew, Furphy, Auld, McLean, Fraser, Bryce, Graham, George, Smith (Shaw).

Forfar Ath (2) 2 *(Whyte 2)*
Stranraer (2) 2 *(Gallagher, Cook) aet*   328
Forfar Ath: Thomson; MacKinnon, Hamill, Hegarty, Adam, Morris, Pryde (Paterson), Holt, Whyte, McPhee, Petrie.
Stranraer: Duffy; McCann (Harkness), Hughes, Spittal, Gallagher, Duncan, Sloan, Grant, Cook, Love, Henderson.
(Stranraer won 7-6 on penalties)

Hamilton A (3) 5 *(Smith 2, McCluskey, Napier 2)*
Alloa (1) 1 *(Henry)*   805
Hamilton A: Ferguson; McKee, Miller, Millen, Weir, Napier, Harris, Reid (Hillcoat), McCluskey (McAnenay), Smith, McDonald.
Alloa: Butter; Newbigging, Lee R, Wilcox, McCulloch, Campbell, Henry (Irvine), Romaines, Black, McAvoy (Bennett), Moffat.

Montrose (1) 2 *(Den Bieman, Rougvie)*
Dumbarton (0) 1 *(Gibson)*   456
Montrose: Larter; Morrison, Fleming, Robertson (McKenzie), Rougvie, Dornan, Maver, Mackay, Wolecki (Allan), King, Den Bieman.
Dumbarton: McFarlane; Marsland, Boyd, Melvin, Martin (Gow), McCracken, McGarvey (Edgar), Dempsey, Gibson, McConville, Willock.

Stenhousemuir (2) 3 *(Bainbridge, Conroy, Speirs)*
Arbroath (1) 2 *(Hunter, Holmes W)*   300
Stenhousemuir: Barnstaple; Cairney, Hallford, Anderson, Tracey, Quinton, Bainbridge, Wilson (Donald), McCormick, Girasoli (Speirs), Conroy.
Arbroath: Balfour; Hamilton, Farnan, Mitchell, Carlin, Martin, Tosh (Joyce), Holmes W, McKenna, Sorbie, Hunter (Morton).

2 OCT

Meadowbank T (0) 1 *(Logan)*
East Fife (1) 2 *(Wilson, Sludden)*   357
Meadowbank T: McQueen; Nicol, Armstrong, Williamson, Grant (Boyd), Coughlin, Logan, Young, McNeill, Irvine (Ryrie), Banks.
East Fife: Charles; Bell, Spence (Taylor PH), Wilson, Beaton, Burns, McBride, Prior, Brown W, Sludden, Allan (Hayton).

SECOND ROUND

15 OCT

Clydebank (1) 1 *(John Dickson)*
Raith R (1) 1 *(Dalziel) aet*   350
Clydebank: Spence; Traynor, Crawford, Maher, McIntosh, Wright, Harvey, Kelly, John Dickson (Sermanni), Henry, Rowe (King).
Raith R: Arthur; McStay, MacLeod, Coyle, Raeside, Young (Dunleavy), Burn, Dalziel, Strang, Brewster, Nelson.
(Raith R won 4-3 on penalties)

Montrose (1) 2 *(Maver, Kerr)*
Albion R (0) 1 *(Cadden)*   463
Montrose: Larter; Morrison, Fleming, Robertson, Rougvie, Dornan (Kerr), Maver, Allan (Fotheringham), McGachie, King, Den Bieman.
Albion R: Connelly; Walsh, McKeown, Easton, McTeague, Clark, Archer, Cadden, Henderson (Pryce), Miller J (Troup), Moore.

Morton (1) 2 *(Mathie, McArthur)*
Kilmarnock (1) 1 *(Burns H) aet*   2864
Morton: Wylie; Collins, Ogg, Rafferty, Doak, Kelly, Mathie, McArthur, Alexander (McDonald), McInnes (Pickering), Lilley.
Kilmarnock: Geddes; MacPherson, McSkimming, Tait, Flexney, Callaghan (Reilly), Mitchell, Burns H (Porteous), Williamson, Burns T, Campbell.

Partick T (0) 1 *(McGlashan)*
Hamilton A (1) 2 *(Reid, McCluskey)*   3000
Partick T: Murdoch; Law, McLaughlin, Farningham, Tierney, Kennedy, Shaw, Johnston, McGlashan, Bell, Irons.
Hamilton A: Ferguson; McKee, Miller, Millen, Weir, McKenzie (Cramb), Harris, Reid, McCluskey, Smith, Stark.

Queen of the S (2) 3 *(Thomson A 2, Mitchell [og])*
Stirling Albion (1) 3 *(Reilly, Watters, Moore) aet* 969
Queen of the S: Davidson; Gordon, McFarlane, Thomson I, McGhie, McGuire D (Fraser), Templeton, Bell, Thomson A, McGuire J, Robertson.
Stirling Albion: McGeown; Mitchell, Watson, Shanks (Conway), Lawrie, Kerr, McInnes, Moore, Watters, Reilly (Docherty A), Docherty R.
(Queen of the S won 5-4 on penalties)

Queen's Park (0) 1 *(O'Brien)*
East Fife (0) 2 *(Hayton, Scott) aet*   600
Queen's Park: Chalmers; Mackay, Stevenson, Elder, Jack, McEntegart, Jackson, O'Brien, McCormick, Mackenzie, Joe McFadyen (O'Neill).
East Fife: Charles; Smith, Spence, Cowell (Wilson), Beaton, Burns, McBride, Prior, Scott, Sludden, Hope (Hayton).

Stenhousemuir (0) 0
Ayr U (1) 2 *(McLean, Graham)*   800
Stenhousemuir: Barnstaple; Clouston, Hallford, Cairney (Bainbridge), Tracey, Anderson, Wilson, Quinton, McCormick, Donald (Speirs), Conroy.
Ayr U: Duncan; Kennedy, Agnew, Furphy, Auld, Hood, McLean, Bryce (Fraser), Graham, George, Smith.

Stranraer (2) 3 *(Harkness, McCann, Henderson)*
Berwick R (1) 1 *(Thorpe)*   450
Stranraer: Duffy; Hughes, Love, McCann, Shirkie, Duncan, McNiven (Cook), Sloan, Harkness (Grant), Ewing, Henderson.
Berwick R: Neilson; McLaren, McGovern (Callachan), Wilson, Cass, Leitch, Scally (Locke), Thorpe, Todd, Ross, Neil.

QUARTER-FINALS

22 OCT

Ayr U (0) 2 *(Auld, Shaw)*
Stranraer (0) 0   2935
Ayr U: Duncan; Kennedy, Agnew, Furphy, Auld, McLean (Fraser), Gardner, Bryce (Smith), Graham, George, Shaw.
Stranraer: Duffy; Hughes, Love, McNiven, Shirkie, McCann, Grant, Duncan, Harkness (Cook), Ewing, Henderson (Walker).

East Fife (1) 2 *(Sludden, Spence)*
Hamilton A (1) 3 *(Smith, McCluskey, Millen)*   1108
East Fife: Charles; Smith, Spence, Wilson, Beaton, Burns (Taylor PH), McBride, Prior, Hayton, Sludden, Hope (Scott).
Hamilton A: Ferguson; McKee, Miller, Millen, Weir, McKenzie, Harris, Reid (McGuigan), McCluskey (Cramb), Smith, Stark.

Montrose (1) 4 *(King 3, McGachie)*
Queen of the S (1) 7 *(Thomson A 2, McGuire J 4, Robertson) aet*   670
Montrose: Larter; Morrison, King, Robertson, Thomson, Dornan, Maver, Allan (Fotheringham), McGachie, Kerr (Chalmers), Den Bieman.
Queen of the S: Davidson; Gordon, McFarlane (Leslie), Sim, McGhie, Thomson I, Templeton, Bell, Thomson A, McGuire J, Robertson.

Morton (1) 2 *(Mathie, Doak)*
Raith R (1) 3 *(Dalziel 3)*   1676
Morton: Wylie; Collins, Ogg (Lilley), Rafferty, Doak, Boag, Mathie, McArthur, Pickering, McInnes, Deeney.
Raith R: Arthur; McStay, MacLeod, Coyle, Dennis, Raeside, Dunleavy, Dalziel, Hetherston (Young), Brewster, Burn (Strang).

SEMI-FINALS

5 NOV

Ayr U (1) 3 *(Graham, Smith 2)*
Queen of the S (2) 2 *(Thomson A 2)*   4254
Ayr U: Duncan; Hood, Agnew, Furphy, Auld, George, Gardner (Smith), Bryce, Graham, Shaw (Brown), Fraser.
Queen of the S: Davidson; Gordon, McFarlane, Sim, Hetherington, Thomson I, Templeton, Bell, Thomson A, McGuire J (Fraser), Robertson.

Hamilton A (0) 2 *(Miller, Weir)*
Raith R (0) 1 *(Dalziel [pen])*   2306
Hamilton A: Monaghan; McKee, Miller, Millen, Weir, McKenzie (McCluskey), Harris, Reid, Clark, Smith, McGuigan (Stark).
Raith R: Arthur; McStay, MacLeod, Coyle, Dennis, Raeside, Sinclair, Dalziel, Hetherston (Strang), Brewster, Burn (Young).

FINAL

8 DEC *at Fir Park*

Hamilton A (1) 1 *(Harris)*
Ayr U (0) 0   9633
Hamilton A: McCulloch; McKee, Millen, Weir, Miller, Reid, Clark, McKenzie, Harris, McCluskey, McDonald.
Ayr U: Purdie; Kennedy, Furphy, Howard, Agnew, Gardner (Shaw), McLean, Smith, Bryce, Graham, Walker.
Referee: L. Mottram (Perth).

WELSH FOOTBALL 1991–92

THE ABACUS LEAGUE

National Division

	P	W	D	L	F	A	Pts
Abergavenny Thursdays	30	23	5	2	64	24	74
Briton Ferry Athletic	30	23	1	6	76	43	70
Aberystwyth Town	30	18	6	6	65	35	60
Haverfordwest County	30	16	7	7	61	41	55
Ton Pentre	30	16	6	8	51	53	54
Maesteg Park Athletic	30	15	6	9	57	37	51
Cwmbran Town	30	11	12	7	50	42	45
Afan Lido	30	12	7	11	54	47	43
Pembroke	30	10	7	13	50	48	37
Llanelli	30	9	6	15	43	61	33
Ebbw Vale	30	8	8	14	38	61	32
Inter Cardiff	30	7	8	15	32	45	29
Caldicot	30	6	6	18	36	60	24
Brecon Corries	30	6	5	19	36	61	23
Bridgend Town	30	4	8	18	35	58	20
Ferndale Athletic	30	4	6	20	31	63	18

Division One

	P	W	D	L	F	A	Pts
Blaenrhondda	32	18	8	6	76	47	62
Morriston Town	32	18	3	11	58	47	57
Ammanford Town	32	16	9	7	55	35	57
Port Talbot	32	15	9	8	57	41	54
Caerleon	32	15	8	9	58	34	53
Pontypridd/Ynys	32	15	4	13	57	53	49
Aberaman	32	14	6	12	52	48	48
Cardiff Civil Service	32	13	9	10	51	48	48
Taffs Well	32	13	7	12	42	41	46
Risca United	32	12	6	14	51	52	42
Llanwern	32	10	9	13	44	44	39
BP	32	11	5	16	47	54	38
Newport YMCA	32	11	5	16	41	54	38
Cardiff Corries	32	9	9	14	54	60	36
Pontllanfraith	32	8	10	14	38	57	34
Seven Sisters	32	8	7	17	37	62	31
Garw	32	5	8	19	30	73	23

Division Two

	P	W	D	L	F	A	Pts
AFC Porth	32	28	3	1	79	20	87
Carmarthen	32	22	6	4	61	19	72
Skewen	32	18	7	7	51	33	61
Tonyrefail	32	16	8	8	54	36	56
Caerau	32	16	8	8	52	39	56
South Wales Police	32	15	8	9	54	39	53
Pontyclun	32	13	9	10	51	39	48
Treharris	32	12	7	13	51	54	43
Pontardawe	32	12	5	15	43	52	41
Pontlottyn	32	10	9	13	42	42	39
Goytre United	32	10	8	14	44	47	38
Milford United	32	11	5	16	48	68	38
Panteg	32	8	5	19	37	63	29
Cardiff Institute	32	7	7	18	41	67	28
AFC Tondu	32	5	9	18	39	61	24
Abercynon	32	6	6	20	38	69	24
Trelewis	32	4	8	20	26	65	20

Abacus Youth Trophy: Cwmbran Town 1, Afan Lido 0.

MANWEB CYMRU ALLIANCE

	P	W	D	L	F	A	Pts
Caersws	30	15	10	5	65	27	55
Llansantffraid	30	15	8	7	58	34	53
Porthmadog	30	14	10	6	63	43	52
Flint Town United	30	14	9	7	58	37	51
Conwy United	30	15	5	10	62	45	50
Connah's Quay Nomads	30	11	12	7	41	33	45
Mostyn	30	13	6	11	52	56	45
Lex	30	11	10	9	44	52	43
Penrhyncoch	30	11	7	12	53	51	40
Mold Alexandra*	30	12	3	15	40	47	36

	P	W	D	L	F	A	Pts
Holywell Town	30	7	10	13	48	49	31
Llanidloes Town	30	8	7	15	37	57	31
Gresford Athletic	30	8	6	16	34	55	30
Carno	30	5	2	23	29	69	17
Brymbo	30	4	2	24	29	108	14
Welshpool Town**	30	20	7	3	74	23	1

* 3 points deducted.
** 66 points deducted.
League Cup: Lex XI 3, Flint Town United 2 (aet), at Brymbo.

RICHARDS THE BUILDERS MID-WALES LEAGUE

	P	W	D	L	F	A	Pts
Knighton Town	30	20	9	1	66	21	69
Morda	30	21	5	4	110	28	68
Caersws	30	18	8	4	72	22	62
Berriew	30	17	8	5	53	25	59
Aberystwyth Town	30	18	3	9	68	44	57
Talgarth	30	15	6	9	65	40	51
Newtown	30	14	9	7	59	34	51
Builth Wells	30	12	8	10	57	38	44
Rhayader Town	30	13	4	13	76	62	43
Penparcau	30	12	6	12	53	59	42
Llandrindod Wells	30	11	8	11	51	45	41
Kington	30	8	3	19	42	68	27
UCW	30	6	2	22	39	85	20
Crickhowell	30	4	8	18	28	73	20
Llanidloes Town	30	2	5	23	19	116	11
Clun Valley	30	1	4	25	21	113	7

SEALINK WELSH ALLIANCE

	P	W	D	L	F	A	Pts
Llangefni Town	28	21	3	4	84	27	66
Felinheli	28	20	5	3	70	35	65
Bangor City	28	18	4	6	70	37	58
Cemaes Bay	28	16	5	7	58	37	53
Llandudno	28	15	7	6	74	41	52
Llanfairpwll PG	28	12	5	11	60	51	41
Pilkingtons	28	9	8	11	40	44	35
Rhydymwyn	28	8	9	11	40	47	33
Conwy United	28	7	10	11	29	41	31
Connah's Quay Nomads*	28	9	6	13	35	51	30
Mochdre	28	7	6	15	40	54	27
L. Llanberis	28	7	5	16	29	62	26
Rhyl	28	7	3	18	28	65	24
Nantle Vale	28	5	7	16	41	58	22
Llanrwst United	28	5	5	18	26	71	20

* 3 points deducted.

READ CONSTRUCTION WELSH NATIONAL LEAGUE (WREXHAM AREA)

Premier Division

	P	W	D	L	F	A	Pts
Wrexham Reserves	26	18	2	6	63	28	56
Ruthin Town	26	17	3	6	58	29	54
Marchwiel Villa	26	17	3	6	47	29	54
New Broughton	26	16	2	8	48	32	50
Chirk AAA	26	14	5	7	46	28	47
Llay RBL	26	12	5	9	43	33	41
Llay Welfare	26	11	5	10	45	49	38
Corwen	26	10	6	10	38	40	36
Penycae	26	8	5	13	37	43	29
Rhostyllen	26	8	4	14	36	42	28
Rhos Aelwyd	26	7	6	13	36	43	27
Buckley	26	7	4	15	38	66	25
Cefn Albion	26	6	4	16	25	54	22
Druids United	26	2	4	20	19	62	10

League Cup Final: Ruthin Town 3, Rhos Aelwyd 2 (aet)

WELSH INTERMEDIATE CUP 1991–92

First Round

Bala Town v Penycae	1-0
Bethesda Athletic v Locomotive Llanberis	
(Bethesda Athletic withdrew, tie awarded to Locomotive Llanberis)	
Builth Wells v Llandrindod Wells	1-0
Cardiff Corinthians v Albion Rovers	1-4
Cardiff Inst. Higher Education v Taffs Well	2-0
Chirk AAA v Rhostyllen Villa	1-1, 3-2
Christchurch v Bryntirion Athletic	1-1, 1-4
Cilfynydd v Tredomen	2-2, 2-3
Corwen Amateurs v New Broughton	0-1
Hirwaun Welfare v Risca United	2-2, 0-3
Hoover Sports v Dinas Powys	3-0
Johnstown Athletic v Rubery Owen Rockwell	1-1, 3-4
Knighton Town v Penparcau	2-0
Llandyrnog United v Rhydymwyn	1-0
Llanfairpwll PG v Blaenau Amateurs	8-0
Llangeinor v Kenfig Hill	7-0
Llanrug United v Cemaes Bay	2-2, 0-3
Llanrwst United v Ruthin Town	0-2
Llantwit Fardre v Treharris Athletic	0-3
Llantwit Major v Pontyclun	0-0, 0-7
Llay Royal British Legion v Druids United	4-0
Llay Welfare v Cefn Albion	4-1
Maltsters Sports v Newcastle Emlyn	3-2
Mochdre v British Aerospace	2-1
Nefyn United v Nantlle Vale	3-0
Newport Corinthians v Croesyceiliog	1-3
Penley v Rhayader Town	2-0
Pilkingtons (St Asaph) v Llandudno	1-0
Pwllheli Borough v Felinheli	1-3
Ragged School v Goytre United	3-0, 2-1
Rhos Aelwyd v Buckley	2-1
Suburbs v BSC Port Talbot	8-0
Trelewis v Penrhiwceiber Rangers	2-2, 1-2

Second Round

Afan Lido v Caldicot Town	0-1
Bala Town v New Broughton	4-4, 1-3 *(aet)*
Blaenrhondda v Maltsters Sports	4-1
Brymbo v Llay Royal British Legion	2-1
Bryntirion Athletic v Albion Rovers	1-1, 0-1 *(aet)*
Builth Wells v Welshpool Town	0-2
Caersws v Brecon Corinthians	3-3, 1-0
Connah's Quay Nomads v Holywell Town	0-0, 0-1
Conwy United v Locomotive Llanberis	3-0
Croesyceiliog v Morriston Town	1-0
Gresford Athletic v Flint Town United	1-1, 1-6
Hoover Sports v Cardiff Inst. Higher Education	4-4, 4-0
Knighton Town v Carno	4-2
Llanfairpwll PG v Felinheli	1-1, 3-2 *(aet)*
Llangeinor v Suburbs	2-3
Llanidloes Town v Penrhyncoch	1-0
Llansantffraid v Morda United	2-1
Llay Welfare v Chirk AAA	1-1, 1-2

Marchwiel Villa v Llandyrnog United	3-2
Mochdre v Penley	1-1, 2-1
Nefyn United v Llangefni Town	1-3
Pilkingtons (St Asaph) v Rubery Owen Rockwell	4-0
Pontyclun v Risca United	0-3
Porthmadog v Cemaes Bay	2-1
Ragged School v Penrhiwceiber Rangers	3-3, 3-1
Rhos Aelwyd v Lex XI	1-2
Ruthin Town v Mold Alexandra	1-3
Tredomen v Treharris Athletic	0-2

Third Round

Abergavenny Thursdays v Porthcawl Town	4-2
Albion Rovers v Caersws	1-1, 0-1
Brymbo v Mostyn	2-4
Chirk AAA v Lex XI	1-1, 2-3
Croesyceiliog v Caldicot Town	1-3
Flint Town United v Pilkingtons (St Asaph)	5-1
Holywell Town v Welshpool Town	1-1, 0-4
Hoover Sports v Treharris Athletic	2-1
Llanfairpwll PG v Knighton Town	2-2, 2-1
Llangefni Town v Mochdre	2-0
Llanidloes Town v Aberystwyth Town	2-1
Llansantffraid v New Broughton	1-0
Marchwiel Villa v Conwy United	0-2
Porthmadog v Mold Alexandra	7-0
Ragged School v Blaenrhondda	1-3
Risca United v Suburbs	1-1, 1-3 *(aet/pens)*

Fourth Round

Abergavenny Thursdays v Hoover Sports	0-1
Blaenrhondda v Llanfairpwll PG	2-0
Caersws v Llanidloes Town	2-0
Conwy United v Llansantffraid	2-1
Flint Town United v Welshpool Town	2-0
Lex XI v Mostyn	4-0
Llangefni Town v Suburbs	3-0
Porthmadog v Caldicot Town	5-0

Fifth Round

Porthmadog v Hoover Sports	5-1
Caersws v Flint Town United	4-2
Lex XI v Conwy United	1-2
Blaenrhondda v Llangefni Town	0-2

Semi-finals

Conwy United v Llangefni Town	0-0, 0-1
(at Y Treaeth, Porthmadog)	
Caersws v Porthmadog	3-1
(at Penrhyncoch FC)	

Final

Caersws v Llangefni Town	1-1, 1-2
(at the Racecourse, Wrexham with the replay at Y Traeth, Porthmadog).	

ALLBRIGHT BITTER WELSH CUP 1991–92

First Round

Afan Lido v Seven Sisters	3-0
Ammanford Town v Carmarthen Town	3-4
Bala Town v New Broughton	1-1, 0-4
Bridgend Town v Ebbw Vale	1-0
Buckley v Brymbo	2-1
Cacrau v Llanwern	0-4
Caerleon v Pontlottyn Blast Furnace	2-1
Cardiff Civil Service v Cardiff Corinthians	3-0
Carno v Llansantffraid	1-2
Cefn Albion v Gresford Athletic	1-2
Cemaes Bay v Conwy United	1-0
Chirk AAA v Lex XI	1-0
Connah's Quay Nomads v Pilkingtons St Asaph	4-1
Cwmbran Town v Newport YMCA	3-2
Ferndale Athletic v Cardiff Inst. Higher Education	10-2
Haverfordwest County v BP Llandarcy	3-0
Inter Cardiff v Caldicot Town	3-3, 3-0
Kidderminster Harriers v Rhayader Town	5-1
Knighton Town v Llanidloes Town	0-0, 2-3

Llandrindod Wells v Brecon Corinthians	1-3
Llandudno v Pwllheli Borough	5-0
Llanelli v Port Talbot Athletic	1-2
Llanrwst United v Rhyl	1-2
Llay Royal British Legion v Rhos Aelwyd	1-0
Maesteg Park Athletic v Trelewis Welfare	8-0
Marchwiel Villa v Llay Welfare	0-0, 4-2
Morriston Town v Pembroke Borough	2-2, 2-1
Nefyn United v Llanfairpwll PG	1-3
Newcastle Emlyn v Stourbridge	3-5
Penrhyncoch v Builth Wells	1-0
Penycae v Johnstown Athletic	5-1
Pontllanfraith v Aberaman	3-0
Porthcawl Town v Pontardawe Athletic	6-1
Porthmadog v Locomotive Llanberis	2-1
Rhydymwyn v Holywell Town	0-2
Risca United v Abercynon Athletic	1-3
Rubery Owen Rockwell v Morda United	1-9
Ruthin Town v British Aerospace	0-1
Skewen Athletic v Briton Ferry Athletic	0-3

Taffs Well v Pontyclun	4-0
Ton Pentre v Stroud	1-0
Tonyrefail Welfare v South Wales Constabulary	3-0
Welshpool Town v Hednesford Town	0-2
(at Hednesford)	

Second Round

Bangor City v Porthmadog	3-1
Brecon Corinthians v Caersws	1-4
British Aerospace v Chirk AAA	1-2
Briton Ferry Athletic v Afan Lido	2-1
Buckley v Llay Royal British Legion	0-3
Caerleon v Ton Petre	2-1
Cardiff Civil Service v Port Talbot Athletic	1-0
Cemaes Bay v Llanfairpwll PG	3-2
Connah's Quay Nomads v Colwyn Bay	1-1, 0-6
Cwmbran Town v Taffs Well	4-1
Flint Town United v Caernarfon Town	2-2, 2-3
Gresford Athletic v Marchwiel Villa	0-2
Haverfordwest County v Abercynon	3-0
Hednesford Town v Penrhyncoch	3-1
Holywell Town v Llandudno	2-2, 3-0
(replay played at Colwyn Bay FC)	
Inter Cardiff v Ferndale Athletic	2-1
Kidderminster Harriers v Morda United	7-1
Llansantffraid v Llanidloes Town	3-1
Maesteg Park Athletic v Llanwern	4-2
Morriston Town v Tonyrefail Welfare	3-0
Mostyn v Rhyl	2-1
New Broughton v Penycae	1-0
Newport AFC v Bridgend Town	3-0
Newtown v Aberystwyth Town	1-2
Pontllanfraith v Abergavenny Thursdays	0-4
Porthcawl Town v Merthyr Tydfil	1-4
Stourbridge v Carmarthen Town	7-1

Third Round

Barry Town v Aberystwyth Town	2-3
Briton Ferry Athletic v Abergavenny Thursdays	3-2
Caersws v Cemaes Bay	1-2
Cardiff City v Newport AFC	3-0
Chirk AAA v Llay Royal British Legion	2-1
Colwyn Bay v Holywell Town	5-1
Cwmbran Town v Maesteg Park Athletic	2-5
Haverfordwest County v Morriston Town	4-1

Hednesford Town v New Broughton	3-0
Inter Cardiff v Caerleon	1-2
Kidderminster Harriers v Llansantffraid	4-1
Marchwiel Villa v Caernarfon Town	0-3
Merthyr Tydfil v Swansea City	0-2
Mostyn v Hereford United	1-3
(played at Flint Town United)	
Stourbridge v Cardiff Civil Service	0-0, 3-1
Wrexham v Bangor City	3-2

Fourth Round

Briton Ferry Athletic v Colwyn Bay	2-4
Caernarfon Town v Aberystwyth Town	0-1
Cardiff City v Stourbridge	3-3, 2-1
Cemaes Bay v Haverfordwest County	1-2
Hereford United v Maesteg Park	1-2
Kidderminster Harriers v Swansea City	1-3
Llay Royal British Legion v Hednesford Town	0-0, 0-3
Wrexham v Caerleon	2-0

Fifth Round

Haverfordwest County v Hednesford Town	0-0, 0-4
Wrexham v Colwyn Bay	0-1*, 1-3
Maesteg Park Athletic v Aberystwyth Town	2-0
Swansea City v Cardiff City	0-1

*Match abandoned due to fog after 63 minutes.

Semi-finals

Cardiff City v Maesteg Park Athletic	0-0, 4-0*
Hednesford Town v Colwyn Bay	1-0, 3-2

*2nd leg played at Ninian Park.

Final: Cardiff City 1, Hednesford Town 0
(at National Stadium, Cardiff, 7 May 1992) Att: 12,000

Cardiff City: Hansbury; Perry, Searle, Gibbins (Gill), Bellamy, Abraham, Ramsey, Griffith (Millar), Pike, Dale, Blake.
Scorer: Dale.

Hednesford Town: Hayward; White (Snaith), Collins, Freeman, Foster, Rudge, Turley (Brown), Walsh, Knight, Burr, O'Connor.

Referee: H. King (Merthyr).

BRITISH GAS WALES YOUTH CUP

First Round

Briton Ferry Athletic v Cwmbran Town	0-3
Caernarfon Town v Llanrwst United Juniors	0-0, 1-2
Caersws v Penrhyncoch	W/O
(tie to Caersws)	
Cogan Coronation v Newport AFC	1-0
Llanidloes Town v Cardiff Civil Service	0-8
Llantwit Fardre v Caldicot Town	0-6
Mynydd Isa Youth v Penyffordd Youth	2-3
Pwllheli Borough v Porthmadog	W/O
(tie to Pwllheli Borough)	
Rhyl v Llanfairpwll	3-3, 4-2 *(aet)*
Tregaron Turfs v Penparcau	1-4
Wrexham Schools v Newtown	1-2

Second Round

Cardiff City v Swansea City	1-0
Cardiff Civil Service v Caldicot Town	3-2
Cogan Coronation v Cwmbran Town	6-2
Hereford United v Caersws	8-1
Llanrwst United Juniors v Hawarden Rangers	2-7
Penparcau v Newtown	2-8
Pwllheli Borough v Penyffordd Youth	1-2
Rhyl v Wrexham	1-3

Third Round

Cardiff City v Hawarden Rangers	4-0
Cogan Coronation v Cardiff Civil Service	2-1
Hereford United v Penyffordd Youth	2-1
Wrexham v Newtown	8-3

Semi-finals

Cogan Coronation v Cardiff City	1-3
(at Ninian Park)	
Wrexham v Hereford United	3-1

Final

Wrexham v Cardiff City	2-1
(played at Rhayader Town FC)	

North East Wales
Goodwins Challenge Cup – Gresford Athletic 3, British Aerospace 2
Horace Wynne Cup – Saltney CC 3, Penley 1
Wrexham League Sunday Challenge Cup – Black Horse FC 5, Green Dragon 0
Presidents Cup – Black Horse FC 4, Gresford Athletic 0
Under 16 Cup – Broughton Villa FC 3, Penyffordd FC 2
Under 14 Cup – Johnstown Youth 2, Broughton Villa FC 1

Gwent County
Senior Cup – Avergavenny Thursdays 2, Cwmbran Town 1
Amateur Cup – Phill 2, Albion Rovers 1

South Wales
Senior Cup – Barry Town 2, Maesteg Park 1
Amateur Cup – Davies Colour 0, Grange Albion 2

Central Wales
Challenge Cup – Caersws 3, Morda United 1
J. Emrys Morgan Cup – Newcastle Emlyn 5, St Dogmaels 1
Youth Cup – Newtown 4, Llanidloes Town 1

West Wales
Senior Cup – Haverfordwest County 3, Ammanford Town 0
Evening Post Intermediate Cup – North End 2, Troestre Sports 1
Youth Cup – Suburbs 1, Morriston Boys Club 0

NORTHERN IRISH FOOTBALL 1991–92

The formidable task confronting Northern Ireland in qualifying for the World Cup final series was again underlined when they drew 2-2 with Lithuania after leading 2-0 in a Group Three tie at Windsor Park, Belfast. A valuable point had been dropped and manager Billy Bingham's hopes of collecting a maximum of eight for the first four matches, all at home, were dashed.

"It is disappointing. Now we must work harder in our remaining fixtures. There is a long way to go yet and I am still confident we can qualify," said Bingham, a pragmatic man and the eternal optimist, whose contract was renewed for another two years in January.

Northern Ireland's performances since Mexico, '86, admittedly a period of transition and rebuilding, have been indifferent, an amalgamation of the good and bad. Consequently, attendances have dwindled to such an extent that the Irish FA secretary David Bowen has revealed that only track advertising and television make Belfast matches financially viable. "Gate receipts don't generate sufficient revenue especially when there is heavy expenditure on away fixtures in a World Cup seven nation Group such as ours", he said.

Because of FIFA's all-seated regulations, Spion Kop and the other open terracing at Windsor Park has been closed for international and European club fixtures, but a new stand on the south side of the stadium is under construction which will bring the seating to 10,500 and the eventual capacity should be around 20,000, a far cry from the immediate post-war era when almost 60,000 watched the British championship series against England and Scotland.

Sponsorship, however, has continued to increase. Vauxhall back the international team and development of the game at all levels; Scottish and Newcastle Brewery have also entered the market along with other established sponsors Smirnoff, TNT, Wilkinson Sword, Cawoods, Budweiser and Bass. In fact, more than £250,000 is pumped into Ulster football, a remarkable figure for a semi-professional set-up.

There was no domination by a single club this season with the trophies spread around the Province. Glentoran won the Smirnoff Irish League, and TNT Gold Cup, Glenavon the Bass Irish Cup, Bangor the Lombard Ulster Cup, Omagh Town the Budweiser, Linfield the Wilkinson Sword League Cup and Cawoods the County Antrim Shield.

Portadown, double winners the previous season, qualified for the UEFA Cup as League runners-up but Linfield, without a major trophy, failed to make it into Europe for the third successive season — an unprecedented happening.

Dundela, managed by Mervyn Bell, were the kings of Irish junior football. They won the Wilkinson B Division and became the first club to go through the programme without a defeat. They also picked up the Smirnoff Knock Out Cup and were named Junior Team of the Year by the Northern Ireland Football Writers Association.

And, of course, there was the usual managerial carousel. Paul Malone moved to Ards from Larne who appointed Gary Erwin as his successor; Ian McFaul (Coleraine), Robbie Barr (Carrick Rangers) and Matt Bradley (Newry Town) resigned while Glenavon sacked Terry Nicholson amidst controversial circumstances; Nicholson has now signed a new three year agreement to take over financially struggling Newry.

There were celebrations, too; Linfield commemorated their seven trophy triumph of 1962 with a glittering banquet at the City Hall, Belfast, while the Glentoran team of 1967, arguably one of the finest in Irish football and which competed in the North American Soccer League as the Detroit Cougars, staged a 25th anniversary reunion in Belfast.

Players, now resident in many parts of the world, were flown to Northern Ireland for the function. A magnificent colour brochure was also produced highlighting the two month 12-match coast-to-coast tour.

MALCOM BRODIE

SMIRNOFF IRISH LEAGUE CHAMPIONSHIP
FINAL TABLE

	P	W	D	L	F	A	Pts
Glentoran	30	24	5	1	78	26	77
Portadown	30	21	2	7	59	19	65
Linfield	30	17	9	4	58	23	60
Larne	30	16	7	7	54	31	55
Glenavon	30	16	4	10	54	36	52
Crusaders	30	14	5	11	55	37	47
Ards	30	10	11	9	50	46	41
Omagh Town	30	10	6	14	51	58	36
Bangor*	30	11	6	13	45	52	36
Ballymena United	30	8	11	11	37	50	35
Ballyclare Comrades	30	8	8	14	37	64	32
Cliftonville	30	7	10	13	27	34	31
Coleraine	30	7	8	15	35	57	29
Newry Town	30	8	5	17	28	57	29
Distillery	30	5	7	18	31	55	22
Carrick Rangers	30	2	8	20	24	78	14

* penalised three points – ineligible player.

BUDWEISER CUP

Final

(The Oval, Belfast, 4 December 1991)

Omagh Town 3 *(McColgan, McCourt, Woodhead)*
Linfield 1 *(McGaughey)* 5000

Omagh Town: McBrearty; McColgan, Coll, McGuiness, McCaul, Dunnion, Woodhead, McCreadie, McCourt, Crilly, Kavanagh.

Linfield: Patterson; Dornan, Easton, Doherty, Jeffrey, Allen (Beatty), Curry, McCormick, McGaughey, Baxter (Hunter), Bailie.

Referee: A Ritchie (Carrickfergus).

Semi-finals Linfield 2 Cliftonville 2 *(Linfield won 7–6 on penalties, at Seaview, Belfast)*
Omagh Town 3 Glentoran 2 *(at Mourneview Park)*

Previous winners: 1988: Glentoran; 1989: Glenavon; 1990: Glentoran; 1991: Portadown

IRISH LEAGUE CHAMPIONSHIP WINNERS

1891	Linfield	1902	Linfield	1912	Glentoran	1927	Belfast Celtic	1938	Belfast Celtic
1892	Linfield	1903	Distillery	1913	Glentoran	1928	Belfast Celtic	1939	Belfast Celtic
1893	Linfield	1904	Linfield	1914	Linfield	1929	Belfast Celtic	1940	Belfast Celtic
1894	Glentoran	1905	Glentoran	1915	Belfast Celtic	1930	Linfield	1948	Belfast Celtic
1895	Linfield	1906	Cliftonville/	1920	Belfast Celtic	1931	Glentoran	1949	Linfield
1896	Distillery		Distillery	1921	Glentoran	1932	Linfield	1950	Linfield
1897	Glentoran	1907	Linfield	1922	Linfield	1933	Belfast Celtic	1951	Glentoran
1898	Linfield	1908	Linfield	1923	Linfield	1934	Linfield	1952	Glenavon
1899	Distillery	1909	Linfield	1924	Queen's Island	1935	Linfield	1953	Glentoran
1900	Belfast Celtic	1910	Cliftonville	1925	Glentoran	1936	Belfast Celtic	1954	Linfield
1901	Distillery	1911	Linfield	1926	Belfast Celtic	1937	Belfast Celtic	1955	Linfield

1956	Linfield	1964	Glentoran	1972	Glentoran	1979	Linfield	1986	Linfield
1957	Glentoran	1965	Derry City	1973	Crusaders	1980	Linfield	1987	Linfield
1958	Ards	1966	Linfield	1974	Coleraine	1981	Glentoran	1988	Glentoran
1959	Linfield	1967	Glentoran	1975	Linfield	1982	Linfield	1989	Linfield
1960	Glenavon	1968	Glentoran	1976	Crusaders	1983	Linfield	1990	Portadown
1961	Linfield	1969	Linfield	1977	Glentoran	1984	Linfield	1991	Portadown
1962	Linfield	1970	Glentoran	1978	Linfield	1985	Linfield	1992	Glentoran
1963	Distillery	1971	Linfield						

LOMBARD ULSTER CUP

Section A	P	W	D	L	F	A	Pts
Ballymena U	3	2	0	1	7	3	6
Portadown	3	2	0	1	7	6	6
Coleraine	3	1	1	1	4	5	4
Ards	3	0	1	2	5	9	1

Section B	P	W	D	L	F	A	Pts
Bangor	3	2	0	1	9	3	6
Crusaders	3	2	0	1	6	4	6
Linfield	3	2	0	1	3	2	6
Carrick Rangers	3	0	0	3	2	11	0

Section C	P	W	D	L	F	A	Pts
Glentoran	3	3	0	0	9	2	9
Cliftonville	3	2	0	1	4	2	6
Distillery	3	0	1	2	1	5	1
Ballyclare Comrades	3	0	1	2	2	7	1

Section D	P	W	D	L	F	A	Pts
Glenavon	3	3	0	0	5	1	9
Newry Town	3	1	1	1	2	2	4
Larne	3	1	0	2	4	4	3
Omagh Town	3	0	1	2	1	5	1

Quarter-finals
Ballymena U 1 Crusaders 1
(Crusaders won 4–2 on penalties)
Bangor 4 Portadown 0; Glentoran 5 Newry Town 0;
Glenavon 2 Cliftonville 1

Semi-finals
Bangor 1 Glenavon 1 (Bangor won 5–3 on penalties)
Crusaders 1 Glentoran 0

Final
(The Oval, Belfast, 2 September 1991)
Bangor 3 *(McCreadie, McCloskey, Caughey)*
Crusaders 1 *(Gardiner)*   3000
Bangor: Eachus; McCartney, Dornan, Gibson, Brown,
O'Connor, McCloskey (Lucas), Hill, McCreadie (Smith),
Caughey, Muldoon.
Crusaders: McKeown; Mallon, Stewart, Burrows J,
Hunter B, Murray (Beckett), Denver, Gardiner, Black-
ledge, Cash (McDonald), Burrows S.
Referee: J. Duffy (Banbridge).

Winners

1949	Linfield	1960	Linfield	1971	Linfield	1982	Glentoran
1950	Larne	1961	Ballymena U	1972	Coleraine	1983	Glentoran
1951	Glentoran	1962	Linfield	1973	Ards	1984	Linfield
1952		1963	Crusaders	1974	Linfield	1985	Coleraine
1953	Glentoran	1964	Linfield	1975	Coleraine	1986	Coleraine
1954	Crusaders	1965	Coleraine	1976	Glentoran	1987	Larne
1955	Glenavon	1966	Glentoran	1977	Linfield	1988	Glentoran
1956	Linfield	1967	Linfield	1978	Linfield	1989	Glentoran
1957	Linfield	1968	Coleraine	1979	Linfield	1990	Portadown
1958	Distillery	1969	Coleraine	1980	Ballymena U	1991	Bangor
1959	Glenavon	1970	Linfield	1981	Glentoran		

TNT GOLD CUP

Section A	P	W	D	L	F	A	Pts
Portadown	3	2	0	1	7	4	6
Distillery	3	2	0	1	6	4	6
Carrick Rangers	3	1	1	1	5	6	4
Newry	3	0	1	2	3	7	1

Section B	P	W	D	L	F	A	Pts
Ballymena United	3	3	0	0	7	0	9
Cliftonville	3	1	1	1	3	2	4
Ards	3	1	0	2	5	6	3
Coleraine	3	0	1	2	3	10	1

Section C	P	W	D	L	F	A	Pts
Linfield	3	2	0	1	8	5	6
Bangor	3	2	0	1	7	5	6
Larne	3	2	0	1	5	6	6
Ballyclare Comrades	3	0	0	3	2	6	0

Section D	P	W	D	L	F	A	Pts
Glentoran	3	2	1	0	11	6	6
Glenavon	3	2	0	1	9	6	6
Crusaders	3	1	1	1	4	5	4
Omagh Town	3	0	0	3	5	12	0

Quarter-finals
Linfield 0 Glenavon 0 (aet; Glenavon won 4–1 on penalties); Glentoran 4 Bangor 1 (aet); Portadown 0 Cliftonville
1; Ballymena United 5 Distillery 0

Semi-finals
Cliftonville 3 Glenavon 2 *(Windsor Park)*
Ballymena United 1 Glentoran 2 *(Seaview, Belfast)*

Final
(Windsor Park, 12th November, 1991)
Glentoran 1 *(Bowers)*
Cliftonville 0   5000
Glentoran: Smyth D; Smyth G, McCaffrey, Morrison,
Devine, Bowers, Campbell, Moore, Macartney, Mathie-
son, Willis (West).
Cliftonville: Rice; Nutt, Loughran, Donnelly, Tabb,
Murray, Macleod, McFadden, Drake, Breslin (O'Kane),
Douglas.
Referee: F. McKnight (Newtownards).

Winners

1946	Belfast Celtic	1958	Coleraine	1970	Linfield	1982	Linfield
1947	Belfast Celtic	1959	Linfield	1971	Linfield	1983	Glentoran
1948	Linfield	1960	Glentown	1972	Portadown	1984	Linfield
1949	Linfield	1961	Linfield	1973	Linfield	1985	Linfield
1950	Linfield	1962	Glentoran	1974	Ards	1986	Crusaders
1951	Glentoran	1963	Linfield	1975	Ballymena U	1987	Glentoran
1952	Portadown	1964	Derry City	1976	Coleraine	1988	Linfield
1953	Ards	1965	Linfield	1977	Glentoran	1989	Linfield
1954	Glenavon	1966	Glentoran	1978	Glentoran	1990	Linfield
1955	Linfield	1967	Linfield	1979	Portadown	1991	Glenavon
1956	Glenavon	1968	Linfield	1980	Linfield	1992	Glenavon
1957	Linfield	1969	Coleraine	1981	Cliftonville		

BASS IRISH CUP 1991–92

First Round

Macosquin v Connor	3-3, 2-7
Barn United v Sirocco Works	3-1
Annalong Swifts v Ballynahinch United	3-3, 4-3
Queen's University v Comber Rec	1-2
Glebe Rangers v AFC	1-3
Tandragee Rovers v Orangefield OB	2-0
Armoy United v Drummond United	3-0
Armagh City v Roe Valley	5-0
Magherafelt Sky Blues v Portstewart	0-4
Fisher Body v GEC	4-3
Cullybackey v Dromara Village	1-6
Institute v Ist Bangor	0-4
H & W Welders v Magherafelt Crusaders	13-0
Dromore Amateurs v Rathfriland Rangers	2-1
Civil Service v Killymoon Rangers	0-1
Armagh Thistle v Ards Rangers	2-5

Second Round

Dervock United v H & W Sports Rec	2-3
Nitos Athletic v Mosside United	2-0
Portstewart v Hanover	1-1, 2-1
Northern Telecom v Annalong Swifts	3-1
H & W Welders v Dromara Village	2-0
Armoy United v Saintfield	2-1
Cromac AFC v Ards Rangers	0-2
Shorts v UUC	4-0
Last Belfast v Barn United	4-0
Dungiven v Drumaness Mills	0-2
Bridgend United v Killymoon Rangers	3-0
Portglenone v Armagh City	2-2, 2-4
Tandragee Rovers v Dromore Amateurs	4-2
Ist Liverpool v Bangor Amateurs	4-3
Southend United v Donard Hospital	1-7
Ist Bangor v Connor	3-2
Islandmagee v Star of the Sea	1-2
AFC v Larne Tech OB	2-1
Comber Rec v Ulster Univ, Jordanstown	1-0
Oxford United Stars v Downshire YM	2-1
Fisher Body v Killyleagh YC	1-5
RUC v Annagh United	2-2, 1-2 (aet)

Third Round

H & W Sports Rec v Star of the Sea	6-0
H & W Welders v Armagh City	1-3
Ist Liverpool v Donard Hospital	0-1
Northern Telecom v Killyleagh YC	1-3
Tandragee Rovers v Nitos Athletic	5-1
Oxford United Stars v Drumaness Mills	2-0
Shorts v Ist Bangor	2-4
Portstewart v Bridgend United	3-2
AFC v Comber Rec	4-3
Annagh United v Armoy United	2-2, 1-3
East Belfast v Ards Rangers	7-0

Fourth Round

Coach United v Armoy United	2-1
Dungannon Swifts v AFC	2-0
FC Enkalon v Donard Hospital	0-5
Banbridge Town v H & W Sports Rec	2-1
Moyola Park v Armagh City	3-3, 4-1
Brantwood v Oxford United Stars	2-2, 1-3
Kilmore Rec v Ballymoney United	3-2
Chimney Corner v Ballinamallard United	0-2

British Telecom v East Belfast	1-1, 2-2
(East Belfast won 4-3 on penalties)	
Crumlin United v Donegal Celtic	0-1
Crewe United v Dunmurry Rec	1-4
Portstewart v Tandragee Rovers	3-1
Tobermore United v Park	2-3
Limavady United v Killyleagh YC	3-1
Loughgall United v Cookstown United	2-1
Dundela v First Bangor	1-0

Fifth Round

Dunmurry Rec v Donard Hospital	4-0
Dungannon Swifts v Coleraine	2-2, 2-0
Moyola Park v Banbridge Town	1-1, 1-2
Ballyclare Comrades v Coach United	4-1
Omagh Town v Port Stewart	3-1
Oxford United Stars v East Belfast	1-0
Linfield v Loughgall United	4-0
Glenavon v Park	4-1
Crusaders v Newry Town	1-1, 3-1
Glentoran v Donegal Celtic	2-0
Portadown v Carrick Rangers	3-0
Kilmore Rec v Cliftonville	0-1
Bangor v Ards	1-2
Dundela v Ballymena United	2-5
Larne v Distillery	1-0
Limavady United v Ballinamallard United	3-1

Sixth Round

Ards v Dunmurry Rec	3-2
Ballyclare Comrades v Oxford United Stars	0-1
Banbridge Town v Linfield	2-2, 0-3
Cliftonville v Larne	2-0
Glentoran v Glenavon	0-0, 0-4
Limavady United v Crusaders	0-0, 0-2
Omagh Town v Ballymena United	1-1, 0-3
Portadown v Dungannon	4-0

Quarter-finals

Portadown v Crusaders	0-1
Glenavon v Ards	3-0
Linfield v Cliftonville	1-0
Ballymena United v Oxford United Stars	4-0

Semi-finals

Linfield v Crusaders (*Oval*)	2-0
Glenavon v Ballymena United (*Windsor Park*)	3-1

Final (*Oval, 2 May 1992*)

Glenavon 2 *(Ferris, McMahon)*
Linfield 1 *(McGaughey)*   14,000
Glenavon: Beck; McCullogh, Scappaticci, Quigley, Byrne, Crawford, McConville, McCoy, McMahon, Ferris (Crowe), Kennedy.
Linfield: Patterson; Dornan, Easton, McConnell, Spiers, Beatty (Hunter), Curry, Doherty (Allen), McGaughey, Baxter, Bailie.
Referee: D. Magill (Belfast).
Play was stopped by the referee for four minutes when Linfield supporters scaled the perimeter wire fencing after McGaughey scored. Fighting broke out and police intervened after missiles were thrown at them. The first half lasted 52 minutes.

IRISH CUP FINALS (from 1946–47)

1946–47	Belfast Celtic 1, Glentoran 0	1963–64	Derry City 2, Glentoran 0	1978–79	Cliftonville 3, Portadown 2
1947–48	Linfield 3, Coleraine 0	1964–65	Coleraine 2, Glenavon 1	1979–80	Linfield 2, Crusaders 0
1948–49	Derry City 3, Glentoran 0	1965–66	Glentoran 2, Linfield 0	1980–81	Ballymena U 1, Glenavon 0
1949–50	Linfield 2, Distillery 1	1966–67	Crusaders 3, Glentoran 1	1981–82	Linfield 2, Coleraine 1
1950–51	Glentoran 3, Ballymena U 1	1967–68	Crusaders 2, Linfield 0	1982–83	Glentoran 1:2, Linfield 1:1
1951–52	Ards 1, Glentoran 0	1968–69	Ards 4, Distillery 2	1983–84	Ballymena U 4,
1952–53	Linfield 5, Coleraine 0	1969–70	Linfield 2, Ballymena U 1		Carrick Rangers 1
1953–54	Derry City 1, Glentoran 0	1970–71	Distillery 3, Derry City 0	1984–85	Glentoran 1:1, Linfield 1:0
1954–55	Dundela 3, Glenavon 0	1971–72	Coleraine 2, Portadown 1	1985–86	Glentoran 2, Coleraine 1
1955–56	Distillery 1, Glentoran 0	1972–73	Glentoran 3, Linfield 2	1986–87	Glentoran 1, Larne 0
1956–57	Glenavon 2, Derry City 0	1973–74	Ards 2, Ballymena U 1	1987–88	Glentoran 1, Glenavon 0
1957–58	Ballymena U 2, Linfield 0	1974–75	Coleraine 1:0:1,	1988–89	Ballymena U 1, Larne 0
1958–59	Glenavon 2, Ballymena U 0		Linfield 1:0:0	1989–90	Glentoran 3, Portadown 0
1959–60	Linfield 5, Ards 1	1975–76	Carrick Rangers 2, Linfield 1	1990–91	Portadown 2, Glenavon 1
1960–61	Glenavon 5, Linfield 1	1976–77	Coleraine 4, Linfield 1	1991–92	Glenavon 2, Linfield 1
1961–62	Linfield 4, Portadown 0	1977–78	Linfield 3, Ballymena U 1		
1962–63	Linfield 2, Distillery 1				

INTERNATIONAL DIRECTORY

The latest available information has been given regarding numbers of clubs and players registered with FIFA, the world governing body. Where known, official colours are listed. With European countries, League tables show a number of signs. * indicates relegated teams, + play-offs, *+ relegated after play-offs. In Yugoslavia, drawn matches result in penalty shoot-outs, the winners receiving a point.

There are 168 FIFA members plus others soon to be admitted. The four home countries, England, Scotland, Northern Ireland and Wales, are dealt with elsewhere in the Yearbook; but basic details appear in this directory.

EUROPE

ALBANIA

Federation Albanaise De Football, Rruga Dervish Hima Nr. 31, Tirana.
Founded: 1930; *Number of Clubs:* 49; *Number of Players:* 5,192; *National Colours:* Red shirts, black shorts, red stockings.
Telephone: 72-56; *Cable:* ALBSPORT TIRANA; *Telex:* 2142.

International matches 1991

France (a) 0-5, Czechoslovakia (h) 0-2, Iceland (h) 1-0, Greece (a) 2-0, Czechoslovakia (a) 1-2.

League Championship wins (1945–92)

Dinamo Tirana 15; Partizan Tirana 14; 17 Nentori 8; Vllaznia 7; Flamurtari 1; Labinoti 1.

Cup wins (1948–92)

Dinamo Tirana 12; Partizan Tirana 12; 17 Nentori 6; Vllaznia 5; Flamurtari 2; Labinoti 1; Elbasan 1.

Final League Table 1991–92

	P	W	D	L	F	A	Pts
Vllaznia	29	19	6	4	60	18	44
Partizani	30	14	10	6	41	25	38
Teuta	30	12	9	9	30	20	33
Besa	30	13	7	10	42	36	33
Dinamo	29	9	13	7	31	20	31
Apolonia	30	11	8	11	32	34	30
Lushnia	29	8	13	8	22	24	29
Elbasan	30	10	8	12	28	29	28
Laci	30	8	12	10	22	27	28
SK Tirana	28	11	5	12	37	30	27
Flamurtari	29	12	9	8	35	30	27
Selenica*	30	10	6	14	34	56	26
Kastrioti	29	10	5	14	34	53	25
Tomori	29	7	12	10	32	32	24
Pogradeci	29	6	12	11	27	39	24
Skenderbeu*	29	4	7	18	16	50	15

Top scorer: Bilali (Vllaznia) 19
Cup Final: Elbasan 2, Besa 1
N.B. Championship not completed.

AUSTRIA

Oesterreichischer Fussball-Bund, Wiener Stadion, Sektor A/F, Meierestrasse, A-1020 Wien.
Founded: 1904; *Number of Clubs:* 2,081; *Number of Players:* 253,576; *National Colours:* White shirts, black shorts, black stockings.
Telephone: 0043-1-217 18; *Cable:* FOOTBALL WIEN; *Telex:* 111919 OEFB A; *Fax:* 0043-1-218 16 32.

International matches 1991

Norway (h) 0-0, Sweden (a) 0-6, Faeroes (h) 3-0, Denmark (a) 1-2, Portugal (a) 1-1, Northern Ireland (a) 1-2, Yugoslavia (h) 0-2.

League Championship wins (1912–92)

Rapid Vienna 29; FK Austria 21; Admira-Energie-Wacker (prev. Sportklub Admira & Admira-Energie) 8; First Vienna 6; Tirol-Svarowski-Innsbruck (prev. Wacker Innsbruck) 7; Wiener Sportklub 3; FAC 1; Hakoah 1; Linz ASK 1; Wacker Vienna 1; WAF 1; Voest Linz 1.

Cup wins (1919–92)

FK Austria 24; Rapid Vienna 13; TS Innsbruck (prev. Wacker Innsbruck) 6; Admira-Energie-Wacker (prev. Sportklub Admira & Admira-Energie) 5; First Vienna 3; Linz ASK 1; Wacker Vienna 1; WAF 1; Wiener Sportklub 1; Graz 1; Stockerau 1.

Qualifying table

	P	W	D	L	F	A	Pts
Austria Salzburg	22	16	2	4	43	18	34
FK Austria	22	14	5	3	51	21	33
Tirol	22	12	5	5	48	34	29
Stahl Linz	22	11	6	5	36	24	28
Rapid	22	10	7	5	37	24	27
Admira Wacker	22	10	7	5	33	22	27
St Polten	22	6	6	10	25	36	18
Vorwaerts	22	7	3	12	28	29	17
Sturm Graz	22	6	3	13	21	36	15
Kremser	22	4	6	12	25	43	14
Vienna	22	4	6	12	20	43	14
Alpine	22	1	6	15	11	48	8

Final table 1991–92

	P	W	D	L	F	A	Pts
FK Austria	14	7	2	5	73	36	33
Austria Salzburg	14	7	2	5	62	37	33
Tirol	14	9	0	5	69	49	33
Admira Wacker	14	7	2	5	57	42	30
Rapid	14	6	2	6	58	40	28
Stahl Linz	14	4	3	7	47	45	25
Vorwaerts	14	5	2	7	44	53	21
St Polten	14	3	3	8	41	54	18

Top scorer: Westerthaler (Tirol) 17
Cup Final: FK Austria 1, Admira Wacker 0

Promotion/Relegation

	P	W	D	L	F	A	Pts
Sturm Graz	14	4	9	1	18	11	17
Molding	14	5	6	3	16	15	16
Linzk	14	5	5	4	19	17	15
Wiener SC	14	5	4	5	23	18	14
Vienna*	14	5	4	5	15	13	14
Alpine*	14	6	2	6	17	20	14
Kremser*	14	3	6	5	22	25	12
Graz AK*	14	3	4	7	12	23	10

BELGIUM

Union Royale Belge Des Societes De Football; Eturl, Association, Rue De La Loi 43, Boite 1, B-1040 Bruxelles.
Founded: 1895; *Number of Clubs:* 2,120; *Number of Players:* 390,468; *National Colours:* Red shirts with tri-coloured trim, red shorts, red stockings with trim.
Telephone: 32 2 477 1211; *Cable:* UBSFA BRUXELLES; *Telex:* 23257 BVBFBF B; *Fax:* 32 2 2147 82391.

International matches 1991

Italy (a) 0-0, Luxembourg (h) 3-0, Wales (h) 1-1,
Germany (a) 0-1, Luxembourg (a) 2-0, Hungary
(a) 2-0, Germany (h) 0-1.

League Championship wins (1896–1992)

Anderlecht 21; Union St Gilloise 11; FC Brugge 9;
Standard Liège 8; Beerschot 7; RC Brussels 6; FC
Liège 5; Daring Brussels 5; Antwerp 4; Mechelen 4;
Lierse SK 3; SV Brugge 3; Beveren 2; RWD
Molenbeek 1.

Cup wins (1954–92)

Anderlecht 7; FC Brugge 5; Standard Liège 4;
Beerschot 2; Waterschei 2; Beveren 2; Gent 2;
Antwerp 2; Lierse SK 1; Racing Doornik 1; Waregem
1; SV Brugge 1; Mechelen 1; FC Liège 1.

Final League Table 1991–92

	P	W	D	L	F	A	Pts
FC Brugge	34	21	11	2	68	29	53
Anderlecht	34	21	7	6	65	26	49
Standard Liège	34	16	14	4	59	26	46
Mechelen	34	15	13	6	47	23	43
Antwerp	34	18	5	11	47	39	41
Gent	34	16	9	9	54	44	41
Lierse SK	34	14	9	11	52	60	37
Ekeren	34	13	11	10	55	45	37
CS Brugge	34	10	14	10	57	56	34
Waregem	34	11	8	15	47	54	31
RWD Molenbeek	34	11	7	16	37	48	29
Beveren	34	9	11	14	42	52	29
FC Liège	34	7	13	14	34	50	27
Charleroi	34	9	9	16	32	43	27
Lokeren	34	8	11	15	38	51	27
Genk	34	8	10	16	32	44	26
Kortrijk*	34	5	10	19	31	72	20
Aalst*	34	4	8	22	18	62	16

Top scorer: Weber (CS Brugge) 26
Cup Final: Antwerp 2, Mechelen 2 *aet*
Antwerp won 5-4 on penalties

BULGARIA

Bulgarian Football Union, Gotcho Gopin 19, 1000 Sofia.
Founded: 1923; *Number of Clubs:* 376; *Number of
Players:* 48,240; *National Colours:* White shirts, green
shorts, red stockings.
Telephone: 87 74 90; *Cable:* BULFUTBOL; *Telex:*
23145 BFS BG; *Fax:* 87 74 90.

International matches 1991

Scotland (a) 1-1, Denmark (a) 1-1, Switzerland (h) 2-3,
San Marino (a) 3-0, Brazil (a) 0-3, Turkey (h) 0-0, Italy
(h) 2-1, San Marino (h) 4-0, Rumania (h) 1-1.

League Championship wins (1925–92)

CSKA Sofia 27; Levski Spartak (prev. Levski Sofia) 16;
Slavia Sofia 6; Vladislav Varna 3; Lokomotiv Sofia 3;
Trakia Plovdiv 2; AS 23 Sofia 1; Botev Plovdiv 1; SC
Sofia 1; Sokol Varna 1; Spartak Plovdiv 1; Tichka
Varna 1; ZSZ Sofia 1; Beroe Stara Zagora 1; Etur 1.

Cup wins (1946–92)

Leuski Sofia 17; CFKA Sredets (prev. CSKA Sofia,
CDNA) 13; Slavia Sofia 6; Lokomotiv Sofia 3; Botev
Plovdiv 1; Spartak Plovdiv 1; Spartak Sofia 1; Marek
Stanke 1; Trakia Plovdiv 1; Spartak Varna 1; Sliven 1.

Final League Table 1991–92

	P	W	D	L	F	A	Pts
CSKA Sofia	30	20	7	3	74	26	47
Levski Sofia	30	19	7	4	54	18	45
Botev Plovdiv	30	13	11	6	46	27	37
Etur	30	12	13	5	35	18	37
Lokomotiv Plovdiv	30	13	9	8	39	24	35
Sliven	30	12	8	10	37	39	32
Lokomotiv Sofia	30	11	9	10	40	37	31
Beroe	30	10	10	10	32	41	30
Yantra	30	8	11	11	24	33	27
Slavia Sofia	30	8	10	12	33	31	26
Tschernomoretz	30	8	9	13	28	43	25
Lokomotiv Gorna	30	8	9	13	22	39	25
Pirin	30	7	9	14	22	34	23
Dobroudja	30	8	7	15	29	48	23
Mineur*	30	5	10	5	19	50	20
Hebar*	30	3	11	16	17	43	17

Top scorer: Sirakov (Levski Sofia) 26
Cup Final: Levski Sofia 5, Pirin 0

CROATIA

Croatian Football Federation, Illica 21/11, CRO-41000
Zagreb, Croatia.
Telephone: 38-41/42 46 47, *Fax:* 38-41/42 46 39.

	P	W	D	L	F	A	Pts
Hajduk Split	22	16	4	2	44	14	36
Zagreb	22	14	5	3	34	9	33
Osijek	22	12	3	7	34	28	27
Inker	22	10	6	6	37	19	26
Hask	22	11	4	7	32	21	26
Rijeka	22	10	5	7	26	23	25
Istra	22	8	5	9	22	27	21
Varteks	22	7	6	9	32	25	20
Cibalia	22	3	9	10	13	24	15
Zadar	22	4	5	13	20	49	13
Dubrovnik*	22	2	7	13	4	36	11
Sibenik*	22	2	7	13	18	41	11

Top scorer: Kozmku (Hajduk Split) 12
Cup Final: Inker 0, 1, Hask 0, 0

CYPRUS

Cyprus Football Association, Stasinos Str. 1, Engomi
152, P.O. Box 5071, Nicosia.
Founded: 1934; *Number of Clubs:* 85; *Number of
Players:* 6,000; *National Colours:* Sky blue shirts, white
shorts, blue and white stockings.
Telephone: (2) 44 53 41, 44 53 42, 45 99 59; *Cable:*
FOOTBALL NICOSIA; *Telex:* 3880 FOOTBALL CY;
Fax: (2) 47 25 44.

International matches 1991

Greece (h) 1-1, Hungary (h) 0-2, Norway (a) 0-3,
USSR (a) 0-4, USSR (h) 0-3, Italy (a) 0-2.

League Championship wins (1935–92)

Omonia 16; Apoel 15; Anorthosis 6; AEL 5; EPA 3;
Olympiakos 3; Pezoporikos 2; Chetin Kayal 1; Trast 1;
Apollon 1.

Cup wins (1935–92)

Apoel 12; Omonia 9; AEL 6; EPA 5; Anorthosis 4;
Apollon 4; Trast 3; Chetin Kayal 2; Olympiakos 1;
Pezoporikos 1; Salamina 1.

Final League Table 1991–92

	P	W	D	L	F	A	Pts
Apoel	26	18	6	2	67	25	60
Anorthosis	26	18	4	4	55	23	58
Apollon	26	16	5	5	53	26	53
Omonia	26	14	7	5	45	28	49
Salamina	26	11	5	10	45	47	38
Pezoporikos	26	10	7	9	37	40	37
AEL	26	10	6	10	37	40	36
EPA	26	8	7	11	37	39	30
Paralimni	26	7	9	10	36	37	30
Aris	26	7	8	12	29	43	29
Evagoras	26	7	6	13	24	37	29
Olympiakos	26	7	5	14	26	42	26
Alki*	26	4	6	16	23	45	18
Aradippu*	26	1	7	18	17	43	10

Top scorer: Dzurjak (Omonia) 21
Cup Final: Apollon 1, Omonia 0

CZECHOSLOVAKIA

Ceskoslovensky Fotbalovy Svaz, Na Porici 12, 11530 Praha 1.
Founded: 1906; *Number of Clubs:* 5,930; *Number of Players:* 375,380; *National Colours:* Red shirts, white shorts, blue stockings.
Telephone: 225836/2350065; *Cable:* SPORTSVAZ PRAHA; *Telex:* 122650 CSTV C.

International matches 1991

Australia (a) 1-0, Thailand (a) 3-2, Australia (a) 2-0, Poland (h) 4-0, Albania (a) 2-0, Iceland (a) 1-0, Switzerland (h) 1-1, France (h) 1-2, Norway (a) 3-2, Albania (h) 2-1, Spain (a) 1-2.

League Championship wins (1926–92)

Sparta Prague 20; Slavia Prague 12; Dukla Prague (prev. UDA) 11; Slovan Bratislava 7; Spartak Trnava 5; Banik Ostrava 3; Inter-Bratislava 1; Spartak Hradec Kralove 1; Viktoria Zizkov 1; Zbrojovka Brno 1; Bohemians 1; Vitkovice 1.

Cup wins (1991–92)

Dukla Prague 8; Sparta Prague 8; Slovan Bratislava 5; Spartak Trnava 4; Banik Ostrava 3; Lokomotiv Kosice 2; TJ Gottwaldov 1; Dunajska Streda 1.

Final League Table 1991–92

	P	W	D	L	F	A	Pts
Slovan Bratislava	30	23	5	2	60	19	51
Sparta Prague	30	22	4	4	68	20	48
Sigma Olomouc	30	17	9	4	60	23	43
Slavia Prague	30	17	7	6	63	26	41
Banik Ostrava	30	13	9	8	50	37	35
Inter Bratislava	30	12	6	12	45	45	30
Tatran Presov	30	12	5	13	33	43	29
Bohemians	30	10	7	13	38	43	27
Dunaiska	30	10	6	14	46	46	26
Vitkovice	30	9	5	16	34	55	23
Dukla Prague	30	6	10	14	30	42	22
Hradec Kralove	30	7	8	15	22	39	22
Budejovice	30	7	8	15	35	59	22
Union Cheb*	30	7	7	16	28	53	21
Spartak Trnava	30	6	9	15	21	59	21
Banska Bystrica*	30	7	5	18	30	54	19

Top scorer: Dubrovsky (Slovan) 25
Cup Final: Sparta Prague 2, Tatran Presov 1

DENMARK

Dansk Boldspil Union, Ved Amagerbanen 15, DK-2300, Copenhagen S.
Founded: 1889; *Number of Clubs:* 1,555; *Number of Players:* 268,517; *National Colours:* Red shirts, white shorts, red stockings.
Telephone: (45) 3195 0511; *Cable:* DANSKBOLDSPIL COPENHAGEN; *Telex:* 15545 DBU DK; *Fax:* (45) 3195 0588.

International matches 1991

Bulgaria (h) 1-1, Yugoslavia (a) 2-1, Austria (h) 2-1, Italy (h) 0-2, Sweden (a) 0-4, Iceland (a) 0-0, Faeroes (a) 4-0, Austria (a) 3-0, Northern Ireland (h) 2-1.

League Championship wins (1913–91)

KB Copenhagen 15; B 93 Copenhagen 9; AB (Akademisk) 9; B 1903 Copenhagen 7; Frem 6; Esbjerg BK 5; Vejle BK 5; AGF Aarhus 5; Brondby 4; Hvidovre 3; Odense BK 3; B 1909 Odense 2; Koge BK 2; Lyngby 2.

Cup wins (1955–91)

Aarhus GF 8; Vejle BK 6; Randers Freja 3; Lyngby 3; BK 09 Odense 2; Aalborg BK 2; Esbjerg BK 2; Frem 2; B 1903 Copenhagen 2; B 93 Copenhagen 1; KB Copenhagen 1; Vanlose 1; Hvidovre 1; Odense BK 1; Brondby 1.

Qualifying table

Lyngby	18	9	6	3	33	18	24
Brondby	18	8	8	2	30	18	24
B 1903	18	8	5	5	32	26	21
Aalborg	18	6	7	5	29	25	19
Aarhus	18	6	6	6	19	20	18
Frem	18	5	7	6	25	27	17
Naestved	18	6	4	8	33	34	16
Silkeborg	18	6	4	8	24	30	16
Vejle	18	6	2	10	24	30	14
Odense	18	4	3	11	28	49	11

Play-offs
(held up by European Championships)
Winners: Lyngby
Top scorer: Moller (Aalborg) 17
Cup Final: Aarhus 3 B 1903 0

Extra League 1991

	P	W	D	L	F	A	Pts
Brondby	18	10	6	2	26	15	26
Lyngby	18	10	4	4	35	18	24
Frem	18	6	7	5	25	24	19
B 1903	18	7	4	7	19	16	18
Aarhus	18	5	8	5	27	26	18
Odense	18	3	11	4	21	20	17
Aalborg	18	6	5	7	29	33	17
Vejle	18	5	6	7	20	22	16
Silkeborg	18	4	7	7	23	33	15
Ikast	18	3	4	11	9	27	10

ENGLAND

The Football Association, 16 Lancaster Gate, London W2 3LW
Founded: 1863; *Number of Clubs:* 42,000; *Number of Players:* 2,250,000; *National Colours:* White shirts, navy blue shorts, white stockings.
Telephone: 071/262 4542; *Cable:* FOOTBALL ASSOCIATION LONDON W2; *Telex:* 261110; *Fax:* 071/402 0486.

ESTONIA

Estonian Football Association, Refati PST 1-376, 200103 Tallinn.
Telephone: 7-0142-238253; *Telex:* 173236 Sport; *Fax:* 7-0142-238387/238355.
Championship with two qualifying groups of seven teams.

FAEROE ISLANDS

Fotboltssamband Foroya, The Faeroes' Football Assn., Gundalur, P.O. Box 1028, FR-110, Torshavn.
Founded: 1979; *Number of Clubs:* 16; *Number of Players:* 1,014.
Telephone: 298 12606; *Telex:* 81332 ITROTT FA; *Fax:* 298 12421.

International matches 1991

Northern Ireland (a) 1-1, Austria (a) 0-3, Turkey (h) 1-1, Northern Ireland (h) 0-5, Denmark (h) 0-4, Yugoslavia (h) 0-2.

Final League Table 1991

	P	W	D	L	F	A	Pts
KI	18	10	4	4	31	19	24
B36	18	10	4	4	37	28	24
GI	18	10	3	5	38	27	23
VB	18	10	3	5	29	19	23
TB	18	9	2	7	29	22	20
HB	18	7	4	7	37	29	18
B68	18	4	8	6	17	21	16
NSI	18	6	3	9	18	25	15
MB*	18	4	4	10	14	28	12
Sumba*	18	2	1	15	19	51	5

Top scorer: Justinussen (GI) 17
Cup Final: B36 1, HB 0

FINLAND

Suomen Palloliitto Finlands Bollfoerbund, Kuparitie 1, P.O. Box 29, SF-00441 Helsinki.
Founded: 1907; *Number of Clubs:* 1,135; *Number of Players:* 66,100; *National Colours:* White shirts, blue shorts, white stockings.
Telephone: 90-56 26 233; *Cable:* SUOMIFOTBOLL HELSINKI; *Telex:* 1001438 SPL SF; *Fax:* 5626413.

International matches 1991

Poland (a) 1-1, Holland (a) 0-2, Malta (h) 2-0, Holland (h) 1-1, Portugal (a) 0-1, Greece (h) 1-1, Greece (a) 0-2.

League Championship wins (1949–91)

Helsinki JK 8; Turun Palloseura 5; Kuopion Palloseura 5; Valkeakosken Haka 4; Kuusysi 4; Lahden Reipas 3; Ilves-Kissat 2; IF Kamraterna 2; Kotkan TP 2; OPS Oulu 2; Torun Pyrkivä 1; IF Kronohagens 1; Helsinki PS 1; Kokkolan PV 1; IF Kamraterna 1; Vasa 1.

Cup wins (1955–91)

Valkeakosken Haka 9; Lahden Reipas 7; Kotkan TP 4; Helsinki JK 3; Mikkelin 2; Kuusysi 2; Kuopion Palloseura 2; Ilves Tampere 2; IFK Abo 1; Drott 1; Helsinki PS 1; Pallo-Peikot 1; Rovaniemi PS 1; TPS Turku 1.

Final League Table 1991

	P	W	D	L	F	A	Pts
Kuusysi	33	16	11	6	56	35	59
MP Mikkeli	33	16	9	8	68	38	57
Haka	33	16	6	11	59	37	54
HJK Helsinki	33	15	7	11	55	38	52
Jaro	33	14	11	8	45	32	52
Ilves	33	13	12	8	51	39	51
Rops Rovaniemi	33	14	8	11	63	51	50
Pori	33	11	10	12	52	44	43
TPS Turku	33	11	10	12	47	56	43
Kups Kuopio	33	7	11	15	35	53	37
OTP Oulu	33	7	11	15	33	53	31
Reipas*	33	2	2	29	17	117	8

Top scorer: Tarkkio (Haka)
Cup Final: TPS Turku 0, Kuusysi 0 *aet*
TPS Turku won 5-3 on penalties

FRANCE

Federation Francaise De Football, 60 Bis Avenue D'Iena, F-75783 Paris, Cedex 16.
Founded: 1919; *Number of Clubs:* 21,629; *Number of Players:* 1,692,205; *National Colours:* Blue shirts, white shorts, red stockings.
Telephone: 44 31 73 00; *Cable:* CEFI PARIS 034; *Telex:* 640000; *Fax:* (1) 4720 8296.

International matches 1991

Spain (h) 3-1, Albania (h) 5-0, Poland (a) 5-1, Czechoslovakia (a) 2-1, Spain (a) 2-1, Iceland (h) 3-1.

League Championship wins (1933–92)

Saint Etienne 10; Olympique Marseille 8; Stade de Reims 6; Nantes 6; AS Monaco 5; OGC Nice 4; Girondins Bordeaux 4; Lille OSC 3; FC Sete 2; Sochaux 2; Racing Club Paris 1; Roubaix-Tourcoing 1; Strasbourg 1; Paris St Germain 1.

Cup wins (1918–92)

Olympique Marseille 10; Saint Etienne 6; Lille OSC 5; Racing Club Paris 5; Red Star 5; AS Monaco 5; Olympique Lyon 4; Girondins Bordeaux 3; CAS Genereaux 2; Nancy 2; OGC Nice 2; Racing Club Strasbourg 2; Sedan 2; FC Sete 2; Stade de Reims 2; SO Montpellier 2; Stade Rennes 2; Paris St Germain 2; AS Cannes 1; Club Français 1; Excelsior Roubaix 1; Le Havre 1; Olympique de Pantin 1; CA Paris 1; Sochaux 1; Toulouse 1; Bastia 1; Nantes 1; Metz 1.

Final League Table 1991–92

	P	W	D	L	F	A	Pts
Marseille	38	23	12	3	67	21	58
Monaco	38	22	8	8	55	33	52
Paris St Germain	38	15	17	6	43	27	47
Auxerre	38	16	12	10	55	32	44
Caen	38	17	10	11	46	45	44
Montpellier	38	12	18	8	40	32	42
Le Havre	38	13	16	9	35	32	42
Lens	38	11	17	10	36	30	39
Nantes	38	12	14	12	37	39	38
St Etienne	38	13	11	14	42	37	37
Toulouse	38	11	14	13	33	40	36
Metz	38	12	11	15	43	43	35
Lille	38	11	13	14	31	34	35
Toulon	38	13	6	19	41	55	32
Nimes	38	9	14	15	31	50	32
Lyon	38	10	11	17	25	39	31
Sochaux	38	9	13	16	35	50	31
Rennes†	38	6	17	15	25	42	29
Cannes*	38	8	12	18	34	48	28
Nancy*	38	10	8	20	43	67	28

Top scorer: Papin (Marseille) 27
Cup Final: not played following semi-final tragedy in Bastia (Corsica)

GEORGIA

Football Federation of Georgia, 5 Shota Iamanidze Stret, Tbillisi 380012, Georgia.
Telephone: 7-883 352 994; *Fax:* 7-883/2 960 820.

GERMANY

Deutsche Fussball-Bund, Otto-Fleck-Schneise 6, Postfach 710265, D-6000, Frankfurt (Main) 71.
Founded: 1900; *Number of Clubs:* 26,760; *Number of Players:* 5,260,320; *National Colours:* White shirts, black shorts, white stockings.
Telephone: (069) 67 880; *Cable:* FUSSBALL FRANKFURT; *Telex:* 4 168 15; *Fax:* (69) 67 88 266.

International matches 1991

USSR (h) 2-1, Belgium (h) 1-0, Wales (a) 0-1, England (a) 1-0, Wales (h) 4-1, Belgium (a) 1-0, Luxemburg (h) 4-0.

League Championship wins (1903–92)

Bayern Munich 12; IFC Nuremberg 9; Schalke 04 7; SV Hamburg 6; Borussia Moenchengladbach 5; VfB Stuttgart 4; VfB Leipzig 3; Sp Vgg Furth 3; Borussia Dortmund 3; IFC Cologne 3; IFC Kaiserslautern 3; Viktoria Berlin 2; Hertha Berlin 2; Hanover 96 2; Dresden SC 2; SV Werder Bremen 2; Munich 1860 1; Union Berlin 1; FC Freiburg 1; Phoenix Karlsruhe 1; Karlsruher FV 1; Holsten Kiel 1; Fortuna Dusseldorf 1; Rapid Vienna 1; VfB Mannheim 1; Rot-Weiss Essen 1; Eintracht Frankfurt 1; Eintracht Brunswick 1.

Cup wins (1935–92)

Bayern Munich 8; IFC Cologne 4; Eintracht Frankfurt 4; IFC Nuremberg 3; SV Hamburg 3; Dresden SC 2; Fortuna Dusseldorf 2; Karlsruhe SC 2; Munich 1860 2; Schalke 04 2; VfB Stuttgart 2; Borussia Moenchengladbach 2; Borussia Dortmund 2; Werder Bremen 2; First Vienna 1; VfB Leipzig 1; Kickers Offenbach 1; Rapid Vienna 1; Rot-Weiss Essen 1; SW Essen 1; Bayer Uerdingen 1; IFC Kaiserslautern 1; Hannover 96 1.

Final League Table 1991–92

	P	W	D	L	F	A	Pts
Stuttgart	38	21	10	7	62	32	52
Borussia Dortmund	38	20	12	6	66	47	52
Eintracht	38	18	14	6	76	41	50
Cologne	38	13	18	7	58	41	44
Kaiserslautern	38	17	10	11	58	42	44
Leverkusen	38	15	13	10	53	49	43
Nuremberg	38	18	7	13	54	51	43
Karlsruhe	38	16	9	13	48	50	41
Werder Bremen	38	11	16	11	44	45	38
Bayern Munich	38	13	10	15	59	61	36
Schalke	38	11	12	15	45	45	34
Hamburg	38	9	16	13	32	43	34
Moenchengladbach	38	10	14	14	36	39	34
Dynamo Dresden	38	12	10	16	34	50	34
Bochum	38	10	13	15	38	55	33
Wattenscheid	38	9	14	15	50	50	32
Stuttgart Kickers*	38	10	11	17	53	64	31
Hansa Rostock*	39	10	11	17	43	55	31
Duisburg*	38	7	16	15	43	55	30
Fortuna Dusseldorf*	38	6	12	20	41	69	24

Top scorer: Walter (Stuttgart) 22
Cup Final: Hannover 96 0, Moenchengladbach 0 *aet* Hannover 96 won 4-3 on penalties

GREECE

Federation Hellenique De Football, Singrou Avenue 137, Athens.
Founded: 1926; *Number of Clubs:* 4,050; *Number of Players:* 180,000; *National Colours:* White shirts, blue shorts, white stockings.
Telephone: 9338850; *Cable:* FOOTBALL ATHENES; *Telex:* 215328; *Fax:* 9359666.

International matches 1991

Portugal (h) 3-2, Cyprus (a) 1-1, Morocco (h) 0-0, Sweden (h) 2-2, Albania (h) 0-2, Finland (a) 1-1, Portugal (a) 0-1, Holland (h) 0-2, Malta (a) 1-1.

League Championship wins (1928–92)

Olympiakos 25; Panathinaikos 16; AEK Athens 9; Aris Salonika 3; PAOK Salonika 2; Larissa 1.

Cup wins (1932–92)

Olympiakos 20; Panathinaikos 13; AEK Athens 9; PAOK Salonika 2; Aris Salonika 1; Ethnikos 1; Iraklis 1; Panionios 1; Kastoria 1; Larissa 1; Ofi Crete 1.

Final League Table 1991–92

	P	W	D	L	F	A	Pts
AEK Athens	34	23	8	3	72	25	54
Olympiakos	34	20	11	3	74	30	51
Panathinaikos	34	21	6	7	66	21	48
PAOK Salonika	34	13	13	8	44	44	39
Apollon	34	14	7	13	35	34	35
Ofi Crete	34	10	14	10	30	29	34
Larissa	34	11	10	13	40	42	32
Iraklis	34	10	11	13	41	41	31
Aris Salonika	34	12	7	15	26	40	31
Athinaikos	34	10	10	14	36	41	30
Korinthos	34	11	8	15	37	47	30
Pierikos	34	11	8	15	41	56	30
Doxa Drama	34	9	11	14	39	38	29
Xanthi	34	13	3	18	36	48	29
Panachaiki	34	12	5	17	42	56	29
Panionios*	34	9	11	14	32	51	29
Panserraikos*	34	9	8	17	29	59	26
Ethnikos*	34	7	11	16	30	48	25

Top scorer: Dimitriadis (AEK Athens) 28
Cup Final: Olympiakos 2, PAOK Salonika 0

HOLLAND

Koninklijke Nederlandsche Voetbalbond,
Woudenbergseweg 56, Postbus 515, NL-3700 AM, Zeist.
Founded: 1889; *Number of Clubs:* 3,097; *Number of Players:* 962,397; *National Colours:* Orange shirts, white shorts, orange stockings.
Telephone: 3429 9211/1268; *Cable:* VOETBAL ZEIST; *Telex:* 40497; *Fax:* 03439 1397.

International matches 1991

Malta (h) 1-0, Finland (h) 2-0, Finland (a) 1-1, Poland (h) 1-1, Portugal (h) 1-0, Greece (a) 2-0.

League Championship wins (1898–1992)

Ajax Amsterdam 23; Feyenoord 13; PSV Eindhoven 13; HVV The Hague 8; Sparta Rotterdam 6; Go Ahead Deventer 4; HBS The Hague 3; Willem II Tilburg 3; RCH Haarlem 2; RAP 2; Heracles 2; ADO The Hague 2; Quick The Hague 1; BVV Schiedam 1; NAC Breda 1; Eindhoven 1; Enschede 1; Volewijckers Amsterdam 1; Limburgia 1; Rapid JC Haarlem 1; DOS Utrecht 1; DWS Amsterdam 1; Haarlem 1; Be Quick Groningen 1; SVV Schiedam 1; AZ 67 Alkmaar 1.

Cup wins (1899–1992)

Ajax Amsterdam 11; Feyenoord 8; PSV Eindhoven 7; Quick The Hague 4; AZ 67 Alkemaar 3; Rotterdam 3; DFC 2; Fortuna Geleen 2; Haarlem 2; HBS The Hague 2; RCH 2; VOC 2; Wageningen 2; Willem II Tilburg 2; FC Den Haag 2; Concordia Rotterdam 1; CVV 1; Eindhoven 1; HVV The Hague 1; Longa 1; Quick Nijmegen 1; RAP 1; Roermond 1; Schoten 1; Velocitas Breda 1; Velocitas Groningen 1; VSV 1; VUC 1; VVV Groningen 1; ZFC 1; NAC Breda 1; Twente Enschede 1; Utrecht 1.

Final League Table 1991–92

	P	W	D	L	F	A	Pts
PSV Eindhoven	34	25	8	1	82	24	58
Ajax	34	25	5	4	83	24	55
Feyenoord	34	20	9	5	54	19	49
Vitesse	34	15	10	9	47	33	40
Groningen	34	14	11	9	44	37	39
Twente	34	13	9	12	53	49	35
Maastricht	34	11	13	10	42	44	35
Sparta	34	11	13	10	50	53	35
Roda	34	12	11	11	41	45	35
RKC Waalwijk	34	10	14	10	50	49	34
Utrecht	34	9	15	10	50	49	34
Willem II	34	11	9	14	44	45	31
Volendam	34	10	8	16	34	50	28
Fortuna Sittard	34	7	11	16	36	50	25
Dordrecht	34	9	7	18	38	64	25
Den Haag	34	6	10	18	34	61	22
Graafschap*	34	6	9	19	29	59	21
Venlo*	34	3	6	25	32	84	12

Top scorer: Bergkamp (Ajax) 24
Cup final: Feyenoord 3, Roda 0

HUNGARY

Magyar Labdarugo Szovetseg, Hungarian Football Federation, Nepkoztarsasag Utja 47, H-1061 Budapest VI.
Founded: 1901; *Number of Clubs:* 1944; *Number of Players* 95,986; *National Colours:* Red shirts, white shorts, green stockings.
Telephone: 36-1-1255 817, 36-1-1420 704; 36-1-1425 103, 36-1-1421 556; *Cable:* MLSZ BUDAPEST; *Telex:* 225782 MLSZ H; *Fax:* 36-1-1425 103.

International matches 1991

India (a) 2-1, Argentina (a) 0-2, Spain (a) 4-2, Cyprus (a) 2-0, USSR (h) 0-1, Italy (a) 1-3, Republic of Ireland (h) 1-2, USSR (a) 2-2, Belgium (h) 0-2, Norway (h) 0-0, Mexico (a) 0-3, El Salvador (a) 1-1.

League Championship wins (1901–92)

Ferencvaros (prev. FRC) 24; MTK-VM Budapest (prev. Hungaria, Bastay and Vörös Lobogo) 19; Ujpest Dozsa 19; Honved 12; Vasas Budapest 6; Csepel 3; Raba Györ (prev. Vasas Györ) 3; BTC 2; Nagyvarad 1.

Cup wins (1910–92)

Farencvaros (prev. FRC) 15; MTK-VM Budapest (prev. Hungaria, Bastay and Vörös Lobogo) 9; Ujpest Dozsa 8; Raba Györ (prev. Vasas Györ) 4; Vasas Budapest 3; Honved 3; Diösgyör 2; Bocskai 1; III Ker 1; Kispesti AC 1; Soroksar 1; Szolnoki MAV 1; Siofok Banyasz 1; Bekescsaba 1; Pecs 1.

Cup not regularly held until 1964

Final League Table 1991–92

	P	W	D	L	F	A	Pts
Ferencvaros	30	18	10	2	61	19	46
Vac Sumsung	30	19	7	4	54	27	45
Honved Kispest	30	19	4	7	61	27	42
Siofok	30	15	6	9	46	34	36
MTK VM	30	14	7	9	44	34	35
Vasas	30	10	13	7	40	29	33
Videoton	30	10	12	8	45	40	32
Ujpest Dozsa	30	8	13	9	41	38	29
Pecs	30	10	9	11	27	34	29
BVSC	30	7	12	11	29	34	26
Raba Gyor	30	8	10	12	34	43	26
Veszprem	30	7	10	13	20	42	24
Haladas+	30	7	8	15	27	42	22
Diosgyor+	30	6	10	14	24	44	22
Tatabanya*	30	6	8	16	27	53	20
Zalaegerszeg*	30	3	7	20	20	60	13

Top scorer: Orosz (Samsung) 16
Cup Final: Ujpest Dozsa 1 Vac Sumsung 0 *aet*

ICELAND

Knattspyrnusamband Island, P.O. Box 8511, 128 Reykjavik.
Founded: 1929; *Number of Clubs:* 73; *Number of Players:* 23,673; *National Colours:* Blue shirts, white shorts, blue stockings.
Telephone: 84 444; *Cable* KSI REYKJAVIK; *Telex:* 2314 ISI IS; *Fax:* 1 68 97 66.

International matches 1991

Malta (a) 4-1, Albania (a) 0-1, Czechoslovakia (h) 0-1, Turkey (h) 5-1, Denmark (h) 0-0, Spain (h) 2-0, France (a) 1-3.

League Championship wins (1912–91)

KR 20; Valur 19; Fram 18; IA Akranes 12; Vikingur 5; IBK Keflavik 3; IBV Vestmann 2; KA Akureyri 1.

Cup wins (1960–91)

KR 7; Fram 7; Valur 7; IA Akranes 5; IBV Vestmann 3; IBA Akureyri 1; Vikingur 1; IBK Keflavik 1.

Final League Table 1991

	P	W	D	L	F	A	Pts
Vikingur	18	12	1	5	36	21	37
Fram	18	11	4	3	29	15	37
KR	18	8	4	6	34	18	28
Valur	18	8	2	8	30	24	26
UBK	18	7	5	6	26	37	26
KA	18	7	4	7	21	23	25
IBV	18	7	3	8	28	36	24
FH	18	6	4	8	26	32	22
Stjarnen*	18	4	6	8	23	27	18
Vidir*	18	2	3	13	17	47	9

Top scorer: Steinsson (Vikingur), Magnusson (FH) 13
Cup Final: Valur 2, FH 1 *aet*

REPUBLIC OF IRELAND

The Football Association of Ireland, (Cumann Peile Na H-Eireann), 80 Merrion Square, South Dublin 2.
Founded: 1921; *Number of Clubs:* 3,190; *Number of Players:* 124,615; *National Colours:* Green shirts, white shorts, green stockings.
Telephone: 76 68 64; *Cable:* SOCCER DUBLIN; *Telex:* 913967 FAI EI; *Fax:* (01) 610 931.

International matches 1991

Wales (a) 3-0, England (a) 1-1, Poland (h) 0-0, Chile (h) 1-1, USA (a) 1-1, Hungary (a) 2-1, Poland (a) 3-3, Turkey (a) 3-1.

League Championship wins (1922–92)

Shamrock Rovers 14; Dundalk 8; Shelbourne 8; Bohemians 7; Waterford 6; Cork United 5; Drumcondra 5; St Patrick's Athletic 4; St James's Gate 2; Cork Athletic 2; Sligo Rovers 2; Limerick 2; Athlone Town 2; Dolphin 1; Cork Hibernians 1; Cork Celtic 1; Derry City 1.

Cup wins (1922–92)

Shamrock Rovers 23; Dundalk 8; Drumcondra 5; Bohemians 5; Shelbourne 3; Cork Athletic 2; Cork United 2; St James's Gate 2; St Patrick's Athletic 2; Cork Hibernians 2; Limerick 2; Waterford 2; Alton United 1; Athlone Town 2; Cork 1; Fordsons 1; Transport 1; Finn Harps 1; Home Farm 1; Sligo 1; UCD 1; Derry City 1; Bray Wanderers 1; Galway United 1.

Final League Table 1991–92

	P	W	D	L	F	A	Pts
Shelbourne	33	21	7	5	57	29	49
Derry City	33	17	10	6	49	21	44
Cork City	33	16	11	6	47	30	43
Dundalk	33	14	12	7	44	31	40
Bohemians	33	14	9	10	45	34	37
Shamrock Rovers	33	9	15	9	33	30	33
St Patrick's Ath	33	9	11	13	38	46	29
Sligo Rovers	33	7	11	15	33	42	25
Drogheda United	33	7	13	13	24	45	25
Bray Wanderers	33	7	10	16	16	38	24
Athlone Town*	33	6	11	16	31	50	23
Galway United*	33	7	8	18	37	58	22

Top scorer: Caulfield (Cork City) 16
Cup Final: Bohemians 1, Cork City 0

ITALY

Federazione Italiana Giuoco Calcio, Via Gregorio Allegri 14, C.P. 2450, 1-00198, Roma.
Founded: 1898; *Number of Clubs:* 20,961; *Number of Players:* 1,420,160; *National Colours:* Blue shirts, white shorts, blue stockings, white trim.
Telephone: 84 911; *Cable:* FEDERCALCIO ROMA; *Telex:* 611438 CALCIO; *Fax:* 06 849 1239.

International matches 1991

Belgium (h) 0-0, Hungary (h) 3-1, Norway (a) 1-2, Denmark (a) 2-0, USSR (h) 1-1, Bulgaria (a) 1-2, USSR (a) 0-0, Norway (h) 1-1, Cyprus (h) 2-0.

League Championship wins (1898–1992)

Juventus 22; Inter-Milan 13; AC Milan 12; Genoa 9; Torino 8; Pro Vercelli 7; Bologna 7; Fiorentina 2; Napoli 2; AS Roma 2; Casale 1; Novese 1; Cagliari 1; Lazio 1; Verona 1; Sampdoria 1.

Cup wins (1922–92)

Juventus 8; AS Roma 7; Torino 4; Fiorentina 4; AC Milan 4; Inter-Milan 3; Napoli 3; Sampdoria 3; Bologna 2; Atalanta 1; Genoa 1; Lazio 1; Vado 1; Venezia 1; Parma 1.

Final League Table 1991–92

	P	W	D	L	F	A	Pts
AC Milan	34	22	12	0	74	21	56
Juventus	34	18	12	4	45	22	48
Torino	34	14	15	5	42	20	43
Napoli	34	15	12	7	56	40	42
Roma	34	13	14	7	37	31	40
Sampdoria	34	11	16	7	38	31	38
Parma	34	11	16	7	32	28	38
Internazionale	34	10	17	7	28	28	37
Foggia	34	12	11	11	58	58	35
Atalanta	34	10	14	10	31	33	34
Lazio	34	11	12	11	43	40	34
Fiorentina	34	10	12	12	44	49	32
Cagliari	34	7	15	12	30	34	29
Genoa	34	9	11	14	35	47	29
Bari*	34	6	10	18	26	47	22
Verona*	34	7	7	20	24	57	21
Cremonese*	34	5	10	19	27	49	20
Ascoli*	34	4	6	24	25	68	14

Top scorer: Van Basten (AC Milan) 25
Cup Final: Parma 0, 2, Juventus 1, 0

LATVIA

The Football Federation of Latvia, 4 Terbatas Str, 226723 Riga.
Telephone: 7-0132-284206; *Telex:* 161183 RITM SU; *Fax:* 7-0132-284412.
Twelve teams in championship.

LIECHTENSTEIN

Liechtensteiner Fussball-Verband, Postfach 165, FL-9490, Vaduz.
Founded: 1933; *Number of Clubs:* 7; *Number of Players:* 1,247; *National Colours:* Blue & red shirts, red shorts, blue stockings.
Telephone: 075 23344; *Cable:* FUSSBALLVERBAND VADUZ; *Telex:* 889 261; *Fax:* 075 28265.

International matches 1991

Switzerland (h) 0-6.

Liechtenstein has no national league. Teams compete in Swiss regional leagues.

LITHUANIA

Lithuanian Football Federation, 6, Zemaites Street, 232675 Vilnius. Championship of 14 teams.
Telephone: 7-0122-261713; *Telex:* 261118 LSK SU; *Fax:* 7-0122-661223.

LUXEMBOURG

Federation Luxembourgeoise De Football, (F.L.F.), 50, Rue De Strasbourg, L-2560, Luxembourg.
Founded: 1908; *Number of Clubs:* 126; *Number of Players:* 21,684; *National Colours:* Red shirts, white shorts, blue stockings.
Telephone: 48 86 65; *Cable:* FOOTBALL LUXEMBOURG; *Telex:* 2426 FLF LU; *Fax:* 400 201.

International matches 1991

Belgium (a) 0-3, Belgium (h) 0-2, Portugal (h) 1-1, Wales (a) 0-1, Germany (a) 0-4.

League Championship wins (1910–92)

Jeunesse Esch 21; Spora Luxembourg 11; Stade Dudelange 10; Red Boys Differdange 6; US Hollerich-Bonnevoie 5; Fola Esch 5; US Luxembourg 5; Avenir Beggen 5; Aris Bonnevoie 3; Progres Niedercorn 3.

Cup wins (1922–92)

Red Boys Differdange 16; Jeunesse Esch 9; US Luxembourg 9; Spora Luxembourg 8; Stade Dudelange 4; Progres Niedercorn 4; Avenir Beggen 4; Fola Esch 3; Alliance Dudelange 2; US Rumelange 2; Aris Bonnevoie 1; US Dudelange 1; Jeunesse Hautcharage 1; National Schiffige 1; Racing Luxembourg 1; SC Tetange 1; Hesperange 1.

Final League Table 1991–92
Qualifying Table

	P	W	D	L	F	A	Pts
Avenir Beggen	18	9	8	1	37	14	26
Jeunesse Esch	18	7	10	1	39	14	24
Union	18	10	4	4	39	22	24
Spora	18	8	7	3	29	18	23
Aris	18	5	7	6	25	25	17
Grevenmacher	18	6	4	8	27	32	16
Red Boys*	18	5	6	7	31	38	16
Hesperange*	18	5	5	8	28	37	15
Wormeldange*	18	3	4	11	15	47	10
Wiltz*	18	3	3	12	20	44	9

Play-Offs

	P	W	D	L	F	A	Pts
Avenir Beggen	10	5	3	2	15	7	26
Union	10	6	2	2	18	15	26
Jeunesse Esch	10	5	1	4	23	12	23
Spora	10	5	2	3	15	17	23
Aris	10	2	2	6	10	16	14
Grevenmacher	10	1	2	7	9	23	12

Top scorer: Marocutti (Union) 19
Cup Final: Avenir Beggen 1, Petange 0
*had to play-off in promotion/relegation sections

MALTA

Malta Football Association, 280 St. Paul Street, Valletta.
Founded: 1900; *Number of Clubs:* 252; *Number of Players:* 5,544; *National Colours:* Red shirts, white shorts, red stockings.
Telephone: 22 26 97; *Cable:* FOOTBALL MALTA VALLETTA; *Telex:* 1752 MALFA MW; *Fax:* 24 51 36.

International matches 1991

Portugal (h) 0-1, Portugal (a) 0-5, Holland (a) 0-1, Iceland (h) 1-4, Finland (a) 0-2, Indonesia (h) 3-0, Egypt (a) 2-5, South Korea (a) 1-1, Libya (h) 2-0, Greece (h) 1-1.

League Championship wins (1910–92)

Floriana 24; Sliema Wanderers 22; Valletta 14; Hibernians 6; Hamrun Spartans 6; Rabat Ajax 2; St George's 1; KOMR 1.

Cup wins (1935–92)

Sliema Wanderers 17; Floriana 16; Valletta 6; Hamrun Spartans 6; Hibernians 5; Gzira United 1; Melita 1; Zurrieq 1; Rabat Ajax 1.

Final League Table 1991–92

	P	W	D	L	F	A	Pts
Valletta	18	15	3	0	45	7	33
Floriana	18	9	6	3	26	12	24
Hamrun Spartans	18	10	3	5	52	28	23
Sliema Wanderers	18	10	3	5	35	18	23
Rabat Ajax	18	6	7	5	31	24	19
Birkirkara	18	4	8	6	16	25	16
Hibernians	18	4	7	7	16	24	15
Zurrieq	18	3	5	10	22	44	11
St Andrew's	18	5	1	12	14	42	11
Mqabba*	18	1	3	14	10	43	5

Top scorer: Sultana (Hamrun Spartans) 22
Cup Final: Hamrun Spartans 3, Valletta 3 *aet*
Hamrun Spartans won 2-1 on penalties

NORTHERN IRELAND

Irish Football Association Ltd, 20 Windsor Avenue, Belfast BT9 6EG.
Founded: 1880; *Number of Clubs:* 1,555; *Number of Players:* 24,558; *National Colours:* Green shirts, white shorts, green stockings.
Telephone: (0232) 66 94 58; *Cable:* FOOTBALL BELFAST; *Telex:* 747317; *Fax:* (0232) 667620.

NORWAY

Norges Fotballforbund Ullevaal Stadion, Postboks 3823, Ulleval Hageby, 0805 Oslo 8.
Founded: 1902; *Number of Clubs:* 1,810; *Number of Players:* 300,000; *National Colours:* Red shirts, white shorts, blue & white stockings.
Telephone: 02 46 98 30; *Cable* FOTBALLFORBUND OSLO; *Telex:* 71722 NFF N; *Fax:* 02 60 82 22.

International matches 1991

Austria (a) 0-0, Cyprus (h) 3-0, Rumania (h) 1-0, Italy (h) 2-1, Sweden (h) 1-2, USSR (h) 0-1, Czechoslovakia (h) 2-3, Hungary (a) 0-0, Italy (a) 1-1.

League Championship wins (1938–91)

Fredrikstad 9; Viking Stavanger 8; Lillestroem 6; Rosenborg Trondheim 6; Valerengen 4; Larvik Turn 3; Brann Bergen 2; Lyn Oslo 2; IK Start 2; Friedig 1; Fram 1; Skeid Oslo 1; Strömsgodset Drammen 1; Moss 1.

Cup wins (1902–91)

Odds Bk, Skien 11; Fredrikstad 10; Lyn Oslo 8; Skeid Oslo 8; Sarpsborg FK 6; Brann Bergen 5; Rosenborg Trondheim 5; Orn F Horten 4; Lillestroem 4; Viking Stavanger 4; Strömsgodset Drammen 4; Frigg 3; Mjondalens F 3; Mercantile 2; Grane Nordstrand 1; Kvik Halden 1; Sparta 1; Gjovik 1; Bodo-Glimt 1; Valerengen 1; Moss 1; Tromso 1; Byrne 1.
(Until 1937 the cup-winners were regarded as champions.)

Final League Table 1991

	P	W	D	L	F	A	Pts
Viking	22	12	5	5	37	27	41
Rosenborg	22	10	6	6	38	28	36
Start	22	10	4	8	31	21	34
Lyn	22	8	10	4	26	26	34
Lillestrom	22	9	4	9	31	27	31
Tromso	22	9	4	9	28	34	31
Molde	22	7	6	9	33	38	27
Kongsvinger	22	7	6	9	26	34	27
Sogndal	22	7	6	9	22	31	27
Brann	22	6	8	8	22	25	26
Fyllingen*	22	6	7	9	21	21	25
Stromsgodset*	22	5	6	11	30	33	21

Top scorer: Loken (Rosenborg) 12
Cup final: Stromsgodset 3, Rosenborg 2

POLAND

Federation Polonaise De Foot-Ball, Al. Ujazdowskie 22, 00-478 Warszawa.
Founded: 1923; *Number of Clubs:* 5,881; *Number of Players:* 317,442; *National Colours:* White shirts, red shorts, white & red stockings.
Telephone: 48-22-28 93 44; 48-22-28 58 21; *Cable:* PEZETPEEN WARSZAWA; *Telex:* 825320 PZPN PL; *Fax:* 48 22 219175.

International matches 1991

Finland (h) 1-1, Czechoslovakia (a) 0-4, Turkey (h) 3-0, Republic of Ireland (a) 0-0, Wales (h) 0-0, France (1-5), Sweden (h) 2-0, Holland (a) 1-1, Republic of Ireland (h) 3-3, England (h) 1-1.

League Championship wins (1921–92)

Gornik Zabrze 14; Ruch Chorzow 13; Wisla Krakow 6; Cracovia 3; Pogon Lwow 4; Legia Warsaw 4; Lech Poznan 4; Warta Poznan 2; Polonia Bytom 2; Stal Mielec 2; Widzew Lodz 2; Garbarnia Krakow 1; Polonia Warsaw 1; LKS Lodz 1; Slask Wroclaw 1; Szombierki Bytom 1; Zaglebie Lubin 1.

Cup wins (1951–92)

Legia Warsaw 9; Gornik Zabrze 6; Zaglebie Sosnowiec 4; Lech Poznan 3; Ruch Chorzow 2; Slask Wroclaw 2; GKS Katowice 2; Gwardia Warsaw 1; LKS Lodz 1; Polonia Warsaw 1; Wisla Krakow 1; Stal Rzeszow 1; Arka Gdynia 1; Lechia Gdansk 1; Widzew Lodz 1; Miedz Legnica 1.

Final League Table 1991–92

	P	W	D	L	F	A	Pts
Lech Poznan	34	19	11	4	66	38	49
Katowice	34	16	12	6	51	29	44
Widzew	34	17	9	8	48	28	43
Gornik Zabrze	34	14	15	5	43	26	43
Ruch	34	13	13	8	43	39	39
Slask	34	15	8	11	42	35	38
Wisla	34	10	14	10	39	35	34
Bydgoszcz	34	11	12	11	43	41	34
Zaglebie Lubin	34	12	10	12	30	31	34
Legia	34	11	11	12	33	33	33
LKS Lodz	34	9	15	10	26	29	33
Hutnik	34	9	14	11	54	46	32
Stal	34	8	16	10	27	28	32
Olimpia	34	8	15	11	34	41	31
Motor Lublin*	34	9	12	13	33	40	30
Wola*	34	8	12	14	23	33	28
Sosnowiec*	34	6	12	16	28	50	24
Debica*	34	2	7	25	15	76	11

Top scorer: Podbrozny (Lech), Wallgora (Hutnik) 20
Cup Final: Miedz Legnica 1, Gornik Zabrze 1 *aet*
Miedz won 4-3 on penalties

PORTUGAL

Federacao Portuguesa De Futebol, Praca De Alegria
N.25, Apartado 21.100, P-1128, Lisboa Codex.
Founded: 1914; *Number of Clubs:* 204; *Number of
Players:* 79,235; *National Colours:* Red shirts, white
shorts, red stockings.
Telephone: 328207/08/09; *Cable:* FUTEBOL LISBOA;
Telex: 13489 FPF P; *Fax:* 346 7231.

International matches 1991

Spain (a) 1-1, Greece (a) 2-3, Northern Ireland (a) 1-3,
Malta (a) 1-0, Malta (h) 5-0, Austria (h) 1-1, Finland
(h) 1-0, Luxembourg (a) 1-1, Holland (a) 0-1, Greece
(h) 1-0.

League Championship wins (1935–92)

Benfica 29; Sporting Lisbon 16; FC Porto 12;
Belenenses 1.

Cup wins (1939–92)

Benfica 21; Sporting Lisbon 11; FC Porto 7; Boavista 4;
Belenenses 3; Vitoria Setubal 2; Academica Coimbra 1;
Leixoes Porto 1; Sporting Braga 1; Amadora 1.

Final League Table 1991–92

	P	W	D	L	F	A	Pts
Porto	34	24	8	2	58	11	56
Benfica	34	17	12	5	62	23	46
Sporting	34	18	8	8	56	26	44
Boavista	34	16	12	6	45	27	44
Guimaraes	34	14	13	7	46	35	41
Maritimo	34	12	11	11	40	38	35
Farense	34	12	11	11	35	33	35
Beira Mar	34	11	10	13	32	41	32
Chaves	34	10	10	14	36	45	30
Estoril	34	10	10	14	34	54	30
Braga	34	12	5	17	41	49	29
Pacos Ferreira	34	10	9	15	31	45	29
Gil Vicente	34	11	7	16	25	43	29
Salgueiros	34	7	14	13	27	35	28
Famalicao	34	9	10	15	27	40	28
Uniao Toriense*	34	8	11	15	37	43	27
Penafiel*	34	7	11	16	30	47	25
Uniao Funchal*	34	9	6	19	30	57	24

Top scorer: Owubokiri (Boavista) 30
Cup Final: Boavista 2, Porto 1

ROMANIA

Federatia Romana De Fotbal, Vasile Conta 16,
Bucharest 70130.
Founded: 1908; *Number of Clubs:* 414; *Number of
Players:* 22,920; *National Colours:* Yellow shirts, blue
shorts, red stockings.
Telephone: 10 70 90; *Cable:* SPORTROM
BUCURESTI-FOTBAL; *Telex:* 11180; *Fax:* 11 70 75
and 11 98 69

International matches 1991

San Marino (a) 3-1, Switzerland (a) 0-0, Spain (a) 2-0,
Norway (a) 0-1, England (a) 2-2, USA (h) 0-2, Scotland
(h) 1-0, Switzerland (h) 1-0, Bulgaria (a) 1-1.

League Championship wins (1910–92)

Steaua Bucharest (prev. CCA) 14; Dinamo Bucharest
14; Venus Bucharest 7, CSC Temesvar 6; UT Arad 6;
Ripensia Temesvar 4; Uni Craiova 4; Petrolul Ploesti 3;
Rapid Bucharest 2; Olimpia Bucharest 2; CAC
Bucharest 2; Arges Pitesti 2; Soc RA Bucharest 1;
Prahova Ploesti 1; CSC Brasov 1; Juventus Bucharest 1;
SSUD Reita 1; Craiova Bucharest 1; Progresul 1;
Ploesti United 1; Unirea Tricolor 1.

Cup wins (1934–92)

Steaua Bucharest (prev. CCA) 18; Rapid Bucharest 9;
Dinamo Bucharest 7; Uni Craiova 5; UT Arad 2;
Progresul 2; Ripensia Temesvar 2; ICO Oradeo 1;
Metal Ochimia Resita 1; Petrolul Ploesti 1; Stinta Cluj
1; Stinta Timisoara 1; Turnu Severin 1; Chimia Rannicu
1; Jiul Petroseni 1; Poli Timisoara 1.

Final League Table 1991–92

	P	W	D	L	F	A	Pts
Dinamo	34	21	13	0	76	23	55
Steaua	34	20	8	6	68	31	48
Elect. Craiova	34	16	7	11	43	28	39
Uni Craiova	34	14	11	9	38	29	39
Timisoara	34	15	9	10	36	34	39
Progresul	34	14	7	13	39	37	35
Rapid	34	13	9	12	34	37	35
Otelul	34	15	5	14	39	46	35
Brasov	34	13	8	13	53	49	34
Petrolul	34	14	6	14	38	49	34
Inter Sibiu	34	13	7	13	41	41	33
Farul	34	14	4	16	40	44	32
Gloria	34	12	7	15	43	39	31
Bacau	34	11	7	16	32	54	29
Sportul	34	10	8	16	37	47	28
Arges*	34	8	8	18	38	52	24
Electromures*	34	8	5	21	31	55	21
Corvinul*	34	6	7	21	35	66	19

Top scorer: Gerstenmajer (Dinamo) 21
Cup Final: Steaua 1, Timisoara 1 *aet*
Steaua won 4-3 on penalties

SAN MARINO

Federazione Sammarinese Giuoco Calcio, Palazzo
C.O.N.S., Via Del Bando 28, 47031 Borgo Maggiore.
Founded: 1931; *Number of Clubs:* 17; *Number of
Players:* 1,033; *Colours:* Blue and white.
Telephone: (0549) 90 22 28 and 90 25 08; *Cable:*
FEDERCALCIO SAN MARINO; *Telex:* 0505 284
CONSMAR SO; *Fax:* 0549 902516.

International matches 1991

Rumania (h) 1-3, Scotland (h) 0-2, Bulgaria (h) 0-3,
Switzerland (a) 0-7, Bulgaria (a) 0-4, Scotland (a) 0-4.

SCOTLAND

The Scottish Football Association Ltd, 6 Park Gardens, Glasgow G3 7YF.
Founded: 1873; *Number of Clubs:* 6,148; *Number of Players:* 135,474; *National Colours:* Dark blue shirts, white shorts, red stockings.
Telephone: 41 332 6372; *Cable:* EXECUTIVE GLASGOW; *Telex:* 778904 SFA G; *Fax:* 41 332 7559.

SLOVENIA

Nogometna Zveza Slovenije, Tabor 14, PP 47, 61004 Ljubljana, Slovenia.
Telephone: 38-61/31 18 88. *Fax:* 38-61/30 23 37.
Championship of 21 teams.

SPAIN

Real Federacion Espanola De Futbol, Calle Alberto Bosch 13, Apartado Postal 347, E-28014 Madrid.
Founded: 1913; *Number of Clubs:* 10,240; *Number of Players:* 408,135; *National Colours:* Red shirts, dark blue shorts, black stockings, yellow trim.
Telephone: 420 13 62; *Cable:* FUTBOL MADRID; *Telex:* 42420 RFEF; *Fax:* 420 20 94.

International matches 1991

Portugal (h) 1-1, France (a) 1-3, Hungary (h) 2-4, Rumania (h) 0-2, Uruguay (h) 2-1, Iceland (a) 0-2, France (h) 1-2, Czechoslovakia (h) 2-1.

League Championship wins (1945–92)

Real Madrid 25; Barcelona 12; Atletico Madrid 8; Athletic Bilbao 8; Valencia 4; Real Sociedad 2; Real Betis 1; Seville 1.

Cup wins (1902–92)

Athletic Bilbao 23; Barcelona 22; Real Madrid 16; Atletico Madrid 8; Valencia 5; Real Union de Irun 3; Seville 3; Real Zaragoza 3; Espanol 2; Arenas 1; Ciclista Sebastian 1; Racing de Irun 1; Vizcaya Bilbao 1; Real Betis 1; Real Sociedad 1.

Final League Table 1991–92

	P	W	D	L	F	A	Pts
Barcelona	38	23	9	6	87	37	55
Real Madrid	38	23	8	7	78	32	54
Atletico Madrid	38	24	5	9	67	35	53
Valencia	38	20	7	11	63	42	47
Real Sociedad	38	16	12	10	44	38	44
Real Zaragoza	38	17	7	14	40	41	41
Albacete	38	16	8	14	45	47	40
Sporting Gijon	38	15	8	15	37	43	38
Burgos	38	12	13	13	40	42	37
Logrones	38	13	10	15	36	51	36
Oviedo	38	14	8	16	41	46	34
Seville	38	13	8	17	48	45	34
Tenerife	38	12	10	16	46	50	34
Athletic Bilbao	38	13	7	18	38	58	33
Osasuna	38	10	13	15	30	40	33
Espanol	38	12	8	18	43	60	32
La Coruna†	38	8	15	15	37	48	31
Cadiz†	38	7	14	17	32	55	28
Valladolid*	38	7	13	18	31	53	27
Mallorca*	38	10	7	21	30	49	27

Top scorer: Manolo (Atletico Madrid)
Cup Final: Atletico Madrid 2, Real Madrid 0

SWEDEN

Svenska Fotbollfoerbundet, Box 1216, S-17123 Solna.
Founded: 1904; *Number of Clubs:* 3,250; *Number of Players:* 485,000; *National Colours:* Yellow shirts, blue shorts, yellow and blue stockings.
Telephone: 8-735 0900; *Cable:* FOOTBALL-S; *Telex:* 17711 FOTBOLL S; *Fax:* 8-27 51 47.

International matches 1991

Greece (a) 2-2, Austria (h) 6-0, Colombia (h) 2-2, USSR (h) 2-3, Denmark (h) 4-0, Norway (a) 2-1, Poland (a) 0-2, Yugoslavia (h) 4-3, Switzerland (a) 1-3.

League Championship wins (1896–1991)

Oergryte IS Gothenburg 14; Malmo FF 13; IFK Gothenburg 13; IFK Norrköping 12; Djurgaarden 8; AIK Stockholm 8; GAIS Gothenburg 6; IF Halsingborg 5; Boras IF Elfsborg 4; Oster Vaxjo 4; Halmstad 2; Atvidaberg 2; IFK Ekilstune 1; IF Gavic Brynas 1; IF Gothenburg 1; Fassbergs 1; Norrköping IK Sleipner 1.

Cup wins (1941–91)

Malmo FF 13; IFK Norrköping 5; AIK Stockholm 4; IFK Gothenburg 4; Atvidaberg 2; Kalmar 2; GAIS Gothenburg 1; IF Halsingborg 1; Raa 1; Landskrona 1; Oster Vaxjo 1; Djurgaarden 1.

Final League Table 1991

Qualifying table

	P	W	D	L	F	A	Pts
IFK Gothenburg	18	9	6	3	29	14	33
Orebro	18	9	6	3	25	17	33
Malmo	18	7	8	3	20	14	29
AIK	18	7	6	5	21	15	27
Djurgaarden	18	6	7	5	27	25	25
Norrkoping	18	5	6	7	24	24	21
Halmstad†	18	5	6	7	22	22	21
GAIS Gothenburg†	18	5	5	8	22	29	20
Osters†	18	3	9	6	23	26	18
Sundsvall†	18	1	7	10	15	42	19

Play-offs

	P	W	D	L	F	A	Pts
IFK Gothenburg	10	6	1	3	14	10	36
Norrkoping	10	6	2	2	18	10	31
Orebro	10	3	2	5	7	13	28
Malmo	10	3	3	4	16	15	27
Djurgaarden	10	3	4	3	16	15	26
AIK	10	3	0	7	10	15	23

Top scorer: Andersson (IFK Gothenburg) 13
Cup Final: IFK Gothenburg 3, AIK 2 *aet*

SWITZERLAND

Association Suisse De Football, Laubeggstrasse 70, B.P. CH-3000, Berne 32.
Founded: 1895; *Number of Clubs:* 1,473; *Number of Players:* 185,286; *National Colours:* Red shirts, white shorts, red stockings.
Telephone: 031-43 51 11; *Cable:* SWISSFOOT BERNE; *Telex:* 912910 SFV CH; *Fax:* (031) 44 33 80.

International matches 1991

USA (a) 1-0, Colombia (a) 3-2, Liechtenstein (a) 6-0, Romania (h) 0-0, Bulgaria (a) 3-2, San Marino (h) 7-0, Czechoslovakia (a) 1-1, Scotland (h) 2-2, Sweden (h) 3-1, Romania (a) 0-1.

League Championship wins (1898–1992)

Grasshoppers 22; Servette 15; Young Boys Berne 11; FC Zurich 9; FC Basle 8; Lausanne 7; La Chaux-de-Fonds 3; FC Lugano 3; Winterthur 3; FX Aarau 2; Neuchatel Xamax 2; FC Anglo-American 1; St Gallen 1; FC Brühl 1; Cantonal-Neuchatel 1; Biel 1; Bellinzona 1; FC Etoile Le Chaux-de-Fonds 1; Lucerne 1; Sion 1.

Cup wins (1926–92)

Grasshoppers 17; Lausanne 7; La Chaux-de-Fonds 6; Young Boys Berne 6; Servette 6; FC Sion 6; FC Basle 5; FC Zurich 5; Lucerne 2; FC Lugano 1; FC Granges 1; St Gallen 1; Urania Geneva 1; Young Fellows Zurich 1; Aarau.

Qualifying Table

	P	W	D	L	F	A	Pts
Lausanne	22	10	10	2	42	17	30
Grasshoppers	22	12	5	5	39	24	29
Sion	22	9	10	3	34	20	28
Servette	22	10	7	5	37	28	27
Neuchatel Xamax	22	9	6	7	28	22	24
St Gallen	22	8	6	8	27	32	22
Young Boys	22	8	5	9	30	30	21
Zurich	22	4	12	6	22	25	20
Lucerne*	22	5	10	7	21	26	20
Lugano*	22	6	8	8	25	36	20
Aarau*	22	3	8	11	21	39	14
Wettingen*	22	1	7	14	18	45	9

Final table

	P	W	D	L	F	A	Pts
Sion	14	7	5	2	23	16	33
Neuchatel Xamax	14	7	5	2	27	16	31
Grasshoppers	14	6	3	5	18	15	30
Young Boys	14	7	3	4	24	16	28
Servette	14	4	5	5	24	22	27
Lausanne	14	2	4	8	11	22	23
Zurich	14	3	6	5	17	27	22
St Gallen	14	3	3	8	18	28	20

Top scorer: Molnar (Servette) 18
Cup Final: Lucerne 3, Lugano 1 *aet*
* had to play-off in promotion/relegation sections

TURKEY

Federation Turque De Football, Konur Sokak No. 10, Ankara — Kizilay.
Founded: 1923; *Number of Clubs:* 230; *Number of Players:* 64,521; *National Colours:* White shirts, white shorts, red and white stockings.
Telephone: 1259182/1259189; *Cable:* FUTBOLSPOR ANKARA; *Telex:* 46308; *Fax:* (4) 117 1090.

International matches 1991

Yugoslavia (h) 1-1, Tunisia (h) 0-0, Poland (a) 0-3, England (h) 0-1, Faeroes (a) 1-1, Iceland (a) 1-5, Bulgaria (a) 0-0, USA (h) 1-1, England (a) 0-1, Republic of Ireland (h) 1-3.

League Championship wins (1960–92)

Fenerbahce 12; Besiktas 9; Galatasaray 8; Trabzonspor 6.

Cup wins (1963–92)

Galatasaray 9; Fenerbahce 4; Besiktas 4; Trabzonspor 4; Goztepe Izmir 2; Atay Ismir 2; Ankaragucu 2; Eskisehirspor 1; Bursapor 1; Genclerbirligi 1; Sakaryaspor 1.

Final League Table 1991–92

	P	W	D	L	F	A	Pts
Besiktas	30	23	7	0	58	20	76
Fenerbahce	30	23	2	5	81	35	71
Galatasaray	30	19	3	8	54	35	60
Trabzonspor	30	16	7	7	56	31	55
Aydinspor	30	12	5	13	36	41	41
Bursapor	30	10	10	10	44	43	40
Ankaragucu	30	10	10	10	43	43	40
Sariyer	30	11	5	14	34	44	38
Altay	30	10	6	14	35	45	36
Genclerbirligi	30	7	13	10	40	46	34
Bakirkoy	30	8	9	13	42	46	33
Konyaspor	30	8	8	14	28	34	32
Gaziantep	30	7	11	12	34	53	32
Boluspor*	30	8	7	15	29	38	31
Adanademirspor*	30	5	9	16	27	61	24
Samsunspor*	30	4	6	20	36	62	18

Top scorer: Aykut (Fenerbahce) 25
Cup Final: Trabzonspor 0, 5, Bursaspor 3, 1

UKRAINE

Football Federation of Ukraine, 42, Kuybysheva Street, 252023 Kiev 23, Ukraine.
Telephone: 7-044/220 1344. *Fax:* 7-044/220 1294.
Two groups of ten teams. Group winners played off: Tavria Simferopol 1, Dynamo Kiev 0.

USSR (now CIS)

USSR Football Federation, Luzhnetskaja Naberezhnaja 8, 119270 Moscow.
Founded: 1912; *Number of Clubs:* 416; *Number of Players:* 4,800,300; *National Colours:* Red shirts, white shorts, red stockings.
Telephone: 201 08 34; *Cable:* SPORTKOMITET SSSR MOSCOW; *Telex:* 411287 PRIZ SU; *Fax:* 2480814.

International matches 1991

Scotland (a) 1-0, Germany (1) 1-2, Hungary (a) 1-0, England (h) 0-1, Argentina (h) 1-1, Cyprus (h) 4-0, Sweden (a) 3-2, Italy (a) 1-1, Norway (a) 1-0, Hungary (h) 2-2, Italy (h) 0-0, Cyprus (a) 3-0.

League Championship wins (1936–91)

Dynamo Kiev 13; Spartak Moscow 12; Dynamo Moscow 11; CSKA Moscow 7; Torpedo Moscow 3; Dynamo Tbilisi 2; Dnepr Dnepropetrovsk 2; Saria Voroshilovgrad 1; Ararat Erevan 1; Dynamo Minsk 1; Zenit Leningrad 1.

Cup wins (1936–91)

Dynamo Kiev 10; Spartak Moscow 10; Torpedo Moscow 6; Dynamo Moscow 6; CSKA Moscow; Donetsk Shaktyor 4; Lokomotiv Moscow 2; Dynamo Tbilisi 2; Ararat Erevan 2; Karpaty Lvov 1; SKA Rostov 1; Zenit Leningrad 1; Metalist Kharkov 1; Dnepr 1.

Final League Table 1991

	P	W	D	L	F	A	Pts
CSKA Moscow	30	17	7	4	57	32	43
Spartak Moscow	30	17	7	6	57	30	41
Torpedo Moscow	30	13	10	7	36	20	36
Chernomorets	30	10	16	4	39	24	36
Dynamo Kiev	30	13	9	8	43	34	35
Dynamo Moscow	30	12	7	11	43	42	31
Ararat Erevan	30	11	7	12	29	36	29
Dynamo Minsk	30	9	11	10	29	31	29
Dnepr	30	9	10	11	31	36	28
Pamir	30	7	13	10	28	32	27
Vladikavkaz	30	9	8	13	33	41	26
Shakhtjor	30	6	14	10	33	41	26
Metallurg	30	9	7	14	27	38	25
Pakhtakor	30	9	7	14	37	45	25
Metallist	30	8	9	13	32	43	25
Lokomotiv	30	5	8	17	18	47	18

Top scorer: Kolyvanov (Dynamo Moscow) 18
CIS Cup Final: Moscow Spartak 2, CSKA Moscow 0
This was the last Soviet championship with teams from Armenia, Belorussia, Russia, Tagikistan, Ukraine and Uzbekistan competing. There are now 15 Leagues operating. In Russia there are two groups of ten.

WALES

The Football Association of Wales Limited, Plymouth Chambers, 3 Westgate Street, Cardiff.
Founded: 1876; *Number of Clubs:* 2,326; *Number of Players:* 53,926; *National Colours:* All red. *Telephone:* 0222 372325; *Telex:* 497 363 FAW G.

YUGOSLAVIA

Yugoslav Football Association, P.O. Box 263, Terazije 35, 11000 Beograd.
Founded: 1919; *Number of Clubs:* 6,532; *Number of Players:* 229,024; *National Colours:* Blue shirts, white shorts, red stockings.
Telephone: 333-433 and 11/334-253; *Cable:* JUGOFUDBAL BEOGRAD; *Telex:* 11666 FSJ YU; *Fax:* 0038-11-33 34 33.

International matches 1991

Turkey (a) 1-1, Northern Ireland (h) 4-1, Denmark (h) 1-2, Faeroes (h) 7-0, Sweden (a) 3-4, Faeroes (a) 2-0, Brazil (a) 1-3, Austria (a) 2-0.

League Championship wins (1923–92)

Red Star Belgrade 19; Partizan Belgrade 11; Hajduk Split 9; Gradjanski Zagreb; BSK Belgrade 5; Dynamo Zagreb 4; Jugoslavija Belgrade 2; Concordia Zagreb 2; FC Sarajevo 2; Vojvodina Novi Sad 2; HASK Zagreb 1; Zeljeznicar 1.

Cup wins (1947–92)

Red Star Belgrade 12; Hajduk Split 9; Dynamo Zagreb 8; Partizan Belgrade 6; BSK Belgrade 2; OFK Belgrade 2; Rejeka 2; Velez Mostar 2; Vardar Skopje 1; Borac Banjaluka 1.

Final League Table 1991–92

	P	W	D*	L	F	A	Pts
Red Star Belgrade	33	23	5	5	77	24	50
Partizan Belgrade	33	21	10	2	59	18	46
Vojvodina	33	19	5	9	45	30	42
OFK Belgrade	33	19	8	6	62	36	41
Proleter	33	16	4	13	40	43	35
Vardar	33	15	6	12	50	34	34
Rad	33	14	3	16	48	43	29
Borac	33	11	10	12	24	32	28
Sarajevo	33	12	6	14	33	45	27
Zemun	33	12	7	14	44	43	26
Raznicki	33	12	5	16	37	45	26
Buducnost	33	12	6	15	30	32	23
Sutjeka	33	11	6	16	40	47	23
Velez Mostar	32	10	5	17	34	53	23
Pelister	33	9	3	21	30	57	20
Spartak	33	7	9	17	27	49	17
Sloboda	31	7	3	21	21	61	16
Zeljeznicar	17	6	3	8	18	24	15

* *drawn games decided by penalty kicks*
Championship not completed because of political situation.
Top scorer: Pancev (Red Star Belgrade) 25
Cup Final: Partizan Belgrade 1, 2, Red Star Belgrade 0, 2

SOUTH AMERICA

ARGENTINA

Asociacion Del Futbol Argentina, Viamonte 1366/76, 1053 Buenos Aires.
Founded: 1893; *Number of Clubs:* 3,035; *Number of Players:* 306,365; *National Colours:* Blue & white shirts, black shorts, white stockings.
Telephone: 40-4276; *Cable:* FUTBOL BUENOS AIRES; *Telex:* 22710 AFA AR; *Fax:* 953 3469 AFA.

BOLIVIA

Federacion Boliviana De Futbol, Av. 16 De Julio No. N. 0782, Casilla Postal No. 474, Cochabamba.
Founded: 1925; *Number of Clubs:* 305; *Number of Players:* 15,290; *National Colours:* Green shirts, white shorts, green stockings.
Telephone: 4-5064; *Cable:* FEDFUTBOL COCHABAMBA; *Telex:* 6239 FEDBOL; *Fax:* 4-7951.

BRAZIL

Confederacao Brasileira De Futebol, Rua Da Alfandega, 70, P.O. Box 1078, 20.070 Rio De Janeiro.
Founded: 1914; *Number of Clubs:* 12,987; *Number of Players:* 551,358; *National Colours:* Yellow shirts, blue shorts, white stockings, green trim.
Telephone: 221/5937; *Cable:* DESPORTOS RIO DE JANEIRO; *Telex:* 2121509 CBDS BR; *Fax:* (021) 252 9294.

CHILE

Federacion De Futbol De Chile, Calle Erasmo Escala No. 1872, Casilla No. 3733, Santiago De Chile.
Founded: 1895; *Number of Clubs:* 4,598; *Number of Players:* 609,724; *National Colours:* Red shirts, blue shorts, white stockings.
Telephone: 696 5381; *Cable:* FEDFUTBOL SANTIAGO DE CHILE; *Telex:* 440474 FEBOL CZ; *Fax:* 698 7082.

COLOMBIA

Federacion Colombiana De Futbol, Avenida 32, No. 16-22, Apartado Aereo No. 17.602, Bogota. D.E.
Founded: 1925; *Number of Clubs:* 3,685; *Number of Players:* 188,050; *National Colours:* Red shirts, blue shorts, tricolour stockings.
Telephone: 245 5370; *Cable:* COLFUTBOL BOGOTA; *Telex:* 45598 COLFU CO.

ECUADOR

Federacion Ecuatoriana De Futbol, Calle Jose Mascote 1.103 (Piso 2), Luque, Casilla 7447, Guayaquil.
Founded: 1925; *Number of Clubs:* 170; *Number of Players:* 15,700; *National Colours:* Yellow shirts, blue shorts, red stockings.
Telephone: 37 16 74; *Cable:* ECUAFUTBOL GUAYAQUIL; *Telex:* 42970 FEECFU ED; *Fax:* (593-4) 373-320.

PARAGUAY

Liga Paraguaya De Futbol, Estadio De Sajonia, Calles Mayor Martinez Y Alejo Garcia, Asuncion.
Founded: 1906; *Number of Clubs:* 1,500; *Number of Players:* 140,000; *National Colours:* Red & white shirts, blue shorts, blue stockings.
Telephone: 81743; *Telex:* 627 PY FUTBOL; *Fax:* 595 21 81743.

PERU

Federacion Peruana De Futbol, Estadio Nacional/Puerto No. 4, Calle Jose Diaz, Lima.
Founded: 1922; *Number of Clubs:* 10,000; *Number of Players:* 325,650; *National Colours:* White shirts, red trim, white shorts, white stockings.
Telephone: 32 05 17; *Cable* FEPEFUTBOL LIMA; *Telex:* 20066 FEPEFUT PE.

URUGUAY

Asociacion Uruguaya De Futbol, Guayabo 1531, Montevideo.
Founded: 1900; *Number of Clubs:* 1,091; *Number of Players:* 134,310; *National Colours:* Light blue shirts, black shorts, black stockings.
Telephone: 40 71 01/06; *Cable:* FUTBOL MONTEVIDEO; *Telex:* AUF UY 22607.

VENEZUELA

Federacion Venezolana De Futbol, Avda Este Estadio Nacional, El Paraiso Apdo. Postal 14160, Candelaria, Caracas.
Founded: 1926; *Number of Clubs:* 1,753; *Number of Players:* 63,175; *National Colours:* Magenta shirts, white shirts, white stockings.
Telephone: 461 80 10; *Cable:* FEVEFUTBOL CARACAS; *Telex:* 26 140 FVFCS VC.

ASIA

AFGHANISTAN

The Football Federation of National Olympic Committee, Kabul.
Founded: 1922; *Number of Clubs:* 30; *Number of Players:* 3,300; *National Colours:* White shirts, white shorts, white stockings.
Telephone: 20579; *Cable:* OLYMPIC KABUL.

BAHRAIN

Bahrain Football Association, P.O. Box 5464, Bahrain.
Founded: 1951; *Number of Clubs:* 25; *Number of Players:* 2,030; *National Colours:* White shirts, red shorts, white stockings.
Telephone: 72 95 63; *Cable:* BAHKORA BAHRAIN; *Telex:* 9040 FAB BN; *Fax:* 729361.

BANGLADESH

Bangladesh Football Federation, Stadium, Dhaka 2.
Founded: 1972; *Number of Clubs:* 1,265; *Number of Players:* 30,385; *National Colours:* Orange shirts, white shorts, green stockings.
Telephone: 23 60 72/23 59 28; *Cable:* FOOTBALFED DHAKA; *Telex:* 642460 BHL BJ.

BRUNEI

Brunei Amateur Football Association, P.O. Box 2010, Bandar Seri Begawan 1920, Brunei Darussalam.
Founded: 1959; *Number of Clubs:* 22; *Number of Players:* 830; *National Colours:* Gold shirts, black shorts, gold stockings.
Telephone: 673-02-24 22 83, 24 31 71; *Cable:* BAFA BRUNEI; *Telex:* dirwyas BU 2575 Attn: BAFA; *Fax:* 673-02-24 23 00.

BURMA (now Myanmar)

Myanmar Football Federation, Aung San Memorial Stadium, Kandawgalay Post Office, Yangon.
Founded: 1947; *Number of Clubs:* 600; *Number of Players:* 21,000; *National Colours:* Red shirts, white shorts, red stockings.
Telephone: 75 249; *Cable:* YANGON MYANMAR; *Telex:* 21218 BRCROS BRN.

CHINA PR

Football Association of The People's Republic of China, 9 Tiyuguan Road, Beijing.
Founded: 1924; *Number of Clubs:* 1,045; *Number of Players:* 2,250,000; *National Colours:* Red shirts, white shorts, red stockings.
Telephone: 01/701 70 18; *Cable:* SPORTSCHINE BEIJING; *Telex:* 22034 ACSF CN; *Fax:* 01/511 25 33.

HONG KONG

The Hong Kong Football Association Ltd, 55 Fat Kwong Street, Homantin, Kowloon, Hong Kong.
Founded: 1914; *Number of Clubs:* 69; *Number of Players:* 3,274; *National Colours:* Red shirts, white shorts, red stockings.
Telephone: 3-712 9122-5; *Cable:* FOOTBALL HONG KONG; *Telex:* 40518 FAHKG HX; *Fax:* 3-760 4303.

INDIA

All India Football Federation, Netaji Indoor Stadium, Eden Gardens, Calcutta 700 021.
Founded: 1937; *Number of Clubs:* 2,000; *Number of Players:* 56,000; *National Colours:* Light blue shirts, white shorts, dark blue stockings.
Telephone: 28 8484; *Cable:* SOCCER CALCUTTA; *Telex:* 212216 MCPL IN.

INDONESIA

All Indonesia Football Federation, Main Stadium Senayan, Gate VII, P.O. Box 2305, Jakarta.
Founded: 1930; *Number of Clubs:* 2,880; *Number of Players:* 97,000; *National Colours:* Red shirts, white shorts, red stockings.
Telephone: 581541/584386; *Cable:* PSSI JAKARTA; *Telex:* 65739 as; *Fax:* (021) 584386.

IRAN

Football Federation of The Islamic Republic of Iran, Ave Varzandeh No. 10, P.O. Box 11/1642, Tehran.
Founded: 1920; *Number of Clubs:* 6,326; *Number of Players:* 306,000; *National Colours:* Green shirts, white shorts, red stockings.
Telephone: (021) 825534; *Cable:* FOOTBALL IRAN — TEHRAN; *Telex:* 212691 VARZ IR.

IRAQ

Iraqi Football Association, Youth City, P.O. Box 484, Baghdad.
Founded: 1948; *Number of Clubs:* 155; *Number of Players:* 4,400; *National Colours:* White shirts, white shorts, white stockings.
Telephone: 772 8430; *Cable:* BALL BAGHDAD; *Telex:* 214074 IRFA IK; *Fax:* 772 84 24.

ISRAEL

Israel Football Association, 12 Carlibach Street, P.O. Box 20188, Tel Aviv 61201.
Founded: 1928; *Number of Clubs:* 544; *Number of Players:* 30,449; *National Colours:* White shirts, blue shorts, white stockings.
Telephone: 56 10 888; *Cable:* CADUREGEL TEL AVIV; *Telex:* 361353 FA; *Fax:* 03 5610838.

JAPAN

The Football Association of Japan, 1-1-1 Jinnan, Shibuya-Ku, Tokyo.
Founded: 1921; *Number of Clubs:* 13,047; *Number of Players:* 358,989; *National Colours:* Blue shirts, white shorts, blue stockings.
Telephone: 03-481-2311; *Cable:* SOCCERJAPAN TOKYO; *Telex:* 2422975 FOTJPN J; *Fax:* 81 3 481 0976.

JORDAN

Jordan Football Association, P.O. Box 1954, Amman.
Founded: 1949; *Number of Clubs:* 98; *Number of Players:* 4,305; *National Colours:* White shirts, white shorts, white stockings.
Telephone: 009626-62 4481, or 62 59 93; *Cable:* JORDAN FOOTBALL ASSOCIATION AM; *Telex:* 22415 FOBALL JO. *Fax:* 009626-62 4454.

KAMPUCHEA

Federation Khmere De Football Association, C.P. 101, Complex Sportif National, Phnom-Penh.
Founded: 1933; *Number of Clubs:* 30; *Number of Players:* 650; *National Colours:* Red shirts, white shorts, red stockings.
Telephone: 22 469; *Cable:* FKFA PHNOMPENH.

KOREA, NORTH

Football Association of The Democratic People's Rep. of Korea, Munsin-Dong 2, Dongdaewon Distr, Pyongyang.
Founded: 1928; *Number of Clubs:* 90; *Number of Players:* 3,420; *National Colours:* Red shirts, white shorts, red stockings.
Telephone: 6-3998; *Cable:* DPR KOREA FOOTBALL PYONGYANG; *Telex:* 5472 KP; *Fax:* 850-2/81 44 03.

KOREA, SOUTH

Korea Football Association, 110-39, Kyeonji-Dong, Chongro-Ku, Seoul.
Founded: 1928; *Number of Clubs:* 476; *Number of Players:* 2,047; *National Colours:* Red shirts, red shorts, red stockings.
Telephone: 02-733-6764; *Cable:* FOOTBALLKOREA SEOUL; *Telex:* KFASEL K 25373; *Fax:* 02 735 2755.

KUWAIT

Kuwait Football Association, Udailiyya, BL. 4, Al-Ittihad St, P.O. Box 2029 (Safat), 13021 Safat.
Founded: 1952; *Number of Clubs:* 14 (senior); *Number of Players:* 1,526; *National Colours:* Blue shirts, white shorts, blue stockings.
Telephone: 00965/255 58 51 or 255 58 39; *Cable:* FOOTKUWAIT; *Telex:* FOOTKUW 22600 KT; *Fax:* 00965/256 37 37.

LAOS

Federation De Foot-Ball Lao, c/o Dir. Des Sports, Education, Physique Et Artistique, Vientiane.
Founded: 1951; *Number of Clubs:* 76; *Number of Players:* 2,060; *National Colours:* Red shirts, white shorts, blue stockings.
Telephone: 27 41; *Cable:* FOOTBALL VIENTIANE.

LEBANON

Federation Libanaise De Football Association, P.O. Box 4732, Omar Ibn Khattab Street, Beirut.
Founded: 1933; *Number of Clubs:* 105; *Number of Players:* 8,125; *National Colours:* Red shirts, white shorts, red stockings.
Telephone: (1) 30 07 60; *Cable:* FOOTBALL BEIRUT; *Telex:* 23001 ALABAL.

MACAO

Associacao De Futebol De Macau (AFM), P.O. Box 920, Macau.
Founded: 1939; *Number of Clubs:* 52; *Number of Players:* 800; *National Colours:* Green shirts, white shorts, green and white stockings.
Telephone: 71 996 (559315); *Cable:* FOOTBALL MACAU.

MALDIVES REPUBLIC

Football Association of Maldives, Attn. Mr. Bandhu Ahamed Saleem, Sports Division, Male.
Founded: 1986; *Number of Clubs:* —; *Number of Players:* —; *National Colours:* Green shirts, white shorts, green and white stockings.
Telephone: 3432; *Telex:* 77039 MINHOM MF; *Fax:* (960) 32 47 39.

MALAYSIA

Football Association of Malaysia, Wisma Fam, Tingkat 4, Jalan SS5A/9, Kelana Jaya, 47301 Petaling, Jaya Selangor.
Founded: 1933; *Number of Clubs:* 450; *Number of Players:* 11,250; *National Colours:* Black and gold shirts, white shorts, black and gold stockings.
Telephone: 03-776 3766; *Cable:* FOOTBALL PETALING JAYA SELANGO; *Telex:* FAM PJ MA 36701; *Fax:* 03-775 7984.

NEPAL

All-Nepal Football Association, Dasharath Rangashala, Tripureshwor, Kathmandu.
Founded: 1951; *Number of Clubs:* 85; *Number of Players:* 2,550; *National Colours:* Red shirts, blue shorts, blue and white stockings.
Telephone: 2-15 703; *Cable:* ANFA KATHMANDU; *Telex:* 2390 NSC NP.

OMAN

Oman Football Association, P.O. Box 6462, Ruwi-Muscat.
Founded: 1978; *Number of Clubs:* 47; *Number of Players:* 2,340; *National Colours:* White shirts, red shorts, white stockings.
Telephone: 70 78 85; *Cable:* FOOTBALL MUSCAT; *Telex:* 3760 FOOTBALL ON; *Fax:* 707829.

PAKISTAN

Pakistan Football Federation, General Secretary, 43 Rettigon Road, Lahore, Pakistan.
Founded: 1948; *Number of Clubs:* 882; *Number of Players:* 21,000; *National Colours:* Green shirts, white shorts, green stockings.
Telephone: 92 42/23 33 48 or 21 06 38; *Cable:* FOOTBALL QUETTA; *Telex:* 47643 PFF PK; *Fax:* 92 42/23 72 97.

PHILIPPINES

Philippine Football Federation, Room 207, Administration Building, Rizal Memorial Sports Complex, Vito Cruz, Metro Manila.
Founded: 1907; *Number of Clubs:* 650; *Number of Players:* 45,000; *National Colours:* Blue shirts, white shorts, blue stockings.
Telephone: 58 83 17; *Cable:* FOOTBALL MANILA; Telex: 63539 ANSCOR PN.

QATAR

Qatar Football Association, P.O. Box 5333, Doha.
Founded: 1960; *Number of Clubs:* 8 (senior); *Number of Players:* 1,380; *National Colours:* White shirts, maroon shorts, white stockings.
Telephone: 351641, 454444; *Cable:* FOOTQATAR DOHA; *Telex:* 4749 QATFOT DH; *Fax:* (0974) 411660.

SAUDI ARABIA

Saudi Arabian Football Federation, North Al-Morabbaa Quarter, P.O. Box 5844, Riyadh 11432.
Founded: 1959; *Number of Clubs:* 120; *Number of Players:* 9,600; *National Colours:* White shirts, white shorts, white stockings.
Telephone: 402 2699; *Cable:* KORA RIYADH; *Telex:* 404300 SAFOTB SJ; *Fax:* 01 402 1276.

SINGAPORE

Football Association of Singapore, Jalan Besar Stadium, Tyrwhitt Road, Singapore 0820.
Founded: 1892; *Number of Clubs:* 250; *Number of Players:* 8,000; *National Colours:* Sky blue shirts, sky blue shorts, sky blue stockings.
Telephone: 293 1477; *Cable:* SOCCER SINGAPORE; *Telex:* SINFA RS 37683.

SRI LANKA

Football Federation of Sri Lanka, No. 2, Old Grand Stand, Race Course — Reid Avenue, Colombo 7.
Founded: 1939; *Number of Clubs:* 600; *Number of Players:* 18,825; *National Colours:* Maroon shirts, white shorts, white stockings.
Telephone: 596179; *Cable:* SOCCER COLOMBO; *Telex:* 21537 METALIX CE; *Fax:* 94-1-580721.

SYRIA

Association Arabe Syrienne De Football, General Sport Fed. Building, October Stadium, Damascus — Baremke.
Founded: 1936; *Number of Clubs:* 102; *Number of Players:* 30,600; *National Colours:* White shirts, white shorts, white stockings.
Telephone: 33 15 11; *Cable:* FOOTBALL DAMASCUS; *Telex:* HOTECH 41 19 35.

THAILAND

The Football Association of Thailand, c/o National Stadium, Rama I Road, Bangkok.
Founded: 1916; *Number of Clubs:* 168; *Number of Players:* 15,000; *National Colours:* Crimson shirts, white shorts, crimson stockings.
Telephone: 02 214 1058; *Cable:* FOOTBALL BANGKOK; *Telex:* 20211 FAT TH; *Fax:* 2154494.

UNITED ARAB EMIRATES

United Arab Emirates Football Association, Post Box 5458, Dubai.
Founded: 1971; *Number of Clubs:* 23 (senior); *Number of Players:* 1,787; *National Colours:* White shirts, white shorts, white stockings.
Telephone: 245 636; *Cable:* FOOTBALL EMIRATES DUBAI; *Telex:* 47623 UAEFA EM; *Fax:* 245 559.

VIETNAM

Association De Football De La Republique Du Viet-Nam, No. 36, Boulevard Tran-Phu, Hanoi. *Founded:* 1962; *Number of Clubs:* 55 (senior); *Number of Players:* 16,000; *National Colours:* Red shirts, white shorts, red stockings. *Telephone:* 5/48 67; *Cable:* AFBVN, 36, TRAN-PHU-HANOI.

YEMEN

Yemen Football Association, P.O. Box 908, Sana'a.
Founded: 1962; *Number of Clubs:* 26; *Number of Players:* 1750; *National Colours:* Green.
Telephone: 00967/2/215720. *Telex:* 2710 YOUTH YE

CONCACAF

ANTIGUA

The Antigua Football Association, P.O. Box 773, St. Johns.
Founded: 1928; *Number of Clubs:* 60; *Number of Players:* 1,008; *National Colours:* Gold shirts, black shorts, black stockings.
Telephone: 809 462 3945; *Cable:* AFA ANTIGUA; *Telex:* 2177 SIDAN AK; *Fax:* 809 462 2649.

BAHAMAS

Bahamas Football Association, P.O. Box N 8434, Nassau, N.P.
Founded: 1967; *Number of Clubs:* 14; *Number of Players:* 700; *National Colours:* Yellow shirts, black shorts, yellow stockings.
Telephone: 809 32 47099; *Cable:* BAHSOCA NASSAU; *Fax:* 809 324 6484.

BARBADOS

Barbados Football Association, P.O. Box 833E, Bridgetown.
Founded: 1910; *Number of Clubs:* 92; *Number of Players:* 1,100; *National Colours;* Royal blue shirts, gold shorts, royal blue stockings.
Telphone: 809 424 4413; *Cable:* FOOTBALL BRIDGETOWN; *Telex:* 2306 SHAMROCK WB; *Fax:* (809) 436 0130.

BELIZE

Belize National Football Association, P.O. Box 1742, Belize City.
Founded: 1986; *National Colours:* Blue shirts, red & white trim, white shorts, blue stockings.
Telephone: 08-2609 or 08 2637; 02 77031 32; 08-2200; *Telex:* 102 FOREIGN BZ.

BERMUDA

The Bermuda Football Association, P.O. Box HM 745, Hamilton 5 HM CX.
Founded: 1928; *Number of Clubs:* 30; *Number of Players:* 1,947; *National Colours:* Blue shirts, white shorts, white stockings.
Telephone: (809) 295 2199; *Cable:* FOOTBALL BERMUDA; *Telex:* 3441 BFA BA; *Fax:* (809) 295 0773.

CANADA

The Canadian Soccer Association, 1600 James Naismith Drive, Gloucester, Ont. K1B 5N4.
Founded: 1912; *Number of Clubs:* 1,600; *Number of Players:* 224,290; *National Colours:* Red shirts, red shorts, red stockings.
Telephone: (613) 748-5667; *Cable:* SOCCANADA OTTAWA; *Telex:* 053-3350; *Fax:* (613) 745-1938.

COSTA RICA

Federacion Costarricense De Futbol, Calle 40-Ave, CTLI, San Jose.
Founded: 1921; *Number of Clubs:* 431; *Number of Players:* 12,429; *National Colours:* Red shirts, blue shorts, white stockings.
Telephone: 22 15 44; *Cable:* FEDEFUTBOL SAN JOSE; *Telex:* 3394 DIDER CR.

CUBA

Asociacion De Futbol De Cuba, c/o Comite Olimpico Cubano, Calle 13 No. 601, Esq. C. Vedado, La Habana, ZP 4.
Founded: 1924; *Number of Clubs:* 70; *Number of Players:* 12,900; *National Colours:* White shirts, blue shorts, white stockings.
Telephone: 40 35 81; *Cable:* FOOTBALL HABANA; *Telex:* 511332 INDER CU.

DOMINICAN REPUBLIC

Federacion Dominicana de Futbol, Apartado De Correos No. 1953, Santo Domingo.
Founded: 1953; *Number of Clubs:* 128; *Number of Players:* 10,706; *National Colours:* Blue shirts, white shorts, red stockings.
Telephone: 542-6923. *Cable:* FEDOFUTBOL SANTO DOMINGO.

EL SALVADOR

Federacion Salvadorena De Futbol, Av. Jm. Delgado, Col. Escalon, Centro Espanol, Apartado 1029, San Salvador.
Founded: 1936; *Number of Clubs:* 944; *Number of Players:* 21,294; *National Colours:* Blue shirts, blue shorts, blue stockings.
Telephone: 23 73 62; *Cable:* FESFUT SAN SALVADOR; *Telex:* 20484 FESFUT SAL.

GRENADA

Grenada Football Association, P.O. Box 326, St. Juilles Street, St. George's.
Founded: 1924; *Number of Clubs:* 15; *Number of Players:* 200; *National Colours:* Green & yellow shirts, red shorts, green & yellow stockings.
Telephone: 1-809/440 1986; *Cable:* GRENBALL GRENADA; *Telex:* 3431 CW BUR; *Fax:* 1-809/440 1986.

GUATEMALA

Federacion Nacional De Futbol De Guatemala C.A., Palacio De Los Deportes, 2 Piso, Zona 4, Guatemala C.A.
Founded: 1933; *Number of Clubs:* 1,611; *Number of Players:* 43,516; *National Colours:* White/blue diagonal striped shirts, blue shorts, white stockings.
Telephone: 362211; *Cable:* FEDFUTBOL GUATEMALA.

GUYANA

Guyana Football Association, P.O. Box 10727 Georgetown.
Founded: 1902; *Number of Clubs:* 103; *Number of Players:* 1,665; *National Colours:* Green & yellow shirts, black shorts, white & green stockings.
Telephone: 02-59458/9; *Cable:* FOOTBALL GUYANA; *Telex:* 2266 RICEBRD GY; *Fax:* (005922) 52169.

HAITI

Federation Haitienne De Football, Stade Sylvio-Cator, Port-Au-Prince.
Founded: 1904; *Number of Clubs:* 40; *Number of Players:* 4,000; *National Colours:* Red shirts, black shorts, red stockings.
Telephone: 2/3237; *Cable:* FEDHAFOOB PORT-AU-PRINCE.

HONDURAS

Federacion Nacional Autonoma De Futbol De Honduras, Apartado Postal 827, Costa Oeste Del Est. Nac, Tegucigalpa, De. C.
Founded: 1951; *Number of Clubs:* 1,050; *Number of Players:* 15,300; *National Colours:* Blue shirts, blue shorts, blue stockings.
Telephone: 32-1897; *Cable* FENAFUTH TEGUCIGALPA; *Telex:* 1209 FENEFUTH; *Fax:* 31 14 28.

JAMAICA

Jamaica Football Federation, Room 9, National Stadium, Kingston 6.
Founded: 1910; *Number of Clubs:* 266; *Number of Players:* 45,200; *National Colours:* Green shirts, black shorts, green & gold stockings.
Cable: FOOTBALL JAMAICA KINGSTON.

MEXICO

Federacion Mexicana De Futbol Asociacion, A.C., Abraham Gonzales 74, C.P. 06600, Col. Juarez, Mexico 6, D.F.
Founded: 1927; *Number of Clubs:* 77 (senior); *Number of Players:* 1,402,270; *National Colours:* Green shirts, white shorts, green stockings.
Telephone: 566 21 55; *Cable:* MEXFUTBOL MEXICO; *Telex:* 1771678 MSUTME; *Fax:* (915) 566 7580.

NETHERLANDS ANTILLES

Nederlands Antiliaanse Voetbal Unie, P.O. Box 341, Curacao, N.A.
Founded: 1921; *Number of Clubs:* 85; *Number of Players:* 4,500; *National Colours:* white shirts, white shorts, white stockings.
Telephone: —; *Cable:* NAVU CURACAO; *Telex:* 1046 ennia na; *Fax:* (599-9) 611173 ennia caribe.

NICARAGUA

Federacion Nicaraguense De Futbol, Inst. Nicaraguense De Deportes, Apartado Postal 976 0 383, Managua.
Founded: 1968; *Number of Clubs:* 31; *Number of Players:* 160 (senior); *National Colours:* Blue shirts, blue shorts, blue stockings.
Telephone: 505 2/66 41 34; *Cable:* FEDEFOOT MANAGUA; *Telex:* 2156 IND NK.

PANAMA

Federacion Nacional De Futbol De Panama, Apdo 1436, Balboa, Ancon., Panama.
Founded: 1937; *Number of Clubs:* 65; *Number of Players:* 4,225; *National Colours:* Red & white shirts, blue shorts, blue stockings.
Telephone: 60 50 32; *Cable:* PANAOLIMPIC PANAMA; *Telex:* 2534 INDE PG; *Fax:* (507) 60 41 66.

PUERTO RICO

Federacion Puertorriquena De Futbol, Coliseo Roberto Clemente, P.O. Box 4355, Hato Rey, 00919-4355.
Founded: 1940; *Number of Clubs:* 175; *Number of Players:* 4,200; *National Colurs:* White & red shirts, blue shorts, white & blue stockings.
Telephone: 766 1461; *Cable:* BORIKENFPF; *Telex:* 3450296; *Fax:* 8660489, 764-2025.

SURINAM

Surinaamse Voetbal Bond, Cultuuruinlaan 7, P.O. Box 1223, Paramaribo.
Founded: 1920; *Number of Clubs:* 168; *Number of Players:* 4,430; *National Colours:* Red shirts, white shorts, white stockings.
Telephone: 73112; *Cable:* SVB Paramaribo.

TRINIDAD AND TOBAGO

Trinidad & Tobago Football Association, Cor. Duke & Scott-Bushe Street, Port of Spain, Trinidad, P.O. Box 400.
Founded: 1906; *Number of Clubs:* 124; *Number of Players:* 5,050; *National Colours:* Red shirts, black shorts, red stockings.
Telephone: 624 5183. *Cable:* TRAFA PORT OF SPAIN; *Telex:* 22652 TRAFA; *Fax:* 627-7661.

USA

United States Soccer Federation, 1750 East Boulder Street, Colorado Springs, CO 80909.
Founded: 1913; *Number of Clubs:* 7,000; *Number of Players:* 1,411,500; *National Colours:* White shirts, blue shorts, red stockings.
Telephone: (719) 578-4678; *Cable:* SOCCERUSA COLORADOSPRINGS; *Telex:* 450024 US SOCCER FED; *Fax:* (719) 578-4636.

Recent additions; ARUBA, SANTA LUCIA, ST. VINCENT and the GRENADINES. Aruba is an island in the Caribbean with 1,500 registered players and 50 clubs. *Colours:* Yellow and blue. St. Lucia is another island in the same area with 4,000 players and 100 clubs. *Colours:* Blue, white and black. St Vincent and the Grenadines is similarly situated and has 5,000 players.

OCEANIA

AUSTRALIA

Australian Soccer Federation, First Floor, 23-25 Frederick Street, Rockdale, NSW 2216.
Founded: 1961; *Number of Clubs:* 6,816; *Number of Players:* 433,957; *National Colours:* Gold shirts, green shorts, white stockings.
Telephone: 29 7026; *Cable:* FOOTBALL SYDNEY; *Telex:* AA 170512; *Fax:* 02 296 556.

FIJI

Fiji Football Association, Mr. J. D. Maharaj, Hon. Secretary Government Bldgs, P.O.B. 2514 Suva.
Founded: 1946; *Number of Clubs;* 140: *Number of Players:* 21,300; *National Colours:* White shirts, black shorts, black stockings.
Telephone: 300453; *Cable:* FOOTSOCCER SUVA; *Telex:* 2366 FJ; *Fax:* 304642.

NEW ZEALAND

New Zealand Football Association, Inc., P.O. Box 62-532, Central Park, Green Lane, Auckland 6.
Founded: 1891; *Number of Clubs:* 312; *Number of Players:* 52,969; *National Colours:* White shirts, black shorts, white stockings.
Telephone: 0-9-525-6120; *Fax:* 0-9-525-6123.

PAPUA-NEW-GUINEA

Papua New Guinea Football (Soccer) Association Inc., P.O. Box 1716, Boroko.
Founded: 1962; *Number of Clubs:* 350; *Number of Players:* 8,250; *National Colours:* Red shirts, black shorts, red stockings.
Telephone: 25 41 09; *Telex:* TOTOTRA NE 23436.

WESTERN SAMOA

Western Samoa Football (Soccer) Association, Min. of Youth, Sports Culture, Private Bag, Apia.
Founded: 1986; *National Colours:* Blue shirts, white shorts, blue and white stockings.
Telephone: 23315; *Telex:* 230 SAMGAMES SX.

Recent additions: SOLOMON ISLANDS, TAHITI and VANUATU. The Solomon Islands are situated in the South Pacific to the south-east of Papua New Guinea. There are 4,000 registered players. Vanuatu was formerly known as the New Hebrides and is a double chain of islands to the south-east of the Solomons. *Colours:* Gold and black.

AFRICA

ALGERIA

Federation Algerienne De Futbol, Route Ahmed Ouaked, Boite Postale No. 39, Alger — Dely Ibrahim.
Founded: 1962; *Number of Clubs:* 780; *Number of Players:* 58,567; *National Colours:* Green shirts, white shorts, red stockings.
Telephone: 799443/796733; *Cable:* FAFOOT ALGER; *Telex:* 61378.

ANGOLA

Federation Angolaise De Football, B.P. 3449, Luanda.
Founded: 1977; *Number of Clubs:* 276; *Number of Players:* 4,269; *National Colours:* Red shirts, black shorts, green stockings.
Telephone: 338635/338233; *Cable:* FUTANGOLA; *Telex:* 4072 CIAM AN.

BENIN

Federation Beninoise De Football, B.P. 965, Cotonou.
Founded: 1968; *Number of Clubs:* 117; *Number of Players:* 6,700; *National Colours:* Green shirts, green shorts, green stockings.
Telephone: 33 05 37; *Cable:* FEBEFOOT COTONOU; *Telex:* 5033 BIMEX COTONOU; *Fax:* 30 02 14.

BOTSWANA

Botswana Football Association, P.O. Box 1396, Gaborone.
Founded: 1976; *National Colours:* Sky blue shirts, white shorts, sky blue stockings. *Cable:* BOTSBALL GABARONE; *Telex:* 2977 BD; *Fax:* (267) 372 911.

BURKINA FASO

Federation Burkinabe De Foot-Ball, B.P. 57, Ouagadougou.
Founded: 1960; *Number of Clubs:* 57; *Number of Players:* 4,672; *National Colours:* Black shirts, white shorts, red stockings.
Telephone: 33 58 20; *Cable:* FEDEFOOT OUAGADOUGOU.

BURUNDI

Federation De Football Du Burundi, B.P. 3426, Bujumbura.
Founded: 1948; *Number of Clubs:* 132; *Number of Players:* 3,930; *National Colours:* Red shirts, white shorts, green stockings.
Telephone: 2 3078; *Cable:* FFB BUJA.

CAMEROON

Federation Camerounaise De Football, B.P. 1116, Yaounde.
Founded: 1960; *Number of Clubs:* 200; *Number of Players:* 9,328; *National Colours:* Green shirts, red shorts, yellow stockings.
Telephone: 22 25 38; *Cable:* FECAFOOT YAOUNDE; *Telex:* JEUNESPO 8568 KN

CAPE VERDE ISLANDS

Federacao Cabo-Verdiana De Futebol, C.P. 234, PRAIA.
Founded: 1986; *National Colours:* Green shirts, green shorts, green stockings.
Telephone: 611362; *Cable:* FCF-CV; *Telex:* 6030 MICDE-CV.

CENTRAL AFRICAN REPUBLIC

Federation Centrafricaine De Football, B.P. 344, Bangui.
Founded: 1937; *Number of Clubs:* 256; *Number of Players:* 7,200; *National Colours:* Grey & blue shirts, white shorts, red stockings.
Telephone: 2141; *Cable:* FOOTBANGUI BANGUI.

CONGO

Federation Congolaise De Football, B.P. 4041, Brazzaville.
Founded: 1962; *Number of Clubs:* 250; *Number of Players:* 5,940; *National Colours:* Red shirts, red shorts, white stockings.
Telephone: 81 51 01; *Cable:* FECOFOOT BRAZZAVILLE; *Telex:* 5210 KG.

EGYPT

Egyptian Football Association, 5, Shareh Gabalaya, Guezira, Al Borg Post Office, Cairo.
Founded: 1921; *Number of Clubs:* 247; *Number of Players:* 19,735; *National Colours:* Red shirts, white shorts, black stockings.
Telephone: 340 1793; *Cable:* KORA CAIRO; *Telex:* 23504 KORA.

ETHIOPIA

Ethiopia Football Federation, Addis Ababa Stadium, P.O. Box 1080, Addis Ababa.
Founded: 1943; *Number of Clubs:* 767; *Number of Players:* 20,594; *National Colours:* Green shirts, yellow shorts, red stockings.
Telephone: 51 44 53 and 51 43 21. *Cable:* FOOTBALL ADDIS ABABA; *Telex:* 21377 NESCO ET.

GABON

Federation Gabonaise De Football, B.P. 181, Libreville.
Founded: 1962; *Number of Clubs:* 320; *Number of Players:* 10,000; *National Colours:* Blue shirts, white shorts, white stockings.
Telephone: 72 22 37; *Cable:* FEGAFOOT LIBREVILLE; *Telex:* 5642 GO.

GAMBIA

Gambia Football Association, P.O. Box 523, Banjul.
Founded: 1952; *Number of Clubs:* 30; *Number of Players:* 860; *National Colours:* White & red shirts, white shorts, white stockings.
Telephone: 958 35; *Cable:* SPORTS GAMBIA BANJUL; *Fax:* GNOSC 220/96270.

GHANA

Ghana Football Association, P.O. Box 1272, Accra.
Founded: 1957; *Number of Clubs:* 347; *Number of Players:* 11,275; *National Colours:* White shirts, white shorts, white stockings.
Telephone: 63 924/7; *Cable:* GFA, ACCRA; *Telex:* 2519 SPORTS GH.

GUINEA

Federation Guineenne De Football, P.O. Box 3645, Conakry.
Founded: 1959; *Number of Clubs:* 351; *Number of Players:* 10,000; *National Colours:* Red shirts, yellow shorts, green stockings.
Telephone: 445041; *Cable:* GUINEFOOT CONAKRY; *Telex:* 22302 MJ.

GUINEA-BISSAU

Federacao De Football Da Guinea-Bissau, Apartado 375, 1035 Bissau-Codex, Rua 4 no 10c.
Founded: 1986; *National Colours:* Green shirts, green shorts, green stockings.
Telephone: 21 25 45; *Cable:* FUTEBOL BISSAU; *Telex:* PAIGC 230 BI.

GUINEA, EQUATORIAL

Federacion Ecuatoguineana De Futbol, Malabo.
Founded: 1986; *National Colours:* All red.
Telephone: 2732; *Cable:* FEGUIFUT/MALABO.

IVORY COAST

Federation Ivoirienne De Football, Stade Felix Houphouet Boigny, B.P. 1202, Abidjan.
Founded: 1960; *Number of Clubs:* 84 (senior); *Number of Players:* 3,655; *National Colours:* Orange shirts, white shorts, green stockings.
Telephone: 22 22 82; *Cable:* FIF ABIDJAN; *Telex:* 22722 FIF CI.

KENYA

Kenya Football Federation, Nyayo National Stadium, P.O. Box 40234, Nairobi.
Founded: 1960; *Number of Clubs:* 351; *Number of Players:* 8,880; *National Colours:* Red shirts, red shorts, red stockings.
Telephone: 340382/339761/9; *Cable:* KEFF NAIROBI; *Telex:* 25784 KFF.

LESOTHO

Lesotho Sports Council, P.O. Box 138, Maseru 100.
Founded: 1932; *Number of Clubs:* 88; *Number of Players:* 2,076; *National Colours:* White shirts, blue shorts, white stockings.
Telephone: 311 291 MASERU; *Cable:* LIPAPALI MASERU; *Telex:* 4493.

LIBERIA

The Liberia Football Association, P.O. Box 1066, Monrovia.
Founded: 1962; *National Colours:* Blue & white shirts, white shorts, blue & white stockings.
Telephone: 22 21 77; *Cable:* LIBFOTASS MONROVIA; *Telex:* 44508 LFA LI.

LIBYA

Libyan Arab Jamahiriya Football Federation, P.O. Box 5137, Tripoli.
Founded: 1963; *Number of Clubs:* 89; *Number of Players:* 2,941; *National Colours:* Green shirts, white shorts, green stockings.
Telephone: 46 610; *Telex:* 20896 KURATP LY.

MADAGASCAR

Federation Malagasy De Football, c/o Comite Nat. De Coordination De Football, B.P. 4409, Antananarivo 101.
Founded: 1961; *Number of Clubs:* 775; *Number of Players:* 23,536; *National Colours:* Red shirts, white shorts, green stockings.
Telephone: 21373; *Telex:* 22264.

MALAWI

Football Association of Malawi, P.O. Box 865, Blantyre.
Founded: 1966; *Number of Clubs:* 465; *Number of Players:* 12,500; *National Colours:* Red shirts, red shorts, red stockings.
Telephone: 636686; *Cable:* FOOTBALL BLANTYRE; *Telex:* 4526 SPORTS MI.

MALI

Federation Malienne De Football, Stade Mamdou Konate, B.P. 1020, Bamako.
Founded: 1960; *Number of Clubs:* 128; *Number of Players:* 5,480; *National Colours:* Green shirts, yellow shorts, red stockings.
Telephone: 22 41 52; *Cable:* MALIFOOT BAMAKO; *Telex:* 0985 1200/1202.

MAURITANIA

Federation De Foot-Ball De La Rep. Isl. De Mauritanie, B.P. 566, Nouakshott.
Founded: 1961; *Number of Clubs:* 59; *Number of Players:* 1,930; *National Colours:* Green and yellow shirts, blue shorts, green stockings.
Telephone: 536 09; *Cable:* FOOTRIM NOUAKSHOTT.

MAURITIUS

Mauritius Football Association, Chancery House, 14 Lislet Geoffroy Street, (2nd Floor, Nos. 303–305), Port Louis.
Founded: 1952; *Number of Clubs:* 397; *Number of Players:* 29,375; *National Colours:* Red shirts, white shorts, red stockings.
Telephone: 212 1418, 212 5771; *Cable:* MFA PORT LOUIS; *Telex:* 4427 MSA IW; *Fax:* (230) 208 41 00.

MOROCCO

Federation Royale Marocaine De Football, Av. Ibn Sina, C.N.S. Bellevue, B.P. 51, Rabat.
Founded: 1955; *Number of Clubs:* 350; *Number of Players:* 19,768; *National Colours:* Red shirts, green shorts, red stockings.
Telephone: 67 27 06/08 or 67 26 07; *Cable:* FERMAFOOT RABAT; *Telex:* 32940 FERMFOOT M. *Fax:* 67 10 70

MOZAMBIQUE

Federacao Mocambicana De Futebol, Av. Samora Machel, 11-2, Caixa Postal 1467, Maputo. *Founded:* 1978; *Number of Clubs:* 144; *National Colours:* Red shirts, red shorts, red stockings. *Telephone:* 26 475; *Cable:* MOCAMBOLA MAPUTC, *Telex:* 6-221/2.

NIGER

Federation Nigerienne De Football, Stade National Niamey, B.P. 10299, Niamey. *Founded:* 1967; *Number of Clubs:* 64; *Number of Players:* 1,525; *National Colours:* Orange shirts, white shorts, green stockings. *Telephone:* 73 31 97; *Cable:* FEDERFOOT NIGER NIAMEY. *Telex:* (975) 5527 or 5349. *Fax:* (00227) 73 55 12.

NIGERIA

Nigeria Football Association National Sports Commission, National Stadium, P.O. Box 466, Lagos. *Founded:* 1945; *Number of Clubs:* 326; *Number of Players:* 80,190; *National Colours:* Green shirts, white shorts, green stockings. *Telephone:* 234-1-83 52 65; *Cable:* FOOTBALL LAGOS; *Telex:* 26570 NFA NG; *Fax:* 234-1-82 49 12.

RWANDA

Federation Rwandaise De Foot-Ball Amateur, B.P. 2000, Kigali. *Founded:* 1972; *Number of Clubs:* 167; *National Colours:* Red shirts, red shorts, red stockings. *Telephone:* 75811 ext. 223; *Cable:* MIJENCOOP KIGALI; *Telex:* 22504 PUBLIC RW. *Fax:* (250) 76574.

SENEGAL

Federation Senegalaise De Football, Stade De L'Amitie, Route De L'Aeroport De Yoff, Dakar. *Founded:* 1960; *Number of Clubs:* 75 (senior); *Number of Players:* 3,977; *National Colours:* Green shirts, yellow shorts, red stockings. *Telephone:* 25 00 57; *Cable:* SENEFOOT DAKAR.

SEYCHELLES

Seychelles Football Federation, P.O. Box 580, Mont Fleuri, Victoria. *Founded:* 1986; *National Colours:* Green shirts, yellow shorts, red stockings. *Telephone:* 24 126; *Telex:* 2271 SZ; *Fax:* 23 518.

ST. THOMAS AND PRINCIPE

Federation Santomense De Fut., P.O. Box 42, Sao Tome. *Founded:* 1986; *National Colours:* Green shirts, green·shorts, green stockings. *Telephone:* 22320; *Telex:* 213 PUBLICO STP.

SIERRA LEONE

Sierra Leone Amateur Football Association, S. Stevens Stadium, Brookfields, P.O. Box 672, Freetown. *Founded:* 1967; *Number of Clubs:* 104; *Number of Players:* 8,120; *National Colours:* Green shirts, white shorts, blue stockings. *Telephone:* 41872; *Cable:* SLAFA FREETOWN; *Telex:* 3210 BOOTH SL.

SOMALIA

Somali Football Federation, Ministry of Sports, C.P. 247, Mogadishu. *Founded:* 1951; *Number of Clubs:* 46 (senior); *Number of Players:* 1,150; *National Colours:* Sky blue shirts, white shorts, white stockings. *Telephone:* 22 273; *Cable:* SOMALIA FOOTBALL MOGADISHU; *Telex:* 3061 SONOC SM.

SUDAN

Sudan Football Association, P.O. Box 437, Khartoum. *Founded:* 1936; *Number of Clubs:* 750; *Number of Players:* 42,200; *National Colours:* White shirts, white shorts, white stockings. *Telephone:* 76 633; *Cable:* ALKOURA, KHARTOUM; *Telex:* 23007 KOR SD.

SWAZILAND

National Football Association of Swaziland, P.O. Box 641, Mbabane. *Founded:* 1976; *Number of Clubs:* 136; *National Colours:* Blue and gold shirts, white shorts, blue and gold stockings. *Telephone:* 46 852; *Telex:* 2245 EXP WD.

TANZANIA

Football Association of Tanzania, P.O. Box 1574, Dar Es Salaam. *Founded:* 1930; *Number of Clubs:* 51; *National Colours:* Yellow shirts, yellow shorts, yellow stockings. *Telephone:* 32 334; *Cable:* FAT DAR ES SALAAM.

TOGO

Federation Togolaise De Football, C.P. 5, Lome. *Founded:* 1960; *Number of Clubs:* 144; *Number of Players:* 4,346; *National Colours:* Red shirts, white shorts, red stockings. *Telephone:* 21 26 98; *Cable:* TOGOFOOT LOME; *Telex:* 5015 CNOT TG.

TUNISIA

Federation Tunisienne De Football, 20 Rue Bilal, El-Menzah VI, Tunis 1004. *Founded:* 1957; *Number of Clubs:* 215; *Number of Players:* 18,300; *National Colours:* Red shirts, white shorts, red stockings. *Telephone:* 23 33 03, 23 35 44; *Cable:* FOOTBALL TUNIS; *Telex:* 14783 FTFOOT TN.

UGANDA

Federation of Uganda Football Associations, P.O. Box 10475, Kampala. *Founded:* 1924; *Number of Clubs:* 400; *Number of Players:* 1,518; *National Colours:* Yellow shirts, black shorts, yellow stockings. *Telephone:* 256 41/25 6021; *Cable:* FUFA KAMPALA; *Telex:* 61272; *Fax:* 256 41/24 55 80.

ZAIRE

Federation Zairoise De Football-Association, Via Agence Zairoise de Presse, Brussels. *Founded:* 1919; *Number of Clubs:* 3,800; *Number of Players:* 64,627; *National Colours:* Green shirts, yellow shorts, yellow stockings. *Cable:* FEZAFA KINSHASA; *Telex:* 63915.

ZAMBIA

Football Association of Zambia, P.O. Box 33474, Lusaka. *Founded:* 1929; *Number of Clubs:* 20 (senior); *Number of Players:* 4,100; *National Colours:* Green shirts, white shorts, black stockings. *Telephone:* 21 11 45; *Cable:* FOOTBALL LUSAKA; *Telex:* 40204.

ZIMBABWE

Zimbabwe Football Association, P.O. Box 8343, Causeway, Harare. *Founded:* 1965; *National Colours:* White shirts, black shorts, black stockings. *Telephone:* 79 12 75/6/7; *Cable:* SOCCER HARARE; *Telex:* 22299 SOCCER ZW; *Fax:* 793 320.

Recent additions: CHAD and SOUTH AFRICA (readmitted). Chad, a landlocked country was once a FIFA member up to·1974 and has now been reaffiliated along with South Africa, a member until 1964.

EUROPEAN CHAMPIONSHIP 1990-92

Qualifying Tournament

GROUP 1

Reykjavik, 30 May 1990, 5250
Iceland (1) 2 *(Gudjohnsen 42, Edvaldsson 88)*
Albania (0) 0
Iceland: Kristinsson B; Thordarson, Edvaldsson, Orlygsson T (Jonsson K 46), Gretarsson, Jonsson Saevar, Berg, Ormslev, Torfarson (Orlygsson O 67), Petursson, Gudjohnsen. .
Albania: Strakosha; Noga (Illiadhe 75), Lekbello, Kovi, Vapa, Jeri, Shehu (Arbete 46), Josa, Millo, Abazi, Demollari.

Reykjavik, 5 September 1990, 8388
Iceland (0) 1 *(Edvaldsson 85)*
France (1) 2 *(Papin 12, Cantona 74)*
Iceland: Sigurdsson; Thrainsson, Edvaldsson, Bergsson, Jonsson Saevar, Orlygsson T (Margeirsson 63), Gretarsson, Thordarson, Ormslev (Kristinsson R 63), Gudjohnsen, Petursson.
France: Martini; Amoros, Boli, Sauzee, Casoni, Blanc (Durand 75), Pardo, Deschamps, Perez, Papin, Cantona (Fernandez 83).

Kosice, 26 September 1990, 30,184
Czechoslovakia (1) 1 *(Danek 43)*
Iceland (0) 0
Czechoslovakia: Stejskal; Kadlec, Kocian, Hipp, Hasek, Bilek (Weiss 67), Kubik, Kula, Moravcik, Skuhravy, Danek.
Iceland: Sirgurdsson; Thrainsson, Bergsson, Edvaldsson, Jonsson Saevar, Kristinsson R (Jonsson K 61), Gretarsson, Thordarson, Jonsson Siggi, Gudjohnsen, Margeirsson (Ormslev 76).

Seville, 10 October 1990, 18,399
Spain (1) 2 *(Butragueno 63, Munoz 66)*
Iceland (0) 1 *(Jonsson Siggi 66)*
Spain: Zubizarreta; Nando, Serna, Rafa Paz (Beguiristain 62), Sanchis, Fernando, Goicoechea, Michel, Butragueno, Martin Vazquez, Carlos (Valverde 71).
Iceland: Sigurdsson; Thrainsson, Edvaldsson, Jonsson K (Gregory 80), Gretarsson, Jonsson Saevar, Bergsson, Jonsson Siggi (Ormslev 72), Gudjohnsen, Thordarson, Margeirsson.

Paris, 13 October 1990, 38,249
France (0) 2 *(Papin 60, 83)*
Czechoslovakia (0) 1 *(Skuhravy 89)*
France: Martini; Boli, Blanc, Casoni, Angloma (Fernandez 52), Deschamps, Sauzee, Durand, Papin, Cantona, Vahirua (Silvestre 85).
Czechoslovakia: Stejskal; Kula, Kadlec, Kocian, Hipp, Moravcik, Chovanec, Kubik (Tittel 85), Bilek (Pecko 82), Skuhravy, Knoflicek.

Prague, 14 November 1990, 21,980
Czechoslovakia (1) 3 *(Danek 16, 67, Moravcik 77)*
Spain (1) 2 *(Roberto 30, Carlos 54)*
Czechoslovakia: Miklosko; Kocian, Kadlec, Hipp, Hasek, Tittel, Moravcik, Kula, Bilek (Belak 80), Danek (Kuka 89), Skuhravy.
Spain: Zubizarreta; Quique, Sanchis, Nando, Serna, Michel (Amor 85), Martin Vazquez, Roberto, Goicoechea, Butragueno, Carlos (Bakero 62).

Tirana, 17 November 1990, 12,972
Albania (0) 0
France (1) 1 *(Boli 25)*
Albania: Arapi; Leskaj (Ferko 46), Stafa, Ibro, Hodja, Lekbello, Zmijani, Demollari, Josa, Kushta, Majaci (Kacaci 56).
France: Martini; Boli, Durand, Casoni, Blanc, Pardo, Deschamps, Sauzee, Tibeuf (Ginola 66), Ferreri, Vahirua (Angloma 82).

Seville, 19 December 1990, 12,625
Spain (4) 9 *(Amor 21, Carlos 24, 65, Butragueno 31, 57, 68, 88, Hierro 40, Bakero 76)*
Albania (0) 0
Spain: Zubizarreta; Sanchis, Alcorta, Goicoechea (Bakero 75), Amor, Hierro, Manolo, Michel (Quique 62), Butragueno, Martin Vazquez, Carlos.

Albania: Arapi; Ibro, Lekbello, Stafa, Kola (Demollari 39), Kushta, Millo, Zmijani, Ferko (Josa 55), Dema, Tahiri.

Paris, 20 February 1991, 45,000
France (1) 3 *(Sauzee 15, Papin 58, Blanc 77)*
Spain (1) 1 *(Bakero 11)*
France: Martini; Amoros, Boli, Casoni, Blanc, Pardo (Fernandez 50), Durand, Sauzee, Papin, Cantona, Vahirua (Deschamps 83).
Spain: Zubizarreta; Quique, Nando, Juanito, Sanchis, Michel, Amor, Vizcaino (Soler 61), Goicoechea, Bakero, Butragueno (Manolo 75).

Paris, 30 March 1991, 25,000
France (4) 5 *(Sauzee 1, 19, Papin 34 (pen), 43, Lekbello 79 (og))*
Albania (0) 0
France: Martini; Amoros, Boli, Blanc, Durand, Fernandez, Sauzee (Deschamps 73), Cocard, Cantona, Papin, Vahirua (Baills 57).
Albania: Nallbani; Zmijani, Lekbello, Vata, Gjergi, Ocelli, Dume, Canaj, Demollari, Tahiri, Kepa.

Tirana, 1 May 1991, 10,000
Albania (0) 0
Czechoslovakia (0) 2 *(Kubik 47, Kuka 67)*
Albania: Nallbani; Zmijani, Dema (Kola 73), Daja, Ocelli, Shpuza, Kushta, Memushi, Barbullushi (Dosti 63), Dume (Kole 70), Milori.
Czechoslovakia: Miklosko; Kula, Kadlec, Hasek (Hapal 19), Grussmann, Tittel, Nemec, Kubik, Kuka, Kukleta (Chylek 84), Moravcik.

Tirana, 26 May 1991, 5000
Albania (0) 1 *(Abazi 56)*
Iceland (0) 0
Albania: Nallbani; Memushi (Josa 17), Ocelli, Lekbello, Shpuza, Daja, Millo, Demollari, Milori, Kushta, Abazi.
Iceland: Sigurdsson; Jonsson Saevar, Bergsson, Gislason, Kristiansson, Kristinsson R (Stefansson 62), Orlygsson T, Thordarson, Gretarsson, Sverrisson, Gregory (Marteinsson 75).

Reykjavik, 5 June 1991, 5000
Iceland (0) 0
Czechoslovakia (1) 1 *(Hasek 15)*
Iceland: Sigurdsson; Jonsson Saevar, Bergsson, Edvaldsson, Gislason, Thordarson, Gretarsson, Orlygsson T, Kristinsson R, Gudjohnsen, Sverrisson (Stefansson 70).
Czechoslovakia: Miklosko; Grussmann, Kocian, Tittel, Hasek, Hapal, Kubik, Kula, Nemec, Danek (Pecko 89), Skuhravy (Kuka 41).

Bratislava, 4 September 1991, 50,000
Czechoslovakia (1) 1 *(Nemecek 21)*
France (0) 2 *(Papin 53, 89)*
Czechoslovakia: Miklosko; Kocian, Tittel, Novotny, Knoflicek (Hapal 80), Kristofik (Frydek 22), Nemecek, Moravcik, Nemec, Pecko, Kuka.
France: Martini; Amoros, Blanc, Angloma (Durand 76), Boli, Casoni, Deschamps, Sauzee, Papin, Cocard (Perez 46), Vahirua.

Reykjavik, 25 September 1991, 8900
Iceland (0) 2 *(Orlygsson T 71, Sverrisson 78)*
Spain (0) 0
Iceland: Kristinsson B; Valsson (Marteinsson 46), Ormslev, Bergsson, Jonsson Saevar, Jonsson K, Jonsson Siggi, Gretarsson, Sverrisson, Thordarson, Orlygsson T, Bjarnason (Magnusson 73).
Spain: Zubizarreta; Abelardo, Eusebio, Sanchis, Solozabal, Michel, Vizcaino, Martin Vazquez (Hierro 67), Goicoechea, Manolo, Butragueno.

Seville, 12 October 1991, 27,500
Spain (1) 1 *(Abelardo 33)*
France (2) 2 *(Fernandez 12, Papin 15)*
Spain: Zubizarreta; Cristobal, Solozabal (Eusebio 46), Abelardo, Sanchis, Vizcaino, Manolo, Bango, Butragueno, Martin Vazquez (Alvaro 73), Hierro.
France: Martini; Amoros, Blanc, Boli, Casoni, Deschamps, Angloma, Fernandez (Durand 82), Perez (Garde 62), Cantona, Papin.

Olomouc, 16 October 1991, 2366
Czechoslovakia (2) 2 *(Kula 35, Lancz 39)*
Albania (0) 1 *(Zmijani 62)*
Czechoslovakia: Miklosko; Jurasko, Tittel, Nemecek, Hapal, Moravcik, Lancz (Sedlacek 64), Frydek, Kula, Danek (Pecko 72), Kuka.
Albania: Strakosha; Zmijani, Lekbello, Kacaj, Cipi, Josa, Milori, Kola (Daja 53), Gjondeda, Abazi, Barbullushi.

Seville, 13 November 1991, 24,500
Spain (1) 2 *(Abelardo 10, Michel 79 (pen))*
Czechoslovakia (0) 1 *(Nemecek 59)*
Spain: Zubizarreta; Abelardo, Soler, Solozabal, Sanchis, Hierro, Moya (Conte 59), Michel, Butragueno, Martin Vazquez (Nadal 46), Vizcaino.
Czechoslovakia: Stejskal; Suchoparek, Glonek, Vlk (Grussmann 65), Kristnu Nemecek, Nemec, Novotny, Pecko, Kula, Dubovsky (Latal 79).

Paris, 20 November 1991, 35,000
France (1) 3 *(Simba 42, Cantona 60, 68)*
Iceland (0) 1 *(Sverrisson 71)*
France: Martini; Amoros, Blanc, Angloma, Casoni (Boli 46), Deschamps, Fernandez, Perez, Cantona, Simba, Vahirua.
Iceland: Kristinsson B; Valsson, Bergsson (Jonsson Saevar 81), Jonsson K, Ormslev, Bjarnason, Orlygsson T, Jonsson Kn, Gudjohnsen, Torfason (Sverrisson 56), Gretarsson.

Albania v Spain, 18 December 1991 not played

	P	W	D	L	F	A	Pts
France	8	8	0	0	20	6	16
Czechoslovakia	8	5	0	3	12	9	10
Spain	7	3	0	4	17	12	6
Iceland	8	2	0	6	7	10	4
Albania	7	1	0	6	2	21	2

France qualified

GROUP 2

Geneva, 12 September 1990, 12,000
Switzerland (1) 2 *(Hottiger 19, Bickel 63)*
Bulgaria (0) 0
Switzerland: Walker; Geiger, Herr, Schepull, Hottiger, Koller, Bickel, Hermann, Sutter A (Piffaretti 88), Knup (Chapuisat 64), Turkyilmaz.
Bulgaria: Valov; Dochev, Zhelev, Iliev, Ivanov, Vasev (Bankov 14), Yanchev, Yordanov, Balakov (Todorov 65), Kostadinov E, Stoichkov.

Hampden Park, 12 September 1990, 12,081
Scotland (1) 2 *(Robertson 37, McCoist 76)*
Romania (1) 1 *(Camataru 13)*
Scotland: Goram; McKimmie, Malpas, McAllister (Nevin 73), Irvine, McLeish, Robertson, McStay, McCoist, MacLeod, Connor (Boyd 59).
Romania: Lung; Petrescu, Klein, Sandoi, Rotariu, Popescu G, Lacatus, Mateut (Sabau 79), Camataru (Raducioiu 62), Hagi, Lupescu.

Bucharest, 17 October 1990, 15,350
Romania (0) 0
Bulgaria (1) 3 *(Sirakov 28, Todorov 48, 76)*
Romania: Stelea; Petrescu, Klein (Sandoi 46), Andone, Rotariu, Popescu G, Lacatus, Sabau, Raducioiu (Balint 46), Hagi, Lupescu.
Bulgaria: Mikhailov; Dochev, Ivanov, Vasev, Iliev, Yankov, Yanchev, Stoichkov, Balakov, Sirakov (Kostadinov E 75), Yordanov (Todorov 46).

Hampden Park, 17 October 1990, 20,740
Scotland (1) 2 *(Robertson 34, McAllister 53)*
Switzerland (0) 1 *(Knup 66)*
Scotland: Goram; McKimmie, Nicol, McCall, McPherson, McLeish, Robertson, McAllister (Collins 79), McCoist, MacLeod, Boyd (Durie 68).
Switzerland: Walker; Piffaretti (Sutter B 80), Schepull (Chassot 73), Herr, Egli, Bickel, Knup, Hermann, Turkyilmaz, Sutter A, Chapuisat.

Sofia, 14 November 1990, 40,000
Bulgaria (0) 1 *(Todorov 74)*
Scotland (1) 1 *(McCoist 9)*
Bulgaria: Mikhailov; Dochev, Mladenov, Yankov, Bankov, Yanchev (Todorov 52), Yordanov, Stoichkov, Penev, Sirakov, Balakov (Kostadinov E 80).

Scotland: Goram; McKimmie, Malpas, McInally, McPherson, Gillespie, Durie (Nevin 67), McAllister, McCoist, McClair, Boyd.

Serravalle, 14 November 1990, 931
San Marino (0) 0
Switzerland (3) 4 *(Sutter A 7, Chapuisat 27, Knup 43, Chassot 87)*
San Marino: Benedettini; Montironi, Guerra, Gobbi, Muccioli (Toccacieli 46), Bonini (Matteoni 46), Zanotti L, Francini, Ceccoli, Pasolini, Macina.
Switzerland: Walker; Hottiger, Geiger, Herr, Sutter B, Bickel (Piffaretti 59), Chapuisat, Hermann, Sutter A, Turkyilmaz (Chassot 46), Knup.

Bucharest, 5 December 1990, 6380
Romania (3) 6 *(Sabau, 2 Mateut 18, Raducioiu 43, Lupescu 56, Badea 77, Petrescu 85)*
San Marino (0) 0
Romania: Prunea; Petrescu, Iovan, Popescu G, Rednic, Sabau, Mateut, Lupescu (Stanici 65), Dumitrescu (Badea 46), Lacatus, Raducioiu.
San Marino: Benedettini; Montironi, Conti, Guerra, Zanotti L, Toccacieli, Matteoni, Ceccoli, Francini, Pasolini (Zanotti P 72), Macina (Bacciocchi 46).

Hampden Park, 27 March 1991, 33,119
Scotland (0) 1 *(Collins 84)*
Bulgaria (0) 1 *(Kostadinov 89)*
Scotland: Goram; McPherson, Malpas, McInally, Gough, McLeish, Strachan (Collins 80), McClair, McCoist, McStay, Durie (Robertson 80).
Bulgaria: Mikhailov; Dochev, Ivanov, Kiriakov, Iliev, Yankov, Kostadinov E, Yordanov, Penev, Sirakov (Alexandrov 86), Balakov (Tanev 86).

Serravalle, 27 March 1991, 745
San Marino (1) 1 *(Pasolini 30 (pen))*
Romania (2) 3 *(Hagi 17 (pen), Raducioiu 45, Matteoni (og) 86)*
San Marino: Benedettini; Canti, Guerra, Gobbi (Toccacieli 74), Muccioli, Matteoni, Francini, Pasolini (Mularoni 89), Ceccoli, Mazza M, Mazza P.
Romania: Prunea; Petrescu, Popescu G (Timofte D 46), Lupescu, Klein, Sandoi, Sabau, Mateut (Timofte I 65), Hagi, Lacatus, Raducioiu.

Neuchatel, 3 April 1991, 15,700
Switzerland (0) 0
Romania (0) 0
Switzerland: Huber; Geiger, Hottiger, Ohrel, Herr, Koller, Bonvin (Bickel 33), Hermann, Aeby, Turkyilmaz (Sutter B 75), Knup.
Romania: Prunea; Petrescu, Klein, Sandoi, Lupescu, Popescu G, Sabau, Hagi (Mateut 85), Lacatus, Radicioiu (Timofte I 89), Timofte D.

Sofia, 1 May 1991, 40,000
Bulgaria (2) 2 *(Kostadinov 11, Sirakov 25)*
Switzerland (0) 3 *(Knup 58, 85, Turkyilmaz 90)*
Bulgaria: Mikhailov; Dochev (Todorov 75), Kiriakov, Yankov, Iliev, Ivanov, Yordanov, Penev, Sirakov (Tanev 65), Balakov, Kostadinov E.
Switzerland: Huber; Egli, Herr, Hottiger, Ohrel, Bonvin, Hermann, Knup (Schepull 87), Koller (Chapuisat 75), Sutter B, Turkyilmaz.

Serravalle, 1 May 1991, 3512
San Marino (0) 0
Scotland (0) 2 *(Strachan 63 (pen), Durie 66)*
San Marino: Benedettini; Canti, Muccioli, Zanotti (Toccacieli 60), Gobbi, Guerra, Ceccoli, Mazza M, Mazza P, Francini, Pasolini (Matteoni 79).
Scotland: Goram; McKimmie, Nicol (Robertson 74), McCall, McPherson, Malpas, Gallacher, Strachan, McClair (Nevin 57), McAllister, Durie.

Serravalle, 22 May 1991, 612
San Marino (0) 0
Bulgaria (2) 3 *(Ivanov 12, Sirakov 19, Penev 59)*
San Marino: Benedettini; Canti, Montironi, Muccioli, Gobbi, Guerra, Ceccoli (Matteoni 82), Mazza M, Mazza P, Francini, Pasolini (Bacciocchi 64).
Bulgaria: Mikhailov; Dimitrov, Ivanov, Kiriakov, Yankov, Anghelov (Todorov 76), Kostadinov E, Gheorghiev, Penev, Sirakov, Yotov (Metkov 56).

St Gallen, 5 June 1991, 12,000
Switzerland (3) 7 *(Knup 2, 86, Hottiger 12, Sutter B 28, Hermann 54, Ohrel 77, Turkyilmaz 89)*
San Marino (0) 0
Switzerland: Huber; Egli (Schepull 74), Herr, Hottiger (Ohrel 74), Hermann, Koller, Sutter A, Sutter B, Turkyilmaz, Knup, Chapuisat.
San Marino: Benedettini; Muccioli, Guerra, Gobbi, Canti, Matteoni (Valentini 46), Mazza M, Francini, Zanotti, Pasolini, Bacciocchi (Malaroni 65).

Berne, 11 September 1991, 48,000
Switzerland (2) 2 *(Chapuisat 30, Hermann 39)*
Scotland (0) 2 *(Durie 47, McCoist 83)*
Switzerland: Huber; Hottiger, Ohrel, Herr, Sforza, Heldmann (Sutter B 64), Knup, Hermann, Turkyilmaz, Sutter A (Bickel 60), Chapuisat.
Scotland: Goram; McKimmie (McClair 66), Boyd, McPherson, Malpas, Strachan, McCall, Nicol, Johnston (McAllister 40), Durie, McCoist.

Sofia, 16 October 1991, 8000
Bulgaria (3) 4 *(Valentini (og) 20, Stoichkov 39 (pen), Yankov 41, Iliev 85)*
San Marino (0) 0
Bulgaria: Mikhailov; Kiriakov, Rakov, Vidov, Iliev, Yankov, Kostadinov E, Stoichkov (Lechkov 69), Penev, Kolev (Yordanov 46), Balakov.
San Marino: Benedettini; Toccacieli, Valentini, Matteoni, Gobbi, Guerra, Mannzaroli, De la Valle, Mazza P, Francini, Pasolini.

Bucharest, 16 October 1991, 30,000
Romania (0) 1 *(Hagi 73 (pen))*
Scotland (0) 0
Romania: Lung; Petrescu, Klein, Sandoi, Lupescu, Popescu G, Lacatus, Timofte D (Timofte I 60), Raducioiu (Dumitrescu 75), Hagi, Munteanu.
Scotland: Goram; McKimmie, Malpas, McCall, McPherson, Levein, Strachan, Galloway (Aitken 70), McClair, Durie, Boyd (Gallacher 59).

Bucharest, 13 November 1991, 35,000
Romania (0) 1 *(Mateut 72)*
Switzerland (0) 0
Romania: Lung; Popescu A, Popescu G, Sandoi, Klein (Munteanu 3), Lupescu, Timofte D (Sabau 46), Hagi, Mateut, Lacatus, Raducioiu.
Switzerland: Huber; Hottiger, Sforza, Herr, Schepull, Ohrel, Sutter B (Bonvin 63), Hermann (Bickel 77), Sutter A, Turkyilmaz, Chapuisat.

Hampden Park, 13 November 1991, 35,170
Scotland (3) 4 *(McStay 10, Gough 31, Durie 37, McCoist 62)*
San Marino (0) 0
Scotland: Goram; McPherson (Johnston 46), Malpas, McAllister, Gough, Levein (Gallacher 60), McCall, Robertson, McCoist, McStay, Durie.
San Marino: Benedettini; Conti, Muccioli, Mazza M, Gobbi, Guerra, Zanotti, Bonini, Mazza P, Francini, Pasolini (Mannzaroli 67).

Sofia, 20 November 1991, 20,000
Bulgaria (0) 1 *(Sirakov 56)*
Romania (1) 1 *(Popescu A 30)*
Bulgaria: Mikhailov; Khubchev, Rakov, Kiriakov, Iliev (Mladenov 57), Yankov, Kostadinov E (Yordanov 69), Stoichkov, Penev, Sirakov, Belakov.
Romania: Lung; Popescu A, Munteanu, Sandoi (Timofte I 68), Lupescu, Popescu G, Lacatus (Dumitrescu 60), Sabau, Raducioiu, Hagi, Mateut.

	P	W	D	L	F	A	Pts
Scotland	8	4	3	1	14	7	11
Switzerland	8	4	2	2	19	7	10
Romania	8	4	2	2	13	7	10
Bulgaria	8	3	3	2	15	8	9
San Marino	8	0	0	8	1	33	0

Scotland qualified

GROUP 3
Moscow, 12 September 1990, 23,000
USSR (1) 2 *(Kanchelskis 22, Kuznetsov 60)*
Norway (0) 0
USSR: Uvarov; Chernishov, Gorlukovich, Kuznetsov O,

Tishenko (Kulkov 79), Shalimov, Mikhailichenko, Kanchelskis, Getsko (Kolivanov 70), Protasov, Dobrovolski.
Norway: Thorstvedt; Lydersen, Pedersen T, Bratseth, Halle, Berg (Pedersen E 61), Ahlsen, Gulbrandsen, Jakobsen, Andersen, Fjortoft (Dahlum 66).

Bergen, 10 October 1990, 6300
Norway 0 (0)
Hungary 0 (0)
Norway: Thorstvedt; Halle, Pedersen T, Bratseth, Lydersen, Pedersen E, Ahlsen, Brandhaug, Jakobsen (Andersen 72), Sorloth, Fjortoft (Dahlum 76).
Hungary: Petry; Monos, Pinter, Szalma, Kovacs E, Limperger, Kiprich (Fodor 79), Kozma, Bognar, Lorincz, Kovacs K (Urbanyi 89).

Budapest, 17 October 1990, 24,600
Hungary (1) 1 *(Disztl L 16)*
Italy (0) 1 *(Baggio R 54)*
Hungary: Petry; Monos, Disztl L, Garaba (Fodor 60), Szalma, Bognar, Limperger, Kiprich, Kozma (Urbanyi 87), Lorincz, Kovacs K.
Italy: Zenga; Bergomi, De Agostini, Baresi, Ferri, Marocchi, Donadoni, De Napoli, Schillaci (Serena 80), Giannini (Berti 87), Baggio R.

Budapest, 31 October 1990, 2300
Hungary (3) 4 *(Lorincz 1, 19, Kiprich 20 (pen), 67 (pen))*
Cyprus (1) 2 *(Xiourouppas 13, Tsolakis 89)*
Hungary: Petry; Disztl L, Monos, Garaba, Limperger, Szalma, Kozma (Fischer 56), Bognar, Lorincz, Kiprich (Rugovics 75), Kovacs K.
Cyprus: Onisiforou; Kalotheou, Miamiliotis, Christodolou, Socratous, Yiangudakis, Andreou (Tsolakis 59), Savva, Kastanas, Constantinou C (Orthanides 73), Xiourouppas.

Rome, 3 November 1990, 52,208
Italy (0) 0
USSR (0) 0
Italy: Zenga; Ferrara, Baresi, Ferri, Maldini, De Napoli, Crippa, De Agostini, Mancini, Schillaci (Serena 70), Baggio R.
USSR: Uvarov; Chernishov, Kulkov, Tsveiba, Shalimov, Aleinikov, Mikhailichenko, Kanchelskis, Getsko (Protasov 67), Mostovoi (Tatarchuk 85), Dobrovolski.

Nicosia, 14 November 1990, 2123
Cyprus (0) 0
Norway (1) 3 *(Sorloth 39, Bohinen 50, Brandhaug 64)*
Cyprus: Charitou; Kalotheou (Kantilos 49), Miamiliotis, Kastanas, Socratous, Yiangudakis, Christodolou, Savva, Tsolakis (Constantinou C 74), Nicolaou, Xiourouppas.
Norway: Thorstvedt; Lydersen, Pedersen T, Bratseth, Lohen (Pedersen E 64), Halle, Brandhaug, Leonhardsen, Bohinen, Sorloth, Dahlum (Fjortoft 80).

Nicosia, 22 December 1990, 9185
Cyprus (0) 0
Italy (3) 4 *(Vierchowod 15, Serena 22, 50, Lombardo 44)*
Cyprus: Onisiforou; Kalotheou, Miamiliotis, Christodolou, Socratous, Yiangudakis, Punnas, Savva (Constantinou C 56), Tsolakis, Nicolaou, Papavasiliu (Xiourouppas 64).
Italy: Zenga; Bergomi, Ferrara, Eranio, Vierchowod, Crippa, Lombardo, Berti, Schillaci, Morocchi, Serena.

Limassol, 3 April 1991, 3000
Cyprus (0) 0
Hungary (2) 2 *(Szalma 15, Kiprich 40)*
Cyprus: Marangos; Constantinou G, Pittas (Kasianos 75), Ioannou, Constantinou C, Yiangudakis, Christofi C, Savva (Sotiriu 83), Savvidis, Nicolaou, Tsolakis.
Hungary: Petry; Monos, Disztl L, Szalma, Nagy, Limperger, Kiprich, Bognar, Fischer (Maroszan 72), Lorincz, Kovacs K.

Budapest, 17 April 1991, 40,000
Hungary (0) 0
USSR (1) 1 *(Mikhailichenko 30)*
Hungary: Petry; Disztl L, Garaba, Limperger, Monos, Kozma (Detari 63), Bognar (Vincze 71), Lorincz, Szalma, Kiprich, Kovacs K.
USSR: Uvarov; Chernishov, Kulkov, Tsveiba, Galiamin, Shalimov, Mikhailichenko, Kanchelskis, Youran (Kuznetsov D 86), Kolivanov, Aleinikov.

Salerno, 1 May 1991, 45,000
Italy (2) 3 *(Donadoni 4, 16, Vialli 56)*
Hungary (0) 1 *(Bognar 66)*
Italy: Zenga; Ferrara (Vierchowod 65), Ferri, Baresi, Maldini, Crippa, De Napoli, Giannini, Donadoni (Eranio 36), Vialli, Mancini.
Hungary: Petry; Monos, Disztl L, Palaczky (Kozma 33), Limperger, Garaba, Kiprich (Gregor 46), Lorincz, Bognar, Detari, Kovacs K.

Oslo, 1 May 1991, 7833
Norway (0) 3 *(Lydersen 49 (pen), Dahlum 65, Sorloth 90)*
Cyprus (0) 0
Norway: Thorstvedt; Pedersen T, Bratseth (Ingebrigtsen 46), Lydersen, Halle (Pedersen E), Ahlsen, Brandhaug, Leonhardsen, Bjornbye, Sorloth, Dahlum.
Cyprus: Charitou; Nicolaou (Sotiriu 89), Constantinou C, Ioannou, Costa, Kalotheou (Constantinou G 84), Savva, Yiangudakis, Pittas, Savvidis, Xiourouppas.

Moscow, 29 May 1991, 20,000
USSR (1) 4 *(Mostovoi 20, Mikhailichenko 51, Korneyev 83, Aleinikov 89)*
Cyprus (0) 0
USSR: Uvarov; Chernishov, Kulkov, Mostovoi (Kuznetsov D 74), Galiamin, Shalimov, Mikhailichenko, Kanchelskis, Aleinikov, Kolivanov, Youran (Korneyev 46).
Cyprus: Charitou; Kalotheou, Pittas, Ioannou, Nicolaou, Yiangudakis, Costa, Christofi C, Savvidis, Christodolou (Constantinou G 88), Xiourouppas (Savva 89).

Oslo, 5 June 1991, 27,500
Norway (2) 2 *(Dahlum 4, Bohinen 24)*
Italy (0) 1 *(Schillaci 79)*
Norway: Thorstvedt; Pedersen T, Ahlsen, Bratseth, Lydersen, Dahlum (Pedersen E 46), Bohinen, Lokken, Ingebrigtsen, Jakobsen, Sorloth.
Italy: Zenga; Baresi, Ferrara, Ferri (Bergomi 89), Maldini, Lombardo, Eranio, De Napoli (Schillaci 53), Crippa, Vialli, Mancini.

Oslo, 28 August 1991, 25,427
Norway (0) 0
USSR (0) 1 *(Mostovoi 74)*
Norway: Thorstvedt; Lydersen, Pedersen T, Bratseth, Nilsen R (Riisnes 66), Lokken, Halle, Leonhardsen, Jakobsen (Skammelsrud 80), Sorloth, Fjortoft.
USSR: Cherchesov; Chernishov, Kulkov, Tsveiba, Kuznetsov O, Shalimov, Mikhailichenko, Kanchelskis (Korneev 71), Aleinikov, Kolivanov, Youran (Mostovoi 46).

Moscow, 25 September 1991, 50,000
USSR (1) 2 *(Shalimov 41 (pen), Kanchelskis 48)*
Hungary (1) 2 *(Kiprich 17, 86)*
USSR: Cherchesov; Chernishov, Kulkov, Tsveiba (Kuznetsov O 20), Galiamin, Shalimov, Mikhailichenko, Kanchelskis, Aleinikov, Kolivanov, Mostovoi (Youran 58).
Hungary: Petry; Monos (Kovacs E 30), Disztl L, Szalma, Linchei, Limperger, Kiprich, Lorincz, Kozma (Fischer 58), Detari, Kovacs K.

Moscow, 12 October 1991, 92,000
USSR (0) 0
Italy (0) 0
USSR: Cherchesov; Chernishov, Kulkov, Kuznetsov O (Tsveiba 46), Galiamin, Shalimov, Mikhailichenko, Kanchelskis, Aleinikov, Protasov (Kuznetsov D 69), Kolivanov.
Italy: Zenga; Ferrara, Maldini, Crippa, Vierchowod, Baresi, Lentini (Lombardo 58), De Napoli, Vialli, Giannini (Mancini 69), Rizzitelli.

Szombathely, 30 October 1991, 10,000
Hungary (0) 0
Norway (0) 0
Hungary: Petry; Pinter, Urban, Lorincz, Nagy, Pisont (Eszenyi 83), Lipcsei (Illes 71), Duro, Detari, Fischer, Kovacs K.
Norway: Grodas; Pedersen T, Bratseth, Ahlsen, Bjornebye, Lokken, Bohinen, Rekdal, Leonnardsen (Ingebrigtsen 78), Jakobsen, Sorloth (Fjortoft 46).

Genoa, 13 November 1991, 30,000
Italy (0) 1 *(Rizzitelli 82)*
Norway (0) 1 *(Jakobsen J-I 60)*
Italy: Pagliuca; Costacurta, Maldini, Berti (De Napoli 66), Ferri, Baresi, Baiano (Rizzitelli 55), Ancelotti, Vialli, Zola, Eranio.
Norway: Thorstvedt; Lokken, Ahlsen, Bratseth, Lydersen, Johnsen R (Pedersen J 46), Rekdal, Ingebrigtsen, Fjortoft, Sorloth, Jakobsen (Berg 77).

Larnaca, 13 November 1991, 4000
Cyprus (0) 0
USSR (1) 3 *(Protasov 27, Youran 79, Kanchelskis 82)*
Cyprus: Charitou; Costa, Pittas, Constantinou C, Socratous, Larkou, Koliandris (Hadjilukas 75), Savva, Savvidis (Sotiriou 46), Ioannou, Charalambous.
USSR: Kharin; Chernishov, Kulkov, Tsveiba, Galiamin, Shalimov, Mikhailichenko, Kanchelskis, Kuznetsov O, Protasov (Mostovoi 70), Kolivanov (Youran 46).

Foggia, 21 December 1991, 26,000
Italy (1) 2 *(Vialli 27, Baggio 55)*
Cyprus (0) 0
Italy: Zenga; Baggio D, Costacurta, Baresi, Maldini, Albertini, Berti, Evani, Zola, Baggio R (Casiraghi 65), Vialli (Baiano 66).
Cyprus: Christofi M; Constantinou G, Pittas, Constantinou C, Nicolaou, Michael (Andreou 62), Koliandris, Savva, Sotiriou, Ioannou (Larkou 80), Charalambous.

	P	W	D	L	F	A	Pts
USSR	8	5	3	0	13	2	13
Italy	8	3	4	1	12	5	10
Norway	8	3	3	2	9	5	9
Hungary	8	2	4	2	10	9	8
Cyprus	8	0	0	8	2	25	0

USSR qualified

GROUP 4
Windsor Park, 12 September 1990, 9008
Northern Ireland (0) 0
Yugoslavia (1) 2 *(Pancev 36, Prosinecki 86)*
Northern Ireland: Kee; Donaghy, Worthington, Taggart, McDonald, Rogan, Dennison (Clarke 66), Wilson D, Dowie, Wilson K, Black.
Yugoslavia: Ivkovic; Spasic, Jozic, Vulic, Hadzibegic, Najdoski, Prosinecki, Savicevic, Pancev (Petrovic 87), Stojkovic, Binic (Stosic 87).

Landskrona, Sweden, 12 September 1990, 1544
Faeroes (0) 1 *(Nielsen 61)*
Austria (0) 0
Faeroes: Knudsen; Jakobsen, Hansen TE, Danielsen, Hansen J, Morkore A, Nielsen, Dam, Hansen A, Reynheim, Morkore K.
Austria: Konsel; Russ, Pecl, Hartmann, Streiter, Peischl, Rodax, Linzmaier, Polster, Herzog (Pacult 63), Reisinger (Wilfurth 63).

Copenhagen, 10 October 1990, 38,500
Denmark (2) 4 *(Laudrup M 8, 48, Elstrup 37, Povlsen 89)*
Faeroes (1) 1 *(Morkore A 21)*
Denmark: Schmeichel; Sivebaek, Nielsen K, Olsen L, Heintze, Bartram, Vilfort, Elstrup (Rasmussen E 73), Povlsen, Laudrup M, Laudrup B.
Faeroes: Knudsen; Jakobsen, Hansen TE, Danielsen, Hansen J, Morkore A (Jarnskor 88), Nielsen, Dam, Hansen A, Reynheim, Morkore K (Mohr 76).

Windsor Park, 17 October 1990, 9079
Northern Ireland (0) 1 *(Clarke 58)*
Denmark (1) 1 *(Bartram 11)*
Northern Ireland: Kee; Donaghy, Worthington, Taggart, McDonald, Rogan, Wilson D, O'Neill C (McBride), Dowie, Clarke, Black.
Denmark: Schmeichel; Sivebaek, Nielsen K, Olsen L, Heintze, Bartram, Larsen J, Vilfort, Povlsen, Laudrup M (Helt 80), Laudrup B (Elstrup 70).

Belgrade, 31 October 1990, 11,422
Yugoslavia (2) 4 *(Pancev 32, 52, 85, Katanec 43)*
Austria (1) 1 *(Ogris A 15)*
Yugoslavia: Ivkovic; Vulic, Spasic, Katanec (Jarni 86), Hadzibegic, Jozic, Prosinecki, Susic (Boban 63), Bazdarevic, Pancev, Vujovic.
Austria: Konsel; Artner, Aigner, Pecl, Streiter, Hortnagl,

Schottel, Herzog (Linzmaier 46), Reisinger, Ogris A (Pacult 52), Polster.

Copenhagen, 14 November 1990, 40,000
Denmark (0) 0
Yugoslavia (0) 2 *(Bazdarevic 77, Jarni 84)*
Denmark: Schmeichel; Sivebaek, Nielsen K, Olsen L, Heintze, Vilfort, Molby Jan (Elstrup 72), Laudrup M, Bartram, Laudrup B, Povlsen (Jensen J 46).
Yugoslavia: Ivkovic; Vulic, Spasic, Hadzibegic, Jarni, Katanec, Jozic, Susic, Bazdarevic, Pancev (Boban 12), Vujovic (Najdoski 89).

Vienna, 14 November 1990, 7062
Austria (0) 0
Northern Ireland (0) 0
Austria: Konsel; Schottel, Pecl, Polger, Artner, Willfurth, Reischl, Linzmaier, Hortnagl, Ogris A, Polster (Pacult 67).
Northern Ireland: Kee; Donaghy, Worthington, Taggart, McDonald, Rogan, Dennison, Wilson D, Clarke (Dowie 62), Wilson K, Black (Morrow 82).

Belgrade, 27 March 1991, 10,000
Yugoslavia (1) 4 *(Binic 35, Pancev 46, 60, 61)*
Northern Ireland (1) 1 *(Hill 45)*
Yugoslavia: Ivkovic; Vulic (Najdoski 85), Jozic, Jarni, Bazdarevic, Spasic, Hadzibegic, Prosinecki, Savicevic, Pancev, Binic.
Northern Ireland: Kee; Fleming, Rogan, Donaghy, Morrow, Hill, Dennison (Quinn 70), Magilton, Dowie, Wilson K (Clarke 60), Black.

Belgrade, 1 May 1991, 26,000
Yugoslavia (0) 1 *(Pancev 50)*
Denmark (1) 2 *(Christensen 31, 62)*
Yugoslavia: Ivkovic; Vulic, Jarni (Najdoski 84), Spasic, Hadzibegic, Jozic, Prosinecki, Savicevic, Pancev, Bazdarevic, Binic.
Denmark: Schmeichel; Sivebaek (Larsen H 54), Nielsen K, Olsen L, Kristensen, Bartram, Jensen J (Goldbaek 82), Christofte, Povlsen, Vilfort, Christensen.

Windsor Park, 1 May 1991, 10,000
Northern Ireland (1) 1 *(Clarke 44)*
Faeroes (0) 1 *(Reynheim 65)*
Northern Ireland: Kee; Donaghy, Worthington, Taggart, McDonald, Magilton, Wilson D (Dennison 83), Clarke, Dowie (Williams 83), Wilson K, Black.
Faeroes: Knudsen; Jakobsen, Hansen TE, Danielsen, Muller, Morkore A, Nielsen, Dam, Hansen A, Reynheim (Thomassen 74), Morkore K (Rasmussen 85).

Belgrade, 16 May 1991, 8000
Yugoslavia (2) 7 *(Najdoski 20, Prosinecki 24, Pancev 50, 74, Vulic 66, Boban 70, Suker 86)*
Faeroes (0) 0
Yugoslavia: Ivkovic (Lazic 80); Stanojkovic, Jarni (Suker 67), Vulic, Najdoski, Spasic, Prosinecki, Boban, Pancev, Savicevic, Mihajlovic.
Faeroes: Knudsen; Jakobsen, Hansen TE, Danielsen, Jarnskor, Morkore A, Nielsen, Dam, Hansen A, Reynheim, Morkore K (Muller 49).

Vienna, 22 May 1991, 13,000
Austria (1) 3 *(Pfeifenberger 13, Streiter 48, Wetl 63)*
Faeroes (0) 0
Austria: Konsel (Wohlfahrt 86); Baur, Russ, Pfeifenberger (Hortnagl 24), Hartmann, Stoger, Schottel, Herzog, Streuter, Wetl, Ogris A.
Faeroes: Knudsen; Jakobsen, Morkore A, Danielsen, Hansen TE, Simonsen, Nielsen, Hansen A, Dam (Thomassen 71), Reynheim, Rasmussen (Mohr 85).

Copenhagen, 5 June 1991, 12,521
Denmark (1) 2 *(Christensen 2, 77)*
Austria (0) 1 *(Ogris E 83)*
Denmark: Schmeichel; Hansen, Nielsen K, Olsen L, Bruun, Vilfort, Larsen H, Nielsen BS, Nielsen C (Goldbaek 46), Povlsen (Rasmussen E 78), Christensen.
Austria: Konrad; Russ (Prosenik 72), Baur, Hartmann, Pfeifenberger, Streiter, Ogris E, Schottel (Hortnagl 66), Herzog, Stoger, Westerhaler.

Landskrona, Sweden, 11 September 1991, 1623
Faeroes (0) 0
Northern Ireland (3) 5 *(Wilson K 7, Clarke 13, 49, 70 (pen), McDonald 15)*

Faeroes: Knudsen; Jakobsen J (Morkore K 78), Hansen TE, Danielsen, Thomassen (Muller 51), Morkore A, Nielsen, Dam, Hansen A, Reynheim, Jonsson.
Northern Ireland: Wright; Donaghy, Morrow, Taggart, McDonald, Magilton, Dennison, Wilson K (O'Neill 70), Dowie, Clarke, Black (McBride 70).

Landskrona, Sweden, 25 September 1991, 2589
Faeroes (0) 0
Denmark (2) 4 *(Christofte 2 (pen), Christensen 7, Pingel 69, Vilfort 76)*
Faeroes: Knudsen (Johannesen 46); Jakobsen, Hansen TE, Danielsen, Morkore K, Dam, Jarnskor, Jonsson (Davidsen 83), Hansen A, Reynheim, Muller.
Denmark: Schmeichel; Sivebaek, Nielsen K, Olsen L, Larsen H, Christofte (Molby John 60), Jensen J, Vilfort, Povlsen, Christensen, Elstrup (Pingel 68).

Vienna, 9 October 1991, 10,000
Austria (0) 0
Denmark (3) 3 *(Artner (og) 10, Povlsen 16, Christensen 37)*
Austria: Konrad; Prosenik, Baur, Resch, Kogler, Schottel (Gschneidter 46), Ogris A, Artner, Herzog, Stoger, Pacult.
Denmark: Schmeichel; Sivebaek, Nielsen K, Olsen L, Larsen H (Jensen B 81), Christofte (Molby John 59), Jensen J, Vilfort, Povlsen, Christensen, Elstrup.

Landskrona, Sweden, 16 October 1991, 2485
Faeroes (0) 0
Yugoslavia (1) 2 *(Jugovic 18, Savicevic 79)*
Faeroes: Knudsen; Jakobsen, Hansen TE, Danielsen, Morkore K, Dam, Morkore A, Jonsson (Jarnskor 88), Hansen A, Reynheim, Muller.
Yugoslavia: Omerovic; Spasic, Hadzibegic, Najdovski, Brnovic, Jugovic, Jokanovic, Bazdarevic, Mihajlovic (Mijatovic 63), Lukic (Stanic 80), Savicevic.

Windsor Park, 16 October 1991, 8000
Northern Ireland (2) 2 *(Dowie 17, Black 40)*
Austria (1) 1 *(Lainer 44)*
Northern Ireland: Wright; Donaghy, Hill, Taggart, Worthington, Dennison, Magilton, Wilson K, Black, Dowie, Clarke (Wilson D 46).
Austria: Knaller; Lainer, Rotter, Hartmann, Kogler, Zsak, Ogris A, Artner, Keglevits (Herzog 62), Stoger (Westerthaler 62), Garger.

Odense, 13 November 1991, 10,881
Denmark (2) 2 *(Povlsen 22, 36)*
Northern Ireland (0) 1 *(Taggart 71)*
Denmark: Schmeichel; Sivebaek, Olsen L, Nielsen K, Vilfort, Christofte, Povlsen, Molby John, Larsen H, Piechnik, Elstrup (Pingel 53).
Northern Ireland: Fettis; Donaghy, Hill, Worthington, McBride, Hughes, Magilton, Wilson K, Black (Dennison 83), Clarke (Dowie 67).

Vienna, 13 November 1991, 8000
Austria (0) 0
Yugoslavia (2) 2 *(Lukic 19, Savicevic 39)*
Austria: Knaller; Zsak, Garger, Kogler, Artner, Gager, Stoger (Keglevits 53), Herzog, Lainer, Ogris A, Westerthaler (Baur 73).
Yugoslavia: Omerovic; Hadzibegic, Vujacic, Milanic, Novak (Brnovic 81), Jokanovic, Savicevic, Bazdarevic, Mihajlovic, Lukic (Mijatovic 46), Pancev.

	P	W	D	L	F	A	Pts
Yugoslavia	8	7	0	1	24	4	14
Denmark	8	6	1	1	18	7	13
Northern Ireland	8	2	3	3	11	7	7
Austria	8	1	1	6	6	14	3
Faeroes	8	1	1	6	3	26	3

Yugoslavia qualified

GROUP 5
Cardiff (Ninian Park), 17 October 1990, 12,000
Wales (1) 3 *(Rush 29, Saunders 86, Hughes 88)*
Belgium (1) 1 *(Versavel 24)*
Wales: Southall; Ratcliffe, Blackmore, Young, Aizlewood, Bodin, Horne, Nicholas, Hughes, Rush, Saunders.
Belgium: Preud'homme; Gerets, Grun, Demol, De Wolf, Versavel, Van der Elst, Scifo, Emmers, Ceulemans, Nilis (Wilmots 75).

Luxembourg, 31 October 1990, 9512
Luxembourg (0) 2 *(Girres 57, Langers 65)*
West Germany (2) 3 *(Klinsmann 16, Bein 30, Voller 49)*
Luxembourg: Van Rijswick; Malget, Petry, Bossi, Birsens, Groff, Hellers, Girres, Salbene (Jeitz 85), Weis, Langers.
West Germany: Illgner; Binz, Berthold, Kohler, Strunz, Hassler, Matthaus, Bein (Reinhardt 73), Brehme, Klinsmann, Voller.

Luxembourg, 14 November 1990, 6800
Luxembourg (0) 0
Wales (1) 1 *(Rush 15)*
Luxembourg: Van Rijswick; Malget, Bossi, Birsens, Petry, Morocutti (Krings 60), Hellers, Girres, Salbene, Weis, Langers.
Wales: Southall; Blackmore, Bodin, Aizlewood, Young, Hughes, Ratcliffe, Horne, Nicholas, Rush (Speed 83), Saunders (Allen 88).

Brussels, 27 February 1991, 24,505
Belgium (3) 3 *(Vandenbergh 7, Ceulemans 17, Scifo 36)*
Luxembourg (0) 0
Belgium: Preud'homme; Grun, Albert, Emmers, Versavel, Dauwen, Scifo, Ceulemans, Degryse, Vandenbergh, Wilmots.
Luxembourg: Koch; Malget (Jeitz 46), Bossi, Birsens, Petry, Groff (Scuto 75), Hellers, Girres, Salbene, Weis, Krings.

Brussels, 27 March 1991, 25,000
Belgium (0) 1 *(Degryse 47)*
Wales (0) 1 *(Saunders 58)*
Belgium: Preud'homme; Gerets, Albert, Grun, Clijsters, Versavel, Van der Elst, Scifo, Degryse, Vandenbergh, Wilmots.
Wales: Southall; Phillips, Ratcliffe, Young, Aizlewood, Bodin, Horne, Nicholas, Hughes, Rush, Saunders.

Hanover, 1 May 1991, 56,000
West Germany (1) 1 *(Matthaus 3)*
Belgium (0) 0
West Germany: Illgner; Berthold, Reuter, Beiersdorfer, Brehme, Hassler, Sammer, Matthaus, Doll, Klinsmann (Helmer 77), Voller (Riedle 88).
Belgium: Preud'homme; Emmers, Crasson, Grun, Albert, Van der Elst, Scifo, Vervoort, Versavel, Degryse, Wilmots (Nilis 77).

Cardiff (Arms Park), 5 June 1991, 38,000
Wales (0) 1 *(Rush 69)*
West Germany (0) 0
Wales: Southall; Phillips, Melville, Bodin, Aizlewood, Ratcliffe, Nicholas, Saunders (Speed 89), Rush, Hughes, Horne.
West Germany: Illgner; Reuter, Brehme, Kohler, Berthold, Buchwald, Helmer, Sammer (Effenberg 76), Matthaus (Doll 46), Klinsmann, Voller.

Luxembourg, 11 September 1991, 9000
Luxembourg (0) 0
Belgium (1) 2 *(Scifo 23, Degryse 48)*
Luxembourg: Van Rijswick; Jeitz, Bossi, Petry, Wolf, Mirsens, Girres, Hellers, Groff, Langers (Thome 66), Morocutti (Krings 77).
Belgium: Preud'homme; Grun (Medved 75), Van der Elst, Demol (Dauwen 79), Borkelmans, Emmers, Staelens, Scifo, Vervoort, Degryse, Nilis.

Nuremberg, 16 October 1991, 46,000
West Germany (3) 4 *(Moller 34, Voller 39, Riedle 44, Doll 69)*
Wales (0) 1 *(Bodin 85 (pen))*
West Germany: Illgner; Binz, Reuter, Kohler, Buchwald, Brehme, Matthaus, Moller, Doll (Effenberg 74), Voller, Riedle (Hassler 65).
Wales: Southall; Ratcliffe, Bodin, Young (Giggs 86), Bowen, Hughes, Melville, Maguire (Speed 46), Horne, Rush, Saunders.

Cardiff (Arms Park), 13 November 1991, 20,000
Wales (0) 1 *(Bodin 82 (pen))*
Luxembourg (0) 0
Wales: Southall; Phillips, Bowen (Bodin 72), Aizlewood, Young, Melville (Giggs 62), Horne, Nicholas, Rush, Hughes, Speed.
Luxembourg: Van Rijswick; Bossi, Birsens, Petry, Wolf,

Girres (Jeitz 87), Hellers, Weis, Groff, Langers (Krings 69), Malget.

Brussels, 20 November 1991, 26,000
Belgium (0) 0
West Germany (1) 1 *(Voller 15)*
Belgium: Preud'homme; Emmers, Grun, Demol (Medved 46), Albert, Borkelmans, Degryse, Scifo, Walem, Boffin, Wilmots (Nilis 67).
West Germany: Illgner; Reuter, Buchwald, Binz, Kohler, Brehme, Doll, Matthaus, Moller (Effenberg 80), Voller, Riedle.

Leverkusen, 17 December 1991, 24,500
West Germany (2) 4 *(Matthaus 15 (pen), Buchwald 44, Riedle 51, Hassler 62)*
Luxembourg (0) 0
West Germany: Illgner; Kohler, Binz, Buchwald, Reuter, Moller (Bein 70), Matthaus, Doll (Hassler 46), Brehme, Riedle, Voller.
Luxembourg: Van Rijswick; Petry, Bossi, Birsens, Girres (Jeitz 83), Weis, Hellers, Groff (Holtz 76), Wolf, Malget, Langers.

	P	W	D	L	F	A	Pts
West Germany	6	5	0	1	13	4	10
Wales	6	4	1	1	8	6	9
Belgium	6	2	1	3	7	6	5
Luxembourg	6	0	0	6	2	14	0

West Germany qualified

GROUP 6
Helsinki, 12 September 1990, 10,242
Finland (0) 0
Portugal (0) 0
Finland: Huttunen; Rinne, Holmgren, Europaeus, Heikkinen, Petaja, Tarkkio (Paavola 73), Litmanen, Jarvinen (Myyry 84), Hjelm, Paatelainen.
Portugal: Silvino; Joao Pinto, Veloso, Ferreira, Venancio, Fonseca (Pacheco 63), Paneira, Andre, Jaime Pacheco, Rui Barros, Rui Aguas (Cadete 46).

Oporto, 17 October 1990, 17,198
Portugal (0) 1 *(Rui Aguas 54)*
Holland (0) 0
Portugal: Silvino; Joao Pinto, Veloso, Venancio, Leal, Paneira, Oceano, Semedo (Ferreira 89), Nelo (Carlos Xavier 87), Rui Aguas, Cadete.
Holland: Van Breukelen; De Boer (Gillhaus 75), Blind, Van Tiggelen (Van't Schip 58), Valckx, Rutjes, Vanenburg, Witschge, Bergkamp, Van Basten, Gullit.

Athens, 31 October 1990, 7768
Greece (2) 4 *(Tsiantakis 37, Karapialis 40, Saravakos 59, Borbokis 88)*
Malta (0) 0
Greece: Papadopoulos T; Apostolakis, Papadopoulos Y, Manolas, Kalitzakis, Tsiantakis, Tsalouhidis, Karapialis, Kofidis, Saravakos, Dimitriadis (Borbokis 31).
Malta: Cini; Carabott, Vella S, Galea, Scerri, Buttigieg, Vella R, Suda (Degiorgio 46), Laferla, Zerafa, Busuttil.

Rotterdam, 21 November 1990, 25,430
Holland (2) 2 *(Bergkamp 7, Van Basten 18)*
Greece (0) 0
Holland: Van Breukelen; De Jong, Blind, Rutjes, Vanenburg, Wouters, Bergkamp (Winter 80), Witschge, Van't Schip, Van Basten, Roy.
Greece: Papadopoulos T; Apostolakis, Papadopoulos Y, Manolas, Kalitzakis, Tsalouhidis, Kofidis (Karageorghiou 53), Karapialis, Tsiantakis, Saravakos, Borbokis.

Ta'Quali, 25 November 1990, 7200
Malta (0) 1 *(Suda 74)*
Finland (0) 1 *(Holmgren 87)*
Malta: Cluett; Buttigieg, Vella S, Galea, Scerri, Vella R, Laferla, Degiorgio, Carabott, Busuttil, Zarb (Suda 71).
Finland: Huttunen; Europaeus, Rinne (Petaja 46), Heikkinen, Holmgren, Myyry, Litmanen, Hjelm, Tauriainen, Tarkkio (Tegelberg 79), Paatelainen.

Ta'Qali, 19 December 1990, 10,254
Malta (0) 0
Holland (3) 8 *(Van Basten 9, 20, 23, 64, 80 (pen)), Winter 53, Bergkamp 60, 66)*

Malta: Cluett; Camilleri E (Suda 46), Camilleri J, Galea, Laferla, Vella S, Carabott, Degiorgio, Scerri, Busuttil, Vella R.
Holland: Van Breukelen; Blind, De Jong, De Boer, Wouters, Koeman E (Winter 46), Bergkamp (Van den Brom 71), Van't Schip, Gullit, Van Basten, Roy.

Athens, 23 January 1991, 20,000

Greece (1) 3 *(Borbokis 7, Manolas 68, Tsalouhidis 85)*

Portugal (1) 2 *(Rui Aguas 18, Futre 62)*

Greece: Sarganis; Apostolakis, Papadopoulos Y, Manolas, Kalitzakis, Tsalouhidis, Kofidis (Athanassiadis 69), Tursunidis, Tsiantakis, Borbokis (Dimitriadis 65), Saravakos.
Portugal: Vitor Baia; Joao Pinto, Veloso, Leal, Venancio, Paneira, Oceano, Rui Barros (Cadete 71), Futre, Rui Aguas, Sousa.

Ta'Qali, 9 February 1991, 5000

Malta (0) 0

Portugal (1) 1 *(Futre 27)*

Malta: Cluett; Vella S, Azzopardi, Galea, Laferla, Buttigieg, Busuttil, Vella R, Suda, Degiorgio, Zerafa.
Portugal: Vitor Baia; Joao Pinto, Leal, Venancio, Veloso, Oceano, Paneira, Rui Barros (Cadete 67), Rui Aguas, Futre (Sousa 63), Semedo.

Oporto, 20 February 1991, 5303

Portugal (3) 5 *(Rui Aguas 5, Leal 33, Paneira 41 (pen), Futre 48, Cadete 81)*

Malta (0) 0

Portugal: Vitor Baia; Joao Pinto (Cadete 46), Leal, Venancio (Madeira 67), Veloso, Oceano, Peneira, Sousa, Rui Aguas, Futre, Semedo.
Malta: Cluett; Vella S, Azzopardi, Camilleri J (Scerri 38), Laferla, Buttigieg, Busuttil, Vella R, Suda (Carabott 51), Degiorgio, Zerafa.

Rotterdam, 13 March 1991, 40,000

Holland (1) 1 *(Van Basten 31 (pen))*

Malta (0) 0

Holland: Van Breukelen; Blind, Vink, De Boer (Kieft 46), Van't Schip, Wouters, Witschge, Gullit, Bergkamp, Van Basten, Roy (Vanenburg 69).
Malta: Cini; Laferla, Camilleri E, Vella S, Brincat (Suda 86), Camilleri J, Azzopardi (Saliba 89), Scerri, Vella R, Degiorgio, Zerafa.

Rotterdam, 17 April 1991, 25,000

Holland (1) 2 *(Van Basten 9, Gullit 75)*

Finland (0) 0

Holland: Van Breukelen; Blind, Vink, De Jong, Gullit, Wouters, Bergkamp (Kieft 72), Witschge, Van't Schip, Van Basten (Rutjes 76), Huistra.
Finland: Huttunen; Kanerva, Heikkinen, Europaeus, Holmgren, Ukkonen, Petaja, Litmanen (Tegelberg 46), Myyry, Tauriainen (Nyssonen 83), Paatelainen.

Helsinki, 16 May 1991, 5150

Finland (0) 2 *(Jarvinen 51, Litmanen 88)*

Malta (0) 0

Finland: Huttunen; Petaja, Holmgren, Heikkinen, Kanerva, Myyry, Litmanen, Ukkonen, Tarkkio (Tauriainen 87), Paatelainen (Paavola 63), Jarvinen.
Malta: Cini; Buttigieg, Brincat, Vella S, Camilleri E (Zerafa 70), Laferla, Busuttil, Vella R, Degiorgio, Scerri, Suda.

Helsinki, 5 June 1991, 21,207

Finland (0) 1 *(Holmgren 78)*

Holland (0) 1 *(De Boer 60)*

Finland: Huttunen; Petaja, Heikkinen, Ukkonen (Hjelm 81), Holmgren, Paavola, Myyry, Litmanen, Jarvinen, Tarkkio, Paatelainen (Tegelberg 66).
Holland: Hiele, Rutjes, Blind, Wouters, De Boer, Koeman R, Winter, Witschge, Van't Schip, Van Basten, Huistra (Kieft 75).

Oporto, 11 September 1991, 30,000

Portugal (1) 1 *(Cesar Brito 22)*

Finland (0) 0

Portugal: Vitor Baia; Joao Pinto, Samuel, Fernando Couto, Leal, Venancio, Cesar Brito (Cadete 80), Rui Barros, Rui Aguas (Oceano 56), Futre, Manuel Guimaraes.
Finland: Huttunen; Tauriainen (Vuorela 59), Holmgren, Heikkinen, Petaja, Pavola, Myyry, Ukkonen (Litmanen 72), Jarvinen, Tarkkio, Paatelainen.

Helsinki, 9 October 1991, 5225

Finland (0) 1 *(Ukkonen 50)*

Greece (0) 1 *(Tsalouhidis 73)*

Finland: Huttunen; Heikkinen, Holmgren, Petaja, Myyry, Jarvinen (Paatelainen 63), Tarkkio (Tegelberg 82), Ukkonen, Hjelm, Litmanen, Vuorela.
Greece: Sarganis; Apostolakis (Athanassiadis 60), Karageorgiou, Mitsibonas, Kalitzakis, Tsalouhidis, Saravakos, Papaioannou, Borbokis (Tursunidis 70), Karapialis,Tsiantakis.

Rotterdam, 16 October 1991, 50,000

Holland (1) 1 *(Witschge 20)*

Portugal (0) 0

Holland: Van Breukelen; Blind, Koeman R, Van Tiggelen, Koeman E, Wouters, Rijkaard (Winter 70), Witschge (Van't Schip 87), Gullit, Van Basten, Bergkamp.
Portugal: Vitor Baia; Joao Pinto, Leal, Venancio, Fernando Couto, Oceano, Peixe (Cesar Brito 80), Rui Barros, Cadete, Futre, Nelo (Figo 56).

Athens, 30 October 1991, 26,000

Greece (0) 2 *(Saravakos 50, Borbokis 52)*

Finland (0) 0

Greece: Sarganis; Apostolakis, Karageorgiou, Mitsibonas, Tsalouhidis, Kalitzakis, Saravakos, Papaioannou, Athanassiadis (Borbokis 46), Karapialis (Tursunidis 73), Tsiantakis
Finland: Holmgren; Huttunen, Heikkinen, Petaja, Vuorela (Paatelainen 54), Huhtamaki (Tegelberg 83), Litmanen, Ukkonen, Jarvinen, Tarkkio, Hjelm.

Lisbon, 20 November 1991, 2000

Portugal (1) 1 *(Joao Pinto II 17)*

Greece (0) 0

Portugal: Vitor Baia; Joao Pinto I, Rui Bento, Fernando Couto, Leal, Peixe, Vitor Paneira (Oceano 46), Rui Barros, Joao Pinto II, Semedo (Figo 15), Rui Aguas.
Greece: Sarganis; Apostolakis, Karageorgiou, Mitsibonas, Tsalouhidis, Kalitzakis, Saravakos, Papaioannou (Athanassiadis 64), Borbokis (Dimitriadis 69), Karapiakis, Tsiantakis.

Salonika, 4 December 1991, 32,500

Greece (0) 0

Holland (1) 2 *(Bergkamp 38, Blind 87)*

Greece: Sarganis; Pavlos, Papaioannou (Karageorgiou 46), Lagonidis, Kalitzakis, Mitsibonas, Tsalouhidis, Saravakos, Papadopoulos Y, Tsiantakis, Nioblias, Karapialis (Tursunidis 61).
Holland: Van Breukelen; Blind, Van Tiggelen, Koeman R, Koeman E, Wouters, Rijkaard (Winter 61), Witschge, Bergkamp, Van Basten, Kieft.

Valletta, 22 December 1991, 8000

Malta (1) 1 *(Sultana 42)*

Greece (0) 1 *(Marinakis 67)*

Malta: Cluett; Brincat, Galea, Vella S, Saliba, Laferla, Busuttil, Vella R (Camilleri J 66), Scerri (Sultana 33), Gregory, Degiorgio.
Greece: Plitsis; Papaioannou, Kapouranis, Mitsibonas, Kalitzakis, Tsalouhidis, Thonis (Giotsas 56), Marangos (Marinakis 44), Dimitriadis, Noblias, Tsiantakis.

	P	W	D	L	F	A	Pts
Holland	8	6	1	1	17	2	13
Portugal	8	5	1	2	11	4	11
Greece	8	3	2	3	11	9	8
Finland	8	1	4	3	5	8	6
Malta	8	0	2	6	2	23	2

Holland qualified

GROUP 7

Wembley, 17 October 1990, 77,040

England (1) 2 *(Lineker 39 (pen), Beardsley 89)*

Poland (0) 0

England: Woods; Dixon, Pearce, Parker, Walker, Wright M, Platt, Gascoigne, Bull (Waddle 56), Lineker (Beardsley 56), Barnes.
Poland: Wandzik; Czachowski, Wdowczyk, Szewczyk, Kaczmarek, Nawrocki, Tarasiewicz, Warzycha R, Furtok (Warzycha K 75), Ziober, Kosecki (Kubicki 85).

Dublin, 17 October 1990, 46,000
Republic of Ireland (2) 5 *(Aldridge 15, 58, 73 (pen), O'Leary 40, Quinn 66)*
Turkey (0) 0
Republic of Ireland: Bonner; Irwin, Staunton, McCarthy, O'Leary, Hughton, Townsend (Moran 73), Houghton, Quinn (Cascarino 66), Aldridge, Sheridan.
Turkey: Engin; Riza, Tugay, Kemal, Gokhan, Erkan (Tanju 46), Bulent, Oguz, Mehmet, Hami, Sercan (Metin 46).

Dublin, 14 November 1990, 45,000
Republic of Ireland (0) 1 *(Cascarino 79)*
England (0) 1 *(Platt 67)*
Republic of Ireland: Bonner; Morris, Staunton, McCarthy, O'Leary, Whelan (McLoughlin 74), McGrath, Houghton, Quinn (Cascarino 62), Aldridge, Townsend.
England: Woods; Dixon, Pearce, Adams, Walker, Wright M, Platt, Cowans, Beardsley, Lineker, McMahon.

Istanbul, 14 November 1990, 4868
Turkey (0) 0
Poland (1) 1 *(Dziekanowski 37)*
Turkey: Engin; Riza, Uiken (Mehmet 67), Bulent, Gokhan, Yusuf, Muhammet (Sercan 67), Unal, Oguz, Tanju, Hami.
Poland: Wandzik; Kubicki, Kaczmarek, Wdowczyk, Warzycha R, Nawrocki, Tarasiewicz, Prusik, Warzycha K, Dziekanowski (Ziober 74), Kosecki.

Wembley, 27 March 1991, 77,753
England (1) 1 *(Dixon 9)*
Republic of Ireland (1) 1 *(Quinn 27)*
England: Seaman; Dixon, Pearce, Adams (Sharpe 46), Walker, Wright M, Robson, Platt, Beardsley, Lineker (Wright I 75), Barnes.
Republic of Ireland: Bonner; Irwin, Staunton, O'Leary, Moran, Townsend, McGrath, Houghton, Quinn, Aldridge (Cascarino 70), Sheedy.

Warsaw, 17 April 1991, 1000
Poland (0) 3 *(Tarasiewicz 75, Urban 81, Kosecki 88)*
Turkey (0) 0
Poland: Wandzik; Kubicki, Kaczmarek (Czachowski 62), Wdowczyk, Jakolcewicz, Warzycha K, Warzycha R, Tarasiewicz, Urban, Kosecki, Ziober (Soczynski 70).
Turkey: Engin; Riza, Tayfun, Gokhan, Kemal, Bulent, Feyyaz (Faruk 80), Muhammet, Mehmet, Tanju, Abdullah (Osman 70).

Dublin, 1 May 1991, 48,000
Republic of Ireland (0) 0
Poland (0) 0
Republic of Ireland: Bonner; Irwin, Staunton, O'Leary, Moran, Townsend, McGrath, Houghton, Quinn (Slaven 70), Aldridge (Cascarino 70), Sheedy.

Poland: Wandzik; Kubicki, Jakolcewicz, Wdowczyk, Soczynski, Warzycha R, Tarasiewicz, Czachowski, Furtok (Kosecki 89), Urban (Warzycha K 88), Szewczyk.

Izmir, 1 May 1991, 20,000
Turkey (0) 0
England (1) 1 *(Wise 32)*
Turkey: Hayrettin; Riza, Ogun, Gokhan, Recap, Muhammet, Unal, Ridvan, Mehmet, Tanju, Ali (Feyyaz 72).
England: Seaman; Dixon; Pearce, Wise, Walker, Pallister, Platt, Thomas G (Hodge 46), Smith, Lineker, Barnes.

Poznan, 16 October 1991, 17,000
Poland (0) 3 *(Czachowski 54, Furtok 76, Urban 87)*
Republic of Ireland (1) 3 *(McGrath 10, Townsend 62, Cascarino 68)*
Poland: Wandzik; Kubicki (Lesiak 32), Czachowski, Soczynski, Wdowczyk, Nawrocki (Skrzypczak 81), Tarasiewicz, Ziober, Urban, Kosecki, Furtok.
Republic of Ireland: Bonner; Morris, Staunton (Phelan 56), Irwin, McGrath, Moran, O'Leary, Sheedy, Keane, Townsend, Cascarino.

Wembley, 16 October 1991, 50,896
England (1) 1 *(Smith 21)*
Turkey (0) 0
England: Woods; Dixon, Pearce, Batty, Walker, Mabbutt, Robson, Platt, Smith, Lineker, Waddle.
Turkey: Hayrettin; Recep, Ogun, Gokhan, Tugay, Turhan, Feyyaz (Hami 76), Riza, Unal, Oguz, Orhan.

Istanbul, 13 November 1991, 42,000
Turkey (1) 1 *(Riza 12 (pen))*
Republic of Ireland (1) 3 *(Byrne 7, 58, Cascarino 55)*
Turkey: Hayrettin; Recep (Bulent 69), Turhan, Gokhan, Tugay, Ogun, Feyyaz (Ridvan 46), Riza, Hami, Oguz, Orhan.
Republic of Ireland: Bonner; Hughton, O'Leary, McCarthy, Phelan, Byrne, McGrath, Staunton, Sheedy, Cascarino, Aldridge.

Poznan, 13 November 1991, 15,000
Poland (1) 1 *(Szewczyk 32)*
England (0) 1 *(Lineker 77)*
Poland: Bako; Warzycha R, Szewczyk (Fedoruk 77), Waldoch, Soczynski, Czachowski, Kosecki, Skrzypczak (Kowalczyk 79), Ziober, Furtok, Urban.
England: Woods; Dixon, Pearce, Gray (Smith 46), Walker, Mabbutt, Platt, Thomas, Rocastle, Lineker, Sinton (Daley 70).

	P	W	D	L	F	A	Pts
England	6	3	3	0	7	3	9
Republic of Ireland	6	2	4	0	13	6	8
Poland	6	2	3	1	8	6	7
Turkey	6	0	0	6	1	14	0

England qualified

EUROPEAN CHAMPIONSHIP 1992

(Final tournament in Sweden)

Denmark's success in the 1992 European Championship blasted a gaping hole through the theory that there has to be endless preparation to achieve victory in an international tournament. Pitchforked into the finals on the exclusion of Yugoslavia, they survived unimpressive performances against England and Sweden before putting their game together against France. Then, despite crippling injuries in the match with Holland they managed to win the resultant penalty shoot-out to reach the final. There they displayed much of the character and determination which has epitomized their football down the years, but above all showed a high skill factor. While this was not as previously revealed in the 1984 European Championship and in the early stages of the 1986 World Cup, it was sufficient to win what was a largely disappointing tournament. The Danish win over Germany in the final was well merited, the Germans being forced to resort to the kind of questionable strong-arm tactics which sadly have risen to the surface in times of stress.

Denmark aside, it was difficult to find anything worth savouring, though Scotland gave everything and fully deserved their one victory over the CIS, who were the least enterprising team in a poor competition. The Scots had in Richard Gough, one of the outstanding players in Sweden.

The Dutch promised much, looked controlled and stylish until unsettled by the swift counter-attacking down the flanks by the Danes. They never recovered their composure and it would have been a travesty of justice had they survived the penalty shoot-out.

For Germany, it was a devastating disappointment to fail in the final. They had lost their inspirational captain and midfield maestro Lothar Matthäus before the tournament began. His successor Rudi Völler lasted one half of the first game before departing with an injured arm and they also suffered injuries to key defenders during the matches in Sweden, but were no more affected than the Danes in this respect.

France, who had been wrongly designated as favourites were clearly well past their peak, but Sweden again showed that the host country has an immense advantage and responded well enough to reach the semi-finals.

For England, it was another failure. Robbed of the services of key players themselves like Paul Gascoigne, John Barnes and Mark Wright, they were never allowed a settled side. Perhaps the saddest sight was the departure from international football of Gary Lineker, withdrawn in the match with Sweden, still one goal short of equalling Bobby Charlton's record of goals.

Group 1

Stockholm, 10 June 1992, 29,860

Sweden (1) 1 *(Eriksson 25)*

France (0) 1 *(Papin 58)*

Sweden: Ravelli; Nilsson R, Eriksson J, Andersson P, Björklund, Schwarz, Ingesson, Thern, Limpar, Brolin, Andersson K (Dahlin 74).
France: Martini; Angloma (Fernandez 66), Amoros, Blanc, Casoni, Boli, Deschamps, Sauzee, Vahirua (Perez 46), Papin, Cantona.
Referee: A. Spirin (CIS).

Malmo, 11 June 1992, 26,385

Denmark (0) 0

England (0) 0

Denmark: Schmeichel; Sivebaek, Nielsen K, Olsen L, Andersen, Christofte, Jensen, Vilfort, Laudrup, Povlsen, Christensen.
England: Woods; Curle (Daley 65), Pearce, Palmer, Keown, Walker, Steven, Platt, Smith, Lineker, Merson (Webb 73).
Referee: J. Blankenstein (Holland).

Malmo, 14 June 1992, 26,535

England (0) 0

France (0) 0

England: Woods; Steven, Pearce, Palmer, Keown, Walker, Batty, Platt, Shearer, Lineker, Sinton.
France: Martini; Amoros, Blanc, Boli, Casoni, Deschamps, Sauzee (Angloma 46), Fernandez (Perez 74), Durand, Cantona, Papin.
Referee: S. Puhl (Hungary).

Stockholm, 14 June 1992, 29,902

Sweden (0) 1 *(Brolin 59)*

Denmark (0) 0

Sweden: Ravelli; Nilsson R, Eriksson J, Andersson P, Björklund, Limpar (Erlingmark 89), Thern, Schwarz, Ingesson, Brolin, Dahlin (Ekstrom 75).
Denmark: Schmeichel; Sivebaek, Nielsen K, Olsen L, Andersen, Christofte, Jensen (Larsen 64), Vilfort, Laudrup, Povlsen, Christensen (Frank 51).
Referee: A. Schmidhuber (Germany).

Malmo, 17 June 1992, 25,763

Denmark (1) 2 *(Larsen 7, Elstrup 77)*

France (0) 1 *(Papin 60)*

Denmark: Schmeichel; Sivebaek, Nielsen K (Piechnik 62), Olsen L, Christofte, Andersen, Larsen, Jensen, Laudrup (Elstrup 69), Frank, Povlsen.
France: Martini; Boli, Blanc, Casoni, Amoros, Deschamps, Perez (Cocard 81), Divert, Papin, Cantona, Vahirua (Fernandez 46).
Referee: H. Forstinger (Austria).

Stockholm, 17 June 1992, 30,126

Sweden (0) 2 *(Eriksson 51, Brolin 82)*

England (1) 1 *(Platt 3)*

Sweden: Ravelli; Nilsson R, Eriksson J, Andersson P, Björklund, Schwarz, Ingesson, Thern, Limpar (Ekstrom 46), Brolin, Dahlin.
England: Woods; Batty, Pearce, Palmer, Keown, Walker, Daley, Webb, Platt, Lineker (Smith 64), Sinton (Merson 79).
Referee: J. Rosa dos Santos (Portugal).

	P	W	D	L	F	A	Pts
Sweden	3	2	1	0	4	2	5
Denmark	3	1	1	1	2	2	3
France	3	0	2	1	2	3	2
England	3	0	2	1	1	2	2

Group 2

Norrkoping, 12 June 1992, 17,410

CIS (0) 1 *(Dobrovolski 62 (pen))*

Germany (0) 1 *(Hässler 90)*

CIS: Kharin; Chernishev, Kuznetsov O, Tsveiba, Kanchelskis, Kuznetsov D, Mikhailichenko, Shalimov (Ivanov 83), Kolyvanov, Dobrovolski, Lyuty (Onopko 46).
Germany: Illgner; Reuter (Klinsmann 62), Kohler, Binz, Buchwald, Brehme, Effenberg, Hässler, Doll, Völler (Möller 46), Riedle.
Referee: G. Biguet (France).

Gothenburg, 12 June 1992, 35,720

Holland (0) 1 *(Bergkamp 76)*

Scotland (0) 0

Holland: Van Breukelen; Van Aerle, Van Tiggelen, Koeman R, Witschge Rob, Wouters (Jonk 55), Bergkamp (Winter 86), Rijkaard, Van Basten, Gullit, Roy.
Scotland: Goram; Gough, McKimmie, McStay, Malpas, McPherson, Durie, McCall, McCoist (Gallacher 75), McClair (Ferguson 79), McAllister.
Referee: B. Karlsson (Sweden).

Gothenburg, 15 June 1992, 34,440

Holland (0) 0

CIS (0) 0

Holland: Van Breukelen; Van Aerle, Van Tiggelen, Koeman R, Witschge Rob, Wouters, Bergkamp, Rijkaard, Van Basten, Gullit (Van't Schip 71), Roy.
CIS: Kharin; Chernishev, Onopko, Tsveiba, Kuznetsov O, Aleinikov (Kuznetsov D 56), Kanchelskis, Youran (Kiryakov 64), Mikhailichenko, Dobrovolski, Kolyvanov.
Referee: P. Mikkelsen (Denmark).

Norrkoping, 15 June 1992, 17,638

Scotland (0) 0

Germany (1) 2 *(Riedle 28, Effenberg 47)*

Scotland: Goram; McKimmie, Malpas, Gough, McPherson, McStay, Durie (Nevin 54), McCall, McClair, McCoist (Gallacher 70), McAllister.
Germany: Illgner; Brehme, Kohler, Binz, Buchwald, Möller, Hässler, Riedle (Reuter 68) (Schulz 74), Sammer, Effenberg, Klinsmann.

Norrkoping, 18 June 1992, 14,660

Scotland (2) 3 *(McStay 6, McClair 17, McAllister 83 (pen))*

CIS (0) 0

Scotland: Goram; McKimmie, Boyd, Gough, McPherson, McAllister, McStay, McCall, McClair, McCoist (McInally 67), Gallacher (Nevin 78).
CIS: Kharin; Chernishev, Tzhadadze, Kuznetsov O, Mikhailichenko, Aleinikov (Kuznetsov D 46), Dobrovolski, Youran, Kanchelskis, Kiryakov (Korneyev 46), Onopko.
Referee: K. Rothlisberger (Switzerland).

Gothenburg, 18 June 1992, 37,725

Holland (2) 3 *(Rijkaard 3, Witschge 15, Bergkamp 73)*

Germany (0) 1 *(Klinsmann 53)*

Holland: Van Breukelen; Der Boer (Winter 62), Van Tiggelen, Koeman R, Rijkaard, Witschge Rob, Wouters, Bergkamp (Bosz 87), Van Basten, Gullit, Roy.
Germany: Illgner; Kohler, Binz (Sammer 46), Frontzeck, Brehme, Effenberg, Hässler, Helmer, Möller, Riedle (Doll 76), Klinsmann.
Referee: P. Pairetto (Italy).

	P	W	D	L	F	A	Pts
Holland	3	2	1	0	4	1	5
Germany	3	1	1	1	4	4	3
Scotland	3	1	0	2	3	3	2
CIS	3	0	2	1	1	4	2

Semi-finals

Stockholm, 21 June 1992, 28,827

Sweden (0) 2 *(Brolin 63 (pen), Andersson 89)*

Germany (1) 3 *(Hassler 11, Riedle 58, 88)*

Sweden: Ravelli; Nilsson R, Eriksson J, Björklund, Ingesson, Thern, Brolin, Andersson K, Dahlin (Ekstrom 72), Ljung, Nilsson J (Limpar 59).
Germany: Illgner; Reuter, Brehme, Kohler, Buchwald, Hässler, Riedle, Helmer, Sammer, Effenberg, Klinsmann.
Referee: T. Lanese (Italy).

Gothenburg, 22 June 1992, 37,450

Denmark (2) 2 *(Larsen 6, 33)*

Holland (1) 2 *(Bergkamp 23, Rijkaard 86)*

Denmark: Schmeichel; Piechnik, Olsen L, Christofte, Sivebaek, Vilfort, Jensen, Laudrup (Elstrup 57), Andersen (Christiansen 70), Larsen, Povlsen.
Holland: Van Breukelen; Van Tiggelen, De Boer (Kieft 46), Koeman R, Rijkaard, Witschge Rob, Wouters, Bergkamp, Van Basten, Gullit, Roy (Van't Schip 116).
aet; Denmark won 5–4 on penalties.
Referee: S. Aladren (Spain).
Penalty shoot-out: Holland: Koeman (scored), Van Basten (shot saved), Bergkamp, Rijkaard, Witschge (scored); *Denmark:* Larsen, Povlsen, Elstrup, Vilfort, Christofte (scored).

Final

Gothenburg, 26 June 1992, 37,800

Denmark (1) 2 *(Jensen 18, Vilfort 78)*

Germany (0) 0

Denmark: Schmeichel; Sivebaek (Christiansen 65), Nielsen K, Olsen L, Christofte, Jensen, Povlsen, Laudrup, Piechnik, Larsen, Vilfort.
Germany: Illgner; Reuter, Brehme, Kohler, Buchwald, Hässler, Riedle, Helmer, Sammer (Doll 46), Effenberg (Thon 78), Klinsmann.
Referee: B. Galler (Switzerland).

N.B. Yugoslavia replaced by Denmark. Germany originally West Germany in draw for qualifying competition. USSR became CIS.

Gary Lineker scores a spectacular late equaliser for England in Poland to enable his country to qualify for the 1992 European Championship finals. (ASP)

Arsenal-bound John Jensen celebrates his goal in the 1992 European Championship final. Denmark beat Germany 2-0. (Colorsport)

EUROPEAN FOOTBALL CHAMPIONSHIP

(formerly EUROPEAN NATIONS' CUP)

Past Finals

Year	Winners		Runners-up		Venue
			Yugoslavia		
1960	USSR	2	1		Paris
1964	Spain	2	USSR	1	Madrid
1968	Italy	2	Yugoslavia	0	Rome
	After 1-1 draw				
1972	W. Germany	3	USSR	0	Brussels
1976	Czechoslovakia	2	W. Germany	2	Belgrade
	(*Czechoslovakia* won on penalties)				
1980	West Germany	2	Belgium	1	Rome
1984	France	2	Spain	0	Paris
1988	Holland	2	USSR	0	Munich

EUROPEAN NATIONS' CUP 1958–60

Preliminary Round

Eire 2, Czechoslovakia 0
Czechoslovakia 4, Eire 0

First Round

France 7, Greece 1
Greece 1, France 1
USSR 3, Hungary 1
Hungary 0, USSR 1
Romania 3, Turkey 0
Turkey 2, Romania 0
Norway 0, Austria 1
Austria 5, Norway 2
Yugoslavia 2, Bulgaria 0
Bulgaria 1, Yugoslavia 1
Portugal 3, East Germany 2
East Germany 0, Portugal 2
Denmark 2, Czechoslovakia 2
Czechoslovakia 5, Denmark 1
Poland 2, Spain 4
Spain 3, Poland 0

Quarter-finals

Portugal 2, Yugoslavia 1
Yugoslavia 5, Portugal 1
France 5, Austria 2
Austria 2, France 4
Romania 0, Czechoslovakia 2
Czechoslovakia 3, Romania 0
USSR w.o. Spain withdrew

Semi-finals

Yugoslavia 5, France 4 (in Paris)
USSR 3, Czechoslovakia 0 (in Marseilles)

Third Place Match (Marseilles)

Czechoslovakia 2, France 0

Final (Paris, 10 July 1960)

USSR (0) 2, Yugoslavia (1) 1 after extra time
USSR: Yachin; Tchekeli, Kroutikov, Voinov, Maslenkin, Netto, Metreveli, Ivanov, Ponedelnik, Bubukin, Meshki.
Yugoslavia: Vidinic; Durkovic, Jusufi, Zanetic, Miladinovic, Perusic, Sekularac, Jerkovic, Galic, Matus, Kostic.
Scorers: Metreveli, Ponedelnik for USSR; Netto (og) for Yugoslavia.

EUROPEAN NATIONS' CUP 1962–64

First Round

Spain 6, Romania 0
Romania 3, Spain 1
Poland 0, Northern Ireland 2

Northern Ireland 2, Poland 0
Denmark 6, Malta 1
Malta 1, Denmark 3
Eire 4, Iceland 2
Iceland 1, Eire 1
Greece withdrew against Albania
East Germany 2, Czechoslovakia 1
Czechoslovakia 1, East Germany 1
Hungary 3, Wales 1
Wales 1, Hungary 1
Italy 6, Turkey 0
Turkey 0, Italy 1
Holland 3, Switzerland 1
Switzerland 1, Holland 1
Norway 0, Sweden 2
Sweden 1, Norway 1
Yugoslavia 3, Belgium 2
Belgium 0, Yugoslavia 1
Bulgaria 3, Portugal 1
Portugal 3, Bulgaria 1
Bulgaria 1, Portugal 0
England 1, France 1
France 5, England 2

Second Round

Spain 1, Northern Ireland 1
Northern Ireland 0, Spain 1
Denmark 4, Albania 0
Albania 1, Denmark 0
Austria 0, Eire 0
Eire 3, Austria 2
East Germany 1, Hungary 2
Hungary 3, East Germany 3
USSR 2, Italy 0
Italy 1, USSR 1
Holland 1, Luxembourg 1
Luxembourg 2, Holland 1
Yugoslavia 0, Sweden 0
Sweden 3, Yugoslavia 2
Bulgaria 1, France 0
France 3, Bulgaria 1

Quarter-finals

Luxembourg 2, Denmark 2
Denmark 3, Luxembourg 3
Denmark 1, Luxembourg 0
Spain 5, Eire 1
Eire 0, Spain 2
France 1, Hungary 3
Hungary 2, France 1
Sweden 1, USSR 1
USSR 3, Sweden 1

Semi-finals

USSR 3, Denmark 0 (in Barcelona)
Spain 2, Hungary 1 (in Madrid)

Third Place Match (Barcelona)

Hungary 3, Denmark 1 after extra time

Final (Madrid, 21 June 1964)

Spain (1) 2, USSR (1) 1

Spain: Iribar; Rivilla, Caleja, Fuste, Olivella, Zoco, Amancio, Pereda, Marcellino, Suarez, Lapetra.
USSR: Yachin; Chustikov, Mudrik, Voronin, Shesternjev, Anitchkin, Chislenko, Ivanov, Ponedelnik, Kornaev, Khusainov.
Scorers: Pereda, Marcellino for Spain; Khusainov for USSR.

EUROPEAN CHAMPIONSHIP 1966–68

Group 1

Eire 0, Spain 0
Eire 2, Turkey 1
Spain 2, Eire 0
Turkey 0, Spain 0
Turkey 2, Eire 1
Eire 0, Czechoslovakia 2
Spain 2, Turkey 0
Czechoslovakia 1, Spain 0
Spain 2, Czechoslovakia 1
Czechoslovakia 3, Turkey 0
Turkey 0, Czechoslovakia 0
Czechoslovakia 1, Eire 2

Group 2

Norway 0, Bulgaria 0
Portugal 1, Sweden 2
Bulgaria 4, Norway 2
Sweden 1, Portugal 1
Norway 1, Portugal 2
Sweden 0, Bulgaria 2
Norway 3, Sweden 1
Sweden 5, Norway 2
Bulgaria 3, Sweden 0
Portugal 2, Norway 1
Bulgaria 1, Portugal 0
Portugal 0, Bulgaria 0

Group 3

Finland 0, Austria 0
Austria 2, Finland 1
Greece 2, Finland 1
Greece 4, Austria 1
Finland 1, Greece 1
Austria 1, USSR 0
USSR 4, Austria 3
Greece 0, USSR 1
USSR 2, Finland 0
Austria 1, Greece 1
Finland 2, USSR 5
USSR 4, Greece 0

Group 4

Albania 0, Yugoslavia 2
West Germany 6, Albania 0
Yugoslavia 1, West Germany 0
West Germany 3, Yugoslavia 1
Yugoslavia 4, Albania 0
Albania 0, West Germany 0

Group 5

Holland 2, Hungary 2
Hungary 6, Denmark 0
Holland 2, Denmark 0
East Germany 4, Holland 3
Hungary 2, Holland 1
Denmark 0, Hungary 2
Denmark 1, East Germany 1
Holland 1, East Germany 0
Hungary 3, East Germany 1
Denmark 3, Holland 2
East Germany 3, Denmark 2
East Germany 1, Hungary 0

Group 6

Cyprus 1, Romania 5
Romania 4, Switzerland 2
Italy 3, Romania 1
Cyprus 0, Italy 2
Romania 7, Cyprus 0

Switzerland 7, Romania 1
Italy 5, Cyprus 0
Switzerland 5, Cyprus 0
Switzerland 2, Italy 2
Italy 4, Switzerland 0
Cyprus 2, Switzerland 1
Romania 0, Italy 1

Group 7

Poland 4, Luxembourg 0
France 2, Poland 1
Luxembourg 0, France 3
Luxembourg 0, Bulgaria 5
Luxembourg 0, Poland 0
Poland 3, Belgium 1
Belgium 2, France 1
Poland 1, France 4
Belgium 2, Poland 4
France 1, Belgium 1
Belgium 3, Luxembourg 0
France 3, Luxembourg 1

Group 8

Northern Ireland 0, England 2
Wales 1, Scotland 1
England 5, Wales 1
Scotland 2, Northern Ireland 1
Northern Ireland 0, Wales 0
England 2, Scotland 3
Wales 0, England 3
Northern Ireland 1, Scotland 0
England 2, Northern Ireland 0
Scotland 3, Wales 2
Scotland 1, England 1
Wales 2, Northern Ireland 0

Quarter-finals

England 1, Spain 0
Spain 1, England 2
Bulgaria 3, Italy 2
Italy 2, Bulgaria 0
France 1, Yugoslavia 1
Yugoslavia 5, France 1
Hungary 2, USSR 0
USSR 3, Hungary 0

Semi-finals

Yugoslavia 1, England 0 (in Florence)
Italy 0, USSR 0 (Italy won toss) (in Naples)

Third Place Match (Rome)

England 2, USSR 0

Final (Rome, 8 June 1968)

Italy (0) 1, Yugoslavia (1) 1
Italy: Zoff; Burgnich, Facchetti, Ferrini, Guarneri, Castano, Domenghini, Juliano, Anastasi, Lodetti, Prati.
Yugoslavia: Pantelic; Fazlagic, Damjanovic, Pavlovic, Paunovic, Holcer, Petkovic, Acimovic, Musemic, Trivic, Dzajic.
Scorers: Domenghini for Italy; Dzajic for Yugoslavia.

Final Replay (Rome, 10 June 1968)

Italy (2) 2, Yugoslavia (0) 0
Italy: Zoff; Burgnich, Facchetti, Rosato, Guarneri, Salvadore, Domenghini, Mazzola, Anastasi, De Sisti, Riva.
Yugoslavia: Pantelic; Fazlagic, Damjanovic, Pavlovic, Paunovic, Holcer, Hosic, Acimovic, Musemic, Trivic, Dzajic.
Scorers: Riva, Anastasi for Italy.

EUROPEAN CHAMPIONSHIP 1970–72

Group 1

Czechoslovakia 1, Finland 1
Romania 3, Finland 0
Wales 0, Romania 0
Wales 1, Czechoslovakia 3
Finland 0, Wales 1
Czechoslovakia 1, Romania 0
Finland 0, Czechoslovakia 4
Finland 0, Romania 4
Wales 3, Finland 0
Czechoslovakia 1, Wales 0
Romania 2, Czechoslovakia 1
Romania 2, Wales 0

Group 2

Norway 1, Hungary 3
France 3, Norway 1
Bulgaria 1, Norway 1
Hungary 1, France 1
Bulgaria 3, Hungary 0
Norway 1, Bulgaria 4
Norway 1, France 3
Hungary 2, Bulgaria 0
France 0, Hungary 2
Hungary 4, Norway 0
France 2, Bulgaria 1
Bulgaria 2, France 1

Group 3

Greece 0, Switzerland 1
Malta 1, Switzerland 2
Malta 0, England 1
England 3, Greece 0
Switzerland 5, Malta 0
England 5, Malta 0
Malta 1, Greece 1
Switzerland 1, Greece 0
Greece 2, Malta 0
Switzerland 2, England 3
England 1, Switzerland 1
Greece 0, England 2

Group 4

Spain 3, Northern Ireland 0
Cyprus 0, Northern Ireland 3
Northern Ireland 5, Cyprus 0
Cyprus 1, USSR 3
Cyprus 0, Spain 2
USSR 2, Spain 1
USSR 6, Cyprus 1
USSR 1, Northern Ireland 0
Northern Ireland 1, USSR 1
Spain 0, USSR 0
Spain 7, Cyprus 0
Northern Ireland 1, Spain 1

Group 5

Denmark 0, Portugal 1
Scotland 1, Denmark 0
Belgium 2, Denmark 0
Belgium 3, Scotland 0
Belgium 3, Portugal 0
Portugal 2, Scotland 0
Denmark 1, Scotland 0
Portugal 5, Denmark 0
Denmark 1, Belgium 2
Scotland 2, Portugal 1
Scotland 1, Belgium 0
Portugal 1, Belgium 1

Group 6

Eire 1, Sweden 1
Sweden 1, Eire 0
Austria 1, Italy 2

Italy 3, Eire 0
Eire 1, Italy 2
Eire 1, Austria 4
Sweden 1, Austria 0
Sweden 0, Italy 0
Austria 1, Sweden 0
Italy 3, Sweden 0
Austria 6, Eire 0
Italy 2, Austria 2

Group 7

Holland 1, Yugoslavia 1
East Germany 1, Holland 0
Luxembourg 0, East Germany 5
Yugoslavia 2, Holland 0
East Germany 2, Luxembourg 1
Luxembourg 0, Yugoslavia 2
Holland 6, Luxembourg 0
East Germany 1, Yugoslavia 2
Holland 3, East Germany 2
Yugoslavia 0, East Germany 0
Yugoslavia 0, Luxembourg 0
Luxembourg 0, Holland 8

Group 8

Poland 3, Albania 0
West Germany 1, Turkey 1
Turkey 2, Albania 1
Albania 0, West Germany 1
Turkey 0, West Germany 3
Albania 1, Poland 1
West Germany 2, Albania 0
Poland 5, Turkey 1
Poland 1, West Germany 3
Albania 3, Turkey 0
West Germany 0, Poland 0
Turkey 1, Poland 0

Quarter-finals

England 1, West Germany 3
Italy 0, Belgium 0
Hungary 1, Romania 1
Yugoslavia 0, USSR 0
West Germany 0, England 0
Belgium 2, Italy 1
USSR 3, Yugoslavia 0
Romania 2, Hungary 2
Play-off: Hungary 2, Romania 1

Semi-finals

USSR 1, Hungary 0 (in Brussels)
West Germany 2, Belgium 1 (in Antwerp)

Third Place Match (Liège)

Belgium 2, Hungary 1

Final (Brussels, 18 June 1972)

West Germany (1) 3, USSR (0) 0
West Germany: Maier; Hottges, Schwarzenbeck,
Beckenbauer, Breitner, Hoeness, Wimmer, Netzer,
Heynckes, Müller, Kremers.
USSR: Rudakov; Dzodzuashvili, Khurtsilava, Kaplichny,
Istomin, Troshkin, Kolotov, Baidachni, Konkov
(Dolmatov), Banishevski (Kozinkievits), Onishenko.
Scorers: Müller 2, Wimmer for West Germany.

EUROPEAN CHAMPIONSHIP 1974–76

Group 1

England 3, Czechoslovakia 0
England 0, Portugal 0
England 5, Cyprus 0
Czechoslovakia 4, Cyprus 0
Czechoslovakia 5, Portugal 0

Cyprus 0, England 1
Cyprus 0, Portugal 2
Czechoslovakia 2, England 1
Portugal 1, Czechoslovakia 1
Portugal 1, England 1
Cyprus 0, Czechoslovakia 3
Portugal 1, Cyprus 0

Group 2

Austria 2, Wales 1
Luxembourg 2, Hungary 4
Wales 2, Hungary 0
Wales 5, Luxembourg 0
Luxembourg 1, Austria 2
Austria 0, Hungary 0
Hungary 1, Wales 2
Luxembourg 1, Wales 3
Hungary 2, Austria 1
Austria 6, Luxembourg 2
Hungary 8, Luxembourg 1
Wales 1, Austria 0

Group 3

Norway 2, Northern Ireland 1
Yugoslavia 3, Norway 1
Sweden 0, Northern Ireland 2
Northern Ireland 1, Yugoslavia 0
Sweden 1, Yugoslavia 2
Norway 1, Yugoslavia 3
Sweden 3, Norway 1
Norway 0, Sweden 2
Northern Ireland 1, Sweden 2
Yugoslavia 3, Sweden 0
Northern Ireland 3, Norway 0
Yugoslavia 1, Northern Ireland 0

Group 4

Denmark 1, Spain 2
Denmark 0, Romania 0
Scotland 1, Spain 2
Spain 1, Scotland 1
Spain 1, Romania 1
Romania 6, Denmark 1
Romania 1, Scotland 1
Denmark 0, Scotland 1
Spain 2, Denmark 0
Scotland 3, Denmark 1
Romania 2, Spain 2
Scotland 1, Romania 1

Group 5

Finland 1, Poland 2
Finland 1, Holland 3
Poland 3, Finland 0
Holland 3, Italy 1
Italy 0, Poland 0
Finland 0, Italy 1
Holland 4, Finland 1
Poland 4, Holland 1
Italy 0, Finland 0
Holland 3, Poland 0
Poland 0, Italy 0
Italy 1, Holland 0

Group 6

Eire 3, USSR 0
Turkey 1, Eire 1
Turkey 2, Switzerland 1
USSR 3, Turkey 0
Switzerland 1, Turkey 1
Eire 2, Switzerland 1
USSR 2, Eire 1
Switzerland 1, Eire 0
Switzerland 0, USSR 1
Eire 4, Turkey 0
USSR 4, Switzerland 1
Turkey 1, USSR 0

Group 7

Iceland 0, Belgium 2
East Germany 1, Iceland 1
Belgium 2, France 1
France 2, East Germany 2
East Germany 0, Belgium 0
Iceland 0, France 0
Iceland 2, East Germany 1
France 3, Iceland 0
Belgium 1, Iceland 0
Belgium 1, East Germany 2
East Germany 2, France 1
France 0, Belgium 0

Group 8

Bulgaria 3, Greece 3
Greece 2, West Germany 2
Greece 2, Bulgaria 1
Malta 0, West Germany 1
Malta 2, Greece 0
Bulgaria 1, West Germany 1
Greece 4, Malta 0
Bulgaria 5, Malta 0
West Germany 1, Greece 1
West Germany 1, Bulgaria 0
Malta 0, Bulgaria 2
West Germany 8, Malta 0

Quarter-finals

Spain 1, West Germany 1
Yugoslavia 2, Wales 0
Czechoslovakia 2, USSR 0
Holland 5, Belgium 0
West Germany 2, Spain 0
USSR 2, Czechoslovakia 2
Wales 1, Yugoslavia 1
Belgium 1, Holland 2

Semi-finals

Czechoslovakia 3, Holland 1 after extra time (in Zagreb)
West Germany 4, Yugoslavia 2 after extra time (in Belgrade)

Third Place Match (Zagreb)

Holland 3, Yugoslavia 2 after extra time

Final (Belgrade, 20 June 1976)

Czechoslovakia (2) 2, West Germany (1) 2
aet; (Czechoslovakia won 5–3 on penalties)
Czechoslovakia: Viktor; Dobias (Vesely F), Pivarnik, Ondrus, Capkovic, Gogh, Moder, Panenka, Svehlic (Jurkemik), Masny, Nehoda.
West Germany: Maier; Vogts, Beckenbauer, Schwarzenbeck, Dietz, Bonhof, Wimmer (Flohe), Müller D, Beer (Bongartz), Hoeness, Holzenbein.
Scorers: Svehlic, Dobias for Czechoslovakia; Müller, Holzenbein for West Germany.

EUROPEAN CHAMPIONSHIP 1978–80

Group 1

Denmark 3, Eire 3
Denmark 3, England 4
Eire 0, Northern Ireland 0
Denmark 2, Bulgaria 2
Eire 1, England 1
Northern Ireland 2, Denmark 1
Bulgaria 0, Northern Ireland 2
England 4, Northern Ireland 0
Northern Ireland 2, Bulgaria 0
Eire 2, Denmark 0
Bulgaria 1, Eire 0
Denmark 4, Northern Ireland 0
Bulgaria 0, England 3
England 1, Denmark 0

Eire 3, Bulgaria 0
Northern Ireland 1, England 5
Bulgaria 3, Denmark 0
Northern Ireland 1, Eire 0
England 2, Bulgaria 0
England 2, Eire 0

Group 2

Norway 0, Austria 2
Belgium 1, Norway 1
Austria 3, Scotland 2
Portugal 1, Belgium 1
Scotland 3, Norway 2
Austria 1, Portugal 2
Portugal 1, Scotland 0
Belgium 1, Austria 1
Austria 0, Belgium 0
Norway 0, Portugal 1
Norway 0, Scotland 4
Austria 4, Norway 0
Norway 1, Belgium 2
Belgium 2, Portugal 0
Scotland 1, Austria 1
Portugal 3, Norway 1
Belgium 2, Scotland 0
Portugal 1, Austria 2
Scotland 1, Belgium 3
Scotland 4, Portugal 1

Group 3

Yugoslavia 1, Spain 2
Romania 3, Yugoslavia 2
Spain 1, Romania 0
Spain 5, Cyprus 0
Cyprus 0, Yugoslavia 3
Romania 2, Spain 2
Cyprus 1, Romania 1
Spain 0, Yugoslavia 1
Yugoslavia 2, Romania 1
Yugoslavia 5, Cyprus 0
Romania 2, Cyprus 0
Cyprus 1, Spain 3

Group 4

Iceland 0, Poland 2
Holland 3, Iceland 0
East Germany 3, Iceland 1
Switzerland 1, Holland 3
Holland 3, East Germany 0
Poland 2, Switzerland 0
Holland 3, Switzerland 0
East Germany 2, Poland 1
Poland 2, Holland 0
Switzerland 0, East Germany 2
Switzerland 2, Iceland 0
Iceland 1, Switzerland 2
Iceland 0, Holland 4
Switzerland 0, Poland 2
Iceland 0, East Germany 3
Poland 1, East Germany 1
Poland 2, Iceland 0
East Germany 5, Switzerland 2
Holland 1, Portugal 1
East Germany 2, Holland 3

Group 5

France 2, Sweden 2
Sweden 1, Czechoslovakia 3
Luxembourg 1, France 3
France 3, Luxembourg 0
Czechoslovakia 2, France 0
Luxembourg 0, Czechoslovakia 3
Sweden 3, Luxembourg 0
Sweden 1, France 3
Czechoslovakia 4, Sweden 1
Luxembourg 1, Sweden 1
France 2, Czechoslovakia 0
Czechoslovakia 4, Luxembourg 0

Group 6

Finland 3, Greece 0
Finland 2, Hungary 1
USSR 2, Greece 0
Hungary 2, USSR 0
Greece 8, Finland 1
Greece 4, Hungary 1
Hungary 0, Greece 0
USSR 2, Hungary 2
Finland 1, USSR 1
Greece 1, USSR 0
Hungary 3, Finland 1
USSR 2, Finland 2

Group 7

Wales 7, Malta 0
Wales 1, Turkey 0
Malta 0, West Germany 0
Turkey 2, Malta 1
Turkey 0, West Germany 0
Wales 0, West Germany 2
Malta 0, Wales 2
West Germany 5, Wales 1
Malta 1, Turkey 2
Turkey 1, Wales 0
West Germany 2, Turkey 0
West Germany 8, Malta 0

Final Tournament
Group 1

West Germany 1, Czechoslovakia 0
Greece 0, Holland 1
West Germany 3, Holland 2
Czechoslovakia 3, Greece 1
Czechoslovakia 1, Holland 1
West Germany 0, Greece 0

Group 2

Belgium 1, England 1
Spain 0, Italy 0
Spain 1, Belgium 2
Italy 1, England 0
England 2, Spain 1
Italy 0, Belgium 0

Third Place Match (Naples)

Italy 1, Czechoslovakia 1
(*aet; Czechoslovakia won 9–8 on penalties*)

Final (Rome, 22 June 1980)

West Germany (1) 2, Belgium (0) 1
West Germany: Schumacher; Briegel, Forster K, Dietz,
Schuster, Rummenigge, Hrubesch, Müller, Aloffs,
Stielike, Kaltz.
Belgium: Pfaff; Gerets, Millecamps, Meeuws, Renquin,
Cools, Van der Eycken, Van Moer, Mommens, Van der
Elst, Ceulemans.
Scorers: Hrubesch 2 for West Germany; Van der Eycken
for Belgium.

EUROPEAN CHAMPIONSHIP 1982–84
Group 1

Belgium 3, Switzerland 0
Scotland 2, East Germany 0
Switzerland 2, Scotland 0
Belgium 3, Scotland 2
East Germany 1, Belgium 2
Scotland 2, Switzerland 2
Belgium 2, East Germany 1
Switzerland 0, East Germany 0
East Germany 3, Switzerland 0
Scotland 1, Belgium 0
Switzerland 3, Belgium 1
East Germany 2, Scotland 1

Group 2

Finland 2, Poland 3
Finland 0, Portugal 2

Portugal 2, Poland 1
USSR 2, Finland 0
Poland 1, Finland 1
USSR 5, Portugal 0
Poland 1, USSR 1
Finland 0, USSR 0
Portugal 5, Finland 0
USSR 2, Poland 0
Poland 0, Portugal 1
Portugal 1, USSR 0

Group 3

Denmark 2, England 2
Luxembourg 0, Greece 2
Luxembourg 1, Denmark 2
Greece 0, England 3
England 9, Luxembourg 0
Luxembourg 2, Hungary 6
England 0, Greece 0
Hungary 6, Luxembourg 2
Denmark 1, Greece 0
England 2, Hungary 0
Hungary 2, Greece 3
Denmark 3, Hungary 1
England 0, Denmark 1
Denmark 6, Luxembourg 0
Hungary 0, England 3
Hungary 1, Denmark 0
Greece 0, Denmark 2
Luxembourg 0, England 4
Greece 2, Hungary 2
Greece 1, Luxembourg 0

Group 4

Wales 1, Norway 0
Norway 3, Yugoslavia 1
Bulgaria 2, Norway 2
Bulgaria 0, Yugoslavia 1
Yugoslavia 4, Wales 4
Wales 1, Bulgaria 0
Norway 1, Bulgaria 2
Norway 0, Wales 0
Yugoslavia 2, Norway 1
Bulgaria 1, Wales 0
Wales 1, Yugoslavia 1
Yugoslavia 3, Bulgaria 2

Group 5

Romania 3, Cyprus 1
Romania 2, Sweden 0
Czechoslovakia 2, Sweden 2
Cyprus 0, Sweden 1
Italy 2, Czechoslovakia 2
Italy 0, Romania 0
Cyprus 1, Italy 1
Cyprus 1, Czechoslovakia 1
Czechoslovakia 6, Cyprus 0
Romania 1, Italy 0
Sweden 5, Cyprus 0
Romania 0, Czechoslovakia 1
Sweden 2, Italy 0
Sweden 0, Romania 1
Sweden 1, Czechoslovakia 0
Italy 0, Sweden 3
Cyprus 0, Romania 1
Czechoslovakia 2, Italy 0
Czechoslovakia 1, Romania 1
Italy 3, Cyprus 1

Group 6

Austria 5, Albania 0
Austria 2, Northern Ireland 0
Turkey 1, Albania 0
Austria 4, Turkey 0
Northern Ireland 1, West Germany 0
Albania 0, Northern Ireland 0
Albania 1, West Germany 2
Northern Ireland 2, Turkey 1

Turkey 0, West Germany 3
Austria 0, West Germany 0
Northern Ireland 1, Albania 0
Albania 1, Turkey 1
Albania 1, Austria 2
Northern Ireland 3, Austria 1
West Germany 3, Austria 0
Turkey 1, Northern Ireland 0
West Germany 5, Turkey 1
Turkey 3, Austria 1
West Germany 0, Northern Ireland 1
West Germany 2, Albania 1

Group 7

Malta 2, Iceland 1
Iceland 1, Holland 1
Holland 2, Eire 1
Eire 2, Iceland 0
Spain 1, Iceland 0
Eire 3, Spain 3
Malta 0, Holland 6
Spain 1, Holland 0
Malta 0, Eire 1
Spain 2, Eire 0
Malta 2, Spain 3
Iceland 0, Spain 1
Iceland 1, Malta 0
Holland 3, Iceland 0
Iceland 0, Eire 3
Eire 2, Holland 3
Holland 2, Spain 1
Eire 8, Malta 0
Holland 5, Malta 0
Spain 12, Malta 1

Final Tournament

Group 1

France 1, Denmark 0
Belgium 2, Yugoslavia 0
France 5, Belgium 0
Denmark 5, Yugoslavia 0
France 3, Yugoslavia 2
Denmark 3, Belgium 2

Group 2

West Germany 0, Portugal 0
Spain 1, Romania 1
Spain 1, Portugal 1
West Germany 2, Romania 1
West Germany 0, Spain 1
Portugal 1, Romania 0

Semi-finals

France 3, Portugal 2
Denmark 1, Spain 1
(aet; Spain won 5–4 on penalties)

Final (Paris, 27 June 1984, 80,000)

France (0) 2, Spain (0) 0
France: Bats; Battiston (Amoros), Le Roux, Bossis, Domergue, Giresse, Platini, Tigana, Fernandez, Lacombe (Genghini), Bellone.
Spain: Arconada; Urquiaga, Salva (Roberto), Gallego, Camacho, Francisco, Julio Alberto (Sarabia), Senor, Victor, Carrasco, Santillana.
Scorers: Platini, Bellone for France.

EUROPEAN CHAMPIONSHIP 1986–88

Group 1

Romania 4, Austria 0
Austria 3, Albania 0
Spain 1, Romania 0
Albania 1, Spain 2
Romania 5, Albania 1
Austria 2, Spain 3

808

Albania 0, Austria 1
Romania 3, Spain 1
Spain 2, Austria 0
Albania 0, Romania 1
Spain 5, Albania 0
Austria 0, Romania 0

Group 2

Sweden 2, Switzerland 0
Portugal 1, Sweden 1
Switzerland 1, Portugal 1
Italy 3, Switzerland 2
Malta 0, Sweden 5
Malta 0, Italy 2
Italy 5, Malta 0
Portugal 0, Italy 1
Portugal 2, Malta 2
Switzerland 4, Malta 1
Sweden 1, Malta 0
Sweden 1, Italy 0
Switzerland 1, Sweden 1
Sweden 0, Portugal 1
Switzerland 0, Italy 0
Portugal 0, Switzerland 0
Italy 2, Sweden 1
Malta 1, Switzerland 1
Italy 3, Portugal 0
Malta 0, Portugal 1

Group 3

Iceland 0, France 0
Iceland 1, USSR 1
Norway 0, East Germany 0
France 0, USSR 2
USSR 4, Norway 0
East Germany 2, Iceland 0
East Germany 0, France 0
France 2, Iceland 0
USSR 2, East Germany 0
Norway 0, USSR 1
Iceland 0, East Germany 6
Norway 2, France 0
USSR 1, France 1
Iceland 2, Norway 1
Norway 0, Iceland 1
East Germany 1, USSR 1
France 1, Norway 1
USSR 2, Iceland 0
East Germany 3, Norway 1
France 0, East Germany 1

Group 4

England 3, Northern Ireland 0
Yugoslavia 4, Turkey 0
England 2, Yugoslavia 0
Turkey 0, Northern Ireland 0
Northern Ireland 0, England 2
Northern Ireland 1, Yugoslavia 2
Turkey 0, England 0
Yugoslavia 3, Northern Ireland 0
England 8, Turkey 0
Yugoslavia 1, England 4
Northern Ireland 1, Turkey 0
Turkey 2, Yugoslavia 3

Group 5

Hungary 0, Holland 1
Poland 2, Greece 1
Greece 2, Hungary 1
Holland 0, Poland 0
Cyprus 2, Greece 4
Cyprus 0, Holland 2
Greece 3, Cyprus 1
Cyprus 0, Hungary 1
Holland 1, Greece 1
Poland 0, Cyprus 0
Greece 1, Poland 0
Holland 2, Hungary 0

Hungary 5, Poland 3
Poland 3, Hungary 2
Hungary 3, Greece 0
Poland 0, Holland 2
Holland 8, Cyprus 0
Cyprus 0, Poland 1
Hungary 1, Cyprus 0
Holland 4, Cyprus 0
Greece 0, Holland 3

Group 6

Finland 1, Wales 1
Czechoslovakia 3, Finland 0
Denmark 1, Finland 0
Czechoslovakia 0, Denmark 0
Wales 4, Finland 0
Finland 0, Denmark 1
Wales 1, Czechoslovakia 1
Denmark 1, Czechoslovakia 1
Wales 1, Denmark 0
Finland 3, Czechoslovakia 0
Denmark 1, Wales 0
Czechoslovakia 2, Wales 0

Group 7

Scotland 0, Bulgaria 0
Belgium 2, Eire 2
Luxembourg 0, Belgium 6
Eire 0, Scotland 0
Scotland 3, Luxembourg 0
Belgium 1, Bulgaria 1
Scotland 0, Eire 1
Belgium 4, Scotland 1
Bulgaria 2, Eire 1
Eire 0, Belgium 0
Luxembourg 1, Bulgaria 4
Bulgaria 3, Luxembourg 0
Luxembourg 0, Eire 2
Eire 2, Luxembourg 1
Bulgaria 2, Belgium 0
Scotland 2, Belgium 0
Eire 2, Bulgaria 0
Belgium 3, Luxembourg 0
Bulgaria 0, Scotland 1
Luxembourg 0, Scotland 0

Final Tournament

Group 1

West Germany 1, Italy 1
Spain 3, Denmark 2
West Germany 2, Denmark 0
Italy 1, Spain 0
West Germany 2, Spain 0
Italy 2, Denmark 0

Group 2

England 0, Eire 1
Holland 0, USSR 1
Holland 3, England 1
Eire 1, USSR 1
England 1, USSR 3
Holland 1, Eire 0

Semi-finals

West Germany 1, Holland 2
USSR 2, Italy 0

Final (Munich, 25 June 1988, 72,308)

Holland (1) 2, USSR (0) 0
Holland: Van Breukelen; Van Aerle, Van Tiggelen, Wouters, Koeman R, Rijkaard, Vanenburg, Gullit, Van Basten, Muhren, Koeman E.
USSR: Dassayev; Khidiatulin, Aleinikov, Mikhailichenko, Litovchenko, Demianenko, Belanov, Gotsmanov (Baltacha 68), Protasov (Pasulko 71), Zavarov, Rats.
Scorers: Gullit, Van Basten for Holland.

THE WORLD CUP 1930–90

Year	Winners		Runners-up		Venue	Attendance	Referee
1930	Uruguay	4	Argentina	2	Montevideo	90,000	Langenus (B)
1934	Italy	2	Czechoslovakia	1	Rome	50,000	Eklind (Se)
	(after extra time)						
1938	Italy	4	Hungary	2	Paris	45,000	Capdeville (F)
1950	Uruguay	2	Brazil	1	Rio de Janeiro	199,854	Reader (E)
1954	West Germany	3	Hungary	2	Berne	60,000	Ling (E)
1958	Brazil	5	Sweden	2	Stockholm	49,737	Guigue (F)
1962	Brazil	3	Czechoslovakia	1	Santiago	68,679	Latychev (USSR)
1966	England	4	West Germany	2	Wembley	93,802	Dienst (Sw)
	(after extra time)						
1970	Brazil	4	Italy	1	Mexico City	107,412	Glockner (EG)
1974	West Germany	2	Holland	1	Munich	77,833	Taylor (E)
1978	Argentina	3	Holland	1	Buenos Aires	77,000	Gonella (I)
	(after extra time)						
1982	Italy	3	West Germany	1	Madrid	90,080	Coelho (Br)
1986	Argentina	3	West Germany	2	Mexico City	114,580	Filho (Br)
1990	West Germany	1	Argentina	0	Rome	73,603	Codesal (Mex)

GOALSCORING AND ATTENDANCES IN WORLD CUP FINAL ROUNDS

	Matches	Goals (avge)	Attendance (avge)
1930, Uruguay	18	70 (3.8)	434,500 (24,138)
1934, Italy	17	70 (4.1)	395,000 (23,235)
1938, France	18	84 (4.6)	483,000 (26,833)
1950, Brazil	22	88 (4.0)	1,337,000 (60,772)
1954, Switzerland	26	140 (5.3)	943,000 (36,270)
1958, Sweden	35	126 (3.6)	868,000 (24,800)
1962, Chile	32	89 (2.7)	776,000 (24,250)
1966, England	32	89 (2.7)	1,614,677 (50,458)
1970, Mexico	32	95 (2.9)	1,673,975 (52,311)
1974, West Germany	38	97 (2.5)	1,774,022 (46,684)
1978, Argentina	38	102 (2.6)	1,610,215 (42,374)
1982, Spain	52	146 (2.8)	1,766,277 (33,967)
1986, Mexico	52	132 (2.5)	2,199,941 (42,307)
1990, Italy	52	115 (2.21)	2,510,686* (48,282)

1994 FIFA WORLD CUP

Qualifying draw for USA 1994

OCEANIA (Members 8, Entries 7)
Either one or no team qualifies
First Round (League System)
Group 1: Australia, Solomon Islands, Western Samoa; *Group 2:* New Zealand, Fiji, Tahiti, Vanuatu.
Two group winners qualify for the **Second Round**. The winner of this Second Round (cup system) will compete against the runner-up of the Concacaf preliminaries, the winner of which will then play the team coming fourth in South America.

ASIA (Members 36, Entries 29)
Two teams qualify
First Round (League System)
Group A: China PR, Iraq, Jordan, Yemen, Pakistan; *Group B:* Iran, Syria, Oman, Chinese Taipei, Myanmar; *Group C:* Korea (North), Qatar, Singapore, Vietnam, Indonesia; *Group D:* Korea (South), Bahrain, Hong Kong, Lebanon, India; *Group E:* Saudi Arabia, Kuwait, Malaysia, Macao; *Group F:* United Arab Emirates, Japan, Thailand, Sri Lanka, Bangladesh.
In the **Second Round** the six group winners will play in one group (league system) home and away games.

CONCACAF (Members 27, Entries 23)
Two or three teams qualify (including USA the hosts)
Preliminary Round (Cup System)
Group North: (A) Bermuda v Haiti; (B) Dominican Republic/Puerto Rico v Jamaica; (C) St Lucia/St Vincent v Cuba; *Group South:* (D) Netherlands Antilles v Antigua; (E) Guyana v Surinam; (F) Barbados v Trinidad and Tobago.
First Round
Central Region: (1) Guatemala v Honduras; (2) Panama v Costa Rica; (3) Nicaragua v El Salvador; *Caribbean Region:* (1) Winner E v Winner C; (2) Winner A v Winner D; (3) Winner F v Winner B.
Second Round (League System)
Group A: Mexico, Winner Central 1, Winner Caribbean 1, Winner Central 2; *Group B:* Canada, Winner Caribbean 2, Winner Central 3, Winner Caribbean 3.

Third Round (League System)
N.B. After elimination games Dominican Republic v Puerto Rico and St Lucia v St Vincent, preliminary round and First Round games according to cup system. Canada and Mexico automatically qualify for the Second Round in two groups of four. Third Round in one group of four. The winners will qualify for the final competition, while the runner-up competes against the winner of the Oceania tournament, the winner of which will play the fourth team from South America.

SOUTH AMERICA (Members 10, Entries 9)
Three or four teams qualify
First Round (League System)
Group A: Argentina, Colombia, Paraguay, Peru; *Group B:* Brazil, Bolivia, Uruguay, Ecuador, Venezuela. The winner in Group A and the winner and runner-up in Group B qualify for the final competition. The runner-up in Group A will have to play the winner of the elimination match between Oceania and Concacaf. Whichever team wins this match will also qualify for the World Cup finals.

AFRICA (Members 48, Entries 37)
Three teams qualify
First Round (League System)
Group A: Algeria, Ghana, Uganda, Burundi; *Group B:* Cameroon, Zaire, Liberia, Swaziland; *Group C:* Egypt, Zimbabwe, Sierra Leone, Angola; *Group D:* Nigeria, Congo, Libya, Togo/Sao Tome; *Group E:* Ivory Coast, Sudan, Niger, Botswana; *Group F:* Morocco, Tunisia, Malawi, Ethiopia; *Group G:* Senegal, Gabon, Mozambique, Mauritania; *Group H:* Zambia, Madagascar, Burkina Faso, Tanzania; *Group I:* Kenya, Guinea, Mali, Gambia.
Elimination match Togo v Sao Tome. First Round in nine groups of four. Group winners to go into **Second Round** in three groups of three. The three group winners qualify for the World Cup finals.

EUROPE/ISRAEL (Members 38+1, Entries 38+1)
Thirteen teams qualify (including Germany as holders)
Group 1: Italy, Scotland, Portugal, Switzerland, Malta, Estonia; *Group 2:* England, Holland, Poland, Norway, Turkey, San Marino; *Group 3:* Spain, Republic of Ireland, Denmark, Northern Ireland, Albania, Lithuania, Latvia; *Group 4:* Belgium, Czechoslovakia, Romania, Wales, Cyprus, Faeroes; *Group 5:* USSR (now CIS), Yugoslavia, Hungary, Greece, Iceland, Luxembourg; *Group 6:* France, Austria, Sweden, Bulgaria, Finland, Israel.
League system with the winner and runner-up of each group plus Germany as holders qualify.

Withdrawals: Cuba, Western Samoa, Sierra Leone

WORLD CUP VENUES USA 1994

Giants Stadium
New York/New Jersey
East Rutherford, New Jersey
Capacity: 76,891
Record attendance: 77,691 New York Cosmos v Fort Lauderdale 14 August 1977
Average July temperature 29.7°C

Robert F Kennedy Memorial Stadium
Washington D.C.
Washington (near Capitol)
Capacity: 56,500
Record attendance: 56,500 (for American football team Washington Redskins)
Average July temperature 31°C

The Citrus Bowl
Orlando, Florida
Orlando, mile west of town centre
Capacity: 70,188
Record attendance: 70,000 (annual Citrus Bowl final)
Average July temperature 26.7°C

Foxboro Stadium
Boston, Massachusetts
Situated between Boston and Providence
Capacity: 61,000
Record attendance: 59,828 (for American football team New England Patriots)
Average July temperature 27.6°C

Pontiac Silverdome
Detroit, Michigan
Pontiac, Michigan
Capacity: 72,794
Record attendance: 82,000 (American football Super Bowl)
Average July temperature 28.3°C

Soldier Field
Chicago, Illinois
On Michigan Lake
Capacity: 66,814
Record attendance: 67,475 (American football team Chicago Bears)
Average July temperature 28.5°C

The Cotton Bowl
Dallas, Texas
Centre of Dallas Fair Park
Capacity: 72,000
Record attendance: 72,000 (American collegiate football)
Average July temperature 36.5°C

The Rose Bowl
Los Angeles, California
Pasadena, outside Los Angeles
Capacity: 102,083
Record attendance: 101,799 (Olympic Soccer final France v Brazil 11 August 1984)
Average July temperature 28.3°C

Stanford Stadium
San Francisco, California
Palo Alto, south of San Francisco
Capacity: 86,019
Record attendance: 84,059 (American football Super Bowl)
Average July temperature 21°C

1994 FIFA WORLD CUP FIXTURES

Preliminary Competition
Europe/Israel (38 + 1 Entries)
13 teams will qualify (including Germany as current champions)

Group 1
(Italy, Scotland, Portugal, Switzerland, Malta, Estonia)
16. 8.92 Estonia v Switzerland
 9. 9.92 Switzerland v Scotland
14.10.92 Italy v Switzerland
14.10.92 Scotland v Portugal
25.10.92 Malta v Estonia
18.11.92 Scotland v Italy
18.11.92 Switzerland v Malta
19.12.92 Malta v Italy
24. 1.93 Malta v Portugal
17. 2.93 Italy v Malta
24. 2.93 Portugal v Italy
24. 3.93 Italy v Malta
31. 3.93 Switzerland v Portugal
14. 4.93 Italy v Estonia
17. 4.93 Malta v Switzerland
28. 4.93 Portugal v Scotland
 1. 5.93 Switzerland v Italy
12. 5.93 Estonia v Malta
19. 5.93 Estonia v Scotland
 2. 6.93 Scotland v Estonia
19. 6.93 Portugal v Malta
 5. 9.93 Estonia v Portugal
 8. 9.93 Scotland v Switzerland
22. 9.93 Estonia v Italy
13.10.93 Italy v Scotland
13.10.93 Portugal v Switzerland
10.11.93 Portugal v Estonia
17.11.93 Italy v Portugal
17.11.93 Malta v Scotland
17.11.93 Switzerland v Estonia

Group 2
(England, Holland, Poland, Norway, Turkey, San Marino)
 9. 9.92 Norway v San Marino
23. 9.92 Norway v Holland
23. 9.92 Poland v Turkey
 7.10.92 San Marino v Norway
14.10.92 England v Norway
14.10.92 Holland v Poland
28.10.92 Turkey v San Marino
18.11.92 England v Turkey
16.12.92 Turkey v Holland
17. 2.93 England v San Marino
24. 2.93 Holland v Turkey
10. 3.93 San Marino v Turkey
24. 3.93 Holland v San Marino
31. 3.93 Turkey v England
28. 4.93 England v Holland
28. 4.93 Norway v Turkey
28. 4.93 Poland v San Marino
19. 5.93 San Marino v Poland
29. 5.93 Poland v England
 2. 6.93 Norway v England
 9. 6.93 Holland v Norway
 8. 9.93 England v Poland
22. 9.93 Norway v Poland
22. 9.93 San Marino v Holland
13.10.93 Holland v England
13.10.93 Poland v Norway
27.10.93 Turkey v Poland
10.11.93 Turkey v Norway
16.11.93 San Marino v England
17.11.93 Poland v Holland

Group 3
(Spain, Republic of Ireland, Denmark, Northern Ireland, Albania, Lithuania, Latvia)
22. 4.92 Spain v Albania
28. 4.92 Northern Ireland v Lithuania
26. 5.92 Republic of Ireland v Albania
 3. 6.92 Albania v Lithuania
12. 8.92 Latvia v Lithuania
26. 8.92 Latvia v Denmark
 9. 9.92 Northern Ireland v Albania
 9. 9.92 Republic of Ireland v Latvia
23. 9.92 Lithuania v Denmark
23. 9.92 Latvia v Spain
14.10.92 Denmark v Republic of Ireland
14.10.92 Northern Ireland v Spain
28.10.92 Lithuania v Latvia
11.11.92 Albania v Latvia
18.11.92 Northern Ireland v Denmark
18.11.92 Spain v Republic of Ireland
16.12.92 Spain v Latvia
17. 2.93 Albania v Northern Ireland
24. 2.93 Spain v Lithuania
31. 3.93 Denmark v Spain
31. 3.93 Republic of Ireland v Northern Ireland
14. 4.93 Denmark v Latvia
14. 4.93 Lithuania v Albania
28. 4.93 Republic of Ireland v Denmark
28. 4.93 Spain v Northern Ireland
15. 5.93 Latvia v Albania
25. 5.93 Lithuania v Northern Ireland
26. 5.93 Albania v Republic of Ireland
 2. 6.93 Denmark v Albania
 2. 6.93 Lithuania v Spain
 2. 6.93 Latvia v Northern Ireland
 9. 6.93 Latvia v Republic of Ireland
16. 6.93 Lithuania v Republic of Ireland
25. 8.93 Denmark v Lithuania
 8. 9.93 Albania v Denmark
 8. 9.93 Northern Ireland v Latvia
 8. 9.93 Republic of Ireland v Lithuania
22. 9.93 Albania v Spain
13.10.93 Denmark v Northern Ireland
13.10.93 Republic of Ireland v Spain
17.11.93 Northern Ireland v Republic of Ireland
17.11.93 Spain v Denmark

Group 4
(Belgium, Czechoslovakia, Romania, Wales, Cyprus, Faeroes)
22. 4.92 Belgium v Cyprus
 6. 5.92 Romania v Faeroes
20. 5.92 Romania v Wales
 3. 6.92 Faeroes v Belgium
17. 6.92 Faeroes v Cyprus
 2. 9.92 Czechoslovakia v Belgium
 9. 9.92 Wales v Faeroes
23. 9.92 Czechoslovakia v Faeroes
14.10.92 Belgium v Romania
14.10.92 Cyprus v Wales
14.11.92 Romania v Czechoslovakia
18.11.92 Wales v Belgium
29.11.92 Cyprus v Romania
14. 2.92 Cyprus v Belgium
24. 3.93 Cyprus v Czechoslovakia
31. 3.93 Belgium v Wales
14. 4.93 Romania v Cyprus
25. 4.93 Cyprus v Faeroes
28. 4.93 Czechoslovakia v Wales
22. 5.93 Belgium v Faeroes
 2. 6.93 Czechoslovakia v Romania
 6. 6.93 Faeroes v Wales
16. 6.93 Faeroes v Czechoslovakia
 8. 9.93 Wales v Czechoslovakia
 8. 9.93 Faeroes v Romania
13.10.93 Romania v Belgium
13.10.93 Wales v Cyprus
27.10.93 Czechoslovakia v Cyprus
17.11.93 Belgium v Czechoslovakia
17.11.93 Wales v Romania

Group 5
(CIS, Yugoslavia, Hungary, Greece, Iceland, Luxembourg)
13. 5.92 Greece v Iceland
 3. 6.92 Hungary v Iceland
 2. 9.92 Iceland v Yugoslavia
 9. 9.92 Luxembourg v Hungary
23. 9.92 Yugoslavia v CIS
 7.10.92 Iceland v Greece
14.10.92 Hungary v Yugoslavia
14.10.92 CIS v Iceland
28.10.92 CIS v Luxembourg
11.11.92 Greece v Hungary
15.11.92 Luxembourg v Yugoslavia
17. 2.93 Greece v Luxembourg
31. 3.93 Hungary v Greece
31. 3.93 Yugoslavia v Luxembourg
14. 4.93 Luxembourg v CIS
28. 4.93 CIS v Hungary
28. 4.93 Yugoslavia v Greece
20. 5.93 Luxembourg v Iceland
23. 5.93 CIS v Greece
 2. 6.93 Iceland v CIS
16. 6.93 Iceland v Hungary
22. 8.93 Yugoslavia v Iceland
 8. 9.93 Hungary v CIS
 8. 9.93 Iceland v Luxembourg
 6.10.93 CIS v Yugoslavia
12.10.93 Luxembourg v Greece
27.10.93 Greece v Yugoslavia
27.10.93 Hungary v Luxembourg
17.11.93 Greece v CIS
17.11.93 Yugoslavia v Hungary

Group 6
(France, Austria, Sweden, Bulgaria, Finland, Israel)
14. 5.92 Finland v Bulgaria
 9. 9.92 Bulgaria v France
 9. 9.92 Finland v Sweden
 7.10.92 Sweden v Bulgaria
14.10.92 France v Austria
28.10.92 Austria v Israel
11.11.92 Israel v Sweden
14.11.92 France v Finland
 2.12.92 Israel v Bulgaria
17. 2.93 Israel v France
27. 3.93 Austria v France
14. 4.93 Austria v Bulgaria
28. 4.93 Bulgaria v Finland
28. 4.93 France v Sweden
12. 5.93 Bulgaria v Israel
13. 5.93 Finland v Austria
19. 5.93 Sweden v Austria
 2. 6.93 Sweden v Israel
16. 6.93 Finland v Israel
22. 8.93 Sweden v France
25. 8.93 Austria v Finland
 8. 9.93 Bulgaria v Sweden
 8. 9.93 Finland v France
13.10.93 Bulgaria v Austria
13.10.93 France v Israel
13.10.93 Sweden v Finland
27.10.93 Israel v Austria
10.11.93 Austria v Sweden
10.11.93 Israel v Finland
17.11.93 France v Bulgaria

Concacaf
(23 Entries)
2 or 3 teams will qualify (including USA as hosts)

Pre-preliminary Round
21. 3.92 Dominican Rep v Puerto Rico : L Livingston, Jamaica
29. 3.92 Puerto Rico v Dominican Rep : E Forbes, Trinidad & Tobago
22. 3.92 St Lucia v St Vincent/Grenada : W Peleris, Haiti
29. 3.92 St Vincent/Grenada v St Lucia : R Ramesh, Trinidad & Tobago

Oceania
(7 Entries)
0 or 1 team will qualify

Group 1: Australia, Tahiti, Solomon Islands
Group 2: New Zealand, Fiji, Vanuatu

 6. 6.92 New Zealand v Fiji
12. 9.92 Fiji v Vanuatu
19. 9.92 Fiji v New Zealand
26. 9.92 Vanuatu v Fiji

Conmebol (South America)
(9 Entries)
3 or 4 teams will qualify

Group A (Argentina, Colombia, Paraguay, Peru)
 1. 8.93 Colombia v Paraguay
 1. 8.93 Peru v Argentina
 8. 8.93 Paraguay v Argentina
 8. 8.93 Peru v Colombia
15. 8.93 Colombia v Argentina
15. 8.93 Paraguay v Peru
22. 8.93 Argentina v Peru
22. 8.93 Paraguay v Colombia
29. 8.93 Argentina v Paraguay
29. 8.93 Colombia v Peru
 5. 9.93 Argentina v Colombia
 5. 9.93 Peru v Paraguay

Group B (Brazil, Uruguay, Ecuador, Bolivia, Venezuela)
18. 7.93 Ecuador v Brazil
18. 7.93 Venezuela v Bolivia
25. 7.93 Bolivia v Brazil
25. 7.93 Venezuela v Uruguay
 1. 8.93 Uruguay v Ecuador
 1. 8.93 Venezuela v Brazil
 8. 8.93 Bolivia v Uruguay
 8. 8.93 Ecuador v Venezuela
15. 8.93 Bolivia v Ecuador
15. 8.93 Uruguay v Brazil
22. 8.93 Bolivia v Venezuela
22. 8.93 Brazil v Ecuador
29. 8.93 Brazil v Bolivia
29. 8.93 Uruguay v Venezuela
 5. 9.93 Brazil v Venezuela
 5. 9.93 Ecuador v Uruguay
12. 9.93 Uruguay v Bolivia
12. 9.93 Venezuela v Ecuador
19. 9.93 Brazil v Uruguay
19. 9.93 Ecuador v Bolivia

WORLD CUP QUALIFYING GAMES PLAYED TO DATE

World Cup qualifying games played to date

Europe

Seville, 22 April 1992, 10,000

Spain (1) 3 *(Michel 2, 66 (pen), Hierro 87)*

Albania (0) 0

Spain: Zubizarreta; Abelardo, Nando, Giner, Michel (Eusebio 85), Amor, Hierro, Vizcaino, Manolo (Bakero 53), Butragueno, Goicoechea.
Albania: Strakosha (Dani 69); Josa (Pegini 55), Kola B, Lekbello, Aya, Abazi, Kushta, Barballushi, Millo, Kola A, Demollari.

Brussels, 22 April 1992, 18,000

Belgium (1) 1 *(Wilmots 24)*

Cyprus (0) 0

Belgium: Preud'homme; Albert, Grun, Van der Elst, Emmers, Scifo, Walem, Boffin (Borkelmans 82), Wilmots (Hofmans 75), Degryse, Oliveira.
Cyprus: Christofi; Costa, Pittas, Constantinou C, Nicolau, Yiangudakis, Ioannou, Larku (Constantinou G 88), Sotiriu, Papavasiliu, Gadjilukas (Panayi 70).

Windsor Park, 28 April 1992, 4500

Northern Ireland (2) 2 *(Wilson 13, Taggart 16)*

Lithuania (1) 2 *(Narberkovas 41, Fridrikas 48)*

Northern Ireland: Fettis; Donaghy (Fleming 46), Taggart, McDonald, Worthington, Black, Magilton, Wilson K, Hughes, Quinn, Dowie (Rogan 80).
Lithuania: Martinkenas; Buzmarkovas, Mika, Janonis, Mazeikis, Tautkas, Urbanas, Fridrikas (Zuta 90), Narbekovas, Baranauskas, Ivanauskas (Danisevicius 89).

Bucharest, 6 May 1992, 10,000

Romania (5) 7 *(Balint 4, 40, 78, Hagi 14, Lacatus 28 (pen), Lupescu 44, Pana 55)*

Faeroes (0) 0

Romania: Stelea; Petrescu, Milhali, Popescu, Munteanu, Pana, Balint, Lupescu (Cheregi 78), Hagi, Lacatus (Gane 63), Rotariu.
Faeroes: Knudsen; Jakobsen, Hansen T, Danielsen, Justiniussen, Morkore A, Jamskor (Nielsen T 50), Dam (Jonsson 60), Hansen A, Reynheim, Muller.

Athens, 13 May 1992, 10,000

Greece (1) 1 *(Sofianidis 28)*

Iceland (0) 0

Greece: Papadopoulos; Apostolakis, Kalitzakis, Manolas, Ntsibonas, Tsaluhidis Y, Tsaluhidis G, Sofianidis, Tursunidis (Noplias 77), Alexandria, Tsdiantakis (Borbokis 60).
Iceland: Kristinsson B; Jonsson Kr, Marteinsson (Magnusson 74), Valsson, Bergsson, Jonsson K, Gudjohnsen, Bjarnasson, Gretarsson, Sverisson, Kristinsson R.

Helsinki, 14 May 1992, 10,000

Finland (0) 0

Bulgaria (2) 3 *(Balakov 16, Kostadinov 25, 85)*

Finland: Huttunen; Pertaja, Holmgren, Heikkinen, Eriksson, Rinne (Huhtamaeki 76), Litmanen, Myyry, Jarvinen, Vanhala (Tegelberg 60), Tarkkio.
Bulgaria: Mikhailov; Ivanov, Tzvetanev, Iliev, Hubchev, Sirakov, Yankov, Stoichkov (Yordanov 69), Peney, Balakov, Kostadinov.

Bucharest, 20 May 1992 23,000

Romania (5) 5 *(Hagi 5, 35, Lupescu 7, 24, Balint 31)*

Wales (0) 1 *(Rush 50)*

Romania: Stelea; Petrescu, Mihali, Belodedici, Munteanu, Sabau (Timofte I 80), Popescu, Lupescu, Hagi (Gerstenmaier 71), Lacatus, Balint.
Wales: Southall; Phillips, Bowen (Blackmore 71), Aizlewood, Melville, Horne, Speed, Pembridge (Giggs 59), Hughes, Rush, Saunders.

Dublin, 26 May 1992, 29,727

Republic of Ireland (0) 2 *(Aldridge 60, McGarth 80)*

Albania (0) 0

Republic of Ireland: Bonner; Irwin, Staunton, O'Leary, McGrath, Townsend, Keane, Houghton, Quinn, Aldridge (Coyne 83), Sheedy (McCarthy 52).
Albania: Dani; Smijani, Qendro (Pali 71), Pegini, Vata, Abazi, Kushta, Vasi, Rrakilli, Zola A (Sokoll 80), Demollari.

Tirana, 3 June 1992, 15,000

Albania (0) 1 *(Abazi 77)*

Lithuania (0) 0

Albania: Dani; Zmijani, Pegini, Lekbello, Vata, Abazi, Kushta, Milori (Rrafi 46), Millo (Fortuzi 89), Vasi, Demollari.
Lithuania: Martinkenas; Buzmarkovas, Sukristovas, Mazekis, Tomas, Danisevicius, Baranauskas, Tautkas (Zuta 82), Urbonas, Ramells (Zadancius 52), Kvitkauskas.

Toftir, 3 June 1992, 5156

Faeroes (0) 0

Belgium (1) 3 *(Albert 30, Wilmosts 65, 71)*

Faeroes: Johannesen; Jakobsen, Hansen T, Danielsen, Jonsson T (Jensen 71), Morkore A (Justinussen 83), Nielsen T, Dam, Hansen A, Reynheim, Muller.
Belgium: Preud'homme; Staelens, Grun, Albert, Emmers, Boffin (Versavel 75), Van der Elst, Denil, Degryse, Scifo, Oliveira (Wilmots 63).

Budapest, 3 June 1992, 10,000

Hungary (1) 1 *(Kiprich 3)*

Iceland (0) 2 *(Orlygsson 51, Magnusson 73)*

Hungary: Petry; Telek, Kovacs E, Lorincz, Simon, Limperger, Pisont (Balog 78), Vincze (Eszenyi 54), Keller, Kiprich, Kovacs K.
Iceland: Kristinsson B; Gretarsson S, (Magnusson 64), Bergsson, Orlygsson, Kristinsson R, Gretarsson A, Valsson, Jonsson Kr, Jonsson K (Bragason 80), Bjarnasson, Marteinsson.

Toftir, 16 June 1992, 4500

Faeroes (0) 0

Cyprus (1) 2 *(Sotiriu 30, Papavasiliu 58)*

Faeroes: Johanen; Jakobsen, Hansen T, Danielsen, Jonsson, Morkore A, Hansen A, Nielsen (Jamskor 62), Rasmussen, Reynheim, Muller (Jensen 66(.
Cyprus: Christofi; Kosta (Larku 46), Pittas, Constantinou C, Nicolau, Yiangudakis, Ioannou Charalambous, Savides, Scotiriu (Panayi 84), Papavasiliu.

Concacaf

Pre-preliminary round
Dominican Republic 1, Puerto Rico 2
Puerto Rico 1, Dominican Republic 1
St Lucia 1, St Vincent 0
St Vincent 3, St Lucia 1

Preliminary round
Bermuda 1, Haiti 0
Haiti 2, Bermuda 1
Jamaica 2, Puerto Rico 1
Puerto Rico 0, Jamaica 3
St Vincent w.o. Cuba withdrew
Netherlands Antilles 1, Antigua 1
Antigua 3, Netherlands Antilles 0
Guyana 1, Surinam 2
Surinam 1, Guyana 1
Barbados 1, Trinidad & Tobago 2
Trinidad & Tobago 3, Barbados 0
Bermuda 3, Antigua 0
Jamaica 1, Puerto Rico 0

Oceania
New Zealand 3, Fiji 0
Vanuatu 1, New Zealand 4
New Zealand 8, Vanuatu 0

BRITISH AND IRISH INTERNATIONAL RESULTS 1872–1992

BRITISH INTERNATIONAL CHAMPIONSHIP 1883–1984

Year	Champions	Pts	Year	Champions	Pts	Year	Champions	Pts
1883–84	Scotland	6	1920–21	Scotland	6	1956–57	England	5
1884–85	Scotland	5	1921–22	Scotland	4	1957–58	England	4
1885–86	England	5	1922–23	Scotland	5		N. Ireland	4
	Scotland	5	1923–24	Wales	6	1958–59	N. Ireland	4
1886–87	Scotland	6	1924–25	Scotland	6		England	4
1887–88	England	6	1925–26	Scotland	6		England	4
1888–89	Scotland	5	1926–27	Scotland	4	1959–60	Scotland	4
1889–90	Scotland	5		England	4		Wales	4
	England	5	1927–28	Wales	5	1960–61	England	6
1890–91	England	6	1928–29	Scotland	6	1961–62	Scotland	6
1891–92	England	6	1929–30	England	6	1962–63	Scotland	6
1892–93	England	6	1930–31	Scotland	4		Scotland	4
1893–94	Scotland	5		England	4	1963–64	England	4
1894–95	England	5	1931–32	England	6		N. Ireland	4
1895–96	Scotland	5	1932–33	Wales	5	1964–65	England	5
1896–97	Scotland	5	1933–34	Wales	5	1965–66	England	5
1897–98	England	6	1934–35	England	4	1966–67	Scotland	5
1898–99	England	6		Scotland	4	1967–68	England	5
1899–1900	Scotland	6	1935–36	Scotland	4	1968–69	England	6
1900–01	England	5	1936–37	Wales	6	1969–70	England	4
1901–02	Scotland	5	1937–38	England	4		Scotland	4
1902–03	England	4	1938–39	England	4		Wales	4
	Ireland	4		Scotland	4	1970–71	England	5
	Scotland	4		Wales	4	1971–72	England	4
1903–04	England	5	1946–47	England	5		Scotland	4
1904–05	England	5	1947–48	England	5	1972–73	England	6
1905–06	England	4	1948–49	Scotland	6	1973–74	England	4
	Scotland	4	1949–50	England	6		Scotland	4
1906–07	Wales	5	1950–51	Scotland	6	1974–75	England	4
1907–08	Scotland	5	1951–52	Wales	5	1975–76	Scotland	6
	England	5		England	5	1976–77	Scotland	5
1908–09	England	6	1952–53	England	4	1977–78	England	6
1909–10	Scotland	4		Scotland	4	1978–79	England	5
1910–11	England	5	1953–54	England	6	1979–80	N. Ireland	5
1911–12	England	5	1954–55	England	6	1980–81	*Not completed*	
	Scotland	5	1955–56	England	3	1981–82	England	6
1912–13	England	4		Scotland	3	1982–83	England	5
1913–14	Ireland	5		Wales	3	1983–84	N. Ireland	3
1919–20	Wales	4		N. Ireland	3			

Note: In the results that follow, wc = World Cup, ec = European Championship. For Ireland, read Northern Ireland from 1921.

ENGLAND v SCOTLAND

Played: 107; England won 43, Scotland won 40, Drawn 24. *Goals:* England 188, Scotland 168.

Year	Venue	E	S	Year	Venue	E	S	Year	Venue	E	S
1872	Glasgow	0	0	1887	Blackburn	2	3	1902	Birmingham	2	2
1873	Kennington Oval	4	2	1888	Glasgow	5	0	1903	Sheffield	1	2
1874	Glasgow	1	2	1889	Kennington Oval	2	3	1904	Glasgow	1	0
1875	Kennington Oval	2	2	1890	Glasgow	1	1	1905	Crystal Palace	1	0
1876	Glasgow	0	3	1891	Blackburn	2	1	1906	Glasgow	1	2
1877	Kennington Oval	1	3	1892	Glasgow	4	1	1907	Newcastle	1	1
1878	Glasgow	2	7	1893	Richmond	5	2	1908	Glasgow	1	1
1879	Kennington Oval	5	4	1894	Glasgow	2	2	1909	Crystal Palace	2	0
1880	Glasgow	4	5	1895	Everton	3	0	1910	Glasgow	0	2
1881	Kennington Oval	1	6	1896	Glasgow	1	2	1911	Everton	1	1
1882	Glasgow	1	5	1897	Crystal Palace	1	2	1912	Glasgow	1	1
1883	Sheffield	2	3	1898	Glasgow	3	1	1913	Chelsea	1	0
1884	Glasgow	0	1	1899	Birmingham	2	1	1914	Glasgow	1	3
1885	Kennington Oval	1	1	1900	Glasgow	1	4	1920	Sheffield	5	4
1886	Glasgow	1	1	1901	Crystal Palace	2	2	1921	Glasgow	0	3

		E	S			E	S			E	S
1922	Aston Villa	0	1	WC1950	Glasgow	1	0	1971	Wembley	3	1
1923	Glasgow	2	2	1951	Wembley	2	3	1972	Glasgow	1	0
1924	Wembley	1	1	1952	Glasgow	2	1	1973	Wembley	5	0
1925	Glasgow	0	2	1953	Wembley	2	2	1973	Glasgow	1	0
1926	Manchester	0	1	WC1954	Glasgow	4	2	1974	Wembley	0	2
1927	Glasgow	2	1	1955	Wembley	7	2	1975	Wembley	5	1
1928	Wembley	1	5	1956	Glasgow	1	1	1976	Glasgow	1	2
1929	Glasgow	0	1	1957	Wembley	2	1	1977	Wembley	1	2
1930	Wembley	5	2	1958	Glasgow	4	0	1978	Glasgow	1	0
1931	Glasgow	0	2	1959	Wembley	1	0	1979	Wembley	3	1
1932	Wembley	3	0	1960	Glasgow	1	1	1980	Glasgow	2	0
1933	Glasgow	1	2	1961	Wembley	9	3	1981	Wembley	0	1
1934	Wembley	3	0	1962	Glasgow	0	2	1982	Glasgow	1	0
1935	Glasgow	0	2	1963	Wembley	1	2	1983	Wembley	2	0
1936	Wembley	1	1	1964	Glasgow	0	1	1984	Glasgow	1	1
1937	Glasgow	1	3	1965	Wembley	2	2	1985	Glasgow	0	1
1938	Wembley	0	1	1966	Glasgow	4	3	1986	Wembley	2	1
1939	Glasgow	2	1	EC1967	Wembley	2	3	1987	Glasgow	0	0
1947	Wembley	1	1	EC1968	Glasgow	1	1	1988	Wembley	1	0
1948	Glasgow	2	0	1969	Wembley	4	1	1989	Glasgow	2	0
1949	Wembley	1	3	1970	Glasgow	0	0				

ENGLAND v WALES

Played: 97; England won 62, Wales won 14, Drawn 21. *Goals:* England 239, Wales 90.

		E	W			E	W			E	W
1879	Kennington Oval	2	1	1911	Millwall	3	0	1955	Cardiff	1	2
1880	Wrexham	3	2	1912	Wrexham	2	0	1956	Wembley	3	1
1881	Blackburn	0	1	1913	Bristol	4	3	1957	Cardiff	4	0
1882	Wrexham	3	5	1914	Cardiff	2	0	1958	Aston Villa	2	2
1883	Kennington Oval	5	0	1920	Highbury	1	2	1959	Cardiff	1	1
1884	Wrexham	4	0	1921	Cardiff	0	0	1960	Wembley	5	1
1885	Blackburn	1	1	1922	Liverpool	1	0	1961	Cardiff	1	1
1886	Wrexham	3	1	1923	Cardiff	2	2	1962	Wembley	4	0
1887	Kennington Oval	4	0	1924	Blackburn	1	2	1963	Cardiff	4	0
1888	Crewe	5	1	1925	Swansea	2	1	1964	Wembley	2	1
1889	Stoke	4	1	1926	Crystal Palace	1	3	1965	Cardiff	0	0
1890	Wrexham	3	1	1927	Wrexham	3	3	EC1966	Wembley	5	1
1891	Sunderland	4	1	1927	Burnley	1	2	EC1967	Cardiff	3	0
1892	Wrexham	2	0	1928	Swansea	3	2	1969	Wembley	2	1
1893	Stoke	6	0	1929	Chelsea	6	0	1970	Cardiff	1	1
1894	Wrexham	5	1	1930	Wrexham	4	0	1971	Wembley	0	0
1894	Queen's Club,			1931	Liverpool	3	1	1972	Cardiff	3	0
	Kensington	1	1	1932	Wrexham	0	0	WC1972	Cardiff	1	0
1896	Cardiff	9	1	1933	Newcastle	1	2	WC1973	Wembley	1	1
1897	Sheffield	4	0	1934	Cardiff	4	0	1973	Wembley	3	0
1898	Wrexham	3	0	1935	Wolverhampton	1	2	1974	Cardiff	2	0
1899	Bristol	4	0	1936	Cardiff	1	2	1975	Wembley	2	2
1900	Cardiff	1	1	1937	Middlesbrough	2	1	1976	Wrexham	2	1
1901	Newcastle	6	0	1938	Cardiff	2	4	1976	Cardiff	1	0
1902	Wrexham	0	0	1946	Manchester	3	0	1977	Wembley	0	1
1903	Portsmouth	2	1	1947	Cardiff	3	0	1978	Cardiff	3	1
1904	Wrexham	2	2	1948	Aston Villa	1	0	1979	Wembley	0	0
1905	Liverpool	3	1	WC1949	Cardiff	4	1	1980	Wrexham	1	4
1906	Cardiff	1	0	1950	Sunderland	4	2	1981	Wembley	0	0
1907	Fulham	1	1	1951	Cardiff	1	1	1982	Cardiff	1	0
1908	Wrexham	7	1	1952	Wembley	5	2	1983	Wembley	2	1
1909	Nottingham	2	0	WC1953	Cardiff	4	1	1984	Wrexham	0	1
1910	Cardiff	1	0	1954	Wembley	3	2				

ENGLAND v IRELAND

Played: 96; England won 74, Ireland won 6, Drawn 16. *Goals:* England 319, Ireland 80.

Year	Venue	E	I	Year	Venue	E	I	Year	Venue	E	I
1882	Belfast	13	0	1914	Middlesbrough	0	3	1957	Wembley	2	3
1883	Liverpool	7	0	1919	Belfast	1	1	1958	Belfast	3	3
1884	Belfast	8	1	1920	Sunderland	2	0	1959	Wembley	2	1
1885	Manchester	4	0	1921	Belfast	1	1	1960	Belfast	5	2
1886	Belfast	6	1	1922	West Bromwich	2	0	1961	Wembley	1	1
1887	Sheffield	7	0	1923	Belfast	1	2	1962	Belfast	3	1
1888	Belfast	5	1	1924	Everton	3	1	1963	Wembley	8	3
1889	Everton	6	1	1925	Belfast	0	0	1964	Belfast	4	3
1890	Belfast	9	1	1926	Liverpool	3	3	1965	Wembley	2	1
1891	Wolverhampton	6	1	1927	Belfast	0	2	EC1966	Belfast	2	0
1892	Belfast	2	0	1928	Everton	2	1	EC1967	Wembley	2	0
1893	Birmingham	6	1	1929	Belfast	3	0	1969	Belfast	3	1
1894	Belfast	2	2	1930	Sheffield	5	1	1970	Wembley	3	1
1895	Derby	9	0	1931	Belfast	6	2	1971	Belfast	1	0
1896	Belfast	2	0	1932	Blackpool	1	0	1972	Wembley	0	1
1897	Nottingham	6	0	1933	Belfast	3	0	1973	Everton	2	1
1898	Belfast	3	2	1935	Everton	2	1	1974	Wembley	1	0
1899	Sunderland	13	2	1935	Belfast	3	1	1975	Belfast	0	0
1900	Dublin	2	0	1936	Stoke	3	1	1976	Wembley	4	0
1901	Southampton	3	0	1937	Belfast	5	1	1977	Belfast	2	1
1902	Belfast	1	0	1938	Manchester	7	0	1978	Wembley	1	0
1903	Wolverhampton	4	0	1946	Belfast	7	2	EC1979	Wembley	4	0
1904	Belfast	3	1	1947	Everton	2	2	1979	Belfast	2	0
1905	Middlesbrough	1	1	1948	Belfast	6	2	EC1979	Belfast	5	1
1906	Belfast	5	0	wc1949	Manchester	9	2	1980	Wembley	1	1
1907	Everton	1	0	1950	Belfast	4	1	1982	Wembley	4	0
1908	Belfast	3	1	1951	Aston Villa	2	0	1983	Belfast	0	0
1909	Bradford	4	0	1952	Belfast	2	2	1984	Wembley	1	0
1910	Belfast	1	1	wc1953	Everton	3	1	wc1985	Belfast	1	0
1911	Derby	2	1	1954	Belfast	2	0	wc1985	Wembley	0	0
1912	Dublin	6	1	1955	Wembley	3	0	EC1986	Wembley	3	0
1913	Belfast	1	2	1956	Belfast	1	1	EC1987	Belfast	2	0

SCOTLAND v WALES

Played: 101; Scotland won 60, Wales won 18, Drawn 23. *Goals:* Scotland 238, Wales 111.

Year	Venue	S	W	Year	Venue	S	W	Year	Venue	S	W
1876	Glasgow	4	0	1910	Kilmarnock	1	0	1955	Glasgow	2	0
1877	Wrexham	2	0	1911	Cardiff	2	2	1956	Cardiff	2	2
1878	Glasgow	9	0	1912	Tynecastle	1	0	1957	Glasgow	1	1
1879	Wrexham	3	0	1913	Wrexham	0	0	1958	Cardiff	3	0
1880	Glasgow	5	1	1914	Glasgow	0	0	1959	Glasgow	1	1
1881	Wrexham	5	1	1920	Cardiff	1	1	1960	Cardiff	0	2
1882	Glasgow	5	0	1921	Aberdeen	2	1	1961	Glasgow	2	0
1883	Wrexham	4	1	1922	Wrexham	1	2	1962	Cardiff	3	2
1884	Glasgow	4	1	1923	Paisley	2	0	1963	Glasgow	2	1
1885	Wrexham	8	1	1924	Cardiff	0	2	1964	Cardiff	2	3
1886	Glasgow	4	1	1925	Tynecastle	3	1	EC1965	Glasgow	4	1
1887	Wrexham	2	0	1926	Cardiff	3	0	EC1966	Cardiff	1	1
1888	Edinburgh	5	1	1927	Glasgow	3	0	1967	Glasgow	3	2
1889	Wrexham	0	0	1928	Wrexham	2	2	1969	Wrexham	5	3
1890	Paisley	5	0	1929	Glasgow	4	2	1970	Glasgow	0	0
1891	Wrexham	4	3	1930	Cardiff	4	2	1971	Cardiff	0	0
1892	Edinburgh	6	1	1931	Glasgow	1	1	1972	Glasgow	1	0
1893	Wrexham	8	0	1932	Wrexham	3	2	1973	Wrexham	2	0
1894	Kilmarnock	5	2	1933	Edinburgh	2	5	1974	Glasgow	2	0
1894	Wrexham	2	2	1934	Cardiff	2	3	1975	Cardiff	2	2
1896	Dundee	4	0	1935	Aberdeen	3	2	1976	Glasgow	3	1
1895	Wrexham	2	2	1936	Cardiff	1	1	wc1977	Glasgow	1	0
1898	Motherwell	5	2	1937	Dundee	1	2	1977	Wrexham	0	0
1899	Wrexham	6	0	1938	Cardiff	1	2	wc1977	Liverpool	2	0
1900	Aberdeen	5	2	1939	Edinburgh	3	2	1978	Glasgow	1	1
1901	Wrexham	1	1	1946	Wrexham	1	3	1979	Cardiff	0	3
1902	Greenock	5	1	1947	Glasgow	1	2	1980	Glasgow	1	0
1903	Cardiff	1	0	wc1948	Cardiff	3	1	1981	Swansea	0	2
1904	Dundee	1	1	1949	Glasgow	2	0	1982	Glasgow	1	0
1905	Wrexham	1	3	1950	Cardiff	3	1	1983	Cardiff	2	0
1906	Edinburgh	0	2	1951	Glasgow	0	1	1984	Glasgow	2	1
1907	Wrexham	0	1	wc1952	Cardiff	2	1	wc1985	Glasgow	0	1
1908	Dundee	2	1	1953	Glasgow	3	3	wc1985	Cardiff	1	1
1909	Wrexham	2	3	1954	Cardiff	1	0				

SCOTLAND v IRELAND

Played: 92; Scotland won 61, Ireland won 15, Drawn 16. *Goals:* Scotland 254, Ireland 81.

Year	Venue	S	I	Year	Venue	S	I	Year	Venue	S	I
1884	Belfast	5	0	1920	Glasgow	3	0	1957	Belfast	1	1
1885	Glasgow	8	2	1921	Belfast	2	0	1958	Glasgow	2	2
1886	Belfast	7	2	1922	Glasgow	2	1	1959	Belfast	4	0
1887	Glasgow	4	1	1923	Belfast	1	0	1960	Glasgow	5	2
1888	Belfast	10	2	1924	Glasgow	2	0	1961	Belfast	6	1
1889	Glasgow	7	0	1925	Belfast	3	0	1962	Glasgow	5	1
1890	Belfast	4	1	1926	Glasgow	4	0	1963	Belfast	1	2
1891	Glasgow	2	1	1927	Belfast	2	0	1964	Glasgow	3	2
1892	Belfast	3	2	1928	Glasgow	0	1	1965	Belfast	2	3
1893	Glasgow	6	1	1929	Belfast	7	3	1966	Glasgow	2	1
1894	Belfast	2	1	1930	Glasgow	3	1	1967	Belfast	0	1
1895	Glasgow	3	1	1931	Belfast	0	0	1969	Glasgow	1	1
1896	Belfast	3	3	1932	Glasgow	3	1	1970	Belfast	1	0
1897	Glasgow	5	1	1933	Belfast	4	0	1971	Glasgow	0	1
1898	Belfast	3	0	1934	Glasgow	1	2	1972	Glasgow	2	0
1899	Glasgow	9	1	1935	Belfast	1	2	1973	Glasgow	1	2
1900	Belfast	3	0	1936	Edinburgh	2	1	1974	Glasgow	0	1
1901	Glasgow	11	0	1937	Belfast	3	1	1975	Glasgow	3	0
1902	Belfast	5	1	1938	Aberdeen	1	1	1976	Glasgow	3	0
1903	Glasgow	0	2	1939	Belfast	2	0	1977	Glasgow	3	0
1904	Dublin	1	1	1946	Glasgow	0	0	1978	Glasgow	1	1
1905	Glasgow	4	0	1947	Belfast	0	2	1979	Glasgow	1	0
1906	Dublin	1	0	1948	Glasgow	3	2	1980	Belfast	0	1
1907	Glasgow	3	0	1949	Belfast	8	2	wc1981	Glasgow	1	1
1908	Dublin	5	0	1950	Glasgow	6	1	1981	Glasgow	2	0
1909	Glasgow	5	0	1951	Belfast	3	0	wc1981	Belfast	0	0
1910	Belfast	0	1	1952	Glasgow	1	1	1982	Belfast	1	1
1911	Glasgow	2	0	1953	Belfast	3	1	1983	Glasgow	0	0
1912	Belfast	4	1	1954	Glasgow	2	2	1984	Belfast	0	2
1913	Dublin	2	1	1955	Belfast	1	2	1992	Glasgow	1	0
1914	Belfast	1	1	1956	Glasgow	1	0				

WALES v IRELAND

Played: 90; Wales won 42, Ireland won 27, Drawn 21. *Goals:* Wales 182, Ireland 127.

Year	Venue	W	I	Year	Venue	W	I	Year	Venue	W	I
1882	Wrexham	7	1	1912	Cardiff	2	3	wc1954	Wrexham	1	2
1883	Belfast	1	1	1913	Belfast	1	0	1955	Belfast	3	2
1884	Wrexham	6	0	1914	Wrexham	1	2	1956	Cardiff	1	1
1885	Belfast	8	2	1920	Belfast	2	2	1957	Belfast	0	0
1886	Wrexham	5	0	1921	Swansea	2	1	1958	Cardiff	1	1
1887	Belfast	1	4	1922	Belfast	1	1	1959	Belfast	1	4
1888	Wrexham	11	0	1923	Wrexham	0	3	1960	Wrexham	3	2
1889	Belfast	3	1	1924	Belfast	1	0	1961	Belfast	5	1
1890	Shrewsbury	5	2	1925	Wrexham	0	0	1962	Cardiff	4	0
1891	Belfast	2	7	1926	Belfast	0	3	1963	Belfast	4	1
1892	Bangor	1	1	1927	Cardiff	2	2	1964	Cardiff	2	3
1893	Belfast	3	4	1928	Belfast	2	1	1965	Belfast	5	0
1894	Swansea	4	1	1929	Wrexham	2	2	1966	Cardiff	1	4
1895	Belfast	2	2	1930	Belfast	0	7	EC1967	Belfast	0	0
1896	Wrexham	6	1	1931	Wrexham	3	2	EC1968	Wrexham	2	0
1897	Belfast	3	4	1932	Belfast	0	4	1969	Belfast	0	0
1898	Llandudno	0	1	1933	Wrexham	4	1	1970	Swansea	1	0
1899	Belfast	0	1	1934	Belfast	1	1	1971	Belfast	0	1
1900	Llandudno	2	0	1935	Wrexham	3	1	1972	Wrexham	0	0
1901	Belfast	1	0	1936	Belfast	2	3	1973	Everton	0	1
1902	Cardiff	0	3	1937	Wrexham	4	1	1974	Wrexham	1	0
1903	Belfast	0	2	1938	Belfast	0	1	1975	Belfast	0	1
1904	Bangor	0	1	1939	Wrexham	3	1	1976	Swansea	1	0
1905	Belfast	2	2	1947	Belfast	1	2	1977	Belfast	1	1
1906	Wrexham	4	4	1948	Wrexham	2	0	1978	Wrexham	1	0
1907	Belfast	3	2	1949	Belfast	2	0	1979	Belfast	1	1
1908	Aberdare	0	1	wc1950	Wrexham	0	0	1980	Cardiff	0	1
1909	Belfast	3	2	1951	Belfast	2	1	1982	Wrexham	3	0
1910	Wrexham	4	1	1952	Swansea	3	0	1983	Belfast	1	0
1911	Belfast	2	1	1953	Belfast	3	2	1984	Swansea	1	1

OTHER BRITISH INTERNATIONAL RESULTS 1908–90

ENGLAND

		v ALBANIA	E	A
wc1989	8 Mar	Tirana	2	0
wc1989	26 Apr	Wembley	5	0

		v ARGENTINA	E	A
1951	9 May	Wembley	2	1
1953	17 May	Buenos Aires	0	0
(abandoned after 21 mins)				
wc1962	2 June	Rancagua	3	1
1964	6 June	Rio de Janeiro	0	1
wc1966	23 July	Wembley	1	0
1974	22 May	Wembley	2	2
1977	12 June	Buenos Aires	1	1
1980	13 May	Wembley	3	1
wc1986	22 June	Mexico City	1	2
1991	25 May	Wembley	2	2

		v AUSTRALIA	E	A
1980	31 May	Sydney	2	1
1983	11 June	Sydney	0	0
1983	15 June	Brisbane	1	0
1983	18 June	Melbourne	1	1
1991	1 June	Sydney	1	0

		v AUSTRIA	E	A
1908	6 June	Vienna	6	1
1908	8 June	Vienna	11	1
1909	1 June	Vienna	8	1
1930	14 May	Vienna	0	0
1932	7 Dec	Chelsea	4	3
1936	6 May	Vienna	1	2
1951	28 Nov	Wembley	2	2
1952	25 May	Vienna	3	2
wc1958	15 June	Boras	2	2
1961	27 May	Vienna	1	3
1962	4 Apr	Wembley	3	1
1965	20 Oct	Wembley	2	3
1967	27 May	Vienna	1	0
1973	26 Sept	Wembley	7	0
1979	13 June	Vienna	3	4

		v BELGIUM	E	B
1921	21 May	Brussels	2	0
1923	19 Mar	Highbury	6	1
1923	1 Nov	Antwerp	2	2
1924	8 Dec	West Bromwich	4	0
1926	24 May	Antwerp	5	3
1927	11 May	Brussels	9	1
1928	19 May	Antwerp	3	1
1929	11 May	Brussels	5	1
1931	16 May	Brussels	4	1
1936	9 May	Brussels	2	3
1947	21 Sept	Brussels	5	2
1950	18 May	Brussels	4	1
1952	26 Nov	Wembley	5	0
wc1954	17 June	Basle	4	4*
1964	21 Oct	Wembley	2	2
1970	25 Feb	Brussels	3	1
EC1980	12 June	Turin	1	1
wc1990	27 June	Bologna	1	0

*After extra time

		v BOHEMIA	E	B
1908	13 June	Prague	4	0

		v BRAZIL	E	B
1956	9 May	Wembley	4	2
wc1958	11 June	Gothenburg	0	0
1959	13 May	Rio de Janeiro	0	2

			E	B
wc1962	10 June	Vina de Mar	1	3
1963	8 May	Wembley	1	1
1964	30 May	Rio de Janeiro	1	5
1969	12 June	Rio de Janeiro	1	2
wc1970	7 June	Guadalajara	0	1
1976	23 May	Los Angeles	0	1
1977	8 June	Rio de Janeiro	0	0
1978	19 Apr	Wembley	1	1
1981	12 May	Wembley	0	1
1984	10 June	Rio de Janeiro	2	0
1987	19 May	Wembley	1	1
1990	28 Mar	Wembley	1	0
1992	17 May	Wembley	1	1

		v BULGARIA	E	B
wc1962	7 June	Rancagua	0	0
1968	11 Dec	Wembley	1	1
1974	1 June	Sofia	1	0
EC1979	6 June	Sofia	3	0
EC1979	22 Nov	Wembley	2	0

		v CAMEROON	E	C
wc1990	1 July	Naples	3	2
1991	6 Feb	Wembley	2	0

		v CANADA	E	C
1986	24 May	Burnaby	1	0

		v CHILE	E	C
wc1950	25 June	Rio de Janeiro	2	0
1953	24 May	Santiago	2	1
1984	17 June	Santiago	0	0
1989	23 May	Wembley	0	0

		v CIS	E	C
1992	29 Apr	Moscow	2	2

		v COLOMBIA	E	C
1970	20 May	Bogota	4	0
1988	24 May	Wembley	1	1

		v CYPRUS	E	C
EC1975	16 Apr	Wembley	5	0
EC1975	11 May	Limassol	1	0

		v CZECHOSLOVAKIA	E	C
1934	16 May	Prague	1	2
1937	1 Dec	Tottenham	5	4
1963	29 May	Bratislava	4	2
1966	2 Nov	Wembley	0	0
wc1970	11 June	Guadalajara	1	0
1973	27 May	Prague	1	1
EC1974	30 Oct	Wembley	3	0
EC1975	30 Oct	Bratislava	1	2
1978	29 Nov	Wembley	1	0
wc1982	20 June	Bilbao	2	0
1990	25 Apr	Wembley	4	2
1992	25 Mar	Prague	2	2

		v DENMARK	E	D
1948	26 Sept	Copenhagen	0	0
1955	2 Oct	Copenhagen	5	1
wc1956	5 Dec	Wolverhampton	5	2
wc1957	15 May	Copenhagen	4	1
1966	3 July	Copenhagen	2	0
EC1978	20 Sept	Copenhagen	4	3
EC1979	12 Sept	Wembley	1	0
EC1982	22 Sept	Copenhagen	2	2

			E	D
EC1983	21 Sept	Wembley	0	1
1988	14 Sept	Wembley	1	0
1989	7 June	Copenhagen	1	1
1990	15 May	Wembley	1	0
EC1992	11 June	Malmo	0	0

v ECUADOR

			E	Ec
1970	24 May	Quito	2	0

v EGYPT

			E	Eg
1986	29 Jan	Cairo	4	0
wc1990	21 June	Cagliari	1	0

v FIFA

			E	FIFA
1938	26 Oct	Highbury	3	0
1953	21 Oct	Wembley	4	4
1963	23 Oct	Wembley	2	1

v FINLAND

			E	F
1937	20 May	Helsinki	8	0
1956	20 May	Helsinki	5	1
1966	26 June	Helsinki	3	0
wc1976	13 June	Helsinki	4	1
wc1976	13 Oct	Wembley	2	1
1982	3 June	Helsinki	4	1
wc1984	17 Oct	Wembley	5	0
wc1985	22 May	Helsinki	1	1
1992	3 June	Helsinki	2	1

v FRANCE

			E	F
1923	10 May	Paris	4	1
1924	17 May	Paris	3	1
1925	21 May	Paris	3	2
1927	26 May	Paris	6	0
1928	17 May	Paris	5	1
1929	9 May	Paris	4	1
1931	14 May	Paris	2	5
1933	6 Dec	Tottenham	4	1
1938	26 May	Paris	4	2
1947	3 May	Highbury	3	0
1949	22 May	Paris	3	1
1951	3 Oct	Highbury	2	2
1955	15 May	Paris	0	1
1957	27 Nov	Wembley	4	0
EC1962	3 Oct	Sheffield	1	1
EC1963	27 Feb	Paris	2	5
wc1966	20 July	Wembley	2	0
1969	12 Mar	Wembley	5	0
wc1982	16 June	Bilbao	3	1
1984	29 Feb	Paris	0	2
1992	19 Feb	Wembley	2	0
EC1992	14 June	Malmo	0	0

v GERMANY

			E	G
1930	10 May	Berlin	3	3
1935	4 Dec	Tottenham	3	0
1938	14 May	Berlin	6	3
1991	11 Sept	Wembley	0	1

v EAST GERMANY

			E	EG
1963	2 June	Leipzig	2	1
1970	25 Nov	Wembley	3	1
1974	29 May	Leipzig	1	1
1984	12 Sept	Wembley	1	0

v WEST GERMANY

			E	WG
1954	1 Dec	Wembley	3	1
1956	26 May	Berlin	3	1
1965	12 May	Nuremberg	1	0
1966	23 Feb	Wembley	1	0
wc1966	30 July	Wembley	4	2*
1968	1 June	Hanover	0	1
wc1970	14 June	Leon	2	3*
EC1972	29 Apr	Wembley	1	3
EC1972	13 May	Berlin	0	0
1975	12 Mar	Wembley	2	0
1978	22 Feb	Munich	1	2
wc1982	29 June	Madrid	0	0
1982	13 Oct	Wembley	1	2
1985	12 June	Mexico City	3	0
1987	9 Sept	Dusseldorf	1	3
wc1990	4 July	Turin	1	1*

After extra time

v GREECE

			E	G
EC1971	21 Apr	Wembley	3	0
EC1971	1 Dec	Athens	2	0
EC1982	17 Nov	Athens	3	0
EC1983	30 Mar	Wembley	0	0
1989	8 Feb	Athens	2	1

v HOLLAND

			E	H
1935	18 May	Amsterdam	1	0
1946	27 Nov	Huddersfield	8	2
1964	9 Dec	Amsterdam	1	1
1969	5 Nov	Amsterdam	1	0
1970	14 Jun	Wembley	0	0
1977	9 Feb	Wembley	0	2
1982	25 May	Wembley	2	0
1988	23 Mar	Wembley	2	2
EC1988	15 June	Dusseldorf	1	3
wc1990	16 June	Cagliari	0	0

v HUNGARY

			E	H
1908	10 June	Budapest	7	0
1909	29 May	Budapest	4	2
1909	31 May	Budapest	8	2
1934	10 May	Budapest	1	2
1936	2 Dec	Highbury	6	2
1953	25 Nov	Wembley	3	6
1954	23 May	Budapest	1	7
1960	22 May	Budapest	0	2
wc1962	31 May	Rancagua	1	2
1965	5 May	Wembley	1	0
1978	24 May	Wembley	4	1
wc1981	6 June	Budapest	3	1
wc1982	18 Nov	Wembley	1	0
EC1983	27 Apr	Wembley	2	0
EC1983	12 Oct	Budapest	3	0
1988	27 Apr	Budapest	0	0
1990	12 Sept	Wembley	1	0
1992	12 May	Budapest	1	0

v ICELAND

			E	I
1982	2 June	Reykjavik	1	1

v REPUBLIC OF IRELAND

			E	RI
1946	30 Sept	Dublin	1	0
1949	21 Sept	Everton	0	2
wc1957	8 May	Wembley	5	1
wc1957	19 May	Dublin	1	1
1964	24 May	Dublin	3	1
1976	8 Sept	Wembley	1	1
EC1978	25 Oct	Dublin	1	1
EC1980	6 Feb	Wembley	2	0
1985	26 Mar	Wembley	2	1
EC1988	12 June	Stuttgart	0	1
wc1990	11 June	Cagliari	1	1
EC1990	14 Nov	Dublin	1	1
EC1991	27 Mar	Wembley	1	1

v ISRAEL

			E	I
1986	26 Feb	Ramat Gan	2	1
1988	17 Feb	Tel Aviv	0	0

820

			E	I
1933	13 May	Rome	1	1
1934	14 Nov	Highbury	3	2
1939	13 May	Milan	2	2
1948	16 May	Turin	4	0
1949	30 Nov	Tottenham	2	0
1952	18 May	Florence	1	1
1959	6 May	Wembley	2	2
1961	24 May	Rome	3	2
1973	14 June	Turin	0	2
1973	14 Nov	Wembley	0	1
1976	28 May	New York	3	2
wc1976	17 Nov	Rome	0	2
wc1977	16 Nov	Wembley	2	0
EC1980	15 June	Turin	0	1
1985	6 June	Mexico City	1	2
1989	15 Nov	Wembley	0	0
wc1990	7 July	Bari	1	2

v ITALY above.

v KUWAIT E K
| wc1982 | 25 June | Bilbao | 1 | 0 |

v LUXEMBOURG E L
1927	21 May	Luxembourg	5	2
wc1960	19 Oct	Luxembourg	9	0
wc1961	28 Sept	Highbury	4	1
wc1977	30 Mar	Wembley	5	0
wc1977	12 Oct	Luxembourg	2	0
EC1982	15 Dec	Wembley	9	0
EC1983	16 Nov	Luxembourg	4	0

v MALAYSIA E M
| 1991 | 12 June | Kuala Lumpur | 4 | 2 |

v MALTA E M
| EC1971 | 3 Feb | Valletta | 1 | 0 |
| EC1971 | 12 May | Wembley | 5 | 0 |

v MEXICO E M
1959	24 May	Mexico City	1	2
1961	10 May	Wembley	8	0
wc1966	16 July	Wembley	2	0
1969	1 June	Mexico City	0	0
1985	9 June	Mexico City	0	1
1986	17 May	Los Angeles	3	0

v MOROCCO E M
| wc1986 | 6 June | Monterrey | 0 | 0 |

v NEW ZEALAND E NZ
| 1991 | 3 June | Auckland | 1 | 0 |
| 1991 | 8 June | Wellington | 2 | 0 |

v NORWAY E N
1937	14 May	Oslo	6	0
1938	9 Nov	Newcastle	4	0
1949	18 May	Oslo	4	1
1966	29 June	Oslo	6	1
wc1980	10 Sept	Wembley	4	0
wc1981	9 Sept	Oslo	1	2

v PARAGUAY E P
| wc1986 | 18 June | Mexico City | 3 | 0 |

v PERU E P
| 1959 | 17 May | Lima | 1 | 4 |
| 1962 | 20 May | Lima | 4 | 0 |

v POLAND E P
1966	5 Jan	Everton	1	1
1966	5 July	Chorzow	1	0
wc1973	6 June	Chorzow	0	2
wc1973	17 Oct	Wembley	1	1

			E	P
wc1986	11 June	Monterrey	3	0
wc1989	3 June	Wembley	3	0
wc1989	11 Oct	Katowice	0	0
EC1990	17 Oct	Wembley	2	0
EC1991	13 Nov	Poznan	1	1

v PORTUGAL E P
1947	25 May	Lisbon	10	0
1950	14 May	Lisbon	5	3
1951	19 May	Everton	5	2
1955	22 May	Oporto	1	3
1958	7 May	Wembley	2	1
wc1961	21 May	Lisbon	1	1
wc1961	25 Oct	Wembley	2	0
1964	17 May	Lisbon	4	3
1964	4 June	São Paulo	1	1
wc1966	26 July	Wembley	2	1
1969	10 Dec	Wembley	1	0
1974	3 Apr	Lisbon	0	0
EC1974	20 Nov	Wembley	0	0
EC1975	19 Nov	Lisbon	1	1
wc1986	3 June	Monterrey	0	1

v ROMANIA E R
1939	24 May	Bucharest	2	0
1968	6 Nov	Bucharest	0	0
1969	15 Jan	Wembley	1	1
wc1970	2 June	Guadalajara	1	0
wc1980	15 Oct	Bucharest	1	2
wc1981	29 April	Wembley	0	0
wc1985	1 May	Bucharest	0	0
wc1985	11 Sept	Wembley	1	1

v SAUDI ARABIA E SA
| 1988 | 16 Nov | Riyadh | 1 | 1 |

v SPAIN E S
1929	15 May	Madrid	3	4
1931	9 Dec	Highbury	7	1
wc1950	2 July	Rio de Janeiro	0	1
1955	18 May	Madrid	1	1
1955	30 Nov	Wembley	4	1
1960	15 May	Madrid	0	3
1960	26 Oct	Wembley	4	2
1965	8 Dec	Madrid	2	0
1967	24 May	Wembley	2	0
EC1968	3 Apr	Wembley	1	0
EC1968	8 May	Madrid	2	1
1980	26 Mar	Barcelona	2	0
EC1980	18 June	Naples	2	1
1981	25 Mar	Wembley	1	2
wc1982	5 July	Madrid	0	0
1987	18 Feb	Madrid	4	2

v SWEDEN E S
1923	21 May	Stockholm	4	2
1923	24 May	Stockholm	3	1
1937	17 May	Stockholm	4	0
1947	19 Nov	Highbury	4	2
1949	13 May	Stockholm	1	3
1956	16 May	Stockholm	0	0
1959	28 Oct	Wembley	2	3
1965	16 May	Gothenburg	2	1
1968	22 May	Wembley	3	1
1979	10 June	Stockholm	0	0
1986	10 Sept	Stockholm	0	1
wc1988	19 Oct	Wembley	0	0
wc1989	6 Sept	Stockholm	0	0
EC1992	17 June	Stockholm	1	2

		v SWITZERLAND	E	S
1933	20 May	Berne	4	0
1938	21 May	Zurich	1	2
1947	18 May	Zurich	0	1
1948	2 Dec	Highbury	6	0
1952	28 May	Zurich	3	0
wc1954	20 June	Berne	2	0
1962	9 May	Wembley	3	1
1963	5 June	Basle	8	1
EC1971	13 Oct	Basle	3	2
EC1971	10 Nov	Wembley	1	1
1975	3 Sept	Basle	2	1
1977	7 Sept	Wembley	0	0
wc1980	19 Nov	Wembley	2	1
wc1981	30 May	Basle	1	2
1988	28 May	Lausanne	1	0

		v TUNISIA	E	T
1990	2 June	Tunis	1	1

		v TURKEY	E	T
wc1984	14 Nov	Istanbul	8	0
wc1985	16 Oct	Wembley	5	0
EC1987	29 Apr	Izmir	0	0
EC1987	14 Oct	Wembley	8	0
EC1991	1 May	Izmir	1	0
EC1991	16 Oct	Wembley	1	0

		v URUGUAY	E	U
1953	31 May	Montevideo	1	2
wc1954	26 June	Basle	2	4
1964	6 May	Wembley	2	1
wc1966	11 July	Wembley	0	0
1969	8 June	Montevideo	2	1
1977	15 June	Montevideo	0	0
1984	13 June	Montevideo	0	2
1990	22 May	Wembley	1	2

		v USA	E	USA
wc1950	29 June	Belo Horizonte	0	1
1953	8 June	New York	6	3
1959	28 May	Los Angeles	8	1
1964	27 May	New York	10	0
1985	16 June	Los Angeles	5	0

		v USSR	E	USSR
1958	18 May	Moscow	1	1
wc1958	8 June	Gothenburg	2	2
wc1958	17 June	Gothenburg	0	1
1958	22 Oct	Wembley	5	0
1967	6 Dec	Wembley	2	2
EC1968	8 June	Rome	2	0
1973	10 June	Moscow	2	1
1984	2 June	Wembley	0	2
1986	26 Mar	Tbilisi	1	0
EC1988	18 June	Frankfurt	1	3
1991	21 May	Wembley	3	1

		v YUGOSLAVIA	E	Y
1939	18 May	Belgrade	1	2
1950	22 Nov	Highbury	2	2
1954	16 May	Belgrade	0	1
1956	28 Nov	Wembley	3	0
1958	11 May	Belgrade	0	5
1960	11 May	Wembley	3	3
1965	9 May	Belgrade	1	1
1966	4 May	Wembley	2	0
EC1968	5 June	Florence	0	1
1972	11 Oct	Wembley	1	1
1974	5 June	Belgrade	2	2
EC1986	12 Nov	Wembley	2	0
EC1987	11 Nov	Belgrade	4	1
1989	13 Dec	Wembley	2	1

SCOTLAND

		v ARGENTINA	S	A
1977	18 June	Buenos Aires	1	1
1979	2 June	Glasgow	1	3
1990	28 Mar	Glasgow	1	0

		v AUSTRALIA	S	A
wc1985	20 Nov	Glasgow	2	0
wc1985	4 Dec	Melbourne	0	0

		v AUSTRIA	S	A
1931	16 May	Vienna	0	5
1933	29 Nov	Glasgow	2	2
1937	9 May	Vienna	1	1
1950	13 Dec	Glasgow	0	1
1951	27 May	Vienna	0	4
wc1954	16 June	Zurich	0	1
1955	19 May	Vienna	4	1
1956	2 May	Glasgow	1	1
1960	29 May	Vienna	1	4
1963	8 May	Glasgow	4	1
(abandoned after 79 mins)				
wc1968	6 Nov	Glasgow	2	1
wc1969	5 Nov	Vienna	0	2
EC1978	20 Sept	Vienna	2	3
EC1979	17 Oct	Glasgow	1	1

		v BELGIUM	S	B
1947	18 May	Brussels	1	2
1948	28 Apr	Glasgow	2	0
1951	20 May	Brussels	5	0
EC1971	3 Feb	Liège	0	3
EC1971	10 Nov	Aberdeen	1	0
1974	2 June	Brussels	1	2
EC1979	21 Nov	Brussels	0	2
EC1979	19 Dec	Glasgow	1	3
EC1982	15 Dec	Brussels	2	3
EC1983	12 Oct	Glasgow	1	1
EC1987	1 Apr	Brussels	1	4
EC1987	14 Oct	Glasgow	2	0

		v BRAZIL	S	B
1966	25 June	Glasgow	1	1
1972	5 July	Rio de Janeiro	0	1
1973	30 June	Glasgow	0	1
wc1974	18 June	Frankfurt	0	0
1977	23 June	Rio de Janeiro	0	2
wc1982	18 June	Seville	1	4
1987	26 May	Glasgow	0	2
wc1990	20 June	Turin	0	1

		v BULGARIA	S	B
1978	22 Feb	Glasgow	2	1
EC1986	10 Sept	Glasgow	0	0
EC1987	11 Nov	Sofia	1	0
EC1990	14 Nov	Sofia	1	1
EC1991	27 Mar	Glasgow	1	1

		v CANADA	S	C
1983	12 June	Vancouver	2	0
1983	16 June	Edmonton	3	0
1983	20 June	Toronto	2	0
1992	21 May	Toronto	3	1

		v CHILE	S	C
1977	15 June	Santiago	4	2
1989	30 May	Glasgow	2	0

		v CIS	S	C
EC1992	18 June	Norrkoping	3	0

		v COLOMBIA	S	C
1988	17 May	Glasgow	0	0

		v COSTA RICA	S	CR
WC1990	11 June	Genoa	0	1

		v CYPRUS	S	C
WC1968	17 Dec	Nicosia	5	0
WC1969	11 May	Glasgow	8	0
WC1989	8 Feb	Limassol	3	2
WC1989	26 Apr	Glasgow	2	1

		v CZECHOSLOVAKIA	S	C
1937	22 May	Prague	3	1
1937	8 Dec	Glasgow	5	0
WC1961	14 May	Bratislava	0	4
WC1961	26 Sept	Glasgow	3	2
WC1961	29 Nov	Brussels	2	4*
1972	2 July	Porto Alegre	0	0
WC1973	26 Sept	Glasgow	2	1
WC1973	17 Oct	Prague	0	1
WC1976	13 Oct	Prague	0	2
WC1977	21 Sept	Glasgow	3	1

After extra time

		v DENMARK	S	D
1951	12 May	Glasgow	3	1
1952	25 May	Copenhagen	2	1
1968	16 Oct	Copenhagen	1	0
EC1970	11 Nov	Glasgow	1	0
EC1971	9 June	Copenhagen	0	1
WC1972	18 Oct	Copenhagen	4	1
WC1972	15 Nov	Glasgow	2	0
EC1975	3 Sept	Copenhagen	1	0
EC1975	29 Oct	Glasgow	3	1
WC1986	4 June	Nezahualcayotl	0	1

		v EGYPT	S	E
1990	16 May	Aberdeen	1	3

		v FINLAND	S	F
1954	25 May	Helsinki	2	1
WC1964	21 Oct	Glasgow	3	1
WC1965	27 May	Helsinki	2	1
1976	8 Sept	Glasgow	6	0
1992	25 Mar	Glasgow	1	1

		v FRANCE	S	F
1930	18 May	Paris	2	0
1932	8 May	Paris	3	1
1948	23 May	Paris	0	3
1949	27 Apr	Glasgow	2	0
1950	27 May	Paris	1	0
1951	16 May	Glasgow	1	0
WC1958	15 June	Orebro	1	2

			S	F
1984	1 June	Marseilles	0	2
WC1989	8 Mar	Glasgow	2	0
WC1989	11 Oct	Paris	0	3

		v GERMANY	S	G
1929	1 June	Berlin	1	1
1936	14 Oct	Glasgow	2	0
EC1992	15 June	Norrkoping	0	2

		v EAST GERMANY	S	EG
1974	30 Oct	Glasgow	3	0
1977	7 Sept	East Berlin	0	1
EC1982	13 Oct	Glasgow	2	0
EC1983	16 Nov	Halle	1	2
1985	16 Oct	Glasgow	0	0
1990	25 Apr	Glasgow	0	1

		v WEST GERMANY	S	WG
1957	22 May	Stuttgart	3	1
1959	6 May	Glasgow	3	2
1964	12 May	Hanover	2	2
WC1969	16 Apr	Glasgow	1	1
WC1969	22 Oct	Hamburg	2	3
1973	14 Nov	Glasgow	1	1
1974	27 Mar	Frankfurt	1	2
1986	8 June	Queretaro	1	2

		v HOLLAND	S	H
1929	4 June	Amsterdam	2	0
1938	21 May	Amsterdam	3	1
1959	27 May	Amsterdam	2	1
1966	11 May	Glasgow	0	3
1968	30 May	Amsterdam	0	0
1971	1 Dec	Rotterdam	1	2
WC1978	11 June	Mendoza	3	2
1982	23 Mar	Glasgow	2	1
1986	29 Apr	Eindhoven	0	0
EC1992	12 June	Gothenburg	0	1

		v HUNGARY	S	H
1938	7 Dec	Glasgow	3	1
1954	8 Dec	Glasgow	2	4
1955	29 May	Budapest	1	3
1958	7 May	Glasgow	1	1
1960	5 June	Budapest	3	3
1980	31 May	Budapest	1	3
1987	9 Sept	Glasgow	2	0

		v ICELAND	S	I
WC1984	17 Oct	Glasgow	3	0
WC1985	28 May	Reykjavik	1	0

		v IRAN	S	I
WC1978	7 June	Cordoba	1	1

		v REPUBLIC OF IRELAND	S	RI
WC1961	3 May	Glasgow	4	1
WC1961	7 May	Dublin	3	0
1963	9 June	Dublin	0	1
1969	21 Sept	Dublin	1	1
EC1986	15 Oct	Dublin	0	0
EC1987	18 Feb	Glasgow	0	1

		v ISRAEL	S	I
WC1981	25 Feb	Tel Aviv	1	0
WC1981	28 Apr	Glasgow	3	1
1986	28 Jan	Tel Aviv	1	0

v ITALY — S / I
1931	20 May	Rome	0	3
wc1965	9 Nov	Glasgow	1	0
wc1965	7 Dec	Naples	0	3
1988	22 Dec	Perugia	0	2

v LUXEMBOURG — S / L
1947	24 May	Luxembourg	6	0
EC1986	12 Nov	Glasgow	3	0
1987	2 Dec	Esch	0	0

v MALTA — S / M
| 1988 | 22 Mar | Valletta | 1 | 1 |
| 1990 | 28 May | Valletta | 2 | 1 |

v NEW ZEALAND — S / NZ
| wc1982 | 15 June | Malaga | 5 | 2 |

v NORWAY — S / N
1929	28 May	Oslo	7	3
1954	5 May	Glasgow	1	0
1954	19 May	Oslo	1	1
1963	4 June	Bergen	3	4
1963	7 Nov	Glasgow	6	1
1974	6 June	Oslo	2	1
EC1978	25 Oct	Glasgow	3	2
EC1979	7 June	Oslo	4	0
wc1988	14 Sept	Oslo	2	1
wc1989	15 Nov	Glasgow	1	1
1992	3 June	Oslo	0	0

v PARAGUAY — S / P
| wc1958 | 11 June | Norrkoping | 2 | 3 |

v PERU — S / P
1972	26 Apr	Glasgow	2	0
wc1978	3 June	Cordoba	1	3
1979	12 Sept	Glasgow	1	1

v POLAND — S / P
1958	1 June	Warsaw	2	1
1960	4 June	Glasgow	2	3
wc1965	23 May	Chorzow	1	1
wc1965	13 Oct	Glasgow	1	2
1980	28 May	Poznan	0	1
wc1990	19 May	Glasgow	1	1

v PORTUGAL — S / P
1950	21 May	Lisbon	2	2
1955	4 May	Glasgow	3	0
1959	3 June	Lisbon	0	1
1966	18 June	Glasgow	0	1
EC1971	21 Apr	Lisbon	0	2
EC1971	13 Oct	Glasgow	2	1
1975	13 May	Glasgow	1	0
EC1978	29 Nov	Lisbon	0	1
EC1980	26 Mar	Glasgow	4	1
wc1980	15 Oct	Glasgow	0	0
wc1981	18 Nov	Lisbon	1	2

v ROMANIA — S / R
EC1975	1 June	Bucharest	1	1
EC1975	17 Dec	Glasgow	1	1
1986	26 Mar	Glasgow	3	0
EC1990	12 Sept	Glasgow	2	1
EC1991	16 Oct	Bucharest	0	1

v SAN MARINO — S / SM
| EC1991 | 1 May | Serravalle | 2 | 0 |
| EC1991 | 13 Nov | Glasgow | 4 | 0 |

v SAUDI ARABIA — S / SA
| 1988 | 17 Feb | Riyadh | 2 | 2 |

v SPAIN — S / Sp
wc1957	8 May	Glasgow	4	2
wc1957	26 May	Madrid	1	4
1963	13 June	Madrid	6	2
1965	8 May	Glasgow	0	0
EC1974	20 Nov	Glasgow	1	2
EC1975	5 Feb	Valencia	1	1
1982	24 Feb	Valencia	0	3
wc1984	14 Nov	Glasgow	3	1
wc1985	27 Feb	Seville	0	1
1988	27 Apr	Madrid	0	0

v SWEDEN — S / Sw
1952	30 May	Stockholm	1	3
1953	6 May	Glasgow	1	2
1975	16 Apr	Gothenburg	1	1
1977	27 Apr	Glasgow	3	1
wc1980	10 Sept	Stockholm	1	0
wc1981	9 Sept	Glasgow	2	0
wc1990	16 June	Genoa	2	1

v SWITZERLAND — S / Sw
1931	24 May	Geneva	3	2
1948	17 May	Berne	1	2
1950	26 Apr	Glasgow	3	1
wc1957	19 May	Basle	2	1
wc1957	6 Nov	Glasgow	3	2
1973	22 June	Berne	0	1
1976	7 Apr	Glasgow	1	0
EC1982	17 Nov	Berne	0	2
EC1983	30 May	Glasgow	2	2
EC1990	17 Oct	Glasgow	2	1
EC1991	11 Sept	Berne	2	2

v TURKEY — S / T
| 1960 | 8 June | Ankara | 2 | 4 |

v URUGUAY — S / U
wc1954	19 June	Basle	0	7
1962	2 May	Glasgow	2	3
1983	21 Sept	Glasgow	2	0
wc1986	13 June	Nezahualcayotl	0	0

v USA — S / USA
| 1952 | 30 Apr | Glasgow | 6 | 0 |
| 1992 | 17 May | Denver | 1 | 0 |

v USSR — S / USSR
1967	10 May	Glasgow	0	2
1971	14 June	Moscow	0	1
wc1982	22 June	Malaga	2	2
1991	6 Feb	Glasgow	0	1

v YUGOSLAVIA — S / Y
1955	15 May	Belgrade	2	2
1956	21 Nov	Glasgow	2	0
wc1958	8 June	Vasteras	1	1
1972	29 June	Belo Horizonte	2	2
wc1974	22 June	Frankfurt	1	1
1984	12 Sept	Glasgow	6	1
wc1988	19 Oct	Glasgow	1	1
wc1989	6 Sept	Zagreb	1	3

v ZAIRE — S / Z
| wc1974 | 14 June | Dortmund | 2 | 0 |

WALES

v ARGENTINA

			W	A
1992	3 June	Tokyo	0	1

v AUSTRIA

			W	A
1954	9 May	Vienna	0	2
EC1955	23 Nov	Wrexham	1	2
EC1974	4 Sept	Vienna	1	2
1975	19 Nov	Wrexham	1	0
1992	29 Apr	Vienna	1	1

v BELGIUM

			W	B
1949	22 May	Liège	1	3
1949	23 Nov	Cardiff	5	1
EC1990	17 Oct	Cardiff	3	1
EC1991	27 Mar	Brussels	1	1

v BRAZIL

			W	B
wc1958	19 June	Gothenburg	0	1
1962	12 May	Rio de Janeiro	1	3
1962	16 May	São Paulo	1	3
1966	14 May	Rio de Janeiro	1	3
1966	18 May	Belo Horizonte	0	1
1983	12 June	Cardiff	1	1
1991	11 Sept	Cardiff	1	0

v BULGARIA

			W	B
EC1983	27 Apr	Wrexham	1	0
EC1983	16 Nov	Sofia	0	1

v CANADA

			W	C
1986	10 May	Toronto	0	2
1986	20 May	Vancouver	3	0

v CHILE

			W	C
1966	22 May	Santiago	0	2

v COSTA RICA

			W	CR
1990	20 May	Cardiff	1	0

v CZECHOSLOVAKIA

			W	C
wc1957	1 May	Cardiff	1	0
wc1957	26 May	Prague	0	2
EC1971	21 Apr	Swansea	1	3
EC1971	27 Oct	Prague	0	1
wc1977	30 Mar	Wrexham	3	0
wc1977	16 Nov	Prague	0	1
wc1980	19 Nov	Cardiff	1	0
wc1981	9 Sept	Prague	0	2
EC1987	29 Apr	Wrexham	1	1
EC1987	11 Nov	Prague	0	2

v DENMARK

			W	D
wc1964	21 Oct	Copenhagen	0	1
wc1965	1 Dec	Wrexham	4	2
EC1987	9 Sept	Cardiff	1	0
EC1987	14 Oct	Copenhagen	0	1
1990	11 Sept	Copenhagen	0	1

v FINLAND

			W	F
EC1971	26 May	Helsinki	1	0
EC1971	13 Oct	Swansea	3	0
EC1987	10 Sept	Helsinki	1	1
EC1987	1 Apr	Wrexham	4	0
wc1988	19 Oct	Swansea	2	2
wc1989	6 Sept	Helsinki	0	1

v FRANCE

			W	F
1933	25 May	Paris	1	1
1939	20 May	Paris	1	2
1953	14 May	Paris	1	6
1982	2 June	Toulouse	1	0

v EAST GERMANY

			W	EG
wc1957	19 May	Leipzig	1	2
wc1957	25 Sept	Cardiff	4	1
wc1969	16 Apr	Dresden	1	2
wc1969	22 Oct	Cardiff	1	3

v WEST GERMANY

			W	WG
1968	8 May	Cardiff	1	1
1969	26 Mar	Frankfurt	1	1
1976	6 Oct	Cardiff	0	2
1977	14 Dec	Dortmund	1	1
EC1979	2 May	Wrexham	0	2
EC1979	17 Oct	Cologne	1	5
wc1989	31 May	Cardiff	0	0
wc1989	15 Nov	Cologne	1	2
EC1991	5 June	Cardiff	1	0
EC1991	16 Oct	Nuremburg	1	4

v GREECE

			W	G
wc1964	9 Dec	Athens	0	2
wc1965	17 Mar	Cardiff	4	1

v HOLLAND

			W	H
wc1988	14 Sept	Amsterdam	0	1
wc1989	11 Oct	Wrexham	1	2
1992	30 May	Utrecht	0	4

v HUNGARY

			W	H
wc1958	8 June	Sanviken	1	1
wc1958	17 June	Stockholm	2	1
1961	28 May	Budapest	2	3
EC1962	7 Nov	Budapest	1	3
EC1963	20 Mar	Cardiff	1	1
EC1974	30 Oct	Cardiff	2	0
EC1975	16 Apr	Budapest	2	1
1985	16 Oct	Cardiff	0	3

v ICELAND

			W	I
wc1980	2 June	Reykjavik	4	0
wc1981	14 Oct	Swansea	2	2
wc1984	12 Sept	Reykjavik	0	1
wc1984	14 Nov	Cardiff	2	1
1991	1 May	Cardiff	1	0

v IRAN

			W	I
1978	18 Apr	Teheran	1	0

v REPUBLIC OF IRELAND

			W	RI
1960	28 Sept	Dublin	3	2
1979	11 Sept	Swansea	2	1
1981	24 Feb	Dublin	3	1
1986	26 Mar	Dublin	1	0
1990	28 Mar	Dublin	0	1
1991	6 Feb	Wrexham	0	3
1992	19 Feb	Dublin	1	0

v ISRAEL

			W	I
wc1958	15 Jan	Tel Aviv	2	0
wc1958	5 Feb	Cardiff	2	6
1984	10 June	Tel Aviv	0	0
1989	8 Feb	Tel Aviv	3	3

v ITALY

			W	I
1965	1 May	Florence	1	4
wc1968	23 Oct	Cardiff	0	1
wc1969	4 Nov	Rome	1	4
1988	4 June	Brescia	1	0

v JAPAN

			W	J
1992	7 June	Matsuyama	1	0

		v KUWAIT	W	K
1977	6 Sept	Wrexham	0	0
1977	20 Sept	Kuwait	0	0

		v LUXEMBOURG	W	L
EC1974	20 Nov	Swansea	5	0
EC1975	1 May	Luxembourg	3	1
EC1990	14 Nov	Luxembourg	1	0
EC1991	13 Nov	Cardiff	1	0

		v MALTA	W	M
EC1978	25 Oct	Wrexham	7	0
EC1979	2 June	Valletta	2	0
1988	1 June	Valletta	3	2

		v MEXICO	W	M
wc1958	11 June	Stockholm	1	1
1962	22 May	Mexico City	1	2

		v NORWAY	W	N
EC1982	22 Sept	Swansea	1	0
EC1983	21 Sept	Oslo	0	0
1984	6 June	Trondheim	0	1
1985	26 Feb	Wrexham	1	1
1985	5 June	Bergen	2	4

		v POLAND	W	P
wc1973	28 Mar	Cardiff	2	0
wc1973	26 Sept	Katowice	0	3
1991	29 May	Radom	0	0

		v PORTUGAL	W	P
1949	15 May	Lisbon	2	3
1951	12 May	Cardiff	2	1

		v ROMANIA	W	R
EC1970	11 Nov	Cardiff	0	0
EC1971	24 Nov	Bucharest	0	2
1983	12 Oct	Wrexham	5	0
1992	20 May	Bucharest	1	5

		v SAUDI ARABIA	W	SA
1986	25 Feb	Dahran	2	1

		v SPAIN	W	S
wc1961	19 Apr	Cardiff	1	2
wc1961	18 May	Madrid	1	1
1982	24 Mar	Valencia	1	1
wc1984	17 Oct	Seville	0	3
wc1985	30 Apr	Wrexham	3	0

		v SWEDEN	W	S
wc1958	15 June	Stockholm	0	0
1988	27 Apr	Stockholm	1	4
1989	26 Apr	Wrexham	0	2
1990	25 Apr	Stockholm	2	4

		v SWITZERLAND	W	S
1949	26 May	Berne	0	4
1951	16 May	Wrexham	3	2

		v TURKEY	W	T
EC1978	29 Nov	Wrexham	1	0
EC1979	21 Nov	Izmir	0	1
wc1980	15 Oct	Cardiff	4	0
wc1981	25 Mar	Ankara	1	0

		v REST OF UNITED KINGDOM	W	UK
1951	5 Dec	Cardiff	3	2
1969	28 July	Cardiff	0	1

		v URUGUAY	W	U
1986	21 Apr	Wrexham	0	0

		v USSR	W	USSR
wc1965	30 May	Moscow	1	2
wc1965	27 Oct	Cardiff	2	1
wc1981	30 May	Wrexham	0	0
wc1981	18 Nov	Tbilisi	0	3
1987	18 Feb	Swansea	0	0

		v YUGOSLAVIA	W	Y
1953	21 May	Belgrade	2	5
1954	22 Nov	Cardiff	1	3
EC1976	24 Apr	Zagreb	0	2
EC1976	22 May	Cardiff	1	1
EC1982	15 Dec	Titograd	4	4
EC1983	14 Dec	Cardiff	1	1
1988	23 Mar	Swansea	1	2

NORTHERN IRELAND

		v ALBANIA	NI	A
wc1965	7 May	Belfast	4	1
wc1965	24 Nov	Tirana	1	1
EC1982	15 Dec	Tirana	0	0
EC1983	27 Apr	Belfast	1	0

		v ALGERIA	NI	A
wc1986	3 June	Guadalajara	1	1

		v ARGENTINA	NI	A
wc1958	11 June	Halmstad	1	3

		v AUSTRALIA	NI	A
1980	11 June	Sydney	2	1
1980	15 June	Melbourne	1	1
1980	18 June	Adelaide	2	1

		v AUSTRIA	NI	A
wc1982	1 July	Madrid	2	2
EC1982	13 Oct	Vienna	0	2

			NI	A
EC1983	21 Sept	Belfast	3	1
EC1990	14 Nov	Vienna	0	0
EC1991	11 Sept	Belfast	2	1

		v BELGIUM	NI	B
wc1976	10 Nov	Liège	0	2
wc1977	16 Nov	Belfast	3	0

		v BRAZIL	NI	B
wc1986	12 June	Guadalajara	0	3

		v BULGARIA	NI	B
wc1972	18 Oct	Sofia	0	3
wc1973	26 Sept	Sheffield	0	0
EC1978	29 Nov	Sofia	2	0
EC1979	2 May	Belfast	2	0

		v CHILE	NI	C
1989	26 May	Belfast	0	1

v CYPRUS

			NI	C
EC1971	3 Feb	Nicosia	3	0
EC1971	21 Apr	Belfast	5	0
wc1973	14 Feb	Nicosia	0	1
wc1973	8 May	London	3	0

v CZECHOSLOVAKIA

			NI	C
wc1958	8 June	Halmstad	1	0
wc1958	17 June	Malmo	2	1*

*After extra time

v DENMARK

			NI	D
EC1978	25 Oct	Belfast	2	1
EC1979	6 June	Copenhagen	0	4
1986	26 Mar	Belfast	1	1
EC1990	17 Oct	Belfast	1	1
EC1991	13 Nov	Odense	1	2

v FAEROES

			NI	F
EC1991	1 May	Belfast	1	1
EC1991	11 Sept	Landskrona	5	0

v FINLAND

			NI	F
wc1984	27 May	Pori	0	1
wc1984	14 Nov	Belfast	2	1

v FRANCE

			NI	F
1951	12 May	Belfast	2	2
1952	11 Nov	Paris	1	3
wc1958	19 June	Norrkoping	0	4
1982	24 Mar	Paris	0	4
wc1982	4 July	Madrid	1	4
1986	26 Feb	Paris	0	0
1988	27 Apr	Belfast	0	0

v GERMANY

			NI	G
1992	2 June	Bremen	1	1

v WEST GERMANY

			NI	WG
wc1958	15 June	Malmo	2	2
wc1960	26 Oct	Belfast	3	4
wc1961	10 May	Hamburg	1	2
1966	7 May	Belfast	0	2
1977	27 Apr	Cologne	0	5
EC1982	17 Nov	Belfast	1	0
EC1983	16 Nov	Hamburg	1	0

v GREECE

			NI	G
wc1961	3 May	Athens	1	2
wc1961	17 Oct	Belfast	2	0
1988	17 Feb	Athens	2	3

v HOLLAND

			NI	H
1962	9 May	Rotterdam	0	4
wc1965	17 Mar	Belfast	2	1
wc1965	7 Apr	Rotterdam	0	0
wc1976	13 Oct	Rotterdam	2	2
wc1977	12 Oct	Belfast	0	1

v HONDURAS

			NI	H
wc1982	21 June	Zaragoza	1	1

v HUNGARY

			NI	H
wc1988	19 Oct	Budapest	0	1
wc1989	6 Sept	Belfast	1	2

v ICELAND

			NI	I
wc1977	11 June	Reykjavik	0	1
wc1977	21 Sept	Belfast	2	0

v REPUBLIC OF IRELAND

			NI	RI
EC1978	20 Sept	Dublin	0	0
EC1979	21 Nov	Belfast	1	0
wc1988	14 Sept	Belfast	0	0
wc1989	11 Oct	Dublin	0	3

v ISRAEL

			NI	I
1968	10 Sept	Jaffa	3	2
1976	3 Mar	Tel Aviv	1	1
wc1980	26 Mar	Tel Aviv	0	0
wc1981	18 Nov	Belfast	1	0
1984	16 Oct	Belfast	3	0
1987	18 Feb	Tel Aviv	1	1

v ITALY

			NI	I
wc1957	25 Apr	Rome	0	1
1957	4 Dec	Belfast	2	2
wc1958	15 Jan	Belfast	2	1
1961	25 Apr	Bologna	2	3

v LITHUANIA

			NI	L
wc1992	28 Apr	Belfast	2	2

v MALTA

			NI	M
1988	21 May	Belfast	3	0
wc1989	26 Apr	Valletta	2	0

v MEXICO

			NI	M
1966	22 June	Belfast	4	1

v MOROCCO

			NI	M
1986	23 Apr	Belfast	2	1

v NORWAY

			NI	N
EC1974	4 Sept	Oslo	1	2
EC1975	29 Oct	Belfast	3	0
1990	27 Mar	Belfast	2	3

v POLAND

			NI	P
EC1962	10 Oct	Katowice	2	0
EC1962	28 Nov	Belfast	2	0
1988	23 Mar	Belfast	1	1
1991	5 Feb	Belfast	3	1

v PORTUGAL

			NI	P
wc1957	16 Jan	Lisbon	1	1
wc1957	1 May	Belfast	3	0
wc1973	28 Mar	Coventry	1	1
wc1973	14 Nov	Lisbon	1	1
wc1980	19 Nov	Lisbon	0	1
wc1981	29 Apr	Belfast	1	0

v ROMANIA

			NI	R
wc1984	12 Sept	Belfast	3	2
wc1985	16 Oct	Bucharest	1	0

v SPAIN

			NI	S
1958	15 Oct	Madrid	2	6
1963	30 May	Bilbao	1	1
1963	30 Oct	Belfast	0	1
EC1970	11 Nov	Seville	0	3
EC1972	16 Feb	Hull	1	1
wc1982	25 June	Valencia	1	0
1985	27 Mar	Palma	0	0
wc1986	7 June	Guadalajara	1	2
wc1988	21 Dec	Seville	0	4
wc1989	8 Feb	Belfast	0	2

v SWEDEN

			NI	S
EC1974	30 Oct	Solna	2	0
EC1975	3 Sept	Belfast	1	2
wc1980	15 Oct	Belfast	3	0
wc1981	3 June	Solna	0	1

v SWITZERLAND

			NI	S
wc1964	14 Oct	Belfast	1	0
wc1964	14 Nov	Lausanne	1	2

		v TURKEY	NI	T
wc1968	23 Oct	Belfast	4	1
wc1968	11 Dec	Istanbul	3	0
EC1983	30 Mar	Belfast	2	1
EC1983	12 Oct	Ankara	0	1
wc1985	1 May	Belfast	2	0
wc1985	11 Sept	Izmir	0	0
EC1986	12 Nov	Izmir	0	0
EC1987	11 Nov	Belfast	1	0

		v URUGUAY	NI	U
1964	29 Apr	Belfast	3	0
1990	18 May	Belfast	1	0

		v USSR	NI	USSR
wc1969	19 Sept	Belfast	0	0
wc1969	22 Oct	Moscow	0	2
EC1971	22 Sept	Moscow	0	1
EC1971	13 Oct	Belfast	1	1

		v YUGOSLAVIA	NI	Y
EC1975	16 Mar	Belfast	1	0
EC1975	19 Nov	Belgrade	0	1
wc1982	17 June	Zaragoza	0	0
EC1987	29 Apr	Belfast	1	2
EC1987	14 Oct	Sarajevo	0	3
EC1990	12 Sept	Belfast	0	2
EC1991	27 Mar	Belgrade	1	4

REPUBLIC OF IRELAND

		v ALBANIA	RI	A
wc1992	26 May	Dublin	2	0

		v ALGERIA	RI	A
1982	28 Apr	Algiers	0	2

		v ARGENTINA	RI	A
1951	13 May	Dublin	0	1
1979	29 May	Dublin	0	0*
1980	16 May	Dublin	0	1

*Not considered a full international

		v AUSTRIA	RI	A
1952	7 May	Vienna	0	6
1953	25 Mar	Dublin	4	0
1958	14 Mar	Vienna	1	3
1962	8 Apr	Dublin	2	3
EC1963	25 Sept	Vienna	0	0
EC1963	13 Oct	Dublin	3	2
1966	22 May	Vienna	0	1
1968	10 Nov	Dublin	2	2
EC1971	30 May	Dublin	1	4
EC1971	10 Oct	Linz	0	6

		v BELGIUM	RI	B
1928	12 Feb	Liège	4	2
1929	30 Apr	Dublin	4	0
1930	11 May	Brussels	3	1
wc1934	25 Feb	Dublin	4	4
1949	24 Apr	Dublin	0	2
1950	10 May	Brussels	1	5
1965	24 Mar	Dublin	0	2
1966	25 May	Liège	3	2
wc1980	15 Oct	Dublin	1	1
wc1981	25 Mar	Brussels	0	1
EC1986	10 Sept	Brussels	2	2
EC1987	29 Apr	Dublin	0	0

		v BRAZIL	RI	B
1974	5 May	Rio de Janeiro	1	2
1982	27 May	Uberlandia	0	7
1987	23 May	Dublin	1	0

		v BULGARIA	RI	B
wc1977	1 June	Sofia	1	2
wc1977	12 Oct	Dublin	0	0
EC1979	19 May	Sofia	0	1
EC1979	17 Oct	Dublin	3	0
wc1987	1 Apr	Sofia	1	2
wc1987	14 Oct	Dublin	2	0

		v CHILE	RI	C
1960	30 Mar	Dublin	2	0
1972	21 June	Recife	1	2
			RI	C
1974	12 May	Santiago	2	1
1982	22 May	Santiago	0	1
1991	22 May	Dublin	1	1

		v CYPRUS	RI	C
wc1980	26 Mar	Nicosia	3	2
wc1980	19 Nov	Dublin	6	0

		v CZECHOSLOVAKIA	RI	C
1938	18 May	Prague	2	2
EC1959	5 Apr	Dublin	2	0
EC1959	10 May	Bratislava	0	4
wc1961	8 Oct	Dublin	1	3
wc1961	29 Oct	Prague	1	7
EC1967	21 May	Dublin	0	2
EC1967	22 Nov	Prague	2	1
wc1969	4 May	Dublin	1	2
wc1969	7 Oct	Prague	0	3
1979	26 Sept	Prague	1	4
1981	29 Apr	Dublin	3	1
1986	27 May	Reykjavik	1	0

		v DENMARK	RI	D
wc1956	3 Oct	Dublin	2	1
wc1957	2 Oct	Copenhagen	2	0
wc1968	4 Dec	Dublin	1	1
	(abandoned after 51 mins)			
wc1969	27 May	Copenhagen	0	2
wc1969	15 Oct	Dublin	1	1
EC1978	24 May	Copenhagen	3	3
EC1979	2 May	Dublin	2	0
wc1984	14 Nov	Copenhagen	0	3
wc1985	13 Nov	Dublin	1	4

		v ECUADOR	RI	E
1972	19 June	Natal	3	2

		v EGYPT	RI	E
wc1990	17 June	Palermo	0	0

		v ENGLAND	RI	E
1946	30 Sept	Dublin	0	1
1949	21 Sept	Everton	2	0
wc1957	8 May	Wembley	1	5
wc1957	19 May	Dublin	1	1
1964	24 May	Dublin	1	3
1976	8 Sept	Wembley	1	1
EC1978	25 Oct	Dublin	1	1
EC1980	6 Feb	Wembley	0	2
1985	26 Mar	Wembley	1	2
EC1988	12 June	Stuttgart	1	0
wc1990	11 June	Cagliari	1	1
EC1990	14 Nov	Dublin	1	1
EC1991	27 Mar	Wembley	1	1

		v FINLAND	RI	F
wc1949	8 Sept	Dublin	3	0
wc1949	9 Oct	Helsinki	1	1
1990	16 May	Dublin	1	1

		v FRANCE	RI	F
1937	23 May	Paris	2	0
1952	16 Nov	Dublin	1	1
wc1953	4 Oct	Dublin	3	5
wc1953	25 Nov	Paris	0	1
wc1972	15 Nov	Dublin	2	1
wc1973	19 May	Paris	1	1
wc1976	17 Nov	Paris	0	2
wc1977	30 Mar	Dublin	1	0
wc1980	28 Oct	Paris	0	2
wc1981	14 Oct	Dublin	3	2
1989	7 Feb	Dublin	0	0

		v GERMANY	RI	G
1935	8 May	Dortmund	1	3
1936	17 Oct	Dublin	5	2
1939	23 May	Bremen	1	1

		v WEST GERMANY	RI	WG
1951	17 Oct	Dublin	3	2
1952	4 May	Cologne	0	3
1955	28 May	Hamburg	1	2
1956	25 Nov	Dublin	3	0
1960	11 May	Dusseldorf	1	0
1966	4 May	Dublin	0	4
1970	9 May	Berlin	1	2
1975	1 Mar	Dublin	1	0†
1979	22 May	Dublin	1	3
1981	21 May	Bremen	0	3†
1989	6 Sept	Dublin	1	1

†v West Germany 'B'

		v HOLLAND	RI	H
1932	8 May	Amsterdam	2	0
1934	8 Apr	Amsterdam	2	5
1935	8 Dec	Dublin	3	5
1955	1 May	Dublin	1	0
1956	10 May	Rotterdam	4	1
wc1980	10 Sept	Dublin	2	1
wc1981	9 Sept	Rotterdam	2	2
EC1982	22 Sept	Rotterdam	1	2
EC1983	12 Oct	Dublin	2	3
EC1988	18 June	Gelsenkirchen	0	1
wc1990	21 June	Palermo	1	1

		v HUNGARY	RI	H
1934	15 Dec	Dublin	2	4
1936	3 May	Budapest	3	3
1936	6 Dec	Dublin	2	3
1939	19 Mar	Cork	2	2
1939	18 May	Budapest	2	2
wc1969	8 June	Dublin	1	2
wc1969	5 Nov	Budapest	0	4
wc1989	8 Mar	Budapest	0	2
wc1989	4 June	Dublin	2	0
1991	11 Sept	Gyor	2	1

		v ICELAND	RI	I
EC1962	12 Aug	Dublin	4	2
EC1962	2 Sept	Reykjavik	1	1
EC1982	13 Oct	Dublin	2	0
EC1983	21 Sept	Reykjavik	3	0
1986	25 May	Reykjavik	2	1

		v IRAN	RI	I
1972	18 June	Recife	2	1

		v N. IRELAND	RI	NI
EC1978	20 Sept	Dublin	0	0
EC1979	21 Nov	Belfast	0	1
wc1988	14 Sept	Belfast	0	0
wc1989	11 Oct	Dublin	3	0

		v ISRAEL	RI	I
1984	4 Apr	Tel Aviv	0	3
1985	27 May	Tel Aviv	0	0
1987	10 Nov	Dublin	5	0

		v ITALY	RI	I
1926	21 Mar	Turin	0	3
1927	23 Apr	Dublin	1	2
EC1970	8 Dec	Rome	0	3
EC1971	10 May	Dublin	1	2
1985	5 Feb	Dublin	1	2
wc 1990	30 June	Rome	0	1
1992	4 June	Foxboro	0	2

		v LUXEMBOURG	RI	L
1936	9 May	Luxembourg	5	1
wc1953	28 Oct	Dublin	4	0
wc1954	7 Mar	Luxembourg	1	0
EC1987	28 May	Luxembourg	2	0
EC1987	9 Sept	Dublin	2	1

		v MALTA	RI	M
EC1983	30 Mar	Valletta	1	0
EC1983	16 Nov	Dublin	8	0
wc1989	28 May	Dublin	2	0
wc1989	15 Nov	Valletta	2	0
1990	2 June	Valletta	3	0

		v MEXICO	RI	M
1984	8 Aug	Dublin	0	0

		v MOROCCO	RI	M
1990	12 Sept	Dublin	1	0

		v NORWAY	RI	N
wc1937	10 Oct	Oslo	2	3
wc1937	7 Nov	Dublin	3	3
1950	26 Nov	Dublin	2	2
1951	30 May	Oslo	3	2
1954	8 Nov	Dublin	2	1
1955	25 May	Oslo	3	1
1960	6 Nov	Dublin	3	1
1964	13 May	Oslo	4	1
1973	6 June	Oslo	1	1
1976	24 Mar	Dublin	3	0
1978	21 May	Oslo	0	0
wc1984	17 Oct	Oslo	0	1
wc1985	1 May	Dublin	0	0
1988	1 June	Oslo	0	0

		v POLAND	RI	P
1938	22 May	Warsaw	0	6
1938	13 Nov	Dublin	3	2
1958	11 May	Katowice	2	2
1958	5 Oct	Dublin	2	2
1964	10 May	Cracow	1	3
1964	25 Oct	Dublin	3	2
1968	15 May	Dublin	2	2
1968	30 Oct	Katowice	0	1
1970	6 May	Dublin	1	2
1970	23 Sept	Dublin	0	2
1973	16 May	Wroclaw	0	2
1973	21 Oct	Dublin	1	0

			RI	P
1976	26 May	Poznan	2	0
1977	24 Apr	Dublin	0	0
1978	12 Apr	Lodz	0	3
1981	23 May	Bydgoszcz	0	3
1984	23 May	Dublin	0	0
1986	12 Nov	Warsaw	0	1
1988	22 May	Dublin	3	1
EC1991	1 May	Dublin	0	0
EC1991	16 Oct	Poznan	3	3

v PORTUGAL

			RI	P
1946	16 June	Lisbon	1	3
1947	4 May	Dublin	0	2
1948	23 May	Lisbon	0	2
1949	22 May	Dublin	1	0
1972	25 June	Recife	1	2
1992	7 June	Boston	2	0

v ROMANIA

			RI	R
1988	23 Mar	Dublin	2	0
wc1990	25 June	Genoa	0	0

v SCOTLAND

			RI	S
wc1961	3 May	Glasgow	1	4
wc1961	7 May	Dublin	0	3
1963	9 June	Dublin	1	0
1969	21 Sept	Dublin	1	1
EC1986	15 Oct	Dublin	0	0
EC1987	18 Feb	Glasgow	1	0

v SPAIN

			RI	S
1931	26 Apr	Barcelona	1	1
1931	13 Dec	Dublin	0	5
1946	23 June	Madrid	1	0
1947	2 Mar	Dublin	3	2
1948	30 May	Barcelona	1	2
1949	12 June	Dublin	1	4
1952	1 June	Madrid	0	6
1955	27 Nov	Dublin	2	2
EC1964	11 Mar	Seville	1	5
EC1964	8 Apr	Dublin	0	2
wc1965	5 May	Dublin	1	0
wc1965	27 Oct	Seville	1	4
wc1965	10 Nov	Paris	0	1
EC1966	23 Oct	Dublin	0	0
EC1966	7 Dec	Valencia	0	2
1977	9 Feb	Dublin	0	1
EC1982	17 Nov	Dublin	3	3
EC1983	27 Apr	Zaragoza	0	2
wc1985	26 May	Cork	0	0
wc1988	16 Nov	Seville	0	2
wc1989	26 Apr	Dublin	1	0

v SWEDEN

			RI	S
wc1949	2 June	Stockholm	1	3
wc1949	13 Nov	Dublin	1	3
1959	1 Nov	Dublin	3	2
1960	18 May	Malmo	1	4
EC1970	14 Oct	Dublin	1	1
EC1970	28 Oct	Malmo	0	1

v SWITZERLAND

			RI	S
1935	5 May	Basle	0	1
1936	17 Mar	Dublin	1	0
1937	17 May	Berne	1	0
1938	18 Sept	Dublin	4	0
1948	5 Dec	Dublin	0	1
EC1975	11 May	Dublin	2	1
EC1975	21 May	Berne	0	1
1980	30 Apr	Dublin	2	0
wc1985	2 June	Dublin	3	0
wc1985	11 Sept	Berne	0	0
1992	25 Mar	Dublin	2	1

v TRINIDAD & TOBAGO

			RI	TT
1982	30 May	Port of Spain	1	2

v TUNISIA

			RI	T
1988	19 Oct	Dublin	4	0

v TURKEY

			RI	T
EC1966	16 Nov	Dublin	2	1
EC1967	22 Feb	Ankara	1	2
EC1974	20 Nov	Izmir	1	1
EC1975	29 Oct	Dublin	4	0
1976	13 Oct	Ankara	3	3
1978	5 Apr	Dublin	4	2
1990	26 May	Izmir	0	0
EC1990	17 Oct	Dublin	5	0
EC1991	13 Nov	Istanbul	3	1

v URUGUAY

			RI	U
1974	8 May	Montevideo	0	2
1986	23 Apr	Dublin	1	1

v USA

			RI	USA
1979	29 Oct	Dublin	3	2
1991	1 June	Boston	1	1
1992	29 Apr	Dublin	4	1
1992	30 May	Washington	1	3

v USSR

			RI	USSR
wc1972	18 Oct	Dublin	1	2
wc1973	13 May	Moscow	0	1
EC1974	30 Oct	Dublin	3	0
EC1975	18 May	Kiev	1	2
wc1984	12 Sept	Dublin	1	0
wc1985	16 Oct	Moscow	0	2
EC1988	15 June	Hanover	1	1
1990	25 Apr	Dublin	1	0

v WALES

			RI	W
1960	28 Sept	Dublin	2	3
1979	11 Sept	Swansea	1	2
1981	24 Feb	Dublin	1	3
1986	26 Mar	Dublin	0	1
1990	28 Mar	Dublin	1	0
1991	6 Feb	Wrexham	3	0
1992	19 Feb	Dublin	0	1

v YUGOSLAVIA

			RI	Y
1955	19 Sept	Dublin	1	4
1988	27 Apr	Dublin	2	0

OTHER INTERNATIONAL MATCHES 1991

January
Spain 1, Portugal 1
Mexico 0, Colombia 0
Australia 0, Czechoslovakia 1

February
Northern Ireland 3, Poland 1
Scotland 1, USSR 0
Australia 0, Czechoslovakia 2
Wales 0, Republic of Ireland 3
England 2, Cameroon 0
Italy 0, Belgium 0
Senegal 0, Ivory Coast 0
Algeria 0, Cameroon 0
Cameroon 2, Ivory Coast 3
Senegal 1, Algeria 3
Argentina 2, Hungary 0
Bermuda 1, USA 0
Turkey 1, Yugoslavia 1
Brazil 1, Paraguay 1
Cyprus 1, Greece 1

March
Algeria 2, Tunisia 1
Liechtenstein 0, Switzerland 6
Argentina 0, Mexico 0
Poland 1, Finland 1
Spain 2, Hungary 4
Germany 2, USSR 1
Argentina 3, Brazil 3
Morocco 0, Greece 0
Czechoslovakia 4, Poland 0
Tunisia 0, Turkey 0

April
Tunisia 0, Algeria 0
Mexico 1, Chile 0
Denmark 1, Bulgaria 1
Spain 0, Romania 2
Brazil 1, Romania 0
Austria 0, Norway 0

May
Wales 1, Iceland 0
Sweden 6, Austria 0
USA 1, Uruguay 0
Mexico 0, Uruguay 2
New Zealand 0, Australia 1
Australia 2, New Zealand 1
USA 0, Argentina 1
Republic of Ireland 1, Chile 1
Norway 1, Romania 0
Brazil 3, Bulgaria 0
Poland 0, Wales 0
Chile 2, Uruguay 1

June
USA 1, Republic of Ireland 1
Australia 0, England 1
New Zealand 0, England 1
Sweden 2, Colombia 2
New Zealand 0, England 2
Italy 2, Denmark 0
Sweden 2, USSR 3
Sweden 4, Denmark 0
Italy 1, USSR 1

Paraguay 0, Bolivia 0
Ecuador 2, Chile 1
Uruguay 0, Peru 0
Ecuador 2, Peru 2
Costa Rica 0, Colombia 1
Uruguay 2, Chile 1
Brazil 1, Argentina 1
Gambia 2, Ghana 3
Chile 3, Ecuador 1

July
Malawi 0, Kenya 2
Gabon 0, Ghana 1
Malawi 1, Kenya 1
Malawi 1, Kenya 1
Faeroes 1, Turkey 1
Iceland 5, Turkey 1
Ivory Coast 0, Guinea 0
Japan 0, South Korea 1

August
Sweden 2, Norway 0
Norway 1, Sweden 2
Malawi 1, Mozambique 0
Malawi 2, Mozambique 0
Czechoslovakia 1, Switzerland 1
Poland 2, Sweden 0
Bulgaria 0, Turkey 0

September
Sweden 4, Yugoslavia 3
Spain 2, Uruguay 1
Turkey 1, USA 1
Portugal 1, Austria 1
Mali 0, Guinea 0
Wales 1, Brazil 0
Hungary 1, Republic of Ireland 2
Holland 1, Poland 1
England 0, Germany 1
Bermuda 1, Jamaica 1
USA 1, Jamaica 0
Norway 2, Czechoslovakia 3
Bulgaria 2, Italy 1

October
Singapore 2, Indonesia 0
Switzerland 3, Sweden 1
Luxembourg 1, Portugal 1
Cyprus 1, Iceland 1
USA 1, North Korea 2

November
Mexico 1, Uruguay 1
Ivory Coast 5, Niger 2
USA 1, Costa Rica 1
Malta 2, Libya 0
Tunisia 5, Ivory Coast 3

December
Egypt 3, Poland 0
Mexico 3, Hungary 0
Egypt 0, Poland 0
Egypt 1, Romania 1
Tunisia 2, Cameroon 2
Malawi 0, Zambia 2

OTHER BRITISH AND IRISH INTERNATIONAL MATCHES 1991–92

Wembley, 11 September 1991, 59,493

England (0) 0

Germany (1) 1 *(Riedle 45)*

England: Woods; Dixon, Dorigo, Batty, Pallister, Parker, Platt, Steven (Stewart 67), Smith, Lineker, Salako (Merson 67).
Germany: Illgner; Binz, Brehme, Kohler, Effenberg, Buchwald, Moller, Hassler, Riedle, Matthaus, Doll (Klinsmann 82).

Gyor, 11 September 1991, 4000

Hungary (0) 1 *(Kovacs K 50)*

Republic of Ireland (0) 2 *(Kelly 51, Sheedy 70)*

Hungary: Petry; Monos (Rugovics 73), Disztl, Csehi, Lipcsei, Lorincz, Kozma, Kovacs E (Berczy 53), Vincze (Eszenyi 63), Detari, Kovacs K.
Republic of Ireland: Bonner; Irwin, Phelan (Morris 81), O'Leary, McCarthy, Sheridan (McLoughlin 46), Keane, Houghton, Quinn, Kelly (Aldridge 63), Sheedy.

Cardiff Arms Park, 11 September 1991, 20,000

Wales (0) 1 *(Saunders 58)*

Brazil (0) 0

Wales: Southall; Pembridge, Bodin (Bowen 67), Aizlewood, Melville, Ratcliffe (Maguire 87), Pascoe (Hodges 76), Horne, Saunders, Hughes, Speed.
Brazil: Taffarel; Cafu (Cassio 60), Cieber, Marcio Santos, Mauro Silva, Jorginho, Moacir (Valdir 60), Geovani (Mazino II 74), Careca, Bebeto, Joao Paulo.

Wembley, 19 February 1992, 58,723

England (1) 2 *(Shearer 44, Lineker 73)*

France (0) 0

England: Woods; Jones, Pearce, Keown, Walker, Wright, Webb, Thomas, Clough, Shearer, Hirst (Lineker 46).
France: Rousset; Amoros, Angloma, Boli, Blanc, Casoni, Deschamps, Fernandez (Durand 71), Papin, Perez (Simba 71), Cantona.

Dublin, 19 February 1992, 15,100

Republic of Ireland (0) 0

Wales (0) 1 *(Pembridge 72)*

Republic of Ireland: Bonner; Morris, Irwin, O'Leary, Daish, Townsend (McLoughlin 46), Phelan (Aldridge 55), Byrne, Keane, Cascarino (Quinn 67), Sheedy.
Wales: Southall; Phillips, Bowen, Aizlewood, Young (Bodin 63), Symons, Horne, Speed (Blackmore 46), Saunders (Nielsen 86), Hughes, Pembridge (Hodges 76).

Hampden Park, 19 February 1992, 13,650

Scotland (1) 1 *(McCoist 11)*

Northern Ireland (0) 0

Scotland: Smith; McKimmie (Durie 46), Robertson D, McPherson, Gough, Malpas, Strachan, McClair (Collins 66), McCoist (Gallacher 46), McAllister, Wright (Robertson J 76).
Northern Ireland: Wright; Donaghy, Worthington, Taggart (Morrow 85), McDonald, Magilton, Black, Wilson K (O'Neil 81), Clarke (Dowie 46), Wilson D, Hughes.

Prague, 25 March 1992, 3300

Czechoslovakia (1) 2 *(Skuhravy 20, Chovanec 58)*

England (1) 2 *(Merson 27, Keown 66)*

Czechoslovakia: Miklosko; Hapal, Kadlec, Kula (Frydek 86), Glonek, Nemecek (Memec 82), Bilek, Chovanec, Kubik, Skuhravy, Knoflicek (Siegel 87).
England: Seaman; Keown, Pearce, Rocastle (Dixon 46), Walker, Mabbutt (Lineker 73), Platt, Merson, Clough (Stewart 46), Hateley, Barnes (Dorigo 52).

Dublin, 25 March 1992, 23,601

Republic of Ireland (1) 2 *(Schepull 27 (og), Aldridge 88 (pen))*

Switzerland (1) 1 *(Whelan 25 (og))*

Republic of Ireland: Bonner; Morris, Phelan, O'Leary, McGrath, Keane, Whelan, McGoldrick (O'Brien 46), Coyne (Aldridge 80), Cascarino, Staunton (Sheedy 55).
Switzerland: Brunner (Pascolo 40); Ohrei (Rothenbuhler 51), Gamperle, Schepull, Egli, Geiger, Piffaretti, Bickel (Heldmann 66), Turkyilmaz, Sutter A, Chapuisat (Dietlin 81).

Hampden Park 25 March 1992, 9275

Scotland (1) 1 *(McStay 24)*

Finland (1) 1 *(Litmanen 41)*

Scotland: Goram; McKimmie, Boyd, Bowman, McPherson, Malpas, Strachan (McAllister 65), McStay, Robertson J (McCoist 54), Collins, Durie.
Finland: Huttunen; Rinne (Nyysonnen 88), Heikkinen, Petaja, Eriksson, Remes, Litmanen, Myyry, Jarvinen, Tarkkio (Vahala 69), Paatelainen.

Moscow, 29 April 1992, 25,000

CIS (1) 2 *(Tzhadadze 43, Kiryakov 55)*

England (1) 2 *(Lineker 15, Steven 71)*

CIS: Kharin; Chernishev, Tzhadadze, Tsveiba, Ledyskhov (Kiryakov 46), Shalimov, Mikhailichenko, Kanchelskis (Karpin 63), Kolyvanov (Lyuty 46), Mostovoi, Youran (Onopko 55).
England: Woods (Martyn 79); Stevens, Sinton (Curle 63), Palmer, Walker, Keown, Platt, Steven (Stewart 77), Shearer (Clough 63), Lineker, Daley.

Dublin, 29 April 1992, 27,000

Republic of Ireland (0) 4 *(Townsend 47, Irwin 52, Quinn 68, Cascarino 87)*

USA (0) 1 *(Wynalda 89)*

Republic of Ireland: Peyton; Morris, Irwin (Milligan 62), O'Leary (Carey 72), McGrath, Townsend, McGoldrick, McLoughlin, Quinn (Cascarino 72), Coyne (Aldridge 82), Staunton.
USA: Meola; Balboa, Savage (Ibsen 72), Armstrong, Doyle, Clavijo, Quinn, Perez (Kinnear 69), Harkes, Wynalda, Vernes (Eck 82).

Vienna, 29 April 1992, 53,000

Austria (0) 1 *(Bauer 59)*

Wales (0) 1 *(Coleman 83)*

Austria: Konsel; Streiter, Rotter, Flogel, Zsak, Prosenik, Ogris (Hasenhutti 44), Stoger, Polster, Herzog (Schottel 79), Gager (Bauer 46).
Wales: Southall; Phillips, Bowen, Aizlewood, Young (Coleman), Blackmore, Goss (Rees 87), Allen (Nogan 75), Roberts, Horne, Hodges (Hall 59).

Budapest, 12 May 1992, 25,000
Hungary (0) 0
England (0) 1 *(Telek 56 (og))*

Hungary: Brochauser; Simon, Telek, Szalma (Kecskes 41), Lorincz, Limperger, Kiprich, Kovacs E, Pisont, Lipcsei, Vincze.
England: Martyn (Seaman 46), Stevens, Dorigo, Curle (Sinton 46), Walker, Keown, Webb (Batty 70), Palmer, Merson (Smith 46), Lineker (Wright 70), Daley.

Wembley, 17 May 1992, 53,428
England (0) 1 *(Platt 49)*
Brazil (1) 1 *(Bebeto 25)*

England: Woods; Stevens, Dorigo (Pearce 72), Palmer, Walker, Keown, Daley (Merson 72), Steven (Webb 46), Platt, Lineker, Sinton (Rocastle 46).
Brazil: Carlos, Winck (Charles 46), Mozer, Ricardo, Mauro Silva, Branco, Bebeto, Henrique (Valdir 74), Renato (Junior 78), Rai, Valdo (Paulo Sergio 72).

Denver, 17 May 1992, 24,157
USA (0) 0
Scotland (1) 1 *(Nevin 7)*

USA: Keller; Balboa, Armstrong, Doyle, Clavijo, Michallik (Gibson 71), Quinn, Henderson, Perez, Kinnear, Wynalda.
Scotland: Marshall; McKimmie, McLaren, McStay (McInally 68), McPherson (Whyte 82), Malpas, Nevin (Ferguson 50), McCall, McClair, McCoist (Bowman 76), McAllister.

Toronto, 21 May 1992, 10,872
Canada (1) 1 *(Catliff 45)*
Scotland (1) 3 *(McAllister 22, 85 (pen), McCoist 68)*

Canada: Forrest; Dasovic, Miller, Samuel, Sarantopoulos, Yallop, Limniatis (Hooper 59), Odinga, Valentine, Catliff (Aunger 78), Mobilio (Bunbury 46).
Scotland: Smith; Boyd, McLaren, McStay, Gough, McPherson, Durie (Malpas 78), McCall (McKimmie 90), Ferguson (McClair 54), McCoist, McAllister.

Utrecht, 30 May 1992, 20,000
Holland (2) 4 *(Gullit 16, 37, Winter 74, Jonk 83)*
Wales (0) 0

Holland: Van Breukelen; Van Aerle, Van Tiggelen (De Boer 17), Blind, Witschge, Wouters (Jonk 74), Bergkamp (Bosz 65), Rijkaard (Winter 46), Van Basten (Kieft 46), Gullit (Van't Schip 46), Roy.
Wales: Southall; Bodin (Phillips 52), Speed, Blackmore (Hughes C 82), Melville, Symons, Horne, Pembridge (Bowen 60), Saunders, Hughes M, Aizlewood.

Washington, 30 May 1992, 35,696
USA (0) 3 *(Perez 54, Balboa 70, Harkes 87)*
Republic of Ireland (0) 1 *(McCarthy 51)*

USA: Meola; Balboa, Doyle, Dooley, Caligiuri, Quinn, Harkes, Ramos (Michallik 78), Murray (Henderson 46) (Clavijo 59), Perez (Stewart 57), Vermes (Wegerle 46).
Republic of Ireland: Peyton; Morris (Irwin 78), Phelan, McGrath, McCarthy, Moran, Houghton, Keane, Quinn, Townsend, Staunton (Coyne 60).

Bremen, 2 June 1992, 24,000
Germany (1) 1 *(Binz 40)*
Northern Ireland (1) 1 *(Hughes 22)*

Germany: Illgner; Reuter, Brehme, Kohler, Binz, Buchwald, Hassler (Doll 46), Voller, Riedle, Sammer (Thom), Effenberg.
Northern Ireland: Wright; Fleming, Worthington, Taggart, McDonald, Donaghy, Black (Morrow 78), Magilton, Clarke (O'Neill 87), Wilson K, Hughes.

Helsinki, 3 June 1992, 16,101
Finland (1) 1 *(Hjelm 27 (pen))*
England (1) 2 *(Platt 45, 62)*

Finland: Huttunen; Rinne (Vanhala 79), Jarvinen, Petaja, Holmgren (Heikkinen 46), Kinnunen, Litmanen (Vurolea 89), Myyry, Hjelm, Tarkkio (Tetelberg 67), Huhtamaki.
England: Woods; Stevens (Palmer 46), Pearce, Keown, Walker, Wright, Platt, Steven (Daley 82), Webb, Lineker, Barnes (Merson 12).

Oslo, 3 June 1992, 8786
Norway (0) 0
Scotland (0) 0

Norway: Grodas; Berg, Bjornebye, Bratseth, Nilsen, Petersen (Mykland 30), Bohinen (Brigtfen 76), Rekdal, Leonhardsen, Dahlum (Flo 73), Strandli.
Scotland: Goram; McLaren, Malpas (McKimmie 68), Gough, McPherson, Boyd, McCall, McStay, McClair (Gallagher 46), McCoist (Durie 46), McAllister (McInally 78).

Gifu (Tokyo), 3 June 1992, 31,000
Argentina (0) 1 *(Batistuta 88)*
Wales (0) 0

Argentina: Islas; Basualdo, Vazquez, Ruggeri, Altamirano, Villarreal, Cagna, Rodriguez (Acosta 55), Franco, Batistuta, Caniggia.
Wales: Southall; Aizlewood, Phillips, Bodin, Blackmore, Symond, Horne, Speed, Saunders, Hughes, Roberts.

Foxboro, 4 June 1992, 34,797
Italy (1) 2 *(Signori 17, Costacurta 67 (pen))*
Republic of Ireland (0) 0

Italy: Zenga; Baresi, Maldine, Costacurta, Bianchi, Galia, Fusi, Carboni, Signori, Mancini (Vialli), Casiraghi.
Republic of Ireland: Bonner; Staunton, Irwin (Peyton), McGrath, O'Leary, McCarthy (McLoughlin), Houghton, McGoldrick (Phelan), Quinn (Coyne), Aldridge (Kelly), Townsend.

Matsuyama, 7 June 1992, 30,000
Japan (0) 0
Wales (1) 1 *(Bowen 40)*

Japan: Maekawa, Meura, Katuya, Horilke, Ahashiratani, Tsunami (Yoshide 60), Ihara, Takeda (Takegi 74), Hirekawi, Moriyasw, Kitazawi.
Wales: Southall; Phillips, Aizlewood (Melville 68), Blackmore, Symons, Bowen, Speed, Horne, Saunders (Pembridge 80), Hughes, Roberts.

Boston, 7 June 1992, 41,227
Portugal (0) 0
Republic of Ireland (1) 2 *(Staunton, Coyne)*

Portugal: Vitor Baia; Leal (Magalhaes), Couto J (Joao Pinto II), Samuel, Couto F, Joao Pinto I, Semedo (Sousa), Filipe, Paneira, Figo (Domingos), Cadete.
Republic of Ireland: Peyton; Staunton, Morris, McGrath, McCarthy, O'Leary, Houghton, McLoughlin, Quinn (Aldridge), Kelly (Coyne), Phelan (McGoldrick).

INTERNATIONAL APPEARANCES

This is a list of full international appearances by Englishmen, Irishmen, Scotsmen and Welshmen in matches against the Home Countries and against foreign nations. It does not include unofficial matches against Commonwealth and Empire countries. The year indicated refers to the season; ie 1992 is the 1991–92 season.

Explanatory code for matches played by all five countries: A represents Austria; Alb, Albania; Alg, Algeria; Arg, Argentina; Aus, Australia; B, Bohemia; Bel, Belgium; Br, Brazil; Bul, Bulgaria; C, CIS; Ca, Canada; Cam, Cameroon; Ch, Chile; Chn, China; Co, Colombia; Cr, Costa Rica; Cy, Cyprus; Cz, Czechoslovakia; D, Denmark; E, England; Ec, Ecuador; Ei, Eire; EG, East Germany; Eg, Egypt; F, France; Fa, Faeroes; Fi, Finland; G, Germany; Gr, Greece; H, Hungary; Ho, Holland; Hon, Honduras; I, Italy; Ic, Iceland; Ir, Iran; Is, Israel; J, Japan; K, Kuwait; L, Luxembourg; Li, Lithuania; M, Mexico; Ma, Malta; Mal, Malaysia; Mor, Morocco; N, Norway; Ni, Northern Ireland; Nz, New Zealand; P, Portugal; Para, Paraguay; Pe, Peru; Pol, Poland; R, Romania; R of E, Rest of Europe; R of UK, Rest of United Kingdom; R of W, Rest of World; S.Ar, Saudi Arabia; S, Scotland; Se, Sweden; Sm, San Marino; Sp, Spain; Sw, Switzerland; T, Turkey; Tr, Trinidad & Tobago; Tun, Tunisia; U, Uruguay; US, United States of America; USSR, Soviet Union; W, Wales; WG, West Germany; Y, Yugoslavia; Z, Zaire.

As at 18 June 1992.

ENGLAND

Abbott, W. (Everton), 1902 v W (1)

A'Court, A. (Liverpool), 1958 v Ni, Br, A, USSR; 1959 v W (5)

Adams, T. A. (Arsenal), 1987 v Sp, T, Br; 1988 v WG, T, Y, Ho, H, S, Co, Sw, Ei, Ho, USSR; 1989 v D, Se, S.Ar.; 1991 v Ei (2) (19)

Adcock, H. (Leicester C), 1929 v F, Bel, Sp; 1930 v Ni, W (5)

Alcock, C. W. (Wanderers), 1875 v S (1)

Alderson, J. T. (C Palace), 1923 v F (1)

Aldridge, A. (WBA), 1888 v Ni; (with Walsall Town Swifts), 1889 v Ni (2)

Allen, A. (Stoke C) 1960 v Se, W, Ni (3)

Allen, A. (Aston Villa), 1888 v Ni (1)

Allen, C. (QPR), 1984 v Br (sub), U, Ch; (with Tottenham H), 1987 v T; 1988 v Is (5)

Allen, H. (Wolverhampton W), 1888 v S, W, Ni; 1889 v S; 1890 v S (5)

Allen, J. P. (Portsmouth), 1934 v Ni, W (2)

Allen, R. (WBA), 1952 v Sw; 1954 v Y, S; 1955 v WG, W (5)

Alsford, W. J. (Tottenham H), 1935 v S (1)

Amos, A. (Old Carthusians), 1885 v S; 1886 v W (2)

Anderson, R. D. (Old Etonians), 1879 v W (1)

Anderson, S. (Sunderland), 1962, v A, S (2)

Anderson, V. (Nottingham F), 1979 v Cz, Se; 1980 v Bul, Sp; 1981 v N, R, W, S; 1982 v Ni, Ic; 1984 v Ni; (with Arsenal), 1985 v T, Ni, Ei, R, Fi, S, M, US; 1986 v USSR, M; 1987 v Se, Ni, I (2), Y, Sp, T; (with Manchester U), 1988 v WG, H, Co (30)

Angus, J. (Burnley), 1961 v A (1)

Armfield, J. C. (Blackpool), 1959 v Br, Pe, M, US; 1960 v Y, Sp, H, S; 1961 v L, P, Sp, M, I, A, W, Ni, S; 1962 v A, Sw, Pe, W, Ni, S, L, P, H, Arg, Bul, Br; 1963 v F (2), Br, EG, Sw, Ni, W, S; 1964 v R of W, W, Ni, S; 1966 v Y, Fi (43)

Armitage, G. H. (Charlton Ath), 1926 v Ni (1)

Armstrong, D. (Middlesbrough), 1980 v Aus; (with Southampton), 1983 v WG; 1984 v W (3)

Armstrong, K. (Chelsea), 1955 v S (1)

Arnold, J. (Fulham), 1933 v S (1)

Arthur, J. W. H. (Blackburn R), 1885 v S, W, Ni; 1886 v S, W; 1887 v W, Ni (7)

Ashcroft, J. (Woolwich Arsenal), 1906 v Ni, W, S (3)

Ashmore, G. S. (WBA), 1926 v Bel (1)

Ashton, C. T. (Corinthians), 1926 v Ni (1)

Ashurst, W. (Notts Co), 1923 v Se (2); 1925 v S, W, Bel (5)

Astall, G. (Birmingham C), 1956 v Fi, WG (2)

Astle, J. (WBA), 1969 v W; 1970 v S, P, Br (sub), Cz (5)

Aston, J. (Manchester U), 1949 v S, W, D, Sw, Se, N, F; 1950 v S, W, Ni, Ei, I, P, Bel, Ch, US; 1951 v Ni (17)

Athersmith, W. C. (Aston Villa), 1892 v Ni, 1897 v S, W, Ni; 1898 v S, W, Ni; 1899 v S, W, Ni; 1900 v S, W (12)

Atyeo, P. J. W. (Bristol C), 1956 v Br, Se, Sp; 1957 v D, Ei (2) (6)

Austin, S. W. (Manchester C), 1926 v Ni (1)

Bach, P. (Sunderland), 1899 v Ni (1)

Bache, J. W. (Aston Villa), 1903 v W; 1904 v W, Ni; 1905 v S; 1907 v Ni; 1910 v Ni; 1911 v S (7)

Baddeley, T. (Wolverhampton W), 1903 v S, Ni; 1904 v S, W, Ni (5)

Bagshaw, J. J. (Derby Co), 1920 v Ni (1)

Bailey, G. R. (Manchester U), 1985 v Ei, M (2)

Bailey, H. P. (Leicester Fosse), 1908 v W, A (2), H, B (5)

Bailey, M. A. (Charlton Ath), 1964 v US; 1965 v W (2)

Bailey, N. C. (Clapham Rovers), 1878 v S; 1879 v S, W; 1880 v S; 1881 v S; 1882 v S, W; 1883 v S, W; 1884 v S, W, Ni; 1885 v S, W, Ni; 1886 v S, W; 1887 v S, W (19)

Baily, E. F. (Tottenham H), 1950 v Sp; 1951 v Y, Ni, W; 1952 v A (2), Sw, W; 1953 v Ni (9)

Bain, J. (Oxford University), 1887 v S (1)

Baker, A. (Arsenal), 1928 v W (1)

Baker, B. H. (Everton), 1921 v Bel; (with Chelsea), 1926 v Ni (2)

Baker, J. H. (Hibernian), 1960 v Y, Sp, H, Ni, S; (with Arsenal) 1966 v Sp, Pol, Ni (8)

Ball, A. J. (Blackpool), 1965 v Y, WG, Se; 1966 v S, Sp, Fi, D, U, Arg, P, WG (2), Pol (2); (with Everton), 1967 v W, S, Ni, A, Cz, Sp; 1968 v W, S, USSR, Sp (2), Y, WG; 1969 v Ni, W, S, R (2), M, Br, U; 1970 v P, Co, Ec, R, Br, Cz (sub), WG, W, S, Bel; 1971 v Ma, EG, Gr, Ma (sub), Ni, S; 1972 v Sw, Gr; (with Arsenal) WG (2), S; 1973 v W (3), Y, S (2), Cz, Ni, Pol; 1974 v P (sub); 1975 v WG, Cy (2), Ni, W, S (72)

Ball, J. (Bury), 1928 v Ni (1)

Balmer, W. (Everton), 1905 v Ni (1)

Bamber, J. (Liverpool), 1921 v W (1)

Bambridge, A. L. (Swifts), 1881 v W; 1883 v W; 1884 v Ni (3)

Bambridge, E. C. (Swifts), 1879 v S; 1880 v S; 1881 v S; 1882 v S, W, Ni; 1883 v W; 1884 v S, W, Ni; 1885 v S, W, Ni; 1886 v S, W; 1887 v S, W, Ni (18)

Bambridge, E. H. (Swifts), 1876 v S (1)

Banks, G. (Leicester C), 1963 v S, Br, Cz, EG; 1964 v W, Ni, S, R of W, U, P (2), US, Arg; 1965 v Ni, S, H, Y, WG, Se; 1966 v Ni, S, Sp, Pol (2), WG (2), Y, Fi, U, M, F, Arg, P; 1967 v Ni, W, S, Cz; (with Stoke C), 1968 v W, Ni, S, USSR (2), Sp, WG, Y; 1969 v Ni, S, R (2), F, U, Br; 1970 v W, Ni, S, Ho, Bel, Co, Ec, R, Br, Cz;

1971 v Gr, Ma (2), Ni, S; 1972 v Sw, Gr, WG (2), W, S (73)

Banks, H. E. (Millwall), 1901 v Ni (1)

Banks, T. (Bolton W), 1958 v USSR (3), Br, A; 1959 v Ni (6)

Bannister, W. (Burnley), 1901 v W; (with Bolton W), 1902 v Ni (2)

Barclay, R. (Sheffield W), 1932 v S; 1933 v Ni; 1936 v S (3)

Barham, M. (Norwich C), 1983 v Aus (2) (2)

Barkas, S. (Manchester C), 1936 v Bel; 1937 v S; 1938 v W, Ni, Cz (5)

Barker, J. (Derby Co), 1935 v I, Ho, S, W, Ni; 1936 v G, A, S, W, Ni; 1937 v W (11)

Barker, R. (Herts Rangers), 1872 v S (1)

Barker, R. R. (Casuals), 1895 v W (1)

Barlow, R. J. (WBA), 1955 v Ni (1)

Barnes, J. (Watford), 1983 v Ni (sub), Aus (sub + 2); 1984 v D, L (sub), F (sub), S, USSR, Br, U, Ch; 1985 v EG, Fi, T, Ni, R, Fi, S, I (sub), M, WG (sub), US (sub); 1986 v R (sub), Is (sub), M (sub), Ca (sub), Arg (sub); 1987 v Se, T (sub), Br; (with Liverpool), 1988 v WG, T, Y, Is, Ho, S, Co, Sw, Ei, Ho, USSR; 1989 v Se, Gr, Alb, Pol, D; 1990 v Se, I, Br, D, U, Tun, Ei, Ho, Eg, Bel, Cam; 1991 v H, Pol, Cam, Ei, T, USSR, Arg; 1992 v Cz, Fi (67)

Barnes, P. S. (Manchester C), 1978 v I, WG, Br, W, S, H; 1979 v D, Ei, Cz, Ni (2), S, Bul, A; (with WBA), 1980 v D, W; 1981 v Sp (sub), Br, W, Sw (sub); (with Leeds U), 1982 v N (sub), Ho (sub) (22)

Barnet, H. H. (Royal Engineers), 1882 v Ni (1)

Barrass, M. W. (Bolton W), 1952 v W, Ni; 1953 v S (3)

Barrett, A. F. (Fulham), 1930 v Ni (1)

Barrett, E. D. (Oldham Ath), 1991 v Nz (1)

Barrett, J. W. (West Ham U), 1929 v Ni (1)

Barry, L. (Leicester C), 1928 v F, Bel; 1929 v F, Bel, Sp (5)

Barson, F. (Aston Villa), 1920 v W (1)

Barton, J. (Blackburn R), 1890 v Ni (1)

Barton, P. H. (Birmingham), 1921 v Bel; 1922 v Ni; 1923 v F; 1924 v Bel, S, W; 1925 v Ni (7)

Bassett, W. I. (WBA), 1888 v Ni, 1889 v S, W; 1890 v S, W; 1891 v S, Ni; 1892 v S; 1893 v S, W; 1894 v S; 1895 v S, Ni; 1896 v S, W, Ni (16)

Bastard, S. R. (Upton Park), 1880 v S (1)

Bastin, C. S. (Arsenal), 1932 v W; 1933 v I, Sw; 1934 v S, Ni, W, H, Cz; 1935 v S, Ni, I; 1936 v S, W, G, A; 1937 v W, Ni; 1938 v S, G, Sw, F (21)

Batty, D. (Leeds U), 1991 v USSR (sub), Arg, Aus, Nz, Mal; 1992 v G, T, H (sub), F, Se (10)

Baugh, R. (Stafford Road), 1886 v Ni; (with Wolverhampton W) 1890 v Ni (2)

Bayliss, A. E. J. M. (WBA), 1891 v Ni (1)

Baynham, R. L. (Luton T), 1956 v Ni, D, Sp (3)

Beardsley, P. A. (Newcastle U), 1986 v Eg (sub), Is, USSR, M, Ca (sub), P (sub), Pol, Para, Arg; 1987 v Ni (2), Y, Sp, Br, S; (with Liverpool), 1988 v WG, T, Y, Is, Ho, H, S, Co, Sw, Ei, Ho; 1989 v D, Se, S.Ar, Gr (sub), Alb (sub + 1), Pol, D; 1990 v Se, Pol, I, Br, U (sub), Tun (sub), Ei, Eg (sub), Cam (sub), WG, I; 1991 v Pol (sub), Ei (2), USSR (sub) (49)

Beasant, D. J. (Chelsea), 1990 v I (sub), W (sub) (2)

Beasley, A. (Huddersfield T), 1939 v S (1)

Beats, W. E. (Wolverhampton W), 1901 v W; 1902 v S (2)

Beattie, T. K. (Ipswich T), 1975 v Cy (2), S; 1976 v Sw, P; 1977 v Fi, I (sub), Ho; 1978 v L (sub) (9)

Becton, F. (Preston NE), 1895 v Ni; (with Liverpool), 1897 v W (2)

Bedford, H. (Blackpool), 1923 v Se; 1925 v Ni (2)

Bell, C. (Manchester C), 1968 v Se, WG; 1969 v W, Bul, F, U, Br; 1970 v Ni (sub), Ho (2), P, Br (sub), Cz, WG (sub); 1972 v Gr, WG (2), W, Ni, S; 1973 v W (3), Y,

S (2), Ni, Cz, Pol; 1974 v A, Pol, I, W, Ni, S, Arg, EG, Bul, Y; 1975 v Cz, P, WG, Cy (2), Ni, S; 1976 v Sw, Cy (48)

Bennett, W. (Sheffield U), 1901 v S, W (2)

Benson, R. W. (Sheffield U), 1913 v Ni (1)

Bentley, R. T. F. (Chelsea), 1949 v Se; 1950 v S, P, Bel, Ch, USA; 1953 v W, Bel; 1955 v W, WG, Sp, P (12)

Beresford, J. (Aston Villa), 1934 v Cz (1)

Berry, A. (Oxford University), 1909 v Ni (1)

Berry, J. J. (Manchester U), 1953 v Arg, Ch, U; 1956 v Se (4)

Bestall, J. G. (Grimsby T), 1935 v Ni (1)

Betmead, H. A. (Grimsby T), 1937 v Fi (1)

Betts, M. P. (Old Harrovians), 1877 v S (1)

Betts, W. (Sheffield W), 1889 v W (1)

Beverley, J. (Blackburn R), 1884 v S, W, Ni (3)

Birkett, R. H. (Clapham Rovers), 1879 v S (1)

Birkett, R. J. E. (Middlesbrough), 1936 v Ni (1)

Birley, F. H. (Oxford University), 1874 v S; (with Wanderers), 1875 v S (2)

Birtles, G. (Nottingham F), 1980 v Arg (sub), I; 1981 v R (3)

Bishop, S. M. (Leicester C), 1927 v S, Bel, L, F (4)

Blackburn, F. (Blackburn R), 1901 v S; 1902 v Ni; 1904 v S (3)

Blackburn, G. F. (Aston Villa), 1924 v F (1)

Blenkinsop, E. (Sheffield W), 1928 v F, Bel; 1929 v S, W, Ni, F, Bel, Sp; 1930 v S, W, Ni, G, A; 1931 v S, W, Ni, F, Bel; 1932 v S, W, Ni, Sp; 1933 v S, W, Ni, A (26)

Bliss, H. (Tottenham H), 1921 v S (1)

Blissett, L. (Watford), 1983 v WG (sub), L, W, Gr (sub), H, Ni, S (sub), Aus (1 + 1 sub); 1984 v D (sub), H, W (sub), S, USSR (14)

Blockley, J. P. (Arsenal), 1973 v Y (1)

Bloomer, S. (Derby Co), 1895 v S, Ni; 1896 v W, Ni; 1897 v S, W, Ni; 1898 v S; 1899 v S, W, Ni; 1900 v S; 1901 v S, W; 1902 v S, W, Ni; 1904 v S; 1905 v S, W, Ni; (with Middlesbrough), 1907 v S, W (23)

Blunstone, F. (Chelsea), 1955 v W, S, F, P; 1957 v Y (5)

Bond, R. (Preston NE), 1905 v Ni, W; 1906 v S, W, Ni; (with Bradford C), 1910 v S, W, Ni (8)

Bonetti, P. P. (Chelsea), 1966 v D; 1967 v Sp, A; 1968 v Sp; 1970 v Ho, P, WG (7)

Bonsor, A. G. (Wanderers), 1873 v S; 1875 v S (2)

Booth, F. (Manchester C), 1905 v Ni (1)

Booth, T. (Blackburn R), 1898 v W; (with Everton), 1903 v S (2)

Bowden, E. R. (Arsenal), 1935 v W, I; 1936 v W, Ni, A; 1937 v H (6)

Bower, A. G. (Corinthians), 1924 v Ni, Bel; 1925 v W, Bel; 1927 v W (5)

Bowers, J. W. (Derby Co), 1934 v S, Ni, W (3)

Bowles, S. (QPR), 1974 v P, W, Ni; 1977 v I, Ho (5)

Bowser, S. (WBA), 1920 v Ni (1)

Boyer, P. J. (Norwich C), 1976 v W (1)

Boyes, W. (WBA), 1935 v Ho; (with Everton), 1939 v W, R of E (3)

Boyle, T. W. (Burnley), 1913 v Ni (1)

Brabrook, P. (Chelsea), 1958 v USSR; 1959 v Ni; 1960 v Sp (3)

Bracewell, P. W. (Everton), 1985 v WG (sub), US; 1986 v Ni (3)

Bradford, G. R. W. (Bristol R), 1956 v D (1)

Bradford, J. (Birmingham), 1924 v Ni; 1925 v Bel; 1928 v S; 1929 v Ni, W, F, Sp; 1930 v S, Ni, G, A; 1931 v W (12)

Bradley, W. (Manchester U), 1959 v I, US, M (sub) (3)

Bradshaw, F. (Sheffield W), 1908 v A (1)

Bradshaw, T. H. (Liverpool), 1897 v Ni (1)

Bradshaw, W. (Blackburn R), 1910 v W, Ni; 1912 v Ni; 1913 v W (4)

Brann, G. (Swifts), 1886 v S, W; 1891 v W (3)

Brawn, W. F. (Aston Villa), 1904 v W, Ni (2)

Bray, J. (Manchester C), 1935 v W; 1936 v S, W, Ni, G; 1937 v S (6)

Brayshaw, E. (Sheffield W), 1887 v Ni (1)

Bridges, B. J. (Chelsea), 1965 v S, H, Y; 1966 v A (4)

Bridgett, A. (Sunderland), 1905 v S; 1908 v S, A (2), H, B; 1909 v Ni, W, H (2), A (11)

Brindle, T. (Darwen), 1880 v S, W (2)

Brittleton, J. T. (Sheffield W), 1912 v S, W, Ni; 1913 v S; 1914 v W (5)

Britton, C. S. (Everton), 1935 v S, W, Ni, I; 1937 v S, Ni, H, N, Se (9)

Broadbent, P. F. (Wolverhampton W), 1958 v USSR, 1959 v S, W, Ni, I, Br; 1960 v S (7)

Broadis, I. A. (Manchester C), 1952 v S, A, I; 1953 v S, Arg, Ch, U, US; (with Newcastle U), 1954 v S, H, Y, Bel, Sw, U (14)

Brockbank, J. (Cambridge University), 1872 v S (1)

Brodie, J. B. (Wolverhampton W), 1889 v S, Ni; 1891 v Ni (3)

Bromilow, T. G. (Liverpool), 1921 v W; 1922 v S, W; 1923 v Bel; 1926 v Ni (5)

Bromley-Davenport, W. E. (Oxford University), 1884 v S, W (2)

Brook, E. F. (Manchester C), 1930 v Ni; 1933 v Sw: 1934 v S, W, Ni, F, H, Cz; 1935 v S, W, Ni, I; 1936 v S, W, Ni; 1937 v H; 1938 v W, Ni (18)

Brooking, T. D. (West Ham U), 1974 v P, Arg, EG, Bul, Y; 1975 v Cz (sub); P; 1976 v P, W, Br, I, Fi; 1977 v Ei, Fi, I, Ho, Ni, W; 1978 v I, WG, W, S (sub), H; 1979 v D, Ei, Ni, W (sub), S, Bul, Se (sub), A; 1980 v D, Ni, Arg (sub), W, Ni, S, Bel, Sp; 1981 v Sw, Sp, R, H; 1982 v H, S, Fi, Sp (sub) (47)

Brooks, J. (Tottenham H), 1957 v W, Y, D (3)

Broome, F. H. (Aston Villa), 1938 v G, Sw, F; 1939 v N, I, R, Y (7)

Brown, A. (Aston Villa), 1882 v S, W, Ni (3)

Brown, A. S. (Sheffield U), 1904 v W; 1906 v Ni (2)

Brown, A. (WBA), 1971 v W (1)

Brown, G. (Huddersfield T), 1927 v S, W, Ni, Bel, L, F; 1928 v W; 1929 v S; (with Aston Villa), 1933 v W (9)

Brown, J. (Blackburn R), 1881 v W; 1882 v Ni; 1885 v S, W, Ni (5)

Brown, J. H. (Sheffield W), 1927 v S, W, Bel, L, F; 1930 v Ni (6)

Brown, K. (West Ham U), 1960 v Ni (1)

Brown, W. (West Ham U), 1924 v Bel (1)

Bruton, J. (Burnley), 1928 v F, Bel; 1929 v S (3)

Bryant, W. I. (Clapton), 1925 v F (1)

Buchan, C. M. (Sunderland), 1913 v Ni; 1920 v W; 1921 v W, Bel; 1923 v F; 1924 v S (6)

Buchanan, W. S. (Clapham R), 1876 v S (1)

Buckley, F. C. (Derby Co), 1914 v Ni (1)

Bull, S. G. (Wolverhampton W), 1989 v S (sub), D (sub); 1990 v Y, Cz, D (sub), U (sub), Tun (sub), Ei (sub), Ho (sub), Eg, Bel (sub); 1991 v H, Pol (13)

Bullock, F. E. (Huddersfield T), 1921 v Ni (1)

Bullock, N. (Bury), 1923 v Bel; 1926 v W; 1927 v Ni (3)

Burgess, H. (Manchester C), 1904 v S, W, Ni; 1906 v S (4)

Burgess, H. (Sheffield W), 1931 v S, Ni, F, Bel (4)

Burnup, C. J. (Cambridge University), 1896 v S (1)

Burrows, H. (Sheffield W), 1934 v H, Cz; 1935 v Ho (3)

Burton, F. E. (Nottingham F), 1889 v Ni (1)

Bury, L. (Cambridge University), 1877 v S; (with Old Etonians), 1879 v W (2)

Butcher, T. (Ipswich T), 1980 v Aus; 1981 v Sp; 1982 v W, S, F, Cz, WG, Sp; 1983 v D, WG, L, W, Gr, H, Ni, S, Aus (3); 1984 v D, H, L, F, Ni; 1985 v EG, Fi, T, Ni, Ei, R, Fi, S, I, WG, US; 1986 v Is, USSR, S, M, Ca, P, Mor, Pol, Para, Arg; (with Rangers), 1987 v Se, Ni (2), Y, Sp, Br, S; 1988 v T, Y; 1989 v D, Se, Gr, Alb (2), Ch, S, Pol, D; 1990 v Se, Pol, I, Y, Br, Cz, D, U, Tun, Ei, Ho, Bel, Cam, WG (77)

Butler, J. D. (Arsenal), 1925 v Bel (1)

Butler, W. (Bolton W), 1924 v S (1)

Byrne, G. (Liverpool), 1963 v S; 1966 v N (2)

Byrne, J. J. (C Palace), 1962 v Ni; (with West Ham U), 1963 v Sw; 1964 v S, U, P (2), Ei, Br, Arg; 1965 v W, S (11)

Byrne, R. W. (Manchester U), 1954 v S, H, Y, Bel, Sw, U; 1955 v S, W, Ni, WG, F, Sp, P; 1956 v S, W, Ni, Br, Se, Fi, WG, D, Sp; 1957 v S, W, Ni, Y, D (2), Ei (2); 1958 v W, Ni, F (33)

Callaghan, I. R. (Liverpool), 1966 v Fi, F; 1978 v Sw, L (4)

Calvey, J. (Nottingham F), 1902 v Ni (1)

Campbell, A. F. (Blackburn R), 1929 v W, Ni; (with Huddersfield T), 1931 v W, S, Ni; 1932 v W, Ni, Sp (8)

Camsell, G. H. (Middlesbrough), 1929 v F, Bel; 1930 v Ni, W; 1934 v F; 1936 v S, G, A, Bel (9)

Capes, A. J. (Stoke C), 1903 v S (1)

Carr, J. (Middlesbrough), 1920 v Ni; 1923 v W (2)

Carr, J. (Newcastle U), 1905 v Ni; 1907 v Ni (2)

Carr, W. H. (Owlerton, Sheffield), 1875 v S (1)

Carter, H. S. (Sunderland), 1934 v S, H; 1936 v G; 1937 v S, Ni, H; (with Derby Co), 1947 v S, W, Ni, Ei, Ho, F, Sw (13)

Carter, J. H. (WBA), 1926 v Bel; 1929 v Bel, Sp (3)

Catlin, A. E. (Sheffield W), 1937 v W, Ni, H, N, Se (5)

Chadwick, A. (Southampton), 1900 v S, W (2)

Chadwick, E. (Everton), 1891 v S, W; 1892 v S; 1893 v S; 1894 v S; 1896 v Ni; 1897 v S (7)

Chamberlain, M (Stoke C), 1983 v L (sub); 1984 v D (sub), S, USSR, Br, U, Ch; 1985 v Fi (sub) (8)

Chambers, H. (Liverpool), 1921 v S, W, Bel; 1923 v S, W, Ni, Bel; 1924 v Ni (8)

Channon, M. R. (Southampton), 1973 v Y, S (2), Ni, W, Cz, USSR, I; 1974 v A, Pol, I, P, W, Ni, S, Arg, EG, Bul, Y; 1975 v Cz, P, WG, Cy (2), Ni (sub), W, S; 1976 v Sw, Cz, P, W, Ni, S, Br, I, Fi; 1977 v Fi, I, L, Ni, W, S, Br (sub), Arg, U; (with Manchester C), 1978 v Sw (46)

Charles, G. A. (Nottingham F), 1991 v Nz, Mal (2)

Charlton, J. (Leeds U), 1965 v S, H, Y, WG, Se; 1966 v W, Ni, S, A, Sp, Pol (2), WG (2), Y, Fi, D, U, M, F, Arg, P; 1967 v W, S, Ni, Cz; 1968 v W, Sp; 1969 v W, R, F; 1970 v Ho (2), P, Cz (35)

Charlton, R. (Manchester U), 1958 v S, P, Y; 1959 v S, W, Ni, USSR, I, Br, Pe, M, US; 1960 v W, S, Se, Y, Sp, H; 1961 v Ni, W, S, L, P, Sp, M, I, A; 1962 v W, Ni, S, A, Sw, Pe, L, P, H, Arg, Bul, Br; 1963 v S, F, Br, Cz, EG, Sw; 1964 v S, W, Ni, R of W, U, P, Ei, Br, Arg, US (sub); 1965 v Ni, S, Ho; 1966 v W, Ni, S, A, Sp, WG (2), Y, Fi, N, Pol, U, M, F, Arg, P; 1967 v Ni, W, S, Cz; 1968 v W, Ni, S, USSR (2), Sp (2), Se, Y; 1969 v S, W, Ni, R (2), Bul, M, Br; 1970 v W, Ni, Ho (2), P, Co, Ec, Cz, R, Br, WG (106)

Charnley, R. O. (Blackpool), 1963 v F (1)

Charsley, C. C. (Small Heath), 1893 v Ni (1)

Chedgzoy, S. (Everton), 1920 v W; 1921 v W, S, Ni; 1922 v Ni; 1923 v S; 1924 v W; 1925 v Ni (8)

Chenery, C. J. (C Palace), 1872 v S; 1873 v S; 1874 v S (3)

Cherry, T. J. (Leeds U), 1976 v W, S (sub), Br, Fi; 1977 v Ei, I, L, Ni, S (sub), Br, Arg, U; 1978 v Sw, L, I, Br, W; 1979 v Cz, W, Se; 1980 v Ei, Arg (sub), W, Ni, S, Aus, Sp (sub) (27)

Chilton, A. (Manchester U), 1951 v Ni; 1952 v F (2)

Chippendale, H. (Blackburn R), 1894 v Ni (1)

Chivers, M. (Tottenham H), 1971 v Ma (2), Gr, Ni, S; 1972 v Sw (1 + 1 sub), Gr, WG (2), Ni (sub), S; 1973 v W (3), S (2), Ni, Cz, Pol, USSR, I; 1974 v A, Pol (24)

Christian, E. (Old Etonians), 1879 v S (1)

Clamp, E. (Wolverhampton W), 1958 v USSR (2), Br, A (4)

836

Clapton, D. R. (Arsenal), 1959 v W (1)

Clare, T. (Stoke C), 1889 v Ni; 1892 v Ni; 1893 v W; 1894 v S (4)

Clarke, A. J. (Leeds U), 1970 v Cz; 1971 v EG, Ma, Ni, W (sub), S (sub); 1973 v S (2), W, Cz, Pol, USSR, I; 1974 v A, Pol, I; 1975 v P; 1976 v Cz, P (sub) (19)

Clarke, H. A. (Tottenham H), 1954 v S (1)

Clay, T. (Tottenham H), 1920 v W; 1922 v W, S, Ni (4)

Clayton, R. (Blackburn R), 1956 v Ni, Br, Se, Fi, WG, Sp; 1957 v S, W, Ni, Y, D (2), Ei (2); 1958 v S, W, Ni, F, P, Y, USSR; 1959 v S, W, Ni, USSR, I, Br, Pe, M, US; 1960 v W, Ni, S, Se, Y (35)

Clegg, J. C. (Sheffield W), 1872 v S (1)

Clegg, W. E. (Sheffield W), 1873 v S; (with Sheffield Albion), 1879 v W (2)

Clemence, R. N. (Liverpool), 1973 v W (2); 1974 v EG, Bul, Y; 1975 v Cz, P, WG, Cy, Ni, W, S; 1976 v Sw, Cz, P, W (2), Ni, S, Br, Fi; 1977 v Ei, Fi, I, Ho, L, S, Br, Arg, U; 1978 v Sw, L, I, WG, Ni, S; 1979 v D, Ei, Ni (2), S, Bul, A (sub); 1980 v D, Bul, Ei, Arg, W, S, Bel, Sp; 1981 v R, Sp, Br, Sw, H; (with Tottenham H), 1982 v N, Ni, Fi; 1983 v L; 1984 v L (61)

Clement, D. T. (QPR), 1976 v W (sub + 1), 1; 1977 v I, Ho (5)

Clough, B. H. (Middlesbrough), 1960 v W, Se (2)

Clough, N. H. (Nottingham F), 1989 v Ch; 1991 v Arg (sub), Aus, Mal; 1992 v F, Cz, C (sub) (7)

Coates, R. (Burnley), 1970 v Ni; 1971 v Gr (sub); (with Tottenham H), Ma, W (7)

Cobbold, W. N. (Cambridge University), 1883 v S, Ni; 1885 v S, Ni; 1886 v S, W; (with Old Carthusians), 1887 v S, W, Ni (9)

Cock, J. G. (Huddersfield T), 1920 v Ni; (with Chelsea), v S (2)

Cockburn, H. (Manchester U), 1947 v W, Ni, Ei; 1948 v S, I; 1949 v S, Ni, D, Sw, Se; 1951 v Arg, P; 1952 v F (13)

Cohen, G. R. (Fulham), 1964 v U, P, Ei, US, Br; 1965 v W, S, Ni, Bel, H, Ho, Y, WG, Se; 1966 v W, S, Ni, A, Sp, Pol (2), WG (2), N, D, U, M, F, Arg, P; 1967 v S, Ni, Cz, Sp; 1968 v W, Ni (37)

Coleclough, H. (C Palace), 1914 v W (1)

Coleman, E. H. (Dulwich Hamlet), 1921 v W (1)

Coleman, J. (Woolwich Arsenal), 1907 v Ni (1)

Common, A. (Sheffield U), 1904 v W, Ni; (with Middlesbrough), 1906 v W (3)

Compton, L. H. (Arsenal), 1951 v W, Y (2)

Conlin, J. (Bradford C), 1906 v S (1)

Connelly, J. M. (Burnley), 1960 v W, N, S, Se; 1962 v W, A, Sw, P; 1963 v W, F; (with Manchester U), 1965 v H, Y, Se; 1966 v W, Ni, S, A, N, D, U (20)

Cook, T. E. R. (Brighton), 1925 v W (1)

Cooper, N. C. (Cambridge University), 1893 v Ni (1)

Cooper, T. (Derby Co), 1928 v Ni; 1929 v W, Ni, S, F, Bel, Sp; 1931 v F; 1932 v W, Sp; 1933 v S; 1934 v S, H, Cz; 1935 v W (15)

Cooper, T. (Leeds U), 1969 v W, S, F, M; 1970 v Ho, Bel, Co, Ec, R, Cz, Br, WG; 1971 v EG, Ma, Ni, W, S; 1972 v Sw (2); 1975 v P (20)

Coppell, S. J. (Manchester U), 1978 v I, WG, Br, W, Ni, S, H; 1979 v D, Ei, Cz, Ni (2), W (sub), S, Bul, A; 1980 v D, Ni, Ei (sub), Sp, Arg, W, S, Bel, I; 1981 v R (sub), Sw, R, Br, W, S, Sw, H; 1982 v H, S, Fi, F, Cz, K, WG; 1983 v L, Gr (42)

Copping, W. (Leeds U), 1933 v I, Sw; 1934 v S, Ni, W, F; (with Arsenal), 1935 v Ni, I; 1936 v A, Bel; 1937 v N, Se, Fi; 1938 v S, W, Ni, Cz; 1939 v W, R of E; (with Leeds U), R (20)

Corbett, B. O. (Corinthians), 1901 v W (1)

Corbett, R. (Old Malvernians), 1903 v W (1)

Corbett, W. S. (Birmingham), 1908 v A, H, B (3)

Corrigan, J. T. (Manchester C), 1976 v I (sub), Br; 1979 v W; 1980 v Ni, Aus; 1981 v W, S; 1982 v W, Ic (9)

Cottee, A. R. (West Ham U), 1987 v Se (sub), Ni (sub); 1988 v H (sub); (with Everton) 1989 v D (sub), Se (sub), Ch (sub), S (7)

Cotterill, G. H. (Cambridge University), 1891 v Ni; (with Old Brightonians), 1892 v W; 1893 v S, Ni (4)

Cottle, J. R. (Bristol C), 1909 v Ni (1)

Cowan, S. (Manchester C), 1926 v Bel; 1930 v A; 1931 v Bel (3)

Cowans, G. (Aston Villa), 1983 v W, H, Ni, S, Aus (3); (with Bari), 1986 v Eg, USSR; (with Aston Villa), 1991 v Ei (10)

Cowell, A. (Blackburn R), 1910 v Ni (1)

Cox, J. (Liverpool), 1901 v Ni; 1902 v S; 1903 v S (3)

Cox, J. D. (Derby Co), 1892 v Ni (1)

Crabtree, J. W. (Burnley), 1894 v Ni; 1895 v Ni, S; (with Aston Villa), 1896 v W, S, Ni; 1899 v S, W, Ni; 1900 v S, W, Ni; 1901 v W; 1902 v W (14)

Crawford, J. F. (Chelsea), 1931 v S (1)

Crawford, R. (Ipswich T), 1962 v Ni, A (2)

Crawshaw, T. H. (Sheffield W), 1895 v Ni; 1896 v S, W, Ni; 1897 v S, W, Ni; 1901 v Ni; 1904 v W, Ni (10)

Crayston, W. J. (Arsenal), 1936 v S, W, G, A, Bel; 1938 v W, Ni, Cz (8)

Creek, F. N. S. (Corinthians), 1923 v F (1)

Cresswell, W. (South Shields), 1921 v W; (with Sunderland), 1923 v F; 1924 v Bel; 1925 v Ni; 1926 v W; 1927 v Ni; (with Everton), 1930 v Ni (7)

Crompton, R. (Blackburn R), 1902 v S, W, Ni; 1903 v S, W; 1904 v S, W, Ni; 1906 v S, W, Ni; 1907 v S, W, Ni; 1908 v S, W, Ni, A (2), H, B; 1909 v S, W, Ni, H (2), A; 1910 v S, W; 1911 v S, W, Ni; 1912 v S, W, Ni; 1913 v S, W, Ni; 1914 v S, W, Ni (41)

Crooks, S. D. (Derby Co), 1930 v S, G, A; 1931 v S, W, Ni, F, Bel; 1932 v S, W, Ni, Sp; 1933 v Ni, W, A; 1934 v S, Ni, W, F, H, Cz; 1935 v Ni; 1936 v S, W; 1937 v W, H (26)

Crowe, C. (Wolverhampton W), 1963 v F (1)

Cuggy, F. (Sunderland), 1913 v Ni; 1914 v Ni (2)

Cullis, S. (Wolverhampton W), 1938 v S, W, Ni, F, Cz; 1939 v S, Ni, R of E, N, I, R, Y (12)

Cunliffe, A. (Blackburn R), 1933 v Ni, W (2)

Cunliffe, D. (Portsmouth), 1900 v Ni (1)

Cunliffe, J. N. (Everton), 1936 v Bel (1)

Cunningham, L. (WBA), 1979 v W, Se, A (sub); (with Real Madrid), 1980 v Ei, Sp (sub); 1981 v R (sub) (6)

Curle, K. (Manchester C), 1992 v C (sub), H, D (3)

Currey, E. S. (Oxford University), 1890 v S, W (2)

Currie, A. W. (Sheffield U), 1972 v Ni; 1973 v USSR, I; 1974 v A, Pol, I; 1976 v Sw; (with Leeds U), 1978 v Br, W (sub), Ni, S, H (sub); 1979 v Cz, Ni (2), W, Se (17)

Cursham, A. W. (Notts Co), 1876 v S; 1877 v S; 1878 v S; 1879 v W; 1883 v S, W (6)

Cursham, H. A. (Notts Co), 1880 v W; 1882 v S, W, Ni; 1883 v S, W, Ni; 1884 v Ni (8)

Daft, H. B. (Notts Co), 1889 v Ni; 1890 v S, W; 1891 v Ni; 1892 v Ni (5)

Daley, A. M. (Aston Villa), 1992 v Pol (sub), C, H, Br, Fi (sub), D (sub), Se (7)

Danks, T. (Nottingham F), 1885 v S (1)

Davenport, P. (Nottingham F), 1985 v Ei (sub) (1)

Davenport, J. K. (Bolton W), 1885 v W; 1890 v Ni (2)

Davis, G. (Derby Co), 1904 v W, Ni (2)

Davis, H. (Sheffield W), 1903 v S, W, Ni (3)

Davison, J. E. (Sheffield W), 1922 v W (1)

Dawson, J. (Burnley), 1922 v S, Ni (2)

Day, S. H. (Old Malvernians), 1906 v Ni, W, S (3)

Dean, W. R. (Everton), 1927 v S, W, F, Bel, L; 1928 v S, W, Ni, F, Bel; 1929 v S, W, Ni; 1931 v S; 1932 v Sp; 1933 v Ni (16)

Deane, B. C. (Sheffield U), 1991 v Nz (sub + 1) (2)

Deeley, N. V. (Wolverhampton W), 1959 v Br, Pe (2)

Devey, J. H. G. (Aston Villa), 1892 v Ni; 1894 v Ni (2)

Devonshire, A. (West Ham U), 1980 v Aus (sub), Ni; 1982 v Ho, Ic; 1983 v WG, W, Gr; 1984 v L (8)

Dewhurst, F. (Preston NE), 1886 v W, Ni; 1887 v S, W, Ni; 1888 v S, W, Ni; 1889 v W (9)

Dewhurst, G. P. (Liverpool Ramblers), 1895 v W (1)

Dickinson, J. W. (Portsmouth), 1949 v N, F; 1950 v S, W, Ei, P, Bel, Ch, US, Sp; 1951 v Ni, W, Y; 1952 v W, Ni, S, A (2), I, Sw; 1953 v W, Ni, S, Bel, Arg, Ch, U, US; 1954 v W, Ni, S, R of E, H (2), Y, Bel, Sw, U; 1955 v Sp, P; 1956 v W, Ni, S, D, Sp; 1957 v W, Y, D (48)

Dimmock, J. H. (Tottenham H), 1921 v S; 1926 v W, Bel (3)

Ditchburn, E. G. (Tottenham H), 1949 v Sw, Se; 1953 v US; 1957 v W, Y, D (6)

Dix, R. W. (Derby Co), 1939 v N (1)

Dixon, J. A. (Notts Co), 1885 v W (1)

Dixon, K. M. (Chelsea), 1985 v M (sub), WG, US; 1986 v Ni, Is, M (sub), Pol (sub); 1987 v Se (8)

Dixon, L. M. (Arsenal), 1990 v Cz; 1991 v H, Pol, Ei (2), Cam, T, Arg; 1992 v G, T, Pol, Cz (sub) (12)

Dobson, A. T. C. (Notts Co), 1882 v Ni; 1884 v S, W, Ni (4)

Dobson, C. F. (Notts Co), 1886 v Ni (1)

Dobson, J. M. (Burnley), 1974 v P, EG, Bul, Y; (with Everton), 1975 v Cz (5)

Doggart, A. G. (Corinthians), 1924 v Bel (1)

Dorigo, A. R. (Chelsea), 1990 v Y (sub), Cz (sub), D (sub), I; 1991 v H (sub), USSR; (with Leeds U), 1992 v G, Cz (sub), H, Br (10)

Dorrell, A. R. (Aston Villa), 1925 v W, Bel, F; 1926 v Ni (4)

Douglas, B. (Blackburn R), 1958 v S, W, Ni, F, P, Y, USSR (2), Br, A; 1959 v S, USSR; 1960 v Y, H; 1961 v Ni, W, S, L, P, Sp, M, I, A; 1962 v W, Ni, S, Pe, L, P, H, Arg, Bul, Br; 1963 v S, Br, Sw (36)

Downs, R. W. (Everton), 1921 v Ni (1)

Doyle, M. (Manchester C), 1976 v W, S (sub), Br, I; 1977 v Ho (5)

Drake, E. J. (Arsenal), 1935 v Ni, I; 1936 v W; 1937 v H; 1938 v F (5)

Ducat, A. (Woolwich Arsenal), 1910 v S, W, Ni; (with Aston Villa), 1920 v S, W; 1921 v Ni (6)

Dunn, A. T. B. (Cambridge University), 1883 v Ni; 1884 v Ni; (with Old Etonians), 1892 v S, W (4)

Duxbury, M. (Manchester U), 1984 v L, F, W, S, USSR, Br, U, Ch; 1985 v EG, Fi (10)

Earle, S. G. J. (Clapton), 1924 v F; (with West Ham U), 1928 v Ni (2)

Eastham, G. (Arsenal), 1963 v Br, Cz, EG; 1964 v W, Ni, S, R of W, U, P, Ei, US, Br, Arg; 1965 v H, WG, Se; 1966 v Sp, Pol, D (19)

Eastham, G. R. (Bolton W), 1935 v Ho (1)

Eckersley, W. (Blackburn R), 1950 v Sp; 1951 v S, Y, Arg, P; 1952 v A (2), Sw; 1953 v Ni, Arg, Ch, U, US; 1954 v W, Ni, R of E, H (17)

Edwards, D. (Manchester U), 1955 v S, F, Sp, P; 1956 v S, Br, Se, Fi, WG; 1957 v S, Ni, Ei (2), D (2); 1958 v W, Ni, F (18)

Edwards, J. H. (Shropshire Wanderers), 1874 v S (1)

Edwards, W. (Leeds U), 1926 v S, W; 1927 v W, Ni, S, F, Bel, L; 1928 v S, F, Bel; 1929 v S, W, Ni; 1930 v W, Ni (16)

Ellerington, W. (Southampton), 1949 v N, F (2)

Elliott, G. W. (Middlesbrough), 1913 v Ni; 1914 v Ni; 1920 v W (3)

Elliott, W. H. (Burnley), 1952 v I, A; 1953 v Ni, W, Bel (5)

Evans, R. E. (Sheffield U), 1911 v S, W, Ni; 1912 v W (4)

Ewer, F. H. (Casuals), 1924 v F; 1925 v Bel (2)

Fairclough, P. (Old Foresters), 1878 v S (1)

Fairhurst, D. (Newcastle U), 1934 v F (1)

Fantham, J. (Sheffield W), 1962 v L (1)

Fashanu, J. (Wimbledon), 1989 v Ch, S (2)

Felton, W. (Sheffield W), 1925 v F (1)

Fenton, M. (Middlesbrough), 1938 v S (1)

Fenwick, T. (QPR), 1984 v W (sub), S, USSR, Br, U, Ch; 1985 v Fi, S, M, US; 1986 v R, T, Ni, Eg, M, P, Mor, Pol, Arg; (with Tottenham H), 1988 v Is (sub) (20)

Field, E. (Clapham Rovers), 1876 v S; 1881 v S (2)

Finney, T. (Preston NE), 1947 v W, Ni, Ei, Ho, F, P; 1948 v S, W, Ni, Bel, Se, I; 1949 v S, W, Ni, Se, N, F; 1950 v S, W, Ni, Ei, I, P, Bel, Ch, US, Sp; 1951 v W, S, Arg, P; 1952 v W, Ni, S, F, I, Sw, A; 1953 v W, Ni, S, Bel, Arg, Ch, U, US; 1954 v W, S, Bel, Sw, U, H, Y; 1955 v WG; 1956 v S, W, Ni, D, Sp; 1957 v S, W, Y, D (2), Ei (2); 1958 v W, S, F, P, Y, USSR (2); 1959 v Ni, USSR (76)

Fleming, H. J. (Swindon T), 1909 v S, H (2); 1910 v W, Ni; 1911 v W, Ni; 1912 v Ni; 1913 v S, W; 1914 v S (11)

Fletcher, A. (Wolverhampton W), 1889 v W; 1890 v W (2)

Flowers, R. (Wolverhampton W), 1955 v F; 1959 v S, W, I, Br, Pe, US, M (sub); 1960 v W, Ni, S, Se, Y, Sp, H; 1961 v Ni, W, S, L, P, Sp, M, I, A; 1962 v W Ni, S, A, Sw, Pe, L, P, H, Arg, Bul, Br; 1963 v Ni, W, S, F (2), Sw; 1964 v Ei, US, P; 1965 v W, Ho, WG; 1966 v N (49)

Forman, Frank (Nottingham F), 1898 v S, Ni; 1899 v S, W, Ni; 1901 v S; 1902 v S, Ni; 1903 v W (9)

Forman, F. R. (Nottingham F), 1899 v S, W, Ni (3)

Forrest, J. H. (Blackburn R), 1884 v W; 1885 v S, W, Ni; 1886 v S, W; 1887 v S, W, Ni; 1889 v S; 1890 v Ni (11)

Fort, J. (Millwall), 1921 v Bel (1)

Foster, R. E. (Oxford University), 1900 v W; (with Corinthians), 1901 v W, Ni, S; 1902 v W (5)

Foster, S. (Brighton & HA), 1982 v Ni, Ho, K (3)

Foulke, W. J. (Sheffield U), 1897 v W (1)

Foulkes, W. A. (Manchester U), 1955 v Ni (1)

Fox, F. S. (Gillingham), 1925 v F (1)

Francis, G. C. J. (QPR), 1975 v Cz, P, W, S; 1976 v Sw, Cz, P, W, Ni, S, Br, Fi (12)

Francis, T. (Birmingham C), 1977 v Ho, L, S, Br; 1978 v Sw, L, I (sub), WG (sub), Br, W, S, H; (with Nottingham F), 1979 v Bul (sub), Se, A (sub); 1980 v Ni, Bul, Sp; 1981 v Sp, R, S (sub), Sw; (with Manchester C), 1982 v N, Ni, W, S (sub), Fi (sub), F, Cz, K, WG, Sp; (with Sampdoria), 1983 v D, Gr, H, Ni, S, Aus (3); 1984 v D, Ni, USSR; 1985 v EG (sub), T (sub), Ni (sub), R, Fi, S, I, M; 1986 v S (52)

Franklin, C. F. (Stoke C), 1947 v S, W, Ni, Ei, Ho, F, Sw, P; 1948 v S, W, Ni, Bel, Se, I; 1949 v S, W, Ni, D, Sw, N, F, Se; 1950 v W, S, Ni, Ei, I (27)

Freeman, B. C. (Everton), 1909 v S, W; (with Burnley), 1912 v S, W, Ni (5)

Froggatt, J. (Portsmouth), 1950 v Ni, I; 1951 v S; 1952 v S, A (2), I, Sw; 1953 v Ni, W, S, Bel, US (13)

Froggatt, R. (Sheffield W), 1953 v W, S, Bel, US (4)

Fry, C. B. (Corinthians), 1901 v Ni (1)

Furness, W. I. (Leeds U), 1933 v I (1)

Galley, T. (Wolverhampton W), 1937 v N, Se (2)

Gardner, T. (Aston Villa), 1934 v Cz; 1935 v Ho (2)

Garfield, B. (WBA), 1898 v Ni (1)

Garratty, W. (Aston Villa), 1903 v W (1)

Garrett, T. (Blackpool), 1952 v S, I; 1954 v W (3)

Gascoigne, P. J. (Tottenham H), 1989 v D (sub), S.Ar (sub), Alb (sub), Ch, S (sub); 1990 v Se (sub), Br (sub), Cz, D, U, Tun, Ei, Ho, Eg, Bel, Cam, WG; 1991 v H, Pol, Cam (20)

Gates, E. (Ipswich T), 1981 v N, R (2)

Gay, L. H. (Cambridge University), 1893 v S; (with Old Brightonians), 1894 v S, W (3)

Geary, F. (Everton), 1890 v Ni; 1891 v S (2)

Geaves, R. L. (Clapham Rovers), 1875 v S (1)

Gee, C. W. (Everton), 1932 v W, Sp; 1937 v Ni (3)

Geldard, A. (Everton), 1933 v I, Sw; 1935 v S; 1938 v Ni (4)

George, C. (Derby Co), 1977 v Ei (1)

George, W. (Aston Villa), 1902 v S, W, Ni (3)

Gibbins, W. V. T. (Clapton), 1924 v F; 1925 v F (2)

Gidman, J. (Aston Villa), 1977 v L (1)

Gillard, I. T. (QPR), 1975 v WG, W; 1976 v Cz (3)

Gilliat, W. E. (Old Carthusians), 1893 v Ni (1)

Goddard, P. (West Ham U), 1982 v lc (sub) (1)

Goodall, F. R. (Huddersfield T), 1926 v S; 1927 v S, F, Bel, L; 1928 v S, W, F, Bel; 1930 v S, G, A; 1931 v S, W, Ni, Bel; 1932 v Ni; 1933 v W, Ni, A, I, Sw; 1934 v W, Ni, F (25)

Goodall, J. (Preston NE), 1888 v S, W; 1889 v S, W; (with Derby Co), 1891 v S, W; 1892 v S; 1893 v W; 1894 v S; 1895 v S, Ni; 1896 v S, W; 1898 v W (14)

Goodhart, H. C. (Old Etonians), 1883 v S, W, Ni (3)

Goodwyn, A. G. (Royal Engineers), 1873 v S (1)

Goodyer, A. C. (Nottingham F), 1879 v S (1)

Gosling, R. C. (Old Etonians), 1892 v W; 1893 v S; 1894 v W; 1895 v W, S (5)

Gosnell, A. A. (Newcastle U), 1906 v Ni (1)

Gough, H. C. (Sheffield U), 1921 v S (1)

Goulden, L. A. (West Ham U), 1937 v Se, N; 1938 v W, Ni, Cz, G, Sw, F; 1939 v S, W, R of E, I, R, Y (14)

Graham, L. (Millwall), 1925 v S, W (2)

Graham, T. (Nottingham F), 1931 v F; 1932 v Ni (2)

Grainger, C. (Sheffield U), 1956 v Br, Se, Fi, WG; 1957 v W, Ni; (with Sunderland), 1957 v S (7)

Gray, A. A. (C Palace), 1992 v Pol (1)

Greaves, J. (Chelsea), 1959 v Pe, M, US; 1960 v W, Se, Y, Sp; 1961 v Ni, W, S, L, P, Sp, I, A; (with Tottenham H), 1962 v S, Sw, Pe, H, Arg, Bul, Br; 1963 v Ni, W, S, F (2), Br, Cz, Sw; 1964 v W, Ni, R of W, P (2), Ei, Br, U, Arg; 1965 v S, Ni, S, Bel, Ho, H, Y; 1966 v W, A, Y, N, D, Pol, U, M, F; 1967 v S, Sp, A (57)

Green, F. T. (Wanderers), 1876 v S (1)

Green, G. H. (Sheffield U), 1925 v F; 1926 v S, Bel, W; 1927 v W, Ni; 1928 v F, Bel (8)

Greenhalgh, E. H. (Notts Co), 1872 v S; 1873 v S (2)

Greenhoff, B. (Manchester U), 1976 v W, Ni; 1977 v Ei, Fi, I, Ho, Ni, W, S, Br, Arg, U; 1978 v Br, W, Ni, S (sub), H (sub); (with Leeds U), 1980 v Aus (sub) (18)

Greenwood, D. H. (Blackburn R), 1882 v S, Ni (2)

Gregory, J. (QPR), 1983 v Aus (3); 1984 v D, H, W (6)

Grimsdell, A. (Tottenham H), 1920 v S, W; 1921 v S, Ni; 1923 v W, Ni (6)

Grosvenor, A. T. (Birmingham), 1934 v Ni, W, F (3)

Gunn, W. (Notts Co), 1884 v S, W (2)

Gurney, R. (Sunderland), 1935 v S (1)

Hacking, J. (Oldham Ath), 1929 v S, W, Ni (3)

Hadley, N. (WBA), 1903 v Ni (1)

Hagan, J. (Sheffield U), 1949 v D (1)

Haines, J. T. W. (WBA), 1949 v Sw (1)

Hall, A. E. (Aston Villa), 1910 v Ni (1)

Hall, G. W. (Tottenham H), 1934 v F; 1938 v S, W, Ni, Cz; 1939 v S, Ni, R of E, I, Y (10)

Hall, J. (Birmingham C), 1956 v S, W, Ni, Br, Se, Fi, WG, D, Sp; 1957 v W, Ni, Y, D (2), Ei (2) (17)

Halse, H. J. (Manchester U), 1909 v A (1)

Hammond, H. E. D. (Oxford University), 1889 v S (1)

Hampson, J. (Blackpool), 1931 v Ni, W; 1933 v A (3)

Hampton, H. (Aston Villa), 1913 v S, W; 1914 v S, W (4)

Hancocks, J. (Wolverhampton W), 1949 v Sw; 1950 v W; 1951 v Y (3)

Hapgood, E. (Arsenal), 1933 v I, Sw; 1934 v S, Ni, W, H, Cz; 1935 v S, Ni, W, I, Ho; 1936 v S, Ni, W, G, A, Bel; 1937 v Fi; 1938 v S, G, Sw, F; 1939 v S, W, Ni, R of E, N, I, Y (30)

Hardinge, H. T. W. (Sheffield U), 1910 v S (1)

Hardman, H. P. (Everton), 1905 v W; 1907 v S, Ni; 1908 v W (4)

Hardwick, G. F. M. (Middlesbrough), 1947 v S, W, Ni, Ei, Ho, F, Sw, P; 1948 v S, W, Ni, Bel, Se (13)

Hardy, H. (Stockport Co), 1925 v Bel (1)

Hardy, S. (Liverpool), 1907 v S, W, Ni; 1908 v S; 1909 v S, W, Ni, H (2), A; 1910 v S, W, Ni; 1912 v Ni; (with Aston Villa), 1913 v S; 1914 v Ni, W, S; 1920 v S, W, Ni (21)

Harford, M. G. (Luton T), 1988 v Is (sub); 1989 v D (2)

Hargreaves, F. W. (Blackburn R), 1880 v W; 1881 v W; 1882 v Ni (3)

Hargreaves, J. (Blackburn R), 1881 v S, W (2)

Harper, E. C. (Blackburn R), 1926 v S (1)

Harris, G. (Burnley), 1966 v Pol (1)

Harris, P. P. (Portsmouth), 1950 v Ei; 1954 v H (2)

Harris, S. S. (Cambridge University), 1904 v S; (with Old Westminsters), 1905 v Ni, W; 1906 v S, W, Ni (6)

Harrison, A. H. (Old Westminsters), 1893 v S, Ni (2)

Harrison, G. (Everton), 1921 v Bel; 1922 v Ni (2)

Harrow, J. H. (Chelsea), 1923 v Ni, Se (2)

Hart, E. (Leeds U), 1929 v W; 1930 v W, Ni; 1933 v S, A; 1934 v S, H, Cz (8)

Hartley, F. (Oxford C), 1923 v F (1)

Harvey, A. (Wednesbury Strollers), 1881 v W (1)

Harvey, J. C. (Everton), 1971 v Ma (1)

Hassall, H. W. (Huddersfield T), 1951 v S, Arg, P; 1952 v F; (with Bolton W), 1954 v Ni (5)

Hateley, M. (Portsmouth), 1984 v USSR (sub), Br, U, Ch; (with AC Milan), 1985 v EG (sub), Fi, Ni, Ei, Fi, S, I, M; 1986 v R, T, Eg, S, M, Ca, P, Mor, Para (sub); 1987 v T (sub), Br (sub), S; (with Monaco), 1988 v WG (sub), Ho (sub), H (sub), Co (sub), Ei (sub), Ho (sub), USSR (sub); (with Rangers), 1992 v Cz (32)

Haworth, G. (Accrington), 1887 v Ni, W, S; 1888 v S; 1890 v S (5)

Hawtrey, J. P. (Old Etonians), 1881 v S, W (2)

Hawkes, R. M. (Luton T), 1907 v Ni; 1908 v A (2), H, B (5)

Haygarth, E. B. (Swifts), 1875 v S (1)

Haynes, J. N. (Fulham), 1955 v Ni; 1956 v S, Ni, Br, Se, Fi, WG, Sp; 1957 v W, Y, D, Ei (2); 1958 v W, Ni, S, F, P, Y, USSR (3), Br, A; 1959 v S, Ni, USSR, I, Br, Pe, M, US; 1960 v Ni, Y, Sp, H; 1961 v Ni, W, S, L, P, Sp, M, I, A; 1962 v W, Ni, S, A, Sw, Pe, P, H, Arg, Bul, Br (56)

Healless, H. (Blackburn R), 1925 v Ni; 1928 v S (2)

Hector, K. J. (Derby Co), 1974 v Pol (sub), I (sub) (2)

Hedley, G. A. (Sheffield U), 1901 v Ni (1)

Hegan, K. E. (Corinthians), 1923 v Bel, F; 1924 v Ni, Bel (4)

Hellawell, M. S. (Birmingham C), 1963 v Ni, F (2)

Henfrey, A. G. (Cambridge University), 1891 v Ni; (with Corinthians), 1892 v W; 1895 v W; 1896 v S, W (5)

Henry, R. P. (Tottenham H), 1963 v F (1)

Heron, F. (Wanderers), 1876 v S (1)

Heron, G. H. H. (Uxbridge), 1873 v S; 1874 v S; (with Wanderers), 1875 v S; 1876 v S; 1878 v S (5)

Hibbert, W. (Bury), 1910 v S (1)

Hibbs, H. E. (Birmingham), 1930 v S, W, A, G; 1931 v S, W, Ni; 1932 v W, Ni, Sp; 1933 v S, W, Ni, A, I, Sw; 1934 v Ni, W, F; 1935 v S, W, Ni, Ho; 1936 v G, W (25)

Hill, F. (Bolton W), 1963 v Ni, W (2)

Hill, G. A. (Manchester U), 1976 v I; 1977 v Ei (sub), Fi (sub), L; 1978 v Sw (sub), L (6)

Hill, J. H. (Burnley), 1925 v W; 1926 v S; 1927 v S, Ni, Bel, F; 1928 v Ni, W; 1929 v F, Bel, Sp (11)

Hill, R. (Luton T), 1983 v D (sub), WG; 1986 v Eg (sub) (3)

Hill, R. H. (Millwall), 1926 v Bel (1)

Hillman, J. (Burnley), 1899 v Ni (1)

Hills, A. F. (Old Harrovians), 1879 v S (1)

Hilsdon, G. R. (Chelsea), 1907 v Ni; 1908 v S, W, Ni, A, H, B; 1909 v Ni (8)

Hine, E. W. (Leicester C), 1929 v W, Ni; 1930 v W, Ni; 1932 v W, Ni (6)

Hinton, A. T. (Wolverhampton W), 1963 v F; (with Nottingham F), 1965 v W, Bel (3)

Hirst, D. E. (Sheffield W), 1991 v Aus, Nz (sub); 1992 v F (3)

Hitchens, G. A. (Aston Villa), 1961 v M, I, A; (with Inter Milan), 1962 v Sw, Pe, H, Br (7)

Hobbis, H. H. F. (Charlton Ath), 1936 v A, Bel (2)

Hoddle, G. (Tottenham H), 1980 v Bul, W, Aus, Sp; 1981 v Sp, W, S; 1982 v N, Ni, W, Ic, Cz (sub), K; 1983 v L (sub), Ni, S; 1984 v H, L, F; 1985 v Ei (sub), S, I (sub), M, WG, US; 1986 v R, T, Ni, Is, USSR, S, M, Ca, P, Mor, Pol, Para, Arg; 1987 v Se, Ni, Y, Sp, T, S; (with Monaco), 1988 v WG, T (sub), Y (sub), Ho (sub), H (sub) Co (sub), Ei (sub), Ho, USSR (53)

Hodge, S. B. (Aston Villa), 1986 v USSR (sub), S, Ca, P (sub), Mor (sub), Pol, Para, Arg; 1987 v Se, Ni, Y; (with Tottenham H), Sp. Ni, T, S; (with Nottingham F), 1989 v D; 1990 v I (sub), Y (sub), Cz, D, U, Tun; 1991 v Cam (sub), T (sub) (24)

Hodgetts, D. (Aston Villa), 1888 v S, W, Ni; 1892 v S, Ni; 1894 v Ni (6)

Hodgkinson, A. (Sheffield U), 1957 v S, Ei (2), D; 1961 v W (5)

Hodgson, G (Liverpool), 1931 v S, Ni, W (3)

Hodkinson, J. (Blackburn R), 1913 v W, S; 1920 v Ni (3)

Hogg, W. (Sunderland), 1902 v S, W, Ni (3)

Holdcroft, G. H. (Preston NE), 1937 v W, Ni (2)

Holden, A. D. (Bolton W), 1959 v S, I, Br, Pe, M (5)

Holden, G. H. (Wednesday OA), 1881 v S; 1884 v S, W, Ni (4)

Holden-White, C. (Corinthians), 1888 v W, S (2)

Holford, T. (Stoke), 1903 v Ni (1)

Holley, G. H. (Sunderland), 1909 v S, W, H (2), A; 1910 v W; 1912 v S, W, NI; 1913 v S (10)

Holliday, E. (Middlesbrough), 1960 v W, Ni, Se (3)

Hollins, J. W. (Chelsea), 1967 v Sp (1)

Holmes, R. (Preston NE), 1888 v Ni; 1891 v S; 1892 v S; 1893 v S, W; 1894 v Ni; 1895 v Ni (7)

Holt, J. (Everton), 1890 v W; 1891 v S, W; 1892 v S, Ni; 1893 v S; 1894 v S, Ni; 1895 v S; (with Reading), 1900 v Ni (10)

Hopkinson, E. (Bolton W), 1958 v W, Ni, S, F, P, Y; 1959 v S, I, Br, Pe, M, US; 1960 v W, Se (14)

Hossack, A. H. (Corinthians), 1892 v W; 1894 v W (2)

Houghton, W. E. (Aston Villa), 1931 v Ni, W, F, Bel; 1932 v S, Ni; 1933 v A (7)

Houlker, A. E. (Blackburn R), 1902 v S; (with Portsmouth), 1903 v S, W; (with Southampton), 1906 v W, Ni (5)

Howarth, R. H. (Preston NE), 1887 v Ni; 1888 v S, W; 1891 v S; (with Everton), 1894 v Ni (5)

Howe, D. (WBA), 1958 v S, W, Ni, F, P, Y, USSR (3), Br, A; 1959 v S, W, Ni, USSR, I, Br, Pe, M, US; 1960 v W, Ni, Se (23)

Howe, J. R. (Derby Co), 1948 v I; 1949 v S, Ni (3)

Howell, L. S. (Wanderers), 1873 v S (1)

Howell, R. (Sheffield U), 1895 v Ni; (with Liverpool) 1899 v S (2)

Hudson, A. A. (Stoke C), 1975 v WG, Cy (2)

Hudson, J. (Sheffield), 1883 v Ni (1)

Hudspeth, F. C. (Newcastle U), 1926 v Ni (1)

Hufton, A. E. (West Ham U), 1924 v Bel; 1928 v S, Ni; 1929 v F, Bel, Sp (6)

Hughes, E. W. (Liverpool), 1970 v W, Ni, S, Ho, P, Bel; 1971 v EG, Ma (2), Gr, W; 1972 v Sw, Gr, WG (2), W, Ni, S; 1973 v W (3), S (2), Pol, USSR, I; 1974 v A, Pol, I, W, Ni, S, Arg, EG, Bul, Y; 1975 v Cz, P, Cy (sub); Ni; 1977 v I, L, W, S, Br, Arg, U; 1978 v Sw, L, I, WG,

Ni, S, H; 1979 v D, Ei, Ni, W, Se; (with Wolverhampton W), 1980 v Sp (sub), Ni, S (sub) (62)

Hughes, L. (Liverpool), 1950 v Ch, US, Sp (3)

Hulme, J. H. A. (Arsenal), 1927 v S, Bel, F; 1928 v S, Ni, W; 1929 v Ni, W; 1933 v S (9)

Humphreys, P. (Notts Co), 1903 v S (1)

Hunt, G. S. (Tottenham H), 1933 v I, Sw, S (3)

Hunt, Rev K. R. G. (Leyton), 1911 v S, W (2)

Hunt, R. (Liverpool), 1962 v A; 1963 v EG; 1964 v S, US, P; 1965 v W; 1966 v S, Sp, Pol (2), WG (2), Fi, N, U, M, F, Arg, P; 1967 v Ni, W, Cz, Sp, A; 1968 v W, Ni, USSR (2) Sp (2), Se, Y; 1969 v R (2) (34)

Hunt, S. (WBA), 1984 v S (sub), USSR (sub) (2)

Hunter, J. (Sheffield Heeley), 1878 v S; 1880 v S, W; 1881 v S, W; 1882 v S, W (7)

Hunter, N. (Leeds U), 1966 v WG, Y, Fi, Sp (sub); 1967 v A; 1968 v Sp, Se, Y, WG, USSR; 1969 v R, W; 1970 v Ho, WG (sub); 1971 v Ma; 1972 v WG (2), W, Ni, S; 1973 v W (2) USSR (sub); 1974 v A, Pol, Ni (sub), S; 1975 v Cz (28)

Hurst, G. C. (West Ham U), 1966 v S, WG (2), Y, Fi, D, Arg, P; 1967 v Ni, W, S, Cz, Sp, A; 1968 v W, Ni, S, Se (sub), WG, USSR (2); 1969 v Ni, S, R (2), Bul, F, M, U, Br; 1970 v W, Ni, S, Ho (1 + 1 sub), Bel, Co, Ec, R, Br, WG; 1971 v EG, Gr, W, S; 1972 v Sw (2), Gr, WG (49)

Iremonger, J. (Nottingham F), 1901 v S; 1902 v Ni (2)

Jack, D. N. B. (Bolton W), 1924 v S, W; 1928 v F; Bel; (with Arsenal), 1930 v S, G, A; 1933 v W, A (9)

Jackson, E. (Oxford University), 1891 v W (1)

Jarrett, B. G. (Cambridge University), 1876 v S; 1877 v S; 1878 v S (3)

Jefferis, F. (Everton), 1912 v S, W (2)

Jezzard, B. A. G. (Fulham), 1954 v H; 1956 v Ni (2)

Johnson, D. E. (Ipswich T), 1975 v W, S; 1976 v Sw; (with Liverpool), 1980 v Ei, Arg, Ni, S, Bel (8)

Johnson, E. (Saltley College), 1880 v W; (with Stoke C), 1884 v Ni (2)

Johnson, J. A. (Stoke C), 1937 v N, Se, Fi, S, Ni (5)

Johnson, T. C. F. (Manchester C), 1926 v Bel; 1930 v W; (with Everton), 1932 v S, Sp; 1933 v Ni (5)

Johnson, W. H. (Sheffield U), 1900 v S, W, Ni; 1903 v S, W, Ni (6)

Johnston, H. (Blackpool), 1947 v S, Ho; 1951 v S; 1953 v Arg, Ch, U, US; 1954 v W, Ni, H (10)

Jones, A. (Walsall Swifts), 1882 v S, W; (with Great Lever), 1883 v S (3)

Jones, H. (Blackburn R), 1927 v S, Bel, L, F; 1928 v S, Ni (6)

Jones, H. (Nottingham F), 1923 v F (1)

Jones, M. D. (Sheffield U), 1965 v WG, Se; (with Leeds U), 1970 v Ho (3)

Jones, R. (Liverpool), 1992 v F (1)

Jones, W. (Bristol C), 1901 v Ni (1)

Jones, W. H. (Liverpool), 1950 v P, Bel (2)

Joy, B. (Casuals), 1936 v Bel (1)

Kail, E. I. L. (Dulwich Hamlet), 1929 v F, Bel, Sp (3)

Kay, A. H. (Everton), 1963 v Sw (1)

Kean, F. W. (Sheffield W), 1923 v S, Bel; 1924 v W; 1925 v Ni; 1926 v Ni, Bel; 1927 v L; (with Bolton W), 1929 v F, Sp (9)

Keegan, J. K. (Liverpool), 1973 v W (2); 1974 v W, Ni, Arg, EG, Bul, Y; 1975 v Cz, WG, Cy (2), Ni, S; 1976 v Sw, Cz, P, W (2), Ni, S, Br, Fi; 1977 v Ei, Fi, I, Ho, L; (with SV Hamburg), W, Br, Arg, U; 1978 v Sw, I, WG, Br, H; 1979 v D, Ei, Cz, Ni, W, S, Bul, Se, A; 1980 v D, Ni, Ei, Sp (2), Arg, Bel, I; (with Southampton), 1981 v Sp, Sw, H; 1982 v N, H, Ni, S, Fi, Sp (sub) (63)

Keen, E. R. L. (Derby Co), 1933 v A; 1937 v W, Ni, H (4)

Kelly, R. (Burnley), 1920 v S; 1921 v S, W, Ni; 1922 v S, W; 1923 v S; 1924 v Ni; 1925 v W, Ni, S; (with Sunderland), 1926 v W; (with Huddersfield T), 1927 v L; 1928 v S (14)

Kennedy, A. (Liverpool), 1984 v Ni, W (2)

Kennedy, R. (Liverpool), 1976 v W (2), Ni, S; 1977 v L, W, S, Br (sub), Arg (sub); 1978 v Sw, L; 1980 v Bul, Sp, Arg, W, Bel (sub), I (17)

Kenyon-Slaney, W. S. (Wanderers), 1873 v S (1)

Keown, M. R. (Everton), 1992 v F, Cz, C, H, Br, Fi, D, F, Se (9)

Kevan, D. T. (WBA), 1957 v S; 1958 v W, Ni, S, P. Y, USSR (3), Br, A; 1959 v M, US; 1961 v M (14)

Kidd, B. (Manchester U), 1970 v Ni, Ec (sub) (2)

King, R. S. (Oxford University), 1882 v Ni (1)

Kingsford, R. K. (Wanderers), 1874 v S (1)

Kingsley, M. (Newcastle U), 1901 v W (1)

Kinsey, G. (Wolverhampton W), 1892 v W; 1893 v S; (with Derby Co), 1896 v W, Ni (4)

Kirchen, A. J. (Arsenal), 1937 v N, Se, Fi (3)

Kirton, W. J. (Aston Villa), 1922 v Ni (1)

Knight, A. E. (Portsmouth), 1920 v Ni (1)

Knowles, C. (Tottenham H), 1968 v USSR, Sp, Se, WG (4)

Labone, B. L. (Everton), 1963 v Ni, W, F; 1967 v Sp, A; 1968 v S, Sp, Se, Y, USSR, WG; 1969 v Ni, S, R, Bul, M, U, Br; 1970 v S, W, Bel, Co, Ec, R, Br, WG (26)

Lampard, F. R. G. (West Ham U), 1973 v Y; 1980 v Aus (2)

Langley, E. J. (Fulham), 1958 v S, P, Y (3)

Langton, R. (Blackburn R), 1947 v W, Ni, Ei, Ho, F, Sw; 1948 v Se; (with Preston NE), 1949 v D, Se; (with Bolton W), 1950 v S; 1951 v Ni (11)

Latchford, R. D. (Everton), 1978 v I, Br, W; 1979 v D, Ei, Cz (sub), Ni (2), W, S, Bul, A (12)

Latheron, E. G. (Blackburn R), 1913 v W; 1914 v Ni (2)

Lawler, C. (Liverpool), 1971 v Ma, W, S; 1972 v Sw (4)

Lawton, T. (Everton), 1939 v S, W, Ni, R of E, N, I, R, Y; (with Chelsea), 1947 v S, W, Ni, Ei, Ho, F, Sw, P; 1948 v W, Ni, Bel; (with Notts Co), 1948 v S, Se, I; 1949 v D (23)

Leach, T. (Sheffield W), 1931 v W, Ni (2)

Leake, A. (Aston Villa), 1904 v S, Ni; 1905 v S, W, Ni (5)

Lee, E. A. (Southampton), 1904 v W (1)

Lee, F. H. (Manchester C), 1969 v Ni, W, S, Bul, F, M, U; 1970 v Ho (2), P, Bel, Co, Ec, R, Br, WG; 1971 v EG, Gr, Ma, Ni, W, S; 1972 v Sw (2), Gr, WG (27)

Lee, J. (Derby Co), 1951 v Ni (1)

Lee, S. (Liverpool), 1983 v Gr, L, W, Gr, H, S, Aus; 1984 v D, H, L, F, Ni, W, Ch (sub) (14)

Leighton, J. E. (Nottingham F), 1886 v Ni (1)

Lilley, H. E. (Sheffield U), 1892 v W (1)

Linacre, H. J. (Nottingham F), 1905 v W, S (2)

Lindley, T. (Cambridge University), 1886 v S, W, Ni; 1887 v S, W, Ni; 1888 v S, W, Ni; (with Nottingham F), 1889 v S; 1890 v S, W; 1891 v Ni (13)

Lindsay, A. (Liverpool), 1974 v Arg, EG, Bul, Y (4)

Lindsay, W. (Wanderers), 1877 v S (1)

Lineker, G. (Leicester C), 1984 v S (sub); 1985 v Ei, R (sub), S (sub), I (sub), WG, US; (with Everton), 1986 v R, T, Ni, Eg, USSR, Ca, P, Mor, Pol, Para, Arg; (with Barcelona), 1987 v Ni (2), Y, Sp, T, Br; 1988 v WG, T, Y, Ho, H, S, Co, Sw, Ei, Ho, USSR; 1989 v Se, S.Ar, Gr, Alb (2), Pol, D; (with Tottenham H) 1990 v Se, Pol, I, Y, Br, Cz, D, U, Tun, Ei, Ho, Eg, Bel, Cam, WG, I; 1991 v H, Pol, Ei (2), Cam, T, Arg, Aus, Nz, Mal; 1992 v G, T, Pol, F (sub), Cz (sub), C, H, Br, Fi, D, F, Se (80)

Lintott, E. H. (QPR), 1908 v S, W, Ni; (with Bradford C), 1909 v S, Ni, H (2) (7)

Lipsham, H. B. (Sheffield U), 1902 v W (1)

Little, B. (Aston Villa), 1975 v W (sub) (1)

Lloyd, L. V. (Liverpool), 1971 v W; 1972 v Sw, Ni; (with Nottingham F), 1980 v W (4)

Lockett, A. (Stoke C), 1903 v Ni (1)

Lodge, L. V. (Cambridge University), 1894 v W; 1895 v S, W; (with Corinthians), 1896 v S, Ni (5)

Lofthouse, J. M. (Blackburn R), 1885 v S, W, Ni; 1887 v S, W; (with Accrington), 1889 v Ni; (with Blackburn R), 1890 v Ni (7)

Lofthouse, N. (Bolton W), 1951 v Y; 1952 v W, Ni, S, A (2), I, Sw; 1953 v W, Ni, S, Bel, Arg, Ch, U, US; 1954 v W, Ni, R of E, Bel, U; 1955 v Ni, S, F, Sp, P; 1956 v W, S, Sp, D, Fi (sub); 1959 v W, USSR (33)

Longworth, E. (Liverpool), 1920 v S; 1921 v Bel; 1923 v S, W, Bel (5)

Lowder, A. (Wolverhampton W), 1889 v W (1)

Lowe, E. (Aston Villa), 1947 v F, Sw, P (3)

Lucas, T. (Liverpool), 1922 v Ni; 1924 v F; 1926 v Bel (3)

Luntley, E. (Nottingham F), 1880 v S, W (2)

Lyttelton, Hon. A. (Cambridge University), 1877 v S (1)

Lyttelton, Hon. E. (Cambridge University), 1878 v S (1)

McCall, J. (Preston NE), 1913 v S, W; 1914 v S; 1920 v S, 1921 v Ni (5)

McDermott, T. (Liverpool), 1978 v Sw, L; 1979 v Ni, W, Se; 1980 v D, Ni (sub), Ei, Ni, S, Bel (sub), Sp; 1981 v N, R, Sw, R (sub), Br, Sw (sub), H; 1982 v N, H, W (sub), Ho, S (sub), Ic (25)

McDonald, C. A. (Burnley), 1958 v USSR (3), Br, A; 1959 v W, Ni, USSR (8)

Macdonald, M. (Newcastle U), 1972 v W, Ni, S (sub); 1973 v USSR (sub); 1974 v P, S (sub), Y (sub); 1975 v WG, Cy (2), Ni; 1976 v Sw (sub), Cz, P (14)

McFarland, R. L. (Derby Co), 1971 v Gr, Ma (2), Ni, S; 1972 v Sw, Gr, WG, S; 1973 v W (3), Ni, S, Cz, Pol, USSR, I; 1974 v A, Pol, I, W, Ni; 1976 v Cz, S; 1977 v Ei, I (28)

McGarry, W.H. (Huddersfield T), 1954 v Sw, U; 1956 v W, D (4)

McGuinness, W. (Manchester U), 1959 v Ni, M (2)

McInroy, A. (Sunderland), 1927 v Ni (1)

McMahon, S. (Liverpool), 1988 v Is, H, Co, USSR; 1989 v D (sub); 1990 v Se, Pol, I, Y (sub), Br, Cz (sub), D, Ei (sub), Eg, Bel, I; 1991 v Ei (17)

McNab, R. (Arsenal), 1969 v Ni, Bul, R (1 + 1 sub) (4)

McNeal, R. (WBA), 1914 v S, W (2)

McNeil, M. (Middlesbrough), 1961 v W, Ni, S, L, P, Sp, M, I; 1962 v L (9)

Mabbutt, G. (Tottenham H), 1983 v WG, Gr, L, W, Gr, H, Ni, S (sub); 1984 v H; 1987 v Y, Ni, T; 1988 v WG; 1992 v T, Pol, Cz (16)

Macaulay, R. H. (Cambridge University), 1881 v S (1)

Macrae, S. (Notts Co), 1883 v S, W, Ni; 1884 v S, W, Ni (6)

Maddison, F. B. (Oxford University), 1872 v S (1)

Madeley, P. E. (Leeds U), 1971 v Ni; 1972 v Sw (2), Gr, WG (2), W, S; 1973 v S, Cz, Pol, USSR, I; 1974 v A, Pol, I; 1975 v Cz, P, Cy; 1976 v Cz, P, Fi; 1977 v Ei, Ho (24)

Magee, T. P. (WBA), 1923 v W, Se; 1925 v S, Bel, F (5)

Makepeace, H. (Everton), 1906 v S; 1910 v S; 1912 v S, W (4)

Male, C. G. (Arsenal), 1935 v S, Ni, I, Ho; 1936 v S, W, Ni, G, A, Bel; 1937 v S, Ni, H, N, Se, Fi; 1939 v I, R, Y (19)

Mannion, W. J. (Middlesbrough), 1947 v S, W, Ni, Ei, Ho, F, Sw, P; 1948 v W, Ni, Bel, Se, I; 1949 v N, F; 1950 v S, Ei, P, Bel, Ch, US; 1951 v Ni, W, S, Y; 1952 v F (26)

Mariner, P. (Ipswich T), 1977 v L (sub), Ni; 1978 v L, W (sub), S; 1980 v W, Ni (sub), S, Aus, I (sub), Sp (sub); 1981 v N, Sw, Sp, Sw, H; 1982 v N, H, Ho, S, Fi, F, Cz, K, WG, Sp; 1983 v D, WG, Gr, W; 1984 v D, H, L; (with Arsenal), 1985 v EG, R (35)

Marsden, J. T. (Darwen), 1891 v Ni (1)

Marsden, W. (Sheffield W), 1930 v W, S, G (3)

Marsh, R. W. (QPR), 1972 v Sw (sub); (with Manchester C), WG (sub + 1), W, Ni, S; 1973 v W (2), Y (9)

Marshall, T. (Darwen), 1880 v W; 1881 v W (2)

Martin, A. (West Ham U), 1981 v Br, S (sub); 1982 v H, Fi; 1983 v Gr, L, W, Gr, H; 1984 v H, L, W; 1985 v Ni; 1986 v Is, Ca, Para; 1987 v Se (17)

Martin, H. (Sunderland), 1914 v Ni (1)

Martyn, A. N. (C Palace), 1992 v C (sub), H (2)

Marwood, B. (Arsenal), 1989 v S.Ar (sub) (1)

Maskrey, H. M. (Derby Co), 1908 v Ni (1)

Mason, C. (Wolverhampton W), 1887 v Ni; 1888 v W; 1890 v Ni (3)

Matthews, R. D. (Coventry C), 1956 v S, Br, Se, WG; 1957 v Ni (5)

Matthews, S. (Stoke C), 1935 v W, I; 1936 v G; 1937 v S; 1938 v S, W, Cz, G, Sw, F; 1939 v S, W, Ni, R of E, N, I, Y; 1947 v S; (with Blackpool), 1947 v Sw, P; 1948 v S, W, Ni, Bel, I; 1949 v S, W, Ni, D, Sw; 1950 v Sp; 1951 v Ni, S; 1954 v Ni, R of E, H, Bel, U; 1955 v Ni, W, S, F, WG, Sp, P; 1956 v W, Br; 1957 v S, W, Ni, Y, D (2), Ei (54)

Matthews, V. (Sheffield U), 1928 v F, Bel (2)

Maynard, W. J. (1st Surrey Rifles), 1872 v S; 1876 v S (2)

Meadows, J. (Manchester C), 1955 v S (1)

Medley, L. D. (Tottenham H), 1951 v Y, W; 1952 v F, A, W, Ni (6)

Meehan, T. (Chelsea), 1924 v Ni (1)

Melia, J. (Liverpool), 1963 v S, Sw (2)

Mercer, D. W. (Sheffield U), 1923 v Ni, Bel (2)

Mercer, J. (Everton), 1939 v S, Ni, I, R, Y (5)

Merrick, G. H. (Birmingham C), 1952 v Ni, S, A (2), I, Sw; 1953 v Ni, W, S, Bel, Arg, Ch, U; 1954 v W, Ni, S, R of E, H (2), Y, Bel, Sw, U (23)

Merson, P. C. (Arsenal), 1992 v G (sub), Cz, H, Br (sub), Fi (sub), D, Se (sub) (7)

Metcalfe, V. (Huddersfield T), 1951 v Arg, P (2)

Mew, J. W. (Manchester U), 1921 v Ni (1)

Middleditch, B. (Corinthians), 1897 v Ni (1)

Milburn, J. E. T. (Newcastle U), 1949 v S, W, Ni, Sw; 1950 v W, P, Bel, Sp; 1951 v W, Arg, P; 1952 v F; 1956 v D (13)

Miller, B. G. (Burnley), 1961 v A (1)

Miller, H. S. (Charlton Ath), 1923 v Se (1)

Mills, G. R. (Chelsea), 1938 v W, Ni, Cz (3)

Mills, M. D. (Ipswich T), 1973 v Y; 1976 v W (2), Ni, S, Br, I (sub), Fi; 1977 v Fi (sub), I, Ni, W, S; 1978 v WG, Br, W, Ni, S, H; 1979 v D, Ei, Ni (2), S, Bul, A; 1980 v D, Ni, Sp (2); 1981 v Sw (2), H; 1982 v N, H, S, Fi, F, Cz, K, WG, Sp (42)

Milne, G. (Liverpool), 1963 v Br, Cz, EG; 1964 v W, Ni, S, R of W, U, P, Ei, Br, Arg; 1965 v Ni, Bel (14)

Milton, C. A. (Arsenal), 1952 v A (1)

Milward, A. (Everton), 1891 v S, W; 1897 v S, W (4)

Mitchell, C. (Upton Park), 1880 v W; 1881 v S; 1883 v S, W; 1885 v W (5)

Mitchell, J. F. (Manchester C), 1925 v Ni (1)

Moffat, H. (Oldham Ath), 1913 v W (1)

Molyneux, G. (Southampton), 1902 v S; 1903 v S, W, Ni (4)

Moon, W. R. (Old Westminsters), 1888 v S, W; 1889 v S, W; 1890 v S, W; 1891 v S (7)

Moore, H. T. (Notts Co), 1883 v Ni; 1885 v W (2)

Moore, J. (Derby Co), 1923 v Se (1)

Moore, R. F. (West Ham U), 1962 v Pe, H, Arg, Bul, Br; 1963 v W, Ni, S, F (2), Br, Cz, EG, Sw; 1964 v W, Ni, S, R of W, U, P (2), Ei, Br, Arg; 1965 v Ni, S, Bel, H, Y, WG, Se; 1966 v W, Ni, S, A, Sp, Pol (2), WG (2), N, D, U, M, F, Arg, P; 1967 v W, Ni, S, Cz, Sp, A; 1968 v W, Ni, S, USSR (2), Sp (2), Se, Y, WG; 1969 v Ni, W, S, R, Bul, F, M, U, Br; 1970 v W, Ni, S, Ho, P, Bel, Co, Ec, R, Br, Cz, WG; 1971 v EG, Gr, Ma, Ni, S; 1972 v Sw (2), Gr, WG (2), W, S; 1973 v W (3), Y, S (2), Ni, Cz, Pol, USSR, I; 1974 v I (108)

Moore, W. G. B. (West Ham U), 1923 v Se (1)

Mordue, J. (Sunderland), 1912 v Ni; 1913 v Ni (2)

Morice, C. J. (Barnes), 1872 v S (1)

Morley, A. (Aston Villa), 1982 v H (sub), Ni, W, Ic; 1983 v D, Gr (6)

Morley, H. (Notts Co), 1910 v Ni (1)

Morren, T. (Sheffield U), 1898 v Ni (1)

Morris, F. (WBA), 1920 v S; 1921 v Ni (2)

Morris, J. (Derby Co), 1949 v N, F; 1950 v Ei (3)

Morris, W. W. (Wolverhampton W), 1939 v S, Ni, R (3)

Morse, H. (Notts Co), 1879 v S (1)

Mort, T. (Aston Villa), 1924 v W, F; 1926 v S (3)

Morten, A. (C Palace), 1873 v S (1)

Mortensen, S. H. (Blackpool), 1947 v P; 1948 v W, S, Ni, Bel, Se, I; 1949 v S, W, Ni, Se, N; 1950 v S, W, Ni, I, P, Bel, Ch, US, Sp; 1951 v S, Arg; 1954 v R of E, H (25)

Morton, J. R. (West Ham U), 1938 v Cz (1)

Mosforth, W. (Sheffield W), 1877 v S; (with Sheffield Albion), 1878 v S; 1879 v S, W; 1880 v S, W; (with Sheffield W), 1881 v W; 1882 v S, W (9)

Moss, F. (Arsenal), 1934 v S, H, Cz; 1935 v I (4)

Moss, F. (Aston Villa), 1922 v S, Ni; 1923 v Ni; 1924 v S, Bel (5)

Mosscrop, E. (Burnley), 1914 v S, W (2)

Mozley, B. (Derby Co), 1950 v W, Ni, Ei (3)

Mullen, J. (Wolverhampton W), 1947 v S; 1949 v N, F; 1950 v Bel (sub), Ch, US; 1954 v W, Ni, S, R of E, Y, Sw (12)

Mullery, A. P. (Tottenham H), 1965 v Ho; 1967 v Sp, A; 1968 v W, Ni, S, USSR, Sp (2), Se, Y; 1969 v Ni, S, R, Bul, F, M, U, Br; 1970 v W, Ni, S (sub), Ho (sub), Bel, P, Co, Ec, R, Cz, WG, Br; 1971 v Ma, EG, Gr; 1972 v Sw (35)

Neal, P. G. (Liverpool), 1976 v W, I; 1977 v W, S, Br, Arg, U; 1978 v Sw, I, WG, Ni, S, H; 1979 v D Ei, Ni (2), S, Bul, A; 1980 v D, Ni, Sp, Arg, W, Bel, I; 1981 v R, Sw, Sp, Br, H; 1982 v N, H, W, Ho, Ic, F (sub), K; 1983 v D, Gr, L, W, Gr, H, Ni, S, Aus (2); 1984 v D (50)

Needham, E. (Sheffield U), 1894 v S; 1895 v S; 1897 v S, W, Ni; 1898 v S, W; 1899 v S, W, Ni; 1900 v S, Ni; 1901 v S, W, Ni; 1902 v W (16)

Newton, K. R. (Blackburn R), 1966 v S, WG; 1967 v Sp, A; 1968 v W, S, Sp, Se, Y, WG; 1969 v Ni, W, S, R, Bul, M, U, Br, F; (with Everton), 1970 v Ni, S, Ho, Co, Ec, R, Cz, WG (27)

Nicholls, J. (WBA), 1954 v S, Y (2)

Nicholson, W. E. (Tottenham H), 1951 v P (1)

Nish, D. J. (Derby Co), 1973 v Ni; 1974 v P, W, Ni, S (5)

Norman, M. (Tottenham H), 1962 v Pe, H, Arg, Bul, Br; 1963 v S, F, Br, Cz, EG; 1964 v W, Ni, S, R of W, U, P (2), US, Br, Arg; 1965 v Ni, Bel, Ho (23)

Nuttall, H. (Bolton W), 1928 v W, Ni; 1929 v S (3)

Oakley, W. J. (Oxford University), 1895 v W; 1896 v S, W, Ni; (with Corinthians), 1897 v S, W, Ni; 1898 v S, W, Ni; 1900 v S, W, Ni; 1901 v S, W, Ni (16)

O'Dowd, J. P. (Chelsea), 1932 v S; 1933 v Ni, Sw (3)

O'Grady, M. (Huddersfield T), 1963 v Ni; (with Leeds U), 1969 v F (2)

Ogilvie, R. A. M. M. (Clapham R), 1874 v S (1)

Oliver, L. F. (Fulham), 1929 v Bel (1)

Olney, B. A. (Aston Villa), 1928 v F, Bel (2)

Osborne, F. R. (Fulham), 1923 v Ni, F; (with Tottenham H), 1925 v Bel; 1926 v Bel (4)

Osborne, R. (Leicester C), 1928 v W (1)

Osgood, P. L. (Chelsea), 1970 v Bel, R (sub), Cz (sub); 1974 v I (4)

Osman, R. (Ipswich T), 1980 v Aus; 1981 v Sp, R, Sw; 1982 v N, Ic; 1983 v D, Aus (3); 1984 v D (11)

Ottaway, C. J. (Oxford University), 1872 v S; 1874 v S (2)

Owen, J. R. B. (Sheffield), 1874 v S (1)

Owen, S. W. (Luton T), 1954 v H, Y, Bel (3)

Page, L. A. (Burnley), 1927 v S, W, Bel, L, F; 1928 v W, Ni (7)

Paine, T. L. (Southampton), 1963 v Cz, EG; 1964 v W, Ni, S, R of W, U, US, P; 1965 v Ni, H, Y, WG, Se; 1966 v W, A, Y, N, M (19)

Pallister, G. A. (Middlesbrough), 1988 v H; 1989 v S.Ar; (with Manchester U), 1991 v Cam (sub), T; 1992 v G (5)

Palmer, C. L. (Sheffield W), 1992 v C, H, Br, Fi (sub), D, F, Se (7)

Pantling, H. H. (Sheffield U), 1924 v Ni (1)

Paravacini, P. J. de (Cambridge University), 1883 v S, W, Ni (3)

Parker, P. A. (QPR), 1989 v Alb (sub), Ch, D; 1990 v Y, U, Ho, Eg, Bel, Cam, WG, I; 1991 v H, Pol, USSR, Aus, Nz; (with Manchester U), 1992 v G (17)

Parker, T. R. (Southampton), 1925 v F (1)

Parkes, P. B. (QPR), 1974 v P (1)

Parkinson, J. (Liverpool), 1910 v S, W (2)

Parr, P. C. (Oxford University), 1882 v W (1)

Parry, E. H. (Old Carthusians), 1879 v W; 1882 v W, S (3)

Parry, R. A. (Bolton W), 1960 v Ni, S (2)

Patchitt, B. C. A. (Corinthians), 1923 v Se (2) (2)

Pawson, F. W. (Cambridge University), 1883 v Ni; (with Swifts), 1885 v Ni (2)

Payne, J. (Luton T), 1937 v Fi (1)

Peacock, A. (Middlesbrough), 1962 v Arg, Bul; 1963 v Ni, W; (with Leeds U), 1966 v W, Ni (6)

Peacock, J. (Middlesbrough), 1929 v F, Bel, Sp (3)

Pearce, S. (Nottingham F), 1987 v Br, S; 1988 v WG (sub), Is, H; 1989 v D, Se, S.Ar, Gr, Alb (2), Ch, S, Pol, D; 1990 v Se, Pol, I, Y, Br, Cz, D, U, Tun, Ei, Ho, Eg, Bel, Cam, WG; 1991 v H, Pol, Ei (2), Cam, T, Arg, Aus, Nz (2), Mal; 1992 v T, Pol, F, Cz, Br (sub), Fi, D, F, Se (50)

Pearson, H. F. (WBA), 1932 v S (1)

Pearson, J. H. (Crewe Alex), 1892 v Ni (1)

Pearson, J. S. (Manchester U), 1976 v W, Ni, S, Br, Fi; 1977 v Ei, Ho (sub), W, S, Br, Arg, U; 1978 v I (sub), WG, Ni (15)

Pearson, S. C. (Manchester U), 1948 v S; 1949 v S, Ni; 1950 v Ni, I; 1951 v P; 1952 v S, I (8)

Pease, W. H. (Middlesbrough), 1927 v W (1)

Pegg, D. (Manchester U), 1957 v Ei (1)

Pejic, M. (Stoke C), 1974 v P, W, Ni, S (4)

Pelly, F. R. (Old Foresters), 1893 v Ni; 1894 v S, W (3)

Pennington, J. (WBA), 1907 v S, W; 1908 v S, W, Ni, A; 1909 v S, W, H (2), A; 1910 v S, W; 1911 v S, W, Ni; 1912 v S, W, Ni; 1913 v S, W; 1914 v S, Ni; 1920 v S, W (25)

Pentland, F. B. (Middlesbrough), 1909 v S, W, H (2), A (5)

Perry, C. (WBA), 1890 v Ni; 1891 v Ni; 1893 v W (3)

Perry, T. (WBA), 1898 v W (1)

Perry, W. (Blackpool), 1956 v Ni, S, Sp (3)

Perryman, S. (Tottenham H), 1982 v Ic (sub) (1)

Peters, M. (West Ham U), 1966 v Y, Fi, Pol, M, F, Arg, P, WG; 1967 v Ni, W, S, Cz; 1968 v W, Ni, S, USSR (2), Sp (2), Se, Y; 1969 v Ni, S, R, Bul, F, M, U, Br; 1970 v Ho (2), P (sub), Bel; (with Tottenham H), W,

Ni, S, Co, Ec, R, Br, Cz, WG; 1971 v EG, Gr, Ma (2), Ni, W, S; 1972 v Sw, Gr, WG (1 + 1 sub), Ni (sub); 1973 v S (2), Ni, W, Cz, Pol, USSR, I; 1974 v A, Pol, I, P, S (67)

Phelan, M. C. (Manchester U), 1990 v I (sub) (1)

Phillips, L. H. (Portsmouth), 1952 v Ni; 1955 v W, WG (3)

Pickering, F. (Everton), 1964 v US; 1965 v Ni, Bel (3)

Pickering, J. (Sheffield U), 1933 v S (1)

Pickering, N. (Sunderland), 1983 v Aus (1)

Pike, T. M. (Cambridge University), 1886 v Ni (1)

Pilkington, B. (Burnley), 1955 v Ni (1)

Plant, J. (Bury), 1900 v S (1)

Platt, D. (Aston Villa), 1990 v I (sub), Y (sub), Br, D (sub), Tun (sub), Ho (sub), Eg (sub), Bel (sub), Cam, WG, I; 1991 v H, Pol, Ei (2), T, USSR, Arg, Aus, Nz (2), Mal; (with Bari), 1992 v G, T, Pol, Cz, C, Br, Fi, D, F, Se (32)

Plum, S. L. (Charlton Ath), 1923 v F (1)

Pointer, R. (Burnley), 1962 v W, L, P (3)

Porteous, T. S. (Sunderland), 1891 v W (1)

Priest, A. E. (Sheffield U), 1900 v Ni (1)

Prinsep, J. F. M. (Clapham Rovers), 1879 v S (1)

Puddefoot, S. C. (Blackburn R), 1926 v S, Ni (2)

Pye, J. (Wolverhampton W), 1950 v Ei (1)

Pym, R. H. (Bolton W), 1925 v S, W; 1926 v W (3)

Quantrill, A. (Derby Co), 1920 v S, W; 1921 v W, Ni (4)

Quixall, A. (Sheffield W), 1954 v W, Ni, R of E; 1955 v Sp, P (sub) (5)

Radford, J. (Arsenal), 1969 v R; 1972 v Sw (sub) (2)

Raikes, G. B. (Oxford University), 1895 v W; 1896 v W, Ni, S (4)

Ramsey, A. E. (Southampton), 1949 v Sw; (with Tottenham H), 1950 v S, I, P, Bel, Ch, US, Sp; 1951 v S, Ni, W, Y, Arg, P; 1952 v S, W, Ni, F, A (2), I, Sw; 1953 v Ni, W, S, Bel, Arg, Ch, U, US; 1954 v R of E, H (32)

Rawlings, A. (Preston NE), 1921 v Bel (1)

Rawlings, W. E. (Southampton), 1922 v S, W (2)

Rawlinson, J. F. P. (Cambridge University), 1882 v Ni (1)

Rawson, H. E. (Royal Engineers), 1875 v S (1)

Rawson, W. S. (Oxford University), 1875 v S; 1877 v S (2)

Read, A. (Tufnell Park), 1921 v Bel (1)

Reader, J. (WBA), 1894 v Ni (1)

Reaney, P. (Leeds U), 1969 v Bul (sub); 1970 v P; 1971 v Ma (3)

Reeves, K. (Norwich C), 1980 v Bul; (with Manchester C), Ni (2)

Regis, C. (WBA), 1982 v Ni (sub), W (sub), Ic; 1983 v WG; (with Coventry C), 1988 v T (sub) (5)

Reid, P. (Everton), 1985 v M (sub), WG, US (sub); 1986 v R, S (sub), Ca (sub), Pol, Para, Arg; 1987 v Br; 1988 v WG, Y (sub), Sw (sub) (13)

Revie, D. G. (Manchester C), 1955 v Ni, S, F; 1956 v W, D; 1957 v Ni (6)

Reynolds, J. (WBA), 1892 v S; 1893 v S, W; (with Aston Villa), 1894 v S, Ni; 1895 v S; 1897 v S, W (8)

Richards, C. H. (Nottingham F), 1898 v Ni (1)

Richards, G. H. (Derby Co), 1909 v A (1)

Richards, J. P. (Wolverhampton W), 1973 v Ni (1)

Richardson, J. R. (Newcastle U), 1933 v I, Sw (2)

Richardson, W. G. (WBA), 1935 v Ho (1)

Rickaby, S. (WBA), 1954 v Ni (1)

Rigby, A. (Blackburn R), 1927 v S, Bel, L, F; 1928 v W (5)

Rimmer, E. J. (Sheffield W), 1930 v S, G, A; 1932 v Sp (4)

Rimmer, J. J. (Arsenal), 1976 v I (1)

Rix, G. (Arsenal), 1981 v N, R, Sw (sub), Br, W, S; 1982

v Ho (sub), Fi (sub), F, Cz, K, WG, Sp; 1983 v D, WG (sub), Gr (sub); 1984 v Ni (17)

Robb, G. (Tottenham H), 1954 v H (1)

Roberts, C. (Manchester U), 1905 v Ni, W, S (3)

Roberts, F. (Manchester C), 1925 v S, W, Bel, F (4)

Roberts, G. (Tottenham H), 1983 v Ni, S; 1984 v F, Ni, S, USSR (6)

Roberts, H. (Arsenal), 1931 v S (1)

Roberts, H. (Millwall), 1931 v Bel (1)

Roberts, R. (WBA), 1887 v S; 1888 v Ni; 1890 v Ni (3)

Roberts, W. T. (Preston NE), 1924 v W, Bel (2)

Robinson, J. (Sheffield W), 1937 v Fi; 1938 v G, Sw; 1939 v W (4)

Robinson, J. W. (Derby Co), 1897 v S, Ni; (with New Brighton Tower), 1898 v S, W, Ni; (with Southampton), 1899 v W, S; 1900 v S, W, Ni; 1901 v Ni (11)

Robson, B. (WBA), 1980 v Ei, Aus; 1981 v N, R, Sw, Sp, R, Br, W, S, Sw, H; 1982 v N; (with Manchester U), H, Ni, W, Ho, S, Fi, F, Cz, WG, Sp; 1983 v D, Gr, L, S; 1984 v H, L, F, Ni, S, USSR, Br, U, Ch; 1985 v EG, Fi, T, Ei, R, Fi, S, M, I, WG, US; 1986 v R, T, Is, M, P, Mor; 1987 v Ni (2), Sp, T, Br, S; 1988 v T, Y, Ho, H, S, Co, Sw, Ei, Ho, USSR; 1989 v S, Se, S.Ar, Gr, Alb (2), Ch, S, Pol, D; 1990 v Pol, I, Y, Cz, U, Tun, Ei, Ho; 1991 v Cam, Ei; 1992 v T (90)

Robson, R. (WBA), 1958 v F, USSR (2), Br, A; 1960 v Sp, H; 1961 v Ni, W, S, L, P, Sp, M, I; 1962 v W, Ni, Sw, L, P (20)

Rocastle, D. (Arsenal), 1989 v D, S.Ar, Gr, Alb (2), Pol (sub), D; 1990 v Se (sub), Pol, Y, D (sub); 1992 v Pol, Cz, Br (sub) (14)

Rose, W. C. (Wolverhampton W), 1884 v S, W, Ni; (with Preston NE), 1886 v Ni; (with Wolverhampton W), 1891 v Ni (5)

Rostron, T. (Darwen), 1881 v S, W (2)

Rowe, A. (Tottenham H), 1934 v F (1)

Rowley, J. F. (Manchester U), 1949 v Sw, Se, F; 1950 v Ni, I; 1952 v S (6)

Rowley, W. (Stoke C), 1889 v Ni; 1892 v Ni (2)

Royle, J. (Everton), 1971 v Ma; 1973 v Y; (with Manchester C), 1976 v Ni (sub), I; 1977 v Fi, L (6)

Ruddlesdin, H. (Sheffield W), 1904 v W, Ni; 1905 v S (3)

Ruffell, J. W. (West Ham U), 1926 v S; 1927 v Ni; 1929 v S, W, Ni; 1930 v W (6)

Russell, B. B. (Royal Engineers), 1883 v W (1)

Rutherford, J. (Newcastle U), 1904 v S; 1907 v S, Ni, W; 1908 v S, Ni, W, A (2), H, B (11)

Sadler, D. (Manchester U), 1968 v Ni, USSR; 1970 v Ec (sub); 1971 v EG (4)

Sagar, C. (Bury), 1900 v Ni; 1902 v W (2)

Sagar, E. (Everton), 1936 v S, Ni, A, Bel (4)

Salako, J. A. (C Palace), 1991 v Aus (sub), Nz (sub + 1), Mal; 1992 v G (5)

Sandford, E. A. (WBA), 1933 v W (1)

Sandilands, R. R. (Old Westminsters), 1892 v W; 1893 v Ni; 1894 v W; 1895 v W; 1896 v W (5)

Sands, J. (Nottingham F), 1880 v W (1)

Sansom, K. (C Palace), 1979 v W; 1980 v Bul, Ei, Arg, W (sub), Ni, S, Bel, I; (with Arsenal), 1981 v N, R, Sw, Sp, R, Br, W, S, Sw; 1982 v Ni, W, Ho, S, Fi, F, Cz, WG, Sp; 1983 v D, WG, Gr, L, Gr, H, Ni, S; 1984 v D, H, L, F, S, USSR, Br, U, Ch; 1985 v EG, Fi, T, Ni, Ei, R, Fi, S, I, M, WG, US; 1986 v R, T, Ni, Eg, Is, USSR, S, M, Ca, P, Mor, Pol, Para, Arg; 1987 v Se, Ni (2), Y, Sp, T; 1988 v WG, T, Y, Ho, S, Co, Sw, Ei, Ho, USSR (86)

Saunders, F. E. (Swifts), 1888 v W (1)

Savage, A. H. (C Palace), 1876 v S (1)

Sayer, J. (Stoke C), 1887 v Ni (1)

Scattergood, E. (Derby Co), 1913 v W (1)

Schofield, J. (Stoke C), 1892 v W; 1893 v W; 1895 v Ni (3)

Scott, L. (Arsenal), 1947 v S, W, Ni, Ei, Ho, F, Sw, P; 1948 v S, W, Ni, Bel, Se, I; 1949 v W, Ni, D (17)

Scott, W. R. (Brentford), 1937 v W (1)

Seaman, D. A. (QPR), 1989 v S.Ar, D (sub); 1990 v Cz (sub); (with Arsenal), 1991 v Cam, Ei, T, Arg; 1992 v Cz, H (sub) (9)

Seddon, J. (Bolton W), 1923 v F, Se (2); 1924 v Bel; 1927 v W; 1929 v S (6)

Seed, J. M. (Tottenham H), 1921 v Bel: 1923 v W, Ni, Bel; 1925 v S (5)

Settle, J. (Bury), 1899 v S, W, Ni; (with Everton), 1902 v S, Ni; 1903 v Ni (6)

Sewell, J. (Sheffield W), 1952 v Ni, A, Sw; 1953 v Ni; 1954 v H (2) (6)

Sewell, W. R. (Blackburn R), 1924 v W (1)

Shackleton, L. F. (Sunderland), 1949 v W, D; 1950 v W; 1955 v W, WG (5)

Sharp, J. (Everton), 1903 v Ni; 1905 v S (2)

Sharpe, L. S. (Manchester U), 1991 v Ei (sub) (1)

Shaw, G. E. (WBA), 1932 v S (1)

Shaw, G. L. (Sheffield U), 1959 v S, W, USSR, I; 1963 v W (5)

Shea, D. (Blackburn R), 1914 v W, Ni (2)

Shearer, A. (Southampton), 1992 v F, C, F (3)

Shellito, K. J. (Chelsea), 1963 v Cz (1)

Shelton A. (Notts Co), 1889 v Ni; 1890 v S, W; 1891 v S, W; 1892 v S (6)

Shelton, C. (Notts Rangers), 1888 v Ni (1)

Shepherd, A. (Bolton W), 1906 v S; (with Newcastle U), 1911 v Ni (2)

Shilton, P. L. (Leicester C), 1971 v EG, W; 1972 v Sw, Ni; 1973 v Y, S (2), Ni, W, Cz, Pol, USSR, I; 1974 v A, Pol, I, W, Ni, S, Arg; (with Stoke C), 1975 v Cy; 1977 v Ni, W; (with Nottingham F), 1978 v W, H; 1979 v Cz, Se, A; 1980 v Ni, Sp, I; 1981 v N, Sw, R; 1982 v H, Ho, S, F, Cz, K, WG, Sp; (with Southampton), 1983 v D, WG, Gr, W, Gr, H, Ni, S, Aus (3); 1984 v D, H, F, Ni, W, S, USSR, Br, U, Ch; 1985 v EG, Fi, T, Ni, R, Fi, S, I, WG; 1986 v R, T, Ni, Eg, Is, USSR, S, M, Ca, P, Mor, Pol, Para, Arg; 1987 v Se, Ni (2), Sp, Br; (with Derby Co), 1988 v WG, T, Y, Ho, S, Co, Sw, Ei, Ho; 1989 v D, Se, Gr, Alb (2), Ch, S, Pol, D; 1990 v Se, Pol, I, Y, Br, Cz, D, U, Tun, Ei, Ho, Eg, Bel, Cam, WG, I (125)

Shimwell, E. (Blackpool), 1949 v Se (1)

Shutt, G. (Stoke C), 1886 v Ni (1)

Silcock, J. (Manchester U), 1921 v S, W; 1923 v Se (3)

Sillett, R. P. (Chelsea), 1955 v F, Sp, P (3)

Simms, E. (Luton T), 1922 v Ni (1)

Simpson, J. (Blackburn R), 1911 v S, W, Ni; 1912 v S, W, Ni; 1913 v S; 1914 v W (8)

Sinton, A. (QPR), 1992 v Pol, C, Br, F, Se (5)

Slater, W. J. (Wolverhampton W), 1955 v W, WG; 1958 v S, P, Y, USSR (3), Br, A; 1959 v USSR; 1960 v S (12)

Smalley, T. (Wolverhampton W), 1937 v W (1)

Smart, T. (Aston Villa), 1921 v S; 1924 v S, W; 1926 v Ni; 1930 v W (5)

Smith, A. (Nottingham F), 1891 v S, W; 1893 v Ni (3)

Smith, A. K. (Oxford University), 1872 v S (1)

Smith, A. M. (Arsenal), 1989 v S.Ar (sub), Gr, Alb (sub), Pol (sub); 1991 v T, USSR, Arg; 1992 v G, T, Pol (sub), H (sub), D, Se (sub) (13)

Smith, B. (Tottenham H), 1921 v S; 1922 v W (2)

Smith, C. E. (C Palace), 1876 v S (1)

Smith, G. O. (Oxford University), 1893 v Ni; 1894 v W, S; 1895 v W; 1896 v Ni, W, S; (with Old Carthusians), 1897 v Ni, W, S; 1898 v Ni, W, S; (with Corinthians); 1899 v Ni, W, S; 1899 v Ni, W, S; 1901 v S (20)

Smith, H. (Reading), 1905 v W, S; 1906 v W, Ni (4)

Smith, J. (WBA), 1920 v Ni; 1923 v Ni (2)

Smith, Joe (Bolton W), 1913 v Ni; 1914 v S, W; 1920 v W, Ni (5)

Smith, J. C. R. (Millwall), 1939 v Ni, N (2)

Smith, J. W. (Portsmouth), 1932 v Ni, W, Sp (3)

Smith, Leslie (Brentford), 1939 v R (1)

Smith, Lionel (Arsenal), 1951 v W; 1952 v W, Ni; 1953 v W, S, Bel (6)

Smith, R, A, (Tottenham H), 1961 v Ni, W, S, L, P, Sp; 1962 v S; 1963 v S, F, Br, Cz, EG; 1964 v W, Ni, R of W (15)

Smith, S. (Aston Villa), 1895 v S (1)

Smith, S. C. (Leicester C), 1936 v Ni (1)

Smith, T. (Birmingham C), 1960 v W, Se (2)

Smith, T. (Liverpool), 1971 v W (1)

Smith, W. H. (Huddersfield T), 1922 v W, S; 1928 v S (3)

Sorby, T. H. (Thursday Wanderers, Sheffield), 1879 v W (1)

Southworth, J. (Blackburn R), 1889 v W; 1891 v W; 1892 v S (3)

Sparks, F. J. (Herts Rangers), 1879 v S; (with Clapham Rovers), 1880 v S, W (3)

Spence, J. W. (Manchester U), 1926 v Bel; 1927 v Ni (2)

Spence, R. (Chelsea), 1936 v A, Bel (2)

Spencer, C. W. (Newcastle U), 1924 v S; 1925 v W (2)

Spencer, H. (Aston Villa), 1897 v S, W; 1900 v W; 1903 v Ni; 1905 v W, S (6)

Spiksley, F. (Sheffield W), 1893 v S, W; 1894 v S, Ni; 1896 v Ni; 1898 v S, W (7)

Spilsbury, B. W. (Cambridge University), 1885 v Ni; 1886 v Ni, S (3)

Spink, N. (Aston Villa), 1983 v Aus (sub) (1)

Spouncer, W. A. (Nottingham F), 1900 v W (1)

Springett, R. D. G. (Sheffield W), 1960 v Ni, S, Y, Sp, H; 1961 v Ni, S, L, P, Sp, M, I, A; 1962 v W, Ni, S, A, Sw, Pe, L, P, H, Arg, Bul, Br; 1963 v Ni, W, F (2), Sw; 1966 v W, A, N (33)

Sproston, B. (Leeds U), 1937 v W; 1938 v S, W, Ni, Cz, G, Sw, F; (with Tottenham H), 1939 v W, R of E; (with Manchester C), N (11)

Squire, R. T. (Cambridge University), 1886 v S, W, Ni (3)

Stanbrough, M. H. (Old Carthusians), 1895 v W (1)

Staniforth, R. (Huddersfield T), 1954 v S, H, Y, Bel, Sw, U; 1955 v W, WG (8)

Starling, R. W. (Sheffield W), 1933 v S; (with Aston Villa), 1937 v S (2)

Statham, D. (WBA), 1983 v W, Aus (2) (3)

Steele, F. C. (Stoke C), 1937 v S, W, Ni, N, Se, Fi (6)

Stein, B. (Luton T), 1984 v F (1)

Stephenson, C. (Huddersfield T), 1924 v W (1)

Stephenson, G. T. (Derby Co), 1928 v F, Bel; (with Sheffield W), 1931 v F (3)

Stephenson, J. E. (Leeds U), 1938 v S; 1939 v Ni (2)

Stepney, A. C. (Manchester U), 1968 v Se (1)

Sterland, M. (Sheffield W), 1989 v S.Ar (1)

Steven, T. M. (Everton), 1985 v Ni, Ei, R, Fi, I, US (sub); 1986 v T (sub), Eg, USSR (sub), M (sub), Pol, Para, Arg; 1987 v Se, Y (sub), Sp (sub); 1988 v T, Y, Ho, H, S, Sw, Ho, USSR; 1989 v S; (with Rangers), 1990 v Cz, Cam (sub), WG (sub), I; 1991 v Cam; (with Marseille), 1992 v G, C, Br, Fi, D, F (36)

Stevens, G. A. (Tottenham H), 1985 v Fi (sub), T (sub), Ni; 1986 v S (sub), M (sub), Mor (sub), Para (sub) (7)

Stevens, M. G. (Everton), 1985 v I, WG; 1986 v R, T, Ni, Eg, Is, S, Ca, P, Mor, Pol, Para, Arg; 1987 v Br, S; 1988 v T, Y, Is, Ho, H (sub), S, Sw, Ei, Ho, USSR; (with Rangers), 1989 v D, Se, Gr, Alb (2), S, Pol; 1990 v Se, Pol, I, Br, D, Tun, Ei, I; 1991 v USSR; 1992 v C, H, Br, Fi (46)

Stewart, P. A. (Tottenham H), 1992 v T (sub), Cz (sub), C (sub) (3)

Stewart, J. (Sheffield W), 1907 v S, W; (with Newcastle U), 1911 v S (3)

Stiles, N. P. (Manchester U), 1965 v S, H, Y, Se; 1966 v W, Ni, S, A, Sp, Pol (2), WG (2), N, D, U, M, F, Arg,

P; 1967 v Ni, W, S, Cz; 1968 v USSR; 1969 v R; 1970 v Ni, S (28)

Stoker, J. (Birmingham), 1933 v W; 1934 v S, H (3)

Storer, H. (Derby Co), 1924 v F; 1928 v Ni (2)

Storey, P. E. (Arsenal), 1971 v Gr, Ni, S; 1972 v Sw, WG, W, Ni, S; 1973 v W (3), Y, S (2), Ni, Cz, Pol, USSR, I (19)

Storey-Moore, I, (Nottingham F), 1970 v Ho (1)

Strange, A. H. (Sheffield W), 1930 v S, A, G; 1931 v S, W, Ni, F, Bel; 1932 v S, W, Ni, Sp; 1933 v S, Ni, A, I, Sw; 1934 v Ni, W, F (20)

Stratford, A. H. (Wanderers), 1874 v S (1)

Streten, B. (Luton T), 1950 v Ni (1)

Sturgess, A. (Sheffield U), 1911 v Ni; 1914 v S (2)

Summerbee, M. G. (Manchester C), 1968 v S, Sp, WG; 1972 v Sw, WG (sub), W, Ni; 1973 v USSR (sub) (8)

Sunderland, A. (Arsenal), 1980 v Aus (1)

Sutcliffe, J. W. (Bolton W), 1893 v W; 1895 v S, Ni; 1901 v S; (with Millwall), 1903 v W (5)

Swan, P. (Sheffield W), 1960 v Y, Sp, H; 1961 v Ni, W, S, L, P, Sp, M, I, A; 1962 v W, Ni, S, A, Sw, L, P (19)

Swepstone, H. A. (Pilgrims), 1880 v S; 1882 v S, W; 1883 v S, W, Ni (6)

Swift, F. V. (Manchester C), 1947 v S, W, Ni, Ei, Ho, F, Sw, P; 1948 v S, W, Ni, Bel, Se, I; 1949 v S, W, Ni, D, N (19)

Tait, G. (Birmingham Excelsior), 1881 v W (1)

Talbot, B. (Ipswich T), 1977 v Ni (sub), S, Br, Arg, U; (with Arsenal), 1980 v Aus (6)

Tambling, R. V. (Chelsea), 1963 v W, F; 1966 v Y (3)

Tate, J. T. (Aston Villa), 1931 v F, Bel; 1933 v W (3)

Taylor, E. (Blackpool), 1954 v H (1)

Taylor, E. H. (Huddersfield T), 1923 v S, W, Ni, Bel; 1924 v S, Ni, F; 1926 v S (8)

Taylor, J. G. (Fulham), 1951 v Arg, P (2)

Taylor, P. H. (Liverpool), 1948 v W, Ni, Se (3)

Taylor, P. J. (C Palace), 1976 v W (sub + 1), Ni, S (4)

Taylor, T. (Manchester U), 1953 v Arg, Ch, U; 1954 v Bel, Sw; 1956 v S, Br, Se, Fi, WG; 1957 v Ni, Y (sub), D (2), Ei (2); 1958 v W, Ni, F (19)

Temple, D. W. (Everton), 1965 v WG (1)

Thickett, H. (Sheffield U), 1899 v S, W (2)

Thomas, D. (Coventry C), 1983 v Aus (1 + 1 sub) (2)

Thomas, D. (QPR), 1975 v Cz (sub), P, Cy (sub + 1), W, S (sub); 1976 v Cz (sub), P (sub) (8)

Thomas, G. R. (C Palace), 1991 v T, USSR, Arg, Aus, Nz (2), Mal; 1992 v Pol, F (9)

Thomas, M. L. (Arsenal), 1989 v S.Ar; 1990 v Y (2)

Thompson, P. (Liverpool), 1964 v P (2), Ei, US, Br, Arg; 1965 v Ni, W, S, Bel, Ho; 1966 v Ni; 1968 v Ni, WG; 1970 v S, Ho (sub) (16)

Thompson, P. B. (Liverpool), 1976 v W (2), Ni, S, Br, I, Fi; 1977 v Fi; 1979 v Ei (sub), Cz, Ni, S, Bul, Se (sub), A; 1980 v D, Ni, Bul, Ei, Sp (2), Arg, W, S, Bel, I; 1981 v N, R, H; 1982 v N, H, W, Ho, S, Fi, F, Cz, K, WG, Sp; 1983 v WG, Gr (42)

Thompson T. (Aston Villa), 1952 v W; (with Preston NE), 1957 v S (2)

Thomson, R. A. (Wolverhampton W), 1964 v Ni, US, P, Arg; 1965 v Bel, Ho, Ni, W (8)

Thornewell, G. (Derby Co), 1923 v Se (2); 1924 v F; 1925 v F (4)

Thornley, I. (Manchester C), 1907 v W (1)

Tilson, S. F. (Manchester C), 1934 v H, Cz; 1935 v W; 1936 v Ni (4)

Titmuss, F. (Southampton), 1922 v W; 1923 v W (2)

Todd, C. (Derby Co), 1972 v Ni; 1974 v P, W, Ni, S, Arg, EG, Bul, Y; 1975 v P (sub), WG, Cy (2), Ni, W, S; 1976 v Sw, Cz, P, Ni, S, Br, Fi; 1977 v Ei, Fi, Ho (sub), Ni (27)

Toone, G. (Notts Co), 1892 v S, W (2)

Topham, A. G. (Casuals), 1894 v W (1)

Topham, R. (Wolverhampton W), 1893 v Ni; (with Casuals) 1894 v W (2)

Towers, M. A. (Sunderland), 1976 v W, Ni (sub), I (3)

Townley, W. J. (Blackburn R), 1889 v W; 1890 v Ni (2)

Townrow, J. E. (Clapton Orient), 1925 v S; 1926 v W (2)

Tremelling, D. R. (Birmingham), 1928 v W (1)

Tresadern, J. (West Ham U), 1923 v S, Se (2)

Tueart, D. (Manchester C), 1975 v Cy (sub), Ni; 1977 v Fi, Ni, W (sub), S (sub) (6)

Tunstall, F. E. (Sheffield U), 1923 v S; 1924 v S, W, Ni, F; 1925 v Ni, S (7)

Turnbull, R. J. (Bradford), 1920 v Ni (1)

Turner, A. (Southampton), 1900 v Ni; 1901 v Ni (2)

Turner, H. (Huddersfield T), 1931 v F, Bel (2)

Turner, J. A. (Bolton W), 1893 v W; (with Stoke C) 1895 v Ni; (with Derby Co) 1898 v Ni (3)

Tweedy, G. J. (Grimsby T), 1937 v H (1)

Ufton, D. G. (Charlton Ath), 1954 v R of E (1)

Underwood A. (Stoke C), 1891 v Ni; 1892 v Ni (2)

Urwin, T. (Middlesbrough), 1923 v Se (2); (with Newcastle U), 1924 v Bel; 1926 v W (4)

Utley, G. (Barnsley), 1913 v Ni (1)

Vaughton, O. H. (Aston Villa), 1882 v S, W, Ni; 1884 v S, W (5)

Veitch, C. C. M. (Newcastle U), 1906 v S, W, Ni; 1907 v S, W; 1909 v W (6)

Veitch, J. G. (Old Westminsters), 1894 v W (1)

Venables, T. F. (Chelsea), 1965 v Ho, Bel (2)

Vidal, R. W. S. (Oxford University), 1873 v S (1)

Viljoen, C. (Ipswich T), 1975 v Ni, W (2)

Viollet, D. S. (Manchester U), 1960 v H; 1962 v L (2)

Von Donop (Royal Engineers), 1873 v S; 1875 v S (2)

Wace, H. (Wanderers), 1878 v S; 1879 v S, W (3)

Waddle, C. R. (Newcastle U), 1985 v Ei, R (sub), Fi (sub), S (sub), I, M (sub), WG, US; (with Tottenham H), 1986 v R, T, Ni, Is, USSR, S, M, Ca, P, Mor, Pol (sub), Arg (sub); 1987 v Se (sub), Ni (2), Y, Sp, T, Br, S; 1988 v WG, Is, H, S (sub), Co, Sw (sub), Ei, Ho (sub); 1989 v Se, S.Ar, Alb (2), Ch, S, Pol, D (sub); (with Marseille), 1990 v Se, Pol, I, Y, Br, D, U, Tun, Ei, Ho, Eg, Bel, Cam, WG, I (sub); 1991 v H (sub), Pol (sub); 1992 v T (62)

Wadsworth, S. J. (Huddersfield T), 1922 v S; 1923 v S, Bel; 1924 v S, Ni; 1925 v S, Ni; 1926 v W; 1927 v Ni (9)

Wainscoat, W. R. (Leeds U), 1929 v S (1)

Waiters, A. K. (Blackpool), 1964 v Ei, Br; 1965 v W, Bel, Ho (5)

Walden, F. I. (Tottenham H), 1914 v S; 1922 v W (2)

Walker, D. S. (Nottingham F), 1989 v D (sub), Se (sub), Gr, Alb (2), Ch, S, Pol, D; 1990 v Se, Pol, I, Y, Br, Cz, D, U, Tun, Ei, Ho, Eg, Bel, Cam, WG, I; 1991 v H, Pol, Ei (2), Cam, T, Arg, Aus, Nz (2), Mal; 1992 v T, Pol, F, Cz, C, H, Br, Fi, D, F, Se (47)

Walker, W. H. (Aston Villa), 1921 v Ni; 1922 v Ni, W, S; 1923 v Se (2); 1924 v S; 1925 v Ni, W, S, Bel, F; 1926 v Ni, W, S; 1927 v Ni, W; 1933 v A (18)

Wall, G. (Manchester U), 1907 v W; 1908 v Ni; 1909 v S; 1910 v W, S; 1912 v S; 1913 v Ni (7)

Wallace, C. W. (Aston Villa), 1913 v W; 1914 v Ni; 1920 v S (3)

Wallace, D. L. (Southampton), 1986 v Eg (1)

Walsh, P. (Luton T), 1983 v Aus (2 + 1 sub) (3)

Walters, A. M. (Cambridge University), 1885 v S, N; 1886 v S; 1887 v S, W; (with Old Carthusians), 1889 v S, W; 1890 v S, W (9)

Walters, K. M. (Rangers), 1991 v Nz (1)

Walters, P. M. (Oxford University), 1885 v S, Ni; (with Old Carthusians), 1886 v S, W, Ni; 1887 v S, W; 1888 v S, Ni; 1889 v S, W; 1890 v S, W (13)

Walton, N. (Blackburn R), 1890 v Ni (1)

Ward, J. T. (Blackburn Olympic), 1885 v W (1)

Ward, P. (Brighton & HA), 1980 v Aus (sub) (1)

Ward, T. V. (Derby Co), 1948 v Bel; 1949 v W (2)

Waring, T. (Aston Villa), 1931 v F, Bel; 1932 v S, W, Ni (5)

Warner, C. (Upton Park), 1878 v S (1)

Warren, B. (Derby Co), 1906 v S, W, Ni; 1907 v S, W, Ni; 1908 v S, W, Ni, A (2), H, B; (with Chelsea), 1909 v S, Ni, W, H (2), A; 1911 v S, Ni, W (22)

Waterfield, G. S. (Burnley), 1927 v W (1)

Watson, D. (Norwich C), 1984 v Br, U, Ch; 1985 v M, US (sub); 1986 v S; (with Everton), 1987 v Ni; 1988 v Is, Ho, S, Sw (sub), USSR (12)

Watson, D. V. (Sunderland), 1974 v P, S (sub), Arg, EG, Bul, Y; 1975 v Cz, P, WG, Cy (2), Ni, W, S; (with Manchester C), 1976 v Sw, Cz (sub), P; 1977 v Ho, L, Ni, W, S, Br, Arg, U; 1978 v Sw, L, I, WG, Br, W, Ni, S, H; 1979 v D, Ei, Cz, Ni (2), W, S, Bul, Se, A; (with Werder Bremen), 1980 v D; (with Southampton), Ni, Bul, Ei, Sp (2), Arg, Ni, S, Bel, I; 1981 v N, R, Sw, R, W, S, Sw, H; (with Stoke C), 1982 v Ni, Ic (65)

Watson, V. M. (West Ham U), 1923 v W, S; 1930 v S, G, A (5)

Watson, W. (Burnley), 1913 v S; 1914 v Ni; 1920 v Ni (3)

Watson, W. (Sunderland), 1950 v Ni, I; 1951 v W, Y (4)

Weaver, S. (Newcastle U), 1932 v S, 1933 v S, Ni (3)

Webb, G. W. (West Ham U), 1911 v S, W (2)

Webb, N. J. (Nottingham F), 1988 v WG (sub), T, Y, Is, Ho, S, Sw, Ei, USSR (sub); 1989 v D, Se, Gr, Alb (2), Ch, S, Pol, D; (with Manchester U), 1990 v Se, I (sub); 1992 v F, H, Br (sub), Fi, D (sub), Se (26)

Webster, M. (Middlesbrough), 1930 v S, A, G (3)

Wedlock, W. J. (Bristol C), 1907 v S, Ni, W; 1908 v S, Ni, W, A (2), H, B; 1909 v S, W, Ni, H (2), A; 1910 v S, W, Ni; 1911 v S, W, Ni; 1912 v S, W, Ni; 1914 v W (26)

Weir, D. (Bolton W), 1889 v S, Ni (2)

Welch, R. de C. (Wanderers), 1872 v S; (with Harrow Chequers), 1874 v S (2)

Weller, K. (Leicester C), 1974 v W, Ni, S, Arg (4)

Welsh, D. (Charlton Ath), 1938 v G, Sw; 1939 v R (3)

West, G. (Everton), 1969 v W, Bul, M (3)

Westwood, R. W. (Bolton W), 1935 v S, W, Ho; 1936 v Ni, G; 1937 v W (6)

Whateley, O. (Aston Villa), 1883 v S, Ni (2)

Wheeler, J. E. (Bolton W), 1955 v Ni (1)

Wheldon, G. F. (Aston Villa), 1897 v Ni; 1898 v S, W, Ni (4)

White, T. A. (Everton), 1933 v I (1)

Whitehead, J. (Accrington), 1893 v W; (with Blackburn R), 1894 v Ni (2)

Whitfeld, H. (Old Etonians), 1879 v W (1)

Whitham, M. (Sheffield U), 1892 v Ni (1)

Whitworth, S. (Leicester C), 1975 v WG, Cy, Ni, W, S; 1976 v Sw, P (7)

Whymark, T. J. (Ipswich T), 1978 v L (sub) (1)

Widdowson, S. W. (Nottingham F), 1880 v S (1)

Wignall, F. (Nottingham F), 1965 v W, Ho (2)

Wilkes, A. (Aston Villa), 1901 v S, W; 1902 v S, W, Ni (5)

Wilkins, R. G. (Chelsea), 1976 v I; 1977 v Ei, Fi, Ni, Br, Arg, U; 1978 v Sw (sub), L, I, WG, W, Ni, S, H; 1979 v D, Ei, Cz, Ni, W, S, Bul, Se (sub), A; (with Manchester U), 1980 v D, Ni, Bul, Sp (2), Arg, W (sub), Ni, S, Bel, I; 1981 v Sp (sub), R, Br, W, S, Sw, H (sub); 1982 v Ni, W, Ho, S, Fi, F, Cz, K, WG, Sp; 1983 v D, WG; 1984 v D, Ni, W, S, USSR, Br, U, Ch; (with AC Milan), 1985 v EG, Fi, T, Ni, Ei, R, Fi, S, I, M; 1986 v T, Ni, Is, Eg, USSR, S, M, Ca, P, Mor; 1987 v Se, Y (sub) (84)

Wilkinson, B. (Sheffield U), 1904 v S (1)

Wilkinson, L. R. (Oxford University), 1891 v W (1)

Williams, B. F. (Wolverhampton W), 1949 v F; 1950 v S, W, Ei, I, P, Bel, Ch, US, Sp; 1951 v Ni, W, S, Y, Arg, P; 1952 v W, F; 1955 v S, WG, F, Sp, P; 1956 v W (24)

Williams, O. (Clapton Orient), 1923 v W, Ni (2)

William, S. (Southampton), 1983 v Aus (1 + 1 sub); 1984 v F; 1985 v EG, Fi, T (6)

Williams, W. (WBA), 1897 v Ni; 1898 v W, Ni, S; 1899 v W, Ni (6)

Williamson, E. C. (Arsenal), 1923 v Se (2) (2)

Williamson, R. G. (Middlesbrough), 1905 v Ni; 1911 v Ni, S, W; 1912 v S, W; 1913 v Ni (7)

Willingham, C. K. (Huddersfield T), 1937 v Fi; 1938 v S, G, Sw, F; 1939 v S, W, Ni, R of E, N, I, Y (12)

Willis, A. (Tottenham H), 1952 v F (1)

Wilshaw, D. J. (Wolverhampton W), 1954 v W, Sw, U; 1955 v S, F, Sp, P; 1956 v W, Ni, Fi, WG; 1957 v Ni (12)

Wilson, C. P. (Hendon), 1884 v S, W (2)

Wilson, C. W. (Oxford University), 1879 v W; 1881 v S (2)

Wilson, G. (Sheffield W), 1921 v S, W, Bel; 1922 v S, Ni; 1923 v S, W, Ni, Bel; 1924 v W, Ni, F (12)

Wilson, G. P. (Corinthians), 1900 v S, W (2)

Wilson, R. (Huddersfield T), 1960 v S, Y, Sp, H; 1962 v W, Ni, S, A, Sw, Pe, P, H, Arg, Bul, Br; 1963 v Ni, F, Br, Cz, EG, Sw; 1964 v W, S, R of W, U, P (2), Ei, Br, Arg; (with Everton) 1965 v S, H, Y, WG, Se; 1966 v WG (sub), W, Ni, A, Sp, Pol (2), Y, Fi, D, U, M, F, Arg, P, WG; 1967 v Ni, W, S, Cz, A; 1968 v Ni, S, USSR (2), Sp (2), Y (63)

Wilson, T. (Huddersfield T), 1928 v S (1)

Winckworth, W. N. (Old Westminsters), 1892 v W; 1893 v Ni (2)

Windridge, J. E. (Chelsea), 1908 v S, W, Ni, A (2), H, B; 1909 v Ni (8)

Wingfield-Stratford, C. V. (Royal Engineers), 1877 v S (1)

Winterburn, N. (Arsenal), 1990 v I (sub) (1)

Wise, D. F. (Chelsea), 1991 v T, USSR, Aus (sub), Nz (2) (5)

Withe, P. (Aston Villa), 1981 v Br, W, S; 1982 v N (sub), W, Ic; 1983 v H, Ni, S; 1984 v H (sub); 1985 v T (11)

Wollaston, C. H. R. (Wanderers), 1874 v S; 1875 v S; 1877 v S; 1880 v S (4)

Wolstenholme, S. (Everton), 1904 v S; (with Blackburn R), 1905 v W, Ni (3)

Wood, H. (Wolverhampton W), 1890 v S, W; 1896 v S (3)

Wood, R. E. (Manchester U), 1955 v Ni, W; 1956 v Fi (3)

Woodcock, A. S. (Nottingham F), 1978 v Ni; 1979 v Ei (sub), Cz, Bul (sub), Se; 1980 v Ni; (with Cologne), Bul, Ei, Sp (2), Arg, Bel, I; 1981 v N, R, Sw, R, W (sub), S; 1982 v Ni (sub), Ho, Fi (sub), WG (sub), Sp; (with Arsenal), 1983 v WG (sub), Gr, L, Gr; 1984 v L,

F (sub), Ni, W, S, Br, U (sub); 1985 v EG, Fi, T, Ni; 1986 v R (sub), T (sub), Is (sub) (42)

Woodger, G. (Oldham Ath), 1911 v Ni (1)

Woodhall, G. (WBA), 1888 v S, W (2)

Woodley, V. R. (Chelsea), 1937 v S, N, Se, Fi; 1938 v S, W, Ni, Cz, G, Sw, F; 1939 v S, W, Ni, R of E, N, I, R, Y (19)

Woods, C. C. E. (Norwich C), 1985 v US; 1986 v Eg (sub), Is (sub), Ca (sub); (with Rangers), 1987 v Y, Sp (sub), Ni (sub), T, S; 1988 v Is, H, Sw (sub), USSR; 1989 v D (sub); 1990 v Br (sub), D (sub); 1991 v H, Pol, Ei, USSR, Aus, Nz (2), Mal; (with Sheffield W), 1992 v G, T, Pol, F, C, Br, Fi, D, F, Se (34)

Woodward, V. J. (Tottenham H), 1903 v S, W, Ni; 1904 v S, Ni; 1905 v S, W, Ni; 1907 v S; 1908 v S, W, Ni, A (2), H, B; 1909 v W, Ni, H (2), A; (with Chelsea), 1910 v Ni; 1911 v W (23)

Woosnam, M. (Manchester C), 1922 v W (1)

Worrall, F. (Portsmouth), 1935 v Ho; 1937 v Ni (2)

Worthington, F. S. (Leicester C), 1974 v Ni (sub), S, Arg, EG, Bul, Y; 1975 v Cz, P (sub) (8)

Wreford-Brown, C. (Oxford University), 1889 v Ni; (with Old Carthusians), 1894 v W; 1895 v W; 1898 v S (4)

Wright, E. G. D. (Cambridge University), 1906 v W (1)

Wright, I. E. (C Palace), 1991 v Cam, Ei (sub), USSR, Nz; (with Arsenal), 1992 v H (sub) (5)

Wright, J. D. (Newcastle U), 1939 v N (1)

Wright, M. (Southampton), 1984 v W; 1985 v EG, Fi, T, Ei, R, I, WG; 1986 v R, T, Ni, Eg, USSR; 1987 v Y, Ni, S; (with Derby Co), 1988 v Is, Ho (sub), Co, Sw, Ei, Ho; 1990 v Cz (sub), Tun (sub), Ho, Eg, Bel, Cam, WG, I; 1991 v H, Pol, Ei (2), Cam, USSR, Arg, Aus, Nz, Mal; (with Liverpool), 1992 v F, Fi (42)

Wright, T. J. (Everton), 1968 v USSR; 1969 v R (2), M (sub), U, Br; 1970 v W, Ho, Bel, R (sub), Br (11)

Wright, W. A. (Wolverhampton W), 1947 v S, W, Ni, Ei, Ho, F, Sw, P; 1948 v S, W, Ni, Bel, Se, I; 1949 v S, W, Ni, D, Sw, Se, N, F; 1950 v S, W, Ni, Ei, I, P, Bel, Ch, US, Sp; 1951 v Ni, S, Arg; 1952 v W, Ni, S, F, A (2), I, Sw; 1953 v Ni, W, S, Bel, Arg, Ch, U, US; 1954 v W, Ni, S, R of E, H (2), Y, Bel, Sw, U; 1955 v W, Ni, S, WG, F, Sp, P; 1956 v Ni, W, S, Br, Se, Fi, WG, D, Sp; 1957 v S, W, Ni, Y, D (2), Ei (2), 1958 v W, Ni, S, P, Y, USSR (3), Br, A, F; 1959 v W, Ni, S, USSR, I, Br, Pe, M, US (105)

Wylie, J. G. (Wanderers), 1878 v S (1)

Yates, J. (Burnley), 1889 v Ni (1)

York, R. E. (Aston Villa), 1922 v S; 1926 v S (2)

Young, A. (Huddersfield T), 1933 v W; 1937 v S, H, N, Se; 1938 v G, Sw, F; 1939 v W (9)

Young, G. M. (Sheffield W), 1965 v W (1)

R. E. Evans also played for Wales against E, Ni, S; J. Reynolds also played for Ireland against E, W, S.

NORTHERN IRELAND

Aherne, T. (Belfast C), 1947 v E; 1948 v S; 1949 v W; (with Luton T), 1950 v W (4)

Alexander, A. (Cliftonville), 1895 v S (1)

Allen, C. A. (Cliftonville), 1936 v E (1)

Allen, J. (Limavady), 1887 v E (1)

Anderson, T. (Manchester U), 1973 v Cy, E, S, W; 1974 v Bul, P; (with Swindon T), 1975 v S (sub); 1976 v Is; 1977 v Ho, Bel, WG, E, S, W, Ic; 1978 v Ic, Ho, Bel; (with Peterborough U), S, E, W; 1979 v D (22)

Anderson, W. (Linfield), 1898 v W, E, S; 1899 v S (4)

Andrews, W. (Glentoran), 1908 v S; (with Grimsby T), 1913 v E, S (3)

Armstrong, G. (Tottenham H), 1977 v WG, E, W (sub), Ic (sub); 1978 v Bel, S, E, W; 1979 v Ei, D, Bul, E, Bul, E, S, W, D; 1980 v E, Ei, Is, S, E, W, Aus (3); 1981 v Se; (with Watford), P, S, P, S, Se; 1982 v S, Is, E, F, W, Y, Hon, Sp, A, F; 1983 v A, T, Alb, S, E, W; (with Real Mallorca), 1984 v A, WG, E, W, Fi; 1985 v R, F, E, Sp; (with WBA), 1986 v T, R (sub), E (sub), F (sub); (with Chesterfield), D (sub), Br (sub) (63)

Baird, G. (Distillery), 1896 v S, E, W (3)

Baird, H. (Huddersfield T), 1939 v E (1)

Balfe, J. (Shelbourne), 1909 v E; 1910 v W (2)

Bambrick, J. (Linfield), 1929 v W, S, E; 1930 v W, S, E; 1932 v W; (with Chelsea), 1935 v W; 1936 v E, S; 1938 v W (11)

Banks, S. J. (Cliftonville), 1937 v W (1)

Barr, H. H. (Linfield), 1962 v E; (with Coventry C), 1963 v E, Pol (3)

Barron, H. (Cliftonville), 1894 v E, W, S; 1895 v S; 1896 v S; 1897 v E, W (7)

Barry, H. (Bohemians), 1900 v S (1)

Baxter, R. A. (Cliftonville), 1887 v S, W (2)

Bennett, L. V. (Dublin University), 1889 v W (1)

Berry, J. (Cliftonville), 1888 v S, W; 1889 v E (3)

Best, G. (Manchester U), 1964 v W, U; 1965 v E, Ho (2), S, Sw (2), Alb; 1966 v S, E, Alb; 1967 v E; 1968 v S; 1969 v S, W, T; 1970 v S, E, W, USSR; 1971 v Cy (2), Sp, E, S, W; 1972 v USSR, Sp; 1973 v Bul; 1974 v P; (with Fulham), 1977 v Ho, Bel, WG; 1978 v Ic, Ho (37)

Bingham, W. L. (Sunderland), 1951 v F; 1952 v E, S, W; 1953 v E, S, F, W; 1954 v E, S, W; 1955 v E, S, W; 1956 v S, W; 1957 v E, S, W, P (2), I; 1958 v S, E, W, I (2), Arg, Cz (2), WG, F; (with Luton T), 1959 v E, S, W, Sp; 1960 v S, E, W; (with Everton), 1961 v E, S, WG (2), Gr, I; 1962 v E, Gr; 1963 v E, S, Pol (2), Sp; (with Port Vale), 1964 v S, E, Sp (56)

Black, J. (Glentoran), 1901 v E (1)

Black, K. (Luton T), 1988 v F (sub), Ma (sub); 1989 v Ei, H, Sp (2), Ch (sub); 1990 v H, N, U; 1991 v Y (2), D, A, Pol, Fa; (with Nottingham F), 1992 v Fa, A, D, S, Li, G (22)

Blair, H. (Portadown), 1931 v S; 1932 v S; (with Swansea), 1934 v S (3)

Blair, J. (Cliftonville), 1907 v W, E, S; 1908 v E, S (5)

Blair R. V. (Oldham Ath), 1975 v Se (sub), S (sub), W; 1976 v Se, Is (5)

Blanchflower, R. D. (Barnsley), 1950 v S, W; 1951 v E, S; (with Aston Villa), F; 1952 v W; 1953 v E, S, W, F; 1954 v E, S, W; (with Tottenham H), 1955 v E, S, W; 1956 v E, S, W; 1957 v E, S, W, I, P (2); 1958 v E, S, W, I (2), Cz (2), Arg, F, WG; 1959 v E, S, W, Sp; 1960 v E, S, W; 1961 v E, S, W, WG (2); 1962 v E, S, W, Gr, Ho; 1963 v E, S, Pol (2) (56)

Blanchflower, J. (Manchester U), 1954 v W; 1955 v E, S; 1956 v S, W; 1957 v S, E, P; 1958 v S, E, I (2) (12)

Bookman, L. O. (Bradford C), 1914 v W; (with Luton T), 1921 v S, W; 1922 v E (4)

Bothwell, A. W. (Ards), 1926 v S, E, W; 1927 v E, W (5)

Bowler, G. C. (Hull C), 1950 v E, S, W (3)

Boyle, P. (Sheffield U), 1901 v E; 1902 v E; 1903 v S, W; 1904 v E (5)

Braithwaite, R. S. (Linfield), 1962 v W; 1963 v P, Sp; (with Middlesbrough), 1964 v W, U; 1965 v E, S, Sw (2), Ho (10)

Breen, T. (Belfast C), 1935 v E, W; 1937 v E, S; (with Manchester U), 1937 v W; 1938 v E, S; 1939 v W, S (9)

Brennan, B. (Bohemians), 1912 v W (1)

Brennan, R. A. (Luton T), 1949 v W; (with Birmingham C), 1950 v E, S, W; (with Fulham), 1951 v E (5)

Briggs, W. R. (Manchester U), 1962 v W; (with Swansea T), 1965 v Ho (2)

Brisby, D. (Distillery), 1891 v S (1)

Brolly, T. (Millwall), 1937 v W; 1938 v W; 1939 v E, W (4)

Brookes, E. A. (Shelbourne), 1920 v S (1)

Brotherston, N. (Blackburn R), 1980 v S, E, W, Aus (3); 1981 v Se, P; 1982 v S, Is, E, F, S, W, Hon (sub), A (sub); 1983 v A (sub), WG, Alb, T, Alb, S (sub), E (sub), W; 1984 v T; 1985 v Is (sub), T (27)

Brown, J. (Glentoran), 1921 v W; (with Tranmere R), 1924 v E, W (3)

Brown, J. (Wolverhampton W), 1935 v E, W; 1936 v E; (with Coventry C), 1937 v E, W; 1938 v S, W; (with Birmingham C), 1939 v E, S, W (10)

Brown, W. G. (Glenavon), 1926 v W (1)

Brown, W. M. (Limavady), 1887 v E (1)

Browne, F. (Cliftonville), 1887 v E, S, W; 1888 v E, S (5)

Browne, R. J. (Leeds U), 1936 v E, W; 1938 v E, W; 1939 v E, S (6)

Bruce, W. (Glentoran), 1961 v S; 1967 v W (2)

Buckle, H. (Cliftonville), 1882 v E (1)

Buckle, H. R. (Sunderland), 1904 v E; (with Bristol R), 1908 v W (2)

Burnett, J. (Distillery), 1894 v E, W, S; (with Glentoran), 1895 v E, W (5)

Burnison, J. (Distillery), 1901 v E, W (2)

Burnison, S. (Distillery), 1908 v E; 1910 v E, S; (with Bradford), 1911 v E, S, W; (with Distillery), 1912 v E; 1913 v W (8)

Burns, J. (Glenavon), 1923 v E (1)

Butler, M. P. (Blackpool), 1939 v W (1)

Campbell, A. C. (Crusaders), 1963 v W; 1965 v Sw (2)

Campbell, D. A. (Nottingham F), 1986 v Mor (sub), Br; 1987 v E (2), T, Y; 1988 v Y (with Charlton Ath), T (sub), Gr (sub), Pol (sub) (10)

Campbell, J. (Cliftonville), 1896 v W; 1897 v E, S, W; (with Distillery), 1898 v E, S, W; (with Cliftonville), 1899 v E; 1900 v E, S; 1901 v S, W; 1902 v S; 1903 v E; 1904 v S (15)

Campbell, J. P. (Fulham), 1951 v E, S (2)

Campbell, R. (Bradford C), 1982 v S, W (sub) (2)

Campbell, W. G. (Dundee), 1968 v S, E; 1969 v T; 1970 v S, W, USSR (6)

Carey, J. J. (Manchester U), 1947 v E, S, W; 1948 v E; 1949 v E, S, W (7)

Carroll, E. (Glenavon), 1925 v S (1)

Casey, T. (Newcastle U), 1955 v W; 1956 v W; 1957 v E, S, W, I, P (2); 1958 v WG, F; (with Portsmouth), 1959 v E, Sp (12)

Cashin, M. (Cliftonville), 1898 v S (1)

Caskey, W. (Derby Co), 1979 v Bul, E, Bul, E, D (sub); 1980 v E (sub); (with Tulsa R), 1982 v F (sub) (7)

Cassidy, T. (Newcastle U), 1971 v E (sub); 1972 v USSR (sub); 1974 v Bul (sub), S, E, W; 1975 v N; 1976 v S, E, W; 1977 v WG (sub); 1980 v E, Ei (sub), Is, S, E, W, Aus (3); (with Burnley), 1981 v Se, P; 1982 v Is, Sp (sub) (24)

Caughey, M. (Linfield), 1986 v F (sub), D (sub) (2)

Chambers, J. (Distillery), 1921 v W; (with Bury), 1928 v E, S, W; 1929 v E, S, W; 1930 v S, W; (with Nottingham F), 1932 v E, S, W (12)

Chatton, H. A. (Partick T), 1925 v E, S; 1926 v E (3)

Christian, J. (Linfield), 1889 v S (1)

Clarke, C. J. (Bournemouth), 1986 v F, D, Mor, Alg (sub), Sp, Br; (with Southampton), 1987 v E, T, Y; 1988 v Y, T, Gr, Pol, F, Ma; 1989 v Ei, H, Sp (1 + 1 sub); (with QPR), Ma, Ch; 1990 v H, Ei, N; (with Portsmouth), 1991 v Y (sub), D, A, Pol, Y (sub), Fa; 1992 v Fa, A, D, S, G (35)

Clarke, R. (Belfast C), 1901 v E, S (2)

Cleary, J. (Glentoran), 1982 v S, W; 1983 v W (sub); 1984 v T (sub); 1985 v Is (5)

Clements, D. (Coventry C), 1965 v W, Ho; 1966 v M; 1967 v S, W; 1968 v S, E; 1969 v T (2), S, W; 1970 v S, E, W, USSR (2); 1971 v Sp, E, S, W, Cy; (with Sheffield W), 1972 v USSR (2), Sp, E, S, W; 1973 v Bul, Cy (2), P, E, S, W; (with Everton), 1974 v Bul, P, S, E, W; 1975 v N, Y, E, S, W; 1976 v Se, Y; (with New York Cosmos), E, W (48)

Clugston, J. (Cliftonville), 1888 v W; 1889 v W, S, E; 1890 v E, S; 1891 v E, W; 1892 v E, S, W; 1893 v E, S, W (14)

Cochrane, D. (Leeds U), 1939 v E, W; 1947 v E, S, W; 1948 v E, S, W; 1949 v S, W; 1950 v S, E (12)

Cochrane, M. (Distillery), 1898 v S, W, E; 1899 v E; 1900 v E, S, W; (with Leicester Fosse), 1901 v S (8)

Cochrane, T. (Coleraine), 1976 v N; (with Burnley), 1978 v S (sub), E (sub), W (sub); 1979 v Ei (sub); (with Middlesbrough), D, Bul, E, Bul, E; 1980 v Is, E (sub), W (sub), Aus (1 + 2 sub); 1981 v Se (sub), P (sub), S, P, S, Se; 1982 v E (sub), F; (with Gillingham), 1984 v S, Fi (sub) (26)

Collins, F. (Celtic), 1922 v S (1)

Condy, J. (Distillery), 1882 v W; 1886 v E, S (3)

Connell, T. (Coleraine), 1978 v W (sub) (1)

Connor, J. (Glentoran), 1901 v S, E; (with Belfast C), 1905 v E, S, W; 1907 v E, S; 1908 v E, S; 1909 v W; 1911 v S, E, W (13)

Connor, M. J. (Brentford), 1903 v S, W; (with Fulham), 1904 v E (3)

Cook, W. (Celtic), 1933 v E, W, S; (with Everton), 1935 v E; 1936 v S, W; 1937 v E, S, W; 1938 v E, S, W; 1939 v E, S, W (15)

Cooke, S. (Belfast YMCA), 1889 v E; (with Cliftonville), 1890 v E, S (3)

Coulter, J. (Belfast C), 1934 v E, S, W; (with Everton), 1935 v E, S, W; 1937 v S, W; (with Grimsby T), 1938 v S, W; (with Chelmsford C), 1939 v S (11)

Cowan, J. (Newcastle U), 1970 v E (sub) (1)

Cowan, T. S. (Queen's Island), 1925 v W (1)

Coyle, F. (Coleraine), 1956 v E, S; 1957 v P; (with Nottingham F), 1958 v Arg (4)

Coyle, L. (Derry C), 1989 v Ch (sub) (1)

Coyle, R. I. (Sheffield W), 1973 v P, Cy (sub), W (sub); 1974 v Bul (sub), P (sub) (5)

Craig, A. B. (Rangers), 1908 v E, S, W; 1909 v S; (with Morton), 1912 v S, W; 1914 v E, S, W (9)

Craig, D. J. (Newcastle U), 1967 v W; 1968 v W; 1969 v T (2), E, S, W; 1970 v E, S, W, USSR; 1971 v Cy (2), S (1 + 1 sub); 1972 v USSR, S (sub); 1973 v Cy (2), E, S, W; 1974 v Bul, P; 1975 v N (25)

Crawford, S. (Distillery), 1889 v E, W; (with Cliftonville), 1891 v E, S, W; 1893 v E, W (7)

Croft, T. (Queen's Island), 1924 v E (1)

Crone, R. (Distillery), 1889 v S; 1890 v E, S, W (4)

Crone, W. (Distillery), 1882 v W; 1884 v E, S, W; 1886 v E, S, W; 1887 v E; 1888 v E, W; 1889 v S; 1890 v W (12)

Crooks, W. (Manchester U), 1922 v W (1)

Crossan, E. (Blackburn R), 1950 v S; 1951 v E; 1955 v W (3)

Crossan, J. A. (Sparta-Rotterdam), 1960 v E; (with Sunderland), 1963 v W, P, Sp; 1964 v E, S, W, U, Sp; 1965 v E, S, Sw (2); (with Manchester C), W, Ho (2), Alb; 1966 v S, E, Alb, WG; 1967 v S; (with Middlesbrough), 1968 v S (24)

Crothers, C. (Distillery), 1907 v W (1)

Cumming, L. (Huddersfield T), 1929 v W, S; (with Oldham Ath), 1930 v E (3)

Cunningham, R. (Ulster), 1892 v S, E, W; 1893 v E (4)

Cunningham, W. E. (St Mirren), 1951 v W; 1953 v E; 1954 v S; 1955 v S; (with Leicester C), 1956 v E, S, W; 1957 v S, W, I, P (2); 1958 v S, W, I, Cz (2), Arg, WG, F; 1959 v E, S, W; 1960 v E, S, W; (with Dunfermline Ath), 1961 v W; 1962 v W, Ho (30)

Curran, S. (Belfast C), 1926 v S, W; 1928 v S (3)

Curran, J. J. (Glenavon), 1922 v W; (with Pontypridd), 1923 v E, S; (with Glenavon), 1924 v E (4)

Cush, W. W. (Glenavon), 1951 v E, S; 1954 v S, E; 1957 v W, I, P (2); (with Leeds U), 1958 v I (2), W, Cz (2), Arg, WG, F; 1959 v E, S, W, Sp; 1960 v E, S, W; (with Portadown), 1961 v WG, Gr; 1962 v Gr (26)

Dalton, W. (YMCA), 1888 v S; (with Linfield), 1890 v S, W; 1891 v S, W; 1892 v E, S, W; 1894 v E, S, W (11)

D'Arcy, S. D. (Chelsea), 1952 v W; 1953 v E; (with Brentford), 1953 v S, W, F (5)

Darling, J. (Linfield), 1897 v E, S; 1900 v S; 1902 v E, S,

W; 1903 v E, S, W; 1905 v E, S, W; 1906 v E, S, W; 1908 v W; 1909 v E; 1910 v E, S, W; 1912 v S (21)

Davey, H. H. (Reading), 1926 v E; 1927 v E, S; 1928 v E; (with Portsmouth), 1928 v W (5)

Davis, T. L. (Oldham Ath), 1937 v E (1)

Davison, J. R. (Cliftonville), 1882 v E, W; 1883 v E, W; 1884 v E, W, S; 1885 v E (8)

Dennison, R. (Wolverhampton W), 1988 v F, Ma; 1989 v H, Sp, Ch (sub); 1990 v Ei, U; 1991 v Y (2), A, Pol, Fa (sub); 1992 v Fa, A, D (sub) (15)

Devine, J. (Glentoran), 1990 v U (sub) (1)

Devine, W. (Limavady), 1886 v E, W; 1887 v W; 1888 v W (4)

Dickson, D. (Coleraine), 1970 v S (sub), W; 1973 v Cy, P (4)

Dickson, T. A. (Linfield), 1957 v S (1)

Dickson, W. (Chelsea), 1951 v W, F; 1952 v E, S, W; 1953 v E, S, W, F; (with Arsenal), 1954 v E, W; 1955 v E (12)

Diffin, W. (Belfast C), 1931 v W (1)

Dill, A. H. (Knock and Down Ath), 1882 v E, W; (with Cliftonville), 1883 v W; 1884 v E, S, W; 1885 v E, S, W (9)

Doherty, I. (Belfast C), 1901 v E (1)

Doherty, J. (Cliftonville), 1933 v E, W (2)

Doherty, L. (Linfield), 1985 v Is; 1988 v T (sub) (2)

Doherty, M. (Distillery), 1938 v S (1)

Doherty, P. D. (Blackpool), 1935 v E, W; 1936 v E, S; (with Manchester C), 1937 v E, W; 1938 v E, S; 1939 v E, W; (with Derby Co), 1947 v E; (with Huddersfield T), 1947 v W; 1948 v E, W; 1949 v S; (with Doncaster R), 1951 v S (16)

Donaghy, M. (Luton T), 1980 v S, E, W; 1981 v Se, P, S (sub); 1982 v S, Is, E, F, S, W, Y, Hon, Sp, F; 1983 v A, WG, Alb, T, Alb, S, E, W; 1984 v A, T, WG, S, E, W, Fi; 1985 v R, Fi, E, Sp, T; 1986 v T, R, E, F, D, Mor, Alg, Sp, Br; 1987 v E (2), T, Is, Y; 1988 v Y, T, Gr, Pol, F, Ma; 1989 v Ei, H; (with Manchester U), Sp (2), Ma, Ch; 1990 v Ei, N; 1991 v Y (2), D, A, Pol, Fa; 1992 v Fa, A, D, S, Li, G (76)

Donnelly, L. (Distillery), 1913 v W (1)

Doran, J. F. (Brighton), 1921 v E; 1922 v E, W (3)

Dougan, A. D. (Portsmouth), 1958 v Cz; (with Blackburn R), 1960 v S; 1961 v E, W, I, Gr; (with Aston Villa), 1963 v S, P (2); (with Leicester C), 1966 v S, E, W, M, Alb, WG; 1967 v E, S; (with Wolverhampton W), 1967 v W; 1968 v S, W, Is; 1969 v T (2), E, S, W; 1970 v S, E, USSR (2); 1971 v Cy (2), Sp, E, S, W; 1972 v USSR (2), E, S, W; 1973 v Bul, Cy (43)

Douglas, J. P. (Belfast C), 1947 v E (1)

Dowd, H. O. (Glenavon), 1974 v W; 1975 v N (sub), Se (3)

Dowie, I. (Luton T), 1990 v N (sub), U; 1991 v Y, D, A (sub); (with West Ham U), Y, Fa; (with Southampton), 1992 v Fa, A, D (sub), S (sub), Li (12)

Duggan, H. A. (Leeds U), 1930 v E; 1931 v E, W; 1933 v E; 1934 v E; 1935 v S, W; 1936 v S (8)

Dunlop, G. (Linfield), 1985 v Is; 1987 v E, Y; 1990 v Ei (4)

Dunne, J. (Sheffield U), 1928 v W; 1931 v W, E; 1932 v E, S; 1933 v E, W (7)

Eames, W. L. E. (Dublin U), 1885 v E, S, W (3)

Eglington, T. J. (Everton), 1947 v S, W; 1948 v E, S, W; 1949 v E (6)

Elder, A. R. (Burnley), 1960 v W; 1961 v S, E, W, WG (2), Gr; 1962 v E, S, Gr; 1963 v E, S, W, P (2), Sp; 1964 v W, U; 1965 v E, S, W, Sw (2), Ho (2), Alb; 1966 v E, S, W, M, Alb; 1967 v E, S, W; (with Stoke C), 1968 v E, W; 1969 v E (sub), S, W; 1970 v USSR (40)

Elleman, A. R. (Cliftonville), 1889 v W; 1890 v E (2)

Elwood, J. H. (Bradford), 1929 v W; 1930 v E (2)

Emerson, W. (Glentoran), 1920 v E, S, W; 1921 v E; 1922

v E, S; (with Burnley), 1922 v W; 1923 v E, S, W; 1924 v E (11)

English, S. (Rangers), 1933 v W, S (2)

Enright, J. (Leeds C), 1912 v S (1)

Falloon, E. (Aberdeen, 1931 v S; 1933 v S (2)

Farquharson, T. G. (Cardiff C), 1923 v S, W; 1924 v E, S, W; 1925 v E, S (7)

Farrell, P. (Distillery), 1901 v S, W (2)

Farrell, P. (Hibernian), 1938 v W (1)

Farrell, P. D. (Everton), 1947 v S, W; 1948 v E, S, W; 1949 v E, W (7)

Feeney, J. M. (Linfield), 1947 v S; (with Swansea T), 1950 v E (2)

Feeney, W. (Glentoran), 1976 v Is (1)

Ferguson, W. (Linfield), 1966 v M; 1967 v E (2)

Ferris, J. (Belfast C), 1920 v E, W; (with Chelsea), 1921 v S, E; (with Belfast C), 1928 v S (5)

Ferris, R. O. (Birmingham C), 1950 v S; 1951 v F; 1952 v S (3)

Fettis, A. (Hull C), 1992 v D, Li (2)

Finney, T. (Sunderland), 1975 v N, E (sub), S, W; 1976 v N, Y, S; (with Cambridge U), 1980 v E, Is, S, E, W, Aus (2) (14)

Fitzpatrick, J. C. (Bohemians), 1896 v E, S (2)

Flack, H. (Burnley), 1929 v S (1)

Fleming, J. G. (Nottingham F), 1987 v E (2), Is, Y; 1988 v T, Gr, Pol; 1989 v Ma, Ch; (with Manchester C), 1990 v H, Ei; (with Barnsley), 1991 v Y; 1992 v Li (sub), G (14)

Forbes, G. (Limavady), 1888 v W; (with Distillery), 1891 v E, S (3)

Forde, J. T. (Ards), 1959 v Sp; 1961 v E, S, WG (4)

Foreman, T. A. (Cliftonville), 1899 v S (1)

Forsyth, J. (YMCA), 1888 v E, S (2)

Fox, W. (Ulster), 1887 v E, S (2)

Fulton, R. P. (Belfast C), 1930 v W; 1931 v E, S, W; 1932 v W, E; 1933 v E, S; 1934 v E, W, S; 1935 v E, W, S; 1936 v S, W; 1937 v E, S, W; 1938 v W (20)

Gaffikin, J. (Linfield Ath), 1890 v S, W; 1891 v S, W; 1892 v E, S, W; 1893 v E, S, W; 1894 v E, S, W; 1895 v E, W (15)

Galbraith, W. (Distillery), 1890 v W (1)

Gallagher, P. (Celtic), 1920 v E, S; 1922 v S; 1923 v S, W; 1924 v S, W; 1925 v S, W, E; (with Falkirk), 1927 v S (11)

Gallogly, C. (Huddersfield T), 1951 v E, S (2)

Gara, A. (Preston NE), 1902 v E, S, W (3)

Gardiner, A. (Cliftonville), 1930 v S, W; 1931 v S; 1932 v E, S (5)

Garrett, J. (Distillery), 1925 v W (1)

Gaston, R. (Oxford U), 1969 v Is (sub) (1)

Gaukrodger, G. (Linfield), 1895 v W (1)

Gaussen, A. W. (Moyola Park), 1884 v E, S; 1888 v E, W; 1889 v E, W (6)

Geary, J. (Glentoran), 1931 v S; 1932 v S (2)

Gibb, J. T. (Wellington Park) 1884 v S, W; 1885 v S, E, W; 1886 v S; 1887 v S, E, W; 1889 v S (10)

Gibb, T. J. (Cliftonville), 1936 v W (1)

Gibson W. K. (Cliftonville), 1894 v S, W, E; 1895 v S; 1897 v W; 1898 v S, W, E; 1901 v S, W, E; 1902 v S, W (13)

Gillespie, R. (Hertford), 1886 v E, S, W; 1887 v E, S, W (6)

Gillespie, W. (Sheffield U), 1913 v E, S; 1914 v E, W; 1920 v S, W; 1921 v E; 1922 v E, S, W; 1923 v E, S, W; 1924 v E, S, W; 1925 v E, S; 1926 v S, W; 1927 v E, W; 1928 v E; 1929 v E; 1931 v E (25)

Gillespie, W. (West Down), 1889 v W (1)

Goodall, A. L. (Derby Co), 1899 v S, W; 1900 v E, W; 1901 v E; 1902 v S; 1903 v E, W; (with Glossop), 1904 v E, W (10)

Goodbody, M. F. (Dublin University), 1889 v E; 1891 v W (2)

Gordon, H. (Linfield), 1891 v S; 1892 v E, S, W; 1893 v E, S, W; 1895 v E, W; 1896 v E, S (11)

Gordon, T. (Linfield), 1894 v W; 1895 v E (2)

Gorman, W. C. (Brentford), 1947 v E, S, W; 1948 v W (4)

Gowdy, J. (Glentoran), 1920 v E; (with Queen's Island), 1924 v W; (with Falkirk), 1926 v E, S; 1927 v E, S (6)

Gowdy, W. A. (Hull C), 1932 v S; (with Sheffield W), 1933 v S; (with Linfield), 1935 v E, S, W; (with Hibernian), 1936 v W (6)

Graham, W. G. L. (Doncaster R), 1951 v W, F; 1952 v E, S, W; 1953 v S, F; 1954 v E, W; 1955 v S, W; 1956 v E, S; 1959 v E (14)

Greer, W. (QPR), 1909 v E, S, W (3)

Gregg, H. (Doncaster R), 1954 v W; 1957 v E, S, W, I, P (2); 1958 v E, I; (with Manchester U), 1958 v Cz, Arg, WG, F, W; 1959 v E, W; 1960 v S, E; 1961 v E, S; 1962 v S, Gr; 1964 v S, E (25)

Hall, G. (Distillery), 1897 v E (1)

Halligan, W. (Derby Co), 1911 v W; (with Wolverhampton W), 1912 v E (2)

Hamill, M. (Manchester U), 1912 v E; 1914 v E, S; (with Belfast C), 1920 v E, S, W; (with Manchester C), 1921 v S (7)

Hamilton, B. (Linfield), 1969 v T; 1971 v Cy (2), E, S, W; (with Ipswich T), 1972 v USSR (1 + 1 sub), Sp; 1973 v Bul, Cy (2), P, E, S, W; 1974 v Bul, S, E, W; 1975 v N, Se, Y, E; 1976 v Se, N, Y; (with Everton), Is, S, E, W; 1977 v Ho, Bel, WG, E, S, W, Ic; (with Millwall), 1978 v S, E, W; 1979 v Ei (sub); (with Swindon T), Bul (2), E, S, W, D; 1980 v Aus (2 sub) (50)

Hamilton, J. (Knock), 1882 v E, W (2)

Hamilton, R. (Distillery), 1908 v W (1)

Hamilton, R. (Rangers), 1928 v S; 1929 v E; 1930 v S, E; 1932 v S (5)

Hamilton, W. (QPR), 1978 v S (sub); (with Burnley), 1980 v S, E, W, Aus (2); 1981 v Se, P, S, P, S, Se; 1982 v S, Is, E, W, Y, Hon, Sp, A, F; 1983 v A, WG, Alb (2), S, E, W; 1984 v A, T, WG, S, E, W, Fi; (with Oxford U), 1985 v R, Sp; 1986 v Mor (sub), Alg, Sp (sub), Br (sub), (41)

Hamilton, W. D. (Dublin Association), 1885 v W (1)

Hamilton, W. J. (Dublin Association), 1885 v W (1)

Hampton, H. (Bradford C), 1911 v E, S, W; 1912 v E, W; 1913 v E, S, W; 1914 v E (9)

Hanna, D. R. A. (Portsmouth), 1899 v W (1)

Hanna, J. (Nottingham F), 1912 v S, W (2)

Hannon, D. J. (Bohemians), 1908 v E, S; 1911 v E, S; 1912 v W; 1913 v E (6)

Harkin, J. T. (Southport), 1968 v W; 1969 v T; (with Shrewsbury T), W (sub); 1970 v USSR; 1971 v Sp (5)

Harland, A. I. (Linfield), 1923 v E (1)

Harris, J. (Cliftonville), 1921 v W (1)

Harris, V. (Shelbourne), 1906 v E; 1907 v E, W; 1908 v E, W, S; (with Everton), 1909 v E, W, S; 1910 v E, S, W; 1911 v E, S, W; 1912 v E; 1913 v E, S; 1914 v S, W (20)

Harvey, M. (Sunderland), 1961 v I; 1962 v Ho; 1963 v W, Sp; 1964 v S, E, W, U, Sp; 1965 v E, S, W, Sw (2), Ho (2), Alb; 1966 v S, E, W, M, Alb, WG; 1967 v E, S; 1968 v E, W; 1969 v Is, T (2), E; 1970 v USSR; 1971 v Cy, W (sub) (34)

Hastings, J. (Knock), 1882 v E, W; (with Ulster), 1883 v W; 1884 v S; 1886 v E, S (7)

Hatton, S. (Linfield), 1963 v S, Pol (2)

Hayes, W. E. (Huddersfield T), 1938 v E, S; 1939 v E, S (4)

Healy, F. (Coleraine), 1982 v S, W, Hon (sub); (with Glentoran), 1983 v A (sub) (4)

Hegan, D. (WBA), 1970 v USSR; (with Wolverhampton W), 1972 v USSR, E, S, W; 1973 v Bul, Cy (7)

Henderson, A. W. (Ulster), 1885 v E, S, W (3)

Hewison, G. (Moyola Park), 1885 v E, S (2)

Hill, C. F. (Sheffield U), 1990 v N, U; 1991 v Pol, Y; 1992 v A, D (6)

Hill, M. J. (Norwich C), 1959 v W; 1960 v W; 1961 v WG; 1962 v S; (with Everton), 1964 v S, E, Sp (7)

Hinton, E. (Fulham), 1947 v S, W; 1948 v S, E, W; (with Millwall), 1951 v W, F (7)

Hopkins, J. (Brighton), 1926 v E (1)

Houston, J. (Linfield), 1912 v S, W; 1913 v W; (with Everton), 1913 v E, S; 1914 v S (6)

Houston, W. (Linfield), 1933 v W (1)

Houston, W. G. (Moyola Park), 1885 v E, S (2)

Hughes, M. E. (Manchester C), 1992 v D, S, Li, G (4)

Hughes, P. (Bury), 1987 v E, T, Is (3)

Hughes, W. (Bolton W), 1951 v W (1)

Humphries, W. (Ards), 1962 v W; (with Coventry C), 1962 v Ho; 1963 v E, S, W, Pol, Sp; 1964 v S, E, Sp; 1965 v S; (with Swansea T), 1965 v W, Ho, Alb (14)

Hunter, A. (Distillery), 1905 v W; 1906 v W, E, S; (with Belfast C), 1908 v W; 1909 v W, E, S (8)

Hunter, A. (Blackburn R), 1970 v USSR; 1971 v Cy (2), E, S, W; (with Ipswich T), 1972 v USSR (2), Sp, E, S, W; 1973 v Bul, Cy (2), P, E, S, W; 1974 v Bul, S, E, W; 1975 v N, Se, Y, E, S, W; 1976 v Se, N, Y, Is, S, E, W; 1977 v Ho, Bel, WG, E, S, W, Ic; 1978 v Ic, Ho, Bel; 1979 v Ei, D, S, W, D; 1980 v E, Ei (53)

Hunter, R. J. (Cliftonville), 1884 v E, S, W (3)

Hunter, V. (Coleraine), 1962 v E; 1964 v Sp (2)

Irvine, R. J. (Linfield), 1962 v Ho; 1963 v E, S, W, Pol (2), Sp; (with Stoke C), 1965 v W (8)

Irvine, R. W. (Everton), 1922 v S; 1923 v E, W; 1924 v E, S; 1925 v E; 1926 v E; 1927 v E, W; 1928 v E, S; (with Portsmouth), 1929 v E; 1930 v S; (with Connah's Quay), 1931 v E; (with Derry C), 1932 v W (15)

Irvine, W. J. (Burnley), 1963 v W, Sp; 1965 v S, W, Sw, Ho (2), Alb; 1966 v S, E, W, M, Alb; 1967 v E, S; 1968 v E, W; (with Preston NE), 1969 v Is, T, E; (with Brighton), 1972 v E, S, W (23)

Irving, S, J. (Dundee), 1923 v S, W; 1924 v S, E, W; 1925 v S, E, W; 1926 v S, W; (with Cardiff C), 1927 v S, E, W; 1928 v S, E, W; (with Chelsea), 1929 v E; 1931 v W (18)

Jackson, T. (Everton), 1969 v Is, E, S, W; 1970 v USSR (1 + 1 sub); (with Nottingham F), 1971 v Sp; 1972 v E, S, W; 1973 v Cy, E, S, W; 1974 v Bul, P, S (sub), E (sub), W (sub); 1975 v N (sub), Se, Y, E, S, W; (with Manchester U); 1976 v Se, N, Y; 1977 v Ho, Bel, WG, E, S, W, Ic (35)

Jamison, J. (Glentoran), 1976 v N (1)

Jennings, P. A. (Watford), 1964 v W, U; (with Tottenham H), 1965 v E, S, Sw (2), Ho, Alb; 1966 v S, E, W, Alb, WG; 1967 v E, S; 1968 v S, E, W; 1969 v Is, T (2), E, S, W; 1970 v S, E, USSR (2); 1971 v Cy (2), E, S, W; 1972 v USSR, Sp, S, E, W; 1973 v Bul, Cy, P, E, S, W; 1974 v P, S, E, W; 1975 v N, Se, Y, E, S, W; 1976 v Se, N, Y, Is, S, E, W; 1977 v Ho, Bel, WG, E, S, W, Ic; (with Arsenal), 1978 v Ic, Ho, Bel; 1979 v Ei, D, Bul, E, Bul, E, S, W, D; 1980 v E, Ei, Is; 1981 v S, P, S, Se; 1982 v S, Is, E, W, Y, Hon, Sp, F; 1983 v Alb, S, E, W; 1984 v A, T, WG, S, W, Fi; 1985 v R, Fi, E, Sp, T; (with Tottenham H), 1986 v T, R, E, F, D; (with Everton), Mor; (with Tottenham H), Alg, Sp, Br (119)

Johnston, H. (Portadown), 1927 v W (1)

Johnston, R. (Old Park), 1885 v S, W (2)

Johnston, S. (Distillery), 1882 v W; 1884 v E; 1886 v E, S (4)

Johnston, S. (Linfield), 1890 v W; 1893 v S, W; 1894 v E (4)

Johnston, S. (Distillery), 1905 v W (1)

Johnston, W. C. (Glenavon), 1962 v W; (with Oldham Ath), 1966 v M (sub) (2)

Jones, J. (Linfield), 1930 v S, W; 1931 v S, W, E; 1932 v S, E; 1933 v S, E, W; 1934 v S, E, W; 1935 v S, E, W; 1936 v E, S; (with Hibernian), 1936 v W; 1937 v E, W, S; (with Glenavon), 1938 v E (23)

Jones, J. (Glenavon), 1956 v W; 1957 v E, W (3)

Jones, S. (Distillery), 1934 v E; (with Blackpool), 1934 v W (2)

Jordan, T. (Linfield), 1895 v E, W (2)

Kavanagh, P. J. (Celtic), 1930 v E (1)

Keane, T. R. (Swansea T), 1949 v S (1)

Kearns, A. (Distillery), 1900 v E, S, W; 1902 v E, S, W (6)

Kee, P. V. (Oxford U), 1990 v N; 1991 v Y (2), D, A, Pol, Fa (7)

Keith, R, M. (Newcastle U), 1958 v E, W, Cz (2), Arg, I, WG, F; 1959 v E, S, W, Sp; 1960 v S, E; 1961 v S, E, W, I, WG (2), Gr; 1962 v W, Ho (23)

Kelly, H. R. (Fulham), 1950 v E, W; (with Southampton), 1951 v E, S (4)

Kelly, J. (Glentoran), 1896 v E (1)

Kelly, J. (Derry C), 1932 v E, W; 1933 v E, W, S; 1934 v W; 1936 v E, S, W; 1937 v S, E (11)

Kelly, P. (Manchester C), 1921 v E (1)

Kelly, P. M. (Barnsley), 1950 v S (1)

Kennedy, A. L. (Arsenal), 1923 v W; 1925 v E (2)

Kernaghan, N. (Belfast C), 1936 v W; 1937 v S; 1938 v E (3)

Kirkwood, H. (Cliftonville), 1904 v W (1)

Kirwan, J. (Tottenham H), 1900 v W; 1902 v E, W; 1903 v E, S, W; 1904 v E, S, W; 1905 v E, S, W; (with Chelsea), 1906 v E, S, W; 1907 v W; (with Clyde), 1909 v S (17)

Lacey, W. (Everton), 1909 v E, S, W; 1910 v E, S, W; 1911 v E, S, W; 1912 v E; (with Liverpool), 1913 v W; 1914 v E, S, W; 1920 v E, S, W; 1921 v E, S, W; 1922 v E, S; (with New Brighton), 1925 v E (23)

Lawther, W. I. (Sunderland), 1960 v W; 1961 v I; (with Blackburn R), 1962 v S, Ho (4)

Leatham, J. (Belfast C), 1939 v W (1)

Ledwidge, J. J. (Shelbourne), 1906 v S, W (2)

Lemon, J. (Glentoran), 1886 v W; 1888 v S; (with Belfast YMCA), 1889 v W (3)

Leslie, W. (YMCA), 1887 v E (1)

Lewis, J. (Glentoran), 1899 v S, E, W; (with Distillery), 1900 v S (4)

Little, J. (Glentoran), 1898 v W (1)

Lockhart, H. (Rossall School), 1884 v W (1)

Lockhart, N. (Linfield), 1947 v E; (with Coventry C), 1950 v W; 1951 v W; 1952 v W; (with Aston Villa), 1954 v S, E; 1955 v W; 1956 v W (8)

Lowther, R. (Glentoran), 1888 v E, S (2)

Loyal, J. (Clarence), 1891 v S (1)

Lutton, R. J. (Wolverhampton W), 1970 v S, E; (with West Ham U), 1973 v Cy (sub), S (sub), W (sub); 1974 v P (6)

Lyner, D. (Glentoran), 1920 v E, W; 1922 v S, W; (with Manchester U), 1923 v E; (with Kilmarnock), 1923 v W (6)

McAdams, W. J. (Manchester C), 1954 v W; 1955 v S; 1957 v E; 1958 v S, I; (with Bolton W), 1961 v E, S, W, I, WG (2), Gr; 1962 v E, Gr; (with Leeds U), Ho (15)

McAlery, J. M. (Cliftonville), 1882 v E, W (2)

McAlinden, J. (Belfast C), 1938 v S; 1939 v S; (with Portsmouth), 1947 v E; (with Southend U), 1949 v E (4)

McAllen, J. (Linfield), 1898 v E; 1899 v E, S, W; 1900 v E, S, W; 1901 v W; 1902 v S (9)

McAlpine, W. J. (Cliftonville), 1901 v S (1)

McArthur, A. (Distillery), 1886 v W (1)

McAuley, J. L. (Huddersfield T), 1911 v E, W; 1912 v E, S; 1913 v E, S (6)

McAuley, P. (Belfast C), 1900 v S (1)

McBride, S. (Glenavon), 1991 v D (sub), Pol (sub); 1992 v Fa (sub), D (4)

McCabe, J. J. (Leeds U), 1949 v S, W; 1950 v E; 1951 v W; 1953 v W; 1954 v S (6)

McCabe, W. (Ulster), 1891 v E (1)

McCambridge, J. (Ballymena), 1930 v S, W; (with Cardiff C), 1931 v W; 1932 v E (4)

McCandless, J. (Bradford), 1912 v W; 1913 v W; 1920 v W, S; 1921 v E (5)

McCandless, W. (Linfield), 1920 v E, W; 1921 v E; (with Rangers), 1921 v W; 1922 v S; 1924 v W, S; 1925 v S; 1929 v W (9)

McCann, P. (Belfast C), 1910 v E, S, W; 1911 v E; (with Glentoran), 1911 v S; 1912 v E; 1913 v W (7)

McCashin, J. (Cliftonville), 1896 v W; 1898 v S, W; 1899 v S (4)

McCavana, W. T. (Coleraine), 1955 v S; 1956 v E, S (3)

McCaw, D. (Distillery), 1882 v E (1)

McCaw, J. H. (Linfield), 1927 v W; 1930 v S; 1931 v E, S, W (5)

McClatchey, J. (Distillery), 1886 v E, S, W (3)

McClatchey, R. (Distillery), 1895 v S (1)

McCleary, J. W. (Cliftonville), 1955 v W (1)

McCleery, W. (Cliftonville), 1922 v N; 1930 v E, W; 1931 v E, S, W; 1932 v S, W; 1933 v E, W (10)

McClelland, J. (Arsenal), 1961 v W, I, WG (2), Gr; (with Fulham), 1967 v M (6)

McClelland, J. (Mansfield T), 1980 v S (sub), Aus (3); 1981 v Se, S; (with Rangers), S, Se; 1982 v S, W, Y, Hon, Sp, A, F; 1983 v A, WG, Alb, T, Alb, S, E, W; 1984 v A, T, WG, S, E, W, Fi; 1985 v R, (with Watford), Fi, Is, E; Sp, T; 1986 v T, F (sub); 1987 v E (2), T, Is, Y; 1988 v T, Gr, F, Ma; 1989 v Ei, H, Sp (2), Ma; (with Leeds U), 1990 v N (53)

McCluggage, A. (Bradford), 1924 v E; (with Burnley), 1927 v S, W; 1928 v S, E, W; 1929 v S, E, W; 1930 v W; 1931 v E, W (12)

McClure, G. (Cliftonville), 1907 v S, W; 1908 v E; (with Distillery), 1909 v E (4)

McConnell, E. (Cliftonville), 1904 v S, W; (with Glentoran), 1905 v S; (with Sunderland), 1906 v E; 1907 v E; 1908 v S, W; (with Sheffield W), 1909 v S, W; 1910 v S, W, E (12)

McConnell, P. (Doncaster R), 1928 v W; (with Southport), 1932 v E (2)

McConnell, W. G. (Bohemians), 1912 v W; 1913 v E, S; 1914 v E, S, W (6)

McConnell, W. H. (Reading), 1925 v W; 1926 v E, W; 1927 v S, W; 1928 v E, W (8)

McCourt, F. J. (Manchester C), 1952 v E, W; 1953 v E, S, W, F (6)

McCoy, J. (Distillery), 1896 v W (1)

McCoy, R. (Coleraine), 1987 v T (sub) (1)

McCracken, R. (C Palace), 1921 v E; 1922 v E, S, W (4)

McCracken, W. (Distillery), 1902 v E, W; 1903 v E; 1904 v E, S, W; (with Newcastle U), 1905 v E, S, W; 1907 v E; 1920 v E; 1922 v E, S, W; (with Hull C), 1923 v S (15)

McCreery, D. (Manchester U), 1976 v S (sub), E, W; 1977 v Ho, Bel, WG, E, S, W, Ic; 1978 v Ic, Ho, Bel, S, E, W; 1979 v Ei, D, Bul, E, Bul, W, D; (with QPR), 1980 v E, Ei, S (sub), E (sub), W (sub), Aus (1 + 1 sub); 1981 v Se (sub), P (sub); (with Tulsa R), S, P, Se; 1982 v S, Is, E (sub), F, Y, Hon, Sp, A, F; (with Newcastle U), v A; 1984 v T (sub); 1985 v R, Sp (sub); 1986 v T (sub), R, E, F, D, Alg, Sp, Br; 1987 v T, E, Y; 1988 v Y; 1989 v Sp, Ma, Ch; (with Hearts), 1990 v H, Ei, N, U (67)

McCrory, S. (Southend U), 1958 v E (1)

McCullough, K. (Belfast C), 1935 v W; 1936 v E; (with Manchester C), 1936 v S; 1937 v E, S (5)

McCullough, W. J. (Arsenal), 1961 v I; 1963 v Sp; 1964 v S, E, W, U, Sp; 1965 v E, Sw; (with Millwall), 1967 v E (10)

McCurdy, C. (Linfield), 1980 v Aus (sub) (1)

McDonald, A. (QPR), 1986 v R, E, F, D, Mor, Alg, Sp, Br; 1987 v E (2), T, Is, Y; 1988 v Y, T, Pol, F, Ma; 1989 v Ei, H, Sp, Ch; 1990 v H, Ei, U; 1991 v Y, D, A, Fa; 1992 v Fa, S, Li, G (33)

McDonald, R. (Rangers), 1930 v S; 1932 v E (2)

McDonnell, J. (Bohemians), 1911 v E, S; 1912 v W; 1913 v W (4)

McElhinney, G. (Bolton W), 1984 v WG, S, E, W, Fi; 1985 v R (6)

McFaul, W. S. (Linfield), 1967 v E (sub); (with Newcastle U), 1970 v W; 1971 v Sp; 1972 v USSR; 1973 v Cy; 1974 v Bul (6)

McGarry, J. K. (Cliftonville), 1951 v W, F, S (3)

McGaughey, M. (Linfield), 1985 v Is (sub) (1)

McGee, G. (Wellington Park), 1885 v E, S, W (3)

McGrath, R. C. (Tottenham H), 1974 v S, E, W; 1975 v N; 1976 v Is (sub); 1977 v Ho; (with Manchester U), Bel, WG, E, S, W, Ic; 1978 v Ic, Ho, Bel, S, E, W; 1979 v Bul (sub), E (2 sub) (21)

McGregor, S. (Glentoran), 1921 v S (1)

McGrillen, J. (Clyde), 1924 v S; (with Belfast C), 1927 v S (2)

McGuire, E. (Distillery), 1907 v S (1)

McIlroy, H. (Cliftonville), 1906 v E (1)

McIlroy, J. (Burnley), 1952 v E, S, W; 1953 v E, S, W; 1954 v E, S, W; 1955 v E, S, W; 1956 v E, S, W; 1957 v E, S, W, I, P (2); 1958 v E, S, W, I (2), Cz (2), Arg, WG, F; 1959 v E, S, W, Sp; 1960 v E, S, W; 1961 v E, W, WG (2), Gr; 1962 v E, S, Gr, Ho; 1963 v E, S, Pol (2); (with Stoke C), 1963 v W; 1966 v S, E, Alb (55)

McIlroy, S. B. (Manchester U), 1972 v Sp, S (sub); 1974 v S, E, W; 1975 v N, Se, Y, E, S, W; 1976 v Se, N, Y, S, E, W; 1977 v Ho, Bel, E, S, W, Ic; 1978 v Ic, Ho, Bel, S, E, W; 1979 v Ei, D, Bul, E, Bul, E, S, W, D; 1980 v E, Ei, Is, S, E, W; 1981 v Se, P, S, P, S, Se; 1982 v S, Is; (with Stoke C), E, F, S, W, Y, Hon, Sp, A, F; 1983 v A, WG, Alb, T, Alb, S, E, W; 1984 v A, T, S, E, W, Fi; 1985 v Fi, E, T; (with Manchester C), 1986 v T, R, E, F, D, Mor, Alg, Sp, Br; 1987 v E (sub) (88)

McIlvenny, J. (Distillery), 1890 v E; 1891 v E (2)

McIlvenny, P. (Distillery), 1924 v W (1)

McKeag, W. (Glentoran), 1968 v S, W (2)

McKee, F. W. (Cliftonville), 1906 v S, W; (with Belfast C), 1914 v E, S, W (5)

McKelvie, H. (Glentoran), 1901 v W (1)

McKenna, J. (Huddersfield), 1950 v E, S, W; 1951 v S, F; 1952 v E (7)

McKenzie, H. (Distillery), 1923 v S (1)

McKenzie, R. (Airdrie), 1967 v W (1)

McKeown, H. (Linfield), 1892 v E, S, W; 1893 v S, W; 1894 v S, W (7)

McKie, H. (Cliftonville), 1895 v E, S, W (3)

McKinney, D. (Hull C), 1921 v S; (with Bradford C), 1924 v S (2)

McKinney, V. J. (Falkirk), 1966 v WG (1)

McKnight, A. (Celtic), 1988 v Y, T, Gr, Pol, F, Ma; (with West Ham U) 1989 v Ei, H, Sp (2) (10)

McKnight, J. (Preston NE), 1912 v S; (with Glentoran), 1913 v S (2)

McLaughlin, J. C. (Shrewsbury T), 1962 v E, S, W, Gr; 1963 v W; (with Swansea T), 1964 v W, U; 1965 v E, W, Sw (2); 1966 v W (12)

McLean, T. (Limavady), 1885 v S (1)

McMahon, J. (Bohemians), 1934 v S (1)

McMaster, G. (Glentoran), 1897 v E, S, W (3)

McMichael, A. (Newcastle U), 1950 v E, S; 1951 v E, S, F; 1952 v E, S, W; 1953 v E, S, W, F; 1954 v E, S, W; 1955 v E, W; 1956 v W; 1957 v E, S, W, I, P (2); 1958 v E, S, W, I (2), Cz (2), Arg, WG, F; 1959 v S, W, Sp; 1960 v E, S, W (40)

McMillan, G. (Distillery), 1903 v E; 1905 v W (2)

McMillan, S. (Manchester U), 1963 v E, S (2)

McMillen, W. S. (Manchester U), 1934 v E; 1935 v S; 1937 v S; (with Chesterfield), 1938 v S, W; 1939 v E, S (7)

McMordie, A. S. (Middlesbrough), 1969 v Is, T (2), E, S, W; 1970 v E, S, W, USSR; 1971 v Cy (2), E, S, W; 1972 v USSR, Sp, E, S, W; 1973 v Bul (21)

McMorran, E. J. (Belfast C), 1947 v E; (with Barnsley), 1951 v E, S, W; 1952 v E, S, W; 1953 v E, S, F; (with Doncaster R), 1953 v W; 1954 v E; 1956 v W; 1957 v I, P (15)

McMullan, D. (Liverpool), 1926 v E, W; 1927 v S (3)

McNally, B. A. (Shrewsbury T), 1986 v Mor; 1987 v T (sub); 1988 v Y, Gr, Ma (sub) (5)

McNinch, J. (Ballymena), 1931 v S; 1932 v S, W (3)

McParland, P. J. (Aston Villa), 1954 v W; 1955 v E, S; 1956 v E, S; 1957 v E, S, W, P; 1958 v E, S, W, I (2), Cz (2), Arg, WG, F; 1959 v E, S, W, Sp; 1960 v E, S, W; 1961 v E, S, W, I, WG (2), Gr; (with Wolverhampton W), 1962 v Ho (34)

McShane, J. (Cliftonville), 1899 v S; 1900 v E, S, W (4)

McVickers, J. (Glentoran), 1888 v E; 1889 v S (2)

McWha, W. B. R. (Knock), 1882 v E, W; (with Cliftonville), 1883 v E, W; 1884 v E; 1885 v E, W (7)

Macartney, A. (Ulster), 1903 v S, W; (with Linfield), 1904 v S, W; (with Everton), 1905 v E, S; (with Belfast C), 1907 v E, S, W; 1908 v E, S, W; (with Glentoran), 1909 v E, S, W (15)

Mackie, J. (Arsenal), 1923 v W; (with Portsmouth), 1935 v S, W (3)

Madden, O. (Norwich C), 1938 v E (1)

Magill, E. J. (Arsenal), 1962 v E, S, Gr; 1963 v E, S, W, Pol (2), Sp; 1964 v E, S, W, U, Sp; 1965 v E, S, Sw (2), Ho, Alb; 1966 v S, E; (with Brighton), 1966 v Alb, W, WG, M (26)

Magilton, J. (Oxford U), 1991 v Pol, Y, Fa; 1992 v Fa, A, D, S, Li, G (9)

Maginnis, H. (Linfield), 1900 v E, S, W; 1903 v S, W; 1904 v E, S, W (8)

Maguire, E. (Distillery), 1907 v S (1)

Mahood, J. (Belfast C), 1926 v S; 1928 v E, S, W; 1929 v E, S, W; 1930 v W; (with Ballymena), 1934 v S (9)

Manderson, R. (Rangers), 1920 v W, S; 1925 v S, E; 1926 v S (5)

Mansfield, J. (Dublin Freebooters), 1901 v E (1)

Martin, C. J. (Glentoran), 1947 v S; (with Leeds U), 1948 v E, S, W; (with Aston Villa), 1949 v E; 1950 v W (6)

Martin, D. (Boness), 1925 v S (1)

Martin, D. C. (Cliftonville), 1882 v E, W; 1883 v E (3)

Martin, D. K. (Belfast C), 1934 v E, S, W; 1935 v S; (with Wolverhampton W), 1935 v E; 1936 v W; (with Nottingham F), 1937 v S; 1938 v E, S; 1939 v S (10)

Mathieson, A. (Luton T), 1921 v W; 1922 v E (2)

Maxwell, J. (Linfield), 1902 v W; 1903 v W, E; (with Glentoran), 1905 v W, S; (with Belfast C), 1906 v W; 1907 v S (7)

Meek, H. L. (Glentoran), 1925 v W (1)

Mehaffy, J. A. C. (Queen's Island), 1922 v W (1)

Meldon, J. (Dublin Freebooters), 1899 v S, W (2)

Mercer, H. V. A. (Linfield), 1908 v E (1)

Mercer, J. T. (Distillery), 1898 v E, S, W; 1899 v E; (with Linfield), 1902 v E, W; (with Distillery), 1903 v S, W; (with Derby Co), 1904 v E, W; 1905 v S (11)

Millar, W. (Barrow), 1932 v W; 1933 v S (2)

Miller, J. (Middlesbrough), 1929 v W, S; 1930 v E (3)

Milligan, D. (Chesterfield), 1939 v W (1)

Milne, R. G. (Linfield), 1894 v E, W; 1895 v E, W;

1896 v E, S, W; 1897 v E, S; 1898 v E, S, W; 1899 v E, W; 1901 v W; 1902 v E, S, W; 1903 v E, S; 1904 v E, S, W; 1906 v E, S, W (27)

Mitchell, C. (Glentoran), 1934 v W (1)

Mitchell, E. J. (Cliftonville), 1933 v S (1)

Mitchell, W. (Distillery), 1932 v E, W; 1933 v E, W; (with Chelsea), 1934 v W, S; 1935 v S, E; 1936 v S, E; 1937 v E, S, W; 1938 v E, S (15)

Molyneux, T. B. (Ligoniel), 1883 v E, W; (with Cliftonville), 1884 v E, W, S; 1885 v E, W; 1886 v E, W, S; 1888 v S (11)

Montgomery, F. J. (Coleraine), 1955 v E (1)

Moore, C. (Glentoran), 1949 v W (1)

Moore, J. (Linfield Ath), 1891 v E, S, W (3)

Moore, P. (Aberdeen), 1933 v E (1)

Moore, T. (Ulster), 1887 v S, W (2)

Moore, W. (Falkirk), 1923 v S (1)

Moorhead, F. W. (Dublin University), 1885 v E (1)

Moorhead, G. (Linfield), 1923 v S; 1928 v S; 1929 v S (3)

Moran, J. (Leeds C), 1912 v S (1)

Moreland, V. (Derby Co), 1979 v Bul (2 sub), E, S; 1980 v E, Ei (6)

Morgan, F. G. (Linfield), 1923 v E; (with Nottingham F), 1924 v S; 1927 v E; 1928 v E, S, W; 1929 v E (7)

Morgan, S. (Port Vale), 1972 v Sp; 1973 v Bul (sub), P, Cy, E, S, W; (with Aston Villa), 1974 v Bul, P, S, E; 1975 v Se; 1976 v Se (sub), N, Y; (with Brighton & HA), S, W (sub); (with Sparta Rotterdam), 1979 v D (18)

Morrison, J. (Linfield Ath), 1891 v E, W (2)

Morrison, T. (Glentoran), 1895 v E, S, W; (with Burnley), 1899 v W; 1900 v W; 1902 v E, S (7)

Morrogh, E. (Bohemians), 1896 v S (1)

Morrow, S. J. (Arsenal), 1990 v U (sub); 1991 v A (sub), Pol, Y; 1992 v Fa, S (sub), G (sub) (7)

Morrow, W. J. (Moyola Park), 1883 v E, W; 1884 v S (3)

Muir, R. (Oldpark), 1885 v S, W (2)

Mullan, G. (Glentoran), 1983 v S, E, W, Alb (sub) (4)

Mulholland, S. (Celtic), 1906 v S, E (2)

Mulligan, J. (Manchester C), 1921 v S (1)

Murphy, J. (Bradford C), 1910 v E, S, W (3)

Murphy, N. (QPR), 1905 v E, S, W (3)

Murray, J. M. (Motherwell), 1910 v E, S; (with Sheffield W), 1910 v W (3)

Napier, R. J. (Bolton W), 1966 v WG (1)

Neill, W. J. T. (Arsenal), 1961 v I, Gr, WG; 1962 v E, S, W, Gr; 1963 v E, W, Pol, Sp; 1964 v S, E, W, U, Sp; 1965 v E, S, W, Sw, Ho (2), Alb; 1966 v S, E, W, Alb, WG, M; 1967 v S, W; 1968 v S, E; 1969 v E, S, W, Is, T (2); 1970 v S, E, W, USSR (2); (with Hull C), 1971 v Cy, Sp; 1972 v USSR, Sp, S, E, W; 1973 v Bul, Cy (2), P, E, S, W (59)

Nelis, P. (Nottingham F), 1923 v E (1)

Nelson, S. (Arsenal), 1970 v W, E (sub); 1971 v Cy, Sp, E, S, W; 1972 v USSR (2), Sp, E, S, W; 1973 v Bul, Cy, P; 1974 v S, E; 1975 v Se, Y; 1976 v Se, N, Is, E; 1977 v Bel (sub), WG, W, Ic; 1978 v Ic, Ho, Bel; 1979 v Ei, D, Bul, E, Bul, E, S, W, D; 1980 v E, Ei, Is; 1981 v S, P, S, Se; (with Brighton & HA), 1982 v E, S, Sp (sub), A (51)

Nicholl, C. J. (Aston Villa), 1975 v Se, Y, E, S, W; 1976 v Se, N, Y, S, E, W; 1977 v W; (with Southampton), 1978 v Bel (sub), S, E, W; 1979 v Ei, Bul, E, Bul, E, W; 1980 v Ei, Is, S, E, W, Aus (3); 1981 v Se, P, S, P, S, Se; 1982 v S, Is, E, F, W, Y, Hon, Sp, A, F; 1983 v S (sub), E, W; (with Grimsby T), 1984 v A, T (51)

Nicholl, H. (Belfast C), 1902 v E, W; 1905 v E (3)

Nicholl, J. M. (Manchester U), 1976 v Is, W (sub); 1977 v Ho, Bel, E, S, W, Ic; 1978 v Ic, Ho, Bel, S, E, W; 1979 v Ei, D, Bul, E, Bul, E, S, W, D; 1980 v E, Ei, Is, S, E, W, Aus (3); 1981 v Se, P, S, P, S, Se; 1982 v S, Is, E; (with Toronto B), F, W, Y, Hon, Sp, A, F;

(with Sunderland), 1983 v A, WG, Alb, T, Alb; (with Toronto B), S, E, W; (with Rangers), 1984 v T, WG, S, E; (with Toronto B), Fi; 1985 v R; (with WBA), Fi, E, Sp, T; 1986 v T, R, E, F, Alg, Sp, Br (73)

Nicholson, J. J. (Manchester U), 1961 v S, W; 1962 v E, W, Gr, Ho; 1963 v E, S, Pol (2); (with Huddersfield T), 1965 v W, Ho (2), Alb; 1966 v S, E, W, Alb, M; 1967 v S, W; 1968 v S, E, W; 1969 v S, E, W, T (2); 1970 v S, E, W, USSR (2); 1971 v Cy (2), E, S, W; 1972 v USSR (2) (41)

Nixon, R. (Linfield), 1914 v S (1)

Nolan-Whelan, J. V. (Dublin Freebooters), 1901 v E, W; 1902 v S, W (4)

O'Brien, M. T. (QPR), 1921 v S; (with Leicester C), 1922 v S, W; 1924 v S, W; (with Hull C), 1925 v S, E, W; 1926 v W; (with Derby Co), 1927 v W (10)

O'Connell, P. (Sheffield W), 1912 v E, S; (with Hull C), 1914 v S, E, W (5)

O'Doherty, A. (Coleraine), 1970 v E, W (sub) (2)

O'Driscoll, J. F. (Swansea T), 1949 v E, S, W (3)

O'Hagan, C. (Tottenham H), 1905 v S, W; 1906 v S, W, E; (with Aberdeen), 1907 v E, S, W; 1908 v S, W; 1909 v E (11)

O'Hagan, W. (St Mirren), 1920 v E, W (2)

O'Hehir, J. C. (Bohemians), 1910 v W (1)

O'Kane, W. J. (Nottingham F), 1970 v E, W, S (sub); 1971 v Sp, E, S, W; 1972 v USSR (2); 1973 v P, Cy; 1974 v Bul, P, S, E, W; 1975 v N, Se, E, S (20)

O'Mahoney, M. T. (Bristol R), 1939 v S (1)

O'Neill, C. (Motherwell), 1989 v Ch (sub); 1990 v Ei (sub); 1991 v D (3)

O'Neill, J. (Leicester C), 1980 v Is, S, E, W, Aus (3); 1981 v P, S, P, S, Se; 1982 v S, Is, E, F, S, F (sub); 1983 v A, WG, Alb, T, Alb, S; 1984 v S (sub); 1985 v Is, Fi, E, Sp, T; 1986 v T, R, E, F, D, Mor, Alg, Sp, Br (39)

O'Neill, J. (Sunderland), 1962 v W (1)

O'Neill, M. A. (Newcastle U), 1988 v Gr, Pol, F, Ma; 1989 v Ei, H, Sp (sub), Sp (sub), Ma (sub), Ch; (with Dundee U), 1990 v H (sub), Ei; 1991 v Pol; 1992 v Fa (sub), S (sub), G (sub) (16)

O'Neill, M. H. (Distillery), 1972 v USSR (sub), (with Nottingham F), Sp (sub), W (sub); 1973 v P, Cy, E, S, W; 1974 v Bul, P, E (sub), W; 1975 v Se, Y, E, S; 1976 v Y; 1977 v E (sub), S; 1978 v Ic, Ho, S, E, W; 1979 v Ei, D, Bul, E, Bul, D; 1980 v Ei, Is, Aus (3); 1981 v Se, P; (with Norwich C), P, S, Se; (with Manchester C), 1982 v S; (with Norwich C), E, F, S, Y, Hon, Sp, A, F; 1983 v A, WG, Alb, T, Alb, S, E; (with Notts Co), 1984 v A, T, WG, E, W, Fi; 1985 v R, Fi (64)

O'Reilly, H. (Dublin Freebooters), 1901 v S, W; 1904 v S (3)

Parke, J. (Linfield), 1964 v S; (with Hibernian), 1964 v E, Sp; (with Sunderland), 1965 v Sw, S, W, Ho (2), Alb; 1966 v WG; 1967 v E, S; 1968 v S, E (14)

Peacock, R. (Celtic), 1952 v S; 1953 v F; 1954 v W; 1955 v E, S; 1956 v E, S; 1957 v W, I, P; 1958 v S, E, W, I (2), Arg, Cz (2), WG; 1959 v E, S, W; 1960 v S, E; 1961 v E, S, I, WG (2), Gr; (with Coleraine), 1962 v S (31)

Peden, J. (Linfield), 1887 v S, W; 1888 v W, E; 1889 v S, E; 1890 v W, S; 1891 v W, E; 1892 v W, E; 1893 v E, S, W; (with Distillery), 1896 v W, E, S; 1897 v W, S; 1898 v W, E, S; (with Linfield), 1899 v W (24)

Penney, S. (Brighton & HA), 1985 v Is; 1986 v T, R, E, F, D, Mor, Alg, Sp; 1987 v E, T, Is; 1988 v Pol, F, Ma; 1989 v Ei, Sp (17)

Percy, J. C. (Belfast YMCA), 1889 v W (1)

Platt, J. A. (Middlesbrough), 1976 v Is (sub); 1978 v S, E, W; 1980 v S, E, W, Aus (3); 1981 v Se, P; 1982 v F, S, W (sub), A; 1983 v A, WG, Alb, T; (with Ballymena

U), 1984 v E, W (sub); (with Coleraine), 1986 v Mor (sub) (23)

Ponsonby, J. (Distillery), 1895 v S; 1896 v E, S, W; 1897 v E, S, W; 1899 v E (8)

Potts, R. M. C. (Cliftonville), 1883 v E, W (2)

Priestley, T. J. (Coleraine), 1933 v S; (with Chelsea), 1934 v E (2)

Pyper, Jas. (Cliftonville), 1897 v S, W; 1898 v S, E, W; 1899 v S; 1900 v E (7)

Pyper, John (Cliftonville), 1897 v E, S, W; 1899 v E, W; 1900 v E, W, S; 1902 v S (9)

Pyper, M. (Linfield), 1932 v W (1)

Quinn, J. M. (Blackburn R), 1985 v Is, Fi, E, Sp, T; 1986 v T, R, E, F, D (sub), Mor (sub); 1987 v E (sub), T; (with Swindon T), 1988 v Y (sub), T, Gr, Pol, F (sub), Ma; (with Leicester C), 1989 v Ei, H (sub), Sp (sub + 1); (with Bradford C), Ma, Ch; 1990 v H; (with West Ham U), N; 1991 v Y (sub); (with Bournemouth), 1992 v Li (29)

Rafferty, P. (Linfield), 1980 v E (sub) (1)

Ramsey, P. (Leicester C), 1984 v A, WG, S; 1985 v Is, E, Sp, T; 1986 v T, Mor; 1987 v Is, E, Y (sub); 1988 v Y; 1989 v Sp (14)

Rankine, J. (Alexander), 1883 v E, W (2)

Raper, E. O. (Dublin University), 1886 v W (1)

Rattray, D. (Avoniel), 1882 v E; 1883 v E, W (3)

Rea, B. (Glentoran), 1901 v E (1)

Redmond, J. (Cliftonville), 1884 v W (1)

Reid, G. H. (Cardiff C), 1923 v S (1)

Reid, J. (Ulster), 1883 v E; 1884 v W; 1887 v S; 1889 v W; 1890 v S, W (6)

Reid, S. E. (Derby Co), 1934 v E, W; 1936 v E (3)

Reid, W. (Hearts), 1931 v E (1)

Reilly, J. (Portsmouth), 1900 v E; 1902 v E (2)

Renneville, W. T. (Leyton), 1910 v S, E, W; (with Aston Villa), 1911 v W (4)

Reynolds, J. (Distillery), 1890 v E, W; (with Ulster), 1891 v E, S, W (5)

Reynolds, R. (Bohemians), 1905 v W (1)

Rice, P. J. (Arsenal), 1969 v Is; 1970 v USSR; 1971 v E, S, W; 1972 v USSR, Sp, E, S, W; 1973 v Bul, Cy, E, S, W; 1974 v Bul, P, S, E, W; 1975 v N, Y, E, S, W; 1976 v Se, N, Y, Is, S, E, W; 1977 v Ho, Bel, WG, E, S, Ic; 1978 v Ic, Ho, Bel; 1979 v Ei, D, E (2), S, W, D; 1980 v E (49)

Roberts, F. C. (Glentoran), 1931 v S (1)

Robinson, P. (Distillery), 1920 v S; (with Blackburn R), 1921 v W (2)

Rogan, A. (Celtic), 1988 v Y (sub), Gr, Pol (sub); 1989 v Ei (sub), H, Sp (2), Ma (sub), Ch; 1990 v H, N (sub), U; 1991 v Y (2), D, A; (with Sunderland), 1992 v Li (sub) (17)

Rollo, D. (Linfield), 1912 v W; 1913 v W; 1914 v W, E; (with Blackburn R), 1920 v S, W; 1921 v E, S, W; 1922 v E; 1923 v E; 1924 v S, W; 1925 v W; 1926 v E; 1927 v E (16)

Rosbotham, A. (Cliftonville), 1887 v E, S, W; 1888 v E, S, W; 1889 v E (7)

Ross, W. E. (Newcastle U), 1969 v Is (1)

Rowley, R. W. M. (Southampton), 1929 v S, W; 1930 v W, E; (with Tottenham H), 1931 v W; 1932 v S (6)

Russell, A. (Linfield), 1947 v E (1)

Russell, S. R. (Bradford C), 1930 v E, S; (with Derry C), 1932 v E (3)

Ryan, R. A. (WBA), 1950 v W (1)

Sanchez, L. P. (Wimbledon), 1987 v T (sub); 1989 v Sp, Ma (3)

Scott, E. (Liverpool), 1920 v S; 1921 v E, S, W; 1922 v E; 1925 v W; 1926 v E, S, W; 1927 v E, S, W; 1928 v E, S, W; 1929 v E, S, W; 1930 v E; 1931 v E; 1932 v

854

W; 1933 v E, S, W; 1934 v E, S, W; (with Belfast C), 1935 v S; 1936 v E, S, W (31)
Scott, J. (Grimsby), 1958 v Cz, F (2)
Scott, J. E. (Cliftonville), 1901 v S (1)
Scott, L. J. (Dublin University), 1895 v S, W (2)
Scott, P. W. (Everton), 1975 v W; 1976 v Y; (with York C), ls, S, E (sub), W; 1978 v S, E, W; (with Aldershot), 1979 v S (sub) (10)
Scott, T. (Cliftonville), 1894 v E, S; 1895 v S, W; 1896 v S, E, W; 1897 v E, W; 1898 v E, S, W; 1900 v W (13)
Scott, W. (Linfield), 1903 v E, S, W; 1904 v E, S, W; (with Everton), 1905 v E, S; 1907 v E, S; 1908 v E, S, W; 1909 v E, S, W; 1910 v E, S; 1911 v E, S, W; 1912 v E; (with Leeds City), 1913 v E, S, W (25)
Scraggs, M. J. (Glentoran), 1921 v W; 1922 v E (2)
Seymour, H. C. (Bohemians), 1914 v W (1)
Seymour, J. (Cliftonville), 1907 v W; 1909 v W (2)
Shanks, T. (Woolwich Arsenal), 1903 v S; 1904 v W; (with Brentford), 1905 v E (3)
Sharkey, P. (Ipswich T), 1976 v S (1)
Sheehan, Dr G. (Bohemians), 1899 v S; 1900 v E, W (3)
Sheridan, J. (Everton), 1903 v W, E, S; 1904 v E, S; (with Stoke C), 1905 v E (6)
Sherrard, J. (Limavady), 1885 v S; 1887 v W; 1888 v W (3)
Sherrard, W. (Cliftonville), 1895 v E, W, S (3)
Sherry, J. J. (Bohemians), 1906 v E; 1907 v W (2)
Shields, J. (Southampton), 1957 v S (1)
Silo, M. (Belfast YMCA), 1888 v E (1)
Simpson, W. J. (Rangers), 1951 v W, F; 1954 v E, S; 1955 v E; 1957 v I, P; 1958 v S, E, W, I; 1959 v S (12)
Sinclair, J. (Knock), 1882 v E, W (2)
Slemin, J. C. (Bohemians), 1909 v W (1)
Sloan, A. S. (London Caledonians), 1925 v W (1)
Sloan, D. (Oxford U), 1969 v Is; 1971 v Sp (2)
Sloan, H. A. de B. (Bohemians), 1903 v E; 1904 v S; 1905 v E; 1906 v W; 1907 v E, W; 1908 v W; 1909 v S (8)
Sloan, J. W. (Arsenal), 1947 v W (1)
Sloan, T. (Cardiff C), 1926 v S, W, E; 1927 v W, S; 1928 v E, W; 1929 v E; (with Linfield), 1930 v W, S; 1931 v S (11)
Sloan, T. (Manchester U), 1979 v S, W (sub), D (sub) (3)
Small, J. (Clarence), 1887 v E (1)
Small, J. M. (Cliftonville), 1893 v E, S, W (3)
Smith, E. E. (Cardiff C), 1921 v S; 1923 v W, E; 1924 v E (4)
Smith, J. (Distillery), 1901 v S, W (2)
Smyth, R. H. (Dublin University), 1886 v W (1)
Smyth S. (Wolverhampton W), 1948 v E, S, W; 1949 v S, W; 1950 v E, S, W; (with Stoke C), 1952 v E (9)
Smyth, W. (Distillery), 1949 v E, S; 1954 v S, E (4)
Snape, A. (Airdrie), 1920 v E (1)
Spence, D. W. (Bury), 1975 v Y, E, S, W; 1976 v Se, Is, E, W, S (sub); (with Blackpool), 1977 v Ho (sub), WG (sub), E (sub), S (sub), W (sub), Ic (sub); 1979 v Ei, D (sub), E (sub), Bul (sub), E (sub), S, W, D; 1980 v Ei; (with Southend U), Is (sub), Aus (sub); 1981 v S (sub), Se (sub); 1982 v F (sub) (29)
Spencer, S. (Distillery), 1890 v E, S; 1892 v E, S, W; 1893 v E (6)
Spiller, E. A. (Cliftonville), 1883 v E, W; 1884 v E, W, S (5)
Stanfield, O. M. (Distillery), 1887 v E, S, W; 1888 v E, S, W; 1889 v E, S, W; 1890 v E, S; 1891 v E, S, W; 1892 v E, S, W; 1893 v E, W; 1894 v E, S, W; 1895 v E, S; 1896 v E, S, W; 1897 v E, S, W (30)
Steele, A. (Charlton Ath), 1926 v W, S; (with Fulham), 1929 v W, S (4)
Stevenson, A. E. (Rangers), 1934 v E, S, W; (with Everton), 1935 v E, S; 1936 v S, W; 1937 v E, W; 1938 v E, W; 1939 v E, S, W; 1947 v S, W; 1948 v S (17)
Stewart, A. (Glentoran), 1967 v W; 1968 v S, E; (with Derby Co), 1968 v W; 1969 v Is, T (1 + 1 sub) (7)

Stewart, D. C. (Hull C), 1978 v Bel (1)
Stewart, I. (QPR), 1982 v F (sub); 1983 v A, WG, Alb, T, Alb, S, E, W; 1984 v A, T, WG, S, E, W, Fi; 1985 v R, Fi, Is, E, Sp, T; (with Newcastle U), 1986 v R, E, D, Mor, Alg (sub), Sp (sub); Br; 1987 v E, Is (sub) (31)
Stewart, R. H. (St Columb's Court), 1890 v E, S, W; (with Cliftonville), 1892 v E, S, W; 1893 v E, W; 1894 v E, S, W (11)
Stewart, T. C. (Linfield), 1961 v W (1)
Swan, S. (Linfield), 1899 v S (1)

Taggart, G. P. (Barnsley), 1990 v N, U; 1991 v Y, D, A, Pol, Fa; 1992 v Fa, A, D, S, Li, G (13)
Taggart, J. (Walsall), 1899 v W (1)
Thompson, F. W. (Cliftonville), 1910 v E, S, W; (with Bradford C), 1911 v E; (with Linfield), v W; 1912 v E, W; 1913 v E, S, W; (with Clyde), 1914 v E, S (12)
Thompson, J. (Belfast Ath), 1889 v S (1)
Thompson, J. (Distillery), 1897 v S (1)
Thunder, P. J. (Bohemians), 1911 v W (1)
Todd, S. J. (Burnley), 1966 v M (sub); 1967 v E; 1968 v W; 1969 v E, S, W; 1970 v S, USSR; (with Sheffield W), 1971 v Cy (2), Sp (sub) (11)
Toner, J. (Arsenal), 1922 v W; 1923 v W; 1924 v W, E; 1925 v E, S; (with St Johnstone), 1927 v E, S (8)
Torrans, R. (Linfield), 1893 v S (1)
Torrans, S. (Linfield), 1889 v S; 1890 v S, W; 1891 v S, W; 1892 v E, S, W; 1893 v E, S; 1894 v E, S, W; 1895 v E; 1896 v E, S, W; 1897 v E, S, W; 1898 v E, S; 1899 v E, W; 1901 v S, W (26)
Trainor, D. (Crusaders), 1967 v W (1)
Tully, C. P. (Celtic), 1949 v E; 1950 v E; 1952 v S; 1953 v E, S, W, F; 1954 v S; 1956 v E; 1959 v Sp (10)
Turner, E. (Cliftonville), 1896 v E, W (2)
Turner, W. (Cliftonville), 1886 v E; 1886 v S; 1888 v S (3)
Twoomey, J. F. (Leeds U), 1938 v W; 1939 v E (2)

Uprichard, W. N. M. C. (Swindon T), 1952 v E, S, W; 1953 v E, S; (with Portsmouth), 1953 v W, F; 1955 v E, S, W; 1956 v E, S, W; 1958 v S, I, Cz; 1959 v S, Sp (18)

Vernon, J. (Belfast C), 1947 v E, S; (with WBA), 1947 v W; 1948 v E, S, W; 1949 v E, S, W; 1950 v E, S; 1951 v E, S, W, F; 1952 v S, E (17)

Waddell, T. M. R. (Cliftonville), 1906 v S (1)
Walker, J. (Doncaster R), 1955 v W (1)
Walker, T. (Bury), 1911 v S (1)
Walsh, D. J. (WBA), 1947 v S, W; 1948 v E, S, W; 1949 v E, S, W; 1950 v W (9)
Walsh, W. (Manchester C), 1948 v E, S, W; 1949 v E, S (5)
Waring, R. (Distillery), 1899 v E (1)
Warren, P. (Shelbourne), 1913 v E, S (2)
Watson, J. (Ulster), 1883 v E, W; 1886 v E, S, W; 1887 v S, W; 1889 v E, W (9)
Watson, P. (Distillery), 1971 v Cy (sub) (1)
Watson, T. (Cardiff C), 1926 v S (1)
Wattle, J. (Distillery), 1899 v E (1)
Webb, C. G. (Brighton), 1909 v S, W; 1911 v S (3)
Weir, E. (Clyde), 1939 v W (1)
Welsh, E. (Carlisle U), 1966 v W, WG, M; 1967 v W (4)
Whiteside, N. (Manchester U), 1982 v Y, Hon, Sp, A, F; 1983 v WG, Alb, T; 1984 v A, T, WG, S, E, W, Fi; 1985 v R, Fi, Is, E, Sp, T; 1986 v R, E, F, D, Mor, Alg, Sp, Br; 1987 v E (2), Is, Y; 1988 v T, Pol, F; (with Everton), 1990 v H, Ei (38)
Whiteside, T. (Distillery), 1891 v E (1)
Whitfield, E. R. (Dublin University), 1886 v W (1)
Williams, J. R. (Ulster), 1886 v E, S (2)
Williams, P. A. (WBA), 1991 v Fa (sub) (1)
Williamson, J. (Cliftonville), 1890 v E; 1892 v S; 1893 v S (3)
Willigham, T. (Burnley), 1933 v W; 1934 v S (2)

855

Willis, G. (Linfield), 1906 v S, W; 1907 v S; 1912 v S (4)
Wilson, D. J. (Brighton & HA), 1987 v T, Is, E (sub); (with Luton T), 1988 v Y, T, Gr, Pol, F, Ma; 1989 v Ei, H, Sp, Ma, Ch; 1990 v H, Ei, N, U; (with Sheffield W), 1991 v Y, D, A, Fa; 1992 v A (sub), S (24)
Wilson, H. (Linfield), 1925 v W (1)
Wilson, K. J. (Ipswich T), 1987 v Is, E, Y; (with Chelsea), 1988 v Y, T, Gr (sub), Pol (sub), F (sub); 1989 v H (sub), Sp (2), Ma, Ch; 1990 v Ei (sub), N, U; 1991 v Y (2), A, Pol, Fa; 1992 v Fa, A, D, S (with Notts Co), Li, G (27)
Wilson, M. (Distillery), 1884 v E, S, W (3)
Wilson, R. (Cliftonville), 1888 v S (1)
Wilson, S. J. (Glenavon), 1962 v S; 1964 v S; (with Falkirk), 1964 v E, W, U, Sp; 1965 v E, Sw; (with Dundee), 1966 v W, WG; 1967 v S; 1968 v E (12)

Wilton, J. M. (St Columb's Court), 1888 v E, W; 1889 v S, E; (with Cliftonville), 1890 v E; (with St Columb's Court), 1892 v W; 1893 v S (7)
Worthington, N. (Sheffield W), 1984 v W, Fi (sub); 1985 v Is, Sp (sub); 1986 v T, R (sub), E (sub), D, Alg, Sp; 1987 v E (2), T, Is, Y; 1988 v Y, T, Gr, Pol, F, Ma; 1989 v Ei, H, Sp, Ma; 1990 v H, Ei, U; 1991 v Y, D, A, Fa; 1992 v A, D, S, Li, G (37)
Wright, J. (Cliftonville), 1906 v E, S, W; 1907 v E, S, W (6)
Wright, T. J. (Newcastle U), 1989 v Ma, Ch; 1990 v H, U; 1992 v Fa, A, S, G (8)

Young, S. (Linfield), 1907 v E, S; 1908 v E, S; (with Airdrie), 1909 v E; 1912 v S; (with Linfield), 1914 v E, S, W (9)

SCOTLAND

Adams, J. (Hearts), 1889 v Ni; 1892 v W; 1893 v Ni (3)
Agnew, W. B. (Kilmarnock), 1907 v Ni; 1908 v W, Ni (3)
Aird, J. (Burnley), 1954 v N (2), A, U (4)
Aitken, A. (Newcastle U), 1901 v E; 1902 v E; 1903 v E, W; 1904 v E; 1905 v E, W; 1906 v E; (with Middlesbrough), 1907 v E, W; 1908 v E; (with Leicester Fosse), 1910 v E; 1911 v E, Ni (14)
Aitken, G. G. (East Fife), 1949 v E, F; 1950 v W, Ni, Sw; (with Sunderland), 1953 v W, Ni; 1954 v E (8)
Aitken, R. (Dumbarton), 1886 v E; 1888 v Ni (2)
Aitken, R. (Celtic), 1980 v Pe (sub), Bel, W (sub), E, Pol; 1983 v Bel, Ca (1 + 1 sub); 1984 v Bel (sub), Ni, W (sub); 1985 v E, Ic; 1986 v W, EG, Aus (2), Is, R, E, D, WG, U; 1987 v Bul, Ei (2), L, Bel, E, Br; 1988 v H, Bel, Bul, L, S.Ar, Ma, Sp, Co, E; 1989 v N, Y, I, Cy, F, Cy, E, Ch; 1990 v F, Sp (sub), N, Arg (sub), Pol, Ma, Cr, Se, Br; (with St Mirren), 1992 v R (sub) (57)
Aitkenhead, W. A. C. (Blackburn R), 1912 v Ni (1)
Albiston, A. (Manchester U), 1982 v Ni; 1984 v U, Bel, EG, W, E; 1985 v Y, Ic, Sp (2), W; 1986 v EG, Ho, U (14)
Alexander, D. (East Stirlingshire), 1894 v W, Ni (2)
Allan, D. S. (Queen's Park), 1885 v E, W; 1886 v W (3)
Allan, G. (Liverpool), 1897 v E (1)
Allan, H. (Hearts), 1902 v W (1)
Allan, J. (Queen's Park), 1887 v E, W (2)
Allan, T. (Dundee), 1974 v WG, N (2)
Ancell, R. F. D. (Newcastle U), 1937 v W, Ni (2)
Anderson, A. (Hearts), 1933 v E; 1934 v A, E, W, Ni; 1935 v E, W, Ni; 1936 v E, W, Ni; 1937 v G, E, W, Ni, A; 1938 v E, W, Ni, Cz, Ho; 1939 v W, H (23)
Anderson, F. (Clydesdale), 1874 v E (1)
Anderson, G. (Kilmarnock), 1901 v Ni (1)
Anderson, H. A. (Raith R), 1914 v W (1)
Anderson, J. (Leicester C), 1954 v Fi (1)
Anderson, K. (Queen's Park), 1896 v Ni; 1898 v E, Ni (3)
Anderson, W. (Queen's Park), 1882 v E; 1883 v E, W; 1884 v E; 1885 v E, W (6)
Andrews, P. (Eastern), 1875 v E (1)
Archibald, A. (Rangers), 1921 v W; 1922 v W, E; 1923 v Ni; 1924 v E W; 1931 v E; 1932 v E (8)
Archibald, S. (Aberdeen), 1980 v P (su); with Tottenham H), Ni, Pol, H; 1981 v Se (sub), Is, Ni, Is, Ni, E; 1982 v Ni, P, Sp (sub), Ho, Nz (sub), Br, USSR; 1983 v EG, Sw (sub), Bel; 1984 v EG, E, F; (with Barcelona), 1985 v Sp, E, Ic (sub); 1986 v WG (27)
Armstrong, M. W. (Aberdeen), 1936 v W, Ni; 1937 v G (3)
Arnott, W. (Queen's Park), 1883 v W; 1884 v E, Ni; 1885 v E, W; 1886 v E; 1887 v E; 1888 v E; 1889 v E; 1890 v E; 1891 v E; 1892 v E; 1893 v E (14)

Auld, J. R. (Third Lanark), 1887 v E, W; 1889 v W (3)
Auld, R. (Celtic), 1959 v H, P; 1960 v W (3)

Baird, A. (Queen's Park), 1892 v Ni; 1894 v W (2)
Baird, D. (Hearts), 1890 v Ni; 1891 v E; 1892 v W (3)
Baird, H. (Airdrieonians), 1956 v A (1)
Baird, J. C. (Vale of Leven), 1876 v E; 1878 v W; 1880 v E (3)
Baird, S. (Rangers), 1957 v Y, Sp (2), Sw, WG; 1958 v F, Ni (7)
Baird, W. U. (St Bernard), 1897 v Ni (1)
Bannon, E. (Dundee U), 1980 v Bel; 1983 v Ni, W, E, Ca; 1984 v EG; 1986 v Is, R, E, D (sub), WG (11)
Barbour, A. (Renton), 1885 v Ni (1)
Barker, J. B. (Rangers), 1893 v W; 1894 v W (2)
Barrett, F. (Dundee), 1894 v Ni; 1895 v W (2)
Battles, B. (Celtic), 1901 v E, W, Ni (3)
Battles, B. jun. (Hearts), 1931 v W (1)
Bauld, W. (Hearts), 1950 v E, Sw, P (3)
Baxter, J. C. (Rangers), 1961 v Ni, Ei (2), Cz; 1962 v Ni, W, E, Cz (2), U; 1963 v W, Ni, E, A, N, Ei, Sp; 1964 v W, E, N, WG; 1965 v W, Ni, Fi; (with Sunderland), 1966 v P, Br, Ni, W, E, I; 1967 v W, E, USSR; 1968 v W (34)
Baxter, R. D. (Middlesbrough), 1939 v E, W, H (3)
Beattie, A. (Preston NE), 1937 v E, A, Cz; 1938 v E; 1939 v W, Ni, H (7)
Beattie, R. (Preston NE), 1939 v W (1)
Begbie, I. (Hearts), 1890 v Ni; 1891 v E; 1892 v W; 1894 v E (4)
Bell, A. (Manchester U), 1912 v Ni (1)
Bell, J. (Dumbarton), 1890 v Ni; 1892 v E; (with Everton), 1896 v E; 1897 v E; 1898 v E; (with Celtic), 1899 v E, W, Ni; 1900 v E, W (10)
Bell, M. (Hearts), 1901 v W (1)
Bell, W. J. (Leeds U), 1966 v P, Br (2)
Bennett, A. (Celtic), 1904 v W; 1907 v Ni; 1908 v W; (with Rangers), 1909 v W, Ni, E; 1910 v E, W; 1911 v E, W; 1913 v Ni (11)
Bennie, R. (Airdrieonians), 1925 v W, Ni; 1926 v Ni (3)
Berry, D. (Queen's Park), 1894 v W; 1899 v W, Ni (3)
Berry, W. H. (Queen's Park), 1888 v E; 1889 v E; 1890 v E; 1891 v E (4)
Bett, J. (Rangers), 1982 v Ho; 1983 v Bel; (with Lokeren), 1984 v Bel, W, E, F; 1985 v Y, Ic, Sp (2), W, E, Ic; (with Aberdeen), 1986 v W, Is, Ho; 1987 v Bel; 1988 v H (sub); 1989 v Y; 1990 v F (sub), N, Arg, Eg, Ma, Cr (25)
Beveridge, W. W. (Glasgow University), 1879 v E, W; 1880 v W (3)
Black, A. (Hearts), 1938 v Cz, Ho; 1939 v H (3)
Black, D. (Hurlford), 1889 v Ni (1)
Black, E. (Metz), 1988 v H (sub), L (sub) (2)

Black, I. H. (Southampton), 1948 v E (1)

Blackburn, J. E. (Royal Engineers), 1873 v E (1)

Blacklaw, A. S. (Burnley), 1963 v N, Sp; 1966 v I (3)

Blackley, J. (Hibernian), 1974 v Cz, E, Bel, Z; 1976 v Sw; 1977 v W, Se (7)

Blair, D. (Clyde), 1929 v W, Ni; 1931 v E, A, I; 1932 v W, Ni; (with Aston Villa), 1933 v W (8)

Blair, J. (Sheffield W), 1920 v E, Ni; (with Cardiff C), 1921 v E; 1922 v E; 1923 v E, W, Ni; 1924 v W (8)

Blair, J. (Motherwell), 1934 v W (1)

Blair, J. A. (Blackpool), 1947 v W (1)

Blair, W. (Third Lanark), 1896 v W (1)

Blessington, J. (Celtic), 1894 v E, Ni; 1896 v E, Ni (4)

Blyth, J. A. (Coventry C), 1978 v Bul, W (2)

Bone, J. (Norwich C), 1972 v Y (sub); 1973 v D (2)

Bowie, J. (Rangers), 1920 v E, Ni (2)

Bowie, W. (Linthouse), 1891 v Ni (1)

Bowman, D. (Dundee U), 1992 V Fi, US (sub) (2)

Bowman, G. A. (Montrose), 1892 v Ni (1)

Boyd, J. M. (Newcastle U), 1934 v Ni (1)

Boyd, R. (Mossend Swifts), 1889 v Ni; 1891 v W (2)

Boyd, T. (Motherwell), 1991 v R (sub), Sw, Bul, USSR; (with Chelsea), 1992 v Sw, R; (with Celtic), Fi, Ca, N, C (10)

Boyd, W. G. (Clyde), 1931 v I, Sw (2)

Brackenbridge, T. (Hearts), 1888 v Ni (1)

Bradshaw, T. (Bury), 1928 v E (1)

Brand, R. (Rangers), 1961 v Ni, Cz, Ei (2); 1962 v Ni, W, Cz, U (8)

Branden, T. (Blackburn R), 1896 v E (1)

Brazil, A. (Ipswich T), 1980 v Pol (sub), H; 1982 v Sp, Ho (sub), Ni, W, E, Nz, USSR (sub); 1983 v EG, Sw, W, E (sub) (13)

Bremner, D. (Hibernian), 1976 v Sw (sub) (1)

Bremner, W. J. (Leeds U), 1965 v Sp; 1966 v E, Pol, P, Br, I (2); 1967 v W, Ni, E; 1968 v W, E; 1969 v W, E, Ni, D, A, WG, Cy (2); 1970 v Ei, WG, A; 1971 v W, E; 1972 v P, Bel, Ho, Ni, W, E, Y, Cz, Br; 1973 v D (2), E (2), Ni (sub), Sw, Br; 1974 v Cz, WG, Ni, W, E, Bel, N, Z, Br, Y; 1975 v Sp (2); 1976 v D (54)

Brennan, F. (Newcastle U), 1947 v W, Ni; 1953 v W, Ni, E; 1954 v Ni, E (7)

Breslin, B. (Hibernian), 1897 v W (1)

Brewster, G. (Everton), 1921 v E (1)

Brogan, J. (Celtic), 1971 v W, Ni, P, E (4)

Brown, A. (Middlesbrough), 1904 v E (1)

Brown, A. (St Mirren), 1890 v W; 1891 v W (2)

Brown, A. D. (East Fife), 1950 v Sw, P, F; (with Blackpool), 1952 v USA, D, Se; 1953 v W; 1954 v W, E, N (2), Fi, A, U (14)

Brown, G. C. P. (Rangers), 1931 v W; 1932 v E, W, Ni; 1933 v E; 1935 v A, E, W; 1936 v E, W; 1937 v G, E, W, Ni, Cz; 1938 v E, W, Cz, Ho (19)

Brown, H. (Partick T), 1947 v W, Bel, L (3)

Brown, J. (Cambuslang), 1890 v W (1)

Brown, J. B. (Clyde), 1939 v W (1)

Brown, J. G. (Sheffield U), 1975 v R (1)

Brown, R. (Dumbarton), 1884 v W, Ni (2)

Brown, R. (Rangers), 1947 v Ni; 1949 v Ni; 1952 v E (3)

Brown, R. jun. (Dumbarton), 1885 v W (1)

Brown, W. D. F. (Dundee), 1958 v F; 1959 v E, W, Ni; (with Tottenham H), 1960 v W, Ni, Pol, A, H, T; 1962 v Ni, W, E, Cz; 1963 v W, Ni, E, A; 1964 v Ni, W, N; 1965 v E, Fi, Pol, Sp; 1966 v Ni, Pol, I (28)

Browning, J. (Celtic), 1914 v W (1)

Brownlie, J. (Hibernian), 1971 v USSR; 1972 v Pe, Ni, E; 1973 v D (2); 1976 v R (7)

Brownlie, J. (Third Lanark), 1909 v E, Ni; 1910 v E, W, Ni; 1911 v W, Ni; 1912 v W, Ni, E; 1913 v W, Ni, E; 1914 v W, Ni, E (16)

Bruce, D. (Vale of Leven), 1890 v W (1)

Bruce, R. F. (Middlesbrough), 1934 v A (1)

Buchan, M. M. (Aberdeen), 1972 v P (sub), Bel; (with

Manchester U), W, Y, Cz, Br; 1973 v D (2), E; 1974 v WG, Ni, W, N, Br, Y; 1975 v EG, Sp, P; 1976 v D, R; 1977 v Fi, Cz, Ch, Arg, Br; 1978 v EG, W (sub), Ni, Pe, Ir, Ho; 1979 v A, N, P (34)

Buchanan, J. (Cambuslang), 1889 v Ni (1)

Buchanan, J. (Rangers), 1929 v E; 1930 v E (2)

Buchanan, P. S. (Chelsea), 1938 v Cz (1)

Buchanan, R. (Abercorn), 1891 v W (1)

Buckley, P. (Aberdeen), 1954 v N; 1955 v W, Ni (3)

Buick, A. (Hearts), 1902 v W, Ni (2)

Burley, G. (Ipswich T), 1979 v W, Ni, E, Arg, N; 1980 v P, Ni, E (sub); Pol; 1982 v W (sub), E (11)

Burns, F. (Manchester U), 1970 v A (1)

Burns, K. (Birmingham C), 1974 v WG; 1975 v EG (sub), Sp (2); 1977 v Cz (sub), W, Se, W (sub); (with Nottingham F), 1978 v Ni (sub), W, E, Pe, Ir; 1979 v N; 1980 v Pe, A, Bel; 1981 v Is, Ni, W (20)

Burns, T. (Celtic), 1981 v Ni; 1982 v Ho (sub), W; 1983 v Bel (sub), Ni, Ca (1 + 1 sub); 1988 v E (sub) (8)

Busby, M. W. (Manchester C), 1934 v W (1)

Cairns, T. (Rangers), 1920 v W; 1922 v E; 1923 v E, W; 1924 v Ni; 1925 v W, E, Ni (8)

Calderhead, D. (Queen of the South), 1889 v Ni (1)

Calderwood, R. (Cartvale), 1885 v Ni, E, W (3)

Caldow, E. (Rangers), 1957 v Sp (2), Sw, WG, E; 1958 v Ni, W, Sw, Par, H, Pol, Y, F; 1959 v E, W, Ni, WG, Ho, P; 1960 v E, W, Ni, A, H, T; 1961 v E, W, Ni, Ei (2), Cz; 1962 v Ni, W, E, Cz (2), U; 1963 v W, Ni, E (40)

Callaghan, P. (Hibernian), 1900 v Ni (1)

Callaghan, W. (Dunfermline Ath), 1970 v Ei (sub), W (2)

Cameron, J. (Rangers), 1886 v Ni (1)

Cameron, J. (Queen's Park), 1896 v Ni (1)

Cameron, J. (St Mirren), 1904 v Ni; (with Chelsea), 1909 v E (2)

Campbell, C. (Queen's Park), 1874 v E; 1876 v W; 1877 v E, W; 1878 v E; 1879 v E; 1880 v E; 1881 v E; 1882 v E, W; 1884 v E; 1885 v E; 1886 v E (13)

Campbell, H. (Renton), 1889 v W (1)

Cambell, Jas (Sheffield W), 1913 v W (1)

Campbell, J. (South Western), 1880 v W (1)

Campbell, J. (Kilmarnock), 1891 v Ni; 1892 v W (2)

Campbell, John (Celtic), 1893 v E, Ni; 1898 v E, Ni; 1900 v E, Ni; 1901 v E, W, Ni; 1902 v W, Ni; 1903 v W (12)

Campbell, John (Rangers), 1899 v E, W, Ni; 1901 v Ni (4)

Campbell, K. (Liverpool), 1920 v E, W, Ni; (with Partick T), 1921 v W, Ni; 1922 v W, Ni, E (8)

Campbell, P. (Rangers), 1878 v W; 1879 v W (2)

Campbell, P. (Morton), 1898 v W (1)

Campbell, R. (Falkirk), 1947 v Bel, L; (with Chelsea), 1950 v Sw, P, F (5)

Campbell, W. (Morton), 1947 v Ni; 1948 v E, Bel, Sw, F (5)

Carabine, J. (Third Lanark), 1938 v Ho; 1939 v E, Ni (3)

Carr, W. M. (Coventry C), 1970 v Ni, W, E; 1971 v D; 1972 v Pe; 1973 v D (sub) (6)

Cassidy, J. (Celtic), 1921 v W, Ni; 1923 v Ni; 1924 v W (4)

Chalmers, S. (Celtic), 1965 v W, Fi; 1966 v P (sub), Br; 1967 v N (5)

Chalmers, W. (Rangers), 1885 v Ni (1)

Chalmers, W. S. (Queen's Park), 1929 v Ni (1)

Chambers, T. (Hearts), 1894 v W (1)

Chaplin, G. D. (Dundee), 1908 v W (1)

Cheyne, A. G. (Aberdeen), 1929 v E, N, G, Ho; 1930 v F (5)

Christie, A. J. (Queen's Park), 1898 v W; 1899 v E, Ni (3)

Christie, R. M. (Queen's Park), 1884 v E (1)

Clark, J. (Celtic), 1966 v Br; 1967 v W, Ni, USSR (4)

Clark, R. B. (Aberdeen), 1968 v W, Ho; 1970 v Ni; 1971

v W, Ni, E, D, P, USSR; 1972 v Bel, Ni, W, E, Cz, Br; 1973 v D, E (17)

Clarke, S. (Chelsea), 1988 v H, Bel, Bul, S.Ar, Ma (5)

Cleland, J. (Royal Albert), 1891 v Ni (1)

Clements, R. (Leith Ath), 1891 v Ni (1)

Clunas, W. L. (Sunderland), 1924 v E; 1926 v W (2)

Collier, W. (Raith R), 1922 v W (1)

Collins, J. (Hibernian), 1988 v S.Ar; 1990 v EG, Pol (sub), Ma (sub); (with Celtic), 1991 v Sw (sub), Bul (sub); 1992 v Ni (sub), Fi (8)

Collins, R. Y. (Celtic), 1951 v W, Ni, A; 1955 v Y, A, H; 1956 v Ni, W; 1957 v E, W, Sp (2), Sw, WG; 1958 v Ni, W, Sw, H, Pol, Y, F, Par; (with Everton), 1959 v E, W, Ni, WG, Ho, P; (with Leeds U), 1965 v E, Pol, Sp (31)

Collins, T. (Hearts), 1909 v W (1)

Colman, D. (Aberdeen), 1911 v E, W, Ni; 1913 v Ni (4)

Colquhoun, E. P. (Sheffield U), 1972 v P, Ho, Pe, Y, Cz, Br; 1973 v D (2), E (9)

Colquhoun, J. (Hearts), 1988 v S.Ar (sub) (1)

Combe, J. R. (Hibernian), 1948 v E, Bel, Sw (3)

Conn, A. (Hearts), 1956 v A (1)

Conn, A. (Tottenham H), 1975 v Ni (sub), E (2)

Connachan, E. D. (Dunfermline Ath), 1962 v Cz, U (2)

Connelly, G. (Celtic), 1974 v Cz, WG (2)

Connolly, J. (Everton), 1973 v Sw (1)

Connor, J. (Airdrieonians), 1886 v Ni (1)

Connor, J. (Sunderland), 1930 v F; 1932 v Ni; 1934 v E; 1935 v Ni (4)

Connor, R. (Dundee), 1986 v Ho; (with Aberdeen), 1988 v S.Ar (sub); 1989 v E; 1991 v R (4)

Cook, W. L. (Bolton W), 1934 v E; 1935 v W, Ni (3)

Cooke, C. (Dundee), 1966 v W, I; (with Chelsea), P, Br; 1968 v E, Ho; 1969 v W, Ni, A, WG (sub), Cy (2); 1970 v A; 1971 v Bel; 1975 v Sp, P (16)

Cooper, D. (Rangers), 1980 v Pe, A (sub); 1984 v W, E; 1985 v Y, Ic, Sp (2), W; 1986 v W (sub), EG, Aus (2), Ho, WG (sub), U (sub); 1987 v Bul, L, Ei, Br; (with Motherwell), 1990 v N, Eg (22)

Cormack, P. B. (Hibernian), 1966 v Br; 1969 v D (sub); 1970 v Ei, WG; (with Nottingham F), 1971 v D (sub), W, P, E; 1972 v Ho (sub) (9)

Cowan, J. (Aston Villa), 1896 v E; 1897 v E; 1898 v E (3)

Cowan, J. (Morton), 1948 v Bel, Sw; F; 1949 v E, W, F; 1950 v E, W, Ni, Sw, P, F; 1951 v E, W, Ni, A (2), D, F, Bel; 1952 v Ni, W, USA, D, Se (25)

Cowan, W. D. (Newcastle U), 1924 v E (1)

Cowie, D. (Dundee), 1953 v E, Se; 1954 v Ni, W, Fi, N, A, U; 1955 v W, Ni, A, H; 1956 v W, A; 1957 v Ni, W; 1958 v H, Pol, Y, Par (20)

Cox, C. J. (Hearts), 1948 v F (1)

Cox, S. (Rangers), 1948 v F; 1949 v E, F; 1950 v E, F, W, Ni, Sw, P; 1951 v E, D, F, Bel, A; 1952 v Ni, W, USA, D, Se; 1953 v W, Ni, E; 1954 v W, Ni, E (25)

Craig, A. (Motherwell), 1929 v N, Ho; 1932 v E (3)

Craig, J. (Celtic), 1977 v Se (sub) (1)

Craig, J. P. (Celtic), 1968 v W (1)

Craig, T. (Rangers), 1927 v Ni; 1928 v Ni; 1929 v N, G, Ho; 1930 v N, E, W (8)

Craig, T. B. (Newcastle U), 1976 v Sw (1)

Crapnell, J. (Airdrieonians), 1929 v E, N, G; 1930 v F; 1931 v Ni, Sw; 1932 v E, F; 1933 v Ni (9)

Crawford, D. (St Mirren), 1894 v W, Ni; 1900 v W (3)

Crawford, J. (Queen's Park), 1932 v F, Ni; 1933 v E, W, Ni (5)

Crerand, P. T. (Celtic), 1961 v Ei (2), Cz; 1962 v Ni, W, E, Cz (2), U; 1963 v W, Ni; (with Manchester U), 1964 v Ni; 1965 v E, Pol, Fi; 1966 v Pol (16)

Cringan, W. (Celtic), 1920 v W; 1922 v E, Ni; 1923 v W, E (5)

Crosbie, J. A. (Ayr U), 1920 v W; (with Birmingham), 1922 v E (2)

Croal, J. A. (Falkirk), 1913 v Ni; 1914 v E, W (3)

Cropley, A. J. (Hibernian), 1972 v P, Bel (2)

Cross, J. H. (Third Lanark), 1903 v Ni (1)

Cruickshank, J. (Hearts), 1964 v WG; 1970 v W, E; 1971 v D, Bel; 1976 v R (6)

Crum, J. (Celtic), 1936 v E; 1939 v Ni (2)

Cullen, M. J. (Luton T), 1956 v A (1)

Cumming, D. S. (Middlesbrough), 1938 v E (1)

Cumming, J. (Hearts), 1955 v E, H, P, Y; 1960 v E, Pol, A, H, T (9)

Cummings, G. (Partick T), 1935 v E; 1936 v W, Ni; (with Aston Villa), E; 1937 v G; 1938 v W, Ni, Cz; 1939 v E (9)

Cunningham, A. N. (Rangers), 1920 v Ni; 1921 v W, E; 1922 v Ni; 1923 v E, W; 1924 v E, Ni; 1926 v E, Ni; 1927 v E, W (12)

Cunningham, W. C. (Preston NE), 1954 v N (2), U, Fi, A; 1955 v W, E, H (8)

Curran, H. P. (Wolverhampton W), 1970 v A; 1971 v Ni, E, D, USSR (sub) (5)

Dalglish, K. (Celtic), 1972 v Bel (sub), Ho; 1973 v D (1 + 1 sub), E (2), W, Ni, Sw, Br; 1974 v Cz (2), WG (2), Ni, W, E, Bel, N (sub), Z, Br, Y; 1975 v EG, Sp (sub + 1), Se, P, W, Ni, E, R; 1976 v D (2), R, Sw, Ni, E; 1977 v Fi, Cz, W (2), Se, Ni, E, Ch, Arg, Br; (with Liverpool), 1978 v EG, Cz, W, Bul, Ni (sub), W, E, Pe, Ir, Ho; 1979 v A, N, P, W, Ni, E, Arg, N; 1980 v Pe, A, Bel (2), P, Ni, W, E, Pol, H; 1981 v Se, P, Is; 1982 v Se, Ni, P (sub), Sp, Ho, Ni, W, E, Nz, Br (sub); 1983 v Bel, Sw; 1984 v U, Bel, EG; 1985 v Y, Ic, Sp, W; 1986 v EG, Aus, R; 1987 v Bul (sub), L (102)

Davidson, D. (Queen's Park), 1878 v W; 1879 v W; 1880 v W; 1881 v E, W (5)

Davidson, J. A. (Partick T), 1954 v N (2), A, U; 1955 v W, Ni, E, H (8)

Davidson, S. (Middlesbrough), 1921 v E (1)

Dawson, A. (Rangers), 1980 v Pol (sub), H; 1983 v Ni, Ca (2) (5)

Dawson, J. (Rangers), 1935 v Ni; 1936 v E; 1937 v G, E, W, Ni, A, Cz; 1938 v W, Ho, Ni; 1939 v E, Ni, H (14)

Deans, J. (Celtic), 1975 v EG, Sp (2)

Delaney, J. (Celtic), 1936 v W, Ni; 1937 v G, E, A, Cz; 1938 v Ni; 1939 v W, Ni; (with Manchester U), 1947 v E; 1948 v E, W, Ni (13)

Devine, A. (Falkirk), 1910 v W (1)

Dewar, G. (Dumbarton), 1888 v Ni; 1889 v E (2)

Dewar, N. (Third Lanark), 1932 v E, F; 1933 v W (3)

Dick, J. (West Ham U), 1959 v E (1)

Dickie, M. (Rangers), 1897 v Ni; 1899 v Ni; 1900 v W (3)

Dickson, W. (Dumbarton), 1888 v Ni (1)

Dickson, W. (Kilmarnock), 1970 v Ni, W, E; 1971 v D, USSR (5)

Divers, J. (Celtic), 1895 v W (1)

Divers, J. (Celtic), 1939 v Ni (1)

Docherty, T. H. (Preston NE), 1952 v W; 1953 v E, Se; 1954 v N (2), A, U; 1955 v W, E, H (2), A; 1957 v E, Y, Sp (2), Sw, WG; 1958 v Ni, W, E, Sw; (with Arsenal), 1959 v W, E, Ni (25)

Dodds, D. (Dundee U), 1984 v U (sub), Ni (2)

Dodds, J. (Celtic), 1914 v E, W, Ni (3)

Doig, J. E. (Arbroath), 1887 v Ni; 1889 v Ni; (with Sunderland), 1896 v E; 1899 v E; 1903 v E (5)

Donachie, W. (Manchester C), 1972 v Pe, Ni, E, Y, Cz, Br; 1973 v D, E, W, Ni; 1974 v Ni; 1976 v R, Ni, W, E; 1977 v Fi, Cz, W (2), Se, Ni, E, Ch, Arg, Br; 1978 v EG, Bul, W, E, Ir, Ho; 1979 v A, N, P (sub) (35)

Donaldson, A. (Bolton W), 1914 v E, Ni, W; 1920 v E, Ni; 1922 v Ni (6)

Donnachie, J. (Oldham Ath), 1913 v E; 1914 v E, Ni (3)

Dougall, C. (Birmingham C), 1947 v W (1)

Dougall, J. (Preston NE), 1939 v E (1)

Dougan, R. (Hearts), 1950 v Sw (1)

Douglas, A. (Chelsea), 1911 v Ni (1)

Douglas, J. (Renfrew), 1880 v W (1)

Dowds, P. (Celtic), 1892 v Ni (1)

Downie, R. (Third Lanark), 1892 v W (1)

Doyle, D. (Celtic), 1892 v E; 1893 v W; 1894 v E; 1895 v E, Ni; 1897 v E; 1898 v E, Ni (8)

Doyle, J. (Ayr U), 1976 v R (1)

Drummond, J. (Falkirk), 1892 v Ni; (with Rangers), 1894 v Ni; 1895 v Ni, E; 1896 v E, Ni; 1897 v Ni; 1898 v E; 1900 v E; 1901 v E; 1902 v E, W, Ni; 1903 v Ni (14)

Dunbar, M. (Cartvale), 1886 v Ni (1)

Duncan, A. (Hibernian), 1975 v P (sub), W, Ni, E, R; 1976 v D (6)

Duncan, D. (Derby Co), 1933 v E, W; 1934 v A, W; 1935 v E, W; 1936 v E, W, Ni; 1937 v G, E, W, Ni; 1938 v W (14)

Duncan, D. M. (East Fife), 1948 v Bel, Sw, F (3)

Duncan, J. (Alexandra Ath), 1878 v W; 1882 v W (2)

Duncan, J. (Leicester C), 1926 v W (1)

Duncanson, J. (Rangers), 1947 v Ni (1)

Dunlop, J. (St Mirren), 1890 v W (1)

Dunlop, W. (Liverpool), 1906 v E (1)

Dunn, J. (Hibernian), 1925 v W, Ni; 1927 v Ni; 1928 v Ni, E; (with Everton), 1929 v W (6)

Durie, G. S. (Chelsea), 1988 v Bul (sub); 1989 v I (sub), Cy; 1990 v Y, EG, Eg, Se; 1991 v Sw (sub), Bul (2), USSR (sub), Sm; (with Tottenham H), 1992 v Sw, R, Sm, Ni (sub), Fi, Ca, N (sub), Ho, G (21)

Durrant, I. (Rangers), 1988 v H, Bel, Ma, Sp; 1989 v N (sub) (5)

Dykes, J. (Hearts), 1938 v Ho; 1939 v Ni (2)

Easson, J. F. (Portsmouth), 1931 v A, Sw; 1934 v W (3)

Ellis, J. (Mossend Swifts), 1892 v Ni (1)

Evans, A. (Aston Villa), 1982 v Ho, Ni, E, Nz (4)

Evans, R. (Celtic), 1949 v E, W, Ni, F; 1950 v W, Ni, Sw, P; 1951 v E, A; 1952 v Ni; 1953 v Se; 1954 v Ni, W, E, N, Fi; 1955 v Ni, P, Y, A, H; 1956 v E, Ni, W, A; 1957 v WG, Sp; 1958 v Ni, W, E, Sw, H, Pol, Y, Par, F; 1959 v E, WG, Ho, P; 1960 v E, Ni, W, Pol; (with Chelsea), 1960 v A, H, T (48)

Ewart, J. (Bradford C), 1921 v E (1)

Ewing, T. (Partick T), 1958 v W, E (2)

Farm, G. N. (Blackpool), 1953 v W, Ni, E, Se; 1954 v Ni, W, E; 1959 v WG, Ho, P (10)

Ferguson, D. (Rangers), 1988 v Ma, Co (sub) (2)

Ferguson, D. (Dundee U), 1992 v US (sub), Ca, Ho (sub) (3)

Ferguson, I. (Rangers), 1989 v I, Cy (sub), F (3)

Ferguson, J. (Vale of Leven), 1874 v E; 1876 v E, W; 1877 v E, W; 1878 v W (6)

Ferguson, R. (Kilmarnock), 1966 v W, E, Ho, P, Br; 1967 v W, Ni (7)

Fernie, W. (Celtic), 1954 v Fi, A, U; 1955 v W, Ni; 1957 v E, Ni, W, Y; 1958 v W, Sw, Par (12)

Findlay, R. (Kilmarnock), 1898 v W (1)

Fitchie, T. T. (Woolwich Arsenal), 1905 v W; 1906 v W, Ni; (with Queen's Park), 1907 v W (4)

Flavell, R. (Airdrieonians), 1947 v Bel, L (2)

Fleck, R. (Norwich C), 1990 v Arg, Se, Br (sub); 1991 v USSR (4)

Fleming, C. (East Fife), 1954 v Ni (1)

Fleming, J. W. (Rangers), 1929 v G, Ho; 1930 v E (3)

Fleming, A. R. (Morton), 1886 v Ni (1)

Forbes, A. R. (Sheffield U), 1947 v Bel, L, E; 1948 v W, Ni, (with Arsenal), 1950 v E, P, F; 1951 v W, Ni, A; 1952 v W, D, Se (14)

Forbes, J. (Vale of Leven), 1884 v E, W, Ni; 1887 v W, E (5)

Ford, D. (Hearts), 1974 v Cz (sub), WG (sub), W (3)

Forrest, J. (Rangers), 1966 v W, I; (with Aberdeen), 1971 v Bel (sub), D, USSR (5)

Forrest, J. (Motherwell), 1958 v E (1)

Forsyth, A. (Partick T), 1972 v Y, Cz, Br; 1973 v D; (with Manchester U), E; 1975 v Sp, Ni (sub), R, EG; 1976 v D (10)

Forsyth, C. (Kilmarnock), 1964 v E; 1965 v W, Ni, Fi (4)

Forsyth, T. (Motherwell), 1971 v D; (with Rangers), 1974 v Cz; 1976 v Sw, Ni, W, E; 1977 v Fi, Se, W, Ni, E, Ch, Arg, Br; 1978 v Cz, W, Ni, W (sub), E, Pe, Ir (sub), Ho (22)

Foyers, R. (St Bernards), 1893 v W; 1894 v W (2)

Fraser, D. M. (WBA), 1968 v Ho; 1969 v Cy (2)

Fraser, J. (Moffat), 1891 v Ni (1)

Fraser, M. J. E. (Queen's Park), 1880 v W; 1882 v W, E; 1883 v W, E (5)

Fraser, J. (Dundee), 1907 v Ni (1)

Fraser, W. (Sunderland), 1955 v W, Ni (2)

Fulton, W. (Abercorn), 1884 v Ni (1)

Fyfe, J. H. (Third Lanark), 1895 v W (1)

Gabriel, J. (Everton), 1961 v W; 1964 v N (sub) (2)

Gallacher, H. K. (Airdrieonians), 1924 v Ni; 1925 v E, W, Ni; 1926 v W; (with Newcastle U), 1926 v E, Ni; 1927 v E, W, Ni; 1928 v E, W; 1929 v E, W, Ni; 1930 v W, Ni, F; (with Chelsea), 1934 v E; (with Derby Co), 1935 v E (20)

Gallacher, K. W. (Dundee U), 1988 v Co, E (sub); 1989 v N, I; (with Coventry C), 1991 v Sm; 1992 v R (sub), Sm (sub), Ni (sub), N (sub), Ho (sub), G (sub), C (12)

Gallacher, P. (Sunderland); 1935 v Ni (1)

Galloway, M. (Celtic), 1992 v R (1)

Galt, J. H. (Rangers), 1908 v W, Ni (2)

Gardiner, I. (Motherwell), 1958 v W (1)

Gardner, D. R. (Third Lanark), 1897 v W (1)

Gardner, R. (Queen's Park), 1872 v E; 1873 v E; (with Clydesdale), 1874 v E; 1875 v E; 1878 v E (5)

Gemmell, S. (St Mirren), 1955 v P, Y (2)

Gemmell, T. (Celtic), 1966 v E; 1967 v W, Ni, E, USSR; 1968 v Ni, E; 1969 v W, Ni, E, D, A, WG, Cy; 1970 v E, Ei, WG; 1971 v Bel (18)

Gemmill, A. (Derby Co), 1971 v Bel; 1972 v P, Ho, Pe, Ni, W, E; 1976 v D, R, Ni, W, E; 1977 v Fi, Cz, W (2), Ni (sub), E (sub), Ch (sub), Arg, Br; 1978 v EG (sub); (with Nottingham F), Bul, Ni, W, E (sub), Pe (sub), Ir, Ho; 1979 v A, N, P, N; (with Birmingham C), 1980 v A, P, Ni, W, E, H; 1981 v Se, P, Is, Ni (43)

Gibb, W. (Clydesdale), 1873 v E (1)

Gibson, D. W. (Leicester C), 1963 v A, N, Ei, Sp; 1964 v Ni; 1965 v W, Fi (7)

Gibson, J. D. (Partick T), 1926 v E; 1927 v E, W, Ni; (with Aston Villa), 1928 v E, W; 1930 v W, Ni (8)

Gibson, N. (Rangers), 1895 v E, Ni; 1896 v E, Ni; 1897 v E, Ni; 1898 v E; 1899 v E, W, Ni; 1900 v E, Ni; 1901 v W; (with Partick T), 1905 v Ni (14)

Gilchrist, J. E. (Celtic), 1922 v E (1)

Gilhooley, M. (Hull C), 1922 v W (1)

Gillespie, G. (Rangers), 1880 v W; 1881 v E, W; 1882 v E; (with Queen's Park), 1886 v W; 1890 v W; 1891 v Ni (7)

Gillespie, G. T. (Liverpool), 1988 v Bel, Bul, Sp; 1989 v N, F, Ch; 1990 v Y, EG, Eg, Pol, Ma, Br (sub); 1991 v Bul (13)

Gillespie, Jas (Third Lanark), 1898 v W (1)

Gillespie. John (Queen's Park), 1896 v W (1)

Gillespie, R. (Queen's Park), 1927 v W; 1931 v W; 1932 v F; 1933 v E (4)

Gillick, T. (Everton), 1937 v A, Cz; 1939 v W, Ni, H (5)

Gilmour, J. (Dundee), 1931 v W (1)

Gilzean, A. J. (Dundee), 1964 v W, E, N, WG; 1965 v Ni, (with Tottenham H), Sp; 1966 v Ni, W, Pol, I; 1968 v W; 1969 v W, E, WG, Cy (2), A (sub); 1970 v Ni, E (sub), WG, A; 1971 v P (22)

Glavin, R. (Celtic), 1977 v Se (1)

Glen, A. (Aberdeen), 1956 v E, Ni (2)

Glen, R. (Renton), 1895 v W; 1896 v W; (with Hibernian), 1900 v Ni (3)

Goram, A. L. (Oldham Ath), 1986 v EG (sub), R, Ho; 1987 v Br; (with Hibernian) 1989 v Y, I; 1990 v EG, Pol, Ma; 1991 v R, Sw, Bul (2), USSR, Sm; (with Rangers), 1992 v Sw, R, Sm, Fi, N, Ho, G, C (23)

Gordon, J. E. (Rangers), 1912 v E, Ni; 1913 v E, Ni, W; 1914 v E, Ni; 1920 v W, E, Ni (10)

Gossland, J. (Rangers), 1884 v Ni (1)

Goudle, J. (Abercorn), 1884 v Ni (1)

Gough, C. R. (Dundee U), 1983 v Sw, Ni, W, E, Ca (3); 1984 v U, Bel, EG, Ni, W, E, F; 1985 v Sp, E, Ic; 1986 v W, EG, Aus, Is, R, E, D, WG, U; (with Tottenham H), 1987 v Bul, L, Ei (2), Bel, E, Br; 1988 v H; (with Rangers), S.Ar, Sp, Co, E; 1989 v Y, I, Cy, F, Cy; 1990 v F, Arg, EG, Eg, Pol, Ma, Cr; 1991 v USSR, Bul; 1992 v Sm, Ni, Ca, N, Ho, G, C (59)

Gourlay, J. (Cambuslang), 1886 v Ni; 1888 v W (2)

Govan, J. (Hibernian), 1948 v E, W, Bel, Sw, F; 1949 v Ni (6)

Gow, D. R. (Rangers), 1888 v E (1)

Gow, J. J. (Queen's Park), 1885 v E (1)

Gow, J. R. (Rangers), 1888 v Ni (1)

Graham, A. (Leeds U), 1978 v EG (sub); 1979 v A (sub), N, W, Ni, E, Arg, N; 1980 v A; 1981 v W (10)

Graham, G. (Arsenal), 1972 v P, SW (sub), Ho, Ni, Y, Cz, Br; 1973 v D (2); (with Manchester U), E, W, Ni, Br (sub) (13)

Graham, J. (Annbank), 1884 v Ni (1)

Graham, J. A. (Arsenal), 1921 v Ni (1)

Grant, J. (Hibernian), 1959 v W, Ni (2)

Grant, P. (Celtic), 1989 v E (sub), Ch (2)

Gray, A. (Hibernian), 1903 v Ni (1)

Gray, A. M. (Aston Villa), 1976 v R, Sw; 1977 v Fi, Cz; 1979 v A, N; (with Wolverhampton W), 1980 v P, E (sub); 1981 v Se, P, Is (sub), Ni; 1982 v Se (sub), Ni (sub); 1983 v Ni, W, E, Ca (1 + 1 sub); (with Everton), 1985 v Ic (20)

Gray, D. (Rangers), 1929 v W, Ni, G, Ho; 1930 v W, E, Ni; 1931 v W; 1933 v W, Ni (10)

Gray, E. (Leeds U), 1969 v E, Cy; 1970 v WG, A; 1971 v W, Ni; 1972 v Bel, Ho; 1976 v W, E; 1977 v Fi, W (12)

Gray, F. T. (Leeds U), 1976 v Sw; 1979 v N, P, W, Ni, E, Arg (sub); (with Nottingham F), 1980 v Bel (sub); 1981 v Se, P, Is, Ni, Is, W; (with Leeds U), Ni, E; 1982 v Se, Ni, P, Sp, Ho, W, Nz, Br, USSR; 1983 v EG, Sw, Bel, Sw, W, E, Ca (32)

Gray, W. (Pollokshields Ath), 1886 v E (1)

Green, A. (Blackpool), 1971 v Bel (sub), P (sub), Ni, E; 1972 v W, E (sub) (6)

Greig, J. (Rangers), 1964 v E, WG; 1965 v W, Ni, E, Fi (2), Sp, Pol; 1966 v Ni, W, E, Pol, I (2), P, Ho, Br; 1967 v W, Ni, E; 1968 v Ni, W, E, Ho; 1969 v W, Ni, E, D, A, WG, Cy (2); 1970 v W, E, Ei, WG, A; 1971 v D, Bel, W (sub), Ni, E; 1976 v D (44)

Groves, W. (Hibernian), 1888 v W; (with Celtic), 1889 v Ni; 1890 v E (3)

Guilliland, W. (Queen's Park), 1891 v W; 1892 v Ni; 1894 v E; 1895 v E (4)

Gunn, B. (Norwich C), 1990 v Eg (1)

Haddock, H. (Clyde), 1955 v E, H (2), P, Y; 1958 v E (6)

Haddow, D. (Rangers), 1894 v E (1)

Haffey, F. (Celtic), 1960 v E; 1961 v E (2)

Hamilton, A. (Queen's Park), 1885 v E, W; 1886 v E; 1888 v E (4)

Hamilton, A. W. (Dundee), 1962 v Cz, U, W, E; 1963 v W, Ni, E, A, N, Ei; 1964 v Ni, W, E, N, WG; 1965 v Ni, W, E, Fi (2), Pol, Sp; 1966 v Pol, Ni (24)

Hamilton, G. (Aberdeen), 1947 v Ni; 1951 v Bel, A; 1954 v N (2) (5)

Hamilton, G. (Port Glasgow Ath), 1906 v Ni (1)

Hamilton, J. (Queen's Park), 1892 v W; 1893 v E, Ni (3)

Hamilton, J. (St Mirren), 1924 v Ni (1)

Hamilton, R. C. (Rangers), 1899 v E, W, Ni; 1900 v W; 1901 v E, Ni; 1902 v W, Ni; 1903 v E; 1904 v Ni; (with Dundee), 1911 v W (11)

Hamilton, T. (Hurlford), 1891 v Ni (1)

Hamilton, T. (Rangers), 1932 v E (1)

Hamilton, W. M. (Hibernian), 1965 v Fi (1)

Hannah, A. B. (Renton), 1888 v W (1)

Hannah, J. (Third Lanark), 1889 v W (1)

Hansen, A. D. (Liverpool), 1979 v W, Arg; 1980 v Bel, P; 1981 v Se, P, Is; 1982 v Se, Ni, P, Sp, Ni (sub), W, E, Nz, Br, USSR; 1983 v EG, Sw, Bel, Sw; 1985 v W (sub); 1986 v R (sub); 1987 v Ei (2), L (26)

Hansen, J. (Partick T), 1972 v Bel (sub), Y (sub) (2)

Harkness, J. D. (Queen's Park), 1927 v E, Ni; 1928 v E; (with Hearts), 1929 v W, E, Ni; 1930 v E, W; 1932 v W, F; 1934 v Ni, W (12)

Harper, J. M. (Aberdeen), 1973 v D (1 + 1 sub); (with Hibernian), 1976 v D; (with Aberdeen), 1978 v Ir (sub) (4)

Harper, W. (Hibernian), 1923 v E, Ni, W; 1924 v E, Ni, W; 1925 v E, Ni, W; (with Arsenal), 1926 v E, Ni (11)

Harris, J. (Partick T), 1921 v W, Ni (2)

Harris, N. (Newcastle U), 1924 v E (1)

Harrower, W. (Queen's Park), 1882 v E; 1884 v Ni; 1886 v W (3)

Hartford, R. A. (WBA), 1972 v Pe, W (sub), E, Y, Cz, Br; (with Manchester C), 1976 v D, R, Ni (sub); 1977 v Cz (sub), W (sub), Se, W, Ni, E, Ch, Arg, Br; 1978 v EG, Cz, W, Bul, W, E, Pe, Ir, Ho; 1979 v A, N, P, W, Ni, E, Arg, N; (with Everton), 1980 v Pe, Bel; 1981 v Ni (sub), Is, W, Ni, E; 1982 v Se; (with Manchester C), Ni, P, Sp, Ni, W, E, Br (50)

Harvey, D. (Leeds U), 1973 v D; 1974 v Cz, WG, Ni, W, E, Bel, Z, Br, Y; 1975 v EG, Sp (2); 1976 v D (2); 1977 v Fi (sub) (16)

Hastings, A. C. (Sunderland), 1936 v Ni; 1938 v Ni (2)

Haughney, M. (Celtic), 1954 v E (1)

Hay, D. (Celtic), 1970 v Ni, W, E; 1971 v D, Bel, W, P, Ni; 1972 v P, Bel, Ho; 1973 v W, Ni, E, Sw, Br; 1974 v Cz (2), WG, Ni, W, E, Bel, N, Z, Br, Y (27)

Hay, J. (Celtic), 1905 v Ni; 1909 v Ni; 1910 v W, Ni, E; 1911 v Ni, E; (with Newcastle U), 1912 v E, W; 1914 v E, Ni (11)

Hegarty, P. (Dundee U), 1979 v W, Ni, E, Arg, N (sub); 1980 v W, E; 1983 v Ni (8)

Heggie, C. (Rangers), 1886 v Ni (1)

Henderson, G. H. (Rangers), 1904 v Ni (1)

Henderson, J. G. (Portsmouth), 1953 v Se; 1954 v Ni, E, N; 1956 v W; (with Arsenal), 1959 v W, Ni (7)

Henderson, W. (Rangers), 1963 v W, Ni, E, A, N, Ei, Sp; 1964 v W, Ni, E, N, WG; 1965 v Fi, Pol, E, Sp; 1966 v Ni, W, Pol, I, Ho; 1967 v W, Ni; 1968 v Ho; 1969 v Ni, E, Cy; 1970 v Ei; 1971 v P (29)

Hepburn, J. (Alloa Ath), 1891 v W (1)

Hepburn, R. (Ayr U), 1932 v Ni (1)

Herd, A. C. (Hearts), 1935 v Ni (1)

Herd, D. G. (Arsenal), 1959 v E, W, Ni; 1961 v E, Cz (5)

Herd, G. (Clyde), 1958 v E; 1960 v H, T; 1961 v W, Ni (5)

Herriot, J. (Birmingham C), 1969 v Ni, E, D, Cy (2), W (sub); 1970 v Ei (sub), WG (8)

Hewie, J. D. (Charlton Ath), 1956 v E, A; 1957 v E, Ni, W, Y, Sp (2), Sw, WG; 1958 v H, Pol, Y, F; 1959 v Ho, P; 1960 v Ni, W, Pol (19)

Higgins, A. (Kilmarnock), 1885 v Ni (1)

Higgins, A. (Newcastle U), 1910 v E, Ni; 1911 v E, Ni (4)

Highet, T. C. (Queen's Park), 1875 v E; 1876 v E, W; 1878 v E (4)

Hill, D. (Rangers), 1881 v E, W; 1882 v W (3)

Hill, D. A. (Third Lanark), 1906 v Ni (1)

Hill, F. R. (Aberdeen), 1930 v F; 1931 v W, Ni (3)

Hill, J (Hearts), 1891 v E; 1892 v W (2)

Hogg, G (Hearts), 1896 v E, Ni (2)

Hogg, J. (Ayr U), 1922 v Ni (1)

Hogg, R. M. (Celtic), 1937 v Cz (1)

Holm, A. H. (Queen's Park), 1882 v W; 1883 v E, W (3)

Holt, D. D. (Hearts), 1963 v A, N, Ei, Sp; 1964 v WG (sub) (5)

Holton, J. A. (Manchester U), 1973 v W, Ni, E, Sw, Br; 1974 v Cz, WG, Ni, W, E, N, Z, Br, Y; 1975 v EG (15)

Hope, R. (WBA), 1968 v Ho; 1969 v D (2)

Houliston, W. (Queen of the South), 1949 v E, Ni, F (3)

Houston, S. M. (Manchester U), 1976 v D (1)

Howden, W. (Partick T), 1905 v Ni (1)

Howe, R. (Hamilton A), 1929 v N, Ho (2)

Howie, J. (Newcastle U), 1905 v E; 1906 v E; 1908 v E (3)

Howie, H. (Hibernian), 1949 v W (1)

Howieson, J. (St Mirren), 1927 v Ni (1)

Hughes, J. (Celtic), 1965 v Pol, Sp; 1966 v Ni, I (2); 1968 v E; 1969 v A; 1970 v Ei (8)

Hughes, W. (Sunderland), 1975 v Se (sub) (1)

Humphries, W. (Motherwell), 1952 v Se (1)

Hunter, A. (Kilmarnock), 1972 v Pe, Y; (with Celtic), 1973 v E; 1974 v Cz (4)

Hunter, J. (Dundee), 1909 v W (1)

Hunter, J. (Third Lanark), 1874 v E; (with Eastern), 1875 v E; (with Third Lanark), 1876 v E; 1877 v W (4)

Hunter, R. (St Mirren), 1890 v Ni (1)

Hunter, W. (Motherwell), 1960 v H, T; 1961 v W (3)

Husband, J. (Partick T), 1947 v W (1)

Hutchison, T. (Coventry C), 1974 v Cz (2), WG (2), Ni, W, Bel (sub), N, Z (sub), Y (sub); 1975 v EG, Sp (2), P, E (sub), R (sub); 1976 v D (17)

Hutton, J. (Aberdeen), 1923 v E, W, Ni; 1924 v Ni; 1926 v W, E, Ni; (with Blackburn R), 1927 v Ni; 1928 v W, Ni (10)

Hutton, J. (St Bernards), 1887 v Ni (1)

Hyslop, T. (Stoke C), 1896 v E; (with Rangers), 1897 v E (2)

Imlach, J. J. S. (Nottingham F), 1958 v H, Pol, Y, F (4)

Imrie, W. N. (St Johnstone), 1929 v N, G (2)

Inglis, J. (Kilmarnock Ath), 1884 v Ni (1)

Inglis, J. (Rangers), 1883 v E, W (2)

Irons, J. H. (Queen's Park), 1900 v W (1)

Irvine, B. (Aberdeen), 1991 v R (1)

Jackson, A. (Cambuslang), 1886 v W; 1888 v Ni (2)

Jackson, A. (Aberdeen), 1925 v E, W, Ni; (with Huddersfield T), 1926 v E, W, Ni; 1927 v W, Ni; 1928 v E, W; 1929 v E, W, Ni; 1930 v E, W, Ni, F (17)

Jackson, C. (Rangers), 1975 v Se, P (sub), W; 1976 v D, R, Ni, W, E (8)

Jackson, J. (Partick T), 1931 v A, I, Sw; 1933 v E; (with Chelsea), 1934 v E; 1935 v E; 1936 v W, Ni (8)

Jackson, T. A. (St Mirren), 1904 v W, E, Ni; 1905 v W; 1907 v W, Ni (6)

James, A. W. (Preston NE), 1926 v W; 1928 v E; 1929 v E, Ni; (with Arsenal), 1930 v E, W, Ni; 1933 v W (8)

Jardine, A. (Rangers), 1971 v D (sub); 1972 v P, Bel, Ho; 1973 v E, Sw, Br; 1974 v Cz (2), WG (2), Ni, W, E, Bel, N, Z, Br, Y; 1975 v EG, Sp (2), Se, P, W, Ni, E; 1977 v Se (sub), Ch (sub), Br (sub); 1978 v Cz, W, Ni, Ir; 1980 v Pe, A, Bel (2) (38)

Jarvie, A. (Airdrieonians), 1971 v P (sub), Ni (sub), E (sub) (3)

Jenkinson, T. (Hearts), 1887 v Ni (1)

Johnston, L. H. (Clyde), 1948 v Bel, Sw (2)

Johnston, M. (Watford), 1984 v W (sub), E (sub), F; (with Celtic), 1985 v Y, Ic, Sp (2), W; 1986 v EG; 1987 v Bul, Ei (2), L; (with Nantes), 1988 v H, Bel, L, S.Ar, Sp, Co, E; 1989 v N, Y, I, Cy, F, Cy, E, Ch (sub); (with Rangers), 1990 v F, N, EG, Pol, Ma, Cr, Se, Br; 1992 v Sw, Sm (sub) (38)

Johnston, R. (Sunderland), 1938 v Cz (1)

Johnston, W. (Rangers), 1966 v W, E, Pol, Ho; 1968 v W, E; 1969 v Ni (sub); 1970 v Ni; 1971 v D; (with WBA), 1977 v Se, W (sub), Ni, E, Ch, Arg, Br; 1978 v EG, Cz, W (2), E, Pe (22)

Johnstone, D. (Rangers), 1973 v W, Ni, E, Sw, Br; 1975 v EG (sub), Se (sub); 1976 v Sw, Ni (sub), E (sub); 1978 v Bul (sub), Ni, W; 1980 v Bel (14)

Johnstone, J. (Abercorn), 1888 v W (1)

Johnstone, J. (Celtic), 1965 v W, Fi; 1966 v E; 1967 v W, USSR; 1968 v W; 1969 v A, WG; 1970 v E, WG; 1971 v D, E; 1972 v P, Bel, Ho, Ni, E (sub); 1974 v W, E, Bel, N; 1975 v EG, Sp (23)

Johnstone, Jas (Kilmarnock), 1894 v W (1)

Johnstone, J. A. (Hearts), 1930 v W; 1933 v W, Ni (3)

Johnstone, R. (Hibernian), 1951 v E, D, F; 1952 v Ni, E; 1953 v E, Se; 1954 v W, E, N, Fi; 1955 v Ni, H; (with Manchester C), 1955 v E; 1956 v E, Ni, W (17)

Johnstone, W. (Third Lanark), 1887 v Ni; 1889 v W; 1890 v E (3)

Jordan, J. (Leeds U), 1973 v E (sub), Sw (sub), Br; 1974 v Cz (sub + 1), WG (sub), Ni (sub), W, E, Bel, N, Z, Br, Y; 1975 v EG, Sp (2); 1976 v Ni, W, E; 1977 v Cz, W, Ni, E; 1978 v EG, Cz, W; (with Manchester U), Bul, Ni, E, Pe, Ir, Ho; 1979 v A, P, W (sub), Ni, E, N; 1980 v Bel, Ni (sub), W, E, Pol; 1981 v Is, W, E; (with AC Milan), 1982 v Se, Ho, W, E, USSR (52)

Kay, J. L. (Queen's Park), 1880 v E; 1882 v E, W; 1883 v E, W; 1884 v W (6)

Keillor, A. (Montrose), 1891 v W; 1892 v Ni; (with Dundee), 1894 v Ni; 1895 v W; 1896 v W; 1897 v W (6)

Keir, L. (Dumbarton), 1885 v W; 1886 v Ni; 1887 v E, W; 1888 v E (5)

Kelly, H. T. (Blackpool), 1952 v USA (1)

Kelly, J. (Renton), 1888 v E; (with Celtic), 1889 v E; 1890 v E; 1892 v E; 1893 v E, Ni; 1894 v W; 1896 v Ni (8)

Kelly, J. C. (Barnsley), 1949 v W, Ni (2)

Kelso, R. (Renton), 1885 v W, Ni; 1886 v W; 1887 v E, W; 1888 v E, Ni; (with Dundee), 1898 v Ni (8)

Kelso, T. (Dundee), 1914 v W (1)

Kennaway, J. (Celtic), 1934 v A (1)

Kennedy, A. (Eastern), 1875 v E; 1876 v E, W; (with Third Lanark), 1878 v E; 1882 v W; 1884 v W (6)

Kennedy, J. (Celtic), 1964 v W, E, WG; 1965 v W, Ni, Fi (6)

Kennedy, J. (Hibernian), 1897 v W (1)

Kennedy, S. (Aberdeen), 1978 v Bul, W, E, Pe, Ho; 1979 v A, P; 1982 v P (sub) (8)

Kennedy, S. (Partick T), 1905 v W (1)

Kennedy, S. (Rangers), 1975 v Se, P, W, Ni, E (5)

Ker, G. (Queen's Park), 1880 v E; 1881 v E, W; 1882 v W, E (5)

Ker, W. (Granville), 1872 v E; (with Queen's Park), 1873 v E (2)

Kerr, A. (Partick T), 1955 v A, H (2)

Kerr, P. (Hibernian), 1924 v Ni (1)

Key, G. (Hearts), 1902 v Ni (1)

Key, W. (Queen's Park), 1907 v Ni (1)

King, A. (Hearts), 1896 v E, W; (with Celtic), 1897 v Ni; 1898 v Ni; 1899 v Ni, W (6)

King, J. (Hamilton A), 1933 v Ni; 1934 v Ni (2)

King, W. S. (Queen's Park), 1929 v W (1)

Kinloch, J. D. (Partick T), 1922 v Ni (1)

Kinnaird, A. F. (Wanderers), 1873 v E (1)

Kinnear, D. (Rangers), 1938 v Cz (1)

Lambie, J. A. (Queen's Park), 1886 v Ni; 1887 v Ni; 1888 v E (3)

Lambie, W. A. (Queen's Park), 1892 v Ni; 1893 v W; 1894 v E; 1895 v E, Ni; 1896 v E, Ni; 1897 v E, Ni (9)

Lamont, D. (Pilgrims), 1885 v Ni (1)

Lang, A. (Dumbarton), 1880 v W (1)

Lang, J. J. (Cydesdale), 1876 v W; (with Third Lanark), 1878 v W (2)

Latta, A. (Dumbarton), 1888 v W; 1889 v E (2)

Law, D. (Huddersfield T), 1959 v W, Ni, Ho, P; 1960 v Ni, W; (with Manchester C), 1960 v E, Pol, A; 1961 v E, Ni; (with Torino), 1962 v Cz (2), E; (with Manchester U), 1963 v W, Ni, E, A, N, Ei, Sp; 1964 v W, E, N, WG; 1965 v W, Ni, E, Fi (2), Pol, Sp; 1966 v Ni, E, Pol; 1967 v W, E, USSR; 1968 v Ni; 1969 v Ni, A, WG; 1972 v Pe, Ni, W, E, Y, Cz, Br; (with Manchester C), 1974 v Cz (2), WG (2), Ni, Z (55)

Law, G. (Rangers), 1910 v E, Ni, W (3)

Law, T. (Chelsea), 1928 v E; 1930 v E (2)

Lawrence, J. (Newcastle U), 1911 v E (1)

Lawrence, T. (Liverpool), 1963 v Ei; 1969 v W, WG (3)

Lawson, D. (St Mirren), 1923 v E (1)

Leckie, R. (Queen's Park), 1872 v E (1)

Leggat, G. (Aberdeen), 1956 v E; 1957 v W; 1958 v Ni, H, Pol, Y, Par; (with Fulham), 1959 v E, W, Ni, WG, Ho; 1960 v E, Ni, W, Pol, A, H (18)

Leighton, J. (Aberdeen), 1983 v EG, Sw, Bel, Sw, W, E, Ca (2); 1984 v U, Bel, Ni, W, E, F; 1985 v Y, Ic, Sp (2), W, E, Ic; 1986 v W, EG, Aus (2), Is, D, WG, U; 1987 v Bul, Ei (2), L, Bel, E; 1988 v H, Bel, Bul, L, S.Ar, Ma, Sp; (with Manchester U), Co, E; 1989 v N, Cy, F, Cy, E, Ch; 1990 v Y, F, N, Arg, Ma (sub), Cr, Se, Br (58)

Lennie, W. (Aberdeen), 1908 v W, Ni (2)

Lennox, R. (Celtic), 1967 v Ni, E, USSR; 1968 v W, L; 1969 v D, A, WG, Cy (sub); 1970 v W (sub) (10)

Leslie, L. G. (Airdrieonians), 1961 v W, Ni, Ei (2), Cz (5)

Levein, C. (Hearts), 1990 v Arg, EG, Eg (sub), Pol, Ma (sub), Se; 1992 v R, Sm (8)

Liddell, W. (Liverpool), 1947 v W, Ni; 1948 v E, W, Ni; 1950 v E, W, P, F; 1951 v W, Ni, E, A; 1952 v W, Ni, E, USA, D, Se; 1953 v W, Ni, E; 1954 v W; 1955 v P, Y, A, H; 1956 v Ni (28)

Liddle, D. (East Fife), 1931 v A, I, Sw (3)

Lindsay, D. (St Mirren), 1903 v Ni (1)

Lindsay, J. (Dumbarton), 1880 v W; 1881 v W, E; 1884 v W, E; 1885 v W, E; 1886 v E (8)

Lindsay, J. (Renton), 1888 v E; 1893 v E, Ni (3)

Linwood, A. B. (Clyde), 1950 v W (1)

Little, R. J. (Rangers), 1953 v Se (1)

Livingstone, G. T. (Manchester C), 1906 v E; (with Rangers), 1907 v W (2)

Lochhead, A. (Third Lanark), 1889 v W (1)

Logan, J. (Ayr U), 1891 v W (1)

Logan, T. (Falkirk), 1913 v Ni (1)

Logie, J. T. (Arsenal), 1953 v Ni (1)

Loney, W. (Celtic), 1910 v W, Ni (2)

Long, H. (Clyde), 1947 v Ni (1)

Longair, W. (Dundee), 1894 v Ni (1)

Lorimer, P. (Leeds U), 1970 v A (sub); 1971 v W, Ni; 1972 v Ni (sub), W, E; 1973 v D (2), E (2); 1974 v WG (sub), E, Bel, N, Z, Br, Y; 1975 v Sp (sub); 1976 v D (2), R (sub) (21)

Love, A. (Aberdeen), 1931 v A, I, Sw (3)

Low, A. (Falkirk), 1934 v Ni (1)

Low, T. P. (Rangers), 1897 v Ni (1)

Low, W. L. (Newcastle U), 1911 v E, W; 1912 v Ni; 1920 v E, Ni (5)

Lowe, J. (Cambuslang), 1891 v Ni (1)

Lowe, J. (St Bernards), 1887 v Ni (1)

Lundie, J. (Hibernian), 1886 v W (1)

Lyall, J. (Sheffield W), 1905 v E (1)

McAdam, J. (Third Lanark), 1880 v W (1)

McAllister, G. (Leicester C), 1990 v EG, Pol, Ma (sub); (with Leeds U), 1991 v R, Sw, Bul, USSR (sub), Sm; 1992 v Sw (sub), Sm, Ni, Fi (sub), US, Ca, N, Ho, G, C (18)

McArthur, D. (Celtic), 1895 v E, Ni; 1899 v W (3)

McAtee, A. (Celtic), 1913 v W (1)

McAulay, J. (Dumbarton), 1882 v W; (with Arthurlie), 1884 v Ni (2)

McAulay, J. (Dumbarton), 1883 v E, W; 1884 v; 1885 v E, W; 1886 v E; 1887 v E, W (8)

McAuley, R. (Rangers), 1932 v Ni, W (2)

McAvennie, F. (West Ham U), 1986 v Aus (2), D (sub), WG (sub); (with Celtic), 1988 v S.Ar (5)

McBain, E. (St Mirren), 1894 v W (1)

McBain, N. (Manchester U), 1922 v E; (with Everton), 1923 v Ni; 1924 v W (3)

McBride, J. (Celtic), 1967 v W, Ni (2)

McBride, P. (Preston NE), 1904 v E; 1906 v E; 1907 v E, W; 1908 v E; 1909 v W (6)

McCall, J. (Renton), 1886 v W; 1887 v E, W; 1888 v E; 1890 v E (5)

McCall, S. M. (Everton), 1990 v Arg, EG, Eg (sub), Pol, Ma, Cr, Se, Br; 1991 v Sw, USSR, Sm; (with Rangers), 1992 v Sw, R, Sm, US, Ca, N, Ho, G, C (20)

McCalliog, J. (Sheffield W), 1967 v E, USSR; 1968 v Ni; 1969 v D; (with Wolverhampton W), 1971 v P (5)

McCallum, N. (Renton), 1888 v Ni (1)

McCann, R. J. (Motherwell), 1959 v WG; 1960 v E, Ni, W; 1961 v E (5)

McCartney, W. (Hibernian), 1902 v Ni (1)

McClair, B. (Celtic), 1987 v L, Ei, E, Br (sub); (with Manchester U), 1988 v Bul, Ma (sub), Sp (sub); 1989 v N, Y, I (sub), Cy, F (sub); 1990 v N (sub), Arg (sub); 1991 v Bul (2), Sm; 1992 v Sw (sub), R, Ni, US, Ca (sub), N, Ho, G, C (26)

McClory, A. (Motherwell), 1927 v W; 1928 v Ni; 1935 v W (3)

McCloy, P. (Ayr U), 1924 v E; 1925 v E (2)

McCloy, P. (Rangers), 1973 v W, Ni, Sw, Br (4)

McCoist, A. (Rangers), 1986 v Ho; 1987 v L (sub), Ei (sub), Bel, E, Br; 1988 v H, Bel, Ma, Sp, Co, E; 1989 v Y (sub), F, Cy, E; 1990 v Y, F, N, EG (sub), Eg, Pol, Ma (sub), Cr (sub), Se (sub), Br; 1991 v R, Sw, Bul (2), USSR; 1992 v Sw, Sm, Ni, Fi (sub), US, Ca, N, Ho, G, C (41)

McColl, A. (Renton), 1888 v Ni (1)

McColl, I. M. (Rangers), 1950 v E, F; 1951 v W, Ni, Bel; 1957 v E, Ni, W, Y, Sp, Sw, WG; 1958 v Ni, E (14)

McColl, R. S. (Queen's Park), 1896 v W, Ni; 1897 v Ni; 1898 v Ni; 1899 v Ni, E, W; 1900 v E, W; 1901 v E, W; (with Newcastle U), 1902 v E; (with Queen's Park), 1908 v Ni (13)

McColl, W. (Renton), 1895 v W (1)

McCombie, A. (Sunderland), 1903 v E, W; (with Newcastle U), 1905 v E, W (4)

McCorkindale, J. (Partick T), 1891 v W (1)

McCormick, R. (Abercorn), 1886 v W (1)

McCrae, D. (St Mirren), 1929 v N, G (2)

McCreadie, A. (Rangers), 1893 v W; 1894 v E (2)

McCreadie, E. G. (Chelsea), 1965 v E, Sp, Fi, Pol; 1966 v P, Ni, W, Pol, I; 1967 v E, USSR; 1968 v Ni, W, E, Ho; 1969 v W, Ni, E, D, A, WG, Cy (2) (23)

McCulloch, D. (Hearts), 1935 v W; (with Brentford), 1936 v E; 1937 v W, Ni; 1938 v Cz; (with Derby Co), 1939 v H, W (7)

MacDonald, A. (Rangers), 1976 v Sw (1)

McDonald, J. (Edinburgh University), 1886 v E (1)

McDonald, J. (Sunderland), 1956 v W, Ni (2)

MacDougall, E. J. (Norwich C) 1975 v Se, P, W, Ni, E; 1976 v D, R (7)

McDougall, J. (Liverpool), 1931 v I, A (2)

McDougall, J. (Airdrieonians), 1926 v Ni (1)

McDougall, J. (Vale of Leven), 1877 v E, W; 1878 v E; 1879 v E, W (5)

McFadyen, W. (Motherwell), 1934 v A, W (2)

Macfarlane, A. (Dundee), 1904 v W; 1906 v W; 1908 v W; 1909 v Ni; 1911 v W (5)

McFarlane, R. (Greenock Morton), 1896 v W (1)

Macfarlane, W. (Hearts), 1947 v L (1)

McGarr, E. (Aberdeen), 1970 v Ei, A (2)

McGarvey, F. P. (Liverpool), 1979 v Ni (sub), Arg; (with Celtic), 1984 v U, Bel (sub), EG (sub), Ni, W (7)

McGeoch, A. (Dumbreck), 1876 v E, W; 1877 v E, W (4)

McGhee, J. (Hibernian), 1886 v W (1)

McGhee, M. (Aberdeen), 1983 v Ca (1 + 1 sub); 1984 v Ni (sub), E (4)

McGonagle, W. (Celtic), 1933 v E; 1934 v A, E, Ni; 1935 v Ni, W (6)

McGrain, D. (Celtic), 1973 v W, Ni, E, Sw, Br; 1974 v Cz (2), WG, W (sub), E, Bel, N, Z, Br, Y; 1975 v Sp, Se, P, W, Ni, E, R; 1976 v D (2), Sw, Ni, W, E; 1977 v Fi, Cz, W (2), Se, Ni, E, Ch, Arg, Br; 1978 v EG, Cz; 1980 v Bel, P, Ni, W, E, Pol, H; 1981 v Se, P, Is, Ni, Is, W (sub), Ni, E; 1982 v Se, Sp, Ho, Ni, E, Nz, USSR (sub) (62)

McGregor, J. C. (Vale of Leven), 1877 v E, W; 1878 v E; 1880 v E (4)

McGrory, J. E. (Kilmarnock), 1965 v Ni, Fi; 1966 v P (3)

McGrory, J. (Celtic), 1928 v Ni; 1931 v E; 1932 v Ni, W; 1933 v E, Ni; 1934 v Ni (7)

McGuire, W. (Beith), 1881 v E, W (2)

McGurk, F. (Birmingham), 1934 v W (1)

McHardy, H. (Rangers), 1885 v Ni (1)

McInally, A. (Aston Villa), 1989 v Cy (sub), Ch; (with Bayern Munich), 1990 v Y (sub), F (sub), Arg, Pol (sub), Ma, Cr (8)

McInally, J. (Dundee U), 1987 v Bel, Br; 1988 v Ma (sub); 1991 v Bul (2); 1992 v US (sub), N (sub), C (sub) (8)

McInally, T. B. (Celtic), 1926 v Ni; 1927 v W (2)

McInnes, T. (Cowlairs), 1889 v Ni (1)

McIntosh, W. (Third Lanark), 1905 v Ni (1)

McIntyre, A. (Vale of Leven), 1878 v E; 1882 v E (2)

McIntyre, H. (Rangers), 1880 v W (1)

McIntyre, J. (Rangers), 1884 v W (1)

McKay, D. (Celtic), 1959 v E, WG, Ho, P; 1960 v E, Pol, A, H, T; 1961 v W, Ni; 1962 v Ni, Cz, U (sub) (14)

Mackay, D. C. (Hearts), 1957 v Sp; 1958 v F; 1959 v W, Ni; (with Tottenham H), 1959 v WG, E; 1960 v W, Ni, A, Pol, H, T; 1961 v W, Ni, E; 1963 v E, A, N; 1964 v Ni, W, N; 1966 v Ni (22)

Mackay, G. (Hearts), 1988 v Bul (sub), L (sub), S.Ar (sub), Ma (4)

McKay, J. (Blackburn R), 1924 v W (1)

McKay, R. (Newcastle U), 1928 v W (1)

McKean, R. (Rangers), 1976 v Sw (1)

McKenzie, D. (Brentford), 1938 v Ni (1)

Mackenzie, J. A. (Partick T), 1954 v W, E, N, Fi, A, U; 1955 v E, H; 1956 v A (9)

McKeown, M. (Celtic), 1889 v Ni; 1890 v E (2)

McKie, J. (East Stirling), 1898 v W (1)

McKillop, T. R. (Rangers), 1938 v Ho (1)

McKimmie, S. (Aberdeen), 1989 v E, Ch; 1990 v Arg, Eg, Cr (sub), Br; 1991 v R, Sw, Bul, Sm; 1992 v Sw, R, Ni, Fi, US, Ca (sub), N (sub), Ho, G, C (20)

McKinlay, D. (Liverpool), 1922 v W, Ni (2)

McKinnon, A. (Queen's Park), 1874 v E (1)

McKinnon, R. (Rangers), 1966 v W, E, I (2), Ho, Br; 1967 v W, Ni, E; 1968 v Ni, W, E, Ho; 1969 v D, A, WG, Cy; 1970 v Ni, W, E, Ei, WG, A; 1971 v D, Bel, P, USSR, D (28)

MacKinnon, W. (Dumbarton), 1883 v E, W; 1884 v E, W (4)

McKinnon, W. W. (Queen's Park), 1872 v E; 1873 v E; 1874 v E; 1875 v E; 1876 v E, W; 1877 v E; 1878 v E; 1879 v E (9)

McLaren, A. (St Johnstone), 1929 v N, G, Ho; 1933 v W, Ni (5)

McLaren, A. (Preston NE), 1947 v E, Bel, L; 1948 v W (4)

McLaren, A. (Hearts), 1992 v US, Ca, N (3)

McLaren, J. (Hibernian), 1888 v W; (with Celtic), 1889 v E; 1890 v E (3)

McLean, A. (Celtic), 1926 v W, Ni; 1927 v W, E (4)

McLean, D. (St Bernards), 1896 v W; 1897 v Ni (2)

McLean, D. (Sheffield W), 1912 v E (1)

McLean, G. (Dundee), 1968 v Ho (1)

McLean, T. (Kilmarnock), 1969 v D, Cy, W; 1970 v Ni, W; 1971 v D (6)

McLeish, A. (Aberdeen), 1980 v F, Ni, W, E, Pol, H; 1981 v Se, Is, Ni, Is, Ni, E; 1982 v Se, Sp, Ni, Br (sub); 1983 v Bel, Sw (sub), W, E, Ca (3); 1984 v U, Bel, EG; Ni, W, E, F; 1985 v Y, Ic, Sp (2), W, E, Ic; 1986 v W, EG, Aus (2), E, Ho, D; 1987 v Bel, E, Br; 1988 v Bel, Bul, L, S.Ar (sub), Ma, Sp, Co, E; 1989 v N, Y, I, Cy, F, Cy, E, Ch; 1990 v Y, F, N, Arg, EG, Eg, Cr, Se, Br; 1991 v R, Sw, USSR, Bul (76)

McLeod, D. (Celtic), 1905 v Ni; 1906 v E, W, Ni (4)

McLeod, J. (Dumbarton), 1888 v Ni; 1889 v W; 1890 v Ni; 1892 v E; 1893 v W (5)

MacLeod, J. M. (Hibernian), 1961 v E, Ei (2), Cz (4)

MacLeod, M. (Celtic), 1985 v E (sub); 1987 v Ei, L, E, Br; (with Borussia Dortmund), 1988 v Co, E; 1989 v I, Ch; 1990 v Y, F, N (sub), Arg, EG, Pol, Se Br; (with Hibernian), 1991 v R, Sw, USSR (sub) (20)

McLeod, W. (Cowlairs), 1886 v Ni (1)

McLintock, A. (Vale of Leven), 1875 v E; 1876 v E; 1880 v E (3)

McLintock, F. (Leicester C), 1963 v N (sub), Ei, Sp; (with Arsenal), 1965 v Ni; 1967 v USSR; 1970 v Ni; 1971 v W, Ni, E (9)

McLuckie, J. S. (Manchester C), 1934 v W (1)

McMahon, A. (Celtic), 1892 v E; 1893 v E, Ni; 1894 v E; 1901 v Ni; 1902 v W (6)

McMenemy, J. (Celtic), 1905 v Ni; 1909 v Ni; 1910 v E, W; 1911 v Ni, W, E; 1912 v W; 1914 v W, Ni, E; 1920 v Ni (12)

McMenemy, J. (Motherwell), 1934 v W (1)

McMillan, J. (St Bernards), 1897 v W (1)

McMillan, I. L. (Airdrieonians), 1952 v E, USA, D; 1955 v E; 1956 v E; (with Rangers), 1961 v Cz (6)

McMillan, T. (Dumbarton), 1887 v Ni (1)

McMullan, J. (Partick T), 1920 v W; 1921 v W, Ni, E; 1924 v E, Ni; 1925 v E; 1926 v W; (with Manchester C), 1926 v E; 1927 v E, W; 1928 v E, W; 1929 v W, E, Ni (16)

McNab, A. (Morton), 1921 v E, Ni (2)

McNab, A. (Sunderland), 1937 v A; (with WBA), 1939 v E (2)

McNab, C. D. (Dundee), 1931 v E, W, A, I, Sw; 1932 v E (6)

McNab, J. S. (Liverpool), 1923 v W (1)

McNair, A. (Celtic), 1906 v W; 1907 v Ni; 1908 v E, W; 1909 v E; 1910 v W; 1912 v E, W, Ni; 1913 v E; 1914 v E, Ni; 1920 v E, W, Ni (15)

McNaught, W. (Raith R), 1951 v A, W, Ni; 1952 v E; 1955 v Ni (5)

McNeil, H. (Queen's Park), 1874 v E; 1875 v E; 1876 v E, W; 1877 v W; 1878 v E; 1879 v E, W; 1881 v E, W (10)

McNeil, M. (Rangers), 1876 v W; 1880 v E (2)

McNeill, W. (Celtic), 1961 v E, Ei (2), Cz; 1962 v Ni, E, Cz, U; 1963 v Ei, Sp; 1964 v W, E, WG; 1965 v E, Fi, Pol, Sp; 1966 v Ni, Pol; 1967 v USSR; 1968 v E; 1969 v Cy, W, E, Cy (sub); 1970 v WG; 1972 v Ni, W, E (29)

McPhail, J. (Celtic), 1950 v W; 1951 v W, Ni, A; 1954 v Ni (5)

McPhail, R. (Airdrieonians), 1927 v E; (with Rangers), 1929 v W; 1931 v E, Ni; 1932 v W, Ni, F; 1933 v E, Ni; 1934 v A, Ni; 1935 v E; 1937 v G, E, Cz; 1938 v W, Ni (17)

McPherson, D. (Kilmarnock), 1892 v Ni (1)

McPherson, D. (Hearts), 1989 v Cy, E; 1990 v N, Ma, Cr,

Se, Br; 1991 v Sw, Bul (2), USSR (sub), Sm; 1992 v
Sw, R, Sm, Ni, Fi, US, Ca, N, Ho, G, C (23)

McPherson, J. (Clydesdale), 1875 v E (1)

McPherson, J. (Vale of Leven), 1879 v E, W; 1880 v E;
1881 v W; 1883 v E, W; 1884 v E; 1885 v Ni (8)

McPherson, J. (Kilmarnock), 1888 v W; (with Cowlairs),
1889 v E; 1890 v Ni, E; (with Rangers), 1892 v W; 1894
v E; 1895 v E, Ni; 1897 v Ni (9)

McPherson, J. (Hearts), 1891 v E (1)

McPherson, R. (Arthurlie), 1882 v E (1)

McQueen, G. (Leeds U), 1974 v Bel; 1975 v Sp (2), P,
W, Ni, E, R; 1976 v D; 1977 v Cz, W (2), Ni, E; 1978
v EG, Cz, W; (with Manchester U), Bul, Ni, W, 1979
v A, N, P, Ni, E, N; 1980 v Pe, A, Bel; 1981 v W (30)

McQueen, M. (Leith Ath), 1890 v W; 1891 v W (2)

McRorie, D. M. (Morton), 1931 v W (1)

McSpadyen, A. (Partick T), 1939 v E, H (2)

McStay, P. (Celtic), 1984 v U, Bel, EG, Ni, W, E (sub);
1985 v Y (sub), Ic, Sp (2), W; 1986 v EG (sub), Aus,
Is, U; 1987 v Bul, Ei (1 + 1 sub), L (sub), Bel, E, Br;
1988 v H, Bel, Bul, L, S.Ar, Sp, Co, E; 1989 v N, Y,
I, Cy, F, Cy, E, Ch; 1990 v Y, F, N, Arg, EG (sub),
Eg, Pol (sub), Ma, Cr, Se (sub), Br; 1991 v R, USSR,
Bul; 1992 v Sm, Fi, US, Ca, N, Ho, G, C (60)

McStay, W. (Celtic), 1921 v W, Ni; 1925 v E, Ni, W; 1926
v E, Ni, W; 1927 v E, Ni, W; 1928 v W, Ni (13)

McTavish, J. (Falkirk), 1910 v Ni (1)

McWhattie, G. C. (Queen's Park), 1901 v W, Ni (2)

McWilliam, P. (Newcastle U), 1905 v E; 1906 v E; 1907
v E, W; 1909 v E, W; 1910 v E; 1911 v W (8)

Macari, L. (Celtic), 1972 v W (sub), E, Y, Cz, Br; 1973
v D; (with Manchester U), E (2), W (sub), Ni (sub);
1975 v Se, P (sub), W, E (sub), R; 1977 v Ni (sub), E
(sub), Ch, Arg; 1978 v EG, W, Bul, Pe (sub), Ir (24)

Macauley, A. R. (Brentford), 1947 v E; (with Arsenal),
1948 v E, W, Ni, Bel, Sw, F (7)

Madden, J. (Celtic), 1893 v W; 1895 v W (2)

Main, F. R. (Rangers), 1938 v W (1)

Main, J. (Hibernian), 1909 v Ni (1)

Maley, W. (Celtic), 1893 v E, Ni (2)

Malpas, M. (Dundee U), 1984 v F; 1985 v E, Ic; 1986 v
W, Aus (2), Is, R, E, Ho, D, WG; 1987 v Bul, Ei, Bel;
1988 v Bel, Bul, L, S.Ar, Ma; 1989 v N, Y, I, Cy, F,
Cy, E, Ch; 1990 v Y, F, N, Eg, Pol, Ma, Cr, Se, Br;
1991 v R, Bul (2), USSR, Sm; 1992 v Sw, R, Sm, Ni,
Fi, US, Ca (sub), N, Ho, G (52)

Marshall, G. (Celtic), 1992 v US (1)

Marshall, H. (Celtic), 1899 v W; 1900 v Ni (2)

Marshall, J. (Middlesbrough), 1921 v E, W, Ni; 1922 v E,
W, Ni; (with Llanelly), 1924 v W (7)

Marshall, J. (Third Lanark), 1885 v Ni; 1886 v W; 1887 v
E, W (4)

Marshall, J. (Rangers), 1932 v E; 1933 v E; 1934 v E (3)

Marshall, R. W. (Rangers), 1892 v Ni; 1894 v Ni (2)

Martin, F. (Aberdeen), 1954 v N (2), A, U; 1955 v E, H
(6)

Martin, N. (Hibernian), 1965 v Fi, Pol; (with Sunderland),
1966 v I (3)

Martis, J. (Motherwell), 1961 v W (1)

Mason, J. (Third Lanark), 1949 v E, W, Ni; 1950 v Ni;
1951 v Ni, Bel, A (7)

Massie, A. (Hearts), 1932 v Ni, W, F; 1933 v Ni; 1934 v
E, Ni; 1935 v E, Ni, W; 1936 v W, Ni; (with Aston
Villa), 1936 v E; 1937 v G, E, W, Ni, A; 1938 v W (18)

Masson, D. S. (QPR), 1976 v Ni, W, E; 1977 v Fi, Cz,
W, Ni, E, Ch, Arg, Br; 1978 v EG, Cz, W; (with Derby
Co), Ni, E, Pe (17)

Mathers, D. (Partick T), 1954 v Fi (1)

Maxwell, W. S. (Stoke C), 1898 v E (1)

May, J. (Rangers), 1906 v W, Ni; 1908 v E, Ni; 1909 v W
(5)

Meechan, P. (Celtic), 1896 v Ni (1)

Meiklejohn, D. D. (Rangers), 1922 v W; 1924 v W; 1925

v W, Ni, E; 1928 v W, Ni; 1929 v E, Ni; 1930 v E, Ni;
1931 v E; 1932 v W, Ni; 1934 v A (15)

Menzies, A. (Hearts), 1906 v E (1)

Mercer, R. (Hearts), 1912 v W; 1913 v Ni (2)

Middleton, R. (Cowdenbeath), 1930 v Ni (1)

Millar, A. (Hearts), 1939 v W (1)

Millar, J. (Rangers), 1897 v E; 1898 v E, W (3)

Millar, J. (Rangers), 1963 v A, Ei (2)

Miller, J. (St Mirren), 1931 v E, I, Sw; 1932 v F; 1934 v
E (5)

Miller, P. (Dumbarton), 1882 v E; 1883 v E, W (3)

Miller, T. (Liverpool), 1920 v E; (with Manchester U),
1921 v E, Ni (3)

Miller, W. (Third Lanark), 1876 v E (1)

Miller, W. (Celtic), 1947 v E, W, Bel, L; 1948 v W, Ni
(6)

Miller, W. (Aberdeen), 1975 v R; 1978 v Bul; 1980 v Bel,
W, E, Pol, H; 1981 v Se, P, Is (sub), Ni, W, Ni, E; 1982
v Ni, P, Ho, Br, USSR; 1983 v EG, Sw (2), W, E, Ca
(3); 1984 v U, Bel, EG, W, E, F; 1985 v Y, Ic, Sp (2),
W, E, Ic; 1986 v W, EG, Aus (2), Is, R, E, Ho, D,
WG, U; 1987 v Bul, E, Br; 1988 v H, L, S.Ar, Ma, Sp,
Co, E; 1989 v N, Y; 1990 v Y, N (65)

Mills, W. (Aberdeen), 1936 v W, Ni; 1937 v W (3)

Milne, J. V. (Middlesbrough), 1938 v E; 1939 v E (2)

Mitchell, D. (Rangers), 1890 v Ni; 1892 v E; 1893 v E,
Ni; 1894 v E (5)

Mitchell, J. (Kilmarnock), 1908 v Ni; 1910 v Ni, W (3)

Mitchell, R. C. (Newcastle U), 1951 v D, F (2)

Mochan, N. (Celtic), 1954 v N, A, U (3)

Moir, W. (Bolton W), 1950 v E (1)

Moncur, R. (Newcastle U), 1968 v Ho; 1970 v Ni, W, E,
Ei; 1971 v D, Bel, W, P, Ni, E, D; 1972 v Pe, Ni, W,
E (16)

Morgan, H. (St Mirren), 1898 v W; (with Liverpool), 1899
v E (2)

Morgan, W. (Burnley), 1968 v Ni; (with Manchester U),
1972 v Pe, Y, Cz, Br; 1973 v D (2), E (2), W, Ni, Sw,
Br; 1974 v Cz (2), WG (2), Ni, Bel (sub), Br, Y (21)

Morris, D. (Raith R), 1923 v Ni; 1924 v E, Ni; 1925 v E,
W, Ni (6)

Morris, H. (East Fife), 1950 v Ni (1)

Morrison, T. (St Mirren), 1927 v E (1)

Morton, A. L. (Queen's Park), 1920 v W, Ni; (with
Rangers), 1921 v E; 1922 v E, W; 1923 v E, W, Ni; 1924
v E, W, Ni; 1925 v E, W, Ni; 1927 v E, Ni; 1928 v E,
W, Ni; 1929 v E, W, Ni; 1930 v E, W, Ni; 1931 v E, W,
Ni; 1932 v E, W, F (31)

Morton, H. A. (Kilmarnock), 1929 v G, Ho (2)

Mudie, J. K. (Blackpool), 1957 v W, Ni, E, Y, Sw, Sp
(2), WG; 1958 v Ni, E, W, Sw, H, Pol, Y, Par, F (17)

Muir, W. (Dundee), 1907 v Ni (1)

Muirhead, T. A. (Rangers), 1922 v Ni; 1923 v E; 1924 v
W; 1927 v Ni; 1928 v Ni; 1929 v W, Ni; 1930 v W (8)

Mulhall, G. (Aberdeen), 1960 v Ni; (with Sunderland),
1963 v Ni; 1964 v Ni (3)

Munro, A. D. (Hearts), 1937 v W, Ni; (with Blackpool),
1938 v Ho (3)

Munro, F. M. (Wolverhampton W), 1971 v Ni (sub), E
(sub), D, USSR; 1975 v Se, W (sub), Ni, E, R (9)

Munro, I. (St Mirren), 1979 v Arg, N; 1980 v Pe, A, Bel,
W, E (7)

Munro, N. (Abercorn), 1888 v W; 1889 v E (2)

Murdoch, J. (Motherwell), 1931 v Ni (1)

Murdoch, R. (Celtic), 1966 v W, E, I (2); 1967 v Ni; 1968
v Ni; 1969 v W, Ni, E, WG, Cy; 1970 v A (12)

Murphy, F. (Celtic), 1938 v Ho (1)

Murray, J. (Renton), 1895 v W (1)

Murray, J. (Hearts), 1958 v E, H, Pol, Y, F (5)

Murray, J. W. (Vale of Leven), 1890 v W (1)

Murray, P. (Hibernian), 1896 v Ni; 1897 v W (2)

Murray, S. (Aberdeen), 1972 v Bel (1)

Mutch, G. (Preston NE), 1938 v E (1)

Napier, C. E. (Celtic), 1932 v E; 1935 v E, W; (with Derby Co), 1937 v Ni, A (5)

Narey, D. (Dundee U), 1977 v Se (sub); 1979 v P, Ni (sub), Arg; 1980 v P, Ni, Pol, H; 1981 v W, E (sub); 1982 v Ho, W, E, Nz (sub), Br, USSR; 1983 v EG, Sw, Bel, Ni, W, E, Ca (3); 1986 v Is, R, Ho, WG, U; 1987 v Bul, E, Bel; 1989 v I, Cy (35)

Neil, R. G. (Hibernian), 1896 v W; (with Rangers), 1900 v W (2)

Neill, R. W. (Queen's Park), 1876 v W; 1877 v E, W; 1878 v W; 1880 v E (5)

Neilles, P. (Hearts), 1914 v W, Ni (2)

Nelson, J. (Cardiff C), 1925 v W, Ni; 1928 v E; 1930 v F (4)

Nevin, P. K. F. (Chelsea), 1986 v R (sub), E (sub); 1987 v L, Ei, Bel (sub); 1988 v L; (with Everton), 1989 v Cy, E; 1991 v R (sub), Bul (sub), Sm (sub); 1992 v US, G (sub), C (sub) (14)

Niblo, T. D. (Aston Villa), 1904 v E (1)

Nibloe, J. (Kilmarnock), 1929 v E, N, Ho; 1930 v W; 1931 v E, Ni, A, I, Sw; 1932 v E, F (11)

Nicholas, C. (Celtic), 1983 v Sw, Ni, E, Ca (3); (with Arsenal), 1984 v Bel, F (sub); 1985 v Y (sub), Ic (sub), Sp (sub), W (sub); 1986 v Is, R (sub), E, D, U (sub); 1987 v Bul, E (sub); (with Aberdeen), 1989 v Cy (sub) (20)

Nicol, S. (Liverpool), 1985 v Y, Ic, Sp, W; 1986 v W, EG, Aus, E, D, WG, U; 1988 v H, Bul, S.Ar, Sp, Co, E; 1989 v N, Y, Cy, F; 1990 v Y, F; 1991 v Sw, USSR, Sm; 1992 v Sw (27)

Nisbet, J. (Ayr U), 1929 v N, G, Ho (3)

Niven, J. B. (Moffatt), 1885 v Ni (1)

O'Donnell, F. (Preston NE), 1937 v E, A, Cz; 1938 v E, W; (with Blackpool), Ho (6)

Ogilvie, D. H. (Motherwell), 1934 v A (1)

O'Hare, J. (Derby Co), 1970 v W, Ni, E; 1971 v D, Bel, W, Ni; 1972 v P, Bel, Ho (sub), Pe, Ni, W (13)

Ormond, W. E. (Hibernian), 1954 v E, N, Fi, A, U; 1959 v E (6)

O'Rourke, F. (Airdrieonians), 1907 v Ni (1)

Orr, J. (Kilmarnock), 1892 v W (1)

Orr, R. (Newcastle U), 1902 v E; 1904 v E (2)

Orr, T. (Morton), 1952 v Ni, W (2)

Orr, W. (Celtic), 1900 v Ni; 1903 v Ni; 1904 v W (3)

Orrock, R. (Falkirk), 1913 v W (1)

Oswald, J. (Third Lanark), 1889 v E; (with St Bernards), 1895 v E; (with Rangers), 1897 v W (3)

Parker, A. H. (Falkirk), 1955 v P, Y, A; 1956 v E, Ni, W, A; 1957 v Ni, W, Y; 1958 v Ni, W, E, Sw; (with Everton), Par (15)

Parlane, D. (Rangers), 1973 v W, Sw, Br; 1975 v Sp (sub), Se, P, W, Ni, E, R; 1976 v D (sub); 1977 v W (12)

Parlane, R. (Vale of Leven), 1878 v W; 1879 v E, W (3)

Paterson, G. D. (Celtic), 1939 v Ni (1)

Paterson, J. (Leicester C), 1920 v E (1)

Paterson, J. (Cowdenbeath), 1931 v A, I, Sw (3)

Paton, A. (Motherwell), 1952 v D, Se (2)

Paton, D. (St Bernards), 1896 v W (1)

Paton, M. (Dumbarton), 1883 v E; 1884 v W; 1885 v W, E; 1886 v E (5)

Paton, R. (Vale of Leven), 1879 v E, W (2)

Patrick, J. (St Mirren), 1897 v E, W (2)

Paul, H. McD. (Queen's Park), 1909 v E, W, Ni (3)

Paul, W. (Partick T), 1888 v W; 1889 v W; 1890 v W (3)

Paul, W. (Dykebar), 1891 v Ni (1)

Pearson, T. (Newcastle U), 1947 v E, Bel (2)

Penman, A. (Dundee), 1966 v Ho (1)

Pettigrew, W. (Motherwell), 1976 v Sw, Ni, W; 1977 v W (sub), Se (5)

Phillips, J. (Queen's Park), 1877 v E, W; 1878 v W (3)

Plenderleith, J. B. (Manchester C), 1961 v Ni (1)

Porteous, W. (Hearts), 1903 v Ni (1)

Pringle, C. (St Mirren), 1921 v W (1)

Provan, D. (Rangers), 1964 v Ni, N; 1966 v I (2), Ho (5)

Provan, D. (Celtic), 1980 v Bel (2 sub), P (sub), Ni (sub); 1981 v Is, W, E; 1982 v Se, P, Ni (10)

Pursell, P. (Queen's Park), 1914 v W (1)

Quinn, J. (Celtic), 1905 v Ni; 1906 v Ni, W; 1908 v Ni, E; 1909 v E; 1910 v E, Ni, W; 1912 v E, W (11)

Quinn, P. (Motherwell), 1961 v E, Ei (2); 1962 v U (4)

Rae, J. (Third Lanark), 1889 v W; 1890 v Ni (2)

Raeside, J. S. (Third Lanark), 1906 v W (1)

Raisbeck, A. G. (Liverpool), 1900 v E; 1901 v E; 1902 v E; 1903 v E, W; 1904 v E; 1906 v E; 1907 v E (8)

Rankin, G. (Vale of Leven), 1890 v Ni; 1891 v E (2)

Rankin, R. (St Mirren), 1929 v N, G, Ho (3)

Redpath, W. (Motherwell), 1949 v W, Ni; 1951 v E, D, F, Bel, A; 1952 v Ni, E (9)

Reid, J. G. (Airdrieonians), 1914 v W; 1920 v W; 1924 v Ni (3)

Reid, R. (Brentford), 1938 v E, Ni (2)

Reid, W. (Rangers), 1911 v E, W, Ni; 1912 v Ni; 1913 v E, W, Ni; 1914 v E, Ni (9)

Reilly, L. (Hibernian), 1949 v E, W, F; 1950 v W, Ni, Sw, F; 1951 v W, E, D, F, Bel, A; 1952 v Ni, W, E, USA, D, Se; 1953 v Ni, W, E, Se; 1954 v W; 1955 v H (2), P, Y, A, E; 1956 v E, W, Ni, A; 1957 v E, Ni, W, Y (38)

Rennie, H. G. (Hearts), 1900 v E, Ni; (with Hibernian), 1901 v E; 1902 v E, Ni, W; 1903 v Ni, W; 1904 v Ni; 1905 v W; 1906 v Ni; 1908 v Ni, W (13)

Renny-Tailyour, H. W. (Royal Engineers), 1873 v E (1)

Rhind, A. (Queen's Park), 1872 v E (1)

Richmond, A. (Queen's Park), 1906 v W (1)

Richmond, J. T. (Clydesdale), 1877 v E; (with Queen's Park), 1878 v E; 1882 v W (3)

Ring, T. (Clyde), 1953 v Se; 1955 v W, Ni, E, H; 1957 v E, Sp (2), Sw, WG; 1958 v Ni, Sw (12)

Rioch, B. D. (Derby Co), 1975 v P, W, Ni, E, R; 1976 v D (2), R, Ni, W, E; 1977 v Fi, Cz, W; (with Everton), W, Ni, E, Ch, Br; 1978 v Cz; (with Derby Co), Ni, E, Pe, Ho (24)

Ritchie, A. (East Stirlingshire), 1891 v W (1)

Ritchie, H. (Hibernian), 1923 v W; 1928 v Ni (2)

Ritchie, J. (Queen's Park), 1897 v W (1)

Ritchie, W. (Rangers), 1962 v U (sub) (1)

Robb, D. T. (Aberdeen), 1971 v W, E, P, D (sub), USSR (5)

Robb, W. (Rangers), 1926 v W; (with Hibernian), 1928 v W (2)

Robertson, A. (Clyde), 1955 v P, A, H; 1958 v Sw, Par (5)

Robertson, D. (Rangers), 1992 v Ni (1)

Robertson, G. (Motherwell), 1910 v W; (with Sheffield W), 1912 v W; 1913 v E, Ni (4)

Robertson, G. (Kilmarnock), 1938 v Cz (1)

Robertson, H. (Dundee), 1962 v Cz (1)

Robertson, J. (Dundee), 1931 v A, I (2)

Robertson, J. (Hearts), 1991 v R, Sw, Bul (sub), Sm (sub); 1992 v Sm, Ni (sub), Fi (7)

Robertson, J. G. (Tottenham H), 1965 v W (1)

Robertson, J. N. (Nottingham F), 1978 v Ni, W (sub), Ir; 1979 v P, N; 1980 v Pe, A, Bel (2), P; 1981 v Se, P, Is, Ni, Is, Ni, E; 1982 v Se, Ni (2), E (sub), Nz, Br, USSR; 1983 v EG, Sw; (with Derby Co), 1984 v U, Bel (28)

Robertson, J. T. (Everton), 1898 v E; (with Southampton), 1899 v E; (with Rangers), 1900 v E, W; 1901 v W, Ni, E; 1902 v W, Ni, E; 1903 v E, W; 1904 v E, W, Ni; 1905 v W (16)

Robertson, P. (Dundee), 1903 v Ni (1)

Robertson, T. (Queen's Park), 1889 v Ni; 1890 v E; 1891 v W; 1892 v Ni (4)

Robertson, T. (Hearts), 1898 v Ni (1)

Robertson, W. (Dumbarton), 1887 v E, W (2)

Robinson, R. (Dundee), 1974 v WG (sub); 1975 v Se, Ni, R (sub) (4)

Rough, A. (Partick T), 1976 v Sw, Ni, W, E; 1977 v Fi, Cz, W (2), Se, Ni, E, Ch, Arg, Br; 1978 v Cz, W, Ni, E, Pe, Ir, Ho; 1979 v A, P, W, Arg, N; 1980 v Pe, A, Bel (2), P, W, E, Pol, H; 1981 v Se, P, Is, Ni, Is, W, E; 1982 v Se, Ni, Sp, Ho, W, E, Nz, Br, USSR; (with Hibernian), 1986 v W (sub), E (53)

Rougvie, D. (Aberdeen), 1984 v Ni (1)

Rowan, A. (Caledonian), 1880 v E; (with Queen's Park), 1882 v W (2)

Russell, D. (Hearts), 1895 v E, Ni; (with Celtic), 1897 v W; 1898 v Ni; 1901 v W, Ni (6)

Russell, J. (Cambuslang), 1890 v Ni (1)

Russell, W. F. (Airdrieonians), 1924 v W; 1925 v E (2)

Rutherford, E. (Rangers), 1948 v F (1)

St John, I. (Motherwell), 1959 v WG; 1960 v E, Ni, W, Pol, A; 1961 v E; (with Liverpool), 1962 v Ni, W, E, Cz (2), U; 1963 v W, Ni, E, N, Ei (sub), Sp; 1964 v Ni; 1965 v E (21)

Sawers, W. (Dundee), 1895 v W (1)

Scarff, P. (Celtic), 1931 v Ni (1)

Schaedler, E. (Hibernian), 1974 v WG (1)

Scott, A. S. (Rangers), 1957 v Ni, Y, WG; 1958 v W, Sw; 1959 v P; 1962 v Ni, W, E, Cz, U; (with Everton), 1964 v W, N; 1965 v Fi; 1966 v P, Br (16)

Scott, J. (Hibernian), 1966 v Ho (1)

Scott, J. (Dundee), 1971 v D (sub), USSR (2)

Scott, M. (Airdrieonians), 1898 v W (1)

Scott, R. (Airdrieonians), 1894 v Ni (1)

Scoular, J. (Portsmouth), 1951 v D, F, A; 1952 v E, USA, D, Se; 1953 v W, Ni (9)

Sellar, W. (Battlefield), 1885 v E; 1886 v E; 1887 v E, W; 1888 v E; (with Queen's Park), 1891 v E; 1892 v E; 1893 v E, Ni (9)

Semple, W. (Cambuslang), 1886 v W (1)

Shankly, W. (Preston NE), 1938 v E; 1939 v E, W, Ni, H (5)

Sharp, G. M. (Everton), 1985 v Ic; 1986 v W, Aus (2 sub), Is, R, U; 1987 v Ei; 1988 v Bel (sub), Bul, L, Ma (12)

Sharp, J. (Dundee), 1904 v W; (with Woolwich Arsenal), 1907 v W, E; 1908 v E; (with Fulham), 1909 v W (5)

Shaw, D. (Hibernian), 1947 v W, Ni; 1948 v E, Bel, Sw, F; 1949 v W, Ni (8)

Shaw, F. W. (Pollokshields Ath), 1884 v E, W (2)

Shaw, J. (Rangers), 1947 v E, Bel, L; 1948 v Ni (4)

Shearer, R. (Rangers), 1961 v E, Ei (2), Cz (4)

Sillars, D. C. (Queen's Park), 1891 v Ni; 1892 v E; 1893 v W; 1894 v E; 1895 v W (5)

Simpson, J. (Third Lanark), 1895 v E, W, Ni (3)

Simpson, J. (Rangers), 1935 v E, W, Ni; 1936 v E, W, Ni; 1937 v G, E, W, Ni, A, Cz; 1938 v W, Ni (14)

Simpson, N. (Aberdeen), 1983 v Ni; 1984 v F (sub); 1987 v E; 1988 v E (4)

Simpson, R. C. (Celtic), 1967 v E, USSR; 1968 v Ni, E; 1969 v A (5)

Sinclair, G. L. (Hearts), 1910 v Ni; 1912 v W, Ni (3)

Sinclair, J. W. E. (Leicester C), 1966 v P (1)

Skene, L. H. (Queen's Park), 1904 v W (1)

Sloan, T. (Third Lanark), 1904 v W (1)

Smellie, R. (Queen's Park), 1887 v Ni; 1888 v W; 1889 v E; 1891 v E; 1893 v E, Ni (6)

Smith, A. (Rangers), 1898 v E; 1900 v E, Ni, W; 1901 v E, Ni, W; 1902 v E, Ni, W; 1903 v E, Ni, W; 1904 v Ni; 1905 v W; 1906 v E, Ni; 1907 v W; 1911 v E, Ni (20)

Smith, D. (Aberdeen), 1966 v Ho; (with Rangers), 1968 v Ho (2)

Smith, G. (Hibernian), 1947 v E, Ni; 1948 v W, Bel, Sw, F; 1952 v E, USA; 1955 v P, Y, A, H; 1956 v E, Ni, W; 1957 v Sp (2), Sw (18)

Smith, H. G. (Hearts), 1988 v S.Ar (sub); 1992 v Ni, Ca (3)

Smith, J. (Rangers), 1935 v Ni; 1938 v Ni (2)

Smith, J. (Ayr U), 1924 v E (1)

Smith, J. (Aberdeen), 1968 v Ho (sub); (with Newcastle U), 1974 v WG, Ni (sub), W (sub) (4)

Smith, J. E. (Celtic), 1959 v H, P (2)

Smith, Jas (Queen's Park), 1872 v E (1)

Smith, John (Mauchline), 1877 v E, W; 1879 v E, W; (with Edinburgh University), 1880 v E; (with Queen's Park), 1881 v W, E; 1883 v E, W; 1884 v E (10)

Smith, N. (Rangers), 1897 v E; 1898 v W; 1899 v E, W, Ni; 1900 v E, W, Ni; 1901 v Ni, W; 1902 v E, Ni (12)

Smith, R. (Queen's Park), 1872 v E; 1873 v E (2)

Smith, T. M. (Kilmarnock), 1934 v E; (with Preston NE), 1938 v E (2)

Somers, P. (Celtic), 1905 v E, Ni; 1907 v Ni; 1909 v W (4)

Somers, W. S. (Third Lanark), 1879 v E, W; (with Queen's Park), 1880 v W (3)

Somerville, G. (Queen's Park), 1886 v E (1)

Souness, G. J. (Middlesbrough), 1975 v EG, Sp, Se; (with Liverpool), 1978 v Bul, W, E (sub), Ho; 1979 v A, N, W, Ni, E; 1980 v Pe, A, Bel, P, Ni; 1981 v P, Is (2); 1982 v Ni, P, Sp, W, E, Nz, Br, USSR; 1983 v EG, Sw, Bel, Sw, W, E, Ca (2 + 1 sub); 1984 v U, Ni, W; (with Sampdoria), 1985 v Y, Ic, Sp (2), W, E, Ic; 1986 v EG, Aus (2), R, E, D, WG (54)

Speedie, D. R. (Chelsea), 1985 v E; 1986 v W, EG (sub), Aus, E; (with Coventry C), 1989 v Y (sub), I (sub), Cy (1 + 1 sub), Ch (10)

Speedie, F. (Rangers), 1903 v E, W, Ni (3)

Speirs, J. H. (Rangers), 1908 v W (1)

Stanton, P. (Hibernian), 1966 v Ho; 1969 v Ni; 1970 v Ei, A; 1971 v D, Bel, P, USSR, D; 1972 v P, Bel, Ho, W; 1973 v W, Ni; 1974 v WG (16)

Stark, J. (Rangers), 1909 v E, Ni (2)

Steel, W. (Morton), 1947 v E, Bel, L; (with Derby Co), 1948 v F, E, W, Ni; 1949 v E, W, Ni, F; 1950 v E, W, Ni, Sw, P, F; (with Dundee), 1951 v W, Ni, E, A (2), D, F, Bel; 1952 v W; 1953 v W, E, Ni, Se (30)

Steele, D. M. (Huddersfield), 1923 v E, W, Ni (3)

Stein, C. (Rangers), 1969 v W, Ni, D, E, Cy (2); 1970 v A (sub), Ni (sub), W, E, Ei, WG; 1971 v D, USSR, Bel, D; 1972 v Cz (sub); (with Coventry C), 1973 v E (2 sub), W (sub), Ni (21)

Stephen, J. F. (Bradford), 1947 v W; 1948 v W (2)

Stevenson, G. (Motherwell), 1928 v W, Ni; 1930 v Ni, E, F; 1931 v E, W; 1932 v W, Ni; 1933 v Ni; 1934 v E; 1935 v Ni (12)

Stewart, A. (Queen's Park), 1888 v Ni; 1889 v W (2)

Stewart, A. (Third Lanark), 1894 v W (1)

Stewart, D. (Dumbarton), 1888 v Ni (1)

Stewart, D. (Queen's Park), 1893 v W; 1894 v Ni; 1897 v Ni (3)

Stewart, D. S. (Leeds U), 1978 v EG (1)

Stewart, G. (Hibernian), 1906 v W, E; (with Manchester C), 1907 v E, W (4)

Stewart, J. (Kilmarnock), 1977 v Ch (sub); (with Middlesbrough), 1979 v N (2)

Stewart, R. (West Ham U), 1981 v W, Ni, E; 1982 v Ni, P, W; 1984 v F; 1987 v Ei (2), L (10)

Stewart, W. E. (Queen's Park), 1898 v Ni; 1900 v Ni (2)

Storrier, D. (Celtic), 1899 v E, W, Ni (3)

Strachan, G. (Aberdeen), 1980 v Ni, W, E, Pol, H (sub); 1981 v Se, P; 1982 v Ni, P, Sp, Ho (sub), Nz, Br, USSR; 1983 v EG, Sw, Bel, Sw, Ni (sub), W, E, Ca (2 + 1 sub); 1984 v EG, Ni, E, F; (with Manchester U), 1985 v Sp (sub), E, Ic; 1986 v W, Aus, R, D, WG, U; 1987 v Bul, Ei (2); 1988 v H; 1989 v F (sub); (with Leeds U), 1990 v F; 1991 v USSR, Bul, Sm; 1992 v Sw, R, Ni, Fi (50)

Sturrock, P. (Dundee U), 1981 v W (sub), Ni, E (sub); 1982 v P, Ni (sub), W (sub), E (sub); 1983 v EG (sub),

Sw, Bel (sub), Ca (3); 1984 v W; 1985 v Y (sub); 1986 v Is (sub), Ho, D, U; 1987 v Bel (20)
Summers, W. (St Mirren), 1926 v E (1)
Symon, J. S. (Rangers), 1939 v H (1)

Tait, T. S. (Sunderland), 1911 v W (1)
Taylor, J. (Queen's Park), 1872 v E; 1873 v E; 1874 v E; 1875 v E; 1876 v E, W (6)
Taylor, J. D. (Dumbarton), 1892 v W; 1893 v W; 1894 v Ni; (with St Mirren), 1895 v Ni (4)
Taylor, W. (Hearts), 1892 v E (1)
Telfer, W. (Motherwell), 1933 v Ni; 1934 v Ni (2)
Telfer, W. D. (St Mirren), 1954 v W (1)
Templeton, R. (Aston Villa), 1902 v E; (with Newcastle U), 1903 v E, W; 1904 v E; (with Woolwich Arsenal), 1905 v W; (with Kilmarnock), 1908 v Ni; 1910 v E, Ni; 1912 v E, Ni; 1913 v W (11)
Thomson, A. (Arthurlie), 1886 v Ni (1)
Thomson, A. (Third Lanark), 1889 v W (1)
Thomson, A. (Airdrieonians), 1909 v Ni (1)
Thomson, A. (Celtic), 1926 v E; 1932 v F; 1933 v W (3)
Thomson, C. (Hearts), 1904 v Ni; 1905 v E, Ni, W; 1906 v W, Ni; 1907 v E, W, Ni; 1908 v E, W, Ni; (with Sunderland), 1909 v W; 1910 v E; 1911 v Ni; 1912 v E, W; 1913 v E, W; 1914 v E, Ni (21)
Thomson, C. (Sunderland), 1937 v Cz (1)
Thomson, D. (Dundee), 1920 v W (1)
Thomson, J. (Celtic), 1930 v F; 1931 v E, W, Ni (4)
Thomson, J. J. (Queen's Park), 1872 v E; 1873 v E; 1874 v E (3)
Thomson, J. R. (Everton), 1933 v W (1)
Thomson, R. (Celtic), 1932 v W (1)
Thomson, R. W. (Falkirk), 1927 v E (1)
Thomson, S. (Rangers), 1884 v W, Ni (2)
Thomson, W. (Dumbarton), 1892 v W; 1893 v W; 1898 v Ni, W (4)
Thomson, W. (Dundee), 1896 v W (1)
Thornton, W. (Rangers), 1947 v W, Ni; 1948 v E, Ni; 1949 v F; 1952 v D, Se (7)
Thomson, W. (St Mirren), 1980 v Ni; 1981 v Ni (sub + 1) 1982 v P; 1983 v Ni, Ca; 1984 v EG (7)
Toner, W. (Kilmarnock), 1959 v W, Ni (2)
Townsley, T. (Falkirk), 1926 v W (1)
Troup, A. (Dundee), 1920 v E; 1921 v W, Ni; 1922 v Ni; (with Everton), 1926 v E (5)
Turnbull, E. (Hibernian), 1948 v Bel, Sw; 1951 v A; 1958 v H, Pol, Y, Par, F (8)
Turner, T. (Arthurlie), 1884 v W (1)
Turner, W. (Pollokshields Ath), 1885 v Ni; 1886 v Ni (2)

Ure, J. F. (Dundee), 1962 v W, Cz; 1963 v W, Ni, E, A, N, Sp; (with Arsenal), 1964 v Ni, N; 1968 v Ni (11)
Urquhart, D. (Hibernian), 1934 v W (1)

Vallance, T. (Rangers), 1877 v E, W; 1878 v E; 1879 v E, W; 1881 v E, W (7)
Venters, A. (Cowdenbeath), 1934 v Ni; (with Rangers), 1936 v E; 1939 v E (3)

Waddell, T. S. (Queen's Park), 1891 v Ni; 1892 v E; 1893 v E, Ni; 1895 v E, Ni (6)
Waddell, W. (Rangers), 1947 v W; 1949 v E, W, Ni, F; 1950 v E, Ni; 1951 v E, D, F, Bel, A; 1952 v Ni, W; 1954 v Ni; 1955 v W, Ni (17)
Wales, H. M. (Motherwell), 1933 v W (1)
Walker, A. (Celtic), 1988 v Co (sub) (1)
Walker, F. (Third Lanark), 1922 v W (1)
Walker, G. (St Mirren), 1930 v F; 1931 v Ni, A, Sw (4)
Walker, J. (Hearts), 1895 v Ni; 1897 v W; 1898 v Ni; (with Rangers), 1904 v W, Ni (5)
Walker, J. (Swindon T), 1911 v E, W, Ni; 1912 v E, W, Ni; 1913 v E, W, Ni (9)

Walker, R. (Hearts), 1900 v E, Ni; 1901 v E, W; 1902 v E, W, Ni; 1903 v E, W, Ni; 1904 v E, W, Ni; 1905 v E, W, Ni; 1906 v Ni; 1907 v E, Ni; 1908 v E, W, Ni; 1909 v E, W; 1912 v E, W, Ni; 1913 v E, W (29)
Walker, T. (Hearts), 1935 v E, W; 1936 v E, W, Ni; 1937 v G, E, W, Ni, A, Cz; 1938 v E, W, Ni, Cz, Ho; 1939 v E, W, Ni, H (20)
Walker, W. (Clyde), 1909 v Ni; 1910 v Ni (2)
Wallace, I. A. (Coventry C), 1978 v Bul; (sub); 1979 v P (sub), W (3)
Wallace, W. S. B. (Hearts), 1965 v Ni; 1966 v E, Ho; (with Celtic), 1967 v E, USSR (sub); 1968 v Ni; 1969 v E (sub) (7)
Wardhaugh, J. (Hearts), 1955 v H; 1957 v Ni (2)
Wark, J. (Ipswich T), 1979 v W, Ni, E, Arg, N (sub); 1980 v Pe, A, Bel (2); 1981 v Is, Ni; 1982 v Se, Sp, Ho, Ni, Nz, Br, USSR; 1983 v EG, Sw (2), Ni, E (sub); 1984 v U, Bel, EG; (with Liverpool), E, F; 1985 v Y (29)
Watson, A. (Queen's Park), 1881 v E, W; 1882 v E (3)
Watson, J. (Sunderland), 1903 v E, W; 1904 v E; 1905 v E; (with Middlesbrough), 1909 v E, Ni (6)
Watson, J. (Motherwell), 1948 v Ni; (with Huddersfield T), 1954 v Ni (2)
Watson, J. A. K. (Rangers), 1878 v W (1)
Watson, P. R. (Blackpool), 1934 v A (1)
Watson, R. (Motherwell), 1971 v USSR (1)
Watson, W. (Falkirk), 1898 v W (1)
Watt, F. (Kilbirnie), 1889 v W, Ni; 1890 v W; 1891 v E (4)
Watt, W. W. (Queen's Park), 1887 v Ni (1)
Waugh, W. (Hearts), 1938 v Cz (1)
Weir, A. (Motherwell), 1959 v WG; 1960 v E, P, A, H, T (6)
Weir, J. (Third Lanark), 1887 v Ni (1)
Weir, J. B. (Queen's Park), 1872 v E; 1874 v E; 1875 v E; 1878 v W (4)
Weir, P. (St Mirren), 1980 v N (sub), W, Pol (sub); H; (with Aberdeen), 1983 v Sw; 1984 v Ni (6)
White, John (Albion R), 1922 v W; (with Hearts), 1923 v Ni (2)
White, J. A. (Falkirk), 1959 v WG, Ho, P; 1960 v Ni; (with Tottenham H), 1960 v W, Pol, A, T; 1961 v W; 1962 v Ni, W, E, Cz (2); 1963 v W, Ni, E; 1964 v Ni, W, E, WG (22)
White, W. (Bolton W), 1907 v E; 1908 v E (2)
Whitelaw, A. (Vale of Leven), 1887 v Ni; 1890 v W (2)
Whyte, D. (Celtic), 1988 v Bel (sub), L; 1989 v Ch (sub); 1992 v US (sub) (4)
Wilson, A. (Sheffield W), 1907 v E; 1908 v E; 1912 v E; 1913 v E, W; 1914 v Ni (6)
Wilson, A. (Portsmouth), 1954 v Fi (1)
Wilson, A. N. (Dunfermline), 1920 v E, W, Ni; 1921 v E, W, Ni; (with Middlesbrough), 1922 v E, W, Ni; 1923 v E, W, Ni (12)
Wilson, D. (Queen's Park), 1900 v W (1)
Wilson, D. (Oldham Ath), 1913 v E (1)
Wilson, D. (Rangers), 1961 v E, W, Ni, Ei (2), Cz; 1962 v Ni, W, E, Cz, U; 1963 v W, E, A, N, Ei, Sp; 1964 v E, WG; 1965 v Ni, E; Fi (22)
Wilson, G. W. (Hearts), 1904 v W; 1905 v E, Ni; 1906 v W; (with Everton), 1907 v E; (with Newcastle U), 1909 v E (6)
Wilson, Hugh, (Newmilns), 1890 v W; (with Sunderland), 1897 v E; (with Third Lanark), 1902 v W; 1904 v Ni (4)
Wilson, I. A. (Leicester C), 1987 v E, Br; (with Everton), 1988 v Bel, Bul, L (5)
Wilson, J. (Vale of Leven), 1888 v W; 1889 v E; 1890 v E; 1891 v E (4)
Wilson, P. (Celtic), 1926 v Ni; 1930 v F; 1931 v Ni; 1933 v E (4)
Wilson, P. (Celtic), 1975 v Sp (sub) (1)
Wilson, R. P. (Arsenal), 1972 v P, Ho (2)

Wiseman, W. (Queen's Park), 1927 v W; 1930 v Ni (2)

Wood, G. (Everton), 1979 v Ni, E, Arg (sub); (with Arsenal), 1982 v Ni (4)

Woodburn, W. A. (Rangers), 1947 v E, Bel, L; 1948 v W, Ni; 1949 v E, F; 1950 v E, W, Ni, P, F; 1951 v E, W, Ni, A (2), D, F, Bel; 1952 v E, W, Ni, USA (24)

Wotherspoon, D. N. (Queen's Park), 1872 v E; 1873 v E (2)

Wright, K. (Hibernian), 1992 v Ni (1)

Wright, T. (Sunderland), 1953 v W, Ni, E (3)

Wylie, T. G. (Rangers), 1890 v Ni (1)

Yeats, R. (Liverpool), 1965 v W; 1966 v I (2)

Yorston, B. C. (Aberdeen), I 931 v Ni (1)

Yorston, H. (Aberdeen), 1955 v W (1)

Young, A. (Hearts), 1960 v E, A (sub), H, T; 1961 v W, Ni; (with Everton), Ei; 1966 v P (8)

Young, A. (Everton), 1905 v E; 1907 v W (2)

Young, G. L. (Rangers), 1947 v E, Ni, Bel, L; 1948 v E, Ni, Bel, Sw, F; 1949 v E, W, Ni, F; 1950 v E, W, Ni, Sw, P, F; 1951 v E, W, Ni, A (2), D, F, Bel; 1952 v E, W, Ni, USA, D, Se; 1953 v W, E, Ni, Se; 1954 v Ni, W; 1955 v W, Ni, P, Y; 1956 v Ni, W, E, A; 1957 v E, Ni, W, Y, Sp, Sw (53)

Young, J. (Celtic), 1906 v Ni (1)

Younger, T. (Hibernian), 1955 v P, Y, A, H; 1956 v E, Ni, W, A; (with Liverpool), 1957 v E, Ni, W, Y, Sp (2), Sw, WG; 1958 v Ni, W, E, Sw, H, Pol, Y, Par (24)

WALES

Adams, H. (Berwyn R), 1882 v Ni, E; (with Druids), 1883 v Ni, E (4)

Aizlewood, M. (Charlton Ath), 1986 v S.Ar, Ca (2); 1987 v Fi; (with Leeds U), USSR, Fi (sub); 1988 v D (sub), Se, Ma, I; 1989 v Ho, Se (sub), WG; (with Bradford C), 1990 v Fi, WG, Ei, Cr; (with Bristol C), 1991 v D, Bel, L, Ei, Bel, Ic, Pol, WG; 1992 v Br, L, Ei, A, R, Ho, Arg, J (33)

Allchurch, I. J. (Swansea T), 1951 v E, Ni, P, Sw; 1952 v E, S, Ni, R of UK; 1953 v S, E, Ni, F, Y; 1954 v S, E, Ni, A; 1955 v S, E, Ni, Y; 1956 v E, S, Ni, A; 1957 v E, S; 1958 v Ni, Is (2), H (2), M, Sw, Br; (with Newcastle U), 1959 v E, S, Ni; 1960 v E, S; 1961 v Ni, H, Sp (2); 1962 v E, S, Br (2), M; (with Cardiff C), 1963 v S, E, Ni, H (2); 1964 v E; 1965 v S, E, Ni, Gr, I, USSR; 1966 (with Swansea T), v USSR, E, S, D, Br (2), Ch (68)

Allchurch, L. (Swansea T), 1955 v Ni; 1956 v A; 1958 v S, Ni, EG, Is; 1959 v S; (with Sheffield U), 1962 v S, Ni, Br; 1964 v E (11)

Allen, B. W. (Coventry C), 1951 v S, E (2)

Allen, M. (Watford), 1986 v S.Ar (sub), Ca (1 + 1 sub); (with Norwich C), 1989 v Is (sub); 1990 v Ho, WG; (with Millwall), Ei, Se, Cr (sub); 1991 v L (sub), Ei (sub); 1992 v A (12)

Arridge, S. (Bootle), 1892 v S, Ni; (with Everton), 1894 v Ni; 1895 v Ni; 1896 v E; (with New Brighton Tower), 1898 v E, Ni; 1899 v E (8)

Astley, D. J. (Charlton Ath), 1931 v Ni; (with Aston Villa), 1932 v E; 1933 v E, S, Ni; 1934 v E, S; 1935 v S; 1936 v E, Ni; (with Derby Co), 1939 v E, S; (with Blackpool), F (13)

Atherton, R. W. (Hibernian), 1899 v E, Ni; 1903 v E, S, Ni; (with Middlesbrough), 1904 v E, S, Ni; 1905 v Ni (9)

Bailiff, W. E. (Llanelly), 1913 v E, S, Ni; 1920 v Ni (4)

Baker, C. W. (Cardiff C), 1958 v M; 1960 v S, Ni; 1961 v S, E, Ei; 1962 v S (7)

Baker, W. G. (Cardiff C), 1948 v Ni (1)

Bamford, T. (Wrexham), 1931 v E, S, Ni; 1932 v Ni; 1933 v F (5)

Barnes, W. (Arsenal), 1948 v E, S, Ni; 1949 v E, S, Ni; 1950 v E, S, Ni, Bel; 1951 v E, S, Ni, P; 1952 v E, S, Ni, R of UK; 1954 v E, S; 1955 v S, Y (22)

Bartley, T. (Glossop NE), 1898 v E (1)

Bastock, A. M. (Shrewsbury), 1892 v Ni (1)

Beadles, G. H. (Cardiff C), 1925 v E, S (2)

Bell, W. S. (Shrewsbury Engineers), 1881 v E, S; (with Crewe Alex), 1886 v E, S, Ni (5)

Bennion, S. R. (Manchester U), 1926 v S; 1927 v S; 1928 v S, E, Ni; 1929 v S, Ni; 1930 v S; 1932 v Ni (10)

Berry, G. F. (Wolverhampton W), 1979 v WG; 1980 v Ei, WG (sub), T; (with Stoke C), 1983 v E (sub) (5)

Blackmore, C. G. (Manchester U), 1985 v N (sub); 1986

v S (sub), H (sub), S.Ar, Ei, U; 1987 v Fi (2), USSR, Cz; 1988 v D (2), Cz, Y, Se, Ma, I; 1989 v Ho, Fi, Is, WG; 1990 v Fi, Ho, WG, Cr; 1991 v Bel, L; 1992 v Ei (sub), A, R (sub), Ho, Arg, J (33)

Blew, H. (Wrexham), 1899 v E, S, Ni; 1902 v S, Ni; 1903 v E, S; 1904 v E, S, Ni; 1905 v S, Ni; 1906 v E, S, Ni; 1907 v S; 1908 v E, S, Ni; 1909 v E, S; 1910 v E (22)

Boden, T. (Wrexham), 1880 v E (1)

Bodin, P. J. (Swindon T), 1990 v Cr; 1991 v D, Bel, L, Ei; (with C Palace), Bel, Ic, Pol, WG; 1992 v Br, G, L (sub); (with Swindon T), Ei (sub), Ho, Arg (15)

Boulter, L. M. (Brentford), 1939 v Ni (1)

Bowdler, H. E. (Shrewsbury), 1893 v S (1)

Bowdler, J. C. H. (Shrewsbury), 1890 v Ni; (with Wolverhampton W), 1891 v Ni, S; 1892 v Ni; (with Shrewsbury), 1894 v E (5)

Bowen, D. L. (Arsenal), 1955 v S, Y; 1957 v Ni, Cz, EG; 1958 v E, S, Ni, EG, Is (2), H (2), M, Se, Br; 1959 v E, S, Ni (19)

Bowen, E. (Druids), 1880 v S; 1883 v S (2)

Bowen, M. R. (Tottenham H), 1986 v Ca (2 sub); (with Norwich C), 1988 v Y (sub); 1989 v Fi (sub), Is, Se, WG (sub); 1990 v Fi (sub), Ho, WG, Se; 1992 v Br (sub), G, L, Ei, A, R, Ho (sub), J (19)

Bowsher, S. J. (Burnley), 1929 v Ni (1)

Boyle, T. (C Palace), 1981 v Ei, S (sub) (2)

Britten, T. J. (Parkgrove), 1878 v S; (with Presteigne), 1880 v S (2)

Brookes, S. J. (Llandudno), 1900 v E, Ni (2)

Brown, A. I. (Aberdare Ath), 1926 v Ni (1)

Bryan, T. (Oswestry), 1886 v E, Ni (2)

Buckland, T. (Bangor), 1899 v E (1)

Burgess, W. A. R. (Tottenham H), 1947 v E, S, Ni; 1948 v E, S; 1949 v E, S, Ni, P, Bel, Sw; 1950 v E, S, Ni, Bel; 1951 v S, Ni, P, Sw; 1952 v E, S, Ni, R of UK; 1953 v S, E, Ni, F, Y; 1954 v E, S, Ni, A (32)

Burke, T. (Wrexham), 1883 v E; 1884 v S; 1885 v E, S, Ni; (with Newton Heath), 1887 v E, S; 1888 v S (8)

Burnett, T. B. (Ruabon), 1877 v S (1)

Burton, A. D. (Norwich C), 1963 v Ni, H; (with Newcastle U), 1964 v E; 1969 v S, E, Ni, I, EG; 1972 v Cz (9)

Butler, J. (Chirk), 1893 v E, S, Ni (3)

Butler, W. T. (Druids), 1900 v S, Ni (2)

Cartwright, L. (Coventry C), 1974 v E (sub), S, Ni; 1976 v S (sub); 1977 v WG (sub); (with Wrexham), 1978 v Ir (sub); 1979 v Ma (7)

Carty, T. — see McCarthy — (Wrexham)

Challen, J. B. (Corinthians), 1887 v E, S; 1888 v E; (with Wellingborough GS), 1890 v E (4)

Chapman, T. (Newtown), 1894 v E, S, Ni; 1895 v S, Ni; (with Manchester C), 1896 v E; 1897 v E (7)

Charles, J. M. (Swansea C), 1981 v Cz, T (sub), S (sub), USSR (sub); 1982 v Ic; 1983 v N (sub), Y (sub), Bul (sub), S, Ni, Br; 1984 v Bul (sub); (with QPR), Y (sub), S; (with Oxford U), 1985 v Ic (sub), Sp, Ic; 1986 v Ei; 1987 v Fi (19)

Charles, M. (Swansea T), 1955 v Ni; 1956 v E, S, A; 1957 v E, Ni, Cz (2), EG; 1958 v E, S, EG, Is (2), H (2), M, Se, Br; 1959 v E, S; (with Arsenal), 1961 v Ni, H, Sp (2); 1962 v E, S; (with Cardiff C), 1962 v Br, Ni; 1963 v S, H (31)

Charles, W. J. (Leeds U), 1950 v Ni; 1951 v Sw; 1953 v Ni, F, Y; 1954 v E, S, Ni, A; 1955 v S, E, Ni, Y; 1956 v E, S, A, Ni; 1957 v E, S, Ni, Cz (2), EG; (with Juventus), 1958 v Is (2), H (2) M, Se; 1960 v S; 1962 v E, Br (2), M; (with Leeds U), 1963 v S; (with Cardiff C), 1964 v S; 1965 v S, USSR (38)

Clarke, R. J. (Manchester C), 1949 v E; 1950 v S, Ni, Bel; 1951 v E, S, Ni, P, Sw; 1952 v S, E, Ni, R of UK; 1953 v S, E; 1954 v E, S, Ni; 1955 v Y, S, E; 1956 v Ni (22)

Coleman, C. (C Palace), 1992 v A (sub) (1)

Collier, D. J. (Grimsby T), 1921 v S (1)

Collins, W. S. (Llanelly), 1931 v S (1)

Conde, C. (Chirk), 1884 v E, S, Ni (3)

Cook, F. C. (Newport Co), 1925 v E, S; (with Portsmouth), 1928 v E, S; 1930 v E, S, Ni; 1932 v E (8)

Crompton, W. (Wrexham), 1931 v E, S, Ni (3)

Cross, E. A. (Wrexham), 1876 v S; 1877 v S (2)

Cross, K. (Druids), 1879 v S; 1881 v E, S (3)

Crowe, V. H. (Aston Villa), 1959 v E, Ni; 1960 v E, Ni; 1961 v S, E, Ni, Ei, H, Sp (2); 1962 v E, S, Br, M; 1963 v H (16)

Cumner, R. H. (Arsenal), 1939 v E, S, Ni (3)

Curtis, A. (Swansea C), 1976 v E, Y (sub), S, Ni, Y (sub), E; 1977 v WG, S (sub), Ni (sub); 1978 v WG, E, S; 1979 v WG, S; (with Leeds U), E, Ni, Ma; 1980 v Ei, WG, T; (with Swansea C), 1982 v Cz, Ic, USSR, Sp, E, S, Ni; 1983 v N; 1984 v R (sub); (with Southampton), S; 1985 v Sp, N (1 + 1 sub); 1986 v H; (with Cardiff C), 1987 v USSR (35)

Curtis, E. R. (Cardiff C), 1928 v S; (with Birmingham), 1932 v S; 1934 v Ni (3)

Daniel, R. W. (Arsenal), 1951 v E, Ni, P; 1952 v E, S, Ni, R of UK; 1953 v S, E, Ni, F, Y; (with Sunderland), 1954 v E, S, Ni; 1955 v E, Ni; 1957 v S, E, Ni, Cz (21)

Darvell, S. (Oxford University), 1897 v S, Ni (2)

Davies, A. (Wrexham), 1876 v S; 1877 v S (2)

Davies, A. (Druids), 1904 v S; (with Middlesbrough), 1905 v S (2)

Davies, A. (Manchester U), 1983 v Ni, Br; 1984 v E, Ni; 1985 v Ic (2), N; (with Newcastle U), 1986 v H; (with Swansea C), 1988 v Ma, I; 1989 v Ho; (with Bradford C), 1990 v Fi, Ei (13)

Davies, A. O. (Barmouth), 1885 v Ni; 1886 v E, S; (with Swifts), 1887 v E, S; 1888 v E, Ni; (with Wrexham), 1889 v S; (with Crewe Alex), 1890 v E (9)

Davies, A. T. (Shrewsbury), 1891 v Ni (1)

Davies, C. (Charlton Ath), 1972 v R (sub) (1)

Davies, D. (Bolton W), 1904 v S, Ni; 1908 v E (sub) (3)

Davies, D. C. (Brecon), 1899 v Ni; (with Hereford), 1900 v Ni (2)

Davies, D. W. (Treharris), 1912 v Ni; (with Oldham Ath), 1913 v Ni (2)

Davies, E. Lloyd (Stoke C), 1904 v E; 1907 v E, S, Ni; (with Northampton T), 1908 v S; 1909 v Ni; 1910 v Ni; 1911 v E, S; 1912 v E, S; 1913 v E, S; 1914 v Ni, E, S (16)

Davies, E. R. (Newcastle U), 1953 v S, E; 1954 v E, S; 1958 v E, EG (6)

Davies, G. (Fulham), 1980 v T, Ic; 1982 v Sp (sub), F (sub); 1983 v E, Bul, S, Ni, Br; 1984 v R (sub), S (sub), E, Ni; 1985 v Ic; (with Manchester C), 1986 v S.Ar, Ei (16)

Davies, Rev. H. (Wrexham), 1928 v Ni (1)

Davies, Idwal (Liverpool Marine), 1923 v S (1)

Davies, J. E. (Oswestry), 1885 v E (1)

Davies, Jas (Wrexham), 1878 v S (1)

Davies, John (Wrexham), 1879 v S (1)

Davies, Jos (Newton Heath), 1888 v E, S, Ni; 1889 v S; 1890 v E; (with Wolverhampton W), 1892 v E; 1893 v E (7)

Davies, Jos (Everton), 1889 v S, Ni; (with Chirk), 1891 v Ni; (with Ardwick), v E, S; (with Sheffield U), 1895 v E, S, Ni; (with Manchester C), 1896 v E; (with Millwall), 1897 v E; (with Reading), 1900 v E (11)

Davies, J. P. (Druids), 1883 v E, Ni (2)

Davies, Ll. (Wrexham), 1907 v Ni; 1910 v Ni, S, E; (with Everton), 1911 v S, Ni; 1912 v Ni, S, E; 1913 v Ni, S, E; 1914 v Ni (13)

Davies, L. S. (Cardiff C), 1922 v E, S, Ni; 1923 v E, S, Ni; 1924 v E, S, Ni; 1925 v S, Ni; 1926 v E, Ni; 1927 v E, Ni; 1928 v S, Ni, E; 1929 v S, Ni, E; 1930 v E, S (23)

Davies, O. (Wrexham), 1890 v S (1)

Davies, R. (Wrexham), 1883 v Ni; 1884 v Ni; 1885 v Ni (3)

Davies, R. (Druids), 1885 v E (1)

Davies, R. O. (Wrexham), 1892 v Ni, E (2)

Davies, R. T. (Norwich C), 1964 v Ni; 1965 v E; 1966 v Br (2), Ch; (with Southampton), 1967 v S, E, Ni; 1968 v S, Ni, WG; 1969 v S, E, Ni, I, WG, R of UK; 1970 v E, S, Ni; 1971 v Cz, S, E, Ni; 1972 v R, E, S, N; (with Portsmouth), 1974 v E (29)

Davies, R. W. (Bolton W), 1964 v E; 1965 v E, S, Ni, D, Gr, USSR; 1966 v E, S, Ni, USSR, D, Br (2), Ch (sub); 1967 v S; (with Newcastle U), E; 1968 v S, Ni, WG; 1969 v S, E, Ni, I; 1970 v EG; 1971 v R, Cz; (with Manchester C), 1972 v E, S, Ni; (with Manchester U), 1973 v E, S (sub), Ni; (with Blackpool), 1974 v Pol (34)

Davies, Stanley (Preston NE), 1920 v E, S, Ni; (with Everton), 1921 v E, S, Ni; (with WBA), 1922 v E, S, Ni; 1923 v S; 1925 v S, Ni; 1926 v S, E, Ni; 1927 v S; 1928 v S; (with Rotherham U), 1930 v Ni (18)

Davies, T. (Oswestry), 1886 v E (1)

Davies, T. (Druids), 1903 v E, Ni, S; 1904 v S (4)

Davies, W. (Wrexham), 1884 v Ni (1)

Davies, W. (Swansea T), 1924 v E, S, Ni; (with Cardiff C), 1925 v E, S, Ni; 1926 v E, S, Ni; 1927 v S; 1928 v Ni; (with Notts Co), 1929 v E, S, Ni; 1930 v E, S, Ni (17)

Davies, William (Wrexham), 1903 v Ni; 1905 v Ni; (with Blackburn R), 1908 v E, S; 1909 v E, S, Ni; 1911 v E, S, Ni; 1912 v Ni (11)

Davies, W. C. (C Palace), 1908 v S; (with WBA), 1909 v E; 1910 v S; (with C Palace), 1914 v E (4)

Davies, W. D. (Everton), 1975 v H, L, S, E, Ni; 1976 v Y (2), E, Ni; 1977 v WG, S (2), Cz, E, Ni; 1978 v K; (with Wrexham), S, Cz, WG, Ir, E, S, Ni; 1979 v Ma, T, WG S, E, Ni, Ma; 1980 v Ei, WG, T, E, S, Ni, Ic; 1981 v T, Cz, Ei, T, S, E, USSR; (with Swansea C), 1982 v Cz, Ic, USSR, Sp, E, S, F; 1983 v Y (52)

Davies, W. H. (Oswestry), 1876 v S; 1877 v S; 1879 v E; 1880 v E (4)

Davies, W. O. (Millwall Ath), 1913 v E, S, Ni; 1914 v S, Ni (5)

Davis, G. (Wrexham), 1978 v Ir, E (sub), Ni (3)

Day, A. (Tottenham H), 1934 v Ni (1)

Deacy, N. (PSV Eindhoven), 1977 v Cz, S, E, Ni; 1978 v K (sub), S (sub), Cz (sub), WG, Ir, S (sub), Ni; (with Beringen), 1979 v T (12)

Dearson, D. J. (Birmingham), 1939 v S, Ni, F (3)

Derrett, S. C. (Cardiff C), 1969 v S, WG; 1970 v I; 1971 v Fi (4)

Dewey, F. T. (Cardiff Corinthians), 1931 v E, S (2)

Dibble, A. (Luton T), 1986 v Ca (1 + 1 sub); (with Manchester C), 1989 v Is (3)

Doughty, J. (Druids), 1886 v S; (with Newton Heath), 1887 v S, Ni; 1888 v E, S, Ni; 1889 v S; 1890 v E (8)

Doughty, R. (Newton Heath and Druids), 1888 v S, Ni (2)

Durban, A. (Derby Co), 1966 v Br (sub); 1967 v Ni; 1968 v E, S, Ni, WG; 1969 v EG, S, E, Ni, WG; 1970 v E, S, Ni, EG, I; 1971 v R, S, E, Ni, Cz, Fi; 1972 v Fi, Cz, E, S, Ni (27)

Dwyer, P. (Cardiff C), 1978 v Ir, E, S, Ni; 1979 v T, S, E, Ni, Ma (sub); 1980 v WG (10)

Edwards; C. (Wrexham), 1878 v S (1)

Edwards, G. (Birmingham C), 1947 v E, S, Ni; 1948 v E, S, Ni; (with Cardiff C), 1949 v Ni, P, Bel, Sw; 1950 v E, S (12)

Edwards, H. (Wrexham Civil Service), 1878 v S; 1880 v E; 1882 v E, S; 1883 v S; 1884 v Ni; 1887 v Ni (7)

Edwards, J. H. (Wanderers), 1876 v S (1)

Edwards, J. H. (Oswestry), 1895 v Ni; 1897 v E, Ni (3)

Edwards, J. H. (Aberystwyth), 1898 v Ni (1)

Edwards, L. T. (Charlton Ath), 1957 v Ni, EG (2)

Edwards, R. I. (Chester), 1978 v K (sub); 1979 v Ma, WG; (with Wrexham), 1980 v T (sub) (4)

Edwards, T. (Linfield), 1932 v S (1)

Egan, W. (Chirk), 1892 v S (1)

Ellis, B. (Motherwell), 1932 v E; 1933 v E, S; 1934 v S; 1936 v E; 1937 v S (6)

Ellis, E. (Nunhead), 1931 v E; (with Oswestry), S; 1932 v Ni (3)

Emanuel, W. J. (Bristol C), 1973 v E (sub), Ni (sub) (2)

England, H. M. (Blackburn R), 1962 v Ni, Br, M; 1963 v Ni, H; 1964 v E, S, Ni; 1965 v E, D, Gr (2), USSR, Ni, I; 1966 v E, S, Ni, USSR, D; (with Tottenham H), 1967 v S, E; 1968 v E, Ni, WG; 1969 v EG; 1970 v R of UK, EG, E, S, Ni, I; 1971 v E; 1972 v Fi, E, S, Ni; 1973 v E (3), S; 1974 v Pol; 1975 v H, L (44)

Evans, B. C. (Swansea C), 1972 v Fi, Cz; 1973 v E (2), Pol, S; (with Hereford U), 1974 v Pol (7)

Evans, D. G. (Reading), 1926 v Ni; 1927 v Ni, E; (with Huddersfield T), 1929 v S (4)

Evans, H. P. (Cardiff C), 1922 v E, S, Ni; 1924 v E, S, Ni (6)

Evans, I. (Crystal Palace), 1976 v A, E, Y (2), E, Ni; 1977 v WG, S (2), Cz, E, Ni; 1978 v K (13)

Evans, J. (Oswestry), 1893 v Ni; 1894 v E, Ni (3)

Evans, J. (Cardiff C), 1912 v Ni; 1913 v Ni; 1914 v S; 1920 v S, Ni; 1922 v Ni; 1923 v E, Ni (8)

Evans, J. H. (Southend U), 1922 v E, S, Ni; 1923 v S (4)

Evans, Len (Aberdare Ath), 1927 v Ni; (with Cardiff C), 1931 v E, S; (with Birmingham), 1934 v Ni (4)

Evans, M. (Oswestry), 1884 v E (1)

Evans, R. (Clapton), 1902 v Ni (1)

Evans, R. E. (Wrexham), 1906 v E, S; (with Aston Villa), Ni; 1907 v E; 1908 v E, S; (with Sheffield U), 1909 v S; 1910 v E, S, Ni (10)

Evans, R. O. (Wrexham), 1902 v Ni; 1903 v E, S, Ni; (with Blackburn R), 1908 v Ni; (with Coventry C), 1911 v E, Ni; 1912 v E, S, Ni (10)

Evans, R. S. (Swansea T), 1964 v Ni (1)

Evans T. J. (Clapton Orient), 1927 v S; 1928 v E, S; (with Newcastle U), Ni (4)

Evans, W. (Tottenham H), 1933 v Ni; 1934 v E, S; 1935 v E; 1936 v E, Ni (6)

Evans, W. A. W. (Oxford University), 1876 v S; 1877 v S (2)

Evans, W. G. (Bootle), 1890 v E; 1891 v E; (with Aston Villa), 1892 v E (3)

Evelyn, E. C. (Crusaders), 1887 v E (1)

Eyton-Jones, J. A. (Wrexham), 1883 v Ni; 1884 v Ni, E, S (4)

Farmer, G. (Oswestry), 1885 v E, S (2)

Felgate, D. (Lincoln C), 1984 v R (sub) (1)

Finnigan, R. J. (Wrexham), 1930 v Ni (1)

Flynn, B. (Burnley), 1975 v L (2 sub), H (sub), S, E, Ni;

1976 v A, E, Y (2), E, Ni; 1977 v WG (sub), S (2), Cz, E, Ni; 1978 v K (2), S; (with Leeds U), Cz, WG, Ir (sub), E, S, Ni; 1979 v Ma, T, S, E, Ni, Ma; 1980 v Ei, WG, E, S, Ni, Ic; 1981 v T, Cz, Ei, T, S, E, USSR; 1982 v Cz, USSR, E, S, Ni, F; 1983 v N; (with Burnley), v Y, E, Bul, S, Ni, Br; 1984 v N, R, Bul, Y, S, N, Is (66)

Ford, T. (Swansea T), 1947 v S; (with Aston Villa), 1947 v Ni; 1948 v S, Ni; 1949 v E, S, Ni, P, Bel, Sw; 1950 v E, S, Ni, Bel; 1951 v S; (with Sunderland), 1951 v E, Ni, P, Sw; 1952 v E, S, Ni, R of UK; 1953 v S, E, Ni, F, Y; (with Cardiff C), 1954 v A; 1955 v S, E, Ni, Y; 1956 v S, Ni, E, A; 1957 v S (38)

Foulkes, H. E. (WBA), 1932 v Ni (1)

Foulkes, W. I. (Newcastle U), 1952 v E, S, Ni, R of UK; 1953 v E, S, F, Y; 1954 v E, S, Ni (11)

Foulkes, W. T. (Oswestry), 1884 v Ni; 1885 v S (2)

Fowler, J. (Swansea T), 1925 v E; 1926 v E, Ni; 1927 v S; 1928 v S; 1929 v E (6)

Garner, J. (Aberystwyth), 1896 v S (1)

Giggs, R. J. (Manchester U), 1992 v G (sub), L (sub), R (sub) (3)

Giles, D. (Swansea C), 1980 v E, S, Ni, Ic; 1981 v T, Cz, T (sub), E (sub), USSR (sub); (with C Palace), 1982 v Sp (sub); 1983 v Ni (sub), Br (12)

Gillam, S. G. (Wrexham), 1889 v S, Ni; (with Shrewsbury T), 1890 v E, Ni; (with Clapton), 1894 v S (5)

Glascodine, G. (Wrexham), 1879 v E (1)

Glover, E. M. (Grimsby T), 1932 v S; 1934 v Ni; 1936 v S; 1937 v E, S, Ni; 1939 v Ni (7)

Godding, G. (Wrexham), 1923 v S, Ni (2)

Godfrey, B. C. (Preston NE), 1964 v Ni; 1965 v D, I (3)

Goodwin, U. (Ruthin), 1881 v E (1)

Goss, J. (Norwich C), 1991 v Ic, Pol (sub); 1992 v A (3)

Gough, R. T. (Oswestry White Star), 1883 v S (1)

Gray, A. (Oldham Ath), 1924 v E, S, Ni; 1925 v E, S, Ni; 1926 v E, S; 1927 v S; (with Manchester C), 1928 v E, S; 1929 v E, S, Ni; (with Manchester Central), 1930 v S; (with Tranmere R), 1932 v E, S, Ni; (with Chester), 1937 v E, S, Ni; 1938 v E, S, Ni (24)

Green, A. W. (Aston Villa), 1901 v Ni; (with Notts Co), 1903 v E, 1904 v S, Ni, 1906 v Ni, E; (with Nottingham F), 1907 v E; 1908 v S (8)

Green, C. R. (Birmingham C), 1965 v USSR, I; 1966 v E, S, USSR, Br (2); 1967 v E; 1968 v E, S, Ni, WG; 1969 v S, I, Ni (sub) (15)

Green, G. H. (Charlton Ath), 1938 v Ni; 1939 v E, Ni, F (4)

Grey, Dr W. (Druids), 1876 v S; 1878 v S (2)

Griffiths, A. T. (Wrexham), 1971 v Cz (sub); 1975 v A, H (2), L (2), E, Ni; 1976 v A, E, S, E (sub), Ni, Y (2); 1977 v WG, S (17)

Griffiths, F. J. (Blackpool), 1900 v E, S (2)

Griffiths, G. (Chirk), 1887 v Ni (1)

Griffiths, J. H. (Swansea T), 1953 v Ni (1)

Griffiths, L. (Wrexham), 1902 v S (1)

Griffiths, M. W. (Leicester C), 1947 v Ni; 1949 v P, Bel; 1950 v E, S, Bel; 1951 v E, Ni, P, Sw; 1954 v A (11)

Griffiths, P. (Chirk), 1884 v E, Ni; 1888 v E; 1890 v S, Ni; 1891 v Ni (6)

Griffiths, P. H. (Everton), 1932 v S (1)

Griffiths, T. P. (Everton), 1927 v E, Ni; 1929 v E; 1930 v E; 1931 v Ni; 1932 v Ni, S, E; (with Bolton W), 1933 v F, E, S, Ni; (with Middlesbrough), 1934 v E, S; 1935 v E, Ni; 1936 v S; (with Aston Villa), Ni; 1937 v E, S, Ni (21)

Hall, G. D. (Chelsea), 1988 v Y (sub), Ma, I; 1989 v Ho, Fi, Is; 1990 v Ei; 1991 v Ei; 1992 v A (sub) (9)

Hallam, J. (Oswestry), 1889 v E (1)

Hanford, H. (Swansea T), 1934 v Ni; 1935 v S; 1936 v E; (with Sheffield W), 1936 v Ni; 1938 v E, S; 1939 v F (7)

Harrington, A. C. (Cardiff C), 1956 v Ni; 1957 v E, S; 1958 v S, Ni, Is (2); 1961 v S, E; 1962 v E, S (11)

Harris, C. S. (Leeds U), 1976 v E, S; 1978 v WG, Ir, E, S, Ni; 1979 v Ma, T, WG, E (sub), Ma; 1980 v Ni (sub), Ic (sub); 1981 v T, Cz (sub), Ei, T, S, E, USSR; 1982 v Cz, Ic, E (sub) (24)

Harris, W. C. (Middlesbrough), 1954 v A; 1957 v EG, Cz; 1958 v E, S, EG (6)

Harrison, W. C. (Wrexham), 1899 v E; 1900 v E, S, Ni; 1901 v Ni (5)

Hayes, A. (Wrexham), 1890 v Ni; 1894 v Ni (2)

Hennessey, W. T. (Birmingham C), 1962 v Ni, Br (2); 1963 v S, E, H (2); 1964 v E, S; 1965 v S, E, D, Gr, USSR; 1966 v E, USSR; (with Nottingham F), 1966 v S, Ni, D, Br (2), Ch; 1967 v S, E; 1968 v E, S, Ni; 1969 v WG, EG, R of UK, EG; (with Derby Co), 1970 v E, S, Ni; 1972 v Fi, Cz, E, S; 1973 v E (39)

Hersee, A. M. (Bangor), 1886 v S, Ni (2)

Hersee, R. (Llandudno), 1886 v Ni (1)

Hewitt, R. (Cardiff C), 1958 v Ni, Is, Se, H, Br (5)

Hewitt, T. J. (Wrexham), 1911 v E, S, Ni; (with Chelsea), 1913 v E, S, Ni; (with South Liverpool), 1914 v E, S (8)

Heywood, D. (Druids), 1879 v E (1)

Hibbott, H. (Newtown Excelsior), 1880 v E, S; (with Newtown), 1885 v S (3)

Higham, G. G. (Oswestry), 1878 v S; 1879 v E (2)

Hill, M. R. (Ipswich T), 1972 v Cz, R (2)

Hockey, T. (Sheffield U), 1972 v Fi, R; 1973 v E (2); (with Norwich C), Pol, S, E, Ni; (with Aston Villa), 1974 v Pol (9)

Hoddinott, T. F. (Watford), 1921 v E, S (2)

Hodges, G. (Wimbledon), 1984 v N (sub), Is (sub); 1987 v USSR, Fi, Cz; (with Newcastle U), 1988 v D (with Watford), D (sub), Cz (sub), Se, Ma (sub), I (sub); 1990 v Se, Cr; (with Sheffield U), 1992 v Br (sub), Ei (sub), A (16)

Hodgkinson, A. V. (Southampton), 1908 v Ni (1)

Holden, A. (Chester C), 1984 v Is (sub) (1)

Hole, B. G. (Cardiff C), 1963 v Ni; 1964 v Ni; 1965 v S, E, Ni, D, Gr (2), USSR, I; 1966 v E, S, Ni, USSR, D, Br (2), Ch; (with Blackburn R), 1967 v S, E, Ni; 1968 v E, S, Ni, WG; (with Aston Villa), 1969 v I, WG, EG; 1970 v I; (with Swansea C), 1971 v R (30)

Hole, W. J. (Swansea T), 1921 v Ni; 1922 v E; 1923 v E, Ni; 1928 v E, S, Ni; 1929 v E, S (9)

Hollins, D. M. (Newcastle U), 1962 v Br (sub), M; 1963 v Ni, H; 1964 v E; 1965 v Ni, Gr, I; 1966 v S, D, Br (11)

Hopkins, I. J. (Brentford), 1935 v S, Ni; 1936 v E, Ni; 1937 v E, S, Ni; 1938 v E, Ni; 1939 v E, S, Ni (12)

Hopkins, J. (Fulham), 1983 v Ni, Br; 1984 v N, R, Bul, Y, S, E, Ni, N, Is; 1985 v Ic (1 + 1 sub), N; (with C Palace), 1990 v Ho, Cr (16)

Hopkins, M. (Tottenham H), 1956 v Ni; 1957 v Ni, S, E, Cz (2), EG; 1958 v S, Ni, EG, Is (2), H (2), M, Se, Br; 1959 v E, S, Ni; 1960 v E, S; 1961 v Ni, H, Sp (2); 1962 v Ni, Br (2), M; 1963 v S, Ni, H (34)

Horne, B. (Portsmouth), 1988 v D (sub), Y, Se (sub), Ma, I; 1989 v Ho, Fi, Is; (with Southampton), Se, WG; 1990 v WG (sub), Ei, Se, Cr; 1991 v D, Bel (2), L, Ei, Ic, Pol, WG; 1992 v Br, G, L, Ei, A, R, Ho, Arg, J (31)

Howell, E. G. (Builth), 1888 v Ni; 1890 v E; 1891 v E (3)

Howells, R. G. (Cardiff C), 1954 v E, S (2)

Hugh, A. R. (Newport Co), 1930 v Ni (1)

Hughes, A. (Rhos), 1894 v E, S (2)

Hughes, A. (Chirk), 1907 v Ni (1)

Hughes, C. M. (Luton T), 1992 v Ho (sub) (1)

Hughes, E. (Everton), 1899 v S, Ni; (with Tottenham H), 1901 v E, S; 1902 v Ni; 1904 v E, Ni, S; 1905 v E, Ni, S; 1906 v E, Ni; 1907 v E (14)

Hughes, E. (Wrexham), 1906 v S; (with Nottingham F), 1906 v Ni; 1908 v S, E; 1910 v Ni, E, S; 1911 v Ni, E,

S; (with Wrexham), 1912 v Ni, E, S; (with Manchester C), 1913 v E, S; 1914 v N (16)

Hughes, F. W. (Northwich Victoria), 1882 v E, Ni; 1883 v E, Ni, S; 1884 v S (6)

Hughes, I. (Luton T), 1951 v E, Ni, P, Sw (4)

Hughes, J. (Cambridge University), 1877 v S; (with Aberystwyth), 1879 v S (2)

Hughes, J. (Liverpool), 1905 v E, S, Ni (3)

Hughes, J. I. (Blackburn R), 1935 v Ni (1)

Hughes, L. M. (Manchester U), 1984 v E, Ni; 1985 v Ic, Sp, Ic, N, S, Sp, N; 1986 v S, H, U; (with Barcelona), 1987 v USSR, Cz; 1988 v D (2), Cz, Se, Ma, I; (with Manchester U), 1989 v Ho, Fi, Is, Se, WG; 1990 v Fi, WG, Cr; 1991 v D, Bel (2), L, Ic, Pol, WG; 1992 v Br, G, L, Ei, R, Ho, Arg, J (43)

Hughes, P. W. (Bangor), 1887 v Ni; 1889 v Ni, E (3)

Hughes, W. (Bootle), 1891 v E; 1892 v S, Ni (3)

Hughes, W. A. (Blackburn R), 1949 v E, Ni, P, Bel, Sw (5)

Hughes, W. M. (Birmingham), 1938 v E, Ni, S; 1939 v E, Ni, S, F; 1947 v E, S, Ni (10)

Humphreys, J. V. (Everton), 1947 v Ni (1)

Humphreys, R. (Druids), 1888 v Ni (1)

Hunter, W. H. (North End, Belfast), 1887 v Ni (1)

Jackett, K. (Watford), 1983 v N, Y, E, Bul, S; 1984 v N, R, Y, S, Ni, N, Is; 1985 v Ic, Sp, Ic, N, S, Sp, N; 1986 v S, H, S.Ar, Ei, Ca (2); 1987 v Fi (2); 1988 v D, Cz, Y, Se (31)

Jackson, W. (St Helens Rec), 1899 v Ni (1)

James, E. (Chirk), 1893 v E, Ni; 1894 v E, S, Ni; 1898 v S, E; 1899 v Ni (8)

James, E. G. (Blackpool), 1966 v Br (2), Ch; 1967 v Ni; 1968 v S; 1971 v Cz, S, E, Ni (9)

James, L. (Burnley), 1972 v Cz, R, S (sub); 1973 v E (3), Pol, S, Ni; 1974 v Pol, E, S, Ni; 1975 v A, H (2), L (2), S, E, Ni; 1976 v A; (with Derby Co), S, E, Y (2), Ni; 1977 v WG, S (2), Cz, E, Ni; 1978 v K (2); (with QPR), WG; (with Burnley), 1979 v T; (with Swansea C), 1980 v E, S, Ni, Ic; 1981 v T, Ei, T, S, E; 1982 v Cz, Ic, USSR, E (sub), S, Ni, F; (with Sunderland), 1983 v E (sub) (54)

James, R. M. (Swansea C), 1979 v Ma, WG (sub), S, E, Ni, Ma; 1980 v WG; 1982 v Cz (sub), Ic, Sp, E, S, Ni, F; 1983 v N, Y, E, Bul; (with Stoke C), 1984 v N, R, Bul, Y, S, E, Ni, N, Is; 1985 v Ic, Sp, Ic; (with QPR), N, S, Sp, N; 1986 v S, S.Ar, Ei, U, Ca (2); 1987 v Fi (2), USSR, Cz; (with Leicester C), 1988 v D (2); (with Swansea C), Y (47)

James, W. (West Ham U), 1931 v Ni; 1932 v Ni (2)

Jarrett, R. H. (Ruthin), 1889 v Ni; 1890 v S (2)

Jarvis, A. L. (Hull C), 1967 v S, E, Ni (3)

Jenkins, E. (Lovell's Ath), 1925 v E (1)

Jenkins, J. (Brighton), 1924 v Ni, E, S; 1925 v S, Ni; 1926 v E, S; 1927 v S (8)

Jenkins, R. W. (Rhyl), 1902 v Ni (1)

Jenkyns, C. A. L. (Small Heath), 1892 v E, S, Ni; 1895 v E; (with Woolwich Arsenal), 1896 v S; (with Newton Heath), 1897 v Ni; (with Walsall), 1898 v S, E (8)

Jennings, W. (Bolton W), 1914 v E, S; 1920 v S; 1923 v Ni, E; 1924 v E, S, Ni; 1927 v S, Ni; 1929 v S (11)

John, R. F. (Arsenal), 1923 v S, Ni; 1925 v Ni; 1926 v E; 1927 v E; 1928 v E, Ni; 1930 v E, S; 1932 v E; 1933 v F, Ni; 1935 v Ni; 1936 v S; 1937 v E (15)

John, W. R. (Walsall), 1931 v Ni; (with Stoke C), 1933 v E, S, Ni, F; 1934 v E, S; (with Preston NE), 1935 v E, S; (with Sheffield U), 1936 v E, S, Ni; (with Swansea T), 1939 v E, S (14)

Johnson, M. G. (Swansea T), 1964 v Ni (1)

Jones, A. (Port Vale), 1987 v Fi, Cz (sub); 1988 v D, (with Charlton Ath), D (sub), Cz (sub); 1990 v Hol (sub) (6)

Jones, A. F. (Oxford University), 1877 v S (1)

Jones, A. T. (Nottingham F), 1905 v E; (with Notts Co), 1906 v E (2)

Jones, Bryn (Wolverhampton W), 1935 v Ni; 1936 v E, S, Ni; 1937 v E, S, Ni; 1938 v E, S, Ni; (with Arsenal), 1939 v E, S, Ni; 1947 v E, S; 1948 v E; 1949 v S (17)

Jones, B. S. (Swansea T), 1963 v S, E, Ni, H (2); 1964 v S, Ni; (with Plymouth Arg), 1965 v D; (with Cardiff C), 1969 v S, E, Ni, I (sub), WG, EG, R of UK (15)

Jones, Charlie (Nottingham F), 1926 v E; 1927 v S, Ni; 1928 v E; (with Arsenal), 1930 v E, S; 1932 v E; 1933 v F (8)

Jones, Cliff (Swansea T), 1954 v A; 1956 v E, Ni, S, A; 1957 v E, S, Ni, Cz (2), EG; 1958 v EG, E, S, Is (2); (with Tottenham H), 1958 v Ni, H (2), M, Se, Br; 1959 v Ni; 1960 v E, S, Ni; 1961 v S, E, Ni, Sp, H, Ei; 1962 v E, Ni, S, Br (2), M; 1963 v S, Ni, H; 1964 v E, S, Ni; 1965 v E, S, Ni, D, Gr (2), USSR, I; 1967 v S, E; 1968 v E, S, WG; (with Fulham), 1969 v I, R of UK (59)

Jones, C. W. (Birmingham), 1935 v Ni; 1939 v F (2)

Jones, D. (Chirk), 1888 v S, Ni; (with Bolton W), 1889 v E, S, Ni; 1890 v E; 1891 v S; 1892 v Ni; 1893 v E; 1894 v E; 1895 v E; 1898 v S; (with Manchester C), 1900 v E, Ni (14)

Jones, D. E. (Norwich C), 1976 v S, E (sub); 1978 v S, Cz, WG, Ir, E; 1980 v E (8)

Jones, D. O. (Leicester C), 1934 v E, Ni; 1935 v E, S; 1936 v E, Ni; 1937 v Ni (7)

Jones, Evan (Chelsea), 1910 v S, Ni, (with Oldham Ath), 1911 v E, S; 1912 v E, S; (with Bolton W), 1914 v Ni (7)

Jones, F. R. (Bangor), 1885 v E, Ni; 1886 v S (3)

Jones, F. W. (Small Heath), 1893 v S (1)

Jones, G. P. (Wrexham), 1907 v S, Ni (2)

Jones, H. (Aberaman), 1902 v Ni (1)

Jones, Humphrey (Bangor), 1885 v E, Ni, S; 1886 v E, Ni, S; (with Queen's Park), 1887 v E; (with East Stirlingshire), 1889 v E, Ni; 1890 v E, S, Ni; (with Queen's Park), 1891 v E, S (14)

Jones, Ivor (Swansea T), 1920 v S, Ni; 1921 v Ni, E; 1922 v S, Ni; (with WBA), 1923 v E, Ni; 1924 v S; 1926 v Ni (10)

Jones, Jeffrey (Llandrindod Wells), 1908 v Ni; 1909 v Ni; 1910 v S (3)

Jones, J. (Druids), 1876 v S (1)

Jones, J. (Berwyn Rangers), 1883 v S, Ni; 1884 v S (3)

Jones, J. (Wrexham), 1925 v Ni (1)

Jones, J. L. (Sheffield U), 1895 v E, S, Ni; 1896 v Ni, S, E; 1897 v Ni, S, E; (with Tottenham H), 1898 v Ni, E, S; 1899 v S, Ni; 1900 v S; 1902 v E, S, Ni; 1904 v E, S, Ni (21)

Jones, J. Love (Stoke C), 1906 v S; (with Middlesbrough), 1910 v Ni (2)

Jones, J. O. (Bangor), 1901 v S, Ni (2)

Jones, J. P. (Liverpool), 1976 v A, E, S; 1977 v WG, S (2) Cz, E, Ni; 1978 v K (2), S, Cz, WG, Ir, E, S, Ni; (with Wrexham), 1979 v Ma, T, WG, S, E, Ni, Ma; 1980 v Ei, WG, T, E, S, Ni, Ic; 1981 v T, Ei, T, S, E, USSR; 1982 v Cz, Ic, USSR, Sp, E, S, Ni, F; 1983 v N; (with Chelsea), v Y, E, Bul, S, Ni, Br; 1984 v N, R, Bul, Y, S, E, Ni, N, Is; 1985 v Ic, N, S, N; (with Huddersfield T), 1986 v S, H, Ei, U, Ca (2) (72)

Jones, J. T. (Stoke C), 1912 v E, S, Ni; 1913 v E, Ni; 1914 v S, Ni; 1920 v E, S, Ni; (with C Palace), 1921 v E, S; 1922 v E, S, Ni (15)

Jones, K. (Aston Villa), 1950 v S (1)

Jones, Leslie J. (Cardiff C), 1933 v F; (with Coventry C), 1935 v Ni; 1936 v S; 1937 v E, S, Ni; (with Arsenal), 1938 v E, S, Ni; 1939 v E, S (11)

Jones, P. W. (Bristol R), 1971 v Fi (1)

Jones, R. (Bangor), 1887 v S; 1889 v E; (with Crewe Alex), 1890 v E (3)

Jones, R. (Leicester Fosse), 1898 v S (1)

Jones, R. (Druids), 1899 v S (1)

Jones, R. (Bangor), 1900 v S, Ni (2)

Jones, R. (Millwall), 1906 v S, Ni (2)

Jones, R. A. (Druids), 1884 v E, Ni, S; 1885 v S (4)

Jones, R. S. (Everton), 1894 v Ni (1)

Jones, S. (Wrexham), 1887 v Ni; (with Chester), 1890 v S (2)

Jones, S. (Wrexham), 1893 v S, Ni; (with Burton Swifts), 1895 v S; 1896 v E, Ni; (with Druids), 1899 v E (6)

Jones, T. (Manchester U), 1926 v Ni; 1927 v E, Ni; 1930 v Ni (4)

Jones, T. D. (Aberdare), 1908 v Ni (1)

Jones, T. G. (Everton), 1938 v Ni; 1939 v E, S, Ni; 1947 v E, S; 1948 v E, S, Ni; 1949 v E, Ni, P, Bel, Sw; 1950 v E, S, Bel (17)

Jones, T. J. (Sheffield W), 1932 v Ni; 1933 v F (2)

Jones, W. E. A. (Swansea T), 1947 v E, S; (with Tottenham H), 1949 v E, S (4)

Jones, W. J. (Aberdare), 1901 v E, S; (with West Ham U), 1902 v E, S (4)

Jones, W. Lot (Manchester C), 1905 v E, Ni; 1906 v E, S, Ni; 1907 v E, S, Ni; 1908 v S; 1909 v E, S, Ni; 1910 v E; 1911 v E; 1913 v E, S; 1914 v S, Ni; (with Southend U), 1920 v E, Ni (20)

Jones, W. P. (Druids), 1889 v E, Ni; (with Wynstay), 1890 v S, Ni (4)

Jones, W. R. (Aberystwyth), 1897 v S (1)

Keenor, F. C. (Cardiff C), 1920 v E, Ni; 1921 v E, Ni, S; 1922 v Ni; 1923 v E, Ni; 1924 v E, Ni, S; 1925 v E, Ni, S; 1926 v S; 1927 v E, Ni, S; 1928 v E, Ni, S; 1929 v E, Ni, S; 1930 v E, Ni, S; 1931 v E, Ni, S; (with Crewe Alex), 1933 v S (32)

Kelly, F. C. (Wrexham), 1899 v S, Ni; (with Druids), 1902 v Ni (3)

Kelsey, A. J. (Arsenal), 1954 v Ni, A; 1955 v S, Ni, Y; 1956 v E, Ni, S, A; 1957 v E, Ni, S, Cz (2), EG; 1958 v E, S, Ni, Is (2), H (2), M, Se, Br; 1959 v E, S; 1960 v E, Ni, S; 1961 v E, Ni, S, H, Sp (2); 1962 v E, S, Ni, Br (2) (41)

Kenrick, S. L. (Druids), 1876 v S; 1877 v S; (with Oswestry), 1879 v E, S; (with Shropshire Wanderers), 1881 v E (5)

Ketley, C. F. (Druids), 1882 v Ni (1)

King, J. (Swansea T), 1955 v E (1)

Kinsey, N. (Norwich C), 1951 v Ni, P, Sw; 1952 v E; (with Birmingham C), 1954 v Ni; 1956 v E, S (7)

Knill, A. R. (Swansea C), 1989 v Ho (1)

Krzywicki, R. L. (Huddersfield T), 1970 v E, S; (with WBA), Ni, EG, I; 1971 v R, Fi; 1972 v Cz (sub) (8)

Lambert, R. (Liverpool), 1947 v S; 1948 v E; 1949 v P, Bel, Sw (5)

Latham, G. (Liverpool), 1905 v E, S; 1906 v S; 1907 v E, S, Ni, 1908 v E; 1909 v Ni; (with Southport Central), 1910 v E; (with Cardiff C), 1913 v Ni (10)

Law, B. J. (QPR), 1990 v Se (1)

Lawrence, E. (Clapton Orient), 1930 v Ni; (with Notts Co), 1932 v S (2)

Lawrence, S. (Swansea T), 1932 v Ni; 1933 v F; 1934 v S, E, Ni; 1935 v E, S; 1936 v S (8)

Lea, A. (Wrexham), 1889 v E; 1891 v S, Ni; 1893 v Ni (4)

Lea, C. (Ipswich T), 1965 v Ni, 1 (2)

Leary, P. (Bangor), 1889 v Ni (1)

Leek, K. (Leicester C), 1961 v S, E, Ni, H, Sp (2); (with Newcastle U), 1962 v S; (with Birmingham C), v Br (sub), M; 1963 v E; 1965 v S, Gr; (with Northampton T), 1965 v Gr (13)

Lever, A. R. (Leicester C), 1953 v S (1)

Lewis, B. (Chester), 1891 v Ni; (with Wrexham), 1892 v S, E, Ni; (with Middlesbrough), 1893 v S, E; (with Wrexham), 1894 v S, E, Ni; 1895 v S (10)

Lewis, D. (Arsenal), 1927 v E; 1928 v Ni; 1930 v E (3)

Lewis, D. (Swansea C), 1983 v Br (sub) (1)

Lewis, D. J. (Swansea T), 1933 v E, S (2)
Lewis, D. M. (Bangor), 1890 v Ni, S (2)
Lewis, J. (Bristol R), 1906 v E (1)
Lewis, J. (Cardiff C), 1926 v S (1)
Lewis, T. (Wrexham), 1881 v E, S (2)
Lewis, W. (Bangor), 1885 v E; 1886 v E, S; 1887 v E, S; 1888 v E; 1889 v E, Ni, S; (with Crewe Alex), 1890 v E; 1891 v E, S; 1892 v E, S, Ni; 1894 v E, S, Ni; (with Chester), 1895 v S, Ni, E; 1896 v E, S, Ni; (with Manchester C), 1897 v E, S; (with Chester), 1898 v Ni (27)
Lewis, W. L. (Swansea T), 1927 v E, Ni; 1928 v E, Ni; 1929 v S; (with Huddersfield T), 1930 v E (6)
Lloyd, B. W. (Wrexham), 1976 v A, E, S (3)
Lloyd, J. W. (Wrexham), 1879 v S; (with Newtown), 1885 v S (2)
Lloyd, R. A. (Ruthin), 1891 v Ni; 1895 v S (2)
Lockley, A. (Chirk), 1898 v Ni (1)
Lovell, S. (C Palace), 1982 v USSR (sub); (with Millwall), 1985 v N; 1986 v S (sub), H (sub), Ca (1 + 1 sub) (6)
Lowrie, G. (Coventry C), 1948 v E, S, Ni; (with Newcastle U), 1949 v P (4)
Lowndes, S. (Newport Co), 1983 v S (sub), Br (sub); (with Millwall), 1985 v N (sub); 1986 v S.Ar (sub), Ei, U, Ca (2); (with Barnsley), 1987 v Fi (sub); 1988 v Se (sub) (10)
Lucas, P. M. (Leyton Orient), 1962 v Ni, M; 1963 v S, E (4)
Lucas, W. H. (Swansea T), 1949 v S, Ni, P, Bel, Sw; 1950 v E; 1951 v E (7)
Lumberg, A. (Wrexham), 1929 v Ni; 1930 v E, S; (with Wolverhampton W), 1932 v S (4)

McCarthy, T. P. (Wrexham), 1889 v Ni (1)
McMillan, R. (Shrewsbury Engineers), 1881 v E, S (2)
Maguire, G. T. (Portsmouth), 1990 v Fi (sub), Ho, WG, Ei, Se; 1992 v Br (sub), G (7)
Mahoney, J. F. (Stoke C), 1968 v E; 1969 v EG; 1971 v Cz; 1973 v E (3), Pol, S, Ni; 1974 v Pol, E, S, Ni; 1975 v A, H (2), L (2), S, E, Ni; 1976 v A, Y (2), E, Ni; 1977 v WG, Cz, S, E, Ni; (with Middlesbrough), 1978 v K (2), S, Cz, Ir, E (sub), S, Ni; 1979 v WG, S, E, Ni, Ma; (with Swansea C), 1980 v Ei, WG, T (sub); 1982 v Ic, USSR; 1983 v Y, E (51)
Martin, T. J. (Newport Co), 1930 v Ni (1)
Marustik, C. (Swansea C), 1982 v Sp, E, S, Ni, F; 1983 v N (6)
Mates, J. (Chirk), 1891 v Ni; 1897 v E, S (3)
Mathews, R. W. (Liverpool), 1921 v Ni; (with Bristol C), 1923 v E; (with Bradford), 1926 v Ni (3)
Matthews, W. (Chester), 1905 v Ni; 1908 v E (2)
Matthias, J. S. (Brymbo), 1896 v S, Ni; (with Shrewsbury), 1897 v E, S; (with Wolverhampton W), 1899 v S (5)
Matthias, T. J. (Wrexham), 1914 v S, E; 1920 v Ni, S, E; 1921 v S, E, Ni; 1922 v S, E, Ni; 1923 v S (12)
Mays, A. W. (Wrexham), 1929 v Ni (1)
Medwin, T. C. (Swansea T), 1953 v Ni, F, Y; (with Tottenham H), 1957 v E, S, Ni, Cz (2), EG; 1958 v E, S, Ni, Is (2), H (2), M, Br; 1959 v E, S, Ni; 1960 v E, S, Ni; 1961 v S, Ei, E, Sp; 1963 v E, H (30)
Melville, A. K. (Swansea C), 1990 v WG, Ei, Se, Cr (sub); (with Oxford U), 1991 v Ic, Pol, WG; 1992 v Br, G, L, R, Ho, J (sub) (13)
Meredith, S. (Chirk), 1900 v S; 1901 v S, E, Ni; (with Stoke C), 1902 v E; 1903 v Ni; 1904 v E; (with Leyton), 1907 v E (8)
Meredith, W. H. (Manchester C), 1895 v E, Ni; 1896 v E, Ni; 1897 v E, Ni, S; 1898 v E, Ni; 1899 v E; 1900 v E, Ni; 1901 v E, Ni; 1902 v E, S; 1903 v E, S, Ni; 1904 v E; 1905 v E, S; (with Manchester U), 1907 v E, S, Ni; 1908 v E, Ni; 1909 v E, S, Ni; 1910 v E, S, Ni; 1911 v E, S, Ni; 1912 v E, S, Ni; 1913 v E, S, Ni; 1914 v E, S, Ni; 1920 v E, S, Ni (48)

Mielczarek, R. (Rotherham U), 1971 v Fi (1)
Millership, H. (Rotherham Co), 1920 v E, S, Ni; 1921 v E, S, Ni (6)
Millington, A. H. (WBA);1963 v S, E, H; (with C Palace), 1965 v E, USSR; (with Peterborough U), 1966 v Ch, Br; 1967 v E, Ni; 1968 v Ni, WG; 1969 v I, EG; (with Swansea T), 1970 v E, S, Ni; 1971 v Cz, Fi; 1972 v Fi (sub), Cz, R (21)
Mills, T. J. (Clapton Orient), 1934 v E, Ni; (with Leicester C), 1935 v E, S (4)
Mills-Roberts, R. H. (St Thomas' Hospital), 1885 v E, S, Ni; 1886 v E; 1887 v E; (with Preston NE), 1888 v E, Ni; (with Llanberis), 1892 v E (8)
Moore, G. (Cardiff C), 1960 v E, S, Ni; 1961 v Ei, Sp; (with Chelsea), 1962 v Br; 1963 v Ni, H; (with Manchester U), 1964 v S, Ni; (with Northampton T), 1966 v Ni, Ch; (with Charlton Ath), 1969 v S, E, Ni, R of UK; 1970 v E, S, Ni, I; 1971 v R (21)
Morgan, J. R. (Cambridge University), 1877 v S; (with Swansea T), 1879 v S; (with Derby School Staff), 1880 v E, S; 1881 v E, S; 1882 v E, S, Ni; (with Swansea T), 1883 v E (10)
Morgan, J. T. (Wrexham), 1905 v Ni (1)
Morgan-Owen, H. (Oxford University), 1901 v E; 1902 v S; 1906 v E, Ni; (with Welshpool), 1907 v S (5)
Morgan-Owen, M. M. (Oxford University), 1897 v S, Ni; 1898 v E, S; 1899 v S; 1900 v E, S; (with Corinthians), 1903 v S; 1906 v S, E, Ni; 1907 v E (12)
Morley, E. J. (Swansea T), 1925 v E; (with Clapton Orient), 1929 v E, S, Ni (4)
Morris, A. G. (Aberystwyth), 1896 v E, Ni, S; (with Swindon T), 1897 v E; 1898 v S; (with Nottingham F), 1899 v E, S; 1903 v E, S; 1905 v E, S; 1907 v E, S; 1908 v E; 1910 v E, S, Ni; 1911 v E, S, Ni; 1912 v E (21)
Morris, C. (Chirk), 1900 v E, S, Ni; (with Derby Co), 1901 v E, S, Ni; 1902 v E, S; 1903 v E, S, Ni; 1904 v Ni; 1905 v E, S, Ni; 1906 v S; 1907 v S; 1908 v E, S; 1909 v E, S, Ni; 1910 v E, S, Ni; (with Huddersfield T), 1911 v E, S, Ni (28)
Morris, E. (Chirk), 1893 v E, S, Ni (3)
Morris, H. (Sheffield U), 1894 v S; (with Manchester C), 1896 v E; (with Grimsby T), 1897 v E (3)
Morris, J. (Oswestry), 1887 v S (1)
Morris, J. (Chirk), 1898 v Ni (1)
Morris, R. (Chirk), 1900 v E, Ni; 1901 v Ni; 1902 v S; (with Shrewsbury T), 1903 v E, Ni (6)
Morris, R. (Druids), 1902 v E, S; (with Newtown), Ni; (with Liverpool), 1903 v S, Ni; 1904 v E, S, Ni; (with Leeds C), 1906 v S; (with Grimsby T), 1907 v Ni; (with Plymouth Arg), 1908 v Ni (11)
Morris, S. (Birmingham), 1937 v E, S; 1938 v E, S; 1939 v F (5)
Morris, W. (Burnley), 1947 v Ni; 1949 v E; 1952 v S, Ni, R of UK (5)
Moulsdale, J. R. B. (Corinthians), 1925 v Ni (1)
Murphy, J. P. (WBA), 1933 v F, E, Ni; 1934 v E, S; 1935 v E, S, Ni; 1936 v E, S, Ni; 1937 v S, Ni; 1938 v E, S (15)

Nardiello, D. (Coventry C), 1978 v Cz, WG (sub) (2)
Neal, J. E. (Colwyn Bay), 1931 v E, S (2)
Neilson, A. B. (Newcastle U), 1992 v Ei (sub) (1)
Newnes, J. (Nelson), 1926 v Ni (1)
Newton, L. F. (Cardiff Corinthians), 1912 v Ni (1)
Nicholas, D. S. (Stoke C), 1923 v S; (with Swansea T), 1927 v E, Ni (3)
Nicholas, P. (C Palace), 1979 v S (sub), Ni (sub), Ma; 1980 v Ei, WG, T, E, S, Ni, Ic; 1981 v T, Cz, E; (with Arsenal), T, S, E, USSR; 1982 v Cz, Ic, USSR, Sp, E, S, Ni, F; 1983 v Y, Bul, S (sub), Ni; 1984 v N, Bul, N, Is; (with C Palace), 1985 v Sp; (with Luton T), N, S, Sp, N; 1986 v S, H, S.Ar, Ei, U, Ca (2); 1987 v Fi (2) USSR, Cz; (with Aberdeen), 1988 v D (2), Cz, Y, Se;

(with Chelsea), 1989 v Ho, Fi, Is, Se, WG; 1990 v Fi, Ho, WG, Ei, Se, Cr; 1991 v D (sub), Bel, L, Ei; (with Watford), Bel, Pol, WG; 1992 v L (73)

Nicholls, J. (Newport Co), 1924 v E, Ni; (with Cardiff C), 1925 v E, S (4)

Niedzwiecki, E. A. (Chelsea), 1985 v N (sub); 1988 v D (2)

Nock, W. (Newtown), 1897 v Ni (1)

Nogan, L. M. (Watford), 1992 v A (sub) (1)

Norman, A. J. (Hull C), 1986 v Ei (sub), U, Ca; 1988 v Ma, I (5)

Nurse, M. T. G. (Swansea T), 1960 v E, Ni; 1961 v S, E, H, Ni, Ei, Sp (2); (with Middlesbrough), 1963 v E, H; 1964 v S (12)

O'Callaghan, E. (Tottenham H), 1929 v Ni; 1930 v S; 1932 v S, E; 1933 v Ni, S, E; 1934 v Ni, S, E; 1935 v E (11)

Oliver, A. (Blackburn R), 1905 v E; (with Bangor), S (2)

O'Sullivan, P. A. (Brighton), 1973 v S (sub); 1976 v S; 1979 v Ma (sub) (3)

Owen, D. (Oswestry), 1879 v E (1)

Owen, E. (Ruthin Grammar School), 1884 v E, Ni, S (3)

Owen, G. (Chirk), 1888 v S; (with Newton Heath), 1889 v S, Ni; 1893 v Ni (4)

Owen, J. (Newton Heath), 1892 v Ni (1)

Owen, Trevor (Crewe Alex), 1899 v E, S (2)

Owen, T. (Oswestry), 1879 v E (1)

Owen, W. (Chirk), 1884 v E; 1885 v Ni; 1887 v E; 1888 v E; 1889 v E, Ni, S; 1890 v S, Ni; 1891 v E, S, Ni; 1892 v E, S; 1893 v S, Ni (16)

Owen, W. P. (Ruthin), 1880 v E, S; 1881 v E, S; 1882 v E, S, Ni; 1883 v E, S; 1884 v E, S, Ni (12)

Owens, J. (Wrexham), 1902 v S (1)

Page, M. E. (Birmingham C), 1971 v Fi; 1972 v S, Ni; 1973 v E (1 + 1 sub), Ni; 1974 v S, Ni; 1975 v H, L, S, E, Ni; 1976 v E, Y (2), E, Ni; 1977 v WG, S; 1978 v K (sub + 1), WG, Ir, E, S; 1979 v Ma, WG (28)

Palmer, D. (Swansea T), 1957 v Cz; 1958 v E, EG (3)

Parris, J. E. (Bradford), 1932 v Ni (1)

Parry, B. J. (Swansea T), 1951 v S (1)

Parry, C. (Everton), 1891 v E, S; 1893 v E; 1894 v E; 1895 v E, S; (with Newtown), 1896 v E, S, Ni; 1897 v Ni; 1898 v E, S, Ni (13)

Parry, E. (Liverpool), 1922 v S; 1923 v E, Ni; 1925 v Ni; 1926 v Ni (5)

Parry, M. (Liverpool), 1901 v E, S, Ni; 1902 v E, S, Ni; 1903 v E, S; 1904 v E, Ni; 1906 v E; 1908 v E, S, Ni; 1909 v E, S (16)

Parry, T. D. (Oswestry), 1900 v E, S, Ni; 1901 v E, S, Ni; 1902 v E (7)

Parry, W. (Newtown), 1895 v Ni (1)

Pascoe, C. (Swansea C), 1984 v N, Is; (with Sunderland), 1989 v Fi, Is, WG (sub); 1990 v Ho (sub), WG (sub); 1991 v Ei, Ic (sub); 1992 v Br (10)

Paul, R. (Swansea T), 1949 v E, S, Ni, P, Sw; 1950 v E, S, Ni, Bel; (with Manchester C), 1951 v S, E, Ni, P, Sw; 1952 v E, S, Ni, R of UK; 1953 v S, E, Ni, F, Y; 1954 v E, S, Ni; 1955 v S, E, Y; 1956 v E, Ni, S, A (33)

Peake, E. (Aberystwyth), 1908 v Ni; (with Liverpool), 1909 v Ni, S, E; 1910 v S, Ni; 1911 v Ni; 1912 v E; 1913 v E, Ni; 1914 v Ni (11)

Peers, E. J. (Wolverhampton W), 1914 v Ni, S, E; 1920 v E, S; 1921 v S, Ni, E, (with Port Vale), 1922 v E, S, Ni, 1923 v E (12)

Pembridge, M. A. (Luton T), 1992 v Br, Ei, R, Ho, J (sub) (5)

Perry, E. (Doncaster R), 1938 v E, S, Ni (3)

Phennah, E. (Civil Service), 1878 v S (1)

Phillips, C. (Wolverhampton W), 1931 v Ni; 1932 v E; 1933 v Ni; 1934 v E, S, Ni; 1935 v E, S, Ni; 1936 v S; (with Aston Villa), 1936 v E, Ni; 1938 v S (13)

Phillips, D. (Plymouth Arg), 1984 v E, Ni, N; (with Manchester C), 1985 v Sp, Ic, S, Sp, N; 1986 v S, H, S.Ar, Ei, U; (with Coventry C), 1987 v Fi, Cz; 1988 v D (2), Cz, Y, Se; 1989 v Se, WG; (with Norwich C), 1990 v Fi, Ho, WG, Ei, Se; 1991 v D, Bel, Ic, Pol, WG; 1992 v L, Ei, A, R, Ho (sub), Arg, J (39)

Phillips, L. (Cardiff C), 1971 v Cz, S, E, Ni; 1972 v Cz, R, S, Ni; 1973 v E; 1974 v Pol (sub), Ni; 1975 v A; (with Aston Villa), H (2), L (2), S, E, Ni; 1976 v A, E, Y (2), E, Ni; 1977 v WG, S (2), Cz, E; 1978 v K (2), S, Cz, WG, E, S; 1979 v Ma; (with Swansea C), T, WG, S, E, Ni, Ma; 1980 v Ei, WG, T, S (sub), Ni, Ic; 1981 v T, Cz, T, S, E, USSR; (with Charlton Ath), 1982 v Cz, USSR (58)

Phillips, T. J. S. (Chelsea), 1973 v E; 1974 v E; 1975 v H (sub); 1978 v K (4)

Phoenix, H. (Wrexham), 1882 v S (1)

Poland, G. (Wrexham), 1939 v Ni, F (2)

Pontin, K. (Cardiff C), 1980 v E (sub), S (2)

Powell, A. (Leeds U), 1947 v E, S; 1948 v E, S, Ni; (with Everton), 1949 v E; 1950 v Bel; (with Birmingham C), 1951 v S (8)

Powell, D. (Wrexham), 1968 v WG; (with Sheffield U), 1969 v S, E, Ni, I, WG; 1970 v E, S, Ni, EG; 1971 v R (11)

Powell, I. V. (QPR), 1947 v E; 1948 v E, S, Ni; (with Aston Villa), 1949 v Bel; 1950 v S, Bel; 1951 v S (8)

Powell, J. (Druids), 1878 v S; 1880 v E, S; 1882 v E, S, Ni; 1883 v E, S, Ni; (with Bolton W), 1884 v E; (with Newton Heath), 1887 v E, S; 1888 v E, S, Ni (15)

Powell, Seth (WBA), 1885 v S; 1886 v E, Ni; 1891 v E, S; 1892 v E, S (7)

Price, H. (Aston Villa), 1907 v S; (with Burton U), 1908 v Ni; (with Wrexham), 1909 v S, E, Ni (5)

Price, J. (Wrexham), 1877 v S; 1878 v S; 1879 v E; 1880 v E, S; 1881 v E, S; (with Druids), 1882 v S, E, Ni; 1883 v S, Ni (12)

Price, P. (Luton T), 1980 v E, S, Ni, Ic; 1981 v T, Cz, Ei, T, S, E, USSR; (with Tottenham H), 1982 v USSR, Sp, F; 1983 v N, Y, E, Bul, S, Ni; 1984 v N, R, Bul, Y, S (sub) (25)

Pring, K. D. (Rotherham U), 1966 v Ch, D; 1967 v Ni (3)

Pritchard, H. K. (Bristol C), 1985 v N (sub) (1)

Pryce-Jones, A. W. (Newtown), 1895 v E (1)

Pryce-Jones, W. E. (Cambridge University), 1887 v S; 1888 v S, E, Ni; 1890 v Ni (5)

Pugh, A. (Rhostyllen), 1889 v S (sub) (1)

Pugh, D. H. (Wrexham), 1896 v S, Ni; 1897 v S, Ni; (with Lincoln C), 1900 v S; 1901 v S, E (7)

Pugsley, J. (Charlton Ath), 1930 v Ni (1)

Pullen, W. J. (Plymouth Arg), 1926 v E (1)

Rankmore, F. E. J. (Peterborough), 1966 v Ch (sub) (1)

Ratcliffe, K. (Everton), 1981 v Cz, Ei, T, S, E, USSR; 1982 v Cz, Ic, USSR, Sp, E; 1983 v Y, E, Bul, S, Ni, Br; 1984 v N, R, Bul, Y, S, E, Ni, N, Is; 1985 v Ic, Sp, Ic, N, S, Sp; 1986 v S, H, S.Ar, U; 1987 v Fi (2), USSR, Cz; 1988 v D (2), Cz; 1989 v Fi, Is, Se, WG; 1990 v Fi; 1991 v D, Bel (2), L, Ei, Ic, Pol, WG; 1992 v Br, G (58)

Rea, J. C. (Aberystwyth), 1894 v Ni, S, E; 1895 v S; 1896 v S, Ni; 1897 v S, Ni; 1898 v Ni (9)

Reece, G. I. (Sheffield U), 1966 v E, S, Ni, USSR; 1967 v S; 1969 v R of UK (sub); 1970 v I (sub); 1971 v S, E, Ni, Fi; 1972 v Fi, R, E (sub), S, Ni; (with Cardiff C), 1973 v E (sub), Ni; 1974 v Pol (sub), E, S, Ni; 1975 v A, H (2), L (2), S, Ni (29)

Reed, W. G. (Ipswich T), 1955. v S, Y (2)

Rees, A. (Birmingham C), 1984 v N (sub) (1)

Rees, J. M. (Luton T), 1992 v A (sub) (1)

Rees, R. R. (Coventry C), 1965 v S, E, Ni, D, Gr (2), I, R; 1966 v S, Ni, R, D, Br (2), Ch; 1967 v E, Ni; 1968 v E, S, Ni; (with WBA), WG; 1969 v I; (with

Nottingham F), 1969 v WG, EG, S (sub), R of UK; 1970 v E, S, Ni, EG, I; 1971 v Cz, R, E (sub), Ni (sub), Fi; 1972 v Cz (sub), R (39)

Rees, W. (Cardiff C), 1949 v Ni, Bel, Sw; (with Tottenham H), 1950 v Ni (4)

Richards, A. (Barnsley), 1932 v S (1)

Richards, D. (Wolverhampton W), 1931 v Ni; 1933 v E, S, Ni; 1934 v E, S, Ni; 1935 v E, S, Ni; 1936 v S; (with Brentford), 1936 v E, Ni; 1937 v S, E; (with Birmingham), Ni; 1938 v E, S, Ni; 1939 v E, S (21)

Richards, G. (Druids), 1899 v E, S, Ni; (with Oswestry), 1903 v Ni; (with Shrewsbury T), 1904 v S; 1905 v Ni (6)

Richards, R. W. (Wolverhampton W), 1920 v E, S; 1921 v Ni; 1922 v E, S; (with West Ham U), 1924 v E, S, Ni; (with Mold), 1926 v S (9)

Richards, S. V. (Cardiff C), 1947 v E (1)

Richards, W. E. (Fulham), 1933 v Ni (1)

Roach, J. (Oswestry), 1885 v Ni (1)

Robbins, W. W. (Cardiff C), 1931 v E, S; 1932 v Ni, E, S; (with WBA), 1933 v F, E, S, Ni; 1934 v S; 1936 v S (11)

Roberts, D. F. (Oxford U), 1973 v Pol, E (sub), Ni; 1974 v E, S; 1975 v A; (with Hull C), L, Ni; 1976 v S, Ni, Y; 1977 v E (sub), Ni; 1978 v K (1 + 1 sub), S, Ni (17)

Roberts, I. W. (Watford), 1990 v Ho; (with Huddersfield T), 1992 v A, Arg, J (4)

Roberts, Jas (Chirk), 1898 v S (1)

Roberts, Jas (Wrexham), 1913 v S, Ni (2)

Roberts, J. (Corwen); 1879 v S, 1880 v. E, S;. 1882 v E, S, Ni; (with Berwyn R), 1883 v E (7)

Roberts, J. (Ruthin), 1881 v S; 1882 v S (2)

Roberts, J. (Bradford C), 1906 v Ni; 1907 v Ni (2)

Roberts, J. G. (Arsenal), 1971 v S, E, Ni, Fi; 1972 v Fi, E, Ni; (with Birmingham C), 1973 v E (2), Pol, S, Ni; 1974 v Pol, E, S, Ni; 1975 v A, H, S, E; 1976 v E, S (22)

Roberts, J. H. (Bolton), 1949 v Bel (1)

Roberts, P. S. (Portsmouth), 1974 v E; 1975 v A, H, L (4)

Roberts, R. (Druids), 1884 v S; (with Bolton W), 1887 v S; 1888 v S, E; 1889 v S, E; 1890 v S; 1892 v Ni; (with Preston NE), S (9)

Roberts; R. (Wrexham), 1886 v Ni; 1887 v Ni (2)

Roberts, R. (Rhos), 1891 v Ni; (with Crewe Alex), 1893 v E (2)

Roberts, W. (Llangollen), 1879 v E, S; 1880 v E, S; (with Berwyn R), 1881 v S; 1883 v S (6)

Roberts, W. (Wrexham), 1886 v E, S, Ni; 1887 v Ni (4)

Roberts, W. H. (Ruthin), 1882 v E, S; 1883 v E, S, Ni; (with Rhyl), 1884 v S (6)

Roberts, W. (Rhyl), 1883 v E (1)

Rodrigues, P. J. (Cardiff C), 1965 v Ni, Gr (2); 1966 v USSR, E, S, D; (with Leicester C), v Ni, Br (2), Ch; 1967 v S; 1968 v E, S, Ni; 1969 v E, Ni, EG, R of UK; 1970 v E, S, Ni, EG; (with Sheffield W), 1971 v R, E, S, Cz, Ni; 1972 v Fi, Cz, R, E, Ni (sub); 1973 v E (3), Pol, S, Ni; 1974 v Pol (40)

Rogers, J. P. (Wrexham), 1896 v E, S, Ni (3)

Rogers, W. (Wrexham), 1931 v E, S (2)

Roose, L. R. (Aberystwyth), 1900 v Ni; (with London Welsh), 1901 v E, S, Ni; (with Stoke C), 1902 v E, S; 1904 v E; (with Everton), 1905 v S, E; (with Stoke C), 1906 v E, S, Ni; 1907 v E, S, Ni; (with Sunderland), 1908 v E, S; 1909 v E, S, Ni; 1910 v E, S, Ni; 1911 v S (24)

Rouse, R. V. (C Palace), 1959 v Ni (1)

Rowlands, A. C. (Tranmere R), 1914 v E (1)

Rowley, T. (Tranmere R), 1959 v Ni (1)

Rush, I. (Liverpool), 1980 v S (sub), Ni; 1981 v E (sub); 1982 v Ic (sub), USSR, E, S, Ni, F; 1983 v N, Y, E, Bul; 1984 v N, R, Bul, Y, S, E, Ni; 1985 v Ic, N, S, Sp; 1986 v S, S.Ar, Ei, U; 1987 v Fi (2), USSR, Cz; (with Juventus), 1988 v D, Cz, Y, Se, Ma, I; (with Liverpool),

1989 v Ho, Fi, Se, WG; 1990 v Fi, Ei; 1991 v D, Bel (2), L, Ei, Pol, WG; 1992 v G, L, R (54)

Russell, M. R. (Merthyr T), 1912 v S, Ni; 1914 v E; (with Plymouth Arg), 1920 v E, S, Ni; 1921 v E, S, Ni; 1922 v E, Ni; 1923 v E, S, Ni; 1924 v E, S, Ni; 1925 v E, S; 1926 v E, S; 1928 v S; 1929 v E (23)

Sabine, H. W. (Oswestry), 1887 v Ni (1)

Saunders, D. (Brighton & HA), 1986 v Ei (sub), Ca (2); 1987 v Fi, USSR (sub); (with Oxford U), 1988 v Y, Se, Ma, I (sub); 1989 v Ho (sub), Fi, Is; (with Derby Co), Se, WG; 1990 v Fi, Ho, WG, Se, Cr; 1991 v D, Bel (2), L, Ei, Ic, Pol, WG; (with Liverpool), 1992 v Br, G, Ei, R, Ho, Arg, J (34)

Savin, G. (Oswestry), 1878 v S (1)

Sayer, P. (Cardiff C), 1977 v Cz, S, E, Ni; 1978 v K (2), S (7)

Scrine, F. H. (Swansea T), 1950 v E, Ni (2)

Sear, C. R. (Manchester C), 1963 v E (1)

Shaw, E. G. (Oswestry), 1882 v Ni; 1884 v S, Ni (3)

Sherwood, A. T. (Cardiff C), 1947 v E, Ni; 1948 v S, Ni; 1949 v E, S, Ni, P, Sw; 1950 v E, S, Ni, Bel; 1951 v E, S, Ni, P, Sw; 1952 v E, S, Ni, R of UK; 1953 v S, E, Ni, F, Y; 1954 v E, S, Ni, A; 1955 v S, E, Y, Ni; 1956 v E, S, Ni, A; (with Newport Co), 1957 v E, S (41)

Shone, W. W. (Oswestry), 1879 v E (1)

Shortt, W. W. (Plymouth Arg), 1947 v Ni; 1950 v Ni, Bel; 1952 v E, S, Ni, R of UK; 1953 v S, E, Ni, F, Y (12)

Showers, D. (Cardiff C), 1975 v E (sub), Ni (2)

Sidlow, C. (Liverpool), 1947 v E, S; 1948 v E, S, Ni; 1949 v S; 1950 v E (7)

Sisson, H. (Wrexham Olympic), 1885 v Ni; 1886 v S, Ni (3)

Slatter, N. (Bristol R), 1983 v S; 1984 v N (sub), Is; 1985 v Ic, Sp, Ic, N, S, Sp, N; (with Oxford U), 1986 v H (sub), S.Ar, Ca (2); 1987 v Fi (sub), Cz; 1988 v D (2), Cz, Ma, I; 1989 v Is (sub) (22)

Smallman, D. P. (Wrexham), 1974 v E (sub), S (sub), Ni; (with Everton), 1975 v H (sub), E, Ni (sub); 1976 v A (7)

Southall, N. (Everton), 1982 v Ni; 1983 v N, E, Bul, S, Ni, Br; 1984 v N, R, Bul, Y, S, E, Ni, N, Is; 1985 v Ic, Sp, Ic, N, S, Sp, N; 1986 v S, H, S.Ar, Ei; 1987 v USSR, Fi, Cz; 1988 v D, Cz, Y, Se; 1989 v Ho, Fi, Se, WG; 1990 v Fi, Ho, WG, Ei, Se, Cr; 1991 v D, Bel (2), L, Ei, Ic, Pol, WG; 1992 v Br, G, L, Ei, A, R, Ho, Arg, J (61)

Speed, G. A. (Leeds U), 1990 v Cr (sub); 1991 v D, L (sub), Ei (sub), Ic, WG (sub); 1992 v Br, G (sub), L, Ei, R, Ho, Arg, J (14)

Sprake, G. (Leeds U), 1964 v S, Ni; 1965 v S, D, Gr; 1966 v E, Ni, USSR; 1967 v S; 1968 v E, S; 1969 v S, E, Ni, WG, R of UK; 1970 v EG, I; 1971 v R, S, E, Ni; 1972 v Fi, E, S, Ni; 1973 v E (2), Pol, S, Ni; 1974 v Pol; (with Birmingham C), S, Ni; 1975 v A, H, L (37)

Stansfield, F. (Cardiff C), 1949 v S (1)

Stevenson, B. (Leeds U), 1978 v Ni; 1979 v Ma, T, S, E, Ni, Ma; 1980 v WG, T, Ic (sub); 1982 v Cz; (with Birmingham C), Sp, S, Ni, F (15)

Stevenson, N. (Swansea C), 1982 v E, S, Ni; 1983 v N (4)

Stitfall, R. F. (Cardiff C), 1953 v E; 1957 v Cz (2)

Sullivan, D. (Cardiff C), 1953 v Ni, F, Y; 1954 v Ni; 1955 v E, Ni; 1957 v E, S; 1958 v Ni, H (2), Se, Br; 1959 v S, Ni; 1960 v E, S (17)

Symons, C. J. (Portsmouth), 1992 v Ei, Ho, Arg, J (4)

Tapscott, D. R. (Arsenal), 1954 v A; 1955 v S, E, Ni, Y; 1956 v E, Ni, S, A; 1957 v Ni, Cz, EG; (with Cardiff C), 1959 v E, Ni (14)

Taylor, J. (Wrexham), 1898 v E (1)

Taylor, O. D. S. (Newtown), 1893 v S, Ni; 1894 v S, Ni (4)

Thomas, C. (Druids), 1899 v Ni; 1900 v S (2)

Thomas, D. A. (Swansea T), 1957 v Cz; 1958 v EG (2)

Thomas, D. S. (Fulham), 1948 v E, S, Ni; 1949 v S (4)

Thomas, E. (Cardiff Corinthians), 1925 v E (1)

Thomas, G. (Wrexham), 1885 v E, S (2)

Thomas, H. (Manchester U), 1927 v E (1)

Thomas, M. (Wrexham), 1977 v WG, S (1 + 1 sub), Ni (sub); 1978 v K (sub), S, Cz, Ir, E, Ni (sub); 1979 v Ma; (with Manchester U), T, WG, Ma (sub); 1980 v Ei, WG (sub), T, E, S, Ni; 1981 v Cz, S, E, USSR; (with Everton), 1982 v Cz; (with Brighton & HA), USSR (sub), Sp, E, S (sub), Ni (sub); 1983 (with Stoke C), v N, Y, E, Bul, S, Ni, Br; 1984 v R, Bul, Y; (with Chelsea), S, E; 1985 v Ic, Sp, Ic, S, Sp, N; 1986 v S; (with WBA), H, S.Ar (sub) (51)

Thomas, M. R. (Newcastle U), 1987 v Fi (1)

Thomas, R. J. (Swindon T), 1967 v Ni; 1968 v WG; 1969 v E, Ni, I, WG, R of UK; 1970 v S, Ni, EG, I; 1971 v S, E, Ni, R, Cz; 1972 v Fi, Cz, R, E, S, Ni; 1973 v E (3), Pol, S, Ni; 1974 v Pol; (with Derby Co), E, S, Ni; 1975 v H (2), L (2), S, E, Ni; 1976 v A, Y, E; 1977 v Cz, S, E, Ni; 1978 v K, S; (with Cardiff Co), Cz (50)

Thomas, T. (Bangor), 1898 v S, Ni (2)

Thomas, W. R. (Newport Co), 1931 v E, S (2)

Thomson, D. (Druids), 1876 v S (1)

Thomson, G. F. (Druids), 1876 v S; 1877 v S (2)

Toshack, J. B. (Cardiff C), 1969 v S, E, Ni, WG, EG, R of UK; 1970 v EG, I; (with Liverpool), 1971 v S, E, Ni, Fi; 1972 v Fi, E; 1973 v E (3), Pol, S; 1975 v A, H (2), L (2), S, E; 1976 v Y (2), E; 1977 v S; 1978 v K (2), S, Cz; (with Swansea C), 1979 v WG (sub), S, E, Ni, Ma; 1980 v WG (40)

Townsend, W. (Newtown), 1887 v Ni; 1893 v Ni (2)

Trainer, H. (Wrexham), 1895 v E, S, Ni (3)

Trainer, J. (Bolton W), 1887 v S; (with Preston NE), 1888 v S; 1889 v E; 1890 v S; 1891 v S; 1892 v Ni, S; 1893 v E; 1894 v Ni, E; 1895 v Ni, E; 1896 v S; 1897 v Ni, S, E; 1898 v S, E; 1899 v Ni, S (20)

Turner, H. G. (Charlton Ath), 1937 v E, S, Ni; 1938 v E, S, Ni; 1939 v Ni, F (8)

Turner, J. (Wrexham), 1892 v E (1)

Turner, R. E. (Wrexham), 1891 v E, Ni (2)

Turner, W. H. (Wrexham), 1887 v E, Ni; 1890 v S; 1891 v E, S (5)

Van Den Hauwe, P. W. R. (Everton), 1985 v Sp; 1986 v S, H; 1987 v USSR, Fi, Cz; 1988 v D (2), Cz, Y, I; 1989 v Fi, Se (13)

Vaughan, Jas (Druids), 1893 v E, S, Ni; 1899 v E (4)

Vaughan, John (Oswestry), 1879 v S; 1880 v S; 1881 v E, S; 1882 v E, S, Ni; 1883 v E, S, Ni; (with Bolton W), 1884 v E (11)

Vaughan, J. O. (Rhyl), 1885 v Ni; 1886 v Ni, E, S (4)

Vaughan, N. (Newport Co), 1983 v Y (sub), Br; 1984 v N; (with Cardiff C), R, Bul, Y, Ni (sub), N, Is; 1985 v Sp (sub) (10)

Vaughan, T. (Rhyl), 1885 v E (1)

Vearncombe, G. (Cardiff C), 1958 v EG; 1961 v Ei (2)

Vernon, T. R. (Blackburn R), 1957 v Ni, Cz (2), EG; 1958 v E, S, EG, Se; 1959 v S; (with Everton), 1960 v Ni; 1961 v S, E, Ei; 1962 v Ni, Br (2), M; 1963 v S, E, H; 1964 v E, S; (with Stoke C), 1965 v Ni, Gr, I; 1966 v E, S, Ni, USSR, D; 1967 v Ni; 1968 v E (32)

Villars, A. K. (Cardiff C), 1974 v E, S, Ni (sub) (3)

Vizard, E. T. (Bolton W), 1911 v E, S, Ni; 1912 v E, S; 1913 v S; 1914 v E, Ni; 1920 v E; 1921 v E, S, Ni; 1922 v E, S; 1923 v E, Ni; 1924 v E, S, Ni; 1926 v E, S; 1927 v S (22)

Walley, J. T. (Watford), 1971 v Cz (1)

Walsh, I. (C Palace), 1980 v Ei, T, E, S, Ic; 1981 v T, Cz, Ei, T, S, E, USSR; 1982 v Cz (sub), Ic; (with Swansea C), Sp, S (sub), Ni (sub), F (18)

Ward, D. (Bristol R), 1959 v E; (with Cardiff C), 1962 v E (2)

Warner, J. (Swansea T), 1937 v E; (with Manchester U), 1939 v F (2)

Warren, F. W. (Cardiff C), 1929 v Ni; (with Middlesbrough), 1931 v Ni; 1933 v F, E; (with Hearts), 1937 v Ni; 1938 v Ni (6)

Watkins, A. E. (Leicester Fosse), 1898 v E, S; (with Aston Villa), 1900 v E, S; (with Millwall), 1904 v Ni (5)

Watkins, W. M. (Stoke C), 1902 v E; 1903 v E, S; (with Aston Villa); 1904 v E, S, Ni; (with Sunderland), 1905 v E, S, Ni; (with Stoke C), 1908 v Ni (10)

Webster, C (Manchester U), 1957 v Cz; 1958 v H, M, Br (4)

Whatley, W. J. (Tottenham H), 1939 v E, S (2)

White, P. F. (London Welsh), 1896 v Ni (1)

Wilcocks, A. R. (Oswestry), 1890 v Ni (1)

Wilding, J. (Wrexham Oympians), 1885 v E, S, Ni; 1886 v E, Ni; (with Bootle), 1887 v E; 1888 v S, Ni; (with Wrexham), 1892 v S (9)

Williams, A. L. (Wrexham), 1931 v E (1)

Williams, B. (Bristol C), 1930 v Ni (1)

Williams, B. D. (Swansea T), 1928 v Ni, E; 1930 v E, S; (with Everton), 1931 v Ni; 1932 v E; 1933 v E, S, Ni; 1935 v Ni (10)

Williams, D. G. (Derby Co), 1988 v Cz, Y, Se, Ma, I; 1989 v Ho, Is, Se, WG; 1990 v Fi, Ho (11)

Williams, D. M. (Norwich C), 1986 v S.Ar (sub), U, Ca (2); 1987 v Fi (5)

Williams, D. R. (Merthyr T), 1921 v E, S; (with Sheffield W), 1923 v S; 1926 v S; 1927 v E, Ni; (with Manchester U), 1929 v E, S (8)

Williams, E. (Crewe Alex), 1893 v E, S (2)

Williams, E. (Druids), 1901 v E, Ni, S; 1902 v E, Ni (5)

Williams, G. (Chirk), 1893 v S; 1894 v S; 1895 v E, S, Ni; 1898 v Ni (6)

Williams, G. E. (WBA), 1960 v Ni; 1961 v S, E, Ei; 1963 v Ni, H; 1964 v E, S, Ni; 1965 v S, E, Ni, D, Gr (2), USSR, I; 1966 v Ni, Br (2), Ch; 1967 v S, E, Ni; 1968 v Ni; 1969 v I (26)

Williams, G. G. (Swansea T), 1961 v Ni, H, Sp (2); 1962 v E (5)

Williams, G. J. J. (Cardiff C), 1951 v Sw (1)

Williams, G. O. (Wrexham), 1907 v Ni (1)

Williams, H. J. (Swansea), 1965 v Gr (2); 1972 v R (3)

Williams, H. T. (Newport Co), 1949 v Ni, Sw; (with Leeds U), 1950 v Ni; 1951 v S (4)

Williams, J. H. (Oswestry), 1884 v E (1)

Williams, J. J. (Wrexham), 1939 v F (1)

Williams, J. T. (Middlesbrough), 1925 v Ni (1)

Williams, J. W. (C Palace), 1912 v S, Ni (2)

Williams, R. (Newcastle U), 1935 v S, E (2)

Williams, R. P. (Caernarvon), 1886 v S (1)

Williams, S. G. (WBA), 1954 v A; 1955 v E, Ni; 1956 v E, S, A; 1958 v E, S, Ni, Is (2), H (2), M, Se, Br; 1959 v E, S, Ni; 1960 v E, S, Ni; 1961 v Ni, Ei, H, Sp (2); 1962 v E, S, Ni, Br (2), M; (with Southampton), 1963 v S, E, H (2); 1964 v E, S; 1965 v S, E, D; 1966 v D (43)

Williams, W. (Druids), 1876 v S; 1878 v S; (with Oswestry), 1879 v E, S; (with Druids), 1880 v E; 1881 v E, S; 1882 v E, S, Ni; 1883 v Ni (11)

Williams, W. (Northampton T), 1925 v S (1)

Witcomb, D. F. (WBA), 1947 v E, S; (with Sheffield W), 1947 v Ni (3)

Woosnam, A. P. (Leyton Orient), 1959 v S; (with West Ham U), E; 1960 v E, S, Ni; 1961 v S, E, Ni, Ei, Sp, H; 1962 v E, S, Ni, Br; (with Aston Villa), 1963 v Ni, H (17)

Woosnam, G. (Newton White Star), 1879 v S (1)

Worthington, T. (Newtown), 1894 v S (1)

Wynn, G. A. (Wrexham), 1909 v E, S, Ni; (with Manchester C), 1910 v E; 1911 v Ni; 1912 v E, S; 1913 v E, S; 1914 v E, S (11)

Wynn, W. (Chirk), 1903 v Ni (1)

Yorath, T. C. (Leeds U), 1970 v I; 1971 v S, E; Ni; 1972 v Cz, E, S, Ni; 1973 v E, Pol, S; 1974 v Pol, E, S, Ni; 1975 v A, H (2), L (2), S; 1976 v A, E, S, Y (2), E, Ni; (with Coventry C), 1977 v WG, S (2), Cz, E, Ni; 1978 v K (2), S, Cz, WG, Ir, E, S, Ni; 1979 v T, WG, S, E, Ni; (with Tottenham H), 1980 v Ei, T, E, S, Ni, Ic; 1981 v T, Cz; (with Vancouver W), Ei, T, USSR (59)

Young, E. (Wimbledon), 1990 v Cr; (with C Palace), 1991 v D, Bel (2), L, Ei; 1992 v G, L, Ei, A (10)

REPUBLIC OF IRELAND

Aherne, T. (Belfast C), 1946 v P, Sp; (with Luton T), 1950 v Fi, E, Fi, Se, Bel; 1951 v N, Arg, N; 1952 v WG (2), A, Sp; 1953 v F; 1954 v F (16)

Aldridge, J. W. (Oxford U), 1986 v W, U, Ic, Cz; 1987 v Bel, S, Pol; (with Liverpool), S, Bul, Bel, Br, L; 1988 v Bul, Pol, N, E, USSR, Ho; 1989 v Ni, Tun, Sp, F, H, Ma (sub), H; 1990 v WG; (with Real Sociedad), Ni, Ma, Fi (sub), T, E, Eg, Ho, R, I; 1991 v T, E (2), Pol; (with Tranmere R), 1992 v H (sub), T, W (sub), Sw (sub), US (sub), Alb, I, P (sub) (47)

Ambrose, P. (Shamrock R), 1955 v N, Ho; 1964 v Pol, N, E (5)

Anderson, J. (Preston NE), 1980 v Cz (sub), US (sub); 1982 v Ch, Br, Tr; (with Newcastle U), 1984 v Chn; 1986 v W, Ic, Cz; 1987 v Bul, Bel, Br, L; 1988 v R (sub), Y (sub); 1989 v Tun (16)

Andrews, P. (Bohemians), 1936 v Ho (1)

Arrigan, T. (Waterford), 1938 v N (1)

Bailham, E. (Shamrock R), 1964 v E (1)

Barber, E. (Shelbourne), 1966 v Sp; (with Birmingham C), 1966 v Bel (2)

Barry, P. (Fordsons), 1928 v Bel; 1929 v Bel (2)

Beglin, J. (Liverpool), 1984 v Chn; 1985 v M, D, I, Is, E, N, Sw; 1986 v Sw, USSR, D, W; 1987 v Bel (sub), S, Pol (15)

Bermingham, J. (Bohemians), 1929 v Bel (1)

Bermingham, P. (St James' Gate), 1935 v H (1)

Braddish, S. (Dundalk), 1978 v Pol (1)

Bonner, P. (Celtic), 1981 v Pol; 1982 v Alg; 1984 v Ma, Is, Chn; 1985 v I, Is, E, N; 1986 v U, Ic; 1987 v Bel (2), S (2), Pol, Bul, Br, L; 1988 v R, Y, N, E, USSR, Ho; 1989 v Sp, F, H, Sp, Ma, H; 1990 v WG, Ni, Ma, W, Fi, T, E, Eg, Ho, R, I; 1991 v Mor, T, E (2), W, Pol, US; 1992 v H, Pol, T, W, Sw, Alb, I (57)

Bradshaw, P. (St James' Gate), 1939 v Sw, Pol, H (2), G (5)

Brady, F. (Fordsons), 1926 v I; 1927 v I (2)

Brady, T. R. (QPR), 1964 v A (2), Sp (2), Pol, N (6)

Brady, W. L. (Arsenal), 1975 v USSR, T, Sw, USSR, Sw, WG; 1976 v T, N, Pol; 1977 v E, T, F (2), Sp, Bul; 1978 v Bul, N; 1979 v Ni, E, D, Bul, WG; 1980 v W, Bul, E, Cy; (with Juventus), 1981 v Ho, Bel, F, Cy, Bel; 1982 v Ho, F, Ch, Br, Tr; 1983 (with Sampdoria), v Ho, Sp, Ic, Ma; 1984 v Ic, Ho, Ma, Pol, Is; (with Internazionale), 1985 v USSR, N, D, I, E, N, Sp, Sw; 1986 v Sw, USSR, D, W; (with Ascoli), 1987 v Bel, S (2), Pol; (with West Ham U), Bul, Bel, Br, L; 1988 v L, Bul; 1989 v F, H (sub), H (sub); 1990 v WG, Fi (72)

Breen, T. (Manchester U), 1937 v Sw, F; (with Shamrock R), 1947 v E, Sp, P (5)

Brennan, F. (Drumcondra), 1965 v Bel (1)

Brennan, S. A. (Manchester U), 1965 v Sp; 1966 v Sp, A, Bel; 1967 v Sp, T, Sp; 1969 v Cz, D, H; 1970 v S, Cz, D, H, Pol (sub), WG; (with Waterford), 1971 v Pol, Se, I (19)

Brown, J. (Coventry C), 1937 v Sw, F (2)

Browne, W. (Bohemians), 1964 v A, Sp, E (3)

Buckley, L. (Shamrock R), 1984 v Pol (sub); (with Waregem), 1985 v M (2)

Burke, F. (Cork), 1934 v Bel (1)

Burke, F. (Cork Ath), 1952 v WG (1)

Burke, J. (Shamrock R), 1929 v Bel (1)

Byrne, A. B. (Southampton), 1970 v D, Pol, WG; 1971 v Pol, Se (2), I (2), A; 1973 v F, USSR (sub), F, N; 1974 v Pol (14)

Byrne, D. (Shelbourne), 1929 v Bel; (with Shamrock R), 1932 v Sp; (with Coleraine), 1934 v Bel (3)

Byrne, J. (Bray Unknowns), 1928 v Bel (1)

Byrne, J. (QPR), 1985 v I, Is (sub), E (sub), Sp (sub); 1987 v S (sub), Bel (sub), Br, L (sub); 1988 v L, Bul (sub), Is, R, Y (sub), Pol (sub); (with Le Havre), 1990 v WG (sub), W, Fi, T (sub), Ma; (with Brighton & HA), 1991 v W; (with Sunderland), 1992 v T, W (22)

Byrne, P. (Shamrock R), 1984 v Pol, Chn; 1985 v M, I; 1986 v D (sub), W (sub), U (sub), Ic (sub), Cz (9)

Byrne, P. (Shelbourne), 1931 v Sp; 1932 v Ho; (with Drumcondra), 1934 v Ho (3)

Byrne, S. (Bohemians), 1931 v Sp (1)

Campbell, A. (Santander), 1985 v I (sub), Is, Sp (3)

Campbell, N. (St Patrick's Ath), 1971 v A (sub); (with Fortuna, Cologne), 1972 v Ir, Ec, Ch, P; 1973 v USSR, F (sub); 1975 v WG; 1976 v N; 1977 v Sp, Bul (sub) (11)

Cannon, H. (Bohemians), 1926 v I; 1928 v Bel (2)

Cantwell, N. (West Ham U), 1954 v L; 1956 v Sp, Ho; 1957 v D, WG, E (2); 1958 v D, Pol, A; 1959 v Pol, Cz (2); 1960 v Se, Ch, Se; 1961 v N; (with Manchester U), S (2); 1962 v Cz (2), A; 1963 v Ic (2), S; 1964 v A, Sp, E; 1965 v Pol, Sp; 1966 v Sp (2), A, Bel; 1967 v Sp, T (36)

Carey, B. P. (Manchester U), 1992 v US (sub) (1)

Carey, J. J. (Manchester U), 1938 v N, Cz, Pol; 1939 v Sw, Pol, H (2), G; 1946 v P, Sp; 1947 v E, Sp, P; 1948 v P, Sp; 1949 v Sw, Bel, P, Se, Sp; 1950 v Fi, E, Fi, Se; 1951 v N, Arg, N; 1953 v F, A (29)

Carolan, J. (Manchester U), 1960 v Se, Ch (2)

Carroll, B. (Shelbourne), 1949 v Bel; 1950 v Fi (2)

Carroll, T. R. (Ipswich T), 1968 v Pol; 1969 v Pol, A, D; 1970 v Cz, Pol, WG; 1971 v Se; (with Birmingham C), 1972 v Ir, Ec, Ch, P; 1973 v USSR (2), Pol, F, N (17)

Cascarino, A. G. (Gillingham), 1986 v Sw, USSR, D; (with Millwall), 1988 v Pol, N (sub), USSR (sub), Ho (sub); 1989 v Ni, Tun, Sp, F, H, Sp, Ma, H; 1990 v WG (sub), Ni, Ma; (with Aston Villa), W, Fi, T, E, Eg, Ho (sub), R (sub), I (sub); 1991 v Mor (sub), T (sub), E (2 sub), Pol (sub), Ch (sub), US; (with Celtic), 1992 v Pol, T; (with Chelsea), W, Sw, US (sub) (38)

Chandler, J. (Leeds U), 1980 v Cz (sub), US (2)

Chatton, H. A. (Shelbourne), 1931 v Sp; (with Dumbarton), 1932 v Sp; (with Cork), 1934 v Ho (3)

Clarke, J. (Drogheda U), 1978 v Pol (sub) (1)

Clarke, K. (Drumcondra), 1948 v P, Sp (2)

Clarke, M. (Shamrock R), 1950 v Bel (1)

Clinton, T. J. (Everton), 1951 v N; 1954 v F, L (3)

Coad, P. (Shamrock R), 1947 v E, Sp, P; 1948 v P, Sp; 1949 v Sw, Bel, P, Se; 1951 v N (sub); 1952 v Sp (11)

Coffey, T. (Drumcondra), 1950 v Fi (1)

Colfer, M. D. (Shelbourne), 1950 v Bel; 1951 v N (2)

Collins, F. (Jacobs), 1927 v I (1)

Conmy, O. M. (Peterborough U), 1965 v Bel; 1967 v Cz; 1968 v Cz, Pol; 1970 v Cz (5)

Connolly, J. (Fordsons), 1926 v I (1)

Connolly, N. (Cork), 1937 v G (1)

Conroy, G. A. (Stoke C), 1970 v Cz, D, H, Pol, WG; 1971 v Pol, Se (2), I; 1973 v USSR, F, USSR, N; 1974 v Pol, Br, U, Ch; 1975 v T, Sw, USSR, Sw, WG; 1976 v T (sub), Pol; 1977 v E, T, Pol (27)

Conway, J. P. (Fulham), 1967 v Sp, T, Sp; 1968 v Cz; 1969 v A (sub), H; 1970 v S, Cz, D, H, Pol, WG; 1971 v I, A; 1974 v U, Ch; 1975 v WG (sub); 1976 v N, Pol; (with Manchester C), 1977 v Pol (20)

Corr, P. J. (Everton), 1949 v P, Sp; 1950 v E, Se (4)

Courtney, E. (Cork U), 1946 v P (1)

Coyne, T. (Celtic), 1992 v Sw, US, Alb (sub), US (sub), I (sub), P (sub) (6)

Cummins, G. P. (Luton T), 1954 v L (2); 1955 v N (2), WG; 1956 v Y, Sp; 1958 v D, Pol, A; 1959 v Pol, Cz (2); 1960 v Se, Ch, WG, Se; 1961 v S (2) (19)

Cuneen, T. (Limerick), 1951 v N (1)

Curtis, D. P. (Shelbourne), 1957 v D, WG; (with Bristol C), 1957 v E (2); 1958 v D, Pol, A; (with Ipswich T), 1959 v Pol; 1960 v Se, Ch, WG, Se; 1961 v N, S; 1962 v A; 1963 v Ic; (with Exeter C), 1964 v A (17)

Cusack, S. (Limerick), 1953 v F (1)

Daish, L. S. (Cambridge U), 1992 v W (1)

Daly, G. A. (Manchester U), 1973 v Pol (sub), N; 1974 v Br (sub), U (sub); 1975 v Sw (sub), WG; 1977 v E, T, F; (with Derby Co), F, Bul; 1978 v Bul, T, D; 1979 v Ni, E, D, Bul; 1980 v Ni, E, Cy, Sw, Arg; (with Coventry C), 1981 v Ho, Bel, Cy, W, Bel, Cz, Pol (sub); 1982 v Alg, Ch, Br, Tr; 1983 v Ho, Sp (sub), Ma; 1984 v ls (sub); (with Birmingham C), 1985 v M (sub), N, Sp, Sw; 1986 v Sw; (with Shrewsbury T), U, Ic (sub), Cz (sub); 1987 v S (sub) (47)

Daly, J. (Shamrock R), 1932 v Ho; 1935 v Sw (2)

Daly, M. (Wolverhampton W), 1978 v T, Pol (2)

Daly, P. (Shamrock R), 1950 v Fi (sub) (1)

Davis, T. L. (Oldham Ath), 1937 v G, H; (with Tranmere R), 1938 v Cz, Pol (4)

Deacy, E. (Aston Villa), 1982 v Alg (sub), Ch, Br, Tr (4)

De Mange, K. J. P. P. (Liverpool), 1987 v Br (sub); (with Hull C), 1989 v Tun (sub) (2)

Dempsey, J. T. (Fulham), 1967 v Sp, Cz; 1968 v Cz, Pol; 1969 v Pol, A, D; (with Chelsea), 1969 v Cz, D; 1970 v H, WG; 1971 v Pol, Se (2), I; 1972 v Ir, Ec, Ch, P (19)

Dennehy, J. (Cork Hibernians), 1972 v Ec (sub), Ch; (with Nottingham F), 1973 v USSR (sub), Pol, F, N; 1974 v Pol (sub); 1975 v T (sub), WG (sub); (with Walsall), 1976 v Pol (sub); 1977 v Pol (sub) (11)

Desmond, P. (Middlesbrough), 1950 v Fi, E, Fi, Se (4)

Devine, J. (Arsenal), 1980 v Cz, Ni; 1981 v Cz; 1982 v Ho, Alg; 1983 v Sp, Ma; (with Norwich C), 1984 v Ic, Ho, Is; 1985 v USSR, N (12)

Donnelly, J. (Dundalk), 1935 v H, Sw, G; 1936 v Ho, Sw, H, L; 1937 v G, H; 1938 v N (10)

Donnelly, T. (Drumcondra), 1938 v N; (Shamrock R), 1939 v Sw (2)

Donovan, D. C. (Everton), 1955 v N, Ho, N, WG; 1957 v E (5)

Donovan, T. (Aston Villa), 1980 v Cz (1)

Dowdall, C. (Fordsons), 1928 v Bel; (with Barnsley), 1929 v Bel; (with Cork), 1931 v Sp (3)

Doyle, C. (Shelbourne), 1959 v Cz (1)

Doyle, D. (Shamrock R), 1926 v I (1)

Doyle, L. (Dolphin), 1932 v Sp (1)

Duffy, B. (Shamrock R), 1950 v Bel (1)

Duggan, H. A. (Leeds U), 1927 v I; 1930 v Bel; 1936 v H, L; (with Newport Co), 1938 v N (5)

Dunne, A. P. (Manchester U), 1962 v A; 1963 v Ic, S; 1964 v A, Sp, Pol, N, E; 1965 v Pol, Sp; 1966 v Sp (2);

A, Bel; 1967 v Sp, T, Sp; 1969 v Pol, D, H; 1970 v H; 1971 v Se, I, A; (with Bolton W), 1974 v Br (sub), U, Ch; 1975 v T, Sw, USSR, Sw, WG; 1976 v T (33)

Dunne, J. (Sheffield U), 1930 v Bel; (with Arsenal), 1936 v Sw, H, L; (with Southampton), 1937 v Sw, F; (with Shamrock R), 1938 v N (2), Cz, Pol; 1939 v Sw, Pol, H (2), G (15)

Dunne, J. C. (Fulham), 1971 v A (1)

Dunne, L. (Manchester C), 1935 v Sw, G (2)

Dunne, P. A. J. (Manchester U), 1965 v Sp; 1966 v Sp (2), WG; 1967 v T (5)

Dunne, S. (Luton T), 1953 v F, A; 1954 v F, L; 1956 v Sp, Ho; 1957 v D, WG, E; 1958 v D, Pol, A; 1959 v Pol; 1960 v WG, Se (15)

Dunne, T. (St Patrick's Ath), 1956 v Ho; 1957 v D, WG (3)

Dunning, P. (Shelbourne), 1971 v Se, I (2)

Dunphy, E. M. (York C), 1966 v Sp; (with Millwall), 1966 v WG; 1967 v T, Sp, T, Cz; 1968 v Cz, Pol; 1969 v Pol, A, D (2), H; 1970 v D, H, Pol, WG (sub); 1971 v Pol, Se (2), 1 (2), A (23)

Dwyer, N. M. (West Ham U), 1960 v Se, Ch, WG, Se; (with Swansea T), 1961 v W, N, S (2); 1962 v Cz (2); 1964 v Pol (sub), N, E; 1965 v Pol (14)

Eccles, P. (Shamrock R), 1986 v U (sub) (1)

Egan, R. (Dundalk), 1929 v Bel (1)

Eglington, T. J. (Shamrock R), 1946 v P, Sp; (with Everton), 1947 v E, Sp, P; 1948 v P; 1949 v Sw, P, Se; 1951 v N, Arg; 1952 v WG (2), A, Sp; 1953 v F, A; 1954 v F, L, F; 1955 v N, Ho, WG; 1956 v Sp (24)

Ellis, P. (Bohemians), 1935 v Sw, G; 1936 v Ho, Sw, L; 1937 v G, H (7)

Fagan, E. (Shamrock R), 1973 v N (sub) (1)

Fagan, F. (Manchester C), 1955 v N; 1960 v Se; (with Derby Co), 1960 v Ch, WG, Se; 1961 v W, N, S (8)

Fagan, K. (Shamrock R), 1926 v I (1)

Fairclough, M. (Dundalk), 1982 v Ch (sub), Tr (sub) (2)

Fallon, S. (Celtic), 1951 v N; 1952 v WG (2), A, Sp; 1953 v F; 1955 v N, WG (8)

Fallon, W. J. (Notts Co), 1935 v H; 1936 v H; 1937 v H, Sw, F; 1939 v Sw, Pol; (with Sheffield W), 1939 v H, G (9)

Farquharson, T. G. (Cardiff C), 1929 v Bel; 1930 v Bel; 1931 v Sp; 1932 v Sp (4)

Farrell, P. (Hibernian), 1937 v Sw, F (2)

Farrell, P. D. (Shamrock R), 1946 v P, Sp; (with Everton), 1947 v Sp, P; 1948 v P, Sp; 1949 v Sw, P (sub), Sp; 1950 v E, Fi, Se; 1951 v Arg, N; 1952 v WG (2), A, Sp; 1953 v F, A; 1954 v F (2); 1955 v N, Ho, WG; 1956 v Y, Sp; 1957 v E (28)

Feenan, J. J. (Sunderland), 1937 v Sw, F (2)

Finucane, A. (Limerick), 1967 v T, Cz; 1969 v Cz, D, H; 1970 v S, Cz; 1971 v Se, I (1 + 1 sub); 1972 v A (11)

Fitzgerald, F. J. (Waterford), 1955 v Ho; 1956 v Ho (2)

Fitzgerald, P. J. (Leeds U), 1961 v W, N, S; 1962 v Cz (2) (5)

Fitzpatrick, K. (Limerick), 1970 v Cz (1)

Fitzsimons, A. G. (Middlesbrough), 1950 v Fi, Bel; 1952 v WG (2), A, Sp; 1953 v F, A; 1954 v F, L, F; 1955 v Ho, N, WG; 1956 v Y, Sp, Ho; 1957 v D, WG, E (2); 1958 v D, Pol, A; 1959 v Pol; (with Lincoln C), 1959 v Cz (26)

Flood, J. J. (Shamrock R), 1926 v I; 1929 v Bel; 1930 v Bel; 1931 v Sp; 1932 v Sp (5)

Fogarty, A. (Sunderland), 1960 v WG, Se; 1961 v S; 1962 v Cz (2); 1963 v Ic (2), S (sub); 1964 v A (2); (with Hartlepools U), Sp (11)

Foley, J. (Cork), 1934 v Bel, Ho; (with Celtic), 1935 v H, Sw, G; 1937 v G, H (7)

Foley, M. (Shelbourne), 1926 v I (1)

Foley, T. C. (Northampton T), 1964 v Sp, Pol, N; 1965 v Pol, Bel; 1966 v Sp (2), WG; 1967 v Cz (9)

878

Foy, T. (Shamrock R), 1938 v N; 1939 v H (2)
Fullam, J. (Preston NE), 1961 v N; (with Shamrock R), 1964 v Sp, Pol, N; 1966 v A, Bel; 1968 v Pol; 1969 v Pol, A, D; 1970 v Cz (sub) (11)
Fullam, R. (Shamrock R), 1926 v I; 1927 v I (2)

Gallagher, C. (Celtic), 1967 v T, Cz (2)
Gallagher, M. (Hibernian), 1954 v L (1)
Gallagher, P. (Falkirk), 1932 v Sp (1)
Galvin, A. (Tottenham H), 1983 v Ho, Ma; 1984 v Ho (sub), Is (sub); 1985 v M, USSR, N, D, I, N, Sp; 1986 v U, Ic, Cz; 1987 v Bel (2), S, Bul, I; (with Sheffield W), 1988 v L, Bul, R, Pol, N, E, USSR, Ho; 1989 v Sp; (with Swindon T), 1990 v WG (29)
Gannon, E. (Notts Co), 1949 v Sw; (with Sheffield W), 1949 v Bel, P, Se, Sp; 1950 v Fi; 1951 v N; 1952 v G, A; 1954 v L, F; 1955 v N; (with Shelbourne), 1955 v N, WG (14)
Gannon, M. (Shelbourne), 1972 v A (1)
Gaskins, P. (Shamrock R), 1934 v Bel, Ho; 1935 v H, Sw, G; (with St James' Gate), 1938 v Cz, Pol (7)
Gavin, J. T. (Norwich C), 1950 v Fi (2); 1953 v F; 1954 v L; (with Tottenham H), 1955 v Ho, WG; (with Norwich C), 1957 v D (7)
Geoghegan, M. (St James' Gate), 1937 v G; 1938 v N (2)
Gibbons, A. (St Patrick's Ath), 1952 v WG; 1954 v L; 1956 v Y, Sp (4)
Gilbert, R. (Shamrock R), 1966 v WG (1)
Giles, C. (Doncaster R), 1951 v N (1)
Giles, M. J. (Manchester U), 1960 v Se, Ch; 1961 v W, N, S (2); 1962 v Cz (2), A; 1963 v Ic, S; (with Leeds U), 1964 v A (2), Sp (2), Pol, N, E; 1965 v Sp; 1966 v Sp (2), A, Bel; 1967 v Sp, T (2); 1969 v A, D, Cz; 1970 v S, Pol, WG; 1971 v I; 1973 v F, USSR; 1974 v Br, U, Ch; 1975 v USSR, T, Sw, USSR, Sw; (with WBA), 1976 v T; 1977 v E, T, F (2), Pol, Bul; (with Shamrock R), 1978 v Bul, T, Pol, N, D; 1979 v Ni, D, Bul, WG (60)
Givens, D. J. (Manchester U), 1969 v D, H; 1970 v S, Cz, D, H; (with Luton T), 1970 v Pol, WG; 1971 v Se, I (2), A; 1972 v Ir, Ec, P; (with QPR), 1973 v F, USSR, Pol, F, N; 1974 v Pol, Br, U, Ch; 1975 v USSR, T, Sw, USSR, Sw, WG; 1976 v T, N, Pol; 1977 v E, T, F (2), Sp, Bul; 1978 v Bul, N, D; (with Birmingham C), 1979 v Ni (sub), E, D, Bul, WG; 1980 v US (sub), Ni (sub), Sw, Arg; 1981 v Ho, Bel, Cy (sub), W; (with Neuchatel X), 1982 v F (sub) (56)
Glen, W. (Shamrock R), 1927 v I; 1929 v Bel; 1930 v Bel; 1932 v Sp; 1936 v Ho, Sw, H, L (8)
Glynn, D. (Drumcondra), 1952 v WG; 1955 v N (2)
Godwin, T. F. (Shamrock R), 1949 v P, Se, Sp; 1950 v Fi, E; (with Leicester C), 1950 v Fi, Se, Bel; 1951 v N; (with Bournemouth), 1956 v Ho; 1957 v E; 1958 v D, Pol (13)
Golding, L. (Shamrock R), 1928 v Bel; 1930 v Bel (2)
Gorman, W. C. (Bury), 1936 v Sw, H, L; 1937 v G, H; 1938 v N, Cz, Pol; 1939 v Sw, Pol, H; (with Brentford), 1947 v E, P (13)
Grace, J. (Drumcondra), 1926 v I (1)
Grealish, A. (Orient), 1976 v N, Pol, D; 1979 v Ni, E, WG; (with Luton T), 1980 v W, Cz, Bul, US, Ni, E, Cy, Sw, Arg; 1981 v Ho, Bel, F, Cy, W, Bel, Pol; (with Brighton & HA), 1982 v Ho, Alg, Ch, Br, Tr; 1983 v Ho, Sp, Ic, Sp; 1984 v Ic, Ho; (with WBA), Pol, Chn; 1985 v M, USSR, N, D, Sp (sub), Sw; 1986 v USSR, D (44)
Gregg, E. (Bohemians), 1978 v Pol, D (sub); 1979 v E (sub), D, Bul, WG; 1980 v W, Cz (9)
Griffith, R. (Walsall), 1935 v H (1)
Grimes, A. A. (Manchester U), 1978 v T, Pol, N (sub); 1980 v Bul, US, Ni, E, Cy; 1981 v Cz, Pol; 1982 v Alg; 1983 v Sp (2); (with Coventry C), 1984 v Pol, Is; (with Luton T), 1988 v L, R (17)

Hale, A. (Aston Villa), 1962 v A; (with Doncaster R), 1963 v Ic; 1964 v Sp (2); (with Waterford), 1967 v Sp; 1968 v Pol (sub); 1969 v Pol, A, D; 1970 v S, Cz; 1971 v Pol (sub); 1972 v A (sub) (13)
Hamilton, T. (Shamrock R), 1959 v Cz (2) (2)
Hand, E. K. (Portsmouth), 1969 v Cz (sub); 1970 v Pol, WG; 1971 v Pol, A; 1973 v USSR, F, USSR, Pol, F; 1974 v Pol, Br, U, Ch; 1975 v T, Sw, USSR, Sw, WG; 1976 v T (20)
Harrington, W. (Cork), 1936 v Ho, Sw, H, L (4)
Hartnett, J. B. (Middlesbrough), 1949 v Sp; 1954 v L (2)
Haverty, J. (Arsenal), 1956 v Ho; 1957 v D, WG, E (2); 1958 v D, Pol, A; 1959 v Pol; 1960 v Se, Ch; 1961 v W, N, S (2); (with Blackburn R), 1962 v Cz (2); (with Millwall), 1963 v S; 1964 v A, Sp, Pol, N, E; (with Celtic), 1965 v Pol; (with Bristol R), 1965 v Sp; (with Shelbourne), 1966 v Sp (2), WG, A, Bel; 1967 v T, Sp (32)
Hayes, A. W. P. (Southampton), 1979 v D (1)
Hayes, W. E. (Huddersfield T), 1947 v E, P (2)
Hayes, W. J. (Limerick), 1949 v Bel (1)
Healey, R. (Cardiff C), 1977 v Pol; 1980 v E (sub) (2)
Heighway, S. D. (Liverpool), 1971 v Pol, Se (2), I, A; 1973 v USSR; 1975 v USSR, T, USSR, WG; 1976 v T, N; 1977 v E, F (2), Sp, Bul; 1978 v Bul, N, D; 1979 v Ni, Bul; 1980 v Bul, US, Ni, E, Cy, Arg; 1981 v Bel, F, Cy, W, Bel; (with Minnesota K), 1982 v Ho (34)
Henderson, B. (Drumcondra), 1948 v P, Sp (2)
Hennessy, J. (Shelbourne), 1956 v Pol, B, Sp; 1966 v WG; (with St Patrick's Ath), 1969 v A (5)
Herrick, J. (Cork Hibernians), 1972 v A, Ch (sub); (with Shamrock R), 1973 v F (sub) (3)
Higgins, J. (Birmingham C), 1951 v Arg (1)
Holmes, J. (Coventry C), 1971 v A (sub); 1973 v F, USSR, Pol, F, N; 1974 v Pol, Br; 1975 v USSR, Sw; 1976 v T, N, Pol; 1977 v E, T, F, Sp; (with Tottenham H), F, Pol, Bul; 1978 v Bul, T, Pol, N, D; 1979 v Ni, E, D, Bul; (with Vancouver W), 1981 v W (30)
Horlecher, A. F. (Bohemians), 1930 v Bel; 1932 v Sp, Ho; 1935 v H; 1936 v Ho, Sw (6)
Houghton, R. J. (Oxford U), 1986 v W, U, Ic, Cz; 1987 v Bel (2), S (2), Pol, L; 1988 v L, Bul; (with Liverpool), Is, Y, N, E, USSR, Ho; 1989 v Ni, Tun, Sp, F, H, Sp, Ma, H; 1990 v Ni, Ma, Fi, E, Eg, Ho, R, I; 1991 v Mor, T, E (2), Pol, Ch, US; 1992 v H, Alb, US, I, P (46)
Howlett, G. (Brighton & HA), 1984 v Chn (sub) (1)
Hoy, M. (Dundalk), 1938 v N; 1939 v Sw, Pol, H (2), G (6)
Hughton, C. (Tottenham H), 1980 v US, E, Sw, Arg; 1981 v Ho, Bel, F, Cy, W, Bel, Pol; 1982 v F; 1983 v Ho, Sp, Ma, Sp; 1984 v Ic, Ho, Ma; 1985 v M (sub), USSR, N, I, Is, E, Sp; 1986 v Sw, USSR, U, Ic; 1987 v Bel, Bul; 1988 v Is, Y, Pol, N, E, USSR, Ho; 1989 v Ni, F, H, Sp, Ma, H; 1990 v W (sub), USSR (sub), Fi, T (sub), Ma (sub); 1991 v T; (with West Ham U), Ch; 1992 v T (53)
Hurley, C. J. (Millwall), 1957 v E; 1958 v D, Pol, A; (with Sunderland), 1959 v Cz (2); 1960 v Se, Ch, WG, Se; 1961 v W, N, S (2); 1962 v Cz (2), A; 1963 v Ic (2), S; 1964 v A (2), Sp (2), Pol, N; 1965 v Sp; 1966 v WG, A, Bel; 1967 v T, Sp, T, Cz; 1968 v Cz, Pol (2); (with Bolton W), 1969 v D, Cz, H (40)
Hutchinson, F. (Drumcondra), 1935 v Sw, G (2)

Irwin, D. J. (Manchester U), 1991 v Mor, T, W, E, Pol, US; 1992 v H, Pol, W, US, Alb, US (sub), I (13)

Jordan, D. (Wolverhampton W), 1937 v Sw, F (2)
Jordan, W. (Bohemians), 1934 v Ho; 1938 v N (2)

Kavanagh, P. J. (Celtic), 1931 v Sp; 1932 v Sp(2)
Keane, R. M. (Nottingham F), 1991 v Ch; 1992 v H, Pol, W, Sw, Alb, US (7)
Keane, T. R. (Swansea T), 1949 v Sw, P, Se, Sp (4)

Kearin, M. (Shamrock R), 1972 v A (1)

Kearns, F. T. (West Ham U), 1954 v L (1)

Kearns, M. (Oxford U), 1970 v Pol (sub); (with Walsall), 1974 v Pol (sub), U, Ch; 1976 v N, Pol; 1977 v E, T, F (2), Sp, Bul; 1978 v N, D; 1979 v Ni, E; (with Wolverhampton W), 1980 v US, Ni (18)

Kelly, D. T. (Walsall), 1988 v Is, R, Y; (with West Ham U), 1989 v Tun (sub); (with Leicester C), 1990 v USSR, Ma; 1991 v Mor, W (sub), Ch, US; 1992 v H; (with Newcastle U), v I (sub), P (13)

Kelly, J. (Derry C), 1932 v Ho; 1934 v Bel; 1936 v Sw, L (4)

Kelly, J. A. (Drumcondra), 1957 v WG, E; (with Preston NE), 1962 v A; 1963 v Ic (2), S; 1964 v A (2), Sp (2), Pol; 1965 v Bel; 1966 v A, Bel; 1967 v Sp (2), T, Cz (2), Pol; 1968 v Pol, A, D, Cz, D, H; 1970 v S, D, H, Pol, WG; 1971 v Pol, Se (2), I (2), A; 1972 v Ir, Ec, Ch, P; 1973 v USSR, F, USSR, Pol, F, N (47)

Kelly, J. P. V. (Wolverhampton W), 1961 v W, N, S; 1962 v Cz (2) (5)

Kelly, M. J. (Portsmouth), 1988 v Y, Pol (sub); 1989 v Tun; 1990 v Mor (4)

Kelly, N. (Nottingham F), 1954 v L (1)

Kendrick, J. (Everton), 1927 v I; 1934 v Bel, Ho; 1936 v Ho (4)

Kennedy, M. F. (Portsmouth), 1986 v Ic, Cz (sub) (2)

Kennedy, W. (St James' Gate), 1932 v Ho; 1934 v Bel, Ho (3)

Keogh, J. (Shamrock R), 1966 v WG (sub) (1)

Keogh, S. (Shamrock R), 1959 v Pol (1)

Kiernan, F. W. (Shamrock R), 1951 v Arg, N; (with Southampton), 1952 v WG (2), A (5)

Kinnear, J. P. (Tottenham H), 1967 v T; 1968 v Cz, Pol; 1969 v A; 1970 v Cz, D, H, Pol; 1971 v Se (sub), I; 1972 v Ir, Ec, Ch, P; 1973 v USSR, F; 1974 v Pol, Br, U, Ch; 1975 v USSR, T, Sw, USSR, WG; (with Brighton & HA), 1976 v T (sub) (26)

Kinsella, J. (Shelbourne), 1928 v Bel (1)

Kinsella, P. (Shamrock R), 1932 v Ho; 1938 v N (2)

Kirkland, A. (Shamrock R), 1927 v I (1)

Lacey, W. (Shelbourne), 1927 v I; 1928 v Bel; 1930 v Bel (3)

Langan, D. (Derby Co), 1978 v T, N; 1980 v Sw, Arg; (with Birmingham C), 1981 v Ho, Bel, F, Cy, W, Bel, Cz, Pol; 1982 v Ho, F; (with Oxford U), 1985 v N, Sp, Sw; 1986 v W, U; 1987 v Bel, S, Pol, Br (sub), L (sub); 1988 v L (25)

Lawler, J. F. (Fulham), 1953 v A; 1954 v L, F; 1955 v N, H, N, WG; 1956 v Y (8)

Lawlor, J. C. (Drumcondra), 1949 v Bel; (with Doncaster R), 1951 v N, Arg (3)

Lawlor, M. (Shamrock R), 1971 v Pol, Se (2), I (sub); 1973 v Pol (5)

Lawrenson, M. (Preston NE), 1977 v Pol; (with Brighton), 1978 v Bul, Pol, N (sub); 1979 v Ni, E; 1980 v E, Cy, Sw; 1981 v Ho, Bel, F, Cy, Pol; (with Liverpool), 1982 v Ho, F; 1983 v Ho, Sp, Ic, Ma, Sp; 1984 v Ic, Ho, Ma, Is; 1985 v USSR, N, D, I, E, N; 1986 v Sw, USSR, D; 1987 v Bel, S; 1988 v Bul, Is (38)

Leech, M. (Shamrock R), 1969 v Cz, D, H; 1972 v A, Ir, Ec, P; 1973 v USSR (sub) (8)

Lennon, C. (St James' Gate), 1935 v H, Sw, G (3)

Lennox, G. (Dolphin), 1931 v Sp; 1932 v Sp (2)

Lowry, D. (St Patrick's Ath), 1962 v A (sub) (1)

Lunn, R. (Dundalk), 1939 v Sw, Pol (2)

Lynch, J. (Cork Bohemians), 1934 v Bel (1)

McAlinden, J. (Portsmouth), 1946 v P, Sp (2)

McCann, J. (Shamrock R), 1957 v WG (1)

McCarthy, J. (Bohemians), 1926 v I; 1928 v Bel; 1930 v Bel (3)

McCarthy, M. (Manchester C), 1984 v Pol, Chn; 1985 v M, D, I, Is, E, Sp, Sw; 1986 v Sw, USSR, W (sub), U, Ic, Cz; 1987 v S (2), Pol, Bul, Bel, Br, L; (with Celtic), 1988 v Bul, Is, R, Y, N, E, USSR, Ho; 1989 v Ni, Tun, Sp, F, H, Sp; (with Lyon), 1990 v WG, Ni, W, USSR, Fi, T, E, Eg, Ho, R, I; (with Millwall), 1991 v Mor, T, E, US; 1992 v H, T, Alb (sub), US, I, P (57)

McCarthy, M. (Shamrock R), 1932 v Ho (1)

McConville, T. (Dundalk), 1972 v A; (with Waterford), 1973 v USSR, F, USSR, Pol, F (6)

McDonagh, Joe (Shamrock R), 1984 v Pol (sub), Ma; 1985 v M (sub) (3)

McDonagh, J. (Everton), 1981 v W, Bel, Cz; (with Bolton W), 1982 v Ho, F, Ch, Br; 1983 v Ho, Sp, Ic, Ma, Sp; (with Notts Co), 1984 v Ic, Ho, Pol; 1985 v M, USSR, N, D, Sp, Sw; 1986 v Sw, USSR, D (24)

McEvoy, M. A. (Blackburn R), 1961 v S (2); 1963 v S; 1964 v A, Sp (2); 1965 v Pol, Bel, Sp; 1966 v Sp (2); 1967 v Sp, T, Cz (17)

McGee, P. (QPR), 1978 v T, N (sub), D (sub); 1979 v Ni, E, D (sub), Bul (sub); 1980 v Cz, Bul; (with Preston NE), US, Ni, Cy, Sw, Arg; 1981 v Bel (sub) (15)

McGoldrick, E. J. (C Palace), 1992 v Sw, US, I, P (sub) (4)

McGowan, D. (West Ham U), 1949 v P, Se, Sp (3)

McGowan, J. (Cork U), 1947 v Sp (1)

McGrath, M. (Blackburn R) 1958 v A; 1959 v Pol, Cz (2); 1960 v Se, WG, Se; 1961 v W; 1962 v Cz (2); 1963 v S; 1964 v A (2), E; 1965 v Pol, Bel, Sp; 1966 v Sp; (with Bradford), 1966 v WG, A, Bel; 1967 v T (22)

McGrath, P. (Manchester U), 1985 v I (sub), Is, E, N (sub), Sw (sub); 1986 v Sw (sub), D, W, Ic, Cz; 1987 v Bel (2), S (2), Pol, Bul, Br, L; 1988 v L, Bul, Y, Pol, N, E, Ho; 1989 v Ni, F, H, Sp, Ma, H; (with Aston Villa), 1990 v WG, Ma, USSR, Fi, T, E, Eg, Ho, R, I; 1991 v E (2), W, Pol, Ch (sub), US; 1992 v Pol, T, Sw, US, Alb, US, I, P (55)

McGuire, W. (Bohemians), 1936 v Ho (1)

McKenzie, G. (Southend U), 1938 v N (2), Cz, Pol; 1939 v Sw, Pol, H (2), G (9)

Mackey, G. (Shamrock R), 1957 v D, WG, E (3)

McLoughlin, A. F. (Swindon T), 1990 v Ma, E (sub), Eg (sub); 1991 v Mor (sub), E (sub); (with Southampton), W, Ch (sub); 1992 v H (sub), W (sub); (with Portsmouth), US, I (sub), P (12)

McLoughlin, F. (Fordsons), 1930 v Bel; (with Cork), 1932 v Sp (2)

McMillan, W. (Belfast Celtic), 1946 v P, Sp (2)

McNally, J. B. (Luton T), 1959 v Cz; 1961 v Sp; 1963 v Ic (3)

Macken, A. (Derby Co), 1977 v Sp (1)

Madden, O. (Cork), 1936 v H (1)

Maguire, J. (Shamrock R), 1929 v Bel (1)

Malone, G. (Shelbourne), 1949 v Bel (1)

Mancini, T. J. (QPR), 1974 v Pol, Br, U, Ch; (with Arsenal), 1975 v USSR (5)

Martin, C. (Bo'ness), 1927 v I (1)

Martin, C. J. (Glentoran), 1946 v P (sub), Sp; 1947 v E; (with Leeds U), 1947 v Sp; 1948 v P, Sp; (with Aston Villa), 1949 v Sw, Bel, P, Se, Sp; 1950 v Fi, E, Fi, Se, Bel; 1951 v Arg; 1952 v WG, A, Sp; 1954 v F (2), L; 1955 v N, Ho, N, WG; 1956 v Y, Sp, Ho (30)

Martin, M. P. (Bohemians), 1972 v A, Ir, Ec, Ch, P; 1973 v USSR; (with Manchester U), 1973 v USSR, Pol, F, N; 1974 v Pol, Br, U, Ch; 1975 v USSR, T, Sw, USSR, Sw, WG; (with WBA), 1976 v T, N, Pol; 1977 v E, T, F (2), Sp, Pol, Bul; (with Newcastle U), 1979 v D, Bul, WG; 1980 v W, Cz, Bul, US, Ni; 1981 v F, Bel, Cz; 1982 v Ho, F, Alg, Ch, Br, Tr; 1983 v Ho, Sp, Ma, Sp (51)

Meagan, M. K. (Everton), 1961 v S; 1962 v A; 1963 v Ic; 1964 v Sp; (with Huddersfield T), 1965 v Bel; 1966 v Sp (2), A, Bel; 1967 v Sp, T, Sp, T, Cz; 1968 v Cz, Pol; (with Drogheda), 1970 v S (17)

Roche, P. J. (Shelbourne), 1972 v A; (with Manchester U), 1975 v USSR, T, Sw, USSR, Sw, WG; 1976 v T (8)

Rogers, E. (Blackburn R), 1968 v Cz, Pol; 1969 v Pol, A, D, Cz, D, H; 1970 v S, D, H; 1971 v I (2), A; (with Charlton Ath), 1972 v Ir, Ec, Ch, P; 1973 v USSR (19)

Ryan, G. (Derby Co), 1978 v T; (with Brighton & HA), 1979 v E, WG; 1980 v W, Cy (sub), Sw, Arg (sub); 1981 v F (sub), Pol (sub); 1982 v Ho (sub), Alg (sub), Ch (sub), Tr; 1984 v Pol, Chn; 1985 v M (16)

Ryan, R. A. (WBA), 1950 v Se, Bel; 1951 v N, Arg, N; 1952 v WG (2), A, Sp; 1953 v F, A; 1954 v F, L, F; 1955 v N; (with Derby Co), 1956 v Sp (16)

Saward, P. (Millwall), 1954 v L; (with Aston Villa), 1957 v E (2); 1958 v D, Pol, A; 1959 v Pol, Cz; 1960 v Se, Ch, WG, Se; 1961 v W, N; (with Huddersfield T), 1961 v S; 1962 v A; 1963 v Ic (2) (18)

Scannell, T. (Southend U), 1954 v L (1)

Scully, P. J. (Arsenal), 1989 v Tun (sub) (1)

Sheedy, K. (Everton), 1984 v Ho (sub), Ma; 1985 v D, I, Is, Sw; 1986 v Sw, D; 1987 v S, Pol; 1988 v Is, R, Pol, E (sub), USSR; 1989 v Ni, Tun, H, Sp, Ma, H; 1990 v Ni, Ma, W (sub), USSR, Fi (sub), T, E, Eg, Ho, R, I; 1991 v W, E, Pol, Ch, US; 1992 v H, Pol, T, W; (with Newcastle U), Sw (sub), Alb (43)

Sheridan, J. J. (Leeds U), 1988 v R, Y, Pol, N (sub); 1989 v Sp; (with Sheffield W), 1990 v W, T (sub), Ma, I (sub); 1991 v Mor (sub), T, Ch, US (sub); 1992 v H (14)

Slaven, B. (Middlesbrough), 1990 v W, Fi, T (sub). Ma; 1991 v W, Pol (sub) (6)

Sloan, J. W. (Arsenal), 1946 v P, Sp (2)

Smyth, M. (Shamrock R), 1969 v Pol (sub) (1)

Squires, J. (Shelbourne), 1934 v Ho (1)

Stapleton, F. (Arsenal), 1977 v T, F, Sp, Bul; 1978 v Bul, N, D; 1979 v Ni, E (sub), D, WG; 1980 v W, Bul, Ni, E, Cy; 1981 v Ho, Bel, F, Cy, Bel, Cz, Pol; (with Manchester U), 1982 v Ho, F, Alg; 1983 v Ho, Sp, Ic, Ma, Sp; 1984 v Ic, Ho, Ma, Pol, Is, Chn; 1985 v N, D, I, Is, E, N, Sw; 1986 v Sw, USSR, D, U, Ic, Cz (sub); 1987 v Bel (2), S (2), Pol, Bul, I; (with Ajax), 1988 v L, Bul, R; (with Derby Co), Y, N, E, USSR, Ho; (with Le Havre), 1989 v F, Sp, Ma; (with Blackburn R), 1990 v WG, Ma (sub) (70)

Staunton, S. (Liverpool), 1989 v Tun, Sp (2), Ma, H; 1990 v WG, Ni, Ma, W, USSR, Fi, T, Ma, E, Eg, Ho, R, I; 1991 v Mor, T, E (2), W, Pol, Ch, US; (with Aston Villa), 1992 v Pol, T, Sw, US, Alb, US, I, P (34)

Stevenson, A. E. (Dolphin), 1932 v Ho; (with Everton), 1947 v E, Sp, P; 1948 v P, Sp; 1949 v Sw (7)

Strahan, F. (Shelbourne), 1964 v Pol, N, E; 1965 v Pol; 1966 v WG (5)

Sullivan, J. (Fordsons), 1928 v Bel (1)

Swan, M. M. G. (Drumcondra), 1960 v Se (sub) (1)

Synnott, N. (Shamrock R), 1978 v T, Pol; 1979 v Ni (3)

Thomas, P. (Waterford), 1974 v Pol, Br (2)

Townsend, A. D. (Norwich C), 1989 v F, Sp (sub), Ma (sub), H; 1990 v WG (sub), Ni, Ma, W, USSR, Fi (sub),

T, Ma (sub), E, Eg, Ho, R, I; (with Chelsea), 1991 v Mor, T, E (2), W, Pol, Ch, US; 1992 v Pol, W, US, Alb, US, I (31)

Traynor, T. J. (Southampton), 1954 v L; 1962 v A; 1963 v Ic (2), S; 1964 v A (2), Sp (8)

Treacy, R. C. P. (WBA), 1966 v WG; 1967 v Sp, Cz; 1968 v Cz; (with Charlton Ath), 1968 v Pol; 1969 v Pol, Cz, D; 1970 v S, D, H (sub), Pol (sub), WG (sub); 1971 v Pol, Se (sub + 1), I, A; (with Swindon T), 1972 v Ir, Ec, Ch, P; 1973 v USSR, F, USSR, Pol, F, N; 1974 v Pol; (with Preston NE), Br; 1975 v USSR, Sw (2), WG; 1976 v T, N (sub), Pol (sub); (with WBA), 1977 v F, Pol; (with Shamrock R), 1978 v T, Pol (2); 1980 v Cz (sub) (43)

Tuohy, L. (Shamrock R), 1956 v Y; 1959 v Cz (2); (with Newcastle U), 1962 v A; 1963 v Ic (2); (with Shamrock R), 1964 v A; 1965 v Bel (8)

Turner, A. (Celtic), 1963 v S; 1964 v Sp (2)

Turner, C. J. (Southend U), 1936 v Sw; 1937 v G, H, Sw, F; (with West Ham U), 1938 v N (2), Cz, Pol; 1939 v H (10)

Vernon, J. (Belfast C), 1946 v P, Sp (2)

Waddock, G. (QPR), 1980 v Sw, Arg; 1981 v W, Pol (sub); 1982 v Alg; 1983 v Ic, Ma, Sp, Ho (sub); 1984 v Ic, Ho, Is; 1985 v I, Is, E, N, Sp; 1986 v USSR; (with Millwall), 1990 v USSR, T (20)

Walsh, D. J. (WBA), 1946 v P, Sp; 1947 v Sp, P; 1948 v P, Sp; 1949 v Sw, P, Se, Sp; 1950 v E, Fi, Se; 1951 v N; (with Aston Villa), v Arg, N; 1952 v Sp; 1953 v A; 1954 v F (2) (20)

Walsh, J. (Limerick), 1982 v Tr (1)

Walsh, M. (Blackpool), 1976 v N, Pol; 1977 v F (sub), Pol; (with Everton), 1979 v Ni (sub); (with QPR), D (sub), Bul, WG (sub); (with Porto), 1981 v Bel (sub), Cz; 1982 v Alg (sub); 1983 v Sp, Ho (sub), Sp (sub); 1984 v Ic (sub), Ma, Pol, Chn; 1985 v USSR, N (sub), D (22)

Walsh, M. (Everton), 1982 v Ch, Br, Tr; 1983 v Sp; (with Norwich C), Ic (5)

Walsh, W. (Manchester C), 1947 v E, Sp, P; 1948 v P, Sp; 1949 v Bel; 1950 v E, Se, Bel (9)

Waters, J. (Grimsby T), 1977 v T; 1980 v Ni (sub) (2)

Watters, F. (Shelbourne), 1926 v I (1)

Weir, E. (Clyde), 1939 v H (2), G (3)

Whelan, R. (St Patrick's Ath), 1964 v A, E (sub) (2)

Whelan, R. (Liverpool), 1981 v Cz (sub); 1982 v Ho (sub), F; 1983 v Ic, Ma, Sp; 1984 v Is; 1985 v USSR, N, I (sub), Is, E, N (sub), Sw (sub); 1986 v USSR (sub), W; 1987 v Bel (sub), S, Bul, Bel, Br, L; 1988 v L, Bul, Pol, N, E, USSR, Ho; 1989 v Ni, F, H, Sp, Ma; 1990 v WG, Ni, Ma, W, Ho (sub); 1991 v Mor, E; 1992 v Sw (42)

Whelan, W. (Manchester U), 1956 v Ho; 1957 v D, E (2) (4)

White, J. J. (Bohemians), 1928 v Bel (1)

Whittaker, R. (Chelsea), 1959 v Cz (1)

Williams, J. (Shamrock R), 1938 v N (1)

BRITISH AND IRISH INTERNATIONAL GOALSCORERS SINCE 1872

Where two players with the same surname and initials have appeared for the same country, and one or both have scored, they have been distinguished by reference to the club which appears *first* against their name in the international appearances section (pages 833–881). Unfortunately, four of the scorers in Scotland's 10-2 victory v Ireland in 1888 are unknown, as is the scorer of one of their nine goals v Wales in March 1878.

ENGLAND

Name	Goals
A'Court, A.	1
Adams, T. A.	4
Adcock, H.	1
Alcock, C. W.	1
Allen, A.	3
Allen, R.	2
Anderson, V.	2
Astall, G.	1
Athersmith, W. C.	3
Atyeo, P. J. W.	5
Bache, J. W.	4
Bailey, N. C.	2
Baily, E. F.	5
Baker, J. H.	3
Ball, A. J.	8
Bambridge, A. L.	1
Bambridge, E. C.	12
Barclay, R.	2
Barnes, J.	10
Barnes, P. S.	4
Barton, J.	1
Bassett, W. I.	7
Bastin, C. S.	12
Beardsley, P. A.	8
Beasley, A.	1
Beattie, T. K.	1
Becton, F.	2
Bedford, H.	1
Bell, C.	9
Bentley, R. T. F.	9
Bishop, S. M.	1
Blackburn, F.	1
Blissett, L.	3
Bloomer, S.	28
Bond, R.	2
Bonsor, A. G.	1
Bowden, E. R.	1
Bowers, J. W.	2
Bowles, S.	1
Bradford, G. R. W.	1
Bradford, J.	7
Bradley, W.	2
Bradshaw, F.	3
Bridges, B. J.	1
Bridgett, A.	3
Brindle, T.	1
Britton, C. S.	1
Broadbent, P. F.	2
Broadis, I. A.	8
Brodie, J. B.	1
Bromley-Davenport, W.	2
Brook, E. F.	10
Brooking, T. D.	5
Brooks, J.	2
Broome, F. H.	3
Brown, A.	4
Brown, A. S.	1
Brown, G.	5
Brown, J.	3
Brown, W.	1
Buchan, C. M.	4
Bull, S. G.	4
Bullock, N.	2
Burgess, H.	4
Butcher, T.	3
Byrne, J. J.	8
Camsell, G. H.	18
Carter, H. S.	7
Carter, J. H.	4
Chadwick, E.	3
Chamberlain, M.	1
Chambers, H.	5
Channon, M. R.	21
Charlton, J.	6
Charlton, R.	49
Chenery, C. J.	1
Chivers, M.	13
Clarke, A. J.	10
Cobbold, W. N.	7
Cock, J. G.	2
Common, A.	2
Connelly, J. M.	7
Coppell, S. J.	7
Cotterill, G. H.	2
Cowans, G.	2
Crawford, R.	1
Crawshaw, T. H.	1
Crayston, W. J.	1
Creek, F. N. S.	1
Crooks, S. D.	7
Currey, E. S.	2
Currie, A. W.	3
Cursham, A. W.	2
Cursham, H. A.	5
Daft, H. B.	3
Davenport, J. K.	2
Davis, G.	1
Davis, H.	1
Day, S. H.	2
Dean, W. R.	18
Devey, J. H. G.	1
Dewhurst, F.	11
Dix, W. R.	1
Dixon, K. M.	4
Dixon, L. M.	1
Douglas, B.	11
Drake, E. J.	6
Ducat, A.	1
Dunn, A. T. B.	2
Eastham, G.	2
Edwards, D.	5
Elliott, W. H.	3
Evans, R. E.	1
Finney, T.	30
Fleming, H. J.	9
Flowers, R.	10
Forman, Frank	1
Forman, Fred	3
Foster, R. E.	3
Francis, G. C. J.	3
Francis, T.	12
Freeman, B. C.	1
Froggatt, J.	2
Froggatt, R.	2
Galley, T.	1
Gascoigne, P. J.	2
Geary, F.	3
Gibbins, W. V. T.	3
Gilliatt, W. E.	3
Goddard, P.	1
Goodall, J.	12
Goodyer, A. C.	1
Gosling, R. C.	2
Goulden, L. A.	4
Grainger, C.	3
Greaves, J.	44
Grosvenor, A. T.	2
Gunn, W.	1
Haines, J. T. W.	2
Hall, G. W.	9
Halse, H. J.	2
Hampson, J.	5
Hampton, H.	2
Hancocks, J.	2
Hardman, H. P.	1
Harris, S. S.	2
Hassall, H. W.	4
Hateley, M.	9
Haynes, J. N.	18
Hegan, K. E.	4
Henfrey, A. G.	2
Hilsdon, G. R.	14
Hine, E. W.	4
Hirst, D. E.	1
Hitchens, G. A.	5
Hobbis, H. H. F.	1
Hoddle, G.	8
Hodgetts, D.	1
Hodgson, G.	1
Holley, G. H.	8
Houghton, W. E.	5
Howell, R.	1
Hughes, E. W.	1
Hulme, J. H. A.	4
Hunt, G. S.	1
Hunt, R.	18
Hunter, N.	2
Hurst, G. C.	24
Jack, D. N. B.	3
Johnson, D. E.	6
Johnson, E.	2
Johnson, J. A.	2
Johnson, T. C. F.	5
Johnson, W. H.	1
Kail, E. I. L.	2
Kay, A. H.	1
Keegan, J. K.	21
Kelly, R.	8
Kennedy, R.	3
Kenyon-Slaney, W. S.	2
Keown, M. R.	1
Kevan, D. T.	8
Kidd, B.	1
Kingsford, R. K.	1
Kirchen, A. J.	2
Kirton, W. J.	1
Langton, R.	1
Latchford, R. D.	5
Latheron, E. G.	1
Lawler, C.	1
Lawton, T.	22
Lee, F.	10
Lee, J.	1
Lee, S.	2
Lindley, T.	15
Lineker, G.	48
Lofthouse, J. M.	3
Lofthouse, N.	30
Hon. A. Lyttelton	1
McCall, J.	1
McDermott, T.	3
Macdonald, M.	6
Mabbutt, G.	1
Mannion, W. J.	11
Mariner, P.	13
Marsh, R. W.	1
Matthews, S.	11
Matthews, V.	1
Medley, L. D.	1
Melia, J.	1
Mercer, D. W.	1
Merson, P. C.	1
Milburn, J. E. T.	10
Miller, H. S.	1
Mills, G. R.	3
Milward, A.	3
Mitchell, C.	5
Moore, J.	1
Moore, R. F.	2
Moore, W. G. B.	2
Morren, T.	1
Morris, F.	1
Morris, J.	3
Mortensen, S. H.	23
Morton, J. R.	1
Mosforth, W.	3
Mullen, J.	6
Mullery, A. P.	1
Neal, P. G.	5
Needham, E.	3
Nicholls, J.	1
Nicholson, W. E.	1
O'Grady, M.	3
Osborne, F. R.	3
Own goals	23
Page, L. A.	1
Paine, T. L.	7
Parry, E. H.	1
Parry, R. A.	1
Pawson, F. W.	1
Payne, J.	2
Peacock, A.	3
Pearce, S.	2
Pearson, J. S.	5
Pearson, S. C.	5
Perry, W.	2
Peters, M.	20
Pickering, F.	5
Platt, D.	11
Pointer, R.	2
Quantrill, A.	1
Ramsay, A. E.	3
Revie, D. G.	4
Reynolds, J.	3
Richardson, J. R.	2
Rigby, A.	3
Rimmer, E. J.	2
Roberts, H.	1
Roberts, W. T.	4
Robinson, J.	3
Robson, B.	26
Robson, R.	4
Rowley, J. F.	6
Royle, J.	2
Rutherford, J.	3
Sagar, C.	1
Sandilands, R. R.	2
Sansom, K.	1
Schofield, J.	1
Seed, J. M.	1
Settle, J.	6
Sewell, J.	3

Shackleton, L. F. 1
Sharp, J. 1
Shearer, A. 1
Shepherd, A. 2
Simpson, J. 1
Smith, A. M. 2
Smith, G. O. 12
Smith, Joe 1
Smith, J. R. 2
Smith, J. W. 4
Smith, R. 13
Smith, S. 1
Sorby, T. H. 1
Southworth, J. 3
Sparks, F. J. 3
Spence, J. W. 1
Spiksley, F. 5
Spilsbury, B. W. 5
Steele, F. C. 8
Stephenson, G. T. 2
Steven, T. M. 4
Stewart, J. 2
Stiles, N. P. 1
Storer, H. 1
Summerbee, M. G. 1

Tambling, R. V. 1
Taylor, P. J. 2
Taylor, T. 16
Thompson, P. B. 1
Thornewell, G. 1
Tilson, S. F. 6
Townley, W. J. 2
Tueart, D. 2

Vaughton, O. H. 6
Veitch, J. G. 3
Violett, D. S. 1

Walker, C. R. 6
Walker, W. H. 9
Wall, G. 2
Wallace, D. 1
Walsh, P. 1
Waring, T. 4
Warren, B. 2
Watson, D. V. 4
Watson, V. M. 4
Webb, G. W. 1
Webb, N. 3
Wedlock, W. J. 2
Weir, D. 2
Weller, K. 1
Welsh, D. 1
Whateley, O. 2
Wheldon, G. F. 6
Whitfield, H. 1
Wignall, F. 2
Wilkes, A. 1
Wilkins, R. G. 3
Willingham, C. K. 1
Wilshaw, D. J. 10
Wilson, D. 1
Wilson, G. P. 1
Winckworth, W. N. 1
Windridge, J. E. 7
Wise, D. F. 1
Withe, P. 1
Wollaston, C. H. R. 1
Wood, H. 1
Woodcock, T. 16
Woodhall, G. 1
Woodward, V. J. 29
Worrall, F. 2
Worthington, F. S. 2
Wright, M. 1
Wright, W. A. 3
Wylie, J. G. 1

Yates, J. 3

NORTHERN IRELAND
Anderson, T. 3
Armstrong, G. 12

Bambrick, J. 12
Barr, H. H. 1
Barron, H. 3
Best, G. 9
Bingham, W. L. 10
Black, K. 1
Blanchflower, D. 2
Blanchflower, J. 1
Brennan, B. 1
Brennan, R. A. 1
Brotherston, N. 3
Brown, J. 1
Browne, F. 2

Campbell, J. 1
Campbell, W. G. 1
Casey, T. 2
Caskey, W. 1
Cassidy, T. 1
Chambers, J. 3
Clarke, C. J. 11
Clements, D. 2
Cochrane, T. 1
Condy, J. 1
Connor, M. J. 1
Coulter, J. 1
Croft, T. 1
Crone, W. 1
Crossan, E. 1
Crossan, J. A. 10
Curran, S. 2
Cush, W. W. 5

Dalton, W. 6
D'Arcy, S. D. 1
Darling, J. 1
Davey, H. H. 1
Davis, T. L. 1
Dill, A. H. 1
Doherty, L. 1
Doherty, P. D. 3
Dougan, A. D. 8
Dowie, I. 1
Dunne, J. 4

Elder, A. R. 1
Emerson, W. 1
English, S. 1

Ferguson, W. 1
Ferris, J. 1
Ferris, R. O. 1
Finney, T. 2

Gaffkin, J. 5
Gara, A. 3
Gawkrodger, G. 1
Gibb, J. T. 2
Gibb, T. J. 1
Gibson, W. K. 1
Gillespie, W. 12
Goodall, A. L. 2

Halligan, W. 1
Hamill, M. 1
Hamilton, B. 4
Hamilton, W. 5
Hannon, D. J. 1
Harkin, J. T. 2
Harvey, M. 3
Hill, C. F. 1
Hughes, M. 1
Humphries, W. 1
Hunter, A. (Distillery) 1
Hunter, A. (Blackburn R)
Irvine, R. W. 3
Irvine, W. J. 8

Johnston, H. 1
Johnston, S. 2
Johnston, W. C. 1
Jones, S. 1
Jones, J. 1

Kelly, J. 4
Kernaghan, N. 2
Kirwan, J. 2

Lacey, W. 3
Lemon, J. 2
Lockhart, N. 3

McAdams, W. J. 7
McAllen, J. 1
McAuley, J. L. 1
McCandless, J. 3
McCaw, J. H. 1
McClelland, J. 1
McCluggage, A. 2
McCracken, W. 1
McCrory, S. 1
McCurdy, C. 1
McDonald, A. 2
McGarry, J. K. 1
McGrath, R. C. 4
McIlroy, J. 10
McIlroy, S. B. 5
McKnight, J. 2
McLaughlin, J. C. 6
McMordie, A. S. 3
McMorran, E. J. 4
McParland, P. J. 10
McWha, W. B. R. 1

Magilton, J. 1
Mahood, J. 2
Martin, D. K. 3
Maxwell, J. 7
Meldon, J. 1
Mercer, J. 1
Mercer, J. T. 1
Millar, W. 1
Milligan, D. 1
Milne, R. G. 2
Molyneux, T. B. 1
Moreland, V. 1
Morgan, S. 3
Morrow, W. J. 1
Murphy, N. 1

Neill, W. J. T. 2
Nelson, S. 1
Nicholl, C. J. 3
Nicholl, J. M. 2
Nicholson, J. J. 6

O'Hagan, C. 2
O'Kane, W. J. 1
O'Neill, J. 1
O'Neill, M. A. 1
O'Neill, M. H. 8
Own goals 5

Peacock, R. 2
Peden, J. 7
Penney, S. 2
Pyper, James 2
Pyper, John 1

Quinn, J. M. 6

Reynolds, J. 1
Rowley, R. W. M. 2

Sheridan, J. 2
Sherrard, J. 1
Simpson, W. J. 5
Sloan, H. A. de B. 4
Smyth, S. 5
Spence, D. W. 3
Stanfield, O. M. 9
Stevenson, A. E. 5
Stewart, I. 2

Taggart, G. P. 4
Thompson, F. W. 2
Tully, C. P. 3
Turner, E. 1

Walker, J. 1

Walsh, D. J. 5
Welsh, E. 1
Whiteside, N. 9
Whiteside, T. 1
Williams, J. R. 1
Williamson, J. 1
Wilson, K, J. 4
Wilson, S. J. 7
Wilton, J. M. 2

Young, S. 2

SCOTLAND
Aitken, R. 1
Aitkenhead, W. A. C. 2
Alexander, D. 1
Allan, D. S. 4
Allan, J. 4
Anderson, F. 1
Anderson, W. 4
Andrews, P. 1
Archibald, A. 1
Archibald, S. 4

Baird, D. 2
Baird, J. C. 2
Baird, S. 2
Bannon, E. 1
Barbour, A. 1
Barker, J. B. 4
Battles, B. Jr 1
Bauld, W. 2
Baxter, J. C. 3
Bell, J. 5
Bennett, A. 2
Berry, D. 1
Bett, J. 1
Beveridge, W. W. 1
Black, A. 3
Black, D. 1
Bone, J. 1
Boyd, R. 2
Boyd, W. G. 1
Brackenridge, T. 1
Brand, R. 8
Brazil, A. 1
Bremner, W. J. 3
Brown, A. D. 6
Buchanan, P. S. 1
Buchanan, R. 1
Buckley, P. 1
Buick, A. 2
Burns, K. 1

Cairns, T. 1
Calderwood, R. 2
Caldow, E. 4
Campbell, C. 1
Campbell, John (*Celtic*) 5
Campbell, John (*Rangers*) 4
Campbell, P. 2
Campbell, R. 1
Cassidy, J. 1
Chalmers, S. 3
Chambers, T. 1
Cheyne, A. G. 4
Christie, A. J. 1
Clunas, W. L. 1
Collins, J. 2
Collins, R. Y. 10
Combe, J. R. 1
Conn, A. 1
Cooper, D. 6
Craig, J. 1
Craig, T. 1
Cunningham, A. N. 5
Curran, H. P. 1

Dalglish, K. 30
Davidson, D. 1
Davidson, J. A. 1
Delaney, J. 3
Devine, A. 1

Name		Name		Name		Name	
Dewar, G.	1	James, A. W.	3	Marshall, H.	1	Taylor, J. D.	1
Dewar, N.	4	Jardine, A.	1	Marshall, J.	1	Templeton, R.	1
Dickson, W.	4	Jenkinson, T.	1	Mason, J.	4	Thomson, A.	1
Divers, J.	1	Johnston, L. H.	1	Massie, A.	1	Thomson, C.	4
Docherty, T. H.	1	Johnston, M.	14	Masson, D. S.	5	Thomson, R.	1
Dodds, D.	1	Johnstone, D.	2	Meiklejohn, D. D.	3	Thomson, W.	1
Donaldson, A.	1	Johnstone, J.	4	Millar, J.	2	Thornton, W.	1
Donnachie, J.	1	Johnstone, Jas.	1	Miller, T.	2		
Dougall, J.	1	Johnstone, R.	9	Miller, W.	1	Waddell, T. S.	1
Drummond, J.	2	Johnstone, W.	1	Mitchell, R. C.	1	Waddell, W.	6
Dunbar, M.	1	Jordan, J.	11	Morgan, W.	1	Walker, J.	2
Duncan, D.	7			Morris, D.	1	Walker, R.	7
Duncan, D. M.	1	Kay, J. L.	5	Morris, H.	3	Walker, T.	9
Duncan, J.	1	Keillor, A.	3	Morton, A. L.	5	Wallace, I. A.	1
Dunn, J.	2	Kelly, J.	1	Mudie, J. K.	9	Wark, J.	7
Durie, G. S.	4	Kelso, J.	1	Mulhall, G.	1	Watson, J. A. K.	1
		Ker, G.	10	Munro, A. D.	1	Watt, F.	2
Easson, J. F.	1	King, A.	1	Munro, N.	1	Watt, W. W.	1
Ellis, J.	1	King, J.	1	Murdoch, R.	5	Weir, A.	1
		Kinnear, D.	1	Murphy, F.	1	Weir, J. B.	2
Ferguson, J.	6			Murray, J.	1	White, J. A.	3
Fernie, W.	1	Lambie, W. A.	5			Wilson, A.	2
Fitchie, T. T.	1	Lang, J. J.	1	Napier, C. E.	3	Wilson, A. N.	13
Flavell, R.	2	Law, D.	30	Narey, D.	1	Wilson, D.	2
Fleming, C.	2	Leggat, G.	8	Neil, R. G.	2	(Queen's Park)	
Fleming, J. W.	3	Lennie, W.	1	Nevin, P.	1	Wilson, D. (Rangers)	9
Fraser, M. J. E.	4	Lennnox, R.	3	Nicholas, C.	5	Wilson, H.	1
		Liddell, W.	6	Nisbet, J.	2	Wylie, T. G.	1
Gallacher, H. K.	23	Lindsay, J.	6				
Gallacher, P.	1	Linwood, A. B.	1	O'Donnell, F.	2	Young, A.	5
Galt, J. H.	1	Logan, J.	1	O'Hare, J.	5		
Gemmell, T. (St Mirren)	1	Lorimer, P.	4	Ormond, W. E.	1	**WALES**	
Gemmell, T. (Celtic)	1	Love, A.	1	O'Rourke, F.	1	Allchurch, I. J.	23
Gemmill, A.	8	Lowe, J. (Cambuslang)	1	Orr, R.	1	Allen, M.	3
Gibb, W.	1	Lowe, J. (St Bernards)	1	Orr, T.	1	Astley, D. J.	12
Gibson, D. W.	3			Oswald, J.	1	Atherton, R. W.	2
Gibson, J. D.	2	McAdam, J.	1	Own goals	14		
Gibson, N.	1	McAllister, G.	4			Bamford, T.	1
Gillespie, Jas.	3	McAulay, J.	1	Parlane, D.	1	Barnes, W.	1
Gillick, T.	3	McAvennie, F.	1	Paul, H. McD.	2	Bodin, P. J.	3
Gilzean, A. J.	10	McCall, J.	1	Paul, W.	6	Boulter, L. M.	1
Gossland, J.	2	McCall, S. M.	1	Pettigrew, W.	2	Bowdler, J. C. H.	3
Goudie, J.	1	McCalliog, J.	1	Provan, D.	1	Bowen, D. L.	1
Gough, C. R.	6	McCallum, N.	1			Bowen, M.	2
Gourlay, J.	1	McClair, B.	1	Quinn, J.	7	Boyle, T.	1
Graham, A.	2	McCoist, A.	12	Quinn, P.	1	Bryan, T.	1
Graham, G.	3	McColl, R. S.	13			Burgess, W. A. R.	1
Gray, A.	7	McCulloch, D.	3			Burke, T.	1
Gray, E.	3	MacDougall, E. J.	3	Rankin, G.	2	Butler, A.	
Gray, F.	1	McDougall, J.	4	Rankin, R.	2		
Greig, J.	3	McFadyen, W.	2	Reid, W.	4	Chapman, T.	2
Groves, W.	5	McFarlane, A.	1	Reilly, L.	22	Charles, J.	1
		McGhee, M.	2	Renny-Tailyour, H. W.	1	Charles, M.	6
Hamilton, G.	4	McGregor, J. C.	1	Richmond, J. T.	1	Charles, W. J.	15
Hamilton, J.	3	McGrory, J.	6	Ring, T.	2	Clarke, R. J.	5
(Queen's Park)		McGuire, W.	1	Rioch, B. D.	6	Coleman, C.	1
Hamilton, R. C.	14	McInally, A.	3	Ritchie, J.	1	Collier, D. J.	1
Harper, J. M.	2	McInnes, T.	2	Robertson, A.	2	Cross, K.	1
Harrower, W.	5	Mackay, D. C.	4	Robertson, J.	2	Cumner, R. H.	6
Hartford, R. A.	3	Mackay, G.	1	Robertson, J. N.	8	Curtis, A.	6
Heggie, C.	5	MacKenzie, J. A.	1	Robertson, J. T.	2	Curtis, E. R.	3
Henderson, J. G.	1	McKie, J.	2	Robertson, T.	1		
Henderson, W.	5	McKimmie, S.	1	Robertson, W.	1	Davies, D. W.	1
Herd, D. G.	4	McKinnon, A.	1	Russell, D.	1	Davies, E. Lloyd	1
Hewie, J. D.	2	McKinnon, R.	1			Davies, G.	2
Higgins, A.	1	McKinnon, W. W.	5	Scott, A. S.	5	Davies, L. S.	6
(Newcastle U)		McLaren, A.	4	Sellar, W.	4	Davies, R. T.	8
Higgins, A. (Kilmarnock)		McLaren, J.	1	Sharp, G.	1	Davies, R. W.	7
	4	McLean, A.	1	Shaw, F. W.	1	Davies, S.	5
Highet, T. C.	1	McLean, T.	1	Simpson, J.	1	Davies, W.	6
Holton, J. A.	2	MacLeod, M.	1	Smith, A.	5	Davies, W. H.	1
Houliston, W.	2	McLintock, F.	1	Smith, G.	4	Davies, William	5
Howie, H.	1	McMahon, A.	6	Smith, J.	1	Davies, W. O.	1
Howie, J.	2	McMenemy, J.	5	Smith, John	12	Deacy, N.	4
Hughes, J.	1	McMillan, I. L.	2	Somerville, G.	1	Doughty, J.	6
Hunter, W.	1	McNeil, H.	5	Souness, G. J.	3	Doughty, R.	2
Hutchison, T.	1	McNeill, W.	3	Speedie, F.	2	Durban, A.	2
Hutton, J.	1	McPhail, J.	3	St John, I.	9	Dwyer, P.	2
Hyslop, T.	1	McPhail, R.	7	Steel, W.	12		
		McPherson, J.	8	Stein, C.	10	Edwards, G.	2
Imrie, W. N.	1	McPherson, R.	1	Stevenson, G.	4	Edwards, R. I.	5
		McQueen, G.	5	Stewart, R.	1	England, H. M.	3
		McStay, P.	9	Stewart, W. E.	1	Evans, I.	1
Jackson, A.	8	Macari, L.	5	Strachan, G.	5	Evans, J.	1
Jackson, C.	1	Madden, J.	5	Sturrock, P.	3	Evans, R. E.	2

Evans, W.	1	Morris, H.	2	Wynn, G. A.	1	Hughton, C.	1

Evans, W. 1
Eyton-Jones, J. A. 1

Flynn, B. 6
Ford, T. 23
Foulkes, W. I. 1
Fowler, J. 3

Giles, D. 2
Glover, E. M. 7
Godfrey, B. C. 2
Green, A. W. 3
Griffiths, A. T. 6
Griffiths, M. W. 2
Griffiths, T. P. 3

Harris, C. S. 1
Hersee, R. 1
Hewitt, R. 1
Hockey, T. 1
Hodges, G. 2
Hole, W. J. 1
Hopkins, I. J. 2
Horne, B. 2
Howell, E. G. 3
Hughes, L. M. 9

James, E. 2
James, L. 10
James, R. 7
Jarrett, R. H. 3
Jenkyns, C. A. 1
Jones, A. 1
Jones, Bryn 6
Jones, B. S. 2
Jones, Cliff 15
Jones, C. W. 1
Jones, D. E. 1
Jones, Evan 1
Jones, H. 1
Jones, I. 1
Jones, J. O. 1
Jones, J. P. 1
Jones, Leslie J. 1
Jones, R. A. 2
Jones, W. L. 6

Keenor, F. C. 2
Krzywicki, R. L. 1

Leek, K. 5
Lewis, B. 3
Lewis, J. 1
Lewis, W. 10
Lewis, W. L. 2
Lovell, S. 1
Lowrie, G. 2

Mahoney, J. F. 1
Mays, A. W. 1
Medwin, T. C. 6
Meredith, W. H. 11
Mills, T. J. 1
Moore, G. 1
Morgan, J. R. 2
Morgan-Owen, H. 1
Morgan-Owen, M. M. 2
Morris, A. G. 9

Morris, H. 2
Morris, R. 1

Nicholas, P. 2

O'Callaghan, E. 3
O'Sullivan, P. A. 1
Owen, G. 2
Owen, W. 4
Owen, W. P. 6
Own goals 12

Palmer, D. 3
Parry, T. D. 3
Paul, R. 1
Peake, E. 1
Pembridge, M. 1
Perry, E. 1
Phillips, C. 5
Phillips, D. 1
Powell, A. 1
Powell, D. 1
Price, J. 4
Price, P. 1
Pryce-Jones, W. E. 3
Pugh, D. H. 2

Reece, G. I. 2
Rees, R. R. 3
Richards, R. W. 1
Roach, J. 2
Robbins, J. W. 4
Roberts, J. (Corwen) 1
Roberts, Jas. 1
Roberts, P. S. 1
Roberts, R. (Druids) 1
Roberts, W. (Llangollen) 2
Roberts, W. (Wrexham) 1
Roberts, W. H. 1
Rush, I. 20
Russell, M. R. 1

Sabine, H. W. 1
Saunders, D. 10
Shaw, E. G. 2
Sisson, H. 4
Slatter, N. 2
Smallman, D. P. 1

Tapscott, D. R. 4
Thomas, M. 4
Thomas, T. 1
Toshack, J. B. 13
Trainer, H. 2

Vaughan, John 2
Vernon, T. R. 8
Vizard, E. T. 1

Walsh, I. 7
Warren, F. W. 3
Watkins, W. M. 4
Wilding, J. 4
Williams, G. E. 1
Williams, G. G. 1
Williams, W. 1
Woosnam, A. P. 4

Wynn, G. A. 1

Yorath, T. C. 2

EIRE
Aldridge, J. 8
Ambrose, P. 1
Anderson, J. 1

Bermingham, P. 1
Bradshaw, P. 4
Brady, L. 9
Brown, D. 1
Byrne, J. (Bray) 1
Byrne, J. (QPR) 5

Cantwell, J. 14
Carey, J. 3
Carroll, T. 1
Cascarino, A. 10
Coad, P. 3
Conroy, T. 2
Conway, J. 3
Coyne, T. 1
Cummings, G. 5
Curtis, D. 8

Daly, G. 13
Davis, T. 4
Dempsey, J. 1
Dennehy, M. 2
Donnelly, J. 3
Donnelly, T. 1
Duffy, B. 1
Duggan, H. 1
Dunne, J. 12
Dunne, L. 1

Eglington, T. 2
Ellis, P. 1

Fagan, F. 5
Fallon, S. 2
Fallon, W. 2
Farrell, P. 3
Fitzgerald, P. 2
Fitzgerald, J. 1
Fitzsimmons, A. 7
Flood, J. J. 4
Fogarty, A. 3
Fullam, J. 1
Fullam, R. 1

Galvin, A. 1
Gavin, M. 2
Geoghegan, M. 2
Giles, J. 5
Givens, D. 19
Glynn, D. 1
Grealish, T. 8
Grimes, A. A. 1

Hale, A. 2
Hand, E. 2
Haverty, J. 3
Holmes, J. 1
Horlacher, A. 2
Houghton, R. 2

Hughton, C. 1
Hurley, C. 2

Irwin, D. 1

Jordan, D. 1

Kelly, D. 7
Kelly, J. 2

Lacey, W. 1
Lawrenson, M. 5
Leech, M. 2

McCann, J. 1
McCarthy, M. 2
McEvoy, A. 6
McGee, P. 4
McGrath, P. 6
Madden, O. 1
Mancini, T. 1
Martin, C. 6
Martin, M. 4
Mooney, J. 1
Moore, P. 7
Moran, K. 6
Moroney, T. 1
Mulligan, P. 1

O'Callaghan, K. 1
O'Connor, T. 2
O'Farrell, F. 2
O'Flanagan, K. 3
O'Keefe, E. 1
O'Leary, D. A. 1
O'Neill, F. 1
O'Reilly, J. 2
O'Reilly, J. 1
Own goals 6

Quinn, N. 8

Ringstead, A. 7
Robinson, M. 4
Rogers, E. 5
Ryan, G. 1
Ryan, R. 3

Sheedy, K. 7
Sheridan, J. 1
Slaven, B. 1
Sloan, W. 1
Squires, J. 1
Stapleton, F. 20
Staunton, S. 2
Strahan, J. 1
Sullivan, J. 1

Townsend, A. D. 2
Treacy, R. 5
Touhy, L. 4

Waddock, G. 3
Walsh, D. 5
Walsh, M. 3
Waters, J. 1
White, J. J. 2
Whelan, R. 3

8th UEFA UNDER-21 TOURNAMENT 1990–92

Group 1 *(Czechoslovakia, Spain, France, Albania, Iceland)*
Iceland (0) 0, Albania (0) 0
Iceland (0) 0, France (0) 1
Czechoslovakia (5) 7, Iceland (0) 0
Spain (2) 2, Iceland (0) 0
France (1) 1, Czechoslovakia (1) 2
Czechoslovakia (3) 3, Spain (0) 1
Albania (0) 0, France (0) 0
Spain (0) 1, Albania (0) 0
France (0) 0, Spain (0) 1
France (0) 3, Albania (0) 0

Albania (1) 1, Czechoslovakia (2) 5
Albania (0) 2, Iceland (0) 1
Iceland (0) 0, Czechoslovakia (1) 1
Czechoslovakia (1) 1, France (0) 0
Iceland (1) 1, Spain (0) 0
Spain (0) 0, France (0) 0
Czechoslovakia (1) 3, Albania (0) 0
Spain (0) 1, Czechoslovakia (1) 1
France (1) 2, Iceland (0) 1
Albania v Spain not played

Group 2 *(Bulgaria, Scotland, Romania, Switzerland)*
Scotland (1) 2, Romania (0) 0
Switzerland (0) 0, Bulgaria (0) 2
Romania (0) 0, Bulgaria (1) 1
Scotland (2) 4, Switzerland (1) 2
Bulgaria (2) 2, Scotland (0) 0
Scotland (1) 1, Bulgaria (0) 0

Switzerland (0) 0, Romania (1) 2
Bulgaria (1) 1, Switzerland (0) 0
Switzerland (0) 0, Scotland (0) 3
Romania (0) 1, Scotland (1) 3
Romania (1) 1, Switzerland (2) 3
Bulgaria (0) 0, Romania (1) 1

Group 3 *(Norway, Italy, USSR, Hungary)*
USSR (1) 2, Norway (0) 2
Norway (2) 3, Hungary (0) 1
Italy (0) 1, Hungary (0) 0
Hungary (0) 0, USSR (0) 0
Italy (0) 1, USSR (0) 0
Norway (2) 6, Italy (0) 0

Italy (0) 1, USSR (0) 0
Norway (0) 0, USSR (1) 1
USSR (0) 2, Hungary (0) 0
USSR (0) 1, Italy (0) 1
Hungary (0) 0, Norway (0) 1
Italy (2) 2, Norway (1) 1

Group 4 *(Denmark, Austria, Yugoslavia, San Marino, Liechtenstein)*
Liechtenstein (0) 0, Austria (3) 6
Austria (6) 10, Liechtenstein (0) 0
San Marino (0) 0, Denmark (1) 3
Yugoslavia (0) 1, Austria (0) 0
Denmark (1) 3, Yugoslavia (0) 0
San Marino (0) 0, Austria (2) 2
Yugoslavia (4) 5, San Marino (0) 0

Austria (0) 3, San Marino (0) 0
Denmark (4) 7, San Marino (0) 0
Yugoslavia (0) 2, Denmark (1) 6
Denmark (0) 1, Austria (1) 1
San Marino (0) 0, Yugoslavia (1) 1
Austria (1) 1, Denmark (1) 1
Austria (0) 1, Yugoslavia (0) 2

Group 5 *(Germany, Luxembourg, Belgium)*
Luxembourg (0) 0, Germany (0) 3
Belgium (0) 2, Luxembourg (0) 0
Germany (1) 3, Belgium (1) 1

Luxembourg (0) 0, Belgium (0) 2
Belgium (0) 0, Germany (0) 3
Germany (1) 3, Luxembourg (0) 0

Group 6 *(Portugal, Holland, Finland, Malta)*
Finland (0) 0, Portugal (1) 1
Portugal (0) 0, Holland (0) 0
Malta (1) 1, Holland (2) 4
Malta (0) 1, Portugal (1) 3
Portugal (2) 2, Malta (0) 0
Holland (3) 7, Malta (0) 1

Holland (0) 1, Finland (0) 0
Finland (0) 1, Holland (0) 7
Finland (1) 3, Malta (0) 1
Portugal (1) 2, Finland (0) 0
Holland (0) 1, Portugal (1) 1
Malta (0) 1, Finland (1) 3

Group 7 *(Poland, England, Republic of Ireland, Turkey)*
England (0) 0, Poland (0) 1
Republic of Ireland (1) 3, Turkey (1) 2
Republic of Ireland (0) 0, England (1) 3
Turkey (0) 0, Poland (0) 1
England (1) 3, Republic of Ireland (0) 0
Poland (1) 2, Turkey (0) 0

Republic of Ireland (0) 1, Poland (0) 2
Turkey (1) 2, England (1) 2
England (0) 2, Turkey (0) 0
Poland (0) 2, Republic of Ireland (0) 0
Poland (1) 2, England (0) 1
Turkey (1) 2, Republic of Ireland (0) 1

Group 8 *(Sweden, Israel, Cyprus, Greece)*
Sweden (2) 5, Greece (0) 0
Cyprus (0) 1, Sweden (0) 1
Greece (2) 2, Israel (1) 2
Israel (1) 4, Cyprus (0) 0
Cyprus (1) 1, Greece (0) 0
Sweden (2) 6, Cyprus (0) 0

Sweden (1) 2, Israel (0) 1
Israel (0) 2, Greece (1) 1
Israel (0) 0, Sweden (0) 0
Greece (0) 1, Sweden (1) 3
Cyprus (0) 1, Israel (1) 2
Greece (2) 2, Cyprus (0) 0

Quarter-finals
Germany (1) 1, Scotland (1) 1
Czechoslovakia (0) 1, Italy (1) 2
Denmark (5) 5, Poland (0) 0
Holland (1) 2, Sweden (1) 1

Scotland (1) 4, Germany (2) 3
Italy (2) 2, Czechoslovakia (0) 0
Poland (0) 1, Denmark (1) 1
Sweden (0) 1, Holland (0) 0

Semi-finals
Denmark (0) 0, Italy (1) 1
Italy (0) 2, Denmark (0) 0

Scotland (0) 0, Sweden (0) 0
Sweden (0) 1, Scotland (0) 0

Final
Italy (0) 2, Sweden (0) 0

Sweden (0) 1, Italy (0) 0

8th UEFA UNDER-18 CHAMPIONSHIP 1990–92

Group 1 *(Israel, Greece, Turkey, Switzerland)*
Greece (1) 1, Switzerland (0) 1
Israel (2) 2, Switzerland (0) 0
Turkey (1) 1, Israel (1) 1
Greece (2) 2, Israel (0) 0
Switzerland (0) 0, Israel (1) 1
Turkey (0) 1, Greece (0) 0

Switzerland (0) 0, Turkey (2) 4
Switzerland (2) 2, Greece (0) 1
Greece (0) 0, Turkey (0) 0
Israel (0) 3, Greece (1) 1
Turkey (0) 1, Switzerland (0) 0
Israel (1) 1, Turkey (1) 1

Group 2 *(Cyprus, Romania, Hungary, Bulgaria)*
Hungary (0) 1, Romania (0) 0
Hungary (0) 0, Cyprus (0) 1
Cyprus (1) 3, Bulgaria (1) 1
Romania (0) 3, Cyprus (0) 2
Bulgaria (0) 0, Cyprus (0) 1
Cyprus (0) 0, Hungary (1) 5

Romania (2) 3, Hungary (0) 1
Romania (1) 1, Bulgaria (0) 1
Hungary (1) 2, Bulgaria (0) 1
Bulgaria (1) 1, Hungary (1) 2
Bulgaria (0) 0, Romania (1) 1
Cyprus (1) 3, Romania (0) 0

Group 3 *(Portugal, France, Denmark, Luxembourg)*
Denmark (2) 7, Luxembourg (0) 0
Portugal (0) 0, France (0) 0
France (0) 2, Denmark (0) 0
Luxembourg (0) 0, Portugal (3) 5
France (0) 0, Portugal (2) 3
Portugal (0) 3, Denmark (0) 0

Luxembourg (0) 0, France (3) 5
Denmark (0) 1, France (1) 2
Portugal (3) 7, Luxembourg (0) 1
France (0) 2, Luxembourg (0) 1
Denmark (0) 0, Portugal (0) 0
Luxembourg (0) 0, Denmark (1) 5

Group 4 *(Italy, Spain, Malta, Germany)*
Italy (2) 9, Malta (0) 0
Spain (0) 0, Italy (1) 2
Malta (0) 1, Spain (0) 1
Italy (0) 0, Spain (0) 0
Malta (0) 0, Germany (0) 1
Germany (2) 4, Malta (0) 0

Spain (0) 1, Germany (1) 3
Germany (0) 0, Italy (0) 0
Spain (0) 0, Malta (0) 0
Italy (1) 2, Germany (0) 2
Germany (2) 3, Spain (0) 0
Malta (0) 0, Italy (2) 2

Group 5 *(England, Belgium, Iceland, Wales)*
Iceland (1) 2, England (1) 3
Belgium (1) 1, Iceland (1) 1
England (0) 0, Belgium (0) 0
Wales (0) 1, Belgium (0) 1
Wales (0) 0, England (0) 1
England (0) 3, Wales (0) 0

Iceland (0) 0, Wales (0) 0
Wales (1) 1, Iceland (1) 2
England (0) 2, Iceland (0) 1
Iceland (0) 2, Belgium (1) 1
Belgium (1) 1, England (0) 0
Belgium (1) 2, Wales (0) 0

Group 6 *(Poland, Republic of Ireland, Scotland, Northern Ireland)*
Northern Ireland (0) 0, Republic of Ireland (1) 2
Poland (0) 1, Scotland (0) 0
Republic of Ireland (2) 2, Scotland (0) 1
Poland (1) 3, Northern Ireland (0) 0
Scotland (0) 0, Northern Ireland (0) 0
Scotland (1) 1, Republic of Ireland (1) 3

Poland (1) 5, Republic of Ireland (0) 0
Republic of Ireland (0) 0, Poland (1) 3
Northern Ireland (0) 0, Poland (1) 1
Scotland (0) 0, Poland (2) 2
Republic of Ireland (1) 2, Northern Ireland (0) 2
Northern Ireland (2) 2, Scotland (1) 2

Group 7 *(Norway, Finland, Holland, Austria)*
Finland (0) 0, Norway (2) 2
Norway (2) 4, Holland (0) 1
Holland (0) 0, Finland (1) 3
Holland (0) 2, Norway (0) 0
Norway (1) 1, Austria (0) 0
Finland (0) 0, Austria (1) 3

Norway (0) 0, Finland (0) 1
Austria (0) 0, Finland (2) 2
Austria (0) 0, Norway (4) 5
Finland (1) 2, Holland (0) 0
Austria (0) 0, Holland (0) 1
Holland (3) 4, Austria (0) 1

Group 8 *(Yugoslavia, USSR, Sweden, Czechoslovakia)*
Yugoslavia (2) 3, USSR (1) 2
Czechoslovakia (0) 2, Sweden (2) 2
USSR (2) 3, Czechoslovakia (0) 0
Sweden (1) 1, Yugoslavia (0) 1
Sweden (1) 2, USSR (0) 2
Czechoslovakia (1) 2, Yugoslavia (0) 0

Sweden (0) 1, Czechoslovakia (0) 1
USSR (2) 4, Yugoslavia (1) 2
Yugoslavia (2) 6, Sweden (2) 4
Yugoslavia (0) 0, Czechoslovakia (0) 0
USSR (1) 2, Sweden (0) 2
Czechoslovakia (2) 2, USSR (1) 2

Final tournament to be held in Germany July 1992

10th UEFA UNDER-16 CHAMPIONSHIP 1992

Group 1: Wales 1, Republic of Ireland 0; Republic of Ireland 2, Wales 0. Republic of Ireland qualified.
Group 2: Iceland 2, Northern Ireland 1; Northern Ireland 2, Iceland 1. Northern Ireland qualified.
Group 3: Malta 0, Holland 6; Holland 2, Malta 0. Holland qualified.
Group 4: Germany 8, Albania 1; Albania v Germany not played.
Group 5: CIS 1, Yugoslavia 1; Yugoslavia 1, CIS 1. Yugoslavia qualified.
Group 6: Turkey 1, Israel 0; Israel 2, Turkey 0. Israel qualified.
Group 7: Luxembourg 0, Spain 5; Spain 3, Luxembourg 1. Spain qualified.
Group 8: France 1, Austria 0; Austria 2, France 5. France qualified.
Group 9: Finland 3, Belgium 0; Belgium 1, Finland 2. Finland qualified.
Group 10: Poland 2, Switzerland 1; Switzerland 1, Italy 0; Italy 3, Switzerland 1; Italy 0, Poland 0; Poland 1, Italy 2; Switzerland 2, Poland 0. Italy qualified.
Group 11: Norway 2, Hungary 2; Hungary 3, Norway 1. Hungary qualified.
Group 12: Czechoslovakia 2, Romania 1; Romania 1, Czechoslovakia 0. Romania qualified.
Group 13: Greece 4, Denmark 1; Denmark 5, Greece 1. Denmark qualified.
Group 14: Bulgaria 0, Scotland 1; Scotland 2, Bulgaria 1. Scotland qualified.
Group 15: Sweden 2, Portugal 0; Portugal 3, Sweden 0. Portugal qualified.

FINAL TOURNAMENT IN CYPRUS

GROUP A

Finland (0) 0, Denmark (0) 1
Yugoslavia (0) 0, Italy (2) 4
Denmark (0) 0, Italy (0) 2

Finland (0) 0, Yugoslavia (2) 2
Denmark (0) 1, Yugoslavia (1) 2
Finland (0) 2, Italy (1) 1

	P	W	D	L	F	A	Pts
Italy	3	2	0	1	7	2	4
Yugoslavia	3	2	0	1	4	5	4
Finland	3	1	0	2	2	4	2
Denmark	3	1	0	2	2	4	2

GROUP B

Republic of Ireland (0) 0, Holland (0) 2
Romania (0) 1, Spain (3) 3
Romania (0) 0, Republic of Ireland (0) 0

Spain (0) 2, Holland (0) 0
Romania (0) 0, Holland (2) 4
Spain (0) 1, Republic of Ireland (0) 1

	P	W	D	L	F	A	Pts
Spain	3	2	1	0	6	2	5
Holland	3	2	0	1	6	2	4
Republic of Ireland	3	0	2	1	1	3	2
Romania	3	0	1	2	1	7	1

GROUP C

Germany (2) 3, Northern Ireland (1) 1
Scotland (2) 3, Cyprus (0) 0
Germany (1) 1, Scotland (0) 0

Northern Ireland (0) 0, Cyprus (0) 0
Germany (1) 2, Cyprus (0) 1
Northern Ireland (0) 1, Scotland (2) 3

	P	W	D	L	F	A	Pts
Germany	3	3	0	0	6	2	6
Scotland	3	2	0	1	6	2	4
Northern Ireland	3	0	1	2	2	6	1
Cyprus	3	0	1	2	1	5	1

GROUP D

France (1) 1, Portugal (0) 2
Israel (2) 3, Hungary (2) 2
France (0) 0, Israel (0) 0

Portugal (0) 1, Hungary (1) 1
France (0) 0, Hungary (0) 1
Portugal (1) 1, Israel (0) 0

	P	W	D	L	F	A	Pts
Portugal	3	2	1	0	4	2	5
Hungary	3	1	1	1	4	4	3
Israel	3	1	1	1	3	3	3
France	3	0	1	2	1	3	1

Semi-finals
Spain (0) 3, Portugal (1) 1
Italy (0) 0, Germany (0) 0
Germany won on penalties.

Third-place match
Italy (0) 1, Portugal (0) 0

Final
Germany (1) 2, Spain (1) 1

ENGLAND UNDER-21 RESULTS 1976–92

EC UEFA Competition for Under-21 Teams

v ALBANIA

Year	Date		Venue	Eng	Alb
EC1989	Mar	7	Shkroda	2	1
EC1989	April	25	Ipswich	2	0

v BULGARIA

				Eng	Bulg
EC1979	June	5	Pernik	3	1
EC1979	Nov	20	Leicester	5	0
1989	June	5	Toulon	2	3

v CZECHOSLOVAKIA

				Eng	Cz
1990	May	28	Toulon	2	1
1992	May	26	Toulon	1	2

v DENMARK

				Eng	Den
EC1978	Sept	19	Hvidovre	2	1
EC1979	Sept	11	Watford	1	0
EC1982	Sept	21	Hvidovre	4	1
EC1983	Sept	20	Norwich	4	1
EC1986	Mar	12	Copenhagen	1	0
EC1986	Mar	26	Manchester	1	1
1988	Sept	13	Watford	0	0

v EAST GERMANY

				Eng	EG
EC1980	April	16	Sheffield	1	2
EC1980	April	23	Jena	0	1

v FINLAND

				Eng	Fin
EC1977	May	26	Helsinki	1	0
EC1977	Oct	12	Hull	8	1
EC1984	Oct	16	Southampton	2	0
EC1985	May	21	Mikkeli	1	3

v FRANCE

				Eng	Fra
EC1984	Feb	28	Sheffield	6	1
EC1984	Mar	28	Rouen	1	0
1987	June	11	Toulon	0	2
EC1988	April	13	Besancon	2	4
EC1988	April	27	Highbury	2	2
1988	June	12	Toulon	2	4
1990	May	23	Toulon	7	3
1991	June	3	Toulon	1	0
1992	May	28	Toulon	0	0

v GERMANY

				Eng	G
1991	Sept	10	Scunthorpe	2	1

v GREECE

				Eng	Gre
EC1982	Nov	16	Piraeus	0	1
EC1983	Mar	29	Portsmouth	2	1
1989	Feb	7	Patras	0	1

v HUNGARY

				Eng	Hun
EC1981	June	5	Keszthely	2	1
EC1981	Nov	17	Nottingham	2	0
EC1983	April	26	Newcastle	1	0
EC1983	Oct	11	Nyiregyhaza	2	0
1990	Sept	11	Southampton	3	1
1992	May	12	Budapest	2	2

v ITALY

				Eng	Italy
EC1978	Mar	8	Manchester	2	1
EC1978	April	5	Rome	0	0
EC1984	April	18	Manchester	3	1
EC1984	May	2	Florence	0	1
EC1986	April	9	Pisa	0	2
EC1986	April	23	Swindon	1	1

v ISRAEL

				Eng	Isr
1985	Feb	27	Tel Aviv	2	1

v MEXICO

				Eng	Mex
1988	June	5	Toulon	2	1
1991	May	29	Toulon	6	0
1992	May	25	Toulon	1	1

v MOROCCO

				Eng	Mor
1987	June	7	Toulon	2	0
1988	June	9	Toulon	1	0

v NORWAY

				Eng	Nor
EC1977	June	1	Bergen	2	1
EC1977	Sept	6	Brighton	6	0
1980	Sept	9	Southampton	3	0
1981	Sept	8	Drammen	0	0

v POLAND

				Eng	Pol
EC1982	Mar	17	Warsaw	2	1
EC1982	April	7	West Ham	2	2
EC1989	June	2	Plymouth	2	1
EC1989	Oct	10	Jastrzebie	3	1
EC1990	Oct	16	Tottenham	0	1
EC1991	Nov	12	Pila	1	2

v PORTUGAL

				Eng	Por
1987	June	13	Toulon	0	0
1990	May	21	Toulon	0	1

v REPUBLIC OF IRELAND

				Eng	RoI
1981	Feb	25	Liverpool	1	0
1985	Mar	25	Portsmouth	3	2
1989	June	9	Toulon	0	0
EC1990	Nov	13	Cork	3	0
EC1991	Mar	26	Brentford	3	0

v ROMANIA

				Eng	Rom
EC1980	Oct	14	Ploesti	0	4
EC1981	April	28	Swindon	3	0
EC1985	April	30	Brasov	0	0
EC1985	Sept	10	Ipswich	3	0

v SENEGAL

				Eng	Sen
1989	June	7	Toulon	6	1
1991	May	27	Toulon	2	1

v SCOTLAND

				Eng	Scot
1977	April	27	Sheffield	1	0
EC1980	Feb	12	Coventry	2	1
EC1980	Mar	4	Aberdeen	0	0
EC1982	April	19	Glasgow	1	0
EC1982	April	28	Manchester	1	1
EC1988	Feb	16	Aberdeen	1	0
EC1988	Mar	22	Nottingham	1	0

v SPAIN

				Eng	Spa
EC1984	May	17	Seville	1	0
EC1984	May	24	Sheffield	2	0
1987	Feb	18	Burgos	2	1

v SWEDEN

				Eng	Swe
1979	June	9	Vasteras	2	1
1986	Sept	9	Ostersund	1	1
EC1988	Oct	18	Coventry	1	1
EC1989	Sept	5	Uppsala	0	1

v SWITZERLAND

				Eng	Swit
EC1980	Nov	18	Ipswich	5	0
EC1981	May	31	Neuenburg	0	0
1988	May	28	Lausanne	1	1

v USA

				Eng	USA
1989	June	11	Toulon	0	2

v TURKEY

				Eng	Tur
EC1984	Nov	13	Bursa	0	0
EC1985	Oct	15	Bristol	3	0
EC1987	April	28	Izmir	0	0
EC1987	Oct	13	Sheffield	1	1
EC1991	April	30	Izmir	2	2
EC1991	Oct	15	Reading	2	0

v USSR

				Eng	USSR
1987	June	9	Toulon	0	0
1988	June	7	Toulon	1	0
1990	May	25	Toulon	2	1
1991	May	31	Toulon	2	1

v WALES

				Eng	Wales
1976	Dec	15	Wolverhampton	0	0
1979	Feb	6	Swansea	1	0
1990	Dec	5	Tranmere	0	0

v WEST GERMANY

				Eng	WG
EC1982	Sept	21	Sheffield	3	1
EC1982	Oct	12	Bremen	2	3
1987	Sept	8	Ludenscheid	0	2

v YUGOSLAVIA

				Eng	Yugo
EC1978	April	19	Novi Sad	1	2
EC1978	May	2	Manchester	1	1
EC1986	Nov	11	Peterborough	1	1
EC1987	Nov	10	Zemun	5	1

BRITISH AND IRISH UNDER-21 TEAMS 1991–92

England Under-21 Internationals
10 Sept
England (1) 2 *(Johnson, Ebbrell)*
Germany (0) 1 *(Stadler)*   6984
England: James; Dodd, Vinnicombe, Ebbrell, Tiler, Warhurst, Johnson, Draper (Matthew), Shearer, Williams P, Campbell.

15 Oct
England (0) 2 *(Shearer 2)*
Turkey (0) 0   7489
England: James; Charles, Vinnicombe, Ebbrell, Tiler, Atherton, Johnson, Matthew (Blake), Shearer, Williams P, Campbell.

12 Nov
Poland (1) 2 *(Juskowiak 2)*
England (0) 1 *(Kitson)*   12,000
England: James; Dodd, Vinnicombe (Atkinson), Blake (Olney), Cundy, Lee, Kitson, Draper, Shearer, Williams P, Johnson.

12 May
Hungary (0) 2 *(Hamori, Harvath)*
England (2) 2 *(Allen, Cole)*   1500
England: Walker; Jackson (Ashcroft), Minto, Sutch, Ehiogu, Hendon (Bazeley), Sheron, Parlour, Cole (Hall), Allen, Heaney.

25 May
Mexico (1) 1 *(Pineda)*
England (1) 1 *(Allen)*
England: Marriott; Jackson, Hendon, Ehiogu, Minto, Sutch, Parlour, Heaney, Johnson, Kitson, Allen.

26 May
England (0) 1 *(Kitson)*
Czechoslovakia (1) 2 *(Neumann, Lerch)*   450
England: Walker; Jackson, Hendon, Ehiogu, Minto (Johnson), Parlour, Sutch (Cole), Clark, Kitson, Allen, Heaney.

28 May
France (0) 0
England (0) 0
England: Walker; Jackson, Hendon, Hall, Ehiogu, Sheron, Parlour (Ramage), Clark, Kitson (Cole), Allen, Heaney.

Scotland Under-21 Internationals
10 Sept
Switzerland (0) 0
Scotland (0) 3 *(Spencer, Creaney, Booth)*   1100
Scotland: Watt; Wright, Cleland, Dennis, Sweeney, Rae, Lambert, Gemmill (O'Donnell), Jess (Spencer), Creaney, Booth.

15 Oct
Romania (0) 1 *(Buia)*
Scotland (1) 3 *(Creaney, Lambert, Bernard)*   5000
Scotland: Watt; Miller, Sweeney, McLaren, Cleland, Lambert, Rae, O'Donnell (Gemmill), Jess, Creaney, Booth (Bernard).

18 Feb
Scotland (2) 3 *(Booth 3)*
Denmark (0) 0   2210
Scotland: Reid (Will); Burley, Beattie (Bowes), Salton, Bollan (Deas), Bernard, O'Neil, O'Donnell, Christie (Hagen), Ferguson, Booth (Hendry).

10 Mar
Germany (1) 1 *(Schmaler)*
Scotland (1) 1 *(Creaney)*   8000
Scotland: Watt; Wright, Cleland, O'Neil, Smith, Fulton (Miller), McKinnon (Bollan), Lambert, Creaney, Jess, O'Donnell.

24 Mar
Scotland (1) 4 *(McKinnon, Creaney, Lambert, Rae)*
Germany (2) 3 *(Kranz, Scholl, Herrlich)*   22,500
Scotland: Watt; McLaren, Wright, Lambert, Smith, Fulton (Rae), Jess (Gemmill), O'Donnell, Creaney, McKinnon, Ferguson.

22 Apr
Scotland (0) 0
Sweden (0) 0   22,500
Scotland: Watt; Wright, McLaren, Cleland, O'Neil (Bernard), Rae, Lambert (O'Donnell), McKinnon, Jess, Ferguson, Creaney.

29 Apr
Sweden (0) 1 *(Rodlund)*
Scotland (0) 0   2376
Scotland: Watt; O'Neil, Wright, McLaren, Cleland, Booth (Jess), Rae, O'Donnell, McKinnon (Gemmill), Creaney, Ferguson.

25 May
USA (2) 5 *(Snow 3, Reyna, Brose)*
Scotland (0) 0
Scotland: Reid; Smith, Salton, Beattie, Roddie, Bernard, Johnson (Donald), Bollan, Booth, Dailly (Hagen), Ferguson.

27 May
Portugal (0) 1 *(Rui Costa)*
Scotland (0) 0
Scotland: Reid; Smith, Salton, Beattie, Bollan, Hagen, Dailly, Johnson (Christie), Roddie (Ferguson), Booth, Donald.

29 May
Yugoslavia (0) 1
Scotland (0) 0
Scotland: Will; Smith, Salton (Donald), Beattie, Bollan, Johnson, Christie, Ferguson, Dickov, Booth, Hagen.

Republic of Ireland Under-21 Internationals
15 Oct
Poland (0) 2 *(Juskowiak 2)*
Republic of Ireland (0) 0   6720
Republic of Ireland: McKenna; McDonald (Cunningham), Fitzgerald, McCarthy, Kenna, Rush, Collins, O'Donoghue, Dunne L (Toal), Arkins, Cousins.

12 Nov
Turkey (1) 2 *(Aydin, Sukur)*
Republic of Ireland (0) 1 *(O'Connor)*   10,000
Republic of Ireland: McKenna; McDonald, Fitzgerald, McCarthy, Kenna, Toal, Collins, O'Donoghue, Dunne L (Rush), O'Connor, Power (Arkins).

24 Mar
Republic of Ireland (1) 1 *(Studer (og))*
Switzerland (0) 1 *(Hohener)*   1500
Republic of Ireland: Connolly; Collins, McCarthy, Carey, Curtis (Byrne), Bacon, Dunne L (Dempsey), Toal, Dunne J, Power (O'Connor), Ampadu (Fenlon).

25 May
Republic of Ireland (1) 3 *(Kinsella, Collins, Power)*
Albania (1) 1 *(Bahali)*   1200
Republic of Ireland: Connolly; Napier, Gillard, McGrath, McCarthy, Curtis, Kinsella, Toal (Collins), Gallen, Power, Dempsey (Brady).

Wales Under-21 International
19 May
Romania (1) 2 *(Gilca, Moisescu (pen))*
Wales (2) 3 *(Jones L 2, Powell)*   1000
Wales: Margetson; Coyne (Powell), Searle, Peters, Ready, Chapple, Hughes, Owen, Jones L, Robinson, Edwards.

1st UNDER-17 WORLD CHAMPIONSHIP

Group A
Italy 0, USA 1
China 1, Argentina 2
Italy 2, China 2
USA 1, Argentina 0
USA 3, China 1
Italy 0, Argentina 0

Group B
Congo 0, Qatar 0
Australia 4, Mexico 3
Congo 0, Australia 2
Qatar 0, Mexico 1
Congo 2, Mexico 1
Qatar 1, Australia 0

Group C
Sudan 4, UAE 1
Germany 0, Brazil 2
Sudan 1, Germany 3
UAE 0, Brazil 4
Sudan 0, Brazil 1
UAE 2, Germany 2

Group D
Ghana 2, Cuba 1
Uruguay 0, Spain 1
Ghana 2, Uruguay 0
Cuba 2, Spain 7
Ghana 1, Spain 1
Cuba 0, Uruguay 1

Quarter-finals
USA 1, Qatar 1 *aet*
Qatar won 5-4 on penalties
Australia 1, Argentina 2
Brazil 1, Ghana 2
Spain 3, Germany 1

Semi-finals
Qatar 0, Ghana 0 *aet*
Ghana won 4-2 on penalties
Argentina 0, Spain 1

Third Place
Qatar 1, Argentina 1 *aet*
Argentina won 4-1 on penalties

Final
Ghana 1, Spain 0

UNDER-21 APPEARANCES 1976–92

ENGLAND

Ablett, G. (Liverpool), 1988 v Fr (1)

Adams, A. (Arsenal), 1985 v Ei, Fi; 1986 v D; 1987 v Se, Y (5)

Adams, N. (Everton), 1987 v Se (1)

Allen, B. (QPR), 1992 v H, M, Cz, F (4)

Allen, C. (QPR), 1980 v EG (sub); (with C Palace), 1981 v N, R (3)

Allen, M. (QPR), 1987 v Se (sub); 1988 v Y (sub) (2)

Allen, P. (West Ham U), 1985 v Ei, R; (with Tottenham H, 1986 v R (3)

Anderson, V. A. (Nottingham F), 1978 v I (1)

Andrews, I. (Leicester C), 1987 v Se (1)

Ashcroft, L. (Preston NE), 1992 v H (sub) (1)

Atherton, P. (Coventry C), 1992 v T (1)

Atkinson, B. (Sunderland), 1991 v W (sub), Sen, M, USSR (sub); F; 1992 v Pol (sub) (6)

Bailey, G. R. (Manchester U), 1979 v W, Bul; 1980 v D, S (2), EG; 1982 v N; 1983 v D, Gr; 1984 v H, F (2), I, Sp (14)

Baker, G. E. (Southampton), 1981 v N, R (2)

Barker, S. (Blackburn R), 1985 v Is (sub), Ei, R; 1986 v I (4)

Bannister, G. (Sheffield W), 1982 v Pol (1)

Barnes, J. (Watford), 1983 v D, Gr (2)

Barnes, P. S. (Manchester C), 1977 v W (sub), S, Fi, N; 1978 v N, Fi, I (2), Y (9)

Barrett, E. D. (Oldham Ath), 1990 v P, F, USSR, Cz (4)

Batty, D. (Leeds U), 1988 v Sw (sub); 1989 v Gr (sub), Bul, Sen, Ei, US; 1990 v Pol (7)

Bazeley, D. S. (Watford), 1992 v H (sub) (1)

Beagrie, P. (Sheffield U), 1988 v WG, T (2)

Beardsmore, R. (Manchester U), 1989 v Gr, Alb (sub), Pol, Bul, USA (5)

Beeston, C (Stoke C), 1988 v USSR (1)

Bertschin, K. E. (Birmingham C), 1977 v S; 1978 v Y (2) (3)

Birtles, G. (Nottingham F), 1980 v Bul, EG (sub) (2)

Blackwell, D. R. (Wimbledon), 1991 v W, T, Sen (sub), M, USSR, F (6)

Blake, M. A. (Aston Villa), 1990 v F (sub), Cz (sub); 1991 v H, Pol, Ei (2), W; 1992 v Pol (8)

Blissett, L. L. (Watford), 1979 v W, Bul (sub), Se; 1980 v D (4)

Bracewell, P. (Stoke C), 1983 v D, Gr (1 + 1 sub), H; 1984 v D, H, F (2), I (2), Sp (2); 1985 v T (13)

Bradshaw, P. W. (Wolverhampton W), 1977 v W, S; 1978 v Fi, Y (4)

Breacker, T. (Luton T), 1986 v I (2) (2)

Brennan, M. (Ipswich T), 1987 v Y, Sp, T, Mor, F (5)

Brightwell, I. (Manchester C), 1989 v D, Alb; 1990 v Se (sub), Pol (4)

Brock, K. (Oxford U), 1984 v I, Sp (2); 1986 v I (4)

Bull, S. G. (Wolverhampton W), 1989 v Alb (2) Pol; 1990 v Se, Pol (5)

Burrows, D. (WBA), 1989 v Se (sub); (with Liverpool), Gr, Alb (2) Pol; 1990 v Se, Pol (7)

Butcher, T. I. (Ipswich T), 1979 v Se; 1980 v D, Bul, S (2), EG (2) (7)

Butters, G. (Tottenham H), 1989 v Bul, Sen (sub), Ei (sub) (3)

Butterworth, I. (Coventry C), 1985 v T, R; (with Nottingham F), 1986 v R, T, D (2), I (2) (8)

Caesar, G. (Arsenal), 1987 v Mor, USSR (sub), F (3)

Callaghan, N. (Watford), 1983 v D, Gr (sub), H (sub); 1984 v D, H, F (2), I, Sp (9)

Campbell, K. J. (Arsenal), 1991 v H, T (sub); 1992 v G, T (4)

Carr, C. (Fulham), 1985 v Ei (sub) (1)

Carr, F. (Nottingham F), 1987 v Se, Y, Sp (sub), Mor, USSR; 1988 v WG (sub), T, Y, F (9)

Caton, T. (Manchester C), 1982 v N, H (sub), Pol (2), S; 1983 v WG (2), Gr; 1984 v D, H, F (2), I (2) (14)

Chamberlain, M. (Stoke C), 1983 v Gr; 1984 v F (sub), I, Sp (4)

Chapman, L. (Stoke C), 1981 v Ei (1)

Charles, G. A. (Nottingham F), 1991 v H, W (sub), Ei; 1992 v T (4)

Chettle, S. (Nottingham F), 1988 v M, USSR, Mor, F; 1989 v D, Se, Gr, Alb (2), Bul; 1990 v Se, Pol (12)

Clark, L. R. (Newcastle U), 1992 v Cz, F (2)

Clough, N. (Nottingham F), 1986 v D (sub); 1987 v Se, Y, T, USSR, F (sub). P; 1988 v WG, T, Y, S (2), M, Mor, F (15)

Cole, A. A. (Arsenal), 1992 v H, Cz (sub), F (sub) (3)

Coney, D. (Fulham), 1985 v T (sub); 1986 v R; 1988 v T, WG (8)

Connor, T. (Brighton & H A), 1987 v Y (1)

Cooke, R. (Tottenham H), 1986 v D (sub) (1)

Cooper, C. (Middlesbrough), 1988 v F (2), M, USSR, Mor; 1989 v D, Se, Gr (8)

Corrigan, J. T. (Manchester C), 1978 v I (2), Y (3)

Cottee, A. (West Ham U), 1985 v Fi (sub), Is (sub), Ei, R, Fi; 1987 v Sp, P; 1988 v WG (8)

Cowans, G. S. (Aston Villa), 1979 v W, Se; 1980 v Bul, EG; 1981 v R (5)

Cranson, I. (Ipswich T), 1985 v Fi, Is, R; 1986 v R, I (5)

Crooks, S. (Stoke C), 1980 v Bul, S (2), EG (sub) (4)

Crossley, M. G. (Nottingham F), 1990 v P, USSR, Cz (3)

Cundy, J. V. (Chelsea), 1991 v Ei (2); 1992 v Pol (3)

Cunningham, L. (WBA), 1977 v S, Fi, N (sub); 1978 v N, Fi, I (6)

Curbishley, L. C. (Birmingham C), 1981 v Sw (1)

Daniel, P. W. (Hull C), 1977 v S, Fi, N; 1978 v Fi, I, Y (2) (7)

Davis, P. (Arsenal), 1982 v Pol, S; 1983 v D, Gr (1 + 1 sub), H (sub); 1987 v T; 1988 v WG, T, Y, Fr (11)

D'Avray, M. (Ipswich T), 1984 v I, Sp (sub) (2)

Deehan, J. M. (Aston Villa), 1977 v N; 1978 v N, Fi, I; 1979 v Bul, Se (sub); 1980 v D (7)

Dennis, M. E. (Birmingham C), 1980 v Bul; 1981 v N, R (3)

Dickens, A. (West Ham U), 1985 v Fi (sub) (1)

Dicks, J. (West Ham U), 1988 v Sw (sub), M, Mor, F (4)

Digby, F. (Swindon T), 1987 v Sp (sub), USSR, P; 1988 v T; 1990 v Pol (5)

Dillon, K. P. (Birmingham C), 1981 v R (1)

Dixon, K. (Chelsea), 1985 v Fi (1)

Dobson, A. (Coventry C), 1989 v Bul, Sen, Ei, US (4)

Dodd, J. R. (Southampton), 1991 v Pol, Ei, T, Sen, M, F; 1992 v G, Pol (8)

Donowa, L. (Norwich C), 1985 v Is, R (sub), Fi (sub) (3)

Dorigo, A. (Aston Villa), 1987 v Se, Sp, T, Mor, USSR, F, P; 1988 v WG, Y, S (2) (11)

Dozzell, J. (Ipswich T), 1987 v Se, Y (sub), Sp, USSR, F, P; 1989 v Se, Gr (sub); 1990 v Se (sub) (9)

Draper, M. A. (Notts Co), 1991 v Ei (sub); 1992 v G, Pol (3)

Duxbury, M. (Manchester U), 1981 v Sw (sub), Ei (sub), R (sub), Sw; 1982 v N; 1983 v WG (2) (7)

Dyson, P. I. (Coventry C), 1981 v N, R, Sw, Ei (4)

Ebbrell, J. (Everton), 1989 v Sen, Ei, US (sub); 1990 v P, F, USSR, Cz; 1991 v H, Pol, Ei, W, T; 1992 v G, T (14)

Ehiogu, U. (Aston Villa), 1992 v H, M, Cz, F (4)

Elliott, P. (Luton T), 1985 v Fi; 1986 v T, D (3)

Ord, R. J. (Sunderland), 1991 v W, M, USSR (3)

Osman, R. C. (Ipswich T), 1979 v W (sub), Se; 1980 v D, S (2), EG (2) (7)

Owen, G. A. (Manchester C), 1977 v S, Fi, N; 1978 v N, Fi, I (2), Y; 1979 v D, W; (with WBA), Bul, Se (sub); 1980 v D, S (2), EG; 1981 v Sw, R; 1982 v N (sub), H; 1983 v WG (2) (22)

Painter, I. (Stoke C), 1986 v I (1)

Palmer, C. (Sheffield W), 1989 v Bul, Sen, Ei, US (4)

Parker, G. (Hull C), 1986 v I (2); (with Nottingham F), v F; 1987 v Se, Y (sub), Sp (6)

Parker, P. (Fulham), 1985 v Fi, T, Is (sub), Ei, R, Fi; 1986 v T, D (8)

Parkes, P. B. F. (QPR), 1979 v D (1)

Parkin, S. (Stoke C), 1987 v Sp (sub); 1988 v WG (sub), T, S (sub), F (5)

Parlour, R. (Arsenal), 1992 v H, M, Cz, F (4)

Peach, D. S. (Southampton), 1977 v S, Fi, N; 1978 v N, I (2) (6)

Peake, A. (Leicester C), 1982 v Pol (1)

Pearce, S. (Nottingham F), 1987 v Y (1)

Pickering N. (Sunderland), 1983 v D (sub), Gr, H; 1984 v F (sub), F, I (2), Sp; 1985 v Is, R, Fi; 1986 v R, T; (with Coventry C), D, I (15)

Platt, D. (Aston Villa), 1988 v M, Mor, F (3)

Porter, G. (Watford), 1987 v Sp (sub), T, Mor, USSR, F, P (sub); 1988 v T (sub), Y, S (2), F, Sw (12)

Pressman, K. (Sheffield W), 1989 v D (sub) (1)

Proctor, M. (Middlesbrough), 1981 v Ei (sub), Sw; 1982 (with Nottingham F), v N, Pol (4)

Ramage, C. D. (Derby Co), 1991 v Pol (sub), W; 1992 v Fr (sub) (3)

Ranson, R. (Manchester C), 1980 v Bul, EG; 1981 v R (sub), R, Sw, (1 + sub), H, Pol (2), S (10)

Redmond, S. (Manchester C), 1988 v F (2), M, USSR, Mor, F; 1989 v D, Se, Gr, Alb (2), Pol; 1990 v Se, Pol (14)

Reeves, K. P. (Norwich C), 1978 v I, Y (2); 1979 v N, W, Bul, Sw; 1980 v D, S; (with Manchester C), EG (10)

Regis, C. (WBA), 1979 v D, Bul, Se; 1980 v S, EG; 1983 v D (6)

Reid, N. S. (Manchester C), 1981 v H (sub); 1982 v H, Pol (2), S (2) (6)

Reid, P. (Bolton W), 1977 v S, Fi, N; 1978 v Fi, I, Y (6)

Richards, J. P. (Wolverhampton W), 1977 v Fi, N (2)

Rideout, P. (Aston Villa), 1985 v Fi, Is, Ei (sub), R; (with Bari), 1986 v D (5)

Ripley, S. (Middlesbrough), 1988 v USSR, F (sub); 1989 v D (sub), Se, Gr, Alb (2); 1990 v Se (8)

Ritchie, A. (Brighton & HA), 1982 v Pol (1)

Rix, G. (Arsenal), 1978 v Fi (sub), Y; 1979 v D, Se; 1980 v D (sub), Bul, S (7)

Robins, M. G. (Manchester U), 1990 v P, F, USSR, Cz; 1991 v H (sub), Pol (6)

Robson, B. (WBA), 1979 v W, Bul (sub), Se; 1980 v D, Bul, S (2) (7)

Robson, S. (Arsenal), 1984 v I; 1985 v Fi, Is, Fi; 1986 v R, I (6)

Robson, S. (West Ham U), 1988 v S, Sw (2)

Rocastle, D. (Arsenal), 1987 v Se, Y, Sp, T; 1988 v WG, T, Y, S (2), F (2 subs), M, USSR, Mor (14)

Rodger, G. (Coventry C), 1987 v USSR, F, P; 1988 v WG (4)

Rosario, R. (Norwich C), 1987 v T (sub), Mor, F, P (sub) (4)

Rowell, G. (Sunderland), 1977 v Fi (1)

Ruddock, N. (Southampton), 1989 v Bul (sub), Sen, Ei, US (4)

Ryan, J. (Oldham Ath), 1983 v H (1)

Samways, V. (Tottenham H), 1988 v Sw (sub); USSR, F; 1989 v D, Se (5)

Sansom, K. G. (C Palace), 1979 v D, W, Bul, Se; 1980 v S (2), EG (2) (8)

Seaman, D. (Birmingham C), 1985 v Fi, T, Is, Ei, R, Fi; 1986 v R, F, D, I (10)

Sedgley, S. (Coventry C), 1987 v USSR, F (sub), P; 1988 v F; 1989 v D (sub), Se, Gr, Alb (2), Pol; (with Tottenham H), 1990 v Se (11)

Sellars, S. (Blackburn R), 1988 v S (sub), F, Sw (3)

Sharpe, L. (Manchester U), 1989 v Gr; 1990 v P (sub), F, USSR, Cz; 1991 v H, Pol (sub), Ei (8)

Shaw, G. R. (Aston Villa), 1981 v Ei, Sw, H; 1982 v H, S; 1983 v WG (2) (7)

Shearer, A. (Southampton), 1991 v Ei (2), W, T, Sen, M, USSR, F; 1992 v G, T, Pol (11)

Shelton, G. (Sheffield W), 1985 v Fi (1)

Sheringham, T. (Millwall), 1988 v Sw (1)

Sheron, M. N. (Manchester C), 1992 v H, F (2)

Sherwood, T. A. (Norwich C), 1990 v P, F, USSR, Cz (4)

Simpson, P. (Manchester C), 1986 v D (sub); 1987 v Y, Mor, F, P (5)

Sims, S. (Leicester C), 1977 v W, S, Fi, N; 1978 v N, Fi, I (2), Y (2) (10)

Sinnott, L. (Watford), 1985 v Is (sub) (1)

Slater, S. I. (West Ham U), 1990 v P, USSR (sub), Cz (sub) (3)

Smith, D. (Coventry C), 1988 v M, USSR (sub), Mor; 1989 v D, Se, Alb (2), Pol; 1990 v Se, Pol (10)

Smith, M. (Sheffield W), 1981 v Ei, R, Sw, H; 1982 v Pol (sub) (5)

Snodin, I. (Doncaster R), 1985 v T, Is, R, Fi (4)

Statham, B. (Tottenham H), 1988 v Sw; 1989 v D (sub), Se (3)

Statham, D. J. (WBA), 1978 v Fi, 1979 v W, Bul, Se; 1980 v D; 1983 v D (6)

Stein, B. (Luton T), 1984 v D, H, I (3)

Sterland, M. (Sheffield W), 1984 v D, H, F (2), I. Sp (2) (7)

Steven, T. (Everton), 1985 v Fi, T (2)

Stevens, G. (Brighton & HA), 1983 v H; (with Tottenham H), 1984 v H, F (1 + sub), I (sub), Sp (1 + sub); 1986 v I (8)

Stewart, P. (Manchester C), 1988 v F (1)

Stuart, G. C. (Chelsea), 1990 v P (sub), F, USSR, Cz; 1991 v T (sub) (5)

Suckling, P. (Coventry C), 1986 v D; (with Manchester C), 1987 v Se (sub), Y, Sp, T; (with C Palace), 1988 v S (2), F (2), Sw (10)

Sunderland, A. (Wolverhampton W), 1977 v W (1)

Swindlehurst, D. (C Palace), 1977 v W (1)

Sutch, D. (Norwich C), 1992 v H, M, Cz (3)

Talbot, B. (Ipswich T), 1977 v W (1)

Thomas, D. (Coventry C), 1981 v Ei; 1983 v WG (2), Gr, H; (with Tottenham H), v I, Sp (7)

Thomas, M. (Luton T), 1986 v T, D, I (3)

Thomas, M. (Arsenal), 1989 v Y, S, F (2), M, USSR, Mor; 1989 v Gr, Alb (2), Pol; 1990 v Se (12)

Thomas, R. E. (Watford), 1990 v P (1)

Thompson, G. L. (Coventry C), 1981 v R, Sw, H; 1982 v N, H, S (6)

Thorn, A. (Wimbledon), 1988 v WG (sub). Y, S, F, Sw (5)

Tiler, C. (Barnsley), 1990 v P, USSR, Cz; 1991 v H, Pol, Ei (2), T, Sen, USSR, F; (with Nottingham F), 1992 v G, T (13)

Venison, B. (Sunderland), 1983 v D, Gr; 1985 v Fi, T, Is, Fi; 1986 v R, T, D (2) (10)

Vinnicombe, C. (Rangers), 1991 v H (sub), Pol, Ei (2), T, Sen, M, USSR (sub), F; 1992 v G, T, Pol (12)

Waddle, C. (Newcastle U), 1985 v Fi (1)

Wallace, D. (Southampton), 1983 v Gr, H; 1984 v D, H, F (2), I, Sp (sub); 1985 v Fi, T, Is; 1986 v R, D, I (14)

Wallace, Ray (Southampton), 1989 v Bul, Sen (sub), Ei; 1990 v Se (4)

Wallace, Rod (Southampton), 1989 v Bul, Ei (sub), US; 1991 v H, Pol, Ei, T, Sen, M, USSR, F (11)

Walker, D. (Nottingham F), 1985 v Fi; 1987 v Se, T; 1988 v WG, T, S (2) (7)

Walker, I. M. (Tottenham H), 1991 v W; 1992 v H, Cz, F (4)

Walsh, G. (Manchester U), 1988 v WG, Y (2)

Walsh, P. M. (Luton T), 1983 v D (sub), Gr (2), H (4)

Walters, K. (Aston Villa), 1984 v D (sub). H (sub); 1985 v Is, Ei, R; 1986 v R, T, D, I (sub) (9)

Ward, P. D. (Brighton & HA), 1978 v N; 1980 v EG (2)

Warhurst, P. (Oldham Ath), 1991 v H, Pol, W, Sen, M (sub), USSR, F (sub); (with Sheffield W), 1992 v G (8)

Watson, D. (Norwich C), 1984 v D, F (2), I (2), Sp (2) (7)

Watson, G. (Sheffield W), 1991 v Sen, USSR (2)

Webb, N. (Portsmouth), 1985 v Ei; (with Nottingham F), 1986 v D (2) (3)

White, D. (Manchester C), 1988 v S (2), F, USSR; 1989 v Se; 1990 v Pol (6)

Whyte, C. (Arsenal), 1982 v S (1 + sub); 1983 v D, Gr (4)

Wicks, S. (QPR), 1982 v S (1)

Wilkins, R. C. (Chelsea), 1977 v W (1)

Wilkinson, P. (Grimsby T), 1985 v Ei, R (sub); (with Everton), 1986 v R (sub), I (4)

Williams, P. (Charlton Ath), 1989 v Bul, Sen, Ei, US (sub) (4)

Williams, P. D. (Derby Co), 1991 v Sen, M, USSR; 1992 v G, T, Pol (6)

Williams, S. C. (Southampton); 1977 v S, Fi, N; 1978 v N, I (1 + sub), Y (2); 1979 v D, Bul, Se (sub); 1980 v D, EG (2) (14)

Winterburn, N. (Wimbledon), 1986 v I (1)

Wise, D. (Wimbledon), 1988 v Sw (1)

Woodcook, A. S. (Nottingham F), 1978 v Fi, I (2)

Woods, C. C. E. (Nottingham F), 1979 v W (sub). Se; (with QPR), 1980 v Bul, EG; 1981 v Sw; (with Norwich C), 1984 v D (6)

Wright, M. (Southampton), 1983 v Gr, H; 1984 v D, H (4)

Wright, W. (Everton), 1979 v D, W, Bul; 1980 v D, S (2) (6)

Yates, D. (Notts Co), 1989 v D (sub), Bul, Sen, Ei, US (5)

SCOTLAND

Aitken, R. (Celtic), 1977 v Cz, W, Sw; 1978 v Cz, W; 1979 v P, N (2); 1980 v Bel, E; 1984 v EG, Y (2); 1985 v WG, Ic, Sp (16)

Albiston, A. (Manchester U), 1977 v Cz, W, Sw; 1978 v Sw, Cz (5)

Archdeacon, O. (Celtic), 1987 v WG (sub) (1)

Archibald, S. (Aberdeen), 1980 v B, E (2), WG; (with Tottenham H), 1981 v D (5)

Bannon, E. J. P. (Hearts), 1979 v US, (with Chelsea), P, N (2); (with Dundee U), 1980 v Bel, WG, E (7)

Beattie, J. (St Mirren), 1992 v D, US, P, Y (4)

Beaumont, D. (Dundee U), 1985 v Ic (1)

Bell, D. (Aberdeen), 1981 v D; 1984 v Y (2)

Bernard, P. R. J. (Oldham Ath), 1992 v R (sub), D, Se (sub), US (4)

Bett, J. (Rangers), 1981 v Se, D; 1982 v Se, D, I, E (2) (7)

Black, E. (Aberdeen), 1983 v EG, Sw (2), Bel; 1985 v Ic, Sp (2), Ic (8)

Blair, A. (Coventry C), 1980 v E; 1981 v Se; (with Aston Villa), 1982 v Se, D, I (5)

Bollan, G. (Dundee U), 1992 v D, G (sub), US, P, Y (5)

Booth, S. (Aberdeen), 1991 v R (sub), Bul (sub + 1), Pol, F (sub); 1992 v Sw, R, D, Se, US, P, Y (12)

Bowes, M. J. (Dunfermline Ath), 1992 v D (sub) (1)

Bowman, D. (Hearts), 1985 v WG (sub) (1)

Boyd, T. (Motherwell), 1987 v WG, Ei (2), Bel; 1988 v Bel (5)

Brazil, A. (Hibernian), 1978 v W (1)

Brazil, A. (Ipswich T), 1979 v N; 1980 v Bel (2), E (2), WG; 1981 v Se; 1982 v Se (8)

Brough, J. (Hearts), 1981 v D (1)

Burley, G. E. (Ipswich T), 1977 v Cz, W, Sw; 1978 v Sw, Cz (5)

Burley, C. (Chelsea), 1992 v D (1)

Burns, H. (Rangers), 1985 v Sp, Ic (sub) (2)

Burns, T. (Celtic), 1977 v Cz, W, E; 1978 v Sw; 1982 v E (5)

Campbell, S. (Dundee), 1989 v N (sub), Y, F (3)

Casey, J. (Celtic), 1978 v W (1)

Christie, M. (Dundee), 1992 v D, P (sub), Y (3)

Clark, R. (Aberdeen), 1977 v Cz, W, Sw (3)

Clarke, S. (St Mirren), 1984 v Bel, EG, Y; 1985 v WG, Ic, Sp (2), Ic (8)

Cleland, A. (Dundee U), 1990 v F, N (2); 1991 v R, Sw, Bul; 1992 v Sw, R, G, Se (2) (11)

Collins, J. (Hibernian), 1988 v Bel, E; 1989 v N, Y, F; 1990 v Y, F, N (8)

Connolly, P. (Dundee U), 1991 v R (sub), Sw, Bul (3)

Connor, R. (Ayr U), 1981 v Se; 1982 v Se (2)

Cooper, D. (Clydebank), 1977 v Cz, W, Sw, E; (with Rangers), 1978 v Sw, Cz (6)

Cooper, N. (Aberdeen), 1982 v D, E (2); 1983 v Bel, EG, Sw (2); 1984 v Bel, EG, Y; 1985 v Ic, Sp, Ic (13)

Crabbe, S. (Hearts), 1990 v Y (sub), F (2)

Craig, T. (Newcastle U), 1977 v E (1)

Crainie, D. (Celtic), 1983 v Sw (sub) (1)

Creaney, G. (Celtic), 1991 v Sw, Bul (2), Pol, F; 1992 v Sw, R, G (2), Se (2) (11)

Dailly, C. (Dundee U), 1991 v R; 1992 v US, P (3)

Dawson, A. (Rangers), 1979 v P, N (2); 1980 v B (2), E (2) WG (8)

Deas, P. A. (St Johnstone), 1992 v D (sub) (1)

Dennis, S. (Raith R), 1992 v Sw (1)

Dickov, P. (Arsenal), 1992 v Y (1)

Dodds, D. (Dundee U), 1978 v W (1)

Donald, G. S. (Hibernian), 1992 v US (sub), P, Y (sub) (3)

Duffy, J. (Dundee), 1987 v Ei (1)

Durie, G. S. (Chelsea), 1987 v WG, Ei, Bel; 1988 v Bel (4)

Durrant, I. (Rangers), 1987 v WG, Ei, Bel; 1988 v E (4)

Doyle, J. (Partick Th), 1981 v D, I (sub) (2)

Ferguson, D. (Rangers), 1987 v WG, Ei, Bel; 1988 v E; 1990 v Y (5)

Ferguson, D. (Dundee U), 1992 v D, G, Se (2) (4)

Ferguson, D. (Manchester U), 1992 v US, P (sub), Y (3)

Ferguson, I. (Dundee), 1983 v EG (sub), Sw (sub); 1984 v Bel (sub), EG (4)

Ferguson, I. (Clyde), 1987 v WG (sub), Ei (with St Mirren), Ei, Bel; 1988 v Bel; (with Rangers), E (sub) (6)

Ferguson, R. (Hamilton A), 1977 v E (1)

Findlay, W. (Hibernian), 1991 v R, Pol, Bul (2), Pol (5)

Fitzpatrick, A. (St Mirren), 1977 v W (sub), Sw (sub), E; 1978 v Sw, Cz (5)

Fleck, R. (Rangers), 1987 v WG (sub), Ei, Bel; (with Norwich C), 1988 v E (2); 1989 v Y (6)

Fridge, L. (St Mirren), 1989 v F; 1990 v Y (2)

Fulton, M. (St Mirren), 1980 v Bel, WG, E; 1981 v Se, D (sub)

Fulton, S. (Celtic), 1991 v R, Sw, Bul, Pol, F; 1992 v G (2) (7)

Gallacher, K. (Dundee U), 1987 v WG, Ei (2), Bel (sub); 1988 v E (2); 1990 v Y (7)

Galloway, M. (Hearts), 1989 v F; (with Celtic), 1990 v N (2)

Geddes, R. (Dundee), 1982 v Se, D, E (2); 1988 v E (5)

Gemmill, S. (Nottingham F), 1992 v Sw, R (sub), G (sub), Se (sub) (4)

Gillespie, G. (Coventry C), 1979 v US; 1980 v E; 1981 v D; 1982 v Se, D, I (2), E (8)

Glover, L. (Nottingham F), 1988 v Bel (sub); 1989 v N; 1990 v Y (3)

Goram, A. (Oldham Ath), 1987 v Ei (1)

Gough, C. R. (Dundee U), 1983 v EG, Sw, Bel; 1984 v Y (2) (5)

Grant, P. (Celtic), 1985 v WG, Ic, Sp; 1987 v WG, Ei (2), Bel; 1988 v Bel, E (2) (10)

Gunn, B. (Aberdeen), 1984 v EG, Y (2); 1985 v WG, Ic, Sp (2), Ic; 1990 v F (9)

Gray, S. (Aberdeen), 1987 v WG (1)

Hagen, D. (Rangers), 1992 v D (sub), US (sub), P, Y (4)

Hamilton, B. (St Mirren), 1989 v Y, F (sub); 1990 v F, N (4)

Hartford, R. A. (Manchester C), 1977 v Sw (1)

Hegarty, P. (Dundee U), 1987 v WG, Bel; 1988 v E (2); 1990 v F, N (4)

Hendry, J. (Tottenham H), 1992 v D (sub) (1)

Hewitt, J. (Aberdeen), 1982 v I; 1983 v EG, Sw (2); 1984 v Bel, Y (sub) (6)

Hogg, G. (Manchester U), 1984 v Y; 1985 v WG, Ic, Sp (4)

Hunter, G. (Hibernian), 1987 v Ei (sub); 1988 v Bel, N (3)

Hunter, P. (East Fife), 1989 v N (sub), F (sub); 1990 v F (sub) (3)

Jardine, I. (Kilmarnock), 1979 v US (1)

Jess, E. (Aberdeen), 1990 v F (sub), N (sub); 1991 v R, Sw, Bul (2), Pol, F; 1992 v Sw, R, G (2), Se (1 + sub) (14)

Johnson, G. I. (Dundee U), 1992 v US, P, Y (3)

Johnston, M. (Partick Th), 1984 v EG (sub); (with Watford), Y (2) (3)

Kirkwood, D. (Hearts), 1990 v Y (1)

Lambert, P. (St Mirren), 1991 v R, Sw, Bul (2), Pol, F; 1992 v Sw, R, G (2), Se (11)

Leighton, J. (Aberdeen), 1982 v I (1)

Levein, C. (Hearts), 1985 v Sp, Ic (2)

Lindsey, J. (Motherwell), 1979 v US (1)

McAllister, G. (Leicester C), 1990 v N (1)

McAlpine, H. (Dundee U), 1983 v EG, Sw (2), Bel; 1984 v Bel (5)

McAvennie, F. (St Mirren), 1982 v I, E; 1985 v Is, Ei, R (5)

McBride, J. (Everton), 1981 v D (1)

McCall, S. (Bradford C), 1988 v E; (with Everton), 1990 v F (2)

McClair, B. (Celtic), 1984 v Bel (sub), EG, Y (1 + sub); 1985 v WG, Ic, Sp, Ic (8)

McCluskey, G. (Celtic), 1979 v US, P; 1980 v Bel, (2); 1982 vD,I(6)

McCoist, A. (Rangers), 1984 v Bel (1)

McCulloch, A. (Kilmarnock), 1981 v Se (1)

McCulloch, I. (Notts Co), 1982 v E (2)

MacDonald, J. (Rangers), 1980 v WG (sub); 1981 v Se; 1982 v Se (sub), L, I (2), E (2 sub) (8)

McGarvey, F. (St Mirren), 1977 v E; 1978 v Cz; (with Celtic), 1982 v D (3)

McGarvey, S. (Manchester U), 1982 v E (sub); 1983 v Bel, Sw; 1984 v Bel (4)

McGhee, M. (Aberdeen), 1981 v D (1)

McGinnis, G. (Dundee U), 1985 v Sp (1)

McInally, J. (Dundee U), 1989 v F (1)

McKimmie, S. (Aberdeen), 1985 v WG, Ic (2) (3)

McKinlay, T. (Dundee), 1984 v EG (sub); 1985 v WG, Ic, Sp (2), Ic (6)

McKinlay, W. (Dundee U), 1989 v N, Y (sub), F; 1990 v Y, F, N (6)

McKinnon, R. (Dundee U), 1991 v R, Pol (sub); 1992 v G (2), Se (2) (6)

McLaren, A. (Hearts), 1989 v F; 1990 v Y, N; 1991 v Sw, Bul, Po1, F; 1992 v R, G, Se (2) (11)

McLaughlin, J. (Morton), 1981 v D; 1982 v Se, D, I, E (2); 1983 v EG, Sw (2), Bel (10)

McLeish, A. (Aberdeen), 1978 v W; 1979 v US; 1980 v Bel, E (2); 1987 v Ei (6)

MacLeod, A. (Hibernian), 1979 v P, N (2) (3)

McLeod, J. (Dundee U), 1989 v N; 1990 v F (2)

MacLeod, M. (Dumbarton), 1979 v US; (with Celtic), P (sub), N (2); 1980 v Bel (5)

McNab, N. (Tottenham H), 1978 v W (1)

McNally, M. (Celtic), 1991 v Bul (1)

McNichol, J. (Brentford), 1979 v P. N (2); 1980 v Bel (2), WG, E (7)

McNiven, D. (Leeds U), 1977 v Cz, W (sub), Sw (sub) (3)

McPherson, D. (Rangers), 1984 v Bel; 1985 v Sp; (with Hearts), 1989 v N, Y (4)

McStay, P. (Celtic), 1983 v EG, Sw (2); 1984 v Y (2) (5)

McWhirter, N. (St Mirren), 1991 v Bul (sub) (1)

Main, A. (Dundee U), 1988 v E; 1989 v Y; 1990 v N (3)

Malpas, M. (Dundee U), 1983 v Bel, Sw (1 + sub); 1984 v Bel, EG, Y (2); 1985 v Sp (8)

May, E. (Hibernian), 1989 v Y (sub), F (2)

Melrose, J. (Partick Th), 1977 v Sw; 1979 v US, P, N (2); 1980 v Bel (sub), WG, E (8)

Miller J. (Aberdeen), 1987 v Ei (sub); 1988 v Bel; (with Celtic) E; 1989 v N, Y; 1990 v F, N (7)

Miller, W. (Aberdeen), 1978 v Sw, Cz (2)

Miller, W. (Hibernian), 1991 v R, Sw, Bul, Pol, F; 1992 v R, G (sub) (7)

Milne, R. (Dundee U), 1982 v Se (sub); 1984 v Bel, EG (3)

Money, I. C. (St Mirren), 1987 v Ei; 1988 v Bel; 1989 v N (3)

Muir, L. (Hibernian), 1977 v Cz (sub) (1)

Narey, D. (Dundee U), 1977 v Cz, Sw; 1978 v Sw, Cz (4)

Nevin, P. (Chelsea), 1985 v WG, Ic, Sp (2), Ic (5)

Nicholas, C. (Celtic), 1981 v Se; 1982 v Se; 1983 v EG, Sw, Bel; (with Arsenal), 1984 v Y (6)

Nicol, S. (Ayr U), 1981 v Se; 1982 v Se, D; (with Liverpool), 1982 v I (2), E (2); 1983 v EG, Sw (2), Bel; 1984 v Bel, EG, Y (14)

Nisbet, S. (Rangers), 1989 v N, Y, F; 1990 v Y, F (5)

O'Donnell, P. (Motherwell), 1992 v Sw (sub), R, D, G (2), Se (1 + sub) (7)

O'Neil, B. (Celtic), 1992 v D, G, Se (2) (4)

O'Neil, J. (Dundee U), 1991 v Bul (sub) (1)

Orr, N. (Morton), 1978 v W (sub); 1979 v US, P, N (2); 1980 v Bel, E (7)

Parlane, D. (Rangers), 1977 v W (1)

Paterson, C. (Hibernian), 1981 v Se; 1982 v I (2)

Payne, G. (Dundee U), 1978 v Sw, Cz, W (3)

Provan, D. (Kilmarnock), 1977 v Cz (sub) (1)

Rae, A. (Millwall), 1991 v Bul (sub + 1), F (sub); 1992 v Sw, R, G (sub), Se (2) (8)

Redford, I. (Rangers), 1981 v Se (sub); 1982 v Se, D, I (2), E (6)

Reid, B. (Rangers), 1991 v F; 1992 v D, US, P (4)

Reid, M. (Celtic), 1982 v E; 1984 v Y (2)

Reid, R. (St Mirren), 1977 v W, Sw, E (3)

Rice, B. (Hibernian), 1985 v WG (1)

Richardson, L. (St Mirren), 1980 v WG, E (sub) (2)

Ritchie, A. (Morton), 1980 v Bel (1)

Robertson, A. (Rangers) 1991 v F (1)
Robertson, C. (Rangers), 1977 v E (sub) (1) .
Robertson, D. (Aberdeen), 1987 v Ei (sub); 1988 v E (2); 1989 v N, Y; 1990 v Y, N (7)
Robertson, J. (Hearts), 1985 v WG, Ic (sub) (2)
Roddie, A. (Aberdeen), 1992 v US, P (2)
Ross, T. W. (Arsenal), 1977 v W (1)
Russell, R. (Rangers), 1978 v W; 1980 v Bel; 1984 v Y (3)

Salton, D. B. (Luton T), 1992 v D, US, P, Y (4)
Shannon, R. (Dundee), 1987 v WG, Ei (2), Bel; 1988 v Bel, E (2) (7)
Sharp, G. (Everton), 1982 v E (1)
Sharp, R. (Dunfermline Ath), 1990 v N (sub); 1991 v R, Sw, Bul (4)
Simpson, N. (Aberdeen), 1982 v I (2), E; 1983 v EG, Sw (2), Bel; 1984 v Bel, EG, Y; 1985 v Sp (11)
Sinclair, G. (Dumbarton), 1977 v E (1)
Smith, B. M. (Celtic), 1992 v G (2), US, P, Y (5)
Smith, G. (Rangers), 1978 v W (1)
Smith, H. G. (Hearts), 1987 v WG, Bel (2)
Sneddon, A. (Celtic), 1979 v US (1)
Speedie, D. (Chelsea), 1985 v Sp (1)
Spencer, J. (Rangers), 1991 v Sw (sub), F; 1992 v Sw (3)
Stanton, P. (Hibernian), 1977 v Cz (1)
Stark, W. (Aberdeen), 1985 v Ic (1)
Stephen, R. (Dundee) 1983 v Be1 (sub) (1)
Stevens, G. (Motherwell), 1977 v E (1)
Stewart, J. (Kilmarnock), 1978 v Sw, Cz; (with Middlesbrough), 1979 v P (3)
Stewart, R. (Dundee U), 1979 v P, N (2); (with West Ham U), 1980 v Bel (2), E (2), WG; 1981 v D; 1982 v I (2), E (12)
Strachan, G. (Aberdeen), 1980 v Bel (1)
Sturrock, P. (Dundee U), 1977 v Cz, W, Sw, E; 1978 v Sw, Cz; 1982 v Se, I, E (9)
Sweeney, S. (Clydebank), 1991 v R, Sw (sub), Bul (2), Pol; 1992 v Sw, R (7)

Thomson, W. (Partick Th), 1977 v E (sub); 1978 v W; (with St Mirren), 1979 v US, N (2); 1980 v Bel (2), E (2), WG (10)
Tolmie, J. (Morton), 1980 v Bel (sub) (1)
Tortolano, J. (Hibernian), 1987 v WG, Ei (2)

Walker, A. (Celtic), 1988 v Bel (1)
Wallace, I. (Coventry C), 1978 v Sw (1)
Walsh, C. (Nottingham F), 1984 v EG, Sw (2). Bel; 1984 v EG (5)
Wark, J. (Ipswich T), 1977 v Cz, W, Sw; 1978 v W; 1979 v P; 1980 v E (2), WG (8)
Watson, A. (Aberdeen), 1981 v Se, D; 1982 v D, I (sub) (4)
Watson, K. (Rangers), 1977 v E; 1978 v Sw (sub) (2)
Watt, M. (Aberdeen), 1991 v R, Sw, Bul (2), Pol, F; 1992 v Sw, R, G (2), Se (2) (12)
Whyte, D. (Celtic), 1987 v Ei (2), Bel; 1988 v E (2); 1989 v N, Y; 1990 v Y, N (9)
Will, J. A. (Arsenal), 1992 v D (sub), Y (2)
Wilson, T. (St Mirren), 1983 v Sw (sub) (1)
Wilson, T. (Nottingham F), 1988 v E; 1989 v N, Y; 1990 v F (4)
Winnie, D. (St Mirren), 1988 v Bel (1)
Wright, P. (Aberdeen), 1989 v Y, F; (with QPR), 1990 v Y (sub) (3)
Wright, S. (Aberdeen), 1991 v Bul, Pol, F; 1992 v Sw, G (2), Se (2) (8)
Wright, T. (Oldham Ath), 1987 v Bel (sub) (1)

WALES

Aizlewood, M. (Luton T), 1979 v E; 1981 v Ho (2)

Balcombe, S. (Leeds U), 1982 v F (sub) (1)
Bater, P. T. (Bristol R), 1977 v E, S (2)
Blackmore, C. (Manchester U), 1984 v N, Bul, Y (3)

Blake, N. (Cardiff C), 1991 v Pol (sub) (1)
Bodin, P. (Cardiff C), 1983 v Y (1)
Bowen, M. (Tottenham H), 1983 v N; 1984 v Bul, Y (3)
Boyle, T. (C Palace), 1982 v F (1)

Cegielski, W. (Wrexham), 1977 v E (sub), S (2)
Chapple, S. R. (Swansea C), 1992 v R (1)
Charles, J. M. (Swansea C), 1979 v E; 1981 v Ho (2)
Clark, J. (Manchester U), 1978 v S; (with Derby Co), 1979 v E (2)
Coleman, C. (Swansea C); 1990 v Pol; 1991 v E, Pol (3)
Coyne, D. (Tranmere R), 1992 v R (1)
Curtis, A. T. (Swansea C), 1977 v E (1)

Davies, A. (Manchester U), 1982 v F (2) Ho; 1983 v N, Y, Bul (6)
Davies, I. C. (Norwich C), 1978 v S (sub) (1)
Deacy, N. (PSV Eindhoven), 1977 v S (1)
Dibble, A. (Cardiff C), 1983 v Bul; 1984 v N, Bul (3)
Doyle, S. C. (Preston NE), 1979 v E (sub); (with Huddersfield T), 1984 v N (2)
Dwyer, P. J. (Cardiff C), 1979 v E (1)

Ebdon, M. (Everton), 1990 v Pol; 1991 v E (2)
Edwards, R. (Bristol C.), 1991 v Pol; 1992 v R (2)
Edwards, R. I. (Chester), 1977 v S; 1978 v W (2)
Evans, A. (Bristol R), 1977 v E (1)

Freestone, R. (Chelsea), 1990 v Pol (1)

Gale, D. (Swansea C), 1983 v Bul; 1984 v N (sub) (2)
Giggs, R. (Manchester U), 1991 v Pol (1)
Giles, D. C. (Cardiff C), 1977 v S; 1978 v S; (with Swansea C), 1981 v Ho; (with C. Palace), 1983 v Y (4)
Giles, P. (Cardiff C), 1982 v F (2), Ho (3)
Graham, D. (Manchester U.), 1991 v E (1)
Griffith, C. (Cardiff C), 1990 v Pol (1)
Griffiths, C. (Shrewsbury T), 1991 v Pol (sub) (1)

Hall, G. D. (Chelsea), 1990 v Pol (1)
Hodges, G. (Wimbledon), 1983 v Y (sub), Bul (sub); 1984 v N, Bul, Y (5)
Holden, A. (Chester C), 1984 v Y (sub) (1)
Hopkins, J. (Fulham), 1982 v F (sub), Ho; 1983 v N, Y, Bul (5)
Hughes, I. (Bury), 1992 v R (1)
Hughes, M. (Manchester U), 1983 v N, Y; 1984 v N. Bul, Y (5)
Hughes, W. (WBA), 1977 v E, S; 1978 v S (3)

Jackett, K. (Watford), 1981 v Ho; 1982 v F (2)
James, R. M. (Swansea C), 1977 v E, S; 1978 v S (3)
Jones, F. (Wrexham), 1981 v Ho (1)
Jones, L. (Cardiff C), 1982 v F (2), Ho (3)
Jones, P. L. (Liverpool), 1992 v R (1)
Jones, V. (Bristol R), 1979 v E; 1981 v Ho (2)

Kendall, M. (Tottenham H), 1978 v S (1)

Law, B. J. (QPR), 1990 v Pol; 1991 v E (2)
Letheran, G. (Leeds U), 1977 v E, S (2)
Lewis, D. (Swansea C), 1982 v F (2), Ho; 1983 v N, Y, Bul; 1984 v N, Bul, Y (9)
Lewis, J. (Cardiff C), 1983 v N (1)
Loveridge, J. (Swansea C), 1982 v Ho; 1983 v N, Bul (3)
Lowndes, S. R. (Newport Co), 1979 v E; 1981 v Ho; (with Millwall), 1984 v Bul, Y (4)

Maddy, P. (Cardiff C), 1982 v Ho; 1983 v N (sub) (2)
Margetson, M. W. (Manchester C), 1992 v R (1)
Marustik, C. (Swansea C), 1982 v F (2); 1983 v Y, Bul; 1984 v N, Bul, Y (7)
Melville, A. K. (Swansea C), 1990 v Pol; (with Oxford U), 1991 v E (2)
Micallef, C. (Cardiff C), 1982 v F, Ho; 1983 v N (3)

Nardiello, D. (Coventry C), 1978 v S (1)
Nicholas, P. (C Palace), 1978 v S; 1979 v E; (with Arsenal), 1982 v F (3)

Nogan, K. (Luton T), 1990 v Pol; 1991 v E (2)
Nogan, L. (Oxford U.) 1991 v E (1)

Owen, G. (Wrexham), 1991 v E (sub), Pol; 1992 v R (3)

Pascoe, C. (Swansea C), 1983 v Bul (sub); 1984 v N (sub), Bul, Y (4)
Pembridge, M. (Luton T), 1991 v Pol (1)
Perry, J. (Cardiff C), 1990 v Pol; 1991 v E, Pol (3)
Peters, M. (Manchester C), 1992 v R (1)
Phillips, D. (Plymouth Arg), 1984 v N, Bul, Y (3)
Phillips, L. (Swansea C), 1979 v E; (with Charlton Ath), 1983 v N (2)
Pontin, K. (Cardiff C), 1978 v S (1)
Powell, L. (Southampton), 1991 v Pol (sub); 1992 v (sub) (2)
Price, P. (Luton T), 1981 v Ho (1)
Pugh, D. (Doncaster R), 1982 v F (2) (2)

Ratcliffe, K. (Everton), 1981 v Ho; 1982 v F (2)
Ready, K. (QPR), 1992 v R (1)
Rees, A. (Birmingham C), 1984 v N (1)
Rees, J. (Luton T), 1990 v Pol; 1991 v E, Pol (3)
Roberts, A. (QPR), 1991 v E, Pol (2)
Roberts, G. (Hull C), 1983 v Bul (1)
Roberts, J. G. (Wrexham), 1977 v E (1)

Robinson, J. (Brighton & HA), 1992 v R (1)
Rush, I. (Liverpool), 1981 v Ho; 1982 v F (2)

Sayer, P. A. (Cardiff C), 1977 v E, S (2)
Searle, D. (Cardiff C), 1991 v Pol (sub); 1992 v R (2)
Slatter, N. (Bristol R), 1983 v N, Y, Bul; 1984 v N, Bul, Y (6)
Speed, G. A. (Leeds U), 1990 v Pol; 1991 v E, Pol (3)
Stevenson, N. (Swansea C), 1982 v F, Ho (2)
Stevenson, W. B. (Leeds U), 1977 v E, S; 1978 v S (3)
Symons, K. (Portsmouth), 1991 v E, Pol (2)

Thomas, Martin R. (Bristol R), 1979 v E; 1981 v Ho (2)
Thomas, Mickey R. (Wrexham), 1977 v E; 1978 v S (2)
Thomas, D. G. (Leeds U), 1977 v E; 1979 v E; 1984 v N (3)
Tibbott, L. (Ipswich T), 1977 v E, S (2)

Vaughan, N. (Newport Co), 1982 v F, Ho (2)

Walsh, I. P. (C Palace), 1979 v E; (with Swansea C), 1983 v Bul (2)
Walton, M. (Norwich C.), 1991 v Pol (sub) (1)
Williams, D. (Bristol R), 1983 v Y (1)
Williams, G. (Bristol R), 1983 v Y, Bul (2)
Wilmot, R. (Arsenal), 1982 v F (2), Ho; 1983 v N, Y; 1984 v Y (6)

ENGLAND B RESULTS 1949–92

Year	Date		Venue	Eng	
			v ALGIERS	Eng	Alg
1990	Dec	11	Algiers	0	0
			v AUSTRALIA	Eng	Aust
1980	Nov	17	Birmingham	1	0
			v CIS	Eng	CIS
1992	April	28	Moscow	1	1
			v CZECHOSLOVAKIA	Eng	Cz
1978	Nov	28	Prague	1	0
1990	April	24	Sunderland	2	0
1992	Mar	24	Budejovice	1	0
			v FINLAND	Eng	Fin
1949	May	15	Helsinki	4	0
			v FRANCE	Eng	Fra
1952	May	22	Le Havre	1	7
1992	Feb	18	Loftus Road	3	0
			v WEST GERMANY	Eng	WG
1954	Mar	24	Gelsenkirchen	4	0
1955	Mar	23	Sheffield	1	1
1978	Feb	21	Augsburg	2	1
			v HOLLAND	Eng	Hol
1949	May	18	Amsterdam	4	0
1950	Feb	22	Newcastle	1	0
1952	Mar	26	Amsterdam	1	0
			v ICELAND	Eng	Ice
1989	May	19	Reykjavik	2	0
1991	April	27	Watford	1	0
			v ITALY	Eng	It
1950	May	11	Milan	0	5
1989	Nov	14	Brighton	1	1
			v LUXEMBOURG	Eng	Lux
1950	May	21	Luxembourg	2	1
			v MALAYSIA	Eng	Mal
1978	May	30	Kuala Lumpur	1	1
			v MALTA	Eng	Mal
1987	Oct	14	Ta'Qali	2	0

Year	Date		Venue	Eng	
			v NEW ZEALAND	Eng	NZ
1978	June	7	Christchurch	4	0
1978	June	11	Wellington	3	1
1978	June	14	Auckland	4	0
1979	Oct	15	Leyton	4	1
1984	Nov	13	Nottingham	2	0
			v NORWAY	Eng	Nor
1989	May	22	Stavanger	1	0
			v REPUBLIC OF IRELAND	Eng	RoI
1990	Mar	27	Cork	1	4
			v SCOTLAND	Eng	Scot
1953	Mar	11	Edinburgh	2	2
1954	Mar	3	Sunderland	1	1
1956	Feb	29	Dundee	2	2
1957	Feb	6	Birmingham	4	1
			v SINGAPORE	Eng	Sin
1978	June	18	Singapore	8	0
			v SPAIN	Eng	Sp
1980	Mar	26	Sunderland	1	0
1981	Mar	25	Granada	2	3
1991*	Dec	18	Castellon	1	1
*Spanish Olympic IX					
			v SWITZERLAND	Eng	Sw
1950	Jan	18	Sheffield	5	0
1954	May	22	Basle	0	2
1956	Mar	21	Southampton	4	1
1989	May	16	Winterthur	2	0
1991	May	20	Walsall	2	1
			v USA	Eng	USA
1980	Oct	14	Manchester	1	0
			v WALES	Eng	Wal
1991	Feb	5	Swansea	1	0
			v YUGOSLAVIA	Eng	Yug
1954	May	16	Ljubljana	1	2
1955	Oct	19	Manchester	5	1
1989	Dec	12	Millwall	2	1

ENGLAND B MATCHES 1991–92

Castellon, 18 December 1991, 4000

Spanish Olympic XI (0) 0

England B (1) 1 *(Merson 43)*

Spanish Olympic XI: Canizares (Rafa 76); Larrainzar (Mariano 46), Angel Luis, Solozabal, Abelardo, Larrazabal, Eskurza (Soler 51), Guardiola (Sanjuan 46), Alfonso, Marino, Luis Enrique (Quico 46).
England B: Seaman; Barrett, Winterburn, Webb, Keown, Curle, Rocastle, Campbell (Slater), Hirst, Palmer, Merson (Deane).

Loftus Road, 18 February 1992, 4827

England B (2) 3 *(Merson 17, Dumas (og) 33, Stewart 70)*

France B (0) 0

England B: Seaman (Coton 46); Curle, Dorigo, Stewart, Mabbutt, Pallister, Ince (Le Tissier 72), Merson, Wright (White 46), Palmer, Sinton.
France B: Olmeta (Lama 46); Sassus, Reynaud, Prunier, Dumas, Silvestre (Laigle 46), Cocard (Partina 65), Dutuel (Djorkaeff 80), Caldararo, Garde, Ginola.

Budejovice, 24 March 1992, 6000

Czechoslovakia B (0) 0

England B (0) 1 *(Smith 74)*

Czechoslovakia B: Molnar (Pribyl 46); Stupala, Suchoparek (Vadura 46), Vrabec (Paktor 46), Silhavy, Mistr (Tejmi 70), Casko, Marosi, Kerbr (Cerny 46), Lancz, Timko (Chvila 46).
England B: Martyn; Barrett, Dicks, Batty, Jobson, Palmer, Sinton, Thomas, Smith (Dorigo 83), Shearer (Hirst 46), Le Tissier.

Moscow, 28 April 1992, 2300

CIS B (0) 1 *(Mamedov 63)*

England B (1) 1 *(Smith 5)*

CIS B: Plotnikov; Gushcin, Mashkarkin, Minko (Pagaev 46), Varalamov, Mamedov, Drozdov (Bavykin 81), Kostijuk (But 46), Fayzullin (Troynin 79), Simutenkov, Skachenko (Beschastnykh 46).
England B: Seaman; Dixon, Dicks, Webb, Mabbutt, Jobson, Rocastle, Beardsley (Le Saux 84), Smith, Thomas, Sharpe (Le Tissier 46).

International Records

MOST GOALS IN AN INTERNATIONAL

England	Malcolm Macdonald (Newcastle U) 5 goals v Cyprus, at Wembley	16.4.1975
	Willie Hall (Tottenham H) 5 goals v Ireland, at Old Trafford	16.11.1938
	G. O. Smith (Corinthians) 5 goals v Ireland, at Sunderland	18.2.1899
	Steve Bloomer (Derby Co) 5 goals* v Wales, at Cardiff	16.3.1896
	Oliver Vaughton (Aston Villa) 5 goals v Ireland, at Belfast	18.2.1882
Scotland	Charles Heggie (Rangers) 5 goals v Ireland, at Belfast	20.3.1886
Ireland	Joe Bambrick (Linfield) 6 goals v Wales, at Belfast	1.2.1930
Wales	James Price (Wrexham) 4 goals v Ireland, at Wrexham	25.2.1882
	Mel Charles (Cardiff C) 4 goals v Ireland, at Cardiff	11.4.1962
	Ian Edwards (Chester) 4 goals v Malta, at Wrexham	25.10.1978

* There are conflicting reports which make it uncertain whether Bloomer scored four or five goals in this game.

MOST GOALS IN AN INTERNATIONAL CAREER

		Goals	Games
England	Bobby Charlton (Manchester U)	49	106
Scotland	Denis Law (Huddersfield T, Manchester C, Torino, Manchester U)	30	55
	Kenny Dalglish (Celtic, Liverpool)	30	102
Ireland	Billy Gillespie (Sheffield U)	12	25
	Joe Bambrick (Linfield, Chelsea)	12	11
	Gerry Armstrong (Tottenham H, Watford, Real Mallorca, WBA, Chesterfield)	12	63
Wales	Trevor Ford (Swansea T, Aston Villa, Sunderland, Cardiff C)	23	38
	Ivor Allchurch (Swansea T, Newcastle U, Cardiff C)	23	68
Republic of Ireland	Frank Stapleton (Arsenal, Manchester U, Ajax, Derby Co, Le Havre, Blackburn R)	20	70

HIGHEST SCORES

World Cup Match	New Zealand	13	Fiji	0	1981
Olympic Games	Denmark	17	France	1	1908
	Germany	16	USSR	0	1912
International Match	Germany	13	Finland	0	1940
	Spain	13	Bulgaria	0	1933
European Cup	Feyenoord	12	K R Reykjavik	2	1969
European Cup-Winners' Cup	Sporting Lisbon	16	Apoel Nicosia	1	1963
Fairs & UEFA Cups	Ajax	14	Red Boys	0	1984

GOALSCORING RECORDS

World Cup Final	Geoff Hurst (England) 3 goals v West Germany	1966
World Cup Final tournament	Just Fontaine (France) 13 goals	1958
Major European Cup game	Lothar Emmerich (Borussia Dortmund) v Floriana in Cup-Winners' Cup – 6 goals	1965
Career	Arthur Friedenreich (Brazil) 1329 goals	1910–30
	Pelé (Brazil) 1281 goals	*1956–78
	Franz 'Bimbo' Binder (Austria, Germany) 1006 goals	1930–50

* Pelé later scored two goals in Testimonial matches making his total 1283.

MOST CAPPED INTERNATIONALS IN BRITISH ISLES

England	Peter Shilton	125 appearances	1970–90
Northern Ireland	Pat Jennings	119 appearances	1964–86
Scotland	Kenny Dalglish	102 appearances	1971–86
Wales	Peter Nicholas	73 appearances	1979–91
Republic of Ireland	Liam Brady	67 appearances	1974–90

TRANSFERS

British moves £2 million and over

£7,000,000 David Platt, Bari to Juventus, May 1992

£5,500,000 David Platt, Aston Villa to Bari, July 1991

£5,500,000 Paul Gascoigne, Tottenham H to Lazio, May 1992

£4,500,000 Chris Waddle, Tottenham H to Marseille, July 1989

£3,200,000 Ian Rush, Liverpool to Juventus, June 1987

£2,900,000 Dean Saunders, Derby Co to Liverpool, July 1991

£2,800,000 Ian Rush, Juventus to Liverpool, August 1988

£2,750,000 Gary Lineker, Everton to Barcelona, June 1986

£2,500,000 Keith Curle, Wimbledon to Manchester C, July 1991

£2,500,000 Ian Wright, Crystal Palace to Arsenal, September 1991

£2,300,000 Mark Hughes, Manchester U to Barcelona, May 1986

£2,300,000 Gary Pallister, Middlesbrough to Manchester U, August 1989

£2,200,000 Tony Cottee, West Ham to Everton, July 1988

£2,200,000 Mark Wright, Derby Co to Liverpool, July 1991

£2,200,000 Gordon Durie, Chelsea to Tottenham H, August 1991

£2,000,000 Paul Gascoigne, Newcastle U to Tottenham H, July 1988

£2,000,000 Teddy Sheringham, Millwall to Nottingham Forest, July 1991

£2,000,000 Darren Anderton, Portsmouth to Tottenham H, May 1992

World records

£13,000,000 Gianluigi Lentini, Torino to AC Milan, June 1992

£12,000,000 Gianluca Vialli, Sampdoria to Juventus, June 1992

£10,000,000 Jean-Pierre Papin, Marseille to AC Milan, June 1992

£8,000,000 Igor Shalimov, Foggia to Internazionalle, June 1992

FA Schools and Youth Games 1991–92

Under-15 Nordic Tournament
7 August 1991 (at Tysvollur)
England (1) 1 *(Walker)*
Denmark (1) 4
England: Hopper; Frost (Smith), Thatcher, Hinshelwood, Faulkner (Holland), Murray, Worrall, Irving, Beech, Walker, Challis.

8 Aug 1991 (at Porsvollur)
England (0) 2 *(Murray, Faulkner)*
Sweden (0) 0
England: Hopper; Faulkner, Challis, Hinshelwood, Holland, Murray, Worrall, Irving (Feltham), Beech (Smith), Walker, Serrant.

10 Aug 1991 (at Tysvollur)
England (1) 3 *(Irving 2, Beech)*
Iceland (0) 2
England: Woods; Holland (Frost), Challis (Thatcher), Hinshelwood, Faulkner, Murray, Worrall, Irving (Smith), Beech (Feltham), Walker, Serrant.

11 Aug 1991 (at Haesteinvolluk)
England (0) 2 *(Serrant, Hinshelwood)*
Norway (1) 1
England: Hopper; Frost (Thatcher), Challis, Hinshelwood, Faulkner, Murray, Worrall, Irving (Feltham), Beech, Walker, Serrant.

12 Aug 1991 (at Porsvollur)
England (2) 3 *(Worrall 2, Hinshelwood)*
Finland (1) 2
England: Hopper; Holland, Challis, Hinshelwood, Faulkner, Murray, Feltham (Woods), Worrall, Beech, Walker, Serrant.

European Youth Championship 1990–92
12 Sept 1991 (at Crystal Palace FC)
England (0) 2 *(Bart-Williams, Myers)*
Iceland (0) 1   1432
England: Stephenson; Watson S (Watson D), Unsworth, Harriott, Basham, Thompson, Bart-Williams, Caskey, Hodges (Marlowe), Myers, Howe.

16 Oct 1991 (at Eernegem)
Belgium (1) 1
England (0) 0
England: Sheppard; Watson S, Unsworth (Marlowe), Pearce, Jackson, Thompson, Bart-Williams (Elliott), Caskey, Shaw, Myers, Howe.

Under-16 friendlies
1 Oct 1991 (at Lilleshall)
England (1) 1 *(Murray)*
Denmark (0) 1   200
England: Hopper; Hinshelwood, Challis, Feltham, Murray, Worrall, Holland (Tierney), Walker, Irving (Smith), Beech (Frost), Serrant.

3 Oct 1991 (at Lilleshall)
England (0) 0
Denmark (0) 1   200
England: Hopper (Woods); Hinshelwood (Holland), Challis, Feltham (Vaughan), Murray, Worrall, Frost (Tierney), Irving (Beech), Smith, Walker, Serrant (Strong).

Under-16 tournament in Italy
15 Oct 1991 (at Alassio)
England (1) 1 *(Irving)*
Scotland (1) 3
England: Woods; Holland (Tierney), Challis, Hinshelwood, Faulkner, Murray, Worrall, Walker, Beech, Irving, Serrant.

16 Oct 1991 (at Cairo)
England (0) 0
Italy (1) 3
England: Pettinger; Holland, Challis, Hinshelwood, Faulkner, Murray (Feltham), Worrall, Walker, Beech (Smith), Irving, Serrant (Frost).

17 Oct 1991 (at Cairo)
England (1) 3 *(Irving 2, Tierney)*
Austria (1) 1
England: Woods (Pettinger); Frost (Holland), Hinshelwood (Serrant), Murray, Feltham, Walker, Worrall, Challis, Irving, Smith (Beech), Tierney.

Under-16 tour
25 Feb 1991 (at Doha)
Qatar (2) 3
England (1) 3 *(Worrall, Challis, Beech)*
England: Hopper (Woods); Hinshelwood, Challis (Thatcher), Murray, Faulkner (Feltham), Worrall (Frost), Holland, Walker, Beech, Irving (Smith), Serrant.

28 Feb 1991 (at Muscat)
Oman (0) 2
England (0) 1 *(Frost)*
England: Hopper; Hinshelwood, Challis, Murray, Faulkner, Worral (Frost), Holland, Walker, Beech, Irving, Serrant.

FA Youth XI friendlies
4 Mar 1992 (at Tiverton)
South-West Counties (0) 1
FA Youth XI (2) 3 *(Twiddy 2, Berry)*   110
FA Youth XI: Bibbo (Draper); Sprod, Benton (Morgan S), Redwood, Berry, Limna, Jones, Morgan J (Mean), Hogg, Twiddy, Darby (Fowler).

9 Mar 1992 (at Bisham Abbey)
FA Youth XI (4) 7 *(Stallard 2, Joachim 2, Brissett, Bryan, 1 own goal)*
Independent Schools XI (0) 0
FA Youth XI: Morgan P; Gallagher, Landon, Blyth, Hutchings, Brissett, Clarke, Canham, Stallard, Cureton, Eadie. Subs (used): Bryan, Day, Joachim.

15 Mar 1992 (at Portsmouth)
FA Youth XI (1) 3 *(Gallen, Druce 2)*
Combined Services Youth (0) 0   100
FA Youth XI: Aouf; Warren, Campbell, Wanless (Sparrow), Patience, Varney, Gallen (Wanless), Ford (Ryan), Druce (Dichio), Dichio, Vincent (Lingley).

ENGLAND YOUTH INTERNATIONAL MATCHES 1947–92

*Professionals.   †Abandoned.   UYT *UEFA Youth Tournament*.   WYT *World Youth Tournament*.

v SCOTLAND

			E	S
1947	25 Oct	Doncaster	4	2
1948	30 Oct	Aberdeen	1	3
UYT1949	21 Apr	Utrecht	0	1
1950	4 Feb	Carlisle	7	1
1951	3 Feb	Kilmarnock	6	1
1952	15 Mar	Sunderland	3	1
1953	7 Feb	Glasgow	4	3
1954	6 Feb	Middlesbrough	2	1
1955	5 Mar	Kilmarnock	3	4
1956	3 Mar	Preston	2	2
1957	9 Mar	Aberdeen	3	1
1958	1 Mar	Hull	2	0
1959	28 Feb	Aberdeen	1	1
1960	27 Feb	Newcastle	1	1
1961	25 Feb	Elgin	3	2
1962	24 Feb	Peterborough	4	2
UYT1963	19 Apr	White City	1	0
1963	18 May	Dumfries	3	1
1964	22 Feb	Middlesbrough	1	1
1965	27 Feb	Inverness	1	2
1966	5 Feb	Hereford	5	3
1967	4 Feb	Aberdeen	0	1
UYT1967	1 Mar	Southampton	1	0
UYT1967	15 Mar	Dundee	0	0
1968	3 Feb	Walsall	0	5
1969	1 Feb	Stranraer	1	1
1970	31 Jan	Derby	1	2
1971	30 Jan	Greenock	1	2
1972	30 Jan	Bournemouth	2	0
1973	20 Jan	Kilmarnock	3	2
1974	26 Jan	Brighton	2	2
UYT1981	27 May	Aachen	0	1
UYT1982	23 Feb	Glasgow	0	1
UYT1982	23 Mar	Coventry	2	2
UYT1983	15 May	Birmingham	4	2
UI61983	5 Oct	Middlesbrough	3	1
UI61983	19 Oct	Motherwell	4	0
UYT1984	27 Nov	Craven Cottage	1	2
1985	8 Apr	Cannes	1	0
1985	25 Mar	Aberdeen	1	4

v WALES

			E	W
1948	28 Feb	High Wycombe	4	2
UYT1948	15 Apr	Shepherds Bush	4	0
1949	26 Feb	Swansea	0	0
1950	25 Feb	Worcester	1	0
1951	17 Feb	Wrexham	1	1
1952	23 Feb	Plymouth	6	0
1953	21 Feb	Swansea	4	2
1954	20 Feb	Derby	2	1
1955	19 Feb	Milford Haven	7	2
1956	18 Feb	Shrewsbury	5	1
1957	9 Feb	Cardiff	7	1
1958	15 Feb	Reading	8	2
1959	14 Feb	Portmadoc	3	0
1960	19 Mar	Canterbury	1	1
1961	18 Mar	Newtown	4	0
1962	17 Mar	Swindon	4	0
1963	16 Mar	Haverfordwest	1	0
1964	15 Mar	Leeds	2	1
1965	20 Mar	Newport	2	2
1966	19 Mar	Northampton	4	1
1967	18 Mar	Cwmbran	3	3
1968	16 Mar	Watford	2	3
1969	15 Mar	Haverfordwest	3	1
UYT1970	25 Feb	Newport	0	0
UYT1970	18 Mar	Leyton	1	2
1970	20 Apr	Reading	0	0
1971	20 Feb	Aberystwyth	1	2
1972	19 Feb	Swindon	4	0
1973	24 Feb	Portmadoc	4	1
UYT1974	9 Jan	West Bromwich	1	0
1974	2 Mar	Shrewsbury	2	1
UYT1974	13 Mar	Cardiff	0	1
UYT1976	11 Feb	Cardiff	1	0
UYT1976	3 Mar	Maine Road	2	3
UYT1977	9 Mar	West Bromwich	1	0
UYT1977	23 Mar	Cardiff	1	1

v NORTHERN IRELAND

			E	NI
1948	15 May	Belfast	2	2
UYT1949	18 Apr	Haarlem	3	3
1949	14 May	Hull	4	2
1950	6 May	Belfast	0	1
1951	5 May	Liverpool	5	2
1952	19 Apr	Belfast	0	2
1953	11 Apr	Wolverhampton	0	0
UYT1954	10 Apr	Bruehl	5	0
1954	8 May	Newtownards	2	2
1955	14 May	Watford	3	0
1956	12 May	Belfast	0	1
1957	11 May	Leyton	6	2
1958	10 May	Bangor	2	4
1959	9 May	Liverpool	5	0
1960	14 May	Portadown	5	2
1961	13 May	Manchester	2	0
1962	12 May	Londonderry	1	2
UYT1963	23 Apr	Wembley	4	0
1963	11 May	Oldham	1	1
1964	25 Jan	Belfast	3	1
1965	22 Jan	Birkenhead	2	3
1966	26 Feb	Belfast	4	0
1967	25 Feb	Stockport	3	0
1968	23 Feb	Belfast	0	2
1969	28 Feb	Birkenhead	0	2
1970	28 Feb	Lurgan	1	3
1971	6 Mar	Blackpool	1	1
1972	11 Mar	Chester	1	1
UYT1972	17 May	Sabadell	4	0
1973	24 Mar	Telford	3	0
1974	19 Apr	Birkenhead	1	2
UYT1975	13 May	Kriens	3	0
UYT1980	16 May	Arnstadt	1	0
UYT1981	11 Feb	Walsall	1	0
UYT1981	11 Mar	Belfast	3	0

v ALGERIA

			E	A
1984	22 Apr	Cannes	3	0

v ARGENTINA

			E	A
*WYT1981	5 Oct	Sydney	1	1

v AUSTRIA

			E	A
UYT1949	19 Apr	Zeist	4	2
UYT1952	17 Apr	Barcelona	5	5
UYT1957	16 Apr	Barcelona	0	3
1958	4 Mar	Highbury	3	2
1958	1 June	Graz	4	3
UYT1960	20 Apr	Vienna	0	1
UYT1964	1 Apr	Rotterdam	2	1
1980	6 Sept	Pazin	0	1
UYT1981	29 May	Bonn	7	0
1981	3 Sept	Umag	3	0
1984	6 Sept	Izola	2	2

v AUSTRALIA

			E	A
*WYT1981	8 Oct	Sydney	1	1

v BELGIUM

			E	B
UYT1948	16 Apr	West Ham	3	1
UYT1951	22 Mar	Cannes	1	1
UYT1953	31 Mar	Brussels	2	0
†1956	7 Nov	Brussels	3	2
1957	13 Nov	Sheffield	2	0
UYT1965	15 Apr	Ludwigshafen	3	0
UYT1969	11 Mar	West Ham	1	0
UYT1969	26 Mar	Waregem	2	0
UYT1972	13 May	Palma	0	0
UYT1973	4 June	Viareggio	0	0
UYT1977	19 May	Lokeren	1	0
1979	17 Jan	Brussels	4	0
1980	8 Sept	Labia	6	1
1983	13 Apr	Birmingham	1	1
1988	20 May	Chatel	0	0
UYT1990	24 July	Nyiregyhaza	1	1
UYT1990	16 Oct	Sunderland	0	0
UYT1991	16 Oct	Eetnegem	0	1

v BRAZIL

			E	B
1986	29 Mar	Cannes	0	0
1986	13 May	Peking	1	2

		v BULGARIA	E	B
UYT1956	28 Mar	Salgotarjan	1	2
UYT1960	16 Apr	Graz	0	1
UYT1962	24 Apr	Ploesti	0	0
UYT1968	7 Apr	Nimes	0	0
UYT1979	31 May	Vienna	0	1

		v CAMEROON	E	C
*WYT1981	3 Oct	Sydney	2	0

		v CHINA	E	C
1983	13 Mar	Cannes	5	1
1985	26 Aug	Baku	0	2
1986	5 May	Peking	1	0

		v CZECHOSLOVAKIA	E	C
UYT1955	7 Apr	Lucca	0	1
UYT1966	21 May	Rijeka	2	3
UYT1969	20 May	Leipzig	3	1
UYT1979	24 May	Bischofshofen	3	0
1979	8 Sept	Pula	1	2
1982	11 Apr	Cannes	0	1
UYT1983	20 May	Highbury	1	1
UYT1989	26 Apr	Bystrica	0	1
UYT1989	14 Nov	Portsmouth	1	0
1989	25 Apr	Wembley	1	1

		v DENMARK	E	D
*1955	1 Oct	Plymouth	9	2
1956	20 May	Esbjerg	2	1
UYT1979	31 Oct	Esbjerg	3	1
UYT1980	26 Mar	Coventry	4	0
*1982	15 July	Stjordal	5	2
1983	16 July	Holbaek	0	1
1987	16 Feb	Maine Road	2	1
1990	28 Mar	Wembley	0	0
1991	6 Feb	Oxford	1	5

		v EGYPT	E	Eg
*WYT1981	11 Oct	Sydney	4	2

		v FINLAND	E	F
UYT1975	19 May	Berne	1	1

		v FRANCE	E	F
1957	24 Mar	Fontainebleau	1	0
1958	22 Mar	Eastbourne	0	1
UYT1966	23 May	Rijeka	1	2
UYT1967	11 May	Istanbul	2	0
*1968	25 Jan	Paris	0	1
UYT1978	8 Feb	Selhurst Park	3	1
UYT1978	1 Mar	Paris	0	0
UYT1979	2 June	Vienna	0	0
1982	12 Apr	Cannes	0	1
1983	2 Apr	Cannes	0	2
UI61984	1 Mar	Watford	4	0
UI61984	21 Mar	Bourg en Bresse	1	1
1984	23 Apr	Cannes	1	2
1986	31 Mar	Cannes	1	2
1986	11 May	Peking	1	1
1988	22 May	Monthey	1	2
UYT1988	15 Nov	Bradford	1	1
UYT1989	11 Oct	Martigues	0	0

		v EAST GERMANY	E	EG
UYT1958	7 Apr	Neunkirchen	1	0
1959	8 Mar	Zwickau	3	4
1960	2 Apr	Portsmouth	1	1
UYT1965	25 Apr	Essen	2	3
UYT1969	22 May	Magdeburg	0	4
UYT1973	10 June	Florence	3	2
UYT1984	25 May	Moscow	1	1
1988	21 May	Monthey	1	0

		v WEST GERMANY	E	WG
UYT1953	4 Apr	Boom	3	1
UYT1954	15 Apr	Gelsenkirchen	2	1
UYT1956	1 Apr	Sztalinvaros	2	1
1957	31 Mar	Oberhausen	4	1
1958	12 Mar	Bolton	1	2
1961	12 Mar	Flensburg	0	2
*1962	31 Mar	Northampton	1	0
*1967	14 Feb	Moenchengladbach	1	0
UYT1972	22 May	Barcelona	2	0
1975	25 Jan	Las Palmas	4	2

1976	14 Nov	Monte Carlo	1	1
UYT1979	28 May	Salzburg	2	0
1979	1 Sept	Pula	1	1
1983	5 Sept	Pazin	2	0

		v GREECE	E	G
UYT1957	18 Apr	Barcelona	2	3
UYT1959	2 Apr	Dimitrovo	4	0
UYT1977	23 May	Beveren	1	1
UI61983	28 July	Puspokladany	1	0
UYT1988	26 Oct	Tranmere	5	0
UYT1989	8 Mar	Xanthi	3	0

		v HOLLAND	E	N
UYT1948	17 Apr	Tottenham	3	2
UYT1951	26 Mar	Cannes	2	1
*1954	21 Nov	Arnhem	2	3
*1955	5 Nov	Norwich	3	1
1957	2 Mar	Brentford	5	5
UYT1957	14 Apr	Barcelona	1	2
1957	2 Oct	Amsterdam	3	2
1961	9 Mar	Utrecht	0	1
*1962	31 Jan	Brighton	4	0
UYT1962	22 Apr	Ploesti	0	3
UYT1963	13 Apr	Wimbledon	5	0
UYT1968	9 Apr	Nimes	1	0
UYT1974	13 Feb	West Bromwich	1	1
UYT1974	27 Feb	The Hague	1	0
UYT1979	23 May	Halle	1	0
1982	9 Apr	Cannes	1	0
1985	7 Apr	Cannes	1	3
1987	1 Aug	Wembley	3	1

		v HUNGARY	E	H
UYT1954	11 Apr	Dusseldorf	1	3
UYT1956	31 Mar	Tatabanya	2	4
*1956	23 Oct	Tottenham	2	1
*1956	25 Oct	Sunderland	2	1
UYT1965	21 Apr	Wuppertal	5	0
UYT1975	16 May	Olten	3	1
UYT1977	10 Oct	Las Palmas	3	0
1979	5 Sept	Pula	2	0
1980	11 Sept	Pula	1	2
1981	7 Sept	Porec	4	0
UI61983	29 July	Debrecen	1	2
1983	3 Sept	Umag	3	2
1986	30 Mar	Cannes	2	0

		v ICELAND	E	I
UYT1973	31 May	Viareggio	2	0
UYT1977	21 May	Turnhout	0	0
UI61983	7 Sept	Reykjavik	2	1
UI61983	19 Sept	Blackburn	4	0
1983	12 Oct	Reykjavik	3	0
1983	1 Nov	Selhurst Park	3	0
UYT1984	16 Oct	Maine Road	5	3
1985	11 Sept	Reykjavik	5	0
UYT1990	12 Sept	Reykjavik	3	2
UYT1991	12 Sept	Crystal Palace	2	1

		v REPUBLIC OF IRELAND	E	RI
UYT1953	5 Apr	Leuven	2	0
UYT1964	30 Mar	Middleburg	6	0
UYT1968	7 Feb	Dublin	0	0
UYT1968	28 Feb	Portsmouth	4	1
UYT1970	14 Jan	Dublin	4	1
UYT1970	4 Feb	Luton	10	0
UYT1975	9 May	Brunnen	1	0
UYT1985	26 Feb	Dublin	1	0
1986	25 Feb	Leeds	2	0
1987	17 Feb	Stoke	2	0
1988	20 Sept	Dublin	2	0

		v ISRAEL	E	I
*1962	20 May	Tel Aviv	3	1
*1962	22 May	Haifa	1	2

		v ITALY	E	I
UYT1958	13 Apr	Luxembourg	0	1
UYT1959	25 Mar	Sofia	0	3
UYT1961	4 Apr	Braga	2	3
UYT1965	23 Apr	Marl-Huels	3	1
UYT1966	25 May	Rijeka	1	1
UYT1967	5 May	Izmir	1	0
1973	14 Feb	Cava dei Tirreni	0	1
1973	14 Mar	Highbury	1	0

UYT1973	6 June	Viareggio	1	0
1978	19 Nov	Monte Carlo	1	2
UYT1979	28 Feb	Rome	1	0
UYT1979	4 Apr	Villa Park	2	0
UYT1983	22 May	Watford	1	1
1983	20 Apr	Cannes	1	0
1985	5 Apr	Cannes	2	2

		v LUXEMBOURG	E	L
UYT1950	25 May	Vienna	1	2
UYT1954	17 Apr	Bad Neuenahr	0	2
1957	2 Feb	West Ham	7	1
1957	17 Nov	Luxembourg	3	0
UYT1958	9 Apr	Esch sur Alzette	5	0
UYT1984	29 May	Moscow	2	0

		v MALTA	E	M
UYT1969	18 May	Wolfen	6	0
UYT1979	26 May	Salzburg	3	0

		v MEXICO	E	M
1983	18 Apr	Cannes	4	0
1985	29 Aug	Baku	0	1
1991	27 Mar	Port of Spain	1	3

		v NORWAY	E	N
*1982	13 July	Levanger	1	4
1983	14 July	Korsor	1	0

		v PARAGUAY	E	P
1985	24 Aug	Baku	2	2

		v POLAND	E	P
UYT1960	18 Apr	Graz	4	2
UYT1964	26 Mar	Breda	1	1
UYT1971	26 May	Presov	0	0
UYT1972	20 May	Valencia	1	0
1975	21 Jan	Las Palmas	1	1
UYT1978	9 May	Chorzow	0	2
1979	3 Sept	Porac	0	1
UYT1980	25 May	Leipzig	2	1
*1982	17 July	Steinkver	3	2
1983	12 July	Slagelse	1	0
1990	15 May	Wembley	3	0

		v PORTUGAL	E	P
UYT1954	18 Apr	Bonn	0	2
UYT1961	2 Apr	Lisbon	0	4
UYT1964	3 Apr	The Hague	4	0
UYT1971	30 May	Prague	3	0
1978	13 Nov	Monte Carlo	2	0
UYT1980	18 May	Rosslau	1	1
1982	7 Apr	Cannes	3	0

		v QATAR	E	Q
*WYT1981	14 Oct	Sydney	1	2
1983	4 Apr	Cannes	1	1

		v ROMANIA	E	R
1957	15 Oct	Tottenham	4	2
UYT1958	11 Apr	Luxembourg	1	0
UYT1959	31 Mar	Pazardjic	1	2
UYT1963	15 Apr	Highbury	3	0
*WYT1981	17 Oct	Adelaide	0	1

		v SAAR	E	S
UYT1954	13 Apr	Dortmund	1	1
UYT1955	9 Apr	Prato	3	1

		v SPAIN	E	S
UYT1952	15 Apr	Barcelona	1	4
1957	26 Sept	Birmingham	4	4
UYT1958	5 Apr	Saarbrucken	2	2
*1958	8 Oct	Madrid	4	2
UYT1961	30 Mar	Lisbon	0	0
*1964	27 Feb	Murcia	2	1
UYT1964	5 Apr	Amsterdam	4	0
UYT1965	17 Apr	Heilbronn	0	0
*1966	30 Mar	Swindon	3	0
UYT1967	7 May	Manisa	2	1
*1971	31 Mar	Pamplona	2	3
*1971	20 Apr	Luton	1	1
1972	9 Feb	Alicante	0	0
1972	15 Mar	Sheffield	4	1
UYT1975	25 Feb	Bristol	1	1
UYT1975	18 Mar	Madrid	1	0
1976	12 Nov	Monte Carlo	3	0

UYT1978	7 May	Bukowno	1	0
1978	17 Nov	Monte Carlo	1	1
UYT1981	25 May	Siegen	1	2
UYT1983	13 May	Stoke	1	0
UYT1990	29 July	Gyula	0	1
1991	25 May	Wembley	1	1
WYT1991	15 June	Faro	0	1

		v SWEDEN	E	S
UYT1971	24 May	Poprad	1	0
1981	5 Sept	Pazin	3	2
1984	10 Sept	Rovinj	1	1
1986	10 Nov	West Bromwich	3	3

		v SWITZERLAND	E	S
UYT1950	26 May	Stockerau	2	1
UYT1951	27 Mar	Nice	3	1
UYT1952	13 Apr	Barcelona	4	0
UYT1955	11 Apr	Florence	0	0
1956	11 Mar	Schaffhausen	2	0
1956	13 Oct	Brighton	2	2
1958	26 May	Zurich	3	0
*1960	8 Oct	Leyton	4	3
*†1962	22 Nov	Coventry	1	0
*1963	21 Mar	Bienne	7	1
UYT1973	2 June	Forte dei Marmi	2	0
UYT1975	11 May	Buochs	4	0
1980	4 Sept	Rovinj	3	0
*1982	6 Sept	Porec	2	0
UI61983	26 July	Hajduboszormeny	4	0
1983	1 Sept	Porec	4	2
1988	19 May	Sion	2	0

		v SYRIA	E	S
WYT1991	18 June	Faro	3	3

		v THAILAND	E	T
1986	7 May	Peking	1	2

		v TRINIDAD & TOBAGO	E	T
1991	25 Mar	Port of Spain	4	0

		v TURKEY	E	T
UYT1959	29 May	Dimitrovo	1	1
UYT1978	5 May	Wodzislaw	1	1

		v URUGUAY	E	U
1977	9 Oct	Las Palmas	1	1
WYT1991	20 June	Faro	0	0

		v USSR	E	U
UYT1963	17 Apr	Tottenham	2	0
UYT1967	13 May	Istanbul	0	1
UYT1968	11 Apr	Nimes	1	1
UYT1971	28 May	Prague	1	1
1978	10 Oct	Las Palmas	1	0
*1982	4 Sept	Umag	1	0
1983	29 Mar	Cannes	0	0
UYT1983	17 May	Aston Villa	0	2
UI61984	3 May	Ludwigsburg	0	2
UYT1984	27 May	Moscow	1	1
1984	8 Sept	Porec	1	0
1985	3 Apr	Cannes	2	1
UYT1990	26 July	Debrecen	1	3

		v WALES	E	W
WYT1991	30 Apr	Wrexham	1	0
UYT1991	22 May	Yeovil	3	0

		v YUGOSLAVIA	E	Y
UYT1953	2 Apr	Liège	1	1
1958	4 Feb	Chelsea	2	2
UYT1962	20 Apr	Ploesti	0	5
UYT1967	9 May	Izmir	1	1
UYT1971	22 May	Bardejor	1	0
UYT1972	18 May	Barcelona	1	0
1976	16 Nov	Monte Carlo	0	3
1978	15 Nov	Monte Carlo	1	1
UYT1980	20 May	Altenburg	2	0
1981	10 Sept	Pula	5	0
*1982	9 Sept	Pula	1	0
UI61983	25 July	Debrecen	4	4
**1983	8 Sept	Pula	2	2
UI61984	5 May	Boblingen	1	0
1984	12 Sept	Buje	1	4

SCHOOLS FOOTBALL 1991–92

ESFA BRITISH GAS TROPHY 1991–92

Fourth Round

Hull v Leicester	1-3
Mid Cheshire v Nottingham	2-0
Leeds v Langbaurgh	3-1
Chester v Newcastle	3-3, 3-3, 5-3
North Sussex v Bromley	4-0
Reading v North Avon	1-1, 3-2
Medway v Bournemouth	1-2
South London v Cardiff	1-2
Croydon v Hackney	0-0, 2-1
North Kent v Southampton	1-3
Sheffield v Chorley	7-0
Wolverhampton v Barnsley	0-2
Liverpool v Kings Norton	2-0
Bolton v Erdington & S	0-0, 3-1
Swansea v M/S Warwicks	3-0
Glos & Forest v Kettering/Corby	1-3

Fifth Round

Leicester v Mid Cheshire	1-1, 1-1, 2-1

Leeds v Chester	3-2
North Sussex v Reading	2-2, 0-1
Bournemouth v Cardiff	5-1
Croydon v Southampton	0-1
Sheffield v Barnsley	2-0
Liverpool v Bolton	0-1
Swansea v Kettering/Corby	1-0

Sixth Round

Leicester v Leeds	0-2
Reading v Bournemouth	3-2
Southampton v Sheffield	2-4
Bolton v Swansea	1-1, 2-1

Semi-finals

Leeds v Reading	1-0
Sheffield v Bolton	3-0

Final

Leeds v Sheffield	1-0, 1-0

ESFA DIAMIK U.16 1991–92

Second Round

West Midlands B v Gloucestershire	1-1, 3-2
Somerset v Oxfordshire	2-3
Devon A v Wiltshire	1-0
Dorset v Sussex A	2-0
Middlesex B v Surrey	3-4
Kent B v Hertfordshire	1-2
Berkshire v Bedfordshire	1-2
Norfolk v Northants	4-4, 0-6
Great Manchester A v Lancashire B	4-1
Lancashire A v Warwickshire	2-4
Merseyside B v Derbyshire	1-0
Cheshire B v Staffordshire B	2-5
Cleveland B v Cumbria	2-2, 2-1
Durham B v Cleveland A	3-1
Humberside B v South Yorkshire A	1-2
Humberside A v South Yorkshire B	1-1, 0-2

Third Round

West Midlands B v Oxfordshire	1-2
Devon A v Dorset	3-2

Surrey v Hertfordshire	1-1, 0-1
Bedfordshire v Northants	1-5
Great Manchester A v Warwickshire	4-4, 1-1, 2-3
Merseyside B v Staffordshire B	4-1
Cleveland B v Durham B	0-3
South Yorkshire A v South Yorkshire B	1-4

Fourth Round

Oxfordshire v Devon A	0-0, 2-3
Hertfordshire v Northants	2-3
Warwickshire v Merseyside B	2-4
Durham B v South Yorkshire B	1-2

Semi-finals

Devon A (Torquay Grammar School) v Northants (Kingsthorpe Upper School, Northampton)	2-1
Merseyside B (De la Salle, Liverpool) v South Yorkshire B (Swinton Comprehensive School)	4-2

Final

Devon A v Merseyside B	2-0

ESFA BARCLAYS BANK U.19 1991–92

Second Round

South Yorkshire v Nottinghamshire	1-2
Lincolnshire A v South Yorkshire B	1-4
Northumberland A v Cleveland	3-1
West Yorkshire B v Durham	0-1
Lincolnshire B v Shropshire	0-1
Cheshire A v West Midlands B	2-2, 2-1
Great Manchester B v Clwyd	3-0
Great Manchester A v Lancashire B	3-2
Middlesex B v Hertfordshire A	2-1
Hampshire A v Inner London A	4-0
Kent A v Essex B	2-3
Norfolk v Hertfordshire B	3-2
Buckinghamshire v Oxfordshire	2-0
Hereford & Worcs v South Glamorgan	2-1
Hampshire B v Devon	1-0
Somerset v Sussex A	0-1

Third Round

Nottinghamshire v South Yorkshire B	1-0
Northumberland A v Durham	3-0

Shropshire v Cheshire A	1-0
Great Manchester B v Great Manchester A	0-1
Middlesex B v Hampshire A	0-1
Essex B v Norfolk	3-0
Buckinghamshire v Hereford & Worcs	0-0, 1-0
Hampshire B v Sussex A	2-1

Fourth Round

Nottinghamshire v Northumberland A	3-0
Shropshire v Great Manchester A	0-0, 0-0, 1-2
Hampshire A v Essex B	1-3
Buckinghamshire v Hampshire B	5-0

Semi-finals

Nottinghamshire (High Pavement College) v Great Manchester A (Winstanley College, Wigan)	1-0
Essex B (Southend High School) v Buckinghamshire (John Hampden School, High Wycombe)	1-2

Final

Nottinghamshire v Buckinghamshire	1-0

ESFA ADIDAS U.19 INTER-COUNTY COMPETITION 1991–92

Round 1
S. Yorkshire (Reg. I) v Merseyside (Reg. II)   2-3

Round 2
Cornwall (Reg. V) v Essex (Reg. IV)   2-1
Nottinghamshire (Reg. III) v
  Merseyside (Reg. II)   0-2

Final:
Merseyside (Reg. II) v Cornwall (Reg. V)   2-0
(at Anfield, Liverpool FC on 2 May 1992)

CENTENARY SHIELD 1991–92 (Under 18)
Wales 1, England 2 – 13 March, Cwmbran
England 2, Switzerland 2 – 28 April, Entlebuch
Switzerland 2, Wales 1 – 5 May

	P	W	D	L	F	A	Pts
Switzerland	2	1	1	0	4	3	3
England	2	1	1	0	4	3	3
Wales	2	0	0	2	2	4	0

ESFA INTER-COUNTY COMPETITION HONOURS LIST

	Winners	*Runners-up*
1978	Devon and South Yorkshire	Joint Holders
1979	Berkshire	Essex
1980	Berkshire	Durham
1981	Merseyside	Middlesex
1982	Humberside	Merseyside
1983	Greater Manchester	Humberside
1984	Hampshire	Durham
1985	Middlesex	Hampshire
1986	Merseyside	Bedfordshire
1987	Northumberland	Hertfordshire
1988	Northumberland	Avon
1989	West Midlands	Lincolnshire
1990	Greater Manchester	Northumberland
1991	Northumberland and Essex	Joint Holders
1992	Merseyside	Cornwall

VICTORY SHIELD 1991–92 (Under-15)

England 2, Wales 2 – 28 February, Burnley
Wales 1, Scotland 1 – 20 March, Swansea
Northern Ireland 3, Scotland 4 – 3 April, Craigavon
Wales 1, Northern Ireland 0 – 8 April, Rhondda
England 3, Northern Ireland 0 – 10 April, Brighton
Scotland 0, England 1 – 1 May, Glasgow

	P	W	D	L	F	A	Pts
England	3	2	1	0	6	2	5
Wales	3	1	2	0	4	3	4
Scotland	3	1	1	1	5	5	3
Northern Ireland	3	0	0	3	3	8	0

ENGLAND'S INTERNATIONAL PROGRAMME 1991–92

Under-15
England 2, Wales 2 – 28 February, Burnley
England 0, Holland 0 – 7 March, Wembley
England 3, Northern Ireland 0 – 10 April, Brighton
Scotland 0, England 1 – 1 May, Ibrox
France 2, England 2 – 5 May, Laon
Germany 1, England 1 – 12 May, Berlin
Germany 4, England 1 – 14 May, Magdeberg

England 1, Italy 1 – 6 June, Wembley

Under-18
England 2, Holland 1 – 3 March, Leicester
Wales 1, England 2 – 13 March, Cwmbran
England 2, Republic of Ireland 1 – 30 March, Yeovil
England 2, Switzerland 2 – 28 April, Entlebuch

THE SMITH CRISPS CUP
(at Wembley)

Semi-finals
Meadowhall Junior School, Rotherham
  v Inglewood Junior School   0-1
Ixworth Middle School v Harmans Water
  Junior School, Bracknell   1-0

Final
Inglewood Junior School, Cumbria
  v Ixworth Middle School, Bury St Edmunds   2-0

3rd /4th place
Harmans Water Junior School
  v Meadowhall Junior School   3-2

THE SMITHS CRISPS INTERNATIONAL SHIELD

England v Italy   1-1

McDONALDS 5-A-SIDE COMPETITION
(at Aston Villa Sports Centre)

Semi-finals
Hemel Hampstead v Norton Priory   3-0
Wood Green v Frederick Gent   1-0

Final
Wood Green High School, Wednesfield
  v Hemel Hempstead School   2-0

OLYMPIC FOOTBALL

Previous medallists

1896 Athens*	1 Denmark 2 Greece	1928 Amsterdam	1 Uruguay 2 Argentina 3 Italy
1990 Paris*	1 Great Britain 2 France	1932 Los Angeles	no tournament
1904 St Louis**	1 Canada 2 USA	1936 Berlin	1 Italy 2 Austria 3 Norway
1908 London	1 Great Britain 2 Denmark 3 Holland	1948 London	1 Sweden 2 Yugoslavia 3 Denmark
1912 Stockholm	1 England 2 Denmark 3 Holland	1952 Helsinki	1 Hungary 2 Yugoslavia 3 Sweden
1920 Antwerp	1 Belgium 2 Spain 3 Holland	1956 Melbourne	1 USSR 2 Yugoslavia 3 Bulgaria
1924 Paris	1 Uruguay 2 Switzerland 3 Sweden	1960 Rome	1 Yugoslavia 2 Denmark 3 Hungary

1964 Tokyo	1 Hungary 2 Czechoslovakia 3 East Germany		
1968 Mexico City	1 Hungary 2 Bulgaria 3 Japan		
1972 Munich	1 Poland 2 Hungary 3 E Germany/USSR		
1976 Montreal	1 East Germany 2 Poland 3 USSR		
1980 Moscow	1 Czechoslovakia 2 East Germany 3 USSR		
1984 Los Angeles	1 France 2 Brazil 3 Yugoslavia		
1988 Seoul	1 USSR 2 Brazil 3 West Germany		

1992 Olympics (in Spain)

* No official tournament
** No official tournament but gold medal later awarded by IOC

OLYMPICS — Qualifiers for Barcelona 1992

Egypt, Morocco, Ghana, Qatar, South Korea, Kuwait, Paraguay, Colombia, USA, Mexico, Spain (hosts), Italy, Australia, Sweden, Denmark, Poland

Draw for the Final Tournament

First Round

Group A
24.7.92 Italy v United States
24.7.92 Poland v Kuwait
27.7.92 Italy v Poland
27.7.92 United States v Kuwait
29.7.92 Italy v Kuwait
29.7.92 United States v Poland

Group B
26.7.92 Ghana v Australia
26.7.92 Denmark v Mexico
28.7.92 Mexico v Australia
28.7.92 Denmark v Ghana
30.7.92 Mexico v Ghana
30.7.92 Denmark v Australia

Group C
24.7.92 Spain v Colombia
24.7.92 Egypt v Qatar
27.7.92 Spain v Egypt
27.7.92 Colombia v Qatar
29.7.92 Spain v Qatar
29.7.92 Colombia v Egypt

Group D
26.7.92 Sweden v Paraguay
26.7.92 Morocco v South Korea
28.7.92 Paraguay v South Korea
28.7.92 Sweden v Morocco
30.7.92 Sweden v South Korea
30.7.92 Paraguay v Morocco

Quater-finals
1.8.92 Winner Gp A v Runner-up Gp B
1.8.92 Winner Gp B v Runner-up Gp A
2.8.92 Winner Gp C v Runner-up Gp D
2.8.92 Winner Gp D v Runner-up Gp C

Semi-finals
5.8.92 Winner q-f 1 v Winner q-f 3
5.8.92 Winner q-f 2 v Winner q-f 4

Third place play-off
7.8.92 Semi-final losers

Final
8.8.92 Semi-final winners

(results in next year's edition)

EUROPEAN CUP

EUROPEAN CUP FINALS 1956–91

Year	Winners		Runners-up		Venue	Attendance	Referee
1956	Real Madrid	4	Reims	3	Paris	38,000	Ellis (E)
1957	Real Madrid	2	Fiorentina	0	Madrid	124,000	Horn (Ho)
1958	Real Madrid	3	AC Milan	2 *(aet)*	Brussels	67,000	Alsteen (Bel)
1959	Real Madrid	2	Reims	0	Stuttgart	80,000	Dutsch (WG)
1960	Real Madrid	7	Eintracht Frankfurt	3	Glasgow	135,000	Mowat (S)
1961	Benfica	3	Barcelona	2	Berne	28,000	Dienst (Sw)
1962	Benfica	5	Real Madrid	3	Amsterdam	65,000	Horn (Ho)
1963	AC Milan	2	Benfica	1	Wembley	45,000	Holland (E)
1964	Internazionale	3	Real Madrid	1	Vienna	74,000	Stoll (A)
1965	Internazionale	1	Benfica	0	Milan	80,000	Dienst (Sw)
1966	Real Madrid	2	Partizan Belgrade	1	Brussels	55,000	Kreitlein (WG)
1967	Celtic	2	Internazionale	1	Lisbon	56,000	Tschenscher (WG)
1968	Manchester U	4	Benfica	1 *(aet)*	Wembley	100,000	Lo Bello (I)
1969	AC Milan	4	Ajax	1	Madrid	50,000	Ortiz (Sp)
1970	Feyenoord	2	Celtic	1 *(aet)*	Milan	50,000	Lo Bello (I)
1971	Ajax	2	Panathinaikos	0	Wembley	90,000	Taylor (E)
1972	Ajax	2	Internazionale	0	Rotterdam	67,000	Helies (F)
1973	Ajax	1	Juventus	0	Belgrade	93,500	Guglovic (Y)
1974	Bayern Munich	1	Atletico Madrid	1	Brussels	65,000	Loraux (Bel)
Replay	Bayern Munich	4	Atletico Madrid	0	Brussels	65,000	Delcourt (Bel)
1975	Bayern Munich	2	Leeds U	0	Paris	50,000	Kitabdjian (F)
1976	Bayern Munich	1	St Etienne	0	Glasgow	54,864	Palotai (H)
1977	Liverpool	3	Moenchengladbach	1	Rome	57,000	Wurtz (F)
1978	Liverpool	1	FC Brugge	0	Wembley	92,000	Corver (Ho)
1979	Nottingham F	1	Malmo	0	Munich	57,500	Linemayr (A)
1980	Nottingham F	1	Hamburg	0	Madrid	50,000	Garrido (P)
1981	Liverpool	1	Real Madrid	0	Paris	48,360	Palotai (H)
1982	Aston Villa	1	Bayern Munich	0	Rotterdam	46,000	Konrath (F)
1983	Hamburg	1	Juventus	0	Athens	75,000	Rainea (R)
1984	Liverpool	1	Roma	1	Rome	69,693	Fredriksson (Se)
	(aet; Liverpool won 4–2 on penalties)						
1985	Juventus	1	Liverpool	0	Brussels	58,000	Daina (Sw)
1986	Steaua Bucharest	0	Barcelona	0	Seville	70,000	Vautrot (F)
	(aet; Steaua won 2–0 on penalties)						
1987	Porto	2	Bayern Munich	1	Vienna	59,000	Ponnet (Bel)
1988	PSV Eindhoven	0	Benfica	0	Stuttgart	70,000	Agnolin (I)
	(aet; PSV won 6–5 on penalties)						
1989	AC Milan	4	Steaua Bucharest	0	Barcelona	97,000	Tritschler (WG)
1990	AC Milan	1	Benfica	0	Vienna	57,500	Kohl (A)
1991	Red Star Belgrade	0	Marseille	0	Bari	56,000	Lanese (I)
	(aet; Red Star won 5–3 on penalties)						

The victorious Barcelona team celebrate with the European Cup after their 1–0 win over Sampdoria at Wembley. (Colorsport)

EUROPEAN CUP 1991–92

First Round, First Leg

Anderlecht (1) 1 *(Degryse 44)*, Grasshoppers (0) 1 *(Nemtsoudis 65)* 10,000
Arsenal (1) 6 *(Linighan 38, Smith 50, 52, 65, 66, Limpar 79)*, FK Austria (0) 1 *(Ogris 56)* 24,124
Barcelona (1) 3 *(Laudrup 24, 46, Goicoechea 75)*, Hansa Rostock (0) 0 78,000
Besiktas (0) 1 *(Mehmet 80 (pen))*, PSV Eindhoven (1) 1 *(Ellerman 27)* 32,500
Brondby (0) 3 *(Christofte 53 (pen), Ekelund 56, Ukechukwu 60)*, Zaglebie Lubin (0) 0 7752
Fram (0) 2 *(Ragnarsson 57, Arnthorsson 62)*, Panathinaikos (1) 2 *(Saravakos 49, 55)* 695
Hamrun Spartans (0) 0, Benfica (4) 6 *(Pacheco 30, Youran 32, 35, 41, 85, Rui Aguas 75)* 6000
HJK Helsinki (0) 0, Kiev Dynamo (0) 1 *(Kovalets 12)* 3032
IFK Gothenburg (0) 0, Flamurtari (0) 0 4252
Kaiserslautern (1) 2 *(Funkel 37 (pen), 73)*, Etur (0) 0 34,000
Kispest Honved (0) 1 *(Negrau 82)*, Dundalk (1) 1 *(McEvoy 27)* 12,000
Red Star Belgrade (2) 4 *(Taniga 15, Stosic 36, Mihajlovic 77, 85)*, Portadown (0) 0 7000 *(in Szeged)*
Sampdoria (2) 5 *(Lombardo 10, 83, Dossena 26, 55, Silas 75)*, Rosenborg (0) 0 25,000
Sparta Prague (1) 1 *(Nemec 19)*, Rangers (0) 0 11,053
Uni Craiova (1) 2 *(Popescu A 21 (pen), Agalliou 69)*, Apollon (0) 0 18,500
Union Luxembourg (0) 0, Marseille (4) 5 *(Papin 11, 31, 85 (pen), Xuereb 14, Sauzee 44)* 9000

First Round, Second Leg

Apollon (1) 3 *(Ptak 9 (pen), Pesirovic 56, 79)*, Uni Craiova (0) 0 10,000
Benfica (0) 4 *(Isaias 52, Cesar Brito 70, Youran 73, Paolo Madeira 75)*, Hamrun Spartans (0) 0 10,000
Dundalk (0) 0, Kispest Honved (2) 2 *(Pisont 24, 29)* 3500
Etur (1) 1 *(Chervenkov 44)*, Kaiserslautern (0) 1 *(Degen 87)* 12,500
FK Austria (0) 1 *(Stoger 78 (pen))*, Arsenal (0) 0 11,000
Flamurtari (1) 1 *(Daulija 26)*, IFK Gothenburg (0) 1 *(Ekstrom 68)* 7000
Grasshoppers (0) 0, Anderlecht (2) 3 *(Nilis 8, 24, 82)* 10,800 *(in Berne)*
Hansa Rostock (0) 1 *(Spies 64)*, Barcelona (0) 0 6000
Kiev Dynamo (1) 3 *(Kovalets 28, Moroz 48, Gritsina 72)*, HJK Helsinki (0) 0 4300
Marseille (1) 5 *(Papin 15, 46, Angloma 56, Eyraud 60, Xuereb 75)*, Union Luxembourg (0) 0 15,000
Panathinaikos (0) 0, Fram (0) 0 50,000
Portadown (0) 0, Red Star Belgrade (2) 4 *(Ratkovic 19, 54, Pancev 38, Radinovic 87)* 5000
PSV Eindhoven (1) 2 *(Vanenburg 25, Kalusha Bwalya 74)*, Besiktas (1) 1 *(Metin 4)* 46,000
Rangers (2) 2 *(McCall 48, 94)*, Sparta Prague (0) 1 *(Nisbet (og) 97)* aet 34,260
Rosenborg (0) 1 *(Strand 83)*, Sampdoria (0) 2 *(Vialli 84, Mancini 89 (pen))* 6705
Zaglebie Lubin (0) 2 *(Czachowski 60, Grech 72)*, Brondby (1) 1 *(Vilfort 28)* 4000

Second Round, First Leg

Barcelona (1) 2 *(Beguiristain 43, 52)*, Kaiserslautern (0) 0 80,000
Benfica (1) 1 *(Isaias 15)*, Arsenal (1) 1 *(Campbell 18)* 80,000
Kiev Dynamo (0) 1 *(Salenko 77 (pen))*, Brondby (1) 1 *(Nielsen 12)* 20,000
Kispest Honved (0) 2 *(Pisont 52, Cservenkai 72)*, Sampdoria (0) 1 *(Cerezo 65)* 10,000
Marseille (1) 3 *(Waddle 34, Papin 55, 59)*, Sparta Prague (0) 2 *(Vrabec 63 (pen), Kukleta 79 (pen))* 10,016
Panathinaikos (2) 2 *(Saravakos 27, Marangos 49)*, IFK Gothenburg (0) 0 60,000
PSV Eindhoven (0) 0, Anderlecht (0) 0 27,000
Red Star Belgrade (1) 3 *(Pancev 15, Lukic 71, Savicevic 85 (pen))*, Apollon (0) 1 *(Ptak 41)* 1500 *(in Szeged)*

Second Round, Second Leg

Anderlecht (1) 2 *(Degryse 10, Boffin 89)*, PSV Eindhoven (0) 0 28,000
Apollon (0) 0, Red Star Belgrade (0) 2 *(Savicevic 47, Lukic 75 (pen))* 10,000
Arsenal (1) 1 *(Pates 20)*, Benfica (1) 3 *(Isaias 36, 109, Kulkov 100)* aet 35,815
Brondby (0) 0, Kiev Dynamo (1) 1 *(Yakovenko 6)* 13,712
IFK Gothenburg (2) 2 *(Svensson 24, Ekstrom 38)*, Panathinaikos (0) 2 *(Saravakos 60, 81 (pen))* 10,684
Kaiserslautern (1) 3 *(Hotic 35, 50, Goldbaek 76)*, Barcelona (0) 1 *(Bakero 89)* 30,200
Sampdoria (2) 3 *(Lombardo 9, Vialli 26, 46)*, Kispest Honved (0) 1 *(Pari (og) 65)* 50,000
Sparta Prague (1) 2 *(Frydek 36, Siegl 69)*, Marseille (0) 1 *(Pele 87)* 32,500

Semi-finals (League system)

Group A

Anderlecht (0) 0, Panathinaikos (0) 0 24,000
Sampdoria (1) 2 *(Mancini 7, Vialli 73)*, Red Star Belgrade (0) 0 30,000
Panathinaikos (0) 0 Sampdoria (0) 0 51,500
Red Star Belgrade (1) 3 *(Ratkovic 19, Ivic 70, Pancev 88)*, Anderlecht (1) 2 *(Lamptey 33, Nilis 55)* 2000 *(in Budapest)*
Anderlecht (0) 3 *(Degryse 53, Nilis 67, 89)*, Sampdoria (1) 2 *(Vialli 26, 67)* 20,000
Panathinaikos (0) 0, Red Star Belgrade (0) 2 *(Pancev 70, 86)* 60,000
Red Star Belgrade (0) 1 *(Mihajlovic 53 (pen))*, Panathinaikos (0) 0 23,000 *(in Sofia)*
Sampdoria (2) 2 *(Lombardo 33, Mancini 35)*, Anderlecht (0) 0 33,874
Panathinaikos (0) 0, Anderlecht (0) 0 17,000
Red Star Belgrade (1) 1 *(Mihajlovic 19)*, Sampdoria (2) 3 *(Katanec 34, Vasilijevic (og) 42, Mancini 77)* 35,000 *(in Sofia)*
Anderlecht (2) 3 *(Oliveira 3, Bosman 44, Degryse 81)*, Red Star Belgrade (1) 2 *(Pancev 5, Cula 80)* 8000
Sampdoria (1) 1 *(Mancini 36)*, Panathinaikos (1) 1 *(Marangos 26)* 39,000

Final table

	P	W	D	L	F	A	Pts
Sampdoria	6	3	2	1	10	5	8
Red Star Belgrade	6	3	0	3	9	10	6
Anderlecht	6	2	2	2	8	9	6
Panathinaikos	6	0	4	2	1	4	4

Group B

Barcelona (2) 3 *(Amor 16, Laudrup 34, Bakero 61)*, Sparta Prague (1) 2 *(Vrabec 18, Nemecek 63)* 82,000
Kiev Dynamo (1) 1 *(Salenko 29)*, Benfica (0) 0 47,500
Benfica (0) 0, Barcelona (0) 0 80,000
Sparta Prague (2) 2 *(Nemecek 13, Vrabec 22)*, Kiev Dynamo (0) 1 *(Saran 55)* 15,000
Benfica (1) 1 *(Pacheco 53 (pen))*, Sparta Prague (1) 1 *(Novotny 32)* 50,000
Kiev Dynamo (0) 0, Barcelona (1) 2 *(Stoichkov 32, 67)* 20,000
Barcelona (0) 3 *(Stoichkov 58, 90, Salinas 87)*, Kiev Dynamo (0) 0 70,000
Sparta Prague (1) 1 *(Chovanec 44)*, Benfica (1) 1 *(Paneira 29)* 29,000
Benfica (1) 5 *(Cesar Brito 25, 62, Isaias 71, Youran 83, 87)*, Kiev Dynamo (0) 0 10,000
Sparta Prague (1) 1 *(Siegl 66)*, Barcelona (0) 0 27,374
Barcelona (2) 2 *(Stoichkov 13, Bakero 23)*, Benfica (1) 1 *(Cesar Brito 27)* 115,000
Kiev Dynamo (1) 1 *(Salenko 82)*, Sparta Prague (0) 0 5000

Final table

	P	W	D	L	F	A	Pts
Barcelona	6	4	1	1	10	4	9
Sparta Prague	6	2	2	2	7	7	6
Benfica	6	1	3	2	8	5	5
Kiev Dynamo	6	2	0	4	3	12	4

European Cup results continued on page 910

EUROPEAN CUP 1991–92 – BRITISH AND IRISH CLUBS

FIRST ROUND, FIRST LEG

17 SEPT

Red Star Belgrade (2) 4 *(Taniga, Stosic, Mihajlovic 2)*
Portadown (0) 0 *in Szeged* 7000
Red Star Belgrade: Lekovic; Radanovic, Taniga, Jugovic, Belodedic, Najdoski, Stosic, Lukic, Ivic (Ivanovic), Ratkovic, Mihajlovic.
Portadown: Keenan; Major, Curliss, Mitchell, Strain, Stewart, Doolin, Russell, Fraser, Cowan, Davidson.

18 SEPT

Arsenal (1) 6 *(Linighan, Smith 4, Limpar)*
FK Austria (0) 1 *(Ogris)* 24,124
Arsenal: Seaman; Dixon, Winterburn, Campbell, Linighan, Adams, Rocastle, Davis, Smith, Merson, Limpar (Groves).
FK Austria: Valov; Sekerlioglu, Pfeffer, Frind, Zsak, Flogel (Schneider), Ogris, Narbekovas, Prosenik, Stoger, Ivanauskas (Hasenhuttl).

Kispest Honved (0) 1 *(Negrau)*
Dundalk (1) 1 *(McEvoy)* 12,000
Kispest Honved: Gulyas; Csabi (Vancea), Csepregi, Berczy, Plokai, Marozsan, Pisont, Kovacs, Csehi (Halami), Negrau, Vincze.
Dundalk: O'Neill; Mackey, Murphy, Hall, Shelley, McNulty, McEvoy, Lawless, Brady (Purdy), Eviston, Hanrahan.

Sparta Prague (1) 1 *(Nemec)*
Rangers (0) 0 11,053
Sparta Prague: Kouba; Hornak, Mistr, Vrabec, Sopko, Nemecek, Nemec, Novotny, Cerny, Siegl, Frydek.
Rangers: Goram; Stevens, Gough, Nisbet, Robertson D, Ferguson (Durrant), McCall, Spackman, McCoist (Brown), Hateley, Huistra.

FIRST ROUND, SECOND LEG

2 OCT

Dundalk (0) 0
Kispest Honved (2) 2 *(Pisont 2)* 3500
Dundalk: O'Neill; Mackey, Coll, Murphy, Shelley, Hanrahan, Lawless, McEvoy, Brady, Eviston, Irwin (Kavanagh).
Kispest Honved: Gulyas; Csabi, Plokai, Csepregi, Kovacs, Csehi, Marozsan (Halami), Berczy, Pisont, Vincze, Negrau (Molmar).

FK Austria (0) 1 *(Stoger (pen))*
Arsenal (0) 0 11,000
FK Austria: Wohlfahrt; Sekerlioglu, Pfeffer, Kern, Zsak, Flogel, Ogris, Narbekovas, Prosenik, Stoger, Ivanauskas.
Arsenal: Seaman; Dixon, Winterburn, Thomas, Linighan, Adams, Rocastle, Campbell, Smith, Merson (Groves), O'Leary.

Portadown (0) 0 5000
Red Star Belgrade (2) 4 *(Ratkovic 2, Pancev, Radinovic)*
Portadown: Keenan; Major, Curliss, Mitchell, Strain, Stewart, Doolin, Russell, Fraser, Cowan, Davidson.
Red Star Belgrade: Lekovic; Nedelikovic, Taniga, Jugovic, Belodedic, Najdoski, Stosic, Lukic, Pancev (Ivic), Ratkovic, Mihajlovic (Radinovic).

Rangers (0) 2 *(McCall 2)*
Sparta Prague (0) 1 *(Nisbet (og)) aet* 34,260
Rangers: Goram; Stevens, Robertson D, Brown (Durrant), Spackman, Nisbet, Kuznetsov, McCall, McCoist (Spencer); Johnston, Mikhailichenko.
Sparta Prague: Kouba; Hornak, Mistr, Vrabec, Sopko, Nemecek, Nemec, Novotny, Cerny (Matta), Siegl, Frydek (Lavicka).

SECOND ROUND, FIRST LEG

23 OCT

Benfica (1) 1 *(Isaias)*
Arsenal (1) 1 *(Campbell)* 80,000
Benfica: Neno; Kulkov, Bento, Madeira, Veloso (Pacheco), Thern, Paneira, Schwarz, Rui Aguas (Cesar Brito), Isaias, Youran.
Arsenal: Seaman; Dixon, Winterburn, Davis, Pates, Adams, Rocastle, Campbell (Groves), Smith, Merson, Limpar (Thomas).

SECOND ROUND, SECOND LEG

6 NOV

Arsenal (1) 1 *(Pates)*
Benfica (1) 3 *(Isaias 2, Kulkov) aet* 35,815
Arsenal: Seaman; Dixon, Winterburn, Davis, Pates, Adams (Bould), Rocastle, Campbell, Smith, Merson, Limpar (Groves).
Benfica: Neno; Kulkov, Madeira, Bento, Veloso, Thern, Paneira, Schwarz, Youran, Costa (Cesar Brito), Isaias (Carlos).

European Cup results continued from page 909

Final: Barcelona (0) 1, Sampdoria (0) 0 *aet*

(at Wembley, 20 May 1992, 70,827)

Barcelona: Zubizarreta; Nando, Ferrer, Koeman, Juan Carlos, Bakero, Salinas (Goicoechea 64), Stoichkov, Laudrup, Guardiola (Alexanco 113), Eusebio. *Scorer:* Koeman 111.
Sampdoria: Pagliuca; Mannini, Katanec, Pari, Vierchowod, Lanna, Lombardo, Cerezo, Vialli (Buso 100), Mancini, Bonetti I (Invernizzi 72).
Referee: Schmidhuber (Germany).

EUROPEAN CUP-WINNERS' CUP

EUROPEAN CUP-WINNERS' CUP FINALS 1961–91

Year	Winners		Runners-up		Venue	Attendance	Referee
1961	Fiorentina	2	Rangers	0 *(1st Leg)*	Glasgow	80,000	Steiner (A)
	Fiorentina	2	Rangers	1 *(2nd Leg)*	Florence	50,000	Hernadi (H)
1962	Atletico Madrid	1	Fiorentina	1	Glasgow	27,389	Wharton (S)
Replay	Atletico Madrid	3	Fiorentina	0	Stuttgart	45,000	Tschenscher (WG)
1963	Tottenham Hotspur	5	Atletico Madrid	1	Rotterdam	25,000	Van Leuwen (Ho)
1964	Sporting Lisbon	3	MTK Budapest	3 *(aet)*	Brussels	9000	Van Nuffel (Bel)
Replay	Sporting Lisbon	1	MTK Budapest	0	Antwerp	18,000	Versyp (Bel)
1965	West Ham U	2	Munich 1860	0	Wembley	100,000	Szolt (H)
1966	Borussia Dortmund	2	Liverpool	1 *(aet)*	Glasgow	41,657	Schwinte (F)
1967	Bayern Munich	1	Rangers	0 *(aet)*	Nuremberg	69,480	Lo Bello (I)
1968	AC Milan	2	Hamburg	0	Rotterdam	60,000	Ortiz (Sp)
1969	Slovan Bratislava	3	Barcelona	2	Basle	40,000	Van Ravens (Ho)
1970	Manchester C	2	Gornik Zabrze	1	Vienna	10,000	Schiller (A)
1971	Chelsea	1	Real Madrid	1 *(aet)*	Athens	42,000	Scheurer (Sw)
Replay	Chelsea	2	Real Madrid	1 *(aet)*	Athens	24,000	Bucheli (Sw)
1972	Rangers	3	Moscow Dynamo	2	Barcelona	35,000	Ortiz (Sp)
1973	AC Milan	1	Leeds U	0	Salonika	45,000	Mihas (Gr)
1974	Magdeburg	2	AC Milan	0	Rotterdam	5000	Van Gemert (Ho)
1975	Dynamo Kiev	3	Ferencvaros	0	Basle	13,000	Davidson (S)
1976	Anderlecht	4	West Ham U	2	Brussels	58,000	Wurtz (F)
1977	Hamburg	2	Anderlecht	0	Amsterdam	65,000	Partridge (E)
1978	Anderlecht	4	Austria/WAC	0	Amsterdam	48,679	Adlinger (WG)
1979	Barcelona	4	Fortuna Dusseldorf	3 *(aet)*	Basle	58,000	Palotai (H)
1980	Valencia	0	Arsenal	0	Brussels	40,000	Christov (Cz)
	(aet; Valencia won 5-4 on penalties)						
1981	Dynamo Tbilisi	2	Carl Zeiss Jena	1	Dusseldorf	9000	Lattanzi (I)
1982	Barcelona	2	Standard Liege	1	Barcelona	100,000	Eschweiler (WG)
1983	Aberdeen	2	Real Madrid	1 *(aet)*	Gothenburg	17,804	Menegali (I)
1984	Juventus	2	Porto	1	Basle	60,000	Prokop (EG)
1985	Everton	3	Rapid Vienna	1	Rotterdam	30,000	Casarin (I)
1986	Dynamo Kiev	3	Atletico Madrid	0	Lyon	39,300	Wohrer (A)
1987	Ajax	1	Lokomotiv Leipzig	0	Athens	35,000	Agnolin (I)
1988	Mechelen	1	Ajax	0	Strasbourg	39,446	Pauly (WG)
1989	Barcelona	2	Sampdoria	0	Berne	45,000	Courtney (E)
1990	Sampdoria	2	Anderlecht	0	Gothenburg	20,103	Galler (Sw)
1991	Manchester U	2	Barcelona	1	Rotterdam	45,000	Karlsson (Se)

Werder Bremen players celebrate the 2-0 win over Monaco in the 1992 European Cup-Winners' Cup Final. (Allsport)

EUROPEAN CUP-WINNERS' CUP 1991–92

Preliminary Round, First Leg

Galway (0) 0, Odense (1) 3 *(Donnerup 39, Nedergaard 46, Elstrup 68)* 4750
Stockerau (0) 0, Tottenham H (1) 1 *(Durie 40)* 15,500

Preliminary Round, Second Leg

Odense (1) 4 *(Nedergaard 35, Hansen 51, Harder 81, Thorup 88)*, Galway (0) 0 1750
Tottenham H (1) 1 *(Mabbutt 41)*, Stockerau (0) 0 28,072

First Round, First Leg

Athinaikos (0) 0, Manchester U (0) 0 9500
Bacau (0) 0, Werder Bremen (3) 6 *(Rufer 8, 13, 32, Bratseth 63, Votava 79, Neubarth 80)* 8000
CSKA Moscow (0) 1 *(Sergeyev 52)*, Roma (0) 2 *(Fakhin (og) 46, Rizzitelli 73)* 60,000
Fyllingen (0) 0 Atletico Madrid (1) 1 *(Manolo 30)* 4333
Glenavon (1) 3 *(Ferguson 32, McBride 60 (pen), Conville 80)*, Ilves (1) 2 *(Aaltonen J 12, Dziadulewicz 78)* 3000
Hajduk Split (0) 1 *(Novakovic 51)*, Tottenham H (0) 0 7000 *(in Linz)*
Katowice (1) 2 *(Szewczyk 42, Wolny 81)*, Motherwell (0) 0 6000
Levski (1) 2 *(Dartilov 36, Bankov 89)*, Ferencvaros (1) 3 *(Desiatric 5, Lipchei 72, 81)* 12,000
Norrkoping (1) 4 *(Karlsson 44, Eriksson 49, Hellstrom 70, Vaatovaara 71 (pen))*, Jeunesse Esch (0) 0 2438
Odense (0) 0, Banik Ostrava (1) 2 *(Skarabela 42, Casko 81)* 2377
Omonia (0) 0, FC Brugge (0) 0 12,000
Partizani (0) 0, Feyenoord (0) 0 15,000
Stahl Eisenhuttenstadt (1) 1 *(Bartz 43)*, Galatasaray (1) 2 *(Kosecki 44, Keser 70)* 10,000
Swansea C (0) 1 *(Legg 71)*, Monaco (2) 2 *(Passi 8 (pen), Rui Barros 27)* 6208
Valletta (0) 0, Porto (2) 3 *(Kostadinov 30, Timofte 39 (pen), Mikhtarski 78)* 1000
Valur (0) 0, Sion (0) 1 *(Rey 80)* 1047

First Round, Second Leg

Atletico Madrid (4) 7 *(Schuster 5, 89, Manolo 18, 34, 87 (pen), Soler 40, Futre 81)*, Fyllingen (0) 2 *(Tengs 54, 68)* 19,600
Banik Ostrava (0) 2 *(Cheylek 81, Steffensen (og) 83)*, Odense (1) 1 *(Bordingaard 8)* 2596
FC Brugge (0) 2 *(Booy 65, Van der Heyden 82)*, Omonia (0) 0 18,000
Ferencvaros (2) 4 *(Lipcsei 1, 89, Albert 28, Deszatnik 57)* Levski (0) 1 *(Dimitrou 73)* 7000
Feyenoord (0) 1 *(Bos 87)*, Partizani (0) 0 20,000
Galatasaray (1) 3 *(Kosecki 20 (pen), Arif 67, Mustafa 87)*, Stahl Eisenhuttenstadt (0) 0 12,000
Ilves (1) 2 *(Mattila 39 (pen), 70)*, Glenavon (0) 1 *(McBride 75)* 3000
Jeunesse Esch (0) 1 *(Marinelli 82)*, Norrkoping (2) 2 *(Eriksson 2, Kvindsal 40)* 1500
Manchester U (0) 2 *(Hughes 109, McClair 111)*, Athinaikos (0) 0 *aet* 35,023
Monaco (5) 8 *(Kendall (og) 6, Fofana 18, Rui Barros 30, Passi 31, 89, Harris (og) 39, Djorkaeff 74, Weah 85)*, Swansea C (0) 0 3000
Motherwell (1) 3 *(Kirk 29, 89, Cusack 86)*, Katowice (0) 1 *(Rzeznicek 67)* 10,032
Porto (0) 1 *(Timofte 89)*, Valletta (0) 0 15,000

Roma (0) 0, CSKA Moscow (1) 1 *(Dimitriev 13)*, 45,000
Sion (1) 1 *(Orlando 78)*, Valur (0) 1 *(Einarsson 67)* 6100
Tottenham H (2) 2 *(Tuttle 6, Durie 14)*, Hajduk Split (0) 0 24,297
Werder Bremen (3) 5 *(Kohn 6, 17, Eilts 9, Bratseth 66, Bode 71)*, Bacau (0) 0 4025

Second Round, First Leg

Atletico Madrid (1) 3 *(Futre 33, 84, Manolo 89)*, Manchester U (0) 0 52,000
Galatasaray (0) 0, Banik Ostrava (0) 1 *(Ollender 68)* 15,000
Ilves (0) 1 *(Czakon 65)*, Roma (1) 1 *(Carnevale 20)* 8727
Katowice (0) 0, FC Brugge (1) 1 *(Staelens 20)* 7000
Norrkoping (1) 1 *(Hellstrom 21)*, Monaco (1) 2 *(Mendy 16, Weah 48)* 4627
Sion (0) 0, Feyenoord (0) 0 12,300
Tottenham H (2) 3 *(Lineker 14, 83, Durie 32)*, Porto (0) 1 *(Kostadinov 51)* 23,621
Werder Bremen (3) 3 *(Neubarth 28, 40, Allofs 33)*, Ferencvaros (1) 2 *(Lipcsei 35, 73)* 7052

Second Round, Second Leg

Banik Ostrava (1) 1 *(Ollender 30)*, Galatasaray (2) 2 *(Yusuf 39, Kosecki 43 (pen))* 5000
FC Brugge (0) 3 *(Verspaille 50, Staelens 64, Schaessens 74)*, Katowice (0) 0 26,000
Ferencvaros (0) 0, Werder Bremen (0) 1 *(Bode 48)* 19,000
Feyenoord (0) 0, Sion (0) 0 *aet Feyenoord won 5-3 on penalties*
Manchester U (1) 1 *(Hughes 4)*, Atletico Madrid (0) 1 *(Schuster 68)* 39,654
Monaco (1) 1 *(Robert 26)*, Norrkoping (0) 0 6000
Porto (0) 0, Tottenham H (0) 0 45,000
Roma (3) 5 *(Giannini 1, Rizzitelli 3, Di Mauro 14, Carnevale 48, 77)*, Ilves (0) 2 *(Czakon 80, 89)* 25,000

Quarter-finals, First Leg

Atletico Madrid (1) 3 *(Schuster 30, Toni 47, Futre 57)*, FC Brugge (2) 2 *(Verspaille 32, Beyens 43)* 55,000
Feyenoord (0) 1 *(Kiprich 56)*, Tottenham H (0) 0 44,000
Roma (0) 0, Monaco (0) 0 40,336
Werder Bremen (0) 2 *(Kohn 78, Bester 85)*, Galatasaray (1) 1 *(Kosecki 33)* 30,000

Quarter-finals, Second Leg

FC Brugge (1) 2 *(Querter 41 (pen), Booy 63)*, Atletico Madrid (1) 1 *(Futre 11)* 22,000
Galatasaray (0) 0, Werder Bremen (0) 0 35,000
Monaco (1) 1 *(Rui Barros 44)*, Roma (0) 0 24,000
Tottenham H (0) 0, Feyenoord (0) 0 29,834

Semi-finals, First Leg

FC Brugge (1) 1 *(Amokachi 5)*, Werder Bremen (0) 0 21,000
Monaco (1) 1 *(Valery 25)*, Feyenoord (1) 1 *(Witschge 8)* 18,000

Semi-finals, Second Leg

Feyenoord (0) 2 *(Witschge 50, Damaschin 84)*, Monaco (1) 2 *(Weah 32, Rui Barros 49)* 38,000
Werder Bremen (1) 2 *(Bode 31, Bockenfeld 60)*, FC Brugge (0) 0 35,000

Final: Werder Bremen (1) 2, Monaco (0) 0

(in Lisbon, 6 May 1992, 16,000)

Werder Bremen: Rollmann; Wolter (Schaaf 34), Borowka, Bratseth, Bode, Bockenfeld, Eilts, Votova, Neubarth (Kohn 75), Allofs, Rufer. *Scorers:* Allofs 41, Rufer 54.
Monaco: Ettori; Valery (Djorkaeff 62), Petis, Mendy, Sonor, Dib, Gnako, Passi, Rui Barros, Weah, Fofana (Clement 59).
Referee: D'Elia (Italy).

EUROPEAN CUP-WINNERS' CUP 1991–92 – BRITISH AND IRISH CLUBS

PRELIMINARY ROUND, FIRST LEG

21 AUG

Galway (0) 0 *at Ballindereen*
Odense (1) 3 *(Donnerup, Nedergaard, Elstrup)* 4750
Galway: McIntyre; Carroll, Rodgers, Cleary, Nolan, Mullan, Wyse, Donohoe, Carpenter, Morris-Burke, Lally (Kearns).
Odense: Hogh; Nedergaard (Hjorth), Gray, Steffenson, Margaard, Helveg, Donnerup, Lund, Hansen, Elstrup, Bordinggard.

Stockerau (0) 0
Tottenham H (1) 1 *(Durie) in Vienna* 15,500
Stockerau: Zajicek; Mazura, Keller, Wenzel, Ostokowski (Flicker), Wacek, Jenisch, Pospisil, Marko (Augustin), Binder, Waliczek.
Tottenham H: Thorstvedt; Fenwick, Van Den Hauwe, Nayim, Howells, Mabbutt, Stewart, Durie, Samways (Hendon), Lineker, Allen.

PRELIMINARY ROUND, SECOND LEG

3 SEPT

Odense (1) 4 *(Nedergaard, Hansen, Harder, Thorup)*
Galway (0) 0 1750
Odense: Hogh; Nedergaard, Gray, Steffenson, Margaard (Helveg), Donnerup, Lund, Hansen, Elstrup, Harder, Thorup.
Galway: McIntyre; Nolan (Morris-Burke), Cleary, Rodgers, Carpenter, Carroll, Mullan, Wyse, Kileen (Kearns), Donohoe, Lally.

4 SEPT

Tottenham H (1) 1 *(Mabbutt)*
Stockerau (0) 0 28,072
Tottenham H: Walker; Fenwick, Van Den Hauwe, Nayim, Howells (Sedgley), Mabbutt, Stewart, Durie, Samways, Lineker (Moran), Bergsson.
Stockerau: Zajicek; Mazura, Keller, Wenzel, Wacek (Van Muysen), Flicker, Jenisch, Pospisil, Marko (Augustin), Binder, Waliczek.

FIRST ROUND, FIRST LEG

17 SEPT

Glenavon (1) 3 *(Ferguson, McBride (pen), Conville)*
Ilves (1) 2 *(Aaltonen J, Dziadulewicz)* 3000
Glenavon: Beck; McKeown, Scappaticci, McCullough, Byrne, Crowe, McCann, McCoy, Ferguson, McBride, Conville.
Ilves: Moilanen; Makela (Nikkila), Aaltonen J, Munnukka, Aaltonen M, Mattila, Juntunen, Dziadulewicz, Hjelm, Ojala, Czakon.

Hajduk Split (0) 1 *(Novakovic)*
Tottenham H (0) 0 *in Linz* 7000
Hajduk Split: Boskovic; Erak, Jarni, Stimac, Jeslinek, Milanko, Novakovic, Mise, Mornar (Abazi), Vucevic, Kozniko (Vukas).
Tottenham H: Walker; Fenwick, Van Den Hauwe, Nayim, Howells (Allen), Mabbutt, Stewart, Durie, Samways, Lineker (Sedgley), Bergsson.

Swansea C (0) 1 *(Legg)*
Monaco (2) 2 *(Passi (pen), Rui Barros)* 6208
Swansea C: Kendall; Jenkins, Thornber, Coughlin, Harris, Davies M, Davey, Davies A, McClean, Connor, Legg.
Monaco: Ettori; Sivebaek, Sonor, Petis, Mendy, Puel, Rui Barros (Gnako), Dib, Weah, Passi, Robert (Djorkaeff).

18 SEPT

Athinaikos (0) 0
Manchester U (0) 0 9500
Athinaikos: Sarganis; Boutzoukas, Kapoyranis, Hatziagelis, Spilliotis, Theodorakos, Hatziraptis (Dimopoulos), Spitsa, Bong, Kolef (Taprazis), Tzalakostas.
Manchester U: Schmeichel; Phelan, Irwin, Bruce, Webb, Pallister, Robins, Ince, McClair, Hughes, Beardsmore (Wallace).

Katowice (1) 2 *(Szewczyk, Wolny)*
Motherwell (0) 0 6000
Katowice: Jojika; Maciejewski, Szewczyk, Lesiak, Grzesik, Strojek, Szyminski (Swierczewski M), Wolcwicz, Walczak (Wolny), Gouruli, Rzeznicek.
Motherwell: Thomson; Griffin, Nijholt, Dolan, Philliben, McCart, Russell, O'Donnell, McLeod (Cusack), Kirk, Cooper.

FIRST ROUND, SECOND LEG

1 OCT

Monaco (5) 8 *(Kendall (og), Fofana, Rui Barros, Passi 2, Harris (og), Djorkaeff, Weah)*
Swansea C (0) 0 3000
Monaco: Ettori; Blondeau, Sonor, Petit, Mendy, Puel, Rui Barros (Djorkaeff), Dib (Robert), Weah, Passi, Fofana.
Swansea: Kendall; Jenkins, Thornber, Coughlin, Harris (Trick), Davies M, Davey (Chapple), Davies A, Gilligan, Raynor, Legg.

2 OCT

Ilves (1) 2 *(Mattila 2 (1 pen))*
Glenavon (0) 1 *(McBride)* 3000
Ilves: Moilanen; Makela, Nikkila (Aaltonen M), Munnukka, Aaltonen J, Mattila, Juntunen, Dziadulewicz, Hjelm, Ojala, Czakon.
Glenavon: Beck; McKeown, Scappaticci, McCullough, Byrne, Crowe (Russell), McCann (Ferris), McCoy, Ferguson, McBride, Conville.

Manchester U (0) 2 *(Hughes, McClair)*
Athinaikos (0) 0 *aet* 35,023
Manchester U: Schmeichel; Phelan, Martin (Beardsmore), Bruce, Kanchelskis, Pallister, Robson, Ince, McClair, Hughes, Wallace (Robins).
Athinaikos: Sarganis; Boutzoukas, Kapoyranis, Hatziagelis, Spilliotis (Zotalis) (Theodorakos), Anastasiou, Hatziraptis, Spitsa, Bak, Tzalakostas, Taprazis.

Motherwell (1) 3 *(Kirk 2, Cusack)*
Katowice (0) 1 *(Rzeznicek)* 10,032
Motherwell: Thomson; Griffin, Nijholt, McCart
(Philliben), Angus (Ferguson), Russell, Dolan, Kirk,
Cusack, Cooper, O'Donnell.
Katowice: Jojika; Maciejewski, Lesiak, Grzesik,
Strojek, Swierczewski P, Wolcwicz, Wolny
(Walczak), Swierczewski M, Rzeznicek, Gouruli.

Tottenham H (2) 2 *(Tuttle, Durie)*
Hajduk Split (0) 0 24,297
Tottenham H: Thorstvedt; Bergsson, Sedgley, Nayim,
Tuttle, Mabbutt, Stewart, Durie, Samways, Lineker,
Allen.
Hajduk Split: Boskovic; Erak (Ladislabic), Jarni,
Stimac, Jeslinek, Bilic, Novakovic, Mise, Milanko,
Vucevic (Abazi), Kozniko.

SECOND ROUND, FIRST LEG

23 OCT

Atletico Madrid (1) 3 *(Futre 2, Manolo)*
Manchester (0) 0 52,000
Atletico Madrid: Abel; Tomas, Soler, Solozabal,
Ferreira, Juanito, Manolo, Schuster, Vizcaino, Futre,
Moya (Lasada).
Manchester U: Schmeichel; Parker, Irwin, Bruce,
Webb, Pallister, Robson, Ince (Martin), McClair,
Hughes, Phelan (Beardsmore).

Tottenham H (2) 3 *(Lineker 2, Durie)*
Porto (0) 1 *(Kostadinov)* 23,621
Tottenham H: Thorstvedt; Edinburgh, Van Den
Hauwe, Sedgley, Walsh (Houghton), Mabbutt,
Stewart, Durie, Samways (Bergsson), Lineker, Allen.
Porto: Vitor Baia; Joao Pinto, Paulo Pareira, Aloisio,
Couto, Filipe, Magalhaes (Toze), Kostadinov,
Timofte (Kiki), Samedo, Andre.

SECOND ROUND, SECOND LEG

6 NOV

Manchester U (1) 1 *(Hughes)*
Atletico Madrid (0) 1 *(Schuster)* 39,654

Manchester U: Walsh; Parker, Blackmore, Bruce,
Webb, Phelan (Martin), Robson, Robins (Pallister),
McClair, Hughes, Giggs.
Atletico Madrid: Abel (Diaz); Tomas, Antonio,
Solozabal, Donato, Juanito, Manolo (Soler),
Schuster, Vizcaino, Futre, Moya.

7 NOV

Porto (0) 0
Tottenham (0) 0 45,000
Porto: Vitor Baia; Joao Pinto, Paulo Pareira, Aloisio,
Couto, Timofte, Toze, Kostadinov, Folha (Andrade),
Samedo (Magalhaes), Andre.
Tottenham H: Thorstvedt; Edinburgh, Van Den
Hauwe, Bergsson, Howells, Mabbutt, Stewart, Durie
(Sedgley), Samways, Lineker (Walsh), Allen.

QUARTER-FINALS, FIRST LEG

4 MAR

Feyenoord (0) 1 *(Kiprich)*
Tottenham H (0) 0 44,000
Feyenoord: De Goey; Fraser, De Wolf, Metgod,
Heus, Scholten, Sabau, Taument, Kiprich, Witschge,
Blinker (Van Gobbel).
Tottenham H: Thorstvedt; Fenwick, Van Den
Hauwe, Sedgley, Howells (Samways), Mabbutt,
Stewart, Durie, Nayim, Lineker (Walsh), Allen.

QUARTER-FINALS, SECOND LEG

18 MAR

Tottenham H (0) 0
Feyenoord (0) 0 29,834
Tottenham H: Thorstvedt; Bergsson, Edinburgh,
Sedgley, Howells (Houghton), Mabbutt, Stewart,
Durie, Nayim (Walsh), Lineker, Allen.
Feyenoord: De Goey; Fraser, De Wolf, Metgod,
Heus, Bosz, Scholten, Sabau (Van Gobbel),
Taument, Witschge, Blinker (Kiprich).

EUROPEAN CUPS DRAW 1992–93

EUROPEAN CUP

Qualifying Round
Shelbourne v Tavria Simferopol; Klaksvikar v Skonto
Riga; Olimpija Ljubljana v Norma Tallinn; Valetta v
Maccabi Tel Aviv.

First Round
Glentoran v Marseille; Rangers v Lyngby; Sion v
Shelbourne or Tavria Simferopol; Stuttgart v Leeds U;
AEK Athens v Apoel; Barcelona v Viking; FC Brugge
v Valetta or Maccabi; FK Austria v CSKA Sofia; IFK
Gothenburg v Besiktas; Kuusysi V Dinamo Bucharest;
Lech Poznan v Klaksvikar or Skonto Riga; AC Milan v
Olimpija Ljubljana or Norma Tallinn; PSV Eindhoven v
Zalgiris Vilnius; Slovan Bratislava v Ferencvaros; Union
Luxembourg v Porto; Vikingur v CSKA Moscow.

CUP-WINNERS' CUP

Qualifying Round
Avenir Beggen v B36 Thorshavn; Branik Maribor v
Hamrun Spartans; Hapoel Petah Tikva v Stromsgodset
Drammen; Vaduz v Chernomorets Odessa.

First Round
Admira Wacker v Cardiff C; Airdrieonians v Sparta
Prague; Glenavon v Antwerp; Liverpool v Apollon
Limassol; Steaua Bucharest v Bohemians Dublin; AIK
Stockholm v Aarhus; Boavista v Valure; Branik Maribor

or Hamrun Spartans v Atletico Madrid; Levski v Lucerne;
Feyenoord v Stromsgodset Drammen or Hapoel Petah
Tikva; Monaco v Miedz Legnica; Moscow Spartak v B36
Thorshavn or Avenir Beggen; Olympiakos v Vaduz or
Chernomorets Odessa; Parma v Ujpest Dozsa;
Trabzonspor v Turku; Werder Bremen v Hannover.

UEFA CUP

First Round
Cologne v Celtic; Hibernian v Anderlecht; Manchester U
v Moscow Torpedo; Sheffield W v Spora; Slavia Prague v
Hearts; Standard Liege v Portadown; Vitesse v Derry
City; Austria Salzburg v Ajax; Benfica v Belvedur Izola;
Caen v Zaragoza; Electroputere Craiova v Panathinaikos;
FC Copenhagen v Mikkelin; Fenerbahce v Botev Plovidiv;
Floriana v Dortmund; Fram v Kaiserslautern;
Grasshoppers v Sporting Lisbon; Guimaraes v Real
Sociedad; Juventus v Anorthosis; Katowice v Galatasaray;
Kiev Dynamo v Rapid Vienna; Lokomotiv Plovdiv v
Auxerre; Mechelen v Orebro; Moscoe Dynamo v
Rosenborg; Norrkoping v Torino; Paris St Germain v
PAOK Salonika; Real Madrid v Politehnica Timisoara;
Sigma Olomouc; Tirol v Roma; VAC Izzo v Groningen;
Valencia v Napoli, Widzew Lodz v Eintracht Frankfurt;
Neuchatel Xamax v Frem.
Qualifying round ties on August 19 and September 2, first
round September 16 and 30.

INTER-CITIES FAIRS & UEFA CUP

FAIRS CUP FINALS 1958–71 *(Winners in italics)*

Year	First Leg	Attendance	Second Leg	Attendance
1958	London 2 Barcelona 2	45,466	*Barcelona* 6 London 0	62,000
1960	Birmingham C 0 Barcelona 0	40,500	*Barcelona* 4 Birmingham C 1	70,000
1961	Birmingham C 2 Roma 2	21,005	*Roma* 2 Birmingham C 0	60,000
1962	Valencia 6 Barcelona 2	65,000	Barcelona 1 *Valencia* 1	60,000
1963	Dynamo Zagreb 1 Valencia 2	40,000	*Valencia* 2 Dynamo Zagreb 0	55,000
1964	*Zaragoza* 2 Valencia 1	50,000	(in Barcelona)	
1965	*Ferencvaros* 1 Juventus 0	25,000	(in Turin)	
1966	Barcelona 0 Zaragoza 1	70,000	Zaragoza 2 *Barcelona* 4	70,000
1967	Dynamo Zagreb 2 Leeds U 0	40,000	Leeds U 0 *Dynamo Zagreb* 0	35,604
1968	Leeds U 1 Ferencvaros 0	25,368	Ferencvaros 0 *Leeds U* 0	70,000
1969	Newcastle U 3 Ujpest Dozsa 0	60,000	Ujpest Dozsa 2 *Newcastle U* 3	37,000
1970	Anderlecht 3 Arsenal 1	37,000	*Arsenal* 3 Anderlecht 0	51,612
1971	Juventus 0 Leeds U 0	42,000		
	(abandoned 51 minutes)			
	Juventus 2 Leeds U 2	42,000	*Leeds U* 1* Juventus 1	42,483

UEFA CUP FINALS 1972–91 *(Winners in italics)*

Year	First Leg	Attendance	Second Leg	Attendance
1972	Wolverhampton W 1 Tottenham H 2	45,000	*Tottenham H* 1 Wolverhampton W 1	48,000
1973	Liverpool 0 Moenchengladbach 0			
	(abandoned 27 minutes)	44,967		
	Liverpool 3 Moenchengladbach 0	41,169	Moenchengladbach 0 *Liverpool* 2	35,000
1974	Tottenham H 2 Feyenoord 2	46,281	*Feyenoord* 2 Tottenham 0	68,000
1975	Moenchengladbach 0 Twente 0	45,000	Twente 1 *Moenchengladbach* 5	24,500
1976	Liverpool 3 FC Brugge 2	56,000	FC Brugge 1 *Liverpool* 1	32,000
1977	Juventus 1 Athletic Bilbao 0	75,000	Athletic Bilbao 2 *Juventus* 1*	43,000
1978	Bastia 0 PSV Eindhoven 0	15,000	*PSV Eindhoven* 3 Bastia 0	27,000
1979	Red Star Belgrade 1 Moenchengladbach 1	87,500	*Moenchengladbach* 1 Red Star Belgrade 0	45,000
1980	Moenchengladbach 3 Eintracht Frankfurt 2	25,000	*Eintracht Frankfurt* 1* Moenchengladbach 0	60,000
1981	Ipswich T 3 AZ 67 Alkmaar 0	27,532	AZ 67 Alkmaar 4 *Ipswich T* 2	28,500
1982	Gothenburg 1 Hamburg 0	42,548	Hamburg 0 *Gothenburg* 3	60,000
1983	Anderlecht 1 Benfica 0	45,000	Benfica 1 *Anderlecht* 1	80,000
1984	Anderlecht 1 Tottenham H 1	40,000	*Tottenham H* 1[1] Anderlecht 1	46,258
1985	Videoton 0 Real Madrid 3	30,000	*Real Madrid* 0 Videoton 1	98,300
1986	Real Madrid 5 Cologne 1	80,000	Cologne 2 *Real Madrid* 0	15,000
1987	Gothenburg 1 Dundee U 0	50,023	Dundee U 1 *Gothenburg* 1	20,911
1988	Espanol 3 Bayer Leverkusen 0	42,000	*Bayer Leverkusen* 3[2] Espanol 0	22,000
1989	Napoli 2 Stuttgart 1	83,000	Stuttgart 3 *Napoli* 3	67,000
1990	Juventus 3 Fiorentina 1	45,000	Fiorentina 0 *Juventus* 0	32,000
1991	Internazionale 2 Roma 0	68,887	Roma 1 *Internazionale* 0	70,901

* won on away goals   [1] *Tottenham H won 4-3 on penalties aet*   [2] *Bayer Leverkusen won 3-2 on penalties aet*

Ajax forward Aron Winter falling over the body of Torino goalkeeper Luca Marchegiani in the second leg of the 1992 UEFA Cup Final. Ajax won on the away goals rule. (Colorsport)

UEFA CUP 1991-92

First Round, First Leg

Aberdeen (0) 0, B 1903 Copenhagen (0) 1 *(Kaus 86)* 13,000

Ajax (0) 3 *(Bergkamp 60, Winter 66, Pettersson 82)*, Orebro (0) 0 17,000 *(in Dusseldorf)*

Anorthosis (0) 1 *(Ombikou 69 (pen))*, Steaua (1) 2 *(Stan 44, Dumitrescu 47)* 12,000

Bangor (0) 0, Olomouc (1) 3 *(Sindelar 33, 46, Kerbr 50)* 3000

Boavista (1) 2 *(Marlon 38, Bamy 57)*, Internazionale (0) 1 *(Fontolan 67)* 20,000

Celtic (2) 2 *(Nicholas 15 (pen), 39)*, Ekeren (0) 0 27,410

Cork C (1) 1 *(Barry 26)*, Bayern Munich (1) 1 *(Effenberg 43)* 8000

CSKA Sofia (0) 0, Parma (0) 0 17,500

Eintracht Frankfurt (4) 6 *(Moller 9, 36, Bein 14, Grundel 32, Yeboah 46, 54)*, Spora (1) 1 *(Rigaud 39 (pen))* 4800

Gent (0) 0, Lausanne (1) 1 *(Cina 40)* 9500

Gijon (0) 2 *(Monchu 64, Luhovy 79)*, Partizan (0) 0 23,600

Groningen (0) 0, Erfurt (1) 1 *(Schmidt 2)* 14,000

Halle (0) 2 *(Wulbier 60, Schulbe 64)*, Moscow Torpedo (0) 1 *(Grishin 65)* 2000

Hamburg (0) 1 *(Eckei 80)*, Gornik Zabrze (0) 1 *(Jegor 50)* 5800

HASK Gradjanski (0) 2 *(Petrovic 60, 81 (pen))*, Trabzonspor (2) 3 *(Cyzio 26, Hami 37, Unal 56)* 1500 *(in Klagenfurt)*

Ikast (0) 0, Auxerre (0) 1 *(Vahirua 67)* 2000

KR Reykjavik (0) 0, Torino (1) 2 *(Mussi 20, Annoni 73)* 1793

Liverpool (2) 6 *(Saunders 12, 77, 85, 86, Houghton 33, 89)*, Kuusysi (1) 1 *(Lehtinen 35)* 17,131

Lyon (1) 1 *(Garde 17)*, Osters (0) 0 20,000

MP Mikkeli (0) 0, Moscow Spartak (2) 2 *(Cherenkov 35, Allen (og) 77)* 4316

Neuchatel Xamax (1) 2 *(Mottiez 43, Hassan I 60)*, Floriana (0) 0 4200

Oviedo (1) 2 *(Bango 44)*, Genoa (0) 0 24,600

PAOK Salonika (1) 1 *(Skartados 40)*, Mechelen (0) 1 *(Ingesson 62)* 17,000

Salgueiros (0) 1 *(Placido 48)*, Cannes (0) 0 6000

Slavia Sofia (1) 1 *(Dermendjiev 43)*, Osasuna (0) 0 5000

Slovan Bratislava (0) 1 *(Dubovsky 69)*, Real Madrid (1) 2 *(Michel 13 (pen), Butragueno 78)* 20,447

Sporting Lisbon (0) 1 *(Yordanov 75)*, Dinamo Bucharest (0) 0 50,000

Sturm Graz (0) 0, Utrecht (0) 1 *(Smolarek 76)* 13,000

Stuttgart (4) 4 *(Sammer 20, Walters 32, Buchwald 35, Walter 39)*, Pecs (0) 1 *(Balog 89)* 7800

Tirol (0) 2 *(Hortnagl 52, Gorosito 54)*, Tromso (0) 1 *(Johansson 39)* 6000

Vac Izzo (0) 1 *(Hahn 61)*, Moscow Dynamo (0) 0 3000

Vllaznia (0) 0, AEK Athens (0) 1 *(Dimitriadis 61)* 17,000

First Round, Second Leg

AEK Athens (1) 2 *(Papaioannu 8, Batista 88)*, Vllaznia (0) 0 22,000

Auxerre (2) 5 *(Vahirua 18, Ferreri 22, 54, Coccard 74, Kovacs 81)*, Ikast (0) 1 *(Hansen 83)* 6500

B 1903 Copenhagen (0) 2 *(Johansen 57, Jensen 87)*, Aberdeen (0) 0 5237

Bayern Munich (0) 2 *(Labbadia 74, Ziege 89 (pen))*, Cork C (0) 0 13,500

Cannes (0) 1 *(Omam Biyik 85)*, Salgueiros (0) 0 *aet Cannes won 4-2 on penalties*

Dinamo Bucharest (0) 2 *(Gerstenmajer 32, 115)*, Sporting Lisbon (0) 0 *aet* 5000

Ekeren (1) 1 *(Schmoller 41)*, Celtic (1) 1 *(Galloway 10)* 7500

Erfurt (0) 1 *(Gottiober 78)*, Groningen (0) 0 4000

Floriana (0) 0, Neuchatel Xamax (0) 0 1000

Genoa (1) 3 *(Skuhravy 20, 89, Caricola 73)*, Oviedo (1) 1 *(Carlos 37)* 50,000

Gornik Zabrze (0) 0, Hamburg (0) 3 *(Von Heesen 61, 80, Spori 84)* 15,000

Internazionale (0) 0, Boavista (0) 0 40,000

Kuusysi (0) 1 *(Belfield 66)*, Liverpool (0) 0 8000

Lausanne (0) 0, Gent (0) 1 *(Medved 60)* aet Gent won 4–1 on penalties 13,100

Mechelen (0) 0, PAOK Salonika (0) 1 *(Borbokis 87)* 8500

Moscow Dynamo (2) 4 *(Kobelev 8 (pen), Kiryakov 30, Kolyvanov 49, 68)*, Vac Izzo (1) 1 *(Romanek 24)* 15,000

Moscow Spartak (1) 3 *(Mostovoi 27, Karpich 57, Radchenko 77)*, MP Mikkeli (1) 1 *(Allen 36)* 6000

Moscow Torpedo (2) 3 *(Agashkov 4 (pen), Chugainov 12, Tishkov 88)*, Halle (0) 0 12,500

Olomouc (1) 3 *(Latal 21, Kerbr 65, Gottwald 68)*, Bangor (0) 0 4445

Orebro (0) 0, Ajax (0) 1 *(Winter 66)* 5561

Osasuna (2) 4 *(Cholo 20, Bustingorri 21, 78, Sola 68)*, Slavia Sofia (0) 0 14,300

Osters (1) 1 *(Jansson 14)*, Lyon (0) 1 *(Roche 53)* 4628

Parma (0) 1 *(Agostini 71)*, CSKA Sofia (0) 1 *(Parushev 88)*, 21,000

Partizan (0) 2 *(Mijatovic 86, Krchmaravic 88)*, Gijon (0) 0 7000 *(in Istanbul)* aet Gijon won 3-2 on penalties

Pecs (1) 2 *(Magyar 18, Mortei 83)*, Stuttgart (0) 2 *(Strehmel 55, Mayer 75)* 4000

Real Madrid (1) 1 *(Alfonso 42)*, Slovan Bratislava (0) 1 *(Lancz 89)* 20,000

Spora (0) 0, Eintracht Frankfurt (2) 5 *(Kruse 32, 61, Weber 44, Schmitt 72, Bein 89)* 1100

Steaua (0) 2 *(Stan 62, 115)*, Anorthosis (0) 2 *(Obicu 53, Ketsbaia 84)* aet 8000

Torino (2) 6 *(Bresciani 14, Policano 44, Martin Vazquez 48, Scifo 52, 64, Carillo 52)*, KR Reykjavik (1) 1 *(Skulasson 16)* 15,000

Trabzonspor (0) 1 *(Hamdi 66)*, HASK Gradjanski (1) 1 *(Petrovic 41)* 12,000

Tromso (1) 1 *(Johansen 39)*, Tirol (1) 1 *(Westerhaler 11)* 6184

Utrecht (0) 3 *(De Kryuff 55, Smolarek 66, Ven de Net 89)*, Sturm Graz (0) 1 *(Devritsj 75)* 16,500

Second Round, First Leg

Auxerre (1) 2 *(Ferreri 41, Kovacs 60)*, Liverpool (0) 0 20,000

B 1903 Copenhagen (1) 6 *(Manniche 38, 64, Nielsen I 56 (pen), Wegner 61, Kaus 77, Uldbjerg 88)*, Bayern Munich (1) 2 *(Mazinho 22, Munch 89)* 12,400

Cannes (0) 0, Moscow Dynamo (1) 1 *(Kiryakov 43)* 7000

Erfurt (1) 1 *(Schulz 39)*, Ajax (0) 2 *(Jonk 46, Bergkamp 76)* 6100

Genoa (2) 3 *(Aguilera 14, 59 (pen), Branco 20)*, Dinamo Bucharest (0) 1 *(Signorini (og) 88)* 40,000

Gent (0) 0, Eintracht Frankfurt (0) 0 5750

Gijon (1) 2 *(Luhovy 44, Stan (og) 89)*, Steaua (1) 2 *(Popa 27, Dimitrescu 59)* 17,000

Hamburg (1) 2 *(Rohde 36, 89)*, CSKA Sofia (0) 0 8120

Lyon (0) 3 *(Bouderbala 59, Bursac 63, Leal 78)*, Trabzonspor (0) 4 *(Seyhmuz 50, Hami 52, 77, Orhan 89)* 25,000

Moscow Spartak (0) 0, AEK Athens (0) 0 25,000

Neuchatel Xamax (3) 5 *(Hassan H 10, 20, 55, 74, Bonvin 38)*, Celtic (0) 1 *(O'Neil 60)* 11,300

Olomouc (0) 2 *(Sindelar 60, Marosi 89)*, Moscow Torpedo (0) 0 5000

Osasuna (0) 0, Stuttgart (0) 0 20,000

PAOK Salonika (0) 0, Tirol (0) 2 *(Westerhaler 52, 78)* behind closed doors

Torino (1) 2 *(Lentini 2, Annoni 69)*, Boavista (0) 0 50,000

Utrecht (1) 1 *(Smolarek 19)*, Real Madrid (1) 3 *(Prosinecki 44, Roest (og) 72, Villaroya 80)* 17,500

Second Round, Second Leg

AEK Athens (0) 2 *(Batista 64, Dimitriadis 75)*, Moscow Spartak (1) 1 *(Mostovoi 15 (pen))* 30,000

Ajax (1) 3 *(Pettersson 30, Blind 58, Van Loen 84)*, Erfurt (0) 0 10,000 *(in Dusseldorf)*

Bayern Munich (1) 1 *(Mazinho 89)*, B 1903 Copenhagen (0) 0 21,000

Boavista (0) 0, Torino (0) 0 10,000

Celtic (0) 1 *(Miller 52)*, Neuchatel Xamax (0) 0 25,454

CSKA Sofia (0) 1 *(Dimitrow 44 (pen))*, Hamburg (1) 4 *(Sporl 34, 83, Furtok 56 (pen), Bode 89)*, 35,000

Dinamo Bucharest (0) 2 *(Gerstenmajer 68, Christea 88)*, Genoa (1) 2 *(Matei 9 (og), Aguilera 55)* 10,000

Eintracht Frankfurt (0) 0, Gent (1) 1 *(Vandenbergh 35)* 11,500

Liverpool (2) 3 *(Molby 4 (pen), Marsh 30, Walters 83)*, Auxerre (0) 0 23,094

Moscow Dynamo (1) 1 *(Kobelev 43 (pen))*, Cannes (1) 1 *(Omam Biyik 9)* 5000

Moscow Torpedo (0) 0, Olomouc (0) 0 14,000

Real Madrid (1) 1 *(Hagi 18)*, Utrecht (0) 0 23,000

Steaua (0) 1 *(Popa 60)*, Gijon (0) 0 18,000

Stuttgart (0) 2 *(Buchwald 80, Sverrisson 89)*, Osasuna (2) 3 *(Urban 8, 47, Merino 17)* 9500

Tirol (1) 2 *(Westerhaler 27, 66)*, PAOK Salonika (0) 0 8000

Trabzonspor (3) 4 *(Hami 17, 80, Hamdi 27, Orhan 45)*, Lyon (1) 1 *(Bursac 41)* 30,000

Third Round, First Leg

AEK Athens (1) 2 *(Batista 21, Sabanadzovic 73)*, Torino (2) 2 *(Casagrande 34, Bresciani 37)* 35,000

B 1903 Copenhagen (1) 1 *(Nielsen I 43)*, Trabzonspor (0) 012,100

Gent (1) 2 *(Vandenbergh 30, Van der Linden 86)*, Moscow Dynamo (0) 0 6000

Hamburg (1) 1 *(Furtok 21)*, Olomouc (2) 2 *(Hapal 10, 45)* 20,000

Neuchatel Xamax (1) 1 *(Hassan I 35)*, Real Madrid (0) 0 20,400

Osasuna (0) 0, Ajax (0) 1 *(Bergkamp 47)* 18,000

Steaua (0) 0, Genoa (1) 1 *(Skuhravy 21)* 23,000

Tirol (0) 0, Liverpool (0) 2 *(Saunders 58, 78)*, 13,500

Third Round, Second Leg

Ajax (1) 1 *(Bergkamp 12)*, Osasuna (0) 0 8000 *(in Dusseldorf)*

Genoa (0) 1 *(Aguilera 59)*, Steaua (0) 0 30,000

Liverpool (1) 4 *(Saunders 39, 57, 68, Venison 84)*, Tirol (0) 0 16,007

Moscow Dynamo (0) 0, Gent (0) 0, 20,000

Olomouc (1) 4 *(Kerbr 13, Hapal 64, Latal 76, Hanus 76)*, Hamburg (0) 1 *(Sporl 60)* 15,000

Real Madrid (0) 4 *(Hassan I (og) 48, Hagi 52, Michel 65 (pen), Sanchis 68)*, Neuchatel Xamax (0) 0 59,000

Torino (0) 1 *(Casagrande 54)*, AEK Athens (0) 0 35,000

Trabzonspor (0) 0, B 1903 Copenhagen (0) 0, 25,000

Quarter-finals, First Leg

B 1903 Copenhagen (0) 0, Torino (1) 2 *(Casagrande 37, Policano 82)* 14,600

Genoa (1) 2 *(Florin 40, Branco 88)*, Liverpool (0) 0 40,000

Gent (0) 0, Ajax (0) 0 15,000

Olomouc (1) 1 *(Hapal 26)*, Real Madrid (1) 1 *(Hierro 45)* 14,000

Quarter-finals, Second Leg

Ajax (2) 3 *(Kreek 7, Bergkamp 10, Jonk 89)*, Gent (0) 0 18,000

Liverpool (0) 1 *(Rush 49)*, Genoa (1) 2 *(Aguilera 28, 72)* 38,840

Real Madrid (0) 1 *(Sanchez 82)*, Olomouc (0) 0 50,000

Torino (1) 1 *(Nielsen I (og) 30)*, B 1903 Copenhagen (0) 0

Semi-finals, First Leg

Genoa (0) 2 *(Aguilera 73, 80)*, Ajax (1) 3 *(Pettersson 1, Roy 60, Winter 88)* 39,000

Real Madrid (0) 2 *(Hagi 60, Hierro 65)*, Torino (0) 1 *(Casagrande 57)* 93,000

Semi-finals, Second Leg

Ajax (0) 1 *(Bergkamp 47)*, Genoa (1) 1 *(Iorio 39)* 48,500

Torino (1) 2 *(Rocha (og) 8, Fusi 76)*, Real Madrid (0) 0 61,000

Final
First Leg: Torino (0) 2, Ajax (1) 2
(in Turin, 29 April 1992, 65,377)

Torino: Marchegiani; Cravero (Bresciani 80), Bruno, Annoni, Benedetti, Venturin, Martin Vazquez, Scifo, Mussi (Sordo 83), Lentini, Casagrande.
Scorer: Casagrande 61, 83.
Ajax: Menzo; Blind, Silooy, Jonk, De Boer, Van't Schip, Winter, Bergkamp, Kreek, Pettersson, Roy (Gronendijk 82).
Scorers: Jonk 44, Pettersson 74 (pen).
Referee: Worrall (England).

Second Leg: Ajax (0) 0, Torino (0) 0
(in Amsterdam, 13 May 1992, 40,000)

Ajax: Menzo; Silooy, Blind, Jonk, De Boer, Winter, Kreek (Vink 80), Alflen, Van't Schip, Pettersson, Roy (Van Loen 65).
Torino: Marchegiani; Mussi, Cravero (Sordo 58), Benedetti, Fusi, Policano, Martin Vazquez, Scifo (Bresciani 62), Venturin, Casagrande, Lentini.
Referee: Petrovic (Yugloslavia).

UEFA CUP 1991–92 – BRITISH AND IRISH CLUBS

FIRST ROUND, FIRST LEG

18 SEPT

Aberdeen (0) 0
B 1903 Copenhagen (0) 1 *(Kaus)*   13,000
Aberdeen: Snelders; Wright (Watson), Irvine,
McKimmie, Connor, Grant, Bett, Ten Caat, Jess,
Van der Ark (Booth), Gillhaus.
B 1903 Copenhagen: Petersen; Wegner, Nielsen I,
Piechnik, Tur, Larsen, Juul, Uldbjerg, Manniche,
Johansen Martin (Kaus), Nielsen L.

Bangor (0) 0
Olomouc (1) 3 *(Sindelar 2, Kerbr)*   3000
Bangor: Eachus; McCartney, Dornan, Gibson,
Brown, O'Connor, McCloskey, Hill, McCreadie,
Caughey, Muldoon (Murphy).
Olomouc: Pribyl; Bokij, Marosi (Kriz), Kotulek,
Vadura, Slaby, Hanus, Gottwald, Kerbr (Mucha),
Sindelar, Hapal.

Celtic (2) 2 *(Nicholas 2 (1 pen))*
Ekeren (0) 0   27,410
Celtic: Bonner; Morris, Whyte, Gillespie (McNally),
Wdowczyk, Fulton, Grant, Collins, Miller, Cascarino
(Coyne), Nicholas.
Ekeren: Vandevalle; Talbut, Snelders, Verstraeten,
Gabbadini, Herreman, Ghislain, Vandersmissen,
Ballenghien, Tahamata, Schmoller.

Cork C (1) 1 *(Barry)*
Bayern Munich (1) 1 *(Effenberg)*   8000
Cork C: Harrington; Murphy, Daly, Bannon, Napier,
Kenneally, Conroy (Crotty), Barry, McCabe,
Caulfield, Morley.
Bayern Munich: Hillringhaus; Berthold, Grahammer,
Kreuzer, Ziege, Bernardo, Bender (Schinto),
Sternkopf (Labbadia), Wohlfarth, Effenberg,
Mazinho.

Liverpool (2) 6 *(Saunders 4, Houghton 2)*
Kuusysi (1) 1 *(Lehtinen)*   17,131
Liverpool: Hooper; Ablett, Burrows, Nicol, Marsh
(Walters), Tanner, Saunders, Houghton, Rush,
McManaman, McMahon.
Kuusysi: Rovio; Remes, Saastamoinen, Jarvinen,
Jantti, Viljanen, Lehtinen (Vehkakoski), Rinne,
Kinnunen, Belfield, Annunen (Glusako).

FIRST ROUND, SECOND LEG

1 OCT

Bayern Munich (0) 2 *(Labbadia, Ziege (pen))*
Cork C (0) 0   13,500
Bayern Munich: Hillringhaus; Berthold, Grahammer,
Schwabl, Ziege, Bender, Sternkopf (Kreuzer),
Pflugler, Labbadia, Effenberg, Mazinho (Wohlfarth).
Cork C: Harrington; Murphy, Daly, Bannon, Napier,
Kenneally, Barry, Conroy, McCabe, Caulfield,
Morley.

Ekeren (1) 1 *(Schmoller)*
Celtic (1) 1 *(Galloway)*   7500
Ekeren: Vandevalle; Talbut, Sabbatini, Herreman,
Verstraeten, Ghislain, Ballenghien, Snelders,
Tahamata, Schmoller, N'Sumbu (Vandersmissen).
Celtic: Bonner; Morris, Whyte, Gillespie, Wdowczy!

(Fulton), Grant, Galloway, O'Neil, Collins, Coyne,
Nicholas (Cascarino).

2 OCT

B 1903 Copenhagen (0) 2 *(Johansen Martin, Jensen)*
Aberdeen (0) 0   5237
B 1903 Copenhagen: Petersen; Wegner, Nielsen I,
Piechnik, Tur, Larsen, Jensen, Uldbjerg, Nielsen K,
Johansen Martin, Johansen Michael.
Aberdeen: Snelders; Watson (Van der Ark), Irvine,
McKimmie, Connor, Van de Ven, Bett, Ten Caat,
Booth (Cameron), Grant, Jess.

Kuusysi (0) 1 *(Belfield)*
Liverpool (0) 0   8000
Kuusysi: Rovio; Remes (Vehkakoski),
Saastamoinen, Jarvinen, Jantti, Viljanen, Lehtinen,
Rantanen (Glouchakov), Kinnunen, Belfield,
Annunen.
Liverpool: Ablett, Burrows (Jones B),
Nicol, Marsh, Harkness, Rosenthal (Carter),
McManaman, Rush, Walters, McMahon.

Olomouc (1) 3 *(Latal, Kerbr, Gottwald)*
Bangor (0) 0   4445
Olomouc: Pribyl; Kover, Marosi, Kotulek, Vadura
(Gottwald), Slaby, Hanus, Latal, Kerbr, Sindelar
(Bokij), Hapal.
Bangor: Eachus; McCartney, Dornan, Gibson,
Brown, O'Connor (Smith), Nelson (Lucas), Woods,
Hill, Caughey, Muldoon.

SECOND ROUND, FIRST LEG

22 OCT

Neuchatel Xamax (3) 5 *(Hassan H 4, Bonvin)*
Celtic (0) 1 *(O'Neil)*   11,300
Neuchatel Xamax: Dalay; Vernier, Fernandez, Luhti,
Ramsay, Perret, Sutter, Rothenbuhler Regis
(Froidevaux), Hassan H (Chasset), Hassan I, Bonvin.
Celtic: Bonner; Grant, Wdowczyk, O'Neil, Whyte,
McNally, Cascarino (Creaney), McStay, Coyne
(Miller), Nicholas, Fulton.

23 OCT

Auxerre (1) 2 *(Ferreri, Kovacs)*
Liverpool (0) 0   20,000
Auxerre: Martini; Kaczmarek (Darras), Prunier,
Roche, Mahe, Guerreiro, Cocard, Dutuel, Kovacs,
Ferreri, Vahirua.
Liverpool: Grobbelaar; Ablett, Burrows, Nicol
(Harkness), McManaman, Tanner, Redknapp
(Marsh), Houghton, Rush, Walters, McMahon.

SECOND ROUND, SECOND LEG

6 NOV

Celtic (0) 1 *(Miller)*
Neuchatel Xamax (0) 0   25,454
Celtic: Bonner; McNally, Galloway, Whyte
(Creaney), Wdowczyk (Cascarino), O'Neil, McStay,
Miller, Nicholas, Coyne, Collins.
Neuchatel Xamax: Dalay; Fasel, Ramzy, Luhti,
Fernandez, Vernier, Perret, Hassan I, Sutter
(Mottiez), Hassan H (Chassot), Bonvin.

Liverpool (2) 3 *(Molby (pen), Marsh, Walters)*
Auxerre (0) 0   23,094
Liverpool: Grobbelaar; Ablett, Burrows, Marsh, Molby, Tanner, McManaman, Houghton, Rush, Walters, McMahon.
Auxerre: Martini; Darras, Kaczmarek (Mazzolini), Roche, Mahe, Guerreiro, Cocard, Dutuel, Kovacs (Otokore), Ferreri, Vahirua.

THIRD ROUND, FIRST LEG

27 NOV

Tirol (0) 0
Liverpool (0) 2 *(Saunders 2)*   13,500
Tirol: Oraze; Hartmann, Russ, Posch, Wazinger, Pacult, Linzmaier, Streiter, Westerhaler, Gorosito, Hortnagl (Kirchler).
Liverpool: Grobbelaar; Harkness, Ablett, Nicol, Wright, Tanner, Saunders, Marsh, McManaman, Molby, McMahon.

THIRD ROUND, SECOND LEG

11 DEC

Liverpool (1) 4 *(Saunders 3, Venison)*
Tirol (0) 0   16,007
Liverpool: Grobbelaar; Harkness (Redknapp), Burrows, Nicol, Wright, Tanner, Saunders, Ablett, McManaman, Molby, Marsh (Venison).

Tirol: Oraze; Hartmann, Wazinger, Posch, Russ, Pacult (Kirchler), Linzmaier, Streiter, Westerhaler, Gorosito, Hortnagl.

QUARTER-FINALS, FIRST LEG

4 MAR

Genoa (1) 2 *(Florin, Branco)*
Liverpool (0) 0   40,000
Genoa: Braglia; Torrente, Branco, Eranio, Collovati, Signorini, Ruotolo, Bortolazzi, Aguilera, Skuhravy, Florin (Onorati).
Liverpool: Hooper; Jones R, Burrows, Nicol, Wright, Marsh, Saunders, Houghton, Walters (Venison), Molby, McManaman.

QUARTER-FINALS, SECOND LEG

18 MAR

Liverpool (0) 1 *(Rush)*
Genoa (1) 2 *(Aguilera 2)*   38,840
Liverpool: Hooper; Jones R (Venison), Burrows, Nicol, Molby, Wright (Tanner), Saunders, Marsh, Rush, Barnes, McManaman.
Genoa: Braglia; Torrente, Branco, Eranio, Collovati, Signorini, Ruotolo, Bortolazzi, Aguilera (Caricola), Skuhravy, Onorati (Florin).

Summary of Appearances

EUROPEAN CUP (1955–92)

English clubs
12 Liverpool
5 Manchester U
3 Nottingham F
2 Derby Co, Wolverhampton W, Everton, Leeds U, Aston Villa, Arsenal
1 Burnley, Tottenham H, Ipswich T, Manchester C

Scottish clubs
15 Celtic
13 Rangers
3 Aberdeen
2 Hearts
1 Dundee, Dundee U, Kilmarnock, Hibernian

Clubs for Northern Ireland
17 Linfield
7 Glentoran
2 Crusaders, Portadown
1 Glenavon, Ards, Distillery, Derry C, Coleraine

Clubs for Eire
7 Shamrock R, Dundalk
6 Waterford
3 Drumcondra
2 Bohemians, Limerick, Athlone T
1 Shelbourne, Cork Hibs, Cork Celtic, Derry C*, Sligo Rovers, St Patrick's Ath

Winners: Celtic 1966–67; Manchester U 1967–68; Liverpool 1976–77, 1977–78, 1980–81, 1983–84; Nottingham F 1978–79, 1979–80; Aston Villa 1981–82

Finalists: Celtic 1969–70; Leeds U 1974–75; Liverpool 1984–85

EUROPEAN CUP-WINNERS' CUP (1960–92)

English clubs
6 Tottenham H
5 Manchester U
4 West Ham U
3 Liverpool
2 Chelsea, Everton, Manchester C
1 Wolverhampton W, Leicester C, WBA, Leeds U, Sunderland, Southampton, Ipswich T, Arsenal

Scottish clubs
10 Rangers
7 Celtic, Aberdeen
2 Dunfermline Ath, Dundee U
1 Dundee, Hibernian, Hearts, St Mirren, Motherwell

Welsh clubs
12 Cardiff C
7 Wrexham, Swansea C
2 Bangor C
1 Borough U, Newport Co, Merthyr Tydfil

Clubs from Northern Ireland
7 Glentoran
4 Ballymena U, Coleraine
3 Crusaders, Glenavon
2 Ards, Linfield
1 Derry C, Distillery, Portadown, Carrick Rangers, Cliftonville

Clubs from Eire
6 Shamrock R
3 Limerick, Waterford, Dundalk
2 Cork Hibs, Bohemians, Galway U
1 Shelbourne, Cork Celtic, St Patrick's Ath, Finn Harps, Home Farm, Sligo Rovers, University College Dublin, Derry C*, Cork City, Bray Wanderers

Winners: Tottenham H 1962–63; West Ham U 1964–65; Manchester C 1969–70; Chelsea 1970–71; Rangers 1971–72; Aberdeen 1982–83; Everton 1984–85; Manchester U 1990–91

Finalists: Rangers 1960–61, 1966–67; Liverpool 1965–66; Leeds U 1972–73; West Ham U 1975–76; Arsenal 1979–80

EUROPEAN FAIRS CUP & UEFA CUP (1955–92)

English clubs
8 Leeds U, Ipswich T
7 Liverpool
6 Everton, Arsenal
5 Manchester U, Southampton, Tottenham H
4 Manchester C, Birmingham C, Newcastle U, Nottingham F, Wolverhampton W, WBA, Aston Villa
3 Chelsea
2 Sheffield W, Stoke C, Derby Co, QPR
1 Burnley, Coventry C, London Rep XI, Watford

Scottish clubs
16 Dundee U
13 Hibernian
11 Aberdeen
8 Rangers
7 Hearts
6 Celtic
5 Dunfermline Ath
4 Dundee
3 St Mirren, Kilmarnock
2 Partick Th
1 Morton, St Johnstone

Clubs from Northern Ireland
11 Glentoran
6 Coleraine
4 Linfield
3 Glenavon
1 Ards, Portadown, Ballymena U, Bangor

Clubs from Eire
7 Bohemians
4 Dundalk
3 Finn Harps, Shamrock R
2 Shelbourne, Drumcondra, St Patrick's Ath
1 Cork Hibs, Athlone T, Limerick, Drogheda U, Galway U, Derry C*, Cork City

Winners: Leeds U 1967–68, 1970–71; Newcastle U 1968–69; Arsenal 1969–70; Tottenham H 1971–72, 1983–84; Liverpool 1972–73, 1975–76; Ipswich T 1980–81

Finalists: London 1955–58; Birmingham C 1958–60, 1960–61; Leeds U 1966–67; Wolverhampton W 1971–72; Tottenham H 1973–74; Dundee U 1986–87

* Now play in League of Ireland.

WOMEN'S NATIONAL LEAGUE

1991–92 will go down as arguably the most historic season in the development of organized women's football in this country. Under the leadership of chairman Tim Stearn and secretary Linda Whitehead the women's game demonstrated its ability to sustain a thriving new National League comprising three divisions of eight clubs. Closely following the guidelines established by clubs outside the Football League, women's football now has its own pyramid with promotion from the grass roots through to a Premier Division organized on a national basis.

The Doncaster Belles, who once again formed the nucleus of the England team, completed a unique League and Cup double. The South Yorkshire club who clinched the League championship with a 100 per cent record, added the Mycil WFA Cup to their list of honours by defeating Red Star Southampton 4-0 in the final which was televised for the fourth year running by Channel 4.

The success of the new competition has led to an expansion of the League structure to 30 clubs in season 1992–93 as women's football aims to consolidate its position as Britain's fastest growing participation sport.

Premier Division

	P	W	D	L	F	A	W	D	L	F	A	GD	Pts
		Home			*Goals*		*Away*			*Goals*			
Doncaster Belles	14	7	0	0	42	2	7	0	0	47	2	+85	28
Red Star Southampton	14	6	0	1	19	7	4	1	2	13	11	+14	21
Wimbledon	14	4	1	2	18	14	4	1	2	16	13	+7	18
Knowsley United	14	2	4	1	15	21	4	1	2	16	9	+1	17
Maidstone Tigresses	14	3	0	4	8	22	0	4	3	5	13	−22	10
Ipswich Town	14	1	2	4	7	18	1	2	4	9	25	−27	8
Millwall Lionesses	14	1	1	5	7	17	1	1	5	4	13	−19	6
Notts Rangers	14	0	2	5	6	20	1	0	6	11	36	−39	4

Division One North

	P	W	D	L	F	A	W	D	L	F	A	GD	Pts
		Home			*Goals*		*Away*			*Goals*			
Bronte	14	5	1	1	27	6	7	0	0	22	2	+41	25
Sheffield Wed.	14	6	0	1	19	3	4	2	1	15	5	+26	22
Davies Argyle*	14	5	1	1	16	9	4	0	3	11	10	+8	17
Wolverhampton	14	3	1	3	16	17	2	1	4	7	13	−7	12
Spondon	14	3	2	2	12	12	1	1	5	11	19	−8	11
Sunderland**	14	3	0	4	13	14	2	1	4	5	26	−22	11
Cowgate Kestrels	14	3	0	4	8	7	2	0	5	11	13	−1	10
Villa Aztecs	14	1	0	6	5	17	0	0	7	3	28	−37	2

* *Davies Argyle deducted 2 points*
** *Sunderland awarded 2 points*

Division One South

	P	W	D	L	F	A	W	D	L	F	A	GD	Pts
		Home			*Goals*		*Away*			*Goals*			
Arsenal	14	7	0	0	58	6	4	3	0	41	5	+88	25
Abbeydale	14	5	2	0	28	3	6	0	1	34	4	+55	24
Hassocks Beacon	14	3	3	1	29	14	4	1	2	28	18	+25	18
Town & County	14	4	1	2	26	16	3	1	3	26	19	+17	16
Reigate	14	3	1	3	23	19	1	2	4	8	19	−7	11
Brighton & Hove Albion	14	2	1	4	13	19	2	0	5	9	31	−28	9
Broadbridge Heath	14	2	0	5	10	30	2	1	4	10	26	−36	9
Milton Keynes	14	0	0	7	0	54	0	0	7	5	65	−114	0

LEADING GOALSCORERS

Karen Walker (Doncaster Belles)	36	Michelle Saunders (Hassocks Beacon)	20
Jo Churchman (Arsenal)	27	Karen Pratt (Hassocks Beacon)	18
Caroline McGloin (Arsenal)	24	Lorraine Robinon (Abbeydale)	18
Naz Ball (Arsenal)	23	Gail Borman (Doncaster Belles)	17
Leslie Saban (Town & County)	20	Jackie Sherrard (Doncaster Belles)	13

NATIONAL LEAGUE CUP

Preliminary Round
Maidstone Tigresses 1, Town & County 2
Milton Keynes 1, Davies Argyle 8

First Round
Abbeydale 5, Town & County 1
Davies Argyle 1, Red Star Southampton 0
Broadbridge Heath 2, Arsenal 12
Hassocks Beacon 0, Wimbledon 1 *aet*
Ipswich T 2, Bronte 1
Reigate 1, Sheffield Weds. 0
Villa Aztecs 1, Brighton & Hove Albion 3
Wolverhampton 0, Millwall Lionesses 1

Quarter-finals
Arsenal 2, Reigate 0
Davies Argyle 2, Abbeydale 1
Ipswich T 2, Brighton & Hove Albion 1
Wimbledon 0, Millwall Lionesses 0 *aet*
(Millwall Lionesses won 5–4 on penalties)

Semi-finals
Arsenal 2, Ipswich T. 0
Davies Argyle 2, Millwall Lionesses 3

Final
Arsenal 1, Millwall Lionesses 0

MYCIL WFA CUP

First Round

GROUP 1
Bridgewater 0, Cardiff 15
Carterton 2, Launton 8
Cheltenham 2, Bournemouth 3
Cirencester 0, Frome 4
Exeter Rangers 0, Oxford 6
Plymouth 2, Bristol Blackwell 5
Salisbury 1, Solent 3
Swindon 3, Newbury 4
Taunton 1, Crewkerne 8
Torquay United 11, Amazons 0
Truro City 6, Bristol United 1
Warmplas Windows 1, Swansea 3

GROUP 2
Beccles 4, Chelmsford 6
Leyton Orient 7, Sporting Kesteven 0
Luton Town 1, Pye 2
Newham 3, Bedford Town Belles 1
Romford withdrew, Canary Rangers
Thetford 0, Suffolk Bluebirds 10
Tower Hamlets withdrew, Norwich Falcons
Woodham Wanderers 0, Southend 12
Wanstead 0, Harlow 0
Wanstead 0, Harlow (Replay) 4
Hornchurch, Byes
Milton Keynes, Byes
Town & County, Byes

GROUP 3
Barnsley 2, Wakefield 5
Bradford City 4, Hull City 1
Middlesbrough 3, Brighouse 0
Newcastle 2, Doncaster Town 1
Scarborough 4, Oakland Rangers 1
Bronte, Byes
Cowgate Kestrels, Byes
Sunderland, Byes

GROUP 4
Sharley Park Spireites 6, Derby County 0
Highfield Rangers 0, Leicester 2
Leyton Linsdale 0, Calverton 6
Millmoor 28, Gresley Rovers 0
Notts County 3, Nettleham 1
Rainworth withdrew, Derby County
Sheffield Weds., Byes
Spondon, Byes

GROUP 5
Bolton 1, Nabwood 2
Rochdale 1, Broadoak 6
Manchester City 1, Huddersfield 4
Bury 0, Preston Rangers 3
Rossendale 1, Tranmere Rovers 2
Manchester United, St Martins withdrew
Wigan 4, Burnley 0
Corinthians 1, Runcorn 6
St Helens 12, Pilkington 0
Liverpool Feds. 0, Wythenshawe 9
Vernon-Carus 0, Ladyblues 1
Blackpool, Byes

GROUP 6
Palace Eagles 5, Winchester 0
Abbey Rangers 1, Corematch 9
Isle of Wight 25, Crowborough 1
Portsmouth 2, Hightown 5
Farnborough 4, Saltdean United 4
Saltdean United 3, Farnborough 1
Brighton & Hove Albion, Byes
Hassocks Beacon, Byes
Crystal Palace, Byes
Maidstone United, Byes
Bromley Borough, Byes
Gosport, Byes
Havant, Byes

GROUP 7
Brentford 4, Hounslow 0
Dunstable 10, Walton & Hersham 0
District Line 4, Slough 0
Hammersmith 0, Watford 24
Reading 0, Wycombe Wanderers 1
Reigate, Byes
Broadbridge Heath, Byes
Binfield, Byes
Bedfont United, Byes
Hemel Hempstead, Byes
Tottenham, Byes

GROUP 8
Kidderminster Harriers 20, Port Vale 0
Birmingham City 2, Crewe 4
Worcester City 4, Bangor 1
Leek Town 8, Telford United 2
St Asaphs 0, Aston Villa 5
Wolverhampton, Byes
Abbeydale, Byes
Villa Aztecs, Byes

Second Round

GROUP 1
Swansea 0, Frome 5
Bristol Blackwell 10, Torquay United 1
Solent 3, Newbury 2
Oxford 2, Truro City 2
Crewkerne 5, Launton 3
Bournemouth 5, Cardiff 0

GROUP 2
Leyton Orient 6, Chelmsford 2
Pye 5, Newham 1
Harlow 2, Milton Keynes 1
Canary Rangers 3, Suffolk Bluebirds 2
Norwich Falcons 2, Southend 5
Hornchurch 3, Town & County 8

GROUP 3
Wakefield 0, Newcastle 1
Bradford 1, Middlesbrough 3
Scarborough 1, Bronte 4
Sunderland 1, Cowgate Kestrels 4

GROUP 4
Sheffield Weds. 11, Notts County 0
Spondon 7, Derby City 1
Millmoor 4, Calverton 1
Sharley Park Spireites 3, Leicester 2

GROUP 5
Runcorn 1, Manchester United 3
Preston Rangers 10, Wythenshawe 1
Wigan 9, Nabwood 0
Broadoak 2, Tranmere Rovers 4
St Helens 2, Blackpool 0
Ladyblues 4, Huddersfield 5

GROUP 6
Saltdean United 4, Gosport 1
Crystal Palace 2, Hassocks Beacon 8
Maidstone United 0, Bromley Borough 11
Havant 0, Hightown 2
Isle of Wight 1, Corematch 3
Palace Eagles 1, Brighton & Hove Albion 5

GROUP 7
Binfield 1, Watford 0
Hemel Hempstead 1, District Line 4
Broadbridge Heath 3, Reigate 4
Brentford 2, Chelsea 10
Wycombe Wanderers 0, Dunstable 3
Tottenham 14, Bedfont United 0

GROUP 8
Worcester City 2, Aston Villa 3
Leek Town 3, Kidderminster Harriers 7
Crewe 5, Villa Aztecs 0
Wolverhampton 0, Abbeydale 3

Third Round

GROUP 1
Bristol Blackwell 7, Bournemouth 0
Solent 11, Crewkerne 0
Oxford 2, Frome 3

GROUP 2
Pye 5, Town & County 3
Harlow 2, Southend 0
Canary Rangers 0, Leyton Orient 7

GROUP 3
Newcastle 2, Bronte 3
Cowgate Kestrels 2, Middlesbrough 4

GROUP 4
Sheffield Weds. 1, Millmoor 2
Sharley Park Spireites 0, Spondon 4

GROUP 5
Preston Rangers 3, Huddersfield 0
Wigan 1, St Helens 4
Tranmere Rovers 3, Manchester United 4

GROUP 6
Hassocks Beacon 6, Brighton & Hove Albion 2
Bromley Borough 6, Corematch 0
Hightown 0, Saltdean United 2

GROUP 7
District Line 7, Tottenham 0
Reigate 2, Dunstable 0
Chelsea 1, Binfield 3

GROUP 8
Aston Villa 1, Crewe 3
Abbeydale 7, Kidderminster Harriers 2

Fourth Round
Arsenal 0, Red Star Southampton 1 *aet*
Middlesbrough 5, Frome 0

Notts Rangers 2, Davies Argyle 0
Bromley Borough 3, Abbeydale 3
Abbeydale 0, Bromley Borough (Replay) 1
Preston Rangers 4, Manchester United 2
Bronte 0, Maidstone Tigresses 0 *aet*
Maidstone Tigresses 2, Bronte (Replay) 1
Saltdean United 4, Pye 0
Ipswich Town 3, Millwall Lionesses 1
Binfield 0, Reigate 3
Hassocks Beacon 2, Bristol Blackwell 1
Leyton Orient 0, Doncaster Belles 14
Solent 1, Spondon 3
St Helens 2, Knowsley United 6
Crewe 1, District Line 5
Leasowe Pacific 5, Millmoor 0
Harlow 1, Wimbledon 6

Fifth Round
Ipswich Town 5, Reigate 2
(First tie postponed)
Maidstone Tigresses 3, Knowsley 2
(First tie postponed)
Middlesbrough 2, Leasowe Pacific 3
Notts Rangers 2, Hassocks Beacon 4
Preston Rangers 0, Doncaster Belles 6
Red Star Southampton 5, Bromley Borough 2 *aet*
Spondon 4, Saltdean United 0
Wimbledon 1, District Line 0

Quarter-finals
Leasowe Pacific 1, Doncaster Belles 5
Maidstone Tigresses 2, Spondon 1
Ipswich T. 1, Red Star Southampton 3
Hassocks Beacon 1, Wimbledon 6

Semi-finals
Doncaster Belles 10, Maidstone Tigresses 1
Red Star Southampton 2, Wimbledon 0

Final
Doncaster Belles 4, Red Star Southampton 0

WOMEN'S WORLD CHAMPIONSHIP

November 1991 in China
Group A
China 4, Norway 0
Denmark 3, New Zealand 0
Norway 4, New Zealand 0
China 2, Denmark 2
China 4, New Zealand 1
Norway 2, Denmark 1

Group B
Japan 0, Brazil 1
Sweden 2, USA 3
Japan 0, Sweden 8
Brazil 0, USA 5
Japan 0, USA 3
Brazil 0, Sweden 2

Group C
Taipei 0, Italy 5
Germany 4, Nigeria 0
Italy 1, Nigeria 0

Taipei 0, Germany 3
Taipei 2, Nigeria 0
Italy 0, Germany 2

Quarter-finals
Denmark 1, Germany 2 *aet*
China 0, Sweden 1
Norway 3, Italy 2 *aet*
USA 7, Taipei 0

Semi-finals
Sweden 1, Norway 4
Germany 2, USA 5

Match for third place
Sweden 4, Germany 0

Final in Guangzhou
Norway 1, USA 2

Official placings: 1 USA; 2 Norway; 3 Sweden; 4 Germany; 5 China; 6 Italy; 7 Denmark; 8 Taipei; 9 Brazil; 10 Nigeria; 11 New Zealand; 12 Japan

5th EUROPEAN CHAMPIONSHIP FOR WOMEN

Group 1
Switzerland 0, Norway 10; Belgium 0, Switzerland 0.

Group 2
Finland 1, Denmark 1; Denmark 4, France 1.

Group 3
England 1, Scotland 0; England 4, Iceland 0; Iceland 1, England 2.

Group 4
Spain 0, Sweden 4; Spain 0, Republic of Ireland 1

Group 5
Greece 0, Romania 0.

Group 6
Yugoslavia and Germany.

Group 7
Poland 1, Czechoslovakia 2; Italy 3, Poland 1.

Group 8
CIS 2, Hungary 1; Bulgaria 0, Hungary 1.

WORLD CLUB CHAMPIONSHIP

Played annually up to 1974 and intermittently until 1979 between the winners of the European Cup and the winners of the South American Champions Cup — known as the Copa Libertadores. In 1980 the winners were decided by one match arranged in Tokyo in February 1981 and the venue has been the same since.

1960 Real Benfica beat Penarol 0-0, 5-1
1961 Penarol beat Benfica 0-1, 5-0, 2-1
1962 Santos beat Benfica 3-2, 5-2
1963 Santos beat AC Milan 2-4, 4-2, 1-0
1964 Inter-Milan beat Independiente 0-1, 2-0, 1-0
1965 Inter-Milan beat Independiente 3-0, 0-0
1966 Penarol beat Real Madrid 2-0, 2-0
1967 Racing Club beat Celtic 0-1, 2-1, 1-0
1968 Estudiantes beat Manchester United 1-0, 1-1
1969 AC Milan beat Estudiantes 3-0, 1-2
1970 Feyenoord beat Estudiantes 2-2, 1-0
1971 Nacional beat Panathinaikos* 1-1, 2-1
1972 Ajax beat Independiente 1-1, 3-0
1973 Independiente beat Juventus* 1-0
1974 Atlético Madrid* beat Independiente 0-1, 2-0
1975 Independiente and Bayern Munich could not agree dates; no matches.
1976 Bayern Munich beat Cruzeiro 2-0, 0-0

1977 Boca Juniors beat Borussia Moenchengladbach* 2-2, 3-0
1978 Not contested
1979 Olimpia beat Malmö* 1-0, 2-1
1980 Nacional beat Nottingham Forest 1-0
1981 Flamengo beat Liverpool 3-0
1982 Penarol beat Aston Villa 2-0
1983 Gremio Porto Alegre beat SV Hamburg 2-1
1984 Independiente beat Liverpool 1-0
1985 Juventus beat Argentinos Juniors 4-2 on penalties after a 2-2 draw
1986 River Plate beat Steaua Bucharest 1-0
1986 FC Porto beat Penarol 2-1 after extra time
1988 Nacional (Uru) beat PSV Eindhoven 7-6 on penalties after 1-1 draw
1989 AC Milan beat Atletico Nacional (Col) 1-0 after extra time
1990 AC Milan beat Olimpia 3-0

*European Cup runners-up; winners declined to take part.

1991

8 December in Tokyo

Red Star Belgrade (1) 3 *(Jugovic 19, 58, Pancev 72)*

Colo Colo (0) 0 60,000

Red Star Belgrade: Milojevic; Radinovic, Vasilijevic, Belodedic, Najdoski, Jugovic, Stosic, Ratkovic, Savicevic, Mihajlovic, Pancev.
Colo Colo: Moron; Garrido, Margas, Miguel Ramirez, Salvatierra (Dabrowski 65), Mendoza, Vilches, Barticciotto, Pizarro, Yanez, Martinez (Rubio 60).
Referee: Rothlisberger (Switzerland).

EUROPEAN SUPER CUP

Played annually between the winners of the European Champions' Cup and the European Cup-Winners' Cup.

Previous Matches

1972 Ajax beat Rangers 3-1, 3-2
1973 Ajax beat AC Milan 0-1, 6-0
1974 Not contested
1975 Dynamo Kiev beat Bayern Munich 1-0, 2-0
1976 Anderlecht beat Bayern Munich 4-1, 1-2
1977 Liverpool beat Hamburg 1-1, 6-0
1978 Anderlecht beat Liverpool 3-1, 1-2
1979 Nottingham F beat Barcelona 1-0, 1-1
1980 Valencia beat Nottingham F 1-0, 1-2
1981 Not contested
1982 Aston Villa beat Barcelona 0-1, 3-0
1983 Aberdeen beat Hamburg 0-0, 2-0
1984 Juventus beat Liverpool 2-0
1985 Juventus v Everton not contested due to UEFA ban on English clubs
1986 Steaua Bucharest beat Dynamo Kiev 1-0
1987 FC Porto beat Ajax 1-0, 1-0
1988 KV Mechelen beat PSV Eindhoven 3-0, 0-1
1989 AC Milan beat Barcelona 1-1, 1-0
1990 AC Milan beat Sampdoria 1-1, 2-0

1991

Old Trafford, 19 November 1991, 22,110

Manchester U (0) 1 *(McClair 67)*

Red Star Belgrade (0) 0

Manchester U: Schmeichel; Martin (Giggs 71), Irwin, Bruce, Webb, Pallister, Kanchelskis, Ince, McClair, Hughes, Blackmore.
Red Star Belgrade: Milojevic; Radinovic, Vasilijevic, Belodedic, Najdoski, Tanjga, Stosic, Jugovic, Pancev, Savicevic (Ivic 82), Mihajlovic.
Referee: Van der Ende (Holland).

SOUTH AMERICA

COPA LIBERTADORES
(South American Cup) 1992

Group 1

	P	W	D	L	F	A	Pts
Newell's (Arg)	8	4	3	1	11	10	11
Univ Catolica (Chi)	8	2	5	1	15	8	9
San Lorenzo (Arg)	8	4	1	3	13	8	9
Colo Colo (Chi)	8	2	4	2	6	7	8
Coquimbo (Chi)	8	1	1	6	6	18	3

Group 2

	P	W	D	L	F	A	Pts
Criciuma (Bra)	6	4	1	1	13	7	9
Sao Paulo (Bra)	6	3	2	1	11	5	8
Bolivar (Bol)	6	2	2	2	9	9	6
San Jose (Bol)	6	0	1	5	5	12	1

Group 3

	P	W	D	L	F	A	Pts
Barcelona (Ecu)	6	4	2	0	11	3	10
Valdez (Ecu)	6	2	2	2	5	4	6
Maritimo (Ven)	6	1	2	3	5	8	4
ULA (Ven)	6	1	2	3	4	10	4

Group 4

	P	W	D	L	F	A	Pts
At Nacional (Col)	6	4	1	1	15	4	9
America (Col)	6	4	0	2	8	7	8
Sp Cristal (Per)	6	2	1	3	6	7	5
Sport Boys (Per)	6	0	2	4	4	15	2

Group 5

	P	W	D	L	F	A	Pts
Cerro Porteno (Para)	6	3	3	0	9	4	9
Nacional (Uru)	6	2	3	1	9	7	7
Defensor (Uru)	6	1	2	3	7	9	4
Sol de America (Para)	6	1	2	3	5	10	4

Second Round First Leg
Univ Catolica 0, America 0
Nacional 0, Sao Paulo 1
Defensor 1, Newell's Old Boys 1
Maritimo 0, At Nacional 0
Bolivar 2, Cerro Porteno 0
San Lorenzo 2, Valdez 0
Sp Cristal 1, Criciuma 2
Colo Colo 1, Barcelona 0

Second Leg
America 1, Univ Catolica 0
Valdez 2, San Lorenzo 0
Sao Paulo 2, Nacional 0
Newell's Old Boys 1, Defensor 0
At Nacional 3, Maritimo 0
Cerro Porteno 3, Bolivar 0
Barcelona 2, Colo Colo 0
Criciuma 3, Cristal 2

Quarter-finals First Leg
Newell's Old Boys 4, San Lorenzo 0
At Nacional 0, America 1
Barcelona 1, Cerro Porteno 1
Sao Paulo 1, Criciuma 0

Second Leg
San Lorenzo 1, Newell's Old Boys 1
Criciuma 1, Sao Paulo 1
America 4, At Nacional 2
Cerro Porteno 1, Barcelona 1

Semi-finals First Leg
Newell's Old Boys 1, America 1
Sao Paulo 3, Barcelona 0

Second Leg
America 1, Newell's Old Boys 1
Barcelona 2, Sao Paulo 0

Final First Leg
Newell's Old Boys 1, Sao Paulo 0

Final Second Leg
Sao Paulo 1, Newell's Old Boys 0
Sao Paulo won 2-0 on penalties

Champions:
Argentina: Newell's Old Boys
Bolivia: Bolivar
Brazil: Bragantino
Chile: Colo Colo
Colombia: Atletico Nacional
Ecuador: Barcelona
Paraguay: Sol de America
Peru: Sporting Cristal
Uruguay: Defensor
Venezuela: ULA Merida

Inter-American Cup
Olimpia (Paraguay) 1,1, America (Mexico) 1,2

South American Super Cup

First Round First Leg
River Plate 2, Gremio 2
Argentinos Juniors 1, Santos 2
Penarol 3, Racing Club 2
Flamengo 1, Estudiantes De La Plata 1
Cruzeiro 0, Colo Colo 0
Boca Juniors 1, Nacional 1

First Round Second Leg
Racing Club 0, Penarol 0
Nacional 2, Boca Juniors 0
Colo Colo 0, Cruzeiro 0
Estudiantes 0, Flamengo 2
Gremio 1, River Plate 1
Santos 0, Argentinos Juniors 0

Second Round First Leg
Penarol 3, Santos 2
River Plate 1, Flamengo 0
Cruzeiro 4, Nacional 0
Independiente 1, Olimpia 1

Second Round Second Leg
Santos 0, Penarol 0
Flamengo 2, River Plate 1
Nacional 3, Cruzeiro 0
Olimpia 2, Independiente 0

Semi-finals First Leg
Cruzeiro 1, Olimpia 1
River Plate 2, Penarol 0

Semi-finals Second Leg
Olimpia 0, Cruzeiro 0
Penarol 1, River Plate 3

Final First Leg
River Plate 2, Cruzeiro 0

Final Second Leg
Cruzeiro 3, River Plate 0

International matches 1991

Argentina
Hungary (h) 2-0; Mexico (h) 0-0; Brazil (h) 3-3; USA (a) 1-0; USSR (n) 1-1; England (a) 2-2; Brazil (a) 1-1; Venezuela (n) 3-0; Chile (a) 1-0; Paraguay (n) 4-1; Peru (n) 3-2; Brazil (n) 3-2; Chile (a) 0-0; Colombia (n) 2-1.

Bolivia
Paraguay (h) 0-1; Paraguay (a) 0-0; Uruguay (n) 1-1; Brazil (n) 1-2; Colombia (n) 0-0; Ecuador (n) 0-4.

Brazil
Paraguay (h) 1-1; Argentina (a) 3-3; Bulgaria (h) 3-0; Argentina (h) 1-1; Bolivia (n) 2-1; Uruguay (n) 1-1; Colombia (n) 0-2; Ecuador (n) 3-1; Argentina (n) 2-3; Colombia (n) 2-0; Chile (a) 2-0; Wales (a) 0-1; Yugoslavia (h) 3-1; Czechoslovakia (h) 2-1.

Chile
Mexico (a) 0-1; Republic of Ireland (a) 1-1; Uruguay (h) 2-1; Ecuador (a) 1-2; Uruguay (a) 1-2; Ecuador (h) 3-1; Venezuela (h) 2-0; Peru (h) 4-2; Argentina (h) 0-1; Paraguay (h) 4-0; Colombia (h) 1-1; Argentina (h) 0-0; Brazil (h) 0-2.

Colombia
Mexico (a) 0-0; Switzerland (n) 2-3; Sweden (a) 2-2; Costa Rica (a) 1-0; Ecuador (n) 1-0; Bolivia (n) 0-0; Brazil (n) 2-0; Uruguay (n) 0-1; Chile (a) 1-1; Brazil (n) 0-2; Argentina (n) 1-2.

Ecuador
Peru (a) 1-0; Chile (h) 2-1; Peru (h) 2-1; Chile (a) 1-3; Colombia (n) 0-1; Uruguay (n) 1-1; Bolivia (n) 4-0; Brazil (n) 1-3.

Paraguay
Brazil (a) 1-1; Bolivia (a) 1-0; Bolivia (h) 0-0; Peru (n) 1-0; Venezuela (n) 5-0; Argentina (n) 1-4; Chile (a) 0-4.

Peru
Ecuador (h) 0-1; Uruguay (h) 1-0; Ecuador (a) 1-2; Paraguay (n) 0-1; Chile (a) 2-4; Venezuela (n) 5-1; Argentina (n) 2-3.

Uruguay
USA (a) 0-1; Mexico (n) 2-0; Costa Rica (a) 1-0; Chile (a) 1-2; Peru (a) 0-1; Chile (h) 2-1; Bolivia (n) 1-1; Ecuador (n) 1-1; Brazil (n) 1-1; Colombia (n) 1-0; Spain (a) 1-2; Mexico (a) 1-1.

Venezuela
Chile (a) 0-2; Argentina (n) 0-3; Paraguay (n) 0-5; Peru (n) 1-5.

AFRICA

AFRICAN NATIONS CUP (in Senegal)

Group A

	P	W	D	L	F	A	Pts
Nigeria	2	2	0	0	4	2	4
Senegal	2	1	0	1	4	2	2
Kenya	2	0	0	2	1	5	0

Group B

	P	W	D	L	F	A	Pts
Cameroon	2	1	1	0	2	1	3
Zaire	2	0	2	0	2	2	2
Morocco	2	0	1	1	1	2	1

Group C

	P	W	D	L	F	A	Pts
Ivory Coast	2	1	1	0	3	0	3
Congo	2	0	2	0	1	1	2
Algeria	2	0	1	1	1	4	1

Group D

	P	W	D	L	F	A	Pts
Ghana	2	2	0	0	2	0	4
Zambia	2	1	0	1	1	1	2
Egypt	2	0	0	2	0	2	0

Quarter-finals
Nigeria 1, Zaire 0
Senegal 0, Cameroon 1
Zambia 0, Ivory Coast 1
Congo 1, Ghana 2

Semi-finals
Ghana 2, Nigeria 1
Cameroon 0, Ivory Coast 0

Third/Fourth place
Cameroon 1, Nigeria 2

Final
Ivory Coast 0, Ghana 0 *aet*
Ivory Coast won 11-10 on penalties

African Champions Cup Final:
Club Africain 6,1, Nakivubo Sports Villa 2,1

East and Central African Cup Final:
Zambia 2, Kenya 0

FOOTBALL AND THE LAW

Football and the law now appear to be as inseparable as Gilbert and Sullivan, with comparable elements of tragi-comedy. They have travelled together for some time since I was advised by senior administrators about a decade ago:

"You lawyers keep out. We can take care of the game without your interference". Well, to paraphrase the song title, 'What a difference a decade makes'.

Last season ended as it began, with the FA in the commercial courts for the second time in 12 months. The first occasion which heralded last season's massive move to end a century-old structure was the FA's battle with the Football League to establish its Premier League. This time ITV sued the FA and the 22 Premier League clubs for alleged breach of confidence by the Premier League, claiming that BSkyB had been tipped off about a new ITV bid for televising the new formation's matches. Mr. Justice Ferris in London's High Court refused to grant an interim injunction to ITV which will now be substituted by a damages claim, linked to a renewal of the restraining claim.

The players, too, have been forced to court. A part-time non-Football League 19 year-old suffered a broken leg from a foul tackle. He sued in the Teeside Crown court and four years later (which is about the time taken generally for serious civil claims to be heard) at the age of 23 received last season £10,000 damages and costs against his opponent, who was doubtless insured. It was made up from £6,000 for pain and suffering and loss of amenity and £4,000 for loss of earning capacity as he was crippled from following his ordinary work.

More publicised was the referee's award of a foul against Torquay United's John Uzzell committed by Brentford's Gary Blissett. This has resulted in a police investigation and the charge of a serious assault which the Crown Prosecution Service has now persuaded local justices in Devon should be tried before a judge and jury in a Crown Court.

No less publicised was the decision of the French authorities to charge the Soccer Federation President, Jean Fournet-Fayard with manslaughter after 15 spectators died and 750 were injured when a temporary stand collapsed in Bastia on May 5: a circumstance similar to the 1902 Ibrox disaster for which, so far as I have been able to trace, no legal proceedings were instituted.

Parliament still has to make up its mind how to operate and create the laws required for the Taylor Report, and FIFA and the International Football Board have tinkered with the playing laws by outlawing the 'back-pass'.

If the English hierarchy had not been so dismissive in by-passing the lawyers a decade ago it is at least arguable that if the dribbling ball player had not been destroyed by the sustained brutal foul play in the Football League system, *football* as distinct from *beefball* could still have survived for the national game.

EDWARD GRAYSON

GM VAUXHALL CONFERENCE 1991-92

Without achieving the excitement which occurred on the last day of the previous season, only goal difference separated Colchester United the champions from Wycombe Wanderers who finished runners-up. Colchester thus returned to the Football League two years after losing their status.

For many weeks of the campaign, these two clubs were given a hard fight of it by Farnborough, thanks to their excellent away record which saw them concede only their first point on their ninth trip. Alas Farnborough were never as potent at home and in fact fell away shortly afterwards.

Both Colchester and Wycombe reported excellent attendances and they shared the top ten gates, although the average for the entire competition was slightly down on 1990-91.

GM VAUXHALL CONFERENCE TABLE 1991-92

| | P | Home | | | Goals | | Away | | | Goals | | |
		W	D	L	F	A	W	D	L	F	A	Pts
Colchester United	42	19	1	1	57	11	9	9	3	41	29	94
Wycombe Wanderers	42	18	1	2	49	13	12	3	6	35	22	94
Kettering Town	42	12	6	3	44	23	8	7	6	28	27	73
Merthyr Tydfil	42	14	4	3	40	24	4	10	7	19	32	68
Farnborough Town	42	8	7	6	36	27	10	5	6	32	26	66
Telford United	42	10	4	7	32	31	9	3	9	30	35	64
Redbridge Forest	42	12	4	5	42	27	6	5	10	27	29	63
Boston United	42	10	4	7	40	35	8	5	8	31	31	63
Bath City	42	8	6	7	27	22	8	6	7	27	29	60
Witton Albion	42	11	6	4	41	26	5	4	12	22	34	58
Northwich Victoria	42	10	4	7	40	25	6	2	13	23	33	54
Welling United	42	8	6	7	40	38	6	6	9	29	41	54
Macclesfield Town	42	7	7	7	25	21	6	6	9	25	29	52
Gateshead	42	8	5	8	22	22	4	7	10	27	35	48
Yeovil Town	42	8	6	7	22	21	3	8	10	18	28	47
Runcorn	42	5	11	5	26	26	6	2	13	24	37	46
Stafford Rangers	42	7	8	6	25	24	3	8	10	16	35	46
Altrincham	42	5	8	8	33	39	6	4	11	28	43	45
Kidderminster Harriers	42	8	6	7	35	32	4	3	14	21	45	45
Slough Town	42	7	3	11	26	39	6	3	12	30	43	45
Cheltenham Town	42	8	5	8	28	35	2	8	11	28	47	43
Barrow	42	5	8	8	29	23	3	6	12	23	49	38

GM VAUXHALL CONFERENCE ATTENDANCES 1991-92

Aggregate 1991-92	Average Gate	% Increase	Gates over 1000	Gates over 2000	Clubs with % Increase
564,045	1221	-14%	41%	14.5%	7

ATTENDANCES BY CLUB 1991-92

Club	Aggregate Attendance 1991-92	Average Gate 1991-92	% Change	Average Gate 1990-91	Gates over 1000
Wycombe Wanderers	75,726	3606	+29	2794	21
Colchester United	73,811	3514	+17	3003	21
Yeovil Town	44,171	2103	-20	2634	21
Kettering Town	38,997	1857	-28	2563	21
Kidderminster Harriers	27,361	1302	+ 9	1197	19
Barrow	26,297	1252	-12	1427	21
Boston United	24,636	1173	-15	1372	12
Telford United	21,826	1039	-12	1186	11
Farnborough Town	20,485	975	+58	616	4
Slough Town	19,416	924	-21	1168	2
Witton Albion	19,182	913	+10	829	4
Cheltenham Town	18,591	885	-14	1029	6
Stafford Rangers	18,342	873	-26	1174	5
Altrincham	18,241	868	-37	1385	5
Welling United	17,648	840	-15	985	3
Northwich Victoria	17,228	820	+10	748	4
Macclesfield Town	15,866	755	-25	1001	3
Redbridge Forest	15,116	719	+114	336	2
Bath City	14,785	704	-20	883	3
Merthyr Tydfil	13,658	650	-21	824	2
Runcorn	13,219	629	-14	729	0
Gateshead	9443	449	-23	586	0

HIGHEST ATTENDANCES 1991-92

7193	Colchester United v Barrow	2.5.92	5083	Colchester United v Wycombe Wanderers	7.12.91
6303	Colchester United v Kettering Town	28.4.92	4773	Colchester United v Redbridge Forest	1.1.92
6035	Wycombe Wanderers v Witton Albion	2.5.92	4283	Wycombe Wanderers v Telford United	12.10.91
5184	Wycombe Wanderers v Colchester United	28.9.91	4263	Wycombe Wanderers v Bath City	20.4.92
5162	Wycombe Wanderers v Slough Town	1.1.92	4148	Colchester United v Merthyr Tydfil	20.4.92

GM VAUXHALL CONFERENCE LEADING GOALSCORERS 1991–92

GMVC			FA	BL	FT
29	Paul Cavell (Redbridge Forest)	+	1	1	2
	Terry Robbins (Welling United)	+	—	—	1
27	Gary Jones (Boston United)	+	2	1	1
26	Roy McDonough (Colchester United)	+	1	—	2
21	Simon Read (Farnborough Town)	+	9	2	3
	Karl Thomas (Witton Albion)	+	3	1	4
20	Steve McGavin (Colchester United)	+	2	2	4
	Dave Webley (Merthyr Tydfil)	+	—	—	—
19	Gary Abbott (Welling United)	+	5	—	1
	Ken McKenna (Altrincham)	+	—	1	—
	Malcolm O'Connor (Northwich Victoria)	+	—	2	1
	Paul Randall (Bath City)	+	3	2	1
18	Jon Graham (Kettering Town)	+	3	—	—
	Keith Scott (Wycombe Wanderers)	+	—	1	1
16	Gary Bennett (Colchester United)	+	—	—	2
	Richard Hill (Kettering Town)	+	1	—	2
	Mickey Spencer (Yeovil Town)	+	1	3	4
	Ceri Williams (Merthyr Tydfil)	+	1	1	1

FA: FA Cup. *BL:* Bob Lord Trophy. *FT:* FA Challenge Trophy.

SPONSORSHIP AWARDS 1991–92

	Vauxhall Motors Sponsorship	Vauxhall Goals Jackpot	Title Award	Sportscast	PPA	Bob Lord Trophy	Fairplay Award	Total
Colchester United	6000	1500	8000	1500	3000	—	—	20,000
Wycombe Wanderers	6000	—	4000	1500	3000	3000	—	17,500
Kettering Town	6000	—	3000	1500	3000	—	—	13,500
Farnborough Town	6000	—	—	1500	3000	—	3000	13,500
Runcorn	6000	—	—	1500	3000	1500	—	12,000
Redbridge Forest	6000	1000	—	1500	3000	—	—	11,500
Northwich Victoria	6000	500	—	1500	3000	—	—	11,000
Slough Town	6000	500	—	1500	3000	—	—	11,000
Welling United	6000	500	—	1500	3000	—	—	11,000
Altrincham	6000	—	—	1500	3000	500	—	11,000
Yeovil Town	6000	—	—	1500	3000	500	—	11,000
Barrow	6000	—	—	1500	3000	—	—	10,500
Bath City	6000	—	—	1500	3000	—	—	10,500
Boston United	6000	—	—	1500	3000	—	—	10,500
Cheltenham Town	6000	—	—	1500	3000	—	—	10,500
Gateshead	6000	—	—	1500	3000	—	—	10,500
Kidderminster Harriers	6000	—	—	1500	3000	—	—	10,500
Macclesfield Town	6000	—	—	1500	3000	—	—	10,500
Merthyr Tydfil	6000	—	—	1500	3000	—	—	10,500
Stafford Rangers	6000	—	—	1500	3000	—	—	10,500
Telford United	6000	—	—	1500	3000	—	—	10,500
Witton Albion	6000	—	—	1500	3000	—	—	10,500

HIGHEST SCORERS

5 Gary Abbott *WELLING UNITED* v Alvechurch (FA Cup Fourth Qualifying Round 26.10.91)
4 Dennis Greene *WYCOMBE WANDERERS* v Altrincham (GM Vauxhall Conference 11.4.92)
Terry Robbins *WELLING UNITED* v Northwich Victoria (GM Vauxhall Conference 26.2.92)
Paul Cavell *REDBRIDGE FOREST* v Cheltenham (GM Vauxhall Conference 29.2.92)
Simon Read *FARNBOROUGH TOWN* v Salisbury (FA Cup Fourth Qualifying Round 26.10.91)
David Leworthy *FARNBOROUGH TOWN* v Macclesfield Town (GM Vauxhall Conference 10.4.92)
Roy McDonough *COLCHESTER UNITED* v Slough (GM Vauxhall Conference 26.8.91)

HIGHEST AGGREGATE SCORES

Altrincham 3-7 Slough Town 19.10.91
Welling United 5-3 Barrow 30.11.91
Kidderminster Harriers 5-3 Gateshead 24.8.91
Macclesfield Town 4-4 Colchester United 25.4.92

LARGEST HOME WINS

Witton Albion 6-0 Stafford Rangers 8.2.92
Wycombe Wanderers 6-1 Telford United 12.10.91
Barrow 6-1 Welling United 28.9.91
Northwich Victoria 6-1 Barrow 24.9.91
Welling United 6-1 Northwich Victoria 26.2.92

LARGEST AWAY WINS

Cheltenham Town 0-7 Redbridge Forest 29.2.92
Redbridge Forest 0-5 Wycombe Wanderers 30.4.92
Slough Town 0-5 Farnborough Town 20.4.92
Welling United 0-5 Bath City 21.3.92

MATCHES WITHOUT DEFEAT

15 Colchester United
12 Colchester United
10 Bath City, Kettering Town, Merthyr Tydfil
9 Redbridge Forest, Stafford Rangers
8 Farnborough Town, Gateshead, Macclesfield Town, Redbridge Forest, Kettering Town

MATCHES WITHOUT A WIN

14 Slough Town
11 Cheltenham Town, Kidderminster Harriers, Redbridge Forest, Witton Albion
10 Yeovil Town
9 Macclesfield Town, Altrincham

CONSECUTIVE CONFERENCE WINS

7 Redbridge Forest, Wycombe Wanderers (twice)
6 Colchester United
5 Telford United, Kettering Town, Colchester United

CONSECUTIVE CONFERENCE DEFEATS

9 Altrincham
6 Slough Town
5 Cheltenham Town, Redbridge Forest, Witton Albion
4 Telford United, Northwich Victoria, Kidderminster Harriers, Farnborough Town, Boston United, Barrow

GM VAUXHALL CONFERENCE 1991–92

APPEARANCES AND GOALSCORERS

ALTRINCHAM
League Appearances: Anderson, G. 31; Berryman, S. 11; Brady, J. 18(3); Burns, P. 8(4); Carter, M. 2(1); Chilton, T. 4; Davies, M. 4; Daws, N. 39(2); Densmore, P. 34(2); Edwards, T. 35(1); Gresly, S. (1); Hayde, M. 9(3); Hughes, M. 9(3); Kilshaw, B. 3(3); Lee, A. 29; Lewis, M. 23(2); McDonald, A. 10(4); Wiggins, H. 24(3); McKenna, K. 35; Miller, T. 1; Reid, A. 33; Roberts, S. 6; Rowlands, P. 22(1); Rudge, S. 20(5); Shaw, N. 24(3); Worrall, S. (1); Wealands, J. 20.
Goals (60): McKenna 19, Anderson 10, Shaw 10, Daws 4, Brady 4, Edwards 2, Lewis 2, McDonald 2, Burns 2, Hughes 2, Reid 1, Rudge 1, Rowlands 1.

BARROW
League Appearances: Atkinson, P. 19(11); Ballantyne, M. 9; Brady, J. 15; Brown, M. 9(7); Burgess, D. 4(8); Campbell, P. (5); Chilton, T. 21; Cowperthwaite, C. 15(1); Doherty, N. 41; Doolan, P. 22(1); Gilmour, B. 2(5); Kelly, N. 21; Knox, S. 13(5); Messenger, G. 32; McDonnell, P. 42; McHugh, S. 7; McNall, K. 18; McPhillips, T. 5; Nolan, D. 7(3); Power, P. 17(1); Proctor, K. 21(2); Rowlands, P. 15; Rutter, M. 5(7); Skivington, G. 32; Slater, P. 36(1); Todhunter, S. 16; Wheatley, D. 18.
Goals (52): Brady 11, Doherty 7, McNall 5, Wheatley 4, Atkinson 3, Brown 3, Cowperthwaite 3, Messenger 3, Rowlands 3, Ballantyne 2, Proctor 2, Slater 2, Gilmore 1, Power 1, own goals 2.

BATH CITY
League Appearances: Bailey, P. 1; Banks, C. 39; Boyle, M. 40; Brown, K. 3; Churchward, A. 31; Cousins, R. 31; Crowley, R. 36; Dick, G. 22; Gill, J. 21; Hedges, I. 40; Hirons, P. 2; Kean, S. 10; Lundon, S. 17; Mings, A. 24; Painter, S. 1; Payne, D. 2; Preston, J. 11; Radford, D. 6; Randall, P. 41; Ricketts, A. 28; Singleton, D. 35; Theobald, A. 2; Weston, I. 25; Withey, G. 39.
Goals (53): Randall 19, Boyle 10, Withey 6, Cousins 3, Hedges 3, Crowley 2, Brown 2, Banks 2, Mings 2, Gill 1, Kean 1, Singleton 1, Weston 1.

BOSTON UNITED
League Appearances: Adams, S. 35; Casey, P. 34; Cavell, P. 11; Collins, S. 38; Hardy, M. 34; Howarth, L. 10; Jones, G. 41; Lamont, L. 1; McGinley, J. 12; McKenna, J. 41; Moore, A. 20; Myles, S. 3; Nesbitt, M. 12; North, M. 1; Nuttell, M. 18; Rafell, S. 22; Retallick, G. 7; Richardson, P. 9; Shirtliff, P. 37; Stoutt, S. 33; Swailes, C. 28; Toone, R. 8.
Goals (68): Jones 27, Nuttell 8, Cavell 7, Stoutt 6, McGinley 5, Hardy 4, Nesbitt 3, Toone 2, Moore 1, Adams 1, Casey 1, Swailes 1, Fletcher 1, North 1.

CHELTENHAM TOWN
League Appearances: Barrett, M. 11; Bloomfield, P. 13(12); Brogan, P. 22(1); Brooks, S. 35; Buckland, M. 29(2); Butler, D. 10; Casey, K. 23; Clark, R. 9; Coates, M. 6; Davies, M. 6; Evans, P. 3; Fox, M. 4; Fry, M. 3; Gansal, M. 2; Gayle, M. 3; Henry, C. 5(2); Horlick, A. (2); Hoult, R. 3; Howells, L. 26; Jordan, N. 8; Lange, T. 6; Livingstone, G. 3; Masefield, P. 7; Matthews, W. 5; Mortimore, P. (2); Nicholls, A. 11; Olson, M. 2; Owen, S. 24; Perrett, D. 11(6); Phillips, S. 1; Powell, B. (1); Purdie, J. 26; Reck, S. 9(3); Smith, J. 15; Smith, N. 17(1); Stobart, L. 16(1); Teggart, D. 6(3); Tester, P. 5(1); Turnbull, P. (3); Willetts, J. (1); Vircavs, A. 34; Warren, C. 1(3); Willetts, K. 40; Wring, J. 4(4).
Goals (56): Willetts 9, Buckland 7, Purdie 7, Smith 6, Brooks 5, Casey 4, Perrett 3, Vircavs 3, Howells 2, Owen 2, Clark 1, Coates 1, Evans 1, Jordan 1, Smith 1, Stobart 1, Turnbull 1, own goal 1.

COLCHESTER UNITED
League Appearances: Abrahams, P. 7; Barrett, S. 42; Bennett, G. 39; Cook, J. 36; Collins, E. 33; Donald, W. 41; Elliott, S. 37; English, T. 38; Goodwin, J. 7; Grainger,
M. 18; Gray, S. 2; Kinsella, M. 42; Martin, D. 9; Masters, M. 15; McDonough, R. 40; McGavin, S. 39; Phillips, I. 6; Restarick, S. 12; Roberts, P. 31; Smith, N. 42; Stewart, I. 10; Walsh, M. 1.
Goals (98): McDonough 26, McGavin 20, Bennett 16, Smith 8, Masters 7, English 6, Kinsella 3, Cook 2, Collins 2, Stewart 2, Barrett 1, Roberts 1, Martin 1, Elliott 1, own goals 2.

FARNBOROUGH TOWN
League Appearances: Baker, K. 35(2); Baker, S. 16; Batey 9; Broome 35(1); Bye 37; Cockram 3(1); Coleman 10; Coles 2(2); Comfort 6(1); Coney 20; Cooper 4; Coombs 8(3); Dalton 9; Doherty 17(3); Fleming 16(7); Hobson 3; Holmes 37(3); Horton 28(10); Hucker 11; Leworthy 19; Lovell 3(5); Power 21; Read 34(2); Rogers 17(4); Stemp, W. 17; Stevens 1(2); Thompson 1; Turkington 7(4); Wigmore 36(2).
Goals (67): Read 21, Leworthy 12, Coney 6, Doherty 5, Holmes 4, Broome 4, Coombs 4, Horton 3, Bye 3, Wigmore 1, Cochram 1, Comfort 1, Cooper 1, Rogers 1.

GATESHEAD
League Appearances: Askew, B. 4; Bell, D. 40; Brabin, G. (2); Butler, C. 21(12); Chambers, S. 10; Corner, D. 35; Cuthbert, S. 10(2); Davies, K. 2(1); Dixon, A. 5; Dixon, K. 9(2); Emson, P. 2(2); Farrey, M. 30(3); Forrest, G. 32(2); Gourlay, A. 2; Granycome, N. 22(2); Grayson, N. 14; Guthrie, S. 4; Halliday, B. 28; Healey, B. 14; Higgins, S. 13; Hopkinson, L. (1); Johnson, I. 7(1); Lamb, A. 26; Leishman, G. 5; Linacre, P. 11(6); Lowery, T. 8; McInerney, I. 2; O'Brien, S. 11(2); Peverell, N. 2(2); Saddington, N. 17; Scope, D. 2; Smith, S. 42; Veart, C. 27(7); Wharton, K. 1; Wheatley, D. 3(5).
Goals (49): Lamb 14, Cuthbert 4, Corner 4, Linacre 4, Butler 4, Grayson 3, Dixon 3, Healey 2, Chambers 2, Veart 1, Halliday 1, Gourlay 1, Dixon, A. 1, Guthrie 1, Emson 1, Granycome 1, Bell 1, Forrest 1.

KETTERING TOWN
League Appearances: Appleby (1); Bancroft 28(3); Barker 4; Bastock 24; Bloodworth 9(2); Brown 38(2); Butterworth 8; Christie 19(1); Cotton 4(2); Cox 1; Culpin 4; Curtis 17; Emson 2(1); Gavin 15; Graham 30(7); Hill 40(2); Howarth 6; Huxford 42; Jones 15(3); Keast 26(7); Nicol 41; North 5(2); Price 18; Shoemake 18; Slack 36(2); Walker 5; Waller 2(3); Walsh 5.
Goals (72): Graham 18, Hill 16, Brown 12, North 7, Christie 5, Gavin 3, Bancroft 3, Nicol 2, Emson 1, Walker 1, Keast 1, Slack 1, Butterworth 1, own goals 2.

KIDDERMINSTER HARRIERS
League Appearances: Barnett, D. 20; Benton, D. 39; Bradley, P. 1; Carroll, M. 6; Coogan, M. 1; Davies, P. 33; Davis, M. 4; Forsyth, R. 15; Grainger, P. 8; Gillett, C. 13; Green, R. 40; Hackett, B. 4; Hadley, D. 17; Hanson, J. 6; Howell, P. 32; Joseph, A. 37; Kurila, A. 6; Lilwall, S. 28; Mackenzie, G. 11; McGrath, J. 35; Mulholland, D. 5; Steadman, D. 2; Taylor, J. 2; Weir, M. 37; Whitehouse, M. 20; Wilcox, B. 32; Wolsey, M. 10.
Goals (55): Whitehouse 10, Howell 9, Humphries 7, Wilcox 5, Davis 4, Grainger 4, Weir 4, Forsyth 3, Lilwall 3, Barnett 2, Benton 1, Joseph 1, Kurila 1, Hadley 1.

MACCLESFIELD TOWN
League Appearances: Ashey, J. 33; Binson, S. 11(2); Boughty, D. 2(3); Clayton, P. 10(22); Dawson, J. 5(14); Doherty, M. 14(2); Dumpsey, M. 32(2); Edwards, E. 38(1); Ellis, R. 15(14); Farrelly, M. 25(3); Farrelly, S. 38; Green, A. 25(1); Hamlon, S. 38; Heesom, D. 11; Hopley, A. 2(4); Imrie, J. 1(1); Johnson, P. 33(1); Kendall, P. 13(2); Lambert, C. 39(2); Miller, I. 2; Rutter, M. 1; Shepherd, G. 31(1); Timmons, T. 31(6); Tobin, S. 8(1); Zelch, A. 4(1).
Goals (47): Lambert 9, Green 7, Doherty 6, Askey 5, Timmons 4, Edwards 3, Bimson 2, Ellis 2, Hopley 2, Hanlon 2, Farrelly 1, Johnson 1, Dumpsey 1, Dawson 1, Clayton 1.

MERTHYR TYDFIL

League Appearances: Abraham, G. 8; Beatty, A. 35(6); Boyle, P. 41; Chiverton, E. 3(12); Coates, M. 7(3); Dauria, D. 31(7); Davey, S. 6(2); Evans, P. 7(4); Fingelly, M. (1); Hemming, C. 10; Hutchison, T. 29(11); James, R. 36; Lewis, R. 23(1); Morgan, J. 1(2); Rogers, K. 27(7); Sherwood, G. 8(5); Thomas, C. (1); Thompson, I. 6(1); Tucker, M. 32(6); Wager, G. 31; Webley, D. 36(4); Williams, C. 37(2); Williams, M. 36(2); Withers, D. 1(7); Wood, G. 11.

Goals (59): Webley 20, Williams 16, Rogers 5, Dauria 5, Tucker 4, Boyle 2, Hutchison 2, Coates 1, Thompson 1, Davey 1, Chiverton 1, Williams 1.

NORTHWICH VICTORIA

League Appearances: Ainsworth, G. 14; Ball, T. 8; Berryman, S. 12; Blain, C. 23(1); Blundell, C. 36; Bullock, T. 22; Butler, B. 34(1); Buxton, S. (1); Donnelly, P. 6(1); Easter, G. 14(1); Edmonson, B. 4(1); Feeley, A. 13; Graham, A. 13(7); Gresly, S. (3); Hackett, L. 1; Hancock, M. 32; Hancock, T. 2; Hemmings, A. 34(5); Holland, S. 7(3); Jones, M. 41; Lanton, D. 2(3); Locke, S. 42; McCormick, M. 5; McIlroy, S. 7; O'Connor, M. 40; O'Gorman, D. 7(1); Stringer, J. 19(1); Wrench, M. 1; Vaughn, G. 22(4).

Goals (63): O'Connor 19, Hemmings 12, Stringer 6, Blain 4, Ainsworth 4, Butler 3, Easter 3, Graham 3, Holland 2, O'Gorman 2, Blundell 1, Edmonson 1, Feeley 1.

REDBRIDGE FOREST

League Appearances: Ashford, N. 9(5); Barrett, K. 10(2); Bennett, I. 18(2); Blackford, G. 21; Broom, J. 19(8); Cavell, P. 28; Cawston, M. (2); Cherry, R. 6(4); Cole, M. 1(4); Conner, S. 42; Davidson, K. 6(16); Docker, I. 6(9); Ebdon, M. 23; Foster, K. 9; Fulling, L. 1(1); Garvey, R. 11(5); Grice, N. 4(2); Hayrettin, H. 5; Hessenthaler, A. 3; Hucker, P. 6; Hopping, A. 1; Jackman, P. 8(1); Jacques, D. 33(2); Mayes, B. 32(3); Owers, A. 7(4); Pamphlett, T. 39; Richardson, P. 27(1); Riley, D. 5; Scott, L. 3; Sowerby, C. 8(3); Shoemake, K. 3; Sullivan, T. (2); Taylor, P. 1(1); Walsh, M. 30(6); Watts, P. 40.

Goals (76): Cavell 29, Walsh 9, Ebdon 7, Mayes 5, Pamphlett 4, Connor 3, Richardson 3, Broom 2, Blackford 2, Riley 2, Garvey 2, Watts 2, Cherry 1, Grice 1, Hessenthaler 1, Hayrettin 1, Sowerby 1.

RUNCORN

League Appearances: Abrahams (5); Bates 31; Brabin 31; Brady 7(3); Byrne 19(1); Carroll 20; Carter 1; Diggle 1(2); Disley 2; Hagan 1(1); Hanchard 5; Harold 32; Hawtin 9(5); Henshaw 7(6); Hill 36; Hughes 2; Imrie 4(1); King (1); Lundon 11(5); McCarty 24; Mullen 36; Palladino 16; Redman 18(7); Richards 14(7); Rigby (2); Routledge 2; Saunders 35; Shaughnessy 37(4); Varden (6); Waring (6); Wall 10; Wellings 9(7); Williams 24; Withers 24(14).

Goals (50): Saunders 12, McCarty 9, Brabin 3, Withers 3, Hill 2, Lundon 2, Redman 2, Abrahams 1, Brady 1, Carroll 1, Disley 1, Hanchard 1, Shaughnessy 1, Wall 1, Wellings 1.

SLOUGH TOWN

League Appearances: Anderson, D. 37; Booker, T. 4; Bunting, T. 27; Burns, P. 3; Dell, T. 5; Donellan, G. 27; Fielder, C. 38; Hemsley, S. 12; Helsley, S. 8; Hickey, S. 8; Knight, T. 22; Joseph, F. 5; Lynch, T. 1; Mallinson, M. 30; McKinnon, P. 35; Moussadick 3; O'Connor, E. 20; Pluckrose, A. 36; Putnam, M. 8; Rake, B. 1; Scott, S. 14; Sitton, J. 4; Sharp, J. 33; Stanley, N. 28; Thompson, S. 23; Turkington 10; Watkiss, R. 9; Whitby, S. 23.

Goals (56): McKinnon 15, Thompson 10, Anderson 8, Pluckrose 6, Donnellan 4, O'Connor 3, Joseph 2, Scott 2, Stanley 2, Mallinson 1, Stacey 1, Turkington 1, og 1.

STAFFORD RANGERS

League Appearances: Anastasi 4(1); Baker (2); Berry 7; Berks, J. 2(1); Berks, P. 11(5); Booth 7(1); Boyle 3; Bradshaw 35; Bremner 7; Brough 5; Brown 5(1); Butterworth 1; Callaghan 7; Dawson 8(1); Devlin 26; Edwards 7; Essex 37; Foreman 10; Harle 5; Harmon 4;

Heggs 4; Hemming 22; Hodkinson 3; Hollier 1; Hope 8(10); Jones 9; Lindsey 8(3); Miller 12(1); Mower 2; Newman 3(3); Palgrave 15(2); Pearson 27(4); Price 42; Roberts 1; Rooney 5(1); Simpson 39; Straw 1(3); Tuohy 12; Wareing (3); Wells 6(1); Whitehouse 1(1); Wilson 5; Withe 2; Wolverson 6; Wood 38(1).

Goals (41): Simpson 6, Foreman 5, Devlin 3, Edwards 3, Wood 3, Winterson 2, Tuohy 2, Palgrave 2, Bradshaw 2, Berks, P. 1, Berry 1, Booth 1, Dawson 1, Essex 1, Heggs 1, Hodkinson 1, Hope 1, Miller 1, Withe 1, og 3.

TELFORD UNITED

League Appearances: Acton, D. 37; Alleyne, R. 7(2); Amos 1(1); Benbow, I. 34(1); Brindley, C. 39; Brown 6(3); Burke 2; Carr 1; Charlton 1; Clarke, S. 20(4); Cooke 3(8); Culpin 1; Downes 1; Duffy 1(1); Dyson 36; Fergusson, S. 23; Fitzpatrick 1(1); Forsythe, R. 9; Garrett, A. 5(4); Gilman, S. 8(1); Grainger 27; Hackett 7(2); Hughes 1; Humphries, J. 30(4); Langford, T. 35(2); Myers, M. 38; Nelson 33; Parrish 15(1); Perks 1; Robinson 1; Ross 3; Ryan 1; Whitehouse 4; Withe, J. 5(6); Whittington 25; Worral 4(5).

Goals (75): Benbow 19, Langford 17, Myers 10, Brindley 6, Dyson 5, Whittington 5, Fergusson 3, Clarke 3, Culpin 2, Alleyne 1, Brown 1, Cooke 1, Parrish 1, Ross 1.

WELLING UNITED

League Appearances: Abboh, D. 1; Abbott, G. 37; Barron, P. 5; Berry, L. 29; Booker, T. 1(3); Brown, W. 24(7); Burgess, R. 7(2); Clemence, N. 29(7); Francis, J. 23; Golley, M. 26(3); Glover, J. 21; Harrison, L. 7; Hone, M. 32(4); Howell, G. 7; Parsons, J. 1; Ransom, N. 39(1); Reynolds, T. 31(1); Robinson, S. 32(1); Robbins, T. 42; Stapley, G. 2; Sullivan, N. 7; White, S. 39.

Goals (69): Robbins 29, Abbott 19, White 4, Ransom 3, Brown 3, Golley 2, Hone 1, Reynolds 1, Clemence 1, Francis 1, Glover 1, Howell 1.

WITTON ALBION

League Appearances: Anderson, S. 30(1); Alford, C. 15(5); Burndred, J. 3; Coathup, L. 25(4); Jim Connor 31(10); Joe Connor 26(2); Cuddy, P. 12(1); Dyson, C. 1(3); Edwards, M. 2(6); Ellis, S. 4(1); Fuller, D. 3; Grimshaw, A. 34; Halliday, M. 17; Heesom, D. 12(1); Hill, J. 9; Hooton, R. 8(1); Hughes, M. 11(1); Hughes, T. 1; Jackson, M. 1; Jarvis, T. (1); Lodge, P. 4; Lutkevitch, M. 20(1); Mason, K. 35; McCluskie, J. 20(10); McDonald, A. 3; McNeilis, S. 39; Morgan, D. 7; Newell, A. 1; Paladino, J. 3; Rose, C. 13; Stewart, G. 29(5); Thomas, K. 34(1); Wilson, P. 5(3); Zelem, A. 3.

Goals (63): Thomas 21, McCluskie 9, Joe Connor 6, Stewart 5, Anderson 5, Alford 4, Grimshaw 3, Lutkevitch 3, McNeilis 2, Jim Connor 1, Ellis 1, Hill 1, Hughes 1, Rose 1.

WYCOMBE WANDERERS

League Appearances: Carroll, D. 37; Case, K. 9(5); Civington, G. 3; Cooper, G. 4(3); Cousins, J. 40; Creaser, G. 42; Crossman, M. 27(1); Deakin, J. 8(5); Gooden, T. 1(6); Greene, D. 11(5); Guppy, S. 38(1); Hutchinson, S. 12(12); Hyde, P. 42; Jackson, P. 7; Kerr, A. 34; Nuttell, M. 9(1); Ryan, K. 10(3); Scott, K. 32(10); Smith, G. 24(2); Stapleton, S. 39; Thompson, S. 11; Walford, S. 6; West, M. 20(3).

Goals (80): Scott 18, Greene 10, West 9, Guppy 7, Nuttell 6, Stapleton 5, Carroll 4, Casey 4, Creaser 4, Hutchinson 4, Kerr 3, Smith 2, Cousins 1, Crossley 1, Ryan 1, Thompson 1.

YEOVIL TOWN

League Appearances: Batty, P. 27(8); Boulton, M. 2(6); Carroll, R. 28(4); Coles, D. 25; Conning, P. 37(1); Cooper, R. 22(6); Dixon, L. (3); Ferns, P. 26(1); Flory, N. 1; Fry, D. 11; Henderson, D. 2(2); Hervin, M. 6; Harrower, S. 37; McDermott, B. 29(4); McEvoy, M. 8(5); Pritchard, H. 8(5); Robinson, D. 14; Rowbotham, J. 5; Rowland, A. 4; Rutter, S. 36(1); Shail, M. 40; Sivell, S. 2; Spencer, M. 39(1); Wallace, A. 32; Wilson, P. 21(1).

Goals (40): Spencer 16, Carroll 6, McDermott 4, Robinson 3, Wallace 3, Boulton 2, Pritchard 2, Conning 1, Rutter 1, Shail 1, Wilson 1.

GM VAUXHALL CONFERENCE: MEMBER CLUBS SEASON 1992–1993

Club: ALTRINCHAM
Colours: Red and black striped shirts, black shorts
Ground: Moss Lane, Altrincham, Cheshire WA15 8AP
Tel: 061-928 1045
Year Formed: 1903
Record Gate: 10,275 (1925 v Sunderland Boys)
Nickname: The Robins
Manager: Gerry Quinn
Secretary: Jean Baldwin

Club: BATH CITY
Colours: Black and white striped shirts, black shorts
Ground: Twerton Park, Bath BA2 1DB
Telephone: 0225 423087 and 313247
Year Formed: 1889
Record Gate: 18,020 (1960 v Brighton)
Nickname: City
Manager: Tony Ricketts
Secretary: Paul Britton

Club: BOSTON UNITED
Colours: Wolves gold shirts, black shorts
Ground: York Street Ground, York Street, Boston, Lincs
Tel: 0205 365524/5
Year Formed: 1934
Record Gate: 10,086 (v Corby Town)
Nickname: The Pilgrims
Manager: Dave Cusack
Secretary: John Blackwell

Club: BROMSGROVE ROVERS
Colours: Green and white striped shirts, black shorts
Ground: Victoria Ground, Birmingham Road, Bromsgrove, Worcs. B61 0DR
Tel: 0527 78260
Year Formed: 1885
Record Gate: 7563 (1957-58 v Worcester City)
Nickname: Rovers
Manager: Bobby Hope
Secretary: B. A. Hewings

Club: DAGENHAM & REDBRIDGE
Colours: Red/blue stripe shirts, royal blue shorts
Ground: Victoria Road Ground, Victoria Road, Dagenham, Essex RM10 7XL
Tel: 081-592 7194, 081-593 3864
Year formed: 1992
Record gate: 2891 (1992 v Wycombe Wanderers)
Nickname: The Stones or The Fords
Manager: John Still
Secretary: K. H. Mizen

Club: FARNBOROUGH TOWN
Colours: Yellow and blue shirts, blue shorts
Ground: John Roberts Ground, Cherrywood Road, Farnborough, Hants GU14 8UD
Tel: 0252 541469
Year Formed: 1967
Record Gate: 3000 (1977 v Billericay T)
Nickname: The Boro
Manager: Ted Pearce
Secretary: Terry Parr

Club: GATESHEAD
Colours: White shirts, black shorts
Ground: International Stadium, Neilson Road, Gateshead NE10 0EF
Telephone: 091-487 7661
Year Formed: 1977 (Reformed)
Record Gate: 20,752 (1937 v Lincoln C)
Nickname: Tynesiders
Manager: Tommy Cassidy
Secretary: Clare Tierney

Club: KETTERING TOWN
Colours: Red and black shirts, black shorts
Ground: Rockingham Road, Kettering, Northants NN16 9AW
Tel: 0536 83028/410815
Year Formed: 1875
Record Gate: 11,536 (1947 v Peterborough)
Nickname: The Poppies
Manager: David Cusack
Secretary: George Ellitson

Club: KIDDERMINSTER HARRIERS
Colours: Red and white shirts, red shorts
Ground: Aggborough, Hoo Road, Kidderminster
Tel: 0562 823931
Year Formed: 1886
Record Gate: 9155 (1948 v Hereford)
Nickname: The Harriers
Manager: Graham Allner
Secretary: Ray Mercer

Club: MACCLESFIELD TOWN
Colours: Royal blue shirts, white shorts
Ground: Moss Rose Ground, London Road, Macclesfield, Cheshire SK11 7SP
Tel: 0625 424324
Year Formed: 1875
Record Gate: 8900 (1968 v Stockport Co)
Nickname: The Silkmen
Manager: Peter Wragg
Secretary: Barry Lingard

Club: MERTHYR TYDFIL
Colours: White/silver/black square shirts, black shorts
Ground: Penydarren Park, Merthyr Tydfil
Tel: 0685 384102
Year Formed: 1945
Record Gate: 21,000 (1949 v Reading)
Nickname: The Martyrs
Manager: Wynford Hopkins
Secretary: Phil Dauncey

Club: NORTHWICH VICTORIA
Colours: Green and white shirts, white
shorts
Ground: The Drill Field, Northwich,
Cheshire CW9 5HN
Tel: 0606 41450
Year Formed: 1874
Record Gate: 11,290 (1949 v Witton A)
Nickname: The Vics
Manager: Sammy McIlroy
Secretary: Derek Nuttall

Club: RUNCORN
Colours: Yellow shirts, green shorts
Ground: Canal Street, Runcorn, Cheshire
Tel: 0928 560076
Year Formed: 1919
Record Gate: 10,011 (1939 v Preston NE)
Nickname: The Linnets
Manager: John Carroll
Secretary: George Worrall

Club: SLOUGH TOWN
Colours: Amber and navy broad hoops,
navy blue shorts
Ground: Wexham Park Stadium,
Wexham Road, Slough SL2 5QR
Tel: 0753 523358
Year Formed: 1890
Record Gate: 8940 (1953 v Pegasus at
Dolphin Stadium); 5000 (1982 v
Millwall at Wexham Stadium)
Nickname: The Rebels
Manager:
Secretary: V. J. McCulloch

Club: STAFFORD RANGERS
Colours: Black and white shirts, white
shorts
Ground: Marston Road, Stafford ST16
3BX
Tel: 0785 42750
Year Formed: 1876
Record Gate: 8536 (1975 v Rotherham)
Nickname: The Boro
Manager: Dennis Booth
Secretary: Angela Meddings

Club: STALYBRIDGE CELTIC
Colours: All royal blue
Ground: Bower Ford, Mottram Road,
Stalybridge, Cheshire SK15 2RT
Tel: 061-338 2828
Year Formed: 1911
Record Gate: 9753 (1922–23 v West
Bromwich Albion)
Nickname: Celtic
Manager: Philip Wilson
Secretary: Martyn Torr

Club: TELFORD UNITED
Colours: White shirts, blue shorts
Ground: Bucks Head, Watling Street,
Telford TF1 2NJ
Tel: 0952 223838

Year Formed: 1877
Record Gate: 13,000 (1935 v Shrewsbury)
Nickname: The Lillywhites
Manager: Gerry Daly
Secretary: Mike Ferriday

Club: WELLING UNITED
Colours: Red shirts, red shorts
Ground: Park View Road Ground,
Welling, Kent
Tel: 081-301 1196
Year Formed: 1963
Record Gate: 4020 (1989 v Gillingham)
Nickname: The Wings
Manager: Nicky Brigden
Secretary: Barrie Hobbins

Club: WITTON ALBION
Colours: Red and white striped shirts,
black shorts
Ground: Wincham Park, Chapel Street,
Wincham, Northwich, Cheshire
CW9 6DA
Tel: 0606 43008
Year Formed: 1890
Record Gate: 10,000 (1948 v Northwich
Victoria)
Nickname: The Albion
Manager: Peter O'Brien
Secretary: David Leather

Club: WOKING
Colours: Red shirts, white shorts
Ground: Kingfield Sports Ground,
Kingfield, Woking, Surrey GU22 9AA
Tel: 0483 772470/776126
Year Formed: 1889
Record Gate: 6000 (1978–79 v Swansea)
Nickname: The Cardinals
Manager: Geoff Chapple
Secretary: Phil Ledger, JP

Club: WYCOMBE WANDERERS
Colours: Light blue and dark blue
quarters, navy blue shorts
Ground: Adams Park, Hillbottom Road,
Sands, High Wycombe HP12 4HJ
Tel: 0494 472100
Year Formed: 1884
Record Gate: 16,000 (1950 v St Albans)
Nickname: The Blues
Manager: Martin O'Neill
Secretary: John Goldsworthy

Club: YEOVIL TOWN
Colours: Green/white striped shirts,
white shorts
Ground: Huish Park, Lufton Way, Yeovil
BA22 8YF
Tel: 0935 23663
Year Formed: 1923
Record Gate: 17,200 (1949 v Sunderland)
Nickname: The Glovers
Manager: Steve Rutter
Secretary: Roger Brinsford

GM VAUXHALL CONFERENCE RESULTS 1991–92

(Home \ Away)	Altrincham	Barrow	Bath City	Boston United	Cheltenham Town	Colchester United	Farnborough Town	Gateshead	Kettering Town	Kidderminster Harriers	Macclesfield Town	Merthyr Tydfil	Northwich Victoria	Redbridge Forest	Runcorn	Slough Town	Stafford Rangers	Telford United	Welling United	Witton Albion	Wycombe Wanderers	Yeovil Town
Altrincham	—	1-1	4-0	2-4	0-2	1-1	3-2	2-1	1-1	1-1	1-1	3-1	1-1	0-1	0-3	2-2	3-0	2-3	1-2	2-2	0-4	2-1
Barrow	0-2	—	2-1	4-1	0-0	5-0	5-0	1-1	3-2	1-2	0-1	2-1	6-1	2-2	2-2	1-0	0-0	4-2	5-3	0-1	0-1	0-0
Bath City	3-2	2-1	—	2-0	5-1	0-0	1-2	0-1	0-1	0-1	0-0	1-1	1-0	0-0	2-1	3-1	0-1	1-2	3-2	0-2	1-1	3-1
Boston United	2-1	2-2	1-0	—	1-1	1-1	4-3	2-1	1-3	1-3	0-1	2-0	1-1	1-4	2-2	3-1	3-1	1-2	1-3	1-0	3-0	1-3
Cheltenham Town	0-2	0-0	1-2	1-1	—	1-1	4-3	2-3	3-1	3-0	2-0	1-2	1-0	0-7	4-1	4-0	0-0	2-0	3-2	0-1	3-0	1-1
Colchester United	3-3	5-0	5-0	4-0	4-0	—	2-3	3-1	3-0	2-0	2-0	0-0	1-0	1-0	0-2	4-0	2-0	2-0	3-1	3-1	3-0	4-0
Farnborough Town	3-0	5-0	1-2	5-0	0-0	2-3	—	1-3	1-3	2-1	4-2	0-0	2-4	1-0	2-1	1-1	1-1	0-2	3-1	1-1	1-3	0-0
Gateshead	5-0	1-1	0-1	2-1	0-2	0-3	0-0	—	0-0	0-3	2-0	2-0	2-0	0-1	1-1	2-1	0-0	0-2	1-1	2-1	2-3	1-0
Kettering Town	5-0	3-2	0-1	1-3	3-0	2-1	1-2	2-1	—	2-1	2-0	3-1	1-0	3-2	3-0	2-3	2-1	3-0	1-1	1-1	1-1	2-0
Kidderminster Harriers	1-0	1-2	0-1	1-3	1-2	2-2	1-1	1-3	2-1	—	1-1	2-2	1-0	5-1	3-0	3-3	1-0	1-2	1-3	1-1	1-0	1-1
Macclesfield Town	1-1	0-1	0-0	3-3	4-4	2-2	1-2	1-0	0-0	0-0	—	3-0	1-0	0-0	0-1	0-1	1-0	1-2	1-3	1-0	3-1	1-2
Merthyr Tydfil	3-1	2-1	1-1	3-1	3-1	2-0	1-0	2-1	4-1	2-1	3-2	—	2-1	2-2	2-0	1-2	1-0	2-2	2-1	1-0	1-2	2-2
Northwich Victoria	1-2	6-1	1-3	1-1	1-1	2-1	2-0	1-1	5-0	3-1	2-1	4-1	—	0-2	3-0	3-0	4-3	3-1	2-0	3-1	0-1	1-0
Redbridge Forest	0-1	2-2	3-1	1-4	1-2	4-0	1-1	1-1	5-0	1-1	0-1	1-1	4-3	—	1-2	4-0	1-0	0-2	2-2	0-1	0-5	0-0
Runcorn	2-2	2-2	0-2	2-2	2-3	4-0	1-1	1-1	4-1	0-0	1-1	3-1	3-1	1-2	—	1-0	1-0	1-2	2-2	0-1	1-2	0-2
Slough Town	2-3	1-0	2-2	3-1	1-2	2-4	0-5	2-0	0-2	3-1	0-3	4-0	4-0	4-0	1-0	—	2-2	0-3	2-2	2-1	0-1	2-2
Stafford Rangers	1-2	0-0	2-0	3-1	3-3	3-3	0-1	1-3	3-1	2-0	0-1	0-0	0-1	3-0	1-0	2-2	—	3-2	0-0	2-1	0-2	1-4
Telford United	2-1	4-2	0-2	1-2	0-3	0-1	1-2	1-1	1-2	3-1	1-2	1-2	1-4	3-3	2-1	2-2	4-1	—	0-0	2-1	1-1	0-0
Welling United	2-2	5-3	0-5	1-3	4-1	2-1	1-0	3-2	1-0	3-2	2-1	6-1	1-1	2-2	1-2	0-2	1-1	3-1	—	2-1	1-3	1-0
Witton Albion	2-0	0-1	2-2	1-0	4-2	2-2	4-1	0-3	2-1	2-0	1-1	4-0	1-1	2-0	1-3	2-1	6-0	1-1	2-2	—	1-2	1-0
Wycombe Wanderers	4-2	3-2	1-0	2-1	3-2	0-1	5-3	0-1	2-1	4-0	2-2	3-2	1-1	1-0	1-0	2-1	3-0	6-1	4-0	4-0	—	3-1
Yeovil Town	2-1	2-0	1-1	1-1	1-0	2-1	2-2	1-0	2-1	2-0	1-1	2-1	2-1	2-1	1-4	1-0	0-1	0-2	3-0	2-1	1-0	—

THE BOB LORD CHALLENGE TROPHY 1991–92

First Round *(two legs)*

Bath City 2 *(Randall 2 pens)*
Slough Town 1 *(Hill)* — 404

Slough Town 2 *(Knight, Joseph)*
Bath City 0 — 584

Cheltenham Town 4 *(Willetts (pen), Casey 2, og)*
Kidderminster H. 2 *(Davies, Humphries)* — 675

Kidderminster H. 3 *(Davies, Howell, Whitehouse)*
Cheltenham Town 1 *(Fox)* — 733
aggregate 5–5 Kidderminster win on away goals

Farnborough Town 3 *(Coombs (pen), Read 2)*
Yeovil Town 2 *(Spencer 2)* — 461

Yeovil Town 3 *(Carroll 2, Boulton)*
Farnborough Town 0 — 1473

Gateshead 3 *(Corner, Bell, Butler)*
Witton Albion 0 — 260

Witton Albion 5 *(Thomas, Hill, Lutkevitch, McCluskie 2)*
Gateshead 0 *aet* — 501

Northwich Victoria 2 *(O'Connor 2)*
Stafford Rangers 0 — 501

Stafford Rangers 1 *(Vaughan)*
Northwich Victoria 1 *(Pearson)* — 540

Redbridge Forest 2 *(Conner, Sowerby)*
Boston United 0 — 202

Boston United 4 *(Shirtliff, P. Casey, Cavell, Jones)*
Redbridge Forest 0 — 746

Byes to Second Round

Altrincham, Barrow, Colchester Utd, Kettering Town, Telford Utd, Macclesfield Town, Merthyr Tydfil, Runcorn, Welling Utd, Wycombe Wanderers

Second Round

Altrincham 2 *(Brady 2)*
Barrow 1 *(Doherty)* — 589

Colchester United 4 *(Collins, McGavin, Kinsella 2)*
Kettering Town 0 — 1296

Merthyr Tydfil 1 *(C. Williams)*
Wycombe Wanderers 3 *(Crossley, Hutchinson, Gooden)* — 526

Northwich Victoria 3 *(Butler, Graham 2)*
Boston United 2 *(Nesbitt 2)* — 474

Runcorn 2 *(Redman, Hawtin)*
Witton Albion 2 *aet (McCluskie 2)* — 850

Witton Albion 0
Runcorn 2 *(Withers, McCarty)* — 503

Slough Town 0
Kidderminster H. 1 *(Howell)* — 408

Telford United 1 *(Brindley)*
Macclesfield Town 2 *aet (Dawson, Timmons)* — 597

Yeovil Town 2 *(Batty, Spencer)*
Welling United 0 — 1340
(First game abandoned after 64 minutes due to rain)

Third Round

Colchester United 2 *(Restarick, McGavin)*
Wycombe Wanderers 6 *(Creaser, Hutchinson 2, West 2, Scott)* — 919

Kidderminster H. 1 *(Howell)*
Yeovil Town 2 *(Cooper, Carroll)* — 681

Macclesfield Town 1 *(Green)*
Altrincham 1 *aet (Hughes)* — 447

Altrincham 3 *(Anderson, Daws, McKenna)*
Macclesfield Town 1 *(Askey)* — 524

Runcorn 2 *(Withers, McCarty)*
Northwich Victoria 1 *(Graham)* — 558

Semi-finals *(two legs)*

Runcorn 2 *(Hill, McCarty)*
Altrincham 1 *(Shaw)* — 532

Altrincham 1 *(Lee)*
Runcorn 3 *(Richards, Disley 2)* — 605

Yeovil Town 0
Wycombe Wanderers 0 — 1816

Wycombe Wanderers 2 *(Creaser, Greene)*
Yeovil Town 0 — 1883

Final *(two legs)*

Runcorn 1 *(Saunders)*
Wycombe Wanderers 0 — 853

Wycombe Wanderers 2 *(Carroll, Guppy)*
Runcorn 0 — 2519
Wycombe Wanderers won 2–1 on aggregate

HFS LOANS LEAGUE 1991–92

PREMIER DIVISION

	P	W	D	L	F	A	Pts
Stalybridge Celtic	42	26	14	2	84	33	92
Marine	42	23	9	10	64	32	78
Morecambe	42	21	13	8	70	44	76
Leek Town	42	21	10	11	62	49	73
Buxton	42	21	9	12	65	47	72
Emley	42	18	11	13	69	47	65
Southport	42	16	17	9	57	48	65
Accrington Stanley	42	17	12	13	78	62	63
Hyde United	42	17	9	16	69	67	60
Fleetwood Town	42	17	8	17	67	64	59
Bishop Auckland	42	16	9	17	48	58	57
Goole Town	42	15	9	18	60	72	54
Horwich RMI	42	13	14	15	44	52	53
Frickley Athletic	42	12	16	14	61	57	52
Droylsden	42	12	14	16	62	72	50
Mossley	42	15	4	23	51	73	49
Whitley Bay	42	13	9	20	53	79	48
Gainsborough Trin.	42	11	13	18	48	63	46
Matlock Town	42	12	9	21	59	87	45
Bangor City	42	11	10	21	46	57	43
Chorley	42	11	9	22	61	82	42
Shepshed Albion	42	6	8	28	46	79	26

FIRST DIVISION

	P	W	D	L	F	A	Pts
Colwyn Bay	42	30	4	8	99	49	94
Winsford United	42	29	6	7	96	41	93
Worksop Town	42	25	5	12	101	51	80
Guiseley	42	22	12	8	93	56	78
Caernarfon Town	42	23	9	10	78	47	78
Bridlington Town	42	22	9	11	86	46	75
Warrington Town	42	20	8	14	79	64	68
Knowsley United	42	18	10	14	69	52	64
Netherfield	42	18	7	17	54	61	61
Harrogate Town	42	14	16	12	73	69	58
Curzon Ashton	42	15	9	18	71	83	54
Farsley Celtic (1)	42	15	9	18	79	101	53
Radcliffe Bor. (3)	42	15	9	18	67	72	51
Newtown	42	15	6	21	60	95	51
Eastwood Town	42	13	11	18	59	70	50
Lancaster City	42	10	19	13	55	62	49
Congleton Town	42	14	5	23	59	81	47
Rhyl	42	11	10	21	59	69	43
Rossendale United	42	9	11	22	61	90	38
Alfreton Town	42	12	2	28	63	98	38
Irlam Town (1)	42	9	7	26	45	95	33
Workington (1)	42	7	8	27	45	99	28

(–) – points deducted for breach of rule.

Leading scorers

Premier Division

40 Chris Camden (Stalybridge Celtic)
31 Steve Holden (Morecambe)
28 Brian Ross (Marine)
25 John Coleman (Morecambe)
21 Paul Beck (Accrington Stanley)
20 Craig Madden (Fleetwood Town)
   Eric Priest (Stalybridge Celtic)
19 Jimmy Clarke (Buxton)
   Paul Kirkham (Hyde United)

First Division

42 Kenny Clark (Worksop Town)
34 Mark Williscroft (Colwyn Bay)
32 Bevan Blackwood (Winsford United)
   Peter Donnelly (Colwyn Bay)
26 Gavin McDonald (Warrington Town)
25 Steve French (Harrogate Town)
24 Mark Tennison (Guiseley)
21 Peter Coyne (Radcliffe Borough)
   Alan Radford (Bridlington Town)

HFS LOANS LEAGUE CHALLENGE CUP

Preliminary Round
Alfreton Town 1, Netherfield 2
Congleton Town 2, Workington 1

First Round
Rhyl 0, Colwyn Bay 7 (*after 1-1 draw*)
Farsley Celtic 4, Bridlington Town 2
Knowsley United 3, Eastwood Town 1
Radcliffe Borough 4, Caernarfon Town 1
Curzon Ashton 1, Warrington Town 0 (*after 0-0 draw*)
Winsford United 4, Newton 1
Guiseley 2, Congleton Town 0
Lancaster City 0, Harrogate Town 3
Rossendale United 3, Irlam Town 0
Worksop Town 1, Netherfield 0

Second Round
Accrington Stanley 1, Southport 2
Chorley 1, Winsford United 3
Curzon Ashton 6, Farsley Celtic 2
Frickley Athletic 2, Worksop Town 1
Harrogate Town 1, Buxton 2
Marine 2, Gainsborough Trinity 0
Radcliffe Borough 0, Goole Town 2
Stalybridge Celtic 4, Leek Town 1
Bishop Auckland 1, Hyde United 0
Colwyn Bay 1, Matlock Town 2
Fleetwood Town 1, Emley 0
Guiseley 6, Bangor City 2
Knowsley United 2, Horwich RMI 1
Morecambe 3, Shepshed Albion 1

Rossendale United 2, Mossley 1
Whitley Bay 1, Droylsden 0

Third Round
Buxton 3, Knowsley United 2
Frickley Athletic 2, Whitley Bay 1
Guiseley 3, Morecambe 3 aet (*after 1-1 draw*)
   (*Guiseley won 4-2 on penalties*)
Matlock Town 1, Rossendale United 0 (*after 1-1 draw*)
Stalybridge Celtic 5, Fleetwood Town 0
Winsford United 1, Marine 3
Curzon Ashton 4, Bishop Auckland 3
Goole Town 1, Southport 0

Fourth Round
Buxton 1, Guiseley 2
Matlock Town 3, Goole Town 2
Curzon Ashton 2, Marine 3
Stalybridge Celtic 0, Frickley Athletic 2

Semi-finals, First Leg
Guiseley 1, Marine 0
Matlock Town 3, Frickley Athletic 2

Semi-finals, Second Leg
Marine 2, Guiseley 0
Frickley Athletic 1, Matlock Town 0 aet
   (*Frickley Athletic won on away goals*)

Final
Marine 1, Frickley Athletic 0 (*at Maine Road*)

HFS LOANS LEAGUE PRESIDENT'S CUP

Final, First Leg
Morecambe 1, Stalybridge Celtic 2

Final, Second Leg
Stalybridge Celtic 0, Morecambe 2

HFS LOANS LEAGUE FIRST DIVISION CUP

Final
Colwyn Bay 3, Worksop Town 1 (*at Stalybridge*)

HFS LOANS LEAGUE—PREMIER DIVISION RESULTS 1991-92

	Accrington Stanley	Bangor City	Bishop Auckland	Buxton	Chorley	Droylsden	Emley	Fleetwood Town	Frickley Athletic	Gainsborough Trinity	Goole Town	Horwich RMI	Hyde United	Leek Town	Marine	Matlock Town	Morecambe	Mossley	Shepshed Albion	Southport	Stalybridge Celtic	Whitley Bay
Accrington Stanley	—	1-0	2-2	1-1	3-2	2-2	2-1	3-0	1-2	1-1	4-0	1-1	1-1	1-0	0-3	2-2	3-1	5-1	3-1	1-1	0-3	3-2
Bangor City	4-3	—	1-1	0-1	1-1	4-0	2-0	0-2	2-1	1-3	2-0	1-2	2-2	0-1	0-2	2-3	0-1	4-0	1-0	1-1	0-1	1-2
Bishop Auckland	0-6	0-0	—	2-0	3-0	1-0	1-1	3-0	1-0	3-1	1-2	1-3	0-1	0-2	3-0	1-1	0-2	1-2	4-1	0-1	1-4	1-1
Buxton	0-1	2-0	2-0	—	4-2	2-0	1-3	1-0	3-0	2-1	1-1	5-0	2-0	3-0	0-3	3-1	1-3	1-3	1-0	1-0	1-2	3-1
Chorley	2-1	4-3	1-0	0-2	—	1-2	0-1	1-0	2-2	3-1	4-4	0-0	2-0	0-2	3-1	2-1	1-2	1-2	1-2	2-2	2-3	1-3
Droylsden	3-2	2-0	1-2	0-0	2-0	—	4-0	1-4	4-2	0-0	3-2	5-1	3-2	2-2	1-1	2-2	0-1	1-4	3-2	1-1	2-2	1-1
Emley	3-1	0-2	4-1	1-2	5-0	1-2	—	4-0	2-0	6-0	2-0	0-0	0-0	0-0	0-1	4-0	3-3	2-1	0-0	3-2	2-2	3-1
Fleetwood Town	2-1	2-1	3-4	1-1	5-0	2-1	1-2	—	2-1	0-1	2-3	1-2	5-1	2-2	0-0	4-0	1-1	3-1	2-0	5-1	0-2	5-0
Frickley Athletic	1-1	2-1	2-0	1-1	1-0	1-1	1-1	3-2	—	0-0	1-2	0-2	3-0	0-1	0-4	2-2	1-1	3-0	6-1	2-0	1-1	4-0
Gainsborough Trinity	0-4	1-1	0-1	0-0	3-1	0-0	0-0	1-1	1-1	—	0-2	4-0	1-0	1-2	0-0	0-1	5-1	0-1	3-1	0-2	3-1	1-3
Goole Town	2-4	0-1	1-2	2-2	4-4	2-2	1-0	2-1	2-2	0-2	—	1-0	0-1	1-1	1-2	3-0	1-2	3-1	0-1	2-1	1-1	1-0
Horwich RMI	1-1	2-2	2-0	0-0	0-0	1-0	3-0	0-1	1-3	4-1	1-0	—	0-2	1-1	1-0	2-1	0-2	1-2	0-0	1-1	0-0	1-0
Hyde United	2-1	0-0	4-0	2-1	1-2	3-1	5-3	7-0	2-1	3-0	1-3	1-1	—	3-0	0-4	3-2	2-2	4-1	3-1	4-0	1-2	0-1
Leek Town	1-0	1-0	1-1	4-1	2-0	2-0	1-1	0-3	1-0	2-1	1-1	3-1	1-0	—	3-2	2-1	0-4	3-2	3-0	3-0	2-3	2-0
Marine	0-1	1-0	0-1	2-0	2-1	3-1	2-0	5-0	1-1	0-0	2-0	2-1	3-3	3-0	—	1-3	3-2	2-1	1-1	1-1	0-0	3-0
Matlock Town	0-4	2-0	0-1	0-2	2-2	3-2	0-3	1-1	1-1	2-1	4-1	1-0	2-0	3-0	0-1	—	0-1	0-2	4-3	3-3	0-3	5-3
Morecambe	4-1	3-0	3-0	2-1	2-1	1-1	0-1	1-2	2-0	1-3	1-1	0-0	2-1	2-2	2-1	3-3	—	1-0	0-2	0-1	0-0	0-1
Mossley	2-2	1-3	0-2	1-3	1-0	3-0	0-3	4-1	1-1	1-1	3-1	1-1	3-0	1-2	0-1	0-1	1-0	—	2-1	0-0	0-1	3-2
Shepshed Albion	4-0	0-0	0-0	2-3	2-3	2-3	3-2	0-1	1-3	2-1	0-1	1-3	1-1	1-2	0-0	4-1	2-4	0-1	—	0-1	3-3	0-1
Southport	2-2	4-0	3-0	2-1	1-1	2-2	2-3	2-0	3-2	1-1	1-1	1-1	1-2	1-0	3-1	2-0	1-1	1-0	3-0	—	0-0	2-0
Stalybridge Celtic	2-1	1-1	0-0	2-2	3-3	2-0	1-0	2-0	2-2	3-0	7-0	2-0	1-2	1-0	3-1	4-0	1-1	5-0	2-1	1-0	—	3-1
Whitley Bay	2-2	0-1	0-2	0-2	0-6	3-1	0-0	0-0	2-2	3-3	2-0	1-3	4-1	0-3	2-2	3-1	1-1	2-1	2-1	1-2	0-2	—

HFS LOANS LEAGUE—FIRST DIVISION RESULTS 1991-92

(Away \ Home)	Alfreton Town	Bridlington Town	Caernarfon Town	Colwyn Bay	Congleton Town	Curzon Ashton	Eastwood Town	Farsley Celtic	Guiseley	Harrogate Town	Irlam Town	Knowsley United	Lancaster City	Netherfield	Newtown	Radcliffe Borough	Rhyl	Rossendale United	Warrington Town	Winsford United	Workington	Worksop Town
Worksop Town	3-0	1-3	1-3	4-2	2-1	0-3	1-2	2-1	1-1	1-1	2-1	0-2	1-2	2-1	1-2	4-1	1-4	0-2	2-1	5-0	0-1	—
Workington	1-3	3-2	5-0	6-1	3-0	6-1	3-1	2-2	6-0	0-2	1-0	3-1	5-1	4-2	2-1	0-1	1-0	1-1	2-2	3-0	—	4-0
Winsford United	2-3	3-1	1-0	1-0	0-2	1-5	1-2	4-5	1-4	1-1	1-4	1-2	0-2	0-1	1-3	1-1	1-2	3-5	3-3	—	3-0	1-2
Warrington Town	1-6	0-2	0-1	1-0	2-3	1-1	1-3	2-5	2-1	1-2	0-1	2-1	3-0	2-1	2-0	2-2	3-1	5-1	—	3-3	1-0	3-0
Rossendale United	0-1	4-0	2-0	1-1	2-0	4-1	4-4	2-4	2-2	4-2	1-2	2-3	2-2	1-0	0-0	3-2	5-1	—	4-0	5-0	1-1	5-1
Rhyl	3-2	4-1	1-1	2-1	2-0	2-1	2-1	3-3	5-2	2-2	1-1	3-0	1-1	0-1	1-0	2-3	—	1-3	2-1	0-0	1-3	1-0
Radcliffe Borough	2-3	1-1	2-0	3-0	3-0	1-0	0-2	2-2	3-1	1-1	3-3	4-1	2-2	1-2	2-0	—	2-1	1-2	2-1	1-0	1-0	1-0
Newtown	4-3	0-1	2-1	3-2	1-2	1-1	2-2	3-2	1-1	2-2	1-3	5-0	0-2	2-0	—	3-1	3-1	2-3	5-1	1-1	0-2	9-0
Netherfield	0-1	0-2	2-1	0-1	1-2	1-1	6-4	3-2	1-0	2-2	1-0	0-0	0-1	—	2-0	3-1	3-1	4-0	0-1	2-1	1-3	5-0
Lancaster City	1-2	2-0	3-2	2-0	0-0	2-3	1-1	1-1	0-1	1-1	1-1	0-0	—	0-2	2-0	5-1	2-3	0-0	1-1	2-0	2-2	1-1
Knowsley United	0-3	1-1	1-3	3-1	0-2	2-0	1-0	0-5	2-0	3-1	1-0	—	0-0	1-2	1-4	4-2	1-1	0-1	3-3	0-2	0-2	4-0
Irlam Town	5-1	3-1	3-0	3-0	2-1	3-1	2-3	2-1	5-0	4-2	—	2-2	4-3	1-1	1-0	1-2	1-0	3-1	3-1	4-0	4-1	6-0
Harrogate Town	3-3	1-1	3-0	1-1	0-1	2-2	0-1	2-3	2-4	—	0-3	2-3	2-0	0-4	0-5	1-1	2-0	1-1	1-1	1-5	5-2	5-0
Guiseley	1-2	4-0	3-0	1-2	0-2	2-2	2-0	1-1	—	0-1	0-1	0-0	2-2	2-2	1-6	1-6	1-2	1-2	1-2	2-2	2-2	3-2
Farsley Celtic	2-4	1-0	0-1	4-1	4-2	1-2	1-2	—	5-0	1-1	2-0	5-3	0-0	1-2	2-4	4-1	0-1	2-1	1-4	2-4	2-2	6-2
Eastwood Town	0-1	5-0	4-1	2-0	1-2	2-0	—	2-3	1-1	3-2	0-4	2-0	1-1	1-1	2-1	1-1	1-1	0-1	3-1	3-1	3-0	0-0
Curzon Ashton	3-1	2-0	2-1	4-3	2-4	—	1-1	4-3	3-2	1-2	0-1	2-2	0-1	1-0	3-1	1-0	3-4	7-0	4-1	1-1	3-0	3-0
Congleton Town	1-0	1-2	2-2	2-1	—	2-0	3-4	1-1	3-1	1-1	3-5	0-0	5-2	3-1	5-1	3-0	1-2	1-2	3-1	4-1	6-2	3-0
Colwyn Bay	0-1	2-0	3-2	—	0-1	2-5	2-2	0-2	2-0	1-4	2-3	0-2	0-2	0-2	1-4	1-4	0-2	1-5	3-3	1-0	1-3	0-1
Caernarfon Town	2-4	0-3	—	1-2	0-2	0-4	0-0	2-5	6-1	3-1	2-1	1-0	2-2	2-2	0-2	0-2	1-2	1-0	0-1	0-0	2-2	2-1
Bridlington Town	2-3	—	0-2	1-4	0-3	0-1	0-1	2-1	1-1	1-1	2-2	2-1	2-2	2-1	0-4	3-1	1-2	1-1	1-1	2-1	0-3	1-3
Alfreton Town	—	8-0	5-2	5-3	3-1	4-1	3-1	2-3	3-1	0-2	1-0	0-1	0-2	3-1	0-1	3-0	3-3	1-2	2-1	1-0	3-2	1-0

BEAZER HOMES LEAGUE 1991–92

Premier Division

	P	W	D	L	F	A	Pts
Bromsgrove Rovers	42	27	9	6	78	34	90
Dover Athletic	42	23	15	4	66	30	84
VS Rugby	42	23	11	8	70	44	80
Bashley	42	22	8	12	70	44	74
Cambridge City	42	18	14	10	71	53	68
Dartford	42	17	15	10	62	45	66
Trowbridge Town	42	17	10	15	69	51	61
Halesowen Town	42	15	15	12	61	49	60
Moor Green	42	15	11	16	61	59	56
Burton Albion	42	15	10	17	59	61	55
Dorchester Town	42	14	13	15	66	73	55
Gloucester City	42	15	9	18	67	70	54
Atherstone United	42	15	8	19	54	66	53
Corby Town	42	13	12	17	66	81	51
Waterlooville	42	13	11	18	43	56	50
Worcester City	42	12	13	17	56	59	49
Crawley Town	42	12	12	18	62	67	48
Chelmsford City	42	12	12	18	49	56	48
Wealdstone	42	13	7	22	52	69	46
Poole Town	42	10	13	19	46	77	43
Fisher Athletic	42	9	11	22	53	89	38
Gravesend & Northfleet	42	8	9	25	39	87	33

Midland Division

	P	W	D	L	F	A	Pts
Solihull Borough	42	29	10	3	92	40	97
Hednesford Town	42	26	13	3	81	37	91
Sutton Coldfield Town	42	21	11	10	71	51	74
Barry Town	42	21	6	15	88	56	69
Bedworth United	42	16	15	11	67	63	63
Nuneaton Borough	42	16	14	12	68	53	62
Tamworth	42	16	12	14	66	52	60
Rushden Town	42	16	12	14	69	63	60
Stourbridge	42	17	8	17	85	62	59
Newport AFC	42	15	13	14	72	60	58
Yate Town	42	14	15	13	65	64	57
Bilston Town	42	15	10	17	56	67	55
Grantham Town	42	11	17	14	59	55	50
King's Lynn	42	13	11	18	61	68	50
Hinckley Town	42	14	8	20	61	87	50
Leicester United	42	12	13	17	56	63	49
Bridgnorth Town	42	12	12	18	61	74	48
Racing Club Warwick	42	11	14	17	45	61	47
Stroud	42	14	4	24	66	88	46
Redditch United	42	12	8	22	52	92	44
Alvechurch	42	11	10	21	54	88	43
Dudley Town	42	8	9	25	41	92	33

Southern Division

	P	W	D	L	F	A	Pts
Hastings Town	42	28	7	7	80	37	91
Weymouth	42	22	12	8	64	35	78
Havant Town	42	21	12	9	67	46	75
Braintree Town	42	21	8	13	77	58	71
Buckingham Town*	42	19	15	8	57	26	69
Andover	42	18	10	14	73	68	64
Ashford Town	42	17	12	13	66	57	63
Sudbury Town	42	18	9	15	70	66	63
Sittingbourne**	42	19	10	13	63	41	61
Burnham	42	15	14	13	57	55	59
Baldock Town	42	16	10	16	62	67	58
Salisbury	42	13	16	13	67	51	55
Hythe Town	42	15	10	17	61	62	55
Margate	42	13	16	13	49	56	55
Newport IOW	42	13	10	19	58	63	49
Dunstable	42	12	12	18	55	67	48
Bury Town	42	14	4	24	52	94	46
Witney Town	42	11	12	19	55	76	45
Fareham Town	42	12	8	22	45	71	44
Erith & Belvedere	42	11	10	21	44	67	43
Canterbury City	42	8	14	20	43	69	38
Gosport Borough	42	6	9	27	32	65	27

* 3 points deducted—ineligible player.
** 6 points deducted—ineligible players.

LEADING GOALSCORERS

Premier Division

A. Diaz (Dorchester Town)	38
C. Hanks (Bromsgrove Rovers)	30
L. Whale (Bashley)	23
T. Rogers (Dover Athletic)	21
G. Manson (Dorchester Town)	20
M. Dent (Poole Town)	19
P. Malcolm (Dover Athletic)	18

Midland Division

C. Burton (Solihull Borough)	28
S. Burr (Hednesford Town)	27
M. Hallam (Leicester United)	26
J. O'Connor (Hednesford Town)	25
C. Summers (Barry Town)	24
G. Hardwick (Bedworth United)	23
K. Thaws (Yate Town)	23

Southern Division

P. Odey (Andover)	29
K. Clark (Whitney Town)	22
S. Tate (Havant Town)	21
D. Arter (Sittingbourne)	19
J. Smith (Salisbury)	19

BEAZER HOMES SOUTHERN LEAGUE PREMIER DIVISION RESULTS 1991–92

	Atherstone United	Bashley	Bromsgrove Rovers	Burton Albion	Cambridge City	Chelmsford City	Corby Town	Crawley Town	Dartford	Dorchester Town	Dover Athletic	Fisher Athletic	Gloucester City	Gravesend & Northfleet	Halesowen Town	Moor Green	Poole Town	Trowbridge Town	VS Rugby	Waterlooville	Wealdstone	Worcester City
Atherstone United	—	1-3	2-0	3-2	0-1	3-0	3-4	1-2	0-0	4-2	1-1	2-2	0-3	2-1	4-0	1-1	3-0	0-3	2-0	1-4	2-0	1-3
Bashley	4-0	—	0-1	1-1	1-1	0-0	3-1	2-0	3-0	0-1	2-0	3-1	2-1	3-0	2-3	3-0	3-0	2-0	3-1	1-2	1-1	2-2
Bromsgrove Rovers	2-0	3-0	—	1-1	0-2	2-1	3-0	5-1	1-0	5-1	0-0	7-0	0-2	1-0	1-0	5-3	3-1	3-1	1-2	1-0	1-0	2-0
Burton Albion	0-2	1-0	3-1	—	2-0	1-2	3-1	1-0	0-1	1-2	0-1	0-2	4-3	2-1	0-0	0-1	5-2	1-3	0-0	0-4	1-1	1-1
Cambridge City	4-1	0-1	1-0	1-1	—	3-0	1-0	1-3	2-0	2-2	2-2	4-0	4-2	3-1	2-1	2-0	5-0	3-0	1-1	0-0	3-0	1-1
Chelmsford City	1-0	1-1	1-1	3-1	6-1	—	1-0	0-0	1-2	0-3	0-1	3-0	0-0	2-3	0-0	3-1	1-1	1-1	1-1	2-3	3-0	0-1
Corby Town	3-1	3-2	1-3	1-2	2-2	1-0	—	3-4	2-2	1-3	1-1	2-1	2-2	2-1	0-4	1-6	2-1	1-1	4-2	1-1	2-6	3-1
Crawley Town	3-1	1-3	0-3	1-2	2-2	3-0	1-1	—	1-1	1-4	0-0	0-0	5-2	2-1	2-0	1-2	3-3	1-0	1-1	2-0	0-1	2-2
Dartford	4-1	1-0	1-2	2-0	2-2	0-2	1-5	3-2	—	1-1	2-1	1-0	5-0	5-0	0-1	1-3	4-0	2-2	2-3	2-1	4-1	1-0
Dorchester Town	0-1	0-1	1-2	0-3	1-3	2-3	0-0	0-4	1-1	—	2-1	3-1	4-2	1-1	0-0	2-2	2-1	3-1	2-1	0-0	2-0	3-3
Dover Athletic	1-0	3-2	2-2	2-1	3-0	3-0	2-1	2-1	1-1	1-1	—	2-0	4-0	3-0	1-1	1-1	1-0	0-4	1-1	1-0	3-0	3-1
Fisher Athletic	0-0	2-3	1-3	1-1	1-1	3-1	2-2	2-2	0-1	6-5	2-3	—	3-0	0-1	0-1	4-0	5-1	0-4	1-3	3-2	0-1	0-1
Gloucester City	2-0	3-1	1-2	2-2	0-0	3-1	3-2	4-1	0-0	2-1	0-4	2-0	—	0-1	1-1	1-1	2-2	2-2	1-2	2-1	3-2	2-0
Gravesend & Northfleet	1-1	1-2	0-1	0-2	2-1	0-1	1-3	1-1	1-1	1-1	0-1	4-2	1-0	—	1-8	1-3	2-3	0-1	2-3	1-0	1-1	0-0
Halesowen Town	1-1	1-2	1-1	4-1	3-2	2-1	1-1	4-2	1-0	2-2	2-0	3-2	1-0	1-1	—	2-0	2-2	1-0	1-2	1-2	1-1	0-0
Moor Green	2-3	2-0	0-1	0-2	2-2	3-2	1-1	1-1	1-3	0-1	1-0	3-0	5-1	2-0	1-1	—	1-2	1-2	0-0	0-0	0-1	2-1
Poole Town	0-1	1-1	0-1	5-3	1-1	0-2	2-2	1-1	0-0	0-1	1-1	1-1	1-1	3-2	3-2	2-2	—	1-0	0-4	0-2	0-1	1-0
Trowbridge Town	0-1	2-0	0-2	3-0	2-1	1-1	2-0	2-1	3-4	0-1	6-0	1-1	1-1	9-0	1-1	2-1	3-1	—	0-1	1-1	3-2	3-2
VS Rugby	1-2	0-2	1-1	1-0	3-1	0-0	0-0	2-1	3-3	3-1	0-1	3-0	2-1	3-1	1-0	2-1	2-2	1-0	—	2-0	3-2	2-0
Waterlooville	3-1	0-0	0-1	0-4	1-1	1-1	1-4	0-2	0-5	2-2	0-2	1-1	1-0	1-0	1-0	0-1	3-1	1-0	0-4	—	0-1	3-1
Wealdstone	1-0	1-2	1-3	1-3	2-0	2-0	3-0	0-2	2-2	2-1	4-4	3-2	0-3	2-1	2-1	1-0	0-1	3-1	0-3	2-0	—	1-4
Worcester City	1-1	1-3	1-1	1-1	2-1	2-1	1-2	2-1	2-0	5-1	1-1	1-1	0-3	6-2	1-2	1-2	0-1	1-2	2-0	0-0	1-0	—

BEAZER HOMES SOUTHERN LEAGUE MIDLAND DIVISION RESULTS 1991-92

	Alvechurch	Barry Town	Bedworth United	Bilston Town	Bridgnorth Town	Dudley Town	Grantham Town	Hednesford Town	Hinckley Town	King's Lynn	Leicester United	Newport AFC	Nuneaton Borough	Racing Club Warwick	Redditch United	Rushden Town	Solihull Borough	Stourbridge	Stroud	Sutton Coldfield Town	Tamworth	Yate Town
Alvechurch	—	0-5	1-3	1-0	2-2	2-1	0-0	1-3	0-0	1-1	1-3	2-0	1-0	1-3	0-0	3-2	2-1	2-4	1-2	2-2	2-3	2-0
Barry Town	2-1	—	3-1	3-1	1-4	0-1	1-3	0-2	1-1	1-1	2-1	2-2	2-2	5-0	4-0	1-0	1-3	2-1	4-1	2-1	0-2	1-2
Bedworth United	1-2	3-1	—	3-3	0-0	2-2	3-2	1-1	3-1	2-2	0-2	3-2	0-0	2-1	1-1	0-0	0-2	1-3	4-1	0-1	1-0	0-0
Bilston Town	1-3	3-1	3-3	—	1-1	1-4	2-2	0-4	1-2	3-1	2-1	2-2	0-1	4-2	1-0	3-0	0-2	0-4	4-1	0-1	2-1	2-1
Bridgnorth Town	2-2	3-0	1-1	1-1	—	3-1	2-4	0-4	2-3	2-0	1-3	1-1	0-1	0-4	2-1	2-1	0-3	0-1	5-2	1-2	1-4	0-0
Dudley Town	0-0	0-6	0-1	0-2	0-1	—	1-1	1-2	0-1	2-0	0-0	2-1	1-1	2-3	1-2	1-4	0-1	2-1	0-1	1-6	2-3	2-3
Grantham Town	2-2	1-1	1-1	1-1	1-2	6-0	—	0-0	2-0	0-0	1-1	3-3	2-2	1-0	2-1	2-1	1-1	0-0	3-1	0-2	3-2	1-2
Hednesford Town	6-0	3-0	0-1	3-0	1-0	0-0	2-1	—	2-0	2-1	3-3	2-1	1-1	2-1	3-0	4-1	4-5	1-1	3-0	1-1	0-0	1-1
Hinckley Town	1-3	1-2	1-3	1-1	2-3	3-0	2-4	2-0	—	0-4	0-0	1-3	2-2	1-4	4-2	1-3	1-2	3-2	3-1	1-2	1-0	4-1
King's Lynn	4-3	3-2	1-1	0-0	0-0	2-0	4-1	1-1	3-1	—	2-5	3-1	2-2	2-1	4-0	3-3	1-3	0-2	2-2	2-2	2-4	1-2
Leicester United	2-0	1-0	1-1	0-0	3-5	5-0	1-3	0-0	1-0	2-5	—	0-0	2-1	1-0	1-2	1-3	1-1	1-1	2-1	2-2	0-1	0-1
Newport AFC	3-0	0-4	3-1	1-1	1-1	1-0	1-0	1-3	2-1	3-1	3-1	—	3-1	5-0	5-0	2-1	1-1	0-4	2-0	1-1	0-3	2-2
Nuneaton Borough	5-2	1-0	2-2	4-1	2-1	0-0	1-0	1-2	5-1	1-0	2-0	2-0	—	0-1	0-1	0-0	0-0	2-2	2-1	0-0	3-3	1-2
Racing Club Warwick	0-0	1-1	0-1	1-2	1-1	3-3	1-1	1-1	2-0	1-0	1-0	0-2	0-0	—	0-1	2-2	0-4	2-0	2-1	0-2	0-0	2-3
Redditch United	1-2	0-4	0-1	1-0	3-2	1-0	1-1	1-1	4-1	0-2	0-1	0-5	0-2	4-1	—	4-4	2-2	2-1	2-0	0-2	1-3	2-0
Rushden Town	1-0	0-3	3-1	3-1	1-1	0-0	2-0	6-1	3-1	2-1	0-1	0-3	2-3	3-1	4-4	—	2-2	3-1	1-0	1-2	3-2	2-0
Solihull Borough	2-1	2-1	2-1	3-1	2-1	3-3	0-2	1-3	1-1	1-1	0-0	3-1	3-1	4-0	1-1	2-0	—	1-0	2-1	3-1	2-1	4-1
Stourbridge	5-1	2-2	2-2	2-1	3-3	4-0	2-0	0-3	0-2	4-0	2-1	2-3	3-1	1-2	5-0	2-3	1-1	—	2-1	0-2	4-1	1-1
Stroud	5-2	2-1	2-6	3-1	4-1	3-1	0-2	2-0	1-2	2-3	5-0	1-1	3-2	0-0	4-5	2-5	1-2	2-1	—	2-1	0-2	1-2
Sutton Coldfield Town	3-2	3-1	2-2	0-1	1-0	1-1	2-0	2-3	2-1	2-1	0-1	1-0	0-0	0-0	3-2	0-0	2-3	2-1	5-0	—	3-2	3-0
Tamworth	2-0	2-3	2-2	1-1	0-0	1-1	2-0	2-3	2-1	2-1	3-0	1-0	1-0	0-1	1-1	1-0	1-1	1-0	4-0	0-1	—	2-2
Yate Town	5-1	0-1	2-2	4-0	0-0	3-3	2-2	1-3	1-1	0-0	1-1	1-5	1-0	1-1	5-0	1-2	3-4	3-1	0-0	3-0	1-3	—

BEAZER HOMES SOUTHERN LEAGUE SOUTHERN DIVISION RESULTS 1991-92

	Andover	Ashford Town	Baldock Town	Braintree Town	Buckingham Town	Burnham	Bury Town	Canterbury City	Dunstable	Erith & Belvedere	Fareham Town	Gosport Borough	Hastings Town	Havant Town	Hythe Town	Margate	Newport IOW	Salisbury	Sittingbourne	Sudbury Town	Weymouth	Witney Town
Andover	—	0-2	2-0	2-5	2-4	2-1	1-2	7-1	3-1	2-0	0-2	0-0	3-1	3-1	2-7	1-3	2-2	1-1	3-2	1-2	3-0	2-1
Ashford Town	2-2	—	2-2	3-1	0-0	1-1	0-3	1-1	1-1	2-1	1-0	2-0	3-4	0-2	2-1	1-1	2-1	2-2	3-1	5-3	0-0	3-0
Baldock Town	2-3	1-0	—	1-3	0-0	2-1	3-2	4-3	1-1	2-0	3-0	1-2	2-1	1-1	2-3	1-1	2-0	1-1	2-3	0-3	2-1	4-1
Braintree Town	1-0	2-0	5-0	—	0-2	4-3	1-3	1-2	7-0	1-0	2-2	1-2	0-2	4-2	2-1	1-1	3-1	2-0	1-1	1-1	0-0	1-0
Buckingham Town	3-0	0-3	2-0	0-2	—	2-2	5-1	3-0	2-1	2-1	1-0	1-1	0-1	2-0	1-1	0-2	1-0	0-0	1-0	5-0	1-1	3-1
Burnham	0-0	2-1	1-2	4-3	2-2	—	2-3	1-0	1-2	1-0	0-0	3-2	1-2	0-0	3-1	1-0	1-3	0-3	3-2	1-1	0-2	2-3
Bury Town	2-0	2-1	0-4	1-3	1-1	1-1	—	1-1	2-5	3-1	3-1	2-0	0-0	0-0	1-0	1-3	1-0	2-0	1-0	5-0	1-2	1-4
Canterbury City	3-3	0-2	1-6	3-4	1-0	0-1	1-1	—	1-1	1-0	1-1	2-0	1-3	4-1	0-3	2-0	3-1	0-0	3-2	1-1	0-1	2-2
Dunstable	2-3	1-2	1-1	1-3	1-0	3-1	2-0	1-0	—	1-3	2-1	0-1	1-2	0-0	1-0	0-0	1-1	1-1	0-0	1-0	0-1	2-2
Erith & Belvedere	1-1	1-1	0-2	0-2	1-1	1-1	0-0	1-0	0-0	—	3-3	2-4	0-4	1-2	0-0	1-3	1-4	0-1	0-1	0-2	0-1	3-1
Fareham Town	0-2	1-3	3-0	1-2	0-3	2-3	1-2	3-2	1-5	1-0	—	4-0	2-2	1-3	0-0	1-1	1-0	0-4	0-3	1-2	1-1	2-1
Gosport Borough	1-2	0-2	0-0	1-2	1-2	0-0	1-1	0-1	0-2	0-1	1-3	—	0-2	1-0	0-1	1-2	2-2	0-3	0-3	3-2	0-1	1-2
Hastings Town	2-0	1-0	2-0	2-0	1-0	2-1	1-2	0-0	3-0	1-1	2-0	2-1	—	0-1	2-3	4-0	3-1	2-1	1-1	3-0	2-0	1-1
Havant Town	1-1	1-0	1-0	3-0	0-3	1-1	5-0	3-1	4-2	1-2	1-1	2-1	3-2	—	3-1	3-1	1-0	3-1	1-0	2-2	1-2	4-1
Hythe Town	1-1	2-2	0-0	2-0	2-0	1-3	3-1	1-0	0-4	1-3	0-1	0-1	0-1	3-1	—	0-1	2-2	1-0	0-0	1-3	0-1	4-4
Margate	1-2	3-2	1-1	1-3	0-0	1-2	1-0	1-0	0-0	5-0	2-2	0-1	1-1	3-3	0-1	—	3-1	1-0	0-0	0-2	1-1	1-0
Newport IOW	0-3	1-3	3-1	2-1	1-1	2-1	4-1	2-2	2-1	0-1	3-0	3-1	0-3	0-0	2-1	0-1	—	1-1	0-1	4-1	0-1	3-1
Salisbury	0-0	3-2	2-3	0-1	0-0	0-0	5-0	3-1	1-2	4-2	0-1	3-2	1-1	0-2	1-1	5-1	2-2	—	0-2	0-0	2-2	1-0
Sittingbourne	1-2	1-0	1-0	2-2	1-0	0-1	3-0	3-0	0-2	2-3	1-0	0-1	2-0	0-1	1-2	1-1	0-2	2-2	—	3-0	2-1	0-0
Sudbury Town	3-1	6-1	4-3	1-2	5-0	1-1	4-0	3-3	0-2	1-1	0-1	1-0	1-2	0-0	2-1	4-0	4-2	1-3	1-6	—	2-0	5-1
Weymouth	1-3	2-1	0-0	2-0	1-0	2-2	5-0	2-0	3-0	4-1	3-0	0-0	1-2	2-2	3-1	3-0	0-0	1-0	0-0	5-3	—	5-1
Witney Town	2-2	0-2	2-0	1-1	3-1	0-2	3-6	1-1	2-2	1-0	2-1	2-0	1-2	2-2	2-0	0-0	4-2	0-3	0-0	1-0	2-1	—

THE BARCLAYS COMMERCIAL SERVICES CUP 1991–92

Preliminary Round
Grantham Town 1,3, Leicester United 2,1
Newport IOW 3,5, Poole Town 3,1

First Round
Dover Athletic 2,2, Sittingbourne 0,0
Canterbury City 2,2, Hastings Town 5,1
Margate 3,0, Erith & Belvedere 2,2
Dartford 3,1, Gravesend & Northfleet 0,3
Buckingham Town 3,3, Burnham 2,2
Chelmsford City 1,0, Bury Town 0,1
   (*Chelmsford City won 5-3 on penalties*)
Crawley Town 3,2, Hythe Town 2,1
Ashford Town 3,0, Fisher Athletic 0,1
King's Lynn 3,1, Sudbury Town 4,3
Braintree Town 2,0, Cambridge City 2,5
Witney Town 0,1, Dunstable 1,3
Wealdstone 2,2, Baldock Town 0,0
VS Rugby 3,4, Rushden Town 1,1
Tamworth 4,3, Hinckley Town 1,0
Nuneaton Borough 1,0, Corby Town 1,2
Atherstone United 0,0, Grantham Town 0,3
Solihull Borough 0,3, Bedworth United 0,1
Bridgnorth Town 4,0, Dudley Town 2,3
Sutton Coldfield Town 0,0, Burton Albion 0,1
Alvechurch 1,3, Redditch United 2,1
Moor Green 2,1, Stourbridge 0,0
Bromsgrove Rovers 3,4, Worcester City 3,1
RC Warwick 1,2, Hednesford Town 2,3
Bilston Town 3,0, Halesowen Town 2,2
Waterlooville 4,2, Bashley 4,0
Salisbury 1,1, Andover 0,0
Newport AFC 0,2, Barry Town 2,1
Trowbridge Town 1,0, Gloucester City 0,2
Havant Town 0,0, Weymouth 0,0
   (*Weymouth won 4-2 on penalties*)
Gosport Borough 0,1, Fareham Town 1,1
Stroud 2,3, Yate Town 3,1
Newport IOW 1,1, Dorchester Town 2,5

Second Round
Dover Athletic 0,1, Hastings Town 0,1
   (*Dover Athletic won on away goals rule*)
Erith & Belvedere 0,0, Dartford 1,4
Buckingham Town 0,1, Chelmsford City 1,1
Crawley Town 1,0, Ashford Town 1,6
Sudbury Town 1,0, Cambridge City 2,4
Dunstable 2,1, Wealdstone 1,4
VS Rugby 2,5, Tamworth 1,1
Corby Town 1,3, Grantham Town 3,2
Solihull Borough 1,4, Dudley Town 2,0
Burton Albion 2,4, Alvechurch 1,2
Moor Green 0,0, Bromsgrove Rovers 0,5
Hednesford Town 3,4, Halesowen Town 0,1
Waterlooville 0,1, Salisbury 2,3
Barry Town 1,0, Gloucester City 1,2
Havant Town 2,2, Fareham Town 1,1
Stroud 1,0, Dorchester Town 2,6

Third Round
Dover Athletic 1,2, Dartford 1,0
Chelmsford City 2,1, Ashford Town 0,1
Cambridge City 1,2, Wealdstone 1,1
VS Rugby 1,1, Grantham Town 1,2
Solihull Borough 0,1, Burton Albion 2,1
Bromsgrove Rovers 1,1, Hednesford Town 1,0
Salisbury 1,2, Gloucester City 2,0
Havant Town 0,2, Dorchester Town 1,2

Fourth Round
Dover Athletic 3,2, Chelmsford City 2,0
Cambridge City 5,2, Grantham Town 0,1
Burton Albion 0,0, Bromsgrove Rovers 6,3
Salisbury 0,0, Dorchester Town 1,2

Semi-finals
Dover Athletic 4,2, Cambridge City 3,0
Bromsgrove Rovers 1,2, Dorchester Town 4,1

Final
Dover Athletic 1,3, Dorchester Town 0,0

DIADORA FOOTBALL LEAGUE 1991–92

Premier Division

	P	Home			Away			Totals			Goals		Pts
		W	D	L	W	D	L	W	D	L	F	A	
Woking	42	16	2	3	14	5	2	30	7	5	96	25	97
Enfield	42	12	4	5	12	3	6	12	4	5	59	45	79
Sutton United	42	11	5	5	8	8	5	19	13	10	88	51	70
Chesham United	42	12	5	4	8	5	8	20	10	12	67	48	70
Wokingham Town	42	9	6	6	10	4	7	19	10	13	73	58	67
Marlow	42	11	5	5	9	2	10	20	7	15	56	50	67
Aylesbury United	42	8	8	5	8	9	4	16	17	9	69	46	65
Carshalton Athletic	42	12	4	5	6	4	11	18	8	16	64	67	62
Dagenham	42	8	9	4	7	7	7	15	16	11	70	59	61
Kingstonian	42	10	2	9	7	6	8	17	8	17	71	65	59
Windsor & Eton	42	7	3	11	8	8	5	15	11	16	56	56	56
Bromley	42	5	5	8	9	4	8	14	12	16	51	57	54
St Albans City	42	5	6	10	9	5	7	14	11	17	66	70	53
Basingstoke Town	42	5	5	8	9	3	9	14	11	17	56	65	53
Grays Athletic	42	7	7	7	7	4	10	14	11	17	53	68	53
Wivenhoe Town	42	11	2	8	5	2	14	16	4	22	56	81	52
Hendon	42	8	3	10	5	6	10	13	9	20	59	73	48
Harrow Borough	42	8	6	7	3	7	11	11	11	13	58	78	46
Hayes	42	7	5	9	3	9	9	10	14	18	52	63	44
Staines Town	42	3	5	13	8	5	8	11	10	21	43	73	43
Bognor Regis Town	42	3	9	9	6	2	13	9	11	22	51	89	38
Bishop's Stortford	42	5	4	12	2	8	11	7	12	23	41	68	33

Division One

	P	Home			Away			Totals			Goals		Pts
		W	D	L	W	D	L	W	D	L	F	A	
Stevenage Borough	40	18	2	0	12	4	4	30	6	4	95	37	96
Yeading	40	13	3	4	11	7	2	24	10	6	83	34	82
Dulwich Hamlet	40	11	5	4	11	4	5	22	9	9	71	40	75
Boreham Wood	40	10	5	5	12	2	6	22	7	11	65	40	73
Wembley	40	11	3	6	10	3	7	21	6	13	54	43	69
Abingdon Town	40	11	4	5	8	4	8	19	8	13	60	47	65
Tooting & Mitcham United	40	9	6	5	7	7	6	16	13	11	57	45	61
Hitchin Town	40	11	5	4	6	5	9	17	10	13	55	45	61
Walton & Hersham	40	7	8	5	8	5	7	15	13	12	62	50	58
Molesey	40	7	3	10	9	6	5	16	9	15	55	61	57
Dorking	40	8	3	9	8	4	8	16	7	17	68	65	55
Barking	40	9	5	6	5	6	9	14	11	15	51	54	53
Chalfont St Peter	40	7	5	8	8	1	11	15	6	19	62	70	51
Leyton-Wingate	40	9	4	7	4	7	9	13	11	16	53	56	50
Uxbridge	40	5	7	8	8	1	11	13	8	19	47	62	47
Maidenhead United	40	5	3	12	8	4	8	13	7	20	52	61	46
Harlow Town	40	4	3	13	7	6	7	11	9	20	50	70	42
Croydon	40	7	3	10	4	3	13	11	6	23	44	68	39
Heybridge Swifts	40	4	4	12	4	5	11	8	9	23	33	71	33
Whyteleafe	40	2	6	12	5	4	11	7	10	23	42	78	31
Aveley	40	6	2	12	2	1	17	8	3	29	33	95	27

Division Two

	P	Home			Away			Totals			Goals		Pts
		W	D	L	W	D	L	W	D	L	F	A	
Purfleet	42	11	5	5	16	3	2	27	8	7	97	48	89
Lewes	42	12	6	3	11	8	2	23	14	5	74	36	83
Billericay Town	42	14	5	2	10	3	8	24	8	10	75	44	80
Leatherhead	42	13	2	6	10	4	7	23	6	13	68	40	75
Ruislip Manor	42	13	3	5	7	6	8	20	9	13	74	51	69
Egham Town	42	10	6	5	9	6	6	19	12	11	81	62	69
Metropolitan Police	42	13	5	3	7	4	10	20	9	13	76	58	69
Saffron Walden Town	42	8	6	7	11	5	5	19	11	12	86	67	68
Hemel Hempstead	42	10	4	7	8	6	7	18	10	14	63	50	64
Hungerford Town	42	9	7	5	9	0	12	18	7	17	53	58	61
Barton Rovers	42	9	5	7	8	3	10	17	8	17	61	64	59
Worthing	42	11	6	4	6	2	13	17	8	17	67	72	59
Witham Town	42	7	7	7	9	4	8	16	11	15	56	61	59
Banstead Athletic	42	7	7	7	9	3	9	16	10	16	69	58	58
Malden Vale	42	12	4	5	3	8	10	15	12	15	63	48	57
Rainham Town	42	9	4	8	5	9	7	14	13	15	53	48	55
Ware	42	8	6	7	3	12	14	14	9	19	58	62	51
Berkhamsted Town	42	10	2	9	3	9	9	13	11	18	56	57	50
Harefield United	42	6	4	11	5	3	13	11	7	24	47	66	40
Southall	42	6	3	12	2	4	15	8	7	27	39	93	31
Southwick	42	3	0	18	3	2	16	6	2	34	29	115	20
Newbury Town	42	2	3	16	2	5	14	4	8	30	30	117	20

Division Three

	P	Home W	D	L	Away W	D	L	Totals W	D	L	Goals F	A	Pts
Edgware Town	40	15	1	4	15	2	3	30	3	7	106	44	93
Chertsey Town	40	16	1	3	13	3	4	29	4	7	115	44	91
Tilbury	40	15	4	1	11	5	4	26	9	5	84	40	87
Hampton	40	15	2	3	11	3	6	26	5	9	93	35	83
Horsham	40	14	2	4	9	6	5	23	8	9	92	51	77
Cove	40	14	3	3	7	6	7	21	9	10	74	49	72
Flackwell Heath	40	11	5	4	8	7	5	19	12	9	78	50	69
Thame United	40	10	2	8	9	5	6	19	7	14	73	46	64
Epsom & Ewell	40	10	7	3	7	4	9	17	11	12	55	50	62
Collier Row	40	11	6	3	6	3	11	17	9	14	67	59	60
Royston Town	40	10	3	7	7	4	9	17	7	16	59	58	58
Kingsbury Town	40	7	8	5	5	2	13	12	10	18	54	61	46
Hertford Town	40	8	6	6	4	4	12	12	10	18	55	73	46
Petersfield United	40	8	3	9	4	6	10	12	9	19	45	67	45
Camberley Town	40	6	3	11	5	5	10	11	8	21	52	69	41
Feltham & Hounslow Borough	40	6	3	11	5	4	11	11	7	22	53	78	40
Bracknell Town	40	7	5	8	3	2	15	10	7	23	48	90	37
Hornchurch	40	5	6	9	3	1	16	8	7	25	40	87	31
Tring Town	40	6	3	11	3	1	16	9	4	27	35	94	31
Clapton	40	6	2	12	3	1	16	9	3	28	47	93	30
Eastbourne United	40	3	2	15	2	3	15	5	5	30	34	121	20

LEADING GOALSCORERS

Premier Division

		Lge	Lge. C	Loc
32	George Friel (Woking)	28	2	2
29	Jimmy Bolton (Carshalton Athletic)	22	6	1
25	Graham Westley (Enfield)	19	5	1
24	Steve Clark (St Albans City)	14	8	2
22	Dominic Feltham (Sutton U)	17	3	2

Division One

		Lge	Lge. C	Loc
36	Martin Gittings (Stevenage Borough)	29	1	6
27	Phil Grainger (Dorking)	22	2	2
22	Steve Portway (Barking)	21		1

Division Two

		Lge	Lge. C	Loc
36	Mark Butler (Egham T)	31	2	3
32	Steve Jones (Billericay Town)	29	3	
28	Richard Camp (Barton R)	25		3
26	Jeff Wood (Purfleet)	22		4

Division Three

		Lge	Lge. C	Loc
31	Nigel Thompson (Cove)	28		3
28	Tony Wood (Flackwell Heath)	27	1	
27	Gary Ewing (Hampton)	27		
	David Whitehead (Hertford Town)	27		

LEADING CLUB GOALSCORERS

Premier Division

	Total	Lge	Lge. C	Loc. C
Aylesbury United (Cliff Hercules)	17	17		
(Daren Collins)	17	17		
Basingstoke Town (Richard Smart)	15	15		
(inc 12 for Kingstonian)				
Bishops Stortford (Peter Petrou)	9	9		
Bognor Regis Town (Kevin Maddock)	9	9		
Bromley (Paul McMenemy)	11	10	1	
Carshalton Ath (Jimmy Bolton)	29	22	6	1
Chesham U (Micky Banton)	14	12	1	1
Dagenham (Leo West)	18	18		
Enfield (Graham Westley)	25	19	5	1
Grays Athletic (Winston Whittingham)	21	18	2	1
Harrow Borough (Steve Conroy)	16	14		2
Hayes (John Lawford)	19	18	1	
(inc 5 Lge and 1 Lge Cup for Bishops Stortford)				
Hendon (Mark Xavier)	18	12	4	2
Kingstonian (Richard Cherry)	19	16	1	2
(inc 1 Lge and 1 Lge Cup for Grays Athletic)				
Marlow (David Lay)	11	10		1
St Albans City (Steve Clark)	24	14	8	2
Staines Town (Gary Crawshaw)	10	10		
Sutton U (Dominic Feltham)	22	17	3	2
Windsor & Eton (Richard Evans)	19	17	2	
Wivenhoe T (Steve Restarick)	11	11		
Woking (George Friel)	32	28	2	2
Wokingham Town (David Thompson)	21	19		2

Division One

	Total	Lge	Lge. C	Loc. C
Abingdon Town (Paul Bradbury)	20	16	3	1
Aveley (Stewart Harvey)	8	8		
Barking (Steve Portway)	22	21		1
Borehamwood (Jimmy Hughes)	15	14	1	
(inc 1 Lge and 1 Lge Cup for Stevenage Borough)				
Chalfont St Peter (Ansill Bushay)	13	13		
(Steve Darlington)	13	13		
Croydon (Matt Norris)	13	12	1	
Dorking (Phil Grainger)	26	22	2	2
Dulwich Hamlet (Matt Norris)	19	18	1	
(inc 12 Lge + 1 Lge Cup for Croydon)				
Harlow Town (Paul Battram)	17	14	1	2
Heybridge Swifts (Wayne Adcock)	7	4	1	2
Hitchin T (Paul Quarmain)	11	11		
Leyton-Wingate (Micky Fredericks)	10	10		
Maidenhead United (Benny Laryea)	18	17		1
Molesey (Michael Rose)	13	11	1	1
Stevenage B (Martin Gittings)	36	29	1	6
Totting & Mitcham United (John Collins)	21	19	2	
Uxbridge (Steve Kuhne)	21	19		2
Walton & Hersham (Justin Mitchell)	11	11		
(Steve Griffiths)	11	11		
(inc 1 Lge for Sutton United)				
Wembley (Kenny Page)	10	9	1	
Whyteleafe (Ian Cox)	9	7	2	
Yeading (Hector Welsh)	17	17		

DIADORA FOOTBALL LEAGUE PREMIER DIVISION RESULTS 1991–92

	Aylesbury United	Basingstoke Town	Bishops Stortford	Bognor Regis Town	Bromley	Carshalton Athletic	Chesham United	Dagenham	Enfield	Grays Athletic	Harrow Borough	Hayes	Hendon	Kingstonian	Marlow	St Albans City	Staines Town	Sutton United	Windsor & Eton	Wivenhoe Town	Woking	Wokingham Town
Aylesbury United	—	2-1	0-0	1-1	1-2	0-0	1-2	1-1	1-1	3-1	7-1	0-0	4-1	0-1	1-0	2-0	0-1	4-4	4-0	1-1	0-4	4-0
Basingstoke Town	0-0	—	1-1	1-1	1-1	1-2	2-2	2-2	1-2	1-2	0-1	4-2	0-1	1-0	2-0	1-1	2-0	0-2	0-2	5-1	0-3	3-3
Bishops Stortford	1-0	0-1	—	1-2	2-3	1-0	0-0	0-4	0-1	3-0	2-0	1-1	3-2	1-3	0-2	1-1	1-2	0-2	1-1	1-2	1-2	1-5
Bognor Regis Town	2-2	1-2	1-1	—	0-0	1-0	0-6	1-0	0-1	2-2	2-2	3-4	1-4	2-2	0-1	2-4	2-2	0-0	0-1	3-0	1-1	1-3
Bromley	0-0	2-0	1-0	1-4	—	3-1	0-1	1-0	0-1	2-3	0-2	0-0	1-1	0-2	0-0	2-0	1-1	2-2	0-1	2-1	0-2	0-0
Carshalton Athletic	1-0	2-1	2-2	1-4	5-1	—	3-0	0-3	1-1	2-1	1-0	3-1	5-4	4-4	2-1	1-2	1-3	2-1	0-1	0-2	0-2	3-2
Chesham United	0-2	2-1	2-1	1-3	1-0	4-0	—	0-1	0-2	2-2	1-0	2-2	0-0	3-2	3-0	3-1	4-0	1-0	0-0	2-1	0-0	4-0
Dagenham	2-4	2-2	3-0	4-1	1-0	1-1	3-0	—	2-1	2-0	5-2	3-3	0-1	1-2	4-1	0-0	1-0	3-1	2-2	2-2	0-0	0-1
Enfield	2-2	0-2	1-0	1-2	1-1	2-1	3-2	3-5	—	2-0	3-0	2-0	1-0	4-0	4-1	0-0	1-0	3-1	0-0	1-0	1-0	0-1
Grays Athletic	3-3	1-0	3-1	1-2	5-1	2-1	1-3	2-1	0-4	—	3-0	2-0	0-0	1-2	1-2	2-0	1-1	0-2	0-0	4-1	0-2	1-1
Harrow Borough	0-4	5-1	3-2	4-1	2-1	1-2	1-1	2-2	1-2	0-2	—	2-4	1-1	1-1	2-1	2-2	6-1	1-1	3-1	1-0	1-3	1-2
Hayes	0-0	0-1	1-0	4-1	1-3	3-2	0-0	4-0	2-0	4-0	1-1	—	3-0	1-1	1-3	0-1	0-1	0-6	0-2	0-2	2-2	0-3
Hendon	1-2	0-2	0-1	3-1	4-1	1-1	2-3	4-0	1-0	2-0	1-1	1-0	—	4-1	1-2	3-5	5-0	0-0	1-1	2-0	0-5	2-1
Kingstonian	0-1	0-1	2-3	3-1	0-2	1-2	3-1	2-2	3-0	4-1	3-1	2-1	5-0	—	4-1	3-5	0-2	0-0	2-0	3-0	1-2	1-2
Marlow	0-0	2-4	1-0	2-1	0-4	4-1	3-0	2-0	0-1	1-0	1-0	4-0	4-0	2-1	—	0-0	4-0	1-0	1-1	1-2	0-3	1-1
St Albans City	3-3	1-1	3-2	2-3	4-2	2-0	1-2	1-2	1-2	1-2	1-2	0-1	1-1	2-2	2-0	—	1-2	1-3	1-1	1-2	1-1	0-3
Staines Town	0-0	4-1	2-2	0-1	0-1	1-2	1-5	1-2	0-1	0-1	6-0	0-0	1-3	1-2	1-0	1-2	—	1-3	0-3	3-0	1-7	2-0
Sutton United	1-2	1-2	2-2	5-0	0-1	2-0	1-1	5-3	0-1	5-0	1-1	3-2	4-2	2-2	3-2	2-3	1-2	—	4-1	4-2	2-0	5-0
Windsor & Eton	2-3	1-3	2-2	1-0	3-2	1-2	1-2	1-2	2-3	1-2	4-0	1-2	1-4	3-0	0-0	2-3	3-1	2-2	—	4-1	0-3	1-0
Wivenhoe Town	0-3	4-1	1-0	4-0	2-4	1-0	1-2	4-0	1-1	1-1	2-1	2-0	1-1	2-0	1-3	1-2	3-0	1-0	0-3	—	2-0	2-0
Woking	2-1	5-0	3-0	3-1	1-2	3-0	2-1	4-0	5-0	1-0	3-1	4-1	1-1	2-0	1-3	4-1	2-2	1-0	0-3	2-0	—	0-1
Wokingham Town	4-0	1-1	0-0	3-1	1-4	0-0	1-0	1-1	2-0	3-1	1-1	5-2	2-1	0-1	2-3	4-1	1-3	3-3	0-1	6-0	0-3	—

DIADORA FOOTBALL LEAGUE DIVISION ONE RESULTS 1991–92

	Abingdon Town	Aveley	Barking	Boreham Wood	Chalfont St Peter	Croydon	Dorking	Dulwich Hamlet	Harlow Town	Heybridge Swifts	Hitchin Town	Leyton-Wingate	Maidenhead United	Molesey	Stevenage Borough	Tooting & Mitcham	Uxbridge	Walton & Hersham	Wembley	Whyteleafe	Yeading
Abingdon Town	—	3-0	2-2	1-2	1-0	1-0	2-0	2-1	2-1	7-1	2-2	0-0	1-2	3-2	4-0	1-1	1-2	1-0	1-0	0-3	1-3
Aveley	0-1	—	2-1	1-2	2-0	0-4	2-0	2-5	0-4	0-0	1-0	1-5	1-0	1-1	0-4	0-2	0-4	1-0	0-2	0-1	0-2
Barking	1-0	5-1	—	2-0	1-0	3-3	2-1	2-0	0-1	1-0	0-2	2-2	2-0	1-1	1-3	0-3	0-1	0-1	1-1	2-1	1-1
Boreham Wood	2-0	4-0	1-1	—	4-2	3-0	3-3	1-1	0-1	0-0	3-0	3-1	1-0	2-0	0-3	4-0	3-0	2-3	1-2	2-2	0-1
Chalfont St Peter	1-3	1-2	1-2	1-1	—	1-1	3-2	1-2	2-0	4-1	1-1	1-2	0-1	2-0	0-0	2-0	2-1	1-1	1-2	2-1	2-4
Croydon	0-0	1-0	1-3	0-1	4-3	—	3-2	0-4	2-0	1-0	2-0	2-0	1-0	0-1	0-1	1-1	1-2	0-3	0-1	2-3	0-3
Dorking	3-0	3-1	2-2	0-1	2-3	1-0	—	3-1	0-3	1-2	4-0	3-3	1-0	0-2	3-1	1-3	0-3	3-0	2-1	0-2	1-1
Dulwich Hamlet	1-1	2-0	3-0	0-1	2-3	1-0	3-4	—	1-0	3-2	3-1	1-0	2-1	0-2	0-1	1-1	2-1	3-0	1-0	1-1	0-0
Harlow Town	1-3	2-3	0-2	0-1	1-3	2-1	0-2	2-0	—	0-1	2-1	2-1	2-2	0-1	0-2	2-2	1-5	2-3	2-5	1-1	1-3
Heybridge Swifts	0-1	2-1	1-1	2-3	2-4	2-0	1-3	0-2	1-1	—	0-0	1-3	0-3	0-1	0-2	2-3	2-0	0-0	1-3	3-1	0-2
Hitchin Town	1-1	5-2	1-0	0-3	1-3	1-1	1-2	0-1	1-1	1-0	—	3-1	2-0	1-1	1-1	0-1	4-0	0-0	4-0	2-0	1-0
Leyton-Wingate	1-0	4-2	0-3	0-2	0-2	1-0	1-2	1-1	0-0	2-0	1-3	—	1-2	2-2	2-2	2-1	4-0	1-3	2-1	3-0	1-0
Maidenhead United	1-2	3-2	4-0	0-2	3-1	0-1	1-3	0-1	3-3	1-1	1-3	3-2	—	1-2	0-3	0-3	2-1	1-2	0-0	1-2	0-2
Molesey	0-2	2-1	4-0	0-1	2-1	2-4	0-3	0-4	1-1	3-1	2-4	0-0	1-3	—	1-1	2-0	4-1	0-3	1-2	2-1	2-4
Stevenage Borough	4-1	5-0	2-0	0-1	5-1	4-2	0-3	1-1	7-1	3-1	3-1	4-1	2-0	3-2	—	2-0	2-0	3-2	2-0	4-0	2-2
Tooting & Mitcham	2-1	3-0	1-1	0-1	1-3	3-2	2-2	1-1	2-3	2-0	0-0	1-0	2-1	0-0	3-1	—	2-0	0-0	0-1	3-1	0-1
Uxbridge	1-2	1-0	0-0	2-3	2-0	1-0	1-1	1-2	1-3	1-1	1-1	0-2	2-2	2-3	1-3	1-1	—	2-1	0-0	2-0	0-3
Walton & Hersham	1-1	4-2	3-2	2-1	1-2	2-0	2-2	0-1	2-2	0-0	2-1	1-1	2-2	0-1	2-3	1-1	4-0	—	0-1	4-1	2-2
Wembley	2-1	3-1	2-1	1-0	2-2	1-0	1-0	3-2	1-0	0-1	3-2	2-1	1-2	0-2	0-1	1-3	0-1	3-0	—	1-1	0-0
Whyteleafe	1-3	1-1	1-3	2-2	2-0	2-3	1-4	1-0	1-3	1-3	0-2	1-1	0-2	1-1	0-1	1-0	1-1	0-3	1-3	—	1-1
Yeading	2-1	3-0	1-0	0-1	5-0	4-2	3-2	0-1	3-0	4-0	0-2	0-0	2-2	6-2	4-0	1-1	1-2	2-0	2-1	5-2	—

DIADORA FOOTBALL LEAGUE DIVISION TWO RESULTS 1991–92

	Banstead Athletic	Barton Rovers	Berkhamsted	Billericay	Egham Town	Harefield United	Hemel Hempstead	Hungerford Town	Leatherhead	Lewes	Malden Vale	Metropolitan Police	Newbury Town	Purfleet	Rainham Town	Ruislip Manor	Saffron Walden	Southall	Southwick	Ware	Witham Town	Worthing
Banstead Athletic	—	1-1	2-2	1-0	0-0	2-1	1-1	0-1	2-1	2-3	3-1	0-1	7-1	3-3	0-0	3-4	1-2	4-1	2-0	1-1	0-1	0-2
Barton Rovers	0-2	—	2-1	0-0	0-1	2-0	0-3	2-1	0-3	0-1	2-1	2-1	1-1	1-2	1-1	1-1	2-3	5-1	3-0	3-0	1-1	3-0
Berkhamsted	3-1	4-1	—	2-3	1-2	1-3	1-2	2-3	1-0	0-0	0-3	3-0	1-1	1-1	0-1	2-5	1-4	2-0	5-1	4-0	2-0	3-0
Billericay	2-0	4-0	2-0	—	2-2	1-1	0-0	4-1	0-3	1-1	3-0	3-2	7-0	0-2	1-1	4-3	2-1	1-0	4-0	1-0	4-1	3-1
Egham Town	3-1	2-1	1-1	1-4	—	1-1	3-1	1-3	0-1	1-1	2-1	4-2	2-0	3-4	1-1	3-2	1-1	5-0	5-4	1-1	5-1	1-3
Harefield United	1-2	0-2	1-1	0-3	0-3	—	4-0	0-1	2-3	2-1	0-0	2-1	2-0	2-4	2-3	0-0	1-1	4-0	5-2	1-2	1-0	0-1
Hemel Hempstead	4-1	0-1	1-0	0-1	0-3	2-0	—	1-3	2-1	3-1	3-1	1-1	6-1	1-1	1-0	2-0	0-1	4-0	0-2	6-3	1-0	2-2
Hungerford Town	0-0	1-1	2-1	2-0	1-3	2-1	2-2	—	0-0	0-0	2-0	1-0	1-1	1-2	2-0	2-1	1-1	1-2	2-1	0-2	0-1	4-1
Leatherhead	0-1	1-0	0-2	1-0	0-3	1-0	4-0	1-0	—	1-1	1-0	0-1	4-0	3-1	1-0	0-3	0-0	4-0	2-1	1-2	2-0	3-0
Lewes	2-2	1-2	3-2	2-1	0-0	4-0	2-0	2-1	1-1	—	1-1	2-2	5-0	1-3	0-0	0-2	4-0	3-0	2-0	1-2	1-0	9-1
Malden Vale	1-0	1-2	3-0	3-0	4-1	4-0	2-0	2-1	1-0	2-3	—	1-1	3-0	0-2	1-1	1-1	4-4	1-1	2-0	3-1	1-2	2-1
Metropolitan Police	3-2	0-0	3-0	1-2	3-3	4-1	1-0	3-2	2-1	2-2	1-1	—	0-0	1-2	2-0	1-0	2-2	6-1	4-1	3-0	5-1	1-0
Newbury Town	1-3	3-5	1-1	1-1	2-1	0-1	1-2	0-2	0-4	0-3	0-4	0-1	—	0-6	1-3	1-2	1-7	1-0	0-3	1-3	2-4	1-2
Purfleet	2-0	5-0	3-1	0-1	4-3	2-2	1-1	1-2	2-3	2-3	1-0	1-3	4-1	—	2-1	1-2	1-2	2-0	4-0	1-1	1-1	2-1
Rainham Town	2-1	0-0	0-0	0-1	0-1	5-1	2-2	0-1	1-1	1-1	1-1	1-1	3-0	1-2	—	2-3	3-2	3-0	0-1	2-1	1-1	2-1
Ruislip Manor	1-0	1-3	0-1	0-1	2-0	1-0	2-2	3-0	3-1	1-1	2-1	3-1	3-0	1-4	1-1	—	1-1	3-0	1-0	4-1	2-0	2-1
Saffron Walden	1-1	1-2	2-0	1-0	1-1	1-0	0-1	4-0	4-2	1-1	4-2	3-2	1-2	1-2	2-2	3-3	—	2-2	5-0	0-4	3-3	3-1
Southall	1-2	2-1	1-1	0-1	1-2	1-0	0-3	2-4	0-0	0-0	0-3	0-4	1-2	0-4	0-0	1-0	2-3	—	7-1	1-0	2-3	2-0
Southwick	1-6	0-3	0-1	0-2	2-5	1-3	0-3	1-0	0-2	0-2	0-3	1-2	1-2	1-2	0-2	0-4	0-2	0-2	—	0-0	0-2	0-4
Ware	1-3	4-1	1-1	4-0	1-0	2-4	1-1	2-0	1-1	1-1	1-1	2-0	3-0	1-4	4-2	2-2	1-6	4-0	9-1	—	1-2	0-1
Witham Town	1-2	2-4	0-0	1-1	1-0	1-0	0-1	2-0	1-1	0-1	1-1	2-3	0-0	2-0	4-2	1-1	1-6	4-0	0-0	2-0	—	1-1
Worthing	1-4	5-1	1-1	5-4	1-1	1-0	1-1	5-1	1-2	2-2	0-0	3-0	4-1	0-4	2-0	2-1	3-2	4-1	1-0	0-1	0-0	—

DIADORA FOOTBALL LEAGUE DIVISION THREE RESULTS 1991-92

	Bracknell Town	Camberley Town	Chertsey Town	Clapton	Collier Row	Cove	Eastbourne United	Edgware Town	Epsom & Ewell	Feltham & Hounslow	Flackwell Heath	Hampton	Hertford Town	Hornchurch	Horsham	Kingsbury Town	Petersfield United	Royston Town	Thame United	Tilbury	Tring Town
Bracknell Town	—	4-2	0-4	1-0	1-1	2-0	4-3	1-5	1-1	1-2	1-3	0-5	0-1	5-1	1-4	2-1	1-1	1-1	1-2	2-2	3-0
Camberley Town	2-3	—	0-2	2-0	0-3	0-1	4-1	2-3	3-1	3-2	2-3	0-1	0-0	2-2	3-1	0-2	1-2	1-2	0-2	0-0	3-0
Chertsey Town	2-0	4-0	—	10-1	1-2	2-1	5-1	4-2	0-1	4-1	2-4	1-3	2-0	4-2	3-4	3-1	1-1	3-0	1-0	4-2	5-0
Clapton	1-0	0-1	10-1	—	3-1	0-3	5-1	0-5	0-1	0-1	4-0	4-0	4-0	0-1	2-2	0-0	1-2	2-0	0-1	0-4	6-0
Collier Row	5-0	1-1	1-2	2-0	—	3-3	3-0	2-2	4-0	1-0	2-1	2-1	6-2	2-0	0-2	4-1	1-1	0-3	3-3	0-0	1-0
Cove	4-0	3-0	2-1	0-3	3-3	—	2-0	1-2	1-3	1-1	4-3	2-1	3-1	2-0	3-0	2-3	0-0	2-0	1-1	2-1	5-0
Eastbourne United	2-1	1-4	0-3	3-0	4-1	1-2	—	1-1	0-1	1-1	1-5	0-6	1-3	2-1	0-1	0-8	2-3	1-3	0-3	0-6	0-3
Edgware Town	2-1	2-1	3-1	4-0	3-0	3-1	9-1	—	2-0	2-0	3-4	2-1	5-0	3-2	2-4	2-0	4-0	2-0	2-3	1-2	5-0
Epsom & Ewell	1-1	1-1	2-3	3-1	2-2	1-1	2-0	0-1	—	3-1	2-2	1-1	3-1	2-0	0-1	2-0	3-1	1-0	1-0	0-0	2-0
Feltham & Hounslow	1-4	2-2	1-3	3-2	1-0	1-1	1-1	0-1	2-0	—	4-3	0-3	1-2	6-0	2-0	1-0	0-1	0-4	1-6	1-2	4-0
Flackwell Heath	3-0	0-1	0-0	4-0	0-3	5-0	1-2	0-1	2-2	3-1	—	2-1	0-0	3-1	3-1	2-0	2-1	2-2	3-1	1-2	2-1
Hampton	4-0	0-0	2-1	3-2	3-2	0-0	5-0	0-1	3-0	2-1	2-1	—	4-2	6-0	0-0	4-1	3-0	2-0	2-0	3-2	1-2
Hertford Town	2-1	6-2	4-1	5-3	4-1	0-3	0-2	0-1	2-2	2-4	0-0	0-3	—	4-1	2-2	2-0	3-0	0-0	0-3	3-0	1-1
Hornchurch	1-1	3-0	1-2	0-1	2-1	1-2	3-0	1-4	1-3	3-4	1-1	1-3	2-0	—	1-1	1-1	3-1	1-0	1-1	0-2	0-1
Horsham	7-0	0-0	0-0	4-1	1-0	4-1	4-0	4-0	5-1	4-2	1-1	1-2	2-1	5-1	—	2-1	3-1	4-2	3-0	2-4	2-0
Kingsbury Town	2-1	0-2	0-2	0-1	0-1	1-0	4-0	0-3	1-1	2-0	1-1	0-0	1-1	1-2	1-0	—	1-1	1-1	2-2	1-2	1-0
Petersfield United	0-1	1-0	1-1	2-0	3-0	2-2	2-2	0-2	0-1	2-2	0-3	2-1	2-0	3-2	1-1	1-5	—	0-3	0-3	2-3	6-1
Royston Town	1-0	2-1	3-1	4-1	0-1	2-3	4-0	0-4	2-1	0-1	1-1	0-2	3-3	1-0	2-4	4-2	3-2	—	0-4	2-2	3-0
Thame United	6-1	2-1	1-0	4-2	4-1	1-0	3-3	1-2	1-0	1-1	1-1	1-1	2-0	0-1	0-1	5-1	4-2	1-2	—	1-3	2-0
Tilbury	2-0	6-1	4-2	4-1	0-1	0-0	3-1	2-1	3-2	2-0	1-1	0-2	3-0	2-0	1-1	3-0	1-0	1-0	2-0	—	3-0
Tring Town	3-1	0-4	5-0	3-3	2-1	0-0	3-1	1-4	1-3	1-0	0-1	0-2	0-2	4-1	2-3	1-2	4-1	0-1	0-0	1-2	—

THE LOCTITE CUP COMPETITION 1991–92

First Round
Aveley 1, St Albans City 6
Aylesbury United 1, Barking 3
Basingstoke Town 1, Croydon 0
Harrow Borough 2, Heybridge Swifts 2 (aet)
 (Harrow Borough won 5–4 on penalties)
Hendon 3, Chalfont St Peter 1
Hitchin Town 0, Abingdon Town 3
Tooting & Mitcham United 1, Stevenage Borough 2 (aet)
Wembley 0, Uxbridge 1
Windsor & Eton 2, Harlow Town 3
Wokingham Town 2, Bishops Stortford 0
Yeading 3, Kingstonian 2 (aet)

Second Round
Barking 1, Dagenham 5
Borehamwood 1, Yeading 2 (aet)
Bromley 0, Bognor Regis Town 1
Dorking 3, Harrow Borough 4
Enfield 2, Molesey 2 (aet)
 (Molesey won 4–2 on penalties)
Harlow Town 2, Hayes 4
Hendon 1, Abingdon Town 2
Leyton-Wingate 0, Chesham United 4
Maidenhead United 2, Basingstoke Town 2 (aet)
 (Basingstoke Town won 3–2 on penalties)
Marlow 1, Carshalton Athletic 2
St Albans City 1, Wokingham Town 3
Staines Town 0, Dulwich Hamlet 3
Sutton United 4, Whyteleafe 0
Uxbridge 4, Grays Athletic 2 (aet)

Wivenhoe Town 0, Stevenage Borough 4
Woking 2, Walton & Hersham 1

Third Round
Carshalton Athletic 2, Abingdon Town 1
Chesham United 2, Woking 5
Dagenham 0, Yeading 2
Dulwich Hamlet 0, Bognor Regis Town 0 (aet)
 (Dulwich Hamlet won 5–4 on penalties)
Harrow Borough 2, Wokingham Town 0
Hayes 1, Uxbridge 3 (aet)
Molesey 4, Stevenage Borough 4 (aet)
 (Molesey won 3–0 on penalties)
Sutton United 3, Basingstoke Town 2

Fourth Round
Dulwich Hamlet 0, Sutton United 0 (aet)
 (Sutton United won 5–4 on penalties)
Harrow Borough 2, Carshalton Athletic 2 (aet)
 (Harrow Borough won 3–1 on penalties)
Molesey 1, Uxbridge 0 (aet)
Woking 1, Yeading 0

Semi-finals
Harrow Borough 0, Woking 2
Sutton United 4, Molesey 1

Final
Sutton United 2, Woking 0
 (at Hayes FC)

THE LOCTITE TROPHY 1991–92

First Round
Banstead Athletic 7, Eastbourne United 1
Barton Rovers 3, Horsham 2 (aet)
Collier Row 4, Lewes 3
Cove 4, Berkhamsted Town 0
Epsom & Ewell 3, Hertford Town 1
Hampton 2, Hornchurch 1
Hemel Hempstead 0, Harefield United 2
Leatherhead 1, Ware 3
Ruislip Manor 1, Witham Town 0
Tilbury 0, Purfleet 2
Tring Town 1, Camberley Town 2

Second Round
Banstead Athletic 0, Southall 1
Barton Rovers 10, Southwick 2
Bracknell Town 1, Newbury Town 1 (aet)
 (Newbury Town won 4–2 on penalties)
Chertsey Town 1, Kingsbury Town 3
Clapton 1, Ruislip Manor 3
Collier Row 2, Saffron Walden Town 4
Cove 2, Hampton 1
Epsom & Ewell 4, Royston Town 1
Flackwell Heath 0, Egham Town 1
Harefield United 2, Camberley Town 1
Hungerford Town 0, Malden Vale 1
Metropolitan Police 1, Feltham & Hounslow Borough 2
Petersfield United 2, Rainham Town 1
Purfleet 2, Edgeware Town 0

Thame United 1, Billericay Town 0
Ware 2, Worthing 3

Third Round
Egham Town 3, Harefield United 0
Epsom & Ewell 0, Cove 1
Feltham & Hounslow Borough 1, Ruislip Manor 3 (aet)
Kingsbury Town 0, Barton Rovers 2
Newbury Town 0, Purfleet 5
Petersfield United 1, Thame United 2
Saffron Walden Town 4, Southall 1
Worthing 0, Malden Vale 3

Fourth Round
Cove 0, Saffron Walden Town 2
Egham Town 2, Thame United 0
Malden Vale 6, Barton Rovers 0
Purfleet 3, Ruislip Manor 0

Semi-finals
Malden Vale 2, Egham Town 2 (aet)
Saffron Walden Town 0, Purfleet 2

Replay
Egham Town 4, Malden Vale 3

Final
Purfleet 3, Egham Town 2
 (at Sutton Utd FC)

THE LOCTITE YOUTH CUP 1991–92

First Round
Chalfont St Peter 0, Kingsbury Town 1
Feltham & Hounslow Borough 5, Egham Town 6
Flackwell Heath 3, Marlow 1
Harrow Borough 1, Clapton 4
Hitchin Town 0, Borehamwood 3
Kingstonian 4, Croydon 1
Lewes 5, Horsham 4
Maidenhead United 4, Bracknell Town 2
Malden Vale 4, Hampton 0
Ruislip Manor 3, Uxbridge 1
Saffron Walden Town 5, Wivenhoe Town 3
Southall 2, Yeading 2 (aet)
 (Yeading won 7–6 on penalties)
Southwick 1, Carshalton Athletic 5
Stevenage Borough 0, St Albans City 18
Sutton United 3, Leatherhead 0

Tring Town 1, Wokingham Town 1 (aet)
 (Wokingham Town won 4–3 on penalties)

Second Round
Billericay Town 3, Leyton-Wingate 3 (aet)
 (Leyton-Wingate won 4–3 on penalties)
Carshalton Athletic 2, Basingstoke Town 1 (aet)
Egham Town 2, Ruislip Manor 4
Epsom & Ewell 0, Bromley 1
Harefield United 0, Clapton 2
Hendon 1, St Albans City 4
Hertford Town 1, Borehamwood 2
 (Ordered to be replayed)
Hertford Town 0, Borehamwood 2
Maidenhead United 2, Flackwell Heath 2 (aet)
 (Maidenhead United won 5–3 on penalties)
Molesey 3, Kingstonian 5

Petersfield United 3, Whyteleafe 2
Saffron Walden Town 13, Witham Town 0
Staines Town 1, Yeading 2
Sutton United 2, Lewes 3
Walton & Hersham 2, Malden Vale 0
Wembley 5, Kingsbury Town 3
Wokingham Town 1, Newbury Town 0

Third Round
Borehamwood 3, St Albans City 3 (aet)
(Borehamwood won 8–7 penalties)
Carshalton Athletic 4, Bromley 3 (aet)
Clapton 3, Wembley 1 (aet)
Kingstonian 2, Petersfield United 1
(Kingstonian removed from competition)
Maidenhead United 0, Wokingham Town 3
Lewes 2, Walton & Hersham 0

Saffron Walden Town 5, Leyton-Wingate 3
Yeading 5, Ruislip Manor 0

Fourth Round
Lewes 3, Borehamwood 1
Saffron Walden Town 0, Clapton 4
Wokingham Town 2, Carshalton Athletic 3 (aet)
Yeading 1, Petersfield United 2

Semi-finals
Carshalton Athletic 1, Clapton 1 (aet)
Lewes 3, Petersfield United 2

Replay
Clapton 4, Carshalton Athletic 1

Final
Clapton 1, Lewes 3
(at Bromley FC)

LEAGUE CUP 1991–92

Preliminary Round
Abingdon Town 2, Hemel Hempstead 0
Barton Rovers 3, Clapton 2
Billericay Town 4, Petersfield United 1
Bracknell Town 0, Harefield United 1
Chertsey Town 1, Tring Town 0
Collier Row 1, Ruislip Manor 4
Eastbourne United 2, Southwick 2 (aet)
Edgware Town 0, Ware 1 (aet)
Hertford Town 2, Purfleet 1
Horsham 4, Feltham & Hounslow Borough 1
Hungerford Town 2, Berkhamsted Town 4
Leatherhead 1, Banstead Athletic 2
Lewes 0, Hornchurch 0 (aet)
Maidenhead United 2, Kingsbury Town 3 (aet)
Malden Vale w/o Vauxhall Motors
Rainham Town 4, Epsom & Ewell 2
(at Epsom & Ewell FC)
Saffron Walden Town 2, Newbury Town 2 (aet)
Southall 3, Metropolitan Police 1
Stevenage Borough 3, Cove 0
Thame United 1, Camberley Town 2
Tilbury 1, Hampton 0
Witham Town 1, Flackwell Heath 2 (aet)
Worthing 1, Egham Town 1 (aet)

Replays
Egham Town 4, Worthing 2
Hornchurch 2, Lewes 3
Newbury Town 0, Saffron Walden Town 2
Southwick 6, Eastbourne United 0

First Round
Abingdon Town 2, Harefield United 0
Aveley 1, Hayes 3
Barking 4, Southwick 3
Banstead Athletic 1, Grays Athletic 2
Barton Rovers 1, Woking 3
Basingstoke Town 1, Dagenham 0
Bishops Stortford 1, Hertford Town 2 (aet)
Carshalton Athletic 3, Croydon 2
Chalfont St Peter 4, Hendon 6 (aet)
Chertsey Town 2, Aylesbury United 0
Chesham United 2, Tooting & Mitcham United 2 (aet)
Dorking 2, Malden Vale 1
Egham Town 2, Borehamwood 0
Harrow Borough 2, Walton & Hersham 1
Heybridge Swifts 1, Kingstonian 0
Hitchin Town 1, Billericay Town 2 (aet)
Lewes 3, Camberley Town 0
Leyton-Wingate 1, Bromley 2
Marlow 2, Wokingham Town 1
Molesey 1, Kingsbury Town 0
Rainham Town 1, Bognor Regis Town 0
(at Purfleet FC)
Royston Town 0, Berkhamsted Town 2
Ruislip Manor 2, St Albans City 3
Saffron Walden Town 0, Enfield 2
Southall 1, Tilbury 3
Staines Town 2, Flackwell Heath 0
Sutton United 2, Stevenage Borough 1
Uxbridge 0, Harlow Town 3
Ware 2, Horsham 2 (aet)
Whyteleafe 2, Wivenhoe Town 1
Windsor & Eton 4, Wembley 1

Yeading 2, Dulwich Hamlet 1 (aet)

Replays
Horsham 1, Ware 2
Tooting & Mitcham United 2, Chesham United 3

Second Round
Abingdon Town 2, Lewes 0
Barking 2, Heybridge Swifts 1
Berkhamsted Town 1, Carshalton Athletic 6
Chertsey Town 1, Enfield 4
Dorking 3, Molesey 3 (aet)
Egham Town 0, Billericay Town 1
(Billericay Town removed from competition)
Harlow Town 0, Grays Athletic 4
Harrow Borough 1, Basingstoke Town 0
Hayes 1, Yeading 0
Hertford Town 0, Sutton United 5
Marlow 3, Windsor & Eton 4 (aet)
St Albans City 4, Bromley 1
Staines Town 0, Chesham United 1
Tilbury 3, Hendon 0
Ware 2, Whyteleafe 1
Woking 4, Rainham Town 1

Replay
Molesey 0, Dorking 2

Third Round
Abingdon Town 1, Sutton United 2
Chesham United 1, Woking 2
Dorking 3, Grays Athletic 4
Enfield 3, Hayes 0
Harrow Borough 0, Carshalton Athletic 1
St Albans City 5, Tilbury 0
Ware 2, Barking 0
Windsor & Eton 0, Egham Town 0 (aet)

Replay
Egham Town 0, Windsor & Eton 0

Second Replay
Egham Town 3, Windsor & Eton 1

Fourth Round
Carshalton Athletic 2, Ware 2 (aet)
Egham Town 1, Grays Athletic 4
Sutton United 2, St Albans City 3 (aet)
Woking 0, Enfield 2

Replay
Ware 1, Carshalton Athletic 0

Semi-finals First Leg
St Albans City 2, Grays Athletic 2
Ware 1, Enfield 2

Semi-finals Second Leg
Enfield 0, Ware 0
(Enfield won 2–1 on agg)
Grays Athletic 1, St Albans City 0
(Grays Athletic won 3–2 on agg)

Final
Enfield 1, Grays Athletic 3
(At Dagenham FC)

952

FA CHALLENGE TROPHY (later known as Vauxhall FA Trophy) 1991–92

First Round Qualifying
Whitby Town v Newcastle Blue Star	2-1
Ferryhill Athletic v Whitley Bay	0-2
Alnwick Town v Southport	0-5
Peterlee Newtown v Murton	0-2
Workington v Northallerton Town	2-2, 0-4
Consett v Shildon	0-3
Brandon United v Spennymoor United	1-1, 0-1
Whickham v North Shields	1-2
Willenhall Town v Colwyn Bay	3-1
Rhyl v Halesowen Town	1-1, 2-1
Moor Green v Radcliffe Borough	5-2
Goole Town v Warrington Town	2-1
Alvechurch v Gainsborough Trinity	0-1
Winsford United v Newtown	3-0
Dudley Town v Redditch United	5-3
Bromsgrove Rovers v Bedworth United	1-1, 2-1
Nuneaton Borough v Marine	0-0, 2-2, 0-1
Eastwood Town v Caernarfon Town	5-1
Worksop Town v Matlock Town	1-1, 3-3, 0-2
Grantham Town v Buxton	0-2
Congleton Town v Atherstone United	0-3
Mossley v Alfreton Town	2-3
Corby Town v Leyton-Wingate	1-3
Stevenage Borough v Wembley	2-3
Chelmsford City v St Albans City	0-1
Vauxhall Motors v Staines Town	
(walkover for Staines Town)	
Barking v Rushden Town	4-2
Hitchin Town v Grays Athletic	2-1
Chalfont St Peter v Stourbridge	3-2
Boreham Wood v Aveley	4-1
Hayes v Baldock Town	3-1
Chesham United v Tamworth	1-0
Yeading v Fareham Town	2-1
Uxbridge v Tooting & Mitcham United	1-2
Molesey v Marlow	2-3
Andover v Bashley	1-2
Bromley v Basingstoke Town	3-0
Gosport Borough v Croydon	4-1
Maidenhead United v Canterbury City	4-0
Erith & Belvedere v Walton & Hersham	3-3, 1-2
Margate v Abingdon Town	1-1, 1-0
Dorking v Bognor Regis Town	2-1
Waterlooville v Crawley Town	3-2
Trowbridge Town v Dorchester Town	1-1, 2-3
Ton Pentre v Barry Town	2-3
Taunton Town v Maesteg Park	6-2
Bideford v Newport AFC	0-1
Bridgend Town v Poole Town	3-1
Cwmbran Town v Salisbury	0-1
(at Salisbury FC)	
Weston-super-Mare v Saltash United	2-2, 3-5

Second Round Qualifying
Southport v North Shields	4-1
Accrington Stanley v Shildon	5-2
Northallerton Town v Whitley Bay	0-0, 3-2
Whitby Town v Murton	5-1
Spennymoor United v Easington Colliery	1-2
Bromsgrove Rovers v Hednesford Town	1-0
Goole Town v Marine	1-3
Alfreton Town v Atherstone United	0-3
Dudley Town v Shepshed Albion	2-1
Eastwood Town v Rhyl	1-2
Droylsden v Winsford United	1-1, 3-1
Willenhall Town v Matlock Town	2-3
Leicester United v Gainsborough Trinity	1-0
Buxton v Moor Green	1-3
Chesham United v Leyton-Wingate	1-0
Barking v Chalfont St Peter	0-2
Staines Town v Heybridge Swifts	0-1
Sutton Coldfield Town v Hayes	2-0
Bishops Stortford v Boreham Wood	1-1, 1-0
Hitchin v St Albans City	2-3
Wembley v Harlow Town	0-0, 1-0
Dorking v Yeading	2-1
Bromley v Maidenhead United	2-0
Bashley v Ashford Town	3-1
Whyteleafe v Margate	1-2
Waterlooville v Walton & Hersham	1-1, 0-4
Gosport Borough v Marlow	0-2
Tooting & Mitcham United v Dulwich Hamlet	3-0

Barry Town v Bridgend Town	2-0
Newport AFC v Saltash United	5-4
Llanelli v Dorchester Town	1-3
Salisbury v Taunton Town	4-1

Third Round Qualifying
Chorley v Frickley Athletic	0-2
Fleetwood Town v Seaham Red Star	4-0
Morecambe v Emley	2-2, 4-2
Northallerton Town v Matlock Town	4-2
Tow Law Town v Bishop Auckland	0-3
(at Crook Town FC)	
Whitby Town v Easington Colliery	1-0
Rhyl v Southport	0-3
Horwich RMI v Marine	1-3
Billingham Synthonia v Droylsden	4-1
South Bank v Bangor City	1-1, 0-1
(1st match at Middlesbrough FC)	
Blyth Spartans v Accrington Stanley	4-0
Fisher Athletic v Bromsgrove Rovers	1-1, 0-2
VS Rugby v Leicester United	2-1
Dudley Town v Worcester City	2-3
Wembley v Chalfont St Peter	2-0
Sutton Coldfield Town v Cambridge City	2-1
Hendon v Wealdstone	0-0, 1-4
Harrow Borough v Bishops Stortford	2-1
Atherstone United v Heybridge Swifts	1-1, 1-0
Burton Albion v Chesham United	0-0, 0-4
Moor Green v Boston United	1-3
Dagenham v St Albans City	3-2
Tooting & Mitcham U v Walton & Hersham	0-0, 1-2
Dorking v Barry Town	2-1
Stroud v Newport AFC	1-3
Windsor & Eton v Sutton United	2-2, 2-4
Gravesend & Northfleet v Marlow	2-1
Bromley v Weymouth	1-0
Wokingham Town v Salisbury	0-0, 0-1
Slough Town v Margate	0-0, 2-1
Bashley v Carshalton Athletic	2-0
Kingstonian v Dorchester Town	3-0

First Round Proper
Witton Albion v Billingham Synthonia	2-2, 2-1
Macclesfield Town v Boston United	0-0, 2-0
Southport v Bishop Auckland	1-0
Northwich Victoria v Hyde United	1-0
Whitby Town v Barrow	0-2
Altrincham v Stalybridge Celtic	1-2
Blyth Spartans v Gateshead	0-0, 0-3
Telford United v Guisborough Town	2-0
Frickley Athletic v Northallerton Town	2-2, 0-1
Fleetwood Town v Morecambe	1-1, 0-1
Bangor City v Gretna	0-0, 2-1
Stafford Rangers v Marine	0-1
Leek Town v Runcorn	3-3, 1-3
Welling United v Dover Athletic	3-2
Wycombe Wanderers v Salisbury	3-0
Woking v Wembley	4-2
Redbridge Forest v Bromsgrove Rovers	1-1, 1-0
Gloucester City v Harrow Borough	1-2
Wivenhoe Town v Marlow	1-0
Sutton Coldfield Town v Farnborough Town	0-3
Colchester United v Kingstonian	2-2, 3-2
VS Rugby v Kettering Town	0-1
Bromley v Worcester City	1-0
Atherstone United v Dorking	1-3
Yeovil Town v Chesham United	3-1
Walton & Hersham v Kidderminster Harriers	0-2
Merthyr Tydfil v Dartford	1-1, 2-1
Aylesbury United v Newport AFC	3-0
Dagenham v Bashley	0-0, 0-2
Sutton United v Bath City	1-2
Enfield v Slough Town	4-0
Cheltenham Town v Wealdstone	3-2

Second Round Proper
Telford United v Northallerton Town	3-0
Morecambe v Welling United	2-1
Runcorn v Kidderminster Harriers	1-1, 2-5
Gateshead v Barrow	1-0
Bromley v Yeovil Town	1-3
Macclesfield Town v Bangor City	1-0
Witton Albion v Aylesbury United	1-0

Northwich Victoria v Cheltenham Town	4-2
Bashley v Kettering Town	2-3
Bath City v Dorking	2-0
Harrow Borough v Stalybridge Celtic	1-3
Marine v Wivenhoe Town	3-0
Farnborough Town v Southport	5-0
Merthyr Tydfil v Colchester United	0-0, 0-1
Wycombe Wanderers v Woking	1-0
Redbridge Forest v Enfield	2-0

Third Round Proper

Northwich Victoria v Macclesfield Town	0-1
Redbridge Forest v Farnborough Town	3-2
Colchester United v Morecambe	3-1
Witton Albion v Stalybridge Celtic	1-0
Telford United v Gateshead	0-0, 1-0
(replay at Blyth Spartans FC)	
Marine v Kettering Town	2-1
Bath City v Wycombe Wanderers	1-1, 0-2
Yeovil Town v Kidderminster Harriers	3-1

Fourth Round Proper

| Marine v Redbridge Forest | 1-1, 1-0 |

Yeovil Town v Macclesfield Town	1-2
Colchester United v Telford United	4-0
Wycombe Wanderers v Witton Albion	1-2

Semi-finals

| Colchester United v Macclesfield Town | 3-0, 1-1 |
| Witton Albion v Marine | 2-2, 4-1 |

FINAL at Wembley

10 MAY

Colchester United (2) 3 *(Masters, Smith, McGavin)*

Witton Albion (0) 1 *(Lutkevitch)* 27,806

Colchester United: Barrett; Donald, Roberts, Kinsella, English, Martin, Cook, Masters, McDonough (Bennett), McGavin, Smith.
Witton Albion: Mason; Halliday, Coathup, McNeilis, Connor Jim, Anderson, Thomas, Rose, Alford, Grimshaw (Connor Joe), Lutkevitch (McCluskie).
Referee: K. Barratt (Coventry).

FA CHALLENGE TROPHY FINALS 1970–91

Year						Year					
1970	Macclesfield T	2	Telford U	0		1981	Bishop's Stortford	1	Sutton U		0
1971	Telford U	3	Hillingdon B	2		1982	Enfield	1	Altrincham	aet	0
1972	Stafford R	3	Barnet	0		1983	Telford U	2	Northwich V		1
1973	Scarborough	2	Wigan Ath	aet 2		1984	Northwich V	2	Bangor C (after 1-1 draw)		1
1974	Morecambe	2	Dartford	1		1985	Wealdstone	2	Boston U		1
1975	Matlock	4	Scarborough	0		1986	Altrincham	1	Runcorn		0
1976	Scarborough	3	Stafford R	aet 2		1987	Kidderminster H	2	Burton A (after 0-0 draw)		1
1977	Scarborough	2	Dagenham	1		1988	Enfield	3	Telford U (after 0-0 draw)		2
1978	Altrincham	3	Leatherhead	1		1989	Telford U	1	Macclesfield T	aet	0
1979	Stafford R	2	Kettering T	0		1990	Barrow	3	Leek T		0
1980	Dagenham	2	Mossley	1		1991	Wycombe W	2	Kidderminster H		1

FA CHALLENGE VASE 1991–92

Extra Preliminary Round

Heaton Stannington v Marske United	0-1
Ponteland United v Sunderland IFG Roker	1-3
Prudhoe East End v Dunston FB	2-7
Whitehaven Miners v Newton Aycliffe	0-4
Pickering Town v Seaton Delaval ST	4-0
Seaton Delaval Amateurs v Sunderland Vaux Ryhope	
	2-0
Heswall v Poulton Victoria	4-0
General Chemicals v Christleton	3-1
Merseyside Police v Westhoughton Town	4-0
Ashville v Bamber Bridge	0-3
Knypersley Victoria v Atherton Collieries	3-4
(at Atherton Collieries FC)	
Waterloo Dock v Cheadle Town	3-1
Redgate Clayton v St Dominics	4-4, 1-7
Newton (WC) v Vauxhall Motors (WC)	1-4
Ayone v Maghull	3-2
(at Maghull FC)	
Kidsgrove Athletic v Leyland DAF	
(walkover for Kidsgrove Athletic)	
Blidworth MW v Brodsworth MW	1-0
Hatfield Main v Immingham Town	2-3
Dunkirk v Lincoln United	1-5
Radford v Louth United	3-2
Priory (Eastwood) v Rossington Main	5-1
Winterton Rangers v Bradford PA	4-1
Nettleham v Tadcaster Albion	0-0, 2-0
Clipstone Welfare v RES Parkgate	1-1, 1-0
Yorkshire Amateur v Worsboro Bridge MW	3-1
Mickleover RBL v Maltby MW	2-1
(at Gresley Rovers FC)	
Liversedge v Kimberley Town	2-1
Stocksbridge Park Steels v Bradley Rangers	2-1
Selby Town v Glasshoughton Welfare	1-4
Shirebrook Colliery v Pontefract Collieries	2-1
Hallam v Hall Road Rangers	2-2, 2-1
(1st match at Hall Road Rangers FC)	
Bloxwich Town v Brackley Town	4-0
Harrowby United v Heath Hayes	5-2
Coleshill Town v Holwell Sports	1-1, 2-3
Oldswinford v Knowle	0-0, 0-1
Oadby Town v Pelsall Villa	1-0
West Bromwich Town v Anstey Nomads	2-2, 0-3
Northfield Town v Tividale	4-0
Burton Park Wanderers v Pegasus Juniors	0-2
Wolverhampton Casuals v Westfields	1-0
Meir KA v Lutterworth Town	2-1
Kings Heath v Highfield Rangers	3-2
(at Knowle FC)	
Stourport Swifts v Bolehall Swifts	2-0
St Andrews v Daventry Town	1-2
Stapenhill v Norton United	6-4
Eccleshall v Hamlet S & L	3-1
Ramsey Town v St Ives Town	2-1
(at St Ives Town FC)	
Diss Town v Clarksteel Yaxley	2-0
Downham Town v Brightlingsea United	1-0
Stansted v Sawbridgeworth Town	2-1
Norwich United v Somersham Town	0-2
Ipswich Wanderers v Wroxham	1-3
(at Wroxham FC)	
Brantham Athletic v Ely City	0-2
Chatteris Town v Woodbridge Town	1-2
Long Sutton Athletic v LBC Ortonians	1-2
Long Buckby v London Colney	2-2, 4-1
Beaconsfield United v Milton Keynes Borough	3-1
Kempston Rovers v Langford	3-0
Wolverton v Brook House	0-3
Biggleswade Town v Wingate & Finchley	0-1
Viking Sports v Amersham Town	3-2
Waltham Abbey v Totternhoe	3-2
The 61 v Cockfosters	1-4
Potters Bar Town v Pirton	1-0
Stotfold v Bowers United	2-1
Winslow United v Rayners Lane	1-3
Brimsdown Rovers v Shillington	2-0
Petersfield United v Bedfont	1-0
Deal Town v Eastbourne Town	1-0
Horley Town v Slade Green	0-3
Ashford Town (Middx) v Hartley Wintney	3-0
Old Salesians v Farleigh Rovers	3-2
Godalming Town v Broadbridge Heath	0-1

Cobham v Ash United	5-1
Sherborne Town v Bicester Town	3-2
Christchurch v Fleet Town	1-3
Oxford City v Wantage Town	3-1
Aerostructures v Milton United	0-1
Ryde Sports v Kintbury Rangers	3-2
AFC Lymington v Bishops Cleeve	5-0
Brockenhurst v BAT	4-0
Flight Refuelling v Harrow Hill	5-1
Bridgwater Town v Brislington	2-0
Cinderford Town v Backwell United	1-1, 2-2, 4-2
Old Georgians v Keynsham Town	0-2
Fairford Town v Larkhall Athletic	2-3
Clandown v Wotton Rovers	1-1, 1-2
Almondsbury Picksons v Cirencester Town	4-4, 1-0
Bemerton Heath Harlequins v Swindon Athletic	2-3
DRG (FP) v Clanfield	3-4
Truro City v St Austell	0-2

Preliminary Round

Evenwood Town v Seaton Delaval Amateurs	1-2
Ashington v Penrith	1-2
Cleator Moor Celtic v Langley Park	2-6
Marske United v West Allotment Celtic	2-1
Hebburn v Norton & Stockton Ancients	2-0
West Auckland Town v Washington	2-0
Willington v Newton Aycliffe	0-4
Annfield Plain v Crook Town	3-1
Shotton Comrades v Durham City	0-6
Chester-le-Street Town v Pickering Town	2-1
Stockton v Dunston FB	1-2
Horden CW v Darlington CB	6-1
Netherfield v Sunderland IFG Roker	1-2
Esh Winning v Bedlington Terriers	1-4
Oldham Town v Newcastle Town	1-2
Vauxhall GM v Rocester	0-0, 0-1
Irlam Town v Heswall	3-2
St Helens Town v Burscough	2-3
Vauxhall Motors (WC) v Atherton LR	1-2
Curzon Ashton v Blackpool (wren) Rovers	0-1
Nantwich Town v Wythenshawe Amateurs	1-1, 1-2
Ashton United v Lancaster City	4-0
Ayone v Bootle	1-1, 3-2
Chadderton v Flixton	4-6
Formby v General Chemicals	1-1, 0-0, 0-1
Clitheroe v Skelmersdale United	2-1
Prescot AFC v Bamber Bridge	1-3
Darwen v St Dominics	1-2
Atherton Collieries v Maine Road	1-1, 1-3
Salford City v Merseyside Police	2-0
Waterloo Dock v Kidsgrove Athletic	1-1, 1-1, 1-1, 1-3
(2nd replay at Knowsley United FC)	
Oakham United v Hallam	1-5
Arnold Town v Lincoln United	0-0, 0-5
Denaby United v Thackley	3-4
Mickleover RBL v Nettleham	3-2
Ossett Albion v Immingham Town	2-5
Clipstone Welfare v Winterton Rangers	0-1
Yorkshire Amateurs v Glasshoughton Welfare	2-3
Armthorpe Welfare v Eccleshill United	4-1
Radford v Harworth CI	1-2
Brigg Town v Shirebrook Colliery	6-1
Priory (Eastwood) v Stocksbridge Park Steels	1-3
Sheffield v Friar Lane OB	2-1
Blidworth MW v Liversedge	1-3
Ilkeston Town v Belper Town	0-3
Stapenhill v Oldbury United	0-2
Wellingborough Town v Northfield Town	1-3
Pegasus Juniors v Northampton Spencer	0-1
Meir KA v Racing Club Warwick	0-1
Eccleshall v Wolverhampton Casuals	2-1
Halesowen Harriers v Holwell Sports	4-2
Daventry Town v West Midlands Police	0-0, 0-0, 1-3
Hinckley v Sandwell Borough	0-1
Bridgnorth Town v Irthlingborough Diamonds	4-1
Malvern Town v Oadby Town	1-0
APV Peterborough City v Stratford Town	1-0
Highgate United v Desborough Town	2-0
Blakenall v Mile Oak Rovers	8-0
Anstey Nomads v Kings Heath	2-1
Harrowby United v Boldmere St Michaels	1-5
Hinckley Town v Walsall Wood	1-0
Solihull Borough v Knowle	6-2

Rushall Olympic v Stourport Swifts — 5-1
Lye Town v Bilston Town — 1-1, 2-5
Wednesfield v Evesham United — 1-3
Bloxwich Town v Chasetown — 0-0, 0-2
Clacton Town v Ely City — 4-3
Canvey Island v Witham Town — 0-1
Boston v Diss Town — 0-1
Eynesbury Rovers v Newmarket Town — 0-0, 0-0, 0-2
Woodbridge Town v Royston Town — 0-1
Halstead Town v Basildon United — 1-3
Ramsey Town v March Town United — 1-2
Mirrlees Blackstone v Lowestoft Town — 1-4
Tiptree United v Downham Town — 3-5
Berkhamsted Town v Soham Town Rangers — 1-0
Stamford Town v Bourne Town — 1-0
Gorleston v Stowmarket Town — 4-2
Stansted v Barton Rovers — 3-0
Bury Town v LBC Ortonians — 1-0
Wroxham v Somersham Town — 3-0
Watton United v Felixstowe Town — 1-2
Rayners Lane v Kingsbury Town — 0-1
Tilbury v Brook House — 5-2
Wingate & Finchley v Hornchurch — 5-0
Waltham Abbey v Leighton Town — 1-0
Brimsdown Rovers v Viking Sports — 0-1
Feltham & Hounslow Borough v Wootton Blue Cross — 5-0
Stotfold v Tring Town — 2-0
Ford United v Metropolitan Police — 2-3
Clapton v Haringey Borough — 1-3
Hertford Town v Beaconsfield United — 4-1
Arlesey Town v Rainham Town — 4-1
Flackwell Heath v Edgware Town — 1-4
Bracknell Town v Hoddesdon Town — 0-1
Kempston Rovers v Cockfosters — 1-3
Welwyn Garden City v Cheshunt — 1-2
Hampton v Ruislip Manor — 1-1, 3-2
Northwood v Long Buckby — 4-1
Letchworth Garden City v Potters Bar Town — 1-1, 1-2
Hemel Hempstead v Barkingside — 4-1
Southall v Eton Manor — 3-2
  (at Eton Manor FC)
Ware v Collier Row — 0-2
Leatherhead v Burnham — 0-1
Worthing v Slade Green — 1-3
Shoreham v Peacehaven & Telscombe — 1-3
Corinthian v Deal Town — 1-0
Wick v Haywards Heath Town — 4-0
Croydon Athletic v Banstead Athletic — 2-4
Horsham v Cove — 5-1
Tunbridge Wells v Cobham — 7-6
Old Salesians v Hailsham Town — 2-7
Chipstead v Burgess Hill Town — 0-4
Herne Bay v Arundel — 8-1
Sittingbourne v Beckenham Town — 3-1
Camberley Town v Southwick — 1-2
Redhill v Alma Swanley — 4-0
Pagham v Horsham YMCA — 3-1
Broadbridge Heath v Oakwood — 0-2
Worthing United v Ringmer — 2-1
Petersfield United v Tonbridge — 1-7
Whitehawk v Ashford Town (Middx) — 2-1
Three Bridges v Darenth Heathside — 2-1
Whitstable Town v Lancing — 4-0
Lewes v Selsey — 0-2
Steyning Town v Epsom & Ewell — 0-3
Egham Town v Malden Vale — 0-1
Portfield v Corinthian Casuals — 0-1
Langney Sports v Eastbourne United — 5-2
Sheppey United v Faversham Town — 1-4
Chichester City v Chatham Town — 3-0
Milton United v Abingdon United — 3-0
Newbury Town v AFC Totton — 3-0
AFC Lymington v Ryde Sports — 1-0
Newport (IW) v Oxford City — 2-0
Sholing Sports v Swanage Town & Herston — 1-2
Thame United v Horndean — 6-0
Brockenhurst v Romsey Town — 1-2
East Cowes Victoria Athletic v Witney Town — 1-2
Fleet Town v Banbury United — 2-2, 3-1
Sherborne Town v First Tower United — 2-2, 2-1
Westbury United v Bournemouth — 0-1
Minehead v Melksham Town — 4-1
Calne Town v Odd Down — 0-1
Glastonbury v Mangotsfield United — 2-4

Clanfield v Devizes Town — 1-3
Chard Town v Swindon Athletic — 2-0
Larkhall Athletic v Bristol Manor Farm — 1-2
Wotton Rovers v Keynsham Town — 2-3
Cinderford Town v Frome Town — 3-0
Shortwood United v Radstock Town — 5-2
Bridgwater Town v Chippenham Town — 0-2
Almondsbury Picksons v Welton Rovers — 0-1
Clevedon Town v Flight Refuelling — 7-1
Exmouth Town v Liskeard Athletic — 1-0
Tiverton Town v Elmore — 3-0
Torrington v Barnstaple Town — 1-1, 2-1
Torpoint Athletic v Ilfracombe Town — 1-0
St Blazey v Crediton United — 1-2
St Austell v Ottery St Mary — 2-0

First Round
West Auckland Town v Horden CW — 1-0
Durham City v Eppleton CW — 2-2, 2-2, 2-1
Seaton Delaval Amateurs v Dunston FB — 1-2
Bedlington Terriers v Newton Aycliffe — 0-1
Penrith v Sunderland IFG Roker — 2-1
Chester-le-Street Town v Langley Park — 3-3, 3-1
Billingham Town v Annfield Plain — 4-3
Hebburn v Marske United — 3-2
Atherton LR v Clitheroe — 2-1
Burscough v Irlam Town — 5-1
Flixton v Kidsgrove Athletic — 1-0
Glossop v Newcastle Town — 0-1
Wythenshawe Amateurs v Eastwood Hanley — 0-2
Salford City v Vauxhall GM — 2-0
Bamber Bridge v St Dominics — 6-1
General Chemicals v Maine Road — 0-1
Rossendale United v Ayone — 5-2
Blackpool (wren) Rovers v Ashton United — 1-2
Lincoln United v Harworth CI — 2-3
Hallam v Ossett Town — 0-1
Glasshoughton Welfare v Belper Town — 0-3
Garforth Town v Heanor Town — 4-1
Mickleover RBL v Borrowash Victoria — 3-4
Liversedge v Rainworth MW — 3-1
Brigg Town v Stocksbridge Park Steels — 5-0
Armthorpe Welfare v Sheffield — 2-4
Harrogate Town v Winterton Rangers — 4-1
Thackley v Immingham Town — 3-1
Shadwell Borough v West Midlands Police — 1-2
Raunds Town v Bridgnorth Town — 1-1, 2-0
Eccleshall v Halesowen Harriers — 4-2
Chasetown v Northampton Spencer — 2-1
Rothwell Town v Evesham United — 1-3
Solihull Borough v Paget Rangers — 4-1
Rushall Olympic v Hinckley Town — 2-1
Boldmere St Michaels v Racing Club Warwick — 0-3
APV Peterborough City v Malvern Town — 3-0
Anstey Nomads v Oldbury United — 4-0
Bilston Town v Highgate United — 1-0
Northfield Town v Blakenall — 1-3
Newmarket Town v Stamford Town — 5-0
Diss Town v Witham Town — 3-1
Downham Town v Felixstowe Town — 3-3, 0-2
Holbeach United v Thetford Town — 2-1
Basildon United v Histon — 5-3
Wroxham v Clacton Town — 3-0
Gorleston v Stansted — 2-1
Berkhamsted Town v Bury Town — 2-0
Kings Lynn v Lowestoft Town — 2-1
Royston Town v March Town United — 2-1
Metropolitan Police v Stotfold — 1-1, 2-0
Burnham Ramblers v Haringey Borough — 2-2, 2-1
Viking Sports v Feltham & Hounslow Borough — 3-1
Collier Row v Wingate & Finchley — 1-0
Purfleet v Southall — 6-0
Northwood v Braintree Town — 7-6
Potters Bar Town v Hampton — 0-0, 1-4
Cheshunt v Waltham Abbey — 2-1
Arlesey Town v Hertford Town — 1-0
Cockfosters v Kingsbury Town — 1-1, 4-1
Hemel Hempstead v Edgware Town — 0-2
Tilbury v Hoddesdon Town — 2-1
Corinthian v Langney Sports — 1-3
Peacehaven & Telscombe v Whitehawk — 5-0
Merstham v Whitstable Town — 0-6
Wick v Sittingbourne — 0-2
Faversham Town v Southwick — 6-0
Tunbridge Wells v Greenwich Borough — 1-2

Three Bridges v Burgess Hill Town	3-3, 1-0
Herne Bay v Hailsham Town	3-1
Worthing United v Selsey	2-1
Havant Town v Redhill	3-2
Pagham v Burnham	1-0
Horsham v Oakwood	1-0
Epsom & Ewell v Chertsey Town	0-2
Slade Green v Chichester City	4-0
Corinthian Casuals v Malden Vale	2-3
Tonbridge v Banstead Athletic	2-1
Sherborne Town v Thatcham Town	0-2
AFC Lymington v Newport (IW)	0-1
Witney Town v Bournemouth	4-3
Didcot Town v Romsey Town	2-1
Fleet Town v Swanage Town & Herston	4-6
Thame United v Milton United	3-0
Newbury Town v Eastleigh	3-0
Welton Rovers v Minehead	1-0
Devizes Town v Chard Town	0-3
Shortwood United v Clevedon Town	3-1
Wellington v Cinderford Town	1-3
Chippenham Town v Bristol Manor Farm	2-0
Keynsham Town v Odd Down	1-0
Mangotsfield United v Wimborne Town	1-2
Torpoint Athletic v St Austell	2-0
Crediton United v Torrington	1-2
Falmouth Town v Tiverton Town	1-3
Exmouth Town v Newquay	0-6

Second Round

Harrogate RA v Penrith	0-1
Great Harwood Town v Farsley Celtic	1-1, 0-4
Dunston FB v Thackley	3-2
Liversedge v Bamber Bridge	3-8
Newton Aycliffe v Hebburn	2-2, 4-2
Chester-le-Street Town v Durham City	2-0
Bridlington Town v Billingham Town	5-0
North Ferriby United v West Auckland Town	1-0
Newcastle Town v Sheffield	3-2
Guiseley v Garforth Town	2-0
Eastwood Hanley v Harrogate Town	4-1
Belper Town v Harworth CI	2-1
Ossett Town v Atherton LR	3-3, 1-3
Flixton v Borrowash Victoria	8-3
Knowsley United v Cammell Laird	1-0
Burscough v Rossendale United	2-0
Ashton United v Maine Road	2-1
Salford City v Brigg Town	0-1
Eccleshall v Wisbech Town	0-2
Gresley Rovers v Blakenall	1-0
Chasetown v Witney Town	3-2
Bilston Town v APV Peterborough City	3-1
Anstey Nomads v Spalding United	3-2
Raunds Town v Holbeach United	3-0
Hinckley Athletic v Hucknall Town	3-2
West Midlands Police v Rushall Olympic	3-1
Racing Club Warwick v Solihull Borough	1-3
Evesham United v Buckingham Town	3-1
Potton United v Walthamstow Pennant	0-4
Diss Town v Viking Sports	4-0
Felixstowe Town v Cheshunt	2-0
Arlesey Town v Newmarket Town	0-2
Great Yarmouth Town v Cockfosters	2-1
Edgware Town v Basildon United	4-3
Burnham Ramblers v East Thurrock United	5-3
Collier Row v Harefield United	4-0
Saffron Walden Town v Wroxham	3-1
Berkhamsted Town v Harwich & Parkeston	2-1
Metropolitan Police v Royston Town	1-0
Gorleston v Hampton	0-2
Haverhill Rovers v Sudbury Town	1-1, 1-2
Billericay Town v Kings Lynn	4-2
Horsham v Littlehampton Town	2-2, 1-0
Sittingbourne v Tilbury	4-2
Malden Vale v Thatcham Town	2-2, 3-2
Hythe Town v Herne Bay	1-1, 2-1
Chertsey Town v Peacehaven & Telscombe	3-2
Faversham Town v Whitstable Town	1-0
Three Bridges v Greenwich Borough	2-0
Langney Sports v Hastings Town	3-3, 1-2
Havant Town v Newport (IW)	1-2
Didcot Town v Worthing United	1-2
Tonbridge v Thame United	1-6
Pagham v Slade Green	3-0
Northwood v Purfleet	3-2

Chippenham Town v Paulton Rovers	1-3
Shortwood United v Bridport	3-1
Torrington v Keynsham Town	1-0
Yate Town v Newbury Town	3-0
Cinderford Town v Newquay	3-1
Wimborne Town v Chard Town	5-2
Hungerford Town v Torpoint Athletic	2-1
Dawlish Town v Welton Rovers	1-2
Tiverton Town v Swanage Town & Herston	2-0

Third Round

Atherton LR v Brigg Town	3-3, 2-3
Farsley Celtic v Guiseley	2-5
Belper Town v Dunston FB	1-1, 0-2
Bridlington Town v Eastwood Hanley	2-3
Chester-le-Street Town v Ashton United	2-1
Newton Aycliffe v Burscough	2-4
Bamber Bridge v Flixton	2-1
North Ferriby United v Knowsley United	1-2
Newcastle Town v Penrith	3-2
Anstey Nomads v Felixstowe Town	2-1
Newmarket Town v Solihull Borough	2-1
Collier Row v West Midlands Police	2-3
Raunds Town v Diss Town	0-2
Walthamstow Pennant v Evesham United	2-3
Edgware Town v Hinckley Athletic	2-1
Wisbech Town v Great Yarmouth Town	2-2, 4-2
Berkhamsted Town v Gresley Rovers	1-2
Burnham Ramblers v Chasetown	2-1
Billericay Town v Bilston Town	2-0
Saffron Walden Town v Sudbury Town	1-2
Hastings Town v Torrington	3-0
Tiverton Town v Sittingbourne	2-3
Pagham v Hythe Town	1-2
Chertsey Town v Cinderford Town	1-1, 0-0, 2-1
Metropolitan Police v Three Bridges	2-0
Welton Rovers v Malden Vale	2-1
Shortwood United v Yate Town	2-3
Hungerford Town v Faversham Town	4-1
Worthing United v Northwood	1-2
Wimborne Town v Horsham	1-0
Hampton v Newport (IW)	0-1
Paulton Rovers v Thame United	4-2

Fourth Round

Dunston FB v Guiseley	1-3
Brigg Town v Bamber Bridge	4-4, 0-1
Newcastle Town v Gresley Rovers	3-2
Burscough v Eastwood Hanley	0-1
Chester-le-Street Town v Knowsley United	1-5
Edgware Town v Welton Rovers	3-1
Sittingbourne v Metropolitan Police	1-2
Anstey Nomads v Diss Town	0-1
Northwood v Chertsey Town	1-4
Wimborne Town v Hastings Town	3-3, 2-1
Sudbury Town v Newmarket Town	3-2
West Midlands Police v Wisbech Town	4-3
Paulton Rovers v Hungerford Town	1-3
Billericay Town v Yate Town	3-4
Newport (IW) v Burnham Ramblers	3-1
Hythe Town v Evesham United	3-3, 0-2

Fifth Round

Chertsey Town v Yate Town	3-1
Guiseley v Edgware Town	4-0
Bamber Bridge v Newport (IW)	2-1
Newcastle Town v Wimborne Town	1-1, 0-1
Hungerford Town v West Midlands Police	0-3
Metropolitan Police v Diss Town	0-2
Knowsley United v Sudbury Town	2-4
Evesham United v Eastwood Hanley	2-1

Sixth Round

Guiseley v Evesham United	4-0
Diss Town v Wimborne Town	0-0, 0-1
West Midlands Police v Sudbury Town	1-2
Chertsey Town v Bamber Bridge	0-1

Semi-finals

Bamber Bridge v Wimborne Town	0-0, 0-2
Guiseley v Sudbury Town	2-2, 3-1

FINAL at Wembley
25 APR
Guiseley **(1) 3** *(Noteman 2, Colville)*
Wimborne Town **(3) 5** *(Richardson, Sturgess 2, Killick 2)*
10,772

Guiseley: Maxted; Atkinson, Hogarth, Tetley (Wilson), Morgan, Brockie, Roberts A, Tennison, Noteman (Colville), Annan, Roberts W.
Wimborne Town: Leonard; Langdown, Beacham, Allan, Taplin, Armes, Richardson, Bridle, Killick, Sturgess, Lynn.
Referee: M. Bodenham (Looe).

FA CHALLENGE VASE FINALS 1975–91

1975 Hoddesdon T	2	Epsom & Ewell	1		
1976 Billericay T	1	Stamford	aet 0		
1977 Billericay T	2	Sheffield (after 1-1 draw)	1		
1978 Blue Star	2	Barton R	1		
1979 Billericay T	4	Almondsbury G	1		
1980 Stamford	2	Guisborough T	0		
1981 Whickham	3	Willenhall T	aet 2		
1982 Forest Green R	3	Rainworth MW	0		
1983 VS Rugby	1	Halesowen T	0		

1984 Stansted	3	Stamford	2
1985 Halesowen T	3	Fleetwood T	1
1986 Halesowen T	3	Southall	0
1987 St Helens T	3	Warrington T	2
1988 Colne D	1	Emley	0
1989 Tamworth	3	Sudbury (after 1-1 draw)	0
1990 Yeading	1	Bridlington T (after 0-0 draw)	
			0
1991 Guiseley	3	Gresley R (after 4-4 draw)	1

FA COUNTY YOUTH CUP

First Round

Northumberland v Cumberland	3-1
East Riding v Durham	0-0, 0-1
Manchester v North Riding	2-3
Cheshire v Derbyshire	2-3
Worcestershire v Staffordshire	1-3
Birmingham v Northamptonshire	8-0
Essex v Norfolk	3-2
Cambridgeshire v Suffolk	4-5
Oxfordshire v Bedfordshire	4-1
Berks & Bucks v Kent	5-1
Army v Sussex	1-7
Devon v Somerset & Avon (Sth)	1-0
Gloucestershire v Cornwall	0-2
Royal Navy v Berks & Bucks	0-2
Wiltshire v Sussex	1-3
Hampshire v Devon	1-2
Dorset v Cornwall	1-0

Second Round

Westmorland v Lancashire	2-3
West Riding v Northumberland	4-3
Sheffield & Hallamshire v Durham	3-1
Liverpool v North Riding	1-1, 2-1
Shropshire v Derbyshire	1-2
Nottinghamshire v Staffordshire	4-1
Lincolnshire v Leicestershire & Rutland	1-3
Herefordshire v Birmingham	0-7
Hertfordshire v Essex	0-1
London v Suffolk	3-4
Surrey v Huntingdonshire	3-1
Middlesex v Oxfordshire	0-3

Third Round

Lancashire v Liverpool	2-0
West Riding v Sheffield & Hallamshire	4-2
Derbyshire v Birmingham	3-3, 3-1
Nottinghamshire v Leicestershire & Rutland	4-3
Essex v Oxfordshire	2-1
Suffolk v Surrey	3-3, 1-2
Berks & Bucks v Dorset	2-0
Sussex v Devon	1-5

Fourth Round

Nottinghamshire v West Riding	3-2
Lancashire v Derbyshire	1-0
Devon v Surrey	0-3
Essex v Berks & Bucks	3-1

Semi-Final

Nottinghamshire v Essex	2-1
Lancashire v Surrey	3-4

Final

Surrey v Nottinghamshire	0-1

FA COUNTY YOUTH CHALLENGE CUP FINALS 1945–91 (aggregate scores)

1945 Staffordshire	3	Wiltshire	2
1946 Berks & Bucks	4	Durham	3
1947 Durham	4	Essex	2
1948 Essex	5	Liverpool	3
1949 Liverpool	4	Middlesex	3
1950 Essex	4	Middlesex	3
1951 Middlesex	3	Leics. & Rutland	1
1952 Sussex	3	Liverpool	1
1953 Sheffield & Hallam	5	Hampshire	3
1954 Liverpool	4	Gloucestershire	1
1955 Bedfordshire	2	Sheffield & Hallam	0
1956 Middlesex	3	Staffordshire	2
1957 Hampshire	4	Cheshire	3
1958 Staffordshire	8	London	0
1959 Birmingham	7	London	5
1960 London	6	Birmingham	4
1961 Lancashire	6	Nottinghamshire	3
1962 Middlesex	6	Nottinghamshire	3
1963 Durham	3	Essex	2
1964 Sheffield & Hallam	1	Birmingham	0
1965 Northumberland	7	Middlesex	4
1966 Leics. & Rutland	6	London	5
1967 Northamptonshire	5	Hertfordshire	4
1968 North Riding	7	Devon	4

1969 Northumberland	1	Sussex	0
(one game only from here)			
1970 Hertfordshire	2	Cheshire	1
1971 Lancashire	2	Gloucestershire	0
1972 Middlesex	2	Liverpool	0
1973 Hertfordshire	3	Northumberland	0
1974 Nottinghamshire	2	London	0
1975 Durham	2	Bedfordshire	1
1976 Northamptonshire	7	Surrey	1
1977 Liverpool	3	Surrey	0
1978 Liverpool	3	Kent	1
1979 Hertfordshire	4	Liverpool	1
1980 Liverpool	2	Lancashire	0
1981 Lancashire	3	East Riding	2
1982 Devon	3	Kent (after 0-0 draw)	2
1983 London	3	Gloucestershire	0
1984 Cheshire	2	Manchester	1
1985 East Riding	2	Middlesex	1
1986 Hertfordshire	4	Manchester	0
1987 North Riding	3	Gloucestershire	1
1988 East Riding	5	Middlesex (after 0-0 draw)	3
1989 Liverpool	2	Hertfordshire	1
1990 Staffordshire	2	Hampshire (after 1-1 draw)	1
1991 Lancashire	6	Surrey	0

FA SUNDAY CUP 1991–92

First Round

Queens Arms v Nenthead	0-4
Dudley & Weetslade v Blyth Waterloo SC	3-2
Mayfield United v Stanton Dale	1-4
Lobster v Whetley Lane	4-0
Carlisle United SC v Iron Bridge	2-4
Lynemouth v Croxteth & Gilmoss RBL	0-4
Framwellgate Moor & Pity Me v Woodlands 84	7-1
Seymour v Hartlepool Lion Hotel	3-5
Western Approaches v Railway Hotel	2-1
Bolton Woods v Oakenshaw	2-2, 0-2
(*Liversedge FC*)	
Littlewoods v B & A Scaffolding	2-3
Rob Roy v Chesterfield Park	
(*walkover for Chesterfield Park*)	
Almithak v AC Sparks	3-2
Netherley RBL v East Bowling Unity	1-1, 3-3, 2-3
(*replay at Crag Road United FC*)	
Hare v Clubmoor Nalgo	2-2, 2-3
(*replay at Nalgo Sports Club*)	
Carnforth v Britannia VNC	2-1
BRNESC v Blue Union	1-3
Baildon Athletic v FC Coachman	1-3
Jolly Farmers v Dock	2-2, 2-1
(*replay at Ashville FC*)	
Radford Park Rangers v Bricklayers Sports	4-5
Altone Steels v Birmingham Celtic	4-0
Kenwick Dynamo v Brookvale Athletic	1-2
Ansells Stockland Star v AD Bulwell	0-2
Dereham Hobbies Sunday v Shouldham Sunday	0-1
Girton Eagles v Watford Labour Club	1-4
Sawston Keys v Gamlingay OB's	3-0
Inter Volante v Cork & Bottle	3-1
(*tie awarded to Cork & Bottle*)	
Boreham Wood Royals v Chequers (Herts)	1-2
Chapel United v Evergreen	2-4
Old Paludians v Broad Plain House	0-5
Sandwell v Olympic Star	2-0
St Joseph's (South Oxhey) v BRSC Aidan	2-1
Theale v Northfield Rangers	1-0
Hanham Sunday v Bedfont Sunday	2-1
Phoenix v Lebeq Tavern	1-2
Bishopstoke AFC v Santogee 66	2-3
Sarton United v Somerset Ambury V & E	1-0
Inter Royalle v Rolls Royce (Sunday)	2-0
Continental v Concord Rangers	0-0, 1-2
(*replay at Thames Road, Canvey Island*)	
Priory Sports v Fryerns Community	2-1
Oxford Road Social v St Clements Hospital	0-3

Second Round

B & A Scaffolding v Green Man 88	3-0
Almithak v Lobster	5-4
Avenue Victoria Lodge v A3	0-1
Eagle-Knowsley v Clubmoor Nalgo	4-1
Nenthead v Northwood	0-1
Hartlepool Lion Hotel v Carnforth	1-0
Jolly Farmers v FC Coachman	
(*walkover for FC Coachman*)	
Blue Union v East Levenshulme	2-2, 3-2
Framwellgate Moor & Pity Me v Dudley & Weetslade	
	2-0
Western Approaches v Oakenshaw	2-3

Toshiba Sharples v Stanton Dale	1-1, 4-5
Humbledon Plains Farm v Croxteth & Gilmoss RBL	2-0
Iron Bridge v Chesterfield Park	3-0
Nicosia v East Bowling Unity	1-1, 2-1
Poringland Wanderers v Marston Sports	2-4
AD Bulwell v Brookvale Athletic	1-2
Sawston Keys v Bournville Warriors	3-2
Cork & Bottle v Lodge Cottrell	0-1
Slade Celtic v Priory Sports	2-2, 1-2
Ford Basildon v Shouldham Sunday	2-1
St Clements Hospital v Chequers (Herts)	0-1
Watford Labour Club v Sandwell	1-4
Bricklayers Sports v Brerton Town	3-2
Altone Steels v St Josephs (Luton)	0-1
Ranelagh Sports v Evergreen	2-0
Sartan United v St Josephs (South Oxhey)	1-0
Ouzavich v Leyton Argyle	3-2
Lee Chapel North v Concord Rangers	2-1
Theale v Lebeq Tavern	3-0
Broad Plain House v Inter Royalle	2-0
Reading Borough v Hanham Sunday	1-2
Collier Row Supporters v Santogee 66	2-1

Third Round

Stantondale v A3	1-2
Iron Bridge v Humbledon Plains Farm	2-0
FC Coachman v Framwellgate More & Pity Me	4-3
Marston Sports v B & A Scaffolding	1-0
Hartlepool Lion Hotel v Almithak	3-2
Northwood v Oakenshaw	2-2, 2-3
Nicosia v Bricklayers Sports	0-1
Blue Union v Eagle-Knowsley	0-1
Ouzavich v Lodge Cottrell	0-2
Theale v Lee Chapel North	3-2
Sandwell v Ranelagh Sports	1-4
Collier Row Supporters v Brookvale Athletic	1-2
Chequers (Herts) v Sawston Keys	2-1
Ford Basildon v Sartan United	1-0
Broad Plain House v Hanham Sunday	0-3
St Josephs (Luton) v Priory Sports	5-1

Fourth Round

Oakenshaw v FC Coachman	2-1
Marston Sports v Hartlepool Lion Hotel	5-3
Iron Bridge v Bricklayers Sports	0-2
A3 v Eagle-Knowsley	2-1
Chequers (Herts) v Theale	2-3
St Josephs (Luton) v Brookvale Athletic	1-0
Ranelagh Sports v Hanham Sunday	2-0
Lodge Cottrell v Ford Basildon	3-0

Fifth Round

Marston Sports v Bricklayers Sports	2-1
A3 v Oakenshaw	1-1, 1-1, 0-2
Lodge Cottrell v Ranelagh Sports	3-0
Theale v St Josephs (Luton)	2-0

Semi-finals

Theale v Oakenshaw	2-2, 2-0
Lodge Cottrell v Marston Sports	0-1

Final

Theale v Marston Sports	3-2

FA SUNDAY CUP FINALS 1965–91

Year	Team	Score	Opponent	Score
1965	London	6	Staffordshire (on aggregate)	2
1966	Unique U	1	Aldridge F	0
1967	Carlton U	2	Stoke W	0
1968	Drovers	2	Brook U	0
1969	Leigh Park	3	Loke U	1
1970	Vention U	1	Unique U	0
1971	Beacontree R	2	Saltley U	0
1972	Newton Unity	4	Springfield C	0
1973	Carlton U	2	Wear Valley	aet 1
1974	Newton Unity	2	Brentford E	0
1975	Fareham T Cent	1	Players Ath E	0
1976	Brandon U	2	Evergreen	1
1977	Langley Park RH	2	Newton Unity	0
1978	Arras	2	Lion R (after 2-2 draw)	1
1979	Lobster	3	Carlton U	2
1980	Fantail	1	Twin Foxes	0
1981	Fantail	1	Mackintosh	0
1982	Dingle Rail	2	Twin Foxes	1
1983	Eagle	2	Lee Chapel (after 1-1 draw)	1
1984	Lee Chapel N	4	Eagle	3
1985	Hobbies	2	Avenue (after 1-1, 2-2 draws)	1
1986	Avenue	1	Glenn Sports	0
1987	Lodge Cottrell	1	Avenue	0
1988	Nexday	2	Sunderland HP	0
1989	Almithak	3	East Levenshulme	1
1990	Humbledon PF	2	Marston Sports	1
1991	Nicosia	3	Ouzavich	2

FA CHALLENGE YOUTH CUP 1991–92

Preliminary Round

South Bank v Marske United	0-2
Billingham Synthonia v Hartlepool United	0-2
Guisborough Town v Stockton	3-1
Accrington Stanley v Flixton	5-1
Huddersfield Town v Lancaster City	8-0
Barrow v Bootle	
(*walkover for Barrow*)	
Rochdale v Preston North End	1-4
Blackpool (wren) Rovers v Rotherham United	1-4
Scarborough v Atherton LR	0-2
Chadderton v Halifax Town	1-4
Wrexham v Stockport County	3-0
Chester City v Warrington Town	1-1
(*at Warrington Town FC*) (*walkover for Warrington Town*)	
Yorkshire Amateurs v Bolton Wanderers	1-2
Marine v Shrewsbury Town	1-1, 0-3
Telford United v Leek Town	7-3
Willenhall Town v Hednesford Town	5-1
Hinckley Town v Leicester United	3-3, 2-3
Burton Albion v Chasetown	4-0
Mile Oak Rovers v Kidderminster Harriers	0-6
Nuneaton Borough v Sutton Coldfield Town	5-0
Tamworth v Corby Town	3-1
Redditch United v Rothwell Town	0-3
Wisbech Town v Lye Town	2-1
Cambridge City v Stowmarket Town	5-1
Witham Town v Brantham Athletic	1-4
Eynesbury Rovers v Norwich City	1-6
Stevenage Borough v Wivenhoe Town	1-2
Bishops Stortford v Hitchin Town	0-4
Letchworth Garden City v Barkingside	6-2
East Thurrock United v Hertford Town	4-1
Tiptree United v Royston Town	1-0
Braintree Town v Welwyn Garden City	2-1
St Albans City v Billericay Town	4-1
Canvey Island v Eton Manor	1-6
Enfield v Clapton	1-3
Buckingham Town v Maidenhead United	2-4
Marlow v Bedfont	1-1, 1-3
Feltham & Hounslow Borough v Harefield United	2-5
Staines Town v Northwood	4-1
Hendon v Leyton-Wingate	1-2
Thamesmead Town v Cheshunt	0-1
(*at Cheshunt FC*)	
Hillingdon Borough v Kingsbury Town	2-2, 3-4
Ruislip Manor v Wembley	3-3, 1-2
Banstead Athletic v Wingate & Finchley	
(*walkover for Wingate & Finchley*)	
Uxbridge v Southall	2-4
Bracknell Town v Chertsey Town	1-0
Wycombe Wanderers v Molesey	5-0
Chatham Town v Herne Bay	1-0
Maidstone United v Bromley	1-4
(*at Bromley FC*)	
Dulwich Hamlet v Fisher Athletic	2-0
(*at Fisher Athletic FC*)	
Three Bridges v Whitehawk	1-0
Farnborough Town v Redhill	10-1
Shoreham v Chipstead	1-1, 6-3
Horsham v Kingstonian	2-10
Walton & Hersham v Steyning Town	1-0
Horsham YMCA v Slough Town	1-2
Sutton United v Croydon	2-1
Langney Sports v Malden Vale	3-5
Havant Town v Worthing	3-1
Thatcham Town v Newbury Town	0-0
(*walkover for Thatcham Town*)	
Hungerford Town v Witney Town	2-4
Romsey Town v Petersfield United	2-4
Basingstoke Town v Horndean	6-0
Worcester City v Evesham United	
(*walkover for Evesham United*)	
Cheltenham Town v Yate Town	5-1
Newport AFC v Gloucester City	1-1, 2-1
Abingdon United v Andover	3-1
Dorchester Town v Frome Town	1-0
Weston-super-Mare v Odd Down	0-1
Torquay United v Bristol Rovers	2-3

First Round Qualifying

Guisborough Town v Netherfield	1-3

Marske United v Hartlepool United	1-3
(*at Hartlepool United FC*)	
Barrow v Preston North End	3-5
Accrington Stanley v Huddersfield Town	0-3
Halifax Town v Wrexham	0-3
Rotherham United v Atherton LR	7-1
Shrewsbury Town v Telford United	4-0
Warrington Town v Bolton Wanderers	0-2
Burton Albion v Kidderminster Harriers	0-1
Willenhall Town v Leicester United	3-0
Rothwell Town v Wisbech Town	6-0
Nuneaton Borough v Tamworth	0-0, 0-2
Norwich City v Wivenhoe Town	9-0
Cambridge City v Brantham Athletic	6-2
East Thurrock United v Tiptree United	6-3
Hitchin Town v Letchworth Garden City	6-3
Eton Manor v Clapton	0-1
Braintree Town v St Albans City	1-1, 2-8
Harefield United v Staines Town	5-1
Maidenhead United v Bedfont	0-1
Kingsbury Town v Wembley	4-4, 1-3
Leyton-Wingate v Cheshunt	0-2
Bracknell Town v Wycombe Wanderers	2-2, 4-6
Wingate & Finchley v Southall	4-2
Dulwich Hamlet v Three Bridges	6-0
Chatham Town v Bromley	1-4
Kingstonian v Walton & Hersham	1-3
Farnborough Town v Shoreham	5-2
Malden Vale v Havant Town	0-3
Slough Town v Sutton United	2-3
Petersfield United v Basingstoke Town	1-6
Thatcham Town v Witney Town	0-2
Newport AFC v Abingdon United	0-0, 1-4
Evesham United v Cheltenham Town	2-4
Bristol Rovers v Bashley	3-3, 1-5
Dorchester Town v Odd Down	0-0, 1-0

Second Round Qualifying

Netherfield v Hartlepool United	0-3
Preston North End v Huddersfield Town	4-1
Wrexham v Rotherham United	0-4
Shrewsbury Town v Bolton Wanderers	1-0
Kidderminster Harriers v Willenhall Town	3-0
Rothwell Town v Tamworth	2-2, 1-2
Norwich City v Cambridge City	5-0
East Thurrock United v Hitchin Town	3-2
Clapton v St Albans City	1-3
Harefield United v Bedfont	0-0, 2-1
Wembley v Cheshunt	1-1, 4-3
Wycombe Wanderers v Wingate & Finchley	3-0
Dulwich Hamlet v Bromley	0-1
Walton & Hersham v Farnborough Town	2-1
Havant Town v Sutton United	2-3
Basingstoke Town v Witney Town	0-2
Abingdon United v Cheltenham Town	1-9
(*at Cheltenham Town FC*)	
Bashley v Dorchester Town	1-1, 3-0

First Round Proper

York City v Blackburn Rovers	1-1, 3-4
Carlisle United v Rotherham United	0-1
Blackpool v Bradford City	2-2, 3-0
Barnsley v Darlington	3-2
Bury v Sunderland	3-3, 0-2
Burnley v Sheffield United	0-2
Oldham Athletic v Wigan Athletic	3-2
Tranmere Rovers v Preston North End	4-1
Shrewsbury Town v Hartlepool United	2-0
Nottingham Forest v Wolverhampton Wanderers	0-0, 0-0, 0-1
Scunthorpe United v Norwich City	0-2
Northampton Town v Stoke City	1-0
Crewe Alexandra v Port Vale	1-0
Mansfield Town v Aston Villa	0-1
Peterborough United v Derby County	1-3
Tamworth v Kidderminster Harriers	1-2
Fulham v Bromley	5-0
Walton & Hersham v Cambridge United	2-2, 0-3
Egham Town v Wimbledon	0-7
Luton Town v East Thurrock United	5-0
Reading v Gillingham	3-1
Sutton United v Wembley	4-3
Harefield United v Charlton Athletic	0-6

Aldershot v Carshalton Athletic	3-4
Whyteleafe v St Albans City	0-2
Wokingham Town v Brighton & Hove Albion	0-2
Epsom & Ewell v Wycombe Wanderers	2-0
Witney Town v Hereford United	1-0
Bashley v Southampton	0-0, 2-1
AFC Bournemouth v Swansea City	2-0
Exeter City v Cheltenham Town	2-2, 1-0
Swindon Town v Bristol City	0-4
Oxford United v Cardiff City	1-2

Second Round Proper

Barnsley v Everton	1-2
Doncaster Rovers v Manchester City	1-1, 0-4
Hull City v Crewe Alexandra	1-1, 0-3
Middlesbrough v Newcastle United	4-0
Sunderland v Manchester United	2-4
Liverpool v Tranmere Rovers	1-2
Blackburn Rovers v Rotherham United	0-2
Sheffield United v Blackpool	5-3
Leeds United v Oldham Athletic	3-3, 2-3
Shrewsbury Town v Sheffield Wednesday	3-0
West Ham United v Kidderminster Harriers	3-0
Northampton Town v Birmingham City	3-0
Notts County v Derby County	0-0, 0-1
Tottenham Hotspur v Coventry City	6-1
West Bromwich Albion v Wolverhampton Wanderers	3-1
Witney Town v Southend United	0-3
Luton Town v Aston Villa	1-0
Watford v Leicester City	2-1
Cambridge United v Colchester United	2-3
Norwich City v Leyton Orient	6-3
Walsall v Ipswich Town	1-0
Sutton United v AFC Bournemouth	1-5
Brighton & Hove Albion v Arsenal	2-5
Portsmouth v Bashley	0-1
Fulham v Brentford	2-2, 0-2
Reading v Carshalton Athletic	3-0
Cardiff City v Queens Park Rangers	0-1
Bristol City v Epsom & Ewell	3-2
Wimbledon v Millwall	2-0
Exeter City v Chelsea	0-4
St Albans City v Plymouth Argyle	0-4
Charlton Athletic v Crystal Palace	0-2

Third Round Proper

Tranmere Rovers v Oldham Athletic	0-0, 1-1, 3-1
Rotherham United v Shrewsbury Town	3-1
Northampton Town v Derby County	1-7
Manchester United v Walsall	2-1
Crewe Alexandra v Middlesbrough	3-2
Manchester City v West Bromwich Albion	1-1, 2-0
Everton v Sheffield United	1-1, 3-2
Reading v West Ham United	2-6

Chelsea v Crystal Palace	0-2
Colchester United v Brentford	1-3
Arsenal v Watford	4-0
Tottenham Hotspur v AFC Bournemouth	7-0
Luton Town v Norwich City	1-1, 1-4
Wimbledon v Bashley	6-0
Southend United v Bristol City	3-0
Plymouth Argyle v Queens Park Rangers	1-3

Fourth Round Proper

Queens Park Rangers v Brentford	5-1
Wimbledon v Norwich City	1-1, 4-3
Southend United v West Ham United	3-3, 1-1, 2-3
Crystal Palace v Crewe Alexandra	2-0
Arsenal v Everton	1-2
Manchester City v Manchester United	1-3
Derby County v Tottenham Hotspur	0-1
Rotherham United v Tranmere Rovers	0-1

Fifth Round Proper

Wimbledon v Queens Park Rangers	2-0
Tottenham Hotspur v Everton	4-0
Crystal Palace v West Ham United	2-0
Manchester United v Tranmere Rovers	2-0

Semi-finals

Wimbledon v Crystal Palace	1-2, 3-3
Manchester United v Tottenham Hotspur	3-0, 2-1

FINAL First Leg

14 APR

Crystal Palace (0) 1 *(McCall)*

Manchester United (2) 3 *(Butt 2, Beckham)*   7825

Crystal Palace: Glass; Clark, Cutler, Holman, Edwards, McPherson (Sparrow), Hawthorne, Rollison, Thompson (McCall), Watts, Ndah.
Manchester United: Pilkington; O'Kane, Switzer, Casper, Neville, Beckham, Butt, Davies, McKee, Savage (Roberts), Thornley.

Second Leg

15 MAY

Manchester United (1) 3 *(Davies, Thornley, McKee)*

Crystal Palace (1) 2 *(McPherson, McCall)*   14,681

Manchester United: Pilkington; O'Kane, Switzer, Casper, Neville, Beckham, Butt, Davies (Gillespie), McKee, Giggs, Thornley (Savage).
Crystal Palace: Glass; Sparrow, Cutler, Holman, Edwards (Watts), McPherson, Hawthorne, Rollison (Daly), McCall, Ndah, Clark.

FA YOUTH CHALLENGE CUP FINALS 1953–91 (aggregate scores)

1953	Manchester U	9	Wolverhampton W	3	1973	Ipswich T	4	Bristol C	1
1954	Manchester U	5	Wolverhampton W	4	1974	Tottenham H	2	Huddersfield T	1
1955	Manchester U	7	WBA	1	1975	Ipswich T	5	West Ham U	1
1956	Manchester U	4	Chesterfield	3	1976	WBA	5	Wolverhampton W	0
1957	Manchester U	8	West Ham U	2	1977	C Palace	1	Everton	0
1958	Wolverhampton W	7	Chelsea	6	1978	C Palace	1	Aston Villa (one game only)	0
1959	Blackburn R	2	West Ham U	1	1979	Millwall	2	Manchester C	0
1960	Chelsea	5	Preston NE	2	1980	Aston Villa	3	Manchester C	2
1961	Chelsea	5	Everton	3	1981	West Ham U	2	Tottenham H	1
1962	Newcastle U	2	Wolverhampton W	1	1982	Watford	7	Manchester U	6
1963	West Ham U	6	Liverpool	5	1983	Norwich C	6	Everton (inc replay)	5
1964	Manchester U	5	West Ham U	2	1984	Everton	4	Stoke C	2
1965	Everton	3	Arsenal	2	1985	Newcastle U	4	Watford	1
1966	Arsenal	5	Sunderland	3	1986	Manchester C	3	Manchester U	1
1967	Sunderland	2	Birmingham C	0	1987	Coventry C	2	Charlton Ath	1
1968	Burnley	3	Coventry C	2	1988	Arsenal	6	Doncaster R	1
1969	Sunderland	6	WBA	3	1989	Watford	2	Manchester C	1
1970	Tottenham H	4	Coventry C	3	1990	Tottenham H	3	Middlesbrough	2
1971	Arsenal	2	Cardiff C	0	1991	Millwall	3	Sheffield W	0
1972	Aston Villa	5	Liverpool	2					

THE NEVILLE OVENDEN FOOTBALL COMBINATION

	P	W	D	L	F	A	Pts
Southampton	38	22	9	7	73	36	75
Chelsea	38	22	7	9	72	43	73
Arsenal	38	22	6	10	80	49	72
Queens Park Rangers	38	22	5	11	76	43	71
Norwich City	38	21	6	11	75	37	69
Luton Town	38	18	8	12	59	51	62
Swindon Town	38	16	8	14	62	60	56
Wimbledon	38	14	12	12	56	44	54
Crystal Palace	38	15	9	14	63	61	54
Ipswich Town	38	15	9	14	65	68	54
Tottenham Hotspur	38	14	11	13	63	54	53
Portsmouth	38	16	2	20	69	75	50
Watford	38	15	3	20	59	69	48
Charlton Athletic	38	13	9	16	50	60	48
Oxford United	38	13	7	18	54	77	46
West Ham United	38	11	11	16	55	64	44
Millwall	38	10	12	16	67	80	42
Fulham	38	11	8	19	39	58	41
Brighton & Hove Albion	38	8	8	22	46	67	32
Reading	38	5	4	29	48	135	19

PONTIN'S CENTRAL LEAGUE

Division One

	P	W	D	L	F	A	Pts
Nottingham Forest	34	23	7	4	81	34	76
Aston Villa	34	19	10	5	62	31	67
Liverpool	34	18	5	11	64	48	59
Blackburn Rovers	34	17	8	9	58	43	59
Leeds United	34	14	11	9	47	41	53
Barnsley	34	15	7	12	54	49	52
Manchester City	34	15	5	14	57	57	50
Manchester United	34	14	6	14	55	50	48
Sunderland	34	12	9	13	52	58	45
Sheffield United	34	10	13	11	48	52	43
Newcastle United	34	12	7	15	60	43	43
Bolton Wanderers	34	10	11	13	52	56	41
Sheffield Wednesday	34	10	9	15	44	49	39
Rotherham United	34	11	4	19	49	72	37
Everton	34	10	7	17	44	67	37
Coventry City	34	7	14	13	42	46	35
West Bromwich Albion	34	10	5	19	43	70	35
Bradford City	34	9	2	23	46	70	29

Division Two

	P	W	D	L	F	A	Pts
Stoke City	34	25	5	4	93	30	80
Wolverhampton Wanderers	34	20	8	6	66	32	68
Leicester City	34	18	8	8	57	29	62
Notts County	34	18	7	9	53	37	61
Huddersfield Town	34	16	8	10	61	46	56
Derby County	34	15	10	9	57	43	55
Burnley	34	14	6	14	48	52	48
Middlesbrough	34	14	4	16	41	52	46
Blackpool	34	13	5	16	51	49	44
Wigan Athletic	34	13	5	16	45	57	44
Scunthorpe United	34	11	10	13	50	68	43
Oldham Athletic	34	12	6	16	56	67	42
Grimsby Town	34	10	8	16	39	45	38
Preston North End	34	10	7	17	36	69	37
Port Vale	34	9	11	14	51	57	36
Mansfield Town*	34	8	7	19	39	54	31
York City	34	9	4	21	33	57	31
Hull City	34	7	9	18	27	59	30

*2 points deducted.

NORTHERN LEAGUE

Division One

	P	W	D	L	F	A	Pts
Gretna	38	25	10	3	81	23	85
Murton	38	23	9	6	83	36	78
Whitby Town	38	23	9	6	74	41	78
Guisborough Town	38	22	10	6	81	36	76
Billingham Synthonia	38	21	6	11	70	44	69
Blyth Spartans	38	19	8	11	63	43	65
South Bank	38	18	9	11	66	48	63
Northallerton Town	38	18	8	12	63	53	62
Consett	38	15	5	18	59	59	50
Tow Law Town	38	13	11	14	59	72	50
Seaham Red Star	38	13	9	16	50	57	48
Peterlee Newtown	38	14	3	21	46	70	45
Newcastle Blue Star*	38	14	5	19	49	52	44
West Auckland Town	38	11	8	19	45	68	41
Brandon United	38	10	10	18	61	75	40
Ferryhill Athletic	38	10	10	18	43	58	40
Easington Colliery	38	11	7	20	42	61	40
Shildon	38	11	7	20	47	83	40
Langley Park	38	7	7	24	50	88	28
Whickham	38	4	5	29	38	93	17

*3 points deducted.

Division Two

	P	W	D	L	F	A	Pts
Stockton	38	27	7	4	102	35	88
Durham City	38	26	9	3	82	24	87
Chester-le-Street Town	38	26	8	4	80	36	86
Hebburn	38	27	4	7	101	44	85
Dunston Fed Breweries	38	26	6	6	104	36	84
Prudhoe East End	38	22	4	12	61	36	70
Billingham Town	38	18	7	13	60	47	61
Crook Town	38	16	9	13	54	53	57
Alnwick Town	38	15	12	11	54	60	57
Ryhope Comm Assoc	38	17	5	16	77	59	56
Esh Winning	38	13	9	16	76	74	48
Ashington	38	13	9	16	50	69	48
Norton & Stockton Anc	38	11	10	17	61	69	43
Shotton Comrades	38	11	6	21	52	66	39
Horden Colliery Welf*	38	10	6	22	52	76	36
Washington	38	8	9	21	36	63	33
Evenwood Town	38	8	7	23	42	105	31
Darlington CB	38	7	4	27	47	97	25
Bedlington Terriers*	38	7	3	28	36	94	21
Willington	38	6	3	29	33	119	21

*3 points deducted.

MIDLAND COMBINATION

Premier Division

	P	W	D	L	F	A	Pts
Evesham United	40	28	7	5	76	31	91
Armitage '90'	40	27	7	6	84	28	88
West Midlands Police	40	24	8	8	86	44	80
Highgate United	40	22	11	7	71	34	77
Sandwell Borough	40	21	8	11	81	45	71
Fershore Town '88'	40	19	11	10	76	41	68
Walsall Wood	40	18	13	9	66	42	67
Stapenhill	40	18	9	13	83	67	63
Boldmere St Michaels	40	17	9	14	69	52	60
Polehall Swifts	40	15	14	11	59	47	59
Northfield Town	40	14	15	11	48	54	57
Coleshill Town	40	12	15	13	46	48	51
Alcester Town	40	11	9	20	53	74	42
Stratford Town	40	11	8	21	47	64	41
Chelmsley Town	40	12	5	23	61	111	41
Knowle	40	10	9	21	59	77	39
Barlestone St Giles	40	10	9	21	39	78	39
Kings Heath	40	8	22	45	68	38
Hinckley FC	40	10	8	22	49	79	38
Bloxwich Town	40	9	8	23	48	83	35
Mile Oak Rovers	40	3	7	30	35	114	16

LANCASHIRE LEAGUE

Division One

	P	W	D	L	F	A	Pts
Crewe Alexandra A	28	22	4	2	84	33	70
Manchester United A	28	18	6	4	69	26	60
Tranmere Rovers A	28	16	4	8	75	38	52
Burnley A	28	14	8	6	79	49	50
Blackburn Rovers A	28	14	5	9	74	56	47
Manchester City A	28	13	6	9	55	30	45
Everton A	28	12	5	11	57	59	41
Bolton Wanderers	28	11	7	10	46	42	40
Liverpool A	28	10	7	11	52	45	37
Marine Reserve	28	8	9	11	58	59	33
Morecambe Reserve	28	9	4	15	42	66	31
Oldham Athletic A	28	8	4	16	45	65	28
Chester City A	28	7	6	15	46	90	27
Preston North End A	28	7	4	17	67	76	25
UMIST	28	1	1	26	12	127	4

Division Two

	P	W	D	L	F	A	Pts
Crewe Alexandra B	30	21	3	6	94	36	66
Manchester United B	30	19	5	6	70	30	62
Blackpool A	30	16	7	7	56	43	55
Liverpool B	30	16	6	8	56	38	54
Tranmere Rovers B	30	16	3	11	56	47	51
Preston North End B	30	15	5	10	63	58	50
Everton B	30	14	4	12	74	51	46
Blackburn Rovers B	30	13	4	13	52	55	43
Carlisle United A	30	11	6	13	61	47	39
Wigan Athletic A	30	10	6	14	50	42	36
Manchester City B	30	10	5	15	38	48	35
Stockport County A	30	10	5	15	51	65	35
Rochdale A	30	8	6	16	43	73	30
Burnley B	30	8	6	16	46	78	30
Bury A	30	7	7	16	50	81	28
Marine Youth	30	6	2	22	34	102	20

BASS NORTH WEST COUNTIES LEAGUE

Division One

	P	W	D	L	F	A	Pts
Ashton United	34	24	5	5	61	31	77
Great Harwood Town	34	22	8	4	68	38	74
Eastwood Hanley	34	18	9	7	54	35	63
Blackpool Rovers	34	16	7	11	73	57	55
Prescot	34	15	6	13	48	43	51
Penrith	34	15	5	14	57	58	50
Skelmersdale United	34	11	11	12	48	52	44
Flixton	34	11	9	14	46	50	42
Clitheroe	34	11	9	14	44	55	42
Darwen	34	10	11	13	56	55	41
Atherton LR	34	11	8	15	38	45	41
Nantwich Town*	34	11	10	13	44	49	40
Vauxhall GM	34	10	10	14	42	51	40
Bacup Borough	34	9	11	14	41	45	38
St Helens Town	34	9	9	16	49	55	36
Maine Road	34	9	9	16	40	60	36
Bradford Park Avenue	34	10	5	19	57	68	35
Bootle	34	9	8	17	41	61	35

*3 points deducted for breach of rule.

Division Two

	P	W	D	L	F	A	Pts
Bamber Bridge	34	25	3	6	97	39	78
Newcastle Town	34	23	6	5	69	26	75
Blackpool Mechanics	34	20	9	5	75	34	69
Burscough	34	19	7	8	82	46	64
Formby	34	17	5	12	49	39	56
Glossop	34	15	9	10	61	44	54
Salford City	34	14	9	11	57	41	51
Castleton Gabriels	34	14	9	11	54	43	51
Cheadle Town	34	15	6	13	53	50	51
Kidsgrove Athletic	34	14	7	13	44	45	49
Chadderton	34	14	6	14	50	48	48
Oldham Town	34	11	8	15	49	62	41
Atherton Collieries	34	12	4	18	51	64	40
Squires Gate	34	11	5	18	45	60	38
Holker OB	34	10	6	18	37	53	36
Maghull	34	7	2	25	38	90	23
Ashton Town	34	4	7	23	47	101	19
Westhoughton Town	34	5	4	25	33	106	19

VAUX WEARSIDE LEAGUE

Division One

	P	W	D	L	F	A	Pts
Eppleton CW	30	22	3	5	79	34	69
Hartlepool Town	30	20	7	3	60	30	67
South Shields	30	21	3	6	90	34	66
Marske United**	30	20	4	6	85	37	58
Annfield Plain	30	17	3	10	57	48	54
Boldonca	30	12	9	9	48	41	45
Wolviston	30	13	5	12	59	55	44
Cleadon SC	30	12	7	11	45	43	43
Newton Aycliffe	30	13	3	14	44	45	42
Vaux Ryhope	30	11	8	11	56	65	41
IFG Roker	30	12	4	14	43	46	40
Cleator Moor	30	8	6	16	43	64	30
Herrington CW	30	7	3	20	32	65	24
Darlington RA*	30	4	9	17	36	66	18
Usworth Vill	30	4	5	21	22	72	17
Newcastle Bohemians	30	3	3	24	27	81	12

**6 points deducted.
*3 points deducted.

Division Two

	P	W	D	L	F	A	Pts
Silksworth	22	15	3	4	70	35	48
Jarrow Roofing	22	15	3	4	53	29	48
Windscale	22	15	0	7	45	39	45
Hebburn Coll	22	13	2	7	45	31	41
Hartlepool BWOB	22	12	1	9	46	29	37
Stanley United	22	9	3	10	29	37	30
Marchon	22	8	4	10	37	41	28
Nissan	22	7	7	8	32	43	28
Esh Albion	22	7	3	12	33	46	24
Wingate	22	6	5	11	28	32	23
Jarrow	22	5	1	16	32	53	16
Sunderland Flo Gas	22	3	2	17	26	61	11

JEWSON SOUTH-WESTERN LEAGUE

	P	W	D	L	F	A	Pts
Falmouth Town	34	26	5	3	91	20	57
Newquay	34	23	5	6	88	31	51
Bugle	34	16	9	9	63	46	41
Truro City	34	14	11	9	74	49	39
Bodmin Town	34	15	9	10	53	51	39
Clyst Rovers	34	15	8	11	59	60	38
Appledore BAAC	34	16	5	13	78	56	37
St Blazey	34	15	6	13	72	67	36
Porthleven	34	14	8	12	77	69	36
Torpoint Athletic	34	14	7	13	49	50	35
Holsworthy	34	9	16	9	37	46	34
Wadebridge Town	34	12	7	15	45	52	31
St Austell	34	10	8	16	45	63	28
Millbrook	34	9	9	16	45	70	27
Launceston	34	8	6	20	45	73	22
Devon/Cornwall Police	34	7	8	19	43	78	22
Tavistock	34	8	5	21	53	79	21
Penzance	34	7	4	23	35	94	18

McEWANS NORTHERN ALLIANCE

Premier Division

	P	W	D	L	F	A	Pts
West Allotment	30	20	4	6	77	26	64
Walker	30	18	4	8	63	35	58
Gillford Park	30	17	5	8	77	35	56
Seaton Delaval AMS	30	15	9	6	62	35	54
Spittal Rovers	30	16	4	10	56	32	52
Seaton Terrace	30	15	6	9	65	45	51
Westerhope	30	13	6	11	48	46	45
Wark	30	12	7	11	62	58	43
Haltwhistle*	30	13	5	12	39	38	41
Ponteland	30	11	7	12	55	46	40
Blyth Kitty Brewster	30	11	7	12	48	54	40
Forest Hall	30	9	8	13	38	55	35
Morpeth	30	8	8	14	38	61	32
Heaton Stannington	30	7	10	13	42	39	31
Swalwell	30	3	7	20	33	72	16
Newbiggin*	30	2	3	25	31	157	6

*3 points deducted.

WEST MIDLANDS LEAGUE

Premier Division

	P	W	D	L	F	A	Pts
Gresley Rovers	36	24	7	5	83	37	79
Paget Rangers	36	20	5	11	81	44	65
Stourport Swifts	36	18	10	8	62	45	64
Blakenall	36	17	10	9	67	49	61
Chasetown	36	17	10	9	47	31	61
Rocester	36	17	8	11	64	52	59
Oldbury United	36	17	7	12	61	47	58
Rushall Olympic	36	16	9	11	61	38	57
Lye Town	36	14	11	11	51	34	53
Halesowen Harriers	36	13	11	12	63	52	50
Willenhall Town	36	14	6	16	56	63	48
Pelsall Villa	36	12	11	13	52	58	47
West Bromwich Town	36	11	11	14	41	60	44
Cradley Town	36	12	7	17	39	56	43
Hinckley Athletic	36	9	7	20	36	56	34
Malvern Town	36	8	9	19	39	79	33
Wednesfield	36	8	8	20	43	69	32
Westfields	36	6	12	18	48	74	30
Oldswinford	36	7	5	24	34	84	26

League Cup
Gresley Rovers 1 Paget Rangers 2

Herefordshire Senior Cup
Westfields 5 Pegasus 0

Division 1

	P	W	D	L	F	A	Pts
Ilkeston Town	38	31	6	1	121	30	99
Darlaston	38	22	11	5	83	34	77
Donnington Wood	38	21	12	5	77	43	75
Gornal Athletic	38	21	8	9	73	41	71
Knypersley Victoria	38	19	9	10	84	54	66
Ettingshall HT	38	15	15	8	60	47	60
Hill Top Rangers	38	17	5	16	75	76	56
Cannock Chase	38	16	7	15	68	71	55
Ludlow Town	38	16	5	17	72	71	53
Moxley Rangers	38	14	9	15	32	42	51
Wolverhampton Casuals	38	13	11	14	51	59	50
Lichfield	38	14	5	19	72	50	47
Tipton Town	38	11	12	15	51	62	45
Wem Town	38	10	10	18	63	73	40
Wolverhampton United	38	8	14	16	63	80	38
Tividale	38	10	6	22	46	72	36
Oldbury United Res	38	8	11	19	64	88	35
Great Wyrley	38	9	6	23	45	86	33
Clancey Dudley	38	8	8	22	49	90	32
Broseley Athletic	38	8	8	22	38	93	32

League Cup
Cannock Chase 1 Ilkeston Town 4 (aet)

Birmingham County FA Challenge Vase
Darlaston 1 Gornal Athletic 1 (aet)
Replay 1-0

WINSTONLEAD KENT LEAGUE

Division One

	P	W	D	L	F	A	Pts
Herne Bay	40	29	6	5	91	34	93
Faversham Town	40	25	11	4	78	33	86
Deal Town	40	26	6	8	119	43	84
Tonbridge	40	26	6	8	93	44	84
Alma Swanley	40	24	11	5	92	49	83
Sheppey United	40	21	11	8	69	44	74
Whitstable	40	21	8	11	70	38	71
Slade Green	40	15	12	13	68	56	57
Greenwich Borough	40	15	10	15	77	62	55
Ramsgate	40	16	7	17	62	58	55
Kent Police	40	14	11	15	60	63	53
Tunbridge Wells	40	15	8	17	61	68	53
Corinthian	40	14	8	18	58	63	50
Beckenham Town	40	12	11	17	51	67	47
Thames Poly	40	8	11	21	43	78	35
Crockenhill	40	7	13	20	48	83	34
Thamesmead Town	40	9	7	24	44	100	34
Cray Wanderers	40	8	7	25	38	84	31
Chatham Town	40	7	10	23	41	89	31
Danson Furness	40	8	7	25	39	94	31
Darenth Heathside	40	6	7	27	42	96	25

Met Police records expunged.

GREAT MILLS LEAGUE

Premier Division

	P	W	D	L	F	A	Pts
Weston Super Mare	40	32	2	6	110	44	98
Clevedon Town	40	28	5	7	90	28	89
Tiverton Town*	40	27	5	8	106	47	85
Bideford	40	25	9	6	102	49	84
Saltash United	40	24	5	11	89	51	77
Plymouth Argyle	40	24	4	12	89	52	76
Taunton Town	40	17	11	12	88	56	62
Mangotsfield United	40	16	13	11	53	39	61
Elmore	40	17	10	13	76	72	61
Paulton Rovers	40	16	11	13	71	60	59
Minehead	40	16	10	14	65	74	58
Liskeard Athletic	40	14	10	16	68	69	52
Dawlish Town	40	15	5	20	77	76	50
Chippenham Town	40	13	7	20	58	95	46
Torrington	40	11	10	19	48	62	43
Bristol Manor Farm	40	10	10	20	42	66	40
Exmouth Town	40	10	8	22	56	97	38
Chard Town	40	8	8	24	48	76	32
Frome Town	40	9	5	25	44	91	32
Welton Rovers	40	8	6	26	32	78	30
Ottery St Mary	40	2	2	36	26	156	8

*1 point deducted.

First Division

	P	W	D	L	F	A	Pts
Westbury United	42	27	10	5	80	39	91
Torquay United	42	26	11	5	96	32	89
Crediton United	42	20	12	10	57	32	72
Bath City	42	22	6	14	91	68	72
Warminster Town	42	19	13	10	80	49	70
Keynsham Town	42	19	13	10	80	69	70
Calne Town	42	20	9	13	73	49	69
Brislington	42	21	6	15	70	51	69
Bridport	42	17	16	9	61	50	67
Ilfracombe Town	42	17	14	11	76	44	65
Odd Down	42	20	5	17	58	46	65
Backwell United	42	17	10	15	64	49	61
Bishop Sutton	42	17	10	15	58	50	61
Glastonbury	42	14	8	20	52	61	50
Larkhall Athletic	42	12	12	18	58	65	48
Radstock Town	42	11	14	17	65	68	47
Barnstaple Town	42	12	8	22	42	55	44
Clandown	42	10	13	19	56	72	43
Wellington	42	9	11	22	42	70	38
Devizes Town	42	8	13	21	57	84	37
Melksham Town	42	8	12	22	44	77	36
Heavitree United	42	2	2	38	26	206	8

JEWSON (EASTERN COUNTIES) LEAGUE

Premier Division

	P	W	D	L	F	A	Pts
Wroxham	42	31	6	5	113	41	99
Stowmarket Town	42	26	9	7	86	50	87
Cornard United	42	24	8	10	85	47	80
Norwich United	42	23	7	12	72	53	76
Wisbech Town	42	23	6	13	86	62	75
Harwich & Parkeston	42	24	2	16	106	61	74
Newmarket Town	42	19	14	9	66	50	71
Haverhill Rovers	42	18	11	13	70	61	65
Halstead Town	42	18	6	18	79	72	60
March Town United	42	15	12	15	64	49	57
Lowestoft Town	42	16	9	17	67	64	57
Gorleston	42	16	8	18	62	54	56
Felixstowe Town	42	14	11	17	55	61	53
Great Yarmouth Town	42	15	6	21	60	71	51
Histon	42	15	5	22	61	89	50
Tiptree United	42	11	16	15	54	70	49
Brantham Athletic	42	12	12	18	51	69	48
Watton United	42	12	9	21	57	70	45
Chatteris Town	42	12	7	23	49	72	43
Brightlingsea United	42	11	9	22	60	83	42
Clacton Town	42	11	9	22	50	90	42
Thetford Town	42	3	4	35	31	135	13

Division One

	P	W	D	L	F	A	Pts
Diss Town	38	28	6	4	105	28	90
Fakenham Town	38	25	7	6	80	35	82
Woodbridge Town	38	19	10	9	70	34	67
Ely City	38	20	6	12	66	52	66
Downham Town	38	19	5	14	68	61	62
Long Sutton Athletic	38	18	7	13	70	58	61
Sudbury Town Reserves	38	17	8	13	72	58	59
Soham Town Rangers	38	16	11	11	70	55	59
Cambridge City Res	38	17	7	14	84	74	58
Somersham Town	38	16	9	13	75	56	57
Hadleigh United	38	17	6	15	59	61	57
Sudbury Wanderers	38	16	6	16	63	62	54
King's Lynn Reserves	38	12	11	15	58	61	47
Warboys Town	38	13	8	17	60	69	47
Ipswich Wanderers	38	10	9	19	47	70	39
Bury Town Reserves	38	10	9	19	45	74	39
Clarksteel Yaxley	38	11	6	21	49	79	39
Swaffham Town	38	11	5	22	53	80	38
Huntingdon United	38	7	7	24	34	90	28
Mildenhall Town	38	2	9	27	31	102	15

CENTRAL MIDLANDS LEAGUE

Supreme Division

	P	W	D	L	F	A	Pts
Lincoln United	34	26	5	3	95	26	83
Hucknall Town	34	22	3	9	86	44	69
Sheffield Aurora	34	22	2	10	68	33	68
Louth United	34	20	6	8	72	41	66
Harworth Colliery Institute	34	20	5	9	76	51	65
Blidworth Welfare	34	16	5	13	46	46	53
Arnold Town	34	15	7	23	73	60	52
Mickleover Royal British Legion	34	16	4	14	72	60	52
Nettleham	34	14	7	13	49	52	49
Priory (Eastwood)	34	14	7	13	50	56	49
Heanor Town	34	13	6	15	48	54	45
Oakham United	34	13	6	15	52	59	45
Borrowash Victoria	34	8	11	15	49	63	35
Shirebrook Colliery	34	10	5	19	51	66	35
Wombwell Town	34	10	4	20	52	71	34
Melton Town	34	7	5	22	42	93	26
Stanton Ilkeston	34	7	4	23	29	78	25
Glapwell	34	3	4	27	44	112	13

Premier Division North

	P	W	D	L	F	A	Pts
Fryston Colliery Welfare	26	20	2	4	75	33	62
Kiveton Park	26	17	4	5	63	29	55
Norton Woodseats	26	14	7	5	58	33	49
Mexborough Town	26	12	8	6	46	31	44
South Normanton Athletic	26	13	5	8	42	32	44
Blackwell Miners League	26	11	6	9	38	44	39
Rossington	26	11	4	11	42	50	37
Lincoln Moorlands	26	9	6	11	44	40	33
Holbrook Miners Welfare	26	8	9	9	35	42	33
Kilburn Miners Welfare	26	8	6	12	56	60	30
Biwater	26	8	4	14	43	41	28
Selston	26	6	6	14	33	60	24
Retford Rail	26	3	6	17	33	70	15
Nuthall	26	4	3	19	34	77	15

Premier Division South

	P	W	D	L	F	A	Pts
Slack & Parr	30	24	3	3	81	23	75
Gedling Town	30	19	6	5	91	42	63
Kimberley Town	30	17	6	7	66	40	57
Highfield Rangers	30	15	8	7	48	28	53
Newhall United	30	17	2	11	63	49	53
Shardlow St James	30	15	4	11	49	38	49
Long Eaton United	30	13	5	12	67	49	44
Derby Carriage & Wagon (Reckitts)	30	14	2	14	47	42	44
Alvaston & Boulton	30	12	6	12	45	44	42
Derby Rolls Royce	30	11	7	12	48	62	40
Radford	30	12	3	15	49	72	39
Leicester Nirvana	30	11	1	18	37	63	34
Brailsford	30	8	5	17	43	74	29
West Hallam	30	7	2	21	38	73	23
Bulwell United	30	6	4	20	46	85	22
Attenborough	30	5	4	21	37	69	19

SPARTAN LEAGUE

Premier Division

	P	W	D	L	F	A	Pts
Northwood	36	26	4	6	97	38	82
Brimsdown Rovers	36	23	7	6	76	28	76
Haringey Borough	36	21	8	7	74	57	71
Brook House	36	21	6	9	68	51	69
Walthamstow Pennant	36	20	8	8	92	35	68
Barkingside	36	19	8	9	56	41	65
Hanwell Town	36	18	7	11	78	41	61
Cheshunt	36	16	12	8	52	31	60
Corinthian Casuals	36	17	3	16	75	44	54
Croydon Athletic	36	16	5	15	66	63	53
Waltham Abbey	36	14	8	14	49	52	50
Cockfosters	36	12	10	14	47	52	46
Hillingdon Borough	36	13	6	17	52	65	45
Beaconsfield United	36	11	8	17	43	69	41
Southgate Athletic	36	11	5	20	41	61	38
Amersham Town	36	7	6	23	33	69	27
North Greenford Utd	36	5	10	21	36	81	25
Beckton United	36	4	8	24	33	100	20
Eltham Town	36	2	3	31	25	115	9

ESSEX SENIOR LEAGUE

Senior Section

	P	W	D	L	F	A	Pts
Ford United	32	20	6	6	64	18	66
Brentwood	32	20	6	6	77	37	66
East Thurrock United	32	19	9	4	62	24	66
Sawbridgeworth Town	32	19	8	5	67	43	65
Canvey Island	32	19	6	7	49	24	63
Basildon United	32	17	5	10	65	39	56
Bowers United	32	15	9	8	49	31	54
Southend Manor	32	14	6	12	62	40	48
Stambridge	32	12	8	12	60	49	44
Woodford Town	32	12	7	13	46	44	43
Concord Rangers	32	10	10	12	39	52	40
Stansted	32	11	6	15	40	50	39
Burnham Ramblers	32	10	4	18	48	71	34
Hullbridge Sports	32	7	7	18	25	63	28
East Ham United	32	7	5	20	35	72	26
Eton Manor	32	5	3	24	24	71	18
Maldon Town	32	1	3	28	20	104	6

EVERARDS BREWERY LEICESTERSHIRE SENIOR LEAGUE

Premier Division	P	W	D	L	F	A	Pts
Holwell Sports	30	21	6	3	97	30	69
St Andrews Social Club	30	19	4	7	65	49	61
Birstall United	30	15	8	7	57	44	53
Anstey Nomads	30	15	6	9	64	38	51
Barwell Athletic	30	12	11	7	56	48	47
Houghton Rangers	30	14	4	12	65	51	46
Lutterworth Town	30	12	10	8	46	39	46
Ibstock Welfare	30	9	15	6	45	39	42
Friar Lane Old Boys	30	10	8	12	63	62	38
Newfoundpool WMC	30	10	8	12	48	50	38
Leics. Constabulary	30	9	9	12	48	52	36
Oadby Town	30	9	8	13	47	60	35
Pedigree Petfoods	30	7	7	16	43	61	28
Syston St Peters	30	8	4	18	49	78	28
Narborough & Lit/trpe	30	5	7	18	38	86	22
Hillcroft	30	3	9	18	30	74	18

Division One	P	W	D	L	F	A	Pts
Burbage Old Boys	34	24	8	2	87	31	80
North Kilworth	34	23	5	6	109	41	74
Downes Sports	34	22	3	9	72	55	69
Barrow Town	34	18	11	5	87	49	65
Ravenstone	34	16	9	9	62	51	57
Kirby Muxloe SC	34	15	10	9	62	52	55
Harborough Town	34	15	8	11	75	64	53
Thringstone	34	14	6	14	51	70	48
Quorn	34	11	11	12	51	54	44
Sileby Town	34	12	5	17	51	53	41
Asfordby Am's	34	11	8	15	58	61	41
Earl Shilton Albion	34	9	11	14	52	75	38
Aylestone Park Old Boys	34	10	7	17	49	82	37
Loughborough Dynamo	34	9	8	17	60	66	35
Anstey Town	34	9	5	20	45	72	32
Leicester YMCA	34	6	10	18	42	72	28
Whetstone Athletic	34	5	12	17	54	74	27
Huncote Sports & Social	34	5	7	22	34	79	22

NORTHERN COUNTIES EAST LEAGUE

Premier Division	P	W	D	L	F	A	Pts
North Shields	36	31	3	2	109	14	96
Sutton Town	36	21	9	6	79	41	72
Denaby United	36	22	3	11	78	47	68
North Ferriby United	36	19	8	9	63	45	65
Spennymoor United	36	17	8	11	61	45	59
Sheffield	36	16	9	11	71	48	57
Maltby MW	36	16	8	12	61	61	56
Brigg Town	36	15	7	14	44	42	52
Thackley	36	14	9	13	45	45	51
Ossett Albion	36	14	8	14	40	51	50
Belper Town	36	12	11	13	48	50	47
Ossett Town	36	11	12	13	48	57	45
Armthorpe Welfare	36	12	9	15	57	67	45
Liversedge	36	11	8	17	54	72	41
Winterton Regulars	36	10	5	21	53	78	35
Pontefract Collieries	36	9	7	20	36	71	34
Eccleshill United	36	7	10	19	38	83	31
Harrogate Railway	36	5	8	23	31	60	23
Glasshoughton Welfare	36	5	8	23	35	74	23

*1 point deducted.

Division One	P	W	D	L	F	A	Pts
Stocksbridge PS	30	19	5	6	71	34	62
Pickering Town	30	19	4	7	84	46	61
Bradley Regulars	30	18	7	5	59	26	61
Yorks Amateurs	30	18	3	9	56	27	57
Hallam	30	17	6	7	57	36	57
Hall Road Regulars	30	17	5	8	68	36	56
Rossington Main	30	13	5	12	44	38	44
RES Parkgate	30	12	5	13	41	59	41
Immingham Town	30	12	4	14	48	64	40
Worsbrough Bridge	30	11	6	13	44	43	39
Garforth Town	30	10	5	15	48	44	35
Tadcaster Albion	30	8	4	18	37	62	28
Selby Town	30	8	4	18	32	67	28
York RI (resigned)	30	6	7	17	32	77	25
Brodsworth MW	30	6	6	18	45	72	24
Hatfield Main*	30	7	2	21	36	71	22

*1 point deducted.

SOUTH EAST COUNTIES LEAGUE

Division One

	P	W	D	L	F	A	Pts
Tottenham Hotspur	30	23	5	2	83	26	51
Arsenal	30	19	5	6	85	48	43
Queens Park Rangers	30	18	3	9	80	51	39
Norwich City	30	16	3	11	56	41	35
Southend United	30	13	8	9	65	56	34
Chelsea	30	15	3	12	52	40	33
Millwall	30	13	6	11	47	41	32
Watford	30	12	6	12	52	47	30
Ipswich Town	30	13	4	13	55	65	30
Fulham	30	11	6	13	47	48	28
West Ham United	30	9	9	12	57	60	27
Leyton Orient	30	11	3	16	55	73	25
Charlton Athletic	30	9	5	16	51	66	23
Gillingham	30	9	2	19	45	82	20
Cambridge United	30	6	4	20	40	85	16
Portsmouth	30	5	4	21	37	78	14

Division Two

	P	W	D	L	F	A	Pts
Crystal Palace	26	18	5	3	69	24	41
Wimbledon	26	16	5	5	71	24	37
Oxford United	26	15	4	7	49	31	34
Luton Town	26	14	6	6	60	45	34
Brentford	26	13	5	8	47	33	31
Southampton	26	11	8	7	32	30	30
Brighton & Hove Albion	26	12	4	10	51	38	28
Bristol City	26	10	5	11	44	45	25
Tottenham Hotspur	26	9	3	14	34	55	21
Swindon Town	26	7	6	13	33	53	20
Reading	26	8	3	15	44	64	19
Bristol Rovers	26	7	2	17	41	86	16
Bournemouth	26	6	3	17	34	50	15
Maidstone United	26	5	3	18	32	60	13

Aldershot's record has been expunged.

HELLENIC LEAGUE

Premier Division	P	W	D	L	F	A	Pts
Shortwood United	34	25	4	5	83	44	79
Cirencester Town	34	23	9	2	73	23	78
Almondsbury Picksons	34	19	7	8	63	38	64
Milton United	34	18	9	7	67	44	63
Cinderford Town	34	16	9	9	57	41	57
Abingdon United	34	17	5	12	54	40	56
Didcot Town	34	16	6	12	70	48	54
Swindon Athletic	34	15	9	10	61	44	54
Bicester Town	34	12	12	10	44	42	48
Banbury United	34	14	5	15	55	55	47
Fairford Town	34	12	9	13	72	55	45
Headington Amateurs	34	10	9	15	48	59	39
Pegasus Juniors	34	11	5	18	66	68	38
Kintbury Rangers	34	9	8	17	47	59	35
Rayners Lane	34	9	8	17	50	75	35
Moreton Town	34	7	4	23	38	100	25
Carterton Town	34	6	6	22	32	74	24
Bishops Cleeve	34	2	6	26	25	96	12

Division One	P	W	D	L	F	A	Pts
Wollen Sports	32	26	4	2	96	28	82
Wantage Town	32	23	6	3	83	32	75
Tuffley Rovers	32	20	8	4	95	34	68
Northleigh	32	20	4	8	84	38	64
Cheltenham Saracens	32	15	7	10	70	45	52
Purton	32	14	7	11	48	40	49
Chipping Norton	32	13	6	13	54	56	45
Highworth Town	32	11	7	14	53	54	40
Cirencester United	32	11	7	14	49	55	40
Lambourn Sports	32	11	7	14	52	74	40
Yarnton	32	11	6	15	42	60	39
Wootton Bassett	32	10	8	14	45	59	38
Easington Sports	32	12	0	20	42	80	36
Kidlington	32	7	9	16	48	70	30
Wallingford Town	32	8	5	19	40	78	29
Clanfield	32	5	10	17	35	66	25
Supermarine	32	3	3	26	20	87	12

SOUTH MIDLANDS LEAGUE

Premier Division

	P	W	D	L	F	A	Pts
Leighton Town	40	29	8	3	98	30	95
MK Borough	40	30	3	7	116	29	93
Biggleswade Town	40	26	6	8	96	38	84
Shillington	40	25	6	9	82	35	81
Wingate & Fin	40	22	10	8	87	51	76
Hoddesdon Town	40	20	13	7	80	42	73
Brache Sparta	40	21	8	11	82	48	71
Leverstock GN	40	21	6	13	63	38	69
Oxford City	40	19	7	14	74	50	64
Langford	40	18	8	14	52	48	62
Potters Bar C	40	17	10	13	76	64	61
Harpenden Town	40	14	11	15	70	63	53
Totternhoe	40	15	4	21	61	84	49
Letchworth GC	40	13	6	21	58	63	45
Pitstone & Ivinghoe	40	12	8	20	63	100	44
Pirton	40	10	11	19	36	61	41
Welwyn Garden City	40	10	10	20	62	87	40
Buckingham A	40	10	6	24	60	77	36
New Bradwell	40	5	8	27	34	93	23
The 61 FC	40	4	5	31	39	114	17
Winslow United	40	2	0	38	20	194	6
Wolverton AFC	0	0	0	0	0	0	0

Division One

	P	W	D	L	F	A	Pts
Ashcroft	38	30	5	3	93	30	95
Luton Old Boys	38	28	7	3	104	41	91
Bedford United	38	28	5	5	118	39	89
Bedford Town	38	26	6	6	100	32	84
Shenley & Loughton	38	20	5	13	85	42	65
Toddington R	38	17	13	8	76	53	64
Delco Products	38	16	6	15	69	59	57
Risborough	38	14	11	13	61	65	53
Ampthill Town	38	14	10	14	65	57	52
Cranfield United	38	13	10	15	62	66	49
Ickleford	38	12	12	14	54	60	48
Tring Athletic	38	12	11	15	57	58	44
Sandy Albion	38	11	8	19	61	87	41
Potters Bar CRS	38	12	4	22	86	99	40
Walden Rangers	38	9	13	16	65	82	40
Flamstead	38	11	7	20	60	87	40
Shefford Town	38	11	7	20	41	72	40
Emberton	38	9	6	23	47	91	33
Caddington	38	4	7	27	40	103	19
Stony Stratford Town	38	2	7	29	41	162	13

HEREWARD SPORTS UNITED COUNTIES LEAGUE

Premier Division

	P	W	D	L	F	A	Pts
Northampton Spencer	46	31	8	7	101	44	101
Raunds	46	27	14	5	94	38	95
Rothwell	46	29	6	11	100	51	93
Bourne	46	27	8	11	113	57	89
Stotfold	46	26	8	12	93	52	86
Mirrless Blackstone	46	23	12	11	77	60	81
Eynesbury	46	22	12	12	82	58	78
Boston	46	21	11	14	79	62	74
Hamlet S & L	46	21	11	14	76	60	74
Arlesey	46	20	12	14	76	65	72
Peterborough City	46	22	5	19	81	66	71
Cogenhoe	46	19	13	14	92	63	70
Potton	46	20	9	27	76	61	69
Daventry	46	18	10	18	71	65	64
Kempston	46	16	15	15	54	51	63
Long Buckby	46	18	9	19	66	67	63
Irthlingborough	46	17	8	21	73	88	59
Desborough	46	13	10	23	57	85	49
Wootton	46	15	3	28	57	85	48
Stamford	46	11	8	27	60	85	41
Spalding	46	10	11	25	59	104	41
Wellingborough	46	7	5	34	45	130	26
Holbeach	46	4	9	33	44	133	21
Brackley	46	3	7	36	39	135	16

Division One

	P	W	D	L	F	A	Pts
Harrowby	34	25	5	4	92	30	80
Newport Pagnell	34	25	5	4	86	44	80
Ramsey	34	23	6	5	95	36	75
St Ives	34	22	6	6	78	32	72
Bugbrooke	34	21	5	8	78	42	68
Higham	34	19	7	8	73	45	64
Ford Sports	34	18	6	10	74	48	60
O N Chenecks	34	16	9	9	61	47	57
Cottingham	34	14	4	16	62	68	46
Thrapston	34	11	6	17	54	70	39
Blisworth	34	11	4	19	50	65	37
Olney	34	10	6	18	53	61	36
Whitworths	34	10	6	18	41	70	36
British Timken	34	9	4	21	65	107	31
Sharnbrook	34	8	5	21	51	77	29
Burton PW	34	6	10	18	38	58	28
Towcester	34	6	6	22	38	72	24
Irchester	34	1	2	31	27	144	5

HIGHLAND LEAGUE

	P	W	D	L	F	A	Pts
Ross County	34	24	3	7	95	43	75
Caledonian	34	22	6	6	93	34	72
Huntly	34	21	7	6	70	43	70
Cove Rangers	34	18	9	7	62	35	63
Keith	34	18	6	10	67	44	60
Lossiemouth	34	17	7	10	62	42	58
Buckie Thistle	34	17	6	11	58	46	57
Elgin City	34	16	6	12	76	51	54
Peterhead	34	16	6	12	61	59	54
Inverness Thistle	34	14	8	12	54	57	50
Forres Mechanics	34	13	8	13	66	62	47
Clachnacuddin	34	11	6	17	43	51	39
Deveronvale	34	12	3	19	41	58	39
Brora Rangers	34	11	5	18	52	67	38
Fraserburgh	34	11	3	20	43	67	36
Fort William	34	8	4	22	48	83	28
Rothes	34	4	4	26	38	99	16
Nairn County	34	3	3	28	23	111	12

AMATEUR FOOTBALL ALLIANCE
1991–92

CUP COMPETITION FINALS

Senior
West Wickham v Midland Bank — 2-1

Greenland Memorial
Old Ignatians v Lancing Old Boys — 1-0

Intermediate
Old Hamptonians 2nd v Old Esthameians 2nd — 2-0

Junior
Hassocks 2nd v Old Aloysians 3rd — 2-0

Minor
Old Esthameians 3rd v Old Finchleians 3rd — 2-0

Senior Novets
Nat West Bank 4th v Lloyds Bank 4th — 3-2

Intermediate Novets
Civil Service 5th v Old Salvatorians 5th — *2-2, 1-3

Junior Novets
Old Salvatorians 9th v Winchmore Hill 7th — 1-0

Veterans
Winchmore Hill Veterans v Old Salesians Veterans — 1-0

Open Veterans
Old Wulfrunians Veterans v Port of London Auth Vets — *1-0

Essex Senior
Old Chigwellians v Old Fairlopians — 2-1

Middlesex Senior
Old Meadonians v Civil Service — 2-1

Surrey Senior
Witan v South Bank Polytechnic — *1-1, 1-0

Essex Intermediate
Old Bealonians 2nd v Old Westhamians 2nd — 2-1

Kent Intermediate
Bank of America 1st v Midland Bank 2nd — 1-0

Middlesex Intermediate
Old Hamptonians 2nd v Winchmore Hill 2nd — *0-0, *2-1

Surrey Intermediate
Old Tenisonians 2nd v Nottsborough 2nd — 4-1

* after extra time

AMATEUR FOOTBALL ALLIANCE SENIOR CUP 1991–92

1st Round Proper
Chertsey O. Salesians 2, National Westminster Bank 5
Witan 0, O. Parkonians 2
West Wickham 1, Wake Green 0
Lensbury 0, O. Bealonians 2
Mill Hill Village 1, Cardinal Manning OB 0
South Bank Polytechnic 2, O. Bromleians 0
O. Finchleians 2, Hale End Athletic 1
Norsemen 3, Duncombe Sports 1
O. Parmiterians 1*:1, O. Grammarians 1*:2
Enfield O. Grammarians 2, O. Esthameians 1
O. Ignatians 3, Lloyds Bank 1
Royal Bank of Scotland 2, British Petroleum 1
Southgate Olympic 0, O. Actonians Assn. 7
Wandsworth Borough 0, Winchmore Hill 1
O. Latymerians 1*a:3, Ulysses 1*a:0
Camdenians 2, Carshalton 9
Glyn O. Boys 1*:2, O. Salesians 1*:0
O. Isleworthians 1, O. Stationers 3
Crouch End Vampires 1*:1*, Hassocks 1*:3*
Albanian 6, Latymer OB 1
O. Tiffinians 5, O. Monovians 0
Economicals 0, Colposa 7
O. Hamptonians 3, O. Owens 2
O. Westminster Citizens 1, Nottsborough 2
Hampstead Heathens 4, O. Southallians 0
St Mary's College 1, O. Elizabethans 2
O. Meadonians 2, Midland Bank 3
O. Chigwellians 2, Leyton County OB 1
O. Brentwoods 2, O. Aloysians 6
O. Kingsburians 1*:2*, E. Barnet O. Grammarians 1*:4*
O. Dorkinians w/o, Opponents disbarred
Civil Service 2, London Airways 0

2nd Round Proper
Nat. W'min. Bank 2*:2, O. Parkonians 2*:3
West Wickham 2, O. Bealonians 1
Mill Hill Village 3, S. Bank Polytechnic 5
O. Finchleians 1, Norsemen 2
O. Grammarians 1, Enfield O. Gramm'ns 3

O. Ignatians 3, Royal Bank of Scotland 2
O. Actonians Assn. 3, Winchmore Hill 2
O. Latymerians 3, Carshalton 1
Glyn O. Boys 0, O. Stationers 1
Hassocks 4, Albanian 1
O. Tiffinians 4, Colposa 0
O. Hamptonians 2, Nottsborough 4
Hampstead Heathens 1, O. Elizabethans 3
Midland Bank 3, O. Chigwellians 2
O. Aloysians 3, E. Barnet O. Grammarians 0
O. Dorkinians 2, Civil Service 5

3rd Round Proper
O. Parkonians 1*:0, West Wickham 1*:1
S. Bank Polytechnic 4, Norsemen 0
Enfield O. Grammarians 1*, O. Ignatians 0*
O. Actonians Assn. 1, O. Latymerians 0
O. Stationers 0, Hassocks 2
O. Tiffinians 0, Nottsborough 1
O. Elizabethans 0, Midland Bank 2
O. Aloysians 2*:2, Civil Service 2*:0

4th Round Proper
West Wickham 1, South Bank Polytechnic 0
Enfield O. Grammarians 2, O. Actonians Assn. 1
Hassocks 1, Nottsborough 2
Midland Bank 2:0, O. Aloysians 2:0
Midland Bank won on penalties

Semi-finals
West Wickham 2*, Enfield O. Grammarians 0*
Nottsborough 0, Midland Bank 4

Final
West Wickham 2, Midland Bank 1

* after extra time
a - abandoned in extra time

REPRESENTATIVE MATCHES

v Cambridge University	Won 2-1	v Royal Air Force FA	Lost 2-3
v Oxford University	Won 3-1	v Sussex County FA	Drawn 2-2
v Army FA	Won 1-0	v London University	Won 2-0
v Royal Navy FA	Lost 1-2		

THE ARTHUR DUNN CUP

Final Tie: Old Chigwellians 3, Old Etonians 1

ARTHURIAN LEAGUE

Premier Division	P	W	D	L	F	A	Pts
Old Chigwellians	16	11	3	2	46	19	25
Old Etonians	16	9	3	4	31	24	21
Old Malvernians	16	8	2	6	27	26	18
Old Cholmeleians	16	6	5	5	30	27	17
Old Reptonians	16	6	4	6	36	25	16
Lancing Old Boys	16	6	2	8	25	28	14
Old Carthusians	16	6	2	8	26	32	14
Old Brentwoods	16	4	4	8	21	31	12
Old Foresters	16	2	3	11	25	55	7

Division One	P	W	D	L	F	A	Pts
Old Wellingburians	16	11	3	2	53	18	25
Old Bradfieldians	19	9	3	4	35	26	21
Old Aldenhamians	16	8	4	4	35	20	20
Old Harrovians	16	6	3	7	27	32	15
Old Haileyburians	16	5	4	7	33	38	14
Old Wykehamists	16	4	5	7	28	37	13
Old Ardinians	16	4	5	7	27	42	13
Old Salopians	16	6	0	10	29	32	12
Old Westminsters	16	5	1	10	26	48	11

Division Two	P	W	D	L	F	A	Pts
Old Welleians	16	11	3	2	53	18	25
Old Carthusians Res	19	9	3	4	35	26	21
Old Cholmeleians Res	16	8	4	4	35	20	20
Old Etonians Res	16	6	3	7	27	32	15
Old Chigwellians Res	16	5	4	7	33	38	14
Old Aldenhamians Res	16	4	5	7	28	37	13
Old Chigwellians 3rd	16	4	5	7	27	42	13
Old Harrovians Res	16	6	0	10	29	32	12
Lancing Old Boys Res	16	5	1	10	26	48	11

Division Three – 9 Teams – won by Old Reptonians Res
Division Four – 9 Teams – won by Lancing Old Boys 3rd
Division Five – 8 Teams – won by Old Wellingburians Res

Junior League Cup
  O. Chigwellians 3rd 0, O. Brentwood Res. 0 (*aet*)
  (Chigwellians won on penalties)

Jin Dixson 6-a-Side Tournament
  O. Chigwellians 2, O. Wellingburians 1

LONDON LEGAL LEAGUE

Division One	P	W	D	L	F	A	Pts
Slaughter & May	22	18	1	3	79	16	37
Wilde Sapte	22	13	6	3	59	25	32
Cameron Markby Hewitt	22	15	1	6	52	34	31
Freshfields	22	12	6	4	60	30	30
Pegasus (Inner Temple)	22	14	1	7	68	34	29
Grays Inn	22	10	6	6	59	36	26
Norton Rose	22	7	3	12	27	50	17
Linklaters & Paines	22	5	5	12	30	51	15
Clifford Chance	22	6	2	14	30	43	14
Lovell White Durrant	22	5	3	14	34	83	13
Titmuss Sainer & Webb	22	6	1	15	17	69	13
Nabarro Nathanson	22	3	1	18	37	81	7

Division Two	P	W	D	L	F	A	Pts
Allen & Overy	22	18	1	3	120	31	37
Macfarlanes	22	17	2	3	70	20	36
Herbert Smith	22	14	2	6	48	34	30
Boodle Hatfield	22	12	4	6	38	26	28
D.J. Freeman & Co	22	10	4	8	53	37	24
McKenna & Co	22	10	2	10	52	62	22
Gouldens	22	9	2	11	45	53	20
Stephenson Harwood	22	8	4	10	38	47	20
Beachcroft Stanleys	22	7	4	11	37	77	18
Taylor Joynson Garrett	22	5	2	15	46	62	12
Denton Hall Burgin & Warrens	22	5	1	16	46	68	11
Baker & McKenzie	22	2	2	18	25	101	6

League Challenge Cup
Grays Inn 0, Freshfields 1

Weavers Arms Cup
Wilde Sapte 4, Pegasus 0

LONDON INSURANCE FA

Division One	P	W	D	L	F	A	Pts
Liverpool Victoria	16	14	1	1	69	23	29
Temple Bar	16	12	1	3	69	19	25
Gaflac	16	8	1	7	44	36	17
Colonial Mutual	16	8	1	7	48	45	17
Granby	16	6	3	7	44	47	15
Eagle Star	16	6	3	7	36	48	15
Sun Alliance	16	4	1	11	24	48	9
Bardhill	16	4	1	11	29	61	9
Bowring	16	4	0	12	26	62	8

Division Two	P	W	D	L	F	A	Pts
Sun Alliance Res	16	11	3	2	58	20	25
Noble Lowndes	16	10	2	4	52	28	22
Temple Bar Res	16	10	2	4	42	27	22
Sedgwick	16	9	1	6	69	37	19
Asphalia	16	9	1	6	47	38	19
Granby Res	16	5	3	8	44	44	13
Norwich Union (London)	16	5	3	8	33	40	13
Liverpool Victoria Res	16	3	1	12	28	76	7
Eagle Star Res	16	2	0	14	20	83	4

Division Three	P	W	D	L	F	A	Pts
Temple Bar 3rd	17	15	1	1	72	15	31
Gaflac Res	18	14	1	3	79	39	29
Sun Alliance 3rd	18	11	0	7	48	43	22
Noble Lowndes Res	18	9	2	7	62	48	20
Bowring Res	18	7	3	8	49	51	17
Guardian Royal Exchange	18	7	3	8	40	45	17
Eagle Star 3rd	18	7	0	11	49	51	14
Temple Bar 4th	18	6	2	10	39	44	14
Liverpool Victoria 3rd	17	3	2	12	46	68	8
Gaflac 3rd	18	2	2	14	25	105	6

Charity Cup – Liverpool Victoria 1, Temple Bar 0
Challenge Cup – Cuaco Res 3, Temple Bar 1
Junior Cup – Sedgwick 5, Eagle Star Res 1
Minor Cup – Temple Bar 3rd 4, Bowring Res 1
W. A. Jewell Memorial Trophy (5-a-Side) – Granby
Sportsmanship Trophy – Colonial Mutual

LONDON BANKS FA

Division One	P	W	D	L	F	A	Pts
Coutts & Co	16	11	2	3	41	24	24
Citibank	16	8	6	2	48	24	22
Hill Samuel Investment Management	16	9	4	3	31	20	22
Allied Irish Bank	16	9	1	6	45	30	19
Kleinwort Benson	16	5	4	7	30	33	14
Credit Suisse	16	5	4	7	31	38	14
Bank of America	16	5	4	7	21	28	14
Chase Manhattan	16	3	2	11	26	47	8
Salomon Brothers	16	2	3	11	27	56	7

Division Two	P	W	D	L	F	A	Pts
MIM	16	14	0	2	59	12	28
Bank of Scotland	16	9	2	5	35	25	20
Manufacturers Hanover Trust	16	9	1	6	43	24	19
Polytechnic	16	6	5	5	25	23	17
Hong Kong Bank	16	7	1	8	38	29	15
National Westminster Bank "A"	16	6	2	8	34	33	14
Coutts & Co Res	16	5	4	7	29	51	14
Union Bank of Switzerland	16	3	7	6	22	40	13
Standard Chartered	16	0	4	12	16	64	4

Division Three	P	W	D	L	F	A	Pts
Nikko Europe	18	15	3	0	76	18	33
Westpack	18	9	5	4	52	30	23
Chase Manhattan Res	18	11	1	6	53	48	23
C. Hoare & Co Res	18	10	2	6	42	28	22
Morgan Stanley	18	8	5	5	40	29	21
Bankers Trust Co	18	6	2	10	34	43	14
Citibank Res	18	5	3	10	33	44	13
National Westminster Bank "B"	18	4	5	9	27	54	13
Bank of America	18	5	1	12	28	52	11
National Westminster Bank "C"	18	2	3	13	24	63	7

Division Four	P	W	D	L	F	A	Pts
Abbey National	14	8	4	2	39	74	20
Morgan Guaranty	14	6	6	2	42	29	17
Scandinavian Bank	14	6	5	3	41	18	16
Australia New Zealand Bank	14	7	1	6	25	26	15
Swiss Bank	14	5	4	5	33	37	14
Manufacturers Hanover Trust Res	14	5	2	7	27	33	12
National Westminster Bank "D"	14	4	3	7	28	38	11
Union Bank of Switzerland Res	14	2	1	11	24	53	5

Division Five 8 Teams – Won by UCB Bank

Challenge Cup – Midland Bank 3, National Westminster Bank 1
Senior Cup – Barclays Bank 3rd 2, National Westminster Bank 3rd 2 (Barclays won on penalties)
Senior Plate – MIM 2, C. Hoare & Co. 1
Minor Cup – Hong Kong Bank 0, National Westminster Bank 5th 1
Junior Cup – Abbey National 2, Morgan Guaranty 1
Junior Plate – Hill Samuel Bank 3, Chase Manhattan Res. 1
Sportsman's Cup – Credit Suisse 3, Abbey National 1
Veterans' Cup – Lloyds Bank 4, Royal Bank of Scotland 2

LONDON OLD BOYS' CUP

Senior
Old Aloysians v Old Ignatians   *0-1
Intermediate
Enfield Old Grammarians Res v Old Meadonians Res   0-2
Junior
Colposa 3rd v Old Aloysians 3rd   1-2
Minor
Old Greenfordians 4th v Old Meadonians 4th   0-5
Novets
Colposa 5th v Enfield Old Grammarians 5th   4-1
Drummond Cup
Old Parmiterians 6th v Enfield Old Grammarians 6th   *0-0, *2-2
(Trophy Shared)
Nemean Cup
Glyn Old Boys 7th. v Albanian 8th   1-3
Veterans
Old Meadonians Veterans v Old Sinjuns Veterans   3-0
* after extra time

THE OLD BOYS' FOOTBALL LEAGUE

Premier Division	P	W	D	L	F	A	Pts
Old Aloysians	20	11	8	1	34	11	30
Enfield Old Grammarians	20	13	3	4	38	27	29
Old Ignatians	20	13	1	6	50	16	27
Old Meadonians	20	10	3	7	40	23	23
Glyn Old Boys	20	9	2	9	32	34	20
Chertsey Old Salesians	20	9	1	10	37	38	19
Old Tenisonians	20	9	0	11	30	40	18
Cardinal Manning Old Boys	20	7	2	11	32	41	16
Old Danes	20	6	3	11	30	44	15
Old Isleworthians	20	4	5	11	30	43	13
Latymer Old Boys	20	3	4	13	19	55	10

Senior Division One	P	W	D	L	F	A	Pts
Old Tiffinians	20	12	6	2	72	22	30
Old Wilsonians	20	13	3	4	43	27	29
Phoenix Old Boys	20	12	4	4	46	23	28
Old Wokingians	20	9	4	7	38	31	22
Old Westhamians	20	8	6	6	34	30	22
Old Suttonians	20	10	2	8	38	36	22
Old Minchendenians	20	6	5	9	41	44	17
Mill Hill County Old Boys	20	7	3	10	31	42	17
Old Salvatorians	20	7	3	10	30	50	17
Old Edmontonians	20	5	3	12	36	64	13
Old Kingsburians	20	1	1	18	25	65	3

Senior Division Two	P	W	D	L	F	A	Pts
Old Tenisonians Res	22	16	2	4	49	20	34
Old Hamptonians	22	12	4	6	52	39	28
Old Tollingtonians	22	9	9	4	41	36	27
John Fisher Old Boys	22	10	6	6	41	47	26
Old Grammarians	22	10	4	8	47	37	24
Clapham Old Xaverians	22	10	3	9	45	45	23
Old Southallians	22	7	8	7	29	30	22
Old Greenfordians	22	8	4	10	47	44	20
Old Alpertonians	22	7	5	10	46	49	19
Old Ignatians Res	22	5	7	10	26	37	17
Old Josephians	22	6	4	12	31	42	16
Old Buckwellians	22	3	2	17	36	64	8

Senior Division Three	P	W	D	L	F	A	Pts
Old Grocers	20	15	2	3	60	19	32
Old Meadonians Res	20	11	5	4	44	34	27
Old Dorkinians	20	10	4	6	53	34	24
Old Manorians	20	10	3	7	50	42	23
Old Vaughanians	20	7	7	6	40	30	21
Enfield Old Grammarians Res	20	8	4	8	31	34	20
Leyton County Old Boys	20	8	3	9	44	46	19
Ravenscroft Old Boys	20	7	2	11	28	34	16
Old Alpertonians Res	20	6	4	10	32	51	16
Old Uffingtonians	20	5	2	13	26	61	12
Chace Old Boys	20	3	4	13	36	59	10

Intermediate Division North – 12 Teams – won by Old Highburians
Intermediate Division South – 12 Teams – won by Old Hamptonians Res
Division One North – 11 Teams – won by Old Camdenians Res
Division One South – 11 Teams – won by Old Thorntonians
Division One West – 11 Teams – won by Chorley Wood Dane Old Boys
Division Two North – 11 Teams – won by Old Edmontonians Res
Division Two South – 11 Teams – won by Old Wokingians 3rd
Division Two West – 12 Teams – won by Old Hamptonians 3rd
Division Three North – 11 Teams – won by Old Minchendenians 4th
Division Three South – 11 Teams – won by Glyn Old Boys 4th
Division Three West – 11 Teams – won by Cardinal Manning Old Boys 3rd
Division Four North – 11 Teams – won by Old Edmontonians 4th
Division Four South – 11 Teams – won by Old Tenisonians 4th
Division Four West – 11 Teams – won by Old Langleyans
Division Five North – 11 Teams – won by Old Minchendenians 6th
Division Five South – 11 Teams – won by Old Dorkinians 4th
Division Five West – 11 Teams – won by Mill Hill County Old Boys 4th
Division Six North – 12 Teams – won by Old Edmontonians 6th
Division Six South – 11 Teams – won by Clapham Old Xaverians 5th
Division Six West – 10 Teams – won by Old Salvatorians 7th
Division Seven North – 12 Teams – won by Old Edmontonians 7th
Division Seven South – 11 Teams – won by Old Sinjuns 5th
Division Seven West – 11 Teams – won by Cardinal Manning Old Boys 5th
Division Eight South – 10 Teams – won by Glyn Old Boys 7th
Division Eight West – 10 Teams – won by Old Salvatorians 9th

SOUTHERN AMATEUR LEAGUE

SENIOR SECTION

Division One	P	W	D	L	F	A	Pts
Old Actonians Association	20	15	2	3	40	13	32
Norsemen	20	10	7	3	34	19	27
Civil Service	20	9	3	8	42	38	21
West Wickham	20	6	9	5	24	20	21
Old Esthameians	20	6	9	5	19	17	21
National Westminster Bank	20	7	6	7	31	30	20
Midland Bank	20	5	8	7	34	36	18
Old Parkonians	20	4	9	7	19	31	17
Carshalton	20	5	7	8	25	38	17
Old Bromleians	20	5	4	11	23	34	14
Winchmore Hill	20	3	6	11	20	35	12

Division Two	P	W	D	L	F	A	Pts
Crouch End Vampires	22	16	6	0	54	20	38
South Bank Polytechnic	22	18	1	3	67	23	37
Lloyds Bank	22	8	7	7	44	38	23
Old Stationers	22	9	5	8	30	27	23
Alexandra Park	22	9	3	10	36	39	21
Polytechnic	22	7	6	9	44	43	20
Barclays Bank	22	8	4	10	39	46	20
Broomfield	22	7	5	10	36	39	19
Southgate Olympic	22	5	7	10	32	34	17
Old Salesians	22	6	4	12	31	52	16
Ibis	22	7	1	14	30	55	15
East Barnet Old Grammarians	22	7	1	14	33	60	15

Division Three	P	W	D	L	F	A	Pts
Lensbury	22	18	2	2	60	21	38
Kew Association	22	16	0	6	66	32	32
Royal Bank of Scotland	22	14	2	6	55	27	30
Old Latymerians	22	13	3	6	42	30	29
Merton	22	13	2	7	40	29	28
Brentham	22	9	3	10	39	34	21
Alleyn Old Boys	22	9	3	10	39	54	21
Old Westminster Citizens	22	8	4	10	42	49	20
Cuaco	22	6	4	12	49	64	16
Old Lyonians	22	5	3	14	35	55	13
Bank of England	22	3	5	14	25	46	11
Reigate Priory	22	1	3	18	16	67	5

RESERVE TEAM SECTION
First Division: – 12 Teams – won by Winchmore Hill Res
Second Division – 11 Teams – won by Old Actonians Association Res
Third Division – 12 Teams – won by Cuaco Res

THIRD TEAM SECTION
First Division – 12 Teams – won by Winchmore Hill 3rd
Second Division – 11 Teams – won by Lloyds Bank 3rd
Third Division – 12 Teams – won by Broomfield 3rd

FOURTH TEAM SECTION
First Division – 12 Teams – won by Winchmore Hill 4th
Second Division – 12 Teams – won by Norsemen 4th
Third Division – 11 Teams – won by Old Westminster Citizens 4th

FIFTH TEAM SECTION
First Division – 12 Teams – won by National Westminster Bank 5th
Second Division – 11 Teams – won by Old Latymerians 5th
Third Division – 8 Teams – won by Alexandra Park 5th

SIXTH TEAM SECTION
First Division – 11 Teams – won by Civil Service 6th
Second Division – 10 Teams – won by Norsemen 6th
Third Division – 9 Teams – won by East Barnet Old Grammarians 6th

SEVENTH TEAM SECTION
First Division – 10 Teams – won by Winchmore Hill 7th
Second Division – 9 Teams – won by Carshalton 7th

EIGHTH & NINTH TEAM SECTION
First Division – 12 Teams – won by Old Stationers 8th
Second Division – 11 Teams – won by Kew Association 9th

SOUTHERN OLYMPIAN LEAGUE

SENIOR SECTION

Division One	P	W	D	L	F	A	Pts
Old Owens	20	13	4	3	53	33	30
Witan	20	11	7	2	57	32	29
Nottsborough	20	10	4	6	53	38	24
Parkfield	20	7	9	4	39	32	23
Old Parmiterians	20	9	3	8	44	41	21
Old Finchleians	20	10	1	9	38	46	21
Old Bealonians	20	6	8	6	34	32	20
Mill Hill Village	20	8	3	9	43	42	19
Southgate County	20	5	4	11	27	42	14
St Mary's College	20	5	3	12	38	47	13
Colposa	20	2	2	16	35	76	6

Division Two	P	W	D	L	F	A	Pts
Old Grammarians	18	11	4	3	42	25	26
Old Fairlopians	18	9	5	4	35	26	23
Hadley	18	10	2	6	36	23	22
Hampstead Heathens	18	6	9	3	39	25	21
Albanian	18	7	4	7	35	34	18
Wandsworth Borough	18	5	5	8	30	32	15
Academicals	18	4	7	7	29	36	15
Pollygons	18	5	5	8	30	51	15
Old Monovians	18	4	5	9	24	36	13
Hale End Athletic	18	4	4	10	18	30	12

Division Three	P	W	D	L	F	A	Pts
Duncombe Sports	20	15	4	1	69	25	34
Ealing Association	20	13	2	5	52	31	28
Ulysses	20	12	3	5	53	24	27
Corinthian-Casuals "A"	20	11	5	4	45	23	27
Old Woodhouseians	20	9	6	5	45	32	24
Old Colfeians	20	9	4	7	31	26	22
Electrosport	20	7	3	10	35	67	17
Brent	20	3	6	11	27	40	12
BBC	20	4	3	13	28	43	11
Birkbeck College	20	5	1	14	24	56	11
Inland Revenue	20	2	3	15	17	59	7

Division Four	P	W	D	L	F	A	Pts
Westerns	20	17	2	1	79	27	36
Pegasus (Inner Temple)	20	13	4	3	81	30	30
London Welsh	20	11	5	4	58	22	27
Fulham Compton Old Boys*	20	11	4	5	50	38	25
London Airways	20	9	3	8	49	40	21
Mayfield Athletic	20	9	2	9	45	44	20
Centymca	20	8	2	10	50	60	18
Tansley	20	6	2	12	40	61	14
Distillers	20	4	3	13	23	66	11
Economicals	20	3	3	14	32	65	9
Bourneside	20	4	0	16	25	79	8

point deducted for breach of rule.

Intermediate Section
Division One – 10 Teams – won by Old Parmiterians Res
Division Two – 10 Teams – won by Nottsborough Res
Division Three – 10 Teams – won by Witan Res
Division Four – 9 Teams – won by Duncombe Sports Res

Junior Section
Division One – 10 Teams – won by Old Parmiterians 3rd
Division Two – 10 Teams – won by Parkfield 4th
Division Three – 10 Teams – won by Witan 3rd
Division Four – 10 Teams – won by Mill Hill Village 5th

Minor Section
Division "A" – 10 Teams – won by Old Owens 3rd
Division "B" – 10 Teams – won by Old Bealonians 5th
Division "C" – 10 Teams – won by Witan 4th
Division "D" – 9 Teams – won by Albanian 8th
Division "E" – 10 Teams – won by Witan 5th
Division "F" – 10 Teams – won by Old Finchleians 8th
Veterans Division – 8 Teams – won by Old Parmiterians Veterans

Senior Challenge Bowl – won by Old Parmiterians
Senior Challenge Shield – won by Nottsborough
Intermediate Challenge Cup – won by Academicals Res
Intermediate Challenge Shield – won by Witan Res
Junior Challenge Cup – won by Colposa 3rd

Junior Challenge Shield – won by Old Parmiterians 3rd
Mander Cup – won by Old Finchleians 4th
Mander Shield – won by Mill Hill Village 4th
Burntwood Trophy – won by Mill Hill Village 5th
Burntwood Shield – won by Old Parmiterians 5th
Thomas Parmiter Cup – won by Parkfield 6th
Thomas Parmiter Shield – won by Old Parmiterians 9th
Veterans' Challenge Cup – won by Colposa Veterans
Veterans' Challenge Shield – won by Tansley Veterans

MIDLAND AMATEUR ALLIANCE

Division One	P	W	D	L	F	A	Pts
Brunts Old Boys	22	17	4	1	71	20	38
Magdala Amateurs	22	16	4	2	113	37	36
Sherwood Amateurs	22	15	6	1	86	32	36
Old Elizabethans	22	16	4	2	71	27	36
Derbyshire Amateurs	22	10	5	7	52	47	25
Bassingfield	22	9	3	10	57	59	21
Lady Bay	22	8	2	12	64	70	18
Kirton BW	22	5	7	10	32	52	17
Tibshelf Old Boys	22	7	2	13	42	53	16
Nottinghamshire	22	4	3	15	22	63	11
FC Toton	22	2	4	16	31	96	8
Beeston OBA	22	0	2	20	18	103	2

Division Two	P	W	D	L	F	A	Pts
Old Elizabethans Res	22	18	3	1	75	13	39
Peoples College	22	16	5	1	67	21	37
Magdala Amateurs Res	22	12	4	6	60	30	28
Old Bemrosians	22	12	4	6	69	44	28
Nottingham Spartan	22	10	3	9	46	48	23
Brunts Old Boys Res	22	9	2	11	53	51	20
Chilwell	22	9	0	13	40	47	18
Lady Bay Res	29	9	2	11	43	61	20
Nottingham Univ Postgraduates	22	5	7	10	40	56	17
Nottinghamshire Res	22	5	4	13	28	66	14
Derbyshire Amateurs Res	22	5	2	15	41	82	12
Heanor Amateurs	22	3	2	17	28	71	8

Division Three	P	W	D	L	F	A	Pts
Sherwood Amateurs Res	18	12	2	4	82	25	26
Tibshelf Old Boys Res	18	11	3	4	43	26	25
Old Elizabethans 3rd	18	8	5	5	32	33	21
County Nalgo	18	9	2	7	29	29	20
Peoples College Res	18	8	4	6	36	36	20
Charnos	18	9	2	7	37	37	20
WB Casuals	18	8	2	8	36	36	18
Bassingfield Res	18	6	4	8	39	39	16
Old Bemrosians Res	18	4	2	12	30	30	10
Beeston OBA Res	18	2	0	16	23	23	2

Division Four	P	W	D	L	F	A	Pts
FC Caplan	20	15	3	2	82	28	33
Woodborough United	20	14	2	4	63	28	30
Derbyshire Amateurs 3rd	20	10	8	2	47	27	28
Monty Hind Old Boys	20	10	4	6	62	47	24
Old Elizabethans 4th	20	10	2	8	43	36	22
Magdala Amateurs 3rd	20	9	4	7	43	43	22
Nottinghamshire 3rd	20	6	5	9	53	63	17
Lady Bay 3rd	20	5	6	9	39	47	16
Old Bemrosians 3rd	20	4	5	11	41	65	13
Tibshelf Old Boys 3rd	20	3	5	12	32	65	11
Peoples College 3rd	20	1	2	17	31	87	4

Division Three – 10 Teams – won by Sherwood Amateurs Res
Division Four – 11 Teams – won by FC Caplan
Senior Cup – won by Sherwood Amateurs
Intermediate Cup – won by Sherwood Amateurs Res
Minor Cup – won by Magdala Amateurs 3rd
Challenge Trophy – won by Sherwood Amateurs
Division Two Challenge Cup – won by Old Elizabethans Res
Division Three Challenge Cup – won by Sherwood Amateurs Res
Division Four Challenge Cup – won by Woodborough United
Supplementary Cup "A" – won by County Nalgo
Supplementary Cup "B" – won by Woodborough United
H B Poole Trophy – won by Old Elizabethans

OLD BOYS' INVITATION CUP

Senior Cup
Old Tenisonians v Old Bromleians — 1-0

Junior Cup
Old Tenisonians Res v Old Latymerians Res — 3-1

Minor Cup
Old Wilsonians 3rd v Old Stationers 3rd — 3-1

4th XI's
Old Esthameians 4th v Old Finchleians 4th — 1-0

5th XI's
Old Stationers 5th v Old Finchleians 5th — 2-1

6th XI's
Old Salesians 6th v Old Wilsonians 6th — 2-1

7th & Lower XI's
Old Finchleians 8th v Old Finchleians 9th — 6-0

Veterans
Old Stationers Veterans v Old Wilsonians Veterans — 3-2

UNIVERSITY FOOTBALL 1991–92

UNIVERSITY OF LONDON INTER-COLLEGIATE LEAGUE 1991–92

Premier Division

	P	W	D	L	F	A	Pts
King's College	16	13	2	1	67	11	28
R. Holloway & Bedford New College	16	12	1	3	47	21	25
Imperial College	16	8	5	3	36	22	21
University College	16	9	3	4	37	31	21
Goldsmiths' College	16	8	2	6	39	23	18
London School of Economics	16	6	0	10	33	47	12
St George's Hospital Medical School	16	3	3	10	17	49	9
Queen Mary Westfield College	16	2	2	12	17	48	6
School of Pharmacy	16	2	0	14	13	54	4

Division One

	P	W	D	L	F	A	Pts
University College Res	18	11	4	3	53	32	26
UMDS	18	12	1	5	44	29	25
R. Holloway & Bedford New College Res	18	11	1	6	58	39	23
St Mary's Hospital Med. Sch.	18	9	4	5	66	41	22
Imperial College Res	18	8	5	5	51	38	21
King's College Res	18	8	3	7	30	26	19
King's College Hospital Med. School	18	6	3	9	42	46	15
Middx/Univ. Coll. Hosp. Med. Schools	18	6	2	10	25	60	14
Royal Free Hospital Sch. of Medicine	18	4	4	10	37	46	12
Queen Mary & Westfield College Res	18	1	1	16	12	61	3

Division Two

	P	W	D	L	F	A	Pts
Ch. Cross & W'min. Hosp. Med. School	18	12	4	2	64	20	28
St. Bartholomew's Hosp. Med. College	18	12	2	4	38	16	26
Imperial College 3rd	18	11	2	5	39	25	24
King's College 3rd	18	9	5	4	52	28	23
R. Sch. of Mines (I.C.)	18	8	2	8	31	33	18
University College 3rd	18	6	4	8	41	49	16
Goldsmith's College 2nd	18	7	1	10	45	34	15
R. London Hosp. Med. College	18	7	1	10	34	53	15
UMDS Res	18	4	0	14	20	62	8
London School of Economics Res	18	3	1	14	22	67	7

Division 3—9 Teams – won by Queen Mary Westfield College 3rd
Division 4—10 Teams – won by Imperial College 4th
Division 5—10 Teams – won by Ch. Cross & W'Min. Hosp. Med. School Res.
Division 6—8 Teams – won by Q. Mary Westfield College

UNIVERSITY MATCH
(4 April 1992, at Craven Cottage, Fulham)
Oxford 2, Cambridge 0

Oxford: S. Mackay; M. Ramsey, M. Sherrell, P. Donovan, P. Dowle, M. Kachingwe, J. Pratt, D. Anderson, J. Dunning, Kevin Knibbs, M. Mellor. *Subs:* D. Austin, G. Brook.
Cambridge: S. Taylor; A. Hunt, D. Pickup, R. Lewis, R. Pearson, D. Friedman, S. Oestmann, A. Davies, M. Deckers, N. Martin, I. Chapman. *Subs:* A. Thompson, M. Butterwick.

COMMERCIAL UNION/UAU 1991–92
First team championship

SOUTH WEST GROUP

Bath 1, Bristol 1
Bath 1, Cranfield 2
Bath 1, Exeter 1
Bath 0, Southampton 3
Bristol 1, Cranfield 0

Bristol 0, Exeter 1
Bristol 1, Southampton 1
Cranfield 1, Exeter 5
Cranfield 1, Southampton 2
Exeter 2, Southampton 1

	P	W	D	L	F	A	Pts
Exeter	4	3	1	0	9	3	7
Southampton	4	3	1	0	7	4	7
Bristol	4	1	2	1	3	3	4
Bath	4	0	2	2	3	7	2
Cranfield	4	1	0	3	4	9	2

SOUTH CENTRAL GROUP

Brunel 2, Imperial 1
Brunel 0, Kings 4
Brunel 2, Reading 0
Brunel 0, RHBNC 0
Imperial 3, Kings 2

Imperial 3, Reading 2
Imperial 2, RHBNC 2
Kings 3, Reading 4
Kings 4, RHBNC 0
Reading 4, RHBNC 1

	P	W	D	L	F	A	Pts
Imperial	4	2	1	1	9	8	5
Brunel	4	2	1	1	4	5	5
Kings	4	2	0	2	13	7	4
Reading	4	2	0	2	10	9	4
RHBNC	4	0	2	2	3	10	2

SOUTH EAST (NORTH) GROUP

Essex 0, East Anglia 1
Essex 4, QMWC 2
Essex 2, UCL 0

East Anglia 4, QMWC 1
East Anglia 4, UCL 0
QMWC 3, UCL 4

	P	W	D	L	F	A	Pts
East Anglia	3	3	0	0	9	1	6
Essex	3	2	0	1	6	3	4
UCL	3	1	0	2	4	9	2
QMWC	3	0	0	3	6	12	0

SOUTH EAST (SOUTH) GROUP

City 0, Kent 3
City 4, LSE 1
City 0, Surrey 4
City 1, Sussex 1
Kent 8, LSE 1

Kent 1, Surrey 3
Kent 1, Sussex 0
LSE 1, Surrey 7
LSE 2, Sussex 3
Surrey 2, Sussex 1

	P	W	D	L	F	A	Pts
Surrey	4	4	0	0	16	3	8
Kent	4	3	0	1	13	4	6
Sussex	4	1	1	2	5	3	3
City	4	1	1	2	5	8	3
LSE	4	0	0	4	5	22	0

WELSH GROUP

Aberystwyth 4, Lampeter 1
Aberystwyth 3, Swansea 1
Aberystwyth 1, UCNW (Bangor) 6
Aberystwyth 0, UWCC 1
Lampeter 1, Swansea 6
Lampeter 0, UCNW (Bangor) 6
Lampeter 0, UWCC 5
Swansea 1, UCNW (Bangor) 0
Swansea 3, UWCC 1
UCNW (Bangor) 2, UWCC 1

	P	W	D	L	F	A	Pts
UCNW (Bangor)	4	3	0	1	14	3	6
Swansea	4	3	0	1	11	5	6
UWCC	4	2	0	2	8	5	4
Aberystwyth	4	2	0	2	8	8	4
Lampeter	4	0	0	4	2	21	0

MIDLANDS GROUP

Aston 3, Birmingham 6
Aston 0, Leicester 2
Aston 0, Loughborough 3
Aston 0, Nottingham 2
Aston 2, Warwick 1
Birmingham 2, Leicester 1
Birmingham 0, Loughborough 1
Birmingham 1, Nottingham 1
Birmingham 3, Warwick 2
Leicester 0, Loughborough 5
Leicester 3, Nottingham 1
Leicester 0, Warwick 2
Loughborough 2, Nottingham 1
Loughborough 2, Warwick 0
Nottingham 1, Warwick 1

	P	W	D	L	F	A	Pts
Loughborough	5	5	0	0	13	1	10
Birmingham	5	4	0	1	13	8	8
Leicester	5	2	0	3	6	10	4
Nottingham	5	1	1	3	6	8	3
Warwick	5	1	1	3	6	8	3
Aston	5	1	0	4	5	14	2

NORTH EAST GROUP

Durham 0, Hull 3
Durham 2, Leeds 1
Durham 3, Newcastle 0
Durham 4, Sheffield 2
Durham 4, York 0
Hull 1, Leeds 3
Hull 0, Newcastle 2
Hull 4, Sheffield 1
Hull 2, York 2
Leeds 1, Newcastle 0
Leeds 1, Sheffield 4
Leeds 4, York 2
Newcastle 2, Sheffield 3
Newcastle 4, York 0
Sheffield 4, York 2

	P	W	D	L	F	A	Pts
Durham	5	4	0	1	13	6	8
Sheffield	5	3	0	2	14	13	6
Leeds	5	3	0	2	10	9	6
Hull	5	2	1	2	10	8	5
Newcastle	5	2	0	3	8	7	4
York	5	0	1	4	6	18	1

NORTH WEST GROUP

Bradford 0, Keele 1
Bradford 1, Lancaster 6
Bradford 0, Liverpool 2
Bradford 1, Manchester 2
Bradford 2, Salford 3
Bradford 3, UMIST 4
Keele 1, Lancaster 0
Keele 1, Liverpool 2
Keele 0, Manchester 4
Keele 4, Salford 2
Keele 2, UMIST 1
Lancaster 0, Liverpool 8
Lancaster 1, Manchester 6
Lancaster 1, Salford 4
Lancaster 3, UMIST 1
Liverpool 3, Manchester 1

Liverpool 3, Salford 2
Liverpool 0, UMIST 1
Manchester 3, Salford 1
Manchester 2, UMIST 2
Salford 1, UMIST 2

	P	W	D	L	F	A	Pts
Liverpool	6	5	0	1	18	5	10
Manchester	6	4	1	1	18	8	9
Keele	6	4	0	2	9	9	8
UMIST	6	3	1	2	11	11	7
Salford	6	2	0	4	13	15	4
Lancaster	6	2	0	4	11	21	4
Bradford	6	0	0	6	7	18	0

Play-off Round
Loughborough 4, City 1
Sheffield 0, Leicester 3
Liverpool 3, Hull 0
Swansea 3, Sussex 4
Exeter 3, Aberystwyth 2
Brunel 3, UWCC 6
Durham 3, UMIST 0
Essex 2, Kings 1
UCNW 0, Bath 1
Kent 1, Bristol 1
Kent won on penalties
Surrey 3, QMWC 1
Southampton 2, UCL 0
Imperial 0, Nottingham 3
Birmingham 0, Keele 1
East Anglia 3, Reading 1
Manchester 1, Leeds 0

Challenge Round
Loughborough 5, Leicester 1
Liverpool 4, Sussex 1
Durham 2, Essex 1
Exeter 3, UWCC 2
Bath 1, Kent 0
Sussex 0, Southampton 2
Nottingham 1, Keele 0
East Anglia 3, Manchester 2

Quarter-finals
Bath 0, Southampton 3
Durham 2, Liverpool 1
Nottingham 3, East Anglia 0
Loughborough 3, Exeter 0

Semi-finals
Southampton 1, Nottingham 2
Durham 3, Loughborough 9 *(aet)*

Final (played at Walsall FC)
Nottingham 1, Loughborough 3

REPRESENTATIVE MATCHES

UAU drew with Luton Town XI 0-0
UAU drew with Tottenham Hotspur XI 1-1
UAU lost to English Schools XI 1-2
UAU lost to Chelsea XI 1-4
UAU beat BCSA 5-1
UAU drew with BPSA 1-1

BUSF TOURNAMENT (IN ULSTER)

Pool A
Scotland 4, NIB 1
Scotland 0, UAU I 2
NIB 0, UAU I 2

Pool B
UAU II 1, NIA 2
UAU II 4, Wales 0
NIA 1, Wales 0

Cross Overs
UAU I 3, Wales 2
NIB 0, NIA 4
Scotland 3, UAU II 0

Play-offs
5/6th NIB 4, Wales 1
3/4th Scotland 2, UAU II 1

Final
UAU I 4, NIA 2

ADDRESSES

The Football Association: R. H. G. Kelly F.C.I.S., 16 Lancaster Gate, London W2 31W

Scotland: J. Farry, 6 Park Gardens, Glasgow G3 7YE. 041-332 6372
Northern Ireland (Irish FA): D. I. Bowen, 20 Windsor Avenue, Belfast BT9 6EG. 0232-669458
Wales: A. Evans, 3 Westgate Street, Cardiff, South Glamorgan CF1 1JF. 0222-372325
Republic of Ireland (FA of Ireland): S. Connolly, 80 Merrion Square South, Dublin 2. 0001-766864

International Federation (FIFA): S. Blatter, FIFA House, Hitzigweg 11, CH-8032 Zurich, Switzerland. 1-384-9595. Fax: 1-384-9696
Union of European Football Associations (UEFA): G. Aigner, PO Box 16, CH-3000 Berne 15, Switzerland. 31-941 41 21. Fax: 31-941 18 38

THE LEAGUES

The Football League: J. D. Dent, F.C.I.S., The Football League, Lytham St Annes, Lancs FY8 1JG. 0253-729421. Telex 67675
The Scottish League: P. Donald, 188 West Regent Street, Glasgow G2 4RY. 041-248 384415
The Irish League: M. Brown, 87 University Street, Belfast BT71 HP. 0232-242888
Football League of Ireland: E. Morris, 80 Merrion Square South, Dublin 2. 0001-765120
GM Vauxhall Conference: P. D. Hunter, 24 Barnehurst Road, Bexleyheath, Kent DA7 6EZ. 0322-521116
Central League: D. J. Grimshaw, 118 St Stephens Road, Deepdale, Preston, Lancs PR1 6TD. 0772-795386
North West Counties League: N. A. Rowles, 845 Liverpool Road, Peel Green, Eccles, Manchester M30 71J. 061-962 4623
Eastern Counties League: C. Lamb, 3 Land Close, Clacton-on-Sea, Essex CO16 8UJ.
Football Combination: N. Chamberlain, 2 Vicarage Close, Old Costessey, Norwich NR8 5DL. 0603-743998
Hellenic League: T. Cuss, 7 Blenheim Road, Kidlington, Oxford OX5 2HP. 08675-5920
Kent League: R. Vintner, The Smithy, The Square, Chilham, Canterbury, Kent CT4 8BY
Lancashire Amateur League: R. G. Bowker, 13 Shores Green Drive, Wincham, Northwich, Cheshire CW9 6EE. 061-480 7723
Lancashire Football League: J. W. Howarth, 465 Whalley Road, Clapton-le-Moors, Accrington, Lancs BB5 5RP. 0254-398957
Leicestershire Senior League: P. Henwood, 450 London Road, Leicester LE2 2PP. Leicester 704121
London Spartan: D. Cordell, 44 Greenleas, Waltham Abbey, Essex. Lea Valley 712428
Manchester League: F. J. Fitzpatrick, 102 Victoria Road, Stretford, Manchester. 061-865 2726
Midland Combination: L. W. James, 175 Barnet Lane, Kingswinford, Brierley Hill, West Midlands. Kingswinford 3459
Mid-Week Football League: N. A. S. Matthews, Cedar Court, Steeple Aston, Oxford. 0869-40347

Northern Premier: R. D. Bayley, 22 Woburn Drive, Hale, Altrincham, Cheshire. 061-980 7007
Northern Intermediate League: G. Thompson, Clegg House, 253 Pitsmoor Road, Sheffield S3 9AQ. 0742-27817
Northern League: T. Golightly, 85 Park Road North, Chester-le-Street, Co. Durham DH3 3SA. 091-388 2056
North Midlands League: G. Thompson, 7 Wren Park Close, Ridgway, Sheffield.
Peterborough and District League: M. J. Croson, 44 Storrington Way, Werrington, Peterborough, Cambs PE4 6QP.
Vauxhall League: N. Robinson, 226 Rye Lane, Peckham SE15 4NL. 081-653 3903
Southern Amateur League: S. J. Lucas, 23 Beaufort Close, North Weald Bassett, Epping, Essex CM16 6JZ. 037882-3932
South-East Counties League: R. A. Bailey, 10 Highlands Road, New Barnet, Herts EN5 5AB. 081-449 5131
Southern League: D. J. Strudwick, 11 Welland Close, Durrington, Worthing, West Sussex BN13 3NR. 0903-267788
South Midlands League: M. Mitchell, 26 Leighton Court, Dunstable, Beds LU6 1EW. 0582-61376
South Western League: R. Lowe, Panorama, Lamerton, Tavistock, Devon PL19 8SD. 0822-61376
United Counties League: R. Gamble, 8 Bostock Avenue, Northampton. 0604-37766
Wearside League: B. Robson, 12 Deneside, Howden-le-Wear, Crook, Co. Durham DL15 8JR. 0388-762034
Western League: M. E. Washer, 126 Chessel Street, Bristol BS3 3DQ. 0272-638308
The Welsh League: K. J. Tucker, 16 The Parade, Merthyr Tydfil, Mid Glamorgan CF47 0ET. 0685-723884
West Midlands Regional League: K. H. Goodfellow, 11 Emsworth Grove, Kings Heath, Birmingham B14 6HY. 021-444 3056
West Yorkshire League: W. Keyworth, 2 Hill Court Grove, Bramley, Yorks L13 2AP. Pudsey 74465
Northern Counties (East): B. Wood, 6 Restmore Avenue, Guiseley, Nr Leeds LS20 9DG. 0943-874558 (home); Bradford 29595 (9 a.m. to 5 p.m.)

COUNTY FOOTBALL ASSOCIATIONS

Bedfordshire: R. G. Berridge, The Limes, 14 Bedford Road, Sandy, Beds SG19 1EL. 0767-680417
Berks and Bucks: W. S. Gosling, 15a London Street, Faringdon, Oxon SN7 8AG. 0367-242099
Birmingham County: M. Pennick, County FA Offices, Rayhall Lane, Great Barr, Birmingham B43 6JE. 021-357 4278
Cambridgeshire: R. E. Rogers, 20 Aingers Road, Histon, Cambridge CB4 4JP. 022023-2803
Cheshire: A. Collins, 50 Ash Grove, Timperley, Altrincham WA15 6JX. 061-980 4706
Cornwall: J. M. Ryder, Penare, 16 Gloweth View, Truro, Cornwall TR1 3JZ.
Cumberland: R. Johnson, 72 Victoria Road, Workington, Cumbria CA14 2QT. 0900-3979
Derbyshire: K. Compton, The Grandstand, Moorways Stadium, Moor Lane, Derby DE2 8FB. 0332-361422
Devon County: C. Squirrel, 51a Wolborough Street, Newton Abbot, Devon TQ12 1JQ. 0626 332077

Dorset County: P. Hough, 9 Parkstone Road, Poole, Dorset BH15 2NN. 0202-746244
Durham: J. R. Walsh, 'Codeslaw', Ferens Park, Durham DH1 1JZ. 0385-48653
East Riding County: D. R. Johnson, 52 Bethune Ave, Hull HU4 7EJ. 0482-641458
Essex County: T. Alexander, 31 Mildmay Road, Chelmsford, Essex CM2 0DN. 0245-357727
Gloucestershire: E. J. Marsh, 46 Douglas Road, Horfield, Bristol BS7 0JD. 0272-519435
Guernsey: M. J. Le Provost, Le Coin, Pleinmont Road, Torteval, Guernsey CI. 0481-65928
Hampshire: R. G. Barnes, 8 Ashwood Gardens, off Winchester Road, Southampton SO9 2UA. 0703-766884
Herefordshire: E. R. Prescott, 7 Kirkland Close, Hampton Park, Hereford HR1 1XP. 0432-51134
Hertfordshire: R. G. Kibble, 4 The Wayside, Leverstock Green, Hemel Hempstead, Herts HP3 8NR. 0442-255918

Huntingdonshire: M. M.Armstrong, 1 Chapel End, Great Giddings, Huntingdon. Cambs PE17 5NP. *08323-262*

Isle of Man: Mrs A. Garrett, 120 Bucks Road, Douglas, IOM. *0624-676349*

Jersey: C. Tostevin, Wellesley, Greve Dazette St Clement, Jersey JE2 6SA. *0534-24929*

Kent County: K. T. Masters, 69 Maidstone Road, Chatham, Kent ME4 6DT. *0634-43824*

Lancashire: J. Kenyon, 31a Wellington St, St John's, Blackburn, Lancs BB1 8AU. *0254-264333/4*

Leicestershire and Rutland: R. E. Barston, Holmes Park, Dog and Gun Lane, Whetstone, Leicester LE8 3LJ. *0533-867828*

Lincolnshire: F. S. Richardson, PO Box 26, 12 Dean Road, Lincoln LN2 4DP. *0522-24917*

Liverpool County: F. L. J. Hunter, 23 Greenfield Road, Old Swann, Liverpool L13 3EN. *051-526 9515*

London: R. S. Ashford, 4 Aldworth Grove, London SE13 6HY. *081-690 9626*

Manchester County: F. Brocklehurst, Sports Complex, Brantingham Road, Chorlton, Manchester M21 1TG. *061-881 0299*

Middlesex County: P. J. Clayton, 30 Rowland Avenue, Kenton, Harrow, Middx HA3 9AF. *081-200 8300*

Norfolk County: R. Kiddell, 39 Beaumont Road, Costessey, Norwich NR5 0HG. *0603-742421*

Northamptonshire: B. Walden, 37 Harding Terrace, Northampton NN1 2PF. *0604-39584*

North Riding County: P. Kirby, 284 Linthorpe Road, Middlesbrough TS1 3QU. *0642-224585*

Northumberland: R. E. Maughan, 3 Osborne Terrace, Jesmond, Newcastle upon Tyne NE2 1NE. *091-297 0101*

Nottinghamshire: W. T. Annable, 7 Clarendon Street, Nottingham NG1 5HS. *0602-418954*

Oxfordshire: P. J. Ladbrook, 3 Wilkins Road, Cowley, Oxford OX4 2HY. *0865-775432*

Sheffield and Hallamshire: G. Thompson, Clegg House, 5 Onslow Road, Sheffield S11 7AF. *0742-670068*

Shropshire: A. W. Brett, 5 Ebnal Road, Shrewsbury SY2 6PW. *0743-56066*

Somerset & Avon (South): Mrs H. Marchment, 30 North Road, Midsomer Norton, Bath BA3 2QQ. *0761-410280*

Staffordshire: G. S. Brookes, 2 Miller Street, Newcastle, Staffs ST5 1HB. *0782-622585*

Suffolk County: W. M. Steward, 2 Millfields, Haughley, Suffolk IP14 3PU. *0449-673481*

Surrey County: L. F. J. Smith, 2 Fairfield Avenue, Horley, Surrey RH6 7PD. *0293-784945*

Sussex County: D. M. Worsfold, County Office, Culver Road, Lancing, Sussex BN15 9AX. *0903-753547*

Westmorland: J. B. Fleming, 101 Burneside Road, Kendal, Cumbria LA9 4RZ. *0539-722915*

West Riding County: R. Carter, Unit 3, Low Mills Road, Wortley, Leeds LS12 4UY. *0532-310101*

Wiltshire: E. M. Parry, 44 Kennet Avenue, Swindon SN2 3LG. *0793-29036*

Worcestershire: P. Rushton, 84 Windermere Drive, Warndon, Worcester WR4 9IB. *0905-51166*

OTHER USEFUL ADDRESSES

Amateur Football Alliance: W. P. Goss, 55 Islington Park Street, London N1 1QB. *071-359 3493*

English Schools FA: M. R. Berry, 4a Eastgate Street, Stafford ST16 2NN. *0785-51142*

Oxford University: S. Morley, The Queen's College, Oxford OX1 4AW.

Cambridge University: Dr A. J. Little, St Catherine's College, Cambridge CB2 1RL.

Army: Major T. C. Knight, Clayton Barracks, Aldershot, Hants GU11 2BG. *0252-24431 Ext 3571*

Royal Air Force: Group Capt P. W. Hilton, Ministry of Defence (Block 10), St Georges Road, Harrogate, N. Yorks HG2 9DB. *0423-793295*

Royal Navy: Lt-Cdr J. Danks, R.N. Sports Office, H.M.S. Temeraire, Portsmouth, Hants PO1 4QS. *0705-822351 Ext 22671*

Universities Athletic Union: G. Gregory-Jones, Suite 36, London Fruit Exchange, Brushfield Street, London E1 6EU. *071-247 3066*

Central Council of Physical Recreation: General Secretary, 70 Brompton Road, London SW3 1HE. *071-584 6651*

British Olympic Association: 6 John Prince's Street, London W1M 0DH. *071-408 2029*

National Federation of Football Supporters' Clubs: Lottery Office: 1 Saville Row, Bath, Avon BA1 2QP. *0224-312247.* Registered Office: 24 South Street, Loughborough, Leics LE11 3EG. *0509-267643*

National Playing Fields Association: Col R. Satterthwaite O.B.E., 578b Catherine Place, London, SW1.

The Scottish Football Commercial Managers Association: J. E. Hillier (Chairman), c/o Keith FC Promotions Office, 60 Union Street, Keith, Banffshire, Scotland.

Professional Footballers' Association: G. Taylor, 2 Oxford Court, Bishopsgate, Off Lower Mosley Street, Manchester M2 3W2. *061-236 0575*

Referees' Association: W. J. Taylor, Cross Offices, Summerhill, Kingswinford, West Midlands DY6 9JE. *0384-288386*

Women's Football Association: Miss L. Whitehead, 448/450 Hanging Ditch, The Corn Exchange, Manchester M4 3ES. *061-832 5911*

The Association of Football League Commercial Managers: G. H. Dimbleby, Secretary WBA FC, The Hawthorns, Halford Lane, West Bromwich B71 4LF.

The Association of Football Statisticians: R. J. Spiller, 22 Bretons, Basildon, Essex SS15 5BY. *0268-416020*

The Football Programme Directory: David Stacey, The Beeches, 66 Southend Road, Wickford, Essex SS11 8EN.

England Football Supporters Association: Publicity Officer, David Stacey, 66 Southend Road, Wickford, Essex SS11 8EN.

The Football League Executive Staffs Association: PO Box 52, Leamington Spa, Warwickshire.

The Ninety-Two Club: 104 Gilda Crescent, Whitchurch, Bristol BS14 9LD.

The Football Trust: Second Floor, Walkden House, 10 Melton Street, London NW1 2EJ. *071-388 4504*

The Football Supporters Association: PO Box 11, Liverpool L26 1XP. *051-709 2594.*

Association of Provincial Football Supporters' Clubs in London: Miss Sallyann Watson, Secretary APFSCIL. 6 Bradshaws Close, Kings Road, London SE25 4ES. *081-676 8390 (home)*

OTHER AWARDS 1991–92

FOOTBALLER OF THE YEAR

The Football Writers' Association Award for the Footballer of the Year went to Gary Lineker of Tottenham Hotspur and England.

Past Winners
1947–48 Stanley Matthews (Blackpool), 1948–49 Johnny Carey (Manchester U), 1949–50 Joe Mercer (Arsenal), 1950–51 Harry Johnston (Blackpool), 1951–52 Billy Wright (Wolverhampton W), 1952–53 Nat Lofthouse (Bolton W), 1953–54 Tom Finney (Preston NE), 1954–55 Don Revie (Manchester C), 1955–56 Bert Trautmann (Manchester C), 1956–57 Tom Finney (Preston NE), 1957–58 Danny Blanchflower (Tottenham H), 1958–59 Syd Owen (Luton T), 1959–60 Bill Slater (Wolverhampton W), 1960–61 Danny Blanchflower (Tottenham H), 1961–62 Jimmy Adamson (Burnley), 1962–63 Stanley Matthews (Stoke C), 1963–64 Bobby Moore (West Ham U), 1964–65 Bobby Collins (Leeds U), 1965–66 Bobby Charlton (Manchester U), 1966–67 Jackie Charlton (Leeds U), 1967–68 George Best (Manchester U), 1968–69 Dave Mackay (Derby Co) shared with Tony Book (Manchester C), 1969–70 Billy Bremner (Leeds U), 1970–71 Frank McLintock (Arsenal), 1971–72 Gordon Banks (Stoke C), 1972–73 Pat Jennings (Tottenham H), 1973–74 Ian Callaghan (Liverpool), 1974–75 Alan Mullery (Fulham), 1975–76 Kevin Keegan (Liverpool), 1976–77 Emlyn Hughes (Liverpool), 1977–78 Kenny Burns (Nottingham F), 1978–79 Kenny Dalglish (Liverpool), 1979–80 Terry McDermott (Liverpool), 1980–81 Frans Thijssen (Ipswich T), 1981–82 Steve Perryman (Tottenham H), 1982–83 Kenny Dalglish (Liverpool), 1983–84 Ian Rush (Liverpool), 1984–85 Neville Southall (Everton), 1985–86 Gary Lineker (Everton), 1986–87 Clive Allen (Tottenham H), 1987–88 John Barnes (Liverpool), 1988–89 Steve Nicol (Liverpool), 1989–90 John Barnes (Liverpool), 1990–91 Gordon Strachan (Leeds).

THE PFA AWARDS 1992

Player of the Year: Gary Pallister (Manchester U).
Previous Winners: 1974 Norman Hunter (Leeds U); 1975 Colin Todd (Derby Co); 1976 Pat Jennings (Tottenham H); 1977 Andy Gray (Aston Villa); 1978 Peter Shilton (Nottingham F); 1979 Liam Brady (Arsenal); 1980 Terry McDermott (Liverpool); 1981 John Wark (Ipswich T); 1982 Kevin Keegan (Southampton); 1983 Kenny Dalglish (Liverpool); 1984 Ian Rush (Liverpool); 1985 Peter Reid (Everton); 1986 Gary Lineker (Everton); 1987 Clive Allen (Tottenham H); 1988 John Barnes (Liverpool); 1989 Mark Hughes (Manchester U); 1990 David Platt (Aston Villa); 1991 Mark Hughes (Manchester U).
Young Player of the Year: Ryan Giggs (Manchester U).
Previous Winners: 1974 Kevin Beattie (Ipswich T); 1975 Mervyn Day (West Ham U); 1976 Peter Barnes (Manchester C); 1977 Andy Gray (Aston Villa); 1978 Tony Woodcock (Nottingham F); 1979 Cyrille Regis (WBA); 1980 Glenn Hoddle (Tottenham H); 1981 Gary Shaw (Aston Villa); 1982 Steve Moran (Southampton); 1983 Ian Rush (Liverpool); 1984 Paul Walsh (Luton T); 1985 Mark Hughes (Manchester U); 1986 Tony Cottee (West Ham U); 1987 Tony Adams (Arsenal); 1988 Paul Gascoigne (Tottenham H); 1989 Paul Merson (Arsenal); 1990 Matthew Le Tissier (Southampton); 1991 Lee Sharpe (Manchester U).
Merit Award: Brian Clough.
Previous Winners: 1974 Bobby Charlton CBE, Cliff Lloyd OBE; 1975 Dennis Law; 1976 George Eastham OBE; 1977 Jack Taylor OBE; 1978 Bill Shankly OBE; 1979 Tom Finney OBE; 1980 Sir Matt Busby CBE; 1981 John Trollope MBE; 1982 Joe Mercer OBE; 1983 Bob Paisley OBE; 1984 Bill Nicholson; 1985 Ron Greenwood; 1986 The 1966 England World Cup team, Sir Alf Ramsey, Harold Shepherdson; 1987 Sir Stanley Matthews; 1988 Billy Bonds MBE; 1989 Nat Lofthouse; 1990 Peter Shilton; 1991 Tommy Hutchison.

HOWARD WILKINSON WINS PERSONAL ACCOLADE FOR LEEDS UNITED TITLE TRIUMPH: HE IS NAMED BARCLAYS BANK MANAGER OF THE YEAR 1992

Howard Wilkinson's achievement in taking Leeds United from the nether regions of the Second Division to the Barclays League title in three and a half years won him the Barclays

Bank Manager of the Year award for 1992. He was named for this prestigious accolade –
the Barclays Trophy and a Barclays Higher Rate Deposit Account cheque for £5,000 – by
a panel of 30 leading football journalists and commentators. The presentation was made
by Mr Alastair Robinson, executive director of Barclays Bank.

It was Wilkinson's 9th managerial award: – his 6th at Leeds United from October 1989
with a Division Two monthly award, followed by 2nd Division Manager of the Season
1990, and overall Manager of the month prizes for November 1990 and October &
November 1991: the first three were at Sheffield Wednesday – Division 2 monthly awards
for September and November 1983 and November 1988.

BARCLAYS BANK DIVISIONAL MANAGERS OF THE SEASON 1991–92

Barclays Bank Divisional Managers of the Season – named in conjunction with The
Football League were: Division Two – John Lyall, Ipswich Town; Division Three – Phil
Holder, Brentford; Division Four – Jimmy Mullen, Burnley.

Each received a Barclays Eagle trophy and a cheque for £1,000.

LEAGUE MANAGERS ACHIEVEMENT AWARD

Barclays Bank announced in May that it had become the official sponsor of the recently-
formed League Managers Association in a three year sponsorship deal. To mark the
arrangement, the Barclays Bank Achievement Award – to be decided by the votes of
members of the LMA – has been introduced to the Barclays Bank Managers Awards
portfolio.

"The award is designed to highlight the efforts of the manager who, in the opinion of
his peers has worked wonders with the resources available to him" explained LMA chief
executive John Camkin.

"It could go to a manager whose team has won a League or Cup trophy. On the other
hand, it may go to someone who has performed a near-miracle to keep his club in its
present division . . or even kept the club afloat by recruitment of youngsters and shrewd
financial dealings.

"For too long these outstanding achievements have gone unrecognised by the game
itself – and the general public. This is an opportunity for managers to honour a colleague
whose work they respect and admire."

The first Barclays Bank Achievement award winner voted by the LMA is Dave Bassett
of Sheffield United, whose second-half of the season run – following a disastrous first half –
kept his club on course for next season's Premier League. He received a cheque for £1,000
and a Barclays Eagle trophy.

BARCLAYS YOUNG EAGLE OF THE YEAR

Roy Keane of Nottingham Forest and the Republic of Ireland – the 20 year-old £25,000
'snip' from Cobh Ramblers in the Opel League of Ireland – was named the Barclays Young
Eagle of the Year by England team manager Graham Taylor, chairman of the voting panel
which includes Jack Charlton, Jimmy Armfield, Trevor Cherry, Stan Cullis, Bill Nicholson,
Bill Dodgin and Terry Yorath. Roy received a Silver Eagle trophy, a replica and a Barclays
Higher Rate Deposit Account cheque for £5,000.

THE SCOTTISH PFA AWARDS 1992

Player of the Year: Premier Division: Ally McCoist (Rangers); First Division: Gordon
Dalziel (Raith R); Second Division: Andy Thomson (Queen of South).
Previous Winners: 1978 Derek Johnstone (Rangers); 1979 Paul Hegarty (Dundee U);
1980 Davie Provan (Celtic); 1981 Sandy Clark (Airdrieonians); 1982 Mark McGhee
(Aberdeen); 1983 Charlie Nicholas (Celtic); 1984 Willie Miller (Aberdeen); 1985 Jim
Duffy (Morton); 1986 Richard Gough (Dundee U); 1987 Brian McClair (Celtic); 1988
Paul McStay (Celtic); 1989 Theo Snelders (Aberdeen); 1990 Jim Bett (Aberdeen);
1991 Paul Elliott (Celtic).
Young Player of the Year: Phil O'Donnell (Motherwell).
Previous Winners: 1978 Graeme Payne (Dundee U); 1979 Graham Stewart (Dundee U);
1980 John MacDonald (Rangers); 1981 Francis McAvennie (St Mirren); 1982 Charlie
Nicholas (Celtic); 1983 Pat Nevin (Clyde); 1984 John Robertson (Hearts); 1985 Craig
Levein (Hearts); 1986 Craig Levein (Hearts); 1987 Robert Fleck (Rangers); 1988
John Collins (Hibernian); 1989 Bill McKinlay (Dundee U); 1990 Scott Crabbe
(Hearts); 1991 Eoin Jess (Aberdeen).

SCOTTISH FOOTBALL WRITERS' ASSOCIATION
Player of the Year 1992 – Ally McCoist (Rangers)

1965 **Billy McNeill** (Celtic)	1979 **Andy Ritchie** (Morton)
1966 **John Greig** (Rangers)	1980 **Gordon Strachan** (Aberdeen)
1967 **Ronnie Simpson** (Celtic)	1981 **Alan Rough** (Partick Th)
1968 **Gordon Wallace** (Raith R)	1982 **Paul Sturrock** (Dundee U)
1969 **Bobby Murdoch** (Celtic)	1983 **Charlie Nicholas** (Celtic)
1970 **Pat Stanton** (Hibernian)	1984 **Willie Miller** (Aberdeen)
1971 **Martin Buchan** (Aberdeen)	1985 **Hamish McAlpine** (Dundee U)
1972 **Dave Smith** (Rangers)	1986 **Sandy Jardine** (Hearts)
1973 **George Connelly** (Celtic)	1987 **Brian McClair** (Celtic)
1974 **Scotland's World Cup Squad**	1988 **Paul McStay** (Celtic)
1975 **Sandy Jardine** (Rangers)	1989 **Richard Gough** (Rangers)
1976 **John Greig** (Rangers)	1990 **Alex McLeish** (Aberdeen)
1977 **Danny McGrain** (Celtic)	1991 **Maurice Malpas** (Dundee U)
1978 **Derek Johnstone** (Rangers)	

EUROPEAN FOOTBALLER OF THE YEAR 1991

French players have never figured very prominently in the annual *France Football* award for the European Footballer of the Year. This year Jean-Pierre Papin of Marseille became the third of his countrymen to achieve the honour following Raymond Kopa in 1958 and Michel Platini three times in succession from 1983–85.

Past winners

1956 **Stanley Matthews** (Blackpool)	1975 **Oleg Blokhin** (Dynamo Kiev)
1957 **Alfredo Di Stefano** (Real Madrid)	1976 **Franz Beckenbauer** (Bayern Munich)
1958 **Raymond Kopa** (Real Madrid)	1977 **Allan Simonsen** (Borussia Moenchengladbach)
1959 **Alfredo Di Stefano** (Real Madrid)	
1960 **Luis Suarez** (Barcelona)	1978 **Kevin Keegan** (SV Hamburg)
1961 **Omar Sivori** (Juventus)	1979 **Kevin Keegan** (SV Hamburg)
1962 **Josef Masopust** (Dukla Prague)	1980 **Karl-Heinz Rummenigge** (Bayern Munich)
1963 **Lev Yashin** (Moscow Dynamo)	
1964 **Denis Law** (Manchester United)	1981 **Karl-Heinz Rummenigge** (Bayern Munich)
1965 **Eusebio** (Benfica)	
1966 **Bobby Charlton** (Manchester United)	1982 **Paolo Rossi** (Juventus)
	1983 **Michel Platini** (Juventus)
1967 **Florian Albert** (Ferencvaros)	1984 **Michel Platini** (Juventus)
1968 **George Best** (Manchester United)	1985 **Michel Platini** (Juventus)
1969 **Gianni Rivera** (AC Milan)	1986 **Igor Belanov** (Dynamo Kiev)
1970 **Gerd Muller** (Bayern Munich)	1987 **Ruud Gullit** (AC Milan)
1971 **Johan Cruyff** (Ajax)	1988 **Marco Van Basten** (AC Milan)
1972 **Franz Beckenbauer** (Bayern Munich)	1989 **Marco Van Basten** (AC Milan)
	1990 **Lothar Matthaus** (Inter-Milan)
1973 **Johan Cruyff** (Barcelona)	
1974 **Johan Cruyff** (Barcelona)	

BARCLAYS BANK MANAGER AWARDS 1991–92
AUGUST
Division 1 – **Alex Ferguson** (Manchester United); *Division 2* – **John Beck** (Cambridge United); *Division 3* – **Terry Cooper** (Birmingham City); *Division 4* – **Billy Ayre** (Blackpool).
SEPTEMBER
Division 1 – **Alex Ferguson** (Manchester United); *Division 2* – **Lennie Lawrence** (Middlesbrough); *Division 3* – **Bobby Gould** (West Bromwich Albion); *Division 4* – **Barry Fry** (Barnet).
OCTOBER
Division 1 – **Howard Wilkinson** (Leeds United); *Division 2* – **Alan Curbishley/Steve Gritt** (Charlton Athletic); *Division 3* – **Terry Cooper** (Birmingham City); *Division 4* – **George Foster** (Mansfield Town).

NOVEMBER
Division 1 – **Howard Wilkinson** (Leeds United); *Division 2* – **David Webb** (Southend United); *Division 3* – **Phil Holder** (Brentford); *Division 4* – **Jimmy Mullen** (Burnley).

DECEMBER
Division 1 – **Alex Ferguson** (Manchester United); *Division 2* – **Graham Turner** (Wolverhampton Wanderers); *Division 3* – **Alan Murray** (Hartlepool United); *Division 4* – **Bill Green** (Scunthorpe United).

JANUARY
Division 1 – **Graeme Souness** (Liverpool); *Division 2* – **Malcolm Crosby** (Sunderland); *Division 3* – **Danny Bergara** (Stockport County); *Division 4* – **Brian Flynn** (Wrexham).

FEBRUARY
Division 1 – **Brian Clough** (Nottingham Forest); *Division 2* – **John Lyall** (Ipswich Town); *Division 3* – **Chris Turner** (Peterborough United); *Division 4* – **Dario Gradi** (Crewe Alexandra).

MARCH
Division 1 – **Gerry Francis** (QPR); *Division 2* – **Alan Curbishley/Steve Gritt** (Charlton Athletic); *Division 3* – **David Philpotts** (Wigan Athletic); *Division 4* – **Phil Henson** (Rotherham United).

APRIL
Division 1 – **Trevor Francis** (Sheffield Wednesday); *Division 2* – **Arthur Cox** (Derby County); *Division 3* – **Phil Holder** (Brentford); *Division 4* – **Steve Thompson** (Lincoln City).

LIST OF REFEREES FOR SEASON 1992–93

Paul Alcock (S. Merstham, Surrey)
David Allison (Lancaster)
Gerald Ashby, (Worcester)
David Axcell, (Southend)
Mike Bailey, (Impington, Cambridge)
Keren Barrett, (Coventry)
Steven Bell, (Huddersfield)
Ray Bigger, (Croydon)
Martin Bodenham, (Looe, Cornwall)
Jim Borrett, (Harleston, Norfolk)
John Brandwood, (Lichfield, Staffs.)
Kevin Breen, (Liverpool)
Alf Buksh, (London)
Keith Burge, (Tonypandy)
Billy Burns, (Scarborough)
Vic Callow, (Solihull)
John Carter, (Christchurch)
Brian Coddington, (Sheffield)
Keith Cooper, (Pontypridd)
Keith Cooper, (Swindon)
Ian Cruikshanks, (Hartlepool)
Paul Danson, (Leicester)
Alan Dawson, (Jarrowe)
Roger Dilkes, (Mossley, Lancs.)
Phil Don, (Hanworth Park, Middlesex)
Steve Dunn, (Bristol)
Paul Durkin, (Portland, Dorset)
David Elleray, (Harrow)
Tom Fitzharris, (Bolton)
Alan Flood, (Stockport)
Peter Foakes, (Clacton-on-Sea)
David Frampton, (Poole, Dorset)
Dermot Gallagher, (Banbury, Oxon.)
Rodger Gifford, (Llanbradach, Mid. Glam.)
Ron Groves, (Weston-Super-Mare)
Allan Gunn, (South Chailey, Sussex)
Keith Hackett, (Sheffield)
Bob Hamer, (Bristol)
Paul Harrison, (Oldham)
Robert Hart, (Darlington)
Ian Hemley, (Ampthill, Beds.)
Ian Hendrick, (Preston)
Brian Hill, (Kettering)
Terry Holbrook, (Walsall)
Mike James, (Horsham)
Peter Jones, (Loughborough)

John Key, (Sheffield)
Howard King, (Merthyr Tydfil)
John Kirkby, (Sheffield)
Ken Leach, (Wolverhampton)
Ray Lewis, (Gt. Bookham, Surrey)
John Lloyd, (Wrexham)
Stephen Lodge, (Barnsley)
Terry Lunt, (Ashton-in-Makerfield, Lancs)
Ken Lupton, (Stockton-on-Tees)
Kevin Lynch, (Lincoln)
John Martin, (Nr. Alton, Hants.)
Roger Milford, (Bristol)
Kelvin Morton, (Bury St. Edmunds)
John Moules, (Erith, Kent)
Bob Nixon, (West Kirkby, Wirrall)
Jim Parker, (Preston)
Roger Pawley, (Cambridge)
Mike Peck, (Kendal)
David Phillips, (Barnsley)
Micky Pierce, (Portsmouth)
Graham Poll, (Berkhamsted)
Graham Pooley, (Bishops Stortford)
Richard Poulain, (Huddersfield)
Ken Redfern, (Whitley Bay)
Mike Reed, (Birmingham)
Jim Rushton, (Stoke-on-Trent)
Paul Scoble, (Portsmouth)
Dave Shadwell, (Bromsgrove)
Ray Shepherd, (Leeds)
Gurnam Singh, (Wolverhampton)
Arthur Smith, (Rubery, Birmingham)
Paul Taylor, (Waltham Cross, Herts.)
Colin Trussell, (Liverpool)
Paul Vanes, (Warley, West Midlands)
Tony Ward, (London)
John Watson, (Whitley Bay)
Trevor West, (Hull)
Clive Wilkes, (Gloucester)
Alan Wilkie, (Chester-le-Street)
Gary Willard, (Worthing, W. Sussex)
Jeff Winter, (Middlesbrough)
Roger Wiseman, (Borehamwood, Herts.)
Eddie Wolstenholme, (Blackburn)
Joe Worrall, (Warrington)
Philip Wright, (Northwich)

RECORDS

Major British Records

HIGHEST WINS

First-Class Match	Arbroath *(Scottish Cup 1st Round)*	36	Bon Accord	0	12 Sept 1885
International Match	England	13	Ireland	0	18 Feb 1882
FA Cup	Preston NE *(1st Round)*	26	Hyde U	0	15 Oct 1887
League Cup	West Ham U *(2nd Round, 2nd Leg)*	10	Bury	0	25 Oct 1983
	Liverpool *(2nd Round, 1st Leg)*	10	Fulham	0	23 Sept 1986

FOOTBALL LEAGUE

Division 1	*(Home)*	WBA	12	Darwen	0	4 April 1892
		Nottingham F	12	Leicester Fosse	0	21 April 1909
	(Away)	Newcastle U	1	Sunderland	9	5 Dec 1908
		Cardiff C	1	Wolverhampton W	9	3 Sept 1955
Division 2	*(Home)*	Newcastle U	13	Newport Co	0	5 Oct 1946
	(Away)	Burslem PV	0	Sheffield U	10	10 Dec 1892
Division 3	*(Home)*	Gillingham	10	Chesterfield	0	5 Sept 1987
	(Away)	Halifax T	0	Fulham	8	16 Sept 1969
Division 3(S)	*(Home)*	Luton T	12	Bristol R	0	13 April 1936
	(Away)	Northampton T	0	Walsall	8	2 Feb 1947
Division 3(N)	*(Home)*	Stockport Co	13	Halifax T	0	6 Jan 1934
	(Away)	Accrington S	0	Barnsley	9	3 Feb 1934
Division 4	*(Home)*	Oldham Ath	11	Southport	0	26 Dec 1962
	(Away)	Crewe Alex	1	Rotherham U	8	8 Sept 1973
Aggregate Division 3(N)		Tranmere R	13	Oldham Ath	4	26 Dec 1935

SCOTTISH LEAGUE

Premier Division	*(Home)*	Aberdeen	8	Motherwell	0	26 March 1979
	(Away)	Hamilton A	0	Celtic	8	5 Nov 1988
Division 1	*(Home)*	Celtic	11	Dundee	0	26 Oct 1895
	(Away)	Airdrieonians	1	Hibernian	11	24 Oct 1950
Division 2	*(Home)*	Airdrieonians	15	Dundee Wanderers	1	1 Dec 1894
	(Away)	Alloa Ath	0	Dundee	10	8 March 1947

LEAGUE CHAMPIONSHIP HAT-TRICKS

Huddersfield T	1923–24 to 1925–26
Arsenal	1932–33 to 1934–35
Liverpool	1981–82 to 1983–84

MOST GOALS FOR IN A SEASON

FOOTBALL LEAGUE

		Goals	*Games*	*Season*
Division 1	Aston V	128	42	1930–31
Division 2	Middlesbrough	122	42	1926–27
Division 3(S)	Millwall	127	42	1927–28
Division 3(N)	Bradford C	128	42	1928–29
Division 3	QPR	111	46	1961–62
Division 4	Peterborough U	134	46	1960–61

SCOTTISH LEAGUE

Premier Division	Rangers	101	44	1991–92
	Dundee U	90	36	1982–83
	Celtic	90	36	1982–83
Division 1	Hearts	132	34	1957–58
Division 2	Raith R	142	34	1937–38
New Division 1	Motherwell	92	39	1981–82
New Division 2	Ayr U	95	39	1987–88

FEWEST GOALS FOR IN A SEASON

FOOTBALL LEAGUE	(minimum 42 games)	Goals	Games	Season
Division 1	Stoke C	24	42	1984–85
Division 2	Watford	24	42	1971–72
Division 3(S)	Crystal Palace	33	42	1950–51
Division 3(N)	Crewe Alex	32	42	1923–24
Division 3	Stockport Co	27	46	1969–70
Division 4	Crewe Alex	29	46	1981–82
SCOTTISH LEAGUE	(minimum 30 games)			
Premier Division	Hamilton A	19	36	1988–89
Division 1	Stirling Alb	18	39	1980–81
	Ayr U	20	34	1966–67
Division 2	Lochgelly U	20	38	1923–24
New Division 1	Stirling Alb	18	39	1980–81
New Division 2	Berwick R	32	39	1987–88

MOST GOALS AGAINST IN A SEASON

FOOTBALL LEAGUE		Goals	Games	Season
Division 1	Blackpool	125	42	1930–31
Division 2	Darwen	141	34	1898–99
Division 3(S)	Merthyr T	135	42	1929–30
Division 3(N)	Nelson	136	42	1927–28
Division 3	Accrington S	123	46	1959–60
Division 4	Hartlepools U	109	46	1959–60
SCOTTISH LEAGUE				
Premier Division	Morton	100	36	1984–85
	Morton	100	44	1987–88
Division 1	Leith Ath	137	38	1931–32
Division 2	Edinburgh C	146	38	1931–32
New Division 1	Queen of the S	99	39	1988–89
New Division 2	Meadowbank Th	89	39	1977–78

FEWEST GOALS AGAINST IN A SEASON

FOOTBALL LEAGUE	(minimum 42 games)	Goals	Games	Season
Division 1	Liverpool	16	42	1978–79
Division 2	Manchester U	23	42	1924–25
Division 3(S)	Southampton	21	42	1921–22
Division 3(N)	Port Vale	21	46	1953–54
Division 3	Middlesbrough	30	46	1986–87
Division 4	Lincoln C	25	46	1980–81
SCOTTISH LEAGUE	(minimum 30 games)			
Premier Division	Rangers	19	36	1989–90
Division 1	Celtic	14	38	1913–14
Division 2	Morton	20	38	1966–67
New Division 1	Hibernian	24	39	1980–81
New Division 2	St Johnstone	24	39	1987–88
	Stirling Alb	24	39	1990–91

MOST POINTS IN A SEASON

FOOTBALL LEAGUE	(under old system)	Points	Games	Season
Division 1	Liverpool	68	42	1978–79
Division 2	Tottenham H	70	42	1919–20
Division 3	Aston V	70	46	1971–72
Division 3(S)	Nottingham F	70	46	1950–51
	Bristol C	70	46	1954–55
Division 3(N)	Doncaster R	72	42	1946–47
Division 4	Lincoln C	74	46	1975–76
FOOTBALL LEAGUE	(three points for a win)			
Division 1	Everton	90	42	1984–85
	Liverpool	90	40	1987–88
Division 2	Chelsea	99	46	1988–89
Division 3	Bournemouth	97	46	1986–87
Division 4	Swindon T	102	46	1985–86
SCOTTISH LEAGUE				
Premier Division	Celtic	72	44	1987–88
	Rangers	72	44	1991–92
Division 1	Rangers	76	42	1920–21
Division 2	Morton	69	38	1966–67
New Division 1	St Mirren	62	39	1976–77
New Division 2	Forfar Ath	63	39	1983–84

FEWEST POINTS IN A SEASON

FOOTBALL LEAGUE	(minimum 34 games)	Points	Games	Season
Division 1	Stoke C	17	42	1984–85
Division 2	Doncaster R	8	34	1904–05
	Loughborough T	8	34	1899–1900
Division 3	Rochdale	21	46	1973–74
	Cambridge U	21	46	1984–85
Division 3(S)	Merthyr T	21	42	1924–25
				& 1929–30
	QPR	21	42	1925–26
Division 3(N)	Rochdale	11	40	1931–32
Division 4	Workington	19	46	1976–77
SCOTTISH LEAGUE	(minimum 30 games)			
Premier Division	St Johnstone	11	36	1975–76
Division 1	Stirling Alb	6	30	1954–55
Division 2	Edinburgh C	7	34	1936–37
New Division 1	Queen of the S	10	39	1988–89
New Division 2	Berwick R	16	39	1987–88
	Stranraer	16	39	1987–88

MOST WINS IN A SEASON

FOOTBALL LEAGUE		Wins	Games	Season
Division 1	Tottenham H	31	42	1960–61
Division 2	Tottenham H	32	42	1919–20
Division 3(S)	Millwall	30	42	1927–28
	Plymouth Arg	30	42	1929–30
	Cardiff C	30	42	1946–47
	Nottingham F	30	46	1950–51
	Bristol C	30	46	1954–55
Division 3(N)	Doncaster R	33	42	1946–47
Division 3	Aston Villa	32	46	1971–72
Division 4	Lincoln C	32	46	1975–76
	Swindon T	32	46	1985–86
SCOTTISH LEAGUE				
Premier Division	Aberdeen	27	36	1984–85
	Rangers	33	44	1991–92
Division 1	Rangers	35	42	1920–21
Division 2	Morton	33	38	1966–67
New Division 1	Motherwell	26	39	1981–82
New Division 2	Forfar Ath	27	39	1983–84
	Ayr U	27	39	1987–88

RECORD HOME WINS IN A SEASON

Brentford won all 21 games in Division 3(S), 1929–30

UNDEFEATED AT HOME

Liverpool 85 games (63 League, 9 League Cup, 7 European, 6 FA Cup), Jan 1978–Jan 1981

RECORD AWAY WINS IN A SEASON

Doncaster R won 18 of 21 games in Division 3(N), 1946–47

FEWEST WINS IN A SEASON

FOOTBALL LEAGUE		Wins	Games	Season
Division 1	Stoke	3	22	1889–90
	Woolwich Arsenal	3	38	1912–13
	Stoke C	3	42	1984–85
Division 2	LoughboroughT	1	34	1899–1900
Division 3(S)	Merthyr T	6	42	1929–30
	QPR	6	42	1925–26
Division 3(N)	Rochdale	4	40	1931–32
Division 3	Rochdale	2	46	1973–74
Division 4	Southport	3	46	1976–77

SCOTTISH LEAGUE

Premier Division	St Johnstone	3	36	1975–76
	Kilmarnock	3	36	1982–83
Division 1	Vale of Leven	0	22	1891–92
Division 2	East Stirlingshire	1	22	1905–06
	Forfar Ath	1	38	1974–75
New Division 1	Queen of the S	2	39	1988–89
New Division 2	Forfar Ath	4	26	1975–76
	Stranraer	4	39	1987–88

MOST DEFEATS IN A SEASON

FOOTBALL LEAGUE		Defeats	Games	Season
Division 1	Stoke C	31	42	1984–85
Division 2	Tranmere R	31	42	1938–39
Division 3	Cambridge U	33	46	1984–85
Division 3(S)	Merthyr T	29	42	1924–25
	Walsall	29	46	1952–53
	Walsall	29	46	1953–54
Division 3(N)	Rochdale	33	40	1931–32
Division 4	Newport Co	33	46	1987–88

SCOTTISH LEAGUE

Premier Division	Morton	29	36	1984–85
Division 1	St Mirren	31	42	1920–21
Division 2	Brechin C	30	36	1962–63
	Lochgelly	30	38	1923–24
New Division 1	Queen of the S	29	39	1988–89
New Division 2	Berwick R	29	39	1987–88

HAT-TRICKS

Career 34 Dixie Dean (Tranmere R, Everton, Notts Co, England)
Division 1 (one season post-war) 6 Jimmy Greaves (Chelsea), 1960–61
Three for one team one match
West, Spouncer, Hooper, Nottingham F v Leicester Fosse, Division 1, 21 April 1909
Barnes, Ambler, Davies, Wrexham v Hartlepools U, Division 4, 3 March 1962
Adcock, Stewart, White, Manchester C v Huddersfield T, Division 2, 7 Nov 1987
Loasby, Smith, Wells, Northampton T v Walsall, Division 3(S), 5 Nov 1927
Bowater, Hoyland, Readman, Mansfield T v Rotherham U, Division 3(N), 27 Dec 1932

FEWEST DEFEATS IN A SEASON

(Minimum 20 games)

FOOTBALL LEAGUE		Defeats	Games	Season
Division 1	Preston NE	0	22	1888–89
	Arsenal	1	38	1990–91
	Liverpool	2	40	1987–88
	Leeds U	2	42	1968–69
Division 2	Liverpool	0	28	1893–94
	Burnley	2	30	1897–98
	Bristol C	2	38	1905–06
	Leeds U	3	42	1963–64
Division 3	QPR	5	46	1966–67
	Bristol R	5	46	1989–90
Division 3(S)	Southampton	4	42	1921–22
	Plymouth Arg	4	42	1929–30
Division 3(N)	Port Vale	3	46	1953–54
	Doncaster R	3	42	1946–47
	Wolverhampton W	3	42	1923–24
Division 4	Lincoln C	4	46	1975–76
	Sheffield U	4	46	1981–82
	Bournemouth	4	46	1981–82

SCOTTISH LEAGUE

Premier Division	Celtic	3	44	1987–88
Division 1	Rangers	1	42	1920–21
Division 2	Clyde	1	36	1956–57
	Morton	1	36	1962–63
	St Mirren	1	36	1967–68
New Division 1	Partick Th	2	26	1975–76
	St Mirren	2	39	1976–77
New Division 2	Raith R	1	26	1975–76
	Clydebank	3	26	1975–76
	Forfar Ath	3	39	1983–84
	Raith R	3	39	1986–87

MOST DRAWN GAMES IN A SEASON

FOOTBALL LEAGUE		*Draws*	*Games*	*Season*
Division 1	Norwich C	23	42	1978–79
Division 4	Exeter C	23	46	1986–87
SCOTTISH LEAGUE				
Premier Division	Hibernian	19	44	1987–88

MOST GOALS IN A GAME

FOOTBALL LEAGUE

Division 1	Ted Drake (Arsenal) 7 goals v Aston Villa	14 Dec 1935
Division 2	Tommy Briggs (Blackburn R) 7 goals v Bristol R	5 Feb 1955
	Neville Coleman (Stoke C) 7 goals v Lincoln C (away)	23 Feb 1957
Division 3(S)	Joe Payne (Luton T) 10 goals v Bristol R	13 April 1936
Division 3(N)	Bunny Bell (Tranmere R) 9 goals v Oldham Ath	26 Dec 1935
Division 3	Steve Earle (Fulham) 5 goals v Halifax T	16 Sept 1969
	Barrie Thomas (Scunthorpe U) 5 goals v Luton T	24 April 1965
	Keith East (Swindon T) 5 goals v Mansfield T	20 Nov 1965
	Alf Wood (Shrewsbury T) 5 goals v Blackburn R	2 Oct 1971
	Tony Caldwell (Bolton W) 5 goals v Walsall	10 Sept 1983
	Andy Jones (Port Vale) 5 goals v Newport Co	4 May 1987
	Steve Wilkinson (Mansfield T) 5 goals v Birmingham C	3 April 1990
Division 4	Bert Lister (Oldham Ath) 6 goals v Southport	26 Dec 1962
FA CUP	Ted MacDougall (Bournemouth) 9 goals v Margate (*1st Round*)	20 Nov 1971
LEAGUE CUP	Frankie Bunn (Oldham Ath) 6 goals v Scarborough	25 Oct 1989
SCOTTISH LEAGUE CUP	Jim Fraser (Ayr U) 5 goals v Dumbarton	13 Aug 1952
SCOTTISH LEAGUE		
Premier Division	Paul Sturrock (Dundee U) 5 goals v Morton	17 Nov 1984
Division 1	Jimmy McGrory (Celtic) 8 goals v Dunfermline Ath	14 Sept 1928
Division 2	Owen McNally (Arthurlie) 8 goals v Armadale	1 Oct 1927
	Jim Dyet (King's Park) 8 goals v Forfar Ath	2 Jan 1930
	John Calder (Morton) 8 goals v Raith R	18 April 1936
	Norman Hayward (Raith R) 8 goals v Brechin C	20 Aug 1937
SCOTTISH CUP	John Petrie (Arbroath) 13 goals v Bon Accord (*1st Round*)	12 Sept 1885

MOST LEAGUE GOALS IN A SEASON

FOOTBALL LEAGUE		*Goals*	*Games*	*Season*
Division 1	Dixie Dean (Everton)	60	39	1927–28
Division 2	George Camsell (Middlesbrough)	59	37	1926–27
Division 3(S)	Joe Payne (Luton T)	55	39	1936–37
Division 3(N)	Ted Harston (Mansfield T)	55	41	1936–37
Division 3	Derek Reeves (Southampton)	39	46	1959–60
Division 4	Terry Bly (Peterborough U)	52	46	1960–61
FA CUP	Sandy Brown (Tottenham H)	15		1900–01
LEAGUE CUP	Clive Allen (Tottenham H)	12		1986–87
SCOTTISH LEAGUE				
Division 1	William McFadyen (Motherwell)	52	34	1931–32
Division 2	Jim Smith (Ayr U)	66	38	1927–28

MOST LEAGUE GOALS IN A CAREER

FOOTBALL LEAGUE		*Goals*	*Games*	*Season*
Arthur Rowley	WBA	4	24	1946–48
	Fulham	27	56	1948–50
	Leicester C	251	303	1950–58
	Shrewsbury T	152	236	1958–65
		434	619	
SCOTTISH LEAGUE				
Jimmy McGrory	Celtic	1	3	1922–23
	Clydebank	13	30	1923–24
	Celtic	396	375	1924–38
		410	408	

MOST CUP GOALS IN A CAREER

FA CUP
Denis Law   41   (Huddersfield T, Manchester C, Manchester U)

A CENTURY OF LEAGUE AND CUP GOALS IN CONSECUTIVE SEASONS

George Camsell	Middlesbrough	59 Lge		5 Cup	1926–27
(101 goals)		33		4	1927–28
Steve Bull	Wolverhampton W	34 Lge		18 Cup	1987–88
(102 goals)		37		13	1988–89

(Camsell's cup goals were all scored in the FA Cup; Bull had 12 in the Sherpa Van Trophy, 3 Littlewoods Cup, 3 FA Cup in 1987–88; 11 Sherpa Van Trophy, 2 Littlewoods Cup in 1988–89.)

LONGEST WINNING SEQUENCE

FOOTBALL LEAGUE		*Games*	*Season*
Division 1	Everton	12	1893–94 (4) and 1894–95 (8)
Division 2	Manchester U	14	1904–05
	Bristol C	14	1905–06
	Preston NE	14	1950–51
Division 3	Reading	13	1985–86
From season's start			
Division 1	Tottenham H	11	1960–61

LONGEST SEQUENCE WITHOUT A WIN FROM SEASON'S START

Division 1	Sheffield U	16	1990–91

LONGEST SEQUENCE OF CONSECUTIVE SCORING (Individual)

FOOTBALL LEAGUE RECORD		
Bill Pendergast (Chester)	15 in 12 games	1938–39

LONGEST WINNING SEQUENCE IN A SEASON

FOOTBALL LEAGUE		*Games*	*Season*
Division 1	Tottenham H	11	1960–61
Division 2	Manchester U	14	1904–05
Division 2	Bristol C	14	1905–06
Division 2	Preston NE	14	1950–51
SCOTTISH LEAGUE			
Division 2	Morton	23	1963–64

LONGEST UNBEATEN SEQUENCE

FOOTBALL LEAGUE		*Games*	*Seasons*
Division 1	Nottingham F	42	Nov 1977–Dec 1978

LONGEST UNBEATEN CUP SEQUENCE

Liverpool   25 rounds   League/Milk Cup   1980–84

LONGEST UNBEATEN SEQUENCE IN A SEASON

FOOTBALL LEAGUE		*Games*	*Season*
Division 1	Burnley	30	1920–21

LONGEST UNBEATEN START TO A SEASON

FOOTBALL LEAGUE		*Games*	*Season*
Division 1	Leeds U	29	1973–74
Division 1	Liverpool	29	1987–88

LONGEST SEQUENCE WITHOUT A WIN IN A SEASON

FOOTBALL LEAGUE		*Games*	*Season*
Division 2	Cambridge U	31	1983–84

LONGEST SEQUENCE OF CONSECUTIVE DEFEATS

FOOTBALL LEAGUE		*Games*	*Season*
Division 2	Darwen	18	1898–99

GOALKEEPING RECORDS (without conceding a goal)

British record *(all competitive games)*
Chris Woods, Rangers, in 1196 minutes from 26 November 1986 to 31 January 1987

Football League
Steve Death, Reading, 1103 minutes from 24 March to 18 August 1979

PENALTIES

Most in a season (individual)		*Goals*	*Season*
Division 1	Francis Lee (Manchester C)	13	1971–72
Most awarded in one game			
Five	Crystal Palace (4 – 1 scored, 3 missed) v Brighton & HA (1 scored), Div 2		1988–89
Most saved in a season			
Division 1	Paul Cooper (Ipswich T)	8 (of 10)	1979–80

MOST LEAGUE APPEARANCES

FOOTBALL LEAGUE
968 Peter Shilton (286 Leicester City, 110 Stoke City, 202 Nottingham Forest, 188 Southampton, 175 Derby County, 7 Plymouth Argyle) 1966–92
824 Terry Paine (7 13 Southampton, 111 Hereford United) 1957–77
795 Tommy Hutchison (165 Blackpool, 314 Coventry City, 46 Manchester City, 92 Burnley 178 Swansea City, also 68 Alloa 1965–68) 1968–91
777 Alan Oakes (565 Manchester City, 211 Chester City, 1 Port Vale) 1959–84
770 John Trollope (all for Swindon Town) 1960–80†
764 Jimmy Dickinson (all for Portsmouth) 1946–65
761 Roy Sproson (all for Port Vale) 1950–72
758 Ray Clemence (48 Scunthorpe United, 470 Liverpool, 240 Tottenham Hotspur) 1966–87
757 Pat Jennings (48 Watford, 472 Tottenham Hotspur, 237 Arsenal) 1963–86
† record for one club

Consecutive
401 Harold Bell (401 Tranmere R; 459 in all games) 1946–55

FA CUP
88 Ian Callaghan (79 Liverpool, 7 Swansea C, 2 Crewe Alex)

Most Senior Matches
1344 Peter Shilton (968 League, 85 FA Cup, 96 League Cup, 125 Internationals, 13 Under-23, 4 Football League XI, 53 others including European Cup, UEFA Cup, World Club Championship, various domestic cup competitions)

MOST CUP WINNERS' MEDALS

FA CUP – 5 medals each

James Forrest (Blackburn R) 1884, 1885, 1886, 1890, 1891
Hon. A. F. Kinnaird (Wanderers) 1873, 1877, 1878, (Old Etonians) 1879, 1882
C. H. R. Wollaston (Wanderers) 1872, 1873, 1876, 1877, 1878

SCOTTISH CUP – 7 medals each

Jimmy McMenemy (Celtic) 1904, 1907, 1908, 1911, 1912, 1914, (Partick Th) 1921
Bob McPhail (Airdieonians) 1924, (Rangers) 1928, 1930, 1932, 1934, 1935, 1936
Billy McNeill (Celtic) 1965, 1967, 1969, 1971, 1972, 1974, 1975

MOST FA CUP FINAL GOALS

Ian Rush (Liverpool): 1986 (2), 1989 (2), 1992 (1)

MOST LEAGUE MEDALS

Phil Neal (Liverpool) 8: 1976, 1977, 1979, 1980, 1982, 1983, 1984, 1986

RECORD ATTENDANCES

Football League	83,260	Manchester U v Arsenal, Maine Road	17.1.1948
Scottish League	118,567	Rangers v Celtic, Ibrox Stadium	2.1.1939
FA Cup Final	126,047*	Bolton W v West Ham U, Wembley	28.4.1923
European Cup	135,826	Celtic v Leeds U, semi-final at Hampden Park	15.4.1970
Scottish Cup	146,433	Celtic v Aberdeen, Hampden Park	24.4.37
World Cup	199,854†	Brazil v Uruguay, Maracana, Rio	16.7.50

* It has been estimated that as many as 70,000 more broke in without paying.
† 173,830 paid.

OTHER RECORDS

YOUNGEST PLAYERS
Football League Albert Geldard, 15 years 158 days, Bradford Park Avenue v Millwall, Division 2, 16.9.29; and Ken Roberts, 15 years 158 days, Wrexham v Bradford Park Avenue, Division 3(N), 1.9.51
Football League scorer
  Ronnie Dix, 15 years 180 days, Bristol Rovers v Norwich City, Division 3(S), 3.3.28.
Division 1
  Derek Forster, 15 years 185 days, Sunderland v Leicester City, 22.8.64.
Division 1 scorer
  Jason Dozzell, 16 years 57 days as substitute Ipswich Town v Coventry City, 4.2.84
Division 1 hat-tricks
  Alan Shearer, 17 years 240 days, Southampton v Arsenal, 9.4.88
  Jimmy Greaves, 17 years 10 months, Chelsea v Portsmouth, 25.12.57 FA Cup (any round)
  Andy Awford, 15 years 88 days as substitute Worcester City v Borehamwood, 3rd Qual. rd, 10.10.87
FA Cup proper
  Scott Endersby, 15 years 288 days, Kettering v Tilbury, 1st rd, 26.11.77
FA Cup Final
  Paul Allen, 17 years 256 days, West Ham United v Arsenal, 1980
FA Cup Final scorer
  Norman Whiteside, 18 years 18 days, Manchester United v Brighton & Hove Albion, 1983
FA Cup Final captain
  David Nish, 21 years 212 days, Leicester City v Manchester City, 1969
League Cup Final scorer
  Norman Whiteside, 17 years 324 days, Manchester United v Liverpool, 1983
League Cup Final captain
  Barry Venison, 20 years 7 months, 8 days, Sunderland v Norwich City, 1985

INTERNATIONALS
England
  Pre-war: James Prinsep (Clapham Rovers) 17 years 252 days, v Scotland, 5.4.1879
  Post-war: Duncan Edwards (Manchester United), 18 years 183 days, v Scotland, 2.4.55
Northern Ireland
  Norman Whiteside (Manchester United), 17 years 42 days, v Yugoslavia, 17.6.82
Scotland
  Johnny Lambie (Queen's Park), 17 years 92 days, v Ireland, 20.3.1886
Wales
  John Charles (Leeds United), 18 years 71 days, v Ireland, 8.3.50
Republic of Ireland
  Jimmy Holmes, 17 years 200 days, v Austria, 30.5.71

OLDEST PLAYERS
Football League
  Neil McBain, 52 years 4 months, New Brighton v Hartlepools United, Div 3(N), 15.3.47 (McBain was New Brighton's manager and had to play in an emergency)
Division 1
  Stanley Matthews, 50 years 5 days, Stoke City v Fulham, 6.2.65
FA Cup Final
  Walter Hampson, 41 years 8 months, Newcastle United v Aston Villa, 1924
FA Cup
  Billy Meredith, 49 years 8 months, Manchester City v Newcastle United, 29.3.24
International debutant
  Leslie Compton, 38 years 2 months, England v Wales, 15. 11.50
International
  Billy Meredith, 45 years 229 days, Wales v England, 15.3.20

SENDINGS-OFF

Season	242 (211 League, 19 FA Cup, 12 Milk Cup)	1982–83
Day	15 (3 League, 12 FA Cup*)	20 Nov 1982
	worst overall FA Cup total	
League	13	14 Dec 1985
FA Cup	Final Kevin Moran, Manchester U v Everton	1985
Wembley	Boris Stankovic, Yugoslavia v Sweden (Olympics)	1948
	Antonio Rattin, Argentina v England (World Cup)	1966
	Billy Bremner (Leeds U) and Kevin Keegan (Liverpool), Charity Shield	1974
	Gilbert Dresch, Luxembourg v England (World Cup)	1977
	Mike Henry, Sudbury T v Tamworth (FA Vase)	1989
Quickest	Ambrose Brown, Wrexham v Hull C (away) Div 3(N): 20 secs	25 Dec 1936
Division 1	Liam O'Brien, Manchester U v Southampton (away): 85 secs	3 Jan 1987
World Cup	Jose Batista, Uruguay v Scotland, Neza, Mexico (World Cup): 55 secs	13 June 1986
Most one game	Four: Crewe Alex (2) v Bradford PA (2) Div 3(N)	8 Jan 1955
	Four: Sheffield U (1) v Portsmouth (3) Div 2	13 Dec 1986
	Four: Port Vale (2) v Northampton T (2) Littlewoods Cup	18 Aug 1987
	Four: Brentford (2) v Mansfield T (2) Div 3	12 Dec 1987

FROM THE CHAPLAIN

QUESTION TIME!

'From *the chaplain*?' someone asks impatiently. 'I thought Vicars only worked on Sundays', quips the humorist. 'Whatever have they got a parson for at a football club?' queries a frankly bemused supporter.

It may come as a surprise to new readers of this page in *Rothmans*, to discover that a substantial number of Football League clubs (and a few in Ireland and Scotland) have chaplains operating within them. But equally a glance through this Yearbook will show that something like a quarter of all the League clubs actually have their origins in a Church or Sunday School or were formed by a clergyman. Thus the game has had a strong ministerial involvement right from the beginning, even if that fact had, formerly, been largely forgotten, and the involvement today of chaplains at nearly forty Football League clubs can only be regarded as natural and wholesome. Indeed, if *we* may now pose the questions for a moment, the issue really becomes: 'With so many clubs benefiting from the involvement of a chaplain and clearly very happy with such a state of affairs, why aren't there even more chaplains?' Equally, 'What has any club got to lose by appointing such a man?' For, although it is sometimes necessary for a chaplain to move away and pass on his responsibilities to a successor, no club that has had such an appointment has ever regretted it, while many of them, right through the Divisions, are positively delighted at their chaplain's contribution to them.

Wicked!

'So, what does he *do*?'

Chaplains are non-assertive most of the time. Unless they have been asked to arrange a club event like a carol service they are low-key individuals who are often quiet and unassuming men, though they are passionate followers of the game and supporters of their club and often possess a wicked sense of humour! They are appointed to assist everyone in and related to football however they can, and they do this in all sorts of ways from providing a listening ear for an overstressed club official to a friendly visit to an injured player who may be feeling anxious, depressed or forgotten.

Someone has used the illustration of the tightrope walker to describe the chaplain's role: below the great man, almost unnoticed and usually quite unnecessary is the safety net. One day he slips and falls . . . but is safely caught – and how thankful he is for that net's presence, just when and where he needed it. That's the chaplain: a friend who is always there, available when life or football goes wrong, a compassionate heart, an experienced carer who is able to bring comfort, encouragement, challenge and support in just the right proportions – and in total confidence if necessary – when those are what is required.

But the chaplain isn't just there for the players in the first team. He is the chaplain for everyone at the club – the office staff, the groundsman and his team, the YTS lads, the stewards and gatemen, and of course the supporters, many of whom view the chaplain as their own personal minister.

'Well, perhaps we'll think about a chaplain at our club.' In that case you might be glad of the assistance of Christians In Sport, who are in touch with all the existing chaplains and could help in making contact with a potential chaplain who would be just right for your club. Please contact them – in confidence of course – at PO Box 93, Oxford OX2 7YP.

OFFICIAL CHAPLAINS TO FOOTBALL LEAGUE CLUBS

Rev Ernie Hume — Sheffield U
Rev John Bingham — Chesterfield
Rev Richard Chewter — Exeter C
Rev Alan Fisher — Bournemouth
Rev Andrew Taggart — Torquay U
Rev David Jeans — Sheffield W
Rev Nigel Sands — Crystal Palace
Very Rev Alan Warren — Leicester C
Rev Phillip Miller — Ipswich T
Rev Allen Bagshawe — Hull C
Rev Tony Adamson — Newcastle U
Rev Derek Cleave — Bristol C
Rev Brian Rice — Hartlepool U
Rev John Boyers — Watford
Rev Michael Chantry — Oxford U
Rev Michael Futers — Derby County
Very Rev Brandon Jackson — Lincoln C
Rev Dick Syms — York City

Rev Dennis Hall — Wigan Ath
Rev William Hall — Middlesbrough
Rev Canon John Hestor — Brighton & HA
Revs Mervyn Terrett and Alan West — Luton T
Rev Jim Rushton — Carlisle U
Rev Robert de Berry — Queen's Park Rangers
Rev Gary Piper — Fulham
Rev Tony Horsfall — Barnsley
Rev Barry Kirk — Reading
Rev Martin Short — Bradford C
Revs Roger Sutton and Justin Dennison — Manchester U
Rev Martin Butt — Walsall
Rev Kevin Tugwell — Cardiff C
Rev Steve Riley — Leeds U
Revs Alan Poulter and Robin Sutton — Tranmere R
Rev Neville Gallagher — Maidstone U
Rev Jeff Banks — Halifax T
Rev Paul Bennett — Swindon T

COACHING AND THE COACHES

The coaching system has undergone many changes in the last few years and is expected to be altered even more radically over the coming seasons. At present those persons wishing to obtain an official coaching qualification will have to pass the tests and examinations set by the Football Association, who pioneered their first educational scheme in 1934 by providing coaching services to grammar schools. Development of both the scheme and the coaches who have come through it, has reached outstanding levels and now there are three tiers of award. The initial award is the Preliminary Certificate; that is followed by the Intermediate Award; whilst the current highest achievement is the Full Coaching Licence. The Director of Coaching Charles Hughes has been instrumental in preparing plans for the future development of the system which is incorporated in the booklet entitled "The Blueprint for the Future of Football" published by the FA. In it are plans to not only keep and upgrade the three previously mentioned awards, but also to promote a final Diploma or Degree in Coaching studies.

Courses for the Preliminary Certificate are in the main run by the County Coaching Associations which are part of the County Football Associations of which there are 43 spread around the country although not necessarily corresponding to geographical boundaries as officially recognized. Historically County FA's date back to the late 19th century and have a number of functions, one of the most important of which is in coaching and education. Each county has an FA Coaching representative and some have an additional Football Development Officer.

Typically, a preliminary course run by a County Association will consist of 26 hours spent during split weeks to assess the student's ability, be they male or female over 17 years of age in practical coaching; the theory of coaching and the Laws of the Game. A student needs to be physically equipped to take part and those with limited experience are advised to undertake an FA Leaders Course before attempting the Preliminary Badge award. Similarly for those wanting to take the subsequent Intermediate and Full Awards, participation on a preparatory course is obligatory unless dispensation is obtained. Both the Intermediate and Advanced or Full Awards Courses take place on a residential basis held at the National Sports Centre, Lilleshall, Shropshire each summer. Full details of everything connected with coaching including a list of coaching books, films and videos can be obtained from the coaching department at the Football Association, 16 Lancaster Gate, London W2 3LW (phone 071-262 4542).

The concept of development of soccer recreation in England and Wales has been split into the twin sections of the programmes for Excellence and for the Community. The full list of the persons in control of these sections designated "directors", starting from the head of coaching and education is as follows:

THE FOOTBALL ASSOCIATION
COACHING AND EDUCATION DEPARTMENT

Director of Coaching and Education: C. F. C. HUGHES, The Football Association, 16 Lancaster Gate, London, W2 3LW. 071-262 4542.
Assistant Director of Coaching and Education — Community Development: R. M. RUSSELL, The Football Association, 16 Lancaster Gate, London, W2 3LW. 071-262 4542.
Assistant Director of Coaching and Education — Excellence: T. PICKERIN, The G. M. Vauxhall Football Association National School, Lilleshall Hall National Sports Centre, near Newport, Shropshire, TF10 9AT. 0952 603136.
Technical Director of The G. M. Vauxhall Football Association National School: K. BLUNT, The G. M. Vauxhall Football Association National School, Lilleshall Hall National Sports Centre, near Newport, Shropshire, TF10 9AT. 0952 603136.
Technical Coordinator for the Programme for Excellence: M. WADSWORTH, The G. M. Vauxhall Football Association National School, Lilleshall Hall National Sports Centre, near Newport, Shropshire, TF10 9AT. 0952 603136.

Regional Directors:

Programme for Community Development

Ted Powell	Regional Director for Community Development – South
Kelly Simmons	Assistant South Regional Director — Women's Football
Colin E. Murphy	Regional Director for Community Development — Midlands
Helen Jevons	Assistant Midlands Regional Director — Women's Football
Ted Copeland	Regional Director for Community Development — North
Julie Fogarty	Assistant North Regional Director — Women's Football

Programme for Excellence

David Burnside	Regional Director for Excellence — South West
Alex Gibson	Regional Director for Excellence — North West
Martin Hunter	Regional Director for Excellence — North East
John Peacock	Regional Director for Excellence — Midlands
Les Reed	Regional Director for Excellence — South and East

National Training Officer for Referees: K. RIDDEN, The Football Association, 16 Lancaster Gate, London, W2 3LW. 071-262 4542.

KEN GOLDMAN

LAWS OF THE GAME

The Laws of the Game and Decisions of the International Board that follow are reproduced with the special permission of FIFA, and the text is the official text as published by FIFA.

LAW I

THE FIELD OF PLAY

The Field of Play and appurtenances shall be as shown in the following plan:

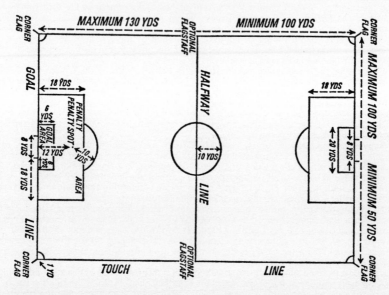

(1) **Dimensions.** The field of play shall be rectangular, its length being not more that 130 yards nor less than 100 yards, and its breadth not more than 100 yards nor less than 50 yards. (In International Matches the length shall be not more than 120 yards nor less than 110 yards and the breadth not more than 80 yards nor less than 70 yards.) The length shall in all cases exceed the breadth.

(2) **Marking.** The field of play shall be marked with distinctive lines, not more than 5 inches in width, not by a V-shaped rut, in accordance with the plan, the longer boundary lines being called the touch-lines and the shorter the goal-lines. A flag on a post not less than 5ft high and having a non-pointed top, shall be placed at each corner; a similar flag-post may be placed opposite the half-way-line on each side of the field of play, not less than 1 yard outside the touch-line. A half-way-line shall be marked out across the field of play. The centre of the field of play shall be indicated by a suitable mark and a circle with a 10 yards radius shall be marked around it.

(3) **The Goal-Area.** At each end of the field of play two lines shall be drawn at right-angles to the goal-line, 6 yards from each goal-post. These shall extend into the field of play for a distance of 6

yards and shall be joined by a line drawn parallel with the goal-line. Each of the spaces enclosed by these goal-lines and the goal-line shall be called a goal-area.

(4) **The Penalty-Area.** At each end of the field of play two lines shall be drawn at right angles to the goal-line, 18 yards from each goal-post. These shall extend into the field of play for a distance of 18 yards and shall be joined by a line drawn parallel with the goal-line. Each of the spaces enclosed by these lines and the goal-line shall be called a penalty-area. A suitable mark shall be made within each penalty area, 12 yards from the mid-point of the goal-line, measured along an undrawn line at right-angles thereto. These shall be the penalty-kick marks. From each penalty-kick mark an arc of a circle, having a radius of 10 yards, shall be drawn outside the penalty-area.

(5) **The Corner Area.** From each corner-flag post a quarter circle, having a radius of 1 yard, shall be drawn inside the field of play.

(6) **The Goals.** The goals shall be placed on the centre of each goal-line and shall consist of two upright posts, equidistant from the corner-flags and 8 yards apart (inside measurement), joined by a horizontal cross-bar the lower edge of which shall be 8ft from the ground. The width and depth

of the goal-posts and the width and depth of the cross-bars shall not exceed 5 inches (12cm). The goal-posts and the cross-bars shall have the same width.

Nets may be attached to the posts, cross-bars and ground behind the goals. They should be appropriately supported and be so placed as to allow the goal-keeper ample room.

Footnote
Goal nets. The use of nets made of hemp, jute or nylon is permitted. The nylon strings may, however, not be thinner than those made of hemp or jute.

Decisions of the International Board

(1) In International Matches the dimensions of the field of play shall be: maximum 110×75 metres; minimum 100×64 metres.

(2) National Associations must adhere strictly to these dimensions. Each National Association organising an International Match must advise the visiting Association, before the match, of the place and the dimensions of the field of play.

(3) The Board has approved this table of measurements for the laws of the Game:

130 yards	. . . 120 metres
120 yards	. . . 110
110 yards	. . . 100
100 yards	. . . 90
80 yards	. . . 75
70 yards	. . . 64
50 yards	. . . 45
18 yards	. . . 16.50
12 yards	. . . 11
10 yards	. . . 9.15
8 yards	. . . 7.32
6 yards	. . . 5.50
1 yard	. . . 1
8 feet	. . . 2.44
5 feet	. . . 1.50
28 inches	. . . 0.71
27 inches	. . . 0.68
9 inches	. . . 0.22
5 inches	. . . 0.12
$\frac{3}{4}$ inch	. . . 0.019
$\frac{1}{2}$ inch	. . . 0.0127
$\frac{3}{8}$ inch	. . . 0.010
14 ounces	. . . 396 grams
16 ounces	. . . 453 grams
15 lb/sq in	. . . 1 kg/cm^2

(4) The goal-line shall be marked the same width as the depth of the goal-posts and the cross-bar, so that the goal-line and goal-post will conform to the same interior and exterior edges.

(5) The 6 yards (for the outline of the goal-area) and the 18 yards (for the outline of the penalty-area) which have to be measured along the goal-line, must start from the inner sides of the goal-posts.

(6) The space within the inside areas of the field of play includes the width of the lines marking these areas.

(7) All Associations shall provide standard equipment, particularly in International Matches, when the laws of the Game must be complied with in every respect and especially with regard to the size of the ball and other equipment which must conform to the regulations. All cases of failure to provide standard equipment must be reported to FIFA.

(8) In a match played under the Rules of a Competition, if the cross-bar becomes displaced or broken, play shall be stopped and the match abandoned unless the cross-bar has been repaired and replaced in position or a new one provided without such being a danger to the players. A rope is not considered to be a satisfactory substitute for a cross-bar.

In a Friendly Match, by mutual consent, play may be resumed without the cross-bar provided it has been removed and no longer constitutes a danger to the players. In these circumstances, a rope may be used as a substitute for a cross-bar. If a rope is not used and the ball crosses the goal-line at a point which in the opinion of the Referee is below where the cross-bar should have been, he shall award a goal.

The game shall be restarted by the Referee dropping the ball at the place where it was when play was stopped.

(9) National Associations may specify such maximum and minimum dimensions for the cross-bars and goal-posts, within the limits laid down in Law I, as they consider appropriate.

(10) Goal-posts and cross-bars must be made of wood, metal or other approved material as decided from time to time by the International FA Board. They may be square, rectangular, round, half-round or elliptical in shape. Goal-posts and cross-bars made of other materials and in other shapes are not permitted. The goal-posts must be of white colour.

(11) 'Curtain-raisers' to International Matches should only be played following agreement on the day of the match, and taking into account the condition of the field of play, between representatives of the two Associations and the Referee (of the International Match).

(12) National Associations, particularly in International Matches, should
— restrict the number of photographers around the field of play.
— have a line ('photographers' line') marked behind the goal-lines at least 2 metres from the corner flag going through a point situated at least 3.5 metres behind the intersection of the goal-line with the line marking the goal area to a point situated at least 6 metres behind the goal-posts.
— prohibit photographers from passing over these lines.
— forbid the use of artificial lighting in the form of 'flashlights'.

LAW II – THE BALL

The ball shall be spherical; the outer casing shall be of leather or other approved materials. No material shall be used in its construction which might prove dangerous to the players.

The circumference of the ball shall not be more than 28in and not less than 27in. The weight of the ball at the start of the game shall not be more than 16oz nor less than 14oz. The pressure shall be equal to 0.6–1.1 atmosphere ($=600$ –1100g/cm^2) at sea level. The ball shall not be changed during the game unless authorised by the Referee.

Decisions of the International Board

---

(1) The ball used in any match shall be considered the property of the Association or Club on whose ground the match is played, and at the close of play it must be returned to the Referee.

(2) The International Board, from time to time, shall decide what constitutes approved materials. Any approved material shall be certified as such by the International Board.

(3) The Board has approved these equivalents of the weights specified in the Law: 14 to 16 ounces = 396 to 453 grams.

(4) If the ball bursts or becomes deflated during the course of a match, the game shall be stopped and restarted by dropping the new ball at the place where the first ball became defective.

(5) If this happens during a stoppage of the game (place-kick, goal-kick, corner-kick, free-kick, penalty-kick or throw-in) the game shall be restarted accordingly.

LAW III – NUMBER OF PLAYERS

(1) A match shall be played by two teams, each consisting of not more than eleven players, one of whom shall be the goalkeeper.

(2) Substitutes may be used in any match played under the rules of an official competition under the jurisdiction of FIFA, Confederations or National Associations, subject to the following conditions:

(a) that the authority of the international association(s) or national association(s) concerned, has been obtained.

(b) that, subject to the restriction contained in the following paragraph (c), the rules of a competition shall state how many, if any, substitutes may be nominated and how many of those nominated may be used.

(c) that a team shall not be permitted to use more than two substitutes in any match, who must be chosen from not more than five players whose names may (subject to the rules of the competition) be required to be given to the referee prior to the commencement of the match.

(3) Substitutes may be used in any other match, provided that the two teams concerned reach agreement on a maximum number, not exceeding five, and that the terms of such agreement are intimated to the Referee, before the match. If the Referee is not informed, or if the teams fail to reach agreement, no more than two substitutes shall be permitted. In all cases, the substitutes must be chosen from not more than five players whose names may be required to be given to the Referee prior to the commencement of the match.

(4) Any of the other players may change places with the goalkeeper, provided that the Referee is informed before the change is made, and provided also, that the change is made during a stoppage in the game.

(5) When a goalkeeper or any other player is to be replaced by a substitute, the following conditions shall be observed.

(a) the Referee shall be informed of the proposed substitution, before it is made.

(b) the substitute shall not enter the field of play until the player he is replacing has left, and then only after having received a signal from the Referee.

(c) he shall enter the field during a stoppage in the game, and at the half-way line.

(d) a player who has been replaced shall not take any further part in the game.

(e) a substitute shall be subject to the authority and jurisdiction of the Referee whether called upon to play or not.

(f) the substitution is completed when the substitute enters the field of play, from which moment he becomes a player and the player whom he is replacing ceases to be a player.
Punishment:

(a) Play shall not be stopped for an infringement of paragraph 4. The players concerned shall be cautioned immediately the ball goes out of play.

(b) If a substitute enters the field of play without the authority of the Referee, play shall be stopped. The substitute shall be cautioned or sent off according to the circumstances. The game shall be restarted by the Referee dropping the ball at the place where it was when play was stopped, unless it was within the goal-area at that time, in which case it shall be dropped on the part of the goal-area line which runs parallel to the goal-line, at the point nearest to where the ball was when play was stopped.

(c) For any other infringement of the Law, the player concerned shall be cautioned, and if the game is stopped by the Referee, to administer the caution, it shall be restarted by an indirect free-kick, to be taken by a player of the opposing team from the place where the ball was when play was stopped. If the free-kick is awarded to a team within its own goal-area, it may be taken from any point within that half of the goal-area in which the ball was when play was stopped.

(d) If a competition's rules require the names of substitutes to be given to the Referee prior to the commencement of the match, then failure to do so will mean no substitutes can be permitted.

(1) The minimum number of players in a team is left to the discretion of National Associations.

(2) The Board is of the opinion that a match should not be considered valid if there are fewer than seven players in either of the teams.

(3) A player who has been ordered off before play begins may be replaced only by one of the named substitutes. The kick-off must not be delayed to allow the substitute to join his team.

A player who has been ordered off after play has started may not be replaced.

A named substitute who has been ordered off, either before or after play has started, may not be replaced (this decision relates only to players who are ordered off under Law XII. It does not apply to players who have infringed Law IV).

(4) A player who has been replaced shall not take any further part in the game.

(5) For any offence committed on the field of play a substitute shall be subject to the same punishment as any other player whether called upon or not.

LAW IV – PLAYERS' EQUIPMENT

(1) (a) The basic compulsory equipment of a player shall consist of a jersey or shirt, shorts, stockings, shinguards and footwear.

(b) A player shall not wear anything which is dangerous to another player.

(2) Shinguards, which must be covered entirely by the stocking, shall be made of a suitable material (rubber, plastic, polyurethane or similar substance) and shall afford a reasonable degree of protection.

(3) Footwear (boots or shoes) must conform to the following standard.

(a) Bars shall be made of leather or rubber and shall be transverse and flat, not less than half an inch in width and shall extend the total width of the sole and be rounded at the corners.

(b) Studs which are independently mounted on the sole and are replaceable shall be made of leather, rubber, aluminium, plastic or similar material and shall be solid. With the exception of that part of the stud forming the base, which shall not protrude from the sole more than one quarter of an inch, studs shall be round in plan and not less than half an inch in diameter. Where studs are tapered, the minimum diameter of any section of the stud must not be less than half an inch. Where metal seating for the screw type is used, this seating must be embedded in the sole of the footwear and any attachment screw shall be part of the stud. Other than the metal seating for the screw type of stud, no metal plates even though covered with leather or rubber shall be worn, neither studs which are threaded to allow them to be screwed on to a base screw that is fixed by nails or otherwise to the soles of footwear, nor studs which, apart from the base, have any form of protruding edge rim or relief marking or ornament should be allowed.

(c) Studs which are moulded as an integral part of the sole and are not replaceable shall be made of rubber, plastic, polyurethene or similar soft materials. Provided that there are no fewer than ten studs on the sole, they shall have a minimum diameter of three-eighths of an inch (10mm). Additional supporting material to stabilise studs of soft materials, and ridges which shall not protrude more than 5mm from the sole and moulded to strengthen it, shall be permitted provided that they are in no way dangerous to other players. In all other respects they shall conform to the general requirements of this Law.

(d) Combined bars and studs may be worn, provided the whole conforms to the general requirements of this Law. Neither bars not studs on the soles or heels shall project more than three-quarters of an inch. If nails are used they shall be driven in flush with the surface.

The goalkeeper shall wear colours which distinguish him from the other players and from the Referee.

Punishment: For any infringement of this Law, the player at fault shall be sent off the field of play to adjust his equipment and he shall not return without first reporting to the Referee, who shall satisfy himself that the player's equipment is in order; the player shall only re-enter the game at a moment when the ball has ceased to be in play.

(1) In International Matches, International Competitions, International Club Competitions and friendly matches between clubs of different National Associations, the Referee, prior to the start of the game, shall inspect the players' equipment and prevent any player whose equipment does not conform to the requirements of this Law from playing until such time as it does comply. The rules of any competition may include a similar provision.

(2) If the Referee finds that a player is wearing articles not permitted by the Laws and which may constitute a danger to other players, he shall order him to take them off. If he fails to carry out the Referee's instruction, the player shall not take part in the match.

(3) A player who has been prevented from taking part in the game or a player who has been sent off the field for infringing Law IV must report to the Referee during a stoppage of the game and may not enter or re-enter the field of play unless and until the Referee has satisfied himself that the player is no longer infringing Law IV.

(4) A player who has been prevented from taking part in a game or who has been sent off because of an infringement of Law IV, and who enters or re-enters the field of play to join or rejoin his team, in breach of the conditions of Law XII(j), shall be cautioned. If the Referee stops the

game to administer the caution, the game shall be restarted by an indirect free-kick, taken by a player of the opposing side, from the place where the ball was when the Referee stopped the game. If the free-kick is awarded to a side within its own goal-area, it may be taken from any point within that half of the goal-area in which the ball was when play was stopped.

LAW V – REFEREES

A Referee shall be appointed to officiate in each game. The authority and the exercise of the powers granted to him by the Laws of the Game commence as soon as he enters the field of play.

His power of penalising shall extend to offences committed when play has been temporarily suspended, or when the ball is out of play. His decision on points of fact connected with the play shall be final, so far as the result of the game is concerned. He shall:

(a) Enforce the Laws.

(b) Refrain from penalising in cases where he is satisified that, by doing so, he would be giving an advantage to the offending team.

(c) Keep a record of the game, act as time-keeper and allow the full or agreed time, adding thereto all time lost through accident or other cause.

(d) Have discretionary power to stop the game for any infringement of the Laws and to suspend or terminate the game whenever, by reason of the elements, interference by spectators, or other cause, he deems such stoppage necessary. In such a case he shall submit a detailed report to the competent authority, within the stipulated time, and in accordance with the provisions set up by the National Association under whose jurisdiction the match was played. Reports will be deemed to be made when received in the ordinary course of post.

(e) From the time he enters the field of play, caution any player guilty of misconduct or ungentlemanly behaviour and, if he persists, suspend him from further participation in the game. In such cases the Referee shall send the name of the offender to the competent authority, within the stipulated time, and in accordance with the provisions set up by the National Association under whose jurisdiction the match was played. Reports will be deemed to be made when received in the ordinary course of post.

(f) Allow no person other than the players and linesmen to enter the field of play without his permission.

(g) Stop the game if, in his opinion, a player has been seriously injured, have the player removed as soon as possible from the field of play, and immediately resume the game. If a player is slightly injured, the game shall not be stopped until the ball has ceased to be in play. A player who is able to go to the touch or goal-line for attention of any kind, shall not be treated on the field of play.

(h) Send off the field of play, any player who, in his opinion, is guilty of violent conduct, serious foul play, or the use of foul or abusive language.

(i) Signal for recommencement of the game after all stoppages.

(j) Decide that the ball provided for a match meets with the requirement of Law II.

Decisions of the International Board

(1) Referees in International Matches shall wear a blazer or blouse the colour of which is distinct from the colours worn by the contesting teams.

(2) Referees for International Matches will be selected from a neutral country unless the countries concerned agree to appoint their own officials.

(3) The Referee must be chosen from the official list of International Referees. This need not apply to Amateur and Youth International Matches.

(4) The Referee shall report to the appropriate authority misconduct or any misdemeanour on the part of spectators, officials, players, named substitutes or other persons which take place either on the field of play or in its vicinity at any time prior to, during, or after the match in question so that appropriate action can be taken by the authority concerned.

(5) Linesmen are assistants of the Referee. In no case shall the Referee consider the intervention of a Linesman if he himself has seen the incident and from his position on the field, is better able to judge. With this reserve, and the Linesman neutral, the Referee can consider the intervention and if the information of the Linesman applies to that phase of the game immediately before the scoring of a goal, the Referee may act thereon and cancel the goal.

(6) The Referee, however, can only reverse his first decision so long as the game has not been restarted.

(7) If the Referee has decided to apply the advantage clause and to let the game proceed, he cannot revoke his decision if the presumed advantage has not been realised, even though he has not, by any gesture, indicated his decision. This does not exempt the offending player from being dealt with by the Referee.

(8) The Laws of the Game are intended to provide that games should be played with as little interference as possible, and in this view it is the duty of Referees to penalise only deliberate breaches of the Law. Constant whistling for trifling and doubtful breaches produces bad feeling and loss of temper on the part of the players and spoils the pleasure of spectators.

(9) By para. (d) of Law V the Referee is empowered to terminate a match in the event of grave disorder, but he has no power or right to decide, in such event, that either team is disqualified and thereby the loser of the match. He must send a detailed report to the proper

authority who alone has power to deal further with the matter.

(10) If a player commits two infringements of a different nature at the same time, the Referee shall punish the more serious offence.

(11) It is the duty of the Referee to act upon the information of neutral Linesmen with regard to incidents that do not come under the personal notice of the Referee.

(12) The Referee shall not allow any person to enter the field until play has stopped, and only then, if he has given him a signal to do so, nor shall he allow coaching from the boundary lines.

LAW VI – LINESMEN

Two Linesmen shall be appointed, whose duty (subject to the decision of the Referee) shall be to indicate when the ball is out of play, which side is entitled to the corner-kick, goal-kick or throw-in, and when a substitute is desired. They shall also assist the Referee to control the game in accordance with the Laws. In the event of undue interference or improper conduct by a Linesman, the Referee shall dispense with his services and arrange a substitute to be appointed. (The matter shall be reported by the Referee to the competent authority.) The Linesmen should be equipped with flags by the Club on whose ground the match is played.

Decisions of the International Board

(1) Linesmen, where neutral, shall draw the Referee's attention to any breach of the Laws of the Game of which they become aware if they consider that the Referee may not have seen it, but the Referee shall always be the judge of the decision to be taken.

(2) National Associations are advised to appoint official Referees of neutral nationality to act as Linesmen in International Matches.

(3) In International Matches, Linesmen's flags shall be of a vivid colour, bright reds and yellows. Such flags are recommended for use in all other matches.

(4) A Linesman may be subject to disciplinary action only upon a report of the Referee for unjustified interference or insufficient assistance.

LAW VII – DURATION OF THE GAME

The duration of the game shall be two equal periods of 45 minutes, unless otherwise mutually agreed upon, subject to the following: (a) Allowance shall be made in either period for all time lost through substitution, the transport from the field of injured players, time-wasting or other cause, the amount of which shall be a matter for the discretion of the Referee; (b) Time shall be extended to permit a penalty-kick being taken at or after the expiration of the normal period in either half.

At half-time the interval shall not exceed five minutes except by consent of the Referee.

Decisions of the International Board

---

(1) If a match has been stopped by the Referee, before the completion of the time specified in the rules, for any reason stated in Law V it must be replayed in full unless the rules of the competition concerned provide for the result of the match at the time of such stoppage to stand.

(2) Players have a right to an interval at half-time.

LAW VIII – THE START OF PLAY

(a) **At the beginning of the game,** choice of ends and the kick-off shall be decided by the toss of a coin. The team winning the toss shall have the option of choice of ends or the kick-off. The Referee having given a signal, the game shall be started by a player taking a place-kick (i.e. a kick at the ball while it is stationary on the ground in the centre of the field of play) into his opponents' half of the field of play. Every player shall be in his own half of the field and every player of the team opposing that of the kicker shall remain not less than 10 yards from the ball until it is kicked-off; it shall not be deemed in play until it has travelled the distance of its own circumference. The kicker shall not play the ball a second time until it has been touched or played by another player.

(b) **After a goal is scored,** the game shall be restarted in like manner by a player of the team losing the goal.

(c) **After half-time:** when restarting after half-time, ends shall be changed and the kick-off shall be taken by a player of the opposite team to that of the player who started the game.

Punishment: For any infringement of this Law, the kick-off shall be retaken, except in the case of the kicker playing the ball again before it has been touched or played by another player; for this offence, an indirect free-kick shall be taken by a player of the opposing team from the place where the infringement occurred, unless the offence is committed by a player in his opponents' goal-area, in which case the free-kick shall be taken from a point anywhere within that half of the goal-area in which the offence occurred. A goal shall not be scored direct from a kick-off.

(d) **After any other temporary suspension:** when restarting the game after a temporary suspension of play from any cause not mentioned elsewhere in these Laws, provided that immediately prior to the suspension the ball has not passed over the touch or goal-lines, the Referee shall drop the ball at the place where it was when play was suspended, unless it was within the goal area at that time, in which case it shall be dropped on that part of the goal area line which runs parallel to the goal-line, at the point nearest to where the ball was when play was stopped. It shall be deemed in play when it has touched the ground; if, however, it goes over the touch or goal-lines after it has been dropped by the Referee, but before it is touched by a player, the Referee shall again drop it. A player shall not play the ball until it has touched the ground. If this section of the Law is not complied with the Referee shall again drop the ball.

(1) If, when the Referee drops the ball, a player infringes any of the Laws before the ball has touched the ground, the player concerned shall be cautioned or sent off the field according to the seriousness of the offence, but a free-kick cannot be awarded to the opposing team because the ball was not in play at the time of the offence. The ball shall therefore be again dropped by the Referee.

(2) Kicking-off by persons other than the players competing in a match is prohibited.

LAW IX – BALL IN AND OUT OF PLAY

The ball is out of play:

(a) When it has wholly crossed the goal-line or touch-line, whether on the ground or in the air.

(b) When the game has been stopped by the Referee.

The ball is in play at all other times from the start of the match to the finish including:

(a) If it rebounds from a goal-post, cross-bar or corner-flag post into the field of play.

(b) If it rebounds off either the Referee or Linesmen when they are in the field of play.

(c) In the event of a supposed infringement of the Laws, until a decision is given.

Decisions of the International Board

(1) The lines belong to the area of which they are the boundaries. In consequence, the touch-lines and the goal-lines belong to the field of play.

LAW X – METHOD OF SCORING

Except as otherwise provided by these Laws, a goal is scored when the whole of the ball has passed over the goal-line, between the goal-posts and under the cross-bar, provided it has not been thrown, carried or intentionally propelled by hand or arm, by a player of the attacking side, except in the case of a goalkeeper, who is within his own penalty-area.

The team scoring the greater number of goals during a game shall be the winner; if no goals, or an equal number of goals are scored, the game shall be termed a 'draw'.

Decisions of the International Board

(1) Law X defines the only method according to which a match is won or drawn; no variation whatsoever can be authorised.

(2) A goal cannot in any case be allowed if the ball has been prevented by some outside agent from passing over the goal-line. If this happens in the normal course of play, other than at the taking of a penalty-kick, the game must be stopped and restarted where the ball came into contact with the interference.

(3) If, when the ball is going into goal, a spectator enters the field before it passes wholly over the goal-line, and tries to prevent a score, a goal shall be allowed if the ball goes into goal unless the spectator has made contact with the ball or has interfered with play, in which case the Referee shall stop the game and restart it by dropping the ball at the place where the contact or interference occurred.

LAW XI – OFF-SIDE

(1) A player is in an off-side position if he is nearer to his opponents' goal-line than the ball, unless:

(a) he is in his own half of the field of play, or

(b) he is not nearer to his opponents' goal-line than at least two of his opponents.

(2) A player shall only be declared off-side and penalised for being in an off-side position if, at the moment the ball touches, or is played by, one of his team, he is, in the opinion of the Referee

(a) interfering with play or with an opponent, or

(b) seeking to gain an advantage by being in that position.

(3) A player shall not be declared off-side by the referee

(a) merely because of his being in an off-side position, or

(b) if he receives the ball, direct from a goal-kick, a corner-kick or a throw-in.

(4) If a player is declared off-side, the Referee shall award an indirect free-kick, which shall be taken by a player of the opposing team from the place where the infringement occurred, unless the offence is committed by a player in his opponents' goal-area, in which case, the free-kick shall be taken from a point anywhere within that half of the goal-area in which the offence occurred.

Decisions of the International Board

(1) Off-side shall not be judged at the moment the player in question receives the ball, but at the moment when the ball is passed to him by one of his own side. A player who is not in an off-side position when one of his colleagues passes the ball to him or takes a free-kick, does not therefore become off-side if he goes forward during the flight of the ball.

(2) A player who is level with the second last opponent or with the last two opponents is not in an off-side position.

LAW XII – FOULS AND MISCONDUCT

A player who intentionally commits any of the following nine offences:

(a) Kicks or attempts to kick an opponent;

(b) Trips an opponent, i.e. throwing or

attempting to throw him by the use of the legs or by stooping in front of or behind him;

(c) Jumps at an opponent;

(d) Charges an opponent in a violent or dangerous manner;

(e) Charges an opponent from behind unless the latter be obstructing;

(f) Strikes or attempts to strike an opponent;

(g) Holds an opponent;

(h) Pushes an opponent;

(i) Handles the ball, i.e. carries, strikes or propels the ball with his hand or arm. (This does not apply to the goalkeeper within his own penalty-area);

shall be penalised by the award of a **direct free-kick** to be taken by the opposing side from the place where the offence occurred, unless the offence is committed by a player in his opponents' goal-area in which case, the free-kick shall be taken from a point anywhere within that half of the goal-area in which the offence occurred.

Should a player of the defending side intentionally commit one of the above nine offences within the penalty-area he shall be penalised by a **penalty-kick.**

A penalty-kick can be awarded irrespective of the position of the ball, if in play, at the time an offence within the penalty-area is committed.

A player committing any of the five following offences:

(1) Playing in a manner considered by the Referee to be dangerous, e.g. attempting to kick the ball while held by the goalkeeper.

(2) Charging fairly, i.e. with the shoulder, when the ball is not within playing distance of the players concerned and they are definitely not trying to play it.

(3) When not playing the ball, intentionally obstructing an opponent, i.e. running between the opponent and the ball, or interposing the body so as to form an obstacle to an opponent.

(4) Charging the goalkeeper except when he

(a) is holding the ball;

(b) is obstructing an opponent;

(c) has passed outside the goal-area.

(5) When playing as goalkeeper and within his own penalty-area

(a) from the moment he takes control of the ball with his hands, he takes more than four steps in any direction whilst holding, bouncing or throwing the ball in the air and catching it again, without releasing it into play, or, having released the ball into play before, during or after the four steps, he touches it again with his hands, before it has been touched or played by another player of the same team outside of the penalty-area or by a player of the opposing team either inside or outside of the penalty-area, or

(b) indulges in tactics which, in the opinion of the Referee, are designed merely to hold up the game and thus waste time and so give an unfair advantage to his own team—shall be penalised by the award of an **indirect free-kick** to be taken by the opposing side from the place where the

infringement occurred, unless the offence is committed by a player in his opponents' goal-area, in which case the free-kick shall be taken from a point anywhere within that half of the goal-area in which the offence occurred.

A player shall be **cautioned** if:

(j) he enters or re-enters the field of play to join or rejoin his team after the game has commenced, or leaves the field of play during the progress of the game (except through accident) without, in either case, first having received a signal from the Referee showing him that he may do so. If the Referee stops the game to administer the caution the game shall be restarted by an indirect free-kick taken by a player of the opposing team from the place where the ball was when the Referee stopped the game. If the free-kick is awarded to a side within its own goal-area it may be taken from any point within the half of the goal-area in which the ball was when play was stopped. If, however, the offending player has committed a more serious offence he shall be penalised according to that section of the law he infringed.

(k) he persistently infringes the Laws of the Game;

(l) he shows by word or action, dissent from any decision given by the Referee;

(m) he is guilty of ungentlemanly conduct.

For any of these last three offences, in addition to the caution, an **indirect free-kick** shall also be awarded to the opposing side from the place where the offence occurred unless a more serious infringement of the Laws of the Game was committed. If the offence is committed by a player in his opponents' goal-area, a free-kick shall be taken from a point anywhere within that half of the goal-area in which the offence occurred.

A player shall be **sent off** the field of play, if:

(n) in the opinion of the Referee he is guilty of violent conduct or serious foul play;

(o) he uses foul or abusive language;

(p) he persists in misconduct after having received a caution.

If play be stopped by reason of a player being ordered from the field for an offence without a separate breach of the Law having been committed, the game shall be resumed by an **indirect free-kick** awarded to the opposing side from the place where the infringement occurred, unless the offence is committed by a player in his opponents' goal-area, in which case the free-kick shall be taken from a point anywhere within that half of the goal-area in which the offence occurred.

Decisions of the International Board

If, in the opinion of the referee, a player who is moving towards his opponents' goal with an obvious opportunity to score a goal is intentionally and physically impeded by unlawful means, i.e. an offence punishable by a free-kick (or a penalty-kick), thus denying the attacking

998

player's team the aforesaid goal-scoring opportunity, the offending player shall be sent off the field of play for serious foul play in accordance with Law XII (n).

(1) If the goalkeeper either intentionally strikes an opponent by throwing the ball vigorously at him or pushes him with the ball while holding it, the Referee shall award a penalty-kick, if the offence took place within the penalty-area.

(2) If a player deliberately turns his back to an opponent when he is about to be tackled, he may be charged but not in a dangerous manner.

(3) In case of body-contact in the goal-area between an attacking player and the opposing goalkeeper not in possession of the ball, the Referee, as sole judge of intention, shall stop the game if, in his opinion, the action of the attacking player was intentional, and award an indirect free-kick.

(4) If a player leans on the shoulders of another player of his own team in order to head the ball, the Referee shall stop the game, caution the player for ungentlemanly conduct and award an indirect free-kick to the opposing side.

(5) A player's obligation when joining or rejoining his team after the start of the match to 'report to the Referee' must be interpreted as meaning 'to draw the attention of the Referee from the touch-line'. The signal from the Referee shall be made by a definite gesture which makes the player understand that he may come into the field of play; it is not necessary for the Referee to wait until the game is stopped (this does not apply in respect of an infringement of Law IV), but the Referee is the sole judge of the moment in which he gives his signal of acknowledgement.

(6) The letter and spirit of Law XII do not oblige the Referee to stop a game to administer a caution. He may, if he chooses, apply the advantage. If he does apply the advantage, he shall caution the player when play stops.

(7) If a player covers up the ball without touching it in an endeavour not to have it played by an opponent, he obstructs but does not infringe Law XII para. 3 because he is already in possession of the ball and covers it for tactical reasons whilst the ball remains within playing distance. In fact, he is actually playing the ball and does not commit an infringement; in this case, the player may be charged because he is in fact playing the ball.

(8) If a player intentionally stretches his arms to obstruct an opponent and steps from one side to the other moving his arms up and down to delay his opponent, forcing him to change course, but does not make 'bodily contact' the Referee shall caution the player for ungentlemanly conduct and award an indirect free-kick.

(9) If a player intentionally obstructs the opposing goalkeeper, in an attempt to prevent him from putting the ball into play in accordance with Law XII, 5(a), the Referee shall award an indirect free-kick.

(10) If, after a Referee has awarded a free-kick a player protests violently by using abusive or foul language and is sent off the field, the free-kick should not be taken until the player has left the field.

(11) Any player, whether he is within or outside the field of play, whose conduct is ungentlemanly or violent, whether or not it is directed towards an opponent, a colleague, the Referee, a Linesman or other person, or who uses foul or abusive language, is guilty of an offence, and shall be dealt with according to the nature of the offence committed.

(12) If, in the opinion of the Referee a goalkeeper intentionally lies on the ball longer than is necessary, he shall be penalised for ungentlemanly conduct and

(a) be cautioned and an indirect free-kick awarded to the opposing team;

(b) in case of repetition of the offence, be sent off the field.

(13) The offence of spitting at opponents, officials or other persons, or similar unseemly behaviour shall be considered as violent conduct within the meaning of section (n) of Law XII.

(14) If, when a Referee is about to caution a player, and before he has done so, the player commits another offence which merits a caution, the player shall be sent off the field of play.

LAW XIII – FREE-KICK

Free-kicks shall be classified under two headings: 'Direct' (from which a goal can be scored direct against the offending side), and 'Indirect' (from which a goal cannot be scored unless the ball has been played or touched by a player other than the kicker before passing through the goal).

When a player is taking a direct or an indirect free-kick inside his own penalty-area, all of the opposing players shall be at least 10 yards (9.15m) from the ball and shall remain outside the penalty area until the ball has been kicked out of the area. The ball shall be in play immediately it has travelled the distance of its own circumference and is beyond the penalty-area. The goalkeeper shall not receive the ball into his hands, in order that he may thereafter kick it into play. If the ball is not kicked direct into play, beyond the penalty-area, the kick shall be retaken.

When a player is taking a direct or an indirect free-kick outside his own penalty-area, all of the opposing players shall be at least ten yards from the ball, until it is in play, unless they are standing on their own goal-line, between the goal-posts. The ball shall be in play when it has travelled the distance of its own circumference.

If a player of the opposing side encroaches into the penalty-area, or within ten yards of the ball, as the case may be, before a free-kick is taken, the Referee shall delay the taking of the kick, until the Law is complied with.

The ball must be stationary when a free-kick is taken, and the kicker shall not play the ball a second time, until it has been touched or played by another player.

Notwithstanding any other reference in these Laws to the point from which a free-kick is to be taken:

1. Any free-kick awarded to the defending team, within its own goal-area, may be taken from any point within that half of the goal-area in which the free-kick has been awarded.

2. Any indirect free-kick awarded to the attacking team within its opponents' goal-area shall be taken from that part of the goal-area line which runs parallel to the goal-line, at the point nearest to where the offence was committed.

Punishment: If the kicker, after taking the free-kick, plays the ball a second time before it has been touched or played by another player an indirect free-kick shall be taken by a player of the opposing team from the spot where the infringement occurred, unless the offence is committed by a player in his opponents' goal-area, in which case the free-kick shall be taken from a point anywhere within that half of the goal-area in which the offence occurred.

course of play, or when time has been extended at half-time or full-time to allow a penalty-kick to be taken or retaken, a goal shall not be nullified if, before passing between the posts and under the cross-bar, the ball touches either or both of the goal-posts or the cross-bar, or the goal-keeper, or any combination of these agencies, providing that no other infringement has occurred.

Punishment: For any infringement of this Law:

(a) by the defending team, the kick shall be retaken if a goal has not resulted.

(b) by the attacking team other than by the player taking the kick, if a goal is scored it shall be disallowed and the kick retaken.

(c) by the player taking the penalty-kick, committed after the ball is in play, a player of the opposing team shall take an indirect free-kick from the spot where the infringement occurred. If, in the case of paragraph (c), the offence is committed by the player in his opponents' goal-area, the free-kick shall be taken from a point anywhere within that half of the goal-area in which the offence occurred.

Decisions of the International Board

(1) In order to distinguish between a direct and indirect free-kick, the Referee, when he awards an indirect free-kick, shall indicate accordingly by raising an arm above his head. He shall keep his arm in that position until the kick has been taken and retain the signal until the ball has been played or touched by another player or goes out of play.

(2) Players who do not retire to the proper distance when a free-kick is taken must be cautioned and on any repetition be ordered off. It is particularly requested of Referees that attempts to delay the taking of a free-kick by encroaching should be treated as serious misconduct.

(3) If, when a free-kick is being taken, any of the players dance about or gesticulate in a way calculated to distract their opponents, it shall be deemed ungentlemanly conduct for which the offender(s) shall be cautioned.

LAW XIV – PENALTY-KICK

A penalty-kick shall be taken from the penalty-mark and, when it is being taken, all players with the exception of the player taking the kick, properly identified, and the opposing goalkeeper, shall be within the field of play but outside the penalty-area, and at least 10 yards from the penalty-mark. The opposing goalkeeper must stand (without moving his feet) on his own goal-line, between the goal-posts, until the ball is kicked. The player taking the kick must kick the ball forward; he shall not play the ball a second time until it has been touched or played by another player. The ball shall be deemed in play directly it is kicked, i.e. when it has travelled the distance of its circumference. A goal may be scored directly from a penalty-kick. When a penalty-kick is being taken during the normal

Decisions of the International Board

(1) When the Referee has awarded a penalty-kick, he shall not signal for it to be taken, until the players have taken up position in accordance with the Law.

(2) (a) If, after the kick has been taken, the ball is stopped in its course towards goal, by an outside agent, the kick shall be retaken.

(b) If, after the kick has been taken, the ball rebounds into play, from the goalkeeper, the cross-bar or a goal-post, and is then stopped in its course by an outside agent, the Referee shall stop play and restart it by dropping the ball at the place where it came into contact with the outside agent.

(3) (a) If, after having given the signal for a penalty-kick to be taken, the Referee sees that the goalkeeper is not in his right place on the goal-line, he shall, nevertheless, allow the kick to proceed. It shall be retaken, if a goal is not scored.

(b) If, after the Referee has given the signal for a penalty-kick to be taken, and before the ball has been kicked, the goalkeeper moves his feet, the Referee shall, nevertheless, allow the kick to proceed. It shall be retaken, if a goal is not scored.

(c) If, after the Referee has given the signal for a penalty-kick to be taken, and before the ball is in play, a player of the defending team encroaches into the penalty-area, or within 10 yards of the penalty-mark, the Referee shall, nevertheless, allow the kick to proceed. It shall be retaken, if a goal is not scored.

The player concerned shall be cautioned.

(4) (a) If, when a penalty-kick is being taken, the player taking the kick is guilty of ungentlemanly conduct, the kick, if already taken, shall be retaken, if a goal is scored.

The player concerned shall be cautioned.

(b) If, after the Referee has given the signal for a penalty-kick to be taken, and before the ball is in play, a colleague of the player taking the kick encroaches into the penalty-area or within ten yards of the penalty-mark, the Referee shall, nevertheless, allow the kick to proceed. If a goal is scored, it shall be disallowed, and the kick retaken.

The player concerned shall be cautioned.

(c) If, in the circumstances described in the foregoing paragraph, the ball rebounds into play from the goalkeeper, the cross-bar or a goal-post and a goal has not been scored, the Referee shall stop the game, caution the player and award an indirect free-kick to the opposing team from the place where the infringement occurred, subject to the over-riding conditions imposed in Law XIII.

(5) (a) If, after the referee has given the signal for a penalty-kick to be taken, and before the ball is in play, the goalkeeper moves from his position on the goal-line, or moves his feet, and a colleague of the kicker encroaches into the penalty-area or within 10 yards of the penalty mark, the kick, if taken, shall be retaken.

The colleague of the kicker shall be cautioned.

(b) If, after the Referee has given the signal for a penalty-kick to be taken, and before the ball is in play, a player of each team encroaches into the penalty area, or within 10 yards of the penalty-mark, the kick if taken, shall be retaken.

The players concerned shall be cautioned.

(6) When a match is extended, at half-time or full-time, to allow a penalty-kick to be taken or retaken, the extension shall last until the moment that the penalty-kick has been completed, i.e. until the Referee has decided whether or not a goal is scored, and the game shall terminate immediately the Referee has made his decision. After the player taking the penalty-kick has put the ball into play, no player other than the defending goalkeeper may play or touch the ball before the kick is completed.

A goal is scored when the ball passes wholly over the goal-line.

(a) direct from the penalty-kick.

(b) having rebounded from either goal-post or the cross-bar, or

(c) having touched or been played by the goalkeeper.

The game shall terminate immediately the Referee has made his decision.

(7) When a penalty-kick is being taken in extended time:

(a) the provisions of all of the foregoing paragraphs, except paragraphs (2)(b) and (4)(c) shall apply in the usual way, and

(b) in the circumstances described in paragraphs (2)(b) and (4)(c) the game shall terminate immediately the ball rebounds from the goalkeeper, the cross-bar or the goal-post.

LAW XV – THROW-IN

When the whole of the ball passes over a touch-line, either on the ground or in the air, it shall be thrown in from the point where it crossed the line, in any direction, by a player of the team opposite to that of the player who last touched it. The thrower at the moment of delivering the ball must face the field of play and part of each foot shall be either on the touch-line or on the ground outside the touch-line. The thrower shall use both hands and shall deliver the ball from behind and over his head. The ball shall be in play immediately it enters the field of play, but the thrower shall not again play the ball until it has been touched or played by another player. A goal shall not be scored direct from a throw-in.

Punishment:

(a) If the ball is improperly thrown in, the throw-in shall be taken by a player of the opposing team.

(b) If the thrower plays the ball a second time before it has been touched or played by another player, an indirect free-kick shall be taken by a player of the opposing team from the place where the infringement occurred, unless the offence is committed by a player in his opponents' goal-area, in which case the free-kick shall be taken from a point anywhere within that half of the goal-area in which the offence occurred.

Decisions of the International Board

(1) If a player taking a throw-in, plays the ball a second time by handling it within the field of play before it has been touched or played by another player, the Referee shall award a direct free-kick.

(2) A player taking a throw-in must face the field of play with some part of his body.

(3) If, when a throw-in is being taken, any of the opposing players dance about or gesticulate in a way calculated to distract or impede the thrower, it shall be deemed ungentlemanly conduct for which the offender(s) shall be cautioned.

(4) A throw-in taken from any position other than the point where the ball passed over the touch-line shall be considered to have been improperly thrown.

LAW XVI – GOAL-KICK

When the whole of the ball passes over the goal-line excluding that portion between the goal-posts, either in the air or on the ground, having last been played by one of the attacking team, it shall be kicked direct into play beyond the penalty-area from a point within that half of the goal-area nearest to where it crossed the line, by a player of the defending team. A goalkeeper shall not receive the ball into his hands from a goal-kick in order that he may thereafter kick it into play. If the ball is not kicked beyond the penalty-area, i.e. direct into play, the kick shall be retaken. The kicker shall not play the ball a second time until it has touched—or been played by—another player. A goal shall not be scored direct from such a kick. Players of the team opposing that of the player taking the goal-kick shall remain outside the penalty-area whilst the kick is being taken.

Punishment: If a player taking a goal-kick plays the ball a second time after it has passed beyond the penalty-area, but before it has touched or been played by another player, an indirect free-kick shall be awarded to the opposing team, to be taken from the place where the infringement occurred, unless the offence is committed by a player in his opponents' goal-area, in which case the free-kick shall be taken from a point anywhere within that half of the goal-area in which the offence occurred.

Decisions of the International Board

(1) When a goal-kick has been taken and the player who has kicked the ball touches it again before it has left the penalty-area, the kick has not been taken in accordance with the Laws and must be retaken.

LAW XVII – CORNER-KICK

When the whole of the ball passes over the goal-line, excluding that portion between the goal-posts, either in the air or on the ground, having last been played by one of the defending team, a member of the attacking team shall take a corner-kick, i.e. the whole of the ball shall be placed within the quarter circle at the nearest corner-flag post, which must not be moved, and it shall be kicked from that position. A goal may be scored direct from such a kick. Players of the team opposing that of the player taking the corner-kick shall not approach within 10 yards of the ball until it is in play, i.e. it has travelled the distance of its own circumference, nor shall the kicker play the ball a second time until it has been touched or played by another player.

Punishment:

(a) If the player who takes the kick plays the ball a second time before it has been touched or played by another player, the Referee shall award an indirect free-kick to the opposing team, to be taken from the place where the infringement occurred, unless the offence is committed by a player in his opponents' goal-area, in which case the free-kick shall be taken from a point anywhere within that half of the goal-area in which the offence occurred.

(b) For any other infringement the kick shall be retaken.

1991 AMENDMENTS

LAW XII – FOULS AND MISCONDUCT

Three new decisions:

Decision No (15): If, in the opinion of the referee, a player who is moving toward his opponents' goal with an obvious opportunity to score a goal is intentionally impeded by an opponent, through unlawful means, i.e. an offence punishable by a free kick (or a penalty kick), thus denying the attacking player's team the aforesaid goal-scoring opportunity, the offending player shall be sent off the field of play for serious foul play in accordance with Law XII (n).

Decision No (16): If, in the opinion of the referee, a player, other than the goalkeeper within his own penalty area, denies his opponents a goal, or an obvious goal-scoring opportunity, by intentionally handling the ball, he shall be sent off the field of play for serious foul play in accordance with Law XII (n).

Decision No (17): The International FA Board is of the opinion that a goalkeeper, in the circumstances described in Law XII 5(a), will be considered to be in control of the ball when he takes possession of the ball by touching it with any part of his hands or arms. Possession of the ball would include the goalkeeper intentionally playing the ball, but would not include circumstances where, in the opinion of the referee, the ball rebounds accidentally from the goalkeeper, for example after he has made a save.

1992 AMENDMENTS

LAW XII – FOULS AND MISCONDUCT

On any occasion when a player deliberately kicks the ball to his own goalkeeper, the goalkeeper is not permitted to touch it with his hands. If, however, the goalkeeper does touch the ball with his hands, he shall be penalised by the award of an indirect free-kick, to be taken by the opposing team from the place where the infringement occurred, subject to the over-riding conditions of Law XIII.

LAW XIII – FREE-KICK

Notwithstanding any other reference in these Laws to the point from which a free-kick is to be taken:

1. Any free-kick awarded to the defending team, within its own goal-area, may be taken from any point within the goal-area.

OBITUARIES

Adams, Ted (b. 30.11.06; d. 28.11.91). Born in the shadow of Anfield this goalkeeper came out of retirement to sign for Burnley and make more than 100 League appearances for them. He was on the books of Liverpool for a time and also played for Barrow, Wrexham and Southport. During the Second World War he guested for New Brighton, Chester and Wrexham.

Alsop, Gilbert (b. Frampton Cotterill, nr. Bristol, September 1908; d. April 1992). Best remembered for his goalscoring feats with Walsall in the 1930s, this powerful centre-forward netted 159 League and Cup goals in two spells with the Saddlers—his best season being 1934–35 when he had 44. Began with Bath City in 1927 and also appeared with Coventry City and West Bromwich Albion before retiring in 1949 and spending more than 20 years on Walsall's ground staff.

Badham, Jack (b. Birmingham 31.1.19; d. January 1992). Joined Birmingham City as an amateur in 1934 but with the war intervening did not turn professional until 1946, making his League debut two years later. Originally a wing-half he made his name as a right-back, but appeared in many other positions. Played in 175 League games before becoming manager of Stourbridge in 1956.

Bastin, Cliff (b. Exeter 14.3.12; d. Exeter 4.12.91). One of the all-time greats, Bastin won every honour open to him before he was 20. Noted for his coolness under pressure and his lethal shot he created a First Division record in 1932–33 by scoring 33 goals from the outside-left position. No wonder his total of 150 League goals is still an Arsenal record. Made League debut with Exeter City at the age of 15 and cost Arsenal £2000 in 1929. Won five League Championship and two FA Cup winners' medals during nearly 18 years with the Gunners. Capped 21 times.

Cliff Bastin   Jack Kelsey

Bigg, Bob (?; d. August 1991). Raiding Crystal Palace outside-left 1934–39. The only Palace winger to notch a hat-trick on the first day of a season. Scored 41 goals.

Compton, Terry (b. Bristol 28.11.31; d. Bristol 6.10.91). A centre-half who had 10 years with Bristol City 1948–58 although the consistent good form of such players as Jack White and Ernie Peacock restricted Compton's League appearances to 45. His best season was 1956–57 when his career was coming to an end.

Combe, Bobby (b. Edinburgh 29.1.24; d. Cyprus 19.11.91). Among the stars of that most successful Hibernian side of the early post-war years, this inside-forward helped them win the League Championship in 1948, 1951 and 1952. Capped as a schoolboy he gained three full caps in 1948. After retiring he was Hibs' assistant trainer and then Dumbarton manager for short spells.

Crapnell, Jimmy (b. Paisley 4.6.03; d. Paisley 24.12.91). One of the smallest full-backs to play for Scotland between the wars, he gained nine caps while with Airdrieonians before being transferred to Motherwell in 1933. After the war he managed Alloa Athletic and St Johnstone.

Davies, Alan (b. Manchester 5.12.61; d. Horton, nr. Swansea 4.2.92). Apprenticed to Manchester United, this midfield player made his League debut with them in May 1982. Gained six Welsh U-21 caps and 11 full caps before his tragic death—found dead in his fume-filled car. Had spells with Newcastle United, Swansea City and Bradford City, as well as on loan to Charlton Athletic and Carlisle United.

Elvy, Reg (b. Leeds 25.11.20; d. Northampton July 1991). Although he had previously made a number of League appearances with Halifax Town and Bolton Wanderers, this lanky goalkeeper really made his name with Blackburn Rovers after he had passed his 31st birthday. Rovers signed him in an injury emergency and he made 192 League appearances for them including 152 without a break. Finished his career at Northampton Town whom he joined in 1956.

Fagan, Willie (b. Musselburgh 20.2.17; d. Wellingborough 29.2.92). Made debut with Glasgow Celtic in 1934–35 and joined Preston 1936. A year later he moved to Liverpool and became an established favourite with that club at centre-forward or inside-left. Was on the losing side in two FA Cup Finals—with Preston 1937 and Liverpool 1950. During the war he played for Scotland and in 1947 he helped Liverpool win the League championship.

Fenton, Ted (b. Forest Gate 1914; d. 12.7.92). First signed for West Ham at the age of 14 and was allowed to develop as a centre-half with Colchester before his League debut as an inside-forward with the Hammers in 1932. Later switched to right-half and was a first team regular until moving to Colchester as player-manager after the war. Returned to Upton Park first as assistant maager, then manager from 1950–61. Also manager of Southend United 1961–65.

Ferrier, Ron (b. Cleethorpes 26.4.14; d. Cleethorpes 11.10.91). After two years with Grimsby Town, he made his League debut with Manchester United in September 1935 as an inside-forward. Once scored seven goals in a game for United's reserves. Oldham Athletic converted him into a centre-forward soon after paying a four-figure fee for him in March 1938 and he became their top scorer. Ended playing career at Lincoln in 1948.

Fogg, William (b. Bangor 1903; d. Birkenhead October 1991). Began as a right-winger with Bangor and had two seasons with Tranmere Rovers 1924–26 before returning to his home-town club. Huddersfield Town brought him back to the Football League in 1928 and he subsequently served Clapton Orient and New Brighton, making a total of 309 League appearances to 1938.

Gallagher, Patsy (b. Bridge of Weir, Renfrewshire 21.8.09; d. Scotland 4.1.92). A typically clever Scottish ball-player he had over 10 seasons with Sunderland 1927–38 before his £5000 transfer to Stoke where injury slowed him down. Was inside-left in the Sunderland side that won the League Championship in 1936 and the FA Cup a year later. One Scottish cap.

Gibson, Colin (b. Normanby 16.9.23; d. Stourbridge 27.3.92). Joined Cardiff City in 1942 and was the only English-born player to appear regularly in the side in their Third Division (South) championship-winning side in 1946–47. A winger, he moved to Newcastle United 1948, Aston Villa 1949, and Lincoln City 1956. Totalled 288 peace-time Football League appearances.

Girling, Howard (b. Birmingham 24.5.22; d. January 1992). Recovered from war wound to play for Crystal Palace as an outside-left 1942–47. Brentford obtained his transfer in February 1947 and he had just over four seasons with them before closing his League career with Bournemouth.

Grieves, Ken (b. Sydney, Australia 27.8.25; d. January 1992). An all-rounder who played cricket for New South Wales 1945–47, Rawtenstall 1947–48, and Lancashire 1949–64 (captain 1963–64) as well as goalkeeper for Bury 1947–49, Bolton Wanderers 1951–55, and Stockport County 1957–58.

Gunson, J. Gordon (b. Chester 1.7.04; d. Broughton, Clwyd, September 1991). League debut with Wrexham 1926 after being on Nelson's books. Snapped up by Sunderland in May 1929, he made 19 League appearances then transferred to Liverpool in March 1930. An ever-present winger in the Liverpool side of 1931–32, he lost his place to Alf Hanson late in the following season and was allowed to leave for Swindon before returning to Wrexham to round off his career in 1935–36. Mistakenly selected to play for Wales before he informed them of his correct place of birth.

Hall, Alex (b. West Calder, nr. Edinburgh 1908; d. Edinburgh 5.9.91). Another member of Sunderland's League Championship and Cup-winning teams of 1936 and 1937 respectively, this full-back was signed from Dunfermline Athletic in 1929. Soon after the outbreak of World War Two he returned to Scotland and played for Hibernian.

Hayhurst, Bert (b. Birdwell, Yorkshire 17.9.05; d. Reading 8.11.91). A product of Frickley Colliery, he developed into an all-rounder, playing cricket for Warwickshire and soccer for Reading whom he joined in 1933 after a season with Luton Town. Became Reading's regular centre-half helping them to reach the FA Cup 5th round in 1935 and making a total of 220 League appearances before retiring during the war.

Hulme, Joe (b. Stafford 26.8.04; d. London 26.9.91). Another star of Arsenal's great trophy-winning side of the 1930s, Joe Hulme was one of the fastest wingers of his generation. Blackburn Rovers introduced him to League football after signing him from York City in 1924 and he was an immediate success. Arsenal obtained his transfer in 1925. In 13 years with the Gunners he scored 107 goals in 333 League games, winning four League Championship, and two FA Cup winners' medals. A surprise move to Huddersfield in January 1938 enabled him to make his fifth Wembley FA Cup Final appearance that year although on the losing side. Capped nine times for England he also played cricket for Middlesex 1929–39, hitting 1000 runs in a season three times.

Jackson, Peter (b. Stoke 23.1.37; d. September 1991). One of a pair of twin brothers (the other is David) who played alongside each other with Wrexham, Bradford City and Tranmere Rovers. Peter began as an amateur with Wrexham in 1954 and was best known as a wing-half with Bradford City where he made over 200 League and Cup appearances between 1954 and 1961 when he moved to Tranmere. In four of those seasons at Bradford City his father was manager.

Jordan, Clarrie (b. South Kirby 20.6.22; d. 24.2.92). Created a club record for Doncaster Rovers by scoring 42 League and Cup goals in 1946–47 when they won the championship of Division 3(N). Transferred to Sheffield Wednesday in February 1948 but his goalscoring talents were not exploited with that club before knee injuries began to affect his play. Had both legs amputated in the mid-1980s.

Kasher, Joseph (b. Crook 14.1.1894; d. January 1992). One of the oldest former Football League players when he died a few days before his 98th birthday. After playing for Willington and Crook Town and serving in World War I he joined Sunderland in 1919. Made 86 First Division appearances at centre-half then moved to Stoke City in 1922. Finished League career with Accrington Stanley 1925–27.

Kelsey, Jack (b. Llansamlet, nr. Swansea 19.11.29; d. 19.3.92). Spotted with junior side Winch Wen, he was signed by Arsenal in 1949 and was eventually acknowledged as one of the safest goalkeepers of his day, going on to make more appearances for the Gunners than any other goalkeeper (over 400 first-team games) before being forced to retire in 1962 because of a back injury. Made 41 appearances for Wales (a record for a goalkeeper) and also represented Great Britain v Rest of Europe in 1955.

Knowles, Cyril (b. Fitzwilliam, nr. Pontefract 17.3.44; d. 31.8.91). Was on both Manchester United's and Wolves' books as a junior before joining Middlesbrough and turning professional in 1962. A full-back who enjoyed attacking, he cost Spurs £45,000 when they secured his transfer in 1964. He played in over 400 League games during 12 years at White Hart Lane, helping his side win the FA Cup in 1967, the League Cup in 1971 and 1973, and the UEFA Cup in 1972, as well as appearing in four full internationals. He managed Darlington, Torquay United and Hartlepool until ill-health forced his retirement.

Leach, Mike (b. London 16.1.47; d. London 13.1.92). A product of Queen's Park Rangers' youth policy in the 1960s, Mike Leach developed from an apprentice and England Youth international to become a real favourite in the attack where he made over 300 League and Cup appearances. After being given a free transfer in March 1978 he played in the USA with Detroit Express and ended his League career with a brief spell at Cambridge United.

Luke, Bill (b. Acklington, Northumberland 1890; d. Northumberland January 1992). Joined Preston North End from Bedlington United in the summer of 1912 and helped them return to the First Division in his one season at Deepdale where he usually played on the right-wing. Joined Hartlepool United in 1913 but a leg injury during World War One ended his career. Was the League's oldest former professional when he died.

McDowall, Les (b. India 25.10.12; d. 18.8.91). Both played in and later managed Manchester City promotion-winning teams. Joined Sunderland from Scottish junior football in 1932 but was given few first-team games before moving to Manchester City in 1938. The war intervened but he was the regular centre-half in the side that won promotion to the First Division in 1947. Appointed Wrexham's player-manager for a brief spell in 1949, he returned to City as manager the following year, steering the club back to the First Division in 1951. Responsible for the development of the "Revie Plan", he remained in charge until 1963 when his resignation followed City's relegation and he became manager of Oldham for two years.

McKennan, Peter (b. Airdrie 16.7.18; d. Dundonald 28.9.91). Whether at inside or centre-forward, this powerfully built player was always difficult to stop. Had his first chance with Partick Thistle at the age of 16 and guested for Chelsea during the war before joining West Bromwich Albion in 1947. Subsequently helped Leicester City, Brentford, Middlesbrough and Oldham Athletic, starring in the "Latics' " side that won promotion to the Second Division in 1953. Was player-coach of Coleraine from 1954 until retiring in 1956. Represented the Scottish League in two games.

Moralee, Matthew (b. Mexborough 21.2.12; d. September 1991). An inside-left best known for his work with Grimsby Town 1931–36, but also appeared with Aston Villa, Leicester City and Shrewsbury Town before returning to his original club, Denaby United, in the early part of the war.

Mudie, Jackie (b. Dundee 10.4.30; d. Stoke-on-Trent 2.3.92). Considering his lack of height and

Joe Hulme

weight, this player was a remarkable success as an inside-forward and centre-forward with Blackpool whom he joined as a 16-year-old amateur in 1946. Made over 300 appearances, scoring 143 League goals, playing in two FA Cup Finals, then transferred to Stoke City in 1961. This skilful player helped the Potters win promotion to the First Division in 1962. Made a short move to Port Vale in November that year. Played in 17 consecutive Scottish internationals.

Oakes, John (b. Northwich 13.9.05; d. Perth, Australia 20.3.92). Signed by Charlton from Aldershot in March 1936 to help clinch promotion to the First Division and remained with them until 1947 when he finished his career with a season at Plymouth Argyle. Appeared in 1946 FA Cup Final at age of 40. Began professional career with Nottingham Forest in 1929 and later served Southend United before scoring 41 goals for Spennymoor in 1933–34. Aldershot turned him into a centre-half during nearly two seasons with them.

Robinson, Ernie (b. Shiney Row, nr. Sunderland 1908; d. Vancouver, Canada July 1991). A right-back who was with Tunbridge Wells, Notts County, Nelson, Barnsley, Sheffield United and Carlisle United between 1928 and the outbreak of the war. Coached in Holland after it. Emigrated to Canada in 1985.

Rudham, "Doug" K. R. (b. Johannesburg 3.5.28; d. Johannesburg August 1991). A goalkeeper who made 66 first team appearances for Liverpool between November 1954 and November 1960 when the Reds were in the Second Division. Capped as an amateur for South Africa.

Stamps, Jackie (b. Maltby 2.12.18; d. Burton-on-Trent November 1991). A tough centre-forward who began with Mansfield Town in 1937, but first attracted attention with New Brighton a year later and was soon snapped up by Derby County scoring two goals on his debut at inside-right. After the war he was regularly scoring goals again for Derby until his transfer to Shrewsbury Town in 1953. Starred in Derby's FA Cup victory in 1946 when he scored two of their goals in extra time to help beat Charlton Athletic. In his later years he was totally blind.

Starling, Ronnie (b. Pelaw, Newcastle-upon-Tyne 11.10.09; d. Sheffield 17.12.91). Had two years with Hull City as an amateur before signing professional in 1927. A clever ball-playing inside-forward he was a delight to watch. Newcastle United made up for missing him as a schoolboy by obtaining his transfer in 1930 but it was as a Sheffield Wednesday player that he really earned fame (FA Cup medal 1935) making 176 League appearances for them from 1932 to 1937 when he moved to Aston Villa and helped them regain First Division status. Retired during the war after guesting for Walsall. Two England caps.

Walker, Willis (b. Gosforth 24.11.1892; d. Keighley 4.12.91). An all-round sportsman who played cricket for Notts (1913–37) and kept goal for either the reserves or first teams of Sheffield United, Doncaster Rovers, Leeds City, South Shields, Bradford PA and Stockport County between 1912 and 1927. He hit 1000 runs in a season 10 times.

Whatmore, Ernie (b. Kidderminster 25.4.1900; d. Kidderminster 30.7.91). Bristol Rovers signed this inside or centre-forward from Shrewsbury in 1923 and he made 134 League appearances for them. Moved to QPR in 1928 and added another 78 League appearances in four seasons.

FA PREMIER LEAGUE
and
BARCLAYS LEAGUE FIXTURES 1992–93

Saturday 15 August 1992
FA Premier League
Arsenal v Norwich C
Chelsea v Oldham Ath
Coventry C v Middlesbrough
Crystal Palace v Blackburn R
Everton v Sheffield W
Ipswich T v Aston Villa
Leeds U v Wimbledon
Sheffield U v Manchester U
Southampton v Tottenham H

Barclays League Division 1
Barnsley v West Ham U
Birmingham C v Notts Co
Brentford v Wolverhampton W
Bristol C v Portsmouth
Charlton Ath v Grimsby T
Leicester C v Luton T
Newcastle U v Southend U
Oxford U v Bristol R
Peterborough U v Derby Co
Swindon T v Sunderland
Tranmere R v Cambridge U
Watford V Millwall

Barclays League Division 2
Bolton W v Huddersfield T
Bradford C v Chester C
Burnley v Swansea C
Exeter C v Rotherham U
Hartlepool U v Reading
Hull C v Stoke C
Leyton O v Brighton & HA
Mansfield T v Plymouth Arg
Port Vale v Fulham
Preston NE v AFC Bournemouth
WBA v Blackpool
Wigan Ath v Stockport Co

Barclays League Division 3
Cardiff C v Darlington
Carlisle U v Walsall
Chesterfield v Barnet
Colchester U v Lincoln C
Crewe Alex v Torquay U
Doncaster R v Bury
Gillingham v Northampton T
Hereford U v Scarborough
Rochdale & Halifax T
Scunthorpe U v Maidstone U
York C v Shrewsbury T

Sunday 16 August 1992
FA Premier League
Nottingham F v Liverpool (4.00)

Monday 17 August 1992
FA Premier League
Manchester C v QPR (7.45)

Tuesday 18 August 1992
FA Premier League
Blackburn R v Arsenal (7.45)
Wimbledon v Ipswich T (8.00)

Barclays League Division 1
Cambridge U v Charlton Ath (7.45)
Wolverhampton W v Leicester C

Wednesday 19 August 1992
FA Premier League
Aston Villa v Leeds U (7.45)

Liverpool v Sheffield U
Manchester U v Everton (8.00)
Middlesbrough v Manchester C (7.45)
Norwich C v Chelsea (7.45)
Oldham Ath v Crystal Palace
QPR v Southampton (7.45)
Sheffield W v Nottingham F (7.45)
Tottenham H v Coventry C (7.45)

Barclays League Division 1
Bristol R v Swindon T (8.00)

Friday 21 August 1992
Barclays League Division 3
Barnet v Colchester U (7.45)
Darlington v Hereford U

Saturday 22 August 1992
FA Premier League
Aston Villa v Southampton
Blackburn R v Manchester C
Manchester U v Ipswich T
Middlesbrough v Leeds U
Norwich C v Everton
Oldham Ath v Nottingham F
QPR v Sheffield U
Sheffield W v Chelsea
Tottenham H v Crystal Palace
Wimbledon v Coventry C

Barclays League Division 1
Bristol R v Brentford
Cambridge U v Birmingham C
Derby Co v Newcastle U
Grimsby T v Watford
Luton T v Bristol C
Millwall v Oxford U
Notts Co v Leicester C
Portsmouth v Barnsley
Southend U v Peterborough U
Sunderland v Tranmere R
West Ham U v Charlton Ath
Wolverhampton W v Swindon T

Barclays League Division 2
AFC Bournemouth v Port Vale
Blackpool v Exeter C
Brighton & HA v Bolton W
Fulham v Preston NE
Huddersfield T v WBA
Hull C v Chester C
Plymouth Arg v Bradford C
Reading v Leyton O
Rotherham U v Hartlepool U
Stockport Co v Burnley
Stoke C v Wigan Ath
Swansea C v Mansfield T

Barclays League Division 3
Bury v Gillingham
Halifax T v Scunthorpe U
Lincoln C v York C
Maidstone U v Carlisle U
Scarborough v Crewe Alex
Shrewsbury T v Doncaster R
Walsall v Cardiff C
Wrexham v Rochdale

Sunday 23 August 1992
FA Premier League
Liverpool v Arsenal (4.00)

Monday 24 August 1992
FA Premier League
Southampton v Manchester U

Tuesday 25 August 1992
FA Premier League
Crystal Palace v Sheffield W (8.00)
Everton v Aston Villa
Ipswich T v Liverpool (7.45)
Leeds U v Tottenham H
Sheffield U v Wimbledon (7.45)

Barclays League Division 1
Charlton Ath v Bristol R (7.45)
Notts Co v Watford (7.45)

Wednesday 26 August 1992
FA Premier League
Arsenal v Oldham Ath (7.45)
Chelsea v Blackburn R
Coventry C v QPR (7.45)
Manchester C v Norwich C (7.45)

Barclays League Division 1
Leicester C v Derby Co (7.45)

Friday 28 August 1992
Barclays League Division 1
Tranmere R v Bristol R

Barclays League Division 2
Hull C v Plymouth Arg

Barclays League Division 3
Crewe Alex v Northampton T

Saturday 29 August 1992
FA Premier League
Arsenal v Sheffield W
Chelsea v QPR
Coventry C v Blackburn R
Crystal Palace v Norwich C
Everton v Wimbledon
Leeds U v Liverpool
Manchester C v Oldham Ath
Nottingham F v Manchester U
Sheffield U v Aston Villa
Southampton v Middlesbrough

Barclays League Division 1
Barnsley v Millwall
Birmingham C v Grimsby T
Brentford v Southend U
Bristol C v Sunderland
Charlton Ath v Luton T
Leicester C v Portsmouth
Newcastle U v West Ham U
Oxford U v Wolverhampton W
Peterborough U v Notts Co
Swindon T v Cambridge U
Watford v Derby Co

Barclays League Division 2
Bolton W v Reading
Bradford C v Brighton & HA
Burnley v Rotherham U
Exeter C v Stoke C
Hartlepool U v Huddersfield T
Leyton O v Blackpool
Mansfield T v Fulham
Port Vale v Stockport Co
Preston NE v Chester C

WBA v AFC Bournemouth
Wigan Ath v Swansea C

Barclays League Division 3
Cardiff C v Halifax T
Carlisle U v Lincoln C
Chesterfield v Bury
Colchester U v Darlington
Doncaster R v Torquay U
Gillingham v Barnet
Hereford U v Walsall
Rochdale v Scarborough
Scunthorpe U v Shrewsbury T
York C v Wrexham

Sunday 30 August 1992

FA Premier League
Ipswich T v Tottenham H (4.00)

Monday 31 August 1992
FA Premier League
Norwich C v Nottingham F (7.45)

Tuesday 1 September 1992
FA Premier League
Liverpool v Southampton
Middlesbrough v Ipswich T
Oldham Ath v Leeds U
Wimbledon v Manchester C (8.00)

Barclays League Division 1
Barnsley v Wolverhampton W (7.45)
Birmingham C v Southend U (8.00)
Brentford v Portsmouth (7.45)

Barclays League Division 2
Bolton W v Blackpool
Exeter C v Brighton & HA
Hartlepool U v Chester C
Hull C v Swansea C
Leyton O v Huddersfield T (7.45)
Mansfield T v AFC Bournemouth
Port Vale v Rotherham U
Wigan Ath v Fulham

Barclays League Division 3
Cardiff C v Northampton T
Carlisle U v Bury
Chesterfield v Darlington
Colchester U v Shrewsbury T (7.45)
Crewe Alex v Halifax T
Doncaster R v Barnet
Gillingham v Wrexham (7.45)
Hereford U v Lincoln C
Rochdale v Maidstone U
Scunthorpe U v Walsall
York C v Torquay U

Wednesday 2 September 1992
FA Premier League
Aston Villa v Chelsea
Manchester U v Crystal Palace (8.00)
QPR v Arsenal (7.45)
Sheffield W v Coventry C (7.45)
Tottenham H v Sheffield U (7.45)

Barclays League Division 1
Newcastle U v Luton T (7.45)

Barclays League Division 2
Bradford C v Stoke C
WBA v Stockport Co

Friday 4 September 1992
Barclays League Division 1
Cambridge U v Brentford (7.45)

Saturday 5 September 1992
FA Premier League
Aston Villa v Crystal Palace
Blackburn R v Nottingham F
Liverpool v Chelsea

Norwich C v Southampton
Oldham Ath v Coventry C
QPR v Ipswich T
Sheffield W v Manchester C
Tottenham H v Everton
Wimbledon v Arsenal

Barclays League Division 1
Bristol R v Newcastle U
Derby Co v Bristol C
Grimsby T v Oxford U
Luton T v Tranmere R
Millwall v Swindon T
Notts Co v Barnsley
Portsmouth v Birmingham C
Southend U v Leicester C
Sunderland v Charlton Ath
West Ham U v Watford
Wolverhampton W v Peterborough
U

Barclays League Division 2
AFC Bournemouth v Hartlepool U
Blackpool v Mansfield T
Brighton & HA v Preston NE
Chester C v Burnley
Fulham v WBA
Plymouth Arg v Leyton O
Reading v Hull C
Rotherham U v Wigan Ath
Stockport Co v Exeter C
Stoke C v Bolton W
Swansea C v Port Vale

Barclays League Division 3
Barnet v Carlisle U
Bury v Colchester U
Darlington v Crewe Alex
Lincoln C v Scunthorpe U
Maidstone U v Chesterfield
Scarborough v Gillingham
Shrewsbury T v Rochdale
Torquay U v Cardiff C
Walsall v York C
Wrexham v Doncaster R

Sunday 6 September 1992
FA Premier League
Manchester U v Leeds U (4.00)

Barclays League Division 2
Huddersfield T v Bradford C (12.30)

Barclays League Division 3
Northampton T v Hereford U (2.00)

Monday 7 September 1992
FA Premier League
Middlesbrough v Sheffield U (7.45)

Tuesday 8 September 1992
Barclays League Division 3
Cardiff C v Carlisle U

Wednesday 9 September 1992
Barclays League Division 2
WBA v Reading

Friday 11 September 1992
Barclays League Division 2
Wigan Ath v Hartlepool U

Saturday 12 September 1992
FA Premier League
Arsenal v Blackburn R
Chelsea v Norwich C
Crystal Palace v Oldham Ath
Everton v Manchester U
Ipswich T v Wimbledon
Manchester C v Middlesbrough
Nottingham F v Sheffield W
Sheffield U v Liverpool
Southampton v QPR

Barclays League Division 1
Barnsley v Derby Co
Brentford v Luton T
Bristol C v Southend U
Charlton Ath v Cambridge U
Leicester C v Wolverhampton W
Millwall v Birmingham C
Newcastle U v Portsmouth
Oxford U v Sunderland
Peterborough U v West Ham U
Swindon T v Bristol R
Tranmere R v Grimsby T
Watford v Notts Co

Barclays League Division 2
AFC Bournemouth v Fulham
Brighton & HA v Huddersfield T
Leyton O v Chester C
Mansfield T v Bradford C
Plymouth Arg v Stoke C
Port Vale v Exeter C
Preston NE v Burnley
Rotherham U v Bolton W
Stockport C v Hull C
Swansea C v Blackpool

Barclays League Division 3
Bury v Barnet
Carlisle U v York C
Colchester U v Walsall
Crewe Alex v Doncaster R
Darlington v Maidstone U
Gillingham v Chesterfield
Lincoln C v Halifax T
Northampton T v Scunthorpe U
Scarborough v Torquay U
Wrexham v Shrewsbury T

Sunday 13 September 1992
FA Premier League
Leeds U v Aston Villa (4.00)

Barclays League Division 3
Hereford U v Cardiff C (12.00)

Monday 14 September 1992
FA Premier League
Coventry C v Tottenham H (7.45)

Tuesday 15 September 1992
FA Premier League
Blackburn R v Everton (7.45)

Barclays League Division 1
Bristol C v West Ham U (7.45)
Oxford U v Cambridge U (7.45)
Peterborough U v Millwall

Barclays League Division 2
Blackpool v AFC Bournemouth
(7.45)
Bolton W v WBA
Burnley v Port Vale
Chester C v Mansfield T
Exeter C v Wigan Ath
Fulham v Swansea C
Hartlepool U v Leyton O
Huddersfield T v Plymouth Arg
Hull C v Preston NE

Barclays League Division 3
Barnet v Northampton T (7.45)
Chesterfield v Crewe Alex
Doncaster R v Colchester U
Halifax T v Darlington
Maidstone U v Lincoln C
Rochdale v Gillingham
Shrewsbury T v Scarborough
Torquay U v Wrexham
Walsall v Bury (7.45)
York C v Hereford U

1008

Wednesday 16 September 1992
Barclays League Division 2
Bradford C v Stockport Co
Reading v Rotherham U (7.45)
Stoke C v Brighton & HA

Friday 18 September 1992
Barclays League Division 1
Southend U v Portsmouth (7.45)
Tranmere R v Charlton Ath

Barclays League Division 3
Doncaster R v Lincoln C

Saturday 19 September 1992
FA Premier League
Aston Villa v Liverpool
Everton v Crystal Palace
Norwich C v Sheffield W
Nottingham F v Coventry C
Oldham Ath v Ipswich T
QPR v Middlesbrough
Sheffield U v Arsenal
Southampton v Leeds U
Tottenham H v Manchester U
Wimbledon v Blackburn R

Barclays League Division 1
Barnsley v Peterborough U
Bristol R v Grimsby T
Cambridge U v Sunderland
Leicester C v Brentford
Luton T v Birmingham C
Millwall v Notts Co
Newcastle U v Bristol C
Swindon T v Oxford U
West Ham U v Derby Co
Wolverhampton W v Watford

Barclays League Division 2
Blackpool v Brighton & HA
Bolton W v AFC Bournemouth
Bradford C v Preston NE
Burnley v Mansfield T
Chester C v Stockport Co
Exeter C v Leyton O
Fulham v Plymouth Arg
Hartlepool U v Port Vale
Huddersfield T v Swansea C
Hull C v Rotherham U
Reading v Wigan Ath
Stoke C v WBA

Barclays League Division 3
Barnet v Hereford U
Cardiff C v Gillingham
Chesterfield v Carlisle U
Halifax T v Scarborough
Maidstone U v Wrexham
Rochdale v Darlington
Scunthorpe U v Crewe Alex
Shrewsbury T v Bury
Torquay U v Northampton T
York C v Colchester U

Sunday 20 September 1992
FA Premier League
Manchester C v Chelsea (4.00)

Friday 25 September 1992
Barclays League Division 2
Stockport Co v Fulham

Barclays League Division 3
Darlington v York C

Saturday 26 September 1992
FA Premier League
Blackburn R v Oldham Ath
Chelsea v Nottingham F
Coventry C v Norwich C
Crystal Palace v Southampton
Ipswich T v Sheffield U

Leeds U v Everton
Liverpool v Wimbledon
Manchester U v QPR
Middlesbrough v Aston Villa

Barclays League Division 1
Birmingham C v Wolverhampton W
Brentford v Millwall
Bristol C v Barnsley
Charlton Ath v Swindon T
Derby Co v Southend U
Grimsby T v Cambridge U
Notts Co v Luton T
Oxford U v Tranmere R
Peterborough U v Newcastle U
Portsmouth v West Ham U
Sunderland v Bristol R
Watford v Leicester C

Barclays League Division 2
AFC Bournemouth v Huddersfield T
Brighton & HA v Reading
Leyton O v Hull C
Mansfield T v Stoke C
Plymouth Arg v Bolton W
Port Vale v Chester C
Preston NE v Hartlepool U
Rotherham U v Blackpool
Swansea C v Bradford C
WBA v Exeter C
Wigan Ath v Burnley

Barclays League Division 3
Bury v Torquay U
Carlisle U v Scunthorpe U
Colchester U v Chesterfield
Crew Alex v Maidstone U
Gillingham v Walsall
Hereford U v Rochdale
Lincoln C v Shrewsbury T
Northampton T v Halifax T
Scarborough v Doncaster R
Wrexham v Barnet

Sunday 27 September 1992
FA Premier League
Sheffield W v Tottenham H (4.00)

Monday 28 September 1992
FA Premier League
Arsenal v Manchester C (7.45)

Tuesday 29 September 1992
Barclays League Division 1
Swindon T v Grimsby T (7.45)
Tranmere R v Notts Co
Watford v Sunderland (7.45)

Barclays League Division 2
Burnley v Plymouth Arg

Friday 2 October 1992
Barclays League Division 2
Reading v Fulham (7.45)

Barclays League Division 3
Darlington v Torquay U

Saturday 3 October 1992
FA Premier League
Arsenal v Chelsea
Blackburn R v Norwich C
Coventry C v Crystal Palace
Ipswich T v Leeds U
Liverpool v Sheffield W
Manchester U v Nottingham F
Middlesbrough v Manchester U
QPR v Tottenham H
Sheffield U v Southampton
Wimbledon v Aston Villa

Barclays League Division 1
Brentford v Newcastle U

Bristol R v Notts Co
Cambridge U v Derby Co
Charlton Ath v Southend U
Grimsby T v Peterborough U
Leicester C v Barnsley
Luton T v Portsmouth
Oxford U v Birmingham C
Sunderland v Millwall (2.00)
Swindon v Watford
Tranmere R v Bristol C
Wolverhampton W v West Ham U

Barclays League Division 2
Burnley v WBA
Chester C v Stoke C
Exeter C v AFC Bournemouth
Hull C v Bradford C
Leyton O v Bolton W
Port Vale v Brighton & HA
Preston NE v Plymouth Arg
Rotherham U v Huddersfield T
Stockport Co v Swansea C
Wigan Ath v Mansfield T

Barclays League Division 3
Barnet v Shrewsbury T
Bury v Scarborough
Cardiff C v Rochdale
Carlisle U v Halifax T
Chesterfield v Scunthorpe U
Gillingham v Crewe Alex
Hereford U v Wrexham
Northampton T v Lincoln C
Walsall v Maidstone U
York C v Doncaster R

Sunday 4 October 1992
FA Premier League
Oldham Ath v Everton (4.00)

Barclays League Division 2
Hartlepool U v Blackpool

Saturday 10 October 1992
Barclays League Division 1
Barnsley v Luton T
Birmingham C v Leicester C
Bristol C v Charlton Ath
Derby Co v Oxford U
Millwall v Cambridge U
Newcastle U v Tranmere R
Notts Co v Grimsby T
Peterborough U v Brentford
Portsmouth v Swindon T
Southend U v Wolverhampton W
Watford v Bristol R
West Ham U v Sunderland

Barclays League Division 2
AFC Bournemouth v Rotherham U
Blackpool v Preston NE
Bolton W v Hartlepool U
Brighton & HA v Wigan Ath
Fulham v Hull C
Huddersfield T v Reading
Mansfield T v Stockport Co
Plymouth Arg v Chester C
Stoke C v Leyton O
Swansea C v Exeter C
WBA v Port Vale

Barclays League Division 3
Crewe Alex v Cardiff C
Doncaster R v Gillingham
Halifax T v Colchester U
Lincoln C v Walsall
Maidstone U v Barnet
Rochdale v Carlisle U
Scarborough v Northampton T
Scunthorpe U v York C
Shrewsbury T v Darlington
Torquay U v Chesterfield (6.30)
Wrexham v Bury

Sunday 11 October 1992
Barclays League Division 2
Bradford C v Burnley (12.00)

Tuesday 13 October 1992
Barclays League Division 3
Northampton T v Chesterfield

Friday 16 October 1992
Barclays League Division 2
Stockport Co v Blackpool

Barclays League Division 3
Colchester U v Crewe Alex (7.45)

Saturday 17 October 1992
FA Premier League
Chelsea v Ipswich T
Crystal Palace v Manchester C
Everton v Coventry C
Leeds U v Sheffield U
Norwich C v QPR
Nottingham F v Arsenal
Sheffield W v Oldham Ath
Southampton v Wimbledon
Tottenham H v Middlesbrough

Barclays League Division 1
Brentford v Watford
Bristol R v West Ham U
Cambridge U v Bristol C
Charlton Ath v Millwall
Grimsby T v Southend U
Leicester C v Peterborough U
Luton T v Derby Co
Oxford U v Barnsley
Swindon T v Notts Co
Tranmere R v Birmingham C
Wolverhampton W v Portsmouth

Barclays League Division 2
Burnley v Fulham
Chester C v Bolton W
Exeter C v Mansfield T
Hartlepool U v Swansea C
Hull C v Huddersfield T
Leyton O v AFC Bournemouth
Port Vale v Plymouth Arg
Preston NE v Stoke C
Reading v Bradford C
Rotherham U v Brighton & HA
Wigan Ath v WBA

Barclays League Division 3
Barnet v Scunthorpe U
Bury v Lincoln C
Cardiff C v Maidstone U
Carlisle U v Wrexham
Chesterfield v Shrewsbury T
Darlington v Scarborough
Hereford U v Torquay U
Northampton T v Doncaster R
Walsall v Halifax T
York C v Rochdale

Sunday 18 October 1992
FA Premier League
Manchester U v Liverpool (4.00)

Barclays League Division 1
Sunderland v Newcastle U (12.00)

Monday 19 October 1992
FA Premier League
Aston Villa v Blackburn R (7.45)

Tuesday 20 October 1992
Barclays League Division 2
Preston NE v Reading

Wednesday 21 October 1992
FA Premier League
Nottingham F v Middlesbrough

Friday 23 October 1992
Barclays League Division 3
Doncaster R v Hereford U

Saturday 24 October 1992
FA Premier League
Arsenal v Everton
Blackburn R v Manchester U
Coventry C v Chelsea
Ipswich T v Crystal Palace
Liverpool v Norwich C
Manchester C v Southampton
Middlesbrough v Sheffield W
Oldham Ath v Aston Villa
QPR v Leeds U
Sheffield U v Nottingham F

Barclays League Division 1
Barnsley v Brentford
Birmingham C v Bristol R
Bristol C v Leicester C
Derby Co v Charlton Ath
Millwall v Wolverhampton W
Newcastle U v Grimsby T
Notts Co v Oxford U
Peterborough U v Luton T
Portsmouth v Sunderland
Watford v Tranmere R
West Ham U v Swindon T

Barclays League Division 2
AFC Bournemouth v Stockport Co
Blackpool v Burnley
Bolton W v Hull C
Bradford C v Leyton O
Brighton & HA v Hartlepool U
Fulham v Chester C
Huddersfield T v Exeter C
Mansfield T v Preston NE
Plymouth Arg v Wigan Ath
Stoke C v Port Vale
Swansea C v Reading
WBA v Rotherham U

Barclays League Division 3
Crewe Alex v Bury
Halifax T v Gillingham
Lincoln C v Barnet
Maidstone U v York C
Rochdale v Walsall
Scarborough v Chesterfield
Scunthorpe U v Colchester U
Shrewsbury T v Cardiff C
Torquay U v Carlisle U
Wrexham v Northampton T

Sunday 25 October 1992
FA Premier League
Wimbledon v Tottenham H (4.00)

Barclays League Division 1
Southend U v Cambridge U (12.00)

Friday 30 October 1992
Barclays League Division 1
Tranmere R v Peterborough U

Barclays League Division 2
Stockport Co v Huddersfield T

Barclays League Division 3
Colchester U v Wrexham (7.45)

Saturday 31 October 1992
FA Premier League
Chelsea v Sheffield U
Everton v Manchester C
Leeds U v Coventry C
Manchester U v Wimbledon

Norwich C v Middlesbrough
Nottingham F v Ipswich T
Sheffield W v Blackburn R
Southampton v Oldham Ath
Tottenham H v Liverpool

Barclays League Division 1
Brentford v Bristol C
Bristol R v Millwall
Cambridge U v West Ham U
Charlton Ath v Birmingham C
Grimsby T v Portsmouth
Leicester C v Newcastle U
Luton T v Southend U
Oxford U v Watford
Sunderland v Notts Co
Swindon T v Barnsley
Wolverhampton W v Derby Co

Barclays League Division 2
Burnley v Stoke C
Chester C v Brighton & HA
Exeter C v Fulham
Hartlepool U v Bradford C
Hull C v WBA
Leyton O v Swansea C
Port Vale v Blackpool
Preston NE v Bolton W
Reading v Plymouth Arg
Rotherham U v Mansfield T
Wigan Ath v AFC Bournemouth

Barclays League Division 3
Barnet v Crewe Alex
Bury v Maidstone U
Cardiff C v Scunthorpe U
Carlisle U v Scarborough
Chesterfield v Rochdale
Darlington v Lincoln C
Gillingham v Torquay U
Hereford U v Halifax T
Northampton T v Shrewsbury T
Walsall v Doncaster R

Sunday 1 November 1992
FA Premier League
Aston Villa v QPR (4.00)

Monday 2 November 1992
FA Premier League
Crystal Palace v Arsenal (8.00)

Tuesday 3 November 1992
Barclays League Division 1
Birmingham C v Newcastle U (8.00)
Bristol R v Barnsley (8.00)
Cambridge U v Luton T (7.45)
Charlton Ath v Leicester C (7.45)
Grimsby T v West Ham U (7.45)
Notts Co v Derby Co (7.45)
Oxford U v Portsmouth (7.45)
Sunderland v Wolverhampton W (7.45)
Swindon T v Brentford (7.45)
Tranmere R v Southend U
Watford v Peterborough U (7.45)

Barclays League Division 2
AFC Bournemouth v Brighton & HA (7.45)
Blackpool v Huddersfield T (7.45)
Burnley v Reading
Exeter C v Bolton W
Fulham v Stoke C
Mansfield T v Hull C
Port Vale v Leyton O
Rotherham U v Chester C
Stockport Co v Preston NE
Swansea C v Plymouth Arg
Wigan Ath v Bradford C

Barclays League Division 3
Barnet v Walsall (7.45)
Bury v York C

Chesterfield v Cardiff C
Colchester U v Carlisle U (7.45)
Doncaster R v Maidstone U
Gillingham v Hereford U (7.45)
Northampton T v Darlington
Scarborough v Lincoln C
Shrewsbury T v Halifax T
Torquay U v Rochdale
Wrexham v Scunthorpe U

Wednesday 4 November 1992
Barclays League Division 1
Millwall v Bristol C (7.45)

Barclays League Division 2
WBA v Hartlepool U

Saturday 7 November 1992
FA Premier League
Arsenal v Coventry C
Aston Villa v Manchester U
Blackburn R v Tottenham H
Chelsea v Crystal Palace
Ipswich T v Southampton
Liverpool v Middlesbrough
Manchester C v Leeds U
Nottingham F v Everton
Oldham Ath v Norwich C
Wimbledon v QPR

Barclays League Division 1
Barnsley v Watford
Brentford v Charlton Ath
Birstol C v Birmingham C
Derby Co v Millwall
Leicester C v Tranmere R
Luton T v Grimsby T
Newcastle U v Swindon T
Peterborough U v Sunderland
Portsmouth v Cambridge U
Southend U v Oxford U
West Ham U v Notts Co
Wolverhampton W v Bristol R

Barclays League Division 2
Bolton W v Port Vale
Bradford C v Fulham
Brighton & HA v Stockport Co
Chester C v Swansea C
Hartlepool U v Exeter C
Huddersfield T v Mansfield T
Hull C v Burnley
Leyton O v WBA
Plymouth Arg v Rotherham U
Preston NE v Wigan Ath
Reading v Blackpool
Stoke C v AFC Bournemouth

Barclays League Division 3
Cardiff C v Colchester U
Carlisle U v Gillingham
Darlington v Bury
Halifax T v Torquay U
Hereford U v Chesterfield
Lincoln C v Wrexham
Maidstone U v Shrewsbury T
Rochdale v Crewe Alex
Scunthorpe U v Doncaster R
Walsall v Scarborough
York C v Barnet

Sunday 8 November 1992
FA Premier League
Sheffield U v Sheffield W (4.00)

Saturday 14 November 1992
Barclays League Division 1
Bristol R v Derby Co
Cambridge U v Barnsley
Charlton Ath v Newcastle U
Grimsby T v Bristol C
Notts Co v Wolverhampton W
Oxford U v Luton T
Sunderland v Leicester C

Swindon T v Southend U
Tranmere R v Brentford
Watford v Portsmouth

Sunday 15 November 1992
Barclays League Division 1
Millwall v West Ham U

Friday 20 November 1992
Barclays League Division 2
Stockport Co v Plymouth Arg
Swansea C v Brighton & HA

Saturday 21 November 1992
FA Premier League
Coventry C v Manchester C
Crystal Palace v Nottingham F
Everton v Chelsea
Leeds U v Arsenal
Manchester U v Oldham Ath
Middlesbrough v Wimbledon
Norwich C v Sheffield U
Sheffield W v Ipswich T
Southampton v Blackburn R
Tottenham H v Aston Villa

Barclays League Division 1
Barnsley v Birmingham C
Brentford v Grimsby T
Bristol C v Swindon T
Derby Co v Sunderland
Leicester C v Cambridge U
Luton T v Millwall
Newcastle U v Watford
Peterborough U v Bristol R
Portsmouth v Tranmere R
Southend U v Notts Co
West Ham U v Oxford U
Wolverhampton W v Charlton Ath

Barclays League Division 2
AFC Bournemouth v Reading
Blackpool v Stoke C
Burnley v Huddersfield T
Exeter C v Chester C
Fulham v Bolton W
Mansfield T v Hartlepool U
Port Vale v Hull C
Rotherham U v Preston NE
WBA v Bradford C
Wigan Ath v Leyton O

Barclays League Division 3
Bury v Hereford U
Colchester U v Rochdale
Crewe Alex v Lincoln C
Doncaster R v Carlisle U
Gillingham v Darlington
Northampton T v York C
Scarborough v Maidstone U
Shrewsbury T v Walsall
Torquay U v Scunthorpe U
Wrexham v Halifax T

Sunday 22 November 1992
Barclays League Division 3
Barnet v Cardiff C (1.00)

Monday 23 November 1992
FA Premier League
QPR v Liverpool (7.45)

Friday 27 November 1992
Barclays League Division 2
Chester C v Wigan Ath

Saturday 28 November 1992
FA Premier League
Arsenal v Manchester U
Aston Villa v Norwich C
Blackburn R v QPR
Chelsea v Leeds U
Ipswich T v Everton

Liverpool v Crystal Palace
Manchester C v Tottenham H
Nottingham F v Southampton
Oldham Ath v Middlesbrough
Sheffield U v Coventry C
Wimbledon v Sheffield W

Barclays League Division 1
Barnsley v Charlton Ath
Brentford v Oxford U
Bristol C v Notts Co
Derby Co v Tranmere R
Leicester C v Bristol R
Luton T v Watford
Newcastle U v Cambridge U
Peterborough U v Swindon T
Portsmouth v Millwall
Southend U v Sunderland
West Ham U v Birmingham C
Wolverhampton W v Grimsby T

Barclays League Division 2
Bolton W v Burnley
Bradford C v Rotherham U
Brighton & HA v Fulham
Hartlepool U v Stockport Co
Huddersfield T v Port Vale
Hull C v Blackpool
Leyton O v Mansfield T
Plymouth Arg v AFC Bournemouth
Preston NE v WBA
Reading v Exeter C
Stoke C v Swansea C

Barclays League Division 3
Cardiff C v Bury
Carlisle U v Northampton T
Darlington v Barnet
Halifax T v Chesterfield
Hereford U v Colchester U
Lincoln C v Gillingham
Maidstone U v Torquay U
Rochdale v Doncaster R
Scunthorpe U v Scarborough
Walsall v Wrexham
York C v Crewe Alex

Friday 4 December 1992
Barclays League Division 1
Tranmere R v West Ham U

Saturday 5 December 1992
FA Premier League
Coventry C v Ipswich T
Crystal Palace v Sheffield U
Leeds U v Nottingham F
Manchester U v Manchester C
Middlesbrough v Blackburn R
Norwich C v Wimbledon
QPR v Oldham Ath
Sheffield W v Aston Villa
Southampton v Arsenal
Tottenham H v Chelsea

Barclays League Division 1
Birmingham C v Brentford
Bristol R v Luton T
Cambridge U v Wolverhampton W
Charlton Ath v Portsmouth
Grimsby T v Leicester C
Millwall v Southend U
Notts Co v Newcastle U
Oxford U v Peterborough U
Sunderland v Barnsley
Swindon T v Derby Co
Watford v Bristol C

Monday 7 December 1992
FA Premier League
Everton v Liverpool (7.45)

Friday 11 December 1992
Barclays League Division 2
Stockport Co v Bolton W

Barclays League Division 3
Colchester U v Torquay U (7.45)
Doncaster R v Cardiff C

Saturday 12 December 1992
FA Premier League
Aston Villa v Nottingham F
Ipswich T v Manchester C
Leeds U v Sheffield W
Liverpool v Blackburn R
Manchester U v Norwich C
Middlesbrough v Chelsea
QPR v Crystal Palace
Sheffield U v Everton
Southampton v Coventry C
Tottenham H v Arsenal
Wimbledon v Oldham Ath

Barclays League Division 1
Barnsley v Newcastle U
Bristol R v Bristol C
Derby Co v Birmingham C
Millwall v Grimsby T
Notts Co v Cambridge U
Oxford U v Leicester C
Peterborough U v Portsmouth
Sunderland v Brentford
Swindon T v Tranmere R
Watford v Charlton Ath
West Ham U v Southend U
Wolverhampton W v Luton T

Barclays League Division 2
Bradford C v AFC Bournemouth
Burnley v Leyton O
Chester C v Reading
Fulham v Rotherham U
Hull C v Exeter C
Mansfield T v Brighton & HA
Plymouth Arg v Hartlepool U
Preston NE v Port Vale
Stoke C v Huddersfield T
Swansea C v WBA
Wigan Ath v Blackpool

Barclays League Division 3
Barnet v Rochdale
Bury v Northampton T
Carlisle U v Crewe Alex
Maidstone U v Halifax T
Scunthorpe U v Hereford U
Shrewsbury T v Gillingham
Walsall v Darlington
Wrexham v Scarborough
York C v Chesterfield

Friday 18 December 1992
Barclays League Division 1
Cambridge U v Bristol R (7.45)

Barclays League Division 2
Leyton O v Preston NE (7.45)
Rotherham U v Swansea C

Barclays League Division 3
Cardiff C v Wrexham
Crewe Alex v Walsall
Gillingham v Colchester U (7.45)

Saturday 19 December 1992
FA Premier League
Arsenal v Middlesbrough
Blackburn R v Sheffield U
Chelsea v Manchester U
Coventry C v Liverpool
Crystal Palace v Leeds U
Everton v Southampton
Manchester C v Aston Villa
Oldham Ath v Tottenham H
Sheffield W v QPR

Barclays League Division 1
Birmingham C v Watford
Bristol C v Peterborough U

Charlton Ath v Oxford U
Grimsby T v Derby Co
Luton T v Sunderland
Newcastle U v Millwall
Portsmouth v Notts Co
Southend U v Barnsley
Tranmere R v Wolverhampton W

Barclays League Division 2
AFC Bournemouth v Hull C
Blackpool v Fulham
Bolton W v Bradford C
Brighton & HA v Plymouth Arg
Exeter C v Burnley
Huddersfield T v Chester C
Port Vale v Wigan Ath
Reading v Stockport Co

Barclays League Division 3
Chesterfield v Doncaster R
Darlington v Scunthorpe U
Halifax T v Bury
Hereford U v Carlisle U
Rochdale v Lincoln C
Scarborough v York C

Sunday 20 December 1992
FA Premier League
Nottingham F v Wimbledon

Barclays League Division 1
Brentford v West Ham U (11.30)
Leicester C v Swindon T

Barclays League Division 2
Hartlepool U v Stoke C
WBA v Mansfield T

Barclays League Division 3
Northampton T v Maidstone U
Torquay U v Shrewsbury T

Monday 21 December 1992
FA Premier League
Norwich C v Ipswich T (7.45)

Saturday 26 December 1992
FA Premier League
Arsenal v Ipswich T (12.00)
Blackburn R v Leeds U
Chelsea v Southampton (12.00)
Coventry C v Aston Villa
Crystal Palace v Wimbledon (12.00)
Everton v Middlesbrough
Manchester C v Sheffield U
Norwich C v Tottenham H
Nottingham F v QPR
Oldham Ath v Liverpool
Sheffield W v Manchester U (12.00)

Barclays League Division 1
Birmingham C v Sunderland
Brentford v Derby Co (12.00)
Bristol C v Oxford U
Cambridge U v Peterborough U
Charlton Ath v West Ham U
Grimsby T v Barnsley
Leicester C v Notts Co (11.30)
Luton T v Swindon T (11.30)
Newcastle U v Wolverhampton W
Portsmouth v Bristol R
Southend U v Watford (12.00)
Tranmere R v Millwall

Barclays League Division 2
AFC Bournemouth v Swansea C
Blackpool v Bradford C
Bolton W v Wigan Ath
Brighton & HA v Burnley
Exeter C v Plymouth Arg (11.00)
Hartlepool U v Hull C
Huddersfield T v Preston NE
Leyton O v Fulham (12.00)
Port Vale v Mansfield T

Reading v Stoke C
Rotherham U v Stockport Co
WBA v Chester C

Barclays League Division 3
Cardiff C v York C
Chesterfield v Lincoln C
Crewe Alex v Wrexham
Darlington v Carlisle U
Gillingham v Maidstone U (11.00)
Halifax T v Doncaster R (12.00)
Hereford U v Shrewsbury T
Northampton T v Colchester U
Rochdale v Scunthorpe U
Scarborough v Barnet
Torquay U v Walsall

Monday 28 December 1992
FA Premier League
Aston Villa v Arsenal
Ipswich T v Blackburn R
Leeds U v Norwich C
Liverpool v Manchester C
Manchester U v Coventry C
Middlesbrough v Crystal Palace
QPR v Everton
Southampton v Sheffield W
Tottenham H v Nottingham F
Wimbledon v Chelsea

Barclays League Division 1
Barnsley v Tranmere R
Bristol R v Southend U
Derby Co v Portsmouth
Millwall v Leicester C
Notts Co v Brentford
Oxford U v Newcastle U
Peterborough U v Charlton Ath
Sunderland v Grimsby T
Watford v Cambridge U
West Ham U v Luton T
Wolverhampton W v Bristol C

Barclays League Division 2
Bradford C v Port Vale
Burnley v AFC Bournemouth
Chester C v Blackpool
Fulham v Hartlepool U
Hull C v Brighton & HA
Mansfield T v Reading
Plymouth Arg v WBA
Preston NE v Exeter C
Stockport Co v Leyton O
Stoke C v Rotherham U
Swansea C v Bolton W
Wigan Ath v Huddersfield T

Barclays League Division 3
Barnet v Torquay U
Bury v Rochdale
Doncaster R v Darlington
Lincoln C v Cardiff C
Maidstone U v Hereford U
Scunthorpe U v Gillingham
Shrewsbury T v Crewe Alex
Walsall v Northampton T
Wrexham v Chesterfield
York C v Halifax T

Tuesday 29 December 1992
FA Premier League
Sheffield U v Oldham Ath (7.45)

Barclays League Division 1
Swindon T v Birmingham C (7.45)

Barclays League Division 3
Colchester U v Scarborough (7.45)

Saturday 2 January 1993
Barclays League Division 1
Birmingham C v Peterborough U

Barclays League Division 2
Blackpool v Swansea C
Bolton W v Rotherham U
Bradford C v Mansfield T
Burnley v Preston NE
Chester C v Leyton O
Exeter C v Port Vale
Fulham v AFC Bournemouth
Hartlepool U v Wigan Ath
Huddersfield T v Brighton & HA
Hull C v Stockport Co
Reading v WBA
Stoke C v Plymouth Arg

Barclays League Division 3
Barnet v Bury
Cardiff C v Hereford U
Chesterfield v Gillingham
Doncaster R v Crewe Alex
Halifax T v Lincoln C
Maidstone U v Darlington
Scunthorpe U v Northampton T
Shrewsbury T v Wrexham
Torquay U v Scarborough
Walsall v Colchester U
York C v Carlisle U

Friday 8 January 1993
Barclays League Division 3
Colchester U v Doncaster R (7.45)
Gillingham v Rochdale (7.45)
Northampton T v Barnet

Saturday 9 January 1993
FA Premier League
Arsenal v Sheffield U
Blackburn R v Wimbledon
Chelsea v Manchester U
Coventry C v Nottingham F
Crystal Palace v Everton
Ipswich T v Oldham Ath
Leeds U v Southampton
Liverpool v Aston Villa
Manchester U v Tottenham H
Middlesbrough v QPR
Sheffield W v Norwich C

Barclays League Division 1
Birmingham C v Luton T
Brentford v Leicester C
Bristol C v Newcastle U
Charlton Ath v Tranmere R
Derby Co v West Ham U
Grimsby T v Bristol R
Notts Co v Millwall
Oxford U v Swindon T
Peterborough U v Barnsley
Portsmouth v Southend U
Sunderland v Cambridge U
Watford v Wolverhampton W

Barclays League Division 2
AFC Bournemouth v Blackpool
Brighton & HA v Stoke C
Leyton O v Hartlepool U
Mansfield T v Chester C
Plymouth Arg v Huddersfield T
Port Vale v Burnley
Preston NE v Hull C
Rotherham U v Reading
Stockport Co v Bradford C
Swansea C v Fulham
WBA v Bolton W
Wigan Ath v Exeter C

Barclays League Division 3
Bury v Walsall
Carlisle U v Cardiff C
Crewe Alex v Chesterfield
Darlington v Halifax T
Hereford U v York C
Lincoln C v Maidstone U
Scarborough v Shrewsbury T
Wrexham v Torquay U

Friday 15 January 1993
Barclays League Division 1
Tranmere R v Oxford U

Saturday 16 January 1993
FA Premier League
Aston Villa v Middlesbrough
Everton v Leeds U
Manchester C v Arsenal
Norwich C v Coventry C
Nottingham F v Chelsea
Oldham Ath v Blackburn R
QPR v Manchester U
Sheffield U v Ipswich T
Southampton v Crystal Palace
Tottenham H v Sheffield W
Wimbledon v Liverpool

Barclays League Division 1
Barnsley v Bristol C
Bristol R v Sunderland
Cambridge U v Grimsby T
Leicester C v Watford
Luton T v Notts Co
Millwall v Brentford
Newcastle U v Peterborough U
Southend U v Derby Co
Swindon T v Charlton Ath
West Ham U v Portsmouth
Wolverhampton W v Birmingham C

Barclays League Division 2
Blackpool v Rotherham U
Bolton W v Plymouth Arg
Bradford C v Swansea C
Burnley v Wigan Ath
Chester C v Port Vale
Exeter C v WBA
Fulham v Stockport Co
Hartlepool U v Preston NE
Huddersfield T v AFC Bournemouth
Hull C v Leyton O
Reading v Brighton & HA
Stoke C v Mansfield T

Barclays League Division 3
Barnet v Wrexham
Chesterfield v Colchester U
Doncaster R v Scarborough
Halifax T v Northampton T
Maidstone U v Crewe Alex
Rochdale v Hereford U
Scunthorpe U v Carlisle U
Shrewsbury T v Lincoln C
Torquay U v Bury
Walsall v Gillingham
York C v Darlington

Wednesday 20 January 1993
Barclays League Division 1
Southend U v Newcastle U (7.45)

Friday 22 January 1993
Barclays League Division 2
Stockport Co v Chester C

Barclays League Division 3
Colchester U v York C (7.45)

Saturday 23 January 1993
Barclays League Division 2
AFC Bournemouth v Bolton W
Brighton & HA v Blackpool
Leyton O v Exeter C
Mansfield T v Burnley
Plymouth Arg v Fulham
Port Vale v Hartlepool U
Preston NE v Bradford C
Rotherham U v Hull C
Swansea C v Huddersfield T
WBA v Stoke C
Wigan Ath v Reading

Barclays League Division 3
Bury v Shrewsbury T
Carlisle U v Chesterfield
Crewe Alex v Scunthorpe U
Darlington v Rochdale
Gillingham v Cardiff C
Hereford U v Barnet
Lincoln C v Doncaster R
Northampton T v Torquay U
Scarborough v Halifax T
Wrexham v Maidstone U

Tuesday 26 January 1993
FA Premier League
Blackburn R v Coventry C (7.45)
Middlesbrough v Southampton
Oldham Ath v Manchester C
Tottenham H v Ipswich T
Wimbledon v Everton (8.00)

Barclays League Division 1
Cambridge U v Oxford U (7.45)
Grimsby T v Swindon T (7.45)
Notts Co v Tranmere R (7.45)
Portsmouth v Brentford (7.45)
Sunderland v Watford (7.45)
Wolverhampton W v Barnsley

Barclays League Division 2
AFC Bournemouth v WBA (7.45)
Blackpool v Leyton O (7.45)
Chester C v Preston NE
Fulham v Mansfield T
Plymouth Arg v Hull C (7.45)
Rotherham U v Burnley
Stockport Co v Port Vale
Swansea C v Wigan Ath

Barclays League Division 3
Barnet v Gillingham (7.45)
Bury v Chesterfield
Darlington v Colchester U
Halifax T v Cardiff C
Lincoln C v Carlisle U
Northampton T v Crewe Alex
Scarborough v Rochdale
Shrewsbury T v Scunthorpe U
Torquay U v Doncaster R
Walsall v Hereford U (7.45)
Wrexham v York C

Wednesday 27 January 1993
FA Premier League
Aston Villa v Sheffield U (7.45)
Liverpool v Leeds U
Manchester U v Nottingham F (8.00)
Norwich C v Crystal Palace (7.45)
QPR v Chelsea (7.45)
Sheffield W v Arsenal (7.45)

Barclays League Division 1
Bristol R v Charlton Ath (8.00)
Derby Co v Leicester C (7.45)
Luton T v Newcastle U (7.45)
Millwall v Peterborough U (7.45)
Southend U v Birmingham C (7.45)
West Ham U v Bristol C (7.45)

Barclays League Division 2
Brighton & HA v Bradford C (7.45)
Huddersfield T v Hartlepool U
Reading v Bolton W (7.45)
Stoke C v Exeter C

Friday 29 January 1993
Barclays League Division 3
Colchester U v Barnet (7.45)
Doncaster R v Shrewsbury T

Saturday 30 January 1993
FA Premier League
Arsenal v Liverpool
Chelsea v Sheffield W

Coventry C v Wimbledon
Crystal Palace v Tottenham H
Everton v Norwich C
Ipswich T v Manchester U
Leeds U v Middlesbrough
Manchester C v Blackburn R
Nottingham F v Oldham Ath
Sheffield U v QPR
Southampton v Aston Villa

Barclays League Division 1
Barnsley v Portsmouth
Birmingham C v Cambridge U
Brentford v Bristol R
Bristol C v Luton T
Charlton Ath v Notts Co
Leicester C v West Ham U
Newcastle U v Derby Co
Oxford U v Millwall
Peterborough U v Southend U
Swindon T v Wolverhampton W
Tranmere R v Sunderland
Watford v Grimsby T

Barclays League Division 2
Bolton W v Brighton & HA
Bradford C v Plymouth Arg
Burnley v Stockport Co
Chester C v Hull C
Exeter C v Blackpool
Hartlepool U v Rotherham U
Leyton O v Reading
Mansfield T v Swansea C
Port Vale v AFC Bournemouth
Preston NE v Fulham
WBA v Huddersfield T
Wigan Ath v Stoke C

Barclays League Division 3
Cardiff C v Walsall
Carlisle U v Maidstone U
Chesterfield v Northampton T
Crewe Alex v Scarborough
Gillingham v Bury
Hereford U v Darlington
Rochdale v Wrexham
Scunthorpe U v Halifax T
York C v Lincoln C

Friday 5 February 1993
Barclays League Division 2
Stockport Co v Wigan Ath
Swansea C v Burnley

Saturday 6 February 1993
FA Premier League
Aston Villa v Ipswich T
Blackburn R v Crystal Palace
Liverpool v Nottingham F
Manchester U v Sheffield U
Middlesbrough v Coventry C
Norwich C v Arsenal
Oldham Ath v Chelsea
QPR v Manchester C
Sheffield W v Everton
Tottenham H v Southampton
Wimbledon v Leeds U

Barclays League Division 1
Bristol R v Oxford U
Cambridge U v Tranmere R
Derby Co v Peterborough U
Grimsby T v Charlton Ath
Luton T v Leicester C
Millwall v Watford
Notts Co v Birmingham C
Portsmouth v Bristol C
Sunderland v Swindon T
West Ham U v Barnsley
Wolverhampton W v Brentford

Barclays League Division 2
AFC Bournemouth v Preston NE
Blackpool v WBA

Brighton & HA v Leyton O
Chester C v Bradford C
Fulham v Port Vale
Huddersfield T v Bolton W
Plymouth Arg v Mansfield T
Reading v Hartlepool U
Rotherham U v Exeter C
Stoke C v Hull C

Barclays League Division 3
Barnet v Chesterfield
Bury v Doncaster R
Darlington v Cardiff C
Halifax T v Rochdale
Lincoln C v Colchester U
Maidstone U v Scunthorpe U
Northampton T v Gillingham
Scarborough v Hereford U
Shrewsbury T v York C
Torquay U v Crewe Alex
Walsall v Carlisle U

Tuesday 9 February 1993
FA Premier League
Arsenal v Wimbledon (7.45)
Crystal Palace v Aston Villa (8.00)
Ipswich T v QPR (7.45)
Leeds U v Manchester U
Sheffield U v Middlesbrough (7.45)

Barclays League Division 1
Birmingham C v Millwall (8.00)
Grimsby T v Tranmere R (7.45)
Portsmouth v Newcastle U (7.45)
Sunderland v Oxford U (7.45)

Wednesday 10 February 1993
FA Premier League
Chelsea v Liverpool
Coventry C v Oldham Ath (7.45)
Everton v Tottenham H
Manchester C v Sheffield W (7.45)
Nottingham F v Blackburn R
Southampton v Norwich C

Barclays League Division 1
Derby Co v Barnsley (7.45)
Luton T v Brentford (7.45)
Southend U v Bristol C (7.45)
West Ham U v Peterborough U (7.45)

Saturday 13 February 1993
FA Premier League
Arsenal v QPR
Chelsea v Aston Villa
Coventry C v Sheffield W
Crystal Palace v Manchester U
Everton v Blackburn R
Ipswich T v Middlesbrough
Leeds U v Oldham Ath
Manchester U v Wimbledon
Nottingham F v Norwich C
Sheffield U v Tottenham H
Southampton v Liverpool

Barclays League Division 1
Barnsley v Notts Co
Birmingham C v Portsmouth
Bristol C v Derby Co
Charlton Ath v Sunderland
Leicester C v Southend U
Newcastle U v Bristol R
Oxford U v Grimsby T
Peterborough U v Wolverhampton W
Swindon T v Millwall
Tranmere R v Luton T
Watford v West Ham U

Barclays League Division 2
Bolton W v Stoke C
Burnley v Chester C
Exeter C v Stockport Co
Hartlepool U v AFC Bournemouth

Hull C v Reading
Leyton O v Plymouth Arg
Mansfield T v Blackpool
Port Vale v Swansea C
Preston NE v Brighton & HA
WBA v Fulham
Wigan Ath v Rotherham U

Barclays League Division 3
Cardiff C v Torquay U
Carlisle U v Barnet
Chesterfield v Maidstone U
Colchester U v Bury
Crewe Alex v Darlington
Doncaster R v Wrexham
Gillingham v Scarborough
Hereford U v Northampton T
Rochdale v Shrewsbury T
Scunthorpe U v Lincoln C
York C v Walsall

Sunday 14 February 1993
Barclays League Division 1
Brentford v Cambridge U (11.30)

Barclays League Division 2
Bradford C v Huddersfield T

Friday 19 February 1993
Barclays League Division 3
Northampton T v Cardiff C

Saturday 20 February 1993
FA Premier League
Aston Villa v Everton
Blackburn R v Chelsea
Liverpool v Ipswich T
Manchester U v Southampton
Middlesbrough v Nottingham F
Norwich C v Manchester C
Oldham Ath v Arsenal
QPR v Coventry C
Sheffield W v Crystal Palace
Tottenham H v Leeds U
Wimbledon v Sheffield U

Barclays League Division 1
Bristol R v Tranmere R
Cambridge U v Swindon T
Derby Co v Watford
Grimsby T v Birmingham C
Luton T v Charlton Ath
Millwall v Barnsley
Notts Co v Peterborough U
Portsmouth v Leicester C
Sunderland v Bristol C
West Ham U v Newcastle U
Wolverhampton W v Oxford U

Barclays League Division 2
AFC Bournemouth v Mansfield T
Blackpool v Bolton W
Brighton & HA v Exeter C
Chester C v Hartlepool U
Fulham v Wigan Ath
Huddersfield T v Leyton O
Plymouth Arg v Burnley
Reading v Preston NE
Rotherham U v Port Vale
Stockport Co v WBA
Stoke C v Bradford C
Swansea C v Hull C

Barclays League Division 3
Barnet v Doncaster R
Bury v Carlisle U
Darlington v Chesterfield
Halifax T v Crewe Alex
Lincoln C v Hereford U
Maidstone U v Rochdale
Shrewsbury T v Colchester U
Torquay U v York C (6.30)
Walsall v Scunthorpe U
Wrexham v Gillingham

Sunday 21 February 1993
Barclays League Division 1
Southend U v Brentford

Friday 26 February 1993
Barclays League Division 2
Rotherham U v AFC Bournemouth
Stockport Co v Mansfield T

Barclays League Division 3
Colchester U v Halifax T (7.45)

Saturday 27 February 1993
FA Premier League
Aston Villa v Wimbledon
Chelsea v Arsenal
Crystal Palace v Coventry C
Everton v Oldham Ath
Leeds U v Ipswich T
Manchester U v Middlesbrough
Norwich C v Blackburn R
Nottingham F v Manchester C
Sheffield W v Liverpool
Southampton v Sheffield U
Tottenham H v QPR

Barclays League Division 1
Brentford v Peterborough U
Bristol R v Watford
Cambridge U v Millwall
Charlton Ath v Bristol C
Grimsby T v Notts Co
Leicester C v Birmingham C
Luton T v Barnsley
Oxford U v Derby Co
Sunderland v West Ham U
Swindon T v Portsmouth
Tranmere R v Newcastle U
Wolverhampton W v Southend U

Barclays League Division 2
Burnley v Bradford C
Chester C v Plymouth Arg
Exeter C v Swansea C
Hartlepool U v Bolton W
Hull C v Fulham
Leyton O v Stoke C
Port Vale v WBA
Preston NE v Blackpool
Reading v Huddersfield T
Wigan Ath v Brighton & HA

Barclays League Division 3
Barnet v Maidstone U
Bury v Wrexham
Cardiff C v Crewe Alex
Carlisle U v Rochdale
Chesterfield v Torquay U
Darlington v Shrewsbury T
Gillingham v Doncaster R
Northampton T v Scarborough
Walsall v Lincoln C
York C v Scunthorpe U

Friday 5 March 1993
Barclays League Division 2
Swansea C v Stockport Co

Barclays League Division 3
Doncaster R v York C

Saturday 6 March 1993
FA Premier League
Arsenal v Nottingham F
Blackburn R v Aston Villa
Coventry C v Everton
Ipswich T v Chelsea
Liverpool v Manchester U
Manchester C v Crystal Palace
Middlesbrough v Tottenham H
Oldham Ath v Sheffield W
QPR v Norwich C
Wimbledon v Southampton

Barclays League Division 1
Barnsley v Leicester C
Birmingham C v Oxford U
Bristol C v Tranmere R
Derby Co v Cambridge U
Millwall v Sunderland
Newcastle U v Brentford
Notts Co v Bristol R
Peterborough U v Grimsby T
Portsmouth v Luton T
Southend U v Charlton Ath
Watford v Swindon T
West Ham U v Wolverhampton W

Barclays League Division 2
AFC Bournemouth v Exeter C
Blackpool v Hartlepool U
Bolton W v Leyton O
Bradford C v Hull C
Brighton & HA v Port Vale
Fulham v Reading
Huddersfield T v Rotherham U
Mansfield T v Wigan Ath
Plymouth Arg v Preston NE
Stoke C v Chester C
WBA v Burnley

Barclays League Division 3
Crewe Alex v Gillingham
Halifax T v Carlisle U
Lincoln C v Northampton T
Maidstone U v Walsall
Rochdale v Cardiff C
Scarborough v Bury
Scunthorpe U v Chesterfield
Shrewsbury T v Barnet
Torquay U v Darlington
Wrexham v Hereford U

Sunday 7 March 1993
FA Premier League
Sheffield U v Leeds U (12.00)

Tuesday 9 March 1993
FA Premier League
Arsenal v Leeds U (7.45)
Blackburn R v Southampton (7.45)
Ipswich T v Sheffield W (7.45)
Oldham Ath v Manchester U
Wimbledon v Middlesbrough (8.00)

Barclays League Division 1
Barnsley v Cambridge U (7.45)
Brentford v Tranmere R (7.45)
Bristol C v Millwall (7.45)
Peterborough U v Birmingham C
Portsmouth v Watford (7.45)
Wolverhampton W v Notts Co

Barclays League Division 2
Bolton W v Mansfield T
Chester C v AFC Bournemouth
Hartlepool U v Burnley
Hull C v Wigan Ath
Leyton O v Rotherham U (7.45)
Plymouth Arg v Blackpool (7.45)
Preston NE v Swansea C

Barclays League Division 3
Cardiff C v Scarborough
Carlisle U v Shrewsbury T
Darlington v Wrexham
Halifax T v Barnet
Hereford U v Crew Alex
Lincoln C v Torquay U
Maidstone U v Colchester U (8.00)
Rochdale v Northampton T
Scunthorpe U v Bury
Walsall v Chesterfield (7.45)
York C v Gillingham

Wednesday 10 March 1993
FA Premier League
Aston Villa v Tottenham H (7.45)

Chelsea v Everton
Liverpool v QPR
Manchester C v Coventry C (7.45)
Nottingham F v Crystal Palace
Sheffield U v Norwich C (7.45)

Barclays League Division 1
Derby Co v Bristol R (7.45)
Leicester C v Sunderland (7.45)
Luton T v Oxford U (7.45)
Newcastle U v Charlton Ath (7.45)
Southend U v Swindon T (7.45)
West Ham U v Grimsby T (7.45)

Barclays League Division 2
Bradford C v Exeter C
Brighton & HA v WBA (7.45)
Huddersfield T v Fulham
Reading v Port Vale (7.45)
Stoke C v Stockport Co

Friday 12 March 1993
Barclays League Division 2
Wigan Ath v Preston NE

Barclays League Division 3
Colchester U v Cardiff C (7.45)
Crewe Alex v Rochdale

Saturday 13 March 1993
FA Premier League
Coventry C v Arsenal
Crystal Palace v Chelsea
Everton v Nottingham F
Leeds U v Manchester C
Manchester U v Aston Villa
Middlesbrough v Liverpool
Norwich C v Oldham Ath
QPR v Wimbledon
Southampton v Ipswich T
Tottenham H v Blackburn R

Barclays League Division 1
Birmingham C v Bristol C
Bristol R v Wolverhampton W
Cambridge U v Portsmouth
Charlton Ath v Brentford
Grimsby T v Luton T
Millwall v Derby Co
Notts Co v West Ham U
Oxford U v Southend
Sunderland v Peterborough U
Swindon T v Newcastle U
Tranmere R v Leicester C
Watford v Barnsley

Barclays League Division 2
AFC Bournemouth v Stoke C
Blackpool v Reading
Burnley v Hull C
Exeter C v Hartlepool U
Fulham v Bradford C
Mansfield T v Huddersfield T
Port Vale v Bolton W
Rotherham U v Plymouth Arg
Stockport Co v Brighton & HA
Swansea C v Chester C
WBA v Leyton O

Barclays League Division 3
Barnet v York C
Bury v Darlington
Chesterfield v Hereford U
Doncaster R v Scunthorpe U
Gillingham v Carlisle U
Scarborough v Walsall
Shrewsbury T v Maidstone U
Torquay U v Halifax T
Wrexham v Lincoln C

Sunday 14 March 1993
FA Premier League
Sheffield W v Sheffield U (12.00)

Tuesday 16 March 1993
Barclays League Division 2
Port Vale v Stoke C (7.45)

Friday 19 March 1993
Barclays League Division 2
Chester C v Rotherham U

Saturday 20 March 1993
FA Premier League
Arsenal v Southampton
Aston Villa v Sheffield W
Blackburn R v Middlesbrough
Chelsea v Tottenham H
Ipswich T v Coventry C
Liverpool v Everton
Manchester C v Manchester U
Nottingham F v Leeds U
Oldham Ath v QPR
Sheffield U v Crystal Palace
Wimbledon v Norwich C

Barclays League Division 1
Barnsley v Sunderland
Brentford v Birmingham C
Bristol C v Watford
Derby Co v Swindon T
Leicester C v Grimsby T
Luton T v Bristol R
Newcastle U v Notts Co
Peterborough U v Oxford U
Portsmouth v Charlton Ath
Southend U v Millwall
West Ham U v Tranmere R
Wolverhampton W v Cambridge U

Barclays League Division 2
Bolton W v Exeter C
Bradford C v Wigan Ath
Brighton & HA v AFC Bournemouth
Hartlepool U v WBA
Huddersfield T v Blackpool
Hull C v Mansfield T
Leyton O v Port Vale
Plymouth Arg v Swansea C
Preston NE v Stockport Co
Reading v Burnley
Stoke C v Fulham

Barclays League Division 3
Cardiff C v Chesterfield
Carlisle U v Colchester U
Darlington v Northampton T
Halifax T v Shrewsbury T
Hereford U v Gillingham
Lincoln C v Scarborough
Maidstone U v Doncaster R
Rochdale v Torquay U
Scunthorpe U v Wrexham
Walsall v Barnet
York C v Bury

Tuesday 23 March 1993
FA Premier League
Crystal Palace v Liverpool (8.00)
Leeds U v Chelsea
Middlesbrough v Oldham Ath
Tottenham H v Manchester C

Barclays League Division 1
Birmingham C v Barnsley (8.00)
Cambridge U v Leicester C (7.45)
Charlton Ath v Wolverhampton W (7.45)
Grimsby T v Brentford (7.45)
Notts Co v Southend U (7.45)
Oxford U v West Ham U (7.45)
Sunderland v Derby Co (7.45)
Swindon T v Bristol C (7.45)
Tranmere R v Portsmouth
Watford v Newcastle U (7.45)

Barclays League Division 2
AFC Bournemouth v Plymouth Arg (7.45)
Blackpool v Hull C (7.45)
Burnley v Bolton W
Exeter C v Reading
Fulham v Brighton & HA
Mansfield T v Leyton O
Port Vale v Huddersfield T
Rotherham U v Bradford C
Stockport Co v Hartlepool U
Swansea C v Stoke C
Wigan Ath v Chester C

Barclays League Division 3
Barnet v Darlington (7.45)
Bury v Cardiff C
Chesterfield v Halifax T
Colchester U v Hereford U (7.45)
Crewe Alex v York C
Doncaster R v Rochdale
Gillingham v Lincoln C (7.45)
Northampton T v Carlisle U
Scarborough v Scunthorpe U
Torquay U v Maidstone U
Wrexham v Walsall

Wednesday 24 March 1993
FA Premier League
Coventry C v Sheffield U (7.45)
Everton v Ipswich T
Manchester U v Arsenal (8.00)
Norwich C v Aston Villa (7.45)
QPR v Blackburn R (7.45)
Sheffield W v Wimbledon (7.45)
Southampton v Nottingham F

Barclays League Division 1
Bristol R v Peterborough U (8.00)
Millwall v Luton T (7.45)

Barclays League Division 2
WBA v Preston NE

Friday 26 March 1993
Barclays League Division 1
Southend U v Tranmere R (7.45)

Barclays League Division 3
Halifax T v Wrexham
York C v Northampton T

Saturday 27 March 1993
Barclays League Division 1
Barnsley v Bristol R
Brentford v Swindon T
Bristol C v Grimsby T
Derby Co v Notts Co
Leicester C v Charlton Ath
Luton T v Cambridge U
Newcastle U v Birmingham C
Peterborough U v Watford
Portsmouth v Oxford U
West Ham U v Millwall
Wolverhampton W v Sunderland

Barclays League Division 2
Bolton W v Fulham
Bradford C v WBA
Brighton & HA v Swansea C
Chester C v Exeter C
Hartlepool U v Mansfield T
Huddersfield T v Burnley
Hull C v Port Vale
Leyton O v Wigan Ath
Plymouth Arg v Stockport Co
Preston NE v Rotherham U
Reading v AFC Bournemouth
Stoke C v Blackpool

Barclays League Division 3
Cardiff C v Barnet
Carlisle U v Doncaster R
Darlington v Gillingham

Hereford U v Bury
Lincoln C v Crewe Alex
Maidstone U v Scarborough
Rochdale v Colchester U
Scunthorpe U v Torquay U
Walsall v Shrewsbury T

Friday 2 April 1993
Barclays League Division 1
Tranmere R v Derby Co

Barclays League Division 2
Fulham v Huddersfield T

Barclays League Division 3
Crewe Alex v Hereford U
Gillingham v York C (7.45)
Northampton T v Rochdale
Wrexham v Darlington

Saturday 3 April 1993
FA Premier League
Arsenal v Tottenham H
Blackburn R v Liverpool
Chelsea v Middlesbrough
Coventry C v Southampton
Crystal Palace v QPR
Everton v Sheffield U
Manchester C v Ipswich T
Norwich C v Manchester U
Nottingham F v Aston Villa
Oldham Ath v Wimbledon
Sheffield W v Leeds U

Barclays League Division 1
Birmingham C v West Ham U
Bristol R v Leicester C
Cambridge U v Newcastle U
Charlton Ath v Barnsley
Grimsby T v Wolverhampton W
Millwall v Portsmouth
Notts Co v Bristol C
Oxford U v Brentford
Sunderland v Southend U
Swindon T v Peterborough U
Watford v Luton T

Barclays League Division 2
AFC Bournemouth v Chester C
Blackpool v Plymouth Arg
Burnley v Hartlepool U
Exeter C v Bradford C
Mansfield T v Bolton W
Port Vale v Reading
Rotherham U v Leyton O
Stockport Co v Stoke C
Swansea C v Preston NE
WBA v Brighton & HA
Wigan Ath v Hull C

Barclays League Division 3
Barnet v Halifax T
Bury v Scunthorpe U
Chesterfield v Walsall
Colchester U v Maidstone U
Scarborough v Cardiff C
Shrewsbury T v Carlisle U
Torquay U v Lincoln C (6.30)

Tuesday 6 April 1993
Barclays League Division 1
Birmingham C v Derby Co (8.00)
Brentford v Sunderland (7.45)
Bristol C v Bristol R (7.45)
Cambridge U v Notts Co (7.45)
Charlton Ath v Watford (7.45)
Grimsby T v Millwall (7.45)
Portsmouth v Peterborough U (7.45)
Tranmere R v Swindon T

Barclays League Division 2
AFC Bournemouth v Bradford C
Blackpool v Wigan Ath (7.45)

Bolton W v Stockport Co
Exeter C v Hull C
Hartlepool U v Plymouth Arg
Leyton O v Burnley (7.45)
Port Vale v Preston NE
Rotherham U v Fulham

Barclays League Division 3
Cardiff C v Doncaster R
Chesterfield v York C
Crewe Alex v Carlisle U
Darlington v Walsall
Gillingham v Shrewsbury T (7.45)
Halifax T v Maidstone U
Hereford U v Scunthorpe U
Northampton T v Bury
Rochdale v Barnet
Scarborough v Wrexham
Torquay U v Colchester U

Wednesday 7 April 1993
Barclays League Division 1
Leicester C v Oxford U (7.45)
Luton T v Wolverhampton W (7.45)
Newcastle U v Barnsley (7.45)
Southend U v West Ham U (7.45)

Barclays League Division 2
Brighton & HA v Mansfield T (7.45)
Huddersfield T v Stoke C
Reading v Chester C (7.45)
WBA v Swansea C

Friday 9 April 1993
FA Premier League
Tottenham H v Norwich C (12.00)

Barclays League Division 2
Stockport Co v Rotherham U

Barclays League Division 3
Colchester U v Northampton T
(7.45)

Saturday 10 April 1993
FA Premier League
Aston Villa v Coventry C
Ipswich T v Arsenal
Leeds U v Blackburn R
Liverpool v Oldham Ath
Manchester U v Sheffield W
Middlesbrough v Everton
QPR v Nottingham F
Sheffield U v Manchester C
Southampton v Chelsea
Wimbledon v Crystal Palace

Barclays League Division 1
Barnsley v Grimsby T
Bristol R v Portsmouth
Derby Co v Brentford
Millwall v Tranmere R
Notts Co v Charlton Ath
Oxford U v Bristol C
Peterborough U v Cambridge U
Sunderland v Birmingham C
Swindon T v Luton T
Watford v Southend U
West Ham U v Leicester C
Wolverhampton W v Newcastle U

Barclays League Division 2
Bradford C v Blackpool
Burnley v Brighton & HA
Chester C v WBA
Fulham v Leyton O
Hull C v Hartlepool U
Mansfield T v Port Vale
Plymouth Arg v Exeter C
Preston NE v Huddersfield T
Stoke C v Reading
Swansea C v AFC Bournemouth
Wigan Ath v Bolton W

Barclays League Division 3
Barnet v Scarborough
Carlisle U v Darlington
Doncaster R v Halifax T
Lincoln C v Chesterfield
Maidstone U v Gillingham
Scunthorpe U v Rochdale
Shrewsbury T v Hereford U
Walsall v Torquay U
Wrexham v Crewe Alex
York C v Cardiff C

Monday 12 April 1993
FA Premier League
Arsenal v Aston Villa
Blackburn R v Ipswich T
Chelsea v Wimbledon
Coventry C v Manchester U
Crystal Palace v Middlesbrough
Everton v QPR
Manchester C v Liverpool
Nottingham F v Tottenham H
Oldham Ath v Sheffield U
Sheffield W v Southampton

Barclays League Division 1
Birmingham C v Swindon T
Brentford v Notts Co
Bristol C v Wolverhampton W
Charlton Ath v Peterborough U
Grimsby T v Sunderland
Newcastle U v Oxford U
Portsmouth v Derby Co
Tranmere R v Barnsley

Barclays League Division 2
Bolton W v Swansea C
Exeter C v Preston NE
Hartlepool U v Fulham
Huddersfield T v Wigan Ath
Leyton O v Stockport Co
Reading v Mansfield T
Rotherham U v Stoke C
WBA v Plymouth Arg

Barclays League Division 3
Cardiff C v Lincoln C
Chesterfield v Wrexham
Crewe Alex v Shrewsbury T
Darlington v Doncaster R
Gillingham v Scunthorpe U
Halifax T v York C
Hereford U v Maidstone U
Northampton T v Walsall
Rochdale v Bury

Tuesday 13 April 1993
Barclays League Division 1
Cambridge U v Watford (7.45)
Leicester C v Millwall (7.45)
Luton T v West Ham U (7.45)

Barclays League Division 2
AFC Bournemouth v Burnley (7.45)
Blackpool v Chester C (7.45)
Port Vale v Bradford C (7.45)

Barclays League Division 3
Scarborough v Colchester U
Torquay U v Barnet

Wednesday 14 April 1993
FA Premier League
Norwich C v Leeds U (7.45)

Barclays League Division 1
Southend U v Bristol R (7.45)

Barclays League Division 2
Brighton & HA v Hull C (7.45)

Friday 16 April 1993
Barclays League Division 2
Stockport Co v Reading

Barclays League Division 3
Colchester U v Gillingham (7.45)

Saturday 17 April 1993
FA Premier League
Aston Villa v Manchester C
Ipswich T v Norwich C
Leeds U v Crystal Palace
Liverpool v Coventry C
Manchester U v Chelsea
Middlesbrough v Arsenal
QPR v Sheffield W
Sheffield U v Blackburn R
Southampton v Everton
Tottenham H v Oldham Ath
Wimbledon v Nottingham F

Barclays League Division 1
Barnsley v Southend U
Bristol R v Cambridge U
Derby Co v Grimsby T
Millwall v Newcastle U
Notts Co v Portsmouth
Oxford U v Charlton Ath
Peterborough U v Bristol C
Sunderland v Luton T
Swindon T v Leicester C
Watford v Birmingham C
West Ham U v Brentford
Wolverhampton W v Tranmere R

Barclays League Division 2
Bradford C v Bolton W
Burnley v Exeter C
Chester C v Huddersfield T
Fulham v Blackpool
Hull C v AFC Bournemouth
Mansfield T v WBA
Plymouth Arg v Brighton & HA
Preston NE v Leyton O
Stoke C v Hartlepool U
Swansea C v Rotherham U
Wigan Ath v Port Vale

Barclays League Division 3
Bury v Halifax T
Carlisle U v Hereford U
Doncaster R v Chesterfield
Lincoln C v Rochdale
Maidstone U v Northampton T
Scunthorpe U v Darlington
Shrewsbury T v Torquay U
Walsall v Crewe Alex
Wrexham v Cardiff C
York C v Scarborough

Friday 23 April 1993
Barclays League Division 1
Southend U v Grimsby T (7.45)

Saturday 24 April 1993
Barclays League Division 1
Barnsley v Oxford U
Birmingham C v Tranmere R
Bristol C v Cambridge U
Derby Co v Luton T
Millwall v Charlton Ath
Notts Co v Swindon T
Peterborough U v Leicester C
Portsmouth v Wolverhampton W
Watford v Brentford
West Ham U v Bristol R

Barclays League Division 2
AFC Bournemouth v Leyton O
Blackpool v Stockport Co
Bolton W v Chester C
Bradford C v Reading
Brighton & HA v Rotherham U

Fulham v Burnley
Huddersfield T v Hull C
Mansfield T v Exeter C
Plymouth Arg v Port Vale
Stoke C v Preston NE
Swansea C v Hartlepool U
WBA v Wigan Ath

Barclays League Division 3
Crewe Alex v Colchester U
Doncaster R v Northampton T
Halifax T v Walsall
Lincoln C v Bury
Maidstone U v Cardiff C
Rochdale v York C
Scarborough v Darlington
Scunthorpe U v Barnet
Shrewsbury T v Chesterfield
Torquay U v Hereford U (6.30)
Wrexham v Carlisle U

Sunday 25 April 1993

Barclays League Division 1
Newcastle U v Sunderland (12.00)

Tuesday 27 April 1993
Barclays League Division 3
Northampton T v Wrexham

Friday 30 April 1993
Barclays League Division 2
Hull C v Bolton W

Saturday 1 May 1993
FA Premier League
Aston Villa v Oldham Ath
Chelsea v Coventry C
Crystal Palace v Ipswich T
Everton v Arsenal
Leeds U v QPR
Manchester U v Blackburn R
Norwich C v Liverpool
Nottingham F v Sheffield U
Sheffield W v Middlesbrough
Southampton v Manchester C
Tottenham H v Wimbledon

Barclays League Division 1
Brentford v Barnsley
Bristol R v Birmingham C
Cambridge U v Southend U
Charlton Ath v Derby Co
Grimsby T v Newcastle U
Leicester C v Bristol C
Luton T v Peterborough U
Oxford U v Notts Co
Sunderland v Portsmouth
Swindon T v West Ham U
Tranmere R v Watford
Wolverhampton W v Millwall

Barclays League Division 2
Burnley v Blackpool
Chester C v Fulham
Exeter C v Huddersfield T
Hartlepool U v Brighton & HA
Leyton O v Bradford C
Preston NE v Mansfield T
Reading v Swansea C
Rotherham U v WBA
Stockport Co v AFC Bournemouth
Wigan Ath v Plymouth Arg

Barclays League Division 3
Barnet v Lincoln C
Bury v Crewe Alex
Cardiff C v Shrewsbury T
Carlisle U v Torquay U
Chesterfield v Scarborough
Colchester U v Scunthorpe U
Gillingham v Halifax T
Hereford U v Doncaster R
Walsall v Rochdale
York C v Maidstone U

Saturday 8 May 1993

FA Premier League
Arsenal v Crystal Palace
Blackburn R v Sheffield W
Coventry C v Leeds U
Ipswich T v Nottingham F
Liverpool v Tottenham H
Manchester C v Everton
Middlesbrough v Norwich C

Oldham Ath v Southampton
QPR v Aston Villa
Sheffield U v Chelsea
Wimbledon v Manchester U

Barclays League Division 1
Barnsley v Swindon T
Birmingham C v Charlton Ath
Bristol C v Brentford
Derby Co v Wolverhampton W
Millwall v Bristol R
Newcastle U v Leicester C
Notts Co v Sunderland
Peterborough U v Tranmere R
Portsmouth v Grimsby T
Southend U v Luton T
Watford v Oxford U
West Ham U v Cambridge U

Barclays League Division 2
AFC Bournemouth v Wigan Ath
Blackpool v Port Vale
Bolton W v Preston NE
Bradford C v Hartlepool U
Brighton & HA v Chester C
Fulham v Exeter C
Huddersfield T v Stockport Co
Mansfield T v Rotherham U
Plymouth Arg v Reading
Stoke C v Burnley
Swansea C v Leyton O
WBA v Hull C

Barclays League Division 3
Crewe Alex v Barnet
Doncaster R v Walsall
Halifax T v Hereford U
Lincoln C v Darlington
Maidstone U v Bury
Rochdale v Chesterfield
Scarborough v Carlisle U
Scunthorpe U v Cardiff C
Shrewsbury T v Northampton T
Torquay U v Gillingham
Wrexham v Colchester U

FA PREMIER LEAGUE FIXTURES 1992–93

	Arsenal	Aston Villa	Blackburn R	Chelsea	Coventry C	Crystal Palace	Everton	Ipswich T	Leeds U	Liverpool	Manchester C	Manchester U	Middlesbrough	Norwich C	Nottingham F	Oldham Ath	QPR	Sheffield U	Sheffield W	Southampton	Tottenham H	Wimbledon
Arsenal	—	12.4	12.9	3.10	7.11	8.5	24.10	26.12	9.3	30.1	28.9	28.11	19.12	15.8	6.3	26.8	13.2	9.1	29.8	20.3	3.4	9.2
Aston Villa	28.12	—	19.10	2.9	10.4	5.9	20.2	6.2	19.8	19.9	17.4	7.11	16.1	28.11	12.12	1.5	1.11	27.1	20.3	22.8	10.3	27.2
Blackburn R	18.8	6.3	—	20.2	26.1	6.2	15.9	12.4	26.12	3.4	22.8	24.10	20.3	3.10	5.9	26.9	28.11	19.12	8.5	9.3	7.11	9.1
Chelsea	27.2	13.2	26.8	—	1.5	7.11	10.3	17.10	28.11	10.2	9.1	19.12	3.4	12.9	26.9	15.8	29.8	31.10	30.1	26.12	20.3	12.4
Coventry C	13.3	26.12	29.8	24.10	—	3.10	6.3	5.12	8.5	19.12	21.11	12.4	15.8	26.9	9.1	10.2	26.8	24.3	13.2	3.4	14.9	30.1
Crystal Palace	2.11	9.2	15.8	13.3	27.2	—	9.1	1.5	19.12	23.3	17.10	13.2	12.4	29.8	21.11	12.9	3.4	5.12	25.8	26.9	30.1	26.12
Everton	1.5	25.8	13.2	21.11	17.10	19.9	—	24.3	16.1	7.12	31.10	12.9	26.12	30.1	13.3	27.2	12.4	3.4	15.8	19.12	10.2	29.8
Ipswich T	10.4	15.8	28.12	6.3	20.3	24.10	28.11	—	3.10	25.8	12.12	30.1	13.2	17.4	8.5	9.1	9.2	26.9	9.3	7.11	30.8	12.9
Leeds U	21.11	13.9	10.4	23.3	31.10	17.4	26.9	27.2	—	29.8	13.3	9.2	30.1	28.12	5.12	13.2	1.5	17.10	12.12	9.1	25.8	15.8
Liverpool	23.8	9.1	12.12	5.9	17.4	28.11	20.3	27.2	27.1	—	28.12	6.3	7.11	24.10	6.2	10.4	10.3	19.8	3.10	1.9	25.8	15.8
Manchester C	16.1	19.12	30.1	20.9	10.3	6.3	8.5	3.4	7.11	12.4	—	28.12	12.9	26.8	3.10	29.8	17.8	26.12	10.2	24.10	28.11	13.2
Manchester U	24.3	13.3	1.5	17.4	28.12	2.9	19.8	22.8	6.9	18.10	5.12	—	27.2	12.12	27.1	21.11	26.9	6.2	10.4	20.2	9.1	31.10
Middlesbrough	17.4	26.9	5.12	12.12	6.2	28.12	10.4	1.9	22.8	13.3	19.8	3.10	—	8.5	31.8	13.3	13.2	7.9	24.10	26.1	6.3	21.11
Norwich C	6.2	24.3	27.2	19.8	16.1	27.1	21.12	14.4	1.5	20.2	3.4	31.10	13.2	—	13.3	23.3	9.1	7.9	19.9	28.11	6.3	21.11
Nottingham F	17.10	3.4	10.2	16.1	19.9	10.3	7.11	31.10	20.3	16.8	3.4	3.4	21.10	13.2	—	31.8	13.3	26.12	1.5	12.9	24.3	20.12
Oldham Ath	20.2	24.10	16.1	6.2	5.9	19.8	4.10	19.9	1.9	26.12	26.1	9.3	28.11	7.11	22.8	—	20.3	12.4	6.3	8.5	19.12	3.4
QPR	2.9	8.5	24.3	27.1	28.11	20.3	28.12	5.9	24.10	23.11	6.2	16.1	19.9	6.3	10.3	5.12	—	22.8	17.4	19.8	3.10	13.3
Sheffield U	19.9	29.8	17.4	8.5	28.11	20.3	28.12	12.1	7.3	12.9	10.4	15.8	9.2	10.3	9.1	29.12	30.1	—	8.11	22.8	3.10	13.3
Sheffield W	27.1	5.12	31.10	22.8	2.9	20.2	6.2	21.11	17.10	3.10	26.12	1.5	9.1	19.8	17.10	29.12	30.1	14.3	—	27.2	12.4	24.3
Southampton	5.12	30.1	21.11	10.4	12.12	16.1	17.4	13.3	19.9	13.2	24.8	1.5	29.8	10.2	24.3	31.10	12.9	27.2	28.12	—	15.8	17.10
Tottenham H	12.12	21.11	13.3	5.12	19.8	22.8	5.9	26.1	20.2	31.10	23.3	19.9	17.10	9.4	28.12	17.4	27.2	2.9	16.1	6.2	—	1.5
Wimbledon	5.9	3.10	19.9	28.12	22.8	10.4	26.1	18.8	6.2	16.1	1.9	8.5	9.3	20.3	17.4	12.12	7.11	20.2	28.11	6.3	25.10	—

BARCLAYS LEAGUE FIXTURES 1992–93

DIVISION ONE

	Barnsley	Birmingham C	Brentford	Bristol C	Bristol R	Cambridge	Charlton Ath	Derby Co	Grimsby T	Leicester C	Luton T	Millwall	Newcastle U	Notts Co	Oxford U	Peterborough U	Portsmouth	Southend U	Sunderland	Swindon T	Tranmere R	Watford	West Ham U	Wolverhampton
Barnsley	—	21.11	24.10	16.1	27.3	9.3	28.11	12.9	10.4	6.3	10.10	29.8	12.12	13.2	24.4	19.9	30.1	17.4	20.3	8.5	28.12	7.11	15.8	1.9
Birmingham C	23.3	—	5.12	13.3	24.10	30.1	8.5	6.4	29.8	10.10	9.1	9.2	3.11	15.8	6.3	2.1	13.2	1.9	26.12	12.4	24.4	19.12	3.4	26.9
Brentford	1.5	20.3	—	31.10	30.1	14.2	7.11	26.12	21.11	9.1	12.9	26.9	3.10	12.4	28.11	27.2	27.2	29.8	6.4	27.3	9.3	7.10	20.12	15.8
Bristol C	26.9	7.11	8.5	—	6.4	24.4	10.10	13.2	21.11	24.10	30.1	26.9	9.1	28.11	26.12	19.12	15.8	12.9	29.8	21.11	6.3	20.3	15.9	12.4
Bristol R	3.11	1.5	22.8	8.12	—	17.4	27.1	14.11	19.9	3.4	5.12	31.10	5.9	3.10	6.2	24.3	10.4	28.12	16.1	19.8	20.2	27.2	17.10	13.3
Cambridge	14.11	22.8	4.9	17.10	8.12	—	18.8	3.10	16.1	3.11	29.8	27.2	3.4	6.4	26.1	26.12	13.3	1.5	19.9	20.2	6.2	13.4	31.10	23.3
Charlton Ath	3.4	31.10	13.3	27.2	27.1	18.8	—	1.5	15.8	3.11	24.4	17.10	14.11	6.4	19.12	12.4	6.3	5.9	23.3	16.1	9.1	20.2	26.12	8.5
Derby Co	10.2	12.12	10.4	5.9	10.3	6.3	24.10	—	1.5	10.10	27.3	7.11	22.8	30.1	19.12	6.2	26.9	2.9	3.10	26.1	28.11	20.2	6.4	8.5
Grimsby T	26.12	20.2	23.3	14.11	19.9	26.9	17.4	27.1	—	5.12	13.3	6.4	1.5	27.3	5.9	3.10	2.9	26.9	28.12	26.1	9.2	22.8	28.11	3.4
Leicester C	3.10	19.9	10.2	22.8	20.3	27.3	2.11	19.12	13.3	—	15.8	13.4	31.10	16.1	10.3	27.1	6.2	31.10	10.3	20.12	5.9	22.8	30.1	12.9
Luton T	27.2	19.9	10.2	4.11	16.1	29.8	24.4	24.3	24.4	15.8	—	21.11	17.4	16.1	10.3	1.5	6.3	31.10	3.10	24.3	5.9	28.12	13.4	24.10
Millwall	20.2	10.2	16.1	4.11	13.2	19.9	27.3	17.10	3.10	13.4	21.11	—	17.4	19.9	22.8	27.1	3.10	5.12	30.1	21.11	13.4	27.3	13.4	27.3
Newcastle U	7.4	3.11	6.3	19.9	27.3	6.3	14.11	17.10	12.4	31.10	27.1	17.4	—	5.12	12.4	16.1	12.9	3.4	26.9	7.11	28.11	6.2	13.3	24.10
Notts Co	5.9	15.8	26.1	19.9	19.9	3.4	6.4	30.1	30.1	5.12	16.1	19.9	1.5	—	24.10	26.12	19.12	9.2	30.10	21.11	26.1	25.8	13.3	9.3
Oxford U	17.10	3.10	10.4	17.4	15.8	10.4	19.12	19.12	27.3	7.4	10.3	22.8	12.4	16.1	—	5.12	12.12	20.3	20.3	9.1	26.9	25.8	27.3	20.2
Peterborough U	9.1	9.3	3.4	10.4	15.8	28.12	6.3	6.2	2.9	26.1	6.2	27.1	26.9	29.8	20.3	—	3.11	13.3	12.9	7.11	8.5	27.3	12.9	13.2
Portsmouth	22.8	5.9	26.1	6.2	26.12	6.2	2.9	9.2	6.3	19.12	9.2	19.12	26.9	19.12	27.3	6.4	—	9.1	24.10	10.10	9.3	27.2	26.9	24.4
Southend U	19.12	27.1	21.2	10.2	25.10	7.11	20.3	12.4	23.4	5.9	8.5	20.3	20.1	21.11	7.11	22.8	18.9	—	28.11	10.3	26.3	26.12	7.4	10.10
Sunderland	5.12	10.4	21.2	20.2	5.9	23.3	5.9	14.11	28.12	14.11	17.4	3.0	18.10	31.10	9.2	13.3	1.5	3.4	—	6.2	22.8	26.1	27.2	3.11
Swindon T	31.10	29.12	3.11	23.3	29.8	3.11	16.1	5.12	29.9	17.4	10.4	26.12	13.3	17.10	19.9	3.4	27.2	14.11	15.8	—	12.12	3.10	1.5	30.1
Tranmere R	12.4	17.10	14.11	3.10	28.8	17.4	18.9	2.4	13.3	13.10	3.4	27.2	29.9	17.10	15.1	3.11	27.2	14.11	15.8	12.12	—	1.5	4.12	19.12
Watford	13.3	17.4	24.4	10.2	28.8	8.5	18.9	2.4	30.1	29.8	3.4	15.8	23.3	12.9	8.5	30.10	14.11	29.9	30.1	6.4	24.10	—	13.2	9.1
West Ham U	6.2	28.11	17.4	27.1	24.4	28.12	26.1	27.2	9.2	12.12	28.12	27.3	20.2	7.11	21.11	10.2	16.1	12.12	27.3	6.2	20.3	13.2	—	6.3
Wolverhampton W	26.1	16.1	6.2	28.12	7.11	20.3	21.11	31.10	28.11	5.9	7.11	1.5	9.3	20.2	5.9	17.10	16.1	12.12	27.3	22.8	17.4	19.9	3.10	—

DIVISION TWO

	Blackpool	Bolton W	Bournemouth	Bradford C	Brighton & HA	Burnley	Chester C	Exeter C	Fulham	Hartlepool U	Huddersfield T	Hull C	Leyton O	Mansfield T	Plymouth Arg	Port Vale	Preston NE	Reading	Rotherham U	Stockport Co	Stoke C	Swansea C	WBA	Wigan Ath
Blackpool	—	20.2	15.9	26.12	19.9	24.10	13.4	22.8	19.12	6.3	3.11	23.3	26.1	5.9	3.4	8.5	10.10	13.3	16.1	24.4	21.11	2.1	6.2	6.4
Bolton W	1.9	—	19.9	19.12	30.1	28.11	24.4	20.3	27.3	10.10	15.8	24.10	6.3	9.3	16.1	7.11	8.5	29.8	10.10	6.4	13.2	12.4	15.9	26.12
Bournemouth	9.1	23.1	—	6.4	3.11	13.4	3.4	6.3	12.9	5.9	26.9	19.12	24.4	20.2	23.3	22.8	6.2	21.11	10.10	24.10	13.3	26.12	26.1	8.5
Bradford C	10.4	17.4	12.12	—	29.8	11.10	15.8	10.3	7.11	8.5	14.2	6.3	24.10	2.1	30.1	28.12	19.9	24.4	28.11	16.9	2.9	16.1	27.3	20.3
Brighton & HA	23.1	22.8	20.3	27.1	—	26.12	8.5	20.2	28.11	24.10	12.9	14.4	6.2	7.4	19.12	6.3	5.9	26.9	24.4	7.11	9.1	27.3	10.3	10.10
Burnley	1.5	23.3	28.12	27.2	26.12	—	13.2	17.4	17.10	3.4	17.4	6.3	7.4	19.9	27.2	16.1	26.1	3.11	29.8	30.1	31.10	31.10	3.10	16.1
Chester C	28.12	17.10	9.3	6.2	31.10	13.2	—	27.3	1.5	20.2	1.5	6.4	19.9	15.9	16.1	2.1	12.4	12.12	19.3	19.9	3.10	15.8	27.2	27.11
Exeter C	30.1	3.11	3.10	3.4	1.9	5.9	27.3	—	31.10	17.4	2.4	10.10	10.4	17.10	26.12	16.1	22.8	23.3	15.8	13.2	29.8	30.1	16.1	15.9
Fulham	17.4	21.11	2.1	13.3	23.3	19.12	21.11	1.5	—	1.5	29.8	26.12	12.12	16.1	19.9	15.9	16.1	6.3	12.12	12.12	3.11	27.2	5.9	20.2
Hartlepool U	4.10	6.2	3.10	16.9	1.5	24.4	24.10	8.5	28.12	—	28.12	2.1	16.1	19.9	6.4	2.1	26.12	15.8	30.1	26.1	20.12	7.11	10.4	2.1
Huddersfield T	20.3	13.2	13.2	6.9	9.3	9.3	1.9	7.11	12.9	28.12	—	29.8	10.4	26.1	19.9	19.9	15.9	13.2	19.9	28.11	7.4	19.9	20.3	12.4
Hull C	28.11	30.4	16.1	3.10	28.12	27.3	22.8	12.12	27.2	10.4	17.10	—	20.2	7.11	16.1	27.3	18.12	30.1	9.3	8.5	15.8	31.10	28.12	9.3
Leyton O	29.8	3.4	17.4	1.5	15.8	7.11	12.9	23.1	26.12	9.1	1.9	26.9	—	28.11	13.2	20.3	24.10	28.12	8.5	12.4	27.2	30.1	7.11	27.3
Mansfield T	13.2	1.9	1.9	12.9	12.12	6.4	9.1	24.4	29.8	21.11	13.3	3.11	28.11	—	15.8	10.4	6.3	8.5	1.9	10.10	26.9	20.3	17.4	6.3
Plymouth Arg	9.3	26.9	28.11	22.8	17.4	23.1	24.4	12.9	23.1	12.12	9.1	5.9	23.3	15.8	—	24.4	6.4	3.4	27.3	27.3	12.9	16.3	28.12	24.10
Port Vale	31.10	13.3	30.1	13.4	3.10	9.1	10.10	28.12	13.2	23.1	23.1	26.1	5.9	10.4	10.4	—	6.4	20.10	20.3	20.3	16.3	13.2	27.2	19.12
Preston NE	27.2	31.10	15.8	23.1	13.2	26.9	26.9	28.11	30.1	26.9	10.4	9.1	17.4	6.3	6.4	6.4	—	20.2	16.9	19.12	17.10	9.3	28.11	7.11
Reading	7.11	27.1	27.3	17.10	16.1	20.3	29.8	27.1	2.10	6.2	27.2	5.9	22.8	31.10	3.10	3.4	21.11	—	16.9	16.9	26.12	1.5	2.1	19.9
Rotherham U	26.9	12.9	26.2	23.3	17.10	12.9	7.4	5.9	6.4	22.8	3.10	22.8	3.4	12.4	31.10	10.3	3.11	9.1	—	26.12	12.4	18.12	1.5	5.9
Stockport Co	16.10	11.12	1.5	9.1	13.3	22.8	3.11	25.9	23.3	23.3	30.10	23.1	23.12	26.2	13.3	20.2	24.4	10.4	9.4	—	3.4	3.10	3.10	5.2
Stoke C	27.3	5.9	7.11	20.2	16.9	8.5	13.3	20.3	20.3	17.4	12.12	6.2	10.10	20.11	2.1	26.1	3.4	24.10	28.12	16.3	—	28.11	19.9	22.8
Swansea C	12.9	28.12	10.4	26.9	20.11	5.2	26.12	10.10	9.1	24.4	23.1	20.2	8.5	22.3	3.11	5.9	24.3	9.9	17.4	5.3	23.3	—	12.12	26.1
WBA	15.8	9.1	29.8	21.11	3.4	6.3	23.3	26.9	28.11	4.11	30.1	8.5	13.3	3.10	12.4	10.10	12.3	23.1	24.10	2.9	23.1	7.4	—	24.4
Wigan Ath	12.12	10.4	31.10	3.11	27.2	26.9	9.1	9.1	11.9	11.9	28.12	3.4	21.11	31.10	1.5	17.4	17.10	13.2	13.2	15.8	30.1	29.8	17.10	—

DIVISION THREE

	Barnet	Bury	Cardiff C	Carlisle U	Chesterfield	Colchester U	Crewe Alex	Darlington	Doncaster R	Gillingham	Halifax T	Hereford U	Lincoln C	Maidstone	Northampton T	Rochdale	Scarborough	Scunthorpe U	Shrewsbury T	Torquay U	Walsall	Wrexham	York C
Barnet	—	2.1	22.11	5.9	6.2	21.8	31.10	23.3	20.2	26.1	3.4	19.9	1.5	27.2	15.9	12.2	10.4	17.10	3.10	28.12	3.11	16.1	13.3
Bury	12.9	—	23.3	20.2	26.1	5.9	1.5	13.3	6.2	22.8	17.4	21.11	17.10	31.10	12.12	28.12	3.10	3.4	23.1	26.9	9.1	27.2	3.11
Cardiff C	27.3	28.11	—	8.9	20.3	7.11	27.2	15.8	6.4	19.9	29.8	2.1	12.4	17.10	1.9	3.10	9.3	31.10	9.3	1.5	30.1	18.12	26.12
Carlisle U	13.2	1.9	9.1	—	23.1	20.3	12.12	10.4	27.3	7.11	3.10	17.4	29.8	30.1	28.11	27.2	31.10	26.9	9.3	1.5	15.8	17.10	12.9
Chesterfield	15.8	29.8	3.11	19.9	—	16.1	15.9	1.9	10.4	2.1	3.10	29.8	26.12	13.2	28.11	27.2	1.5	3.10	17.10	27.2	3.4	12.4	6.4
Colchester U	29.1	13.2	12.3	3.11	26.9	—	16.10	29.8	8.1	16.4	23.3	13.3	15.8	3.4	30.1	31.10	29.12	1.5	1.9	11.12	12.9	30.10	22.1
Crewe Alex	8.5	24.10	10.10	6.4	9.1	24.4	—	13.2	12.9	6.3	26.2	23.3	3.4	26.9	9.4	21.11	30.1	23.1	1.9	15.8	18.12	26.12	23.3
Darlington	28.11	7.11	6.2	26.12	9.1	24.4	5.9	—	12.4	27.3	1.9	21.8	31.10	12.9	28.8	12.3	17.10	23.1	12.4	2.10	6.4	9.3	25.9
Doncaster R	1.9	15.8	11.12	21.11	17.4	15.9	2.1	28.12	—	10.10	10.4	23.10	18.9	20.3	24.4	23.3	16.1	13.3	29.1	29.8	8.5	13.2	5.3
Gillingham	29.8	30.1	23.1	13.3	12.9	18.12	3.10	21.11	27.2	—	1.5	3.11	18.9	3.11	15.8	8.1	13.2	12.4	6.4	31.10	26.9	1.9	2.4
Halifax T	9.3	19.12	26.1	6.3	28.11	10.10	20.2	15.9	26.12	24.10	—	8.5	2.1	6.4	16.1	6.2	19.9	22.8	20.3	7.11	24.4	26.3	12.4
Hereford U	23.1	24.4	13.9	19.12	7.11	6.2	27.3	28.12	23.1	20.3	31.10	—	1.9	12.4	13.2	26.9	15.8	6.4	26.12	17.10	29.8	3.10	9.1
Lincoln C	24.10	24.4	28.12	26.1	10.4	6.2	27.3	28.12	20.3	28.11	13.2	9.1	—	12.4	6.3	17.4	20.3	5.9	26.9	9.3	10.10	7.11	22.8
Maidstone	10.10	8.5	24.4	22.8	5.9	9.3	16.1	2.1	20.3	10.4	13.2	20.2	15.9	—	17.4	20.2	27.3	6.2	7.11	28.11	6.3	19.9	24.10
Northampton T	8.1	6.4	19.2	23.3	13.10	26.12	26.1	3.11	17.10	6.2	26.9	6.9	3.10	20.12	—	2.4	27.2	12.9	31.10	23.1	12.4	27.4	21.11
Rochdale	6.4	12.4	6.3	10.10	8.5	7.11	7.11	19.9	28.11	5.9	15.8	16.1	19.12	1.9	9.3	—	29.8	26.12	13.2	20.3	24.10	30.1	24.4
Scarborough	26.12	6.3	3.4	8.5	24.10	27.3	22.8	24.4	26.9	5.9	23.1	6.2	3.11	21.11	9.3	10.10	—	23.3	9.1	12.9	13.3	6.4	19.12
Scunthorpe U	24.4	9.3	8.5	16.1	6.3	24.10	19.9	17.4	7.11	28.12	30.1	12.12	13.2	15.8	2.1	10.4	28.11	—	29.8	27.3	1.9	20.3	10.10
Shrewsbury T	6.3	19.9	24.10	3.4	24.4	20.2	28.12	10.10	22.8	12.12	3.11	10.4	16.1	13.3	8.5	5.9	15.9	26.1	—	17.4	21.11	2.1	6.2
Torquay U	13.4	16.1	5.9	24.10	10.10	6.4	6.2	3.11	26.1	8.5	13.3	24.4	3.4	23.3	19.9	3.11	2.1	21.11	20.12	—	26.12	15.9	20.2
Walsall	20.3	15.9	22.8	6.2	9.3	2.1	17.4	12.12	31.10	16.1	17.10	26.1	27.2	3.10	28.12	1.5	7.11	20.2	27.3	10.4	—	28.11	5.9
Wrexham	26.9	10.10	17.4	24.4	28.12	10.4	8.5	9.3	2.4	20.2	21.11	6.3	13.3	23.1	24.10	22.8	12.12	3.11	12.9	9.1	23.3	—	26.1
York C	7.11	20.3	10.4	2.1	12.12	19.9	28.11	16.1	3.10	9.3	28.12	15.9	30.1	1.5	26.3	17.10	17.4	27.2	15.8	1.9	13.2	29.8	—

High-flying Leeds striker Lee Chapman had the misfortune to break his wrist after falling awkwardly in the FA Cup tie with Manchester United. Leeds lost 1–0. (Allsport)

Ipswich Town players David Linighan, Chris Kiwomya and Romeo Zondervan celebrate winning the Second Division championship. (Allsport)

THE FOOTBALL ASSOCIATION
FIXTURE PROGRAMME—SEASON 1992–93

August
1 Sat   Official Opening of Season
8 Sat   FA Charity Shield
15 Sat   Premier League & Football League Season
           commences
22 Sat
29 Sat   FA Challenge Cup Preliminary Round
31 Mon   Bank Holiday

September
5 Sat   FA Challenge Vase Extra Preliminary Round
9 Wed   International Date
12 Sat   FA Challenge Cup 1st Round Qualifying
           FA Youth Challenge Cup Preliminary Round*
16 Wed   EC/ECWC/UEFA 1st Round (1st Leg)
19 Sat   FA Challenge Trophy—1st Round Qualifying
26 Sat   FA Challenge Cup 2nd Round Qualifying
30 Wed   EC/ECWC/UEFA 1st Round (2nd Leg)

October
3 Sat   FA Challenge Vase Preliminary Round
           FA Youth Challenge Cup 1st Round Qualifying*
10 Sat   FA Challenge Cup 3rd Round Qualifying
11 Sun   FA Sunday Cup First Round
14 Wed   England v Norway (World Cup)
17 Sat   FA Challenge Trophy 2nd Round Qualifying
           FA Youth Challenge Cup 2nd Round
           Qualifying*
           FA County Youth Challenge Cup 1st Round*
21 Sat   EC/ECWC/UEFA 2nd Round (1st Leg)
24 Sat   FA Challenge Cup 4th Round Qualifying
31 Sat   FA Challenge Vase 1st Round

November
4 Wed   EC/ECWC/UEFA 2nd Round (2nd Leg)
7 Sat
8 Sun   FA Sunday Cup 2nd Round
14 Sat   FA Challenge Cup 1st Round Proper
           FA Youth Challenge Cup 1st Round Proper*
18 Wed   England v Turkey (World Cup)
21 Sat   FA Challenge Vase 2nd Round
25 Wed   UEFA Cup 3rd Round (1st Leg)
           FA Challenge Cup 1st Round Proper (Replay)
28 Sat   FA Challenge Trophy 3rd Round Qualifying
           FA County Youth Challenge Cup 2nd Round*

December
5 Sat   FA Challenge Cup 2nd Round Proper
6 Sun   FA Sunday Cup 3rd Round
9 Wed   UEFA Cup 3rd Round (2nd Leg)
12 Sat   FA Challenge Vase 3rd Round
           FA Youth Challenge Cup 2nd Round Proper*
16 Wed   FA Challenge Cup 2nd Round Proper (Replay)
19 Sat
25 Fri   Christmas Day
26 Sat   Boxing Day
28 Mon   Bank Holiday

January
1 Fri   New Year's Day
2 Sat   FA Challenge Cup 3rd Round Proper
9 Sat   FA Challenge Trophy 1st Round Proper
13 Wed   FA Challenge Cup 3rd Round Proper (Replay)

16 Sat   FA Challenge Vase 4th Round
           FA Youth Challenge Cup 3rd Round Proper*
           FA County Youth Challenge Cup 3rd Round*
17 Sun   FA Sunday Cup 4th Round
23 Sat   FA Challenge Cup 4th Round Proper
30 Sat   FA Challenge Trophy 2nd Round Proper

February
3 Wed   FA Challenge Cup 4th Round Proper (Replay)
6 Sat   FA Challenge Vase 5th Round
           FA Youth Challenge Cup 4th Round Proper*
13 Sat   FA Challenge Cup 5th Round Proper
14 Sun   FA Sunday Cup 5th Round
17 Wed   England v San Marino (World Cup)
20 Sat   FA Challenge Trophy 3rd Round Proper
           FA County Youth Challenge Cup 4th Round*
24 Wed   FA Challenge Cup 5th Round Proper (Replay)
27 Sat   FA Challenge Vase Sixth Round

March
3 Wed   EC/ECWC/UEFA Quarter-final (First Leg)
6 Sat   FA Challenge Cup 6th Round Proper
           FA Youth Challenge Cup 5th Round Proper*
13 Sat   FA Challenge Trophy 4th Round Proper
17 Wed   EC/ECWC/UEFA Quarter-final (2nd Leg)
           FA Challenge Cup 6th Round Proper (Replay)
20 Sat   FA Challenge Vase Semi-final (First Leg)
           FA County Youth Challenge Cup Semi-final*
21   FA Sunday Cup Semi-final
27 Sat   FA Challenge Vase Semi-final (2nd Leg)
31 Wed   Turkey v England (World Cup)

April
3 Sat   FA Challenge Trophy Semi-final (First Leg)
           FA Youth Challenge Cup Semi-final*
4 Sun   FA Challenge Cup Semi-final
7 Wed   EC/ECWC/UEFA Semi-final (First Leg)
9 Fri   Good Friday
10 Sat   FA Challenge Trophy Semi-final (Second Leg)
12 Mon   Easter Monday
14 Wed   FA Challenge Cup Semi-final (Replay)
17 Sat
21 Wed   EC/ECWC/UEFA Semi-final (Second Leg)
24 Sat   FA Challenge Vase Final (provisional date)
28 Wed   England v Holland (World Cup)

May
1 Sat   Rugby League Final
           FA County Youth Challenge Cup Final*
2 Sun   FA Sunday Cup Final
3 Mon   Bank Holiday
5 Wed   UEFA Cup Final (First Leg)
8 Sat   FA Challenge Trophy Final (provisional date)
           FA Youth Challenge Cup Final*
12 Wed   European Cup-Winners' Cup Final
15 Sat   FA Challenge Cup Final
18 Tue   International Date
19 Wed   UEFA Cup Final (Second Leg)
21 Fri   International Date
23 Sun   International Date
26 Wed   European Champion Clubs' Cup Final
29 Sat   Poland v England (World Cup)

June
2 Wed   Norway v England (World Cup)
Closing dates of rounds

ROTHMANS RUGBY LEAGUE YEARBOOK 1992–93
                    Edited by Raymond Fletcher and David Howes   £14.99

ROTHMANS RUGBY UNION YEARBOOK 1992–93
                              Edited by Stephen Jones   £14.99

PLAYFAIR FOOTBALL ANNUAL 1992–93 Edited by Jack Rollin   £3.99

PLAYFAIR NON-LEAGUE FOOTBALL ANNUAL 1992–93
                              Edited by Bruce Smith   £3.99

WILLIE CARSON: THE ILLUSTRATED BIOGRAPHY by Michael Seely   £9.99

Headline offers an exciting range of quality titles by both established and new authors available from:

Headline Book Publishing PLC
Cash Sales Department,
PO Box 11,
Falmouth,
Cornwall TR10 9EN

Alternatively, you may fax your order to the above address:
Fax No. 0326 376423.

Payments can be made as follows: cheque, postal order (payable to Headline Book Publishing PLC) or by
credit cards, Visa/Access. Do not send cash or currency. UK and BFPO customers: please send a cheque
or postal order (no currency) and allow £1.00 for postage and packing for the first book plus 50p for each
additional book up to a maximum charge of £3.00.

Overseas customers, including Ireland, please allow £2.00 for postage and packing for the first book, £1.00
for the second book, and 50p for each additional book.

NAME (Block Letters) ....

ADDRESS...

....

....

I enclose my remittance for ....

I wish to pay by Visa/Access card

Number..

Card expiry date ....